W9-CZL-347

The
College Blue Book®

39th Edition

Distance Learning Programs

The College Blue Book®

39th Edition

Distance Learning Programs

MACMILLAN REFERENCE USA
A part of Gale, Cengage Learning

Detroit • New York • San Francisco • New Haven, Conn • Waterville, Maine • London

The College Blue Book, 39th Edition
Volume 6

Project Editor: Bohdan Romaniuk

Editorial Support Services: Wayne Fong

Composition and Electronic Prepress: Gary Leach

Manufacturing: Rita Wimberley

Product Management: Jerry Moore

Distance Learning program data provided by Peterson's Publishing, a Nelnet company (www.petersonspublishing.com).

Gale
27500 Drake Rd.
Farmington Hills, MI, 48331-3535

ISBN-13: 978-0-02-866155-1 (6 vol. set)
ISBN-10: 0-02-866155-9 (6 vol. set)
ISBN-13: 978-0-02-866161-2 (vol. 6)
ISBN-10: 0-02-866161-3 (vol. 6)

ISSN 1556-0570

This title is also available as an e-book.
ISBN-13: 978-0-02-866173-5 (set)
ISBN-10: 0-02-866173-7 (set)
Contact your Gale sales representative for ordering information.

Printed in the United States of America
1 2 3 4 5 6 7 15 14 13 12 11

TABLE OF CONTENTS

HOW TO USE THIS GUIDE

INSTITUTION PROFILES AND SPECIAL MESSAGES

Here, in alphabetical order, you'll find more than 900 institutions offering postsecondary education at a distance. Each profile covers such items as accreditation information, availability of financial aid, degrees and awards offered, course subject areas offered outside of degree programs, and the person or office to contact for program information.

For each institution, specific degrees and award programs are listed, followed by a list of subjects for which individual courses (undergraduate, graduate, and noncredit) are offered.

INSTITUTIONAL INFORMATION

The sections here describe overall characteristics of an institution and its distance learning offerings, featuring key facts and figures about the institutions, including:

- Institution Web site
- Background information on the institution
- Type of accreditation held by the institution
- When distance learning courses were first offered at the institution
- Number of students enrolled in distance learning courses
- Availability of financial aid
- Services available to distance learners
- Person or office to contact for more information about the institution's distance learning courses

DEGREES AND AWARDS

This part of the profile lists each program leading to a degree or certificate that can be completed entirely at a distance. Programs are grouped by the level of award: associate degrees, baccalaureate degrees, graduate degrees, undergraduate certificates, and graduate certificates.

COURSE SUBJECT AREAS OFFERED OUTSIDE OF DEGREE PROGRAMS

Listed here are the general subject areas in which the institution offers courses at a distance. Subjects are divided into those offered for undergraduate credit and for graduate credit and those that are noncredit. Note that this is not a listing of course titles; you will need to contact the institution for a detailed list of courses offered.

APPENDIX

The **Appendix** lists resources that can give you more information on subjects presented in previous sections of this guide.

GLOSSARY

With the **Glossary**, you'll be able to learn all the pertinent terms from A to Z.

INDEXES

If you are interested in locating a certificate or degree program in a specific field of study, refer to the index of **Institutions Offering Degree and Certificate Programs.** Here you'll find institutions offering everything from accounting to theological and ministerial studies.

If it is individual courses you're looking for, the index of **Non-Degree-Related Course Subject Areas** will guide you to institutions offering credit and noncredit courses at either the undergraduate or graduate level.

The **Geographical Listing of Distance Learning Programs** lets you find programs that are offered by institutions that are located near you. Keep in mind that most institutions' offerings are available nationally, and sometimes internationally. See individual listings for details.

DATA COLLECTION PROCEDURES

The information provided in these profiles was collected during the summer of 2011 by way of a survey posted online for colleges and universities. With minor exceptions, all data included in this edition have been submitted by officials at the schools themselves. In addition, many of the institutions that submitted data were contacted directly by the Peterson's research staff to verify unusual figures, resolve discrepancies, and obtain additional data. All usable information received in time for publication has been included. The omission of any particular item from an index or profile listing signifies that the item is either not applicable to that institution or that data were not available. Although Peterson's has every reason to believe that the information presented in this guide is accurate, students should check with each college or university to verify such figures as tuition and fees, which may have changed since the publication of this guide.

CRITERIA FOR INCLUSION IN THIS BOOK

In the research for this guide, the following definition of distance learning was used: a planned teaching/learning experience in which teacher and students are separated by physical distance and use any of a wide spectrum of media. This definition is based on the one developed by the University of Wisconsin Extension.

The College Blue Book: Distance Learning Programs profiles more than 900 institutions of higher education currently offering courses or entire programs at a distance. To be included, all U.S. institutions must have full accreditation or candidate-for-accreditation (preaccreditation) status granted by an institutional or specialized accrediting body recognized by the U.S. Department of Education or the Council for Higher Education Accreditation. The six U.S. regional accrediting associations are: the New England Association of Schools and Colleges, Middle States Association of Colleges and Schools, North Central Association of Colleges and Schools, Northwest Commission on Colleges and Universities, Southern Association of Colleges and Schools, and Western Association of Schools and Colleges. Approval by state educational agencies is conferred separately on some distance education courses. Canadian institutions must be chartered and authorized to grant degrees by the provincial government, be affiliated with a chartered institution, or be accredited by a recognized U.S. accrediting body.

WHAT IS DISTANCE LEARNING?

One student is a busy professional who needs to update work-related skills by taking a couple of computer applications courses in his spare time. Another student, a working mother, never finished her bachelor's degree and would love to have that diploma and get a better job. A third student attends a local community college, but what he'd really like is a degree offered by a four-year institution halfway across the country—without moving. Another would-be student is employed full-time in a field in which a master's degree, perhaps even a doctorate, would really give her career a boost. What all these diverse people have in common is an already full life. For them, disrupting family and work by commuting to sometimes distant on-campus classes on a rigid schedule is simply not a workable option. Instead, students like these are turning to distance learning in order to pursue their educational goals. For many people, and perhaps you, distance learning is a blessing—it means you can get the education you need, which might otherwise be difficult or impossible to obtain in the traditional manner.

What, exactly, is distance learning (also called distance education)? Broadly defined, distance learning is the delivery of educational programs to students who are off site. In a distance learning course, the instructor is not in the same place as the student; the students may be widely separated by geography and time; and the instructor and students communicate with each other using various means, from the U.S. mail to the Internet. Students who take a distance education course are called distance learners, whether they live 300 miles from the university or right across the street.

Distance learning makes use of many technologies, and courses are structured in many different ways. Adding to the variety of distance learning programs provided by traditional institutions of higher education are programs offered by new types of institutions, many worthy, others known as diploma mills, that help to fuel the growth in distance education. With so many technologies, courses, programs, and institutions involved in distance education, your distance learning options can be confusing at first. However, it's critical that you understand what distance education involves and which institutions offer a solid education *before* you enroll. That way you'll be sure that you spend your effort, time, and money wisely on a reputable education.

In this section, we'll give you an overview of distance learning; in "Is Distance Learning Right for You?", we'll help you determine whether or not distance education is right for you; and then in later sections we'll give you enough background and guidance so you can make an informed choice when selecting a program. We'll also provide suggestions for handling the application process, paying for your education, and making the most of your distance learning experience.

A BRIEF HISTORY OF DISTANCE EDUCATION

In the last five to ten years, distance education has mushroomed, so it's easy to think of it as a completely recent phenomenon. However, today's distance education, based primarily on video and Internet technologies, has its roots in the correspondence courses that arose in the late 1800s. Instructors would send print materials to students by mail, and students would do their assignments and return them by mail. Correspondence courses were asynchronous; that is, the student was not tied to the instructor's timetable. He or she would do the work when it was convenient. Correspondence courses still exist, mostly for single courses, but they have lost ground over the last seventy years to more modern technologies. The first generation of technology that began to supplant correspondence courses was radio in the 1930s, followed by broadcast television in the 1950s and 1960s. Radio and television courses provided one-way communication, and so they were most suitable for delivering information from the faculty to the students. Typically, there was only minimal interaction between instructor and students, and there was no interaction at all among students. Another constraint on radio and television courses was time. Broadcast courses are synchronous; students had to be listening to the radio or watching television when the course was broadcast, or they would miss the class.

In the 1960s and '70s, the advent of cable television, audiocassette recorders, and videocassette recorders solved the time problem posed by the earlier broadcast courses. Courses could be broadcast over cable channels several times so students could watch at their convenience. With a VCR or tape recorder, a student could record a lecture or class session when it was broadcast and view or hear it at any time. In fact, recorders made broadcasting unnecessary. The content of a course could be recorded on an audiocassette or videotape and sent to students, who could listen or view it when they had time. Although recording technology provided convenience for students, because courses are asynchronous, it did not solve the major drawback of broadcast courses—the lack of interaction among faculty members and students.

Beginning in the 1980s, the personal computer, two-way audio and videoconferencing, and the Internet greatly expanded the scope of distance education. With these new technologies, much more information could be conveyed from the faculty to students. More importantly, two-way communication became possible, using interactive video technology or e-mail, newsgroups, bulletin boards, and chat rooms on the Internet. Today, distance education makes use of a wide range of technologies.

INSTRUCTIONAL TECHNOLOGIES IN DISTANCE LEARNING

Today's distance learning courses can be divided into several main categories according to the primary technologies they use to deliver instruction: print-based courses, audio-based courses, video-based courses, and Internet-based courses. The audio, video, and Internet courses all have variations that are synchronous—classes take place at specific times only—and asynchronous—classes that occur at flexible times that may be more convenient for the student.

PRINT-BASED COURSES

Correspondence courses use print materials as the medium of instruction. Students receive the materials by mail at the start of the course and return completed assignments by mail. Sometimes fax machines are used to speed up the delivery of assignments, and the telephone can be used if communication between instructor and student is necessary. Patti Iversen, who lives in Montana, completed part of her Bachelor of Science in Nursing degree from the University of Mary in North Dakota by correspondence course. "The correspondence courses offered no direct contact with the instructor or other students," she recalls. "I purchased a syllabus and book and was otherwise on my own." In addition to the lack of interaction between instructor and students, correspondence courses have the disadvantage of being slow. The low-tech nature of a print-based course means lots of delay between assignments and feedback. Of course, the low-tech nature of the course is an advantage, too. Students don't have to invest in expensive technology and can do their work anywhere. Even though print materials continue to play a very important role in distance learning, they are now usually supplemented by more modern instructional technologies.

AUDIO-BASED COURSES

Audio-based courses may involve two-way communication, as in audio or phone conferencing; or they may involve one-way communication, including radio broadcast and prerecorded CDs sent to students. Fritz J. Messere, Professor of Communication Studies at the State University of New York at Oswego, recalls the first time, in 1981, he was involved in teaching a course that used phone conferencing. Once a week, faculty members and students from ten universities as well as representatives from the Federal Communications Commission "met" for a class. "The first three weeks were chaotic," recalls Messere. "We didn't know who was talking." However, they worked out a plan in which a different faculty member moderated the session each week by asking questions. At midsession there was a break, followed by a round-robin discussion, in which each site participated in a predetermined sequence.

According to the National Center for Education Statistics of the U.S. Department of Education, audio-based technologies are not widely used today, with only about 12 percent of institutions of higher learning reporting their use as the primary means of delivering a course. Instead, audio technologies may be used to supplement the main technology used in the course. For example, in an Internet-based distance education course, students and professors may call one another periodically.

VIDEO-BASED COURSES

Video-based technologies include two-way interactive video conferencing, one-way video with two-way audio, one-way live video, and one-way prerecorded videotapes or DVDs provided to students. Of these, two-way interactive video and prerecorded videos are the most popular. Of the institutions of higher learning surveyed by the U.S. Department of Education, 54 percent used two-way interactive video and 47 percent used prerecorded videos as the primary mode of instructional delivery in their distance education courses.

Two-Way Interactive Video

A course taught by means of two-way interactive video takes place simultaneously in two or more sites. The instructor is located in the home site with a group of students, and other students are located in satellite sites, often with a facilitator to help out. Each site has TV monitors or large screens on which the instructor and students can be viewed. One student in a biology of horticulture course at the University of Cincinnati described the technology used in her course: "Both [home and satellite] classrooms are set up with cameras and two video screens each, which show what is going on in both classrooms. There is a technical assistant present in each location, one on the main campus to set things up and work with the camera, etc., and another in the remote location to set equipment up and to adjust settings should there be any problems." The course itself was conducted as a lecture: "For the most part, the instructor lectures, with students occasionally asking or answering questions. When any student speaks in class, they press a button on a little apparatus on the desk in front of them, which makes the camera point to them as they speak and allows their voice to be transmitted to the other location." Quizzes and exams are faxed to the satellite site and faxed back or mailed by an assistant when they are completed. Like the best classroom teaching, two-way interactive video works well when the instructor is comfortable with "performing" on camera. "You have to keep students at all sites involved with you by making the lecture as entertaining as possible," says Dr. Larry Anthony, former Academic Director of the Addiction Studies and Treatment program at the University of Cincinnati. "I've had to adapt my teaching to the medium. For example, instead of using overheads as I might in a regular classroom, I'm more inclined to use a series of PowerPoint slides because they're more entertaining."

Two-way interactive video bridges geographical distances but not time. Students must be in a particular place at a particular time to take the course.

Prerecorded Video

A far less sophisticated, though almost as popular, means of instruction is prerecorded video. Each course session is videotaped and mailed to off-site students. To supplement this, the course may have a Web site where notes and assignments are posted, or these may be mailed to the off-site students along with the tapes or DVDs. If students have any questions, they can call or e-mail the instructor after they view the video. For many students, the lack of interactivity is made up for by the benefit of "attending" class at their own convenience. Nicole DeRaleau, who received her Master of Engineering degree at Worcester Polytechnic Institute in Massachusetts, says, "Watching the videotaped class was really not very different from sitting in class, except that I couldn't raise my hand and ask questions." On the other hand, she points out that the asynchronous nature of prerecorded video was an

The time and place dimensions of various distance learning instructional technologies.

	Specific place	**Any place**
Any time (asynchronous)		◆ Online courses (newsgroups, bulletin boards, Web sites, e-mail) ◆ CD-ROMs, DVDs ◆ Videotapes ◆ Audiotapes, CDs ◆ Correspondence courses
Specific time (synchronous)	◆ Two-way interactive videoconferencing ◆ Two-way interactive audioconferencing ◆ Traditional on-campus classes	◆ Online course (interactive computer conferencing, chat rooms, MUDs, MOOs) ◆ Radio broadcasts ◆ TV broadcasts, satellite, and cable

advantage: "I could watch half a class at one sitting, and the other half at a later time. I often worked late, and I didn't have to worry about missing class."

INTERNET-BASED COURSES

Today many distance learning courses, called online courses or e-learning, are offered over the Internet. Some online courses use synchronous, "real-time" instruction based primarily on interactive computer conferencing or chat rooms. However, most Internet-based courses use asynchronous instruction, making use of online course management systems, Web sites, e-mail, electronic mailing lists, newsgroups, bulletin boards, and messaging programs.

In asynchronous online courses, instructors post instructional material and assignments, including text, images, video, audio, and even interactive simulations, on the course Web site. Using messaging systems, newsgroups, or bulletin boards, they can start online discussions by posting a comment or question; students can log on using a password and join the discussion at their convenience. In some courses there may be periodic "real-time" interaction in chat rooms or interactive environments like MUDS (multiple-user dungeons) and MOOs (multiple-object orientations). Feedback and guidance to individual students can be done by e-mail or telephone. Note that most of the interaction in an online course is text-based; instructors and students communicate primarily through the keyboarded word. Joanne Simon Walters, who earned a Master of Business Administration degree from the University of Phoenix Online, describes the setup of her courses: "We used newsgroup folders—the main classroom, a chat room, a course material folder, an assignment folder, and four study group folders. We posted a minimum of three messages per day to the main folder in which that week's readings were discussed. In those messages we encouraged other students to share ideas, experiences, and opinions on various topics . . . ." Besides this seminar-style interaction, there were many assignments, according to Walters. "We also submitted weekly summaries, one graded group assignment, and two personal assignments weekly." Needless to say, students must have a computer with the appropriate software and Internet access in order to take an Internet-based course. The cost of technology aside, online distance learning programs have considerable advantages. Because the course material stays online for a period of time, students can log on at their own convenience. "There are time stamps on everything they submit," says Michael S. Ameigh, Assistant Provost for Budget and Operations and Associate Professor of Communication Studies at the State University of New York at Oswego. "I can see that students are often working in the middle of the night." This flexibility is one of the main attractions of online courses for students, but it can also be its main disadvantage. "It's a common misperception that online courses can be dropped into and out of," says Claudine SchWeber, Ph.D., Chair, Doctor of Management Program and former Associate Provost, Distance Education & Lifelong Learning at the University of Maryland University College. Without class sessions to attend at scheduled times, the impetus to log on and do course work must come from within, which requires a great deal of self-discipline.

To help ensure that students keep up, many instructors structure the learning environment by setting weekly deadlines for reading lectures and completing assignments, requiring group projects, and making participation in online discussions mandatory. "I personally contact students who do not participate," says Fritz Messere, who has been teaching broadcasting and business courses online for several years. "Students must interact with me in order to pass the course." At the University of Phoenix Online, students are required to log on to a course and post messages five days out of seven as one of the requirements for passing. In online courses with participation requirements, the amount of interaction between the faculty and students is far greater than in a large lecture class held on campus. There's no lying low in the back of the classroom in a well-run online course.

MIXING THE TECHNOLOGIES

Many courses use a combination of technologies as well as print materials. For example, at Southwest Texas State University, a course in geography for elementary and high school teachers begins with a videoconference, with the instructor introducing himself or herself and outlining the course requirements. A printed study guide with all assigned readings and activities is distributed to all participants at the first session. Teachers who cannot get to a videoconferencing site are sent a video of the first session along with the study guide. After the first session, the course moves online. Using chat rooms, threaded discussions, and e-mail, participants do their assignments and group projects and interact online. Assignments are snail-mailed to the faculty member. Finally, the class concludes with another synchronous videoconference or recorded video.

This course may be unusual in that it combines two of the major distance learning technologies, but it is not unusual to find courses that use one of the major technologies and supplement it with another. For example, e-mail is used for individual student-instructor communication in most courses, even if the course is conducted by two-way interactive video or prerecorded video.

FUTURE TRENDS

Today, online instruction, two-way interactive video, and one-way prerecorded video are the most popular instructional technologies in distance education. According to the Department of Education's National Center for Education Statistics, colleges and universities are planning to increase their use of Internet-based instruction and two-way interactive video. Prerecorded video is likely to decrease in popularity. The explosive growth in distance learning in the last five years has come primarily from online courses, and that is likely to continue. With better databases and other sources of information continuing to appear on the Internet, ease of access to reliable data will increase. Also, high bandwidth technologies make individualized, customized, and live video interactions possible, with lengthy video programming available. Online distance learning is also causing a shift to a more collaborative learning model. "Because of the nature of online resources and communication, the faculty is no longer the one authoritative voice," explains Dr. Claudine SchWeber of the University of Maryland University College. An undergraduate there agrees. "Students learn from each other as well as from the instructor and course materials," she commented. "Instructors who are comfortable with online technology . . . create a classroom environment that is interactive, inviting, stimulating, motivating, and lively." Another interesting trend to note is the incorporation of the new instructional technologies in conventional, classroom-based courses. "What we are finding is that our distance technology is having an impact on the way we teach on-campus courses to undergraduate and graduate students," comments McRae C. Banks II, Professor of Entrepreneurship and Strategy and Department Head of the Department of Management at Worcester Polytechnic Institute in Massachusetts. "As one example, some faculty members have students take online quizzes before each class period . . . . Before the professor goes into class, he or she knows what areas the students understand and what areas are troubling them. Now more time can be spent where the students are having difficulty." Other professors hold office hours or help sessions in chat rooms when they are at home or out of town at conferences. Still others require students to respond to each class lecture by posting a comment to a discussion group. "For us, the bottom line is finding ways to enhance the educational experience for students," says Banks.

WHAT CAN YOU LEARN VIA DISTANCE EDUCATION?

The short answer is almost anything. You can take a single course in almost any field, or earn a certificate or degree in many fields, by distance education. Next, we'll give you an overview of what's available, and in "What Can You Study via Distance Learning?" we'll discuss these programs in more detail.

COURSE OFFERINGS

According to the U.S. Department of Education's National Center for Education Statistics (2008), in the 2006–07 academic year, 66 percent of the 4,160 two-year and four-year Title IV degree-granting postsecondary institutions in the United States offered college-level distance education courses. The overall percentage included 97 percent of public two-year institutions, 18 percent of private for-profit two-year institutions, 89 percent of public four-year institutions, 53 percent of private not-for-profit institutions, and 70 percent of private for-profit four-year institutions.

As you can see in the chart on the next page, 65 percent of the institutions reported college-level credit-granting distance education courses, and 23 percent reported noncredit distance education courses. There were approximately 12.2 million enrollments (or registrations) in college-level credit-granting distance education courses in 2006–07. Of these enrollments, 77 percent were reported in online courses, 12 percent were reported in hybrid/blended online courses, and 10 percent were reported in other types of distance education courses.

In 2006–07, there were approximately 11,200 college-level programs that were designed to be completed totally through distance education; 66 percent of these programs were reported as degree programs, and 34 percent were reported as certificate programs.

Asynchronous (not simultaneous or real-time) Internet-based technologies were cited as the most widely used technology for the instructional delivery of distance education courses; they were used to a large extent in 75 percent of the institutions that offered college-level credit-granting distance education courses and to a moderate extent in 17 percent of the institutions offering college-level credit-granting distance education courses. The most common factors cited as affecting distance education decisions to a major extent were meeting student demand for flexible schedules, providing access to college for

Total number of two-year and four-year Title IV degree-granting postsecondary institutions, and percent that offered distance education courses, by course type and institutional type: 2006–07

Institution type	Total number of institutions	Percent offered any distance education courses	Percent offered college-level distance education courses	Percent offered noncredit distance education courses
All institution types	4,200	66	65	23
Public two-year	1,000	97	97	50
Private for-profit two-year	500	18	16	Reporting standards not met
Public four-year	600	89	88	42
Private not-for-profit four-year	1,500	53	53	10
Private for-profit four-year	300	70	70	2

Source: U.S. Department of Education, National Center for Education Statistics (2008).

students who would otherwise not have access, making more courses available, and seeking to increase student enrollment. Of the courses offered, the greatest number are generally found in fields that are part of a general undergraduate education, such as English, humanities, and the social and behavioral sciences; physical and life sciences; and mathematics. However, in the fields of education, engineering, and library and information sciences, more courses are offered at the graduate/first-professional level than at the undergraduate level. According to the Department of Education, there are three likely reasons for this: the emphasis on graduate education in these fields, the suitability of course content for distance education, and the likelihood that groups of students would be located in particular places, such as a school district or engineering firm, to receive broadcast or interactive video courses.

DEGREE AND CERTIFICATE PROGRAMS

Many institutions of higher learning simply offer a smorgasbord of distance education courses that can be taken for credit. An increasing number of institutions, however, have taken distance education to the next step; they have begun to offer undergraduate and graduate certificate and degree programs that can be completed entirely by distance education. For example, a student with an associate degree from a local community college can go on to earn a baccalaureate degree from a four-year institution by distance learning, without relocating. Or a working professional can earn a master's degree or professional certificate on a part-time basis through distance learning. Recently, there has been a phenomenal increase in the number of degree and certificate programs available through distance learning. Most degree and certificate programs are in the fields of liberal/general studies, business and management, health professions, education, and engineering.

WHO OFFERS DISTANCE LEARNING?

The better question might be, "Who doesn't?" With lifelong learning becoming commonplace and communications technologies improving rapidly, the demand for distance education has grown dramatically, and with it the number and variety of providers. The first group of providers consists of the traditional colleges, universities, graduate schools, community colleges, technical schools, and vocational schools. These providers range from schools only their neighbors have heard of to household names like Stanford, Virginia Tech, and the University of California, to name just a few. The challenges posed by distance education have forced colleges and universities to be creative in their approaches. Some schools have formed partnerships with cable companies, public broadcasting services, satellite broadcasters, and online education companies to deliver high-quality distance education. Colleges and universities also partner with corporations to deliver courses and degree programs to employees. For example, the University of Cincinnati's College of Pharmacy offers courses and a master's degree program via distance learning to employees of Procter & Gamble Pharmaceuticals Norwich, New York, location as well as other P&G sites.

Many schools have formed consortia, or collaborative groups, within a state or region or even internationally, which enables students to take courses as needed from all the participating institutions. An example of a consortium is the University of Texas (UT) TeleCampus, which does not confer degrees but supports the participating University of Texas campuses, which do award degrees.

A few colleges and universities are virtual, meaning they don't have a campus. These schools offer most or all of their instruction by means of distance education, providing complete degree programs. The University of Phoenix Online and Walden University are two well-known examples.

Finally, there are many online purveyors of noncredit distance education courses on subjects that range from candlemaking and beauty secrets to C++ programming and Spanish. These courses may be fun and even instructive, but they won't contribute to your formal educational credentials.

We'll discuss the providers of distance education more fully in "Who Offers Distance Education?"

HOW EFFECTIVE IS DISTANCE LEARNING?

There is a great deal of interest in the effectiveness of distance learning. Research into this subject is largely anecdotal and much of it is out-of-date, given the rapid development of instructional technology in the last few years. However, Thomas L. Russell, in a widely quoted report entitled *The No Significant Difference Phenomenon*, concluded from a review of 355 research studies and summaries published between 1928 and 1999 that the learning outcomes (test scores and course grades) of distance learning and traditional students are similar. In addition, Russell found that distance learners themselves have positive attitudes toward distance education and are generally satisfied with it. There are a number of questions regarding the effectiveness of distance education that have not yet been answered by the research. For example, how do the different learning styles of students relate to the use of particular technologies? How do individual differences among students affect their ability to learn by distance education? Why do more students drop out of distance education courses than drop out of traditional courses? What types of content are most suitable for distance learning? Common sense suggests that distance education is more effective for some people than for others, the different instructional technologies are more effective with different types of learners, and some subjects are more suitable for distance education than other subjects.

Some educators are not fans of distance education, believing that technology, no matter how sophisticated, cannot substitute the face-to-face interactions of a community of teachers and learners. Even proponents of distance learning concede that students who have the time and money for a traditional on-campus education should go for it. "Technology can't provide the intangible experiences of campus life, especially on the undergraduate level," comments Robert V. Steiner, former Associate Director of Leadership Programs and Distance Learning at Columbia University's Teachers College. "However, distance education is extremely helpful for adult learners who need to get their education in a flexible manner."

Barbara Lockee, Virginia Tech's distance learning program developer and professor of instructional technology, agrees. "Distance education has the increased potential to reach new audiences that haven't had access to higher education," says Lockee. "Because of the changing needs of our work force, people who are employed need ongoing, lifelong education. So new higher-ed participants are in their 30s and beyond, and many probably have their undergraduate degree but need skills to be successful in the information age."

Distance education may have benefits beyond accessibility, flexibility, and convenience. For example, when asked to compare the experiences of teaching a course to a single classroom of students and by two-way interactive video, Larry Anthony indicated that the students in the distance learning course had the richer experience. "We were hearing from people in different parts of the country," he explained. "In addiction studies, there are different cultural issues and problems in different places. In terms of diversity, the distance learning class was great." Kevin Ruthen, who earned a Master of Science degree in information resource management from Syracuse University, also thought that distance education had added to the value of his degree: "The students and professors . . . were all different ages, from many professional fields, and from many regions of the world," he recalls. "I learned a tremendous amount and gained many different perspectives due to this diversity as opposed to what would be, in my opinion, a less diverse class environment in an on-campus class."

PURSUING YOUR EDUCATION BY DISTANCE LEARNING

Still interested in distance learning? Then the next question is: What's involved in finding a reputable distance education program and getting in? A lot. The first, and perhaps the most important part of this process, is a combination of introspection and research. You are going to have to assess yourself and what's out there to find a good match. You'll have to answer questions like: What are my professional goals? What are my interests and abilities? Which courses or certificate or degree programs will help me achieve my goals? Am I prepared for higher education in this field? What must I do to improve my qualifications? Do I have the motivation, personal characteristics, and skills that will enable me to learn at a distance? In "Is Distance Learning Right for You?", we will help you assess the advantages and disadvantages of distance learning as well as your strengths and weaknesses; this will enable you to decide whether or not distance education is for you. Then in "What Can You Study via Distance Learning?", we'll describe the different degree and certificate programs that are available, what's involved in transferring credits, and how you may be able to earn credits for prior learning and life experience. In "Who Offers Distance Education?", we'll describe the various types of distance learning providers. We'll give you suggestions on how to find out more about programs and institutions.

Once you've done your research on distance education programs, on what basis should you evaluate them? In addition to finding out the all-important accreditation status of the programs in which you are interested, you'll have to find out what each program is really like and whether it's a good match for you. Will the program help you achieve your educational and professional goals? Is the instructional technology a comfortable match for you? "Selecting a Good Distance Learning Program" discusses these issues and provides a checklist of factors you should consider when you evaluate distance education programs.

Once you've identified the programs to which you will apply, what standardized qualifying exams, if any, will you need to take? What should you do to prepare for the SAT*, Graduate Record Examinations (GRE®), or one of the graduate admissions examinations used by many of the professional schools? You will have to find out what each program requires as part of its application and what the deadlines are. You may have to write a personal statement so that the admissions committee can evaluate your background. You will have to ask instructors or colleagues to write letters of recommendation. In "Taking Standardized Admissions Tests" and "Applying for Admission to Degree Programs" we will describe the process in more detail and give you suggestions on how to prepare applications that will gain you admission.

How are you going to pay for your education? If you are planning to attend part-time while working, that may not be a problem. But for full-time students, financing a distance degree program can be complicated. You will have to figure out how much money you will need, find possible sources of aid, and apply for them. "Paying for Your Education" covers financing your distance education.

Finally, in "Succeeding as a Distance Learner," some of the students we interviewed and surveyed will share more of their experiences and offer additional advice on succeeding in a distance education program.

In the pages that follow, there are many suggestions for accomplishing all of the tasks involved in selecting and applying to distance learning programs. Not all the advice will be applicable to everyone. Still, this book will provide you with an overview of what you will need to know. And it will indicate what you will need to find out on your own to ensure that your distance education does all that you hope it will do.

*SAT is a registered trademark of the College Board, which was not involved in the production of, and does not endorse, this book.
GRE® is a registered trademark of Educational Testing Service (ETS). This book is not endorsed or approved by ETS.

IS DISTANCE LEARNING RIGHT FOR YOU?

Distance learning can satisfy a wide range of needs for many people in diverse circumstances, but it's not for everyone. Some students don't have the study skills or self-discipline to succeed as a distance learner. Others are interested in a field of study or a degree that is not offered via distance learning. Still, for most people distance learning has the potential to open up new possibilities in higher education. For many adult students, the advantages of distance learning far outweigh the disadvantages. In this section, we'll discuss the pros and cons of distance learning and help you assess whether or not distance learning is right for you.

THE ADVANTAGES OF DISTANCE LEARNING

Distance learning has many benefits. That's why distance learning programs meet the needs of so many different people of all ages, genders, professions, and educational backgrounds.

As you read the following list of distance learning benefits, ask yourself if any of them provide a way to overcome an obstacle that is standing in your way when you think about going back to school. Do any of these advantages make continuing your education a real possibility right now, rather than a vague goal for sometime in the future?

Here are the benefits of distance learning in general:

- **Distance learning breaks down time barriers.** In most distance learning programs, you don't have to be at a certain place at a certain time. You can learn when it's convenient for you, so you can fit your education into a busy work and home life. You only take as many courses as you can handle at a time, and sometimes you can start whenever you like instead of at the beginning of a semester.
- **Distance learning breaks down geographical barriers.** Whether you are logging on to a course from your own computer at home or traveling a short distance to a satellite classroom, distance education makes your geographical distance from a college or university irrelevant. Students who live in remote areas, who don't have time to commute to a campus, and who travel a lot on business benefit from this aspect of distance education.
- **Distance learning goes at your own pace.** Distance learning is ideal for students who like to set their own pace and who learn best on their own. As you work through course material, you can spend more time on difficult concepts and less time on easier ones. Although you are likely to have weekly or other periodic deadlines, as long as you make them, you can approach the work at a pace that suits your schedule.
- **Distance learning can save money.** Although the tuition and fees for distance learning courses are usually comparable to those charged for on-campus courses, you can save money on child care, gas, parking, and other commuting costs. In addition, you generally don't have to take time off from work to attend class.
- **Distance learning fits individual needs.** You can often tailor a program to fit your particular educational and professional goals and take courses from various institutions if necessary.
- **Distance learning provides freedom of choice.** Since you are not confined to schools within easy commuting distance, you are able to consider distance learning programs at reputable colleges and universities around the country and the world.
- **Distance learning teaches more than just the course material.** Depending on the type of program you take, distance learning can improve your computer, Internet, reading, writing, and oral communication skills, which benefits you no matter what kind of career you pursue.
- **Distance learning broadens your perspective.** Often, your classmates will be from diverse backgrounds and places. You will interact with a more diverse group of people than you would normally find on most campuses.

Refer to Figure 2-1 for the specific advantages of each of the major distance learning instructional technologies.

THE DISADVANTAGES OF DISTANCE LEARNING

Before you think that distance learning is the solution to all problems of access to education, know that it does have its drawbacks. Consider whether or not any of the following general disadvantages would cause you to eliminate distance learning from your education plans. For disadvantages specific to a particular instructional technology, refer to Figure 2-1.

- **Distance learning requires a high degree of discipline and self-motivation.** Dropout rates are higher for distance learning programs than for campus-based programs. No doubt, some dropouts are students who did not realize that distance learning requires as much, if not more, time than a traditional on-campus class. For older distance education students, it's easy for work or family needs to take priority over education. Many distance learners drop out because the distance course is the easiest thing to let go of when things get too hectic.
- **Distance learning can be lonely.** Some people need the face-to-face interaction that a traditional classroom provides. Even though instructors may try to overcome social isolation in distance learning courses, for some students there is simply not enough social contact to keep them enthusiastic and motivated.
- **Distance learning can take longer.** Because distance learning is self-motivated, it's easier to give in to other demands on your time and postpone taking courses, increasing the time it takes to complete a degree program.
- **Distance learning students may get poor student services.** On-campus students have convenient access to the library, academic advisers, job placement services, tutoring, and student centers. Many distance learning programs offer student services

Figure 2-1: Specific Advantages and Disadvantages of the Major Distance Learning Technologies

Distance Learning Technology	Advantages	Disadvantages
Online	▲Course work can be done at any time of day or night. ▲Any computer with Internet access can be used. ▲Courses can easily be taken from more than one school. ▲Computer skills are developed. ▲There are no commuting costs.	▼Lots of self-discipline and motivation are needed. ▼A computer with Internet access is needed. ▼Social interaction is online only.
Two-way interactive videoconferencing	▲There is access to courses at distant campuses. ▲Social interaction is most similar to that of a traditional classroom. ▲There is no cost to the student for technology.	▼Classes are held at particular times and places.
Videotapes or DVDs of class sessions	▲Course work can be done at any time of day or night. ▲Any TV and VCR or DVD player can be used. ▲There are no commuting costs.	▼Lots of self-discipline and motivation are needed. ▼Social interaction is minimal. ▼Distance learners are several days behind on-campus class.

such as online library access and registration, but in most schools the services still can't compare to those available to on-campus students.

- **Distance learning students miss the college experience.** College campuses offer a lot more than classes, with cultural and sports activities, dorm life, faculty-student interaction, and the opportunity to form lifelong friendships. Although this is not an important consideration for most older distance learners, younger students that pursue an undergraduate education may find the on-campus experience too valuable to pass up.
- **A traditional college degree is a better choice to meet some future goals.** Although distance learning is becoming more mainstream and is usually accepted by employers, as long as it is from a reputable institution, it is still regarded by some in the traditional academic community as inferior. Thus, a traditional degree may be more valuable if you are considering applying in the future to the more prestigious graduate and professional programs, including law school and medical school.

ASSESSING YOURSELF

With the advantages and disadvantages of distance learning in mind, you should take some time to honestly answer the following questions. Consider your own goals, circumstances, personality, skills, social support, and comfort with technology to determine whether or not you are a good candidate for distance learning.

GOALS

What are your educational and professional goals?

First you must determine your educational and professional goals. Ask yourself what you would like to be doing in five or ten years, and then determine what courses or degree programs will help you achieve your goals. Do you need a course to update your skills, a certificate to provide professional credentials, or a degree to solidify or advance your professional standing?

For example, when Head Start announced that an associate degree in early childhood education would soon be a requirement for its teachers, Angela Butcher had a problem. Butcher, who was teaching at Jackson-Vinton Community Action Head Start in Ohio, just had a high school diploma. "I was so scared of losing my job. Going to a college campus (the closest is 45 minutes away) after working 8 hours a day and finding a sitter for my 2 children because my husband works second shift—it was just impossible to even think about doing it. Then my director received a brochure about the distance learning program at the University of Cincinnati and asked if I would like to give college a shot that way." Butcher continues, "I felt this was a true gift to help me to [keep] the profession that is dear to me."

For Butcher, the goal was crystal clear and the means of achieving that goal fell into place quite nicely. However, for any student, it's important to know what you hope to accomplish by undertaking any degree program. "Make sure you have your goals defined," advises Scott Garrod, a who earned a master's degree in business from Syracuse University. "Then the decision between a distance or traditional [program] will be easy." Keep in mind that in some fields a distance education degree is not as acceptable as it is in others. Although most business employers don't make any distinctions between distance and on-campus degrees, as long as they are from reputable institutions, in academia and some professions employers may not be so accommodating. Be sure you understand what academic credentials will carry weight in the field in which you are interested.

Why are you considering distance education?

Do you have a busy schedule full of commitments to work, family, and community? If so, your top reason for enrolling in a distance education course or program may be the flexibility it offers. The ability to do course work at your own convenience is the key consideration for most distance learners.

"My schedule does not permit consistent attendance in a traditional classroom," comments one 46-year-old undergraduate. "As a consultant, I may be required to spend up to 60 hours at a client site . . . . As a parent, I have many commitments that would take priority over my attending class." She continues, "The online program at the University of Maryland University College offers me maximum flexibility in which to pursue my educational goals without interfering with the rest of my crazy schedule." Another student, Kimberly Foreman, who studied for a Master of Healthcare Administration from Seton Hall University's online program in New Jersey, investigated several programs. "Traditional on-campus evening classes interfered with work and family obligations. The weekend programs still required that I be at a certain place at a certain time, and this was also inconvenient," she explains. "I wanted flexibility and a program that allowed me to be self-directed but still have interaction with faculty members and classmates." The online program she found at Seton Hall met her needs.

Some students need the flexibility of distance education because their work involves a great deal of travel. "With my job, travel is a requirement . . . sometimes unpredictable travel," says Scott Garrod of Syracuse University. "So a distance learning program that was not classroom-dependent was a great alternative." Another student, Paul Nashawaty, explains, "My profession had me traveling around and moving from place to place." Nashawaty, who earned a Master of Business Administration from Worcester Polytechnic Institute in Massachusetts, concluded, "It would have been very difficult for me to transfer from school to school."

Other students enroll in distance education courses and programs because they live too far from the institutions of higher learning that offer the education they need. These are students for whom the word "distance" in distance learning has a literal meaning. "My husband is a farmer, so my family is not mobile," explains Patti Iversen, a nurse who lives in Montana and earned a Master of Science in Nursing degree (family nurse-practitioner) from Gonzaga University in Spokane, Washington. "I live in a rural community, and the closest colleges and universities are 250 to 300 miles from my home. I did not want to leave my family for extended periods of time in order to meet my educational and career objectives." For Iversen, distance learning was the only way to achieve her goals.

"I wanted a degree from a respected and vigorous program but didn't want to move my family or quit my job," says Lara Hollenczer, a marketing manager who lives in Maryland and earned a master's degree in communications management from Syracuse University in New York. Distance learning provided the means to earn the degree she wanted without disrupting her work and family life. So, when you consider taking a course or enrolling in a degree program, ask yourself whether flexibility of time and place is critical for you. If flexibility is one of your top needs, distance learning may be the right choice for you.

PERSONAL ATTITUDES AND SKILLS

Are you prepared to do as much work as you would have to do in a traditional course, and perhaps more?

Many people believe that distance learning is an easier or faster way to earn a degree. This is because in recent years many fraudulent distance learning schools have sprung up, promising degrees in little or no time for little or no work. These diploma mills have given rise to the false perception that distance learning degrees are somehow easier to earn than degrees earned the traditional way. However, distance learning courses and degree programs offered by reputable schools require just as much time and effort as their on-campus counterparts.

"Some students think that an online course is cybersurfing for credit," says Michael S. Ameigh, Assistant Provost for Budget and Operations and Associate Professor of Communication Studies at the State University of New York at Oswego. "But an online course is actually more work than if students took the course in the classroom." That's because online instructors often require a certain amount of participation from students in order to pass the course, whereas most classroom instructors do not demand participation from students beyond completing the assignments and exams. So, at the beginning of each course, Ameigh tries to weed out students who think that online learning is easier than conventional courses. He provides a 6-minute "welcome document," a streaming media PowerPoint presentation with narration that gives an overview of what the course covers and what he expects of students. In courses taken by distance learners and on-campus students, instructors make no distinctions between distance learners and traditional students when it comes to the course work that they must do. For example, in Gonzaga University's undergraduate and graduate nursing programs, "Course requirements for students at a distance are identical to those for their on-campus colleagues," according to Dale Ann Abendroth, Ph.D., RN, Assistant Professor of Nursing.

From the student's perspective, a high-quality distance education course is as rigorous as a traditional course. "Certainly the expectations of the instructor and the volume of readings and assignments were as stringent, or even more so, than on-site courses I have taken," comments a high school librarian of her Rutgers University postgraduate course in critical issues for the wired classroom. "Be prepared for a great deal of work. It seems to me that more work is assigned than in a 'regular' class, so students shouldn't perceive distance learning as an easy way out. It isn't!"

Do you have the time-management skills necessary to juggle work, home, and school responsibilities?

As we have seen, a distance learning course or program takes as much time as a traditional one, and sometimes more. So ask yourself, do you have enough time to take a distance learning course or courses? Will you be able to juggle your course work, professional work, family obligations, and community activities to make time for all your responsibilities? "I've seen students register for four or five classes in a semester and try to work full-time," says Patti Wolf, Assistant Dean, John L. Grove College of Business, Shippensburg University and former Associate Professor of Information Systems Management at the University of Maryland University College. "Many of these students underestimated the time required for their online courses and ended up doing poorly." Wolf adds, "You should expect to spend as much time online (or otherwise preparing for class) as you would in a traditional classroom." Distance learner Patti Iversen advises students to "be realistic about the amount of time that will be needed for study and travel, if required [for programs with residency periods]."

In addition to having enough time to do the course work, students have to be able to plan their time, make a schedule, and stick to it. "The biggest problem I see among my students is an inability to budget their time," says Wolf. "They get to the third week of class and realize that it's Saturday night and they haven't done their homework."

Iversen agrees. "Failure to adequately anticipate and plan for the rigors of independent learning leads to frustration and poor outcomes," she warns. Even though many courses, like Wolf's, are set up in weekly blocks to help students pace themselves, it's still up to the student to make time to log on or watch the video and do the assignments.

Do you have the discipline and self-motivation to work regularly if you don't have to show up for class at a given time and place?

When we asked students and faculty members what personal qualities a distance learner needs, most people mentioned discipline and self-motivation as the keys to success. "Success as a distance learner requires more self-discipline and greater ability to learn autonomously than site-based learning," claims distance learner Patti Iversen. Paul Nashawaty echoes her remarks, "You must keep on top of the workload and try not to slack off," he says. "Discipline was my number-one factor for success in this program." A University of Maryland University College undergraduate agrees, "Students [must] have the discipline to complete course work studies and assignments on time and independently without the in-person reminders that come with regularly scheduled class meetings." When you are considering distance education, ask yourself whether or not you have the qualities needed to see it through. According to Denise Petrosino, a certified public accountant who was enrolled in a master's in organizational management at the University of Phoenix Online, "As long as you are goal-oriented and self-motivated, you can do it."

Do you have the initiative and assertiveness needed to succeed in a distance learning environment?

Initiative and assertiveness are qualities needed for success in distance learning. Students need to take the initiative to ask questions and resolve problems that the instructor may not be able to perceive.

In addition, students in distance learning courses need to be assertive in order to make themselves known to the instructor and to other students. For example, in an online course, a student who never participates in threaded discussions tends to "disappear." "In the online environment, students have to be assertive," says Michael S. Ameigh of the State University of New York at Oswego. "Otherwise we don't know who they are." Similarly, in a prerecorded video course, a student who never contacts the instructor has little presence in the instructor's mind. Of course, initiative and assertiveness are pluses for traditional on-campus students, too. The student who speaks up in class is more likely to have a good learning experience and succeed in a course than the student who sits silently in the back of the room. For many adults, maturity brings assertiveness. "My students are a professional group," says Dale Ann Abendroth, Assistant Professor of Nursing at Gonzaga University. "It's rare that I have a wallflower in a course."

YOUR ACADEMIC AND PROFESSIONAL SKILLS

Do you have sound study skills, including reading, researching, writing papers, and taking exams?

Good study skills are a necessary prerequisite for distance learning. In fact, many institutions that offer distance learning courses and degree programs require that students have taken at least some college-level courses before they enroll in a distance education degree program. For example, some distance education bachelor's programs prefer students with an associate degree from a community college or a certain minimum number of undergraduate credit hours. In this way, they ensure that students are ready to tackle course work via distance learning without needing much help with basic study skills.

For graduate programs, it is simply assumed that students have the necessary study skills and are ready to undertake graduate-level work. Laurie Noe, who earned an Ed.D. in management of children and youth programs from Nova Southeastern University, explains, "You are required to produce papers, take tests, conduct research, and formulate and state your opinions just as if you were in a traditional setting."

Do you have good communication skills? Can you present yourself well in writing? Can you speak up on camera?

Good communication skills—reading, writing, listening, and speaking—are necessary to succeed in all types of distance learning courses and programs. However, different distance learning technologies emphasize different communication skills.

"Online students have to be reasonably articulate in the written mode of communication," explains Claudine SchWeber, Associate Provost for Distance Education and Lifelong Learning at the University of Maryland University College. That's because virtually all communication in an online course takes place through the written word, therefore you must be comfortable with reading messages and responding in writing.

For some people, this is ideal. "Students who are petrified to talk in class often find it easy to communicate in writing online. They can make well-reasoned, thought-out responses to the discussion," explains Patti Wolf, formerly of the University of Maryland University College. "One of the things that happens online is that people who talk little in the classroom feel more comfortable and tend to communicate well," says Karen Novick, Associate Dean for Administration and Student Services at Rutgers University's School of Communication and Information. Robert V. Steiner, who directed the distance learning project at Teachers College, Columbia University, also agrees. "For some students, online learning may provide a more comfortable environment in which to express themselves. Students can reflect on what they want to say before they post a message." On the other hand, some students are simply more visual and more oriented to getting information via television rather than the written word. For them, two-way interactive video is a more comfortable way to communicate. It's easier for these students to speak up and communicate with people they can see and hear rather than to write messages to unseen students and instructors. "Once students get used to being on camera, they react fairly normally," says Larry Anthony, former Director of the Addiction Studies Program at the University of Cincinnati. Of course, students who take courses via video still need written communication skills because most of their assignments and exams are in writing.

If you are pursuing a degree or certificate to improve your professional standing, do you have the background that may be required?

Many graduate-level professional programs require that students have worked in the field for several years before they apply. For example, many programs that offer a Master in Business Administration prefer students who have demonstrated their professional capabilities through several years of work. Graduate-level work in other fields, such as nursing, social work, and education, often requires related work experience. Be sure you have the necessary professional background for the programs you are considering.

SOCIAL FACTORS

Do you have the support of your family and employers?

As you have realized by now, a distance learning course or program can be challenging. Taking such a course or program means that you will be working harder than ever, so having the backing of your family and employer can be very helpful. "It's important to have a good support group behind you," says Barbara Rosenbaum, who earned a master's degree in communications management from Syracuse University. "My husband, friends, family, and colleagues helped me keep my energy and focus up." Distance learner Patti Iversen agrees. "A local support network is a valuable asset in helping to overcome the occasional slump in motivation that occurs over time."

Are you comfortable with the social interaction that is characteristic of distance learning? Can you overcome or accept the social isolation that often occurs?

The issue of social interaction and isolation is complex because different factors, including instructional technology, personality, and life circumstances, influence how each person reacts to the social element of distance learning.

Instructional technology. As we saw when we discussed communication skills, each distance learning technology draws on particular skills. Similarly, each distance learning technology offers a different type of social interaction. Let's look at each major distance learning technology to get a better idea of how it affects the social elements of distance education.

The technology that offers a social experience most similar to that of the conventional classroom is two-way interactive video. Even though the students may be geographically distant from one another, communication is in real time, people can see one another, and the feeling of social isolation is minimized. Kenneth Wachter, Professor of Demography and Statistics at the University of California, Berkeley, offered an advanced postgraduate course in mathematical demography via two-way interactive video to students at Berkeley and UCLA. He was delighted by how the two groups of students were brought together. "The thing that works best is the human back and forth," says Wachter.

Online courses can also offer social interaction, but in a new and, to some, unfamiliar form. "At first it is strange e-mailing someone you don't know. However, you get to know the person via e-mail just as you would talking or writing a letter," explains an undergraduate at the University of Maryland University College. "In the cybercafes that are provided for classmates, we talk about class work, movies, music, time management, and sports. It helps bring the class together socially." Denise Petrosino, who was enrolled in a master's program in organizational management at the University of Phoenix Online, agrees. "If you have a fear of limited interaction with the teacher and students, you can put that aside because I believe that we learn more about our teacher and classmates in the online program than in the live classroom," says Petrosino. "The reason I say this is because you get to read all correspondence between students and teacher."

In courses in which class videos are mailed to off-site students, the sense of social isolation is the most pronounced. That's because these courses often do not provide a means for ongoing discussion between off-site students, on-site students, and instructors. "The professors do not know much about the distance students' personalities, or even what they look like," explains Nicole DeRaleau, who lives in Connecticut and was a Master of Engineering student at Worcester Polytechnic Institute in Massachusetts. "Their interaction with us was minimal, and the closest form of personal interaction was a telephone call, which was almost always initiated by the student." Note that some courses that rely on video for instructional delivery are now moving online as well, establishing class bulletin boards on which discussions can take place, thus improving the social interaction of the off-site students.

Personality. The second factor that influences how social interaction and social isolation are perceived is an individual's personality—one person's social isolation is another person's cherished privacy. For some people, the type of interaction that characterizes distance learning is not enough to overcome a sense of social isolation. "Eye contact, vocal inflection, body language—all these elements of communication are missing [online]," explains Robert V. Steiner, who directed the distance learning project at Teachers College, Columbia University. "For some people, the sense of isolation can be significant." As a student at the University of Phoenix Online, Joanne Simon Walters dealt with this reality of online classes. "I like to talk, so for me, the social interaction was lacking." Another distance learner thinks that people who are "social butterflies" will find the social interactions of distance learning unfulfilling.

On the other hand, people who are not especially extroverted may find distance learning suits them. They can participate, especially in online courses, without risking too much personal revelation.

Personal circumstances. How important is social interaction? Clearly, there must be enough interaction to facilitate learning. But for many adult students, the lack of social interaction is simply not a problem.

"For the most part, I feel detached from the class itself, and that is okay," says Brigit Dolan, a nurse who lives in Boise, Idaho, and is enrolled in Gonzaga University's Master of Science in Nursing program in Spokane, Washington. In this program, students are required to attend classes three times per semester. The remaining classes are mailed to them on video. "I feel okay to share my ideas and experiences when I'm there, but I'm fulfilled enough in other areas of my life that I don't yearn for that much interaction from my school life . . . . I just do my work, communicate with my professors and classmates occasionally, and that's about it." Like Brigit Dolan, most adult students are not looking for the social life and collegiality that are characteristics of the on-campus undergraduate experience. A librarian taking a postgraduate course at Rutgers University explains, "I don't think social interaction is a high priority in the kind of postgrad courses I take; we all have jobs and personal lives, and time is precious." Carla Gentry, a nurse enrolled in a distance learning master's program, agrees. "At my stage in life, I am not going to school for the social benefits."

How well do you work with others?

After the discussion of social interaction and social isolation, you may wonder why working well with others is important in the distance learning environment. The reason is that many instructors try to overcome the potential social isolation of the distance education course by assigning group work, thus forcing people to interact with each other.

Doing a group project in a distance learning class is challenging. The first challenge is to coordinate the activities of a group of people who are extremely busy, geographically distant from one another, and doing their work at different hours of the day and night. The second challenge is to get a group of distance learners to work together. "Since distance learners are so independent and self-motivated, they also like to do things their own way," says Brigit Dolan, who finds group projects the most challenging aspect of distance education. Trust, cooperation, and flexibility are key.

TECHNOLOGY ISSUES

Do you have the technical skills, or the willingness to acquire these skills, that may be required of a distance learning program?

Those of you who see yourselves as technologically challenged may have been dismayed by the discussion in "What Is Distance Learning?" of the technology involved in many distance learning courses. Don't be. Remember that the technology is just a tool, a means to an end, and it can be learned.

In fact, some distance learning technology is not particularly advanced from the user's point of view. For example, in two-way interactive video courses, all you have to do is learn to activate the microphone (some even activate automatically when you speak) and watch the video monitors. For prerecorded video, you just pop in the DVD and turn on the TV. Online courses do involve a little more technological savvy. However, consider the experience of one librarian who was taking a traditional on-campus postgraduate course at Rutgers University. "My first online course was thrust upon me," she recalls. The instructor, who developed a serious health problem that prevented her from coming in to class, gave students the option of continuing online. "I, on my own, would never have chosen this mode; I was too computer-illiterate at that time. However, I quickly found that the technical skills required were really not onerous at all and that I could master them easily . . . . If I can succeed—no spring chicken with little technology experience—anyone can." Denise Petrosino agrees. "You do not have to be a technical genius to go to school online. If you have a computer, can log onto the Web, and know how to use e-mail, you are set."

Do you have or are you willing to gain access to the necessary equipment, which may include a computer, DVD drive, television, DVD player, or fax machine?

Most people own a television and DVD player, so these are not usually items that a new distance learner needs to purchase. However, investing in the proper computer hardware and software for a distance education program can be costly. Even if you already own a computer with Internet access, you may have to upgrade your hardware or Internet browser or purchase additional software in order to meet the minimum technical requirements of a course.

Can you tolerate dealing with technology problems?

Technology sometimes fails, and distance learners have to learn how to cope when it does. Many schools offer technical support for distance learners, and sometimes problems can be solved quickly. But if your computer system crashes for a week, you'll have to find other alternatives until you can fix the problem. "Students should be comfortable with the technology triad—fax, phone, and computer," says Claudine SchWeber of the University of Maryland University College. "Then if one goes down, they have other channels of communication."

A MINI SELF-ASSESSMENT

If you do an Internet search using the phrase "distance learning self-assessment," you will find dozens of brief quizzes designed to evaluate whether or not distance learning suits your personality, skills, and learning style. Most are posted on the Web sites of colleges and universities that offer distance education courses. For example, the Community College of Baltimore County's self-assessment test can be found at www.ccbcmd.edu/distance/assess.html, and St. Louis Community College offers its self-assessment at http://www.stlcc.edu/distance_learning/READI_assessment.html.

For your convenience, we've provided a brief self-assessment. Although most of the online quizzes focus on Internet-based courses, this assessment is broader. Take it and see how you do!

DISTANCE LEARNING SELF-ASSESSMENT

1. When I think about how I learn, I think:
   (A) I learn best independently. I am self-motivated and like to work at my own pace. I don't need a lot of handholding.
   (B) I like to work independently, but I like to get some feedback once in a while on how I'm doing. I don't need a lot of support, just a little help every once in a while.
   (C) I can work independently, but I want to know where I stand. I like to be in an interactive situation where I get regular feedback on how I am doing.
   (D) I need lots of interaction with my teachers and peers. I like the give and take of the classroom setting. It keeps me engaged in my classes.

2. When I think about learning through different media, such as the Internet or videoconferencing, I think:
   (A) It would be exciting to be able to do my work through a different medium. The idea of sitting in a classroom does nothing for me.
   (B) I am open to the idea of trying something different, like an Internet class. I would like to see how it would work for me.
   (C) I'm not sure that I would be ready to work that independently. When I think of furthering my education, I see myself in a more traditional setting.
   (D) I absolutely want a traditional learning experience. I want to be in a classroom setting and experience all that school has to offer.
3. When I think about interacting with my teachers, I think:
   (A) I don't really care whether or not I have any face-to-face contact with my teachers. As long as I'm getting the kind of information I need to be successful in my classes, I can be satisfied as a student.
   (B) I don't need a great deal of direct contact with my teachers. I'm a good, independent worker. I do want to be able to ask for help and direction when I need it.
   (C) I don't need to be in a situation where I have daily conversations with my teachers, but I do like to know that they are there if I need them. I find a good teacher really helps me get excited about a topic.
   (D) I really value my contacts with my teachers. I like to be able to engage in a dialogue in the classroom. A good teacher helps me connect to the subject.
4. When I think about trying to do schoolwork at home, I think:
   (A) I have a great setup at home, which is conducive to studying. I like the idea of being able to work in my own space and at my own pace.
   (B) I can work fairly well at home, I just have to make sure that I don't get too distracted by what is going on around me.
   (C) I could work at home, but I really don't see that as an ideal situation. There is too much going on, and I would be able to concentrate better in a classroom or library setting.
   (D) There is no way I want to learn from home. I want to get out of the house and be in a classroom with other students.
5. When it comes to setting my schedule for learning and studying, I think:
   (A) I need as much flexibility as I can get. I've got a lot of other things going on in my life, and I'd really like to be able to work at my own pace.
   (B) I would like to have some flexibility in scheduling my classes, but I don't want to drag it out either. I want to get through my education as quickly as possible.
   (C) I like the idea of having my time fairly structured. If I don't have someone pushing me along, it may take me longer than I want to get through school.
   (D) I need to have a structured schedule to keep me on task.
6. When I think about the traditional education experience, I think:
   (A) Campus or classroom life doesn't really appeal to me at this stage in my life. I don't need or want the experience, for example, of living in a dorm or sitting in a classroom. I want to find an alternative way of earning my degree or certificate.
   (B) I'm not sure if I want to commit to the classroom experience. It may work for me, but I'm willing to look at other ways of earning a degree.
   (C) I think I would be happier if I were on a campus somewhere. I think I'd probably regret missing out on the learning experience. I wouldn't rule out the notion of being a commuter, though.
   (D) I really want a traditional learning experience where I can get away from home. I'm at a point in my life where that seems to be the logical next step for me.

To evaluate your readiness for distance education, count the number of (A)s, (B)s, (C)s, and (D)s among your responses. If most of your answers were

- (A)—you should carefully investigate distance education as an option for continuing your education.
- (B)—you should investigate whether distance learning programs are suitable for meeting at least part of your educational needs. For example, you may want to complete a significant portion of your academic work through a distance learning program but still allow yourself time for some of your work to be completed in a traditional classroom setting.
- (C)—you're probably better-suited for a traditional campus-based college experience than a distance learning environment. However, some course work through a distance learning program may be a great way to supplement your on-campus course work. You should probably look for a program that will provide you with faculty or mentor feedback on a regular basis.
- (D)—you are clearly suited for a traditional classroom setting where you can have more immediate interaction with your teachers and peers. This is not to say that you may not find distance learning programs useful at some point in the future, but it sounds like you need something more hands-on so you can get immediate feedback in the classroom while enjoying the other benefits of college life.

CONCLUSION

As you have seen in this section, distance learning is not for those who lack motivation or need other people to keep them on task. On the other hand, it is perfectly suited for those who have definite educational and professional goals, are committed to getting an education, are focused and organized, can persevere when things get tough, and need the flexibility that distance education offers.

Finding the time in a busy schedule to successfully complete distance learning courses is a challenge for most adults. It's easy for work and family obligations to take precedence over getting an education. Still, distance learning makes it possible for many adults who cannot regularly attend on-campus classes to get a high-quality education. As one undergraduate distance learner commented, "For working adults (and particularly working parents), distance learning may provide the best means for obtaining an undergraduate or graduate degree from a highly respected university without interfering with life's other commitments."

WHAT CAN YOU STUDY VIA DISTANCE LEARNING?

If you are interested in pursuing your education by distance learning, you are not limited to a few specialized courses or degree programs. Actually, almost every course, certificate, and degree program that you can take on campus is also available in a distance learning format. There are exceptions, of course. Degree programs in subjects that require laboratory work or performance, for example, cannot usually be done completely at a distance. Still, distance education spans a wide range of offerings, from accredited graduate-level degree programs to self-help and hobby courses. Although some programs and courses are limited to residents of certain states or regions, many are available nationwide and internationally.

In this section we will focus on programs and courses offered by institutions of higher education, including technical institutes, community colleges, four-year colleges, and universities. Figure 3-1 shows how higher education is structured in the United States, and how distance learning programs and courses are available at most levels of postsecondary education. The exceptions are some professional degrees, such as doctor of medicine, and postdoctoral study and research. Another partial exception is the law degree (LL.B., J.D.). Although you can acquire a law degree via distance learning, at the time this book was published, no distance learning law program had been accredited by the American Bar Association. Thus, a person with a law degree from an unaccredited distance learning program will not be able to take the bar exam in most states. The accreditation issue is important in many fields besides law, and we will examine it more closely in "Selecting a Good Distance Learning Program." In this section we'll simply things to give you an overview of the degrees, certificates, and courses that are available via distance learning and guidance on how to find programs and courses of interest to you.

UNDERGRADUATE DEGREE PROGRAMS

Today you can earn an associate or bachelor's degree entirely by distance learning. You may also be able to shorten the time it takes to earn a degree if you transfer college credits from other institutions of higher learning, earn credits through equivalency exams, or present a portfolio of your accomplishments. For adults, earning credits for past academic and other work can cut a year or more off the time it takes to earn an undergraduate degree. So don't be shy about negotiating for credits with the school in which you plan to enroll—the time and money you save may be considerable.

ASSOCIATE DEGREE

The degree conferred by community colleges is the associate degree. Students enrolled full-time can earn an associate degree in two years, but part-time students may take much longer to earn the 60 to 64 credits required. The two most common associate degrees are the Associate of Arts (A.A.) and the Associate of Science (A.S.), although there are many other titles that range from Associate of Business Administration (A.B.A.) to Associate of General Studies (A.G.S.). Distance learning associate degrees are offered in a wide range of fields, including liberal arts, business, computer science, and health professions. Many students who have earned an associate degree go on to apply those credits toward a bachelor's degree.

BACHELOR'S DEGREE

The bachelor's degree is recognized worldwide as the first university degree a student earns. In the United States, the bachelor's degree is conferred by four-year colleges, universities, and technical institutes. Although students enrolled full-time can earn the degree in four years, many actually take up to six years. Part-time students take longer, of course, to earn the 120 to 128 credits required for the bachelor's degree.

In most colleges and universities, the course of study that leads to a bachelor's degree consists of concentrated work in a "major" such as psychology or business and wide-ranging work in a variety of subjects—the liberal arts—to give students a broad foundation of knowledge. However, some bachelor's degree programs focus on intensive study in a particular field without the broad liberal arts background.

The most common bachelor's degrees are the Bachelor of Arts (B.A.) and the Bachelor of Science (B.S.), although there are scores of other titles in use as well. Distance learning bachelor's degrees are offered in many fields, including business, engineering, computer science, economics, English, history, nursing, psychology, and telecommunications. Some colleges and universities offer interdisciplinary degrees, such as environmental studies or arts management, and some permit students to design their own interdisciplinary program.

TRANSFERRING CREDITS

Adult students who have earned some college credits during the course of their career can decrease the time it takes to earn an undergraduate degree by transferring the credits they've earned to a degree program. Many institutions of higher learning will accept transfer credits toward a degree. *Since each school's requirements vary, it's important to check before you enroll.* The school may have rules regarding the maximum number of transfer credits and the types of courses for which credit will be granted. Consult the academic advising office before you register.

EARNING CREDITS BY TAKING EXAMS

It's also possible to earn credit for prior learning if you take examinations to assess your knowledge and skills. For example, if you have worked in the human resources department of a large organization for years, you may know a lot about human resource

Figure 3–1: The Structure of Higher Education in the U.S.

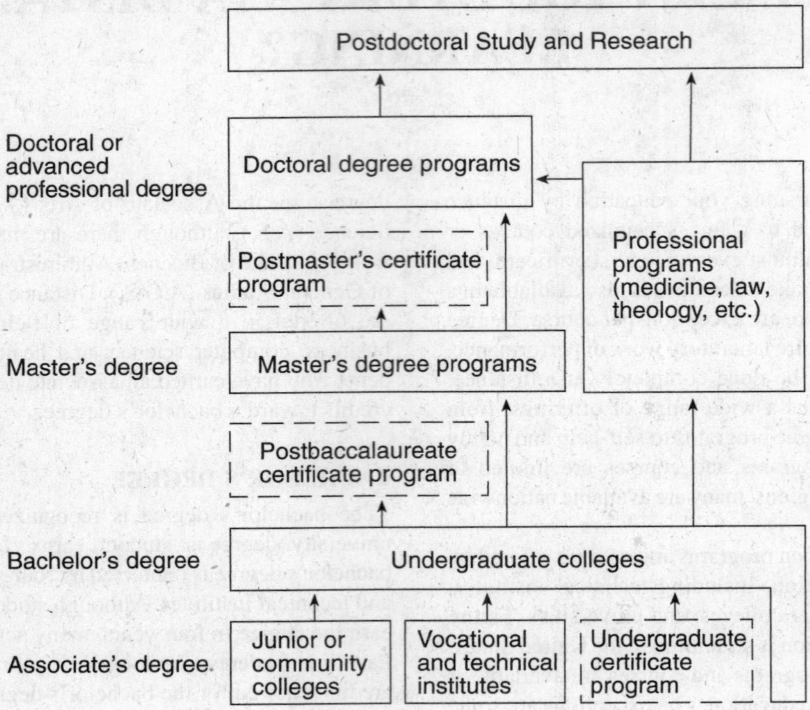

Structure of higher education in the United States. Note that the arrows indicate common pathways of students, but not the only possible pathway. *Source:* Adapted from U.S. Department of Education, National Center for Educational Statistics.

management. If you take and pass a college-level exam in human resource management, you can earn 3 credits toward your degree—without taking a course or paying tuition. Although some schools have developed their own equivalency exams, most schools accept the results of examinations taken through national programs.

CLEP Exams. The most well-known of the national equivalency exam programs is the College-Level Examination Program (CLEP), which is administered by the College Entrance Examination Board and recognized by about 2,900 colleges and universities. Most of the CLEP tests are multiple-choice exams, and some are multiple-choice and essay. There are five general exams: social sciences and history, English composition, humanities, college mathematics, and natural sciences. In addition, there are about thirty specific subject area tests, including American government, Spanish, principles of management, and introductory sociology. A good score on an exam is worth between 3 and 12 credits, it depends on the exam and the credits accepted by your school.

Earning credits by scoring well on equivalency exams can save you both time and tuition money. If you'd like more information about the CLEP exams, visit the College Board Web site at www.collegeboard.org/clep, e-mail them at clep@info.collegeboard.org, or call 800-257-9558.

Excelsior College Examinations. The Excelsior College Examination series, formerly the Regents College Examination series, is similar to the CLEP exams. The series consists of about forty subject area equivalency examinations that are 3 or 4 hours long. Subjects include anatomy and physiology, auditing, organizational behavior, and educational psychology; and the exams are recognized by over 900 colleges and universities. For more information, visit the Excelsior College Web site at www.excelsior.edu, e-mail them at testadmn@excelsior.edu, or call 888-647-2388 (toll-free).

DSSTs. Another series of equivalency exams are the DSSTs. The DSSTs are examinations offered by Prometric. These tests were originally developed for military personnel but are now available for civilians as well. The tests are similar to the CLEP exams, but there are some subject areas not offered by CLEP, such as geography, criminal justice, marketing, technical writing, and ethics in America.

For more information about the DSSTs, you can check the Web site at www.getcollegecredit.com, send an e-mail to getcollegecredit@prometric.com, or call 877-471-9860 (toll-free).

GRE Subject Tests. The Graduate Record Examination (GRE) Subject Tests, administered by the Educational Testing Service (ETS), assess knowledge that would ordinarily be acquired during the course of majoring in a subject as an undergraduate. The subjects include biochemistry, cell and molecular biology; biology; chemistry; computer science; literature in English; mathematics; physics; and psychology.

For more information about the GRE Subject Tests, visit the GRE online site at www.gre.org or call 609-771-7670 or 866-473-4373.

EARNING CREDITS FOR LIFE EXPERIENCE

Many undergraduate degree programs, especially those designed for adults, give credit for knowledge and skills you've gained through life experience. Although the knowledge usually comes through paid employment, it can also be acquired through volunteer work, company or military training courses, travel, recreational activities and hobbies, and reading.

There is a catch, of course—you must document the specifics of what you have learned. It's simply not enough to say that you learned about marketing while selling widgets for XYZ Company. Instead, you must demonstrate what you have learned about pricing, promotion, and product mix; for example, showing plans for a marketing campaign. Thus, to earn credit for life experience, you should assemble a file, or portfolio, of information about your work and other accomplishments. The file may include writing samples, awards, taped presentations or performances, copies of speeches, newspaper articles, official job descriptions, military records, works of art, designs, blueprints, films, or photographs. Your portfolio is then evaluated by an institution's faculty. A student can earn as many as 30 credits—one quarter the number needed for a bachelor's degree—as the result of a good portfolio review. For example, through a portfolio evaluation, a senior marketing executive in her forties earned 30 credits, mostly in marketing and communications, toward her distance learning bachelor's degree from University of Maryland University College. For more information about assessment opportunities for adult learners, check the Web site of the Council for Adult and Experiential Learning (CAEL) at www.cael.org or call 312-499-2600.

Credit for Work Training. Since 1974, thousands of employees have been earning college credit for selected educational programs sponsored by businesses, industry, professional associations, labor unions, and government agencies. The American Council on Education's College Credit Recommendation Service evaluates such programs according to established college-level criteria and recommends college credit for those programs that measure up to these standards. You can check their Web site at www.acenet.edu, e-mail them at credit@ace.nche.edu, or call 866-205-6267.

Credit for Military Training. Service in the military, specialized training, and occupational experience have the potential to earn you college credit. Many military programs have already been evaluated in terms of their equivalency to college credit. The institutions that belong to Servicemembers Opportunity Colleges (SOC) have agreed to assess students' prior learning and accept each other's credits in transfer. To find out more, check the SOC Web site at www.soc.aascu.org, e-mail them at socmail@aascu.org, or call 800-368-5622 (toll-free).

GRADUATE DEGREE PROGRAMS

MASTER'S DEGREE

The master's degree is the first academic or professional degree earned after the bachelor's degree. A traditional, full-time master's degree student may take a year or two to earn the required 30 credits. Part-time students usually take longer; it depends on the design of the degree program. In some master's degree programs, students are simply expected to take advanced-level courses and perhaps pass a culminating exam. In others, original research and a thesis are also required. Some distance learning master's degree programs have a brief residency requirement. Students usually earn a Master of Arts (M.A.), a Master of Science (M.S.), or a Master of Business Administration (M.B.A.) degree.

At the time this book was published, distance learning master's degree programs outnumbered other distance learning degree programs by a considerable margin. Most of these degree programs are professional in nature and are designed for working adults with experience in the field. If you are interested in a master's degree in library science, business, or education, you are in luck. These are fields in which there are many distance master's degree programs from which to choose.

However, if you are looking for a distance learning master's degree program in an academic field, such as English language and literature, chemistry, or ethnic and cultural studies, your choices are far more limited. That's because most master's programs in academic fields are campus based.

Another type of master's degree that is offered via distance learning is the interdisciplinary degree. Some are offered in liberal studies or humanities and are granted for advanced study and a culminating project or thesis. Others combine academic and professional areas of study. Still others are offered in broad subject areas like environmental studies, in which students are expected to design their own course of study based on their particular interests.

In the future, the number of distance academic and interdisciplinary master's degree programs is likely to increase, but far more slowly than the number of professional degree programs, for which the demand is much greater.

DOCTORAL DEGREE

The doctoral degree, the highest degree awarded, is earned after an advanced course of study that usually culminates in original research and a dissertation, an extended written work. The traditional on-campus doctoral student takes four to ten years to complete the degree, but many distance learning doctoral programs are structured to streamline the process. Thus, some doctoral degrees can be earned in as little as three years. Most distance learning doctoral programs, even those offered by virtual universities like the University of Phoenix Online, have a brief residency requirement. The Doctor of Philosophy (Ph.D.) is the most common doctoral degree; it is awarded in fields that range from philosophy to geology to communication. Other frequently awarded doctoral degrees include the Doctor of Education (Ed.D.), Doctor of Business Administration (D.B.A.), Doctor of Engineering (Eng.D.), and Doctor of Psychology (Psy.D.). There are far fewer distance learning doctoral programs than master's programs. However, you can find programs in a wide range of fields, although the number of programs within each field may be limited. You can earn a distance learning doctoral degree in fields as diverse as business, engineering, computer science, counseling psychology, instructional technology, education, human services, library science, English literature, management, pharmacy, and public policy. As with distance learning master's degrees, distance learning doctoral degrees tend to be professional rather than academic. Many of these degree programs are designed with the professional working adult in mind.

EARNING GRADUATE-LEVEL CREDIT FOR KNOWLEDGE AND EXPERIENCE

There is disagreement among institutions of higher education about whether to award graduate-level credit for knowledge acquired outside academia. At present, many graduate schools do not offer credit to students for knowledge and experience acquired before enrollment in the program, no matter how deep or extensive that knowledge and experience may be. However, other less conservative institutions are more open to granting graduate credit for life experience. Check with the schools and programs in which you are interested to see what their policies are.

CERTIFICATE PROGRAMS

Distance learning certificate programs can train you for a new career or give you a foundation in a new subject even if you've already earned a college degree in an entirely different field. A certificate program usually consists of around six to ten courses, all focused on a single profession or subject, and it can be earned at the undergraduate or graduate level. Some schools now offer a portion of a master's or other degree as a certificate. This allows you to take part of the full degree curriculum and either stop at the certification level or proceed through for the entire degree. If this is an option that interests you, be sure to consider the admissions requirements carefully. If you think you may matriculate through to the entire degree, be sure you understand the admissions requirements for each program because they may differ.

PROFESSIONAL CERTIFICATE PROGRAMS

To give you just a few examples of professional certificate programs offered via distance learning, within the engineering profession there are certificates in computer-integrated manufacturing, systems engineering, and fire-protection engineering. In business, there are distance learning certificate programs in information technology and health services management. In education, distance learning certificates include early reading instruction, children's literature, and English as a second language. In health care, certificates include medical assisting, home health nursing, and health-care administration. In law, distance learning certificates are offered in paralegal/legal assistant studies and legal issues for business professionals.

Professional certificate programs are often designed with the help of professional associations and licensing boards, and thus encompass real-world, practical knowledge. Many are designed to prepare students for professional certification or licensure. At the end of the program, the student sits for an exam and earns a state-recognized certificate from a certifying agency or licensing board. *If this is your goal, you should make sure that the certification program you want to take meets the certifying agency or licensing board's requirements.* That way, you won't waste your time or money completing a program that won't help you meet your ultimate professional goals.

CERTIFICATE PROGRAMS IN ACADEMIC SUBJECTS

Less common, but still available via distance learning, are undergraduate and graduate certificate programs in many academic subjects. At the undergraduate level, you can earn a certificate in areas such as American studies, Chinese language and literature, English composition, creative writing, ethnic and cultural studies, general studies, humanities, and liberal arts and sciences. If you later enroll in an undergraduate degree program, you may be able to apply the credits earned in a certificate program toward your degree.

At the graduate level, you can earn a certificate via distance learning in subjects like biology, English language and literature, geography, physiological psychology, religious studies, and statistics.

INDIVIDUAL COURSES

If you are seeking to update your professional skills, acquire specialized knowledge, earn a few credits toward a degree, or simply take a class for your own pleasure, individual distance learning courses may be for you. Many institutions of higher education venture into distance learning by offering a few classes scattered throughout various departments. As their experience with distance education increases, they begin to offer complete programs of study. Thus, if you are interested in just taking a few courses, you have the widest range of choices. You can find individual courses in subjects that range from accounting to animal sciences and from art history to aviation—and that's just a random sample beginning with the letter *A*.

There are several options that may be open to you when you take an individual course, such as taking the course for credit, taking it without earning credit, or earning Continuing Education Units (CEUs). The option you select depends on your purpose for taking the course.

TAKING A COURSE FOR CREDIT

If you are enrolled in a degree program and need a few credits, taking a distance learning course may help you satisfy your degree requirements. Your own college or university may offer courses via distance learning. In fact, students enrolled in conventional on-campus degree programs sometimes take distance learning courses from their schools when they go home for the summer. For example, Iowa's Drake University offers online summer courses to its students.

If your own institution does not offer suitable distance learning courses, you may be able to take a distance education course from any regionally accredited college or university and get credit for it. You may even be able to save some tuition money if you select a course at a community college or a less expensive four-year college or university. The credits you earn will probably be transferable to the institution in which you are enrolled. *But before you enroll in a course at another college or university, be sure to check with your own school to make sure it will accept the credits.* Many colleges and universities require that you obtain a minimum number of credits from core courses and courses in your major in order to earn their degree. To avoid losing time and money on a course that won't be recognized by your school, it's wise to check with your academic adviser and work out a degree plan before you take courses from other institutions. If you are not currently enrolled in a degree program but think you may be in the future, taking a couple of distance education courses for credit is a good way to see whether or not a distance education degree program is for you. Later you may be able to apply the credits toward your degree.

NONCREDIT COURSES

If learning for the sake of learning or acquiring specific professional knowledge is your goal, taking a distance education course on a noncredit basis may be the way to go. Such courses may help you prepare for a new career or study for professional licensure and certification.

Just as you can audit an on-campus course for a lesser charge than if you were taking the course for credit, you can audit a distance learning course as well. Students who audit a course don't receive a grade, so they are not usually required to turn in assignments or take exams. Still, many do so in order to maximize the learning experience.

CONTINUING EDUCATION UNITS

Distance learning is a good option for working adults whose professions require continuing education, even after they've earned their degree, certificate, or license. Many states mandate continuing education for people in professions such as teaching, nursing, and accounting. For example, New Jersey requires teachers to complete 100 hours of professional development work every five years. Professionals in engineering, business, and computer science may also opt to keep up with developments in their field through distance learning. If you take a distance learning course for professional enhancement, you don't necessarily have to earn regular college credits for it. Instead, you may be able to earn CEUs. The CEU system is a nationally recognized program that provides a standardized measure for accumulating, transferring, and recognizing participation in continuing education programs. One CEU is defined as 10 contact hours of participation in an organized continuing education experience under responsible sponsorship, capable direction, and qualified instruction. Some institutions will permit you to take courses for continuing education credits rather than for regular credit or no credit. It is still important to take the courses from a properly accredited program, however, so that employers and professional agencies will recognize them.

FINDING PROGRAMS AND COURSES

THE INTERNET

The Internet is an excellent place to start your search for information about distance learning courses and programs. One Internet database is the International Distance Learning Course Finder, provided by International Where and How. When you search for a course, you can specify course subject, course name, country, or institution; and you can narrow the search by language of instruction, mode of instructional technology, and type of credit you are seeking. The Course Finder seems to work well for locating individual courses, but it seems less efficient when asked to locate degree programs.

If you have particular institutions in mind, you can log on to their Web sites to find out about their distance learning courses and degrees. Some of these sites provide distance learning self-assessments and explanations of course delivery systems as well as academic information about courses and programs.

PRINT DIRECTORIES

Print directories are another excellent source of information about distance education courses and degree programs, although one should adhere to this word of caution about using the print directories: There are many directories still in libraries and bookstores that were published recently but are already quite out of date. So many new distance learning courses and degree programs are being offered each year that you must make sure you consult the most recent directories. Otherwise, you may miss the ideal course or program for you.

WHO OFFERS DISTANCE EDUCATION?

As communication technologies have improved and the need for continuous lifelong learning has increased, the nature of postsecondary education has begun to change. Traditional colleges and universities, which used to be the sole purveyors of higher education, now find themselves competing with a range of unconventional providers, including corporate universities, for-profit virtual universities, and unaffiliated distance learning providers. From the student's point of view, the array of institutions that offer distance learning can be confusing. What difference does it make to you whether you take a distance learning course or program from a traditional college, through a consortium of institutions of higher education, from one of the new virtual universities, or from an unaffiliated online provider?

Whether or not the institution matters depends on your purpose. If you just take a few courses for professional development or for your own pleasure and never plan to seek certification or college credit, then your choice of institution is not critical. You can just choose the distance learning provider that seems to have the courses that best suit your informal needs. However, if you plan to earn college credit, professional certification, or a degree, your choice of provider becomes much more important. You must choose an institution whose courses and degrees are widely recognized and accepted in your field. That may mean sticking to the accredited bricks-and-mortar colleges for distance learning programs, or it may mean enrolling in an innovative degree program from a virtual university only a few years old. In this section, we'll describe some of the institutions and partnerships that offer distance learning in order to acquaint you with the variety of providers that exists. In the next section, we will explain some criteria that you can use to evaluate distance education offerings.

TRADITIONAL COLLEGES AND UNIVERSITIES

The most familiar group of distance education providers consists of the traditional colleges, universities, graduate schools, community colleges, technical schools, and vocational schools. In these institutions, distance education arose as individual administrators and faculty members took the initiative to use new technologies to deliver off-campus instruction to students. As the number of courses grew, many institutions developed whole degree programs as the next step.

Among the traditional colleges and universities, public institutions are more likely to offer distance education courses and degree programs than private institutions. In addition, larger institutions are more likely to have distance learning offerings than smaller institutions.

The greatest advantage that most traditional colleges and universities bring to the distance education field is that they are established, well-known institutions with reputable faculty members and lots of experience in education. In other words, they enter the distance learning market with solid educational credentials. If they fall short, it is likely to be in the areas of instructional and information technology. Because a lot of distance education courses are developed ad hoc, the quality of the instructional technology may vary considerably, even from one course to another within the same school. In addition, traditional colleges and universities may fall short in information technology support for faculty members and students. For example, the Gartner Group, an information technology research organization, recommends that organizations have one information technology staff person for every 50 to 75 users. In contrast, colleges and universities report an average of one technical support person for every 150 to 800 users. Recognizing this shortcoming, many colleges and universities have established policies and procedures to set up instructional technology standards and consistency, and they have increased their technical resources and training efforts to support faculty members and students. In addition, because developing high-quality distance education courses and programs is time-consuming and expensive, colleges and universities have begun to form partnerships to pool their resources. These partnerships, called consortia, have quickly developed into major players in the world of distance higher education.

CONSORTIA

Distance learning consortia are associations or partnerships of higher education institutions that have agreed to cooperate to provide distance learning courses and resources. Most consortia are designed to provide students with a greater selection of both courses and faculty expertise than is available at a single institution. Some consortia also offer centralized student and faculty support services. Just as there are many variations on the basic on-campus program, there are many distance education consortium models too.

It's important to remember that most distance learning consortia are not degree-granting institutions to which the student applies. Though there are exceptions to this, as in the case of Western Governors University and National Technological University (discussed later in the section), students normally apply directly to at least one school in the consortium as a means of accessing the resources of other member institutions.

Almost without exception, accredited universities in consortia have roughly the same application procedures and admissions requirements for distance degree programs as for traditional campus-based programs. In general, minimum grade point averages, standardized test scores of a certain percentile, and letters of recommendation or intent are required for both bachelor's and master's degree programs. The exception is the competency-based program that waives academic credentials and previous schooling and instead uses workplace experience and learned skill-based assessments to place students. So why do you need to know about consortia if you probably will never apply to one? The answer is that by enrolling in a college or university degree program, you may find yourself in a consortium without even realizing it, especially if you attend a state university.

TYPES OF CONSORTIA

Over the last few years, several types of consortia have emerged as the most successful and most popular distance education models. Among them are statewide consortia of public universities and colleges, statewide consortia of public and private institutions, regional consortia, and consortia of peer institutions of higher education.

Statewide Consortia of Public Colleges and Universities. On the tightly focused side of the spectrum, a consortium may consist of the campuses of a single state university system. Students access the distance learning offerings of the various state colleges through a portal sometimes referred to as a virtual university.

A good example of a public statewide consortium is the University of Texas TeleCampus collaboration, which consists of fifteen UT campuses (www.telecampus.utsystem.edu). In collaborative degree plans offered via the TeleCampus, you may apply to one school, take courses from several partner institutions, use centralized support services, and receive a fully accredited degree from the "home" campus to which you originally applied. The TeleCampus serves as both a portal to distance education offerings in the Texas system and as a centralized point of service.

Many other states operate or develop consortia of their public colleges and universities, including Connecticut, Illinois, Kansas, Massachusetts, Michigan, New Jersey, New York, Ohio, Oklahoma, Oregon, South Dakota, and Tennessee. All have arrangements in place whereby students can take some transferable credits online from more than one institution and apply them to a degree at their home institution.

Statewide Consortia of Public and Private Colleges and Universities. Broadening the scope a bit is the statewide consortium that includes both public and private institutions of higher education. Students in the state can use a single Web site to select distance education courses offered by member colleges and universities. If you are enrolled in a degree program at one member institution, you have access to distance learning courses given by other member institutions. Although the consortia members typically work together to maximize the transferability of credits from one college or university to another, it is still usually up to you to ensure that credits earned elsewhere can be applied to your home institution's degree.

For example, Kentucky Virtual Campus (KYVC) encompasses more than fifty institutions in the state of Kentucky, ranging from universities to technical colleges (www.kyvu.org). Each member institution charges its own tuition rates for in-state and out-of-state students. In addition to maintaining a centralized Internet directory of all distance learning courses offered in Kentucky, KYVC offers exceptional student support services. For example, you can fill out a common form to apply online to any of the fifty member institutions. Once you are admitted to the KYVC system, you have centralized online access to every library book in the system as well as online access to the full text of 5,000 journals. If you wish to check out a book, it will be sent to the nearest public library, where you can pick it up free of charge. If there is no library nearby, the book will be sent by courier to your home or office. Your academic records will be maintained by each institution at which you take a course, but also by KYVC, which will keep your complete records from all institutions.

Regional Consortia. Regional consortia include institutions of higher education from more than one state. Such consortia may involve public institutions, private institutions, or a mix of both. The Southern Regional Education Board (SREB) launched the Electronic Campus in 1998 and now offers more than 3,200 courses from 262 colleges and universities in sixteen states (www.electroniccampus.org). The Electronic Campus attempts to guarantee a standard of quality in the courses it lists by reviewing them to make sure they are well set up and supported by adequate services. It does not judge curriculum (it leaves that to member institutions) nor does it list courses in their first year of instruction.

From the Electronic Campus Web site, you can identify distance learning programs and courses that are available from all member institutions. For more detailed information, you can search the site by college or university, discipline, level, and state, including course descriptions and how the programs and courses are delivered. You can also connect directly to a particular college or university to learn about registration, enrollment, and cost.

The Electronic Campus system is administratively decentralized. The acceptance of transfer credits and the use of credits for program requirements are determined by the college or university in which the student is enrolled. Likewise, all institutions set their own levels for in-state and out-of-state tuition, maintain individual student records, and determine policy with respect to access to their own student services. Therefore, if you take three classes from three different institutions you might have to be admitted to all three, pay three different tuition rates, and contact all three institutions for your academic records. A unique model of regional distance education collaboration, consisting of members from nineteen states, is Western Governors University (www.wgu.edu). Unlike most other virtual universities that serve as the hub of a consortium, WGU enrolls its own students and grants its own degrees by assessing students' knowledge through competency-based examinations. WGU does not teach its own courses, but it provides its students with access to courses from member institutions.

Other regional consortia include the National Universities Degree Consortium, a collaboration of ten accredited universities from across the United States (www.nudc.org); and the Canadian Virtual University, which includes seven universities across Canada (www.cvu-uvc.ca). Today, students can even choose to participate in a global consortium like CREAD, the inter-American nonprofit distance education consortium, based at Nova Southeastern University in South Florida.

Consortia of Peer Institutions of Higher Education. Groups of institutions sometimes form consortia because they have a common orientation or complementary strengths from which students might benefit.

For example, the Jesuit Distance Education Network (JesuitNET) of the Association of Jesuit Colleges and Universities seeks to expand the array of learning options for students on its twenty-eight campuses throughout the United States (www.ajcunet.edu). Through the JesuitNET system, a student enrolled at any member institution is able to take fully transferable online courses at any other member institution. Tuition rates are set by individual colleges and universities. Through its Web site, JesuitNET promotes these schools' online degree and certificate programs as well as individual courses.

PROS AND CONS OF CONSORTIA LEARNING MODELS

One obvious advantage of consortia is the pooling of resources. More university partners translates to more choices in curriculum, and often a shared expense in developing instructional design and technology. Consortia can offer a centralized database or course schedule that allows you to find members' courses easily rather than having to search many institutions' materials and Web sites for what you need. You may also have the chance to choose from among a group of respected faculty members from within the consortia, which allows you to find the teachers with expertise most closely suited to your academic and professional interests. This large sampling of faculty members tends to offer a more diverse worldview in the classroom. And, a consortium can often provide essential student services on a scale not fiscally achievable by a single university. For example, a dozen universities can pool resources for a much broader digital library than any single school could supply on its own.

However, from the student's point of view, consortia can have problems, many of which can be attributed to their relative newness. The most critical of these for students are problems with transferring credits. Other drawbacks may include large class sizes and problems in communication.

Problems with Transferring Credits. One problem that sometimes comes up for students trying to earn an entire degree, or part of a degree, online is that their home institution may require a minimum number of "home" credits, yet it may not offer enough courses via distance learning for a student to meet that minimum. "I am concerned because [my home campus] offers a limited number of online classes," says Andrea Bessel, who earned a bachelor's degree in business administration with a concentration in finance. Bessel, who works full time and preferred the convenience of online to on-campus courses, took classes from several institutions in the State University of New York (SUNY) Learning Network (www.sln.suny.edu). "It was great that other SUNY campuses offered more courses," continues Bessel, "but I was concerned about accumulating too many transfer credits—you were only allowed so many."

In the future, this problem is likely to arise less often for several reasons. First, as distance education degree programs become more common and well known, students are likely to search them out and apply directly to the institution that offers them. In contrast, like many other students, Bessel applied to her local state college campus and only later discovered that taking online courses within the statewide system was much more convenient than traveling to class. Second, individual institutions will continue to add to their distance education offerings, broadening the course choices for their "home" students. And third, some state systems and other consortia may eventually decide to liberalize their rules on transfer credit maximums within the consortium as the demand for distance degrees increases.

Indeed, some consortia have already succeeded in solving credit transfer problems, and others are addressing the challenge of reconciling differing credit transfer policies and logistics. *However, to ensure that any courses you take will successfully transfer from one institution to another (and ultimately toward your degree), you should secure an academic adviser at the start of your program and investigate the transferability of credits before you register for courses at other institutions within the consortium.* Serving as your own adviser brings the risk that some courses may ultimately not transfer toward your degree.

Large Class Size. Because so many students have access to courses in a consortium, online classes may reach an unmanageable size if limits are not placed on the student-to-teacher ratio. Many schools now adopt a ceiling on the number of students allowed in an online class, with teaching assistants or subsections of the course added for each additional set of students. This is vital to the processing of information and interaction required in the successful online course. Faculty members often find that a class of 25 students is quite manageable, but more may become problematic.

Miscommunication. Communication may be difficult in a consortium. The larger the consortium, the more likely that many universities or university systems are involved, and therefore you may need to communicate with several institutions that have differing policies and procedures. Additional communication snags can arise when you try to move your student records from one campus to the next. Some consortia have spent considerable time, effort, and money to make this tedious and laborious process appear seamless to you as a student. For those that have not, you should be prepared to take a proactive stance in helping to see that your records are successfully moved from one department, college, or university to another.

COMPARING THE SINGLE UNIVERSITY TO THE CONSORTIUM

A student who is looking for a learning community with school pride and a great deal of local loyalty may find the multicampus environment of a consortium less desirable than the collegiality of the single university environment. In today's workplace and economy, however, many students opt for the flexibility and increased curriculum choices of a consortium over an individual school. Many consortia have succeeded in creating a sense of community for learners, and many more are attempting to do so. The high level of dialogue in the online environment can often build friendships, connections, and communities not achieved in a traditional environment. A single university can offer you the chance to immerse yourself in one department (of your major, for example), but a consortium can offer a wider variety of choices in mentors and philosophies. As a student, you should think about which you'd prefer.

VIRTUAL UNIVERSITIES

In recent years, the development of communication technology has led to a new type of institution called a virtual university. It's a school without a campus that delivers instruction and degree programs exclusively via technology and usually for a profit. The University of Phoenix Online, Walden University, the United

States Open University, and Jones International University are all examples of virtual universities. Some of these institutions have years of experience in distance learning and have evolved as the technologies have changed. For example, Walden University is nearly 40 years old, and the University of Phoenix Online was established in 1989 as an offshoot of the University of Phoenix, which was founded in 1976. Others, like the United States Open University, are newer with a much shorter track record. What most of these institutions have in common is a focus on education for adults. Their course offerings, degree programs, and student services are all geared toward the busy working adult who needs the flexibility of distance education. For example, courses at the University of Phoenix Online are delivered via the Internet. Students take one 5-week course at a time, which allows them to focus their effort intensively on one subject. Student services can be accessed via the university Web site. "We are customer-service oriented," says Russell Paden, Vice President of Academic Operations at the University of Phoenix Online. "We make things easy and convenient for the student." Virtual universities have a mixed reputation in the world of higher education. Although their degrees are accepted by many employers, they are often looked down upon by traditional academics. A few are regionally accredited, some are too new to be accredited, and some are modern versions of the old diploma mills (see "Selecting a Good Distance Learning Program" for more on accreditation).

From a student's point of view, then, the biggest disadvantage of a virtual university may be its less-than-stellar educational reputation, whether deserved or not. A great advantage of the best of these institutions, however, is that they tend to be sophisticated in terms of instructional technology and design and technical support. To the student, this can mean ease, convenience, and flexibility.

THE NEW ONLINE PROVIDERS

The growth of the distance learning market in higher education, continuing education, and training has attracted investors and educators who are eager to provide courses to adults, primarily via the Internet. There are many of these startup ventures, and they take many forms. The following are examples to illustrate:

- The Global Education Network (GEN) offers distance education courses from some of the top colleges in the United States, including Brown, Wellesley, and Williams.
- KaplanCollege.com offers graduate courses for teachers through the John F. Kennedy University.

In the coming years, the new online providers will begin to sort themselves out as some models succeed and some fail. If you are taking courses through your employer or for personal reasons, you may find that one of these companies has courses that meet your needs. If, however, you are looking for a degree program, you are better off sticking with well-established institutions of higher education, at least at present.

SELECTING A GOOD DISTANCE LEARNING PROGRAM

As a prospective distance learning student, you should begin to evaluate programs in which you are interested as much as you would any campus-based, traditional program. The first question, of course, is: Does the curriculum meet your educational and professional goals? If it doesn't, there's not much point in looking into that program any further, however flexible and convenient it seems. If the program does seem to meet your educational needs, then the real work of evaluating it must begin.

Distance education students need to be especially concerned about the quality of the programs they are considering for two main reasons. First, there are a lot of diploma mills out there. As we've seen, there has been a proliferation of distance learning degree programs spurred by the Internet. Many are legitimate, but some are not. As one distance bachelor's degree student put it, "Admission to some online programs consists of nothing more than your name, date of birth, and a check." In fact, to demonstrate how easy it is to set up an online "university" that looks authentic, Emir Mohammed created a Web site for Oxford Open University, a fictitious virtual university, complete with a list of imaginary faculty members with degrees from bogus institutions. So if you run across a school that promises you a degree for little time, effort, or money, be cautious. If it sounds too good to be true, it probably is.

The second reason distance learning students must be especially careful about quality is that in many quarters, distance degrees are still considered the poor relations of degrees earned on campus. "One area of confusion for working adult students is the reaction to distance learning from traditional academia," says Russell Paden, Vice President of Academic Operations for the University of Phoenix Online. "Although attitudes are changing, some in the traditional academic world still think their way is the only way." Robert V. Steiner, who directed the distance learning project at Teachers College, Columbia University, agrees. "For better or worse, justly or not," he says, "there continues to be a perception that distance education degree programs are inferior to traditional programs." Fritz J. Messere, Professor of Communication Studies at the State University of New York at Oswego, thinks that in five or six years, that attitude will change. "When we see what the people with distance degrees actually accomplish in the future, our reluctance to acknowledge that these are real degrees and meaningful educational experiences will disappear."

However, in the meantime you need to evaluate each distance education program that looks promising to ensure that its certificate or degree will be of value to you in the future. What can you do to ensure that a distance credential will be recognized in the academic, professional, and/or business communities? What can you do to assess whether or not the program and the university are of high quality? Basically, you must do a lot of research. You must gather information from the program, university, accrediting agencies, professional associations, faculty, current and former students, and colleagues. Only then can you make an informed decision about whether a program is good as well as right for you.

To guide you in this task, this section describes some of the criteria you should keep in mind as you evaluate each distance education program. *Pay particular attention to the sections on reputation and accreditation.* More than any other factors, a school and program's reputation and accreditation status can serve as benchmarks of quality that will affect the value of your degree.

REPUTATION

"Look for a brand name—a recognized university," suggests Fritz J. Messere of SUNY Oswego. For many students, the reputation of the school is the paramount factor in selecting a program. Sonja Cole, a middle-school media specialist who enrolled in a continuing professional education program at Rutgers University in New Jersey, explains, "I know that Rutgers has an excellent reputation for academic rigor, so I assumed that their online courses would be just as challenging and stimulating." She continues, "The most important factor to me was the reputation of the school, because distance learning programs are not always taken seriously by administrators and business people . . . . If you can say you took distance courses at a very reputable school, they will be more likely to give you credit." Not only should you consider the reputation of a university in general, you should consider the reputation of a distance degree from a university *in your field*. For example, if you plan to earn a bachelor's degree at a distance to prepare for graduate work, find out whether or not graduate programs in your field will accept an undergraduate distance degree, even from a reputable institution.

"If you are in doubt about the validity of a distance degree in your chosen field, ask around," advises Patti Wolf, former Associate Professor of Information Systems Management at University of Maryland University College. When Wolf was looking for a doctoral program for herself, almost all of her colleagues advised her that a distance degree would not be as well accepted in her chosen career as a traditional degree. Another doctoral student, who is earning an Ed.D. from a relatively new virtual university, regrets that "the one thing I didn't do [was] speak to administrators in local universities to review the reputation of the school I finally chose. Even though the program is still exactly what I wanted and the convenience, schedule, and costs meet my needs, the public perception of this program is not wonderful." Carla Gentry, who earned a distance master's degree in nursing (nurse-practitioner) at Gonzaga University in Washington, puts the importance of reputation succinctly: "You wouldn't want to spend all that time and money and then find out that the degree isn't worth anything."

ACCREDITATION

The accreditation status of a college, university, or program can give you an indication of its general quality and reputation. But just what does accreditation mean, and how does it affect distance learners?

WHAT IS ACCREDITATION?

In the United States, authority over postsecondary educational institutions is decentralized. The states, not the federal government, have the authority to regulate educational institutions within their borders, and as a consequence, standards and quality vary considerably for "state-approved" schools. You will find many state-approved schools that are not accredited, and many that are.

In order to ensure a basic level of quality, the practice of accrediting institutions arose. Private, nongovernmental educational agencies with a regional or national scope have adopted standards to evaluate whether or not colleges and universities provide educational programs at basic levels of quality. Institutions that seek accreditation conduct an in-depth self-study to measure their performance against the standards. The accrediting agency then conducts an on-site evaluation and either awards accreditation or preaccreditation status—or denies accreditation. Periodically the agency reevaluates each institution to make sure its continued accreditation is warranted. So accreditation is not a one-shot deal—an institution must maintain high standards or it runs the risk of jeopardizing its accreditation status as a result of one of the periodic evaluations.

Seeking accreditation is entirely voluntary on the part of the institution of higher education. The initial accreditation process takes a long time—as much as five or ten years—and it costs money. You can see that a very new school will not have been in operation long enough to be accredited.

INSTITUTIONAL AND SPECIALIZED ACCREDITATION

There are two basic types of accreditation: institutional accreditation and specialized accreditation. Institutional accreditation is awarded to an institution by one of six regional accrediting agencies and many national accrediting agencies, such as the Distance Education and Training Council. The regional accrediting agencies play the largest role in institutional accreditation (see the Appendix for a list of the regional accrediting agencies). If a college or university is regionally accredited, that means that the institution as a whole has met the accrediting agency's standards. Within the institution, particular programs and departments contribute to the institution's objectives at varying levels of quality. There are several benefits of enrolling in a program at a regionally accredited college or university:

- You are assured of a basic level of quality education and services.
- Any credits you earn are more likely to be transferable to other regionally accredited institutions, although we've seen that each institution makes its own decisions on transfer credits on a case-by-case basis.
- Any certificate or degree you earn is more likely to be recognized by other colleges and universities and by employers as a legitimate credential.
- You may qualify for federal loans and grants because regionally accredited institutions are eligible to participate in Title IV financial aid programs (see "Paying for Your Education" for more on financial aid).

In contrast to institutional accreditation, specialized accreditation usually applies to a single department, program, or school that is part of a larger institution of higher education. The accredited unit may be as big as a college within a university or as small as a curriculum within a field of study. Most specialized accrediting agencies review units within institutions that are regionally accredited, although some also accredit freestanding institutions. There are specialized accrediting agencies in almost fifty fields, including allied health, art and design, Bible college education, business, engineering, law, marriage and family therapy, nursing, psychology, and theology. Specialized accreditation may or may not be a consideration for you when you evaluate distance education programs. That's because the role of specialized accreditation varies considerably depending on the field of study. In some professional fields, you must have a degree or certificate from a program with specialized accreditation in order to take qualifying exams or practice the profession. In other fields, specialized accreditation has little or no effect on your ability to work. Thus, it's especially important that you find out what role accreditation plays in your field since it may affect your professional future as well as the quality of your education.

CHECKING ON A SCHOOL AND ITS ACCREDITORS

Since accreditation is awarded by private organizations, any group can hang out a shingle and proclaim itself an accrediting agency. Some diploma mills, for example, have been known to create their own accrediting agency and then proclaim themselves "accredited." So how can you tell (1) if the school or college in which you are interested is regionally accredited, (2) if the program has the specialized accreditation you need, and (3) if the agencies that have accredited the school and program are legitimate? Of course, you can simply ask the school or program, but since accreditation is so important, it's probably a lot wiser to check elsewhere.

First, check with the regional accrediting agency that covers the state in which the school is located. Then check with any specialized accrediting agency that may assess the particular program in which you are interested.

To find out if an accrediting agency is legitimate and nationally recognized, you can consult the Council for Higher Education Accreditation (CHEA), a private agency that accredits the accreditors (www.chea.org). Or you can check with the U.S. Department of Education. Their Web site has a complete list of institutional and specialized accrediting agencies recognized by the federal government (www.ed.gov/admins/finaid/accred/index.html). This Web site will also tell you whether or not accreditation by a particular agency makes the school eligible to participate in federal financial aid programs. A list of regional and specialized accrediting agencies, with contact information, is also provided in the *Additional Resources* section.

CHECKING ON CANADIAN INSTITUTIONS OF HIGHER EDUCATION

In Canada, as in the United States, there is no centralized governmental accrediting agency. Instead, the provincial governments evaluate the quality of university programs in each province, with a few nationwide agencies evaluating professional programs. To check on a Canadian university, you can contact the appropriate provincial department of education. To get general information about accreditation in Canada, visit the Web site of the Council of Ministers of Education at www.cmec.ca. Their Web site also has contact information and links to the provincial departments of education.

CHECKING ON AN UNACCREDITED INSTITUTION

As we've seen, seeking accreditation is a voluntary process, and some legitimate schools choose not to undertake it. In addition, the newer virtual universities may not have been around long enough to be accredited. So what can you do to make sure a school is legitimate if it is not accredited?

First, you can call the state agency with jurisdiction over higher education in the state in which the school is located. The agency can at least tell you whether or not the school is operating with a legitimate charter, and it may be able to tell you if any complaints have been lodged or legal action taken against it. Second, you can call the school and ask why it is not accredited and whether the school has plans to seek accreditation. If the school tells you it has applied for accreditation, double-check its status with the agency it names. Third, you can consult with people in your field about the school's reputation and the value of its degree. Remember, in some fields, a degree from an unaccredited school or program will bar you from professional licensure and practice. So keep in mind that enrolling in an unaccredited school or program can be risky. If you can avoid it, do so.

ACCREDITATION ISSUES RELATING TO DISTANCE EDUCATION

In the United States during the 1990s, controversy arose over the accreditation of online programs within traditional universities and the accreditation of completely virtual universities. On the one hand, many felt that online degree programs should be evaluated using the same criteria as other degree programs within institutions of higher education. Others thought that new standards were needed to properly evaluate distance education.

Although this issue has not yet been settled, the six regional accrediting agencies have proposed uniform guidelines for evaluating distance education. The impetus for this move is the fact that many distance education programs cross regional borders; the agencies want to ensure that similar standards are adopted across the country. Among the proposed criteria specific to accrediting distance education are faculty control of course content, technical and program support for both faculty members and students, and evaluation and assessment methods for measuring student learning. However, until these or other guidelines are accepted, distance education programs will continue to be evaluated using the same criteria as on-campus programs.

PROGRAM QUALITY

The reputation of a college or university and its accreditation status can give you a broad idea of its standing in the academic and professional world. If you are pursuing a graduate degree or know your field of interest as an undergraduate, it's important to separate the reputation of the program or department in which you are interested from the reputation of the university to which it belongs. Granted, in many cases, both the program and the university will have similar reputations. But in some cases, you may find a below-average program at an excellent university or an above-average program at a university with a lesser reputation.

Keep in mind that you should be looking for a high-quality curriculum and good faculty; the fact that the program is taught at a distance should be secondary. "I chose this program because it would have been one of my top three choices if I had decided to pursue a full-time [on-campus] master's program," explains Lara Hollenczer, who earned a distance master's degree in communications management at Syracuse University. Hollenczer suggests talking to professors and current students to get a better idea of a program in which you are interested.

ACADEMIC QUALITY

One way to assess the quality of a program, as we have seen, is to find out whether or not it is accredited by a specialized agency—if that applies in your field. But there are other ways to assess a program's academic quality. First, look at the curriculum. Does it cover what you need to learn? Is the syllabus up to date? For one master's degree student in nursing (family nurse practitioner studies), the quality of the curriculum was the factor that led her to choose Gonzaga University. "I definitely wanted to know that when I graduated I would have a good education and know what I was doing," she explains.

Next, check some of the program's student data. For example, what percentage of students who enroll actually complete the degree? What percentage of students are employed in a field relating to their studies? What are some of the program's graduates doing today? A program with a high completion rate and successful graduates is preferable to one with a high dropout rate.

FACULTY

Second, check out the faculty members. What are their credentials? What are their areas of expertise? Are they well regarded in their field? If the program is professional in nature, look for faculty members with a blend of academic background and professional experience. If the program is academic, you should find out whether tenure-track professors with Ph.D.'s teach both the on-campus and distance courses or if distance courses are relegated to part-time adjunct faculty members and/or assistants. Finally, evaluate whether or not the faculty is experienced both with the course content and with the instructional medium. If a program looks interesting to you, get in touch with a couple of faculty members to discuss it. You can tell a lot about a program by whether or not the faculty members are willing to take some time to talk to prospective students.

EXPERIENCE WITH ADULT LEARNERS

A third area of concern is the program's experience with adult learners. If you're an adult learner and choose to enroll in a college oriented to young undergraduates, you may find yourself struggling to cope. "My concern would be that in some programs the adult learner is an afterthought," says Claudine SchWeber, Associate Provost, Distance Education and Lifelong Learning at University of Maryland University College. "Adults are more critical consumers, and that won't fly these days." Working adult students have different needs than full-time on-campus students, and assessing the degree to which a program takes those needs into account can help you decide whether or not a program is a good match for you.

For Robin Barnes, who earned a distance master's degree in nursing (family nurse-practitioner studies) at Gonzaga University, the flexibility of the faculty in dealing with adult students was extremely important. "We were adult learners who had lives and jobs outside of school. If we needed more time for a paper due to work schedules or a family crisis, the instructors were very understanding." Carla Gentry, in the same program, agrees. "The most important factor to me was the flexibility of the program and the staff's willingness to work with my schedule."

INSTRUCTIONAL DESIGN AND TECHNOLOGY

There are several areas that fall under the broad category of instructional design and technology that you should assess for each program you consider.

IS THE INSTRUCTIONAL TECHNOLOGY A GOOD MATCH FOR THE CONTENT?

Your first concern in the area of instructional design and technology should be whether or not the delivery system and the content are a good match. "How can you evaluate whether the technology and content mesh?" asks Robert V. Steiner of Teacher's College, Columbia University. "Online courses are more suitable for knowledge-intensive fields like business and engineering," he points out. "Subjects involving skills development and human interaction are more difficult to convey online." So, for example, in many behavioral sciences courses that involve clinical components, you need to be able to watch human interaction. In many science courses, you need to be able to do lab work. Such courses are more suited to two-way interactive video or on-campus formats than to the online format.

IS THE INSTRUCTIONAL TECHNOLOGY A GOOD MATCH FOR YOU?

Your second consideration is whether or not the instructional technology is a good match for your skills, personality, and learning style. In "Is Distance Learning Right for You?", we covered the pros and cons of the various technologies and described the skills and temperaments best suited to each.

If you are uncertain about your ability to adapt to a program's instructional technology, there are several things you can do. "If possible, take a tour of the technology being used before you enroll," advises Patti Wolf formerly of University of Maryland University College. Many institutional Web sites offer short demos, previews, or tutorials so you can get an idea of what the instructional technology will be like. For example, if you are interested in a distance program at Penn State, you can take a sample course on its World Campus Web site. If the programs in which you are interested do not offer such amenities, ask previous students how the instructional technology worked and what level of expertise is necessary. If technology is an area of particular concern for you, you might even consider a trial run. "I would recommend taking one course before deciding to apply to a school, to see if the style works for the individual," suggests Nicole DeRaleau, who earned an environmental engineering master's degree from Worcester Polytechnic Institute. "If it doesn't work, then perhaps the credits can be transferred and there is no major loss."

HOW RELIABLE IS THE TECHNOLOGY?

On a related note, because distance students depend on technology, it's important that it be reliable. Not only will you depend on your own computer, DVD player, or TV, but you will depend on the institution's technology, too. Ask current students what their experiences have been. Does the server often go down? Are there frequent problems with camera equipment or satellite transmissions?

If the program is newly formatted for distance education, be prepared for some technological bugs to be worked out on your watch. If the prospect of participating in a maiden voyage is too anxiety-provoking, look for programs that have been running for at least a year.

Last, find out what technical support is offered to students. The best setup is free technical support accessed via a toll-free number 24 hours a day, seven days a week.

HOW DO THE FACULTY AND STUDENTS INTERACT?

You should also investigate how the communication and social issues involved in distance learning are dealt with in the programs in which you are interested. (For a review of these issues, see "Is Distance Learning Right for You?") For example, how do students and faculty members communicate? Will you be expected to log on to an online course at specific times or at your convenience? Will you be expected to participate in online discussions a certain number of times during the course? For example, at the University of Phoenix Online, students are expected to log on and participate five days out of seven. At other schools, participation requirements may be program-wide or set by individual instructors.

Another question to ask is: What is done to overcome the distance learner's social isolation? Some programs do little; others rely on group work to forge a community of learning; and still others use a cohort format, in which a group of students enrolls in a program at the same time and proceeds through it together at the same pace.

Pay particular attention to the faculty-to-student ratio in online courses. If there are more than 25 to 30 students per instructor, you're not likely to get much individual attention.

ADVISING AND OTHER SERVICES

Academic advising is one of the most important student services for distance learners, especially if you are seeking to transfer credits or earn credits through examinations or from life experience to apply to a degree. Check what advising services are offered to distance learners, and see how easy they are to access. "I tested academic advising services," reports a distance learning undergraduate at University of Maryland University College. "That was important to me because I've been out of college for such a long time and I needed some help in selecting courses to complete requirements." Advising is also of particular interest to students in a consortium. If you are interested in a program that is part of a consortium, find out if the consortium offers advising or mentoring to help you navigate among institutions and to guide your overall progress.

Other support services that are important to distance education students are libraries, bookstores, administrative support, record keeping, and technical support. Many institutions and consortia offer online and telephone access to these services for distance students. In particular, access to an online library is extremely important, especially if you don't live near a good college or university library. Find out what type of access is offered, what the library's resources are, how materials are delivered, and if training on how to use an online library is offered.

If the program in which you are interested is part of a consortium, be sure you understand how each of these student services is handled. In some cases you will have access only to your home institution's services; in other cases you will have access to the services of all member institutions.

Another thing to watch out for is the extent to which the institution as a whole has kept up with an innovative degree program. For example, at many universities, distance learning courses and programs originate in a couple of departments eager to pursue new ways of educating. However, the university's centralized academic and administrative services may lag behind, leaving distance students to struggle with a system not designed for their needs.

As you investigate a program and its services, keep in mind that the way you are treated as a prospective student can tell you something about what you will encounter once enrolled. "Look at the responsiveness of the institution," advises Robert V. Steiner of Teacher's College, Columbia University, "and ask yourself, 'How client-centered is that program?'"

RESIDENCY REQUIREMENT

Some programs, especially doctoral programs, have a residency requirement for distance learning students. The requirement may be several campus visits during the course of a semester, or a brief on-site meeting at the start of a semester. Some residency periods may last up to a week or two. In addition, you may have to travel to the campus to take exams, or you may be able to take them locally with a proctor. Be sure you understand what the on-site requirements of a program are and whether or not you can fulfill them.

TIME FRAMES

Check to see how much time you have to complete a certificate or degree program, and decide whether or not the time frame meets your needs. Some programs have a generous upper limit on the number of years you may take to complete a degree, which allows you to proceed at your own pace. Other programs may be structured on an accelerated or cohort model, with a timetable and lots of interim deadlines. If that's the case, make sure your own schedule can accommodate this. For example, if a program goes year-round and you are usually at a cabin in the woods without Internet access every summer, the program is not a good match for your lifestyle. In addition, if you are considering an accelerated or cohort degree program, make sure you have the support of your family, who may not get much attention from you during this period.

COST

The cost of a distance education degree or certificate program is often the same for on-campus and distance students. However, there are some things you should look out for:

- If you enroll in a consortium, member institutions may charge tuition at different rates.
- If you enroll in a public university, you will probably be charged out-of-state tuition if you are not a state resident.
- Some institutions charge an extra technology fee to cover the costs associated with distance education.
- If there is a residency period, you should plan on spending money for travel, accommodations, and meals.
- If you enroll in an online program, you need to budget for hardware, software, and Internet access as well as books.
- If you are interested in receiving federal financial aid, you must be enrolled in an institution accredited by one of the regional accrediting agencies or certain of the specialized agencies approved by the U.S. Department of Education (check their Web site at www.ed.gov/admins/finaid/accred/index.html).

YOUR PERSONAL CHECKLIST

This section discusses many factors that you can consider when evaluating a distance education program. Here is a checklist to sum up the criteria you should keep in mind:

- ✔ The institution's reputation
- ✔ Institutional (regional) accreditation
- ✔ Specialized accreditation, if applicable
- ✔ The program's quality: curriculum, faculty, and responsiveness to adult learners
- ✔ A good match between instructional technology and content
- ✔ A good match between instructional technology and your skills, personality, and learning style
- ✔ Interaction among students and faculty members
- ✔ Reliability of technology and good technical support
- ✔ Academic advising services
- ✔ Other support services: library, bookstore, administrative support, and record keeping
- ✔ Residency requirements, if any
- ✔ Time frame for completing certificate or degree
- ✔ Cost

Although we have described many factors, in the end there may be only three or four aspects of a program that really concern you. You may be more interested in a program's reputation than in any other factor. Or accreditation may be the most important issue for you. Perhaps you are concerned about finding a good match between your personality and learning style and the instructional design of a program. That is why the self-assessment you did while reading "Is Distance Learning Right for You?" is so crucial, since you can now focus on what's important to you when you evaluate distance programs.

So remember, keep your own educational, professional, and personal needs in the forefront during the selection process. Choosing a good program not only means choosing a high-quality program; it also means choosing a program that's a good match for you.

TAKING STANDARDIZED ADMISSIONS TESTS

For some people, the prospect of taking one of the standardized admissions tests is enough to make them put aside the idea of earning a degree indefinitely. You may be anxious about taking the SAT, Graduate Record Examinations (GRE), or one of the professional exams, but if you have chosen to apply to a program that requires an admissions test, there is no way of avoiding the experience. Many undergraduate programs require the SAT or ACT. Graduate programs often require the GRE or a professional examination, and some require a subject area test and writing assessment as well. Finally, if you are not a native speaker of English, you may need to pass a test of English language proficiency. So unless you've chosen to apply to programs that do not require an examination, you are going to have to take at least one exam—and do well on it.

Note that community colleges and many programs designed specifically for adult learners, including some distance learning programs, do not require a standardized admissions test as part of the application process. Therefore, the first thing you should do is to determine which exam(s), if any, you are expected to take. This information should appear in the packet that accompanies the program's application form. If you do not yet have this material, you should simply call the admissions office or program and ask or check the program's Web site. Once you know which exam you must take, contact the testing service that gives the exam and request registration materials or register online. Information on contacting the testing services appears in the Appendix.

Before we go into detail about the tests, it might be helpful to discuss how an admissions committee might use your score. The role played by the SAT or ACT on the undergraduate level is similar to the GRE or GMAT on the graduate level. These tests provide a benchmark. Essentially, your test score is one of the few objective bits of information in your application that can be used to gauge where you fall in the range of applicants. A few programs, especially the top professional programs that receive many more applicants than they can admit, may use the score as a means of reducing the applicant pool. If your score is below their cutoff, they will not even look at the rest of your application. But most programs are much more flexible in the way they evaluate scores. If your score is low, you may still be considered for admission, especially if your grade point average is high, your work experience is relevant, or your application is otherwise strong. Others will index your exam score and your grade point average to arrive at a more balanced number. Some programs offer a conditional admission when a standardized exam score is low. In order to earn an unconditional admission, you may have to retake the exam to boost your score or achieve a certain GPA in the first courses you take.

Basically, you should regard taking a standardized admissions test as an opportunity to improve your application. And that means you must take the test with plenty of time left to meet application deadlines (see "Taking Standardized Admissions Tests" and "Applying for Admission to Degree Programs" for more information on applying). That way, if you take the test early and are disappointed with the results, you will have time to retake it. Note that test registration deadlines precede test dates by about six weeks and that you must also allow a few weeks after the testing date for score reporting.

You must also prepare. Thorough preparation, including taking practice tests, can add points to your score by refreshing your memory and giving you experience with test taking. Preparation is especially important if you have been out of school for a long time. As one student who had been out of school for twenty years put it, "Logarithms?! Geometry rules?!" If this sounds like you, you may need to do a quick recap of high school mathematics to do well on the mathematics portion of the SAT, ACT, GRE, or GMAT. And you may have forgotten what test taking is like, but if you study and practice it will help you overcome any weaknesses you may have. We'll discuss ways to prepare for the exams later in this section after we describe the various tests.

UNDERGRADUATE ADMISSIONS TESTS

Bachelor's degree programs that require a standardized admissions test will usually accept either the SAT or the ACT. Some programs will also require SAT Subject Tests in specific subjects.

THE SAT: A TEST OF REASONING

The SAT, which is administered by the Educational Testing Service (ETS) for the College Board, tests your critical reading, writing, and math reasoning skills. These are analytical skills developed over time both in school and at work; the test does not assess your knowledge of specific content areas.

The SAT is a 3-hour-and-45-minute paper test divided into ten sections: three critical reading sections, three math sections, three writing sections, and one unscored experimental section. The 25-minute essay will always be the first section of the test. The unscored section will be an unidentified math, critical reading, or writing multiple choice section.

Critical Reading Sections. The critical reading sections of the SAT test your ability to understand and analyze what you read, see relationships between the parts of a sentence, and understand word meaning in context. In other words, they test your language skills. Two of the critical reading sections last 25 minutes, and the third lasts 20 minutes. There are two types of questions:

- Passage-based reading questions measure your ability to read, understand, and think analytically about a single reading passage or a pair of passages. Reading passages range from 100 to 850 words.
- Sentence-completion questions assess your ability to understand the meaning of words and to recognize correct grammatical patterns.

Math Sections. The math sections of the SAT assess your ability to solve arithmetic, algebra I, algebra II, and geometry problems. The test does not include trigonometry or calculus. Each section lasts 20 or 25 minutes, and there are two main types of questions:

- 44 multiple-choice questions with five choices test your ability to solve math problems.
- 10 questions require a student-generated answer.

Writing Sections. The writing sections include multiple-choice questions and a 25-minute essay. The multiple-choice questions assess your ability to improve sentences and paragraphs and to identify grammatical errors. The short essay assesses your ability to organize and express your ideas clearly. The multiple-choice sections last 25 and 10 minutes and have three main types of questions:

- Improving sentences
- Improving paragraphs
- Identifying sentence errors

Note that you are permitted to bring, in the College Board's words, "almost any four-function, scientific, or graphing calculator" to use on the math sections. According to the College Board, students who use a calculator do slightly better because they do not make computational errors.

Tips for Taking the SAT. It pays to familiarize yourself with the test directions and typical question format beforehand so you don't waste precious testing time trying to figure out what to do (see the section below on test preparation). Because the sections appear in a paper booklet, you can do the questions in a section in any order. For that reason, it makes sense to answer the easy questions first and place a check mark beside the hard questions. Later, if you have time, you can return to the hard questions.

The way the SAT is scored should also influence your approach. First, you are awarded one point for each correct answer. But you lose a fraction of a point for each incorrect answer, except on the student-response questions in the math section. On those questions, you do not lose points for an incorrect answer. If you omit a question, you are not penalized. This means that guessing is only worth it if you can eliminate one or two choices as clearly wrong, improving your odds of picking the correct answer. So if a question and its choices are truly mysterious to you, skip it. The test booklet can be used for computations and notes. Don't make any extra marks on the answer sheet, because it's read by a machine that cannot tell the difference between an answer and a doodle.

THE SAT SUBJECT TESTS

The SAT Subject Tests are 1-hour subject area tests that assess your knowledge of a particular content area taught in high school. The questions are primarily multiple choice. The subject areas include literature in English, U.S. history, world history, two mathematics tests, biology, chemistry, and physics. There are reading-only language tests in French, German, modern Hebrew, Italian, Latin, and Spanish. Finally, there are reading and listening language tests in Chinese, French, German, Japanese, Korean, and Spanish.

THE ACT

The ACT is an admissions exam consisting of four tests: English, reading, mathematics, science, and an optional writing test. The examination takes about 3½ to 4 hours, and it includes 215 multiple-choice questions with either four or five answer choices, as well as an optional 30-minute essay. Since you are not penalized for an incorrect answer on the ACT, you should answer all the questions even if you have to guess.

Unlike the SAT, the ACT is not an aptitude test. Instead, it is based on the high school English, math, and science curriculum. The questions are directly related to what you learned in high school.

GRADUATE ADMISSIONS TESTS

If you apply to graduate school, you may need to take one of the graduate admissions tests. There are two types of Graduate Record Examinations: the General Test, which is usually referred to as the GRE, and the Subject Tests. Each of these tests has a different purpose, and you may need to take more than one of them. If so, try not to schedule two tests on the same day. The experience may be more arduous than you anticipate. Another general admissions test that is sometimes required instead of the GRE is the Miller Analogies Test. In addition, there are specialized exams required for admission to various professional programs.

THE GENERAL TEST (GRE)

According to ETS, the GRE "measures verbal, quantitative, and analytical reasoning skills that have been developed over a long period of time and are not necessarily related to any field of study." Like the SAT, the GRE is a test designed to assess whether you have the aptitude for higher-level study. Even though the GRE may not have subject area relevance, it can indicate that you are capable of doing the difficult reading, synthesizing, and writing demanded of most graduate students.

The test is divided into three separately timed parts, and all the questions are multiple choice: (1) a 30-minute verbal reasoning section with 30 questions, (2) a 45-minute quantitative reasoning section with 28 questions, and (3) an analytical writing section with two questions: an issue task (45 minutes) and an argument task (30 minutes). The parts may be presented in any order. In addition, an unidentified verbal, quantitative, or analytical section that doesn't count in your score may be included. You won't have any way to tell which of the duplicated sections is the "real" one, so you should complete all sections carefully. Finally, another section, on which ETS is still doing research, may also appear. This section will be identified as such and will not count toward your score. ETS tells test-takers to plan to spend 2½ to 4 hours at the testing site.

Introduced on August 1, 2011, the GRE revised General Test features new types of questions that more closely reflect the kind of thinking and the skills you need to succeed in today's demanding graduate and business school programs. The GRE revised General Test is divided into three areas of assessment: Analytical Writing, Verbal Reasoning, and Quantitative Reasoning. The first section will always be Analytical Writing. The other sections may appear in any order.

The **Analytical Writing** section assesses your ability to think critically and transfer your ideas into well-developed, well-reasoned, and well-supported writing. There are two tasks for this section of the test: an Argument Task and an Issue Task.

The first requires that you analyze someone else's argument and the second that you build your own argument either in support of or in disagreement with an opinion, policy, recommendation, or claim. Thus, the GRE assesses your ability to develop and support your own ideas and your ability to analyze another's argument and his or her supporting evidence. In addition, you will also be expected to sustain well-focused and coherent writing and control the elements of standard written English.

You won't have a choice of tasks in either section; there will only be one prompt to answer for each task. In addition, the tasks are more specific and completing them will rely on your ability to think critically and write analytically.

The **Verbal Reasoning** sections of the GRE revised General Test assess your ability to understand, analyze, and apply information found in the types of reading you'll be doing in graduate school. According to ETS, the questions ôbetter measure your ability to understand what you read and how you apply your reasoning skills.ö Among the questions you'll find are ones that ask you to reason from incomplete data; analyze and draw conclusions; identify author's assumptions and perspectives; distinguish major and minor points; understand the structure of a text; understand the meaning of words, sentences, and passages; and understand multiple levels of meaning.

Three types of questions appear in the Verbal Reasoning section: Reading Comprehension, Text Completion, and Sentence Equivalence.

The reading comprehension questions are further divided into multiple-choice questions—select one answer choice; multiple-choice questions—select one or more answer choices; and select-in-passage questions. The text completion questions may require one, two, or three answers, whereas each sentence equivalence question requires two answers.

The **Quantitative Reasoning** sections measure your ability to understand, interpret, and analyze quantitative information; use mathematical models to solve problems; and apply basic mathematical knowledge and skills. The Quantitative Reasoning section requires basic knowledge in arithmetic, algebra, geometry, and data analysis. In the new GRE General Test the subject matter of the questions emphasize real-world scenarios and data interpretation.

The purpose of the on-screen calculator is to de-emphasize computation and emphasize the thought processes used to determine what the question is asking and how to go about finding the answer. While you'll find that the traditional multiple-choice question is the format used for the majority of questions, some multiple-choice questions will ask you to select one or more answers and the numeric entry questions provide no answer options from which to choose.

The Quantitative Reasoning section consists of four types of questions: Multiple-choice questions—select one answer choice; Multiple-choice questions—select one or more answer choices; Quantitative comparison questions; and Numeric entry questions. With the exception of quantitative comparison questions, the questions in the Quantitative Reasoning sections may also appear as part of a data interpretation set: a group of questions that refer to the same tables, graphs, or other data presentation.

Tips for Taking the GRE. The GRE is now given only in computer format except in areas of the world where computer-based testing is not available. The test is somewhat different from the old paper-and-pencil test. At the start of each section, you are given questions of moderate difficulty. The computer uses your responses to each question and its information about the test's structure to decide which question to give you next. If your responses continue to be correct, the computer "rewards" you by giving you a harder question. On the other hand, if you answer incorrectly, the next question will typically be easier. In short, the computer uses a cumulative assessment of your performance along with information about the test's design to decide which question you get next.

One result of this format is that you cannot skip a question. The computer needs your answer to a question before it can give you the next one. So you must answer or you get a "no score." In addition, this format means you cannot go back to a previous question to change your answer. The computer has already taken your answer and used it to give you subsequent questions. No backtracking is possible once you've entered and confirmed your answer. This also means that each person's test is different. Even if two people start with the same item set in the basic test section, once they differ on an answer, the subsequent portion of the test will branch differently.

According to ETS, even though people take different tests, their scores are comparable. This is because the characteristics of the questions answered correctly and incorrectly, including their difficulty levels, are taken into account in the calculation of the score. In addition, ETS claims that the computer-based test scores are also comparable to the old paper-and-pencil test scores.

One benefit of the computer-based format is that when you finish, you can cancel the test results—before seeing them—if you feel you've done poorly. If you do decide to keep the test, then you can see your unofficial scores right away. In addition, official score reporting is relatively fast—ten to fifteen days.

A drawback of the format, besides the fact that you cannot skip questions, is that some of the readings, graphs, and questions are too large to appear on the screen in their entirety. You have to scroll up and down to see the whole item. Likewise, referring to a passage or graph while answering a question means that you must scroll up. In addition, you can't underline sentences in a passage or make marks in the margin as you could on the paper test. To make up for this, ETS provides scratch paper that you can use to make notes and do calculations.

To help test-takers accustom themselves to the computerized format, ETS provides a tutorial that you may complete before starting on the actual test. The tutorial familiarizes you with the use of a mouse, the conventions of pointing, clicking, and scrolling and the format of the test. If you are familiar with computers, the tutorial will take you less than one-half hour. If you are not, you are permitted to spend more time on it. According to ETS, the system is easy to use, even for a person with no previous computer experience. However, if you are not accustomed to computers, you would be far better off if you practice your basic skills before you get to the testing site. Although in theory a mouse is easy to use, novices often have trouble getting the cursor to go where they want it to go. The last thing you want to deal with while taking the GRE is a wild mouse and accidental clicking on the wrong answers. If it's any consolation, no knowledge of the keyboard is required—everything is accomplished by pointing and clicking.

GRE SUBJECT AREA TESTS

The subject area tests are achievement tests, and they test your content knowledge of particular subjects. There are eight subject area tests, and they are given in paper-and-pencil format only. The subjects include biochemistry, cell and molecular biology; biology; chemistry; computer science; literature in English; mathematics; physics; and psychology. The subject area tests assume a level of knowledge consistent with majoring in a subject or at least having an extensive background in it. ETS suggests allowing about 3½ hours at the testing site for a subject area test.

Unlike the General Test, which is given many times year round, the subject tests are given only three times a year. Keep in mind that because the tests are paper-based, it takes four to six weeks for your scores to be mailed to your designated institutions. Because the tests are given infrequently and score reporting is slow, be sure you plan ahead carefully so your test results will arrive before your deadlines.

MILLER ANALOGIES TEST

The Miller Analogies Test (MAT), which is run by Harcourt Assessment, is accepted by more than 2,300 graduate school programs. It is a test of mental ability given entirely in the form of analogies. For example, the analogies may tap your knowledge of fine arts, literature, mathematics, natural science, and social science.

On the MAT, you have 60 minutes to solve 120 problems. The test is given on an as-needed basis at more than 500 test centers in the United States, Canada, and overseas.

PROFESSIONAL SCHOOL EXAMS

Professional graduate programs are likely to require you to take the appropriate graduate admissions test. The major tests are the Graduate Management Admissions Test (GMAT) for business school applicants; the Law School Admissions Test (LSAT) for law school applicants; and the Medical College Admissions Test (MCAT) for medical school applicants. However, there are also specialized graduate admissions tests in the fields of dentistry, veterinary science, pharmacy, optometry, and education.

Graduate Management Admissions Test. The test most likely to be taken by prospective distance learning students is the GMAT. It is run by the Graduate Management Admissions Council and administered by Pearson VUE. Like the GRE, the GMAT is a computer-based test. It is designed to help schools of business assess applicants' aptitude for graduate-level programs in business and management.

The GMAT tests verbal, quantitative, and analytic writing skills:

- In the Verbal section, you will be asked to understand and evaluate written English. There are 41 multiple-choice questions of three basic types: reading comprehension, critical reasoning, and sentence correction. You have 75 minutes to complete this section.
- The Quantitative section tests your basic math skills, understanding of elementary mathematical concepts, and ability to solve quantitative problems. There are 37 multiple-choice questions of two basic types: data sufficiency and problem solving. You have 75 minutes to complete this section.
- The Analytical Writing Assessment measures your ability to think critically and communicate in writing. There are two essay topics, and you are allowed 30 minutes each to respond. You must analyze an issue and an argument in this section of the test.

TESTS OF ENGLISH LANGUAGE PROFICIENCY

Regardless of whether you're applying to an undergraduate or graduate program, if your native language is not English, you may be required to take the Test of English as a Foreign Language (TOEFL) or Test of Spoken English (TSE) in order to determine your readiness to take courses in English. Both tests are administered by ETS.

The TOEFL is given in computer-based form throughout most of the world. Like the computer-based GRE, the TOEFL does not require previous computer experience. You are given the opportunity to practice on the computer before the test begins. The TOEFL has four sections—listening, reading, structure, and writing—and it lasts about 4 hours.

The TSE evaluates your ability to speak English. During the test, which takes about a half hour, you answer questions that are presented in written and recorded form. Your responses are recorded; there is no writing required on this test. The TSE is not given in as many locations as the TOEFL, so you may have to travel a considerable distance to take it.

PREPARING FOR A STANDARDIZED TEST

You can improve your scores and reduce your test anxiety by preparing for the exams you need to take. At the very least, preparation will mean that you are familiar with the test instructions and the types of questions you will be asked. If your computer skills need improvement, adequate preparation will mean that you focus on the questions rather than struggle with the mouse when you take the computer-based tests. For achievement tests such as the subject area tests, you will actually need to study content. There are many ways you can prepare for the tests, but whichever method you choose, start early.

- **Practice by taking old tests.** You can check the Web sites of the various tests to download or request practice tests, or you can buy practice test books at a bookstore. You'll find free sample test questions on many other Web sites, including Peterson's (www.petersonspublishing.com).
- **Use test-preparation workbooks.** These books give information and test-taking strategies, as well as practice items. There are many workbooks on the market, some with CD-ROMs, that will help you prepare for an admissions test. You'll find a long list of titles to choose from in Peterson's online bookstore at www.petersonspublishing.com.
- **Use test-preparation software.** Test-preparation software is becoming more popular as more of the tests shift to computerized format. You can purchase the software in just about any computer software store. You can also take practice tests online at www.petersonspublishing.com/testprep.

- **Take a test-preparation course.** If you don't trust yourself to stick with a self-study program using practice tests, workbooks, or software, sign up for a review course such as those given by Kaplan. Although the courses are much more expensive than the do-it-yourself approach, they may be worth it if they make you study.
- **If your math is rusty, study math content.** According to the College Board, people who study math boost their scores more than people who focus only on test-taking skills.

For a list of test-preparation resources, see the Appendix.

REDUCING TEST ANXIETY

The best way to reduce test anxiety is to be thoroughly prepared. If you are well-acquainted with the format, directions, and types of questions you will encounter, you will not need to waste precious testing time puzzling over these aspects of the exam. In addition to thorough preparation, here are some suggestions to reduce the stress of taking the exam.

- Get a good night's rest and don't tank up on caffeinated beverages—they will only make you feel more stressed.
- Make sure you've got all the things you will need, including your admission ticket and proper identification; pencils and erasers if you are taking a paper-based test; and a calculator, if one is permitted.
- Dress in layers so you will be prepared for a range of room temperatures.
- Get to the testing site at least a half an hour early. Make sure you know the way, and leave yourself plenty of time to get there.
- Pace yourself during the exam. Know how the exam is scored so you can plan your approach.
- Last, try to keep things in perspective. Remember, the exam score is just one item on your application.

We'll discuss the remaining parts of an application in the next section.

APPLYING FOR ADMISSION TO DEGREE PROGRAMS

Now that you have narrowed your selection of programs and ascertained whether or not you need to take a standardized admissions test, it's time to prepare and assemble your applications. If you have not already done so, request an application and information packet from each program to which you plan to apply, download these items from their Web sites, or review them online.

When you look over these materials, you will see that there may be a lot of work involved in applying to a degree program. It may take you a few months to register for and take standardized tests and to assemble and submit all the necessary information, especially if you're an international student or you've been out of school for a few years. Because the process can be complicated and time consuming, you should start well ahead of time. Even if you apply to a certificate program or an associate degree program at a community college, a process that is typically less complicated, you should still make sure to start in time.

DEADLINES

For programs at traditional colleges and universities, application deadlines for fall admission may range from August (one full year prior to your planned enrollment) to late spring or summer for programs with rolling admissions. However, most programs require that you submit your application between January and March of the year in which you wish to start. For certificate programs and at community colleges, the deadlines may be later.

At some of the online universities, students can start their studies at any time of year. For example, at Walden University you can start on the first of any month. At Walden, the deadline for application materials is the first of the month two months prior to the month of enrollment.

Different programs have different deadlines. So be careful when you check the deadlines in the application materials from your various programs. And remember, the deadlines are not suggestions. One student applying to a traditional university who mistook a March deadline for May recalls that "not only would they not consider my application, but they wouldn't refund my application fee, either. I had to reapply the next year and pay again to be considered for their program." So don't be careless about dates—double-check them. Make a checklist like Figure 7-1 to help you keep track of things and stay on top of deadlines.

Application Checklist. Keep track of your applications by inserting a check mark or a completion date in the appropriate column or row. Note that the last four items are financial aid documents, which will be discussed in "Paying for Your Education."

PARTS OF AN APPLICATION

For each program to which you apply, you will have to submit a number of items to make your application complete. For most bachelor's and graduate degree programs, these include:

- Standardized admissions test scores (see "Taking Standardized Admissions Tests")
- An application form
- Your high school, undergraduate, or other transcripts
- Letters of recommendation
- Personal essay(s)

In addition, if you are seeking credit for life experience, an assessment portfolio will be required (see "What Can You Study via Distance Learning?"). A personal interview may be required for some programs, although for most, an interview is optional. A program may require additional items, such as a resume or arts portfolio.

For most associate degree programs at community colleges, the application is much simpler. Typically, it consists of just an application form; you may not even need to submit high school transcripts. For certificate programs, the application may consist of an application form and one or two other items.

Because requirements vary so widely, be sure you read the admissions information thoroughly so you understand what each program expects of you. Since each program may require a slightly different set of items, be sure your checklist reflects this in order to keep track of what you'll need to do.

We'll discuss the main elements of an application below; we'll cover financial aid applications in the next section.

THE APPLICATION FORM

On the application form, you provide basic information such as the program or department to which you are applying; your name, date of birth, social security number, address, and contact information; your citizenship status; your demographic background (usually optional); your current employer and position; your educational background; names of people who are providing references (ask them first!); and admissions test dates. Sometimes the application form also includes a section for applying for financial aid. However, a separate application form for financial aid may be necessary. Be sure you understand what forms you need to submit and to whom if you are applying for aid.

If you use a paper application, you should type the information on the form. If a typewriter is not available, then print your entries neatly. Be sure you do not accidentally omit information, and double-check that there are no spelling errors. "Photocopy the application and fill the copy out," suggests a graduate student in engineering at Worcester Polytechnic Institute. "Make sure it is clear and concise, and then copy it onto the actual form."

If you decide to apply online, don't just sit at the computer and dash off the application. Download the application form, fill it in, then proofread it carefully. Only then should you transmit it, being sure to keep a copy. Note that if you apply to an online degree program and the school does not offer an online application, you

Figure 7–1: Application Checklist

Item	Program 1		Program 2		Program 3	
	Date Due/Date Completed		Date Due/Date Completed		Date Due/Date Completed	
Application form						
Test scores requested						
Transcripts requested						
Letters of recommendation solicited						
Letters of recommendation follow-up						
Personal essay(s)						
Application fee						
Other items required (specify)						
Application submitted						
Application follow-up						
FAFSA						
Other financial aid forms						
Financial aid supporting documents						
Financial aid application follow-up						

should think twice about applying. The lack of an online application is probably indicative of the low level of online student services you can expect once you are enrolled.

Many undergraduate colleges accept a common application form in place of their own. This means that most of the fields you will need to fill in will be the same for all of the schools that accept the common application. You may have to fill out a supplementary form for a college if you use one of these standardized forms. Using a standardized application form lets you concentrate on being organized and writing good essays.

TRANSCRIPTS

As proof of your academic background, you will need to submit official transcripts from each high school (for undergraduate programs), college, and university you have attended, even if you have taken just one course from that institution. To request official transcripts, contact your high school's guidance office or the registrars of your undergraduate college and other institutions you have attended. Be sure to allow two or three months for your request to be processed. It will save time if you call ahead to find out what the fee for each transcript is and what information they need to pull your file and send the transcript to the proper recipient. Then you can enclose a check for that amount with your written request.

Since many schools will send the transcripts directly to the admissions offices of the programs to which you are applying, you may also want to request an unofficial copy of your transcript. You can use this copy for your own reference during the application process.

When you review your transcripts, look for weaknesses that may need explaining, even if they occurred years ago. For example, a low GPA one semester, a very poor grade in a course, or even a below-average overall GPA may hurt your chances of acceptance unless you have a good reason for them. You can explain any shortfalls in your transcripts in your personal essay, cover letter, or addendum to the application.

LETTERS OF RECOMMENDATION

You will probably have to provide letters of recommendation for each program to which you apply. These letters are important, because like the personal essay, they give the members of the admissions committee a more personal view of you than is possible from your grades and test scores. Good letters of recommendation can tremendously increase your chances of admission, and lukewarm letters can harm your application. So it's important to approach the task of choosing and preparing your letter writers in a thoughtful and timely fashion.

In fact, it's a good idea to start asking for references a few months before your application deadline. Professionals and professors are extremely busy people, and the more time that you can give them to work on your recommendation, the better it will reflect who you are. Starting early will also give you an opportunity to follow up with your recommenders well before the application deadlines.

CHOOSING PEOPLE TO WRITE RECOMMENDATIONS

If possible, at least one of your recommendations should be from a teacher or professor, because (1) they are in the best position to judge you as a potential student and (2) members of the admissions committee will consider them peers and so be more inclined to trust their judgment of you.

If you cannot make up the full complement of letters from faculty members or if you are applying to professional programs, you can ask employers or people who know you in a professional capacity to write references for you. In fact, if you are applying to professional programs, having letters of recommendation from those already practicing in the field is a plus.

When you are trying to decide who to ask for recommendations, keep these criteria in mind. The people you ask should

- have a high opinion of you.
- know you well, preferably in more than one context.
- be familiar with your field.
- be familiar with the programs to which you apply.
- have taught a large number of students (or have managed a large number of employees) so they have a good basis upon which to compare you (favorably!) to your peers.
- be known by the admissions committee as someone whose opinion can be trusted.
- have good writing skills.
- be reliable enough to write and mail the letter on time.

A tall order? Yes. It's likely that no one person you choose will meet all these criteria, but try to find people who come close to this ideal.

APPROACHING YOUR LETTER WRITERS

Once you've decided who you plan to ask for references, be diplomatic. Don't simply show up in their offices, ask them to write a letter, and give them the letter of recommendation forms. Plan your approach so that you leave the potential recommender, as well as yourself, a graceful "out" in case the recommender reacts less than enthusiastically.

On your first approach, you should remind the person about who you are (if necessary) and then ask if they think they can write you a good letter of recommendation. This gives the person a chance to say no. If the person agrees, but hesitates or seems to be lukewarm, you can thank them for agreeing to help you. Later, you can write them a note saying that you won't need a letter of recommendation after all. On the other hand, if the person seems genuinely pleased to help you, you can then make an appointment to give them the letter of recommendation forms and the other information they will need.

WAIVING YOUR RIGHT TO SEE A LETTER

The letter of recommendation forms in your application packets contain a waiver. If you sign the waiver, you give up your right to see the letter of recommendation. Before you decide whether or not to sign it, discuss the waiver with each person who is writing you a reference. Some people will write you a reference only if you agree to sign the waiver and they can be sure the letter is confidential. This does not necessarily mean they intend to write a negative letter; instead, it means that they think a confidential letter will carry more weight with the admissions committee. In fact, they are right. A confidential letter usually has more validity in the eyes of the admissions committee. From the committee's point of view, an "open" letter may be less than candid because the letter writer knew you were going to read it. So, in general, it's better for you to waive your right to see a letter. If this makes you anxious in regard to a particular recommender, then do not choose that person to write a letter.

HELPING YOUR LETTER WRITERS

Once a faculty member or employer has agreed to write a letter of recommendation for you, he or she wants to write something positive on your behalf. No matter how great you are, this won't be possible if the letter writer cannot remember you and your accomplishments very well.

So when you meet with your letter writers to give them the letter of recommendation forms, use this opportunity to provide them with information about yourself. Bring a resume that highlights your academic, professional, and personal accomplishments. List the course or courses you took with them, the grades you got, and any significant work you did, such as a big research paper or presentation. The resume can be the basis of a conversation you have with the letter writer that amplifies your notable accomplishments.

What should you do if the letter writer asks *you* to draft the letter? Accept gracefully. Then pretend you are the writer, and craft a letter extolling your virtues and accomplishments in detail. Remember, if the letter writer does not like what you've written, he or she is free to change it in the final draft.

You can help your letter writers by filling in as much of the information as you can on the letter of recommendation forms. It's also a nice gesture to provide stamped, addressed envelopes for the letters if they are to be mailed directly to the programs or to you for inclusion in your application. Be sure your letter writers understand what their deadlines are. In other words, do everything you can to expedite the process, especially since you may be approaching people who are already extremely busy.

Last, send thank-you notes to professors and employers who have come through for you with letters of recommendation. Cementing good relationships now can only help you in the future.

IF YOU'VE BEEN OUT OF SCHOOL FOR YEARS

What should you do if you have been out of school for years and have lost touch with your teachers and professors? There are several things you can do to overcome the problems associated with the passage of time.

First, if a teacher or professor is still at your alma mater, you can get in touch by mail or e-mail, remind the person of who you are, describe what you've done since they taught you and what your plans for school are, and include a resume. Tell the instructor what you remember most about the courses you took with him or her. Most people keep their course records for at least a few years and can look up your grades. If you are still near your high school or undergraduate institution, you can make your approach in person. Once you've made this initial approach, you can then call and ask if the person thinks he or she can write a strong recommendation for you.

Another strategy if you've been out of school for a while is to obtain letters of recommendation from faculty members teaching in the programs to which you plan to apply. In order to obtain such a letter, you may have to take a course in the program before you enroll so that the faculty member gets to know you. Members of an admissions committee will hesitate to reject a candidate who has been strongly recommended by one of their colleagues.

Finally, if you are having trouble recruiting teachers and professors to recommend you, call the programs to which you are applying and ask what their policy is for applicants in your situation. Many programs designed for adult learners, especially the professional programs, allow you to use letters from employers. But remember, if you apply to an academic rather than a professional program, letters from employers will not carry as much weight as letters from faculty members.

THE PERSONAL ESSAY

The application to a degree program is not all numbers and outside evaluations. Schools are also interested in finding out about you as an individual and in more intangible qualities, like your ability to write a good essay. Thus, the personal essay is the part of the application in which you can take control and demonstrate who you are and why you deserve to be admitted. Other parts of your application—test scores, grade point average, and transcripts—may reflect your academic ability, but not much else. The letters of recommendation are beyond your control once you've chosen the writers. But a good personal essay can make you stand out. It can show the qualities that will make you an excellent student and professional. In other words, the essay is your showcase and you should make the most of it. Even if you can write superb prose in your sleep, you still need to know *what* to write. In this section, you'll get a step-by-step guide to preparing the personal essay.

REQUIREMENTS VARY

The essays required of applicants vary widely. For some programs, you may just have to explain in one or two paragraphs why you want to go to that school. For others, you may have to write on a more creative topic, such as the person who influenced you the most. Still for others, such as graduate business programs, the application may call for two, three, or even more essays on different topics. Business schools and programs pay a lot of attention to the personal essay because professional experience is an important criterion for admission, and this is best reflected in the essays.

The admissions committee gleans a lot of information from *what* you write. But they can also tell a lot from *how* you write. If your writing is clear and conveys your ideas effectively, you are demonstrating your ability to communicate. If your writing is free of grammatical and spelling errors, you are demonstrating your attention to detail. Good writing skills are essential for a student in any field, so a poorly written essay can hurt an application. A well-written statement, on the other hand, will help your case.

THINK BEFORE YOU WRITE

Do you remember the self-assessment you did in "Is Distance Learning Right for You?" You answered many difficult questions about your goals, interests, strengths, and weaknesses in order to decide if pursuing an education through distance learning was right for you. If you did an honest and thorough job of assessing yourself then, you will have already thought through many of the issues you will now need to address when you write your personal essay.

Things to Think About. Your self-assessment should make it easier for you to get a handle on issues such as:

- your personal and professional goals and their relationship to your education
- how you came to be interested in a particular field and why you think you are well suited for it
- aspects of your life that make you uniquely qualified to pursue study in this field
- experiences or qualities that distinguish you from other applicants
- unusual hardships or obstacles that you've had to overcome
- unusual accomplishments, whether personal, professional, or academic
- professional experiences that have contributed to your personal growth
- how your skills and personal characteristics would contribute to your success in a distance learning degree program

In addition, when you researched and evaluated programs to which you would apply, you learned a lot about the programs that were good matches for you. In your essay, you may also have to address issues like

- what appeals to you about a particular program.
- how your interests and strengths match their needs.

Be Yourself . . . The most common piece of advice from most admissions directors about writing the personal essay is to be yourself. Remember, you are seeking to be accepted by a program that is a good match for you. If you disguise who you really are in an effort to impress an admissions committee, you are doing yourself—and the school—a disservice. So, be honest. If you demonstrate self-knowledge by presenting your strengths as well as your limitations, your essay will be a true reflection of who you are.

. . . But Be Diplomatic. Honesty is important, but so is diplomacy. Try not to reveal weaknesses in your personality such as laziness, dishonesty, or selfishness. Don't say you want to enroll in a program just because it's online or you know you can get in. Even though these things may be true, they are not reasons with which the admissions committee will necessarily be sympathetic. Instead, frame your points in a positive light: you can fulfill the admission requirements because you have the proper prerequisites, and you know of its reputation for quality online teaching.

WRITE A STRONG OPENING

When you write your essay, put yourself in the position of an admissions committee member who may be reading fifty essays a day. By the end of all this reading, this poor individual may be bored to tears and would be pleased by any essay that simply engages his or her interest. How are you going to accomplish this? By writing an opening that grabs the reader's attention.

Describe an Important Experience. Instead of beginning with, "I want to go to school because . . ." try to engage the reader with something significant. For example, was there an experience that led you to make the decision to pursue your education? If so, describe it.

The opening is also the place where you can set forth any unusual experience you have had that contributed significantly to the person you are today. The experience may be growing up poor, being an Olympic athlete, or moving to the United States at the age of fourteen. Whatever the experience is, show how it has formed your character and life and how it relates to the education you want to pursue now.

Be Specific. What if you have not had a defining moment or experience that sparked your interest in further education? Then write an opening that is specific enough to have some real interest. The key is to remember that specific details are usually more interesting than general statements. Use concrete examples of your successes and action verbs to describe events. Be specific and you'll have a better chance of connecting with your readers.

TELL HOW YOUR STORY INTERSECTS WITH THEIRS

If you apply to several programs, you will be tempted to write a boilerplate essay. Resist the temptation. Admissions committees grow adept at picking out the generic personal statements.

Remember that when you were evaluating programs you were looking for a good match for you. The personal essay is the place where you can explain to the admissions committee why you are a good match for that school. The story of your intellectual and professional development and your goals should culminate in your reasons for choosing this particular program. Your reasons should reflect a knowledge of the program.

Use the Brochure or Catalog as a Resource. You can use the knowledge you've gained from researching the program if you don't know it firsthand to explain why you want to enroll in a program. In particular, the program brochure or catalog can be a good resource when you write this section of the essay. It's important to know what a school has to offer before you write the essay. The admissions committee members will be looking for a good fit for their program.

In addition to identifying the tangible characteristics of a program, you can also get a sense of its philosophy and values from the brochure or catalog.

DESCRIBE YOUR GOALS

In most essays, you will have to explain how a degree will help you achieve your goals. Even if you are not exactly sure what you want to do professionally, describe what you might be interested in doing once you receive the degree. Indicating that you have a purpose in obtaining a degree shows that you are focused and motivated and have a real sense of the possibilities.

EXPLAIN SHORTCOMINGS IN YOUR BACKGROUND

There is a difference of opinion on whether or not the personal essay is the place to explain any weaknesses in your academic or professional preparation if you are not directly asked to do so. Some people think that the essay should concentrate on a positive presentation of your qualifications. They feel that an explanation of poor standardized test scores, for example, belongs in an addendum or cover letter. Others think that the essay is the place to address your application's weaknesses.

Perhaps a good rule of thumb is to address any weaknesses or shortcomings that are directly relevant to your proposed studies in the essay. On the other hand, if the weak spot in your application is not directly related to your field of study, you may prefer to address it in an addendum or cover letter. For example, if when you were a college freshman you had a poor GPA, you can explain this separately. Try to put a positive spin on it, too. Explain, for example, how your GPA in your major was much higher, or how your GPA improved as you matured. Essentially, your decision as to where to address your weaknesses will depend on their importance and relevance to your pursuit of a degree.

EDIT YOUR DRAFTS

Follow the Instructions. When you sit down to draft your essay, the first thing you should make sure is that you are *answering the question posed on the application*. Be sure you read the instructions for each program's personal statement carefully. Small differences in wording can affect how you approach writing the essay.

Don't Write Too Much or Too Little. The second thing you should keep in mind as you begin your draft is the length of the essay. Often, the length is specified. What should you do if length is not specified? Write one to two typed pages. An essay that is shorter than one page does not allow room for you to develop your ideas, and an essay that is longer than two pages becomes a chore for the admissions committee to read. Don't play with font size, either, in order to get the statement to come out the right length. Admissions officers don't really want to read eight-point type. Stick with a basic font, such as Times New Roman, and keep the size between 10 and 12 points. If the essay asks for a specific word count, follow it to the letter. If you come in over or under by 10 words or so, don't worry too much about it. But if you're 100 or more words short or long, you'll have some adding or cutting to do.

Finally, when you write your first draft, do not waste space by repeating information that the admissions committee can get from other parts of your application, such as your transcript or resume. Use the essay to provide new information or to highlight particular accomplishments.

Review the First Draft. Once you have drafted your essay, read the question again. Has your draft answered the question fully? If the essay is incomplete, go back and fill in the missing material. Then ask people for feedback. Although your spouse and friends may be helpful, you may get more valuable suggestions from faculty members or colleagues who know you and who also know what a personal essay should be like. Ask whether you've included things you should leave out or should add things you've forgotten. Is the tone right? Have you achieved the right balance between boasting and being too modest? Are there any problems with organization, clarity, grammar, or spelling?

Prepare the Final Draft. Once you've revised the essay, set it aside for a couple of days. Then proofread it with a fresh eye. If you are satisfied with your final draft, ask someone else to proofread it for you. The final draft should be absolutely free of grammar and spelling errors, so do not rely on grammar or spellcheckers to find all the errors. Once you are done, be sure to keep backup files as well as a hard copy. Although you won't be able to use the whole essay for all your applications, you may be able to use parts of it. If you do work this way, be absolutely sure when you submit the final essays to different programs that you have not made any embarrassing cutting and pasting mistakes.

Finally, if you submit the statement on separate sheets of paper rather than on the application form itself, put your name, social security number, and the question at the top of the essay and type "see attached essay" on the application form.

MAKE IT YOURS

If after reading this section you are still daunted by the prospect of writing your personal statement, just put the whole task aside for a few days. You will find that the ideas and suggestions you've just read will trigger some mental activity and that soon you will have some ideas of your own to jot down.

Remember, also, that it's not necessary to have an exotic background or a dramatic event to recount in order to write a good essay and gain admission to a program. Admissions committees look for diversity—in gender, race, ethnicity, nationality, and socioeconomic status—to name some obvious characteristics. But they are also looking for people with diverse life experiences to add richness to their student body. Your background, which may seem perfectly ordinary to you, nevertheless has unique and relevant elements that can be assets to the program you choose. Your task is to identify and build upon these elements to persuade the admissions committee that you should be selected.

INTERVIEWS

Interviews are rarely a requirement of the distance education application process. However, if you think you do well in interviews, you can call each program and ask for an interview. A good interview may be an opportunity to sway the admissions committee in your favor. Human nature being what it is, an excellent half-hour interview may loom larger than years of average grades in the minds of those who evaluate your application.

Most interviewers are interested in the way you approach problems, think, and articulate your ideas, and so they will concentrate on questions that will reveal these aspects of your character and not on questions that test your technical knowledge. They may ask you controversial questions or give you hypothetical problems to solve. Or they may ask about your professional goals, motivation for study, and areas of interest—much of the same material that is in a typical personal essay. Remember that interviewers are interested more in how you think than in what you think.

When you prepare for an interview, it would be helpful if you have already written your personal essay, because the thought processes involved in preparing the essay will help you articulate many of the issues that are likely to come up in an interview. It is also helpful to do your homework on the program, so if the opportunity arises for you to ask questions, you can do so intelligently. Last, be sure you are dressed properly. That means dress as if you are going to a professional job interview.

SUBMITTING YOUR APPLICATION

As we mentioned at the beginning of this section, you should submit your completed applications well before they are due. *Be sure to keep a copy of everything.* That way, you won't lose hours of work if the application gets lost. You can either mail the application to the admissions office or file portions of it online through the programs' Web sites. Remember, however, that some elements of the application, such as the official transcripts, will still need to be mailed in paper form. Note also that most schools that accept online applications simply print them and process them as if they had come in by regular mail.

Try to submit all of your materials at once, which simplifies the task of compiling and tracking your application at the admissions office. If that's impossible, as it is for many students, keep track of missing items and forward them as soon as possible. Remember that if items are missing, your application is likely just to sit in the admissions office.

FOLLOWING UP

It's important that you check up on the status of your applications, especially if you don't receive acknowledgment that an application is complete. Give the admissions office a couple of weeks to process your application, and then call or send an e-mail to find out whether or not it's complete. For some schools, you can check the status of your application online through their Web sites. Usually the missing items are transcripts or letters of recommendation.

IN SUMMARY

Preparing a thorough, focused, and well-written application is one of the most important tasks you will ever undertake. A good application can gain you admission to a program that can help you achieve your goals. "The application process is just one of those hoops you have to jump through to get where you want to go," advises a distance learning student at Gonzaga University. With your destination in mind, work on your applications as if they are the most important things you can possibly be doing, because they are.

PAYING FOR YOUR EDUCATION

Pursuing a certificate or degree can cost a lot of money, but it is usually money well spent. On average, people with undergraduate and graduate degrees make more money than those who do not have these credentials. Still, the question remains: How are you going to pay for school and support yourself (and perhaps your family) at the same time?

Most adult distance learning students solve the problem of paying for their education by continuing to work full-time and attending school part time. As one student put it, "I work and I pay as I go." Although attending part-time does not cut the total cost of your certificate or degree, it does have the advantage of spreading your costs over a longer period and enables you to pay for your education out of your current income. Note, however, that attending school less than half-time will disqualify you from most forms of financial aid.

In this section, we'll discuss ways to pay for your education, both by looking for low-cost alternatives and by finding financial aid. We'll discuss types and sources of aid, where you can find information about financial aid, and the application process. Finally, we'll describe some of the tax issues that may be relevant to students pursuing higher education.

LOOKING FOR LOW-COST ALTERNATIVES

There are ways you can cut the cost of your education, even before you look for sources of financial aid. These include attending a community college rather than a four-year college and attending a public institution of higher education rather than a private one.

COMMUNITY COLLEGE VERSUS FOUR-YEAR COLLEGE

If you are an undergraduate pursuing a bachelor's degree, you could consider enrolling at a community college for your first two years of study. Most community colleges charge less tuition than four-year colleges do. Toward the end of your second year of study, you can apply to a four-year college as a transfer student and complete your bachelor's degree there.

PUBLIC VERSUS PRIVATE COLLEGE OR UNIVERSITY

Since four-year public colleges and universities get most of their support from government funding, they are less expensive than private colleges and universities. Public colleges and universities usually have two scales for tuition and fees—one for out-of-state residents and a much less expensive scale for state residents.

With so much money at stake, and if moving is an option for you, it is definitely worthwhile to find out how you can establish residency in the state in which you plan to get your degree. You may simply have to reside in the state for a year—your first year of school—in order to be considered a legal resident. But being a resident while a student may not count, and you may have to move to the state a year before you plan to enroll. The legal residency requirements of each state vary, so be sure you have the right information if you decide to pursue this strategy.

TYPES OF FINANCIAL AID

Before we get into a discussion of the various sources of financial aid, it would be helpful to understand some basics. For example, financial aid can be classified in a few ways. First, it can be categorized by type of aid:

- **Grants, scholarships,** and **fellowships** are gifts that do not have to be repaid. These words are used somewhat interchangeably; there is no real difference among them, except that scholarships are usually awarded to undergraduates and fellowships are awarded to graduate students.
- **Loans** are awards that do have to be repaid, with interest, either while you are in school or after you leave school, depending on the terms of the loan. If you consider loans, note that financial aid counselors recommend that your total student debt payment should not exceed 8 to 15 percent of your projected monthly income after you receive your degree.
- **Work-study awards** are amounts you earn through part-time work in a federal aid program.
- **Reimbursements**, generally from employers, repay you for amounts you've already spent on tuition.

You can also classify financial aid according to the reason the student is awarded the aid:

- **Need-based aid** is financial aid awarded on the basis of your financial need. It may take the form of grants, loans, or work-study.
- **Merit-based aid** is funding awarded on the basis of academic merit, regardless of financial need.

A subset of merit-based aid is student profile-based aid—financial aid to students because of their identities. For example, some scholarships are targeted for veterans, minorities, or women; and others are targeted for people with very specific qualifications that the philanthropist wants to reward, such as an Eagle Scout studying labor relations.

A third way to classify financial aid is by its source. The major sources of aid for students are as follows:

- The **federal government**, by far the largest disburser of financial aid—over $50 billion to more than 8.5 million students each year
- **State governments**, some of which have large financial aid programs

- **Private sources of aid**, which include colleges and universities, employers, foundations, service organizations, national scholarship and fellowship programs, home equity loans, and private loan programs

THE LANGUAGE OF FINANCIAL AID

There's some financial aid jargon that you'll have to master in order to understand need-based financial aid programs. Some terms that you'll see frequently include the following:

- **Enrollment status**—Whether you are enrolled full time, three-quarter time, half time, or less than half time in a degree or certificate program. Your status affects your eligibility for most types of aid.
- **Expected Family Contribution (EFC)**—This is the amount you and your family are expected to contribute to the cost of your education per academic year. If you are a dependent, *family* means you and your parents; if you are independent, this means you and your spouse, if you are married. The formula was established by the U.S. Congress to help estimate federal aid amounts for eligible students, and it is used by college financial aid offices as well as the U.S. Department of Education.
- **Cost of attendance**—The total cost—tuition, fees, living expenses, books, supplies, and miscellaneous expenses—of attending a particular school for an academic year. Each school estimates its own cost of attendance, and you can find out what it is if you check your admissions information packet or call the financial aid office. Distance learners should make sure that technology costs are included in the school's cost of attendance and in their own budgets. The cost of transportation, hotels, and meals during residency periods, if any, should also be accounted for in the cost of attendance.
- **Financial need**—The amount of money you need to be given or loaned or that you will earn through work-study in order to attend your school. It is calculated by subtracting your EFC from your cost of attendance:

  Cost of Attendance
  – Expected Family Contribution
  = Financial Need

  Note that your financial need will differ from program to program. That's because the cost of attendance will vary from school to school, but your EFC will remain the same, whether you attend the local community college or an expensive private university.

FEDERAL FINANCIAL AID

As we've mentioned, the U.S. government is the largest player in the financial aid arena, and most of your financial aid is likely to come from this source. The federal government provides need-based aid in the form of grants, work-study programs, and loans. Up-to-date information about federal financial aid programs can be found at the U.S. Department of Education's Web site, www.studentaid.ed.gov, or by calling 800-4-FEDAID (toll-free). Eligibility issues relevant to distance learners and some of the basics of federal aid are discussed below. Note that some of these eligibility criteria may change as distance degrees become more common and financial aid programs are modified to reflect the new realities.

ARE YOU ELIGIBLE FOR FEDERAL FINANCIAL AID?

Your financial need is just one criterion used to determine whether or not you are eligible to receive aid from the federal government. In addition, you must

- have a high school diploma or GED or pass a test approved by the Department of Education.
- be enrolled in a degree or certificate program.
- be enrolled in an eligible institution (see below).
- be a U.S. citizen or eligible noncitizen.
- have a Social Security number.
- register with the Selective Service if required.
- maintain satisfactory academic progress once you are in school.

If you have been convicted under federal or state laws of the sale or possession of illegal drugs, you may not be eligible to participate in federal financial aid programs. Call the Federal Student Aid Information Center at 800-4-FEDAID (toll-free) for further information.

If you are not sure if you qualify as an eligible noncitizen, call the financial aid office of the school you plan to attend.

INSTITUTIONAL ELIGIBILITY: AN ISSUE PERTINENT TO DISTANCE LEARNERS

In order to participate in federal financial aid programs, an institution of higher learning must fulfill the criteria established by Congress for the disbursement of Title IV funds, as federal student aid is officially known. There are many complex regulations that establish institutional eligibility. Of these, several may apply to institutions that offer certificates or degrees at a distance. For example, in order to be eligible to participate in federal financial aid programs, an institution must be accredited by an agency—other than the Distance Education and Training Council (DETC)—recognized by the U.S. Department of Education. The reason that schools accredited only by the DETC are not eligible is that they are classified as "correspondence schools," and schools that teach primarily by correspondence are ineligible according to the law. In order to qualify to disburse Title IV aid, an institution must teach at least 50.1 percent of its classes in the traditional classroom or must be classified as an independent study institution rather than a correspondence school. Other requirements for participation in federal financial aid programs involve the academic schedule; for example, there must be a thirty-week academic year, a template that doesn't fit some of the new virtual universities.

The Distance Education Demonstration Program. The rules governing federal aid were originally promulgated to prevent fraud and to assure that funds would be provided to students at schools that met certain standards. However, with the growth of distance education, these regulations are increasingly becoming obstacles to provide aid to students at legitimate but innovative institutions. Recognizing this, Congress established the Distance Education Demonstration Program under the direction of the Department of Education. "The purpose of the Distance Education Demonstration Program is to collect data that will provide some understanding of what constitutes quality in distance education," explains Marianne R. Phelps, former special assistant to the assistant secretary for postsecondary education. "Congress needs information in order to become comfortable with the risks involved in funding distance education." Under this program, the department is permitted to waive some of the Title IV regulations, if necessary, for the fifteen participating institutions of higher education. Eventually, the experiences and data generated by the Distance Education Demonstration Program may provide a basis for a review of current rules and regulations.

Determining the Eligibility Status of an Institution or Program. In the meantime, what can you do to make sure that the school and program in which you are interested are eligible to participate in federal financial aid programs? The simple answer, of course, is call them and ask. However, you can also do some double-checking on your own to confirm what the school tells you.

If you plan to enroll in a regionally accredited traditional college or university, you can safely assume that the institution as a whole is eligible to participate in federal aid programs—since distance certificates and degrees are likely to be a very small proportion of its overall offerings (see "Selecting a Good Distance Learning Program" for a discussion of accreditation). However, because institutions have the discretion to exclude specific programs, you should double-check to see if the school disperses federal aid to students enrolled in programs that interest you. Call the financial aid office and ask. If you are not sure of the accreditation status, and therefore the Title IV status, of the school in which you are interested, first check with the school to find out which agencies, if any, have accredited it. Then visit the Department of Education's Web site to check on the accrediting agencies. The department lists the accrediting agencies of which it approves, and in its short description of each agency, it indicates whether or not the institutions it accredits qualify for Title IV funding. You can then call the accrediting agency to make sure it has indeed accredited the school or program in which you are interested.

FEDERAL AID PROGRAMS

Once you've established the eligibility of the institution and program in which you are interested, you may want to check the federal aid programs in which they participate. Not all schools participate in all the available programs.

Among the federal aid programs are Pell Grants, Federal Supplemental Educational Opportunity Grants, work-study, and William D. Ford Direct Loans (commonly called Stafford loans), and Perkins Loans.

Pell Grants. Pell Grants, which do not have to be repaid, are awarded to undergraduate students on the basis of need, even if they are enrolled less than half time. In some cases, a student enrolled in a postbaccalaureate teacher certification program may be awarded a Pell Grant. There are no Pell Grants for other graduate students.

The maximum amount of the Pell Grant changes each year and depends on annual funding allocations by Congress. The maximum award for the school year 2010–11 is $5,550. The amount of an award depends on a combination of your financial need, your costs to attend school, your enrollment status as a full-time or part-time student, and whether or not you plan to study for a full academic year or less.

If you are awarded a Pell Grant, the money can be applied directly to your school costs or be paid to you directly or some combination of these methods. Your school must inform you on how it will be disbursing your grant. Disbursements must occur at least once per term or a minimum of twice a year.

Federal Supplemental Educational Opportunity Grants. Federal Supplemental Educational Opportunity Grants (FSEOGs) are awards to undergraduates with exceptional financial need, even if they are enrolled less than half time. These grants generally go to Pell Grant recipients with the lowest EFC. The amount of an FSEOG ranges from $100 to $4,000 per year.

Unlike the Pell Grant program, which provides funds to each eligible student, the FSEOG program is campus-based. This means that the federal government awards each participating institution a certain amount of money, and the school's financial aid office decides how to allocate it. When the school uses up its funding for the year, there are no more FSEOGs awarded. Check with your school to see whether or not it participates in this program.

Federal Work-Study Program. Some colleges and universities participate in the federal work-study program, which provides part-time jobs in public and private nonprofit organizations to both undergraduate and graduate students who demonstrate financial need. The government pays up to 75 percent of your wages, and your employer pays the balance. The value of a work-study job depends on your need, the other elements in your financial aid package, and the amount of money the school has to offer. Not all universities have work-study funds, and some that do have the funds limit their use to undergraduates.

If you receive work-study funds, you may be able to use them in a job that is related to your field. You will have to check with the financial aid office to find out what jobs are available, whether or not you can use the funds in a job you find elsewhere, and what bureaucratic requirements you will have to satisfy.

Direct Loan Program. The Direct Loan is borrowed directly from the U.S. Department of Education through the college's financial aid office.

You are eligible to borrow under this loan program if you are enrolled at least half time and have financial need remaining after your EFC, Pell Grant eligibility, and aid from other sources are subtracted from your annual cost of attendance. Depending on your need, you may be eligible for a subsidized loan in which the government pays the interest that accrues while you are enrolled at least half time. If you cannot demonstrate sufficient financial need according to government criteria, you may still be able to borrow, but your loan will be unsubsidized. This means that interest will accrue on the loan while you are still in school unless you arrange to pay it during this period.

In both types of loans, repayment of the principal as well as future interest begins six months after you are last enrolled on at least a half-time basis. Undergraduates may borrow a maximum of $5,500 to $12,500 per year, depending on the year of undergrad education. Graduate students may borrow up to $20,500 per year up to a maximum of $138,500 (or $224,000 for health professionals), which includes any undergraduate loans you may still have. Currently Stafford loans have a fixed interest rate determined by loan type and first disbursement date. Subsidized Stafford loans to undergraduates first disbursed on or after July 1, 2010, have a fixed interest rate of 4.5%. All other Stafford loans first disbursed on or after July 1, 2006, have a fixed interest rate of 6.8%.

Perkins Loan Program. Another source of federal funds is the Perkins Loan program. The Perkins Loan is available to both undergraduate and graduate students who demonstrate exceptional financial need, whether enrolled full-time or part-time, and it is administered by each individual college or university. In some cases, schools reserve Perkins Loans for undergraduates. If you are an undergraduate eligible for a Perkins Loan, you may be able to borrow up to $5,500 per year with a $27,500 maximum. An eligible graduate student may be able to borrow up to $8,000 per year with a $60,000 maximum including undergraduate and graduate Perkins borrowing.

At present, the interest rate is 5 percent, and no interest accrues while you are enrolled in school at least half time. You must start repaying the loan nine months after you are last enrolled on a half-time basis. This loan is the best deal offered by the government.

REPAYING YOUR FEDERAL LOANS

After you graduate, leave school, or drop below half-time status, you will have a grace period of either six or nine months before loan payments start. During the grace period, you will be sent information about payment plans and your first payment due date. You can repay the loan over a maximum of ten years with a $50 minimum monthly payment, with a graduated plan in which the payments start out low and gradually increase, or with a plan that bases your payments on your income level.

You can also consolidate all your outstanding federal loans into one loan. Having one loan to repay will minimize the chances of administrative error and allow you to write one check per month rather than several.

If you have trouble repaying your federal loans, you may qualify for a deferment or forbearance on your loan. During a deferment, payments are suspended, and if the loan is subsidized, interest does not accrue. During forbearance, payments are postponed or reduced. Repayment assistance may be available if you serve in the military.

STATE AID PROGRAMS

Some states offer financial aid to state residents that attend school in-state, some offer aid to state residents that attend school in-state or elsewhere, and some offer aid to students that attend school in their state regardless of their residency status. Contact your state scholarship office directly to find out what's available and whether you are eligible to apply. Telephone numbers are listed in the Appendix.

PRIVATE SOURCES OF FINANCIAL AID

In addition to the federal government, other organizations provide financial aid to students. These include your school, national and local organizations, private lenders, employers, internships, and cooperative education programs.

THE COLLEGE OR UNIVERSITY

Second only to the federal government in the amount of financial aid disbursed yearly are colleges and universities. Many of these institutions award both need-based and merit-based aid to deserving students. To find out more about the types of aid that the school you are interested in disburses, contact the financial aid office.

NATIONAL AND LOCAL ORGANIZATIONS

Foundations, nonprofit organizations, churches, service and fraternal organizations, professional associations, corporations, unions, and many other national and local organizations award grants to students of higher education. Many of these awards go to students who fit a certain profile, but many of them are open to anyone who applies. The drawback of this type of aid is that you have to locate it and apply on your own.

PRIVATE LENDERS

Many students borrow from private lenders, whether through alternative loan programs, home equity loans, or other types of loans.

Alternative Loan Programs. In addition to the federal loan programs, there are many private alternative loan programs designed to help students. Most private loan programs disburse funds based on your creditworthiness rather than your financial need. Some loan programs target all types of students; others are designed specifically for graduate or professional students. In addition, you can use other types of private loans not specifically designed for education to help finance your degree. For more information, check with your bank and your school's financial aid office.

Home Equity Loans. For students who own their own homes, a home equity loan or line of credit can be an attractive financing alternative to private loan programs. Some of these loans are offered at low rates and allow you to defer payment of the principal for years. In addition, if you use the loan to pay for educational expenses, the interest on the loan is tax deductible.

Credit Cards. Whatever you do, do not use your credit cards to borrow money for school on a long-term basis. The interest rates and finance charges will be high, and the balance will grow astronomically. Credit cards are useful to pay tuition and fees if you (1) can pay the balance in full, (2) expect a student loan to come through shortly, (3) expect your employer to reimburse your costs. Otherwise, avoid them.

INTERNSHIPS AND COOPERATIVE EDUCATION PROGRAMS

In addition to the federal work-study program, there are other employment opportunities that may help you finance your education. Internships with organizations outside the university can provide money as well as practical experience in your field. As an intern, you are usually paid by the outside organization, and you may or may not get credit for the work you do. Although they have been common in the professional programs, such as design and business, for years, lately internships have been growing in popularity in academic programs as well.

In cooperative education programs, you usually alternate periods of full-time work in your field with periods of full-time study. You are paid for the work you do, and you may or may not get academic credit for it as well.

Internship and cooperative education programs may be administered in your department or by a separate office, so you will have to ask to find out.

EMPLOYER REIMBURSEMENT

If you work full time and attend school part time, you may be reimbursed for part or all of your tuition by your employer. Many employers require that you receive a minimum grade in order to qualify for reimbursement. Keep in mind, however, that your employer will withhold taxes and other deductions when it reimburses you, and you will have to make up the difference. Check with your employer before you enroll; some employers reimburse tuition only for job-related courses. Others will not reimburse employees for distance learning courses.

Some large corporations that consider job-related certificate and degrees as forms of employee training may underwrite the entire cost of a program. For example, AT&T paid Denise Petrosino's tuition directly to the University of Phoenix Online. "As long as I maintained a B average, I had 100 percent coverage," explains Petrosino, who earned a master's degree in organizational management.

LOCATING INFORMATION ABOUT FINANCIAL AID

Finding information about financial aid can be a challenge. There is no one central clearinghouse for information about financial aid for undergraduate and graduate study. You are going to have to check a number of different sources to get the full picture on possible sources of aid that are available for you. We'll discuss a few of them here, but for a list of financial aid resources, see the Appendix.

THE GOVERNMENT

The best source of information on federal aid for students is the U.S. government itself. The federal aid programs are administered by the U.S. Department of Education. You can contact them through their Web site, by telephone, or by mail. (See the Appendix for specifics.) Remember, however, that not all colleges and universities participate in each federal program, so if a particular federal aid program interests you, you will have to contact your school's financial aid office to make sure it's available.

If you are a graduate student, you should note that many agencies of the federal government offer fellowships to graduate students in related fields. Contact the agencies that are relevant to your field of study for further information.

For information on state aid, contact your state agency of higher education (see the Appendix).

THE COLLEGE OR UNIVERSITY

At a small college, the financial aid office is usually the source of all financial aid information. However, at a university, there is more than one office involved with student aid, and thus more than one source of information about it. Each university has a different administrative structure, so you will have to figure out the offices you will most likely need to contact. These may include:

- **The financial aid office.** The university-wide financial aid office is generally the best source of information about federal and private loan programs as well as university-based grants and federal work-study assistance. They may also be able to steer you to other sources of information.
- **The college or school's administrative office.** The next place to check is the administrative office of the college or school to which you are applying. For example, you may be applying for a master's degree in special education. This department may be under the jurisdiction of the College of Education. That office may or may not administer grants to the students of the college. Call to find out.
- **The office of the graduate school.** If you are a graduate student, it pays to check this administrative office; it may or may not have funding to award. If it does, the fellowships or grants are likely to be awarded on a university-wide, competitive basis.
- **The specific program or department to which you are applying.** Often a program brochure describes the types of aid that the department awards its students. If you cannot find this information in the materials you have, then call the program and ask. You'll be able to find out about program aid from this source.

It's important to check with all these offices to see what's available. It's also important to be proactive and call the financial aid office as well as other offices to find out your chances of receiving aid.

THE INTERNET

The Internet is an excellent source of information about all types of financial aid. One of the best places to start your Internet search for financial aid is the Financial Aid Information Page at www.finaid.org. This site has a great deal of information about the different types of financial aid and provides links to other relevant sites as well. It provides a good overview of the financial aid situation. In addition, the site offers several calculators that enable you to estimate many useful figures, including your EFC, projected costs of attendance, and future student loan payments. There are also a number of searchable databases of national scholarships and fellowships on the Internet. One searchable database of financial aid resources can be found on Peterson's Web site (www.petersons.com/finaid), which lists millions of sources of aid totaling billions of dollars. Another scholarship database is FastWeb at www.fastweb.com. On each of these sites, you'll need to answer a questionnaire about your educational background, field of study, and personal characteristics. When you are done, the database is searched to match your data with eligibility requirements of several hundred thousand fellowships and scholarships. You are then given a list of possible fellowships and scholarships to pursue on your own. There is no cost for either of these services.

There are a few things you should beware of when using Internet search services. First, a searchable database is only as good as its index, so you may find yourself getting some odd matches. In addition, most searchable databases of scholarships and fellowships are designed primarily for undergraduates, so the number of potential matches for a graduate student is far fewer than the several hundred thousand sources of aid that a database may contain. Finally, some of these

Internet search services charge a fee. Given the amount of free information that's available, both on the Internet and in libraries, it's not necessary to pay for this type of research.

PRINT DIRECTORIES

Although the searchable databases on the Internet are easy to use, it's still a good idea to check print directories of national scholarships, grants, and fellowships. These directories have indexes that make locating potential sources of funds easy. Scholarships, grants, and fellowships are indexed by field of study as well as by type of student. So, for example, you can search for all funding related to the study of Latin America or electrical engineering. Or you can search for funding that is targeted to Hispanic students, disabled students, or adult students. It's a good idea just to browse, too, in case something catches your eye.

There are quite a few directories that you can consult. For undergraduates, Peterson's *Scholarships, Grants, & Prizes* lists many private sources of aid, and Peterson's *College Money Handbook* covers college and university sources of financial aid. For graduate students, the *Annual Register of Grant Support: A Directory of Funding Sources*, published by the National Register Publishing Company, is a comprehensive guide to awards from the government, foundations, and business and professional organizations.

APPLYING FOR FINANCIAL AID

Depending on your personal situation and the requirements of the school, you may have to submit just one or a number of applications for financial aid. If you apply for need-based aid, university merit aid, national scholarships and fellowships, or private loan programs, you will have several application forms to deal with. However many applications you must submit, start the process early.

DEADLINES

"I cannot overemphasize the importance of applying early," says Emerelle McNair, former Director of Scholarships and Financial Aid at Southern Polytechnic State University in Georgia. "Most awards are made in spring for the following academic year." Be sure you've picked the correct deadlines from your program application information packet. *Students applying for financial aid often have an earlier deadline for the entire application.* If you look for sources of aid outside the program and university, such as national scholarships and fellowships, then it is even more important to start your research early—a full year or more before you plan to enroll.

Remember, it can easily take months to fill out applications and assemble all the supporting data for a financial aid request. You may need to submit income tax forms, untaxed income verification, asset verification, and documents that support any special circumstances you are claiming. For private scholarship applications, you may need to write an essay and provide letters of recommendation. So give yourself plenty of time to submit the initial application. Later, if you are asked to provide additional information or supporting documents, do so as quickly as possible.

THE FAFSA

The Free Application for Federal Student Aid (FAFSA) is the only form you will need to apply for most federal need-based aid programs and state aid programs as well. FAFSA is used by both undergraduate and graduate students. The FAFSA form is issued annually by the Department of Education at the end of each calendar year (see www.fafsa.ed.gov), and it is available both in paper and online. You use it to report financial data from the previous year in order to be considered for aid in the school year that starts the following fall. It's much easier to fill out the FAFSA if you have already done your federal income tax forms for the year, but since most schools require you to file the FAFSA in January or February, that may be difficult. If your federal income tax return is not done, use estimates so you can file the FAFSA on time. You can amend it later if necessary. Because the FAFSA is designed for undergraduate students who are dependent on their parents, if you are a working adult student you may find you are having difficulty interpreting some of the questions or that the questions do not cover all your circumstances. If there is information about your financial situation that is not elicited by the FAFSA but that you feel is germane to your application, then explain the circumstances in a separate letter to the financial aid office of the schools to which you apply. Suppose, for example, that you have been working full-time for a few years but you are planning to quit your job and attend school full-time. You would complete the FAFSA using the previous year's full-time income figures, but this would not be an accurate reflection of your financial situation during the following school year because your income will drop precipitously. In such a case, you would notify the financial aid office so that it can make a professional judgment as to whether or not your need should be revised upward.

After you submit the FAFSA, you will receive a Student Aid Report (SAR), an acknowledgment that includes a summary of the data you have sent them. Check to make sure the information is accurate and that the schools you have chosen to have the data sent to are correctly listed. If there are errors, make corrections right away. The SAR will also show your EFC, the amount you and your spouse (or parents if you are still a dependent) will be expected to contribute. This information is used by each school to calculate your financial need (cost of attendance minus EFC) and to award need-based aid.

SCHOOL'S FINANCIAL AID APPLICATION FORM OR CSS PROFILE®

A school may require that you submit a separate financial aid application in addition to the program application and the FAFSA. If you do not see such a form in the program application packet, call the admissions office to find out whether or not you need to obtain it from another office.

Some schools do not have their own financial aid application form. Instead, they require you to submit a standardized form, the College Scholarship Service's (CSS) Financial Aid PROFILE. This form is similar to the FAFSA, but it is used to award university aid.

THE PROGRAM APPLICATION

For many schools, the program application is the main application for university-based aid. Much of the nonfederal university-based aid for incoming students is determined by the admissions committee's assessment of the merit of program applications. So a strong program application, submitted on time, will improve your chances of getting aid from the program or university. Since you cannot predict which elements of your application will be weighted most heavily by a given admissions committee, do your best on all of them.

NATIONAL AND PRIVATE SCHOLARSHIP AND FELLOWSHIP APPLICATIONS

If you apply for national and/or private scholarships and fellowships, you will have to submit separate applications for each one to the awarding organizations. Follow instructions carefully, making sure you meet all deadlines. Some scholarship applications can be as elaborate as program applications, with letters of recommendation and essays, so allow yourself a lot of time to complete them.

FOLLOWING UP

Just as you do with your program application, follow up with your financial aid applications as well. If you do not receive the SAR, an acknowledgment that your FAFSA form was received, within a few weeks of filing the FAFSA, check on its status. In addition, call the university offices with which you are dealing to make sure everything is proceeding smoothly.

TAX BENEFITS FOR STUDENTS

Whether or not you receive financial aid, there are many recently enacted tax benefits for adults who want to return to school (as well as for parents who send or plan to send their children to college). In effect, these tax cuts make the first two years of college universally available, and they give many more working adults the financial means to go back to school. About 12.9 million students benefit—5.8 million under the HOPE Scholarship tax credit and 7.1 million under the Lifetime Learning tax credit. Countless others benefit from new rules concerning Individual Retirement Accounts (IRAs) and state tuition savings plans as well as from deductions on student loan interest and employer reimbursements for education expenses.

THE AMERICAN OPPORTUNITY CREDIT

The American Opportunity Credit (formerly the Hope Credit) can be claimed for expenses for the first four years of postsecondary education. This is a change from the previous Hope Credit. The American Opportunity Credit is also different from the Hope Credit in that it includes expenses for course-related books, supplies, and equipment. It is a tax credit of up to $2,500 of the cost of qualifying tuition and expenses, and up to 40% of the credit is refundable (up to $1,000).

Eligibility also differs from the former Hope Credit. A taxpayer who pays qualified tuition and related expenses and whose federal income tax return has a modified adjusted gross income of $80,000 or less ($160,000 or less for joint filers) is eligible for the credit. The credit is reduced if a taxpayer's modified adjusted gross income exceeds those amounts. A taxpayer whose modified adjusted gross income is greater than $90,000 ($180,000 for joint filers) cannot benefit from this credit.

THE LIFETIME LEARNING TAX CREDIT

The Lifetime Learning tax credit is targeted toward adults who want to go back to school, change careers, or take a course or two to upgrade their skills as well as to college juniors, seniors, and graduate and professional degree students. A family may receive a 20 percent tax credit for the first $10,000 of tuition and required fees, up to $2,000.

The Lifetime Learning tax credit is available for tuition and required fees less grants, scholarships, and other tax-free educational assistance. The maximum credit is determined on a per-taxpayer (family) basis, regardless of the number of postsecondary students in the family, and it is phased out at the same income levels as the American Opportunity Credit.

INDIVIDUAL RETIREMENT ACCOUNTS

Since January 1, 1998, taxpayers have been able to withdraw funds from an IRA, without penalty, for their own higher education expenses or those of their spouse, child, or even grandchild. However, you do have to pay income taxes on the amount you withdraw.

In addition, for each child under age 18, families may deposit $500 per year into an education IRA in the child's name. Earnings in the education IRA accumulate tax-free, and no taxes are due upon withdrawal if the money is used to pay for postsecondary tuition and required fees (less grants, scholarships, and other tax-free educational assistance), books, equipment, and eligible room and board expenses. Once the child reaches age 30, his or her education IRA must be closed or transferred to a younger member of the family.

A taxpayer's ability to contribute to an education IRA is phased out when the taxpayer is a joint filer with an adjusted gross income between $190,000 and $220,000, or a single filer with an adjusted gross income between $95,000 and $110,000. There are a few restrictions. For example, a student who receives the tax-free distributions from an education IRA may not, in the same year, benefit from the HOPE Scholarship or Lifetime Learning tax credits.

STATE TUITION PLANS

When a family uses a qualified state-sponsored tuition plan to save for college, no tax is due in connection with the plan until the time of withdrawal. Families can now use these plans to save not only for tuition but also for certain room and board expenses for students who attend college on at least a half-time basis. Tuition and required fees paid with withdrawals from a qualified state tuition plan are eligible for the HOPE Scholarship tax credit and Lifetime Learning tax credit.

TAX-DEDUCTIBLE STUDENT LOAN INTEREST

For many graduates, one of the first financial obligations is to repay their student loans. The student loan interest deduction reduces the burden of the repayment obligation by allowing students or their families to take a tax deduction for interest paid in the first 60 months of repayment on student loans. The deduction is available even if an individual does not itemize other deductions.

You can claim the deduction if all of the following apply: (1) You paid interest on a qualified student loan in the previous tax year; (2) Your filing status is not married filing separately; (3)

Your modified adjusted gross income is less than $70,000 ($145,000 if filing jointly); and (4) You and your spouse, if filing jointly, cannot be claimed as dependents on someone else's return. A qualified student loan is a loan you took out solely to pay qualified higher education expenses. See the instructions for Form 1040 to determine if your expenses qualify.

TAX-DEDUCTIBLE EMPLOYER REIMBURSEMENTS

If you take undergraduate courses and your employer reimburses you for education-related expenses, you may be able to exclude up to $5,250 of employer-provided education benefits from your income. Reimbursement for graduate and professional courses is not eligible for this exclusion and is counted as taxable income.

COMMUNITY SERVICE LOAN FORGIVENESS

This provision excludes from your income any student loan amounts forgiven by nonprofit, tax-exempt charitable, or educational institutions for borrowers who take community-service jobs that address unmet community needs. For example, a recent graduate who takes a low-paying job in a rural school will not owe any additional income tax if in recognition of this service her college or another charity forgives a loan it made to her to help pay her college costs. This provision applies to loans forgiven after August 5, 1997.

FOR ADDITIONAL INFORMATION

The tax issues relating to higher education are discussed in more detail in Internal Revenue Service Publication 970, *Tax Benefits for Higher Education.* To obtain a copy, visit the Internal Revenue Service Web site at www.irs.gov or call 800-829-3676 (toll-free).

PAYING FOR SCHOOL IS POSSIBLE

You can see that it *is* possible to find the financial aid that will help you pay for school. You will have to be persistent in your search for funds. You may have to spend time working on financial aid research and applications. You may have to borrow money. And once you enter a program, you may have to simplify your lifestyle in order to cut your expenses.

But if you really want to earn a degree or certificate, you can find the financial help that will make it possible. Be realistic about your needs, leave yourself enough time to complete all the paperwork, and do your homework. Now is a good time to look back on all the reasons why you want to continue your education—to remind yourself why it's worth it.

SUCCEEDING AS A DISTANCE LEARNER

Congratulations! You have weathered the selection and application process and you are about to embark on a new phase of your education. As you will soon find out for yourself, taking courses at a distance is not like going to class on campus. Distance learners often have the convenience of setting their own hours and pacing themselves in their studies. As we have seen in previous sections, the instructional technology lends itself to innovative approaches to teaching and learning, including more student participation and collaboration, especially in online courses. You'll find that because you work at a distance you will have more time to reflect about and respond to what you learn as well as to take part in discussions. You may be surprised at the ways in which the community of learning develops in a well-run distance course.

Of course, distance learners face a few challenges unique to the instructional design of distance courses. As a distance learner, you'll be expected to organize your time, work independently as well as collaboratively, take the initiative in your studies, and monitor your own progress, all while mastering the technology and using it as a valuable tool for learning.

So, in addition to the basic study skills you would need to earn any degree—reading, writing, analytical thinking, and test-taking skills—you will need other skills and strategies to succeed at distance learning. In this section we'll give you some suggestions and tips from successful distance learners that will help you become a more effective and successful student yourself.

MASTERING THE TECHNOLOGY

We'll start with technology, because success in distance learning depends first upon reliable technology that you understand how to use. Once you've mastered the technology, it will recede into the background and become something you simply use and even take for granted.

HAVING THE RIGHT EQUIPMENT

Before you start a course, make sure you have the technological tools you will need to participate in discussions and complete assignments. Most programs provide a list of technical requirements ahead of time. If your course is online, get a list of the hardware and software required, and make sure the computer you plan to use is properly equipped and that you have a reliable Internet service provider. If you take a course via broadcast or video, learn how to use your DVR and DVD player. If you have to buy equipment, don't skimp on specifications to save a few dollars now. The money you spend now to make sure you have the appropriate hardware and software is money well spent, because you'll find it much easier to get your work done properly if you are not struggling with inadequate machinery.

IMPROVING YOUR TECHNOLOGY SKILLS

If you have the proper equipment but think you may not be up to speed technologically, try to improve your technology skills before courses start. As we discussed in "Selecting a Good Distance Learning Program," many colleges offer online tutorials or sample minicourses that you can take if you feel you need some practice with the technology before you actually take your first course. "I am a computer novice and never realized the extent of the computer's online capabilities until I had to learn about it through trial and error," reports a language arts literacy teacher who took a graduate course online from Rutgers University. "This was very frustrating." So if you have the opportunity for a sample course or practice session before courses begin, take it.

TIPS FOR SUCCEEDING WITH TECHNOLOGY

To master the technology involved in your distance courses:

- Make sure you have the appropriate hardware and software for your courses, and don't skimp on the specifications if you need to purchase any items.
- Take a tutorial or sample minicourse ahead of time to familiarize yourself with the instructional technology.
- Allow yourself extra time at the beginning of the course to navigate the technology.
- Keep copies of your assignments and back up your computer files.
- Ask for help when you need it. Well-run distance programs have technological support via telephone seven days a week, 24 hours a day.

Remember, the technology involved in distance learning is a tool that anyone can master—it just may take some effort.

LEARNING ABOUT LIBRARY RESOURCES

Once you've got the technology working for you, the next resource you need to familiarize yourself with is the library. Understanding how to use a library is important to any student's success, but it is especially important for distance students who may not be able to get to a good bricks-and-mortar university library to get the materials they need.

TAKING AN ORIENTATION PROGRAM

One of the first things you should check before courses begin is whether or not a library services orientation program designed for distance students is available. If it is, sign up to take the orientation right away. "An early orientation to library resources, particularly interlibrary loans, is needed for those who can't physically access a library," recommends Kurt Krause, a hotel manager who took an online hospitality management course from

Virginia Tech. Learning about library services through an orientation program will save you time later on when you actually need to do research for a course.

LEARNING WHAT'S AVAILABLE ONLINE

Although the Internet has revolutionized the way we look for and store information, don't make the mistake of thinking that all the information you will need is available on the Internet. True, many journals, databases, catalogs, and newspapers are instantaneously available online, and you can access them directly or through the university library if a subscription is needed. However, the material that's available online is only a fraction of the total resources of a library. Books, for example, are still primarily in print form. Many academic journals provide only abstracts (not full-text articles) online, and a few are not online at all. Reference services may be available only face-to-face or by telephone. And reserve collections may or may not be available online. So one of the first tasks you face is to learn just what you can access online via the university library or directly on the Internet and what you must access in paper, microform, or other physical media.

PLANNING AHEAD TO GET THE MATERIALS YOU NEED

The reason you will need to know what your research resources are fairly early in the game is that you will have to plan ahead if you need to access nondigitized (paper) information at a distance, especially if the material needs to be secured via interlibrary loan. "Because I did not have physical access to a medical library in my community, I had to organize my data collection for assigned papers early in the semester," explains Patti Iversen. "The biggest handicap was the time delay in ordering and receiving full-text articles. A time lapse of three weeks from time of request to delivery of articles was common." You can see the need to plan ahead under these circumstances.

TIPS FOR SUCCEEDING WITH LIBRARY RESOURCES

In order to be prepared for course work, early in the term or, even better, before the term starts:

- **Take a library orientation if one is available.** If there is no formal distance orientation, call the library and ask for an informal orientation.
- **Check your local public and university libraries.** Find out what resources they have and whether or not you can arrange access.
- **Check each course syllabus very early in the term.** Determine whether you can obtain everything you will need online or whether you will have to make other arrangements for some items.
- **Use the reference services of your university library.** Ask for help. Reference librarians are there to help you, even if it's by e-mail or over the phone.

MANAGING YOUR TIME

"If you are a student at any college, there is one thing you just don't have enough of....TIME! Everything is about time," says Cena Barber, who took online courses toward her degree in political science and history at Drake University in Iowa. For students who have family and work responsibilities as well, lack of time is a particularly acute problem. "With life's challenges, kids, family, job—it's hard to keep your studies a high priority," explains Scott Garrod, who earned a master's degree in business from Syracuse University. "When your 4-year-old wants a story read, do you have to study your accounting? That's an easy choice, but it means making up the accounting at a later time."

GENERAL TIPS FOR MANAGING YOUR TIME

Not having enough time is a common problem. Distance learners can approach this problem in several ways:

- **Be realistic about how many courses you can handle.** If you work and/or have a family, you will have relatively little time to spend on schoolwork. Start out with one or two courses at a time, and then if you feel you can increase your courseload, do so. This is especially important if you take a distance course for the first time and don't know exactly what to expect.
- **Set up a regular time to study, but expect to be interrupted.** If you have a study schedule, you are more likely to get your schoolwork done, but be sure to leave some extra time. Unless you live alone, you'll need time for your family commitments. Young kids, especially, don't much care what you are doing when they need a parent, so if possible try to schedule study time when they are not around.
- **Set up a regular place to study.** Although it may be difficult if you are doing schoolwork at home, try to establish a study area that's yours alone to use. If possible, the area should be quiet and free of distractions. "Since you are doing the work at home you can be easily distracted," explains Andrea Bessel, who earned a bachelor's degree in business administration from the State University of New York at Oswego. "A lot of times something came up and I ended up setting my homework aside, which was not a good habit to get into." So if necessary, do schoolwork at your local public library or from work if your employer permits it.
- **Set priorities on what you have to do.** Make judgments about what you need to do, and then spend your time on activities that are the most important and must be done first. Get used to the fact that you may have to postpone some tasks.
- **Set deadlines.** Distance learning can be very unstructured, so you probably will have to be your own taskmaster. "I learned that I had to set deadlines for myself," says Brigit Dolan, who earned a master's degree from Gonzaga University in Washington, "or I never got anything done."
- **Don't procrastinate.** "Procrastination is your worst enemy," claims Robin Barnes, who earned a master's degree in nursing (family nurse-practitioner) from Gonzaga University.
- **Use time-management tools to help you schedule your time.** Planners, whether paper or electronic, can help you allocate time and keep track of deadlines. "To do" lists can help you manage your short-term commitments.

MANAGING TIME IN ONLINE COURSES

In addition to the lack of time that all students contend with, online distance learners face unique challenges associated with time, namely, managing the flexibility of the online format and dealing with lag time when communicating with students and faculty members.

MANAGING THE FLEXIBILITY OF ONLINE COURSES

Flexibility is a unique advantage that attracts people to asynchronous courses, especially online courses. But flexibility can have a downside as well. "The best thing about distance learning is the freedom to set one's own hours for study and learning. The worst thing about distance learning is the freedom to set one's own hours for study and learning!" exclaims a middle school language arts literacy teacher taking an online graduate course from Rutgers. "Although it hasn't happened to me, it is easy to put aside work and projects for the course when one is not locked into a regular schedule. I can see how one could easily fall behind through a lack of discipline." So you can see that you'll have to use your time-management skills to take advantage of the flexibility and not let it take advantage of you.

MANAGING THE AMOUNT OF TIME SPENT ONLINE

Not only does the flexibility of online courses mean that you need discipline to log on regularly, but once you are connected you have, in theory, as much time as you want to spend on the course. Cena Barber points out, "There is no time limit as to how long the class lasts. It could be 5 minutes one day and 5 hours the next." Unless you are careful, it's easy to spend more time than you really have on an online course, so before you log on, decide how much time you have to spend during that session.

GETTING ACCUSTOMED TO THE PACE

Another difference between online and traditional courses that comes as a surprise to many students is the pace at which discussions proceed. In an online course, there is a time interval between when you post a message and when you get a response—in an asynchronous discussion group—or when you send an e-mail and get a reply. Hours, even days, may elapse between exchanges on a topic, and it can take a while to get used to the slow progress of communication.

The time delay sometimes becomes a problem when students work on a group project with deadlines. "Given the time lag, it took ever so much more time to get anything done if you had to collaborate with anyone," explains a library media specialist taking an online postgraduate course from Rutgers. "When would they open the discussion thread? When would they respond? These were frustrations that I hadn't counted on and found difficult to deal with." To solve these problems, groups working on projects often communicate by telephone or in real-time chat rooms.

TIPS FOR MANAGING TIME IN ONLINE COURSES

Given the asynchronous nature of online courses, you will not be able to completely solve the time problems they pose. However, you can minimize or avoid them to some degree.

- **Set a schedule for logging on.** Even though no one may have given you a daily class schedule, you will benefit if you work one out for yourself. "You should become accustomed to getting online on a regular basis," advises a computer studies major at University of Maryland University College. "I log on each day to see what is new."
- **Limit the amount of time you will spend online at one session.** The limit might be 1 hour, for example. On some days that will be too much time, and on others, too little, but at least you will have a benchmark to aim for.
- **Don't fret about the time delays in asynchronous discussions.** Before you know it, you will have become used to this method of communication and it will no longer seem odd.
- **Use a chat room or the telephone when asynchronous communication becomes too slow.** You can make an appointment to meet in a chat room or have a teleconference if group work needs to be accomplished more efficiently. If e-mailing a fellow student or the instructor takes too long, try telephoning.

MANAGING TIME IN VIDEOTAPED COURSES

Students that take courses in which on-campus lectures are videotaped and mailed to them face a different set of time-management challenges. First, the weekly video may take a considerable amount of time to watch. And second, the taping, duplicating, and delivery time means that distance students lag behind on-campus students in the same course.

SCHEDULING TIME TO WATCH THE VIDEOS

Depending on the course load, students that take videotaped courses may find themselves with 3 to 12 hours or more of videos to watch each week on top of their assignments. Essentially, the amount of time is the same as it would be if they had to attend classes. Since they don't have to attend classes, inexperienced students may put off watching the videos, thinking they can catch up at a later date. "In the first semester, the learning curve is steep," comments Dale Ann Abendroth, assistant professor of nursing at Gonzaga University. "So I set up my assignments to force students into a pattern of watching the videotapes." If you have a savvy instructor, the assignments will put you on a schedule. If the instructor doesn't take a structured approach, you will need to plan a regular schedule to watch the videos in order to keep up with the course work.

MANAGING THE DELAY BETWEEN DISTANCE AND ON-CAMPUS STUDENTS

In videotaped courses, the distance students are a half-week to a week behind the on-campus students. "It can get a little confusing when reading topics don't correspond with lecture topics because the tapes arrive one week later than the class," explains Carla Gentry, who earned a Master of Science in Nursing (family nurse-practitioner) from Gonzaga University. If the course also has a Web-based component, the distance students have to cope with joining the Web-based discussion group and receiving the readings before the videotaped lectures arrive.

Schools do try to solve this time-delay problem, with mixed success. "Throughout the semester, we'd have a one-week lag on assignment due dates (in comparison to the students who are actually in class on campus)," explains Nicole DeRaleau, who earned a master's degree in engineering from Worcester Polytechnic Institute in Massachusetts. "At the end of the semester, however, we would have a one-week disadvantage because the whole class had to turn in final assignments, projects, and finals on the same date in order to get grades done on time," says DeRaleau. "This was *very* stressful." In contrast, at Gonzaga University's nursing program, distance students are permitted to take their final exams in their local communities a few days later than the on-campus students. "These are logistical problems that both the faculty and students become accustomed to solving," explains Abendroth.

TIPS FOR MANAGING TIME IN VIDEOTAPED COURSES

There are a couple of things you can do to manage your time if you take videotaped courses:

- **Set a schedule for watching the videos.** Even though you don't have to show up for class, you still need to put in classroom time in front of your own TV. If you're good at multitasking, you can follow Brigit Dolan's lead. "Sometimes I was able to pick up my house while listening and taking in the information," explains the former graduate student.
- **Keep up with your course work.** Since at times you may need to complete assignments or take exams with less lead time than on-campus students have, it's imperative that you keep up with the work on a regular basis. You may face an end-of-term time crunch, so study regularly throughout the course to minimize its effect.

COMMUNICATING WITH FACULTY

When you are a distance learner you can't just raise your hand and ask a question or stay after class to talk with the instructor. Even in two-way interactive video classes, which are more similar to traditional classes than other distance learning formats, there can be difficulties in communicating with an instructor at a remote location. "It can be a little more inconvenient to speak with your instructor if you need to ask about something you wouldn't ask in front of the whole class," reports a horticulture student taking a two-way interactive video course from the University of Cincinnati.

For students in online and videotaped courses, communicating with an instructor can be slow. "Sometimes you do more self-teaching because you cannot just drop into the instructor's office," explains Robin Barnes. "You may have to wait a day or two for an answer to a question. Have patience and be kind to yourself." However, you can use technology to your advantage in communicating with faculty members. E-mail, for example, is an excellent way to contact a faculty member to find out what his or her expectations are, to clarify assignments, or simply to ask a question. You may not get a response immediately, but most faculty members will answer their e-mail within a day or two. In fact, you should make a point of communicating with your instructor in distance courses. "Be sure to communicate regularly with your professor because [the course] can seem pretty far removed if you are not getting feedback every week or so," advises Sonja Cole, a middle school media specialist who took online courses from Rutgers.

TIPS FOR COMMUNICATING WITH FACULTY MEMBERS

To ensure you get the input an instructor can provide and to make yourself known, here are some strategies for communicating with faculty members:

- **Participate in online discussion groups.** Although your instructor may not comment all the time, he or she is following the class's discussions and will get to know you there.
- **Participate in class discussions in two-way interactive video courses.** It's easy to "hide in the back of the class" if you attend a course in a remote location, but you'll get more out of the class if you respond to the instructor and the class discussion.
- **Be assertive in communicating with your instructors.** "You have to take the initiative," advises a distance learning student. "If you do not make sure that you get the best learning opportunity that you can, no one is going to do that for you." Remember, most faculty members are more than happy to help their students.
- **Use e-mail or the telephone.** If you need to communicate with the instructor privately, use e-mail or the telephone. Most faculty members will respond within a day or two.

REACHING OUT TO YOUR FELLOW STUDENTS

Just as you should take the initiative in communicating with your instructors, you should also be proactive in communicating with fellow students. Communicating with your peers has two benefits: it helps you feel connected to the learning community and it enables you to learn from your fellow students. In addition, establishing good communication with fellow students is key to successful collaborative efforts.

MAKING CONNECTIONS WITH THE LEARNING COMMUNITY

"I made a conscious effort to build relationships with other students and to keep e-mail contact with them," explains Patti Iversen, who lives in Montana and took distance courses from Gonzaga University in Washington. "This allowed each of us the opportunity to get feedback and commiserate." Another student, who is earning a bachelor's degree in information systems management from University of Maryland University College, reports, "My experience with fellow classmates in the online classroom has been very positive. I have found that establishing relationships, despite the fact that they are short-lived, has aided me." During periods when your motivation flags, this connection with others in your courses can help energize you and put you back on track.

TAKING ADVANTAGE OF WHAT YOUR PEERS HAVE TO OFFER

Your fellow students can be resources for you. Many distance students are adults with considerable life and professional experience, so they can contribute as much as they learn from the interactions in a course. According to Michael Olsen, who taught distance courses on the hospitality industry at Virginia Tech, students in his courses were "mature, industry-experienced professionals who came extremely well prepared. They were good contributors and they were not afraid to interact." Scott Garrod, who earned a master's degree in business from Syracuse University, liked the broad range of people he met through his distance courses. "You do not develop deep relationships," he explains, "but in a distance program you meet a wider range of individuals across multiple countries and careers."

Since all this knowledge and experience is within easy reach, you should take advantage of it. "You need to read through the responses that others post on the Web, so that you actually gain something from the forum discussion," explains Beth Grote, a Drake University graduate who took a course online. Some students do more than simply participate in class and in online discussion groups—they form study groups of their own. "You just have to make it a point to form an Internet study group," suggests Robin Barnes. "We would try to converse once a week, more often if we were working on a project."

WORKING ON GROUP PROJECTS

Since instructors often assign group projects in distance courses to help forge a community of learners, you will probably find yourself working with others much more frequently than you did in your past on-campus classes. According to several distance students we surveyed, doing group projects well is one of the most challenging aspects of distance learning. Often the logistics of getting a group of busy working adults in different time zones to meet at an appointed time in a chat room or be available for a conference call can be daunting. In some online courses, separate discussion groups are formed so group members can communicate asynchronously. "You need to have lots of patience and dedication," warns Kevin Ruthen, who earned a master's degree in information resource management from Syracuse University. "Interaction in an online environment can often be more time-consuming than an on-campus meeting."

And the problems of interaction are not limited to time factors. In the online environment, it's sometimes difficult for a group to coalesce and assign roles and tasks to its members. "In one of my courses, members tiptoed around each other, no one wanting to seem overbearing and declare themselves the leader, boss, facilitator, whatever. But we really needed one," explains a library media specialist taking online courses from Rutgers. "It took quite a while for a shakedown to occur so that some work could be accomplished." She continues, "Another problem was what to do about members of the team who were unproductive. It's very hard to prod people over the Internet. On the other hand, since you don't have the opportunity for meandering, off-topic conversations that start in on-site classes, things move swiftly, on schedule."

TIPS FOR COMMUNICATING WELL WITH YOUR PEERS

To make the most of your interactions with your fellow students, you can use these suggestions:

- **Participate.** You should participate in discussions, whether they are in class in two-way interactive video courses or are online. You will get a lot more out of your courses if you take an active part. In addition, you will get to know the other students and they will get to know you.
- **Share your knowledge and experiences.** Don't assume you have nothing to offer. Most adults have plenty of experience and knowledge that can be of value to others.
- **If you need support from other students, ask for it.** Everyone runs into occasional problems in a course, even if the problem is simply feeling overwhelmed by the amount of work you have to do. Communicating with other students can help you solve problems and get back on track, or it can simply make you feel better because you've let off some steam.
- **Use various forms of communication as needed.** Don't feel limited to class time or discussion groups. You can e-mail or call people with whom you'd like to converse in private. Remember, other distance students may feel somewhat disconnected from the group, too, and they will probably welcome an overture from you.
- **Be assertive.** When you work in a group, be assertive about what you can contribute. If the group is not making progress, try to use some of your leadership skills to get things moving.

ENLISTING YOUR FAMILY'S SUPPORT

One of the main benefits of most distance learning courses is that you can take the course from home. But unless you live alone, that means that you are working from a shared space in the presence of your family. Not only do they have to cope with the fact that you have less time for them, but they have to watch you be inaccessible—not an easy task. Therefore you should make sure you enlist the support and cooperation of your family; having their support will make your life—and theirs—much easier.

One distance student made her education something of a family enterprise. "I worked full-time, and I was blessed with a wonderful, supportive husband and the 2 greatest children one could ever dream of," says LaVonne Johnson, who earned a master's degree in nursing from Gonzaga University. "We were in this together—everyone helping on some level," she continues, "My husband cooked, cleaned, did laundry, and would even proof papers. My 13-year-old daughter was a great help around the house, and my 16-year-old son was always helping with PowerPoint projects, statistical analysis, and Excel graphs. Needless-to-say, in return I tried really hard not to impact my family any more than they already were, and we got by."

IN CONCLUSION

Distance learning is challenging, but with motivation, self-discipline, and the support of family, coworkers, and fellow students, you can succeed in your courses and earn a certificate or degree if that's your goal. Perhaps the best summation of distance education we encountered from the scores of students we surveyed came from Patti Iversen:

> Distance learning isn't for the faint of heart or those who require considerable reinforcement to remain on task. It is sometimes difficult for others to recognize the challenges of the distance learner, as job, family, and community activities all continue as before. Finding a way to carve out of a busy schedule the time necessary to successfully complete courses that seem relatively invisible is a big challenge. At the same time, there is

absolutely no way that I could have hoped to accomplish the goal that I have set for myself except as a distance learner. I am able to stretch and grow, professionally and personally, while continuing to live a lifestyle that I value immensely. It isn't always an easy task—it is often rigorous and sometimes frustrating—but distance learning has opened a gate of opportunity for me that previously was inaccessible.

Distance learning can provide that opportunity for you as well.

ADDITIONAL RESOURCES

WHAT IS DISTANCE LEARNING?

You can find countless sources of information about distance learning by doing an Internet search. One Web site that lists links to distance learning resources is www.dmoz.org/Reference/Education/Distance_Learning. Some other good sources of information include the following:

The Chronicle of Higher Education
1255 23rd Street, NW
Washington, DC 20037
Phone: 202-466-1000
E-mail: circulation@chronicle.com
Web: http://chronicle.com

Russell, Thomas L. *The No Significant Difference Phenomenon.* Available at teleeducation.nb.ca/nosignificantdifference/.

2010 Distance Education Survey Results, Trends in eLearning: Tracking the Impact of eLearning at Community Colleges
Instructional Technology Council.
http://www.itcnetwork.org/attachments/article/87/ITCAnnualSurveyMay2011Final.pdf

IS DISTANCE LEARNING RIGHT FOR YOU?

Sometimes it helps to have some objective help when you are assessing your goals, aptitudes, strengths, and weaknesses:

National Board for Certified Counselors
3 Terrace Way, Suite D
Greensboro, NC 27403-3660
Phone: 800-398-5389 (toll-free)
E-mail: nbcc@nbcc.org
Web: www.nbcc.org

WHAT CAN YOU STUDY VIA DISTANCE LEARNING?

Print Directories

Guide to Distance Learning Programs in Canada 2001. Education International, 2001.

Equivalency Examinations

College Level Examination Program (CLEP)
P.O. Box 6600
Princeton, NJ 08541-6600
Phone: 609-771-7865
E-mail: clep@info.collegeboard.org
Web: www.collegeboard.org/clep

CLEP Success. Lawrenceville, NJ: Peterson's, 2009.

Master the CLEP, 12th edition, Peterson's, 2011.

DSST Exams
Phone: 877-471-9860 (toll-free)
E-mail: getcollegecredit@prometric.com
Web: www.getcollegecredit.com

Excelsior College Examination Program (formerly Regents College Examinations)
Test Administration Office
Excelsior College
7 Columbia Circle
Albany, NY 12203-5159
Phone: 888-647–2388 (toll-free)
E-mail: testadmn@excelsior.edu
Web: www.excelsior.edu/

GRE Subject Area Tests
GRE-ETS
P.O. Box 6000
Princeton, NJ 08541-6000
Phone: 609-771-7670
E-mail: gre-info@ets.org
Web: www.gre.org

Assessment for Life Experience

Council for Adult and Experiential Learning (CAEL)
55 East Monroe Street, Suite 1930
Chicago, IL 60603
Phone: 312-499-2600
E-mail: cael@cael.org
Web: www.cael.org

Credit for Work Training

American Council on Education
Center for Adult Learning Educational Credentials
One Dupont Circle NW
Washington, DC 20036
Phone: 202-939-9475
E-mail: credit@ace.nche.edu
Web: www.acenet.edu

Credit for Military Training

Servicemembers Opportunities Colleges
1307 New York Avenue NW, fifth floor
Washington, DC 20005-4701
Phone: 800-368-5622 (toll-free)
E-mail: socmail@aascu.org
Web: www.soc.aascu.org

SELECTING A GOOD DISTANCE LEARNING PROGRAM

The names and contact information of all agencies recognized by the U.S. Department of Education (www.ed.gov/offices/OPE/accreditation/natlagencies.html) and the Council for Higher Education Accreditation (www.chea.org) are listed below.

Institutional Accrediting Agencies—Regional

Middle States Association of Colleges and Schools

Accredits institutions in Delaware, District of Columbia, Maryland, New Jersey, New York, Pennsylvania, Puerto Rico, and the Virgin Islands.

Dr. Elizabeth Sibolski, President
Commission on Higher Education
3624 Market Street
Philadelphia, PA 19104-2680
Phone: 267-284-5000
Fax: 215-662-5501
E-mail: info@msache.org
Web: www.msache.org

New England Association of Schools and Colleges

Accredits institutions in Connecticut, Maine, Massachusetts, New Hampshire, Rhode Island, and Vermont.

Barbara E. Brittingham, Director
Commission on Institutions of Higher Education
209 Burlington Road
Bedford, MA 01730-1433
Phone: 781-271-0022
Fax: 781-271-0950
E-mail: kwillis@neasc.org
Web: www.neasc.org

North Central Association of Colleges and Schools

Accredits institutions in Arizona, Arkansas, Colorado, Illinois, Indiana, Iowa, Kansas, Michigan, Minnesota, Missouri, Nebraska, New Mexico, North Dakota, Ohio, Oklahoma, South Dakota, West Virginia, Wisconsin, and Wyoming.

Dr. Sylvia Manning, Executive Director
The Higher Learning Commission
230 South LaSalle Street, Suite 7-500
Chicago, IL 60604-1413
Phone: 800-621-7440
Fax: 312-263-7462
E-mail: smanning@hlcommission.org
Web: www.ncahigherlearningcommission.org

Northwest Commission on Colleges and Universities

Accredits institutions in Alaska, Idaho, Montana, Nevada, Oregon, Utah, and Washington.

Dr. Sandra E. Elman, Executive Director
Commission on Colleges
8060 165th Avenue, NE, Ste 100
Redmond, WA 98052
Phone: 425-558-4224
Fax: 425-376-0596
E-mail: selman@nwccu.org
Web: www.nwccu.org

Southern Association of Colleges and Schools

Accredits institutions in Alabama, Florida, Georgia, Kentucky, Louisiana, Mississippi, North Carolina, South Carolina, Tennessee, Texas, and Virginia.

Belle Wheelan, President
Commission on Colleges
1866 Southern Lane
Decatur, GA 30033-4097
Phone: 404-679-4500
Fax: 404-679-4558
E-mail: questions@sacscoc.org
Web: www.sacscoc.org

Western Association of Schools and Colleges

Accredits institutions in California, Guam, and Hawaii.

Ralph Wolff, President and Executive Director
Accrediting Commission for Senior Colleges and Universities
985 Atlantic Avenue, Suite 100
Alameda, CA 94501
Phone: 510-748-9001
Fax: 510-748-9797
E-mail: rwolff@wascsenior.org
Web: www.wascweb.org

Institutional Accrediting Agencies—Other

Accrediting Council for Independent Colleges and Schools

Albert C. Gray, Ph.D., Executive Director
750 First Street, NE, Suite 980
Washington, DC 20002-4241
Phone: 202-336-6780
Fax: 202-842-2593
E-mail: info@acics.org
Web: www.acics.org

Distance Education and Training Council

Michael P. Lambert, Executive Secretary
1601 Eighteenth Street, NW
Washington, DC 20009-2529
Phone: 202-234-5100
Fax: 202-332-1386
E-mail: brianna@detc.org
Web: www.detc.org

Specialized Accrediting Agencies

Acupuncture

William W. Goding, MEd, RRT; Interim Executive Director
Accreditation Commission for Acupuncture and Oriental Medicine
14502 Greenview Drive
Suite 300B
Laurel, MD 20708
Phone: 301-313-0855
Fax: 301-313-0912
E-mail: info@acaom.org
Web: www.acaom.org

Art and Design

Samuel Hope, Executive Director
National Association of Schools of Art and Design
11250 Roger Bacon Drive, Suite 21
Reston, VA 20190
Phone: 703-437-0700
Fax: 703-437-6312
E-mail: info@arts-accredit.org
Web: www.arts-accredit.org

Chiropractic

Lee Van Dusen, President
The Council on Chiropractic Education
8049 North 85th Way
Scottsdale, AZ 85258-4321
Phone: 480-443-8877
Fax: 480-483-7333
E-mail: cce@cce-usa.org
Web: www.cce-usa.org

Clinical Laboratory Science

Dianne M. Cearlock, CEO
National Accrediting Agency for Clinical Laboratory Sciences
5600 N. River Road
Rosemont, IL 60018
Phone: 312-714-8880
Fax: 312-714-8886
E-mail: info@naacls.org
Web: www.naacls.org

Dance

Samuel Hope, Executive Director
National Association of Schools of Dance
11250 Roger Bacon Drive, Suite 21
Reston, VA 20190
Phone: 703-437-0700
Fax: 703-437-6312
E-mail: info@arts-accredit.org
Web: www.arts-accredit.org

Dentistry

Anthony Ziebert, Director Commission on Dental Accreditation
American Dental Association
211 East Chicago Avenue, Suite 1900
Chicago, IL 60611
Phone: 312-440-4643
Fax: 312-440-2800
E-mail: accreditation@ada.org
Web: www.ada.org

Dietetics

Dr. Ulric K. Chung, Executive Director
American Dietetic Association
Commission on Accreditation for Dietetics Education
120 South Riverside Plaza
Suite 2000
Chicago, Illinois 60606-6995
Phone: 800-877-1600
Fax: 312-899-4817
E-mail: cade@eatright.org
Web: www.eatright.org/cade

Education

Arthur Wise, President
National Council for Accreditation of Teacher Education
2010 Massachusetts Avenue, NW
Washington, DC 20036-1023
Phone: 202-466-7496
Fax: 202-296-6620
E-mail: info@ncate.org
Web: www.ncate.org

Engineering

Michael Milligan, Executive Director
Accreditation Board for Engineering and Technology, Inc.
111 Market Place, Suite 1050
Baltimore, MD 21202
Phone: 410-347-7700
Fax: 410-625-2238
E-mail: accreditation@abet.org
Web: www.abet.org

Environment

National Environmental Health Science and Protection Accreditation Council
720 South Colorado Boulevard, Suite 970-S
Denver, CO 80246-1925
Phone: 303-756-9090
Fax: 303-691-9490
E-mail: staff@neha.org
Web: www.neha.org/AccredCouncil.html

Forestry

Michael T. Goergen, Jr., Executive Vice President and CEO
Committee on Education
Society of American Foresters
5400 Grosvenor Lane
Bethesda, MD 20814-2198
Phone: 301-897-8720 Ext. 119
Fax: 301-897-3690
E-mail: clearkt@safnet.org
Web: www.safnet.org

Health Services Administration

John S. Lloyd, President and CEO
Commission on Accreditatino of Healthcare Management Education
2111 Wilson Boulevard
Suite 700
Washington, DC 20001-4510
Phone: 703-351-5010
Fax: 703-991-5989
E-mail: info@cahme.org
Web: www.cahme.org

Interior Design

Holly Mattson, Director
Council for Interior Design Accreditation
206 Grandville Avenue, Suite 350
Grand Rapids, MI 49503-2920
Phone: 616-458-0400
Fax: 616-458-0460
E-mail: info@accredit-id.org
Web: www.accredit-id.org

Journalism and Mass Communications

Susanne Shaw, Executive Director
Accrediting Council on Education in Journalism and Mass Communications
School of Journalism
Stauffer-Flint Hall
University of Kansas
Lawrence, KS 66045
Phone: 785-864-3973
Fax: 785-864-5225
E-mail: sshaw@kuhub.cc.ukans.edu
Web: www.ukans.edu/~acejmc

Landscape Architecture

Ronald C. Leighton, Accreditation Manager
Landscape Architectural Accreditation Board
American Society of Landscape Architects
636 I Street, NW
Washington, DC 20001-3736
Phone: 202-898-2444
Fax: 202-898-1185
E-mail: rleighton@asla.org
Web: www.asla.org

Law

Hulett H. Askew, Consultant on Legal Education
American Bar Association
321 North Clark Street, 21st Floor
Chicago, Illinois 60654
Phone: 312-988-6738
Fax: 312-988-5681
E-mail: legaled@americanbar.org
Web: www.abanet.org/legaled/

Library

Karen O'Brien, Director
Office for Accreditation
American Library Association
50 East Huron Street
Chicago, Illinois 60611
Phone: 800-545-2433 Ext. 2432
Fax: 312-280-2433
E-mail: accred@ala.org
Web: www.ala.org/accreditation/

Marriage and Family Therapy

Jeff S. Harmon, Director of Accreditation Services
Commission on Accreditation for Marriage and Family Therapy Education
American Association for Marriage and Family Therapy
112 South Alfred Street
Alexandria, Virginia 22314-3061
Phone: 703-838-9808
Fax: 703-838-9805
E-mail: coa@aamft.org
Web: www.aamft.org

Medical Illustration

Commission on Accreditation of Allied Health Education Programs (CAAHEP)
Kathleen Megivern, Executive Director
1361 Park Street
Clearwater, Florida 33756
Phone: 727-210-2350
Fax: 727-210-2354
E-mail: mail@caahep.org
Web: www.caahep.org

Medicine

Liaison Committee on Medical Education (LCME)
In even-numbered years beginning each July 1, contact:
Dan Hunt, Secretary
Association of American Medical Colleges
2450 N Street, NW
Washington, DC 20037
Phone: 202-828-0596
Fax: 202-828-1125
E-mail: dhunt@aamc.org
Web: www.lcme.org

In odd-numbered years beginning each July 1, contact:
Barbara Barzansky, Secretary
American Medical Association
Council on Medical Education
515 North State Street
Chicago, Illinois 60654
Phone: 312-464-4933
Fax: 312-464-5830
E-mail: lcme@aamc.org
Web: www.ama-assn.org

Music

Samuel Hope, Executive Director
National Association of Schools of Music (NASM)
Commission on Accreditation
11250 Roger Bacon Drive, Suite 21
Reston, Virginia 20190
Phone: 703-437-0700
Fax: 703-437-6312
E-mail: info@arts-accredit.org
Web: www.arts-accredit.org

Naturopathic Medicine

Daniel Seitz, Executive Director
Council on Naturopathic Medical Education
P.O. Box 178
Great Barrington, Massachusetts 01230
Phone: 413-528-8877
Fax: 413-528-8880
E-mail: council@cnme.org
Web: www.cnme.org

Nurse Anesthesia

Francis R. Gerbasi, Executive Director
Council on Accreditation of Nurse Anesthesia Educational Programs
American Association of Nurse Anesthetists
222 South Prospect Avenue, Suite 304
Park Ridge, Illinois 60068
Phone: 847-692-7050 Ext. 1154
Fax: 847-692-6968
E-mail: info@aana.com
Web: www.aana.com

Nurse Education

Jennifer L. Butlin, Director
Commission on Collegiate Nursing Education (CCNE)
One Dupont Circle, NW, Suite 530
Washington, DC 20036-1120
Phone: 202-887-6791
Fax: 202-887-8476
E-mail: jbutlin@aacn.nche.edu
Web: www.aacn.nche.edu/accreditation

Nurse Midwifery

Susan E. Stone, Chair
Accreditation Commission for Midwifery Education
American College of Nurse-Midwives
Nurse-Midwifery Program
8403 Colesville Road, Suite 1550
Silver Spring, Maryland 20910
Phone: 240-485-1800
Fax: 240-485-1818
E-mail: susan.stone@frontierschool.edu
Web: www.midwife.org/acme

Jo Anne Myers-Ciecko, Executive Director
Midwifery Education Accreditation Council
P.O. Box 984
La Conner, Washington 98257
Phone: 360-466-2080
Fax: 480-907-2936
E-mail: info@meacschools.org
Web: www.meacschools.org

Nurse Practitioner

Susan Wysocki, President and CEO
National Association of Nurse Practitioners in Women's Health
Council on Accreditation
505 C Street, NE
Washington, DC 20002
Phone: 202-543-9693
Fax: 202-543-9858
E-mail: info@npwh.org
Web: www.npwh.org

Nursing

Sharon J. Tanner, Executive Director
National League for Nursing Accrediting Commission (NLNAC)
3343 Peachtree Road, NE, Suite 500
Atlanta, Georgia 30326
Phone: 404-975-5000
Fax: 404-975-5020
E-mail: nlnac@nlnac.org
Web: www.nlnac.org

Occupational Therapy

Neil Harvison, Director of Accreditation
American Occupational Therapy Association
4720 Montgomery Lane
P.O. Box 31220
Bethesda, Maryland 20824-1220
Phone: 301-652-2682 Ext. 2912
Fax: 301-652-7711
E-mail: nharvison@aota.org
Web: www.aota.org

Optometry

Joyce L. Urbeck, Administrative Director
Accreditation Council on Optometric Education
American Optometric Association (AOA)
243 North Lindbergh Boulevard
St. Louis, Missouri 63141
Phone: 314-991-4000 Ext. 246
Fax: 314-991-4101
E-mail: ACOE@aoa.org
Web: www.theacoe.org

Osteopathic Medicine

Konrad C. Miskowicz-Retz, Director
Department of Accreditation
Commission on Osteopathic College Accreditation
American Osteopathic Association
142 East Ontario Street
Chicago, Illinois 60611
Phone: 312-202-8048
Fax: 312-202-8202
E-mail: kretz@osteopathic.org
Web: www.osteopathic.org

Pharmacy

Peter H. Vlasses, Executive Director
Accreditation Council for Pharmacy Education
135 S. LaSalle Street, Suite 4100
Chicago, Illinois 60603-4810
Phone: 312-664-3575
Fax: 312-664-4652
E-mail: csinfo@acpe-accredit.org
Web: www.acpe-accredit.org

Physical Therapy

Mary Jane Harris, Director
Commission on Accreditation in Physical Therapy Education
American Physical Therapy Association (APTA)
1111 North Fairfax Street
Alexandria, Virginia 22314
Phone: 703-706-3245
Fax: 703-684-7343
E-mail: accreditation@apta.org
Web: www.apta.org

Physician Assistant Studies

John E. McCarty, Executive Director
Accreditation Review Commission on Education for the Physician Assistant, Inc. (ARC-PA)
12000 Findley Road, Suite 150
Johns Creek, Georgia 30097
Phone: 770-476-1224
Fax: 770-476-1738
E-mail: johnmccarty@arc-pa.org
Web: www.arc-pa.org

Planning

Shonagh Merits, Executive Director
American Institute of Certified Planners/Association of Collegiate Schools of Planning/American Planning Association
Planning Accreditation Board (PAB)
53 W. Jackson Boulevard, Suite 1315
Chicago, Illinois 60604
Phone: 312-334-1271
Fax: 312-334-1273
E-mail: pab@planning.org
Web: www.planningaccreditation.org

Podiatric Medicine

Alan R. Tinkleman, Executive Director
Council on Podiatric Medical Education
American Podiatric Medical Association
9312 Old Georgetown Road
Bethesda, Maryland 20814-1621
Phone: 301-571-9200
Fax: 301-571-4903
E-mail: artinkleman@apma.org
Web: www.cpme.org

Psychology and Counseling

Susan Zlotlow, Executive Director
Office of Program Consultation and Accreditation
American Psychological Association
750 First Street, NE
Washington, DC 20002-4242
Phone: 202-336-5979
Fax: 202-336-5978
E-mail: apaaccred@apa.org
Web: www.apa.org/ed/accreditation

Carol L. Bobby, Executive Director
Council for Accreditation of Counseling and Related Educational Programs
1001 North Fairfax Street, Suite 510
Alexandria, Virginia 22314
Phone: 703-535-5990
Fax: 703-739-6209
E-mail: cacrep@cacrep.org
Web: www.cacrep.org

Public Affairs and Administration

Crystal Calarusse, Executive Director
Commission on Peer Review and Accreditation
National Association of Schools of Public Affairs and Administration
1029 Vermont Avenue, NW, Suite 1100
Washington, DC 20005
Phone: 202-628-8965
Fax: 202-626-4978
E-mail: copra@naspaa.org
Web: www.naspaa.org

Public Health

Laura Rasar King, Executive Director
Council on Education for Public Health
800 Eye Street, NW, Suite 202
Washington, DC 20001-3710
Phone: 202-789-1050
Fax: 202-789-1895
E-mail: Lking@ceph.org
Web: www.ceph.org

Rehabilitation Education

Tom Evenson, President
Council on Rehabilitation Education (CORE)
Commission on Standards and Accreditation
1699 Woodfield Road, Suite 300
Schaumburg, Illinois 60173
Phone: 847-944-1345
Fax: 847-944-1346
E-mail: evenson@unt.edu
Web: www.core-rehab.org

Social Work

Stephen M. Holloway, Director of Accreditation
Commission on Accreditation
Council on Social Work Education
1701 Duke Street, Suite 200
Alexandria, Virginia 22314
Phone: 703-519-2044
Fax: 703-683-8080
E-mail: sholloway@cswe.org
Web: www.cswe.org

Speech-Language Pathology and Audiology

Patrima L. Tice, Director of Accreditation
American Speech-Language-Hearing Association
2200 Research Boulevard
Rockville, Maryland 20850-3289
Phone: 301-296-5796
Fax: 301-296-8750
E-mail: ptice@asha.org
Web: www.asha.org

Teacher Education

James G. Cibulka, President
National Council for Accreditation of Teacher Education
2010 Massachusetts Avenue, NW, Suite 500
Washington, DC 20036-1023
Phone: 202-466-7496
Fax: 202-296-6620
E-mail: ncate@ncate.org
Web: www.ncate.org

Frank B. Murray, President
Teacher Education Accreditation Council (TEAC)
Accreditation Committee
One Dupont Circle, Suite 320
Washington, DC 20036-0110
Phone: 202-466-7236
Fax: 202-466-7238
E-mail: frank@teac.org
Web: www.teac.org

Technology

Dr. Michale S. McComis, Executive Director
Accrediting Commission of Career Schools and Colleges (ACCSC)
2101 Wilson Boulevard, Suite 302
Arlington, Virginia 22201
Phone: 703-247-4212
Fax: 703-247-4533
E-mail: mccomis@accsc.org
Web: www.accsc.org

Theater

Samuel Hope, Executive Director
National Association of Schools of Theatre
Commission on Accreditation
11250 Roger Bacon Drive, Suite 21
Reston, Virginia 20190
Phone: 703-437-0700
Fax: 703-437-6312
E-mail: info@arts-accredit.org
Web: www.arts-accredit.org

Theology

Bernard Fryshman, Executive Vice President
Association of Advanced Rabbinical and Talmudic Schools (AARTS)
Accreditation Commission
11 Broadway, Suite 405
New York, New York 10004
Phone: 212-363-1991
Fax: 212-533-5335
E-mail: BFryshman@nyit.edu

Daniel O. Aleshire, Executive Director
Association of Theological Schools in the United States and Canada (ATS)
Commission on Accrediting
10 Summit Park Drive
Pittsburgh, Pennsylvania 15275-1110
Phone: 412-788-6505
Fax: 412-788-6510
E-mail: ats@ats.edu
Web: www.ats.edu

T. Paul Boatner, President
Transnational Association of Christian Colleges and Schools
Accreditation Commission
15935 Forest Road
Forest, Virginia 24551
Phone: 434-525-9539
Fax: 434-525-9538
E-mail: info@tracs.org
Web: www.tracs.org

Veterinary Medicine

Elizabeth Sabin, Director
Education and Research Division
American Veterinary Medical Association
Council on Education
1931 North Meacham Road, Suite 100
Schaumburg, Illinois 60173
Phone: 847-925-8070
Fax: 847-925-9329
E-mail: info@avma.org
Web: www.avma.org

Accreditation in Canada

To get general information about accreditation in Canada, visit the Web site of the Council of Ministers of Education. Their Web site also has contact information and links to the provincial departments of education.

Council of Ministers of Education, Canada
95 St. Clair Avenue West, Suite 1106
Toronto, Ontario
Canada M4V 1N6
Phone: 416-962-8100
Fax: 416-962-2800
E-mail: information@cmec.ca
Web: www.cmec.ca

Other Resources for Evaluating Programs

Bear, Mariah P., John Bear, and John B. Bear. *Bear's Guide to Earning Degrees By Distance Learning, 16th ed.* Ten Speed Press, 2006.

Quality on the Line: Benchmarks for Success in Internet-Based Distance Education. Washington, DC: The Institute for Higher Education Policy, March 2000. Available at www.ihep.com/qualityonline.pdf.

TAKING STANDARDIZED ADMISSIONS TESTS

SAT

For information about the SAT, contact the College Board:

SAT Program
The College Board
P.O. Box 025505
Miami, FL 33102
Phone: 866-756-7346 (in the U.S.);
212-713-7789 (international)
E-mail: sat@info.collegeboard.org
Web: www.collegeboard.org

The College Board offers free preparation advice and practice tests. The Web site also offers other test-preparation materials, including books, videos, and software, for a charge. Order at www.collegeboard.org or call 609-771-7243:

ACT

ACT Registration
P.O. Box 414
Iowa City, IA 52243-0414
Phone: 319-337-1270
Web: www.act.org/aap

The Web site offers test-preparation strategies, sample questions, and information about other ACT resources.

ACT Inc., *The Real ACT with CD.* Lawrenceville, NJ: Peterson's, 2010.

GRE

For information about the GRE, contact the Educational Testing Service:

GRE-ETS
P.O. Box 6000
Princeton, NJ 08541-6000
Phone: 609-771-7670
E-mail: gre-info@ets.org
Web site (GRE Online): www.gre.org

The Web site offers a lot of material that can be downloaded: information bulletins, practice tests, descriptions of the subject area tests, and preparation software. Order from ETS at www.gre.org:

GRE Big Book

GRE Powerprep Software. Includes test preparation for both the General Test and the Writing Assessment.

GRE Practicing to Take the General Test

Practice Books for Subject Area Tests

MAT

Pearson
19500 Bulverde Road
San Antonio, TX 78259
Phone: 800-622-3231 (toll-free);
210-339-8710
Web: www.milleranalogies.com

GMAT

GMAT
The Graduate Management Admission Council
11921 Freedom Drive, Suite 300
Reston, Virginia 20190
Phone: 703-668-9600
E-mail: contact via Web site
Web: www.gmac.com

TOEFL

Information on the TOEFL can be obtained from the Educational Testing Service:

TOEFL
P.O. Box 6151
Princeton, NJ 08541-6151
Phone: 609-771-7100
E-mail: toefl@ets.org
Web: www.toefl.org

APPLYING FOR ADMISSION TO DEGREE PROGRAMS

Davidson, Wilma, and Susan McCloskey. *Writing a Winning College Application Essay.* Lawrenceville, NJ: Peterson's, 2002.

Hayden, Thomas C. *Insider's Guide to College Admissions.* Lawrenceville, NJ: Peterson's, 2000.

Stewart, Mark Alan *How to Write the Perfect Personal Statement, 4th ed.* Lawrenceville, NJ: Peterson's, 2009. Lots of suggestions, both from the author and admissions representatives of graduate and professional schools, along with many sample essays.

PAYING FOR YOUR EDUCATION

General Information

Financial Aid Information Page (www.finaid.org). The best place to start an Internet search for financial aid information.

National Association of Student Financial Aid Administrators (www.nasfaa.org). Lots of essays explain various aspects of financial aid, including educational tax credits.

State Residency

Todd, Daryl F., Jr. *How to Cut Tuition: The Complete Guide to In-State Tuition.* Linwood, NJ: Atlantic Educational Publishing, 1997.

Federal Aid

Federal Student Aid Information Center
P.O. Box 84
Washington, DC 20044-0084
Phone: 800-4-FED-AID (toll-free) (general information, assistance, and publications)
Web sites:
General information and home page: www.ed.gov/studentaid

For a copy of *Financial Aid: The Student Guide:* www.ed.gov/prog_info/SFA/StudentGuide.

For the FAFSA, go to FAFSA Online: www.fafsa.ed.gov.

For more on the Distance Education Demonstration Program: www.ed.gov/offices/OPE/PPI/DistEd/proginfo.html.

State Agencies of Higher Education

Alabama: 334-242-1998
Alaska: 907-465-2962
Arizona: 602-258-2435
Arkansas: 501-371-2000
California: 916-526-7590
Colorado: 303-866-2723
Connecticut: 860-947-1800
Delaware: 800-292-7935 (toll-free)
District of Columbia: 202-727-6436
Florida: 888-827-2004 (toll-free)
Georgia: 770-724-9000
Hawaii: 808-956-8213
Idaho: 208-334-2270
Illinois: 800-899-4722 (toll-free)
Indiana: 317-464-4400
Iowa: 515-725-3400
Kansas: 785-296-3421
Kentucky: 800-928-8926 (toll-free)
Louisiana: 800-259-5626 Ext. 1012 (toll-free)
Maine: 800-228-3734 (toll-free)
Maryland: 410-260-4500
Massachusetts: 617-994-6950
Michigan: 800-642-5626 (toll-free)
Minnesota: 800-657-3866 (toll-free)
Mississippi: 601-432-6623
Missouri: 800-473-6757 (toll-free)
Montana: 406-444-6570
Nebraska: 402-471-2847
Nevada: 775-687-9228
New Hampshire: 603-271-2555
New Jersey: 800-792-8670 (toll-free)
New Mexico: 800-279-9777 (toll-free)
New York: 888-697-4372 (toll-free)
North Carolina: 866-866-2362 (toll-free)
North Dakota: 701-328-4114
Ohio: 888-833-1133 (toll-free)
Oklahoma: 800-858-1840 (toll-free)
Oregon: 800-452-8807 (toll-free)
Pennsylvania: 717-787-5041
Rhode Island: 800-922-9855 (toll-free)
South Carolina: 803-737-2260
South Dakota: 605-773-3455
Tennessee: 615-741-3605
Texas: 800-242-3062 (toll-free)
Utah: 801-321-7103
Vermont: 800-642-3177 (toll-free)
Virginia: 804-225-2600
Washington: 360-753-7800
West Virginia: 304-558-0699
Wisconsin: 608-267-2206
Wyoming: 307-777-7763
Guam: 671-475-0457
Northern Marianas: 670-234-6128
Puerto Rico: 787-641-7100
Republic of Palau: 680-488-2471
Virgin Islands: 340-774-0100

CSS Financial Aid Profile

Contact the College Scholarship Service at www.collegeboard.org or 305-829-9793.

Grants, Fellowships, and Scholarships

AJR Newslink (www.newslink.org). Awards, grants, and scholarships for journalism students.

Annual Register of Grant Support: A Directory of Funding Sources. Wilmette, IL.: National Register Publishing Company.

Corporate Foundation Profiles. New York: Foundation Center, 1999 (http://fdncenter.org or 212-620-4230).

FastWeb (http://fastweb.com). Online searchable database of scholarships and fellowships.

How to Get Money for College: Financing Your Future Beyond Federal Aid 2012. Lawrenceville, NJ: Peterson's, 2011.

Scholarships, Grants, & Prizes 2012. Lawrenceville, NJ: Peterson's, 2011.

Cooperative Education

Re, Joseph M. *Earn and Learn.* Octameron Associates, 1997.

Credit Reporting Agencies

It's a good idea to check your credit rating before you apply for any loans. Call first to find out if there is a fee.

Experian
P.O. Box 9530
Allen, TX 75013
Phone: 888-397-3742 (toll-free)

Equifax
P.O. Box 740241
Atlanta, GA 30374
Phone: 800-685-1111 (toll-free)

CSC Credit Services
Consumer Assistance Center
652 N. Sam Houston Parkway E.
Houston, TX 77060
Phone: 800-305-7868 (toll-free)

Trans Union Corporation
2 Baldwin Place
Chester, PA 19022
Phone: 800-888-4213 (toll-free)

Tax Issues

Educational Expenses, IRS Publication 508.

Tax Benefits for Higher Education. IRS Publication 970.

To get a copy of these publications, visit the Internal Revenue Service Web site at www.irs.ustreas.gov/prod/forms_pubs/pubs or call 800-829-3676 (toll-free).

Women, Minority Students, Disabled Students, and Veterans

Bruce-Young, Doris M., and William C. Young. *Higher Education Money Book for Women and Minorities.* Young Enterprises International, 1997.

Minority and Women's Complete Scholarship Book; plus Scholarships for Religious Affiliations and People with Disabilities. Sourcebooks, 1998.

Olson, Elizabeth A. *Dollars for College (Women).* Garrett Park Press, 1995.

Saludos Web Education Center (www.saludos.com). Internships and scholarships targeted to Hispanic Americans as well as those not considering race or ethnicity.

Schlachter, Gail Ann, and R. David Weber. *Financial Aid for African Americans, 2009–2011.* Reference Service Press, 2009.

Schlachter, Gail Ann, and R. David Weber. *Financial Aid for the Disabled and Their Families, 2008–2010.* Reference Service Press, 2008.

Schlachter, Gail Ann, and R. David Weber. *Financial Aid for Veterans, Military Personnel, and Their Dependents, 2008–2010.* Reference Service Press, 2008.

Schlachter, Gail Ann. *Directory of Financial Aid for Women, 2009–2011.* Reference Service Press, 2009.

International Students

Funding for U.S. Study—A Guide for International Students and Professionals and *Financial Resources for International Study*. New York: Institute of International Education (www.iiebooks.org).

SUCCEEDING AS A DISTANCE LEARNER

Peterson's *How to Master Online Learning.* Lawrenceville, NJ; 2010.

Bruno, Frank J. *Going Back to School: College Survival Strategies for Adult Students.* New York, Arco, 1998.

GLOSSARY

accreditation—in the United States, the process by which private, nongovernmental educational agencies with regional or national scope certify that colleges and universities provide educational programs at basic levels of quality

ACT—a standardized undergraduate admissions test that is based on the typical high school curriculum

associate degree—a degree awarded upon the successful completion of a prebaccalaureate-level program, usually consisting of two years of full-time study at the college level

asynchronous—not simultaneous or concurrent; for example, discussion groups in online courses are asynchronous because students can log on and post messages at any time

audioconferencing—electronic meeting in which participants in remote locations can communicate with one another using phones

bachelor's degree—a degree awarded upon the successful completion of about four years of full-time study at the college level

bandwidth—the width of frequencies required to transmit a communications signal without too much distortion; video, animation, and sound require more bandwidth than text

broadband—a high-speed, high-capacity transmission channel carried on coaxial or fiber-optic cable; it has a higher *bandwidth* than telephone lines and so can transmit more data more quickly than telephone lines

broadcast radio and television—radio and television programs sent out over the airwaves; one of the earliest distance learning technologies still used today

browser—a computer program used to view, download, upload, or otherwise access documents (sites) on the World Wide Web

bulletin board—a site on the Internet where people can post messages

cable television—television programming transmitted over optical fiber, coaxial, or twisted pair (telephone) cables

CD-ROM—compact disc, read-only memory; an optical storage technology that allows you to store and play back data

certificate—an educational credential awarded upon completion of a structured curriculum, typically including several courses but lasting for a period of time less than that required for a degree

certification—the awarding of a credential, usually by a professional or industry group, usually after a course of study and the passing of an exam

chat room—a site on the Internet in which people can communicate synchronously by typing messages to one another

CLEP—the College Level Examination Program, administered by the College Board, that tests students' subject knowledge in order to award college-level credit for noncollegiate learning

common application form—a standardized basic admissions application form, available online, that is used by many colleges

consortium—a group of colleges and universities that pool resources to enable students to take courses as needed from all participating institutions

continuing education unit—10 contact hours of participation in an organized continuing education program; a nationwide, standardized measure of continuing education courses

correspondence course—individual or self-guided study by mail from a college or university for which credit is typically granted through written assignments and proctored examinations; also referred to as *independent study*

correspondence school—a school whose primary means of delivering instruction is via *correspondence courses*

cost of attendance—the total cost, including tuition, fees, living expenses, books, supplies, and miscellaneous expenses, of attending a particular school for an academic year

distance learning—the delivery of educational programs to students who are off site; also called *distance education*

doctoral degree—the highest degree awarded upon demonstrated mastery of a subject, including the ability to do scholarly research

DSSTs—a series of equivalency examinations used originally by the U.S. Department of Defense but now available to civilians as well

DVD—digital video disc; an optical storage technology that allows you to store and retrieve audio and video data

DVR—digital video recorder

e-learning—distance learning via the Internet; sometimes called *online learning*

e-mail—text or other messages sent over the Internet

enrollment status—whether a student is enrolled full-time, three-quarter-time, half-time, or less than half-time in a degree or certificate program

equivalency examination—an examination similar to the final exam of a college-level course; if you pass, you may be awarded college-level credit; for example, the CLEP and DSST exams

Excelsior College Examinations—a series of equivalency examinations administered by Excelsior College; formerly the Regents College Examinations

Expected Family Contribution (EFC)—the amount a student and his or her family are expected to contribute to the cost of the student's education per academic year

FAFSA—the Free Application for Federal Student Aid; needed to apply for federal aid programs

fax machine—a telecopying device that transmits written or graphic material over telephone lines to produce a hard copy at a remote location

Federal Supplemental Educational Opportunity Grant (FSEOG)—a federal grant awarded to students that demonstrate the greatest financial need

Federal Work-Study Program—provides part-time jobs in public and private nonprofit organizations to both undergraduate and graduate students who demonstrate financial need; the government pays up to 75 percent of the student's wages, and the employer pays the balance

fellowship—monies to be used for a student's education that does not have to be repaid; also called a *grant* or *scholarship*

financial need—the amount of money a student needs to be given or loaned or to earn through work-study, in order to attend school for one year, calculated by subtracting Expected Family Contribution (EFC) from cost of attendance

first-professional degree—a degree awarded upon the successful completion of a program of study (for which a bachelor's degree is normally the prerequisite) that prepares a student for a specific profession

GMAT—the Graduate Management Admissions Test, a standardized test used by many graduate programs in business

graduate degree—a degree awarded upon the successful completion of a program of study at the postbaccalaureate level; usually a master's or doctoral degree

grant—monies to be used for a student's education that do not have to be repaid; also called a *scholarship* or *fellowship*

GRE General Test—the Graduate Record Examinations General Test, which tests verbal, quantitative, and analytical skills; usually taken by prospective graduate students

GRE Subject Area Tests—examinations that assess knowledge usually acquired in college-level courses

instructional design—the way course content is organized for the learner; it varies from one distance technology to another

Internet—the global computer network of networks that allows for the transmission of words, images, and sound to anyone with an Internet connection; one of the major instructional delivery systems for distance learning

Internet service provider (ISP)—a company such as AOL or Earthlink that serves as a gateway to the Internet; by subscribing to its service, an individual can connect to the Internet

life experience—a basis for earning college credit, usually demonstrated by means of a portfolio

LSAT—the Law School Admissions Test, taken by law school applicants

master's degree—a degree awarded upon the successful completion of a program of study beyond the baccalaureate level that typically requires one or two years of full-time study

MAT—the Miller Analogies Test, a standardized admissions test used by some graduate programs

MCAT—the Medical College Admissions Test, taken by medical school applicants

merit-based aid—funding awarded on the basis of academic merit, regardless of financial need

modem—MOdulator DEModulator; a device that allows a computer to connect with other computers (and therefore the Internet) over telephone lines; the faster the modem speed, the faster data is transmitted

need-based aid—financial aid awarded on the basis of financial need; it may take the form of grants, loans, or work-study

online course—a course offered primarily over the Internet

online learning—distance learning via the Internet; sometimes called *e-learning*

Pell Grant—a federal grant that is awarded to students on the basis of financial need

Perkins Loan—a loan offered by the federal government to students with exceptional financial need

PowerPoint—a software program that enables the user to prepare slides with text, graphics, and sound; often used by instructors in their class presentations

PROFILE®—the financial aid application service of the College Board is a standardized financial aid application form used by many colleges and universities

SAT—a standardized undergraduate admissions test

SAT Subject Tests—subject area tests that assess high school–level knowledge; used by some schools for undergraduate admissions

satellite television—programming beamed to an orbiting satellite, then retrieved by one or more ground-based satellite dishes

scholarship—monies to be used for a student's education that do not have to be repaid; also called a *grant* or *fellowship*

Stafford Loan—a subsidized or unsubsidized loan that is offered by the federal government

streaming video—high *bandwidth* video data transmission

synchronous—occurring simultaneously, in real time

Title IV funds—federal money disbursed to eligible students through eligible, accredited institutions of higher learning or directly from the government

TOEFL—the Test of English as a Foreign Language, taken by students who are not native speakers of English

two-way interactive video—two-way communication of video and audio signals so that people in remote locations can see and hear one another

videoconferencing—one-way video and two-way audio transmission, or two-way video transmission conducted via satellite; instructors and students can communicate between remote locations

videotaped lecture—recording of an on-campus lecture or class session; usually mailed to distance learners enrolled in the course

virtual university—a college or university that offers most or all of its instruction exclusively via technology and usually for a profit

whiteboard—a program that allows multiple users at their own computers to draw and write comments on the same document

work-study award—an amount a student earns through part-time work as part of the Federal Work-Study Program

Institution Profiles

This section contains factual profiles of institutions, with a focus on their distance learning programs. Each profile covers such items as accreditation information, availability of financial aid, degree and certificate programs offered, non-degree-related course topics offered, and whom to contact for program information.

The profile information presented here was collected during the summer of 2011 via an online survey for distance learning programs and is arranged alphabetically.

ABILENE CHRISTIAN UNIVERSITY
Abilene, Texas
Instructional Technology
http://www.acu.edu/graduate/degree-programs/online-programs/index.html

Abilene Christian University was founded in 1906. It is accredited by Southern Association of Colleges and Schools. It first offered distance learning courses in 1996. In fall 2010, there were 400 students enrolled in distance learning courses. Institutionally administered financial aid is available to distance learners.

Services Distance learners have accessibility to academic advising, bookstore, campus computer network, career placement assistance, e-mail services, library services, tutoring.

Contact Mr. David Pittman, Director of Graduate Recruiting, Abilene Christian University, ACU Box 29000, Admissions and Recruiting, Abilene, TX 79699-9201. Telephone: 325-674-2656. Fax: 325-674-2130. E-mail: david.pittman@acu.edu.

DEGREES AND AWARDS
Certificate Conflict Resolution and Reconciliation; Leadership of Digital Learning; Superintendent Certification
MA Conflict Resolution and Reconciliation
MEd Curriculum and Instruction in Digital Learning; Curriculum and Instruction in Special Education; Curriculum and Instruction; Higher Education; Leadership of Learning Digital Learning; Leadership of Learning
MS Organizational and Human Resource Development (OHRD)

COURSE SUBJECT AREAS OFFERED OUTSIDE OF DEGREE PROGRAMS
Undergraduate—biblical studies; business/corporate communications; communication and media; economics; education; English.
Graduate—biblical studies; education; human development, family studies, and related services.

ACADEMY COLLEGE
Minneapolis, Minnesota
http://www.academycollege.edu

Academy College was founded in 1936. It is accredited by Accrediting Council for Independent Colleges and Schools. It first offered distance learning courses in 2005. In fall 2010, there were 111 students enrolled in distance learning courses. Institutionally administered financial aid is available to distance learners.

Services Distance learners have accessibility to academic advising, bookstore, campus computer network, career placement assistance, library services.

Contact Ms. Tracey Schantz, Campus Director, Academy College, 1101 East 78th Street, Suite 100, Bloomington, MN 55420. Telephone: 952-851-0066. Fax: 952-851-0094. E-mail: admissions@academycollege.edu.

DEGREES AND AWARDS
BSBA Business Administration

ACADEMY OF ART UNIVERSITY
San Francisco, California
http://online.academyart.edu

Academy of Art University was founded in 1929. It is accredited by Accrediting Council for Independent Colleges and Schools. It first offered distance learning courses in 2002. In fall 2010, there were 8,662 students enrolled in distance learning courses. Institutionally administered financial aid is available to distance learners.

Services Distance learners have accessibility to academic advising, bookstore, campus computer network, career placement assistance, e-mail services, tutoring.

Contact Admissions, Academy of Art University, 79 New Montgomery Street, San Francisco, CA 94105. Telephone: 800-544-2787. E-mail: info@academyart.edu.

DEGREES AND AWARDS
AA Advertising; Animation and Visual Effects; Fashion; Fine Art; Game Design; Graphic Design; Illustration; Industrial Design; Interior Architecture and Design; Motion Pictures and Television; Music for Visual Media; Photography; Web Design and New Media
BA Multimedia Communications
BFA Advertising; Animation and Visual Effects; Fashion; Fine Art; Game Design; Graphic Design; Illustration; Industrial Design; Interior Architecture and Design; Motion Pictures and Television; Music for Visual Media; Photography; Web Design and New Media
MA Multimedia Communications
MFA Advertising; Animation and Visual Effects; Fashion; Fine Art; Game Design; Graphic Design; Illustration; Industrial Design; Interior Architecture and Design; Motion Pictures and Television; Music for Visual Media; Photography; Web Design and New Media

COURSE SUBJECT AREAS OFFERED OUTSIDE OF DEGREE PROGRAMS
Undergraduate—apparel and textiles; communication and media; design and applied arts; film/video and photographic arts; fine and studio arts; graphic communications; interior architecture; visual and performing arts.
Graduate—apparel and textiles; communication and media; design and applied arts; film/video and photographic arts; fine and studio arts; graphic communications; interior architecture; visual and performing arts.

ACADIA UNIVERSITY
Wolfville, Nova Scotia, Canada
Division of Continuing and Distance Education
http://openacadia.ca

Acadia University was founded in 1838. It is provincially chartered. It first offered distance learning courses in 1968. In fall 2010, there were 1,000 students enrolled in distance learning courses. Institutionally administered financial aid is available to distance learners.

Services Distance learners have accessibility to academic advising, bookstore, campus computer network, e-mail services, library services, tutoring.

Contact Ms. Helen Tidcombe, Student Services Representative, Acadia University, Open Acadia, 38 Crowell Drive, Wolfville, NS B4P 2R6, Canada. Telephone: 800-565-6568. Fax: 902-585-1068. E-mail: openacadia@acadiau.ca.

DEGREES AND AWARDS
Programs offered do not lead to a degree or other formal award.

COURSE SUBJECT AREAS OFFERED OUTSIDE OF DEGREE PROGRAMS
Undergraduate—accounting and computer science; accounting and related services; astronomy and astrophysics; biblical studies; bilingual, multilingual, and multicultural education; biology; business administration, management and operations; business/commerce; business/corporate communications; business, management, and marketing related; business/managerial economics; chemistry; computer and information sciences; computer and information sciences and support services related; computer programming; computer science; economics; education; educational/instructional media design; education related; English; English language and literature related; English or French as a second or foreign language (teaching); foods, nutrition, and related services; geography and cartography; geological and earth sciences/geosciences; gerontology; history; languages (foreign languages related); liberal arts and sciences, general studies and humanities; linguistic, comparative, and related language studies; management sciences and quantitative methods; marketing; mathematics and computer science; microbiological sciences and immunology; multi/interdisciplinary studies related; music; nutrition sciences; philosophy; physics; political science and government; psychology; psychology related; social sciences; social sciences related; sociology; sociology and anthropology; special education.
Graduate—educational assessment, evaluation, and research; educational/instructional media design; education related.
Non-credit—mathematics.

ADAMS STATE COLLEGE
Alamosa, Colorado
Extended Studies
http://exstudies.adams.edu

Adams State College was founded in 1921. It is accredited by North Central Association of Colleges and Schools. It first offered distance learning courses in 1978. In fall 2010, there were 2,000 students enrolled in distance learning courses. Institutionally administered financial aid is available to distance learners.

Services Distance learners have accessibility to academic advising, bookstore, e-mail services, library services.

Contact Ms. Kaycee Gilmore-Holman, Student Advisor, Adams State College, Extended Studies, 208 Edgemont Boulevard, Alamosa, CO 81102. Telephone: 800-548-6679. Fax: 719-587-7974. E-mail: ascadvisor@adams.edu.

DEGREES AND AWARDS

AA General Education requirements

AS General Education requirements

BA Business Administration; Interdisciplinary Studies; Interdisciplinary Studies; Sociology

BS Business Administration

COURSE SUBJECT AREAS OFFERED OUTSIDE OF DEGREE PROGRAMS

Undergraduate—accounting and related services; agricultural business and management; business/commerce; business/corporate communications; business, management, and marketing related; business/managerial economics; criminal justice and corrections; criminology; English language and literature related; finance and financial management services; history; human resources management; legal studies (non-professional general, undergraduate); marketing; mathematics; sociology.

Graduate—education.

Non-credit—accounting and related services; business/commerce; computer software and media applications; data processing; entrepreneurial and small business operations; gerontology; linguistic, comparative, and related language studies; sales merchandising, and related marketing operations (general); sales, merchandising and related marketing operations (specialized).

AIB COLLEGE OF BUSINESS
Des Moines, Iowa
http://www.aib.edu/Admissions/OnlineClasses/tabid/159/Default.aspx

AIB College of Business was founded in 1921. It is accredited by North Central Association of Colleges and Schools. It first offered distance learning courses in 2001. In fall 2010, there were 500 students enrolled in distance learning courses. Institutionally administered financial aid is available to distance learners.

Services Distance learners have accessibility to academic advising, bookstore, campus computer network, career placement assistance, e-mail services, library services, tutoring.

Contact Ms. Shirlee Krouch, Admissions Counselor, AIB College of Business, 2500 Fleur Drive, Des Moines, IA 50321. Telephone: 800-444-1921. Fax: 515-244-6773. E-mail: krouchs@aib.edu.

DEGREES AND AWARDS

AAS Accounting and Business Leadership; Accounting and Financial Services; Accounting and Information Technology; Accounting; Business Administration and Financial Services; Business Administration and Information Technology; Business Administration and International Business; Business Administration and Leadership; Business Administration–Sales and Marketing; Business Administration; General Studies; Health Information Management; Sports and Event Management; Steno Transcription; Voice Captioning; Voice Court Reporting; Voice Transcription

BS Accounting; Business Administration

ALBERTUS MAGNUS COLLEGE
New Haven, Connecticut
http://www.albertus.edu/

Albertus Magnus College was founded in 1925. It is accredited by New England Association of Schools and Colleges. It first offered distance learning courses in 1998. In fall 2010, there were 998 students enrolled in distance learning courses. Institutionally administered financial aid is available to distance learners.

Services Distance learners have accessibility to academic advising, bookstore, campus computer network, career placement assistance, e-mail services, library services, tutoring.

Contact Bob Hubbard, Director of Academic Computer Programs, Albertus Magnus College, 700 Prospect Street, New Haven, CT 06511. Telephone: 203-773-8595. Fax: 203-773-8588. E-mail: rhubbard@albertus.edu.

DEGREES AND AWARDS

MBA Management

COURSE SUBJECT AREAS OFFERED OUTSIDE OF DEGREE PROGRAMS

Undergraduate—accounting and computer science; biology; business, management, and marketing related; communication and media; computer systems analysis; criminal justice and corrections; finance and financial management services; liberal arts and sciences, general studies and humanities; mathematics; philosophy and religious studies related; political science and government; sociology; statistics.

Graduate—business, management, and marketing related; education; human services; liberal arts and sciences, general studies and humanities.

ALCORN STATE UNIVERSITY
Alcorn State, Mississippi
Office of Academic Technologies
http://blackboard.alcorn.edu

Alcorn State University was founded in 1871. It is accredited by Southern Association of Colleges and Schools. It first offered distance learning courses in 1997. In fall 2010, there were 1,104 students enrolled in distance learning courses. Institutionally administered financial aid is available to distance learners.

Services Distance learners have accessibility to academic advising, bookstore, campus computer network, e-mail services, library services.

Contact Dr. Samuel L. White, Vice President for Academic Affairs, Alcorn State University, 1000 ASU Drive, #569, Alcorn State, MS 39096-7500. Telephone: 601-877-6142. Fax: 601-877-6256. E-mail: slwhite@alcorn.edu.

DEGREES AND AWARDS

BSN Nursing–BSN-RN On Line Program

MSN Nurse Educator

MSWEL Workforce Education Leadership (MSN)

COURSE SUBJECT AREAS OFFERED OUTSIDE OF DEGREE PROGRAMS

Undergraduate—accounting and computer science; accounting and related services; agriculture and agriculture operations related; business, management, and marketing related; engineering; finance and financial management services; history; human resources management; marketing; music; physical sciences; taxation.

Graduate—biological and biomedical sciences related; business, management, and marketing related; education; engineering technologies related; finance and financial management services; marketing; physical sciences.

ALLEN COLLEGE
Waterloo, Iowa
http://www.allencollege.edu/

Allen College was founded in 1989. It is accredited by North Central Association of Colleges and Schools. It first offered distance learning courses in 2000. In fall 2010, there were 450 students enrolled in distance learning courses. Institutionally administered financial aid is available to distance learners.

Services Distance learners have accessibility to academic advising, bookstore, campus computer network, career placement assistance, e-mail services, library services, tutoring.

Contact Ms. Brenda Colleen Barnes, Director, Medical Laboratory Science Program and Assistant Professor, Allen College, 1825 Logan Avenue, Waterloo, IA 50703. Telephone: 319-226-2082. Fax: 319-226-2051. E-mail: barnesbc@ihs.org.

DEGREES AND AWARDS
BHS Medical Laboratory Science
BSN Nursing–Bachelor of Science in Nursing
MSN Nursing

ALLEN COMMUNITY COLLEGE
Iola, Kansas
http://www.allencc.edu

Allen Community College was founded in 1923. It is accredited by North Central Association of Colleges and Schools. It first offered distance learning courses in 2001. In fall 2010, there were 1,500 students enrolled in distance learning courses. Institutionally administered financial aid is available to distance learners.

Services Distance learners have accessibility to academic advising, bookstore, campus computer network, career placement assistance, e-mail services, library services, tutoring.

Contact Ann Lindbloom, Online Coordinator, Allen Community College, PO Box 66, Burlingame, KS 66413. Telephone: 785-654-2416. E-mail: alindbloom@allencc.edu.

DEGREES AND AWARDS
Programs offered do not lead to a degree or other formal award.

COURSE SUBJECT AREAS OFFERED OUTSIDE OF DEGREE PROGRAMS
Undergraduate—accounting and computer science; agricultural business and management; agriculture; allied health and medical assisting services; anthropology; behavioral sciences; biological and physical sciences; biology; business administration, management and operations; business/commerce; business, management, and marketing related; business/managerial economics; cell biology and anatomical sciences; computer and information sciences; computer software and media applications; criminal justice and corrections; data entry/microcomputer applications; economics; English; geography and cartography; health aides/attendants/orderlies; health and physical education/fitness; history; mathematics; mathematics and statistics related; music; nutrition sciences; philosophy; physical sciences; political science and government; psychology; psychology related; sociology; statistics.

ALPENA COMMUNITY COLLEGE
Alpena, Michigan
http://www.alpenacc.edu

Alpena Community College was founded in 1952. It is accredited by North Central Association of Colleges and Schools. It first offered distance learning courses in 1997. In fall 2010, there were 264 students enrolled in distance learning courses. Institutionally administered financial aid is available to distance learners.

Services Distance learners have accessibility to academic advising, bookstore, e-mail services, library services, tutoring.

Contact Dr. Mark Curtis, Vice President for Academic and Student Affairs, Alpena Community College, 665 Johnson Street, Alpena, MI 49707. Telephone: 989-358-7458. Fax: 989-358-7568. E-mail: curtism@alpenacc.edu.

DEGREES AND AWARDS
Certificate Corrections Officer Academic program

COURSE SUBJECT AREAS OFFERED OUTSIDE OF DEGREE PROGRAMS
Undergraduate—computer/information technology administration and management; computer systems networking and telecommunications; construction trades related; criminal justice and corrections; electrical engineering technologies; English; English language and literature related; fine and studio arts; health and medical administrative services; mathematics; philosophy; political science and government; psychology; sociology.

Non-credit—building/construction finishing, management, and inspection; construction trades related; heavy/industrial equipment maintenance technologies; work and family studies.

ALVIN COMMUNITY COLLEGE
Alvin, Texas
Instructional Services
http://www.alvincollege.edu/de/default.htm

Alvin Community College was founded in 1949. It is accredited by Southern Association of Colleges and Schools. It first offered distance learning courses in 1995. In fall 2010, there were 1,272 students enrolled in distance learning courses. Institutionally administered financial aid is available to distance learners.

Services Distance learners have accessibility to academic advising, bookstore, career placement assistance, e-mail services, library services, tutoring.

Contact Mrs. Dena L. Faust, Director of Distance Education, Alvin Community College, 3110 Mustang Road, Alvin, TX 77511. Telephone: 281-756-3728. Fax: 281-756-3880. E-mail: dfaust@alvincollege.edu.

DEGREES AND AWARDS
AA Psychology/Sociology
AAS Management Development

COURSE SUBJECT AREAS OFFERED OUTSIDE OF DEGREE PROGRAMS
Undergraduate—anthropology; applied mathematics; archeology; biology; business administration, management and operations; business operations support and assistant services; computer and information sciences; computer/information technology administration and management; computer programming; computer science; computer software and media applications; curriculum and instruction; economics; English; geography and cartography; geological and earth sciences/geosciences; history; liberal arts and sciences, general studies and humanities; mathematics; mathematics and computer science; mathematics and statistics related; psychology; psychology related.

Non-credit—business operations support and assistant services; computer and information sciences; computer and information sciences and support services related.

AMBERTON UNIVERSITY
Garland, Texas
http://www.amberton.edu/

Amberton University was founded in 1971. It is accredited by Southern Association of Colleges and Schools. It first offered distance learning courses in 1992. In fall 2010, there were 887 students enrolled in distance learning courses. Institutionally administered financial aid is available to distance learners.

Services Distance learners have accessibility to academic advising, bookstore, library services.

Contact Dr. Jo Lynn Loyd, Vice President, Strategic Services, Amberton University, 1700 Eastgate Drive, Garland, TX 75041. Telephone: 972-279-6511 Ext. 126. Fax: 972-279-9773. E-mail: jloyd@amberton.edu.

DEGREES AND AWARDS
BBA Management
MA Professional Development

MBA Management
MS Human Relations and Business

COURSE SUBJECT AREAS OFFERED OUTSIDE OF DEGREE PROGRAMS
Undergraduate—accounting and related services; business administration, management and operations.
Graduate—business administration, management and operations.

THE AMERICAN COLLEGE
Bryn Mawr, Pennsylvania
http://www.theamericancollege.edu/
The American College was founded in 1927. It is accredited by Middle States Association of Colleges and Schools. It first offered distance learning courses in 1961. In fall 2010, there were 30,000 students enrolled in distance learning courses. Institutionally administered financial aid is available to distance learners.
Services Distance learners have accessibility to academic advising, bookstore, library services.
Contact Office of Student Services, The American College, 270 South Bryn Mawr Avenue, Bryn Mawr, PA 19010. Telephone: 888-263-7265. Fax: 610-526-1465. E-mail: studentservices@theamericancollege.edu.

DEGREES AND AWARDS
Certificate CFP(r) Certification Curriculum
Diploma Chartered Advisor for Senior Living (CASL) designation; Chartered Financial Consultant (ChFC(r)) designation; Chartered Healthcare Consultant -ChHC(tm); Chartered Leadership Fellow(r) (CLF(r)) designation; Chartered Life Underwriter (CLU(r)) designation; Financial Services Specialist (FSS); LUTC Fellow Designation; Registered Employee Benefits Consultant(r) (REBC(r)) designation; Registered Health Underwriter(r) (RHU(r)) designation
Advanced Graduate Diploma Chartered Advisor in Philanthropy(r)(CAP) designation
Graduate Certificate Business Succession Planning; Charitable Planning; Estate Planning and Taxation; Financial Planning–Graduate Financial Planning track
MSFS Financial Services
MSM Leadership

COURSE SUBJECT AREAS OFFERED OUTSIDE OF DEGREE PROGRAMS
Undergraduate—business administration, management and operations; business/commerce; finance and financial management services; gerontology; human resources management; insurance; sales, merchandising and related marketing operations (specialized); taxation.
Graduate—business administration, management and operations; business/commerce; finance and financial management services; human resources management; insurance; taxation.

AMERICAN GRADUATE UNIVERSITY
Covina, California
http://www.agu.edu/
American Graduate University is accredited by Distance Education and Training Council. It first offered distance learning courses in 1975. In fall 2010, there were 956 students enrolled in distance learning courses. Institutionally administered financial aid is available to distance learners.
Services Distance learners have accessibility to academic advising, bookstore, library services.
Contact Ms. Marie J. Sirney, Executive Vice President, American Graduate University, 733 North Dodsworth Avenue, Covina, CA 91724. Telephone: 626-966-4576 Ext. 1003. Fax: 626-915-1709. E-mail: mariesirney@agu.edu.

DEGREES AND AWARDS
MAM Acquisition Management–Master of Acquisition Management
MBA Acquisition and Contracting concentration or Project Management concentration; General Management
MCM Contract Management–Master of Contract Management
MPM Project Management–Master of Project Management
MSM Supply Management

COURSE SUBJECT AREAS OFFERED OUTSIDE OF DEGREE PROGRAMS
Graduate—accounting and related services; business administration, management and operations; business/corporate communications; business/managerial economics.

AMERICAN UNIVERSITY
Washington, District of Columbia
http://www.american.edu/onlinelearning
American University was founded in 1893. It is accredited by Middle States Association of Colleges and Schools. It first offered distance learning courses in 2004. In fall 2010, there were 36 students enrolled in distance learning courses.
Services Distance learners have accessibility to academic advising, bookstore, campus computer network, career placement assistance, e-mail services, library services.
Contact Online Learning, American University, 4400 Massachusetts Avenue, NW, Washington, DC 20016. Telephone: 202-885-2150. E-mail: onlinelearning@american.edu.

DEGREES AND AWARDS
Programs offered do not lead to a degree or other formal award.

COURSE SUBJECT AREAS OFFERED OUTSIDE OF DEGREE PROGRAMS
Undergraduate—anthropology; chemistry; communication and journalism related; criminology; education; English language and literature related; finance and financial management services; health and physical education/fitness; history; international business; international relations and national security studies; literature; political science and government; psychology.
Graduate—communication and journalism related; criminology; education; English language and literature related; health and physical education/fitness; international relations and national security studies; political science and government; psychology.

AMRIDGE UNIVERSITY
Montgomery, Alabama
Extended Learning Program
http://www.amridgeuniversity.edu
Amridge University was founded in 1967. It is accredited by Southern Association of Colleges and Schools. It first offered distance learning courses in 1993. In fall 2010, there were 749 students enrolled in distance learning courses. Institutionally administered financial aid is available to distance learners.
Services Distance learners have accessibility to academic advising, bookstore, career placement assistance, library services, tutoring.
Contact Carl Byrd, Call Center Coordinator, Amridge University, 1200 Taylor Road, Montgomery, AL 36117. Telephone: 800-351-4040 Ext. 7569. Fax: 334-387-3878. E-mail: carlbyrd@amridgeuniversity.edu.

DEGREES AND AWARDS
AA Liberal Studies
BA Biblical Studies
BS Business Administration/General Business; Business Administration/Information Communication; Business Administration/Information Systems Management; Human Development; Human Resource Leadership; Liberal Studies; Management Communication; Ministry/Bible; Public Safety and Business/Organization Security; Public Safety and Criminal Justice; Public Safety and Homeland Security
MA Behavioral Leadership and Management; Biblical Exposition; Biblical Studies; Historical and Theological Studies; Marriage and Family Therapy; Practical Ministry; Professional Counseling
MDiv Marriage and Family Therapy; Ministerial Leadership; Ministry; Pastoral Counseling; Professional Counseling

MS Leadership and Management; Ministerial Leadership; Pastoral Counseling
DMin Christian Ministry; Family Therapy
PhD Biblical Studies; Family Therapy

COURSE SUBJECT AREAS OFFERED OUTSIDE OF DEGREE PROGRAMS

Undergraduate—human services; liberal arts and sciences, general studies and humanities; missionary studies and missiology; pastoral counseling and specialized ministries; philosophy and religious studies related; religious studies; theological and ministerial studies.
Graduate—human services; missionary studies and missiology; pastoral counseling and specialized ministries; philosophy and religious studies related; religious studies; theological and ministerial studies.
Non-credit—human services; liberal arts and sciences, general studies and humanities; missionary studies and missiology; pastoral counseling and specialized ministries; philosophy and religious studies related; religious studies; theological and ministerial studies.

ANAHEIM UNIVERSITY
Anaheim, California
http://www.anaheim.edu

Anaheim University first offered distance learning courses in 1998. In fall 2010, there were 682 students enrolled in distance learning courses. Institutionally administered financial aid is available to distance learners.
Services Distance learners have accessibility to academic advising, bookstore, campus computer network, career placement assistance, e-mail services, library services, tutoring.
Contact Ms. Valda D. Judd, Administrative Director, Anaheim University, Office of Admissions, Room 110, 1240 South State College Boulevard, Anaheim, CA 92806. Telephone: 714-772-3330. Fax: 714-772-3331. E-mail: admissions@anaheim.edu.

DEGREES AND AWARDS

MA Teaching English to Speakers of Other Languages (TESOL)
MBA Online Global; Sustainable Management

COURSE SUBJECT AREAS OFFERED OUTSIDE OF DEGREE PROGRAMS

Graduate—business, management, and marketing related; English or French as a second or foreign language (teaching).
Non-credit—English or French as a second or foreign language (teaching).

ANDERSON UNIVERSITY
Anderson, Indiana
http://www.anderson.edu/sot/academics/onlinemts/index.html

Anderson University was founded in 1917. It is accredited by North Central Association of Colleges and Schools. It first offered distance learning courses in 1999. In fall 2010, there were 18 students enrolled in distance learning courses. Institutionally administered financial aid is available to distance learners.
Services Distance learners have accessibility to academic advising, bookstore, campus computer network, e-mail services, library services, tutoring.
Contact Dr. John H. Aukerman, Director of Distance Education, Anderson University, 1100 East 5th Street, Anderson, IN 46012. Telephone: 765-641-4530. Fax: 765-641-3005. E-mail: jhaukerman@anderson.edu.

DEGREES AND AWARDS

MA Christian Ministry

ANDERSON UNIVERSITY
Anderson, South Carolina
http://www.andersonuniversity.edu/#myGallery-picture(3)

Anderson University was founded in 1911. It is accredited by Southern Association of Colleges and Schools. It first offered distance learning courses in 2005. In fall 2010, there were 1,270 students enrolled in distance learning courses. Institutionally administered financial aid is available to distance learners.
Services Distance learners have accessibility to academic advising, bookstore, campus computer network, career placement assistance, e-mail services, library services.
Contact Mrs. Kathy G. Kay, Associate Director of Graduate and Evening Admissions, Anderson University, 316 Boulevard, Anderson, SC 29621. Telephone: 864-231-2020. Fax: 864-231-2115. E-mail: kkay@andersonuniversity.edu.

DEGREES AND AWARDS

BBA Healthcare Management
BCJ Criminal Justice
BCM Christian Studies
BSHS Behavioral Science; Human Services
MBA Business Administration
MMin Ministry

COURSE SUBJECT AREAS OFFERED OUTSIDE OF DEGREE PROGRAMS

Undergraduate—biology; business administration, management and operations; computer and information sciences; criminal justice and corrections; education; English; health services/allied health/health sciences; mathematics; political science and government; psychology; religious studies; sociology.
Graduate—business administration, management and operations; education; religious studies.

ANDOVER NEWTON THEOLOGICAL SCHOOL
Newton Centre, Massachusetts
http://www.ants.edu

Andover Newton Theological School was founded in 1807. It is accredited by New England Association of Schools and Colleges. It first offered distance learning courses in 1999. In fall 2010, there were 150 students enrolled in distance learning courses. Institutionally administered financial aid is available to distance learners.
Services Distance learners have accessibility to academic advising, bookstore, campus computer network, e-mail services, library services.
Contact Dr. Jeffrey Jones, Director of Distance Learning, Andover Newton Theological School, 210 Herrick Road, Newton Centre, MA 02459. Telephone: 617-964-1100 Ext. 2364. E-mail: jjones@ants.edu.

DEGREES AND AWARDS

Programs offered do not lead to a degree or other formal award.

COURSE SUBJECT AREAS OFFERED OUTSIDE OF DEGREE PROGRAMS

Graduate—biblical studies; history; missionary studies and missiology; pastoral counseling and specialized ministries; religious education; religious studies; theological and ministerial studies; theology and religious vocations related.
Non-credit—biblical studies; religious education; religious studies.

ANDREW JACKSON UNIVERSITY
Birmingham, Alabama
http://www.aju.edu/

Andrew Jackson University was founded in 1994. It is accredited by Distance Education and Training Council. It first offered distance learning courses in 1994. In fall 2010, there were 550 students enrolled in distance learning courses. Institutionally administered financial aid is available to distance learners.
Services Distance learners have accessibility to academic advising, bookstore, library services.
Contact Mrs. Tammy J. Kassner, Director of Admissions, Andrew Jackson University, 2919 John Hawkins Parkway, Birmingham, AL 35244. Telephone: 205-588-2827 Ext. 1. Fax: 877-737-6217. E-mail: admissions@aju.edu.

DEGREES AND AWARDS

AS Business; Communication; Criminal Justice; Psychology
BA Communications
BS Business, Entrepreneurship concentration; Business, General Business concentration; Business, Management/Leadership concentration; Business, Sales and Sales Management; Criminal Justice

MBA Entrepreneurship concentration; Finance concentration; Health Services Management concentration; Human Resource Management concentration; Management Concentration; Marketing concentration; Sales Management concentration; Strategic Leadership concentration
MPA Public Administration
MS Criminal Justice

COURSE SUBJECT AREAS OFFERED OUTSIDE OF DEGREE PROGRAMS

Undergraduate—business administration, management and operations; communication and media; criminal justice and corrections; entrepreneurial and small business operations.
Graduate—business administration, management and operations; criminal justice and corrections; entrepreneurial and small business operations; finance and financial management services; human resources management; public administration; sales, merchandising and related marketing operations (specialized).

ANDREWS UNIVERSITY
Berrien Springs, Michigan
http://www.andrews.edu/dlit

Andrews University was founded in 1874. It is accredited by North Central Association of Colleges and Schools. It first offered distance learning courses in 1997. In fall 2010, there were 125 students enrolled in distance learning courses. Institutionally administered financial aid is available to distance learners.
Services Distance learners have accessibility to academic advising, campus computer network, e-mail services, library services, tutoring.
Contact Mrs. Marsha Jean Beal, Director of the Center for Distance Learning and Instructional Technology, Andrews University, Room #304, James White Library, Berrien Springs, MI 49104-0074. Telephone: 269-471-6200. Fax: 269-471-6166. E-mail: bealmj@andrews.edu.

DEGREES AND AWARDS

AA Liberal Arts, General Studies, Humanities
BA Liberal Arts, General Studies, Humanities; Theological Studies
BS Liberal Arts, General Studies, Humanities
Ed S Curriculum and Instruction
MA Educational Administration
MAE Curriculum and Instruction
MS Nursing Education
EdD Curriculum and Instruction
PhD Curriculum and Instruction

COURSE SUBJECT AREAS OFFERED OUTSIDE OF DEGREE PROGRAMS

Undergraduate—area studies; astronomy and astrophysics; biblical studies; geography and cartography; history; languages (Romance languages); mathematics and statistics related; religious studies; sociology.
Graduate—education; religious studies.

ANGELINA COLLEGE
Lufkin, Texas
Continuing Education
http://www.angelina.edu

Angelina College was founded in 1968. It is accredited by Southern Association of Colleges and Schools. It first offered distance learning courses in 1990. In fall 2010, there were 5,800 students enrolled in distance learning courses. Institutionally administered financial aid is available to distance learners.
Services Distance learners have accessibility to academic advising, bookstore, campus computer network, e-mail services, library services, tutoring.
Contact Ms. Judith A. Wright, Coordinator of Off-Campus and Distance Learning, Angelina College, 3500 South First Street, P.O. Box 1768, Lufkin, TX 75902-1768. Telephone: 936-633-5392. Fax: 936-633-3235. E-mail: jwright@angelina.edu.

DEGREES AND AWARDS

Programs offered do not lead to a degree or other formal award.

COURSE SUBJECT AREAS OFFERED OUTSIDE OF DEGREE PROGRAMS

Undergraduate—accounting and related services; allied health and medical assisting services; behavioral sciences; biology; business/commerce; business/corporate communications; computer and information sciences; computer programming; computer software and media applications; criminal justice and corrections; drama/theatre arts and stagecraft; economics; electrical engineering technologies; health and physical education/fitness; health professions related; history; human biology; human services; legal studies (non-professional general, undergraduate); liberal arts and sciences, general studies and humanities; music; political science and government; psychology; sociology; visual and performing arts related.
Non-credit—biology/biotechnology laboratory technician; microbiological sciences and immunology; teaching assistants/aides.

ANGELO STATE UNIVERSITY
San Angelo, Texas
http://www.angelo.edu/

Angelo State University was founded in 1928. It is accredited by Southern Association of Colleges and Schools. It first offered distance learning courses in 2000. In fall 2010, there were 2,712 students enrolled in distance learning courses. Institutionally administered financial aid is available to distance learners.
Services Distance learners have accessibility to academic advising, bookstore, campus computer network, career placement assistance, e-mail services, library services, tutoring.
Contact Dr. Nancy Allen, Associate Vice President, Academic and Student Affairs, Angelo State University, 2601 West Avenue North, ASU Station #11008, San Angelo, TX 76909. Telephone: 325-942-2723 Ext. 298. Fax: 325-942-2128. E-mail: nancy.allen@angelo.edu.

DEGREES AND AWARDS

BSN Nursing–RN to BSN
Certification Education
MA Curriculum and Instruction
MEd Education
MS Applied Psychology
MSN Nursing–RN to MSN

COURSE SUBJECT AREAS OFFERED OUTSIDE OF DEGREE PROGRAMS

Undergraduate—business, management, and marketing related; communication and journalism related; computer and information sciences; computer science; economics; English; international business; mathematics; music; philosophy; political science and government; psychology; real estate; sociology.
Graduate—communication and journalism related; economics; English; psychology.

ANNE ARUNDEL COMMUNITY COLLEGE
Arnold, Maryland
Distance Learning Center
http://www.aacc.edu/virtualcampus

Anne Arundel Community College was founded in 1961. It is accredited by Middle States Association of Colleges and Schools. It first offered distance learning courses in 1981. In fall 2010, there were 5,863 students enrolled in distance learning courses. Institutionally administered financial aid is available to distance learners.
Services Distance learners have accessibility to academic advising, bookstore, campus computer network, career placement assistance, e-mail services, library services, tutoring.
Contact Ms. Patty McCarthy-O'Neill, Distance Learning Coordinator, Anne Arundel Community College, 101 College Parkway, Arnold, MD 21012-1895. Telephone: 410-777-2514. Fax: 410-777-2691. E-mail: pmmccarthyoneill@aacc.edu.

DEGREES AND AWARDS
AA Transfer Studies
AAS Business Management; Computer Information Systems, Programming/ Analysis option; General Technology
AS Business Administration transfer; Computer Science Transfer, Management Information Systems option

COURSE SUBJECT AREAS OFFERED OUTSIDE OF DEGREE PROGRAMS
Undergraduate—accounting and related services; allied health and medical assisting services; applied mathematics; behavioral sciences; biological and physical sciences; business administration, management and operations; business, management, and marketing related; business/ managerial economics; chemistry; communication and media; computer and information sciences; computer science; criminal justice and corrections; economics; finance and financial management services; geography and cartography; health and physical education/fitness; history; hospitality administration; intercultural/multicultural and diversity studies; legal studies (non-professional general, undergraduate); legal support services; marketing; mathematics and statistics related; philosophy; political science and government; social sciences related; sociology; statistics.
Non-credit—business, management, and marketing related; computer and information sciences; finance and financial management services; health services/allied health/health sciences; history; languages (foreign languages related).

ANTELOPE VALLEY COLLEGE
Lancaster, California

Antelope Valley College was founded in 1929. It is accredited by Western Association of Schools and Colleges. It first offered distance learning courses in 1996. Institutionally administered financial aid is available to distance learners.
Services Distance learners have accessibility to bookstore, career placement assistance, e-mail services, library services, tutoring.
Contact Dr. Jackie Fisher, Vice President of Academic Affairs, Antelope Valley College, 3041 West Avenue K, Lancaster, CA 93536-5426. Telephone: 661-722-6304. Fax: 661-722-6324. E-mail: jfisher@avc.edu.

DEGREES AND AWARDS
Programs offered do not lead to a degree or other formal award.

COURSE SUBJECT AREAS OFFERED OUTSIDE OF DEGREE PROGRAMS
Undergraduate—accounting and related services; astronomy and astrophysics; biology; business, management, and marketing related; chemistry; computational science; computer and information sciences; computer and information sciences and support services related; economics; English; English language and literature related; family and consumer sciences/ human sciences; film/video and photographic arts; geological and earth sciences/geosciences; health and physical education/fitness; history; human development, family studies, and related services; library science related; mathematics; nutrition sciences; political science and government; psychology; real estate; sociology.

ANTIOCH UNIVERSITY MIDWEST
Yellow Springs, Ohio
http://midwest.antioch.edu

Antioch University Midwest was founded in 1988. It is accredited by North Central Association of Colleges and Schools. It first offered distance learning courses in 1988. In fall 2010, there were 114 students enrolled in distance learning courses. Institutionally administered financial aid is available to distance learners.
Services Distance learners have accessibility to academic advising, bookstore, campus computer network, e-mail services, library services.
Contact Mr. Seth Gordon, Assistant Director of Admissions, Antioch University Midwest, 900 Dayton Street, Yellow Springs, OH 45387. Telephone: 937-769-1825. Fax: 937-769-1804. E-mail: sgordon@ antioch.edu.

DEGREES AND AWARDS
MA Community Change and Civic Leadership; Conflict Analysis and Engagement; Individualized Liberal and Professional Studies (various self-designed topics); Management

COURSE SUBJECT AREAS OFFERED OUTSIDE OF DEGREE PROGRAMS
Graduate—business administration, management and operations; education.

APPALACHIAN STATE UNIVERSITY
Boone, North Carolina
http://www.distance.appstate.edu/

Appalachian State University was founded in 1899. It is accredited by Southern Association of Colleges and Schools. It first offered distance learning courses in 1960. In fall 2010, there were 1,500 students enrolled in distance learning courses. Institutionally administered financial aid is available to distance learners.
Services Distance learners have accessibility to academic advising, bookstore, campus computer network, career placement assistance, e-mail services, library services, tutoring.
Contact Dr. Mary F. Englebert, Director, Office of Distance Education, Appalachian State University, Office of Distance Education, ASU Box 32054, Boone, NC 28608. Telephone: 828-262-6519. E-mail: englebertmf@appstate.edu.

DEGREES AND AWARDS
BS Business Education; Health Promotion
BSBA Management
License Curriculum post-Masters; School Administration
Graduate Certificate Appalachian Studies; Distance Education–Online Teaching and Learning; Gerontology; Sociology
MA Educational Media, Instructional Technology specialist (Computers); Educational Media, New Media and Global Education
MLS School and Public Library

AQUINAS INSTITUTE OF THEOLOGY
St. Louis, Missouri
http://www.ai.edu/

Aquinas Institute of Theology was founded in 1925. It is accredited by North Central Association of Colleges and Schools. It first offered distance learning courses in 1995. In fall 2010, there were 150 students enrolled in distance learning courses. Institutionally administered financial aid is available to distance learners.
Services Distance learners have accessibility to academic advising, campus computer network, e-mail services, library services.
Contact Ms. Mary Ann Steiner, Assistant to the Academic Dean, Aquinas Institute of Theology, 23 South Spring Avenue, St. Louis, MO 63108. Telephone: 314-256-8873. E-mail: steiner@ai.edu.

DEGREES AND AWARDS
MA General degree program; Health Care Mission; Pastoral Studies

COURSE SUBJECT AREAS OFFERED OUTSIDE OF DEGREE PROGRAMS
Graduate—theology and religious vocations related.

ARAPAHOE COMMUNITY COLLEGE
Littleton, Colorado
Educational Technology
http://www.arapahoe.edu

Arapahoe Community College was founded in 1965. It is accredited by North Central Association of Colleges and Schools. It first offered distance learning courses in 1985. In fall 2010, there were 3,938 students enrolled in distance learning courses. Institutionally administered financial aid is available to distance learners.
Services Distance learners have accessibility to academic advising, bookstore, campus computer network, e-mail services, library services.

Contact Lee Christopher, eLearning Manager, Arapahoe Community College, 5900 South Santa Fe Drive, Littleton, CO 80160. Telephone: 303-797-5965. Fax: 303-797-5700 Ext. 6700. E-mail: lee.christopher@arapahoe.edu.

DEGREES AND AWARDS

AAS Financial Services; Health Information Technology; Mortuary Science; Physical Therapist Assistant–Military Completer Program

COURSE SUBJECT AREAS OFFERED OUTSIDE OF DEGREE PROGRAMS

Undergraduate—accounting and computer science; accounting and related services; allied health and medical assisting services; allied health diagnostic, intervention, and treatment professions; anthropology; apparel and textiles; applied mathematics; architecture related; astronomy and astrophysics; audiovisual communications technologies; behavioral sciences; biochemistry, biophysics and molecular biology; bioethics/medical ethics; biology; business administration, management and operations; business/corporate communications; business, management, and marketing related; chemistry; clinical/medical laboratory science/research; communication and journalism related; communication and media; communications technology; computer and information sciences; computer and information sciences and support services related; computer/information technology administration and management; computer programming; computer science; computer software and media applications; computer systems analysis; computer systems networking and telecommunications; construction management; criminal justice and corrections; economics; education; educational administration and supervision; education related; education (specific levels and methods); education (specific subject areas); electrical engineering technologies; engineering technologies related; English; English language and literature related; entrepreneurial and small business operations; ethnic, cultural minority, gender, and group studies; film/video and photographic arts; finance and financial management services; funeral service and mortuary science; geography and cartography; geological and earth sciences/geosciences; geological/geophysical engineering; graphic communications; health aides/attendants/orderlies; health and medical administrative services; health and physical education/fitness; health/medical preparatory programs; health professions related; health services/allied health/health sciences; history; homeland security, law enforcement, firefighting and protective services related; human biology; human development, family studies, and related services; information science/studies; insurance; journalism; languages (Romance languages); languages (South Asian); legal professions and studies related; legal studies (non-professional general, undergraduate); legal support services; liberal arts and sciences, general studies and humanities; literature; management information systems; marketing; mathematics; mathematics and computer science; mathematics and statistics related; music; pharmacology and toxicology; pharmacy, pharmaceutical sciences, and administration; philosophy; physics; political science and government; psychology; psychology related; public health; public relations, advertising, and applied communication related; publishing; real estate; sales merchandising, and related marketing operations (general); sales, merchandising and related marketing operations (specialized); social and philosophical foundations of education; social sciences; sociology; sociology and anthropology; statistics; teaching assistants/aides; telecommunications management; vehicle maintenance and repair technologies; visual and performing arts.

ARIZONA WESTERN COLLEGE
Yuma, Arizona
http://www.azwestern.edu

Arizona Western College was founded in 1962. It is accredited by North Central Association of Colleges and Schools. It first offered distance learning courses in 1992. In fall 2010, there were 4,203 students enrolled in distance learning courses. Institutionally administered financial aid is available to distance learners.

Services Distance learners have accessibility to academic advising, bookstore, campus computer network, career placement assistance, e-mail services, library services, tutoring.

Contact Jana L. Moore, Associate Dean of Distance Education, Arizona Western College, PO Box 929, Yuma, AZ 85366-0929. Telephone: 928-317-6052. E-mail: jana.moore@azwestern.edu.

DEGREES AND AWARDS

AA Administration of Justice Studies; Education–Elementary; Education–Secondary; General Studies
AAS Business, general
AGS General Studies
AS General Studies

COURSE SUBJECT AREAS OFFERED OUTSIDE OF DEGREE PROGRAMS

Undergraduate—accounting and related services; business/commerce; computer and information sciences; criminal justice and corrections; English; fire protection; liberal arts and sciences, general studies and humanities.

ARKANSAS STATE UNIVERSITY
Jonesboro, Arkansas
Center for Regional Programs
http://www2.astate.edu/a/regional-programs/

Arkansas State University was founded in 1909. It is accredited by North Central Association of Colleges and Schools. It first offered distance learning courses in 1988. In fall 2010, there were 2,000 students enrolled in distance learning courses. Institutionally administered financial aid is available to distance learners.

Services Distance learners have accessibility to academic advising, bookstore, campus computer network, e-mail services, library services.

Contact Dr. Beverly Boals Gilbert, Dean, Continuing Education and Community Outreach, Arkansas State University, Continuing Education and Community Outreach, Box 2260, State University, AR 72467. Telephone: 870-972-3052. Fax: 870-972-3849. E-mail: bboals@astate.edu.

DEGREES AND AWARDS

Programs offered do not lead to a degree or other formal award.

COURSE SUBJECT AREAS OFFERED OUTSIDE OF DEGREE PROGRAMS

Undergraduate—accounting and related services; agricultural business and management; agriculture; bilingual, multilingual, and multicultural education; business administration, management and operations; business/corporate communications; business, management, and marketing related; computer/information technology administration and management; criminal justice and corrections; curriculum and instruction; economics; education; educational administration and supervision; engineering related; funeral service and mortuary science; human resources management; languages (foreign languages related); marketing; mathematics; military science, leadership and operational art related; registered nursing, nursing administration, nursing research and clinical nursing; social work; sociology.

Graduate—agriculture; business, management, and marketing related; curriculum and instruction; educational administration and supervision.

ARKANSAS STATE UNIVERSITY–BEEBE
Beebe, Arkansas
http://www.asub.edu/distance-learning/

Arkansas State University–Beebe was founded in 1927. It is accredited by North Central Association of Colleges and Schools. It first offered distance learning courses in 1999. In fall 2010, there were 1,600 students enrolled in distance learning courses. Institutionally administered financial aid is available to distance learners.

Services Distance learners have accessibility to academic advising, bookstore, e-mail services, library services, tutoring.

Contact Rhonda Durham, Director of Distance Learning, Arkansas State University–Beebe, PO Box 1000, Beebe, AR 72012. Telephone: 501-882-4442. Fax: 501-882-4403. E-mail: rsdurham@asub.edu.

DEGREES AND AWARDS

AA Liberal Arts

COURSE SUBJECT AREAS OFFERED OUTSIDE OF DEGREE PROGRAMS

Undergraduate—accounting and related services; agricultural business and management; business administration, management and operations; business/corporate communications; business, management, and marketing related; communication and media; computer and information sciences; computer programming; criminal justice and corrections; data entry/microcomputer applications; ecology, evolution, systematics, and population biology; economics; English; geography and cartography; geological and earth sciences/geosciences; history; mathematics; music; philosophy; physical sciences; political science and government; psychology; sociology; statistics; visual and performing arts.

ARKANSAS STATE UNIVERSITY–MOUNTAIN HOME
Mountain Home, Arkansas
http://www.asumh.edu

Arkansas State University–Mountain Home was founded in 2000. It is accredited by North Central Association of Colleges and Schools. It first offered distance learning courses in 2000. In fall 2010, there were 824 students enrolled in distance learning courses. Institutionally administered financial aid is available to distance learners.

Services Distance learners have accessibility to academic advising, bookstore, campus computer network, career placement assistance, e-mail services, library services, tutoring.

Contact Mr. Scott Raney, Director of Student Services, Arkansas State University–Mountain Home, 1600 South College Street, Mountain Home, AR 72653. Telephone: 870-508-6168. Fax: 870-508-6284. E-mail: sraney@asumh.edu.

DEGREES AND AWARDS

AA General degree

COURSE SUBJECT AREAS OFFERED OUTSIDE OF DEGREE PROGRAMS

Undergraduate—accounting and computer science; biology; business administration, management and operations; computer science; drama/theatre arts and stagecraft; economics; health professions related; history; liberal arts and sciences, general studies and humanities; mathematics.

ARKANSAS TECH UNIVERSITY
Russellville, Arkansas
Virtual Learning Center
http://www.atu.edu/etech/

Arkansas Tech University was founded in 1909. It is accredited by North Central Association of Colleges and Schools. It first offered distance learning courses in 1996. In fall 2010, there were 3,049 students enrolled in distance learning courses. Institutionally administered financial aid is available to distance learners.

Services Distance learners have accessibility to academic advising, bookstore, campus computer network, career placement assistance, e-mail services, library services.

Contact Admissions Office, Arkansas Tech University, 1605 Coliseum Drive, Suite 141, Russellville, AR 72801. Telephone: 479-968-0343. Fax: 479-964-0522. E-mail: tech.enroll@atu.edu.

DEGREES AND AWARDS

AS Early Childhood Education
BS Early Childhood Education; Emergency Administration and Management
MS College Student Personnel; Emergency Management and Homeland Security

COURSE SUBJECT AREAS OFFERED OUTSIDE OF DEGREE PROGRAMS

Undergraduate—agriculture; biology; business administration, management and operations; computer and information sciences; educational/instructional media design; education related; education (specific levels and methods); education (specific subject areas); electrical, electronics and communications engineering; English language and literature related; health and medical administrative services; history; homeland security, law enforcement, firefighting and protective services related; hospitality administration; journalism; marketing; mathematics; mechanic and repair technologies related; music; physical sciences; political science and government; psychology; rehabilitation and therapeutic professions.

Graduate—educational administration and supervision; educational/instructional media design; education related; education (specific subject areas); journalism.

ASBURY UNIVERSITY
Wilmore, Kentucky
http://www.asbury.edu

Asbury University was founded in 1890. It is accredited by Southern Association of Colleges and Schools. It first offered distance learning courses in 2006. Institutionally administered financial aid is available to distance learners.

Services Distance learners have accessibility to academic advising, bookstore, campus computer network, career placement assistance, e-mail services, library services, tutoring.

Contact Mrs. Theresa Scates, Online Campus Director, Asbury University, One Macklem Drive, Wilmore, KY 40390. Telephone: 859-858-3511 Ext. 2400. E-mail: theresa.scates@asbury.edu.

DEGREES AND AWARDS

Programs offered do not lead to a degree or other formal award.

COURSE SUBJECT AREAS OFFERED OUTSIDE OF DEGREE PROGRAMS

Undergraduate—biblical studies; business, management, and marketing related; economics; English language and literature related; history; philosophy; psychology; religious studies; sociology.

Graduate—education; educational administration and supervision; education (specific levels and methods).

ASHLAND UNIVERSITY
Ashland, Ohio
http://www.ashland.edu/graduate/online-programs

Ashland University was founded in 1878. It is accredited by North Central Association of Colleges and Schools. It first offered distance learning courses in 2000. In fall 2010, there were 789 students enrolled in distance learning courses. Institutionally administered financial aid is available to distance learners.

Services Distance learners have accessibility to academic advising, bookstore, campus computer network, career placement assistance, e-mail services, library services, tutoring.

Contact Dr. Greg Gerrick, Dean, Graduate School, Ashland University, 401 College Avenue, Ashland, OH 44805. Telephone: 419-289-5657. Fax: 419-289-5949. E-mail: ggerrick@ashland.edu.

DEGREES AND AWARDS

BSN Nursing–RN to BSN Track
Certificate Gerontology
Diploma Christian Studies
Endorsement Nursing–School Nurse Licensure; Technology Facilitator
MBA Executive Management
MFA Creative Writing

COURSE SUBJECT AREAS OFFERED OUTSIDE OF DEGREE PROGRAMS

Undergraduate—accounting and computer science; biological and physical sciences; business, management, and marketing related; chemistry; communication and journalism related; communication and media; computer/information technology administration and management; computer science; economics; education; English language and literature related; gerontology; history; management information systems; mathematics and computer science; philosophy and religious studies related; psychology; religious studies.

Graduate—biblical studies; education; theological and ministerial studies.

ASSUMPTION COLLEGE
Worcester, Massachusetts
Graduate School
http://graduate.assumption.edu/rehabilitation-counseling/online-master-arts-program-rehabilitation-counseling

Assumption College was founded in 1904. It is accredited by New England Association of Schools and Colleges. It first offered distance learning courses in 2007. In fall 2010, there were 54 students enrolled in distance learning courses. Institutionally administered financial aid is available to distance learners.

Services Distance learners have accessibility to academic advising, bookstore, campus computer network, career placement assistance, e-mail services, library services.

Contact Ms. Adrian O. Dumas, Director of Graduate Enrollment Management and Services, Assumption College, 500 Salisbury Street, Worcester, MA 01609. Telephone: 508-767-7387. Fax: 508-767-7030. E-mail: graduate@assumption.edu.

DEGREES AND AWARDS

MA Rehabilitation Counseling

ATHABASCA UNIVERSITY
Athabasca, Alberta, Canada
http://www.athabascau.ca/

Athabasca University was founded in 1970. It is provincially chartered. It first offered distance learning courses in 1972. In fall 2010, there were 37,000 students enrolled in distance learning courses. Institutionally administered financial aid is available to distance learners.

Services Distance learners have accessibility to academic advising, bookstore, campus computer network, library services, tutoring.

Contact Information Centre, Athabasca University, 1 University Drive, Athabasca, AB T9S 3A3, Canada. Telephone: 800-788-9041. Fax: 780-675-6437.

DEGREES AND AWARDS

BA Anthropology (3 year); Anthropology (4 year); Canadian Studies (4 year); English (3 year); English (4 year); French (3 year); French (4 year); History (3 year); History (4 year); Human Resources Management/Marketing (3 year); Human Resources Management/Marketing (4 year) and post-Diploma; Human Resources and Labour Relations and post-Diploma; Humanities (3 year); Humanities (4 year); Indigenous Nations and Organizations; Information Systems (3 year); Information Systems (4 year); Labour Studies (3 year); Labour Studies (4 year); Management post-Diploma (3 year); Management post-Diploma (4 year); Political Economy (3 year); Political Economy (4 year); Political Science (3 year); Political Science (4 year); Psychology (3 year); Psychology (4 year); Sociology (3 year); Sociology (4 year); Women's Studies (3 year); Women's Studies (4 year)

BComm Bcomm–Accounting and post-diploma major; Bcomm–Financial Services and post-diploma major; Bcomm–General and post-diploma; Bcomm–e-Commerce and post-diploma major

BGS Applied Studies; Arts and Science

BN Nursing–post-LPN; Nursing–post-RN

BPA Communication Studies; Criminal Justice; Governance, Law, and Management; Human Services

BS BSc and BSc post-diploma; Computing and Information Systems–post-Diploma; Computing and Information Systems; Health Administration post-Diploma; Health Administration; Human Science–post-Diploma; Human Science

Certificate Accounting; Accounting, advanced; Administration; Career Development; Computers and Management Information Systems; Computing and Information Systems; Counseling Women; E-Commerce; English Language Studies; Financial Services; French Language Proficiency; Health Development Administration; Heritage Resources Management; Human Resources and Labour Relations; Labour Studies; Management Applications; Management Foundations; Marketing; Public Administration

Diploma Arts; Inclusive Education

Advanced Graduate Diploma Counseling post-Graduate certificate; Distance Education (Technology); Human Resource Management; Instructional Design; Legislative Design; Management; Nursing–Nursing Practice, advanced

Graduate Certificate Instructional Design

MA Integrated Studies

MBA Business Administration; Energy Elective; Project Management

MC Collaborative

MDE Distance Education

MHS Health Studies

MN Nursing

MSIS Information Systems; Information Systems

DBA Business Administration

EdD Education

COURSE SUBJECT AREAS OFFERED OUTSIDE OF DEGREE PROGRAMS

Undergraduate—accounting and computer science; accounting and related services; anthropology; astronomy and astrophysics; behavioral sciences; biological and biomedical sciences related; biological and physical sciences; biology; business administration, management and operations; business/commerce; business/corporate communications; business, management, and marketing related; business/managerial economics; chemistry; communication and journalism related; communication and media; communication disorders sciences and services; communications technology; community organization and advocacy; computer and information sciences; computer and information sciences and support services related; computer/information technology administration and management; computer programming; computer science; computer software and media applications; computer systems analysis; computer systems networking and telecommunications; criminal justice and corrections; criminology; data processing; demography and population; economics; education; educational assessment, evaluation, and research; English; English language and literature related; environmental control technologies; finance and financial management services; fine and studio arts; foods, nutrition, and related services; geography and cartography; geological and earth sciences/geosciences; health and medical administrative services; health/medical preparatory programs; health professions related; history; human development, family studies, and related services; human resources management; human services; international relations and national security studies; journalism; legal studies (non-professional general, undergraduate); linguistic, comparative, and related language studies; management information systems; marketing; mathematics; mathematics and computer science; mental and social health services and allied professions; music; natural resources conservation and research; natural resources management and policy; philosophy; philosophy and religious studies related; physical sciences; plant sciences; political science and government; psychology; psychology related; public administration; public health; public policy analysis; public relations, advertising, and applied communication related; sales merchandising, and related marketing operations (general); social sciences; sociology; statistics.

Graduate—accounting and related services; agricultural business and management; business administration, management and operations; business/corporate communications; business, management, and marketing related; business/managerial economics; community organization and advocacy; computer and information sciences; computer and information sciences and support services related; computer/information technology administration and management; computer science; computer systems analysis; curriculum and instruction; economics; educational administration and supervision; educational assessment, evaluation, and research; education related; health/medical preparatory programs; health professions related; history; human development, family studies, and related services; human resources management; human services; information science/studies; international business; international relations and national security studies; management information systems; management sciences and quantitative methods; marketing; mathematics and computer science; mental and social health services and allied professions; philosophy; political science and government; psychology; public administration; public administration and social service professions related; public health; public policy analysis; public relations, advertising, and applied communication related; sales merchandising, and related mar-

keting operations (general); sales, merchandising and related marketing operations (specialized); social sciences; social sciences related; social work; sociology; special education; taxation.
Non-credit—accounting and related services; anthropology; astronomy and astrophysics; biology; building/construction finishing, management, and inspection; business administration, management and operations; business/commerce; business/corporate communications; business, management, and marketing related; business/managerial economics; business operations support and assistant services; chemistry; city/urban, community and regional planning; communication and media; communication disorders sciences and services; communications technology; community organization and advocacy; computer and information sciences; computer/information technology administration and management; computer programming; computer science; computer software and media applications; computer systems analysis; criminal justice and corrections; criminology; data entry/microcomputer applications; data processing; economics; educational administration and supervision; educational assessment, evaluation, and research; educational/instructional media design; education related; English; English or French as a second or foreign language (teaching); environmental control technologies; ethnic, cultural minority, gender, and group studies; finance and financial management services; fine and studio arts; foods, nutrition, and related services; geological and earth sciences/geosciences; gerontology; health professions related; history; human development, family studies, and related services; human resources management; human services; international business; international relations and national security studies; journalism; liberal arts and sciences, general studies and humanities; linguistic, comparative, and related language studies; management information systems; management sciences and quantitative methods; marketing; mathematics; mathematics and computer science; mental and social health services and allied professions; music; philosophy; philosophy and religious studies related; physical sciences; political science and government; psychology; public administration; public administration and social service professions related; public health; public policy analysis; public relations, advertising, and applied communication related; radio, television, and digital communication; sales merchandising, and related marketing operations (general); sales, merchandising and related marketing operations (specialized); science technologies related; science, technology and society; social and philosophical foundations of education; social sciences; social sciences related; social work; sociology; statistics; taxation.

ATLANTIC CAPE COMMUNITY COLLEGE
Mays Landing, New Jersey
Academic Computing and Distance Education
http://www.atlantic.edu/online

Atlantic Cape Community College was founded in 1964. It is accredited by Middle States Association of Colleges and Schools. It first offered distance learning courses in 1984. In fall 2010, there were 3,593 students enrolled in distance learning courses. Institutionally administered financial aid is available to distance learners.
Services Distance learners have accessibility to academic advising, bookstore, campus computer network, career placement assistance, e-mail services, library services, tutoring.
Contact Otto Hernandez, Associate Dean of Aviation, Technical Studies Institute, and GIS Programs, Atlantic Cape Community College, 5100 Black Horse Pike, Mays Landing, NJ 08330. Telephone: 609-343-4978. Fax: 609-343-5122. E-mail: hernandez@atlantic.edu.

DEGREES AND AWARDS

AA Business; History; Literature; Psychology; Social Science
AAS Business Administration; Computer Programming; Computer Systems Support; Office Systems Technology
AS Business Administration; Computer Information Systems; General Studies

COURSE SUBJECT AREAS OFFERED OUTSIDE OF DEGREE PROGRAMS

Undergraduate—criminology; education; health and physical education/fitness; hospitality administration; music; philosophy and religious studies; visual and performing arts related.

A.T. STILL UNIVERSITY OF HEALTH SCIENCES
Mesa, Arizona
Arizona School of Health Sciences
http://www.atsu.edu/ashs/online_programs/index.htm

A.T. Still University of Health Sciences was founded in 1892. It is accredited by North Central Association of Colleges and Schools. It first offered distance learning courses in 1995. In fall 2010, there were 178 students enrolled in distance learning courses. Institutionally administered financial aid is available to distance learners.
Services Distance learners have accessibility to academic advising, bookstore, campus computer network, e-mail services, library services, tutoring.
Contact Grecia Koenecke, Admissions Coordinator, A.T. Still University of Health Sciences, 5845 East Still Circle, Suite 213, Mesa, AZ 85206. Telephone: 877-469-2878. Fax: 480-219-6122. E-mail: gkoenecke@atsu.edu.

DEGREES AND AWARDS

MS Human Movement; Occupational Therapy (Advanced Masters of Science); Physician Assistant Studies
DH Sc Health Science
DPT Transitional Doctor of Physical Therapy

COURSE SUBJECT AREAS OFFERED OUTSIDE OF DEGREE PROGRAMS

Non-credit—health professions related.

A.T. STILL UNIVERSITY OF HEALTH SCIENCES
Kirksville, Missouri
School of Health Management
http://www.atsu.edu/shm/index.htm

A.T. Still University of Health Sciences was founded in 1892. It is accredited by North Central Association of Colleges and Schools. It first offered distance learning courses in 1999. In fall 2010, there were 119 students enrolled in distance learning courses. Institutionally administered financial aid is available to distance learners.
Services Distance learners have accessibility to academic advising, bookstore, campus computer network, e-mail services, library services.
Contact Mrs. Sarah Elizabeth Spencer, Associate Director of Admissions, A.T. Still University of Health Sciences, 210 A.S. Osteopathy Street, Kirksville, MO 63501. Telephone: 660-626-2820 Ext. 2669. Fax: 660-626-2826. E-mail: sspencer@atsu.edu.

DEGREES AND AWARDS

MHA Health Administration
MPH Public Health
DH Ed Health Education

AUBURN UNIVERSITY
Auburn University, Alabama
Distance Learning/Outreach Technology
http://www.distance.auburn.edu

Auburn University was founded in 1856. It is accredited by Southern Association of Colleges and Schools. It first offered distance learning courses in 1975. In fall 2010, there were 1,786 students enrolled in distance learning courses. Institutionally administered financial aid is available to distance learners.
Services Distance learners have accessibility to academic advising, bookstore, campus computer network, career placement assistance, e-mail services, library services.
Contact Mrs. Ernestine Morris-Stinson, Administrator I, Auburn University, 282 Thach Concourse, Foy Hall, Auburn University, AL 36849. Telephone: 866-684-5131. Fax: 334-844-3125. E-mail: audl@auburn.edu.

DEGREES AND AWARDS

Certificate Dietary Management; Emergency Management; Project Management Prep
EMBA Business Administration; Physicians Executive MBA

Ed S Business and Marketing Education; Foreign Language
MA Early Childhood Intervention
MAE Aerospace Engineering; Foreign Language
MAg Agriculture
MBA Business Administration
MBA/M Acc Accountancy
MBA/MSMIS Management Information Systems Dual Degree program
MBE Business Education
MCE Chemical Engineering; Civil Engineering
MCSE Computer Science and Engineering
MD/MBA Physicians Executive
MEd Business Education; Collaborative Teacher and Early Childhood Education; Music; Rehabilitation Counseling
MISE Industrial and Systems Engineering
MME Materials Engineering; Mechanical Engineering
MS Agronomy and Soil Science; Hotel and Restaurant Management
PharmD Pharmacy

COURSE SUBJECT AREAS OFFERED OUTSIDE OF DEGREE PROGRAMS

Undergraduate—agriculture; animal sciences; communication and media; communication disorders sciences and services; computer science; film/video and photographic arts; geological and earth sciences/geosciences; health and physical education/fitness; plant sciences; statistics.
Graduate—accounting and related services; aerospace, aeronautical and astronautical engineering; agricultural and domestic animal services; agricultural and food products processing; agricultural production; business administration, management and operations; civil engineering; civil engineering technologies; computer science; education; education related; education (specific levels and methods); education (specific subject areas); engineering-related fields; engineering science; foods, nutrition, and related services; pharmacy, pharmaceutical sciences, and administration; special education.
Non-credit—animal sciences; computer/information technology administration and management; construction management; data processing; engineering; foods, nutrition, and related services; languages (foreign languages related); surveying engineering; veterinary biomedical and clinical sciences.

AUSTIN PEAY STATE UNIVERSITY
Clarksville, Tennessee
http://www.apsu.edu/

Austin Peay State University was founded in 1927. It is accredited by Southern Association of Colleges and Schools. It first offered distance learning courses in 1996. In fall 2010, there were 5,567 students enrolled in distance learning courses. Institutionally administered financial aid is available to distance learners.
Services Distance learners have accessibility to academic advising, bookstore, campus computer network, career placement assistance, e-mail services, library services, tutoring.
Contact Mrs. Melissa Conwell, APSU Online Advisor, Austin Peay State University, PO Box 4717, Clarksville, TN 37044. Telephone: 931-221-6484. Fax: 931-221-6485. E-mail: conwellm@apsu.edu.

DEGREES AND AWARDS

AS Liberal Arts
BA Communication Arts (BA, BS)–Information Specialist
BA/BS Political Science
BPS Professional Studies, APSU (organizational forensics minor available); Regents Online degree program
BS Computer Science–Information Systems; Criminal Justice–Homeland Security; Nursing–RN to BSN completion track
MA Communication Arts–Corporate Communication; Education Curriculum and Instruction; Industrial-Organizational Psychology; Military History
MS Health and Human Performance, Health Leadership–Health Administration
MSM Management

COURSE SUBJECT AREAS OFFERED OUTSIDE OF DEGREE PROGRAMS

Graduate—communication and journalism related; health and physical education/fitness.
Non-credit—accounting and computer science; allied health and medical assisting services; alternative and complementary medical support services; American Sign Language (ASL); bilingual, multilingual, and multicultural education; business administration, management and operations; business/commerce; business/corporate communications; business, management, and marketing related; business/managerial economics; business operations support and assistant services; computer and information sciences; computer and information sciences and support services related; computer engineering technologies; computer software and media applications; computer systems analysis; computer systems networking and telecommunications; construction management; construction trades related; crafts, folk art and artisanry; criminal justice and corrections; dental support services and allied professions; design and applied arts; dispute resolution; education; education related; English or French as a second or foreign language (teaching); entrepreneurial and small business operations; family and consumer economics; fine and studio arts; health professions related; health services/allied health/health sciences; heating, air conditioning, ventilation and refrigeration maintenance technology; homeland security, law enforcement, firefighting and protective services related; insurance; intercultural/multicultural and diversity studies; languages (foreign languages related); languages (Romance languages); legal professions and studies related; legal support services; marketing; real estate; sales merchandising, and related marketing operations (general); sales, merchandising and related marketing operations (specialized); sustainability studies.

AVILA UNIVERSITY
Kansas City, Missouri
http://www.avila.edu/

Avila University was founded in 1916. It is accredited by North Central Association of Colleges and Schools. It first offered distance learning courses in 1999. In fall 2010, there were 229 students enrolled in distance learning courses. Institutionally administered financial aid is available to distance learners.
Services Distance learners have accessibility to academic advising, bookstore, campus computer network, e-mail services, library services.
Contact Dr. Steve Iliff, Dean of the School of Professional Studies, Avila University, 11901 Wornall Road, Kansas City, MO 64145. Telephone: 816-501-3763. Fax: 816-941-4650. E-mail: steve.iliff@avila.edu.

DEGREES AND AWARDS

Programs offered do not lead to a degree or other formal award.

COURSE SUBJECT AREAS OFFERED OUTSIDE OF DEGREE PROGRAMS

Undergraduate—biological and physical sciences; business administration, management and operations; business, management, and marketing related; economics; English language and literature related; health and medical administrative services; international business; multi/interdisciplinary studies related; psychology.

BAKER COLLEGE ONLINE
http://www.BakerCollegeOnline.com

Baker College Online first offered distance learning courses in 1994. In fall 2010, there were 7,000 students enrolled in distance learning courses. Institutionally administered financial aid is available to distance learners.
Services Distance learners have accessibility to academic advising, bookstore, campus computer network, career placement assistance, e-mail services, library services, tutoring.
Contact Mr. Chuck J. Gurden, Vice President, Graduate and Online Admissions, Baker College Online, 1116 West Bristol Road, Flint, MI 48507. Telephone: 800-469-4062. Fax: 810-766-4399. E-mail: adm-ol@baker.edu.

DEGREES AND AWARDS

AAS Applied Science
ABA Business Administration
BBA Business Administration
BGS General Studies
BS Psychology
MBA Business Administration
MSCS Information Systems
DBA Business Administration

COURSE SUBJECT AREAS OFFERED OUTSIDE OF DEGREE PROGRAMS

Undergraduate—accounting and computer science; computer science; finance and financial management services; human resources management; management information systems; marketing.

Graduate—accounting and related services; business, management, and marketing related; finance and financial management services; health services/allied health/health sciences; human resources management; marketing.

BAKKE GRADUATE UNIVERSITY
Seattle, Washington
http://www.bgu.edu

Bakke Graduate University was founded in 1990. It is accredited by Transnational Association of Christian Colleges and Schools. It first offered distance learning courses in 1995. In fall 2010, there were 25 students enrolled in distance learning courses. Institutionally administered financial aid is available to distance learners.

Services Distance learners have accessibility to academic advising, bookstore, e-mail services, library services.

Contact Ms. Addie Tolle, Registrar, Bakke Graduate University, 1013 Eighth Avenue, Suite 401, Seattle, WA 98104. Telephone: 206-264-9100 Ext. 110. Fax: 206-264-8828. E-mail: addiet@bgu.edu.

DEGREES AND AWARDS

Programs offered do not lead to a degree or other formal award.

COURSE SUBJECT AREAS OFFERED OUTSIDE OF DEGREE PROGRAMS

Graduate—biblical studies; business administration, management and operations; entrepreneurial and small business operations; religious studies; theological and ministerial studies; theology and religious vocations related; urban studies/affairs.

BALDWIN-WALLACE COLLEGE
Berea, Ohio
http://www.bw.edu/resources/infotech/depts/edserv/distance_learning/

Baldwin-Wallace College was founded in 1845. It is accredited by North Central Association of Colleges and Schools. It first offered distance learning courses in 2005. In fall 2010, there were 429 students enrolled in distance learning courses. Institutionally administered financial aid is available to distance learners.

Services Distance learners have accessibility to academic advising, bookstore, campus computer network, career placement assistance, e-mail services, library services, tutoring.

Contact Mrs. Nancy Jirousek, Director of Adult and Continuing Education/Veterans Services, Baldwin-Wallace College, 275 Eastland Road, Berea, OH 44017. Telephone: 440-826-2298. Fax: 440-826-2054. E-mail: njirouse@bw.edu.

DEGREES AND AWARDS

BA Organizational Leadership
License Mild/Moderate Intervention Specialist License
MBA Management (Hybrid)

COURSE SUBJECT AREAS OFFERED OUTSIDE OF DEGREE PROGRAMS

Undergraduate—applied mathematics; business administration, management and operations; business, management, and marketing related; computer science; finance and financial management services; health and physical education/fitness; history; human resources management; music; political science and government; sociology.

Graduate—business administration, management and operations; special education.

BALL STATE UNIVERSITY
Muncie, Indiana
School of Extended Education
http://www.bsu.edu/distance

Ball State University was founded in 1918. It is accredited by North Central Association of Colleges and Schools. It first offered distance learning courses in 1984. In fall 2010, there were 3,523 students enrolled in distance learning courses. Institutionally administered financial aid is available to distance learners.

Services Distance learners have accessibility to academic advising, bookstore, campus computer network, career placement assistance, e-mail services, library services, tutoring.

Contact Nancy Prater, Director of Marketing and Communications, Ball State University, School of Extended Education, Carmichael Hall, Room 200, Muncie, IN 47306. Telephone: 765-285-9042. Fax: 765-285-7161. E-mail: nprater@bsu.edu.

DEGREES AND AWARDS

AA General Studies
AS Business Administration Management
BGS General Studies
BSN Nursing–RN to Bachelor of Science in Nursing
License Gifted and Talented Education; Principal's License
CCCPE Emerging Media Journalism
Ed S School Superintendency
MA Applied Behavior Analysis, Autism emphasis; Career and Technical Education; Educational Psychology, Gifted and Talented Education specialization; Executive Development for Public Service; Interior Design option; Physical Education, Coaching specialization; Public Relations; Secondary Education; Special Education; Technology Education
MAE Business and Marketing Education; Educational Administration and Supervision; Elementary Education
MBA Business Administration
MS Interior Design option
MSN Nursing
DNP Nursing Practice

COURSE SUBJECT AREAS OFFERED OUTSIDE OF DEGREE PROGRAMS

Undergraduate—business, management, and marketing related; computer science; criminal justice and corrections; journalism.

Graduate—behavioral sciences; communication and journalism related; communications technology; education; education related; health and medical administrative services; health professions related; information science/studies; management information systems; public health; public relations, advertising, and applied communication related; real estate; sales merchandising, and related marketing operations (general); special education.

Non-credit—communication and journalism related.

BAPTIST BIBLE COLLEGE OF PENNSYLVANIA
Clarks Summit, Pennsylvania
http://www.bbc.edu/online.asp

Baptist Bible College of Pennsylvania was founded in 1932. It is accredited by Association for Biblical Higher Education. It first offered distance learning courses in 1998. In fall 2010, there were 355 students enrolled in distance learning courses. Institutionally administered financial aid is available to distance learners.

Services Distance learners have accessibility to academic advising, bookstore, career placement assistance, e-mail services, library services.

Contact Ms. Erica Vail, Distance Learning Facilitator, Baptist Bible College of Pennsylvania, 538 Venard Road, Clarks Summit, PA 18411. Telephone: 570-585-9226. Fax: 570-585-9359. E-mail: evail@bbc.edu.

DEGREES AND AWARDS

MA Bible
MCP Counseling Ministries
MDiv Divinity
MMin Ministry
MSE Teacher Education
DMin Leadership in Ministry
PhD Biblical Studies

COURSE SUBJECT AREAS OFFERED OUTSIDE OF DEGREE PROGRAMS

Undergraduate—animal sciences; astronomy and astrophysics; biblical studies; biology; business administration, management and operations; cell biology and anatomical sciences; history; mathematics and statistics related; pastoral counseling and specialized ministries; philosophy and religious studies related; religious studies; statistics; theological and ministerial studies; theology and religious vocations related.
Graduate—animal sciences; astronomy and astrophysics; biblical studies; biology; cell biology and anatomical sciences; computer and information sciences and support services related; mathematics and statistics related; philosophy and religious studies related; religious studies; theological and ministerial studies; theology and religious vocations related.

THE BAPTIST COLLEGE OF FLORIDA
Graceville, Florida
Division of Distance Learning
http://www.baptistcollege.edu

The Baptist College of Florida was founded in 1943. It is accredited by Southern Association of Colleges and Schools. It first offered distance learning courses in 1999. In fall 2010, there were 150 students enrolled in distance learning courses. Institutionally administered financial aid is available to distance learners.
Services Distance learners have accessibility to academic advising, bookstore, campus computer network, career placement assistance, e-mail services, library services, tutoring.
Contact Dr. David Coggins, Director of Distance Learning, The Baptist College of Florida, 5400 College Drive, Graceville, FL 32440. Telephone: 850-263-3261 Ext. 482. Fax: 850-263-7506. E-mail: jdcoggins @baptistcollege.edu.

DEGREES AND AWARDS

AD Divinity
BA Christian Studies; Ministry Studies

COURSE SUBJECT AREAS OFFERED OUTSIDE OF DEGREE PROGRAMS

Undergraduate—biblical studies; business administration, management and operations; computer software and media applications; mathematics; music; philosophy and religious studies related.

BAPTIST MISSIONARY ASSOCIATION THEOLOGICAL SEMINARY
Jacksonville, Texas
http://bmats.edu

Baptist Missionary Association Theological Seminary was founded in 1955. It is accredited by Southern Association of Colleges and Schools. It first offered distance learning courses in 2000. In fall 2010, there were 25 students enrolled in distance learning courses. Institutionally administered financial aid is available to distance learners.
Services Distance learners have accessibility to academic advising, bookstore, library services.
Contact Dr. Philip W. Attebery, Dean/Registrar, Baptist Missionary Association Theological Seminary, 1530 East Pine Street, Jacksonville, TX 75766. Telephone: 903-586-2501. Fax: 903-586-0378. E-mail: bmatsem@bmats.edu.

DEGREES AND AWARDS

Programs offered do not lead to a degree or other formal award.

COURSE SUBJECT AREAS OFFERED OUTSIDE OF DEGREE PROGRAMS

Undergraduate—religious education; religious studies; theological and ministerial studies; theology and religious vocations related.
Graduate—religious education; religious studies; theological and ministerial studies; theology and religious vocations related.
Non-credit—theological and ministerial studies; theology and religious vocations related.

BARCLAY COLLEGE
Haviland, Kansas
Online Program
http://www.barclaycollege.edu

Barclay College was founded in 1917. It is accredited by Association for Biblical Higher Education. It first offered distance learning courses in 2008. In fall 2010, there were 59 students enrolled in distance learning courses. Institutionally administered financial aid is available to distance learners.
Services Distance learners have accessibility to academic advising, bookstore, campus computer network, e-mail services, library services.
Contact Dr. Glenn Leppert, Registrar, Barclay College, 607 North Kingman, Haviland, KS 67059-0288. Telephone: 620-862-5252 Ext. 46. Fax: 620-862-5242. E-mail: registrar@barclaycollege.edu.

DEGREES AND AWARDS

BS Christian Ministry Leadership; Psychology
BSc Biblical Studies

COURSE SUBJECT AREAS OFFERED OUTSIDE OF DEGREE PROGRAMS

Undergraduate—behavioral sciences; biblical studies; education related; English; mathematics; missionary studies and missiology; physical sciences; psychology; religious/sacred music; sociology; theological and ministerial studies.

BELHAVEN UNIVERSITY
Jackson, Mississippi
http://online.belhaven.edu

Belhaven University was founded in 1883. It is accredited by Southern Association of Colleges and Schools. It first offered distance learning courses in 2006. In fall 2010, there were 245 students enrolled in distance learning courses. Institutionally administered financial aid is available to distance learners.
Services Distance learners have accessibility to academic advising, campus computer network, e-mail services, library services.
Contact Jenny Mixon, Director of Graduate and Online Admission, Belhaven University, 1500 Peachtree Street, Box 279, Jackson, MS 39202. Telephone: 601-965-7043. Fax: 601-968-8946. E-mail: jmixon @belhaven.edu.

DEGREES AND AWARDS

AA General Studies
BS Management
MBA/Diploma Business Administration
MPA Public Administration

COURSE SUBJECT AREAS OFFERED OUTSIDE OF DEGREE PROGRAMS

Undergraduate—business administration, management and operations; liberal arts and sciences, general studies and humanities.
Graduate—business administration, management and operations; education.

BELLEVUE COLLEGE
Bellevue, Washington
Telecommunications Program–Distance Learning Department
http://bellevuecollege.edu/distance/

Bellevue College was founded in 1966. It is accredited by Northwest Commission on Colleges and Universities. It first offered distance learning courses in 1980. In fall 2010, there were 6,000 students enrolled in distance learning courses. Institutionally administered financial aid is available to distance learners.

Services Distance learners have accessibility to academic advising, bookstore, campus computer network, e-mail services, library services, tutoring.

Contact Liz Anderson, Director of Distance Education, Bellevue College, 3000 Landerholm Circle SE, Bellevue, WA 98007-6484. Telephone: 425-564-2438. Fax: 425-564-5564. E-mail: liz.anderson@bellevuecollege.edu.

DEGREES AND AWARDS
AA General Studies
AAS Transfer degree for Business Students; Transfer degree
Certificate of Achievement Business Intelligence Developer
Certificate Administrative Assistant; Bookkeeping–Paraprofessional Accounting program; Business Intelligence Analyst; Business Software Specialist–Business Technology Systems; Database User Specialist; Introductory C++ Programming; Office Assistant
Certification Business Software Specialist, Advanced

COURSE SUBJECT AREAS OFFERED OUTSIDE OF DEGREE PROGRAMS
Undergraduate—accounting and related services; anthropology; archeology; astronomy and astrophysics; atmospheric sciences and meteorology; biology; botany/plant biology; business administration, management and operations; business/commerce; business/corporate communications; business, management, and marketing related; business/managerial economics; business operations support and assistant services; chemistry; communication and media; computer and information sciences; computer and information sciences and support services related; computer programming; computer science; computer software and media applications; criminal justice and corrections; criminology; ecology, evolution, systematics, and population biology; economics; education; English; English language and literature related; entrepreneurial and small business operations; ethnic, cultural minority, gender, and group studies; fire protection; geography and cartography; geological and earth sciences/geosciences; health professions related; history; languages (foreign languages related); liberal arts and sciences, general studies and humanities; management information systems; marketing; mathematics; mathematics and statistics related; medieval and Renaissance studies; music; natural sciences; nutrition sciences; philosophy; physical sciences; physical sciences related; plant sciences; political science and government; psychology; psychology related; social sciences; social sciences related; sociology; statistics.

BELMONT TECHNICAL COLLEGE
St. Clairsville, Ohio
http://www.btc.edu

Belmont Technical College was founded in 1971. It is accredited by North Central Association of Colleges and Schools. It first offered distance learning courses in 1999. In fall 2010, there were 354 students enrolled in distance learning courses. Institutionally administered financial aid is available to distance learners.

Services Distance learners have accessibility to academic advising, bookstore, campus computer network, career placement assistance, e-mail services, library services, tutoring.

Contact Amy E. Leoni, E-Learning Coordinator, Belmont Technical College, 120 Fox Shannon Place, St. Clairsville, OH 43950. Telephone: 740-695-9500 Ext. 1186. Fax: 740-695-2247. E-mail: aleoni@btc.edu.

DEGREES AND AWARDS
AAS Information Technology and Information Services Library Paraprofessional

COURSE SUBJECT AREAS OFFERED OUTSIDE OF DEGREE PROGRAMS
Undergraduate—accounting and computer science; accounting and related services; computer and information sciences; computer and information sciences and support services related; computer programming; computer science; computer software and media applications; English; English language and literature related; health services/allied health/health sciences; information science/studies; library and archives assisting; library science related; philosophy; physical sciences; psychology; sociology; statistics.

BENNINGTON COLLEGE
Bennington, Vermont
http://www.bennington.edu/go/graduate/ma-in-teaching-a-second-language

Bennington College was founded in 1932. It is accredited by New England Association of Schools and Colleges. It first offered distance learning courses in 2001. In fall 2010, there were 21 students enrolled in distance learning courses. Institutionally administered financial aid is available to distance learners.

Services Distance learners have accessibility to academic advising, library services, tutoring.

Contact Nancy Pearlman, Assistant Director of Programs in Teacher Education, Bennington College, One College Drive, Bennington, VT 05201. Telephone: 802-440-4710. Fax: 802-440-4383. E-mail: matsl@bennington.edu.

DEGREES AND AWARDS
Programs offered do not lead to a degree or other formal award.

COURSE SUBJECT AREAS OFFERED OUTSIDE OF DEGREE PROGRAMS
Graduate—education; languages (foreign languages related).

BERKLEE COLLEGE OF MUSIC
Boston, Massachusetts
Berkleemusic
http://www.berkleemusic.com

Berklee College of Music was founded in 1945. It is accredited by New England Association of Schools and Colleges. It first offered distance learning courses in 2002. In fall 2010, there were 2,689 students enrolled in distance learning courses. Institutionally administered financial aid is available to distance learners.

Services Distance learners have accessibility to academic advising, bookstore, library services.

Contact Dorothy Lannon, Continuing Education Registrar, Berklee College of Music, 1140 Boylston Street, MS-855, Boston, MA 02215. Telephone: 617-747-2146. Fax: 617-747-2149. E-mail: registrar@berkleemusic.com.

DEGREES AND AWARDS
Programs offered do not lead to a degree or other formal award.

COURSE SUBJECT AREAS OFFERED OUTSIDE OF DEGREE PROGRAMS
Undergraduate—business/commerce; music; visual and performing arts.
Non-credit—business/commerce; music; visual and performing arts.

BETHEL UNIVERSITY
McKenzie, Tennessee
http://www.bethel-college.edu/

Bethel University was founded in 1842. It is accredited by Southern Association of Colleges and Schools. It first offered distance learning courses in 1998. In fall 2010, there were 2,500 students enrolled in distance learning courses. Institutionally administered financial aid is available to distance learners.

Services Distance learners have accessibility to academic advising, bookstore, campus computer network, career placement assistance, e-mail services, library services, tutoring.

Contact Mrs. Lisa Vaughn, Director of Student Affairs, Educational Outreach, Bethel University, 325 Cherry Avenue, McKenzie, TN 38201. Telephone: 731-352-4000. Fax: 731-352-4069. E-mail: vaughnl@bethel-college.edu.

DEGREES AND AWARDS
BCJ Criminal Justice
BS Management and Organizational Development
MBA Business Administration

COURSE SUBJECT AREAS OFFERED OUTSIDE OF DEGREE PROGRAMS
Undergraduate—biology; business administration, management and operations; criminal justice and corrections; education; geography and cartography.
Graduate—business, management, and marketing related; education.

BEULAH HEIGHTS UNIVERSITY
Atlanta, Georgia
http://www.beulah.org/
Beulah Heights University was founded in 1918. It is accredited by Association for Biblical Higher Education. It first offered distance learning courses in 2000. In fall 2010, there were 300 students enrolled in distance learning courses. Institutionally administered financial aid is available to distance learners.
Services Distance learners have accessibility to academic advising, bookstore, campus computer network, e-mail services, library services.
Contact Mr. John Dreher, Director of Admissions, Beulah Heights University, 892 Berne Street SE, PO Box 18145, Atlanta, GA 30316. Telephone: 404-627-2681 Ext. 117. Fax: 404-627-0702. E-mail: john.dreher@beulah.org.

DEGREES AND AWARDS
Programs offered do not lead to a degree or other formal award.

COURSE SUBJECT AREAS OFFERED OUTSIDE OF DEGREE PROGRAMS
Undergraduate—applied mathematics; biblical studies; communication and media; computer science; English; ethnic, cultural minority, gender, and group studies; human development, family studies, and related services; liberal arts and sciences, general studies and humanities; mathematics; pastoral counseling and specialized ministries; philosophy; political science and government; religious education.
Graduate—biblical studies; business administration, management and operations; pastoral counseling and specialized ministries; religious studies.

BIG BEND COMMUNITY COLLEGE
Moses Lake, Washington
http://www.bigbend.edu
Big Bend Community College was founded in 1962. It is accredited by Northwest Commission on Colleges and Universities. It first offered distance learning courses in 2000. In fall 2010, there were 1,000 students enrolled in distance learning courses. Institutionally administered financial aid is available to distance learners.
Services Distance learners have accessibility to academic advising, bookstore, campus computer network, e-mail services, library services, tutoring.
Contact Dean Tim S. Fuhrman, Dean of Library Resources, Big Bend Community College, 7662 Chanute Street NE, Moses Lake, WA 98837. Telephone: 509-793-2350. Fax: 509-762-2402. E-mail: timf@bigbend.edu.

DEGREES AND AWARDS
Programs offered do not lead to a degree or other formal award.

COURSE SUBJECT AREAS OFFERED OUTSIDE OF DEGREE PROGRAMS
Undergraduate—accounting and related services; allied health and medical assisting services; anthropology; behavioral sciences; business/commerce; chemistry; crafts, folk art and artisanry; dietetics and clinical nutrition services; economics; English; English language and literature related; geological and earth sciences/geosciences; history; library science and administration; mathematics; natural sciences; philosophy and religious studies related; physical sciences.

BLACKHAWK TECHNICAL COLLEGE
Janesville, Wisconsin
http://www.blackhawk.edu
Blackhawk Technical College was founded in 1968. It is accredited by North Central Association of Colleges and Schools. It first offered distance learning courses in 2000. In fall 2010, there were 807 students enrolled in distance learning courses. Institutionally administered financial aid is available to distance learners.
Services Distance learners have accessibility to academic advising, bookstore, campus computer network, career placement assistance, e-mail services, library services.
Contact Linda Brown, Enrollment Services Manager, Blackhawk Technical College, 6004 South County Road G, PO Box 5009, Janesville, WI 53547-5009. Telephone: 608-757-7670. Fax: 608-743-4407. E-mail: lbrown@blackhawk.edu.

DEGREES AND AWARDS
Programs offered do not lead to a degree or other formal award.

COURSE SUBJECT AREAS OFFERED OUTSIDE OF DEGREE PROGRAMS
Undergraduate—accounting and related services; agricultural business and management; allied health and medical assisting services; business administration, management and operations; business, management, and marketing related; business operations support and assistant services; clinical/medical laboratory science/research; computer and information sciences and support services related; computer programming; computer systems networking and telecommunications; criminal justice and corrections; culinary arts and related services; dental support services and allied professions; education (specific levels and methods); electromechanical instrumentation and maintenance technologies; fire protection; health and medical administrative services; heating, air conditioning, ventilation and refrigeration maintenance technology; legal support services; marketing; mechanical engineering related technologies.
Non-credit—apparel and textiles; business operations support and assistant services; computer software and media applications; crafts, folk art and artisanry; criminal justice and corrections; drafting/design engineering technologies; film/video and photographic arts; fire protection; foods, nutrition, and related services; human development, family studies, and related services; languages (foreign languages related); leatherworking and upholstery; real estate; sales, merchandising and related marketing operations (specialized); woodworking.

BLACKSTONE CAREER INSTITUTE
Allentown, Pennsylvania
http://www.blackstone.edu
Blackstone Career Institute first offered distance learning courses in 2001. In fall 2010, there were 1,842 students enrolled in distance learning courses. Institutionally administered financial aid is available to distance learners.
Services Distance learners have accessibility to academic advising.
Contact Adria Wetherhold, Assistant Director of Education, Blackstone Career Institute, 1011 Brookside Road, Suite 300, Allentown, PA 18106. Telephone: 610-871-0031 Ext. 249. Fax: 610-871-0034. E-mail: awetherhold@blackstone.edu.

DEGREES AND AWARDS
Programs offered do not lead to a degree or other formal award.

COURSE SUBJECT AREAS OFFERED OUTSIDE OF DEGREE PROGRAMS
Undergraduate—allied health and medical assisting services; legal research and advanced professional studies; legal support services.

Non-credit—allied health and medical assisting services; legal support services.

BLESSING-RIEMAN COLLEGE OF NURSING
Quincy, Illinois
http://www.brcn.edu

Blessing-Rieman College of Nursing was founded in 1985. It is accredited by North Central Association of Colleges and Schools. In fall 2010, there were 30 students enrolled in distance learning courses. Institutionally administered financial aid is available to distance learners.

Services Distance learners have accessibility to academic advising, bookstore, campus computer network, e-mail services, library services.

Contact Rachel Cramsey, Registrar, Blessing-Rieman College of Nursing, PO Box 7005, Broadway at 11th, Quincy, IL 62305-7005. Telephone: 217-228-5520 Ext. 6962. Fax: 217-223-1781. E-mail: rcramsey@brcn.edu.

DEGREES AND AWARDS

BSN Nursing–RN to BSN

BLOOMFIELD COLLEGE
Bloomfield, New Jersey
http://www.bloomfield.edu/

Bloomfield College was founded in 1868. It is accredited by Middle States Association of Colleges and Schools. It first offered distance learning courses in 1997. In fall 2010, there were 451 students enrolled in distance learning courses. Institutionally administered financial aid is available to distance learners.

Services Distance learners have accessibility to campus computer network, career placement assistance, e-mail services, library services.

Contact Dr. Marion Terenzio, Vice President for Academic Affairs, Bloomfield College, 467 Franklin Street, Bloomfield, NJ 07003. Telephone: 973-748-9000 Ext. 226. Fax: 973-743-3998. E-mail: marion_terenzio@bloomfield.edu.

DEGREES AND AWARDS

Programs offered do not lead to a degree or other formal award.

COURSE SUBJECT AREAS OFFERED OUTSIDE OF DEGREE PROGRAMS

Undergraduate—accounting and related services; business administration, management and operations; business, management, and marketing related; business/managerial economics; communication and journalism related; computer and information sciences; computer systems analysis; computer systems networking and telecommunications; economics; education; English; English language and literature related; health professions related; history; human development, family studies, and related services; human resources management; marketing; political science and government; psychology; sociology; visual and performing arts related.

Graduate—accounting and related services.

BLOOMSBURG UNIVERSITY OF PENNSYLVANIA
Bloomsburg, Pennsylvania
School of Graduate Studies
http://www.bloomu.edu

Bloomsburg University of Pennsylvania was founded in 1839. It is accredited by Middle States Association of Colleges and Schools. It first offered distance learning courses in 1983. In fall 2010, there were 236 students enrolled in distance learning courses. Institutionally administered financial aid is available to distance learners.

Services Distance learners have accessibility to academic advising, bookstore, campus computer network, career placement assistance, e-mail services, library services.

Contact Mr. Thomas Fletcher, Director, Corporate and Continuing Education, Bloomsburg University of Pennsylvania, 700 West Main Street, Bloomsburg, PA 17815-1301. Telephone: 570-389-5161. Fax: 570-389-5060. E-mail: tfletche@bloomu.edu.

DEGREES AND AWARDS

MS Instructional Technology Education Specialist; Radiologist Assistant

COURSE SUBJECT AREAS OFFERED OUTSIDE OF DEGREE PROGRAMS

Undergraduate—business, management, and marketing related; statistics.

Graduate—business, management, and marketing related; curriculum and instruction; educational/instructional media design.

Non-credit—communications technologies and support services related.

BLUEFIELD COLLEGE
Bluefield, Virginia
http://www.bluefield.edu/inspire/

Bluefield College was founded in 1922. It is accredited by Southern Association of Colleges and Schools. It first offered distance learning courses in 1990. In fall 2010, there were 249 students enrolled in distance learning courses. Institutionally administered financial aid is available to distance learners.

Services Distance learners have accessibility to academic advising, bookstore, campus computer network, e-mail services, library services, tutoring.

Contact Mrs. Cathy Payne, Director of inSPIRE Admissions West, Bluefield College, 3000 College Drive, Bluefield, VA 24605. Telephone: 276-326-4233. Fax: 276-326-4395. E-mail: cpayne@bluefield.edu.

DEGREES AND AWARDS

BA/BS Criminal Justice/Public Safety; Management and Leadership
BS Behavioral Science/Human Services

COURSE SUBJECT AREAS OFFERED OUTSIDE OF DEGREE PROGRAMS

Undergraduate—biblical studies; communication and journalism related; English; fine and studio arts; health and physical education/fitness; history; literature; mathematics; science technologies; social sciences.

BOB JONES UNIVERSITY
Greenville, South Carolina
http://www.bju.edu/bjuonline/

Bob Jones University was founded in 1927. It is accredited by Transnational Association of Christian Colleges and Schools. It first offered distance learning courses in 1986. In fall 2010, there were 605 students enrolled in distance learning courses. Institutionally administered financial aid is available to distance learners.

Services Distance learners have accessibility to academic advising, bookstore, campus computer network, career placement assistance, e-mail services, library services.

Contact Mr. Gary Deedrick, Director of Admission, Bob Jones University, 1700 Wade Hampton Boulevard, Greenville, SC 29614. Telephone: 800-252-6363. Fax: 800-232-9258. E-mail: admission@bju.edu.

DEGREES AND AWARDS

MA Biblical Studies
MEd Teaching and Learning

COURSE SUBJECT AREAS OFFERED OUTSIDE OF DEGREE PROGRAMS

Undergraduate—accounting and related services; biblical studies; business administration, management and operations; English; English or French as a second or foreign language (teaching); history; human resources management; marketing; mathematics; philosophy; psychology related; religious studies; social sciences; theological and ministerial studies.

Graduate—biblical studies; education; educational administration and supervision; English; English or French as a second or foreign language (teaching); history; religious studies; theological and ministerial studies.

BOISE STATE UNIVERSITY
Boise, Idaho
Division of Extended Studies
http://www.boisestate.edu/distance

Boise State University was founded in 1932. It is accredited by Northwest Commission on Colleges and Universities. It first offered distance learning courses in 1980. In fall 2010, there were 5,190 students enrolled in distance learning courses. Institutionally administered financial aid is available to distance learners.

Services Distance learners have accessibility to academic advising, bookstore, campus computer network, career placement assistance, e-mail services, library services, tutoring.

Contact Kelley Brandt, Assistant Director, Boise State University, 220 East Parkcenter Boulevard, Department of Distance Education, Boise, ID 83706-3940. Telephone: 208-426-5962. Fax: 208-426-3467. E-mail: distanceed@boisestate.edu.

DEGREES AND AWARDS

BSN Nursing–RN to BS Online degree completion option

BSRC Respiratory Care degree completion program

Graduate Certificate Human Performance Technology; Online Teaching; School Technology Coordination; Technology Integration; Workplace E-Learning and Performance Support; Workplace Instructional Design

MET Educational Technology

MN Nursing

MS Instructional and Performance Technology

MSE Educational Technology

MSN Nursing

COURSE SUBJECT AREAS OFFERED OUTSIDE OF DEGREE PROGRAMS

Undergraduate—accounting and related services; allied health and medical assisting services; allied health diagnostic, intervention, and treatment professions; anthropology; behavioral sciences; biological and physical sciences; biology; building/construction finishing, management, and inspection; business administration, management and operations; business/corporate communications; business, management, and marketing related; business/managerial economics; business operations support and assistant services; chemistry; classical and ancient studies; computer and information sciences and support services related; criminal justice and corrections; criminology; curriculum and instruction; economics; education; educational assessment, evaluation, and research; educational/instructional media design; education related; education (specific levels and methods); education (specific subject areas); electrical engineering technologies; engineering related; English; English language and literature related; entrepreneurial and small business operations; geography and cartography; geological and earth sciences/geosciences; health and medical administrative services; health/medical preparatory programs; health professions related; health services/allied health/health sciences; history; human biology; human development, family studies, and related services; human resources management; languages (foreign languages related); languages (Romance languages); liberal arts and sciences, general studies and humanities; library science related; marketing; mathematics; medical illustration and informatics; medieval and Renaissance studies; movement and mind-body therapies and education; music; nutrition sciences; philosophy; physics; psychology; registered nursing, nursing administration, nursing research and clinical nursing; rhetoric and composition/writing studies; social sciences; social sciences related; social work; sociology; special education; statistics; visual and performing arts related.

Graduate—allied health and medical assisting services; audiovisual communications technologies; cognitive science; communications technologies and support services related; communications technology; criminal justice and corrections; criminology; educational/instructional media design; education related; health and medical administrative services; human resources management; management sciences and quantitative methods; registered nursing, nursing administration, nursing research and clinical nursing; social work.

Non-credit—education related.

BOSSIER PARISH COMMUNITY COLLEGE
Bossier City, Louisiana
BPCC Distance Learning Program/Institutional Advancement
http://www.bpcc.edu

Bossier Parish Community College was founded in 1967. It is accredited by Southern Association of Colleges and Schools. It first offered distance learning courses in 1995. In fall 2010, there were 3,947 students enrolled in distance learning courses. Institutionally administered financial aid is available to distance learners.

Services Distance learners have accessibility to academic advising, bookstore, campus computer network, career placement assistance, e-mail services, library services, tutoring.

Contact Kathleen Gay, Dean of Educational Technology, Bossier Parish Community College, 6220 East Texas Street, Bossier City, LA 71111. Telephone: 318-678-6136. Fax: 318-678-6407. E-mail: kgay@bpcc.edu.

DEGREES AND AWARDS

AAS CIT Cyber; Computer Information Systems; Healthcare Management; Telecommunications

AD Criminal Justice

AGS General Studies

COURSE SUBJECT AREAS OFFERED OUTSIDE OF DEGREE PROGRAMS

Undergraduate—allied health and medical assisting services; applied mathematics; behavioral sciences; biological and biomedical sciences related; biological and physical sciences; communications technology; computer and information sciences; computer and information sciences and support services related; computer science; computer software and media applications; computer systems networking and telecommunications; criminal justice and corrections; curriculum and instruction; education; education related; English; film/video and photographic arts; fine and studio arts; fire protection; food science and technology; geography and cartography; health and medical administrative services; history; linguistic, comparative, and related language studies; mathematics; mathematics and statistics related; pharmacy, pharmaceutical sciences, and administration; psychology related; sociology.

Non-credit—carpentry; computer and information sciences; computer programming; computer software and media applications; computer systems analysis; crafts, folk art and artisanry; culinary arts and related services; dance; design and applied arts; education; film/video and photographic arts; fishing and fisheries sciences and management; health aides/attendants/orderlies; hospitality administration; human resources management; real estate; religious education; sales, merchandising and related marketing operations (specialized).

BOSTON ARCHITECTURAL COLLEGE
Boston, Massachusetts
http://www.the-bac.edu/

Boston Architectural College was founded in 1889. It is accredited by New England Association of Schools and Colleges. It first offered distance learning courses in 2000. In fall 2010, there were 250 students enrolled in distance learning courses. Institutionally administered financial aid is available to distance learners.

Services Distance learners have accessibility to academic advising, career placement assistance, e-mail services, library services, tutoring.

Contact Ms. Jane Toland, Head of Continuing Education Programs and Curriculum, Boston Architectural College, 320 Newbury Street, Boston, MA 02115. Telephone: 617-585-0101. Fax: 617-585-0121. E-mail: ce@the-bac.edu.

DEGREES AND AWARDS

Certificate Sustainable Design

M Arch Architecture

MDS Historic Preservation; Sustainable Design

COURSE SUBJECT AREAS OFFERED OUTSIDE OF DEGREE PROGRAMS

Undergraduate—architectural engineering; architectural engineering technologies; architectural sciences and technology; architecture; architecture related; ecology, evolution, systematics, and population biology; environmental design; heating, air conditioning, ventilation and refrigeration maintenance technology; interior architecture.

Graduate—architectural engineering; architectural engineering technologies; architectural sciences and technology; architecture; architecture related; ecology, evolution, systematics, and population biology; environmental design; heating, air conditioning, ventilation and refrigeration maintenance technology; interior architecture.

Non-credit—architectural engineering; architectural engineering technologies; architectural sciences and technology; architecture; architecture related; ecology, evolution, systematics, and population biology; environmental design; heating, air conditioning, ventilation and refrigeration maintenance technology; interior architecture.

BOSTON UNIVERSITY
Boston, Massachusetts
Boston University Online
http://www.bu.edu/online

Boston University was founded in 1839. It is accredited by New England Association of Schools and Colleges. It first offered distance learning courses in 2001. In fall 2010, there were 3,500 students enrolled in distance learning courses. Institutionally administered financial aid is available to distance learners.

Services Distance learners have accessibility to academic advising, bookstore, campus computer network, e-mail services, library services, tutoring.

Contact Andrew Hinkell, Administrative Coordinator, Boston University, Office of Distance Education, 1010 Commonwealth Avenue, Boston, MA 02215. Telephone: 617-358-1960. Fax: 617-358-1961. E-mail: disted@bu.edu.

DEGREES AND AWARDS

BLS Undergraduate degree completion program

Certificate Genealogical Research; Professional Investigation

CCCPE Paralegal

Graduate Certificate Clinical Investigation; Database Management and Business Intelligence; Digital Forensics; Entrepreneurship; Information Security; Information Technology Project Management; Information Technology; Information Technology, Advanced; Instructional Technology; International Marketing Management; Physical Education, Health Education, Coaching; Project Management; Risk Management and Organizational Continuity

MAEd Art Education

MCJ Criminal Justice

MM Music Education

MPM Project Management

MSCS Computer Information Systems–Master of Science in Computer Information Systems

MSFS Banking and Financial Services Management (MSBFM)

MSHA Health Communication

MSHRM Human Resource Management

MSM Business Continuity, Security, and Risk Management; Insurance Management–Master of Science in Insurance Management

MSMM International Marketing Management

MSW Social Work

DPT Physical Therapy

OTD Occupational Therapy

PhD Doctor of Music Arts in Music Education

COURSE SUBJECT AREAS OFFERED OUTSIDE OF DEGREE PROGRAMS

Graduate—business, management, and marketing related; computer systems networking and telecommunications; curriculum and instruction; educational/instructional media design; entrepreneurial and small business operations.

Non-credit—finance and financial management services; legal support services.

BOWLING GREEN STATE UNIVERSITY
Bowling Green, Ohio
http://cobl.bgsu.edu/index.php

Bowling Green State University was founded in 1910. It is accredited by North Central Association of Colleges and Schools. It first offered distance learning courses in 1998. In fall 2010, there were 2,036 students enrolled in distance learning courses. Institutionally administered financial aid is available to distance learners.

Services Distance learners have accessibility to academic advising, bookstore, campus computer network, career placement assistance, e-mail services, library services, tutoring.

Contact Ms. Rebekah Patterson, Secretary, Center for Online and Blended Learning, Bowling Green State University, 104 University Hall, Bowling Green, OH 43403. Telephone: 419-372-6792. Fax: 419-372-4867. E-mail: rpatter@bgsu.edu.

DEGREES AND AWARDS

BLS Liberal Studies–Bachelor of Liberal Studies online degree program

BS Fire Administration; Technological Education, advanced

BSN Nursing–RN/BSN completion

BST Quality Systems

Graduate Certificate Autism Spectrum Disorders; Computer Technology Endorsement; Food and Nutrition; International Scientific and Technical Communication; Ohio Reading Endorsement program; Quality Systems; Women's Studies certificate

MA English

MAT Biology, Interdisciplinary Science specialization

MBA Executive Master of Business Administration; Executive Master of Organization Development

MEd Classroom Technology; Curriculum and Teaching; Special Education, Assistive Technology specialization

MFHD Food and Nutrition

MS Criminal Justice

PhD Technology Management

COURSE SUBJECT AREAS OFFERED OUTSIDE OF DEGREE PROGRAMS

Undergraduate—area studies; astronomy and astrophysics; atmospheric sciences and meteorology; biology; business administration, management and operations; classical and ancient studies; communication and media; communication disorders sciences and services; communications technologies and support services related; computer science; cultural studies/critical theory and analysis; curriculum and instruction; education; education related; English language and literature related; environmental design; ethnic, cultural minority, gender, and group studies; family and consumer sciences/human sciences; film/video and photographic arts; fine and studio arts; geography and cartography; geological and earth sciences/geosciences; gerontology; health and physical education/fitness; health professions related; health services/allied health/health sciences; history; human services; interdisciplinary studies; international/global studies; journalism; languages (foreign languages related); liberal arts and sciences, general studies and humanities; literature; management sciences and quantitative methods; mathematics; medical clinical sciences/graduate medical studies; music; natural resources management and policy; nutrition sciences; parks, recreation and leisure; philosophy; physics; political science and government; psychology; public health; social sciences; sociology.

Graduate—area studies; educational/instructional media design; history; mathematics; music; parks, recreation and leisure facilities management.

Non-credit—business/commerce; computer and information sciences and support services related; computer software and media applications; construction trades related; fire protection; health professions related; hospitality administration; natural resources management and policy.

BRADLEY UNIVERSITY

Peoria, Illinois
Division of Continuing Education and Professional Development
http://www.bradley.edu/classes/

Bradley University was founded in 1897. It is accredited by North Central Association of Colleges and Schools. It first offered distance learning courses in 1985. In fall 2010, there were 387 students enrolled in distance learning courses. Institutionally administered financial aid is available to distance learners.

Services Distance learners have accessibility to academic advising, bookstore, campus computer network, career placement assistance, e-mail services, library services.

Contact Kathie Beaty, Registrar, Bradley University, Peoria, IL 61625. E-mail: kbeaty@bradley.edu.

DEGREES AND AWARDS

MSEE Electrical Engineering
MSME Mechanical Engineering

COURSE SUBJECT AREAS OFFERED OUTSIDE OF DEGREE PROGRAMS

Undergraduate—business, management, and marketing related; communication and media; computer and information sciences; education; English; family and consumer sciences/human sciences; health services/allied health/health sciences; international business; psychology; social work; sociology; theological and ministerial studies.

Graduate—education; electrical engineering technologies; health and medical administrative services; health services/allied health/health sciences; political science and government.

BRANDEIS UNIVERSITY

Waltham, Massachusetts
http://www.brandeis.edu/gps/

Brandeis University was founded in 1948. It is accredited by New England Association of Schools and Colleges. It first offered distance learning courses in 1999. In fall 2010, there were 202 students enrolled in distance learning courses. Institutionally administered financial aid is available to distance learners.

Services Distance learners have accessibility to academic advising, bookstore, campus computer network, e-mail services, library services.

Contact Frances Stearns, Associate Director of Admissions and Student Services, Brandeis University, MS 084, 415 South Street, Waltham, MA 02454-9110. Telephone: 781-736-8785. Fax: 781-736-3420. E-mail: gps@brandeis.edu.

DEGREES AND AWARDS

MS Health and Medical Informatics; Information Assurance; Information Technology Management; Management of Projects and Programs; Virtual Team Management and Communication
MSE Software Engineering

BRAZOSPORT COLLEGE

Lake Jackson, Texas
http://www.brazosport.edu/

Brazosport College was founded in 1968. It is accredited by Southern Association of Colleges and Schools. It first offered distance learning courses in 1997. In fall 2010, there were 2,400 students enrolled in distance learning courses. Institutionally administered financial aid is available to distance learners.

Services Distance learners have accessibility to academic advising, bookstore, campus computer network, e-mail services, library services, tutoring.

Contact Mr. Terry Comingore, Director, Learning Services, Brazosport College, 500 College Drive, Lake Jackson, TX 77566. Telephone: 979-230-3318. Fax: 979-230-3348. E-mail: terry.comingore@brazosport.edu.

DEGREES AND AWARDS

AA General Education
BAT Applied Technology

COURSE SUBJECT AREAS OFFERED OUTSIDE OF DEGREE PROGRAMS

Undergraduate—accounting and related services; biology; business administration, management and operations; business, management, and marketing related; chemistry; computer and information sciences; criminal justice and corrections; economics; education; fine and studio arts; geography and cartography; history; industrial production technologies; international business; mathematics; music; nutrition sciences; political science and government; psychology.

BRENAU UNIVERSITY

Gainesville, Georgia
Department of Distance Learning
http://online.brenau.edu

Brenau University was founded in 1878. It is accredited by Southern Association of Colleges and Schools. It first offered distance learning courses in 1998. In fall 2010, there were 979 students enrolled in distance learning courses. Institutionally administered financial aid is available to distance learners.

Services Distance learners have accessibility to academic advising, bookstore, campus computer network, career placement assistance, e-mail services, library services, tutoring.

Contact Dr. David L. Barnett, Associate Vice President for Nonresidential Programs, Brenau University, 500 Washington Street SE, Gainesville, GA 30501. Telephone: 770-534-6257. Fax: 770-718-5329. E-mail: dlbarnett@brenau.edu.

DEGREES AND AWARDS

AA Liberal Studies
BA Organizational Leadership
BBA Accounting; Business
BS Human Resources Management
BSN Nursing–RN to BSN
Ed S Early Childhood Education; Middle Grades
MBA Accounting; Business Administration; Healthcare Management; Insurance Management; Project Management
MEd Early Childhood Education; Middle Grades Education
MS Applied Gerontology

COURSE SUBJECT AREAS OFFERED OUTSIDE OF DEGREE PROGRAMS

Undergraduate—accounting and related services; allied health and medical assisting services; anthropology; astronomy and astrophysics; business administration, management and operations; business/commerce; business/corporate communications; business, management, and marketing related; business/managerial economics; communication and media; computer and information sciences; criminal justice and corrections; criminology; curriculum and instruction; design and applied arts; economics; education; educational administration and supervision; educational assessment, evaluation, and research; educational/instructional media design; education related; education (specific levels and methods); education (specific subject areas); English; English language and literature related; geography and cartography; health/medical preparatory programs; health professions related; history; human development, family studies, and related services; human resources management; information science/studies; international business; journalism; legal studies (nonprofessional general, undergraduate); liberal arts and sciences, general studies and humanities; linguistic, comparative, and related language studies; management information systems; management sciences and quantitative methods; marketing; mathematics; mathematics and statistics related; museum studies; music; peace studies and conflict resolution; pharmacology and toxicology; philosophy; political science and government; psychology; psychology related; public administration; public administration and social service professions related; public relations, advertising, and applied communication related; sales, merchandising and related marketing operations (specialized); social and philosophical foundations of education; social sciences; sociology; special education; statistics; taxation; visual and performing arts related.

Graduate—accounting and related services; allied health diagnostic, intervention, and treatment professions; business administration, management and operations; business/commerce; business/corporate communications; business, management, and marketing related; business/managerial economics; computer and information sciences; economics; education; educational administration and supervision; educational assessment, evaluation, and research; education related; finance and financial management services; health and medical administrative services; health professions related; international business; management information systems; management sciences and quantitative methods; marketing; rehabilitation and therapeutic professions; sales merchandising, and related marketing operations (general); sales, merchandising and related marketing operations (specialized); taxation.

BREWTON-PARKER COLLEGE
Mt. Vernon, Georgia
http://www.bpc.edu/

Brewton-Parker College was founded in 1904. It is accredited by Southern Association of Colleges and Schools. It first offered distance learning courses in 2002. In fall 2010, there were 156 students enrolled in distance learning courses. Institutionally administered financial aid is available to distance learners.

Services Distance learners have accessibility to academic advising, bookstore, campus computer network, e-mail services, library services.

Contact Mrs. Sandra Clay, Director of Admissions, Brewton-Parker College, #2011, PO Box 197, Mount Vernon, GA 30445. Telephone: 912-583-3247. Fax: 912-583-4498. E-mail: sclay@bpc.edu.

DEGREES AND AWARDS

Programs offered do not lead to a degree or other formal award.

COURSE SUBJECT AREAS OFFERED OUTSIDE OF DEGREE PROGRAMS

Undergraduate—accounting and related services; business administration, management and operations; business, management, and marketing related; education; information science/studies; management information systems; religious studies.

BRIAR CLIFF UNIVERSITY
Sioux City, Iowa
http://www.briarcliff.edu/

Briar Cliff University was founded in 1930. It is accredited by North Central Association of Colleges and Schools. It first offered distance learning courses in 1994. In fall 2010, there were 70 students enrolled in distance learning courses. Institutionally administered financial aid is available to distance learners.

Services Distance learners have accessibility to academic advising, bookstore, campus computer network, career placement assistance, e-mail services, library services.

Contact Ms. Sharisue Wilcoxon, Vice President of Enrollment Management, Briar Cliff University, 3303 Rebecca Street, Sioux City, IA 51104-2100. Telephone: 712-279-5200. Fax: 712-279-5410. E-mail: sharisue.wilcoxon@briarcliff.edu.

DEGREES AND AWARDS

BA Accounting; Business Administration and Management; Education; Human Resources Management

Graduate Certificate Human Resources Management

MAE Education

BRIDGEWATER STATE UNIVERSITY
Bridgewater, Massachusetts
Continuing and Distance Education
http://www.bridgew.edu/cde

Bridgewater State University was founded in 1840. It is accredited by New England Association of Schools and Colleges. It first offered distance learning courses in 1996. In fall 2010, there were 2,725 students enrolled in distance learning courses. Institutionally administered financial aid is available to distance learners.

Services Distance learners have accessibility to bookstore, campus computer network, e-mail services, library services.

Contact Dr. Mary W. Fuller, Director of Continuing and Distance Education, Bridgewater State University, John Joseph Moakley Center, 100 Burrill Avenue, Bridgewater, MA 02325. Telephone: 508-531-6141. Fax: 508-531-6121. E-mail: mfuller@bridgew.edu.

DEGREES AND AWARDS

Programs offered do not lead to a degree or other formal award.

COURSE SUBJECT AREAS OFFERED OUTSIDE OF DEGREE PROGRAMS

Undergraduate—accounting and computer science; anthropology; business/corporate communications; business/managerial economics; communication and journalism related; communication and media; communication disorders sciences and services; computer/information technology administration and management; criminal justice and corrections; curriculum and instruction; economics; education; educational administration and supervision; educational assessment, evaluation, and research; entrepreneurial and small business operations; ethnic, cultural minority, gender, and group studies; geography and cartography; geological and earth sciences/geosciences; marketing; music; political science and government; psychology; sociology; special education.

Graduate—communication and media; economics; educational administration and supervision; linguistic, comparative, and related language studies; psychology; special education.

BRIGHAM YOUNG UNIVERSITY
Provo, Utah
Independent Study
http://elearn.byu.edu

Brigham Young University was founded in 1875. It is accredited by Northwest Commission on Colleges and Universities. It first offered distance learning courses in 1921. In fall 2010, there were 100,000 students enrolled in distance learning courses. Institutionally administered financial aid is available to distance learners.

Services Distance learners have accessibility to academic advising, bookstore, e-mail services, library services, tutoring.

Contact Customer Support, Brigham Young University, BYU Independent Study, 120 Morris Center (MORC), Provo, UT 84602-0300. Telephone: 800-914-8931. Fax: 801-422-0102. E-mail: indstudy@byu.edu.

DEGREES AND AWARDS

Programs offered do not lead to a degree or other formal award.

COURSE SUBJECT AREAS OFFERED OUTSIDE OF DEGREE PROGRAMS

Undergraduate—accounting and related services; anthropology; astronomy and astrophysics; biological and biomedical sciences related; biology; botany/plant biology; business administration, management and operations; business/corporate communications; business, management, and marketing related; chemical engineering; chemistry; civil engineering; communication and media; communication disorders sciences and services; curriculum and instruction; dance; drama/theatre arts and stagecraft; economics; education; educational administration and supervision; education related; food science and technology; geography and cartography; geological and earth sciences/geosciences; health and physical education/fitness; history; information science/studies; languages (Germanic); languages (Middle/Near Eastern and Semitic); languages (Romance languages); liberal arts and sciences, general studies and

humanities; marketing; mathematics and statistics related; microbiological sciences and immunology; music; philosophy; philosophy and religious studies related; physical sciences; physics; political science and government; psychology; religious education; religious studies; social work; sociology; special education; statistics; work and family studies.
Non-credit—computer and information sciences; computer software and media applications; English language and literature related; history; human development, family studies, and related services; religious studies.

BRIGHAM YOUNG UNIVERSITY–IDAHO
Rexburg, Idaho
Online Learning
http://www.byui.edu/online

Brigham Young University–Idaho was founded in 1888. It is accredited by Northwest Commission on Colleges and Universities. It first offered distance learning courses in 2000. Institutionally administered financial aid is available to distance learners.
Services Distance learners have accessibility to academic advising, bookstore, campus computer network, e-mail services, library services, tutoring.
Contact Mr. Jason Meldrum, Online Degrees Coordinator, Brigham Young University–Idaho, Rexburg, ID 83440. E-mail: meldrumj@byui.edu.

DEGREES AND AWARDS

AAS Administative Assistant/Office Management
AGS General Studies
BSc Applied Management
BUS University Studies

COURSE SUBJECT AREAS OFFERED OUTSIDE OF DEGREE PROGRAMS

Undergraduate—accounting and computer science; accounting and related services; architecture; arts, entertainment, and media management; behavioral sciences; biblical studies; bilingual, multilingual, and multicultural education; biological and biomedical sciences related; biological and physical sciences; biology; business administration, management and operations; business, management, and marketing related; classical and ancient studies; communication and journalism related; communication and media; computer software and media applications; curriculum and instruction; drama/theatre arts and stagecraft; economics; education; English; English language and literature related; family and consumer economics; family and consumer sciences/human sciences; foods, nutrition, and related services; geological and earth sciences/geosciences; health professions related; history; human resources management; interior architecture; languages (foreign languages related); languages (Romance languages); library science related; literature; mathematics; mathematics and statistics related; music; natural sciences; philosophy; philosophy and religious studies; physics; political science and government; psychology; publishing; radio, television, and digital communication; religious education; religious studies; sales merchandising, and related marketing operations (general); social sciences; social work; sociology; statistics.

BROCK UNIVERSITY
St. Catharines, Ontario, Canada
Centre for Adult Education and Community Outreach, Faculty of Education
http://www.brocku.ca/education/futurestudents/adulted/bachelor-of-ed-in-adult-education

Brock University was founded in 1964. It is provincially chartered. It first offered distance learning courses in 1993. In fall 2010, there were 500 students enrolled in distance learning courses. Institutionally administered financial aid is available to distance learners.
Services Distance learners have accessibility to academic advising, bookstore, campus computer network, career placement assistance, e-mail services, library services.
Contact Sandra Plavinskis, Coordinator of B.Ed. in Adult Education Degree and Certificate Programs, Brock University, Centre for Adult Education and Community Outreach, Faculty of Education, St. Catharines, ON L2S 3A1, Canada. Telephone: 905-688-5550 Ext. 4308. Fax: 905-984-4842. E-mail: adulted@brocku.ca.

DEGREES AND AWARDS

BEd Adult Education (BEd in Adult Education)
Certificate Adult Education

COURSE SUBJECT AREAS OFFERED OUTSIDE OF DEGREE PROGRAMS

Undergraduate—education; education related.

BRONX COMMUNITY COLLEGE OF THE CITY UNIVERSITY OF NEW YORK
Bronx, New York
http://www.bcc.cuny.edu/DistanceLearning/Default.cfm

Bronx Community College of the City University of New York was founded in 1959. It is accredited by Middle States Association of Colleges and Schools. It first offered distance learning courses in 2000. In fall 2010, there were 1,100 students enrolled in distance learning courses. Institutionally administered financial aid is available to distance learners.
Services Distance learners have accessibility to academic advising, bookstore, campus computer network, career placement assistance, e-mail services, library services, tutoring.
Contact Dr. Howard Wach, Director of the Office of Instructional Technology, Bronx Community College of the City University of New York, 2155 University Avenue, Bronx, NY 10453. Telephone: 718-289-5655. E-mail: howard.wach@bcc.cuny.edu.

DEGREES AND AWARDS

Programs offered do not lead to a degree or other formal award.

COURSE SUBJECT AREAS OFFERED OUTSIDE OF DEGREE PROGRAMS

Undergraduate—accounting and computer science; accounting and related services; allied health and medical assisting services; allied health diagnostic, intervention, and treatment professions; animal sciences; anthropology; astronomy and astrophysics; biology; botany/plant biology; chemistry; communication and media; computer and information sciences; computer science; criminal justice and corrections; data processing; education; English; geography and cartography; history; homeland security, law enforcement, firefighting and protective services related; human services; languages (foreign languages related); marketing; mathematics; mathematics and computer science; mechanical engineering related technologies; music; nuclear engineering technologies; pharmacy, pharmaceutical sciences, and administration; philosophy; physics; psychology; sociology; taxation.

BROOKDALE COMMUNITY COLLEGE
Lincroft, New Jersey
Telecourse Program–Division of Arts and Communication
http://www.brookdalecc.edu/pages/200.asp

Brookdale Community College was founded in 1967. It is accredited by Middle States Association of Colleges and Schools. It first offered distance learning courses in 1974. In fall 2010, there were 2,500 students enrolled in distance learning courses. Institutionally administered financial aid is available to distance learners.
Services Distance learners have accessibility to bookstore, campus computer network, e-mail services, library services, tutoring.
Contact Norah Kerr-McCurry, Director, Brookdale Community College, Teaching and Learning Center, 765 Newman Springs Road, Lincroft, NJ 07738. Telephone: 732-224-2089. Fax: 732-224-2001. E-mail: nkerr-mccurry@brookdalecc.edu.

DEGREES AND AWARDS

AA Business Administration; English; History; Liberal Arts; Psychology; Social Sciences; Sociology

COURSE SUBJECT AREAS OFFERED OUTSIDE OF DEGREE PROGRAMS

Undergraduate—accounting and related services; anthropology; biology; business administration, management and operations; chemistry; criminal justice and corrections; drama/theatre arts and stagecraft; English; marketing; mathematics; philosophy and religious studies related; social sciences related; sociology.

BROWARD COLLEGE
Fort Lauderdale, Florida
Instructional Technology
http://www.broward.edu/elearning

Broward College was founded in 1960. It is accredited by Southern Association of Colleges and Schools. It first offered distance learning courses in 1978. In fall 2010, there were 8,686 students enrolled in distance learning courses. Institutionally administered financial aid is available to distance learners.

Services Distance learners have accessibility to academic advising, bookstore, e-mail services, library services, tutoring.

Contact Jean Griffin, eLearning Coordinator, Broward College, 3501 Southwest Davie Road, Building 17, Room 226, Davie, FL 33314. Telephone: 954-201-6564. Fax: 954-201-6398. E-mail: jgriffin@broward.edu.

DEGREES AND AWARDS

AA Accounting; Business Administration; Criminal Justice; Elementary Education; English; Liberal Arts; Pre-Law

AS Accounting Technology; Aviation Operations; Business Administration; Emergency Management

Certificate Accounting Applications; Business Management; Business Specialist–Small Business Management; Customer Service; Emergency Management; Information Technology Support–MS Office Specialist; Medical Office Management; Office Management; Office Specialist; Office Support

COURSE SUBJECT AREAS OFFERED OUTSIDE OF DEGREE PROGRAMS

Undergraduate—anthropology; biology; business/commerce; computer science; economics; education related; entrepreneurial and small business operations; geography and cartography; geological and earth sciences/geosciences; health and physical education/fitness; history; languages (Romance languages); legal studies (non-professional general, undergraduate); marketing; mathematics and statistics related; philosophy; philosophy and religious studies related; psychology; sociology; statistics.

BRYAN COLLEGE
Dayton, Tennessee
http://www.bryan.edu/online_learning.html

Bryan College was founded in 1930. It is accredited by Southern Association of Colleges and Schools. It first offered distance learning courses in 2005. In fall 2010, there were 150 students enrolled in distance learning courses. Institutionally administered financial aid is available to distance learners.

Services Distance learners have accessibility to bookstore, campus computer network, e-mail services, library services.

Contact Charlene Armstrong, Coordinator of Online Learning, Bryan College, PO Box 7000, Dayton, TN 37321. Telephone: 423-775-7558. Fax: 423-775-7512. E-mail: online@bryan.edu.

DEGREES AND AWARDS

BS Business Administration–Organizational Leadership

COURSE SUBJECT AREAS OFFERED OUTSIDE OF DEGREE PROGRAMS

Undergraduate—biblical studies; biology; English language and literature related; history; mathematics; psychology.

BRYANT & STRATTON ONLINE
Lackawanna, New York
http://www.bryantstratton.edu

Bryant & Stratton Online is accredited by Middle States Association of Colleges and Schools. It first offered distance learning courses in 1997. In fall 2010, there were 2,300 students enrolled in distance learning courses. Institutionally administered financial aid is available to distance learners.

Services Distance learners have accessibility to academic advising, bookstore, campus computer network, career placement assistance, e-mail services, library services, tutoring.

Contact Scott Traylor, Associate Campus Director, Bryant & Stratton Online, Sterling Park, 200 Redtail, Orchard Park, NY 14127. Telephone: 716-677-8800 Ext. 241. Fax: 716-677-8899. E-mail: online@bryantstratton.edu.

DEGREES AND AWARDS

AAS Accounting Online; Administrative Assistant; Business Online; Criminal Justice; Human Resources Specialist; IT-Networking; IT-Security; Interactive Media Design Online; Medical Administrative Assistant; Medical Reimbursement and Coding; Paralegal Online

BBA Business Administration

BS Criminal Justice; Financial Services; Health Services Administration

COURSE SUBJECT AREAS OFFERED OUTSIDE OF DEGREE PROGRAMS

Undergraduate—business administration, management and operations; business/commerce; business/corporate communications; criminology; finance and financial management services; health and medical administrative services; legal support services.

Non-credit—business administration, management and operations; business/commerce; business/corporate communications; criminology; finance and financial management services; health and medical administrative services; legal support services.

BRYANT UNIVERSITY
Smithfield, Rhode Island
http://www.bryant.edu/wps/wcm/connect/Bryant/Divisions/Academic%20Affairs/EDC/Programs/e-Learning%20Programs/

Bryant University was founded in 1863. It is accredited by New England Association of Schools and Colleges. It first offered distance learning courses in 2001. In fall 2010, there were 155 students enrolled in distance learning courses. Institutionally administered financial aid is available to distance learners.

Services Distance learners have accessibility to campus computer network, library services.

Contact Jennifer Doherty, E-Learning Coordinator, Bryant University, 1150 Douglas Pike, Smithfield, RI 02917. Telephone: 401-232-6501. E-mail: jdohert2@bryant.edu.

DEGREES AND AWARDS

Programs offered do not lead to a degree or other formal award.

COURSE SUBJECT AREAS OFFERED OUTSIDE OF DEGREE PROGRAMS

Graduate—economics; statistics.

Non-credit—accounting and computer science; accounting and related services; business administration, management and operations; business/commerce; business/corporate communications; business, management, and marketing related; business/managerial economics; finance and financial management services; human resources management; insurance; management information systems; management sciences and quantitative methods; taxation.

BUENA VISTA UNIVERSITY
Storm Lake, Iowa
Master of Education
http://www.bvu.edu/learn/who_we_are/locations/online.dot

Buena Vista University was founded in 1891. It is accredited by North Central Association of Colleges and Schools. It first offered distance learning courses in 2004. In fall 2010, there were 13 students enrolled in distance learning courses. Institutionally administered financial aid is available to distance learners.

Services Distance learners have accessibility to academic advising, bookstore, campus computer network, career placement assistance, e-mail services, library services, tutoring.

Contact Laura Harris, BVU Online, Buena Vista University, 610 West 4th Street, Storm Lake, IA 50588. Telephone: 712-749-1893. Fax: 712-749-1241. E-mail: harrisl@bvu.edu.

DEGREES AND AWARDS

MEd Curriculum and Instruction–Effective Teaching and Instructional Leadership emphasis; Curriculum and Instruction–Teaching English as a Second Language emphasis

COURSE SUBJECT AREAS OFFERED OUTSIDE OF DEGREE PROGRAMS

Undergraduate—accounting and related services; business administration, management and operations; business/commerce; business/corporate communications; business, management, and marketing related; business/managerial economics; communication and journalism related; communication and media; criminal justice and corrections; curriculum and instruction; education; English; finance and financial management services; marketing; political science and government; psychology.

Graduate—curriculum and instruction; education; English or French as a second or foreign language (teaching).

BUFFALO STATE COLLEGE, STATE UNIVERSITY OF NEW YORK
Buffalo, New York
http://www.buffalostate.edu/continuingstudies

Buffalo State College, State University of New York was founded in 1867. It is accredited by Middle States Association of Colleges and Schools. It first offered distance learning courses in 1998. In fall 2010, there were 500 students enrolled in distance learning courses. Institutionally administered financial aid is available to distance learners.

Services Distance learners have accessibility to academic advising, bookstore, career placement assistance, e-mail services, library services.

Contact Dr. Margaret A. Shaw-Burnett, Associate Vice President, Academic Affairs, Continuing Professional Studies, Buffalo State College, State University of New York, 1300 Elmwood Avenue, Cleveland Hall 210, Buffalo, NY 14222. Telephone: 716-878-5907. Fax: 716-878-5930. E-mail: shawma@buffalostate.edu.

DEGREES AND AWARDS

CAGS Adult Education; Creativity and Change Leadership; Human Resource Development

MS Adult Education; Creative Studies

COURSE SUBJECT AREAS OFFERED OUTSIDE OF DEGREE PROGRAMS

Undergraduate—anthropology; business, management, and marketing related; communication and media; computer science; criminal justice and corrections; design and applied arts; dietetics and clinical nutrition services; economics; education; education related; English; history; political science and government.

Graduate—education; education related.

BURLINGTON COLLEGE
Burlington, Vermont
Independent Degree Program (IDP)
http://www.burlington.edu

Burlington College was founded in 1972. It is accredited by New England Association of Schools and Colleges. It first offered distance learning courses in 1993. In fall 2010, there were 15 students enrolled in distance learning courses. Institutionally administered financial aid is available to distance learners.

Services Distance learners have accessibility to academic advising, career placement assistance, e-mail services, library services, tutoring.

Contact Ms. Gillian Homsted, Director of Admissions, Burlington College, 351 North Avenue, Burlington, VT 05401. Telephone: 802-862-9616 Ext. 104. Fax: 802-660-4331. E-mail: admissions@burlington.edu.

DEGREES AND AWARDS

BA Cinema Studies; Documentary Studies; Expressive Arts; Fine Arts; Human Services; Integral Psychology; Inter-American Studies; International Relations and Diplomacy; Legal and Justice Studies; Media Activism; Photography; Psychology; Self-Designed Major; Transpersonal Psychology; Writing and Literature
BFA Film; Graphic Design; Photography
MA Self-Designed Major

COURSE SUBJECT AREAS OFFERED OUTSIDE OF DEGREE PROGRAMS

Undergraduate—communication and journalism related; communication and media; community organization and advocacy; crafts, folk art and artisanry; criminal justice and corrections; criminology; design and applied arts; English; English language and literature related; ethnic, cultural minority, gender, and group studies; film/video and photographic arts; fine and studio arts; graphic communications; history; human development, family studies, and related services; human services; intercultural/multicultural and diversity studies; interdisciplinary studies; international/global studies; journalism; legal professions and studies related; legal studies (non-professional general, undergraduate); legal support services; liberal arts and sciences, general studies and humanities; literature; movement and mind-body therapies and education; multi/interdisciplinary studies related; peace studies and conflict resolution; philosophy; philosophy and religious studies related; political science and government; psychology; psychology related; social sciences; social sciences related; social work; sociology; somatic bodywork and related therapeutic services; theology and religious vocations related; visual and performing arts; visual and performing arts related; woodworking.

Graduate—multi/interdisciplinary studies related.

BURLINGTON COUNTY COLLEGE
Pemberton, New Jersey
Distance Learning Office
http://staff.bcc.edu/distance

Burlington County College was founded in 1966. It is accredited by Middle States Association of Colleges and Schools. It first offered distance learning courses in 1978. In fall 2010, there were 2,922 students enrolled in distance learning courses. Institutionally administered financial aid is available to distance learners.

Services Distance learners have accessibility to academic advising, bookstore, career placement assistance, e-mail services, library services, tutoring.

Contact Ms. Kathleen Devone, Coordinator of Distance Learning, Burlington County College, 601 Pemberton-Browns Mills Road, Pemberton, NJ 08068. Telephone: 609-894-9311 Ext. 1790. Fax: 609-894-4189. E-mail: dlearn@bcc.edu.

DEGREES AND AWARDS

AA Liberal Arts (Education); Liberal Arts (Psychology); Liberal Arts
AAS Liberal Arts and Sciences (Business Management Technology)
AS Liberal Arts and Sciences (Accounting); Liberal Arts and Sciences (Business Administration); Liberal Arts and Sciences

COURSE SUBJECT AREAS OFFERED OUTSIDE OF DEGREE PROGRAMS

Undergraduate—accounting and computer science; accounting and related services; allied health diagnostic, intervention, and treatment professions; anthropology; astronomy and astrophysics; biological and physical sciences; biology; business administration, management and operations; business/commerce; business/corporate communications; business, management, and marketing related; business/managerial economics; business operations support and assistant services; communication and media; computer and information sciences; computer software and media applications; criminal justice and corrections; criminology; culinary arts and related services; ecology, evolution, systematics, and population biology; economics; education; education related; English; English language and literature related; film/video and photographic arts; fine and studio arts; food science and technology; foods, nutrition, and related services; health and medical administrative services; health professions related; history; hospitality administration; human development, family studies, and related services; human services; international business; legal studies (non-professional general, undergraduate); management sciences and quantitative methods; marketing; mathematics; mathematics and computer science; mathematics and statistics related; music; physical sciences; political science and government; psychology; psychology related; social and philosophical foundations of education; social sciences; social sciences related; sociology; statistics.

BUTLER COMMUNITY COLLEGE
El Dorado, Kansas
http://www.butlercc.edu/

Butler Community College was founded in 1927. It is accredited by North Central Association of Colleges and Schools. It first offered distance learning courses in 1998. In fall 2010, there were 4,000 students enrolled in distance learning courses. Institutionally administered financial aid is available to distance learners.

Services Distance learners have accessibility to academic advising, bookstore, campus computer network, e-mail services, library services, tutoring.

Contact Ms. Meg McGranaghan, Director, Instructional Technology, Butler Community College, 901 South Haverhill Road, El Dorado, KS 67042. Telephone: 316-322-3345. Fax: 316-322-3315. E-mail: megmcg@butlercc.edu.

DEGREES AND AWARDS

AA History; Liberal Arts; Philosophy and Religion
AAS Marketing and Management
AGS Liberal Arts
AS History; Liberal Arts; Software Development

COURSE SUBJECT AREAS OFFERED OUTSIDE OF DEGREE PROGRAMS

Undergraduate—accounting and computer science; accounting and related services; agricultural and domestic animal services; agricultural and food products processing; agricultural business and management; allied health and medical assisting services; allied health diagnostic, intervention, and treatment professions; anthropology; applied mathematics; arts, entertainment, and media management; astronomy and astrophysics; atmospheric sciences and meteorology; behavioral sciences; biological and physical sciences; biology; business administration, management and operations; business, management, and marketing related; chemistry; communication and journalism related; computer programming; computer science; computer software and media applications; computer systems networking and telecommunications; criminal justice and corrections; criminology; data entry/microcomputer applications; drafting/design engineering technologies; economics; education; English; entrepreneurial and small business operations; fine and studio arts; fire protection; geological and earth sciences/geosciences; gerontology; health and physical education/fitness; health professions related; history; hospitality administration; human development, family studies, and related services; human resources management; liberal arts and sciences, general studies and humanities; marketing; mathematics; mathematics and statistics related; music; nutrition sciences; philosophy; philosophy and religious studies related; physical sciences; physical sciences related; physics; political science and government; psychology; public health; religious studies; social sciences; social sciences related; social work; sociology; statistics.

BUTLER COUNTY COMMUNITY COLLEGE
Butler, Pennsylvania
http://www.bc3.edu/onlinelearning

Butler County Community College was founded in 1965. It is accredited by Middle States Association of Colleges and Schools. It first offered distance learning courses in 1998. In fall 2010, there were 900 students enrolled in distance learning courses. Institutionally administered financial aid is available to distance learners.

Services Distance learners have accessibility to academic advising, bookstore, career placement assistance, e-mail services, library services, tutoring.

Contact Mrs. Ann McCandless, Dean of Educational Technology, Butler County Community College, PO Box 1203, Butler, PA 16003. Telephone: 888-826-2829 Ext. 8523. Fax: 724-285-6047. E-mail: ann.mccandless@bc3.edu.

DEGREES AND AWARDS

Programs offered do not lead to a degree or other formal award.

COURSE SUBJECT AREAS OFFERED OUTSIDE OF DEGREE PROGRAMS

Undergraduate—accounting and related services; allied health and medical assisting services; applied mathematics; biology; business administration, management and operations; business, management, and marketing related; chemistry; communication and media; computer programming; computer science; computer systems networking and telecommunications; criminology; data entry/microcomputer applications; economics; education; finance and financial management services; fire protection; foods, nutrition, and related services; health and physical education/fitness; history; human resources management; marketing; mathematics; music; philosophy; philosophy and religious studies related; political science and government; psychology; sociology.

Non-credit—communication and media; computer software and media applications; crafts, folk art and artisanry; culinary arts and related services; design and applied arts; film/video and photographic arts; finance and financial management services; graphic communications; real estate.

CABRILLO COLLEGE
Aptos, California
Instruction, Transfer and Distance Education
http://www.cabrillo.edu/services/disted/

Cabrillo College was founded in 1959. It is accredited by Western Association of Schools and Colleges. It first offered distance learning courses in 1994. In fall 2010, there were 3,500 students enrolled in distance learning courses. Institutionally administered financial aid is available to distance learners.

Services Distance learners have accessibility to academic advising, bookstore, career placement assistance, e-mail services, library services, tutoring.

Contact Francine Van Meter, Director, Teaching and Learning Center, Cabrillo College, 6500 Soquel Drive, Aptos, CA 95003. Telephone: 831-479-6191. Fax: 831-479-5721. E-mail: francine.vanmeter@cabrillo.edu.

DEGREES AND AWARDS

AA Accounting; Business; Liberal Arts; Liberal Arts
AS Computer Applications and Business Technology; Criminal Justice

COURSE SUBJECT AREAS OFFERED OUTSIDE OF DEGREE PROGRAMS

Undergraduate—accounting and computer science; accounting and related services; allied health and medical assisting services; anthropology; biological and biomedical sciences related; biological and physical sciences; business/commerce; cell biology and anatomical sciences; communication and journalism related; computer and information sciences; computer science; criminal justice and corrections; culinary arts and related services; English; film/video and photographic arts; fire protection; foods, nutrition, and related services; geography and cartography; geological and earth sciences/geosciences; health professions related; history; journalism; languages (Romance languages); legal studies (non-professional general, undergraduate); library science related; mathematics; music; philosophy; philosophy and religious studies related; physical sciences; real estate; sociology; visual and performing arts related.

CALDWELL COLLEGE
Caldwell, New Jersey
Center for Continuing Education
http://www.caldwell.edu/adult-ed/external.html

Caldwell College was founded in 1939. It is accredited by Middle States Association of Colleges and Schools. It first offered distance learning courses in 1979. In fall 2010, there were 500 students enrolled in distance learning courses. Institutionally administered financial aid is available to distance learners.

Services Distance learners have accessibility to academic advising, bookstore, campus computer network, career placement assistance, e-mail services, library services, tutoring.

Contact Ms. Jennifer M. Kim, Director of Advisement, Caldwell College, 120 Bloomfield Avenue, Caldwell, NJ 07006. Telephone: 973-618-3680. E-mail: jkim@caldwell.edu.

DEGREES AND AWARDS

BA Criminal Justice; English; Foreign Language; History; Multidisciplinary Studies/Humanities; Multidisciplinary Studies/Social Science/Fire Science; Multidisciplinary Studies/Social Science/Pharmacy Management; Multidisciplinary Studies/Social Sciences; Political Science; Psychology; Sociology; Theology

BS Accounting; Business Administration; Financial Economics; International Business; Management; Marketing

COURSE SUBJECT AREAS OFFERED OUTSIDE OF DEGREE PROGRAMS

Undergraduate—accounting and related services; business administration, management and operations; communication and journalism related; computer and information sciences and support services related; criminal justice and corrections; economics; information science/studies; mathematics and computer science; political science and government; psychology; religious studies; sociology.

Graduate—accounting and related services; business administration, management and operations; educational administration and supervision; psychology.

CALIFORNIA STATE UNIVERSITY, CHICO
Chico, California
Center for Regional and Continuing Education
http://rce.csuchico.edu/online

California State University, Chico was founded in 1887. It is accredited by Western Association of Schools and Colleges. It first offered distance learning courses in 1975. In fall 2010, there were 2,000 students enrolled in distance learning courses. Institutionally administered financial aid is available to distance learners.

Services Distance learners have accessibility to academic advising, bookstore, campus computer network, career placement assistance, e-mail services, library services, tutoring.

Contact Mr. Jeffrey S. Layne, Program Director, California State University, Chico, Chico, CA 95929-0250. Telephone: 530-898-6105. Fax: 530-898-4020. E-mail: jlayne@csuchico.edu.

DEGREES AND AWARDS

BA Liberal Studies; Social Science; Sociology
BSN Nursing
MN Nursing

COURSE SUBJECT AREAS OFFERED OUTSIDE OF DEGREE PROGRAMS

Undergraduate—agriculture; anthropology; behavioral sciences; communication and media; curriculum and instruction; dance; education; English; ethnic, cultural minority, gender, and group studies; geography and cartography; geological and earth sciences/geosciences; health and medical administrative services; health services/allied health/health sciences; history; human development, family studies, and related services; liberal arts and sciences, general studies and humanities; linguistic, comparative, and related language studies; philosophy; political science and government; psychology; religious studies; social sciences; social work; sociology.

Graduate—education.

CALIFORNIA STATE UNIVERSITY, DOMINGUEZ HILLS
Carson, California
Distance Learning
http://dominguezonline.csudh.edu

California State University, Dominguez Hills was founded in 1960. It is accredited by Western Association of Schools and Colleges. It first offered distance learning courses in 1974. In fall 2010, there were 4,000 students enrolled in distance learning courses. Institutionally administered financial aid is available to distance learners.

Services Distance learners have accessibility to academic advising, bookstore, campus computer network, e-mail services, library services, tutoring.

Contact Registration Department, California State University, Dominguez Hills, College of Extended and International Education, 1000 East Victoria Street, Carson, CA 90747. Telephone: 310-243-3741. Fax: 310-516-3971. E-mail: eeinfo@csudh.edu.

DEGREES AND AWARDS

BS Applied Studies; Nursing completion program; Quality Assurance

Certificate of Completion Quality Assurance

Certificate Assistive Technology; Community College Teaching; Production and Inventory Control; Purchasing

CCCPE Administrative Medical Specialist, Medical Billing and Coding certificate; Coding for the Physician's Office, Advanced; Home Inspection; Hospital Coding and CCS Prep, Advanced; Medical Billing and Coding; Medical Transcription; Paralegal certificate; Paralegal certificate, Advanced; Technical Writing

MA Humanities; Negotiation, Conflict Resolution, and Peacebuilding

MBA Business Administration

MPA Public Administration

MS Nursing; Quality Assurance

COURSE SUBJECT AREAS OFFERED OUTSIDE OF DEGREE PROGRAMS

Undergraduate—biology; education; educational administration and supervision; education related; landscape architecture; music; physics.

Non-credit—accounting and related services; alternative and complementary medicine and medical systems; business/corporate communications; business, management, and marketing related; communication and journalism related; computer and information sciences; computer/information technology administration and management; design and applied arts; dietetics and clinical nutrition services; education; educational administration and supervision; environmental control technologies; film/video and photographic arts; finance and financial management services; fine and studio arts; gerontology; graphic communications; health and medical administrative services; history; human resources management; mathematics; museum studies; music; personal and culinary services related; psychology related; quality control and safety technologies; sales merchandising, and related marketing operations (general); sales, merchandising and related marketing operations (specialized).

CALIFORNIA STATE UNIVERSITY, EAST BAY
Hayward, California
Online Campus
http://www.csueastbay.edu/online/

California State University, East Bay was founded in 1957. It is accredited by Western Association of Schools and Colleges. It first offered distance learning courses in 1998. In fall 2010, there were 5,523 students enrolled in distance learning courses. Institutionally administered financial aid is available to distance learners.

Services Distance learners have accessibility to academic advising, bookstore, campus computer network, career placement assistance, e-mail services, library services, tutoring.

Contact Andrea Lum, Special Assistant, California State University, East Bay, Academic Programs and Graduate Studies, 25800 Carlos Bee Boulevard, Hayward, CA 94542. Telephone: 510-885-4519. Fax: 510-885-4777. E-mail: andrea.lum@csueastbay.edu.

DEGREES AND AWARDS

BA Human Development

BS Business Administration; Hospitality and Tourism; Recreation

MS Ed Online Teaching and Learning option

MS Educational Leadership; Recreation and Tourism; Taxation

COURSE SUBJECT AREAS OFFERED OUTSIDE OF DEGREE PROGRAMS

Undergraduate—anthropology; arts, entertainment, and media management; computer systems networking and telecommunications; criminology; English language and literature related; ethnic, cultural minority, gender, and group studies; geography and cartography; geological and earth sciences/geosciences; health services/allied health/health sciences; history; library science related; mathematics; physics; public policy analysis; sociology.

Graduate—arts, entertainment, and media management; museum studies.

CALIFORNIA STATE UNIVERSITY, MONTEREY BAY
Seaside, California
http://extended.csumb.edu/onlinecourseschedules.htm

California State University, Monterey Bay was founded in 1994. It is accredited by Western Association of Schools and Colleges. It first offered distance learning courses in 2000. In fall 2010, there were 464 students enrolled in distance learning courses. Institutionally administered financial aid is available to distance learners.

Services Distance learners have accessibility to academic advising, bookstore, campus computer network, career placement assistance, e-mail services, library services, tutoring.

Contact Karen Sellick, Distributed Learning and Extended Education Analyst, California State University, Monterey Bay, 100 Campus Center, Seaside, CA 93955. Telephone: 831-582-4142. Fax: 831-582-4502. E-mail: karen_sellick@csumb.edu.

DEGREES AND AWARDS

EMBA Online Executive MBA

COURSE SUBJECT AREAS OFFERED OUTSIDE OF DEGREE PROGRAMS

Undergraduate—computer science; education related; film/video and photographic arts; geological and earth sciences/geosciences; languages (Romance languages); music; parks, recreation and leisure; social sciences.

Graduate—business administration, management and operations; education.

CALIFORNIA STATE UNIVERSITY, SACRAMENTO
Sacramento, California
Distance and Distributed Education
http://www.csus.edu/atcs/

California State University, Sacramento was founded in 1947. It is accredited by Western Association of Schools and Colleges. It first offered distance learning courses in 1986. In fall 2010, there were 5,000 students enrolled in distance learning courses. Institutionally administered financial aid is available to distance learners.

Services Distance learners have accessibility to academic advising, bookstore, campus computer network, e-mail services, library services, tutoring.

Contact Dr. Jean-Pierre Raymond Bayard, Assistant Vice President, Academic Affairs Technology Initiatives/Director of Academic Technology and Creative Services, California State University, Sacramento, 6000 J Street, Sacramento, CA 95819. Telephone: 916-278-3370. Fax: 916-278-5143. E-mail: bayardj@csus.edu.

DEGREES AND AWARDS

Programs offered do not lead to a degree or other formal award.

COURSE SUBJECT AREAS OFFERED OUTSIDE OF DEGREE PROGRAMS

Undergraduate—accounting and related services; anthropology; business/corporate communications; business, management, and marketing related; clinical/medical laboratory science/research; computer and information sciences; computer software and media applications; criminal justice and corrections; economics; foods, nutrition, and related services; geological and earth sciences/geosciences; gerontology; health and physical education/fitness; history; human development, family studies, and related services; journalism; languages (Romance languages); management information systems; mathematics; medieval and Renaissance studies; music; psychology; real estate; sales merchandising, and related marketing operations (general); sociology; special education; statistics.

Graduate—business, management, and marketing related; educational assessment, evaluation, and research; educational/instructional media design; electrical, electronics and communications engineering; public policy analysis.

CALIFORNIA STATE UNIVERSITY, SAN BERNARDINO
San Bernardino, California
http://odl.csusb.edu/

California State University, San Bernardino was founded in 1965. It is accredited by Western Association of Schools and Colleges. It first offered distance learning courses in 1988. In fall 2010, there were 1,408 students enrolled in distance learning courses. Institutionally administered financial aid is available to distance learners.

Services Distance learners have accessibility to academic advising, bookstore, e-mail services, library services.

Contact Dr. James Michael Monaghan, Assistant Vice President of Academic Technology and Distributed Learning, California State University, San Bernardino, 5500 University Parkway, San Bernardino, CA 92407. Telephone: 909-537-7439. Fax: 909-537-7637. E-mail: monaghan@csusb.edu.

DEGREES AND AWARDS

BSN Nursing–Online RN to BSN

MA Criminal Justice; Education–Career and Technical Education (EVOC); Education–Instructional Technology (ETEC); Education–Reading Education (ERDG); Special Education–Level II credential ESPE; Teaching English to Speakers of Other Languages (TESOL)

MPA Public Administration

MSN Nursing

COURSE SUBJECT AREAS OFFERED OUTSIDE OF DEGREE PROGRAMS

Undergraduate—accounting and computer science; accounting and related services; Air Force ROTC; allied health and medical assisting services; astronomy and astrophysics; bilingual, multilingual, and

multicultural education; business administration, management and operations; business, management, and marketing related; communication and journalism related; communication and media; communications technology; criminal justice and corrections; economics; education; educational/instructional media design; education related; education (specific subject areas); English; ethnic, cultural minority, gender, and group studies; finance and financial management services; languages (foreign languages related); liberal arts and sciences, general studies and humanities; mathematics; multi/interdisciplinary studies related; political science and government; psychology; social work; visual and performing arts.
Graduate—allied health diagnostic, intervention, and treatment professions; communication and media; communications technology; criminal justice and corrections; education; educational/instructional media design; education (specific subject areas); public administration.
Non-credit—education related.

CALIFORNIA STATE UNIVERSITY, SAN MARCOS
San Marcos, California
Extended Studies
http://www.csusm.edu/el

California State University, San Marcos was founded in 1990. It is accredited by Western Association of Schools and Colleges. It first offered distance learning courses in 1997. In fall 2010, there were 500 students enrolled in distance learning courses. Institutionally administered financial aid is available to distance learners.
Services Distance learners have accessibility to academic advising, bookstore, campus computer network, career placement assistance, e-mail services, library services, tutoring.
Contact Ms. Veronica Martinelli, Program Coordinator, California State University, San Marcos, 333 South Twin Oaks Valley Road, San Marcos, CA 92096. Telephone: 760-750-8717. Fax: 760-750-3138. E-mail: vmartine@csusm.edu.

DEGREES AND AWARDS
Programs offered do not lead to a degree or other formal award.

COURSE SUBJECT AREAS OFFERED OUTSIDE OF DEGREE PROGRAMS
Undergraduate—accounting and computer science; allied health and medical assisting services; applied mathematics; business administration, management and operations; business operations support and assistant services; computer and information sciences and support services related; computer programming; education (specific subject areas); mathematics; social work.
Graduate—education related; education (specific subject areas).
Non-credit—accounting and computer science; business/commerce; communication and journalism related; computer and information sciences; drama/theatre arts and stagecraft; family and consumer economics; fine and studio arts; health/medical preparatory programs; health services/allied health/health sciences; languages (foreign languages related); mathematics; philosophy; psychology related; work and family studies.

CAMPBELLSVILLE UNIVERSITY
Campbellsville, Kentucky
http://www.campbellsville.edu/

Campbellsville University was founded in 1906. It is accredited by Southern Association of Colleges and Schools. It first offered distance learning courses in 1999. In fall 2010, there were 600 students enrolled in distance learning courses. Institutionally administered financial aid is available to distance learners.
Services Distance learners have accessibility to academic advising, bookstore, campus computer network, career placement assistance, e-mail services, library services.
Contact Ms. Monica Bamwine, Coordinator of Academic Outreach, Campbellsville University, 1 University Drive, Campbellsville, KY 42718-2799. Telephone: 270-789-5221. Fax: 270-789-5550. E-mail: mkbamwine@campbellsville.edu.

DEGREES AND AWARDS
MBA Business Administration
MRS Master of Theology
MSE Special Education

COURSE SUBJECT AREAS OFFERED OUTSIDE OF DEGREE PROGRAMS
Undergraduate—business, management, and marketing related; computer and information sciences; geological and earth sciences/geosciences; music; philosophy; religious studies; social work; sociology; special education.
Graduate—business administration, management and operations; educational administration and supervision; religious studies; social work; special education.

CANISIUS COLLEGE
Buffalo, New York
On-Line Graduate Programs
http://www.canisius.edu/education/onlinemasters.asp

Canisius College was founded in 1870. It is accredited by Middle States Association of Colleges and Schools. It first offered distance learning courses in 2002. In fall 2010, there were 641 students enrolled in distance learning courses. Institutionally administered financial aid is available to distance learners.
Services Distance learners have accessibility to academic advising, bookstore, campus computer network, career placement assistance, e-mail services, library services, tutoring.
Contact Mr. James D. Bagwell, Director, Graduate Admissions, Canisius College, 2001 Main Street (LY120), Buffalo, NY 14208-1098. Telephone: 800-950-2505. Fax: 716-888-3290. E-mail: graded@canisius.edu.

DEGREES AND AWARDS
Certification Educational Administration and Supervision New York State School Building Leader; Educational Administration and Supervision New York State School District Leader
MS Ed Online Master of Science in Literacy; Online Master of Science in Physical Education
MSE Online Master of Science in Sport Administration

COURSE SUBJECT AREAS OFFERED OUTSIDE OF DEGREE PROGRAMS
Undergraduate—biology; business, management, and marketing related; communication and media; education (specific levels and methods); English; languages (Romance languages).
Graduate—behavioral sciences; curriculum and instruction; education; educational assessment, evaluation, and research; education related; education (specific levels and methods); education (specific subject areas); health and physical education/fitness; international business; social work; student counseling and personnel services.

CAPE FEAR COMMUNITY COLLEGE
Wilmington, North Carolina
http://cfcc.edu

Cape Fear Community College was founded in 1959. It is accredited by Southern Association of Colleges and Schools. It first offered distance learning courses in 1988. In fall 2010, there were 4,367 students enrolled in distance learning courses. Institutionally administered financial aid is available to distance learners.
Services Distance learners have accessibility to academic advising, bookstore, campus computer network, career placement assistance, e-mail services, library services, tutoring.
Contact Dr. Larolyn Zylicz, Department Chair, Distance Learning, Cape Fear Community College, 411 North Front Street, Wilmington, NC 28401. Telephone: 910-362-7245. Fax: 910-362-7152. E-mail: lzylicz@cfcc.edu.

DEGREES AND AWARDS
AA General Studies

COURSE SUBJECT AREAS OFFERED OUTSIDE OF DEGREE PROGRAMS

Undergraduate—accounting and related services; business, management, and marketing related; computer and information sciences; computer engineering technologies; computer systems networking and telecommunications; criminal justice and corrections; data entry/microcomputer applications; economics; education; film/video and photographic arts; health services/allied health/health sciences; legal studies (non-professional general, undergraduate); legal support services; marketing.
Non-credit—business/commerce; human resources management.

CAPITAL COMMUNITY COLLEGE
Hartford, Connecticut
Distance Learning Class
http://ccc.commnet.edu/

Capital Community College was founded in 1946. It is accredited by New England Association of Schools and Colleges. It first offered distance learning courses in 1998. In fall 2010, there were 335 students enrolled in distance learning courses. Institutionally administered financial aid is available to distance learners.
Services Distance learners have accessibility to academic advising, bookstore, career placement assistance, library services, tutoring.
Contact Mr. Michael Kriscenski, Distance Learning Counselor, Capital Community College, 950 Main Street, Hartford, CT 06103. Telephone: 860-906-5040. E-mail: mkriscenski@ccc.commnet.edu.

DEGREES AND AWARDS

AS Computer Information System; General Studies

COURSE SUBJECT AREAS OFFERED OUTSIDE OF DEGREE PROGRAMS

Undergraduate—accounting and related services; allied health diagnostic, intervention, and treatment professions; behavioral sciences; biology; business administration, management and operations; business/commerce; business, management, and marketing related; business/managerial economics; communication and media; computer and information sciences; computer/information technology administration and management; computer software and media applications; criminology; economics; English; English language and literature related; genetics; health services/allied health/health sciences; history; human development, family studies, and related services; human resources management; human services; marketing; political science and government; psychology; social sciences; sociology.

CARDINAL STRITCH UNIVERSITY
Milwaukee, Wisconsin
http://www.stritch.edu/

Cardinal Stritch University was founded in 1937. It is accredited by North Central Association of Colleges and Schools. It first offered distance learning courses in 1995. In fall 2010, there were 100 students enrolled in distance learning courses. Institutionally administered financial aid is available to distance learners.
Services Distance learners have accessibility to academic advising, bookstore, campus computer network, career placement assistance, e-mail services, library services, tutoring.
Contact Mr. John Mueller, Vice President, Enrollment Management, Cardinal Stritch University, 6801 North Yates Road, Milwaukee, WI 53217. Telephone: 414-410-4059. E-mail: jpmueller@stritch.edu.

DEGREES AND AWARDS

BS Business Management; Public Safety Management; Strategic Management Information Systems
MA Special Education
MBA Business Administration
MEd Education; Instructional Technology

COURSE SUBJECT AREAS OFFERED OUTSIDE OF DEGREE PROGRAMS

Graduate—education; educational administration and supervision.
Non-credit—business administration, management and operations; computer software and media applications; family and consumer sciences/human sciences business services.

CARLETON UNIVERSITY
Ottawa, Ontario, Canada
Instructional Television
http://www.carleton.ca/cuol

Carleton University was founded in 1942. It is provincially chartered. It first offered distance learning courses in 1978. In fall 2010, there were 5,000 students enrolled in distance learning courses. Institutionally administered financial aid is available to distance learners.
Services Distance learners have accessibility to academic advising, bookstore, campus computer network, e-mail services, library services.
Contact Maria Brockelhurst, CUOL Student Centre Services Coordinator, Carleton University, D299 Loeb Building, 1125 Colonel By Drive, Ottawa, ON K1S 5B6, Canada. Telephone: 613-520-2600 Ext. 8905. Fax: 613-520-4456. E-mail: maria_brockelhurst@carleton.ca.

DEGREES AND AWARDS

Programs offered do not lead to a degree or other formal award.

COURSE SUBJECT AREAS OFFERED OUTSIDE OF DEGREE PROGRAMS

Undergraduate—accounting and related services; astronomy and astrophysics; biology; chemistry; criminology; economics; English; geography and cartography; history; legal studies (non-professional general, undergraduate); political science and government; psychology; religious studies; social work.
Graduate—architecture related; fire protection.

CARLOW UNIVERSITY
Pittsburgh, Pennsylvania
http://www.carlow.edu/

Carlow University was founded in 1929. It is accredited by Middle States Association of Colleges and Schools. It first offered distance learning courses in 1997. In fall 2010, there were 147 students enrolled in distance learning courses. Institutionally administered financial aid is available to distance learners.
Services Distance learners have accessibility to academic advising, bookstore, campus computer network, career placement assistance, e-mail services, library services, tutoring.
Contact Susan Shutter, Senior Director of Admissions, Carlow University, 3333 Fifth Avenue, Pittsburgh, PA 15213. Telephone: 412-578-8764. E-mail: admissions@carlow.edu.

DEGREES AND AWARDS

Certificate Human Resource Management Technology
MBA Business Administration, Executive Management, Innovation, and Technology concentrations
MS Fraud and Forensics

COURSE SUBJECT AREAS OFFERED OUTSIDE OF DEGREE PROGRAMS

Undergraduate—communication and media; economics; education (specific subject areas); English; health professions related; history; information science/studies; management information systems; philosophy; psychology; sociology.
Graduate—health professions related; human resources management; psychology.

CARL SANDBURG COLLEGE
Galesburg, Illinois
http://www.sandburg.edu

Carl Sandburg College was founded in 1967. It is accredited by North Central Association of Colleges and Schools. It first offered distance learning courses in 1986. In fall 2010, there were 400 students enrolled in distance learning courses. Institutionally administered financial aid is available to distance learners.
Services Distance learners have accessibility to academic advising, bookstore, campus computer network, career placement assistance, e-mail services, library services.

Contact Carol Kreider, Director of Admissions, Carl Sandburg College, 2400 Tom L. Wilson Boulevard, Galesburg, IL 61401. Telephone: 309-341-5234. Fax: 309-344-3291. E-mail: ckreider@sandburg.edu.

DEGREES AND AWARDS

Programs offered do not lead to a degree or other formal award.

COURSE SUBJECT AREAS OFFERED OUTSIDE OF DEGREE PROGRAMS

Undergraduate—accounting and related services; allied health and medical assisting services; cell biology and anatomical sciences; computer science; computer software and media applications; computer systems networking and telecommunications; drama/theatre arts and stagecraft; education; English; fine and studio arts; geography and cartography; health services/allied health/health sciences; music; psychology; social sciences; sociology; vehicle maintenance and repair technologies.

CARROLL UNIVERSITY

Waukesha, Wisconsin

http://www.carrollu.edu/academics/online

Carroll University was founded in 1846. It is accredited by North Central Association of Colleges and Schools. It first offered distance learning courses in 1995. In fall 2010, there were 513 students enrolled in distance learning courses. Institutionally administered financial aid is available to distance learners.

Services Distance learners have accessibility to academic advising, bookstore, campus computer network, career placement assistance, e-mail services, library services, tutoring.

Contact Ms. Linda J. Sklander, Director of Admissions, Carroll University, 100 North East Avenue, Waukesha, WI 53186. Telephone: 262-524-7228. E-mail: sklander@carrollu.edu.

DEGREES AND AWARDS

Programs offered do not lead to a degree or other formal award.

COURSE SUBJECT AREAS OFFERED OUTSIDE OF DEGREE PROGRAMS

Undergraduate—accounting and computer science; business, management, and marketing related; communication and media; computer science; economics; English; finance and financial management services; history; philosophy; religious education; sociology.

Graduate—computer science; computer software and media applications; education (specific subject areas).

CASCADIA COMMUNITY COLLEGE

Bothell, Washington

http://www.cascadia.edu/

Cascadia Community College was founded in 1999. It is accredited by Northwest Commission on Colleges and Universities. It first offered distance learning courses in 2001. In fall 2010, there were 1,200 students enrolled in distance learning courses. Institutionally administered financial aid is available to distance learners.

Services Distance learners have accessibility to academic advising, bookstore, campus computer network, e-mail services, library services, tutoring.

Contact Norm Wright, Distance Advising, Cascadia Community College, 18345 Campus Way NE, Bothell, WA 98011. Telephone: 425-352-8147. E-mail: nwright@cascadia.ctc.edu.

DEGREES AND AWARDS

AA Integrated Studies–Associate in Integrated Studies (DTA); Integrated Studies–Associate in Integrated Studies (DTA); Integrated Studies–Associate in Integrated Studies (DTA)

COURSE SUBJECT AREAS OFFERED OUTSIDE OF DEGREE PROGRAMS

Undergraduate—accounting and computer science; accounting and related services; American Sign Language (ASL); anthropology; archeology; astronomy and astrophysics; biological and physical sciences; biology; botany/plant biology; business administration, management and operations; chemistry; communication and journalism related; communication and media; computer and information sciences and support services related; computer software and media applications; drama/theatre arts and stagecraft; ecology, evolution, systematics, and population biology; economics; education related; English; English language and literature related; foods, nutrition, and related services; geography and cartography; geological and earth sciences/geosciences; history; intercultural/multicultural and diversity studies; international/global studies; mathematics; mathematics and computer science; music; natural sciences; nutrition sciences; philosophy; physics; plant sciences; political science and government; psychology; psychology related; social sciences; sociology; statistics; zoology/animal biology.

THE CATHOLIC DISTANCE UNIVERSITY

Hamilton, Virginia

http://www.cdu.edu/

The Catholic Distance University was founded in 1983. It is accredited by Distance Education and Training Council. It first offered distance learning courses in 1983. In fall 2010, there were 500 students enrolled in distance learning courses. Institutionally administered financial aid is available to distance learners.

Services Distance learners have accessibility to academic advising, bookstore, campus computer network, e-mail services, library services.

Contact Ms. Carol Ciullo, Director of Admissions, The Catholic Distance University, 120 East Colonial Highway, Hamilton, VA 20158. Telephone: 888-254-4238 Ext. 700. Fax: 540-338-4788. E-mail: cciullo@cdu.edu.

DEGREES AND AWARDS

BA Theology
Certification Catechist certificate, Advanced
Diploma Catechetical diploma
MA Theology

COURSE SUBJECT AREAS OFFERED OUTSIDE OF DEGREE PROGRAMS

Undergraduate—philosophy and religious studies related; theological and ministerial studies; theology and religious vocations related.

Graduate—philosophy and religious studies related; religious education; religious studies; theological and ministerial studies; theology and religious vocations related.

Non-credit—philosophy and religious studies related; religious education; religious studies; theological and ministerial studies; theology and religious vocations related.

CAYUGA COUNTY COMMUNITY COLLEGE

Auburn, New York

http://www.cayuga-cc.edu/

Cayuga County Community College was founded in 1953. It is accredited by Middle States Association of Colleges and Schools. It first offered distance learning courses in 1998. In fall 2010, there were 2,000 students enrolled in distance learning courses. Institutionally administered financial aid is available to distance learners.

Services Distance learners have accessibility to academic advising, bookstore, career placement assistance, e-mail services, library services, tutoring.

Contact Ed Kowalski, Director of Distance Learning, Cayuga County Community College, 197 Franklin Street, Auburn, NY 13021. Telephone: 315-255-1743. Fax: 315-255-2117. E-mail: kowalskie@cayuga-cc.edu.

DEGREES AND AWARDS

AA Liberal Arts and Humanities
AAS Business Administration; Criminal Justice/Corrections; Criminal Justice/Police
AS Business Administration; Liberal Arts and Sciences, Mathematics, and Science

COURSE SUBJECT AREAS OFFERED OUTSIDE OF DEGREE PROGRAMS

Undergraduate—accounting and related services; anthropology; behavioral sciences; biological and biomedical sciences related; biological and physical sciences; biological/biosystems engineering; biology; business administration, management and operations; business/commerce; business/corporate communications; business, management, and marketing related; business/managerial economics; business operations support and assistant services; cell biology and anatomical sciences; communication and journalism related; communication and media; communications technology; computer and information sciences; computer and information sciences and support services related; computer programming; computer science; computer software and media applications; computer systems analysis; computer systems networking and telecommunications; criminal justice and corrections; criminology; data entry/microcomputer applications; economics; education related; English; English language and literature related; entrepreneurial and small business operations; ethnic, cultural minority, gender, and group studies; film/video and photographic arts; health and physical education/fitness; history; information science/studies; languages (Romance languages); liberal arts and sciences, general studies and humanities; management information systems; marketing; mathematics; mathematics and computer science; mathematics and statistics related; microbiological sciences and immunology; music; pharmacology and toxicology; political science and government; psychology; psychology related; radio, television, and digital communication; real estate; real estate development; science technologies related; social sciences; social sciences related; sociology; sociology and anthropology; statistics.

CEDARVILLE UNIVERSITY
Cedarville, Ohio
http://www.cedarville.edu/

Cedarville University was founded in 1887. It is accredited by North Central Association of Colleges and Schools. It first offered distance learning courses in 1999. In fall 2010, there were 493 students enrolled in distance learning courses. Institutionally administered financial aid is available to distance learners.

Services Distance learners have accessibility to academic advising, bookstore, campus computer network, career placement assistance, e-mail services, library services.

Contact Mr. Philip James Schanely, Manager, Center for Teaching and Learning, Cedarville University, 251 North Main Street, Cedarville, OH 45314. Telephone: 937-766-3759. E-mail: philschanely@cedarville.edu.

DEGREES AND AWARDS

Programs offered do not lead to a degree or other formal award.

COURSE SUBJECT AREAS OFFERED OUTSIDE OF DEGREE PROGRAMS

Undergraduate—accounting and computer science; accounting and related services; anthropology; archeology; biblical studies; bioethics/medical ethics; biological and physical sciences; biology; business/corporate communications; communication and journalism related; drafting/design engineering technologies; education; English; English language and literature related; finance and financial management services; geography and cartography; geological and earth sciences/geosciences; history; mathematics; social sciences; social work; sociology; soil sciences; special education.

Graduate—education.

CENTENARY COLLEGE
Hackettstown, New Jersey
http://www.centenarycollege.edu/cms/en/prospective-students/online-programs

Centenary College was founded in 1867. It is accredited by Middle States Association of Colleges and Schools. It first offered distance learning courses in 2003. In fall 2010, there were 120 students enrolled in distance learning courses. Institutionally administered financial aid is available to distance learners.

Services Distance learners have accessibility to academic advising, bookstore, campus computer network, career placement assistance, e-mail services, library services, tutoring.

Contact Carlene Colston, Enrollment Manager, Centenary College, Adult and Professional Programs, 300 Littleton Road, Parsippany, NJ 07054. Telephone: 877-437-3746 Ext. 5067. Fax: 973-257-8960 Ext. 5067. E-mail: colstonc@centenarycollege.edu.

DEGREES AND AWARDS

AA Liberal Arts
BBA Business Administration
MBA Business Administration

CENTRAL BIBLE COLLEGE
Springfield, Missouri
http://www.cbcag.edu/

Central Bible College was founded in 1922. It is accredited by Association for Biblical Higher Education. It first offered distance learning courses in 2001. In fall 2010, there were 190 students enrolled in distance learning courses. Institutionally administered financial aid is available to distance learners.

Services Distance learners have accessibility to academic advising, bookstore, campus computer network, e-mail services, library services.

Contact Lisa Dreckman, Admission Counselor, Central Bible College, 3000 North Grant Avenue, Springfield, MO 65803. Telephone: 417-833-2551 Ext. 1354. Fax: 417-221-7154. E-mail: ldreckman@cbcag.edu.

DEGREES AND AWARDS

AA Biblical Studies; Church Leadership
BA Biblical Studies; Church Leadership

COURSE SUBJECT AREAS OFFERED OUTSIDE OF DEGREE PROGRAMS

Undergraduate—biblical studies; biological and physical sciences; education; history; missionary studies and missiology; pastoral counseling and specialized ministries; philosophy and religious studies related; religious education; religious studies; theological and ministerial studies; theology and religious vocations related.

CENTRAL CAROLINA COMMUNITY COLLEGE
Sanford, North Carolina
http://www.cccc.edu/de

Central Carolina Community College was founded in 1962. It is accredited by Southern Association of Colleges and Schools. It first offered distance learning courses in 1997. In fall 2010, there were 2,649 students enrolled in distance learning courses. Institutionally administered financial aid is available to distance learners.

Services Distance learners have accessibility to academic advising, bookstore, campus computer network, career placement assistance, e-mail services, library services, tutoring.

Contact Ms. Rory Dutterer, Distance Education Counselor, Central Carolina Community College, 1105 Kelly Drive, Sanford, NC 27330. Telephone: 919-718-7511. Fax: 919-718-7380. E-mail: rdutterer@cccc.edu.

DEGREES AND AWARDS

AA University Transfer
AAS General degree; General degree; General degree
AS University Transfer

Certificate Various Subjects–BioQuality, Entrepreneur, Human Resources Management; Various Subjects–Income Tax Preparer, Library Services, Manager Trainee; Various Subjects–Medical Transcription, Networking; Various Subjects–Payroll Accounting, Small Business Financial Advisor I and II

COURSE SUBJECT AREAS OFFERED OUTSIDE OF DEGREE PROGRAMS

Undergraduate—accounting and related services; agriculture; anthropology; biblical studies; biological and physical sciences; biotechnology; business/commerce; business, management, and marketing related; business operations support and assistant services; chemistry; computer programming; computer science; criminal justice and corrections; drama/theatre arts and stagecraft; economics; education; electrical engineering technologies; English; health and physical education/fitness; history; languages (foreign languages related); library science related; marketing; mathematics; sociology.

Non-credit—clinical/medical laboratory science/research; computer and information sciences; criminal justice and corrections; management information systems.

CENTRAL CAROLINA TECHNICAL COLLEGE
Sumter, South Carolina
http://www.cctech.edu

Central Carolina Technical College was founded in 1963. It is accredited by Southern Association of Colleges and Schools. It first offered distance learning courses in 1995. In fall 2010, there were 1,100 students enrolled in distance learning courses. Institutionally administered financial aid is available to distance learners.

Services Distance learners have accessibility to academic advising, bookstore, campus computer network, career placement assistance, e-mail services, library services, tutoring.

Contact Ms. Susan McMaster, Vice President, Academic Affairs, Central Carolina Technical College, 492 North Guignard Drive, Sumter, SC 29150. Telephone: 803-778-1961 Ext. 311. Fax: 803-778-7896. E-mail: mcmastersm@cctech.edu.

DEGREES AND AWARDS

AA the Arts

Certificate Medical Record Coding certificate; Wastewater Operator certificate; Water Operator certificate

COURSE SUBJECT AREAS OFFERED OUTSIDE OF DEGREE PROGRAMS

Undergraduate—accounting and related services; agriculture; allied health and medical assisting services; business administration, management and operations; business operations support and assistant services; computer/information technology administration and management; criminal justice and corrections; data entry/microcomputer applications; economics; English; environmental/environmental health engineering; forestry; history; legal studies (non-professional general, undergraduate); marketing; mathematics; music; natural resources conservation and research; psychology; religious studies; sociology.

CENTRALIA COLLEGE
Centralia, Washington
Distance Learning
http://cconline.centralia.edu

Centralia College was founded in 1925. It is accredited by Northwest Commission on Colleges and Universities. It first offered distance learning courses in 1975. In fall 2010, there were 400 students enrolled in distance learning courses. Institutionally administered financial aid is available to distance learners.

Services Distance learners have accessibility to academic advising, bookstore, campus computer network, career placement assistance, e-mail services, library services, tutoring.

Contact Eric Richardson, eLearning Coordinator, Centralia College, 600 Centralia College Boulevard, Centralia, WA 98531. Telephone: 360-736-9391 Ext. 374. E-mail: erichardson@centralia.edu.

DEGREES AND AWARDS

AA Criminal Justice emphasis; Criminal Justice

AGS General Studies

COURSE SUBJECT AREAS OFFERED OUTSIDE OF DEGREE PROGRAMS

Undergraduate—accounting and related services; anthropology; business administration, management and operations; business, management, and marketing related; chemistry; computer software and media applications; criminal justice and corrections; education; English; geography and cartography; geological and earth sciences/geosciences; health and physical education/fitness; history; human development, family studies, and related services; liberal arts and sciences, general studies and humanities; library science related; management information systems; mathematics; philosophy; political science and government; psychology; real estate; social sciences; sociology; statistics.

Non-credit—computer and information sciences; computer programming; computer software and media applications; computer systems analysis; data entry/microcomputer applications; management information systems; real estate; sales, merchandising and related marketing operations (specialized).

CENTRAL MICHIGAN UNIVERSITY
Mount Pleasant, Michigan
Off-Campus Programs
http://www.cel.cmich.edu/default.html

Central Michigan University was founded in 1892. It is accredited by North Central Association of Colleges and Schools. It first offered distance learning courses in 1971. In fall 2010, there were 8,000 students enrolled in distance learning courses. Institutionally administered financial aid is available to distance learners.

Services Distance learners have accessibility to academic advising, bookstore, campus computer network, career placement assistance, e-mail services, library services, tutoring.

Contact Ms. Amy Darnell, Coordinator of Recruitment Services, Central Michigan University, 802 Industrial Drive, Mount Pleasant, MI 48858. Telephone: 800-950-1144 Ext. 3860. E-mail: whitf1am@cmich.edu.

DEGREES AND AWARDS

BS Administration–Building Code Administration; Administration–Organizational Administration; Community Development, Community Services major; Community Development, Health Sciences major; Community Development, Public Administration major; Education; Information Technology; Integrated Leadership Studies major; Psychology major

Ed S General Educational Administration

MA Counseling; Education; Reading and Literacy K-12; School Principalship; Sport Administration

MAE Educational Leadership, Charter School Administration emphasis; Technology

MAEd Guidance and Development

MBA Logistics Management concentration; MIS concentration, SAP emphasis; Value Driven Organization

MPA Public Administration

MS Administration–Health Services Administration concentration; Administration–Human Resource Administration; Administration–Information Resource Management concentration; Administration–Leadership concentration; Administration–Public Administration concentration; Nutrition and Dietetics

DHA Healthcare Administration

EdD Education Ladder Specialist program

COURSE SUBJECT AREAS OFFERED OUTSIDE OF DEGREE PROGRAMS

Undergraduate—accounting and computer science; allied health and medical assisting services; architecture related; behavioral sciences; building/construction finishing, management, and inspection; business administration, management and operations; business/commerce; business/corporate communications; business, management, and marketing related; business/managerial economics; business operations support and assistant services; community organization and advocacy; construction management; construction trades; economics; family and consumer sciences/human sciences; family and consumer sciences/human sciences related; health and medical administrative services; health and physical education/fitness; health professions related; health services/allied health/health sciences; human development, family studies, and related services; human resources management; human services; marketing; multi/interdisciplinary studies related; political science and government; psychology; psychology related; public administration; public administration and social service professions related; public policy analysis; work and family studies.

Graduate—accounting and computer science; behavioral sciences; business administration, management and operations; business/commerce; business/corporate communications; business, management, and marketing related; business/managerial economics; communication and journalism related; communications technology; computer and information sciences; computer and information sciences and support services related; computer systems analysis; curriculum and instruction; dietetics and clinical nutrition services; economics; education (specific levels and methods); education (specific subject areas); entrepreneurial and small business operations; finance and financial management services; food science and technology; foods, nutrition, and related services; health and medical administrative services; health professions related; hospitality administration; human resources management; management information systems; management sciences and quantitative methods; marketing; multi/interdisciplinary studies related; nutrition sciences; political science and government; public administration; public administration and social service professions related; public policy analysis; public relations, advertising, and applied communication related; sales merchandising, and related marketing operations (general).

Non-credit—building/construction finishing, management, and inspection; business/commerce; construction trades; data entry/microcomputer applications; education; education related; education (specific levels and methods); education (specific subject areas); environmental design; health and medical administrative services; health professions related; pharmacy, pharmaceutical sciences, and administration; science technologies related.

CENTRAL NEW MEXICO COMMUNITY COLLEGE
Albuquerque, New Mexico
http://www.cnm.edu/depts/dl

Central New Mexico Community College was founded in 1965. It is accredited by North Central Association of Colleges and Schools. It first offered distance learning courses in 1997. In fall 2010, there were 6,656 students enrolled in distance learning courses. Institutionally administered financial aid is available to distance learners.

Services Distance learners have accessibility to academic advising, bookstore, campus computer network, career placement assistance, e-mail services, library services, tutoring.

Contact Ms. Audrey Gramstad, Administrative Director, Distance Learning and Instructional Support, Central New Mexico Community College, Distance Learning Office, 525 Buena Vista SE, Albuquerque, NM 87106. Telephone: 505-224-4246. Fax: 505-224-3321. E-mail: agramstad@cnm.edu.

DEGREES AND AWARDS
AA Liberal Arts
AAS Business Administration; Office Administration

COURSE SUBJECT AREAS OFFERED OUTSIDE OF DEGREE PROGRAMS
Undergraduate—accounting and related services; biology; building/construction finishing, management, and inspection; business administration, management and operations; business/commerce; business, management, and marketing related; business/managerial economics; business operations support and assistant services; clinical/medical laboratory science/research; communication and media; computer and information sciences; computer programming; criminal justice and corrections; culinary arts and related services; data processing; economics; English; entrepreneurial and small business operations; fire protection; foods, nutrition, and related services; information science/studies; international business; legal studies (non-professional general, undergraduate); mathematics; microbiological sciences and immunology; philosophy; psychology; real estate; sales merchandising, and related marketing operations (general); sociology.

CENTRAL OREGON COMMUNITY COLLEGE
Bend, Oregon
Open Campus Distance Learning Program
http://www.cocc.edu/

Central Oregon Community College was founded in 1949. It is accredited by Northwest Commission on Colleges and Universities. It first offered distance learning courses in 1996. In fall 2010, there were 1,194 students enrolled in distance learning courses. Institutionally administered financial aid is available to distance learners.

Services Distance learners have accessibility to academic advising, bookstore, campus computer network, e-mail services, library services, tutoring.

Contact Barbara Klett, Instructional Technology Coordinator, Central Oregon Community College, 2600 NW College Way, Bend, OR 97701. Telephone: 541-383-7785. E-mail: bklett@cocc.edu.

DEGREES AND AWARDS
Programs offered do not lead to a degree or other formal award.

COURSE SUBJECT AREAS OFFERED OUTSIDE OF DEGREE PROGRAMS
Undergraduate—air transportation; allied health and medical assisting services; biology; business administration, management and operations; computer and information sciences; geological and earth sciences/geosciences; health and physical education/fitness; health services/allied health/health sciences; history; liberal arts and sciences, general studies and humanities; library science and administration; mathematics.

Non-credit—business administration, management and operations; business/corporate communications; business, management, and marketing related; business operations support and assistant services; computer software and media applications.

CENTRAL PENNSYLVANIA COLLEGE
Summerdale, Pennsylvania
http://www.centralpenn.edu/admissions/online/

Central Pennsylvania College was founded in 1881. It is accredited by Middle States Association of Colleges and Schools. It first offered distance learning courses in 2003. In fall 2010, there were 906 students enrolled in distance learning courses. Institutionally administered financial aid is available to distance learners.

Services Distance learners have accessibility to academic advising, bookstore, campus computer network, career placement assistance, e-mail services, library services, tutoring.

Contact Kristen Markus, Online Enrollment Director, Central Pennsylvania College, College Hill and Valley Roads, Summerdale, PA 17093. Telephone: 717-728-2288. E-mail: kristenmarkus@centralpenn.edu.

DEGREES AND AWARDS
AS Accounting; Computer Information Systems; Criminal Justice; Entrepreneurship and Small Business; Marketing

BS Accounting; Business Administration; Corporate Communications; Criminal Justice Administration; Homeland Security Management; Information Technology

COURSE SUBJECT AREAS OFFERED OUTSIDE OF DEGREE PROGRAMS
Undergraduate—accounting and computer science; criminology; human resources management.

CENTRAL TEXAS COLLEGE
Killeen, Texas
Distance Education and Educational Technology
http://online.ctcd.edu

Central Texas College was founded in 1967. It is accredited by Southern Association of Colleges and Schools. It first offered distance learning courses in 1972. In fall 2010, there were 15,144 students enrolled in distance learning courses. Institutionally administered financial aid is available to distance learners.

Services Distance learners have accessibility to academic advising, bookstore, career placement assistance, library services, tutoring.

Contact Mrs. Kimberley Christian, Coordinator, Recruiting and Retention, Central Texas College, PO Box 1800, Killeen, TX 76540. Telephone: 254-526-1223. Fax: 254-526-1751. E-mail: kimberley.christian@ctcd.edu.

DEGREES AND AWARDS
AA General Studies; Interdisciplinary Studies; Social Science
AAS Applied Management (non-Texas locations); Applied Management with Computer Applications (non-Texas students only); Applied Technology; At-Risk Youth specialization; Business Management Marketing and Sales Management; Business Management; Chemical Dependency specialization; Computer Science–Information Security Management; Computer Science–Information Technology; Criminal Justice Corrections specialization; Criminal Justice; Executive Assistant; Homeland Security and Emergency Management; Hospitality Management–Food and Beverage Management; Hospitality Management–Hotel Management Specialization; Hospitality Management–Restaurant and Culinary Management; Network Systems Administrator; Office Management; Social Work specialization
AS Business Administration
Certificate At-Risk Youth specialization; Business Management Marketing and Sales; Business Management; Chemical Dependency specialization–Advanced certificate; Computer Helpdesk Specialist; Criminal Justice Addictions; Criminal Justice Corrections specialization; Criminal Justice Studies specialization; Homeland Security and Emergency Management; Hospitality Management–Food and Beverage Management; Hospitality Management–Property Management Advanced; Hospitality Management–Rooms Division; Information Security Management Specialist; Medical Office Specialist; Medical Transcription; Microsoft Information Technology Server Administrator; Network Specialist; Office Assistant; Office Management Levels 1 and 2; Software Applications Specialist; Web Design Basics

COURSE SUBJECT AREAS OFFERED OUTSIDE OF DEGREE PROGRAMS
Undergraduate—accounting and computer science; accounting and related services; allied health and medical assisting services; anthropology; applied mathematics; biblical studies; business administration, management and operations; business/corporate communications; business, management, and marketing related; business/managerial economics; business operations support and assistant services; communication and media; computer and information sciences; computer and information sciences and support services related; computer programming; computer science; computer software and media applications; computer systems analysis; computer systems networking and telecommunications; criminal justice and corrections; criminology; culinary arts and related services; economics; education; English; English language and literature related; entrepreneurial and small business operations; ethnic, cultural minority, gender, and group studies; family and consumer sciences/human sciences; fine and studio arts; fire protection; foods, nutrition, and related services; geography and cartography; health and physical education/fitness; health professions related; history; hospitality administration; human resources management; legal studies (non-professional general, undergraduate); management information systems; marketing; mathematics; mathematics and computer science; mathematics and statistics related; mental and social health services and allied professions; multi/interdisciplinary studies related; music; philosophy; philosophy and religious studies related; political science and government; psychology; psychology related; public administration; real estate; sales, merchandising and related marketing operations (specialized); social sciences; social sciences related; social work; sociology; statistics.

CENTRAL VIRGINIA COMMUNITY COLLEGE
Lynchburg, Virginia
Learning Resources
http://www.cvcc.vccs.edu

Central Virginia Community College was founded in 1966. It is accredited by Southern Association of Colleges and Schools. It first offered distance learning courses in 1984. In fall 2010, there were 2,337 students enrolled in distance learning courses. Institutionally administered financial aid is available to distance learners.

Services Distance learners have accessibility to academic advising, bookstore, campus computer network, e-mail services, library services, tutoring.

Contact Susan S. Beasley, Distance Education Coordinator, Central Virginia Community College, 3506 Wards Road, Lynchburg, VA 24502. Telephone: 434-832-7742. Fax: 434-832-7881. E-mail: beasleys@cvcc.vccs.edu.

DEGREES AND AWARDS
Programs offered do not lead to a degree or other formal award.

COURSE SUBJECT AREAS OFFERED OUTSIDE OF DEGREE PROGRAMS
Undergraduate—accounting and related services; agricultural business and management; allied health and medical assisting services; applied mathematics; astronomy and astrophysics; biology; business administration, management and operations; business operations support and assistant services; chemistry; computer and information sciences; computer software and media applications; economics; education related; English; health professions related; history; information science/studies; library science related; marketing; mathematics; music; nutrition sciences; philosophy; political science and government; psychology; psychology related; religious studies; social sciences related; sociology.

CENTRAL WASHINGTON UNIVERSITY
Ellensburg, Washington
Center for Learning Technologies
http://www.cwu.edu/~media/

Central Washington University was founded in 1891. It is accredited by Northwest Commission on Colleges and Universities. It first offered distance learning courses in 1996. In fall 2010, there were 1,200 students enrolled in distance learning courses. Institutionally administered financial aid is available to distance learners.

Services Distance learners have accessibility to academic advising, bookstore, campus computer network, career placement assistance, e-mail services, library services.

Contact Tracy Terrell, Registrar, Central Washington University, Mitchell Hall, 400 East University Way, Ellensburg, WA 98926-7465. Telephone: 509-963-3076. Fax: 509-963-3022. E-mail: reg@cwu.edu.

DEGREES AND AWARDS
BAS Information Technology and Administrative Management
MS Physical Education, Health, and Leisure Studies

COURSE SUBJECT AREAS OFFERED OUTSIDE OF DEGREE PROGRAMS
Undergraduate—accounting and related services; anthropology; biology; business administration, management and operations; business/commerce; business/corporate communications; chemistry; communication and journalism related; computer/information technology administration and management; computer software and media applications; criminal justice and corrections; economics; education; educational/instructional media design; education (specific levels and methods); education (specific subject areas); English; family and consumer sciences/human sciences related; geography and cartography; history; human development, family studies, and related services; human resources management; legal studies (non-professional general, undergraduate); management information systems; marketing; nutrition sciences; philosophy and religious studies related; psychology; psychology related; social sciences related; sociology.

Graduate—accounting and related services; business administration, management and operations; education; health and physical education/ fitness.

CENTRAL WYOMING COLLEGE
Riverton, Wyoming
Distance Education and Extended Studies
http://www.cwc.edu

Central Wyoming College was founded in 1966. It is accredited by North Central Association of Colleges and Schools. It first offered distance learning courses in 1983. In fall 2010, there were 858 students enrolled in distance learning courses. Institutionally administered financial aid is available to distance learners.

Services Distance learners have accessibility to academic advising, bookstore, campus computer network, e-mail services, library services, tutoring.

Contact Retha Reinke, Distance Education Technician, Central Wyoming College, 2660 Peck Avenue, Riverton, WY 82501. Telephone: 307-855-2124. Fax: 307-855-2065. E-mail: rreinke@cwc.edu.

DEGREES AND AWARDS

AA General Studies

COURSE SUBJECT AREAS OFFERED OUTSIDE OF DEGREE PROGRAMS

Undergraduate—accounting and related services; agricultural and domestic animal services; biology; chemistry; communication and media; computer and information sciences; computer science; data entry/ microcomputer applications; economics; education (specific subject areas); fine and studio arts; geography and cartography; health and physical education/fitness; languages (American Indian/Native American); library science and administration; mathematics; mechanics and repair; music; political science and government; psychology; religious studies; social sciences; sociology; vehicle maintenance and repair technologies; zoology/ animal biology.

Non-credit—agricultural and domestic animal services; air transportation; animal sciences; applied horticulture and horticultural business services; botany/plant biology; business operations support and assistant services; computer software and media applications; culinary arts and related services; dance; data entry/microcomputer applications; design and applied arts; drama/theatre arts and stagecraft; electrical and power transmission installation; electrical/electronics maintenance and repair technology; film/video and photographic arts; finance and financial management services; fine and studio arts; food science and technology; foods, nutrition, and related services; graphic communications; health and physical education/fitness; health professions related; health services/ allied health/health sciences; history; landscape architecture; languages (foreign languages related); mechanics and repair; mental and social health services and allied professions; movement and mind-body therapies and education; music; nutrition sciences; personal and culinary services related; precision metal working; psychology; vehicle maintenance and repair technologies; veterinary biomedical and clinical sciences; visual and performing arts; visual and performing arts related; wildlife and wildlands science and management; woodworking.

CERRITOS COLLEGE
Norwalk, California
Distributed Education Program
http://www.cerritos.edu/de

Cerritos College was founded in 1956. It is accredited by Western Association of Schools and Colleges. It first offered distance learning courses in 1985. In fall 2010, there were 11,000 students enrolled in distance learning courses. Institutionally administered financial aid is available to distance learners.

Services Distance learners have accessibility to academic advising, bookstore, e-mail services, library services.

Contact Yvette Juarez, Program Assistant, Distance Education, Cerritos College, 11110 Alondra Boulevard, Norwalk, CA 90650. Telephone: 562-860-2451 Ext. 2405. Fax: 562-467-5091. E-mail: yjuarez@cerritos.edu.

DEGREES AND AWARDS

Programs offered do not lead to a degree or other formal award.

COURSE SUBJECT AREAS OFFERED OUTSIDE OF DEGREE PROGRAMS

Undergraduate—accounting and computer science; accounting and related services; anthropology; business/commerce; business operations support and assistant services; curriculum and instruction; data entry/ microcomputer applications; history; journalism; legal studies (non-professional general, undergraduate); management information systems; psychology; radio, television, and digital communication; real estate; sociology; woodworking; zoology/animal biology.

CHAMBERLAIN COLLEGE OF NURSING
St. Louis, Missouri
http://www.chamberlain.edu/home.html

Chamberlain College of Nursing was founded in 1889. It is accredited by North Central Association of Colleges and Schools. It first offered distance learning courses in 2000. In fall 2010, there were 7,451 students enrolled in distance learning courses. Institutionally administered financial aid is available to distance learners.

Services Distance learners have accessibility to academic advising, bookstore, library services.

Contact Evan Celing, Director of Admissions, Chamberlain College of Nursing, 11830 Westline Industrial Drive, Suite 106, St. Louis, MO 63146. Telephone: 888-673-3879. E-mail: eceling@chamberlain.edu.

DEGREES AND AWARDS

BSN Nursing–Fast Track RN to BSN degree completion program
MSN Nursing

CHAMINADE UNIVERSITY OF HONOLULU
Honolulu, Hawaii
http://www.chaminade.edu/

Chaminade University of Honolulu was founded in 1955. It is accredited by Western Association of Schools and Colleges. It first offered distance learning courses in 1997. In fall 2010, there were 800 students enrolled in distance learning courses. Institutionally administered financial aid is available to distance learners.

Services Distance learners have accessibility to academic advising, bookstore, campus computer network, e-mail services, library services.

Contact Morris Lee, Director of Adult Evening and Online Programs, Chaminade University of Honolulu, 3140 Waialae Avenue, Honolulu, HI 96816-1578. Telephone: 808-735-4755. Fax: 808-735-4766. E-mail: online@chaminade.edu.

DEGREES AND AWARDS

Programs offered do not lead to a degree or other formal award.

COURSE SUBJECT AREAS OFFERED OUTSIDE OF DEGREE PROGRAMS

Undergraduate—business administration, management and operations; criminal justice and corrections; education; English; history; political science and government; psychology.

Graduate—criminal justice and corrections; education; religious studies.

CHAMPLAIN COLLEGE
Burlington, Vermont
Continuing Education Division
http://www.online.champlain.edu

Champlain College was founded in 1878. It is accredited by New England Association of Schools and Colleges. It first offered distance learning courses in 1993. In fall 2010, there were 800 students enrolled in distance learning courses. Institutionally administered financial aid is available to distance learners.

Services Distance learners have accessibility to academic advising, bookstore, campus computer network, career placement assistance, e-mail services, library services, tutoring.

Contact Bridget Baldwin, Director of CPS Admissions, Champlain College, Division of CPS, 246 South Willard Street, Burlington, VT 05401. Telephone: 888-545-3459. Fax: 802-865-6447. E-mail: cps@champlain.edu.

DEGREES AND AWARDS

AS Accounting; Business Management; Health Informatics; Software Development; Web Design and Development

BS Accounting; Business Management; Computer Forensics and Digital Investigations; Computer and Information Systems; Health Informatics; Healthcare Management; Integrated Studies; Management Information Systems; Network Security and Administration; Software Development; Web Design and Development

Certificate .Net Technology; Accounting–Cost; Accounting–Forensic; Accounting–Managerial; Accounting; Accounting, advanced; C++; Computer Forensics and Digital Investigations; Computer Networking; Data Coding and Classification; Data Systems and Technology; Healthcare Management; Human Resource Management; Information Security; Internet Marketing; Java Development; Linux Administration, Security and Support; Management; Mobile Programming; Organizational Development; PHP Programming; Small Business and Entrepreneurship; Software Development; System Administration; Web Design; Web Infrastructure; Web Programming

MBA Business Administration

MEd Early Childhood Education

MS Digital Forensics Management; Digital Forensics Management; Healthcare Management; Law; Law; Law; Managing Innovation and Information Technology; Mediation and Applied Conflict Studies

COURSE SUBJECT AREAS OFFERED OUTSIDE OF DEGREE PROGRAMS

Undergraduate—accounting and related services; business administration, management and operations; business/commerce; business/corporate communications; chemistry; communication and journalism related; communication and media; computer and information sciences; computer and information sciences and support services related; computer/information technology administration and management; computer programming; computer software and media applications; computer systems networking and telecommunications; economics; English; entrepreneurial and small business operations; finance and financial management services; geography and cartography; history; human resources management; international business; liberal arts and sciences, general studies and humanities; mathematics; mathematics and computer science; physical sciences; psychology; public relations, advertising, and applied communication related; sociology.

Graduate—business/commerce; business, management, and marketing related; business/managerial economics; health and medical administrative services; information science/studies.

CHARTER OAK STATE COLLEGE
New Britain, Connecticut
http://www.charteroak.edu/

Charter Oak State College was founded in 1973. It is accredited by New England Association of Schools and Colleges. It first offered distance learning courses in 1992. In fall 2010, there were 2,278 students enrolled in distance learning courses. Institutionally administered financial aid is available to distance learners.

Services Distance learners have accessibility to academic advising, bookstore, e-mail services, library services, tutoring.

Contact Dr. Dana Wilkie, Dean of Undergraduate Programs, Charter Oak State College, 55 Paul J. Manafort Drive, New Britain, CT 06053. Telephone: 860-832-3835. E-mail: dwilkie@charteroak.edu.

DEGREES AND AWARDS

AA General Studies

AS General Studies

BA General Studies

BS General Studies

COURSE SUBJECT AREAS OFFERED OUTSIDE OF DEGREE PROGRAMS

Undergraduate—accounting and related services; behavioral sciences; biology/biotechnology laboratory technician; business administration, management and operations; business, management, and marketing related; communication and media; computer and information sciences; computer systems networking and telecommunications; criminology; educational administration and supervision; educational/instructional media design; English language and literature related; finance and financial management services; foods, nutrition, and related services; genetics; geological and earth sciences/geosciences; health services/allied health/health sciences; management information systems; marketing; mathematics; mathematics and statistics related; philosophy; philosophy and religious studies related; political science and government; psychology; psychology related; public administration; public administration and social service professions related; social sciences; social sciences related; sociology; statistics.

Non-credit—health professions related; pharmacy, pharmaceutical sciences, and administration.

CHATHAM UNIVERSITY
Pittsburgh, Pennsylvania
http://www.chatham.edu/ccps

Chatham University was founded in 1869. It is accredited by Middle States Association of Colleges and Schools. It first offered distance learning courses in 2005. In fall 2010, there were 400 students enrolled in distance learning courses. Institutionally administered financial aid is available to distance learners.

Services Distance learners have accessibility to academic advising, bookstore, campus computer network, career placement assistance, e-mail services, library services, tutoring.

Contact Mr. David A. Vey, Admission Support Specialist, Chatham University, College for Continuing and Professional Studies, Woodland Road, Pittsburgh, PA 15232. Telephone: 412-365-1448. Fax: 412-365-1720. E-mail: ccps@chatham.edu.

DEGREES AND AWARDS

BSN Nursing–RN to BSN

Graduate Certificate Infant Mental Health

M Arch Master of Science in Interior Architecture

MFA Creative Writing (Low-Residency MFA)

MPW Professional Writing

DNP Nursing Practice

OTD Professional Doctor of Occupational Therapy

COURSE SUBJECT AREAS OFFERED OUTSIDE OF DEGREE PROGRAMS

Undergraduate—accounting and related services; behavioral sciences; biochemistry, biophysics and molecular biology; biology; business, management, and marketing related; business/managerial economics; chemistry; communication and journalism related; computer and information sciences and support services related; economics; education; engineering; English; environmental design; film/video and photographic arts; history; human services; interior architecture; international business; languages (Romance languages); legal professions and studies related; marketing; mathematics; museum studies; music; physics; political science and government; psychology; religious studies; social work; visual and performing arts.

Graduate—accounting and related services; biology; business administration, management and operations; business operations support and assistant services; education; film/video and photographic arts; interior architecture; landscape architecture; physical sciences; teaching assistants/aides.

Non-credit—computer software and media applications.

CHATTANOOGA STATE COMMUNITY COLLEGE
Chattanooga, Tennessee
Distance Learning Program
http://www.chattanoogastate.edu/cde/

Chattanooga State Community College was founded in 1965. It is accredited by Southern Association of Colleges and Schools. It first offered distance learning courses in 1979. In fall 2010, there were 2,500 students enrolled in distance learning courses. Institutionally administered financial aid is available to distance learners.

Services Distance learners have accessibility to academic advising, bookstore, campus computer network, career placement assistance, e-mail services, library services, tutoring.

Contact Tim Dills, Assistant Director, Center for Distributed Education, Chattanooga State Community College, 4501 Amnicola Highway, Chattanooga, TN 37406-1097. Telephone: 423-697-2592. Fax: 423-697-4479. E-mail: tim.dills@chattanoogastate.edu.

DEGREES AND AWARDS
Programs offered do not lead to a degree or other formal award.

COURSE SUBJECT AREAS OFFERED OUTSIDE OF DEGREE PROGRAMS
Undergraduate—accounting and computer science; accounting and related services; allied health and medical assisting services; American Sign Language (ASL); behavioral sciences; biblical studies; biology; building/construction finishing, management, and inspection; business administration, management and operations; business/commerce; business, management, and marketing related; chemistry; communication and media; computer and information sciences; computer science; dental support services and allied professions; economics; education; English; finance and financial management services; fire protection; geography and cartography; health and medical administrative services; health/medical preparatory programs; health professions related; history; liberal arts and sciences, general studies and humanities; marketing; mathematics; mathematics and statistics related; music; philosophy; philosophy and religious studies related; physics; political science and government; psychology; religious studies; sociology; statistics.

CHEMEKETA COMMUNITY COLLEGE
Salem, Oregon
Chemeketa Online
http://online.chemeketa.edu

Chemeketa Community College was founded in 1955. It is accredited by Northwest Commission on Colleges and Universities. It first offered distance learning courses in 1979. In fall 2010, there were 5,636 students enrolled in distance learning courses. Institutionally administered financial aid is available to distance learners.

Services Distance learners have accessibility to academic advising, bookstore, e-mail services, library services, tutoring.

Contact Kathy Roberts, Online Assistant, Chemeketa Community College, 4000 Lancaster Drive NE, PO Box 14007, Salem, OR 97309-7070. Telephone: 503-399-7873. E-mail: kathy.roberts@chemeketa.edu.

DEGREES AND AWARDS
AA Oregon Transfer
AAS Accounting; Fire Protection Technology–Fire Prevention; Fire Protection Technology–Fire Suppression; Hospitality Management; Management; Speech/Language Pathology Assistant; Tourism and Travel Management
AGS General Studies
AS Business
Certificate of Completion Oregon Transfer Module
Certificate Business Software; Hospitality Management; Speech/Language Pathology Assistant; Tourism and Travel Management

COURSE SUBJECT AREAS OFFERED OUTSIDE OF DEGREE PROGRAMS
Undergraduate—accounting and related services; allied health and medical assisting services; anthropology; applied mathematics; archeology; astronomy and astrophysics; biological and biomedical sciences related; biological and physical sciences; biology; business administration, management and operations; business/commerce; business/corporate communications; business, management, and marketing related; business operations support and assistant services; chemistry; computer and information sciences; computer and information sciences and support services related; computer programming; computer science; computer software and media applications; computer systems networking and telecommunications; criminal justice and corrections; criminology; curriculum and instruction; data entry/microcomputer applications; drafting/design engineering technologies; economics; education; education related; ethnic, cultural minority, gender, and group studies; fine and studio arts; fire protection; foods, nutrition, and related services; geography and cartography; geological and earth sciences/geosciences; health and physical education/fitness; health professions related; history; hospitality administration; human development, family studies, and related services; information science/studies; liberal arts and sciences, general studies and humanities; management information systems; mathematics; mathematics and computer science; mathematics and statistics related; music; philosophy; philosophy and religious studies related; physical sciences; physical sciences related; political science and government; psychology; psychology related; religious studies; sales merchandising, and related marketing operations (general); sales, merchandising and related marketing operations (specialized); social sciences; social sciences related; sociology; statistics.

CINCINNATI CHRISTIAN UNIVERSITY
Cincinnati, Ohio
Correspondence Department
http://www.ccuniversity.edu/elearn

Cincinnati Christian University was founded in 1924. It is accredited by Association for Biblical Higher Education. It first offered distance learning courses in 1980. In fall 2010, there were 272 students enrolled in distance learning courses. Institutionally administered financial aid is available to distance learners.

Services Distance learners have accessibility to academic advising, bookstore, campus computer network, e-mail services, library services, tutoring.

Contact Suzanne Faber, Director of Distance Education Development, Cincinnati Christian University, 2700 Glenway Avenue, Cincinnati, OH 45204-3200. Telephone: 513-244-8475. Fax: 513-244-8123. E-mail: suzanne.faber@ccuniversity.edu.

DEGREES AND AWARDS
Programs offered do not lead to a degree or other formal award.

COURSE SUBJECT AREAS OFFERED OUTSIDE OF DEGREE PROGRAMS
Undergraduate—biblical studies; education; history.
Graduate—biblical studies; education; history; religious studies.

CINCINNATI STATE TECHNICAL AND COMMUNITY COLLEGE
Cincinnati, Ohio
http://www.cincinnatistate.edu/real-world-academics/distance-learning/

Cincinnati State Technical and Community College was founded in 1966. It is accredited by North Central Association of Colleges and Schools. It first offered distance learning courses in 1995. In fall 2010, there were 3,463 students enrolled in distance learning courses. Institutionally administered financial aid is available to distance learners.

Services Distance learners have accessibility to academic advising, bookstore, campus computer network, e-mail services, library services, tutoring.

Contact Ms. Gaby Boeckermann, Director of Admissions, Cincinnati State Technical and Community College, 3520 Central Parkway, Cincinnati, OH 45223. Telephone: 513-569-1550. E-mail: gaby.boeckermann@cincinnatistate.edu.

DEGREES AND AWARDS

Programs offered do not lead to a degree or other formal award.

COURSE SUBJECT AREAS OFFERED OUTSIDE OF DEGREE PROGRAMS

Undergraduate—accounting and related services; allied health and medical assisting services; audiovisual communications technologies; bioethics/medical ethics; biology; biomedical/medical engineering; business administration, management and operations; business/commerce; business/corporate communications; business, management, and marketing related; business operations support and assistant services; cell biology and anatomical sciences; civil engineering technologies; communication and media; computer and information sciences; computer and information sciences and support services related; computer/information technology administration and management; computer software and media applications; computer systems networking and telecommunications; data processing; dietetics and clinical nutrition services; education (specific subject areas); engineering technologies related; health aides/attendants/orderlies; health and medical administrative services; health professions related; history; homeland security, law enforcement, firefighting and protective services related; information science/studies; management information systems; mechanical engineering related technologies; physiology, pathology and related sciences; psychology; sociology.

CITRUS COLLEGE

Glendora, California

Distance Education

http://www.citruscollege.com

Citrus College was founded in 1915. It is accredited by Western Association of Schools and Colleges. It first offered distance learning courses in 1996. In fall 2010, there were 2,800 students enrolled in distance learning courses. Institutionally administered financial aid is available to distance learners.

Services Distance learners have accessibility to bookstore, campus computer network, e-mail services, library services.

Contact Ms. Lari Kirby, Distance Education Supervisor, Citrus College, 1000 West Foothill Boulevard, Glendora, CA 91741-1899. Telephone: 626-914-8569. E-mail: online@citruscollege.edu.

DEGREES AND AWARDS

Programs offered do not lead to a degree or other formal award.

COURSE SUBJECT AREAS OFFERED OUTSIDE OF DEGREE PROGRAMS

Undergraduate—accounting and computer science; anthropology; astronomy and astrophysics; behavioral sciences; biological and physical sciences; biology; business/commerce; communication and media; computer and information sciences; computer programming; criminal justice and corrections; economics; English; history; journalism; liberal arts and sciences, general studies and humanities; mathematics; music; philosophy; political science and government; psychology; psychology related; real estate; social sciences; sociology.

CITY COLLEGES OF CHICAGO SYSTEM

Chicago, Illinois

Center for Distance Learning

http://cdl.ccc.edu

City Colleges of Chicago System first offered distance learning courses in 1956. In fall 2010, there were 4,853 students enrolled in distance learning courses. Institutionally administered financial aid is available to distance learners.

Services Distance learners have accessibility to bookstore, campus computer network, e-mail services, library services, tutoring.

Contact Ms. Martha Madkins, Associate Dean, City Colleges of Chicago System, 6343 South Halsted Street, Center for Distance Learning, Chicago, IL 60621. Telephone: 773-487-3718. Fax: 312-553-5987. E-mail: mmadkins2@ccc.edu.

DEGREES AND AWARDS

Programs offered do not lead to a degree or other formal award.

COURSE SUBJECT AREAS OFFERED OUTSIDE OF DEGREE PROGRAMS

Undergraduate—accounting and computer science; accounting and related services; anthropology; architecture; biology; business administration, management and operations; business/commerce; business, management, and marketing related; communication and journalism related; computer and information sciences; computer science; economics; fine and studio arts; geography and cartography; history; homeland security, law enforcement, firefighting and protective services related; languages (foreign languages related); languages (Romance languages); liberal arts and sciences, general studies and humanities; literature; marketing; mathematics; mathematics and computer science; mathematics and statistics related; multi/interdisciplinary studies related; music; natural sciences; nutrition sciences; philosophy; philosophy and religious studies related; physical sciences; physical sciences related; political science and government; psychology; psychology related; public relations, advertising, and applied communication related; social sciences; sociology; sociology and anthropology; statistics; visual and performing arts.

CITY UNIVERSITY OF SEATTLE

Bellevue, Washington

Distance Learning Option

http://www.cityu.edu

City University of Seattle was founded in 1973. It is accredited by Northwest Commission on Colleges and Universities. It first offered distance learning courses in 1985. In fall 2010, there were 1,200 students enrolled in distance learning courses. Institutionally administered financial aid is available to distance learners.

Services Distance learners have accessibility to academic advising, bookstore, e-mail services, library services, tutoring.

Contact Office of Admissions, City University of Seattle, 11900 NE First Street, Bellevue, WA 98005. Telephone: 800-422-4898. Fax: 425-709-5361. E-mail: info@cityu.edu.

DEGREES AND AWARDS

AS General Studies

BA Psychology–Applied Psychology

BS Accounting; Business Administration (Information Systems/Technology emphasis); Business Administration (Marketing emphasis); Business Administration (Project Management emphasis); Business Administration–E-Commerce emphasis (Bulgaria); Business Administration–General Management emphasis; Business Administration–Human Resource emphasis; Business Administration–Individualized Study emphasis; Computer Systems (Networking/Telecommunications emphasis); General Studies

Certificate Accounting; Marketing; Networking/Telecommunications; Project Management

Graduate Certificate Financial Management; General Management; Information Systems; Marketing; Project Management; Sustainable Business; Technology Management

MA Leadership

MBA Business Administration

MEd Educational Leadership–Administrator certification; Leadership; Reading and Literacy

MS Project Management; Technology Management

COURSE SUBJECT AREAS OFFERED OUTSIDE OF DEGREE PROGRAMS

Undergraduate—accounting and related services; communication and journalism related; communication and media; computer systems networking and telecommunications; criminal justice and corrections; economics; English; history; human services; marketing; mathematics; mathematics and statistics related; philosophy; psychology; psychology related.

CITY VISION COLLEGE
Kansas City, Missouri
http://www.cityvision.edu

City Vision College is accredited by Distance Education and Training Council. It first offered distance learning courses in 1998. In fall 2010, there were 54 students enrolled in distance learning courses. Institutionally administered financial aid is available to distance learners.

Services Distance learners have accessibility to academic advising, bookstore.

Contact Rev. Theresa McLoyd, Director of Admissions, City Vision College, PO Box 413188, 712 East 31st Street, Kansas City, MO 64141-3188. Telephone: 816-960-2008. Fax: 816-569-0223. E-mail: tmcloyd@cityvision.edu.

DEGREES AND AWARDS

BA Missions
BS Addiction Studies; Nonprofit Management

CLACKAMAS COMMUNITY COLLEGE
Oregon City, Oregon
Learning Resources
http://depts.clackamas.edu/dl/

Clackamas Community College was founded in 1966. It is accredited by Northwest Commission on Colleges and Universities. It first offered distance learning courses in 1997. In fall 2010, there were 3,200 students enrolled in distance learning courses. Institutionally administered financial aid is available to distance learners.

Services Distance learners have accessibility to academic advising, bookstore, campus computer network, career placement assistance, e-mail services, library services, tutoring.

Contact Steve Beining, Director of Distance Learning, Clackamas Community College, 19600 South Molalla Avenue, Oregon City, OR 97045. Telephone: 503-594-3223. E-mail: sbeining@clackamas.edu.

DEGREES AND AWARDS

Programs offered do not lead to a degree or other formal award.

COURSE SUBJECT AREAS OFFERED OUTSIDE OF DEGREE PROGRAMS

Undergraduate—accounting and computer science; accounting and related services; allied health and medical assisting services; astronomy and astrophysics; biology; building/construction finishing, management, and inspection; business administration, management and operations; business, management, and marketing related; chemistry; computer science; criminal justice and corrections; education; environmental/environmental health engineering; human development, family studies, and related services; legal professions and studies related; mathematics; music; physics.

CLARION UNIVERSITY OF PENNSYLVANIA
Clarion, Pennsylvania
Extended Studies and Distance Learning Department
http://www.clarion.edu/virtualcampus

Clarion University of Pennsylvania was founded in 1867. It is accredited by Middle States Association of Colleges and Schools. It first offered distance learning courses in 1996. In fall 2010, there were 1,397 students enrolled in distance learning courses. Institutionally administered financial aid is available to distance learners.

Services Distance learners have accessibility to academic advising, bookstore, campus computer network, e-mail services, library services, tutoring.

Contact Ms. Lynne M. Lander Fleisher, Director of Virtual Campus, Clarion University of Pennsylvania, Office of Extended Programs, 840 Wood Street, Clarion, PA 16214. Telephone: 814-393-2778. Fax: 814-393-2779. E-mail: lfleisher@clarion.edu.

DEGREES AND AWARDS

AA Arts and Sciences
AS Allied Health; Early Childhood Education
BLS Liberal Studies, Business Administration minor; Liberal Studies, Communication concentration; Liberal Studies, Community Service concentration; Liberal Studies, Library Science concentration; Liberal Studies, Psychology minor; Liberal Studies, Women's Studies concentration
BS Medical Imaging
BSN Nursing
Certification Early Childhood Directors Credential Renewal program; Early Childhood Directors Credential program; Instructional Technology Specialist
Endorsement CPA Exam Eligibility program; Early Childhood CDA Credential Renewal program; Radiologic Sciences prerequisite program
MBA Business Administration
MLS Library Science
MS Mass Media Arts and Journalism; Rehabilitative Science
MSN Nursing–Family Nurse Practitioner

COURSE SUBJECT AREAS OFFERED OUTSIDE OF DEGREE PROGRAMS

Undergraduate—allied health and medical assisting services; atmospheric sciences and meteorology; biology; chemistry; clinical/medical laboratory science/research; communication and media; computer science; dental support services and allied professions; economics; education; education related; health and physical education/fitness; health services/allied health/health sciences; languages (foreign languages related); legal professions and studies related; library science and administration; music; philosophy; psychology; real estate; visual and performing arts related.
Graduate—business administration, management and operations; communication and journalism related; communication and media; education; library science and administration; rehabilitation and therapeutic professions.
Non-credit—real estate.

CLARKSON COLLEGE
Omaha, Nebraska
Office of Distance Education
http://www.clarksoncollege.edu

Clarkson College was founded in 1888. It is accredited by North Central Association of Colleges and Schools. It first offered distance learning courses in 1986. In fall 2010, there were 820 students enrolled in distance learning courses. Institutionally administered financial aid is available to distance learners.

Services Distance learners have accessibility to academic advising, bookstore, campus computer network, career placement assistance, e-mail services, library services, tutoring.

Contact Ms. Denise A. Work, Director, Admissions, Clarkson College, 101 South 42nd Street, Omaha, NE 68131-2379. Telephone: 402-552-3100. Fax: 402-552-6067. E-mail: admiss@clarksoncollege.edu.

DEGREES AND AWARDS

AD Health Information Technology
BS Health Care Business, Health Information Administration; Health Care Business, Management major; Medical Imaging
BSN Nursing–RN to BSN
Certificate Health Information Management; Imaging Informatics
MS Health Care Administration
MSN Health Care Administration; Nursing Education; Nursing and Adult Nurse Practitioner; Nursing–Family Nurse Practitioner

CLARK STATE COMMUNITY COLLEGE
Springfield, Ohio
Alternative Methods of Instructional Delivery
http://www.clarkstate.edu/online_learning.php

Clark State Community College was founded in 1962. It is accredited by North Central Association of Colleges and Schools. It first offered distance learning courses in 1996. In fall 2010, there were 1,836 students enrolled in distance learning courses. Institutionally administered financial aid is available to distance learners.

Services Distance learners have accessibility to academic advising, bookstore, campus computer network, career placement assistance, e-mail services, library services, tutoring.

Contact Amy Sues, Coordinator of Advising, Clark State Community College, PO Box 570, Springfield, OH 45501-0570. Telephone: 937-328-3867. Fax: 937-328-3853. E-mail: suesa@clarkstate.edu.

DEGREES AND AWARDS

AA University Transfer
AAB Accounting; Court Reporting/Captioning; Human Resource Management option; Logistics and Supply Chain Management option; Management; Marketing and E-Business option; Office Administration
AAS Medical Laboratory Technology; Nursing–Registered Nursing; Physical Therapist Assistant
AS University Transfer

COURSE SUBJECT AREAS OFFERED OUTSIDE OF DEGREE PROGRAMS

Undergraduate—accounting and computer science; agricultural business and management; allied health and medical assisting services; applied horticulture and horticultural business services; behavioral sciences; biological and physical sciences; biology; biology/biotechnology laboratory technician; business administration, management and operations; business/commerce; cell biology and anatomical sciences; chemistry; communication and media; computer software and media applications; English; health professions related; psychology; sociology.
Non-credit—computer and information sciences; computer software and media applications; transportation and materials moving related.

CLARY SAGE COLLEGE
Tulsa, Oklahoma
http://www.clarysagecollege.com/

Clary Sage College is accredited by Accrediting Council for Independent Colleges and Schools. It first offered distance learning courses in 2008. In fall 2010, there were 7 students enrolled in distance learning courses. Institutionally administered financial aid is available to distance learners.
Services Distance learners have accessibility to academic advising, campus computer network, career placement assistance, library services, tutoring.
Contact Rebecca Banuelos, Admissions Representative, Clary Sage College, 3131 South Sheridan, Tulsa, OK 74145. Telephone: 918-298-8200. Fax: 918-298-0099. E-mail: admissions@clarysagecollege.com.

DEGREES AND AWARDS

Programs offered do not lead to a degree or other formal award.

COURSE SUBJECT AREAS OFFERED OUTSIDE OF DEGREE PROGRAMS

Undergraduate—cosmetology and related personal grooming services.

CLATSOP COMMUNITY COLLEGE
Astoria, Oregon
http://www.clatsopcc.edu

Clatsop Community College was founded in 1958. It is accredited by Northwest Commission on Colleges and Universities. It first offered distance learning courses in 1986. In fall 2010, there were 205 students enrolled in distance learning courses. Institutionally administered financial aid is available to distance learners.
Services Distance learners have accessibility to bookstore, e-mail services, library services.
Contact Kirsten Horning, Distance Education Coordinator, Clatsop Community College, 1680 Lexington Avenue, Astoria, OR 97103. Telephone: 503-338-2341. Fax: 503-325-5738. E-mail: khorning@clatsopcc.edu.

DEGREES AND AWARDS

Programs offered do not lead to a degree or other formal award.

COURSE SUBJECT AREAS OFFERED OUTSIDE OF DEGREE PROGRAMS

Undergraduate—accounting and related services; business administration, management and operations; criminal justice and corrections; economics; English language and literature related; health and physical education/fitness; history; literature; mathematics; psychology; sociology; statistics.

CLEAR CREEK BAPTIST BIBLE COLLEGE
Pineville, Kentucky
http://ccbbc.educampusonline.com

Clear Creek Baptist Bible College was founded in 1926. It is accredited by Association for Biblical Higher Education. It first offered distance learning courses in 2002. In fall 2010, there were 100 students enrolled in distance learning courses. Institutionally administered financial aid is available to distance learners.
Services Distance learners have accessibility to academic advising, bookstore, campus computer network, career placement assistance, e-mail services, library services, tutoring.
Contact Rev. Billy Howell, Director of Admissions, Clear Creek Baptist Bible College, 300 Clear Creek Road, Pineville, KY 40977. Telephone: 606-337-3196 Ext. 103. Fax: 606-337-2372. E-mail: bhowell@ccbbc.edu.

DEGREES AND AWARDS

BA Ministry

COURSE SUBJECT AREAS OFFERED OUTSIDE OF DEGREE PROGRAMS

Undergraduate—biblical studies; theological and ministerial studies; theology and religious vocations related.
Non-credit—biblical studies; theological and ministerial studies; theology and religious vocations related.

CLEARY UNIVERSITY
Ann Arbor, Michigan
http://www.cleary.edu

Cleary University was founded in 1883. It is accredited by North Central Association of Colleges and Schools. It first offered distance learning courses in 1994. In fall 2010, there were 762 students enrolled in distance learning courses. Institutionally administered financial aid is available to distance learners.
Services Distance learners have accessibility to academic advising, bookstore, campus computer network, career placement assistance, e-mail services, library services, tutoring.
Contact Carrie Bonofiglio, Director of Admissions, Cleary University, 3750 Cleary Drive, Howell, MI 48843. Telephone: 888-525-3279. E-mail: admissions@cleary.edu.

DEGREES AND AWARDS

AAS Information Technology
MBA Business Administration

COURSE SUBJECT AREAS OFFERED OUTSIDE OF DEGREE PROGRAMS

Undergraduate—computer and information sciences and support services related.
Graduate—finance and financial management services; sustainability studies.

CLEMSON UNIVERSITY
Clemson, South Carolina
Distance Education, Educational Technology Services
http://www.clemson.edu/ccit/learning_tech/distance_ed/index.html

Clemson University was founded in 1889. It is accredited by Southern Association of Colleges and Schools. It first offered distance learning courses in 1988. In fall 2010, there were 4,534 students enrolled in distance learning courses. Institutionally administered financial aid is available to distance learners.
Services Distance learners have accessibility to academic advising, bookstore, campus computer network, career placement assistance, e-mail services, library services.

Contact Debra Charles, Manager, Instructional Services, Clemson University, 433 Brackett Hall, PO Box 342803, Clemson, SC 29634-2803. Telephone: 864-444-5077. Fax: 864-656-0750. E-mail: debm@clemson.edu.

DEGREES AND AWARDS

MCSM Construction Science and Management
MHRM Human Resource Development
MPA Public Administration
MS Biological Sciences; Youth Development
MSE Industrial Engineering

COURSE SUBJECT AREAS OFFERED OUTSIDE OF DEGREE PROGRAMS

Undergraduate—astronomy and astrophysics; biological and physical sciences; biology; business/commerce; communication and media; construction management; economics; electrical engineering technologies; marketing; mathematics; music; nutrition sciences; parks, recreation and leisure; physics; public administration; sociology.
Graduate—agriculture; animal sciences; biological and physical sciences; biology; business administration, management and operations; communication and media; construction management; electrical engineering technologies; English; history; human resources management; nutrition sciences; public administration; statistics.
Non-credit—accounting and related services; allied health and medical assisting services; biological and physical sciences; biology; building/construction finishing, management, and inspection; business/commerce; business, management, and marketing related; business operations support and assistant services; communication and media; computer and information sciences; computer programming; computer software and media applications; computer systems networking and telecommunications; construction engineering technologies; data entry/microcomputer applications; data processing; languages (Romance languages); legal professions and studies related; mathematics; public administration; publishing; teaching assistants/aides.

CLEVELAND COMMUNITY COLLEGE
Shelby, North Carolina
Distance Learning Program
http://www.clevelandcommunitycollege.edu

Cleveland Community College was founded in 1965. It is accredited by Southern Association of Colleges and Schools. It first offered distance learning courses in 1999. In fall 2010, there were 1,500 students enrolled in distance learning courses. Institutionally administered financial aid is available to distance learners.
Services Distance learners have accessibility to academic advising, bookstore, e-mail services, library services, tutoring.
Contact Melody Heflin, Academic Advisor, Student Success Center, Cleveland Community College, 137 South Post Road, Shelby, NC 28152. Telephone: 704-484-6085. Fax: 704-484-4072. E-mail: heflinm@clevelandcommunitycollege.edu.

DEGREES AND AWARDS

Programs offered do not lead to a degree or other formal award.

COURSE SUBJECT AREAS OFFERED OUTSIDE OF DEGREE PROGRAMS

Undergraduate—accounting and computer science; accounting and related services; biology; biology/biotechnology laboratory technician; biotechnology; business administration, management and operations; business/commerce; business, management, and marketing related; business/managerial economics; computer and information sciences; computer/information technology administration and management; computer programming; computer software and media applications; computer systems networking and telecommunications; criminal justice and corrections; economics; education; education related; electrical/electronics maintenance and repair technology; English; entrepreneurial and small business operations; finance and financial management services; fire protection; history; holocaust and related studies; human development, family studies, and related services; literature; mathematics; music; psychology; psychology related; sales merchandising, and related marketing operations (general); social sciences; sociology; statistics; teaching assistants/aides.
Non-credit—fire protection.

CLEVELAND INSTITUTE OF ELECTRONICS
Cleveland, Ohio
http://www.cie-wc.edu

Cleveland Institute of Electronics was founded in 1934. It is accredited by Distance Education and Training Council. It first offered distance learning courses in 1941. In fall 2010, there were 1,731 students enrolled in distance learning courses. Institutionally administered financial aid is available to distance learners.
Services Distance learners have accessibility to academic advising, bookstore, e-mail services, library services, tutoring.
Contact Guidance Counselor, Cleveland Institute of Electronics, 1776 East 17th Street, Cleveland, OH 44114. Telephone: 216-781-9400. Fax: 216-781-0331. E-mail: instruct@cie-wc.edu.

DEGREES AND AWARDS

AAS Computer Information Technology and Systems Management; Electronic Engineering Technology; Software Engineering
Diploma A+ Certification and Computer Technology; Broadcast Engineering; Computer Programming with Java and C#; Electronics Engineering; Electronics Technology and Advanced Troubleshooting; Electronics Technology with Digital Microprocessor Lab; Electronics Technology with FCC License Preparation; Electronics Technology with Laboratory; Industrial Electronics with PLC Technology; Introduction to Computers and Microsoft Office; Introduction to Home Automation Installation; Network+ Certification and Computer Technology; Wireless and Electronic Communications

COURSE SUBJECT AREAS OFFERED OUTSIDE OF DEGREE PROGRAMS

Undergraduate—communication and media; computer engineering; electrical engineering technologies; engineering; social sciences related.
Non-credit—accounting and computer science; computer/information technology administration and management; computer programming; computer science; computer software and media applications; data entry/microcomputer applications; electrical and power transmission installation; electrical/electronics maintenance and repair technology; mechanical engineering related technologies; mechanic and repair technologies related; mechanics and repair.

CLEVELAND STATE COMMUNITY COLLEGE
Cleveland, Tennessee
Instructional Computer Technology Center of Emphasis
http://www.clevelandstatecc.edu

Cleveland State Community College was founded in 1967. It is accredited by Southern Association of Colleges and Schools. It first offered distance learning courses in 1998. In fall 2010, there were 800 students enrolled in distance learning courses. Institutionally administered financial aid is available to distance learners.
Services Distance learners have accessibility to academic advising, bookstore, campus computer network, career placement assistance, e-mail services, library services, tutoring.
Contact Dr. Jerry L. Faulkner, Vice President for Academic Affairs, Cleveland State Community College, 3535 Adkisson Drive, PO Box 3570, Cleveland, TN 37320-3570. Telephone: 423-472-4171 Ext. 381. Fax: 423-478-6254. E-mail: jfaulkner01@clevelandstatecc.edu.

DEGREES AND AWARDS

Programs offered do not lead to a degree or other formal award.

COURSE SUBJECT AREAS OFFERED OUTSIDE OF DEGREE PROGRAMS

Undergraduate—accounting and related services; allied health and medical assisting services; biological and physical sciences; business/commerce; computer and information sciences; data entry/microcomputer

applications; education; history; mathematics; music; pharmacology and toxicology; physics; psychology; sociology; statistics.
Non-credit—accounting and computer science; accounting and related services; applied mathematics; audiovisual communications technologies; behavioral sciences; biological and physical sciences; business administration, management and operations; business/commerce; business, management, and marketing related; chemistry; communication and journalism related; communication and media; computer and information sciences; computer and information sciences and support services related; computer software and media applications; economics; education related; family and consumer economics; film/video and photographic arts; finance and financial management services; foods, nutrition, and related services.

CLINTON COMMUNITY COLLEGE
Plattsburgh, New York
http://www.clinton.edu/onlinelearning

Clinton Community College was founded in 1969. It is accredited by Middle States Association of Colleges and Schools. It first offered distance learning courses in 2000. In fall 2010, there were 310 students enrolled in distance learning courses. Institutionally administered financial aid is available to distance learners.
Services Distance learners have accessibility to academic advising, bookstore, campus computer network, career placement assistance, e-mail services, library services.
Contact Prof. Vicky Sloan, Distance Learning Coordinator, Clinton Community College, 136 Clinton Point Drive, Plattsburgh, NY 12901. Telephone: 518-562-4281. E-mail: vicky.sloan@clinton.edu.

DEGREES AND AWARDS
AA Liberal Arts/Humanities and Social Science
AAS Business
AS Business Administration

COURSE SUBJECT AREAS OFFERED OUTSIDE OF DEGREE PROGRAMS
Undergraduate—accounting and related services; applied mathematics; biological and physical sciences; business administration, management and operations; business/corporate communications; computer and information sciences; computer programming; criminal justice and corrections; economics; English; health services/allied health/health sciences; history; human development, family studies, and related services; human services; liberal arts and sciences, general studies and humanities; music; political science and government; psychology; sociology; statistics.

CLOVIS COMMUNITY COLLEGE
Clovis, New Mexico
http://www.clovis.edu/

Clovis Community College was founded in 1990. It is accredited by North Central Association of Colleges and Schools. It first offered distance learning courses in 1990. In fall 2010, there were 525 students enrolled in distance learning courses. Institutionally administered financial aid is available to distance learners.
Services Distance learners have accessibility to academic advising, bookstore, e-mail services, library services, tutoring.
Contact Mr. John Hansen, Recruitment Coordinator, Clovis Community College, 417 Schepps Boulevard, Clovis, NM 88101. Telephone: 575-769-4912. Fax: 575-769-4190. E-mail: john.hansen@clovis.edu.

DEGREES AND AWARDS
AAS Criminal Justice; Health Information Technology

COURSE SUBJECT AREAS OFFERED OUTSIDE OF DEGREE PROGRAMS
Undergraduate—accounting and computer science; biblical studies; biology; business administration, management and operations; chemistry; communication and media; computer and information sciences; criminal justice and corrections; economics; electrical/electronics maintenance and repair technology; English; fine and studio arts; history; human biology; languages (Romance languages); legal studies (nonprofessional general, undergraduate); mathematics; mathematics and statistics related; political science and government; psychology; religious studies; sociology; sociology and anthropology; statistics.

COASTAL CAROLINA UNIVERSITY
Conway, South Carolina
http://www.coastal.edu/dl/

Coastal Carolina University was founded in 1954. It is accredited by Southern Association of Colleges and Schools. It first offered distance learning courses in 1997. In fall 2010, there were 825 students enrolled in distance learning courses. Institutionally administered financial aid is available to distance learners.
Services Distance learners have accessibility to academic advising, bookstore, campus computer network, career placement assistance, e-mail services, library services, tutoring.
Contact Ms. Jennifer M. Shinaberger, Assistant Director for Distance Learning and TEAL Center, Coastal Carolina University, PO Box 261954, Conway, SC 29528-6054. Telephone: 843-349-2737. E-mail: jshinabe@coastal.edu.

DEGREES AND AWARDS
Programs offered do not lead to a degree or other formal award.

COURSE SUBJECT AREAS OFFERED OUTSIDE OF DEGREE PROGRAMS
Undergraduate—biology; communication and journalism related; computer science; education; English; fine and studio arts; health and physical education/fitness; history; journalism; marine sciences; political science and government; psychology; religious studies.
Graduate—education.

COGSWELL POLYTECHNICAL COLLEGE
Sunnyvale, California
http://www.cogswell.edu/fireScience.html

Cogswell Polytechnical College was founded in 1887. It is accredited by Western Association of Schools and Colleges. It first offered distance learning courses in 1981. In fall 2010, there were 110 students enrolled in distance learning courses. Institutionally administered financial aid is available to distance learners.
Services Distance learners have accessibility to academic advising, bookstore, campus computer network, e-mail services, library services.
Contact Ms. Milla Zlatanov, Data Manager, Cogswell Polytechnical College, 1175 Bordeaux Drive, Sunnyvale, CA 94089. Telephone: 408-541-0100 Ext. 133. Fax: 408-747-0764. E-mail: mzlatanov@cogswell.edu.

DEGREES AND AWARDS
BS Fire Administration, Fire Prevention and Technology

COURSE SUBJECT AREAS OFFERED OUTSIDE OF DEGREE PROGRAMS
Undergraduate—fire protection; public administration.

COLEMAN UNIVERSITY
San Diego, California
http://www.coleman.edu

Coleman University was founded in 1963. It is accredited by Accrediting Council for Independent Colleges and Schools. It first offered distance learning courses in 2001. In fall 2010, there were 250 students enrolled in distance learning courses. Institutionally administered financial aid is available to distance learners.
Services Distance learners have accessibility to academic advising, bookstore, career placement assistance, e-mail services, library services.
Contact Karen Hynes, Registrar, Coleman University, 8888 Balboa Avenue, San Diego, CA 92123. Telephone: 858-499-0202. Fax: 858-499-0233. E-mail: khynes@coleman.edu.

DEGREES AND AWARDS

Programs offered do not lead to a degree or other formal award.

COURSE SUBJECT AREAS OFFERED OUTSIDE OF DEGREE PROGRAMS

Undergraduate—accounting and related services; business administration, management and operations; computer and information sciences; computer/information technology administration and management; computer programming; English; history; human resources management; marketing; mathematics; philosophy; physical sciences; psychology; statistics.

Graduate—business administration, management and operations; business/commerce; business/corporate communications; marketing.

THE COLLEGE AT BROCKPORT, STATE UNIVERSITY OF NEW YORK

Brockport, New York

http://www.brockport.edu/

The College at Brockport, State University of New York was founded in 1867. It is accredited by Middle States Association of Colleges and Schools. It first offered distance learning courses in 2000. In fall 2010, there were 475 students enrolled in distance learning courses. Institutionally administered financial aid is available to distance learners.

Services Distance learners have accessibility to bookstore, campus computer network, career placement assistance, e-mail services, library services.

Contact Dr. Karen Schuhle-Williams, Director of Special Sessions and Programs, The College at Brockport, State University of New York, 350 New Campus Drive, Brockport, NY 14589. Telephone: 585-395-5724. Fax: 585-395-5542. E-mail: kschuhle@brockport.edu.

DEGREES AND AWARDS

Programs offered do not lead to a degree or other formal award.

COURSE SUBJECT AREAS OFFERED OUTSIDE OF DEGREE PROGRAMS

Undergraduate—business administration, management and operations; communication and journalism related; communication and media; computer science; computer software and media applications; education; English language and literature related; health professions related; psychology related; social sciences; social work.

Graduate—English or French as a second or foreign language (teaching); health services/allied health/health sciences; liberal arts and sciences, general studies and humanities; parks, recreation and leisure; parks, recreation and leisure facilities management; social work.

COLLEGE OF EMMANUEL AND ST. CHAD

Saskatoon, Saskatchewan, Canada

http://usask.ca/stu/emmanuel

College of Emmanuel and St. Chad was founded in 1879. It is provincially chartered. It first offered distance learning courses in 1995. In fall 2010, there were 1 students enrolled in distance learning courses. Institutionally administered financial aid is available to distance learners.

Services Distance learners have accessibility to academic advising, bookstore, campus computer network, library services.

Contact Ms. Colleen Walker, Registrar, College of Emmanuel and St. Chad, 114 Seminary Crescent, Saskatoon, SK S7N 0X3, Canada. Telephone: 306-975-1558. Fax: 306-934-2683. E-mail: colleen.walker@usask.ca.

DEGREES AND AWARDS

Programs offered do not lead to a degree or other formal award.

COURSE SUBJECT AREAS OFFERED OUTSIDE OF DEGREE PROGRAMS

Graduate—biblical studies; theological and ministerial studies; theology and religious vocations related.

COLLEGE OF SAINT MARY

Omaha, Nebraska

http://www.csm.edu/

College of Saint Mary was founded in 1923. It is accredited by North Central Association of Colleges and Schools. It first offered distance learning courses in 2001. In fall 2010, there were 132 students enrolled in distance learning courses. Institutionally administered financial aid is available to distance learners.

Services Distance learners have accessibility to academic advising, bookstore, campus computer network, career placement assistance, e-mail services, library services, tutoring.

Contact Dr. Christine Pharr, Vice President for Academic Affairs, College of Saint Mary, 7000 Mercy Road, Omaha, NE 68106. Telephone: 402-399-2693 E-mail: cpharr@csm.edu.

DEGREES AND AWARDS

Programs offered do not lead to a degree or other formal award.

COURSE SUBJECT AREAS OFFERED OUTSIDE OF DEGREE PROGRAMS

Undergraduate—business, management, and marketing related; economics; educational assessment, evaluation, and research; English language and literature related; health professions related; physical sciences; psychology; sociology; special education.

Graduate—health professions related; special education.

THE COLLEGE OF ST. SCHOLASTICA

Duluth, Minnesota

Graduate Studies

http://www.css.edu/online.xml

The College of St. Scholastica was founded in 1912. It is accredited by North Central Association of Colleges and Schools. It first offered distance learning courses in 1986. In fall 2010, there were 700 students enrolled in distance learning courses. Institutionally administered financial aid is available to distance learners.

Services Distance learners have accessibility to academic advising, bookstore, campus computer network, career placement assistance, e-mail services, library services, tutoring.

Contact Kris Carlson, Online Admissions Representative, The College of St. Scholastica, 1200 Kenwood Avenue, Duluth, MN 55811. Telephone: 218-723-7062. Fax: 877-723-7062. E-mail: cssonline@css.edu.

DEGREES AND AWARDS

BS Nursing–RN to BS completion
BSc Health Information Management
Certificate Educational Technology; Healthcare Informatics; Information Technology Leadership
MA Information Technology Leadership
MEd Education
MS Health Information Management
DPT Transitional Doctor of Physical Therapy

COURSE SUBJECT AREAS OFFERED OUTSIDE OF DEGREE PROGRAMS

Undergraduate—biology; computer and information sciences; economics; gerontology; health and medical administrative services; music; psychology.

Graduate—biology; curriculum and instruction; health and medical administrative services; library science related; music.

COLLEGE OF SAN MATEO

San Mateo, California

http://www.collegeofsanmateo.edu

College of San Mateo was founded in 1922. It is accredited by Western Association of Schools and Colleges. It first offered distance learning courses in 1977. In fall 2010, there were 1,600 students enrolled in distance learning courses. Institutionally administered financial aid is available to distance learners.

Services Distance learners have accessibility to academic advising, bookstore, campus computer network, e-mail services, library services.

Contact Mr. Ronald Andrade, Program Services Coordinator, College of San Mateo, 1700 West Hillsdale Boulevard, San Mateo, CA 94402-3784. Telephone: 650-524-6933. Fax: 650-726-7443. E-mail: andrader@smccd.edu.

DEGREES AND AWARDS

AA Accounting; Natural Sciences, Social Science, and Humanities

AS Computer Science Applications and Development

COURSE SUBJECT AREAS OFFERED OUTSIDE OF DEGREE PROGRAMS

Undergraduate—accounting and related services; astronomy and astrophysics; biology; business/commerce; business/corporate communications; computer and information sciences; computer programming; computer software and media applications; film/video and photographic arts; languages (Romance languages); mathematics; nutrition sciences; philosophy; political science and government; psychology; sociology; statistics.

COLLEGE OF SOUTHERN MARYLAND
La Plata, Maryland
Distance Learning Department
http://www.csmd.edu

College of Southern Maryland was founded in 1958. It is accredited by Middle States Association of Colleges and Schools. It first offered distance learning courses in 1980. In fall 2010, there were 4,525 students enrolled in distance learning courses. Institutionally administered financial aid is available to distance learners.

Services Distance learners have accessibility to academic advising, bookstore, campus computer network, career placement assistance, e-mail services, library services, tutoring.

Contact Paul Toscano, Lead Distance Learning Coordinator, College of Southern Maryland, 8730 Mitchell Road, PO Box 910, La Plata, MD 20646-0910. Telephone: 301-934-7615. Fax: 301-934-7699. E-mail: info@csmd.edu.

DEGREES AND AWARDS

AA Arts and Sciences–Applied Science and Technology; Arts and Sciences–Arts and Humanities; Arts and Sciences–Social Sciences; Arts and Sciences; General Studies

AAS Computer Information Systems; Information Services Technology–Web Developer; Information Services Technology; Management Development

AS Business Administration–Technical Management; Business Administration

Certificate Accounting, advanced; Accounting, basic; General Studies; Information Services Technology; Management Development–Marketing; Management Development; Web Developer

COURSE SUBJECT AREAS OFFERED OUTSIDE OF DEGREE PROGRAMS

Undergraduate—accounting and related services; astronomy and astrophysics; biology; business/commerce; business/corporate communications; communication and media; computer systems analysis; computer systems networking and telecommunications; criminal justice and corrections; economics; education related; fine and studio arts; geography and cartography; health and physical education/fitness; history; human development, family studies, and related services; human resources management; information science/studies; international business; languages (Romance languages); legal studies (non-professional general, undergraduate); marketing; mathematics; mathematics and statistics related; philosophy; philosophy and religious studies related; physics; political science and government; psychology; sociology; statistics.

Non-credit—business administration, management and operations; communication and journalism related; computer/information technology administration and management; construction trades; education; health and medical administrative services; health professions related.

COLLEGE OF THE DESERT
Palm Desert, California
http://collegeofthedesert.edu/

College of the Desert was founded in 1959. It is accredited by Western Association of Schools and Colleges. It first offered distance learning courses in 1998. In fall 2010, there were 2,000 students enrolled in distance learning courses. Institutionally administered financial aid is available to distance learners.

Services Distance learners have accessibility to campus computer network, e-mail services, library services.

Contact Mr. Farley Herzek, Vice President, Academic Affairs, College of the Desert, 43500 Monterey Avenue, Palm Desert, CA 92260. Telephone: 760-773-2506. E-mail: fherzek@collegeofthedesert.edu.

DEGREES AND AWARDS

Programs offered do not lead to a degree or other formal award.

COLLEGE OF THE HUMANITIES AND SCIENCES, HARRISON MIDDLETON UNIVERSITY
Tempe, Arizona
http://www.hmu.edu

College of the Humanities and Sciences, Harrison Middleton University was founded in 1998. It is accredited by Distance Education and Training Council. It first offered distance learning courses in 2000. In fall 2010, there were 500 students enrolled in distance learning courses. Institutionally administered financial aid is available to distance learners.

Services Distance learners have accessibility to academic advising, e-mail services, library services, tutoring.

Contact Deborah A. Deacon, Dean of Graduate Studies, College of the Humanities and Sciences, Harrison Middleton University, 1105 East Broadway Road, Tempe, AZ 85282. Telephone: 877-248-6724. Fax: 800-762-1622. E-mail: ddeacon@hmu.edu.

DEGREES AND AWARDS

AA Humanities
BA Humanities
MA Imaginative Literature; Jurisprudence; Natural Science; Philosophy and Religion; Social Science
MAE Education
EdD Education

COURSE SUBJECT AREAS OFFERED OUTSIDE OF DEGREE PROGRAMS

Undergraduate—biology; history; languages (foreign languages related); languages (Romance languages); mathematics; philosophy; social sciences.

Graduate—education related; English language and literature related; mathematics; philosophy and religious studies related; social sciences related.

COLLEGE OF THE SISKIYOUS
Weed, California
Distance Learning
http://www.siskiyous.edu/distancelearning/

College of the Siskiyous was founded in 1957. It is accredited by Western Association of Schools and Colleges. It first offered distance learning courses in 1975. In fall 2010, there were 785 students enrolled in distance learning courses. Institutionally administered financial aid is available to distance learners.

Services Distance learners have accessibility to academic advising, bookstore, career placement assistance, e-mail services, library services, tutoring.

Contact Nancy Shepard, Telecommunications Specialist, College of the Siskiyous, 800 College Avenue, Weed, CA 96094. Telephone: 530-938-5520. E-mail: distlearn@siskiyous.edu.

DEGREES AND AWARDS

AA Early Childhood Education

COURSE SUBJECT AREAS OFFERED OUTSIDE OF DEGREE PROGRAMS

Undergraduate—accounting and related services; anthropology; business/commerce; business/corporate communications; communication and media; computer science; education; English language and literature related; family and consumer economics; health and physical education/fitness; history; liberal arts and sciences, general studies and humanities; mathematics; nutrition sciences; political science and government; psychology; social sciences; student counseling and personnel services; teaching assistants/aides.

COLORADO MOUNTAIN COLLEGE
Glenwood Springs, Colorado
Online Learning
http://www.coloradomtn.edu/online_learning/

Colorado Mountain College was founded in 1965. It is accredited by North Central Association of Colleges and Schools. It first offered distance learning courses in 1985. In fall 2010, there were 1,400 students enrolled in distance learning courses. Institutionally administered financial aid is available to distance learners.

Services Distance learners have accessibility to academic advising, bookstore, e-mail services, library services.

Contact Mr. Daryl D. Yarrow, CEO of Online Learning, Colorado Mountain College, 831 Grand Avenue, Glenwood Springs, CO 81601. Telephone: 800-621-8559 Ext. 8336. Fax: 970-947-8307. E-mail: distance@coloradomtn.edu.

DEGREES AND AWARDS

AA Generalist
AGS Generalist

COURSE SUBJECT AREAS OFFERED OUTSIDE OF DEGREE PROGRAMS

Undergraduate—accounting and related services; anthropology; astronomy and astrophysics; biology; business/commerce; business/corporate communications; chemistry; computer science; computer software and media applications; economics; education related; fine and studio arts; geography and cartography; health and medical administrative services; health professions related; history; hospitality administration; languages (foreign languages related); legal studies (non-professional general, undergraduate); liberal arts and sciences, general studies and humanities; library science related; mathematics and statistics related; philosophy; psychology; sociology; statistics.

COLORADO STATE UNIVERSITY
Fort Collins, Colorado
College of Business
http://www.CSUcis.com

Colorado State University was founded in 1870. It is accredited by North Central Association of Colleges and Schools. It first offered distance learning courses in 1970. In fall 2010, there were 50 students enrolled in distance learning courses. Institutionally administered financial aid is available to distance learners.

Services Distance learners have accessibility to academic advising, bookstore, campus computer network, career placement assistance, e-mail services, library services, tutoring.

Contact Ms. Claire Pettner, MSBA-CIS Graduate Advisor, Colorado State University, College of Business, 1201 Campus Delivery, 210 Rockwell Hall West, Fort Collins, CO 80523-1201. Telephone: 866-491-2746 Ext. 1. Fax: 970-491-3949. E-mail: claire.pettner@colostate.edu.

DEGREES AND AWARDS

MBA Business Administration–Distance MBA program;
MSBA Computer Information Systems

COURSE SUBJECT AREAS OFFERED OUTSIDE OF DEGREE PROGRAMS

Graduate—computer and information sciences; computer and information sciences and support services related.

COLORADO STATE UNIVERSITY
Fort Collins, Colorado
Division of Continuing Education
http://www.online.colostate.edu

Colorado State University was founded in 1870. It is accredited by North Central Association of Colleges and Schools. It first offered distance learning courses in 1967. In fall 2010, there were 2,974 students enrolled in distance learning courses. Institutionally administered financial aid is available to distance learners.

Services Distance learners have accessibility to academic advising, bookstore, campus computer network, e-mail services, library services.

Contact Ms. Jenny Hannifin, Student Engagement Coordinator, Colorado State University, CSU OnlinePlus, Division of Continuing Education, 1040 Campus Delivery, Fort Collins, CO 80523-1040. Telephone: 970-491-2665. E-mail: jenny.hannifin@colostate.edu.

DEGREES AND AWARDS

BA Liberal Arts
BS Agricultural Business; Fire and Emergency Services Administration; Human Development and Family Studies
Certificate of Completion Veterinary Medicine Online
Certificate Applied Statistics and Data Analysis; Child Care Training; Community-Based Development; Construction Management; Core Business Competencies; Ergonomics; Finance; Fire and Emergency Services Administration (FESA); Green Building; Green Homes; Interior Design for High School Teachers; Literacy Instruction Authorization; Mediation; Natural Resources and the Environment; Organizational Development; Organizational Learning and Performance; Performance Management; Postsecondary Teaching; Project Management; Psychological Measurement and Methodologies; Regulary Affairs; Residential Interiors; Seed Technology Education; Society of Human Resource Management Learning System (SHRM); Statistical Theory and Method; Sustainable Military Land Management; Systems Engineering; Teaching with Technology and Distance Learning
EMBA Business Administration
Graduate Certificate Computer Information Systems; Computer Systems and Security; Science Instruction, Advanced; Software Engineering; Student Affairs in Higher Education; Water Resources; Workplace Learning and Performance
MAIOP Master of Applied Industrial/Organizational Psychology
MAg Agricultural Extension Education; Integrated Resource Management (IRM)
MBA Business Administration
MBA/MS Computer Information Systems
MCS Computer Science
ME Biomedical Engineering specialization; Civil Engineering; Engineering Management program; Materials Engineering; Systems Engineering
MEd Adult Education and Training (AET); Educational Leadership, Renewal, and Change; Organizational Performance and Change (OPC)
MEngr Industrial Engineering and Operations Research
MM Music Therapy
MS Ed Natural Sciences Education
MS Dietetics (Food Science and Nutrition); Mechanical Engineering (Engineering Management); Merchandising; Rangeland Ecosystem Science; Statistics; Student Affairs in Higher Education
MSW Social Work
PhD College and University Leadership; Organizational Performance and Change (OPC)

COLORADO TECHNICAL UNIVERSITY COLORADO SPRINGS
Colorado Springs, Colorado
http://www.coloradotech.edu/

Colorado Technical University Colorado Springs was founded in 1965. It is accredited by North Central Association of Colleges and Schools. It first offered distance learning courses in 2003. Institutionally administered financial aid is available to distance learners.

Services Distance learners have accessibility to academic advising, bookstore, campus computer network, career placement assistance, e-mail services, library services, tutoring.

Contact Admissions Department, Colorado Technical University Colorado Springs, 4435 North Chestnut Street, Suite E, Colorado Springs, CO 80907. Telephone: 800-416-8904. E-mail: info@ctuonline.edu.

DEGREES AND AWARDS

AS Accounting; Business Administration; General Studies; Health Administration Services
BS Accounting; Criminal Justice–Homeland Security and Emergency Management concentration; Criminal Justice–Human Services concentration; Criminal Justice; Finance; Financial Forensics; Financial Planning; Health Services Administration; Information Technology–Data Management specialization; Information Technology–Software Application Programming specialization; Information Technology–Web Development specialization; Information Technology; Information Technology, Network Management specialization; Information Technology, Security specialization; Information Technology, Software Systems Engineering specialization; Management; Nursing; Psychology
BSBA Finance concentration; Health Care Management concentration; Human Resource Management concentration; Information Technology concentration; International Business concentration; Management concentration; Marketing concentration; Project Management concentration; Property Management concentration
EMBA Executive Master of Business Administration
MBA Accounting concentration; Enviromental and Social Sustainability concentration; Finance concentration; Health Care Management concentration; Human Resource Management concentration; Logistics and Supply Chain Management concentration; Marketing concentration; Mediation and Dispute Resolution concentration; Operations Management concentration; Technology Management concentration
MS Systems Engineering
MSCJ General
MSCS Computer Systems Security; Database Systems; Software Engineering
MSIT Data Management Technology; Network Management; Security Management
MSM Enterprise Information Systems; Homeland Security; Information Systems Security concentration; Information Technology Management concentration; Organizational Leadership and Change; Project Management concentration

COLUMBIA BASIN COLLEGE
Pasco, Washington
http://www.columbiabasin.edu/distance/

Columbia Basin College was founded in 1955. It is accredited by Northwest Commission on Colleges and Universities. It first offered distance learning courses in 1995. In fall 2010, there were 461 students enrolled in distance learning courses. Institutionally administered financial aid is available to distance learners.

Services Distance learners have accessibility to academic advising, bookstore, career placement assistance, e-mail services, library services, tutoring.

Contact Jerry Lewis, Director of eLearning, Columbia Basin College, 2600 North 20th Avenue, Pasco, WA 99301. Telephone: 509-542-4465. Fax: 509-546-0401. E-mail: jlewis@columbiabasin.edu.

DEGREES AND AWARDS

AAB Business
AAS Business, Humanities, Social Sciences

COURSE SUBJECT AREAS OFFERED OUTSIDE OF DEGREE PROGRAMS

Undergraduate—accounting and related services; anthropology; behavioral sciences; business administration, management and operations; business/commerce; business operations support and assistant services; communication and media; computer and information sciences and support services related; computer programming; computer science; computer software and media applications; economics; English; ethnic, cultural minority, gender, and group studies; fine and studio arts; geography and cartography; health and physical education/fitness; history; mathematics; mathematics and statistics related; political science and government; psychology; sociology.

COLUMBIA COLLEGE
Columbia, Missouri
http://www.ccis.edu/online/

Columbia College was founded in 1851. It is accredited by North Central Association of Colleges and Schools. It first offered distance learning courses in 2000. In fall 2010, there were 10,468 students enrolled in distance learning courses. Institutionally administered financial aid is available to distance learners.

Services Distance learners have accessibility to academic advising, bookstore, campus computer network, career placement assistance, e-mail services, library services, tutoring.

Contact Ms. Marilyn Whitehead, Director of Administration, Online Campus, Columbia College, 1001 Rogers Street, Attention: Online Campus, Columbia, MO 65216. Telephone: 573-875-7246. Fax: 573-875-7445. E-mail: mawhitehead@ccis.edu.

DEGREES AND AWARDS

AA General Studies
AGS General Studies
AS Business Administration; Computer Information Systems; Criminal Justice; Environmental Studies; Fire Service Administration; Human Services
BA American Studies; Business Administration; Criminal Justice Administration; History; Human Services; Psychology; Sociology
BGS General Studies
BS Business Administration; Computer Information Systems; Management Information Systems
MA Military Studies
MAT Education
MBA Business Administration
MSCJ Criminal Justice Administration

COURSE SUBJECT AREAS OFFERED OUTSIDE OF DEGREE PROGRAMS

Undergraduate—accounting and related services; anthropology; arts, entertainment, and media management; astronomy and astrophysics; behavioral sciences; biological and biomedical sciences related; business administration, management and operations; business/commerce; business, management, and marketing related; chemistry; computer and information sciences; criminal justice and corrections; cultural studies/critical theory and analysis; curriculum and instruction; economics; education; English; entrepreneurial and small business operations; finance and financial management services; geography and cartography; history; human services; marketing; mathematics; mathematics and computer science; multi/interdisciplinary studies related; music; philosophy and religious studies related; physical sciences; political science and government; psychology; psychology related; religious studies; sales merchandising, and related marketing operations (general); social sciences related; sociology.

Graduate—business administration, management and operations; business, management, and marketing related; business/managerial economics; criminal justice and corrections; education; educational assessment, evaluation, and research; history; philosophy; political science and government.

COLUMBIA-GREENE COMMUNITY COLLEGE
Hudson, New York
Educational Technology Center
http://blackboard.sunycgcc.edu/

Columbia-Greene Community College was founded in 1969. It is accredited by Middle States Association of Colleges and Schools. It first offered distance learning courses in 1995. In fall 2010, there were 201 students enrolled in distance learning courses. Institutionally administered financial aid is available to distance learners.

Services Distance learners have accessibility to campus computer network, e-mail services, library services.

Contact Ms. Carol Doerfer, Assistant Dean, Columbia-Greene Community College, Room 110, 4400 Route 23, Hudson, NY 12534. Telephone: 518-828-4181 Ext. 3350. Fax: 518-828-8543. E-mail: doerfer@sunycgcc.edu.

DEGREES AND AWARDS

Programs offered do not lead to a degree or other formal award.

COURSE SUBJECT AREAS OFFERED OUTSIDE OF DEGREE PROGRAMS

Undergraduate—business administration, management and operations; computer programming; psychology; sociology.

COLUMBIA INTERNATIONAL UNIVERSITY
Columbia, South Carolina
Distance Education Center
http://www.ciu.edu/distance

Columbia International University was founded in 1923. It is accredited by Association for Biblical Higher Education. It first offered distance learning courses in 1978. In fall 2010, there were 900 students enrolled in distance learning courses. Institutionally administered financial aid is available to distance learners.

Services Distance learners have accessibility to academic advising, bookstore, campus computer network, career placement assistance, e-mail services, library services, tutoring.

Contact Mrs. Alisa Fulton, Assessment and Student Services Coordinator, Columbia International University, 7435 Monticello Road, Columbia, SC 29203. Telephone: 803-807-5731. Fax: 803-223-2502. E-mail: distance@ciu.edu.

DEGREES AND AWARDS

Programs offered do not lead to a degree or other formal award.

COURSE SUBJECT AREAS OFFERED OUTSIDE OF DEGREE PROGRAMS

Undergraduate—biblical studies; missionary studies and missiology; religious studies; theological and ministerial studies; theology and religious vocations related.

Graduate—anthropology; biblical studies; curriculum and instruction; education; educational administration and supervision; education related; history; languages (classics and classical); linguistic, comparative, and related language studies; missionary studies and missiology; religious studies; theological and ministerial studies; theology and religious vocations related.

Non-credit—anthropology; biblical studies; education; languages (classics and classical); missionary studies and missiology; religious studies; theological and ministerial studies; theology and religious vocations related.

COLUMBIA SOUTHERN UNIVERSITY
Orange Beach, Alabama
http://www.columbiasouthern.edu

Columbia Southern University was founded in 1993. It is accredited by Distance Education and Training Council. It first offered distance learning courses in 1993. In fall 2010, there were 17,594 students enrolled in distance learning courses. Institutionally administered financial aid is available to distance learners.

Services Distance learners have accessibility to academic advising, bookstore, library services, tutoring.

Contact Admissions Department, Columbia Southern University, 21982 University Lane, Orange Beach, AL 36561. Telephone: 251-981-3771. Fax: 251-981-3815. E-mail: admissions@columbiasouthern.edu.

DEGREES AND AWARDS

AA General Education

AAS Business; Criminal Justice; Fire Science

BS Business Administration; Criminal Justice Administration; Environmental Management; Fire Science; Health Care Administration; Human Resource Management; Information Technology; Occupational Safety and Health; Occupational Safety and Health/Fire Science; Organizational Leadership; Psychology

BSBA Finance; Hospitality and Tourism; Information Technology; International Management; Management; Marketing; Project Management; Sport Management

MBA Business Administration; Finance; Health Care Management; Human Resource Management; Marketing; Project Management; Public Administration

MS Criminal Justice Administration; Emergency Services Management; Occupational Safety and Health; Occupational Safety and Health/Environmental Management; Organizational Leadership

DBA Business Administration

COLUMBIA UNIVERSITY
New York, New York
Columbia Video Network
http://www.cvn.columbia.edu

Columbia University was founded in 1754. It is accredited by Middle States Association of Colleges and Schools. It first offered distance learning courses in 1986. In fall 2010, there were 335 students enrolled in distance learning courses. Institutionally administered financial aid is available to distance learners.

Services Distance learners have accessibility to academic advising, bookstore, campus computer network, career placement assistance, e-mail services, library services.

Contact Distance Learning Recruiter, Columbia University, 540 Mudd Building, 500 West 120th Street, MC 4719, New York, NY 10027. Telephone: 212-854-6447. Fax: 212-854-2325. E-mail: info@cvn.columbia.edu.

DEGREES AND AWARDS

Certificate of Achievement Applied Mathematics; Applied Physics; Business and Technology; Civil Engineering; Construction Management; Earth and Environmental Engineering; Financial Engineering; Industrial Engineering; Information Systems; Intelligent Systems; Manufacturing Engineering; Materials Science and Engineering; Multimedia Networking; Nanotechnology; Networking and Systems; New Media Engineering; Operations Research; Systems Engineering; Telecommunications; Wireless and Mobile Networking

MBA/MS Business and Operations Research dual degrees

MS Applied Mathematics; Applied Physics; Biomedical Engineering; Chemical Engineering; Civil Engineering–Construction Engineering and Management; Civil Engineering; Computer Science; Earth and Environmental Engineering; Electrical Engineering; Engineering Management Systems–Logistics and Supply Chain Optimization; Engineering Management Systems–Risk and Revenue Management; Materials Science and Engineering; Mechanical Engineering; Operations Research–Methods in Finance; Operations Research

PD Computer Systems Engineering; Electrical Engineering; Industrial Engineering; Mechanical Engineering

DES Civil Engineering; Computer Science; Earth and Environmental Engineering; Electrical Engineering; Materials Science and Engineering; Mechanical Engineering

COURSE SUBJECT AREAS OFFERED OUTSIDE OF DEGREE PROGRAMS

Undergraduate—computer science; electrical, electronics and communications engineering; mathematics; mathematics and computer science; mathematics and statistics related.

Graduate—applied mathematics; biomedical/medical engineering; business administration, management and operations; business operations support and assistant services; ceramic sciences and engineering; chemical engineering; civil engineering; computer and information sciences; computer engineering; computer engineering technologies; computer programming; computer science; computer software and media applications; computer systems analysis; computer systems networking and telecommunications; construction engineering; construction engineering technologies; construction management; electrical, electronics and communications engineering; electrical engineering technologies; electromechanical engineering; electromechanical instrumentation and maintenance technologies; engineering; engineering mechanics; engineering-related technologies; entrepreneurial and small business operations; environmental control technologies; environmental design; environmental/environmental health engineering; finance and financial management services; industrial engineering; manufacturing engineering; materials sciences; mathematics and computer science; mechanical engineering; mechanical engineering related technologies; operations research; physical science technologies; physics; systems engineering.

Non-credit—applied mathematics; biomathematics, bioinformatics, and computational biology; business administration, management and operations; civil engineering; computer and information sciences; computer engineering; computer engineering technologies; computer programming; computer science; computer software and media applications; computer systems analysis; computer systems networking and telecommunications; construction engineering; construction engineering technologies; construction management; electrical, electronics and communications engineering; electrical engineering technologies; electromechanical instrumentation and maintenance technologies; engineering; engineering mechanics; engineering related; engineering-related fields; engineering-related technologies; engineering technologies related; environmental control technologies; environmental design; environmental/environmental health engineering; industrial engineering; management sciences and quantitative methods; manufacturing engineering; materials engineering; materials sciences; mathematics and computer science; mechanical engineering; mechanical engineering related technologies; nanotechnology; physics; systems engineering.

COLUMBUS STATE COMMUNITY COLLEGE
Columbus, Ohio
Global Campus
http://www.cscc.edu

Columbus State Community College was founded in 1963. It is accredited by North Central Association of Colleges and Schools. It first offered distance learning courses in 1980. In fall 2010, there were 16,000 students enrolled in distance learning courses. Institutionally administered financial aid is available to distance learners.

Services Distance learners have accessibility to academic advising, bookstore, campus computer network, career placement assistance, e-mail services, library services, tutoring.

Contact Dr. Suzanne Patzer, Interim Director for Instructional Technologies and Distance Learning, Columbus State Community College, Center for Teaching and Learning Innovation, 339 Cleveland Avenue, Columbus, OH 43215. Telephone: 614-287-5748. E-mail: spatzer@cscc.edu.

DEGREES AND AWARDS

AA General Studies

AAS Accounting; Business Management; Digital Design and Graphics; Digital Photography; Exercise Science; Finance; Geographic Information Systems; Health Information Management Technology; Interactive Media; Marketing; Medical Laboratory Technology; Nursing; Retail Management; Supply Chain Management

CCCPE 3-D Visualization; Accounting concentration; Bookkeeping; Complementary Care; Desktop Publishing; Digital Design; Digital Media; Direct Marketing; Geographic Information Systems; Health Care Manager; Health and Safety Training for Hazardous Waste Operations; Histology; International Commerce certificate; Leadership Skills Development; Medical Coding; Nonprofit Management; Nurse Aide; Nursing–Registered Nurse First Assistant; Occupational Health and Safety certificate; Office Specialist; Patient Care Skills; Photography; Photoshop for Illustration and Design; Photoshop for Photographers; Pre-MBA (Business Management); Pre-MBA (Marketing); Purchasing; Rich Media Communication; Sleep Study; Strategic Procurement; Supply Chain Management; Sustainable Building; System Z; Taxation Specialist; Visual Communication; Web Communication

COURSE SUBJECT AREAS OFFERED OUTSIDE OF DEGREE PROGRAMS

Undergraduate—accounting and related services; allied health and medical assisting services; allied health diagnostic, intervention, and treatment professions; anthropology; architecture; astronomy and astrophysics; biological and biomedical sciences related; biology; business administration, management and operations; business/corporate communications; business operations support and assistant services; cell biology and anatomical sciences; chemistry; classical and ancient studies; communication and journalism related; communication and media; computer and information sciences; computer programming; computer software and media applications; computer systems networking and telecommunications; construction management; culinary arts and related services; dental support services and allied professions; design and applied arts; drafting/design engineering technologies; drama/theatre arts and stagecraft; economics; engineering mechanics; engineering technologies related; English; English language and literature related; English or French as a second or foreign language (teaching); environmental control technologies; ethnic, cultural minority, gender, and group studies; film/video and photographic arts; finance and financial management services; fire protection; foods, nutrition, and related services; geography and cartography; geological and earth sciences/geosciences; graphic communications; health aides/attendants/orderlies; health and medical administrative services; health and physical education/fitness; health professions related; health services/allied health/health sciences; history; hospitality administration; human resources management; intercultural/multicultural and diversity studies; international business; international relations and national security studies; landscape architecture; languages (foreign languages related); languages (Germanic); languages (Romance languages); legal studies (non-professional general, undergraduate); legal support services; marketing; materials sciences; mathematics; mechanical engineering; mechanical engineering related technologies; mental and social health services and allied professions; music; natural sciences; nuclear and industrial radiologic technologies; nutrition sciences; pharmacology and toxicology; philosophy; philosophy and religious studies related; physics; political science and government; psychology; public relations, advertising, and applied communication related; quality control and safety technologies; real estate; sales merchandising, and related marketing operations (general); science technologies related; social sciences related; sociology; taxation; vehicle maintenance and repair technologies; veterinary biomedical and clinical sciences; visual and performing arts related.

COLUMBUS STATE UNIVERSITY
Columbus, Georgia
Distance Learning Design & Delivery Services
http://www.columbusstate.edu

Columbus State University was founded in 1958. It is accredited by Southern Association of Colleges and Schools. It first offered distance learning courses in 1991. In fall 2010, there were 2,188 students enrolled in distance learning courses. Institutionally administered financial aid is available to distance learners.

Services Distance learners have accessibility to academic advising, bookstore, campus computer network, career placement assistance, e-mail services, library services, tutoring.

Contact Dr. Wayne Slabon, Director, Distance Learning, Columbus State University, Distance Learning Design and Delivery, 4225 University Avenue, Columbus, GA 31907. Telephone: 706-569-3455. Fax: 706-565-4032. E-mail: slabon_wayne@columbusstate.edu.

DEGREES AND AWARDS

BA Communications major; Liberal Arts

BS Information Technology

MAT Secondary Math and Science Education

MBA Georgia WebMBA

MEd Accomplished Teaching; Educational Leadership

MPA Government Administration

MS Computer Science–Applied Computer Science

COURSE SUBJECT AREAS OFFERED OUTSIDE OF DEGREE PROGRAMS

Undergraduate—computer science; education; liberal arts and sciences, general studies and humanities; psychology; sociology.

Graduate—business administration, management and operations; computer programming; education (specific subject areas).

COMMUNITY COLLEGE OF ALLEGHENY COUNTY
Pittsburgh, Pennsylvania
http://www.ccac.edu/

Community College of Allegheny County was founded in 1966. It is accredited by Middle States Association of Colleges and Schools. It first offered distance learning courses in 1997. Institutionally administered financial aid is available to distance learners.

Services Distance learners have accessibility to academic advising, bookstore, campus computer network, career placement assistance, e-mail services, library services, tutoring.

Contact Sharon Gregory-Brown, Senior Secretary, Community College of Allegheny County, 800 Allegheny Avenue, OCS Room 123, Pittsburgh, PA 15233. Telephone: 412-237-2239. Fax: 412-237-8187. E-mail: sgregory-brown@ccac.edu.

DEGREES AND AWARDS

Programs offered do not lead to a degree or other formal award.

COURSE SUBJECT AREAS OFFERED OUTSIDE OF DEGREE PROGRAMS

Undergraduate—accounting and computer science; anthropology; biology; business administration, management and operations; computer science; criminal justice and corrections; dietetics and clinical nutrition services; economics; education; English; fire protection; foods, nutrition, and related services; health and physical education/fitness; history; homeland security; journalism; legal support services; mathematics; philosophy; physics; political science and government; psychology; sociology.

COMMUNITY COLLEGE OF BEAVER COUNTY
Monaca, Pennsylvania
http://www.ccbc.edu

Community College of Beaver County was founded in 1966. It is accredited by Middle States Association of Colleges and Schools. It first offered distance learning courses in 1998. In fall 2010, there were 500 students enrolled in distance learning courses. Institutionally administered financial aid is available to distance learners.

Services Distance learners have accessibility to academic advising, bookstore, campus computer network, e-mail services, library services, tutoring.

Contact Mr. Scott Ensworth, Dean of Student Services, Community College of Beaver County, 1 Campus Drive, Student Services Center, Monaca, PA 15061-2588. Telephone: 724-480-3364. Fax: 724-775-4687. E-mail: scott.ensworth@ccbc.edu.

DEGREES AND AWARDS

Programs offered do not lead to a degree or other formal award.

COURSE SUBJECT AREAS OFFERED OUTSIDE OF DEGREE PROGRAMS

Undergraduate—accounting and computer science; air transportation; behavioral sciences; business administration, management and operations; business, management, and marketing related; business/managerial economics; computer and information sciences; computer programming; computer science; computer software and media applications; criminal justice and corrections; economics; education; English; fine and studio arts; history; liberal arts and sciences, general studies and humanities; mathematics; nutrition sciences; philosophy; psychology; psychology related; social sciences; social sciences related; sociology; statistics.

Non-credit—accounting and computer science; business administration, management and operations; business/commerce; business/corporate communications; business, management, and marketing related; business/managerial economics; business operations support and assistant services; computer and information sciences; computer science; computer software and media applications; entrepreneurial and small business operations; graphic communications.

CONCORDIA UNIVERSITY, ST. PAUL
St. Paul, Minnesota
http://www.csp.edu

Concordia University, St. Paul was founded in 1893. It is accredited by North Central Association of Colleges and Schools. It first offered distance learning courses in 1998. In fall 2010, there were 1,150 students enrolled in distance learning courses. Institutionally administered financial aid is available to distance learners.

Services Distance learners have accessibility to academic advising, bookstore, campus computer network, e-mail services, library services, tutoring.

Contact Ms. Kimberly Craig, Director, Graduate and Undergraduate Accelerated Admission, Concordia University, St. Paul, 275 Syndicate Street North, St. Paul, MN 55104-5494. Telephone: 800-333-4705. Fax: 651-603-6320. E-mail: craig@csp.edu.

DEGREES AND AWARDS

BA Accounting; Child Development; Criminal Justice; Exercise Science in Kinesiology; Family Life Education; Food Retail Management; Human Resource Management; Information Technology Management; Marketing and Innovation Management; Organizational Management and Leadership

BS Pulmonary Science

MA Christian Outreach; Classroom Instruction; Criminal Justice Leadership; Family Life Education; Human Resource Management; Leadership and Management; Sports Management; Strategic Communication Management

MAE Differentiated Instruction; Early Childhood; Educational Leadership

MBA Business Administration; Health Care Management

COURSE SUBJECT AREAS OFFERED OUTSIDE OF DEGREE PROGRAMS

Undergraduate—business/commerce; education; human development, family studies, and related services; sociology.

Graduate—business/commerce; education; human development, family studies, and related services; sociology.

Non-credit—business/commerce; communication and media; fine and studio arts; mathematics and computer science; social sciences.

CONCORDIA UNIVERSITY WISCONSIN
Mequon, Wisconsin
Continuing Education Division
http://www.cuw.edu

Concordia University Wisconsin was founded in 1881. It is accredited by North Central Association of Colleges and Schools. It first offered distance learning courses in 1994. In fall 2010, there were 1,600 students enrolled in distance learning courses. Institutionally administered financial aid is available to distance learners.

Services Distance learners have accessibility to academic advising, bookstore, campus computer network, career placement assistance, e-mail services, library services, tutoring.

Contact Sarah Pecor, Director of E-Learning, Concordia University Wisconsin, 12800 North Lake Shore Drive, Mequon, WI 53097. Telephone: 262-243-4257. Fax: 262-243-4459. E-mail: sarah.pecor@cuw.edu.

DEGREES AND AWARDS

AA Lay Ministry

BA Business Management

BSN Nursing–BSN completion for RN's

MBA Business Administration

MS Curriculum and Instruction; Education Administration; Education Counseling; Reading

MSN Nursing

DNP Nurse Practice

COURSE SUBJECT AREAS OFFERED OUTSIDE OF DEGREE PROGRAMS

Undergraduate—accounting and related services; business, management, and marketing related; computer science; economics; finance and financial management services; history; management sciences and quantitative methods; marketing.

Graduate—business administration, management and operations; curriculum and instruction; educational administration and supervision; education related.

CORNELL UNIVERSITY
Ithaca, New York
Cornell Office of Distance Learning
http://www.sce.cornell.edu/dl/

Cornell University was founded in 1865. It is accredited by Middle States Association of Colleges and Schools. It first offered distance learning courses in 1997. Institutionally administered financial aid is available to distance learners.

Services Distance learners have accessibility to academic advising, bookstore, campus computer network, e-mail services, library services.

Contact Special Programs Director, Cornell University, B20 Day Hall, Ithaca, NY 14853. Telephone: 607-255-7259. Fax: 607-255-9697. E-mail: cusp@cornell.edu.

DEGREES AND AWARDS

Programs offered do not lead to a degree or other formal award.

COURSE SUBJECT AREAS OFFERED OUTSIDE OF DEGREE PROGRAMS

Undergraduate—anthropology; biological/biosystems engineering; economics; environmental design; health professions related; management sciences and quantitative methods; marketing; public health; sociology; statistics.

Graduate—anthropology; marketing; public health; sociology; statistics.

CORNING COMMUNITY COLLEGE
Corning, New York
Open Learning Program
http://www.corning-cc.edu

Corning Community College was founded in 1956. It is accredited by Middle States Association of Colleges and Schools. It first offered distance learning courses in 1996. In fall 2010, there were 1,188 students enrolled in distance learning courses. Institutionally administered financial aid is available to distance learners.

Services Distance learners have accessibility to academic advising, bookstore, campus computer network, career placement assistance, e-mail services, library services, tutoring.

Contact Dr. James Jansen, Associate Dean of Academic Affairs, Corning Community College, 1 Academic Drive, Corning, NY 14830-3297. Telephone: 607-962-9140. Fax: 607-962-9577. E-mail: jjansen5@corning-cc.edu.

DEGREES AND AWARDS

Programs offered do not lead to a degree or other formal award.

COURSE SUBJECT AREAS OFFERED OUTSIDE OF DEGREE PROGRAMS

Undergraduate—accounting and computer science; accounting and related services; applied mathematics; business administration, management and operations; business/managerial economics; business operations support and assistant services; chemistry; computer programming; computer science; computer software and media applications; computer systems networking and telecommunications; criminal justice and corrections; design and applied arts; economics; education; educational assessment, evaluation, and research; English; English language and literature related; fine and studio arts; graphic communications; health and physical education/fitness; history; hospitality administration; human services; mathematics; philosophy; psychology; sociology.

COSSATOT COMMUNITY COLLEGE OF THE UNIVERSITY OF ARKANSAS
De Queen, Arkansas
Division of Distance Education
http://cccua.edu

Cossatot Community College of the University of Arkansas was founded in 1991. It is accredited by North Central Association of Colleges and Schools. It first offered distance learning courses in 1997. In fall 2010, there were 600 students enrolled in distance learning courses. Institutionally administered financial aid is available to distance learners.

Services Distance learners have accessibility to academic advising, bookstore, career placement assistance, e-mail services, library services, tutoring.

Contact Dr. Maria S. Parker, Vice Chancellor of Academic Services, Cossatot Community College of the University of Arkansas, PO Box 960, DeQueen, AR 71832. Telephone: 870-584-4471. Fax: 870-642-3320. E-mail: mparker@cccua.edu.

DEGREES AND AWARDS

AA University Transfer
AAS Business Management
AGS General Studies

COURSE SUBJECT AREAS OFFERED OUTSIDE OF DEGREE PROGRAMS

Undergraduate—accounting and related services; agricultural business and management; biology; botany/plant biology; business/commerce; business/corporate communications; business/managerial economics; communication and media; computer and information sciences; computer programming; economics; education; English language and literature related; fine and studio arts; fire protection; health and physical education/fitness; history; human development, family studies, and related services; mathematics; psychology; sociology.

Non-credit—accounting and related services; business administration, management and operations; business/commerce; business/corporate communications; business, management, and marketing related; business/managerial economics; business operations support and assistant services; computer and information sciences; computer and information sciences and support services related; computer engineering; computer/information technology administration and management; computer programming; computer science; computer software and media applications; electrical and power transmission installation; electrical, electronics and communications engineering; electrical/electronics maintenance and repair technology; electrical engineering technologies; electromechanical instrumentation and maintenance technologies; management information systems; management sciences and quantitative methods; marketing; sales merchandising, and related marketing operations (general); sales, merchandising and related marketing operations (specialized); special education.

COVENANT THEOLOGICAL SEMINARY
St. Louis, Missouri
External Studies Office
http://www.covenantseminary.edu/academics/degreeprograms/distanceeducation/

Covenant Theological Seminary was founded in 1956. It is accredited by North Central Association of Colleges and Schools. It first offered distance learning courses in 1989. In fall 2010, there were 185 students enrolled in distance learning courses. Institutionally administered financial aid is available to distance learners.

Services Distance learners have accessibility to academic advising, bookstore, campus computer network, career placement assistance, e-mail services, library services, tutoring.

Contact Mr. Jeremy Kicklighter, Director of Admissions, Covenant Theological Seminary, 12330 Conway Road, St. Louis, MO 63141. Telephone: 800-264-8064. Fax: 314-434-4819. E-mail: admissions@covenantseminary.edu.

DEGREES AND AWARDS

Programs offered do not lead to a degree or other formal award.

COURSE SUBJECT AREAS OFFERED OUTSIDE OF DEGREE PROGRAMS

Graduate—biblical studies; history; missionary studies and missiology; religious education; religious/sacred music; religious studies; theological and ministerial studies; theology and religious vocations related.

Non-credit—biblical studies; history; missionary studies and missiology; religious education; religious/sacred music; religious studies; theological and ministerial studies; theology and religious vocations related.

CROWN COLLEGE
St. Bonifacius, Minnesota
Crown College Online
http://www.crown.edu/ags

Crown College was founded in 1916. It is accredited by North Central Association of Colleges and Schools. It first offered distance learning courses in 2000. In fall 2010, there were 317 students enrolled in distance learning courses. Institutionally administered financial aid is available to distance learners.

Services Distance learners have accessibility to academic advising, bookstore, campus computer network, career placement assistance, e-mail services, library services, tutoring.

Contact James Hunter, Director of AGS Enrollment, Crown College, 8700 College View Drive, St. Bonifacius, MN 55375. Telephone: 952-446-4300. Fax: 952-446-4461. E-mail: hunterj@crown.edu.

DEGREES AND AWARDS

AA General Studies
AS Christian Ministries
BA Strategic Communication
BS Business Administration; Christian Ministry; Psychology/Counseling
BSN Nursing–BSN Completion
Certificate Bible
Graduate Certificate International Educator's certificate; Transformational Leadership
MA Christian Studies; Instructional Leadership; International Leadership Studies; Ministry Leadership; Organizational Leadership
MBA Business Administration

COURSE SUBJECT AREAS OFFERED OUTSIDE OF DEGREE PROGRAMS

Undergraduate—accounting and related services; missionary studies and missiology; pastoral counseling and specialized ministries; philosophy and religious studies related; religious education; religious studies.

Graduate—biblical studies; education; educational administration and supervision; education related; intercultural/multicultural and diversity studies; international and comparative education; international/global studies; missionary studies and missiology; philosophy and religious studies related; theological and ministerial studies.

CULVER-STOCKTON COLLEGE
Canton, Missouri
http://www.culver.edu/

Culver-Stockton College was founded in 1853. It is accredited by North Central Association of Colleges and Schools. It first offered distance learning courses in 2002. In fall 2010, there were 42 students enrolled in distance learning courses. Institutionally administered financial aid is available to distance learners.

Services Distance learners have accessibility to academic advising, bookstore, campus computer network, career placement assistance, e-mail services, library services, tutoring.

Contact Dr. David W. Wilson, Interim Dean of the College, Culver-Stockton College, One College Hill, Canton, MO 63435. Telephone: 573-288-6325. Fax: 573-288-6616. E-mail: dwilson@culver.edu.

DEGREES AND AWARDS

BS Business

COURSE SUBJECT AREAS OFFERED OUTSIDE OF DEGREE PROGRAMS

Undergraduate—accounting and related services; biology; business administration, management and operations; economics; education; English; geography and cartography; history; management information systems; mathematics; natural sciences; philosophy; political science and government; psychology; religious studies.

CUMBERLAND UNIVERSITY
Lebanon, Tennessee
Master of Arts in Education
http://www.cumberland.edu/

Cumberland University was founded in 1842. It is accredited by Southern Association of Colleges and Schools. It first offered distance learning courses in 1999. In fall 2010, there were 140 students enrolled in distance learning courses. Institutionally administered financial aid is available to distance learners.

Services Distance learners have accessibility to academic advising, bookstore, campus computer network, career placement assistance, e-mail services, library services, tutoring.

Contact Debbie Whitaker, Program Coordinator, Cumberland University, One Cumberland Square, Lebanon, TN 37087-3408. Telephone: 800-467-0562 Ext. 1217. Fax: 877-217-5284. E-mail: dwhitaker@cumberland.edu.

DEGREES AND AWARDS

MAE Education

COURSE SUBJECT AREAS OFFERED OUTSIDE OF DEGREE PROGRAMS

Graduate—education.

DABNEY S. LANCASTER COMMUNITY COLLEGE
Clifton Forge, Virginia
http://www.dslcc.edu

Dabney S. Lancaster Community College was founded in 1964. It is accredited by Southern Association of Colleges and Schools. It first offered distance learning courses in 1998. In fall 2010, there were 700 students enrolled in distance learning courses. Institutionally administered financial aid is available to distance learners.

Services Distance learners have accessibility to campus computer network, career placement assistance, e-mail services, library services, tutoring.

Contact Billy Ould, AV/IT Specialist, Dabney S. Lancaster Community College, PO Box 1000, Dabney Lane, Clifton Forge, VA 24422. Telephone: 540-863-2869. E-mail: would@dslcc.edu.

DEGREES AND AWARDS

Programs offered do not lead to a degree or other formal award.

COURSE SUBJECT AREAS OFFERED OUTSIDE OF DEGREE PROGRAMS

Undergraduate—accounting and computer science; accounting and related services; alternative and complementary medicine and medical systems; applied mathematics; biochemistry, biophysics and molecular biology; business, management, and marketing related; criminal justice and corrections; economics; English; English language and literature related; history; human development, family studies, and related services; mathematics; mathematics and statistics related; nutrition sciences; psychology; psychology related.

Non-credit—accounting and computer science; communications technology; computer and information sciences; culinary arts and related services.

DAKOTA COLLEGE AT BOTTINEAU
Bottineau, North Dakota
http://www.dakotacollege.edu

Dakota College at Bottineau was founded in 1906. It is accredited by North Central Association of Colleges and Schools. It first offered distance learning courses in 2000. In fall 2010, there were 260 students enrolled in distance learning courses. Institutionally administered financial aid is available to distance learners.

Services Distance learners have accessibility to academic advising, bookstore, e-mail services, library services.

Contact Kayla O'Toole, Distance Education Specialist, Dakota College at Bottineau, 105 Simrall Boulevard, Bottineau, ND 58318. Telephone: 888-918-5623. E-mail: kayla.otoole@dakotacollege.edu.

DEGREES AND AWARDS

AA Liberal Arts
AAS Accounting Technician; Administrative Assistant; Advertising and Marketing; Caregiver Services–Adult; Caregiver Services–Child; Medical Administrative Assistant; Medical Assistant; Paraeducation; Recreation Management
Certificate of Completion Bookkeeping; Caregiver Services–Child; Grounds Work Skills, basic; Medical Coding; Medical Transcription; Recreation Management
Certificate Paraeducation
Diploma Advertising and Marketing; Bookkeeping; Caregiver Services–Adult; Medical Assistant; Medical Coding; Medical Transcription; Reception Services; Urban Forestry Technology

COURSE SUBJECT AREAS OFFERED OUTSIDE OF DEGREE PROGRAMS

Undergraduate—accounting and computer science; accounting and related services; allied health and medical assisting services; applied horticulture and horticultural business services; behavioral sciences; biological and biomedical sciences related; botany/plant biology; business administration, management and operations; business, management, and marketing related; business operations support and assistant services; chemistry; clinical/medical laboratory science/research; computer and information sciences; computer and information sciences and support services related; data entry/microcomputer applications; economics; education; education related; foods, nutrition, and related services; forestry; gerontology; health and medical administrative services; health and physical education/fitness; health/medical preparatory programs; health professions related; health services/allied health/health sciences; history; human resources management; human services; liberal arts and sciences, general studies and humanities; marketing; mathematics; mathematics and computer science; natural sciences; parks, recreation and leisure; parks, recreation and leisure facilities management; parks, recreation, leisure, and fitness studies related; pharmacology and toxicology; physical sciences; plant sciences; psychology; psychology related; public administration; religious education; science technologies related; social sciences; soil sciences; teaching assistants/aides.

DAKOTA STATE UNIVERSITY
Madison, South Dakota
Extended Programs
http://www.dsu.edu/disted/index.aspx

Dakota State University was founded in 1881. It is accredited by North Central Association of Colleges and Schools. It first offered distance learning courses in 1991. In fall 2010, there were 1,193 students enrolled in distance learning courses. Institutionally administered financial aid is available to distance learners.
Services Distance learners have accessibility to academic advising, bookstore, campus computer network, career placement assistance, e-mail services, library services, tutoring.
Contact Ms. Susan Eykamp, Distance Education Specialist, Extended Programs, Dakota State University, 820 North Washington Avenue, Tunheim Classroom Building, Madison, SD 57042-1799. Telephone: 800-641-4309. Fax: 605-256-5095. E-mail: dsuinfo@dsu.edu.

DEGREES AND AWARDS

AA General Studies
AS Application Programming; Business Management; Health Information Technology; Network and System Administration
BBA Management Information Systems; Management; Marketing
BEd Elementary Education/Special Education
BGS General Studies
BS Computer Information Systems; Computer Science; Health Information Administration; Professional and Technical Communication
Certificate Healthcare Coding; Programming and Systems Development
MS Educational Technology; Health Informatics; Information Assurance and Computer Security
MSIS Information Systems
DSc IS Information Systems

COURSE SUBJECT AREAS OFFERED OUTSIDE OF DEGREE PROGRAMS

Undergraduate—accounting and related services; biology; business administration, management and operations; communications technology; computer and information sciences; computer and information sciences and support services related; computer/information technology administration and management; computer programming; computer science; computer systems analysis; economics; education related; English; English language and literature related; fine and studio arts; health and medical administrative services; health and physical education/fitness; human resources management; information science/studies; languages (foreign languages related); linguistic, comparative, and related language studies; mathematics; music; nutrition sciences; physics; political science and government; psychology; sociology; special education.
Graduate—computer and information sciences; computer and information sciences and support services related; educational/instructional media design; education related; health and medical administrative services; information science/studies.

DAKOTA WESLEYAN UNIVERSITY
Mitchell, South Dakota
http://www.dwu.edu/

Dakota Wesleyan University was founded in 1885. It is accredited by North Central Association of Colleges and Schools. It first offered distance learning courses in 2002. In fall 2010, there were 103 students enrolled in distance learning courses. Institutionally administered financial aid is available to distance learners.
Services Distance learners have accessibility to academic advising, bookstore, campus computer network, e-mail services, library services.
Contact Karen A. Knoell, Registrar, Dakota Wesleyan University, 1200 West University Avenue, Mitchell, SD 57301. Telephone: 605-995-2647. Fax: 605-995-2643. E-mail: kaknoell@dwu.edu.

DEGREES AND AWARDS

Programs offered do not lead to a degree or other formal award.

COURSE SUBJECT AREAS OFFERED OUTSIDE OF DEGREE PROGRAMS

Undergraduate—business administration, management and operations; education; health professions related; philosophy; psychology; sociology.
Graduate—educational administration and supervision; education related.

DALLAS BAPTIST UNIVERSITY
Dallas, Texas
Dallas Baptist University Online (DBU Online)
http://online.dbu.edu

Dallas Baptist University was founded in 1965. It is accredited by Southern Association of Colleges and Schools. It first offered distance learning courses in 1998. In fall 2010, there were 2,139 students enrolled in distance learning courses. Institutionally administered financial aid is available to distance learners.
Services Distance learners have accessibility to academic advising, bookstore, campus computer network, career placement assistance, e-mail services, library services, tutoring.
Contact Ms. Judy Yi, Online Student Coordinator, Dallas Baptist University, Online Education, 3000 Mountain Creek Parkway, Dallas, TX 75211-9299. Telephone: 800-460-8188. Fax: 214-333-5373. E-mail: online@dbu.edu.

DEGREES AND AWARDS

AA General degree
ABA Business Administration
ABS Biblical Studies
BA Biblical Studies

BAS Christian Ministries (Business concentration only); Communication; Criminal Justice; Health Care Management; Interdisciplinary Studies–8 concentrations; Psychology; Sociology
BBA Management Information Systems; Management; Marketing
BBS Business Administration; Management Information Systems; Management; Marketing
Certificate Health Care Management; Information Systems and Technology; Management Practices
Graduate Certificate Childhood Ministry Leadership; Health Care Management; Higher Education Administration; Human Resource Management; Information Systems and Technology; Management; Marketing; Ministry Leadership in Business Ministry; Project Management; School Principalship
MA Professional Development in Church Leadership; Professional Development in Criminal Justice; Professional Development in Finance; Professional Development in Higher Education; Professional Development in Leadership Studies; Professional Development in Management Information Systems; Professional Development in Management; Professional Development in Marketing; Worship Leadership
MACE Adult Ministry; Business Ministry concentration; Childhood Ministry concentration; Christian Education and Childhood Ministry; Collegiate Ministry concentration; Dual MACE Student Ministry and Masters of Arts in Management; Dual MACE/MBA; Family Ministry concentration; General concentration; Student Ministry (Youth and Collegiate); Worship Ministry concentration
MAM Dual M.Ed.–Curriculum and Instruction and MAM; Dual Master of Arts in Management and Master of Education in Higher Education; Health Care Management; Human Resource Management; Management, general
MAT Distance Learning specialization
MBA Dual Master of Arts in Christian Education–Childhood Ministry/Master of Business Administration; Finance Accelerated BBS/MBA; Finance; Health Care Management Accelerated BBS/MBA; Health Care Management; International Business Accelerated BBS/MBA; International Business; Management Accelerated BBA/MBA; Management Accelerated BBS/MBA; Management Information Systems Accelerated BBS/MBA; Management Information Systems; Management; Marketing Accelerated BBS/MBA; Marketing; Project Management Accelerated BBS/MBA; Project Management
MBA/M Ed Dual degree program; Educational Leadership
MEd Curriculum and Instruction, Distance Learning specialization; Curriculum and Instruction, Supervision specialization; Curriculum and Instruction/Educational Leadership Dual degree; Educational Leadership; Higher Education Administration Track, Distance Learning specialization; Higher Education Administration Track, Interdisciplinary Studies
MLA Interdisciplinary track; Single Discipline Track–Christian Ministry

COURSE SUBJECT AREAS OFFERED OUTSIDE OF DEGREE PROGRAMS

Undergraduate—accounting and computer science; accounting and related services; atmospheric sciences and meteorology; behavioral sciences; biblical studies; biological and physical sciences; biology; business administration, management and operations; business/commerce; business/corporate communications; business, management, and marketing related; business/managerial economics; communication and journalism related; communication and media; communications technologies and support services related; communications technology; computer and information sciences; computer and information sciences and support services related; computer science; computer software and media applications; computer systems analysis; computer systems networking and telecommunications; criminal justice and corrections; criminology; curriculum and instruction; economics; education; educational assessment, evaluation, and research; education related; education (specific levels and methods); education (specific subject areas); English; English language and literature related; English or French as a second or foreign language (teaching); finance and financial management services; fine and studio arts; geological and earth sciences/geosciences; graphic communications; health and physical education/fitness; health professions related; history; human development, family studies, and related services; human resources management; international agriculture; languages (classics and classical); liberal arts and sciences, general studies and humanities; management information systems; marketing; mathematics; mathematics and statistics related; missionary studies and missiology; natural sciences; philosophy; philosophy and religious studies related; political science and government; psychology; psychology related; public health; religious education; religious studies; sales merchandising, and related marketing operations (general); social sciences; social sciences related; social work; sociology; special education; statistics; theological and ministerial studies; theology and religious vocations related.
Graduate—accounting and related services; business administration, management and operations; business/commerce; business/corporate communications; business, management, and marketing related; business/managerial economics; computer and information sciences; computer/information technology administration and management; computer software and media applications; computer systems analysis; computer systems networking and telecommunications; criminal justice and corrections; criminology; curriculum and instruction; economics; education; educational administration and supervision; educational assessment, evaluation, and research; educational/instructional media design; education related; education (specific levels and methods); English or French as a second or foreign language (teaching); entrepreneurial and small business operations; finance and financial management services; history; human resources management; information science/studies; international business; liberal arts and sciences, general studies and humanities; management information systems; management sciences and quantitative methods; marketing; missionary studies and missiology; philosophy and religious studies related; religious education; religious studies; sales merchandising, and related marketing operations (general); statistics; theological and ministerial studies.

DALLAS CHRISTIAN COLLEGE
Dallas, Texas
http://www.dallas.edu/Online/index.cfm

Dallas Christian College was founded in 1950. It is accredited by Association for Biblical Higher Education. It first offered distance learning courses in 2001. In fall 2010, there were 90 students enrolled in distance learning courses. Institutionally administered financial aid is available to distance learners.
Services Distance learners have accessibility to academic advising, bookstore, career placement assistance, e-mail services, library services, tutoring.
Contact Ms. Brittany C. Burnette, Associate Director of Admissions, Dallas Christian College, 2700 Christian Parkway, Dallas, TX 75234. Telephone: 800-688-1029 Ext. 161. E-mail: bburnette@dallas.edu.

DEGREES AND AWARDS

BS Management and Ethics; Ministry and Leadership

COURSE SUBJECT AREAS OFFERED OUTSIDE OF DEGREE PROGRAMS

Undergraduate—accounting and related services; biblical studies; business, management, and marketing related; interdisciplinary studies; liberal arts and sciences, general studies and humanities; pastoral counseling and specialized ministries; philosophy and religious studies; theological and ministerial studies; theology and religious vocations related.

DANVILLE COMMUNITY COLLEGE
Danville, Virginia
Learning Resource Center
http://www.dcc.vccs.edu

Danville Community College was founded in 1967. It is accredited by Southern Association of Colleges and Schools. It first offered distance learning courses in 1990. In fall 2010, there were 1,500 students enrolled in distance learning courses. Institutionally administered financial aid is available to distance learners.
Services Distance learners have accessibility to academic advising, bookstore, career placement assistance, e-mail services, library services, tutoring.

Contact Mr. William L. Dey, Director of Learning Resources and Distance Learning, Danville Community College, 1008 South Main Street, Danville, VA 24541. Telephone: 434-797-8454. Fax: 434-797-8415. E-mail: wdey@dcc.vccs.edu.

DEGREES AND AWARDS
AAS Marketing, Electronic Commerce specialization

COURSE SUBJECT AREAS OFFERED OUTSIDE OF DEGREE PROGRAMS
Undergraduate—accounting and related services; allied health and medical assisting services; allied health diagnostic, intervention, and treatment professions; applied mathematics; behavioral sciences; biological and biomedical sciences related; biology; business administration, management and operations; business/commerce; business, management, and marketing related; business operations support and assistant services; communication and media; computer programming; computer science; computer software and media applications; criminal justice and corrections; criminology; dental support services and allied professions; dentistry and oral sciences (advanced/graduate); design and applied arts; drafting/design engineering technologies; education; educational/ instructional media design; engineering; engineering related; engineering-related fields; English; English language and literature related; foods, nutrition, and related services; geography and cartography; graphic communications; health and physical education/fitness; health professions related; history; human development, family studies, and related services; liberal arts and sciences, general studies and humanities; marketing; mathematics; mathematics and computer science; natural sciences; nutrition sciences; political science and government; psychology; social sciences; sociology; theological and ministerial studies.

DAVIDSON COUNTY COMMUNITY COLLEGE
Lexington, North Carolina
http://www.davidsonccc.edu

Davidson County Community College was founded in 1958. It is accredited by Southern Association of Colleges and Schools. It first offered distance learning courses in 2003. Institutionally administered financial aid is available to distance learners.
Services Distance learners have accessibility to academic advising, bookstore, campus computer network, career placement assistance, e-mail services, library services, tutoring.
Contact Lori S. Blevins, Director of Admissions, Davidson County Community College, PO Box 1287, Lexington, NC 27293. Telephone: 336-249-8186 Ext. 6240. Fax: 336-224-0240. E-mail: lblevins@davidsonccc.edu.

DEGREES AND AWARDS
Programs offered do not lead to a degree or other formal award.

COURSE SUBJECT AREAS OFFERED OUTSIDE OF DEGREE PROGRAMS
Undergraduate—biological and physical sciences; cosmetology and related personal grooming services; criminal justice and corrections; data entry/microcomputer applications; education; health services/allied health/ health sciences; history; languages (Romance languages); linguistic, comparative, and related language studies; mathematics; pharmacy, pharmaceutical sciences, and administration; psychology; religious studies; sociology.

DAWSON COMMUNITY COLLEGE
Glendive, Montana
Continuing and Extension Education Department
http://www.dawson.edu

Dawson Community College was founded in 1940. It is accredited by Northwest Commission on Colleges and Universities. It first offered distance learning courses in 1990. In fall 2010, there were 45 students enrolled in distance learning courses. Institutionally administered financial aid is available to distance learners.
Services Distance learners have accessibility to academic advising, bookstore, e-mail services, library services, tutoring.
Contact Mrs. MaryAnn Vester, Director of Continuing Education and Outreach, Dawson Community College, 300 College Drive, Glendive, MT 59330. Telephone: 406-377-3396 Ext. 409. Fax: 406-377-8132. E-mail: mare@dawson.edu.

DEGREES AND AWARDS
AA General Studies
AAS Business Management; Criminal Justice; Early Childhood Education; Law Enforcement
AS General Studies

COURSE SUBJECT AREAS OFFERED OUTSIDE OF DEGREE PROGRAMS
Undergraduate—agricultural business and management; agriculture; anthropology; biology; business administration, management and operations; communication and media; computer software and media applications; criminal justice and corrections; fine and studio arts; psychology; sociology.

DAYTONA STATE COLLEGE
Daytona Beach, Florida
College of Online Studies
http://online.DaytonaState.edu

Daytona State College was founded in 1958. It is accredited by Southern Association of Colleges and Schools. It first offered distance learning courses in 1974. In fall 2010, there were 4,500 students enrolled in distance learning courses. Institutionally administered financial aid is available to distance learners.
Services Distance learners have accessibility to academic advising, bookstore, campus computer network, e-mail services, library services, tutoring.
Contact Dr. Robert Saum, Dean, College of Online Studies, Daytona State College, PO Box 2811, 1200 West International Speedway Boulevard, Daytona Beach, FL 32120-2811. Telephone: 386-506-3484. Fax: 386-506-4601. E-mail: saumr@daytonastate.edu.

DEGREES AND AWARDS
AA Liberal Arts (in state); Liberal Arts (out of state)
AS Accounting Technology (in state); Accounting Technology (out of state); Business Administration (in state); Business Administration (out of state); Office Administration (in state); Office Administration (out of state)
BAS Management and Supervision (in state); Management and Supervision (out of state)
BSET Engineering Technology (in state); Engineering Technology (out of state)

COURSE SUBJECT AREAS OFFERED OUTSIDE OF DEGREE PROGRAMS
Undergraduate—accounting and computer science; allied health and medical assisting services; behavioral sciences; biological and physical sciences; business, management, and marketing related; computer programming; criminal justice and corrections; economics; education; educational/instructional media design; English; English language and literature related; history; languages (foreign languages related); mathematics; music; philosophy; taxation; visual and performing arts.

DEFIANCE COLLEGE
Defiance, Ohio
Design for Leadership
http://www.defiance.edu/pages/design_for_leadership.html

Defiance College was founded in 1850. It is accredited by North Central Association of Colleges and Schools. It first offered distance learning courses in 1971. In fall 2010, there were 20 students enrolled in distance learning courses. Institutionally administered financial aid is available to distance learners.
Services Distance learners have accessibility to academic advising, campus computer network, career placement assistance, e-mail services, library services, tutoring.

Contact Dr. Marian R. Plant, Coordinator, Design for Leadership, Defiance College, 701 North Clinton Street, Defiance, OH 43512. Telephone: 419-783-2465. Fax: 419-784-0426. E-mail: design@defiance.edu.

DEGREES AND AWARDS

AA Christian Religious Education
BA Christian Religious Education
Certificate Church Education; Youth Ministry Leadership

COURSE SUBJECT AREAS OFFERED OUTSIDE OF DEGREE PROGRAMS

Undergraduate—biblical studies; religious education; theological and ministerial studies; theology and religious vocations related.

DELGADO COMMUNITY COLLEGE
New Orleans, Louisiana
Community Campus
http://www.dcc.edu/

Delgado Community College was founded in 1921. It is accredited by Southern Association of Colleges and Schools. It first offered distance learning courses in 1989. In fall 2010, there were 4,015 students enrolled in distance learning courses. Institutionally administered financial aid is available to distance learners.

Services Distance learners have accessibility to academic advising, bookstore, e-mail services, library services, tutoring.

Contact Tanisca Wilson, Assistant Director of Admission, Delgado Community College, New Orleans, LA 70119. Telephone: 504-671-5014. E-mail: tjones3@dcc.edu.

DEGREES AND AWARDS

AAS Administrative Office Technologies; Care and Development of Young Children; Computer information Technology
AS Accounting; Business Administration

COURSE SUBJECT AREAS OFFERED OUTSIDE OF DEGREE PROGRAMS

Undergraduate—accounting and computer science; biological and physical sciences; business administration, management and operations; business, management, and marketing related; business/managerial economics; computer and information sciences; criminal justice and corrections; economics; English; finance and financial management services; fine and studio arts; history; legal studies (non-professional general, undergraduate); liberal arts and sciences, general studies and humanities; mathematics; philosophy and religious studies related.

DENVER SEMINARY
Littleton, Colorado
http://www.denverseminary.edu

Denver Seminary was founded in 1950. It is accredited by North Central Association of Colleges and Schools. It first offered distance learning courses in 1988. In fall 2010, there were 143 students enrolled in distance learning courses. Institutionally administered financial aid is available to distance learners.

Services Distance learners have accessibility to academic advising, bookstore, career placement assistance, library services.

Contact Dr. Venita Doughty, Director of Educational Technology, Denver Seminary, 6399 South Santa Fe Drive, Littleton, CO 80120. Telephone: 303-762-6933. Fax: 303-761-8060. E-mail: venita.doughty@denverseminary.edu.

DEGREES AND AWARDS

Programs offered do not lead to a degree or other formal award.

COURSE SUBJECT AREAS OFFERED OUTSIDE OF DEGREE PROGRAMS

Graduate—biblical studies; history; philosophy and religious studies related; religious education; religious studies; theological and ministerial studies.

DEPAUL UNIVERSITY
Chicago, Illinois
Office of Distance Learning
http://www.depaul.edu/admission/types_of_admission/index.asp

DePaul University was founded in 1898. It is accredited by North Central Association of Colleges and Schools. It first offered distance learning courses in 1994. In fall 2010, there were 3,384 students enrolled in distance learning courses. Institutionally administered financial aid is available to distance learners.

Services Distance learners have accessibility to academic advising, bookstore, campus computer network, career placement assistance, e-mail services, library services, tutoring.

Contact Admissions, DePaul University, One East Jackson Boulevard, Chicago, IL 60604-2287. Telephone: 312-362-8300. E-mail: admission@depaul.edu.

DEGREES AND AWARDS

BA Liberal Arts, general
Certificate Financial Planning; Mastery in Prior Learning Assessment; Practical Internet Marketing; Prior Learning Assessment; Professional in Human Resources; Project Management; Wealth Management; e-Financial Planning
MA Curriculum Studies; Educational Leadership; Information Technology
MS Accountancy; Applied Technology; Business Information Technology; Computational Finance; Computer Science; Computer, Information, and Network Security; E-Commerce Technology; Human-Computer Interaction; IT Project Management; Information Systems; Network Engineering and Management; Predictive Analytics; Public Administration, International Public Management specialization; Public Service Management; Software Engineering; Taxation

COURSE SUBJECT AREAS OFFERED OUTSIDE OF DEGREE PROGRAMS

Undergraduate—computer and information sciences and support services related; computer programming; computer science; computer software and media applications; computer systems networking and telecommunications; education; information science/studies; intercultural/multicultural and diversity studies; liberal arts and sciences, general studies and humanities; psychology; religious studies.

Graduate—accounting and related services; computer programming; computer science; computer software and media applications; computer systems networking and telecommunications; educational administration and supervision; education (specific subject areas); finance and financial management services; information science/studies; management sciences and quantitative methods; marketing; public administration and social service professions related.

Non-credit—alternative and complementary medical support services; finance and financial management services; human resources management; management sciences and quantitative methods.

DEPAUL UNIVERSITY
Chicago, Illinois
School for New Learning
http://www.snlonline.depaul.edu

DePaul University was founded in 1898. It is accredited by North Central Association of Colleges and Schools. It first offered distance learning courses in 2001. In fall 2010, there were 941 students enrolled in distance learning courses. Institutionally administered financial aid is available to distance learners.

Services Distance learners have accessibility to academic advising, bookstore, campus computer network, career placement assistance, e-mail services, library services, tutoring.

Contact Admission Counselor, DePaul University, 1 East Jackson Boulevard, Chicago, IL 60604. Telephone: 312-362-6338. E-mail: adultenrollment@depaul.edu.

DEGREES AND AWARDS

BA Individualized Focus Area

COURSE SUBJECT AREAS OFFERED OUTSIDE OF DEGREE PROGRAMS

Undergraduate—liberal arts and sciences, general studies and humanities; science, technology and society; social sciences related.

DePAUL UNIVERSITY
Chicago, Illinois
SPS Online
http://spsonline.info/

DePaul University was founded in 1898. It is accredited by North Central Association of Colleges and Schools. It first offered distance learning courses in 2004. In fall 2010, there were 150 students enrolled in distance learning courses. Institutionally administered financial aid is available to distance learners.

Services Distance learners have accessibility to academic advising, bookstore, campus computer network, career placement assistance, e-mail services, library services, tutoring.

Contact Dr. J. Patrick Murphy, CM, Director, School of Public Service, DePaul University, 14 East Jackson Boulevard, Suite 1600, Chicago, IL 60604. Telephone: 312-362-5608. Fax: 312-362-5506. E-mail: jpmurphy@depaul.edu.

DEGREES AND AWARDS

MNM Nonprofit Management
MPA Public Administration
MS Public Service Management (MPS) Online

COURSE SUBJECT AREAS OFFERED OUTSIDE OF DEGREE PROGRAMS

Graduate—community organization and advocacy; economics; human services; international and comparative education; international/global studies; international relations and national security studies; public administration; public administration and social service professions related; public policy analysis; urban studies/affairs.

DeVRY UNIVERSITY ONLINE
Addison, Illinois
http://www.devry.edu/online

DeVry University Online was founded in 2000. It is accredited by North Central Association of Colleges and Schools. In fall 2010, there were 37,505 students enrolled in distance learning courses. Institutionally administered financial aid is available to distance learners.

Services Distance learners have accessibility to academic advising, bookstore, career placement assistance, e-mail services, library services.

Contact Sarah Penn, Director of Admissions Online, DeVry University Online, 1200 East Diehl Road, Naperville, IL 60563. Telephone: 630-645-6170. E-mail: spenn@devry.edu.

DEGREES AND AWARDS

AAS Accounting; Electronics and Computer Technology; Health Information Technology; Network Systems Administration; Web Graphic Design
BS Computer Engineering Technology; Computer Information Systems; Electronics Engineering Technology; Game and Simulation Programming; Justice Administration; Liberal Studies; Management; Multimedia Design and Development; Network and Communications Management; Technical Management
BSBA Business Administration
MAFM Accounting and Financial Management
MBA Business Administration
MHRM Human Resource Management
MISM Information Systems Management
MPA Public Administration
MPM Project Management
MS Educational Technology
MSEE Electrical Engineering
MTM Network and Communications Management

COURSE SUBJECT AREAS OFFERED OUTSIDE OF DEGREE PROGRAMS

Undergraduate—accounting and related services; biological and biomedical sciences related; business/commerce; communication and media; computer and information sciences; economics; legal studies (nonprofessional general, undergraduate); liberal arts and sciences, general studies and humanities; marketing; mathematics.

Graduate—accounting and related services; business/commerce; communication and media; communications technology; computer and information sciences; computer systems networking and telecommunications; economics; entrepreneurial and small business operations; finance and financial management services; health professions related; human resources management; marketing; mathematics; public administration; taxation.

DICKINSON STATE UNIVERSITY
Dickinson, North Dakota
http://www.dickinsonstate.edu/extendedlearning/

Dickinson State University was founded in 1918. It is accredited by North Central Association of Colleges and Schools. It first offered distance learning courses in 1998. In fall 2010, there were 600 students enrolled in distance learning courses. Institutionally administered financial aid is available to distance learners.

Services Distance learners have accessibility to academic advising, bookstore, campus computer network, career placement assistance, e-mail services, library services, tutoring.

Contact Mr. John Hurlimann, Director, Dickinson State University, 291 Campus Drive, CB 183, Dickinson, ND 58601. Telephone: 701-483-2166. Fax: 701-483-2028. E-mail: john.hurlimann@dickinsonstate.edu.

DEGREES AND AWARDS

AA General Program
AS Agricultural Sales and Services–Equine option
BA Composite Social Science; English
BAS Applied Science; Applied Science
BPS University Studies
BS Accounting; Business Administration; Computer Science; Computer Technology Management; Education–Elementary Education; Finance; Finance; History; Human Resource Management; Human Resource Management; International Business; International Business; Secondary Education–Composite Social Science; Secondary Education–English; Secondary Education–History; Secondary Education–Math
BUS University Studies

COURSE SUBJECT AREAS OFFERED OUTSIDE OF DEGREE PROGRAMS

Undergraduate—accounting and computer science; accounting and related services; agricultural and domestic animal services; agriculture; behavioral sciences; biology; business administration, management and operations; business/corporate communications; business, management, and marketing related; communication and media; computer science; computer software and media applications; data entry/microcomputer applications; economics; education; educational administration and supervision; education related; education (specific levels and methods); education (specific subject areas); English; entrepreneurial and small business operations; geological and earth sciences/geosciences; history; holocaust and related studies; international business; marketing; music; political science and government; psychology; real estate; sociology; statistics.

DOMINICAN COLLEGE
Orangeburg, New York

Dominican College was founded in 1952. It is accredited by Middle States Association of Colleges and Schools. It first offered distance learning courses in 2000. In fall 2010, there were 784 students enrolled in distance learning courses. Institutionally administered financial aid is available to distance learners.

Services Distance learners have accessibility to academic advising, bookstore, campus computer network, career placement assistance, e-mail services, library services.

Contact Ms. Joyce Elbe, Director of Admissions, Dominican College, DePorres Hall, 470 Western Highway, Orangeburg, NY 10962. Telephone: 866-432-4636. Fax: 845-365-3151. E-mail: joyce.elbe@dc.edu.

DEGREES AND AWARDS
MSE Teacher of Blind and/or Visually Impaired
DPT Transitional Doctor of Physical Therapy

COURSE SUBJECT AREAS OFFERED OUTSIDE OF DEGREE PROGRAMS
Undergraduate—allied health diagnostic, intervention, and treatment professions; biology; business, management, and marketing related; criminology; education; English; history; psychology; sociology.
Graduate—allied health and medical assisting services; education.

DRAKE UNIVERSITY
Des Moines, Iowa
Distance Learning Program
http://www.drake.edu

Drake University was founded in 1881. It is accredited by North Central Association of Colleges and Schools. It first offered distance learning courses in 1997. In fall 2010, there were 2,000 students enrolled in distance learning courses. Institutionally administered financial aid is available to distance learners.
Services Distance learners have accessibility to academic advising, bookstore, campus computer network, e-mail services, library services.
Contact Mr. Charles Sengstock, Director of Extension Education, Drake University, School of Education, 3206 University Avenue, Des Moines, IA 50311. Telephone: 515-271-2184. E-mail: charles.sengstrock@drake.edu.

DEGREES AND AWARDS
Programs offered do not lead to a degree or other formal award.

COURSE SUBJECT AREAS OFFERED OUTSIDE OF DEGREE PROGRAMS
Undergraduate—accounting and related services; biochemistry, biophysics and molecular biology; business administration, management and operations; business/commerce; business/managerial economics; communication and journalism related; communication and media; computer and information sciences; economics; education; education related; education (specific subject areas); English; history; human resources management; information science/studies; international relations and national security studies; journalism; legal research and advanced professional studies; liberal arts and sciences, general studies and humanities; management information systems; management sciences and quantitative methods; marketing; mathematics and computer science; pharmacy, pharmaceutical sciences, and administration; political science and government; psychology; psychology related; public relations, advertising, and applied communication related; social sciences related; special education; visual and performing arts related.
Graduate—accounting and computer science; business administration, management and operations; business/commerce; economics; education; education (specific subject areas); finance and financial management services; health professions related; health services/allied health/health sciences; human resources management; information science/studies; insurance; journalism; pharmacy, pharmaceutical sciences, and administration; political science and government; psychology; public administration; public administration and social service professions related; public health; public relations, advertising, and applied communication related; rehabilitation and therapeutic professions.

DREW UNIVERSITY
Madison, New Jersey
http://www.drew.edu/theo.aspx

Drew University was founded in 1867. It is accredited by Middle States Association of Colleges and Schools. It first offered distance learning courses in 1998. In fall 2010, there were 108 students enrolled in distance learning courses. Institutionally administered financial aid is available to distance learners.
Services Distance learners have accessibility to academic advising, bookstore, campus computer network, e-mail services, library services.
Contact Dr. Carl Savage, Director, Doctor of Ministry Program, Drew University, 36 Madison Avenue, 12 CAMPUS, Madison, NJ 07940. Telephone: 973-408-3630. Fax: 973-408-3178. E-mail: csavage@drew.edu.

DEGREES AND AWARDS
Programs offered do not lead to a degree or other formal award.

COURSE SUBJECT AREAS OFFERED OUTSIDE OF DEGREE PROGRAMS
Graduate—theological and ministerial studies.
Non-credit—theological and ministerial studies.

DREXEL UNIVERSITY
Philadelphia, Pennsylvania
E-Learning
http://www.drexel.com/petersons

Drexel University was founded in 1891. It is accredited by Middle States Association of Colleges and Schools. It first offered distance learning courses in 1997. In fall 2010, there were 3,500 students enrolled in distance learning courses. Institutionally administered financial aid is available to distance learners.
Services Distance learners have accessibility to academic advising, bookstore, career placement assistance, e-mail services, library services, tutoring.
Contact Drexel University Online, Drexel University, One Drexel Plaza, 3001 Market Street, Suite 300, Philadelphia, PA 19104. Telephone: 877-215-0009. Fax: 215-895-0525. E-mail: info@drexel.com.

DEGREES AND AWARDS
BS Business Administration; Communication; Communications and Applied Technology; Computing and Security Technology; Criminal Justice; Education; General Studies–Individualized Studies; General Studies, Business minor; Health Services Administration; Professional Studies; Property Management; Psychology
BSN Nursing–RN to BSN
Certificate Clinical Trials Research; Complementary and Integrative Therapies; Creativity Studies; Education–Graduate Intern Teaching certificate; Education–post-Bachelor's Teaching certificate; Emergency Management; Epidemiology and Biostatistics; Gaming and Casino Operations; Healthcare Informatics; Instructional Technology Specialist; Medical Billing and Coding; Nursing Education and Faculty Role; Nursing Leadership in Health Systems Management; Nursing–Innovation and Intra/Entrepreneurship in Advanced Nursing Practice; Retail Leadership; Teaching English as a Second Language (TESL)
CAGS Information Studies and Technology
Graduate Certificate Autism Spectrum Disorders; Community College Administration and Leadership; Computing Security Technology; Construction Management; Creativity Studies; E-Learning Leadership; Engineering Management; Gaming and Casino Operations; Homeland Security Management; Mathematics Learning and Teaching; Real Estate; Special Education certification; Student Development and Affairs; Sustainability and Green Construction
MBA Business Administration; Pharmaceutical Management
MHS Physician Assistant post-Professional program
MS Arts Administration; Business Analytics; Clinical Research Organization and Management; Clinical Research for Health Professionals; Communication; Computer Science; Construction Management; Creativity and Innovation; Educational Administration–Collaborative Leadership; Electrical Engineering; Engineering Management; Engineering Technology; Global and International Education; Health Informatics; Higher Education; Hospitality Management; Human Resource Development; Information Systems; Learning Technologies; Library and Information Science; Math Learning and Teaching; Professional Studies; Project Management; Property Management; Software Engineering; Special Education; Sport Management; Teaching, Learning, and Curriculum
MSN Clinical Trials Research; Nursing Education and Faculty Role; Nursing Leadership in Health Systems Management; Nursing–Acute Care Nurse Practitioner; Nursing–Adult Psychiatric Mental Health Nurse Practitioner; Nursing–Innovation and Intra/Entrepreneurship in Advanced

Nursing Practice; Nursing–RN-MSN Bridge program; Nursing–Women's Health Nurse Practitioner; Pediatric Primary Care
PMC Archival Studies Specialist; Competitive Intelligence and Knowledge Management Specialist; Digital Libraries specialist; Innovation and Intra/Entrepreneurship in Advanced Nursing Practice; Medical Family Therapy; Nursing Education and Faculty Role; Nursing–Adult Psychiatric Mental Health Nurse Practitioner; Youth Services Specialist
DNP Nursing Practice

COURSE SUBJECT AREAS OFFERED OUTSIDE OF DEGREE PROGRAMS

Undergraduate—apparel and textiles; business administration, management and operations; business/commerce; business, management, and marketing related; communications technologies and support services related; computer and information sciences; computer science; finance and financial management services; health professions related; health services/allied health/health sciences; marketing; psychology; sales merchandising, and related marketing operations (general).
Graduate—alternative and complementary medical support services; alternative and complementary medicine and medical systems; business administration, management and operations; business/commerce; business/corporate communications; business, management, and marketing related; clinical/medical laboratory science/research; computer and information sciences; computer and information sciences and support services related; computer engineering; computer engineering technologies; computer science; construction management; curriculum and instruction; education; educational administration and supervision; educational assessment, evaluation, and research; educational/instructional media design; education related; education (specific levels and methods); education (specific subject areas); electrical, electronics and communications engineering; electrical engineering technologies; engineering; engineering related; engineering-related fields; engineering-related technologies; engineering science; engineering technologies related; engineering technology; English or French as a second or foreign language (teaching); entrepreneurial and small business operations; finance and financial management services; health professions related; hospitality administration; information science/studies; international and comparative education; international/global studies; library science and administration; library science related; management information systems; marketing; parks, recreation and leisure facilities management; pharmacology and toxicology; public health; public policy analysis; real estate; sales merchandising, and related marketing operations (general); sales, merchandising and related marketing operations (specialized); science technologies related; statistics; teaching assistants/aides.

DREXEL UNIVERSITY
Philadelphia, Pennsylvania
LeBow College of Business
http://www.lebow.drexel.edu/Prospects/MBA/online.php

Drexel University was founded in 1891. It is accredited by Middle States Association of Colleges and Schools. It first offered distance learning courses in 1998. In fall 2010, there were 353 students enrolled in distance learning courses. Institutionally administered financial aid is available to distance learners.
Services Distance learners have accessibility to academic advising, bookstore, campus computer network, career placement assistance, e-mail services, library services.
Contact Mr. John Adamski, Director, Graduate Admissions, Drexel University, 207 Matheson Hall, 3141 Chestnut Street, Philadelphia, PA 19104. Telephone: 215-895-6804. Fax: 215-895-1725. E-mail: mba@drexel.edu.

DEGREES AND AWARDS

MBA Business; Pharmaceutical Management

COURSE SUBJECT AREAS OFFERED OUTSIDE OF DEGREE PROGRAMS

Undergraduate—accounting and related services; business administration, management and operations; business/commerce; business/managerial economics; entrepreneurial and small business operations; management sciences and quantitative methods; marketing.
Graduate—accounting and related services; business administration, management and operations; business, management, and marketing related; business/managerial economics; computer/information technology administration and management; entrepreneurial and small business operations; finance and financial management services; international business; management sciences and quantitative methods; marketing; operations research.
Non-credit—accounting and computer science; business/commerce; economics; entrepreneurial and small business operations; finance and financial management services; international business; management information systems; management sciences and quantitative methods; statistics.

DRURY UNIVERSITY
Springfield, Missouri
http://www.drury.edu/online

Drury University was founded in 1873. It is accredited by North Central Association of Colleges and Schools. It first offered distance learning courses in 1999. In fall 2010, there were 1,500 students enrolled in distance learning courses. Institutionally administered financial aid is available to distance learners.
Services Distance learners have accessibility to academic advising, bookstore, campus computer network, e-mail services, library services, tutoring.
Contact Mr. Steve Hynds, Director for Online Education, Drury University, 900 North Benton Avenue, Springfield, MO 65802. Telephone: 417-873-7406. E-mail: grader@drury.edu.

DEGREES AND AWARDS

AS Criminal Justice; English; Environmental Studies Management; General Studies; History; Psychology
BGS General Studies
MEd Instructional Math; Instructional Technology

COURSE SUBJECT AREAS OFFERED OUTSIDE OF DEGREE PROGRAMS

Undergraduate—accounting and related services; behavioral sciences; biology; business, management, and marketing related; chemistry; communication and media; computer and information sciences; criminology; English; geography and cartography; history; legal studies (nonprofessional general, undergraduate); liberal arts and sciences, general studies and humanities; management information systems; marketing; mathematics; music; natural resources and conservation related; philosophy and religious studies related; physical sciences; political science and government; psychology; religious studies; social sciences; sociology.
Graduate—communication and media; criminology; education.
Non-credit—criminal justice and corrections.

DUKE UNIVERSITY
Durham, North Carolina
Nicholas School of the Environment
http://www.nicholas.duke.edu/del/del-mem

Duke University was founded in 1838. It is accredited by Southern Association of Colleges and Schools. It first offered distance learning courses in 2004. In fall 2010, there were 29 students enrolled in distance learning courses. Institutionally administered financial aid is available to distance learners.
Services Distance learners have accessibility to academic advising, bookstore, campus computer network, career placement assistance, e-mail services, library services.
Contact Director, Duke Environmental Leadership Program, Duke University, Nicholas School of the Environment, Box 90328, Durham, NC 27708-0328. Telephone: 919-613-8082. Fax: 919-613-9002. E-mail: del@nicholas.duke.edu.

DEGREES AND AWARDS

MEM Duke Environmental Leadership Master of Environmental Management

COURSE SUBJECT AREAS OFFERED OUTSIDE OF DEGREE PROGRAMS

Graduate—ecology, evolution, systematics, and population biology; management sciences and quantitative methods; natural resources and conservation related; natural resources conservation and research; natural resources management and policy; natural sciences.

DUQUESNE UNIVERSITY
Pittsburgh, Pennsylvania
Center for Distance Learning
http://www.duq.edu/online/

Duquesne University was founded in 1878. It is accredited by Middle States Association of Colleges and Schools. It first offered distance learning courses in 1996. In fall 2010, there were 900 students enrolled in distance learning courses. Institutionally administered financial aid is available to distance learners.

Services Distance learners have accessibility to academic advising, bookstore, campus computer network, career placement assistance, e-mail services, library services, tutoring.

Contact Ruth Newberry, Director, Educational Technology, Duquesne University, Rockwell Hall, 600 Forbes Avenue, Pittsburgh, PA 15282. Telephone: 412-396-1813. Fax: 412-396-5144. E-mail: edtech@duq.edu.

DEGREES AND AWARDS

BS Degree completion program; Humane Leadership
BSN Nursing–RN to BSN/MSN
Certificate Nursing–post-BSN
Graduate Certificate Nursing–post-Masters; Organizational Leadership in Animal Advocacy
MA Leadership and Liberal Studies
MLD Leadership, Global Leadship concentration
MS Community Leadership; Leadership and Business Ethics; Leadership and Information Technology–Masters of Leadership and Information Technology; Music Education–Masters in Music Education; Sports Leadership
MSN Nursing; Nursing
DNP Nursing
PhD Nursing–Doctor of Nursing Practice; Nursing

COURSE SUBJECT AREAS OFFERED OUTSIDE OF DEGREE PROGRAMS

Undergraduate—fine and studio arts; theological and ministerial studies; theology and religious vocations related.

Graduate—curriculum and instruction; education; educational/instructional media design; music; pastoral counseling and specialized ministries; public policy analysis.

Non-credit—animal sciences; computer and information sciences; legal support services.

D'YOUVILLE COLLEGE
Buffalo, New York
Distance Learning
http://ddl.dyc.edu

D'Youville College was founded in 1908. It is accredited by Middle States Association of Colleges and Schools. It first offered distance learning courses in 1996. In fall 2010, there were 2,000 students enrolled in distance learning courses. Institutionally administered financial aid is available to distance learners.

Services Distance learners have accessibility to academic advising, bookstore, campus computer network, e-mail services, library services.

Contact Dr. John T. Murphy, Director of Instructional Support Services and Distance Education, D'Youville College, 320 Porter Avenue, Buffalo, NY 14201. Telephone: 716-829-8147. Fax: 716-829-7760. E-mail: murphyj@dyc.edu.

DEGREES AND AWARDS

Programs offered do not lead to a degree or other formal award.

COURSE SUBJECT AREAS OFFERED OUTSIDE OF DEGREE PROGRAMS

Undergraduate—accounting and computer science; accounting and related services; biological and physical sciences; business administration, management and operations; business, management, and marketing related; clinical/medical laboratory science/research; computer and information sciences; computer/information technology administration and management; economics; education; education (specific subject areas); health professions related; history; human resources management; international business; international/global studies; natural sciences; physics; political science and government; social sciences; special education; statistics.

Graduate—biological and biomedical sciences related; biological and physical sciences; business/commerce; business/managerial economics; cognitive science; education; health and medical administrative services; information science/studies; international business; medical clinical sciences/graduate medical studies; nutrition sciences; social and philosophical foundations of education; special education; statistics.

EARLHAM SCHOOL OF RELIGION
Richmond, Indiana
http://esr.earlham.edu

Earlham School of Religion was founded in 1960. It first offered distance learning courses in 2001. In fall 2010, there were 105 students enrolled in distance learning courses. Institutionally administered financial aid is available to distance learners.

Services Distance learners have accessibility to academic advising, bookstore, campus computer network, e-mail services, library services.

Contact Valerie Hurwitz, Director of Recruitment and Admissions, Earlham School of Religion, 228 College Avenue, Richmond, IN 47374. Telephone: 800-432-1377. Fax: 765-983-1688. E-mail: hurwiva@earlham.edu.

DEGREES AND AWARDS

MA ESR Access
MDiv ESR Access

COURSE SUBJECT AREAS OFFERED OUTSIDE OF DEGREE PROGRAMS

Graduate—biblical studies; pastoral counseling and specialized ministries; peace studies and conflict resolution; religious education; religious studies; theological and ministerial studies; theology and religious vocations related.

EAST CENTRAL COMMUNITY COLLEGE
Decatur, Mississippi
Adult and Continuing Education
http://www.eccc.edu

East Central Community College was founded in 1928. It is accredited by Southern Association of Colleges and Schools. It first offered distance learning courses in 2000. In fall 2010, there were 855 students enrolled in distance learning courses. Institutionally administered financial aid is available to distance learners.

Services Distance learners have accessibility to academic advising, bookstore, campus computer network, e-mail services, library services, tutoring.

Contact Dr. Chris C. Jenkins, Dean of eLearning Education, East Central Community College, PO Box 129, Decatur, MS 39327. Telephone: 601-635-6322. Fax: 601-635-4011. E-mail: cjenkins@eccc.edu.

DEGREES AND AWARDS

Programs offered do not lead to a degree or other formal award.

COURSE SUBJECT AREAS OFFERED OUTSIDE OF DEGREE PROGRAMS

Undergraduate—accounting and computer science; allied health and medical assisting services; biblical studies; biological and physical sciences; business administration, management and operations; chemistry;

computer and information sciences; economics; education; English; history; mathematics; music; physical sciences; psychology; sociology.

EASTERN ILLINOIS UNIVERSITY
Charleston, Illinois
School of Continuing Education
http://www.eiu.edu/~adulted/

Eastern Illinois University was founded in 1895. It is accredited by North Central Association of Colleges and Schools. It first offered distance learning courses in 1994. In fall 2010, there were 1,200 students enrolled in distance learning courses. Institutionally administered financial aid is available to distance learners.

Services Distance learners have accessibility to academic advising, bookstore, campus computer network, career placement assistance, e-mail services, library services, tutoring.

Contact Dr. William Hine, Dean, School of Continuing Education, Eastern Illinois University, 600 Lincoln Avenue, Charleston, IL 61920. Telephone: 217-581-6644. E-mail: wchine@eiu.edu.

DEGREES AND AWARDS

BA General Studies
BS Nursing; Organizational and Professional Development

COURSE SUBJECT AREAS OFFERED OUTSIDE OF DEGREE PROGRAMS

Undergraduate—area studies; astronomy and astrophysics; biological and biomedical sciences related; biological and physical sciences; biology; communication and journalism related; economics; education; education (specific subject areas); English language and literature related; family and consumer economics; geological and earth sciences/geosciences; health and physical education/fitness; health services/allied health/health sciences; history; human development, family studies, and related services; human resources management; industrial production technologies; journalism; mathematics and statistics related; parks, recreation and leisure; philosophy; physical sciences; physics; psychology; social sciences; social sciences related.

Graduate—communication disorders sciences and services; computer/information technology administration and management; educational administration and supervision; family and consumer economics; health and physical education/fitness; human development, family studies, and related services; psychology.

Non-credit—legal support services.

EASTERN KENTUCKY UNIVERSITY
Richmond, Kentucky
Continuing Education and Outreach
http://www.eku.edu/onlinelearning/

Eastern Kentucky University was founded in 1906. It is accredited by Southern Association of Colleges and Schools. It first offered distance learning courses in 1995. In fall 2010, there were 4,500 students enrolled in distance learning courses. Institutionally administered financial aid is available to distance learners.

Services Distance learners have accessibility to academic advising, bookstore, campus computer network, career placement assistance, e-mail services, library services, tutoring.

Contact William St. Pierre, System Director for Credit Programs, Eastern Kentucky University, 202 Perkins Building, 521 Lancaster Avenue, Richmond, KY 40475. Telephone: 859-622-8342. Fax: 859-622-6205. E-mail: bill.stpierre@eku.edu.

DEGREES AND AWARDS

BCJ Law Enforcement
BS Corrections and Juvenile Justice; Fire and Safety Engineering Technology; Homeland Security; Occupational Safety
MS Corrections and Juvenile Justice; Safety, Security, and Emergency Management

COURSE SUBJECT AREAS OFFERED OUTSIDE OF DEGREE PROGRAMS

Undergraduate—accounting and computer science; anthropology; biological and physical sciences; biology; communication and journalism related; curriculum and instruction; economics; educational administration and supervision; fine and studio arts; geography and cartography; health professions related; history; journalism; marketing; mathematics; mathematics and statistics related; philosophy; philosophy and religious studies related; political science and government; radio, television, and digital communication; social work.

Graduate—business administration, management and operations; curriculum and instruction; educational administration and supervision; library science and administration; public health; special education.

EASTERN MENNONITE UNIVERSITY
Harrisonburg, Virginia
Eastern Mennonite Seminary
http://www.emu.edu/seminary/distance-learning/

Eastern Mennonite University was founded in 1917. It is accredited by Southern Association of Colleges and Schools. It first offered distance learning courses in 1997. In fall 2010, there were 30 students enrolled in distance learning courses. Institutionally administered financial aid is available to distance learners.

Services Distance learners have accessibility to academic advising, bookstore, campus computer network, career placement assistance, e-mail services, library services.

Contact Don Yoder, Director of Admissions, Eastern Mennonite University, 1200 Park Road, Harrisonburg, VA 22802-2462. Telephone: 540-432-4257. Fax: 540-432-4598. E-mail: semadmiss@emu.edu.

DEGREES AND AWARDS

Programs offered do not lead to a degree or other formal award.

COURSE SUBJECT AREAS OFFERED OUTSIDE OF DEGREE PROGRAMS

Graduate—biblical studies; missionary studies and missiology; pastoral counseling and specialized ministries; peace studies and conflict resolution; philosophy; philosophy and religious studies related; religious studies; theological and ministerial studies.

EASTERN OREGON UNIVERSITY
La Grande, Oregon
Division of Distance Education
http://www.eou.edu/advising/

Eastern Oregon University was founded in 1929. It is accredited by Northwest Commission on Colleges and Universities. It first offered distance learning courses in 1978. In fall 2010, there were 1,800 students enrolled in distance learning courses. Institutionally administered financial aid is available to distance learners.

Services Distance learners have accessibility to academic advising, bookstore, campus computer network, career placement assistance, e-mail services, library services.

Contact Liz Burton, Director of Academic Advising, Eastern Oregon University, Academic Advising, One University Boulevard, La Grande, OR 97850-2899. Telephone: 800-544-2195. Fax: 541-962-3359. E-mail: eburton@eou.edu.

DEGREES AND AWARDS

BA English Literature; Physical Activity and Health; Psychology
BS Anthropology/Sociology; Business Administration; Business and Economics; Fire Services Administration; Liberal Studies; Philosophy, Politics, and Economics; Physical Activity and Health; Psychology

COURSE SUBJECT AREAS OFFERED OUTSIDE OF DEGREE PROGRAMS

Undergraduate—accounting and related services; agricultural business and management; anthropology; biology; botany/plant biology; business/commerce; chemistry; computer science; criminology; drama/theatre arts and stagecraft; economics; English; English language and literature

related; geography and cartography; health and physical education/fitness; music; philosophy; physics; political science and government; psychology.
Graduate—education related.

EASTERN UNIVERSITY
St. Davids, Pennsylvania
http://www.eastern.edu/

Eastern University was founded in 1952. It is accredited by Middle States Association of Colleges and Schools. It first offered distance learning courses in 2000. In fall 2010, there were 941 students enrolled in distance learning courses. Institutionally administered financial aid is available to distance learners.
Services Distance learners have accessibility to academic advising, bookstore, campus computer network, career placement assistance, e-mail services, library services, tutoring.
Contact Kate Fuerst, Associate Registrar, Accelerated and Online Programs, Eastern University, 1300 Eagle Road, St. Davids, PA 19087-3696. Telephone: 610-341-4392 Fax: 610-341-5998 E-mail: kfuerst@eastern.edu.

DEGREES AND AWARDS
AA Liberal Arts, General Studies
BA Organizational Leadership
BS Business Administration
MA Organizational Leadership; Urban Studies
MEd Multicultural Education with ESL or TESOL
MS Nonprofit Management
DA Marriage and Family
PhD Organizational Leadership

COURSE SUBJECT AREAS OFFERED OUTSIDE OF DEGREE PROGRAMS
Undergraduate—biblical studies.
Non-credit—biblical studies.

EASTERN WASHINGTON UNIVERSITY
Cheney, Washington
Division for International and Educational Outreach
http://www.ewu.edu/dieo

Eastern Washington University was founded in 1882. It is accredited by Northwest Commission on Colleges and Universities. It first offered distance learning courses in 1965. In fall 2010, there were 900 students enrolled in distance learning courses. Institutionally administered financial aid is available to distance learners.
Services Distance learners have accessibility to academic advising, bookstore, campus computer network, career placement assistance, e-mail services, library services, tutoring.
Contact Laurie Charles, Advisor, Eastern Washington University, Division for International and Educational Outreach, 300 Senior Hall, Cheney, WA 99004-2442. Telephone: 800-924-6606. Fax: 509-359-6257. E-mail: gothedistance@ewu.edu.

DEGREES AND AWARDS
MS Dental Hygiene

COURSE SUBJECT AREAS OFFERED OUTSIDE OF DEGREE PROGRAMS
Undergraduate—accounting and related services; allied health diagnostic, intervention, and treatment professions; city/urban, community and regional planning; communication and media; communication disorders sciences and services; education; education (specific subject areas); English; ethnic, cultural minority, gender, and group studies; family and consumer sciences/human sciences; fine and studio arts; foods, nutrition, and related services; geography and cartography; health and medical administrative services; health and physical education/fitness; history; human resources management; journalism; languages (Romance languages); liberal arts and sciences, general studies and humanities; management information systems; music; parks, recreation and leisure; philosophy; political science and government; psychology; public administration and social service professions related; religious studies; social sciences; social work; sociology.
Graduate—social work; urban studies/affairs.
Non-credit—allied health and medical assisting services; allied health diagnostic, intervention, and treatment professions; business administration, management and operations; business/commerce; business/corporate communications; business, management, and marketing related; education; health and physical education/fitness; human resources management; international business; languages (foreign languages related); manufacturing engineering; real estate; sales merchandising, and related marketing operations (general).

EASTERN WEST VIRGINIA COMMUNITY AND TECHNICAL COLLEGE
Moorefield, West Virginia
http://www.easternwv.edu

Eastern West Virginia Community and Technical College was founded in 1999. It is accredited by North Central Association of Colleges and Schools. It first offered distance learning courses in 2001. In fall 2010, there were 371 students enrolled in distance learning courses. Institutionally administered financial aid is available to distance learners.
Services Distance learners have accessibility to academic advising, bookstore, library services, tutoring.
Contact Laurel Godlove, Academic Services Program Coordinator, Eastern West Virginia Community and Technical College, 316 Eastern Drive, Moorefield, WV 26836. Telephone: 304-434-8000 Ext. 244. Fax: 304-434-7000. E-mail: lgodlove@eastern.wvnet.edu.

DEGREES AND AWARDS
Programs offered do not lead to a degree or other formal award.

COURSE SUBJECT AREAS OFFERED OUTSIDE OF DEGREE PROGRAMS
Undergraduate—accounting and computer science; business administration, management and operations; business, management, and marketing related; business operations support and assistant services; computer and information sciences; computer/information technology administration and management; economics; English; entrepreneurial and small business operations; history; liberal arts and sciences, general studies and humanities; marketing; mathematics; mathematics and statistics related; music; philosophy; political science and government; psychology; real estate; social sciences; sociology; statistics.

EASTERN WYOMING COLLEGE
Torrington, Wyoming
Outreach
http://ewc.wy.edu

Eastern Wyoming College was founded in 1948. It is accredited by North Central Association of Colleges and Schools. It first offered distance learning courses in 1990. In fall 2010, there were 287 students enrolled in distance learning courses. Institutionally administered financial aid is available to distance learners.
Services Distance learners have accessibility to academic advising, bookstore, e-mail services, library services, tutoring.
Contact Aaron Bahmer, Instructional Technologist, Eastern Wyoming College, 3200 West C Street, Torrington, WY 82240. Telephone: 307-532-8284. Fax: 307-532-8229. E-mail: aaron.bahmer@ewc.wy.edu.

DEGREES AND AWARDS
AA Criminal Justice; Early Childhood Education; Interdisciplinary Studies
AAS Business Administration
AS Interdisciplinary Studies
CCCPE Criminal Justice–Corrections certificate

COURSE SUBJECT AREAS OFFERED OUTSIDE OF DEGREE PROGRAMS
Undergraduate—accounting and related services; agricultural business and management; agriculture; anthropology; biology; business adminis-

tration, management and operations; business/commerce; communication and media; computer and information sciences; computer software and media applications; criminal justice and corrections; economics; education; education (specific levels and methods); English; entrepreneurial and small business operations; family and consumer sciences/human sciences; geological and earth sciences/geosciences; health and physical education/fitness; history; marketing; mathematics; nutrition sciences; philosophy and religious studies related; political science and government; psychology; sociology; special education; veterinary biomedical and clinical sciences; zoology/animal biology.

EAST GEORGIA COLLEGE
Swainsboro, Georgia
http://www.ega.edu

East Georgia College was founded in 1973. It is accredited by Southern Association of Colleges and Schools. It first offered distance learning courses in 1997. In fall 2010, there were 857 students enrolled in distance learning courses. Institutionally administered financial aid is available to distance learners.

Services Distance learners have accessibility to academic advising, bookstore, campus computer network, e-mail services, library services.

Contact Mr. David Gribbin, Institutional Research Director, East Georgia College, 131 College Circle, Swainsboro, GA 30401. Telephone: 478-289-2047. Fax: 478-289-2057. E-mail: dgribbin@ega.edu.

DEGREES AND AWARDS
AA Online Associate of Arts Degree

COURSE SUBJECT AREAS OFFERED OUTSIDE OF DEGREE PROGRAMS
Undergraduate—biology; business administration, management and operations; economics; education; English; history; literature; mathematics; political science and government; statistics.

EAST LOS ANGELES COLLEGE
Monterey Park, California
http://www.elac.edu

East Los Angeles College was founded in 1945. It is accredited by Western Association of Schools and Colleges. It first offered distance learning courses in 1998. In fall 2010, there were 3,746 students enrolled in distance learning courses. Institutionally administered financial aid is available to distance learners.

Services Distance learners have accessibility to academic advising, bookstore, career placement assistance, e-mail services, library services, tutoring.

Contact Ms. Pauletta Daw, Distance Education Coordinator, East Los Angeles College, 1301 Avenida Cesar Chavez, Monterey Park, CA 91754. Telephone: 323-415-5313. E-mail: dawpe@elac.edu.

DEGREES AND AWARDS
Programs offered do not lead to a degree or other formal award.

COURSE SUBJECT AREAS OFFERED OUTSIDE OF DEGREE PROGRAMS
Undergraduate—accounting and computer science; anthropology; applied mathematics; arts, entertainment, and media management; behavioral sciences; bilingual, multilingual, and multicultural education; business administration, management and operations; business/corporate communications; business, management, and marketing related; computer and information sciences; computer and information sciences and support services related; criminal justice and corrections; criminology; cultural studies/critical theory and analysis; data entry/microcomputer applications; family and consumer economics; fine and studio arts; foods, nutrition, and related services; health and physical education/fitness; history; liberal arts and sciences, general studies and humanities; management information systems; mathematics; music; philosophy; psychology; visual and performing arts.

EDGECOMBE COMMUNITY COLLEGE
Tarboro, North Carolina
http://www.edgecombe.edu

Edgecombe Community College was founded in 1968. It is accredited by Southern Association of Colleges and Schools. It first offered distance learning courses in 1991. In fall 2010, there were 2,369 students enrolled in distance learning courses. Institutionally administered financial aid is available to distance learners.

Services Distance learners have accessibility to academic advising, bookstore, campus computer network, career placement assistance, e-mail services, library services, tutoring.

Contact Mr. Richard Greene, Distance Learning Director, Edgecombe Community College, 225 Tarboro Street, Rocky Mount, NC 27801. Telephone: 252-823-5166 Ext. 340. Fax: 252-985-2212. E-mail: greener@edgecombe.edu.

DEGREES AND AWARDS
AA Early Childhood Education
AAB Business Administration
AAS Health Information Technology

COURSE SUBJECT AREAS OFFERED OUTSIDE OF DEGREE PROGRAMS
Undergraduate—accounting and related services; business administration, management and operations; business/commerce; business/corporate communications; business, management, and marketing related; computer and information sciences; computer and information sciences and support services related; computer/information technology administration and management; computer programming; computer software and media applications; computer systems analysis; computer systems networking and telecommunications; data entry/microcomputer applications; education (specific subject areas); ethnic, cultural minority, gender, and group studies; health and medical administrative services; health/medical preparatory programs; history; human development, family studies, and related services; management information systems; psychology; sociology.

Non-credit—accounting and related services; business administration, management and operations; business/commerce; business/corporate communications; business, management, and marketing related; business/managerial economics; business operations support and assistant services; communication and media; computer and information sciences; computer and information sciences and support services related; computer/information technology administration and management; computer programming; computer science; computer software and media applications; data entry/microcomputer applications; English; health and medical administrative services; management information systems; sales, merchandising and related marketing operations (specialized).

EDISON STATE COMMUNITY COLLEGE
Piqua, Ohio
http://www.edisonohio.edu/

Edison State Community College was founded in 1973. It is accredited by North Central Association of Colleges and Schools. It first offered distance learning courses in 1987. In fall 2010, there were 1,292 students enrolled in distance learning courses. Institutionally administered financial aid is available to distance learners.

Services Distance learners have accessibility to academic advising, bookstore, campus computer network, career placement assistance, e-mail services, library services, tutoring.

Contact Cecelia Green, Director of Distance Learning, Edison State Community College, 1973 Edison Drive, Piqua, OH 45356. Telephone: 937-778-8600 Ext. 7883. E-mail: cgreen@edisonohio.edu.

DEGREES AND AWARDS
AA General degree
AAB Medical Office Assistant

COURSE SUBJECT AREAS OFFERED OUTSIDE OF DEGREE PROGRAMS
Undergraduate—accounting and related services; allied health and medical assisting services; anthropology; biblical studies; biology; business

administration, management and operations; business/commerce; business/corporate communications; business, management, and marketing related; business operations support and assistant services; cell biology and anatomical sciences; chemistry; communication and media; computer and information sciences; computer engineering; computer/information technology administration and management; computer programming; computer science; computer software and media applications; computer systems analysis; computer systems networking and telecommunications; criminal justice and corrections; criminology; design and applied arts; drama/theatre arts and stagecraft; ecology, evolution, systematics, and population biology; economics; English; fine and studio arts; geological and earth sciences/geosciences; history; human development, family studies, and related services; human resources management; human services; industrial production technologies; literature; management information systems; marketing; mathematics; mathematics and computer science; philosophy; philosophy and religious studies; philosophy and religious studies related; physics; psychology; psychology related; public relations, advertising, and applied communication related; religious studies; social sciences; sociology; statistics.
Non-credit—computer and information sciences; computer/information technology administration and management; computer software and media applications.

ELAINE P. NUNEZ COMMUNITY COLLEGE
Chalmette, Louisiana
http://www.nunez.edu

Elaine P. Nunez Community College was founded in 1992. It is accredited by Southern Association of Colleges and Schools. It first offered distance learning courses in 1998. In fall 2010, there were 483 students enrolled in distance learning courses. Institutionally administered financial aid is available to distance learners.
Services Distance learners have accessibility to e-mail services, library services.
Contact Mr. Ron Chapman, E-Learning Coordinator, Elaine P. Nunez Community College, 3710 Paris Road, Chalmette, LA 70043. Telephone: 504-278-6282. Fax: 504-278-6284. E-mail: rchapman@nunez.edu.

DEGREES AND AWARDS
Programs offered do not lead to a degree or other formal award.

COURSE SUBJECT AREAS OFFERED OUTSIDE OF DEGREE PROGRAMS
Undergraduate—accounting and related services; business/commerce; computer and information sciences and support services related; economics; education related; English; fine and studio arts; health and medical administrative services; history; industrial production technologies; mathematics; nutrition sciences; psychology; sociology.

EL CAMINO COLLEGE
Torrance, California
Distance Education
http://www.elcamino.edu/Library/DistanceEd

El Camino College was founded in 1947. It is accredited by Western Association of Schools and Colleges. It first offered distance learning courses in 1970. In fall 2010, there were 1,327 students enrolled in distance learning courses. Institutionally administered financial aid is available to distance learners.
Services Distance learners have accessibility to academic advising, campus computer network, career placement assistance, e-mail services, library services, tutoring.
Contact Mr. Howard G. Story, Distance Education and Media Coordinator, El Camino College, Schauerman Library, 16007 Crenshaw Boulevard, Torrance, CA 90506. Telephone: 310-660-6453. Fax: 310-660-3593 Ext. 6712. E-mail: hstory@elcamino.edu.

DEGREES AND AWARDS
Programs offered do not lead to a degree or other formal award.

COURSE SUBJECT AREAS OFFERED OUTSIDE OF DEGREE PROGRAMS
Undergraduate—anthropology; astronomy and astrophysics; biological and biomedical sciences related; economics; geological and earth sciences/geosciences; health and physical education/fitness; human development, family studies, and related services; journalism; music; philosophy; political science and government; psychology; social sciences related; sociology.

ELLIS UNIVERSITY
Chicago, Illinois
http://www.ellis.edu

Ellis University is accredited by Distance Education and Training Council. It first offered distance learning courses in 2008. In fall 2010, there were 914 students enrolled in distance learning courses. Institutionally administered financial aid is available to distance learners.
Services Distance learners have accessibility to academic advising, bookstore, campus computer network, career placement assistance, e-mail services, library services, tutoring.
Contact Mr. LePra George, Assistant Director of Admissions, Ellis University, 111 North Canal Street, Suite 380, Chicago, IL 60606. Telephone: 312-669-5273 Fax: 312-669-6514. E-mail: lgeorge@ellis.edu.

DEGREES AND AWARDS
AA Child Development

AAS Paralegal Studies

BA Child Development; Paralegal Studies

BPS Hospitality Management; Interdisciplinary Studies

BS Accounting; Business Administration; Criminal Justice; Management of Information Systems

MA Business Communications; Education

MBA Business Administration

MS Instructional Technology

MSM Management

ELMIRA COLLEGE
Elmira, New York
http://www.elmira.edu/

Elmira College was founded in 1855. It is accredited by Middle States Association of Colleges and Schools. It first offered distance learning courses in 2000. In fall 2010, there were 120 students enrolled in distance learning courses. Institutionally administered financial aid is available to distance learners.
Services Distance learners have accessibility to academic advising, bookstore, campus computer network, e-mail services, library services.
Contact Dean Elizabeth A. Lambert, Dean of Continuing Education and Graduate Studies, Elmira College, One Park Place, Elmira, NY 14901. Telephone: 607-735-1825. Fax: 607-735-1150. E-mail: elambert@elmira.edu.

DEGREES AND AWARDS
Programs offered do not lead to a degree or other formal award.

COURSE SUBJECT AREAS OFFERED OUTSIDE OF DEGREE PROGRAMS
Undergraduate—biology; management information systems; philosophy and religious studies.

Graduate—biology; business, management, and marketing related; business/managerial economics; education; education related; health and medical administrative services; homeland security; management information systems; psychology.

EMORY UNIVERSITY
Atlanta, Georgia
Rollins School of Public Health
http://www.sph.emory.edu/cmph

Emory University was founded in 1836. It is accredited by Southern Association of Colleges and Schools. It first offered distance learning courses in 1997. In fall 2010, there were 134 students enrolled in distance learning courses. Institutionally administered financial aid is available to distance learners.

Services Distance learners have accessibility to academic advising, bookstore, campus computer network, career placement assistance, e-mail services, library services.

Contact Mrs. Melissa Krancer, Associate Director of Academic Programs, Emory University, 1518 Clifton Road, RSPH, Atlanta, GA 30322. Telephone: 404-727-9489. Fax: 404-727-9853. E-mail: mkrance@emory.edu.

DEGREES AND AWARDS

MPH Applied Epidemiology; Applied Public Health Informatics; Healthcare Outcomes; Prevention Science

COURSE SUBJECT AREAS OFFERED OUTSIDE OF DEGREE PROGRAMS

Graduate—behavioral sciences; public health.

EMPORIA STATE UNIVERSITY
Emporia, Kansas
Office of Lifelong Learning
http://emporia.edu/distance

Emporia State University was founded in 1863. It is accredited by North Central Association of Colleges and Schools. It first offered distance learning courses in 1970. In fall 2010, there were 2,263 students enrolled in distance learning courses. Institutionally administered financial aid is available to distance learners.

Services Distance learners have accessibility to academic advising, bookstore, campus computer network, career placement assistance, e-mail services, library services.

Contact Jan Farwell, Assistant Director, Distance Education, Emporia State University, 8400 West 110th Street, Suite 150, Overland Park, KS 66210. Telephone: 913-338-4378. Fax: 913-338-1434. E-mail: jfarwell@emporia.edu.

DEGREES AND AWARDS

BEd Elementary Education
BGS Integrated Studies
BS Information Resource Studies
BSBA Business
MA Teaching English to Speakers of Other Languages
MBE Business Education
MLS Library and Information Science
MS Curriculum and Instruction; Educational Administration; Instructional Design and Technology; Physical Education; Physical Sciences (Earth Science emphasis); School Counseling (K-12); Special Education (Adaptive)
MSE Early Childhood Education; Master Teacher Elementary

ENDICOTT COLLEGE
Beverly, Massachusetts
http://www.endicott.edu/gps

Endicott College was founded in 1939. It is accredited by New England Association of Schools and Colleges. It first offered distance learning courses in 2003. In fall 2010, there were 333 students enrolled in distance learning courses. Institutionally administered financial aid is available to distance learners.

Services Distance learners have accessibility to academic advising, bookstore, campus computer network, career placement assistance, e-mail services, library services, tutoring.

Contact Dr. Mary Huegel, Dean of School of Graduate and Professional Studies, Endicott College, 376 Hale Street, Beverly, MA 01915. Telephone: 978-232-2084. Fax: 978-232-3000. E-mail: mhuegel@endicott.edu.

DEGREES AND AWARDS

MBA Business Administration
MEd Athletic Administration; Integrative Learning; Montessori Integrative Learning

COURSE SUBJECT AREAS OFFERED OUTSIDE OF DEGREE PROGRAMS

Undergraduate—business administration, management and operations; business/commerce; business, management, and marketing related; economics; education; English; geography and cartography; human development, family studies, and related services; industrial production technologies; management information systems; management sciences and quantitative methods; natural sciences; nutrition sciences; psychology; social sciences.
Graduate—behavioral sciences; business/commerce; computer and information sciences; education.
Non-credit—business/commerce.

ENTERPRISE STATE COMMUNITY COLLEGE
Enterprise, Alabama
http://www.escc.edu

Enterprise State Community College was founded in 1965. It is accredited by Southern Association of Colleges and Schools. It first offered distance learning courses in 2000. In fall 2010, there were 390 students enrolled in distance learning courses. Institutionally administered financial aid is available to distance learners.

Services Distance learners have accessibility to academic advising, bookstore, campus computer network, career placement assistance, e-mail services, library services, tutoring.

Contact Dr. Jean A. Johnson, Distance Learning Coordinator, Enterprise State Community College, PO Box 1300, Enterprise, AL 36331. Telephone: 334-347-2623 Ext. 2316. E-mail: jjohnson@escc.edu.

DEGREES AND AWARDS

Programs offered do not lead to a degree or other formal award.

COURSE SUBJECT AREAS OFFERED OUTSIDE OF DEGREE PROGRAMS

Undergraduate—accounting and computer science; accounting and related services; applied mathematics; business, management, and marketing related; communication and media; computer and information sciences; computer and information sciences and support services related; computer science; computer software and media applications; data entry/microcomputer applications; economics; English; history; liberal arts and sciences, general studies and humanities; music; physical sciences; psychology; psychology related; sociology; visual and performing arts related.

ERIE COMMUNITY COLLEGE
Buffalo, New York
http://www.ecc.edu/

Erie Community College was founded in 1971. It is accredited by Middle States Association of Colleges and Schools. It first offered distance learning courses in 1992. In fall 2010, there were 795 students enrolled in distance learning courses. Institutionally administered financial aid is available to distance learners.

Services Distance learners have accessibility to academic advising, bookstore, campus computer network, career placement assistance, e-mail services, library services, tutoring.

Contact Ms. Martha Dixon, Director, Distance Learning, Erie Community College, 4041 Southwestern Boulevard, Orchard Park, NY 14127. Telephone: 716-851-1939. Fax: 716-270-2859. E-mail: dixon@ecc.edu.

DEGREES AND AWARDS

AA Liberal Arts and Science/Humanities and Social Science

AAS Business–Business Administration; Business–Office Management; Criminal Justice–Law Enforcement; Telecommunications Technology–Verizon
AS Business–Business Administration (transfer option); Criminal Justice; Liberal Arts and Science–General Studies; Physical Education Studies
Certificate Computer Applications for the Office; GIS Software Application Specialist; Homeland Security

COURSE SUBJECT AREAS OFFERED OUTSIDE OF DEGREE PROGRAMS

Undergraduate—accounting and related services; allied health diagnostic, intervention, and treatment professions; anthropology; archeology; biological and biomedical sciences related; business operations support and assistant services; chemistry; clinical/medical laboratory science/research; computer/information technology administration and management; computer science; computer software and media applications; computer systems analysis; criminal justice and corrections; culinary arts and related services; data entry/microcomputer applications; dietetics and clinical nutrition services; drama/theatre arts and stagecraft; economics; education; education related; education (specific subject areas); English; English language and literature related; finance and financial management services; fine and studio arts; fire protection; geography and cartography; health and medical administrative services; health and physical education/fitness; history; hospitality administration; human resources management; international relations and national security studies; journalism; languages (Romance languages); legal professions and studies related; liberal arts and sciences, general studies and humanities; marketing; mathematics; music; natural resources conservation and research; nutrition sciences; philosophy; physiology, pathology and related sciences; political science and government; psychology; registered nursing, nursing administration, nursing research and clinical nursing; religious studies; social sciences related; sociology; statistics.

ERIE COMMUNITY COLLEGE, NORTH CAMPUS
Williamsville, New York
http://www.ecc.edu/

Erie Community College, North Campus was founded in 1946. It is accredited by Middle States Association of Colleges and Schools. It first offered distance learning courses in 1990. In fall 2010, there were 1,692 students enrolled in distance learning courses. Institutionally administered financial aid is available to distance learners.
Services Distance learners have accessibility to academic advising, bookstore, campus computer network, career placement assistance, e-mail services, library services, tutoring.
Contact Ms. Martha Dixon, Director, Distance Learning, Erie Community College, North Campus, 4041 Southwestern Boulevard, Orchard Park, NY 14127. Telephone: 716-851-1939. Fax: 716-270-2859. E-mail: dixon@ecc.edu.

DEGREES AND AWARDS

AA Liberal Arts and Science/Humanities and Social Science
AAS Business–Business Administration; Business–Office Management; Criminal Justice–Law Enforcement; Telecommunications Technology–Verizon
AS Business–Business Administration (transfer option); Criminal Justice; Liberal Arts and Science–General Studies; Physical Education Studies
Certificate Computer Applications for the Office; GIS Software Application Specialist; Homeland Security

COURSE SUBJECT AREAS OFFERED OUTSIDE OF DEGREE PROGRAMS

Undergraduate—accounting and related services; allied health diagnostic, intervention, and treatment professions; anthropology; archeology; biological and biomedical sciences related; business operations support and assistant services; chemistry; clinical/medical laboratory science/research; computer/information technology administration and management; computer science; computer software and media applications; computer systems analysis; criminal justice and corrections; culinary arts and related services; data entry/microcomputer applications; dietetics and clinical nutrition services; drama/theatre arts and stagecraft; economics; education; education related; education (specific subject areas); English; English language and literature related; finance and financial management services; fine and studio arts; fire protection; geography and cartography; health and medical administrative services; health and physical education/fitness; history; hospitality administration; human resources management; international relations and national security studies; journalism; languages (Romance languages); legal professions and studies related; liberal arts and sciences, general studies and humanities; marketing; mathematics; music; natural resources conservation and research; nutrition sciences; philosophy; physiology, pathology and related sciences; political science and government; psychology; registered nursing, nursing administration, nursing research and clinical nursing; religious studies; social sciences related; sociology; statistics.

ERIE COMMUNITY COLLEGE, SOUTH CAMPUS
Orchard Park, New York
http://www.ecc.edu/

Erie Community College, South Campus was founded in 1974. It is accredited by Middle States Association of Colleges and Schools. It first offered distance learning courses in 1991. In fall 2010, there were 875 students enrolled in distance learning courses. Institutionally administered financial aid is available to distance learners.
Services Distance learners have accessibility to academic advising, bookstore, campus computer network, career placement assistance, e-mail services, library services, tutoring.
Contact Ms. Martha Dixon, Director, Distance Learning, Erie Community College, South Campus, 4041 Southwestern Boulevard, Orchard Park, NY 14127. Telephone: 716-851-1939. Fax: 716-270-2859. E-mail: dixon@ecc.edu.

DEGREES AND AWARDS

AA Liberal Arts and Science/Humanities and Social Science
AAS Business–Business Administration; Business–Office Management; Criminal Justice–Law Enforcement; Telecommunications Technology–Verizon
AS Business–Business Administration (transfer option); Criminal Justice; Liberal Arts and Science–General Studies; Physical Education Studies
Certificate Computer Applications for the Office; GIS Software Application Specialist; Homeland Security

COURSE SUBJECT AREAS OFFERED OUTSIDE OF DEGREE PROGRAMS

Undergraduate—accounting and related services; allied health diagnostic, intervention, and treatment professions; anthropology; archeology; biological and biomedical sciences related; business operations support and assistant services; chemistry; clinical/medical laboratory science/research; computer/information technology administration and management; computer science; computer software and media applications; computer systems analysis; criminal justice and corrections; culinary arts and related services; data entry/microcomputer applications; dietetics and clinical nutrition services; drama/theatre arts and stagecraft; economics; education; education related; education (specific subject areas); English; English language and literature related; finance and financial management services; fine and studio arts; fire protection; geography and cartography; health and medical administrative services; health and physical education/fitness; history; hospitality administration; human resources management; international relations and national security studies; journalism; languages (Romance languages); legal professions and studies related; liberal arts and sciences, general studies and humanities; marketing; mathematics; music; natural resources conservation and research; nutrition sciences; philosophy; physiology, pathology and related sciences; political science and government; psychology; registered nursing, nursing administration, nursing research and clinical nursing; religious studies; social sciences related; sociology; statistics.

ERIKSON INSTITUTE

Chicago, Illinois

http://www.erikson.edu/default/academics/onlineofferings.aspx

Erikson Institute was founded in 1966. It is accredited by North Central Association of Colleges and Schools. It first offered distance learning courses in 2001. In fall 2010, there were 40 students enrolled in distance learning courses. Institutionally administered financial aid is available to distance learners.

Services Distance learners have accessibility to academic advising, bookstore, campus computer network, career placement assistance, e-mail services, library services, tutoring.

Contact Ms. Valerie Williams, Associate Director, Admission and Multicultural Student Affairs, Erikson Institute, 451 North LaSalle Street, Chicago, IL 60654-4510. Telephone: 312-893-7142. Fax: 312-755-1672. E-mail: vwilliams@erikson.edu.

DEGREES AND AWARDS

MS Early Childhood Education

COURSE SUBJECT AREAS OFFERED OUTSIDE OF DEGREE PROGRAMS

Graduate—family and consumer sciences/human sciences.
Non-credit—family and consumer sciences/human sciences.

EVEREST UNIVERSITY

Melbourne, Florida

http://www.cci.edu

Everest University was founded in 1953. It is accredited by Accrediting Council for Independent Colleges and Schools. It first offered distance learning courses in 1999. In fall 2010, there were 150 students enrolled in distance learning courses. Institutionally administered financial aid is available to distance learners.

Services Distance learners have accessibility to academic advising, bookstore, campus computer network, career placement assistance, library services, tutoring.

Contact Mrs. Alicia Ellegood, Online Learning Coordinator, Everest University, 2401 North Harbor City Boulevard, Melbourne, FL 32935. Telephone: 321-253-2929 Ext. 166. Fax: 321-255-2017. E-mail: aellegoo@cci.edu.

DEGREES AND AWARDS

AS Business Administration

EXCELSIOR COLLEGE

Albany, New York

Learning Services

http://www.excelsior.edu

Excelsior College was founded in 1970. It is accredited by Middle States Association of Colleges and Schools. It first offered distance learning courses in 1971. In fall 2010, there were 29,939 students enrolled in distance learning courses. Institutionally administered financial aid is available to distance learners.

Services Distance learners have accessibility to academic advising, bookstore, career placement assistance, library services, tutoring.

Contact Annette Jeffes, Assistant Vice President and Director of Admissions, Excelsior College, 7 Columbia Circle, Albany, NY 12203. Telephone: 518-464-8500. Fax: 518-464-8777. E-mail: ajeffes@excelsior.edu.

DEGREES AND AWARDS

AA Liberal Arts
AAS Administrative/Management Studies; Nursing; Technical Studies
AS Business; Computer Software; Electronics Technology; Nuclear Engineering Technology; Nursing; Science; Technology
BA Liberal Arts; Liberal Studies
BS Accounting; Accounting, NYS CPA track; Business, general; Criminal Justice; Electrical Engineering Technology; Finance; Global Business; Health Sciences; Hotel, Restaurant and Tourism Management; Information Technology; Management Information Systems; Management of Human Resources; Marketing; Nuclear Engineering Technology; Operations Management; Risk Management and Insurance; Science
BSN Nursing
BST Technology
MA Liberal Studies
MBA Business
MS Nursing

COURSE SUBJECT AREAS OFFERED OUTSIDE OF DEGREE PROGRAMS

Undergraduate—accounting and computer science; behavioral sciences; biology; business administration, management and operations; business, management, and marketing related; computer and information sciences; computer software and media applications; criminal justice and corrections; English; health/medical preparatory programs; history; international/global studies; liberal arts and sciences, general studies and humanities; management information systems; mathematics; nuclear engineering technologies; psychology.
Graduate—business administration, management and operations; health/medical preparatory programs; liberal arts and sciences, general studies and humanities.

FAULKNER UNIVERSITY

Montgomery, Alabama

http://www.faulkner.edu

Faulkner University was founded in 1942. It is accredited by Southern Association of Colleges and Schools. It first offered distance learning courses in 1996. In fall 2010, there were 64 students enrolled in distance learning courses. Institutionally administered financial aid is available to distance learners.

Services Distance learners have accessibility to academic advising, bookstore, campus computer network, career placement assistance, e-mail services, library services.

Contact Dr. Marci M. Johns, Professor of Legal Studies and Criminal Justice, Faulkner University, 5345 Atlanta Highway, Montgomery, AL 36109-3398. Telephone: 334-386-7304. Fax: 334-386-7281. E-mail: mjohns@faulkner.edu.

DEGREES AND AWARDS

MC Counseling
MH Master of Letters
MS Justice Administration (Master of Justice Administration)

COURSE SUBJECT AREAS OFFERED OUTSIDE OF DEGREE PROGRAMS

Undergraduate—biblical studies; computer and information sciences; cultural studies/critical theory and analysis; English; history; information science/studies; liberal arts and sciences, general studies and humanities; psychology.
Graduate—criminal justice and corrections; liberal arts and sciences, general studies and humanities; psychology related.

FAYETTEVILLE STATE UNIVERSITY

Fayetteville, North Carolina

http://www.uncfsu.edu/onlineeducation

Fayetteville State University was founded in 1867. It is accredited by Southern Association of Colleges and Schools. It first offered distance learning courses in 1999. In fall 2010, there were 2,000 students enrolled in distance learning courses. Institutionally administered financial aid is available to distance learners.

Services Distance learners have accessibility to academic advising, bookstore, campus computer network, career placement assistance, e-mail services, library services, tutoring.

Contact Mr. Wes Brown, Online Advisor, Fayetteville State University, Continuing Education Building, 1200 Murchison Road, Fayetteville, NC 28301. Telephone: 910-672-2571. Fax: 910-672-1491. E-mail: wkbrown01@uncfsu.edu.

DEGREES AND AWARDS

Programs offered do not lead to a degree or other formal award.

COURSE SUBJECT AREAS OFFERED OUTSIDE OF DEGREE PROGRAMS

Undergraduate—business/commerce; computer science; criminal justice and corrections; education (specific levels and methods); psychology; sociology; special education.

Graduate—business administration, management and operations; criminal justice and corrections; education; history; social work; special education.

FERRIS STATE UNIVERSITY

Big Rapids, Michigan

http://www.ferris.edu/online

Ferris State University was founded in 1884. It is accredited by North Central Association of Colleges and Schools. It first offered distance learning courses in 1991. In fall 2010, there were 2,749 students enrolled in distance learning courses. Institutionally administered financial aid is available to distance learners.

Services Distance learners have accessibility to academic advising, bookstore, campus computer network, career placement assistance, e-mail services, library services.

Contact Cheryl Cluchey, Assistant Dean, Ferris State University, 410 Oak Street, Alumni 113, Big Rapids, MI 49307. Telephone: 231-591-3811. Fax: 231-591-3539. E-mail: clucheyc@ferris.edu.

DEGREES AND AWARDS

BS Allied Health Sciences; Dental Hygiene; HVACR Engineering Technology; Nuclear Medicine Technology
BSN Nursing
MBA Business Administration
MS Nursing

COURSE SUBJECT AREAS OFFERED OUTSIDE OF DEGREE PROGRAMS

Undergraduate—accounting and computer science; allied health and medical assisting services; allied health diagnostic, intervention, and treatment professions; bioethics/medical ethics; biological and physical sciences; business administration, management and operations; business, management, and marketing related; business/managerial economics; communication and journalism related; computer science; criminal justice and corrections; culinary arts and related services; economics; education; English; English language and literature related; ethnic, cultural minority, gender, and group studies; finance and financial management services; geography and cartography; heating, air conditioning, ventilation and refrigeration maintenance technology; history; intercultural/multicultural and diversity studies; languages (foreign languages related); mathematics and statistics related; nuclear and industrial radiologic technologies; physics; political science and government; social sciences related; statistics.

Graduate—business administration, management and operations; computer/information technology administration and management; education; educational administration and supervision; ophthalmic and optometric support services and allied professions; registered nursing, nursing administration, nursing research and clinical nursing.

FIELDING GRADUATE UNIVERSITY

Santa Barbara, California

http://www.fielding.edu/

Fielding Graduate University was founded in 1974. It is accredited by Western Association of Schools and Colleges. It first offered distance learning courses in 1974. In fall 2010, there were 1,541 students enrolled in distance learning courses. Institutionally administered financial aid is available to distance learners.

Services Distance learners have accessibility to academic advising, bookstore, e-mail services, library services.

Contact Kathy Belway, Admissions Assistant, Fielding Graduate University, 2112 Santa Barbara Street, Santa Barbara, CA 93105-3538. Telephone: 800-340-1099. Fax: 805-687-9793. E-mail: admission@fielding.edu.

DEGREES AND AWARDS

Certificate Clinical Psychology respecialization; Evidence-Based Coaching; Integral Studies; Organization Management and Development; Teaching in the Virtual Classroom
Graduate Certificate Sustainability Leadership
MA Media Psychology and Social Change; Organization Management and Development
EdD Educational Leadership and Change
PhD Clinical Psychology; Human and Organizational Development; Media Psychology

COURSE SUBJECT AREAS OFFERED OUTSIDE OF DEGREE PROGRAMS

Graduate—business administration, management and operations; education; human development, family studies, and related services; psychology.

FINGER LAKES COMMUNITY COLLEGE

Canandaigua, New York

http://www.flcc.edu

Finger Lakes Community College was founded in 1965. It is accredited by Middle States Association of Colleges and Schools. It first offered distance learning courses in 1995. In fall 2010, there were 1,133 students enrolled in distance learning courses. Institutionally administered financial aid is available to distance learners.

Services Distance learners have accessibility to academic advising, bookstore, campus computer network, career placement assistance, e-mail services, library services, tutoring.

Contact Ms. Bonnie Ritts, Director of Admissions, Finger Lakes Community College, 3325 Marvin Sands Drive, Canandaigua, NY 14424. Telephone: 585-394-3500 Ext. 7278. Fax: 585-394-5005. E-mail: admissions@flcc.edu.

DEGREES AND AWARDS

AA Liberal Arts and Sciences
AAS Business Administration; Electronic Commerce; Tourism Management
AS Business Administration; Sports and Tourism

COURSE SUBJECT AREAS OFFERED OUTSIDE OF DEGREE PROGRAMS

Undergraduate—accounting and computer science; biology; business/commerce; business/corporate communications; communication and journalism related; computer and information sciences; computer/information technology administration and management; computer programming; criminal justice and corrections; economics; education; health and physical education/fitness; history; languages (Romance languages); legal studies (non-professional general, undergraduate); liberal arts and sciences, general studies and humanities; marketing; mathematics and statistics related; nutrition sciences; philosophy; physics; psychology; sales, merchandising and related marketing operations (specialized); sociology.

Non-credit—computer software and media applications.

FITCHBURG STATE UNIVERSITY

Fitchburg, Massachusetts

Division of Graduate and Continuing Education

http://www.fitchburgstate.edu/

Fitchburg State University was founded in 1894. It is accredited by New England Association of Schools and Colleges. It first offered distance learning courses in 1989. In fall 2010, there were 1,200 students enrolled in distance learning courses. Institutionally administered financial aid is available to distance learners.

Services Distance learners have accessibility to academic advising, bookstore, campus computer network, career placement assistance, e-mail services, library services, tutoring.

Contact Michael B. Leamy, EdD, Distance Education Coordinator, Fitchburg State University, 160 Pearl Street, Fitchburg, MA 01420. Telephone: 978-665-4783. Fax: 978-665-3658. E-mail: mleamy1@fitchburgstate.edu.

DEGREES AND AWARDS
MBA Business Administration
MEd Elementary Education; Secondary Education
MSN Nursing–Master of Science in Forensic Nursing

COURSE SUBJECT AREAS OFFERED OUTSIDE OF DEGREE PROGRAMS
Undergraduate—accounting and computer science; behavioral sciences; biological and physical sciences; business administration, management and operations; communication and media; computer science; education; education related; English; human resources management; industrial production technologies; legal studies (non-professional general, undergraduate); mathematics; mathematics and computer science; music; social sciences; sociology; special education; statistics.
Graduate—accounting and computer science; behavioral sciences; business administration, management and operations; communication and media; computer science; education; educational administration and supervision; education related; finance and financial management services; industrial production technologies; social sciences.

FIVE TOWNS COLLEGE
Dix Hills, New York
http://www.ftc.edu

Five Towns College was founded in 1972. It is accredited by Middle States Association of Colleges and Schools. It first offered distance learning courses in 2002. In fall 2010, there were 375 students enrolled in distance learning courses. Institutionally administered financial aid is available to distance learners.
Services Distance learners have accessibility to campus computer network, e-mail services, library services.
Contact Mr. Jerry Cohen, Dean of Enrollment, Five Towns College, 305 North Service Road, Dix Hills, NY 11746. Telephone: 631-424-7000 Ext. 2121. Fax: 631-656-2172. E-mail: jcohen@ftc.edu.

DEGREES AND AWARDS
Programs offered do not lead to a degree or other formal award.

COURSE SUBJECT AREAS OFFERED OUTSIDE OF DEGREE PROGRAMS
Undergraduate—biology; business/commerce; business, management, and marketing related; communication and media; computer and information sciences; education; information science/studies; liberal arts and sciences, general studies and humanities; music; psychology; sociology.
Graduate—education; music.

FLORIDA HOSPITAL COLLEGE OF HEALTH SCIENCES
Orlando, Florida
Distance Learning Programs
http://www.onlinenursing.FHCHS.edu

Florida Hospital College of Health Sciences was founded in 1913. It is accredited by Southern Association of Colleges and Schools. It first offered distance learning courses in 2000. In fall 2010, there were 2,000 students enrolled in distance learning courses. Institutionally administered financial aid is available to distance learners.
Services Distance learners have accessibility to academic advising, bookstore, e-mail services, library services, tutoring.
Contact Enrollment Office, Director of Admissions, Florida Hospital College of Health Sciences, Off-Site Admissions Office, 2145 MetroCenter Boulevard, Suite 400, Orlando, FL 32835. Fax: 888-768-6276. E-mail: admissionsbsn@onlinenursing.fhchs.edu.

DEGREES AND AWARDS
BS Diagnostic Medical Sonography
BSN Nursing–RN to BSN
BSRS Radiologic Sciences

COURSE SUBJECT AREAS OFFERED OUTSIDE OF DEGREE PROGRAMS
Undergraduate—biological and biomedical sciences related; health professions related; legal studies (non-professional general, undergraduate); liberal arts and sciences, general studies and humanities; mathematics.

FLORIDA INSTITUTE OF TECHNOLOGY
Melbourne, Florida
University College–Online Learning Division–Virtual Campus
http://es.fit.edu/dl/

Florida Institute of Technology was founded in 1958. It is accredited by Southern Association of Colleges and Schools. It first offered distance learning courses in 1995. In fall 2010, there were 6,841 students enrolled in distance learning courses. Institutionally administered financial aid is available to distance learners.
Services Distance learners have accessibility to academic advising, bookstore, career placement assistance, e-mail services, library services, tutoring.
Contact Ms. Penny Vassar, Director, Virtual Campus, Florida Institute of Technology, 150 West University Boulevard, Melbourne, FL 32901. Telephone: 888-225-2239. Fax: 864-226-2258. E-mail: pvassar@fit.edu.

DEGREES AND AWARDS
MPA Public Administration
MS Acquisition and Contract Management; Computer Information Systems; Human Resources Management; Logistics Management–Humanitarian and Disaster Relief Logistics concentration; Logistics Management; Management–Acquisition and Contract Management concentration; Management–Human Resources Management concentration; Management–Information Systems concentration; Management–Logistics Management concentration; Management–Transportation Management concentration; Management–eBusiness concentration; Management; Material Acquisition Management; Operations Research; Project Management; Project Management, Information Systems concentration; Project Management, Operations Research concentration; Systems Management; Systems Management, Operations Research concentration

COURSE SUBJECT AREAS OFFERED OUTSIDE OF DEGREE PROGRAMS
Graduate—business administration, management and operations; business/commerce; human resources management; information science/studies; quality control and safety technologies; systems science and theory; transportation and materials moving related.
Non-credit—behavioral sciences; psychology related.

FLORIDA STATE UNIVERSITY
Tallahassee, Florida
Academic and Professional Program Services
http://distance.fsu.edu

Florida State University was founded in 1851. It is accredited by Southern Association of Colleges and Schools. It first offered distance learning courses in 1987. In fall 2010, there were 4,000 students enrolled in distance learning courses. Institutionally administered financial aid is available to distance learners.
Services Distance learners have accessibility to academic advising, bookstore, campus computer network, career placement assistance, e-mail services, library services.
Contact Lea Ann Gates, Assistant Director, Distance Learning Support Services, Florida State University, Office of Distance Learning, C3500 University Center, Tallahassee, FL 32306-2550. Telephone: 850-644-7536. Fax: 850-644-5803. E-mail: lselman@campus.fsu.edu.

DEGREES AND AWARDS
BS Computer Science; Criminology; Interdisciplinary Social Science; Software Engineering
Graduate Certificate Communication Disorders; Emergency Management
MBA Business Administration
MS Criminology, Criminal Justice Studies major; Educational Leadership/Administration; Higher Education; Information Studies; Instructional Systems; Instructional Systems, Open and Distance Learning major; Instructional Systems, Performance Improvement and Human Resource Development major; Management Information Systems; Risk Management/Insurance; Special Education; Speech Language Pathology; Teaching (MOST)
MSN Nurse Educator
MSW Social Work

COURSE SUBJECT AREAS OFFERED OUTSIDE OF DEGREE PROGRAMS
Undergraduate—classical and ancient studies; communication and media; criminology; economics; geography and cartography; political science and government; public administration; sociology; urban studies/affairs.
Graduate—communication disorders sciences and services; computer and information sciences; educational/instructional media design; human resources management; information science/studies; library science related; public administration; social work; special education.
Non-credit—building/construction finishing, management, and inspection; computer/information technology administration and management; computer software and media applications; finance and financial management services.

FLORIDA TECH UNIVERSITY ONLINE
Tampa, Florida
http://online.fit.edu

Florida Tech University Online first offered distance learning courses in 1995. In fall 2010, there were 6,841 students enrolled in distance learning courses. Institutionally administered financial aid is available to distance learners.
Services Distance learners have accessibility to academic advising, bookstore, career placement assistance, e-mail services, library services, tutoring.
Contact Mr. Brian Ehrlich, Director, Online Program Administration, Florida Tech University Online, 150 West University Boulevard, Melbourne, FL 32901. Telephone: 321-422-5137. Fax: 321-574-1498. E-mail: behrlich@fit.edu.

DEGREES AND AWARDS
AA Accounting; Applied Psychology; Business Administration; Criminal Justice; Healthcare Management; Liberal Arts; Marketing
AS Computer Information Systems
BA Accounting; Applied Psychology; Applied Psychology, Child Advocacy concentration; Applied Psychology, Clinical Psychology concentration; Applied Psychology, Forensic Psychology concentration; Applied Psychology, Human Factors concentration; Applied Psychology, Organizational Psychology concentration; Business Administration, Accounting concentration; Business Administration, Computer Information Systems concentration; Business Administration, Healthcare Management concentration; Business Administration, Management concentration; Business Administration, Marketing concentration; Criminal Justice
BS Computer Information Systems
MBA Accounting; Business Administration; Business Administration, Accounting and Finance concentration; Business Administration, Healthcare Management concentration; Business Administration, Information Technology Management concentration; Business Administration, Management concentration; Business Administration, Marketing concentration; Business Administration, Project Management concentration; Finance; Internet Marketing
MSIT Information Technology

FONTBONNE UNIVERSITY
St. Louis, Missouri
http://www.fontbonne.edu/

Fontbonne University was founded in 1917. It is accredited by North Central Association of Colleges and Schools. It first offered distance learning courses in 2000. In fall 2010, there were 693 students enrolled in distance learning courses. Institutionally administered financial aid is available to distance learners.
Services Distance learners have accessibility to academic advising, bookstore, campus computer network, e-mail services, library services, tutoring.
Contact Admissions Office, Fontbonne University, 6800 Wydown Boulevard, St. Louis, MO 63105. Telephone: 314-889-1400 Ext. 5222. E-mail: online@fontbonne.edu.

DEGREES AND AWARDS
MAEd Teaching of Reading
MM Management
MS Computer Education; Supply Chain Management

COURSE SUBJECT AREAS OFFERED OUTSIDE OF DEGREE PROGRAMS
Undergraduate—business administration, management and operations; communication and media; computer and information sciences; economics; family and consumer sciences/human sciences; history; library science and administration; mathematics; mathematics and statistics related; philosophy; psychology; religious studies; sociology.
Graduate—business administration, management and operations; communication disorders sciences and services; education; family and consumer sciences/human sciences.

FORT HAYS STATE UNIVERSITY
Hays, Kansas
Virtual College
http://www.fhsu.edu/virtualcollege

Fort Hays State University was founded in 1902. It is accredited by North Central Association of Colleges and Schools. It first offered distance learning courses in 1987. In fall 2010, there were 6,965 students enrolled in distance learning courses. Institutionally administered financial aid is available to distance learners.
Services Distance learners have accessibility to academic advising, bookstore, campus computer network, career placement assistance, e-mail services, library services, tutoring.
Contact Mrs. Hayley Bieker, Virtual College Online Student Communication Strategist, Fort Hays State University, 600 Park Street, Hays, KS 67601-4099. Telephone: 785-628-4291. Fax: 785-628-4037. E-mail: hjbieker@fhsu.edu.

DEGREES AND AWARDS
AGS General Studies
BA Political Science; Sociology
BBA Management Information Systems; Management–Human Resources concentration; Management; Marketing; Tourism and Hospitality Management
BGS General Studies; Military Specialties
BS Business Education–Business Teacher Licensure; Business Education–Corporate Communication; Business Education–Training and Development; Early Childhood Unified; Education TEAM Honors; Elementary Education TEAM K-6, Special Education minor; Elementary Education; Information Networking and Telecommunications (Computer Networking and Telecommunications concentration); Information Networking and Telecommunications (Web Development concentration); Justice Studies; Medical Diagnostic Imaging; Organizational Leadership; Technology Leadership
BSN Nursing–RN to BSN
Certificate Accounting; Adult Care Home Administration; Business Information Systems; Cardiovascular Interventional Technology (CVIT); Community Development; Community Health Promotion; Community Health; Computed Tomography (CT); Consumer Health; Corrections; Customer Service; E-Commerce Web Development; Emergency Services

Leadership; Geographic Information Systems (GIS); Globalization and Culture Change; Grant Proposal Writing and Program Evaluation; Healthy Aging; Human Resource Management; International Studies; Internetworking; Justice Networking; Law Enforcement; Law and the Courts; Leadership; Life Stages and Transitions; Magnetic Resonance Imaging (MRI); Management; Marketing; Nursing–post-Masters Nursing Administration; Nursing–post-Masters Nursing Education; Operations Management; Pre-Law; Public Administration; Sociology of Medicine and Aging; Tourism and Hospitality Leadership; Tourism and Hospitality Management; Tourism and Hospitality Marketing; Victim Advocacy; Web Development; Women's Imaging; Women's and Gender Studies

Certification Addictions Counseling certification program; Computer Science–Cisco Certified Network Associate Preparation, Military; Computer Science–Cisco Certified Network Associate Preparation, accelerated

Endorsement Adaptive Special Education; Building Leadership-Principal; District Leadership-Superintendent; English Speakers of Other Languages; Gifted Education; Library Media Specialist; Reading Specialist; School Counselor

Ed S Educational Administration major

Graduate Certificate Adult Care Home Administration; Business; Business, Advanced; Human Resource Management; Management Information Systems; Organizational Leadership; Tourism and Hospitality Leadership (Graduate/Industry)

MBA Leadership

MLS Liberal Studies

MS Counseling; Education; Educational Administration; Health and Human Performance; Instructional Technology; Special Education

MSN Nursing Administration; Nursing Education; Nursing–Family Nurse Practitioner track

PSM Health Care Administration; Health Care Administration

COURSE SUBJECT AREAS OFFERED OUTSIDE OF DEGREE PROGRAMS

Undergraduate—accounting and computer science; biological and physical sciences; business administration, management and operations; communication and journalism related; communication disorders sciences and services; computer and information sciences; criminal justice and corrections; economics; educational administration and supervision; education related; English; geological and earth sciences/geosciences; health and physical education/fitness; history; information science/studies; languages (foreign languages related); liberal arts and sciences, general studies and humanities; marketing; mathematics and computer science; multi/interdisciplinary studies related; music; philosophy; physics; political science and government; psychology; sociology; special education.

Graduate—education related; education (specific subject areas); health and physical education/fitness; liberal arts and sciences, general studies and humanities; multi/interdisciplinary studies related; special education.

Non-credit—accounting and computer science; accounting and related services; business administration, management and operations; communication and journalism related; economics; management information systems; sales merchandising, and related marketing operations (general).

FORT VALLEY STATE UNIVERSITY
Fort Valley, Georgia
http://www.fvsu.edu/

Fort Valley State University was founded in 1895. It is accredited by Southern Association of Colleges and Schools. It first offered distance learning courses in 1998. In fall 2010, there were 421 students enrolled in distance learning courses. Institutionally administered financial aid is available to distance learners.

Services Distance learners have accessibility to academic advising, campus computer network, e-mail services, library services.

Contact Ms. Karen Watson, Assistant Coordinator of Online Instruction, Fort Valley State University, 1005 State University Drive, Department of Mathematics and Computer Science, Fort Valley, GA 31030. Telephone: 478-825-6999. Fax: 478-825-6286. E-mail: watsonk@fvsu.edu.

DEGREES AND AWARDS

BA Criminal Justice; English, Technical and Professional Writing concentration; Political Science; Psychology

MS Rehabilitation Counseling and Case Management

COURSE SUBJECT AREAS OFFERED OUTSIDE OF DEGREE PROGRAMS

Undergraduate—accounting and computer science; accounting and related services; agricultural and food products processing; agricultural business and management; agricultural engineering; animal sciences; behavioral sciences; biology; business, management, and marketing related; business/managerial economics; chemistry; communication and media; computer and information sciences; computer science; criminal justice and corrections; curriculum and instruction; drama/theatre arts and stagecraft; electrical engineering technologies; health and physical education/fitness; history; international relations and national security studies; languages (foreign languages related); liberal arts and sciences, general studies and humanities; marketing; mathematics; political science and government; psychology; social work; sociology.

Graduate—animal sciences; biotechnology; environmental/environmental health engineering; mental and social health services and allied professions; rehabilitation and therapeutic professions.

Non-credit—education related.

FRAMINGHAM STATE UNIVERSITY
Framingham, Massachusetts
Division of Academic Technology and Distance Learning
http://www.framingham.edu/online-learning/index.html

Framingham State University was founded in 1839. It is accredited by New England Association of Schools and Colleges. It first offered distance learning courses in 1998. In fall 2010, there were 1,604 students enrolled in distance learning courses. Institutionally administered financial aid is available to distance learners.

Services Distance learners have accessibility to academic advising, bookstore, campus computer network, career placement assistance, e-mail services, library services, tutoring.

Contact Ms. Robin Robinson, Director, Education Technology and Support, Framingham State University, 100 State Street, PO Box 9101, Framingham, MA 01701-9101. Telephone: 508-626-4688. E-mail: rrobinson@framingham.edu.

DEGREES AND AWARDS

BA Liberal Studies

Graduate Certificate Instructional Technology Proficiency; Merchandising; Nutrition Education

MA Educational Leadership

MBA Business Administration (hybrid program)

MEd Curriculum and Instructional Technology; Educational Technology; Elementary Education; Nutrition Education–Nutrition Education Specialist; Nutrition Education–School Nutrition Specialist; Science, Technology, Engineering, and Math 1-6 (hybrid)

MSN Nursing Education or Leadership (hybrid program)

COURSE SUBJECT AREAS OFFERED OUTSIDE OF DEGREE PROGRAMS

Undergraduate—anthropology; biology; business administration, management and operations; communication and media; computer science; economics; English; foods, nutrition, and related services; geological and earth sciences/geosciences; history; mathematics; music; philosophy; political science and government; psychology; sociology.

Graduate—business administration, management and operations; business, management, and marketing related; education; education (specific subject areas); finance and financial management services; foods, nutrition, and related services; special education.

FRANCISCAN UNIVERSITY OF STEUBENVILLE
Steubenville, Ohio
Distance Learning
http://www.franciscan.edu/distancelearning

Franciscan University of Steubenville was founded in 1946. It is accredited by North Central Association of Colleges and Schools. It first offered distance learning courses in 1995. In fall 2010, there were 350 students enrolled in distance learning courses. Institutionally administered financial aid is available to distance learners.

Services Distance learners have accessibility to academic advising, bookstore, e-mail services, library services.

Contact Ms. Virginia Garrison, Coordinator, Franciscan University of Steubenville, Distance Learning, 1235 University Boulevard, Steubenville, OH 43952. Telephone: 800-466-8336. Fax: 740-284-7037. E-mail: distance@franciscan.edu.

DEGREES AND AWARDS

MA Theology
MS Ed Teaching Online concentration

COURSE SUBJECT AREAS OFFERED OUTSIDE OF DEGREE PROGRAMS

Undergraduate—philosophy; theological and ministerial studies.
Graduate—education; educational/instructional media design; theological and ministerial studies.
Non-credit—philosophy; theological and ministerial studies.

FRANKLIN PIERCE UNIVERSITY
Rindge, New Hampshire
http://www.franklinpierce.edu/academics/online/index.htm

Franklin Pierce University was founded in 1962. It is accredited by New England Association of Schools and Colleges. It first offered distance learning courses in 2004. In fall 2010, there were 295 students enrolled in distance learning courses. Institutionally administered financial aid is available to distance learners.

Services Distance learners have accessibility to academic advising, bookstore, campus computer network, career placement assistance, e-mail services, library services, tutoring.

Contact Dr. John Ragsdale, Jr., Franklin Pierce University Online Programs, Franklin Pierce University, 670 North Commercial Street, Manchester, NH 03101. Telephone: 603-626-4972. E-mail: ragsdalej@franklinpierce.edu.

DEGREES AND AWARDS

AA Criminal Justice; General Studies; Human Services; Management; Marketing
BA American Studies; Criminal Justice
BA/BS Integrated Studies
BS General Studies; Management; Marketing
Certificate Accounting; Human Services; Management; Marketing; Paralegal
Graduate Certificate Emerging Network Technologies; Health Practice Management; Human Resource Management
MBA Energy and Sustainability Studies; Energy and Sustainability Studies; Energy and Sustainability Studies; Health Administration; Human Resource Management; Leadership; Sports Management; Sports Management
MEd Curriculum and Instruction (optional Literacy focus); Elementary Education (K-8) degree and certification; General Special Education with Emotional/Behavioral Disabilities (K-12); General Special Education with Learning Disabilities (K-12); Middle/Secondary Education in Biology (7-12), English (5-12), or Social Studies (5-12)
MS Information Technology Management

COURSE SUBJECT AREAS OFFERED OUTSIDE OF DEGREE PROGRAMS

Undergraduate—accounting and related services; behavioral sciences; business administration, management and operations; business/managerial economics; communication and media; computer and information sciences; criminal justice and corrections; economics; homeland security, law enforcement, firefighting and protective services related; human services; marketing; mathematics; mathematics and statistics related; psychology; social sciences related.

Graduate—accounting and computer science; allied health and medical assisting services; business administration, management and operations; business/managerial economics; communication disorders sciences and services; communications technology; computer and information sciences; computer/information technology administration and management; computer systems networking and telecommunications; education; education (specific levels and methods); education (specific subject areas); health and medical administrative services; health professions related; health services/allied health/health sciences; human resources management; information science/studies; management sciences and quantitative methods; marketing; mathematics and statistics related; natural resources and conservation related; natural resources management and policy; natural sciences; parks, recreation and leisure facilities management; psychology related; public administration and social service professions related; public relations, advertising, and applied communication related; social sciences related; statistics.

FREED-HARDEMAN UNIVERSITY
Henderson, Tennessee
http://www.fhu.edu/

Freed-Hardeman University was founded in 1869. It is accredited by Southern Association of Colleges and Schools. It first offered distance learning courses in 2005. Institutionally administered financial aid is available to distance learners.

Services Distance learners have accessibility to academic advising, campus computer network, e-mail services, library services.

Contact Dr. C.J. Vires, Vice President for Academics, Freed-Hardeman University, 158 East Main Street, Henderson, TN 38340. Telephone: 731-989-6004. E-mail: cvires@fhu.edu.

DEGREES AND AWARDS

MBA Business Administration

COURSE SUBJECT AREAS OFFERED OUTSIDE OF DEGREE PROGRAMS

Graduate—biblical studies.

FREE WILL BAPTIST BIBLE COLLEGE
Nashville, Tennessee
http://online.fwbbc.edu

Free Will Baptist Bible College was founded in 1942. It is accredited by Association for Biblical Higher Education. It first offered distance learning courses in 1998. In fall 2010, there were 55 students enrolled in distance learning courses. Institutionally administered financial aid is available to distance learners.

Services Distance learners have accessibility to academic advising, bookstore, career placement assistance, e-mail services, library services.

Contact Mrs. Jena Simpson, Online Learning/Adult Studies, Free Will Baptist Bible College, 3606 West End Avenue, Nashville, TN 37205. Telephone: 615-844-5226. E-mail: jenasimpson@fwbbc.edu.

DEGREES AND AWARDS

AS Ministry

COURSE SUBJECT AREAS OFFERED OUTSIDE OF DEGREE PROGRAMS

Undergraduate—biblical studies; religious studies; theological and ministerial studies; theology and religious vocations related.
Non-credit—biblical studies; religious studies; theological and ministerial studies; theology and religious vocations related.

FRIENDS UNIVERSITY
Wichita, Kansas
http://learnonline.friends.edu

Friends University was founded in 1898. It is accredited by North Central Association of Colleges and Schools. It first offered distance learning courses in 2005. In fall 2010, there were 303 students enrolled in distance learning courses. Institutionally administered financial aid is available to distance learners.

Services Distance learners have accessibility to academic advising, bookstore, campus computer network, career placement assistance, e-mail services, library services, tutoring.

Contact Ms. Jeanette Hanson, Executive Director, Adult Recruitment, Friends University, 2100 West University Avenue, Wichita, KS 67213. Telephone: 316-295-5485. Fax: 316-295-5050. E-mail: jeanette@friends.edu.

DEGREES AND AWARDS
BBA Business Management
BS Computer Information Systems; Organization Management and Leadership
MAT Teaching
MBA Business Administration
MMIS Management Information Systems

COURSE SUBJECT AREAS OFFERED OUTSIDE OF DEGREE PROGRAMS
Undergraduate—applied mathematics; biology; communication and media; computer science; economics; English; English language and literature related; fine and studio arts; history; mathematics; philosophy; political science and government; psychology; religious studies; sociology.

FRONT RANGE COMMUNITY COLLEGE
Westminster, Colorado
Distance Learning Office
http://frontrange.edu/online

Front Range Community College was founded in 1968. It is accredited by North Central Association of Colleges and Schools. It first offered distance learning courses in 1986. In fall 2010, there were 4,288 students enrolled in distance learning courses. Institutionally administered financial aid is available to distance learners.

Services Distance learners have accessibility to academic advising, bookstore, campus computer network, e-mail services, library services, tutoring.

Contact Kae Novak, Online Student Success Coordinator, Front Range Community College, 3645 West 112th Avenue, Westminster, CO 80031. Telephone: 303-404-5470. Fax: 303-404-5156. E-mail: karen.novak@frontrange.edu.

DEGREES AND AWARDS
AAS Accounting; Business; Computer Information Systems
Certificate Accounting; Management Basics; Marketing Basics; Programming; Web Authoring

COURSE SUBJECT AREAS OFFERED OUTSIDE OF DEGREE PROGRAMS
Undergraduate—accounting and related services; allied health and medical assisting services; alternative and complementary medicine and medical systems; anthropology; biological and physical sciences; biology; business administration, management and operations; business, management, and marketing related; business operations support and assistant services; chemistry; classical and ancient studies; communication and journalism related; communication and media; computer and information sciences; computer programming; computer science; computer software and media applications; criminal justice and corrections; criminology; data entry/microcomputer applications; data processing; economics; education; English; entrepreneurial and small business operations; geography and cartography; graphic communications; health professions related; history; hospitality administration; human development, family studies, and related services; human resources management; journalism; languages (Romance languages); legal professions and studies related; marketing; mathematics; mathematics and statistics related; music; nutrition sciences; pharmacology and toxicology; philosophy; philosophy and religious studies related; physics; psychology; religious studies; sociology; statistics.

FROSTBURG STATE UNIVERSITY
Frostburg, Maryland
http://www.frostburg.edu/

Frostburg State University was founded in 1898. It is accredited by Middle States Association of Colleges and Schools. It first offered distance learning courses in 1995. In fall 2010, there were 1,488 students enrolled in distance learning courses. Institutionally administered financial aid is available to distance learners.

Services Distance learners have accessibility to academic advising, bookstore, campus computer network, career placement assistance, e-mail services, library services.

Contact Brian Wilson, Distance Learning Specialist, Frostburg State University, Academic Computing & Instructional Technologies, Pullen Hall, Frostburg, MD 21532. Telephone: 301-687-3188. E-mail: bwilson@frostburg.edu.

DEGREES AND AWARDS
BSN Nursing
MBA Management
MS Park and Recreation Resource Management

COURSE SUBJECT AREAS OFFERED OUTSIDE OF DEGREE PROGRAMS
Undergraduate—accounting and related services; computer and information sciences; criminal justice and corrections; electrical, electronics and communications engineering; engineering; English; history; mathematics; mechanical engineering; music; physical sciences; political science and government; psychology; sociology.

Graduate—business administration, management and operations; curriculum and instruction; educational administration and supervision; educational assessment, evaluation, and research; marketing; psychology.

FULLER THEOLOGICAL SEMINARY
Pasadena, California
http://fuller.edu/fulleronline/

Fuller Theological Seminary was founded in 1947. It is accredited by Western Association of Schools and Colleges. It first offered distance learning courses in 1995. In fall 2010, there were 675 students enrolled in distance learning courses. Institutionally administered financial aid is available to distance learners.

Services Distance learners have accessibility to academic advising, bookstore, e-mail services, library services, tutoring.

Contact Dr. Kevin Osborn, Executive Director of Distributed Learning, Fuller Theological Seminary, 135 North Oakland Avenue, Pasadena, CA 91182. Telephone: 626-584-5262. Fax: 626-304-3740. E-mail: osborn@fuller.edu.

DEGREES AND AWARDS
MA Global Leadership

COURSE SUBJECT AREAS OFFERED OUTSIDE OF DEGREE PROGRAMS
Graduate—missionary studies and missiology; psychology; religious studies; social sciences related; theology and religious vocations related.

Non-credit—missionary studies and missiology; religious studies; social sciences; theological and ministerial studies.

GADSDEN STATE COMMUNITY COLLEGE

Gadsden, Alabama
Distance Learning
http://www.gadsdenstate.edu/academics/elearning/index.php

Gadsden State Community College was founded in 1965. It is accredited by Southern Association of Colleges and Schools. It first offered distance learning courses in 1978. In fall 2010, there were 1,900 students enrolled in distance learning courses. Institutionally administered financial aid is available to distance learners.

Services Distance learners have accessibility to academic advising, bookstore, campus computer network, career placement assistance, e-mail services, library services.

Contact Ms. Sara W. Brenizer, Associate Dean, Distance Learning, Gadsden State Community College, PO Box 227, 1001 Wallace Drive, 240 B Inzer Hall, Gadsden, AL 35902. Telephone: 256-439-6833. Fax: 256-549-8466. E-mail: sbrenizer@gadsdenstate.edu.

DEGREES AND AWARDS

AAS Child Development
AGS General Studies
AS Business Administration

COURSE SUBJECT AREAS OFFERED OUTSIDE OF DEGREE PROGRAMS

Undergraduate—accounting and computer science; biology; business administration, management and operations; business/managerial economics; chemistry; computer science; cosmetology and related personal grooming services; criminal justice and corrections; economics; education related; English; fishing and fisheries sciences and management; geological and earth sciences/geosciences; health and physical education/fitness; health services/allied health/health sciences; history; human services; mathematics; music; nutrition sciences; philosophy; political science and government; psychology; sociology.

GANNON UNIVERSITY

Erie, Pennsylvania
Center for Adult Learning
http://online.gannon.edu/online-degrees

Gannon University was founded in 1925. It is accredited by Middle States Association of Colleges and Schools. It first offered distance learning courses in 1976. In fall 2010, there were 260 students enrolled in distance learning courses. Institutionally administered financial aid is available to distance learners.

Services Distance learners have accessibility to academic advising, bookstore, campus computer network, career placement assistance, e-mail services, library services.

Contact Ms. Virginia P. Arp, Director, Center for Excellence in Teaching and Learning, Gannon University, 109 University Square, Erie, PA 16541. Telephone: 814-871-5788. E-mail: arp001@gannon.edu.

DEGREES AND AWARDS

BSN Nursing
MBA Business Administration
MPA Public Administration
MSEM Engineering Management

COURSE SUBJECT AREAS OFFERED OUTSIDE OF DEGREE PROGRAMS

Undergraduate—accounting and related services; biblical studies; biology; business/commerce; business/corporate communications; criminal justice and corrections; criminology; economics; education; educational administration and supervision; educational/instructional media design; English; finance and financial management services; foods, nutrition, and related services; history; international business; legal studies (non-professional general, undergraduate); literature; marketing; mathematics; music; philosophy; psychology; religious studies; special education; statistics.

Graduate—business/commerce; education; human resources management; international business.

GARDEN CITY COMMUNITY COLLEGE

Garden City, Kansas
http://www.gcccks.edu

Garden City Community College was founded in 1919. It is accredited by North Central Association of Colleges and Schools. It first offered distance learning courses in 1999. In fall 2010, there were 212 students enrolled in distance learning courses. Institutionally administered financial aid is available to distance learners.

Services Distance learners have accessibility to academic advising, bookstore, career placement assistance, e-mail services, library services, tutoring.

Contact Ryan Ruda, Dean of Student Services, Garden City Community College, 801 Campus Drive, Garden City, KS 67846. Telephone: 620-276-9597. Fax: 620-276-9573. E-mail: ryan.ruda@gcccks.edu.

DEGREES AND AWARDS

AA General degree
AGS General degree
AS General degree

GARRETT COLLEGE

McHenry, Maryland
http://www.garrettcollege.edu

Garrett College was founded in 1966. It is accredited by Middle States Association of Colleges and Schools. It first offered distance learning courses in 1994. In fall 2010, there were 239 students enrolled in distance learning courses. Institutionally administered financial aid is available to distance learners.

Services Distance learners have accessibility to academic advising, bookstore, e-mail services, library services.

Contact Rachelle Davis, Director of Admissions, Garrett College, 687 Mosser Road, McHenry, MD 21541. Telephone: 301-387-3739. Fax: 301-387-3038. E-mail: admissions@garrettcollege.edu.

DEGREES AND AWARDS

AGS General Studies

GASTON COLLEGE

Dallas, North Carolina
http://www.gaston.edu

Gaston College was founded in 1963. It is accredited by Southern Association of Colleges and Schools. It first offered distance learning courses in 1997. In fall 2010, there were 2,500 students enrolled in distance learning courses. Institutionally administered financial aid is available to distance learners.

Services Distance learners have accessibility to academic advising, bookstore, campus computer network, career placement assistance, library services, tutoring.

Contact Mrs. Kimberly C. Gelsinger, Director of Distance Education, Gaston College, 201 Highway 321 South, Dallas, NC 28034. Telephone: 704-922-6515. Fax: 704-922-6443. E-mail: gelsinger.kim@gaston.edu.

DEGREES AND AWARDS

AAS Criminal Justice Technology; Dietetic Technician
AD Education, general

COURSE SUBJECT AREAS OFFERED OUTSIDE OF DEGREE PROGRAMS

Undergraduate—accounting and related services; allied health and medical assisting services; biological and biomedical sciences related; business/commerce; business/corporate communications; business, management, and marketing related; chemistry; communication and media; communications technology; computer and information sciences; computer programming; computer software and media applications; computer systems networking and telecommunications; criminal justice and corrections; criminology; education (specific subject areas); English; geography and cartography; geological and earth sciences/geosciences; human development, family studies, and related services; information science/studies; legal studies (non-professional general, undergraduate);

liberal arts and sciences, general studies and humanities; management information systems; mathematics; psychology; psychology related; sociology.

GATEWAY COMMUNITY COLLEGE
New Haven, Connecticut
http://www.gwcc.commnet.edu/

Gateway Community College was founded in 1992. It is accredited by New England Association of Schools and Colleges. It first offered distance learning courses in 1999. In fall 2010, there were 1,196 students enrolled in distance learning courses. Institutionally administered financial aid is available to distance learners.

Services Distance learners have accessibility to academic advising, career placement assistance, e-mail services, library services, tutoring.

Contact Ms. Kim Shea, Director of Admissions, Gateway Community College, 60 Sargent Drive, New Haven, CT 06511. Telephone: 203-285-2011. Fax: 203-285-2018. E-mail: kshea@gwcc.commnet.edu.

DEGREES AND AWARDS

Programs offered do not lead to a degree or other formal award.

COURSE SUBJECT AREAS OFFERED OUTSIDE OF DEGREE PROGRAMS

Undergraduate—business/commerce; English language and literature related; health/medical preparatory programs; history; mathematics; microbiological sciences and immunology; philosophy; physical sciences; physiology, pathology and related sciences; psychology; sales merchandising, and related marketing operations (general); social sciences.

GENESEE COMMUNITY COLLEGE
Batavia, New York
Information Technology and Distance Learning
http://www.genesee.edu/DL

Genesee Community College was founded in 1966. It is accredited by Middle States Association of Colleges and Schools. It first offered distance learning courses in 1987. In fall 2010, there were 1,610 students enrolled in distance learning courses. Institutionally administered financial aid is available to distance learners.

Services Distance learners have accessibility to academic advising, bookstore, campus computer network, career placement assistance, e-mail services, library services, tutoring.

Contact Ms. Judith M. Littlejohn, Academic Support/Distance Learning Advisor, Genesee Community College, 1 College Road, Batavia, NY 14020-9704. Telephone: 585-343-0055 Ext. 6158. Fax: 585-343-0433. E-mail: jmlittlejohn@genesee.edu.

DEGREES AND AWARDS

AA Liberal Arts–Humanities and Social Science
AAS Business Administration; Criminal Justice; Entrepreneurship; Individualized Studies
AS Business Administration; Criminal Justice; Economic Crime Investigation; General Studies; Teacher Education Transfer

COURSE SUBJECT AREAS OFFERED OUTSIDE OF DEGREE PROGRAMS

Undergraduate—accounting and related services; anthropology; business/commerce; business, management, and marketing related; computer and information sciences; criminal justice and corrections; economics; education; education related; English language and literature related; gerontology; history; hospitality administration; marketing; mathematics; mathematics and statistics related; music; political science and government; psychology; psychology related; sales merchandising, and related marketing operations (general); social sciences; sociology; statistics.

Non-credit—business administration, management and operations; computer and information sciences and support services related; entrepreneurial and small business operations.

GEORGE FOX UNIVERSITY
Newberg, Oregon

George Fox University was founded in 1891. It is accredited by Northwest Commission on Colleges and Universities. It first offered distance learning courses in 1997. In fall 2010, there were 628 students enrolled in distance learning courses. Institutionally administered financial aid is available to distance learners.

Services Distance learners have accessibility to academic advising, bookstore, e-mail services, library services, tutoring.

Contact Admissions, George Fox University, 414 North Meridian Street, Newberg, OR 97132. Telephone: 800-765-4369. E-mail: admissions@georgefox.edu.

DEGREES AND AWARDS

BA Management and Organizational Leadership–Adult Degree Completion
MA Ministry Leadership; Spiritual Formation; Theological Studies
MDiv Divinity
DBA Business Administration
DMin Leadership and Spiritual Formation; Leadership in Emerging Culture–Global Missional Leadership; Leadership in Emerging Culture–Semiotics and Future Studies

COURSE SUBJECT AREAS OFFERED OUTSIDE OF DEGREE PROGRAMS

Undergraduate—biblical studies; business administration, management and operations; English; history; marketing; mathematics; music; psychology; religious studies; sociology; visual and performing arts.

Graduate—business administration, management and operations; educational administration and supervision; educational assessment, evaluation, and research; pastoral counseling and specialized ministries; theology and religious vocations related.

GEORGIA COLLEGE & STATE UNIVERSITY
Milledgeville, Georgia
http://www.gcsu.edu/

Georgia College & State University was founded in 1889. It is accredited by Southern Association of Colleges and Schools. It first offered distance learning courses in 1995. In fall 2010, there were 355 students enrolled in distance learning courses. Institutionally administered financial aid is available to distance learners.

Services Distance learners have accessibility to bookstore, campus computer network, career placement assistance, e-mail services, library services.

Contact Ms. Kate Marshall, Graduate Admissions Coordinator, Georgia College & State University, Campus Box 107, Milledgeville, GA 31061. Telephone: 478-445-1184. Fax: 478-445-1336. E-mail: kate.marshall@gcsu.edu.

DEGREES AND AWARDS

MBA Web MBA
MMT Music Therapy

COURSE SUBJECT AREAS OFFERED OUTSIDE OF DEGREE PROGRAMS

Undergraduate—health and physical education/fitness; health professions related.

Graduate—education; health professions related.

GEORGIA HIGHLANDS COLLEGE
Rome, Georgia
Division of Academic Success and eLearning
http://www.highlands.edu/site/division-of-academic-success-and-elearning

Georgia Highlands College was founded in 1970. It is accredited by Southern Association of Colleges and Schools. It first offered distance learning courses in 1977. In fall 2010, there were 1,000 students enrolled in distance learning courses. Institutionally administered financial aid is available to distance learners.

Services Distance learners have accessibility to academic advising, bookstore, campus computer network, e-mail services, library services, tutoring.

Contact Dr. Jeffrey Linek, Director of eLearning for Academics, Georgia Highlands College, Cartersville Campus, 5441 Highway 20 NE, Cartersville, GA 30121. Telephone: 678-872-8065. Fax: 678-872-8057. E-mail: jlinek@highlands.edu.

DEGREES AND AWARDS

Programs offered do not lead to a degree or other formal award.

COURSE SUBJECT AREAS OFFERED OUTSIDE OF DEGREE PROGRAMS

Undergraduate—allied health and medical assisting services; biology; economics; education (specific levels and methods); English; English language and literature related; health and physical education/fitness; history; mathematics; psychology.

GEORGIA INSTITUTE OF TECHNOLOGY

Atlanta, Georgia

Center for Distance Learning

http://www.dlpe.gatech.edu/dl/

Georgia Institute of Technology was founded in 1885. It is accredited by Southern Association of Colleges and Schools. It first offered distance learning courses in 1977. In fall 2010, there were 1,250 students enrolled in distance learning courses. Institutionally administered financial aid is available to distance learners.

Services Distance learners have accessibility to academic advising, bookstore, campus computer network, e-mail services, library services.

Contact Ms. Tanya Krawiec, Academic Program Manager, Georgia Institute of Technology, 84 5th Street NW, Room 013, Atlanta, GA 30308-1031. Telephone: 404-894-3378. Fax: 404-894-8924. E-mail: tanya.krawiec@dlpe.gatech.edu.

DEGREES AND AWARDS

MS Aerospace Engineering; Applied Systems Engineering emphasis, Professional Masters Degree; Computational Science and Engineering (CSE); Electrical Engineering; Industrial and Systems Engineering; Information Security; Integrated Facility and Property Management; Mechanical Engineering; Medical Physics; Operations Research

COURSE SUBJECT AREAS OFFERED OUTSIDE OF DEGREE PROGRAMS

Undergraduate—engineering; mathematics.

Graduate—aerospace, aeronautical and astronautical engineering; applied mathematics; architectural engineering; architecture related; biomedical/medical engineering; building/construction finishing, management, and inspection; civil engineering; computer and information sciences; computer engineering; computer engineering technologies; computer science; computer systems analysis; environmental/environmental health engineering; mathematics; mechanical engineering.

Non-credit—aerospace, aeronautical and astronautical engineering; civil engineering; computer engineering; environmental/environmental health engineering; mathematics; mechanical engineering.

GEORGIAN COURT UNIVERSITY

Lakewood, New Jersey

http://www.georgian.edu

Georgian Court University was founded in 1908. It is accredited by Middle States Association of Colleges and Schools. It first offered distance learning courses in 2004. In fall 2010, there were 890 students enrolled in distance learning courses. Institutionally administered financial aid is available to distance learners.

Services Distance learners have accessibility to bookstore, campus computer network, career placement assistance, e-mail services, library services.

Contact Mr. Patrick Givens, Assistant Director of Graduate Admissions, Georgian Court University, 900 Lakewood Avenue, Lakewood, NJ 08701-2697. Telephone: 732-987-2736. Fax: 732-987-2084 E-mail: givensp@georgian.edu.

DEGREES AND AWARDS

MA Administration and Leadership

COURSE SUBJECT AREAS OFFERED OUTSIDE OF DEGREE PROGRAMS

Undergraduate—biological and physical sciences; business administration, management and operations; communication and media; education; educational administration and supervision; fine and studio arts; history; languages (foreign languages related); liberal arts and sciences, general studies and humanities; mathematics; philosophy; religious studies.

Graduate—biological and biomedical sciences related; business, management, and marketing related; education; health professions related.

GEORGIA STATE UNIVERSITY

Atlanta, Georgia

Division of Distance and Distributed Learning

http://www.gsu.edu/enrollment/online_courses.html

Georgia State University was founded in 1913. It is accredited by Southern Association of Colleges and Schools. It first offered distance learning courses in 1996. In fall 2010, there were 2,787 students enrolled in distance learning courses. Institutionally administered financial aid is available to distance learners.

Services Distance learners have accessibility to academic advising, bookstore, campus computer network, e-mail services, library services.

Contact Office of the Registrar, Georgia State University, PO Box 4017, Atlanta, GA 30302. Telephone: 404-413-2600. E-mail: onestopshop@gsu.edu.

DEGREES AND AWARDS

MAT Reading, Language, and Literacy Education

MEd Mathematics Education; Reading, Language, and Literacy Education; Science Education

MS Instructional Technology; Measurement and Statistics

PhD Nursing

COURSE SUBJECT AREAS OFFERED OUTSIDE OF DEGREE PROGRAMS

Undergraduate—computer and information sciences; education related; finance and financial management services; health professions related; health services/allied health/health sciences; hospitality administration; languages (Romance languages); mathematics; nutrition sciences; political science and government; psychology.

Graduate—business administration, management and operations; educational/instructional media design; education (specific levels and methods); education (specific subject areas); health and physical education/fitness; health services/allied health/health sciences; nutrition sciences.

GLENVILLE STATE COLLEGE

Glenville, West Virginia

http://www.glenville.edu/

Glenville State College was founded in 1872. It is accredited by North Central Association of Colleges and Schools. It first offered distance learning courses in 1997. In fall 2010, there were 580 students enrolled in distance learning courses. Institutionally administered financial aid is available to distance learners.

Services Distance learners have accessibility to academic advising, bookstore, campus computer network, career placement assistance, e-mail services, library services, tutoring.

Contact Dr. John Peek, Provost and Senior Vice President, Glenville State College, Office of Academic Affairs, 200 High Street, Glenville, WV 26351. Telephone: 304-462-6111. Fax: 304-462-8619. E-mail: john.peek@glenville.edu.

DEGREES AND AWARDS

Programs offered do not lead to a degree or other formal award.

COURSE SUBJECT AREAS OFFERED OUTSIDE OF DEGREE PROGRAMS

Undergraduate—business, management, and marketing related; computer software and media applications; criminal justice and corrections; economics; education (specific subject areas); English; finance and financial management services; history; mathematics and statistics related; physical sciences; political science and government; psychology; sociology; special education.

GLOBAL UNIVERSITY
Springfield, Missouri
http://www.globaluniversity.edu/

Global University was founded in 1948. It is accredited by Distance Education and Training Council. It first offered distance learning courses in 1948. In fall 2010, there were 12,857 students enrolled in distance learning courses. Institutionally administered financial aid is available to distance learners.

Services Distance learners have accessibility to academic advising, bookstore, e-mail services, library services.

Contact Rev. Todd Waggoner, Director of Enrollment and International Student Services, Global University, 1211 South Glenstone Avenue, Springfield, MO 65804. Telephone: 800-443-1083 Ext. 2335. Fax: 417-863-9621. E-mail: twaggoner@globaluniversity.edu.

DEGREES AND AWARDS

AA Bible/Theology; Church Ministries; Religious Studies

BA Bible and Theology (Second BA degree); Bible and Theology (Three-Year BA degree); Bible and Theology; Intercultural Studies Second BA degree; Intercultural Studies Three-Year BA degree; Intercultural Studies; Religious Education Three-Year BA degree; Religious Education

Certificate Bible Interpreter (Undergraduate certificate I); Bible and Theology; Center For Native Leadership Development; Christian Communicator (Undergraduate certificate II); Christian Mission (Undergraduate certificate III)

Diploma Bible and Doctrine; Center For Native Leadership Development–Ministerial Studies; Christian Service; Church Ministries; Ministerial Studies Level One (Certified Minister); Ministerial Studies Level Three (Ordained Minister); Ministerial Studies Level Two (Licensed Minister); Ministry; Royal Rangers Organizational Leaders–Bronze Tier; Royal Rangers Organizational Leaders–Gold Tier; Royal Rangers Organizational Leaders–Platinum Tier; Royal Rangers Organizational Leaders–Silver Tier; Theology; Urban Bible Training

MA Ministerial Studies–Broad Field Plan; Ministerial Studies–Education concentration; Ministerial Studies–Intercultural Studies; Ministerial Studies–Leadership concentration

MABS Broad Field Plan; New Testament concentration

MDiv Divinity

COURSE SUBJECT AREAS OFFERED OUTSIDE OF DEGREE PROGRAMS

Undergraduate—biblical studies; education; ethnic, cultural minority, gender, and group studies; history; human services; intercultural/multicultural and diversity studies; international relations and national security studies; liberal arts and sciences, general studies and humanities; missionary studies and missiology; multi/interdisciplinary studies related; pastoral counseling and specialized ministries; philosophy; philosophy and religious studies related; psychology; psychology related; religious education; religious/sacred music; religious studies; social sciences; social sciences related; sociology; theological and ministerial studies; theology and religious vocations related.

Graduate—biblical studies; curriculum and instruction; education; educational administration and supervision; educational assessment, evaluation, and research; education related; history; intercultural/multicultural and diversity studies; international/global studies; international relations and national security studies; missionary studies and missiology; pastoral counseling and specialized ministries; peace studies and conflict resolution; philosophy; philosophy and religious studies related; religious education; religious studies; social and philosophical foundations of education; theological and ministerial studies; theology and religious vocations related.

Non-credit—biblical studies; missionary studies and missiology; pastoral counseling and specialized ministries; philosophy and religious studies related; religious education; religious studies; theological and ministerial studies; theology and religious vocations related.

GODDARD COLLEGE
Plainfield, Vermont
Distance Learning Programs
http://www.goddard.edu

Goddard College was founded in 1938. It is accredited by New England Association of Schools and Colleges. It first offered distance learning courses in 1963. In fall 2010, there were 804 students enrolled in distance learning courses. Institutionally administered financial aid is available to distance learners.

Services Distance learners have accessibility to academic advising, bookstore, campus computer network, e-mail services, library services.

Contact Josh Castle, Associate Dean and Registrar, Goddard College, 123 Pitkin Road, Plainfield, VT 05667. Telephone: 800-906-8312. Fax: 802-454-1029. E-mail: admissions@goddard.edu.

DEGREES AND AWARDS

BA Education; Health Arts and Sciences; Individualized Studies; Sustainability

BFA Creative Writing

MA Education; Health Arts and Sciences; Individualized Studies; Psychology and Counseling; Sustainable Business and Communities

MFA Creative Writing; Interdisciplinary Arts

COURSE SUBJECT AREAS OFFERED OUTSIDE OF DEGREE PROGRAMS

Undergraduate—anthropology; architectural history and criticism; area studies; behavioral sciences; city/urban, community and regional planning; classical and ancient studies; communication and journalism related; communication and media; community organization and advocacy; curriculum and instruction; drama/theatre arts and stagecraft; economics; education; education related; education (specific levels and methods); English; English language and literature related; ethnic, cultural minority, gender, and group studies; fine and studio arts; history; intercultural/multicultural and diversity studies; international/global studies; liberal arts and sciences, general studies and humanities; linguistic, comparative, and related language studies; movement and mind-body therapies and education; music; peace studies and conflict resolution; philosophy; physical sciences; political science and government; psychology; psychology related; science, technology and society; social sciences; social sciences related; sociology; sustainability studies.

Graduate—anthropology; community organization and advocacy; dance; drama/theatre arts and stagecraft; education; education related; education (specific levels and methods); education (specific subject areas); entrepreneurial and small business operations; environmental design; fine and studio arts; liberal arts and sciences, general studies and humanities; movement and mind-body therapies and education; natural resources and conservation related; natural resources conservation and research; peace studies and conflict resolution; political science and government; psychology; psychology related; public health; public policy analysis; science, technology and society; social and philosophical foundations of education; social sciences related; sociology; somatic bodywork and related therapeutic services; urban studies/affairs; visual and performing arts; work and family studies.

GOD'S BIBLE SCHOOL AND COLLEGE
Cincinnati, Ohio
http://www.gbs.edu/adep

God's Bible School and College was founded in 1900. It is accredited by Association for Biblical Higher Education. It first offered distance learning courses in 2001. In fall 2010, there were 70 students enrolled in distance learning courses. Institutionally administered financial aid is available to distance learners.

Services Distance learners have accessibility to academic advising, bookstore, campus computer network, e-mail services, library services, tutoring.

Contact Ms. Betty J. Cochran, Aldersgate Distance Education Program Coordinator, God's Bible School and College, 1810 Young Street, Cincinnati, OH 45202. Telephone: 513-763-6652. Fax: 513-258-0675. E-mail: bcochran@gbs.edu.

DEGREES AND AWARDS
AA Bible and Theology
BA Church and Family Ministry; Ministerial Education

COURSE SUBJECT AREAS OFFERED OUTSIDE OF DEGREE PROGRAMS
Undergraduate—biblical studies; theological and ministerial studies; theology and religious vocations related.

GOLDEN GATE BAPTIST THEOLOGICAL SEMINARY
Mill Valley, California
http://www.ggbts.edu/

Golden Gate Baptist Theological Seminary was founded in 1944. It is accredited by Western Association of Schools and Colleges. It first offered distance learning courses in 2006. In fall 2010, there were 194 students enrolled in distance learning courses. Institutionally administered financial aid is available to distance learners.

Services Distance learners have accessibility to academic advising, bookstore, library services.

Contact Dr. Rick Durst, Director of Online Learning, Golden Gate Baptist Theological Seminary, 201 Seminary Drive, Mill Valley, CA 94941. Telephone: 415-380-1535. E-mail: ecampus@ggbts.edu.

DEGREES AND AWARDS
Programs offered do not lead to a degree or other formal award.

COURSE SUBJECT AREAS OFFERED OUTSIDE OF DEGREE PROGRAMS
Graduate—theological and ministerial studies; theology and religious vocations related.

GONZAGA UNIVERSITY
Spokane, Washington
School of Professional Studies
http://www.gonzaga.edu/

Gonzaga University was founded in 1887. It is accredited by Northwest Commission on Colleges and Universities. It first offered distance learning courses in 1995. In fall 2010, there were 1,000 students enrolled in distance learning courses. Institutionally administered financial aid is available to distance learners.

Services Distance learners have accessibility to academic advising, bookstore, campus computer network, career placement assistance, e-mail services, library services, tutoring.

Contact Distance Learning Programs, Gonzaga University, East 502 Boone, Spokane, WA 99258. Telephone: 866-295-3105.

DEGREES AND AWARDS
MA Communication and Leadership Studies; Organizational Leadership
MS Nursing

GOUCHER COLLEGE
Baltimore, Maryland
Center for Graduate and Professional Studies
http://www.goucher.edu

Goucher College was founded in 1885. It is accredited by Middle States Association of Colleges and Schools. It first offered distance learning courses in 1995. In fall 2010, there were 220 students enrolled in distance learning courses. Institutionally administered financial aid is available to distance learners.

Services Distance learners have accessibility to academic advising, bookstore, campus computer network, e-mail services, library services.

Contact Ms. Megan Cornett, Director of Marketing and Communications, Goucher College, Welch Center for Graduate and Professional Studies, 1021 Dulaney Valley Road, Baltimore, MD 21204. Telephone: 410-337-6200. Fax: 410-337-6085. E-mail: mcornett@goucher.edu.

DEGREES AND AWARDS
MA Arts Administration; Cultural Sustainability; Digital Arts; Historic Preservation
MFA Creative Nonfiction

COURSE SUBJECT AREAS OFFERED OUTSIDE OF DEGREE PROGRAMS
Graduate—education.

GOVERNORS STATE UNIVERSITY
University Park, Illinois
School of Extended Learning
http://www.govst.edu

Governors State University was founded in 1969. It is accredited by North Central Association of Colleges and Schools. It first offered distance learning courses in 1981. In fall 2010, there were 1,458 students enrolled in distance learning courses. Institutionally administered financial aid is available to distance learners.

Services Distance learners have accessibility to academic advising, bookstore, career placement assistance, e-mail services, library services, tutoring.

Contact Veronica Williams, Director, Continuing Education, Governors State University, 1 University Parkway, University Park, IL 60484. Telephone: 708-534-4099. Fax: 708-534-8458. E-mail: vwilliams@govst.edu.

DEGREES AND AWARDS
BA Interdisciplinary Studies

COURSE SUBJECT AREAS OFFERED OUTSIDE OF DEGREE PROGRAMS
Undergraduate—accounting and related services; anthropology; communication and media; fine and studio arts; geography and cartography; marketing; psychology; social work; sociology.
Graduate—anthropology; fine and studio arts; social work; sociology.
Non-credit—communication and media; criminal justice and corrections; education; educational assessment, evaluation, and research; education related; health professions related.

GRACE COLLEGE
Winona Lake, Indiana
http://www.grace.edu/academics/online-programs

Grace College was founded in 1948. It is accredited by North Central Association of Colleges and Schools. It first offered distance learning courses in 1999. In fall 2010, there were 64 students enrolled in distance learning courses. Institutionally administered financial aid is available to distance learners.

Services Distance learners have accessibility to academic advising, bookstore, campus computer network, career placement assistance, e-mail services, library services.

Contact Mr. Matt Carlton, Enrollment Counselor Department of Online Education, Grace College, 200 Seminary Drive, Winona Lake, IN 46590. Telephone: 888-249-0533. Fax: 574-372-5182. E-mail: matthew.carlton@grace.edu.

DEGREES AND AWARDS

BA/BS Management
MA Clinical Mental Health Counseling; Interpersonal Relations; Ministry Studies

GRACELAND UNIVERSITY
Lamoni, Iowa
Distance Learning
http://www.graceland.edu

Graceland University was founded in 1895. It is accredited by North Central Association of Colleges and Schools. It first offered distance learning courses in 1988. In fall 2010, there were 824 students enrolled in distance learning courses. Institutionally administered financial aid is available to distance learners.
Services Distance learners have accessibility to academic advising, bookstore, campus computer network, e-mail services, library services, tutoring.
Contact Drew Schaefer, Director of Marketing, Graceland University, 1401 West Truman Road, Independence, MO 64050. Telephone: 800-833-0524. Fax: 816-833-2990. E-mail: dschaefe@graceland.edu.

DEGREES AND AWARDS

BA Health Care Management
BSN Nursing
MEd Curriculum and Instruction: A Collaborative Approach; Differentiated Instruction; Management in the Inclusive Classroom; Mild/Moderate Special Education, 5-12; Mild/Moderate Special Education, K-8; Technology Integration
MSN Nurse Educator; Nursing–Family Nurse Practitioner
PMC Nurse Educator; Nursing–Family Nurse Practitioner

COURSE SUBJECT AREAS OFFERED OUTSIDE OF DEGREE PROGRAMS

Undergraduate—behavioral sciences; biochemistry, biophysics and molecular biology; biology; business administration, management and operations; chemistry; computer and information sciences; drama/theatre arts and stagecraft; history; information science/studies; marketing; microbiological sciences and immunology; psychology; sociology; statistics.
Graduate—education; religious studies.

GRAND VALLEY STATE UNIVERSITY
Allendale, Michigan
Division of Continuing Education
http://www.gvsu.edu/online/

Grand Valley State University was founded in 1960. It is accredited by North Central Association of Colleges and Schools. In fall 2010, there were 500 students enrolled in distance learning courses. Institutionally administered financial aid is available to distance learners.
Services Distance learners have accessibility to academic advising, bookstore, campus computer network, career placement assistance, e-mail services, library services, tutoring.
Contact Sandy Becker, Distance Education Department, Grand Valley State University, 401 West Fulton, DeVos Center, 289C DEV, Grand Rapids, MI 49504. Telephone: 616-331-6616. Fax: 616-331-6501. E-mail: beckers@gvsu.edu.

DEGREES AND AWARDS

MEd Educational Technology

COURSE SUBJECT AREAS OFFERED OUTSIDE OF DEGREE PROGRAMS

Undergraduate—accounting and related services; business administration, management and operations; criminal justice and corrections; liberal arts and sciences, general studies and humanities; sociology.
Graduate—accounting and related services; business administration, management and operations; communication and media; education; public administration; social work; sociology; special education.

GRANITE STATE COLLEGE
Concord, New Hampshire
http://www.granite.edu

Granite State College was founded in 1972. It is accredited by New England Association of Schools and Colleges. It first offered distance learning courses in 1999. In fall 2010, there were 897 students enrolled in distance learning courses. Institutionally administered financial aid is available to distance learners.
Services Distance learners have accessibility to academic advising, bookstore, e-mail services, library services, tutoring.
Contact Ms. Jane Williamson, Admissions Coordinator, Granite State College, 8 Old Suncook Road, Concord, NH 03301. Telephone: 888-228-3000. Fax: 603-513-1386. E-mail: jane.williamson@granite.edu.

DEGREES AND AWARDS

AA General Studies
AS Behavioral Science; Business
BA Individualized Studies; Liberal Studies
BS Applied Studies, Allied Health Services option; Applied Studies, Education and Training option; Applied Studies, Management option; Behavioral Science; Business Management; Criminal Justice; Criminal Justice, Administration option; Health Care Management; Individualized Studies
MS Project Management

COURSE SUBJECT AREAS OFFERED OUTSIDE OF DEGREE PROGRAMS

Undergraduate—area studies; behavioral sciences; business administration, management and operations; business, management, and marketing related; communication and media; computer/information technology administration and management; computer programming; computer systems analysis; criminal justice and corrections; curriculum and instruction; education (specific levels and methods); English; English language and literature related; finance and financial management services; health and medical administrative services; history; human development, family studies, and related services; human resources management; liberal arts and sciences, general studies and humanities; management information systems; management sciences and quantitative methods; mathematics; mathematics and statistics related; mental and social health services and allied professions; multi/interdisciplinary studies related; psychology related; social sciences.
Graduate—education (specific subject areas); special education.
Non-credit—education related; family and consumer sciences/human sciences; health services/allied health/health sciences; intercultural/multicultural and diversity studies.

GRANTHAM UNIVERSITY
Kansas City, Missouri
http://www.grantham.edu/

Grantham University was founded in 1951. It is accredited by Distance Education and Training Council. It first offered distance learning courses in 1990. In fall 2010, there were 11,837 students enrolled in distance learning courses. Institutionally administered financial aid is available to distance learners.
Services Distance learners have accessibility to academic advising, bookstore, career placement assistance, e-mail services, library services, tutoring.
Contact Mr. Jared Parlette, Senior Admissions Manager, Grantham University, 7200 NW 86th Street, Kansas City, MO 64153. Telephone: 800-955-2527. Fax: 816-595-5757. E-mail: admissions@grantham.edu.

DEGREES AND AWARDS

AA Business Administration; Business Management; Criminal Justice; Engineering Management Technology; General Studies; Multidisciplinary Studies
AAS Medical Coding and Billing

AS Computer Science; Electronics and Computer Engineering Technology

BA Criminal Justice; General Studies

BS Accounting; Business Administration Human Resources Management; Business Administration; Business Management; Computer Engineering Technology; Computer Science; Electronics Engineering Technology; Engineering Management Technology; Health Systems Management; Information Systems Security; Information Systems; Multidisciplinary Studies

BSN Nursing–RN to BSN degree completion program

MBA Business Administration; Information Management; Project Management

MHA Healthcare Administration

MS Business Intelligence; Health Systems Management; Information Management Technology; Information Management–Project Management; Information Technology; Performance Improvement

MSN Case Management; Nursing Education; Nursing Informatics; Nursing Management and Organizational Leadership; Nursing–RN to MSN Degree completion program

COURSE SUBJECT AREAS OFFERED OUTSIDE OF DEGREE PROGRAMS

Undergraduate—accounting and related services; business administration, management and operations; business/commerce; business, management, and marketing related; business/managerial economics; chemistry; computer and information sciences; computer engineering; computer engineering technologies; computer/information technology administration and management; computer programming; computer science; computer software and media applications; computer systems analysis; computer systems networking and telecommunications; criminal justice and corrections; data entry/microcomputer applications; economics; electrical, electronics and communications engineering; electrical engineering technologies; engineering; finance and financial management services; health and medical administrative services; health professions related; history; human resources management; information science/studies; legal studies (non-professional general, undergraduate); management information systems; marketing; mathematics; mathematics and computer science; mathematics and statistics related; physics; psychology; psychology related; sales merchandising, and related marketing operations (general); sociology.

Graduate—accounting and related services; business/managerial economics; communications technology; finance and financial management services; health professions related; human resources management; management information systems; marketing; systems engineering.

GREENVILLE TECHNICAL COLLEGE
Greenville, South Carolina
Distance Learning
http://www.gvltec.edu

Greenville Technical College was founded in 1962. It is accredited by Southern Association of Colleges and Schools. It first offered distance learning courses in 1990. In fall 2010, there were 7,270 students enrolled in distance learning courses. Institutionally administered financial aid is available to distance learners.

Services Distance learners have accessibility to academic advising, bookstore, campus computer network, career placement assistance, e-mail services, library services, tutoring.

Contact Mr. Christopher Satterfield, Academic Advisor, Distance Education, Greenville Technical College, PO Box 5616, Greenville, SC 29606-5616. Telephone: 864-250-8393. Fax: 864-250-8085. E-mail: chris.satterfield@gvltec.edu.

DEGREES AND AWARDS

AA the Arts

AAS Computer Technology (Programming emphasis); Health Information Management; Management; Marketing

AS General degree

COURSE SUBJECT AREAS OFFERED OUTSIDE OF DEGREE PROGRAMS

Undergraduate—accounting and computer science; astronomy and astrophysics; business, management, and marketing related; computer programming; economics; English language and literature related; fine and studio arts; history; human services; languages (foreign languages related); marketing; mathematics; music; philosophy and religious studies related; physics; political science and government; psychology; sociology.

HAGERSTOWN COMMUNITY COLLEGE
Hagerstown, Maryland
http://www.hagerstowncc.edu/

Hagerstown Community College was founded in 1946. It is accredited by Middle States Association of Colleges and Schools. It first offered distance learning courses in 1998. In fall 2010, there were 189 students enrolled in distance learning courses. Institutionally administered financial aid is available to distance learners.

Services Distance learners have accessibility to bookstore, library services.

Contact Samantha Willard, Office Associate/Test Center Technician, Hagerstown Community College, Continuing Education, 11400 Robinwood Drive, Hagerstown, MD 21742. Telephone: 301-790-2800 Ext. 413. Fax: 301-733-4229. E-mail: slwillard@hagerstowncc.edu.

DEGREES AND AWARDS

Programs offered do not lead to a degree or other formal award.

COURSE SUBJECT AREAS OFFERED OUTSIDE OF DEGREE PROGRAMS

Non-credit—accounting and related services; allied health and medical assisting services; business, management, and marketing related; computer programming; computer software and media applications; computer systems networking and telecommunications; culinary arts and related services; publishing.

HANNIBAL-LAGRANGE UNIVERSITY
Hannibal, Missouri
http://www.hlg.edu/

Hannibal-LaGrange University was founded in 1858. It is accredited by North Central Association of Colleges and Schools. It first offered distance learning courses in 2005. In fall 2010, there were 67 students enrolled in distance learning courses. Institutionally administered financial aid is available to distance learners.

Services Distance learners have accessibility to academic advising, bookstore, campus computer network, career placement assistance, e-mail services, library services, tutoring.

Contact Jill Arnold, Director of Online Programs, Hannibal-LaGrange University, 2800 Palmyra Road, Hannibal, MO 63401. Telephone: 573-221-3675. E-mail: jarnold@hlg.edu.

DEGREES AND AWARDS

BSN Nursing

COURSE SUBJECT AREAS OFFERED OUTSIDE OF DEGREE PROGRAMS

Undergraduate—arts, entertainment, and media management; biology; education (specific subject areas); English; history; mathematics; music; psychology; religious education.

HARCUM COLLEGE
Bryn Mawr, Pennsylvania
http://www.harcum.edu/

Harcum College was founded in 1915. It is accredited by Middle States Association of Colleges and Schools. It first offered distance learning courses in 2002. In fall 2010, there were 950 students enrolled in distance learning courses. Institutionally administered financial aid is available to distance learners.

Services Distance learners have accessibility to academic advising, bookstore, campus computer network, e-mail services, library services, tutoring.

Contact Mr. Timothy Strong Ely, Assistant Vice President for Online Education and Instructional Design, Harcum College, 750 Montgomery Avenue, Bryn Mawr, PA 19010. Telephone: 610-526-6053. Fax: 610-526-6031. E-mail: tely@harcum.edu.

DEGREES AND AWARDS

AS Histotechnology; Medical Laboratory Technician; Neurodiagnostic Technology

COURSE SUBJECT AREAS OFFERED OUTSIDE OF DEGREE PROGRAMS

Undergraduate—accounting and computer science; allied health and medical assisting services; allied health diagnostic, intervention, and treatment professions; behavioral sciences; biological and physical sciences; biology; business administration, management and operations; business, management, and marketing related; business/managerial economics; economics; English; liberal arts and sciences, general studies and humanities; marketing; mathematics; natural sciences; psychology; sociology.

HARFORD COMMUNITY COLLEGE
Bel Air, Maryland
http://www.harford.edu/eLearning

Harford Community College was founded in 1957. It is accredited by Middle States Association of Colleges and Schools. It first offered distance learning courses in 1999. In fall 2010, there were 2,800 students enrolled in distance learning courses. Institutionally administered financial aid is available to distance learners.

Services Distance learners have accessibility to academic advising, bookstore, campus computer network, career placement assistance, e-mail services, library services, tutoring.

Contact LeRoy Trusty, Director of E-Learning, Harford Community College, 401 Thomas Run Road, Bel Air, MD 21015. Telephone: 443-412-2145. Fax: 443-412-2481. E-mail: letrusty@harford.edu.

DEGREES AND AWARDS

AA General Studies
ABA Business Administration

COURSE SUBJECT AREAS OFFERED OUTSIDE OF DEGREE PROGRAMS

Undergraduate—biology; chemistry; education (specific subject areas); English; history; mathematics; psychology; social sciences related.

Non-credit—computer and information sciences; computer programming; computer systems networking and telecommunications; real estate.

HARRISBURG AREA COMMUNITY COLLEGE
Harrisburg, Pennsylvania
Distance Education Office
http://www.hacc.edu/VirtualCampus

Harrisburg Area Community College was founded in 1964. It is accredited by Middle States Association of Colleges and Schools. It first offered distance learning courses in 1987. In fall 2010, there were 5,300 students enrolled in distance learning courses. Institutionally administered financial aid is available to distance learners.

Services Distance learners have accessibility to academic advising, bookstore, career placement assistance, library services, tutoring.

Contact Mr. Robert Karas, Counselor, Harrisburg Area Community College, 1 HACC Drive, Harrisburg, PA 17110. Telephone: 717-231-1300 Ext. 1509. Fax: 717-909-1493. E-mail: rdkaras@hacc.edu.

DEGREES AND AWARDS

Programs offered do not lead to a degree or other formal award.

COURSE SUBJECT AREAS OFFERED OUTSIDE OF DEGREE PROGRAMS

Undergraduate—accounting and related services; allied health and medical assisting services; anthropology; applied mathematics; astronomy and astrophysics; behavioral sciences; biological and physical sciences; business administration, management and operations; business/commerce; business, management, and marketing related; business/managerial economics; computer programming; computer science; computer software and media applications; criminal justice and corrections; economics; engineering; English; environmental/environmental health engineering; finance and financial management services; foods, nutrition, and related services; geography and cartography; geological and earth sciences/geosciences; gerontology; history; information science/studies; library science related; marketing; mathematics; mathematics and computer science; microbiological sciences and immunology; philosophy; physical sciences; psychology; public health; sociology and anthropology; statistics.

HARTFORD SEMINARY
Hartford, Connecticut
http://www.hartsem.edu/academic/distance.htm

Hartford Seminary was founded in 1834. It is accredited by New England Association of Schools and Colleges. It first offered distance learning courses in 2002. In fall 2010, there were 65 students enrolled in distance learning courses. Institutionally administered financial aid is available to distance learners.

Services Distance learners have accessibility to academic advising, bookstore, library services, tutoring.

Contact Dr. Scott Thumma, Director of Distance Education, Hartford Seminary, 77 Sherman Street, Hartford, CT 06105. Telephone: 860-509-9571. E-mail: sthumma@hartsem.edu.

DEGREES AND AWARDS

Programs offered do not lead to a degree or other formal award.

COURSE SUBJECT AREAS OFFERED OUTSIDE OF DEGREE PROGRAMS

Graduate—pastoral counseling and specialized ministries; religious studies.

Non-credit—religious studies.

HAYWOOD COMMUNITY COLLEGE
Clyde, North Carolina
http://www.haywood.edu

Haywood Community College was founded in 1964. It is accredited by Southern Association of Colleges and Schools. It first offered distance learning courses in 1992. In fall 2010, there were 1,632 students enrolled in distance learning courses. Institutionally administered financial aid is available to distance learners.

Services Distance learners have accessibility to academic advising, bookstore, career placement assistance, e-mail services, library services, tutoring.

Contact Debbie Rowland, Coordinator of Admissions, Haywood Community College, 185 Freedlander Drive, Clyde, NC 28716. Telephone: 828-627-4646. Fax: 828-627-4513. E-mail: drowland@haywood.edu.

DEGREES AND AWARDS

AA General degree
AAS Accounting; Business Administration; Criminal Justice Technology; Early Childhood Education–Administration track; Early Childhood Education–College Transfer track; Early Childhood Education–Early Childhood Education track; Early Childhood Education–Infant and Toddler track; Early Childhood Education–Special Education track; Entrepreneurship; Financial Services; General Occupational Technology; Medical Office Administration; Office Administration–Legal; Office Administration
Certificate Forestry Technology–Natural Resources Specialist; Geospatial Technology–Advanced Geospatial Specialist; Geospatial Technology–Global Positioning Systems Specialist; Geospatial Technology–Property Mapping Specialist; Low Impact Development–LID Specialist

COURSE SUBJECT AREAS OFFERED OUTSIDE OF DEGREE PROGRAMS

Undergraduate—accounting and related services; animal sciences; anthropology; applied horticulture and horticultural business services;

behavioral sciences; business administration, management and operations; business/commerce; computer and information sciences; computer engineering technologies; computer/information technology administration and management; computer programming; computer science; computer software and media applications; computer systems analysis; computer systems networking and telecommunications; construction engineering; construction management; construction trades; construction trades related; cosmetology and related personal grooming services; criminal justice and corrections; criminology; data entry/microcomputer applications; economics; education; education related; engineering; engineering technologies related; English; English language and literature related; entrepreneurial and small business operations; finance and financial management services; fine and studio arts; forestry; health and physical education/fitness; history; human development, family studies, and related services; information science/studies; liberal arts and sciences, general studies and humanities; management information systems; mathematics; mathematics and computer science; music; natural resources and conservation related; natural resources conservation and research; natural resources management and policy; natural sciences; parks, recreation and leisure; parks, recreation and leisure facilities management; parks, recreation, leisure, and fitness studies related; plant sciences; political science and government; psychology; religious studies; social sciences; social sciences related; sociology; soil sciences; teaching assistants/aides; wildlife and wildlands science and management.

HEARTLAND COMMUNITY COLLEGE
Normal, Illinois
http://www.heartland.edu

Heartland Community College was founded in 1990. It is accredited by North Central Association of Colleges and Schools. It first offered distance learning courses in 1991. In fall 2010, there were 1,358 students enrolled in distance learning courses. Institutionally administered financial aid is available to distance learners.

Services Distance learners have accessibility to academic advising, bookstore, career placement assistance, e-mail services, library services, tutoring.

Contact Dan Hagberg, Dean for Online Learning & Instructional Technology, Heartland Community College, 1500 West Raab Road, Normal, IL 61761. Telephone: 309-268-8662. Fax: 309-268-7989. E-mail: dan.hagberg@heartland.edu.

DEGREES AND AWARDS
Programs offered do not lead to a degree or other formal award.

COURSE SUBJECT AREAS OFFERED OUTSIDE OF DEGREE PROGRAMS
Undergraduate—accounting and related services; anthropology; business/commerce; communication and media; computer science; economics; education; English; foods, nutrition, and related services; health services/allied health/health sciences; history; human development, family studies, and related services; mathematics; mathematics and statistics related; music; political science and government; psychology; sociology.

Non-credit—business/commerce; computer software and media applications; English or French as a second or foreign language (teaching).

HERITAGE CHRISTIAN UNIVERSITY
Florence, Alabama
Distance Learning
http://www.hcu.edu

Heritage Christian University was founded in 1971. It is accredited by Association for Biblical Higher Education. It first offered distance learning courses in 1992. In fall 2010, there were 37 students enrolled in distance learning courses. Institutionally administered financial aid is available to distance learners.

Services Distance learners have accessibility to academic advising, bookstore, campus computer network, career placement assistance, e-mail services, library services, tutoring.

Contact Brad McKinnon, Admissions Counselor, Heritage Christian University, PO Box HCU, Florence, AL 35630-0051. Telephone: 800-367-3565 Ext. 226. Fax: 256-766-9289. E-mail: bmckinnon@hcu.edu.

DEGREES AND AWARDS
AA Bible; Biblical Studies; Theology
BA Bible; Biblical Studies; Theology
MA Bible; Biblical Studies

HERITAGE COLLEGE
Denver, Colorado
http://www.heritage-education.com/

Heritage College was founded in 1986. It is accredited by Accrediting Commission of Career Schools and Colleges. It first offered distance learning courses in 2002. In fall 2010, there were 400 students enrolled in distance learning courses. Institutionally administered financial aid is available to distance learners.

Services Distance learners have accessibility to academic advising, campus computer network, career placement assistance, e-mail services, library services, tutoring.

Contact Ms. Jamie Valencia, Director of Admissions, Heritage College, 12 Lakeside Lane, Denver, CO 80212. Telephone: 303-477-7240 Ext. 10140. Fax: 303-477-7276. E-mail: jamiev@heritage-education.com.

DEGREES AND AWARDS
AGS Structured Learning
AIS Hospital and Health Services Management

COURSE SUBJECT AREAS OFFERED OUTSIDE OF DEGREE PROGRAMS
Undergraduate—health services/allied health/health sciences.
Non-credit—health services/allied health/health sciences.

HERKIMER COUNTY COMMUNITY COLLEGE
Herkimer, New York
Internet Academy
http://www.ia.herkimer.edu

Herkimer County Community College was founded in 1966. It is accredited by Middle States Association of Colleges and Schools. It first offered distance learning courses in 1997. In fall 2010, there were 1,500 students enrolled in distance learning courses. Institutionally administered financial aid is available to distance learners.

Services Distance learners have accessibility to academic advising, bookstore, career placement assistance, e-mail services, library services, tutoring.

Contact Ms. Linda C. Lamb, Associate Dean of Continuing Education/Internet Academy, Herkimer County Community College, 100 Reservoir Road, Herkimer, NY 13550. Telephone: 315-866-0300 Ext. 8442. Fax: 315-866-0402. E-mail: internetacademy@herkimer.edu.

DEGREES AND AWARDS
AA Liberal Arts and Sciences–General Studies; Liberal Arts and Sciences–Humanities; Liberal Arts and Sciences–Social Science
AAS Business Administration; Business–Accounting; Business–Health Services Management Technology; Business–Human Resource Management; Business–Marketing; Business–Small Business Management; Criminal Justice; Human Services; Paralegal; Travel and Tourism–Hospitality and Events Management
AS Business Administration; Business–Accounting; Business–Business Administration; Criminal Justice; Criminal Justice–Cybersecurity; Criminal Justice–Economic Crime
Certificate Medical Coder/Transcriptionist; Small Business Management; Teaching Assistant

COURSE SUBJECT AREAS OFFERED OUTSIDE OF DEGREE PROGRAMS
Undergraduate—accounting and related services; biology; business administration, management and operations; business/commerce; business/corporate communications; computer and information sciences; com-

puter software and media applications; computer systems networking and telecommunications; criminal justice and corrections; English; entrepreneurial and small business operations; human resources management; human services; liberal arts and sciences, general studies and humanities; mathematics and computer science; psychology; sales, merchandising and related marketing operations (specialized).

HERZING UNIVERSITY ONLINE
Milwaukee, Wisconsin
http://www.herzingonline.edu

Herzing University Online is accredited by North Central Association of Colleges and Schools. It first offered distance learning courses in 2003. In fall 2010, there were 3,000 students enrolled in distance learning courses. Institutionally administered financial aid is available to distance learners.

Services Distance learners have accessibility to academic advising, bookstore, campus computer network, career placement assistance, e-mail services, library services, tutoring.

Contact Mr. Ben Nirschl, Director of Admissions, Herzing University Online, W140 N8917 Lilly Road, Menomonee Falls, WI 53051. Telephone: 866-508-0748 Ext. 840. E-mail: bnirschl@onl.herzing.edu.

DEGREES AND AWARDS

AD Business Management; Graphic Design; Health Information Management; Information Technology Administration and Management; Insurance Billing and Coding Specialist; Legal Studies; Medical Assisting Services; Medical Office Administration; Public Safety; Software Development

BS Accounting; Business Management; Business Management, Business Administration concentration; Business Management, Entrepreneurial Studies concentration; Business Management, Human Resource Development concentration; Criminal Justice; Criminal Justice, Homeland Security concentration; Graphic Design; Graphic Design, Print Design concentration; Graphic Design, Web Design concentration; Health Information Management; Healthcare Management; Homeland Security and Public Safety; Information Technology Administration and Management; Legal Studies; Nursing Bridge program; Software Development; Technology Management; Technology Management, Computer Science minor

Diploma Bookkeeping and Payroll Accounting; Insurance Billing and Coding Specialist; Medical Assisting Services; Medical Office Administration

MBA Business Administration dual concentration; Business Administration; Business Administration, Accounting concentration; Business Administration, Business Management concentration; Business Administration, Healthcare Management concentration; Business Administration, Human Resources concentration; Business Administration, Marketing concentration; Business Administration, Project Management concentration; Business Administration, Technology Management concentration

MSN Nursing, Nursing Education concentration; Nursing, Nursing Management concentration

HIBBING COMMUNITY COLLEGE
Hibbing, Minnesota
http://www.hibbing.edu

Hibbing Community College was founded in 1916. It is accredited by North Central Association of Colleges and Schools. It first offered distance learning courses in 2002. In fall 2010, there were 1,153 students enrolled in distance learning courses. Institutionally administered financial aid is available to distance learners.

Services Distance learners have accessibility to academic advising, bookstore, campus computer network, e-mail services, library services, tutoring.

Contact Mr. Michael Raich, Dean of Academic Affairs, Hibbing Community College, 1515 East 25th Street, Hibbing, MN 55746-3300. Telephone: 218-262-7000. Fax: 218-262-6717. E-mail: michaelraich@hibbing.edu.

DEGREES AND AWARDS

AA General degree; Medical Lab Tech

COURSE SUBJECT AREAS OFFERED OUTSIDE OF DEGREE PROGRAMS

Undergraduate—accounting and related services; anthropology; biological and physical sciences; business administration, management and operations; business, management, and marketing related; chemistry; clinical/medical laboratory science/research; computer and information sciences; computer programming; computer science; computer software and media applications; criminal justice and corrections; culinary arts and related services; data entry/microcomputer applications; economics; fine and studio arts; foods, nutrition, and related services; health/medical preparatory programs; history; information science/studies; intercultural/multicultural and diversity studies; liberal arts and sciences, general studies and humanities; mathematics; multi/interdisciplinary studies related; music; philosophy; political science and government; psychology; social sciences; sociology.

Non-credit—accounting and related services; computer and information sciences; computer software and media applications; real estate.

HILLSBOROUGH COMMUNITY COLLEGE
Tampa, Florida
Distance Learning Office
http://www.hccfl.edu/distance-learning.apx

Hillsborough Community College was founded in 1968. It is accredited by Southern Association of Colleges and Schools. It first offered distance learning courses in 1971. Institutionally administered financial aid is available to distance learners.

Services Distance learners have accessibility to academic advising, bookstore, career placement assistance, e-mail services, library services, tutoring.

Contact Melissa Zucal, Distance Learning Manager, Hillsborough Community College, 39 Columbia, Suite 714, Tampa, FL 33606. Telephone: 813-259-6531. Fax: 813-259-6536. E-mail: mzucal@hccfl.edu.

DEGREES AND AWARDS

Programs offered do not lead to a degree or other formal award.

COURSE SUBJECT AREAS OFFERED OUTSIDE OF DEGREE PROGRAMS

Undergraduate—applied mathematics; astronomy and astrophysics; biology; business administration, management and operations; business/commerce; communication and media; computer and information sciences; computer/information technology administration and management; computer programming; computer science; computer software and media applications; criminal justice and corrections; economics; English; finance and financial management services; fire protection; geological and earth sciences/geosciences; geological/geophysical engineering; health professions related; human development, family studies, and related services; legal studies (non-professional general, undergraduate); marketing; nutrition sciences; ophthalmic and optometric support services and allied professions; political science and government; psychology; sociology.

HOBE SOUND BIBLE COLLEGE
Hobe Sound, Florida
Department of External Studies
http://www.hobeonline.com

Hobe Sound Bible College was founded in 1960. It is accredited by Association for Biblical Higher Education. It first offered distance learning courses in 1993. In fall 2010, there were 100 students enrolled in distance learning courses. Institutionally administered financial aid is available to distance learners.

Services Distance learners have accessibility to academic advising, bookstore, e-mail services, library services.

Contact Mr. Dalbert N. Walker, Dean of Adult Distributed Education, Hobe Sound Bible College, PO Box 1065, Hobe Sound, FL 33475. Telephone: 772-546-5534 Ext. 1014. Fax: 772-545-1422. E-mail: dalbertwalker@hsbc.edu.

DEGREES AND AWARDS

AA Ministerial Studies
BA Christian Studies, general; Ministerial Studies; Ministerial Studies

COURSE SUBJECT AREAS OFFERED OUTSIDE OF DEGREE PROGRAMS

Undergraduate—biblical studies; education (specific levels and methods); missionary studies and missiology; pastoral counseling and specialized ministries; philosophy and religious studies related.
Non-credit—biblical studies; education; missionary studies and missiology; pastoral counseling and specialized ministries; philosophy and religious studies related.

HOCKING COLLEGE
Nelsonville, Ohio
Instructional Development
http://online.hocking.edu/

Hocking College was founded in 1968. It is accredited by North Central Association of Colleges and Schools. It first offered distance learning courses in 1998. In fall 2010, there were 1,076 students enrolled in distance learning courses. Institutionally administered financial aid is available to distance learners.
Services Distance learners have accessibility to academic advising, campus computer network, e-mail services, library services.
Contact Carolyn Tripp, Online Learning Director, Hocking College, Office of Educational Outreach, Oakely 210, 3301 Hocking Parkway, Nelsonville, OH 45764. Telephone: 740-753-6151. E-mail: tripp_c@hocking.edu.

DEGREES AND AWARDS

Programs offered do not lead to a degree or other formal award.

COURSE SUBJECT AREAS OFFERED OUTSIDE OF DEGREE PROGRAMS

Undergraduate—accounting and computer science; allied health and medical assisting services; cell biology and anatomical sciences; communication and media; economics; English; health/medical preparatory programs; hospitality administration; liberal arts and sciences, general studies and humanities; mathematics; psychology; social sciences; visual and performing arts related.

HODGES UNIVERSITY
Naples, Florida
http://www.hodges.edu/admissions/distanceEducation

Hodges University was founded in 1990. It is accredited by Southern Association of Colleges and Schools. It first offered distance learning courses in 1995. In fall 2010, there were 1,500 students enrolled in distance learning courses. Institutionally administered financial aid is available to distance learners.
Services Distance learners have accessibility to academic advising, bookstore, campus computer network, career placement assistance, e-mail services, library services, tutoring.
Contact Ms. Jane Trembath, Director of Distance Admissions, Hodges University, 2655 Northbrooke Drive, Naples, FL 34119. Telephone: 866-684-6689. Fax: 866-684-6064. E-mail: jtrembath@hodges.edu.

DEGREES AND AWARDS

AS Business Administration; Criminal Justice; Health Information Technology; Interdisciplinary Studies; Management; Paralegal Studies
BS Applied Psychology; Criminal Justice; Health Administration; Information Systems Management; Interdisciplinary Studies; Legal Studies; Management
BSBA Business Administration
MBA Business Administration
MISM Information Systems Management
MPA Public Administration
MPS Professional Studies
MSCJ Criminal Justice
MSM Management

HOFSTRA UNIVERSITY
Hempstead, New York
http://www.hofstra.edu/Academics/dl/index.html

Hofstra University was founded in 1935. It is accredited by Middle States Association of Colleges and Schools. It first offered distance learning courses in 2002. In fall 2010, there were 410 students enrolled in distance learning courses. Institutionally administered financial aid is available to distance learners.
Services Distance learners have accessibility to academic advising, bookstore, campus computer network, career placement assistance, e-mail services, library services.
Contact Mr. Ron Chalmers, Manager, Instructional Design Team, Hofstra University, 203 McEwen Hall, 125 Hofstra University, Hempstead, NY 11549-1000. Telephone: 516-463-4532. E-mail: fcsrac@hofstra.edu.

DEGREES AND AWARDS

CAGS Gifted Education (NY State)
MBA Strategic Business Management
MS Ed Educational Leadership and Policy Studies (Higher Education)
MS Computer Science

COURSE SUBJECT AREAS OFFERED OUTSIDE OF DEGREE PROGRAMS

Undergraduate—accounting and computer science; anthropology; behavioral sciences; biochemistry, biophysics and molecular biology; biological and biomedical sciences related; biology; business administration, management and operations; business, management, and marketing related; business/managerial economics; communication and journalism related; communication and media; communication disorders sciences and services; communications technology; computer and information sciences; computer science; education; English; English language and literature related; film/video and photographic arts; health professions related; history; international business; international/global studies; journalism; languages (foreign languages related); languages (Romance languages); liberal arts and sciences, general studies and humanities; marketing; philosophy; philosophy and religious studies related; political science and government; psychology; radio, television, and digital communication; statistics.
Graduate—accounting and related services; biology; business, management, and marketing related; computer and information sciences; computer science; education; educational administration and supervision; gerontology; languages (Romance languages); legal studies (non-professional general, undergraduate); marketing; special education; statistics.
Non-credit—computer science; education; insurance.

HOLY APOSTLES COLLEGE AND SEMINARY
Cromwell, Connecticut
http://www.holyapostles.edu

Holy Apostles College and Seminary was founded in 1956. It is accredited by New England Association of Schools and Colleges. It first offered distance learning courses in 1998. In fall 2010, there were 160 students enrolled in distance learning courses. Institutionally administered financial aid is available to distance learners.
Services Distance learners have accessibility to academic advising, library services, tutoring.
Contact Mr. Robert Mish, Distance Learning Coordinator, Holy Apostles College and Seminary, 33 Prospect Hill Road, Cromwell, CT 06416. Telephone: 860-632-3015. Fax: 860-632-3083. E-mail: distancelearn@holyapostles.edu.

DEGREES AND AWARDS

MA Philosophy; Theology

COURSE SUBJECT AREAS OFFERED OUTSIDE OF DEGREE PROGRAMS

Graduate—philosophy and religious studies related.

HOLYOKE COMMUNITY COLLEGE
Holyoke, Massachusetts
http://webtide.hccdl.org

Holyoke Community College was founded in 1946. It is accredited by New England Association of Schools and Colleges. It first offered distance learning courses in 1999. In fall 2010, there were 1,780 students enrolled in distance learning courses. Institutionally administered financial aid is available to distance learners.

Services Distance learners have accessibility to academic advising, bookstore, campus computer network, career placement assistance, e-mail services, library services, tutoring.

Contact Gloria A. DeFillipo, Dean of Distance Education, Holyoke Community College, 303 Homestead Avenue, Holyoke, MA 01040. Telephone: 413-552-2236. Fax: 413-552-2045. E-mail: gdefillipo@hcc.edu.

DEGREES AND AWARDS
Programs offered do not lead to a degree or other formal award.

COURSE SUBJECT AREAS OFFERED OUTSIDE OF DEGREE PROGRAMS
Undergraduate—accounting and computer science; applied mathematics; business administration, management and operations; business, management, and marketing related; communication and media; computer science; criminal justice and corrections; criminology; data entry/microcomputer applications; economics; English language and literature related; geography and cartography; history; hospitality administration; human resources management; human services; mathematics; music; nutrition sciences; political science and government; psychology; sociology; special education; statistics.

HOPE INTERNATIONAL UNIVERSITY
Fullerton, California
Distance Learning Department
http://www.hiu.edu

Hope International University was founded in 1928. It is accredited by Association for Biblical Higher Education. It first offered distance learning courses in 1994. In fall 2010, there were 511 students enrolled in distance learning courses. Institutionally administered financial aid is available to distance learners.

Services Distance learners have accessibility to academic advising, bookstore, career placement assistance, e-mail services, library services.

Contact Teresa Smith, Director of Admissions, Graduate and Adult Programs, Hope International University, 2500 East Nutwood Avenue, Fullerton, CA 92831. Telephone: 714-879-3901 Ext. 7371. Fax: 714-681-7450. E-mail: spsadmissions@hiu.edu.

DEGREES AND AWARDS
AA General Education
BS Business Administration; Christian Ministry; Human Development; Intercultural Studies
MA Christian Leadership; Educational Administration; Missions/Intercultural Studies; Worship
MBA/MSM General Management; International Development; Marketing Management; Non-Profit Management
MEd Education

COURSE SUBJECT AREAS OFFERED OUTSIDE OF DEGREE PROGRAMS
Undergraduate—anthropology; behavioral sciences; biblical studies; business, management, and marketing related; economics; history; human development, family studies, and related services; intercultural/multicultural and diversity studies; liberal arts and sciences, general studies and humanities; philosophy; psychology; religious studies; sociology.

Graduate—agricultural business and management; biblical studies; business administration, management and operations; education; psychology; religious studies; theological and ministerial studies; urban studies/affairs.

Non-credit—biblical studies; ethnic, cultural minority, gender, and group studies; history; psychology; religious studies.

HOPKINSVILLE COMMUNITY COLLEGE
Hopkinsville, Kentucky
http://hopkinsville.kctcs.edu/academics/distance_online_learning.aspx

Hopkinsville Community College was founded in 1965. It is accredited by Southern Association of Colleges and Schools. It first offered distance learning courses in 2000. In fall 2010, there were 2,061 students enrolled in distance learning courses. Institutionally administered financial aid is available to distance learners.

Services Distance learners have accessibility to academic advising, bookstore, campus computer network, career placement assistance, e-mail services, library services, tutoring.

Contact Dr. Lance Roland Angell, Dean, Institutional Effectiveness, Hopkinsville Community College, ADM 212, 720 North Drive, PO Box 2100, Hopkinsville, KY 42241-2100. Telephone: 270-707-3709. Fax: 270-885-5755. E-mail: lance.angell@kctcs.edu.

DEGREES AND AWARDS
Programs offered do not lead to a degree or other formal award.

COURSE SUBJECT AREAS OFFERED OUTSIDE OF DEGREE PROGRAMS
Undergraduate—accounting and computer science; architectural engineering technologies; arts, entertainment, and media management; astronomy and astrophysics; biology; business, management, and marketing related; chemistry; classical and ancient studies; communication and journalism related; computer engineering; computer science; criminal justice and corrections; economics; education; education related; English language and literature related; family and consumer economics; geography and cartography; history; human services; mathematics and statistics related; music; philosophy; physics; psychology related; sociology; statistics.

Non-credit—accounting and related services; business administration, management and operations; computer and information sciences; design and applied arts; health professions related; languages (foreign languages related); legal professions and studies related; teaching assistants/aides.

HOUSTON COMMUNITY COLLEGE SYSTEM
Houston, Texas
Distance Education Department
http://de.hccs.edu

Houston Community College System was founded in 1971. It is accredited by Southern Association of Colleges and Schools. It first offered distance learning courses in 1985. In fall 2010, there were 12,390 students enrolled in distance learning courses. Institutionally administered financial aid is available to distance learners.

Services Distance learners have accessibility to academic advising, bookstore, e-mail services, library services, tutoring.

Contact Ms. Eva Gonzalez, Program Coordinator, Distance Education, Houston Community College System, 3100 Main Street, MC 1740, Houston, TX 77002. Telephone: 713-718-5152. Fax: 713-718-5388. E-mail: eva.gonzalez@hccs.edu.

DEGREES AND AWARDS
Programs offered do not lead to a degree or other formal award.

COURSE SUBJECT AREAS OFFERED OUTSIDE OF DEGREE PROGRAMS
Undergraduate—accounting and related services; anthropology; astronomy and astrophysics; biology; biotechnology; business administration, management and operations; chemistry; computer/information technology administration and management; computer science; criminology; economics; film/video and photographic arts; fine and studio arts; fire protection; foods, nutrition, and related services; geography and cartography; history; human development, family studies, and related services; human resources management; human services; languages (Romance

languages); management information systems; marketing; mathematics; mathematics and statistics related; philosophy; physical sciences; political science and government; psychology; real estate; sociology.

HUNTINGTON COLLEGE OF HEALTH SCIENCES
Knoxville, Tennessee
http://www.hchs.edu

Huntington College of Health Sciences was founded in 1984. It is accredited by Distance Education and Training Council. It first offered distance learning courses in 1985. In fall 2010, there were 600 students enrolled in distance learning courses. Institutionally administered financial aid is available to distance learners.
Services Distance learners have accessibility to academic advising, bookstore, e-mail services, library services.
Contact Kim Galyon, Director of Admissions, Huntington College of Health Sciences, 1204 D Kenesaw Avenue, Knoxville, TN 37919. Telephone: 800-290-4226. Fax: 865-524-8339. E-mail: studentservices@hchs.edu.

DEGREES AND AWARDS
AS Nutrition
BAS Health Sciences
MS Nutrition–Master of Science of Nutrition

COURSE SUBJECT AREAS OFFERED OUTSIDE OF DEGREE PROGRAMS
Undergraduate—biochemistry, biophysics and molecular biology; biological and physical sciences; biology; cell biology and anatomical sciences; chemistry; English; foods, nutrition, and related services; marketing; mathematics; nutrition sciences; physiology, pathology and related sciences; psychology.
Graduate—chemistry; foods, nutrition, and related services; health professions related; nutrition sciences.
Non-credit—foods, nutrition, and related services; health professions related.

HUSTON-TILLOTSON UNIVERSITY
Austin, Texas

Huston-Tillotson University was founded in 1875. It is accredited by Southern Association of Colleges and Schools. In fall 2010, there were 130 students enrolled in distance learning courses. Institutionally administered financial aid is available to distance learners.
Services Distance learners have accessibility to e-mail services, library services.
Contact Ms. Janice Smith, Assistant Professor of Instructional Technology and Coordinator of Distance Education, Huston-Tillotson University, 900 Chicon Street, Austin, TX 78702. Telephone: 512-505-3165. Fax: 512-505-3190. E-mail: jsmith@htu.edu.

DEGREES AND AWARDS
Programs offered do not lead to a degree or other formal award.

COURSE SUBJECT AREAS OFFERED OUTSIDE OF DEGREE PROGRAMS
Undergraduate—criminal justice and corrections; education; English; sociology.

ILLINOIS CENTRAL COLLEGE
East Peoria, Illinois
http://www.icc.edu

Illinois Central College was founded in 1967. It is accredited by North Central Association of Colleges and Schools. It first offered distance learning courses in 1998. In fall 2010, there were 3,500 students enrolled in distance learning courses. Institutionally administered financial aid is available to distance learners.
Services Distance learners have accessibility to academic advising, bookstore, campus computer network, career placement assistance, e-mail services, library services, tutoring.
Contact Patrice Hess, Interim Associate Dean of Online Learning, Illinois Central College, 1 College Drive, East Peoria, IL 61635. Telephone: 309-694-5295. Fax: 309-694-8567. E-mail: phess@icc.edu.

DEGREES AND AWARDS
AS General Studies
Certificate Emergency Management

ILLINOIS EASTERN COMMUNITY COLLEGES, FRONTIER COMMUNITY COLLEGE
Fairfield, Illinois
http://www.iecc.edu/fcc

Illinois Eastern Community Colleges, Frontier Community College was founded in 1976. It is accredited by North Central Association of Colleges and Schools. It first offered distance learning courses in 1994. In fall 2010, there were 152 students enrolled in distance learning courses. Institutionally administered financial aid is available to distance learners.
Services Distance learners have accessibility to academic advising, bookstore, campus computer network, career placement assistance, e-mail services, library services, tutoring.
Contact Mr. Bob Boyles, Dean of Instruction, Illinois Eastern Community Colleges, Frontier Community College, 2 Frontier Drive, Fairfield, IL 62837. Telephone: 618-842-3711 Ext. 4000. Fax: 618-842-6340. E-mail: boylesr@iecc.edu.

DEGREES AND AWARDS
AAS Administrative Information Tech D219; Science and Arts Transfer Degree D111
AGS General Studies Degree D595
AS Transfer Degree D110

COURSE SUBJECT AREAS OFFERED OUTSIDE OF DEGREE PROGRAMS
Undergraduate—accounting and computer science; allied health and medical assisting services; business/commerce; foods, nutrition, and related services; health and physical education/fitness; human biology; marketing; nutrition sciences; physiology, pathology and related sciences.

ILLINOIS EASTERN COMMUNITY COLLEGES, LINCOLN TRAIL COLLEGE
Robinson, Illinois
http://www.iecc.edu/ltc

Illinois Eastern Community Colleges, Lincoln Trail College was founded in 1969. It is accredited by North Central Association of Colleges and Schools. It first offered distance learning courses in 1994. In fall 2010, there were 496 students enrolled in distance learning courses. Institutionally administered financial aid is available to distance learners.
Services Distance learners have accessibility to academic advising, bookstore, campus computer network, career placement assistance, e-mail services, library services, tutoring.
Contact Ms. Kathy Harris, Dean of Instruction, Illinois Eastern Community Colleges, Lincoln Trail College, 11220 State Highway 1, Robinson, IL 62454. Telephone: 618-544-7423. E-mail: harrisk@iecc.edu.

DEGREES AND AWARDS
AAS Administrative Information Tech D219; Science and Arts Transfer Degree D111
AGS General Studies Degree D595
AS Transfer Degree D110

COURSE SUBJECT AREAS OFFERED OUTSIDE OF DEGREE PROGRAMS
Undergraduate—accounting and computer science; astronomy and astrophysics; business/commerce; computer software and media applications; computer systems networking and telecommunications; geography and cartography; health professions related; mathematics; psychology; psychology related.

ILLINOIS EASTERN COMMUNITY COLLEGES, OLNEY CENTRAL COLLEGE

Olney, Illinois

http://www.iecc.edu/occ

Illinois Eastern Community Colleges, Olney Central College was founded in 1962. It is accredited by North Central Association of Colleges and Schools. It first offered distance learning courses in 1994. In fall 2010, there were 608 students enrolled in distance learning courses. Institutionally administered financial aid is available to distance learners.

Services Distance learners have accessibility to academic advising, bookstore, campus computer network, career placement assistance, e-mail services, library services, tutoring.

Contact Mr. Rodney Ranes, President, Illinois Eastern Community Colleges, Olney Central College, 305 North West Street, Olney, IL 62450. Telephone: 618-395-7777 Ext. 2002. Fax: 618-395-5212. E-mail: ranesr@iecc.edu.

DEGREES AND AWARDS

AAS Accounting and Computing Degree D140; Administrative Information Tech D219; Medical Office Assistant Degree D190; Science and Arts Transfer Degree D111

AGS General Studies Degree D595

AS Transfer Degree D110

COURSE SUBJECT AREAS OFFERED OUTSIDE OF DEGREE PROGRAMS

Undergraduate—accounting and computer science; accounting and related services; business/commerce; communication and media; computer and information sciences; economics; liberal arts and sciences, general studies and humanities; mathematics; psychology; social sciences.

ILLINOIS EASTERN COMMUNITY COLLEGES, WABASH VALLEY COLLEGE

Mount Carmel, Illinois

http://www.iecc.edu/wvc

Illinois Eastern Community Colleges, Wabash Valley College was founded in 1960. It is accredited by North Central Association of Colleges and Schools. It first offered distance learning courses in 1994. In fall 2010, there were 315 students enrolled in distance learning courses. Institutionally administered financial aid is available to distance learners.

Services Distance learners have accessibility to academic advising, bookstore, campus computer network, career placement assistance, e-mail services, library services, tutoring.

Contact Mr. Wayne Morris, Interim Dean of Instruction, Illinois Eastern Community Colleges, Wabash Valley College, 2200 College Drive, Mount Carmel, IL 62863. Telephone: 618-262-8641. E-mail: morrisw@iecc.edu.

DEGREES AND AWARDS

AAS Administrative Information Tech D219; Science and Arts Transfer Degree D111

AGS General Studies Degree D595

AS Transfer Degree D110

COURSE SUBJECT AREAS OFFERED OUTSIDE OF DEGREE PROGRAMS

Undergraduate—accounting and related services; business/commerce; chemistry; history; human resources management; liberal arts and sciences, general studies and humanities; mathematics; mathematics and statistics related; psychology; statistics.

ILLINOIS INSTITUTE OF TECHNOLOGY

Chicago, Illinois

IIT Online

http://www.iit-online.iit.edu

Illinois Institute of Technology was founded in 1890. It is accredited by North Central Association of Colleges and Schools. It first offered distance learning courses in 1976. In fall 2010, there were 1,293 students enrolled in distance learning courses. Institutionally administered financial aid is available to distance learners.

Services Distance learners have accessibility to academic advising, bookstore, campus computer network, career placement assistance, e-mail services, library services.

Contact Mr. Charles Scott, IIT Online Student Services Manager, Illinois Institute of Technology, 10 West 31st Street, Room 103, Stuart Building, Chicago, IL 60616-3793. Telephone: 312-567-5217. Fax: 312-567-5913. E-mail: scott@iit.edu.

DEGREES AND AWARDS

BAT Bachelor of Industrial Technology and Operations
Graduate Certificate Analytical Method Development; Analytical Spectroscopy; Chromatography; Computer Network Security Technologies; Information Systems; Radiologic Physics; Synthesis and Characterization of Inorganic Material; Synthesis and Characterization of Inorganic and Organic Materials; Synthesis and Characterization of Organic Materials
M Ch E Chemical Engineering
MB Biology
MCC Computer Science
MChem Analytical Chemistry; Material and Chemical Synthesis
ME Computer Engineering; Master of Biomedical Imaging and Signals; Telecommunications and Software Engineering
MECE Electrical and Computer Engineering; Master of Network Engineering; Master of VLSI and Microelectronics
MEE Master of Power Engineering
MEM Electricity Markets
MHP Health Physics
MITM Information Technology and Management
MITO Industrial Technology and Operations
MME Master of Manufacturing Engineering via the Internet
MS Computer Science; Electrical Engineering
MTEL Master of Telecommunications and Software Engineering

ILLINOIS STATE UNIVERSITY

Normal, Illinois

Extended University

http://www.provost.ilstu.edu/

Illinois State University was founded in 1857. It is accredited by North Central Association of Colleges and Schools. It first offered distance learning courses in 1994. In fall 2010, there were 1,870 students enrolled in distance learning courses. Institutionally administered financial aid is available to distance learners.

Services Distance learners have accessibility to academic advising, bookstore, campus computer network, career placement assistance, e-mail services, library services.

Contact Mandy Chapman, Coordinator of Academic Services, Illinois State University, Campus Box 4000, Normal, IL 61790. Telephone: 309-438-7018. E-mail: achapma@ilstu.edu.

DEGREES AND AWARDS

BA/BS RHIM-HIM Online Sequence
BSN Nursing–RN to BSN

COURSE SUBJECT AREAS OFFERED OUTSIDE OF DEGREE PROGRAMS

Undergraduate—business, management, and marketing related; communication and journalism related; communication and media; communication disorders sciences and services; criminal justice and corrections; curriculum and instruction; education; education related; English; family

and consumer economics; health professions related; intercultural/multicultural and diversity studies; linguistic, comparative, and related language studies; mathematics.
Graduate—agriculture; chemistry; curriculum and instruction; educational administration and supervision; history; library science related; marketing; mathematics; special education.

ILLINOIS VALLEY COMMUNITY COLLEGE
Oglesby, Illinois
Learning Technologies
http://www.ivcc.edu

Illinois Valley Community College was founded in 1924. It is accredited by North Central Association of Colleges and Schools. It first offered distance learning courses in 1984. In fall 2010, there were 900 students enrolled in distance learning courses.
Services Distance learners have accessibility to academic advising, bookstore, career placement assistance, e-mail services, library services.
Contact Emily Vescogni, Director, Illinois Valley Community College, 815 North Orlando Smith Avenue, Oglesby, IL 61348. Telephone: 815-224-0462. Fax: 815-224-3033. E-mail: emily_vescogni@ivcc.edu.

DEGREES AND AWARDS
Programs offered do not lead to a degree or other formal award.

COURSE SUBJECT AREAS OFFERED OUTSIDE OF DEGREE PROGRAMS
Undergraduate—accounting and related services; biological and physical sciences; business/corporate communications; business, management, and marketing related; computer/information technology administration and management; computer software and media applications; drafting/design engineering technologies; economics; education; English; ethnic, cultural minority, gender, and group studies; film/video and photographic arts; geography and cartography; geological and earth sciences/geosciences; health professions related; health services/allied health/health sciences; liberal arts and sciences, general studies and humanities; mathematics; political science and government; psychology; psychology related; social sciences; sociology.
Non-credit—business administration, management and operations; health professions related.

INDIANA STATE UNIVERSITY
Terre Haute, Indiana
Office of Distance Support Services
http://www.indstate.edu/distance

Indiana State University was founded in 1865. It is accredited by North Central Association of Colleges and Schools. It first offered distance learning courses in 1969. In fall 2010, there were 2,700 students enrolled in distance learning courses. Institutionally administered financial aid is available to distance learners.
Services Distance learners have accessibility to academic advising, bookstore, campus computer network, career placement assistance, e-mail services, library services.
Contact Office of Admissions, Indiana State University, Erickson Hall, Room 114, Terre Haute, IN 47809. Telephone: 800-468-6478. Fax: 812-237-8023. E-mail: studentservices@indstate.edu.

DEGREES AND AWARDS
BS Adult and Career Education; Business Administration; Criminology and Criminal Justice; Electronics Engineering Technology; Human Resource Development; Insurance and Risk Management; Mechanical Engineering Technology; Nursing–LPN-BS; Nursing–RN to BS; Technology Management
Certificate Corrections; Law Enforcement; Post-Secondary Facilitator; Private Security and Loss Prevention
License Career and Technical Education Business License; Driver Education Instructor; Middle/Secondary Teaching; School Administration; Visual Impairment
Graduate Certificate Gifted and Talented; Human Resource Development; Public Administration; Public Librarian Level IV; Public Personnel Administration; School Library Media Services; Teaching English as a Second or Foreign Language
MA Criminology and Criminal Justice
MPA Public Administration
MS Criminology and Criminal Justice; Electronics and Computer Technology; Health Sciences, Public Health concentration; Health and Safety (Occupational Safety Management specialization); Human Resource Development; Nursing–Nursing Administration specialization; Nursing–Nursing Education specialization; Student Affairs and Higher Education; Student Affairs and Higher Education
DNP Nursing Practice
PhD Technology Management

COURSE SUBJECT AREAS OFFERED OUTSIDE OF DEGREE PROGRAMS
Undergraduate—accounting and computer science; accounting and related services; aerospace, aeronautical and astronautical engineering; biological and physical sciences; biology; botany/plant biology; business administration, management and operations; business/commerce; business, management, and marketing related; business operations support and assistant services; chemistry; computer programming; computer science; construction engineering technologies; construction management; criminal justice and corrections; criminology; curriculum and instruction; drafting/design engineering technologies; economics; education; education related; electrical engineering technologies; engineering-related technologies; English; finance and financial management services; geography and cartography; health and physical education/fitness; history; human resources management; human services; insurance; library science related; management information systems; marketing; mathematics; mathematics and computer science; mathematics and statistics related; mechanical engineering related technologies; music; psychology; sociology.
Graduate—bilingual, multilingual, and multicultural education; criminal justice and corrections; criminology; curriculum and instruction; education; educational administration and supervision; educational assessment, evaluation, and research; educational/instructional media design; education related; education (specific levels and methods); education (specific subject areas); electrical, electronics and communications engineering; electrical engineering technologies; electromechanical instrumentation and maintenance technologies; English or French as a second or foreign language (teaching); finance and financial management services; human resources management; library science related; public administration; public administration and social service professions related; special education; student counseling and personnel services.

INDIANA TECH
Fort Wayne, Indiana
Independent Study
http://www.indianatech.edu/online

Indiana Tech was founded in 1930. It is accredited by North Central Association of Colleges and Schools. It first offered distance learning courses in 1982. In fall 2010, there were 1,082 students enrolled in distance learning courses. Institutionally administered financial aid is available to distance learners.
Services Distance learners have accessibility to academic advising, bookstore, campus computer network, career placement assistance, e-mail services, library services, tutoring.
Contact Warrior Information Network, Indiana Tech, 1600 East Washington Boulevard, Fort Wayne, IN 46803. Telephone: 888-832-4742. Fax: 888-832-4844. E-mail: win@indianatech.edu.

DEGREES AND AWARDS
AS Accounting; Business Administration–Management; Business Administration–Production Management; Criminal Justice; General Studies
BS Accounting; Business Administration–Health Care Administration; Business Administration–Human Resources; Business Administration–Management; Business Administration–Marketing; Criminal Justice–Crime Analysis; Criminal Justice–Criminal Justice Administration; Criminal Justice–Rehabilitative Services; Management–Information Systems; Organizational Leadership; Psychology

MBA Business Administration and Accounting; Business Administration and Health Care Management; Business Administration and Human Resources; Business Administration and Marketing; Business Administration–Management
MS Organizational Leadership; Police Administration
MSE Engineering Management
MSM Business Administration and Management
PhD Global Leadership–Academic Administration; Global Leadership–Organizational Management

INDIANA UNIVERSITY OF PENNSYLVANIA
Indiana, Pennsylvania
School of Continuing Education
http://www.iup.edu/distance/

Indiana University of Pennsylvania was founded in 1875. It is accredited by Middle States Association of Colleges and Schools. It first offered distance learning courses in 1990. In fall 2010, there were 1,873 students enrolled in distance learning courses. Institutionally administered financial aid is available to distance learners.
Services Distance learners have accessibility to academic advising, bookstore, campus computer network, career placement assistance, e-mail services, library services.
Contact Mr. Stephen Anspacher, Coordinator of Distance Education, Indiana University of Pennsylvania, Distance Learning and Continuing Education, Keith Hall 100, Indiana, PA 15705. Telephone: 724-357-2292. E-mail: stephen.anspacher@iup.edu.

DEGREES AND AWARDS
Certification Information Assurance certificate of recognition
Graduate Certificate Safety Sciences
MA Criminology
MS Safety Science

COURSE SUBJECT AREAS OFFERED OUTSIDE OF DEGREE PROGRAMS
Undergraduate—accounting and related services; anthropology; arts, entertainment, and media management; business, management, and marketing related; communication and media; computer science; criminology; education; English; finance and financial management services; foods, nutrition, and related services; health and physical education/fitness; hospitality administration; information science/studies; journalism; management information systems; marketing; mathematics; music; philosophy; physics; political science and government; psychology.
Graduate—anthropology; business, management, and marketing related; criminal justice and corrections; criminology; education; engineering-related fields; English; foods, nutrition, and related services; health and physical education/fitness; liberal arts and sciences, general studies and humanities; mathematics; music; physics; political science and government; science technologies related; student counseling and personnel services.

INDIANA UNIVERSITY–PURDUE UNIVERSITY FORT WAYNE
Fort Wayne, Indiana
http://new.ipfw.edu/online

Indiana University–Purdue University Fort Wayne was founded in 1917. It is accredited by North Central Association of Colleges and Schools. It first offered distance learning courses in 1996. In fall 2010, there were 5,968 students enrolled in distance learning courses. Institutionally administered financial aid is available to distance learners.
Services Distance learners have accessibility to bookstore, campus computer network, e-mail services, library services.
Contact Karen VanGorder, Director of Online Learning, Indiana University–Purdue University Fort Wayne, 2101 East Coliseum Boulevard, Fort Wayne, IN 46805. Telephone: 260-481-6016. Fax: 260-481-6949. E-mail: vangordk@ipfw.edu.

DEGREES AND AWARDS
BGS General Studies–Associate of Arts and Bachelor of General Studies

COURSE SUBJECT AREAS OFFERED OUTSIDE OF DEGREE PROGRAMS
Undergraduate—accounting and related services; anthropology; architectural engineering technologies; astronomy and astrophysics; biology; business/commerce; chemistry; communication and journalism related; communication and media; computer science; economics; education; engineering; English; fine and studio arts; geological and earth sciences/geosciences; history; human services; industrial engineering; journalism; manufacturing engineering; mathematics; music; pharmacology and toxicology; philosophy; philosophy and religious studies related; physics; political science and government; psychology; registered nursing, nursing administration, nursing research and clinical nursing; sociology.
Graduate—business administration, management and operations; educational administration and supervision; registered nursing, nursing administration, nursing research and clinical nursing.
Non-credit—allied health and medical assisting services; business, management, and marketing related; manufacturing engineering; pharmacy, pharmaceutical sciences, and administration.

INDIANA UNIVERSITY SYSTEM
Bloomington, Indiana
School of Continuing Studies
http://scs.indiana.edu

Indiana University System is accredited by North Central Association of Colleges and Schools. It first offered distance learning courses in 1995. In fall 2010, there were 3,500 students enrolled in distance learning courses. Institutionally administered financial aid is available to distance learners.
Services Distance learners have accessibility to academic advising, bookstore, campus computer network, e-mail services, library services.
Contact Peer Advisor, Indiana University System, 408 North Union Street, Bloomington, IN 47405. Telephone: 800-334-1011. Fax: 812-855-8680. E-mail: scs@indiana.edu.

DEGREES AND AWARDS
Certificate Accounting–Healthcare Accounting and Financial Management; Distance Education
MS Adult Education

INDIANA WESLEYAN UNIVERSITY
Marion, Indiana
http://www.indwes.edu

Indiana Wesleyan University was founded in 1920. It is accredited by North Central Association of Colleges and Schools. It first offered distance learning courses in 1996. In fall 2010, there were 6,388 students enrolled in distance learning courses. Institutionally administered financial aid is available to distance learners.
Services Distance learners have accessibility to academic advising, bookstore, campus computer network, career placement assistance, e-mail services, library services, tutoring.
Contact Mrs. Leslie Zolman, Director of Admissions, Indiana Wesleyan University, 1900 West 50th Street, Marion, IN 46953. Telephone: 866-IWU-4YOU. Fax: 765-677-2541. E-mail: aes@indwes.edu.

DEGREES AND AWARDS
AS Accounting; Business; Christian Ministries; Computer Information Technology; Criminal Justice; General Studies
BS Accounting; Addictions Counseling; Biblical Studies; Business Information Systems; Criminal Justice; General Studies; Management; Marketing; Nursing–RN to BS completion
BSBA Business Administration
Certificate Communications; Criminal Justice; Human Services; Nursing–Parish Nursing; Religious Studies
License Career Builders for Educators; Exceptional Learners Education; Transition to Teaching
CAGS Addictions Counseling
CCCPE General Studies
Graduate Certificate Accounting; Health Care Management; Human Resources; Nursing–post-Masters Primary Care Nursing

MA Addictions Counseling; Ministry (Ministerial Leadership and Youth Ministry concentrations); Organizational Leadership; Student Development Counseling and Administration
MBA Business Administration; Virtual MBA (Executive Management); Virtual MBA (International Business); Xpress
MDiv Ministry
MEd Education
MSM Management
MSN Nursing Administration; Nursing Education; Nursing–Primary Care Nursing
EdD Organizational Leadership

COURSE SUBJECT AREAS OFFERED OUTSIDE OF DEGREE PROGRAMS

Undergraduate—biblical studies; business administration, management and operations; communication and media; computer and information sciences; computer software and media applications; criminal justice and corrections; fine and studio arts; history; languages (foreign languages related); liberal arts and sciences, general studies and humanities; mathematics; music; philosophy; psychology.
Graduate—biblical studies; liberal arts and sciences, general studies and humanities; mathematics; mathematics and computer science; mathematics and statistics related; multi/interdisciplinary studies related; music; philosophy; philosophy and religious studies; philosophy and religious studies related; psychology; psychology related; public administration and social service professions related; public policy analysis; public relations, advertising, and applied communication related; religious education; religious/sacred music; religious studies; sales merchandising, and related marketing operations (general); sales, merchandising and related marketing operations (specialized); science technologies; science technologies related; science, technology and society; social sciences; social sciences related; sociology; statistics; theological and ministerial studies; theology and religious vocations related; veterinary biomedical and clinical sciences.

INSTITUTE FOR CHRISTIAN STUDIES
Toronto, Ontario, Canada
http://www.icscanada.edu

Institute for Christian Studies was founded in 1967. It is provincially chartered. It first offered distance learning courses in 1990. In fall 2010, there were 7 students enrolled in distance learning courses. Institutionally administered financial aid is available to distance learners.
Services Distance learners have accessibility to academic advising, e-mail services, library services.
Contact Mr. Shawn Stovell, Associate Academic Dean/Registrar, Institute for Christian Studies, 229 College Street, Suite 100, Toronto, ON M5T 1R4, Canada. Telephone: 888-326-5347 Ext. 239. Fax: 416-979-2332. E-mail: sstovell@icscanada.edu.

DEGREES AND AWARDS

MWS Education

COURSE SUBJECT AREAS OFFERED OUTSIDE OF DEGREE PROGRAMS

Graduate—education related; philosophy; philosophy and religious studies related; political science and government; theological and ministerial studies.

INTER AMERICAN UNIVERSITY OF PUERTO RICO, SAN GERMÁN CAMPUS
San Germán, Puerto Rico
http://www.sg.inter.edu/

Inter American University of Puerto Rico, San Germán Campus was founded in 1912. It is accredited by Middle States Association of Colleges and Schools. It first offered distance learning courses in 1997. In fall 2010, there were 646 students enrolled in distance learning courses. Institutionally administered financial aid is available to distance learners.
Services Distance learners have accessibility to campus computer network, e-mail services, library services.
Contact Prof. Luis M. Zornosa, Distance Learning Coordinator, Inter American University of Puerto Rico, San Germán Campus, PO Box 5100, Department of Management and Entrepreneurial Sciences, San Germán, PR 00683. Telephone: 787-264-1912 Ext. 7407. E-mail: lzornosa@sg.inter.edu.

DEGREES AND AWARDS

Programs offered do not lead to a degree or other formal award.

COURSE SUBJECT AREAS OFFERED OUTSIDE OF DEGREE PROGRAMS

Undergraduate—accounting and computer science; behavioral sciences; business/managerial economics; computer and information sciences; computer science; education (specific levels and methods); engineering; engineering related; English language and literature related; finance and financial management services; health and physical education/fitness; history; liberal arts and sciences, general studies and humanities; management information systems; marketing; music; philosophy and religious studies related; social sciences.
Graduate—accounting and related services; business administration, management and operations; business, management, and marketing related; business/managerial economics; library science and administration; management information systems.

IONA COLLEGE
New Rochelle, New York
http://www.iona.edu

Iona College was founded in 1940. It is accredited by Middle States Association of Colleges and Schools. It first offered distance learning courses in 1999. In fall 2010, there were 141 students enrolled in distance learning courses. Institutionally administered financial aid is available to distance learners.
Services Distance learners have accessibility to academic advising, bookstore, campus computer network, career placement assistance, e-mail services, library services, tutoring.
Contact Mr. Kevin Cavanagh, Assistant Vice President for College Admissions, Iona College, Admissions, 715 North Avenue, New Rochelle, NY 10801. Telephone: 914-633-2502. Fax: 914-633-2642. E-mail: kcavanagh@iona.edu.

DEGREES AND AWARDS

Programs offered do not lead to a degree or other formal award.

COURSE SUBJECT AREAS OFFERED OUTSIDE OF DEGREE PROGRAMS

Undergraduate—business administration, management and operations; business/corporate communications; business, management, and marketing related; business operations support and assistant services; communication and journalism related; communication and media; computer and information sciences and support services related; computer programming; computer software and media applications; economics; entrepreneurial and small business operations; finance and financial management services; health and medical administrative services; health professions related; health services/allied health/health sciences; international business; legal studies (non-professional general, undergraduate); liberal arts and sciences, general studies and humanities; management information systems; marketing; mathematics; philosophy; philosophy and religious studies related; psychology; psychology related; science, technology and society; social work.
Graduate—business administration, management and operations; business/commerce; business/corporate communications; business, management, and marketing related; business/managerial economics; communication and journalism related; communications technologies and support services related; computer and information sciences; computer engineering technologies; computer/information technology administration and management; computer science; computer software and media applications; computer systems analysis; computer systems networking and telecommunications; economics; education; educational administration and supervision; educational assessment, evaluation, and research; educational/instructional media design; education related; education (specific levels and methods); education (specific subject areas); finance and financial

management services; health and medical administrative services; health professions related; health services/allied health/health sciences; history; human resources management; information science/studies; international business; journalism; languages (Romance languages); legal professions and studies related; management information systems; marketing; psychology; public relations, advertising, and applied communication related.

IOWA LAKES COMMUNITY COLLEGE
Estherville, Iowa
http://www.iowalakes.edu

Iowa Lakes Community College was founded in 1967. It is accredited by North Central Association of Colleges and Schools. It first offered distance learning courses in 1999. In fall 2010, there were 2,000 students enrolled in distance learning courses. Institutionally administered financial aid is available to distance learners.

Services Distance learners have accessibility to academic advising, bookstore, campus computer network, career placement assistance, e-mail services, library services, tutoring.

Contact Ms. Theresa Zeigler, Distance and Global Education Director, Iowa Lakes Community College, 300 South 18th Street, Estherville, IA 51334. Telephone: 712-362-2604 Ext. 148. Fax: 712-362-8363. E-mail: tzeigler@iowalakes.edu.

DEGREES AND AWARDS
AA Liberal Arts, general

COURSE SUBJECT AREAS OFFERED OUTSIDE OF DEGREE PROGRAMS
Undergraduate—accounting and computer science; accounting and related services; agricultural business and management; agriculture and agriculture operations related; biological and biomedical sciences related; biology; business, management, and marketing related; business/managerial economics; chemistry; communications technology; computer software and media applications; criminal justice and corrections; English language and literature related; history; human biology; languages (foreign languages related); liberal arts and sciences, general studies and humanities; mathematics; music; philosophy and religious studies; physical sciences related; psychology related; science technologies related; social sciences; sociology and anthropology.

Non-credit—computer software and media applications.

IOWA VALLEY COMMUNITY COLLEGE DISTRICT
Marshalltown, Iowa
http://www.iavalley.edu/

Iowa Valley Community College District first offered distance learning courses in 1999. In fall 2010, there were 1,104 students enrolled in distance learning courses. Institutionally administered financial aid is available to distance learners.

Services Distance learners have accessibility to bookstore, campus computer network, e-mail services, library services, tutoring.

Contact Dr. Chris A. Russell, Chief Academic Officer, Iowa Valley Community College District, 3700 South Center Street, Marshalltown, IA 50158. Telephone: 641-844-5716. E-mail: chris.russell@iavalley.edu.

DEGREES AND AWARDS
AA the Arts

COURSE SUBJECT AREAS OFFERED OUTSIDE OF DEGREE PROGRAMS
Undergraduate—accounting and related services; behavioral sciences; biological and biomedical sciences related; business, management, and marketing related; communication and media; criminal justice and corrections; economics; education; history; management sciences and quantitative methods; mathematics; nutrition sciences; philosophy and religious studies related; psychology; sociology; statistics.

ITASCA COMMUNITY COLLEGE
Grand Rapids, Minnesota
http://www.itascacc.edu

Itasca Community College was founded in 1922. It is accredited by North Central Association of Colleges and Schools. It first offered distance learning courses in 2006. In fall 2010, there were 200 students enrolled in distance learning courses. Institutionally administered financial aid is available to distance learners.

Services Distance learners have accessibility to academic advising, bookstore, campus computer network, e-mail services.

Contact Ms. Gwen Litchke, Registrar, Itasca Community College, 1851 East Highway 169, Grand Rapids, MN 55744. Telephone: 218-322-2329. Fax: 218-322-2332. E-mail: glitchke@itascacc.edu.

DEGREES AND AWARDS
Programs offered do not lead to a degree or other formal award.

COURSE SUBJECT AREAS OFFERED OUTSIDE OF DEGREE PROGRAMS
Undergraduate—biology; computer science; health/medical preparatory programs; history; industrial production technologies; natural sciences.

ITHACA COLLEGE
Ithaca, New York
http://www.ithaca.edu/gps

Ithaca College was founded in 1892. It is accredited by Middle States Association of Colleges and Schools. It first offered distance learning courses in 2006. In fall 2010, there were 50 students enrolled in distance learning courses. Institutionally administered financial aid is available to distance learners.

Services Distance learners have accessibility to academic advising, e-mail services, library services.

Contact Jennifer Wofford, PhD, Graduate and Professional Studies, Ithaca College, Ithaca, NY 14850. E-mail: jwofford@ithaca.edu.

DEGREES AND AWARDS
Programs offered do not lead to a degree or other formal award.

COURSE SUBJECT AREAS OFFERED OUTSIDE OF DEGREE PROGRAMS
Undergraduate—anthropology; biology; communication and media; economics; health services/allied health/health sciences; journalism; marketing; mathematics; philosophy; political science and government; religious education; sociology.

JACKSONVILLE STATE UNIVERSITY
Jacksonville, Alabama
Office of Distance Education
http://www.jsu.edu/distance

Jacksonville State University was founded in 1883. It is accredited by Southern Association of Colleges and Schools. It first offered distance learning courses in 1994. In fall 2010, there were 3,281 students enrolled in distance learning courses. Institutionally administered financial aid is available to distance learners.

Services Distance learners have accessibility to academic advising, bookstore, career placement assistance, e-mail services, library services, tutoring.

Contact Ms. Gina Glass, Secretary to the Associate Vice President of Distance Education, Jacksonville State University, Office of Distance Education, 700 Pelham Road North, Jacksonville, AL 36265-1602. Telephone: 256-782-8172. Fax: 256-782-8128. E-mail: dlinfo@jsu.edu.

DEGREES AND AWARDS
BS Business/Management; Emergency Management (Homeland Security minor); Emergency Management (Public Safety Communications minor); Family and Consumer Sciences, Child Development concentration
BSN Nursing–RN to BSN STEP program

Graduate Certificate Emergency Management; Geographical Information Systems; Nursing Education
MBA Business Administration
MPA Emergency Management; Geographical Information Systems; Sport Management
MS Computer Systems and Software Design; Emergency Management; Manufacturing Systems Technology
MSE Collaborative 6-12; Collaborative K-6; Early Childhood Education; Instructional Leadership; Library Media; Physical Education
MSN Nursing–RN to BSN to MSN STEP program; Nursing

COURSE SUBJECT AREAS OFFERED OUTSIDE OF DEGREE PROGRAMS

Undergraduate—accounting and computer science; accounting and related services; anthropology; applied mathematics; atmospheric sciences and meteorology; behavioral sciences; biological and biomedical sciences related; biological and physical sciences; biology; biology/biotechnology laboratory technician; biopsychology; business administration, management and operations; business/commerce; business/corporate communications; business, management, and marketing related; business/managerial economics; chemistry; computer and information sciences; computer and information sciences and support services related; computer/information technology administration and management; computer programming; computer science; computer software and media applications; computer systems analysis; computer systems networking and telecommunications; criminal justice and corrections; criminology; curriculum and instruction; data processing; economics; education; educational administration and supervision; educational assessment, evaluation, and research; educational/instructional media design; education related; education (specific levels and methods); education (specific subject areas); engineering; English; English language and literature related; environmental control technologies; family and consumer economics; family and consumer sciences/human sciences; family and consumer sciences/human sciences business services; family and consumer sciences/human sciences related; finance and financial management services; foods, nutrition, and related services; genetics; geography and cartography; geological and earth sciences/geosciences; gerontology; health and physical education/fitness; health professions related; history; homeland security, law enforcement, firefighting and protective services related; human development, family studies, and related services; information science/studies; international business; languages (foreign languages related); liberal arts and sciences, general studies and humanities; management information systems; management sciences and quantitative methods; marketing; mathematics; mathematics and computer science; mathematics and statistics related; music; nutrition sciences; physical sciences; physics; political science and government; psychology; psychology related; public administration; public administration and social service professions related; quality control and safety technologies; sales merchandising, and related marketing operations (general); sales, merchandising and related marketing operations (specialized); science, technology and society; social and philosophical foundations of education; social sciences; social work; sociology; special education; statistics; student counseling and personnel services; visual and performing arts; visual and performing arts related.
Graduate—accounting and computer science; accounting and related services; behavioral sciences; biology; business administration, management and operations; business/commerce; business/corporate communications; business, management, and marketing related; business/managerial economics; chemistry; computer and information sciences; computer and information sciences and support services related; computer engineering; computer/information technology administration and management; computer programming; computer science; computer software and media applications; computer systems analysis; computer systems networking and telecommunications; criminal justice and corrections; criminology; curriculum and instruction; economics; education; educational administration and supervision; educational assessment, evaluation, and research; educational/instructional media design; education related; education (specific levels and methods); education (specific subject areas); environmental control technologies; family and consumer sciences/human sciences related; finance and financial management services; fire protection; geography and cartography; geological and earth sciences/geosciences; health and physical education/fitness; health professions related; homeland security, law enforcement, firefighting and protective services related; human development, family studies, and related services; human resources management; information science/studies; liberal arts and sciences, general studies and humanities; management information systems; management sciences and quantitative methods; marketing; mathematics and computer science; pharmacology and toxicology; physical sciences; political science and government; psychology; psychology related; public administration; public administration and social service professions related; quality control and safety technologies; sales merchandising, and related marketing operations (general); sales, merchandising and related marketing operations (specialized); science, technology and society; social and philosophical foundations of education; social sciences; social work; sociology; special education; statistics.

JAMES A. RHODES STATE COLLEGE
Lima, Ohio
http://www.rhodesstate.edu

James A. Rhodes State College was founded in 1971. It is accredited by North Central Association of Colleges and Schools. It first offered distance learning courses in 1991. In fall 2010, there were 1,432 students enrolled in distance learning courses. Institutionally administered financial aid is available to distance learners.
Services Distance learners have accessibility to academic advising, bookstore, campus computer network, career placement assistance, e-mail services, library services, tutoring.
Contact Chad Teman, Admissions, James A. Rhodes State College, 4240 Campus Drive, Lima, OH 45804. Telephone: 419-995-8010. Fax: 419-995-8098. E-mail: teman.c@rhodesstate.edu.

DEGREES AND AWARDS

AAB Business Administration; Business Management; Marketing
AAS Corrections; Emergency Medical Services program; Industrial Engineering Technology; Occupational Therapy Assistant; Physical Therapist Assistant; Radiographic Imaging; Respiratory Care
ATS Concrete

COURSE SUBJECT AREAS OFFERED OUTSIDE OF DEGREE PROGRAMS

Undergraduate—accounting and related services; allied health and medical assisting services; business/commerce; business operations support and assistant services; civil engineering technologies; communication and media; computer programming; computer software and media applications; construction trades related; criminal justice and corrections; dental support services and allied professions; design and applied arts; education (specific levels and methods); electrical/electronics maintenance and repair technology; engineering technologies related; finance and financial management services; geography and cartography; health/medical preparatory programs; health professions related; human services; legal studies (non-professional general, undergraduate); liberal arts and sciences, general studies and humanities; physiology, pathology and related sciences; psychology related; quality control and safety technologies; sales merchandising, and related marketing operations (general); sales, merchandising and related marketing operations (specialized); social sciences related.
Non-credit—manufacturing engineering.

JAMES MADISON UNIVERSITY
Harrisonburg, Virginia
Distance Learning Center, Office of Continuing Education
http://cit.jmu.edu/online_learning/

James Madison University was founded in 1908. It is accredited by Southern Association of Colleges and Schools. It first offered distance learning courses in 1996. In fall 2010, there were 881 students enrolled in distance learning courses. Institutionally administered financial aid is available to distance learners.
Services Distance learners have accessibility to academic advising, bookstore, campus computer network, career placement assistance, e-mail services, library services.

Contact Ms. Andrea Adams, Assistant Director, Faculty Development and E-Learning Programs, James Madison University, Center for Instructional Technology, Carrier Library, MSC 1702, Harrisonburg, VA 22807. Telephone: 540-568-6568. Fax: 540-568-6734. E-mail: adamsah@jmu.edu.

DEGREES AND AWARDS

MBA Information Security
MC Sc Information Security
MS Health Science/Dietetics; Speech-Language Pathology

COURSE SUBJECT AREAS OFFERED OUTSIDE OF DEGREE PROGRAMS

Undergraduate—accounting and related services; biology; business/commerce; communication and media; communications technology; criminal justice and corrections; education (specific levels and methods); English; fine and studio arts; geological and earth sciences/geosciences; health and physical education/fitness; health professions related; history; human resources management; linguistic, comparative, and related language studies; mathematics and statistics related; music; nutrition sciences; philosophy; psychology; sociology; statistics.
Graduate—business administration, management and operations; computer science; health and medical administrative services; health professions related; nutrition sciences; special education.
Non-credit—business administration, management and operations; business/managerial economics; computer and information sciences; education (specific subject areas); health and medical administrative services; international/global studies; manufacturing engineering; medical clinical sciences/graduate medical studies; special education; student counseling and personnel services.

JAMESTOWN COLLEGE
Jamestown, North Dakota

Jamestown College was founded in 1883. It is accredited by North Central Association of Colleges and Schools. It first offered distance learning courses in 2011. In fall 2010, there were 25 students enrolled in distance learning courses. Institutionally administered financial aid is available to distance learners.
Services Distance learners have accessibility to bookstore, e-mail services.
Contact Ms. Tena Lawrence, Dean of Enrollment Management, Jamestown College, 6080 College Lane, Jamestown, ND 58405. Telephone: 701-252-3467 Ext. 5562. Fax: 701-253-4318. E-mail: tlawrenc@jc.edu.

DEGREES AND AWARDS

Programs offered do not lead to a degree or other formal award.

COURSE SUBJECT AREAS OFFERED OUTSIDE OF DEGREE PROGRAMS

Undergraduate—behavioral sciences; biological and physical sciences; business administration, management and operations; chemistry; computer science; English; history.

JAMESTOWN COMMUNITY COLLEGE
Jamestown, New York
Distance Education
http://www.sunyjcc.edu/online

Jamestown Community College was founded in 1950. It is accredited by Middle States Association of Colleges and Schools. It first offered distance learning courses in 1995. In fall 2010, there were 1,013 students enrolled in distance learning courses. Institutionally administered financial aid is available to distance learners.
Services Distance learners have accessibility to academic advising, bookstore, campus computer network, career placement assistance, e-mail services, library services, tutoring.
Contact Admissions Office, Jamestown Community College, 525 Falconer Street, PO Box 20, Jamestown, NY 14702-0020. Telephone: 800-388-8557 Ext. 1001. Fax: 716-338-1450. E-mail: admissions@mail.sunyjcc.edu.

DEGREES AND AWARDS

AA Individual Studies; Individual Studies
AAS Business–Business Administration; Individual Studies; Information Technology
AS Computer Science
CCCPE Individual Studies; Information Technology; Psychology of the Workplace

COURSE SUBJECT AREAS OFFERED OUTSIDE OF DEGREE PROGRAMS

Undergraduate—accounting and computer science; accounting and related services; biblical studies; business administration, management and operations; business/commerce; business/corporate communications; business, management, and marketing related; business/managerial economics; business operations support and assistant services; communication and media; computer and information sciences; computer and information sciences and support services related; computer engineering; computer engineering technologies; computer/information technology administration and management; computer programming; computer science; computer software and media applications; computer systems analysis; computer systems networking and telecommunications; criminal justice and corrections; criminology; English; English language and literature related; entrepreneurial and small business operations; history; human development, family studies, and related services; human resources management; human services; languages (foreign languages related); liberal arts and sciences, general studies and humanities; marketing; mathematics; mathematics and computer science; pharmacology and toxicology; psychology; psychology related; statistics.
Non-credit—accounting and related services; business administration, management and operations; business/commerce; business/corporate communications; business, management, and marketing related; business operations support and assistant services; communication and media; computer and information sciences; computer and information sciences and support services related; computer software and media applications; computer systems networking and telecommunications; entrepreneurial and small business operations; finance and financial management services; food science and technology; health and medical administrative services; human resources management; human services; journalism; liberal arts and sciences, general studies and humanities; linguistic, comparative, and related language studies; marketing; psychology related; real estate; sociology.

JEFFERSON COMMUNITY COLLEGE
Watertown, New York
Division of Continuing Education
http://www.sunyjefferson.edu

Jefferson Community College was founded in 1961. It is accredited by Middle States Association of Colleges and Schools. It first offered distance learning courses in 1995. In fall 2010, there were 1,532 students enrolled in distance learning courses. Institutionally administered financial aid is available to distance learners.
Services Distance learners have accessibility to academic advising, bookstore, career placement assistance, e-mail services, library services, tutoring.
Contact Gina Costanzo, Distance Learning Coordinator, Jefferson Community College, 1220 Coffeen Street, Watertown, NY 13601. Telephone: 315-786-2440. Fax: 315-786-0158. E-mail: gcostanzo@sunyjefferson.edu.

DEGREES AND AWARDS

AA Individual Studies; Liberal Arts–Humanities and Social Science
AAS Individual Studies
AS Business Administration; Criminal Justice; Individual Studies

COURSE SUBJECT AREAS OFFERED OUTSIDE OF DEGREE PROGRAMS

Undergraduate—accounting and related services; anthropology; behavioral sciences; biology; business administration, management and operations; business, management, and marketing related; chemistry; economics; English; geological and earth sciences/geosciences; health and physical education/fitness; history; mathematics and statistics related; psychology; social sciences; sociology.

Non-credit—computer software and media applications.

JOHN A. LOGAN COLLEGE
Carterville, Illinois
Learning Resources
http://www.jalc.edu

John A. Logan College was founded in 1967. It is accredited by North Central Association of Colleges and Schools. It first offered distance learning courses in 1998. In fall 2010, there were 1,000 students enrolled in distance learning courses. Institutionally administered financial aid is available to distance learners.

Services Distance learners have accessibility to academic advising, campus computer network, career placement assistance, e-mail services, library services.

Contact Mr. Terry Crain, Dean of Student Services, John A. Logan College, 700 Logan College Road, Carterville, IL 62918. Telephone: 618-985-2828 Ext. 8221. E-mail: janeminton@jalc.edu.

DEGREES AND AWARDS

AA General degree

COURSE SUBJECT AREAS OFFERED OUTSIDE OF DEGREE PROGRAMS

Undergraduate—accounting and computer science; accounting and related services; allied health and medical assisting services; American Sign Language (ASL); anthropology; astronomy and astrophysics; biological and physical sciences; biology; business, management, and marketing related; business/managerial economics; computer and information sciences; computer and information sciences and support services related; computer science; computer software and media applications; computer systems networking and telecommunications; data processing; dental support services and allied professions; design and applied arts; education; education related; English; English language and literature related; film/video and photographic arts; history; liberal arts and sciences, general studies and humanities; literature; marketing; mathematics; mathematics and computer science; music; physics; political science and government; psychology; religious studies.

JOHN JAY COLLEGE OF CRIMINAL JUSTICE OF THE CITY UNIVERSITY OF NEW YORK
New York, New York
http://www.jjay.cuny.edu

John Jay College of Criminal Justice of the City University of New York was founded in 1964. It is accredited by Middle States Association of Colleges and Schools. It first offered distance learning courses in 1999. In fall 2010, there were 2,288 students enrolled in distance learning courses. Institutionally administered financial aid is available to distance learners.

Services Distance learners have accessibility to academic advising, bookstore, campus computer network, e-mail services, library services.

Contact Katherine Killoran, Director of Undergraduate Studies, John Jay College of Criminal Justice of the City University of New York, 899 Tenth Avenue, Room 532T, New York, NY 10019-1107. Telephone: 212-237-8263. Fax: 212-237-8919. E-mail: kkilloran@jjay.cuny.edu.

DEGREES AND AWARDS

Programs offered do not lead to a degree or other formal award.

COURSE SUBJECT AREAS OFFERED OUTSIDE OF DEGREE PROGRAMS

Undergraduate—area studies; computer and information sciences and support services related; English language and literature related; history; homeland security, law enforcement, firefighting and protective services related; legal professions and studies related; multi/interdisciplinary studies related; psychology; public administration and social service professions related; social sciences.

Graduate—health professions related; homeland security, law enforcement, firefighting and protective services related; psychology; public administration and social service professions related.

THE JOHNS HOPKINS UNIVERSITY
Baltimore, Maryland
Bloomberg School of Public Health
http://distance.jhsph.edu

The Johns Hopkins University was founded in 1876. It is accredited by Middle States Association of Colleges and Schools. It first offered distance learning courses in 1997. In fall 2010, there were 1,200 students enrolled in distance learning courses. Institutionally administered financial aid is available to distance learners.

Services Distance learners have accessibility to academic advising, bookstore, campus computer network, career placement assistance, e-mail services, library services, tutoring.

Contact Mr. David Earle, Academic Administrator, The Johns Hopkins University, 615 North Wolfe Street, Room W1015, Baltimore, MD 21205. Telephone: 410-955-1291. E-mail: dearle@jhsph.edu.

DEGREES AND AWARDS

Certificate Public Health Practice Training certificate; Public Health Training certificate; Quantitative Methods in Public Health Training certificate

MD/Dr PH Public Health, part-time

MHS Occupational and Environmental Hygiene, part-time/Internet-based Master of Science in Public Health (MSPH)

MPH Public Health, part-time/Internet-based

COURSE SUBJECT AREAS OFFERED OUTSIDE OF DEGREE PROGRAMS

Graduate—behavioral sciences; demography and population; foods, nutrition, and related services; genetics; health and medical administrative services; health services/allied health/health sciences; human biology; management information systems; management sciences and quantitative methods; mathematics and statistics related; mental and social health services and allied professions; public health; public policy analysis; statistics.

THE JOHNS HOPKINS UNIVERSITY
Baltimore, Maryland
Engineering for Professionals
http://www.ep.jhu.edu

The Johns Hopkins University was founded in 1876. It is accredited by Middle States Association of Colleges and Schools. It first offered distance learning courses in 2000. In fall 2010, there were 400 students enrolled in distance learning courses. Institutionally administered financial aid is available to distance learners.

Services Distance learners have accessibility to academic advising, bookstore, campus computer network, e-mail services, library services.

Contact Ms. Artie Kennedy, Admissions Coordinator, The Johns Hopkins University, 6810 Deerpath Road, Suite 100, Elkridge, MD 21075. Telephone: 410-516-2300. E-mail: jhep@jhu.edu.

DEGREES AND AWARDS

MS Bioinformatics; Computer Science; Environmental Engineering and Science; Environmental Planning and Management; Information Assurance; Information Systems Engineering; Systems Engineering

COURSE SUBJECT AREAS OFFERED OUTSIDE OF DEGREE PROGRAMS

Graduate—applied mathematics; chemical engineering; computer and information sciences; computer engineering; computer/information technology administration and management; computer programming; computer systems networking and telecommunications; electrical, electronics and communications engineering; electrical engineering technologies; engineering-related fields; engineering science; environmental/environmental health engineering; information science/studies.

JOHNSON STATE COLLEGE
Johnson, Vermont
External Degree Program
http://jsc.edu/edp

Johnson State College was founded in 1828. It is accredited by New England Association of Schools and Colleges. It first offered distance learning courses in 1998. In fall 2010, there were 400 students enrolled in distance learning courses. Institutionally administered financial aid is available to distance learners.

Services Distance learners have accessibility to academic advising, bookstore, career placement assistance, e-mail services, library services.

Contact Ms. Rhonda Osgood, Staff Assistant, EDP, Johnson State College, External Degree Program, 337 College Hill, Johnson, VT 05656. Telephone: 802-635-1290. E-mail: rhonda.osgood@jsc.edu.

DEGREES AND AWARDS

BA Business Management; Professional Studies

COURSE SUBJECT AREAS OFFERED OUTSIDE OF DEGREE PROGRAMS

Undergraduate—anthropology; applied mathematics; behavioral sciences; biopsychology; business administration, management and operations; business, management, and marketing related; education; English; English language and literature related; environmental/environmental health engineering; history; human resources management; psychology; religious studies; sociology; special education.

JOHNSON UNIVERSITY
Knoxville, Tennessee
Distance Learning Office
http://www.JohnsonU.edu

Johnson University was founded in 1893. It is accredited by Association for Biblical Higher Education. It first offered distance learning courses in 1988. In fall 2010, there were 77 students enrolled in distance learning courses. Institutionally administered financial aid is available to distance learners.

Services Distance learners have accessibility to academic advising, bookstore, campus computer network, e-mail services, library services.

Contact Dr. John C. Ketchen, Director of Distance Learning, Johnson University, 7900 Johnson Drive, Knoxville, TN 37998. Telephone: 865-251-2254. Fax: 865-251-2285. E-mail: mketchen@johnsonu.edu.

DEGREES AND AWARDS

MA New Testament

COURSE SUBJECT AREAS OFFERED OUTSIDE OF DEGREE PROGRAMS

Undergraduate—biblical studies; English or French as a second or foreign language (teaching); missionary studies and missiology; music; pastoral counseling and specialized ministries; religious studies.

Graduate—biblical studies.

JOHNSTON COMMUNITY COLLEGE
Smithfield, North Carolina
http://www.johnstoncc.edu/

Johnston Community College was founded in 1969. It is accredited by Southern Association of Colleges and Schools. It first offered distance learning courses in 1997. In fall 2010, there were 2,750 students enrolled in distance learning courses.

Services Distance learners have accessibility to academic advising, bookstore, e-mail services, library services, tutoring.

Contact Terri Lee, Director, Instructional Technology and Distance Education, Johnston Community College, PO Box 2350, Smithfield, NC 27577. Telephone: 919-209-2177. Fax: 919-209-2110. E-mail: tslee@johnstoncc.edu.

DEGREES AND AWARDS

Programs offered do not lead to a degree or other formal award.

COURSE SUBJECT AREAS OFFERED OUTSIDE OF DEGREE PROGRAMS

Undergraduate—accounting and computer science; accounting and related services; biology; business administration, management and operations; business, management, and marketing related; chemistry; computer and information sciences; computer systems networking and telecommunications; criminal justice and corrections; economics; education; education (specific levels and methods); English; English language and literature related; geography and cartography; geological and earth sciences/geosciences; health and medical administrative services; history; human biology; languages (Romance languages); legal support services; literature; marketing; mathematics; music; philosophy; philosophy and religious studies; psychology; religious studies; sociology.

JONES INTERNATIONAL UNIVERSITY
Centennial, Colorado
http://www.jiu.edu

Jones International University was founded in 1995. It is accredited by North Central Association of Colleges and Schools. It first offered distance learning courses in 1995. In fall 2010, there were 7,674 students enrolled in distance learning courses. Institutionally administered financial aid is available to distance learners.

Services Distance learners have accessibility to academic advising, bookstore, e-mail services, library services, tutoring.

Contact Admission Counselor, Jones International University, 9697 East Mineral Avenue, Centennial, CO 80112. Telephone: 800-811-5663. Fax: 303-799-0966. E-mail: info@international.edu.

DEGREES AND AWARDS

AA Business Administration

BA Business Communication

BBA Business Administration

Ed S K-12 Education Leadership

MA Business Communication

MBA Business Administration

MEd Adult Education and Leadership; Education–K-12 Educators and Administration

DBA Business Administration

EdD Adult Education Leadership; K-12 Education Leadership

COURSE SUBJECT AREAS OFFERED OUTSIDE OF DEGREE PROGRAMS

Undergraduate—business administration, management and operations; business/corporate communications; communications technology; computer/information technology administration and management; computer software and media applications; computer systems networking and telecommunications; entrepreneurial and small business operations; human resources management; international business; multi/interdisciplinary studies related.

Graduate—business/corporate communications; business, management, and marketing related; communication and journalism related; computer software and media applications; computer systems networking and telecommunications; educational/instructional media design; education related; entrepreneurial and small business operations; international business; library science related; multi/interdisciplinary studies related; peace studies and conflict resolution; public relations, advertising, and applied communication related.

J. SARGEANT REYNOLDS COMMUNITY COLLEGE
Richmond, Virginia
Division of Instructional Technologies and Distance Education
http://www.reynolds.edu

J. Sargeant Reynolds Community College was founded in 1972. It is accredited by Southern Association of Colleges and Schools. It first offered distance learning courses in 1980. In fall 2010, there were 4,992 students enrolled in distance learning courses. Institutionally administered financial aid is available to distance learners.

Services Distance learners have accessibility to academic advising, bookstore, campus computer network, e-mail services, library services, tutoring.

Contact M.R. Macbeth, Coordinator of Center for Distance Learning, J. Sargeant Reynolds Community College, Center for Distance Learning, PO Box 85622, Richmond, VA 23285-5622. Telephone: 804-523-5612. Fax: 804-371-3822. E-mail: distance-ed@reynolds.edu.

DEGREES AND AWARDS
AAS Early Childhood Development; Medical Laboratory Technology; Opticianry; Respiratory Therapy
AS Business Administration
Certificate Early Childhood Development; Early Childhood Education; Hospitality Leadership; Hotel Rooms Division Management; Opticians Apprentice; Respiratory Therapy–Advanced Practice; Sleep Technology for Polysomnography; eCommerce

COURSE SUBJECT AREAS OFFERED OUTSIDE OF DEGREE PROGRAMS
Undergraduate—accounting and related services; biology; business administration, management and operations; business, management, and marketing related; business operations support and assistant services; chemistry; computer science; computer software and media applications; criminal justice and corrections; economics; education; food science and technology; health and physical education/fitness; history; human development, family studies, and related services; information science/studies; linguistic, comparative, and related language studies; marketing; mathematics; philosophy; political science and government; psychology; social sciences related; sociology.

JUDSON COLLEGE
Marion, Alabama
Distance Learning Program
http://www.judson.edu

Judson College was founded in 1838. It is accredited by Southern Association of Colleges and Schools. It first offered distance learning courses in 1976. In fall 2010, there were 70 students enrolled in distance learning courses. Institutionally administered financial aid is available to distance learners.

Services Distance learners have accessibility to academic advising, bookstore, campus computer network, career placement assistance, e-mail services, library services.

Contact Mr. Bradley A. Moore, Director of Distance Learning, Judson College, 302 Bibb Street, Marion, AL 36756. Telephone: 800-447-9472 Ext. 5169. Fax: 334-683-5169. E-mail: bmoore3@judson.edu.

DEGREES AND AWARDS
BA Business; Criminal Justice; Education–Secondary Education; English; History; Music; Psychology; Religious Studies
BMin Ministry Studies
BS Business; Criminal Justice; Education; Psychology

COURSE SUBJECT AREAS OFFERED OUTSIDE OF DEGREE PROGRAMS
Undergraduate—behavioral sciences; biblical studies; bioethics/medical ethics; biological and physical sciences; business administration, management and operations; criminal justice and corrections; ecology, evolution, systematics, and population biology; economics; education; education (specific levels and methods); education (specific subject areas); English; history; music; philosophy and religious studies related; political science and government; psychology; social sciences; sociology.

JUDSON UNIVERSITY
Elgin, Illinois
Division of Continuing Education
http://www.judsonU.edu

Judson University was founded in 1963. It is accredited by North Central Association of Colleges and Schools. It first offered distance learning courses in 1998. In fall 2010, there were 200 students enrolled in distance learning courses. Institutionally administered financial aid is available to distance learners.

Services Distance learners have accessibility to academic advising, bookstore, campus computer network, career placement assistance, e-mail services, library services, tutoring.

Contact Martha Johnson, Director of Online Education and Instructional Technology, Judson University, 1151 North State Street, Elgin, IL 60123. Telephone: 847-628-2583. Fax: 847-628-1007. E-mail: mjohnson@judsonu.edu.

DEGREES AND AWARDS
BA Management and Leadership
MA Organizational Leadership

COURSE SUBJECT AREAS OFFERED OUTSIDE OF DEGREE PROGRAMS
Undergraduate—astronomy and astrophysics; biblical studies; communication and media; computer software and media applications; data entry/microcomputer applications; English; English language and literature related; fine and studio arts; history; human services; liberal arts and sciences, general studies and humanities; mathematics; political science and government; psychology; public relations, advertising, and applied communication related; sociology.

KANSAS STATE UNIVERSITY
Manhattan, Kansas
Division of Continuing Education, Continuing Learning
http://www.distance.k-state.edu

Kansas State University was founded in 1863. It is accredited by North Central Association of Colleges and Schools. It first offered distance learning courses in 1971. In fall 2010, there were 8,000 students enrolled in distance learning courses. Institutionally administered financial aid is available to distance learners.

Services Distance learners have accessibility to academic advising, bookstore, campus computer network, career placement assistance, e-mail services, library services, tutoring.

Contact Peggy Blanken, Call Center Supervisor, Kansas State University, Division of Continuing Education, 1615 Anderson Avenue, Manhattan, KS 66502. Telephone: 785-532-5575. Fax: 785-532-5637. E-mail: informationdce@k-state.edu.

DEGREES AND AWARDS
BS Animal Science and Industry; Dietetics; Early Childhood Education; Family Studies and Human Services; Food Science and Industry; General Business; Interdisciplinary Social Science; Technology Management
Certificate Conflict Resolution; Food Science; Transportation Engineering
Endorsement ESL Endorsement in Elementary and Secondary Education; Reading Specialist
Specialized diploma Animal Science and Industry Undergraduate minor; Business Undergraduate minor; Conflict Analysis and Trauma Studies Undergraduate minor; Nuclear Engineering Undergraduate Minor
Graduate Certificate Academic Advising; Applied Statistics; Business Administration; Conflict Resolution; Educational Computing, Design, and Online Learning/Classroom Technology; Food Safety and Defense; Food Science; Gerontology; Horticultural Therapy; Management of Animal Health Related Organizations; Occupational Health Psychology; Organizational Leadership; Personal Financial Planning; Public Administration; Youth Development

MAg Agribusiness
MEngr Operations Research
MS Academic Advising; Adult and Continuing Education; Agribusiness; Chemical Engineering; Civil Engineering; Community Development; Dietetics; Educational Administration; Educational Computing, Design, and Online Learning/Classroom Technology; Electrical Engineering; Engineering Management; English as a Second Language; Food Science and Industry; Gerontology; Mechanical Engineering; Merchandising; Operations Research; Personal Financial Planning; Psychology, Industrial and Organizational Psychology emphasis; Software Engineering; Youth Development
PhD Personal Financial Planning

COURSE SUBJECT AREAS OFFERED OUTSIDE OF DEGREE PROGRAMS

Undergraduate—accounting and computer science; accounting and related services; agricultural and domestic animal services; agricultural and food products processing; agricultural business and management; agricultural production; agriculture; agriculture and agriculture operations related; animal sciences; apparel and textiles; applied horticulture and horticultural business services; behavioral sciences; biochemistry, biophysics and molecular biology; biological and physical sciences; biology; business administration, management and operations; business/commerce; business, management, and marketing related; chemical engineering; chemistry; civil engineering; civil engineering technologies; community organization and advocacy; computer and information sciences; computer and information sciences and support services related; computer engineering; computer engineering technologies; computer/information technology administration and management; computer programming; computer science; computer software and media applications; criminal justice and corrections; criminology; curriculum and instruction; dietetics and clinical nutrition services; ecology, evolution, systematics, and population biology; economics; education; educational administration and supervision; educational/instructional media design; education (specific levels and methods); education (specific subject areas); electrical, electronics and communications engineering; electrical engineering technologies; engineering; engineering mechanics; engineering related; engineering-related fields; engineering-related technologies; engineering science; engineering technologies related; engineering technology; English; English or French as a second or foreign language (teaching); ethnic, cultural minority, gender, and group studies; family and consumer sciences/human sciences; family and consumer sciences/human sciences related; finance and financial management services; food science and technology; foods, nutrition, and related services; geography and cartography; geological and earth sciences/geosciences; gerontology; ground transportation; history; hospitality administration; human development, family studies, and related services; human resources management; industrial engineering; information science/studies; liberal arts and sciences, general studies and humanities; management information systems; manufacturing engineering; marketing; mechanical engineering; mechanical engineering related technologies; multi/interdisciplinary studies related; music; natural resources and conservation related; natural resources conservation and research; natural resources management and policy; natural sciences; nuclear engineering; nutrition sciences; physical sciences; physical sciences related; political science and government; psychology; psychology related; public administration; public administration and social service professions related; public health; social sciences; social sciences related; sociology; statistics; veterinary biomedical and clinical sciences; work and family studies.

Graduate—agricultural and food products processing; agricultural business and management; agricultural public services; agriculture; agriculture and agriculture operations related; animal sciences; apparel and textiles; business administration, management and operations; business/commerce; business, management, and marketing related; business/managerial economics; business operations support and assistant services; chemical engineering; civil engineering; civil engineering technologies; community organization and advocacy; computer and information sciences; computer and information sciences and support services related; computer engineering; computer engineering technologies; computer/information technology administration and management; computer programming; computer science; computer software and media applications; curriculum and instruction; dietetics and clinical nutrition services; education; educational administration and supervision; educational/instructional media design; education related; education (specific levels and methods); education (specific subject areas); electrical, electronics and communications engineering; electrical engineering technologies; engineering; engineering mechanics; engineering related; engineering-related fields; engineering-related technologies; engineering science; engineering technology; English or French as a second or foreign language (teaching); family and consumer sciences/human sciences; family and consumer sciences/human sciences related; finance and financial management services; food science and technology; foods, nutrition, and related services; gerontology; ground transportation; hospitality administration; human development, family studies, and related services; human resources management; industrial engineering; industrial production technologies; management information systems; manufacturing engineering; mechanical engineering; mechanical engineering related technologies; nuclear engineering; operations research; plant sciences; psychology; psychology related; public administration; public administration and social service professions related; public health; quality control and safety technologies; veterinary biomedical and clinical sciences.

Non-credit—agricultural and domestic animal services; agricultural and food products processing; agricultural business and management; agricultural production; agricultural public services; agriculture; agriculture and agriculture operations related; animal sciences; apparel and textiles; applied horticulture and horticultural business services; botany/plant biology; business administration, management and operations; business/commerce; business, management, and marketing related; business/managerial economics; curriculum and instruction; dietetics and clinical nutrition services; education; educational administration and supervision; educational assessment, evaluation, and research; education related; education (specific levels and methods); education (specific subject areas); family and consumer economics; family and consumer sciences/human sciences; family and consumer sciences/human sciences related; finance and financial management services; food science and technology; foods, nutrition, and related services; legal professions and studies related; legal support services; social sciences related; veterinary biomedical and clinical sciences; work and family studies; zoology/animal biology.

KAPLAN UNIVERSITY ONLINE
Fort Lauderdale, Florida
http://www.kaplan.edu/

Kaplan University Online first offered distance learning courses in 1999. In fall 2010, there were 72,271 students enrolled in distance learning courses. Institutionally administered financial aid is available to distance learners.

Services Distance learners have accessibility to academic advising, bookstore, career placement assistance, e-mail services, library services, tutoring.

Contact Information, Kaplan University Online, 6301 Kaplan University Avenue, Fort Lauderdale, FL 33309. Telephone: 866-527-5268. E-mail: infoku@kaplan.edu.

DEGREES AND AWARDS

AAS Accounting; Business Administration/Management; Computer Forensics; Computer Information Systems; Criminal Justice; Early Childhood Development; Educational Paraprofessional; Fire Science; Health Information Technology; Human Services; Medical Assisting; Medical Office Management; Medical Transcription; Nursing; Paralegal Studies; Public Administration
AS Interdisciplinary Studies
BS Accounting; Business; Communication; Criminal Justice Administration and Management; Criminal Justice; Early Childhood Development; Environmental Policy and Management; Fire Science; Fire and Emergency Management; Health Care Administration; Health Information Management; Health Science; Health and Wellness; Human Services; Information Technology; International and Comparative Criminal Justice; Legal Studies; Liberal Studies; Nutrition Science; Paralegal Studies; Political Science; Professional Studies; Psychology; Public Administration and Policy; Public Health
BSN Nursing

Certificate Accounting; Computer Forensics post-Baccalaureate; Corrections certificate; Crime Scene Technician; Entrepreneurship for Growth Ventures; Entrepreneurship for New Ventures; Human Resources; Information Security; Information Technology Pathway; Internet and Website Development; Introduction to Computer Programming Language; Legal Secretary; Linux System Administration post-Baccalaureate certificate; Management and Supervision certificate in Criminal Justice; National Security Administration post-Baccalaureate certificate; Nursing–Adult Nurse Practitioner; Nursing–Family Nurse Practitioner; Oracle Database Administration post-Baccalaureate certificate; Pathway to Paralegal post-Baccalaureate certificate; Private Security Management; Private Security; Project Management; Teaching with Technology
Graduate Certificate Nurse Administrator; Nurse Educator; Nurse Informatics
MAT Teaching
MBA Business Administration
MHA Health Care Administration
MPA Public Administration
MPH Public Health
MS Accounting; Criminal Justice; Environmental Policy; Fire and Emergency Services; Health Education; Homeland Security and Emergency Management; Information Technology; Legal Studies; Management; Psychology
MSE Education; Higher Education; Instructional Technology
MSN Nursing

KAUAI COMMUNITY COLLEGE
Lihue, Hawaii
University Center-Kauai
http://info.kauai.hawaii.edu/uckauai/

Kauai Community College was founded in 1965. It is accredited by Western Association of Schools and Colleges. It first offered distance learning courses in 1988. In fall 2010, there were 150 students enrolled in distance learning courses. Institutionally administered financial aid is available to distance learners.

Services Distance learners have accessibility to academic advising, bookstore, campus computer network, e-mail services, library services, tutoring.

Contact Ms. Pua Palmeira, University Center-Distance Education, Kauai Community College, 3-1901 Kaumualii Highway, Lihue, HI 96766-9500. Telephone: 808-245-8330. Fax: 808-245-0101. E-mail: marlapua@hawaii.edu.

DEGREES AND AWARDS
Programs offered do not lead to a degree or other formal award.

COURSE SUBJECT AREAS OFFERED OUTSIDE OF DEGREE PROGRAMS
Undergraduate—accounting and related services; business administration, management and operations; education; psychology; public administration; public health; social sciences.
Graduate—accounting and related services; education (specific subject areas); library science and administration; social work.

KEAN UNIVERSITY
Union, New Jersey
http://www.kean.edu/~de/

Kean University was founded in 1855. It is accredited by Middle States Association of Colleges and Schools. It first offered distance learning courses in 1998. In fall 2010, there were 1,091 students enrolled in distance learning courses. Institutionally administered financial aid is available to distance learners.

Services Distance learners have accessibility to bookstore, campus computer network, e-mail services, library services.

Contact Dr. Mark Lender, Vice President of Academic Affairs, Kean University, 1000 Morris Avenue, Office of Academic Affairs, Union, NJ 07083. Telephone: 908-737-7030. Fax: 908-737-7035. E-mail: mlender@kean.edu.

DEGREES AND AWARDS
Programs offered do not lead to a degree or other formal award.

COURSE SUBJECT AREAS OFFERED OUTSIDE OF DEGREE PROGRAMS
Undergraduate—accounting and related services; business administration, management and operations; education (specific levels and methods); education (specific subject areas); finance and financial management services; fine and studio arts; history; marketing; mathematics; parks, recreation and leisure facilities management; philosophy and religious studies; political science and government; sociology; special education.
Graduate—accounting and related services; educational administration and supervision; education (specific levels and methods); special education.
Non-credit—accounting and related services; alternative and complementary medical support services; biological and biomedical sciences related; business administration, management and operations; business, management, and marketing related; communication and journalism related; computer and information sciences; computer programming; computer software and media applications; education; English language and literature related; English or French as a second or foreign language (teaching); family and consumer sciences/human sciences; film/video and photographic arts; finance and financial management services; fine and studio arts; health and physical education/fitness; health professions related; languages (East Asian); languages (Romance languages); legal professions and studies related; mathematics; music; parks, recreation and leisure; personal and culinary services related; visual and performing arts; work and family studies.

KETTERING UNIVERSITY
Flint, Michigan
Graduate School
http://kettering.edu/graduate

Kettering University was founded in 1919. It is accredited by North Central Association of Colleges and Schools. It first offered distance learning courses in 1982. In fall 2010, there were 1,100 students enrolled in distance learning courses. Institutionally administered financial aid is available to distance learners.

Services Distance learners have accessibility to academic advising, bookstore, campus computer network, e-mail services, library services.

Contact Joanne Allen, Publications Coordinator, Kettering University, 1700 University Avenue, Flint, MI 48504-4898. Telephone: 866-584-7237 Ext. 5. Fax: 810-762-9935. E-mail: gradoff@kettering.edu.

DEGREES AND AWARDS
MBA General concentration; Health Care Systems Management; IT concentration; Leadership; Manufacturing Engineering (Industrial and Manufacturing Engineering concentration); Mechanical Design (ME concentration); Power Electronics and Machine Drives (EE concentration); Supply Chain Management; Systems Engineering (Industrial and Manufacturing Engineering concentration)
MS Manufacturing Operations; Operations Management
MSE Electrical and Computer Engineering concentration; Manufacturing Engineering concentration; Mechanical Cognate; Mechanical Design concentration; Sustainable Energy and Hybrid Technology
MSEM Engineering Management

COURSE SUBJECT AREAS OFFERED OUTSIDE OF DEGREE PROGRAMS
Non-credit—business administration, management and operations; business, management, and marketing related; computer/information technology administration and management; electrical, electronics and communications engineering; engineering; engineering related; engineering-related fields; industrial engineering; management information systems; management sciences and quantitative methods; manufacturing engineering; mathematics and statistics related; mechanical engineering; quality control and safety technologies.

KEYSTONE COLLEGE

La Plume, Pennsylvania

http://www.keystone.edu/academics/onlinelearning/index.htm

Keystone College was founded in 1868. It is accredited by Middle States Association of Colleges and Schools. It first offered distance learning courses in 2005. In fall 2010, there were 369 students enrolled in distance learning courses. Institutionally administered financial aid is available to distance learners.

Services Distance learners have accessibility to bookstore, campus computer network, e-mail services, library services, tutoring.

Contact Cheryl Guse, Coordinator of Online Learning, Keystone College, La Plume, PA 18440. Telephone: 570-945-8422. E-mail: cheryl.guse@keystone.edu.

DEGREES AND AWARDS

AS Business Administration
BSc Business

COURSE SUBJECT AREAS OFFERED OUTSIDE OF DEGREE PROGRAMS

Undergraduate—accounting and computer science; behavioral sciences; biology; business administration, management and operations; business, management, and marketing related; communication and journalism related; communication and media; computer/information technology administration and management; criminal justice and corrections; criminology; economics; education (specific subject areas); English; geological and earth sciences/geosciences; health and physical education/fitness; history; human resources management; interdisciplinary studies; liberal arts and sciences, general studies and humanities; marketing; mathematics; mathematics and statistics related; nutrition sciences; political science and government; psychology; social sciences related.

KILIAN COMMUNITY COLLEGE

Sioux Falls, South Dakota

http://www.kilian.edu

Kilian Community College was founded in 1977. It is accredited by North Central Association of Colleges and Schools. It first offered distance learning courses in 2002. In fall 2010, there were 49 students enrolled in distance learning courses. Institutionally administered financial aid is available to distance learners.

Services Distance learners have accessibility to e-mail services, library services.

Contact Ms. Mary Klockman, Director of Admissions, Kilian Community College, 300 East 6th Street, Sioux Falls, SD 57103. Telephone: 605-221-3100. Fax: 605-336-2606. E-mail: mklockman@kilian.edu.

DEGREES AND AWARDS

Programs offered do not lead to a degree or other formal award.

COURSE SUBJECT AREAS OFFERED OUTSIDE OF DEGREE PROGRAMS

Undergraduate—accounting and computer science; business administration, management and operations; computer and information sciences; human resources management.

KIRKWOOD COMMUNITY COLLEGE

Cedar Rapids, Iowa

http://www.kirkwood.edu

Kirkwood Community College was founded in 1966. It is accredited by North Central Association of Colleges and Schools. It first offered distance learning courses in 1980. In fall 2010, there were 5,800 students enrolled in distance learning courses. Institutionally administered financial aid is available to distance learners.

Services Distance learners have accessibility to academic advising, bookstore, campus computer network, career placement assistance, e-mail services, library services, tutoring.

Contact Alan Peterka, Anytime/Anywhere Department Coordinator, Kirkwood Community College, 6301 Kirkwood Boulevard SW, 214 Linn Hall, Cedar Rapids, IA 52406. Telephone: 319-398-1248. Fax: 319-398-5492. E-mail: alan.peterka@kirkwood.edu.

DEGREES AND AWARDS

AA Liberal Arts
AAS Health Information Technology Online; Management Online
AS Business Administration Online

COURSE SUBJECT AREAS OFFERED OUTSIDE OF DEGREE PROGRAMS

Undergraduate—accounting and related services; anthropology; biology; business administration, management and operations; business operations support and assistant services; chemistry; communication and media; computer software and media applications; criminal justice and corrections; criminology; economics; education (specific subject areas); film/video and photographic arts; health/medical preparatory programs; history; human resources management; human services; journalism; management information systems; mathematics; music; philosophy and religious studies related; psychology; psychology related; religious studies; sociology; statistics; veterinary biomedical and clinical sciences.

Non-credit—business/commerce; computer and information sciences; computer software and media applications; computer systems analysis; computer systems networking and telecommunications; data entry/microcomputer applications; data processing.

KIRTLAND COMMUNITY COLLEGE

Roscommon, Michigan

http://www.kirtland.edu/online-learning/

Kirtland Community College was founded in 1966. It is accredited by North Central Association of Colleges and Schools. It first offered distance learning courses in 1996. In fall 2010, there were 123 students enrolled in distance learning courses. Institutionally administered financial aid is available to distance learners.

Services Distance learners have accessibility to academic advising, bookstore, e-mail services, library services, tutoring.

Contact Mrs. Kerry L. Hannah, eLearning Coordinator, Kirtland Community College, 10775 North St. Helen Road, Roscommon, MI 48653. Telephone: 989-275-5000 Ext. 423. Fax: 989-275-6775. E-mail: kerry.hannah@kirtland.edu.

DEGREES AND AWARDS

AAB General Business
AD Nursing–LPN to RN
Certificate Bookkeeping; Entrepreneurship

COURSE SUBJECT AREAS OFFERED OUTSIDE OF DEGREE PROGRAMS

Undergraduate—accounting and related services; allied health and medical assisting services; biology; business administration, management and operations; business/commerce; business, management, and marketing related; business operations support and assistant services; psychology; sales, merchandising and related marketing operations (specialized).

LABETTE COMMUNITY COLLEGE

Parsons, Kansas

http://www.labette.edu

Labette Community College was founded in 1923. It is accredited by North Central Association of Colleges and Schools. It first offered distance learning courses in 1985. In fall 2010, there were 1,147 students enrolled in distance learning courses. Institutionally administered financial aid is available to distance learners.

Services Distance learners have accessibility to academic advising, bookstore, campus computer network, e-mail services, library services, tutoring.

Contact Ms. Elizabeth Ann Walker, Outreach Director, Labette Community College, 200 South 14th Street, Parsons, KS 67357. Telephone: 620-820-1221. Fax: 620-421-4481. E-mail: elizabethw@labette.edu.

DEGREES AND AWARDS

AA History; Multi-Cultural International Studies; Philosophy; Philosophy
AAS Financial Services
AGS General Studies

COURSE SUBJECT AREAS OFFERED OUTSIDE OF DEGREE PROGRAMS

Undergraduate—allied health diagnostic, intervention, and treatment professions; business/managerial economics; communication and media; computer programming; computer science; computer software and media applications; computer systems networking and telecommunications; criminology; finance and financial management services; fine and studio arts; genetics; geography and cartography; health and physical education/fitness; health/medical preparatory programs; history; human resources management; liberal arts and sciences, general studies and humanities; management information systems; mathematics; mathematics and statistics related; music; physical sciences; political science and government; psychology; sociology.
Non-credit—human resources management.

LACKAWANNA COLLEGE
Scranton, Pennsylvania
Distance Learning Center
http://www.lackawanna.edu

Lackawanna College was founded in 1894. It is accredited by Middle States Association of Colleges and Schools. It first offered distance learning courses in 1994. In fall 2010, there were 302 students enrolled in distance learning courses. Institutionally administered financial aid is available to distance learners.
Services Distance learners have accessibility to academic advising, bookstore, career placement assistance, e-mail services, library services.
Contact Mrs. Melanie A. Kowalski, Director of MIS, Lackawanna College, 501 Vine Street, Scranton, PA 18509. Telephone: 570-504-1583. Fax: 570-961-7877. E-mail: kowalskim@lackawanna.edu.

DEGREES AND AWARDS

Programs offered do not lead to a degree or other formal award.

COURSE SUBJECT AREAS OFFERED OUTSIDE OF DEGREE PROGRAMS

Undergraduate—accounting and computer science; audiovisual communications technologies; behavioral sciences; business administration, management and operations; communication and journalism related; communication and media; criminal justice and corrections; economics; education; English; history; human services; mathematics; psychology; public administration; social sciences; sociology; statistics.

LAKEHEAD UNIVERSITY
Thunder Bay, Ontario, Canada
Part-Time Studies
http://cedl.lakeheadu.ca

Lakehead University was founded in 1965. It is provincially chartered. It first offered distance learning courses in 1987. In fall 2010, there were 1,995 students enrolled in distance learning courses. Institutionally administered financial aid is available to distance learners.
Services Distance learners have accessibility to academic advising, bookstore, campus computer network, career placement assistance, e-mail services, library services, tutoring.
Contact Continuing Education and Distributed Learning, Lakehead University, Advanced Technology and Academic Centre, 955 Oliver Road, Thunder Bay, ON P7B 5E1, Canada. Telephone: 807-346-7730. Fax: 807-343-8008. E-mail: cedl@lakeheadu.ca.

DEGREES AND AWARDS

BA General Studies
Certificate Dementia Studies Interdisciplinary certificate; Palliative Care Interdisciplinary certificate
MEd Education
MPH Health Studies; Nursing
PhD Education Studies

COURSE SUBJECT AREAS OFFERED OUTSIDE OF DEGREE PROGRAMS

Undergraduate—anthropology; biology; chemistry; English; English language and literature related; geography and cartography; health professions related; history; mathematics; philosophy and religious studies; political science and government; psychology; social work; visual and performing arts.
Non-credit—visual and performing arts related.

LAKE-SUMTER COMMUNITY COLLEGE
Leesburg, Florida
http://www.lscc.edu

Lake-Sumter Community College was founded in 1962. It is accredited by Southern Association of Colleges and Schools. It first offered distance learning courses in 1986. In fall 2010, there were 3,200 students enrolled in distance learning courses. Institutionally administered financial aid is available to distance learners.
Services Distance learners have accessibility to academic advising, bookstore, e-mail services, library services, tutoring.
Contact Ms. Becky Fudge, Senior Staff Assistant, Lake-Sumter Community College, 9501 Highway 441, Leesburg, FL 34788. Telephone: 352-365-3665. E-mail: admissinquiry@lscc.edu.

DEGREES AND AWARDS

Programs offered do not lead to a degree or other formal award.

COURSE SUBJECT AREAS OFFERED OUTSIDE OF DEGREE PROGRAMS

Undergraduate—business administration, management and operations; business/commerce; business/corporate communications; business, management, and marketing related; computer software and media applications; economics; education; English language and literature related; foods, nutrition, and related services; health and medical administrative services; health/medical preparatory programs; library science and administration; physical sciences; psychology; psychology related.

LAKE SUPERIOR COLLEGE
Duluth, Minnesota
http://www.lsc.edu/e-campus/

Lake Superior College was founded in 1995. It is accredited by North Central Association of Colleges and Schools. It first offered distance learning courses in 1997. In fall 2010, there were 2,600 students enrolled in distance learning courses. Institutionally administered financial aid is available to distance learners.
Services Distance learners have accessibility to academic advising, bookstore, campus computer network, career placement assistance, e-mail services, library services, tutoring.
Contact Melissa Leno, Enrollment Services Specialist, Lake Superior College, 2101 Trinity Road, Duluth, MN 55811. Telephone: 218-733-5903. E-mail: m.leno@lsc.edu.

DEGREES AND AWARDS

AA Liberal Education
AAS Accountant; Network Administration; Paralegal Studies
AS Accountant; Business Administration; Paralegal Studies
Certificate Administrative Support–Legal Secretary; CISCO Network Associate; Hemodialysis Patient Care Technician; Microcomputer Office Specialist; Microsoft Systems Administrator; Professional Bookkeeper

COURSE SUBJECT AREAS OFFERED OUTSIDE OF DEGREE PROGRAMS

Undergraduate—accounting and related services; anthropology; astronomy and astrophysics; biological and physical sciences; business/commerce; business/corporate communications; business operations support and assistant services; communication and media; computer and information sciences; computer software and media applications; economics; fine and studio arts; geography and cartography; geological and earth sciences/geosciences; health/medical preparatory programs; health professions related; history; liberal arts and sciences, general studies and humanities; mathematics; philosophy and religious studies related; physical sciences; political science and government; psychology; sociology.

LAMAR STATE COLLEGE–ORANGE

Orange, Texas

http://www.lsco.edu

Lamar State College–Orange was founded in 1969. It is accredited by Southern Association of Colleges and Schools. It first offered distance learning courses in 1999. In fall 2010, there were 698 students enrolled in distance learning courses. Institutionally administered financial aid is available to distance learners.

Services Distance learners have accessibility to academic advising, bookstore, campus computer network, career placement assistance, e-mail services, library services.

Contact Dr. Sribhagyam Srinivasan, Instructional Designer, Lamar State College–Orange, 410 Front Street, Orange, TX 77630. Telephone: 409-882-3958. Fax: 409-882-3985. E-mail: sribhagyam.srinivasan@lsco.edu.

DEGREES AND AWARDS

Programs offered do not lead to a degree or other formal award.

COURSE SUBJECT AREAS OFFERED OUTSIDE OF DEGREE PROGRAMS

Undergraduate—allied health and medical assisting services; behavioral sciences; bioethics/medical ethics; biology; business administration, management and operations; business, management, and marketing related; computer programming; computer science; computer systems networking and telecommunications; crafts, folk art and artisanry; drama/theatre arts and stagecraft; economics; education (specific levels and methods); English language and literature related; environmental control technologies; finance and financial management services; health/medical preparatory programs; history; nutrition sciences; psychology; quality control and safety technologies; visual and performing arts related.

LAMAR STATE COLLEGE–PORT ARTHUR

Port Arthur, Texas

Academic Division

http://www.lamarpa.edu/

Lamar State College–Port Arthur was founded in 1909. It is accredited by Southern Association of Colleges and Schools. It first offered distance learning courses in 1996. In fall 2010, there were 1,000 students enrolled in distance learning courses. Institutionally administered financial aid is available to distance learners.

Services Distance learners have accessibility to academic advising, bookstore, campus computer network, e-mail services, library services.

Contact Dr. William Beauregard Duncan, Distance Learning Coordinator, Lamar State College–Port Arthur, PO Box 310, Port Arthur, TX 77641. Telephone: 409-984-6349. Fax: 409-984-6000. E-mail: duncanwb@lamarpa.edu.

DEGREES AND AWARDS

AAS Upward Mobility Nursing program

COURSE SUBJECT AREAS OFFERED OUTSIDE OF DEGREE PROGRAMS

Undergraduate—behavioral sciences; biological and biomedical sciences related; business administration, management and operations; computer and information sciences; computer programming; computer science; computer software and media applications; computer systems networking and telecommunications; data entry/microcomputer applications; economics; English; fine and studio arts; foods, nutrition, and related services; health professions related; mathematics; philosophy; philosophy and religious studies related; psychology.

Non-credit—allied health and medical assisting services; allied health diagnostic, intervention, and treatment professions; alternative and complementary medical support services; alternative and complementary medicine and medical systems; business administration, management and operations; business/commerce; business, management, and marketing related; business/managerial economics; business operations support and assistant services; computer and information sciences; computer/information technology administration and management; computer programming; computer science; computer software and media applications; computer systems analysis; computer systems networking and telecommunications; data entry/microcomputer applications; data processing; entrepreneurial and small business operations; finance and financial management services; health aides/attendants/orderlies; human resources management; information science/studies; management information systems; marketing; public relations, advertising, and applied communication related; sales merchandising, and related marketing operations (general); sales, merchandising and related marketing operations (specialized).

LANDER UNIVERSITY

Greenwood, South Carolina

http://www.lander.edu/ucg

Lander University was founded in 1872. It is accredited by Southern Association of Colleges and Schools. It first offered distance learning courses in 2002. In fall 2010, there were 50 students enrolled in distance learning courses. Institutionally administered financial aid is available to distance learners.

Services Distance learners have accessibility to academic advising, bookstore, campus computer network, career placement assistance, e-mail services, library services.

Contact Ms. Lori S. Micke, Coordinator, UCG Programs, Lander University, University Center of Greenville, 225 South Pleasantburg Drive, Greenville, SC 29607. Telephone: 864-250-8920. Fax: 864-250-8924. E-mail: lmicke@lander.edu.

DEGREES AND AWARDS

Programs offered do not lead to a degree or other formal award.

COURSE SUBJECT AREAS OFFERED OUTSIDE OF DEGREE PROGRAMS

Undergraduate—criminal justice and corrections; political science and government; public administration; sociology.

Graduate—education (specific levels and methods).

LANSING COMMUNITY COLLEGE

Lansing, Michigan

Virtual College

http://www.lcc.edu/elearning

Lansing Community College was founded in 1957. It is accredited by North Central Association of Colleges and Schools. It first offered distance learning courses in 1979. In fall 2010, there were 9,249 students enrolled in distance learning courses. Institutionally administered financial aid is available to distance learners.

Services Distance learners have accessibility to academic advising, bookstore, campus computer network, e-mail services, library services, tutoring.

Contact Ms. Michelle Detering, Academic Advisor and Online Student Support Specialist, Lansing Community College, 1130 Academic Advising, PO Box 40010, Lansing, MI 48901-7210. Telephone: 517-483-5324. Fax: 517-483-1970. E-mail: deterim@lcc.edu.

DEGREES AND AWARDS

AA Business (pre-transfer); Criminal Justice; Economics; Foreign Language; Interdisciplinary Humanities; Liberal Arts; Psychology; Social Science; Sociology

AD Business; Computer Programmer/Analyst; Criminal Justice–Law Enforcement; E-Business; Financial Institutions; General Studies; International Business

Certificate of Achievement E-Business; Transfer Studies

Certificate of Completion Computer Programmer/Analyst; Computer Readiness for Workplace; Computer Technology Basics; Correctional

Officer; Financial Institutions; Microsoft Office Specialist certification preparation; Taking Initiative for Management Effectiveness; Web Site Developer

COURSE SUBJECT AREAS OFFERED OUTSIDE OF DEGREE PROGRAMS

Undergraduate—accounting and related services; allied health and medical assisting services; anthropology; architecture; astronomy and astrophysics; biology; business administration, management and operations; business/commerce; business, management, and marketing related; business operations support and assistant services; chemistry; computer and information sciences; computer and information sciences and support services related; computer/information technology administration and management; computer programming; computer science; computer software and media applications; computer systems analysis; criminal justice and corrections; criminology; data entry/microcomputer applications; data processing; design and applied arts; economics; education; education related; English; foods, nutrition, and related services; geography and cartography; health professions related; history; hospitality administration; international business; languages (foreign languages related); languages (Germanic); languages (Romance languages); legal studies (non-professional general, undergraduate); linguistic, comparative, and related language studies; marketing; mathematics; mathematics and computer science; mathematics and statistics related; multi/interdisciplinary studies related; music; natural resources and conservation related; natural resources conservation and research; natural sciences; philosophy; philosophy and religious studies related; physical sciences; physical sciences related; political science and government; psychology; psychology related; real estate; sales merchandising, and related marketing operations (general); science technologies related; social sciences; social sciences related; sociology; statistics; visual and performing arts.

LA ROCHE COLLEGE
Pittsburgh, Pennsylvania
http://www.laroche.edu/graduate/online-learning.htm

La Roche College was founded in 1963. It is accredited by Middle States Association of Colleges and Schools. It first offered distance learning courses in 2004. In fall 2010, there were 332 students enrolled in distance learning courses. Institutionally administered financial aid is available to distance learners.

Services Distance learners have accessibility to academic advising, bookstore, career placement assistance, e-mail services, library services.

Contact Ms. Hope Schiffgens, Director of Graduate Studies and Adult Education, La Roche College, 9000 Babcock Boulevard, Pittsburgh, PA 15237. Telephone: 412-536-1266. Fax: 412-536-1283. E-mail: hope.schiffgens@laroche.edu.

DEGREES AND AWARDS

BSN Nursing
MSN Nursing

COURSE SUBJECT AREAS OFFERED OUTSIDE OF DEGREE PROGRAMS

Undergraduate—business, management, and marketing related; business/managerial economics; communication and journalism related; communications technologies and support services related; computer and information sciences; finance and financial management services; history; human resources management; liberal arts and sciences, general studies and humanities; mathematics; multi/interdisciplinary studies related; philosophy and religious studies related; psychology; social sciences; theology and religious vocations related; visual and performing arts.

Graduate—human resources management.

LASELL COLLEGE
Newton, Massachusetts
Graduate and Professional Studies in Management
http://www.lasell.edu/Admissions/Graduate-Admission/Masters-Degrees-and-Graduate-Certificates.html?ctschool=lasell&cttype=referral&ctsource=peterdist

Lasell College was founded in 1851. It is accredited by New England Association of Schools and Colleges. It first offered distance learning courses in 2005. In fall 2010, there were 215 students enrolled in distance learning courses. Institutionally administered financial aid is available to distance learners.

Services Distance learners have accessibility to academic advising, e-mail services, library services.

Contact Ms. Adrienne Franciosi, Director of Graduate Admission, Lasell College, 1844 Commonwealth Avenue, Newton, MA 02466. Telephone: 617-242-2214. Fax: 617-243-2450. E-mail: gradinfo@lasell.edu.

DEGREES AND AWARDS

Graduate Certificate Elder Care Administration; Elder Care Marketing; Fundraising Management; Human Resources Management; Integrated Marketing Communication; Management; Marketing; Non-Profit Management; Project Management; Public Relations; Sport Hospitality Management; Sport Leadership; Sport Non-Profit Management
MS Sport Management–Sport Hospitality Management; Sport Management–Sport Leadership; Sport Management–Sport Non-Profit Management
MSC Integrated Marketing Communication; Public Relations
MSM Elder Care Administration; Elder Care Marketing; Fundraising Management; Human Resources Management; Management; Marketing; Non-Profit Management; Project Management

LA SIERRA UNIVERSITY
Riverside, California
http://www.lasierra.edu/index.php?id=digitallearning

La Sierra University was founded in 1922. It is accredited by Western Association of Schools and Colleges. It first offered distance learning courses in 1999. In fall 2010, there were 100 students enrolled in distance learning courses. Institutionally administered financial aid is available to distance learners.

Services Distance learners have accessibility to academic advising, bookstore, campus computer network, e-mail services, library services, tutoring.

Contact Mr. Dean W. Hunt, EdD, Digital Learning Director, La Sierra University, 4500 Riverwalk Parkway, Riverside, CA 92505. Telephone: 951-785-2984. Fax: 951-785-2316. E-mail: dhunt@lasierra,edu.

DEGREES AND AWARDS

MA Curriculum and Instruction–Educational Technology
MAT Teaching

COURSE SUBJECT AREAS OFFERED OUTSIDE OF DEGREE PROGRAMS

Undergraduate—education (specific levels and methods); education (specific subject areas).
Graduate—educational/instructional media design; education related; education (specific levels and methods); education (specific subject areas).
Non-credit—special education.

LASSEN COMMUNITY COLLEGE DISTRICT
Susanville, California
Office of Distance Learning
http://www.lassencollege.edu

Lassen Community College District was founded in 1925. It is accredited by Western Association of Schools and Colleges. It first offered distance learning courses in 2005. In fall 2010, there were 1,258 students enrolled in distance learning courses. Institutionally administered financial aid is available to distance learners.

Services Distance learners have accessibility to academic advising, bookstore, campus computer network, career placement assistance, e-mail services, library services, tutoring.

Contact Brenda Hoffman, Correspondence Technician, Lassen Community College District, PO Box 3000, Susanville, CA 96130. Telephone: 530-251-8875. Fax: 530-251-8825. E-mail: bhoffman@lassencollege.edu.

DEGREES AND AWARDS

Programs offered do not lead to a degree or other formal award.

COURSE SUBJECT AREAS OFFERED OUTSIDE OF DEGREE PROGRAMS

Undergraduate—anthropology; business administration, management and operations; English; history; political science and government; psychology; sociology.

LAUREL UNIVERSITY
High Point, North Carolina
http://www.laureluniversity.edu

Laurel University was founded in 1932. It is accredited by Association for Biblical Higher Education. It first offered distance learning courses in 2004. In fall 2010, there were 75 students enrolled in distance learning courses. Institutionally administered financial aid is available to distance learners.

Services Distance learners have accessibility to academic advising, bookstore, career placement assistance, e-mail services, library services.

Contact Mr. Jeremy Reese, Director of Admissions, Laurel University, 1215 Eastchester Drive, High Point, NC 27265. Telephone: 336-887-3000. Fax: 855-528-3538. E-mail: admissions@laureluniversity.edu.

DEGREES AND AWARDS

AA Ministry
BA Bible and Theology; Christian Counseling; Christian Ministry; Elementary Christian School Teacher Education; Management and Business Ethics; Pastoral Ministries
MA Theological Studies
MAEd Christian School Education
MBA Business Administration

COURSE SUBJECT AREAS OFFERED OUTSIDE OF DEGREE PROGRAMS

Undergraduate—American Sign Language (ASL); anthropology; biology; English language and literature related; geography and cartography; intercultural/multicultural and diversity studies; languages (classics and classical); literature; mathematics and computer science; music.

LAWRENCE TECHNOLOGICAL UNIVERSITY
Southfield, Michigan
http://www.ltu.edu/ltuonline/

Lawrence Technological University was founded in 1932. It is accredited by North Central Association of Colleges and Schools. It first offered distance learning courses in 1998. In fall 2010, there were 623 students enrolled in distance learning courses. Institutionally administered financial aid is available to distance learners.

Services Distance learners have accessibility to academic advising, bookstore, campus computer network, career placement assistance, e-mail services, library services, tutoring.

Contact Dr. Richard Bush, Director, eLearning Services, Lawrence Technological University, 21000 West Ten Mile Road, Southfield, MI 48075. Telephone: 248-204-2380. Fax: 248-204-2389. E-mail: elearning@ltu.edu.

DEGREES AND AWARDS

BS Information Technology
CCCPE Architecture Management; Building Information Modeling and Computer Visualization certificate; Non-Profit Management and Leadership; Project Management; Workplace Technologies
MBA Business Administration
MBA/M Arch Master of Architecture
MEM Engineering Management
MET Educational Technology Training and Performance Improvement program

COURSE SUBJECT AREAS OFFERED OUTSIDE OF DEGREE PROGRAMS

Undergraduate—architecture; business administration, management and operations; computer/information technology administration and management; human resources management; mathematics and statistics related; psychology related.

Graduate—accounting and related services; architecture related; business administration, management and operations; computer/information technology administration and management; educational/instructional media design; engineering; finance and financial management services; human resources management; information science/studies; international business; management information systems; marketing.

LEHIGH UNIVERSITY
Bethlehem, Pennsylvania
Office of Distance Learning
http://www.distance.lehigh.edu

Lehigh University was founded in 1865. It is accredited by Middle States Association of Colleges and Schools. It first offered distance learning courses in 1992. In fall 2010, there were 700 students enrolled in distance learning courses. Institutionally administered financial aid is available to distance learners.

Services Distance learners have accessibility to academic advising, bookstore, campus computer network, career placement assistance, e-mail services, library services, tutoring.

Contact Lisa Moughan, Marketing Coordinator, Lehigh University, 436 Brodhead Avenue, Bethlehem, PA 18015. Telephone: 610-758-4372. Fax: 610-758-4190. E-mail: lim2@lehigh.edu.

DEGREES AND AWARDS

Certificate Project Management; Supply Chain Management
Graduate Certificate Regulatory Affairs
MBA Business Administration
ME Chemical Engineering; Polymer Science and Engineering
MME Mechanical Engineering (MS or MEng)
MS Chemistry; Manufacturing Systems Engineering; Molecular Biology; Polymer Science and Engineering

COURSE SUBJECT AREAS OFFERED OUTSIDE OF DEGREE PROGRAMS

Graduate—biological and physical sciences; business administration, management and operations; cell biology and anatomical sciences; chemical engineering; chemistry; polymer/plastics engineering.

Non-credit—business administration, management and operations; business/corporate communications; chemical engineering; chemistry; polymer/plastics engineering.

LEHMAN COLLEGE OF THE CITY UNIVERSITY OF NEW YORK
Bronx, New York
http://www.lehman.cuny.edu/online-education/students/index.php

Lehman College of the City University of New York was founded in 1931. It is accredited by Middle States Association of Colleges and Schools. It first offered distance learning courses in 1997. In fall 2010, there were 2,333 students enrolled in distance learning courses. Institutionally administered financial aid is available to distance learners.

Services Distance learners have accessibility to bookstore, campus computer network, e-mail services, library services, tutoring.

Contact Ms. Carol Weisz, Associate Director of Online Education, Lehman College of the City University of New York, 250 Bedford Park Boulevard West, Bronx, NY 10468. Telephone: 718-960-5871. Fax: 718-951-4738. E-mail: carol.weisz@lehman.cuny.edu.

DEGREES AND AWARDS

Programs offered do not lead to a degree or other formal award.

COURSE SUBJECT AREAS OFFERED OUTSIDE OF DEGREE PROGRAMS

Undergraduate—accounting and related services; biology; business administration, management and operations; business, management, and marketing related; chemistry; computer science; dance; economics; English; geography and cartography; history; journalism; languages (Romance languages); political science and government.

LENOIR COMMUNITY COLLEGE

Kinston, North Carolina

Distance Learning Services

http://www.lenoircc.edu

Lenoir Community College was founded in 1960. It is accredited by Southern Association of Colleges and Schools. It first offered distance learning courses in 1997. In fall 2010, there were 2,127 students enrolled in distance learning courses. Institutionally administered financial aid is available to distance learners.

Services Distance learners have accessibility to academic advising, bookstore, campus computer network, career placement assistance, e-mail services, library services, tutoring.

Contact Mrs. Deborah Jo W. Wilson, Director of Distance Education, Lenoir Community College, PO Box 188, 231 Highway 58 South, Kinston, NC 28502-0188. Telephone: 252-527-6223 Ext. 516. Fax: 252-527-6879. E-mail: jwilson@lenoircc.edu.

DEGREES AND AWARDS

AA the Arts
AAS Accounting; Business Administration; Global Logistics

COURSE SUBJECT AREAS OFFERED OUTSIDE OF DEGREE PROGRAMS

Undergraduate—allied health and medical assisting services; behavioral sciences; biblical studies; bilingual, multilingual, and multicultural education; biological and physical sciences; biology; business, management, and marketing related; computer and information sciences; computer engineering technologies; computer programming; criminal justice and corrections; curriculum and instruction; economics; education; education related; English; fine and studio arts; history; linguistic, comparative, and related language studies; mathematics and statistics related; psychology.

LESLEY UNIVERSITY

Cambridge, Massachusetts

http://web.lesley.edu/admissions/online.asp

Lesley University was founded in 1909. It is accredited by New England Association of Schools and Colleges. It first offered distance learning courses in 1996. In fall 2010, there were 500 students enrolled in distance learning courses. Institutionally administered financial aid is available to distance learners.

Services Distance learners have accessibility to academic advising, bookstore, campus computer network, career placement assistance, e-mail services, library services, tutoring.

Contact Ms. Sabina Petrucci, Assistant Director of Academic Advising and Student Services, Lesley University, e-Learning and Instructional Support, 29 Everett Street, Cambridge, MA 02138. Telephone: 617-349-8301. Fax: 617-349-8917. E-mail: spetrucc@lesley.edu.

DEGREES AND AWARDS

BS Management Online; Psychology
MEd Individually Designed; Mathematics Education (1-8); Science in Education; Technology in Education
MS Ecological Teaching and Learning
PhD Educational Studies, Adult Learning specialization

COURSE SUBJECT AREAS OFFERED OUTSIDE OF DEGREE PROGRAMS

Undergraduate—business, management, and marketing related; psychology.

Graduate—curriculum and instruction; education; educational administration and supervision; educational/instructional media design; education related; education (specific levels and methods); education (specific subject areas); English or French as a second or foreign language (teaching); mathematics; special education.

LETOURNEAU UNIVERSITY

Longview, Texas

Adult Education Degree Programs

http://adults.letu.edu/

LeTourneau University was founded in 1946. It is accredited by Southern Association of Colleges and Schools. It first offered distance learning courses in 1999. In fall 2010, there were 965 students enrolled in distance learning courses. Institutionally administered financial aid is available to distance learners.

Services Distance learners have accessibility to academic advising, bookstore, campus computer network, career placement assistance, e-mail services, library services, tutoring.

Contact Dr. Carol Green, Vice President for the School of Graduate and Professional Studies, LeTourneau University, 2100 South Mobberly Avenue, Longview, TX 75602. Telephone: 903-233-4060. Fax: 903-233-4001. E-mail: carolgreen@letu.edu.

DEGREES AND AWARDS

AIS Interdisciplinary Studies
BBA Business Administration
BBM Business Management
BPsych Psychology
BS Teacher Education
BSHS Human Services
MA Psychology
MBA Business Administration
MBOL Masters of Strategic Leadership
MEd Online Master in Education
MSE Engineering

COURSE SUBJECT AREAS OFFERED OUTSIDE OF DEGREE PROGRAMS

Undergraduate—biblical studies; biology; business administration, management and operations; curriculum and instruction; economics; education related; education (specific levels and methods); education (specific subject areas); English; geography and cartography; history; human development, family studies, and related services; mathematics; psychology.

Graduate—business administration, management and operations; engineering; psychology.

LEWIS-CLARK STATE COLLEGE

Lewiston, Idaho

Distance Learning

http://www.lcsc.edu/dl

Lewis-Clark State College was founded in 1893. It is accredited by Northwest Commission on Colleges and Universities. It first offered distance learning courses in 1995. In fall 2010, there were 3,208 students enrolled in distance learning courses. Institutionally administered financial aid is available to distance learners.

Services Distance learners have accessibility to academic advising, bookstore, campus computer network, career placement assistance, e-mail services, library services.

Contact Carolyn D. Quintero, Coordinator, Faculty/Student Services, Lewis-Clark State College, 500 Eighth Avenue, Lewiston, ID 83501. Telephone: 208-792-2239. Fax: 208-792-2444. E-mail: cdquintero@lcsc.edu.

DEGREES AND AWARDS

AA Liberal Arts
AAS Early Childhood Development; Web Development
AS Business Administration; Entrepreneurship
BAS Early Childhood Development; Web Development

BS Business Administration; Interdisciplinary Studies; Management

BSN Nursing

Certification Secondary Education

COURSE SUBJECT AREAS OFFERED OUTSIDE OF DEGREE PROGRAMS

Undergraduate—accounting and related services; anthropology; biology; business administration, management and operations; business/corporate communications; business, management, and marketing related; business/managerial economics; business operations support and assistant services; communication and media; community organization and advocacy; computer and information sciences and support services related; computer programming; computer science; computer systems analysis; criminal justice and corrections; criminology; data entry/microcomputer applications; data processing; economics; education; educational assessment, evaluation, and research; education related; education (specific levels and methods); education (specific subject areas); English; English language and literature related; entrepreneurial and small business operations; finance and financial management services; foods, nutrition, and related services; gerontology; graphic communications; health and medical administrative services; health/medical preparatory programs; history; hospitality administration; human resources management; languages (foreign languages related); liberal arts and sciences, general studies and humanities; literature; marketing; mathematics; mathematics and statistics related; natural sciences; philosophy; political science and government; practical nursing, vocational nursing and nursing assistants; psychology; psychology related; social sciences; social sciences related; social work; sociology; sociology and anthropology; special education.

Non-credit—allied health and medical assisting services.

LEWIS UNIVERSITY
Romeoville, Illinois
http://www.lewisu.edu/

Lewis University was founded in 1932. It is accredited by North Central Association of Colleges and Schools. It first offered distance learning courses in 1999. Institutionally administered financial aid is available to distance learners.

Services Distance learners have accessibility to academic advising, bookstore, campus computer network, career placement assistance, e-mail services, library services, tutoring.

Contact Dr. Michele Young, Special Assistant to the Provost, Lewis University, 500 Independence Boulevard, Romeoville, IL 60446. Telephone: 815-836-5517. Fax: 815-838-8990. E-mail: youngmi@lewisu.edu.

DEGREES AND AWARDS

BA Fire Service Administration

MA Organizational Leadership

MS Aviation and Transportation; Criminal/Social Justice; Information Security; Public Safety Administration

MSN Nursing

COURSE SUBJECT AREAS OFFERED OUTSIDE OF DEGREE PROGRAMS

Undergraduate—alternative and complementary medicine and medical systems; biological and physical sciences; data entry/microcomputer applications; fine and studio arts; history; human biology; intercultural/multicultural and diversity studies; liberal arts and sciences, general studies and humanities; literature; music; philosophy and religious studies related; political science and government; sociology; visual and performing arts related.

LIBERTY UNIVERSITY
Lynchburg, Virginia
Distance Learning Program
http://www.luonline.com/

Liberty University was founded in 1971. It is accredited by Southern Association of Colleges and Schools. It first offered distance learning courses in 1985. In fall 2010, there were 45,902 students enrolled in distance learning courses. Institutionally administered financial aid is available to distance learners.

Services Distance learners have accessibility to academic advising, bookstore, campus computer network, career placement assistance, e-mail services, library services, tutoring.

Contact Jay Bridge, Director of Admissions, Liberty University, 1971 University Boulevard, Lynchburg, VA 24502-2269. Telephone: 800-424-9595. Fax: 800-628-7977. E-mail: luoadmissions@liberty.edu.

DEGREES AND AWARDS

AA Accounting; Business; Criminal Justice; General Studies; Management Information Systems; Paralegal Studies; Psychology; Religion

BS Accounting; Aeronautics; Business Administration; Business; Criminal Justice; Interdisciplinary Studies; Management Information Systems; Paralegal Studies; Psychology; Religion

BSN Nursing–RN to BSN

Ed S Education Specialist

MA Christian Leadership; Discipleship Ministries; Evangelism and Church Planting; Human Services; Intercultural Studies; Management and Leadership; Marriage and Family Therapy; Pastoral Counseling; Professional Counseling; Theological Studies; Worship Studies

MAR Religion

MAT Teaching

MBA Business Administration

MDiv Divinity

MEd Education

MS Accounting

MSN Nursing

DMin Ministry

EdD Education

PhD Counseling

COURSE SUBJECT AREAS OFFERED OUTSIDE OF DEGREE PROGRAMS

Undergraduate—accounting and related services; biblical studies; biology; business/commerce; business/corporate communications; business, management, and marketing related; business/managerial economics; communication and media; computer/information technology administration and management; criminal justice and corrections; economics; education; history; marketing; philosophy; psychology; religious studies; social sciences; theology and religious vocations related.

Graduate—accounting and related services; biblical studies; business administration, management and operations; business, management, and marketing related; curriculum and instruction; educational administration and supervision; educational assessment, evaluation, and research; educational/instructional media design; education related; education (specific levels and methods); education (specific subject areas); English; family and consumer sciences/human sciences; legal professions and studies related; psychology; religious studies; special education; theological and ministerial studies; theology and religious vocations related.

LIFE PACIFIC COLLEGE
San Dimas, California
School of Distance Learning
http://www.lifepacific.edu/distance

Life Pacific College was founded in 1923. It is accredited by Association for Biblical Higher Education. It first offered distance learning courses in 1924. In fall 2010, there were 300 students enrolled in distance learning courses. Institutionally administered financial aid is available to distance learners.

Services Distance learners have accessibility to academic advising, bookstore, career placement assistance, library services.

Contact Brian Tomhave, Director, Life Pacific College, 1100 West Covina Boulevard, San Dimas, CA 91773. Telephone: 877-851-0900. Fax: 909-706-3099. E-mail: distance@lifepacific.edu.

DEGREES AND AWARDS

AA Biblical Studies
BA Ministry and Leadership degree completion program
MA Strategic Leadership, Ministry emphasis

COURSE SUBJECT AREAS OFFERED OUTSIDE OF DEGREE PROGRAMS

Undergraduate—biblical studies; philosophy and religious studies related; theological and ministerial studies.
Non-credit—biblical studies; religious studies.

LIMESTONE COLLEGE
Gaffney, South Carolina
Extended Campus Internet Program
http://www.limestone.edu/extended-campus

Limestone College was founded in 1845. It is accredited by Southern Association of Colleges and Schools. It first offered distance learning courses in 1997. In fall 2010, there were 2,662 students enrolled in distance learning courses. Institutionally administered financial aid is available to distance learners.
Services Distance learners have accessibility to academic advising, bookstore, campus computer network, career placement assistance, e-mail services, library services, tutoring.
Contact Mrs. Katie Jones, Academic Advisor/Blackboard Trainer, Limestone College, Extended Campus, 1115 College Drive, Gaffney, SC 29340-3799. Telephone: 864-488-4597. Fax: 864-488-4595. E-mail: kphillips@limestone.edu.

DEGREES AND AWARDS

AA Business Administration; Liberal Studies
AS Computer Science Information Technology; Computer Science Programming
BA Criminal Justice; Liberal Studies; Psychology
BS Business Administration; Computer Science; Health Care Administration; Human Resources; Liberal Studies

LINCOLN CHRISTIAN UNIVERSITY
Lincoln, Illinois
Distance Learning
http://www.lincolnchristian.edu

Lincoln Christian University was founded in 1944. It is accredited by Association for Biblical Higher Education. It first offered distance learning courses in 1993. In fall 2010, there were 252 students enrolled in distance learning courses. Institutionally administered financial aid is available to distance learners.
Services Distance learners have accessibility to academic advising, bookstore, campus computer network, e-mail services, library services.
Contact Admissions, Lincoln Christian University, 100 Campus View Drive, Lincoln, IL 62656. Telephone: 217-732-3168 Ext. 2315. E-mail: admissions@lincolnchristian.edu.

DEGREES AND AWARDS

BA Christian Ministry; Human Services; Leadership and Management
MA Bible and Theology; Organizational Leadership; Teaching English to Speakers of Other Languages (TESOL)

COURSE SUBJECT AREAS OFFERED OUTSIDE OF DEGREE PROGRAMS

Undergraduate—biblical studies; business, management, and marketing related; education; English or French as a second or foreign language (teaching); history; mathematics; missionary studies and missiology; religious studies; social sciences; theological and ministerial studies; theology and religious vocations related.
Graduate—biblical studies; English or French as a second or foreign language (teaching); languages (Middle/Near Eastern and Semitic); religious education; religious studies; theological and ministerial studies.
Non-credit—biblical studies; religious studies; theological and ministerial studies.

LINDENWOOD UNIVERSITY
St. Charles, Missouri
http://www.lindenwood.edu/online/

Lindenwood University was founded in 1827. It is accredited by North Central Association of Colleges and Schools. It first offered distance learning courses in 2002. In fall 2010, there were 471 students enrolled in distance learning courses. Institutionally administered financial aid is available to distance learners.
Services Distance learners have accessibility to academic advising, bookstore, campus computer network, career placement assistance, e-mail services, library services, tutoring.
Contact Dr. Edward Perantoni, Director of Distance Learning, Lindenwood University, 209 South Kingshighway, St. Charles, MO 63301. Telephone: 636-949-4705. Fax: 636-949-4989. E-mail: eperantoni@lindenwood.edu.

DEGREES AND AWARDS

BA Criminal Justice
MA Education Technology; Nonprofit Administration
MBA Business Administration
MFA Writing

COURSE SUBJECT AREAS OFFERED OUTSIDE OF DEGREE PROGRAMS

Undergraduate—accounting and related services; astronomy and astrophysics; biology; criminal justice and corrections; criminology; education related; English language and literature related; fine and studio arts; geological and earth sciences/geosciences; health and physical education/fitness; history; literature; philosophy; political science and government; psychology; social work; sociology.
Graduate—education; educational administration and supervision; educational assessment, evaluation, and research; educational/instructional media design; education related; psychology related.

LIPSCOMB UNIVERSITY
Nashville, Tennessee
http://www.lipscomb.edu/

Lipscomb University was founded in 1891. It is accredited by Southern Association of Colleges and Schools. It first offered distance learning courses in 1999. In fall 2010, there were 735 students enrolled in distance learning courses. Institutionally administered financial aid is available to distance learners.
Services Distance learners have accessibility to academic advising, bookstore, campus computer network, career placement assistance, e-mail services, library services.
Contact Mary Owen Holmes, Recruiter, Adult Degree Program, Lipscomb University, One University Park Drive, Nashville, TN 37204. Telephone: 615-966-5279. E-mail: holmesmm@lipscomb.edu.

DEGREES AND AWARDS

Programs offered do not lead to a degree or other formal award.

COURSE SUBJECT AREAS OFFERED OUTSIDE OF DEGREE PROGRAMS

Undergraduate—accounting and computer science; accounting and related services; biblical studies; business administration, management and operations; education; English; legal studies (non-professional general, undergraduate); marketing; music; nutrition sciences; philosophy.
Graduate—accounting and related services; biblical studies; business administration, management and operations; education; educational administration and supervision; educational assessment, evaluation, and research; finance and financial management services; marketing; peace studies and conflict resolution; psychology.

LOCK HAVEN UNIVERSITY OF PENNSYLVANIA
Lock Haven, Pennsylvania
http://ecampus.lhup.edu/

Lock Haven University of Pennsylvania was founded in 1870. It is accredited by Middle States Association of Colleges and Schools. It first offered distance learning courses in 1995. In fall 2010, there were 1,000 students enrolled in distance learning courses. Institutionally administered financial aid is available to distance learners.

Services Distance learners have accessibility to academic advising, bookstore, campus computer network, e-mail services, library services, tutoring.

Contact Vicki Paulina, Office of Academic Technology, Lock Haven University of Pennsylvania, Court House Annex, Lock Haven, PA 17745. Telephone: 570-484-3059. Fax: 570-484-2404. E-mail: vpaulina@lhup.edu.

DEGREES AND AWARDS
MEd Alternative Education; Teaching and Learning
MHS Physician Assistant
MLA Liberal Arts

COURSE SUBJECT AREAS OFFERED OUTSIDE OF DEGREE PROGRAMS
Undergraduate—anthropology; applied mathematics; bioethics/medical ethics; business, management, and marketing related; communication and media; computer programming; criminology; education; English language and literature related; film/video and photographic arts; fine and studio arts; foods, nutrition, and related services; geography and cartography; health and physical education/fitness; health/medical preparatory programs; health services/allied health/health sciences; history; marketing; music; philosophy and religious studies; political science and government; psychology; social and philosophical foundations of education; sociology; sociology and anthropology; statistics; visual and performing arts related.
Graduate—communication and media; curriculum and instruction; education; educational administration and supervision; health professions related; liberal arts and sciences, general studies and humanities; public health; science, technology and society.
Non-credit—allied health and medical assisting services; business/commerce; computer and information sciences and support services related; construction trades; education; legal professions and studies related.

LONG BEACH CITY COLLEGE
Long Beach, California
http://de.lbcc.edu

Long Beach City College was founded in 1927. It is accredited by Western Association of Schools and Colleges. It first offered distance learning courses in 1980. In fall 2010, there were 3,660 students enrolled in distance learning courses. Institutionally administered financial aid is available to distance learners.

Services Distance learners have accessibility to academic advising, bookstore, career placement assistance, library services.

Contact Ms. Wendi Lopez, Distance Learning Specialist II, Long Beach City College, 4901 East Carson Street, Y-10, Long Beach, CA 90808. Telephone: 562-938-4025. Fax: 562-938-4014. E-mail: de@lbcc.edu.

DEGREES AND AWARDS
Programs offered do not lead to a degree or other formal award.

COURSE SUBJECT AREAS OFFERED OUTSIDE OF DEGREE PROGRAMS
Undergraduate—accounting and related services; anthropology; astronomy and astrophysics; biology; business administration, management and operations; business, management, and marketing related; computer and information sciences; computer and information sciences and support services related; computer programming; computer science; computer software and media applications; computer systems networking and telecommunications; dance; design and applied arts; drafting/design engineering technologies; drama/theatre arts and stagecraft; economics; electrical/electronics maintenance and repair technology; English; English or French as a second or foreign language (teaching); film/video and photographic arts; finance and financial management services; foods, nutrition, and related services; geography and cartography; graphic communications; health and physical education/fitness; health/medical preparatory programs; history; human development, family studies, and related services; international business; journalism; legal professions and studies related; liberal arts and sciences, general studies and humanities; library science and administration; marketing; mathematics; mathematics and computer science; mathematics and statistics related; movement and mind-body therapies and education; music; nutrition sciences; pharmacology and toxicology; philosophy; political science and government; psychology; radio, television, and digital communication; real estate; registered nursing, nursing administration, nursing research and clinical nursing; social sciences; sociology; statistics.

LONG ISLAND UNIVERSITY AT RIVERHEAD
Riverhead, New York
Homeland Security Management Institute
http://www.liu.edu/homeland

Long Island University at Riverhead first offered distance learning courses in 2005. In fall 2010, there were 145 students enrolled in distance learning courses. Institutionally administered financial aid is available to distance learners.

Services Distance learners have accessibility to academic advising, e-mail services, library services.

Contact Dr. Vincent Henry, Director/Associate Professor, Long Island University at Riverhead, 121 Speonk-Riverhead Road, LIU Building, Riverhead, NY 11901. Telephone: 631-259-9074. Fax: 631-259-9055. E-mail: vincent.henry@liu.edu.

DEGREES AND AWARDS
MS Homeland Security Mangement

COURSE SUBJECT AREAS OFFERED OUTSIDE OF DEGREE PROGRAMS
Graduate—homeland security; homeland security, law enforcement, firefighting and protective services related.

LOS ANGELES HARBOR COLLEGE
Wilmington, California
Distance Education Programs
http://www.lahc.edu/harboronline.html

Los Angeles Harbor College was founded in 1949. It is accredited by Western Association of Schools and Colleges. It first offered distance learning courses in 1996. In fall 2010, there were 1,800 students enrolled in distance learning courses. Institutionally administered financial aid is available to distance learners.

Services Distance learners have accessibility to bookstore, campus computer network, e-mail services, library services, tutoring.

Contact Dr. Robert Richards, Associate Dean, Research and Planning, Los Angeles Harbor College, 1111 Figueroa Place, Wilmington, CA 90744. Telephone: 310-233-4044. Fax: 310-233-4661. E-mail: richarr@lahc.edu.

DEGREES AND AWARDS
Programs offered do not lead to a degree or other formal award.

COURSE SUBJECT AREAS OFFERED OUTSIDE OF DEGREE PROGRAMS
Undergraduate—accounting and related services; business/commerce; computer and information sciences; computer programming; criminal justice and corrections; criminology; economics; English; English language and literature related; fire protection; health services/allied health/health sciences; history; library science related; linguistic, comparative, and related language studies; political science and government; psychology; real estate; sociology.

LOS ANGELES TRADE-TECHNICAL COLLEGE
Los Angeles, California
http://moodle.lattc.edu

Los Angeles Trade-Technical College was founded in 1925. It is accredited by Western Association of Schools and Colleges. It first offered distance learning courses in 1986. In fall 2010, there were 600 students enrolled in distance learning courses. Institutionally administered financial aid is available to distance learners.

Services Distance learners have accessibility to academic advising, bookstore, campus computer network, e-mail services, library services.

Contact Ms. Linda Delzeit, Online Coordinator, Los Angeles Trade-Technical College, 400 West Washington Boulevard, Los Angeles, CA 90015. Telephone: 213-763-3733. Fax: 213-406-1237. E-mail: delzeil@lattc.edu.

DEGREES AND AWARDS
AA Liberal Arts, General

COURSE SUBJECT AREAS OFFERED OUTSIDE OF DEGREE PROGRAMS
Undergraduate—anthropology; astronomy and astrophysics; business, management, and marketing related; computer software and media applications; construction trades; criminal justice and corrections; English; English language and literature related; film/video and photographic arts; geography and cartography; health and physical education/fitness; heating, air conditioning, ventilation and refrigeration maintenance technology; history; human development, family studies, and related services; liberal arts and sciences, general studies and humanities; marketing; mathematics; mathematics and statistics related; political science and government; psychology; public relations, advertising, and applied communication related; sales merchandising, and related marketing operations (general); sociology; statistics.

LOUISIANA STATE UNIVERSITY AND AGRICULTURAL AND MECHANICAL COLLEGE
Baton Rouge, Louisiana
Independent Study
http://www.outreach.lsu.edu/idl

Louisiana State University and Agricultural and Mechanical College was founded in 1860. It is accredited by Southern Association of Colleges and Schools. It first offered distance learning courses in 1924. In fall 2010, there were 9,000 students enrolled in distance learning courses. Institutionally administered financial aid is available to distance learners.

Services Distance learners have accessibility to bookstore, e-mail services, library services.

Contact Sunny Zeringue, Learner Services Coordinator, Louisiana State University and Agricultural and Mechanical College, Independent and Distance Learning, 1225 Pleasant Hall, Baton Rouge, LA 70803. Telephone: 800-234-5046. Fax: 225-578-3090. E-mail: answers@outreach.lsu.edu.

DEGREES AND AWARDS
Programs offered do not lead to a degree or other formal award.

COURSE SUBJECT AREAS OFFERED OUTSIDE OF DEGREE PROGRAMS
Undergraduate—accounting and related services; anthropology; biology; business administration, management and operations; cell biology and anatomical sciences; communication and media; criminology; curriculum and instruction; drama/theatre arts and stagecraft; ecology, evolution, systematics, and population biology; economics; education; educational assessment, evaluation, and research; education related; education (specific levels and methods); education (specific subject areas); English; English language and literature related; ethnic, cultural minority, gender, and group studies; finance and financial management services; fine and studio arts; geography and cartography; geological and earth sciences/geosciences; health and physical education/fitness; history; journalism; languages (classics and classical); languages (Germanic); languages (Romance languages); library science related; linguistic, comparative, and related language studies; management information systems; management sciences and quantitative methods; marketing; mathematics; mathematics and statistics related; mechanical engineering; music; physical sciences; physics; political science and government; psychology; psychology related; social sciences; social sciences related; sociology; statistics.

Non-credit—biology; English; mathematics.

LOUISIANA STATE UNIVERSITY AT EUNICE
Eunice, Louisiana
Continuing Education
http://www.lsue.edu/elearning

Louisiana State University at Eunice was founded in 1967. It is accredited by Southern Association of Colleges and Schools. It first offered distance learning courses in 1996. In fall 2010, there were 634 students enrolled in distance learning courses. Institutionally administered financial aid is available to distance learners.

Services Distance learners have accessibility to academic advising, bookstore, campus computer network, career placement assistance, e-mail services, library services, tutoring.

Contact Dr. Kenneth Elliott, Assistant Director of Continuing Education, Louisiana State University at Eunice, PO Box 1129, Eunice, LA 70535. Telephone: 337-550-1390. Fax: 337-550-1393. E-mail: kelliott@lsue.edu.

DEGREES AND AWARDS
AAS Fire and Emergency Services

AS Criminal Justice

COURSE SUBJECT AREAS OFFERED OUTSIDE OF DEGREE PROGRAMS
Undergraduate—agriculture; agriculture and agriculture operations related; allied health and medical assisting services; biology; business administration, management and operations; business, management, and marketing related; business/managerial economics; business operations support and assistant services; computer software and media applications; criminal justice and corrections; education; geography and cartography; health and medical administrative services; health professions related; health services/allied health/health sciences; history; hospitality administration; information science/studies; marketing; mathematics; psychology.

LOURDES COLLEGE
Sylvania, Ohio
http://www.lourdes.edu

Lourdes College was founded in 1958. It is accredited by North Central Association of Colleges and Schools. It first offered distance learning courses in 2005. In fall 2010, there were 386 students enrolled in distance learning courses. Institutionally administered financial aid is available to distance learners.

Services Distance learners have accessibility to academic advising, campus computer network, career placement assistance, e-mail services, library services.

Contact Amy Mergen, Director of Admissions, Lourdes College, 6832 Convent Boulevard, Sylvania, OH 43560. Telephone: 419-824-3677. Fax: 419-824-3916. E-mail: amergen@lourdes.edu.

DEGREES AND AWARDS
Programs offered do not lead to a degree or other formal award.

COURSE SUBJECT AREAS OFFERED OUTSIDE OF DEGREE PROGRAMS
Undergraduate—business, management, and marketing related; education; fine and studio arts; history; philosophy; sociology; theological and ministerial studies.

LOYOLA UNIVERSITY NEW ORLEANS
New Orleans, Louisiana
Off-Campus Learning Program
http://css.loyno.edu/nursing/distance-learning-program

Loyola University New Orleans was founded in 1912. It is accredited by Southern Association of Colleges and Schools. It first offered distance learning courses in 1991. In fall 2010, there were 38 students enrolled in distance learning courses. Institutionally administered financial aid is available to distance learners.

Services Distance learners have accessibility to academic advising, bookstore, campus computer network, career placement assistance, e-mail services, library services, tutoring.

Contact Distance Learning Program, Loyola University New Orleans, New Orleans, LA 70118. Telephone: 504-865-3043.

DEGREES AND AWARDS

BSN Nursing–RN to BSN
MSN Health Care Systems Management

COURSE SUBJECT AREAS OFFERED OUTSIDE OF DEGREE PROGRAMS

Undergraduate—criminal justice and corrections; English; history; literature; philosophy and religious studies; social sciences.

LUNA COMMUNITY COLLEGE
Las Vegas, New Mexico
http://www.luna.edu

Luna Community College is accredited by North Central Association of Colleges and Schools. It first offered distance learning courses in 2004. In fall 2010, there were 380 students enrolled in distance learning courses. Institutionally administered financial aid is available to distance learners.

Services Distance learners have accessibility to academic advising, campus computer network, career placement assistance, e-mail services, library services, tutoring.

Contact Lorraine Martinez, Director of Title V, Luna Community College, 366 Luna Drive, Las Vegas, NM 87701. Telephone: 505-454-5375. E-mail: lomartinez@luna.edu.

DEGREES AND AWARDS

AAS Business Administration; General Agriculture; Military Studies

COURSE SUBJECT AREAS OFFERED OUTSIDE OF DEGREE PROGRAMS

Undergraduate—accounting and computer science; agricultural business and management; agriculture; allied health and medical assisting services; behavioral sciences; business administration, management and operations; business/commerce; business/managerial economics; communication and media; computational science; computer and information sciences; curriculum and instruction; economics; education; English; fire protection; health services/allied health/health sciences; history; languages (foreign languages related); liberal arts and sciences, general studies and humanities; management information systems; marketing; mathematics; military science, leadership and operational art related; nutrition sciences; psychology; teaching assistants/aides.

LUZERNE COUNTY COMMUNITY COLLEGE
Nanticoke, Pennsylvania
Telecollege
http://www.luzerne.edu/

Luzerne County Community College was founded in 1966. It is accredited by Middle States Association of Colleges and Schools. It first offered distance learning courses in 1981. In fall 2010, there were 12,000 students enrolled in distance learning courses. Institutionally administered financial aid is available to distance learners.

Services Distance learners have accessibility to academic advising, bookstore, campus computer network, career placement assistance, e-mail services, library services.

Contact Mr. Barry E. Cipala, Director of the Distance Learning Center, Luzerne County Community College, 1333 South Prospect Street, Nanticoke, PA 18634. Telephone: 570-740-0559 Ext. 559. Fax: 570-740-0295. E-mail: bcipala@luzerne.edu.

DEGREES AND AWARDS

AAS Business; General degree
AS General Studies

COURSE SUBJECT AREAS OFFERED OUTSIDE OF DEGREE PROGRAMS

Undergraduate—business administration, management and operations; liberal arts and sciences, general studies and humanities.
Non-credit—computer software and media applications.

LYNN UNIVERSITY
Boca Raton, Florida
The Institute for Distance Learning
http://www.lynn.edu/distancelearning

Lynn University was founded in 1962. It is accredited by Southern Association of Colleges and Schools. It first offered distance learning courses in 1998. In fall 2010, there were 450 students enrolled in distance learning courses. Institutionally administered financial aid is available to distance learners.

Services Distance learners have accessibility to academic advising, bookstore, campus computer network, career placement assistance, e-mail services, library services, tutoring.

Contact Ms. Ioulia Nikiforova-Bohannan, Assistant Director of Admissions, Lynn University, 3601 North Military Trail, Boca Raton, FL 33431. Telephone: 561-237-7803. Fax: 561-237-7100. E-mail: inikiforova@lynn.edu.

DEGREES AND AWARDS

BS Business Administration; Criminal Justice; Psychology
Certification Emergency and Disaster Management
Graduate Certificate Emergency and Disaster Management
MBA Aviation Management; Financial Valuation and Investment Management; Hospitality Management; International Business; Marketing; Mass Communication and Media Management; Sports and Athletics Administration
MEd Educational Leadership, Higher Education Administration specialization; Educational Leadership, School Administration specialization
MS Criminal Justice Administration; Emergency Planning and Administration

MACON STATE COLLEGE
Macon, Georgia
Office of Distance Learning
http://www.maconstate.edu

Macon State College was founded in 1968. It is accredited by Southern Association of Colleges and Schools. It first offered distance learning courses in 1997. In fall 2010, there were 2,000 students enrolled in distance learning courses. Institutionally administered financial aid is available to distance learners.

Services Distance learners have accessibility to academic advising, bookstore, campus computer network, career placement assistance, e-mail services, library services, tutoring.

Contact Office of Admissions, Macon State College, 100 College Station Drive, Macon, GA 31206. Telephone: 478-471-2800. E-mail: admissions@maconstate.edu.

DEGREES AND AWARDS

BST Information Technology

COURSE SUBJECT AREAS OFFERED OUTSIDE OF DEGREE PROGRAMS

Undergraduate—accounting and computer science; accounting and related services; applied mathematics; biology; business/commerce; business/corporate communications; business, management, and marketing related; communication and media; computer and information sciences; computer/information technology administration and management; computer programming; computer software and media applications; computer systems analysis; computer systems networking and telecommunications; education; education (specific levels and methods); English; graphic communications; health and medical administrative services; health professions related; health services/allied health/health sciences; history; information science/studies; mathematics; mathematics and computer science; mathematics and statistics related; political science and government; psychology; public administration and social service professions related; public health; statistics.

MAHARISHI UNIVERSITY OF MANAGEMENT
Fairfield, Iowa
Distance MBA Program
http://www.mum.edu

Maharishi University of Management was founded in 1971. It is accredited by North Central Association of Colleges and Schools. It first offered distance learning courses in 1995. In fall 2010, there were 419 students enrolled in distance learning courses. Institutionally administered financial aid is available to distance learners.

Services Distance learners have accessibility to academic advising, e-mail services.

Contact Dr. Dennis Heaton, Dean of Distance Education, Maharishi University of Management, 1000 North Fourth Street, Fairfield, IA 52557. Telephone: 641-472-1191. E-mail: distance@mum.edu.

DEGREES AND AWARDS

MBA Business Administration

COURSE SUBJECT AREAS OFFERED OUTSIDE OF DEGREE PROGRAMS

Undergraduate—accounting and related services; alternative and complementary medicine and medical systems; finance and financial management services.

Graduate—accounting and related services; business, management, and marketing related; computer and information sciences; finance and financial management services; health professions related.

Non-credit—accounting and related services; finance and financial management services; philosophy and religious studies related; physics.

MALONE UNIVERSITY
Canton, Ohio
Malone University Online Learning
http://www.malone.edu/online

Malone University was founded in 1892. It is accredited by North Central Association of Colleges and Schools. It first offered distance learning courses in 1999. In fall 2010, there were 600 students enrolled in distance learning courses. Institutionally administered financial aid is available to distance learners.

Services Distance learners have accessibility to academic advising, bookstore, career placement assistance, e-mail services, library services.

Contact Sharon Purvis, Online Coordinator, Malone University, 2600 Cleveland Avenue, Canton, OH 44709. Telephone: 330-471-8423. Fax: 330-471-8570. E-mail: distancelearning@malone.edu.

DEGREES AND AWARDS

BA Business Management

COURSE SUBJECT AREAS OFFERED OUTSIDE OF DEGREE PROGRAMS

Undergraduate—biblical studies; biology; business administration, management and operations; business/commerce; communication and journalism related; communication and media; educational/instructional media design; fine and studio arts; health and physical education/fitness; history; human development, family studies, and related services; liberal arts and sciences, general studies and humanities; philosophy; political science and government; psychology; social sciences related; sociology.

Graduate—biblical studies; business administration, management and operations; clinical, counseling and applied psychology.

MANSFIELD UNIVERSITY OF PENNSYLVANIA
Mansfield, Pennsylvania
Center for Lifelong Learning
http://cll.mansfield.edu

Mansfield University of Pennsylvania was founded in 1857. It is accredited by Middle States Association of Colleges and Schools. It first offered distance learning courses in 1995. In fall 2010, there were 2,332 students enrolled in distance learning courses. Institutionally administered financial aid is available to distance learners.

Services Distance learners have accessibility to academic advising, bookstore, campus computer network, career placement assistance, e-mail services, library services, tutoring.

Contact Brian D. Barden, Executive Director of Enrollment Services, Mansfield University of Pennsylvania, South Hall, Mansfield, PA 16933. Telephone: 570-662-4813. Fax: 570-662-4121. E-mail: bbarden@mansfield.edu.

DEGREES AND AWARDS

BA Art History

BSN Nursing–RN to BSN

MOL Organizational Leadership

MSE Library and Information Technologies–School Library and Information Technologies

MSN Nursing Education

COURSE SUBJECT AREAS OFFERED OUTSIDE OF DEGREE PROGRAMS

Undergraduate—accounting and related services; anthropology; business administration, management and operations; communication and journalism related; computer and information sciences; criminal justice and corrections; economics; education; education (specific subject areas); English; English language and literature related; history; liberal arts and sciences, general studies and humanities; marketing; mathematics; music; nutrition sciences; psychology; sociology.

Graduate—business/corporate communications; education; educational assessment, evaluation, and research; library science and administration; social sciences related.

Non-credit—accounting and computer science; accounting and related services; agricultural and food products processing; allied health and medical assisting services; applied mathematics; business/corporate communications; communication and journalism related; communications technology; computer and information sciences; computer and information sciences and support services related; computer programming; computer software and media applications; computer systems analysis; computer systems networking and telecommunications; construction engineering technologies; construction trades; criminal justice and corrections; data entry/microcomputer applications; data processing; dental support services and allied professions; education related; film/video and photographic arts; fine and studio arts; foods, nutrition, and related services; health and medical administrative services; heating, air conditioning, ventilation and refrigeration maintenance technology; hospitality administration; legal professions and studies related; legal studies (non-professional general, undergraduate); management information systems; marketing; nutrition sciences; pharmacy, pharmaceutical sciences, and administration; publishing; sales merchandising, and related marketing operations (general); social work.

MARIAN UNIVERSITY
Fond du Lac, Wisconsin
http://www.marianuniversity.edu/

Marian University was founded in 1936. It is accredited by North Central Association of Colleges and Schools. It first offered distance learning courses in 2000. In fall 2010, there were 741 students enrolled in distance learning courses. Institutionally administered financial aid is available to distance learners.

Services Distance learners have accessibility to academic advising, bookstore, campus computer network, career placement assistance, e-mail services, library services.

Contact Ms. Cheryl Teichmiller, Registrar, Marian University, 45 South National Avenue, Fond du Lac, WI 54935. Telephone: 800-262-7426 Ext. 7618. Fax: 920-926-6708. E-mail: cteichmiller@marianuniversity.edu.

DEGREES AND AWARDS

MAE Differentiated Instruction for At-Risk Learners (DIAL); Educational Technology; Teacher Education certification program
MS Criminal Justice Leadership; Grief and Bereavement

COURSE SUBJECT AREAS OFFERED OUTSIDE OF DEGREE PROGRAMS

Undergraduate—business administration, management and operations; computer and information sciences; criminal justice and corrections; education; English; finance and financial management services; homeland security; languages (Romance languages); marketing; philosophy; physical sciences; psychology; social work; sociology; theological and ministerial studies.
Graduate—curriculum and instruction; education; educational/instructional media design; health professions related.
Non-credit—health professions related.

MARIST COLLEGE
Poughkeepsie, New York
School of Management
http://www.marist.edu/gpp/distancelearning/

Marist College was founded in 1929. It is accredited by Middle States Association of Colleges and Schools. It first offered distance learning courses in 1998. In fall 2010, there were 1,949 students enrolled in distance learning courses. Institutionally administered financial aid is available to distance learners.
Services Distance learners have accessibility to academic advising, bookstore, campus computer network, career placement assistance, e-mail services, library services.
Contact Sharone Wellington-deAnda, Project Coordinator, Global and Professional, Marist College, School of Global and Professional Programs, Poughkeepsie, NY 12601. Telephone: 845-575-3202. Fax: 845-575-3262. E-mail: distancelearning@marist.edu.

DEGREES AND AWARDS

BA Liberal Studies
BS Liberal Studies
MA Communication; Educational Psychology
MBA Business Administration
MPA Public Administration
MS Information Systems; Technology Management

COURSE SUBJECT AREAS OFFERED OUTSIDE OF DEGREE PROGRAMS

Undergraduate—accounting and related services; business, management, and marketing related; economics; finance and financial management services; legal studies (non-professional general, undergraduate); statistics.
Graduate—accounting and related services; business administration, management and operations; business, management, and marketing related; business/managerial economics; finance and financial management services; international business; management sciences and quantitative methods; marketing.

MARLBORO COLLEGE GRADUATE COLLEGE
Brattleboro, Vermont
http://gradschool.marlboro.edu

Marlboro College Graduate College first offered distance learning courses in 1997. In fall 2010, there were 110 students enrolled in distance learning courses. Institutionally administered financial aid is available to distance learners.
Services Distance learners have accessibility to academic advising, career placement assistance, e-mail services, library services, tutoring.
Contact Joe Heslin, Graduate Admissions Director, Marlboro College Graduate College, 28 Vernon Street, Suite 120, Brattleboro, VT 05301. Telephone: 888-258-5665 Ext. 209. Fax: 802-258-9201. E-mail: jheslin@gradschool.marlboro.edu.

DEGREES AND AWARDS

Programs offered do not lead to a degree or other formal award.

COURSE SUBJECT AREAS OFFERED OUTSIDE OF DEGREE PROGRAMS

Undergraduate—accounting and computer science; business administration, management and operations; business/corporate communications; business, management, and marketing related; computer and information sciences; computer/information technology administration and management; computer programming; computer science; computer software and media applications; computer systems analysis; computer systems networking and telecommunications; entrepreneurial and small business operations; finance and financial management services; information science/studies; management information systems; marketing.
Non-credit—business administration, management and operations; business/commerce; communications technologies and support services related; communications technology; computer and information sciences; computer and information sciences and support services related; computer/information technology administration and management; computer software and media applications; education; educational administration and supervision; educational assessment, evaluation, and research; educational/instructional media design; education related; health and medical administrative services; health professions related; health services/allied health/health sciences; public health.

MARQUETTE UNIVERSITY
Milwaukee, Wisconsin
http://www.marquette.edu/

Marquette University was founded in 1881. It is accredited by North Central Association of Colleges and Schools. It first offered distance learning courses in 1997. In fall 2010, there were 25 students enrolled in distance learning courses. Institutionally administered financial aid is available to distance learners.
Services Distance learners have accessibility to academic advising, bookstore, campus computer network, e-mail services, library services.
Contact Heidi Schweizer, E-Learning Director, Marquette University, PO Box 1881, 320(f) Raynor Library, Center for Teaching and Learning, Milwaukee, WI 53201. Telephone: 414-288-8811. Fax: 414-288-3945. E-mail: heidi.schweizer@marquette.edu.

DEGREES AND AWARDS

EMBA Executive Master of Business Administration
MACE Christian Doctrine

COURSE SUBJECT AREAS OFFERED OUTSIDE OF DEGREE PROGRAMS

Undergraduate—anthropology; applied mathematics; biological and physical sciences; business, management, and marketing related; communication and journalism related; communication and media; criminal justice and corrections; criminology; education; English; history; mathematics and computer science; philosophy; psychology; sociology; sociology and anthropology; theology and religious vocations related.
Graduate—computer and information sciences; education; health services/allied health/health sciences.

MARSHALL UNIVERSITY
Huntington, West Virginia
Distributed Education Technology
http://www.marshall.edu/muonline

Marshall University was founded in 1837. It is accredited by North Central Association of Colleges and Schools. It first offered distance learning courses in 1986. In fall 2010, there were 6,385 students enrolled in distance learning courses. Institutionally administered financial aid is available to distance learners.
Services Distance learners have accessibility to academic advising, bookstore, campus computer network, career placement assistance, e-mail services, library services, tutoring.

Contact Crystal Stewart, Program Manager, Marshall University, One John Marshall Drive, Drinko Library 313A, Huntington, WV 25755-2140. Telephone: 304-696-2970. Fax: 304-696-3229. E-mail: crystal.stewart@marshall.edu.

DEGREES AND AWARDS

BA Regents Bachelor of Arts

MEd Elementary or Secondary Education

COURSE SUBJECT AREAS OFFERED OUTSIDE OF DEGREE PROGRAMS

Undergraduate—accounting and related services; anthropology; business administration, management and operations; business/managerial economics; chemistry; communication and journalism related; communication and media; computer and information sciences; computer and information sciences and support services related; computer engineering; economics; geography and cartography; health professions related; history; journalism; library science and administration; management information systems; marketing; mathematics; mathematics and computer science; mathematics and statistics related; philosophy; philosophy and religious studies; psychology; social work; sociology; statistics; visual and performing arts.

Graduate—accounting and related services; computer and information sciences; educational administration and supervision; educational assessment, evaluation, and research; education related; history; marketing; social work; sociology; visual and performing arts.

MARY BALDWIN COLLEGE
Staunton, Virginia
Adult Degree Program
http://www.mbc.edu/adp

Mary Baldwin College was founded in 1842. It is accredited by Southern Association of Colleges and Schools. It first offered distance learning courses in 1977. In fall 2010, there were 760 students enrolled in distance learning courses. Institutionally administered financial aid is available to distance learners.

Services Distance learners have accessibility to academic advising, bookstore, campus computer network, career placement assistance, e-mail services, library services, tutoring.

Contact Drema Hernandez, Adult Degree Program, Mary Baldwin College, ADP House, Staunton, VA 24401. Telephone: 800-822-2460. Fax: 540-887-7265. E-mail: adp@mbc.edu.

DEGREES AND AWARDS

BA Liberal Arts

BA/BS Liberal Arts

COURSE SUBJECT AREAS OFFERED OUTSIDE OF DEGREE PROGRAMS

Undergraduate—accounting and related services; business administration, management and operations; communication and media; criminal justice and corrections; economics; education; education (specific subject areas); English; health and medical administrative services; history; human resources management; liberal arts and sciences, general studies and humanities; marketing; multi/interdisciplinary studies related; philosophy; philosophy and religious studies related; political science and government; psychology; religious studies; social work; sociology.

Graduate—education; education related; education (specific levels and methods); education (specific subject areas).

Non-credit—business administration, management and operations; health professions related; sales merchandising, and related marketing operations (general).

MARYGROVE COLLEGE
Detroit, Michigan
Master in the Art of Teaching Program
http://www.marygrove.edu

Marygrove College was founded in 1905. It is accredited by North Central Association of Colleges and Schools. It first offered distance learning courses in 1989. In fall 2010, there were 1,670 students enrolled in distance learning courses. Institutionally administered financial aid is available to distance learners.

Services Distance learners have accessibility to academic advising, bookstore, campus computer network, e-mail services, library services, tutoring.

Contact Ms. Karen Wood, Chief Marketing and Communications Officer, Marygrove College, 8425 West McNichols, Detroit, MI 48221. Telephone: 313-927-1446. Fax: 313-927-1345. E-mail: kwood@marygrove.edu.

DEGREES AND AWARDS

MA Educational Leadership

MAT Teacher Education

MEd Educational Technology

COURSE SUBJECT AREAS OFFERED OUTSIDE OF DEGREE PROGRAMS

Undergraduate—education (specific subject areas).

Graduate—education (specific subject areas).

MARYLHURST UNIVERSITY
Marylhurst, Oregon
Department of Distance Learning
http://online.marylhurst.edu

Marylhurst University was founded in 1893. It is accredited by Northwest Commission on Colleges and Universities. It first offered distance learning courses in 1996. In fall 2010, there were 1,686 students enrolled in distance learning courses. Institutionally administered financial aid is available to distance learners.

Services Distance learners have accessibility to academic advising, bookstore, campus computer network, career placement assistance, library services, tutoring.

Contact Chris Sweet, Director of Admissions, Marylhurst University, 17600 Pacific Highway, Marylhurst, OR 97036. Telephone: 503-699-6268. E-mail: csweet@marylhurst.edu.

DEGREES AND AWARDS

BA Interdisciplinary Studies

BS Business and Leadership; Business and Management; Real Estate

MBA Business Administration; Sustainable Business

COURSE SUBJECT AREAS OFFERED OUTSIDE OF DEGREE PROGRAMS

Undergraduate—biblical studies; business/corporate communications; business, management, and marketing related; communication and media; English; English language and literature related; film/video and photographic arts; gerontology; intercultural/multicultural and diversity studies; liberal arts and sciences, general studies and humanities; mathematics; natural sciences; philosophy and religious studies related; physical sciences related; psychology; religious studies; social sciences related; theological and ministerial studies.

Graduate—biblical studies; education; education related; gerontology; liberal arts and sciences, general studies and humanities; religious studies; theological and ministerial studies; theology and religious vocations related.

MARYMOUNT UNIVERSITY
Arlington, Virginia
http://www.marymount.edu/

Marymount University was founded in 1950. It is accredited by Southern Association of Colleges and Schools. It first offered distance learning courses in 1999. In fall 2010, there were 40 students enrolled in distance learning courses. Institutionally administered financial aid is available to distance learners.

Services Distance learners have accessibility to academic advising, bookstore, campus computer network, career placement assistance, e-mail services, library services, tutoring.

Contact Ms. Francesca Reed, Director, Graduate Admissions, Marymount University, 2807 North Glebe Road, Arlington, VA 22207. Telephone: 703-284-5901. Fax: 703-527-3815. E-mail: francesca.reed@marymount.edu.

DEGREES AND AWARDS
BSN Nursing–RN to BSN
MA Criminal Justice Administration and Policy
MEd Administration and Supervision

COURSE SUBJECT AREAS OFFERED OUTSIDE OF DEGREE PROGRAMS
Graduate—business administration, management and operations; business/commerce; business, management, and marketing related; computer science; education; information science/studies.

MARYVILLE UNIVERSITY OF SAINT LOUIS
St. Louis, Missouri
http://www.maryville.edu/

Maryville University of Saint Louis was founded in 1872. It is accredited by North Central Association of Colleges and Schools. It first offered distance learning courses in 2002. In fall 2010, there were 106 students enrolled in distance learning courses. Institutionally administered financial aid is available to distance learners.

Services Distance learners have accessibility to academic advising, campus computer network, e-mail services.

Contact Ms. Chris Bretz, Enrollment Specialist, Adult and Continuing Education, Maryville University of Saint Louis, 12250 Weber Hill Road, Suite 105, Sunset Hills, MO 63127. Telephone: 314-529-9488. Fax: 314-529-9908. E-mail: cbretz@maryville.edu.

DEGREES AND AWARDS
Programs offered do not lead to a degree or other formal award.

COURSE SUBJECT AREAS OFFERED OUTSIDE OF DEGREE PROGRAMS
Undergraduate—accounting and computer science; business, management, and marketing related; business operations support and assistant services; communication and media; computer and information sciences; computer/information technology administration and management; computer programming; computer software and media applications; data entry/microcomputer applications; data processing; finance and financial management services; marketing; sales merchandising, and related marketing operations (general).

Non-credit—accounting and related services; business administration, management and operations; business/corporate communications; communications technology; computer and information sciences; computer software and media applications; computer systems analysis; computer systems networking and telecommunications; data entry/microcomputer applications; data processing; entrepreneurial and small business operations; human development, family studies, and related services; human resources management; journalism; languages (foreign languages related); management information systems; marketing; public relations, advertising, and applied communication related.

MASSACHUSETTS COLLEGE OF ART AND DESIGN
Boston, Massachusetts
Graduate and Continuing Education
http://www.massart.edu/ce

Massachusetts College of Art and Design was founded in 1873. It is accredited by New England Association of Schools and Colleges. It first offered distance learning courses in 2005. In fall 2010, there were 50 students enrolled in distance learning courses. Institutionally administered financial aid is available to distance learners.

Services Distance learners have accessibility to academic advising, bookstore, campus computer network, e-mail services, library services.

Contact Joe Doucette, Advisor, Massachusetts College of Art and Design, 621 Huntington Avenue, Boston, MA 02115. Telephone: 617-879-7165. Fax: 617-879-7171. E-mail: joe.doucette@massart.edu.

DEGREES AND AWARDS
Programs offered do not lead to a degree or other formal award.

COURSE SUBJECT AREAS OFFERED OUTSIDE OF DEGREE PROGRAMS
Undergraduate—architectural history and criticism; architecture; design and applied arts; liberal arts and sciences, general studies and humanities; social sciences; visual and performing arts.

Graduate—liberal arts and sciences, general studies and humanities; social sciences; visual and performing arts.

MASTER'S COLLEGE AND SEMINARY
Toronto, Ontario, Canada
http://www.mcs.edu/

Master's College and Seminary was founded in 1939. It is provincially chartered. It first offered distance learning courses in 1996. In fall 2010, there were 173 students enrolled in distance learning courses. Institutionally administered financial aid is available to distance learners.

Services Distance learners have accessibility to academic advising, bookstore, e-mail services, library services.

Contact Rev. Merv Anthony, Director of Student Services and Registrar, Master's College and Seminary, 282 Cummer Avenue, Toronto, ON M2M 2E7, Canada. Telephone: 800-295-6368 Ext. 224. Fax: 416-482-7004. E-mail: merv.anthony@mcs.edu.

DEGREES AND AWARDS
Programs offered do not lead to a degree or other formal award.

COURSE SUBJECT AREAS OFFERED OUTSIDE OF DEGREE PROGRAMS
Undergraduate—biblical studies; pastoral counseling and specialized ministries; philosophy and religious studies related; religious education; religious studies; theological and ministerial studies; theology and religious vocations related.

MAYVILLE STATE UNIVERSITY
Mayville, North Dakota
Enrollment Services Office
http://www.mayvillestate.edu

Mayville State University was founded in 1889. It is accredited by North Central Association of Colleges and Schools. It first offered distance learning courses in 1999. In fall 2010, there were 463 students enrolled in distance learning courses. Institutionally administered financial aid is available to distance learners.

Services Distance learners have accessibility to academic advising, bookstore, campus computer network, career placement assistance, e-mail services, library services.

Contact Ms. Misti Wuori, Director of Admissions and Extended Learning, Mayville State University, 330 Third Street NE, Mayville, ND 58257. Telephone: 701-788-4631. Fax: 701-788-4748. E-mail: misti.wuori@mayvillestate.edu.

DEGREES AND AWARDS

AA Early Childhood Education
BA Early Childhood Education
BEd Early Elementary Education; Elementary Education; Mathematics Education
BS Business Administration (Bachelor of Applied Science); Business Administration; Mathematics
BUS General Studies

COURSE SUBJECT AREAS OFFERED OUTSIDE OF DEGREE PROGRAMS

Undergraduate—accounting and related services; biology; business administration, management and operations; chemistry; education; human development, family studies, and related services; library science and administration; mathematics.

McDANIEL COLLEGE
Westminster, Maryland
Graduate and Professional Studies
http://www.mcdaniel.edu

McDaniel College was founded in 1867. It is accredited by Middle States Association of Colleges and Schools. It first offered distance learning courses in 1999. Institutionally administered financial aid is available to distance learners.

Services Distance learners have accessibility to academic advising, bookstore, e-mail services, library services.

Contact Ms. Crystal L. Perry, Administrator of Graduate Records, McDaniel College, Office of Graduate Admissions, Academic Hall, 210, 2 College Hill, Westminster, MD 21157. Telephone: 410-857-2513. Fax: 410-857-2515. E-mail: cperry@mcdaniel.edu.

DEGREES AND AWARDS

Graduate Certificate Gerontology
MS Gerontology

COURSE SUBJECT AREAS OFFERED OUTSIDE OF DEGREE PROGRAMS

Undergraduate—communication and media.

Graduate—educational assessment, evaluation, and research; educational/instructional media design; education related; gerontology.

McDOWELL TECHNICAL COMMUNITY COLLEGE
Marion, North Carolina
Educational Programs
http://www.mcdowelltech.edu/

McDowell Technical Community College was founded in 1964. It is accredited by Southern Association of Colleges and Schools. It first offered distance learning courses in 1991. In fall 2010, there were 600 students enrolled in distance learning courses. Institutionally administered financial aid is available to distance learners.

Services Distance learners have accessibility to academic advising, campus computer network, e-mail services, library services, tutoring.

Contact Joan E. Weiler, Director of Distance Education, McDowell Technical Community College, 54 College Drive, Marion, NC 28752-9724. Telephone: 828-652-0651. Fax: 828-659-1077. E-mail: jweiler@mcdowelltech.edu.

DEGREES AND AWARDS

Programs offered do not lead to a degree or other formal award.

COURSE SUBJECT AREAS OFFERED OUTSIDE OF DEGREE PROGRAMS

Undergraduate—accounting and related services; allied health and medical assisting services; business administration, management and operations; business/commerce; computer systems networking and telecommunications; education; education (specific levels and methods); English language and literature related; information science/studies; liberal arts and sciences, general studies and humanities; mathematics and statistics related; psychology related; social sciences.

McKENDREE UNIVERSITY
Lebanon, Illinois
Master of Business Administration Program
http://www.mckendree.edu/academics/remote_learning_special_programs.aspx

McKendree University was founded in 1828. It is accredited by North Central Association of Colleges and Schools. It first offered distance learning courses in 2009. In fall 2010, there were 129 students enrolled in distance learning courses. Institutionally administered financial aid is available to distance learners.

Services Distance learners have accessibility to academic advising, bookstore, campus computer network, e-mail services, library services, tutoring.

Contact Patty Aubel, Graduate Admission Counselor, McKendree University, 701 College Road, Lebanon, IL 62254. Telephone: 618-537-6943. Fax: 618-537-6410. E-mail: plaubel@mckendree.edu.

DEGREES AND AWARDS

MAEd Higher Education Administrative Services
MBA Business Administration
MSN Nursing

COURSE SUBJECT AREAS OFFERED OUTSIDE OF DEGREE PROGRAMS

Undergraduate—accounting and computer science; allied health diagnostic, intervention, and treatment professions; business administration, management and operations; business, management, and marketing related; computer and information sciences; computer/information technology administration and management; computer programming; computer science; economics; education; English; marketing; mathematics and statistics related; psychology; sociology.

Graduate—accounting and related services; allied health diagnostic, intervention, and treatment professions; business, management, and marketing related; business/managerial economics; education; educational administration and supervision; educational assessment, evaluation, and research.

McMURRY UNIVERSITY
Abilene, Texas
http://www.mcm.edu

McMurry University was founded in 1923. It is accredited by Southern Association of Colleges and Schools. It first offered distance learning courses in 2000. In fall 2010, there were 244 students enrolled in distance learning courses. Institutionally administered financial aid is available to distance learners.

Services Distance learners have accessibility to academic advising, bookstore, e-mail services, library services.

Contact Mrs. Vicki Dunnam, Online Educational Design Support Specialist, McMurry University, Box 207, McMurry Station, Abilene, TX 79697. Telephone: 325-793-4987. E-mail: dunnam.vicki@mcm.edu.

DEGREES AND AWARDS

Programs offered do not lead to a degree or other formal award.

COURSE SUBJECT AREAS OFFERED OUTSIDE OF DEGREE PROGRAMS

Undergraduate—biblical studies; biochemistry, biophysics and molecular biology; biology; business administration, management and operations; business/managerial economics; chemistry; computer/information technology administration and management; curriculum and instruction; drama/theatre arts and stagecraft; education; education (specific levels and methods); English; health and physical education/fitness; history; languages (foreign languages related); management information systems; mathematics; psychology; religious studies.

McNEESE STATE UNIVERSITY
Lake Charles, Louisiana
Division of Continuing Education and Distance Learning
http://www.mcneese.edu/elearning

McNeese State University was founded in 1939. It is accredited by Southern Association of Colleges and Schools. It first offered distance learning courses in 1998. In fall 2010, there were 3,908 students enrolled in distance learning courses. Institutionally administered financial aid is available to distance learners.

Services Distance learners have accessibility to academic advising, bookstore, campus computer network, career placement assistance, e-mail services, library services, tutoring.

Contact Dr. Helen B. Ware, Director of Electronic Learning, McNeese State University, Box 93325, Lake Charles, LA 70609. Telephone: 337-475-5126. Fax: 337-475-5539. E-mail: hware@mcneese.edu.

DEGREES AND AWARDS
BA Sociology
BS Criminal Justice; Family and Consumer Sciences
Certification School Library certification
MS Nursing

COURSE SUBJECT AREAS OFFERED OUTSIDE OF DEGREE PROGRAMS
Undergraduate—business administration, management and operations; communication and media; computer and information sciences; criminal justice and corrections; education; educational administration and supervision; electrical engineering technologies; engineering; English; family and consumer economics; geological and earth sciences/geosciences; health and physical education/fitness; history; languages (foreign languages related); legal studies (non-professional general, undergraduate); library science and administration; marketing; mathematics; music; psychology; special education; visual and performing arts related; work and family studies.

Graduate—education; educational administration and supervision; education (specific subject areas); psychology.

Non-credit—accounting and related services; allied health and medical assisting services; audiovisual communications technologies; computer and information sciences and support services related; computer programming; computer software and media applications; computer systems analysis; computer systems networking and telecommunications; dental support services and allied professions; health and medical administrative services; pharmacy, pharmaceutical sciences, and administration.

MEDICAL COLLEGE OF WISCONSIN
Milwaukee, Wisconsin
Master of Public Health Degree Programs
http://www.mcw.edu/mph

Medical College of Wisconsin was founded in 1913. It is accredited by North Central Association of Colleges and Schools. It first offered distance learning courses in 1986. In fall 2010, there were 80 students enrolled in distance learning courses. Institutionally administered financial aid is available to distance learners.

Services Distance learners have accessibility to academic advising, bookstore, campus computer network, career placement assistance, e-mail services, library services.

Contact Brandon Clark, Program Coordinator, MPH Degree Program, Medical College of Wisconsin, Institute for Health and Society, 8701 Watertown Plank Road, Milwaukee, WI 53226. Telephone: 414-456-4510. Fax: 414-456-6160. E-mail: mph@mcw.edu.

DEGREES AND AWARDS
Graduate Certificate Public Health
MPH Public Health

COURSE SUBJECT AREAS OFFERED OUTSIDE OF DEGREE PROGRAMS
Graduate—accounting and related services; behavioral sciences; bioethics/medical ethics; community organization and advocacy; educational assessment, evaluation, and research; environmental/environmental health engineering; health and medical administrative services; health professions related; public health.

MEDICAL UNIVERSITY OF SOUTH CAROLINA
Charleston, South Carolina
Distance Education
http://academicdepartments.musc.edu/ets/de/

Medical University of South Carolina was founded in 1824. It is accredited by Southern Association of Colleges and Schools. It first offered distance learning courses in 1997. In fall 2010, there were 758 students enrolled in distance learning courses. Institutionally administered financial aid is available to distance learners.

Services Distance learners have accessibility to academic advising, campus computer network, e-mail services, library services, tutoring.

Contact Mr. Geoffrey A. Freeman, Director of Distance Education, Medical University of South Carolina, 45 Courtenay Drive, MSC 951, Charleston, SC 29425. Telephone: 843-792-9133. Fax: 843-792-1506. E-mail: freemang@musc.edu.

DEGREES AND AWARDS
BSN Nursing–Accelerated Bachelor of Science in Nursing
MAS Research Administration
MHA Executive Program
MSN Nursing
DHA Health Administration
DNP Nursing

MEMORIAL UNIVERSITY OF NEWFOUNDLAND
St. John's, Newfoundland and Labrador, Canada
Distance Education and Learning Technologies
http://www.distance.mun.ca

Memorial University of Newfoundland was founded in 1925. It is provincially chartered. It first offered distance learning courses in 1969. In fall 2010, there were 4,159 students enrolled in distance learning courses. Institutionally administered financial aid is available to distance learners.

Services Distance learners have accessibility to academic advising, bookstore, e-mail services, library services.

Contact May Stafford, Client Relations, Memorial University of Newfoundland, G.A. Hickman Building, ED-2000, St. John's, NF A1B 3X8, Canada. Telephone: 709-864-8700. E-mail: mstaffor@mun.ca.

DEGREES AND AWARDS
BA Police Studies
BBA Business Administration
BN Nursing–post-RN
BS Maritime Studies–Bachelor of Maritime Studies (BMS); Technology–Bachelor Technology (BTech)
Certificate Business Administration; Career Development; Criminology; Library Studies; Newfoundland Studies; Public Administration
Diploma Business Administration
MEd Counseling Psychology; Curriculum Teaching and Learning Studies; Educational Leadership Studies; Information Technology; Postsecondary Studies
MN Nursing
MPE Physical Education
MSW Social Work

COURSE SUBJECT AREAS OFFERED OUTSIDE OF DEGREE PROGRAMS
Undergraduate—anthropology; biology; business administration, management and operations; computer science; economics; education; education related; engineering; English; library science and administration; mathematics; philosophy; political science and government; psychology; religious studies; social work; sociology; statistics.

Graduate—criminology; education related; library science and administration; social work.

MERCER COUNTY COMMUNITY COLLEGE
Trenton, New Jersey
http://www.mccc.edu/programs_tvc.shtml

Mercer County Community College was founded in 1966. It is accredited by Middle States Association of Colleges and Schools. It first offered distance learning courses in 1998. In fall 2010, there were 2,500 students enrolled in distance learning courses. Institutionally administered financial aid is available to distance learners.

Services Distance learners have accessibility to academic advising, bookstore, career placement assistance, e-mail services, library services, tutoring.

Contact Michael Sullivan, Coordinator, Mercer County Community College, 1200 Old Trenton Road, Trenton, NJ 08690. Telephone: 609-570-3315. E-mail: sullivam@mccc.edu.

DEGREES AND AWARDS
AA Liberal Arts and Sciences
AAS Business Management

COURSE SUBJECT AREAS OFFERED OUTSIDE OF DEGREE PROGRAMS
Undergraduate—accounting and related services; allied health diagnostic, intervention, and treatment professions; anthropology; business/commerce; business, management, and marketing related; business/managerial economics; communication and media; computer and information sciences; computer and information sciences and support services related; computer programming; computer software and media applications; criminology; economics; education; English; health and physical education/fitness; health/medical preparatory programs; history; languages (Romance languages); legal studies (non-professional general, undergraduate); library science related; marketing; mathematics; mathematics and statistics related; nutrition sciences; philosophy; philosophy and religious studies; plant sciences; psychology related; social sciences; sociology.

Non-credit—computer/information technology administration and management; computer systems networking and telecommunications; finance and financial management services.

MERCY COLLEGE
Dobbs Ferry, New York
Mercy Online
http://www.mercy.edu/academics/mercy-online/

Mercy College was founded in 1951. It is accredited by Middle States Association of Colleges and Schools. It first offered distance learning courses in 1990. In fall 2010, there were 3,038 students enrolled in distance learning courses. Institutionally administered financial aid is available to distance learners.

Services Distance learners have accessibility to academic advising, bookstore, campus computer network, career placement assistance, e-mail services, library services, tutoring.

Contact Ms. Mary Lozina, Mercy Online Director, Mercy College, 555 Broadway, Dobbs Ferry, NY 10522. Telephone: 914-674-7651. Fax: 914-674-7240. E-mail: mlozina@mercy.edu.

DEGREES AND AWARDS
BA Behavioral Science; English; History; Psychology
BS Behavioral Science; Business Administration–Finance; Business Administration–International Business; Business Administration–Management; Business Administration–Marketing; Business Administration–Sport Management; Business Administration; Computer Information Systems; Computer Science; Criminal Justice; Cybersecurity; Legal Studies; Mathematics; Nursing; Organizational Management; Psychology; Sociology
MA English Literature
MBA Business Administration
MPA Health Services Management
MS Adolescence Education and Students with Disabilities; Adolescence Education, Grades 7-12; Childhood Education and Students with Disabilities; Childhood Education, Grade 1-6; Counseling; Cybersecurity; Cybersecurty (Combined BS/MS); Early Childhood Education and Students with Disabilities; Early Childhood Education, Birth—Grade 2; Health Services Management; Human Resource Management; Marriage and Family Therapy; Middle Childhood Education and Students with Disabilities; Middle Childhood Education, Grades 5-9; Nursing Administration; Nursing Education; Organizational Leadership; Psychology; School Building Leadership; Teaching English to Speakers of Other Languages; Teaching Literacy, Birth to Grade 12; Web Strategy and Design

MERCY COLLEGE OF NORTHWEST OHIO
Toledo, Ohio
http://www.mercycollege.edu/

Mercy College of Northwest Ohio was founded in 1993. It is accredited by North Central Association of Colleges and Schools. It first offered distance learning courses in 2005. In fall 2010, there were 756 students enrolled in distance learning courses. Institutionally administered financial aid is available to distance learners.

Services Distance learners have accessibility to academic advising, bookstore, career placement assistance, e-mail services, library services, tutoring.

Contact Mr. Daniel W. Hoppe, Jr., Director of Distance Education, Chair of Healthcare Administration Program, Mercy College of Northwest Ohio, 2221 Madison Avenue, Toledo, OH 43604. Telephone: 419-251-1714. Fax: 419-251-1570. E-mail: daniel.hoppe@mercycollege.edu.

DEGREES AND AWARDS
Programs offered do not lead to a degree or other formal award.

COURSE SUBJECT AREAS OFFERED OUTSIDE OF DEGREE PROGRAMS
Undergraduate—allied health and medical assisting services; arts, entertainment, and media management; bioethics/medical ethics; biology; chemistry; data entry/microcomputer applications; English language and literature related; fine and studio arts; health professions related; intercultural/multicultural and diversity studies; interdisciplinary studies; liberal arts and sciences, general studies and humanities; mathematics; nutrition sciences; psychology; religious studies; social sciences; statistics.

Non-credit—allied health and medical assisting services; biological and physical sciences; business operations support and assistant services; data entry/microcomputer applications; health and medical administrative services; mathematics.

MESA COMMUNITY COLLEGE
Mesa, Arizona
http://www.mesacc.edu/mcconline/

Mesa Community College was founded in 1965. It is accredited by North Central Association of Colleges and Schools. It first offered distance learning courses in 1998. In fall 2010, there were 7,000 students enrolled in distance learning courses. Institutionally administered financial aid is available to distance learners.

Services Distance learners have accessibility to academic advising, bookstore, campus computer network, career placement assistance, e-mail services, library services, tutoring.

Contact Alicia Barnett, Distance Learning Advisor, Mesa Community College, 1833 West Southern Avenue, Mesa, AZ 85202. Telephone: 480-461-7924. E-mail: mcconline@mcmail.maricopa.edu.

DEGREES AND AWARDS
Programs offered do not lead to a degree or other formal award.

COURSE SUBJECT AREAS OFFERED OUTSIDE OF DEGREE PROGRAMS
Undergraduate—biology; business administration, management and operations; communication and media; computer/information technology administration and management; computer programming; computer science; computer software and media applications; criminal justice and corrections; economics; English; family and consumer sciences/human sciences related; foods, nutrition, and related services; health/medical

preparatory programs; health professions related; history; linguistic, comparative, and related language studies; mathematics; political science and government; religious studies.

MESA STATE COLLEGE
Grand Junction, Colorado
Continuing Education Center
http://www.mesastate.edu/online/index.html

Mesa State College was founded in 1925. It is accredited by North Central Association of Colleges and Schools. It first offered distance learning courses in 1996. In fall 2010, there were 1,742 students enrolled in distance learning courses. Institutionally administered financial aid is available to distance learners.

Services Distance learners have accessibility to academic advising, bookstore, campus computer network, career placement assistance, e-mail services, library services, tutoring.

Contact Jared Meier, Director of Admissions, Mesa State College, 1100 North Avenue, Grand Junction, CO 81501. Telephone: 800-982-6372. Fax: 970-248-1613. E-mail: admissions@mesastate.edu.

DEGREES AND AWARDS

AA Social Science
AS Sport Management
BA Liberal Arts, Elementary Education licensure
BAS Public Adminstration/Public Safety; Radiologic Technology
BS Nursing; Sport Management

COURSE SUBJECT AREAS OFFERED OUTSIDE OF DEGREE PROGRAMS

Undergraduate—accounting and related services; arts, entertainment, and media management; biology; business administration, management and operations; chemistry; criminal justice and corrections; dance; education; English; English language and literature related; fine and studio arts; health and physical education/fitness; history; management sciences and quantitative methods; mathematics; music; political science and government; psychology; social sciences; sociology; visual and performing arts.

Graduate—business administration, management and operations; education.

METROPOLITAN COMMUNITY COLLEGE–PENN VALLEY
Kansas City, Missouri
Distance Education and Media
http://distance.mcckc.edu

Metropolitan Community College–Penn Valley was founded in 1969. It is accredited by North Central Association of Colleges and Schools. It first offered distance learning courses in 1998. In fall 2010, there were 6,300 students enrolled in distance learning courses. Institutionally administered financial aid is available to distance learners.

Services Distance learners have accessibility to academic advising, bookstore, e-mail services, library services, tutoring.

Contact Kenneth Peters, Student Support Specialist, Metropolitan Community College–Penn Valley, 3201 Southwest Trafficway, Kansas City, MO 64111-2764. Telephone: 816-604-4490. Fax: 816-759-4673. E-mail: kenneth.peters@mcckc.edu.

DEGREES AND AWARDS

AA General AA–Transfer emphasis

COURSE SUBJECT AREAS OFFERED OUTSIDE OF DEGREE PROGRAMS

Undergraduate—accounting and related services; biology; computer science; criminal justice and corrections; economics; education; engineering; engineering science; fire protection; geography and cartography; history; human development, family studies, and related services; mathematics; philosophy; physical sciences; psychology; sociology.

MGH INSTITUTE OF HEALTH PROFESSIONS
Boston, Massachusetts
http://www.mghihp.edu/

MGH Institute of Health Professions was founded in 1977. It is accredited by New England Association of Schools and Colleges. It first offered distance learning courses in 2000. In fall 2010, there were 474 students enrolled in distance learning courses. Institutionally administered financial aid is available to distance learners.

Services Distance learners have accessibility to academic advising, bookstore, campus computer network, e-mail services, library services, tutoring.

Contact Ms. Maureen R. Judd, Director of Admissions, MGH Institute of Health Professions, 36 1st Avenue, Boston, MA 02129-4557. Telephone: 617-726-6069. Fax: 617-726-8010. E-mail: mjudd@mghihp.edu.

DEGREES AND AWARDS

Certificate Medical Imaging post-Baccalaureate certificate
DPT Physical Therapy–Transitional Doctor of Physical Therapy

COURSE SUBJECT AREAS OFFERED OUTSIDE OF DEGREE PROGRAMS

Undergraduate—chemistry; communication disorders sciences and services; microbiological sciences and immunology; nutrition sciences; physiology, pathology and related sciences; statistics.

Graduate—communication disorders sciences and services; health professions related.

MIAMI DADE COLLEGE
Miami, Florida
Virtual College
http://virtual.mdc.edu

Miami Dade College was founded in 1960. It is accredited by Southern Association of Colleges and Schools. It first offered distance learning courses in 1997. In fall 2010, there were 8,000 students enrolled in distance learning courses. Institutionally administered financial aid is available to distance learners.

Services Distance learners have accessibility to academic advising, bookstore, e-mail services, library services, tutoring.

Contact Lloyd Hollingsworth, Student Services Coordinator, Miami Dade College, 300 NE 2nd Avenue, Miami, FL 33132-2297. Telephone: 305-237-3873. Fax: 305-237-3863. E-mail: lholling@mdc.edu.

DEGREES AND AWARDS

AA Pre-Bachelor of Arts
AS Business Administration

COURSE SUBJECT AREAS OFFERED OUTSIDE OF DEGREE PROGRAMS

Undergraduate—accounting and computer science; accounting and related services; arts, entertainment, and media management; atmospheric sciences and meteorology; behavioral sciences; biblical studies; biological and biomedical sciences related; biological and physical sciences; biology; business administration, management and operations; business, management, and marketing related; business/managerial economics; computer and information sciences; computer programming; computer science; computer software and media applications; criminal justice and corrections; criminology; data entry/microcomputer applications; dietetics and clinical nutrition services; ecology, evolution, systematics, and population biology; economics; education; education related; English; English language and literature related; foods, nutrition, and related services; health and medical administrative services; health/medical preparatory programs; health professions related; health services/allied health/health sciences; history; hospitality administration; human biology; human development, family studies, and related services; international relations and national security studies; liberal arts and sciences, general studies and humanities; library science related; management sciences and quantitative methods; marine sciences; marketing; mathematics; mathematics and computer science; mathematics and statistics related; music; natural sciences; philosophy; philosophy and religious studies related; physical sciences; physical sciences related; physics;

political science and government; psychology; psychology related; religious education; religious studies; social and philosophical foundations of education; social sciences; sociology; statistics; taxation.
Non-credit—health professions related.

MIAMI UNIVERSITY–REGIONAL CAMPUSES
Oxford, Ohio
http://www.regionals.muohio.edu/elearning/

Miami University–Regional Campuses first offered distance learning courses in 1996. In fall 2010, there were 1,800 students enrolled in distance learning courses. Institutionally administered financial aid is available to distance learners.
Services Distance learners have accessibility to academic advising, bookstore, campus computer network, career placement assistance, e-mail services, library services, tutoring.
Contact Mr. Michael Judge, Regional Director of E-Learning Initiatives, Miami University–Regional Campuses, 1601 University Boulevard, Hamilton, OH 45011. Telephone: 513-785-3259. E-mail: elearning@muohio.edu.

DEGREES AND AWARDS
AAB Business Management Technology
BS Engineering Technology Bachelor completion program
BSN Nursing–RN-BSN completion program

COURSE SUBJECT AREAS OFFERED OUTSIDE OF DEGREE PROGRAMS
Undergraduate—business administration, management and operations; chemistry; criminal justice and corrections; electrical engineering technologies; electromechanical instrumentation and maintenance technologies; engineering technologies related; history; liberal arts and sciences, general studies and humanities; philosophy; physics; psychology; social sciences related; sociology; statistics.

MICHIGAN STATE UNIVERSITY COLLEGE OF LAW
East Lansing, Michigan
http://www.law.msu.edu

Michigan State University College of Law was founded in 1891. It is accredited by Association of American Law Schools. It first offered distance learning courses in 1999. In fall 2010, there were 14 students enrolled in distance learning courses. Institutionally administered financial aid is available to distance learners.
Services Distance learners have accessibility to academic advising, campus computer network, career placement assistance, e-mail services, library services.
Contact Kathleen Payne, Associate Dean for Academic Affairs, Michigan State University College of Law, 368 Law College Building, East Lansing, MI 48824. Telephone: 517-432-6926 Fax: 517-432-6801. E-mail: payneka@law.msu.edu.

DEGREES AND AWARDS
Programs offered do not lead to a degree or other formal award.

COURSE SUBJECT AREAS OFFERED OUTSIDE OF DEGREE PROGRAMS
Graduate—legal professions and studies related; legal research and advanced professional studies; legal support services.
Non-credit—legal professions and studies related; legal research and advanced professional studies; legal studies (non-professional general, undergraduate); legal support services.

MICHIGAN TECHNOLOGICAL UNIVERSITY
Houghton, Michigan
Sponsored Educational Programs
http://techonline.mtu.edu

Michigan Technological University was founded in 1885. It is accredited by North Central Association of Colleges and Schools. It first offered distance learning courses in 1984. In fall 2010, there were 274 students enrolled in distance learning courses. Institutionally administered financial aid is available to distance learners.
Services Distance learners have accessibility to academic advising, bookstore, e-mail services, library services.
Contact Ms. Patricia A. Lins, Director, Educational Technology/Online Learning, Michigan Technological University, Educational Technology/Online Learning, 1400 Townsend Drive, Houghton, MI 49931. Telephone: 906-487-2925. Fax: 906-487-2787. E-mail: plins@mtu.edu.

DEGREES AND AWARDS
Certificate Electric Power Engineering; Electric Power, Advanced
MBA Business Administration
ME Hybrid Vehicle Engineering emphasis, Professional Masters Program
MS Electrical Engineering; Mechanical Engineering
MSE Applied Science Education
PhD Mechanical Engineering

COURSE SUBJECT AREAS OFFERED OUTSIDE OF DEGREE PROGRAMS
Undergraduate—arts, entertainment, and media management; astronomy and astrophysics; business, management, and marketing related; chemical engineering; chemistry; communication and media; computer and information sciences; electrical, electronics and communications engineering; forestry; materials sciences; mathematics and statistics related; mechanical engineering; physics; psychology; surveying engineering.
Graduate—biological and biomedical sciences related; business, management, and marketing related; economics; education (specific subject areas); electrical, electronics and communications engineering; geological and earth sciences/geosciences; interdisciplinary studies; materials sciences; mechanical engineering; surveying engineering.
Non-credit—computer and information sciences; electrical, electronics and communications engineering; forestry; materials sciences; mechanical engineering.

MID-CONTINENT UNIVERSITY
Mayfield, Kentucky
http://www.midcontinent.edu/online

Mid-Continent University was founded in 1949. It is accredited by Southern Association of Colleges and Schools. It first offered distance learning courses in 2003. In fall 2010, there were 776 students enrolled in distance learning courses. Institutionally administered financial aid is available to distance learners.
Services Distance learners have accessibility to academic advising, bookstore, library services.
Contact Mrs. Traci Wallrauch, Director of Online Operations, Mid-Continent University, 99 Powell Road East, Mayfield, KY 42066. Telephone: 270-247-8521 Ext. 624. Fax: 270-247-9400. E-mail: twallrauch@midcontinent.edu.

DEGREES AND AWARDS
Programs offered do not lead to a degree or other formal award.

COURSE SUBJECT AREAS OFFERED OUTSIDE OF DEGREE PROGRAMS
Undergraduate—biblical studies; business administration, management and operations; liberal arts and sciences, general studies and humanities; psychology.

MIDDLESEX COMMUNITY COLLEGE
Middletown, Connecticut
http://www.mxctc.commnet.edu/distance

Middlesex Community College was founded in 1966. It is accredited by New England Association of Schools and Colleges. It first offered distance learning courses in 1999. In fall 2010, there were 750 students enrolled in distance learning courses. Institutionally administered financial aid is available to distance learners.
Services Distance learners have accessibility to academic advising, bookstore, campus computer network, e-mail services, library services, tutoring.
Contact Dr. Yi Guan-Raczkowski, Director of Distance Learning, Middlesex Community College, 100 Training Hill Road, Middletown, CT 06457. Telephone: 860-343-5783. E-mail: yguan@mxcc.commnet.edu.

DEGREES AND AWARDS

AGS General Studies

COURSE SUBJECT AREAS OFFERED OUTSIDE OF DEGREE PROGRAMS

Undergraduate—accounting and computer science; anthropology; biology; business administration, management and operations; business, management, and marketing related; communication and journalism related; communication and media; computer and information sciences; criminology; economics; education; English language and literature related; foods, nutrition, and related services; history; human services; management information systems; marketing; mathematics; philosophy; psychology; social sciences; social work; sociology; special education; statistics.

MIDDLESEX COMMUNITY COLLEGE
Bedford, Massachusetts
http://www.middlesex.mass.edu/online

Middlesex Community College was founded in 1970. It is accredited by New England Association of Schools and Colleges. It first offered distance learning courses in 1996. In fall 2010, there were 5,000 students enrolled in distance learning courses. Institutionally administered financial aid is available to distance learners.

Services Distance learners have accessibility to academic advising, bookstore, campus computer network, e-mail services, library services, tutoring.

Contact Sanford A. Arbogast, Academic Technology Analyst, Middlesex Community College, Academic Resources Building, Springs Road, Bedford, MA 01730. Telephone: 781-280-3739. Fax: 781-280-3771. E-mail: arbogasts@middlesex.mass.edu.

DEGREES AND AWARDS

AA Liberal Arts and Sciences

AAS Liberal Studies

ABA Accounting; Business Administration Career; Hospitality Management; Small Business Administration

AS Business Administration transfer; Criminal Justice–Administration option; Criminal Justice–Law Enforcement option; Fire Protection; Psychology

Certificate Liberal Studies; Small Business Management

COURSE SUBJECT AREAS OFFERED OUTSIDE OF DEGREE PROGRAMS

Undergraduate—accounting and related services; anthropology; behavioral sciences; bilingual, multilingual, and multicultural education; biological and biomedical sciences related; biological and physical sciences; biology; business administration, management and operations; business/commerce; business/corporate communications; business, management, and marketing related; business/managerial economics; chemistry; communication and journalism related; communication and media; communications technology; computer and information sciences; computer and information sciences and support services related; computer programming; computer science; computer software and media applications; criminal justice and corrections; criminology; data entry/microcomputer applications; dental support services and allied professions; economics; education; education (specific levels and methods); education (specific subject areas); English; English language and literature related; ethnic, cultural minority, gender, and group studies; fine and studio arts; fire protection; foods, nutrition, and related services; geography and cartography; history; hospitality administration; human resources management; human services; journalism; languages (foreign languages related); languages (Romance languages); legal professions and studies related; legal studies (non-professional general, undergraduate); liberal arts and sciences, general studies and humanities; linguistic, comparative, and related language studies; marketing; mathematics; mathematics and computer science; mathematics and statistics related; museum studies; natural sciences; pharmacology and toxicology; philosophy; philosophy and religious studies related; physical sciences; political science and government; psychology; psychology related; public health; public relations, advertising, and applied communication related; publishing; radio, television, and digital communication; social sciences; social sciences related; sociology; statistics; taxation.

Non-credit—business administration, management and operations; business/commerce; computer software and media applications; computer systems analysis; finance and financial management services; fine and studio arts; gerontology.

MIDDLE TENNESSEE STATE UNIVERSITY
Murfreesboro, Tennessee
College of Continuing Education and Distance Learning
http://www.mtsu.edu/universitycollege

Middle Tennessee State University was founded in 1911. It is accredited by Southern Association of Colleges and Schools. It first offered distance learning courses in 1994. In fall 2010, there were 9,923 students enrolled in distance learning courses. Institutionally administered financial aid is available to distance learners.

Services Distance learners have accessibility to academic advising, bookstore, campus computer network, e-mail services, library services, tutoring.

Contact Dr. Dianna Rust, Associate Dean, Distance Education and Non-Traditional Programs, Middle Tennessee State University, 1301 East Main Street, MTSU Box 54, Murfreesboro, TN 37132. Telephone: 615-898-5611. Fax: 615-896-7925. E-mail: drust@mtsu.edu.

DEGREES AND AWARDS

BS Liberal Studies; Professional Studies, Information Technology concentration; Professional Studies, Organizational Leadership concentration; Psychology

BSN Nursing

Ed S Curriculum and Instruction (English as a Second Language); Education Specialist (Technology and Curriculum Design)

MEd Teaching and Learning, advanced studies

MPS Professional Studies, Strategic Leadership concentration

MSN Nursing

COURSE SUBJECT AREAS OFFERED OUTSIDE OF DEGREE PROGRAMS

Undergraduate—accounting and computer science; accounting and related services; aerospace, aeronautical and astronautical engineering; agricultural business and management; astronomy and astrophysics; business administration, management and operations; business/corporate communications; communication and media; computer and information sciences; criminal justice and corrections; economics; education; English; family and consumer sciences/human sciences; food science and technology; geological and earth sciences/geosciences; health and physical education/fitness; human development, family studies, and related services; human resources management; journalism; liberal arts and sciences, general studies and humanities; marketing; mathematics; nutrition sciences; political science and government; psychology; radio, television, and digital communication; sales merchandising, and related marketing operations (general); social sciences; social work; sociology.

Graduate—aerospace, aeronautical and astronautical engineering; economics; educational assessment, evaluation, and research; library science and administration; marketing; mathematics; special education.

Non-credit—allied health and medical assisting services; bilingual, multilingual, and multicultural education; business administration, management and operations; business/commerce; business/corporate communications; business, management, and marketing related; business/managerial economics; city/urban, community and regional planning; computer and information sciences; computer/information technology administration and management; computer programming; computer science; computer software and media applications; computer systems networking and telecommunications; crafts, folk art and artisanry; culinary arts and related services; fine and studio arts; human resources management; linguistic, comparative, and related language studies; management information systems; real estate; sales, merchandising and related marketing operations (specialized).

MIDLAND COLLEGE
Midland, Texas
Distance Learning Program
http://www.midland.edu

Midland College was founded in 1969. It is accredited by Southern Association of Colleges and Schools. It first offered distance learning courses in 1996. In fall 2010, there were 1,800 students enrolled in distance learning courses. Institutionally administered financial aid is available to distance learners.

Services Distance learners have accessibility to academic advising, bookstore, campus computer network, career placement assistance, e-mail services, library services, tutoring.

Contact Mr. Ryan Gibbs, Director, Admissions and Recruitment, Midland College, 3600 North Garfield Street, Midland, TX 79705. Telephone: 432-685-5502. Fax: 432-685-6401. E-mail: rgibbs@midland.edu.

DEGREES AND AWARDS

AAS Diesel Technology; Energy Technology–Petroleum Energy Technician or Wind Energy Technician; Fire Protection Technology

COURSE SUBJECT AREAS OFFERED OUTSIDE OF DEGREE PROGRAMS

Undergraduate—accounting and related services; business/commerce; business/corporate communications; business/managerial economics; business operations support and assistant services; computer and information sciences; computer software and media applications; education (specific levels and methods); English; gerontology; health and medical administrative services; health and physical education/fitness; health professions related; history; journalism; languages (Romance languages); legal studies (non-professional general, undergraduate); mathematics and statistics related; music; philosophy and religious studies related; sociology; statistics.

Non-credit—business administration, management and operations; business operations support and assistant services; computer and information sciences; computer and information sciences and support services related; computer systems analysis; computer systems networking and telecommunications; cosmetology and related personal grooming services; criminal justice and corrections; fire protection; gerontology; health professions related; vehicle maintenance and repair technologies.

MIDSTATE COLLEGE
Peoria, Illinois
http://www.midstate.edu/

Midstate College was founded in 1888. It is accredited by North Central Association of Colleges and Schools. It first offered distance learning courses in 1999. In fall 2010, there were 456 students enrolled in distance learning courses. Institutionally administered financial aid is available to distance learners.

Services Distance learners have accessibility to academic advising, bookstore, career placement assistance, e-mail services, library services, tutoring.

Contact Ms. April Bimrose, Admissions Representative, Midstate College, 411 West Northmoor Road, Peoria, IL 61614. Telephone: 309-692-4092 Ext. 1090. Fax: 309-692-3893. E-mail: admissions@midstate.edu.

DEGREES AND AWARDS

BBA Business Administration

COURSE SUBJECT AREAS OFFERED OUTSIDE OF DEGREE PROGRAMS

Undergraduate—accounting and related services; allied health and medical assisting services; applied mathematics; business, management, and marketing related; computer and information sciences; computer software and media applications; psychology.

MID-STATE TECHNICAL COLLEGE
Wisconsin Rapids, Wisconsin
Information Services
http://mstc.edu/academics/distanceed.htm

Mid-State Technical College was founded in 1917. It is accredited by North Central Association of Colleges and Schools. It first offered distance learning courses in 1996. In fall 2010, there were 1,225 students enrolled in distance learning courses. Institutionally administered financial aid is available to distance learners.

Services Distance learners have accessibility to academic advising, bookstore, career placement assistance, e-mail services, library services, tutoring.

Contact Lea Ann Turner, Learning Technology Manager, Mid-State Technical College, 500 32nd Street North, Wisconsin Rapids, WI 54494. Telephone: 715-422-5480. Fax: 715-422-5609. E-mail: leaann.turner@mstc.edu.

DEGREES AND AWARDS

AAS Biomedical Informatics Technician; Clinical Research Coordinator; Supervisory Management

COURSE SUBJECT AREAS OFFERED OUTSIDE OF DEGREE PROGRAMS

Undergraduate—agriculture; allied health and medical assisting services; biology; business administration, management and operations; civil engineering; civil engineering technologies; computer and information sciences; computer and information sciences and support services related; cosmetology and related personal grooming services; forestry; health services/allied health/health sciences; microbiological sciences and immunology; sociology; statistics; systems engineering.

MIDWAY COLLEGE
Midway, Kentucky
http://www.midway.edu/

Midway College was founded in 1847. It is accredited by Southern Association of Colleges and Schools. It first offered distance learning courses in 2003. In fall 2010, there were 680 students enrolled in distance learning courses. Institutionally administered financial aid is available to distance learners.

Services Distance learners have accessibility to academic advising, bookstore, e-mail services, library services.

Contact Patti Kirk, Admissions Counselor/Recruiter, Midway College, 512 East Stephens Street, Midway, KY 40347. Telephone: 800-952-4122. E-mail: midwayonlinecollege@midway.edu.

DEGREES AND AWARDS

AA Business Administration
AS Medical Assisting; Medical Coding
BA Business Administration; Education; Health Care Administration; Psychology; Public Safety–Criminal Justice

COURSE SUBJECT AREAS OFFERED OUTSIDE OF DEGREE PROGRAMS

Undergraduate—accounting and related services; biological and physical sciences; computer science; economics; education related; finance and financial management services; geography and cartography; mathematics; music; psychology; religious studies.

Graduate—business administration, management and operations; business, management, and marketing related; business/managerial economics.

MIDWESTERN STATE UNIVERSITY
Wichita Falls, Texas
http://www.mwsu.edu/

Midwestern State University was founded in 1922. It is accredited by Southern Association of Colleges and Schools. It first offered distance learning courses in 1972. In fall 2010, there were 850 students enrolled in distance learning courses. Institutionally administered financial aid is available to distance learners.

Services Distance learners have accessibility to academic advising, bookstore, campus computer network, career placement assistance, e-mail services, library services.

Contact Dr. Pamela Morgan, Director of Extended Education, Midwestern State University, 3410 Taft Boulevard, Wichita Falls, TX 76308-2099. Telephone: 940-397-4785. Fax: 940-397-4868. E-mail: pamela.morgan@mwsu.edu.

DEGREES AND AWARDS

BAA Arts and Science–Applied Arts and Sciences
BSRS Radiologic Sciences
MAE Educational Leadership
MS Radiologic Sciences (Education or Administration major)

COURSE SUBJECT AREAS OFFERED OUTSIDE OF DEGREE PROGRAMS

Undergraduate—business/commerce; business/corporate communications; communication and media; computer and information sciences; criminal justice and corrections; education; geography and cartography; health professions related; liberal arts and sciences, general studies and humanities; political science and government; psychology related; public administration; sociology.
Graduate—education related; health professions related.

MIDWIVES COLLEGE OF UTAH
Salt Lake City, Utah
http://www.midwifery.edu

Midwives College of Utah was founded in 1980. It is accredited by Midwifery Education Accreditation Council. It first offered distance learning courses in 1980. In fall 2010, there were 150 students enrolled in distance learning courses. Institutionally administered financial aid is available to distance learners.
Services Distance learners have accessibility to academic advising, bookstore, campus computer network, e-mail services, library services, tutoring.
Contact Cindy Winward, Administrative Assistant, Midwives College of Utah, 1174 East Graystone Way, Suite 2, Salt Lake City, UT 84106. Telephone: 866-680-2756. Fax: 866-207-2024. E-mail: office@midwifery.edu.

DEGREES AND AWARDS

Programs offered do not lead to a degree or other formal award.

COURSE SUBJECT AREAS OFFERED OUTSIDE OF DEGREE PROGRAMS

Undergraduate—education.
Graduate—education.
Non-credit—education.

MILWAUKEE SCHOOL OF ENGINEERING
Milwaukee, Wisconsin
MSOE-TV
http://www.msoe.edu/admiss

Milwaukee School of Engineering was founded in 1903. It is accredited by North Central Association of Colleges and Schools. It first offered distance learning courses in 1989. In fall 2010, there were 235 students enrolled in distance learning courses. Institutionally administered financial aid is available to distance learners.
Services Distance learners have accessibility to academic advising, bookstore, campus computer network, career placement assistance, e-mail services, library services.
Contact Ms. Mary Nielsen, Registrar, Milwaukee School of Engineering, 1025 North Broadway, Milwaukee, WI 53202-3109. Telephone: 414-277-7216. Fax: 414-277-6914. E-mail: nielsen@msoe.edu.

DEGREES AND AWARDS

Programs offered do not lead to a degree or other formal award.

COURSE SUBJECT AREAS OFFERED OUTSIDE OF DEGREE PROGRAMS

Undergraduate—business, management, and marketing related; computer and information sciences; management information systems.
Graduate—business administration, management and operations; business/commerce; business/managerial economics.

MINNEAPOLIS COLLEGE OF ART AND DESIGN
Minneapolis, Minnesota
MCAD Distance Learning
http://online.mcad.edu

Minneapolis College of Art and Design was founded in 1886. It is accredited by North Central Association of Colleges and Schools. It first offered distance learning courses in 1995. In fall 2010, there were 200 students enrolled in distance learning courses. Institutionally administered financial aid is available to distance learners.
Services Distance learners have accessibility to academic advising, bookstore, campus computer network, career placement assistance, e-mail services, library services, tutoring.
Contact Rebecca J. Alm, Senior Director of Learning Resources, Minneapolis College of Art and Design, 2501 Stevens Avenue, Minneapolis, MN 55404. Telephone: 612-874-3658. Fax: 612-874-3704. E-mail: rebecca_alm@mcad.edu.

DEGREES AND AWARDS

Programs offered do not lead to a degree or other formal award.

COURSE SUBJECT AREAS OFFERED OUTSIDE OF DEGREE PROGRAMS

Undergraduate—design and applied arts; film/video and photographic arts; fine and studio arts; visual and performing arts related.
Graduate—design and applied arts; education (specific subject areas); fine and studio arts; visual and performing arts related.
Non-credit—design and applied arts; film/video and photographic arts; fine and studio arts; visual and performing arts related.

MINNESOTA SCHOOL OF BUSINESS–ONLINE
Richfield, Minnesota
http://www.msbcollege.edu

Minnesota School of Business–Online first offered distance learning courses in 2000. In fall 2010, there were 1,080 students enrolled in distance learning courses. Institutionally administered financial aid is available to distance learners.
Services Distance learners have accessibility to academic advising, bookstore, career placement assistance, e-mail services, library services, tutoring.
Contact Network Admissions Support, Minnesota School of Business–Online, 1401 West 76th Street, Suite 300, Richfield, MN 55423. Telephone: 877-609-8889. E-mail: admissions.support@msbcollege.edu.

DEGREES AND AWARDS

AAS Accounting and Tax Program; Business Administration; Cosmetology Business; Criminal Justice; Health Fitness Specialist; Information Technology; Management Accounting; Paralegal; Sales and Marketing; Transportation Business
BS Accounting; Business Administration; Business Management; Criminal Justice; Health Care Management; Health Fitness Specialist; Information Technology; Media Business; Paralegal
Certificate Post-Baccalaureate certificate
Diploma Accounting; Business Administrative Assistant
MBA Business Administration
MS Health Fitness Management
MSM Management

COURSE SUBJECT AREAS OFFERED OUTSIDE OF DEGREE PROGRAMS

Undergraduate—accounting and computer science; accounting and related services; agricultural and domestic animal services; agricultural business and management; allied health and medical assisting services; business administration, management and operations; business/commerce; business/corporate communications; business, management, and marketing related; business/managerial economics; business operations support and assistant services; communication and journalism related; communication and media; computer and information sciences; computer and information sciences and support services related; computer/information technology administration and management; computer programming; computer science; computer software and media applications; computer systems analysis; computer systems networking and telecommunications; cosmetology and related personal grooming services; criminal justice and corrections; criminology; data entry/microcomputer applications; data processing; family and consumer economics; family and consumer sciences/human sciences; family and consumer sciences/human sciences business services; family and consumer sciences/human sciences related; foods, nutrition, and related services; health and medical administrative services; health and physical education/fitness; health services/allied health/health sciences; homeland security; homeland security, law enforcement, firefighting and protective services related; hospitality administration; human development, family studies, and related services; human resources management; legal support services; marketing; transportation and materials moving related.

MINNESOTA SCHOOL OF BUSINESS–RICHFIELD
Richfield, Minnesota
http://www.msbcollege.edu

Minnesota School of Business–Richfield was founded in 1877. It is accredited by Accrediting Council for Independent Colleges and Schools. It first offered distance learning courses in 2000. In fall 2010, there were 1,080 students enrolled in distance learning courses. Institutionally administered financial aid is available to distance learners.

Services Distance learners have accessibility to academic advising, campus computer network, career placement assistance, e-mail services, library services, tutoring.

Contact Chris Schmitz, Director of Admissions, Minnesota School of Business–Richfield, 1401 West 76th Street, Suite 400, Richfield, MN 55423. Telephone: 877-609-8889. E-mail: cschmitz@msbcollege.edu.

DEGREES AND AWARDS
AAS Accounting and Tax Specialist; Business Administration; Cosmetology Business; Health Fitness Specialist; Information Technology; Management Accounting; Paralegal; Transportation Business

BS Accounting; Business Administration; Business Management; Health Care Management; Health Fitness Specialist; Information Technology; Paralegal

MBA Business Administration

MSM Health Fitness Management; Management

COURSE SUBJECT AREAS OFFERED OUTSIDE OF DEGREE PROGRAMS
Undergraduate—accounting and related services; animal sciences; biology; business administration, management and operations; communication and media; computer science; entrepreneurial and small business operations; health and medical administrative services; international business; legal professions and studies related; legal studies (nonprofessional general, undergraduate); liberal arts and sciences, general studies and humanities; mathematics; taxation; veterinary biomedical and clinical sciences.

Graduate—business administration, management and operations.

MINOT STATE UNIVERSITY
Minot, North Dakota
Continuing Education
http://www.minotstateu.edu/online

Minot State University was founded in 1913. It is accredited by North Central Association of Colleges and Schools. It first offered distance learning courses in 1991. In fall 2010, there were 1,356 students enrolled in distance learning courses. Institutionally administered financial aid is available to distance learners.

Services Distance learners have accessibility to academic advising, bookstore, campus computer network, career placement assistance, e-mail services, library services, tutoring.

Contact Jolina Miller, Online Program Coordinator, Minot State University, Center for Extended Learning, 500 University Avenue West, Minot, ND 58707. Telephone: 701-858-3430. Fax: 701-858-4343. E-mail: online@minotstateu.edu.

DEGREES AND AWARDS
AS Developmental Disabilities

BAS Applied Business Information Technology; Applied Management

BGS General Studies

BS International Business; Management Information Systems; Management; Marketing

BSN Nursing for Registered Nurses

CAGS Knowledge Management

CCCPE Application Software Specialist; Developmental Disabilities; Web Development

MS Information Systems; Management

COURSE SUBJECT AREAS OFFERED OUTSIDE OF DEGREE PROGRAMS
Undergraduate—accounting and related services; anthropology; computer programming; computer science; criminal justice and corrections; curriculum and instruction; economics; education; education (specific levels and methods); English; entrepreneurial and small business operations; finance and financial management services; health services/allied health/health sciences; history; human resources management; information science/studies; international business; liberal arts and sciences, general studies and humanities; literature; marketing; mathematics; mathematics and statistics related; philosophy; political science and government; psychology; psychology related; public health; social sciences; sociology; special education; statistics.

Graduate—mathematics; special education.

MISERICORDIA UNIVERSITY
Dallas, Pennsylvania
http://www.misericordia.edu/

Misericordia University was founded in 1924. It is accredited by Middle States Association of Colleges and Schools. It first offered distance learning courses in 1994. In fall 2010, there were 637 students enrolled in distance learning courses. Institutionally administered financial aid is available to distance learners.

Services Distance learners have accessibility to academic advising, bookstore, campus computer network, career placement assistance, e-mail services, library services, tutoring.

Contact Mr. Alex Sergay, Manager, Online Learning Systems, Misericordia University, Center for Adult and Continuing Education, 301 Lake Street, Dallas, PA 18612. Telephone: 570-674-6726. E-mail: asergay@misericordia.edu.

DEGREES AND AWARDS
BS Business Administration; Diagnostic Medical Sonography; Professional Studies

BSN Nursing–RN to BSN

MBA Business Administration

MS Organizational Management

DPT Transitional Doctorate of Physical Therapy (tDPT)

OTD Occupational Therapy

COURSE SUBJECT AREAS OFFERED OUTSIDE OF DEGREE PROGRAMS
Undergraduate—English language and literature related; fine and studio arts; management information systems; philosophy; political science and government; psychology; religious studies; sociology; statistics.

Graduate—curriculum and instruction; education; gerontology.

MISSISSIPPI COLLEGE
Clinton, Mississippi
http://www.mc.edu/online/

Mississippi College was founded in 1826. It is accredited by Southern Association of Colleges and Schools. It first offered distance learning courses in 2006. In fall 2010, there were 478 students enrolled in distance learning courses. Institutionally administered financial aid is available to distance learners.

Services Distance learners have accessibility to academic advising, bookstore, campus computer network, career placement assistance, e-mail services, library services.

Contact Mr. Kyle Brantley, Interim Director of Admissions, Mississippi College, Office of Enrollment Services, Box 4026, 1 Nelson Hall, Clinton, MS 39058. Telephone: 601-925-7634. Fax: 601-925-3950. E-mail: enrollment-services@mc.edu.

DEGREES AND AWARDS

BSN Nursing–Online RN-to-BSN Track

MHSA Health Services Administration

MS Higher Education Administration

COURSE SUBJECT AREAS OFFERED OUTSIDE OF DEGREE PROGRAMS

Undergraduate—accounting and related services; biology; computer science; criminal justice and corrections; economics; health and physical education/fitness; history; legal professions and studies related; management information systems; mathematics; music; visual and performing arts.

Graduate—biology; business administration, management and operations; criminal justice and corrections; education; management information systems.

MISSISSIPPI STATE UNIVERSITY
Mississippi State, Mississippi
Division of Academic Outreach & Continuing Education
http://www.distance.msstate.edu

Mississippi State University was founded in 1878. It is accredited by Southern Association of Colleges and Schools. It first offered distance learning courses in 1987. In fall 2010, there were 1,700 students enrolled in distance learning courses. Institutionally administered financial aid is available to distance learners.

Services Distance learners have accessibility to academic advising, bookstore, campus computer network, career placement assistance, e-mail services, library services.

Contact Dr. Laura A. Crittenden, Manager, Office of Academic Outreach, Mississippi State University, Division of Academic Outreach and Continuing Education, 365 Barr Avenue, PO Box 5247, Mississippi State, MS 39762-5247. Telephone: 662-325-2677. Fax: 662-325-2657. E-mail: lcrittenden@aoce.msstate.edu.

DEGREES AND AWARDS

BS Elementary Education; Geosciences; Interdisciplinary Studies

Certificate Geosciences, Broadcast Meteorology; Geosciences, Operational Meteorology; Geospatial and Remote Sensing

Graduate Certificate Business Administration; Diversity certificate program; Geospatial and Remote Sensing; Vision Specialist

M Eng Engineering

MA Interdisciplinary Sciences

MAT Community College Instruction; Secondary Education

MBA Business Administration; Project Management

MS Food Science, Nutrition, and Health Promotion; Forestry; General Biology–Teachers in Biology; Geosciences, Teachers in Geoscience; Industrial Engineering; Workforce Education Leadership

MSIS Information Systems

PhD Community College Leadership; Computer Engineering; Electrical Engineering; Engineering, Industrial Engineering concentration

COURSE SUBJECT AREAS OFFERED OUTSIDE OF DEGREE PROGRAMS

Undergraduate—accounting and computer science; accounting and related services; biological and physical sciences; biology; communication and journalism related; communication and media; computer and information sciences; computer science; curriculum and instruction; educational/instructional media design; education related; education (specific levels and methods); education (specific subject areas); fine and studio arts; forestry; geological and earth sciences/geosciences; human development, family studies, and related services; insurance; landscape architecture; mathematics; multi/interdisciplinary studies related; physical sciences related; physics; special education; statistics; zoology/animal biology.

Graduate—agriculture; business administration, management and operations; business/commerce; business/managerial economics; chemical engineering; civil engineering; computer engineering; computer science; curriculum and instruction; educational administration and supervision; educational assessment, evaluation, and research; educational/instructional media design; education (specific subject areas); electrical, electronics and communications engineering; engineering; engineering technologies related; health professions related; public administration.

MISSOURI BAPTIST UNIVERSITY
St. Louis, Missouri
http://www.mobap.edu/distance-learning

Missouri Baptist University was founded in 1964. It is accredited by North Central Association of Colleges and Schools. It first offered distance learning courses in 2000. In fall 2010, there were 900 students enrolled in distance learning courses. Institutionally administered financial aid is available to distance learners.

Services Distance learners have accessibility to academic advising, bookstore, campus computer network, career placement assistance, e-mail services, library services, tutoring.

Contact Dr. Greg Comfort, Director of Distance Learning, Missouri Baptist University, One College Park Drive, St. Louis, MO 63141-8698. Telephone: 314-392-2282. Fax: 314-434-7596. E-mail: distancelearning@mobap.edu.

DEGREES AND AWARDS

MS Sport Management

MSE Curriculum and Instruction

COURSE SUBJECT AREAS OFFERED OUTSIDE OF DEGREE PROGRAMS

Undergraduate—biblical studies; biology; business administration, management and operations; chemistry; computer and information sciences; educational administration and supervision; education (specific subject areas); religious studies.

Graduate—educational administration and supervision; education (specific subject areas); library science and administration; religious education; religious studies.

MISSOURI UNIVERSITY OF SCIENCE AND TECHNOLOGY
Rolla, Missouri
Extended Programs
http://dce.mst.edu

Missouri University of Science and Technology was founded in 1870. It is accredited by North Central Association of Colleges and Schools. It first offered distance learning courses in 1985. In fall 2010, there were 650 students enrolled in distance learning courses. Institutionally administered financial aid is available to distance learners.

Services Distance learners have accessibility to academic advising, bookstore, campus computer network, career placement assistance, e-mail services, library services.

Contact Ms. Sue Turner, Director of Distance and Continuing Education, Missouri University of Science and Technology, 216 Centennial Hall, 300 West 12th Street, Rolla, MO 65409. Telephone: 573-341-4550. Fax: 573-341-4992. E-mail: suet@mst.edu.

DEGREES AND AWARDS

MBA Business Administration
MEG Geotechnics
MEngr Manufacturing Engineering; Mining Engineering
MS IST Information Science and Technology
MS Systems Engineering
MSAE Aerospace Engineering
MSCE Civil Engineering
MSCPE Computer Engineering
MSCS Computer Science
MSE Engineering Management; Environmental Engineering
MSEE Electrical Engineering
MSME Mechanical Engineering

COURSE SUBJECT AREAS OFFERED OUTSIDE OF DEGREE PROGRAMS

Graduate—business administration, management and operations; business, management, and marketing related; civil engineering; civil engineering technologies; computer and information sciences; computer science; electrical, electronics and communications engineering; electrical engineering technologies; engineering; engineering mechanics; engineering-related technologies; engineering science; engineering technologies related; information science/studies; manufacturing engineering; mechanical engineering; mechanical engineering related technologies; mining and mineral engineering; quality control and safety technologies; systems engineering.

Non-credit—aerospace, aeronautical and astronautical engineering; business administration, management and operations; business, management, and marketing related; chemistry; civil engineering; civil engineering technologies; computer and information sciences; computer science; electrical/electronics maintenance and repair technology; electrical engineering technologies; engineering; engineering related; engineering-related fields; engineering-related technologies; entrepreneurial and small business operations; environmental/environmental health engineering; geological and earth sciences/geosciences; materials engineering; mining and mineral engineering; quality control and safety technologies; surveying engineering; systems engineering; transportation and materials moving related.

MITCHELL TECHNICAL INSTITUTE
Mitchell, South Dakota
http://www.mitchelltech.edu

Mitchell Technical Institute was founded in 1968. It is accredited by North Central Association of Colleges and Schools. It first offered distance learning courses in 1994. In fall 2010, there were 20 students enrolled in distance learning courses. Institutionally administered financial aid is available to distance learners.

Services Distance learners have accessibility to academic advising, bookstore, career placement assistance, e-mail services, library services.

Contact John J. Heemstra, Outreach Coordinator, Mitchell Technical Institute, 821 North Capital Street, Mitchell, SD 57301. Telephone: 605-995-3065. Fax: 605-995-3067. E-mail: john.heemstra@mitchelltech.edu.

DEGREES AND AWARDS

Programs offered do not lead to a degree or other formal award.

COURSE SUBJECT AREAS OFFERED OUTSIDE OF DEGREE PROGRAMS

Undergraduate—electrical and power transmission installation; electrical, electronics and communications engineering.

Non-credit—agricultural business and management; agriculture and agriculture operations related; business, management, and marketing related; business operations support and assistant services; computer and information sciences; computer software and media applications; data entry/microcomputer applications; entrepreneurial and small business operations; health professions related; heating, air conditioning, ventilation and refrigeration maintenance technology; quality control and safety technologies.

MONMOUTH UNIVERSITY
West Long Branch, New Jersey
http://www.monmouth.edu/

Monmouth University was founded in 1933. It is accredited by Middle States Association of Colleges and Schools. It first offered distance learning courses in 1998. In fall 2010, there were 345 students enrolled in distance learning courses. Institutionally administered financial aid is available to distance learners.

Services Distance learners have accessibility to academic advising, bookstore, campus computer network, career placement assistance, e-mail services, library services.

Contact Robert D. McCaig, EdD, Vice President for Enrollment Management, Monmouth University, 400 Cedar Avenue, West Long Branch, NJ 07764-1898. Telephone: 732-571-3413. Fax: 732-263-5101. E-mail: rmccaig@monmouth.edu.

DEGREES AND AWARDS

Graduate Certificate Educational Technology; Homeland Security
MS Ed Special Education/Autism track

COURSE SUBJECT AREAS OFFERED OUTSIDE OF DEGREE PROGRAMS

Undergraduate—education.

Graduate—criminal justice and corrections; education; health services/allied health/health sciences; psychology.

MONROE COLLEGE
New Rochelle, New York
http://www.monroecollege.edu/online

Monroe College was founded in 1983. It first offered distance learning courses in 2000. In fall 2010, there were 1,454 students enrolled in distance learning courses. Institutionally administered financial aid is available to distance learners.

Services Distance learners have accessibility to academic advising, bookstore, campus computer network, career placement assistance, e-mail services, library services, tutoring.

Contact Brent Passey, Director of Online Admissions, Monroe College, 2501 Jerome Avenue, Bronx, NY 10468. Telephone: 646-393-8267. E-mail: bpassey@monroecollege.edu.

DEGREES AND AWARDS

AAS Business Administration; Hospitality Management; Information Technology; Medical Administration
AS Criminal Justice
BBA Business Management; Health Services Administration; Hospitality Management; Information Technology
BS Criminal Justice; Public Health
MBA Business Management
MS Criminal Justice

COURSE SUBJECT AREAS OFFERED OUTSIDE OF DEGREE PROGRAMS

Undergraduate—accounting and computer science; allied health and medical assisting services; behavioral sciences; business administration, management and operations; business, management, and marketing related; business/managerial economics; computer and information sciences; computer/information technology administration and management; computer programming; computer systems analysis; computer systems networking and telecommunications; criminal justice and corrections; criminology; economics; English; entrepreneurial and small business operations; finance and financial management services; health and medical administrative services; hospitality administration; human resources management; international business; management information systems; marketing; mathematics; mathematics and statistics related; philosophy; political science and government; psychology; social sciences; social sciences related; sociology; statistics; student counseling and personnel services; taxation.

MONROE COMMUNITY COLLEGE

Rochester, New York

http://www.monroecc.edu/

Monroe Community College was founded in 1961. It is accredited by Middle States Association of Colleges and Schools. It first offered distance learning courses in 1997. In fall 2010, there were 3,178 students enrolled in distance learning courses. Institutionally administered financial aid is available to distance learners.

Services Distance learners have accessibility to academic advising, bookstore, campus computer network, career placement assistance, e-mail services, library services.

Contact Peggy VanKirk, Coordinator of Online Services, Monroe Community College, 1000 East Henrietta Road, Rochester, NY 14623-5780. Telephone: 585-292-3441. Fax: 585-292-3855. E-mail: pvankirk@monroecc.edu.

DEGREES AND AWARDS

AAS Criminal Justice
AS Business Administration; Liberal Arts
Certificate Dental Assisting

COURSE SUBJECT AREAS OFFERED OUTSIDE OF DEGREE PROGRAMS

Undergraduate—accounting and related services; biology; business/commerce; communication and media; criminal justice and corrections; dental support services and allied professions; liberal arts and sciences, general studies and humanities; mathematics; psychology; public relations, advertising, and applied communication related; social sciences.

MONROE COUNTY COMMUNITY COLLEGE

Monroe, Michigan

http://www.monroeccc.edu

Monroe County Community College was founded in 1964. It is accredited by North Central Association of Colleges and Schools. It first offered distance learning courses in 2000. In fall 2010, there were 768 students enrolled in distance learning courses. Institutionally administered financial aid is available to distance learners.

Services Distance learners have accessibility to academic advising, bookstore, campus computer network, career placement assistance, e-mail services, library services, tutoring.

Contact Mr. Mark Hall, Director of Admissions and Guidance Services, Monroe County Community College, 1555 South Raisinville Road, Monroe, MI 48161. Telephone: 734-384-4261. Fax: 734-242-9711. E-mail: mhall@monroeccc.edu.

DEGREES AND AWARDS

Programs offered do not lead to a degree or other formal award.

COURSE SUBJECT AREAS OFFERED OUTSIDE OF DEGREE PROGRAMS

Undergraduate—business/commerce; computer and information sciences; computer software and media applications; economics; mathematics; political science and government; psychology; work and family studies.

MONTANA STATE UNIVERSITY–GREAT FALLS COLLEGE OF TECHNOLOGY

Great Falls, Montana

Distance Learning Department

http://distance.msugf.edu

Montana State University–Great Falls College of Technology was founded in 1969. It is accredited by Northwest Commission on Colleges and Universities. It first offered distance learning courses in 1997. In fall 2010, there were 1,401 students enrolled in distance learning courses. Institutionally administered financial aid is available to distance learners.

Services Distance learners have accessibility to academic advising, bookstore, career placement assistance, e-mail services, library services, tutoring.

Contact Ms. Karen K. Vosen, Distance Education Student Support Coordinator, Montana State University–Great Falls College of Technology, 2100 16th Avenue South, Great Falls, MT 59405. Telephone: 406-771-4440. Fax: 406-771-4317. E-mail: kvosen@msugf.edu.

DEGREES AND AWARDS

AA Education, general
AAS Business Administration–Management; Health Information Technology; Medical Billing and Coding; Medical Transcription
AS Education, general
Certificate of Completion General Studies–Montana University System General Core
Certificate Health Information Coding Specialist; Medical Billing Specialist; Medical Transcription

MONTCALM COMMUNITY COLLEGE

Sidney, Michigan

http://www.montcalm.edu/

Montcalm Community College was founded in 1965. It is accredited by North Central Association of Colleges and Schools. It first offered distance learning courses in 2002. In fall 2010, there were 628 students enrolled in distance learning courses. Institutionally administered financial aid is available to distance learners.

Services Distance learners have accessibility to academic advising, bookstore, career placement assistance, e-mail services, library services.

Contact Debra Alexander, Associate Dean of Student Services, Montcalm Community College, 2800 College Drive, Sidney, MI 48885-9723. Telephone: 989-328-1250. Fax: 989-328-2950. E-mail: admissions@montcalm.edu.

DEGREES AND AWARDS

Programs offered do not lead to a degree or other formal award.

COURSE SUBJECT AREAS OFFERED OUTSIDE OF DEGREE PROGRAMS

Undergraduate—accounting and related services; biology; business administration, management and operations; business/commerce; computer programming; criminal justice and corrections; data entry/microcomputer applications; economics; English; international business; psychology.

Non-credit—accounting and related services; business administration, management and operations; computer and information sciences; health professions related.

MONTGOMERY COMMUNITY COLLEGE

Troy, North Carolina

http://www.montgomery.edu

Montgomery Community College was founded in 1967. It is accredited by Southern Association of Colleges and Schools. It first offered distance learning courses in 2000. In fall 2010, there were 450 students enrolled in distance learning courses. Institutionally administered financial aid is available to distance learners.

Services Distance learners have accessibility to academic advising, bookstore, campus computer network, career placement assistance, e-mail services, library services, tutoring.

Contact Thomas M. Sargent, Director of Distance Learning and Professional Development, Montgomery Community College, 1011 Page Street, Troy, NC 27371. Telephone: 910-576-6222 Ext. 217. Fax: 910-576-2176. E-mail: sargentt@montgomery.edu.

DEGREES AND AWARDS

AA General Studies
AAB Business Administration; Hunting and Shooting Sports Management
AAS Criminal Justice

COURSE SUBJECT AREAS OFFERED OUTSIDE OF DEGREE PROGRAMS

Undergraduate—accounting and related services; allied health and medical assisting services; business administration, management and

operations; business/commerce; business, management, and marketing related; business/managerial economics; business operations support and assistant services; computer and information sciences; computer software and media applications; criminal justice and corrections; English; human resources management; liberal arts and sciences, general studies and humanities; psychology; religious education; sociology.
Non-credit—allied health and medical assisting services; biblical studies; business administration, management and operations; business/corporate communications; computer and information sciences; computer software and media applications; English.

MONTGOMERY COUNTY COMMUNITY COLLEGE
Blue Bell, Pennsylvania
Learning Resources Unit
http://www.mc3.edu/academics/online

Montgomery County Community College was founded in 1964. It is accredited by Middle States Association of Colleges and Schools. It first offered distance learning courses in 1992. In fall 2010, there were 3,559 students enrolled in distance learning courses. Institutionally administered financial aid is available to distance learners.
Services Distance learners have accessibility to academic advising, bookstore, campus computer network, career placement assistance, e-mail services, library services, tutoring.
Contact Ms. Kimberly Springfield, e-Learning Administrative Support Assistant, Montgomery County Community College, 340 DeKalb Pike, Blue Bell, PA 19422. Telephone: 215-619-7345. Fax: 215-619-7167. E-mail: kspringf@mc3.edu.

DEGREES AND AWARDS
AA Education in the Early Years–Birth through Fourth Grade; Liberal Studies; Secondary Education; Social Science
AAS Criminal Justice; Management; Marketing; Office Administration
AGS General Studies
AS Business Administration; Business Administration, International option; Computer Science; Management Information Systems
Certificate Business Management; International Studies; Office Administration (Specialty Certificate); Office Administration

COURSE SUBJECT AREAS OFFERED OUTSIDE OF DEGREE PROGRAMS
Undergraduate—accounting and related services; anthropology; astronomy and astrophysics; biology; business administration, management and operations; business/commerce; computer and information sciences; computer programming; computer science; computer software and media applications; criminology; dental support services and allied professions; economics; education; geography and cartography; geological and earth sciences/geosciences; health professions related; history; liberal arts and sciences, general studies and humanities; marketing; mathematics; nutrition sciences; philosophy; psychology; sociology; statistics.
Non-credit—accounting and related services; business operations support and assistant services; health and medical administrative services; health professions related.

MOODY BIBLE INSTITUTE
Chicago, Illinois
Moody Bible Institute External Studies Division
http://www.moody.edu/distancelearning/

Moody Bible Institute was founded in 1886. It is accredited by Association for Biblical Higher Education. It first offered distance learning courses in 1941. In fall 2010, there were 1,500 students enrolled in distance learning courses. Institutionally administered financial aid is available to distance learners.
Services Distance learners have accessibility to academic advising, career placement assistance, e-mail services, library services.
Contact John Engelkemier, Manager of Operations, Moody Bible Institute, 820 North LaSalle Boulevard, Chicago, IL 60610. Telephone: 800-758-6352. Fax: 312-329-2081. E-mail: mdlc@moody.edu.

DEGREES AND AWARDS
ABS Biblical Studies
BS Biblical Studies; Ministry Leadership
Certificate Biblical Studies

COURSE SUBJECT AREAS OFFERED OUTSIDE OF DEGREE PROGRAMS
Undergraduate—biblical studies; languages (classics and classical); philosophy; philosophy and religious studies related; physical sciences; psychology; religious education; religious studies; theological and ministerial studies; theology and religious vocations related.
Graduate—biblical studies; religious studies; theological and ministerial studies; theology and religious vocations related.
Non-credit—biblical studies; religious studies; theological and ministerial studies.

MOORPARK COLLEGE
Moorpark, California
http://www.moorparkcollege.edu

Moorpark College was founded in 1967. It is accredited by Western Association of Schools and Colleges. It first offered distance learning courses in 1978. In fall 2010, there were 3,845 students enrolled in distance learning courses. Institutionally administered financial aid is available to distance learners.
Services Distance learners have accessibility to academic advising, bookstore, career placement assistance, e-mail services, library services, tutoring.
Contact Richard Torres, Outreach Coordinator, Moorpark College, 7075 Campus Road, Moorpark, CA 93021. Telephone: 805-378-1400. E-mail: mcoutreach@vcccd.edu.

DEGREES AND AWARDS
AS Health Information Management

COURSE SUBJECT AREAS OFFERED OUTSIDE OF DEGREE PROGRAMS
Undergraduate—accounting and computer science; accounting and related services; allied health and medical assisting services; allied health diagnostic, intervention, and treatment professions; anthropology; behavioral sciences; biological and physical sciences; biology; business/commerce; business, management, and marketing related; communication and journalism related; communication and media; computer and information sciences; criminal justice and corrections; economics; education related; English; geography and cartography; health services/allied health/health sciences; journalism; languages (classics and classical); languages (foreign languages related); languages (Romance languages); mathematics; music; nutrition sciences; philosophy; philosophy and religious studies related; physical sciences; political science and government; psychology; sociology; statistics.

MORAINE PARK TECHNICAL COLLEGE
Fond du Lac, Wisconsin
http://www.morainepark.edu

Moraine Park Technical College was founded in 1967. It is accredited by North Central Association of Colleges and Schools. It first offered distance learning courses in 1999. In fall 2010, there were 6,400 students enrolled in distance learning courses. Institutionally administered financial aid is available to distance learners.
Services Distance learners have accessibility to academic advising, bookstore, campus computer network, career placement assistance, e-mail services, library services, tutoring.
Contact Catherine Werner, Instructional Delivery Technologies Specialist, Moraine Park Technical College, 2151 North Main Street, West Bend, WI 53090. Telephone: 262-335-5824. E-mail: cwerner@morainepark.edu.

DEGREES AND AWARDS
AAS Health Information Technology; Information Technology–Applications Developer; Instructional Assistant; Leadership Development
AD Accounting; Business Management; Water Quality
Technical Certificate Information Technology–Web Designer/Developer; Medical Transcription

MORNINGSIDE COLLEGE
Sioux City, Iowa
http://webs.morningside.edu/gradedu/index.htm

Morningside College was founded in 1894. It is accredited by North Central Association of Colleges and Schools. It first offered distance learning courses in 2003. In fall 2010, there were 1,018 students enrolled in distance learning courses. Institutionally administered financial aid is available to distance learners.
Services Distance learners have accessibility to academic advising, bookstore, campus computer network, e-mail services, library services, tutoring.
Contact Janice Petersen, Secretary, Graduate Studies–Education, Morningside College, 1501 Morningside Avenue, Sioux City, IA 51106. Telephone: 712-274-5000 Ext. 5375. E-mail: petersen@morningside.edu.

DEGREES AND AWARDS
MAT Education

MOTLOW STATE COMMUNITY COLLEGE
Tullahoma, Tennessee
Academic Affairs
http://www.mscc.edu

Motlow State Community College was founded in 1969. It is accredited by Southern Association of Colleges and Schools. It first offered distance learning courses in 1996. In fall 2010, there were 635 students enrolled in distance learning courses. Institutionally administered financial aid is available to distance learners.
Services Distance learners have accessibility to academic advising, bookstore, campus computer network, career placement assistance, e-mail services, library services, tutoring.
Contact Ms. Bonny Copenhaver, Provost and Vice President for Student Affairs, Motlow State Community College, PO Box 8500, Lynchburg, TN 37352-8500. Telephone: 931-393-1696. Fax: 931-393-1681. E-mail: bcopenhaver@mscc.edu.

DEGREES AND AWARDS
AAS Business Technology; Nursing; Web Technology

COURSE SUBJECT AREAS OFFERED OUTSIDE OF DEGREE PROGRAMS
Undergraduate—computer and information sciences; economics; management information systems; mathematics; statistics.

MOUNTAIN EMPIRE COMMUNITY COLLEGE
Big Stone Gap, Virginia
Office of Continuing and Distance Education
http://www.mecc.edu/distance/index.html

Mountain Empire Community College was founded in 1972. It is accredited by Southern Association of Colleges and Schools. It first offered distance learning courses in 1979. In fall 2010, there were 2,483 students enrolled in distance learning courses. Institutionally administered financial aid is available to distance learners.
Services Distance learners have accessibility to academic advising, bookstore, campus computer network, career placement assistance, e-mail services, library services, tutoring.
Contact Susan Kennedy, Coordinator of Distance Education, Mountain Empire Community College, 3441 Mountain Empire Road, Big Stone Gap, VA 24219. Telephone: 276-523-7488. Fax: 276-523-7486. E-mail: skennedy@me.vccs.edu.

DEGREES AND AWARDS
AAS Accounting; Administrative Support Technology–Medical Office specialist; Administrative Support Technology; Business Administration; Correctional Services; General Studies; Liberal Arts; Water/Wastewater specialization
Certificate Career Studies–Accounting; Career Studies–Child Development; Career Studies–Computer Software Specialist; Career Studies–Geographical Information Systems; Career Studies–Health Information Technology; Career Studies–Legal Office Assisting; Career Studies–Medical Records Clerk; Career Studies–Medical Transcriptionist; Career Studies–Office Automation Specialist; Career Studies–Personal Computing for Home and Office; Career Studies–Wastewater Plant Operator; Career Studies–Water Plant Operator; Career Studies–Word Processing; Clerical Assistant

COURSE SUBJECT AREAS OFFERED OUTSIDE OF DEGREE PROGRAMS
Undergraduate—accounting and related services; astronomy and astrophysics; atmospheric sciences and meteorology; biology; business/commerce; communication and media; computer and information sciences; criminal justice and corrections; criminology; economics; fine and studio arts; geological and earth sciences/geosciences; health and physical education/fitness; history; human development, family studies, and related services; languages (Romance languages); legal studies (non-professional general, undergraduate); linguistic, comparative, and related language studies; marketing; mathematics; music; psychology; religious studies; sociology.

MOUNTAIN STATE UNIVERSITY
Beckley, West Virginia
The School of Extended and Distance Learning
http://www.mountainstate.edu

Mountain State University was founded in 1933. It is accredited by North Central Association of Colleges and Schools. It first offered distance learning courses in 1992. In fall 2010, there were 3,000 students enrolled in distance learning courses. Institutionally administered financial aid is available to distance learners.
Services Distance learners have accessibility to academic advising, bookstore, e-mail services, library services, tutoring.
Contact Ms. Donna Sibray, Distance Learning Assistant, Mountain State University, PO Box 9003, Beckley, WV 25802-9003. Telephone: 304-929-1688. Fax: 304-929-1604. E-mail: dsibray@mountainstate.edu.

DEGREES AND AWARDS
AA General Studies
AAS Early Childhood Development
AS Accounting; Business Administration–Finance; Business Administration–Health Care Management; Business Administration–Hospitality; Business Administration–Human Resource Management; Business Administration–Management; Business Administration–Marketing; Computer Science; Criminal Justice; Diagnostic Medical Sonography; EMS; Education Teacher Prep; Information Technology; Legal Studies; Medical Assisting; Wildlife Management
BA Psychology
BA/BS Liberal Studies
BS Accounting; Airline Transport Professional; Aviation; Business Administration–Finance; Business Administration–Health Care Management; Business Administration–Hospitality; Business Administration–Human Resource Management; Business Administration–Management; Business Administration–Marketing; Business Studies; Computer Science; Criminal Justice; Diagnostic Medical Sonography; Health Sciences; Information Technology; Legal Studies; Organizational Leadership; Organizational Leadership, Criminal Justice Administration concentration; Organizational Leadership, Hospitality Leadership concentration
Certificate Certified Medical Transcription
Certification Diagnostic Medical Sonography; Medical Coding and Billing; Phlebotomy
MA Psychology
MS Strategic Leadership
MSN Nurse Anesthesia concentration

PD Executive Leadership (DEL)
PMC Nurse Anesthesia concentration

COURSE SUBJECT AREAS OFFERED OUTSIDE OF DEGREE PROGRAMS

Undergraduate—accounting and related services; astronomy and astrophysics; biochemistry, biophysics and molecular biology; biology; botany/plant biology; business administration, management and operations; business/commerce; business, management, and marketing related; cell biology and anatomical sciences; chemistry; criminal justice and corrections; criminology; ecology, evolution, systematics, and population biology; economics; English language and literature related; finance and financial management services; fine and studio arts; geography and cartography; gerontology; health and medical administrative services; history; insurance; international business; legal studies (non-professional general, undergraduate); liberal arts and sciences, general studies and humanities; management information systems; marketing; mathematics; mathematics and statistics related; microbiological sciences and immunology; music; philosophy; philosophy and religious studies related; physical sciences; physics; physiology, pathology and related sciences; psychology; social sciences; social sciences related; social work; sociology; statistics.
Graduate—criminal justice and corrections; health and medical administrative services; multi/interdisciplinary studies related; psychology; psychology related.

MOUNT ALLISON UNIVERSITY
Sackville, New Brunswick, Canada
Continuing and Distance Education
http://www.mta.ca/conted/index.html

Mount Allison University was founded in 1839. It is provincially chartered. It first offered distance learning courses in 1965. In fall 2010, there were 100 students enrolled in distance learning courses. Institutionally administered financial aid is available to distance learners.
Services Distance learners have accessibility to academic advising, bookstore, campus computer network, e-mail services, library services, tutoring.
Contact Ms. Heather Patterson, Director, Mount Allison University, Continuous Learning, 62 York Street, Sackville, NB E4L 1E2, Canada. Telephone: 506-364-2266. Fax: 506-364-2272. E-mail: hpatters@mta.ca.

DEGREES AND AWARDS
Programs offered do not lead to a degree or other formal award.

COURSE SUBJECT AREAS OFFERED OUTSIDE OF DEGREE PROGRAMS

Undergraduate—biology; business/commerce; economics; English; geological and earth sciences/geosciences; languages (Romance languages); mathematics; physics; psychology; religious education; sociology.

MOUNT MARTY COLLEGE
Yankton, South Dakota
http://www.mtmc.edu/admission/pre-college/duel-cretid.aaspx

Mount Marty College was founded in 1936. It is accredited by North Central Association of Colleges and Schools. It first offered distance learning courses in 2003. In fall 2010, there were 242 students enrolled in distance learning courses. Institutionally administered financial aid is available to distance learners.
Services Distance learners have accessibility to campus computer network, e-mail services, library services.
Contact Paula Tacke, Director of Admissions, Mount Marty College, 1105 West 8th Street, Yankton, SD 57078. Telephone: 605-668-1545. Fax: 605-668-1508. E-mail: paula.tacke@mtmc.edu.

DEGREES AND AWARDS
Programs offered do not lead to a degree or other formal award.

COURSE SUBJECT AREAS OFFERED OUTSIDE OF DEGREE PROGRAMS

Undergraduate—English; mathematics; psychology; sociology.

MOUNT MARY COLLEGE
Milwaukee, Wisconsin
http://www.mtmary.edu

Mount Mary College was founded in 1913. It is accredited by North Central Association of Colleges and Schools. It first offered distance learning courses in 2008. In fall 2010, there were 17 students enrolled in distance learning courses. Institutionally administered financial aid is available to distance learners.
Services Distance learners have accessibility to academic advising, bookstore, campus computer network, career placement assistance, e-mail services, library services, tutoring.
Contact Mount Mary College. Telephone: 414-258-4810.

DEGREES AND AWARDS
Programs offered do not lead to a degree or other formal award.

COURSE SUBJECT AREAS OFFERED OUTSIDE OF DEGREE PROGRAMS

Undergraduate—education; health professions related; history; philosophy; political science and government.
Graduate—education; fine and studio arts; health professions related.

MOUNT OLIVE COLLEGE
Mount Olive, North Carolina
http://www.moc.edu

Mount Olive College was founded in 1951. It is accredited by Southern Association of Colleges and Schools. It first offered distance learning courses in 2003. In fall 2010, there were 927 students enrolled in distance learning courses. Institutionally administered financial aid is available to distance learners.
Services Distance learners have accessibility to academic advising, bookstore, campus computer network, career placement assistance, e-mail services, library services, tutoring.
Contact Mrs. Georgette M. Prichard, Manager of Enrollment Information, Mount Olive College, Office of Admissions, 634 Henderson Street, Mount Olive, NC 28365. Telephone: 800-653-0854 Ext. 1204. Fax: 919-658-9816. E-mail: gprichard@moc.edu.

DEGREES AND AWARDS
Programs offered do not lead to a degree or other formal award.

COURSE SUBJECT AREAS OFFERED OUTSIDE OF DEGREE PROGRAMS

Undergraduate—accounting and computer science; biblical studies; biology; business administration, management and operations; criminal justice and corrections; criminology; economics; education; English language and literature related; health and physical education/fitness; history; liberal arts and sciences, general studies and humanities; management information systems; mathematics; music; parks, recreation, leisure, and fitness studies related; psychology; religious studies.

MOUNT SAINT VINCENT UNIVERSITY
Halifax, Nova Scotia, Canada
Distance Learning and Continuing Education
http://www.msvu.ca/distance

Mount Saint Vincent University was founded in 1873. It is provincially chartered. It first offered distance learning courses in 1980. In fall 2010, there were 900 students enrolled in distance learning courses. Institutionally administered financial aid is available to distance learners.
Services Distance learners have accessibility to academic advising, bookstore, campus computer network, e-mail services, library services.
Contact Client Service Assistant, Mount Saint Vincent University, 166 Bedford Highway, Halifax, NS B3M 2J6, Canada. Telephone: 902-457-6511. Fax: 902-443-2135. E-mail: distance@msvu.ca.

DEGREES AND AWARDS
BA Liberal Arts and General Studies
BBA Business Administration; Marketing
BTHM Tourism and Hospitality Management
Certificate Accounting; Gerontology; Information Technology Management
MEd Education

MOUNT WACHUSETT COMMUNITY COLLEGE
Gardner, Massachusetts
Division of Continuing Education
http://www.mwcc.edu

Mount Wachusett Community College was founded in 1963. It is accredited by New England Association of Schools and Colleges. It first offered distance learning courses in 1994. In fall 2010, there were 2,111 students enrolled in distance learning courses. Institutionally administered financial aid is available to distance learners.
Services Distance learners have accessibility to academic advising, bookstore, campus computer network, career placement assistance, e-mail services, library services, tutoring.
Contact Ms. Deborah Brennan, Distance Learning Administrative Assistant, Mount Wachusett Community College, 444 Green Street, Gardner, MA 01440. Telephone: 978-630-9275. Fax: 978-630-9537. E-mail: dbrennan@mwcc.mass.edu.

DEGREES AND AWARDS
AS Broadcasting and Electronic Media, Photography concentration (BCTP); Business Administration–Career (BAC); Business Administration–Career, Accounting concentration (BACA); Business Administration–Transfer (BA); Computer Information Systems (CIS); Fire Science Technology (FS); General Studies (GS); General Studies–Allied Health concentration (GSAH); Human Services (HS); Liberal Arts and Sciences (LAS); Liberal Arts and Sciences–Communications track (LAC); Liberal Arts and Sciences–Pre-Engineering Track (LAER); Paralegal Studies (PLD)

COURSE SUBJECT AREAS OFFERED OUTSIDE OF DEGREE PROGRAMS
Undergraduate—biology; business administration, management and operations; communication and journalism related; computer programming; computer software and media applications; criminal justice and corrections; criminology; economics; film/video and photographic arts; history; human development, family studies, and related services; human resources management; human services; journalism; legal professions and studies related; management information systems; marketing; mathematics; mathematics and statistics related; mental and social health services and allied professions; political science and government; psychology; social sciences; sociology; statistics.
Non-credit—accounting and computer science; business administration, management and operations; business, management, and marketing related; business operations support and assistant services; computer and information sciences; computer software and media applications; entrepreneurial and small business operations; environmental design; film/video and photographic arts; finance and financial management services; gerontology; health professions related; heating, air conditioning, ventilation and refrigeration maintenance technology; hospitality administration; human resources management; languages (foreign languages related); marketing; music; pharmacy, pharmaceutical sciences, and administration; veterinary biomedical and clinical sciences.

MURRAY STATE COLLEGE
Tishomingo, Oklahoma
http://www.mscok.edu

Murray State College was founded in 1908. It is accredited by North Central Association of Colleges and Schools. It first offered distance learning courses in 1996. In fall 2010, there were 1,128 students enrolled in distance learning courses. Institutionally administered financial aid is available to distance learners.
Services Distance learners have accessibility to academic advising, campus computer network, career placement assistance, e-mail services, library services, tutoring.
Contact Mr. Michael Van Burrell, Distance Learning Coordinator, Murray State College, One Murray Campus, Tishomingo, OK 73460. Telephone: 580-371-2371 Ext. 123. Fax: 580-371-9844. E-mail: mburrell@mscok.edu.

DEGREES AND AWARDS
Programs offered do not lead to a degree or other formal award.

COURSE SUBJECT AREAS OFFERED OUTSIDE OF DEGREE PROGRAMS
Undergraduate—accounting and computer science; allied health and medical assisting services; applied mathematics; behavioral sciences; biological and physical sciences; biology; business administration, management and operations; business/corporate communications; computer software and media applications; criminal justice and corrections; finance and financial management services; history; marketing; mathematics; music; physical sciences; political science and government.

MURRAY STATE UNIVERSITY
Murray, Kentucky
Continuing Education
http://www.murraystate.edu/distancelearning

Murray State University was founded in 1922. It is accredited by Southern Association of Colleges and Schools. It first offered distance learning courses in 1990. In fall 2010, there were 1,705 students enrolled in distance learning courses. Institutionally administered financial aid is available to distance learners.
Services Distance learners have accessibility to academic advising, bookstore, campus computer network, career placement assistance, e-mail services, library services.
Contact Lisa O'Neal, Coordinator of Distance Learning, Murray State University, 303 Sparks Hall, CEAO, Murray, KY 42071-0009. Telephone: 270-809-2159. Fax: 270-809-3593. E-mail: loneal1@murraystate.edu.

DEGREES AND AWARDS
BIS Integrated Studies (Bachelor of Integrated Studies)
BS Telecommunications Systems Management
BSBA Business Administration
Certification Library Media +30 Certification Program for Rank I; Library Media +30 Certification Program for Rank I for Certified School Media Librarians
Endorsement English as a Second Language Endorsement for Kentucky Teachers; Gifted and Talented Certificate Endorsement for Kentucky Teachers; Instruction Computer Technology certificate endorsement for Kentucky Teachers
MAEd Education/Reading and Writing
MBA Business Administration
MIT Teaching English to Speakers of Other Languages
MN Academic Nurse Educator option
MSN Nursing–Clinical Nurse Specialist option
MTM Telecommunications Systems Management

COURSE SUBJECT AREAS OFFERED OUTSIDE OF DEGREE PROGRAMS
Undergraduate—accounting and related services; agricultural production; agriculture; anthropology; applied mathematics; biology; business administration, management and operations; business/corporate communications; business, management, and marketing related; business/managerial economics; chemistry; communication and journalism related; community organization and advocacy; computer and information sciences; criminal justice and corrections; curriculum and instruction; economics; education; education related; English; geography and cartography; health and medical administrative services; history; journalism; philosophy; philosophy and religious studies related; public administration; social sciences related; social work.
Graduate—agriculture; business administration, management and operations; business/commerce; business, management, and marketing related; computer/information technology administration and management; English; English language and literature related; English or French as a second or

foreign language (teaching); human development, family studies, and related services; marketing; psychology related; public administration.

Non-credit—business administration, management and operations; computer programming; health and medical administrative services.

NAROPA UNIVERSITY
Boulder, Colorado
Outreach Office
http://www.naropa.edu/distancelearning

Naropa University was founded in 1974. It is accredited by North Central Association of Colleges and Schools. It first offered distance learning courses in 1999. In fall 2010, there were 200 students enrolled in distance learning courses. Institutionally administered financial aid is available to distance learners.

Services Distance learners have accessibility to academic advising, bookstore, career placement assistance, e-mail services, library services.

Contact Jirka Hladis, Director of Distance Learning Curriculum Development, Naropa University, 2130 Arapahoe Avenue, Boulder, CO 80302. Telephone: 303-245-4702. E-mail: jirka@naropa.edu.

DEGREES AND AWARDS

MA Contemplative Education; Transpersonal Psychology; Transpersonal Psychology, Ecopsychology concentration

MFA Creative Writing

COURSE SUBJECT AREAS OFFERED OUTSIDE OF DEGREE PROGRAMS

Undergraduate—ethnic, cultural minority, gender, and group studies; liberal arts and sciences, general studies and humanities; multi/interdisciplinary studies related; philosophy and religious studies related; psychology; religious studies.

Graduate—education; English; languages (East Asian); liberal arts and sciences, general studies and humanities; multi/interdisciplinary studies related; psychology related; religious education.

Non-credit—area studies; education; education related; ethnic, cultural minority, gender, and group studies; human development, family studies, and related services; philosophy; philosophy and religious studies related; psychology; psychology related; religious education; religious/sacred music; religious studies; theological and ministerial studies; theology and religious vocations related.

NASHVILLE STATE TECHNICAL COMMUNITY COLLEGE
Nashville, Tennessee
http://www.nscc.edu

Nashville State Technical Community College was founded in 1970. It is accredited by Southern Association of Colleges and Schools. It first offered distance learning courses in 1998. In fall 2010, there were 4,700 students enrolled in distance learning courses. Institutionally administered financial aid is available to distance learners.

Services Distance learners have accessibility to academic advising, bookstore, campus computer network, career placement assistance, e-mail services, library services, tutoring.

Contact Doug Jameson, Coordinator of Online Learning, Nashville State Technical Community College, 120 White Bridge Road, Nashville, TN 37209. Telephone: 615-353-3461. Fax: 615-353-3774. E-mail: doug.jameson@nscc.edu.

DEGREES AND AWARDS

AA General Studies; University Parallel

AAS Business Management; Computer Accounting; General Technology; General degree; Office Administration

AS University Parallel

Technical Certificate Accounting Technology; Administrative Assistant; Early Childhood Education

COURSE SUBJECT AREAS OFFERED OUTSIDE OF DEGREE PROGRAMS

Undergraduate—accounting and computer science; allied health and medical assisting services; biology; botany/plant biology; business, management, and marketing related; computer programming; education (specific subject areas); entrepreneurial and small business operations; homeland security; liberal arts and sciences, general studies and humanities; marketing; mathematics; philosophy; psychology related; social work; sociology; special education.

Non-credit—allied health and medical assisting services; business, management, and marketing related; business operations support and assistant services; computer and information sciences; computer systems networking and telecommunications; criminal justice and corrections; education (specific subject areas); health services/allied health/health sciences; liberal arts and sciences, general studies and humanities; marketing; plant sciences; social work.

NASSAU COMMUNITY COLLEGE
Garden City, New York
Office of Distance Education
http://www.ncc.edu

Nassau Community College was founded in 1959. It is accredited by Middle States Association of Colleges and Schools. It first offered distance learning courses in 1991. In fall 2010, there were 4,000 students enrolled in distance learning courses. Institutionally administered financial aid is available to distance learners.

Services Distance learners have accessibility to academic advising, bookstore, campus computer network, e-mail services, library services.

Contact Prof. Arthur L. Friedman, EdD, Coordinator, Distance Education, Nassau Community College, One Education Drive, Garden City, NY 11530-6793. Telephone: 516-572-7883. Fax: 516-572-0690. E-mail: arthur.friedman@ncc.edu.

DEGREES AND AWARDS

Programs offered do not lead to a degree or other formal award.

COURSE SUBJECT AREAS OFFERED OUTSIDE OF DEGREE PROGRAMS

Undergraduate—accounting and related services; anthropology; apparel and textiles; astronomy and astrophysics; atmospheric sciences and meteorology; behavioral sciences; biology; business administration, management and operations; business/commerce; computer and information sciences; economics; English language and literature related; entrepreneurial and small business operations; foods, nutrition, and related services; geological and earth sciences/geosciences; health and physical education/fitness; history; languages (Romance languages); legal studies (non-professional general, undergraduate); marketing; mathematics; mathematics and statistics related; music; nutrition sciences; physical sciences related; psychology; psychology related; sociology; statistics.

Non-credit—English; mathematics.

NATIONAL-LOUIS UNIVERSITY
Chicago, Illinois
http://www.nl.edu/

National-Louis University was founded in 1886. It is accredited by North Central Association of Colleges and Schools. It first offered distance learning courses in 1998. In fall 2010, there were 964 students enrolled in distance learning courses. Institutionally administered financial aid is available to distance learners.

Services Distance learners have accessibility to academic advising, bookstore, campus computer network, e-mail services, library services, tutoring.

Contact Mr. Stephen Neer, Director, Academic Advising, National-Louis University, 122 South Michigan Avenue, Chicago, IL 60603. Telephone: 312-261-3031. Fax: 312-261-3031. E-mail: stephen.neer@nl.edu.

DEGREES AND AWARDS

BS Healthcare Leadership; Management Information Systems; Management

MEd Adult Education; Early Childhood Administration; Interdisciplinary Studies in Curriculum and Instruction; Technology in Education
MS Management

NATIONAL UNIVERSITY
La Jolla, California
NU Online
http://www.nu.edu

National University was founded in 1971. It is accredited by Western Association of Schools and Colleges. It first offered distance learning courses in 1994. In fall 2010, there were 19,069 students enrolled in distance learning courses. Institutionally administered financial aid is available to distance learners.

Services Distance learners have accessibility to academic advising, bookstore, campus computer network, career placement assistance, e-mail services, library services, tutoring.

Contact Mr. James Wilson, Associate Regional Dean, Online, National University, 3570 Aero Court, Room #207, San Diego, CA 92123. Telephone: 866-682-2237 Ext. 3531. Fax: 858-309-3540. E-mail: jwilson@nu.edu.

DEGREES AND AWARDS

AA General Studies; Health Care Administration
BA Arabic Studies; Comparative Literature; Early Childhood Development; English–Single Subject Preparation in English; English; Global Studies; History; Management; Marketing; Psychology; Sociology
BBA Business Administration
BS Accountancy; Allied Health; Computer Science; Construction Engineering; Criminal Justice Administration; Financial Management; Information Systems; Information Technology Management; Nursing; Organizational Behavior; Software Engineering
Certificate Early Childhood Special Education
Certification Administrative Services certificate; Education–Level I Education Specialist Credential–Mild/Mod; Education–TED Multiple or Single Subject Teaching Credential
EMBA Executive Master of Business Administration (Spanish version)
Graduate Certificate Supply Chain Management
MA English; Human Behavior; Human Resource Management and Organizational Development; Management
MAT Teaching
MBA Business Administration; Business Administration
MBA/MHA Health Care Administration
MEd Cross-Cultural Teaching
MFA Creative Writing; Digital Cinema
MPA Public Administration
MS Computer Science; Educational Administration and Administrative Services; Educational Technology; Educational and Instructional Technology; Electronic Business; Engineering Management; Forensic Sciences–Master of Forensic Sciences; Homeland Security and Safety Engineering; Information Systems; Organizational Leadership; Special Education and Level I Specialist Credential Mild/Moderate; Technology Management

COURSE SUBJECT AREAS OFFERED OUTSIDE OF DEGREE PROGRAMS

Undergraduate—accounting and related services; allied health and medical assisting services; biological and physical sciences; building/construction finishing, management, and inspection; business administration, management and operations; business/commerce; communications technology; computer software and media applications; construction engineering technologies; criminal justice and corrections; education; English; history; information science/studies; international/global studies; management sciences and quantitative methods; psychology; public administration.

Graduate—accounting and related services; business administration, management and operations; business/commerce; computer and information sciences; computer programming; computer science; computer software and media applications; computer systems analysis; criminology; education; educational administration and supervision; educational/instructional media design; education (specific subject areas); human resources management; public administration; special education.

NAUGATUCK VALLEY COMMUNITY COLLEGE
Waterbury, Connecticut
http://www.nvcc.commnet.edu

Naugatuck Valley Community College was founded in 1992. It is accredited by New England Association of Schools and Colleges. It first offered distance learning courses in 1998. In fall 2010, there were 1,392 students enrolled in distance learning courses. Institutionally administered financial aid is available to distance learners.

Services Distance learners have accessibility to academic advising, bookstore, campus computer network, career placement assistance, e-mail services, library services, tutoring.

Contact Ms. Stacey L. Williams, Director of Distance Learning, Naugatuck Valley Community College, 750 Chase Parkway, Waterbury, CT 06708. Telephone: 203-575-8182. E-mail: swilliams@nvcc.commnet.edu.

DEGREES AND AWARDS

Programs offered do not lead to a degree or other formal award.

COURSE SUBJECT AREAS OFFERED OUTSIDE OF DEGREE PROGRAMS

Undergraduate—accounting and computer science; accounting and related services; aerospace, aeronautical and astronautical engineering; applied mathematics; astronomy and astrophysics; audiovisual communications technologies; behavioral sciences; biology; business administration, management and operations; business, management, and marketing related; business/managerial economics; business operations support and assistant services; chemistry; communication and journalism related; communication and media; computer and information sciences; computer science; computer software and media applications; computer systems networking and telecommunications; criminal justice and corrections; culinary arts and related services; data entry/microcomputer applications; economics; engineering technology; English; English language and literature related; fine and studio arts; health professions related; hospitality administration; human development, family studies, and related services; insurance; legal research and advanced professional studies; legal studies (non-professional general, undergraduate); liberal arts and sciences, general studies and humanities; mathematics; music; nutrition sciences; pharmacology and toxicology; philosophy; psychology; real estate; sales, merchandising and related marketing operations (specialized); social work; sociology; statistics; vehicle maintenance and repair technologies; visual and performing arts related.

Non-credit—accounting and related services; crafts, folk art and artisanry; dance; data entry/microcomputer applications; data processing; education; health and physical education/fitness; health/medical preparatory programs; real estate.

NAZARENE BIBLE COLLEGE
Colorado Springs, Colorado
http://online.nbc.edu

Nazarene Bible College was founded in 1967. It is accredited by Association for Biblical Higher Education. It first offered distance learning courses in 1998. In fall 2010, there were 900 students enrolled in distance learning courses. Institutionally administered financial aid is available to distance learners.

Services Distance learners have accessibility to academic advising, bookstore, career placement assistance, e-mail services, library services, tutoring.

Contact Scott E. McConnaughey, Online Team Manager, Nazarene Bible College, 1111 Academy Park Loop, Colorado Springs, CO 80910. Telephone: 719-884-5035. Fax: 719-884-5039. E-mail: semcconnaughey@nbc.edu.

DEGREES AND AWARDS

Programs offered do not lead to a degree or other formal award.

NEBRASKA CHRISTIAN COLLEGE
Papillion, Nebraska
http://www.nechristian.edu

Nebraska Christian College was founded in 1944. It is accredited by Association for Biblical Higher Education. It first offered distance learning courses in 2000. In fall 2010, there were 15 students enrolled in distance learning courses. Institutionally administered financial aid is available to distance learners.

Services Distance learners have accessibility to academic advising, bookstore, campus computer network, career placement assistance, e-mail services.

Contact Dr. Mark S. Krause, Academic Dean, Nebraska Christian College, 12550 South 114th Street, Papillion, NE 68046. Telephone: 402-935-9400. Fax: 402-935-9500. E-mail: mkrause@nechristian.edu.

DEGREES AND AWARDS
Programs offered do not lead to a degree or other formal award.

COURSE SUBJECT AREAS OFFERED OUTSIDE OF DEGREE PROGRAMS
Undergraduate—religious studies; theological and ministerial studies; theology and religious vocations related.

NEW ENGLAND COLLEGE OF BUSINESS AND FINANCE
Boston, Massachusetts
http://www.necb.edu/

New England College of Business and Finance was founded in 1909. It is accredited by New England Association of Schools and Colleges. It first offered distance learning courses in 2002. In fall 2010, there were 1,000 students enrolled in distance learning courses. Institutionally administered financial aid is available to distance learners.

Services Distance learners have accessibility to academic advising, bookstore, e-mail services, library services, tutoring.

Contact Eric Ledlum, Enrollment Advisor, New England College of Business and Finance, 10 High Street, Suite 204, Boston, MA 02110. Telephone: 800-997-1673 Fax: 617-951-2533. E-mail: eric.ledlum@necb.edu.

DEGREES AND AWARDS
AS Business Administration
CCCPE Accounting and Finance; Banking Studies; Branch Management; Commercial Lending; Financial Services Studies; Forensic Accounting; Mutual Funds and Investments

COURSE SUBJECT AREAS OFFERED OUTSIDE OF DEGREE PROGRAMS
Undergraduate—accounting and related services; business administration, management and operations; business, management, and marketing related; business operations support and assistant services; computer and information sciences; economics; English; finance and financial management services; history; insurance; mathematics and statistics related; statistics.

Non-credit—accounting and related services; business administration, management and operations; business/commerce; business, management, and marketing related; business/managerial economics; business operations support and assistant services; finance and financial management services.

NEW ENGLAND INSTITUTE OF TECHNOLOGY
Warwick, Rhode Island
http://blackboard.neit.edu

New England Institute of Technology was founded in 1940. It is accredited by New England Association of Schools and Colleges. It first offered distance learning courses in 1996. In fall 2010, there were 110 students enrolled in distance learning courses. Institutionally administered financial aid is available to distance learners.

Services Distance learners have accessibility to academic advising, bookstore, campus computer network, career placement assistance, e-mail services, library services, tutoring.

Contact Mr. Michael Caruso, Admissions Officer, New England Institute of Technology, 2500 Post Road, Warwick, RI 02886. Telephone: 401-739-5000 Ext. 3411. E-mail: mcaruso@neit.edu.

DEGREES AND AWARDS
AS Information Technology

COURSE SUBJECT AREAS OFFERED OUTSIDE OF DEGREE PROGRAMS
Undergraduate—communications technology; computer and information sciences; engineering technology; English language and literature related; mathematics; physics; physiology, pathology and related sciences; psychology; sociology; statistics.

NEW JERSEY CITY UNIVERSITY
Jersey City, New Jersey
Continuing Education
http://newlearning.njcu.edu

New Jersey City University was founded in 1927. It is accredited by Middle States Association of Colleges and Schools. It first offered distance learning courses in 1997. In fall 2010, there were 2,159 students enrolled in distance learning courses. Institutionally administered financial aid is available to distance learners.

Services Distance learners have accessibility to bookstore, e-mail services, library services.

Contact Marie A. Fosello, Director of Online Learning, New Jersey City University, 2039 Kennedy Boulevard, Jersey City, NJ 07305-1597. Telephone: 201-200-3449. Fax: 201-200-2188. E-mail: conted@njcu.edu.

DEGREES AND AWARDS
MA Educational Technology
MS Accounting

COURSE SUBJECT AREAS OFFERED OUTSIDE OF DEGREE PROGRAMS
Undergraduate—arts, entertainment, and media management; biology; business administration, management and operations; computer science; criminal justice and corrections; economics; education; English; fire protection; geological and earth sciences/geosciences; health services/allied health/health sciences; history; mathematics; physics; political science and government; psychology; security policy and strategy; sociology; special education.

Graduate—business administration, management and operations; education; educational administration and supervision; health services/allied health/health sciences; mathematics; security policy and strategy; special education.

NEWMAN THEOLOGICAL COLLEGE
Edmonton, Alberta, Canada
http://www.newman.edu

Newman Theological College was founded in 1969. It is provincially chartered. It first offered distance learning courses in 1987. In fall 2010, there were 22 students enrolled in distance learning courses. Institutionally administered financial aid is available to distance learners.

Services Distance learners have accessibility to academic advising, bookstore, campus computer network, e-mail services, library services, tutoring.

Contact Maria Saulnier, Registrar, Newman Theological College, 10012 84 Street NW, Edmonton, AB T6A 0B2, Canada. Telephone: 780-392-2450 Ext. 5227. Fax: 780-462-4013. E-mail: registrar@newman.edu.

DEGREES AND AWARDS
Certificate Theological Studies
Advanced Graduate Diploma Religious Education

COURSE SUBJECT AREAS OFFERED OUTSIDE OF DEGREE PROGRAMS

Undergraduate—theological and ministerial studies.
Graduate—religious education.
Non-credit—theological and ministerial studies.

NEW MEXICO HIGHLANDS UNIVERSITY
Las Vegas, New Mexico
http://www.nmhu.edu/

New Mexico Highlands University was founded in 1893. It is accredited by North Central Association of Colleges and Schools. It first offered distance learning courses in 1996. In fall 2010, there were 600 students enrolled in distance learning courses. Institutionally administered financial aid is available to distance learners.

Services Distance learners have accessibility to academic advising, bookstore, campus computer network, career placement assistance, e-mail services, library services, tutoring.

Contact Miss Evonne Roybal-Tafoya, Director of Educational Outreach Services, New Mexico Highlands University, Educational Outreach Services, Box 9000, Las Vegas, NM 87701. Telephone: 505-454-3271. Fax: 505-454-3066. E-mail: roybal_ej@nmhu.edu.

DEGREES AND AWARDS

BSN Nursing, BSN
MA Human Performance and Sport Accelerated Masters Program

COURSE SUBJECT AREAS OFFERED OUTSIDE OF DEGREE PROGRAMS

Undergraduate—accounting and related services; bilingual, multilingual, and multicultural education; business administration, management and operations; business/commerce; business, management, and marketing related; business/managerial economics; computer science; criminology; curriculum and instruction; education; educational administration and supervision; education related; management information systems; management sciences and quantitative methods; social work; special education.

Graduate—accounting and related services; bilingual, multilingual, and multicultural education; business administration, management and operations; business/commerce; business, management, and marketing related; business/managerial economics; curriculum and instruction; education; educational administration and supervision; education related; education (specific subject areas); English or French as a second or foreign language (teaching); management information systems; special education.

NEW MEXICO JUNIOR COLLEGE
Hobbs, New Mexico
http://www.nmjc.edu

New Mexico Junior College was founded in 1965. It is accredited by North Central Association of Colleges and Schools. It first offered distance learning courses in 2001. In fall 2010, there were 1,300 students enrolled in distance learning courses. Institutionally administered financial aid is available to distance learners.

Services Distance learners have accessibility to academic advising, bookstore, campus computer network, career placement assistance, e-mail services, library services, tutoring.

Contact Mr. Jeff McCool, Dean of Training and Outreach, New Mexico Junior College, 5317 Lovington Highway, Hobbs, NM 88240. Telephone: 575-492-4711. Fax: 575-492-4727. E-mail: jmccool@nmjc.edu.

DEGREES AND AWARDS

AA Business; Criminal Justice; Education, Early Childhood
AAS Energy Technology

COURSE SUBJECT AREAS OFFERED OUTSIDE OF DEGREE PROGRAMS

Undergraduate—accounting and computer science; allied health and medical assisting services; biology; business administration, management and operations; communication and journalism related; communication and media; computer software and media applications; criminal justice and corrections; design and applied arts; economics; education related; geological and earth sciences/geosciences; history; mathematics; mathematics and statistics related; nuclear and industrial radiologic technologies; psychology; social sciences; sociology.

Non-credit—building/construction finishing, management, and inspection; business/corporate communications; business, management, and marketing related; dance; entrepreneurial and small business operations; languages (foreign languages related).

NEW MEXICO STATE UNIVERSITY
Las Cruces, New Mexico
Office of Distance Education and Weekend College
http://distance.nmsu.edu

New Mexico State University was founded in 1888. It is accredited by North Central Association of Colleges and Schools. It first offered distance learning courses in 1989. In fall 2010, there were 9,500 students enrolled in distance learning courses. Institutionally administered financial aid is available to distance learners.

Services Distance learners have accessibility to academic advising, bookstore, campus computer network, career placement assistance, e-mail services, library services, tutoring.

Contact Jeanette Jones, Distance Education Program Facilitator, New Mexico State University, College of Extended Learning, Distance Education, PO Box 30001, MSC 3CEL, Las Cruces, NM 88003-8001. Telephone: 575-646-4692. Fax: 575-646-2044. E-mail: distance@nmsu.edu.

DEGREES AND AWARDS

BA Sociology
BBA General Business; Marketing
BCJ Criminal Justice
BS Elementary Education; Hotel, Restaurant, and Tourism Management; Information and Communication Technology
BSN Nursing
Certificate Online Teaching and Learning; Systems Engineering
Endorsement Information Technology Coordinator; Reading; School Library Media Specialist
License Educational Administrative Licensure; Elementary Licensure (post-BA); Special Education Alternative licensure
MA Agricultural and Extension Educator; Community College and University Administration emphasis; Counseling and Guidance (Guidance and Human Relations specialization); Education Curriculum and Instruction Early Childhood Education; Sociology; Spanish
MAE Curriculum and Instruction emphasis; Learning Technologies emphasis; Pk-12 Educational Administration
MAT Online Teaching emphasis; Teaching of Science
MCJ Criminal Justice
MM Music Education
MS Industrial Engineering
MSW Social Work
EdD Educational Administration (Educational Leadership)
PhD Curriculum and Instruction, Learning Technologies emphasis; Nursing

COURSE SUBJECT AREAS OFFERED OUTSIDE OF DEGREE PROGRAMS

Undergraduate—accounting and related services; anthropology; business administration, management and operations; business/commerce; business, management, and marketing related; computer/information technology administration and management; computer science; criminal justice and corrections; curriculum and instruction; educational assessment, evaluation, and research; educational/instructional media design; foods, nutrition, and related services; history; human services; industrial engineering; international business; languages (Romance languages); liberal arts and sciences, general studies and humanities; marketing; mathematics; mathematics and statistics related; mental and social health services and allied professions; music; psychology; public health; sociology; wildlife and wildlands science and management.

Graduate—criminal justice and corrections; education related; industrial engineering; manufacturing engineering; mechanical engineering; nutrition sciences; public health; sociology; special education.

NEW MEXICO STATE UNIVERSITY
Las Cruces, New Mexico
Doña Ana Community College
http://Dacc.nmsu.edu

New Mexico State University was founded in 1888. It is accredited by North Central Association of Colleges and Schools. It first offered distance learning courses in 1998. In fall 2010, there were 603 students enrolled in distance learning courses. Institutionally administered financial aid is available to distance learners.

Services Distance learners have accessibility to academic advising, bookstore, campus computer network, career placement assistance, e-mail services.

Contact Dr. Margaret Lovelace, Special Assistant to the President, New Mexico State University, 3400 South Espina, PO Box 30001, MSC 3DA, Las Cruces, NM 88003-8001. Telephone: 575-527-7520. Fax: 575-527-7764. E-mail: mlovelac@nmsu.edu.

DEGREES AND AWARDS
AAS Library Science

COURSE SUBJECT AREAS OFFERED OUTSIDE OF DEGREE PROGRAMS
Undergraduate—allied health and medical assisting services; anthropology; biology; business administration, management and operations; business, management, and marketing related; computer and information sciences; economics; education; film/video and photographic arts; fire protection; health professions related; languages (Romance languages); library science and administration; mathematics; music; nutrition sciences; philosophy; sociology; statistics.

NEW MEXICO STATE UNIVERSITY–ALAMOGORDO
Alamogordo, New Mexico
http://nmsua.edu

New Mexico State University–Alamogordo was founded in 1958. It is accredited by North Central Association of Colleges and Schools. It first offered distance learning courses in 1997. In fall 2010, there were 1,136 students enrolled in distance learning courses. Institutionally administered financial aid is available to distance learners.

Services Distance learners have accessibility to academic advising, bookstore, campus computer network, e-mail services, library services.

Contact Dr. Debra Teachman, Vice President of Academic Affairs, New Mexico State University–Alamogordo, Academic Office, 2400 North Scenic Drive, Alamogordo, NM 88310. Telephone: 575-439-3621. Fax: 575-439-3622. E-mail: teachman@nmsua.nmsu.edu.

DEGREES AND AWARDS
Programs offered do not lead to a degree or other formal award.

COURSE SUBJECT AREAS OFFERED OUTSIDE OF DEGREE PROGRAMS
Undergraduate—applied mathematics; biomedical/medical engineering; chemistry; computer and information sciences; economics; legal studies (non-professional general, undergraduate); liberal arts and sciences, general studies and humanities; philosophy; psychology.

NEW MEXICO STATE UNIVERSITY–CARLSBAD
Carlsbad, New Mexico
http://www.cavern.nmsu.edu/

New Mexico State University–Carlsbad was founded in 1950. It is accredited by North Central Association of Colleges and Schools. It first offered distance learning courses in 2000. In fall 2010, there were 900 students enrolled in distance learning courses. Institutionally administered financial aid is available to distance learners.

Services Distance learners have accessibility to bookstore, campus computer network, e-mail services, library services.

Contact Paula Wallace, Educational Technology Specialist, New Mexico State University–Carlsbad, Office 2G, Learning Technology Center, 1500 University Drive, Carlsbad, NM 88220. Telephone: 575-234-9261. Fax: 575-234-9262. E-mail: paulwall@nmsu.edu.

DEGREES AND AWARDS
Programs offered do not lead to a degree or other formal award.

COURSE SUBJECT AREAS OFFERED OUTSIDE OF DEGREE PROGRAMS
Undergraduate—allied health and medical assisting services; anthropology; applied mathematics; biological and physical sciences; biology; building/construction finishing, management, and inspection; business administration, management and operations; business/commerce; business, management, and marketing related; cell biology and anatomical sciences; computer and information sciences; computer software and media applications; economics; education; English; finance and financial management services; geological and earth sciences/geosciences; geological/geophysical engineering; history; human biology; human development, family studies, and related services; human services; languages (foreign languages related); marketing; mathematics; mental and social health services and allied professions; physical sciences; physics; political science and government; psychology; public health; social sciences; social work; statistics.

NEW MEXICO STATE UNIVERSITY–GRANTS
Grants, New Mexico
http://grants.nmsu.edu

New Mexico State University–Grants was founded in 1968. It is accredited by North Central Association of Colleges and Schools. It first offered distance learning courses in 2000. In fall 2010, there were 250 students enrolled in distance learning courses. Institutionally administered financial aid is available to distance learners.

Services Distance learners have accessibility to academic advising, bookstore, campus computer network, e-mail services, library services.

Contact Dr. Harry Sheski, Vice President for Academic Affairs, New Mexico State University–Grants, 1500 North 3rd Street, Grants, NM 87020. Telephone: 505-287-7981. Fax: 505-287-2329. E-mail: hsheski@nmsu.edu.

DEGREES AND AWARDS
Programs offered do not lead to a degree or other formal award.

COURSE SUBJECT AREAS OFFERED OUTSIDE OF DEGREE PROGRAMS
Undergraduate—accounting and related services; biology; business administration, management and operations; computer science; criminal justice and corrections; education; geography and cartography; health professions related; history; mathematics; political science and government; social work; sociology.

NEW ORLEANS BAPTIST THEOLOGICAL SEMINARY
New Orleans, Louisiana
NOBTS Virtual Campus/NOBTS Extension Center System
http://www.nobts.edu

New Orleans Baptist Theological Seminary was founded in 1917. It is accredited by Southern Association of Colleges and Schools. It first offered distance learning courses in 2000. In fall 2010, there were 225 students enrolled in distance learning courses. Institutionally administered financial aid is available to distance learners.

Services Distance learners have accessibility to academic advising, bookstore, campus computer network, library services.

Contact Dr. Craig Price, Associate Dean of Online Learning, New Orleans Baptist Theological Seminary, 3939 Gentilly Boulevard, New Orleans, LA 70126. Telephone: 504-282-4455. E-mail: cprice@nobts.edu.

DEGREES AND AWARDS
Programs offered do not lead to a degree or other formal award.

COURSE SUBJECT AREAS OFFERED OUTSIDE OF DEGREE PROGRAMS
Undergraduate—biblical studies; languages (classics and classical); psychology; religious education; religious/sacred music; religious studies.

Graduate—biblical studies; psychology; religious education; religious/sacred music; religious studies.
Non-credit—biblical studies; religious education; religious/sacred music; religious studies.

NEW RIVER COMMUNITY COLLEGE
Dublin, Virginia
Distance Education and Off-Campus Services
http://de.nr.edu

New River Community College was founded in 1969. It is accredited by Southern Association of Colleges and Schools. It first offered distance learning courses in 1980. In fall 2010, there were 1,200 students enrolled in distance learning courses. Institutionally administered financial aid is available to distance learners.
Services Distance learners have accessibility to academic advising, bookstore, e-mail services, library services.
Contact Diane Viers, Media Specialist, New River Community College, PO Box 1127, 5251 College Drive, Dublin, VA 24084. Telephone: 540-674-3600 Ext. 4341. Fax: 540-674-3626. E-mail: dviers@nr.edu.

DEGREES AND AWARDS
AAS Administrative Support Technology; Education; General Studies

COURSE SUBJECT AREAS OFFERED OUTSIDE OF DEGREE PROGRAMS
Undergraduate—accounting and related services; American Sign Language (ASL); biological and physical sciences; biology; business, management, and marketing related; chemistry; computer programming; computer science; criminal justice and corrections; economics; English; entrepreneurial and small business operations; finance and financial management services; history; human services; legal studies (nonprofessional general, undergraduate); marketing; mathematics; music; philosophy; psychology; sociology; statistics.

NEW YORK INSTITUTE OF TECHNOLOGY
Old Westbury, New York
On-Line Campus
http://www.nyit.edu/academics/nyit_online

New York Institute of Technology was founded in 1955. It is accredited by Middle States Association of Colleges and Schools. It first offered distance learning courses in 1984. In fall 2010, there were 1,522 students enrolled in distance learning courses. Institutionally administered financial aid is available to distance learners.
Services Distance learners have accessibility to campus computer network, career placement assistance, e-mail services, library services.
Contact Ms. Kathleen Lyons, Associate Director of Admissions, New York Institute of Technology, 1855 Broadway, New York, NY 10023. Telephone: 212-261-1528. E-mail: klyons@nyit.edu.

DEGREES AND AWARDS
BA Interdisciplinary Studies
BPS Hospitality Management; Interdisciplinary Studies
BS Interdisciplinary Studies
MS Adolescence Education Specialist in Science 7-12; Adolescence Education, Specialist in Mathematics 7-12; Childhood Education; Clinical Nutrition; Energy Management; Instructional Technology

NEW YORK MEDICAL COLLEGE
Valhalla, New York
School of Health Sciences and Practice
http://www.nymc.edu/shsp

New York Medical College was founded in 1860. It is accredited by Middle States Association of Colleges and Schools. It first offered distance learning courses in 2006. In fall 2010, there were 150 students enrolled in distance learning courses. Institutionally administered financial aid is available to distance learners.
Services Distance learners have accessibility to academic advising, bookstore, campus computer network, career placement assistance, e-mail services, library services, tutoring.
Contact Ms. Pamela Suett, Director of Recruitment, New York Medical College, Institute of Public Health, School of Health Sciences and Practice Building, Valhalla, NY 10595. Telephone: 914-594-4759. Fax: 914-594-4292. E-mail: shsp_online@nymc.edu.

DEGREES AND AWARDS
Graduate Certificate Emergency Preparedness; Global Health; Industrial Hygiene
MPH Environmental Health Science; Health Policy and Management

COURSE SUBJECT AREAS OFFERED OUTSIDE OF DEGREE PROGRAMS
Graduate—environmental/environmental health engineering; health professions related; public health.

NICHOLS COLLEGE
Dudley, Massachusetts
http://www.nichols.edu/eveningonline/online/index.html

Nichols College was founded in 1815. It is accredited by New England Association of Schools and Colleges. It first offered distance learning courses in 1999. In fall 2010, there were 520 students enrolled in distance learning courses. Institutionally administered financial aid is available to distance learners.
Services Distance learners have accessibility to academic advising, bookstore, career placement assistance, e-mail services, library services, tutoring.
Contact Nora Luquer, Assistant Director of Enrollment Services, Nichols College, 124 Center Road, Dudley, MA 01571. Telephone: 508-213-2059. E-mail: nora.luquer@nichols.edu.

DEGREES AND AWARDS
ABA General Business
BSBA Criminal Justice Management; Finance; General Business; Marketing
MBA Business Administration–Traditional MBA; Security Management; Sport Management
MOL Organizational Leadership

COURSE SUBJECT AREAS OFFERED OUTSIDE OF DEGREE PROGRAMS
Undergraduate—accounting and related services; business administration, management and operations; business, management, and marketing related; business/managerial economics; computer and information sciences; criminal justice and corrections; economics; English; finance and financial management services; history; human resources management; marketing; mathematics; mathematics and statistics related; music; physical sciences; political science and government; psychology; psychology related; religious studies; sociology; statistics.
Graduate—accounting and computer science; business administration, management and operations; business/commerce; business/corporate communications; business, management, and marketing related; business/managerial economics; business operations support and assistant services; criminal justice and corrections; economics; human resources management; information science/studies; international business; management sciences and quantitative methods; marketing; mathematics and statistics related; statistics.

NICOLET AREA TECHNICAL COLLEGE
Rhinelander, Wisconsin
http://www.nicoletcollege.edu

Nicolet Area Technical College was founded in 1968. It is accredited by North Central Association of Colleges and Schools. It first offered distance learning courses in 1997. In fall 2010, there were 960 students enrolled in distance learning courses. Institutionally administered financial aid is available to distance learners.
Services Distance learners have accessibility to academic advising, bookstore, campus computer network, career placement assistance, e-mail services, library services.

Contact Susan A. Kordula, Director of Admissions, Nicolet Area Technical College, PO Box 518, Rhinelander, WI 54501. Telephone: 715-365-4464. E-mail: skordula@nicoletcollege.edu.

DEGREES AND AWARDS

AAS Business Management

COURSE SUBJECT AREAS OFFERED OUTSIDE OF DEGREE PROGRAMS

Undergraduate—accounting and related services; allied health and medical assisting services; biological and biomedical sciences related; business administration, management and operations; business/commerce; communication and media; computer software and media applications; economics; English language and literature related; ethnic, cultural minority, gender, and group studies; geography and cartography; geological and earth sciences/geosciences; health/medical preparatory programs; history; human development, family studies, and related services; liberal arts and sciences, general studies and humanities; mathematics; political science and government; psychology; sales, merchandising and related marketing operations (specialized); social sciences; sociology.

NIPISSING UNIVERSITY
North Bay, Ontario, Canada
Centre for Continuing Education
http://www.nipissingu.ca/cftl

Nipissing University was founded in 1992. It is provincially chartered. It first offered distance learning courses in 1997. In fall 2010, there were 450 students enrolled in distance learning courses. Institutionally administered financial aid is available to distance learners.

Services Distance learners have accessibility to academic advising, bookstore, e-mail services, library services, tutoring.

Contact Flexible Learning Clerk, Nipissing University, 100 College Drive, Box 5002, North Bay, ON P1B 8L7, Canada. Telephone: 705-474-3450 Ext. 4343. Fax: 705-475-0264. E-mail: cftl@nipissingu.ca.

DEGREES AND AWARDS

BComm Commerce

COURSE SUBJECT AREAS OFFERED OUTSIDE OF DEGREE PROGRAMS

Undergraduate—accounting and related services; business administration, management and operations; business/commerce; business, management, and marketing related; economics; English; finance and financial management services; history; human resources management; international business; management sciences and quantitative methods; marketing; mathematics; philosophy; physics.

NORTH ARKANSAS COLLEGE
Harrison, Arkansas
Articulated Programs and Distance Learning
http://www.northark.edu/

North Arkansas College was founded in 1974. It is accredited by North Central Association of Colleges and Schools. It first offered distance learning courses in 1988. In fall 2010, there were 450 students enrolled in distance learning courses. Institutionally administered financial aid is available to distance learners.

Services Distance learners have accessibility to bookstore, campus computer network, e-mail services, library services, tutoring.

Contact Ms. Valerie C. Martin, Director of Online Learning, North Arkansas College, 1515 Pioneer Drive, Harrison, AR 72601. Telephone: 870-391-3263. Fax: 870-391-3250. E-mail: vmartin@northark.edu.

DEGREES AND AWARDS

Programs offered do not lead to a degree or other formal award.

COURSE SUBJECT AREAS OFFERED OUTSIDE OF DEGREE PROGRAMS

Undergraduate—accounting and related services; allied health and medical assisting services; anthropology; biological and physical sciences; business/corporate communications; computer/information technology administration and management; computer programming; economics; education related; fine and studio arts; health and physical education/fitness; history; human resources management; management information systems; mathematics; philosophy; psychology; social sciences related; statistics.

NORTH CAROLINA CENTRAL UNIVERSITY
Durham, North Carolina
http://www.nccu.edu/

North Carolina Central University was founded in 1910. It is accredited by Southern Association of Colleges and Schools. It first offered distance learning courses in 1997. In fall 2010, there were 2,461 students enrolled in distance learning courses. Institutionally administered financial aid is available to distance learners.

Services Distance learners have accessibility to academic advising, bookstore, campus computer network, e-mail services, library services, tutoring.

Contact Paulette Morrison-Danner, Faculty and Student Support Coordinator, North Carolina Central University, Division of Extended Studies, 2047 H.M. Michaux Education, Jr. Building, Durham, NC 27707. Telephone: 919-530-7442. Fax: 919-530-5220. E-mail: pscotton@wpo.nccu.edu.

DEGREES AND AWARDS

BBA Hospitality and Tourism Administration
BS Birth to Kindergarten Education (B-K); Criminal Justice; Nursing–RN to BSN
Certificate Recreation Management
MA Online Instructional Design
MEd Communications Disorders
MLS Library Science
MS Information Science

COURSE SUBJECT AREAS OFFERED OUTSIDE OF DEGREE PROGRAMS

Undergraduate—apparel and textiles; biological and physical sciences; business/commerce; communication and journalism related; communication and media; criminal justice and corrections; education; educational administration and supervision; educational assessment, evaluation, and research; English; family and consumer sciences/human sciences; management information systems.

Graduate—communication disorders sciences and services; educational/instructional media design; library science and administration; parks, recreation and leisure facilities management; sales, merchandising and related marketing operations (specialized); special education.

Non-credit—allied health diagnostic, intervention, and treatment professions; linguistic, comparative, and related language studies; mathematics.

NORTH CAROLINA STATE UNIVERSITY
Raleigh, North Carolina
Distance Education
http://distance.ncsu.edu

North Carolina State University was founded in 1887. It is accredited by Southern Association of Colleges and Schools. It first offered distance learning courses in 1976. In fall 2010, there were 7,774 students enrolled in distance learning courses. Institutionally administered financial aid is available to distance learners.

Services Distance learners have accessibility to academic advising, bookstore, campus computer network, career placement assistance, e-mail services, library services, tutoring.

Contact Melissa M. Williford, Director, Distance Education Administrative Services, North Carolina State University, Campus Box 7113, DELTA, Venture II, Suite 500, Raleigh, NC 27695-7113. Telephone: 919-515-9032. Fax: 919-515-6668. E-mail: melissa_williford@ncsu.edu.

DEGREES AND AWARDS

BA Leadership in the Public Sector

Certificate Agricultural Business Management post-Baccalaureate certificate; Agricultural Business Management; Agronomic Crop Production; Animal Nutrition; Computer Programming; Fabric Manufacturing; Feed Milling; Food Safety Manager's Certificate; General Horticulture; HACCP (Hazard Analysis and Critical Control Points); Plant Pests, Pathogens, and People; Soil Science; Textiles Fundamentals
License Business and Marketing Education Initial Licensure program; Licensure in Education for Agricultural Professionals
Graduate Certificate Biological and Agricultural Engineering; Community College Teaching; E-Learning; Geographic Information Systems; Horticulture Science; Nonwoven Science and Technology; Training and Development
MAT Teaching
MBAE Biological and Agricultural Engineering
MCE Chemical Engineering; Civil Engineering
MCS Computer Science
ME Engineering Online
MEE Environmental Engineering
MEd Curriculum and Instruction, Business and Marketing Education concentration; Instructional Technology; Training and Development
MIE Industrial Engineering
MME Master of Integrated Manufacturing Systems Engineering
MMSE Materials Science and Engineering
MS Animal Science; Computer Networking; Curriculum and Instruction, Business and Marketing Education concentration; Environmental Assessment; Family Life and Youth Development; Forest Biomaterials; Geospatial Information Science and Technology; Horticultural Science; Instructional Technology; Nutrition; Parks, Recreation, Tourism and Sport Management; Textile Chemistry
MSAE Aerospace Engineering
MSE Agricultural Education; Master of Nuclear Engineering
MSEE Electrical Engineering
MSME Mechanical Engineering
MT Textiles Off-campus Programs (TOP)

COURSE SUBJECT AREAS OFFERED OUTSIDE OF DEGREE PROGRAMS

Undergraduate—accounting and related services; agricultural and domestic animal services; agricultural and food products processing; agricultural production; agriculture; animal sciences; anthropology; apparel and textiles; bioethics/medical ethics; biological and physical sciences; biology; botany/plant biology; business administration, management and operations; business/commerce; business, management, and marketing related; chemistry; communication and journalism related; communication and media; computer programming; design and applied arts; economics; education (specific subject areas); English; English language and literature related; English or French as a second or foreign language (teaching); environmental/environmental health engineering; ethnic, cultural minority, gender, and group studies; foods, nutrition, and related services; forestry; genetics; geological and earth sciences/geosciences; health and physical education/fitness; health professions related; history; human resources management; landscape architecture; languages (Germanic); languages (Modern Greek); languages (Romance languages); languages (South Asian); marketing; mathematics; microbiological sciences and immunology; multi/interdisciplinary studies related; music; natural sciences; nutrition sciences; parks, recreation and leisure facilities management; parks, recreation, leisure, and fitness studies related; philosophy; physical sciences; physics; plant sciences; political science and government; psychology; science, technology and society; social sciences; social work; sociology; sociology and anthropology; soil sciences; statistics; textile sciences and engineering; zoology/animal biology.

Graduate—agricultural and food products processing; agriculture; agriculture and agriculture operations related; animal sciences; biological and physical sciences; business administration, management and operations; curriculum and instruction; education; educational administration and supervision; educational/instructional media design; education (specific subject areas); engineering; family and consumer sciences/human sciences; food science and technology; foods, nutrition, and related services; geography and cartography; nutrition sciences; parks, recreation and leisure facilities management; plant sciences; social work; soil sciences; statistics; work and family studies.

NORTH CAROLINA WESLEYAN COLLEGE
Rocky Mount, North Carolina
http://www.ncwc.edu/adult

North Carolina Wesleyan College was founded in 1956. It is accredited by Southern Association of Colleges and Schools. It first offered distance learning courses in 2003. In fall 2010, there were 120 students enrolled in distance learning courses. Institutionally administered financial aid is available to distance learners.
Services Distance learners have accessibility to academic advising, bookstore, campus computer network, career placement assistance, e-mail services, library services, tutoring.
Contact Dr. Evan Duff, Vice President of Adult Education, North Carolina Wesleyan College, 3400 North Wesleyan Drive, Rocky Mount, NC 27804. Telephone: 252-985-5100 Ext. 5263. E-mail: eduff@ncwc.edu.

DEGREES AND AWARDS

BA Criminal Justice; Psychology; Religious Studies
BS Accounting; Business Administration; Computer Information Systems; Elementary Education

NORTH CENTRAL STATE COLLEGE
Mansfield, Ohio
http://www.ncstatecollege.edu/online

North Central State College was founded in 1961. It is accredited by North Central Association of Colleges and Schools. It first offered distance learning courses in 1994. In fall 2010, there were 650 students enrolled in distance learning courses. Institutionally administered financial aid is available to distance learners.
Services Distance learners have accessibility to academic advising, bookstore, campus computer network, career placement assistance, e-mail services, library services, tutoring.
Contact Mike Welker, Interim Director, Distance Learning, North Central State College, Distance Learning Department, 2441 Kenwood Circle, Mansfield, OH 44901. Telephone: 419-755-4706. Fax: 419-755-5674. E-mail: mwelker@ncstatecollege.edu.

DEGREES AND AWARDS

Programs offered do not lead to a degree or other formal award.

COURSE SUBJECT AREAS OFFERED OUTSIDE OF DEGREE PROGRAMS

Undergraduate—accounting and computer science; allied health and medical assisting services; behavioral sciences; biological and physical sciences; business administration, management and operations; business/corporate communications; criminal justice and corrections; international business.
Non-credit—accounting and computer science; accounting and related services; allied health and medical assisting services; alternative and complementary medicine and medical systems; business/commerce; computer and information sciences; computer and information sciences and support services related; computer programming; education related; engineering-related technologies; entrepreneurial and small business operations; family and consumer sciences/human sciences; foods, nutrition, and related services; gerontology; health professions related; languages (Romance languages).

NORTH CENTRAL TEXAS COLLEGE
Gainesville, Texas
http://www.nctcecampus.info

North Central Texas College was founded in 1924. It is accredited by Southern Association of Colleges and Schools. It first offered distance learning courses in 1999. In fall 2010, there were 2,251 students enrolled in distance learning courses. Institutionally administered financial aid is available to distance learners.
Services Distance learners have accessibility to academic advising, bookstore, e-mail services, library services, tutoring.

Contact Debbie J. Huffman, Dean of eLearning, North Central Texas College, 1525 West California Street, Gainesville, TX 76240. Telephone: 940-668-7731 Ext. 4475. Fax: 940-668-6490. E-mail: dhuffman@nctc.edu.

DEGREES AND AWARDS

Programs offered do not lead to a degree or other formal award.

COURSE SUBJECT AREAS OFFERED OUTSIDE OF DEGREE PROGRAMS

Undergraduate—agricultural business and management; biology; business administration, management and operations; business, management, and marketing related; business operations support and assistant services; computer and information sciences; computer/information technology administration and management; computer software and media applications; criminal justice and corrections; criminology; dance; data entry/microcomputer applications; economics; education; English; English language and literature related; fine and studio arts; history; mathematics; music; nutrition sciences; political science and government; practical nursing, vocational nursing and nursing assistants; psychology; registered nursing, nursing administration, nursing research and clinical nursing; social sciences; sociology.

NORTH DAKOTA STATE COLLEGE OF SCIENCE
Wahpeton, North Dakota
http://www.ndscs.edu/

North Dakota State College of Science was founded in 1903. It is accredited by North Central Association of Colleges and Schools. It first offered distance learning courses in 1968. In fall 2010, there were 1,481 students enrolled in distance learning courses. Institutionally administered financial aid is available to distance learners.

Services Distance learners have accessibility to academic advising, bookstore, career placement assistance, e-mail services, library services, tutoring.

Contact Ms. Margaret Wall, Dean of Extended Learning, North Dakota State College of Science, 800 Sixth Street North, Wahpeton, ND 58076-0002. Telephone: 701-671-2430. Fax: 701-671-2146. E-mail: margaret.wall@ndscs.edu.

DEGREES AND AWARDS

AA Liberal Arts and Science/Liberal Studies

AAS Architectural Drafting and Estimating Technology; Business Management, eBusiness emphasis; Business Technology Management; Construction Management Technology; Health Information Technician; Pharmacy Technician

AS Nursing–Bridge to ASN Nursing

Certificate Computer Information Systems–Web Design/Web Developer; HIT–Medical Coding; Medical Transcription

COURSE SUBJECT AREAS OFFERED OUTSIDE OF DEGREE PROGRAMS

Undergraduate—accounting and related services; allied health and medical assisting services; applied mathematics; biology; business administration, management and operations; business, management, and marketing related; chemistry; civil engineering technologies; computer and information sciences; computer and information sciences and support services related; computer/information technology administration and management; computer programming; drafting/design engineering technologies; economics; English; foods, nutrition, and related services; health and medical administrative services; health and physical education/fitness; health professions related; history; marketing; mathematics; microbiological sciences and immunology; psychology; psychology related; social sciences; sociology.

NORTH DAKOTA STATE UNIVERSITY
Fargo, North Dakota
Division of Distance and Continuing Education
http://www.ndsu.edu/dce

North Dakota State University was founded in 1890. It is accredited by North Central Association of Colleges and Schools. It first offered distance learning courses in 1998. Institutionally administered financial aid is available to distance learners.

Services Distance learners have accessibility to academic advising, bookstore, career placement assistance, e-mail services, library services, tutoring.

Contact Connie Jadrny, Marketing, Recruitment, and Public Relations Coordinator, North Dakota State University, Department 2020, PO Box 6050, Fargo, ND 58108-6050. Telephone: 701-231-7015. Fax: 701-231-7016. E-mail: connie.jadrny@ndsu.edu.

DEGREES AND AWARDS

BA Sociology

BS Health Communication; Human Development and Family Science, Child Development option; Human Development and Family Science, Family Science option; Journalism, Broadcasting, and Mass Communication Technologies; Public Relations and Advertising; Sociology

BSN Nursing–LPN to BSN; Nursing–RN to BSN

BUS University Studies

Graduate Certificate Family Financial Planning; Food Protection; Gerontology; Merchandising; Software Engineering; Transportation Leadership; Transportation and Urban Systems

MA Community Development; Mass Communication; Speech Communication

MS Community Development; Construction Management; Family and Consumer Science Education; Health, Nutrition, and Exercise Science, Dietetics option; Human Development and Family Science, Family Financial Planning option; Human Development and Family Science, Gerontology option; Human Development and Family Science, Youth Development option; Mass Communication; Merchandising; Speech Communication; Transportation and Urban Systems

MSE Software Engineering

MTUS Transportation and Urban Systems

COURSE SUBJECT AREAS OFFERED OUTSIDE OF DEGREE PROGRAMS

Undergraduate—accounting and related services; animal sciences; anthropology; apparel and textiles; applied mathematics; arts, entertainment, and media management; biology; botany/plant biology; chemistry; communication and journalism related; communication and media; computer and information sciences; computer programming; computer science; computer software and media applications; computer systems analysis; construction management; criminal justice and corrections; data entry/microcomputer applications; economics; education; education related; English; English language and literature related; ethnic, cultural minority, gender, and group studies; family and consumer economics; family and consumer sciences/human sciences; family and consumer sciences/human sciences related; film/video and photographic arts; food science and technology; foods, nutrition, and related services; genetics; history; homeland security; hospitality administration; human development, family studies, and related services; interdisciplinary studies; journalism; liberal arts and sciences, general studies and humanities; literature; marketing; mathematics; multi/interdisciplinary studies related; music; plant sciences; psychology; psychology related; public relations, advertising, and applied communication related; rural sociology; sales merchandising, and related marketing operations (general); sociology; sociology and anthropology; work and family studies; zoology/animal biology.

Graduate—apparel and textiles; building/construction finishing, management, and inspection; business administration, management and operations; business/corporate communications; business, management, and marketing related; city/urban, community and regional planning; communication and journalism related; communication and media; communications technology; computer engineering; computer programming; computer science; computer software and media applications; computer systems analysis; curriculum and instruction; dietetics and clinical nutrition services; economics; education; educational administration and supervision; educational assessment, evaluation, and research; educational/instructional media design; education related; education (specific levels and methods); education (specific subject areas); family and consumer economics; family and consumer sciences/human sciences; family and consumer sciences/human sciences business services; family and consumer sciences/human sciences related; finance and financial management services; food science and technology; foods, nutrition, and related services; gerontology; health professions related; health services/allied health/health sciences; history; human development, family studies, and related services; journalism; liberal arts and sciences, general studies and humanities; microbiological sciences and immunology; music; natural resources management and policy; nutrition sciences; psychology; public relations, advertising, and applied communication related; rhetoric and composition/writing studies; rural sociology; sales merchandising, and related marketing operations (general); sales, merchandising and related marketing operations (specialized); transportation and materials moving related; work and family studies.

Non-credit—allied health and medical assisting services; business administration, management and operations; business/commerce; business/corporate communications; business, management, and marketing related; business operations support and assistant services; communication and journalism related; communication and media; communications technology; computer and information sciences; computer programming; computer science; computer software and media applications; data entry/microcomputer applications; film/video and photographic arts; finance and financial management services; human development, family studies, and related services; human resources management; legal support services; literature; marketing; sales merchandising, and related marketing operations (general); sales, merchandising and related marketing operations (specialized); telecommunications management.

NORTHEASTERN STATE UNIVERSITY
Tahlequah, Oklahoma
Center for Academic Technology and Distance Learning
http://arapaho.nsuok.edu/~ctl/atc_files

Northeastern State University was founded in 1846. It is accredited by North Central Association of Colleges and Schools. It first offered distance learning courses in 1998. In fall 2010, there were 3,573 students enrolled in distance learning courses. Institutionally administered financial aid is available to distance learners.

Services Distance learners have accessibility to academic advising, bookstore, campus computer network, career placement assistance, e-mail services, library services, tutoring.

Contact Dr. Charles T. Ziehr, Assistant Vice President for Teaching and Learning, Northeastern State University, 600 North Grand Avenue, Administration 122, Tahlequah, OK 74464. Telephone: 918-444-2065. Fax: 918-458-2061. E-mail: ziehr@nsuok.edu.

DEGREES AND AWARDS

BSN Nursing–Nursing for Registered Nurses

COURSE SUBJECT AREAS OFFERED OUTSIDE OF DEGREE PROGRAMS

Undergraduate—accounting and related services; anthropology; biology; business administration, management and operations; computer systems networking and telecommunications; criminal justice and corrections; education; educational administration and supervision; educational assessment, evaluation, and research; educational/instructional media design; education (specific subject areas); English; finance and financial management services; hospitality administration; human resources management; languages (Germanic); legal studies (non-professional general, undergraduate); linguistic, comparative, and related language studies; marketing; sociology; special education.

Graduate—business administration, management and operations; educational administration and supervision; English.

NORTHEASTERN UNIVERSITY
Boston, Massachusetts
Distance Learning Center
http://www.northeastern.edu/online

Northeastern University was founded in 1898. It is accredited by New England Association of Schools and Colleges. It first offered distance learning courses in 1984. In fall 2010, there were 3,049 students enrolled in distance learning courses. Institutionally administered financial aid is available to distance learners.

Services Distance learners have accessibility to academic advising, bookstore, campus computer network, career placement assistance, e-mail services, library services, tutoring.

Contact Denise Weir, Director, NU Online, Northeastern University, 360 Huntington Avenue, 40 BV, Boston, MA 02115. Telephone: 617-373-7563. E-mail: d.weir@neu.edu.

DEGREES AND AWARDS

AS Accounting; Business Administration; Finance; Human Resources Management; Liberal Arts

BS English; Environmental Studies Policy; Finance and Accounting Management; Health Management; History; Human Services; Information Technology; Leadership; Liberal Arts–Business minor; Liberal Studies; Management; Operations Technology; Organizational Communications; Political Science; Psychology; Public Affairs; Sociology; Technical Communications

BSN Nursing

Certificate Accounting; Accounting, Advanced; Paralegal–Credit; Paralegal–noncredit

Graduate Certificate Adult and Organizational Learning; Biopharmaceutical Domestic Regulatory Affairs; Biopharmaceutical International Regulatory Affairs; Construction Management; Distance Learning; Forensic Accounting; Geographic Information Systems; Global Studies and International Affairs; Health Informatics; Health Management; Higher Education Administration; Human Resources Management; Leadership; Medical Devices Regulatory Affairs; Nonprofit Management; Organizational Communications; Project Management; Remote Sensing; TESOL

MEd Higher Education Administration; Learning and Instruction; Special Education specialization

MPA Public Administration

MPS Geographic Information Technology; Informatics

MS Applied Nutrition; Corporate and Organizational Communication; Criminal Justice Leadership; Health Informatics; Human Services; Information Assurance; Leadership; Nonprofit Management; Project Management; Regulatory Affairs for Drugs, Biologics, and Medical Devices; Respiratory Care Leadership; Sports Leadership; Sports Leadership; Technical Communications; Technology Commercialization

DPT Transitional Doctor of Physical Therapy

EdD Education

NORTHERN KENTUCKY UNIVERSITY
Highland Heights, Kentucky
Educational Outreach
http://nkuonline.nku.edu/

Northern Kentucky University was founded in 1968. It is accredited by Southern Association of Colleges and Schools. It first offered distance learning courses in 1983. In fall 2010, there were 2,500 students enrolled in distance learning courses. Institutionally administered financial aid is available to distance learners.

Services Distance learners have accessibility to academic advising, bookstore, campus computer network, career placement assistance, e-mail services, library services, tutoring.

Contact Kristen Lovett, Associate Director of Educational Outreach, Northern Kentucky University, Educational Outreach, CA 270, Nunn Drive, Highland Heights, KY 41099-5700. Telephone: 859-392-2409. Fax: 859-392-2416. E-mail: edoutreach@nku.edu.

DEGREES AND AWARDS

AA Criminal Justice

BA Communication Studies; Criminal Justice; Organizational Leadership

BS Construction Management–Surveying; Library Informatics
BSN Nursing–RN to BSN
Certificate Entrepreneurship; Nurse Practitioner Advancement
Endorsement Gifted and Talented Education
Graduate Certificate Business Informatics; Health Informatics
MA Integrative Studies
MAE Education; Teacher as Leader
MS Business Informatics; Health Informatics
MSN Nursing
DNP Nursing Practice

COURSE SUBJECT AREAS OFFERED OUTSIDE OF DEGREE PROGRAMS

Undergraduate—communication and media; criminal justice and corrections; entrepreneurial and small business operations; health professions related; information science/studies; liberal arts and sciences, general studies and humanities; library science related.
Graduate—education related; health services/allied health/health sciences; information science/studies.

NORTHERN STATE UNIVERSITY
Aberdeen, South Dakota
Continuing Education
http://www.northern.edu

Northern State University was founded in 1901. It is accredited by North Central Association of Colleges and Schools. It first offered distance learning courses in 1994. In fall 2010, there were 667 students enrolled in distance learning courses. Institutionally administered financial aid is available to distance learners.
Services Distance learners have accessibility to academic advising, bookstore, career placement assistance, e-mail services, library services, tutoring.
Contact Dr. Sharon Paranto, Director of Extended Studies, Northern State University, 1200 South Jay Street, Aberdeen, SD 57401-7198. Telephone: 605-626-2568. Fax: 605-626-2542. E-mail: parantos@northern.edu.

DEGREES AND AWARDS

AA General Studies
AS Banking and Financial Services
BGS General Studies
BS Banking and Financial Services; Management; Marketing

COURSE SUBJECT AREAS OFFERED OUTSIDE OF DEGREE PROGRAMS

Undergraduate—accounting and related services; biological and physical sciences; biology; business administration, management and operations; business/commerce; business, management, and marketing related; computer and information sciences; economics; education; educational administration and supervision; English; gerontology; health and physical education/fitness; international business; languages (foreign languages related); liberal arts and sciences, general studies and humanities; library science and administration; management information systems; marketing; mathematics; mathematics and statistics related; music; psychology; sociology.
Graduate—education.

NORTH GEORGIA COLLEGE & STATE UNIVERSITY
Dahlonega, Georgia
E-Learning/Opportunity Services
http://www.northgeorgia.edu

North Georgia College & State University was founded in 1873. It is accredited by Southern Association of Colleges and Schools. It first offered distance learning courses in 1998. In fall 2010, there were 1,306 students enrolled in distance learning courses. Institutionally administered financial aid is available to distance learners.
Services Distance learners have accessibility to academic advising, bookstore, e-mail services, library services, tutoring.
Contact Irene Kokkala, Director of Center of Teaching and Learning Excellence, North Georgia College & State University, 82 College Circle, Dahlonega, GA 30597. Telephone: 706-864-1862. E-mail: ikokkala@northgeorgia.edu.

DEGREES AND AWARDS

BSN Nursing
MA International Affairs
MEd Middle Grades Math and Science

COURSE SUBJECT AREAS OFFERED OUTSIDE OF DEGREE PROGRAMS

Undergraduate—biological and biomedical sciences related; business, management, and marketing related; computer and information sciences; finance and financial management services; history; languages (foreign languages related); liberal arts and sciences, general studies and humanities; marketing; psychology; social sciences; visual and performing arts.
Graduate—biological and biomedical sciences related; education; history.
Non-credit—education; education (specific subject areas).

NORTH HENNEPIN COMMUNITY COLLEGE
Brooklyn Park, Minnesota
http://www.nhcc.edu

North Hennepin Community College was founded in 1966. It is accredited by North Central Association of Colleges and Schools. It first offered distance learning courses in 1997. In fall 2010, there were 2,321 students enrolled in distance learning courses. Institutionally administered financial aid is available to distance learners.
Services Distance learners have accessibility to academic advising, bookstore, career placement assistance, e-mail services, library services, tutoring.
Contact Jenna Schnell, Counseling and Advising/Online Advisor, North Hennepin Community College, 7411 85th Avenue North, Brooklyn Park, MN 55445. Telephone: 763-493-0522. Fax: 763-424-0929. E-mail: jenna.schnell@nhcc.edu.

DEGREES AND AWARDS

AA History; Liberal Arts
AAS Business Computer Systems and Management
AS Business Computer Systems and Management; Business Management

COURSE SUBJECT AREAS OFFERED OUTSIDE OF DEGREE PROGRAMS

Undergraduate—accounting and related services; biology; building/construction finishing, management, and inspection; business/commerce; chemistry; communication and media; computer and information sciences; construction engineering technologies; economics; education; engineering; English; fine and studio arts; geography and cartography; health and physical education/fitness; health services/allied health/health sciences; languages (foreign languages related); legal studies (nonprofessional general, undergraduate); liberal arts and sciences, general studies and humanities; marketing; mathematics and computer science; music; philosophy; physics; political science and government; psychology; sociology; visual and performing arts.
Non-credit—accounting and computer science; accounting and related services; business administration, management and operations; business/commerce; business/corporate communications; business, management, and marketing related; communication and journalism related; computer and information sciences; computer and information sciences and support services related; computer science; computer software and media applications; computer systems networking and telecommunications; English or French as a second or foreign language (teaching); health services/allied health/health sciences; languages (foreign languages related); liberal arts and sciences, general studies and humanities; marketing; science technologies related.

NORTH IOWA AREA COMMUNITY COLLEGE

Mason City, Iowa

http://www.niacc.edu

North Iowa Area Community College was founded in 1918. It is accredited by North Central Association of Colleges and Schools. It first offered distance learning courses in 1989. Institutionally administered financial aid is available to distance learners.

Services Distance learners have accessibility to academic advising, bookstore, e-mail services, library services.

Contact Ms. Michelle Petznick, Registrar, North Iowa Area Community College, 500 College Drive, Mason City, IA 50401. Telephone: 641-422-4205. Fax: 641-422-4112. E-mail: petznmic@niacc.edu.

DEGREES AND AWARDS

AA General online degree program

COURSE SUBJECT AREAS OFFERED OUTSIDE OF DEGREE PROGRAMS

Undergraduate—accounting and related services; applied mathematics; biology; business/commerce; business, management, and marketing related; chemistry; economics; education; English language and literature related; finance and financial management services; geography and cartography; history; human resources management; insurance; marketing; mathematics; philosophy; psychology; social sciences; statistics; visual and performing arts.

Non-credit—computer software and media applications; health professions related; human development, family studies, and related services; insurance; real estate.

NORTH LAKE COLLEGE

Irving, Texas

http://www.northlakecollege.edu

North Lake College was founded in 1977. It is accredited by Southern Association of Colleges and Schools. It first offered distance learning courses in 1995. In fall 2010, there were 2,168 students enrolled in distance learning courses. Institutionally administered financial aid is available to distance learners.

Services Distance learners have accessibility to academic advising, bookstore, career placement assistance, e-mail services, library services, tutoring.

Contact Ms. Shirley Thompson, Professor, North Lake College, Irving, TX 75052. E-mail: sthompson@dcccd.edu.

DEGREES AND AWARDS

AA General Studies

AAS Business Administration; Business Office Systems and Support–Executive Assistant; Electronic Commerce; Logistics Technology; Management; Mortgage Banking; Real Estate

AS General Studies

COURSE SUBJECT AREAS OFFERED OUTSIDE OF DEGREE PROGRAMS

Undergraduate—accounting and related services; bilingual, multilingual, and multicultural education; biological and physical sciences; biology; business/commerce; business, management, and marketing related; chemistry; communications technology; computer and information sciences; computer programming; computer systems networking and telecommunications; economics; education; English; history; human development, family studies, and related services; languages (Romance languages); mathematics; music; philosophy; physics; political science and government; psychology; real estate; sociology; statistics; transportation and materials moving related.

Non-credit—real estate.

NORTH SEATTLE COMMUNITY COLLEGE

Seattle, Washington

Distance Learning Office

http://www.virtualcollege.org

North Seattle Community College was founded in 1970. It is accredited by Northwest Commission on Colleges and Universities. It first offered distance learning courses in 1993. In fall 2010, there were 2,813 students enrolled in distance learning courses. Institutionally administered financial aid is available to distance learners.

Services Distance learners have accessibility to academic advising, bookstore, campus computer network, career placement assistance, e-mail services, library services, tutoring.

Contact Terre O'Malley, Program Assistant, North Seattle Community College, North's e-Learning Support Center, 9600 College Way North, LB2237, Seattle, WA 98103. Telephone: 206-934-3738. Fax: 206-985-3984. E-mail: north.elearning@seattlecolleges.edu.

DEGREES AND AWARDS

AA General Studies

COURSE SUBJECT AREAS OFFERED OUTSIDE OF DEGREE PROGRAMS

Undergraduate—accounting and computer science; accounting and related services; allied health and medical assisting services; allied health diagnostic, intervention, and treatment professions; anthropology; applied mathematics; astronomy and astrophysics; biochemistry, biophysics and molecular biology; bioethics/medical ethics; biological and physical sciences; biology; business administration, management and operations; business/commerce; business, management, and marketing related; chemistry; computer programming; computer software and media applications; computer systems networking and telecommunications; drama/theatre arts and stagecraft; economics; English; English language and literature related; foods, nutrition, and related services; geological and earth sciences/geosciences; health and medical administrative services; heating, air conditioning, ventilation and refrigeration maintenance technology; history; human development, family studies, and related services; international business; liberal arts and sciences, general studies and humanities; library science and administration; library science related; mathematics; music; philosophy; psychology; sociology; statistics.

NORTH SHORE COMMUNITY COLLEGE

Danvers, Massachusetts

Distance Learning

http://www.northshore.edu/distance

North Shore Community College was founded in 1965. It is accredited by New England Association of Schools and Colleges. It first offered distance learning courses in 1986. In fall 2010, there were 1,500 students enrolled in distance learning courses. Institutionally administered financial aid is available to distance learners.

Services Distance learners have accessibility to academic advising, bookstore, campus computer network, e-mail services, library services, tutoring.

Contact Ms. Michelle Mabee, Administrative Assistant, Academic Technology and Distance Learning, North Shore Community College, 1 Ferncroft Road, Danvers, MA 01923. Telephone: 781-477-2172. Fax: 781-586-8453. E-mail: tlemoi@northshore.edu.

DEGREES AND AWARDS

AA Business Administration; Liberal Arts

AS Fire Protection and Safety Technology

Certificate Web Development

COURSE SUBJECT AREAS OFFERED OUTSIDE OF DEGREE PROGRAMS

Undergraduate—biology; business/commerce; computer science; film/video and photographic arts; history; languages (Romance languages); legal studies (non-professional general, undergraduate); marketing; mathematics; mathematics and statistics related; music; psychology; social sciences related; sociology; statistics.

Non-credit—business/commerce; business operations support and assistant services; communication and media; computer and information sciences; computer software and media applications; computer systems networking and telecommunications; entrepreneurial and small business operations.

NORTHWEST ARKANSAS COMMUNITY COLLEGE
Bentonville, Arkansas
Northwest Arkansas Distance Education
http://www.nwacc.edu/disted

NorthWest Arkansas Community College was founded in 1989. It is accredited by North Central Association of Colleges and Schools. It first offered distance learning courses in 1997. In fall 2010, there were 2,500 students enrolled in distance learning courses. Institutionally administered financial aid is available to distance learners.

Services Distance learners have accessibility to academic advising, bookstore, career placement assistance, e-mail services, library services, tutoring.

Contact Kate M. Burkes, PhD, Director of Distance Learning, NorthWest Arkansas Community College, BH 2425, One College Drive, Bentonville, AR 72712. Telephone: 479-619-4299. Fax: 479-619-4383. E-mail: kburkes@nwacc.edu.

DEGREES AND AWARDS

AA Transfer degree
AAS Environmental and Regulatory Science

COURSE SUBJECT AREAS OFFERED OUTSIDE OF DEGREE PROGRAMS

Undergraduate—accounting and related services; agricultural and food products processing; agriculture; allied health diagnostic, intervention, and treatment professions; apparel and textiles; applied mathematics; behavioral sciences; biology; business administration, management and operations; business/corporate communications; business, management, and marketing related; business operations support and assistant services; chemistry; communication and media; computer and information sciences; computer and information sciences and support services related; computer/information technology administration and management; computer programming; computer software and media applications; computer systems networking and telecommunications; criminal justice and corrections; culinary arts and related services; economics; English; English language and literature related; entrepreneurial and small business operations; fine and studio arts; fire protection; food science and technology; foods, nutrition, and related services; geography and cartography; geological and earth sciences/geosciences; health and physical education/fitness; health professions related; health services/allied health/health sciences; history; hospitality administration; international business; legal studies (non-professional general, undergraduate); liberal arts and sciences, general studies and humanities; mathematics; music; nutrition sciences; personal and culinary services related; philosophy; political science and government; psychology; psychology related; social sciences; social sciences related; sociology.

Non-credit—mathematics.

NORTHWESTERN CONNECTICUT COMMUNITY COLLEGE
Winsted, Connecticut
http://www.nwctc.commnet.edu/distancelearning/

Northwestern Connecticut Community College was founded in 1965. It is accredited by New England Association of Schools and Colleges. It first offered distance learning courses in 1997. In fall 2010, there were 533 students enrolled in distance learning courses. Institutionally administered financial aid is available to distance learners.

Services Distance learners have accessibility to academic advising, bookstore, e-mail services, library services, tutoring.

Contact Beverly J. King, Director, Education Technology/Distance Learning, Northwestern Connecticut Community College, Park Place East, Winsted, CT 06098. Telephone: 860-738-6323. E-mail: bking@nwcc.commnet.edu.

DEGREES AND AWARDS

Programs offered do not lead to a degree or other formal award.

COURSE SUBJECT AREAS OFFERED OUTSIDE OF DEGREE PROGRAMS

Undergraduate—allied health and medical assisting services; biological and physical sciences; business, management, and marketing related; computer and information sciences; education (specific levels and methods); English or French as a second or foreign language (teaching); geography and cartography; history; mathematics; philosophy; psychology; science, technology and society; sociology.

Non-credit—computer and information sciences; computer software and media applications.

NORTHWESTERN MICHIGAN COLLEGE
Traverse City, Michigan
Distance Education Services
http://www.nmc.edu/online/

Northwestern Michigan College was founded in 1951. It is accredited by North Central Association of Colleges and Schools. It first offered distance learning courses in 1982. In fall 2010, there were 2,024 students enrolled in distance learning courses. Institutionally administered financial aid is available to distance learners.

Services Distance learners have accessibility to academic advising, bookstore, campus computer network, career placement assistance, e-mail services, library services, tutoring.

Contact Janet Oliver, Director, Northwestern Michigan College, Educational Media Technologies, 1701 East Front Street, Traverse City, MI 49686. Telephone: 231-995-1076. Fax: 231-995-1080. E-mail: joliver@nmc.edu.

DEGREES AND AWARDS

AAS Business Administration; Education, general transfer
AD Nursing
AGS General Studies (AGS)
Certificate Office Applications Specialist

COURSE SUBJECT AREAS OFFERED OUTSIDE OF DEGREE PROGRAMS

Undergraduate—accounting and related services; anthropology; biology; business administration, management and operations; business/corporate communications; business, management, and marketing related; chemistry; computer and information sciences; computer and information sciences and support services related; computer programming; computer software and media applications; computer systems networking and telecommunications; criminal justice and corrections; economics; English language and literature related; history; legal studies (non-professional general, undergraduate); mathematics and statistics related; music; pharmacology and toxicology; philosophy; physics; psychology; psychology related; sociology; statistics.

NORTHWESTERN OKLAHOMA STATE UNIVERSITY
Alva, Oklahoma
http://www.nwosu.edu/

Northwestern Oklahoma State University was founded in 1897. It is accredited by North Central Association of Colleges and Schools. It first offered distance learning courses in 2004. In fall 2010, there were 1,000 students enrolled in distance learning courses. Institutionally administered financial aid is available to distance learners.

Services Distance learners have accessibility to academic advising, bookstore, campus computer network, career placement assistance, e-mail services, library services, tutoring.

Contact Mr. Jake G. Boedecker, Coordinator of Distance Learning, Northwestern Oklahoma State University, 709 Oklahoma Boulevard, Alva, OK 73717. Telephone: 580-327-8180. E-mail: jgboedecker@nwosu.edu.

DEGREES AND AWARDS

Programs offered do not lead to a degree or other formal award.

COURSE SUBJECT AREAS OFFERED OUTSIDE OF DEGREE PROGRAMS

Undergraduate—accounting and computer science; accounting and related services; business administration, management and operations; business/commerce; business/corporate communications; communication and media; criminal justice and corrections; curriculum and instruction; education; English; history; public relations, advertising, and applied communication related; sociology.

Graduate—bilingual, multilingual, and multicultural education; business administration, management and operations; educational administration and supervision; education related.

NORTHWEST-SHOALS COMMUNITY COLLEGE

Muscle Shoals, Alabama

http://www.nwscc.edu/distanceeducation/

Northwest-Shoals Community College was founded in 1963. It is accredited by Southern Association of Colleges and Schools. It first offered distance learning courses in 1999. In fall 2010, there were 920 students enrolled in distance learning courses. Institutionally administered financial aid is available to distance learners.

Services Distance learners have accessibility to academic advising, bookstore, campus computer network, e-mail services, library services.

Contact Ms. April Cookson, Distance Education Coordinator, Northwest-Shoals Community College, PO Box 2545, Muscle Shoals, AL 35662. Telephone: 256-331-5395. Fax: 256-331-5347. E-mail: cookson@nwscc.edu.

DEGREES AND AWARDS

AS Business Administration; General Education

COURSE SUBJECT AREAS OFFERED OUTSIDE OF DEGREE PROGRAMS

Undergraduate—accounting and computer science; business administration, management and operations; computer and information sciences; cosmetology and related personal grooming services; criminal justice and corrections; criminology; data entry/microcomputer applications; data processing; education; education (specific subject areas); English; geography and cartography; health and physical education/fitness; health services/allied health/health sciences; history; literature; mathematics; music; natural sciences; political science and government; psychology; religious studies; sociology; statistics.

NORTHWEST STATE COMMUNITY COLLEGE

Archbold, Ohio

http://www.northweststate.edu/

Northwest State Community College was founded in 1968. It is accredited by North Central Association of Colleges and Schools. It first offered distance learning courses in 2007. In fall 2010, there were 2,500 students enrolled in distance learning courses. Institutionally administered financial aid is available to distance learners.

Services Distance learners have accessibility to academic advising, bookstore, campus computer network, career placement assistance, e-mail services, library services, tutoring.

Contact Debra Beach, Coordinator of Instructional Support and Distance Learning, Northwest State Community College, State Route 22600, Archbold, OH 43502. Telephone: 419-267-1361. E-mail: dbeach@northweststate.edu.

DEGREES AND AWARDS

Programs offered do not lead to a degree or other formal award.

COURSE SUBJECT AREAS OFFERED OUTSIDE OF DEGREE PROGRAMS

Undergraduate—accounting and computer science; allied health and medical assisting services; applied mathematics.

NOTRE DAME COLLEGE

South Euclid, Ohio

http://www.notredamecollege.edu/adult

Notre Dame College was founded in 1922. It is accredited by North Central Association of Colleges and Schools. It first offered distance learning courses in 2006. In fall 2010, there were 477 students enrolled in distance learning courses. Institutionally administered financial aid is available to distance learners.

Services Distance learners have accessibility to academic advising, bookstore, career placement assistance, e-mail services, library services, tutoring.

Contact Mrs. Anne Marie Hodges, Finn Center, Associate Director of Faculty and Student Support, Notre Dame College, 4545 College Road, South Euclid, OH 44121. Telephone: 216-373-6378. Fax: 216-381-3802. E-mail: ahodges@ndc.edu.

DEGREES AND AWARDS

MA Security Policy Studies

MEd Education

COURSE SUBJECT AREAS OFFERED OUTSIDE OF DEGREE PROGRAMS

Undergraduate—accounting and computer science; applied mathematics; behavioral sciences; business administration, management and operations; computer science; economics; English; history; holocaust and related studies; management information systems; marketing; mathematics; microbiological sciences and immunology; music; natural sciences; philosophy and religious studies; psychology; sociology; statistics.

Non-credit—education; education (specific levels and methods); homeland security; intelligence, command control and information.

NOVA SCOTIA AGRICULTURAL COLLEGE

Truro, Nova Scotia, Canada

Center for Continuing and Distance Education

http://www.nsac.ca/cde

Nova Scotia Agricultural College was founded in 1905. It is provincially chartered. It first offered distance learning courses in 1996. In fall 2010, there were 45 students enrolled in distance learning courses. Institutionally administered financial aid is available to distance learners.

Services Distance learners have accessibility to academic advising, bookstore, e-mail services, library services.

Contact Mrs. Pamela Doyle, Administrative Assistant, Nova Scotia Agricultural College, PO Box 550, 23 Sheep Hill Lane, Truro, NS B2N 5E3, Canada. Telephone: 902-893-6666. Fax: 902-895-5528. E-mail: cde@nsac.ca.

DEGREES AND AWARDS

Programs offered do not lead to a degree or other formal award.

COURSE SUBJECT AREAS OFFERED OUTSIDE OF DEGREE PROGRAMS

Undergraduate—agricultural and domestic animal services; agricultural business and management; agricultural production; agriculture; animal sciences; plant sciences.

Non-credit—agriculture; animal sciences; plant sciences.

NOVA SOUTHEASTERN UNIVERSITY

Fort Lauderdale, Florida

Masters in Clinical Vision Research

http://www.nova.edu/cvr

Nova Southeastern University was founded in 1964. It is accredited by Southern Association of Colleges and Schools. It first offered distance learning courses in 2002. In fall 2010, there were 10 students enrolled in distance learning courses. Institutionally administered financial aid is available to distance learners.

Services Distance learners have accessibility to academic advising, bookstore, campus computer network, e-mail services, library services.

Contact Josephine Shallo-Hoffmann, Chair of Research and Graduate Programs, Nova Southeastern University, 3200 South University Drive, Fort Lauderdale, FL 33328. Telephone: 954-262-4226. Fax: 954-262-3875. E-mail: shoffman@nova.edu.

DEGREES AND AWARDS

MS Clinical Vision Research

COURSE SUBJECT AREAS OFFERED OUTSIDE OF DEGREE PROGRAMS

Graduate—medical clinical sciences/graduate medical studies.
Non-credit—medical clinical sciences/graduate medical studies.

NYACK COLLEGE
Nyack, New York
http://nyackonline.org/

Nyack College was founded in 1882. It is accredited by Middle States Association of Colleges and Schools. It first offered distance learning courses in 1999. In fall 2010, there were 200 students enrolled in distance learning courses.
Services Distance learners have accessibility to academic advising, bookstore, career placement assistance, library services.
Contact Office of Admissions, Nyack College, 1 South Boulevard, Nyack, NY 10960. Telephone: 800-336-9225. E-mail: enroll@nyack.edu.

DEGREES AND AWARDS

Programs offered do not lead to a degree or other formal award.

COURSE SUBJECT AREAS OFFERED OUTSIDE OF DEGREE PROGRAMS

Undergraduate—behavioral sciences; biblical studies; business administration, management and operations; communication and media; education; education related; education (specific levels and methods); English; English language and literature related; history; mathematics; music; philosophy; philosophy and religious studies related; political science and government; psychology; religious studies; social work; theological and ministerial studies; theology and religious vocations related.
Graduate—biblical studies; business administration, management and operations; education; education related; missionary studies and missiology; religious studies; theological and ministerial studies; theology and religious vocations related.

OAKLAND COMMUNITY COLLEGE
Bloomfield Hills, Michigan
http://www.oaklandcc.edu

Oakland Community College was founded in 1964. It is accredited by North Central Association of Colleges and Schools. It first offered distance learning courses in 2000. In fall 2010, there were 2,407 students enrolled in distance learning courses. Institutionally administered financial aid is available to distance learners.
Services Distance learners have accessibility to bookstore, e-mail services, library services.
Contact Douglas L. Riddering, Counselor, Oakland Community College, 2900 Featherstone Road, Building B, Room 231, Auburn Hills, MI 48326-2845. Telephone: 248-232-4358. Fax: 248-232-4355. E-mail: dlridder@oaklandcc.edu.

DEGREES AND AWARDS

Programs offered do not lead to a degree or other formal award.

COURSE SUBJECT AREAS OFFERED OUTSIDE OF DEGREE PROGRAMS

Undergraduate—accounting and computer science; biology; business administration, management and operations; computer and information sciences; computer programming; computer software and media applications; computer systems analysis; construction trades; criminal justice and corrections; drafting/design engineering technologies; English language and literature related; film/video and photographic arts; health and medical administrative services; health and physical education/fitness; history; human resources management; library and archives assisting; marketing; mathematics; mathematics and statistics related; natural resources and conservation related; nutrition sciences; parks, recreation, leisure, and fitness studies related; philosophy; psychology; public health; social sciences; sociology.

OAKLAND UNIVERSITY
Rochester, Michigan
http://www.oakland.edu/elis

Oakland University was founded in 1957. It is accredited by North Central Association of Colleges and Schools. It first offered distance learning courses in 1995. In fall 2010, there were 3,187 students enrolled in distance learning courses. Institutionally administered financial aid is available to distance learners.
Services Distance learners have accessibility to academic advising, bookstore, campus computer network, career placement assistance, e-mail services, library services, tutoring.
Contact Oakland University, 2200 North Squirrel Road, Rochester, MI 48309-4401. Telephone: 248-370-4566.

DEGREES AND AWARDS

BIS Integrative Studies
BS Occupational Safety and Health; Nursing RN/BSN
CAGS Adult/Gerontological Nurse Practitioner post-Graduate certificate; Autism Spectrum Disorder (ASD) endorsement; Education Specialist in K-12 Leadership; Family Nurse Practitioner post-Graduate certificate; International Baccalaureate certificate; Nurse Anesthesia post-Graduate certificate; Nursing Education post-Baccalaureate certificate; Nursing Education post-Graduate certificate; Oncology Rehabilitation certificate
CCCPE Continuing Education–Animal Assisted Therapy certificate; Continuing Education–Songwriting certificate
MEd Special Education; Teacher Leadership
MS Safety Management
MSE Engineering Management
MSN Adult Health Clinical Nurse Specialist; Adult/Gerontological Nurse Practitioner; Family Nurse Practitioner; Nurse Anesthesia; Nursing Education; Nursing RN/MSN
DNP Nursing

OAKTON COMMUNITY COLLEGE
Des Plaines, Illinois
http://www.oakton.edu/distancelearning

Oakton Community College was founded in 1969. It is accredited by North Central Association of Colleges and Schools. It first offered distance learning courses in 1975. In fall 2010, there were 2,500 students enrolled in distance learning courses. Institutionally administered financial aid is available to distance learners.
Services Distance learners have accessibility to academic advising, bookstore, career placement assistance, e-mail services, library services, tutoring.
Contact Ms. Robin Nash, Manager of Alternative Education, Oakton Community College, 1600 East Golf Road, Des Plaines, IL 60016. Telephone: 847-635-1971. Fax: 847-635-1987. E-mail: rnash@oakton.edu.

DEGREES AND AWARDS

AA Arts
AS Science

COURSE SUBJECT AREAS OFFERED OUTSIDE OF DEGREE PROGRAMS

Undergraduate—accounting and related services; anthropology; applied mathematics; area studies; astronomy and astrophysics; behavioral sciences; biological and physical sciences; business/commerce; business/corporate communications; chemistry; communication and journalism related; communication and media; computer and information sciences; computer science; computer software and media applications; data entry/microcomputer applications; drama/theatre arts and stagecraft; economics; engineering; English; film/video and photographic arts; genetics; geography and cartography; graphic communications; health and medical administrative services; health professions related; health services/allied health/health sciences; history; holocaust and related studies; human development, family studies, and related services; international business; journalism; languages (Germanic); languages (Romance languages); languages (Southeast Asian and Australasian/Pacific); legal studies (non-professional general, undergraduate); liberal arts and sciences, general studies and humanities; library science related; linguistic, comparative, and related language studies; marketing; mathematics; mechanical engineering; pharmacy, pharmaceutical sciences, and administration; philosophy; philosophy and religious studies related; physical sciences; political science and government; psychology; radio, television, and digital communication; sales merchandising, and related marketing operations (general); social sciences; sociology; statistics.

Non-credit—business/commerce; communication and journalism related; computer and information sciences; culinary arts and related services; data entry/microcomputer applications; family and consumer economics; languages (Romance languages).

OCEAN COUNTY COLLEGE
Toms River, New Jersey
http://www.ocean.edu/academics/distance_learning/distance_learning_form_completed.htm

Ocean County College was founded in 1964. It is accredited by Middle States Association of Colleges and Schools. It first offered distance learning courses in 2000. In fall 2010, there were 2,013 students enrolled in distance learning courses. Institutionally administered financial aid is available to distance learners.

Services Distance learners have accessibility to academic advising, bookstore, campus computer network, e-mail services, library services.

Contact Mr. Jeff Harmon, Associate Director of E-Learning, Ocean County College, College Drive, PO Box 2001, Toms River, NJ 08754-2001. Telephone: 732-255-0400 Ext. 2499. Fax: 732-255-0524. E-mail: jharmon@ocean.edu.

DEGREES AND AWARDS
AS Business Administration; Computer Science; Criminal Justice; General Studies; Homeland Security

COURSE SUBJECT AREAS OFFERED OUTSIDE OF DEGREE PROGRAMS
Undergraduate—accounting and related services; biology; business administration, management and operations; computer and information sciences; computer software and media applications; economics; education related; English; health and physical education/fitness; history; intercultural/multicultural and diversity studies; liberal arts and sciences, general studies and humanities; marketing; mathematics; philosophy; physics; psychology; psychology related; social sciences; sociology; statistics.

ODESSA COLLEGE
Odessa, Texas
Division of Distance Education
http://www.odessa.edu

Odessa College was founded in 1946. It is accredited by Southern Association of Colleges and Schools. It first offered distance learning courses in 1986. In fall 2010, there were 2,972 students enrolled in distance learning courses. Institutionally administered financial aid is available to distance learners.

Services Distance learners have accessibility to academic advising, bookstore, campus computer network, career placement assistance, e-mail services, library services, tutoring.

Contact Corey Davis, Executive Director OC Global, Odessa College, 201 West University, Odessa, TX 79764. Telephone: 432-335-6781. Fax: 432-335-6667. E-mail: cdavis@odessa.edu.

DEGREES AND AWARDS
ASAST Occupational Safety and Health Technology

COURSE SUBJECT AREAS OFFERED OUTSIDE OF DEGREE PROGRAMS
Undergraduate—accounting and related services; allied health and medical assisting services; biology; business/commerce; business, management, and marketing related; business operations support and assistant services; communication and journalism related; computer and information sciences; computer and information sciences and support services related; computer science; economics; English; environmental control technologies; environmental/environmental health engineering; mathematics; mathematics and statistics related; sociology.

Non-credit—business administration, management and operations; business, management, and marketing related; computer software and media applications; linguistic, comparative, and related language studies; sales, merchandising and related marketing operations (specialized).

THE OHIO STATE UNIVERSITY
Columbus, Ohio
Technology Enhanced Learning and Research (TELR)
http://telr.osu.edu

The Ohio State University was founded in 1870. It is accredited by North Central Association of Colleges and Schools. It first offered distance learning courses in 1995. In fall 2010, there were 4,819 students enrolled in distance learning courses. Institutionally administered financial aid is available to distance learners.

Services Distance learners have accessibility to academic advising, bookstore, campus computer network, e-mail services, library services, tutoring.

Contact Mr. Michael Hofherr, Director for Learning Technologies, The Ohio State University, Learning Technology, 1858 Neil Avenue Mall, 418 Thompson Library, Columbus, OH 43210. Telephone: 614-247-6819. Fax: 614-292-7081. E-mail: hofherr.3@osu.edu.

DEGREES AND AWARDS
EMBA Business Administration

MSE Welding Engineering

DNP Nursing Practice Doctorate

COURSE SUBJECT AREAS OFFERED OUTSIDE OF DEGREE PROGRAMS
Undergraduate—agriculture; allied health and medical assisting services; anthropology; behavioral sciences; biology; business/commerce; chemistry; classical and ancient studies; computer and information sciences; dental support services and allied professions; ecology, evolution, systematics, and population biology; education; education related; education (specific levels and methods); education (specific subject areas); engineering related; family and consumer economics; family and consumer sciences/human sciences related; finance and financial management services; food science and technology; forestry; health professions related; human development, family studies, and related services; languages (foreign languages related); linguistic, comparative, and related language studies; mathematics; music; nutrition sciences; pharmacy, pharmaceutical sciences, and administration; plant sciences; political science and government; psychology; social sciences; social work; sociology; sociology and anthropology; visual and performing arts related.

Graduate—allied health and medical assisting services; allied health diagnostic, intervention, and treatment professions; business administration, management and operations; city/urban, community and regional planning; education; educational administration and supervision; education related; engineering related; health professions related; history; mechanical engineering; nuclear engineering; nutrition sciences; plant sciences; social work.

Non-credit—gerontology; mental and social health services and allied professions; special education.

OHIO UNIVERSITY
Athens, Ohio
Lifelong Learning
http://www.outreach.ohio.edu/index.htm

Ohio University was founded in 1804. It is accredited by North Central Association of Colleges and Schools. It first offered distance learning courses in 1941. In fall 2010, there were 4,200 students enrolled in distance learning courses. Institutionally administered financial aid is available to distance learners.

Services Distance learners have accessibility to academic advising, bookstore, career placement assistance, e-mail services, library services, tutoring.

Contact Ms. Carissa Anderson, eLearning OHIO, Ohio University, 128 Haning Hall, 1 Ohio University, Athens, OH 45701. Telephone: 800-444-2910 Ext. 34768. Fax: 740-593-2901. E-mail: independent.study@ohio.edu.

DEGREES AND AWARDS

AA Arts and Humanities; Social Sciences
AIS Individualized Studies
AS Mathematics; Natural Science
BCJ Criminal Justice
BGS Specialized Studies
BSAST Technical and Applied Studies
BSN Nursing–RN to BSN

COURSE SUBJECT AREAS OFFERED OUTSIDE OF DEGREE PROGRAMS

Undergraduate—accounting and related services; biological and physical sciences; biology; business/commerce; business operations support and assistant services; communication and media; criminal justice and corrections; criminology; drama/theatre arts and stagecraft; economics; English; English language and literature related; ethnic, cultural minority, gender, and group studies; family and consumer sciences/human sciences; geography and cartography; history; human resources management; journalism; linguistic, comparative, and related language studies; literature; marketing; mathematics; mathematics and statistics related; philosophy; philosophy and religious studies related; physics; psychology; sales, merchandising and related marketing operations (specialized); sociology; sociology and anthropology.

Non-credit—accounting and related services; business administration, management and operations; business/commerce; business, management, and marketing related; computer and information sciences and support services related; education related; languages (Romance languages); legal support services.

OKEFENOKEE TECHNICAL COLLEGE
Waycross, Georgia
http://www.okefenokeetech.edu

Okefenokee Technical College is accredited by Council on Occupational Education. It first offered distance learning courses in 1999. In fall 2010, there were 760 students enrolled in distance learning courses. Institutionally administered financial aid is available to distance learners.

Services Distance learners have accessibility to academic advising, bookstore, career placement assistance, e-mail services, library services, tutoring.

Contact Amanda Morris Dryden, Coordinator of Distance Education and Web Master, Okefenokee Technical College, 1701 Carswell Avenue, Waycross, GA 31503. Telephone: 912-287-5851. Fax: 912-287-4865. E-mail: amorris@okefenokeetech.edu.

DEGREES AND AWARDS

Programs offered do not lead to a degree or other formal award.

COURSE SUBJECT AREAS OFFERED OUTSIDE OF DEGREE PROGRAMS

Undergraduate—allied health and medical assisting services; business, management, and marketing related; computer and information sciences.

Non-credit—allied health and medical assisting services; business, management, and marketing related; computer and information sciences.

OKLAHOMA PANHANDLE STATE UNIVERSITY
Goodwell, Oklahoma
http://www.opsu.edu/

Oklahoma Panhandle State University was founded in 1909. It is accredited by North Central Association of Colleges and Schools. It first offered distance learning courses in 1992. In fall 2010, there were 441 students enrolled in distance learning courses. Institutionally administered financial aid is available to distance learners.

Services Distance learners have accessibility to academic advising, bookstore, campus computer network, e-mail services, library services.

Contact Bobby Jenkins, Registrar, Oklahoma Panhandle State University, PO Box 430, Goodwell, OK 73939. Telephone: 580-349-1376. E-mail: bjenkins@opsu.edu.

DEGREES AND AWARDS

Programs offered do not lead to a degree or other formal award.

COURSE SUBJECT AREAS OFFERED OUTSIDE OF DEGREE PROGRAMS

Undergraduate—accounting and computer science; accounting and related services; behavioral sciences; biological and physical sciences; biology; business administration, management and operations; business, management, and marketing related; chemistry; computer and information sciences; economics; English; English language and literature related; history; mathematics; music; natural sciences; physical sciences; political science and government; psychology; social sciences; sociology.

OKLAHOMA STATE UNIVERSITY
Stillwater, Oklahoma
Distance Learning
http://is.okstate.edu

Oklahoma State University was founded in 1890. It is accredited by North Central Association of Colleges and Schools. It first offered distance learning courses in 1945. In fall 2010, there were 3,500 students enrolled in distance learning courses. Institutionally administered financial aid is available to distance learners.

Services Distance learners have accessibility to bookstore, campus computer network, e-mail services.

Contact Jenny England, Administrative Support Specialist, Oklahoma State University, 309 Wes Watkins Center, Stillwater, OK 74078. Telephone: 405-744-6390. Fax: 405-744-3420. E-mail: ics-inf@okstate.edu.

DEGREES AND AWARDS

Programs offered do not lead to a degree or other formal award.

COURSE SUBJECT AREAS OFFERED OUTSIDE OF DEGREE PROGRAMS

Undergraduate—agricultural and domestic animal services; agricultural and food products processing; agricultural production; animal sciences; anthropology; applied horticulture and horticultural business services; applied mathematics; atmospheric sciences and meteorology; business administration, management and operations; business/corporate communications; business, management, and marketing related; classical and ancient studies; education related; English language and literature related; fire protection; foods, nutrition, and related services; geography and cartography; gerontology; history; human resources management; languages (Germanic); languages (Romance languages); liberal arts and sciences, general studies and humanities; literature; management information systems; marketing; mathematics; mathematics and statistics related; music; nutrition sciences; plant sciences; political science and government; psychology; sales merchandising, and related marketing operations (general); sales, merchandising and related marketing operations (specialized); statistics.

Non-credit—fire protection.

OLYMPIC COLLEGE

Bremerton, Washington

http://www.oc.ctc.edu/

Olympic College was founded in 1946. It is accredited by Northwest Commission on Colleges and Universities. It first offered distance learning courses in 1995. In fall 2010, there were 1,500 students enrolled in distance learning courses. Institutionally administered financial aid is available to distance learners.

Services Distance learners have accessibility to academic advising, bookstore, campus computer network, e-mail services, library services.

Contact Cara J. Lunsford, Media Assistant, Olympic College, Media Services and Distance Learning, 1600 Chester Avenue, Bremerton, WA 98337-1699. Telephone: 360-475-7773. Fax: 360-475-7775. E-mail: cjlunsford@olympic.edu.

DEGREES AND AWARDS

Programs offered do not lead to a degree or other formal award.

COURSE SUBJECT AREAS OFFERED OUTSIDE OF DEGREE PROGRAMS

Undergraduate—accounting and related services; anthropology; business administration, management and operations; business/corporate communications; business, management, and marketing related; business/managerial economics; business operations support and assistant services; chemistry; communication and media; computer and information sciences; computer and information sciences and support services related; computer programming; economics; education (specific subject areas); English; English language and literature related; entrepreneurial and small business operations; fine and studio arts; fire protection; health and medical administrative services; history; human development, family studies, and related services; liberal arts and sciences, general studies and humanities; marketing; mathematics; political science and government; practical nursing, vocational nursing and nursing assistants; psychology related; radio, television, and digital communication; sociology.

ORANGE COAST COLLEGE

Costa Mesa, California

http://www.orangecoastcollege.com

Orange Coast College was founded in 1947. It is accredited by Western Association of Schools and Colleges. It first offered distance learning courses in 1998. In fall 2010, there were 4,633 students enrolled in distance learning courses. Institutionally administered financial aid is available to distance learners.

Services Distance learners have accessibility to academic advising, bookstore, e-mail services, library services, tutoring.

Contact Ms. Sheri Sterner, Administrative Director of Institutional Effectiveness, Orange Coast College, 2701 Fairview Road, Costa Mesa, CA 92626. Telephone: 714-432-5081. E-mail: ssterner@occ.cccd.edu.

DEGREES AND AWARDS

Programs offered do not lead to a degree or other formal award.

COURSE SUBJECT AREAS OFFERED OUTSIDE OF DEGREE PROGRAMS

Undergraduate—accounting and related services; allied health and medical assisting services; anthropology; biology; business, management, and marketing related; communication and journalism related; computer and information sciences; computer/information technology administration and management; computer programming; computer software and media applications; drafting/design engineering technologies; English; film/video and photographic arts; food science and technology; foods, nutrition, and related services; health and physical education/fitness; history; hospitality administration; human development, family studies, and related services; mathematics; music; physics; political science and government; psychology; real estate.

OREGON COAST COMMUNITY COLLEGE

Newport, Oregon

http://www.oregoncoastcc.org

Oregon Coast Community College was founded in 1987. It first offered distance learning courses in 1997. In fall 2010, there were 242 students enrolled in distance learning courses. Institutionally administered financial aid is available to distance learners.

Services Distance learners have accessibility to academic advising.

Contact Maggie Gray, Advising Specialist, Oregon Coast Community College, 400 SE College Way, Newport, OR 97366. Telephone: 541-867-8512. Fax: 541-574-7159. E-mail: mgray@occc.cc.or.us.

DEGREES AND AWARDS

Programs offered do not lead to a degree or other formal award.

COURSE SUBJECT AREAS OFFERED OUTSIDE OF DEGREE PROGRAMS

Undergraduate—accounting and computer science; allied health and medical assisting services; biological and physical sciences; history; literature; mathematics; physical sciences; psychology; social sciences; sociology; statistics.

OREGON HEALTH & SCIENCE UNIVERSITY

Portland, Oregon

School of Nursing

http://www.ohsu.edu/xd/education/schools/school-of-nursing/

Oregon Health & Science University was founded in 1974. It is accredited by Northwest Commission on Colleges and Universities. It first offered distance learning courses in 1992. In fall 2010, there were 200 students enrolled in distance learning courses. Institutionally administered financial aid is available to distance learners.

Services Distance learners have accessibility to academic advising, bookstore, campus computer network, career placement assistance, e-mail services, library services, tutoring.

Contact Ms. Tami Buedefeldt, Office Manager for Student Affairs and Admissions, Oregon Health & Science University, SoN Office of Admissions, Mail Code SN-ADM, 3455 SW US Veterans Hospital Road, Portland, OR 97239-2941. Telephone: 503-494-7725. Fax: 503-494-6433. E-mail: proginfo@ohsu.edu.

DEGREES AND AWARDS

BSN Nursing

MPH Primary Health Care and Health Disparities

OREGON INSTITUTE OF TECHNOLOGY

Klamath Falls, Oregon

http://www.oit.edu/distance-education

Oregon Institute of Technology was founded in 1947. It is accredited by Northwest Commission on Colleges and Universities. It first offered distance learning courses in 1997. In fall 2010, there were 887 students enrolled in distance learning courses. Institutionally administered financial aid is available to distance learners.

Services Distance learners have accessibility to academic advising, bookstore, campus computer network, career placement assistance, e-mail services, library services, tutoring.

Contact Barb DeKalb, Director of Distance Education, Oregon Institute of Technology, 3201 Campus Drive, Klamath Falls, OR 97601. Telephone: 541-885-1142. Fax: 541-885-1139. E-mail: barb.dekalb@oit.edu.

DEGREES AND AWARDS

AAS Polysomnographic Technology

BS Allied Health Management; Dental Hygiene–Dental Hygiene degree completion; Information Technology Online; Operations Management; Radiological Science–Radiological Science degree completion; Respiratory Care; Ultrasound–degree completion in Ultrasound, Echocardiography option; Ultrasound–degree completion in Ultrasound, Vascular Technology option

BSc Diagnostic Medical Sonography
Certificate of Completion Polysomnographic Technology
MS Manufacturing Engineering Technology

COURSE SUBJECT AREAS OFFERED OUTSIDE OF DEGREE PROGRAMS

Undergraduate—accounting and related services; anthropology; business administration, management and operations; business/commerce; computer/information technology administration and management; economics; management information systems; mathematics; psychology; social sciences.

OREGON STATE UNIVERSITY
Corvallis, Oregon
Extended Campus
http://ecampus.oregonstate.edu

Oregon State University was founded in 1868. It is accredited by Northwest Commission on Colleges and Universities. It first offered distance learning courses in 1986. In fall 2010, there were 4,200 students enrolled in distance learning courses. Institutionally administered financial aid is available to distance learners.

Services Distance learners have accessibility to academic advising, bookstore, campus computer network, career placement assistance, e-mail services, library services, tutoring.

Contact Ecampus Student Services Center, Oregon State University, 4943 The Valley Library, Corvallis, OR 97331-4504. Telephone: 800-667-1465. Fax: 541-737-2734. E-mail: ecampus@oregonstate.edu.

DEGREES AND AWARDS

BA Liberal Studies; Political Science–Online; Political Science
BA/BS General Anthropology; Sociology; Women Studies
BS Agriculture, general; Environmental Economics and Policy; Environmental Sciences; Fisheries and Wildlife Online; General Horticulture; Horticulture, general; Human Development and Family Sciences; Liberal Studies; Natural Resources; Political Science–Online; Political Science
Certificate of Completion Management and Human Resource Skills for Pharmacists
Endorsement ESOL/Bilingual Education
License Continuing Teaching Licensure
Graduate Certificate Fisheries Management; GIScience Professional certificate; Sustainable Natural Resources; Water Conflict Management
MAT Early Childhood/Elementary Education
MEd Adult Education; Education
MHP Radiation Health Physics
MS Master of Natural Resources; Radiation Health Physics
EdD Community College Leadership concentration
PhD Community College Leadership concentration; Counseling

COURSE SUBJECT AREAS OFFERED OUTSIDE OF DEGREE PROGRAMS

Undergraduate—agricultural business and management; agriculture; agriculture and agriculture operations related; American Sign Language (ASL); anthropology; applied horticulture and horticultural business services; applied mathematics; atmospheric sciences and meteorology; botany/plant biology; business/commerce; business/corporate communications; chemistry; communication and media; ecology, evolution, systematics, and population biology; economics; education; education related; English; English language and literature related; ethnic, cultural minority, gender, and group studies; fishing and fisheries sciences and management; forestry; geography and cartography; geological and earth sciences/geosciences; health and medical administrative services; health services/allied health/health sciences; history; human development, family studies, and related services; landscape architecture; languages (foreign languages related); languages (Germanic); languages (Romance languages); liberal arts and sciences, general studies and humanities; mathematics and statistics related; natural resources and conservation related; natural resources conservation and research; natural resources management and policy; philosophy; philosophy and religious studies related; plant sciences; political science and government; psychology; sales merchandising, and related marketing operations (general); science, technology and society; social sciences related; sociology; soil sciences; statistics; wildlife and wildlands science and management.

Graduate—education; educational administration and supervision; education related; education (specific levels and methods); education (specific subject areas); English or French as a second or foreign language (teaching); environmental/environmental health engineering; foods, nutrition, and related services; geography and cartography; geological and earth sciences/geosciences; health and medical administrative services; health professions related; natural resources conservation and research; natural resources management and policy; nuclear and industrial radiologic technologies; public health.

Non-credit—business, management, and marketing related; communication and media; computer software and media applications; English; family and consumer economics; film/video and photographic arts; fine and studio arts; health and medical administrative services; human resources management; languages (Romance languages); linguistic, comparative, and related language studies; pharmacology and toxicology; pharmacy, pharmaceutical sciences, and administration; psychology; sales, merchandising and related marketing operations (specialized).

OUACHITA TECHNICAL COLLEGE
Malvern, Arkansas
http://www.otcweb.edu

Ouachita Technical College was founded in 1972. It is accredited by North Central Association of Colleges and Schools. It first offered distance learning courses in 1998. In fall 2010, there were 330 students enrolled in distance learning courses. Institutionally administered financial aid is available to distance learners.

Services Distance learners have accessibility to academic advising, bookstore, campus computer network, career placement assistance, e-mail services, library services, tutoring.

Contact Mr. Tony Hunnicutt, Distance Learning Coordinator, Ouachita Technical College, One College Circle, Malvern, AR 72104. Telephone: 501-337-5000 Ext. 1106. Fax: 501-337-9382. E-mail: thunnicutt@otcweb.edu.

DEGREES AND AWARDS

AA Education, general
AAS Criminal Justice

COURSE SUBJECT AREAS OFFERED OUTSIDE OF DEGREE PROGRAMS

Undergraduate—behavioral sciences; biological and physical sciences; biology; business administration, management and operations; computer and information sciences; computer software and media applications; computer systems networking and telecommunications; criminal justice and corrections; history; human resources management; liberal arts and sciences, general studies and humanities; mathematics; philosophy; political science and government; psychology; social sciences; sociology.

OXNARD COLLEGE
Oxnard, California
http://www.oxnardcollege.edu

Oxnard College was founded in 1975. It is accredited by Western Association of Schools and Colleges. It first offered distance learning courses in 1997. In fall 2010, there were 1,119 students enrolled in distance learning courses. Institutionally administered financial aid is available to distance learners.

Services Distance learners have accessibility to academic advising, bookstore, e-mail services, library services.

Contact Dr. Erika Endrijonas, Executive Vice President for Student Learning, Oxnard College, 4000 South Rose Avenue, Oxnard, CA 93033. Telephone: 805-986-5814. Fax: 805-986-5914. E-mail: endrijonas@vcccd.edu.

DEGREES AND AWARDS

Programs offered do not lead to a degree or other formal award.

COURSE SUBJECT AREAS OFFERED OUTSIDE OF DEGREE PROGRAMS

Undergraduate—accounting and related services; anthropology; applied mathematics; area studies; bilingual, multilingual, and multicultural education; biological and biomedical sciences related; biology; botany/plant biology; business administration, management and operations; business/corporate communications; business, management, and marketing related; business operations support and assistant services; chemistry; communication and media; computer and information sciences; computer engineering; computer/information technology administration and management; computer programming; computer science; computer software and media applications; computer systems analysis; computer systems networking and telecommunications; criminal justice and corrections; data entry/microcomputer applications; economics; English; environmental control technologies; fine and studio arts; geological and earth sciences/geosciences; history; human services; languages (foreign languages related); legal studies (non-professional general, undergraduate); marketing; mathematics; mechanic and repair technologies related; microbiological sciences and immunology; music; philosophy; physical sciences; physics; political science and government; psychology; public relations, advertising, and applied communication related; radio, television, and digital communication; sales, merchandising and related marketing operations (specialized); sociology.

OZARKS TECHNICAL COMMUNITY COLLEGE
Springfield, Missouri
http://www.otc.edu

Ozarks Technical Community College was founded in 1990. It is accredited by North Central Association of Colleges and Schools. It first offered distance learning courses in 2000. In fall 2010, there were 4,200 students enrolled in distance learning courses. Institutionally administered financial aid is available to distance learners.

Services Distance learners have accessibility to academic advising, bookstore, career placement assistance, e-mail services, library services, tutoring.

Contact Mr. C. DeWitt Salley, Jr., Director of Online Teaching and Learning, Ozarks Technical Community College, 1001 East Chestnut Expressway, Springfield, MO 65802. Telephone: 417-447-8199. Fax: 417-447-8818. E-mail: salleyc@otc.edu.

DEGREES AND AWARDS

AA General Education; Teaching

AAS Accounting; Business Technology; Business and Marketing

COURSE SUBJECT AREAS OFFERED OUTSIDE OF DEGREE PROGRAMS

Undergraduate—accounting and computer science; allied health and medical assisting services; anthropology; behavioral sciences; biochemistry, biophysics and molecular biology; biological and physical sciences; business administration, management and operations; business/commerce; business/corporate communications; business, management, and marketing related; cell biology and anatomical sciences; communication and media; computer and information sciences; criminal justice and corrections; criminology; culinary arts and related services; data processing; drama/theatre arts and stagecraft; economics; education; educational/instructional media design; education related; English; family and consumer economics; foods, nutrition, and related services; geography and cartography; history; human resources management; languages (Germanic); liberal arts and sciences, general studies and humanities; mathematics; music; philosophy; philosophy and religious studies related; political science and government; psychology; religious studies; social sciences; sociology; theology and religious vocations related; urban studies/affairs; visual and performing arts related; work and family studies.

PACE UNIVERSITY
New York, New York
Online Pace
http://www.online.pace.edu

Pace University was founded in 1906. It is accredited by Middle States Association of Colleges and Schools. It first offered distance learning courses in 1997. In fall 2010, there were 4,264 students enrolled in distance learning courses. Institutionally administered financial aid is available to distance learners.

Services Distance learners have accessibility to academic advising, bookstore, campus computer network, career placement assistance, e-mail services, library services, tutoring.

Contact Ms. Danielle Plass, Manager, Online Support Services, Pace University, One Pace Plaza, New York, NY 10038. Telephone: 212-346-1471. E-mail: dplass@pace.edu.

DEGREES AND AWARDS

AS Applied Information Technology, Telecommunications degree

BS Organizational Communications; Professional Technology Studies; Telecommunications

Graduate Certificate Business Aspects of Publishing; Internet Technologies; Telecommunications

MA Nursing Education

MBA Business Administration–e.MBA

MS Internet Technology for E-Commerce; Publishing

DPS Computing

COURSE SUBJECT AREAS OFFERED OUTSIDE OF DEGREE PROGRAMS

Undergraduate—accounting and related services; anthropology; bilingual, multilingual, and multicultural education; biological and physical sciences; biology; business administration, management and operations; business/commerce; chemistry; communication and journalism related; communication and media; community organization and advocacy; computer and information sciences and support services related; computer programming; computer science; computer software and media applications; computer systems networking and telecommunications; criminal justice and corrections; criminology; economics; education; education (specific subject areas); English; ethnic, cultural minority, gender, and group studies; finance and financial management services; fine and studio arts; history; information science/studies; international business; languages (foreign languages related); legal studies (non-professional general, undergraduate); linguistic, comparative, and related language studies; marketing; mathematics; mathematics and statistics related; multi/interdisciplinary studies related; physical sciences; political science and government; psychology; science, technology and society; social sciences; sociology; statistics; visual and performing arts.

Graduate—bilingual, multilingual, and multicultural education; business administration, management and operations; business/commerce; community organization and advocacy; computer and information sciences; computer and information sciences and support services related; computer/information technology administration and management; computer programming; computer software and media applications; computer systems analysis; computer systems networking and telecommunications; curriculum and instruction; education; educational administration and supervision; educational assessment, evaluation, and research; educational/instructional media design; education related; health and medical administrative services; health/medical preparatory programs; information science/studies; management information systems; marketing; public administration; publishing; student counseling and personnel services.

Non-credit—business/commerce; computer and information sciences; education; liberal arts and sciences, general studies and humanities; personal and culinary services related.

PACIFIC STATES UNIVERSITY
Los Angeles, California
http://www.psuca.edu/online/

Pacific States University was founded in 1928. It is accredited by Accrediting Council for Independent Colleges and Schools. It first offered distance learning courses in 2003. In fall 2010, there were 1 students enrolled in distance learning courses. Institutionally administered financial aid is available to distance learners.

Services Distance learners have accessibility to academic advising, library services, tutoring.

Contact Mr. Rex K. Lu, Coordinator, Pacific States University, 3450 Wilshire Boulevard, Suite 500, Los Angeles, CA 90010. Telephone: 323-731-2383 Ext. 209. Fax: 323-731-7276. E-mail: rex@psuca.edu.

DEGREES AND AWARDS

MBAIB International Business

COURSE SUBJECT AREAS OFFERED OUTSIDE OF DEGREE PROGRAMS

Undergraduate—accounting and related services; business, management, and marketing related; economics.

Graduate—accounting and computer science; business administration, management and operations; business/commerce; business/managerial economics; economics; finance and financial management services; human resources management; international business; marketing.

PAINE COLLEGE
Augusta, Georgia
http://www.paine.edu/academics/online.aspx

Paine College was founded in 1882. It is accredited by Southern Association of Colleges and Schools. It first offered distance learning courses in 2005. In fall 2010, there were 162 students enrolled in distance learning courses. Institutionally administered financial aid is available to distance learners.

Services Distance learners have accessibility to academic advising, bookstore, campus computer network, career placement assistance, e-mail services, library services, tutoring.

Contact Mr. Andre Farley, Dean of Online and Blended Programs, Paine College, 1235 15th Street, Augusta, GA 30901. Telephone: 706-793-2030. Fax: 706-793-7596. E-mail: afarley@paine.edu.

DEGREES AND AWARDS

Programs offered do not lead to a degree or other formal award.

COURSE SUBJECT AREAS OFFERED OUTSIDE OF DEGREE PROGRAMS

Undergraduate—area studies; English language and literature related; history; languages (Iranian/Persian); mathematics; philosophy; political science and government; psychology.

PALM BEACH STATE COLLEGE
Lake Worth, Florida
http://www.palmbeachstate.edu/eLearning.xml

Palm Beach State College was founded in 1933. It is accredited by Southern Association of Colleges and Schools. It first offered distance learning courses in 1997. In fall 2010, there were 7,500 students enrolled in distance learning courses. Institutionally administered financial aid is available to distance learners.

Services Distance learners have accessibility to academic advising, bookstore, career placement assistance, e-mail services, library services, tutoring.

Contact Ms. Anne Guiler, Course Management Administrator, Palm Beach State College, 4200 Congress Avenue, Lake Worth, FL 33461. Telephone: 561-868-4088. E-mail: guilera@palmbeachstate.edu.

DEGREES AND AWARDS

Programs offered do not lead to a degree or other formal award.

COURSE SUBJECT AREAS OFFERED OUTSIDE OF DEGREE PROGRAMS

Undergraduate—accounting and related services; anthropology; astronomy and astrophysics; biological and physical sciences; business/commerce; chemistry; communication and media; computer and information sciences; economics; education; electrical engineering technologies.

PAMLICO COMMUNITY COLLEGE
Grantsboro, North Carolina
http://www.pamlicocc.edu/

Pamlico Community College was founded in 1963. It is accredited by Southern Association of Colleges and Schools. It first offered distance learning courses in 1999. In fall 2010, there were 300 students enrolled in distance learning courses. Institutionally administered financial aid is available to distance learners.

Services Distance learners have accessibility to academic advising, bookstore, campus computer network, career placement assistance, e-mail services, library services, tutoring.

Contact Ms. Kathleen Mayo, Distance Learning Coordinator, Pamlico Community College, PO Box 185, Grantsboro, NC 28529. Telephone: 252-249-1851 Ext. 3012. Fax: 252-249-2377. E-mail: kmayo@pamlicocc.edu.

DEGREES AND AWARDS

Programs offered do not lead to a degree or other formal award.

COURSE SUBJECT AREAS OFFERED OUTSIDE OF DEGREE PROGRAMS

Undergraduate—accounting and computer science; accounting and related services; allied health and medical assisting services; applied mathematics; behavioral sciences; biological and physical sciences; biology; business administration, management and operations; business/commerce; business, management, and marketing related; business/managerial economics; chemistry; communications technology; computer and information sciences; computer and information sciences and support services related; computer/information technology administration and management; computer programming; computer software and media applications; computer systems networking and telecommunications; cosmetology and related personal grooming services; criminal justice and corrections; criminology; data entry/microcomputer applications; education; education related; education (specific levels and methods); electrical/electronics maintenance and repair technology; electrical engineering technologies; English; English language and literature related; fire protection; health aides/attendants/orderlies; health and medical administrative services; health services/allied health/health sciences; history; marketing; masonry; mathematics; mathematics and computer science; mathematics and statistics related; psychology; psychology related; science technologies related; sociology.

THE PARALEGAL INSTITUTE, INC.
Phoenix, Arizona
http://www.theparalegalinstitute.com/

The Paralegal Institute, Inc. was founded in 1974. It is accredited by Distance Education and Training Council. It first offered distance learning courses in 1979. In fall 2010, there were 350 students enrolled in distance learning courses. Institutionally administered financial aid is available to distance learners.

Services Distance learners have accessibility to academic advising, e-mail services, tutoring.

Contact Brooke Laing, Director of Admissions, The Paralegal Institute, Inc., 7332 East Butherus Drive, Suite 102, Scottsdale, AZ 85260. Telephone: 800-354-1254. Fax: 602-212-0502. E-mail: blaing@theparalegalinstitute.edu.

DEGREES AND AWARDS

AA Criminal Justice; Paralegal

COURSE SUBJECT AREAS OFFERED OUTSIDE OF DEGREE PROGRAMS

Undergraduate—criminal justice and corrections; legal studies (non-professional general, undergraduate).

PARIS JUNIOR COLLEGE

Paris, Texas

Http://www.parisjc.edu

Paris Junior College was founded in 1924. It is accredited by Southern Association of Colleges and Schools. It first offered distance learning courses in 1999. In fall 2010, there were 1,600 students enrolled in distance learning courses. Institutionally administered financial aid is available to distance learners.

Services Distance learners have accessibility to academic advising, bookstore, e-mail services, library services.

Contact Mrs. Shelia Reece, Director of Admissions, Paris Junior College, 2400 Clarksville Street, Paris, TX 75460. Telephone: 903-782-0425. Fax: 903-782-0427. E-mail: sreece@parisjc.edu.

DEGREES AND AWARDS

Programs offered do not lead to a degree or other formal award.

COURSE SUBJECT AREAS OFFERED OUTSIDE OF DEGREE PROGRAMS

Undergraduate—agriculture; allied health and medical assisting services; biological and physical sciences; biology; business/commerce; communication and journalism related; criminal justice and corrections; drama/theatre arts and stagecraft; economics; education; education related; education (specific levels and methods); English; health services/allied health/health sciences; history; languages (foreign languages related); microbiological sciences and immunology; plant sciences; psychology; sociology.

Non-credit—accounting and computer science; allied health and medical assisting services; American Sign Language (ASL); area studies; behavioral sciences; bilingual, multilingual, and multicultural education; business administration, management and operations; business/commerce; business operations support and assistant services; communications technology; computer and information sciences; construction trades related; design and applied arts; education related; finance and financial management services; health aides/attendants/orderlies; hospitality administration; languages (foreign languages related); legal professions and studies related; mathematics; music; public administration; real estate.

PASCO-HERNANDO COMMUNITY COLLEGE

New Port Richey, Florida

http://www.phcc.edu

Pasco-Hernando Community College was founded in 1972. It is accredited by Southern Association of Colleges and Schools. It first offered distance learning courses in 1993. In fall 2010, there were 2,602 students enrolled in distance learning courses. Institutionally administered financial aid is available to distance learners.

Services Distance learners have accessibility to academic advising, bookstore, campus computer network, career placement assistance, e-mail services, library services, tutoring.

Contact Adm. Cheryl Sandoe, Assistant Dean of Academic Technology, Pasco-Hernando Community College, 10230 Ridge Road, New Port Richey, FL 34654-5199. Telephone: 727-816-3367. Fax: 727-816-3300. E-mail: sandoec@phcc.edu.

DEGREES AND AWARDS

AA the Arts

COURSE SUBJECT AREAS OFFERED OUTSIDE OF DEGREE PROGRAMS

Undergraduate—accounting and related services; biology; business administration, management and operations; computer and information sciences; education related; legal support services; mathematics and statistics related; nutrition sciences; physical sciences; psychology; social sciences related; sociology.

Non-credit—business/corporate communications; computer and information sciences; computer programming; computer software and media applications; education; education related; education (specific subject areas); English; family and consumer economics; health and medical administrative services; health professions related; health services/allied health/health sciences; insurance; legal studies (non-professional general, undergraduate); personal and culinary services related; real estate; sales merchandising, and related marketing operations (general); sales, merchandising and related marketing operations (specialized).

PEIRCE COLLEGE

Philadelphia, Pennsylvania

Peirce College Non-Traditional Education

http://www.peirce.edu

Peirce College was founded in 1865. It is accredited by Middle States Association of Colleges and Schools. It first offered distance learning courses in 1996. In fall 2010, there were 1,812 students enrolled in distance learning courses. Institutionally administered financial aid is available to distance learners.

Services Distance learners have accessibility to academic advising, bookstore, career placement assistance, e-mail services, library services, tutoring.

Contact Ms. Nadine M. Maher, Dean, Enrollment Management, Peirce College, 1420 Pine Street, Philadelphia, PA 19102. Telephone: 888-467-3472 Ext. 9214. Fax: 215-670-9366. E-mail: info@peirce.edu.

DEGREES AND AWARDS

AA General Studies

AS Business Administration–Business Law concentration; Business Administration–Entrepreneurship/Small Business Management concentration; Business Administration–Management concentration; Business Administration–Marketing concentration; Health Information Technology; Information Technology; Paralegal Studies

BS Accounting; Business Administration–Business Law concentration; Business Administration–Entrepreneurship/Small Business Management concentration; Business Administration–Management concentration; Business Administration–Marketing concentration; Business Administration–Professional Studies concentration; Healthcare Administration; Human Resource Management; Information Technology–Desktop Applications for Business concentration; Information Technology–Information Security concentration; Information Technology–Networking, Administration, and Security concentration; Information Technology–Programming and Application Development concentration; Information Technology–Technology Management concentration; Paralegal Studies

Certificate Business Administration–Business Law concentration; Certified Information Systems Security Professional (CISSP); Information Technology–.NET Programming concentration; Information Technology–Help Desk Technician concentration; Paralegal Studies

COURSE SUBJECT AREAS OFFERED OUTSIDE OF DEGREE PROGRAMS

Undergraduate—economics; English; history; liberal arts and sciences, general studies and humanities; mathematics and statistics related; philosophy; psychology; sociology.

PELLISSIPPI STATE TECHNICAL COMMUNITY COLLEGE

Knoxville, Tennessee

Educational Technology Services

http://www.pstcc.edu/online

Pellissippi State Technical Community College was founded in 1974. It is accredited by Southern Association of Colleges and Schools. It first offered distance learning courses in 1991. In fall 2010, there were 2,700 students enrolled in distance learning courses. Institutionally administered financial aid is available to distance learners.

Services Distance learners have accessibility to academic advising, bookstore, campus computer network, career placement assistance, e-mail services, library services, tutoring.

Contact Dr. Dennis Adams, Dean of Instructional Services, Pellissippi State Technical Community College, 10915 Hardin Valley Road, Knoxville, TN 37933. Telephone: 865-694-6593. E-mail: dadams@pstcc.edu.

DEGREES AND AWARDS

AAS Web Technology

COURSE SUBJECT AREAS OFFERED OUTSIDE OF DEGREE PROGRAMS

Undergraduate—accounting and related services; allied health and medical assisting services; anthropology; archeology; behavioral sciences; biology; botany/plant biology; business administration, management and operations; business/commerce; business, management, and marketing related; communication and media; computer and information sciences; computer software and media applications; drama/theatre arts and stagecraft; English; history; human resources management; languages (Romance languages); marketing; mathematics and statistics related; music; philosophy; philosophy and religious studies related; physics; psychology; public relations, advertising, and applied communication related; sociology; statistics; visual and performing arts related.

PENINSULA COLLEGE
Port Angeles, Washington
http://pencol.edu/

Peninsula College was founded in 1961. It is accredited by Northwest Commission on Colleges and Universities. It first offered distance learning courses in 1994. In fall 2010, there were 3,899 students enrolled in distance learning courses. Institutionally administered financial aid is available to distance learners.

Services Distance learners have accessibility to academic advising, bookstore, career placement assistance, library services, tutoring.

Contact Vicki Sievert, eLearning Coordinator, Peninsula College, 1502 East Lauridsen Boulevard, Port Angeles, WA 98362. Telephone: 360-417-6272. Fax: 360-457-8100. E-mail: vsievert@pencol.edu.

DEGREES AND AWARDS

AA Liberal Arts

AAS Criminal Justice

COURSE SUBJECT AREAS OFFERED OUTSIDE OF DEGREE PROGRAMS

Undergraduate—accounting and related services; allied health and medical assisting services; anthropology; astronomy and astrophysics; biochemistry, biophysics and molecular biology; biological and physical sciences; business administration, management and operations; business/commerce; business, management, and marketing related; chemistry; communication and journalism related; computer and information sciences; computer software and media applications; criminal justice and corrections; dental support services and allied professions; economics; education; entrepreneurial and small business operations; geological and earth sciences/geosciences; health and physical education/fitness; health professions related; history; human development, family studies, and related services; information science/studies; journalism; liberal arts and sciences, general studies and humanities; mathematics; mathematics and computer science; mathematics and statistics related; music; natural sciences; nutrition sciences; pharmacology and toxicology; philosophy; physical sciences; political science and government; psychology; social sciences; sociology.

Non-credit—allied health and medical assisting services; computer and information sciences; computer and information sciences and support services related; computer software and media applications; construction trades; construction trades related; crafts, folk art and artisanry; data entry/microcomputer applications; film/video and photographic arts; fine and studio arts; fishing and fisheries sciences and management; foods, nutrition, and related services.

PENN STATE UNIVERSITY PARK
State College, Pennsylvania
Department of Distance Education/World Campus
http://www.worldcampus.psu.edu

Penn State University Park was founded in 1855. It is accredited by Middle States Association of Colleges and Schools. It first offered distance learning courses in 1998. In fall 2010, there were 8,000 students enrolled in distance learning courses. Institutionally administered financial aid is available to distance learners.

Services Distance learners have accessibility to academic advising, bookstore, campus computer network, e-mail services, library services.

Contact Penn State World Campus Adult Learner Services, Penn State University Park, 128 Outreach Building, 100 Innovation Boulevard, University Park, PA 16802. Telephone: 800-252-3592. Fax: 814-865-3290. E-mail: psuwd@psu.edu.

DEGREES AND AWARDS

AA Letters, Arts, and Sciences

AS Business Administration; Human Development and Family Studies; Information Sciences and Technology; Turfgrass Science and Management

BA Law and Society; Letters, Arts, and Sciences; Political Science; Psychology

BS Business; Criminal Justice; Information Sciences and Technology; Organizational Leadership; Psychology; Turfgrass Science

BSN Nursing–RN to BSN

Certificate Adult Development and Aging; Children, Youth, and Family Services; Digital Arts; Information Science and Technology; Labor Studies and Employment Relations; Nursing Management; Organizational Communication; SAP (Systems, Applications and Products in Data Processing); Turfgrass Management; Turfgrass Management, Advanced; Weather Forecasting

Certification Special Education Supervisory certificate

Graduate Certificate Applied Behavior Analysis for Special Education; Applied Statistics; Autism; Children's Literature; Community and Economic Development; Distance Education; Educational Technology Integration; Family Literacy; Geographic Information Systems; Geospatial Intelligence; Homeland Security and Defense; Institutional Research; Nursing–Geriatric Nursing Education; Project Management; Reading Instruction for Special Education (RISE); Supply Chain Management

MA Geographic Information Systems

MAS Applied Statistics

MBA iMBA

ME Systems Engineering

MEM Engineering Management

MEd Adult Education; Curriculum and Instruction–Children's Literature; Earth Sciences; Instructional Systems–Educational Technology

MPA Public Administration

MPM Project Management

MPS Art Education; Community and Economic Development; Homeland Security; Human Resources and Employment Relations; Information Sciences; Supply Chain Management; Turfgrass Management

MSE Software Engineering

COURSE SUBJECT AREAS OFFERED OUTSIDE OF DEGREE PROGRAMS

Undergraduate—criminal justice and corrections; human development, family studies, and related services; human resources management; information science/studies; landscape architecture; legal professions and studies related; legal studies (non-professional general, undergraduate); liberal arts and sciences, general studies and humanities; management information systems; parks, recreation and leisure facilities management; personal and culinary services related; psychology; psychology related.

Graduate—business administration, management and operations; business, management, and marketing related; community organization and advocacy; computer and information sciences; curriculum and instruction; educational assessment, evaluation, and research; educational/instructional media design; education (specific subject areas); geography and cartography; geological and earth sciences/geosciences; health services/allied health/health sciences; human resources management; special education; statistics; systems engineering.

PENNSYLVANIA COLLEGE OF TECHNOLOGY
Williamsport, Pennsylvania
http://www.pct.edu/oit/distance/

Pennsylvania College of Technology was founded in 1965. It is accredited by Middle States Association of Colleges and Schools. It first offered distance learning courses in 1996. In fall 2010, there were 717 students enrolled in distance learning courses. Institutionally administered financial aid is available to distance learners.

Services Distance learners have accessibility to academic advising, bookstore, campus computer network, career placement assistance, e-mail services, library services, tutoring.

Contact Paula Neal, Distance Learning Services Assistant, Pennsylvania College of Technology, One College Avenue, DIF #50, Williamsport, PA 17701. Telephone: 570-320-8019. Fax: 570-321-5559. E-mail: distancelearning@pct.edu.

DEGREES AND AWARDS
BS Applied Health Studies; Automotive Technology Management; Dental Hygiene; Health Information Management; Nursing; Technology Management; Web Design and Multimedia

COURSE SUBJECT AREAS OFFERED OUTSIDE OF DEGREE PROGRAMS
Undergraduate—accounting and related services; architecture; biological and biomedical sciences related; biology; building/construction finishing, management, and inspection; business/commerce; business/corporate communications; chemistry; computer and information sciences; construction engineering technologies; dental support services and allied professions; English language and literature related; environmental/environmental health engineering; finance and financial management services; fine and studio arts; geological and earth sciences/geosciences; health professions related; history; international business; marketing; mathematics; philosophy and religious studies related; statistics.

PERELANDRA COLLEGE
La Mesa, California
http://www.perelandra.edu

Perelandra College is accredited by Distance Education and Training Council. It first offered distance learning courses in 2002. In fall 2010, there were 12 students enrolled in distance learning courses. Institutionally administered financial aid is available to distance learners.

Services Distance learners have accessibility to academic advising, bookstore, career placement assistance, tutoring.

Contact Ken Kuhlken, President, Perelandra College, 8697-C La Mesa Boulevard, PMB 21, La Mesa, CA 91942. Telephone: 619-335-0441. Fax: 619-512-4291. E-mail: ken@perelandra.edu.

DEGREES AND AWARDS
BA Writing
MA Counseling; Creative Writing

COURSE SUBJECT AREAS OFFERED OUTSIDE OF DEGREE PROGRAMS
Undergraduate—English; English language and literature related.
Graduate—English; English language and literature related.

PERU STATE COLLEGE
Peru, Nebraska
http://www.peru.edu/distanceeducation/

Peru State College was founded in 1867. It is accredited by North Central Association of Colleges and Schools. It first offered distance learning courses in 2000. In fall 2010, there were 1,520 students enrolled in distance learning courses. Institutionally administered financial aid is available to distance learners.

Services Distance learners have accessibility to academic advising, bookstore, campus computer network, career placement assistance, e-mail services, library services, tutoring.

Contact Ms. Laura Roberts, Director of Offutt Operations and Online Services, Peru State College, PO Box 10, 600 Hoyt Street, Peru, NE 68421. Telephone: 888-258-5558. Fax: 402-872-2435. E-mail: lroberts@peru.edu.

DEGREES AND AWARDS
BA Business Administration; Criminal Justice; Education; Liberal Arts; Psychology
BAS Business Administration–Management
BS Business Administration; Criminal Justice; Education; Psychology
MS Ed Curriculum and Instruction
MSM Entrepreneurial and Economic Development

COURSE SUBJECT AREAS OFFERED OUTSIDE OF DEGREE PROGRAMS
Undergraduate—accounting and computer science; biology; business administration, management and operations; business, management, and marketing related; computer/information technology administration and management; computer science; criminal justice and corrections; economics; education; education (specific levels and methods); English; history; liberal arts and sciences, general studies and humanities; mathematics; music; philosophy; physical sciences; political science and government; psychology; sociology.
Graduate—business, management, and marketing related; education.

PHILADELPHIA UNIVERSITY
Philadelphia, Pennsylvania
http://www.philau.edu/

Philadelphia University was founded in 1884. It is accredited by Middle States Association of Colleges and Schools. It first offered distance learning courses in 1998. In fall 2010, there were 244 students enrolled in distance learning courses. Institutionally administered financial aid is available to distance learners.

Services Distance learners have accessibility to academic advising, bookstore, campus computer network, career placement assistance, e-mail services, library services, tutoring.

Contact Mr. Jack Klett, Director of Graduate Admissions, Philadelphia University, School House Lane and Henry Avenue, Philadelphia, PA 19144. Telephone: 215-951-2943. E-mail: gradadms@philau.edu.

DEGREES AND AWARDS
Certificate Nurse Midwifery
Graduate Certificate Sustainable Practices
MS Disaster Medicine and Management; Midwifery

COURSE SUBJECT AREAS OFFERED OUTSIDE OF DEGREE PROGRAMS
Undergraduate—accounting and related services; business administration, management and operations; economics; finance and financial management services; history; legal studies (non-professional general, undergraduate); management information systems; management sciences and quantitative methods; marketing; operations research; psychology; sociology; statistics.
Graduate—accounting and related services; apparel and textiles; environmental design; finance and financial management services; international business; management information systems; management sciences and quantitative methods; marketing; rehabilitation and therapeutic professions; statistics.

PHOENIX COLLEGE
Phoenix, Arizona

Phoenix College was founded in 1920. It is accredited by North Central Association of Colleges and Schools. It first offered distance learning courses in 2002. In fall 2010, there were 2,830 students enrolled in distance learning courses. Institutionally administered financial aid is available to distance learners.

Services Distance learners have accessibility to academic advising, e-mail services, library services, tutoring.

Contact Kurt Chambers, Faculty, Phoenix College, 1202 West Thomas Road, Phoenix, AZ 85013. Telephone: 602-285-7265. E-mail: kurt.chambers@pcmail.maricopa.edu.

DEGREES AND AWARDS
Programs offered do not lead to a degree or other formal award.

COURSE SUBJECT AREAS OFFERED OUTSIDE OF DEGREE PROGRAMS
Undergraduate—accounting and related services; anthropology; behavioral sciences; biology; business, management, and marketing related; chemistry; computer science; construction trades; criminal justice and corrections; dental support services and allied professions; economics; education; English; foods, nutrition, and related services; history; languages (foreign languages related); legal professions and studies related; library science and administration; marketing; mathematics; parks, recreation, leisure, and fitness studies related; philosophy; political science and government; psychology; real estate; religious studies; sociology.
Non-credit—accounting and related services; business, management, and marketing related; business operations support and assistant services; computer and information sciences and support services related; finance and financial management services; fine and studio arts; languages (Romance languages); marketing; real estate; sales merchandising, and related marketing operations (general).

PIEDMONT BAPTIST COLLEGE AND GRADUATE SCHOOL
Winston-Salem, North Carolina
http://www.pbc.edu

Piedmont Baptist College and Graduate School was founded in 1947. It is accredited by Transnational Association of Christian Colleges and Schools. It first offered distance learning courses in 2001. In fall 2010, there were 77 students enrolled in distance learning courses. Institutionally administered financial aid is available to distance learners.
Services Distance learners have accessibility to academic advising, bookstore, campus computer network, e-mail services, library services.
Contact Mrs. Angela Hoover, Director of Admissions, Piedmont Baptist College and Graduate School, 420 South Broad Street, Winston-Salem, NC 27101. Telephone: 336-714-7927. E-mail: hoovera@pbc.edu.

DEGREES AND AWARDS
AA Bible; Christian Ministries
BA Bible–Selected Minor, Bible for College Graduates, Christian Ministries with two minors
Certificate Biblical Foundations
MABS Biblical Studies

COURSE SUBJECT AREAS OFFERED OUTSIDE OF DEGREE PROGRAMS
Undergraduate—biblical studies; pastoral counseling and specialized ministries; religious studies; theological and ministerial studies.
Graduate—biblical studies; theological and ministerial studies.

PIEDMONT COMMUNITY COLLEGE
Roxboro, North Carolina
http://www.piedmont.cc.edu

Piedmont Community College was founded in 1970. It is accredited by Southern Association of Colleges and Schools. It first offered distance learning courses in 1989. In fall 2010, there were 721 students enrolled in distance learning courses. Institutionally administered financial aid is available to distance learners.
Services Distance learners have accessibility to academic advising, bookstore, campus computer network, career placement assistance, e-mail services, library services, tutoring.
Contact Libbie McPhaul-Moore, Distance Education Coordinator/Instructor, Piedmont Community College, PO Box 1197, Roxboro, NC 27573. Telephone: 336-599-1181 Ext. 445. Fax: 336-599-9146. E-mail: mcphaul@piedmontcc.edu.

DEGREES AND AWARDS
AA University Transfer
AAS Accounting; Business Administration; Information Systems; Web Technologies
Certificate Accounting; Business Administration; Information Systems; Marketing
Diploma Business Administration; Information Systems

COURSE SUBJECT AREAS OFFERED OUTSIDE OF DEGREE PROGRAMS
Undergraduate—accounting and computer science; biology; biotechnology; business operations support and assistant services; computer programming; criminal justice and corrections; entrepreneurial and small business operations; history; human services; marketing; mathematics and statistics related; psychology; social work; sociology.

PIKES PEAK COMMUNITY COLLEGE
Colorado Springs, Colorado
Learning Technologies
http://www.ppcc.edu

Pikes Peak Community College was founded in 1968. It is accredited by North Central Association of Colleges and Schools. It first offered distance learning courses in 1978. In fall 2010, there were 4,000 students enrolled in distance learning courses. Institutionally administered financial aid is available to distance learners.
Services Distance learners have accessibility to academic advising, bookstore, campus computer network, e-mail services, library services, tutoring.
Contact Julie Witherow, Director of eLearning/Distance Education, Pikes Peak Community College, 5675 South Academy Boulevard, Colorado Springs, CO 80906-5498. Telephone: 719-502-3049. Fax: 719-502-3556. E-mail: julie.witherow@ppcc.edu.

DEGREES AND AWARDS
AA General degree
AAS Criminal Justice; Fire Science Technology

COURSE SUBJECT AREAS OFFERED OUTSIDE OF DEGREE PROGRAMS
Undergraduate—accounting and related services; anthropology; astronomy and astrophysics; biological and physical sciences; business administration, management and operations; business/commerce; business/corporate communications; business/managerial economics; business operations support and assistant services; computer and information sciences and support services related; computer programming; computer science; computer software and media applications; computer systems networking and telecommunications; criminal justice and corrections; criminology; design and applied arts; drama/theatre arts and stagecraft; economics; English; fire protection; geography and cartography; history; journalism; marketing; natural resources and conservation related; natural resources conservation and research; political science and government; psychology; radio, television, and digital communication; sociology.

PINE TECHNICAL COLLEGE
Pine City, Minnesota
Distance Education Center
http://www.pinetech.edu

Pine Technical College was founded in 1965. It is accredited by North Central Association of Colleges and Schools. It first offered distance learning courses in 1985. In fall 2010, there were 413 students enrolled in distance learning courses. Institutionally administered financial aid is available to distance learners.
Services Distance learners have accessibility to academic advising, bookstore, campus computer network, e-mail services, library services, tutoring.
Contact Nancy Mach, Dean of Student Services, Pine Technical College, 900 4th Street SE, Pine City, MN 55063. Telephone: 320-629-5173. Fax: 320-629-5101. E-mail: machn@pinetech.edu.

DEGREES AND AWARDS

Programs offered do not lead to a degree or other formal award.

COURSE SUBJECT AREAS OFFERED OUTSIDE OF DEGREE PROGRAMS

Undergraduate—American Sign Language (ASL); business, management, and marketing related; computer programming; health professions related; mathematics; public administration and social service professions related.

Non-credit—health professions related.

PITT COMMUNITY COLLEGE

Greenville, North Carolina

Distance Education Department

http://www.pittcc.edu

Pitt Community College was founded in 1961. It is accredited by Southern Association of Colleges and Schools. It first offered distance learning courses in 1996. In fall 2010, there were 6,881 students enrolled in distance learning courses. Institutionally administered financial aid is available to distance learners.

Services Distance learners have accessibility to academic advising, bookstore, career placement assistance, e-mail services, library services, tutoring.

Contact Mr. Don Hazelwood, Director of Instructional Technology and Distance Education, Pitt Community College, Highway 11 South, PO Drawer 7007, Greenville, NC 27835-7007. Telephone: 252-493-7608. E-mail: dphazelwood179@my.pittcc.edu.

DEGREES AND AWARDS

AAS Business Administration–Marketing and Advertising; Business Administration; Computer Programming; Health Information Technology; Healthcare Management Technology; Industrial Management Technology; Medical Office Administration; Office Administation

Certificate Accounting–Basic Accounting certification; Administrative Manager's certificate; Business Administration–Human Resources Management; Computer Software Applications; Healthcare Leadership and Management; Healthcare Management; Information Systems Technology; Management Application and Principles; Marketing; Object-Oriented Programming; Office Technology Skills, Basic

COURSE SUBJECT AREAS OFFERED OUTSIDE OF DEGREE PROGRAMS

Undergraduate—accounting and related services; biochemistry, biophysics and molecular biology; biology; international business; legal studies (non-professional general, undergraduate); marketing; mental and social health services and allied professions; philosophy and religious studies related; sociology.

PITTSBURGH TECHNICAL INSTITUTE

Oakdale, Pennsylvania

http://www.pti.edu/online

Pittsburgh Technical Institute was founded in 1946. It is accredited by Middle States Association of Colleges and Schools. It first offered distance learning courses in 2001. In fall 2010, there were 146 students enrolled in distance learning courses. Institutionally administered financial aid is available to distance learners.

Services Distance learners have accessibility to academic advising, bookstore, career placement assistance, e-mail services, library services, tutoring.

Contact Jeff Leedstrom, Director of Adult Enrollment, Pittsburgh Technical Institute, 1111 McKee Road, Oakdale, PA 15071. Telephone: 412-809-5100. Fax: 412-809-5351. E-mail: leedstrom.jeff@pti.edu.

DEGREES AND AWARDS

AS Online Business Administration–Management; Online Safety and Security Administration

Certificate Medical Coding

COURSE SUBJECT AREAS OFFERED OUTSIDE OF DEGREE PROGRAMS

Undergraduate—business administration, management and operations; computer/information technology administration and management; drafting/design engineering technologies; electrical, electronics and communications engineering; health professions related; heating, air conditioning, ventilation and refrigeration maintenance technology; mathematics; physics.

PITTSBURG STATE UNIVERSITY

Pittsburg, Kansas

http://www.pittstate.edu/

Pittsburg State University was founded in 1903. It is accredited by North Central Association of Colleges and Schools. It first offered distance learning courses in 1994. In fall 2010, there were 638 students enrolled in distance learning courses. Institutionally administered financial aid is available to distance learners.

Services Distance learners have accessibility to academic advising, bookstore, campus computer network, career placement assistance, e-mail services, library services.

Contact Ms. B.B. Stotts, Director, Pittsburg State University, Continuing and Graduate Studies, 1701 South Broadway, Pittsburg, KS 66762. Telephone: 620-235-4181. Fax: 620-235-4219. E-mail: bstotts@pittstate.edu.

DEGREES AND AWARDS

BSN Nursing–RN to BSN

MA History

MS Educational Technology; Engineering Technology; Health, Human Performance and Recreation; Human Resource Development

MSE English as a Second Language; Reading Specialist

COURSE SUBJECT AREAS OFFERED OUTSIDE OF DEGREE PROGRAMS

Undergraduate—accounting and related services; biology; building/construction finishing, management, and inspection; business, management, and marketing related; communication and journalism related; computer and information sciences; construction engineering technologies; criminal justice and corrections; curriculum and instruction; design and applied arts; economics; education; engineering technologies related; English; family and consumer sciences/human sciences business services; health and physical education/fitness; history; marketing; mathematics; philosophy; physiology, pathology and related sciences; psychology; social sciences.

Graduate—communication and journalism related; construction management; curriculum and instruction; design and applied arts; education; educational administration and supervision; education (specific levels and methods); engineering technologies related; history; human resources management; library science related; psychology; special education.

PORTLAND COMMUNITY COLLEGE

Portland, Oregon

Distance Learning Department

http://www.distance.pcc.edu

Portland Community College was founded in 1961. It is accredited by Northwest Commission on Colleges and Universities. It first offered distance learning courses in 1981. In fall 2010, there were 5,732 students enrolled in distance learning courses. Institutionally administered financial aid is available to distance learners.

Services Distance learners have accessibility to academic advising, bookstore, campus computer network, career placement assistance, e-mail services, library services, tutoring.

Contact Dennis Hitchcox, Programming Coordinator, Distance Education, Portland Community College, PO Box 19000, Portland, OR 97280-0990. Telephone: 503-977-4655. Fax: 503-977-4858. E-mail: dhitchco@pcc.edu.

DEGREES AND AWARDS

AAS Management and Supervisory Development
AGS General Studies
ASAST Computer Information Systems–Network Administration; Gerontology; Medical Laboratory Technology
Certificate Medical Assisting
Certification Computer Information Systems E-Commerce–Design and Development track

COURSE SUBJECT AREAS OFFERED OUTSIDE OF DEGREE PROGRAMS

Undergraduate—accounting and computer science; air transportation; animal sciences; applied mathematics; archeology; architecture; astronomy and astrophysics; audiovisual communications technologies; biology; business administration, management and operations; business/commerce; business, management, and marketing related; business/managerial economics; chemistry; computer programming; computer science; computer software and media applications; computer systems analysis; computer systems networking and telecommunications; criminal justice and corrections; curriculum and instruction; dental support services and allied professions; economics; education; education related; English; fire protection; foods, nutrition, and related services; geography and cartography; gerontology; history; human development, family studies, and related services; human resources management; intercultural/multicultural and diversity studies; liberal arts and sciences, general studies and humanities; library science and administration; management sciences and quantitative methods; manufacturing engineering; marketing; mathematics; mathematics and computer science; mathematics and statistics related; mechanical engineering related technologies; mechanic and repair technologies related; medieval and Renaissance studies; music; nutrition sciences; peace studies and conflict resolution; philosophy; philosophy and religious studies related; physical sciences; physical sciences related; physics; political science and government; psychology; psychology related; real estate; social sciences; social sciences related; sociology; statistics; work and family studies.
Non-credit—accounting and computer science; accounting and related services; agriculture and agriculture operations related; apparel and textiles; architecture related; building/construction finishing, management, and inspection; business administration, management and operations; business/commerce; business, management, and marketing related; homeland security, law enforcement, firefighting and protective services related; journalism; languages (foreign languages related); legal professions and studies related; mechanic and repair technologies related; medieval and Renaissance studies; multi/interdisciplinary studies related; parks, recreation and leisure; parks, recreation, leisure, and fitness studies related; personal and culinary services related; philosophy and religious studies related; physiology, pathology and related sciences; precision production related; psychology related; public administration and social service professions related; public relations, advertising, and applied communication related; real estate; science technologies related; social sciences related; theology and religious vocations related; visual and performing arts related.

PORTLAND STATE UNIVERSITY
Portland, Oregon
Independent Study
http://www.istudy.pdx.edu

Portland State University was founded in 1946. It is accredited by Northwest Commission on Colleges and Universities. In fall 2010, there were 1,500 students enrolled in distance learning courses. Institutionally administered financial aid is available to distance learners.
Services Distance learners have accessibility to bookstore, e-mail services, library services.
Contact Elizabeth Harrison, Office Manager, Portland State University, School of Extended Studies, Independent Study Program, PO Box 1491, Portland, OR 97207-1491. Telephone: 800-547-8887 Ext. 54865. Fax: 503-725-4880. E-mail: istudy@pdx.edu.

DEGREES AND AWARDS

Programs offered do not lead to a degree or other formal award.

COURSE SUBJECT AREAS OFFERED OUTSIDE OF DEGREE PROGRAMS

Undergraduate—chemistry; criminal justice and corrections; economics; English; geological and earth sciences/geosciences; history; mathematics and statistics related; psychology; sociology; statistics.

PRAIRIE BIBLE INSTITUTE
Three Hills, Alberta, Canada
Prairie Distance Education
http://www.prairie.edu/distanceed

Prairie Bible Institute was founded in 1922. It is provincially chartered. It first offered distance learning courses in 1950. In fall 2010, there were 250 students enrolled in distance learning courses. Institutionally administered financial aid is available to distance learners.
Services Distance learners have accessibility to academic advising, campus computer network, career placement assistance, e-mail services, library services.
Contact Mrs. Connie Nyman, Student Services Coordinator, Prairie Bible Institute, Prairie Distance Education, Box 4000, Three Hills, AB T0M 2N0, Canada. Telephone: 800-785-4226. Fax: 403-443-3037. E-mail: distance.ed@prairie.edu.

DEGREES AND AWARDS

AA Religious Studies
BA Bible, Theology, Ministry
Certificate Bible
Diploma Theological Studies (Graduate)
Graduate Certificate Theological Studies

COURSE SUBJECT AREAS OFFERED OUTSIDE OF DEGREE PROGRAMS

Undergraduate—anthropology; biblical studies; history; missionary studies and missiology; music; philosophy and religious studies related; psychology; theological and ministerial studies.
Graduate—anthropology; biblical studies; missionary studies and missiology; theological and ministerial studies.

PRAIRIE VIEW A&M UNIVERSITY
Prairie View, Texas
Office of Distance Learning
http://dl.pvamu.edu

Prairie View A&M University was founded in 1878. It is accredited by Southern Association of Colleges and Schools. It first offered distance learning courses in 1992. In fall 2010, there were 1,875 students enrolled in distance learning courses. Institutionally administered financial aid is available to distance learners.
Services Distance learners have accessibility to bookstore, campus computer network, e-mail services, library services.
Contact Dr. John R. Williams, Director, Office of Distance Learning, Prairie View A&M University, PO Box 519, MS 1210, Prairie View, TX 77446. Telephone: 936-261-3283. Fax: 936-261-3289. E-mail: jrwilliams@pvamu.edu.

DEGREES AND AWARDS

BSN Nursing–RN
MA Counseling
MBA General Business Administration
MEd Educational Administration
MS Juvenile Justice
MSN Nursing–Family Nurse Practitioner

COURSE SUBJECT AREAS OFFERED OUTSIDE OF DEGREE PROGRAMS

Undergraduate—accounting and computer science; architecture; business, management, and marketing related; communication and journalism related; computer engineering technologies; economics; English language and literature related; finance and financial management services; history; information science/studies; languages (foreign languages related); materials engineering; mechanical engineering; sociology.

Graduate—computer/information technology administration and management; criminal justice and corrections; economics; education; ethnic, cultural minority, gender, and group studies; finance and financial management services; management information systems; marketing; psychology.

PRATT COMMUNITY COLLEGE
Pratt, Kansas
http://www.prattcc.edu

Pratt Community College was founded in 1938. It is accredited by North Central Association of Colleges and Schools. It first offered distance learning courses in 1999. In fall 2010, there were 500 students enrolled in distance learning courses. Institutionally administered financial aid is available to distance learners.

Services Distance learners have accessibility to academic advising, bookstore, campus computer network, career placement assistance, e-mail services, library services, tutoring.

Contact Dr. Jim Stratford, Vice President for Instruction, Pratt Community College, 348 NE SR 61, Pratt, KS 67124. Telephone: 620-450-2121 Ext. 121. Fax: 620-672-5288. E-mail: jims@prattcc.edu.

DEGREES AND AWARDS
Programs offered do not lead to a degree or other formal award.

COURSE SUBJECT AREAS OFFERED OUTSIDE OF DEGREE PROGRAMS
Undergraduate—accounting and related services; allied health and medical assisting services; biology; business administration, management and operations; chemistry; communication and media; computer systems networking and telecommunications; criminal justice and corrections; economics; education; electrical and power transmission installation; history; liberal arts and sciences, general studies and humanities; mathematics; music; political science and government; psychology; social sciences related; sociology.

PRESCOTT COLLEGE
Prescott, Arizona
http://www.prescott.edu/

Prescott College was founded in 1966. It is accredited by North Central Association of Colleges and Schools. It first offered distance learning courses in 1978. In fall 2010, there were 600 students enrolled in distance learning courses. Institutionally administered financial aid is available to distance learners.

Services Distance learners have accessibility to academic advising, bookstore, e-mail services, library services, tutoring.

Contact Ted Bouras, Director of Admissions, Adult and Graduate Degree Programs, Prescott College, 220 Grove Avenue, Prescott, AZ 86301. Telephone: 877-350-2100 Ext. 2106. Fax: 928-776-5242. E-mail: tbouras@prescott.edu.

DEGREES AND AWARDS
BA Adventure Education; Business; Counseling Psychology/Human Services; Creative Writing; Cultural and Regional Studies; Education; Elementary Education; Environmental Studies; History; Humanities; Management; Music; Natural Resources and Conservation; Political Science; Special Education; Sustainable Community Development
Certification Teacher certification
MA Adventure Education; Alternative Energy Systems; Anthropology; Art History; Art Therapy; Arts Management; Bilingual Education; Counseling and Psychology; Counseling–School Guidance Counseling; Cultural Studies; Ecology; Education; Educational Administration; Environmental Education; Environmental Studies; Equine Assisted Mental Health; Film and Cinema Studies; Fire Science; Foreign Languages; Gay and Lesbian Studies; Gender Studies; Higher Education Administration; Humanities; Land Use Planning; Mental Health Counseling; Museum Studies; Natural Resources and Conservation; Peace Studies; Philosophy; Photography; Playwriting and Screenwriting; Religious Studies; Sustainability Education; Sustainable Community Development; Wetlands Management; Wildlife Management
PhD Sustainability Education

COURSE SUBJECT AREAS OFFERED OUTSIDE OF DEGREE PROGRAMS
Graduate—communication and media; community organization and advocacy; education; ethnic, cultural minority, gender, and group studies; history; human development, family studies, and related services; human services; movement and mind-body therapies and education; natural resources and conservation related; natural resources management and policy; parks, recreation and leisure facilities management; peace studies and conflict resolution; philosophy and religious studies related; psychology; wildlife and wildlands science and management.
Non-credit—alternative and complementary medical support services; audiovisual communications technologies; behavioral sciences; business, management, and marketing related; communication and media; community organization and advocacy; crafts, folk art and artisanry; culinary arts and related services; dance; design and applied arts; education related; entrepreneurial and small business operations; environmental design; ethnic, cultural minority, gender, and group studies; film/video and photographic arts; health and physical education/fitness; languages (foreign languages related); movement and mind-body therapies and education; music; woodworking.

PRESENTATION COLLEGE
Aberdeen, South Dakota
http://www.presentation.edu/

Presentation College was founded in 1951. It is accredited by North Central Association of Colleges and Schools. It first offered distance learning courses in 1994. In fall 2010, there were 500 students enrolled in distance learning courses. Institutionally administered financial aid is available to distance learners.

Services Distance learners have accessibility to academic advising, bookstore, campus computer network, career placement assistance, e-mail services, library services, tutoring.

Contact JoEllen Lindner, Vice President for Enrollment and Student Retention Services, Presentation College, 1500 North Main Street, Aberdeen, SD 57401. Telephone: 605-229-8492. Fax: 605-229-8425. E-mail: joellen.lindner@presentation.edu.

DEGREES AND AWARDS
AS Medical Office Administration; Surgical Technology Completion program
BS Business Completion; Nursing–AD-LPN to BSN Nursing completion; Nursing–LPN Certificate to BSN Nursing completion; Nursing–RN to BSN completion; Radiologic Technology completion program
Certificate Medical Coding

COURSE SUBJECT AREAS OFFERED OUTSIDE OF DEGREE PROGRAMS
Undergraduate—American Sign Language (ASL); business administration, management and operations; health and medical administrative services; mathematics; psychology; religious studies; statistics.

PROVIDENCE COLLEGE
Providence, Rhode Island
http://www.providence.edu/sce

Providence College was founded in 1917. It is accredited by New England Association of Schools and Colleges. It first offered distance learning courses in 1999. In fall 2010, there were 179 students enrolled in distance learning courses.

Services Distance learners have accessibility to academic advising, bookstore, campus computer network, e-mail services, library services, tutoring.

Contact Jennifer Andrews, Academic Adviser, Providence College, School of Continuing Education, One Cunningham Square, Providence, RI 02918. Telephone: 401-865-2487. E-mail: jandrew6@providence.edu.

DEGREES AND AWARDS
Programs offered do not lead to a degree or other formal award.

COURSE SUBJECT AREAS OFFERED OUTSIDE OF DEGREE PROGRAMS

Undergraduate—astronomy and astrophysics; biology; business administration, management and operations; communication and media; cultural studies/critical theory and analysis; education; English; history; interdisciplinary studies; liberal arts and sciences, general studies and humanities; literature; philosophy; psychology; sociology; theological and ministerial studies.

Non-credit—religious education; religious studies.

PROVIDENCE COLLEGE AND THEOLOGICAL SEMINARY
Otterburne, Manitoba, Canada
Department of Continuing Education
http://www.providencecollege.ca

Providence College and Theological Seminary was founded in 1925. It is provincially chartered. It first offered distance learning courses in 1975. In fall 2010, there were 50 students enrolled in distance learning courses. Institutionally administered financial aid is available to distance learners.

Services Distance learners have accessibility to academic advising, bookstore, campus computer network, career placement assistance, e-mail services, library services.

Contact Ms. Cherry Wiebe, Director of Recruitment and Admissions, Providence College and Theological Seminary, 10 College Crescent, Otterburne, MB R0A 1G0, Canada. Telephone: 204-433-7488. Fax: 204-433-7158. E-mail: info@prov.ca.

DEGREES AND AWARDS

Programs offered do not lead to a degree or other formal award.

COURSE SUBJECT AREAS OFFERED OUTSIDE OF DEGREE PROGRAMS

Undergraduate—anthropology; biblical studies; business administration, management and operations; communication and media; education related; English language and literature related; English or French as a second or foreign language (teaching); history; interdisciplinary studies; mathematics; music; philosophy; psychology; social sciences; social work; sociology; theological and ministerial studies; theology and religious vocations related.

Graduate—biblical studies; education related; missionary studies and missiology; pastoral counseling and specialized ministries; religious studies; theological and ministerial studies; theology and religious vocations related.

Non-credit—biblical studies; education related; human resources management; missionary studies and missiology; pastoral counseling and specialized ministries; religious/sacred music; theological and ministerial studies; theology and religious vocations related.

PULASKI TECHNICAL COLLEGE
North Little Rock, Arkansas
http://www.pulaskitech.edu

Pulaski Technical College was founded in 1945. It is accredited by North Central Association of Colleges and Schools. It first offered distance learning courses in 1999. In fall 2010, there were 5,100 students enrolled in distance learning courses. Institutionally administered financial aid is available to distance learners.

Services Distance learners have accessibility to bookstore, campus computer network, e-mail services, library services, tutoring.

Contact Mr. Jason Green, Distance Learning Director, Pulaski Technical College, 3000 West Scenic Drive, North Little Rock, AR 72118. Telephone: 501-812-2716. Fax: 501-771-2844. E-mail: jkgreen@pulaskitech.edu.

DEGREES AND AWARDS

AA General Education

COURSE SUBJECT AREAS OFFERED OUTSIDE OF DEGREE PROGRAMS

Undergraduate—accounting and computer science; accounting and related services; allied health and medical assisting services; anthropology; applied mathematics; biology; business administration, management and operations; business/commerce; business operations support and assistant services; computer and information sciences; computer systems networking and telecommunications; data entry/microcomputer applications; data processing; economics; education; education related; English; family and consumer economics; health and medical administrative services; history; languages (foreign languages related); legal professions and studies related; legal studies (non-professional general, undergraduate); liberal arts and sciences, general studies and humanities; mathematics; mathematics and computer science; natural sciences; philosophy; physical sciences; political science and government; psychology; religious studies; social sciences; sociology; visual and performing arts.

PURDUE UNIVERSITY
West Lafayette, Indiana
Distance Education Services
http://www.continuinged.purdue.edu

Purdue University was founded in 1869. It is accredited by North Central Association of Colleges and Schools. It first offered distance learning courses in 1968. In fall 2010, there were 4,000 students enrolled in distance learning courses. Institutionally administered financial aid is available to distance learners.

Services Distance learners have accessibility to academic advising, e-mail services, library services.

Contact Robin E. Cunningham, Associate Director, Distance Learning, Purdue University, 128 Memorial Mall, West Lafayette, IN 47907-2034. Telephone: 765-494-2975. Fax: 765-496-6384. E-mail: rec@purdue.edu.

DEGREES AND AWARDS

AS Veterinarian Technician
EMBA Business Management
Graduate Certificate Aviation Leadership; Vet Homeland Security
MBA/MS MS Agribusiness/MBA Business
MS Ed Learning Design and Technology
MS Aviation Technology concentration; Building Construction Management; Industrial Engineering
MSCE Civil Engineering
MSE Engineering
MSEE Electrical and Computer Engineering
MSME Mechanical Engineering

COURSE SUBJECT AREAS OFFERED OUTSIDE OF DEGREE PROGRAMS

Undergraduate—animal sciences; business/corporate communications; communication and journalism related; health professions related; history; sociology; veterinary biomedical and clinical sciences.

Graduate—business administration, management and operations; curriculum and instruction; engineering.

Non-credit—agriculture; engineering.

QUEEN'S UNIVERSITY AT KINGSTON
Kingston, Ontario, Canada
Continuing and Distance Studies
http://www.queensu.ca/cds

Queen's University at Kingston was founded in 1841. It is provincially chartered. It first offered distance learning courses in 1911. In fall 2010, there were 1,500 students enrolled in distance learning courses. Institutionally administered financial aid is available to distance learners.

Services Distance learners have accessibility to academic advising, bookstore, campus computer network, career placement assistance, e-mail services, library services, tutoring.

Contact Wilma Fernetich, Advisor, Continuing and Distance Studies, Queen's University at Kingston, Kingston, ON K7L 2N6, Canada. Telephone: 613-533-6000 Ext. 77770. Fax: 613-533-6805. E-mail: fernetic@post.queensu.ca.

DEGREES AND AWARDS

Programs offered do not lead to a degree or other formal award.

COURSE SUBJECT AREAS OFFERED OUTSIDE OF DEGREE PROGRAMS

Undergraduate—biology; business/commerce; cell biology and anatomical sciences; chemistry; classical and ancient studies; cognitive science; cultural studies/critical theory and analysis; economics; English language and literature related; ethnic, cultural minority, gender, and group studies; geography and cartography; history; neurobiology and neurosciences; nutrition sciences; pharmacology and toxicology; philosophy; physics; physiology, pathology and related sciences; psychology; social sciences related; sociology; statistics.

QUINCY UNIVERSITY
Quincy, Illinois
http://www.quincy.edu/

Quincy University was founded in 1860. It is accredited by North Central Association of Colleges and Schools.

Contact Mrs. Syndi Peck, Vice President of Enrollment Management, Quincy University, 1800 College Avenue, Quincy, IL 62301-2699. Telephone: 217-228-5210. Fax: 217-228-5479. E-mail: admissions@quincy.edu.

DEGREES AND AWARDS

Programs offered do not lead to a degree or other formal award.

COURSE SUBJECT AREAS OFFERED OUTSIDE OF DEGREE PROGRAMS

Undergraduate—accounting and related services; business, management, and marketing related; communication and journalism related; education; human services; microbiological sciences and immunology; philosophy.
Graduate—education.

QUINEBAUG VALLEY COMMUNITY COLLEGE
Danielson, Connecticut
http://www.qvcc.commnet.edu/

Quinebaug Valley Community College was founded in 1971. It is accredited by New England Association of Schools and Colleges. It first offered distance learning courses in 1998. In fall 2010, there were 400 students enrolled in distance learning courses. Institutionally administered financial aid is available to distance learners.

Services Distance learners have accessibility to academic advising, library services, tutoring.

Contact Ms. Sarah Hendricks, Assistant Director of Admissions, Quinebaug Valley Community College, 742 Upper Maple Street, Danielson, CT 06239. Telephone: 860-412-7225. Fax: 860-412-7222. E-mail: shendricks@qvcc.commnet.edu.

DEGREES AND AWARDS

Programs offered do not lead to a degree or other formal award.

COURSE SUBJECT AREAS OFFERED OUTSIDE OF DEGREE PROGRAMS

Undergraduate—anthropology; biological and physical sciences; business, management, and marketing related; education; engineering; English language and literature related; health and medical administrative services; history; human services; liberal arts and sciences, general studies and humanities; materials sciences; nutrition sciences; political science and government; polymer/plastics engineering; social sciences; sociology.
Non-credit—accounting and computer science; allied health and medical assisting services; business/corporate communications; computer and information sciences and support services related; computer software and media applications; dental support services and allied professions; dietetics and clinical nutrition services; health and medical administrative services; legal professions and studies related; personal and culinary services related; pharmacy, pharmaceutical sciences, and administration; polymer/plastics engineering; real estate; sales merchandising, and related marketing operations (general); veterinary biomedical and clinical sciences.

QUINNIPIAC UNIVERSITY
Hamden, Connecticut
http://www.quinnipiac.edu/quonline

Quinnipiac University was founded in 1929. It is accredited by New England Association of Schools and Colleges. It first offered distance learning courses in 2001. In fall 2010, there were 653 students enrolled in distance learning courses. Institutionally administered financial aid is available to distance learners.

Services Distance learners have accessibility to academic advising, bookstore, campus computer network, career placement assistance, e-mail services, library services, tutoring.

Contact Adm. Valerie Schlesinger, Director of Admissions, Quinnipiac University, 275 Mount Carmel Avenue, Hamden, CT 06518. Telephone: 203-582-8200. E-mail: valerie.schlesinger@quinnipiac.edu.

DEGREES AND AWARDS

BS Organizational Leadership
MBA Business Administration
MS Higher Education Leadership Professional focus; Human Resource Leadership Professional focus; Information Technology Leadership Professional focus; Insurance Leadership Professional focus; Organizational Leadership, general degree
MSC Interactive Communications

COURSE SUBJECT AREAS OFFERED OUTSIDE OF DEGREE PROGRAMS

Undergraduate—accounting and computer science; applied mathematics; behavioral sciences; biological and physical sciences; biology; business/managerial economics; chemistry; communication and journalism related; communication and media; computer science; history; management information systems; political science and government.
Graduate—accounting and computer science; accounting and related services; business, management, and marketing related; business/managerial economics; communication and journalism related; communication and media; communications technologies and support services related; computer and information sciences; education related; finance and financial management services; journalism; management information systems.
Non-credit—education.

QUINSIGAMOND COMMUNITY COLLEGE
Worcester, Massachusetts
http://www.qcc.edu

Quinsigamond Community College was founded in 1963. It is accredited by New England Association of Schools and Colleges. It first offered distance learning courses in 2001. In fall 2010, there were 1,920 students enrolled in distance learning courses. Institutionally administered financial aid is available to distance learners.

Services Distance learners have accessibility to academic advising, bookstore, campus computer network, career placement assistance, e-mail services, library services, tutoring.

Contact Paula Moseley, Enrollment Counselor (Senior Admissions Counselor), Quinsigamond Community College, 670 West Boylston Street, Worcester, MA 01606. Telephone: 508-854-7558. E-mail: paulajm@qcc.mass.edu.

DEGREES AND AWARDS

AA Early Childhood Education–Career option; General Studies; Liberal Arts
AAS Telecommunications Technology
AS Business Administration Career; Business Administration Transfer; Computer Information Systems–Applications Specialist option; Com-

puter Information Systems–Programming option; Computer Systems Engineering Technology–Computer Forensics option; Criminal Justice; Electronics Technology–Biomedical Instrument option and Electronics Technician option; Fire Science; Hotel and Restaurant Management–Hospitality option and Food service option; Human Services; Manufacturing Technolgy; Medical Support Specialist, Medical Assisting option; Paramedic Technology

COURSE SUBJECT AREAS OFFERED OUTSIDE OF DEGREE PROGRAMS

Undergraduate—accounting and computer science; allied health and medical assisting services; applied mathematics; behavioral sciences; biological and physical sciences; business, management, and marketing related; computer and information sciences; computer programming; criminal justice and corrections; economics; English; fire protection; history; human services; liberal arts and sciences, general studies and humanities; mathematics; psychology; sociology.

Non-credit—accounting and related services; business, management, and marketing related; computer and information sciences and support services related; entrepreneurial and small business operations; graphic communications; health services/allied health/health sciences; legal professions and studies related; sales merchandising, and related marketing operations (general); teaching assistants/aides; veterinary biomedical and clinical sciences.

RANDOLPH COMMUNITY COLLEGE
Asheboro, North Carolina
Virtual Campus
http://moodle.randolph.edu

Randolph Community College was founded in 1962. It is accredited by Southern Association of Colleges and Schools. It first offered distance learning courses in 1998. In fall 2010, there were 2,500 students enrolled in distance learning courses. Institutionally administered financial aid is available to distance learners.

Services Distance learners have accessibility to academic advising, bookstore, e-mail services, library services, tutoring.

Contact Tracy A. Emerson, Distance Education Technical Specialist, Randolph Community College, 629 Industrial Park Avenue, PO Box 1009, Asheboro, NC 27205. Telephone: 336-633-0263. Fax: 336-629-4695. E-mail: taemerson@randolph.edu.

DEGREES AND AWARDS

AA College Transfer degree

AAS Accounting; Business Administration; Criminal Justice; Information Systems; Office Systems Technology

COURSE SUBJECT AREAS OFFERED OUTSIDE OF DEGREE PROGRAMS

Undergraduate—accounting and related services; computer and information sciences; computer software and media applications; criminal justice and corrections; economics; education (specific subject areas); ethnic, cultural minority, gender, and group studies; finance and financial management services; history; human development, family studies, and related services; human services; languages (foreign languages related); legal studies (non-professional general, undergraduate); marketing; mathematics; music; philosophy and religious studies related; psychology; sociology.

Non-credit—accounting and related services; allied health and medical assisting services; allied health diagnostic, intervention, and treatment professions; biology; business operations support and assistant services; clinical/medical laboratory science/research; computer and information sciences; computer software and media applications; gerontology; human services; languages (foreign languages related); legal support services; pharmacy, pharmaceutical sciences, and administration.

RAPPAHANNOCK COMMUNITY COLLEGE
Glenns, Virginia
Distance Learning
http://www.rappahannock.edu

Rappahannock Community College was founded in 1970. It is accredited by Southern Association of Colleges and Schools. It first offered distance learning courses in 1995. In fall 2010, there were 1,300 students enrolled in distance learning courses. Institutionally administered financial aid is available to distance learners.

Services Distance learners have accessibility to academic advising, bookstore, campus computer network, career placement assistance, e-mail services, library services, tutoring.

Contact Kristy Walker, Assistant for Distance Learning and Technology, Rappahannock Community College, 52 Campus Drive, Warsaw, VA 22572. Telephone: 804-333-6786. Fax: 804-333-6784. E-mail: kwalker@rappahannock.edu.

DEGREES AND AWARDS

AAS General Studies

Certificate Administrative Support; Bookkeeping/Accounting

COURSE SUBJECT AREAS OFFERED OUTSIDE OF DEGREE PROGRAMS

Undergraduate—accounting and related services; allied health and medical assisting services; astronomy and astrophysics; business administration, management and operations; business/corporate communications; criminal justice and corrections; education; fine and studio arts; geological and earth sciences/geosciences; health and physical education/fitness; history; mathematics; psychology; religious studies; sociology.

READING AREA COMMUNITY COLLEGE
Reading, Pennsylvania
http://www.racc.edu

Reading Area Community College was founded in 1971. It is accredited by Middle States Association of Colleges and Schools. It first offered distance learning courses in 1986. In fall 2010, there were 920 students enrolled in distance learning courses. Institutionally administered financial aid is available to distance learners.

Services Distance learners have accessibility to academic advising, bookstore, campus computer network, e-mail services, library services, tutoring.

Contact Ms. Mary Ellen G. Heckman, Assistant Dean of Library Services and Learning Resources, Reading Area Community College, 10 South Second Street, PO Box 1706, Reading, PA 19603. Telephone: 610-372-4721 Ext. 5061. E-mail: mheckman@racc.edu.

DEGREES AND AWARDS

AGS General Studies

COURSE SUBJECT AREAS OFFERED OUTSIDE OF DEGREE PROGRAMS

Undergraduate—accounting and related services; business administration, management and operations; business/commerce; computer and information sciences; drama/theatre arts and stagecraft; economics; English language and literature related; film/video and photographic arts; human development, family studies, and related services; languages (Romance languages); library science related; marketing; mathematics; psychology; sociology; statistics.

Non-credit—allied health and medical assisting services; business, management, and marketing related.

REGENT COLLEGE
Vancouver, British Columbia, Canada
http://www.regent-college.edu/distance

Regent College was founded in 1968. It is provincially chartered. It first offered distance learning courses in 1998. In fall 2010, there were 99 students enrolled in distance learning courses. Institutionally administered financial aid is available to distance learners.

Services Distance learners have accessibility to academic advising, bookstore, campus computer network, library services, tutoring.

Contact Fiona Broadhead, Administrative Assistant, Regent College, 5800 University Boulevard, Vancouver, BC V6T 2E4, Canada. Telephone: 604-224-3245. Fax: 604-224-3097. E-mail: distance.education @regent-college.edu.

DEGREES AND AWARDS

Programs offered do not lead to a degree or other formal award.

COURSE SUBJECT AREAS OFFERED OUTSIDE OF DEGREE PROGRAMS

Graduate—biblical studies; religious education; religious studies; theological and ministerial studies; theology and religious vocations related.
Non-credit—biblical studies; religious education; religious studies; theological and ministerial studies; theology and religious vocations related.

REGENT UNIVERSITY
Virginia Beach, Virginia
Distance Education
http://www.regent.edu

Regent University was founded in 1977. It is accredited by Southern Association of Colleges and Schools. It first offered distance learning courses in 1989. In fall 2010, there were 4,092 students enrolled in distance learning courses. Institutionally administered financial aid is available to distance learners.
Services Distance learners have accessibility to academic advising, bookstore, campus computer network, career placement assistance, e-mail services, library services, tutoring.
Contact Mr. Matthew Chadwick, Director of Enrollment Management, Regent University, 1000 Regent University Drive, LIB 102, Virginia Beach, VA 23464. Telephone: 800-373-5504. Fax: 757-352-4381. E-mail: admissions@regent.edu.

DEGREES AND AWARDS

AA Accounting; Business; Christian Studies; Criminal Justice; General Studies; History; Human Resource Management; Information Systems; International Business; Marketing; Psychology
BA Animation; Biblical and Theological Studies; Christian Ministry; Cinema-Television; Communication; English; Government; History; Religious Studies; Theater
BS Business; Criminal Justice; Elementary Education; Information Systems Technology; Interdisciplinary Studies; Mathematics; Organizational Leadership and Management; Psychology
Certificate TESOL
CAGS Education; Leadership
Ed S Special Education Leadership
Graduate Certificate Leadership
MA Biblical Studies; Cinema Arts; Clinical Mental Health Counseling; Clinical Psychology; Communication; Counseling; Government; Human Services Counseling; Journalism; Organizational Leadership; Practical Theology; Strategic Foresight; Television Arts; Theater Arts
MBA Business Administration
MDiv Practical Theology
MEd Career Switcher with Licensure; Christian School Program; Cross-Categorical Special Education; Educational Leadership; Elementary Education Licensure; Individualized degree program; Leadership in Character Education; Leadership in Mathematics Education; Student Affairs; TESOL
DMin Ministry–Leadership and Renewal
DSL Strategic Leadership
EdD Education
PhD Communication; Counseling Education and Supervision; Organizational Leadership; Renewal Studies

COURSE SUBJECT AREAS OFFERED OUTSIDE OF DEGREE PROGRAMS

Undergraduate—accounting and related services; biblical studies; business administration, management and operations; business/commerce; business, management, and marketing related; communication and journalism related; communication and media; communications technology; criminal justice and corrections; drama/theatre arts and stagecraft; education; English; film/video and photographic arts; history; human resources management; information science/studies; international business; management information systems; marketing; mathematics; natural sciences; physical sciences; political science and government; psychology; religious studies; social sciences; theological and ministerial studies; theology and religious vocations related; visual and performing arts.
Graduate—accounting and related services; biblical studies; business administration, management and operations; business/commerce; business, management, and marketing related; communication and journalism related; communication and media; communications technology; education; educational administration and supervision; film/video and photographic arts; international business; journalism; legal professions and studies related; legal research and advanced professional studies; legal support services; mental and social health services and allied professions; missionary studies and missiology; pastoral counseling and specialized ministries; political science and government; psychology; public administration; public policy analysis; religious education; religious studies; theological and ministerial studies; theology and religious vocations related; visual and performing arts.

REINHARDT UNIVERSITY
Waleska, Georgia
http://ru.learninghouse.com

Reinhardt University was founded in 1883. It is accredited by Southern Association of Colleges and Schools. It first offered distance learning courses in 2007. In fall 2010, there were 152 students enrolled in distance learning courses. Institutionally administered financial aid is available to distance learners.
Services Distance learners have accessibility to academic advising, bookstore, campus computer network, career placement assistance, e-mail services, library services, tutoring.
Contact Dr. Thomas Reed, Coordinator of Online Instruction, Reinhardt University, 7300 Reinhardt Circle, Waleska, GA 30183-2981. Telephone: 770-720-9196. Fax: 770-720-5602. E-mail: tmr@reinhardt.edu.

DEGREES AND AWARDS

Programs offered do not lead to a degree or other formal award.

COURSE SUBJECT AREAS OFFERED OUTSIDE OF DEGREE PROGRAMS

Undergraduate—accounting and related services; arts, entertainment, and media management; business administration, management and operations; business, management, and marketing related; business operations support and assistant services; economics; English; history; religious studies.

REND LAKE COLLEGE
Ina, Illinois
Learning Resource Center
http://www.rlc.edu

Rend Lake College was founded in 1967. It is accredited by North Central Association of Colleges and Schools. It first offered distance learning courses in 1995. In fall 2010, there were 204 students enrolled in distance learning courses. Institutionally administered financial aid is available to distance learners.
Services Distance learners have accessibility to academic advising, bookstore, campus computer network, career placement assistance, e-mail services, library services, tutoring.
Contact Mrs. Krystal N. Reagan, Distance Learning and Media Technology Specialist, Rend Lake College, 468 North Ken Gray Parkway, Ina, IL 62846. Telephone: 618-437-5321 Ext. 1299. Fax: 618-437-5677. E-mail: reagank@rlc.edu.

DEGREES AND AWARDS

Programs offered do not lead to a degree or other formal award.

COURSE SUBJECT AREAS OFFERED OUTSIDE OF DEGREE PROGRAMS

Undergraduate—accounting and computer science; accounting and related services; anthropology; business administration, management and operations; business/commerce; business/corporate communications;

business, management, and marketing related; business/managerial economics; business operations support and assistant services; computer/information technology administration and management; computer programming; computer science; computer software and media applications; computer systems analysis; computer systems networking and telecommunications; criminal justice and corrections; dietetics and clinical nutrition services; economics; education; English; family and consumer economics; family and consumer sciences/human sciences business services; film/video and photographic arts; finance and financial management services; foods, nutrition, and related services; geography and cartography; geological and earth sciences/geosciences; health and physical education/fitness; health services/allied health/health sciences; history; international/global studies; liberal arts and sciences, general studies and humanities; management information systems; marketing; mathematics; microbiological sciences and immunology; music; nutrition sciences; philosophy; philosophy and religious studies related; plant sciences; political science and government; psychology; psychology related; real estate; religious studies; social sciences; sociology; work and family studies.
Non-credit—accounting and related services; business administration, management and operations; business/commerce; business operations support and assistant services; computer software and media applications; entrepreneurial and small business operations; human resources management; languages (foreign languages related); sales merchandising, and related marketing operations (general).

RESEARCH COLLEGE OF NURSING
Kansas City, Missouri
College of Nursing
http://www.researchcollege.edu/

Research College of Nursing was founded in 1980. It is accredited by North Central Association of Colleges and Schools. It first offered distance learning courses in 2000. In fall 2010, there were 100 students enrolled in distance learning courses. Institutionally administered financial aid is available to distance learners.
Services Distance learners have accessibility to academic advising, campus computer network, e-mail services.
Contact Ms. Leslie Ann Mendenhall, Director of Transfer and Graduate Recruitment, Research College of Nursing, 2525 East Meyer Boulevard, Kansas City, MO 64132. Telephone: 816-995-2820. Fax: 816-995-2813. E-mail: leslie.mendenhall@researchcollege.edu.

DEGREES AND AWARDS
MSN Executive Nurse Practice

COURSE SUBJECT AREAS OFFERED OUTSIDE OF DEGREE PROGRAMS
Undergraduate—physiology, pathology and related sciences.
Graduate—pharmacology and toxicology; physiology, pathology and related sciences.

THE RICHARD STOCKTON COLLEGE OF NEW JERSEY
Pomona, New Jersey
Office of Distance Education
http://www.stockton.edu/distance

The Richard Stockton College of New Jersey was founded in 1969. It is accredited by Middle States Association of Colleges and Schools. It first offered distance learning courses in 1996. In fall 2010, there were 2,013 students enrolled in distance learning courses. Institutionally administered financial aid is available to distance learners.
Services Distance learners have accessibility to academic advising, bookstore, campus computer network, e-mail services, library services.
Contact Dennis Fotia, Assistant Director of Distance Education, The Richard Stockton College of New Jersey, PO Box 195, Pomona, NJ 08240-0195. Telephone: 609-652-4580. Fax: 609-626-5562. E-mail: dennis.fotia@stockton.edu.

DEGREES AND AWARDS
Programs offered do not lead to a degree or other formal award.

COURSE SUBJECT AREAS OFFERED OUTSIDE OF DEGREE PROGRAMS
Undergraduate—accounting and computer science; anthropology; applied mathematics; area studies; audiovisual communications technologies; behavioral sciences; business administration, management and operations; communication and media; criminal justice and corrections; criminology; curriculum and instruction; education; ethnic, cultural minority, gender, and group studies; film/video and photographic arts; foods, nutrition, and related services; health professions related; international business; liberal arts and sciences, general studies and humanities; marketing; mathematics and statistics related; nutrition sciences; psychology; psychology related; public health; sociology; special education; statistics.
Graduate—allied health and medical assisting services; business, management, and marketing related; holocaust and related studies; information science/studies; marketing.
Non-credit—accounting and related services; agricultural and food products processing; allied health and medical assisting services; film/video and photographic arts; library science and administration; marketing; radio, television, and digital communication; real estate; sales merchandising, and related marketing operations (general); teaching assistants/aides.

RICHMOND COMMUNITY COLLEGE
Hamlet, North Carolina
http://www.richmondcc.edu/

Richmond Community College was founded in 1964. It is accredited by Southern Association of Colleges and Schools. It first offered distance learning courses in 2000. In fall 2010, there were 630 students enrolled in distance learning courses. Institutionally administered financial aid is available to distance learners.
Services Distance learners have accessibility to academic advising, bookstore, e-mail services, library services, tutoring.
Contact Ms. Sharon Goodman, Director of Counseling, Richmond Community College, PO Box 1189, Hamlet, NC 28345. Telephone: 910-410-1734. Fax: 910-582-7102. E-mail: sharong@richmondcc.edu.

DEGREES AND AWARDS
Programs offered do not lead to a degree or other formal award.

COURSE SUBJECT AREAS OFFERED OUTSIDE OF DEGREE PROGRAMS
Undergraduate—accounting and computer science; allied health and medical assisting services; business administration, management and operations; business/managerial economics; communication and media; computer science; criminal justice and corrections; economics; education; English; psychology; sociology.
Non-credit—allied health and medical assisting services; business operations support and assistant services; computer software and media applications; criminal justice and corrections; education; languages (foreign languages related).

RIDER UNIVERSITY
Lawrenceville, New Jersey
http://www.rider.edu/ccs

Rider University was founded in 1865. It is accredited by Middle States Association of Colleges and Schools. In fall 2010, there were 218 students enrolled in distance learning courses. Institutionally administered financial aid is available to distance learners.
Services Distance learners have accessibility to academic advising, bookstore, e-mail services, library services.
Contact Dean Boris Vilic, Dean, College of Continuing Studies, Rider University, 2083 Lawrenceville Road, Lawrenceville, NJ 08648. Telephone: 609-896-5033. Fax: 609-896-5261. E-mail: bvilic@rider.edu.

DEGREES AND AWARDS
BS Business Administration

RIO HONDO COLLEGE
Whittier, California
http://www.riohondo.edu/

Rio Hondo College was founded in 1960. It is accredited by Western Association of Schools and Colleges. It first offered distance learning courses in 1998. In fall 2010, there were 11,065 students enrolled in distance learning courses. Institutionally administered financial aid is available to distance learners.

Services Distance learners have accessibility to academic advising, bookstore, campus computer network, library services, tutoring.

Contact Judy Pearson, Director of Admissions and Records, Rio Hondo College, 3600 Workman Mill Road, Whittier, CA 90601. Telephone: 562-692-0921 Ext. 4639. E-mail: jpearson@riohondo.edu.

DEGREES AND AWARDS

Programs offered do not lead to a degree or other formal award.

COURSE SUBJECT AREAS OFFERED OUTSIDE OF DEGREE PROGRAMS

Undergraduate—accounting and related services; anthropology; archeology; business, management, and marketing related; computer and information sciences; computer programming; criminal justice and corrections; economics; education related; English; fine and studio arts; fire protection; geological and earth sciences/geosciences; health and medical administrative services; health and physical education/fitness; history; international business; languages (Romance languages); library science and administration; library science related; marketing; mathematics; political science and government; psychology; sociology.

RIVERSIDE COMMUNITY COLLEGE DISTRICT
Riverside, California
Open Campus
http://www.opencampus.com

Riverside Community College District was founded in 1916. It is accredited by Western Association of Schools and Colleges. It first offered distance learning courses in 1982. In fall 2010, there were 16,000 students enrolled in distance learning courses. Institutionally administered financial aid is available to distance learners.

Services Distance learners have accessibility to academic advising, bookstore, campus computer network, career placement assistance, e-mail services, library services.

Contact Col. Glen L. Brady, Director, Distance Education/Open Campus, Riverside Community College District, Open Campus, 1533 Spruce Street, Riverside, CA 92507. Telephone: 951-222-8561. Fax: 951-686-4122. E-mail: glen.brady@rccd.edu.

DEGREES AND AWARDS

Programs offered do not lead to a degree or other formal award.

COURSE SUBJECT AREAS OFFERED OUTSIDE OF DEGREE PROGRAMS

Undergraduate—accounting and related services; American Sign Language (ASL); anthropology; architectural history and criticism; architecture; astronomy and astrophysics; biology; business administration, management and operations; business/commerce; communication and media; computer and information sciences; computer science; computer systems networking and telecommunications; criminology; economics; English; film/video and photographic arts; geography and cartography; graphic communications; history; hospitality administration; human resources management; languages (classics and classical); languages (foreign languages related); languages (Middle/Near Eastern and Semitic); legal support services; library science and administration; linguistic, comparative, and related language studies; marketing; mathematics; music; nutrition sciences; philosophy; political science and government; psychology; radio, television, and digital communication; real estate; religious studies; sociology; transportation and materials moving related; visual and performing arts; work and family studies.

Non-credit—mathematics.

RIVIER COLLEGE
Nashua, New Hampshire
http://Rivier.edu/

Rivier College was founded in 1933. It is accredited by New England Association of Schools and Colleges. It first offered distance learning courses in 2006. In fall 2010, there were 600 students enrolled in distance learning courses. Institutionally administered financial aid is available to distance learners.

Services Distance learners have accessibility to academic advising, bookstore, campus computer network, career placement assistance, e-mail services, library services, tutoring.

Contact Mr. Mat Kitredge, Director of Graduate and Undergraduate Admissions, Rivier College, 420 South Main Street, Nashua, NH 03060. Telephone: 603-897-8229. Fax: 603-897-8811. E-mail: mkitredge@rivier.edu.

DEGREES AND AWARDS

BA Psychology
BS Nursing

COURSE SUBJECT AREAS OFFERED OUTSIDE OF DEGREE PROGRAMS

Undergraduate—behavioral sciences; business administration, management and operations; communication and media; economics; English; history; philosophy; physics; psychology; registered nursing, nursing administration, nursing research and clinical nursing; religious studies; sociology.

Graduate—business administration, management and operations; education.

ROBERT MORRIS UNIVERSITY
Moon Township, Pennsylvania
Department of Enrollment Management
http://www.rmu.edu/web/cms/fully-online/Pages/default.aspx

Robert Morris University was founded in 1921. It is accredited by Middle States Association of Colleges and Schools. It first offered distance learning courses in 1999. In fall 2010, there were 3,628 students enrolled in distance learning courses. Institutionally administered financial aid is available to distance learners.

Services Distance learners have accessibility to academic advising, bookstore, campus computer network, career placement assistance, e-mail services, library services, tutoring.

Contact Ms. Constance Barlamas, Admissions Counselor, Online Programs, Robert Morris University, 6001 University Boulevard, Moon Township, PA 15108. Telephone: 412-397-5224. E-mail: onlineadmissions@rmu.edu.

DEGREES AND AWARDS

BA Professional and Technical Writing
BS Applied Psychology; Health Services Administration; Organizational Studies
MBA General Management
MS Business, Computer/Information Tech; Instructional Leadership; Organizational Studies

COURSE SUBJECT AREAS OFFERED OUTSIDE OF DEGREE PROGRAMS

Undergraduate—accounting and related services; biological and biomedical sciences related; business, management, and marketing related; communication and journalism related; computer systems analysis; education; English; environmental/environmental health engineering; finance and financial management services; health and medical administrative services; history; legal studies (non-professional general, undergraduate); management information systems; marketing; mathematics and statistics related; multi/interdisciplinary studies related; physical sciences; psychology; social sciences.

Graduate—computer and information sciences; curriculum and instruction; management information systems; multi/interdisciplinary studies related.

ROCHESTER INSTITUTE OF TECHNOLOGY
Rochester, New York
Graduate Enrollment Services
http://www.rit.edu/online

Rochester Institute of Technology was founded in 1829. It is accredited by Middle States Association of Colleges and Schools. It first offered distance learning courses in 1979. In fall 2010, there were 4,500 students enrolled in distance learning courses. Institutionally administered financial aid is available to distance learners.

Services Distance learners have accessibility to academic advising, bookstore, campus computer network, career placement assistance, e-mail services, library services.

Contact Ms. Diane Ellison, Director, Office of Part-time and Graduate Enrollment Services, Rochester Institute of Technology, Bausch & Lomb Center, 58 Lomb Memorial Drive, Rochester, NY 14623. Telephone: 585-475-2229. Fax: 585-475-7164. E-mail: opes@rit.edu.

DEGREES AND AWARDS
AAS Applied Arts and Science
BS Arts and Science–Applied Arts and Science
Certificate Fundamentals of Manufacturing Management; Health Systems Administration; International Logistics and Transportation Management; Public Relations Communications–Professional Writing; Quality Management; Small Business Management; Technical Communication, Basic; Technical Communications, advanced
Diploma Applied Arts and Science
Graduate Certificate Elements of Health Care Leadership; Health Systems Finance; Network Planning and Design; Networking and Systems Administration; Project Management; Senior Living Management; Statistical Methods for Product and Process Improvement; Statistical Quality; Strategic Training; Technical Information Design
MEngr Microelectronics Manufacturing Engineering
MS Applied Statistics; Environmental Health and Safety Management; Facility Management; Health Systems Administration; Imaging Science; Manufacturing Leadership; Networking and Systems Administration; Product Development; Professional Studies; Service Leadership and Innovation; Telecommunications Engineering Technology

COURSE SUBJECT AREAS OFFERED OUTSIDE OF DEGREE PROGRAMS
Undergraduate—anthropology; architectural engineering; behavioral sciences; biology; business administration, management and operations; business/corporate communications; business, management, and marketing related; chemistry; communication and journalism related; communication and media; graphic communications; health services/allied health/health sciences; hospitality administration; human resources management; international business; multi/interdisciplinary studies related; political science and government; psychology; sociology; statistics.
Graduate—business administration, management and operations; business, management, and marketing related; communication and media; computer and information sciences; computer/information technology administration and management; construction management; environmental/environmental health engineering; health professions related; health services/allied health/health sciences; hospitality administration; industrial engineering; mathematics; statistics.

ROCKINGHAM COMMUNITY COLLEGE
Wentworth, North Carolina
http://www.rockinghamcc.edu

Rockingham Community College was founded in 1964. It is accredited by Southern Association of Colleges and Schools. It first offered distance learning courses in 1997. Institutionally administered financial aid is available to distance learners.

Services Distance learners have accessibility to academic advising, bookstore, e-mail services, library services.

Contact Dr. Jan Overman, Vice President for Academic Affairs, Rockingham Community College, PO Box 38, Wentworth, NC 27375-0038. Telephone: 336-342-4261 Ext. 2138. Fax: 336-349-9986. E-mail: overmanj@rockinghamcc.edu.

DEGREES AND AWARDS
Programs offered do not lead to a degree or other formal award.

COURSE SUBJECT AREAS OFFERED OUTSIDE OF DEGREE PROGRAMS
Undergraduate—business/commerce; computer software and media applications; data entry/microcomputer applications; economics.
Non-credit—allied health diagnostic, intervention, and treatment professions; bilingual, multilingual, and multicultural education; business administration, management and operations; business/commerce; business/corporate communications; business, management, and marketing related; business/managerial economics; business operations support and assistant services; communication and journalism related; communication and media; communications technology; computer and information sciences; computer programming; computer science; computer software and media applications; computer systems analysis; computer systems networking and telecommunications; data entry/microcomputer applications; data processing; design and applied arts; entrepreneurial and small business operations; finance and financial management services; fire protection; human services; industrial production technologies; international business; management information systems; management sciences and quantitative methods; marketing; public health; sales merchandising, and related marketing operations (general); sales, merchandising and related marketing operations (specialized).

ROCKLAND COMMUNITY COLLEGE
Suffern, New York
Telecourse and Distance Learning Department
http://www.sunyrockland.edu/academics/distance-learning

Rockland Community College was founded in 1959. It is accredited by Middle States Association of Colleges and Schools. It first offered distance learning courses in 1985. In fall 2010, there were 950 students enrolled in distance learning courses. Institutionally administered financial aid is available to distance learners.

Services Distance learners have accessibility to academic advising, bookstore, campus computer network, career placement assistance, e-mail services, library services, tutoring.

Contact Mr. Rick Echevarria, Administrative Assistant, Rockland Community College, 145 College Road, Room 8300, Suffern, NY 10901. Telephone: 845-574-4713. E-mail: rechevar@sunyrockland.edu.

DEGREES AND AWARDS
Programs offered do not lead to a degree or other formal award.

COURSE SUBJECT AREAS OFFERED OUTSIDE OF DEGREE PROGRAMS
Undergraduate—anthropology; biology; business/commerce; chemistry; computer science; economics; English; finance and financial management services; fine and studio arts; geography and cartography; health/medical preparatory programs; health professions related; history; liberal arts and sciences, general studies and humanities; marketing; mathematics; philosophy; physical sciences; political science and government; psychology; social sciences related.
Graduate—economics; statistics.

ROGERS STATE UNIVERSITY
Claremore, Oklahoma
Distance Learning
http://www.rsuonline.edu

Rogers State University was founded in 1909. It is accredited by North Central Association of Colleges and Schools. It first offered distance learning courses in 1989. In fall 2010, there were 941 students enrolled in distance learning courses. Institutionally administered financial aid is available to distance learners.

Services Distance learners have accessibility to academic advising, bookstore, career placement assistance, e-mail services, library services.

Contact Kari Johnson, Online Counselor, Rogers State University, 1701 West Will Rogers Boulevard, Claremore, OK 74017. Telephone: 918-343-7726. Fax: 918-343-7595. E-mail: online@rsu.edu.

DEGREES AND AWARDS

AA Business Administration; Liberal Arts–English or Global Humanities option
AAS Applied Technology
AS Computer Science
BA Liberal Arts–English or Global Humanities option
BS Business Administration–Management option; Business Information Technology–Computer Network Administration or Software Development and Multimedia option; Organizational Leadership–Business Studies, Communications Strategies, Liberal Studies, or Social Studies focus
BTECH Applied Technology

COURSE SUBJECT AREAS OFFERED OUTSIDE OF DEGREE PROGRAMS

Undergraduate—accounting and related services; biology; business administration, management and operations; computer/information technology administration and management; criminal justice and corrections; engineering-related technologies; English; fine and studio arts; geological and earth sciences/geosciences; health professions related; history; languages (Romance languages); liberal arts and sciences, general studies and humanities; marketing; mathematics; music; nutrition sciences; philosophy; political science and government; psychology related; social sciences; sociology.

ROGER WILLIAMS UNIVERSITY
Bristol, Rhode Island
School of Continuing Studies
http://scs.rwu.edu

Roger Williams University was founded in 1956. It is accredited by New England Association of Schools and Colleges. It first offered distance learning courses in 1974. In fall 2010, there were 330 students enrolled in distance learning courses. Institutionally administered financial aid is available to distance learners.

Services Distance learners have accessibility to academic advising, bookstore, campus computer network, career placement assistance, e-mail services, library services.

Contact John Stout, Dean, School of Continuing Studies, Roger Williams University, 150 Washington Street, Providence, RI 02903. Telephone: 401-254-3530. Fax: 401-254-3560. E-mail: jstout@rwu.edu.

DEGREES AND AWARDS

BGS Health Care Administration; Industrial Technology; Social and Health Services; Technology Leadership and Management
BS Criminal Justice; Paralegal Studies; Public Administration
MPA Public Administration
MS Criminal Justice; Leadership

COURSE SUBJECT AREAS OFFERED OUTSIDE OF DEGREE PROGRAMS

Undergraduate—criminal justice and corrections; criminology; finance and financial management services; history; legal studies (non-professional general, undergraduate); physical sciences related; sociology.

ROSALIND FRANKLIN UNIVERSITY OF MEDICINE AND SCIENCE
North Chicago, Illinois
http://www.rosalindfranklin.edu

Rosalind Franklin University of Medicine and Science was founded in 1912. It is accredited by North Central Association of Colleges and Schools. It first offered distance learning courses in 1993. In fall 2010, there were 146 students enrolled in distance learning courses. Institutionally administered financial aid is available to distance learners.

Services Distance learners have accessibility to academic advising, bookstore, campus computer network, e-mail services, library services, tutoring.

Contact Ms. Laura Nelson, Administrative Assistant, Rosalind Franklin University of Medicine and Science, 3333 Green Bay Road, North Chicago, IL 60064-3095. Telephone: 847-578-3310. Fax: 847-578-8623. E-mail: distance.education@rosalindfranklin.edu.

DEGREES AND AWARDS

CAGS Healthcare Administration and Management; Women's Health
MS Clinical Nutrition/Nutrition Education; Healthcare Administration and Management; Women's Health
DPT Physical Therapy–post-Professional Doctor of Physical Therapy
PhD Interprofessional Healthcare Studies

ROSEMONT COLLEGE
Rosemont, Pennsylvania
Schools of Graduate and Professional Studies
http://www.rosemont.edu/gps2/online/MBA.php

Rosemont College was founded in 1921. It is accredited by Middle States Association of Colleges and Schools. It first offered distance learning courses in 2008. In fall 2010, there were 122 students enrolled in distance learning courses. Institutionally administered financial aid is available to distance learners.

Services Distance learners have accessibility to academic advising, bookstore, campus computer network, career placement assistance, e-mail services, library services, tutoring.

Contact Ms. Meghan Mellinger, Admissions Counselor, Rosemont College, 1400 Montgomery Avenue, Rosemont, PA 19010. Telephone: 610-527-0200 Ext. 2596. Fax: 610-520-4399. E-mail: admissions@rosemont.edu.

DEGREES AND AWARDS

MBA Business Administration

COURSE SUBJECT AREAS OFFERED OUTSIDE OF DEGREE PROGRAMS

Undergraduate—business, management, and marketing related.
Graduate—publishing.

ROSE STATE COLLEGE
Midwest City, Oklahoma
Academic Affairs
http://www.rose.edu/dl/

Rose State College was founded in 1968. It is accredited by North Central Association of Colleges and Schools. It first offered distance learning courses in 1972. In fall 2010, there were 2,709 students enrolled in distance learning courses. Institutionally administered financial aid is available to distance learners.

Services Distance learners have accessibility to academic advising, bookstore, campus computer network, career placement assistance, e-mail services, library services, tutoring.

Contact Chris Meyer, Director, Instructional Technology, Rose State College, Learning Resources Center, 6420 SE 15th Street, Midwest City, OK 73110. Telephone: 405-733-7913. E-mail: cmeyer@rose.edu.

DEGREES AND AWARDS

AA Business; English; History; Liberal Arts; Social Sciences
AAS Library Technical Assistant

COURSE SUBJECT AREAS OFFERED OUTSIDE OF DEGREE PROGRAMS

Undergraduate—accounting and computer science; accounting and related services; allied health and medical assisting services; allied health diagnostic, intervention, and treatment professions; alternative and complementary medical support services; alternative and complementary medicine and medical systems; apparel and textiles; audiovisual communications technologies; biology; business administration, management and operations; business/commerce; business/corporate communications; business, management, and marketing related; business/managerial economics; communication and journalism related; computer/information technology administration and management; computer programming; computer science; computer software and media applications; computer systems analysis; computer systems networking and telecommunica-

tions; criminal justice and corrections; economics; English; English language and literature related; foods, nutrition, and related services; geography and cartography; geological and earth sciences/geosciences; geological/geophysical engineering; graphic communications; health and physical education/fitness; health/medical preparatory programs; health professions related; health services/allied health/health sciences; history; information science/studies; legal professions and studies related; legal research and advanced professional studies; legal studies (non-professional general, undergraduate); liberal arts and sciences, general studies and humanities; library and archives assisting; library science and administration; library science related; marketing; mathematics; philosophy; philosophy and religious studies related; physical sciences; physical sciences related; political science and government; psychology; psychology related; social sciences; social sciences related; sociology.
Non-credit—health and physical education/fitness.

ROWAN-CABARRUS COMMUNITY COLLEGE
Salisbury, North Carolina
http://www.rccc.edu

Rowan-Cabarrus Community College was founded in 1963. It is accredited by Southern Association of Colleges and Schools. It first offered distance learning courses in 1991. In fall 2010, there were 3,000 students enrolled in distance learning courses. Institutionally administered financial aid is available to distance learners.
Services Distance learners have accessibility to academic advising, bookstore, campus computer network, career placement assistance, e-mail services, library services, tutoring.
Contact Educational Resource Services Office, Rowan-Cabarrus Community College, Salisbury, NC 28145. Telephone: 704-637-0760 Ext. 3713. E-mail: distance_ed@rccc.edu.

DEGREES AND AWARDS
AA Arts (Associate and pre-major Associate)
AAS Business Administration

COURSE SUBJECT AREAS OFFERED OUTSIDE OF DEGREE PROGRAMS
Undergraduate—accounting and related services; astronomy and astrophysics; biology; business administration, management and operations; computer and information sciences; computer/information technology administration and management; computer software and media applications; criminal justice and corrections; criminology; economics; education; English; history; human development, family studies, and related services; industrial engineering; philosophy and religious studies related; physical sciences; psychology; sales merchandising, and related marketing operations (general); sociology.
Non-credit—accounting and related services; business/commerce; computer and information sciences; computer software and media applications; computer systems networking and telecommunications; education related; languages (Romance languages); legal professions and studies related; sales, merchandising and related marketing operations (specialized).

ROWAN UNIVERSITY
Glassboro, New Jersey
http://www.rowan.edu/colleges/cgce

Rowan University was founded in 1923. It is accredited by Middle States Association of Colleges and Schools. It first offered distance learning courses in 2007. In fall 2010, there were 185 students enrolled in distance learning courses. Institutionally administered financial aid is available to distance learners.
Services Distance learners have accessibility to academic advising, bookstore, campus computer network, career placement assistance, e-mail services, library services, tutoring.
Contact Saudia Beverly, Recruitment Specialist, Rowan University, Shpeen Hall, 3rd Floor, 201 Mullica Hill Road, Glassboro, NJ 08028. Telephone: 856-256-5147. E-mail: beverly@rowan.edu.

DEGREES AND AWARDS
BLS Liberal Studies
M Eng Engineering Management
MBA Business Administration
MEd Teacher Leadership

COURSE SUBJECT AREAS OFFERED OUTSIDE OF DEGREE PROGRAMS
Undergraduate—liberal arts and sciences, general studies and humanities.
Graduate—business administration, management and operations; education; engineering.

SACRAMENTO CITY COLLEGE
Sacramento, California
Distance/Online Education
http://saccity-online.org/de

Sacramento City College was founded in 1916. It is accredited by Western Association of Schools and Colleges. It first offered distance learning courses in 1986. In fall 2010, there were 5,683 students enrolled in distance learning courses. Institutionally administered financial aid is available to distance learners.
Services Distance learners have accessibility to academic advising, bookstore, campus computer network, e-mail services, library services, tutoring.
Contact Mr. David Martin, Instructional Development Specialist, Center for Online and Virtual Education, Sacramento City College, 3835 Freeport Boulevard, Sacramento, CA 95822. Telephone: 916-650-2726. E-mail: martind@scc.losrios.edu.

DEGREES AND AWARDS
Programs offered do not lead to a degree or other formal award.

COURSE SUBJECT AREAS OFFERED OUTSIDE OF DEGREE PROGRAMS
Undergraduate—accounting and computer science; accounting and related services; allied health and medical assisting services; allied health diagnostic, intervention, and treatment professions; alternative and complementary medical support services; American Sign Language (ASL); anthropology; applied mathematics; astronomy and astrophysics; audiovisual communications technologies; behavioral sciences; bilingual, multilingual, and multicultural education; biological and biomedical sciences related; biological and physical sciences; biology; business administration, management and operations; business/commerce; business/corporate communications; business, management, and marketing related; business/managerial economics; business operations support and assistant services; cell biology and anatomical sciences; chemistry; classical and ancient studies; clinical/medical laboratory science/research; communication and journalism related; communication and media; communications technologies and support services related; communications technology; computer and information sciences; computer and information sciences and support services related; computer engineering; computer engineering technologies; computer/information technology administration and management; computer programming; computer science; computer software and media applications; computer systems analysis; computer systems networking and telecommunications; cosmetology and related personal grooming services; criminal justice and corrections; cultural studies/critical theory and analysis; data entry/microcomputer applications; dental support services and allied professions; design and applied arts; drafting/design engineering technologies; drama/theatre arts and stagecraft; economics; electrical, electronics and communications engineering; electrical/electronics maintenance and repair technology; electrical engineering technologies; electromechanical engineering; electromechanical instrumentation and maintenance technologies; English; English or French as a second or foreign language (teaching); ethnic, cultural minority, gender, and group studies; family and consumer economics; family and consumer sciences/human sciences; family and consumer sciences/human sciences business services; family and consumer sciences/human sciences related; film/video and photographic arts; finance and financial management services; foods, nutrition, and related services; geography and cartography; geological and earth sciences/

geosciences; gerontology; graphic communications; health and physical education/fitness; health professions related; health services/allied health/ health sciences; heating, air conditioning, ventilation and refrigeration maintenance technology; history; human biology; human development, family studies, and related services; human services; information science/ studies; interdisciplinary studies; journalism; languages (Iranian/Persian); library and archives assisting; library science and administration; library science related; literature; marketing; mathematics; mathematics and computer science; mathematics and statistics related; music; nutrition sciences; philosophy; philosophy and religious studies; philosophy and religious studies related; physical sciences; physical sciences related; physiology, pathology and related sciences; political science and government; psychology; psychology related; public policy analysis; real estate; real estate development; rhetoric and composition/writing studies; social sciences; social sciences related; sociology; sociology and anthropology; statistics; transportation and materials moving related; vehicle maintenance and repair technologies; visual and performing arts.

THE SAGE COLLEGES
Troy, New York

The Sage Colleges is accredited by Middle States Association of Colleges and Schools. It first offered distance learning courses in 1999. In fall 2010, there were 669 students enrolled in distance learning courses. Institutionally administered financial aid is available to distance learners.
Services Distance learners have accessibility to academic advising, campus computer network, e-mail services.
Contact Dr. Connell Frazer, Director of Sage Online, The Sage Colleges, 65 1st Street, Troy, NY 12180. Telephone: 518-244-4580. Fax: 518-244-2400. E-mail: frazec@sage.edu.

DEGREES AND AWARDS
MS Applied Behavior Analysis and Autism; Masters in Teaching Excellence
DPT Transitional Doctorate of Physical Therapy

COURSE SUBJECT AREAS OFFERED OUTSIDE OF DEGREE PROGRAMS
Undergraduate—biological and biomedical sciences related; business, management, and marketing related; computer and information sciences; education; English language and literature related; health professions related; legal professions and studies related; philosophy; psychology.
Graduate—education; health professions related.

ST. AMBROSE UNIVERSITY
Davenport, Iowa
http://www.sau.edu/

St. Ambrose University was founded in 1882. It is accredited by North Central Association of Colleges and Schools. It first offered distance learning courses in 1990. In fall 2010, there were 314 students enrolled in distance learning courses. Institutionally administered financial aid is available to distance learners.
Services Distance learners have accessibility to academic advising, bookstore, campus computer network, career placement assistance, e-mail services, library services.
Contact Ms. Linda M. Eisenlauer, Director of the Center for Instructional Design and Technology, St. Ambrose University, 518 West Locust Street, Davenport, IA 52803. Telephone: 563-333-6496. Fax: 563-333-6125. E-mail: eisenlauerlindam@sau.edu.

DEGREES AND AWARDS
Programs offered do not lead to a degree or other formal award.

COURSE SUBJECT AREAS OFFERED OUTSIDE OF DEGREE PROGRAMS
Undergraduate—accounting and related services; economics; education (specific subject areas); English; history; international/global studies; management sciences and quantitative methods; marketing; philosophy; sociology.
Graduate—business administration, management and operations; education (specific subject areas).

ST. ANDREW'S COLLEGE
Saskatoon, Saskatchewan, Canada
http://www.usask.ca/stu/standrews

St. Andrew's College is provincially chartered. It first offered distance learning courses in 1997. In fall 2010, there were 14 students enrolled in distance learning courses. Institutionally administered financial aid is available to distance learners.
Services Distance learners have accessibility to academic advising, campus computer network, e-mail services, library services.
Contact Colleen Walker, Registrar, St. Andrew's College, 1121 College Drive, Saskatoon, SK S7N 0W3, Canada. Telephone: 306-966-5244. Fax: 306-966-8981. E-mail: standrews.registrar@usask.ca.

DEGREES AND AWARDS
Programs offered do not lead to a degree or other formal award.

COURSE SUBJECT AREAS OFFERED OUTSIDE OF DEGREE PROGRAMS
Graduate—religious education; religious studies; theological and ministerial studies; theology and religious vocations related.

ST. CLAIR COUNTY COMMUNITY COLLEGE
Port Huron, Michigan
http://www.SC4.edu/onlinelearning

St. Clair County Community College was founded in 1923. It is accredited by North Central Association of Colleges and Schools. It first offered distance learning courses in 2000. In fall 2010, there were 947 students enrolled in distance learning courses. Institutionally administered financial aid is available to distance learners.
Services Distance learners have accessibility to academic advising, bookstore, career placement assistance, e-mail services, library services, tutoring.
Contact Debra Lacey, eLearning Coordinator, St. Clair County Community College, 323 Erie Street, PO Box 5015, Port Huron, MI 48061-5015. Telephone: 810-989-5525. E-mail: dlacey@sc4.edu.

DEGREES AND AWARDS
AA General degree
AD Business (transfer program); General Education; Nursing–AAS Nursing, Health Care Provider to RN Articulation

COURSE SUBJECT AREAS OFFERED OUTSIDE OF DEGREE PROGRAMS
Undergraduate—accounting and related services; astronomy and astrophysics; business administration, management and operations; business/ corporate communications; chemistry; communication and journalism related; computer and information sciences; economics; education (specific levels and methods); electrical engineering technologies; geography and cartography; history; mathematics; political science and government; psychology; social sciences; sociology; statistics.

ST. CLOUD STATE UNIVERSITY
St. Cloud, Minnesota
Center for Continuing Studies
http://www.stcloudstate.edu/continuingstudies

St. Cloud State University was founded in 1869. It is accredited by North Central Association of Colleges and Schools. It first offered distance learning courses in 1975. In fall 2010, there were 3,200 students enrolled in distance learning courses. Institutionally administered financial aid is available to distance learners.
Services Distance learners have accessibility to academic advising, bookstore, campus computer network, career placement assistance, e-mail services, library services, tutoring.
Contact Mr. Michael Evans, Associate Director for e-Student Services, St. Cloud State University, 720 4th Avenue South, St. Cloud, MN 56301. Telephone: 320-308-3081. Fax: 320-308-5041. E-mail: mjevans@stcloudstate.edu.

DEGREES AND AWARDS

AA Liberal Arts
BA Criminal Justice Studies
BEd Special Education
BGS Community Psychology; Self-Designed program
MA Teaching English as a Second Language
MBA Business Administration
MS Behavior Analysis; Criminal Justice Studies; Educational Administration; Higher Education Administration
MSE Special Education

COURSE SUBJECT AREAS OFFERED OUTSIDE OF DEGREE PROGRAMS

Undergraduate—anthropology; astronomy and astrophysics; biology; botany/plant biology; chemistry; communication and media; criminal justice and corrections; economics; educational administration and supervision; English; environmental/environmental health engineering; history; management information systems; mathematics; philosophy; physics; psychology; social sciences related; sociology; special education; statistics.
Graduate—behavioral sciences; criminal justice and corrections; psychology related; statistics.

SAINT FRANCIS UNIVERSITY
Loretto, Pennsylvania
Academic Affairs
http://www.francis.edu

Saint Francis University was founded in 1847. It is accredited by Middle States Association of Colleges and Schools. It first offered distance learning courses in 1995. In fall 2010, there were 350 students enrolled in distance learning courses. Institutionally administered financial aid is available to distance learners.
Services Distance learners have accessibility to academic advising, bookstore, campus computer network, career placement assistance, e-mail services, library services, tutoring.
Contact Dr. Peter Skoner, Associate Provost, Saint Francis University, 313 Scotus Hall, PO Box 600, Loretto, PA 15940. Telephone: 814-472-3085. Fax: 814-472-3365. E-mail: pskoner@francis.edu.

DEGREES AND AWARDS

MHS Health Sciences
MMS Medicine

COURSE SUBJECT AREAS OFFERED OUTSIDE OF DEGREE PROGRAMS

Undergraduate—accounting and computer science; accounting and related services; behavioral sciences; biblical studies; bioethics/medical ethics; biological and biomedical sciences related; biological and physical sciences; biology; business administration, management and operations; business/commerce; business/corporate communications; business, management, and marketing related; business/managerial economics; business operations support and assistant services; cell biology and anatomical sciences; chemistry; computer and information sciences; computer and information sciences and support services related; computer/information technology administration and management; computer science; data entry/microcomputer applications; English; English language and literature related; health/medical preparatory programs; health professions related; health services/allied health/health sciences; history; human resources management; information science/studies; management information systems; marketing; philosophy; philosophy and religious studies related; physical sciences; physical sciences related; physics; political science and government; psychology; religious studies; social work; sociology; statistics.
Graduate—bioethics/medical ethics; business administration, management and operations; business/commerce; business/corporate communications; business, management, and marketing related; business/managerial economics; health/medical preparatory programs; health professions related; health services/allied health/health sciences; human resources management; information science/studies; management information systems; management sciences and quantitative methods; marketing; pharmacology and toxicology.
Non-credit—religious education; religious studies.

ST. GREGORY'S UNIVERSITY
Shawnee, Oklahoma
http://www.stgregorys.edu/

St. Gregory's University was founded in 1875. It is accredited by North Central Association of Colleges and Schools. It first offered distance learning courses in 2009. In fall 2010, there were 10 students enrolled in distance learning courses. Institutionally administered financial aid is available to distance learners.
Services Distance learners have accessibility to academic advising, bookstore, campus computer network, e-mail services, library services.
Contact Mrs. Kay Stith, Associate Dean for Academic Services/Registrar, St. Gregory's University, 1900 West MacArthur, Shawnee, OK 74804. Telephone: 405-878-5434. E-mail: kkstith@stgregorys.edu.

DEGREES AND AWARDS

Programs offered do not lead to a degree or other formal award.

COURSE SUBJECT AREAS OFFERED OUTSIDE OF DEGREE PROGRAMS

Undergraduate—accounting and computer science; behavioral sciences; English; history; mathematics; philosophy; psychology; social sciences.

ST. JOHN FISHER COLLEGE
Rochester, New York
http://www.sjfc.edu/

St. John Fisher College was founded in 1948. It is accredited by Middle States Association of Colleges and Schools. It first offered distance learning courses in 2004. In fall 2010, there were 32 students enrolled in distance learning courses. Institutionally administered financial aid is available to distance learners.
Services Distance learners have accessibility to academic advising, bookstore, campus computer network, career placement assistance, e-mail services, library services, tutoring.
Contact Mr. Jose Perales, Director of Graduate Admissions, St. John Fisher College, 3690 East Avenue, Rochester, NY 14618. Telephone: 585-385-8161. Fax: 585-385-8344. E-mail: grad@sjfc.edu.

DEGREES AND AWARDS

Programs offered do not lead to a degree or other formal award.

COURSE SUBJECT AREAS OFFERED OUTSIDE OF DEGREE PROGRAMS

Undergraduate—economics; English; sociology.
Graduate—business, management, and marketing related; health professions related.

ST. JOHN'S UNIVERSITY
Queens, New York
Online Learning
http://www.stjohns.edu/distancelearning

St. John's University was founded in 1870. It is accredited by Middle States Association of Colleges and Schools. It first offered distance learning courses in 1994. In fall 2010, there were 1,490 students enrolled in distance learning courses. Institutionally administered financial aid is available to distance learners.
Services Distance learners have accessibility to academic advising, bookstore, campus computer network, career placement assistance, e-mail services, library services, tutoring.
Contact Dr. Jeffery E. Olson, Associate Provost, Online Learning and Services, St. John's University, 8000 Utopia Parkway, Queens, NY 11439. Telephone: 718-990-5705. Fax: 718-990-5689. E-mail: distancelearning@stjohns.edu.

DEGREES AND AWARDS
AA Liberal Studies
AS Business; Criminal Justice
BA Liberal Studies
BS Administrative Studies; Criminal Justice
MA Liberal Studies
MS Ed School Building Leader in Educational Administration and Supervision; Teaching Children with Disabilities in Childhood Education
PMC School District Leader Advanced certificate

COURSE SUBJECT AREAS OFFERED OUTSIDE OF DEGREE PROGRAMS
Undergraduate—accounting and related services; anthropology; biology; business administration, management and operations; communication and journalism related; computer science; criminal justice and corrections; economics; education; English; finance and financial management services; history; languages (Romance languages); legal studies (non-professional general, undergraduate); marketing; mathematics; pharmacy, pharmaceutical sciences, and administration; philosophy; physics; political science and government; psychology; science technologies related; sociology; theology and religious vocations related.
Graduate—business, management, and marketing related; criminal justice and corrections; economics; education; educational administration and supervision; educational assessment, evaluation, and research; educational/instructional media design; education related; education (specific levels and methods); education (specific subject areas); finance and financial management services; liberal arts and sciences, general studies and humanities; library science and administration.

ST. JOHN'S UNIVERSITY
Queens, New York
The School of Education
http://www.stjohns.edu/distancelearning

St. John's University was founded in 1870. It is accredited by Middle States Association of Colleges and Schools. It first offered distance learning courses in 1994. In fall 2010, there were 300 students enrolled in distance learning courses. Institutionally administered financial aid is available to distance learners.
Services Distance learners have accessibility to academic advising, bookstore, campus computer network, career placement assistance, e-mail services, library services, tutoring.
Contact Dr. Kelly K. Ronayne, Associate Dean, St. John's University, 8000 Utopia Parkway, Sullivan Hall, G9, Queens, NY 11439. Telephone: 718-990-2304. Fax: 718-990-2343. E-mail: graded@stjohns.edu.

DEGREES AND AWARDS
MS Ed School Building Leader in Educational Administration and Supervision; Teaching Children with Disabilities in Childhood Education
PMC School District Leader Advanced certificate

COURSE SUBJECT AREAS OFFERED OUTSIDE OF DEGREE PROGRAMS
Graduate—education; educational administration and supervision; educational assessment, evaluation, and research; educational/instructional media design; education related; education (specific levels and methods); education (specific subject areas); library science and administration.

ST. JOSEPH'S COLLEGE, LONG ISLAND CAMPUS
Patchogue, New York
http://www. sjcny.edu/omop

St. Joseph's College, Long Island Campus was founded in 1916. It is accredited by Middle States Association of Colleges and Schools. It first offered distance learning courses in 1999. In fall 2010, there were 743 students enrolled in distance learning courses. Institutionally administered financial aid is available to distance learners.
Services Distance learners have accessibility to academic advising, bookstore, career placement assistance, e-mail services, library services, tutoring.
Contact Ms. Shannon M. O'Neill, Assistant Dean, St. Joseph's College, Long Island Campus, 155 West Roe Boulevard, Patchogue, NY 11772. Telephone: 631-687-2678. Fax: 631-447-5192. E-mail: smoneill@sjcny.edu.

DEGREES AND AWARDS
BS Organizational Management
Certificate Human Resources; Leadership and Supervision
EMBA Business Administration

COURSE SUBJECT AREAS OFFERED OUTSIDE OF DEGREE PROGRAMS
Undergraduate—biology; English; history; human services; liberal arts and sciences, general studies and humanities; psychology; religious studies; social sciences.
Graduate—business administration, management and operations; human resources management.

ST. JOSEPH'S COLLEGE, NEW YORK
Brooklyn, New York
http://www.sjcny.edu/omop

St. Joseph's College, New York was founded in 1916. It is accredited by Middle States Association of Colleges and Schools. It first offered distance learning courses in 1999. In fall 2010, there were 743 students enrolled in distance learning courses. Institutionally administered financial aid is available to distance learners.
Services Distance learners have accessibility to academic advising, bookstore, career placement assistance, e-mail services, library services, tutoring.
Contact Ms. Shannon M. O'Neill, Assistant Dean, St. Joseph's College, New York, 155 West Roe Boulevard, Patchogue, NY 11772. Telephone: 631-687-2678. Fax: 631-447-5192. E-mail: smoneill@sjcny.edu.

DEGREES AND AWARDS
BS Organizational Management
Certificate Human Resources; Leadership and Supervision
EMBA Business Administration

COURSE SUBJECT AREAS OFFERED OUTSIDE OF DEGREE PROGRAMS
Undergraduate—biology; English; history; liberal arts and sciences, general studies and humanities; marketing; psychology; religious studies; social sciences.
Graduate—business administration, management and operations; human resources management.

SAINT JOSEPH'S COLLEGE OF MAINE
Standish, Maine
Graduate & Professional Studies
http://online.sjcme.edu

Saint Joseph's College of Maine was founded in 1912. It is accredited by New England Association of Schools and Colleges. It first offered distance learning courses in 1976. In fall 2010, there were 2,300 students enrolled in distance learning courses. Institutionally administered financial aid is available to distance learners.
Services Distance learners have accessibility to academic advising, bookstore, campus computer network, e-mail services, library services.
Contact Lynne Robinson, Director of Admissions, Saint Joseph's College of Maine, 278 Whites Bridge Road, Standish, ME 04084-5263. Telephone: 800-752-4723. Fax: 207-892-7480. E-mail: info@sjcme.edu.

DEGREES AND AWARDS
AS Adult Education and Training specialization; Business Administration; Criminal Justice; General Studies; Human Services; Psychology; Radiologic Science Administration
BA Adult Religious Education/Theology Studies

BS Adult Education and Training; Business Administration; Criminal Justice; General Studies; Health Administration; Human Services; Long-Term Care Administration; Psychology; Radiological Science Administration
BSBA Business Administration
BSN Nursing–RN to BSN
Certificate Adult Education and Training; Long-Term Care Administration
Certification Health Administration
Graduate Certificate Nursing Administration and Leadership; Nursing and Health Care Education
MAFM Accountancy
MAPT Pastoral Theology
MBA Quality Leadership
MBA/MHA Nursing and Health Administration
MBA/MSN Health Administration and Nursing
MSE Education
MSHA Health Administration
MSN Nursing/Family Nurse Practitioner

COURSE SUBJECT AREAS OFFERED OUTSIDE OF DEGREE PROGRAMS

Undergraduate—behavioral sciences; business administration, management and operations; criminal justice and corrections; human services; psychology; registered nursing, nursing administration, nursing research and clinical nursing; religious studies; social sciences; theology and religious vocations related.
Graduate—accounting and related services; business administration, management and operations; business, management, and marketing related; education; educational administration and supervision; health and medical administrative services; health professions related; management sciences and quantitative methods; registered nursing, nursing administration, nursing research and clinical nursing; theology and religious vocations related.

SAINT LEO UNIVERSITY
Saint Leo, Florida
Center for Distance Learning
http://online.saintleo.edu

Saint Leo University was founded in 1889. It is accredited by Southern Association of Colleges and Schools. It first offered distance learning courses in 1998. In fall 2010, there were 10,866 students enrolled in distance learning courses. Institutionally administered financial aid is available to distance learners.
Services Distance learners have accessibility to academic advising, bookstore, campus computer network, career placement assistance, e-mail services, library services, tutoring.
Contact Ms. Tonya Chestnut, Admissions Coordinator, Saint Leo University, Center for Online Learning, MC 2260, PO Box 6665, Saint Leo, FL 33574-6665. Telephone: 888-875-8265. Fax: 352-588-4793. E-mail: tonya.chestnut@saintleo.edu.

DEGREES AND AWARDS

AA Criminal Justice; Liberal Arts
AAB Business Administration
BA Accounting; Business Administration, Accounting concentration; Business Administration, Management concentration; Business Administration, Marketing concentration; Criminal Justice; Criminal Justice, Criminalistics concentration; Criminal Justice, Homeland Security concentration; Human Resources Administration; International Hospitality and Tourism Management; Liberal Studies; Psychology; Sociology
BS Computer Information Systems; Health Care Management
CAGS Accounting; Criminal Justice Management; Health Care Management; Information Security Management; Instructional Design; Marketing
Ed S Educational Leadership; Higher Education Leadership
MBA Accounting concentration; General track; Health Care Management concentration; Human Resources Administration concentration; Information Security Management concentration; Marketing concentration; Sport Business concentration
MEd Educational Leadership concentration; Exceptional Student Education concentration; Instructional Leadership concentration
MS Criminal Justice; Criminal Justice, Critical Incident Management concentration; Criminal Justice, Forensic Science concentration; Critical Incident Management; Instructional Design
MSW Clinical Practice concentration, Advanced

COURSE SUBJECT AREAS OFFERED OUTSIDE OF DEGREE PROGRAMS

Undergraduate—accounting and related services; biological and physical sciences; business administration, management and operations; computer/information technology administration and management; criminal justice and corrections; economics; education; English; fine and studio arts; geography and cartography; health and medical administrative services; history; human resources management; marketing; mathematics; music; natural sciences; philosophy; political science and government; psychology; religious studies; social sciences; sociology.

ST. LOUIS COMMUNITY COLLEGE
St. Louis, Missouri
Office of the Vice Chancellor for Academic and Student Affairs
http://www.stlcc.edu/Distance_Learning

St. Louis Community College is accredited by North Central Association of Colleges and Schools. It first offered distance learning courses in 1973. In fall 2010, there were 7,000 students enrolled in distance learning courses. Institutionally administered financial aid is available to distance learners.
Services Distance learners have accessibility to academic advising, bookstore, campus computer network, career placement assistance, e-mail services, library services, tutoring.
Contact Philip D. Hanson, Senior Project Associate, Distance Education, St. Louis Community College, Office of the Vice Chancellor for Academic and Student Affairs, 300 South Broadway, St. Louis, MO 63102. Telephone: 314-539-5185. Fax: 314-539-5443. E-mail: phanson@stlcc.edu.

DEGREES AND AWARDS

AAS Criminal Justice–Law; Information Reporting
CCCPE Business Administration; CART/Captioning; Funeral Directing

COURSE SUBJECT AREAS OFFERED OUTSIDE OF DEGREE PROGRAMS

Undergraduate—accounting and computer science; anthropology; biological and physical sciences; business, management, and marketing related; communication and journalism related; computer and information sciences; computer and information sciences and support services related; computer software and media applications; data entry/microcomputer applications; funeral service and mortuary science; history; languages (Romance languages); marketing; mathematics; philosophy and religious studies related; political science and government; psychology related; sociology.
Non-credit—business administration, management and operations; business/commerce; business, management, and marketing related; computer and information sciences; management information systems.

SAINT LOUIS UNIVERSITY
St. Louis, Missouri
School of Nursing
http://nursing.slu.edu/

Saint Louis University was founded in 1818. It is accredited by North Central Association of Colleges and Schools. It first offered distance learning courses in 1997. In fall 2010, there were 600 students enrolled in distance learning courses. Institutionally administered financial aid is available to distance learners.
Services Distance learners have accessibility to academic advising, bookstore, campus computer network, career placement assistance, e-mail services, library services, tutoring.

Contact Mr. Scott Ragsdale, Recruitment Specialist, Saint Louis University, 3525 Caroline Street, St. Louis, MO 63104-1099. Telephone: 314-977-8995. Fax: 314-977-8949. E-mail: slunurse@slu.edu.

DEGREES AND AWARDS

BSN Nursing–RN to BSN
MSN Nursing
PMC Nursing
DNP Nursing
PhD Nursing

SAINT MARY-OF-THE-WOODS COLLEGE
Saint Mary-of-the-Woods, Indiana
Woods External Degree Program
http://www.smwc.edu

Saint Mary-of-the-Woods College was founded in 1840. It is accredited by North Central Association of Colleges and Schools. It first offered distance learning courses in 1973. In fall 2010, there were 1,300 students enrolled in distance learning courses. Institutionally administered financial aid is available to distance learners.

Services Distance learners have accessibility to academic advising, bookstore, career placement assistance, e-mail services, library services, tutoring.

Contact Alicia Holloway, Assistant Director of Admission, Saint Mary-of-the-Woods College, Office of Distance Admission, 122 Guerin Hall, Saint Mary-of-the-Woods, IN 47876. Telephone: 800-499-0373. Fax: 812-535-1010. E-mail: wedadms@smwc.edu.

DEGREES AND AWARDS

AA Humanities; Paralegal Studies
AS Accounting; Business, general; Early Childhood/Child Development
BA Creative Writing; Criminal Justice; English; History and Political Studies; Humanities; Journalism; Mathematics; Paralegal Studies; Professional Writing; Social Science/History; Theology
BS Accounting Information Systems; Accounting; Business Administration; Computer Information Systems; Digital Media Communication; Education–Kindergarten-Elementary Education; Education–Middle School/High School Special Education; Education–Preschool-Grade 3 Education/Mild Intervention; Human Resource Management; Human Services; Marketing; Psychology; Secondary Education–English; Secondary Education–Mathematics; Secondary Education–Social Studies
Certificate Paralegal Studies
MA Art Therapy; Earth Literacy; Music Therapy; Pastoral Theology
MEd Education
MLD Leadership Development

COURSE SUBJECT AREAS OFFERED OUTSIDE OF DEGREE PROGRAMS

Undergraduate—accounting and related services; business administration, management and operations; business/commerce; computer and information sciences; education; education related; education (specific levels and methods); education (specific subject areas); history; human resources management; human services; journalism; liberal arts and sciences, general studies and humanities; marketing; mathematics; political science and government; psychology; social sciences related; special education; theology and religious vocations related.

Graduate—business administration, management and operations; business, management, and marketing related; education; education related; music; natural resources and conservation related; psychology related; theological and ministerial studies; theology and religious vocations related.

ST. MARY'S UNIVERSITY
San Antonio, Texas
Graduate School
http://www.stmarytx.edu

St. Mary's University was founded in 1852. It is accredited by Southern Association of Colleges and Schools. It first offered distance learning courses in 1998. In fall 2010, there were 117 students enrolled in distance learning courses. Institutionally administered financial aid is available to distance learners.

Services Distance learners have accessibility to academic advising, bookstore, campus computer network, career placement assistance, e-mail services, library services.

Contact Dr. Henry Flores, Dean of the Graduate School, St. Mary's University, One Camino Santa Maria, Box 43, San Antonio, TX 78228. Telephone: 210-436-3101. Fax: 210-431-2220. E-mail: hflores@stmarytx.edu.

DEGREES AND AWARDS

MA International Relations

COURSE SUBJECT AREAS OFFERED OUTSIDE OF DEGREE PROGRAMS

Graduate—business administration, management and operations; pastoral counseling and specialized ministries; theological and ministerial studies.

SAINT PAUL COLLEGE–A COMMUNITY & TECHNICAL COLLEGE
St. Paul, Minnesota
http://www.saintpaul.edu

Saint Paul College–A Community & Technical College was founded in 1919. It is accredited by North Central Association of Colleges and Schools. It first offered distance learning courses in 1999. In fall 2010, there were 650 students enrolled in distance learning courses. Institutionally administered financial aid is available to distance learners.

Services Distance learners have accessibility to academic advising, bookstore, campus computer network, career placement assistance, e-mail services, library services, tutoring.

Contact Enrollment Services, Saint Paul College–A Community & Technical College, 235 Marshall Avenue, St. Paul, MN 55102. Telephone: 800-227-6029. Fax: 651-846-1555. E-mail: admissions@saintpaul.edu.

DEGREES AND AWARDS

AA Liberal Arts and Sciences
CCCPE Human Resources Professional certificate

COURSE SUBJECT AREAS OFFERED OUTSIDE OF DEGREE PROGRAMS

Undergraduate—accounting and computer science; anthropology; behavioral sciences; biological and physical sciences; biology; business administration, management and operations; business/corporate communications; business, management, and marketing related; business operations support and assistant services; cell biology and anatomical sciences; chemistry; communication and journalism related; communication and media; computer/information technology administration and management; computer programming; computer science; computer software and media applications; culinary arts and related services; economics; education; English; ethnic, cultural minority, gender, and group studies; foods, nutrition, and related services; graphic communications; health services/allied health/health sciences; history; hospitality administration; human resources management; information science/studies; intercultural/multicultural and diversity studies; international business; liberal arts and sciences, general studies and humanities; management information systems; marketing; mathematics; natural sciences; nutrition sciences; philosophy; political science and government; psychology; science, technology and society; sociology.

ST. PETERSBURG COLLEGE
St. Petersburg, Florida
Electronic Campus
http://www.spcollege.edu/ecampus/

St. Petersburg College was founded in 1927. It is accredited by Southern Association of Colleges and Schools. It first offered distance learning courses in 1970. In fall 2010, there were 32,450 students enrolled in distance learning courses. Institutionally administered financial aid is available to distance learners.

Services Distance learners have accessibility to academic advising, bookstore, career placement assistance, e-mail services, library services, tutoring.

Contact Audra Liswith, Curriculum Support Specialist, St. Petersburg College, 9200 113th Street North, Seminole, FL 33773. Telephone: 727-394-6270. E-mail: liswith.audra@spcollege.edu.

DEGREES AND AWARDS

AA General Program
AS Crime Scene Technology; Emergency Administration and Management; Fire Science; Funeral Services; Health Information Management; Healthcare Informatics; Medical Laboratory Technology; Veterinary Technology
BAS Banking; Business Administration; Dental Hygiene; Health Services Administration; International Business; Management and Organizational Leadership; Public Safety Administration; Sustainability Management; Technology Management; Veterinary Technology
Certificate Computer-Related Crime Investigations; Crime Scene Technology; Critical Care (advanced technical certification); Emergency Administration and Management; Emergency Care; Fire Inspector I; Fire Inspector II; Fire Investigator I; Fire Officer I; Fire Officer II; Gangs Enforcement Management; Healthcare Informatics; Medical Coder; Sepsis Awareness and Education; Veterinary Hospital Management

COURSE SUBJECT AREAS OFFERED OUTSIDE OF DEGREE PROGRAMS

Undergraduate—accounting and related services; allied health diagnostic, intervention, and treatment professions; anthropology; archeology; area studies; astronomy and astrophysics; behavioral sciences; biblical studies; biological and physical sciences; biology; business administration, management and operations; business/commerce; business/corporate communications; chemistry; communication and media; computer science; criminal justice and corrections; economics; education; educational assessment, evaluation, and research; educational/instructional media design; education (specific levels and methods); entrepreneurial and small business operations; finance and financial management services; fine and studio arts; funeral service and mortuary science; geography and cartography; history; hospitality administration; liberal arts and sciences, general studies and humanities; linguistic, comparative, and related language studies; mathematics; microbiological sciences and immunology; music; philosophy; political science and government; psychology; special education; wildlife and wildlands science and management.
Non-credit—accounting and computer science; air transportation; building/construction finishing, management, and inspection; business/corporate communications; communication and media; computer and information sciences; computer/information technology administration and management; data entry/microcomputer applications; data processing; education; educational administration and supervision; educational assessment, evaluation, and research; educational/instructional media design; electrical/electronics maintenance and repair technology; environmental design; film/video and photographic arts; finance and financial management services; funeral service and mortuary science; ground transportation; health and physical education/fitness; insurance; languages (foreign languages related); management information systems; parks, recreation and leisure; real estate; vehicle maintenance and repair technologies; work and family studies.

ST. PHILIP'S COLLEGE
San Antonio, Texas
http://www.alamo.edu/spc/admin/distance/default.aspx

St. Philip's College was founded in 1898. It is accredited by Southern Association of Colleges and Schools. It first offered distance learning courses in 1991. In fall 2010, there were 3,444 students enrolled in distance learning courses. Institutionally administered financial aid is available to distance learners.
Services Distance learners have accessibility to academic advising, bookstore, campus computer network, career placement assistance, e-mail services, library services, tutoring.
Contact Ms. Belinda Esqueda, Distance Learning Support Specialist, St. Philip's College, 1801 Martin Luther King Drive, San Antonio, TX 78203. Telephone: 210-483-2239. Fax: 210-486-2130. E-mail: besqueda@alamo.edu.

DEGREES AND AWARDS

Programs offered do not lead to a degree or other formal award.

COURSE SUBJECT AREAS OFFERED OUTSIDE OF DEGREE PROGRAMS

Undergraduate—accounting and computer science; accounting and related services; behavioral sciences; biology; business/commerce; chemistry; computer software and media applications; criminology; economics; English; history; mathematics; social sciences.

ST. STEPHEN'S COLLEGE
Edmonton, Alberta, Canada
http://www.ualberta.ca/ST.STEPHENS/

St. Stephen's College was founded in 1912. It is provincially chartered. It first offered distance learning courses in 1995. In fall 2010, there were 64 students enrolled in distance learning courses. Institutionally administered financial aid is available to distance learners.
Services Distance learners have accessibility to academic advising, bookstore, library services.
Contact Kelly Parson, Assistant Registrar, St. Stephen's College, 8810 112th Street, Edmonton, AB T6G 2J6, Canada. Telephone: 780-439-7311. Fax: 780-433-8875. E-mail: kparson@ualberta.ca.

DEGREES AND AWARDS

Programs offered do not lead to a degree or other formal award.

COURSE SUBJECT AREAS OFFERED OUTSIDE OF DEGREE PROGRAMS

Graduate—biblical studies; philosophy and religious studies related; psychology related; religious studies; theological and ministerial studies.

SAINT VINCENT COLLEGE
Latrobe, Pennsylvania
http://www.stvincent.edu/

Saint Vincent College was founded in 1846. It is accredited by Middle States Association of Colleges and Schools.
Contact Dr. John Smetanka, Vice President for Academic Affairs and Academic Dean, Saint Vincent College, Latrobe, PA 15650. E-mail: john.smetanka@stvincent.edu.

DEGREES AND AWARDS

Programs offered do not lead to a degree or other formal award.

COURSE SUBJECT AREAS OFFERED OUTSIDE OF DEGREE PROGRAMS

Undergraduate—education.

SALEM COMMUNITY COLLEGE
Carneys Point, New Jersey
http://www.salemcc.edu

Salem Community College was founded in 1972. It is accredited by Middle States Association of Colleges and Schools. It first offered distance learning courses in 1997. In fall 2010, there were 173 students enrolled in distance learning courses. Institutionally administered financial aid is available to distance learners.
Services Distance learners have accessibility to academic advising, e-mail services, library services, tutoring.
Contact Ms. Karen Mattison, Manager of Academic Technology, Salem Community College, 460 Hollywood Avenue, Carneys Point, NJ 08069. Telephone: 856-351-2727. E-mail: kmattison@salemcc.edu.

DEGREES AND AWARDS

Programs offered do not lead to a degree or other formal award.

COURSE SUBJECT AREAS OFFERED OUTSIDE OF DEGREE PROGRAMS

Undergraduate—arts, entertainment, and media management; bioethics/medical ethics; biological and physical sciences; computer/information technology administration and management; ethnic, cultural minority, gender, and group studies; history; philosophy.

SALVE REGINA UNIVERSITY

Newport, Rhode Island
Extension Study
http://www.salve.edu

Salve Regina University was founded in 1934. It is accredited by New England Association of Schools and Colleges. It first offered distance learning courses in 1985. In fall 2010, there were 450 students enrolled in distance learning courses. Institutionally administered financial aid is available to distance learners.

Services Distance learners have accessibility to academic advising, bookstore, campus computer network, career placement assistance, e-mail services, library services.

Contact Tiffany K. McClanaghan, Associate Director of Professional and Graduate Studies, Salve Regina University, 100 Ochre Point Avenue, Newport, RI 02840-4192. Telephone: 401-341-2198. Fax: 401-341-2973. E-mail: tiffany.mcclanaghan@salve.edu.

DEGREES AND AWARDS

BS Business
Certificate Management
MA Humanities; International Relations; Rehabilitation Counseling
MBA Business Administration
MS Administration of Justice; Management

COURSE SUBJECT AREAS OFFERED OUTSIDE OF DEGREE PROGRAMS

Graduate—business administration, management and operations; business/commerce; health and medical administrative services; international relations and national security studies; rehabilitation and therapeutic professions.

Non-credit—business/commerce; health and medical administrative services; human resources management.

SAM HOUSTON STATE UNIVERSITY

Huntsville, Texas
Correspondence Course Division
http://cor.shsu.edu

Sam Houston State University was founded in 1879. It is accredited by Southern Association of Colleges and Schools. It first offered distance learning courses in 1953. In fall 2010, there were 1,200 students enrolled in distance learning courses. Institutionally administered financial aid is available to distance learners.

Services Distance learners have accessibility to bookstore, e-mail services, library services.

Contact Gail M. Wright, Correspondence Course Coordinator, Sam Houston State University, Box 2536, Huntsville, TX 77341-2536. Telephone: 936-294-1003. Fax: 936-294-3703. E-mail: cor_gmw@shsu.edu.

DEGREES AND AWARDS

Programs offered do not lead to a degree or other formal award.

COURSE SUBJECT AREAS OFFERED OUTSIDE OF DEGREE PROGRAMS

Undergraduate—agricultural business and management; anthropology; business, management, and marketing related; chemistry; economics; English; family and consumer economics; film/video and photographic arts; finance and financial management services; food science and technology; foods, nutrition, and related services; geological and earth sciences/geosciences; gerontology; health professions related; history; legal studies (non-professional general, undergraduate); marketing; mathematics and statistics related; nutrition sciences; philosophy; political science and government; psychology; sociology; statistics.

SAMPSON COMMUNITY COLLEGE

Clinton, North Carolina
http://www.sampsoncc.edu

Sampson Community College was founded in 1965. It is accredited by Southern Association of Colleges and Schools. It first offered distance learning courses in 1999. In fall 2010, there were 600 students enrolled in distance learning courses. Institutionally administered financial aid is available to distance learners.

Services Distance learners have accessibility to academic advising, e-mail services, library services.

Contact Mr. Lewis Phillip Gravis, Director of Distance Learning, Sampson Community College, 1801 Sunset Avenue, PO Box 318, Clinton, NC 28329. Telephone: 910-592-8081 Ext. 2040. Fax: 910-592-9864. E-mail: lgravis@sampsoncc.edu.

DEGREES AND AWARDS

Programs offered do not lead to a degree or other formal award.

COURSE SUBJECT AREAS OFFERED OUTSIDE OF DEGREE PROGRAMS

Undergraduate—accounting and related services; agricultural and food products processing; agricultural production; agriculture and agriculture operations related; animal sciences; behavioral sciences; bilingual, multilingual, and multicultural education; business administration, management and operations; business/managerial economics; computer and information sciences; computer and information sciences and support services related; computer systems networking and telecommunications; criminal justice and corrections; data entry/microcomputer applications; finance and financial management services; history; human development, family studies, and related services; psychology; sociology.

Non-credit—computer and information sciences.

SAMUEL MERRITT UNIVERSITY

Oakland, California
Academic Affairs
http://www.samuelmerritt.edu

Samuel Merritt University was founded in 1909. It is accredited by Western Association of Schools and Colleges. It first offered distance learning courses in 2001. Institutionally administered financial aid is available to distance learners.

Services Distance learners have accessibility to academic advising, bookstore, campus computer network, e-mail services, library services, tutoring.

Contact Mr. John Garten-Shuman, Vice President of Enrollment Services, Samuel Merritt University, Peralta Pavillion, 450 30th Street, Oakland, CA 94609. Telephone: 800-607-6377. Fax: 510-869-6525. E-mail: jgartens@samuelmerritt.edu.

DEGREES AND AWARDS

MSN Nursing

SAN BERNARDINO VALLEY COLLEGE

San Bernardino, California
Distance Education Office
http://www.valleycollege.edu/

San Bernardino Valley College was founded in 1926. It is accredited by Western Association of Schools and Colleges. It first offered distance learning courses in 1986. In fall 2010, there were 5,579 students enrolled in distance learning courses. Institutionally administered financial aid is available to distance learners.

Services Distance learners have accessibility to academic advising, bookstore, campus computer network, career placement assistance, e-mail services, library services, tutoring.

Contact Ms. Trelisa Glazatov, System Administrator, San Bernardino Valley College, 441 West 8th Street, San Bernardino, CA 92401. Telephone: 909-384-4303. Fax: 909-885-3035. E-mail: tglazato@sbccd.cc.ca.us.

DEGREES AND AWARDS

Programs offered do not lead to a degree or other formal award.

COURSE SUBJECT AREAS OFFERED OUTSIDE OF DEGREE PROGRAMS

Undergraduate—accounting and related services; anthropology; astronomy and astrophysics; biology; business administration, management and operations; business, management, and marketing related; chemistry; communication and journalism related; criminal justice and corrections; economics; English; fine and studio arts; history; human development, family studies, and related services; liberal arts and sciences, general studies and humanities; mathematics and statistics related; philosophy and religious studies related; political science and government; psychology related; radio, television, and digital communication; real estate; social sciences related; sociology.

SAN DIEGO COMMUNITY COLLEGE DISTRICT
San Diego, California
http://www.sdccdonline.net

San Diego Community College District first offered distance learning courses in 2001. In fall 2010, there were 9,848 students enrolled in distance learning courses. Institutionally administered financial aid is available to distance learners.

Services Distance learners have accessibility to academic advising, bookstore, library services, tutoring.

Contact Dr. Andrea Henne, Dean, Online and Distributed Learning, San Diego Community College District, 3375 Camino del Rio South, Suite 125, San Diego, CA 92108. Telephone: 619-388-6750. E-mail: ahenne @sdccd.edu.

DEGREES AND AWARDS

AA Communication Studies; Psychology; Social and Behavioral Sciences

AS Accounting; Administration of Justice Law Enforcement specialization; Business Administration; Business Management; Computer Business Technology Administrative Assistant; Computer Business Technology Microcomputer Applications; Computer and Information Sciences; Military Leadership

COURSE SUBJECT AREAS OFFERED OUTSIDE OF DEGREE PROGRAMS

Undergraduate—accounting and computer science; accounting and related services; air transportation; allied health and medical assisting services; allied health diagnostic, intervention, and treatment professions; American Sign Language (ASL); anthropology; apparel and textiles; applied mathematics; astronomy and astrophysics; audiovisual communications technologies; behavioral sciences; biological and physical sciences; biology; business administration, management and operations; business/commerce; business/corporate communications; business, management, and marketing related; business/managerial economics; business operations support and assistant services; chemistry; cognitive science; communication and journalism related; communication and media; communications technology; computer and information sciences; computer and information sciences and support services related; computer/information technology administration and management; computer programming; computer science; computer software and media applications; computer systems networking and telecommunications; criminal justice and corrections; data entry/microcomputer applications; economics; education; education related; engineering related; English; English language and literature related; fine and studio arts; fire protection; genetics; health and physical education/fitness; health professions related; history; information science/studies; intercultural/multicultural and diversity studies; journalism; legal studies (non-professional general, undergraduate); liberal arts and sciences, general studies and humanities; library science and administration; library science related; marketing; mathematics; mathematics and computer science; mathematics and statistics related; music; natural sciences; nutrition sciences; philosophy; physical sciences; physical sciences related; physics; political science and government; psychology; psychology related; public administration and social service professions related; real estate; social sciences; social sciences related; sociology; statistics.

Non-credit—accounting and computer science; apparel and textiles; computer and information sciences; computer science; computer software and media applications; health and physical education/fitness; music.

SAN DIEGO STATE UNIVERSITY
San Diego, California
Academic Affairs
http://interwork.sdsu.edu/cdl

San Diego State University was founded in 1897. It is accredited by Western Association of Schools and Colleges. It first offered distance learning courses in 1984. In fall 2010, there were 971 students enrolled in distance learning courses. Institutionally administered financial aid is available to distance learners.

Services Distance learners have accessibility to academic advising, bookstore, e-mail services, library services, tutoring.

Contact Ms. Francesca Ringland, Director, Credit Community Education, College of Education, San Diego State University, 5500 Campanile Drive, San Diego, CA 92182. Telephone: 619-594-2193. E-mail: ringland@mail.sdsu.edu.

DEGREES AND AWARDS

Certificate Instructional Technology

MA Education Leadership–Pacific Cohorts

MAE Educational Technology

MS Biomedical Quality Systems; Regulatory Affairs; Rehabilitation Counseling

COURSE SUBJECT AREAS OFFERED OUTSIDE OF DEGREE PROGRAMS

Undergraduate—anthropology; biology; building/construction finishing, management, and inspection; business/commerce; business, management, and marketing related; computer engineering; criminal justice and corrections; economics; education; educational/instructional media design; education related; education (specific levels and methods); education (specific subject areas); English; ethnic, cultural minority, gender, and group studies; geography and cartography; geological and earth sciences/geosciences; gerontology; history; human development, family studies, and related services; journalism; marketing; mechanical engineering; parks, recreation, leisure, and fitness studies related; philosophy; physiology, pathology and related sciences; psychology; religious studies; social work; special education.

Graduate—educational administration and supervision; educational/instructional media design; education (specific levels and methods).

Non-credit—business/commerce; computer programming; computer software and media applications; education; film/video and photographic arts; geological and earth sciences/geosciences; history.

SAN JACINTO COLLEGE DISTRICT
Pasadena, Texas
Distance Learning
http://www.sanjac.edu

San Jacinto College District was founded in 1961. It is accredited by Southern Association of Colleges and Schools. It first offered distance learning courses in 1985. In fall 2010, there were 6,363 students enrolled in distance learning courses. Institutionally administered financial aid is available to distance learners.

Services Distance learners have accessibility to academic advising, bookstore, campus computer network, e-mail services, library services, tutoring.

Contact Mrs. Niki Whiteside, Vice President, Educational Technology, San Jacinto College District, 4624 Fairmont Parkway, Suite 203, Pasadena, TX 77504. Telephone: 281-991-2660. Fax: 281-998-6130. E-mail: niki.whiteside@sjcd.edu.

DEGREES AND AWARDS

AAS Accounting; Criminal Justice–Law Enforcement option; Criminal Justice–Social Services option

Certificate Accounting; Accounting; Air Conditioning Technology; Business Office Technology, Accounting speciality; Business Office

Technology, General Office speciality; Business Office Technology, Legal Secretary speciality; Core Criminal Justice; General Office Clerk; Law Enforcement Option; Management Specialty

COURSE SUBJECT AREAS OFFERED OUTSIDE OF DEGREE PROGRAMS
Undergraduate—accounting and related services; air transportation; allied health and medical assisting services; anthropology; applied mathematics; audiovisual communications technologies; behavioral sciences; bilingual, multilingual, and multicultural education; biology; business/commerce; business, management, and marketing related; computer and information sciences; computer science; computer software and media applications; criminal justice and corrections; criminology; culinary arts and related services; drafting/design engineering technologies; economics; education; English; English language and literature related; fine and studio arts; fire protection; food science and technology; geography and cartography; health and medical administrative services; health and physical education/fitness; health professions related; health services/allied health/health sciences; history; homeland security; human development, family studies, and related services; legal support services; marketing; mathematics; music; philosophy; psychology; psychology related; public administration; public relations, advertising, and applied communication related; real estate; social sciences related; sociology; statistics.

SANTA FE COMMUNITY COLLEGE
Santa Fe, New Mexico
Department of Distance Learning
http://www.sfcc.edu/distance_learning

Santa Fe Community College was founded in 1983. It is accredited by North Central Association of Colleges and Schools. It first offered distance learning courses in 1998. In fall 2010, there were 2,270 students enrolled in distance learning courses. Institutionally administered financial aid is available to distance learners.
Services Distance learners have accessibility to academic advising, bookstore, e-mail services, library services, tutoring.
Contact Carla Slentz, Title V Director and Administrative Associate for Vice President of Academic and Student Affairs, Santa Fe Community College, 6401 Richards Avenue, Santa Fe, NM 87508. Telephone: 505-428-1166. E-mail: carla.slentz@sfcc.edu.

DEGREES AND AWARDS
Programs offered do not lead to a degree or other formal award.

COURSE SUBJECT AREAS OFFERED OUTSIDE OF DEGREE PROGRAMS
Undergraduate—accounting and computer science; allied health and medical assisting services; allied health diagnostic, intervention, and treatment professions; American Sign Language (ASL); anthropology; apparel and textiles; architectural sciences and technology; business administration, management and operations; computer software and media applications; criminal justice and corrections; dental support services and allied professions; design and applied arts; economics; education (specific subject areas); environmental design; foods, nutrition, and related services; geological and earth sciences/geosciences; health and physical education/fitness; history; hospitality administration; human services; languages (Romance languages); legal support services; mathematics; music; philosophy; political science and government; psychology; social work; sociology.

SANTA MONICA COLLEGE
Santa Monica, California
SMC Online
http://smconline.org

Santa Monica College was founded in 1929. It is accredited by Western Association of Schools and Colleges. It first offered distance learning courses in 1999. Institutionally administered financial aid is available to distance learners.
Services Distance learners have accessibility to academic advising, bookstore, e-mail services, library services.
Contact Julie Yarrish, Associate Dean of Online Services and Support, Santa Monica College, 1900 Pico Boulevard, Santa Monica, CA 90405. Telephone: 310-434-3762. E-mail: yarrish_julie@smc.edu.

DEGREES AND AWARDS
Programs offered do not lead to a degree or other formal award.

COURSE SUBJECT AREAS OFFERED OUTSIDE OF DEGREE PROGRAMS
Undergraduate—accounting and computer science; accounting and related services; allied health diagnostic, intervention, and treatment professions; architectural history and criticism; architecture; behavioral sciences; biochemistry, biophysics and molecular biology; biological and physical sciences; biology; botany/plant biology; business administration, management and operations; business/commerce; business/corporate communications; business, management, and marketing related; cell biology and anatomical sciences; communication and journalism related; communication and media; computer programming; computer science; ecology, evolution, systematics, and population biology; economics; education; English; entrepreneurial and small business operations; foods, nutrition, and related services; geological and earth sciences/geosciences; health services/allied health/health sciences; history; intercultural/multicultural and diversity studies; journalism; languages (foreign languages related); library science and administration; marketing; music; nutrition sciences; pharmacology and toxicology; psychology; sociology.

SANTA ROSA JUNIOR COLLEGE
Santa Rosa, California
http://online.santarosa.edu/

Santa Rosa Junior College was founded in 1918. It is accredited by Western Association of Schools and Colleges. It first offered distance learning courses in 1989. In fall 2010, there were 5,000 students enrolled in distance learning courses. Institutionally administered financial aid is available to distance learners.
Services Distance learners have accessibility to academic advising, bookstore, campus computer network, e-mail services, library services.
Contact Dr. W. Cherry Li-Bugg, Dean, Learning Resources and Educational Technology, Santa Rosa Junior College, 1501 Mendocino Avenue, Santa Rosa, CA 95401. Telephone: 707-527-4392. Fax: 707-527-4545. E-mail: wli-bugg@santarosa.edu.

DEGREES AND AWARDS
AA Humanities; Liberal Studies; Psychology; Social and Behavioral Sciences
AS Interactive Media Design; Real Estate

COURSE SUBJECT AREAS OFFERED OUTSIDE OF DEGREE PROGRAMS
Undergraduate—accounting and related services; allied health and medical assisting services; anthropology; astronomy and astrophysics; atmospheric sciences and meteorology; behavioral sciences; business administration, management and operations; business/commerce; business/corporate communications; business operations support and assistant services; communication and journalism related; communication and media; communications technology; computer and information sciences; computer and information sciences and support services related; computer programming; computer science; computer software and media applications; computer systems networking and telecommunications; criminal justice and corrections; criminology; culinary arts and related services; economics; English; ethnic, cultural minority, gender, and group studies; family and consumer sciences/human sciences; fire protection; food science and technology; geological and earth sciences/geosciences; graphic communications; health professions related; human development, family studies, and related services; information science/studies; intercultural/multicultural and diversity studies; international/global studies; journalism; languages (foreign languages related); liberal arts and sciences, general studies and humanities; library science and administration; library science related; marketing; mathematics; multi/interdisciplinary studies related; philosophy; psychology; psychology related; real estate; sociology; visual and performing arts.

SAUK VALLEY COMMUNITY COLLEGE
Dixon, Illinois
http://www.svcc.edu/

Sauk Valley Community College was founded in 1965. It is accredited by North Central Association of Colleges and Schools. It first offered distance learning courses in 1993. In fall 2010, there were 725 students enrolled in distance learning courses. Institutionally administered financial aid is available to distance learners.

Services Distance learners have accessibility to academic advising, bookstore, e-mail services, library services.

Contact Alan Pfeifer, Dean of Information Services, Sauk Valley Community College, 173 Illinois Route 2, Dixon, IL 61021. Telephone: 815-288-5511 Ext. 218. Fax: 815-288-5958. E-mail: pfeifer@svcc.edu.

DEGREES AND AWARDS

Programs offered do not lead to a degree or other formal award.

COURSE SUBJECT AREAS OFFERED OUTSIDE OF DEGREE PROGRAMS

Undergraduate—accounting and related services; biology; business administration, management and operations; business/commerce; business operations support and assistant services; chemistry; computer and information sciences; computer and information sciences and support services related; computer/information technology administration and management; computer programming; computer software and media applications; criminal justice and corrections; criminology; economics; history; international business; mathematics and statistics related; psychology; sociology.

Non-credit—computer and information sciences.

SAVANNAH COLLEGE OF ART AND DESIGN
Savannah, Georgia
http://www.scad.edu

Savannah College of Art and Design was founded in 1978. It is accredited by Southern Association of Colleges and Schools. It first offered distance learning courses in 2003. In fall 2010, there were 493 students enrolled in distance learning courses. Institutionally administered financial aid is available to distance learners.

Services Distance learners have accessibility to academic advising, bookstore, campus computer network, career placement assistance, e-mail services, library services, tutoring.

Contact Ms. Nior Gonzales, Director of eLearning Recruitment, Savannah College of Art and Design, PO Box 3146, Savannah, GA 31402-3146. Telephone: 912-596-2794. Fax: 912-525-5986. E-mail: ngonzale@scad.edu.

DEGREES AND AWARDS

BA Advertising; Graphic Design; Interactive Design and Game Development; Photography; Sequential Art

BFA Graphic Design

Certificate Digital Publishing

Graduate Certificate Digital Publishing Management; Historic Preservation; Interactive Design; Typeface Design

MA Arts Administration; Design Management; Digital Photography; Graphic Design; Historic Preservation; Illustration Design; Illustration; Interactive Design and Game Development; Interior Design; International Preservation; Motion Media Design; Painting

MAT Art; Drama

MFA Graphic Design; Interactive Design and Game Development; Painting

COURSE SUBJECT AREAS OFFERED OUTSIDE OF DEGREE PROGRAMS

Undergraduate—fine and studio arts.

Graduate—fine and studio arts.

SEMINOLE STATE COLLEGE OF FLORIDA
Sanford, Florida
Distance Learning Department
http://www.seminolestate.edu/dl/

Seminole State College of Florida was founded in 1966. It is accredited by Southern Association of Colleges and Schools. It first offered distance learning courses in 1970. In fall 2010, there were 5,721 students enrolled in distance learning courses. Institutionally administered financial aid is available to distance learners.

Services Distance learners have accessibility to academic advising, bookstore, campus computer network, career placement assistance, e-mail services, library services, tutoring.

Contact Mrs. Margaret Taylor, Distance Learning Support Specialist, Seminole State College of Florida, Distance Learning Department, 100 Weldon Boulevard, Sanford, FL 32773. Telephone: 407-708-2424. Fax: 407-708-2547. E-mail: dl@seminolestate.edu.

DEGREES AND AWARDS

AA General Studies

AS Accounting Technology; Business Administration; Business Management, Marketing and Administration; Computer Information Systems Technology–Networking specialization; Computer Information Systems Technology–Programming specialization; Computer Information Technology; Computer Programming and Analysis (web programming specialization); Computer Programming and Analysis; Criminal Justice Technology; Early Childhood Management; Fire Science Technology; Network Services Technology; Office Administration

Certificate Computer Programming; Health Information Management–Medical Information Coder/Biller; International Business; Management; Marketing; Microsoft Certified Systems Administrator; Microsoft Certified Systems Engineer; Web Development

Certification Computer Engineering CISCO/CCNA

Technical Certificate Accounting Applications; Accounting Operations; Accounting Specialist; Childcare Center Management specialization; Early Childhood Education Preschool specialization; Human Resources Administrator; Office Management; Office Software Applications; Office Specialist; Office Support; Wireless and Advanced

COURSE SUBJECT AREAS OFFERED OUTSIDE OF DEGREE PROGRAMS

Undergraduate—accounting and related services; anthropology; biological and physical sciences; business administration, management and operations; computer/information technology administration and management; computer programming; computer systems networking and telecommunications; criminology; economics; English; fire protection; history; marketing; mathematics and statistics related; nutrition sciences; psychology; public health; sociology.

Non-credit—computer programming; education (specific levels and methods); entrepreneurial and small business operations; ethnic, cultural minority, gender, and group studies; international business; marketing.

SESSIONS COLLEGE FOR PROFESSIONAL DESIGN
Tempe, Arizona
http://sessions.edu

Sessions College for Professional Design is accredited by Distance Education and Training Council. It first offered distance learning courses in 1997. In fall 2010, there were 1,500 students enrolled in distance learning courses. Institutionally administered financial aid is available to distance learners.

Services Distance learners have accessibility to academic advising, campus computer network, e-mail services.

Contact Admissions Advisor, Sessions College for Professional Design, 314 South Mill Avenue, Suite 300, Tempe, AZ 85281. Telephone: 800-258-4115. Fax: 480-212-1704. E-mail: admissions@sessions.edu.

DEGREES AND AWARDS

AD Graphic Design; Web Design

COURSE SUBJECT AREAS OFFERED OUTSIDE OF DEGREE PROGRAMS

Undergraduate—audiovisual communications technologies; design and applied arts; film/video and photographic arts; fine and studio arts; graphic communications; marketing; publishing; visual and performing arts related.

Non-credit—audiovisual communications technologies; design and applied arts; film/video and photographic arts; fine and studio arts; marketing; publishing.

SETON HALL UNIVERSITY
South Orange, New Jersey
MA in Counseling
http://www.shu.edu>o¢ounselor

Seton Hall University was founded in 1856. It is accredited by Middle States Association of Colleges and Schools. It first offered distance learning courses in 1999. In fall 2010, there were 250 students enrolled in distance learning courses. Institutionally administered financial aid is available to distance learners.

Services Distance learners have accessibility to academic advising, bookstore, campus computer network, career placement assistance, e-mail services, library services.

Contact Rosalie Maiorella, Program Director, Seton Hall University, 400 South Orange Avenue, South Orange, NJ 07046. Telephone: 973-761-9325. E-mail: rosalie.maiorella@shu.edu.

DEGREES AND AWARDS

MA Counseling; School Counseling

MHA Healthcare Administration–Master of Healthcare Administration

COURSE SUBJECT AREAS OFFERED OUTSIDE OF DEGREE PROGRAMS

Graduate—communication and media; educational administration and supervision; health professions related; student counseling and personnel services.

SETON HALL UNIVERSITY
South Orange, New Jersey
MA in Health Administration
http://www.shu.edu/go/mha

Seton Hall University was founded in 1856. It is accredited by Middle States Association of Colleges and Schools. It first offered distance learning courses in 1998. In fall 2010, there were 120 students enrolled in distance learning courses. Institutionally administered financial aid is available to distance learners.

Services Distance learners have accessibility to academic advising, bookstore, campus computer network, career placement assistance, e-mail services, library services.

Contact Anne Hewitt, PhD, Director of Graduate Studies, Healthcare Administration, Seton Hall University, 400 South Orange Avenue, South Orange, NJ 07079. Telephone: 973-761-9510. Fax: 973-275-2463. E-mail: mha@shu.edu.

DEGREES AND AWARDS

MHA Healthcare Administration

COURSE SUBJECT AREAS OFFERED OUTSIDE OF DEGREE PROGRAMS

Graduate—business administration, management and operations; business/corporate communications; business, management, and marketing related.

SETON HALL UNIVERSITY
South Orange, New Jersey
MA in Strategic Communication and Leadership
http://www.shu.edu/go/mascl

Seton Hall University was founded in 1856. It is accredited by Middle States Association of Colleges and Schools. It first offered distance learning courses in 1998. In fall 2010, there were 100 students enrolled in distance learning courses. Institutionally administered financial aid is available to distance learners.

Services Distance learners have accessibility to academic advising, bookstore, campus computer network, career placement assistance, e-mail services, library services.

Contact Dr. Richard Dool, Director of Graduate Studies, Communication, Seton Hall University, 400 South Orange Avenue, South Orange, NJ 07079. Telephone: 973-313-6237. Fax: 973-761-9234. E-mail: mascl@shu.edu.

DEGREES AND AWARDS

MA Strategic Communication and Leadership

COURSE SUBJECT AREAS OFFERED OUTSIDE OF DEGREE PROGRAMS

Graduate—business/corporate communications; health and medical administrative services; health professions related.

SETON HILL UNIVERSITY
Greensburg, Pennsylvania
Academic Affairs
http://www.setonhill.edu

Seton Hill University was founded in 1883. It is accredited by Middle States Association of Colleges and Schools. It first offered distance learning courses in 1999. In fall 2010, there were 100 students enrolled in distance learning courses. Institutionally administered financial aid is available to distance learners.

Services Distance learners have accessibility to academic advising, bookstore, campus computer network, career placement assistance, e-mail services, library services, tutoring.

Contact Ms. Tracey L. Bartos, Director of Graduate and Adult Studies, Seton Hill University, 1 Seton Hill Drive, Greensburg, PA 15601. Telephone: 724-838-4283. Fax: 724-830-1891. E-mail: bartos@setonhill.edu.

DEGREES AND AWARDS

Certificate Genocide and Holocaust Studies

MAE Inclusive Education

COURSE SUBJECT AREAS OFFERED OUTSIDE OF DEGREE PROGRAMS

Undergraduate—accounting and computer science; business/commerce; communication and journalism related; computer and information sciences; education related; history; holocaust and related studies; human resources management; languages (foreign languages related); liberal arts and sciences, general studies and humanities; mathematics and statistics related; philosophy; political science and government; psychology; religious education; religious studies; special education; statistics.

Graduate—accounting and related services; communications technology; education; educational/instructional media design; holocaust and related studies.

Non-credit—human resources management; sales, merchandising and related marketing operations (specialized).

SHASTA BIBLE COLLEGE
Redding, California
Individualized Distance Learning
http://www.shasta.edu

Shasta Bible College was founded in 1971. It is accredited by Transnational Association of Christian Colleges and Schools. It first offered distance learning courses in 1999. In fall 2010, there were 15 students enrolled in distance learning courses. Institutionally administered financial aid is available to distance learners.

Services Distance learners have accessibility to academic advising, bookstore, e-mail services, library services.

Contact Mrs. Faith McCarthy, Registrar, Shasta Bible College, 2951 Goodwater Avenue, Redding, CA 96002. Telephone: 530-221-4275 Ext. 26. Fax: 530-221-6929. E-mail: registrar@shasta.edu.

DEGREES AND AWARDS
BA Christian Professional Studies
MA Christian Ministries; Christian Ministries
MDiv Divinity
MS School and Church Administration

COURSE SUBJECT AREAS OFFERED OUTSIDE OF DEGREE PROGRAMS
Undergraduate—biblical studies; education related; religious studies.
Graduate—educational administration and supervision; education related.
Non-credit—biblical studies; education related.

SHAWNEE STATE UNIVERSITY
Portsmouth, Ohio
Department of Nursing
http://www.shawnee.edu/acad/hs/bsn/index.html

Shawnee State University was founded in 1986. It is accredited by North Central Association of Colleges and Schools. It first offered distance learning courses in 1997. In fall 2010, there were 466 students enrolled in distance learning courses. Institutionally administered financial aid is available to distance learners.

Services Distance learners have accessibility to bookstore, e-mail services, library services.

Contact Dr. Mattie Burton, Chair, Nursing, Shawnee State University, 940 Second Street, Health Sciences Building, Room 121, Portsmouth, OH 45662. Telephone: 740-351-3378. E-mail: mburton@shawnee.edu.

DEGREES AND AWARDS
BSN Nursing

COURSE SUBJECT AREAS OFFERED OUTSIDE OF DEGREE PROGRAMS
Undergraduate—business administration, management and operations; business, management, and marketing related; engineering-related technologies; health and physical education/fitness; health services/allied health/health sciences; psychology.

SHIPPENSBURG UNIVERSITY OF PENNSYLVANIA
Shippensburg, Pennsylvania
Extended Studies
http://www.ship.edu/extended/

Shippensburg University of Pennsylvania was founded in 1871. It is accredited by Middle States Association of Colleges and Schools. It first offered distance learning courses in 1998. In fall 2010, there were 119 students enrolled in distance learning courses. Institutionally administered financial aid is available to distance learners.

Services Distance learners have accessibility to academic advising, bookstore, campus computer network, career placement assistance, e-mail services, library services, tutoring.

Contact Dr. Christina M. Sax, Associate Provost and Dean of Academic Outreach and Innovation, Shippensburg University of Pennsylvania, 1871 Old Main Drive, Shippensburg, PA 17257-2299. Telephone: 717-477-1348. Fax: 717-477-4050. E-mail: extended@ship.edu.

DEGREES AND AWARDS
Certificate Business–Advanced Studies in Business
MBA Business Administration

COURSE SUBJECT AREAS OFFERED OUTSIDE OF DEGREE PROGRAMS
Undergraduate—accounting and related services; biology; communication and media; computer engineering; computer science; criminal justice and corrections; economics; education; English; finance and financial management services; fine and studio arts; geography and cartography; history; information science/studies; international business; management information systems; management sciences and quantitative methods; marketing; mathematics; mathematics and computer science; music; philosophy; physics; political science and government; psychology; social work; sociology; special education.
Graduate—accounting and related services; biology; business administration, management and operations; communication and media; criminal justice and corrections; education; English; entrepreneurial and small business operations; fine and studio arts; geography and cartography; history; information science/studies; international business; management information systems; management sciences and quantitative methods; marketing; political science and government; psychology; social work; sociology; special education.

SIENA HEIGHTS UNIVERSITY
Adrian, Michigan
http://www.sienaheights.edu/

Siena Heights University was founded in 1919. It is accredited by North Central Association of Colleges and Schools. It first offered distance learning courses in 1995. In fall 2010, there were 450 students enrolled in distance learning courses. Institutionally administered financial aid is available to distance learners.

Services Distance learners have accessibility to academic advising, bookstore, e-mail services, library services.

Contact Lori Timmis, Assistant Dean for the College for Professional Studies, Siena Heights University, 1247 East Siena Heights Drive, Adrian, MI 49221. Telephone: 517-264-7195. E-mail: ltimmis@sienaheights.edu.

DEGREES AND AWARDS
BA Multidisciplinary Studies
BAS Applied Science
BBA Business Administration

COURSE SUBJECT AREAS OFFERED OUTSIDE OF DEGREE PROGRAMS
Undergraduate—business administration, management and operations; business, management, and marketing related; health professions related; liberal arts and sciences, general studies and humanities; philosophy and religious studies related; social sciences related.

SIMMONS COLLEGE
Boston, Massachusetts
http://www.simmons.edu/shs

Simmons College was founded in 1899. It is accredited by New England Association of Schools and Colleges. It first offered distance learning courses in 2001. In fall 2010, there were 87 students enrolled in distance learning courses. Institutionally administered financial aid is available to distance learners.

Services Distance learners have accessibility to academic advising, bookstore, campus computer network, e-mail services, library services, tutoring.

Contact Ms. Yolanda Mendez Rainey, Administrative Assistant, Simmons College, 300 The Fenway, Boston, MA 02115-5898. Telephone: 617-521-2518. Fax: 617-521-3044. E-mail: yolanda.rainey@simmons.edu.

DEGREES AND AWARDS
CAGS Health Professions Education; Sports Nutrition
DNP Nursing–Doctor of Nursing Practice

DPT Bridge Doctor of Physical Therapy

COURSE SUBJECT AREAS OFFERED OUTSIDE OF DEGREE PROGRAMS

Non-credit—psychology related; statistics.

SINCLAIR COMMUNITY COLLEGE
Dayton, Ohio
Distance Learning Division
http://www.sinclair.edu/online

Sinclair Community College was founded in 1887. It is accredited by North Central Association of Colleges and Schools. It first offered distance learning courses in 1979. In fall 2010, there were 6,116 students enrolled in distance learning courses. Institutionally administered financial aid is available to distance learners.

Services Distance learners have accessibility to academic advising, bookstore, career placement assistance, e-mail services, library services, tutoring.

Contact Mrs. Elizabeth A. Burns, SinclairOnline Program Coordinator, Sinclair Community College, Distance Learning Programs and Support (14-223), 444 West Third Street, Dayton, OH 45402. Telephone: 937-512-5224. Fax: 937-512-2891. E-mail: elizabeth.burns@sinclair.edu.

DEGREES AND AWARDS

AA Liberal Arts and Sciences; Liberal Arts, History emphasis; Liberal Arts, Psychology emphasis
AAS Business Management; Health Information Management
AS Business Administration; Liberal Arts and Sciences
Certificate Business Management; Medical Coding and Billing Specialist; Pharmacy Technician; Software Applications for the Professional

COURSE SUBJECT AREAS OFFERED OUTSIDE OF DEGREE PROGRAMS

Undergraduate—accounting and computer science; accounting and related services; allied health and medical assisting services; applied mathematics; audiovisual communications technologies; behavioral sciences; bilingual, multilingual, and multicultural education; biological and biomedical sciences related; biological and physical sciences; biology; business administration, management and operations; business/commerce; business, management, and marketing related; business/managerial economics; chemistry; civil engineering; classical and ancient studies; communication and journalism related; communication and media; communications technology; computer and information sciences; computer and information sciences and support services related; computer programming; computer science; computer software and media applications; computer systems networking and telecommunications; cultural studies/critical theory and analysis; data entry/microcomputer applications; data processing; drafting/design engineering technologies; drama/theatre arts and stagecraft; economics; education; English; English language and literature related; entrepreneurial and small business operations; ethnic, cultural minority, gender, and group studies; family and consumer sciences/human sciences related; finance and financial management services; fine and studio arts; health and medical administrative services; health/medical preparatory programs; health services/allied health/health sciences; history; human biology; human resources management; human services; intercultural/multicultural and diversity studies; interdisciplinary studies; international business; international/global studies; languages (foreign languages related); legal studies (non-professional general, undergraduate); liberal arts and sciences, general studies and humanities; literature; management information systems; marketing; mathematics; mathematics and computer science; mathematics and statistics related; music; natural sciences; pharmacology and toxicology; pharmacy, pharmaceutical sciences, and administration; philosophy; philosophy and religious studies; philosophy and religious studies related; physical sciences related; physics; political science and government; psychology; psychology related; public administration; social and philosophical foundations of education; social sciences; social sciences related; sociology; sociology and anthropology; statistics; visual and performing arts; visual and performing arts related.

SIOUX FALLS SEMINARY
Sioux Falls, South Dakota
http://www.sfseminary.edu/learning/

Sioux Falls Seminary was founded in 1858. It is accredited by North Central Association of Colleges and Schools. It first offered distance learning courses in 2000. In fall 2010, there were 55 students enrolled in distance learning courses. Institutionally administered financial aid is available to distance learners.

Services Distance learners have accessibility to academic advising, bookstore, campus computer network, career placement assistance, e-mail services, library services.

Contact Mr. Nathan M. Helling, Director of Enrollment, Sioux Falls Seminary, 2100 South Summit Avenue, Sioux Falls, SD 57105. Telephone: 605-336-6588 Ext. 2718. Fax: 605-335-9090. E-mail: nhelling@sfseminary.edu.

DEGREES AND AWARDS

Programs offered do not lead to a degree or other formal award.

COURSE SUBJECT AREAS OFFERED OUTSIDE OF DEGREE PROGRAMS

Graduate—education (specific subject areas); religious/sacred music; theological and ministerial studies; theology and religious vocations related.

SLIPPERY ROCK UNIVERSITY OF PENNSYLVANIA
Slippery Rock, Pennsylvania
http://academics.sru.edu/cfit/distance_education/

Slippery Rock University of Pennsylvania was founded in 1889. It is accredited by Middle States Association of Colleges and Schools. It first offered distance learning courses in 1995. In fall 2010, there were 1,348 students enrolled in distance learning courses. Institutionally administered financial aid is available to distance learners.

Services Distance learners have accessibility to academic advising, bookstore, campus computer network, career placement assistance, e-mail services, library services, tutoring.

Contact Ms. Mimi Campbell, Associate Director of Admissions, Slippery Rock University of Pennsylvania, 1 Morrow Way, Office of Admissions, Slippery Rock, PA 16057. Telephone: 724-738-2015. Fax: 724-738-2913. E-mail: asktherock@sru.edu.

DEGREES AND AWARDS

BSN Nursing

MA Criminal Justice

MEd Environmental Education; Math and Science (K-8); Special Education, Master Teacher or Supervision

MS Park and Resource Management

COURSE SUBJECT AREAS OFFERED OUTSIDE OF DEGREE PROGRAMS

Undergraduate—accounting and related services; business administration, management and operations; chemistry; communication and media; computer and information sciences; criminal justice and corrections; criminology; ecology, evolution, systematics, and population biology; education; education related; geography and cartography; geological and earth sciences/geosciences; health professions related; languages (foreign languages related); languages (Germanic); literature; music; philosophy; political science and government; social work; special education; statistics; taxation.

Graduate—criminal justice and corrections; criminology; education; education related; education (specific subject areas); geological and earth sciences/geosciences; parks, recreation and leisure facilities management; special education.

SONOMA STATE UNIVERSITY
Rohnert Park, California
Liberal Studies Special Sessions Degree Programs
http://www.sonoma.edu/exed

Sonoma State University was founded in 1960. It is accredited by Western Association of Schools and Colleges. It first offered distance learning courses in 1996. In fall 2010, there were 500 students enrolled in distance learning courses. Institutionally administered financial aid is available to distance learners.

Services Distance learners have accessibility to academic advising, bookstore, campus computer network, career placement assistance, e-mail services, library services.

Contact Beth Warner, Academic Program Coordinator, Sonoma State University, School of Extended Education, 1801 East Cotati Avenue, Rohnert Park, CA 94928-3609. Telephone: 707-664-3977. Fax: 707-664-2613. E-mail: beth.warner@sonoma.edu.

DEGREES AND AWARDS

BA Liberal Studies

COURSE SUBJECT AREAS OFFERED OUTSIDE OF DEGREE PROGRAMS

Undergraduate—educational/instructional media design; education related; education (specific levels and methods); environmental design; peace studies and conflict resolution.

Graduate—psychology; psychology related.

Non-credit—business administration, management and operations; business/corporate communications; business, management, and marketing related; computer/information technology administration and management; computer software and media applications; computer systems networking and telecommunications; construction engineering technologies; construction management; environmental design; landscape architecture.

SOUTHEAST ARKANSAS COLLEGE
Pine Bluff, Arkansas
http://www.seark.edu/

Southeast Arkansas College was founded in 1991. It is accredited by North Central Association of Colleges and Schools. It first offered distance learning courses in 1995. In fall 2010, there were 508 students enrolled in distance learning courses. Institutionally administered financial aid is available to distance learners.

Services Distance learners have accessibility to bookstore, career placement assistance, e-mail services, library services.

Contact Kathleen Boyle, Coordinator of Distance Learning, Southeast Arkansas College, 1900 Hazel Street, Pine Bluff, AR 71603. Telephone: 870-543-5992. Fax: 870-543-5992. E-mail: kboyle@seark.edu.

DEGREES AND AWARDS

Programs offered do not lead to a degree or other formal award.

COURSE SUBJECT AREAS OFFERED OUTSIDE OF DEGREE PROGRAMS

Undergraduate—anthropology; applied mathematics; business administration, management and operations; business/commerce; business/corporate communications; business, management, and marketing related; business/managerial economics; computer/information technology administration and management; computer programming; computer science; computer software and media applications; computer systems analysis; computer systems networking and telecommunications; criminal justice and corrections; criminology; data entry/microcomputer applications; economics; education (specific subject areas); electromechanical instrumentation and maintenance technologies; English; English language and literature related; entrepreneurial and small business operations; fire protection; foods, nutrition, and related services; geography and cartography; health and physical education/fitness; health professions related; health services/allied health/health sciences; history; insurance; international business; marketing; mathematics; mathematics and computer science; mathematics and statistics related; psychology; real estate; sociology; statistics.

Non-credit—teaching assistants/aides.

SOUTHEAST COMMUNITY COLLEGE AREA
Lincoln, Nebraska
http://thehub.southeast.edu

Southeast Community College Area first offered distance learning courses in 1998. In fall 2010, there were 3,200 students enrolled in distance learning courses. Institutionally administered financial aid is available to distance learners.

Services Distance learners have accessibility to academic advising, bookstore, career placement assistance, e-mail services, library services, tutoring.

Contact Robert D. Morgan, Beatrice Campus Director/Dean of Distance Learning, Southeast Community College Area, 4771 West Scott Road, Beatrice, NE 68310. Telephone: 402-228-8272. Fax: 402-228-2218. E-mail: bmorgan@southeast.edu.

DEGREES AND AWARDS

AAS Business Administration; Early Childhood; Medical Assisting; Radiologic Technology program; Respiratory Care; Surgical Technology
Certification Food Service Training Program
Diploma Medical Assisting
License Nursing Home Administration

COURSE SUBJECT AREAS OFFERED OUTSIDE OF DEGREE PROGRAMS

Undergraduate—accounting and related services; biological and biomedical sciences related; business administration, management and operations; business/commerce; business/corporate communications; economics; English; foods, nutrition, and related services; health and medical administrative services; health professions related; history; human services; liberal arts and sciences, general studies and humanities; mathematics; philosophy; psychology; sales, merchandising and related marketing operations (specialized).

Non-credit—management sciences and quantitative methods; mathematics.

SOUTHEASTERN COMMUNITY COLLEGE
Whiteville, North Carolina
http://www.sccnc.edu

Southeastern Community College was founded in 1964. It is accredited by Southern Association of Colleges and Schools. It first offered distance learning courses in 1998. In fall 2010, there were 5,000 students enrolled in distance learning courses. Institutionally administered financial aid is available to distance learners.

Services Distance learners have accessibility to academic advising, bookstore, career placement assistance, e-mail services, library services, tutoring.

Contact Ms. Angela Phillips, e-Learning Specialist, Southeastern Community College, PO Box 151, Whiteville, NC 28472. Telephone: 910-642-7141 Ext. 229. Fax: 910-642-0353. E-mail: anphillips@sccnc.edu.

DEGREES AND AWARDS

AA Business Administration; College Transfer degree; Elementary, Middle Grades, and Special Education
AAB Business Administration
AAS Electronic Commerce

COURSE SUBJECT AREAS OFFERED OUTSIDE OF DEGREE PROGRAMS

Undergraduate—accounting and related services; allied health and medical assisting services; biology; business administration, management and operations; business/commerce; business/managerial economics; chemistry; communication and journalism related; communication and media; computer and information sciences; computer science; computer software and media applications; computer systems networking and telecommunications; criminal justice and corrections; data processing; economics; education; English; geography and cartography; health and medical administrative services; history; marketing; mathematics; music;

philosophy; philosophy and religious studies related; physics; psychology; social sciences; sociology; zoology/animal biology.

SOUTHEASTERN ILLINOIS COLLEGE
Harrisburg, Illinois
Distance Learning
http://www.sic.edu/onlinedegree

Southeastern Illinois College was founded in 1960. It is accredited by North Central Association of Colleges and Schools. It first offered distance learning courses in 1988. In fall 2010, there were 1,250 students enrolled in distance learning courses. Institutionally administered financial aid is available to distance learners.

Services Distance learners have accessibility to academic advising, bookstore, campus computer network, career placement assistance, e-mail services, library services, tutoring.

Contact Mrs. Karla J. Lewis, Distance Learning Specialist, Southeastern Illinois College, 3575 College Road, Harrisburg, IL 62946. Telephone: 618-252-5400 Ext. 2265. Fax: 618-252-2713. E-mail: karla.lewis@sic.edu.

DEGREES AND AWARDS
AA General degree
AAS Early Childhood Education

COURSE SUBJECT AREAS OFFERED OUTSIDE OF DEGREE PROGRAMS
Undergraduate—behavioral sciences; biotechnology; business/commerce; communication and journalism related; computer and information sciences; computer software and media applications; data entry/microcomputer applications; economics; education; English; family and consumer sciences/human sciences related; health professions related; history; mathematics; music; philosophy; political science and government; psychology; religious studies; sociology; statistics.

SOUTHEASTERN OKLAHOMA STATE UNIVERSITY
Durant, Oklahoma
http://www.se.edu/online-learning

Southeastern Oklahoma State University was founded in 1909. It is accredited by North Central Association of Colleges and Schools. It first offered distance learning courses in 2000. In fall 2010, there were 2,042 students enrolled in distance learning courses. Institutionally administered financial aid is available to distance learners.

Services Distance learners have accessibility to academic advising, bookstore, campus computer network, career placement assistance, e-mail services, library services, tutoring.

Contact Dr. Linda Kallam, Director of Online Learning, Southeastern Oklahoma State University, 1405 North 4th, PMB 4178, Durant, OK 74701. Telephone: 580-745-2682. Fax: 580-745-7458. E-mail: lkallam@se.edu.

DEGREES AND AWARDS
Programs offered do not lead to a degree or other formal award.

COURSE SUBJECT AREAS OFFERED OUTSIDE OF DEGREE PROGRAMS
Undergraduate—accounting and related services; air transportation; astronomy and astrophysics; behavioral sciences; biology; business administration, management and operations; business/commerce; business, management, and marketing related; communication and media; computer and information sciences; computer science; criminal justice and corrections; criminology; economics; education related; finance and financial management services; gerontology; health and physical education/fitness; history; languages (American Indian/Native American); languages (Romance languages); marketing; mathematics; music; physical sciences; political science and government; psychology; quality control and safety technologies; sociology; statistics.
Graduate—accounting and related services; educational administration and supervision; educational assessment, evaluation, and research; education related; education (specific subject areas); health and physical education/fitness; quality control and safety technologies; special education.
Non-credit—accounting and related services; computer software and media applications; computer systems networking and telecommunications; crafts, folk art and artisanry; culinary arts and related services; dance; drama/theatre arts and stagecraft; education related; family and consumer economics; film/video and photographic arts; health and physical education/fitness; languages (Romance languages); nutrition sciences.

SOUTHEAST MISSOURI STATE UNIVERSITY
Cape Girardeau, Missouri
Southeast Online
http://online.semo.edu

Southeast Missouri State University was founded in 1873. It is accredited by North Central Association of Colleges and Schools. It first offered distance learning courses in 1999. In fall 2010, there were 2,231 students enrolled in distance learning courses. Institutionally administered financial aid is available to distance learners.

Services Distance learners have accessibility to academic advising, bookstore, campus computer network, career placement assistance, e-mail services, library services, tutoring.

Contact Mrs. Robin Adkison Grebing, Director of Southeast Online, Southeast Missouri State University, Kent Library, Room 305, Mail Stop 4650, Cape Girardeau, MO 63701. Telephone: 573-986-7306. Fax: 573-986-6858. E-mail: rgrebing@semo.edu.

DEGREES AND AWARDS
BGS General Studies
BS Industrial Technology; Interdisciplinary Studies
BSBA Organizational Administration
BSN Nursing–RN to BSN completion
MA Teaching English to Speakers of Other Languages
MAEd Educational Technology–Master of Arts in Secondary Education
MBA General Management option
MSCJ Criminal Justice

SOUTHERN ADVENTIST UNIVERSITY
Collegedale, Tennessee
http://www.southern.edu/online/Pages/default.aspx

Southern Adventist University was founded in 1892. It is accredited by Southern Association of Colleges and Schools. It first offered distance learning courses in 2006. In fall 2010, there were 192 students enrolled in distance learning courses. Institutionally administered financial aid is available to distance learners.

Services Distance learners have accessibility to academic advising, bookstore, e-mail services, library services.

Contact Lisa Hess, Administrative Assistant and Academic Advisor, Southern Adventist University, PO Box 370, Online Campus, Collegedale, TN 37315. Telephone: 423-236-2087. E-mail: online@southern.edu.

DEGREES AND AWARDS
Programs offered do not lead to a degree or other formal award.

COURSE SUBJECT AREAS OFFERED OUTSIDE OF DEGREE PROGRAMS
Undergraduate—chemistry; education related; English; finance and financial management services; health services/allied health/health sciences; history; mathematics and statistics related; philosophy and religious studies; physical sciences; psychology; registered nursing, nursing administration, nursing research and clinical nursing; religious/sacred music; social work; sociology; statistics.
Graduate—business administration, management and operations; business, management, and marketing related; education; educational administration and supervision; educational assessment, evaluation, and research; educational/instructional media design; education (specific levels and methods); education (specific subject areas); social work.

SOUTHERN ARKANSAS UNIVERSITY–MAGNOLIA
Magnolia, Arkansas
http://www.saumag.edu/

Southern Arkansas University–Magnolia was founded in 1909. It is accredited by North Central Association of Colleges and Schools. It first offered distance learning courses in 1998. In fall 2010, there were 1,021 students enrolled in distance learning courses. Institutionally administered financial aid is available to distance learners.

Services Distance learners have accessibility to academic advising, bookstore, campus computer network, career placement assistance, e-mail services, library services.

Contact Mrs. Kathy Cole, Coordinator of Online Faculty Training, Southern Arkansas University–Magnolia, PO Box 9302, Magnolia, AR 71754. Telephone: 870-235-4168. Fax: 870-235-5227. E-mail: kscole@saumag.edu.

DEGREES AND AWARDS

MBA Business Administration

MEd Curriculum and Instruction

MSS Kinesiology–Coaching

COURSE SUBJECT AREAS OFFERED OUTSIDE OF DEGREE PROGRAMS

Undergraduate—accounting and computer science; business, management, and marketing related; curriculum and instruction; education related; education (specific levels and methods); education (specific subject areas); finance and financial management services; health/medical preparatory programs; health professions related; health services/allied health/health sciences; liberal arts and sciences, general studies and humanities; management information systems; marketing; music; psychology; psychology related.

Graduate—agriculture; business administration, management and operations; clinical, counseling and applied psychology; computer and information sciences; curriculum and instruction; education; educational administration and supervision; education related; education (specific levels and methods); education (specific subject areas); English or French as a second or foreign language (teaching); library science related; mathematics; physical sciences; public administration; student counseling and personnel services.

SOUTHERN CONNECTICUT STATE UNIVERSITY
New Haven, Connecticut
http://www.southernct.edu

Southern Connecticut State University was founded in 1893. It is accredited by New England Association of Schools and Colleges. In fall 2010, there were 882 students enrolled in distance learning courses. Institutionally administered financial aid is available to distance learners.

Contact Christine Barrett, Interim Assistant Dean for Special Programs, Southern Connecticut State University, 501 Crescent Street, New Haven, CT 06515. Telephone: 203-392-6195. Fax: 203-392-5252. E-mail: barrettc@southernct.edu.

DEGREES AND AWARDS

MLS Library Science

COURSE SUBJECT AREAS OFFERED OUTSIDE OF DEGREE PROGRAMS

Undergraduate—communication and media; management information systems; political science and government; psychology; sociology; visual and performing arts.

Graduate—education; management information systems; social work; sociology.

SOUTHERN ILLINOIS UNIVERSITY CARBONDALE
Carbondale, Illinois
Office of Distance Education
http://www.dce.siu.edu/siuconnected

Southern Illinois University Carbondale was founded in 1869. It is accredited by North Central Association of Colleges and Schools. It first offered distance learning courses in 1981. In fall 2010, there were 1,325 students enrolled in distance learning courses. Institutionally administered financial aid is available to distance learners.

Services Distance learners have accessibility to academic advising, bookstore, campus computer network, e-mail services, library services, tutoring.

Contact Gayla Stoner, Administration, Southern Illinois University Carbondale, Office of Distance Education and Off-Campus Programs, Mail Code 6513, Carbondale, IL 62901. Telephone: 618-453-4033. E-mail: gstoner@siu.edu.

DEGREES AND AWARDS

BS Information Systems Technology

COURSE SUBJECT AREAS OFFERED OUTSIDE OF DEGREE PROGRAMS

Undergraduate—agricultural business and management; agricultural engineering; agricultural mechanization; agriculture; anthropology; architectural history and criticism; architectural sciences and technology; architecture; behavioral sciences; biological and biomedical sciences related; biological and physical sciences; biology; business/commerce; business, management, and marketing related; computer and information sciences; computer/information technology administration and management; criminal justice and corrections; criminology; drama/theatre arts and stagecraft; educational administration and supervision; education related; education (specific subject areas); English; finance and financial management services; geography and cartography; health/medical preparatory programs; history; information science/studies; insurance; journalism; landscape architecture; languages (East Asian); languages (Romance languages); management sciences and quantitative methods; marketing; mathematics; mathematics and statistics related; music; philosophy; philosophy and religious studies related; plant sciences; political science and government; quality control and safety technologies; real estate; religious studies; sales merchandising, and related marketing operations (general); social sciences; sociology; zoology/animal biology.

Graduate—agricultural engineering; anthropology; education; rehabilitation and therapeutic professions.

Non-credit—marketing.

SOUTHERN ILLINOIS UNIVERSITY EDWARDSVILLE
Edwardsville, Illinois
Office of Continuing Education
http://www.siue.edu/educationaloutreach

Southern Illinois University Edwardsville was founded in 1957. It is accredited by North Central Association of Colleges and Schools. It first offered distance learning courses in 1994. In fall 2010, there were 518 students enrolled in distance learning courses. Institutionally administered financial aid is available to distance learners.

Services Distance learners have accessibility to academic advising, bookstore, campus computer network, career placement assistance, e-mail services, library services, tutoring.

Contact Mary C. Ettling, Assistant Director, Office of Educational Outreach, Southern Illinois University Edwardsville, Campus Box 1084, Edwardsville, IL 62026. Telephone: 618-650-3215. Fax: 618-650-2629. E-mail: mawalke@siue.edu.

DEGREES AND AWARDS

BS Nursing–RN to BS option

MS Health Care and Nursing Administration; Nurse Educator; Nursing–Family Nurse Practitioner

COURSE SUBJECT AREAS OFFERED OUTSIDE OF DEGREE PROGRAMS

Undergraduate—computer science; economics; education; engineering; English; geography and cartography; mathematics; music; philosophy; political science and government.

Graduate—education; information science/studies.

SOUTHERN MAINE COMMUNITY COLLEGE
South Portland, Maine
http://www.smccme.edu/ecampus/

Southern Maine Community College was founded in 1946. It is accredited by New England Association of Schools and Colleges. It first offered distance learning courses in 1999. In fall 2010, there were 3,500 students enrolled in distance learning courses. Institutionally administered financial aid is available to distance learners.

Services Distance learners have accessibility to academic advising, campus computer network, e-mail services, library services, tutoring.

Contact Enrollment Services, Southern Maine Community College, 2 Fort Road, South Portland, ME 04106. Telephone: 207-741-5800. E-mail: menrollmentservices@smccme.edu.

DEGREES AND AWARDS
AA Liberal Studies concentration

COURSE SUBJECT AREAS OFFERED OUTSIDE OF DEGREE PROGRAMS
Undergraduate—allied health and medical assisting services; biology; criminology; culinary arts and related services; dietetics and clinical nutrition services; economics; English; history; human resources management; mathematics; psychology; social sciences.

SOUTHERN METHODIST UNIVERSITY
Dallas, Texas
School of Engineering–Distance Learning
http://www.lyle.smu.edu

Southern Methodist University was founded in 1911. It is accredited by Southern Association of Colleges and Schools. It first offered distance learning courses in 1968. In fall 2010, there were 500 students enrolled in distance learning courses. Institutionally administered financial aid is available to distance learners.

Services Distance learners have accessibility to academic advising, bookstore, campus computer network, e-mail services, library services, tutoring.

Contact Mrs. Abigail L. Smith, Assistant Director, Graduate Distance and Military Education, Southern Methodist University, PO Box 750335, Dallas, TX 75275-0335. Telephone: 214-768-4661. Fax: 214-768-8874. E-mail: abigails@lyle.smu.edu.

DEGREES AND AWARDS
MS Computer Engineering; Computer Science; Environmental Engineering; Environmental Science (Environmental Systems Management major); Environmental Science (Hazardous and Waste Materials Management major); Environmental Science; Information Engineering and Management; Manufacturing Systems Management; Operations Research; Security Engineering; Software Engineering; Systems Engineering; Telecommunications
MSCE Civil Engineering
MSEE Electrical Engineering
MSEM Engineering Management
MSME Mechanical Engineering

COURSE SUBJECT AREAS OFFERED OUTSIDE OF DEGREE PROGRAMS
Graduate—civil engineering; civil engineering technologies; computer and information sciences; computer and information sciences and support services related; computer engineering; computer engineering technologies; computer/information technology administration and management; computer science; computer software and media applications; computer systems networking and telecommunications; construction engineering; electrical, electronics and communications engineering; electrical engineering technologies; engineering mechanics; engineering related; engineering-related fields; engineering-related technologies; engineering science; engineering technologies related; engineering technology; environmental design; environmental/environmental health engineering; industrial engineering; information science/studies; mechanical engineering; mechanical engineering related technologies; systems engineering.

SOUTHERN NEW HAMPSHIRE UNIVERSITY
Manchester, New Hampshire
SNHU Online
http://www.snhu.edu/online

Southern New Hampshire University was founded in 1932. It is accredited by New England Association of Schools and Colleges. It first offered distance learning courses in 1996. In fall 2010, there were 18,000 students enrolled in distance learning courses. Institutionally administered financial aid is available to distance learners.

Services Distance learners have accessibility to academic advising, bookstore, campus computer network, career placement assistance, e-mail services, library services, tutoring.

Contact Centralized Admissions Team, Southern New Hampshire University, College of Online and Continuing Education, 33 South Commercial Street, Suite 203, Manchester, NH 03101-2626. Telephone: 866-860-0449. Fax: 603-645-9706. E-mail: online@snhu.edu.

DEGREES AND AWARDS
AA Liberal Arts
AS Accounting; Business Administration; Computer Information Technology; Fashion Merchandising; Marketing
BA Advertising; Communications; Community Sociology; Creative Writing; Creative Writing (Fiction concentration); Creative Writing (Non-Fiction concentration); Creative Writing (Poetry concentration); Creative Writing (Screenwriting); English Language and Literature; History; Psychology (Child and Adolescent Development concentration); Psychology; Social Science
BS Accounting; Accounting/Finance; Accounting/Information Systems; Advertising; Business Administration (Human Resource Management concentration); Business Administration (Organizational Leadership concentration); Business Administration (Small Business Management concentration); Business Administration; Business Studies (Accounting concentration); Business Studies (Business Administration concentration); Business Studies (Business Finance concentration); Business Studies (Computer Information Technology concentration); Business Studies (Human Resource Management concentration); Business Studies (International Management concentration); Business Studies (Marketing concentration); Business Studies (Organizational Leadership concentration); Business Studies (Small Business Management concentration); Computer Information Technology (Game Design and Development); Computer Information Technology (Network and Telecommunications concentration); Computer Information Technology (Software Development); Computer Information Technology (Web Design and Development); Computer Information Technology; Computer Information Technology (Cyber Security concentration); Computer Information Technology (Database Management concentration); Finance/Economics; International Business; Justice Studies; Marketing; Retail Management; Technical Management
Certificate Accounting; Business Information Systems; Human Resource Management
Graduate Certificate Accounting; Finance; Human Resource Management; Integrated Marketing Communications; International Business; Marketing; Microfinance Management; Operations Management; Sport Management; Training and Development
MBA Global MBA
MS Accounting; Accounting/Finance; Business Education; Community Economic Development; Finance; Justice Studies; Marketing; Operations and Project Management; Organizational Leadership; Sport Management

COURSE SUBJECT AREAS OFFERED OUTSIDE OF DEGREE PROGRAMS
Undergraduate—accounting and computer science; accounting and related services; business administration, management and operations; business/commerce; business/corporate communications; business, management, and marketing related; communication and journalism related; communication and media; computer and information sciences; eco-

nomics; English language and literature related; entrepreneurial and small business operations; finance and financial management services; human resources management; information science/studies; international relations and national security studies; liberal arts and sciences, general studies and humanities; marketing; psychology; social sciences.
Graduate—accounting and computer science; accounting and related services; business administration, management and operations; business/commerce; business/corporate communications; business, management, and marketing related; criminal justice and corrections; human resources management; international business; international/global studies; marketing; operations research.

SOUTHERN OREGON UNIVERSITY
Ashland, Oregon
Extended Campus Programs
http://www.sou.edu/distancelearning

Southern Oregon University was founded in 1926. It is accredited by Northwest Commission on Colleges and Universities. It first offered distance learning courses in 1992. In fall 2010, there were 1,100 students enrolled in distance learning courses. Institutionally administered financial aid is available to distance learners.
Services Distance learners have accessibility to academic advising, bookstore, campus computer network, e-mail services, library services, tutoring.
Contact Jennifer McVay-Dyche, Director of Distance Education, Southern Oregon University, Distance Education Center, 1250 Siskiyou Boulevard, Ashland, OR 97520. Telephone: 541-552-8290. Fax: 541-552-8290. E-mail: mcvaydycj@sou.edu.

DEGREES AND AWARDS

BS Business Administration; Criminal Justice; Early Childhood Development
MAT Special Education
MEd Continuing Teaching License

COURSE SUBJECT AREAS OFFERED OUTSIDE OF DEGREE PROGRAMS

Undergraduate—accounting and related services; business administration, management and operations; business, management, and marketing related; computer science; criminal justice and corrections; criminology; economics; education; education (specific levels and methods); health and physical education/fitness; history; human services; mathematics; music; philosophy; political science and government; psychology; special education; visual and performing arts related.
Graduate—accounting and related services; business administration, management and operations; education; education (specific subject areas).

SOUTHERN UNION STATE COMMUNITY COLLEGE
Wadley, Alabama
http://www.suscc.edu

Southern Union State Community College was founded in 1922. It is accredited by Southern Association of Colleges and Schools. It first offered distance learning courses in 2001. In fall 2010, there were 1,000 students enrolled in distance learning courses. Institutionally administered financial aid is available to distance learners.
Services Distance learners have accessibility to academic advising, bookstore, campus computer network, career placement assistance, e-mail services, library services, tutoring.
Contact Mr. Adam McGhee, Coordinator of Distance Education, Southern Union State Community College, 1701 Lafayette Parkway, Opelika, AL 36801. Telephone: 334-745-6437 Ext. 5414. E-mail: amcghee@suscc.edu.

DEGREES AND AWARDS

AAS AAS

COURSE SUBJECT AREAS OFFERED OUTSIDE OF DEGREE PROGRAMS

Undergraduate—accounting and computer science; accounting and related services; applied mathematics; arts, entertainment, and media management; bilingual, multilingual, and multicultural education; biochemistry, biophysics and molecular biology; biological and biomedical sciences related; biological and physical sciences; biology; business/commerce; business/corporate communications; business, management, and marketing related; business/managerial economics; business operations support and assistant services; computer science; finance and financial management services; history; languages (classics and classical); legal professions and studies related; mathematics; real estate; sociology.

SOUTHERN UNIVERSITY AT NEW ORLEANS
New Orleans, Louisiana
http://www.suno.edu

Southern University at New Orleans was founded in 1959. It is accredited by Southern Association of Colleges and Schools. It first offered distance learning courses in 2003. In fall 2010, there were 1,322 students enrolled in distance learning courses. Institutionally administered financial aid is available to distance learners.
Services Distance learners have accessibility to academic advising, bookstore, career placement assistance, e-mail services, library services, tutoring.
Contact Dr. David S. Adegboye, Vice Chancellor for Academic Affairs, Southern University at New Orleans, 6400 Press Drive, New Orleans, LA 70126. Telephone: 504-286-5000 Ext. 5381. E-mail: dadegboye@suno.edu.

DEGREES AND AWARDS

BGS General Studies
BS Criminal Justice; Early Childhood Education
MA Museum Studies

COURSE SUBJECT AREAS OFFERED OUTSIDE OF DEGREE PROGRAMS

Undergraduate—biology; business/managerial economics; chemistry; communication and journalism related; computer systems analysis; economics; English; family and consumer economics; fine and studio arts; geography and cartography; geological and earth sciences/geosciences; history; management information systems; mathematics; philosophy; physical sciences; political science and government; public administration; social work.
Graduate—business, management, and marketing related; criminal justice and corrections; social work.

SOUTH PIEDMONT COMMUNITY COLLEGE
Polkton, North Carolina
http://www.spcc.edu

South Piedmont Community College was founded in 1962. It is accredited by Southern Association of Colleges and Schools. It first offered distance learning courses in 1982. In fall 2010, there were 1,600 students enrolled in distance learning courses. Institutionally administered financial aid is available to distance learners.
Services Distance learners have accessibility to academic advising, bookstore, e-mail services, library services.
Contact Ms. Ann Teal, Administrative Assistant to Dean of Learning Technologies and Accountability, South Piedmont Community College, PO Box 126, 680 Highway 74 West, Polkton, NC 28135. Telephone: 704-272-5436. E-mail: ateal@spcc.edu.

DEGREES AND AWARDS

AAS Early Childhood Education

COURSE SUBJECT AREAS OFFERED OUTSIDE OF DEGREE PROGRAMS

Undergraduate—accounting and computer science; accounting and related services; allied health and medical assisting services; allied health diagnostic, intervention, and treatment professions; applied mathematics; behavioral sciences; biological and biomedical sciences related; biology; biotechnology; business administration, management and operations; business/commerce; business, management, and marketing related;

business/managerial economics; carpentry; cell biology and anatomical sciences; chemistry; communication and journalism related; communication and media; communications technology; computer and information sciences; computer and information sciences and support services related; computer/information technology administration and management; computer programming; computer science; computer software and media applications; computer systems networking and telecommunications; criminal justice and corrections; dietetics and clinical nutrition services; economics; education; educational administration and supervision; education related; education (specific levels and methods); education (specific subject areas); electrical/electronics maintenance and repair technology; English; English language and literature related; entrepreneurial and small business operations; finance and financial management services; foods, nutrition, and related services; geography and cartography; health professions related; health services/allied health/ health sciences; heating, air conditioning, ventilation and refrigeration maintenance technology; history; human development, family studies, and related services; human services; intercultural/multicultural and diversity studies; legal professions and studies related; marketing; mathematics; mathematics and statistics related; music; psychology; psychology related; religious studies; social sciences; sociology; special education; statistics; teaching assistants/aides.

Non-credit—health aides/attendants/orderlies.

SOUTH SUBURBAN COLLEGE
South Holland, Illinois
http://www.ssc.edu

South Suburban College was founded in 1927. It is accredited by North Central Association of Colleges and Schools. Institutionally administered financial aid is available to distance learners.

Services Distance learners have accessibility to e-mail services, library services, tutoring.

Contact Admissions, South Suburban College, 15800 South State Street, South Holland, IL 60473. Telephone: 708-210-5718. E-mail: admissions@ssc.edu.

DEGREES AND AWARDS
Programs offered do not lead to a degree or other formal award.

COURSE SUBJECT AREAS OFFERED OUTSIDE OF DEGREE PROGRAMS
Undergraduate—accounting and computer science; behavioral sciences; biology; business administration, management and operations; computer and information sciences; computer science; English language and literature related; legal professions and studies related; legal support services; mathematics; mathematics and computer science; philosophy.

SOUTHWESTERN ADVENTIST UNIVERSITY
Keene, Texas
Adult Degree Program
http://www.swau.edu/admissions/apply-to-southwestern

Southwestern Adventist University was founded in 1894. It is accredited by Southern Association of Colleges and Schools. It first offered distance learning courses in 1978. In fall 2010, there were 86 students enrolled in distance learning courses. Institutionally administered financial aid is available to distance learners.

Services Distance learners have accessibility to academic advising, bookstore, e-mail services, library services.

Contact Dr. Robert Gardner, Director, Southwestern Adventist University, Adult Degree Program, 100 West Hillcrest Drive, Keene, TX 76059. Telephone: 817-202-6204. Fax: 817-202-6777. E-mail: adp@swau.edu.

DEGREES AND AWARDS
BA History; Religion; Social Sciences; Theology

BS Business Management; Elementary Education; General Studies; Psychology; Social Sciences

COURSE SUBJECT AREAS OFFERED OUTSIDE OF DEGREE PROGRAMS
Undergraduate—English; theological and ministerial studies.

Graduate—business, management, and marketing related; education.

SOUTHWESTERN BAPTIST THEOLOGICAL SEMINARY
Fort Worth, Texas
Department of Continuing Education
http://swbts.edu

Southwestern Baptist Theological Seminary was founded in 1908. It is accredited by Southern Association of Colleges and Schools. It first offered distance learning courses in 2000. In fall 2010, there were 502 students enrolled in distance learning courses. Institutionally administered financial aid is available to distance learners.

Services Distance learners have accessibility to academic advising, bookstore, campus computer network, career placement assistance, e-mail services, library services.

Contact Dr. Jim Wicker, Director of Web-Based Education, Southwestern Baptist Theological Seminary, PO Box 22147, Fort Worth, TX 76122. Telephone: 817-923-1921 Ext. 6805. Fax: 817-921-8760. E-mail: jwicker@swbts.edu.

DEGREES AND AWARDS
Programs offered do not lead to a degree or other formal award.

COURSE SUBJECT AREAS OFFERED OUTSIDE OF DEGREE PROGRAMS
Undergraduate—biblical studies; religious education; religious studies; theological and ministerial studies.

Graduate—biblical studies; educational administration and supervision; educational assessment, evaluation, and research; educational/instructional media design; education related; human development, family studies, and related services; linguistic, comparative, and related language studies; pastoral counseling and specialized ministries; philosophy and religious studies related; psychology related; religious education; religious/sacred music; religious studies; theological and ministerial studies; theology and religious vocations related.

SOUTHWESTERN COLLEGE
Winfield, Kansas
Southwestern College Online
http://www.southwesterncollege.org

Southwestern College was founded in 1885. It is accredited by North Central Association of Colleges and Schools. It first offered distance learning courses in 2001. In fall 2010, there were 1,674 students enrolled in distance learning courses. Institutionally administered financial aid is available to distance learners.

Services Distance learners have accessibility to academic advising, bookstore, career placement assistance, library services, tutoring.

Contact Gail Cullen, Director of Academic Affairs, Southwestern College, 2040 South Rock Road, Wichita, KS 67207. Telephone: 888-684-5335 Ext. 203. Fax: 316-688-5218. E-mail: gail.cullen@sckans.edu.

DEGREES AND AWARDS
BA Pastoral Studies; Security Management; Youth Ministry

BS Accounting; Business Administration; Business Quality Management; Computer Operations Technology; Computer Programming Technology; Criminal Justice; Healthcare Administration; Human Resource Development; Nursing–RN to BSN; Operations Management; Strategic Leadership

MA Specialized Ministries–Youth and Young Adult Ministry; Teaching

MBA Business Administration

MS Leadership; Management; Security Administration

SOUTHWESTERN COMMUNITY COLLEGE
Creston, Iowa
http://www.swcciowa.edu

Southwestern Community College was founded in 1966. It is accredited by North Central Association of Colleges and Schools. It first offered distance learning courses in 2000. In fall 2010, there were 679 students enrolled in distance learning courses. Institutionally administered financial aid is available to distance learners.

Services Distance learners have accessibility to academic advising, bookstore, campus computer network, e-mail services, library services, tutoring.

Contact Doug Greene, Director of Distance Learning, Southwestern Community College, 1501 West Townline Street, Creston, IA 50801. Telephone: 641-782-7081 Ext. 324. Fax: 641-782-3312. E-mail: greene@swcciowa.edu.

DEGREES AND AWARDS
AA General degree; Liberal Arts
AS General degree

COURSE SUBJECT AREAS OFFERED OUTSIDE OF DEGREE PROGRAMS
Undergraduate—accounting and related services; area studies; biology; cell biology and anatomical sciences; fine and studio arts; geography and cartography; journalism; mathematics and statistics related; music; philosophy and religious studies related; sociology.

SOUTHWESTERN OKLAHOMA STATE UNIVERSITY
Weatherford, Oklahoma
Tele-Learning
http://www.swosu.edu/distance/

Southwestern Oklahoma State University was founded in 1901. It is accredited by North Central Association of Colleges and Schools. It first offered distance learning courses in 1981. In fall 2010, there were 1,300 students enrolled in distance learning courses. Institutionally administered financial aid is available to distance learners.

Services Distance learners have accessibility to academic advising, bookstore, e-mail services, library services, tutoring.

Contact Ms. Paige Ingraham, Administrative Assistant, Southwestern Oklahoma State University, Center for Distance Education, 100 Campus Drive, Weatherford, OK 73096. Telephone: 580-774-3149. E-mail: distance@swosu.edu.

DEGREES AND AWARDS
BBA Finance; Management; Marketing
BSN Nursing RN/BSN
MBA Business Administration
MEd School Administration; School Counseling
MS Business Administration

SOUTHWEST MISSISSIPPI COMMUNITY COLLEGE
Summit, Mississippi
http://www.smcc.edu

Southwest Mississippi Community College was founded in 1918. It is accredited by Southern Association of Colleges and Schools. It first offered distance learning courses in 2001. In fall 2010, there were 350 students enrolled in distance learning courses. Institutionally administered financial aid is available to distance learners.

Services Distance learners have accessibility to academic advising, bookstore, campus computer network, e-mail services, library services, tutoring.

Contact Ms. Alicia Shows, Distance Learning Coordinator, Southwest Mississippi Community College, 1156 College Drive, Summit, MS 39666. Telephone: 601-276-3718. Fax: 601-276-3888. E-mail: showsa@smcc.edu.

DEGREES AND AWARDS
AA General

SOUTHWEST VIRGINIA COMMUNITY COLLEGE
Richlands, Virginia
Audiovisual and Distance Education Services
http://desweb.sw.edu/

Southwest Virginia Community College was founded in 1968. It is accredited by Southern Association of Colleges and Schools. It first offered distance learning courses in 1991. In fall 2010, there were 2,200 students enrolled in distance learning courses. Institutionally administered financial aid is available to distance learners.

Services Distance learners have accessibility to academic advising, bookstore, campus computer network, career placement assistance, e-mail services, library services, tutoring.

Contact Mrs. Sylvia Dye, Office Manager, Distance and Distributed Learning, Southwest Virginia Community College, PO Box SVCC, Richlands, VA 24641. Telephone: 276-964-7279. Fax: 276-964-7686. E-mail: sylvia.dye@sw.edu.

DEGREES AND AWARDS
AAS Arts and Science degree program

AS General Studies

Certificate Network and Internet Administration

COURSE SUBJECT AREAS OFFERED OUTSIDE OF DEGREE PROGRAMS
Undergraduate—history; languages (Romance languages); mathematics and statistics related; sociology; statistics.

Non-credit—computer and information sciences and support services related.

SOUTHWEST WISCONSIN TECHNICAL COLLEGE
Fennimore, Wisconsin
http://www.swtc.edu/

Southwest Wisconsin Technical College was founded in 1967. It is accredited by North Central Association of Colleges and Schools. It first offered distance learning courses in 1989. In fall 2010, there were 800 students enrolled in distance learning courses. Institutionally administered financial aid is available to distance learners.

Services Distance learners have accessibility to academic advising, bookstore, career placement assistance, e-mail services, library services, tutoring.

Contact Kristal Davenport, Instructional Technology Support Specialist, Southwest Wisconsin Technical College, 1800 Bronson Boulevard, Fennimore, WI 53809. Telephone: 608-822-2426. Fax: 608-822-6019. E-mail: kdavenport@swtc.edu.

DEGREES AND AWARDS
Diploma Medical Transcription

Technical Certificate Medical Coding Specialist

COURSE SUBJECT AREAS OFFERED OUTSIDE OF DEGREE PROGRAMS
Undergraduate—accounting and related services; allied health and medical assisting services; applied mathematics; behavioral sciences; business/corporate communications; business, management, and marketing related; business/managerial economics; communication and journalism related; communication and media; computer and information sciences; computer programming; computer software and media applications; computer systems networking and telecommunications; cosmetology and related personal grooming services; culinary arts and related services; curriculum and instruction; economics; educational/instructional media design; ethnic, cultural minority, gender, and group studies; finance and financial management services; foods, nutrition, and related services; health aides/attendants/orderlies; health/medical preparatory programs; hospitality administration; human resources management; management information systems; mathematics; mathematics and statistics related; practical nursing, vocational nursing and nursing assistants; psychology; social sciences; sociology; statistics.

SPARTANBURG COMMUNITY COLLEGE

Spartanburg, South Carolina

http://online.sccsc.edu

Spartanburg Community College was founded in 1961. It is accredited by Southern Association of Colleges and Schools. It first offered distance learning courses in 1997. In fall 2010, there were 1,200 students enrolled in distance learning courses. Institutionally administered financial aid is available to distance learners.

Services Distance learners have accessibility to academic advising, bookstore, campus computer network, career placement assistance, e-mail services, library services, tutoring.

Contact Mr. Neil Griffin, Director of SCCOnline, Spartanburg Community College, PO Box 4386, Business I-85 and New Cut Road, Spartanburg, SC 29305-4386. Telephone: 864-592-4961. Fax: 864-592-4941. E-mail: griffinn@sccsc.edu.

DEGREES AND AWARDS

AA University Transfer Program (Liberal Arts)

AAS Basic Interperting (American Sign Language); Management with Fire Services Electives; Management with Marketing Electives; Management

AS University Transfer Program (Science)

COURSE SUBJECT AREAS OFFERED OUTSIDE OF DEGREE PROGRAMS

Undergraduate—accounting and related services; American Sign Language (ASL); applied mathematics; biology; business administration, management and operations; business/commerce; business, management, and marketing related; chemistry; computer and information sciences; computer software and media applications; culinary arts and related services; data entry/microcomputer applications; dental support services and allied professions; education; English; history; hospitality administration; liberal arts and sciences, general studies and humanities; mathematics; mathematics and statistics related; music; philosophy; plant sciences; psychology; sales merchandising, and related marketing operations (general); social sciences; sociology; statistics; visual and performing arts.

Non-credit—accounting and related services; applied mathematics; business, management, and marketing related; computer and information sciences; computer programming; computer software and media applications; criminal justice and corrections; culinary arts and related services; education related; finance and financial management services; health and medical administrative services; health professions related; human resources management; languages (Romance languages); legal support services; mathematics; music; real estate; sales merchandising, and related marketing operations (general).

SPENCERIAN COLLEGE

Louisville, Kentucky

http://sullivan.angellearning.com

Spencerian College was founded in 1892. It is accredited by Accrediting Council for Independent Colleges and Schools. It first offered distance learning courses in 1999. In fall 2010, there were 500 students enrolled in distance learning courses. Institutionally administered financial aid is available to distance learners.

Services Distance learners have accessibility to academic advising, bookstore, campus computer network, career placement assistance, e-mail services, library services.

Contact Ms. Kathleen M. Belanger, Director of Admissions, Spencerian College, 4627 Dixie Highway, Louisville, KY 40216. Telephone: 502-447-1000. Fax: 502-447-4574. E-mail: kbelanger@spencerian.edu.

DEGREES AND AWARDS

AAS Various programs

Certificate Various programs

Diploma Various programs

SPERTUS INSTITUTE OF JEWISH STUDIES

Chicago, Illinois

http://www.spertus.edu/

Spertus Institute of Jewish Studies was founded in 1924. It is accredited by North Central Association of Colleges and Schools. It first offered distance learning courses in 1994. In fall 2010, there were 250 students enrolled in distance learning courses. Institutionally administered financial aid is available to distance learners.

Services Distance learners have accessibility to academic advising, library services.

Contact Dr. Dean Bell, Dean and Chief Academic Officer, Spertus Institute of Jewish Studies, 610 South Michigan Avenue, Chicago, IL 60605. Telephone: 312-322-1791. Fax: 312-922-6406. E-mail: college@spertus.edu.

DEGREES AND AWARDS

MS Jewish Education–Master of Science in Jewish Education (MSJE)

MSJS Jewish Studies

DJS Jewish Studies

SPOKANE COMMUNITY COLLEGE

Spokane, Washington

http://www.scc.spokane.edu/

Spokane Community College was founded in 1963. It is accredited by Northwest Commission on Colleges and Universities. In fall 2010, there were 4,500 students enrolled in distance learning courses. Institutionally administered financial aid is available to distance learners.

Services Distance learners have accessibility to academic advising, bookstore, career placement assistance, e-mail services, library services, tutoring.

Contact Ruth Perkins, eLearning Helpdesk Technician, Spokane Community College, 1810 North Greene Street, MS 2150, Spokane, WA 99217. Telephone: 509-533-8240. Fax: 509-533-7192. E-mail: rperkins@scc.spokane.edu.

DEGREES AND AWARDS

AAS Accounting Assistant; Administrative Assistant; Administrative Office Management; Customer Service Representative; Legal Administrative Assistant; Office Information Systems

COURSE SUBJECT AREAS OFFERED OUTSIDE OF DEGREE PROGRAMS

Undergraduate—accounting and computer science; allied health and medical assisting services; American Sign Language (ASL); anthropology; applied horticulture and horticultural business services; applied mathematics; arts, entertainment, and media management; astronomy and astrophysics; biology; business administration, management and operations; business/corporate communications; business, management, and marketing related; business/managerial economics; business operations support and assistant services; chemistry; communication and media; computer and information sciences; computer/information technology administration and management; computer programming; computer science; computer software and media applications; computer systems networking and telecommunications; criminal justice and corrections; culinary arts and related services; data entry/microcomputer applications; data processing; dental support services and allied professions; economics; English; English language and literature related; English or French as a second or foreign language (teaching); health and medical administrative services; health and physical education/fitness; health services/allied health/health sciences; history; languages (foreign languages related); languages (Romance languages); legal professions and studies related; legal support services; liberal arts and sciences, general studies and humanities; marketing; mathematics; mathematics and computer science; mathematics and statistics related; music; natural resources and conservation related; philosophy; psychology; social sciences related; sociology; sociology and anthropology.

Non-credit—allied health and medical assisting services; health professions related.

SPOON RIVER COLLEGE

Canton, Illinois

http://www.src.edu/

Spoon River College was founded in 1959. It is accredited by North Central Association of Colleges and Schools. It first offered distance learning courses in 1998. In fall 2010, there were 435 students enrolled in distance learning courses. Institutionally administered financial aid is available to distance learners.

Services Distance learners have accessibility to academic advising, bookstore, career placement assistance, e-mail services, library services, tutoring.

Contact Ms. Lara Dively, Advisor, Spoon River College, 23235 North County 22, Canton, IL 61520. Telephone: 800-334-7337. Fax: 309-649-6215. E-mail: info@src.edu.

DEGREES AND AWARDS

Programs offered do not lead to a degree or other formal award.

COURSE SUBJECT AREAS OFFERED OUTSIDE OF DEGREE PROGRAMS

Undergraduate—accounting and related services; allied health and medical assisting services; biology; chemistry; communication and journalism related; communication and media; ecology, evolution, systematics, and population biology; economics; education; English; fine and studio arts; graphic communications; health professions related; human development, family studies, and related services; microbiological sciences and immunology; philosophy and religious studies related; social sciences; statistics.

SPRING ARBOR UNIVERSITY

Spring Arbor, Michigan

http://www.arbor.edu/sauonline

Spring Arbor University was founded in 1873. It is accredited by North Central Association of Colleges and Schools. It first offered distance learning courses in 1998. In fall 2010, there were 361 students enrolled in distance learning courses. Institutionally administered financial aid is available to distance learners.

Services Distance learners have accessibility to academic advising, bookstore, campus computer network, e-mail services, library services.

Contact Brenda Collins, SAUonline Support Specialist, Spring Arbor University, 106 East Main Street, Suite #7, Spring Arbor, MI 49283. Telephone: 517-750-6565. Fax: 517-750-2618. E-mail: bcollins@arbor.edu.

DEGREES AND AWARDS

BS Organizational Management

MA Spiritual Formation and Leadership

MAE Education

MBA Business

MCS Communication

MSM Management

MSN Nursing

COURSE SUBJECT AREAS OFFERED OUTSIDE OF DEGREE PROGRAMS

Undergraduate—accounting and computer science; business administration, management and operations; communication and journalism related; computer software and media applications; criminal justice and corrections; economics; education (specific subject areas); English; finance and financial management services; geography and cartography; history; hospitality administration; human resources management; marketing; music; philosophy; psychology; religious studies; social sciences; social work; sociology; special education.

STANLY COMMUNITY COLLEGE

Albemarle, North Carolina

http://www.stanly.edu

Stanly Community College was founded in 1971. It is accredited by Southern Association of Colleges and Schools. It first offered distance learning courses in 1990. In fall 2010, there were 3,200 students enrolled in distance learning courses. Institutionally administered financial aid is available to distance learners.

Services Distance learners have accessibility to academic advising, bookstore, campus computer network, career placement assistance, e-mail services, library services, tutoring.

Contact Dennis Souther, Dean of Stanly Online, Stanly Community College, 141 College Drive, Albemarle, NC 28001. Telephone: 704-991-0280. Fax: 704-991-0255. E-mail: dsouther5612@stanly.edu.

DEGREES AND AWARDS

AA General degree

AAS Accounting; Business Administration; Criminal Justice Technology; Cyber Crime Technology; Early Childhood Associate; Human Services; Information Systems Security; Network Technology

COURSE SUBJECT AREAS OFFERED OUTSIDE OF DEGREE PROGRAMS

Undergraduate—accounting and related services; allied health diagnostic, intervention, and treatment professions; applied mathematics; biological and biomedical sciences related; biology; business administration, management and operations; computer and information sciences; computer and information sciences and support services related; computer systems networking and telecommunications; criminal justice and corrections; economics; finance and financial management services; human development, family studies, and related services; human services; management information systems; marketing; mathematics; philosophy and religious studies related; political science and government; psychology; religious studies; sociology.

STATE UNIVERSITY OF NEW YORK AT NEW PALTZ

New Paltz, New York

Center for Continuing and Professional Education

http://www.newpaltz.edu/regionaled

State University of New York at New Paltz was founded in 1828. It is accredited by Middle States Association of Colleges and Schools. It first offered distance learning courses in 1995. In fall 2010, there were 448 students enrolled in distance learning courses. Institutionally administered financial aid is available to distance learners.

Services Distance learners have accessibility to bookstore, campus computer network, career placement assistance, e-mail services, library services.

Contact Helise Winters, Director, Extension and Distance Learning, State University of New York at New Paltz, 1 Hawk Drive, Suite 9, New Paltz, NY 12561-2443. Telephone: 845-257-2894. Fax: 845-257-2899. E-mail: edl@newpaltz.edu.

DEGREES AND AWARDS

Programs offered do not lead to a degree or other formal award.

COURSE SUBJECT AREAS OFFERED OUTSIDE OF DEGREE PROGRAMS

Undergraduate—anthropology; biology; communication and media; communication disorders sciences and services; computer science; curriculum and instruction; economics; geography and cartography; geological and earth sciences/geosciences; history; mathematics; philosophy; psychology; public relations, advertising, and applied communication related; social and philosophical foundations of education; sociology.

Graduate—computer science; education.

STATE UNIVERSITY OF NEW YORK AT OSWEGO
Oswego, New York
Office of Distance Learning
http://www.oswego.edu/extended_learning/online_degrees.html

State University of New York at Oswego was founded in 1861. It is accredited by Middle States Association of Colleges and Schools. It first offered distance learning courses in 1995. In fall 2010, there were 900 students enrolled in distance learning courses. Institutionally administered financial aid is available to distance learners.

Services Distance learners have accessibility to academic advising, bookstore, campus computer network, career placement assistance, e-mail services, library services, tutoring.

Contact Mr. Thomas Ingram, Director of Academic Planning, State University of New York at Oswego, Division of Extended Learning, 151 Campus Center, Oswego, NY 13126. Telephone: 315-312-2270. Fax: 315-312-3078. E-mail: extlearn@oswego.edu.

DEGREES AND AWARDS
BA Broadcasting and Mass Communications; Public Justice
BS Vocational Teacher Preparation
MS Vocational Teacher Preparation

COURSE SUBJECT AREAS OFFERED OUTSIDE OF DEGREE PROGRAMS
Undergraduate—accounting and computer science; anthropology; applied mathematics; archeology; arts, entertainment, and media management; behavioral sciences; biology; business administration, management and operations; business/commerce; business/managerial economics; chemistry; communication and journalism related; communication and media; computer and information sciences; computer science; computer systems networking and telecommunications; criminal justice and corrections; drama/theatre arts and stagecraft; economics; education (specific subject areas); English; geological and earth sciences/geosciences; health services/allied health/health sciences; history; information science/studies; international business; international/global studies; journalism; liberal arts and sciences, general studies and humanities; literature; marketing; mathematics; music; philosophy; philosophy and religious studies related; psychology; public relations, advertising, and applied communication related; sociology; visual and performing arts.

Graduate—accounting and related services; anthropology; business administration, management and operations; communication and media; curriculum and instruction; education; educational administration and supervision; gerontology; history; psychology.

STATE UNIVERSITY OF NEW YORK AT PLATTSBURGH
Plattsburgh, New York
Distance Learning Office
http://www.plattsburgh.edu/academics/onlinelearning

State University of New York at Plattsburgh was founded in 1889. It is accredited by Middle States Association of Colleges and Schools. It first offered distance learning courses in 1990. In fall 2010, there were 815 students enrolled in distance learning courses. Institutionally administered financial aid is available to distance learners.

Services Distance learners have accessibility to academic advising, bookstore, campus computer network, career placement assistance, e-mail services, library services, tutoring.

Contact Ms. Holly B. Heller-Ross, Associate Dean, Library and Information Services, State University of New York at Plattsburgh, Feinberg Library, 2 Draper Avenue, Plattsburgh, NY 12901. Telephone: 518-564-5192. Fax: 518-564-4236. E-mail: hellerhb@plattsburgh.edu.

DEGREES AND AWARDS
BS Nursing

COURSE SUBJECT AREAS OFFERED OUTSIDE OF DEGREE PROGRAMS
Undergraduate—anthropology; biochemistry, biophysics and molecular biology; biology; biopsychology; business administration, management and operations; education; education related; English; entrepreneurial and small business operations; ethnic, cultural minority, gender, and group studies; geological and earth sciences/geosciences; health and physical education/fitness; health professions related; history; languages (Romance languages); library science related; marketing; mathematics; music; political science and government; psychology related; sales, merchandising and related marketing operations (specialized); social sciences; sociology; statistics; work and family studies.

Graduate—business administration, management and operations; education; educational administration and supervision; educational/instructional media design; education related; entrepreneurial and small business operations; special education.

STATE UNIVERSITY OF NEW YORK COLLEGE AT CORTLAND
Cortland, New York
SUNY Cortland eLearning
http://www2.cortland.edu/offices/information-resources/index.dot

State University of New York College at Cortland was founded in 1868. It is accredited by Middle States Association of Colleges and Schools. It first offered distance learning courses in 1997. In fall 2010, there were 429 students enrolled in distance learning courses.

Services Distance learners have accessibility to academic advising, bookstore, campus computer network, career placement assistance, e-mail services, library services, tutoring.

Contact Ms. Amy L. Berg, Associate Provost, Information Resources, State University of New York College at Cortland, PO Box 2000, Cortland, NY 13045. Telephone: 607-753-5942. Fax: 607-753-5985. E-mail: amy.berg@cortland.edu.

DEGREES AND AWARDS
Programs offered do not lead to a degree or other formal award.

COURSE SUBJECT AREAS OFFERED OUTSIDE OF DEGREE PROGRAMS
Undergraduate—communication and media; computer software and media applications; English language and literature related; political science and government; psychology.

Graduate—business, management, and marketing related; education; education (specific subject areas); health services/allied health/health sciences; psychology.

STATE UNIVERSITY OF NEW YORK COLLEGE AT ONEONTA
Oneonta, New York
Academic Support Services
http://www.oneonta.edu

State University of New York College at Oneonta was founded in 1889. It is accredited by Middle States Association of Colleges and Schools. It first offered distance learning courses in 1999. In fall 2010, there were 59 students enrolled in distance learning courses. Institutionally administered financial aid is available to distance learners.

Services Distance learners have accessibility to bookstore, campus computer network, e-mail services, library services.

Contact Ms. Michelle W. Thibault, Director of Continuing Education and Summer Session, State University of New York College at Oneonta, 135 Netzer Administration Building, Oneonta, NY 13820. Telephone: 607-436-2548. Fax: 607-436-2548. E-mail: thibaumw@oneonta.edu.

DEGREES AND AWARDS
License Dietetic Internship program
MS Nutrition and Dietetics

COURSE SUBJECT AREAS OFFERED OUTSIDE OF DEGREE PROGRAMS
Undergraduate—ethnic, cultural minority, gender, and group studies.

Graduate—education; foods, nutrition, and related services.

STATE UNIVERSITY OF NEW YORK COLLEGE AT POTSDAM

Potsdam, New York

http://www.potsdam.edu/academics/online

State University of New York College at Potsdam was founded in 1816. It is accredited by Middle States Association of Colleges and Schools. It first offered distance learning courses in 2002. In fall 2010, there were 115 students enrolled in distance learning courses. Institutionally administered financial aid is available to distance learners.

Services Distance learners have accessibility to academic advising, bookstore, campus computer network, e-mail services, library services.

Contact Katie Logan, Keyboard Specialist II, Office of Extended Education, State University of New York College at Potsdam, 44 Pierrepont Avenue, Potsdam, NY 13676. Telephone: 315-267-2166. Fax: 315-267-3088. E-mail: logankm@potsdam.edu.

DEGREES AND AWARDS

Programs offered do not lead to a degree or other formal award.

COURSE SUBJECT AREAS OFFERED OUTSIDE OF DEGREE PROGRAMS

Undergraduate—anthropology; behavioral sciences; biology; business administration, management and operations; business, management, and marketing related; business/managerial economics; communication and journalism related; data processing; economics; education (specific subject areas); entrepreneurial and small business operations; geography and cartography; geological and earth sciences/geosciences; languages (foreign languages related); management information systems; music; physical sciences; psychology; sociology.

Graduate—education (specific levels and methods).

Non-credit—accounting and related services; business administration, management and operations; business/commerce; communication and media; computer and information sciences; computer programming; computer software and media applications; culinary arts and related services; data entry/microcomputer applications; entrepreneurial and small business operations; finance and financial management services; languages (Romance languages); linguistic, comparative, and related language studies; sales, merchandising and related marketing operations (specialized).

STATE UNIVERSITY OF NEW YORK COLLEGE OF AGRICULTURE AND TECHNOLOGY AT MORRISVILLE

Morrisville, New York

http://www.morrisville.edu/

State University of New York College of Agriculture and Technology at Morrisville was founded in 1908. It is accredited by Middle States Association of Colleges and Schools. It first offered distance learning courses in 1997. In fall 2010, there were 700 students enrolled in distance learning courses. Institutionally administered financial aid is available to distance learners.

Services Distance learners have accessibility to academic advising, bookstore, campus computer network, career placement assistance, e-mail services, library services.

Contact Office of Admission, State University of New York College of Agriculture and Technology at Morrisville, Morrisville, NY 13408. Telephone: 315-684-6046. Fax: 315-684-6427. E-mail: admissions@morrisville.edu.

DEGREES AND AWARDS

Programs offered do not lead to a degree or other formal award.

COURSE SUBJECT AREAS OFFERED OUTSIDE OF DEGREE PROGRAMS

Undergraduate—accounting and computer science; accounting and related services; agricultural business and management; agriculture; business/commerce; computer/information technology administration and management; computer software and media applications; English language and literature related; entrepreneurial and small business operations; hospitality administration; management sciences and quantitative methods; mathematics; psychology.

STATE UNIVERSITY OF NEW YORK COLLEGE OF ENVIRONMENTAL SCIENCE & FORESTRY, RANGER SCHOOL

Wanakena, New York

http://www.esf.edu/outreach

State University of New York College of Environmental Science & Forestry, Ranger School was founded in 1912. It is accredited by Middle States Association of Colleges and Schools. It first offered distance learning courses in 2008. In fall 2010, there were 30 students enrolled in distance learning courses. Institutionally administered financial aid is available to distance learners.

Contact Dr. Richard Beal, Assistant Dean of Educational Outreach, State University of New York College of Environmental Science & Forestry, Ranger School, 222 Marshall Hall, 1 Forestry Road, Syracuse, NY 13110. Telephone: 315-470-6817. E-mail: rebeal@esf.edu.

DEGREES AND AWARDS

Programs offered do not lead to a degree or other formal award.

COURSE SUBJECT AREAS OFFERED OUTSIDE OF DEGREE PROGRAMS

Undergraduate—environmental/environmental health engineering.

Graduate—education related.

STATE UNIVERSITY OF NEW YORK COLLEGE OF TECHNOLOGY AT CANTON

Canton, New York

SUNY Canton Online

http://www.canton.edu

State University of New York College of Technology at Canton was founded in 1906. It is accredited by Middle States Association of Colleges and Schools. It first offered distance learning courses in 1998. In fall 2010, there were 1,816 students enrolled in distance learning courses. Institutionally administered financial aid is available to distance learners.

Services Distance learners have accessibility to academic advising, bookstore, career placement assistance, e-mail services, library services.

Contact Pamela Enser, Registrar, State University of New York College of Technology at Canton, 34 Cornell Drive, Canton, NY 13617. Telephone: 315-386-7647. Fax: 315-379-3819. E-mail: enserp@canton.edu.

DEGREES AND AWARDS

BBA Finance; Management

BS Nursing

BTECH Alternative and Renewable Energy Systems; Criminal Investigation; Dental Hygiene; Emergency Management; Graphic and Multimedia Design; Health Care Management; Law Enforcement Leadership; Legal Studies; Veterinary Services Management

COURSE SUBJECT AREAS OFFERED OUTSIDE OF DEGREE PROGRAMS

Undergraduate—accounting and related services; animal sciences; business administration, management and operations; computer and information sciences; criminal justice and corrections; economics; engineering; engineering technology; English; health and medical administrative services; history; physical sciences; psychology; social sciences.

STATE UNIVERSITY OF NEW YORK EMPIRE STATE COLLEGE

Saratoga Springs, New York

Center for Distance Learning

http://www.esc.edu/cdl

State University of New York Empire State College was founded in 1971. It is accredited by American Association of Colleges of Nursing. It first offered distance learning courses in 1979. In fall 2010, there were 8,150 students enrolled in distance learning courses. Institutionally administered financial aid is available to distance learners.

Services Distance learners have accessibility to academic advising, bookstore, campus computer network, career placement assistance, e-mail services, library services, tutoring.

Contact Ms. Shelly B. Dixon, Director of Outreach, State University of New York Empire State College, 111 West Avenue, Saratoga Springs, NY 12866. Telephone: 518-587-2100 Ext. 2300. Fax: 518-587-2660. E-mail: cdladvisor@esc.edu.

DEGREES AND AWARDS

AA Business, Management, and Economics; Cultural Studies; Educational Studies; Historical Studies; Human Development; Interdisciplinary Studies; Labor Studies; Science, Math, and Technology; Social Theory, Social Structure, and Change; the Arts

AAB Community and Human Services

AS Business, Management, and Economics; Cultural Studies; Educational Studies; Historical Studies; Human Development; Interdisciplinary Studies; Labor Studies; Science, Math, and Technology; Social Theory, Social Structure, and Change; the Arts

BA Business, Management, and Economics; Community and Human Services; Cultural Studies; Educational Studies; Historical Studies; Human Development; Interdisciplinary Studies; Labor Studies; Science, Math, and Technology; Social Theory, Social Structure, and Change; the Arts

BPS Business, Management, and Economics

BS Business, Management, and Economics; Community and Human Services; Cultural Studies; Educational Studies; Historical Studies; Human Development; Interdisciplinary Studies; Labor Studies; Science, Math, and Technology; Social Theory, Social Structure, and Change; the Arts

BSN Nursing

MA Liberal Studies; Policy Studies

MAT Teaching

MBA Business Administration

COURSE SUBJECT AREAS OFFERED OUTSIDE OF DEGREE PROGRAMS

Undergraduate—accounting and related services; biology; communication and media; computer/information technology administration and management; criminal justice and corrections; education; finance and financial management services; fire protection; history; human development, family studies, and related services; international business; legal studies (non-professional general, undergraduate); management information systems; mathematics and statistics related; political science and government; sociology; statistics.

Graduate—business/commerce; education; political science and government; social sciences.

STATE UNIVERSITY OF NEW YORK INSTITUTE OF TECHNOLOGY

Utica, New York

Program in Health Services Administration

http://www.sunyit.edu/programs/graduate/mbahsm/

State University of New York Institute of Technology was founded in 1966. It is accredited by Middle States Association of Colleges and Schools. It first offered distance learning courses in 1998. Institutionally administered financial aid is available to distance learners.

Services Distance learners have accessibility to academic advising, bookstore, campus computer network, career placement assistance, e-mail services, library services.

Contact Ms. Maryrose Raab, Graduate Center Coodinator, State University of New York Institute of Technology, 100 Seymour Road, Utica, NY 13502. Telephone: 315-792-7215. Fax: 315-792-7837. E-mail: maryrose.raab@sunyit.edu.

DEGREES AND AWARDS

Programs offered do not lead to a degree or other formal award.

COURSE SUBJECT AREAS OFFERED OUTSIDE OF DEGREE PROGRAMS

Undergraduate—accounting and related services; business administration, management and operations; business/commerce; communication and media; health and medical administrative services; health professions related; human resources management.

Graduate—accounting and related services; business administration, management and operations; business/commerce; communication and media; health and medical administrative services; health professions related; human resources management; taxation.

STATE UNIVERSITY OF NEW YORK INSTITUTE OF TECHNOLOGY

Utica, New York

Program in Technology Management

http://www.sunyit.edu/programs/graduate/mbatm/

State University of New York Institute of Technology was founded in 1966. It is accredited by Middle States Association of Colleges and Schools. It first offered distance learning courses in 1988. Institutionally administered financial aid is available to distance learners.

Services Distance learners have accessibility to academic advising, bookstore, campus computer network, career placement assistance, e-mail services, library services.

Contact Ms. Maryrose Raab, Graduate Center Coordinator, State University of New York Institute of Technology, 100 Seymour Road, Utica, NY 13502. Telephone: 315-792-7347. Fax: 315-792-7837. E-mail: gradcenter@sunyit.edu.

DEGREES AND AWARDS

MBA Technology Management

COURSE SUBJECT AREAS OFFERED OUTSIDE OF DEGREE PROGRAMS

Graduate—accounting and computer science; business administration, management and operations; business, management, and marketing related; business/managerial economics; economics; finance and financial management services; health and medical administrative services; health services/allied health/health sciences; human resources management; legal studies (non-professional general, undergraduate); management information systems; management sciences and quantitative methods; sales merchandising, and related marketing operations (general); sales, merchandising and related marketing operations (specialized).

STATE UNIVERSITY OF NEW YORK INSTITUTE OF TECHNOLOGY

Utica, New York

Program in Information and Design Technology

http://www.sunyit.edu/programs/graduate/idt/

State University of New York Institute of Technology was founded in 1966. It is accredited by Middle States Association of Colleges and Schools. It first offered distance learning courses in 1988. Institutionally administered financial aid is available to distance learners.

Services Distance learners have accessibility to academic advising, bookstore, campus computer network, career placement assistance, e-mail services, library services.

Contact Ms. Maryrose Raab, Graduate Center Coordinator, State University of New York Institute of Technology, 100 Seymour Road, Utica, NY 13502. Telephone: 315-792-7347. Fax: 315-792-7837. E-mail: gradcenter@sunyit.edu.

DEGREES AND AWARDS
MS Information Design and Technology

COURSE SUBJECT AREAS OFFERED OUTSIDE OF DEGREE PROGRAMS
Graduate—communication and media; communications technology; educational/instructional media design; graphic communications; information science/studies; radio, television, and digital communication.

STATE UNIVERSITY OF NEW YORK INSTITUTE OF TECHNOLOGY
Utica, New York
Program in Health Information Management
http://www.sunyit.edu/undergraduate/him

State University of New York Institute of Technology was founded in 1966. It is accredited by Middle States Association of Colleges and Schools. It first offered distance learning courses in 1988. In fall 2010, there were 123 students enrolled in distance learning courses. Institutionally administered financial aid is available to distance learners.
Services Distance learners have accessibility to academic advising, bookstore, campus computer network, career placement assistance, e-mail services, library services.
Contact Ms. Jennifer Phelan-Ninh, Admissions, State University of New York Institute of Technology, 100 Seymour Road, Utica, NY 13502. Telephone: 315-792-7500. Fax: 315-792-7837. E-mail: admissions@sunyit.edu.

DEGREES AND AWARDS
Programs offered do not lead to a degree or other formal award.

COURSE SUBJECT AREAS OFFERED OUTSIDE OF DEGREE PROGRAMS
Undergraduate—accounting and related services; business, management, and marketing related; health professions related; health services/allied health/health sciences; human resources management.

STATE UNIVERSITY OF NEW YORK INSTITUTE OF TECHNOLOGY
Utica, New York
Program in Nursing Education
http://www.sunyit.edu/programs/graduate/nur/nursing_education

State University of New York Institute of Technology was founded in 1966. It is accredited by Middle States Association of Colleges and Schools. It first offered distance learning courses in 1988. Institutionally administered financial aid is available to distance learners.
Services Distance learners have accessibility to academic advising, bookstore, campus computer network, career placement assistance, e-mail services, library services.
Contact Ms. Maryrose Raab, Graduate Center Coordinator, State University of New York Institute of Technology, 100 Seymour Road, Utica, NY 13502. Telephone: 315-792-7347. Fax: 315-792-7837. E-mail: gradcenter@sunyit.edu.

DEGREES AND AWARDS
MS Nursing Education

STATE UNIVERSITY OF NEW YORK INSTITUTE OF TECHNOLOGY
Utica, New York
Program in Nursing Administration
http://www.sunyit.edu/programs/graduate/nur/nurse_admin

State University of New York Institute of Technology was founded in 1966. It is accredited by Middle States Association of Colleges and Schools. It first offered distance learning courses in 1988. Institutionally administered financial aid is available to distance learners.
Services Distance learners have accessibility to academic advising, bookstore, campus computer network, career placement assistance, e-mail services, library services.
Contact Ms. Maryrose Raab, Graduate Center Coordinator, State University of New York Institute of Technology, 100 Seymour Road, Utica, NY 13502. Telephone: 315-792-7347. Fax: 315-792-7837. E-mail: gradcenter@sunyit.edu.

DEGREES AND AWARDS
MS Nursing Administration

STATE UNIVERSITY OF NEW YORK INSTITUTE OF TECHNOLOGY
Utica, New York
Program in Nurse Practitioner
http://www.sunyit.edu/undergraduate.nur.nursing_program

State University of New York Institute of Technology was founded in 1966. It is accredited by Middle States Association of Colleges and Schools. It first offered distance learning courses in 1988. Institutionally administered financial aid is available to distance learners.
Services Distance learners have accessibility to academic advising, bookstore, campus computer network, career placement assistance, e-mail services, library services.
Contact Ms. Jennifer Phelan-Ninh, Admissions, State University of New York Institute of Technology, 100 Seymour Road, Utica, NY 13502. Telephone: 315-792-7500. Fax: 315-792-7837. E-mail: admissions@sunyit.edu.

DEGREES AND AWARDS
BS Nursing

STATE UNIVERSITY OF NEW YORK INSTITUTE OF TECHNOLOGY
Utica, New York
Program in Adult Nurse Practitioner
http://www.sunyit.edu/programs/graduate/nur/adult_nurse_prac

State University of New York Institute of Technology was founded in 1966. It is accredited by Middle States Association of Colleges and Schools. It first offered distance learning courses in 1988. Institutionally administered financial aid is available to distance learners.
Services Distance learners have accessibility to academic advising, bookstore, campus computer network, career placement assistance, e-mail services.
Contact Mr. Kyle Johnson, Associate Provost of Information and Learning Resources, State University of New York Institute of Technology, 100 Seymour Road, Utica, NY 13502. Telephone: 315-792-7193. Fax: 315-792-7517. E-mail: online@sunyit.edu.

DEGREES AND AWARDS
MS Nursing–Adult Nurse Practitioner

STATE UNIVERSITY OF NEW YORK INSTITUTE OF TECHNOLOGY
Utica, New York
Program in Family Nurse Practitioner
http://www.sunyit.edu/programs/graduate/nur/family_nurse_prac

State University of New York Institute of Technology was founded in 1966. It is accredited by Middle States Association of Colleges and Schools. It first offered distance learning courses in 1988. Institutionally administered financial aid is available to distance learners.
Services Distance learners have accessibility to academic advising, bookstore, campus computer network, career placement assistance, e-mail services, library services.
Contact Ms. Maryrose Raab, Graduate Center Coordinator, State University of New York Institute of Technology, 100 Seymour Road, Utica, NY 13502. Telephone: 315-792-7347. Fax: 315-792-7837. E-mail: gradcenter@sunyit.edu.

DEGREES AND AWARDS

MS Nursing–Family Nurse Practitioner; Nursing–Family Nurse Practitioner

STATE UNIVERSITY OF NEW YORK INSTITUTE OF TECHNOLOGY
Utica, New York
Program in Gerontological Nurse Practitioner
http://www.sunyit.edu/programs/graduate/nur/gerontology_nurse_prac

State University of New York Institute of Technology was founded in 1966. It is accredited by Middle States Association of Colleges and Schools. It first offered distance learning courses in 1988. Institutionally administered financial aid is available to distance learners.

Services Distance learners have accessibility to academic advising, bookstore, campus computer network, career placement assistance, e-mail services, library services.

Contact Ms. Maryrose Raab, Graduate Center Coordinator, State University of New York Institute of Technology, 100 Seymour Road, Utica, NY 13502. Telephone: 315-792-7347. Fax: 315-792-7837. E-mail: gradcenter@sunyit.edu.

DEGREES AND AWARDS

MS Nursing–Gerontological Nurse Practitioner

STATE UNIVERSITY OF NEW YORK INSTITUTE OF TECHNOLOGY
Utica, New York
Program in Accountancy
http://www.sunyit.edu/programs/graduate/msacc/

State University of New York Institute of Technology was founded in 1966. It is accredited by Middle States Association of Colleges and Schools. It first offered distance learning courses in 1998. Institutionally administered financial aid is available to distance learners.

Services Distance learners have accessibility to academic advising, bookstore, campus computer network, career placement assistance, e-mail services, library services.

Contact Ms. Maryrose Raab, Graduate Center Coordinator, State University of New York Institute of Technology, 100 Seymour Road, Utica, NY 13502. Telephone: 315-792-7215. Fax: 315-792-7837. E-mail: maryrose.raab@sunyit.edu.

DEGREES AND AWARDS

MS Accountancy

COURSE SUBJECT AREAS OFFERED OUTSIDE OF DEGREE PROGRAMS

Graduate—accounting and computer science; accounting and related services; business administration, management and operations; business, management, and marketing related; business/managerial economics; economics; finance and financial management services; management information systems; management sciences and quantitative methods; taxation.

STEPHEN F. AUSTIN STATE UNIVERSITY
Nacogdoches, Texas
http://sfaonline.sfasu.edu/

Stephen F. Austin State University was founded in 1923. It is accredited by Southern Association of Colleges and Schools. It first offered distance learning courses in 1993. In fall 2010, there were 2,100 students enrolled in distance learning courses. Institutionally administered financial aid is available to distance learners.

Services Distance learners have accessibility to academic advising, bookstore, campus computer network, career placement assistance, e-mail services, library services, tutoring.

Contact Andra Floyd, Distance Education Support Specialist, Stephen F. Austin State University, SFA Box 13038, Nacogdoches, TX 75962. Telephone: 936-468-1919. Fax: 936-468-1308. E-mail: sfaonline@sfasu.edu.

DEGREES AND AWARDS

BS Child and Family Development–Head Start completion; Interdisciplinary Studies EC-6, 4-8

BSN Nursing–RN to BSN transition program

Certificate ESL certification; Elementary Education (post-Baccalaureate certification); Executive Hospitality Supervision; Hospitality Administration

Graduate Certificate Master Reading Teacher

MA Music Education

MEd Educational Leadership, Principal certification

MPA Public Administration

MS Human Sciences; Resource Interpretation

COURSE SUBJECT AREAS OFFERED OUTSIDE OF DEGREE PROGRAMS

Undergraduate—accounting and related services; agriculture; astronomy and astrophysics; business administration, management and operations; business/corporate communications; curriculum and instruction; economics; family and consumer economics; finance and financial management services; foods, nutrition, and related services; hospitality administration; mathematics; music; psychology; sales, merchandising and related marketing operations (specialized); social work; special education.

Graduate—educational administration and supervision; education related; education (specific levels and methods); forestry; music; psychology; public administration; special education.

STEPHENS COLLEGE
Columbia, Missouri
Division of Graduate and Continuing Studies
http://www.stephens.edu/gcs

Stephens College was founded in 1833. It is accredited by North Central Association of Colleges and Schools. It first offered distance learning courses in 1970. In fall 2010, there were 260 students enrolled in distance learning courses. Institutionally administered financial aid is available to distance learners.

Services Distance learners have accessibility to academic advising, bookstore, e-mail services, library services.

Contact Ms. Jennifer Deaver, Associate Director of Recruitment, Stephens College, 1200 East Broadway, Box 2083, Columbia, MO 65215. Telephone: 800-388-7579. Fax: 573-876-7290. E-mail: online@stephens.edu.

DEGREES AND AWARDS

Programs offered do not lead to a degree or other formal award.

COURSE SUBJECT AREAS OFFERED OUTSIDE OF DEGREE PROGRAMS

Undergraduate—accounting and related services; behavioral sciences; biological and biomedical sciences related; biological and physical sciences; biology; business administration, management and operations; business/commerce; business/corporate communications; business, management, and marketing related; communication and journalism related; communication and media; computer and information sciences; computer and information sciences and support services related; computer software and media applications; data entry/microcomputer applications; education; education related; education (specific levels and methods); English; English language and literature related; entrepreneurial and small business operations; ethnic, cultural minority, gender, and group studies; finance and financial management services; health and medical administrative services; health professions related; history; human resources management; liberal arts and sciences, general studies and humanities; marketing; mathematics and statistics related; natural sciences; pharmacology and toxicology; philosophy; physiology, pathology and related sciences; psychology; psychology related; public administration; public administration and social service professions related; public relations, advertising, and applied communication related; social sciences; social sciences related; statistics.

Graduate—accounting and related services; business administration, management and operations; business/commerce; business, management, and marketing related; business/managerial economics; curriculum and instruction; education; education related; education (specific levels and methods); entrepreneurial and small business operations; finance and financial management services; human resources management; marketing; psychology; psychology related.

STONY BROOK UNIVERSITY, STATE UNIVERSITY OF NEW YORK

Stony Brook, New York
Electronic Extension Program
http://www.stonybrook.edu/spd/online/

Stony Brook University, State University of New York was founded in 1957. It is accredited by Middle States Association of Colleges and Schools. It first offered distance learning courses in 1996. In fall 2010, there were 900 students enrolled in distance learning courses. Institutionally administered financial aid is available to distance learners.

Services Distance learners have accessibility to academic advising, bookstore, campus computer network, e-mail services, library services.

Contact Kim Giacalone, Associate Director, Stony Brook University, State University of New York, School of Professional Development, N 213 SBS Building, Stony Brook, NY 11794-4310. Telephone: 631-632-9484. Fax: 631-632-9046. E-mail: kim.giacalone@stonybrook.edu.

DEGREES AND AWARDS

Certificate Educational Leadership

Graduate Certificate Coaching; Human Resource Management

MA Higher Education Administration; Liberal Studies

MPS Professional Studies

COURSE SUBJECT AREAS OFFERED OUTSIDE OF DEGREE PROGRAMS

Graduate—education; educational administration and supervision; education (specific subject areas); English language and literature related; human resources management; liberal arts and sciences, general studies and humanities.

SUFFOLK UNIVERSITY

Boston, Massachusetts
Suffolk MBA Online
http://www.suffolk.edu/mbaonline

Suffolk University was founded in 1906. It is accredited by New England Association of Schools and Colleges. It first offered distance learning courses in 1999. In fall 2010, there were 300 students enrolled in distance learning courses. Institutionally administered financial aid is available to distance learners.

Services Distance learners have accessibility to academic advising, bookstore, campus computer network, career placement assistance, e-mail services, library services.

Contact Dr. Lillian M. Hallberg, Assistant Dean of Graduate Programs and Dean of MBA Programs, Suffolk University, 8 Ashburton Place, Boston, MA 02108. Telephone: 617-573-8306. Fax: 617-573-8653. E-mail: lhallber@suffolk.edu.

DEGREES AND AWARDS

MBA Accelerated MBA for Attorneys; Accelerated MBA for CPAs; Business Administration

COURSE SUBJECT AREAS OFFERED OUTSIDE OF DEGREE PROGRAMS

Graduate—accounting and related services; business, management, and marketing related; entrepreneurial and small business operations; finance and financial management services; human resources management; international business; management information systems; marketing; taxation.

SULLIVAN COUNTY COMMUNITY COLLEGE

Loch Sheldrake, New York
http://www.sunysullivan.edu/

Sullivan County Community College was founded in 1962. It is accredited by Middle States Association of Colleges and Schools. It first offered distance learning courses in 2002. In fall 2010, there were 169 students enrolled in distance learning courses. Institutionally administered financial aid is available to distance learners.

Services Distance learners have accessibility to academic advising, bookstore, career placement assistance, e-mail services, library services, tutoring.

Contact Office of Workforce Development, Continuing Education, and Lifelong Learning, Sullivan County Community College, 112 College Road, Loch Sheldrake, NY 12759. Telephone: 845-434-5750 Ext. 4398. Fax: 845-434-4806. E-mail: scccworkforce@sullivan.suny.edu.

DEGREES AND AWARDS

Programs offered do not lead to a degree or other formal award.

COURSE SUBJECT AREAS OFFERED OUTSIDE OF DEGREE PROGRAMS

Undergraduate—accounting and computer science; accounting and related services; astronomy and astrophysics; behavioral sciences; business administration, management and operations; business, management, and marketing related; business operations support and assistant services; computer and information sciences; computer programming; economics; English; geological and earth sciences/geosciences; history; liberal arts and sciences, general studies and humanities; literature; mathematics; music; physical sciences; psychology; social sciences.

Non-credit—accounting and computer science; behavioral sciences; biological and physical sciences; business administration, management and operations; communication and journalism related; computer software and media applications; computer systems networking and telecommunications; construction trades related; education; education related; electrical engineering technologies; engineering; English; entrepreneurial and small business operations; environmental control technologies; environmental design; gerontology; health professions related; legal professions and studies related.

SUMMIT PACIFIC COLLEGE

Abbotsford, British Columbia, Canada
http://www.summitpacific.ca

Summit Pacific College was founded in 1941. It is provincially chartered. It first offered distance learning courses in 1999. In fall 2010, there were 100 students enrolled in distance learning courses. Institutionally administered financial aid is available to distance learners.

Services Distance learners have accessibility to academic advising, bookstore, career placement assistance, library services, tutoring.

Contact Rev. Robert McIntyre, Director, Distance Education, Summit Pacific College, 35235 Straiton Road, PO Box 1700, Abbotsford, BC V2S 7E7, Canada. Telephone: 604-851-7228. Fax: 604-853-8951. E-mail: distanceed@summitpacific.ca.

DEGREES AND AWARDS

Programs offered do not lead to a degree or other formal award.

COURSE SUBJECT AREAS OFFERED OUTSIDE OF DEGREE PROGRAMS

Undergraduate—biblical studies; pastoral counseling and specialized ministries; religious education; religious studies; theological and ministerial studies.

Non-credit—biblical studies; religious education; religious studies; theological and ministerial studies.

SYRACUSE UNIVERSITY
Syracuse, New York
Martin J. Whitman School of Management
http://whitman.syr.edu/mba/imba

Syracuse University was founded in 1870. It is accredited by Middle States Association of Colleges and Schools. It first offered distance learning courses in 1977. In fall 2010, there were 250 students enrolled in distance learning courses. Institutionally administered financial aid is available to distance learners.

Services Distance learners have accessibility to academic advising, bookstore, campus computer network, e-mail services, library services.

Contact Joshua LaFave, Director of Graduate Enrollment, Syracuse University, 721 University Avenue, Suite 315, Syracuse, NY 13244-2450. Telephone: 315-443-3497. Fax: 315-443-9517. E-mail: jjlafave@syr.edu.

DEGREES AND AWARDS
MBA iMBA
MS iMS Accounting; iMS in Supply Chain Management

SYRACUSE UNIVERSITY
Syracuse, New York
School of Information Studies
http://www.ischool.syr.edu

Syracuse University was founded in 1870. It is accredited by Middle States Association of Colleges and Schools. It first offered distance learning courses in 1993. In fall 2010, there were 375 students enrolled in distance learning courses. Institutionally administered financial aid is available to distance learners.

Services Distance learners have accessibility to academic advising, bookstore, campus computer network, career placement assistance, e-mail services, library services, tutoring.

Contact Sue Corieri, Director of Enrollment Management, Syracuse University, School of Information Studies, 245 Hinds Hall, Syracuse, NY 13244. Telephone: 315-443-2575. Fax: 315-443-5806. E-mail: sbcorier@syr.edu.

DEGREES AND AWARDS
CAGS Digital Libraries; Information Security Management; Information Systems and Telecommunications Management; School Media
EMS Information Management
MLIS Library and Information Science
MS Information Management
MTM Telecommunications and Network Management
DPS Information Studies

COURSE SUBJECT AREAS OFFERED OUTSIDE OF DEGREE PROGRAMS
Graduate—communications technology; computer and information sciences; computer/information technology administration and management; computer software and media applications; computer systems analysis; computer systems networking and telecommunications; data processing; information science/studies; library and archives assisting; library science and administration; library science related; management information systems; systems science and theory.

SYRACUSE UNIVERSITY
Syracuse, New York
University College
http://uc.syr.edu/

Syracuse University was founded in 1870. It is accredited by Middle States Association of Colleges and Schools. It first offered distance learning courses in 1966. In fall 2010, there were 1,000 students enrolled in distance learning courses. Institutionally administered financial aid is available to distance learners.

Services Distance learners have accessibility to academic advising, bookstore, campus computer network, career placement assistance, e-mail services, library services.

Contact Dr. Geraldine de Berly, Senior Associate Dean, University College, Syracuse University, 700 University Avenue, Suite 403, Syracuse, NY 13244-2530. Telephone: 315-443-5753. Fax: 315-443-4410. E-mail: gdeberly@uc.syr.edu.

DEGREES AND AWARDS
CAGS Digital Libraries; Information Security Management; Information Systems and Telecommunications Management; School Media
MBA iMBA
MS Communications Management; Information Management; Library and Information Science in School Media; Library and Information Science; Social Sciences; Telecommunications and Network Management

COURSE SUBJECT AREAS OFFERED OUTSIDE OF DEGREE PROGRAMS
Undergraduate—biological and physical sciences; business, management, and marketing related; computer and information sciences; English language and literature related; ethnic, cultural minority, gender, and group studies; liberal arts and sciences, general studies and humanities; science, technology and society; social sciences; statistics; visual and performing arts related.
Graduate—anthropology; business administration, management and operations; communication and media; computer and information sciences; computer/information technology administration and management; computer systems networking and telecommunications; ethnic, cultural minority, gender, and group studies; history; information science/studies; library science and administration; library science related; management information systems; sociology; visual and performing arts related.

TABOR COLLEGE
Hillsboro, Kansas
http://www.tabor.edu/

Tabor College was founded in 1908. It is accredited by North Central Association of Colleges and Schools. It first offered distance learning courses in 2009. In fall 2010, there were 45 students enrolled in distance learning courses. Institutionally administered financial aid is available to distance learners.

Services Distance learners have accessibility to academic advising, campus computer network, e-mail services, library services.

Contact Adam Penner, Director of Enrollment, Tabor College, 7348 West 21st Street, Wichita, KS 67205. Telephone: 316-729-6333. E-mail: agsinfo@tabor.edu.

DEGREES AND AWARDS
Programs offered do not lead to a degree or other formal award.

COURSE SUBJECT AREAS OFFERED OUTSIDE OF DEGREE PROGRAMS
Undergraduate—health/medical preparatory programs; health professions related; health services/allied health/health sciences; history; liberal arts and sciences, general studies and humanities; literature; multi/interdisciplinary studies related; psychology; registered nursing, nursing administration, nursing research and clinical nursing; social sciences; sociology; statistics.

TAFT COLLEGE
Taft, California
http://www.taftcollege.edu

Taft College was founded in 1922. It is accredited by Western Association of Schools and Colleges. It first offered distance learning courses in 1997. In fall 2010, there were 3,000 students enrolled in distance learning courses. Institutionally administered financial aid is available to distance learners.

Services Distance learners have accessibility to academic advising, bookstore, campus computer network, e-mail services, library services, tutoring.

Contact Linda West, Distance Learning Coordinator, Taft College, 29 Emmons Park Drive, Taft, CA 93268. Telephone: 661-763-7831. Fax: 661-763-7703. E-mail: lwest@taft.org.

DEGREES AND AWARDS

AA Business Administration; Liberal Arts
AS Business, general; Criminal Justice Administration; Early Childhood Education; Management

COURSE SUBJECT AREAS OFFERED OUTSIDE OF DEGREE PROGRAMS

Undergraduate—accounting and related services; applied mathematics; biological and physical sciences; business administration, management and operations; business/commerce; computer science; criminal justice and corrections; economics; English; English language and literature related; geological and earth sciences/geosciences; history; human development, family studies, and related services; mathematics; mathematics and statistics related; psychology; psychology related; social sciences; social sciences related; sociology; statistics.

TARLETON STATE UNIVERSITY
Stephenville, Texas
Center for Instructional Technology and Distributed Education
http://online.tarleton.edu

Tarleton State University was founded in 1899. It is accredited by Southern Association of Colleges and Schools. It first offered distance learning courses in 1994. In fall 2010, there were 3,000 students enrolled in distance learning courses. Institutionally administered financial aid is available to distance learners.
Services Distance learners have accessibility to academic advising, bookstore, campus computer network, career placement assistance, e-mail services, library services, tutoring.
Contact Ms. Jana Holland, Manager, Tarleton State University e-Campus Outreach, Tarleton State University, Box T-0011, Stephenville, TX 76402. Telephone: 817-732-7300. E-mail: holland@tarleton.edu.

DEGREES AND AWARDS

MBA Business Administration
MCJ Criminal Justice
MS Agricultural Education; Educational Psychology–Experimental Psychology
MSHRM Human Resource Management
MSIS Information Sciences
MSM Management and Leadership

COURSE SUBJECT AREAS OFFERED OUTSIDE OF DEGREE PROGRAMS

Undergraduate—accounting and related services; agriculture and agriculture operations related; applied mathematics; business/commerce; business, management, and marketing related; business/managerial economics; computer programming; computer software and media applications; curriculum and instruction; economics; education; educational administration and supervision; educational/instructional media design; education (specific levels and methods); English; family and consumer sciences/human sciences related; health and physical education/fitness; history; mathematics and statistics related; physical sciences; political science and government; psychology related.
Graduate—computer and information sciences; computer and information sciences and support services related; computer/information technology administration and management; computer programming; computer science; computer software and media applications; computer systems analysis; computer systems networking and telecommunications; curriculum and instruction; education; educational administration and supervision; educational assessment, evaluation, and research; education related; education (specific levels and methods); education (specific subject areas); health and physical education/fitness; history; human resources management; information science/studies; marketing; physical sciences; psychology; social sciences; special education.
Non-credit—accounting and related services; business/commerce; business/corporate communications; business operations support and assistant services; computer programming; computer software and media applications; data entry/microcomputer applications; human development, family studies, and related services; human resources management; languages (foreign languages related); linguistic, comparative, and related language studies; real estate.

TAYLOR UNIVERSITY
Fort Wayne, Indiana
Taylor University Online
http://www.taylor.edu/online

Taylor University was founded in 1938. It is accredited by North Central Association of Colleges and Schools. It first offered distance learning courses in 1941. In fall 2010, there were 524 students enrolled in distance learning courses. Institutionally administered financial aid is available to distance learners.
Services Distance learners have accessibility to academic advising, bookstore, e-mail services, library services, tutoring.
Contact Carrie L. Meyer, Director of Online Learning and Instructional Technology, Taylor University, 3201 Stellhorn Road, Fort Wayne, IN 46815. Telephone: 260-744-8750. Fax: 260-744-8796. E-mail: online@taylor.edu.

DEGREES AND AWARDS

AA Biblical Studies; Justice Administration–Public Policy concentration; Justice Administration, Ministry concentration; Liberal Arts–History concentration; Liberal Arts, Business concentration; Liberal Arts, Christian Ministries concentration; Liberal Arts, Discipleship concentration; Liberal Arts, Professional Writing concentration; Liberal Arts, Social Science concentration
BBA Business Administration
Certificate Biblical Studies; Biblical and Cultural Leadership; Christian Worker; Justice and Ministry; Leadership Development; Missions Studies; Professional Writing

COURSE SUBJECT AREAS OFFERED OUTSIDE OF DEGREE PROGRAMS

Undergraduate—area studies; behavioral sciences; biblical studies; biological and physical sciences; biology; business administration, management and operations; business/commerce; business, management, and marketing related; business/managerial economics; communication and journalism related; computer and information sciences; computer/information technology administration and management; computer science; criminal justice and corrections; economics; education; educational/instructional media design; education related; English; fine and studio arts; geography and cartography; history; information science/studies; journalism; liberal arts and sciences, general studies and humanities; management information systems; marketing; mathematics; medieval and Renaissance studies; missionary studies and missiology; multi/interdisciplinary studies related; music; pastoral counseling and specialized ministries; peace studies and conflict resolution; philosophy; philosophy and religious studies related; physical sciences; physical sciences related; political science and government; psychology; psychology related; religious education; religious/sacred music; religious studies; social sciences; social sciences related; social work; sociology; theological and ministerial studies; theology and religious vocations related.

TEMPLE UNIVERSITY
Philadelphia, Pennsylvania
Online Learning Program
http://www.temple.edu/distanceandsummer

Temple University was founded in 1884. It is accredited by Middle States Association of Colleges and Schools. It first offered distance learning courses in 1995. In fall 2010, there were 1,610 students enrolled in distance learning courses. Institutionally administered financial aid is available to distance learners.
Services Distance learners have accessibility to academic advising, bookstore, campus computer network, career placement assistance, e-mail services, library services, tutoring.

Contact Dr. Dominique Monolescu Kliger, Distance Learning Program Director, Temple University, 1301 Cecil B. Moore Avenue, 671 Ritter Annex Building, Philadelphia, PA 19122. Telephone: 215-204-2712. Fax: 215-204-2666. E-mail: online@temple.edu.

DEGREES AND AWARDS

BSN Nursing–RN to BSN completion program
MBA Fox Online MBA Program
MS/MPH QA/RA Program
DPT Physical Therapy
OTD Occupational Therapy

COURSE SUBJECT AREAS OFFERED OUTSIDE OF DEGREE PROGRAMS

Undergraduate—anthropology; architecture; business administration, management and operations; communication and media; communications technology; crafts, folk art and artisanry; economics; education; educational/instructional media design; engineering; film/video and photographic arts; health professions related; journalism; languages (foreign languages related); liberal arts and sciences, general studies and humanities; multi/interdisciplinary studies related; music; physics; psychology; sales, merchandising and related marketing operations (specialized).
Graduate—accounting and related services; business administration, management and operations; business/commerce; communication and media; communications technology; economics; education; educational administration and supervision; health professions related; journalism; music; physical sciences; social work.
Non-credit—business/corporate communications; economics; landscape architecture; languages (Romance languages).

TEXAS A&M UNIVERSITY–CORPUS CHRISTI

Corpus Christi, Texas
http://www.tamucc.edu/

Texas A&M University–Corpus Christi was founded in 1947. It is accredited by Southern Association of Colleges and Schools. It first offered distance learning courses in 1976. In fall 2010, there were 1,164 students enrolled in distance learning courses. Institutionally administered financial aid is available to distance learners.
Services Distance learners have accessibility to academic advising, bookstore, campus computer network, career placement assistance, e-mail services, library services, tutoring.
Contact Dr. Lauren Cifuentes, Director of Distance Education, Texas A&M University–Corpus Christi, 6300 Ocean Drive, Unit 5758, Corpus Christi, TX 78412-5758. Telephone: 361-825-5709. Fax: 361-825-2496. E-mail: lauren.cifuentes@tamucc.edu.

DEGREES AND AWARDS

BSN Nursing
MS Geospatial Surveying Engineering (GSEN)
MSN Nursing Administration

COURSE SUBJECT AREAS OFFERED OUTSIDE OF DEGREE PROGRAMS

Undergraduate—accounting and related services; statistics.
Graduate—accounting and related services; economics; education related; marketing.

TEXAS CHRISTIAN UNIVERSITY

Fort Worth, Texas
Cyberlearning
http://tcuglobal.edu

Texas Christian University was founded in 1873. It is accredited by Southern Association of Colleges and Schools. It first offered distance learning courses in 1999. In fall 2010, there were 330 students enrolled in distance learning courses. Institutionally administered financial aid is available to distance learners.
Services Distance learners have accessibility to academic advising, bookstore, campus computer network, career placement assistance, e-mail services, library services, tutoring.
Contact Mrs. Romana J. Hughes, Assistant Director of Learning Resources, Texas Christian University, Box 298970, Fort Worth, TX 76129. Telephone: 817-257-7434. Fax: 817-257-7393. E-mail: r.hughes@tcu.edu.

DEGREES AND AWARDS

Advanced Graduate Diploma Liberal Arts–Master of Liberal Arts
MSN Nursing
DNP Nursing

TEXAS STATE TECHNICAL COLLEGE WEST TEXAS

Sweetwater, Texas
http://www.sweetwater.tstc.edu/

Texas State Technical College West Texas was founded in 1970. It is accredited by Southern Association of Colleges and Schools. It first offered distance learning courses in 1995. In fall 2010, there were 350 students enrolled in distance learning courses. Institutionally administered financial aid is available to distance learners.
Services Distance learners have accessibility to academic advising, bookstore, career placement assistance, e-mail services, library services.
Contact Ken Woods, Director of Distance Learning, Texas State Technical College West Texas, 300 College Drive, Sweetwater, TX 79556. Telephone: 915-235-7326. Fax: 915-235-7309. E-mail: ken.woods@sweetwater.tstc.edu.

DEGREES AND AWARDS

AAS Digital Imaging and Design

COURSE SUBJECT AREAS OFFERED OUTSIDE OF DEGREE PROGRAMS

Undergraduate—computer and information sciences.
Non-credit—graphic communications.

TEXAS STATE UNIVERSITY–SAN MARCOS

San Marcos, Texas
Correspondence and Extension Studies
http://www.correspondence.txstate.edu

Texas State University–San Marcos was founded in 1899. It is accredited by Southern Association of Colleges and Schools. It first offered distance learning courses in 1953. In fall 2010, there were 1,400 students enrolled in distance learning courses. Institutionally administered financial aid is available to distance learners.
Services Distance learners have accessibility to bookstore, campus computer network, e-mail services, library services, tutoring.
Contact Carolyn Bettelheim, Administrative Assistant, Texas State University–San Marcos, Office of Distance and Extended Learning, 302 ASB North, 601 University Drive, San Marcos, TX 78666. Telephone: 512-245-2322. Fax: 512-245-8934. E-mail: corrstudy@txstate.edu.

DEGREES AND AWARDS

Programs offered do not lead to a degree or other formal award.

COURSE SUBJECT AREAS OFFERED OUTSIDE OF DEGREE PROGRAMS

Undergraduate—allied health and medical assisting services; behavioral sciences; biological and physical sciences; biology; business/commerce; cell biology and anatomical sciences; criminology; dance; English; English language and literature related; fine and studio arts; health and medical administrative services; health professions related; history; journalism; languages (Romance languages); legal professions and studies related; liberal arts and sciences, general studies and humanities; mathematics; mathematics and computer science; music; philosophy; political science and government; psychology; psychology related; social sciences; social sciences related; sociology.
Graduate—mathematics.

TEXAS WOMAN'S UNIVERSITY
Denton, Texas
http://www.twu.edu/de

Texas Woman's University was founded in 1901. It is accredited by Southern Association of Colleges and Schools. It first offered distance learning courses in 1994. In fall 2010, there were 7,439 students enrolled in distance learning courses. Institutionally administered financial aid is available to distance learners.

Services Distance learners have accessibility to academic advising, bookstore, campus computer network, career placement assistance, e-mail services, library services, tutoring.

Contact Ms. Laura Macsas, DE Senior Administrative Assistant, Texas Woman's University, PO Box 425649, Denton, TX 76204. Telephone: 940-898-3409. Fax: 940-898-3416. E-mail: de@twu.edu.

DEGREES AND AWARDS

BA/BS Criminal Justice
BAS Health Studies
BBA Human Resource Management; Management; Marketing
BGS General Studies
BS Dental Hygiene (RDH to BS); Health Studies
BSN Nursing–RN to BS in Nursing
EMBA Business Administration
MA Drama; Library Science
MAT Teaching
MEd Reading Education
MLS Library Science
MOT COTA to MOT
MS Education of the Deaf; Family Studies; Food Systems Administration (Nutrition and Food Sciences); Health Studies; Kinesiology (All Area Coaching); Kinesiology (Softball Coaching); Kinesiology (Sport Management); Nursing (Health Systems Management); Nutrition; Speech-Language Pathology
MSN Nursing Education
PhD Nursing; Occupational Therapy

COURSE SUBJECT AREAS OFFERED OUTSIDE OF DEGREE PROGRAMS

Undergraduate—business administration, management and operations; computer and information sciences; English; family and consumer economics; health and physical education/fitness; health services/allied health/health sciences; history; sociology; visual and performing arts.

Graduate—bilingual, multilingual, and multicultural education; business administration, management and operations; business/commerce; communication disorders sciences and services; education; education related; family and consumer economics; health and physical education/fitness; health services/allied health/health sciences; library science and administration; nutrition sciences; rehabilitation and therapeutic professions; sociology; visual and performing arts.

Non-credit—business administration, management and operations; computer software and media applications; engineering; English; insurance; legal professions and studies related; real estate.

THIEL COLLEGE
Greenville, Pennsylvania
http://www.thiel.edu/outreach/adult-distance-education.htm

Thiel College was founded in 1866. It is accredited by Middle States Association of Colleges and Schools. It first offered distance learning courses in 2006. Institutionally administered financial aid is available to distance learners.

Services Distance learners have accessibility to academic advising, bookstore, career placement assistance, e-mail services, tutoring.

Contact Dr. Jennifer S. Griffin, Assistant Academic Dean, Thiel College, 75 College Avenue, Greenville, PA 16125. Telephone: 724-589-2069. Fax: 724-589-2021. E-mail: jgriffin@thiel.edu.

DEGREES AND AWARDS

Programs offered do not lead to a degree or other formal award.

COURSE SUBJECT AREAS OFFERED OUTSIDE OF DEGREE PROGRAMS

Undergraduate—accounting and related services; business, management, and marketing related; communication and journalism related; communication and media; computer software and media applications; health and physical education/fitness; history; mathematics and statistics related; neurobiology and neurosciences.

THOMAS EDISON STATE COLLEGE
Trenton, New Jersey
DIAL–Distance and Independent Adult Learning
http://www.tesc.edu

Thomas Edison State College was founded in 1972. It is accredited by Middle States Association of Colleges and Schools. It first offered distance learning courses in 1972. In fall 2010, there were 18,736 students enrolled in distance learning courses. Institutionally administered financial aid is available to distance learners.

Services Distance learners have accessibility to academic advising, library services.

Contact Mr. David Hoftiezer, Director of Admissions, Thomas Edison State College, 101 West State Street, Trenton, NJ 08608-1176. Telephone: 888-442-8372. Fax: 609-984-8447. E-mail: admissions@tesc.edu.

DEGREES AND AWARDS

AA Human Services–Associate of Arts in Human Services (AAHS); Liberal Arts/General Studies
AAS Administrative Studies; Applied Computer Studies; Applied Electronic Studies; Applied Health Studies; Aviation Support; Construction and Facility Support; Criminal Justice; Dental Hygiene (through UMDNJ); Electrical/Mechanical Systems and Maintenance; Environmental, Safety, and Security Technology; Mechanics and Maintenance; Occupational Studies
AS Business Administration (ASBA)
ASAST Air Traffic Control; Architectural Design; Aviation Flight Technology; Aviation Maintenance Technology; Biomedical Electronics; Civil and Construction Engineering Technology; Clinical Lab Science; Computer Science Technology; Electrical Technology; Electronic Engineering Technology; Engineering Graphics; Environmental Sciences; Fire Protection Science; Kitchen and Bath Design; Laboratory Animal Science; Manufacturing Engineering Technology; Mechanical Engineering Technology; Medical Imaging; Nuclear Engineering Technology; Nuclear Medicine Technology; Polysomnography (ASAST); Radiation Protection; Radiation Therapy; Respiratory Care; Surveying; Technical Studies (ASAST)
ASNSM Biology; Computer Science; Mathematics
BA Anthropology; Art; Biology; Communications; Computer Science; Criminal Justice; Economics; English; Environmental Studies; Foreign Language; History; Humanities; Journalism; Labor Studies; Liberal Studies; Mathematics; Music; Natural Sciences/Mathematics; Philosophy; Photography; Political Science; Psychology; Religion; Social Sciences; Sociology; Theater
BS Homeland Security and Emergency Preparedness; Organizational Leadership (BSOL)
BSAST Air Traffic Control; Architectural Design; Automotive Performance Technology (BSAST); Aviation Flight Technology; Aviation Maintenance Technology; Biomedical Electronics; Civil Engineering Technology; Clinical Lab Science; Computer Science Technology; Construction; Dental Hygiene; Diagnostic Medical Sonography (BSAT); Electrical Technology; Electronic Engineering Technology; Energy Utility Technology; Engineering Graphics; Environmental Sciences; Fire Protection Science; Health Service Technology; Information Technology; Kitchen and Bath Design; Laboratory Animal Science; Manufacturing Engineering Technology; Mechanical Engineering Technology; Medical Imaging; Nuclear Engineering Technology; Nuclear Medicine Technology; Radiation Protection; Radiation Therapy; Respiratory Care; Surveying; Technical Studies
BSBA Accounting; Computer Information Systems; Entrepreneurship; Finance; Financial Institution Management; General Management; Hospital Health Care Administration; Hospitality Management; Human

Resources Management/Organizational Management; International Business; Marketing; Operations Management; Public Administration; Real Estate
BSHS Administration of Justice; Child Development Services; Community Services; Emergency Disaster Services; Gerontology; Health Services Administration; Health Services; Health and Nutrition Counseling; Human Services; Legal Services; Mental Health and Rehabilitation Services; Recreation Services; Social Services Administration; Social Services for Special Populations; Social Services
BSHeS Allied Dental Education (with UMDNJ); Coordinated Dietetic Science (with UMDNJ); Health Services Education and Management (with UMDNJ); Imaging Sciences, Advanced (with UMDNJ)
BSN Nursing
Certificate Accounting pre-Associate certificate; Clinical Trials Management post-Baccalaureate certificate; Computer Aided Design pre-Associate certificate; Computer Information Systems pre-Associate certificate; Computer Science pre-Associate certificate; Dental Assistant pre-Associate certificate (jointly sponsored by UMDNJ and TESC); E-Commerce pre-Associate certificate; Electronics pre-Associate certificate; Finance Pre-Associate certificate; Fitness and Wellness Services pre-Associate certificate; Homeland Security post-Baccalaureate certificate; Human Resource Management post-Baccalaureate certificate; Human Resource Management pre-Associate certificate; Imaging Science Pre-Associate certificate; Labor Studies Pre-Associate certificate; Marketing pre-Associate certificate; Online Learning and Teaching post-Baccalaureate certificate; Operations Management pre-Associate certificate; Organizational Management and Leadership post-Baccalaureate certificate; Public Administration Pre-Associate certificate; Public Service Leadership post-Baccalaureate certificate
Graduate Certificate Nursing–post-Masters certificate in Nurse Educator
MA Liberal Studies
MAEd Educational Leadership (MAEdL)
MS Master of Science in Applied Science and Technology in Clinical Trials (MSAST); Master of Science in Applied Science and Technology in Technical Studies (MSAST)
MSHRM Human Resources Management
MSM Environmental Policy/Environmental Justice; Information Technology for Public Service; Management; Nonprofit Management; Public Finance; Public Health/Public Policy; Public Service Administration and Leadership; Public Service Community and Economic Development
MSN Nursing

THREE RIVERS COMMUNITY COLLEGE
Norwich, Connecticut
http://www.trcc.commnet.edu/

Three Rivers Community College was founded in 1963. It is accredited by New England Association of Schools and Colleges. It first offered distance learning courses in 2000. In fall 2010, there were 1,151 students enrolled in distance learning courses. Institutionally administered financial aid is available to distance learners.
Services Distance learners have accessibility to academic advising, bookstore, campus computer network, career placement assistance, library services, tutoring.
Contact Mr. Kem Barfield, Director of Educational Technology, Three Rivers Community College, 574 New London Turnpike, Norwich, CT 06360. Telephone: 860-383-5215. E-mail: kbarfield@trcc.commnet.edu.

DEGREES AND AWARDS
AS Computer Support Specialist; Criminal Justice; General Studies

COURSE SUBJECT AREAS OFFERED OUTSIDE OF DEGREE PROGRAMS
Undergraduate—accounting and related services; business administration, management and operations; computer and information sciences; education (specific subject areas); environmental/environmental health engineering; history; mathematics; nutrition sciences; psychology; sociology.
Non-credit—allied health and medical assisting services; computer software and media applications.

TOCCOA FALLS COLLEGE
Toccoa Falls, Georgia
http://www.tfc.edu/online

Toccoa Falls College was founded in 1907. It is accredited by Association for Biblical Higher Education. It first offered distance learning courses in 2005. In fall 2010, there were 40 students enrolled in distance learning courses. Institutionally administered financial aid is available to distance learners.
Services Distance learners have accessibility to academic advising, bookstore, campus computer network, e-mail services, library services, tutoring.
Contact Michael Shiflet, Admissions Counselor, Toccoa Falls College, 107 North Chapel Drive, PO Box 800899, Toccoa Falls, GA 30598. Telephone: 706-886-7299 Ext. 4575. Fax: 706-393-6012. E-mail: michaels@tfc.edu.

DEGREES AND AWARDS
AA General Studies
BA/BS Ministry Leadership; Youth Ministries
BBA Nonprofit Business Administration
CBS College Level Instruction with Maximum Bible (CLIMB)

COURSE SUBJECT AREAS OFFERED OUTSIDE OF DEGREE PROGRAMS
Undergraduate—accounting and computer science; anthropology; biblical studies; business administration, management and operations; business, management, and marketing related; education; history; liberal arts and sciences, general studies and humanities; mathematics; philosophy; psychology; religious education; religious studies; statistics; theological and ministerial studies.

TOMPKINS CORTLAND COMMUNITY COLLEGE
Dryden, New York
Instructional and Learning Resources
http://portal.tc3.edu/Wiki/myWeb%20Courses%20FAQ/Home.aspx

Tompkins Cortland Community College was founded in 1968. It is accredited by Middle States Association of Colleges and Schools. It first offered distance learning courses in 1997. In fall 2010, there were 1,500 students enrolled in distance learning courses. Institutionally administered financial aid is available to distance learners.
Services Distance learners have accessibility to academic advising, bookstore, career placement assistance, e-mail services, library services, tutoring.
Contact Tony DeFranco, Coordinator of Learning Technology Services, Tompkins Cortland Community College, 170 North Street, PO Box 139, Dryden, NY 13053. Telephone: 607-844-8211 Ext. 4399. Fax: 607-844-9665. E-mail: defrant@tc3.edu.

DEGREES AND AWARDS
AAS Business Administration–Applied Management; Chemical Dependency Studies Counseling; Hotel and Restaurant Management; Paralegal Studies

COURSE SUBJECT AREAS OFFERED OUTSIDE OF DEGREE PROGRAMS
Undergraduate—accounting and related services; biotechnology; business/commerce; business/corporate communications; communication and media; computer and information sciences; computer programming; computer software and media applications; criminal justice and corrections; education (specific levels and methods); English; ethnic, cultural minority, gender, and group studies; fine and studio arts; hospitality administration; human services; international business; legal studies (non-professional general, undergraduate); management sciences and quantitative methods; marketing; mathematics; mental and social health services and allied professions; psychology; psychology related; sociology; visual and performing arts.
Non-credit—business, management, and marketing related; business operations support and assistant services; computer software and media applications; computer systems networking and telecommunications; data processing.

TRIDENT TECHNICAL COLLEGE

Charleston, South Carolina

http://www.tridenttech.edu

Trident Technical College was founded in 1964. It is accredited by Southern Association of Colleges and Schools. It first offered distance learning courses in 1991. In fall 2010, there were 14,000 students enrolled in distance learning courses. Institutionally administered financial aid is available to distance learners.

Services Distance learners have accessibility to academic advising, bookstore, campus computer network, career placement assistance, e-mail services, library services.

Contact Dr. Roscoe Thornthwaite, Dean of Distance Learning and Broadcast Services, Trident Technical College, 7000 Rivers Avenue, Charleston, SC 29406. Telephone: 843-574-6474. Fax: 843-574-6595. E-mail: roscoe.thornthwaite@tridenttech.edu.

DEGREES AND AWARDS

Programs offered do not lead to a degree or other formal award.

COURSE SUBJECT AREAS OFFERED OUTSIDE OF DEGREE PROGRAMS

Undergraduate—accounting and related services; business administration, management and operations; business/commerce; business/managerial economics; business operations support and assistant services; computer and information sciences; computer/information technology administration and management; computer programming; computer software and media applications; computer systems networking and telecommunications; criminal justice and corrections; data entry/microcomputer applications; economics; history; human development, family studies, and related services; human services; management information systems; mathematics; philosophy; psychology; quality control and safety technologies; sociology; visual and performing arts.

TRINE UNIVERSITY

Angola, Indiana

http://www.trine.edu/

Trine University was founded in 1884. It is accredited by North Central Association of Colleges and Schools. It first offered distance learning courses in 1995. In fall 2010, there were 359 students enrolled in distance learning courses. Institutionally administered financial aid is available to distance learners.

Services Distance learners have accessibility to academic advising, bookstore, career placement assistance, e-mail services, library services.

Contact Mr. David Wood, Dean, School of Professional Studies, Trine University, 1 University Avenue, Angola, IN 46703. Telephone: 260-665-4600. Fax: 260-665-4309. E-mail: woodd@trine.edu.

DEGREES AND AWARDS

AD Accounting; Business Administration; Engineering Technology

BA General Studies

BBA Business

BPS Applied Management

BS Communication; Computer Science; Criminal Justice; Emergency Management; Engineering Technology; Psychology

ME Biomechanical Engineering; Civil Engineering; Mechanical Engineering

MS Criminal Justice; Leadership

COURSE SUBJECT AREAS OFFERED OUTSIDE OF DEGREE PROGRAMS

Undergraduate—accounting and related services; business administration, management and operations; business/commerce; economics; fine and studio arts; geological and earth sciences/geosciences; history; legal studies (non-professional general, undergraduate); liberal arts and sciences, general studies and humanities; marketing; mathematics; social sciences.

TRINIDAD STATE JUNIOR COLLEGE

Trinidad, Colorado

Telecommunications and Distance Learning

http://www.trinidadstate.edu

Trinidad State Junior College was founded in 1925. It is accredited by North Central Association of Colleges and Schools. It first offered distance learning courses in 1992. In fall 2010, there were 873 students enrolled in distance learning courses. Institutionally administered financial aid is available to distance learners.

Contact Ms. Kimberlee Dawn VanOrden, Distance Learning Proctor/Polycom Liaison, Trinidad State Junior College, 600 Prospect #352, Trinidad, CO 81082. Telephone: 719-846-5728. Fax: 719-846-5477. E-mail: kimberlee.vanorden@trinidadstate.edu.

DEGREES AND AWARDS

Programs offered do not lead to a degree or other formal award.

COURSE SUBJECT AREAS OFFERED OUTSIDE OF DEGREE PROGRAMS

Undergraduate—geography and cartography; human development, family studies, and related services; psychology; sociology.

TRINITY COLLEGE OF NURSING AND HEALTH SCIENCES

Rock Island, Illinois

http://www.trinityqc.com/college/default.htm

Trinity College of Nursing and Health Sciences was founded in 1994. It is accredited by North Central Association of Colleges and Schools. It first offered distance learning courses in 2003. In fall 2010, there were 87 students enrolled in distance learning courses. Institutionally administered financial aid is available to distance learners.

Services Distance learners have accessibility to academic advising, bookstore, campus computer network, e-mail services, library services.

Contact Lori Perez, Admissions Representative, Trinity College of Nursing and Health Sciences, 2122 25th Avenue, Rock Island, IL 61201. Telephone: 309-779-7812. Fax: 309-779-7748. E-mail: perezlj@ihs.org.

DEGREES AND AWARDS

Programs offered do not lead to a degree or other formal award.

COURSE SUBJECT AREAS OFFERED OUTSIDE OF DEGREE PROGRAMS

Undergraduate—health professions related.

TRINITY INTERNATIONAL UNIVERSITY

Deerfield, Illinois

Division of Open Studies

http://www.tiu.edu/divinity/academics/mode/distance/?

Trinity International University was founded in 1897. It is accredited by North Central Association of Colleges and Schools. It first offered distance learning courses in 1985. In fall 2010, there were 150 students enrolled in distance learning courses. Institutionally administered financial aid is available to distance learners.

Services Distance learners have accessibility to academic advising, bookstore, campus computer network, e-mail services, library services, tutoring.

Contact Mr. Jonathan M. Kimmel, Distance Education Coordinator, Trinity International University, 2065 Half Day Road, Deerfield, IL 60015. Telephone: 847-317-6554. Fax: 847-317-6509. E-mail: jon@trinet.tiu.edu.

DEGREES AND AWARDS

Programs offered do not lead to a degree or other formal award.

COURSE SUBJECT AREAS OFFERED OUTSIDE OF DEGREE PROGRAMS

Graduate—biblical studies; missionary studies and missiology; religious education; religious studies; theological and ministerial studies.

TUNXIS COMMUNITY COLLEGE

Farmington, Connecticut

http://www.tunxis.commnet.edu/online

Tunxis Community College was founded in 1969. It is accredited by New England Association of Schools and Colleges. It first offered distance learning courses in 1996. In fall 2010, there were 1,100 students enrolled in distance learning courses. Institutionally administered financial aid is available to distance learners.

Services Distance learners have accessibility to academic advising, bookstore, library services, tutoring.

Contact Peter McCluskey, Director of Admissions, Tunxis Community College, 271 Scott Swamp Road, Farmington, CT 06032. Telephone: 860-255-3563. E-mail: tx-admissions@txcc.commnet.edu.

DEGREES AND AWARDS

AA Criminal Justice; General Studies/Liberal Arts

Certificate Corrections pre-certification

COURSE SUBJECT AREAS OFFERED OUTSIDE OF DEGREE PROGRAMS

Undergraduate—anthropology; business administration, management and operations; communication and media; computer and information sciences; computer systems networking and telecommunications; criminal justice and corrections; criminology; dental support services and allied professions; English; history; linguistic, comparative, and related language studies; management information systems; music; philosophy; psychology; sociology.

Non-credit—business/commerce; computer and information sciences; criminal justice and corrections; education related; information science/studies.

TYLER JUNIOR COLLEGE

Tyler, Texas

Learning Resources

http://www.tjc.edu/de

Tyler Junior College was founded in 1926. It is accredited by Southern Association of Colleges and Schools. It first offered distance learning courses in 1969. In fall 2010, there were 7,005 students enrolled in distance learning courses. Institutionally administered financial aid is available to distance learners.

Services Distance learners have accessibility to academic advising, bookstore, career placement assistance, e-mail services, library services, tutoring.

Contact Gay Howard, Secretary of Learning Resources, Tyler Junior College, PO Box 9020, Tyler, TX 75711. Telephone: 903-510-2529. Fax: 903-510-2643. E-mail: ghow@tjc.edu.

DEGREES AND AWARDS

AA Education; General Studies; Government; Liberal Arts–English; Psychology; Social Work; Sociology

AAS Business Management; Health Information Technology

AS Health and Kinesiology–Kinesiology

Certificate Medical Office Management

COURSE SUBJECT AREAS OFFERED OUTSIDE OF DEGREE PROGRAMS

Undergraduate—accounting and related services; astronomy and astrophysics; biology; business administration, management and operations; business/commerce; business/corporate communications; business operations support and assistant services; cell biology and anatomical sciences; computer and information sciences; computer and information sciences and support services related; computer/information technology administration and management; computer programming; computer science; computer software and media applications; computer systems analysis; computer systems networking and telecommunications; criminal justice and corrections; economics; education; educational/instructional media design; fine and studio arts; fire protection; health services/allied health/health sciences; history; languages (Romance languages); legal studies (non-professional general, undergraduate); legal support services; liberal arts and sciences, general studies and humanities; mathematics and statistics related; music; political science and government; psychology; sociology.

Non-credit—accounting and related services; business administration, management and operations; business/commerce; computer and information sciences; computer programming; computer software and media applications; educational/instructional media design; information science/studies; management information systems.

UNIFICATION THEOLOGICAL SEMINARY

Barrytown, New York

http://www.uts.edu

Unification Theological Seminary was founded in 1975. It is accredited by Middle States Association of Colleges and Schools. It first offered distance learning courses in 1994. In fall 2010, there were 30 students enrolled in distance learning courses. Institutionally administered financial aid is available to distance learners.

Services Distance learners have accessibility to academic advising, bookstore, e-mail services, library services.

Contact Mrs. Davetta Ogunlola, Director of Admissions, Unification Theological Seminary, 4 West 43rd Street, New York, NY 10036. Telephone: 212-563-6647 Ext. 105. Fax: 212-563-6431. E-mail: d.ogunlola@uts.edu.

DEGREES AND AWARDS

Programs offered do not lead to a degree or other formal award.

COURSE SUBJECT AREAS OFFERED OUTSIDE OF DEGREE PROGRAMS

Graduate—biblical studies; history; languages (East Asian); philosophy; philosophy and religious studies related; theological and ministerial studies.

Non-credit—biblical studies; history; languages (East Asian); philosophy; philosophy and religious studies related; theological and ministerial studies.

UNION COLLEGE

Barbourville, Kentucky

http://online.unionky.edu/

Union College was founded in 1879. It is accredited by Southern Association of Colleges and Schools. It first offered distance learning courses in 2003. In fall 2010, there were 564 students enrolled in distance learning courses. Institutionally administered financial aid is available to distance learners.

Services Distance learners have accessibility to academic advising, bookstore, campus computer network, career placement assistance, e-mail services, library services.

Contact Dr. Jerry Jackson, Dean of Enrollment, Union College, Union College, 310 College Street, Barbourville, KY 40906. Telephone: 606-546-4151. E-mail: jjackson@unionky.edu.

DEGREES AND AWARDS

MA Education; Psychology

COURSE SUBJECT AREAS OFFERED OUTSIDE OF DEGREE PROGRAMS

Undergraduate—psychology; psychology related.

Graduate—psychology; psychology related.

UNION COUNTY COLLEGE

Cranford, New Jersey

http://www.ucc.edu/DistanceEducation

Union County College was founded in 1933. It is accredited by Middle States Association of Colleges and Schools. It first offered distance learning courses in 1991. In fall 2010, there were 6,646 students enrolled in distance learning courses. Institutionally administered financial aid is available to distance learners.

Services Distance learners have accessibility to academic advising, bookstore, campus computer network, e-mail services, library services, tutoring.

Contact Dr. Barbara Gaba, Provost and Associate Vice President of Academic Affairs, Union County College, 40 West Jersey Street, Elizabeth, NJ 07201. Telephone: 908-965-6091.

DEGREES AND AWARDS

AAS Business Management; Computer Science
AS Information Systems Technology; Liberal Studies
Certificate Office Professional

COURSE SUBJECT AREAS OFFERED OUTSIDE OF DEGREE PROGRAMS

Undergraduate—accounting and related services; allied health and medical assisting services; American Sign Language (ASL); astronomy and astrophysics; biology; business administration, management and operations; business, management, and marketing related; chemistry; communication and media; computer and information sciences; computer science; criminal justice and corrections; drafting/design engineering technologies; economics; engineering; English; fine and studio arts; history; liberal arts and sciences, general studies and humanities; mathematics; physical sciences; physics; political science and government; psychology; sociology.

UNION INSTITUTE & UNIVERSITY
Cincinnati, Ohio
http://www.myunion.edu

Union Institute & University was founded in 1969. It is accredited by North Central Association of Colleges and Schools. It first offered distance learning courses in 1993. In fall 2010, there were 1,800 students enrolled in distance learning courses. Institutionally administered financial aid is available to distance learners.
Services Distance learners have accessibility to academic advising, bookstore, career placement assistance, e-mail services, library services.
Contact Admissions, Union Institute & University, 440 East McMillan Street, Cincinnati, OH 45206. Telephone: 800-486-3116. Fax: 513-861-0779. E-mail: admissions@myunion.edu.

DEGREES AND AWARDS

BA Liberal Arts and Sciences
BS Multiple majors
MA Arts and Social Sciences (multiple concentrations)
MEd Education
EdD Education
PhD Interdisciplinary Studies
Psy D Psychology

COURSE SUBJECT AREAS OFFERED OUTSIDE OF DEGREE PROGRAMS

Undergraduate—liberal arts and sciences, general studies and humanities.
Graduate—education; psychology.

UNION PRESBYTERIAN SEMINARY
Richmond, Virginia
http://www.upsem.edu

Union Presbyterian Seminary was founded in 1812. It is accredited by Southern Association of Colleges and Schools. It first offered distance learning courses in 1988. In fall 2010, there were 25 students enrolled in distance learning courses. Institutionally administered financial aid is available to distance learners.
Services Distance learners have accessibility to academic advising, campus computer network, e-mail services, library services.
Contact Mrs. Kate Fiedler Boswell, Director of Admissions, Union Presbyterian Seminary, 3401 Brook Road, Richmond, VA 23227. Telephone: 804-278-4222. Fax: 800-665-8679. E-mail: kboswell@upsem.edu.

DEGREES AND AWARDS

MACE Christian Education

COURSE SUBJECT AREAS OFFERED OUTSIDE OF DEGREE PROGRAMS

Graduate—pastoral counseling and specialized ministries; religious education; theology and religious vocations related.
Non-credit—religious education; religious studies; theology and religious vocations related.

UNION UNIVERSITY
Jackson, Tennessee
http://www.uu.edu/

Union University was founded in 1823. It is accredited by Southern Association of Colleges and Schools. It first offered distance learning courses in 1999. In fall 2010, there were 3,500 students enrolled in distance learning courses. Institutionally administered financial aid is available to distance learners.
Services Distance learners have accessibility to academic advising, bookstore, campus computer network, career placement assistance, e-mail services, library services.
Contact Ms. Robin Navel, Director of Online Instruction and Training, Union University, 1050 Union University Drive, Jackson, TN 38305. Telephone: 731-661-5402. E-mail: rnavel@uu.edu.

DEGREES AND AWARDS

BSN Nursing
EdD Higher Education–School Administration

COURSE SUBJECT AREAS OFFERED OUTSIDE OF DEGREE PROGRAMS

Undergraduate—accounting and computer science; behavioral sciences; biological and physical sciences; business, management, and marketing related; computer science; education; library science and administration; management information systems; marketing; mathematics and computer science; medical clinical sciences/graduate medical studies; physical science technologies; physics; psychology; religious studies.
Graduate—education; educational administration and supervision; educational assessment, evaluation, and research; health professions related; religious studies.
Non-credit—religious studies.

UNITED STATES SPORTS ACADEMY
Daphne, Alabama
Continuing Education and Distance Learning
http://www.ussa.edu

United States Sports Academy was founded in 1972. It is accredited by Southern Association of Colleges and Schools. It first offered distance learning courses in 1995. In fall 2010, there were 1,200 students enrolled in distance learning courses. Institutionally administered financial aid is available to distance learners.
Services Distance learners have accessibility to academic advising, bookstore, campus computer network, e-mail services, library services, tutoring.
Contact Dr. Craig Bogar, Dean of Student Services, United States Sports Academy, One Academy Drive, Daphne, AL 36526-7055. Telephone: 800-223-2668 Ext. 7147. Fax: 251-625-1035. E-mail: cbogar@ussa.edu.

DEGREES AND AWARDS

BS Sports Coaching; Sports Management; Sports Studies
Certification Coaching–National Coaching certification; International Sport diploma; Sports Coaching (International certification); Sports Coaching; Sports Management (International certification); Sports Management; Sports Medicine
MSS Sports Coaching; Sports Fitness; Sports Management; Sports Medicine; Sports Studies
EdD Sports Management–Olympic emphasis; Sports Management

COURSE SUBJECT AREAS OFFERED OUTSIDE OF DEGREE PROGRAMS

Undergraduate—business, management, and marketing related; health and physical education/fitness.

Graduate—business administration, management and operations; entrepreneurial and small business operations; health and physical education/fitness; health professions related; marketing.

Non-credit—business, management, and marketing related; health and physical education/fitness; parks, recreation and leisure; parks, recreation and leisure facilities management; parks, recreation, leisure, and fitness studies related.

UNIVERSIDAD DEL TURABO

Gurabo, Puerto Rico

Universidad del Turabo was founded in 1972. It is accredited by Middle States Association of Colleges and Schools. It first offered distance learning courses in 2001. In fall 2010, there were 140 students enrolled in distance learning courses. Institutionally administered financial aid is available to distance learners.

Services Distance learners have accessibility to academic advising, campus computer network, e-mail services, library services.

Contact Dr. Vigin A. Dones, Associate Dean of Business Administration, Universidad del Turabo, PO Box 3030, University Station, Gurabo, PR 00778. Telephone: 787-743-7979 Ext. 4978. E-mail: vdones@suagm.edu.

DEGREES AND AWARDS

MBA Business Administration

UNIVERSITY AT ALBANY, STATE UNIVERSITY OF NEW YORK

Albany, New York

http://www.albany.edu/its/distance_learning.htm

University at Albany, State University of New York was founded in 1844. It is accredited by Middle States Association of Colleges and Schools. In fall 2010, there were 600 students enrolled in distance learning courses. Institutionally administered financial aid is available to distance learners.

Services Distance learners have accessibility to academic advising, bookstore, e-mail services, library services.

Contact Admissions, University at Albany, State University of New York, Albany, NY 12222. E-mail: ugadmissions@albany.edu or graduate@uamail.albany.edu.

DEGREES AND AWARDS

Certificate Public Health–Fundamentals and Principles

MS Childhood Education (Literacy); Curriculum Development and Instructional Technology; Early Childhood (Literacy)

COURSE SUBJECT AREAS OFFERED OUTSIDE OF DEGREE PROGRAMS

Undergraduate—anthropology; astronomy and astrophysics; business administration, management and operations; communication and journalism related; communication and media; computer and information sciences; computer/information technology administration and management; computer programming; computer science; criminal justice and corrections; criminology; curriculum and instruction; English; history; intercultural/multicultural and diversity studies; mathematics; music; physics; political science and government; social sciences; social sciences related; sociology.

Graduate—computer and information sciences; computer and information sciences and support services related; computer/information technology administration and management; information science/studies; social work.

THE UNIVERSITY OF AKRON

Akron, Ohio

Information Services

http://www.uakron.edu

The University of Akron was founded in 1870. It is accredited by North Central Association of Colleges and Schools. It first offered distance learning courses in 1994. In fall 2010, there were 27,000 students enrolled in distance learning courses. Institutionally administered financial aid is available to distance learners.

Services Distance learners have accessibility to academic advising, bookstore, campus computer network, career placement assistance, e-mail services, library services, tutoring.

Contact Ms. Holly Harris Bane, Associate Vice President, Strategic Initiatives and Engagement, The University of Akron, Buchtel Hall 102, Akron, OH 44325-4703. Telephone: 330-972-7508. Fax: 330-972-8699. E-mail: harrisb@uakron.edu.

DEGREES AND AWARDS

MET Educational/Instructional Technology (Masters in Instructional Technology)

MS Education; Nursing; Social Work

COURSE SUBJECT AREAS OFFERED OUTSIDE OF DEGREE PROGRAMS

Undergraduate—accounting and related services; allied health and medical assisting services; allied health diagnostic, intervention, and treatment professions; anthropology; archeology; Army ROTC; astronomy and astrophysics; audiovisual communications technologies; behavioral sciences; bilingual, multilingual, and multicultural education; biochemistry, biophysics and molecular biology; biological and physical sciences; biology; botany/plant biology; business administration, management and operations; business/commerce; business/corporate communications; business, management, and marketing related; business/managerial economics; business operations support and assistant services; cell biology and anatomical sciences; chemistry; city/urban, community and regional planning; civil engineering; civil engineering technologies; communication and journalism related; communication and media; community organization and advocacy; computer and information sciences; computer science; computer software and media applications; computer systems networking and telecommunications; criminal justice and corrections; criminology; curriculum and instruction; design and applied arts; drama/theatre arts and stagecraft; economics; education; educational administration and supervision; educational assessment, evaluation, and research; educational/instructional media design; education related; education (specific levels and methods); education (specific subject areas); engineering related; engineering technology; English; English language and literature related; English or French as a second or foreign language (teaching); ethnic, cultural minority, gender, and group studies; family and consumer sciences/human sciences; finance and financial management services; fire protection; foods, nutrition, and related services; geography and cartography; geological and earth sciences/geosciences; health and medical administrative services; health/medical preparatory programs; health professions related; health services/allied health/health sciences; history; homeland security, law enforcement, firefighting and protective services related; hospitality administration; human resources management; journalism; languages (East Asian); languages (Germanic); languages (Romance languages); liberal arts and sciences, general studies and humanities; linguistic, comparative, and related language studies; mathematics; mathematics and computer science; mathematics and statistics related; microbiological sciences and immunology; music; peace studies and conflict resolution; pharmacy, pharmaceutical sciences, and administration; philosophy; philosophy and religious studies related; physical sciences; physical sciences related; political science and government; polymer/plastics engineering; psychology; public administration; public administration and social service professions related; real estate; sales merchandising, and related marketing operations (general); sales, merchandising and related marketing operations (specialized); social and philosophical foundations of education; social sciences; social work; sociology; special education; statistics; taxation; urban studies/affairs; visual and performing arts; zoology/animal biology.

Graduate—accounting and related services; applied mathematics; bilingual, multilingual, and multicultural education; business administration, management and operations; communication disorders sciences and services; computer and information sciences; computer software and media applications; curriculum and instruction; drama/theatre arts and stagecraft; economics; education; educational administration and supervision; educational assessment, evaluation, and research; educational/instructional media design; education related; education (specific levels and methods); education (specific subject areas); engineering; English; English language and literature related; health professions related; history; human resources management; human services; information science/studies; legal research and advanced professional studies; mathematics; mathematics and computer science; mathematics and statistics related; political science and government; psychology; psychology related; public administration; public health; social and philosophical foundations of education; social work; special education; statistics; taxation; urban studies/affairs.

Non-credit—allied health and medical assisting services; business administration, management and operations; business/commerce; communications technology; computer and information sciences; computer and information sciences and support services related; computer/information technology administration and management; computer programming; computer science; computer software and media applications; computer systems analysis; computer systems networking and telecommunications; curriculum and instruction; data entry/microcomputer applications; data processing; educational/instructional media design; education related; education (specific levels and methods); entrepreneurial and small business operations; health aides/attendants/orderlies; health and medical administrative services; health and physical education/fitness; health/medical preparatory programs; health professions related; human resources management; information science/studies.

THE UNIVERSITY OF ALABAMA IN HUNTSVILLE
Huntsville, Alabama
Engineering Management Distance Learning Programs
http://www.engdl.uah.edu/

The University of Alabama in Huntsville was founded in 1950. It is accredited by Southern Association of Colleges and Schools. It first offered distance learning courses in 1992. In fall 2010, there were 294 students enrolled in distance learning courses. Institutionally administered financial aid is available to distance learners.

Services Distance learners have accessibility to academic advising, bookstore, campus computer network, career placement assistance, e-mail services, library services.

Contact Dr. Sherri Restauri Carson, Program Manager for Distance Learning College of Engineering, The University of Alabama in Huntsville, N147 Olin B. King Technology Hall, 301 Sparkman Drive, Huntsville, AL 35899. Telephone: 256-824-7391. Fax: 256-824-6608. E-mail: sherri.restauri@uah.edu.

DEGREES AND AWARDS

MS Modeling and Simulation; Operations Research; Software Engineering

MSE Engineering Management; Industrial Engineering; Missile Systems Engineering; Rotorcraft Systems Engineering; Systems Engineering

PhD Engineering Management; Industrial Engineering; Systems Engineering

COURSE SUBJECT AREAS OFFERED OUTSIDE OF DEGREE PROGRAMS

Graduate—accounting and related services; aerospace, aeronautical and astronautical engineering; behavioral sciences; business administration, management and operations; business, management, and marketing related; business/managerial economics; civil engineering; civil engineering technologies; computer engineering; computer engineering technologies; computer science; economics; engineering; engineering mechanics; environmental/environmental health engineering; industrial engineering; management sciences and quantitative methods; manufacturing engineering; marketing; materials sciences; mathematics and statistics related; mechanical engineering; operations research; psychology; psychology related; quality control and safety technologies; statistics; systems engineering.

UNIVERSITY OF ALASKA FAIRBANKS
Fairbanks, Alaska
Center for Distance Education and Independent Learning
http://distance.uaf.edu

University of Alaska Fairbanks was founded in 1917. It is accredited by Northwest Commission on Colleges and Universities. It first offered distance learning courses in 1964. In fall 2010, there were 1,763 students enrolled in distance learning courses. Institutionally administered financial aid is available to distance learners.

Services Distance learners have accessibility to academic advising, bookstore, campus computer network, e-mail services, library services, tutoring.

Contact Krystal Huwe, Communications, University of Alaska Fairbanks, PO Box 756700, Fairbanks, AK 99775. Telephone: 800-277-8060. Fax: 907-479-3443. E-mail: distance@uaf.edu.

DEGREES AND AWARDS

AAS Applied Business

COURSE SUBJECT AREAS OFFERED OUTSIDE OF DEGREE PROGRAMS

Undergraduate—accounting and computer science; accounting and related services; allied health and medical assisting services; allied health diagnostic, intervention, and treatment professions; anthropology; applied mathematics; astronomy and astrophysics; behavioral sciences; bilingual, multilingual, and multicultural education; biological and physical sciences; biology; botany/plant biology; business administration, management and operations; business/commerce; business, management, and marketing related; business/managerial economics; business operations support and assistant services; clinical, counseling and applied psychology; cognitive science; communication and journalism related; communication and media; communications technologies and support services related; communications technology; computational science; computer and information sciences; computer and information sciences and support services related; computer engineering; computer programming; computer science; computer software and media applications; criminal justice and corrections; criminology; curriculum and instruction; data entry/microcomputer applications; data processing; design and applied arts; drafting/design engineering technologies; drama/theatre arts and stagecraft; economics; education; educational administration and supervision; educational assessment, evaluation, and research; education related; English; English language and literature related; entrepreneurial and small business operations; ethnic, cultural minority, gender, and group studies; film/video and photographic arts; finance and financial management services; fine and studio arts; fishing and fisheries sciences and management; food science and technology; foods, nutrition, and related services; geography and cartography; geological and earth sciences/geosciences; gerontology; health and medical administrative services; health/medical preparatory programs; health professions related; health services/allied health/health sciences; history; human development, family studies, and related services; human resources management; information science/studies; intercultural/multicultural and diversity studies; interdisciplinary studies; international business; journalism; languages (classics and classical); languages (Romance languages); legal studies (nonprofessional general, undergraduate); liberal arts and sciences, general studies and humanities; library science and administration; library science related; linguistic, comparative, and related language studies; literature; management information systems; management sciences and quantitative methods; marine sciences; marketing; mathematics; mathematics and computer science; mathematics and statistics related; mental and social health services and allied professions; music; natural resources and conservation related; natural resources management and policy; natural sciences; nutrition sciences; philosophy and religious studies related; physical sciences; physical sciences related; political science and government; practical nursing, vocational nursing and nursing assistants; psychology; psychology related; public administration; public administration and social service professions related; public health; public relations, advertising, and applied communication related; radio, television, and digital communication; real estate; real estate development; rehabilitation and therapeutic professions; research and experimental psychology; rhetoric and composition/writing studies; rural sociology; sales merchandising, and related marketing operations (general); social

and philosophical foundations of education; social sciences; social sciences related; social work; sociology; sociology and anthropology; statistics; teaching assistants/aides; visual and performing arts related; wildlife and wildlands science and management; work and family studies.
Graduate—computer and information sciences; curriculum and instruction; educational administration and supervision; education related; education (specific levels and methods); human development, family studies, and related services; intercultural/multicultural and diversity studies; legal professions and studies related; psychology; psychology related.

UNIVERSITY OF ALASKA, PRINCE WILLIAM SOUND COMMUNITY COLLEGE
Valdez, Alaska
http://www.pwscc.edu

University of Alaska, Prince William Sound Community College was founded in 1978. It is accredited by Northwest Commission on Colleges and Universities. It first offered distance learning courses in 1996. In fall 2010, there were 200 students enrolled in distance learning courses. Institutionally administered financial aid is available to distance learners.
Services Distance learners have accessibility to academic advising, bookstore, e-mail services, library services.
Contact Ms. Robyn Paul, Advisor, University of Alaska, Prince William Sound Community College, PO Box 97, Valdez, AK 99686. Telephone: 907-834-1626. Fax: 907-834-1691. E-mail: rkpaul@pwscc.edu.

DEGREES AND AWARDS
AA General Studies

COURSE SUBJECT AREAS OFFERED OUTSIDE OF DEGREE PROGRAMS
Undergraduate—accounting and computer science; allied health and medical assisting services; allied health diagnostic, intervention, and treatment professions; behavioral sciences; biology; communication and media; communication disorders sciences and services; computer and information sciences; English language and literature related; human services; liberal arts and sciences, general studies and humanities; outdoor education; parks, recreation and leisure facilities management.

UNIVERSITY OF ALBERTA
Edmonton, Alberta, Canada
Master of Arts in Communications & Technology
http://www.mact.ca

University of Alberta was founded in 1906. It is provincially chartered. It first offered distance learning courses in 2000. In fall 2010, there were 90 students enrolled in distance learning courses. Institutionally administered financial aid is available to distance learners.
Services Distance learners have accessibility to academic advising, bookstore, campus computer network, career placement assistance, e-mail services, library services, tutoring.
Contact Eileen Crookes, Program Coordinator, University of Alberta, 10230 Jasper Avenue, Edmonton, AB T5J 4P6, Canada. Telephone: 780-492-1501. Fax: 780-492-0627. E-mail: eileen.crookes@ualberta.ca.

DEGREES AND AWARDS
MA Communications and Technology

THE UNIVERSITY OF ARIZONA
Tucson, Arizona
Extended University, Distance Learning Program
http://www.outreachcollege.arizona.edu/dist/

The University of Arizona was founded in 1885. It is accredited by North Central Association of Colleges and Schools. It first offered distance learning courses in 1972. In fall 2010, there were 900 students enrolled in distance learning courses. Institutionally administered financial aid is available to distance learners.
Services Distance learners have accessibility to bookstore, campus computer network, e-mail services, library services.
Contact Colleen Reed, Program Coordinator, The University of Arizona, PO Box 210158, University Services Building, Room 301, Tucson, AZ 85721-0158. Telephone: 520-626-2079. Fax: 520-626-1102. E-mail: distance@email.arizona.edu.

DEGREES AND AWARDS
Graduate Certificate Digital Information Management; Gerontology; Optical Sciences
MEngr Engineering
MS Optical Sciences

COURSE SUBJECT AREAS OFFERED OUTSIDE OF DEGREE PROGRAMS
Undergraduate—agriculture; agriculture and agriculture operations related; behavioral sciences; computer science; family and consumer sciences/human sciences; history.
Graduate—education (specific levels and methods); engineering; engineering mechanics; gerontology; industrial engineering; library science and administration; mechanical engineering; public health; special education.

THE UNIVERSITY OF ARIZONA
Tucson, Arizona
Independent Study through Correspondence
http://www.outreachcollege.arizona.edu

The University of Arizona was founded in 1885. It is accredited by North Central Association of Colleges and Schools. It first offered distance learning courses in 1915. In fall 2010, there were 1,600 students enrolled in distance learning courses. Institutionally administered financial aid is available to distance learners.
Services Distance learners have accessibility to bookstore, e-mail services, library services.
Contact Mrs. Tammy Weingart, Office Specialist, The University of Arizona, University Services Building, 888 North Euclid, #301, Tucson, AZ 85721. Telephone: 520-626-4228. Fax: 520-626-3269. E-mail: tjweinga@email.arizona.edu.

DEGREES AND AWARDS
Programs offered do not lead to a degree or other formal award.

COURSE SUBJECT AREAS OFFERED OUTSIDE OF DEGREE PROGRAMS
Undergraduate—accounting and computer science; animal sciences; anthropology; atmospheric sciences and meteorology; cell biology and anatomical sciences; civil engineering technologies; family and consumer sciences/human sciences business services; geography and cartography; geological and earth sciences/geosciences; history; mathematics; physics; political science and government; psychology; sociology.
Graduate—family and consumer economics; geological and earth sciences/geosciences.

UNIVERSITY OF ARKANSAS AT LITTLE ROCK
Little Rock, Arkansas
Extended Programs
http://ualr.edu/extendedprograms

University of Arkansas at Little Rock was founded in 1927. It is accredited by North Central Association of Colleges and Schools. It first offered distance learning courses in 1975. In fall 2010, there were 4,935 students enrolled in distance learning courses. Institutionally administered financial aid is available to distance learners.
Services Distance learners have accessibility to academic advising, bookstore, e-mail services, library services.
Contact Donna Rae Eldridge, Director of Online and Off-Campus Programs, University of Arkansas at Little Rock, UALR Extended Programs, 2801 South University Avenue, Little Rock, AR 72204. Telephone: 501-569-3003. Fax: 501-569-8560. E-mail: dreldridge@ualr.edu.

DEGREES AND AWARDS

BA Criminal Justice; Liberal Arts; Mathematics
BBA Management
BS Community Health Promotion; Mathematics
BSN Nursing
MA Orientation and Mobility; Rehabilitation Counseling
MEd Learning Systems Technology
MS Criminal Justice

COURSE SUBJECT AREAS OFFERED OUTSIDE OF DEGREE PROGRAMS

Undergraduate—accounting and related services; American Sign Language (ASL); anthropology; archeology; astronomy and astrophysics; atmospheric sciences and meteorology; biology; botany/plant biology; building/construction finishing, management, and inspection; business administration, management and operations; business, management, and marketing related; communication and journalism related; communication and media; construction management; construction trades related; criminal justice and corrections; criminology; data entry/microcomputer applications; economics; education; education related; education (specific levels and methods); English; English language and literature related; ethnic, cultural minority, gender, and group studies; finance and financial management services; foods, nutrition, and related services; genetics; geography and cartography; geological and earth sciences/geosciences; gerontology; health and physical education/fitness; health professions related; health services/allied health/health sciences; history; human resources management; journalism; languages (foreign languages related); liberal arts and sciences, general studies and humanities; management information systems; marketing; mathematics; mathematics and statistics related; multi/interdisciplinary studies related; music; philosophy; philosophy and religious studies related; physical sciences; physical sciences related; political science and government; psychology; psychology related; real estate; religious studies; social work; sociology; statistics.
Graduate—biology; business administration, management and operations; business, management, and marketing related; criminal justice and corrections; economics; education; educational administration and supervision; educational assessment, evaluation, and research; educational/instructional media design; education related; education (specific levels and methods); English; finance and financial management services; gerontology; history; human resources management; languages (foreign languages related); marketing; mathematics; political science and government; real estate; rehabilitation and therapeutic professions; social and philosophical foundations of education; social work; special education.

UNIVERSITY OF ATLANTA
Atlanta, Georgia
http://www.uofa.edu

University of Atlanta is accredited by Distance Education and Training Council. It first offered distance learning courses in 2006. In fall 2010, there were 792 students enrolled in distance learning courses. Institutionally administered financial aid is available to distance learners.
Services Distance learners have accessibility to academic advising, bookstore, campus computer network, career placement assistance, e-mail services, library services, tutoring.
Contact Bill Kay, Vice President for Enrollment Management, University of Atlanta, University Headquarters, 6685 Peachtree Industrial Boulevard, Atlanta, GA 30360. Telephone: 404-424-8410 Ext. 3131. E-mail: bkay@uofa.edu.

DEGREES AND AWARDS

BS Business Administration–Finance; Business Administration–International Business; Business Administration–Management; Business Administration–Marketing; Computer Science; Criminal Justice; Healthcare Administration; Human Resource Management; Management Information Systems
EMBA Business Administration
Graduate Certificate Healthcare Administration; Information Technology for Management; Program Management master certificate
MBA Business Administration
MS Business Administration–Finance; Business Administration–International Business; Business Administration–Management; Business Administration–Marketing; Computer Science; Criminal Justice; Educational Leadership; Healthcare Administration; Human Resource Management; Management Information Systems
DBA Managerial Science

COURSE SUBJECT AREAS OFFERED OUTSIDE OF DEGREE PROGRAMS

Undergraduate—health professions related; information science/studies.

UNIVERSITY OF BALTIMORE
Baltimore, Maryland
UBOnline
http://www.ubalt.edu/admissions

University of Baltimore was founded in 1925. It is accredited by Middle States Association of Colleges and Schools. It first offered distance learning courses in 1999. In fall 2010, there were 1,800 students enrolled in distance learning courses. Institutionally administered financial aid is available to distance learners.
Services Distance learners have accessibility to academic advising, bookstore, campus computer network, career placement assistance, e-mail services, library services, tutoring.
Contact Lenora Giles, ELearning Counselor, University of Baltimore, 1420 North Charles Street, Baltimore, MD 21201. Telephone: 877-APPLY-UB. Fax: 410-837-4793. E-mail: admissions@ubalt.edu.

DEGREES AND AWARDS

BS Business Administration
MBA Business Administration
MPA Public Administration

COURSE SUBJECT AREAS OFFERED OUTSIDE OF DEGREE PROGRAMS

Undergraduate—health and medical administrative services.
Graduate—health and medical administrative services; legal professions and studies related.

UNIVERSITY OF BRIDGEPORT
Bridgeport, Connecticut
Office of Distance Learning
http://www.bridgeport.edu/online

University of Bridgeport was founded in 1927. It is accredited by New England Association of Schools and Colleges. It first offered distance learning courses in 1997. In fall 2010, there were 350 students enrolled in distance learning courses. Institutionally administered financial aid is available to distance learners.
Services Distance learners have accessibility to academic advising, bookstore, campus computer network, e-mail services, library services, tutoring.
Contact Claude A. Perrottet, Coordinator, Distance Learning Programs, University of Bridgeport, 126 Park Avenue, Bridgeport, CT 06604. Telephone: 203-576-4853. Fax: 203-576-4537. E-mail: ubonline@bridgeport.edu.

DEGREES AND AWARDS

BS Dental Hygiene Online (degree completion program); General Studies
Certification Marriage Education (for credit); Marriage Education (non-credit)
MS Computer Science; Dental Hygiene; Human Nutrition; Technology Management

COURSE SUBJECT AREAS OFFERED OUTSIDE OF DEGREE PROGRAMS

Undergraduate—business/commerce; business, management, and marketing related; dental support services and allied professions; economics; entrepreneurial and small business operations; foods, nutrition, and related services; history; human development, family studies, and related services; human services; liberal arts and sciences, general studies and

humanities; mathematics and statistics related; music; philosophy; philosophy and religious studies related; political science and government; psychology; religious studies; sales merchandising, and related marketing operations (general); social sciences; sociology.
Graduate—foods, nutrition, and related services.
Non-credit—human development, family studies, and related services.

THE UNIVERSITY OF BRITISH COLUMBIA
Vancouver, British Columbia, Canada
Distance Education and Technology
http://ctlt.ubc.ca

The University of British Columbia was founded in 1915. It is provincially chartered. It first offered distance learning courses in 1949. In fall 2010, there were 6,000 students enrolled in distance learning courses. Institutionally administered financial aid is available to distance learners.
Services Distance learners have accessibility to academic advising, bookstore, campus computer network, career placement assistance, e-mail services, library services, tutoring.
Contact Paul Poole, Program Manager, Non-degree Studies, The University of British Columbia, Enrollment Services, 1874 East Mall, Room 2016, Brock Hall, Vancouver, BC V6T 1Z1, Canada. Telephone: 604-822-9836. Fax: 604-822-5945. E-mail: paul.poole@ubc.ca.

DEGREES AND AWARDS
Programs offered do not lead to a degree or other formal award.

COURSE SUBJECT AREAS OFFERED OUTSIDE OF DEGREE PROGRAMS
Undergraduate—agricultural business and management; agriculture; allied health diagnostic, intervention, and treatment professions; animal sciences; area studies; biology; civil engineering; computer and information sciences; dental support services and allied professions; English; environmental control technologies; ethnic, cultural minority, gender, and group studies; film/video and photographic arts; foods, nutrition, and related services; forestry; geography and cartography; geological and earth sciences/geosciences; history; landscape architecture; languages (East Asian); languages (Romance languages); library science related; medical clinical sciences/graduate medical studies; medieval and Renaissance studies; metallurgical engineering; music; philosophy; political science and government; psychology; rehabilitation and therapeutic professions; social work; soil sciences.
Graduate—library science related; medical clinical sciences/graduate medical studies.

UNIVERSITY OF CALGARY
Calgary, Alberta, Canada
Teaching and Learning Centre at University of Calgary
http://tlc.ucalgary.ca

University of Calgary was founded in 1945. It is provincially chartered. It first offered distance learning courses in 1977.
Services Distance learners have accessibility to academic advising, bookstore, campus computer network, career placement assistance, e-mail services, library services.
Contact J. Carruthers, E-Learning Coordinator, University of Calgary, 2500 University Drive NW, Calgary, AB T2N 1N4, Canada. Telephone: 403-220-7364. E-mail: carruthe@ucalgary.ca.

DEGREES AND AWARDS
BCR Community Rehabilitation
Certificate Adult Learning, Adult and Community Education specialization; Adult Learning, Workplace Learning specialization; Adult Learning, e-Learning specialization; Human Resource Management; Security Management certificate; Teacher Assistant; Teaching Second Language
MEd Education–Master of Education

COURSE SUBJECT AREAS OFFERED OUTSIDE OF DEGREE PROGRAMS
Undergraduate—social work.

Graduate—education; educational administration and supervision; educational assessment, evaluation, and research; educational/instructional media design; social work.
Non-credit—education (specific levels and methods).

UNIVERSITY OF CALIFORNIA, DAVIS
Davis, California
UC Davis Extension
http://extension.ucdavis.edu/unit/online_learning/

University of California, Davis was founded in 1905. It is accredited by Western Association of Schools and Colleges. It first offered distance learning courses in 1987. In fall 2010, there were 600 students enrolled in distance learning courses. Institutionally administered financial aid is available to distance learners.
Services Distance learners have accessibility to academic advising, bookstore, library services.
Contact Bill Heekin, Director of Student Services, University of California, Davis, 1333 Research Park Drive, Davis, CA 95618. Telephone: 530-757-8777. Fax: 530-757-8696. E-mail: bheekin@ucde.ucdavis.edu.

DEGREES AND AWARDS
Programs offered do not lead to a degree or other formal award.

COURSE SUBJECT AREAS OFFERED OUTSIDE OF DEGREE PROGRAMS
Undergraduate—computer systems analysis; education; education (specific subject areas); food science and technology; health professions related; languages (Romance languages); legal professions and studies related; legal support services; management sciences and quantitative methods; natural resources and conservation related; natural resources management and policy; peace studies and conflict resolution; public health.
Non-credit—allied health and medical assisting services; construction trades related; education; education related; education (specific levels and methods); food science and technology; health professions related; languages (Romance languages); legal professions and studies related; legal support services; natural resources management and policy; public health.

UNIVERSITY OF CALIFORNIA, RIVERSIDE
Riverside, California
University Extension
http://www.extension.ucr.edu

University of California, Riverside was founded in 1954. It is accredited by Western Association of Schools and Colleges. It first offered distance learning courses in 1994. In fall 2010, there were 650 students enrolled in distance learning courses. Institutionally administered financial aid is available to distance learners.
Services Distance learners have accessibility to academic advising, bookstore, library services.
Contact Brian Reilly, Distance Learning Coordinator, University of California, Riverside, 1200 University Avenue, Riverside, CA 92507. Telephone: 951-827-1067. E-mail: breilly@ucx.ucr.edu.

DEGREES AND AWARDS
Programs offered do not lead to a degree or other formal award.

COURSE SUBJECT AREAS OFFERED OUTSIDE OF DEGREE PROGRAMS
Non-credit—agriculture and agriculture operations related; applied horticulture and horticultural business services; atmospheric sciences and meteorology; computer software and media applications; education related; geography and cartography; plant sciences.

UNIVERSITY OF CENTRAL FLORIDA
Orlando, Florida
Center for Distributed Learning
http://online.ucf.edu

University of Central Florida was founded in 1963. It is accredited by Southern Association of Colleges and Schools. It first offered distance learning courses in 1996. In fall 2010, there were 20,053 students enrolled in distance learning courses. Institutionally administered financial aid is available to distance learners.

Services Distance learners have accessibility to academic advising, bookstore, campus computer network, e-mail services, library services.

Contact Mr. Robert Reed, Associate Director, University of Central Florida, 3100 Technology Parkway, Suite 234, Orlando, FL 32826-3271. Telephone: 407-823-4910. Fax: 407-207-4911. E-mail: reed@ucf.edu.

DEGREES AND AWARDS

BA Interdisciplinary Studies; Political Science

BS Health Services Administration; Interdisciplinary Studies; Technical Education and Industry Training

BSN Nursing

Graduate Certificate Applied Operations Research; Autism Spectrum Disorders; Community College Education; Construction Engineering; Corrections Leadership; Design for Usability; Gifted Education; Health Care Informatics; Industrial Ergonomics and Safety; Initial Teacher Professional Preparation; Instructional Design for Simulations; Instructional/Educational Technology; Mathematics; Nonprofit Management; Nursing Education; Nursing–Clinical Nurse Leader; Police Leadership; Pre-Kindergarten Handicapped endorsement; Professional Writing; Project Engineering; Public Administration; Quality Assurance; Special Education; Structural Engineering; Systems Engineering; Systems Simulation for Engineers; Transportation Engineering; Urban Education; e-Learning Professional Development

MA Applied Learning and Instruction; Career and Technical Education; English, Technical Communication track; Instructional Technology/Media

MEd Exceptional Education

MM Nonprofit Management

MS Civil Engineering; Criminal Justice; Digital Forensics; Environmental Engineering; Forensic Science; Health Sciences, Executive Health Services Administration; Industrial Engineering

MSAE Aerospace Engineering

MSCE Civil Engineering

MSME Mechanical Engineering

MSN Nursing

PSM Health Care Informatics; Modeling and Simulation

DNP Nursing Practice

COURSE SUBJECT AREAS OFFERED OUTSIDE OF DEGREE PROGRAMS

Undergraduate—history; legal professions and studies related; philosophy and religious studies related; psychology; sociology; statistics.

UNIVERSITY OF CINCINNATI
Cincinnati, Ohio
Distance Learning Programs
http://www.uc.edu/distance

University of Cincinnati was founded in 1819. It is accredited by North Central Association of Colleges and Schools. It first offered distance learning courses in 1984. Institutionally administered financial aid is available to distance learners.

Services Distance learners have accessibility to academic advising, bookstore, campus computer network, e-mail services, library services, tutoring.

Contact Dr. Melody Clark, Academic Director, Distance Learning, University of Cincinnati, PO Box 210635, Cincinnati, OH 45221-0635. E-mail: melody.clark@uc.edu.

DEGREES AND AWARDS

AAS Early Childhood Education; Fire Science Technology

BEd Early Childhood Education

BS Clinical Laboratory Science; Fire Science Technology; Health Information Management; Special Education–Sign Language Interpreting track (Bachelor completion program); Substance Abuse Counseling

Certificate Curriculum and Instruction in Medical Education for Healthcare Professionals; Medical Biller/Coder; Postsecondary Literacy Instruction; Software Productivity

MEd Curriculum and Instruction (for Health Care Professionals); Curriculum and Instruction–General Studies; Educational Leadership

MS Criminal Justice; Pharmaceutical Sciences, Cosmetic Science emphasis

MSN Nurse Midwifery; Nursing Administration; Nursing–Adult Nurse Practitioner; Nursing–Clinical Nurse Specialist/Nurse Educator; Nursing–Family Nurse Practitioner; Nursing–Psychiatric Clinical Nurse Specialist; Nursing–Psychiatric Nurse Practitioner; Women's Health Nurse Practitioner

COURSE SUBJECT AREAS OFFERED OUTSIDE OF DEGREE PROGRAMS

Undergraduate—accounting and related services; anthropology; business/commerce; communication disorders sciences and services; computer and information sciences; computer software and media applications; criminal justice and corrections; economics; education; engineering related; English; geography and cartography; geological and earth sciences/geosciences; history; liberal arts and sciences, general studies and humanities; mathematics; philosophy; philosophy and religious studies related; psychology.

Graduate—communication disorders sciences and services; criminal justice and corrections; curriculum and instruction; education related; engineering related; pharmacy, pharmaceutical sciences, and administration.

Non-credit—accounting and computer science; accounting and related services; business/commerce; business operations support and assistant services; computer and information sciences; computer programming; publishing; real estate.

UNIVERSITY OF CINCINNATI RAYMOND WALTERS COLLEGE
Cincinnati, Ohio
Outreach and Continuing Education
http://www.rwc.uc.edu/oce/index.html

University of Cincinnati Raymond Walters College was founded in 1967. It is accredited by North Central Association of Colleges and Schools. It first offered distance learning courses in 1995. In fall 2010, there were 1,265 students enrolled in distance learning courses. Institutionally administered financial aid is available to distance learners.

Services Distance learners have accessibility to academic advising, bookstore, campus computer network, career placement assistance, e-mail services, library services, tutoring.

Contact Ms. Janice Ooten, Program Manager, University of Cincinnati Raymond Walters College, 9555 Plainfield Road, Cincinnati, OH 45236-1096. Telephone: 513-936-1533. Fax: 513-745-8315. E-mail: janice.ooten@uc.edu.

DEGREES AND AWARDS

Programs offered do not lead to a degree or other formal award.

COURSE SUBJECT AREAS OFFERED OUTSIDE OF DEGREE PROGRAMS

Undergraduate—allied health and medical assisting services; American Sign Language (ASL); audiovisual communications technologies; behavioral sciences; biology; business/commerce; business, management, and marketing related; computer/information technology administration and management; computer software and media applications; film/video and photographic arts; health professions related; nuclear and industrial radiologic technologies; psychology; sociology.

UNIVERSITY OF COLORADO AT COLORADO SPRINGS

Colorado Springs, Colorado

http://www.uccs.edu/distance

University of Colorado at Colorado Springs was founded in 1965. It is accredited by North Central Association of Colleges and Schools. It first offered distance learning courses in 1996. Institutionally administered financial aid is available to distance learners.

Services Distance learners have accessibility to academic advising, bookstore, campus computer network, e-mail services, library services.

Contact Ries Carley, Director, Campus Wide Extended Studies, University of Colorado at Colorado Springs, 1420 Austin Bluffs Parkway, Colorado Springs, CO 80918. Telephone: 719-255-5178. E-mail: carley.ries@uccs.edu.

DEGREES AND AWARDS

BA Nursing–RN to BSN
BA/BS Allied Health Completion
Endorsement Gifted and Talented Endorsement; Special Education Endorsement
License Principal Licensure; Principal Licensure
Graduate Certificate Correctional Health; Disaster Public Health; Early Literacy; Instructional Technology; International Business English certificate; Nursing Education; Nursing–Forensic Nursing; Nursing–Gerontological Nursing; Nursing–Holistic Nursing; Systems Engineering; Teaching English as a Second Language/Foreign Language
MA Curriculum and Instruction; Leadership Education and Principal licensure; Leadership; Special Education
MBA Business Administration
MBA/Certificate Business Administration; Finance; Healthcare Administration; International Business; Management; Marketing; Project Management; Space Systems Management; Technology Management
ME Engineering Management; Space Operations; Systems Engineering
MPA Public Administration
MSN Nurse Practitioner and Clinical Specialist
DNP Nursing

COURSE SUBJECT AREAS OFFERED OUTSIDE OF DEGREE PROGRAMS

Undergraduate—biological and biomedical sciences related; chemistry; communication and media; economics; geography and cartography; gerontology; health professions related; history; languages (Middle/Near Eastern and Semitic); mathematics; mechanical engineering; psychology; sociology.

Graduate—aerospace, aeronautical and astronautical engineering; business/commerce; criminal justice and corrections; educational administration and supervision; finance and financial management services; gerontology; health and medical administrative services; health professions related; mechanical engineering; pharmacy, pharmaceutical sciences, and administration; public administration.

Non-credit—accounting and computer science; accounting and related services; allied health and medical assisting services; business/corporate communications; communication and journalism related; computer and information sciences and support services related; computer programming; computer software and media applications; English language and literature related; graphic communications; health and medical administrative services; journalism.

UNIVERSITY OF COLORADO BOULDER

Boulder, Colorado

Center for Advanced Engineering and Technology Education (CAETE)

http://CUEngineeringOnline.colorado.edu

University of Colorado Boulder was founded in 1876. It is accredited by North Central Association of Colleges and Schools. It first offered distance learning courses in 1983. In fall 2010, there were 509 students enrolled in distance learning courses. Institutionally administered financial aid is available to distance learners.

Services Distance learners have accessibility to academic advising, bookstore, campus computer network, career placement assistance, e-mail services, library services.

Contact Robin M.W. McClanahan, Marketing Manager, University of Colorado Boulder, CAETE, 435 UCB, Boulder, CO 80309. Telephone: 303-492-0212. Fax: 303-492-5987. E-mail: caete@colorado.edu.

DEGREES AND AWARDS

Graduate Certificate Astrodynamics and Satellite Navigation Systems; Computer and Network Security; Computer and Network Security; Energy Communication Networks; Engineering Entrepreneurship; Engineering Management; Leadership and Ethical Decision Making; Managing Applied Research; Managing Research and Development; Network Architecture; Performance Excellence; Power Electronics; Project Management; Quality Systems and Engineering; Software Engineering; Technology Ventures and Product Management; Telecommunications Policy; Wireless Network and Technologies
ME Computer Science; Electrical and Computer Engineering; Engineering Management; Telecommunications
MS Aerospace Engineering; Electrical and Computer Engineering; Telecommunications

COURSE SUBJECT AREAS OFFERED OUTSIDE OF DEGREE PROGRAMS

Graduate—aerospace, aeronautical and astronautical engineering; biomedical/medical engineering; civil engineering; computer engineering; computer science; computer systems networking and telecommunications; electrical engineering technologies; engineering related; environmental/environmental health engineering; management sciences and quantitative methods; mechanical engineering.

Non-credit—aerospace, aeronautical and astronautical engineering; biomedical/medical engineering; civil engineering; computer engineering; computer science; computer systems networking and telecommunications; electrical engineering technologies; engineering related; environmental/environmental health engineering; management information systems; mechanical engineering.

UNIVERSITY OF DENVER

Denver, Colorado

University College

http://www.universitycollege.du.edu

University of Denver was founded in 1864. It is accredited by North Central Association of Colleges and Schools. It first offered distance learning courses in 1996. In fall 2010, there were 400 students enrolled in distance learning courses. Institutionally administered financial aid is available to distance learners.

Services Distance learners have accessibility to academic advising, bookstore, campus computer network, career placement assistance, e-mail services, library services.

Contact Mr. Mark Guthrie, Director of Enrollment and Advising, University of Denver, 2211 South Josephine, Denver, CO 80208. Telephone: 303-871-7582. Fax: 303-871-3070. E-mail: maguthri@du.edu.

DEGREES AND AWARDS

BA Degree completion program
Certificate Alternative Dispute Resolution; Applied Communication; Arts Development and Program Management; Arts, Literature, and Culture; Creative Writing; Database Design and Administration; Emergency Planning and Response; Energy and Sustainability; Environmental Assessment of Nuclear Power; Environmental Health and Safety; Environmental Management; Environmental Policy; Fundraising and Philanthropy; Geographic Information Systems; Global Human Resources; Global Issues; Healthcare Policy, Law, and Ethics; Human Capacity in Organizations; Human Resource Management and Development; Information Security; Information Systems Security; Knowledge Based Organizations; Medical and Healthcare Information Technologies; Natural Resource Management; Organizational Development and Training; Organizational Security; Project Management; Public Relations and Marketing; Software Design and Programming; Strategic Innovation and Change; Strategic Management of Healthcare; Technology Management; Telecommunications Management; Telecommunications Technology; Visual Art and Design; Web Design and Development; World History and Culture
MLS Arts and Culture; Global Affairs

MPS Healthcare Leadership; Leadership and Organizations; Organizational and Professional Communication; Strategic Human Resource Management
MS Geographic Information Science; Master of Applied Science in Environmental Policy and Management; Master of Applied Science in Information and Communications Technology; Master of Applied Science in Security Management

COURSE SUBJECT AREAS OFFERED OUTSIDE OF DEGREE PROGRAMS
Undergraduate—business/corporate communications; public policy analysis; science, technology and society; social sciences related.
Graduate—business administration, management and operations; communication and media; computer and information sciences; computer and information sciences and support services related; computer/information technology administration and management; computer systems networking and telecommunications; liberal arts and sciences, general studies and humanities; linguistic, comparative, and related language studies; natural resources management and policy.

UNIVERSITY OF DUBUQUE
Dubuque, Iowa
Professional Programs
http://www.dbq.edu/
University of Dubuque was founded in 1852. It is accredited by North Central Association of Colleges and Schools. It first offered distance learning courses in 2007. In fall 2010, there were 126 students enrolled in distance learning courses. Institutionally administered financial aid is available to distance learners.
Services Distance learners have accessibility to academic advising, bookstore, campus computer network, career placement assistance, e-mail services, library services, tutoring.
Contact Dr. Gail Hodge, Associate Dean for Professional Programs, University of Dubuque, 2000 University Avenue, Dubuque, IA 52001. Telephone: 563-589-3349. Fax: 563-589-3416. E-mail: ghodge@dbq.edu.

DEGREES AND AWARDS
Programs offered do not lead to a degree or other formal award.

COURSE SUBJECT AREAS OFFERED OUTSIDE OF DEGREE PROGRAMS
Undergraduate—air transportation; arts, entertainment, and media management; biology; business, management, and marketing related; communication and media; computer and information sciences; computer/information technology administration and management; criminology; design and applied arts; education; English language and literature related; environmental/environmental health engineering; history; marketing; mathematics; music; nutrition sciences; psychology; religious studies; rhetoric and composition/writing studies; sociology; special education.

UNIVERSITY OF DUBUQUE
Dubuque, Iowa
Theological Seminary
http://udts.dbq.edu/DistanceED.cfm
University of Dubuque was founded in 1852. It is accredited by North Central Association of Colleges and Schools. It first offered distance learning courses in 2000. In fall 2010, there were 210 students enrolled in distance learning courses. Institutionally administered financial aid is available to distance learners.
Services Distance learners have accessibility to academic advising, bookstore, campus computer network, career placement assistance, e-mail services, library services.
Contact Ms. Margaret (Peggy) Sell, Director of Seminary Admissions, University of Dubuque, 2000 University Avenue, Dubuque, IA 52001. Telephone: 800-369-8987. Fax: 563-589-3110. E-mail: psell@dbq.edu.

DEGREES AND AWARDS
Certificate Commissioned Lay Pastor
MAMC Missional Christianity
MDiv Distance M.Div.; Unclassified Student status

COURSE SUBJECT AREAS OFFERED OUTSIDE OF DEGREE PROGRAMS
Graduate—missionary studies and missiology; theological and ministerial studies.
Non-credit—biblical studies; pastoral counseling and specialized ministries; religious education; theology and religious vocations related.

UNIVERSITY OF EVANSVILLE
Evansville, Indiana
http://www.evansville.edu/
University of Evansville was founded in 1854. It is accredited by North Central Association of Colleges and Schools. It first offered distance learning courses in 2004. In fall 2010, there were 40 students enrolled in distance learning courses. Institutionally administered financial aid is available to distance learners.
Services Distance learners have accessibility to bookstore, campus computer network, e-mail services, library services.
Contact Mrs. Carla S. Doty, Director, Adult Education, University of Evansville, 1800 Lincoln Avenue, Evansville, IN 47722. Telephone: 812-488-2982. Fax: 812-488-2432. E-mail: cd39@evansville.edu.

DEGREES AND AWARDS
Programs offered do not lead to a degree or other formal award.

COURSE SUBJECT AREAS OFFERED OUTSIDE OF DEGREE PROGRAMS
Undergraduate—accounting and related services; business administration, management and operations; communication and media; curriculum and instruction; educational assessment, evaluation, and research; health/medical preparatory programs.
Graduate—health and medical administrative services.
Non-credit—accounting and computer science; allied health and medical assisting services; business operations support and assistant services; computer and information sciences and support services related; data entry/microcomputer applications; finance and financial management services.

THE UNIVERSITY OF FINDLAY
Findlay, Ohio
Global Campus
http://www.findlay.edu
The University of Findlay was founded in 1882. It is accredited by North Central Association of Colleges and Schools. It first offered distance learning courses in 1998. In fall 2010, there were 535 students enrolled in distance learning courses. Institutionally administered financial aid is available to distance learners.
Services Distance learners have accessibility to academic advising, bookstore, campus computer network, career placement assistance, e-mail services, library services, tutoring.
Contact Mrs. Heather L. Riffle, Assistant Director, Graduate and Professional Studies, The University of Findlay, 1000 North Main Street, Findlay, OH 45840. Telephone: 419-434-4600. Fax: 419-434-5517. E-mail: riffle@findlay.edu.

DEGREES AND AWARDS
BS Business Management; Environmental, Safety, and Health Management
MAE Education
MBA Business Administration
MS Environmental, Safety, and Health Management

COURSE SUBJECT AREAS OFFERED OUTSIDE OF DEGREE PROGRAMS

Undergraduate—accounting and related services; biblical studies; business administration, management and operations; business/commerce; business/managerial economics; chemistry; communication and journalism related; computer science; criminal justice and corrections; criminology; economics; ethnic, cultural minority, gender, and group studies; fine and studio arts; history; human resources management; international business; marketing; mathematics; philosophy and religious studies related; religious studies; social sciences; sociology; statistics; visual and performing arts.

Graduate—accounting and related services; business administration, management and operations; business/corporate communications; business/managerial economics; educational assessment, evaluation, and research; educational/instructional media design; environmental control technologies; human resources management; marketing; public administration; sales merchandising, and related marketing operations (general).

Non-credit—business, management, and marketing related; business/managerial economics; management information systems; management sciences and quantitative methods.

UNIVERSITY OF FLORIDA
Gainesville, Florida
Distance Learning
http://www.distancelearning.ufl.edu

University of Florida was founded in 1853. It is accredited by Southern Association of Colleges and Schools. It first offered distance learning courses in 1996. In fall 2010, there were 5,212 students enrolled in distance learning courses. Institutionally administered financial aid is available to distance learners.

Services Distance learners have accessibility to academic advising, bookstore, campus computer network, career placement assistance, e-mail services, library services, tutoring.

Contact Ken Nanni, Director, Distance Learning, University of Florida, PO Box 113172, Gainesville, FL 32611-3175. Telephone: 352-392-1711. E-mail: knanni@dce.ufl.edu.

DEGREES AND AWARDS

BS Applied Physiology and Kinesiology; Business Administration; Fire and Emergency Services; Health Education; Sports Management

Certificate Executive EMS Officer; Geomatics; Landscape Pest Management; Pest Control Technology; Urban Pest Management

Ed S Curriculum and Instruction; Special Education

Graduate Certificate Construction Project Management; Emergency Services Disaster Management; Environmental Forensics; Environmental Policy Management; Family Financial Planning; Forensic DNA and Serology; Forensic Death Investigation; Forensic Drug Chemistry; Forensic Toxicology; Geographic Information Systems; Geriatric Care Management; Health Care Risk Management; Landscape Pest Management; Non-Profit Management; Pest Control Technology; Pharmaceutical Chemistry; Public Health; Soil Ecosystems Services; Sustainable Construction; Sustainable Land Resources and Nutrient Management; Urban Pest Management; Wetland and Water Resource Management

MA Art Education; Latin

MBA Business Administration

MCM International Construction Management

MEd Curriculum and Instruction; Special Education

MHS Occupational Therapy

MS Agricultural Education and Communication; Architectural Studies–Sustainable Design; Civil Engineering; Computer Engineering; Electrical and Computer Engineering; Entomology; Environmental Engineering Sciences; Industrial and Systems Engineering; Information Systems and Operations Management; Materials Science and Engineering; Mechanical and Aerospace Engineering; Pest Management; Pharmaceutical Chemistry; Pharmaceutical Outcomes and Policy; Pharmaceutical Science–Forensic DNA and Serology; Pharmaceutical Science–Forensic Drug Chemistry; Pharmaceutical Science–Forensic Science; Soil and Water Science, Environmental Science; Veterinary Medical Sciences–Forensic Toxicology; Water, Wastewater, and Stormwater Engineering

MSWREE Water Resources Planning and Management

EdD Educational Leadership; Educational Technology; Higher Education Administration

PhD Audiology; Classical Civilization; Latin and Roman Studies

PharmD Pharmacy, First Professional degree; Pharmacy, Working Professional

COURSE SUBJECT AREAS OFFERED OUTSIDE OF DEGREE PROGRAMS

Undergraduate—agricultural and domestic animal services; agricultural and food products processing; agricultural business and management; agricultural production; agricultural public services; agriculture; agriculture and agriculture operations related; anthropology; applied horticulture and horticultural business services; applied mathematics; astronomy and astrophysics; biblical studies; biochemistry, biophysics and molecular biology; biology; botany/plant biology; business administration, management and operations; business/commerce; business, management, and marketing related; chemistry; communication and journalism related; communication and media; criminal justice and corrections; criminology; ecology, evolution, systematics, and population biology; economics; education; educational assessment, evaluation, and research; education (specific subject areas); English; English language and literature related; English or French as a second or foreign language (teaching); entrepreneurial and small business operations; finance and financial management services; fire protection; food science and technology; foods, nutrition, and related services; forestry; geography and cartography; geological and earth sciences/geosciences; gerontology; history; human development, family studies, and related services; human resources management; insurance; international business; journalism; languages (classics and classical); languages (Germanic); languages (Romance languages); legal studies (non-professional general, undergraduate); liberal arts and sciences, general studies and humanities; linguistic, comparative, and related language studies; management sciences and quantitative methods; marketing; mathematics; mathematics and statistics related; multi/interdisciplinary studies related; natural resources and conservation related; natural resources management and policy; nutrition sciences; parks, recreation and leisure; parks, recreation and leisure facilities management; parks, recreation, leisure, and fitness studies related; philosophy; philosophy and religious studies related; political science and government; psychology; psychology related; public administration; public relations, advertising, and applied communication related; real estate; religious studies; sales merchandising, and related marketing operations (general); social and philosophical foundations of education; social sciences related; sociology; soil sciences; statistics; textile sciences and engineering.

Graduate—agricultural business and management; agricultural mechanization; agricultural public services; agriculture; audiovisual communications technologies; biological and biomedical sciences related; biology/biotechnology laboratory technician; building/construction finishing, management, and inspection; business, management, and marketing related; civil engineering; classical and ancient studies; communication and media; communications technology; computer and information sciences; computer engineering; computer programming; computer science; computer software and media applications; computer systems analysis; computer systems networking and telecommunications; construction management; curriculum and instruction; ecology, evolution, systematics, and population biology; education; educational administration and supervision; educational assessment, evaluation, and research; educational/instructional media design; education related; education (specific levels and methods); education (specific subject areas); engineering; environmental control technologies; food science and technology; foods, nutrition, and related services; genetics; gerontology; health/medical preparatory programs; materials engineering; materials sciences; natural resources and conservation related; natural resources management and policy; parks, recreation and leisure facilities management; soil sciences; special education; statistics; veterinary biomedical and clinical sciences.

Non-credit—environmental control technologies; foods, nutrition, and related services; gerontology; insurance; medical clinical sciences/graduate medical studies; nutrition sciences; pharmacology and toxicology; pharmacy, pharmaceutical sciences, and administration.

UNIVERSITY OF FLORIDA
Gainesville, Florida
UF EDGE
http://www.ufedge.ufl.edu

University of Florida was founded in 1853. It is accredited by Southern Association of Colleges and Schools. It first offered distance learning courses in 1964. In fall 2010, there were 500 students enrolled in distance learning courses. Institutionally administered financial aid is available to distance learners.

Services Distance learners have accessibility to academic advising, bookstore, campus computer network, career placement assistance, e-mail services, library services, tutoring.

Contact Pamela Simon, Program Assistant, University of Florida, College of Engineering, 109 CSE, PO Box 116100, Gainesville, FL 32611-6100. Telephone: 352-392-9670. Fax: 352-846-2255. E-mail: phs@ufl.edu.

DEGREES AND AWARDS

MS Civil Engineering; Computer Engineering (Bioinformatics track); Computer Engineering (General track); Electrical and Computer Engineering; Environmental Engineering (Systems Ecology and Ecological Engineering track); Environmental Engineering (Water Resources Planning and Management track); Environmental Engineering (Water, Wastewater, and Stormwater Engineering track); Materials Science and Engineering; Mechanical and Aerospace Engineering (Dynamics and Control track); Mechanical and Aerospace Engineering (Fundamentals of Thermal Fluids Transport track); Mechanical and Aerospace Engineering (Solid Mechanics and Design track); Systems Engineering

COURSE SUBJECT AREAS OFFERED OUTSIDE OF DEGREE PROGRAMS

Graduate—civil engineering; computer engineering; engineering; environmental/environmental health engineering; industrial engineering; materials sciences; mechanical engineering; systems engineering.

Non-credit—aerospace, aeronautical and astronautical engineering; civil engineering; computer engineering; engineering; environmental/environmental health engineering; industrial engineering; materials engineering; materials sciences; mechanical engineering; systems engineering.

UNIVERSITY OF GREAT FALLS
Great Falls, Montana
Center for Distance Learning
http://www.ugf.edu/distancelearning/

University of Great Falls was founded in 1932. It is accredited by Northwest Commission on Colleges and Universities. It first offered distance learning courses in 1979. In fall 2010, there were 68 students enrolled in distance learning courses. Institutionally administered financial aid is available to distance learners.

Services Distance learners have accessibility to academic advising, bookstore, campus computer network, career placement assistance, e-mail services, library services, tutoring.

Contact Jim Gretch, Director of Distance Learning, University of Great Falls, 1301 20th Street South, Great Falls, MT 59405. Telephone: 406-791-5320. Fax: 406-791-5394. E-mail: jgretch@ugf.edu.

DEGREES AND AWARDS

AA Addictions Counseling; Criminal Justice; Paralegal Studies

BA Criminal Justice; Paralegal Studies; Psychology

MA Criminal Justice Administration; Secondary Teaching

MAM Organizational Management

COURSE SUBJECT AREAS OFFERED OUTSIDE OF DEGREE PROGRAMS

Undergraduate—biological and physical sciences; computer and information sciences; computer science; computer software and media applications; criminal justice and corrections; English; fine and studio arts; health and physical education/fitness; history; human services; legal studies (non-professional general, undergraduate); liberal arts and sciences, general studies and humanities; mathematics; mathematics and statistics related; natural sciences; philosophy and religious studies related; psychology; social sciences; sociology; theological and ministerial studies.

Graduate—criminal justice and corrections; education (specific levels and methods); human services; psychology.

UNIVERSITY OF HAWAII AT HILO
Hilo, Hawaii
http://hilo.hawaii.edu/academics/dl/

University of Hawaii at Hilo was founded in 1970. It is accredited by Western Association of Schools and Colleges. It first offered distance learning courses in 1994. Institutionally administered financial aid is available to distance learners.

Services Distance learners have accessibility to academic advising, bookstore, campus computer network, career placement assistance, e-mail services, library services.

Contact Dr. Candace Wheeler, Distance Learning Coordinator, University of Hawaii at Hilo, 200 West Kiwili Street, Hilo, HI 96720. Telephone: 808-974-7664. Fax: 808-933-8863. E-mail: mcandace@hawaii.edu.

DEGREES AND AWARDS

Programs offered do not lead to a degree or other formal award.

COURSE SUBJECT AREAS OFFERED OUTSIDE OF DEGREE PROGRAMS

Undergraduate—anthropology; behavioral sciences; education; geological and earth sciences/geosciences; health services/allied health/health sciences; marine sciences; psychology.

UNIVERSITY OF HOUSTON
Houston, Texas
Division of Educational Technology and Outreach
http://distance.uh.edu

University of Houston was founded in 1927. It is accredited by Southern Association of Colleges and Schools. It first offered distance learning courses in 1983. In fall 2010, there were 10,840 students enrolled in distance learning courses. Institutionally administered financial aid is available to distance learners.

Services Distance learners have accessibility to academic advising, bookstore, campus computer network, e-mail services, library services.

Contact Distance Education Student Services, University of Houston, Educational Technology and University Outreach, 111 C.N. Hilton, Houston, TX 77204-3051. Telephone: 713-743-3327. Fax: 713-743-3300. E-mail: deservices@uh.edu.

DEGREES AND AWARDS

BA History; Psychology

BS Psychology; Retailing and Consumer Science

MA Mathematics

MEd Physical Education

MS Future Studies

COURSE SUBJECT AREAS OFFERED OUTSIDE OF DEGREE PROGRAMS

Undergraduate—anthropology; communication and media; dance; English; health and physical education/fitness; history; hospitality administration; liberal arts and sciences, general studies and humanities; philosophy and religious studies related; sales, merchandising and related marketing operations (specialized).

Graduate—business/commerce; computer science; hospitality administration; human resources management; mathematics.

UNIVERSITY OF HOUSTON–DOWNTOWN
Houston, Texas
http://www.uhd.edu/academic/distance/welcome.html

University of Houston–Downtown was founded in 1974. It is accredited by Southern Association of Colleges and Schools. It first offered distance learning courses in 1994. In fall 2010, there were 3,326 students enrolled in distance learning courses. Institutionally administered financial aid is available to distance learners.

Services Distance learners have accessibility to academic advising, bookstore, campus computer network, career placement assistance, e-mail services, library services, tutoring.

Contact Mr. Louis Evans, Executive Director of Distance Education, University of Houston–Downtown, One Main Street, Suite S-950, Houston, TX 77002. Telephone: 713-221-8003. Fax: 713-221-8922. E-mail: evansl@uhd.edu.

DEGREES AND AWARDS
BA Interdisciplinary Studies; Mathematics
BAAS Applied Administration; Criminal Justice; Safety Management
BBA Accounting; Computer Information Systems; Finance; General Business; Management; Marketing; Supply Chain Management
BS Biological and Physical Sciences; Criminal Justice; Interdisciplinary Studies; Psychology
MAT Teaching
MSCJ Criminal Justice

COURSE SUBJECT AREAS OFFERED OUTSIDE OF DEGREE PROGRAMS
Undergraduate—accounting and related services; biology; business administration, management and operations; business, management, and marketing related; chemistry; communication and media; computer/information technology administration and management; computer science; criminal justice and corrections; drama/theatre arts and stagecraft; economics; education; engineering technology; English; finance and financial management services; fine and studio arts; history; languages (foreign languages related); liberal arts and sciences, general studies and humanities; management information systems; mathematics; music; natural sciences; philosophy; political science and government; psychology; social sciences; sociology; statistics.
Graduate—criminal justice and corrections.

UNIVERSITY OF HOUSTON–VICTORIA
Victoria, Texas
http://www.uhv.edu/

University of Houston–Victoria was founded in 1973. It is accredited by Southern Association of Colleges and Schools. It first offered distance learning courses in 1996. In fall 2010, there were 3,000 students enrolled in distance learning courses. Institutionally administered financial aid is available to distance learners.

Services Distance learners have accessibility to academic advising, bookstore, campus computer network, career placement assistance, e-mail services, library services, tutoring.

Contact Dr. Holly Verhasselt, Executive Assistant to Provost, University of Houston–Victoria, 3007 North Ben Wilson, Victoria, TX 77901-4450. Telephone: 361-570-4365. Fax: 361-580-5514. E-mail: verhasselth@uhv.edu.

DEGREES AND AWARDS
BA History
BBA Business, general; Management; Marketing
BS Criminal Justice; Psychology
MBA Business Administration; Global MBA
MEd Special Education
MS Computer Information System; Economic Development and Entrepreneurship

COURSE SUBJECT AREAS OFFERED OUTSIDE OF DEGREE PROGRAMS
Undergraduate—accounting and related services; biology; communication and journalism related; computer and information sciences; criminal justice and corrections; education; history; psychology.
Graduate—accounting and related services; business administration, management and operations; computer and information sciences; education; entrepreneurial and small business operations; history; psychology.

UNIVERSITY OF IDAHO
Moscow, Idaho
Engineering Outreach
http://eo.uidaho.edu

University of Idaho was founded in 1889. It is accredited by Northwest Commission on Colleges and Universities. It first offered distance learning courses in 1976. In fall 2010, there were 297 students enrolled in distance learning courses. Institutionally administered financial aid is available to distance learners.

Services Distance learners have accessibility to academic advising, bookstore, campus computer network, career placement assistance, e-mail services, library services.

Contact Ms. Diane Bancke, Administrative Manager, University of Idaho, Engineering Outreach, PO Box 441014, Moscow, ID 83844-1014. Telephone: 800-824-2889. Fax: 208-885-9249. E-mail: outreach@uidaho.edu.

DEGREES AND AWARDS
Certificate Analog Integrated Circuit Design; Applied Geotechnics; Electric Machines and Drives; Power System Protection and Relaying; Secure and Dependable Computing Systems; Semiconductor Theory and Devices; Six Sigma Innovation and Design; Statistics; Structural Engineering; Water Resources Engineering
MAT Teaching Mathematics
MEngr Biological and Agricultural Engineering (Water Management emphasis); Civil Engineering; Computer Engineering; Electrical Engineering; Engineering Management; Mechanical Engineering
MS Biological and Agricultural Engineering (Water Management emphasis); Computer Engineering; Computer Science; Electrical Engineering; Geological Engineering

COURSE SUBJECT AREAS OFFERED OUTSIDE OF DEGREE PROGRAMS
Undergraduate—agricultural engineering; applied mathematics; biology; civil engineering; computer engineering; computer science; computer systems networking and telecommunications; electrical, electronics and communications engineering; electrical engineering technologies; engineering; engineering science; engineering technology; environmental/environmental health engineering; materials engineering; mathematics; mathematics and computer science; mathematics and statistics related; mechanical engineering; mechanical engineering related technologies; psychology; statistics.
Graduate—accounting and computer science; agricultural engineering; applied mathematics; business administration, management and operations; business, management, and marketing related; civil engineering; computer engineering; computer science; electrical engineering technologies; engineering; engineering technology; environmental/environmental health engineering; geological/geophysical engineering; mathematics; mathematics and computer science; mathematics and statistics related; mechanical engineering; mechanical engineering related technologies; psychology; statistics.

UNIVERSITY OF IDAHO
Moscow, Idaho
Independent Study in Idaho
http://www.uidaho.edu/isi

University of Idaho was founded in 1889. It is accredited by Northwest Commission on Colleges and Universities. It first offered distance learning courses in 1973. In fall 2010, there were 779 students enrolled in distance learning courses. Institutionally administered financial aid is available to distance learners.

Services Distance learners have accessibility to bookstore, e-mail services, library services.

Contact Sherrie Metlen, Program Manager, University of Idaho, Independent Study in Idaho, PO Box 443081, Moscow, ID 83844-3081. Telephone: 877-464-3246. Fax: 208-885-5738. E-mail: indepst@uidaho.edu.

DEGREES AND AWARDS

Programs offered do not lead to a degree or other formal award.

COURSE SUBJECT AREAS OFFERED OUTSIDE OF DEGREE PROGRAMS

Undergraduate—accounting and computer science; accounting and related services; anthropology; behavioral sciences; business/commerce; computer programming; economics; education; education related; education (specific levels and methods); English; English language and literature related; environmental/environmental health engineering; family and consumer economics; family and consumer sciences/human sciences related; finance and financial management services; foods, nutrition, and related services; health professions related; history; human development, family studies, and related services; journalism; languages (classics and classical); languages (Germanic); languages (Romance languages); liberal arts and sciences, general studies and humanities; library science and administration; library science related; marketing; mathematics and statistics related; microbiological sciences and immunology; music; nutrition sciences; philosophy; philosophy and religious studies related; physics; political science and government; psychology; psychology related; real estate; social sciences; social sciences related; sociology; statistics; visual and performing arts related.

Graduate—library science and administration; library science related.

UNIVERSITY OF ILLINOIS AT CHICAGO

Chicago, Illinois

School of Continuing Studies

http://www.uiconline.uic.edu

University of Illinois at Chicago was founded in 1946. It is accredited by North Central Association of Colleges and Schools. It first offered distance learning courses in 1998. In fall 2010, there were 4,827 students enrolled in distance learning courses. Institutionally administered financial aid is available to distance learners.

Services Distance learners have accessibility to academic advising, bookstore, campus computer network, e-mail services, library services.

Contact UIC Online Programs, University of Illinois at Chicago, School of Continuing Studies, MC 140, 1333 South Halsted Street, Suite 205, Chicago, IL 60607. Telephone: 312-355-0423. Fax: 312-413-9730. E-mail: online@uic.edu.

DEGREES AND AWARDS

BBA Business Administration degree completion

BS Health Information Management degree completion

BSN Nursing–BSN Completion Program for RNs

Certificate Administrative Nursing Leadership; Advanced Practice Cardiometabolic; Advanced Practice Palliative Care; Bioinformatics; Clinical Research Methods; Community Public Health Practice, Advanced; Community Public Health Practice, basic; Educational Research Methods; Electromagnetics Technology; Emergency Management and Continuity Planning; Engineering Law and Management; Environmental Health Informatics; Health Informatics; Health Information Management; Nursing–Advanced Practice Forensic Nurse; Nursing–School Nurse; Patient Safety, Error Science, and Full Disclosure; Public Health Geographic Information Systems; Public Health Informatics; Public Health Management; Survey Research Methods; Teaching/Learning in Nursing and Health Sciences; Wireless Communications Technology; e-Government

MEd Measurement, Evaluation, Statistics and Assessment

MEngr Engineering

MHPE Health Professions Education

MPH Community Health Sciences; Health Policy and Administration; Public Health Informatics

MS Health Informatics; Patient Safety Leadership

PMC Health Informatics

DNP Nursing

COURSE SUBJECT AREAS OFFERED OUTSIDE OF DEGREE PROGRAMS

Undergraduate—business administration, management and operations; engineering; health professions related; health services/allied health/health sciences.

Graduate—accounting and related services; biomedical/medical engineering; business administration, management and operations; business/commerce; business, management, and marketing related; business/managerial economics; chemical engineering; clinical/medical laboratory science/research; computer and information sciences; computer science; economics; educational assessment, evaluation, and research; education (specific subject areas); electrical, electronics and communications engineering; electrical engineering technologies; engineering; engineering related; engineering technology; finance and financial management services; health professions related; health services/allied health/health sciences; information science/studies; marketing; medical illustration and informatics; pharmacy, pharmaceutical sciences, and administration; public administration; public health; social work; statistics.

Non-credit—allied health and medical assisting services; business administration, management and operations; business/commerce; business, management, and marketing related; health professions related; marketing; pharmacy, pharmaceutical sciences, and administration; public administration and social service professions related; public health; social work.

UNIVERSITY OF ILLINOIS AT SPRINGFIELD

Springfield, Illinois

Office of Technology-Enhanced Learning

http://online.uis.edu

University of Illinois at Springfield was founded in 1969. It is accredited by North Central Association of Colleges and Schools. It first offered distance learning courses in 1984. In fall 2010, there were 2,852 students enrolled in distance learning courses. Institutionally administered financial aid is available to distance learners.

Services Distance learners have accessibility to academic advising, bookstore, campus computer network, career placement assistance, e-mail services, library services, tutoring.

Contact Dr. Ray Schroeder, Director of Office of Technology and Enhanced Learning, University of Illinois at Springfield, OTEL, Brookens, Room 426, One University Plaza, MS BRK 425, Springfield, IL 62703-5407. Telephone: 217-206-7531. Fax: 217-206-7539. E-mail: schroeder.ray@uis.edu.

DEGREES AND AWARDS

BA English; History; Liberal Studies; Mathematical Sciences; Philosophy

BBA Business Administration

BS Computer Science

MA Environmental Studies–Sustainable Development and Policy; Legal Studies; Liberal and Integrative Studies; Teacher Leadership

MPA Public Administration

MPH Public Health

MS Computer Science; Human Services–Social Services Administration concentration; Management Information Systems

COURSE SUBJECT AREAS OFFERED OUTSIDE OF DEGREE PROGRAMS

Undergraduate—accounting and related services; biology; business administration, management and operations; business, management, and marketing related; chemistry; clinical/medical laboratory science/research; communication and journalism related; communication and media; computer science; criminal justice and corrections; economics; education related; English; fine and studio arts; history; languages (foreign languages related); legal studies (non-professional general, undergraduate); liberal arts and sciences, general studies and humanities; mathematics; multi/interdisciplinary studies related; philosophy; political science and government; psychology; psychology related; social work; sociology; visual and performing arts.

Graduate—biology; business administration, management and operations; communication and media; computer science; education related;

environmental/environmental health engineering; history; human services; legal professions and studies related; management information systems; political science and government; public administration; public administration and social service professions related; public health.

UNIVERSITY OF ILLINOIS AT URBANA–CHAMPAIGN
Champaign, Illinois
College of Engineering
http://online.engineering.illinois.edu

University of Illinois at Urbana–Champaign was founded in 1867. It is accredited by North Central Association of Colleges and Schools. It first offered distance learning courses in 1998. In fall 2010, there were 250 students enrolled in distance learning courses. Institutionally administered financial aid is available to distance learners.

Services Distance learners have accessibility to academic advising, bookstore, campus computer network, career placement assistance, e-mail services, library services.

Contact Mr. Frank M. Hoskinson, Interim Director of Engineering Online Programs, University of Illinois at Urbana–Champaign, Office of Continuing Engineering Education, 400 Engineering Hall, MC-268, 1308 West Green Street, Urbana, IL 61801. Telephone: 217-333-6634. Fax: 217-333-0015. E-mail: ocee@illinois.edu.

DEGREES AND AWARDS

Graduate Certificate Business Management for Engineers; Computer Security; Environmental and Water Resources Engineering; Information Systems; Materials Engineering; Materials Failure Analysis; Networks and Distributed Systems; Software Engineering; Strategic Technology Management; System Software; Systems Engineering

MCS Computer Science–Master of Computer Science

MSME Mechanical Engineering

COURSE SUBJECT AREAS OFFERED OUTSIDE OF DEGREE PROGRAMS

Undergraduate—business, management, and marketing related; electrical engineering technologies; engineering related; management sciences and quantitative methods.

Graduate—civil engineering; computer science; computer systems analysis; computer systems networking and telecommunications; data processing; engineering; entrepreneurial and small business operations; genetics; management sciences and quantitative methods; materials engineering; materials sciences; mathematics; mechanical engineering; systems engineering.

Non-credit—engineering; genetics; management sciences and quantitative methods; mechanical engineering.

UNIVERSITY OF ILLINOIS AT URBANA–CHAMPAIGN
Champaign, Illinois
Curriculum, Technology, and Education Reform Program
http://education.illinois.edu/online/cter/

University of Illinois at Urbana–Champaign was founded in 1867. It is accredited by North Central Association of Colleges and Schools. It first offered distance learning courses in 1999. In fall 2010, there were 48 students enrolled in distance learning courses. Institutionally administered financial aid is available to distance learners.

Services Distance learners have accessibility to academic advising, campus computer network, e-mail services, library services, tutoring.

Contact Ms. Helen Katz, Office Support Specialist, University of Illinois at Urbana–Champaign, Educational Psychology, 225 Education Building, 1310 South 6th Street, Champaign, IL 61820. Telephone: 217-333-5242. Fax: 217-244-7620. E-mail: hnkatz@illinois.edu.

DEGREES AND AWARDS

MEd Curriculum, Technology, and Education Reform (CTER); Quantitative Literacy

COURSE SUBJECT AREAS OFFERED OUTSIDE OF DEGREE PROGRAMS

Graduate—computer software and media applications; educational/instructional media design.

Non-credit—computer software and media applications; educational/instructional media design.

UNIVERSITY OF ILLINOIS AT URBANA–CHAMPAIGN
Champaign, Illinois
Graduate School of Library and Information Science
http://www.lis.illinois.edu/

University of Illinois at Urbana–Champaign was founded in 1867. It is accredited by North Central Association of Colleges and Schools. It first offered distance learning courses in 1996. In fall 2010, there were 400 students enrolled in distance learning courses. Institutionally administered financial aid is available to distance learners.

Services Distance learners have accessibility to academic advising, bookstore, campus computer network, career placement assistance, e-mail services, library services, tutoring.

Contact Penny Ames, GSLIS Admissions, University of Illinois at Urbana–Champaign, 501 East Daniel Street, Champaign, IL 61820. Telephone: 800-982-0914. Fax: 217-244-3302. E-mail: lis-apply@uiuc.edu.

DEGREES AND AWARDS

CAGS Library and Information Science

MS Library and Information Science

COURSE SUBJECT AREAS OFFERED OUTSIDE OF DEGREE PROGRAMS

Graduate—communications technology; computer and information sciences; computer/information technology administration and management; computer software and media applications; educational/instructional media design; library science and administration; science, technology and society.

Non-credit—computer and information sciences; library science and administration; science, technology and society.

UNIVERSITY OF ILLINOIS AT URBANA–CHAMPAIGN
Champaign, Illinois
Online & Continuing Education
http://oce.illinois.edu

University of Illinois at Urbana–Champaign was founded in 1867. It is accredited by North Central Association of Colleges and Schools. It first offered distance learning courses in 1995. Institutionally administered financial aid is available to distance learners.

Services Distance learners have accessibility to academic advising, bookstore, campus computer network, career placement assistance, e-mail services, library services, tutoring.

Contact Dr. Faye Lesht, Head, Academic Outreach, University of Illinois at Urbana–Champaign, 901 West University Avenue, MC-260, Urbana, IL 61801-2777. Telephone: 217-333-3061. Fax: 217-265-4114. E-mail: oce-info@illinois.edu.

DEGREES AND AWARDS

Certificate Environmental Sustainability; NetMath

Certification Library and Information Science, K-12

Endorsement Bilingual/ESL; Middle Grades

CAGS Educational Organization and Leadership; Library and Information Science

Graduate Certificate Business Management for Engineers; Community College Teaching and Learning; Computer Science/Computer Security; Computer Science/Information Systems; Computer Science/Networks and Distributed Systems; Computer Science/Software Engineering; Computer Science/System Software; Crop Sciences; Environmental and Water Resources Engineering; Horticulture; Human Resource Development;

Mechanical Engineering/Materials Failure Analysis; Mechanical Engineering/Materials; Strategic Technology Management; Systems Engineering; eLearning

MCS Computer Science

MEd Education Policy, Organization, and Leadership (EPOL), eLearning concentration; Education Psychology, Quantitative Literacy specialization; Educational Organization and Leadership, Educational Leadership and Policy emphasis; Educational Organization and Leadership/Educational Administration; Educational Policy Studies, Diversity and Equity Issues in Education emphasis; Educational Policy Studies, Global Studies in Education emphasis; Educational Policy Studies, New Learning and New Literacies emphasis; Educational Psychology, Curriculum, Technology, and Education Reform emphasis; Human Resource Education, Community College Teaching and Learning concentration; Human Resource Education, Health Profession Education emphasis; Human Resource Education, Human Resource Development concentration; Special Education

MLIS LEEP–Library and Information Science

MS Agricultural Education; Crop Sciences; Food Science and Human Nutrition; Health Communication; Natural Resources and Environmental Sciences; Recreation, Sport, and Tourism

MSME Mechanical Engineering

MSW Campus and Community track

EdD Educational Organization and Leadership (School Executive Leadership), Educational Administration concentration; Educational Organization and Leadership, Community College Executive Leadership with Higher Education concentration

COURSE SUBJECT AREAS OFFERED OUTSIDE OF DEGREE PROGRAMS

Undergraduate—agricultural business and management; agriculture and agriculture operations related; anthropology; atmospheric sciences and meteorology; biology; botany/plant biology; business administration, management and operations; business/corporate communications; business, management, and marketing related; chemistry; classical and ancient studies; communication and journalism related; communication and media; dance; economics; education; education related; education (specific subject areas); English; English language and literature related; ethnic, cultural minority, gender, and group studies; history; human development, family studies, and related services; intercultural/multicultural and diversity studies; international/global studies; journalism; languages (foreign languages related); languages (Romance languages); liberal arts and sciences, general studies and humanities; mathematics; mathematics and computer science; mathematics and statistics related; parks, recreation and leisure; physiology, pathology and related sciences; plant sciences; political science and government; psychology; psychology related; public relations, advertising, and applied communication related; sociology; sociology and anthropology; special education; visual and performing arts.

Graduate—agricultural and food products processing; agriculture; bilingual, multilingual, and multicultural education; computer and information sciences; computer/information technology administration and management; computer science; computer systems networking and telecommunications; curriculum and instruction; education; educational administration and supervision; educational assessment, evaluation, and research; education related; education (specific subject areas); engineering; engineering-related fields; engineering science; environmental/environmental health engineering; health and medical administrative services; health professions related; health services/allied health/health sciences; human resources management; international/global studies; liberal arts and sciences, general studies and humanities; library science and administration; library science related; materials engineering; mathematics; mechanical engineering; natural resources and conservation related; natural resources conservation and research; natural resources management and policy; parks, recreation and leisure; parks, recreation and leisure facilities management; parks, recreation, leisure, and fitness studies related; plant sciences; social work; sociology and anthropology; soil sciences; special education.

Non-credit—mathematics.

THE UNIVERSITY OF KANSAS
Lawrence, Kansas
http://www.ContinuingEd.ku.edu/is

The University of Kansas was founded in 1866. It is accredited by North Central Association of Colleges and Schools. In fall 2010, there were 2,000 students enrolled in distance learning courses. Institutionally administered financial aid is available to distance learners.

Services Distance learners have accessibility to academic advising, bookstore, library services.

Contact Enrollment Coordinator, The University of Kansas, KUCE Independent Study, 1515 Saint Andrews Drive, Lawrence, KS 66047. Telephone: 785-864-7886. Fax: 785-864-7895. E-mail: enroll@ku.edu.

DEGREES AND AWARDS

Programs offered do not lead to a degree or other formal award.

COURSE SUBJECT AREAS OFFERED OUTSIDE OF DEGREE PROGRAMS

Undergraduate—anthropology; atmospheric sciences and meteorology; biology; classical and ancient studies; curriculum and instruction; economics; English; ethnic, cultural minority, gender, and group studies; geography and cartography; geological and earth sciences/geosciences; history; human development, family studies, and related services; liberal arts and sciences, general studies and humanities; mathematics; political science and government; psychology; religious studies; sociology; statistics.

Graduate—behavioral sciences; curriculum and instruction; educational administration and supervision; history; psychology; special education.

UNIVERSITY OF LETHBRIDGE
Lethbridge, Alberta, Canada
http://www.uleth.ca/

University of Lethbridge was founded in 1967. It is provincially chartered. It first offered distance learning courses in 2001. In fall 2010, there were 482 students enrolled in distance learning courses. Institutionally administered financial aid is available to distance learners.

Services Distance learners have accessibility to academic advising, bookstore, campus computer network, career placement assistance, e-mail services, library services, tutoring.

Contact Inquiries, University of Lethbridge, 4401 University Drive, Lethbridge, AB T1K 3M4, Canada. Telephone: 403-329-2233. E-mail: inquiries@uleth.ca.

DEGREES AND AWARDS

Programs offered do not lead to a degree or other formal award.

COURSE SUBJECT AREAS OFFERED OUTSIDE OF DEGREE PROGRAMS

Undergraduate—arts, entertainment, and media management; computer software and media applications; education related; management information systems; management sciences and quantitative methods.

Graduate—education; educational administration and supervision; educational assessment, evaluation, and research; education related.

UNIVERSITY OF LOUISVILLE
Louisville, Kentucky
Division of Distance and Continuing Education
http://www.louisville.edu/online

University of Louisville was founded in 1798. It is accredited by Southern Association of Colleges and Schools. It first offered distance learning courses in 1992. In fall 2010, there were 2,000 students enrolled in distance learning courses. Institutionally administered financial aid is available to distance learners.

Services Distance learners have accessibility to academic advising, bookstore, campus computer network, career placement assistance, e-mail services, library services, tutoring.

Contact Shelly Reid, Program Coordinator Senior, University of Louisville, Office of Online Learning (Delphi Center), Burhans Hall, Shelby

Campus, Louisville, KY 40292. Telephone: 502-852-6456. Fax: 502-852-8573. E-mail: online@louisville.edu.

DEGREES AND AWARDS

BA Communication

BS Administration of Justice; Communication; Nursing–RN to Bachelor of Science in Nursing; Workforce Leadership

Certificate Equine Business

Graduate Certificate Data Mining; Network and Information Security

MA Higher Education Administration

MS Administration of Justice; Civil Engineering, Transportation Engineering specialization; Computer Science; Human Resource Education

COURSE SUBJECT AREAS OFFERED OUTSIDE OF DEGREE PROGRAMS

Undergraduate—anthropology; archeology; astronomy and astrophysics; behavioral sciences; drama/theatre arts and stagecraft; English; ethnic, cultural minority, gender, and group studies; geography and cartography; health and physical education/fitness; languages (classics and classical); philosophy; political science and government; psychology; sociology; statistics.

Graduate—bioethics/medical ethics; communication and media; education; educational administration and supervision; educational assessment, evaluation, and research; education related; human resources management; social work; special education.

Non-credit—business, management, and marketing related; human resources management.

UNIVERSITY OF MAINE
Orono, Maine
Continuing Education Division
http://LearnOnline.umaine.edu

University of Maine was founded in 1865. It is accredited by New England Association of Schools and Colleges. It first offered distance learning courses in 1989. In fall 2010, there were 4,000 students enrolled in distance learning courses. Institutionally administered financial aid is available to distance learners.

Services Distance learners have accessibility to academic advising, bookstore, campus computer network, e-mail services, library services.

Contact Jeffrey St. John, Director, Continuing and Distance Education, University of Maine, 5713 Chadbourne Hall, Orono, ME 04469-5713. Telephone: 207-581-3142. Fax: 207-581-3141. E-mail: jeffrey.stjohn@umit.maine.edu.

DEGREES AND AWARDS

BUS University Studies

Certificate Maine Studies

COURSE SUBJECT AREAS OFFERED OUTSIDE OF DEGREE PROGRAMS

Undergraduate—accounting and related services; area studies; biology; civil engineering technologies; communication disorders sciences and services; computer and information sciences and support services related; education (specific subject areas); English or French as a second or foreign language (teaching); ethnic, cultural minority, gender, and group studies; languages (foreign languages related); mechanical engineering; music; plant sciences; psychology; public administration; sociology; special education; visual and performing arts.

Graduate—animal sciences; anthropology; business/commerce; civil engineering; education; liberal arts and sciences, general studies and humanities; mechanical engineering; social work.

UNIVERSITY OF MAINE AT AUGUSTA
Augusta, Maine
University of Maine System Network for Education and Technology (UNET)
http://www.uma.maine.edu

University of Maine at Augusta was founded in 1965. It is accredited by New England Association of Schools and Colleges. It first offered distance learning courses in 1986. In fall 2010, there were 3,000 students enrolled in distance learning courses. Institutionally administered financial aid is available to distance learners.

Services Distance learners have accessibility to academic advising, bookstore, campus computer network, e-mail services, library services, tutoring.

Contact Sheri Fraser, Director of Academic and Career Advising, University of Maine at Augusta, 46 University Drive, Augusta, ME 04330. Telephone: 207-621-3390. Fax: 207-621-3171. E-mail: fraser@maine.edu.

DEGREES AND AWARDS

AA Liberal Studies

AS Business Administration; Computer Information Systems; Justice Studies; Library and Information Services; Medical Laboratory Technology; Mental Health and Human Services

BA Liberal Studies

BBA Business Administration

BS Accounting; Applied Science–Bachelor of Applied Science; Computer Information Systems; Justice Studies; Library and Information Services; Management; Mental Health and Human Services

COURSE SUBJECT AREAS OFFERED OUTSIDE OF DEGREE PROGRAMS

Undergraduate—accounting and related services; American Sign Language (ASL); anthropology; applied mathematics; behavioral sciences; business administration, management and operations; business/commerce; business/corporate communications; business, management, and marketing related; business/managerial economics; business operations support and assistant services; communication and media; computer and information sciences; computer and information sciences and support services related; computer software and media applications; criminal justice and corrections; criminology; economics; English; family and consumer sciences/human sciences; finance and financial management services; health professions related; history; human development, family studies, and related services; human resources management; human services; information science/studies; languages (Romance languages); liberal arts and sciences, general studies and humanities; library science and administration; library science related; management sciences and quantitative methods; marketing; mathematics; mathematics and statistics related; mental and social health services and allied professions; music; nutrition sciences; philosophy; physical sciences; political science and government; psychology; social sciences; social sciences related; sociology; statistics; taxation.

Non-credit—mental and social health services and allied professions; security policy and strategy.

UNIVERSITY OF MAINE AT FORT KENT
Fort Kent, Maine
http://www.umfk.maine.edu/distance/

University of Maine at Fort Kent was founded in 1878. It is accredited by New England Association of Schools and Colleges. It first offered distance learning courses in 1989. In fall 2010, there were 400 students enrolled in distance learning courses. Institutionally administered financial aid is available to distance learners.

Services Distance learners have accessibility to academic advising, bookstore, campus computer network, career placement assistance, e-mail services, library services, tutoring.

Contact Jill M. Cairns, Admissions Director, University of Maine at Fort Kent, 23 University Drive, Fort Kent, ME 04743. Telephone: 207-834-7602. Fax: 207-834-7609. E-mail: umfkadm@maine.edu.

DEGREES AND AWARDS

AA General Studies, Accounting Sequence; General Studies, Criminal Justice Sequence

AS Information Security

BS Business Management; Rural Public Safety Administration

BSN Nursing–RN to BSN

BUS University Studies

COURSE SUBJECT AREAS OFFERED OUTSIDE OF DEGREE PROGRAMS

Undergraduate—anthropology; astronomy and astrophysics; behavioral sciences; business/commerce; business, management, and marketing related; communication and media; computer and information sciences; criminal justice and corrections; economics; education related; education (specific levels and methods); English; geography and cartography; geological and earth sciences/geosciences; health professions related; history; liberal arts and sciences, general studies and humanities; music; philosophy; political science and government; psychology; public administration; public policy analysis; real estate; sociology; special education.

UNIVERSITY OF MAINE AT MACHIAS
Machias, Maine
Distance Learning
http://www.umm.maine.edu/distance-ed.html

University of Maine at Machias was founded in 1909. It is accredited by New England Association of Schools and Colleges. It first offered distance learning courses in 1990. In fall 2010, there were 900 students enrolled in distance learning courses. Institutionally administered financial aid is available to distance learners.

Services Distance learners have accessibility to academic advising, bookstore, campus computer network, career placement assistance, e-mail services, library services, tutoring.

Contact Linda Schofield, Instructional Technologist, University of Maine at Machias, Distance Education, Torrey Hall, 9 O'Brien Avenue, Machias, ME 04654. Telephone: 207-255-1241. Fax: 207-255-4864. E-mail: lschof@maine.edu.

DEGREES AND AWARDS

BA Psychology and Community Studies

BS Business and Entrepreneurial Studies

BUS Business; Special Education

Certificate of Completion Entrepreneurship

Certificate Human Resource Management; Marketing

COURSE SUBJECT AREAS OFFERED OUTSIDE OF DEGREE PROGRAMS

Undergraduate—accounting and computer science; American Sign Language (ASL); behavioral sciences; bioethics/medical ethics; business administration, management and operations; business/commerce; business, management, and marketing related; communication and media; criminology; curriculum and instruction; economics; education; education related; education (specific levels and methods); education (specific subject areas); English; English language and literature related; entrepreneurial and small business operations; film/video and photographic arts; foods, nutrition, and related services; health and physical education/fitness; history; human biology; human resources management; human services; liberal arts and sciences, general studies and humanities; literature; mathematics; molecular medicine; natural resources and conservation related; nutrition sciences; pharmacology and toxicology; philosophy; political science and government; psychology; psychology related; rural sociology; social sciences; sociology; sociology and anthropology; statistics.

UNIVERSITY OF MANAGEMENT AND TECHNOLOGY
Arlington, Virginia
http://www.umtweb.edu

University of Management and Technology was founded in 1998. It is accredited by Distance Education and Training Council. It first offered distance learning courses in 1998. In fall 2010, there were 6,820 students enrolled in distance learning courses. Institutionally administered financial aid is available to distance learners.

Services Distance learners have accessibility to academic advising, bookstore, library services, tutoring.

Contact Dr. J. Davidson Frame, Academic Dean, University of Management and Technology, 1901 Fort Myer Drive, Suite 700, Arlington, VA 22209. Telephone: 703-516-0035. Fax: 703-516-0985. E-mail: davidson.frame@umtweb.edu.

DEGREES AND AWARDS

ABA Business Administration

AS Computer Science; Criminal Justice; Engineering Management; General Studies; Information Technology

BBA Criminal Justice Administration; Engineering Management; Health Administration; Human Resources Management; Information Technology Management; International Management; Management; Marketing Management

BS Computer Science–Information Systems; Computer Science–Information Technology; Computer Science–Software Engineering; Computer Science; Criminal Justice; Engineering Management; General Studies; Health Administration; Information Technology

Certificate Business Management; Health Administration; Human Resources Management; Information Technology

Graduate Certificate Acquisition Management; Information Technology; Project Management; Public Administration

MBA Management; Project Management

MHA Health Administration

MPA Criminal Justice Administration; Public Administration

MS Information Technology–IT Management; Information Technology–IT Project Management; Information Technology–Management Information Systems

MSCJ Homeland Security

MSCS Computer Science; Software Engineering

MSE Engineering Management

MSM Acquisition Management; Criminal Justice Administration; Management; Project Management

DBA Business Administration

COURSE SUBJECT AREAS OFFERED OUTSIDE OF DEGREE PROGRAMS

Undergraduate—accounting and computer science; applied mathematics; behavioral sciences; business administration, management and operations; business, management, and marketing related; computer and information sciences; computer/information technology administration and management; computer programming; computer science; computer software and media applications; computer systems analysis; computer systems networking and telecommunications; criminal justice and corrections; criminology; economics; English; finance and financial management services; health professions related; history; human resources management; international business; international/global studies; management information systems; management sciences and quantitative methods; mathematics; psychology; public administration; science technologies related; science, technology and society; statistics.

Graduate—accounting and computer science; business administration, management and operations; business/commerce; criminal justice and corrections; criminology; economics; health professions related; linguistic, comparative, and related language studies; management information systems; psychology.

UNIVERSITY OF MANITOBA
Winnipeg, Manitoba, Canada
Distance and Online Education
http://www.umanitoba.ca/distance

University of Manitoba was founded in 1877. It is provincially chartered. It first offered distance learning courses in 1950. In fall 2010, there were 7,000 students enrolled in distance learning courses. Institutionally administered financial aid is available to distance learners.

Services Distance learners have accessibility to academic advising, bookstore, campus computer network, e-mail services, library services.

Contact Student Support, University of Manitoba, Distance and Online Education, 188D Extended Education Complex, Winnipeg, MB R3T 2N2, Canada. Telephone: 204-474-8012. Fax: 204-474-7660. E-mail: de_info@umanitoba.ca.

DEGREES AND AWARDS
BA General degree and Advanced degree; Geography
BSW Social Work
Graduate Certificate Education post-Baccalaureate diploma

UNIVERSITY OF MARY
Bismarck, North Dakota
http://www.umary.edu/

University of Mary was founded in 1959. It is accredited by North Central Association of Colleges and Schools. It first offered distance learning courses in 2005. In fall 2010, there were 750 students enrolled in distance learning courses. Institutionally administered financial aid is available to distance learners.

Services Distance learners have accessibility to academic advising, bookstore, campus computer network, career placement assistance, e-mail services, library services.

Contact Toni Stanton, Distance Education Administrative Assistant, University of Mary, 7500 University Drive, Bismarck, ND 58504. Telephone: 701-355-8353. Fax: 701-255-7687. E-mail: thstanton@umary.edu.

DEGREES AND AWARDS
BS Accounting; Business; College Studies; Marketing; Nursing; Organizational Leadership
MBA Accountancy; Executive MBA; Health Care Administration; Human Resource Management; Management
MEd Curriculum, Instruction and Assessment
MPM Project Management
MS Strategic Leadership
MSN Nurse Administrator; Nursing–Family Nurse Practitioner

COURSE SUBJECT AREAS OFFERED OUTSIDE OF DEGREE PROGRAMS
Undergraduate—accounting and related services; anthropology; arts, entertainment, and media management; business administration, management and operations; business, management, and marketing related; chemistry; communication and journalism related; computer/information technology administration and management; English language and literature related; history; mathematics and statistics related; philosophy; physiology, pathology and related sciences; political science and government; social sciences; sociology; theological and ministerial studies.
Graduate—philosophy; psychology.

UNIVERSITY OF MARYLAND, BALTIMORE
Baltimore, Maryland
Master's Program in Nursing
http://nursing.umaryland.edu/

University of Maryland, Baltimore was founded in 1807. It is accredited by Middle States Association of Colleges and Schools.

Services Distance learners have accessibility to academic advising, bookstore, campus computer network, career placement assistance, e-mail services, library services, tutoring.

Contact Dr. Patricia Morton, Associate Dean, Academic Affairs, University of Maryland, Baltimore, 655 West Lombard Street, Room 505K, Baltimore, MD 21201. Telephone: 410-706-4378. E-mail: morton@son.umaryland.edu.

DEGREES AND AWARDS
BSN Nursing–RN to BSN
MS Nursing
DNP Nursing
PhD Nursing

UNIVERSITY OF MARYLAND UNIVERSITY COLLEGE
Adelphi, Maryland
http://www.umuc.edu

University of Maryland University College was founded in 1947. It is accredited by Middle States Association of Colleges and Schools. It first offered distance learning courses in 1993. In fall 2010, there were 37,977 students enrolled in distance learning courses. Institutionally administered financial aid is available to distance learners.

Services Distance learners have accessibility to academic advising, bookstore, campus computer network, career placement assistance, e-mail services, library services, tutoring.

Contact Enrollment Specialist, University of Maryland University College, 3501 University Boulevard East, Adelphi, MD 20783. Telephone: 800-888-UMUC. Fax: 301-985-7884. E-mail: enroll@umuc.edu.

DEGREES AND AWARDS
BA Asian Studies; Communication Studies; English; History; Humanities
BS Accounting; Business Administration; Computer Information Technology; Computer Science; Computer Studies; Computer and Information Science; Criminal Justice; Emergency Management; Environmental Management; Finance; Fire Science; Gerontology; Global Business and Public Policy; Homeland Security; Human Resource Management; Information Systems Management; Investigative Forensics; Legal Studies; Management Studies; Marketing; Political Science; Psychology; Social Science
BSc Cybersecurity
Graduate Certificate Accounting and Information Technology; Accounting; Bioinformatics; Biotechnology Management; Chief Information Officer (CIO); Criminal Justice Management; Database Systems Technologies; Distance Education Leadership and E-learning; Distance Education, Globalization, and Development; E-Learning and Instructional Systems Design; Environmental Management; Financial Management in Organizations; Foundations of Distance Education and E-learning; Foundations of Human Resource Management; Foundations of Information Technology; Health Care Administration; Homeland Security Management; Informatics; Information Assurance; Integrated Direct Marketing; Integrative Supply Chain Management; International Marketing; International Trade; Leadership and Management; Library and Intellectual Property in DE and E-learning; Nonprofit and Association Financial Management; Policy and Management in Distance Education and E-learning; Project Management; Public Relations; Software Engineering; Systems Analysis; Teaching and Training at a Distance; Technology in Distance Education and E-learning; Telecommunications Management
MAT Teaching
MBA Business Administration
MDE Master of Distance Education and E-learning
MEd Instructional Technology
MIM International Management
MS Accounting and Financial Management; Accounting and Information Technology; Biotechnology; Cybersecurity Policy; Cybersecurity; Environmental Management; Financial Management and Information Systems; Health Administration Informatics; Health Care Administration; Information Technology; Management; Technology Management
DM Management

UNIVERSITY OF MARY WASHINGTON
Fredericksburg, Virginia
http://www.umw.edu/distance

University of Mary Washington was founded in 1908. It is accredited by Southern Association of Colleges and Schools. It first offered distance learning courses in 2008. In fall 2010, there were 152 students enrolled in distance learning courses. Institutionally administered financial aid is available to distance learners.

Services Distance learners have accessibility to academic advising, bookstore, campus computer network, career placement assistance, e-mail services, library services, tutoring.

Contact Dr. John Morello, Associate Provost, University of Mary Washington, 1301 College Avenue, Fredericksburg, VA 22401. Telephone: 540-654-1269. E-mail: jmorello@umw.edu.

DEGREES AND AWARDS
Programs offered do not lead to a degree or other formal award.

COURSE SUBJECT AREAS OFFERED OUTSIDE OF DEGREE PROGRAMS
Undergraduate—accounting and related services; business, management, and marketing related; computer science; economics; legal studies (nonprofessional general, undergraduate); psychology.

Graduate—business administration, management and operations; business/corporate communications; business, management, and marketing related; computer and information sciences; computer/information technology administration and management; curriculum and instruction; education; engineering; management information systems; management sciences and quantitative methods; marketing; special education.

UNIVERSITY OF MASSACHUSETTS BOSTON
Boston, Massachusetts
Corporate, Continuing and Distance Education
http://uc.umb.edu/dl

University of Massachusetts Boston was founded in 1964. It is accredited by New England Association of Schools and Colleges. It first offered distance learning courses in 2001. In fall 2010, there were 2,000 students enrolled in distance learning courses. Institutionally administered financial aid is available to distance learners.

Services Distance learners have accessibility to academic advising, bookstore, campus computer network, career placement assistance, e-mail services, library services, tutoring.

Contact Mr. Jason Mauricio Campos, Manager of Online Education, University of Massachusetts Boston, University College, 100 Morrissey Boulevard, Boston, MA 02125-3393. Telephone: 617-287-7912. Fax: 617-287-7922. E-mail: jason.campos@umb.edu.

DEGREES AND AWARDS
BA Community Studies completer program
BS Nursing–RN to BS
Certificate Fundamentals of Information Technology; Gerontological Social Policy; Gerontology–Frank J. Manning Certificate in Gerontology
Graduate Certificate Critical and Creative Thinking (Focus on Creativity at Work); Education–Adapting Curriculum Frameworks for All Learners; Education–Technology, Learning, and Leadership; Gerontology–Management of Aging Services track; Global Post-Disaster Studies (Reconstruction with Vulnerable Populations); Instructional Technology Design; Science in a Changing World; Special Education–Orientation and Mobility; Vision Rehabilitation Therapy specialization
MA Critical and Creative Thinking; Linguistics–Applied Linguistics, ESL concentration; Science in a Changing World
MEd Instructional Design; School Counseling; Special Education–Orientation and Mobility; Special Education–Teaching of Students with Visual Impairments; Vision Rehabilitation Therapy specialization
MS Family Therapy; Gerontology–Management of Aging Services track; Mental Health Counseling; Rehabilitation Counseling
PMC Nursing–Clinical Nurse Specialist (CNS) post-Masters; Nursing–Gerontological/Adult and Family Nurse Practitioner
DNP Nursing–post-Masters Doctor of Nursing Practice

COURSE SUBJECT AREAS OFFERED OUTSIDE OF DEGREE PROGRAMS
Undergraduate—anthropology; archeology; biology; business administration, management and operations; chemistry; classical and ancient studies; communication and media; community organization and advocacy; computer and information sciences; computer/information technology administration and management; criminal justice and corrections; economics; education related; English; environmental/environmental health engineering; geography and cartography; gerontology; health and physical education/fitness; history; international relations and national security studies; languages (classics and classical); languages (Romance languages); liberal arts and sciences, general studies and humanities; linguistic, comparative, and related language studies; management information systems; marketing; mathematics; music; natural resources and conservation related; nutrition sciences; philosophy; physics; political science and government; psychology; social sciences; sociology; statistics; visual and performing arts.

Graduate—classical and ancient studies; criminal justice and corrections; education; educational/instructional media design; education (specific subject areas); English; gerontology; history; international relations and national security studies; languages (classics and classical); languages (Romance languages); linguistic, comparative, and related language studies; marketing; natural resources conservation and research; psychology; rehabilitation and therapeutic professions; sociology; special education; statistics; student counseling and personnel services.

Non-credit—business, management, and marketing related; human services.

UNIVERSITY OF MASSACHUSETTS LOWELL
Lowell, Massachusetts
Continuing Studies and Corporate Education
http://continuinged.uml.edu/online

University of Massachusetts Lowell was founded in 1894. It is accredited by New England Association of Schools and Colleges. It first offered distance learning courses in 1995. In fall 2010, there were 4,000 students enrolled in distance learning courses. Institutionally administered financial aid is available to distance learners.

Services Distance learners have accessibility to academic advising, bookstore, campus computer network, e-mail services, library services.

Contact Amy Yacus, Assistant Director of Marketing and Outreach, University of Massachusetts Lowell, One University Avenue, Lowell, MA 01854-2881. Telephone: 800-480-3190. Fax: 978-934-4064. E-mail: amy_yacus@uml.edu.

DEGREES AND AWARDS
AS Information Technology
BA Liberal Arts (BLA); Psychology
BS Information Technology; Information Technology, Business minor
Certificate Contemporary Communications; Data/Telecommunications; Information Technology; Multimedia Applications; Paralegal Studies; Security Management and Homeland Security; UNIX; Website Design and Development
Graduate Certificate Behavioral Intervention in Autism; Clinical Pathology; Domestic Violence Prevention; Forensic Criminology; Foundations of Business; Laboratory and Biological Safety; Network Security; Plastics Engineering Fundamentals; Security Studies; Sleep and Sleep Disorders in Health and Disease; Systems Models and Management; Victim Studies
MA Criminal Justice
MBA Business Administration
MEd Curriculum and Instruction; Educational Administration; Reading and Language

COURSE SUBJECT AREAS OFFERED OUTSIDE OF DEGREE PROGRAMS
Non-credit—business administration, management and operations; business, management, and marketing related; educational/instructional media design; education related.

UNIVERSITY OF MEMPHIS
Memphis, Tennessee
Extended Programs
http://ecampus.memphis.edu

University of Memphis was founded in 1912. It is accredited by Southern Association of Colleges and Schools. It first offered distance learning courses in 1991. In fall 2010, there were 5,331 students enrolled in distance learning courses. Institutionally administered financial aid is available to distance learners.
Services Distance learners have accessibility to academic advising, bookstore, campus computer network, career placement assistance, e-mail services, library services, tutoring.
Contact Dr. Vicki Sallis Murrell, Assistant Dean, University of Memphis, 201 Brister Hall, Memphis, TN 38152. Telephone: 901-678-8900. Fax: 901-678-4049. E-mail: vmurrell@memphis.edu.

DEGREES AND AWARDS
BA African American Studies; Communication; English (African-American Literature and Technical Writing); History; Journalism (Public Relations concentration); Philosophy; Psychology
BBA Accountancy; Finance and Real Estate; Management Information Systems (MIS); Management; Marketing and Supply Chain Management
BSN Nursing–RN to BSN
Certificate Real Estate Professional certificate
Graduate Certificate Engineering Project Management; English as a Second Language (ESL); Instructional Design and Technology (IDT); Leadership; Literacy, Leadership, and Coaching; Local Government Management
MA English (ESL); History; Journalism; Liberal Studies
MAT Secondary Education; Special Education
MBA Business Administration
MHA Health Administration
MPH Public Health
MS Applied Computer Science; Educational Psychology; Health Promotion; ICL–Instruction and Curriculum Leadership, Reading concentration; ICL–Instruction and Curriculum Leadership, School Library Specialist; ICL–Instruction and Curriculum Leadership, Secondary; Instructional Design and Technology (IDT); Leadership; Sports Commerce
EdD Higher and Adult Education

COURSE SUBJECT AREAS OFFERED OUTSIDE OF DEGREE PROGRAMS
Undergraduate—biology; business administration, management and operations; business/corporate communications; computer and information sciences; computer/information technology administration and management; criminal justice and corrections; curriculum and instruction; English; fire protection; health and physical education/fitness; history; journalism; multi/interdisciplinary studies related; music; psychology; public administration; public relations, advertising, and applied communication related.
Graduate—communication and media; educational administration and supervision; educational/instructional media design; English; journalism; public relations, advertising, and applied communication related.
Non-credit—computer and information sciences; human resources management; human services.

UNIVERSITY OF MICHIGAN
Ann Arbor, Michigan
College of Engineering
http://interpro.engin.umich.edu

University of Michigan was founded in 1817. It is accredited by North Central Association of Colleges and Schools. It first offered distance learning courses in 1996. In fall 2010, there were 750 students enrolled in distance learning courses. Institutionally administered financial aid is available to distance learners.
Services Distance learners have accessibility to academic advising, bookstore, campus computer network, career placement assistance, e-mail services, library services, tutoring.
Contact Ed Borbely, Director, University of Michigan, CoE, 2401 Plymouth Road, Suite A/B, Ann Arbor, MI 48105-1093. Telephone: 734-647-7171. E-mail: borbely@umich.edu.

DEGREES AND AWARDS
ME Automotive Engineering; Energy Systems; Global Automotive and Manufacturing Engineering; Manufacturing Engineering; Pharmaceutical Engineering
MEngr Automotive Engineering

COURSE SUBJECT AREAS OFFERED OUTSIDE OF DEGREE PROGRAMS
Non-credit—finance and financial management services; health and medical administrative services; human computer interaction; industrial engineering; manufacturing engineering; mathematics and statistics related; nanotechnology; quality control and safety technologies.

UNIVERSITY OF MICHIGAN–DEARBORN
Dearborn, Michigan
http://www.engin.umd.umich.edu/DLN/

University of Michigan–Dearborn was founded in 1959. It is accredited by North Central Association of Colleges and Schools. It first offered distance learning courses in 2003. In fall 2010, there were 300 students enrolled in distance learning courses. Institutionally administered financial aid is available to distance learners.
Services Distance learners have accessibility to academic advising, bookstore, campus computer network, e-mail services, library services.
Contact Susan Guinn, Distance Learning Program Manager, University of Michigan–Dearborn, College of Engineering and Computer Science, 4901 Evergreen Road, 2010 PEC, Dearborn, MI 48128-1491. Telephone: 313-593-4000. Fax: 313-593-4070. E-mail: sguinn@umich.edu.

DEGREES AND AWARDS
MS Computer Information Science; Engineering Management; Information Systems and Technology; Program and Project Management; Software Engineering
MSE Automotive Systems Engineering; Computer Engineering; Electrical Engineering; Industrial and Systems Engineering; Mechanical Engineering

COURSE SUBJECT AREAS OFFERED OUTSIDE OF DEGREE PROGRAMS
Undergraduate—computer and information sciences; computer science.
Graduate—computer and information sciences; computer engineering; computer science; engineering; engineering science; mechanical engineering.
Non-credit—engineering science.

UNIVERSITY OF MICHIGAN–FLINT
Flint, Michigan
Distance Learning Program
http://online.umflint.edu/

University of Michigan–Flint was founded in 1956. It is accredited by North Central Association of Colleges and Schools. It first offered distance learning courses in 2000. In fall 2010, there were 3,446 students enrolled in distance learning courses. Institutionally administered financial aid is available to distance learners.
Services Distance learners have accessibility to academic advising, bookstore, campus computer network, career placement assistance, e-mail services, library services.
Contact Theresa Stevens, Assistant Director, University of Michigan–Flint, Office of Extended Learning, Flint, MI 48502. Telephone: 810-237-6600. Fax: 810-766-6803. E-mail: tmsteven@umflint.edu.

DEGREES AND AWARDS
BA Journalism
BAS Africana Studies, Communication, English, Healthcare, History or Psychology concentration
BBA Business Administration

BSN Nursing
Certificate Africana Studies
MA Technology in Education (Global)
MBA Business Administration
MPA Educational Administration–WebPlus! MPA Program
MS Computer and Information Systems
DNP Nursing Practice
DPT Transitional Doctor of Physical Therapy

COURSE SUBJECT AREAS OFFERED OUTSIDE OF DEGREE PROGRAMS

Undergraduate—accounting and related services; allied health diagnostic, intervention, and treatment professions; business/commerce; communication and journalism related; computer science; education; health and medical administrative services; health/medical preparatory programs; health professions related; history; information science/studies; journalism; languages (Romance languages); linguistic, comparative, and related language studies; management sciences and quantitative methods; marketing; mathematics; political science and government; public relations, advertising, and applied communication related; social sciences; social work; statistics; visual and performing arts.
Graduate—accounting and related services; business administration, management and operations; education; educational administration and supervision; health and medical administrative services; health professions related; human resources management; management sciences and quantitative methods; marketing.
Non-credit—accounting and related services; business administration, management and operations; business/commerce; business/corporate communications; business, management, and marketing related; computer software and media applications; educational administration and supervision; educational assessment, evaluation, and research; educational/instructional media design; education (specific subject areas); management information systems; sales, merchandising and related marketing operations (specialized); teaching assistants/aides.

UNIVERSITY OF MINNESOTA, CROOKSTON
Crookston, Minnesota
Office of Continuing Education
http://www.umcrookston.edu/online

University of Minnesota, Crookston was founded in 1966. It is accredited by North Central Association of Colleges and Schools. It first offered distance learning courses in 1990. In fall 2010, there were 750 students enrolled in distance learning courses. Institutionally administered financial aid is available to distance learners.
Services Distance learners have accessibility to academic advising, bookstore, campus computer network, career placement assistance, e-mail services, library services, tutoring.
Contact Michelle Christopherson, Director, Center for Adult Learning, University of Minnesota, Crookston, 208 Selvig Hall, 2900 University Avenue, Crookston, MN 56716-5001. Telephone: 218-281-8679. Fax: 218-281-8676. E-mail: mchristo@umn.edu.

DEGREES AND AWARDS

BS Accounting; Applied Health (BAH); Applied Studies Online; Business Online; Communication; Health Management; Information Technology Management; Manufacturing Management (BMM); Marketing

COURSE SUBJECT AREAS OFFERED OUTSIDE OF DEGREE PROGRAMS

Undergraduate—accounting and computer science; accounting and related services; agricultural and food products processing; biology; business administration, management and operations; computer and information sciences; data entry/microcomputer applications; data processing; economics; English language and literature related; entrepreneurial and small business operations; foods, nutrition, and related services; health and medical administrative services; history; industrial production technologies; information science/studies; management information systems; manufacturing engineering; marketing; mathematics; microbiological sciences and immunology; philosophy; physics; psychology; sociology; statistics.

UNIVERSITY OF MINNESOTA, DULUTH
Duluth, Minnesota
http://www.d.umn.edu/ce/distanceeducation/online/index.html

University of Minnesota, Duluth was founded in 1947. It is accredited by North Central Association of Colleges and Schools. It first offered distance learning courses in 1980. In fall 2010, there were 700 students enrolled in distance learning courses. Institutionally administered financial aid is available to distance learners.
Services Distance learners have accessibility to academic advising, bookstore, campus computer network, career placement assistance, e-mail services, library services.
Contact Joanne Gerber, Program Coordinator, University of Minnesota, Duluth, 104 Darland Administration, 1049 University Drive, Duluth, MN 55812. Telephone: 218-726-6797. E-mail: jgerber@d.umn.edu.

DEGREES AND AWARDS

Programs offered do not lead to a degree or other formal award.

COURSE SUBJECT AREAS OFFERED OUTSIDE OF DEGREE PROGRAMS

Undergraduate—anthropology; astronomy and astrophysics; criminology; education (specific levels and methods); education (specific subject areas); health and physical education/fitness; history; music; philosophy; psychology; social work; sociology; special education; statistics.
Graduate—education (specific subject areas); special education.
Non-credit—education; education related; education (specific subject areas).

UNIVERSITY OF MINNESOTA, MORRIS
Morris, Minnesota
Online Learning Program
http://onlinelearning.morris.umn.edu/

University of Minnesota, Morris was founded in 1959. It is accredited by North Central Association of Colleges and Schools. It first offered distance learning courses in 1997. In fall 2010, there were 75 students enrolled in distance learning courses. Institutionally administered financial aid is available to distance learners.
Services Distance learners have accessibility to academic advising, bookstore, campus computer network, e-mail services, library services.
Contact Ms. Chlene L. Anderson, Online Learning Coordinator, University of Minnesota, Morris, 314 Behmler Hall, 600 East 4th Street, Morris, MN 56267. Telephone: 320-589-6461. Fax: 320-589-6399. E-mail: onlinelearning@morris.umn.edu.

DEGREES AND AWARDS

Programs offered do not lead to a degree or other formal award.

COURSE SUBJECT AREAS OFFERED OUTSIDE OF DEGREE PROGRAMS

Undergraduate—education; education (specific subject areas); English; geography and cartography; international and comparative education; mathematics; multi/interdisciplinary studies related; political science and government; psychology; sociology; statistics.

UNIVERSITY OF MINNESOTA, TWIN CITIES CAMPUS
Minneapolis, Minnesota
School of Nursing
http://www.nursing.umn.edu/

University of Minnesota, Twin Cities Campus was founded in 1851. It is accredited by North Central Association of Colleges and Schools. It first offered distance learning courses in 2000. In fall 2010, there were 289 students enrolled in distance learning courses. Institutionally administered financial aid is available to distance learners.
Services Distance learners have accessibility to academic advising, bookstore, campus computer network, e-mail services, library services.

Contact Recruiter, University of Minnesota, Twin Cities Campus, 5-160 Weaver Densford Hall, 308 Harvard Street SE, Minneapolis, MN 55455. Telephone: 612-625-7980. Fax: 612-625-7727. E-mail: sonstudentinfo @umn.edu.

DEGREES AND AWARDS

MS Nurse Midwifery; Nursing–Public Health Nursing; Nursing–Women's Health Care Nurse Practitioner; Psych Mental Health

DNP Adult Health/Gerontological CNS; Health Innovation and Leadership; Informatics; Integrative Health and Healing; Midwifery; Nurse Anesthesia; Nursing–Adult/Gerontological Nurse Practitioner; Nursing–Adult/Women's Health Nurse Practitioner; Nursing–Family Nurse Practitioner; Nursing–Pediatric CNS; Nursing–Pediatric Nurse Practitioner; Nursing–Psychiatric Mental Health CNS; Nursing–Public Health Nursing; Nursing–Public Health Nursing-Adolescent Health; Nursing–post-Master's DNP

UNIVERSITY OF MISSOURI–KANSAS CITY
Kansas City, Missouri
Interactive Video Network
http://www.umkc.edu/ia

University of Missouri–Kansas City was founded in 1929. It is accredited by North Central Association of Colleges and Schools. It first offered distance learning courses in 1988. In fall 2010, there were 6,000 students enrolled in distance learning courses. Institutionally administered financial aid is available to distance learners.

Services Distance learners have accessibility to academic advising, bookstore, campus computer network, e-mail services, library services, tutoring.

Contact Molly Mead, Instructional Designer, University of Missouri–Kansas City, Fine Arts Building, 5100 Rockhill Road, Kansas City, MO 64112. Telephone: 816-235-6595. Fax: 816-235-1170. E-mail: meadmo @umkc.edu.

DEGREES AND AWARDS

BA Bachelor of Liberal Arts and Sciences/Liberal Studies

BS Dental Hygiene degree completion program

BSN Nursing–RN-BSN

Ed S District Level Administration

MS Dental Hygiene Education

MSN Nurse Educator, Pediatric Nurse Practitioner, Women's Health Nurse Practitioner, or Neonatal Nurse Practitioner emphasis

DNP Nursing Practice

PhD Nursing Science

COURSE SUBJECT AREAS OFFERED OUTSIDE OF DEGREE PROGRAMS

Undergraduate—accounting and computer science; communication and journalism related; communication and media; communications technology; computer and information sciences; computer and information sciences and support services related; computer engineering; computer engineering technologies; computer/information technology administration and management; computer programming; computer science; computer systems networking and telecommunications; economics; English; history; liberal arts and sciences, general studies and humanities; mathematics; music; philosophy; political science and government; psychology related; social sciences related; visual and performing arts.

Graduate—dentistry and oral sciences (advanced/graduate); education; educational administration and supervision; educational assessment, evaluation, and research; education related; education (specific levels and methods); liberal arts and sciences, general studies and humanities; mechanical engineering; sociology.

Non-credit—business administration, management and operations; dental support services and allied professions; education.

THE UNIVERSITY OF MONTANA WESTERN
Dillon, Montana
School of Outreach
http://outreach.umwestern.edu

The University of Montana Western was founded in 1893. It is accredited by Northwest Commission on Colleges and Universities. It first offered distance learning courses in 1989. In fall 2010, there were 600 students enrolled in distance learning courses. Institutionally administered financial aid is available to distance learners.

Services Distance learners have accessibility to academic advising, bookstore, campus computer network, career placement assistance, e-mail services, library services.

Contact Vickie Lansing, Director of Continuing Education and Extension Programs, The University of Montana Western, 710 South Atlantic Street, Dillon, MT 59725. Telephone: 406-683-7304. Fax: 406-683-7809. E-mail: v_lansing@umwestern.edu.

DEGREES AND AWARDS

AAS Early Childhood Education

BS Early Childhood Education; Elementary Education

Certification Child Development Associate

COURSE SUBJECT AREAS OFFERED OUTSIDE OF DEGREE PROGRAMS

Undergraduate—business, management, and marketing related; computer software and media applications; education; education (specific levels and methods); geological and earth sciences/geosciences; history; liberal arts and sciences, general studies and humanities; library science related; mathematics; philosophy; psychology.

Non-credit—computer software and media applications; legal professions and studies related.

UNIVERSITY OF NEBRASKA AT KEARNEY
Kearney, Nebraska
eCampus
http://ecampus.unk.edu

University of Nebraska at Kearney was founded in 1903. It is accredited by North Central Association of Colleges and Schools. It first offered distance learning courses in 1986. In fall 2010, there were 2,000 students enrolled in distance learning courses. Institutionally administered financial aid is available to distance learners.

Services Distance learners have accessibility to academic advising, bookstore, campus computer network, career placement assistance, e-mail services, library services, tutoring.

Contact Gloria Vavricka, Director of eCampus, University of Nebraska at Kearney, Communications Center, 3rd Floor, 1910 University Drive, Kearney, NE 68849-4220. Telephone: 308-865-8390. Fax: 308-865-8090. E-mail: vavrickag@unk.edu.

DEGREES AND AWARDS

BA Early Childhood Unified

BS Business Administration; Organizational Communication Comprehensive option; Sociology

Certificate Post-Baccalaureate

Endorsement Driver Education (Undergraduate); English as a Second Language (Graduate); Gifted (Graduate); Mild/Moderate 7-12 (UG and G); Mild/Moderate K-6 (UG and G); School Librarian (Graduate); Vocational Diversified Occupations (UG & G)

Ed S Education Specialist–School Superintendent

MA Graduate History

MAE Art Education; Curriculum and Instruction; Educational Administration–Supervisor of Special Education; Music Education; Reading PK-12; School Principalship–PreK-8 or 7-12; Special Education (Gifted, Advanced Pract., Mild/Moderate Disabilities)

MS Biology

MSE Instructional Technology

UNIVERSITY OF NEVADA, RENO
Reno, Nevada
Independent Study and Division of Continuing Education
http://istudy.unr.edu

University of Nevada, Reno was founded in 1874. It is accredited by Northwest Commission on Colleges and Universities. It first offered distance learning courses in 1944. In fall 2010, there were 3,500 students enrolled in distance learning courses. Institutionally administered financial aid is available to distance learners.

Services Distance learners have accessibility to bookstore, campus computer network, e-mail services, library services.

Contact Shannon Brown, Assistant Director for Online Instruction, University of Nevada, Reno, Independent Learning, Mail Stop 0050, Reno, NV 89557. Telephone: 775-784-4652. Fax: 775-784-1280. E-mail: shannonb@unr.edu.

DEGREES AND AWARDS
EMBA Online Executive MBA
MAEd Literacy Studies
MEd Equity and Diversity in Educational Settings
DNP Nursing Practice

COURSE SUBJECT AREAS OFFERED OUTSIDE OF DEGREE PROGRAMS
Undergraduate—accounting and related services; anthropology; area studies; business/commerce; business/managerial economics; communication and media; computer and information sciences; criminal justice and corrections; curriculum and instruction; economics; education related; English; English or French as a second or foreign language (teaching); fine and studio arts; health professions related; history; holocaust and related studies; information science/studies; intercultural/multicultural and diversity studies; journalism; languages (Romance languages); liberal arts and sciences, general studies and humanities; library science and administration; library science related; linguistic, comparative, and related language studies; marketing; mathematics; music; psychology; public health; social work; sociology; statistics.

Graduate—curriculum and instruction; education; education related; ethnic, cultural minority, gender, and group studies; library science and administration; psychology related.

UNIVERSITY OF NEW ENGLAND
Biddeford, Maine
Distance Learning Programs
http://distance.une.edu/com/online

University of New England was founded in 1831. It is accredited by New England Association of Schools and Colleges. It first offered distance learning courses in 2002. In fall 2010, there were 2,000 students enrolled in distance learning courses. Institutionally administered financial aid is available to distance learners.

Services Distance learners have accessibility to academic advising, e-mail services, tutoring.

Contact Dr. Rebecca J. Rowe, Assistant Director of COM Distance Education, University of New England, COM Distance Education, 11 Hills Beach Road, Biddeford, ME 04005. Telephone: 207-581-1173. E-mail: rrowe@une.edu.

DEGREES AND AWARDS
Programs offered do not lead to a degree or other formal award.

COURSE SUBJECT AREAS OFFERED OUTSIDE OF DEGREE PROGRAMS
Undergraduate—biochemistry, biophysics and molecular biology; biology; chemistry; health/medical preparatory programs; health professions related; microbiological sciences and immunology; physics; physiology, pathology and related sciences; psychology; statistics.

UNIVERSITY OF NEW HAVEN
West Haven, Connecticut
http://www.newhaven.edu/

University of New Haven was founded in 1920. It is accredited by New England Association of Schools and Colleges. It first offered distance learning courses in 2000. In fall 2010, there were 127 students enrolled in distance learning courses. Institutionally administered financial aid is available to distance learners.

Services Distance learners have accessibility to bookstore, campus computer network, e-mail services, library services.

Contact Mr. Ira Kleinfeld, Associate Provost, University of New Haven, 300 Boston Post Road, West Haven, CT 06516. Telephone: 203-932-7063. E-mail: ikleinfeld@newhaven.edu.

DEGREES AND AWARDS
Programs offered do not lead to a degree or other formal award.

COURSE SUBJECT AREAS OFFERED OUTSIDE OF DEGREE PROGRAMS
Undergraduate—accounting and related services; business administration, management and operations; business/commerce; business, management, and marketing related; communication and journalism related; communication and media; criminal justice and corrections; dental support services and allied professions; dietetics and clinical nutrition services; economics; engineering; English; English language and literature related; ethnic, cultural minority, gender, and group studies; human resources management; legal studies (non-professional general, undergraduate); management sciences and quantitative methods; marketing; mathematics and statistics related; nutrition sciences; philosophy; public administration; public health; public policy analysis; sociology.

Graduate—accounting and related services; business administration, management and operations; communications technology; criminal justice and corrections; education; education (specific subject areas); history; human resources management; international business; legal studies (non-professional general, undergraduate); mathematics and statistics related; statistics; taxation.

UNIVERSITY OF NORTH ALABAMA
Florence, Alabama
Educational Technology Services/Distance Learning
http://distance.una.edu

University of North Alabama was founded in 1830. It is accredited by Southern Association of Colleges and Schools. It first offered distance learning courses in 1997. In fall 2010, there were 4,056 students enrolled in distance learning courses. Institutionally administered financial aid is available to distance learners.

Services Distance learners have accessibility to academic advising, bookstore, campus computer network, career placement assistance, e-mail services, library services, tutoring.

Contact Ms. Bonnie Coats, Coordinator of Distance Learning Outreach, University of North Alabama, UNA Box 5005, Florence, AL 35632-0001. Telephone: 877-765-6110. Fax: 256-718-3923. E-mail: bdcoats@una.edu.

DEGREES AND AWARDS
BIS Sociology
BS Sociology
BSN Nursing–RN to BSN
MBA Business Administration–Online MBA program

COURSE SUBJECT AREAS OFFERED OUTSIDE OF DEGREE PROGRAMS
Undergraduate—accounting and related services; area studies; business, management, and marketing related; communication and media; computer and information sciences; criminal justice and corrections; economics; education; English; film/video and photographic arts; finance and financial management services; foods, nutrition, and related services; geography and cartography; gerontology; history; marketing; mathematics; philosophy; political science and government; psychology; social work; sociology.

Graduate—accounting and related services; area studies; business administration, management and operations; business/commerce; education; English; geography and cartography.

THE UNIVERSITY OF NORTH CAROLINA AT ASHEVILLE

Asheville, North Carolina

http://agc.unca.edu/distedcourses

The University of North Carolina at Asheville was founded in 1927. It is accredited by Southern Association of Colleges and Schools. It first offered distance learning courses in 2000. In fall 2010, there were 350 students enrolled in distance learning courses. Institutionally administered financial aid is available to distance learners.

Services Distance learners have accessibility to academic advising, e-mail services, library services.

Contact Mrs. Susan E. Allman, Director of Distance Education, The University of North Carolina at Asheville, One University Heights, CPO#2140, Asheville, NC 28804. Telephone: 828-232-5122. Fax: 828-251-6618. E-mail: sallman@unca.edu.

DEGREES AND AWARDS

Programs offered do not lead to a degree or other formal award.

COURSE SUBJECT AREAS OFFERED OUTSIDE OF DEGREE PROGRAMS

Undergraduate—behavioral sciences; biology; design and applied arts; education; English; environmental/environmental health engineering; ethnic, cultural minority, gender, and group studies; languages (foreign languages related); languages (Romance languages); mathematics; physics; political science and government; psychology; religious studies; social sciences; social sciences related; statistics.

Graduate—education related; ethnic, cultural minority, gender, and group studies; health services/allied health/health sciences; liberal arts and sciences, general studies and humanities; science technologies related.

Non-credit—education.

THE UNIVERSITY OF NORTH CAROLINA AT CHAPEL HILL

Chapel Hill, North Carolina

The William and Ida Friday Center for Continuing Education

http://fridaycenter.unc.edu

The University of North Carolina at Chapel Hill was founded in 1789. It is accredited by Southern Association of Colleges and Schools. It first offered distance learning courses in 1941. In fall 2010, there were 4,000 students enrolled in distance learning courses. Institutionally administered financial aid is available to distance learners.

Services Distance learners have accessibility to academic advising, bookstore, career placement assistance, library services.

Contact Carol McDonnell, Student Services Manager, The University of North Carolina at Chapel Hill, CB #1020, Chapel Hill, NC 27599-1020. Telephone: 800-862-5669. Fax: 919-962-5549. E-mail: carol_mcdonnell@unc.edu.

DEGREES AND AWARDS

Programs offered do not lead to a degree or other formal award.

COURSE SUBJECT AREAS OFFERED OUTSIDE OF DEGREE PROGRAMS

Undergraduate—accounting and related services; anthropology; area studies; astronomy and astrophysics; biology; business administration, management and operations; business/corporate communications; chemistry; communication and media; computer and information sciences; criminal justice and corrections; drama/theatre arts and stagecraft; economics; ethnic, cultural minority, gender, and group studies; fine and studio arts; foods, nutrition, and related services; geography and cartography; geological and earth sciences/geosciences; history; hospitality administration; journalism; languages (classics and classical); languages (foreign languages related); languages (Romance languages); languages (Slavic, Baltic, and Albanian); mathematics and statistics related; music; parks, recreation and leisure; philosophy; physics; political science and government; psychology; religious studies; sociology; statistics.

Non-credit—business/corporate communications; business, management, and marketing related; ethnic, cultural minority, gender, and group studies; fine and studio arts; history; music; philosophy; political science and government.

THE UNIVERSITY OF NORTH CAROLINA AT CHARLOTTE

Charlotte, North Carolina

Continuing Education, Extension and Summer Programs

http://distanceed.uncc.edu/

The University of North Carolina at Charlotte was founded in 1946. It is accredited by Southern Association of Colleges and Schools. It first offered distance learning courses in 1998. In fall 2010, there were 1,215 students enrolled in distance learning courses. Institutionally administered financial aid is available to distance learners.

Services Distance learners have accessibility to academic advising, bookstore, campus computer network, career placement assistance, e-mail services, library services, tutoring.

Contact Dr. Dennis L. McElhoe, Director of Credit Programs, Extended Academic Programs, The University of North Carolina at Charlotte, Credit Programs, 1017 Colvard Hall, 9201 University City Boulevard, Charlotte, NC 28223-0001. Telephone: 704-687-4594. E-mail: dmcelhoe@uncc.edu.

DEGREES AND AWARDS

BA Child and Family Development; Elementary Education

BS Respiratory Therapy

BSET Electrical Engineering Technology; Fire Science

BSN Nursing–RN to BSN completion

Graduate Certificate Education, Academically or Intellectually Gifted Add-On Teacher Licensure; Education, Middle and Secondary Education Teacher Licensure; Information Security and Privacy; Instructional Systems Technology; Nursing Administration; Nursing Education; School Counseling (post-Masters); Special Education, Adapted Curriculum; Special Education, General Curriculum Teacher licensure

MAT Middle Grades and Secondary Education; Special Education (K-12)–General Curriculum

MEd Education, Middle Grades; Instructional Systems Technology; Reading, Language, and Literacy

MS Engineering Management

MSA Education and School Administration

MSN Community and Public Health; Nursing Administration; Nursing Education

COURSE SUBJECT AREAS OFFERED OUTSIDE OF DEGREE PROGRAMS

Undergraduate—education; engineering technology.

Graduate—education; educational administration and supervision; educational/instructional media design; engineering; information science/studies.

THE UNIVERSITY OF NORTH CAROLINA WILMINGTON

Wilmington, North Carolina

Division of Academic Affairs

http://www.uncw.edu/extension

The University of North Carolina Wilmington was founded in 1947. It is accredited by Southern Association of Colleges and Schools. It first offered distance learning courses in 1992. In fall 2010, there were 1,007 students enrolled in distance learning courses. Institutionally administered financial aid is available to distance learners.

Services Distance learners have accessibility to academic advising, bookstore, campus computer network, career placement assistance, e-mail services, library services, tutoring.

Contact Dr. George W. Ayers, Director, Interim, The University of North Carolina Wilmington, Administration Building, Room 23, 444 Western

Boulevard, Jacksonville, NC 28546. Telephone: 910-455-2310. Fax: 910-451-5266. E-mail: ayersg@uncw.edu.

DEGREES AND AWARDS

Programs offered do not lead to a degree or other formal award.

COURSE SUBJECT AREAS OFFERED OUTSIDE OF DEGREE PROGRAMS

Undergraduate—business administration, management and operations; criminal justice and corrections; education (specific subject areas); English; history; philosophy and religious studies related; psychology; social work.
Graduate—chemistry; education (specific subject areas); liberal arts and sciences, general studies and humanities.

UNIVERSITY OF NORTH DAKOTA

Grand Forks, North Dakota

Division of Continuing Education

http://www.distance.und.edu

University of North Dakota was founded in 1883. It is accredited by North Central Association of Colleges and Schools. It first offered distance learning courses in 1970. In fall 2010, there were 2,741 students enrolled in distance learning courses. Institutionally administered financial aid is available to distance learners.
Services Distance learners have accessibility to academic advising, bookstore, campus computer network, career placement assistance, e-mail services, library services, tutoring.
Contact Ms. Heidi Flaten, Assistant Director, Academic Planning, University of North Dakota, Harrington Hall, Room 225, 3264 Campus Road, Stop 9021, Grand Forks, ND 58202-9021. Telephone: 800-342-8230. Fax: 701-777-3348. E-mail: heidi.flaten@email.und.edu.

DEGREES AND AWARDS

BA Communication; Psychology; Social Science
BGS General Studies
BS Chemical Engineering; Civil Engineering; Communication; Electrical Engineering; Mechanical Engineering; Nursing–RN to BSN; Psychology
Graduate Certificate Autistic Spectrum Disorders; Environmental Engineering; Geographic Information Sciences; Health Administration; Instructional Design and Technology; Policy Analysis; Public Administration
MA Counseling (K-12 school emphasis); Forensic Psychology
MBA Business Administration
MEd Education Leadership; English Language Learner (ELL); Instructional Design and Technology; Special Education
MPA Public Administration
MS Applied Economics; Aviation; Early Childhood Education; Elementary Education; Instructional Design and Technology; Nursing–Family Nurse Practitioner specialization; Nursing–Gerontological Nursing specialization; Nursing–RN to MS; Public Health specialization, Advanced; Space Studies; Special Education
MSN Nursing–Education specialization
MSW Social Work
EdD Educational Leadership
PhD Higher Education; Nursing

COURSE SUBJECT AREAS OFFERED OUTSIDE OF DEGREE PROGRAMS

Undergraduate—accounting and related services; anthropology; behavioral sciences; bilingual, multilingual, and multicultural education; business administration, management and operations; business, management, and marketing related; business/managerial economics; chemical engineering; chemistry; civil engineering; communication and journalism related; communication and media; computer and information sciences; computer systems analysis; criminal justice and corrections; dietetics and clinical nutrition services; economics; education; education related; education (specific levels and methods); education (specific subject areas); engineering; English; geography and cartography; geological and earth sciences/geosciences; health professions related; history; linguistic, comparative, and related language studies; mathematics; mechanical engineering; pharmacology and toxicology; philosophy and religious studies related; physical sciences; physics; political science and government; psychology; psychology related; religious studies; social sciences; social sciences related; social work; sociology; statistics.
Graduate—business administration, management and operations; economics; education; educational administration and supervision; educational assessment, evaluation, and research; educational/instructional media design; education related; education (specific subject areas); English or French as a second or foreign language (teaching); environmental/environmental health engineering; health professions related; management sciences and quantitative methods; psychology; public administration; public administration and social service professions related; public health; public policy analysis; social work; special education; student counseling and personnel services.
Non-credit—computer programming; computer software and media applications; graphic communications; health and medical administrative services; health professions related; heating, air conditioning, ventilation and refrigeration maintenance technology; human resources management; legal support services; mathematics; real estate.

UNIVERSITY OF NORTHERN IOWA

Cedar Falls, Iowa

Division of Continuing Education

http://www.uni.edu/continuinged/

University of Northern Iowa was founded in 1876. It is accredited by North Central Association of Colleges and Schools. It first offered distance learning courses in 1941. In fall 2010, there were 1,200 students enrolled in distance learning courses. Institutionally administered financial aid is available to distance learners.
Services Distance learners have accessibility to academic advising, bookstore, campus computer network, career placement assistance, e-mail services, library services, tutoring.
Contact Dr. Kent Johnson, Acting Dean, Continuing Education and Special Programs, University of Northern Iowa, 2637 Hudson Road, Cedar Falls, IA 50614-0223. Telephone: 319-273-2122. Fax: 319-273-2872. E-mail: kent.johnson@uni.edu.

DEGREES AND AWARDS

BLS Liberal Studies
MA Instructional Techology; Philanthropy and Nonprofit Development; Teaching English in Secondary Schools (TESS); Teaching English to Speakers of Other Languages (TESOL)
MAE Elementary Education; Professional Development for Teachers

COURSE SUBJECT AREAS OFFERED OUTSIDE OF DEGREE PROGRAMS

Undergraduate—accounting and related services; area studies; communication and media; criminology; economics; education; education related; education (specific levels and methods); education (specific subject areas); English; family and consumer economics; foods, nutrition, and related services; geography and cartography; health and physical education/fitness; human development, family studies, and related services; marketing; mathematics; mathematics and statistics related; music; psychology; religious studies; social and philosophical foundations of education; social sciences related; social work; sociology; statistics.
Graduate—classical and ancient studies; criminology; curriculum and instruction; education; education related; education (specific levels and methods); education (specific subject areas); geography and cartography; religious studies; social work; sociology.

UNIVERSITY OF NORTH FLORIDA

Jacksonville, Florida

http://www.unf.edu/distancelearning/

University of North Florida was founded in 1965. It is accredited by Southern Association of Colleges and Schools. It first offered distance learning courses in 1997. In fall 2010, there were 2,194 students enrolled in distance learning courses. Institutionally administered financial aid is available to distance learners.
Services Distance learners have accessibility to academic advising, bookstore, campus computer network, career placement assistance, e-mail services, library services, tutoring.

Contact Ms. Deb Miller, Director, Center for Instruction and Research Technology, University of North Florida, Center for Instruction and Research Technology, 1 UNF Drive, Building 1, Room 1800, Jacksonville, FL 32224-7699. Telephone: 904-620-1416. E-mail: dfmiller@unf.edu.

DEGREES AND AWARDS

MAE Educational Technology Leadership
MEd School Leadership; Special Education, American Sign Language (ASL)/English Interpreting concentration
DNP Nursing–Clinical Nursing

COURSE SUBJECT AREAS OFFERED OUTSIDE OF DEGREE PROGRAMS

Undergraduate—accounting and related services; American Sign Language (ASL); anthropology; building/construction finishing, management, and inspection; computer and information sciences; computer engineering; computer/information technology administration and management; computer programming; criminal justice and corrections; dietetics and clinical nutrition services; education; engineering; engineering mechanics; English language and literature related; health and medical administrative services; health professions related; health services/allied health/health sciences; music; nutrition sciences; philosophy; psychology; public health; registered nursing, nursing administration, nursing research and clinical nursing; religious studies; social work; sociology; sociology and anthropology; special education.
Graduate—building/construction finishing, management, and inspection; dietetics and clinical nutrition services; education; educational administration and supervision; educational/instructional media design; education related; health and medical administrative services; health/medical preparatory programs; mechanical engineering; nutrition sciences; philosophy; public health; registered nursing, nursing administration, nursing research and clinical nursing.

UNIVERSITY OF OREGON
Eugene, Oregon
Distance Education
http://de.uoregon.edu

University of Oregon was founded in 1872. It is accredited by Northwest Commission on Colleges and Universities. It first offered distance learning courses in 1996. In fall 2010, there were 1,165 students enrolled in distance learning courses. Institutionally administered financial aid is available to distance learners.
Services Distance learners have accessibility to academic advising, bookstore, campus computer network, e-mail services, library services.
Contact Ms. Sonya Faust, Credit Programs Coordinator, University of Oregon, Distance Education, 1277 University of Oregon, Eugene, OR 97403-1277. Telephone: 541-346-4231. Fax: 541-346-3545. E-mail: disted@uoregon.edu.

DEGREES AND AWARDS

MS Applied Information Management

COURSE SUBJECT AREAS OFFERED OUTSIDE OF DEGREE PROGRAMS

Undergraduate—accounting and related services; architecture related; astronomy and astrophysics; business administration, management and operations; curriculum and instruction; economics; education (specific levels and methods); environmental design; ethnic, cultural minority, gender, and group studies; geography and cartography; geological and earth sciences/geosciences; linguistic, comparative, and related language studies; literature; multi/interdisciplinary studies related; physics; political science and government; science, technology and society; special education; visual and performing arts related.
Graduate—architecture related; business administration, management and operations; curriculum and instruction; education (specific levels and methods); environmental design; geography and cartography; information science/studies; management information systems; special education.

UNIVERSITY OF PENNSYLVANIA
Philadelphia, Pennsylvania
Distance Education
http://www.sas.upenn.edu/lps/online

University of Pennsylvania was founded in 1740. It is accredited by Middle States Association of Colleges and Schools. It first offered distance learning courses in 2009. In fall 2010, there were 200 students enrolled in distance learning courses. Institutionally administered financial aid is available to distance learners.
Services Distance learners have accessibility to academic advising, bookstore, campus computer network, career placement assistance, e-mail services, library services.
Contact Dr. Jacqueline P. Candido, SAS Online Learning Manager, University of Pennsylvania, College of Liberal and Professional Studies, 3440 Market Street, Suite 100, Philadelphia, PA 19104-3335. Telephone: 215-898-4970. Fax: 215-573-2053. E-mail: candido@sas.upenn.edu.

DEGREES AND AWARDS

Programs offered do not lead to a degree or other formal award.

COURSE SUBJECT AREAS OFFERED OUTSIDE OF DEGREE PROGRAMS

Undergraduate—classical and ancient studies; English; liberal arts and sciences, general studies and humanities; mathematics; music; social sciences.

UNIVERSITY OF PITTSBURGH AT BRADFORD
Bradford, Pennsylvania
http://www.upb.pitt.edu/

University of Pittsburgh at Bradford was founded in 1963. It is accredited by Middle States Association of Colleges and Schools. It first offered distance learning courses in 1995. In fall 2010, there were 602 students enrolled in distance learning courses. Institutionally administered financial aid is available to distance learners.
Services Distance learners have accessibility to academic advising, bookstore, campus computer network, career placement assistance, e-mail services, library services, tutoring.
Contact Mr. Bernie Picklo, Academic Technology Integrator, University of Pittsburgh at Bradford, 300 Campus Drive, Bradford, PA 16701-2898. Telephone: 814-362-7644. Fax: 814-362-5279. E-mail: bjp47@pitt.edu.

DEGREES AND AWARDS

Programs offered do not lead to a degree or other formal award.

COURSE SUBJECT AREAS OFFERED OUTSIDE OF DEGREE PROGRAMS

Undergraduate—anthropology; astronomy and astrophysics; business, management, and marketing related; chemistry; communication and media; criminal justice and corrections; economics; education; English; health and physical education/fitness; petroleum engineering; philosophy; physics; psychology; sociology; visual and performing arts.

UNIVERSITY OF ST. AUGUSTINE FOR HEALTH SCIENCES
St. Augustine, Florida
Division of Distance Education
http://www.usa.edu

University of St. Augustine for Health Sciences was founded in 1978. It is accredited by Distance Education and Training Council. It first offered distance learning courses in 1979. In fall 2010, there were 553 students enrolled in distance learning courses. Institutionally administered financial aid is available to distance learners.
Services Distance learners have accessibility to academic advising, bookstore, e-mail services, library services, tutoring.
Contact Ms. Dian Hartley, Associate Vice President of Student Services, University of St. Augustine for Health Sciences, 1 University Boulevard, St. Augustine, FL 32086. Telephone: 904-826-0084 Ext. 207. Fax: 904-826-0085. E-mail: info@usa.edu.

DEGREES AND AWARDS
DH Sc Health Science
DPT Transitional Doctor of Physical Therapy
EdD Education
OTD Transitional Doctor of Occupational Therapy

COURSE SUBJECT AREAS OFFERED OUTSIDE OF DEGREE PROGRAMS
Graduate—rehabilitation and therapeutic professions.
Non-credit—health professions related.

UNIVERSITY OF ST. FRANCIS
Joliet, Illinois
http://www.stfrancis.edu/

University of St. Francis was founded in 1920. It is accredited by North Central Association of Colleges and Schools. It first offered distance learning courses in 1997. In fall 2010, there were 1,519 students enrolled in distance learning courses. Institutionally administered financial aid is available to distance learners.
Services Distance learners have accessibility to academic advising, bookstore, campus computer network, career placement assistance, e-mail services, library services, tutoring.
Contact Ms. Sandra Sloka, Director, Graduate and Degree Completion Admissions, University of St. Francis, 500 Wilcox Street, Joliet, IL 60435. Telephone: 800-735-7500. Fax: 815-740-5032. E-mail: ssloka@stfrancis.edu.

DEGREES AND AWARDS
BS Health Care Leadership; Management; Organizational Leadership
BSN Nursing Fast Track
MBA Business Administration
MS Health Administration; Teaching and Learning; Training and Development
MSM Management
MSN Clinical Specialist; Nurse Practitioner
DNP Nursing

COURSE SUBJECT AREAS OFFERED OUTSIDE OF DEGREE PROGRAMS
Undergraduate—accounting and related services; business administration, management and operations; computer and information sciences; education; English; health professions related; history; marketing; mathematics; philosophy and religious studies related; psychology; social sciences.
Graduate—business administration, management and operations; educational assessment, evaluation, and research; health and medical administrative services.

UNIVERSITY OF ST. THOMAS
Houston, Texas

University of St. Thomas was founded in 1947. It is accredited by Southern Association of Colleges and Schools. It first offered distance learning courses in 2001. In fall 2010, there were 60 students enrolled in distance learning courses. Institutionally administered financial aid is available to distance learners.
Services Distance learners have accessibility to academic advising, bookstore, career placement assistance, e-mail services, library services.
Contact Arthur Ortiz, Director of Freshman Admissions, University of St. Thomas, 3800 Montrose Boulevard, Houston, TX 77006. Telephone: 713-525-3500. Fax: 713-525-3558. E-mail: admissions@stthom.edu.

DEGREES AND AWARDS
MEd Online Masters of Education

COURSE SUBJECT AREAS OFFERED OUTSIDE OF DEGREE PROGRAMS
Graduate—education.

UNIVERSITY OF SAN FRANCISCO
San Francisco, California
http://www.usfca.edu/bps/

University of San Francisco was founded in 1855. It is accredited by Western Association of Schools and Colleges. It first offered distance learning courses in 2001. In fall 2010, there were 119 students enrolled in distance learning courses. Institutionally administered financial aid is available to distance learners.
Services Distance learners have accessibility to academic advising, bookstore, campus computer network, e-mail services, library services.
Contact Jennifer E. Turpin, PhD, Provost and Vice President for Academic Affairs, University of San Francisco, 2130 Fulton Street, San Francisco, CA 94117-1080. Telephone: 415-422-6136. E-mail: provost@usfca.edu.

DEGREES AND AWARDS
Programs offered do not lead to a degree or other formal award.

COURSE SUBJECT AREAS OFFERED OUTSIDE OF DEGREE PROGRAMS
Undergraduate—area studies; business administration, management and operations; business/managerial economics; visual and performing arts.

UNIVERSITY OF SASKATCHEWAN
Saskatoon, Saskatchewan, Canada
Distance Learning, Off-Campus and Certificate Programs
http://www.ccde.usask.ca

University of Saskatchewan was founded in 1907. It is provincially chartered. It first offered distance learning courses in 1941. In fall 2010, there were 1,500 students enrolled in distance learning courses. Institutionally administered financial aid is available to distance learners.
Services Distance learners have accessibility to academic advising, bookstore, campus computer network, e-mail services, library services, tutoring.
Contact Ms. Grace Milashenko, Independent Studies Coordinator, University of Saskatchewan, Centre for Continuing and Distance Education, 427 Williams Building, 221 Cumberland Avenue North, Saskatoon, SK S7N 1M3, Canada. Telephone: 306-966-5562. Fax: 306-966-5590. E-mail: grace.milashenko@usask.ca.

DEGREES AND AWARDS
Programs offered do not lead to a degree or other formal award.

COURSE SUBJECT AREAS OFFERED OUTSIDE OF DEGREE PROGRAMS
Undergraduate—agricultural business and management; agriculture; anthropology; archeology; computer science; curriculum and instruction; economics; educational/instructional media design; education related; education (specific levels and methods); education (specific subject areas); English; English or French as a second or foreign language (teaching); geography and cartography; geological and earth sciences/geosciences; history; liberal arts and sciences, general studies and humanities; mathematics; music; political science and government; psychology; religious studies; sociology; sociology and anthropology; special education.
Graduate—education related.
Non-credit—agricultural business and management; agriculture and agriculture operations related; applied horticulture and horticultural business services; botany/plant biology; educational/instructional media design; education related; education (specific subject areas); English or French as a second or foreign language (teaching); landscape architecture; soil sciences.

THE UNIVERSITY OF SCRANTON

Scranton, Pennsylvania

http://matrix.scranton.edu/academics/cgce/online%20admissions.shtml/

The University of Scranton was founded in 1888. It is accredited by Middle States Association of Colleges and Schools. It first offered distance learning courses in 2004. In fall 2010, there were 1,200 students enrolled in distance learning courses. Institutionally administered financial aid is available to distance learners.

Services Distance learners have accessibility to academic advising, bookstore, campus computer network, career placement assistance, e-mail services, library services.

Contact Regina Bennett, Assistant Dean, Online Programs, The University of Scranton, Scranton, PA 18510. Telephone: 570-941-4281. E-mail: bennettr1@scranton.edu.

DEGREES AND AWARDS

MBA Enterprise Resource Planning; Online MBA in Health Care Management; Online MBA; Operations Management

MS Education–Curriculum and Instruction; Educational Supervision; Human Resources

DPT Transition Doctor of Physical Therapy

COURSE SUBJECT AREAS OFFERED OUTSIDE OF DEGREE PROGRAMS

Graduate—educational administration and supervision.

UNIVERSITY OF SOUTH ALABAMA

Mobile, Alabama

USA Online

http://usaonline.southalabama.edu

University of South Alabama was founded in 1963. It is accredited by Southern Association of Colleges and Schools. It first offered distance learning courses in 1999. In fall 2010, there were 4,465 students enrolled in distance learning courses. Institutionally administered financial aid is available to distance learners.

Services Distance learners have accessibility to academic advising, bookstore, e-mail services, library services.

Contact Norma Jean Tanner, Director of Admissions, University of South Alabama, MH 2500, Mobile, AL 36688-0002. Telephone: 251-460-6141. Fax: 251-460-7876. E-mail: admiss@usouthal.edu.

DEGREES AND AWARDS

BA/BS Interdisplinary Studies

BS Information Systems

BSBA General Business

BSN Nursing

Certification Educational Media (Library Media); English Speaking Other Languages (ESOL); Reading Specialist

MEd Educational Administration; Educational Media (Library Media); Reading Specialist; Secondary Education, English Speaking Other Language (ESOL) major

MS Instructional Design and Development

MSN Nursing

DNP Nursing

COURSE SUBJECT AREAS OFFERED OUTSIDE OF DEGREE PROGRAMS

Undergraduate—biological and biomedical sciences related; communication and journalism related; computer and information sciences; education; engineering; gerontology; psychology; sociology.

Graduate—biology; educational administration and supervision; educational/instructional media design; education (specific levels and methods); gerontology; sociology; special education.

UNIVERSITY OF SOUTH CAROLINA SUMTER

Sumter, South Carolina

http://www.uscsumter.edu/

University of South Carolina Sumter was founded in 1966. It is accredited by Southern Association of Colleges and Schools. It first offered distance learning courses in 1993. In fall 2010, there were 170 students enrolled in distance learning courses. Institutionally administered financial aid is available to distance learners.

Services Distance learners have accessibility to academic advising, bookstore, campus computer network, e-mail services, library services.

Contact Mr. Keith Britton, Director of Admissions, University of South Carolina Sumter, 200 Miller Road, Sumter, SC 29150. Telephone: 803-938-3882. E-mail: kbritton@uscsumter.edu.

DEGREES AND AWARDS

Programs offered do not lead to a degree or other formal award.

COURSE SUBJECT AREAS OFFERED OUTSIDE OF DEGREE PROGRAMS

Undergraduate—accounting and related services; business/managerial economics; education; history; political science and government; psychology related; social sciences; sociology.

THE UNIVERSITY OF SOUTH DAKOTA

Vermillion, South Dakota

Division of Continuing and Distance Education

http://www.usd.edu/cde

The University of South Dakota was founded in 1862. It is accredited by North Central Association of Colleges and Schools. It first offered distance learning courses in 1957. In fall 2010, there were 4,264 students enrolled in distance learning courses. Institutionally administered financial aid is available to distance learners.

Services Distance learners have accessibility to academic advising, bookstore, campus computer network, career placement assistance, e-mail services, library services, tutoring.

Contact Recruitment Coordinator, The University of South Dakota, Division of Continuing and Distance Education, 414 East Clark Street, Vermillion, SD 57069. Telephone: 800-233-7937. Fax: 605-677-6118. E-mail: cde@usd.edu.

DEGREES AND AWARDS

AA General Studies

BGS General Studies

BS Alcohol and Drug Studies; Health Sciences; Nursing

Certificate Alcohol and Drug Studies

Ed S Educational Administration/Elementary School Principal; Educational Administration/Pre-K-12 Principal; Educational Administration/School District Superintendent; Educational Administration/Secondary School Principal

Graduate Certificate Alcohol and Drug Studies; Disaster Mental Health; Literacy Leadership and Coaching; Long-Term Care Management

MA Addiction Studies; Educational Administration/Adult and Higher Education; Educational Administration/Elementary School Principal; Educational Administration/Pre-K-12 Principal; Educational Administration/School District Superintendent; Educational Administration/Secondary School Principal

MBA Business Administration; Health Services Administration specialization

MPA Executive Master of Public Administration

MS Technology for Education and Training

MSA Administration/Alcohol and Drug Studies specialization; Administration/Criminal Justice specialization; Administration/Health Services Administration specialization; Administration/Interdisciplinary Studies specialization; Administration/Long-Term Care Administration specialization; Administration/Organizational Leadership specialization

DPT Transitional Doctorate of Physical Therapy

COURSE SUBJECT AREAS OFFERED OUTSIDE OF DEGREE PROGRAMS

Undergraduate—accounting and computer science; behavioral sciences; biology; business administration, management and operations; business/commerce; business, management, and marketing related; business/managerial economics; business operations support and assistant services; chemistry; criminal justice and corrections; criminology; drama/theatre arts and stagecraft; education; English; history; liberal arts and sciences, general studies and humanities; mathematics; microbiological sciences and immunology; music; physical sciences; physiology, pathology and related sciences; psychology; public relations, advertising, and applied communication related; social sciences related; sociology; statistics.

Graduate—accounting and computer science; business administration, management and operations; business/corporate communications; business, management, and marketing related; business/managerial economics; criminal justice and corrections; economics; education; education related; education (specific levels and methods); education (specific subject areas); health professions related; human resources management; liberal arts and sciences, general studies and humanities; public administration; public administration and social service professions related.

UNIVERSITY OF SOUTHERN CALIFORNIA
Los Angeles, California
Technology Enhanced Learning and Distance Learning Initiative
http://uscnow.usc.edu/

University of Southern California was founded in 1880. It is accredited by Western Association of Schools and Colleges. It first offered distance learning courses in 1972. In fall 2010, there were 2,500 students enrolled in distance learning courses. Institutionally administered financial aid is available to distance learners.

Services Distance learners have accessibility to academic advising, bookstore, campus computer network, career placement assistance, e-mail services, library services, tutoring.

Contact Susan Metros, Deputy CIO, Technology Enhanced Learning, University of Southern California, Los Angeles, CA 90089-2812. Telephone: 213-821-8084. E-mail: smetros@usc.edu.

DEGREES AND AWARDS

Graduate Certificate Astronautical Engineering; Clinical Research Design and Management; Engineering Technology Commercialization; Food Safety; Geographic Information Science and Technology; Gerontology; Network Centric Systems; Patient and Product Safety; Petroleum Engineering (Smart Oilfield Technologies); Preclinical Drug Development; Regulatory and Clinical Affairs; Systems Architecting and Engineering

MA Aging Services Management; Gerontology; Long-Term Care Administration; Teaching of English to Speakers of Other Languages (TESOL); Teaching

MCM Construction Management

MEDED Academic Medicine

MS Aerospace Engineering; Aerospace and Mechanical Engineering (Computational Fluid and Solid Mechanics); Aerospace and Mechanical Engineering (Dynamics and Control); Astronautical Engineering; Biomedical Engineering (Medical Imaging and Imaging Informatics); Biomedical Engineering; Chemical Engineering; Civil Engineering (Construction Engineering); Civil Engineering (Structural Engineering); Civil Engineering (Transportation Engineering); Computer Engineering; Computer Science (Computer Networks); Computer Science (Computer Security); Computer Science (Multimedia and Creative Technologies); Computer Science (Software Engineering); Computer Science; Electrical Engineering (Computer Networks); Electrical Engineering (Electric Power); Electrical Engineering (Multimedia and Creative Technologies); Electrical Engineering (VLSI Design); Electrical Engineering; Engineering Management; Environmental Engineering; Financial Engineering; Geographic Information Science and Technology; Green Technologies; Health Systems Management Engineering; Industrial and Systems Engineering; Materials Engineering; Mechanical Engineering; Medical Device and Diagnostic Engineering; Operations Research Engineering; Petroleum Engineering (Smart Oilfield Technologies); Petroleum Engineering; Product Development Engineering; Regulatory Science; Systems Architecting and Engineering

MSW Social Work

COURSE SUBJECT AREAS OFFERED OUTSIDE OF DEGREE PROGRAMS

Undergraduate—gerontology.

Graduate—education; engineering; geography and cartography; medical clinical sciences/graduate medical studies; pharmacy, pharmaceutical sciences, and administration; social work.

UNIVERSITY OF SOUTHERN MAINE
Portland, Maine
USU Distance Learning Program
http://www.usm.maine.edu/online

University of Southern Maine was founded in 1878. It is accredited by New England Association of Schools and Colleges. It first offered distance learning courses in 1983. In fall 2010, there were 2,983 students enrolled in distance learning courses. Institutionally administered financial aid is available to distance learners.

Services Distance learners have accessibility to academic advising, bookstore, campus computer network, career placement assistance, e-mail services, library services, tutoring.

Contact Ms. Amy Gieseke, Coordinator of Online Student Services/Student Sucess Advisor, University of Southern Maine, PO Box 9300, Portland, ME 04104-9300. Telephone: 207-780-5921. Fax: 207-228-8094. E-mail: agieseke@usm.maine.edu.

DEGREES AND AWARDS

BA Communication

BS Leadership and Organizational Studies; Nursing and RN to BS

Certificate Creative Leadership and Global Strategy; Leadership Studies

Certification Education–Unified K-8 General and Special Education

CAGS Adult Learning

MA Leadership Studies

MS Adult and Higher Education

MSE Teaching and Learning

COURSE SUBJECT AREAS OFFERED OUTSIDE OF DEGREE PROGRAMS

Undergraduate—accounting and computer science; accounting and related services; American Sign Language (ASL); animal sciences; anthropology; applied mathematics; arts, entertainment, and media management; behavioral sciences; bilingual, multilingual, and multicultural education; business administration, management and operations; business/managerial economics; classical and ancient studies; communication and media; criminology; data processing; economics; English; English language and literature related; ethnic, cultural minority, gender, and group studies; geological and earth sciences/geosciences; health professions related; history; human resources management; interdisciplinary studies; liberal arts and sciences, general studies and humanities; marketing; mathematics; mathematics and statistics related; movement and mind-body therapies and education; music; philosophy; political science and government; psychology; registered nursing, nursing administration, nursing research and clinical nursing; social sciences; sociology; statistics.

Graduate—education; educational assessment, evaluation, and research; public policy analysis; social work.

UNIVERSITY OF SOUTHERN MISSISSIPPI
Hattiesburg, Mississippi
Department of Continuing Education
http://www.usm.edu/elo/

University of Southern Mississippi was founded in 1910. It is accredited by Southern Association of Colleges and Schools. It first offered distance learning courses in 1993. In fall 2010, there were 4,442 students enrolled in distance learning courses. Institutionally administered financial aid is available to distance learners.

Services Distance learners have accessibility to academic advising, bookstore, campus computer network, career placement assistance, e-mail services, library services.

Contact Eagle Learning Online, University of Southern Mississippi, Learning Enhancement Center, 118 College Drive, #9649, Hattiesburg, MS 39406-0001. Telephone: 601-266-5518. Fax: 601-266-4560. E-mail: elo@usm.edu.

DEGREES AND AWARDS

BS Construction Technology; Elementary Education (Teacher Assistant program); Special Education
BSN Nursing (RN completion)
MAT Teaching of Languages (MATL)
MEd Educational Administration and Supervision; Music Education–Master of Music Education
MLIS Library Information Science
MPH Health Services Administration
MS Child and Family Studies; Economic Development; Instructional Technology; Polymer Science and Engineering; Special Education; Sport Coaching Education; Sport Management; Workforce Training and Development
PhD Human Capital Development; Instructional Technology and Design; International Development

COURSE SUBJECT AREAS OFFERED OUTSIDE OF DEGREE PROGRAMS

Undergraduate—accounting and related services; economics; educational administration and supervision; educational assessment, evaluation, and research; education related; engineering technologies related; English; foods, nutrition, and related services; geography and cartography; health professions related; human development, family studies, and related services; liberal arts and sciences, general studies and humanities; library science related; linguistic, comparative, and related language studies; management information systems; marketing; mathematics and statistics related; microbiological sciences and immunology; music; philosophy and religious studies related; social work; sociology; special education.
Graduate—biochemistry, biophysics and molecular biology; biology; city/urban, community and regional planning; construction engineering technologies; curriculum and instruction; education; educational administration and supervision; educational assessment, evaluation, and research; human development, family studies, and related services; linguistic, comparative, and related language studies; marketing; music; parks, recreation, leisure, and fitness studies related; public health; social and philosophical foundations of education; social work; special education; statistics.

THE UNIVERSITY OF TENNESSEE AT CHATTANOOGA

Chattanooga, Tennessee
UTC Continuing Education
http://www.utc.edu/ce

The University of Tennessee at Chattanooga was founded in 1886. It is accredited by Southern Association of Colleges and Schools. It first offered distance learning courses in 1993. In fall 2010, there were 1,500 students enrolled in distance learning courses. Institutionally administered financial aid is available to distance learners.
Services Distance learners have accessibility to academic advising, bookstore, career placement assistance, e-mail services, library services.
Contact Ms. Tonya P. Botts, Distance Learning Manager, The University of Tennessee at Chattanooga, 615 McCallie Avenue, Department 5255, Chattanooga, TN 37403. Telephone: 423-755-4344. Fax: 423-425-4170. E-mail: tonya-botts@utc.edu.

DEGREES AND AWARDS

MEM Engineering Management
MEd Education
DPT Physical Therapy

COURSE SUBJECT AREAS OFFERED OUTSIDE OF DEGREE PROGRAMS

Undergraduate—computer science; criminal justice and corrections; education; education (specific levels and methods); health and physical education/fitness.
Graduate—education; political science and government.
Non-credit—computer software and media applications; human resources management; journalism; sales, merchandising and related marketing operations (specialized).

THE UNIVERSITY OF TENNESSEE AT MARTIN

Martin, Tennessee
Office of Extended Campus and Continuing Education
http://www.utm.edu

The University of Tennessee at Martin was founded in 1900. It is accredited by Southern Association of Colleges and Schools. It first offered distance learning courses in 1992. In fall 2010, there were 1,517 students enrolled in distance learning courses. Institutionally administered financial aid is available to distance learners.
Services Distance learners have accessibility to academic advising, bookstore, campus computer network, career placement assistance, e-mail services, library services.
Contact Dr. Tommy Cates, Executive Director of Extended Campus and Online Studies, The University of Tennessee at Martin, Extended Campus and Online Studies, 227 Administration Building, Martin, TN 38238-5050. Telephone: 731-881-7764. Fax: 731-881-3589. E-mail: tcates@utm.edu.

DEGREES AND AWARDS

BS Nursing
BSBA Management
BUS University Studies
MBA Banking and Financial Services Professionals
MS Ed Counseling; Educational Leadership
MS Agriculture and Natural Resources Systems Management; Family and Consumer Sciences
MSE Interdisciplinary; Teaching–Curriculum and Instruction

COURSE SUBJECT AREAS OFFERED OUTSIDE OF DEGREE PROGRAMS

Graduate—education (specific subject areas); English or French as a second or foreign language (teaching); special education.
Non-credit—accounting and related services; business administration, management and operations; computer and information sciences; crafts, folk art and artisanry; criminal justice and corrections; education; education (specific levels and methods); human development, family studies, and related services.

THE UNIVERSITY OF TENNESSEE SPACE INSTITUTE

Tullahoma, Tennessee
Distance and Continuing Education
http://www.utsi.edu/em

The University of Tennessee Space Institute is accredited by Southern Association of Colleges and Schools. It first offered distance learning courses in 1982. In fall 2010, there were 150 students enrolled in distance learning courses. Institutionally administered financial aid is available to distance learners.
Services Distance learners have accessibility to academic advising, e-mail services, library services.
Contact Ms. Charlotte Henley, Administrative Specialist, The University of Tennessee Space Institute, 411 B.H. Goethert Parkway, Mailstop 19, Tullahoma, TN 37388-9700. Telephone: 931-393-7293. Fax: 931-393-7201. E-mail: chenley@utsi.edu.

DEGREES AND AWARDS

MS Aviation Systems; Industrial Engineering/Engineering Management
PhD Industrial Engineering/Engineering Management

COURSE SUBJECT AREAS OFFERED OUTSIDE OF DEGREE PROGRAMS

Graduate—aerospace, aeronautical and astronautical engineering; materials engineering; mathematics; mechanical engineering; physics.

THE UNIVERSITY OF TEXAS AT ARLINGTON
Arlington, Texas
Center for Distance Education
http://distance.uta.edu

The University of Texas at Arlington was founded in 1895. It is accredited by Southern Association of Colleges and Schools. It first offered distance learning courses in 1973. In fall 2010, there were 23,500 students enrolled in distance learning courses. Institutionally administered financial aid is available to distance learners.

Services Distance learners have accessibility to academic advising, bookstore, campus computer network, e-mail services, library services, tutoring.

Contact Dr. Pete Smith, Assistant Vice President of Academic Affairs, The University of Texas at Arlington, Box 19027, Arlington, TX 76019. Telephone: 817-272-5727. Fax: 817-272-5728. E-mail: info@distance.uta.edu.

DEGREES AND AWARDS
BA Criminology and Criminal Justice (completion degree)
BSN Nursing–Bachelor of Science in Nursing (BSN); Nursing–RN to BSN, Registered Nurse to Bachelor of Science in Nursing
MBA Management, general
ME Aerospace Engineering; Computer Science and Engineering; Mechanical Engineering
MEd Curriculum and Instruction–Mathematics Education; Curriculum and Instruction–Science Education; Curriculum and Instruction/Reading; Educational Leadership and Policy Studies
MPA Public Administration
MS Industrial Engineering
MSCE Civil Engineering
MSEE Electrical Engineering
MSN Nursing Administration

COURSE SUBJECT AREAS OFFERED OUTSIDE OF DEGREE PROGRAMS
Undergraduate—accounting and computer science; accounting and related services; anthropology; biological and biomedical sciences related; biology; business, management, and marketing related; communication and journalism related; communication and media; computer/information technology administration and management; criminology; drama/theatre arts and stagecraft; economics; fine and studio arts; health and physical education/fitness; languages (Romance languages); political science and government; social work; sociology.
Graduate—aerospace, aeronautical and astronautical engineering; curriculum and instruction; engineering mechanics; environmental/environmental health engineering; finance and financial management services; mechanical engineering; political science and government; social work.
Non-credit—social work.

THE UNIVERSITY OF TEXAS AT BROWNSVILLE
Brownsville, Texas
Online Learning
http://www.utb.edu

The University of Texas at Brownsville was founded in 1973. It is accredited by Southern Association of Colleges and Schools. It first offered distance learning courses in 2003. In fall 2010, there were 3,332 students enrolled in distance learning courses. Institutionally administered financial aid is available to distance learners.

Services Distance learners have accessibility to academic advising, bookstore, campus computer network, career placement assistance, e-mail services, library services, tutoring.

Contact Mr. Rene Sainz, Assistant Director, ITS Online Learning, The University of Texas at Brownsville, 80 Fort Brown, Brownsville, TX 78520. Telephone: 956-882-6695. Fax: 956-882-6751. E-mail: rene.sainz@utb.edu.

DEGREES AND AWARDS
BA Applied Business Technology; Interdisciplinary Studies; Legal Studies
BAT Computer Information System Technology; Health Services Technology; Workforce Leadership and Supervision
BS Criminal Justice; Nursing
Certification Master Technology Teacher; Polysomnography; Spanish Translation; e-Learning
MBA Business Administration
MEd Educational Technology
MS Mathematics

COURSE SUBJECT AREAS OFFERED OUTSIDE OF DEGREE PROGRAMS
Undergraduate—behavioral sciences; bilingual, multilingual, and multicultural education; computer science; curriculum and instruction; mathematics; mathematics and statistics related; social sciences related.
Graduate—education related.
Non-credit—accounting and related services; business administration, management and operations; computer software and media applications; computer systems networking and telecommunications; criminal justice and corrections; culinary arts and related services; dance; foods, nutrition, and related services; ground transportation; real estate.

THE UNIVERSITY OF TEXAS AT DALLAS
Richardson, Texas
Global On-Line MBA
http://www.som.utdallas.edu/onlinePrograms/globalMbaOnline/

The University of Texas at Dallas was founded in 1969. It is accredited by Southern Association of Colleges and Schools. It first offered distance learning courses in 1999. In fall 2010, there were 234 students enrolled in distance learning courses. Institutionally administered financial aid is available to distance learners.

Services Distance learners have accessibility to academic advising, campus computer network, e-mail services, library services.

Contact Corina Cantua, Advisor, The University of Texas at Dallas, 800 West Campbell Road, Mail Station 20, Richardson, TX 75080-3021. Telephone: 972-883-5963. Fax: 972-883-6425. E-mail: corina.cantua@utdallas.edu.

DEGREES AND AWARDS
MBA Global MBA On-line
MS Accounting; Project Management
MSIT Information Technology Management

COURSE SUBJECT AREAS OFFERED OUTSIDE OF DEGREE PROGRAMS
Graduate—accounting and computer science; accounting and related services; business administration, management and operations; business/commerce; business, management, and marketing related; business/managerial economics; economics; entrepreneurial and small business operations; finance and financial management services; health and medical administrative services; international business; international/global studies; management information systems; management sciences and quantitative methods; marketing; operations research; statistics.
Non-credit—clinical, counseling and applied psychology; management sciences and quantitative methods; manufacturing engineering; marketing.

THE UNIVERSITY OF TEXAS OF THE PERMIAN BASIN
Odessa, Texas
REACH Program Center
http://reach.utpb.edu/

The University of Texas of the Permian Basin was founded in 1969. It is accredited by Southern Association of Colleges and Schools. It first offered distance learning courses in 1996. In fall 2010, there were 1,837 students enrolled in distance learning courses. Institutionally administered financial aid is available to distance learners.

Services Distance learners have accessibility to academic advising, bookstore, e-mail services, library services, tutoring.

Contact Scott Smiley, Director, The University of Texas of the Permian Basin, 4901 East University Boulevard, Odessa, TX 79762. Telephone: 432-552-2608. Fax: 432-552-2605. E-mail: smiley_s@utpb.edu.

DEGREES AND AWARDS
BA Humanities; Sociology
BAAS Industrial Technology
BS Criminal Justice
CAGS Autism and Developmental Disabilities in Early Childhood
MA Educational Leadership; English as a Second Language Education; Special Education
MBA Business Administration
MS Kinesiology; Kinesiology

COURSE SUBJECT AREAS OFFERED OUTSIDE OF DEGREE PROGRAMS
Undergraduate—applied mathematics; behavioral sciences; bilingual, multilingual, and multicultural education; business, management, and marketing related; chemistry; communication and journalism related; communication and media; computer and information sciences; computer science; criminal justice and corrections; curriculum and instruction; education; education related; education (specific levels and methods); education (specific subject areas); English; English language and literature related; English or French as a second or foreign language (teaching); environmental control technologies; fine and studio arts; health and physical education/fitness; history; human development, family studies, and related services; industrial production technologies; liberal arts and sciences, general studies and humanities; management sciences and quantitative methods; mathematics; mathematics and computer science; music; political science and government; psychology; social work; sociology; visual and performing arts.
Graduate—accounting and related services; curriculum and instruction; education; educational administration and supervision; education related; education (specific levels and methods); education (specific subject areas); English language and literature related; finance and financial management services; health and physical education/fitness; marketing; psychology; special education; statistics.

UNIVERSITY OF THE INCARNATE WORD
San Antonio, Texas
Virtual University
http://online.uiw.edu

University of the Incarnate Word was founded in 1881. It is accredited by Southern Association of Colleges and Schools. It first offered distance learning courses in 2000. In fall 2010, there were 2,000 students enrolled in distance learning courses. Institutionally administered financial aid is available to distance learners.
Services Distance learners have accessibility to academic advising, bookstore, campus computer network, career placement assistance, e-mail services, library services, tutoring.
Contact Admissions Counselor, University of the Incarnate Word, CPO #312, 4301 Broadway, San Antonio, TX 78209. Telephone: 877-870-1875. Fax: 210-829-2756. E-mail: eapadmission@uiwtx.edu.

DEGREES AND AWARDS
AA Business; Information Systems; Liberal Studies
BA Administration; Human Resources; Organizational Development; Religious Studies
BAA Applied Arts and Sciences (BAAS)
BS Criminal Justice; Psychology
BSBA Business Administration in Accounting; Business Administration in Banking and Finance; Business Administration in General Business; Business Administration in Information Systems; Business Administration in International Business; Business Administration in Management; Business Administration in Marketing
MA Administration in Communication Arts; Administration in Healthcare Administration; Applied Administration; Organizational Development
MBA General Program; International
MEd Teacher Leadership

COURSE SUBJECT AREAS OFFERED OUTSIDE OF DEGREE PROGRAMS
Non-credit—legal professions and studies related; legal research and advanced professional studies; legal support services.

UNIVERSITY OF THE PACIFIC
Stockton, California
Center for Professional and Continuing Education
http://www.pacific.edu/cpce

University of the Pacific was founded in 1851. It is accredited by Western Association of Schools and Colleges. It first offered distance learning courses in 1995. In fall 2010, there were 1,700 students enrolled in distance learning courses. Institutionally administered financial aid is available to distance learners.
Contact Matt Van Donsel, Coordinator for Program Development and Management, University of the Pacific, 3601 Pacific Avenue, Stockton, CA 95211. Telephone: 209-946-2424 Ext. 65040. Fax: 209-946-3916. E-mail: cpce@pacific.edu.

DEGREES AND AWARDS
Programs offered do not lead to a degree or other formal award.

COURSE SUBJECT AREAS OFFERED OUTSIDE OF DEGREE PROGRAMS
Undergraduate—behavioral sciences; communication and media; dance; English; history; journalism; movement and mind-body therapies and education; music.
Graduate—curriculum and instruction; education related; education (specific subject areas).
Non-credit—behavioral sciences; entrepreneurial and small business operations; legal professions and studies related.

UNIVERSITY OF THE SCIENCES IN PHILADELPHIA
Philadelphia, Pennsylvania
http://www.usciences.edu

University of the Sciences in Philadelphia was founded in 1821. It is accredited by Middle States Association of Colleges and Schools. It first offered distance learning courses in 2000. In fall 2010, there were 186 students enrolled in distance learning courses. Institutionally administered financial aid is available to distance learners.
Services Distance learners have accessibility to academic advising, bookstore, campus computer network, e-mail services, library services.
Contact Ms. Dianna Collins, Executive Director of Admissions, University of the Sciences in Philadelphia, 600 South 43rd Street, Philadelphia, PA 19104-4418. Telephone: 215-596-8556. Fax: 215-895-1185. E-mail: graduate@usciences.edu.

DEGREES AND AWARDS
MBA Pharmaceutical Business
MS Biomedical Writing

COURSE SUBJECT AREAS OFFERED OUTSIDE OF DEGREE PROGRAMS
Undergraduate—information science/studies.
Graduate—allied health diagnostic, intervention, and treatment professions; health professions related; health services/allied health/health sciences; information science/studies; marketing.

UNIVERSITY OF THE SOUTHWEST
Hobbs, New Mexico
http://www.usw.edu/

University of the Southwest was founded in 1962. It is accredited by North Central Association of Colleges and Schools. It first offered distance learning courses in 1994. In fall 2010, there were 307 students enrolled in distance learning courses. Institutionally administered financial aid is available to distance learners.
Services Distance learners have accessibility to academic advising, bookstore, campus computer network, e-mail services, library services, tutoring.

Contact Evelyn Rising, Registrar, University of the Southwest, 6610 North Lovington Highway, Hobbs, NM 88240. Telephone: 575-492-2119. Fax: 575-392-6006. E-mail: erising@usw.edu.

DEGREES AND AWARDS

BS Criminal Justice

MBA Business Administration

MSE Counseling (Mental Health); Curriculum and Instruction–Reading; Curriculum and Instruction; Early Childhood Education; Educational Administration; Educational Diagnostician; School Business Administration; School Counseling; Special Education

COURSE SUBJECT AREAS OFFERED OUTSIDE OF DEGREE PROGRAMS

Undergraduate—accounting and related services; biblical studies; bilingual, multilingual, and multicultural education; biology; business administration, management and operations; business, management, and marketing related; computer and information sciences; criminal justice and corrections; criminology; economics; education; education (specific levels and methods); education (specific subject areas); English language and literature related; geological and earth sciences/geosciences; history; psychology; religious studies; social sciences related; sociology; special education.

Graduate—business administration, management and operations; curriculum and instruction; education; educational administration and supervision; education related; education (specific subject areas).

THE UNIVERSITY OF TOLEDO
Toledo, Ohio
Division of Distance and eLearning
http://www.utoledo.edu/dl/

The University of Toledo was founded in 1872. It is accredited by North Central Association of Colleges and Schools. It first offered distance learning courses in 1998. In fall 2010, there were 6,503 students enrolled in distance learning courses. Institutionally administered financial aid is available to distance learners.

Services Distance learners have accessibility to academic advising, bookstore, campus computer network, career placement assistance, e-mail services, library services, tutoring.

Contact Mr. James Ham, Learning Ventures, The University of Toledo, 2801 West Bancroft Street, Memorial Field House, Room 3015-C (Mail Stop 129), Toledo, OH 43606-3390. Telephone: 419-530-8835. Fax: 419-530-8836. E-mail: utdl@utoledo.edu.

DEGREES AND AWARDS

AD Accounting Technology; Business Management Technology; Computer Software Specialist; FastTrack Business Management Technology; Information Services and Support; Interdisciplinary Technical Studies; Programming and Software Development

BA Interdisciplinary Studies Program; Liberal Studies

BBA Applied Organization Technology

BEd Early Childhood Education–FastTrack degree completion

BS Computer Science and Engineering Technology; Criminal Justice; Health Care Administration; Health Information Administration; Information Technology

BSN Nursing–RN to BSN

CAGS Contemporary Gerontological Practice; Elder Law; Health Information Administration; Nursing Education

Graduate Certificate Patient Advocate

MA Recreation Administration

MEd Early Childhood Education; Physical Education, Adapted Physical Education track (APE); Special Education Early Childhood

MLS Liberal Studies

MSE Engineering

MSN Nurse Educator

DNP Nursing Practice

UNIVERSITY OF TORONTO
Toronto, Ontario, Canada
School of Continuing Studies
http://learn.utoronto.ca

University of Toronto was founded in 1827. It is provincially chartered. It first offered distance learning courses in 1944. In fall 2010, there were 5,000 students enrolled in distance learning courses. Institutionally administered financial aid is available to distance learners.

Services Distance learners have accessibility to academic advising, bookstore, e-mail services.

Contact Margaret White, Program Assistant, University of Toronto, School of Continuing Studies, 158 St. George Street, Toronto, ON M5S 2V8, Canada. Telephone: 416-978-7697. Fax: 416-978-5673. E-mail: margaret.white@utoronto.ca.

DEGREES AND AWARDS

Programs offered do not lead to a degree or other formal award.

COURSE SUBJECT AREAS OFFERED OUTSIDE OF DEGREE PROGRAMS

Non-credit—accounting and related services; business administration, management and operations; business/corporate communications; business, management, and marketing related; business/managerial economics; communication and media; computer/information technology administration and management; economics; finance and financial management services; human resources management; insurance; languages (East Asian); languages (foreign languages related); languages (Germanic); languages (Romance languages); languages (South Asian); management information systems; management sciences and quantitative methods; marketing; taxation.

UNIVERSITY OF UTAH
Salt Lake City, Utah
Distance Education
http://distance.utah.edu

University of Utah was founded in 1850. It is accredited by Northwest Commission on Colleges and Universities. It first offered distance learning courses in 1941. In fall 2010, there were 1,000 students enrolled in distance learning courses. Institutionally administered financial aid is available to distance learners.

Services Distance learners have accessibility to bookstore.

Contact Michelle Lynch, Program Coordinator, University of Utah, 1901 East South Campus Drive, Room 1215, Salt Lake City, UT 84112-9359. Telephone: 800-467-8839. Fax: 801-581-6267. E-mail: distance@aoce.utah.edu.

DEGREES AND AWARDS

Programs offered do not lead to a degree or other formal award.

COURSE SUBJECT AREAS OFFERED OUTSIDE OF DEGREE PROGRAMS

Undergraduate—anthropology; biology; chemistry; economics; education (specific subject areas); finance and financial management services; fine and studio arts; foods, nutrition, and related services; history; mathematics; mathematics and statistics related; music; political science and government; psychology; social sciences; special education; statistics.

Non-credit—real estate.

UNIVERSITY OF VIRGINIA
Charlottesville, Virginia
Educational Technologies
http://www.scps.virginia.edu/

University of Virginia was founded in 1819. It is accredited by Southern Association of Colleges and Schools. It first offered distance learning courses in 1983. In fall 2010, there were 1,537 students enrolled in distance learning courses. Institutionally administered financial aid is available to distance learners.

Services Distance learners have accessibility to academic advising, bookstore, e-mail services, library services.

Contact AnnMarie Black, Office of Admissions, University of Virginia, 104 Midmont Lane, Charlottesville, VA 22904. Telephone: 434-982-3200. Fax: 434-924-3587. E-mail: ab3f@virginia.edu.

DEGREES AND AWARDS
ME Engineering

COURSE SUBJECT AREAS OFFERED OUTSIDE OF DEGREE PROGRAMS
Undergraduate—accounting and related services; computer/information technology administration and management.
Graduate—education; human resources management; information science/studies; marketing; public administration.

UNIVERSITY OF WATERLOO
Waterloo, Ontario, Canada
Centre for Extended Learning
http://extendedlearning.uwaterloo.ca

University of Waterloo was founded in 1957. It is provincially chartered. It first offered distance learning courses in 1968. In fall 2010, there were 4,600 students enrolled in distance learning courses. Institutionally administered financial aid is available to distance learners.
Services Distance learners have accessibility to academic advising, bookstore, campus computer network, e-mail services, library services, tutoring.
Contact Learner Support Services, University of Waterloo, Centre for Extended Learning, Waterloo, ON N2L 3G1, Canada. Telephone: 519-888-4002. Fax: 519-746-4607. E-mail: extendedlearning@uwaterloo.ca.

DEGREES AND AWARDS
BA English; Liberal Studies; Philosophy; Social Development Studies
BSc General non-major
Certificate French Language, Level 1 or Level 2; Studies of Child Abuse
Diploma General Studies in Social Work
MEB Environment and Business
MMSc Management of Technology
MMT Mathematics for Teachers
MPH Public Health

COURSE SUBJECT AREAS OFFERED OUTSIDE OF DEGREE PROGRAMS
Undergraduate—accounting and related services; anthropology; area studies; astronomy and astrophysics; biblical studies; biochemistry, biophysics and molecular biology; biological and biomedical sciences related; biological and physical sciences; biology; business/managerial economics; cell biology and anatomical sciences; chemistry; community organization and advocacy; computer and information sciences; computer science; ecology, evolution, systematics, and population biology; economics; ethnic, cultural minority, gender, and group studies; finance and financial management services; geological and earth sciences/geosciences; gerontology; history; human development, family studies, and related services; insurance; international relations and national security studies; languages (foreign languages related); languages (Germanic); languages (Slavic, Baltic, and Albanian); legal studies (non-professional general, undergraduate); liberal arts and sciences, general studies and humanities; linguistic, comparative, and related language studies; mathematics; mathematics and statistics related; medieval and Renaissance studies; microbiological sciences and immunology; multi/interdisciplinary studies related; peace studies and conflict resolution; philosophy; philosophy and religious studies related; physical sciences; physics; physiology, pathology and related sciences; psychology; psychology related; religious studies; social sciences; social sciences related; social work; sociology; statistics.
Graduate—business administration, management and operations; curriculum and instruction; management information systems; mathematics and statistics related; public health; sustainability studies.
Non-credit—accounting and related services; business administration, management and operations; business/corporate communications; chemistry; communication and media; communications technology; computer programming; computer software and media applications; computer systems networking and telecommunications; data processing; graphic communications; human resources management; languages (foreign languages related); marketing; mathematics and statistics related; physics; publishing.

THE UNIVERSITY OF WEST ALABAMA
Livingston, Alabama
http://www.uwa.edu/Online_Education

The University of West Alabama was founded in 1835. It is accredited by Southern Association of Colleges and Schools. It first offered distance learning courses in 2002. In fall 2010, there were 3,000 students enrolled in distance learning courses. Institutionally administered financial aid is available to distance learners.
Services Distance learners have accessibility to academic advising, bookstore, campus computer network, e-mail services, library services.
Contact Online Advisor, The University of West Alabama, Station #46, Livingston, AL 35470. Telephone: 877-892-1835. E-mail: online@uwa.edu.

DEGREES AND AWARDS
BBA Accounting; Business Administration
BS Technology
Ed S Collaborative Special Education; Counseling (non-certification); Early Childhood Education; Elementary Education; Instructional Leadership; Library Media; School Counseling; Teacher Leader
MAT Non-certification; Teaching certification
MC Ed College Student Development; Counseling/Psychology; General Education; Guidance and Counseling; Library Media
MEd Early Childhood Education; Elementary Education; Library Media; School Counseling; Secondary Education; Special Education

COURSE SUBJECT AREAS OFFERED OUTSIDE OF DEGREE PROGRAMS
Undergraduate—behavioral sciences; biology; botany/plant biology; communication and journalism related; economics; education; English; history; marketing; psychology; social sciences; sociology; special education.

THE UNIVERSITY OF WESTERN ONTARIO
London, Ontario, Canada
http://www.uwo.ca/

The University of Western Ontario was founded in 1878. It is provincially chartered. In fall 2010, there were 9,818 students enrolled in distance learning courses. Institutionally administered financial aid is available to distance learners.
Services Distance learners have accessibility to academic advising, bookstore, campus computer network, career placement assistance, e-mail services, library services.
Contact Ms. Debbie Sims, Supervisor, Distance Studies, The University of Western Ontario, Western Student Services Building, RM 2140, London, ON N6A 3K7, Canada. Telephone: 519-661-2111 Ext. 85130. Fax: 519-661-3615. E-mail: dsims@uwo.ca.

DEGREES AND AWARDS
BA English; French; Sociology
Certificate Writing

UNIVERSITY OF WEST FLORIDA
Pensacola, Florida
Online Campus/Academic Technology Center
http://onlinecampus.uwf.edu

University of West Florida was founded in 1963. It is accredited by Southern Association of Colleges and Schools. It first offered distance learning courses in 1995. In fall 2010, there were 5,500 students enrolled in distance learning courses. Institutionally administered financial aid is available to distance learners.
Services Distance learners have accessibility to academic advising, bookstore, campus computer network, career placement assistance, e-mail services, library services, tutoring.

Contact Mr. John Carey, Director, UWF Online Campus Student Support Center, University of West Florida, 11000 University Parkway, Building 77, Room 149, Pensacola, FL 32514. Telephone: 850-474-7209. Fax: 850-474-2807. E-mail: jcarey@uwf.edu.

DEGREES AND AWARDS

BA Exceptional Student Education
BS Career and Technical Studies Education–Vocational Program Development; Career and Technical Studies Education–Vocational Teacher Education; Health Sciences, Allied Health; Health Sciences, Health Care Professional; Health Sciences, Medical Information Technology; IIT Networking and Telecommunications; Information Engineering Technology; Maritime Studies; Oceanography
MA Special Education
MEd Career and Technical Education (CTE); Education and Training Management Subspecialty/Human Performance Technology; Education and Training Management Subspecialty/Instructional Technology; Education–Comprehensive Masters in Education; Instructional Technology
MS Mathematics; Public Health
MSA Acquisition and Contract Administration; Biomedical/Pharmaceutical; Criminal Justice Administration; Database Administration; Health Care Administration; Human Performance Technology; Leadership; Nursing Administration; Public Administration; Software Engineering Administration
MSN Nursing

COURSE SUBJECT AREAS OFFERED OUTSIDE OF DEGREE PROGRAMS

Undergraduate—anthropology; archeology; biological and biomedical sciences related; biology; business/corporate communications; communication and media; communications technology; computer programming; computer science; computer software and media applications; computer systems networking and telecommunications; data entry/microcomputer applications; economics; engineering technologies related; English; fine and studio arts; history; liberal arts and sciences, general studies and humanities; mathematics; mathematics and statistics related; philosophy; physical sciences; physical sciences related; political science and government; religious studies; statistics.
Graduate—accounting and computer science; allied health diagnostic, intervention, and treatment professions; behavioral sciences; business administration, management and operations; computer science; educational/instructional media design; education related; health services/allied health/health sciences; information science/studies; political science and government; public administration and social service professions related; special education.
Non-credit—business, management, and marketing related; communications technology; computer engineering; education related; education (specific subject areas); human resources management.

UNIVERSITY OF WEST GEORGIA
Carrollton, Georgia
http://distance.westga.edu/

University of West Georgia was founded in 1933. It is accredited by Southern Association of Colleges and Schools. It first offered distance learning courses in 1997. In fall 2010, there were 4,644 students enrolled in distance learning courses. Institutionally administered financial aid is available to distance learners.
Services Distance learners have accessibility to academic advising, bookstore, career placement assistance, e-mail services, library services, tutoring.
Contact Janet P. Gubbins, Director, Distance and Distributed Ed Center, University of West Georgia, Honors House, Maple Street, Carrollton, GA 30117. Telephone: 678-839-0630. Fax: 678-839-0636. E-mail: jgubbins @westga.edu.

DEGREES AND AWARDS

BS Criminology
CCCPE School Library Media Add-on
Ed S Media major (School Library Media and Instructional Technology tracks); Special Education
MAT Teaching in Secondary Mathematics and Science
MBA Georgia WebMBA
MEd Media major (School Library Media and Instructional Technology tracks)
MSCS Applied Computer Science
MSN The Health Systems Leadership Track–Leader/Manager, Clinical Nurse Leader, Nursing Education track
PMC Nursing Education
EdD School Improvement

COURSE SUBJECT AREAS OFFERED OUTSIDE OF DEGREE PROGRAMS

Undergraduate—accounting and computer science; anthropology; applied mathematics; biology; business administration, management and operations; business, management, and marketing related; communication and media; computer and information sciences; computer science; criminal justice and corrections; curriculum and instruction; economics; education; educational/instructional media design; education related; education (specific levels and methods); English; geological and earth sciences/geosciences; history; languages (foreign languages related); library science and administration; marketing; mathematics; philosophy; philosophy and religious studies related; physics; political science and government; psychology; social sciences related; sociology; special education.
Graduate—applied mathematics; bilingual, multilingual, and multicultural education; business administration, management and operations; computer and information sciences; curriculum and instruction; education; educational administration and supervision; educational assessment, evaluation, and research; educational/instructional media design; education related; education (specific levels and methods); English or French as a second or foreign language (teaching); geography and cartography; geological and earth sciences/geosciences; health/medical preparatory programs; health services/allied health/health sciences; management information systems; mathematics; psychology related; social sciences; sociology; special education.
Non-credit—education (specific levels and methods).

UNIVERSITY OF WINDSOR
Windsor, Ontario, Canada
Continuing Education
http://www.uwindsor.ca/registrar/distance-education

University of Windsor was founded in 1857. It is provincially chartered. It first offered distance learning courses in 1985. In fall 2010, there were 1,750 students enrolled in distance learning courses. Institutionally administered financial aid is available to distance learners.
Services Distance learners have accessibility to academic advising, bookstore, campus computer network, career placement assistance, e-mail services, library services, tutoring.
Contact Mr. Marty Lowman, Supervisor, Student Information Resource Centre (SIRC), University of Windsor, Windsor, ON N9B 3P4, Canada. Telephone: 519-253-3000 Ext. 1414. Fax: 519-971-3623. E-mail: askme@uwindsor.ca.

DEGREES AND AWARDS

Programs offered do not lead to a degree or other formal award.

COURSE SUBJECT AREAS OFFERED OUTSIDE OF DEGREE PROGRAMS

Undergraduate—accounting and related services; arts, entertainment, and media management; biology; business administration, management and operations; computer science; economics; history; mathematics and statistics related; natural sciences; political science and government; science, technology and society.
Non-credit—education (specific levels and methods).

THE UNIVERSITY OF WINNIPEG

Winnipeg, Manitoba, Canada

http://ctlt.uwinnipeg.ca/

The University of Winnipeg was founded in 1967. It is provincially chartered. It first offered distance learning courses in 1992. In fall 2010, there were 1,200 students enrolled in distance learning courses. Institutionally administered financial aid is available to distance learners.

Services Distance learners have accessibility to academic advising, bookstore, campus computer network, career placement assistance, e-mail services, library services, tutoring.

Contact D. Laube, Manager of Programs, The University of Winnipeg, The Centre for Teaching, Learning, and Technology, Room 4C68, 515 Portage Avenue, Winnipeg, MB R3B 2E9, Canada. Telephone: 204-786-9849. Fax: 204-783-3116. E-mail: d.laube@uwinnipeg.ca.

DEGREES AND AWARDS

Programs offered do not lead to a degree or other formal award.

COURSE SUBJECT AREAS OFFERED OUTSIDE OF DEGREE PROGRAMS

Undergraduate—accounting and related services; biology; chemistry; criminal justice and corrections; ecology, evolution, systematics, and population biology; English; environmental/environmental health engineering; geography and cartography; liberal arts and sciences, general studies and humanities; physics; religious studies; social sciences; sociology.

UNIVERSITY OF WISCONSIN COLLEGES

Madison, Wisconsin

UWC On-line

http://online.uwc.edu/

University of Wisconsin Colleges is accredited by North Central Association of Colleges and Schools. It first offered distance learning courses in 1998. In fall 2010, there were 1,400 students enrolled in distance learning courses. Institutionally administered financial aid is available to distance learners.

Services Distance learners have accessibility to academic advising, bookstore, campus computer network, e-mail services, library services, tutoring.

Contact Ms. Bethany Gordy, Senior Instructional Designer, University of Wisconsin Colleges, 505 South Rosa Road, Suite 200, Madison, WI 53719. Telephone: 608-265-0768. Fax: 608-262-7872. E-mail: bethany.gordy@uwc.edu.

DEGREES AND AWARDS

AAS Liberal Arts

COURSE SUBJECT AREAS OFFERED OUTSIDE OF DEGREE PROGRAMS

Undergraduate—anthropology; biology; business/commerce; chemistry; communication and journalism related; economics; English; ethnic, cultural minority, gender, and group studies; geography and cartography; geological and earth sciences/geosciences; history; journalism; mathematics; mathematics and computer science; mathematics and statistics related; music; natural sciences; philosophy; political science and government; psychology; social sciences; sociology; statistics; visual and performing arts related.

Non-credit—English; mathematics.

UNIVERSITY OF WISCONSIN–GREEN BAY

Green Bay, Wisconsin

BSN–LINC Online RN–BSN Program

http://www.uwgb.edu/nursing/

University of Wisconsin–Green Bay was founded in 1968. It is accredited by North Central Association of Colleges and Schools. It first offered distance learning courses in 2000. In fall 2010, there were 226 students enrolled in distance learning courses. Institutionally administered financial aid is available to distance learners.

Services Distance learners have accessibility to academic advising, bookstore, campus computer network, e-mail services, library services.

Contact Jennifer Schwahn, Advisor, University of Wisconsin–Green Bay, 2420 Nicolet Drive, Rose Hall 325, Green Bay, WI 54311-7001. Telephone: 920-465-2826. Fax: 920-465-2854. E-mail: schwahnj@uwgb.edu.

DEGREES AND AWARDS

BSN Nursing–Professional Program in Nursing

COURSE SUBJECT AREAS OFFERED OUTSIDE OF DEGREE PROGRAMS

Undergraduate—chemistry; ethnic, cultural minority, gender, and group studies; fine and studio arts; gerontology; health/medical preparatory programs; health services/allied health/health sciences; human development, family studies, and related services; intercultural/multicultural and diversity studies; medical clinical sciences/graduate medical studies; natural sciences; pharmacology and toxicology; philosophy; public health; social sciences related; statistics.

UNIVERSITY OF WISCONSIN–LA CROSSE

La Crosse, Wisconsin

http://www.uwlax.edu/

University of Wisconsin–La Crosse was founded in 1909. It is accredited by North Central Association of Colleges and Schools. It first offered distance learning courses in 1995. In fall 2010, there were 400 students enrolled in distance learning courses. Institutionally administered financial aid is available to distance learners.

Services Distance learners have accessibility to academic advising, bookstore, campus computer network, career placement assistance, e-mail services, library services, tutoring.

Contact Brian Udermann, Director of Online Education, University of Wisconsin–La Crosse, 1725 State Street, La Crosse, WI 54601. Telephone: 608-785-8181. E-mail: udermann.bria@uwlax.edu.

DEGREES AND AWARDS

Certificate Medical Dosimetry
MEd Professional Development Learning Community Program
MS Medical Dosimetry; Student Affairs Administration in Higher Education

COURSE SUBJECT AREAS OFFERED OUTSIDE OF DEGREE PROGRAMS

Undergraduate—health professions related; history; insurance; international/global studies; liberal arts and sciences, general studies and humanities; linguistic, comparative, and related language studies; ophthalmic and optometric support services and allied professions; psychology; sociology and anthropology.

Graduate—accounting and related services; business administration, management and operations; economics; finance and financial management services; microbiological sciences and immunology; parks, recreation and leisure facilities management; sales merchandising, and related marketing operations (general).

UNIVERSITY OF WISCONSIN–MADISON

Madison, Wisconsin

http://www.wisc.edu/

University of Wisconsin–Madison was founded in 1848. It is accredited by North Central Association of Colleges and Schools. It first offered distance learning courses in 1991. In fall 2010, there were 2,289 students enrolled in distance learning courses.

Services Distance learners have accessibility to academic advising, bookstore, campus computer network, e-mail services, library services.

Contact Student Application Contact, University of Wisconsin–Madison, Madison, WI 53706. Telephone: 608-263-2400.

DEGREES AND AWARDS

BS Nursing
Certificate of Completion Distance Education
Certificate Laboratory Quality Management
MA Library and Information Studies
ME Engineering–Engine Systems; Engineering–Polymer Science

MEngr Professional Practice; Technical Japanese
MPAS Physician Assistant Studies
MS Computer Engineering; Educational Psychology, Professional Educator option; Electrical Engineering; Manufacturing Systems Engineering
PharmD Pharmacy

UNIVERSITY OF WISCONSIN MBA CONSORTIUM
http://www.wisconsinonlinemba.org/

University of Wisconsin MBA Consortium first offered distance learning courses in 1997. In fall 2010, there were 425 students enrolled in distance learning courses. Institutionally administered financial aid is available to distance learners.
Services Distance learners have accessibility to academic advising, bookstore, campus computer network, career placement assistance, e-mail services, library services.
Contact Jan M. Stewart, Program Associate, University of Wisconsin MBA Consortium, Schneider Hall 215, 105 Garfield Avenue, Eau Claire, WI 54702-4004. Telephone: 888-832-7090. Fax: 715-836-3923. E-mail: stewarjm@uwec.edu.

DEGREES AND AWARDS
MBA Business Administration

COURSE SUBJECT AREAS OFFERED OUTSIDE OF DEGREE PROGRAMS
Graduate—accounting and related services; economics; finance and financial management services; management information systems; management sciences and quantitative methods; marketing.

UNIVERSITY OF WISCONSIN–MILWAUKEE
Milwaukee, Wisconsin
Distance Learning and Instructional Support
http://www4.uwm.edu/SCE/

University of Wisconsin–Milwaukee was founded in 1956. It is accredited by North Central Association of Colleges and Schools. Institutionally administered financial aid is available to distance learners.
Contact Latonia Pernell, Distance Education Program Coordinator, University of Wisconsin–Milwaukee, 161 West Wisconsin Avenue, #6000, Milwaukee, WI 53203. Telephone: 414-227-3336. Fax: 414-227-3330. E-mail: ldglass@uwm.edu.

DEGREES AND AWARDS
Programs offered do not lead to a degree or other formal award.

COURSE SUBJECT AREAS OFFERED OUTSIDE OF DEGREE PROGRAMS
Non-credit—behavioral sciences; business/corporate communications; education (specific levels and methods); human services; science technologies related.

UNIVERSITY OF WISCONSIN–MILWAUKEE
Milwaukee, Wisconsin
School of Information Studies
http://www.sois.uwm.edu

University of Wisconsin–Milwaukee was founded in 1956. It is accredited by North Central Association of Colleges and Schools. It first offered distance learning courses in 1998. In fall 2010, there were 700 students enrolled in distance learning courses. Institutionally administered financial aid is available to distance learners.
Services Distance learners have accessibility to academic advising, bookstore, campus computer network, career placement assistance, e-mail services, library services.
Contact Dr. Betsy A. Schoeller, Distance Education Coordinator, University of Wisconsin–Milwaukee, 510 Bolton Hall, Milwaukee, WI 53211. Telephone: 414-229-2944. Fax: 414-229-4848. E-mail: schoeller@sois.uwm.edu.

DEGREES AND AWARDS
MLIS Library and Information Science

COURSE SUBJECT AREAS OFFERED OUTSIDE OF DEGREE PROGRAMS
Undergraduate—computer and information sciences; information science/studies; library science related.
Graduate—business, management, and marketing related; computer and information sciences; information science/studies; library science and administration.

UNIVERSITY OF WISCONSIN–PARKSIDE
Kenosha, Wisconsin
http://www.uwp.edu/

University of Wisconsin–Parkside was founded in 1968. It is accredited by North Central Association of Colleges and Schools. It first offered distance learning courses in 1996. In fall 2010, there were 104 students enrolled in distance learning courses. Institutionally administered financial aid is available to distance learners.
Services Distance learners have accessibility to academic advising, bookstore, campus computer network, career placement assistance, e-mail services, library services, tutoring.
Contact Dirk Baldwin, Associate Dean of School of Business and Technology, University of Wisconsin–Parkside, 900 Wood Road, PO Box 2000, Kenosha, WI 53141-2000. Telephone: 262-595-2046. Fax: 262-595-2680. E-mail: dirk.baldwin@uwp.edu.

DEGREES AND AWARDS
BS Sustainable Management
MBA Business Administration

COURSE SUBJECT AREAS OFFERED OUTSIDE OF DEGREE PROGRAMS
Undergraduate—business administration, management and operations; computer science; languages (foreign languages related).

UNIVERSITY OF WISCONSIN–PLATTEVILLE
Platteville, Wisconsin
Bachelor of Science in Business Administration at a Distance
http://www.uwplatt.edu/disted/business-administration.html

University of Wisconsin–Platteville was founded in 1866. It is accredited by North Central Association of Colleges and Schools. It first offered distance learning courses in 1978. In fall 2010, there were 1,073 students enrolled in distance learning courses. Institutionally administered financial aid is available to distance learners.
Services Distance learners have accessibility to academic advising, bookstore, campus computer network, career placement assistance, e-mail services, library services.
Contact Clint Nemitz, Admission Specialist, Online Bachelor of Science in Business Administration, University of Wisconsin–Platteville, 2100 Ullsvik Hall, 1 University Plaza, Platteville, WI 53818-3099. Telephone: 800-362-5460. Fax: 608-342-1071. E-mail: nemitzc@uwplatt.edu.

DEGREES AND AWARDS
BSBA Business Administration
Certificate Human Resource Management; International Business; Leadership and Human Performance; Marketing

COURSE SUBJECT AREAS OFFERED OUTSIDE OF DEGREE PROGRAMS
Non-credit—business administration, management and operations.

UNIVERSITY OF WISCONSIN–PLATTEVILLE
Platteville, Wisconsin
Distance Learning Center
http://www.uwplatt.edu/disted/

University of Wisconsin–Platteville was founded in 1866. It is accredited by North Central Association of Colleges and Schools. It first offered distance learning courses in 1978. In fall 2010, there were 1,073 students enrolled in distance learning courses. Institutionally administered financial aid is available to distance learners.

Services Distance learners have accessibility to academic advising, bookstore, campus computer network, career placement assistance, e-mail services, library services.

Contact Clint Nemitz, Admission Specialist, University of Wisconsin–Platteville, 2100 Ullsvik Hall, 1 University Plaza, Platteville, WI 53818-3099. Telephone: 800-362-5460. Fax: 608-342-1071. E-mail: nemitzc@uwplatt.edu.

DEGREES AND AWARDS

BS Business Administration; Criminal Justice
Certificate Human Resource Management; International Business; Leadership and Human Performance; Marketing
Advanced Graduate Diploma Criminal Justice
Graduate Certificate Engineering Management; Geotechnical Engineering; Project Management; Project Management, Advanced; Structural Engineering; Structural/Geotechnical Engineering
MS Criminal Justice; Engineering; Project Management

COURSE SUBJECT AREAS OFFERED OUTSIDE OF DEGREE PROGRAMS

Non-credit—business administration, management and operations; criminal justice and corrections; engineering.

UNIVERSITY OF WISCONSIN–PLATTEVILLE
Platteville, Wisconsin
Master of Science in Education, Adult Education at a Distance
http://www.uwplatt.edu/mse/AdultEd.htm

University of Wisconsin–Platteville was founded in 1866. It is accredited by North Central Association of Colleges and Schools. It first offered distance learning courses in 1978. In fall 2010, there were 40 students enrolled in distance learning courses. Institutionally administered financial aid is available to distance learners.

Services Distance learners have accessibility to academic advising, bookstore, campus computer network, career placement assistance, e-mail services, library services.

Contact Dr. Patricia Bromley, Program Director, University of Wisconsin–Platteville, 2100 Ullsvik Hall, 1 University Plaza, Platteville, WI 53818-3099. Telephone: 800-362-5460. Fax: 608-342-1071. E-mail: disted@uwplatt.edu.

DEGREES AND AWARDS

MSE Adult Education

UNIVERSITY OF WISCONSIN–PLATTEVILLE
Platteville, Wisconsin
Online Bachelor of Science in Criminal Justice
http://www.uwplatt.edu/disted/criminal-justice.html

University of Wisconsin–Platteville was founded in 1866. It is accredited by North Central Association of Colleges and Schools. It first offered distance learning courses in 1978. In fall 2010, there were 1,073 students enrolled in distance learning courses. Institutionally administered financial aid is available to distance learners.

Services Distance learners have accessibility to academic advising, bookstore, campus computer network, career placement assistance, e-mail services, library services.

Contact Clint Nemitz, Admission Specialist, Online Bachelor of Science in Criminal Justice, University of Wisconsin–Platteville, 2100 Ullsvik Hall, 1 University Plaza, Platteville, WI 53818-3099. Telephone: 800-362-5460. Fax: 608-342-1071. E-mail: nemitzc@uwplatt.edu.

DEGREES AND AWARDS

BS Criminal Justice

COURSE SUBJECT AREAS OFFERED OUTSIDE OF DEGREE PROGRAMS

Non-credit—criminal justice and corrections; criminology.

UNIVERSITY OF WISCONSIN–PLATTEVILLE
Platteville, Wisconsin
Online Master of Science in Criminal Justice Program
http://www.uwplatt.edu/disted/criminal-justice-MS.html

University of Wisconsin–Platteville was founded in 1866. It is accredited by North Central Association of Colleges and Schools. It first offered distance learning courses in 1978. In fall 2010, there were 1,073 students enrolled in distance learning courses. Institutionally administered financial aid is available to distance learners.

Services Distance learners have accessibility to academic advising, bookstore, campus computer network, career placement assistance, e-mail services, library services.

Contact Clint Nemitz, Admission Specialist, Online Master of Science in Criminal Justice, University of Wisconsin–Platteville, 2100 Ullsvik Hall, 1 University Plaza, Platteville, WI 53818-3099. Telephone: 800-362-5460. Fax: 608-342-1071. E-mail: nemitzc@uwplatt.edu.

DEGREES AND AWARDS

Advanced Graduate Diploma Criminal Justice
CGMS Child Advocacy Studies certificate (CAST)
MSCJ Criminal Justice

COURSE SUBJECT AREAS OFFERED OUTSIDE OF DEGREE PROGRAMS

Non-credit—criminal justice and corrections; criminology; social work.

UNIVERSITY OF WISCONSIN–PLATTEVILLE
Platteville, Wisconsin
Online Master of Science in Project Management Program
http://www.uwplatt.edu/disted/project-management.html

University of Wisconsin–Platteville was founded in 1866. It is accredited by North Central Association of Colleges and Schools. It first offered distance learning courses in 1978. In fall 2010, there were 1,073 students enrolled in distance learning courses. Institutionally administered financial aid is available to distance learners.

Services Distance learners have accessibility to academic advising, bookstore, campus computer network, career placement assistance, e-mail services, library services.

Contact Clint Nemitz, Admission Specialist, Online Master of Science in Project Management, University of Wisconsin–Platteville, 2100 Ullsvik Hall, 1 University Plaza, Platteville, WI 53818-3099. Telephone: 800-362-5460. Fax: 608-342-1071. E-mail: nemitzc@uwplatt.edu.

DEGREES AND AWARDS

CAGS Project Management
Graduate Certificate Project Management
MS Project Management

COURSE SUBJECT AREAS OFFERED OUTSIDE OF DEGREE PROGRAMS

Non-credit—business administration, management and operations; business, management, and marketing related.

UNIVERSITY OF WISCONSIN–PLATTEVILLE
Platteville, Wisconsin
Online Master of Science in Engineering Program
http://www.uwplatt.edu/disted/engineering.html

University of Wisconsin–Platteville was founded in 1866. It is accredited by North Central Association of Colleges and Schools. It first offered distance learning courses in 1978. In fall 2010, there were 1,073 students enrolled in distance learning courses. Institutionally administered financial aid is available to distance learners.

Services Distance learners have accessibility to academic advising, bookstore, campus computer network, career placement assistance, e-mail services, library services.

Contact Clint Nemitz, Admission Specialist, Online Master of Science in Engineering, University of Wisconsin–Platteville, 2100 Ullsvik Hall, 1 University Plaza, Platteville, WI 53818-3099. Telephone: 800-362-5460. Fax: 608-342-1071. E-mail: nemitzc@uwplatt.edu.

DEGREES AND AWARDS

Graduate Certificate Engineering Management; Geotechnical Engineering; Structural Engineering; Structural/Geotechnical Engineering
MSE Engineering

COURSE SUBJECT AREAS OFFERED OUTSIDE OF DEGREE PROGRAMS

Non-credit—civil engineering; industrial engineering; mechanical engineering.

UNIVERSITY OF WISCONSIN–STOUT
Menomonie, Wisconsin
Office of Continuing Education
http://www.uwstout.edu/de

University of Wisconsin–Stout was founded in 1891. It is accredited by North Central Association of Colleges and Schools. It first offered distance learning courses in 1980. In fall 2010, there were 6,857 students enrolled in distance learning courses. Institutionally administered financial aid is available to distance learners.
Services Distance learners have accessibility to academic advising, bookstore, campus computer network, career placement assistance, e-mail services, library services, tutoring.
Contact Sandra White, Credit Outreach Program Manager III, University of Wisconsin–Stout, Online and Credit Outreach, 140 Vocational Rehabilitation Building, Menomonie, WI 54751-0790. Telephone: 715-232-1610. Fax: 715-232-3385. E-mail: whites@uwstout.edu.

DEGREES AND AWARDS

BS Engineering Technology; Golf Enterprise Management; Human Development and Family Studies; Information and Communication Technologies; Management; Manufacturing Engineering; Sustainable Management
Certificate Gaming Management; Human Resource Management; Quality Management; Sustainable Enterprise Management; Sustainable Management Science
Certification Early Childhood/Middle Childhood; Instructional Technology Coordinator; Reading Teacher certification; Traffic Safety Education
Graduate Certificate E-Learning and Online Teaching; Instructional Design
MS Career and Technical Education; Education; Information Communication Technologies; Manufacturing Engineering; Technology Management; Training and Development; Vocational Rehabilitation Counseling

COURSE SUBJECT AREAS OFFERED OUTSIDE OF DEGREE PROGRAMS

Undergraduate—business, management, and marketing related; chemistry; economics; education; human resources management.
Graduate—business administration, management and operations; education; human resources management; science technologies related.
Non-credit—education (specific levels and methods); human development, family studies, and related services.

UNIVERSITY OF WISCONSIN–STOUT
Menomonie, Wisconsin
Program in Vocational Rehabilitation
http://www.uwstout.edu/programs/msvr/

University of Wisconsin–Stout was founded in 1891. It is accredited by North Central Association of Colleges and Schools. It first offered distance learning courses in 2002. In fall 2010, there were 55 students enrolled in distance learning courses. Institutionally administered financial aid is available to distance learners.
Services Distance learners have accessibility to academic advising, bookstore, campus computer network, career placement assistance, e-mail services, library services.
Contact Debra Homa, PhD, Online Vocational Rehabilitation Program Director, University of Wisconsin–Stout, 221 10th Avenue East, Department of Rehabilitation and Counseling, Menomonie, WI 54751. Telephone: 715-232-1113. Fax: 715-232-2356. E-mail: homad@uwstout.edu.

DEGREES AND AWARDS

MS Vocational Rehabilitation–Rehabilitation Counseling

UNIVERSITY OF WISCONSIN–SUPERIOR
Superior, Wisconsin
http://www.uwsuper.edu/distancelearning

University of Wisconsin–Superior was founded in 1893. It is accredited by North Central Association of Colleges and Schools. It first offered distance learning courses in 1978. In fall 2010, there were 300 students enrolled in distance learning courses. Institutionally administered financial aid is available to distance learners.
Services Distance learners have accessibility to academic advising, bookstore, campus computer network, career placement assistance, e-mail services, library services, tutoring.
Contact Peter D. Nordgren, Associate Dean for Distance Learning, University of Wisconsin–Superior, Distance Learning Center, Belknap and Catlin, PO Box 2000, Superior, WI 54880-4500. Telephone: 877-528-6597. Fax: 715-394-8139. E-mail: pnordgre@uwsuper.edu.

DEGREES AND AWARDS

BS Communicating Arts, Speech Communication concentration; Elementary Education; Individually Designed major; Sustainable Management

COURSE SUBJECT AREAS OFFERED OUTSIDE OF DEGREE PROGRAMS

Undergraduate—accounting and computer science; astronomy and astrophysics; biology; business administration, management and operations; communication and journalism related; communication and media; curriculum and instruction; education; English; fine and studio arts; history; human services; legal studies (non-professional general, undergraduate); library science and administration; mathematics and computer science; physical sciences; social sciences.
Graduate—education; educational administration and supervision; education (specific subject areas); library science and administration.
Non-credit—legal studies (non-professional general, undergraduate); legal support services.

UPPER IOWA UNIVERSITY
Fayette, Iowa
Center for Distance Education
http://www.uiu.edu

Upper Iowa University was founded in 1857. It is accredited by North Central Association of Colleges and Schools. It first offered distance learning courses in 1973. In fall 2010, there were 3,000 students enrolled in distance learning courses. Institutionally administered financial aid is available to distance learners.
Services Distance learners have accessibility to academic advising, bookstore, campus computer network, career placement assistance, e-mail services, library services, tutoring.
Contact Dawn Novak, Admissions Coordinator, Center for Distance Education, Upper Iowa University, PO Box 1861, Fayette, IA 52142. Telephone: 800-603-3756. Fax: 563-425-5353. E-mail: distance@uiu.edu.

DEGREES AND AWARDS

AA Business, general; Liberal Arts
BS Accounting; Business Administration; Criminal Justice; Emergency and Disaster Management; Financial Management; Health Services Administration; Human Resources Management; Human Services; Management Information Systems; Management; Marketing; Psychology; Public Administration; Public Administration–Fire Science emphasis; Public Administration–Law Enforcement emphasis; Social Sciences

Certificate Emergency and Disaster Management; Human Resources Management; Marketing; Organizational Communications; Organizational Leadership

MBA Business Administration, Accounting emphasis; Business Administration, Corporate Financial Management emphasis; Business Administration, Global Business emphasis; Business Administration, Human Resources Management emphasis; Business Administration, Organizational Development emphasis; Business Administration, Quality Management emphasis

MHEA Community and Technical College emphasis; Leadership emphasis

MPA Public Administration, General Study emphasis; Public Administration, Government Administration emphasis; Public Administration, Health and Human Services emphasis; Public Administration, Justice and Homeland Security emphasis; Public Administration, Nonprofit Organizations emphasis; Public Administration, Public Personnel Management emphasis

COURSE SUBJECT AREAS OFFERED OUTSIDE OF DEGREE PROGRAMS

Undergraduate—accounting and related services; astronomy and astrophysics; biology; business administration, management and operations; business/corporate communications; business, management, and marketing related; communication and media; criminal justice and corrections; criminology; English; entrepreneurial and small business operations; finance and financial management services; health professions related; health services/allied health/health sciences; history; human resources management; human services; international business; legal studies (nonprofessional general, undergraduate); liberal arts and sciences, general studies and humanities; management information systems; management sciences and quantitative methods; marketing; mathematics; mathematics and statistics related; natural sciences; philosophy and religious studies related; physical sciences; political science and government; psychology; psychology related; public administration; public administration and social service professions related; public relations, advertising, and applied communication related; social sciences; social sciences related; sociology; statistics.

Graduate—accounting and related services; business administration, management and operations; business, management, and marketing related; business/managerial economics; human resources management.

Non-credit—accounting and computer science; accounting and related services; biological and physical sciences; biology; communication and media; history; international business; management information systems; marketing; political science and government; psychology; public administration; sociology; statistics.

UTAH STATE UNIVERSITY
Logan, Utah
Independent and Distance Education
http://distance.usu.edu

Utah State University was founded in 1888. It is accredited by Northwest Commission on Colleges and Universities. It first offered distance learning courses in 1911. In fall 2010, there were 12,109 students enrolled in distance learning courses. Institutionally administered financial aid is available to distance learners.

Services Distance learners have accessibility to academic advising, bookstore, campus computer network, e-mail services, library services.

Contact Staff Assistant, Regional Campuses and Distance Education, Utah State University, 5055 Old Main Hill, Logan, UT 84322-5055. Telephone: 800-233-2137. Fax: 435-797-1399. E-mail: distance.info@usu.edu.

DEGREES AND AWARDS

AS Deafblindness Preservice Training; General Studies

BS Agribusiness; Communicative Disorders and Deaf Education (Second Bachelors); Communicative Disorders and Deaf Education; Economics; Family Life Studies; Psychology

ME Electrical or Computer Engineering

MEd Instructional Technology and Learning Sciences–Educational Technology specialization

MS Applied Environmental Geoscience; English/Technical Writing specialization online; Instructional Technology and Learning Sciences

MSRC Rehabilitation Counseling

COURSE SUBJECT AREAS OFFERED OUTSIDE OF DEGREE PROGRAMS

Undergraduate—accounting and related services; American Sign Language (ASL); anthropology; applied mathematics; biology; business administration, management and operations; business, management, and marketing related; business operations support and assistant services; chemistry; communication and journalism related; communication disorders sciences and services; data entry/microcomputer applications; data processing; economics; English; family and consumer economics; family and consumer sciences/human sciences; geography and cartography; geological and earth sciences/geosciences; history; human development, family studies, and related services; human resources management; journalism; liberal arts and sciences, general studies and humanities; mathematics; mathematics and computer science; mathematics and statistics related; music; philosophy; physical sciences; physics; psychology; social sciences; social work; sociology; special education; statistics.

Graduate—agriculture and agriculture operations related; business administration, management and operations; computer programming; computer science; computer software and media applications; computer systems analysis; computer systems networking and telecommunications; curriculum and instruction; education; educational administration and supervision; educational assessment, evaluation, and research; educational/instructional media design; education (specific levels and methods); education (specific subject areas); English; family and consumer sciences/human sciences; human development, family studies, and related services; human resources management; library science related; psychology; rehabilitation and therapeutic professions; social sciences related; social work; special education.

UTICA COLLEGE
Utica, New York
http://www.uticaonline.edu/

Utica College was founded in 1946. It is accredited by Middle States Association of Colleges and Schools. It first offered distance learning courses in 2000. In fall 2010, there were 2,410 students enrolled in distance learning courses. Institutionally administered financial aid is available to distance learners.

Services Distance learners have accessibility to academic advising, bookstore, campus computer network, e-mail services, library services, tutoring.

Contact Dr. James Brown, Assistant Vice President for Strategic Initiatives, Utica College, 1600 Burrstone Road, Office of Graduate and Extended Studies, Utica, NY 13502. Telephone: 315-792-3001. Fax: 315-792-3002. E-mail: jbrown@utica.edu.

DEGREES AND AWARDS

BS Criminal Justice–Economic Crime Investigation; Cybersecurity and Information Assurance

Certificate Financial Crime Investigation

MBA Business Administration–Economic Crime and Fraud Management; Business Administration–Professional Accountancy

MS Cybersecurity Intelligence and Forensics; Economic Crime Management

DPT Physical Therapy–Transitional Doctorate of Physical Therapy

COURSE SUBJECT AREAS OFFERED OUTSIDE OF DEGREE PROGRAMS

Undergraduate—biology; economics; English; gerontology; liberal arts and sciences, general studies and humanities; mathematics; psychology.

Graduate—history; liberal arts and sciences, general studies and humanities; philosophy.

VALENCIA COLLEGE
Orlando, Florida
http://valenciacc.edu

Valencia College was founded in 1967. It is accredited by Southern Association of Colleges and Schools. It first offered distance learning courses in 1997. In fall 2010, there were 13,709 students enrolled in distance learning courses. Institutionally administered financial aid is available to distance learners.

Services Distance learners have accessibility to academic advising, bookstore, campus computer network, career placement assistance, e-mail services, library services.

Contact Visit Valencia, Valencia College, 1800 South Kirkman Road, Orlando, FL 32811. Fax: 407-299-5000. E-mail: ask@valencia.com.

DEGREES AND AWARDS

Programs offered do not lead to a degree or other formal award.

COURSE SUBJECT AREAS OFFERED OUTSIDE OF DEGREE PROGRAMS

Undergraduate—allied health and medical assisting services; allied health diagnostic, intervention, and treatment professions; anthropology; arts, entertainment, and media management; behavioral sciences; biological and physical sciences; biology; business administration, management and operations; business, management, and marketing related; chemistry; communication and journalism related; communications technology; computer and information sciences; computer/information technology administration and management; computer programming; computer science; criminal justice and corrections; criminology; culinary arts and related services; data entry/microcomputer applications; economics; education; education related; English; family and consumer economics; film/video and photographic arts; fine and studio arts; food science and technology; foods, nutrition, and related services; geography and cartography; health professions related; health services/allied health/health sciences; history; interdisciplinary studies; legal professions and studies related; legal studies (non-professional general, undergraduate); liberal arts and sciences, general studies and humanities; literature; marketing; mathematics; mathematics and computer science; mathematics and statistics related; medieval and Renaissance studies; nutrition sciences; personal and culinary services related; physical sciences; political science and government; psychology; psychology related; registered nursing, nursing administration, nursing research and clinical nursing; social sciences; sociology; statistics; visual and performing arts.

VALLEY CITY STATE UNIVERSITY
Valley City, North Dakota
North Dakota Interactive Video Network
http://distancelearning.vcsu.edu

Valley City State University was founded in 1890. It is accredited by North Central Association of Colleges and Schools. It first offered distance learning courses in 2000. In fall 2010, there were 912 students enrolled in distance learning courses. Institutionally administered financial aid is available to distance learners.

Services Distance learners have accessibility to academic advising, bookstore, campus computer network, career placement assistance, e-mail services, library services.

Contact Misty Lindgren, Administrative Assistant for the Office of Graduate Studies and Research, Valley City State University, 101 College Street SW, Valley City, ND 58072. Telephone: 701-845-7303. Fax: 701-845-7305. E-mail: misty.lindgren@vcsu.edu.

DEGREES AND AWARDS

BS Business Education; English Education; History Education; Music; Professional Communication; Technology Education
BSc Career and Technical Education
CAGS Library and Information Technologies; Teaching English Language Learners
MEd Education

COURSE SUBJECT AREAS OFFERED OUTSIDE OF DEGREE PROGRAMS

Undergraduate—business administration, management and operations; business, management, and marketing related; communication and journalism related; education; education (specific subject areas); health and physical education/fitness; library science and administration; library science related; marketing; psychology.

VANDERBILT UNIVERSITY
Nashville, Tennessee
MS in Nursing
http://www.nursing.vanderbilt.edu

Vanderbilt University was founded in 1873. It is accredited by Southern Association of Colleges and Schools. It first offered distance learning courses in 1996. In fall 2010, there were 340 students enrolled in distance learning courses. Institutionally administered financial aid is available to distance learners.

Services Distance learners have accessibility to academic advising, bookstore, campus computer network, career placement assistance, e-mail services, library services.

Contact Admissions Counselor, Vanderbilt University, Godchaux Hall 207, 461 21st Avenue South, Nashville, TN 37240. Telephone: 888-333-9192. Fax: 615-343-0333. E-mail: vusn-admissions@vanderbilt.edu.

DEGREES AND AWARDS

MSN Health Systems Management; Nurse Midwifery; Nursing Informatics; Nursing–Acute Care Nurse Practitioner; Nursing–Adult Nurse Practitioner; Nursing–Adult/Gerontological Nurse Practitioner; Nursing–Adult/Palliative Care Nurse Practitioner; Nursing–Family Nurse Practitioner; Nursing–Neonatal Nurse Practitioner; Nursing–Pediatric Nurse Practitioner; Nursing–Psychiatric Mental Health Nurse Practitioner; Women's Health Nurse Practitioner
DNP Nursing Practice
PhD Nursing Science

VANGUARD UNIVERSITY OF SOUTHERN CALIFORNIA
Costa Mesa, California
http://www.vanguard.edu/cdp

Vanguard University of Southern California was founded in 1920. It is accredited by Western Association of Schools and Colleges. It first offered distance learning courses in 2002. In fall 2010, there were 250 students enrolled in distance learning courses. Institutionally administered financial aid is available to distance learners.

Services Distance learners have accessibility to academic advising, bookstore, campus computer network, career placement assistance, e-mail services, library services, tutoring.

Contact Ms. Janae McCabe, Student Advisor, Vanguard University of Southern California, 55 Fair Drive, Costa Mesa, CA 92626. Telephone: 714-668-6130 Ext. 6116. E-mail: shari.farris@vanguard.edu.

DEGREES AND AWARDS

BA Early Childhood Education

COURSE SUBJECT AREAS OFFERED OUTSIDE OF DEGREE PROGRAMS

Undergraduate—curriculum and instruction; education; educational administration and supervision; education related; human development, family studies, and related services.

VERMONT TECHNICAL COLLEGE
Randolph Center, Vermont
http://www.vtc.edu

Vermont Technical College was founded in 1866. It is accredited by New England Association of Schools and Colleges. It first offered distance learning courses in 1996. In fall 2010, there were 457 students enrolled in distance learning courses. Institutionally administered financial aid is available to distance learners.

Services Distance learners have accessibility to academic advising, bookstore, campus computer network, career placement assistance, e-mail services, library services.

Contact Michael Dempsey, Registrar, Vermont Technical College, PO Box 500, Randolph Center, VT 05061. Telephone: 802-728-1303. Fax: 802-728-1597. E-mail: mdempsey@vtc.vsc.edu.

DEGREES AND AWARDS

Programs offered do not lead to a degree or other formal award.

COURSE SUBJECT AREAS OFFERED OUTSIDE OF DEGREE PROGRAMS

Undergraduate—allied health and medical assisting services; computer science; English.

VINCENNES UNIVERSITY

Vincennes, Indiana

Distance Education/Degree Completion

http://www.vinu.edu/distance

Vincennes University was founded in 1801. It is accredited by North Central Association of Colleges and Schools. It first offered distance learning courses in 1989. In fall 2010, there were 2,222 students enrolled in distance learning courses. Institutionally administered financial aid is available to distance learners.

Services Distance learners have accessibility to academic advising, bookstore, campus computer network, career placement assistance, e-mail services, library services, tutoring.

Contact Mrs. Shanni E. Simmons, Director of Distance Education, Vincennes University, 1002 North First Street, Vincennes, IN 47591. Telephone: 812-888-4026. Fax: 812-888-2054. E-mail: ssimmons@vinu.edu.

DEGREES AND AWARDS

AA Behavioral Sciences; Behavioral Sciences, Psychology concentration; Behavioral Sciences, Sociology concentration; Liberal Arts

AAS Accounting; Administrative Office Technology; Business Management; Computer Programming; Funeral Service Education; General Studies–Business Studies; General Studies; Law Enforcement Studies; Pharmacy Technician; Technology Apprenticeship–General Studies option

AS Behavioral Science, Psychology concentration; Behavioral Sciences; Behavioral Sciences, Sociology concentration; Business Administration; Funeral Service Education; General Studies; Health Information Management; Information Technology; Law Enforcement Studies; Liberal Arts, Social Science concentration; Social Work; Supply Chain Logistics Management; Technology Apprenticeship

BS Homeland Security and Public Safety

Certificate Behavioral Science–Substance Abuse certificate; Collegiate Studies; Community Rehabilitation; Directed Studies

COURSE SUBJECT AREAS OFFERED OUTSIDE OF DEGREE PROGRAMS

Undergraduate—accounting and related services; allied health and medical assisting services; applied mathematics; behavioral sciences; business administration, management and operations; business/commerce; business, management, and marketing related; business operations support and assistant services; chemistry; computer and information sciences; computer/information technology administration and management; criminal justice and corrections; economics; education; entrepreneurial and small business operations; fire protection; funeral service and mortuary science; history; homeland security; information science/studies; liberal arts and sciences, general studies and humanities; mathematics; pharmacy, pharmaceutical sciences, and administration; psychology; rehabilitation and therapeutic professions; sales, merchandising and related marketing operations (specialized); social sciences; social work; sociology.

WAKE TECHNICAL COMMUNITY COLLEGE

Raleigh, North Carolina

http://www.waketech.edu

Wake Technical Community College was founded in 1958. It is accredited by Southern Association of Colleges and Schools. It first offered distance learning courses in 1986. In fall 2010, there were 7,102 students enrolled in distance learning courses. Institutionally administered financial aid is available to distance learners.

Services Distance learners have accessibility to academic advising, bookstore, campus computer network, career placement assistance, e-mail services, library services, tutoring.

Contact Diana Osborne, Head, Distance Education Support Department, Wake Technical Community College, Main Campus, 9101 Fayetteville Road, Raleigh, NC 27603-5696. Telephone: 919-866-5616. Fax: 919-773-6190. E-mail: dgosborne@waketech.edu.

DEGREES AND AWARDS

AA the Arts

AAS Business Administration, Human Resources Management; Criminal Justice Technology; Global Logistics Technology; Industrial Engineering Technology; Mechanical Engineering Technology; Medical Office Administration; Office Administration–Legal; Office Administration; Web Technologies

AGS General Education

Certificate Accounting Core; CISCO Certified Network Associate; E-Commerce; Early Childhood Education; Global Logistics Technology–Distribution Management; Global Logistics Technology; Graphics and Design; Human Resources Administration; Human Resources Management; IT Foundations; IT Support Management; Income Tax Preparer; Industrial Engineering Technology, Advanced Quality; Industrial Engineering Technology, Industrial Management; Industrial Engineering Technology, Manufacturing Process Control; Industrial Engineering Technology, Quality Assurance; Infant/Toddler Care; Java Programming; Legal Office; Mechanical Drafting Technology; Mechanical Engineering Technology–Engineering Fundamentals; Mechanical Engineering Technology–Engineering Management; Mechanical Engineering Technology–Materials Engineering; Mechanical Engineering Technology–Mechanical Design; Mechanical Engineering Technology–Thermal Mechanics; Medical Billing and Coding; Medical Document Specialist; Medical Office Specialist; Microsoft Application Specialist; Microsoft Certified Systems Administrator; Office Specialist; Oracle DBA Programming; Oracle Developer; Payroll Accounting Clerk; Spreadsheet Management; Visual C# Programming; Web Designer; Web Designer; Web Developer; Web Technologies–E-Commerce Programming; Word Processing and Publications

Diploma Office Administration

COURSE SUBJECT AREAS OFFERED OUTSIDE OF DEGREE PROGRAMS

Undergraduate—accounting and related services; allied health and medical assisting services; anthropology; architectural sciences and technology; astronomy and astrophysics; biology; biotechnology; business administration, management and operations; business operations support and assistant services; chemistry; civil engineering technologies; computer and information sciences and support services related; computer engineering technologies; computer programming; computer software and media applications; computer systems analysis; computer systems networking and telecommunications; construction management; construction trades; cosmetology and related personal grooming services; criminal justice and corrections; culinary arts and related services; data entry/microcomputer applications; data processing; dental support services and allied professions; drafting/design engineering technologies; drama/theatre arts and stagecraft; economics; education (specific levels and methods); electrical/electronics maintenance and repair technology; electrical engineering technologies; geological and earth sciences/geosciences; gerontology; health and physical education/fitness; health services/allied health/health sciences; heating, air conditioning, ventilation and refrigeration maintenance technology; heavy/industrial equipment maintenance technologies; history; hospitality administration; human resources management; human services; landscape architecture; liberal arts and sciences, general studies and humanities; marketing; mathematics; music; philosophy; physics; political science and government; psychology; religious studies; social work; sociology; surveying engineering; transportation and materials moving related.

Non-credit—accounting and related services; business administration, management and operations; business operations support and assistant services; computer and information sciences and support services related; computer programming; computer software and media applications; data entry/microcomputer applications; data processing; education related; entrepreneurial and small business operations; family and consumer economics; film/video and photographic arts; finance and financial management services; graphic communications; health and physical education/fitness; health professions related; health services/allied health/health sciences; languages (foreign languages related); languages

(Romance languages); legal studies (non-professional general, undergraduate); legal support services; marketing; publishing; sales merchandising, and related marketing operations (general); sales, merchandising and related marketing operations (specialized).

WALDEN UNIVERSITY
Minneapolis, Minnesota
http://www.WaldenU.edu/

Walden University was founded in 1970. It is accredited by North Central Association of Colleges and Schools. It first offered distance learning courses in 1970. In fall 2010, there were 47,456 students enrolled in distance learning courses. Institutionally administered financial aid is available to distance learners.

Services Distance learners have accessibility to academic advising, bookstore, campus computer network, e-mail services, library services, tutoring.

Contact Reena Lichtenfeld, Director of Admissions, Walden University, 650 South Exeter Street, Baltimore, MD 21202. Telephone: 800-925-3368. E-mail: admissions@waldenu.edu.

DEGREES AND AWARDS

BS Accounting; Business Administration; Child Development; Communications; Computer Information Systems; Criminal Justice; Educational Studies; Health Studies; Healthcare Management; Information Technology; Instructional Design and Technology; Interdisciplinary Studies; Political Science and Public Administration; Psychology
BSN Nursing
Certificate Homeland Security; Instructional Design post-Bachelor's certificate; Nursing Education; Nursing Informatics; Nursing Leadership and Management; Organizational Psychology and Development post-Bachelor's specialized learning certificate; Post-Doctoral specialized learning certificate; Psychology post-Doctoral certificate (respecialization); Teaching Online post-Masters Specialized Learning certificate
Ed S Adminstration Leadership for Teacher and Learning; Curriculum, Instruction, and Professional Development; Education Technology; Educational Leadership and Administration (Principal Preparation); Special Education; Teacher Leadership
Graduate Certificate Applied Project Management post-Bachelor's; Clinical Research and Administration post-Bachelor's; College Teaching and Learning post-Bachelor's; Criminal Justice post-Bachelor's; Enrollment Management and Institutional Marketing post-Bachelor's; Government Management post-Bachelor's; Homeland Security post-Bachelor's; Nonprofit Management post-Bachelor's; Professional Development post-Bachelor's; Project Management post-Bachelor's, Advanced; Public Management and Leadership post-Bachelor's; Public Policy post-Bachelor's; Strategic Planning and Public Policy post-Bachelor's
MAT Teacher Preparation post-Baccalaureate
MBA Business Administration
MHA Healthcare Administration
MISM Information Systems Management
MPA Public Administration
MPH Public Health
MS Accounting and Management; Accounting; Adult Learning; Clinical Research Administration; Early Childhood Studies; Education; Forensic Psychology; Health Informatics; Higher Education; Human Resource Management; Instructional Design and Technology; Leadership; Management; Marriage, Couple, and Family Counseling; Mental Health Counseling; Nonprofit Management and Leadership; Nursing–BSN track; Nursing–RN track; Project Management; Psychology; Special Education Endorsement programs (with MS Education)
DBA Business Administration
EdD Education
PhD Counselor Education and Supervision; Education; Health Services; Human Services; Management; Psychology; Public Health; Public Policy and Administration

COURSE SUBJECT AREAS OFFERED OUTSIDE OF DEGREE PROGRAMS

Graduate—business, management, and marketing related; education; engineering related; health professions related; psychology.

WALLA WALLA UNIVERSITY
College Place, Washington
http://www.wallawalla.edu/academics/distance-learning-d2l/

Walla Walla University was founded in 1892. It is accredited by Northwest Commission on Colleges and Universities.

Contact Sylvia Nosworthy, Director of Distance Learning, Walla Walla University, College Place, WA 99324. Telephone: 509-527-2781. E-mail: sylvia.nosworthy@wallawalla.edu.

DEGREES AND AWARDS

Programs offered do not lead to a degree or other formal award.

COURSE SUBJECT AREAS OFFERED OUTSIDE OF DEGREE PROGRAMS

Undergraduate—biblical studies; English language and literature related; music; psychology; social work.
Graduate—education.

WASHINGTON STATE UNIVERSITY
Pullman, Washington
Online Degree Programs
http://online.wsu.edu

Washington State University was founded in 1890. It is accredited by Northwest Commission on Colleges and Universities. It first offered distance learning courses in 1991. In fall 2010, there were 3,200 students enrolled in distance learning courses. Institutionally administered financial aid is available to distance learners.

Services Distance learners have accessibility to academic advising, bookstore, campus computer network, career placement assistance, e-mail services, library services, tutoring.

Contact Student Services, Washington State University, 104 Van Doren Hall, PO Box 645220, Pullman, WA 99164-5220. Telephone: 800-222-4978. Fax: 509-335-4850. E-mail: online@wsu.edu.

DEGREES AND AWARDS

BA Business Administration–Accounting; Business Administration–Management Information Systems; Business Administration–Management and Operations; Criminal Justice; Human Development; Humanities; Social Sciences
BSN Nursing–RN to BSN
Certificate Organic Agriculture; Professional Writing
Graduate Certificate Bioethics; Early Childhood Leadership and Administration; Molecular Biosciences
MS Agriculture
PSM Professional Science

COURSE SUBJECT AREAS OFFERED OUTSIDE OF DEGREE PROGRAMS

Undergraduate—anthropology; economics; English; history; marketing; mathematics; political science and government; psychology; sociology.

WAYLAND BAPTIST UNIVERSITY
Plainview, Texas
http://www.wbu.edu/

Wayland Baptist University was founded in 1908. It is accredited by Southern Association of Colleges and Schools. It first offered distance learning courses in 1998. In fall 2010, there were 2,408 students enrolled in distance learning courses. Institutionally administered financial aid is available to distance learners.

Services Distance learners have accessibility to academic advising, bookstore, e-mail services, library services.

Contact Mr. Jay Sample, Virtual Campus Director, Wayland Baptist University, 1900 West 7th Street, CMB 420, Plainview, TX 79072. Telephone: 806-291-1725. Fax: 806-291-1957. E-mail: samplej@wbu.edu.

DEGREES AND AWARDS

AAS Applied Science
BAS Applied Science
BCM Christian Ministry
BSN Nursing
MA English; History; Management
MBA Business Administration
MCM Christian Ministry
MEd Education
MPA Public Administration

COURSE SUBJECT AREAS OFFERED OUTSIDE OF DEGREE PROGRAMS

Undergraduate—accounting and related services; business administration, management and operations; communication and media; criminal justice and corrections; economics; education related; finance and financial management services; geography and cartography; geological and earth sciences/geosciences; health and medical administrative services; history; management information systems; marketing; music; physical sciences; political science and government; psychology; religious education; religious studies; sociology.
Graduate—accounting and related services; business administration, management and operations; economics; education related; health and medical administrative services; human resources management; management information systems; multi/interdisciplinary studies related; public administration; religious education; religious studies.

WAYNE COMMUNITY COLLEGE
Goldsboro, North Carolina
http://www.waynecc.edu

Wayne Community College was founded in 1957. It is accredited by Southern Association of Colleges and Schools. It first offered distance learning courses in 1998. In fall 2010, there were 4,500 students enrolled in distance learning courses. Institutionally administered financial aid is available to distance learners.
Services Distance learners have accessibility to academic advising, bookstore, career placement assistance, e-mail services, library services, tutoring.
Contact Michelle Turnage, Director, Educational Support Technology, Wayne Community College, 3000 Wayne Memorial Drive, Goldsboro, NC 27533. Telephone: 919-735-5151 Ext. 7023. Fax: 919-736-9425. E-mail: shell@waynecc.edu.

DEGREES AND AWARDS

AA General degree
AAS Accounting; Agribusiness Technology; Applied Animal Science Technology; Business Administration; Business Administration/Marketing and Retailing; Business Administration/Operations Management; Computer Information Technology; Computer-Intergrated Machining Technology; Criminal Justice Technology; Criminal Justice Technology/Latent Evidence; Electronics Engineering Technology; Emergency Preparedness Technology; General Occupational Technology; Healthcare Management Technology; Human Services Technology; Human Services/Substance Abuse; Information Systems Security; Mechanical Engineering Technology; Medical Assisting; Medical Assisting/Advanced Standing Alternative for Medical Office Admin or Medical Transcription; Medical Office Adminstration; Networking Technology; Office Administration Technology; Sustainabilty Technology; Turfgrass Management Technology
AGS General Education

COURSE SUBJECT AREAS OFFERED OUTSIDE OF DEGREE PROGRAMS

Undergraduate—agricultural business and management; agricultural production; business administration, management and operations; business/commerce; computer/information technology administration and management; computer software and media applications; computer systems networking and telecommunications; criminal justice and corrections; data processing; drafting/design engineering technologies; economics; education related; education (specific subject areas); electrical engineering technologies; English; forestry; heating, air conditioning, ventilation and refrigeration maintenance technology; history; industrial production technologies; liberal arts and sciences, general studies and humanities; management information systems; mechanical engineering related technologies; mechanic and repair technologies related; science, technology and society; special education; sustainability studies; vehicle maintenance and repair technologies; visual and performing arts; work and family studies.
Non-credit—accounting and computer science; allied health and medical assisting services; bilingual, multilingual, and multicultural education; business/corporate communications; business, management, and marketing related; carpentry; computer and information sciences and support services related; computer software and media applications; construction trades; cosmetology and related personal grooming services; crafts, folk art and artisanry; criminal justice and corrections; dental support services and allied professions; drafting/design engineering technologies; electrical/electronics maintenance and repair technology; fire protection; real estate; vehicle maintenance and repair technologies.

WAYNE STATE COLLEGE
Wayne, Nebraska
Regional Education and Distance Learning
http://www.wsc.edu

Wayne State College was founded in 1910. It is accredited by North Central Association of Colleges and Schools. It first offered distance learning courses in 1997. In fall 2010, there were 1,255 students enrolled in distance learning courses. Institutionally administered financial aid is available to distance learners.
Services Distance learners have accessibility to academic advising, bookstore, campus computer network, career placement assistance, e-mail services, library services.
Contact Ms. Lisa Reynolds, Assistant Director of Continuing Education, Wayne State College, 1111 Main Street, Wayne, NE 68787. Telephone: 402-375-7215. Fax: 402-375-7204. E-mail: lireyno1@wsc.edu.

DEGREES AND AWARDS

Ed S School Administration/Educational Leadership
MBA Business Administration
MS Organizational Management

COURSE SUBJECT AREAS OFFERED OUTSIDE OF DEGREE PROGRAMS

Undergraduate—business administration, management and operations; criminal justice and corrections; economics; education; education (specific subject areas); English; industrial production technologies; multi/interdisciplinary studies related; natural sciences; physical sciences; physics; special education.
Graduate—business administration, management and operations; communications technologies and support services related; criminal justice and corrections; economics; education; educational administration and supervision; education (specific subject areas); industrial production technologies; mathematics; parks, recreation and leisure facilities management; psychology; special education.

WAYNE STATE UNIVERSITY
Detroit, Michigan
Educational Outreach
http://online.wayne.edu

Wayne State University was founded in 1868. It is accredited by North Central Association of Colleges and Schools. It first offered distance learning courses in 1967. In fall 2010, there were 4,509 students enrolled in distance learning courses. Institutionally administered financial aid is available to distance learners.
Services Distance learners have accessibility to academic advising, bookstore, campus computer network, career placement assistance, e-mail services, library services, tutoring.
Contact Dr. James Mazoue, Director of Online Programs, Wayne State University, 169 Purdy/Kresge Library, Detroit, MI 48202. Telephone: 313-577-4873. Fax: 313-577-6777. E-mail: jmazoue@wayne.edu.

DEGREES AND AWARDS

BSW Social Work
MBA Business Administration
MEd Career Education; Instructional Technology
MLIS Library and Information Science

COURSE SUBJECT AREAS OFFERED OUTSIDE OF DEGREE PROGRAMS

Undergraduate—anthropology; cell biology and anatomical sciences; communication and media; computer and information sciences; computer programming; computer science; computer software and media applications; computer systems networking and telecommunications; criminal justice and corrections; dance; dietetics and clinical nutrition services; economics; education; electrical engineering technologies; engineering-related fields; engineering technology; English; film/video and photographic arts; finance and financial management services; food science and technology; foods, nutrition, and related services; geological and earth sciences/geosciences; health and physical education/fitness; health services/allied health/health sciences; history; information science/studies; languages (Slavic, Baltic, and Albanian); liberal arts and sciences, general studies and humanities; music; nutrition sciences; physical sciences; political science and government; psychology; social sciences; social work; sociology; sociology and anthropology; urban studies/affairs.
Graduate—accounting and related services; anthropology; bilingual, multilingual, and multicultural education; biomedical/medical engineering; business administration, management and operations; business, management, and marketing related; business/managerial economics; cell biology and anatomical sciences; communication and media; computer and information sciences; computer programming; computer software and media applications; education; educational administration and supervision; educational assessment, evaluation, and research; finance and financial management services; health and physical education/fitness; health services/allied health/health sciences; history; human resources management; information science/studies; legal research and advanced professional studies; library science and administration; marketing; music; nutrition sciences; psychology; rehabilitation and therapeutic professions; social work; special education; visual and performing arts.

WEBBER INTERNATIONAL UNIVERSITY
Babson Park, Florida
http://www.webber.edu/e-LearningProgram/

Webber International University was founded in 1927. It is accredited by Southern Association of Colleges and Schools. It first offered distance learning courses in 2008. In fall 2010, there were 51 students enrolled in distance learning courses. Institutionally administered financial aid is available to distance learners.
Services Distance learners have accessibility to academic advising, bookstore, campus computer network, career placement assistance, e-mail services, library services, tutoring.
Contact Mrs. Treasa McLean, Director, Webber International University, 1201 North Scenic Highway, Babson Park, FL 33827. Telephone: 863-638-2984. E-mail: mcleantj@webber.edu.

DEGREES AND AWARDS

BA/BS General Business

COURSE SUBJECT AREAS OFFERED OUTSIDE OF DEGREE PROGRAMS

Undergraduate—accounting and computer science; accounting and related services; arts, entertainment, and media management; behavioral sciences; business administration, management and operations; business/commerce; business/corporate communications; business, management, and marketing related; business/managerial economics; computer and information sciences; computer and information sciences and support services related; computer/information technology administration and management; computer programming; computer science; computer software and media applications; computer systems analysis; economics; English; English or French as a second or foreign language (teaching); ethnic, cultural minority, gender, and group studies; film/video and photographic arts; finance and financial management services; marketing; parks, recreation and leisure; parks, recreation and leisure facilities management; psychology; sociology.
Graduate—computer and information sciences; international business; international/global studies; marketing.

WEBSTER UNIVERSITY
St. Louis, Missouri
Online Learning Center
http://www.webster.edu/online

Webster University was founded in 1915. It is accredited by North Central Association of Colleges and Schools. It first offered distance learning courses in 1998. In fall 2010, there were 5,074 students enrolled in distance learning courses. Institutionally administered financial aid is available to distance learners.
Services Distance learners have accessibility to academic advising, bookstore, career placement assistance, e-mail services, library services, tutoring.
Contact Sarah Nandor, Director of Admissions, Webster University, 470 East Lockwood Avenue, St. Louis, MO 63119. Telephone: 314-968-7109. Fax: 314-246-7122. E-mail: nandor@webster.edu.

DEGREES AND AWARDS

BSN Nursing–RN to BSN
Certificate Gerontology; Online Teaching and Learning; Web Site Design; Web Site Development
Ed S Educational Leadership; School Systems, Superintendency, and Leadership; Technology Leadership
Graduate Certificate Decision Support Systems; Government Contracting; Web Services
MA Business and Organizational Security Management; Communication Arts; Communications Management; Education and Innovation; Gerontology; Human Resources Development; Human Resources Management; Information Technology Management; International Relations; Management and Leadership; Media Communications; Procurement and Acquisitions Management; Public Relations; Social Science Education
MBA Business Administration
MET Educational Technology
MS Environmental Management; Finance

COURSE SUBJECT AREAS OFFERED OUTSIDE OF DEGREE PROGRAMS

Undergraduate—computer and information sciences; languages (foreign languages related); mathematics; philosophy; public relations, advertising, and applied communication related; religious education.
Graduate—business, management, and marketing related; communication and journalism related; computer and information sciences and support services related; education; educational administration and supervision; finance and financial management services; homeland security, law enforcement, firefighting and protective services related; international/global studies; international relations and national security studies; management information systems; marketing; special education.

WESTCHESTER COMMUNITY COLLEGE
Valhalla, New York
http://www.sunywcc.edu/

Westchester Community College was founded in 1946. It is accredited by Middle States Association of Colleges and Schools. It first offered distance learning courses in 1997. In fall 2010, there were 2,573 students enrolled in distance learning courses. Institutionally administered financial aid is available to distance learners.
Services Distance learners have accessibility to academic advising, bookstore, e-mail services, library services, tutoring.
Contact Margi Winters, PhD, Assistant Dean for Distance Learning, Westchester Community College, 75 Grasslands Road, Valhalla, NY 10595. Telephone: 914-606-8677. Fax: 914-606-8550. E-mail: margi.winters@sunywcc.edu.

DEGREES AND AWARDS

AA Liberal Arts/Humanities; Liberal Arts/Social Science
AAS Computer Security and Forensics
Certificate Computer Programming

COURSE SUBJECT AREAS OFFERED OUTSIDE OF DEGREE PROGRAMS

Undergraduate—accounting and related services; anthropology; behavioral sciences; biological and physical sciences; biology; business/commerce; business, management, and marketing related; chemistry; communication and media; computer and information sciences; computer and information sciences and support services related; computer programming; computer science; computer systems analysis; computer systems networking and telecommunications; criminal justice and corrections; culinary arts and related services; data processing; dietetics and clinical nutrition services; economics; English; English language and literature related; geography and cartography; health and physical education/fitness; history; human development, family studies, and related services; management information systems; marketing; mathematics; mathematics and computer science; music; natural sciences; nutrition sciences; philosophy; philosophy and religious studies related; political science and government; psychology; religious studies; sales, merchandising and related marketing operations (specialized); social sciences; sociology; work and family studies.

WESTERN CAROLINA UNIVERSITY
Cullowhee, North Carolina
Continuing Education and Summer School
http://edoutreach.wcu.edu

Western Carolina University was founded in 1889. It is accredited by Southern Association of Colleges and Schools. It first offered distance learning courses in 1997. In fall 2010, there were 1,722 students enrolled in distance learning courses. Institutionally administered financial aid is available to distance learners.

Services Distance learners have accessibility to academic advising, bookstore, campus computer network, career placement assistance, e-mail services, library services, tutoring.

Contact Ms. Amy Fahey, Student Services, Western Carolina University, 138 Camp Building, Cullowhee, NC 28723. Telephone: 828-227-2737. Fax: 828-227-7115. E-mail: acfahey@email.wcu.edu.

DEGREES AND AWARDS

BEd Birth–Kindergarten (BS); Elementary Education
BS Criminal Justice; Emergency Medical Care; Engineering Technology Program; Public Safety and Security Management
BSBA Entrepreneurship
BSN Nursing–RN to BSN
Certificate Culturally Based Native Health
MAT Special Education
MBA Master of Entrepreneurship (ME Program)
MCM Construction Management Program
MPM Project Management
MS Human Resources; Two-Year Community College Administration program
MSA School Administration Program
MSN Nurse Administration; Nurse Educator track
PMC Construction Management–Land Development; Nurse Educator post-Graduate Program; Project Management post-Baccalaureate

COURSE SUBJECT AREAS OFFERED OUTSIDE OF DEGREE PROGRAMS

Undergraduate—education; educational administration and supervision; education related; education (specific levels and methods); special education.

Graduate—educational administration and supervision; education (specific levels and methods); human resources management.

Non-credit—educational administration and supervision; education (specific levels and methods); education (specific subject areas); finance and financial management services; management sciences and quantitative methods.

WESTERN INTERNATIONAL UNIVERSITY
Phoenix, Arizona

Western International University was founded in 1978. It is accredited by North Central Association of Colleges and Schools. It first offered distance learning courses in 2001. Institutionally administered financial aid is available to distance learners.

Services Distance learners have accessibility to academic advising, bookstore, campus computer network, career placement assistance, e-mail services, library services.

Contact Mr. JR Porter, Faculty Technology Manageer, Western International University, 9215 North Black Canyon Highway, Phoenix, AZ 85021-2718. Telephone: 602-429-1007. Fax: 602-749-0752. E-mail: jr.porter@west.edu.

DEGREES AND AWARDS

AA Business
BA Behavioral Science; Criminal Behavior; Human Resource Management; Legal Studies; Professional Communications
BS Accounting; Business Administration; Business; Informatics; Management
MA Human Dynamics; Innovative Leadership
MBA Finance; International Business; Management; Marketing
MPA Public Administration
MS Information Systems Engineering

WESTERN KENTUCKY UNIVERSITY
Bowling Green, Kentucky
Distance Learning
http://www.wku.edu/online

Western Kentucky University was founded in 1906. It is accredited by Southern Association of Colleges and Schools. It first offered distance learning courses in 1999. In fall 2010, there were 5,795 students enrolled in distance learning courses. Institutionally administered financial aid is available to distance learners.

Services Distance learners have accessibility to academic advising, bookstore, career placement assistance, e-mail services, library services, tutoring.

Contact Ms. Cindy Troutman, Assistant Director, Distance Learning, Western Kentucky University, Distance Learning, 1906 College Heights Boulevard, 31084, Bowling Green, KY 42101-1084. Telephone: 270-745-2106. Fax: 270-745-2107. E-mail: cindy.troutman@wku.edu.

DEGREES AND AWARDS

AAS Paramedicine completion
AD Office Systems Technology
AS Interdisciplinary Early Childhood Education
BA Sociology
BS Computer Information Technology; Consumer and Family Sciences, Child Studies emphasis; Technology Management
Certificate Canadian Studies; Family Home Visiting; International Student Services
Endorsement Gifted and Talented Graduate Teaching Endorsement
Graduate Certificate Autism Spectrum Disorders; Instructional Design; Leadership; Women's Studies
MA Criminology; History; Mathematics Education; Social Responsibility and Sustainable Communities
MAE Adult Education; Instructional Design; Literacy Education
MBA eMBA
MS Biology; Communication Disorders; Library Media Education; Physical Education Pedagogy; Technology Management

COURSE SUBJECT AREAS OFFERED OUTSIDE OF DEGREE PROGRAMS

Undergraduate—accounting and computer science; behavioral sciences; biblical studies; biological and physical sciences; biology; cell biology and anatomical sciences; chemistry; community organization and advocacy; computer and information sciences; computer and information sciences and support services related; computer/information technology administration and management; computer science; computer systems networking and telecommunications; crafts, folk art and artisanry; criminal justice and corrections; criminology; curriculum and instruction; dance; data entry/microcomputer applications; data processing; demography and population; ecology, evolution, systematics, and population biology; economics; education; education related; education (specific levels and methods); education (specific subject areas); English; English language and literature related; English or French as a second or foreign language (teaching); ethnic, cultural minority, gender, and group studies; family and consumer sciences/human sciences; family and consumer sciences/human sciences business services; family and consumer sciences/human sciences related; fine and studio arts; foods, nutrition, and related services; geography and cartography; gerontology; graphic communications; health and medical administrative services; health and physical education/fitness; health/medical preparatory programs; health professions related; health services/allied health/health sciences; historic preservation and conservation; history; human development, family studies, and related services; human resources management; human services; information science/studies; international business; international/global studies; international relations and national security studies; journalism; languages (foreign languages related); legal professions and studies related; legal studies (non-professional general, undergraduate); legal support services; liberal arts and sciences, general studies and humanities; library science and administration; library science related; linguistic, comparative, and related language studies; management information systems; marketing; mathematics; mathematics and computer science; mathematics and statistics related; mental and social health services and allied professions; multi/interdisciplinary studies related; music; natural resources and conservation related; natural resources conservation and research; natural resources management and policy; natural sciences; nutrition sciences; parks, recreation and leisure; parks, recreation and leisure facilities management; parks, recreation, leisure, and fitness studies related; philosophy; philosophy and religious studies related; physical sciences; physical sciences related; physical science technologies; plant sciences; political science and government; psychology; psychology related; public administration; public health; public policy analysis; public relations, advertising, and applied communication related; radio, television, and digital communication; real estate; religious education; religious studies; sales merchandising, and related marketing operations (general); science technologies related; science, technology and society; social and philosophical foundations of education; social sciences; social sciences related; social work; sociology; soil sciences; statistics; student counseling and personnel services; theology and religious vocations related; visual and performing arts; visual and performing arts related; wildlife and wildlands science and management; work and family studies.

Graduate—behavioral sciences; biological and biomedical sciences related; biological and physical sciences; biology; business administration, management and operations; business/corporate communications; business, management, and marketing related; cell biology and anatomical sciences; criminal justice and corrections; criminology; curriculum and instruction; design and applied arts; ecology, evolution, systematics, and population biology; economics; education; educational administration and supervision; educational assessment, evaluation, and research; educational/instructional media design; education related; education (specific levels and methods); education (specific subject areas); English language and literature related; ethnic, cultural minority, gender, and group studies; family and consumer economics; historic preservation and conservation; history; human development, family studies, and related services; human services; intercultural/multicultural and diversity studies; international and comparative education; international business; library science and administration; library science related; mathematics; mathematics and computer science; microbiological sciences and immunology; multi/interdisciplinary studies related; museum studies; nutrition sciences; physical sciences; plant sciences; political science and government; psychology; psychology related; public administration; public administration and social service professions related; public health; science, technology and society; social and philosophical foundations of education; social sciences; social sciences related; social work; sociology; special education; statistics; student counseling and personnel services; systems science and theory; work and family studies.

WESTERN MICHIGAN UNIVERSITY
Kalamazoo, Michigan
Department of Distance Education
http://www.wmich.edu/online/

Western Michigan University was founded in 1903. It is accredited by North Central Association of Colleges and Schools. It first offered distance learning courses in 1996. In fall 2010, there were 2,204 students enrolled in distance learning courses. Institutionally administered financial aid is available to distance learners.

Services Distance learners have accessibility to academic advising, bookstore, career placement assistance, e-mail services, library services.

Contact Mrs. Cathy Smith, Administrative Specialist, Western Michigan University, Extended University Programs, 1903 West Michigan Avenue, Kalamazoo, MI 49008-5230. Telephone: 269-387-4164. Fax: 269-387-4226. E-mail: cathleen.smith@wmich.edu.

DEGREES AND AWARDS

BS Child and Family Development; Family Studies; Manufacturing Engineering

Graduate Certificate Educational Technology

MA Career and Technical Education; Educational Technology; Orientation and Mobility; Science Education; Teaching Children who are Visually Impaired; Teaching Children who are Visually Impaired/Orientation and Mobility–MA/MA Dual Degree; Vision Rehabilitation Therapy

COURSE SUBJECT AREAS OFFERED OUTSIDE OF DEGREE PROGRAMS

Undergraduate—alternative and complementary medical support services; alternative and complementary medicine and medical systems; anthropology; education; educational/instructional media design; ethnic, cultural minority, gender, and group studies; family and consumer economics; family and consumer sciences/human sciences; family and consumer sciences/human sciences related; history; human development, family studies, and related services; industrial engineering; manufacturing engineering; medieval and Renaissance studies; music; philosophy; political science and government; rehabilitation and therapeutic professions; religious studies; social work; sociology; work and family studies.

Graduate—alternative and complementary medical support services; curriculum and instruction; education; educational administration and supervision; educational assessment, evaluation, and research; educational/instructional media design; education related; education (specific levels and methods); family and consumer economics; family and consumer sciences/human sciences; health and physical education/fitness; science, technology and society; work and family studies.

WESTERN SEMINARY
Portland, Oregon
Center for Lifelong Learning
http://www.westernseminary.edu

Western Seminary was founded in 1927. It is accredited by Northwest Commission on Colleges and Universities. It first offered distance learning courses in 1981. In fall 2010, there were 173 students enrolled in distance learning courses. Institutionally administered financial aid is available to distance learners.

Services Distance learners have accessibility to academic advising, bookstore, career placement assistance, e-mail services, library services.

Contact James Stewart, Director of Distance Education, Western Seminary, 5511 SE Hawthorne Boulevard, Portland, OR 97215. Telephone: 877-517-1800. Fax: 503-517-1801. E-mail: jstewart@westernseminary.edu.

DEGREES AND AWARDS

Programs offered do not lead to a degree or other formal award.

COURSE SUBJECT AREAS OFFERED OUTSIDE OF DEGREE PROGRAMS

Graduate—biblical studies; religious education; religious studies; theological and ministerial studies; theology and religious vocations related.
Non-credit—biblical studies; religious education; religious studies; theological and ministerial studies; theology and religious vocations related.

WESTERN TEXAS COLLEGE
Snyder, Texas
http://ecampus.wtc.edu

Western Texas College was founded in 1969. It is accredited by Southern Association of Colleges and Schools. It first offered distance learning courses in 2003. In fall 2010, there were 1,200 students enrolled in distance learning courses. Institutionally administered financial aid is available to distance learners.
Services Distance learners have accessibility to academic advising, bookstore, e-mail services, library services.
Contact Tammy Wesson, Director of Distance Learning, Western Texas College, 6200 College Avenue, Snyder, TX 79549. Telephone: 325-574-7630. Fax: 866-264-6967. E-mail: twesson@wtc.edu.

DEGREES AND AWARDS

AA General degree
AAS Business Technology

COURSE SUBJECT AREAS OFFERED OUTSIDE OF DEGREE PROGRAMS

Undergraduate—agriculture; behavioral sciences; biology; chemistry; computer science; design and applied arts; education; English; history; landscape architecture; mathematics; natural sciences; physical sciences; radio, television, and digital communication; social sciences.

WESTERN WYOMING COMMUNITY COLLEGE
Rock Springs, Wyoming
Extended Education
http://www.wwcc.wy.edu/dist_ed/

Western Wyoming Community College was founded in 1959. It is accredited by North Central Association of Colleges and Schools. It first offered distance learning courses in 1988. In fall 2010, there were 1,400 students enrolled in distance learning courses. Institutionally administered financial aid is available to distance learners.
Services Distance learners have accessibility to academic advising, bookstore, campus computer network, career placement assistance, e-mail services, library services, tutoring.
Contact Nancy Johnson, Director of Distance Education, Western Wyoming Community College, 2500 College Drive, C-571, PO Box 428, Rock Springs, WY 82902. Telephone: 307-382-1757. Fax: 307-382-1812. E-mail: njohnson@wwcc.wy.edu.

DEGREES AND AWARDS

AA General Studies
AAS Office Information Systems
AS Accounting; Business Administration; Computer Information Systems; Economics; General Studies; Marketing
Certificate Accounting; Western American Studies
Certification Web Site Development certificate

COURSE SUBJECT AREAS OFFERED OUTSIDE OF DEGREE PROGRAMS

Undergraduate—accounting and related services; anthropology; applied mathematics; biological and physical sciences; business administration, management and operations; business/commerce; business operations support and assistant services; communication and journalism related; computer science; computer software and media applications; economics; education (specific levels and methods); ethnic, cultural minority, gender, and group studies; history; philosophy; psychology; social work; sociology.

WEST HILLS COMMUNITY COLLEGE
Coalinga, California
Learning Resources Division
http://www.westhillscollege.com/

West Hills Community College was founded in 1932. It is accredited by Western Association of Schools and Colleges. It first offered distance learning courses in 1989. In fall 2010, there were 3,000 students enrolled in distance learning courses. Institutionally administered financial aid is available to distance learners.
Services Distance learners have accessibility to academic advising, bookstore, campus computer network, career placement assistance, e-mail services, library services, tutoring.
Contact M. Susan Whitener, Associate Vice Chancellor of Educational Planning, West Hills Community College, 9900 Cody Avenue, Coalinga, CA 93210. Telephone: 559-925-3404. Fax: 559-925-3830. E-mail: susanwhitener@whccd.edu.

DEGREES AND AWARDS

AA Administration of Justice–Correctional Science; Administration of Justice–Law Enforcement; Computer Information Systems; Liberal Arts–Arts and Humanities emphasis (Coalinga campus-based); Liberal Arts–Arts and Humanities emphasis (Lemoore campus-based); Liberal Arts–Math and Science emphasis (Coalinga campus-based); Liberal Arts–Math and Science emphasis (Lemoore campus-based); Liberal Arts–Social Science emphasis (Lemoore campus-based); Liberal Arts–Social and Behavioral Science emphasis (Coalinga campus-based); Psychology; Social Science
AS Administration of Justice–Correctional Science; Administration of Justice–Law Enforcement; Computer Information Systems
Certificate of Completion Child Development Certificate–School-Age (Coalinga Campus-based); Web Developer (Lemoore campus-based)

COURSE SUBJECT AREAS OFFERED OUTSIDE OF DEGREE PROGRAMS

Undergraduate—behavioral sciences; bilingual, multilingual, and multicultural education; biological and physical sciences; biology; business administration, management and operations; business, management, and marketing related; business/managerial economics; classical and ancient studies; computer and information sciences; computer and information sciences and support services related; computer/information technology administration and management; criminal justice and corrections; economics; education; education related; English; English language and literature related; entrepreneurial and small business operations; ethnic, cultural minority, gender, and group studies; geological and earth sciences/geosciences; health and physical education/fitness; health/medical preparatory programs; health professions related; health services/allied health/health sciences; history; human development, family studies, and related services; information science/studies; intercultural/multicultural and diversity studies; liberal arts and sciences, general studies and humanities; management information systems; mathematics; mathematics and computer science; mathematics and statistics related; microbiological sciences and immunology; multi/interdisciplinary studies related; music; natural sciences; nutrition sciences; philosophy; physical sciences; physical sciences related; political science and government; psychology; psychology related; social sciences; social sciences related; social work; sociology; statistics.

WEST LOS ANGELES COLLEGE
Culver City, California
Distance Learning Center
http://www.wlac.edu/online

West Los Angeles College was founded in 1969. It is accredited by Western Association of Schools and Colleges. It first offered distance learning courses in 1999. In fall 2010, there were 4,608 students enrolled in distance learning courses. Institutionally administered financial aid is available to distance learners.
Services Distance learners have accessibility to academic advising, bookstore, campus computer network, career placement assistance, e-mail services, library services, tutoring.

Contact Mr. Eric Jean Ichon, Dean of Distance Learning and Instructional Technology, West Los Angeles College, 9000 Overland Avenue, HLRC 4A, Culver City, CA 90230. Telephone: 310-287-4305. Fax: 310-287-4418. E-mail: ichone@wlac.edu.

DEGREES AND AWARDS

AA Accounting; Business Administration; English; Liberal Arts; Marketing; Real Estate; Travel; Travel
AAB Business
Certificate of Achievement Accounting; Advanced Travel; Business; Computer Network and Security Management; Real Estate
Certificate of Completion Advanced Travel
Certificate Jewish Studies; Travel, basic
Technical Certificate Computer Network Management; Computer Network and Information System Security

COURSE SUBJECT AREAS OFFERED OUTSIDE OF DEGREE PROGRAMS

Undergraduate—accounting and computer science; air transportation; allied health and medical assisting services; anthropology; applied mathematics; behavioral sciences; business administration, management and operations; business/commerce; business, management, and marketing related; business/managerial economics; business operations support and assistant services; computer and information sciences; computer/information technology administration and management; computer science; criminal justice and corrections; data entry/microcomputer applications; dental support services and allied professions; dentistry and oral sciences (advanced/graduate); design and applied arts; drama/theatre arts and stagecraft; economics; education; education (specific levels and methods); education (specific subject areas); English; English language and literature related; fire protection; foods, nutrition, and related services; health and physical education/fitness; health/medical preparatory programs; health services/allied health/health sciences; history; information science/studies; international relations and national security studies; languages (East Asian); languages (foreign languages related); languages (South Asian); languages (Southeast Asian and Australasian/Pacific); legal professions and studies related; legal studies (non-professional general, undergraduate); legal support services; liberal arts and sciences, general studies and humanities; library science and administration; library science related; marketing; mathematics; music; philosophy; political science and government; psychology; real estate; sales, merchandising and related marketing operations (specialized); social sciences; social sciences related; visual and performing arts; work and family studies.

WESTMORELAND COUNTY COMMUNITY COLLEGE
Youngwood, Pennsylvania
Learning Resources
http://wccc.edu

Westmoreland County Community College was founded in 1970. It is accredited by Middle States Association of Colleges and Schools. It first offered distance learning courses in 1987. In fall 2010, there were 2,500 students enrolled in distance learning courses. Institutionally administered financial aid is available to distance learners.

Services Distance learners have accessibility to academic advising, bookstore, campus computer network, career placement assistance, e-mail services, library services, tutoring.

Contact Ms. Kathleen A. Keefe, Director of Learning Resources and Special Projects, Westmoreland County Community College, 145 Pavilion Lane, Youngwood, PA 15697. Telephone: 724-925-4101. Fax: 724-925-1150. E-mail: keefek@wccc.edu.

DEGREES AND AWARDS

AA Business Administration
AAS Business Management

COURSE SUBJECT AREAS OFFERED OUTSIDE OF DEGREE PROGRAMS

Undergraduate—accounting and related services; biology; business/commerce; business operations support and assistant services; communication and journalism related; communications technology; computer software and media applications; computer systems networking and telecommunications; education related; film/video and photographic arts; fine and studio arts; health and medical administrative services; human development, family studies, and related services; legal studies (non-professional general, undergraduate); mechanical engineering; philosophy; psychology; real estate; religious studies; sociology.
Non-credit—computer and information sciences.

WEST SHORE COMMUNITY COLLEGE
Scottville, Michigan
http://www.westshore.edu

West Shore Community College was founded in 1967. It is accredited by North Central Association of Colleges and Schools. It first offered distance learning courses in 1998. In fall 2010, there were 400 students enrolled in distance learning courses. Institutionally administered financial aid is available to distance learners.

Services Distance learners have accessibility to academic advising, bookstore, career placement assistance, e-mail services, library services, tutoring.

Contact Patti Davidson, Director of Distance Learning, West Shore Community College, 3000 North Stiles Road, Scottville, MI 49454-0277. Telephone: 231-843-5830. Fax: 231-843-5830. E-mail: pldavidson@westshore.edu.

DEGREES AND AWARDS

AGS General Studies

COURSE SUBJECT AREAS OFFERED OUTSIDE OF DEGREE PROGRAMS

Undergraduate—biology; botany/plant biology; business administration, management and operations; business, management, and marketing related; computer and information sciences; criminal justice and corrections; geological and earth sciences/geosciences; history; liberal arts and sciences, general studies and humanities; marketing; mathematics; mathematics and statistics related; music; public relations, advertising, and applied communication related; sociology.

WEST TEXAS A&M UNIVERSITY
Canyon, Texas
http://wtclass.wtamu.edu/default.asp

West Texas A&M University was founded in 1909. It is accredited by Southern Association of Colleges and Schools. It first offered distance learning courses in 1997. In fall 2010, there were 782 students enrolled in distance learning courses. Institutionally administered financial aid is available to distance learners.

Services Distance learners have accessibility to academic advising, bookstore, campus computer network, career placement assistance, e-mail services, library services.

Contact Mr. Shawn Thomas, Director, Admissions, West Texas A&M University, Office of Admissions, WTAMU Box 60907, Canyon, TX 79016-0001. Telephone: 806-651-2020. Fax: 806-651-5285. E-mail: admissions@mail.wtamu.edu.

DEGREES AND AWARDS

BCJ Administration emphasis
BGS General Studies
BSN Nursing–RN to BSN completion
MA Teaching
MBA Business Administration
MEd Administration; Curriculum and Instruction; Educational Diagnostician; Instructional Technology; Reading
MS Agricultural Business Economics

COURSE SUBJECT AREAS OFFERED OUTSIDE OF DEGREE PROGRAMS

Undergraduate—criminal justice and corrections; education.
Graduate—accounting and computer science; educational assessment, evaluation, and research; education (specific subject areas).

WEST VIRGINIA NORTHERN COMMUNITY COLLEGE

Wheeling, West Virginia

http://www.wvncc.edu/

West Virginia Northern Community College was founded in 1972. It is accredited by North Central Association of Colleges and Schools. It first offered distance learning courses in 1988. In fall 2010, there were 538 students enrolled in distance learning courses. Institutionally administered financial aid is available to distance learners.

Services Distance learners have accessibility to academic advising, bookstore, campus computer network, career placement assistance, e-mail services, library services, tutoring.

Contact Kimberly Patterson, Instructional Designer/Distance Education Coordinator, West Virginia Northern Community College, 1704 Market Street, Wheeling, WV 26003. Telephone: 304-214-8907. E-mail: kpatterson@wvncc.edu.

DEGREES AND AWARDS

Programs offered do not lead to a degree or other formal award.

COURSE SUBJECT AREAS OFFERED OUTSIDE OF DEGREE PROGRAMS

Undergraduate—allied health and medical assisting services; biology; business administration, management and operations; chemistry; computer software and media applications; criminal justice and corrections; economics; history; mathematics and statistics related; microbiological sciences and immunology; physics; political science and government; psychology; psychology related; social sciences; sociology.

Non-credit—accounting and computer science; computer and information sciences; real estate.

WEST VIRGINIA STATE UNIVERSITY

Institute, West Virginia

http://www.wvstateu.edu/

West Virginia State University was founded in 1891. It is accredited by North Central Association of Colleges and Schools. It first offered distance learning courses in 1998. In fall 2010, there were 424 students enrolled in distance learning courses. Institutionally administered financial aid is available to distance learners.

Services Distance learners have accessibility to academic advising, bookstore, campus computer network, career placement assistance, e-mail services, library services, tutoring.

Contact Dr. John Teeuwissen, Assistant Vice President for Academic Affairs, West Virginia State University, 131 Ferrell Hall, PO Box 1000, Institute, WV 25112. Telephone: 304-766-3147. Fax: 304-766-4251. E-mail: johntee@wvstateu.edu.

DEGREES AND AWARDS

Programs offered do not lead to a degree or other formal award.

COURSE SUBJECT AREAS OFFERED OUTSIDE OF DEGREE PROGRAMS

Undergraduate—business administration, management and operations; chemistry; communication and journalism related; communication and media; criminology; economics; education; English; film/video and photographic arts; fine and studio arts; gerontology; health and physical education/fitness; health professions related; social work; statistics; visual and performing arts related.

Graduate—communication and media; criminal justice and corrections; film/video and photographic arts.

WEST VIRGINIA UNIVERSITY

Morgantown, West Virginia

Extended Learning

http://elearn.wvu.edu/

West Virginia University was founded in 1867. It is accredited by North Central Association of Colleges and Schools. It first offered distance learning courses in 1987. In fall 2010, there were 6,533 students enrolled in distance learning courses. Institutionally administered financial aid is available to distance learners.

Services Distance learners have accessibility to academic advising, bookstore, campus computer network, career placement assistance, e-mail services, library services, tutoring.

Contact Ms. Cindy K. Hart, Director of WVU Online Programs, West Virginia University, 707 Allen Hall, PO Box 6808, Morgantown, WV 26506-6808. Telephone: 304-293-3852. Fax: 304-293-3853. E-mail: lkhart@mail.wvu.edu.

DEGREES AND AWARDS

BA Multidisciplinary Studies; Regents Bachelor of Arts
BSN Nursing–RN to BSN
Certificate Integrated Marketing Communications
EMBA Business Administration
Graduate Certificate Digital Marketing Communications; Emergency Medicine certificate program; Nonprofit Management; Software Engineering; Software Engineering
MA Elementary Education; Instructional Design and Technology; Secondary Education Science emphasis; Secondary Education Social Studies emphasis; Special Education; Special Education, Autism Spectrum Disorder certification; Special Education, Early Intervention/Early Childhood certification; Special Education, Gifted Education certification; Special Education, Low Vision/Blindness certification; Special Education, Multicategorical certification; Special Education, Severe/Multiple Disabilities certification
MLS Legal Studies
MPH Public Health
MS Athletic Coaching; Integrated Marketing Communications; Rehabilitation Counseling; Safety Management; School Health Education; Software Engineering; Sports Management
MSE Physical Education Teacher Education
MSN Nursing
DNP Nursing Practice

COURSE SUBJECT AREAS OFFERED OUTSIDE OF DEGREE PROGRAMS

Graduate—computer engineering technologies; computer science; engineering technologies related; marketing.

Non-credit—business, management, and marketing related; computer software and media applications; education; education related; education (specific subject areas); engineering related; finance and financial management services; food science and technology; foods, nutrition, and related services; health professions related; health services/allied health/health sciences; human services; legal support services; management information systems; pharmacy, pharmaceutical sciences, and administration; veterinary biomedical and clinical sciences.

WHARTON COUNTY JUNIOR COLLEGE

Wharton, Texas

http://www.wcjc.edu/

Wharton County Junior College was founded in 1946. It is accredited by Southern Association of Colleges and Schools. It first offered distance learning courses in 1993. In fall 2010, there were 1,300 students enrolled in distance learning courses. Institutionally administered financial aid is available to distance learners.

Services Distance learners have accessibility to academic advising, bookstore, e-mail services, library services, tutoring.

Contact Ms. Lisa Shoppa, Distance Learning Support Specialist, Wharton County Junior College, 911 Boling Highway, Wharton, TX 77488. Telephone: 979-532-6929. Fax: 979-532-6567. E-mail: lisas@wcjc.edu.

DEGREES AND AWARDS

AA General Studies

COURSE SUBJECT AREAS OFFERED OUTSIDE OF DEGREE PROGRAMS

Undergraduate—accounting and computer science; allied health and medical assisting services; behavioral sciences; biology; business administration, management and operations; business/commerce; business, management, and marketing related; computer and information sciences; computer science; computer software and media applications; computer systems networking and telecommunications; criminal justice and corrections; English; English language and literature related; geological and earth sciences/geosciences; history; liberal arts and sciences, general studies and humanities; marketing; psychology; sociology.

WHEELING JESUIT UNIVERSITY
Wheeling, West Virginia
http://www.wju.edu/adulted/

Wheeling Jesuit University was founded in 1954. It is accredited by North Central Association of Colleges and Schools. It first offered distance learning courses in 2000. In fall 2010, there were 305 students enrolled in distance learning courses. Institutionally administered financial aid is available to distance learners.

Services Distance learners have accessibility to academic advising, bookstore, campus computer network, career placement assistance, e-mail services, library services, tutoring.

Contact Rebecca Forney, Dean of Enrollment Management, Wheeling Jesuit University, 316 Washington Avenue, Wheeling, WV 26003. Telephone: 304-243-2284. Fax: 304-243-2397. E-mail: bforney@wju.edu.

DEGREES AND AWARDS

BSN Nursing–RN to MSN
CCCPE Teaching certification, accelerated
MAE Masters in Education Leadership
MSN Nursing

COURSE SUBJECT AREAS OFFERED OUTSIDE OF DEGREE PROGRAMS

Undergraduate—education; health professions related.
Graduate—education; health professions related.

WICHITA STATE UNIVERSITY
Wichita, Kansas
Media Resources Center
http://webs.wichita.edu/?u=mrcwebtelecourse&p=/index

Wichita State University was founded in 1895. It is accredited by North Central Association of Colleges and Schools. It first offered distance learning courses in 1982. In fall 2010, there were 1,600 students enrolled in distance learning courses. Institutionally administered financial aid is available to distance learners.

Services Distance learners have accessibility to bookstore, e-mail services, library services.

Contact Mary Morriss, Telecourse Coordinator, Wichita State University, 1845 Fairmount Street, Wichita, KS 67260-0057. Telephone: 316-978-7766. Fax: 316-978-3560. E-mail: patricia.morriss@wichita.edu.

DEGREES AND AWARDS

Programs offered do not lead to a degree or other formal award.

COURSE SUBJECT AREAS OFFERED OUTSIDE OF DEGREE PROGRAMS

Undergraduate—anthropology; biology; business administration, management and operations; communication and media; criminal justice and corrections; dental support services and allied professions; education; electrical engineering technologies; English; ethnic, cultural minority, gender, and group studies; family and consumer economics; geography and cartography; gerontology; health services/allied health/health sciences; history; mathematics; music; philosophy; psychology; sociology.
Graduate—business administration, management and operations; criminal justice and corrections; education; fine and studio arts; gerontology; health services/allied health/health sciences; music; psychology; social sciences.

WIDENER UNIVERSITY
Chester, Pennsylvania
http://www.widener.edu/uc

Widener University was founded in 1821. It is accredited by Middle States Association of Colleges and Schools. It first offered distance learning courses in 1996. In fall 2010, there were 368 students enrolled in distance learning courses. Institutionally administered financial aid is available to distance learners.

Services Distance learners have accessibility to academic advising, bookstore, campus computer network, career placement assistance, e-mail services, library services.

Contact Dr. Emily C. Richardson, Dean, University College, Widener University, One University Place, Chester, PA 19013. Telephone: 610-499-4282. E-mail: ecrichardson@widener.edu.

DEGREES AND AWARDS

AA Liberal Arts
AS Allied Health; General Studies
BA Liberal Studies; Organizational Development and Leadership
BS Allied Health; Professional Studies

WILFRID LAURIER UNIVERSITY
Waterloo, Ontario, Canada
Office of Teaching Support Services
http://www.wlu.ca/onlinelearning

Wilfrid Laurier University was founded in 1911. It is provincially chartered. It first offered distance learning courses in 1978. In fall 2010, there were 3,000 students enrolled in distance learning courses. Institutionally administered financial aid is available to distance learners.

Services Distance learners have accessibility to academic advising, bookstore, campus computer network, career placement assistance, e-mail services, library services.

Contact Lisa Fanjoy, Manager, Distance and Continuing Education, Wilfrid Laurier University, Office of Teaching Support Services, 75 University Avenue West, Waterloo, ON N2L 3C5, Canada. Telephone: 519-884-0710 Ext. 4106. Fax: 519-884-6063. E-mail: lfanjoy@wlu.ca.

DEGREES AND AWARDS

BA General Studies

COURSE SUBJECT AREAS OFFERED OUTSIDE OF DEGREE PROGRAMS

Undergraduate—accounting and related services; anthropology; astronomy and astrophysics; biology; biopsychology; botany/plant biology; business/commerce; communication and media; economics; English; finance and financial management services; fine and studio arts; geography and cartography; geological and earth sciences/geosciences; history; languages (Germanic); languages (Romance languages); philosophy; psychology; psychology related; religious studies; social work; sociology; visual and performing arts.

WILKES COMMUNITY COLLEGE
Wilkesboro, North Carolina
Individualized Studies Department
http://www.wilkescc.edu

Wilkes Community College was founded in 1965. It is accredited by Southern Association of Colleges and Schools. It first offered distance learning courses in 1984. In fall 2010, there were 1,739 students enrolled in distance learning courses. Institutionally administered financial aid is available to distance learners.

Services Distance learners have accessibility to academic advising, bookstore, campus computer network, career placement assistance, e-mail services, library services.

Contact Debi McGuire, Director of Distance Learning, Wilkes Community College, PO Box 120, Wilkesboro, NC 28697. Telephone: 336-838-6524. E-mail: debi.mcguire@wilkescc.edu.

DEGREES AND AWARDS

AA Arts
AAS Business Administration

COURSE SUBJECT AREAS OFFERED OUTSIDE OF DEGREE PROGRAMS

Undergraduate—accounting and related services; biology; business administration, management and operations; business/commerce; business, management, and marketing related; business/managerial economics; communication and media; communications technology; computer and information sciences; computer and information sciences and support services related; computer programming; computer science; data processing; drama/theatre arts and stagecraft; education related; English;

English language and literature related; ethnic, cultural minority, gender, and group studies; fine and studio arts; history; human development, family studies, and related services; management information systems; marketing; mathematics; philosophy and religious studies related; physical sciences; psychology; psychology related; public relations, advertising, and applied communication related; religious studies; sales, merchandising and related marketing operations (specialized); sociology.

WILLIAMSON CHRISTIAN COLLEGE
Franklin, Tennessee
http://www.williamsoncc.edu

Williamson Christian College was founded in 1997. It is accredited by Association for Biblical Higher Education. It first offered distance learning courses in 2000. In fall 2010, there were 15 students enrolled in distance learning courses. Institutionally administered financial aid is available to distance learners.

Services Distance learners have accessibility to academic advising, bookstore, career placement assistance, e-mail services, library services.

Contact Dr. Sharon Landers, Executive Vice President of Academic Affairs, Williamson Christian College, 200 Seaboard Lane, Franklin, TN 37067. Telephone: 615-771-7821. Fax: 615-771-7810. E-mail: sharon@williamsoncc.edu.

DEGREES AND AWARDS
BS Leadership and Ministry; Management and Ethics

COURSE SUBJECT AREAS OFFERED OUTSIDE OF DEGREE PROGRAMS
Undergraduate—biblical studies; religious studies; theological and ministerial studies.

WINDWARD COMMUNITY COLLEGE
Kaneohe, Hawaii

Windward Community College was founded in 1972. It is accredited by Western Association of Schools and Colleges. It first offered distance learning courses in 2001. In fall 2010, there were 600 students enrolled in distance learning courses. Institutionally administered financial aid is available to distance learners.

Services Distance learners have accessibility to academic advising, bookstore, career placement assistance, e-mail services, library services, tutoring.

Contact Dr. Ann Lemke, Counselor, Windward Community College, 45-720 Kea'ahala Road, Kaneohe, HI 96744. Telephone: 808-235-7448. E-mail: lemke@hawaii.edu.

DEGREES AND AWARDS
Programs offered do not lead to a degree or other formal award.

COURSE SUBJECT AREAS OFFERED OUTSIDE OF DEGREE PROGRAMS
Undergraduate—accounting and computer science; animal sciences; anthropology; chemistry; computer and information sciences; economics; English; family and consumer sciences/human sciences; health/medical preparatory programs; political science and government; sociology.

WINSTON-SALEM STATE UNIVERSITY
Winston-Salem, North Carolina
http://www.wssu.edu/academics/lifelong-learning/distance-learning/default.aspx

Winston-Salem State University was founded in 1892. It is accredited by Southern Association of Colleges and Schools. It first offered distance learning courses in 1996. In fall 2010, there were 3,500 students enrolled in distance learning courses. Institutionally administered financial aid is available to distance learners.

Services Distance learners have accessibility to academic advising, bookstore, campus computer network, e-mail services, library services, tutoring.

Contact Mrs. Myra Reid, Student Support Manager, Winston-Salem State University, Division of Lifelong Learning, NASS, Anderson Center, Suite 137, Office 115, Winston-Salem, NC 27110. Telephone: 336-750-2633. Fax: 336-750-2636. E-mail: reidmy@wssu.edu.

DEGREES AND AWARDS
BIS Integrative Studies
BS Clinical Laboratory Science; Education—Birth to Kindergarten Education (lateral entry/certification)
BSN Nursing RN/BSN
Certificate Computer Programming (post-Baccalaureate)

COURSE SUBJECT AREAS OFFERED OUTSIDE OF DEGREE PROGRAMS
Undergraduate—allied health and medical assisting services; behavioral sciences; biological and physical sciences; business administration, management and operations; business/commerce; computer programming; criminal justice and corrections; curriculum and instruction; education; English; geological and earth sciences/geosciences; gerontology; health and physical education/fitness; history; interdisciplinary studies; liberal arts and sciences, general studies and humanities; mathematics and computer science; microbiological sciences and immunology; music; philosophy and religious studies; political science and government; registered nursing, nursing administration, nursing research and clinical nursing; social and philosophical foundations of education; social sciences; sociology.
Graduate—education; rehabilitation and therapeutic professions.
Non-credit—business, management, and marketing related.

WISCONSIN INDIANHEAD TECHNICAL COLLEGE
Shell Lake, Wisconsin
http://www.witc.edu

Wisconsin Indianhead Technical College was founded in 1912. It is accredited by North Central Association of Colleges and Schools. It first offered distance learning courses in 1991. In fall 2010, there were 2,400 students enrolled in distance learning courses. Institutionally administered financial aid is available to distance learners.

Services Distance learners have accessibility to academic advising, bookstore, career placement assistance, e-mail services, library services, tutoring.

Contact Dr. Diane Vertin, Vice President, Academic Affairs, Wisconsin Indianhead Technical College, 600 North 21st Street, Superior, WI 54880. Telephone: 715-394-6677 Ext. 6214. E-mail: diane.vertin@witc.edu.

DEGREES AND AWARDS
AA Accounting; Administrative Professional; Early Childhood Education; Information Technology–Web Analyst; Marketing; Marketing; Medical Administrative Specialist; Occupational Therapy Assistant; Paramedic Technician; Supervisory Management
AD Business Management; Finance
Diploma Accounting Assistant; Dietary Manager; EMT-Paramedic; Office Support Specialist

COURSE SUBJECT AREAS OFFERED OUTSIDE OF DEGREE PROGRAMS
Undergraduate—accounting and related services; agricultural and food products processing; agricultural business and management; agriculture; applied mathematics; business administration, management and operations; business/commerce; business operations support and assistant services; communication and media; computer and information sciences; computer programming; foods, nutrition, and related services; human development, family studies, and related services; psychology; public relations, advertising, and applied communication related; sales, merchandising and related marketing operations (specialized); sociology; statistics.
Non-credit—accounting and related services; agricultural and food products processing; agricultural business and management; agriculture; applied mathematics; business administration, management and operations; business/commerce; business operations support and assistant services; communication and media; computer and information sciences;

computer programming; foods, nutrition, and related services; human development, family studies, and related services; psychology; public relations, advertising, and applied communication related; sales, merchandising and related marketing operations (specialized); sociology; statistics.

WORCESTER POLYTECHNIC INSTITUTE
Worcester, Massachusetts
Advanced Distance Learning Network
http://www.online.wpi.edu

Worcester Polytechnic Institute was founded in 1865. It is accredited by New England Association of Schools and Colleges. It first offered distance learning courses in 1979. In fall 2010, there were 500 students enrolled in distance learning courses. Institutionally administered financial aid is available to distance learners.

Services Distance learners have accessibility to academic advising, bookstore, campus computer network, career placement assistance, e-mail services, library services.

Contact Pamela Shelley, Associate Director, Worcester Polytechnic Institute, 100 Institute Road, Worcester, MA 01609-2280. Telephone: 508-831-6789. E-mail: online@wpi.edu.

DEGREES AND AWARDS

CGMS Management
Graduate Certificate Environmental Engineering; Fire Protection Engineering
MBA Management
MIT Information Technology Management
MS Environmental Engineering; Fire Protection Engineering; Operations Design and Leadership; Power Systems Engineering; System Dynamics; Systems Engineering
MSMM Marketing and Technology Innovation

COURSE SUBJECT AREAS OFFERED OUTSIDE OF DEGREE PROGRAMS

Graduate—business administration, management and operations; engineering; environmental/environmental health engineering; fire protection; marketing; systems engineering; systems science and theory.

WORCESTER STATE UNIVERSITY
Worcester, Massachusetts
http://www.worcester.edu/

Worcester State University was founded in 1874. It is accredited by New England Association of Schools and Colleges. It first offered distance learning courses in 2000. In fall 2010, there were 943 students enrolled in distance learning courses. Institutionally administered financial aid is available to distance learners.

Services Distance learners have accessibility to academic advising, bookstore, campus computer network, career placement assistance, e-mail services, library services, tutoring.

Contact Dr. William White, Associate Vice President for Continuing Education and Outreach/Dean of Graduate Studies, Worcester State University, Office of Graduate and Continuing Education, 486 Chandler Street, Worcester, MA 01602-2597. Telephone: 508-929-8811. Fax: 508-929-8100. E-mail: wwhite@worcester.edu.

DEGREES AND AWARDS

Programs offered do not lead to a degree or other formal award.

COURSE SUBJECT AREAS OFFERED OUTSIDE OF DEGREE PROGRAMS

Undergraduate—business administration, management and operations; communication and media; computer and information sciences; criminal justice and corrections; economics; English; health professions related; history; mathematics; philosophy; psychology; sociology; statistics; visual and performing arts.
Graduate—education; English; health professions related; history.
Non-credit—business administration, management and operations; communication and media; computer and information sciences; computer science; entrepreneurial and small business operations; film/video and photographic arts; human resources management; human services; public relations, advertising, and applied communication related.

XAVIER UNIVERSITY
Cincinnati, Ohio
http://www.xavier.edu/

Xavier University was founded in 1831. It is accredited by North Central Association of Colleges and Schools. It first offered distance learning courses in 1999. In fall 2010, there were 181 students enrolled in distance learning courses. Institutionally administered financial aid is available to distance learners.

Services Distance learners have accessibility to bookstore, career placement assistance, e-mail services, library services.

Contact Kandi Stinson, Associate Provost for Academic Affairs, Xavier University, 3800 Victory Parkway, Cincinnati, OH 45207. Telephone: 513-745-4286. Fax: 513-745-4223. E-mail: stinson@xavier.edu.

DEGREES AND AWARDS

Programs offered do not lead to a degree or other formal award.

COURSE SUBJECT AREAS OFFERED OUTSIDE OF DEGREE PROGRAMS

Undergraduate—management information systems.
Graduate—business administration, management and operations; education; practical nursing, vocational nursing and nursing assistants.

YALE UNIVERSITY
New Haven, Connecticut
School of Nursing
http://www.nursing.yale.edu/

Yale University was founded in 1701. It is accredited by New England Association of Schools and Colleges. It first offered distance learning courses in 2006. In fall 2010, there were 11 students enrolled in distance learning courses. Institutionally administered financial aid is available to distance learners.

Services Distance learners have accessibility to academic advising, bookstore, campus computer network, career placement assistance, e-mail services, library services, tutoring.

Contact Ms. Melissa Pucci, Director of Admissions, Yale University, PO Box 9740, New Haven, CT 06536. Telephone: 203-737-1793. Fax: 203-737-5409. E-mail: melissa.pucci@yale.edu.

DEGREES AND AWARDS

MSN Nursing Management, Policy, and Leadership program

YAVAPAI COLLEGE
Prescott, Arizona
http://www.yc.edu

Yavapai College was founded in 1966. It is accredited by North Central Association of Colleges and Schools. It first offered distance learning courses in 2000. In fall 2010, there were 3,000 students enrolled in distance learning courses. Institutionally administered financial aid is available to distance learners.

Services Distance learners have accessibility to academic advising, bookstore, campus computer network, e-mail services, library services, tutoring.

Contact Admissions, Yavapai College, 1100 East Sheldon Street, Prescott, AZ 86301. E-mail: admissions@yc.edu.

DEGREES AND AWARDS

Programs offered do not lead to a degree or other formal award.

COURSE SUBJECT AREAS OFFERED OUTSIDE OF DEGREE PROGRAMS

Undergraduate—accounting and computer science; agricultural and domestic animal services; agriculture; allied health and medical assisting services; anthropology; biology; business, management, and marketing related; communication and journalism related; communications technology; computer/information technology administration and management; criminal justice and corrections; education; English; ethnic, cultural minority, gender, and group studies; fire protection; history; human development, family studies, and related services; mathematics; music; psychology; sociology.

YORK COLLEGE OF PENNSYLVANIA
York, Pennsylvania
Special Programs
http://www.ycp.edu

York College of Pennsylvania was founded in 1787. It is accredited by Middle States Association of Colleges and Schools. It first offered distance learning courses in 1981. In fall 2010, there were 300 students enrolled in distance learning courses. Institutionally administered financial aid is available to distance learners.

Services Distance learners have accessibility to academic advising, bookstore, campus computer network, career placement assistance, e-mail services, library services, tutoring.

Contact Leroy M. Keeney, Director, Office of Community Education, York College of Pennsylvania, 1 Country Club Road, York, PA 17403. Telephone: 717-815-1451. Fax: 717-849-1670. E-mail: oced@ycp.edu.

DEGREES AND AWARDS

Programs offered do not lead to a degree or other formal award.

COURSE SUBJECT AREAS OFFERED OUTSIDE OF DEGREE PROGRAMS

Undergraduate—business/commerce.

Graduate—business/commerce; business, management, and marketing related; education related.

Non-credit—accounting and related services; business administration, management and operations; business/commerce; business/corporate communications; business, management, and marketing related; communication and media; finance and financial management services; management information systems; sales, merchandising and related marketing operations (specialized).

YORK COUNTY COMMUNITY COLLEGE
Wells, Maine
http://www.yccc.edu

York County Community College was founded in 1994. It is accredited by New England Association of Schools and Colleges. It first offered distance learning courses in 1999. In fall 2010, there were 300 students enrolled in distance learning courses. Institutionally administered financial aid is available to distance learners.

Services Distance learners have accessibility to academic advising, bookstore, e-mail services, library services, tutoring.

Contact Fred Quistgard, Director of Admissions, York County Community College, 112 College Drive, Wells, ME 04090. Telephone: 207-646-9282 Ext. 311. Fax: 207-641-0837. E-mail: fquistgard@yccc.edu.

DEGREES AND AWARDS

AAS Business Administration

COURSE SUBJECT AREAS OFFERED OUTSIDE OF DEGREE PROGRAMS

Undergraduate—accounting and related services; applied mathematics; business administration, management and operations; business/commerce; business/corporate communications; business, management, and marketing related; business operations support and assistant services; computer and information sciences; computer/information technology administration and management; computer programming; computer software and media applications; English language and literature related; human development, family studies, and related services; psychology; religious studies; sociology.

YORK TECHNICAL COLLEGE
Rock Hill, South Carolina
Distance Learning Department
http://www.yorktech.edu

York Technical College was founded in 1961. It is accredited by Southern Association of Colleges and Schools. It first offered distance learning courses in 1995. In fall 2010, there were 2,500 students enrolled in distance learning courses. Institutionally administered financial aid is available to distance learners.

Services Distance learners have accessibility to academic advising, bookstore, career placement assistance, e-mail services, library services, tutoring.

Contact Ms. Ginger Dewey, Department Manager, York Technical College, 452 South Anderson Road, Rock Hill, SC 29730. Telephone: 803-327-8038. Fax: 803-981-7193. E-mail: gdewey@yorktech.edu.

DEGREES AND AWARDS

Programs offered do not lead to a degree or other formal award.

COURSE SUBJECT AREAS OFFERED OUTSIDE OF DEGREE PROGRAMS

Undergraduate—accounting and related services; biological and physical sciences; business administration, management and operations; business/commerce; computer science; criminal justice and corrections; criminology; economics; English; environmental/environmental health engineering; history; marketing; mathematics; music; philosophy; psychology; sociology.

Non-credit—computer and information sciences and support services related.

YORK UNIVERSITY
Toronto, Ontario, Canada
http://www.yorku.ca/

York University was founded in 1959. It is provincially chartered. It first offered distance learning courses in 1994. In fall 2010, there were 8,000 students enrolled in distance learning courses. Institutionally administered financial aid is available to distance learners.

Services Distance learners have accessibility to academic advising, bookstore, campus computer network, e-mail services, library services, tutoring.

Contact Ms. Amalia Syligardakis, Manager, e-Learning Services, York University, e-Services Office, 4700 Keele Street, Room 2120, TEL Building, Toronto, ON M3J 1P3, Canada. Telephone: 416-736-2100 Ext. 30705. Fax: 416-736-5637. E-mail: amalias@yorku.ca.

DEGREES AND AWARDS

BBA Administrative Studies

COURSE SUBJECT AREAS OFFERED OUTSIDE OF DEGREE PROGRAMS

Undergraduate—accounting and related services; business administration, management and operations; business/corporate communications; business/managerial economics; communication and media; economics; English language and literature related; film/video and photographic arts; geography and cartography; health professions related; history; human development, family studies, and related services; human resources management; liberal arts and sciences, general studies and humanities; management sciences and quantitative methods; marketing; mathematics; philosophy; political science and government; psychology related; public administration; public administration and social service professions related; religious studies; social sciences; social work; sociology; statistics; visual and performing arts related.

YOUNGSTOWN STATE UNIVERSITY
Youngstown, Ohio
http://web.ysu.edu/de

Youngstown State University was founded in 1908. It is accredited by North Central Association of Colleges and Schools. It first offered distance learning courses in 1999. In fall 2010, there were 1,033 students enrolled in distance learning courses. Institutionally administered financial aid is available to distance learners.

Services Distance learners have accessibility to academic advising, bookstore, campus computer network, career placement assistance, e-mail services, library services, tutoring.

Contact Dr. Annette M. Burden, Associate Professor and Interim Director of Distance Education, Youngstown State University, Department of Mathematics and Statistics, One University Plaza, Youngstown, OH 44555-0001. Telephone: 330-941-1526. Fax: 330-941-3195. E-mail: amburden@ysu.edu.

DEGREES AND AWARDS

BS Applied Mathematics; Applied Science–Community Health; Criminal Justice (BSAS); Public Health (BSAS)
BSN Nursing–RN to BSN
Certificate Computer Teacher Education; Health Profeessions; Reading Teacher Education
License Educational Technology Endorsement; Literacy Specialist
MHSA Master of Health and Human Services
MPH Public Health
MS Statistics
MSE Computer Teacher Education; Early Childhood Education

COURSE SUBJECT AREAS OFFERED OUTSIDE OF DEGREE PROGRAMS

Undergraduate—accounting and computer science; business, management, and marketing related; communication and journalism related; computer/information technology administration and management; criminal justice and corrections; economics; engineering related; English language and literature related; foods, nutrition, and related services; geological and earth sciences/geosciences; health and physical education/fitness; health professions related; history; languages (classics and classical); liberal arts and sciences, general studies and humanities; mathematics; natural sciences; nutrition sciences; philosophy; philosophy and religious studies related; psychology related; rhetoric and composition/writing studies; social sciences related.

Graduate—educational administration and supervision; educational/instructional media design; health professions related; mathematics and statistics related; public administration; public health.

Non-credit—accounting and related services; allied health and medical assisting services; business administration, management and operations; business, management, and marketing related; business/managerial economics; business operations support and assistant services; computer and information sciences; computer software and media applications; computer systems networking and telecommunications; English language and literature related; entrepreneurial and small business operations; health and medical administrative services; public relations, advertising, and applied communication related; sales, merchandising and related marketing operations (specialized).

Indexes

INSTITUTIONS OFFERING DEGREE AND CERTIFICATE PROGRAMS

Index of degree and certificate programs offered by institutions. A=Associate degree; B=Bachelor's degree; GC=Graduate certificate; M=Master's degree; UC=Undergraduate certificate

.NET TECHNOLOGY

Champlain College (UC)

3-D VISUALIZATION

Columbus State Community College (GC)

A+ CERTIFICATION AND COMPUTER TECHNOLOGY

Cleveland Institute of Electronics (UC)

AAS

Southern Union State Community College (A)

ACADEMIC ADVISING

Kansas State University (GC,M)

ACADEMIC MEDICINE

University of Southern California (M)

ACADEMIC NURSE EDUCATOR OPTION

Murray State University (M)

ACCELERATED MBA FOR ATTORNEYS

Suffolk University (M)

ACCELERATED MBA FOR CPAS

Suffolk University (M)

ACCOMPLISHED TEACHING

Columbus State University (M)

ACCOUNTANCY

Auburn University (M)
DePaul University (M)
National University (B)
Saint Joseph's College of Maine (M)
State University of New York Institute of Technology (M)
University of Mary (M)
University of Memphis (B)

ACCOUNTANT

Lake Superior College (A)

ACCOUNTING

AIB College of Business (A,B)
Athabasca University (UC)
Brenau University (B,M)
Briar Cliff University (B)
Broward College (A)
Cabrillo College (A)
Caldwell College (B)
Central Pennsylvania College (A,B)
Champlain College (UC,A,B)
Chemeketa Community College (A)
City University of Seattle (UC,B)
Clark State Community College (A)
College of San Mateo (A)
Colorado Technical University Colorado Springs (A,B)
Columbus State Community College (A)
Concordia University, St. Paul (B)
Delgado Community College (A)
DeVry University Online (A)
Dickinson State University (B)
Ellis University (B)
Excelsior College (B)
Florida Tech University Online (A,B,M)
Fort Hays State University (UC)
Franklin Pierce University (UC)
Front Range Community College (UC,A)
Grantham University (B)
Haywood Community College (A)
Herzing University Online (B)
Indiana Tech (A,B)
Indiana Wesleyan University (GC,A,B)
Kaplan University Online (UC,A,B,M)
Lenoir Community College (A)
Liberty University (A,B,M)
Middlesex Community College (A)
Minnesota School of Business–Online (UC,B)
Minnesota School of Business–Richfield (B)
Moraine Park Technical College (A)
Mountain Empire Community College (A)
Mountain State University (A,B)
Mount Saint Vincent University (UC)
New Jersey City University (M)
North Carolina Wesleyan College (B)
Northeastern University (UC,A)
Ozarks Technical Community College (A)
Peirce College (B)
Piedmont Community College (UC,A)
Randolph Community College (A)
Regent University (A)
Saint Leo University (GC,B)
Saint Mary-of-the-Woods College (A,B)
San Diego Community College District (A)
San Jacinto College District (UC,A)
Southern New Hampshire University (UC,GC,A,B,M)
Southwestern College (B)
Stanly Community College (A)
Thomas Edison State College (B)
Trine University (A)
University of Houston–Downtown (B)
University of Maine at Augusta (B)
University of Mary (B)
University of Maryland University College (GC,B)
University of Minnesota, Crookston (B)
The University of Texas at Dallas (M)
The University of West Alabama (B)
Upper Iowa University (B)
Vincennes University (A)
Walden University (B,M)
Wayne Community College (A)
Western International University (B)
Western Wyoming Community College (UC,A)
West Los Angeles College (UC,A)
Wisconsin Indianhead Technical College (A)

ACCOUNTING AND BUSINESS LEADERSHIP

AIB College of Business (A)

ACCOUNTING AND COMPUTING DEGREE D140

Illinois Eastern Community Colleges, Olney Central College (A)

ACCOUNTING AND FINANCE

New England College of Business and Finance (GC)

ACCOUNTING AND FINANCIAL MANAGEMENT

DeVry University Online (M)
University of Maryland University College (M)

ACCOUNTING AND FINANCIAL SERVICES

AIB College of Business (A)

ACCOUNTING AND INFORMATION TECHNOLOGY

AIB College of Business (A)
University of Maryland University College (GC,M)

ACCOUNTING AND MANAGEMENT

Walden University (M)

ACCOUNTING AND TAX PROGRAM

Minnesota School of Business–Online (A)

ACCOUNTING AND TAX SPECIALIST

Minnesota School of Business–Richfield (A)

ACCOUNTING APPLICATIONS

Broward College (UC)
Seminole State College of Florida (UC)

ACCOUNTING ASSISTANT

Spokane Community College (A)
Wisconsin Indianhead Technical College (UC)

ACCOUNTING CONCENTRATION

Colorado Technical University Colorado Springs (M)
Columbus State Community College (GC)
Saint Leo University (M)

ACCOUNTING CORE

Wake Technical Community College (UC)

ACCOUNTING INFORMATION SYSTEMS

Saint Mary-of-the-Woods College (B)

ACCOUNTING ONLINE

Bryant & Stratton Online (A)

ACCOUNTING OPERATIONS

Seminole State College of Florida (UC)

ACCOUNTING PRE-ASSOCIATE CERTIFICATE

Thomas Edison State College (UC)

ACCOUNTING SPECIALIST

Seminole State College of Florida (UC)

ACCOUNTING TECHNICIAN

Dakota College at Bottineau (A)

ACCOUNTING TECHNOLOGY

Broward College (A)
Nashville State Technical Community College (UC)
Seminole State College of Florida (A)
The University of Toledo (A)

ACCOUNTING TECHNOLOGY (IN STATE)

Daytona State College (A)

ACCOUNTING TECHNOLOGY (OUT OF STATE)

Daytona State College (A)

ACCOUNTING–BASIC ACCOUNTING CERTIFICATION

Pitt Community College (UC)

ACCOUNTING–COST

Champlain College (UC)

ACCOUNTING–FORENSIC

Champlain College (UC)

ACCOUNTING–HEALTHCARE ACCOUNTING AND FINANCIAL MANAGEMENT

Indiana University System (UC)

ACCOUNTING–MANAGERIAL

Champlain College (UC)

ACCOUNTING, ADVANCED

Athabasca University (UC)
Champlain College (UC)
College of Southern Maryland (UC)

ACCOUNTING, ADVANCED

Northeastern University (UC)

ACCOUNTING, BASIC

College of Southern Maryland (UC)

ACCOUNTING, NYS CPA TRACK

Excelsior College (B)

ACCOUNTING/FINANCE

Southern New Hampshire University (B,M)

ACCOUNTING/INFORMATION SYSTEMS

Southern New Hampshire University (B)

ACQUISITION AND CONTRACT ADMINISTRATION

University of West Florida (M)

ACQUISITION AND CONTRACT MANAGEMENT

Florida Institute of Technology (M)

ACQUISITION AND CONTRACTING CONCENTRATION OR PROJECT MANAGEMENT CONCENTRATION

American Graduate University (M)

ACQUISITION MANAGEMENT

University of Management and Technology (GC,M)

ACQUISITION MANAGEMENT–MASTER OF ACQUISITION MANAGEMENT

American Graduate University (M)

ADAPTIVE SPECIAL EDUCATION

Fort Hays State University (UC)

ADDICTION STUDIES

City Vision College (B)
The University of South Dakota (M)

ADDICTIONS COUNSELING

Indiana Wesleyan University (GC,B,M)
University of Great Falls (A)

ADDICTIONS COUNSELING CERTIFICATION PROGRAM

Fort Hays State University (UC)

ADMINISTATIVE ASSISTANT/ OFFICE MANAGEMENT

Brigham Young University–Idaho (A)

ADMINISTRATION

Athabasca University (UC)
University of the Incarnate Word (B)
West Texas A&M University (M)

ADMINISTRATION AND LEADERSHIP

Georgian Court University (M)

ADMINISTRATION AND SUPERVISION

Marymount University (M)

ADMINISTRATION EMPHASIS

West Texas A&M University (B)

ADMINISTRATION IN COMMUNICATION ARTS

University of the Incarnate Word (M)

ADMINISTRATION IN HEALTHCARE ADMINISTRATION

University of the Incarnate Word (M)

ADMINISTRATION OF JUSTICE

Salve Regina University (M)
Thomas Edison State College (B)
University of Louisville (B,M)

ADMINISTRATION OF JUSTICE LAW ENFORCEMENT SPECIALIZATION

San Diego Community College District (A)

ADMINISTRATION OF JUSTICE STUDIES

Arizona Western College (A)

ADMINISTRATION OF JUSTICE–CORRECTIONAL SCIENCE

West Hills Community College (A)

ADMINISTRATION OF JUSTICE–LAW ENFORCEMENT

West Hills Community College (A)

ADMINISTRATION–BUILDING CODE ADMINISTRATION

Central Michigan University (B)

ADMINISTRATION–HEALTH SERVICES ADMINISTRATION CONCENTRATION

Central Michigan University (M)

ADMINISTRATION–HUMAN RESOURCE ADMINISTRATION

Central Michigan University (M)

ADMINISTRATION–INFORMATION RESOURCE MANAGEMENT CONCENTRATION

Central Michigan University (M)

ADMINISTRATION–LEADERSHIP CONCENTRATION

Central Michigan University (M)

ADMINISTRATION–ORGANIZATIONAL ADMINISTRATION

Central Michigan University (B)

ADMINISTRATION–PUBLIC ADMINISTRATION CONCENTRATION

Central Michigan University (M)

ADMINISTRATION/ALCOHOL AND DRUG STUDIES SPECIALIZATION

The University of South Dakota (M)

ADMINISTRATION/CRIMINAL JUSTICE SPECIALIZATION

The University of South Dakota (M)

ADMINISTRATION/HEALTH SERVICES ADMINISTRATION SPECIALIZATION

The University of South Dakota (M)

ADMINISTRATION/INTERDISCIPLINARY STUDIES SPECIALIZATION

The University of South Dakota (M)

ADMINISTRATION/LONG-TERM CARE ADMINISTRATION SPECIALIZATION

The University of South Dakota (M)

ADMINISTRATION/ORGANIZATIONAL LEADERSHIP SPECIALIZATION

The University of South Dakota (M)

ADMINISTRATIVE ASSISTANT

Bellevue College (UC)
Bryant & Stratton Online (A)
Dakota College at Bottineau (A)
Nashville State Technical Community College (UC)
Spokane Community College (A)

ADMINISTRATIVE INFORMATION TECH D219

Illinois Eastern Community Colleges, Frontier Community College (A)
Illinois Eastern Community Colleges, Lincoln Trail College (A)
Illinois Eastern Community Colleges, Olney Central College (A)
Illinois Eastern Community Colleges, Wabash Valley College (A)

ADMINISTRATIVE MANAGER'S CERTIFICATE

Pitt Community College (UC)

ADMINISTRATIVE MEDICAL SPECIALIST, MEDICAL BILLING AND CODING CERTIFICATE

California State University, Dominguez Hills (GC)

ADMINISTRATIVE NURSING LEADERSHIP

University of Illinois at Chicago (UC)

ADMINISTRATIVE OFFICE MANAGEMENT

Spokane Community College (A)

ADMINISTRATIVE OFFICE TECHNOLOGIES

Delgado Community College (A)

ADMINISTRATIVE OFFICE TECHNOLOGY

Vincennes University (A)

ADMINISTRATIVE PROFESSIONAL

Wisconsin Indianhead Technical College (A)

ADMINISTRATIVE SERVICES CERTIFICATE

National University (UC)

ADMINISTRATIVE STUDIES

St. John's University (B)
Thomas Edison State College (A)
York University (B)

ADMINISTRATIVE SUPPORT

Rappahannock Community College (UC)

ADMINISTRATIVE SUPPORT TECHNOLOGY

Mountain Empire Community College (A)
New River Community College (A)

ADMINISTRATIVE SUPPORT TECHNOLOGY–MEDICAL OFFICE SPECIALIST

Mountain Empire Community College (A)

ADMINISTRATIVE SUPPORT–LEGAL SECRETARY

Lake Superior College (UC)

ADMINISTRATIVE/MANAGEMENT STUDIES

Excelsior College (A)

ADMINSTRATION LEADERSHIP FOR TEACHER AND LEARNING

Walden University (M)

ADOLESCENCE EDUCATION AND STUDENTS WITH DISABILITIES

Mercy College (M)

ADOLESCENCE EDUCATION SPECIALIST IN SCIENCE 7-12

New York Institute of Technology (M)

ADOLESCENCE EDUCATION, GRADES 7-12

Mercy College (M)

ADOLESCENCE EDUCATION, SPECIALIST IN MATHEMATICS 7-12

New York Institute of Technology (M)

ADULT AND CAREER EDUCATION

Indiana State University (B)

ADULT AND CONTINUING EDUCATION

Kansas State University (M)

ADULT AND HIGHER EDUCATION

University of Southern Maine (M)

ADULT AND ORGANIZATIONAL LEARNING

Northeastern University (GC)

ADULT CARE HOME ADMINISTRATION

Fort Hays State University (UC,GC)

ADULT DEVELOPMENT AND AGING

Penn State University Park (UC)

ADULT EDUCATION

Brock University (UC)
Buffalo State College, State University of New York (GC,M)
Indiana University System (M)
National-Louis University (M)
Oregon State University (M)
Penn State University Park (M)
University of Wisconsin–Platteville (M)
Western Kentucky University (M)

ADULT EDUCATION (BED IN ADULT EDUCATION)

Brock University (B)

ADULT EDUCATION AND LEADERSHIP

Jones International University (M)

ADULT EDUCATION AND TRAINING

Saint Joseph's College of Maine (UC,B)

ADULT EDUCATION AND TRAINING (AET)

Colorado State University (M)

ADULT EDUCATION AND TRAINING SPECIALIZATION

Saint Joseph's College of Maine (A)

ADULT EDUCATION LEADERSHIP

Jones International University (D)

ADULT HEALTH CLINICAL NURSE SPECIALIST

Oakland University (M)

ADULT HEALTH/ GERONTOLOGICAL CNS

University of Minnesota, Twin Cities Campus (D)

ADULT LEARNING

University of Southern Maine (GC)
Walden University (M)

ADULT LEARNING, ADULT AND COMMUNITY EDUCATION SPECIALIZATION

University of Calgary (UC)

ADULT LEARNING, E-LEARNING SPECIALIZATION

University of Calgary (UC)

ADULT LEARNING, WORKPLACE LEARNING SPECIALIZATION

University of Calgary (UC)

ADULT MINISTRY

Dallas Baptist University (M)

ADULT RELIGIOUS EDUCATION/ THEOLOGY STUDIES

Saint Joseph's College of Maine (B)

ADULT/GERONTOLOGICAL NURSE PRACTITIONER

Oakland University (M)

ADULT/GERONTOLOGICAL NURSE PRACTITIONER POST-GRADUATE CERTIFICATE

Oakland University (GC)

ADVANCED PRACTICE CARDIOMETABOLIC

University of Illinois at Chicago (UC)

ADVANCED PRACTICE PALLIATIVE CARE

University of Illinois at Chicago (UC)

ADVANCED TRAVEL

West Los Angeles College (UC)

ADVENTURE EDUCATION

Prescott College (B,M)

ADVERTISING

Academy of Art University (A,B,M)
Savannah College of Art and Design (B)
Southern New Hampshire University (B)

ADVERTISING AND MARKETING

Dakota College at Bottineau (UC,A)

AERONAUTICS

Liberty University (B)

AEROSPACE AND MECHANICAL ENGINEERING (COMPUTATIONAL FLUID AND SOLID MECHANICS)

University of Southern California (M)

AEROSPACE AND MECHANICAL ENGINEERING (DYNAMICS AND CONTROL)

University of Southern California (M)

AEROSPACE ENGINEERING

Auburn University (M)
Georgia Institute of Technology (M)
Missouri University of Science and Technology (M)
North Carolina State University (M)
University of Central Florida (M)
University of Colorado Boulder (M)
University of Southern California (M)
The University of Texas at Arlington (M)

AFRICAN AMERICAN STUDIES

University of Memphis (B)

AFRICANA STUDIES

University of Michigan–Flint (UC)

AFRICANA STUDIES, COMMUNICATION, ENGLISH, HEALTHCARE, HISTORY OR PSYCHOLOGY CONCENTRATION

University of Michigan–Flint (B)

AGING SERVICES MANAGEMENT

University of Southern California (M)

AGRIBUSINESS

Kansas State University (M)
Utah State University (B)

AGRIBUSINESS TECHNOLOGY

Wayne Community College (A)

AGRICULTURAL EDUCATION

North Carolina State University (M)

AGRICULTURAL AND EXTENSION EDUCATOR

New Mexico State University (M)

AGRICULTURAL BUSINESS

Colorado State University (B)

AGRICULTURAL BUSINESS ECONOMICS

West Texas A&M University (M)

AGRICULTURAL BUSINESS MANAGEMENT

North Carolina State University (UC)

AGRICULTURAL BUSINESS MANAGEMENT POST-BACCALAUREATE CERTIFICATE

North Carolina State University (UC)

AGRICULTURAL EDUCATION

Tarleton State University (M)
University of Illinois at Urbana–Champaign (M)

AGRICULTURAL EDUCATION AND COMMUNICATION

University of Florida (M)

AGRICULTURAL EXTENSION EDUCATION

Colorado State University (M)

AGRICULTURAL SALES AND SERVICES–EQUINE OPTION

Dickinson State University (A)

AGRICULTURE

Auburn University (M)
Washington State University (M)

AGRICULTURE AND NATURAL RESOURCES SYSTEMS MANAGEMENT

The University of Tennessee at Martin (M)

AGRICULTURE, GENERAL

Oregon State University (B)

AGRONOMIC CROP PRODUCTION

North Carolina State University (UC)

AGRONOMY AND SOIL SCIENCE

Auburn University (M)

AIR CONDITIONING TECHNOLOGY

San Jacinto College District (UC)

AIR TRAFFIC CONTROL

Thomas Edison State College (A,B)

AIRLINE TRANSPORT PROFESSIONAL

Mountain State University (B)

ALCOHOL AND DRUG STUDIES

The University of South Dakota (UC,GC,B)

ALLIED DENTAL EDUCATION (WITH UMDNJ)

Thomas Edison State College (B)

ALLIED HEALTH

Clarion University of Pennsylvania (A)
National University (B)
Widener University (A,B)

ALLIED HEALTH COMPLETION

University of Colorado at Colorado Springs (B)

ALLIED HEALTH MANAGEMENT

Oregon Institute of Technology (B)

ALLIED HEALTH SCIENCES

Ferris State University (B)

ALTERNATIVE AND RENEWABLE ENERGY SYSTEMS

State University of New York College of Technology at Canton (B)

ALTERNATIVE DISPUTE RESOLUTION

University of Denver (UC)

ALTERNATIVE EDUCATION

Lock Haven University of Pennsylvania (M)

ALTERNATIVE ENERGY SYSTEMS

Prescott College (M)

AMERICAN STUDIES

Columbia College (B)
Franklin Pierce University (B)

ANALOG INTEGRATED CIRCUIT DESIGN

University of Idaho (UC)

ANALYTICAL CHEMISTRY

Illinois Institute of Technology (M)

ANALYTICAL METHOD DEVELOPMENT

Illinois Institute of Technology (GC)

ANALYTICAL SPECTROSCOPY

Illinois Institute of Technology (GC)

ANIMAL NUTRITION

North Carolina State University (UC)

ANIMAL SCIENCE

North Carolina State University (M)

ANIMAL SCIENCE AND INDUSTRY

Kansas State University (B)

ANIMAL SCIENCE AND INDUSTRY UNDERGRADUATE MINOR

Kansas State University (UC)

ANIMATION

Regent University (B)

ANIMATION AND VISUAL EFFECTS

Academy of Art University (A,B,M)

ANTHROPOLOGY

Prescott College (M)
Thomas Edison State College (B)

ANTHROPOLOGY (3 YEAR)

Athabasca University (B)

ANTHROPOLOGY (4 YEAR)

Athabasca University (B)

ANTHROPOLOGY/SOCIOLOGY

Eastern Oregon University (B)

APPALACHIAN STUDIES

Appalachian State University (GC)

APPLICATION PROGRAMMING

Dakota State University (A)

APPLICATION SOFTWARE SPECIALIST

Minot State University (GC)

APPLIED ADMINISTRATION

University of Houston–Downtown (B)
University of the Incarnate Word (M)

APPLIED ANIMAL SCIENCE TECHNOLOGY

Wayne Community College (A)

APPLIED ARTS AND SCIENCE

Rochester Institute of Technology (UC,A)

APPLIED ARTS AND SCIENCES (BAAS)

University of the Incarnate Word (B)

APPLIED BEHAVIOR ANALYSIS AND AUTISM

The Sage Colleges (M)

APPLIED BEHAVIOR ANALYSIS FOR SPECIAL EDUCATION

Penn State University Park (GC)

APPLIED BEHAVIOR ANALYSIS, AUTISM EMPHASIS

Ball State University (M)

APPLIED BUSINESS

University of Alaska Fairbanks (A)

APPLIED BUSINESS INFORMATION TECHNOLOGY

Minot State University (B)

APPLIED BUSINESS TECHNOLOGY

The University of Texas at Brownsville (B)

APPLIED COMMUNICATION

University of Denver (UC)

APPLIED COMPUTER SCIENCE

University of Memphis (M)
University of West Georgia (M)

APPLIED COMPUTER STUDIES

Thomas Edison State College (A)

APPLIED ECONOMICS

University of North Dakota (M)

APPLIED ELECTRONIC STUDIES

Thomas Edison State College (A)

APPLIED ENVIRONMENTAL GEOSCIENCE

Utah State University (M)

APPLIED EPIDEMIOLOGY

Emory University (M)

APPLIED GEOTECHNICS

University of Idaho (UC)

APPLIED GERONTOLOGY

Brenau University (M)

APPLIED HEALTH (BAH)

University of Minnesota, Crookston (B)

APPLIED HEALTH STUDIES

Pennsylvania College of Technology (B)
Thomas Edison State College (A)

APPLIED INFORMATION MANAGEMENT

University of Oregon (M)

APPLIED INFORMATION TECHNOLOGY, TELECOMMUNICATIONS DEGREE

Pace University (A)

APPLIED LEARNING AND INSTRUCTION

University of Central Florida (M)

APPLIED MANAGEMENT

Brigham Young University–Idaho (B)
Minot State University (B)
Trine University (B)

APPLIED MANAGEMENT (NON-TEXAS LOCATIONS)

Central Texas College (A)

APPLIED MANAGEMENT WITH COMPUTER APPLICATIONS (NON-TEXAS STUDENTS ONLY)

Central Texas College (A)

APPLIED MATHEMATICS

Columbia University (UC,M)
Youngstown State University (B)

APPLIED NUTRITION

Northeastern University (M)

APPLIED OPERATIONS RESEARCH

University of Central Florida (GC)

APPLIED ORGANIZATION TECHNOLOGY

The University of Toledo (B)

APPLIED PHYSICS

Columbia University (UC,M)

APPLIED PHYSIOLOGY AND KINESIOLOGY

University of Florida (B)

APPLIED PROJECT MANAGEMENT POST-BACHELOR'S

Walden University (GC)

APPLIED PSYCHOLOGY

Angelo State University (M)
Florida Tech University Online (A,B)
Hodges University (B)
Robert Morris University (B)

APPLIED PSYCHOLOGY, CHILD ADVOCACY CONCENTRATION

Florida Tech University Online (B)

APPLIED PSYCHOLOGY, CLINICAL PSYCHOLOGY CONCENTRATION

Florida Tech University Online (B)

APPLIED PSYCHOLOGY, FORENSIC PSYCHOLOGY CONCENTRATION

Florida Tech University Online (B)

APPLIED PSYCHOLOGY, HUMAN FACTORS CONCENTRATION

Florida Tech University Online (B)

APPLIED PSYCHOLOGY, ORGANIZATIONAL PSYCHOLOGY CONCENTRATION

Florida Tech University Online (B)

APPLIED PUBLIC HEALTH INFORMATICS

Emory University (M)

APPLIED SCIENCE

Baker College Online (A)
Dickinson State University (B)
Siena Heights University (B)
Wayland Baptist University (A,B)

APPLIED SCIENCE EDUCATION

Michigan Technological University (M)

APPLIED SCIENCE–BACHELOR OF APPLIED SCIENCE

University of Maine at Augusta (B)

APPLIED SCIENCE–COMMUNITY HEALTH

Youngstown State University (B)

APPLIED STATISTICS

Kansas State University (GC)
Penn State University Park (GC,M)
Rochester Institute of Technology (M)

APPLIED STATISTICS AND DATA ANALYSIS

Colorado State University (UC)

APPLIED STUDIES

Athabasca University (B)
California State University, Dominguez Hills (B)

APPLIED STUDIES ONLINE

University of Minnesota, Crookston (B)

APPLIED STUDIES, ALLIED HEALTH SERVICES OPTION

Granite State College (B)

APPLIED STUDIES, EDUCATION AND TRAINING OPTION

Granite State College (B)

APPLIED STUDIES, MANAGEMENT OPTION

Granite State College (B)

APPLIED SYSTEMS ENGINEERING EMPHASIS, PROFESSIONAL MASTERS DEGREE

Georgia Institute of Technology (M)

APPLIED TECHNOLOGY

Brazosport College (B)
Central Texas College (A)
DePaul University (M)
Rogers State University (A,B)

ARABIC STUDIES

National University (B)

ARCHITECTURAL DESIGN

Thomas Edison State College (A,B)

ARCHITECTURAL DRAFTING AND ESTIMATING TECHNOLOGY

North Dakota State College of Science (A)

ARCHITECTURAL STUDIES–SUSTAINABLE DESIGN

University of Florida (M)

ARCHITECTURE

Boston Architectural College (M)

ARCHITECTURE MANAGEMENT

Lawrence Technological University (GC)

ARCHIVAL STUDIES SPECIALIST

Drexel University (GC)

ART

Savannah College of Art and Design (M)
Thomas Edison State College (B)

ART EDUCATION

Boston University (M)
Penn State University Park (M)
University of Florida (M)
University of Nebraska at Kearney (M)

ART HISTORY

Mansfield University of Pennsylvania (B)
Prescott College (M)

ART THERAPY

Prescott College (M)
Saint Mary-of-the-Woods College (M)

ARTS

Athabasca University (UC)
Oakton Community College (A)
Wilkes Community College (A)

ARTS (ASSOCIATE AND PRE-MAJOR ASSOCIATE)

Rowan-Cabarrus Community College (A)

ARTS ADMINISTRATION

Drexel University (M)
Goucher College (M)
Savannah College of Art and Design (M)

ARTS AND CULTURE

University of Denver (M)

ARTS AND HUMANITIES

Ohio University (A)

ARTS AND SCIENCE

Athabasca University (B)

ARTS AND SCIENCE DEGREE PROGRAM

Southwest Virginia Community College (A)

ARTS AND SCIENCE–APPLIED ARTS AND SCIENCES

Midwestern State University (B)
Rochester Institute of Technology (B)

ARTS AND SCIENCES

Clarion University of Pennsylvania (A)
College of Southern Maryland (A)

ARTS AND SCIENCES–APPLIED SCIENCE AND TECHNOLOGY

College of Southern Maryland (A)

ARTS AND SCIENCES–ARTS AND HUMANITIES

College of Southern Maryland (A)

ARTS AND SCIENCES–SOCIAL SCIENCES

College of Southern Maryland (A)

ARTS AND SOCIAL SCIENCES (MULTIPLE CONCENTRATIONS)

Union Institute & University (M)

ARTS DEVELOPMENT AND PROGRAM MANAGEMENT

University of Denver (UC)

ARTS MANAGEMENT

Prescott College (M)

ARTS, LITERATURE, AND CULTURE

University of Denver (UC)

ASIAN STUDIES

University of Maryland University College (B)

ASSISTIVE TECHNOLOGY

California State University, Dominguez Hills (UC)

ASTRODYNAMICS AND SATELLITE NAVIGATION SYSTEMS

University of Colorado Boulder (GC)

ASTRONAUTICAL ENGINEERING

University of Southern California (GC,M)

AT-RISK YOUTH SPECIALIZATION

Central Texas College (UC,A)

ATHLETIC ADMINISTRATION

Endicott College (M)

ATHLETIC COACHING

West Virginia University (M)

AUDIOLOGY

University of Florida (D)

AUTISM

Penn State University Park (GC)

AUTISM AND DEVELOPMENTAL DISABILITIES IN EARLY CHILDHOOD

The University of Texas of the Permian Basin (GC)

AUTISM SPECTRUM DISORDER (ASD) ENDORSEMENT

Oakland University (GC)

AUTISM SPECTRUM DISORDERS

Bowling Green State University (GC)
Drexel University (GC)
University of Central Florida (GC)
Western Kentucky University (GC)

AUTISTIC SPECTRUM DISORDERS
University of North Dakota (GC)

AUTOMOTIVE ENGINEERING
University of Michigan (M)

AUTOMOTIVE PERFORMANCE TECHNOLOGY (BSAST)
Thomas Edison State College (B)

AUTOMOTIVE SYSTEMS ENGINEERING
University of Michigan–Dearborn (M)

AUTOMOTIVE TECHNOLOGY MANAGEMENT
Pennsylvania College of Technology (B)

AVIATION
Mountain State University (B)
University of North Dakota (M)

AVIATION AND TRANSPORTATION
Lewis University (M)

AVIATION FLIGHT TECHNOLOGY
Thomas Edison State College (A,B)

AVIATION LEADERSHIP
Purdue University (GC)

AVIATION MAINTENANCE TECHNOLOGY
Thomas Edison State College (A,B)

AVIATION MANAGEMENT
Lynn University (M)

AVIATION OPERATIONS
Broward College (A)

AVIATION SUPPORT
Thomas Edison State College (A)

AVIATION SYSTEMS
The University of Tennessee Space Institute (M)

AVIATION TECHNOLOGY CONCENTRATION
Purdue University (M)

BACHELOR OF INDUSTRIAL TECHNOLOGY AND OPERATIONS
Illinois Institute of Technology (B)

BACHELOR OF LIBERAL ARTS AND SCIENCES/LIBERAL STUDIES
University of Missouri–Kansas City (B)

BANKING
St. Petersburg College (B)

BANKING AND FINANCIAL SERVICES
Northern State University (A,B)

BANKING AND FINANCIAL SERVICES MANAGEMENT (MSBFM)
Boston University (M)

BANKING AND FINANCIAL SERVICES PROFESSIONALS
The University of Tennessee at Martin (M)

BANKING STUDIES
New England College of Business and Finance (GC)

BASIC INTERPERTING (AMERICAN SIGN LANGUAGE)
Spartanburg Community College (A)

BCOMM–ACCOUNTING AND POST-DIPLOMA MAJOR
Athabasca University (B)

BCOMM–E-COMMERCE AND POST-DIPLOMA MAJOR
Athabasca University (B)

BCOMM–FINANCIAL SERVICES AND POST-DIPLOMA MAJOR
Athabasca University (B)

BCOMM–GENERAL AND POST-DIPLOMA
Athabasca University (B)

BEHAVIOR ANALYSIS
St. Cloud State University (M)

BEHAVIORAL INTERVENTION IN AUTISM
University of Massachusetts Lowell (GC)

BEHAVIORAL LEADERSHIP AND MANAGEMENT
Amridge University (M)

BEHAVIORAL SCIENCE
Anderson University (B)
Granite State College (A,B)
Mercy College (B)
Western International University (B)

BEHAVIORAL SCIENCE–SUBSTANCE ABUSE CERTIFICATE
Vincennes University (UC)

BEHAVIORAL SCIENCE, PSYCHOLOGY CONCENTRATION
Vincennes University (A)

BEHAVIORAL SCIENCE/HUMAN SERVICES
Bluefield College (B)

BEHAVIORAL SCIENCES
Vincennes University (A)

BEHAVIORAL SCIENCES, PSYCHOLOGY CONCENTRATION
Vincennes University (A)

BEHAVIORAL SCIENCES, SOCIOLOGY CONCENTRATION
Vincennes University (A)

BIBLE
Baptist Bible College of Pennsylvania (M)
Crown College (UC)
Heritage Christian University (A,B,M)
Piedmont Baptist College and Graduate School (A)
Prairie Bible Institute (UC)

BIBLE AND DOCTRINE
Global University (UC)

BIBLE AND THEOLOGY
Global University (UC,B)
God's Bible School and College (A)
Laurel University (B)
Lincoln Christian University (M)

BIBLE AND THEOLOGY (SECOND BA DEGREE)
Global University (B)

BIBLE AND THEOLOGY (THREE-YEAR BA DEGREE)
Global University (B)

BIBLE INTERPRETER (UNDERGRADUATE CERTIFICATE I)
Global University (UC)

BIBLE–SELECTED MINOR, BIBLE FOR COLLEGE GRADUATES, CHRISTIAN MINISTRIES WITH TWO MINORS

Piedmont Baptist College and Graduate School (B)

BIBLE, THEOLOGY, MINISTRY

Prairie Bible Institute (B)

BIBLE/THEOLOGY

Global University (A)

BIBLICAL AND CULTURAL LEADERSHIP

Taylor University (UC)

BIBLICAL AND THEOLOGICAL STUDIES

Regent University (B)

BIBLICAL EXPOSITION

Amridge University (M)

BIBLICAL FOUNDATIONS

Piedmont Baptist College and Graduate School (UC)

BIBLICAL STUDIES

Amridge University (B,M,D)
Baptist Bible College of Pennsylvania (D)
Barclay College (B)
Bob Jones University (M)
Central Bible College (A,B)
Dallas Baptist University (A,B)
Heritage Christian University (A,B,M)
Indiana Wesleyan University (B)
Life Pacific College (A)
Moody Bible Institute (UC,A,B)
Piedmont Baptist College and Graduate School (M)
Regent University (M)
Taylor University (UC,A)

BILINGUAL EDUCATION

Prescott College (M)

BILINGUAL/ESL

University of Illinois at Urbana–Champaign (UC)

BIOETHICS

Washington State University (GC)

BIOINFORMATICS

The Johns Hopkins University (M)
University of Illinois at Chicago (UC)
University of Maryland University College (GC)

BIOLOGICAL AND AGRICULTURAL ENGINEERING

North Carolina State University (GC,M)

BIOLOGICAL AND AGRICULTURAL ENGINEERING (WATER MANAGEMENT EMPHASIS)

University of Idaho (M)

BIOLOGICAL AND PHYSICAL SCIENCES

University of Houston–Downtown (B)

BIOLOGICAL SCIENCES

Clemson University (M)

BIOLOGY

Illinois Institute of Technology (M)
Thomas Edison State College (A,B)
University of Nebraska at Kearney (M)
Western Kentucky University (M)

BIOLOGY, INTERDISCIPLINARY SCIENCE SPECIALIZATION

Bowling Green State University (M)

BIOMECHANICAL ENGINEERING

Trine University (M)

BIOMEDICAL ELECTRONICS

Thomas Edison State College (A,B)

BIOMEDICAL ENGINEERING

Columbia University (M)
University of Southern California (M)

BIOMEDICAL ENGINEERING (MEDICAL IMAGING AND IMAGING INFORMATICS)

University of Southern California (M)

BIOMEDICAL ENGINEERING SPECIALIZATION

Colorado State University (M)

BIOMEDICAL INFORMATICS TECHNICIAN

Mid-State Technical College (A)

BIOMEDICAL QUALITY SYSTEMS

San Diego State University (M)

BIOMEDICAL WRITING

University of the Sciences in Philadelphia (M)

BIOMEDICAL/PHARMACEUTICAL

University of West Florida (M)

BIOPHARMACEUTICAL DOMESTIC REGULATORY AFFAIRS

Northeastern University (GC)

BIOPHARMACEUTICAL INTERNATIONAL REGULATORY AFFAIRS

Northeastern University (GC)

BIOTECHNOLOGY

University of Maryland University College (M)

BIOTECHNOLOGY MANAGEMENT

University of Maryland University College (GC)

BIRTH TO KINDERGARTEN EDUCATION (B-K)

North Carolina Central University (B)

BIRTH–KINDERGARTEN (BS)

Western Carolina University (B)

BOOKKEEPING

Columbus State Community College (GC)
Dakota College at Bottineau (UC)
Kirtland Community College (UC)

BOOKKEEPING AND PAYROLL ACCOUNTING

Herzing University Online (UC)

BOOKKEEPING–PARAPROFESSIONAL ACCOUNTING PROGRAM

Bellevue College (UC)

BOOKKEEPING/ACCOUNTING

Rappahannock Community College (UC)

BRANCH MANAGEMENT

New England College of Business and Finance (GC)

BRIDGE DOCTOR OF PHYSICAL THERAPY

Simmons College (D)

BROAD FIELD PLAN

Global University (M)

BROADCAST ENGINEERING

Cleveland Institute of Electronics (UC)

BROADCASTING AND ELECTRONIC MEDIA, PHOTOGRAPHY CONCENTRATION (BCTP)

Mount Wachusett Community College (A)

BROADCASTING AND MASS COMMUNICATIONS

State University of New York at Oswego (B)

BSC AND BSC POST-DIPLOMA

Athabasca University (B)

BUILDING CONSTRUCTION MANAGEMENT

Purdue University (M)

BUILDING INFORMATION MODELING AND COMPUTER VISUALIZATION CERTIFICATE

Lawrence Technological University (GC)

BUILDING LEADERSHIP-PRINCIPAL

Fort Hays State University (UC)

BUSINESS

Andrew Jackson University (A)
Atlantic Cape Community College (A)
Brenau University (B)
Cabrillo College (A)
Chemeketa Community College (A)
Clinton Community College (A)
Columbia Basin College (A)
Columbia Southern University (A)
Culver-Stockton College (B)
Drexel University (M)
Emporia State University (B)
Excelsior College (A,M)
Fort Hays State University (GC)
Front Range Community College (A)
Granite State College (A)
Indiana Wesleyan University (A)
Judson College (B)
Kaplan University Online (B)
Keystone College (B)
Lansing Community College (A)
Liberty University (A,B)
Luzerne County Community College (A)
New Mexico Junior College (A)
Penn State University Park (B)
Prescott College (B)
Regent University (A,B)
Rose State College (A)
St. John's University (A)
Salve Regina University (B)
Spring Arbor University (M)
Trine University (B)
University of Maine at Machias (B)
University of Mary (B)
University of the Incarnate Word (A)
Western International University (A,B)
West Los Angeles College (UC,A)

BUSINESS (PRE-TRANSFER)

Lansing Community College (A)

BUSINESS (TRANSFER PROGRAM)

St. Clair County Community College (A)

BUSINESS ADMINISTRATION

Academy College (B)
Adams State College (B)
AIB College of Business (A,B)
Anderson University (M)
Athabasca University (M,D)
Atlantic Cape Community College (A)
Auburn University (M)
Baker College Online (A,B,M,D)
Ball State University (M)
Belhaven University (M)
Bethel University (M)
Brenau University (M)
Brookdale Community College (A)
Broward College (A)
Bryant & Stratton Online (B)
Caldwell College (B)
California State University, Dominguez Hills (M)
California State University, East Bay (B)
Campbellsville University (M)
Cardinal Stritch University (M)
Cayuga County Community College (A)
Centenary College (B,M)
Central New Mexico Community College (A)
Central Pennsylvania College (B)
Central Texas College (A)
Champlain College (M)
City University of Seattle (M)
Clarion University of Pennsylvania (M)
Cleary University (M)
Clinton Community College (A)
College of Southern Maryland (A)
Colorado State University (M)
Colorado Technical University Colorado Springs (A)
Columbia College (A,B,M)
Columbia Southern University (B,M,D)
Concordia University, St. Paul (M)
Concordia University Wisconsin (M)
Crown College (B,M)
Dallas Baptist University (A,B)
Delgado Community College (A)
DeVry University Online (B,M)
Dickinson State University (B)
Drexel University (B,M)
Eastern Oregon University (B)
Eastern University (B)
Eastern Wyoming College (A)
Edgecombe Community College (A)
Ellis University (B,M)
Endicott College (M)
Everest University (A)
Ferris State University (M)
Finger Lakes Community College (A)
Fitchburg State University (M)
Florida State University (M)
Florida Tech University Online (A,M)
Freed-Hardeman University (M)
Friends University (M)
Gadsden State Community College (A)
Gannon University (M)
Genesee Community College (A)
George Fox University (D)
Grantham University (A,B,M)
Harford Community College (A)
Haywood Community College (A)
Herkimer County Community College (A)
Herzing University Online (M)
Hodges University (A,B,M)
Hope International University (B)
Indiana State University (B)
Indiana Wesleyan University (B,M)
Jacksonville State University (M)
James A. Rhodes State College (A)
Jefferson Community College (A)
Jones International University (A,B,M,D)
J. Sargeant Reynolds Community College (A)
Kansas State University (GC)
Kaplan University Online (M)
Keystone College (A)
Lake Superior College (A)
Laurel University (M)
Lawrence Technological University (M)
Lehigh University (M)
Lenoir Community College (A)
LeTourneau University (B,M)
Lewis-Clark State College (A,B)
Liberty University (B,M)
Limestone College (A,B)
Lindenwood University (M)
Luna Community College (A)
Lynn University (B)
Maharishi University of Management (M)
Marist College (M)
Marylhurst University (M)
Mayville State University (B)
McKendree University (M)
Memorial University of Newfoundland (UC,B)
Mercy College (B,M)
Miami Dade College (A)
Michigan Technological University (M)
Midstate College (B)
Midway College (A,B)
Minnesota School of Business–Online (A,B,M)
Minnesota School of Business–Richfield (A,B,M)
Misericordia University (B,M)
Mississippi State University (GC,M)
Missouri University of Science and Technology (M)
Monroe College (A)
Monroe Community College (A)
Montgomery Community College (A)
Montgomery County Community College (A)
Mountain Empire Community College (A)
Mount Saint Vincent University (B)
Murray State University (B,M)
National University (B,M)
New England College of Business and Finance (A)
North Carolina Wesleyan College (B)
Northeastern University (A)
North Lake College (A)
North Shore Community College (A)
Northwestern Michigan College (A)
Northwest-Shoals Community College (A)
Ocean County College (A)
The Ohio State University (M)
Penn State University Park (A)
Peru State College (B)
Piedmont Community College (UC,A)
Pitt Community College (A)
Quinnipiac University (M)

Randolph Community College (A)
Regent University (M)
Rider University (B)
Rogers State University (A)
Rosemont College (M)
Rowan-Cabarrus Community College (A)
Rowan University (M)
St. Cloud State University (M)
St. Joseph's College, Long Island Campus (M)
St. Joseph's College, New York (M)
Saint Joseph's College of Maine (A,B)
Saint Leo University (A)
St. Louis Community College (GC)
Saint Mary-of-the-Woods College (B)
St. Petersburg College (B)
Salve Regina University (M)
San Diego Community College District (A)
Seminole State College of Florida (A)
Shippensburg University of Pennsylvania (M)
Siena Heights University (B)
Sinclair Community College (A)
Southeast Community College Area (A)
Southeastern Community College (A)
Southern Arkansas University–Magnolia (M)
Southern New Hampshire University (A,B)
Southern Oregon University (B)
Southwestern College (B,M)
Southwestern Oklahoma State University (M)
Stanly Community College (A)
State University of New York Empire State College (M)
Suffolk University (M)
Taft College (A)
Tarleton State University (M)
Taylor University (B)
Texas Woman's University (M)
Trine University (A)
Universidad del Turabo (M)
University of Atlanta (M)
University of Baltimore (B,M)
University of Colorado at Colorado Springs (M)
The University of Findlay (M)
University of Florida (B,M)
University of Houston–Victoria (M)
University of Illinois at Springfield (B)
University of Maine at Augusta (A,B)
University of Management and Technology (A,D)
University of Maryland University College (B,M)
University of Massachusetts Lowell (M)
University of Memphis (M)
University of Michigan–Flint (B,M)
University of Nebraska at Kearney (B)
University of North Dakota (M)
University of St. Francis (M)
The University of South Dakota (M)
The University of Texas at Brownsville (M)
The University of Texas of the Permian Basin (M)
University of the Southwest (M)
The University of West Alabama (B)
University of Wisconsin MBA Consortium (M)
University of Wisconsin–Parkside (M)
University of Wisconsin–Platteville (B)
University of Wisconsin–Platteville (B)
Upper Iowa University (B)
Vincennes University (A)
Walden University (B,M,D)
Wayland Baptist University (M)
Wayne Community College (A)
Wayne State College (M)
Wayne State University (M)
Webster University (M)
Western International University (B)
Western Wyoming Community College (A)
West Los Angeles College (A)
Westmoreland County Community College (A)
West Texas A&M University (M)
West Virginia University (M)
Wilkes Community College (A)
York County Community College (A)

BUSINESS ADMINISTRATION (ASBA)

Thomas Edison State College (A)

BUSINESS ADMINISTRATION (BACHELOR OF APPLIED SCIENCE)

Mayville State University (B)

BUSINESS ADMINISTRATION (HUMAN RESOURCE MANAGEMENT CONCENTRATION)

Southern New Hampshire University (B)

BUSINESS ADMINISTRATION (HYBRID PROGRAM)

Framingham State University (M)

BUSINESS ADMINISTRATION (IN STATE)

Daytona State College (A)

BUSINESS ADMINISTRATION (INFORMATION SYSTEMS/ TECHNOLOGY EMPHASIS)

City University of Seattle (B)

BUSINESS ADMINISTRATION (MARKETING EMPHASIS)

City University of Seattle (B)

BUSINESS ADMINISTRATION (ORGANIZATIONAL LEADERSHIP CONCENTRATION)

Southern New Hampshire University (B)

BUSINESS ADMINISTRATION (OUT OF STATE)

Daytona State College (A)

BUSINESS ADMINISTRATION (PROJECT MANAGEMENT EMPHASIS)

City University of Seattle (B)

BUSINESS ADMINISTRATION (SMALL BUSINESS MANAGEMENT CONCENTRATION)

Southern New Hampshire University (B)

BUSINESS ADMINISTRATION AND ACCOUNTING

Indiana Tech (M)

BUSINESS ADMINISTRATION AND FINANCIAL SERVICES

AIB College of Business (A)

BUSINESS ADMINISTRATION AND HEALTH CARE MANAGEMENT

Indiana Tech (M)

BUSINESS ADMINISTRATION AND HUMAN RESOURCES

Indiana Tech (M)

BUSINESS ADMINISTRATION AND INFORMATION TECHNOLOGY

AIB College of Business (A)

BUSINESS ADMINISTRATION AND INTERNATIONAL BUSINESS

AIB College of Business (A)

BUSINESS ADMINISTRATION AND LEADERSHIP

AIB College of Business (A)

BUSINESS ADMINISTRATION AND MANAGEMENT

Briar Cliff University (B)
Indiana Tech (M)

BUSINESS ADMINISTRATION AND MARKETING

Indiana Tech (M)

BUSINESS ADMINISTRATION CAREER

Middlesex Community College (A)
Quinsigamond Community College (A)

BUSINESS ADMINISTRATION DEGREE COMPLETION

University of Illinois at Chicago (B)

BUSINESS ADMINISTRATION DUAL CONCENTRATION

Herzing University Online (M)

BUSINESS ADMINISTRATION HUMAN RESOURCES MANAGEMENT

Grantham University (B)

BUSINESS ADMINISTRATION IN ACCOUNTING

University of the Incarnate Word (B)

BUSINESS ADMINISTRATION IN BANKING AND FINANCE

University of the Incarnate Word (B)

BUSINESS ADMINISTRATION IN GENERAL BUSINESS

University of the Incarnate Word (B)

BUSINESS ADMINISTRATION IN INFORMATION SYSTEMS

University of the Incarnate Word (B)

BUSINESS ADMINISTRATION IN INTERNATIONAL BUSINESS

University of the Incarnate Word (B)

BUSINESS ADMINISTRATION IN MANAGEMENT

University of the Incarnate Word (B)

BUSINESS ADMINISTRATION IN MARKETING

University of the Incarnate Word (B)

BUSINESS ADMINISTRATION MANAGEMENT

Ball State University (A)

BUSINESS ADMINISTRATION ONLINE

Kirkwood Community College (A)

BUSINESS ADMINISTRATION TRANSFER

Anne Arundel Community College (A)
Middlesex Community College (A)

BUSINESS ADMINISTRATION TRANSFER

Quinsigamond Community College (A)

BUSINESS ADMINISTRATION–ACCOUNTING

Washington State University (B)

BUSINESS ADMINISTRATION–APPLIED MANAGEMENT

Tompkins Cortland Community College (A)

BUSINESS ADMINISTRATION–BUSINESS LAW CONCENTRATION

Peirce College (UC,A,B)

BUSINESS ADMINISTRATION–CAREER (BAC)

Mount Wachusett Community College (A)

BUSINESS ADMINISTRATION–CAREER, ACCOUNTING CONCENTRATION (BACA)

Mount Wachusett Community College (A)

BUSINESS ADMINISTRATION–DISTANCE MBA PROGRAM

Colorado State University (M)

BUSINESS ADMINISTRATION–E-COMMERCE EMPHASIS (BULGARIA)

City University of Seattle (B)

BUSINESS ADMINISTRATION–E. MBA

Pace University (M)

BUSINESS ADMINISTRATION–ECONOMIC CRIME AND FRAUD MANAGEMENT

Utica College (M)

BUSINESS ADMINISTRATION–ENTREPRENEURSHIP/SMALL BUSINESS MANAGEMENT CONCENTRATION

Peirce College (A,B)

BUSINESS ADMINISTRATION–FINANCE

Mercy College (B)
Mountain State University (A,B)
University of Atlanta (B,M)

BUSINESS ADMINISTRATION–GENERAL MANAGEMENT EMPHASIS

City University of Seattle (B)

BUSINESS ADMINISTRATION–HEALTH CARE ADMINISTRATION

Indiana Tech (B)

BUSINESS ADMINISTRATION–HEALTH CARE MANAGEMENT

Mountain State University (A,B)

BUSINESS ADMINISTRATION–HOSPITALITY

Mountain State University (A,B)

BUSINESS ADMINISTRATION–HUMAN RESOURCE EMPHASIS

City University of Seattle (B)

BUSINESS ADMINISTRATION–HUMAN RESOURCE MANAGEMENT

Mountain State University (A,B)

BUSINESS ADMINISTRATION–HUMAN RESOURCES

Indiana Tech (B)

BUSINESS ADMINISTRATION–HUMAN RESOURCES MANAGEMENT

Pitt Community College (UC)

BUSINESS ADMINISTRATION–INDIVIDUALIZED STUDY EMPHASIS

City University of Seattle (B)

BUSINESS ADMINISTRATION–INTERNATIONAL BUSINESS

Mercy College (B)
University of Atlanta (B,M)

BUSINESS ADMINISTRATION–MANAGEMENT

Indiana Tech (A,B,M)
Mercy College (B)
Montana State University–Great Falls College of Technology (A)
Mountain State University (A,B)
Peru State College (B)
University of Atlanta (B,M)

BUSINESS ADMINISTRATION–MANAGEMENT AND OPERATIONS

Washington State University (B)

BUSINESS ADMINISTRATION–MANAGEMENT CONCENTRATION

Peirce College (A,B)

BUSINESS ADMINISTRATION–MANAGEMENT INFORMATION SYSTEMS

Washington State University (B)

BUSINESS ADMINISTRATION–MANAGEMENT OPTION

Rogers State University (B)

BUSINESS ADMINISTRATION–MARKETING

Indiana Tech (B)
Mercy College (B)
Mountain State University (A,B)
University of Atlanta (B,M)

BUSINESS ADMINISTRATION–MARKETING AND ADVERTISING

Pitt Community College (A)

BUSINESS ADMINISTRATION–MARKETING CONCENTRATION

Peirce College (A,B)

BUSINESS ADMINISTRATION–ONLINE MBA PROGRAM

University of North Alabama (M)

BUSINESS ADMINISTRATION–ORGANIZATIONAL LEADERSHIP

Bryan College (B)

BUSINESS ADMINISTRATION–PRODUCTION MANAGEMENT

Indiana Tech (A)

BUSINESS ADMINISTRATION–PROFESSIONAL ACCOUNTANCY

Utica College (M)

BUSINESS ADMINISTRATION–PROFESSIONAL STUDIES CONCENTRATION

Peirce College (B)

BUSINESS ADMINISTRATION–SALES AND MARKETING

AIB College of Business (A)

BUSINESS ADMINISTRATION–SPORT MANAGEMENT

Mercy College (B)

BUSINESS ADMINISTRATION–TECHNICAL MANAGEMENT

College of Southern Maryland (A)

BUSINESS ADMINISTRATION–TRADITIONAL MBA

Nichols College (M)

BUSINESS ADMINISTRATION–TRANSFER (BA)

Mount Wachusett Community College (A)

BUSINESS ADMINISTRATION, ACCOUNTING AND FINANCE CONCENTRATION

Florida Tech University Online (M)

BUSINESS ADMINISTRATION, ACCOUNTING CONCENTRATION

Florida Tech University Online (B)
Herzing University Online (M)
Saint Leo University (B)

BUSINESS ADMINISTRATION, ACCOUNTING EMPHASIS

Upper Iowa University (M)

BUSINESS ADMINISTRATION, BUSINESS MANAGEMENT CONCENTRATION

Herzing University Online (M)

BUSINESS ADMINISTRATION, COMPUTER INFORMATION SYSTEMS CONCENTRATION

Florida Tech University Online (B)

BUSINESS ADMINISTRATION, CORPORATE FINANCIAL MANAGEMENT EMPHASIS

Upper Iowa University (M)

BUSINESS ADMINISTRATION, EXECUTIVE MANAGEMENT, INNOVATION, AND TECHNOLOGY CONCENTRATIONS

Carlow University (M)

BUSINESS ADMINISTRATION, GLOBAL BUSINESS EMPHASIS

Upper Iowa University (M)

BUSINESS ADMINISTRATION, HEALTHCARE MANAGEMENT CONCENTRATION

Florida Tech University Online (B,M)
Herzing University Online (M)

BUSINESS ADMINISTRATION, HUMAN RESOURCES CONCENTRATION

Herzing University Online (M)

BUSINESS ADMINISTRATION, HUMAN RESOURCES MANAGEMENT

Wake Technical Community College (A)

BUSINESS ADMINISTRATION, HUMAN RESOURCES MANAGEMENT EMPHASIS

Upper Iowa University (M)

BUSINESS ADMINISTRATION, INFORMATION TECHNOLOGY MANAGEMENT CONCENTRATION

Florida Tech University Online (M)

BUSINESS ADMINISTRATION, INTERNATIONAL OPTION

Montgomery County Community College (A)

BUSINESS ADMINISTRATION, MANAGEMENT CONCENTRATION

Florida Tech University Online (B,M)
Saint Leo University (B)

BUSINESS ADMINISTRATION, MARKETING CONCENTRATION

Florida Tech University Online (B,M)
Herzing University Online (M)
Saint Leo University (B)

BUSINESS ADMINISTRATION, ORGANIZATIONAL DEVELOPMENT EMPHASIS

Upper Iowa University (M)

BUSINESS ADMINISTRATION, PROJECT MANAGEMENT CONCENTRATION

Florida Tech University Online (M)
Herzing University Online (M)

BUSINESS ADMINISTRATION, QUALITY MANAGEMENT EMPHASIS

Upper Iowa University (M)

BUSINESS ADMINISTRATION, TECHNOLOGY MANAGEMENT CONCENTRATION

Herzing University Online (M)

BUSINESS ADMINISTRATION/GENERAL BUSINESS

Amridge University (B)

BUSINESS ADMINISTRATION/INFORMATION COMMUNICATION

Amridge University (B)

BUSINESS ADMINISTRATION/INFORMATION SYSTEMS MANAGEMENT

Amridge University (B)

BUSINESS ADMINISTRATION/ MANAGEMENT

Kaplan University Online (A)

BUSINESS ADMINISTRATION/ MARKETING AND RETAILING

Wayne Community College (A)

BUSINESS ADMINISTRATION/ OPERATIONS MANAGEMENT

Wayne Community College (A)

BUSINESS ADMINISTRATIVE ASSISTANT

Minnesota School of Business–Online (UC)

BUSINESS ANALYTICS

Drexel University (M)

BUSINESS AND ECONOMICS

Eastern Oregon University (B)

BUSINESS AND ENTREPRENEURIAL STUDIES

University of Maine at Machias (B)

BUSINESS AND LEADERSHIP

Marylhurst University (B)

BUSINESS AND MANAGEMENT

Marylhurst University (B)

BUSINESS AND MARKETING

Ozarks Technical Community College (A)

BUSINESS AND MARKETING EDUCATION

Auburn University (M)
Ball State University (M)

BUSINESS AND MARKETING EDUCATION INITIAL LICENSURE PROGRAM

North Carolina State University (UC)

BUSINESS AND OPERATIONS RESEARCH DUAL DEGREES

Columbia University (M)

BUSINESS AND ORGANIZATIONAL SECURITY MANAGEMENT

Webster University (M)

BUSINESS AND TECHNOLOGY

Columbia University (UC)

BUSINESS ASPECTS OF PUBLISHING

Pace University (GC)

BUSINESS COMMUNICATION

Jones International University (B,M)

BUSINESS COMMUNICATIONS

Ellis University (M)

BUSINESS COMPLETION

Presentation College (B)

BUSINESS COMPUTER SYSTEMS AND MANAGEMENT

North Hennepin Community College (A)

BUSINESS CONTINUITY, SECURITY, AND RISK MANAGEMENT

Boston University (M)

BUSINESS EDUCATION

Appalachian State University (B)
Auburn University (M)
Emporia State University (M)
Southern New Hampshire University (M)
Valley City State University (B)

BUSINESS EDUCATION–BUSINESS TEACHER LICENSURE

Fort Hays State University (B)

BUSINESS EDUCATION–CORPORATE COMMUNICATION

Fort Hays State University (B)

BUSINESS EDUCATION–TRAINING AND DEVELOPMENT

Fort Hays State University (B)

BUSINESS INFORMATICS

Northern Kentucky University (GC,M)

BUSINESS INFORMATION SYSTEMS

Fort Hays State University (UC)
Indiana Wesleyan University (B)
Southern New Hampshire University (UC)

BUSINESS INFORMATION TECHNOLOGY

DePaul University (M)

BUSINESS INFORMATION TECHNOLOGY–COMPUTER NETWORK ADMINISTRATION OR SOFTWARE DEVELOPMENT AND MULTIMEDIA OPTION

Rogers State University (B)

BUSINESS INTELLIGENCE

Grantham University (M)

BUSINESS INTELLIGENCE ANALYST

Bellevue College (UC)

BUSINESS INTELLIGENCE DEVELOPER

Bellevue College (UC)

BUSINESS MANAGEMENT

Anne Arundel Community College (A)
Broward College (UC)
Cardinal Stritch University (B)
Central Texas College (UC,A)
Champlain College (A,B)
Columbus State Community College (A)
Concordia University Wisconsin (B)
Cossatot Community College of the University of Arkansas (A)
Dakota State University (A)
Dawson Community College (A)
Friends University (B)
Granite State College (B)
Grantham University (A,B)
Herzing University Online (A,B)
James A. Rhodes State College (A)
Johnson State College (B)
LeTourneau University (B)
Malone University (B)
Mercer County Community College (A)
Minnesota School of Business–Online (B)
Minnesota School of Business–Richfield (B)
Monroe College (B,M)
Montgomery County Community College (UC)
Moraine Park Technical College (A)
Nashville State Technical Community College (A)
Nicolet Area Technical College (A)
North Hennepin Community College (A)
Purdue University (M)
San Diego Community College District (A)
Sinclair Community College (UC,A)
Southwestern Adventist University (B)
Tyler Junior College (A)
Union County College (A)
The University of Findlay (B)
University of Maine at Fort Kent (B)
University of Management and Technology (UC)
Vincennes University (A)
Westmoreland County Community College (A)
Wisconsin Indianhead Technical College (A)

BUSINESS MANAGEMENT FOR ENGINEERS

University of Illinois at Urbana–Champaign (GC)

University of Illinois at Urbana–Champaign (GC)

BUSINESS MANAGEMENT MARKETING AND SALES

Central Texas College (UC)

BUSINESS MANAGEMENT MARKETING AND SALES MANAGEMENT

Central Texas College (A)

BUSINESS MANAGEMENT TECHNOLOGY

Miami University–Regional Campuses (A)
The University of Toledo (A)

BUSINESS MANAGEMENT, BUSINESS ADMINISTRATION CONCENTRATION

Herzing University Online (B)

BUSINESS MANAGEMENT, EBUSINESS EMPHASIS

North Dakota State College of Science (A)

BUSINESS MANAGEMENT, ENTREPRENEURIAL STUDIES CONCENTRATION

Herzing University Online (B)

BUSINESS MANAGEMENT, HUMAN RESOURCE DEVELOPMENT CONCENTRATION

Herzing University Online (B)

BUSINESS MANAGEMENT, MARKETING AND ADMINISTRATION

Seminole State College of Florida (A)

BUSINESS MINISTRY CONCENTRATION

Dallas Baptist University (M)

BUSINESS OFFICE SYSTEMS AND SUPPORT–EXECUTIVE ASSISTANT

North Lake College (A)

BUSINESS OFFICE TECHNOLOGY, ACCOUNTING SPECIALITY

San Jacinto College District (UC)

BUSINESS OFFICE TECHNOLOGY, GENERAL OFFICE SPECIALITY

San Jacinto College District (UC)

BUSINESS OFFICE TECHNOLOGY, LEGAL SECRETARY SPECIALITY

San Jacinto College District (UC)

BUSINESS ONLINE

Bryant & Stratton Online (A)
University of Minnesota, Crookston (B)

BUSINESS QUALITY MANAGEMENT

Southwestern College (B)

BUSINESS SOFTWARE

Chemeketa Community College (UC)

BUSINESS SOFTWARE SPECIALIST–BUSINESS TECHNOLOGY SYSTEMS

Bellevue College (UC)

BUSINESS SOFTWARE SPECIALIST, ADVANCED

Bellevue College (UC)

BUSINESS SPECIALIST–SMALL BUSINESS MANAGEMENT

Broward College (UC)

BUSINESS STUDIES

Mountain State University (B)

BUSINESS STUDIES (ACCOUNTING CONCENTRATION)

Southern New Hampshire University (B)

BUSINESS STUDIES (BUSINESS ADMINISTRATION CONCENTRATION)

Southern New Hampshire University (B)

BUSINESS STUDIES (BUSINESS FINANCE CONCENTRATION)

Southern New Hampshire University (B)

BUSINESS STUDIES (COMPUTER INFORMATION TECHNOLOGY CONCENTRATION)

Southern New Hampshire University (B)

BUSINESS STUDIES (HUMAN RESOURCE MANAGEMENT CONCENTRATION)

Southern New Hampshire University (B)

BUSINESS STUDIES (INTERNATIONAL MANAGEMENT CONCENTRATION)

Southern New Hampshire University (B)

BUSINESS STUDIES (MARKETING CONCENTRATION)

Southern New Hampshire University (B)

BUSINESS STUDIES (ORGANIZATIONAL LEADERSHIP CONCENTRATION)

Southern New Hampshire University (B)

BUSINESS STUDIES (SMALL BUSINESS MANAGEMENT CONCENTRATION)

Southern New Hampshire University (B)

BUSINESS SUCCESSION PLANNING

The American College (GC)

BUSINESS TECHNOLOGY

Motlow State Community College (A)
Ozarks Technical Community College (A)
Western Texas College (A)

BUSINESS TECHNOLOGY MANAGEMENT

North Dakota State College of Science (A)

BUSINESS UNDERGRADUATE MINOR

Kansas State University (UC)

BUSINESS–ACCOUNTING

Herkimer County Community College (A)

BUSINESS–ADVANCED STUDIES IN BUSINESS

Shippensburg University of Pennsylvania (UC)

BUSINESS–BUSINESS ADMINISTRATION

Erie Community College (A)
Erie Community College, North Campus (A)
Erie Community College, South Campus (A)
Herkimer County Community College (A)
Jamestown Community College (A)

BUSINESS–BUSINESS ADMINISTRATION (TRANSFER OPTION)

Erie Community College (A)
Erie Community College, North Campus (A)
Erie Community College, South Campus (A)

BUSINESS–HEALTH SERVICES MANAGEMENT TECHNOLOGY

Herkimer County Community College (A)

BUSINESS–HUMAN RESOURCE MANAGEMENT
Herkimer County Community College (A)

BUSINESS–MARKETING
Herkimer County Community College (A)

BUSINESS–OFFICE MANAGEMENT
Erie Community College (A)
Erie Community College, North Campus (A)
Erie Community College, South Campus (A)

BUSINESS–SMALL BUSINESS MANAGEMENT
Herkimer County Community College (A)

BUSINESS, ADVANCED
Fort Hays State University (GC)

BUSINESS, COMPUTER/ INFORMATION TECH
Robert Morris University (M)

BUSINESS, ENTREPRENEURSHIP CONCENTRATION
Andrew Jackson University (B)

BUSINESS, GENERAL
Arizona Western College (A)
Excelsior College (B)
Saint Mary-of-the-Woods College (A)
Taft College (A)
University of Houston–Victoria (B)
Upper Iowa University (A)

BUSINESS, GENERAL BUSINESS CONCENTRATION
Andrew Jackson University (B)

BUSINESS, HUMANITIES, SOCIAL SCIENCES
Columbia Basin College (A)

BUSINESS, MANAGEMENT, AND ECONOMICS
State University of New York Empire State College (A,B)

BUSINESS, MANAGEMENT/ LEADERSHIP CONCENTRATION
Andrew Jackson University (B)

BUSINESS, SALES AND SALES MANAGEMENT
Andrew Jackson University (B)

BUSINESS/MANAGEMENT
Jacksonville State University (B)

C++
Champlain College (UC)

CAMPUS AND COMMUNITY TRACK
University of Illinois at Urbana–Champaign (M)

CANADIAN STUDIES
Western Kentucky University (UC)

CANADIAN STUDIES (4 YEAR)
Athabasca University (B)

CARDIOVASCULAR INTERVENTIONAL TECHNOLOGY (CVIT)
Fort Hays State University (UC)

CARE AND DEVELOPMENT OF YOUNG CHILDREN
Delgado Community College (A)

CAREER AND TECHNICAL EDUCATION
Ball State University (M)
University of Central Florida (M)
University of Wisconsin–Stout (M)
Valley City State University (B)
Western Michigan University (M)

CAREER AND TECHNICAL EDUCATION (CTE)
University of West Florida (M)

CAREER AND TECHNICAL EDUCATION BUSINESS LICENSE
Indiana State University (UC)

CAREER AND TECHNICAL STUDIES EDUCATION–VOCATIONAL PROGRAM DEVELOPMENT
University of West Florida (B)

CAREER AND TECHNICAL STUDIES EDUCATION–VOCATIONAL TEACHER EDUCATION
University of West Florida (B)

CAREER BUILDERS FOR EDUCATORS
Indiana Wesleyan University (UC)

CAREER DEVELOPMENT
Athabasca University (UC)
Memorial University of Newfoundland (UC)

CAREER EDUCATION
Wayne State University (M)

CAREER STUDIES–ACCOUNTING
Mountain Empire Community College (UC)

CAREER STUDIES–CHILD DEVELOPMENT
Mountain Empire Community College (UC)

CAREER STUDIES–COMPUTER SOFTWARE SPECIALIST
Mountain Empire Community College (UC)

CAREER STUDIES–GEOGRAPHICAL INFORMATION SYSTEMS
Mountain Empire Community College (UC)

CAREER STUDIES–HEALTH INFORMATION TECHNOLOGY
Mountain Empire Community College (UC)

CAREER STUDIES–LEGAL OFFICE ASSISTING
Mountain Empire Community College (UC)

CAREER STUDIES–MEDICAL RECORDS CLERK
Mountain Empire Community College (UC)

CAREER STUDIES–MEDICAL TRANSCRIPTIONIST
Mountain Empire Community College (UC)

CAREER STUDIES–OFFICE AUTOMATION SPECIALIST
Mountain Empire Community College (UC)

CAREER STUDIES–PERSONAL COMPUTING FOR HOME AND OFFICE
Mountain Empire Community College (UC)

CAREER STUDIES–WASTEWATER PLANT OPERATOR
Mountain Empire Community College (UC)

CAREER STUDIES–WATER PLANT OPERATOR
Mountain Empire Community College (UC)

CAREER STUDIES–WORD PROCESSING
Mountain Empire Community College (UC)

CAREER SWITCHER WITH LICENSURE

Regent University (M)

CAREGIVER SERVICES–ADULT

Dakota College at Bottineau (UC,A)

CAREGIVER SERVICES–CHILD

Dakota College at Bottineau (UC,A)

CART/CAPTIONING

St. Louis Community College (GC)

CASE MANAGEMENT

Grantham University (M)

CATECHETICAL DIPLOMA

The Catholic Distance University (UC)

CATECHIST CERTIFICATE, ADVANCED

The Catholic Distance University (UC)

CENTER FOR NATIVE LEADERSHIP DEVELOPMENT

Global University (UC)

CENTER FOR NATIVE LEADERSHIP DEVELOPMENT–MINISTERIAL STUDIES

Global University (UC)

CERTIFIED INFORMATION SYSTEMS SECURITY PROFESSIONAL (CISSP)

Peirce College (UC)

CERTIFIED MEDICAL TRANSCRIPTION

Mountain State University (UC)

CFP(R) CERTIFICATION CURRICULUM

The American College (UC)

CHARITABLE PLANNING

The American College (GC)

CHARTERED ADVISOR FOR SENIOR LIVING (CASL) DESIGNATION

The American College (UC)

CHARTERED ADVISOR IN PHILANTHROPY(R)(CAP) DESIGNATION

The American College (GC)

CHARTERED FINANCIAL CONSULTANT (CHFC(R)) DESIGNATION

The American College (UC)

CHARTERED HEALTHCARE CONSULTANT -CHHC(TM)

The American College (UC)

CHARTERED LEADERSHIP FELLOW(R) (CLF(R)) DESIGNATION

The American College (UC)

CHARTERED LIFE UNDERWRITER (CLU(R)) DESIGNATION

The American College (UC)

CHEMICAL DEPENDENCY SPECIALIZATION

Central Texas College (A)

CHEMICAL DEPENDENCY SPECIALIZATION–ADVANCED CERTIFICATE

Central Texas College (UC)

CHEMICAL DEPENDENCY STUDIES COUNSELING

Tompkins Cortland Community College (A)

CHEMICAL ENGINEERING

Auburn University (M)
Columbia University (M)
Illinois Institute of Technology (M)
Kansas State University (M)
Lehigh University (M)
North Carolina State University (M)
University of North Dakota (B)
University of Southern California (M)

CHEMISTRY

Lehigh University (M)

CHIEF INFORMATION OFFICER (CIO)

University of Maryland University College (GC)

CHILD ADVOCACY STUDIES CERTIFICATE (CAST)

University of Wisconsin–Platteville (GC)

CHILD AND FAMILY DEVELOPMENT

The University of North Carolina at Charlotte (B)
Western Michigan University (B)

CHILD AND FAMILY DEVELOPMENT–HEAD START COMPLETION

Stephen F. Austin State University (B)

CHILD AND FAMILY STUDIES

University of Southern Mississippi (M)

CHILD CARE TRAINING

Colorado State University (UC)

CHILD DEVELOPMENT

Concordia University, St. Paul (B)
Ellis University (A,B)
Gadsden State Community College (A)
Walden University (B)

CHILD DEVELOPMENT ASSOCIATE

The University of Montana Western (UC)

CHILD DEVELOPMENT CERTIFICATE–SCHOOL-AGE (COALINGA CAMPUS-BASED)

West Hills Community College (UC)

CHILD DEVELOPMENT SERVICES

Thomas Edison State College (B)

CHILDCARE CENTER MANAGEMENT SPECIALIZATION

Seminole State College of Florida (UC)

CHILDHOOD EDUCATION

New York Institute of Technology (M)

CHILDHOOD EDUCATION (LITERACY)

University at Albany, State University of New York (M)

CHILDHOOD EDUCATION AND STUDENTS WITH DISABILITIES

Mercy College (M)

CHILDHOOD EDUCATION, GRADE 1-6

Mercy College (M)

CHILDHOOD MINISTRY CONCENTRATION

Dallas Baptist University (M)

CHILDHOOD MINISTRY LEADERSHIP

Dallas Baptist University (GC)

CHILDREN'S LITERATURE
Penn State University Park (GC)

CHILDREN, YOUTH, AND FAMILY SERVICES
Penn State University Park (UC)

CHRISTIAN COMMUNICATOR (UNDERGRADUATE CERTIFICATE II)
Global University (UC)

CHRISTIAN COUNSELING
Laurel University (B)

CHRISTIAN DOCTRINE
Marquette University (M)

CHRISTIAN EDUCATION
Union Presbyterian Seminary (M)

CHRISTIAN EDUCATION AND CHILDHOOD MINISTRY
Dallas Baptist University (M)

CHRISTIAN LEADERSHIP
Hope International University (M)
Liberty University (M)

CHRISTIAN MINISTRIES
Crown College (A)
Indiana Wesleyan University (A)
Piedmont Baptist College and Graduate School (A)
Shasta Bible College (M)

CHRISTIAN MINISTRIES (BUSINESS CONCENTRATION ONLY)
Dallas Baptist University (B)

CHRISTIAN MINISTRY
Amridge University (D)
Anderson University (M)
Crown College (B)
Hope International University (B)
Laurel University (B)
Lincoln Christian University (B)
Regent University (B)
Wayland Baptist University (B,M)

CHRISTIAN MINISTRY LEADERSHIP
Barclay College (B)

CHRISTIAN MISSION (UNDERGRADUATE CERTIFICATE III)
Global University (UC)

CHRISTIAN OUTREACH
Concordia University, St. Paul (M)

CHRISTIAN PROFESSIONAL STUDIES
Shasta Bible College (B)

CHRISTIAN RELIGIOUS EDUCATION
Defiance College (A,B)

CHRISTIAN SCHOOL EDUCATION
Laurel University (M)

CHRISTIAN SCHOOL PROGRAM
Regent University (M)

CHRISTIAN SERVICE
Global University (UC)

CHRISTIAN STUDIES
Anderson University (B)
Ashland University (UC)
The Baptist College of Florida (B)
Crown College (M)
Regent University (A)

CHRISTIAN STUDIES, GENERAL
Hobe Sound Bible College (B)

CHRISTIAN WORKER
Taylor University (UC)

CHROMATOGRAPHY
Illinois Institute of Technology (GC)

CHURCH AND FAMILY MINISTRY
God's Bible School and College (B)

CHURCH EDUCATION
Defiance College (UC)

CHURCH LEADERSHIP
Central Bible College (A,B)

CHURCH MINISTRIES
Global University (UC,A)

CINEMA ARTS
Regent University (M)

CINEMA STUDIES
Burlington College (B)

CINEMA-TELEVISION
Regent University (B)

CISCO CERTIFIED NETWORK ASSOCIATE
Wake Technical Community College (UC)

CISCO NETWORK ASSOCIATE
Lake Superior College (UC)

CIT CYBER
Bossier Parish Community College (A)

CIVIL AND CONSTRUCTION ENGINEERING TECHNOLOGY
Thomas Edison State College (A)

CIVIL ENGINEERING
Auburn University (M)
Colorado State University (M)
Columbia University (UC,M,D)
Kansas State University (M)
Missouri University of Science and Technology (M)
North Carolina State University (M)
Purdue University (M)
Southern Methodist University (M)
Trine University (M)
University of Central Florida (M)
University of Florida (M)
University of Florida (M)
University of Idaho (M)
University of North Dakota (B)
The University of Texas at Arlington (M)

CIVIL ENGINEERING (CONSTRUCTION ENGINEERING)
University of Southern California (M)

CIVIL ENGINEERING (STRUCTURAL ENGINEERING)
University of Southern California (M)

CIVIL ENGINEERING (TRANSPORTATION ENGINEERING)
University of Southern California (M)

CIVIL ENGINEERING TECHNOLOGY
Thomas Edison State College (B)

CIVIL ENGINEERING–CONSTRUCTION ENGINEERING AND MANAGEMENT
Columbia University (M)

CIVIL ENGINEERING, TRANSPORTATION ENGINEERING SPECIALIZATION
University of Louisville (M)

CLASSICAL CIVILIZATION

University of Florida (D)

CLASSROOM INSTRUCTION

Concordia University, St. Paul (M)

CLASSROOM TECHNOLOGY

Bowling Green State University (M)

CLERICAL ASSISTANT

Mountain Empire Community College (UC)

CLINICAL INVESTIGATION

Boston University (GC)

CLINICAL LAB SCIENCE

Thomas Edison State College (A,B)

CLINICAL LABORATORY SCIENCE

University of Cincinnati (B)
Winston-Salem State University (B)

CLINICAL MENTAL HEALTH COUNSELING

Grace College (M)
Regent University (M)

CLINICAL NUTRITION

New York Institute of Technology (M)

CLINICAL NUTRITION/NUTRITION EDUCATION

Rosalind Franklin University of Medicine and Science (M)

CLINICAL PATHOLOGY

University of Massachusetts Lowell (GC)

CLINICAL PRACTICE CONCENTRATION, ADVANCED

Saint Leo University (M)

CLINICAL PSYCHOLOGY

Fielding Graduate University (D)
Regent University (M)

CLINICAL PSYCHOLOGY RESPECIALIZATION

Fielding Graduate University (UC)

CLINICAL RESEARCH ADMINISTRATION

Walden University (M)

CLINICAL RESEARCH AND ADMINISTRATION POST-BACHELOR'S

Walden University (GC)

CLINICAL RESEARCH COORDINATOR

Mid-State Technical College (A)

CLINICAL RESEARCH DESIGN AND MANAGEMENT

University of Southern California (GC)

CLINICAL RESEARCH FOR HEALTH PROFESSIONALS

Drexel University (M)

CLINICAL RESEARCH METHODS

University of Illinois at Chicago (UC)

CLINICAL RESEARCH ORGANIZATION AND MANAGEMENT

Drexel University (M)

CLINICAL SPECIALIST

University of St. Francis (M)

CLINICAL TRIALS MANAGEMENT POST-BACCALAUREATE CERTIFICATE

Thomas Edison State College (UC)

CLINICAL TRIALS RESEARCH

Drexel University (UC,M)

CLINICAL VISION RESEARCH

Nova Southeastern University (M)

COACHING

Stony Brook University, State University of New York (GC)

COACHING–NATIONAL COACHING CERTIFICATION

United States Sports Academy (UC)

CODING FOR THE PHYSICIAN'S OFFICE, ADVANCED

California State University, Dominguez Hills (GC)

COLLABORATIVE

Athabasca University (M)

COLLABORATIVE 6-12

Jacksonville State University (M)

COLLABORATIVE K-6

Jacksonville State University (M)

COLLABORATIVE SPECIAL EDUCATION

The University of West Alabama (M)

COLLABORATIVE TEACHER AND EARLY CHILDHOOD EDUCATION

Auburn University (M)

COLLEGE AND UNIVERSITY LEADERSHIP

Colorado State University (D)

COLLEGE LEVEL INSTRUCTION WITH MAXIMUM BIBLE (CLIMB)

Toccoa Falls College (UC)

COLLEGE STUDENT DEVELOPMENT

The University of West Alabama (M)

COLLEGE STUDENT PERSONNEL

Arkansas Tech University (M)

COLLEGE STUDIES

University of Mary (B)

COLLEGE TEACHING AND LEARNING POST-BACHELOR'S

Walden University (GC)

COLLEGE TRANSFER DEGREE

Randolph Community College (A)
Southeastern Community College (A)

COLLEGIATE MINISTRY CONCENTRATION

Dallas Baptist University (M)

COLLEGIATE STUDIES

Vincennes University (UC)

COMMERCE

Nipissing University (B)

COMMERCIAL LENDING

New England College of Business and Finance (GC)

COMMISSIONED LAY PASTOR

University of Dubuque (UC)

COMMUNICATING ARTS, SPEECH COMMUNICATION CONCENTRATION

University of Wisconsin–Superior (B)

COMMUNICATION

Andrew Jackson University (A)
Dallas Baptist University (B)
Drexel University (B,M)
Kaplan University Online (B)
Marist College (M)
Regent University (B,M,D)
Spring Arbor University (M)
Trine University (B)
University of Louisville (B)
University of Memphis (B)
University of Minnesota, Crookston (B)
University of North Dakota (B)
University of Southern Maine (B)

COMMUNICATION AND LEADERSHIP STUDIES

Gonzaga University (M)

COMMUNICATION ARTS

Webster University (M)

COMMUNICATION ARTS (BA, BS)–INFORMATION SPECIALIST

Austin Peay State University (B)

COMMUNICATION ARTS–CORPORATE COMMUNICATION

Austin Peay State University (M)

COMMUNICATION DISORDERS

Florida State University (GC)
Western Kentucky University (M)

COMMUNICATION STUDIES

Athabasca University (B)
Northern Kentucky University (B)
San Diego Community College District (A)
University of Maryland University College (B)

COMMUNICATIONS

Andrew Jackson University (B)
Indiana Wesleyan University (UC)
Southern New Hampshire University (B)
Thomas Edison State College (B)
Walden University (B)

COMMUNICATIONS AND APPLIED TECHNOLOGY

Drexel University (B)

COMMUNICATIONS AND TECHNOLOGY

University of Alberta (M)

COMMUNICATIONS DISORDERS

North Carolina Central University (M)

COMMUNICATIONS MAJOR

Columbus State University (B)

COMMUNICATIONS MANAGEMENT

Syracuse University (M)
Webster University (M)

COMMUNICATIVE DISORDERS AND DEAF EDUCATION

Utah State University (B)

COMMUNICATIVE DISORDERS AND DEAF EDUCATION (SECOND BACHELORS)

Utah State University (B)

COMMUNITY AND ECONOMIC DEVELOPMENT

Penn State University Park (GC,M)

COMMUNITY AND HUMAN SERVICES

State University of New York Empire State College (A,B)

COMMUNITY AND PUBLIC HEALTH

The University of North Carolina at Charlotte (M)

COMMUNITY AND TECHNICAL COLLEGE EMPHASIS

Upper Iowa University (M)

COMMUNITY CHANGE AND CIVIC LEADERSHIP

Antioch University Midwest (M)

COMMUNITY COLLEGE ADMINISTRATION AND LEADERSHIP

Drexel University (GC)

COMMUNITY COLLEGE AND UNIVERSITY ADMINISTRATION EMPHASIS

New Mexico State University (M)

COMMUNITY COLLEGE EDUCATION

University of Central Florida (GC)

COMMUNITY COLLEGE INSTRUCTION

Mississippi State University (M)

COMMUNITY COLLEGE LEADERSHIP

Mississippi State University (D)

COMMUNITY COLLEGE LEADERSHIP CONCENTRATION

Oregon State University (D)

COMMUNITY COLLEGE TEACHING

California State University, Dominguez Hills (UC)
North Carolina State University (GC)

COMMUNITY COLLEGE TEACHING AND LEARNING

University of Illinois at Urbana–Champaign (GC)

COMMUNITY DEVELOPMENT

Fort Hays State University (UC)
Kansas State University (M)
North Dakota State University (M)

COMMUNITY DEVELOPMENT, COMMUNITY SERVICES MAJOR

Central Michigan University (B)

COMMUNITY DEVELOPMENT, HEALTH SCIENCES MAJOR

Central Michigan University (B)

COMMUNITY DEVELOPMENT, PUBLIC ADMINISTRATION MAJOR

Central Michigan University (B)

COMMUNITY ECONOMIC DEVELOPMENT

Southern New Hampshire University (M)

COMMUNITY HEALTH

Fort Hays State University (UC)

COMMUNITY HEALTH PROMOTION

Fort Hays State University (UC)
University of Arkansas at Little Rock (B)

COMMUNITY HEALTH SCIENCES

University of Illinois at Chicago (M)

COMMUNITY LEADERSHIP

Duquesne University (M)

COMMUNITY PSYCHOLOGY

St. Cloud State University (B)

COMMUNITY PUBLIC HEALTH PRACTICE, ADVANCED

University of Illinois at Chicago (UC)

COMMUNITY PUBLIC HEALTH PRACTICE, BASIC

University of Illinois at Chicago (UC)

COMMUNITY REHABILITATION

University of Calgary (B)
Vincennes University (UC)

COMMUNITY SERVICES

Thomas Edison State College (B)

COMMUNITY SOCIOLOGY

Southern New Hampshire University (B)

COMMUNITY STUDIES COMPLETER PROGRAM

University of Massachusetts Boston (B)

COMMUNITY-BASED DEVELOPMENT

Colorado State University (UC)

COMPARATIVE LITERATURE

National University (B)

COMPETITIVE INTELLIGENCE AND KNOWLEDGE MANAGEMENT SPECIALIST

Drexel University (GC)

COMPLEMENTARY AND INTEGRATIVE THERAPIES

Drexel University (UC)

COMPLEMENTARY CARE

Columbus State Community College (GC)

COMPOSITE SOCIAL SCIENCE

Dickinson State University (B)

COMPUTATIONAL FINANCE

DePaul University (M)

COMPUTATIONAL SCIENCE AND ENGINEERING (CSE)

Georgia Institute of Technology (M)

COMPUTED TOMOGRAPHY (CT)

Fort Hays State University (UC)

COMPUTER ACCOUNTING

Nashville State Technical Community College (A)

COMPUTER AIDED DESIGN PRE-ASSOCIATE CERTIFICATE

Thomas Edison State College (UC)

COMPUTER AND INFORMATION SCIENCE

University of Maryland University College (B)

COMPUTER AND INFORMATION SCIENCES

San Diego Community College District (A)

COMPUTER AND INFORMATION SYSTEMS

Champlain College (B)
University of Michigan–Flint (M)

COMPUTER AND NETWORK SECURITY

University of Colorado Boulder (GC)

COMPUTER APPLICATIONS AND BUSINESS TECHNOLOGY

Cabrillo College (A)

COMPUTER APPLICATIONS FOR THE OFFICE

Erie Community College (UC)
Erie Community College, North Campus (UC)
Erie Community College, South Campus (UC)

COMPUTER BUSINESS TECHNOLOGY ADMINISTRATIVE ASSISTANT

San Diego Community College District (A)

COMPUTER BUSINESS TECHNOLOGY MICROCOMPUTER APPLICATIONS

San Diego Community College District (A)

COMPUTER EDUCATION

Fontbonne University (M)

COMPUTER ENGINEERING

Illinois Institute of Technology (M)
Mississippi State University (D)
Missouri University of Science and Technology (M)
Southern Methodist University (M)
University of Florida (M)
University of Idaho (M)
University of Michigan–Dearborn (M)
University of Southern California (M)
University of Wisconsin–Madison (M)

COMPUTER ENGINEERING (BIOINFORMATICS TRACK)

University of Florida (M)

COMPUTER ENGINEERING (GENERAL TRACK)

University of Florida (M)

COMPUTER ENGINEERING CISCO/ CCNA

Seminole State College of Florida (UC)

COMPUTER ENGINEERING TECHNOLOGY

DeVry University Online (B)
Grantham University (B)

COMPUTER FORENSICS

Kaplan University Online (A)

COMPUTER FORENSICS AND DIGITAL INVESTIGATIONS

Champlain College (UC,B)

COMPUTER FORENSICS POST-BACCALAUREATE

Kaplan University Online (UC)

COMPUTER HELPDESK SPECIALIST

Central Texas College (UC)

COMPUTER INFORMATION SCIENCE

University of Michigan–Dearborn (M)

COMPUTER INFORMATION SYSTEM

Capital Community College (A)
University of Houston–Victoria (M)

COMPUTER INFORMATION SYSTEM TECHNOLOGY

The University of Texas at Brownsville (B)

COMPUTER INFORMATION SYSTEMS

Atlantic Cape Community College (A)
Bossier Parish Community College (A)
Central Pennsylvania College (A)
College of Southern Maryland (A)
Colorado State University (GC,M)
Colorado State University (M)
Columbia College (A,B)
Dakota State University (B)
DeVry University Online (B)
Florida Institute of Technology (M)
Florida Tech University Online (A,B)
Friends University (B)
Front Range Community College (A)
Kaplan University Online (A)
Mercy College (B)
North Carolina Wesleyan College (B)
Saint Leo University (B)
Saint Mary-of-the-Woods College (B)
Thomas Edison State College (B)
University of Houston–Downtown (B)
University of Maine at Augusta (A,B)
Walden University (B)

Western Wyoming Community College (A)
West Hills Community College (A)

COMPUTER INFORMATION SYSTEMS (CIS)

Mount Wachusett Community College (A)

COMPUTER INFORMATION SYSTEMS E-COMMERCE–DESIGN AND DEVELOPMENT TRACK

Portland Community College (UC)

COMPUTER INFORMATION SYSTEMS PRE-ASSOCIATE CERTIFICATE

Thomas Edison State College (UC)

COMPUTER INFORMATION SYSTEMS TECHNOLOGY–NETWORKING SPECIALIZATION

Seminole State College of Florida (A)

COMPUTER INFORMATION SYSTEMS TECHNOLOGY–PROGRAMMING SPECIALIZATION

Seminole State College of Florida (A)

COMPUTER INFORMATION SYSTEMS–APPLICATIONS SPECIALIST OPTION

Quinsigamond Community College (A)

COMPUTER INFORMATION SYSTEMS–MASTER OF SCIENCE IN COMPUTER INFORMATION SYSTEMS

Boston University (M)

COMPUTER INFORMATION SYSTEMS–NETWORK ADMINISTRATION

Portland Community College (A)

COMPUTER INFORMATION SYSTEMS–PROGRAMMING OPTION

Quinsigamond Community College (A)

COMPUTER INFORMATION SYSTEMS–WEB DESIGN/WEB DEVELOPER

North Dakota State College of Science (UC)

COMPUTER INFORMATION SYSTEMS, PROGRAMMING/ ANALYSIS OPTION

Anne Arundel Community College (A)

COMPUTER INFORMATION TECHNOLOGY

Delgado Community College (A)

COMPUTER INFORMATION TECHNOLOGY

Indiana Wesleyan University (A)
Seminole State College of Florida (A)
Southern New Hampshire University (A,B)
University of Maryland University College (B)
Wayne Community College (A)
Western Kentucky University (B)

COMPUTER INFORMATION TECHNOLOGY (GAME DESIGN AND DEVELOPMENT)

Southern New Hampshire University (B)

COMPUTER INFORMATION TECHNOLOGY (NETWORK AND TELECOMMUNICATIONS CONCENTRATION)

Southern New Hampshire University (B)

COMPUTER INFORMATION TECHNOLOGY (SOFTWARE DEVELOPMENT)

Southern New Hampshire University (B)

COMPUTER INFORMATION TECHNOLOGY (WEB DESIGN AND DEVELOPMENT)

Southern New Hampshire University (B)

COMPUTER INFORMATION TECHNOLOGY AND SYSTEMS MANAGEMENT

Cleveland Institute of Electronics (A)

COMPUTER INFORMATION TECHONLOLGY (CYBER SECURITY CONCENTRATION)

Southern New Hampshire University (B)

COMPUTER INFORMATION TECHONLOLGY (DATABASE MANAGEMENT CONCENTRATION)

Southern New Hampshire University (B)

COMPUTER NETWORK AND INFORMATION SYSTEM SECURITY

West Los Angeles College (UC)

COMPUTER NETWORK AND SECURITY MANAGEMENT

West Los Angeles College (UC)

COMPUTER NETWORK MANAGEMENT

West Los Angeles College (UC)

COMPUTER NETWORK SECURITY TECHNOLOGIES

Illinois Institute of Technology (GC)

COMPUTER NETWORKING

Champlain College (UC)
North Carolina State University (M)

COMPUTER OPERATIONS TECHNOLOGY

Southwestern College (B)

COMPUTER PROGRAMMER/ ANALYST

Lansing Community College (UC,A)

COMPUTER PROGRAMMING

Atlantic Cape Community College (A)
North Carolina State University (UC)
Pitt Community College (A)
Seminole State College of Florida (UC)
Vincennes University (A)
Westchester Community College (UC)

COMPUTER PROGRAMMING (POST-BACCALAUREATE)

Winston-Salem State University (UC)

COMPUTER PROGRAMMING AND ANALYSIS

Seminole State College of Florida (A)

COMPUTER PROGRAMMING AND ANALYSIS (WEB PROGRAMMING SPECIALIZATION)

Seminole State College of Florida (A)

COMPUTER PROGRAMMING TECHNOLOGY

Southwestern College (B)

COMPUTER PROGRAMMING WITH JAVA AND C#

Cleveland Institute of Electronics (UC)

COMPUTER READINESS FOR WORKPLACE

Lansing Community College (UC)

COMPUTER SCIENCE

Colorado State University (M)
Columbia University (M,D)
Dakota State University (B)
DePaul University (M)
Dickinson State University (B)

Drexel University (M)
Florida State University (B)
Grantham University (A,B)
Hofstra University (M)
Illinois Institute of Technology (M)
Jamestown Community College (A)
The Johns Hopkins University (M)
Limestone College (B)
Mercy College (B)
Missouri University of Science and Technology (M)
Montgomery County Community College (A)
Mountain State University (A,B)
National University (B,M)
North Carolina State University (M)
Ocean County College (A)
Rogers State University (A)
Southern Methodist University (M)
Thomas Edison State College (A,B)
Trine University (B)
Union County College (A)
University of Atlanta (B,M)
University of Bridgeport (M)
University of Colorado Boulder (M)
University of Idaho (M)
University of Illinois at Springfield (B,M)
University of Illinois at Urbana–Champaign (M)
University of Louisville (M)
University of Management and Technology (A,B,M)
University of Maryland University College (B)
University of Southern California (M)

COMPUTER SCIENCE (COMPUTER NETWORKS)

University of Southern California (M)

COMPUTER SCIENCE (COMPUTER SECURITY)

University of Southern California (M)

COMPUTER SCIENCE (MULTIMEDIA AND CREATIVE TECHNOLOGIES)

University of Southern California (M)

COMPUTER SCIENCE (SOFTWARE ENGINEERING)

University of Southern California (M)

COMPUTER SCIENCE AND ENGINEERING

Auburn University (M)
The University of Texas at Arlington (M)

COMPUTER SCIENCE AND ENGINEERING TECHNOLOGY

The University of Toledo (B)

COMPUTER SCIENCE APPLICATIONS AND DEVELOPMENT

College of San Mateo (A)

COMPUTER SCIENCE INFORMATION TECHNOLOGY

Limestone College (A)

COMPUTER SCIENCE PRE-ASSOCIATE CERTIFICATE

Thomas Edison State College (UC)

COMPUTER SCIENCE PROGRAMMING

Limestone College (A)

COMPUTER SCIENCE TECHNOLOGY

Thomas Edison State College (A,B)

COMPUTER SCIENCE TRANSFER, MANAGEMENT INFORMATION SYSTEMS OPTION

Anne Arundel Community College (A)

COMPUTER SCIENCE–APPLIED COMPUTER SCIENCE

Columbus State University (M)

COMPUTER SCIENCE–CISCO CERTIFIED NETWORK ASSOCIATE PREPARATION, ACCELERATED

Fort Hays State University (UC)

COMPUTER SCIENCE–CISCO CERTIFIED NETWORK ASSOCIATE PREPARATION, MILITARY

Fort Hays State University (UC)

COMPUTER SCIENCE–INFORMATION SECURITY MANAGEMENT

Central Texas College (A)

COMPUTER SCIENCE–INFORMATION SYSTEMS

Austin Peay State University (B)
University of Management and Technology (B)

COMPUTER SCIENCE–INFORMATION TECHNOLOGY

Central Texas College (A)
University of Management and Technology (B)

COMPUTER SCIENCE–MASTER OF COMPUTER SCIENCE

University of Illinois at Urbana–Champaign (M)

COMPUTER SCIENCE–SOFTWARE ENGINEERING

University of Management and Technology (B)

COMPUTER SCIENCE/COMPUTER SECURITY

University of Illinois at Urbana–Champaign (GC)

COMPUTER SCIENCE/ INFORMATION SYSTEMS

University of Illinois at Urbana–Champaign (GC)

COMPUTER SCIENCE/NETWORKS AND DISTRIBUTED SYSTEMS

University of Illinois at Urbana–Champaign (GC)

COMPUTER SCIENCE/SOFTWARE ENGINEERING

University of Illinois at Urbana–Champaign (GC)

COMPUTER SCIENCE/SYSTEM SOFTWARE

University of Illinois at Urbana–Champaign (GC)

COMPUTER SECURITY

University of Illinois at Urbana–Champaign (GC)

COMPUTER SECURITY AND FORENSICS

Westchester Community College (A)

COMPUTER SOFTWARE

Excelsior College (A)

COMPUTER SOFTWARE APPLICATIONS

Pitt Community College (UC)

COMPUTER SOFTWARE SPECIALIST

The University of Toledo (A)

COMPUTER STUDIES

University of Maryland University College (B)

COMPUTER SUPPORT SPECIALIST

Three Rivers Community College (A)

COMPUTER SYSTEMS (NETWORKING/ TELECOMMUNICATIONS EMPHASIS)

City University of Seattle (B)

COMPUTER SYSTEMS AND SECURITY

Colorado State University (GC)

COMPUTER SYSTEMS AND SOFTWARE DESIGN

Jacksonville State University (M)

COMPUTER SYSTEMS ENGINEERING

Columbia University (M)

COMPUTER SYSTEMS ENGINEERING TECHNOLOGY–COMPUTER FORENSICS OPTION

Quinsigamond Community College (A)

COMPUTER SYSTEMS SECURITY

Colorado Technical University Colorado Springs (M)

COMPUTER SYSTEMS SUPPORT

Atlantic Cape Community College (A)

COMPUTER TEACHER EDUCATION

Youngstown State University (UC,M)

COMPUTER TECHNOLOGY (PROGRAMMING EMPHASIS)

Greenville Technical College (A)

COMPUTER TECHNOLOGY BASICS

Lansing Community College (UC)

COMPUTER TECHNOLOGY ENDORSEMENT

Bowling Green State University (GC)

COMPUTER TECHNOLOGY MANAGEMENT

Dickinson State University (B)

COMPUTER, INFORMATION, AND NETWORK SECURITY

DePaul University (M)

COMPUTER-INTERGRATED MACHINING TECHNOLOGY

Wayne Community College (A)

COMPUTER-RELATED CRIME INVESTIGATIONS

St. Petersburg College (UC)

COMPUTERS AND MANAGEMENT INFORMATION SYSTEMS

Athabasca University (UC)

COMPUTING

Pace University (D)

COMPUTING AND INFORMATION SYSTEMS

Athabasca University (UC,B)

COMPUTING AND INFORMATION SYSTEMS–POST-DIPLOMA

Athabasca University (B)

COMPUTING AND SECURITY TECHNOLOGY

Drexel University (B)

COMPUTING SECURITY TECHNOLOGY

Drexel University (GC)

CONCRETE

James A. Rhodes State College (A)

CONFLICT ANALYSIS AND ENGAGEMENT

Antioch University Midwest (M)

CONFLICT ANALYSIS AND TRAUMA STUDIES UNDERGRADUATE MINOR

Kansas State University (UC)

CONFLICT RESOLUTION

Kansas State University (UC,GC)

CONFLICT RESOLUTION AND RECONCILIATION

Abilene Christian University (UC,M)

CONSTRUCTION

Thomas Edison State College (B)

CONSTRUCTION AND FACILITY SUPPORT

Thomas Edison State College (A)

CONSTRUCTION ENGINEERING

National University (B)
University of Central Florida (GC)

CONSTRUCTION MANAGEMENT

Colorado State University (UC)
Columbia University (UC)
Drexel University (GC,M)
North Dakota State University (M)
Northeastern University (GC)
University of Southern California (M)

CONSTRUCTION MANAGEMENT PROGRAM

Western Carolina University (M)

CONSTRUCTION MANAGEMENT TECHNOLOGY

North Dakota State College of Science (A)

CONSTRUCTION MANAGEMENT–LAND DEVELOPMENT

Western Carolina University (GC)

CONSTRUCTION MANAGEMENT–SURVEYING

Northern Kentucky University (B)

CONSTRUCTION PROJECT MANAGEMENT

University of Florida (GC)

CONSTRUCTION SCIENCE AND MANAGEMENT

Clemson University (M)

CONSTRUCTION TECHNOLOGY

University of Southern Mississippi (B)

CONSUMER AND FAMILY SCIENCES, CHILD STUDIES EMPHASIS

Western Kentucky University (B)

CONSUMER HEALTH

Fort Hays State University (UC)

CONTEMPLATIVE EDUCATION

Naropa University (M)

CONTEMPORARY COMMUNICATIONS

University of Massachusetts Lowell (UC)

CONTEMPORARY GERONTOLOGICAL PRACTICE

The University of Toledo (GC)

CONTINUING EDUCATION–ANIMAL ASSISTED THERAPY CERTIFICATE

Oakland University (GC)

CONTINUING EDUCATION–SONGWRITING CERTIFICATE

Oakland University (GC)

CONTINUING TEACHING LICENSE

Southern Oregon University (M)

CONTINUING TEACHING LICENSURE

Oregon State University (UC)

CONTRACT MANAGEMENT–MASTER OF CONTRACT MANAGEMENT

American Graduate University (M)

COORDINATED DIETETIC SCIENCE (WITH UMDNJ)

Thomas Edison State College (B)

CORE BUSINESS COMPETENCIES

Colorado State University (UC)

CORE CRIMINAL JUSTICE

San Jacinto College District (UC)

CORPORATE AND ORGANIZATIONAL COMMUNICATION

Northeastern University (M)

CORPORATE COMMUNICATIONS

Central Pennsylvania College (B)

CORRECTIONAL HEALTH

University of Colorado at Colorado Springs (GC)

CORRECTIONAL OFFICER

Lansing Community College (UC)

CORRECTIONAL SERVICES

Mountain Empire Community College (A)

CORRECTIONS

Fort Hays State University (UC)
Indiana State University (UC)
James A. Rhodes State College (A)

CORRECTIONS AND JUVENILE JUSTICE

Eastern Kentucky University (B,M)

CORRECTIONS CERTIFICATE

Kaplan University Online (UC)

CORRECTIONS LEADERSHIP

University of Central Florida (GC)

CORRECTIONS OFFICER ACADEMIC PROGRAM

Alpena Community College (UC)

CORRECTIONS PRE-CERTIFICATION

Tunxis Community College (UC)

COSMETOLOGY BUSINESS

Minnesota School of Business–Online (A)
Minnesota School of Business–Richfield (A)

COTA TO MOT

Texas Woman's University (M)

COUNSELING

Athabasca University (M)
Central Michigan University (M)
Faulkner University (M)
Fort Hays State University (M)
Liberty University (D)
Mercy College (M)
Oregon State University (D)
Perelandra College (M)
Prairie View A&M University (M)
Regent University (M)
Seton Hall University (M)
The University of Tennessee at Martin (M)

COUNSELING (K-12 SCHOOL EMPHASIS)

University of North Dakota (M)

COUNSELING (MENTAL HEALTH)

University of the Southwest (M)

COUNSELING (NON-CERTIFICATION)

The University of West Alabama (M)

COUNSELING AND GUIDANCE (GUIDANCE AND HUMAN RELATIONS SPECIALIZATION)

New Mexico State University (M)

COUNSELING AND PSYCHOLOGY

Prescott College (M)

COUNSELING EDUCATION AND SUPERVISION

Regent University (D)

COUNSELING MINISTRIES

Baptist Bible College of Pennsylvania (M)

COUNSELING POST-GRADUATE CERTIFICATE

Athabasca University (GC)

COUNSELING PSYCHOLOGY

Memorial University of Newfoundland (M)

COUNSELING PSYCHOLOGY/HUMAN SERVICES

Prescott College (B)

COUNSELING WOMEN

Athabasca University (UC)

COUNSELING–SCHOOL GUIDANCE COUNSELING

Prescott College (M)

COUNSELING/PSYCHOLOGY

The University of West Alabama (M)

COUNSELOR EDUCATION AND SUPERVISION

Walden University (D)

COURT REPORTING/CAPTIONING

Clark State Community College (A)

CPA EXAM ELIGIBILITY PROGRAM

Clarion University of Pennsylvania (UC)

CREATIVE LEADERSHIP AND GLOBAL STRATEGY

University of Southern Maine (UC)

CREATIVE NONFICTION

Goucher College (M)

CREATIVE STUDIES

Buffalo State College, State University of New York (M)

CREATIVE WRITING

Ashland University (M)
Goddard College (B,M)
Naropa University (M)
National University (M)
Perelandra College (M)
Prescott College (B)
Saint Mary-of-the-Woods College (B)
Southern New Hampshire University (B)
University of Denver (UC)

CREATIVE WRITING (FICTION CONCENTRATION)

Southern New Hampshire University (B)

CREATIVE WRITING (LOW-RESIDENCY MFA)

Chatham University (M)

CREATIVE WRITING (NON-FICTION CONCENTRATION)

Southern New Hampshire University (B)

CREATIVE WRITING (POETRY CONCENTRATION)

Southern New Hampshire University (B)

CREATIVE WRITING (SCREENWRITING)

Southern New Hampshire University (B)

CREATIVITY AND CHANGE LEADERSHIP

Buffalo State College, State University of New York (GC)

CREATIVITY AND INNOVATION

Drexel University (M)

CREATIVITY STUDIES

Drexel University (UC,GC)

CRIME SCENE TECHNICIAN

Kaplan University Online (UC)

CRIME SCENE TECHNOLOGY

St. Petersburg College (UC,A)

CRIMINAL BEHAVIOR

Western International University (B)

CRIMINAL INVESTIGATION

State University of New York College of Technology at Canton (B)

CRIMINAL JUSTICE

Anderson University (B)
Andrew Jackson University (A,B,M)
Athabasca University (B)
Bethel University (B)
Bossier Parish Community College (A)
Boston University (M)
Bowling Green State University (M)
Broward College (A)
Bryant & Stratton Online (A,B)
Cabrillo College (A)
Caldwell College (B)
California State University, San Bernardino (M)
Centralia College (A)
Central Pennsylvania College (A)
Central Texas College (A)
Clovis Community College (A)
Colorado Technical University Colorado Springs (B)
Columbia College (A)
Columbia Southern University (A)
Concordia University, St. Paul (B)
Dallas Baptist University (B)
Dawson Community College (A)
Drexel University (B)
Drury University (A)
Eastern Wyoming College (A)
Ellis University (B)
Erie Community College (A)
Erie Community College, North Campus (A)
Erie Community College, South Campus (A)
Excelsior College (B)
Florida Tech University Online (A,B)
Fort Valley State University (B)
Franklin Pierce University (A,B)
Genesee Community College (A)
Granite State College (B)
Grantham University (A,B)
Herkimer County Community College (A)
Herzing University Online (B)
Hodges University (A,B,M)
Indiana Tech (A)
Indiana Wesleyan University (UC,A,B)
Jefferson Community College (A)
Judson College (B)
Kaplan University Online (A,B,M)
Lansing Community College (A)
Liberty University (A,B)
Limestone College (B)
Lindenwood University (B)
Louisiana State University at Eunice (A)
Lynn University (B)
McNeese State University (B)
Mercy College (B)
Minnesota School of Business–Online (A,B)
Monroe College (A,B,M)
Monroe Community College (A)
Montgomery Community College (A)
Montgomery County Community College (A)
Mountain State University (A,B)
New Mexico Junior College (A)
New Mexico State University (B,M)
North Carolina Central University (B)
North Carolina Wesleyan College (B)
Northern Kentucky University (A,B)
Ocean County College (A)
Ohio University (B)
Ouachita Technical College (A)
The Paralegal Institute, Inc. (A)
Peninsula College (A)
Penn State University Park (B)
Peru State College (B)
Pikes Peak Community College (A)
Quinsigamond Community College (A)
Randolph Community College (A)
Regent University (A,B)
Roger Williams University (B,M)
St. John's University (A,B)
Saint Joseph's College of Maine (A,B)
Saint Leo University (A,B,M)
Saint Mary-of-the-Woods College (B)
Slippery Rock University of Pennsylvania (M)
Southeast Missouri State University (M)
Southern Oregon University (B)
Southern University at New Orleans (B)
Southwestern College (B)
Tarleton State University (M)
Texas Woman's University (B)
Thomas Edison State College (A,B)
Three Rivers Community College (A)
Trine University (B,M)
Tunxis Community College (A)
University of Arkansas at Little Rock (B,M)
University of Atlanta (B,M)
University of Central Florida (M)
University of Cincinnati (M)
University of Great Falls (A,B)
University of Houston–Downtown (B,M)
University of Houston–Victoria (B)
University of Management and Technology (A,B)
University of Maryland University College (B)
University of Massachusetts Lowell (M)
The University of Texas at Brownsville (B)
The University of Texas of the Permian Basin (B)
University of the Incarnate Word (B)
University of the Southwest (B)
The University of Toledo (B)
University of Wisconsin–Platteville (GC)
University of Wisconsin–Platteville (M)
University of Wisconsin–Platteville (B)
Upper Iowa University (B)
Walden University (B)
Washington State University (B)
Western Carolina University (B)

CRIMINAL JUSTICE (BSAS)

Youngstown State University (B)

CRIMINAL JUSTICE ADDICTIONS

Central Texas College (UC)

CRIMINAL JUSTICE ADMINISTRATION

Central Pennsylvania College (B)
Columbia College (B,M)
Columbia Southern University (B,M)
Lynn University (M)
National University (B)
Taft College (A)
University of Great Falls (M)
University of Management and Technology (B,M)
University of West Florida (M)

CRIMINAL JUSTICE ADMINISTRATION AND MANAGEMENT

Kaplan University Online (B)

CRIMINAL JUSTICE ADMINISTRATION AND POLICY

Marymount University (M)

CRIMINAL JUSTICE CORRECTIONS SPECIALIZATION

Central Texas College (UC,A)

CRIMINAL JUSTICE EMPHASIS

Centralia College (A)

CRIMINAL JUSTICE LEADERSHIP

Concordia University, St. Paul (M)
Marian University (M)
Northeastern University (M)

CRIMINAL JUSTICE MANAGEMENT

Nichols College (B)
Saint Leo University (GC)
University of Maryland University College (GC)

CRIMINAL JUSTICE POST-BACHELOR'S

Walden University (GC)

CRIMINAL JUSTICE STUDIES

St. Cloud State University (B,M)

CRIMINAL JUSTICE STUDIES SPECIALIZATION

Central Texas College (UC)

CRIMINAL JUSTICE TECHNOLOGY

Gaston College (A)
Haywood Community College (A)
Seminole State College of Florida (A)
Stanly Community College (A)
Wake Technical Community College (A)
Wayne Community College (A)

CRIMINAL JUSTICE TECHNOLOGY/LATENT EVIDENCE

Wayne Community College (A)

CRIMINAL JUSTICE– CRIME ANALYSIS

Indiana Tech (B)

CRIMINAL JUSTICE–ADMINISTRATION OPTION

Middlesex Community College (A)

CRIMINAL JUSTICE–CORRECTIONS CERTIFICATE

Eastern Wyoming College (GC)

CRIMINAL JUSTICE–CRIMINAL JUSTICE ADMINISTRATION

Indiana Tech (B)

CRIMINAL JUSTICE–CYBERSECURITY

Herkimer County Community College (A)

CRIMINAL JUSTICE–ECONOMIC CRIME

Herkimer County Community College (A)

CRIMINAL JUSTICE–ECONOMIC CRIME INVESTIGATION

Utica College (B)

CRIMINAL JUSTICE–HOMELAND SECURITY

Austin Peay State University (B)

CRIMINAL JUSTICE–HOMELAND SECURITY AND EMERGENCY MANAGEMENT CONCENTRATION

Colorado Technical University Colorado Springs (B)

CRIMINAL JUSTICE–HUMAN SERVICES CONCENTRATION

Colorado Technical University Colorado Springs (B)

CRIMINAL JUSTICE–LAW

St. Louis Community College (A)

CRIMINAL JUSTICE–LAW ENFORCEMENT

Erie Community College (A)
Erie Community College, North Campus (A)
Erie Community College, South Campus (A)
Lansing Community College (A)

CRIMINAL JUSTICE–LAW ENFORCEMENT OPTION

Middlesex Community College (A)
San Jacinto College District (A)

CRIMINAL JUSTICE–REHABILITATIVE SERVICES

Indiana Tech (B)

CRIMINAL JUSTICE–SOCIAL SERVICES OPTION

San Jacinto College District (A)

CRIMINAL JUSTICE, ADMINISTRATION OPTION

Granite State College (B)

CRIMINAL JUSTICE, CRIMINALISTICS CONCENTRATION

Saint Leo University (B)

CRIMINAL JUSTICE, CRITICAL INCIDENT MANAGEMENT CONCENTRATION

Saint Leo University (M)

CRIMINAL JUSTICE, FORENSIC SCIENCE CONCENTRATION

Saint Leo University (M)

CRIMINAL JUSTICE, HOMELAND SECURITY CONCENTRATION

Herzing University Online (B)
Saint Leo University (B)

CRIMINAL JUSTICE/ CORRECTIONS

Cayuga County Community College (A)

CRIMINAL JUSTICE/POLICE

Cayuga County Community College (A)

CRIMINAL JUSTICE/PUBLIC SAFETY

Bluefield College (B)

CRIMINAL/SOCIAL JUSTICE

Lewis University (M)

CRIMINOLOGY

Florida State University (B)
Indiana University of Pennsylvania (M)
Memorial University of Newfoundland (UC)
University of West Georgia (B)
Western Kentucky University (M)

CRIMINOLOGY AND CRIMINAL JUSTICE

Indiana State University (B,M)

CRIMINOLOGY AND CRIMINAL JUSTICE (COMPLETION DEGREE)

The University of Texas at Arlington (B)

CRIMINOLOGY, CRIMINAL JUSTICE STUDIES MAJOR

Florida State University (M)

CRITICAL AND CREATIVE THINKING

University of Massachusetts Boston (M)

CRITICAL AND CREATIVE THINKING (FOCUS ON CREATIVITY AT WORK)

University of Massachusetts Boston (GC)

CRITICAL CARE (ADVANCED TECHNICAL CERTIFICATION)

St. Petersburg College (UC)

CRITICAL INCIDENT MANAGEMENT

Saint Leo University (M)

CROP SCIENCES

University of Illinois at Urbana–Champaign (GC,M)

CROSS-CATEGORICAL SPECIAL EDUCATION

Regent University (M)

CROSS-CULTURAL TEACHING

National University (M)

CULTURAL AND REGIONAL STUDIES

Prescott College (B)

CULTURAL STUDIES

Prescott College (M)
State University of New York Empire State College (A,B)

CULTURAL SUSTAINABILITY

Goucher College (M)

CULTURALLY BASED NATIVE HEALTH

Western Carolina University (UC)

CURRICULUM AND INSTRUCTION

Abilene Christian University (M)
Andrews University (M,D)
Angelo State University (M)
Concordia University Wisconsin (M)
Emporia State University (M)
Missouri Baptist University (M)
Peru State College (M)
Southern Arkansas University–Magnolia (M)
University of Colorado at Colorado Springs (M)
University of Florida (M)
University of Massachusetts Lowell (M)
University of Nebraska at Kearney (M)
University of the Southwest (M)
West Texas A&M University (M)

CURRICULUM AND INSTRUCTION (ENGLISH AS A SECOND LANGUAGE)

Middle Tennessee State University (M)

CURRICULUM AND INSTRUCTION (FOR HEALTH CARE PROFESSIONALS)

University of Cincinnati (M)

CURRICULUM AND INSTRUCTION (OPTIONAL LITERACY FOCUS)

Franklin Pierce University (M)

CURRICULUM AND INSTRUCTION EMPHASIS

New Mexico State University (M)

CURRICULUM AND INSTRUCTION IN DIGITAL LEARNING

Abilene Christian University (M)

CURRICULUM AND INSTRUCTION IN MEDICAL EDUCATION FOR HEALTHCARE PROFESSIONALS

University of Cincinnati (UC)

CURRICULUM AND INSTRUCTION IN SPECIAL EDUCATION

Abilene Christian University (M)

CURRICULUM AND INSTRUCTION–CHILDREN'S LITERATURE

Penn State University Park (M)

CURRICULUM AND INSTRUCTION–EDUCATIONAL TECHNOLOGY

La Sierra University (M)

CURRICULUM AND INSTRUCTION–EFFECTIVE TEACHING AND INSTRUCTIONAL LEADERSHIP EMPHASIS

Buena Vista University (M)

CURRICULUM AND INSTRUCTION–GENERAL STUDIES

University of Cincinnati (M)

CURRICULUM AND INSTRUCTION–MATHEMATICS EDUCATION

The University of Texas at Arlington (M)

CURRICULUM AND INSTRUCTION–READING

University of the Southwest (M)

CURRICULUM AND INSTRUCTION–SCIENCE EDUCATION

The University of Texas at Arlington (M)

CURRICULUM AND INSTRUCTION–TEACHING ENGLISH AS A SECOND LANGUAGE EMPHASIS

Buena Vista University (M)

CURRICULUM AND INSTRUCTION, BUSINESS AND MARKETING EDUCATION CONCENTRATION

North Carolina State University (M)

CURRICULUM AND INSTRUCTION, DISTANCE LEARNING SPECIALIZATION

Dallas Baptist University (M)

CURRICULUM AND INSTRUCTION, LEARNING TECHNOLOGIES EMPHASIS

New Mexico State University (D)

CURRICULUM AND INSTRUCTION, SUPERVISION SPECIALIZATION

Dallas Baptist University (M)

CURRICULUM AND INSTRUCTION/ EDUCATIONAL LEADERSHIP DUAL DEGREE

Dallas Baptist University (M)

CURRICULUM AND INSTRUCTION/ READING

The University of Texas at Arlington (M)

CURRICULUM AND INSTRUCTION: A COLLABORATIVE APPROACH

Graceland University (M)

CURRICULUM AND INSTRUCTIONAL TECHNOLOGY

Framingham State University (M)

CURRICULUM AND TEACHING

Bowling Green State University (M)

CURRICULUM DEVELOPMENT AND INSTRUCTIONAL TECHNOLOGY

University at Albany, State University of New York (M)

CURRICULUM POST-MASTERS

Appalachian State University (UC)

CURRICULUM STUDIES

DePaul University (M)

CURRICULUM TEACHING AND LEARNING STUDIES

Memorial University of Newfoundland (M)

CURRICULUM, INSTRUCTION AND ASSESSMENT

University of Mary (M)

CURRICULUM, INSTRUCTION, AND PROFESSIONAL DEVELOPMENT

Walden University (M)

CURRICULUM, TECHNOLOGY, AND EDUCATION REFORM (CTER)

University of Illinois at Urbana–Champaign (M)

CUSTOMER SERVICE

Broward College (UC)
Fort Hays State University (UC)

CUSTOMER SERVICE REPRESENTATIVE

Spokane Community College (A)

CYBER CRIME TECHNOLOGY

Stanly Community College (A)

CYBERSECURITY

Mercy College (B,M)
University of Maryland University College (B,M)

CYBERSECURITY AND INFORMATION ASSURANCE

Utica College (B)

CYBERSECURITY INTELLIGENCE AND FORENSICS

Utica College (M)

CYBERSECURITY POLICY

University of Maryland University College (M)

CYBERSECURTY (COMBINED BS/MS)

Mercy College (M)

DATA CODING AND CLASSIFICATION

Champlain College (UC)

DATA MANAGEMENT TECHNOLOGY

Colorado Technical University Colorado Springs (M)

DATA MINING

University of Louisville (GC)

DATA SYSTEMS AND TECHNOLOGY

Champlain College (UC)

DATA/TELECOMMUNICATIONS

University of Massachusetts Lowell (UC)

DATABASE ADMINISTRATION

University of West Florida (M)

DATABASE DESIGN AND ADMINISTRATION

University of Denver (UC)

DATABASE MANAGEMENT AND BUSINESS INTELLIGENCE

Boston University (GC)

DATABASE SYSTEMS

Colorado Technical University Colorado Springs (M)

DATABASE SYSTEMS TECHNOLOGIES

University of Maryland University College (GC)

DATABASE USER SPECIALIST

Bellevue College (UC)

DEAFBLINDNESS PRESERVICE TRAINING

Utah State University (A)

DECISION SUPPORT SYSTEMS

Webster University (GC)

DEGREE COMPLETION PROGRAM

Duquesne University (B)
University of Denver (B)

DEMENTIA STUDIES INTERDISCIPLINARY CERTIFICATE

Lakehead University (UC)

DENTAL ASSISTANT PRE-ASSOCIATE CERTIFICATE (JOINTLY SPONSORED BY UMDNJ AND TESC)

Thomas Edison State College (UC)

DENTAL ASSISTING

Monroe Community College (UC)

DENTAL HYGIENE

Eastern Washington University (M)
Ferris State University (B)
Pennsylvania College of Technology (B)
St. Petersburg College (B)
State University of New York College of Technology at Canton (B)
Thomas Edison State College (B)
University of Bridgeport (M)

DENTAL HYGIENE (RDH TO BS)

Texas Woman's University (B)

DENTAL HYGIENE (THROUGH UMDNJ)

Thomas Edison State College (A)

DENTAL HYGIENE DEGREE COMPLETION PROGRAM

University of Missouri–Kansas City (B)

DENTAL HYGIENE EDUCATION

University of Missouri–Kansas City (M)

DENTAL HYGIENE ONLINE (DEGREE COMPLETION PROGRAM)

University of Bridgeport (B)

DENTAL HYGIENE–DENTAL HYGIENE DEGREE COMPLETION

Oregon Institute of Technology (B)

DESIGN FOR USABILITY

University of Central Florida (GC)

DESIGN MANAGEMENT

Savannah College of Art and Design (M)

DESKTOP PUBLISHING

Columbus State Community College (GC)

DEVELOPMENTAL DISABILITIES

Minot State University (GC,A)

DIAGNOSTIC MEDICAL SONOGRAPHY

Florida Hospital College of Health Sciences (B)
Misericordia University (B)
Mountain State University (UC,A,B)
Oregon Institute of Technology (B)

DIAGNOSTIC MEDICAL SONOGRAPHY (BSAT)

Thomas Edison State College (B)

DIESEL TECHNOLOGY

Midland College (A)

DIETARY MANAGEMENT

Auburn University (UC)

DIETARY MANAGER

Wisconsin Indianhead Technical College (UC)

DIETETIC INTERNSHIP PROGRAM

State University of New York College at Oneonta (UC)

DIETETIC TECHNICIAN
Gaston College (A)

DIETETICS
Kansas State University (B,M)

DIETETICS (FOOD SCIENCE AND NUTRITION)
Colorado State University (M)

DIFFERENTIATED INSTRUCTION
Concordia University, St. Paul (M)
Graceland University (M)

DIFFERENTIATED INSTRUCTION FOR AT-RISK LEARNERS (DIAL)
Marian University (M)

DIGITAL ARTS
Goucher College (M)
Penn State University Park (UC)

DIGITAL CINEMA
National University (M)

DIGITAL DESIGN
Columbus State Community College (GC)

DIGITAL DESIGN AND GRAPHICS
Columbus State Community College (A)

DIGITAL FORENSICS
Boston University (GC)
University of Central Florida (M)

DIGITAL FORENSICS MANAGEMENT
Champlain College (M)

DIGITAL IMAGING AND DESIGN
Texas State Technical College West Texas (A)

DIGITAL INFORMATION MANAGEMENT
The University of Arizona (GC)

DIGITAL LIBRARIES
Syracuse University (GC)
Syracuse University (GC)

DIGITAL LIBRARIES SPECIALIST
Drexel University (GC)

DIGITAL MARKETING COMMUNICATIONS
West Virginia University (GC)

DIGITAL MEDIA
Columbus State Community College (GC)

DIGITAL MEDIA COMMUNICATION
Saint Mary-of-the-Woods College (B)

DIGITAL PHOTOGRAPHY
Columbus State Community College (A)
Savannah College of Art and Design (M)

DIGITAL PUBLISHING
Savannah College of Art and Design (UC)

DIGITAL PUBLISHING MANAGEMENT
Savannah College of Art and Design (GC)

DIRECT MARKETING
Columbus State Community College (GC)

DIRECTED STUDIES
Vincennes University (UC)

DISASTER MEDICINE AND MANAGEMENT
Philadelphia University (M)

DISASTER MENTAL HEALTH
The University of South Dakota (GC)

DISASTER PUBLIC HEALTH
University of Colorado at Colorado Springs (GC)

DISCIPLESHIP MINISTRIES
Liberty University (M)

DISTANCE EDUCATION
Athabasca University (M)
Indiana University System (UC)
Penn State University Park (GC)
University of Wisconsin–Madison (UC)

DISTANCE EDUCATION (TECHNOLOGY)
Athabasca University (GC)

DISTANCE EDUCATION LEADERSHIP AND E-LEARNING
University of Maryland University College (GC)

DISTANCE EDUCATION–ONLINE TEACHING AND LEARNING
Appalachian State University (GC)

DISTANCE EDUCATION, GLOBALIZATION, AND DEVELOPMENT
University of Maryland University College (GC)

DISTANCE LEARNING
Northeastern University (GC)

DISTANCE LEARNING SPECIALIZATION
Dallas Baptist University (M)

DISTANCE M.DIV.
University of Dubuque (M)

DISTRICT LEADERSHIP-SUPERINTENDENT
Fort Hays State University (UC)

DISTRICT LEVEL ADMINISTRATION
University of Missouri–Kansas City (M)

DIVERSITY CERTIFICATE PROGRAM
Mississippi State University (GC)

DIVINITY
Baptist Bible College of Pennsylvania (M)
The Baptist College of Florida (A)
George Fox University (M)
Global University (M)
Liberty University (M)
Shasta Bible College (M)

DOCTOR OF MUSIC ARTS IN MUSIC EDUCATION
Boston University (D)

DOCUMENTARY STUDIES
Burlington College (B)

DOMESTIC VIOLENCE PREVENTION
University of Massachusetts Lowell (GC)

DRAMA
Savannah College of Art and Design (M)
Texas Woman's University (M)

DRIVER EDUCATION (UNDERGRADUATE)
University of Nebraska at Kearney (UC)

DRIVER EDUCATION INSTRUCTOR
Indiana State University (UC)

DUAL DEGREE PROGRAM
Dallas Baptist University (M)

DUAL M.ED.–CURRICULUM AND INSTRUCTION AND MAM
Dallas Baptist University (M)

DUAL MACE STUDENT MINISTRY AND MASTERS OF ARTS IN MANAGEMENT
Dallas Baptist University (M)

DUAL MACE/MBA
Dallas Baptist University (M)

DUAL MASTER OF ARTS IN CHRISTIAN EDUCATION–CHILDHOOD MINISTRY/MASTER OF BUSINESS ADMINISTRATION
Dallas Baptist University (M)

DUAL MASTER OF ARTS IN MANAGEMENT AND MASTER OF EDUCATION IN HIGHER EDUCATION
Dallas Baptist University (M)

DUKE ENVIRONMENTAL LEADERSHIP MASTER OF ENVIRONMENTAL MANAGEMENT
Duke University (M)

E-BUSINESS
Lansing Community College (UC,A)

E-COMMERCE
Athabasca University (UC)
Wake Technical Community College (UC)

E-COMMERCE PRE-ASSOCIATE CERTIFICATE
Thomas Edison State College (UC)

E-COMMERCE TECHNOLOGY
DePaul University (M)

E-COMMERCE WEB DEVELOPMENT
Fort Hays State University (UC)

E-FINANCIAL PLANNING
DePaul University (UC)

E-GOVERNMENT
University of Illinois at Chicago (UC)

E-LEARNING
North Carolina State University (GC)
The University of Texas at Brownsville (UC)

E-LEARNING AND INSTRUCTIONAL SYSTEMS DESIGN
University of Maryland University College (GC)

E-LEARNING AND ONLINE TEACHING
University of Wisconsin–Stout (GC)

E-LEARNING LEADERSHIP
Drexel University (GC)

E-LEARNING PROFESSIONAL DEVELOPMENT
University of Central Florida (GC)

EARLY CHILDHOOD
Concordia University, St. Paul (M)
Southeast Community College Area (A)

EARLY CHILDHOOD (LITERACY)
University at Albany, State University of New York (M)

EARLY CHILDHOOD ADMINISTRATION
National-Louis University (M)

EARLY CHILDHOOD ASSOCIATE
Stanly Community College (A)

EARLY CHILDHOOD CDA CREDENTIAL RENEWAL PROGRAM
Clarion University of Pennsylvania (UC)

EARLY CHILDHOOD DEVELOPMENT
J. Sargeant Reynolds Community College (UC,A)
Kaplan University Online (A,B)
Lewis-Clark State College (A,B)
Mountain State University (A)
National University (B)
Southern Oregon University (B)

EARLY CHILDHOOD DIRECTORS CREDENTIAL PROGRAM
Clarion University of Pennsylvania (UC)

EARLY CHILDHOOD DIRECTORS CREDENTIAL RENEWAL PROGRAM
Clarion University of Pennsylvania (UC)

EARLY CHILDHOOD EDUCATION
Arkansas Tech University (A,B)
Brenau University (M)
Champlain College (M)
Clarion University of Pennsylvania (A)
College of the Siskiyous (A)
Dawson Community College (A)
Eastern Wyoming College (A)
Edgecombe Community College (A)
Emporia State University (M)
Erikson Institute (M)
Jacksonville State University (M)
J. Sargeant Reynolds Community College (UC)
Kansas State University (B)
Mayville State University (A,B)
Nashville State Technical Community College (UC)
Southeastern Illinois College (A)
Southern University at New Orleans (B)
South Piedmont Community College (A)
Taft College (A)
University of Cincinnati (A,B)
The University of Montana Western (A,B)
University of North Dakota (M)
University of the Southwest (M)
The University of Toledo (M)
The University of West Alabama (M)
Vanguard University of Southern California (B)
Wake Technical Community College (UC)
Wisconsin Indianhead Technical College (A)
Youngstown State University (M)

EARLY CHILDHOOD EDUCATION AND STUDENTS WITH DISABILITIES
Mercy College (M)

EARLY CHILDHOOD EDUCATION PRESCHOOL SPECIALIZATION
Seminole State College of Florida (UC)

EARLY CHILDHOOD EDUCATION–ADMINISTRATION TRACK
Haywood Community College (A)

EARLY CHILDHOOD EDUCATION–CAREER OPTION
Quinsigamond Community College (A)

EARLY CHILDHOOD EDUCATION–COLLEGE TRANSFER TRACK
Haywood Community College (A)

EARLY CHILDHOOD EDUCATION–EARLY CHILDHOOD EDUCATION TRACK
Haywood Community College (A)

EARLY CHILDHOOD EDUCATION–FASTTRACK DEGREE COMPLETION

The University of Toledo (B)

EARLY CHILDHOOD EDUCATION–INFANT AND TODDLER TRACK

Haywood Community College (A)

EARLY CHILDHOOD EDUCATION–SPECIAL EDUCATION TRACK

Haywood Community College (A)

EARLY CHILDHOOD EDUCATION, BIRTH—GRADE 2

Mercy College (M)

EARLY CHILDHOOD INTERVENTION

Auburn University (M)

EARLY CHILDHOOD LEADERSHIP AND ADMINISTRATION

Washington State University (GC)

EARLY CHILDHOOD MANAGEMENT

Seminole State College of Florida (A)

EARLY CHILDHOOD SPECIAL EDUCATION

National University (UC)

EARLY CHILDHOOD STUDIES

Walden University (M)

EARLY CHILDHOOD UNIFIED

Fort Hays State University (B)
University of Nebraska at Kearney (B)

EARLY CHILDHOOD/CHILD DEVELOPMENT

Saint Mary-of-the-Woods College (A)

EARLY CHILDHOOD/ ELEMENTARY EDUCATION

Oregon State University (M)

EARLY CHILDHOOD/MIDDLE CHILDHOOD

University of Wisconsin–Stout (UC)

EARLY ELEMENTARY EDUCATION

Mayville State University (B)

EARLY LITERACY

University of Colorado at Colorado Springs (GC)

EARTH AND ENVIRONMENTAL ENGINEERING

Columbia University (UC,M,D)

EARTH LITERACY

Saint Mary-of-the-Woods College (M)

EARTH SCIENCES

Penn State University Park (M)

ECOLOGICAL TEACHING AND LEARNING

Lesley University (M)

ECOLOGY

Prescott College (M)

ECOMMERCE

J. Sargeant Reynolds Community College (UC)

ECONOMIC CRIME INVESTIGATION

Genesee Community College (A)

ECONOMIC CRIME MANAGEMENT

Utica College (M)

ECONOMIC DEVELOPMENT

University of Southern Mississippi (M)

ECONOMIC DEVELOPMENT AND ENTREPRENEURSHIP

University of Houston–Victoria (M)

ECONOMICS

Lansing Community College (A)
Thomas Edison State College (B)
Utah State University (B)
Western Wyoming Community College (A)

EDUCATION

Angelo State University (UC,M)
Athabasca University (D)
Briar Cliff University (B,M)
Cardinal Stritch University (M)
Central Michigan University (B,M)
The College of St. Scholastica (M)
College of the Humanities and Sciences, Harrison Middleton University (M,D)
Columbia College (M)
Cumberland University (M)
Drexel University (B)
Ellis University (M)
Fort Hays State University (M)
Goddard College (B,M)
Hope International University (M)
Indiana Wesleyan University (M)
Institute for Christian Studies (M)
Judson College (B)
Kaplan University Online (M)
Lakehead University (M)
Liberty University (M,D)
Midway College (B)
Morningside College (M)
Mount Saint Vincent University (M)
New River Community College (A)
Northeastern University (D)
Northern Kentucky University (M)
Notre Dame College (M)
Oregon State University (M)
Peru State College (B)
Prescott College (B,M)
Regent University (GC,D)
Saint Joseph's College of Maine (M)
Saint Mary-of-the-Woods College (M)
Spring Arbor University (M)
Tyler Junior College (A)
Union College (M)
Union Institute & University (M,D)
The University of Akron (M)
The University of Findlay (M)
University of St. Augustine for Health Sciences (D)
The University of Tennessee at Chattanooga (M)
University of Wisconsin–Stout (M)
Valley City State University (M)
Walden University (M,D)
Wayland Baptist University (M)

EDUCATION—BIRTH TO KINDERGARTEN EDUCATION (LATERAL ENTRY/ CERTIFICATION)

Winston-Salem State University (B)

EDUCATION ADMINISTRATION

Concordia University Wisconsin (M)

EDUCATION AND INNOVATION

Webster University (M)

EDUCATION AND SCHOOL ADMINISTRATION

The University of North Carolina at Charlotte (M)

EDUCATION AND TRAINING MANAGEMENT SUBSPECIALTY/ HUMAN PERFORMANCE TECHNOLOGY

University of West Florida (M)

EDUCATION AND TRAINING MANAGEMENT SUBSPECIALTY/ INSTRUCTIONAL TECHNOLOGY

University of West Florida (M)

EDUCATION COUNSELING

Concordia University Wisconsin (M)

EDUCATION CURRICULUM AND INSTRUCTION

Austin Peay State University (M)

EDUCATION CURRICULUM AND INSTRUCTION EARLY CHILDHOOD EDUCATION

New Mexico State University (M)

EDUCATION IN THE EARLY YEARS–BIRTH THROUGH FOURTH GRADE

Montgomery County Community College (A)

EDUCATION LADDER SPECIALIST PROGRAM

Central Michigan University (D)

EDUCATION LEADERSHIP

University of North Dakota (M)

EDUCATION LEADERSHIP–PACIFIC COHORTS

San Diego State University (M)

EDUCATION OF THE DEAF

Texas Woman's University (M)

EDUCATION POLICY, ORGANIZATION, AND LEADERSHIP (EPOL), ELEARNING CONCENTRATION

University of Illinois at Urbana–Champaign (M)

EDUCATION POST-BACCALAUREATE DIPLOMA

University of Manitoba (GC)

EDUCATION PSYCHOLOGY, QUANTITATIVE LITERACY SPECIALIZATION

University of Illinois at Urbana–Champaign (M)

EDUCATION SPECIALIST

Liberty University (M)

EDUCATION SPECIALIST –SCHOOL SUPERINTENDENT

University of Nebraska at Kearney (M)

EDUCATION SPECIALIST (TECHNOLOGY AND CURRICULUM DESIGN)

Middle Tennessee State University (M)

EDUCATION SPECIALIST IN K-12 LEADERSHIP

Oakland University (GC)

EDUCATION STUDIES

Lakehead University (D)

EDUCATION TEACHER PREP

Mountain State University (A)

EDUCATION TEAM HONORS

Fort Hays State University (B)

EDUCATION TECHNOLOGY

Lindenwood University (M)
Walden University (M)

EDUCATION–ADAPTING CURRICULUM FRAMEWORKS FOR ALL LEARNERS

University of Massachusetts Boston (GC)

EDUCATION–CAREER AND TECHNICAL EDUCATION (EVOC)

California State University, San Bernardino (M)

EDUCATION–COMPREHENSIVE MASTERS IN EDUCATION

University of West Florida (M)

EDUCATION–CURRICULUM AND INSTRUCTION

The University of Scranton (M)

EDUCATION–ELEMENTARY

Arizona Western College (A)

EDUCATION–ELEMENTARY EDUCATION

Dickinson State University (B)

EDUCATION–GRADUATE INTERN TEACHING CERTIFICATE

Drexel University (UC)

EDUCATION–INSTRUCTIONAL TECHNOLOGY (ETEC)

California State University, San Bernardino (M)

EDUCATION–K-12 EDUCATORS AND ADMINISTRATION

Jones International University (M)

EDUCATION–KINDERGARTEN-ELEMENTARY EDUCATION

Saint Mary-of-the-Woods College (B)

EDUCATION–LEVEL I EDUCATION SPECIALIST CREDENTIAL–MILD/MOD

National University (UC)

EDUCATION–MASTER OF EDUCATION

University of Calgary (M)

EDUCATION–MIDDLE SCHOOL/HIGH SCHOOL SPECIAL EDUCATION

Saint Mary-of-the-Woods College (B)

EDUCATION–POST-BACHELOR'S TEACHING CERTIFICATE

Drexel University (UC)

EDUCATION–PRESCHOOL-GRADE 3 EDUCATION/MILD INTERVENTION

Saint Mary-of-the-Woods College (B)

EDUCATION–READING EDUCATION (ERDG)

California State University, San Bernardino (M)

EDUCATION–SECONDARY

Arizona Western College (A)
Judson College (B)

EDUCATION–TECHNOLOGY, LEARNING, AND LEADERSHIP

University of Massachusetts Boston (GC)

EDUCATION–TED MULTIPLE OR SINGLE SUBJECT TEACHING CREDENTIAL

National University (UC)

EDUCATION–UNIFIED K-8 GENERAL AND SPECIAL EDUCATION

University of Southern Maine (UC)

EDUCATION, ACADEMICALLY OR INTELLECTUALLY GIFTED ADD-ON TEACHER LICENSURE

The University of North Carolina at Charlotte (GC)

EDUCATION, EARLY CHILDHOOD

New Mexico Junior College (A)

EDUCATION, GENERAL

Gaston College (A)
Montana State University–Great Falls College of Technology (A)
Ouachita Technical College (A)

EDUCATION, GENERAL TRANSFER

Northwestern Michigan College (A)

EDUCATION, MIDDLE AND SECONDARY EDUCATION TEACHER LICENSURE

The University of North Carolina at Charlotte (GC)

EDUCATION, MIDDLE GRADES

The University of North Carolina at Charlotte (M)

EDUCATION/READING AND WRITING

Murray State University (M)

EDUCATIONAL ADMINISTRATION

Andrews University (M)
Emporia State University (M)
Fort Hays State University (M)
Hope International University (M)
Kansas State University (M)
Prairie View A&M University (M)
Prescott College (M)
St. Cloud State University (M)
University of Massachusetts Lowell (M)
University of South Alabama (M)
University of the Southwest (M)

EDUCATIONAL ADMINISTRATION (EDUCATIONAL LEADERSHIP)

New Mexico State University (D)

EDUCATIONAL ADMINISTRATION AND ADMINISTRATIVE SERVICES

National University (M)

EDUCATIONAL ADMINISTRATION AND SUPERVISION

Ball State University (M)
University of Southern Mississippi (M)

EDUCATIONAL ADMINISTRATION AND SUPERVISION NEW YORK STATE SCHOOL BUILDING LEADER

Canisius College (UC)

EDUCATIONAL ADMINISTRATION AND SUPERVISION NEW YORK STATE SCHOOL DISTRICT LEADER

Canisius College (UC)

EDUCATIONAL ADMINISTRATION MAJOR

Fort Hays State University (M)

EDUCATIONAL ADMINISTRATION– SUPERVISOR OF SPECIAL EDUCATION

University of Nebraska at Kearney (M)

EDUCATIONAL ADMINISTRATION– COLLABORATIVE LEADERSHIP

Drexel University (M)

EDUCATIONAL ADMINISTRATION–WEBPLUS! MPA PROGRAM

University of Michigan–Flint (M)

EDUCATIONAL ADMINISTRATION/ ADULT AND HIGHER EDUCATION

The University of South Dakota (M)

EDUCATIONAL ADMINISTRATION/ ELEMENTARY SCHOOL PRINCIPAL

The University of South Dakota (M)

EDUCATIONAL ADMINISTRATION/ PRE-K-12 PRINCIPAL

The University of South Dakota (M)

EDUCATIONAL ADMINISTRATION/ SCHOOL DISTRICT SUPERINTENDENT

The University of South Dakota (M)

EDUCATIONAL ADMINISTRATION/ SECONDARY SCHOOL PRINCIPAL

The University of South Dakota (M)

EDUCATIONAL ADMINISTRATIVE LICENSURE

New Mexico State University (UC)

EDUCATIONAL AND INSTRUCTIONAL TECHNOLOGY

National University (M)

EDUCATIONAL COMPUTING, DESIGN, AND ONLINE LEARNING/ CLASSROOM TECHNOLOGY

Kansas State University (GC,M)

EDUCATIONAL DIAGNOSTICIAN

University of the Southwest (M)
West Texas A&M University (M)

EDUCATIONAL LEADERSHIP

California State University, East Bay (M)
Columbus State University (M)
Concordia University, St. Paul (M)
Dallas Baptist University (M)
DePaul University (M)
Framingham State University (M)
Marygrove College (M)
Midwestern State University (M)
Regent University (M)
Saint Leo University (M)
Stony Brook University, State University of New York (UC)
University of Atlanta (M)
University of Cincinnati (M)
University of Florida (D)
University of North Dakota (D)
The University of Tennessee at Martin (M)
The University of Texas of the Permian Basin (M)
Webster University (M)

EDUCATIONAL LEADERSHIP (MAEDL)

Thomas Edison State College (M)

EDUCATIONAL LEADERSHIP AND ADMINISTRATION (PRINCIPAL PREPARATION)

Walden University (M)

EDUCATIONAL LEADERSHIP AND CHANGE

Fielding Graduate University (D)

EDUCATIONAL LEADERSHIP AND POLICY STUDIES

The University of Texas at Arlington (M)

EDUCATIONAL LEADERSHIP AND POLICY STUDIES (HIGHER EDUCATION)

Hofstra University (M)

EDUCATIONAL LEADERSHIP CONCENTRATION

Saint Leo University (M)

EDUCATIONAL LEADERSHIP STUDIES
Memorial University of Newfoundland (M)

EDUCATIONAL LEADERSHIP–ADMINISTRATOR CERTIFICATION
City University of Seattle (M)

EDUCATIONAL LEADERSHIP, CHARTER SCHOOL ADMINISTRATION EMPHASIS
Central Michigan University (M)

EDUCATIONAL LEADERSHIP, HIGHER EDUCATION ADMINISTRATION SPECIALIZATION
Lynn University (M)

EDUCATIONAL LEADERSHIP, PRINCIPAL CERTIFICATION
Stephen F. Austin State University (M)

EDUCATIONAL LEADERSHIP, RENEWAL, AND CHANGE
Colorado State University (M)

EDUCATIONAL LEADERSHIP, SCHOOL ADMINISTRATION SPECIALIZATION
Lynn University (M)

EDUCATIONAL LEADERSHIP/ ADMINISTRATION
Florida State University (M)

EDUCATIONAL MEDIA (LIBRARY MEDIA)
University of South Alabama (UC,M)

EDUCATIONAL MEDIA, INSTRUCTIONAL TECHNOLOGY SPECIALIST (COMPUTERS)
Appalachian State University (M)

EDUCATIONAL MEDIA, NEW MEDIA AND GLOBAL EDUCATION
Appalachian State University (M)

EDUCATIONAL ORGANIZATION AND LEADERSHIP
University of Illinois at Urbana–Champaign (GC)

EDUCATIONAL ORGANIZATION AND LEADERSHIP (SCHOOL EXECUTIVE LEADERSHIP), EDUCATIONAL ADMINISTRATION CONCENTRATION
University of Illinois at Urbana–Champaign (D)

EDUCATIONAL ORGANIZATION AND LEADERSHIP, COMMUNITY COLLEGE EXECUTIVE LEADERSHIP WITH HIGHER EDUCATION CONCENTRATION
University of Illinois at Urbana–Champaign (D)

EDUCATIONAL ORGANIZATION AND LEADERSHIP, EDUCATIONAL LEADERSHIP AND POLICY EMPHASIS
University of Illinois at Urbana–Champaign (M)

EDUCATIONAL ORGANIZATION AND LEADERSHIP/EDUCATIONAL ADMINISTRATION
University of Illinois at Urbana–Champaign (M)

EDUCATIONAL PARAPROFESSIONAL
Kaplan University Online (A)

EDUCATIONAL POLICY STUDIES, DIVERSITY AND EQUITY ISSUES IN EDUCATION EMPHASIS
University of Illinois at Urbana–Champaign (M)

EDUCATIONAL POLICY STUDIES, GLOBAL STUDIES IN EDUCATION EMPHASIS
University of Illinois at Urbana–Champaign (M)

EDUCATIONAL POLICY STUDIES, NEW LEARNING AND NEW LITERACIES EMPHASIS
University of Illinois at Urbana–Champaign (M)

EDUCATIONAL PSYCHOLOGY
Marist College (M)
University of Memphis (M)

EDUCATIONAL PSYCHOLOGY–EXPERIMENTAL PSYCHOLOGY
Tarleton State University (M)

EDUCATIONAL PSYCHOLOGY, CURRICULUM, TECHNOLOGY, AND EDUCATION REFORM EMPHASIS
University of Illinois at Urbana–Champaign (M)

EDUCATIONAL PSYCHOLOGY, GIFTED AND TALENTED EDUCATION SPECIALIZATION
Ball State University (M)

EDUCATIONAL PSYCHOLOGY, PROFESSIONAL EDUCATOR OPTION
University of Wisconsin–Madison (M)

EDUCATIONAL RESEARCH METHODS
University of Illinois at Chicago (UC)

EDUCATIONAL STUDIES
State University of New York Empire State College (A,B)
Walden University (B)

EDUCATIONAL STUDIES, ADULT LEARNING SPECIALIZATION
Lesley University (D)

EDUCATIONAL SUPERVISION
The University of Scranton (M)

EDUCATIONAL TECHNOLOGY
Boise State University (M)
The College of St. Scholastica (UC)
Dakota State University (M)
DeVry University Online (M)
Framingham State University (M)
Grand Valley State University (M)
Marian University (M)
Marygrove College (M)
Monmouth University (GC)
National University (M)
New Jersey City University (M)
Pittsburg State University (M)
San Diego State University (M)
University of Florida (D)
The University of Texas at Brownsville (M)
Webster University (M)
Western Michigan University (GC,M)

EDUCATIONAL TECHNOLOGY ENDORSEMENT
Youngstown State University (UC)

EDUCATIONAL TECHNOLOGY INTEGRATION
Penn State University Park (GC)

EDUCATIONAL TECHNOLOGY LEADERSHIP
University of North Florida (M)

EDUCATIONAL TECHNOLOGY TRAINING AND PERFORMANCE IMPROVEMENT PROGRAM
Lawrence Technological University (M)

EDUCATIONAL TECHNOLOGY–MASTER OF ARTS IN SECONDARY EDUCATION
Southeast Missouri State University (M)

EDUCATIONAL/INSTRUCTIONAL TECHNOLOGY (MASTERS IN INSTRUCTIONAL TECHNOLOGY)
The University of Akron (M)

ELDER CARE ADMINISTRATION
Lasell College (GC,M)

ELDER CARE MARKETING
Lasell College (GC,M)

ELDER LAW
The University of Toledo (GC)

ELEARNING
University of Illinois at Urbana–Champaign (GC)

ELECTRIC MACHINES AND DRIVES
University of Idaho (UC)

ELECTRIC POWER ENGINEERING
Michigan Technological University (UC)

ELECTRIC POWER, ADVANCED
Michigan Technological University (UC)

ELECTRICAL AND COMPUTER ENGINEERING
Illinois Institute of Technology (M)
Purdue University (M)
University of Colorado Boulder (M)
University of Florida (M)

ELECTRICAL AND COMPUTER ENGINEERING CONCENTRATION
Kettering University (M)

ELECTRICAL ENGINEERING
Bradley University (M)
Columbia University (M,D)
DeVry University Online (M)
Drexel University (M)
Georgia Institute of Technology (M)
Illinois Institute of Technology (M)
Kansas State University (M)
Michigan Technological University (M)
Mississippi State University (D)
Missouri University of Science and Technology (M)
North Carolina State University (M)
Southern Methodist University (M)
University of Idaho (M)
University of Michigan–Dearborn (M)
University of North Dakota (B)
University of Southern California (M)
The University of Texas at Arlington (M)
University of Wisconsin–Madison (M)

ELECTRICAL ENGINEERING (COMPUTER NETWORKS)
University of Southern California (M)

ELECTRICAL ENGINEERING (ELECTRIC POWER)
University of Southern California (M)

ELECTRICAL ENGINEERING (MULTIMEDIA AND CREATIVE TECHNOLOGIES)
University of Southern California (M)

ELECTRICAL ENGINEERING (VLSI DESIGN)
University of Southern California (M)

ELECTRICAL ENGINEERING TECHNOLOGY
Excelsior College (B)
The University of North Carolina at Charlotte (B)

ELECTRICAL OR COMPUTER ENGINEERING
Utah State University (M)

ELECTRICAL TECHNOLOGY
Thomas Edison State College (A,B)

ELECTRICAL/MECHANICAL SYSTEMS AND MAINTENANCE
Thomas Edison State College (A)

ELECTRICITY MARKETS
Illinois Institute of Technology (M)

ELECTROMAGNETICS TECHNOLOGY
University of Illinois at Chicago (UC)

ELECTRONIC BUSINESS
National University (M)

ELECTRONIC COMMERCE
Finger Lakes Community College (A)
North Lake College (A)
Southeastern Community College (A)

ELECTRONIC ENGINEERING TECHNOLOGY
Cleveland Institute of Electronics (A)
Thomas Edison State College (A,B)

ELECTRONICS AND COMPUTER ENGINEERING TECHNOLOGY
Grantham University (A)

ELECTRONICS AND COMPUTER TECHNOLOGY
DeVry University Online (A)
Indiana State University (M)

ELECTRONICS ENGINEERING
Cleveland Institute of Electronics (UC)

ELECTRONICS ENGINEERING TECHNOLOGY
DeVry University Online (B)
Grantham University (B)
Indiana State University (B)
Wayne Community College (A)

ELECTRONICS PRE-ASSOCIATE CERTIFICATE
Thomas Edison State College (UC)

ELECTRONICS TECHNOLOGY
Excelsior College (A)

ELECTRONICS TECHNOLOGY AND ADVANCED TROUBLESHOOTING
Cleveland Institute of Electronics (UC)

ELECTRONICS TECHNOLOGY WITH DIGITAL MICROPROCESSOR LAB
Cleveland Institute of Electronics (UC)

ELECTRONICS TECHNOLOGY WITH FCC LICENSE PREPARATION
Cleveland Institute of Electronics (UC)

ELECTRONICS TECHNOLOGY WITH LABORATORY
Cleveland Institute of Electronics (UC)

ELECTRONICS TECHNOLOGY–BIOMEDICAL INSTRUMENT OPTION AND ELECTRONICS TECHNICIAN OPTION
Quinsigamond Community College (A)

ELEMENTARY CHRISTIAN SCHOOL TEACHER EDUCATION

Laurel University (B)

ELEMENTARY EDUCATION

Ball State University (M)
Broward College (A)
Emporia State University (B)
Fitchburg State University (M)
Fort Hays State University (B)
Framingham State University (M)
Mayville State University (B)
Mississippi State University (B)
New Mexico State University (B)
North Carolina Wesleyan College (B)
Prescott College (B)
Regent University (B)
Southwestern Adventist University (B)
The University of Montana Western (B)
The University of North Carolina at Charlotte (B)
University of North Dakota (M)
University of Northern Iowa (M)
The University of West Alabama (M)
University of Wisconsin–Superior (B)
Western Carolina University (B)
West Virginia University (M)

ELEMENTARY EDUCATION (K-8) DEGREE AND CERTIFICATION

Franklin Pierce University (M)

ELEMENTARY EDUCATION (POST-BACCALAUREATE CERTIFICATION)

Stephen F. Austin State University (UC)

ELEMENTARY EDUCATION (TEACHER ASSISTANT PROGRAM)

University of Southern Mississippi (B)

ELEMENTARY EDUCATION LICENSURE

Regent University (M)

ELEMENTARY EDUCATION TEAM K-6, SPECIAL EDUCATION MINOR

Fort Hays State University (B)

ELEMENTARY EDUCATION/ SPECIAL EDUCATION

Dakota State University (B)

ELEMENTARY LICENSURE (POST-BA)

New Mexico State University (UC)

ELEMENTARY OR SECONDARY EDUCATION

Marshall University (M)

ELEMENTARY, MIDDLE GRADES, AND SPECIAL EDUCATION

Southeastern Community College (A)

ELEMENTS OF HEALTH CARE LEADERSHIP

Rochester Institute of Technology (GC)

EMBA

Western Kentucky University (M)

EMERGENCY ADMINISTRATION AND MANAGEMENT

Arkansas Tech University (B)
St. Petersburg College (UC,A)

EMERGENCY AND DISASTER MANAGEMENT

Lynn University (UC,GC)
Upper Iowa University (UC,B)

EMERGENCY CARE

St. Petersburg College (UC)

EMERGENCY DISASTER SERVICES

Thomas Edison State College (B)

EMERGENCY MANAGEMENT

Auburn University (UC)
Broward College (UC,A)
Drexel University (UC)
Florida State University (GC)
Illinois Central College (UC)
Jacksonville State University (GC,M)
State University of New York College of Technology at Canton (B)
Trine University (B)
University of Maryland University College (B)

EMERGENCY MANAGEMENT (HOMELAND SECURITY MINOR)

Jacksonville State University (B)

EMERGENCY MANAGEMENT (PUBLIC SAFETY COMMUNICATIONS MINOR)

Jacksonville State University (B)

EMERGENCY MANAGEMENT AND CONTINUITY PLANNING

University of Illinois at Chicago (UC)

EMERGENCY MANAGEMENT AND HOMELAND SECURITY

Arkansas Tech University (M)

EMERGENCY MEDICAL CARE

Western Carolina University (B)

EMERGENCY MEDICAL SERVICES PROGRAM

James A. Rhodes State College (A)

EMERGENCY MEDICINE CERTIFICATE PROGRAM

West Virginia University (GC)

EMERGENCY PLANNING AND ADMINISTRATION

Lynn University (M)

EMERGENCY PLANNING AND RESPONSE

University of Denver (UC)

EMERGENCY PREPAREDNESS

New York Medical College (GC)

EMERGENCY PREPAREDNESS TECHNOLOGY

Wayne Community College (A)

EMERGENCY SERVICES DISASTER MANAGEMENT

University of Florida (GC)

EMERGENCY SERVICES LEADERSHIP

Fort Hays State University (UC)

EMERGENCY SERVICES MANAGEMENT

Columbia Southern University (M)

EMERGING MEDIA JOURNALISM

Ball State University (GC)

EMERGING NETWORK TECHNOLOGIES

Franklin Pierce University (GC)

EMS

Mountain State University (A)

EMT-PARAMEDIC

Wisconsin Indianhead Technical College (UC)

ENERGY AND SUSTAINABILITY

University of Denver (UC)

ENERGY AND SUSTAINABILITY STUDIES

Franklin Pierce University (M)

ENERGY COMMUNICATION NETWORKS

University of Colorado Boulder (GC)

ENERGY ELECTIVE

Athabasca University (M)

ENERGY MANAGEMENT

New York Institute of Technology (M)

ENERGY SYSTEMS

University of Michigan (M)

ENERGY TECHNOLOGY

New Mexico Junior College (A)

ENERGY TECHNOLOGY–PETROLEUM ENERGY TECHNICIAN OR WIND ENERGY TECHNICIAN

Midland College (A)

ENERGY UTILITY TECHNOLOGY

Thomas Edison State College (B)

ENGINEERING

LeTourneau University (M)
Mississippi State University (M)
Purdue University (M)
The University of Arizona (M)
University of Illinois at Chicago (M)
The University of Toledo (M)
University of Virginia (M)
University of Wisconsin–Platteville (M)
University of Wisconsin–Platteville (M)

ENGINEERING ENTREPRENEURSHIP

University of Colorado Boulder (GC)

ENGINEERING GRAPHICS

Thomas Edison State College (A,B)

ENGINEERING LAW AND MANAGEMENT

University of Illinois at Chicago (UC)

ENGINEERING MANAGEMENT

Drexel University (GC,M)
Gannon University (M)
Indiana Tech (M)
Kansas State University (M)
Kettering University (M)
Lawrence Technological University (M)
Missouri University of Science and Technology (M)
National University (M)
Oakland University (M)
Penn State University Park (M)
Rowan University (M)
Southern Methodist University (M)
The University of Alabama in Huntsville (M,D)
University of Colorado at Colorado Springs (M)
University of Colorado Boulder (GC,M)
University of Idaho (M)
University of Management and Technology (A,B,M)
University of Michigan–Dearborn (M)
The University of North Carolina at Charlotte (M)
University of Southern California (M)
The University of Tennessee at Chattanooga (M)
University of Wisconsin–Platteville (GC)

ENGINEERING MANAGEMENT PROGRAM

Colorado State University (M)

ENGINEERING MANAGEMENT SYSTEMS–LOGISTICS AND SUPPLY CHAIN OPTIMIZATION

Columbia University (M)

ENGINEERING MANAGEMENT SYSTEMS–RISK AND REVENUE MANAGEMENT

Columbia University (M)

ENGINEERING MANAGEMENT TECHNOLOGY

Grantham University (A,B)

ENGINEERING ONLINE

North Carolina State University (M)

ENGINEERING PROJECT MANAGEMENT

University of Memphis (GC)

ENGINEERING TECHNOLOGY

Drexel University (M)
Pittsburg State University (M)
Trine University (A,B)
University of Wisconsin–Stout (B)

ENGINEERING TECHNOLOGY (IN STATE)

Daytona State College (B)

ENGINEERING TECHNOLOGY (OUT OF STATE)

Daytona State College (B)

ENGINEERING TECHNOLOGY BACHELOR COMPLETION PROGRAM

Miami University–Regional Campuses (B)

ENGINEERING TECHNOLOGY COMMERCIALIZATION

University of Southern California (GC)

ENGINEERING TECHNOLOGY PROGRAM

Western Carolina University (B)

ENGINEERING–ENGINE SYSTEMS

University of Wisconsin–Madison (M)

ENGINEERING–POLYMER SCIENCE

University of Wisconsin–Madison (M)

ENGINEERING, INDUSTRIAL ENGINEERING CONCENTRATION

Mississippi State University (D)

ENGLISH

Bowling Green State University (M)
Brookdale Community College (A)
Broward College (A)
Caldwell College (B)
Dickinson State University (B)
Drury University (A)
Judson College (B)
Mercy College (B)
National University (B,M)
Northeastern University (B)
Regent University (B)
Rose State College (A)
Saint Mary-of-the-Woods College (B)
Thomas Edison State College (B)
University of Illinois at Springfield (B)
University of Maryland University College (B)
University of Waterloo (B)
The University of Western Ontario (B)
Wayland Baptist University (M)
West Los Angeles College (A)

ENGLISH (3 YEAR)

Athabasca University (B)

ENGLISH (4 YEAR)

Athabasca University (B)

ENGLISH (AFRICAN-AMERICAN LITERATURE AND TECHNICAL WRITING)

University of Memphis (B)

ENGLISH (ESL)

University of Memphis (M)

ENGLISH AS A SECOND LANGUAGE

Kansas State University (M)
Pittsburg State University (M)

ENGLISH AS A SECOND LANGUAGE (ESL)

University of Memphis (GC)

ENGLISH AS A SECOND LANGUAGE (GRADUATE)

University of Nebraska at Kearney (UC)

ENGLISH AS A SECOND LANGUAGE EDUCATION

The University of Texas of the Permian Basin (M)

ENGLISH AS A SECOND LANGUAGE ENDORSEMENT FOR KENTUCKY TEACHERS

Murray State University (UC)

ENGLISH EDUCATION

Valley City State University (B)

ENGLISH LANGUAGE AND LITERATURE

Southern New Hampshire University (B)

ENGLISH LANGUAGE LEARNER (ELL)

University of North Dakota (M)

ENGLISH LANGUAGE STUDIES

Athabasca University (UC)

ENGLISH LITERATURE

Eastern Oregon University (B)
Mercy College (M)

ENGLISH SPEAKERS OF OTHER LANGUAGES

Fort Hays State University (UC)

ENGLISH SPEAKING OTHER LANGUAGES (ESOL)

University of South Alabama (UC)

ENGLISH–SINGLE SUBJECT PREPARATION IN ENGLISH

National University (B)

ENGLISH, TECHNICAL AND PROFESSIONAL WRITING CONCENTRATION

Fort Valley State University (B)

ENGLISH, TECHNICAL COMMUNICATION TRACK

University of Central Florida (M)

ENGLISH/TECHNICAL WRITING SPECIALIZATION ONLINE

Utah State University (M)

ENROLLMENT MANAGEMENT AND INSTITUTIONAL MARKETING POST-BACHELOR'S

Walden University (GC)

ENTERPRISE INFORMATION SYSTEMS

Colorado Technical University Colorado Springs (M)

ENTERPRISE RESOURCE PLANNING

The University of Scranton (M)

ENTOMOLOGY

University of Florida (M)

ENTREPRENEURIAL AND ECONOMIC DEVELOPMENT

Peru State College (M)

ENTREPRENEURSHIP

Boston University (GC)
Genesee Community College (A)
Haywood Community College (A)
Kirtland Community College (UC)
Lewis-Clark State College (A)
Northern Kentucky University (UC)
Thomas Edison State College (B)
University of Maine at Machias (UC)
Western Carolina University (B)

ENTREPRENEURSHIP AND SMALL BUSINESS

Central Pennsylvania College (A)

ENTREPRENEURSHIP CONCENTRATION

Andrew Jackson University (M)

ENTREPRENEURSHIP FOR GROWTH VENTURES

Kaplan University Online (UC)

ENTREPRENEURSHIP FOR NEW VENTURES

Kaplan University Online (UC)

ENVIROMENTAL AND SOCIAL SUSTAINABILITY CONCENTRATION

Colorado Technical University Colorado Springs (M)

ENVIRONMENT AND BUSINESS

University of Waterloo (M)

ENVIRONMENTAL AND REGULATORY SCIENCE

NorthWest Arkansas Community College (A)

ENVIRONMENTAL AND WATER RESOURCES ENGINEERING

University of Illinois at Urbana–Champaign (GC)
University of Illinois at Urbana–Champaign (GC)

ENVIRONMENTAL ASSESSMENT

North Carolina State University (M)

ENVIRONMENTAL ASSESSMENT OF NUCLEAR POWER

University of Denver (UC)

ENVIRONMENTAL ECONOMICS AND POLICY

Oregon State University (B)

ENVIRONMENTAL EDUCATION

Prescott College (M)
Slippery Rock University of Pennsylvania (M)

ENVIRONMENTAL ENGINEERING

Missouri University of Science and Technology (M)
North Carolina State University (M)
Southern Methodist University (M)
University of Central Florida (M)
University of North Dakota (GC)
University of Southern California (M)
Worcester Polytechnic Institute (GC,M)

ENVIRONMENTAL ENGINEERING (SYSTEMS ECOLOGY AND ECOLOGICAL ENGINEERING TRACK)

University of Florida (M)

ENVIRONMENTAL ENGINEERING (WATER RESOURCES PLANNING AND MANAGEMENT TRACK)

University of Florida (M)

ENVIRONMENTAL ENGINEERING (WATER, WASTEWATER, AND STORMWATER ENGINEERING TRACK)

University of Florida (M)

ENVIRONMENTAL ENGINEERING AND SCIENCE

The Johns Hopkins University (M)

ENVIRONMENTAL ENGINEERING SCIENCES
University of Florida (M)

ENVIRONMENTAL FORENSICS
University of Florida (GC)

ENVIRONMENTAL HEALTH AND SAFETY
University of Denver (UC)

ENVIRONMENTAL HEALTH AND SAFETY MANAGEMENT
Rochester Institute of Technology (M)

ENVIRONMENTAL HEALTH INFORMATICS
University of Illinois at Chicago (UC)

ENVIRONMENTAL HEALTH SCIENCE
New York Medical College (M)

ENVIRONMENTAL MANAGEMENT
Columbia Southern University (B)
University of Denver (UC)
University of Maryland University College (GC,B,M)
Webster University (M)

ENVIRONMENTAL PLANNING AND MANAGEMENT
The Johns Hopkins University (M)

ENVIRONMENTAL POLICY
Kaplan University Online (M)
University of Denver (UC)

ENVIRONMENTAL POLICY AND MANAGEMENT
Kaplan University Online (B)

ENVIRONMENTAL POLICY MANAGEMENT
University of Florida (GC)

ENVIRONMENTAL POLICY/ ENVIRONMENTAL JUSTICE
Thomas Edison State College (M)

ENVIRONMENTAL SCIENCE
Southern Methodist University (M)

ENVIRONMENTAL SCIENCE (ENVIRONMENTAL SYSTEMS MANAGEMENT MAJOR)
Southern Methodist University (M)

ENVIRONMENTAL SCIENCE (HAZARDOUS AND WASTE MATERIALS MANAGEMENT MAJOR)
Southern Methodist University (M)

ENVIRONMENTAL SCIENCES
Oregon State University (B)
Thomas Edison State College (A,B)

ENVIRONMENTAL STUDIES
Columbia College (A)
Prescott College (B,M)
Thomas Edison State College (B)

ENVIRONMENTAL STUDIES MANAGEMENT
Drury University (A)

ENVIRONMENTAL STUDIES POLICY
Northeastern University (B)

ENVIRONMENTAL STUDIES–SUSTAINABLE DEVELOPMENT AND POLICY
University of Illinois at Springfield (M)

ENVIRONMENTAL SUSTAINABILITY
University of Illinois at Urbana–Champaign (UC)

ENVIRONMENTAL, SAFETY, AND HEALTH MANAGEMENT
The University of Findlay (B,M)

ENVIRONMENTAL, SAFETY, AND SECURITY TECHNOLOGY
Thomas Edison State College (A)

EPIDEMIOLOGY AND BIOSTATISTICS
Drexel University (UC)

EQUINE ASSISTED MENTAL HEALTH
Prescott College (M)

EQUINE BUSINESS
University of Louisville (UC)

EQUITY AND DIVERSITY IN EDUCATIONAL SETTINGS
University of Nevada, Reno (M)

ERGONOMICS
Colorado State University (UC)

ESL CERTIFICATION
Stephen F. Austin State University (UC)

ESL ENDORSEMENT IN ELEMENTARY AND SECONDARY EDUCATION
Kansas State University (UC)

ESOL/BILINGUAL EDUCATION
Oregon State University (UC)

ESR ACCESS
Earlham School of Religion (M)

ESTATE PLANNING AND TAXATION
The American College (GC)

EVANGELISM AND CHURCH PLANTING
Liberty University (M)

EVIDENCE-BASED COACHING
Fielding Graduate University (UC)

EXCEPTIONAL EDUCATION
University of Central Florida (M)

EXCEPTIONAL LEARNERS EDUCATION
Indiana Wesleyan University (UC)

EXCEPTIONAL STUDENT EDUCATION
University of West Florida (B)

EXCEPTIONAL STUDENT EDUCATION CONCENTRATION
Saint Leo University (M)

EXECUTIVE ASSISTANT
Central Texas College (A)

EXECUTIVE DEVELOPMENT FOR PUBLIC SERVICE
Ball State University (M)

EXECUTIVE EMS OFFICER
University of Florida (UC)

EXECUTIVE HOSPITALITY SUPERVISION
Stephen F. Austin State University (UC)

EXECUTIVE LEADERSHIP (DEL)
Mountain State University (M)

EXECUTIVE MANAGEMENT
Ashland University (M)

EXECUTIVE MASTER OF BUSINESS ADMINISTRATION
Bowling Green State University (M)
Colorado Technical University Colorado Springs (M)
Marquette University (M)

EXECUTIVE MASTER OF BUSINESS ADMINISTRATION (SPANISH VERSION)
National University (M)

EXECUTIVE MASTER OF ORGANIZATION DEVELOPMENT
Bowling Green State University (M)

EXECUTIVE MASTER OF PUBLIC ADMINISTRATION
The University of South Dakota (M)

EXECUTIVE MBA
University of Mary (M)

EXECUTIVE NURSE PRACTICE
Research College of Nursing (M)

EXECUTIVE PROGRAM
Medical University of South Carolina (M)

EXERCISE SCIENCE
Columbus State Community College (A)

EXERCISE SCIENCE IN KINESIOLOGY
Concordia University, St. Paul (B)

EXPRESSIVE ARTS
Burlington College (B)

FABRIC MANUFACTURING
North Carolina State University (UC)

FACILITY MANAGEMENT
Rochester Institute of Technology (M)

FAMILY AND CONSUMER SCIENCE EDUCATION
North Dakota State University (M)

FAMILY AND CONSUMER SCIENCES
McNeese State University (B)
The University of Tennessee at Martin (M)

FAMILY AND CONSUMER SCIENCES, CHILD DEVELOPMENT CONCENTRATION
Jacksonville State University (B)

FAMILY FINANCIAL PLANNING
North Dakota State University (GC)
University of Florida (GC)

FAMILY HOME VISITING
Western Kentucky University (UC)

FAMILY LIFE AND YOUTH DEVELOPMENT
North Carolina State University (M)

FAMILY LIFE EDUCATION
Concordia University, St. Paul (B,M)

FAMILY LIFE STUDIES
Utah State University (B)

FAMILY LITERACY
Penn State University Park (GC)

FAMILY MINISTRY CONCENTRATION
Dallas Baptist University (M)

FAMILY NURSE PRACTITIONER
Oakland University (M)

FAMILY NURSE PRACTITIONER POST-GRADUATE CERTIFICATE
Oakland University (GC)

FAMILY STUDIES
Texas Woman's University (M)
Western Michigan University (B)

FAMILY STUDIES AND HUMAN SERVICES
Kansas State University (B)

FAMILY THERAPY
Amridge University (D)
University of Massachusetts Boston (M)

FASHION
Academy of Art University (A,B,M)

FASHION MERCHANDISING
Southern New Hampshire University (A)

FASTTRACK BUSINESS MANAGEMENT TECHNOLOGY
The University of Toledo (A)

FEED MILLING
North Carolina State University (UC)

FILM
Burlington College (B)

FILM AND CINEMA STUDIES
Prescott College (M)

FINANCE
Colorado State University (UC)
Colorado Technical University Colorado Springs (B)
Columbia Southern University (B,M)
Columbus State Community College (A)
Dallas Baptist University (M)
Dickinson State University (B)
Excelsior College (B)
Florida Tech University Online (M)
Nichols College (B)
Northeastern University (A)
Southern New Hampshire University (GC,M)
Southwestern Oklahoma State University (B)
State University of New York College of Technology at Canton (B)
Thomas Edison State College (B)
University of Colorado at Colorado Springs (M)
University of Houston–Downtown (B)
University of Maryland University College (B)
Webster University (M)
Western International University (M)
Wisconsin Indianhead Technical College (A)

FINANCE ACCELERATED BBS/MBA
Dallas Baptist University (M)

FINANCE AND ACCOUNTING MANAGEMENT
Northeastern University (B)

FINANCE AND REAL ESTATE
University of Memphis (B)

FINANCE CONCENTRATION
Andrew Jackson University (M)
Colorado Technical University Colorado Springs (B,M)

FINANCE PRE-ASSOCIATE CERTIFICATE
Thomas Edison State College (UC)

FINANCE/ECONOMICS
Southern New Hampshire University (B)

FINANCIAL CRIME INVESTIGATION
Utica College (UC)

FINANCIAL ECONOMICS

Caldwell College (B)

FINANCIAL ENGINEERING

Columbia University (UC)
University of Southern California (M)

FINANCIAL FORENSICS

Colorado Technical University Colorado Springs (B)

FINANCIAL INSTITUTION MANAGEMENT

Thomas Edison State College (B)

FINANCIAL INSTITUTIONS

Lansing Community College (UC,A)

FINANCIAL MANAGEMENT

City University of Seattle (GC)
National University (B)
Upper Iowa University (B)

FINANCIAL MANAGEMENT AND INFORMATION SYSTEMS

University of Maryland University College (M)

FINANCIAL MANAGEMENT IN ORGANIZATIONS

University of Maryland University College (GC)

FINANCIAL PLANNING

Colorado Technical University Colorado Springs (B)
DePaul University (UC)

FINANCIAL PLANNING–GRADUATE FINANCIAL PLANNING TRACK

The American College (GC)

FINANCIAL SERVICES

The American College (M)
Arapahoe Community College (A)
Athabasca University (UC)
Bryant & Stratton Online (B)
Haywood Community College (A)
Labette Community College (A)

FINANCIAL SERVICES SPECIALIST (FSS)

The American College (UC)

FINANCIAL SERVICES STUDIES

New England College of Business and Finance (GC)

FINANCIAL VALUATION AND INVESTMENT MANAGEMENT

Lynn University (M)

FINE ARTS

Academy of Art University (A,B,M)
Burlington College (B)

FIRE ADMINISTRATION

Bowling Green State University (B)

FIRE ADMINISTRATION, FIRE PREVENTION AND TECHNOLOGY

Cogswell Polytechnical College (B)

FIRE AND EMERGENCY MANAGEMENT

Kaplan University Online (B)

FIRE AND EMERGENCY SERVICES

Kaplan University Online (M)
Louisiana State University at Eunice (A)
University of Florida (B)

FIRE AND EMERGENCY SERVICES ADMINISTRATION

Colorado State University (B)

FIRE AND EMERGENCY SERVICES ADMINISTRATION (FESA)

Colorado State University (UC)

FIRE AND SAFETY ENGINEERING TECHNOLOGY

Eastern Kentucky University (B)

FIRE INSPECTOR I

St. Petersburg College (UC)

FIRE INSPECTOR II

St. Petersburg College (UC)

FIRE INVESTIGATOR I

St. Petersburg College (UC)

FIRE OFFICER I

St. Petersburg College (UC)

FIRE OFFICER II

St. Petersburg College (UC)

FIRE PROTECTION

Middlesex Community College (A)

FIRE PROTECTION AND SAFETY TECHNOLOGY

North Shore Community College (A)

FIRE PROTECTION ENGINEERING

Worcester Polytechnic Institute (GC,M)

FIRE PROTECTION SCIENCE

Thomas Edison State College (A,B)

FIRE PROTECTION TECHNOLOGY

Midland College (A)

FIRE PROTECTION TECHNOLOGY–FIRE PREVENTION

Chemeketa Community College (A)

FIRE PROTECTION TECHNOLOGY–FIRE SUPPRESSION

Chemeketa Community College (A)

FIRE SCIENCE

Columbia Southern University (A,B)
Kaplan University Online (A,B)
Prescott College (M)
Quinsigamond Community College (A)
St. Petersburg College (A)
University of Maryland University College (B)
The University of North Carolina at Charlotte (B)

FIRE SCIENCE TECHNOLOGY

Pikes Peak Community College (A)
Seminole State College of Florida (A)
University of Cincinnati (A,B)

FIRE SCIENCE TECHNOLOGY (FS)

Mount Wachusett Community College (A)

FIRE SERVICE ADMINISTRATION

Columbia College (A)
Lewis University (B)

FIRE SERVICES ADMINISTRATION

Eastern Oregon University (B)

FISHERIES AND WILDLIFE ONLINE

Oregon State University (B)

FISHERIES MANAGEMENT

Oregon State University (GC)

FITNESS AND WELLNESS SERVICES PRE-ASSOCIATE CERTIFICATE

Thomas Edison State College (UC)

FOOD AND NUTRITION

Bowling Green State University (GC,M)

FOOD PROTECTION

North Dakota State University (GC)

FOOD RETAIL MANAGEMENT

Concordia University, St. Paul (B)

FOOD SAFETY

University of Southern California (GC)

FOOD SAFETY AND DEFENSE

Kansas State University (GC)

FOOD SAFETY MANAGER'S CERTIFICATE

North Carolina State University (UC)

FOOD SCIENCE

Kansas State University (UC,GC)

FOOD SCIENCE AND HUMAN NUTRITION

University of Illinois at Urbana–Champaign (M)

FOOD SCIENCE AND INDUSTRY

Kansas State University (B,M)

FOOD SCIENCE, NUTRITION, AND HEALTH PROMOTION

Mississippi State University (M)

FOOD SERVICE TRAINING PROGRAM

Southeast Community College Area (UC)

FOOD SYSTEMS ADMINISTRATION (NUTRITION AND FOOD SCIENCES)

Texas Woman's University (M)

FOREIGN LANGUAGE

Auburn University (M)
Caldwell College (B)
Lansing Community College (A)
Thomas Edison State College (B)

FOREIGN LANGUAGES

Prescott College (M)

FORENSIC ACCOUNTING

New England College of Business and Finance (GC)
Northeastern University (GC)

FORENSIC CRIMINOLOGY

University of Massachusetts Lowell (GC)

FORENSIC DEATH INVESTIGATION

University of Florida (GC)

FORENSIC DNA AND SEROLOGY

University of Florida (GC)

FORENSIC DRUG CHEMISTRY

University of Florida (GC)

FORENSIC PSYCHOLOGY

University of North Dakota (M)
Walden University (M)

FORENSIC SCIENCE

University of Central Florida (M)

FORENSIC SCIENCES–MASTER OF FORENSIC SCIENCES

National University (M)

FORENSIC TOXICOLOGY

University of Florida (GC)

FOREST BIOMATERIALS

North Carolina State University (M)

FORESTRY

Mississippi State University (M)

FORESTRY TECHNOLOGY–NATURAL RESOURCES SPECIALIST

Haywood Community College (UC)

FOUNDATIONS OF BUSINESS

University of Massachusetts Lowell (GC)

FOUNDATIONS OF DISTANCE EDUCATION AND E-LEARNING

University of Maryland University College (GC)

FOUNDATIONS OF HUMAN RESOURCE MANAGEMENT

University of Maryland University College (GC)

FOUNDATIONS OF INFORMATION TECHNOLOGY

University of Maryland University College (GC)

FOX ONLINE MBA PROGRAM

Temple University (M)

FRAUD AND FORENSICS

Carlow University (M)

FRENCH

The University of Western Ontario (B)

FRENCH (3 YEAR)

Athabasca University (B)

FRENCH (4 YEAR)

Athabasca University (B)

FRENCH LANGUAGE PROFICIENCY

Athabasca University (UC)

FRENCH LANGUAGE, LEVEL 1 OR LEVEL 2

University of Waterloo (UC)

FUNDAMENTALS OF INFORMATION TECHNOLOGY

University of Massachusetts Boston (UC)

FUNDAMENTALS OF MANUFACTURING MANAGEMENT

Rochester Institute of Technology (UC)

FUNDRAISING AND PHILANTHROPY

University of Denver (UC)

FUNDRAISING MANAGEMENT

Lasell College (GC,M)

FUNERAL DIRECTING

St. Louis Community College (GC)

FUNERAL SERVICE EDUCATION

Vincennes University (A)

FUNERAL SERVICES

St. Petersburg College (A)

FUTURE STUDIES

University of Houston (M)

GAME AND SIMULATION PROGRAMMING

DeVry University Online (B)

GAME DESIGN

Academy of Art University (A,B,M)

GAMING AND CASINO OPERATIONS

Drexel University (UC,GC)

GAMING MANAGEMENT

University of Wisconsin–Stout (UC)

GANGS ENFORCEMENT MANAGEMENT

St. Petersburg College (UC)

GAY AND LESBIAN STUDIES

Prescott College (M)

GENDER STUDIES

Prescott College (M)

GENEALOGICAL RESEARCH

Boston University (UC)

GENERAL

Colorado Technical University Colorado Springs (M)
Southwest Mississippi Community College (A)

GENERAL AA–TRANSFER EMPHASIS

Metropolitan Community College–Penn Valley (A)

GENERAL AGRICULTURE

Luna Community College (A)

GENERAL ANTHROPOLOGY

Oregon State University (B)

GENERAL BIOLOGY–TEACHERS IN BIOLOGY

Mississippi State University (M)

GENERAL BUSINESS

Kansas State University (B)
Kirtland Community College (A)
New Mexico State University (B)
Nichols College (A,B)
University of Houston–Downtown (B)
University of South Alabama (B)
Webber International University (B)

GENERAL BUSINESS ADMINISTRATION

Prairie View A&M University (M)

GENERAL CONCENTRATION

Dallas Baptist University (M)
Kettering University (M)

GENERAL DEGREE

Arkansas State University–Mountain Home (A)
Central Carolina Community College (A)
Dallas Baptist University (A)
Edison State Community College (A)
Garden City Community College (A)
Greenville Technical College (A)
Haywood Community College (A)
Hibbing Community College (A)
John A. Logan College (A)
Luzerne County Community College (A)
Nashville State Technical Community College (A)
Pikes Peak Community College (A)
St. Clair County Community College (A)
Southeastern Illinois College (A)
Southwestern Community College (A)
Stanly Community College (A)
Wayne Community College (A)
Western Texas College (A)

GENERAL DEGREE AND ADVANCED DEGREE

University of Manitoba (B)

GENERAL DEGREE PROGRAM

Aquinas Institute of Theology (M)

GENERAL EDUCATION

Brazosport College (A)
Columbia Southern University (A)
Hope International University (A)
Northwest-Shoals Community College (A)
Ozarks Technical Community College (A)
Pulaski Technical College (A)
St. Clair County Community College (A)
The University of West Alabama (M)
Wake Technical Community College (A)
Wayne Community College (A)

GENERAL EDUCATION REQUIREMENTS

Adams State College (A)

GENERAL EDUCATIONAL ADMINISTRATION

Central Michigan University (M)

GENERAL HORTICULTURE

North Carolina State University (UC)
Oregon State University (B)

GENERAL MANAGEMENT

American Graduate University (M)
City University of Seattle (GC)
Hope International University (M)
Robert Morris University (M)
Thomas Edison State College (B)

GENERAL MANAGEMENT OPTION

Southeast Missouri State University (M)

GENERAL NON-MAJOR

University of Waterloo (B)

GENERAL OCCUPATIONAL TECHNOLOGY

Haywood Community College (A)
Wayne Community College (A)

GENERAL OFFICE CLERK

San Jacinto College District (UC)

GENERAL ONLINE DEGREE PROGRAM

North Iowa Area Community College (A)

GENERAL PROGRAM

Dickinson State University (A)
St. Petersburg College (A)
University of the Incarnate Word (M)

GENERAL SPECIAL EDUCATION WITH EMOTIONAL/BEHAVIORAL DISABILITIES (K-12)

Franklin Pierce University (M)

GENERAL SPECIAL EDUCATION WITH LEARNING DISABILITIES (K-12)

Franklin Pierce University (M)

GENERAL STUDIES

AIB College of Business (A)
Arizona Western College (A)
Atlantic Cape Community College (A)
Baker College Online (B)
Ball State University (A,B)
Belhaven University (A)
Bellevue College (A)
Bossier Parish Community College (A)
Brigham Young University–Idaho (A)
Cape Fear Community College (A)
Capital Community College (A)
Centralia College (A)
Central Texas College (A)
Central Wyoming College (A)
Charter Oak State College (A,B)
Chemeketa Community College (A)
City University of Seattle (A,B)
College of Southern Maryland (UC,A)
Colorado Technical University Colorado Springs (A)
Columbia College (A,B)
Columbus State Community College (A)
Cossatot Community College of the University of Arkansas (A)
Crown College (A)
Dakota State University (A,B)
Dawson Community College (A)
Drury University (A,B)
Eastern Illinois University (B)
Fort Hays State University (A,B)
Franklin Pierce University (A,B)
Gadsden State Community College (A)
Garrett College (A)
Genesee Community College (A)
Granite State College (A)
Grantham University (A,B)
Harford Community College (A)

Illinois Central College (A)
Indiana Tech (A)
Indiana Wesleyan University (GC,A,B)
Labette Community College (A)
Lakehead University (B)
Lansing Community College (A)
Liberty University (A)
Luzerne County Community College (A)
Mayville State University (B)
Middlesex Community College (A)
Minot State University (B)
Montgomery Community College (A)
Montgomery County Community College (A)
Mountain Empire Community College (A)
Mountain State University (A)
Nashville State Technical Community College (A)
New River Community College (A)
Northern State University (A,B)
North Lake College (A)
North Seattle Community College (A)
Ocean County College (A)
Peirce College (A)
Portland Community College (A)
Quinsigamond Community College (A)
Rappahannock Community College (A)
Reading Area Community College (A)
Regent University (A)
Saint Joseph's College of Maine (A,B)
Seminole State College of Florida (A)
Southeast Missouri State University (B)
Southern University at New Orleans (B)
Southwestern Adventist University (B)
Southwest Virginia Community College (A)
Texas Woman's University (B)
Three Rivers Community College (A)
Toccoa Falls College (A)
Trine University (B)
Tyler Junior College (A)
University of Alaska, Prince William Sound Community College (A)
University of Bridgeport (B)
University of Management and Technology (A,B)
University of North Dakota (B)
The University of South Dakota (A,B)
Utah State University (A)
Vincennes University (A)
Western Wyoming Community College (A)
West Shore Community College (A)
West Texas A&M University (B)
Wharton County Junior College (A)
Widener University (A)
Wilfrid Laurier University (B)

GENERAL STUDIES (AGS)

Northwestern Michigan College (A)

GENERAL STUDIES (GS)

Mount Wachusett Community College (A)
National University (A)

GENERAL STUDIES DEGREE D595

Illinois Eastern Community Colleges, Frontier Community College (A)
Illinois Eastern Community Colleges, Lincoln Trail College (A)
Illinois Eastern Community Colleges, Olney Central College (A)
Illinois Eastern Community Colleges, Wabash Valley College (A)

GENERAL STUDIES IN SOCIAL WORK

University of Waterloo (UC)

GENERAL STUDIES–ALLIED HEALTH CONCENTRATION (GSAH)

Mount Wachusett Community College (A)

GENERAL STUDIES–ASSOCIATE OF ARTS AND BACHELOR OF GENERAL STUDIES

Indiana University–Purdue University Fort Wayne (B)

GENERAL STUDIES–BUSINESS STUDIES

Vincennes University (A)

GENERAL STUDIES–INDIVIDUALIZED STUDIES

Drexel University (B)

GENERAL STUDIES–MONTANA UNIVERSITY SYSTEM GENERAL CORE

Montana State University–Great Falls College of Technology (UC)

GENERAL STUDIES, ACCOUNTING SEQUENCE

University of Maine at Fort Kent (A)

GENERAL STUDIES, BUSINESS MINOR

Drexel University (B)

GENERAL STUDIES; CRIMINAL JUSTICE SEQUENCE

University of Maine at Fort Kent (A)

GENERAL STUDIES/LIBERAL ARTS

Tunxis Community College (A)

GENERAL TECHNOLOGY

Anne Arundel Community College (A)
Nashville State Technical Community College (A)

GENERAL TRACK

Saint Leo University (M)

GENERALIST

Colorado Mountain College (A)

GENOCIDE AND HOLOCAUST STUDIES

Seton Hill University (UC)

GEOGRAPHIC INFORMATION SCIENCE

University of Denver (M)

GEOGRAPHIC INFORMATION SCIENCE AND TECHNOLOGY

University of Southern California (GC,M)

GEOGRAPHIC INFORMATION SCIENCES

University of North Dakota (GC)

GEOGRAPHIC INFORMATION SYSTEMS

Columbus State Community College (GC,A)
Fort Hays State University (UC)
Jacksonville State University (GC,M)
North Carolina State University (GC)
Northeastern University (GC)
Penn State University Park (GC,M)
University of Denver (UC)
University of Florida (GC)

GEOGRAPHIC INFORMATION TECHNOLOGY

Northeastern University (M)

GEOGRAPHY

University of Manitoba (B)

GEOLOGICAL ENGINEERING

University of Idaho (M)

GEOMATICS

University of Florida (UC)

GEORGIA WEBMBA

Columbus State University (M)
University of West Georgia (M)

GEOSCIENCES

Mississippi State University (B)

GEOSCIENCES, BROADCAST METEOROLOGY

Mississippi State University (UC)

GEOSCIENCES, OPERATIONAL METEOROLOGY

Mississippi State University (UC)

GEOSCIENCES, TEACHERS IN GEOSCIENCE

Mississippi State University (M)

GEOSPATIAL AND REMOTE SENSING

Mississippi State University (UC,GC)

GEOSPATIAL INFORMATION SCIENCE AND TECHNOLOGY

North Carolina State University (M)

GEOSPATIAL INTELLIGENCE

Penn State University Park (GC)

GEOSPATIAL SURVEYING ENGINEERING (GSEN)

Texas A&M University–Corpus Christi (M)

GEOSPATIAL TECHNOLOGY–ADVANCED GEOSPATIAL SPECIALIST

Haywood Community College (UC)

GEOSPATIAL TECHNOLOGY–GLOBAL POSITIONING SYSTEMS SPECIALIST

Haywood Community College (UC)

GEOSPATIAL TECHNOLOGY–PROPERTY MAPPING SPECIALIST

Haywood Community College (UC)

GEOTECHNICAL ENGINEERING

University of Wisconsin–Platteville (GC)

GEOTECHNICS

Missouri University of Science and Technology (M)

GERIATRIC CARE MANAGEMENT

University of Florida (GC)

GERONTOLOGICAL SOCIAL POLICY

University of Massachusetts Boston (UC)

GERONTOLOGY

Appalachian State University (GC)
Ashland University (UC)
Kansas State University (GC,M)
McDaniel College (GC,M)
Mount Saint Vincent University (UC)
North Dakota State University (GC)
Portland Community College (A)
Thomas Edison State College (B)
The University of Arizona (GC)
University of Maryland University College (B)
University of Southern California (GC,M)
Webster University (UC,M)

GERONTOLOGY–FRANK J. MANNING CERTIFICATE IN GERONTOLOGY

University of Massachusetts Boston (UC)

GERONTOLOGY–MANAGEMENT OF AGING SERVICES TRACK

University of Massachusetts Boston (GC,M)

GIFTED (GRADUATE)

University of Nebraska at Kearney (UC)

GIFTED AND TALENTED

Indiana State University (GC)

GIFTED AND TALENTED CERTIFICATE ENDORSEMENT FOR KENTUCKY TEACHERS

Murray State University (UC)

GIFTED AND TALENTED EDUCATION

Ball State University (UC)
Northern Kentucky University (UC)

GIFTED AND TALENTED ENDORSEMENT

University of Colorado at Colorado Springs (UC)

GIFTED AND TALENTED GRADUATE TEACHING ENDORSEMENT

Western Kentucky University (UC)

GIFTED EDUCATION

Fort Hays State University (UC)
University of Central Florida (GC)

GIFTED EDUCATION (NY STATE)

Hofstra University (GC)

GIS SOFTWARE APPLICATION SPECIALIST

Erie Community College (UC)
Erie Community College, North Campus (UC)
Erie Community College, South Campus (UC)

GISCIENCE PROFESSIONAL CERTIFICATE

Oregon State University (GC)

GLOBAL AFFAIRS

University of Denver (M)

GLOBAL AND INTERNATIONAL EDUCATION

Drexel University (M)

GLOBAL AUTOMOTIVE AND MANUFACTURING ENGINEERING

University of Michigan (M)

GLOBAL BUSINESS

Excelsior College (B)

GLOBAL BUSINESS AND PUBLIC POLICY

University of Maryland University College (B)

GLOBAL HEALTH

New York Medical College (GC)

GLOBAL HUMAN RESOURCES

University of Denver (UC)

GLOBAL ISSUES

University of Denver (UC)

GLOBAL LEADERSHIP

Fuller Theological Seminary (M)

GLOBAL LEADERSHIP–ACADEMIC ADMINISTRATION

Indiana Tech (D)

GLOBAL LEADERSHIP–ORGANIZATIONAL MANAGEMENT

Indiana Tech (D)

GLOBAL LOGISTICS

Lenoir Community College (A)

GLOBAL LOGISTICS TECHNOLOGY

Wake Technical Community College (UC,A)

GLOBAL LOGISTICS TECHNOLOGY–DISTRIBUTION MANAGEMENT

Wake Technical Community College (UC)

GLOBAL MBA

Southern New Hampshire University (M)
University of Houston–Victoria (M)

GLOBAL MBA ON-LINE
The University of Texas at Dallas (M)

GLOBAL POST-DISASTER STUDIES (RECONSTRUCTION WITH VULNERABLE POPULATIONS)
University of Massachusetts Boston (GC)

GLOBAL STUDIES
National University (B)

GLOBAL STUDIES AND INTERNATIONAL AFFAIRS
Northeastern University (GC)

GLOBALIZATION AND CULTURE CHANGE
Fort Hays State University (UC)

GOLF ENTERPRISE MANAGEMENT
University of Wisconsin–Stout (B)

GOVERNANCE, LAW, AND MANAGEMENT
Athabasca University (B)

GOVERNMENT
Regent University (B,M)
Tyler Junior College (A)

GOVERNMENT ADMINISTRATION
Columbus State University (M)

GOVERNMENT CONTRACTING
Webster University (GC)

GOVERNMENT MANAGEMENT POST-BACHELOR'S
Walden University (GC)

GRADUATE HISTORY
University of Nebraska at Kearney (M)

GRANT PROPOSAL WRITING AND PROGRAM EVALUATION
Fort Hays State University (UC)

GRAPHIC AND MULTIMEDIA DESIGN
State University of New York College of Technology at Canton (B)

GRAPHIC DESIGN
Academy of Art University (A,B,M)
Burlington College (B)
Herzing University Online (A,B)
Savannah College of Art and Design (B,M)
Sessions College for Professional Design (A)

GRAPHIC DESIGN, PRINT DESIGN CONCENTRATION
Herzing University Online (B)

GRAPHIC DESIGN, WEB DESIGN CONCENTRATION
Herzing University Online (B)

GRAPHICS AND DESIGN
Wake Technical Community College (UC)

GREEN BUILDING
Colorado State University (UC)

GREEN HOMES
Colorado State University (UC)

GREEN TECHNOLOGIES
University of Southern California (M)

GRIEF AND BEREAVEMENT
Marian University (M)

GROUNDS WORK SKILLS, BASIC
Dakota College at Bottineau (UC)

GUIDANCE AND COUNSELING
The University of West Alabama (M)

GUIDANCE AND DEVELOPMENT
Central Michigan University (M)

HACCP (HAZARD ANALYSIS AND CRITICAL CONTROL POINTS)
North Carolina State University (UC)

HEALTH ADMINISTRATION
Athabasca University (B)
A.T. Still University of Health Sciences (M)
Franklin Pierce University (M)
Hodges University (B)
Medical University of South Carolina (D)
Saint Joseph's College of Maine (UC,B,M)
University of Management and Technology (UC,B,M)
University of Memphis (M)
University of North Dakota (GC)
University of St. Francis (M)

HEALTH ADMINISTRATION AND NURSING
Saint Joseph's College of Maine (M)

HEALTH ADMINISTRATION INFORMATICS
University of Maryland University College (M)

HEALTH ADMINISTRATION POST-DIPLOMA
Athabasca University (B)

HEALTH ADMINISTRATION SERVICES
Colorado Technical University Colorado Springs (A)

HEALTH AND HUMAN PERFORMANCE
Fort Hays State University (M)

HEALTH AND HUMAN PERFORMANCE, HEALTH LEADERSHIP–HEALTH ADMINISTRATION
Austin Peay State University (M)

HEALTH AND KINESIOLOGY–KINESIOLOGY
Tyler Junior College (A)

HEALTH AND MEDICAL INFORMATICS
Brandeis University (M)

HEALTH AND NUTRITION COUNSELING
Thomas Edison State College (B)

HEALTH AND SAFETY (OCCUPATIONAL SAFETY MANAGEMENT SPECIALIZATION)
Indiana State University (M)

HEALTH AND SAFETY TRAINING FOR HAZARDOUS WASTE OPERATIONS
Columbus State Community College (GC)

HEALTH AND WELLNESS
Kaplan University Online (B)

HEALTH ARTS AND SCIENCES
Goddard College (B,M)

HEALTH CARE ADMINISTRATION
Clarkson College (M)
Columbia Southern University (B)
Fort Hays State University (M)
Kaplan University Online (B,M)
Limestone College (B)
Midway College (B)
National University (A,M)
Roger Williams University (B)
University of Mary (M)
University of Maryland University College (GC,M)

The University of Toledo (B)
University of West Florida (M)

HEALTH CARE AND NURSING ADMINISTRATION

Southern Illinois University Edwardsville (M)

HEALTH CARE BUSINESS, HEALTH INFORMATION ADMINISTRATION

Clarkson College (B)

HEALTH CARE BUSINESS, MANAGEMENT MAJOR

Clarkson College (B)

HEALTH CARE INFORMATICS

University of Central Florida (GC,M)

HEALTH CARE LEADERSHIP

University of St. Francis (B)

HEALTH CARE MANAGEMENT

Columbia Southern University (M)
Concordia University, St. Paul (M)
Dallas Baptist University (UC,GC,B,M)
Graceland University (B)
Granite State College (B)
Indiana Wesleyan University (GC)
Minnesota School of Business–Online (B)
Minnesota School of Business–Richfield (B)
Saint Leo University (GC,B)
State University of New York College of Technology at Canton (B)

HEALTH CARE MANAGEMENT ACCELERATED BBS/MBA

Dallas Baptist University (M)

HEALTH CARE MANAGEMENT CONCENTRATION

Colorado Technical University Colorado Springs (B,M)
Saint Leo University (M)

HEALTH CARE MANAGER

Columbus State Community College (GC)

HEALTH CARE MISSION

Aquinas Institute of Theology (M)

HEALTH CARE RISK MANAGEMENT

University of Florida (GC)

HEALTH CARE SYSTEMS MANAGEMENT

Kettering University (M)
Loyola University New Orleans (M)

HEALTH COMMUNICATION

Boston University (M)
North Dakota State University (B)
University of Illinois at Urbana–Champaign (M)

HEALTH DEVELOPMENT ADMINISTRATION

Athabasca University (UC)

HEALTH EDUCATION

A.T. Still University of Health Sciences (D)
Kaplan University Online (M)
University of Florida (B)

HEALTH FITNESS MANAGEMENT

Minnesota School of Business–Online (M)
Minnesota School of Business–Richfield (M)

HEALTH FITNESS SPECIALIST

Minnesota School of Business–Online (A,B)
Minnesota School of Business–Richfield (A,B)

HEALTH INFORMATICS

Champlain College (A,B)
Dakota State University (M)
Drexel University (M)
Northeastern University (GC,M)
Northern Kentucky University (GC,M)
University of Illinois at Chicago (UC,GC,M)
Walden University (M)

HEALTH INFORMATION ADMINISTRATION

Dakota State University (B)
The University of Toledo (GC,B)

HEALTH INFORMATION CODING SPECIALIST

Montana State University–Great Falls College of Technology (UC)

HEALTH INFORMATION MANAGEMENT

AIB College of Business (A)
Clarkson College (UC)
The College of St. Scholastica (B,M)
Greenville Technical College (A)
Herzing University Online (A,B)
Kaplan University Online (B)
Moorpark College (A)
Pennsylvania College of Technology (B)
St. Petersburg College (A)
Sinclair Community College (A)
University of Cincinnati (B)
University of Illinois at Chicago (UC)
Vincennes University (A)

HEALTH INFORMATION MANAGEMENT DEGREE COMPLETION

University of Illinois at Chicago (B)

HEALTH INFORMATION MANAGEMENT TECHNOLOGY

Columbus State Community College (A)

HEALTH INFORMATION MANAGEMENT–MEDICAL INFORMATION CODER/BILLER

Seminole State College of Florida (UC)

HEALTH INFORMATION TECHNICIAN

North Dakota State College of Science (A)

HEALTH INFORMATION TECHNOLOGY

Arapahoe Community College (A)
Clarkson College (A)
Clovis Community College (A)
Dakota State University (A)
DeVry University Online (A)
Edgecombe Community College (A)
Hodges University (A)
Kaplan University Online (A)
Montana State University–Great Falls College of Technology (A)
Moraine Park Technical College (A)
Peirce College (A)
Pitt Community College (A)
Tyler Junior College (A)

HEALTH INFORMATION TECHNOLOGY ONLINE

Kirkwood Community College (A)

HEALTH INNOVATION AND LEADERSHIP

University of Minnesota, Twin Cities Campus (D)

HEALTH MANAGEMENT

Northeastern University (GC,B)
University of Minnesota, Crookston (B)

HEALTH PHYSICS

Illinois Institute of Technology (M)

HEALTH POLICY AND ADMINISTRATION

University of Illinois at Chicago (M)

HEALTH POLICY AND MANAGEMENT

New York Medical College (M)

HEALTH PRACTICE MANAGEMENT

Franklin Pierce University (GC)

HEALTH PROFESSIONS

Youngstown State University (UC)

HEALTH PROFESSIONS EDUCATION

Simmons College (GC)
University of Illinois at Chicago (M)

HEALTH PROMOTION

Appalachian State University (B)
University of Memphis (M)

HEALTH SCIENCE

A.T. Still University of Health Sciences (D)
Kaplan University Online (B)
University of St. Augustine for Health Sciences (D)

HEALTH SCIENCE/DIETETICS

James Madison University (M)

HEALTH SCIENCES

Excelsior College (B)
Huntington College of Health Sciences (B)
Mountain State University (B)
Saint Francis University (M)
The University of South Dakota (B)

HEALTH SCIENCES, ALLIED HEALTH

University of West Florida (B)

HEALTH SCIENCES, EXECUTIVE HEALTH SERVICES ADMINISTRATION

University of Central Florida (M)

HEALTH SCIENCES, HEALTH CARE PROFESSIONAL

University of West Florida (B)

HEALTH SCIENCES, MEDICAL INFORMATION TECHNOLOGY

University of West Florida (B)

HEALTH SCIENCES, PUBLIC HEALTH CONCENTRATION

Indiana State University (M)

HEALTH SERVICE TECHNOLOGY

Thomas Edison State College (B)

HEALTH SERVICES

Thomas Edison State College (B)
Walden University (D)

HEALTH SERVICES ADMINISTRATION

Bryant & Stratton Online (B)
Colorado Technical University Colorado Springs (B)
Drexel University (B)
Mississippi College (M)
Monroe College (B)
Robert Morris University (B)
St. Petersburg College (B)
Thomas Edison State College (B)
University of Central Florida (B)
University of Southern Mississippi (M)
Upper Iowa University (B)

HEALTH SERVICES ADMINISTRATION SPECIALIZATION

The University of South Dakota (M)

HEALTH SERVICES EDUCATION AND MANAGEMENT (WITH UMDNJ)

Thomas Edison State College (B)

HEALTH SERVICES MANAGEMENT

Mercy College (M)

HEALTH SERVICES MANAGEMENT CONCENTRATION

Andrew Jackson University (M)

HEALTH SERVICES TECHNOLOGY

The University of Texas at Brownsville (B)

HEALTH STUDIES

Athabasca University (M)
Lakehead University (M)
Texas Woman's University (B,M)
Walden University (B)

HEALTH SYSTEMS ADMINISTRATION

Rochester Institute of Technology (UC,M)

HEALTH SYSTEMS FINANCE

Rochester Institute of Technology (GC)

HEALTH SYSTEMS MANAGEMENT

Grantham University (B,M)
Vanderbilt University (M)

HEALTH SYSTEMS MANAGEMENT ENGINEERING

University of Southern California (M)

HEALTH, HUMAN PERFORMANCE AND RECREATION

Pittsburg State University (M)

HEALTH, NUTRITION, AND EXERCISE SCIENCE, DIETETICS OPTION

North Dakota State University (M)

HEALTHCARE ADMINISTRATION

Central Michigan University (D)
Grantham University (M)
Peirce College (B)
Seton Hall University (M)
Southwestern College (B)
University of Atlanta (GC,B,M)
University of Colorado at Colorado Springs (M)
Walden University (M)

HEALTHCARE ADMINISTRATION AND MANAGEMENT

Rosalind Franklin University of Medicine and Science (GC,M)

HEALTHCARE ADMINISTRATION–MASTER OF HEALTHCARE ADMINISTRATION

Seton Hall University (M)

HEALTHCARE CODING

Dakota State University (UC)

HEALTHCARE INFORMATICS

The College of St. Scholastica (UC)
Drexel University (UC)
St. Petersburg College (UC,A)

HEALTHCARE LEADERSHIP

National-Louis University (B)
University of Denver (M)

HEALTHCARE LEADERSHIP AND MANAGEMENT

Pitt Community College (UC)

HEALTHCARE MANAGEMENT

Anderson University (B)
Bossier Parish Community College (A)
Brenau University (M)
Champlain College (UC,B,M)
Florida Tech University Online (A)
Herzing University Online (B)
Pitt Community College (UC)
Walden University (B)

HEALTHCARE MANAGEMENT TECHNOLOGY

Pitt Community College (A)
Wayne Community College (A)

HEALTHCARE OUTCOMES

Emory University (M)

HEALTHCARE POLICY, LAW, AND ETHICS

University of Denver (UC)

HEALTHY AGING

Fort Hays State University (UC)

HEMODIALYSIS PATIENT CARE TECHNICIAN

Lake Superior College (UC)

HERITAGE RESOURCES MANAGEMENT

Athabasca University (UC)

HIGHER AND ADULT EDUCATION

University of Memphis (D)

HIGHER EDUCATION

Abilene Christian University (M)
Drexel University (M)
Florida State University (M)
Kaplan University Online (M)
University of North Dakota (D)
Walden University (M)

HIGHER EDUCATION ADMINISTRATION

Dallas Baptist University (GC)
Mississippi College (M)
Northeastern University (GC,M)
Prescott College (M)
St. Cloud State University (M)
Stony Brook University, State University of New York (M)
University of Florida (D)
University of Louisville (M)

HIGHER EDUCATION ADMINISTRATION TRACK, DISTANCE LEARNING SPECIALIZATION

Dallas Baptist University (M)

HIGHER EDUCATION ADMINISTRATION TRACK, INTERDISCIPLINARY STUDIES

Dallas Baptist University (M)

HIGHER EDUCATION ADMINISTRATIVE SERVICES

McKendree University (M)

HIGHER EDUCATION LEADERSHIP

Saint Leo University (M)

HIGHER EDUCATION LEADERSHIP PROFESSIONAL FOCUS

Quinnipiac University (M)

HIGHER EDUCATION–SCHOOL ADMINISTRATION

Union University (D)

HISTOLOGY

Columbus State Community College (GC)

HISTORIC PRESERVATION

Boston Architectural College (M)
Goucher College (M)
Savannah College of Art and Design (GC,M)

HISTORICAL AND THEOLOGICAL STUDIES

Amridge University (M)

HISTORICAL STUDIES

State University of New York Empire State College (A,B)

HISTORY

Atlantic Cape Community College (A)
Brookdale Community College (A)
Butler Community College (A)
Caldwell College (B)
Columbia College (B)
Dickinson State University (B)
Drury University (A)
Judson College (B)
Labette Community College (A)
Mercy College (B)
National University (B)
Northeastern University (B)
North Hennepin Community College (A)
Pittsburg State University (M)
Prescott College (B)
Regent University (A,B)
Rose State College (A)
Southern New Hampshire University (B)
Southwestern Adventist University (B)
Thomas Edison State College (B)
University of Houston (B)
University of Houston–Victoria (B)
University of Illinois at Springfield (B)
University of Maryland University College (B)
University of Memphis (B,M)
Wayland Baptist University (M)
Western Kentucky University (M)

HISTORY (3 YEAR)

Athabasca University (B)

HISTORY (4 YEAR)

Athabasca University (B)

HISTORY AND POLITICAL STUDIES

Saint Mary-of-the-Woods College (B)

HISTORY EDUCATION

Valley City State University (B)

HISTOTECHNOLOGY

Harcum College (A)

HIT–MEDICAL CODING

North Dakota State College of Science (UC)

HOME INSPECTION

California State University, Dominguez Hills (GC)

HOMELAND SECURITY

Colorado Technical University Colorado Springs (M)
Eastern Kentucky University (B)
Erie Community College (UC)
Erie Community College, North Campus (UC)
Erie Community College, South Campus (UC)
Monmouth University (GC)
Ocean County College (A)
Penn State University Park (M)
University of Management and Technology (M)
University of Maryland University College (B)
Walden University (UC)

HOMELAND SECURITY AND DEFENSE

Penn State University Park (GC)

HOMELAND SECURITY AND EMERGENCY MANAGEMENT

Central Texas College (UC,A)
Kaplan University Online (M)

HOMELAND SECURITY AND EMERGENCY PREPAREDNESS

Thomas Edison State College (B)

HOMELAND SECURITY AND PUBLIC SAFETY

Herzing University Online (B)
Vincennes University (B)

HOMELAND SECURITY AND SAFETY ENGINEERING

National University (M)

HOMELAND SECURITY MANAGEMENT

Central Pennsylvania College (B)
Drexel University (GC)
University of Maryland University College (GC)

HOMELAND SECURITY MANGEMENT

Long Island University at Riverhead (M)

HOMELAND SECURITY POST-BACCALAUREATE CERTIFICATE

Thomas Edison State College (UC)

HOMELAND SECURITY POST-BACHELOR'S

Walden University (GC)

HORTICULTURAL SCIENCE

North Carolina State University (M)

HORTICULTURAL THERAPY

Kansas State University (GC)

HORTICULTURE

University of Illinois at Urbana–Champaign (GC)

HORTICULTURE SCIENCE

North Carolina State University (GC)

HORTICULTURE, GENERAL

Oregon State University (B)

HOSPITAL AND HEALTH SERVICES MANAGEMENT

Heritage College (A)

HOSPITAL CODING AND CCS PREP, ADVANCED

California State University, Dominguez Hills (GC)

HOSPITAL HEALTH CARE ADMINISTRATION

Thomas Edison State College (B)

HOSPITALITY ADMINISTRATION

Stephen F. Austin State University (UC)

HOSPITALITY AND TOURISM

California State University, East Bay (B)
Columbia Southern University (B)

HOSPITALITY AND TOURISM ADMINISTRATION

North Carolina Central University (B)

HOSPITALITY LEADERSHIP

J. Sargeant Reynolds Community College (UC)

HOSPITALITY MANAGEMENT

Chemeketa Community College (UC,A)
Drexel University (M)
Ellis University (B)
Lynn University (M)
Middlesex Community College (A)
Monroe College (A,B)
New York Institute of Technology (B)
Thomas Edison State College (B)

HOSPITALITY MANAGEMENT–FOOD AND BEVERAGE MANAGEMENT

Central Texas College (UC,A)

HOSPITALITY MANAGEMENT–HOTEL MANAGEMENT SPECIALIZATION

Central Texas College (A)

HOSPITALITY MANAGEMENT–PROPERTY MANAGEMENT ADVANCED

Central Texas College (UC)

HOSPITALITY MANAGEMENT–RESTAURANT AND CULINARY MANAGEMENT

Central Texas College (A)

HOSPITALITY MANAGEMENT–ROOMS DIVISION

Central Texas College (UC)

HOTEL AND RESTAURANT MANAGEMENT

Auburn University (M)
Tompkins Cortland Community College (A)

HOTEL AND RESTAURANT MANAGEMENT–HOSPITALITY OPTION AND FOOD SERVICE OPTION

Quinsigamond Community College (A)

HOTEL ROOMS DIVISION MANAGEMENT

J. Sargeant Reynolds Community College (UC)

HOTEL, RESTAURANT AND TOURISM MANAGEMENT

Excelsior College (B)

HOTEL, RESTAURANT, AND TOURISM MANAGEMENT

New Mexico State University (B)

HUMAN AND ORGANIZATIONAL DEVELOPMENT

Fielding Graduate University (D)

HUMAN BEHAVIOR

National University (M)

HUMAN CAPACITY IN ORGANIZATIONS

University of Denver (UC)

HUMAN CAPITAL DEVELOPMENT

University of Southern Mississippi (D)

HUMAN DEVELOPMENT

Amridge University (B)
California State University, East Bay (B)
Hope International University (B)
State University of New York Empire State College (A,B)
Washington State University (B)

HUMAN DEVELOPMENT AND FAMILY SCIENCE, CHILD DEVELOPMENT OPTION

North Dakota State University (B)

HUMAN DEVELOPMENT AND FAMILY SCIENCE, FAMILY FINANCIAL PLANNING OPTION

North Dakota State University (M)

HUMAN DEVELOPMENT AND FAMILY SCIENCE, FAMILY SCIENCE OPTION

North Dakota State University (B)

HUMAN DEVELOPMENT AND FAMILY SCIENCE, GERONTOLOGY OPTION

North Dakota State University (M)

HUMAN DEVELOPMENT AND FAMILY SCIENCE, YOUTH DEVELOPMENT OPTION

North Dakota State University (M)

HUMAN DEVELOPMENT AND FAMILY SCIENCES

Oregon State University (B)

HUMAN DEVELOPMENT AND FAMILY STUDIES

Colorado State University (B)
Penn State University Park (A)
University of Wisconsin–Stout (B)

HUMAN DYNAMICS

Western International University (M)

HUMAN MOVEMENT

A.T. Still University of Health Sciences (M)

HUMAN NUTRITION

University of Bridgeport (M)

HUMAN PERFORMANCE AND SPORT ACCELERATED MASTERS PROGRAM

New Mexico Highlands University (M)

HUMAN PERFORMANCE TECHNOLOGY

Boise State University (GC)
University of West Florida (M)

HUMAN RELATIONS AND BUSINESS

Amberton University (M)

HUMAN RESOURCE DEVELOPMENT

Buffalo State College, State University of New York (GC)
Clemson University (M)
Drexel University (M)
Indiana State University (GC,B,M)
Pittsburg State University (M)
Southwestern College (B)
University of Illinois at Urbana–Champaign (GC)

HUMAN RESOURCE EDUCATION

University of Louisville (M)

HUMAN RESOURCE EDUCATION, COMMUNITY COLLEGE TEACHING AND LEARNING CONCENTRATION

University of Illinois at Urbana–Champaign (M)

HUMAN RESOURCE EDUCATION, HEALTH PROFESSION EDUCATION EMPHASIS

University of Illinois at Urbana–Champaign (M)

HUMAN RESOURCE EDUCATION, HUMAN RESOURCE DEVELOPMENT CONCENTRATION

University of Illinois at Urbana–Champaign (M)

HUMAN RESOURCE LEADERSHIP

Amridge University (B)

HUMAN RESOURCE LEADERSHIP PROFESSIONAL FOCUS

Quinnipiac University (M)

HUMAN RESOURCE MANAGEMENT

Athabasca University (GC)
Boston University (M)
Champlain College (UC)
Columbia Southern University (B,M)
Concordia University, St. Paul (B,M)
Dallas Baptist University (GC,M)
DeVry University Online (M)
Dickinson State University (B)
Fort Hays State University (UC,GC)
Franklin Pierce University (GC,M)
Mercy College (M)
Peirce College (B)
Regent University (A)
Saint Mary-of-the-Woods College (B)
Southern New Hampshire University (UC,GC)
Stony Brook University, State University of New York (GC)
Tarleton State University (M)
Texas Woman's University (B)
University of Atlanta (B,M)
University of Calgary (UC)
University of Maine at Machias (UC)
University of Mary (M)
University of Maryland University College (B)
University of Wisconsin–Platteville (UC)
University of Wisconsin–Stout (UC)
Walden University (M)
Western International University (B)

HUMAN RESOURCE MANAGEMENT AND DEVELOPMENT

University of Denver (UC)

HUMAN RESOURCE MANAGEMENT AND ORGANIZATIONAL DEVELOPMENT

National University (M)

HUMAN RESOURCE MANAGEMENT CONCENTRATION

Andrew Jackson University (M)
Colorado Technical University Colorado Springs (B,M)

HUMAN RESOURCE MANAGEMENT OPTION

Clark State Community College (A)

HUMAN RESOURCE MANAGEMENT POST-BACCALAUREATE CERTIFICATE

Thomas Edison State College (UC)

HUMAN RESOURCE MANAGEMENT PRE-ASSOCIATE CERTIFICATE

Thomas Edison State College (UC)

HUMAN RESOURCE MANAGEMENT TECHNOLOGY

Carlow University (UC)

HUMAN RESOURCES

Indiana Wesleyan University (GC)
Kaplan University Online (UC)
Limestone College (B)
St. Joseph's College, Long Island Campus (UC)
St. Joseph's College, New York (UC)
The University of Scranton (M)
University of the Incarnate Word (B)
Western Carolina University (M)

HUMAN RESOURCES ADMINISTRATION

Saint Leo University (B)
Wake Technical Community College (UC)

HUMAN RESOURCES ADMINISTRATION CONCENTRATION

Saint Leo University (M)

HUMAN RESOURCES ADMINISTRATOR

Seminole State College of Florida (UC)

HUMAN RESOURCES AND EMPLOYMENT RELATIONS

Penn State University Park (M)

HUMAN RESOURCES AND LABOUR RELATIONS

Athabasca University (UC)

HUMAN RESOURCES AND LABOUR RELATIONS AND POST-DIPLOMA

Athabasca University (B)

HUMAN RESOURCES DEVELOPMENT

Webster University (M)

HUMAN RESOURCES MANAGEMENT

Brenau University (B)
Briar Cliff University (GC,B)
Florida Institute of Technology (M)
Lasell College (GC,M)
Northeastern University (GC,A)
Thomas Edison State College (M)
University of Management and Technology (UC,B)
Upper Iowa University (UC,B)
Wake Technical Community College (UC)
Webster University (M)

HUMAN RESOURCES MANAGEMENT/MARKETING (3 YEAR)

Athabasca University (B)

HUMAN RESOURCES MANAGEMENT/MARKETING (4 YEAR) AND POST-DIPLOMA

Athabasca University (B)

HUMAN RESOURCES MANAGEMENT/ ORGANIZATIONAL MANAGEMENT
Thomas Edison State College (B)

HUMAN RESOURCES PROFESSIONAL CERTIFICATE
Saint Paul College–A Community & Technical College (GC)

HUMAN RESOURCES SPECIALIST
Bryant & Stratton Online (A)

HUMAN SCIENCE
Athabasca University (B)

HUMAN SCIENCE–POST-DIPLOMA
Athabasca University (B)

HUMAN SCIENCES
Stephen F. Austin State University (M)

HUMAN SERVICES
Anderson University (B)
Athabasca University (B)
Burlington College (B)
Columbia College (A,B)
Franklin Pierce University (UC,A)
Herkimer County Community College (A)
Indiana Wesleyan University (UC)
Kaplan University Online (A,B)
LeTourneau University (B)
Liberty University (M)
Lincoln Christian University (B)
Northeastern University (B,M)
Quinsigamond Community College (A)
Saint Joseph's College of Maine (A,B)
Saint Mary-of-the-Woods College (B)
Stanly Community College (A)
Thomas Edison State College (B)
Upper Iowa University (B)
Walden University (D)

HUMAN SERVICES (HS)
Mount Wachusett Community College (A)

HUMAN SERVICES COUNSELING
Regent University (M)

HUMAN SERVICES TECHNOLOGY
Wayne Community College (A)

HUMAN SERVICES–ASSOCIATE OF ARTS IN HUMAN SERVICES (AAHS)
Thomas Edison State College (A)

HUMAN SERVICES–SOCIAL SERVICES ADMINISTRATION CONCENTRATION
University of Illinois at Springfield (M)

HUMAN SERVICES/SUBSTANCE ABUSE
Wayne Community College (A)

HUMAN-COMPUTER INTERACTION
DePaul University (M)

HUMANE LEADERSHIP
Duquesne University (B)

HUMANITIES
California State University, Dominguez Hills (M)
College of the Humanities and Sciences, Harrison Middleton University (A,B)
Prescott College (B,M)
Saint Mary-of-the-Woods College (A,B)
Salve Regina University (M)
Santa Rosa Junior College (A)
Thomas Edison State College (B)
University of Maryland University College (B)
The University of Texas of the Permian Basin (B)
Washington State University (B)

HUMANITIES (3 YEAR)
Athabasca University (B)

HUMANITIES (4 YEAR)
Athabasca University (B)

HUNTING AND SHOOTING SPORTS MANAGEMENT
Montgomery Community College (A)

HVACR ENGINEERING TECHNOLOGY
Ferris State University (B)

HYBRID VEHICLE ENGINEERING EMPHASIS, PROFESSIONAL MASTERS PROGRAM
Michigan Technological University (M)

ICL–INSTRUCTION AND CURRICULUM LEADERSHIP, READING CONCENTRATION
University of Memphis (M)

ICL–INSTRUCTION AND CURRICULUM LEADERSHIP, SCHOOL LIBRARY SPECIALIST
University of Memphis (M)

ICL–INSTRUCTION AND CURRICULUM LEADERSHIP, SECONDARY
University of Memphis (M)

IIT NETWORKING AND TELECOMMUNICATIONS
University of West Florida (B)

ILLUSTRATION
Academy of Art University (A,B,M)
Savannah College of Art and Design (M)

ILLUSTRATION DESIGN
Savannah College of Art and Design (M)

IMAGINATIVE LITERATURE
College of the Humanities and Sciences, Harrison Middleton University (M)

IMAGING INFORMATICS
Clarkson College (UC)

IMAGING SCIENCE
Rochester Institute of Technology (M)

IMAGING SCIENCE PRE-ASSOCIATE CERTIFICATE
Thomas Edison State College (UC)

IMAGING SCIENCES, ADVANCED (WITH UMDNJ)
Thomas Edison State College (B)

IMBA
Penn State University Park (M)
Syracuse University (M)

IMS ACCOUNTING
Syracuse University (M)

IMS IN SUPPLY CHAIN MANAGEMENT
Syracuse University (M)

INCLUSIVE EDUCATION
Athabasca University (UC)
Seton Hill University (M)

INCOME TAX PREPARER
Wake Technical Community College (UC)

INDIGENOUS NATIONS AND ORGANIZATIONS
Athabasca University (B)

INDIVIDUAL STUDIES
Jamestown Community College (GC,A)
Jefferson Community College (A)

INDIVIDUALIZED DEGREE PROGRAM
Regent University (M)

INDIVIDUALIZED FOCUS AREA

DePaul University (B)

INDIVIDUALIZED LIBERAL AND PROFESSIONAL STUDIES (VARIOUS SELF-DESIGNED TOPICS)

Antioch University Midwest (M)

INDIVIDUALIZED STUDIES

Genesee Community College (A)
Goddard College (B,M)
Granite State College (B)
Ohio University (A)

INDIVIDUALLY DESIGNED

Lesley University (M)

INDIVIDUALLY DESIGNED MAJOR

University of Wisconsin–Superior (B)

INDUSTRIAL AND SYSTEMS ENGINEERING

Auburn University (M)
Georgia Institute of Technology (M)
University of Florida (M)
University of Michigan–Dearborn (M)
University of Southern California (M)

INDUSTRIAL DESIGN

Academy of Art University (A,B,M)

INDUSTRIAL ELECTRONICS WITH PLC TECHNOLOGY

Cleveland Institute of Electronics (UC)

INDUSTRIAL ENGINEERING

Clemson University (M)
Columbia University (UC,M)
Mississippi State University (M)
New Mexico State University (M)
North Carolina State University (M)
Purdue University (M)
The University of Alabama in Huntsville (M,D)
University of Central Florida (M)
The University of Texas at Arlington (M)

INDUSTRIAL ENGINEERING AND OPERATIONS RESEARCH

Colorado State University (M)

INDUSTRIAL ENGINEERING TECHNOLOGY

James A. Rhodes State College (A)
Wake Technical Community College (A)

INDUSTRIAL ENGINEERING TECHNOLOGY, ADVANCED QUALITY

Wake Technical Community College (UC)

INDUSTRIAL ENGINEERING TECHNOLOGY, INDUSTRIAL MANAGEMENT

Wake Technical Community College (UC)

INDUSTRIAL ENGINEERING TECHNOLOGY, MANUFACTURING PROCESS CONTROL

Wake Technical Community College (UC)

INDUSTRIAL ENGINEERING TECHNOLOGY, QUALITY ASSURANCE

Wake Technical Community College (UC)

INDUSTRIAL ENGINEERING/ ENGINEERING MANAGEMENT

The University of Tennessee Space Institute (M,D)

INDUSTRIAL ERGONOMICS AND SAFETY

University of Central Florida (GC)

INDUSTRIAL HYGIENE

New York Medical College (GC)

INDUSTRIAL MANAGEMENT TECHNOLOGY

Pitt Community College (A)

INDUSTRIAL TECHNOLOGY

Roger Williams University (B)
Southeast Missouri State University (B)
The University of Texas of the Permian Basin (B)

INDUSTRIAL TECHNOLOGY AND OPERATIONS

Illinois Institute of Technology (M)

INDUSTRIAL-ORGANIZATIONAL PSYCHOLOGY

Austin Peay State University (M)

INFANT MENTAL HEALTH

Chatham University (GC)

INFANT/TODDLER CARE

Wake Technical Community College (UC)

INFORMATICS

Northeastern University (M)
University of Maryland University College (GC)
University of Minnesota, Twin Cities Campus (D)
Western International University (B)

INFORMATION AND COMMUNICATION TECHNOLOGIES

University of Wisconsin–Stout (B)

INFORMATION AND COMMUNICATION TECHNOLOGY

New Mexico State University (B)

INFORMATION ASSURANCE

Brandeis University (M)
The Johns Hopkins University (M)
Northeastern University (M)
University of Maryland University College (GC)

INFORMATION ASSURANCE AND COMPUTER SECURITY

Dakota State University (M)

INFORMATION ASSURANCE CERTIFICATE OF RECOGNITION

Indiana University of Pennsylvania (UC)

INFORMATION COMMUNICATION TECHNOLOGIES

University of Wisconsin–Stout (M)

INFORMATION DESIGN AND TECHNOLOGY

State University of New York Institute of Technology (M)

INFORMATION ENGINEERING AND MANAGEMENT

Southern Methodist University (M)

INFORMATION ENGINEERING TECHNOLOGY

University of West Florida (B)

INFORMATION MANAGEMENT

Grantham University (M)
Syracuse University (M)

INFORMATION MANAGEMENT TECHNOLOGY

Grantham University (M)

INFORMATION MANAGEMENT-PROJECT MANAGEMENT

Grantham University (M)

INFORMATION NETWORKING AND TELECOMMUNICATIONS (COMPUTER NETWORKING AND TELECOMMUNICATIONS CONCENTRATION)

Fort Hays State University (B)

INFORMATION NETWORKING AND TELECOMMUNICATIONS (WEB DEVELOPMENT CONCENTRATION)

Fort Hays State University (B)

INFORMATION REPORTING

St. Louis Community College (A)

INFORMATION RESOURCE STUDIES

Emporia State University (B)

INFORMATION SCIENCE

North Carolina Central University (M)

INFORMATION SCIENCE AND TECHNOLOGY

Missouri University of Science and Technology (M)
Penn State University Park (UC)

INFORMATION SCIENCES

Penn State University Park (M)
Tarleton State University (M)

INFORMATION SCIENCES AND TECHNOLOGY

Penn State University Park (A,B)

INFORMATION SECURITY

Boston University (GC)
Champlain College (UC)
Georgia Institute of Technology (M)
James Madison University (M)
Kaplan University Online (UC)
Lewis University (M)
University of Denver (UC)
University of Maine at Fort Kent (A)

INFORMATION SECURITY AND PRIVACY

The University of North Carolina at Charlotte (GC)

INFORMATION SECURITY, MANAGEMENT

Saint Leo University (GC)
Syracuse University (GC)

INFORMATION SECURITY MANAGEMENT CONCENTRATION

Saint Leo University (M)

INFORMATION SECURITY MANAGEMENT SPECIALIST

Central Texas College (UC)

INFORMATION SERVICES AND SUPPORT

The University of Toledo (A)

INFORMATION SERVICES TECHNOLOGY

College of Southern Maryland (UC,A)

INFORMATION SERVICES TECHNOLOGY–WEB DEVELOPER

College of Southern Maryland (A)

INFORMATION STUDIES

Florida State University (M)
Syracuse University (D)

INFORMATION STUDIES AND TECHNOLOGY

Drexel University (GC)

INFORMATION SYSTEMS

Athabasca University (M)
Baker College Online (M)
City University of Seattle (GC)
Columbia University (UC)
Dakota State University (M,D)
DePaul University (M)
Drexel University (M)
Grantham University (B)
Illinois Institute of Technology (GC)
Marist College (M)
Minot State University (M)
Mississippi State University (M)
National University (B,M)
Piedmont Community College (UC,A)
Randolph Community College (A)
Regent University (A)
University of Illinois at Urbana–Champaign (GC)
University of South Alabama (B)
University of the Incarnate Word (A)

INFORMATION SYSTEMS (3 YEAR)

Athabasca University (B)

INFORMATION SYSTEMS (4 YEAR)

Athabasca University (B)

INFORMATION SYSTEMS AND OPERATIONS MANAGEMENT

University of Florida (M)

INFORMATION SYSTEMS AND TECHNOLOGY

Dallas Baptist University (UC,GC)
University of Michigan–Dearborn (M)

INFORMATION SYSTEMS AND TELECOMMUNICATIONS MANAGEMENT

Syracuse University (GC)

INFORMATION SYSTEMS ENGINEERING

The Johns Hopkins University (M)
Western International University (M)

INFORMATION SYSTEMS MANAGEMENT

DeVry University Online (M)
Hodges University (B,M)
University of Maryland University College (B)
Walden University (M)

INFORMATION SYSTEMS SECURITY

Grantham University (B)
Stanly Community College (A)
University of Denver (UC)
Wayne Community College (A)

INFORMATION SYSTEMS SECURITY CONCENTRATION

Colorado Technical University Colorado Springs (M)

INFORMATION SYSTEMS TECHNOLOGY

Pitt Community College (UC)
Regent University (B)
Southern Illinois University Carbondale (B)
Union County College (A)

INFORMATION TECHNOLOGY

Boston University (GC)
Central Michigan University (B)
Central Pennsylvania College (B)
Cleary University (A)
Colorado Technical University Colorado Springs (B)
Columbia Southern University (B)
Columbus State University (B)
DePaul University (M)
Excelsior College (B)
Florida Tech University Online (M)
Grantham University (M)
Jamestown Community College (GC,A)
Kaplan University Online (B,M)
Lawrence Technological University (B)
Macon State College (B)
Memorial University of Newfoundland (M)
Minnesota School of Business–Online (A,B)
Minnesota School of Business–Richfield (A,B)
Monroe College (A,B)
Mountain State University (A,B)
New England Institute of Technology (A)
Northeastern University (B)
Peirce College (A)
Thomas Edison State College (B)
University of Management and Technology (UC,GC,A,B)
University of Maryland University College (M)
University of Massachusetts Lowell (UC,A,B)
The University of Toledo (B)

Vincennes University (A)
Walden University (B)

INFORMATION TECHNOLOGY ADMINISTRATION AND MANAGEMENT

Herzing University Online (A,B)

INFORMATION TECHNOLOGY AND ADMINISTRATIVE MANAGEMENT

Central Washington University (B)

INFORMATION TECHNOLOGY AND INFORMATION SERVICES LIBRARY PARAPROFESSIONAL

Belmont Technical College (A)

INFORMATION TECHNOLOGY AND MANAGEMENT

Illinois Institute of Technology (M)

INFORMATION TECHNOLOGY CONCENTRATION

Colorado Technical University Colorado Springs (B)

INFORMATION TECHNOLOGY COORDINATOR

New Mexico State University (UC)

INFORMATION TECHNOLOGY FOR MANAGEMENT

University of Atlanta (GC)

INFORMATION TECHNOLOGY FOR PUBLIC SERVICE

Thomas Edison State College (M)

INFORMATION TECHNOLOGY LEADERSHIP

The College of St. Scholastica (UC,M)

INFORMATION TECHNOLOGY LEADERSHIP PROFESSIONAL FOCUS

Quinnipiac University (M)

INFORMATION TECHNOLOGY MANAGEMENT

Brandeis University (M)
Concordia University, St. Paul (B)
Franklin Pierce University (M)
Mount Saint Vincent University (UC)
National University (B)
University of Management and Technology (B)
University of Minnesota, Crookston (B)
The University of Texas at Dallas (M)
Webster University (M)
Worcester Polytechnic Institute (M)

INFORMATION TECHNOLOGY MANAGEMENT CONCENTRATION

Colorado Technical University Colorado Springs (M)

INFORMATION TECHNOLOGY ONLINE

Oregon Institute of Technology (B)

INFORMATION TECHNOLOGY PATHWAY

Kaplan University Online (UC)

INFORMATION TECHNOLOGY PROJECT MANAGEMENT

Boston University (GC)

INFORMATION TECHNOLOGY SUPPORT–MS OFFICE SPECIALIST

Broward College (UC)

INFORMATION TECHNOLOGY–.NET PROGRAMMING CONCENTRATION

Peirce College (UC)

INFORMATION TECHNOLOGY–APPLICATIONS DEVELOPER

Moraine Park Technical College (A)

INFORMATION TECHNOLOGY–DATA MANAGEMENT SPECIALIZATION

Colorado Technical University Colorado Springs (B)

INFORMATION TECHNOLOGY–DESKTOP APPLICATIONS FOR BUSINESS CONCENTRATION

Peirce College (B)

INFORMATION TECHNOLOGY–HELP DESK TECHNICIAN CONCENTRATION

Peirce College (UC)

INFORMATION TECHNOLOGY–INFORMATION SECURITY CONCENTRATION

Peirce College (B)

INFORMATION TECHNOLOGY–IT MANAGEMENT

University of Management and Technology (M)

INFORMATION TECHNOLOGY–IT PROJECT MANAGEMENT

University of Management and Technology (M)

INFORMATION TECHNOLOGY–MANAGEMENT INFORMATION SYSTEMS

University of Management and Technology (M)

INFORMATION TECHNOLOGY–NETWORKING, ADMINISTRATION, AND SECURITY CONCENTRATION

Peirce College (B)

INFORMATION TECHNOLOGY–PROGRAMMING AND APPLICATION DEVELOPMENT CONCENTRATION

Peirce College (B)

INFORMATION TECHNOLOGY–SOFTWARE APPLICATION PROGRAMMING SPECIALIZATION

Colorado Technical University Colorado Springs (B)

INFORMATION TECHNOLOGY–TECHNOLOGY MANAGEMENT CONCENTRATION

Peirce College (B)

INFORMATION TECHNOLOGY–WEB ANALYST

Wisconsin Indianhead Technical College (A)

INFORMATION TECHNOLOGY–WEB DESIGNER/DEVELOPER

Moraine Park Technical College (UC)

INFORMATION TECHNOLOGY–WEB DEVELOPMENT SPECIALIZATION

Colorado Technical University Colorado Springs (B)

INFORMATION TECHNOLOGY, ADVANCED

Boston University (GC)

INFORMATION TECHNOLOGY, BUSINESS MINOR

University of Massachusetts Lowell (B)

INFORMATION TECHNOLOGY, NETWORK MANAGEMENT SPECIALIZATION

Colorado Technical University Colorado Springs (B)

INFORMATION TECHNOLOGY, SECURITY SPECIALIZATION

Colorado Technical University Colorado Springs (B)

INFORMATION TECHNOLOGY, SOFTWARE SYSTEMS ENGINEERING SPECIALIZATION

Colorado Technical University Colorado Springs (B)

INITIAL TEACHER PROFESSIONAL PREPARATION

University of Central Florida (GC)

INNOVATION AND INTRA/ ENTREPRENEURSHIP IN ADVANCED NURSING PRACTICE

Drexel University (GC)

INNOVATIVE LEADERSHIP

Western International University (M)

INSTITUTIONAL RESEARCH

Penn State University Park (GC)

INSTRUCTION COMPUTER TECHNOLOGY CERTIFICATE ENDORSEMENT FOR KENTUCKY TEACHERS

Murray State University (UC)

INSTRUCTIONAL AND PERFORMANCE TECHNOLOGY

Boise State University (M)

INSTRUCTIONAL ASSISTANT

Moraine Park Technical College (A)

INSTRUCTIONAL DESIGN

Athabasca University (GC)
Saint Leo University (GC,M)
University of Massachusetts Boston (M)
University of Wisconsin–Stout (GC)
Western Kentucky University (GC,M)

INSTRUCTIONAL DESIGN AND DEVELOPMENT

University of South Alabama (M)

INSTRUCTIONAL DESIGN AND TECHNOLOGY

Emporia State University (M)
University of North Dakota (GC,M)
Walden University (B,M)
West Virginia University (M)

INSTRUCTIONAL DESIGN AND TECHNOLOGY (IDT)

University of Memphis (GC,M)

INSTRUCTIONAL DESIGN FOR SIMULATIONS

University of Central Florida (GC)

INSTRUCTIONAL DESIGN POST-BACHELOR'S CERTIFICATE

Walden University (UC)

INSTRUCTIONAL LEADERSHIP

Crown College (M)
Jacksonville State University (M)
Robert Morris University (M)
The University of West Alabama (M)

INSTRUCTIONAL LEADERSHIP CONCENTRATION

Saint Leo University (M)

INSTRUCTIONAL MATH

Drury University (M)

INSTRUCTIONAL SYSTEMS

Florida State University (M)

INSTRUCTIONAL SYSTEMS TECHNOLOGY

The University of North Carolina at Charlotte (GC,M)

INSTRUCTIONAL SYSTEMS–EDUCATIONAL TECHNOLOGY

Penn State University Park (M)

INSTRUCTIONAL SYSTEMS, OPEN AND DISTANCE LEARNING MAJOR

Florida State University (M)

INSTRUCTIONAL SYSTEMS, PERFORMANCE IMPROVEMENT AND HUMAN RESOURCE DEVELOPMENT MAJOR

Florida State University (M)

INSTRUCTIONAL TECHNOLOGY

Boston University (GC)
Cardinal Stritch University (M)
Drury University (M)
Ellis University (M)
Fort Hays State University (M)
Georgia State University (M)
Kaplan University Online (M)
New York Institute of Technology (M)
North Carolina State University (M)
San Diego State University (UC)
University of Colorado at Colorado Springs (GC)
University of Maryland University College (M)
University of Nebraska at Kearney (M)
University of Southern Mississippi (M)
University of West Florida (M)
Wayne State University (M)
West Texas A&M University (M)

INSTRUCTIONAL TECHNOLOGY AND DESIGN

University of Southern Mississippi (D)

INSTRUCTIONAL TECHNOLOGY AND LEARNING SCIENCES

Utah State University (M)

INSTRUCTIONAL TECHNOLOGY AND LEARNING SCIENCES–EDUCATIONAL TECHNOLOGY SPECIALIZATION

Utah State University (M)

INSTRUCTIONAL TECHNOLOGY COORDINATOR

University of Wisconsin–Stout (UC)

INSTRUCTIONAL TECHNOLOGY DESIGN

University of Massachusetts Boston (GC)

INSTRUCTIONAL TECHNOLOGY EDUCATION SPECIALIST

Bloomsburg University of Pennsylvania (M)

INSTRUCTIONAL TECHNOLOGY PROFICIENCY

Framingham State University (GC)

INSTRUCTIONAL TECHNOLOGY SPECIALIST

Clarion University of Pennsylvania (UC)
Drexel University (UC)

INSTRUCTIONAL TECHNOLOGY/ MEDIA

University of Central Florida (M)

INSTRUCTIONAL TECHOLOGY

University of Northern Iowa (M)

INSTRUCTIONAL/EDUCATIONAL TECHNOLOGY

University of Central Florida (GC)

INSURANCE AND RISK MANAGEMENT
Indiana State University (B)

INSURANCE BILLING AND CODING SPECIALIST
Herzing University Online (UC,A)

INSURANCE LEADERSHIP PROFESSIONAL FOCUS
Quinnipiac University (M)

INSURANCE MANAGEMENT
Brenau University (M)

INSURANCE MANAGEMENT–MASTER OF SCIENCE IN INSURANCE MANAGEMENT
Boston University (M)

INTEGRAL PSYCHOLOGY
Burlington College (B)

INTEGRAL STUDIES
Fielding Graduate University (UC)

INTEGRATED DIRECT MARKETING
University of Maryland University College (GC)

INTEGRATED FACILITY AND PROPERTY MANAGEMENT
Georgia Institute of Technology (M)

INTEGRATED LEADERSHIP STUDIES MAJOR
Central Michigan University (B)

INTEGRATED MARKETING COMMUNICATION
Lasell College (GC,M)

INTEGRATED MARKETING COMMUNICATIONS
Southern New Hampshire University (GC)
West Virginia University (UC,M)

INTEGRATED RESOURCE MANAGEMENT (IRM)
Colorado State University (M)

INTEGRATED STUDIES
Athabasca University (M)
Champlain College (B)
Emporia State University (B)
Franklin Pierce University (B)
Murray State University (B)

INTEGRATED STUDIES–ASSOCIATE IN INTEGRATED STUDIES (DTA)
Cascadia Community College (A)

INTEGRATIVE HEALTH AND HEALING
University of Minnesota, Twin Cities Campus (D)

INTEGRATIVE LEARNING
Endicott College (M)

INTEGRATIVE STUDIES
Northern Kentucky University (M)
Oakland University (B)
Winston-Salem State University (B)

INTEGRATIVE SUPPLY CHAIN MANAGEMENT
University of Maryland University College (GC)

INTELLIGENT SYSTEMS
Columbia University (UC)

INTER-AMERICAN STUDIES
Burlington College (B)

INTERACTIVE COMMUNICATIONS
Quinnipiac University (M)

INTERACTIVE DESIGN
Savannah College of Art and Design (GC)

INTERACTIVE DESIGN AND GAME DEVELOPMENT
Savannah College of Art and Design (B,M)

INTERACTIVE MEDIA
Columbus State Community College (A)

INTERACTIVE MEDIA DESIGN
Santa Rosa Junior College (A)

INTERACTIVE MEDIA DESIGN ONLINE
Bryant & Stratton Online (A)

INTERCULTURAL STUDIES
Global University (B)
Hope International University (B)
Liberty University (M)

INTERCULTURAL STUDIES SECOND BA DEGREE
Global University (B)

INTERCULTURAL STUDIES THREE-YEAR BA DEGREE
Global University (B)

INTERDISCIPLINARY
The University of Tennessee at Martin (M)

INTERDISCIPLINARY ARTS
Goddard College (M)

INTERDISCIPLINARY EARLY CHILDHOOD EDUCATION
Western Kentucky University (A)

INTERDISCIPLINARY HUMANITIES
Lansing Community College (A)

INTERDISCIPLINARY SCIENCES
Mississippi State University (M)

INTERDISCIPLINARY SOCIAL SCIENCE
Florida State University (B)
Kansas State University (B)

INTERDISCIPLINARY STUDIES
Adams State College (B)
Central Texas College (A)
Eastern Wyoming College (A)
Ellis University (B)
Governors State University (B)
Hodges University (A,B)
Kaplan University Online (A)
LeTourneau University (A)
Lewis-Clark State College (B)
Liberty University (B)
Marylhurst University (B)
Mississippi State University (B)
New York Institute of Technology (B)
Regent University (B)
Southeast Missouri State University (B)
State University of New York Empire State College (A,B)
Union Institute & University (D)
University of Central Florida (B)
University of Houston–Downtown (B)
The University of Texas at Brownsville (B)
Walden University (B)

INTERDISCIPLINARY STUDIES EC-6, 4-8
Stephen F. Austin State University (B)

INTERDISCIPLINARY STUDIES IN CURRICULUM AND INSTRUCTION
National-Louis University (M)

INTERDISCIPLINARY STUDIES PROGRAM
The University of Toledo (B)

INTERDISCIPLINARY STUDIES–8 CONCENTRATIONS

Dallas Baptist University (B)

INTERDISCIPLINARY TECHNICAL STUDIES

The University of Toledo (A)

INTERDISCIPLINARY TRACK

Dallas Baptist University (M)

INTERDISPLINARY STUDIES

University of South Alabama (B)

INTERIOR ARCHITECTURE AND DESIGN

Academy of Art University (A,B,M)

INTERIOR DESIGN

Savannah College of Art and Design (M)

INTERIOR DESIGN FOR HIGH SCHOOL TEACHERS

Colorado State University (UC)

INTERIOR DESIGN OPTION

Ball State University (M)

INTERNATIONAL

University of the Incarnate Word (M)

INTERNATIONAL AFFAIRS

North Georgia College & State University (M)

INTERNATIONAL AND COMPARATIVE CRIMINAL JUSTICE

Kaplan University Online (B)

INTERNATIONAL BACCALAUREATE CERTIFICATE

Oakland University (GC)

INTERNATIONAL BUSINESS

Caldwell College (B)
Dallas Baptist University (M)
Dickinson State University (B)
Lansing Community College (A)
Lynn University (M)
Minot State University (B)
Pacific States University (M)
Regent University (A)
St. Petersburg College (B)
Seminole State College of Florida (UC)
Southern New Hampshire University (GC,B)
Thomas Edison State College (B)
University of Colorado at Colorado Springs (M)
University of Wisconsin–Platteville (UC)
Western International University (M)

INTERNATIONAL BUSINESS ACCELERATED BBS/MBA

Dallas Baptist University (M)

INTERNATIONAL BUSINESS CONCENTRATION

Colorado Technical University Colorado Springs (B)

INTERNATIONAL BUSINESS ENGLISH CERTIFICATE

University of Colorado at Colorado Springs (GC)

INTERNATIONAL COMMERCE CERTIFICATE

Columbus State Community College (GC)

INTERNATIONAL CONSTRUCTION MANAGEMENT

University of Florida (M)

INTERNATIONAL DEVELOPMENT

Hope International University (M)
University of Southern Mississippi (D)

INTERNATIONAL EDUCATOR'S CERTIFICATE

Crown College (GC)

INTERNATIONAL HOSPITALITY AND TOURISM MANAGEMENT

Saint Leo University (B)

INTERNATIONAL LEADERSHIP STUDIES

Crown College (M)

INTERNATIONAL LOGISTICS AND TRANSPORTATION MANAGEMENT

Rochester Institute of Technology (UC)

INTERNATIONAL MANAGEMENT

Columbia Southern University (B)
University of Management and Technology (B)
University of Maryland University College (M)

INTERNATIONAL MARKETING

University of Maryland University College (GC)

INTERNATIONAL MARKETING MANAGEMENT

Boston University (GC,M)

INTERNATIONAL PRESERVATION

Savannah College of Art and Design (M)

INTERNATIONAL RELATIONS

St. Mary's University (M)
Salve Regina University (M)
Webster University (M)

INTERNATIONAL RELATIONS AND DIPLOMACY

Burlington College (B)

INTERNATIONAL SCIENTIFIC AND TECHNICAL COMMUNICATION

Bowling Green State University (GC)

INTERNATIONAL SPORT DIPLOMA

United States Sports Academy (UC)

INTERNATIONAL STUDENT SERVICES

Western Kentucky University (UC)

INTERNATIONAL STUDIES

Fort Hays State University (UC)
Montgomery County Community College (UC)

INTERNATIONAL TRADE

University of Maryland University College (GC)

INTERNET AND WEBSITE DEVELOPMENT

Kaplan University Online (UC)

INTERNET MARKETING

Champlain College (UC)
Florida Tech University Online (M)

INTERNET TECHNOLOGIES

Pace University (GC)

INTERNET TECHNOLOGY FOR E-COMMERCE

Pace University (M)

INTERNETWORKING

Fort Hays State University (UC)

INTERPERSONAL RELATIONS

Grace College (M)

INTERPROFESSIONAL HEALTHCARE STUDIES

Rosalind Franklin University of Medicine and Science (D)

INTRODUCTION TO COMPUTER PROGRAMMING LANGUAGE
Kaplan University Online (UC)

INTRODUCTION TO COMPUTERS AND MICROSOFT OFFICE
Cleveland Institute of Electronics (UC)

INTRODUCTION TO HOME AUTOMATION INSTALLATION
Cleveland Institute of Electronics (UC)

INTRODUCTORY C++ PROGRAMMING
Bellevue College (UC)

INVESTIGATIVE FORENSICS
University of Maryland University College (B)

IT CONCENTRATION
Kettering University (M)

IT FOUNDATIONS
Wake Technical Community College (UC)

IT PROJECT MANAGEMENT
DePaul University (M)

IT SUPPORT MANAGEMENT
Wake Technical Community College (UC)

IT-NETWORKING
Bryant & Stratton Online (A)

IT-SECURITY
Bryant & Stratton Online (A)

JAVA DEVELOPMENT
Champlain College (UC)

JAVA PROGRAMMING
Wake Technical Community College (UC)

JEWISH EDUCATION–MASTER OF SCIENCE IN JEWISH EDUCATION (MSJE)
Spertus Institute of Jewish Studies (M)

JEWISH STUDIES
Spertus Institute of Jewish Studies (M,D)
West Los Angeles College (UC)

JOURNALISM
Regent University (M)
Saint Mary-of-the-Woods College (B)
Thomas Edison State College (B)
University of Memphis (M)
University of Michigan–Flint (B)

JOURNALISM (PUBLIC RELATIONS CONCENTRATION)
University of Memphis (B)

JOURNALISM, BROADCASTING, AND MASS COMMUNICATION TECHNOLOGIES
North Dakota State University (B)

JURISPRUDENCE
College of the Humanities and Sciences, Harrison Middleton University (M)

JUSTICE ADMINISTRATION
DeVry University Online (B)
Faulkner University (M)

JUSTICE ADMINISTRATION–PUBLIC POLICY CONCENTRATION
Taylor University (A)

JUSTICE ADMINISTRATION, MINISTRY CONCENTRATION
Taylor University (A)

JUSTICE AND MINISTRY
Taylor University (UC)

JUSTICE NETWORKING
Fort Hays State University (UC)

JUSTICE STUDIES
Fort Hays State University (B)
Southern New Hampshire University (B,M)
University of Maine at Augusta (A,B)

JUVENILE JUSTICE
Prairie View A&M University (M)

K-12 EDUCATION LEADERSHIP
Jones International University (M,D)

KINESIOLOGY
The University of Texas of the Permian Basin (M)

KINESIOLOGY (ALL AREA COACHING)
Texas Woman's University (M)

KINESIOLOGY (SOFTBALL COACHING)
Texas Woman's University (M)

KINESIOLOGY (SPORT MANAGEMENT)
Texas Woman's University (M)

KINESIOLOGY–COACHING
Southern Arkansas University–Magnolia (M)

KITCHEN AND BATH DESIGN
Thomas Edison State College (A,B)

KNOWLEDGE BASED ORGANIZATIONS
University of Denver (UC)

KNOWLEDGE MANAGEMENT
Minot State University (GC)

LABOR STUDIES
State University of New York Empire State College (A,B)
Thomas Edison State College (B)

LABOR STUDIES AND EMPLOYMENT RELATIONS
Penn State University Park (UC)

LABOR STUDIES PRE-ASSOCIATE CERTIFICATE
Thomas Edison State College (UC)

LABORATORY AND BIOLOGICAL SAFETY
University of Massachusetts Lowell (GC)

LABORATORY ANIMAL SCIENCE
Thomas Edison State College (A,B)

LABORATORY QUALITY MANAGEMENT
University of Wisconsin–Madison (UC)

LABOUR STUDIES
Athabasca University (UC)

LABOUR STUDIES (3 YEAR)
Athabasca University (B)

LABOUR STUDIES (4 YEAR)
Athabasca University (B)

LAND USE PLANNING
Prescott College (M)

LANDSCAPE PEST MANAGEMENT
University of Florida (UC,GC)

LATIN
University of Florida (M)

LATIN AND ROMAN STUDIES
University of Florida (D)

LAW
Champlain College (M)

LAW AND SOCIETY
Penn State University Park (B)

LAW AND THE COURTS
Fort Hays State University (UC)

LAW ENFORCEMENT
Dawson Community College (A)
Eastern Kentucky University (B)
Fort Hays State University (UC)
Indiana State University (UC)

LAW ENFORCEMENT LEADERSHIP
State University of New York College of Technology at Canton (B)

LAW ENFORCEMENT OPTION
San Jacinto College District (UC)

LAW ENFORCEMENT STUDIES
Vincennes University (A)

LAY MINISTRY
Concordia University Wisconsin (A)

LEADERSHIP
The American College (M)
City University of Seattle (M)
Fort Hays State University (UC,M)
Franklin Pierce University (M)
Kettering University (M)
Northeastern University (GC,B,M)
Regent University (GC)
Roger Williams University (M)
Southwestern College (M)
Trine University (M)
University of Colorado at Colorado Springs (M)
University of Memphis (GC,M)
University of West Florida (M)
Walden University (M)
Western Kentucky University (GC)

LEADERSHIP AND BUSINESS ETHICS
Duquesne University (M)

LEADERSHIP AND ETHICAL DECISION MAKING
University of Colorado Boulder (GC)

LEADERSHIP AND HUMAN PERFORMANCE
University of Wisconsin–Platteville (UC)

LEADERSHIP AND INFORMATION TECHNOLOGY–MASTERS OF LEADERSHIP AND INFORMATION TECHNOLOGY
Duquesne University (M)

LEADERSHIP AND LIBERAL STUDIES
Duquesne University (M)

LEADERSHIP AND MANAGEMENT
Amridge University (M)
Concordia University, St. Paul (M)
Lincoln Christian University (B)
University of Maryland University College (GC)

LEADERSHIP AND MINISTRY
Williamson Christian College (B)

LEADERSHIP AND ORGANIZATIONAL STUDIES
University of Southern Maine (B)

LEADERSHIP AND ORGANIZATIONS
University of Denver (M)

LEADERSHIP AND SPIRITUAL FORMATION
George Fox University (D)

LEADERSHIP AND SUPERVISION
St. Joseph's College, Long Island Campus (UC)
St. Joseph's College, New York (UC)

LEADERSHIP DEVELOPMENT
Moraine Park Technical College (A)
Saint Mary-of-the-Woods College (M)
Taylor University (UC)

LEADERSHIP EDUCATION AND PRINCIPAL LICENSURE
University of Colorado at Colorado Springs (M)

LEADERSHIP EMPHASIS
Upper Iowa University (M)

LEADERSHIP IN CHARACTER EDUCATION
Regent University (M)

LEADERSHIP IN EMERGING CULTURE–GLOBAL MISSIONAL LEADERSHIP
George Fox University (D)

LEADERSHIP IN EMERGING CULTURE–SEMIOTICS AND FUTURE STUDIES
George Fox University (D)

LEADERSHIP IN MATHEMATICS EDUCATION
Regent University (M)

LEADERSHIP IN MINISTRY
Baptist Bible College of Pennsylvania (D)

LEADERSHIP IN THE PUBLIC SECTOR
North Carolina State University (B)

LEADERSHIP OF DIGITAL LEARNING
Abilene Christian University (UC)

LEADERSHIP OF LEARNING
Abilene Christian University (M)

LEADERSHIP OF LEARNING DIGITAL LEARNING
Abilene Christian University (M)

LEADERSHIP SKILLS DEVELOPMENT
Columbus State Community College (GC)

LEADERSHIP STUDIES
University of Southern Maine (UC,M)

LEADERSHIP, GLOBAL LEADSHIP CONCENTRATION
Duquesne University (M)

LEARNING AND INSTRUCTION
Northeastern University (M)

LEARNING DESIGN AND TECHNOLOGY
Purdue University (M)

LEARNING SYSTEMS TECHNOLOGY
University of Arkansas at Little Rock (M)

LEARNING TECHNOLOGIES
Drexel University (M)

LEARNING TECHNOLOGIES EMPHASIS

New Mexico State University (M)

LEEP–LIBRARY AND INFORMATION SCIENCE

University of Illinois at Urbana–Champaign (M)

LEGAL ADMINISTRATIVE ASSISTANT

Spokane Community College (A)

LEGAL AND JUSTICE STUDIES

Burlington College (B)

LEGAL OFFICE

Wake Technical Community College (UC)

LEGAL SECRETARY

Kaplan University Online (UC)

LEGAL SERVICES

Thomas Edison State College (B)

LEGAL STUDIES

Herzing University Online (A,B)
Hodges University (B)
Kaplan University Online (B,M)
Mercy College (B)
Mountain State University (A,B)
State University of New York College of Technology at Canton (B)
University of Illinois at Springfield (M)
University of Maryland University College (B)
The University of Texas at Brownsville (B)
Western International University (B)
West Virginia University (M)

LEGISLATIVE DESIGN

Athabasca University (GC)

LETTERS, ARTS, AND SCIENCES

Penn State University Park (A,B)

LIBERAL AND INTEGRATIVE STUDIES

University of Illinois at Springfield (M)

LIBERAL ARTS

Arkansas State University–Beebe (A)
Austin Peay State University (A)
Brookdale Community College (A)
Broward College (A)
Burlington County College (A)
Butler Community College (A)
Cabrillo College (A)
Centenary College (A)
Central New Mexico Community College (A)
Colorado State University (B)
Columbus State University (B)
Dakota College at Bottineau (A)
Excelsior College (A,B)
Florida Tech University Online (A)
Kirkwood Community College (A)
Lansing Community College (A)
Lewis-Clark State College (A)
Lock Haven University of Pennsylvania (M)
Mary Baldwin College (B)
Monroe Community College (A)
Mountain Empire Community College (A)
Northeastern University (A)
North Hennepin Community College (A)
North Shore Community College (A)
Peninsula College (A)
Peru State College (B)
Quinsigamond Community College (A)
Rose State College (A)
St. Cloud State University (A)
Saint Leo University (A)
Southern New Hampshire University (A)
Southwestern Community College (A)
Taft College (A)
University of Arkansas at Little Rock (B)
University of Wisconsin Colleges (A)
Upper Iowa University (A)
Vincennes University (A)
West Los Angeles College (A)
Widener University (A)

LIBERAL ARTS (BLA)

University of Massachusetts Lowell (B)

LIBERAL ARTS (EDUCATION)

Burlington County College (A)

LIBERAL ARTS (IN STATE)

Daytona State College (A)

LIBERAL ARTS (OUT OF STATE)

Daytona State College (A)

LIBERAL ARTS (PSYCHOLOGY)

Burlington County College (A)

LIBERAL ARTS AND GENERAL STUDIES

Mount Saint Vincent University (B)

LIBERAL ARTS AND HUMANITIES

Cayuga County Community College (A)

LIBERAL ARTS AND SCIENCE–GENERAL STUDIES

Erie Community College (A)
Erie Community College, North Campus (A)
Erie Community College, South Campus (A)

LIBERAL ARTS AND SCIENCE/ HUMANITIES AND SOCIAL SCIENCE

Erie Community College (A)
Erie Community College, North Campus (A)
Erie Community College, South Campus (A)

LIBERAL ARTS AND SCIENCE/ LIBERAL STUDIES

North Dakota State College of Science (A)

LIBERAL ARTS AND SCIENCES

Burlington County College (A)
Finger Lakes Community College (A)
Mercer County Community College (A)
Middlesex Community College (A)
Saint Paul College–A Community & Technical College (A)
Sinclair Community College (A)
Union Institute & University (B)

LIBERAL ARTS AND SCIENCES (ACCOUNTING)

Burlington County College (A)

LIBERAL ARTS AND SCIENCES (BUSINESS ADMINISTRATION)

Burlington County College (A)

LIBERAL ARTS AND SCIENCES (BUSINESS MANAGEMENT TECHNOLOGY)

Burlington County College (A)

LIBERAL ARTS AND SCIENCES (LAS)

Mount Wachusett Community College (A)

LIBERAL ARTS AND SCIENCES–COMMUNICATIONS TRACK (LAC)

Mount Wachusett Community College (A)

LIBERAL ARTS AND SCIENCES–GENERAL STUDIES

Herkimer County Community College (A)

LIBERAL ARTS AND SCIENCES–HUMANITIES

Herkimer County Community College (A)

LIBERAL ARTS AND SCIENCES–PRE-ENGINEERING TRACK (LAER)

Mount Wachusett Community College (A)

LIBERAL ARTS AND SCIENCES–SOCIAL SCIENCE

Herkimer County Community College (A)

LIBERAL ARTS AND SCIENCES, MATHEMATICS, AND SCIENCE

Cayuga County Community College (A)

LIBERAL ARTS–ARTS AND HUMANITIES EMPHASIS (COALINGA CAMPUS-BASED)

West Hills Community College (A)

LIBERAL ARTS–ARTS AND HUMANITIES EMPHASIS (LEMOORE CAMPUS-BASED)

West Hills Community College (A)

LIBERAL ARTS–BUSINESS MINOR

Northeastern University (B)

LIBERAL ARTS–ENGLISH

Tyler Junior College (A)

LIBERAL ARTS–ENGLISH OR GLOBAL HUMANITIES OPTION

Rogers State University (A,B)

LIBERAL ARTS–HISTORY CONCENTRATION

Taylor University (A)

LIBERAL ARTS–HUMANITIES AND SOCIAL SCIENCE

Genesee Community College (A)
Jefferson Community College (A)

LIBERAL ARTS–MASTER OF LIBERAL ARTS

Texas Christian University (GC)

LIBERAL ARTS–MATH AND SCIENCE EMPHASIS (COALINGA CAMPUS-BASED)

West Hills Community College (A)

LIBERAL ARTS–MATH AND SCIENCE EMPHASIS (LEMOORE CAMPUS-BASED)

West Hills Community College (A)

LIBERAL ARTS–SOCIAL AND BEHAVIORAL SCIENCE EMPHASIS (COALINGA CAMPUS-BASED)

West Hills Community College (A)

LIBERAL ARTS–SOCIAL SCIENCE EMPHASIS (LEMOORE CAMPUS-BASED)

West Hills Community College (A)

LIBERAL ARTS, BUSINESS CONCENTRATION

Taylor University (A)

LIBERAL ARTS, CHRISTIAN MINISTRIES CONCENTRATION

Taylor University (A)

LIBERAL ARTS, DISCIPLESHIP CONCENTRATION

Taylor University (A)

LIBERAL ARTS, ELEMENTARY EDUCATION LICENSURE

Mesa State College (B)

LIBERAL ARTS, GENERAL

DePaul University (B)
Iowa Lakes Community College (A)

LIBERAL ARTS, GENERAL

Los Angeles Trade-Technical College (A)

LIBERAL ARTS, GENERAL STUDIES

Eastern University (A)

LIBERAL ARTS, GENERAL STUDIES, HUMANITIES

Andrews University (A,B)

LIBERAL ARTS, HISTORY EMPHASIS

Sinclair Community College (A)

LIBERAL ARTS, PROFESSIONAL WRITING CONCENTRATION

Taylor University (A)

LIBERAL ARTS, PSYCHOLOGY EMPHASIS

Sinclair Community College (A)

LIBERAL ARTS, SOCIAL SCIENCE CONCENTRATION

Taylor University (A)
Vincennes University (A)

LIBERAL ARTS/GENERAL STUDIES

Thomas Edison State College (A)

LIBERAL ARTS/HUMANITIES

Westchester Community College (A)

LIBERAL ARTS/HUMANITIES AND SOCIAL SCIENCE

Clinton Community College (A)

LIBERAL ARTS/SOCIAL SCIENCE

Westchester Community College (A)

LIBERAL EDUCATION

Lake Superior College (A)

LIBERAL STUDIES

Amridge University (A,B)
Brenau University (A)
California State University, Chico (B)
DeVry University Online (B)
Eastern Oregon University (B)
Excelsior College (B,M)
Fort Hays State University (M)
Framingham State University (B)
Granite State College (B)
Kaplan University Online (B)
Limestone College (A,B)
Marist College (B)
Middlesex Community College (UC,A)
Middle Tennessee State University (B)
Montgomery County Community College (A)
Mountain State University (B)
Northeastern University (B)
Oregon State University (B)
Rowan University (B)
St. John's University (A,B,M)
Saint Leo University (B)
Santa Rosa Junior College (A)
Sonoma State University (B)
State University of New York Empire State College (M)
Stony Brook University, State University of New York (M)
Thomas Edison State College (B,M)
Union County College (A)
University of Illinois at Springfield (B)
University of Maine at Augusta (A,B)
University of Memphis (M)
University of Northern Iowa (B)
University of the Incarnate Word (A)
The University of Toledo (B,M)
University of Waterloo (B)
Widener University (B)

LIBERAL STUDIES CONCENTRATION

Southern Maine Community College (A)

LIBERAL STUDIES–BACHELOR OF LIBERAL STUDIES ONLINE DEGREE PROGRAM

Bowling Green State University (B)

LIBERAL STUDIES, BUSINESS ADMINISTRATION MINOR

Clarion University of Pennsylvania (B)

LIBERAL STUDIES, COMMUNICATION CONCENTRATION

Clarion University of Pennsylvania (B)

LIBERAL STUDIES, COMMUNITY SERVICE CONCENTRATION

Clarion University of Pennsylvania (B)

LIBERAL STUDIES, LIBRARY SCIENCE CONCENTRATION

Clarion University of Pennsylvania (B)

LIBERAL STUDIES, PSYCHOLOGY MINOR

Clarion University of Pennsylvania (B)

LIBERAL STUDIES, WOMEN'S STUDIES CONCENTRATION

Clarion University of Pennsylvania (B)

LIBRARY AND INFORMATION SCIENCE

Drexel University (M)
Emporia State University (M)
Syracuse University (M)
University of Illinois at Urbana–Champaign (GC)
University of Illinois at Urbana–Champaign (M)
University of Wisconsin–Milwaukee (M)
Wayne State University (M)

LIBRARY AND INFORMATION SCIENCE IN SCHOOL MEDIA

Syracuse University (M)

LIBRARY AND INFORMATION SCIENCE, K-12

University of Illinois at Urbana–Champaign (UC)

LIBRARY AND INFORMATION SERVICES

University of Maine at Augusta (A,B)

LIBRARY AND INFORMATION STUDIES

University of Wisconsin–Madison (M)

LIBRARY AND INFORMATION TECHNOLOGIES

Valley City State University (GC)

LIBRARY AND INFORMATION TECHNOLOGIES–SCHOOL LIBRARY AND INFORMATION TECHNOLOGIES

Mansfield University of Pennsylvania (M)

LIBRARY AND INTELLECTUAL PROPERTY IN DE AND E-LEARNING

University of Maryland University College (GC)

LIBRARY INFORMATICS

Northern Kentucky University (B)

LIBRARY INFORMATION SCIENCE

University of Southern Mississippi (M)

LIBRARY MEDIA

Jacksonville State University (M)
The University of West Alabama (M)

LIBRARY MEDIA +30 CERTIFICATION PROGRAM FOR RANK I

Murray State University (UC)

LIBRARY MEDIA +30 CERTIFICATION PROGRAM FOR RANK I FOR CERTIFIED SCHOOL MEDIA LIBRARIANS

Murray State University (UC)

LIBRARY MEDIA EDUCATION

Western Kentucky University (M)

LIBRARY MEDIA SPECIALIST

Fort Hays State University (UC)

LIBRARY SCIENCE

Clarion University of Pennsylvania (M)
New Mexico State University (A)
North Carolina Central University (M)
Southern Connecticut State University (M)
Texas Woman's University (M)

LIBRARY STUDIES

Memorial University of Newfoundland (UC)

LIBRARY TECHNICAL ASSISTANT

Rose State College (A)

LICENSURE IN EDUCATION FOR AGRICULTURAL PROFESSIONALS

North Carolina State University (UC)

LIFE STAGES AND TRANSITIONS

Fort Hays State University (UC)

LINGUISTICS–APPLIED LINGUISTICS, ESL CONCENTRATION

University of Massachusetts Boston (M)

LINUX ADMINISTRATION, SECURITY AND SUPPORT

Champlain College (UC)

LINUX SYSTEM ADMINISTRATION POST-BACCALAUREATE CERTIFICATE

Kaplan University Online (UC)

LITERACY EDUCATION

Western Kentucky University (M)

LITERACY INSTRUCTION AUTHORIZATION

Colorado State University (UC)

LITERACY LEADERSHIP AND COACHING

The University of South Dakota (GC)

LITERACY SPECIALIST

Youngstown State University (UC)

LITERACY STUDIES

University of Nevada, Reno (M)

LITERACY, LEADERSHIP, AND COACHING

University of Memphis (GC)

LITERATURE

Atlantic Cape Community College (A)

LOCAL GOVERNMENT MANAGEMENT

University of Memphis (GC)

LOGISTICS AND SUPPLY CHAIN MANAGEMENT CONCENTRATION

Colorado Technical University Colorado Springs (M)

LOGISTICS AND SUPPLY CHAIN MANAGEMENT OPTION

Clark State Community College (A)

LOGISTICS MANAGEMENT

Florida Institute of Technology (M)

LOGISTICS MANAGEMENT CONCENTRATION

Central Michigan University (M)

LOGISTICS MANAGEMENT–HUMANITARIAN AND DISASTER RELIEF LOGISTICS CONCENTRATION

Florida Institute of Technology (M)

LOGISTICS TECHNOLOGY

North Lake College (A)

LONG-TERM CARE ADMINISTRATION

Saint Joseph's College of Maine (UC,B)
University of Southern California (M)

LONG-TERM CARE MANAGEMENT

The University of South Dakota (GC)

LOW IMPACT DEVELOPMENT–LID SPECIALIST

Haywood Community College (UC)

LUTC FELLOW DESIGNATION

The American College (UC)

MAGNETIC RESONANCE IMAGING (MRI)

Fort Hays State University (UC)

MAINE STUDIES

University of Maine (UC)

MANAGEMENT

Albertus Magnus College (M)
Amberton University (B,M)
Antioch University Midwest (M)
Appalachian State University (B)
Athabasca University (GC)
Austin Peay State University (M)
Belhaven University (B)
Caldwell College (B)
Champlain College (UC)
Chemeketa Community College (A)
Clark State Community College (A)
Colorado Technical University Colorado Springs (B)
Columbia Southern University (B)
Dakota State University (B)
Dallas Baptist University (GC,B,M)
DeVry University Online (B)
Ellis University (M)
Florida Institute of Technology (M)
Fontbonne University (M)
Fort Hays State University (UC,B)
Franklin Pierce University (UC,A,B)
Frostburg State University (M)
Grace College (B)
Greenville Technical College (A)
Hodges University (A,B,M)
Indiana Wesleyan University (B,M)
Kaplan University Online (M)
Lasell College (GC,M)
Lewis-Clark State College (B)
Minnesota School of Business–Online (M)
Minnesota School of Business–Richfield (M)
Minot State University (B,M)
Montgomery County Community College (A)
National-Louis University (B,M)
National University (B,M)
Northeastern University (B)
Northern State University (B)
North Lake College (A)
Prescott College (B)
Salve Regina University (UC,M)
Seminole State College of Florida (UC)
Southwestern College (M)
Southwestern Oklahoma State University (B)
Spartanburg Community College (A)
Spring Arbor University (M)
State University of New York College of Technology at Canton (B)
Taft College (A)
Texas Woman's University (B)
Thomas Edison State College (M)
University of Arkansas at Little Rock (B)
University of Colorado at Colorado Springs (M)
University of Houston–Downtown (B)
University of Houston–Victoria (B)
University of Maine at Augusta (B)
University of Management and Technology (B,M)
University of Mary (M)
University of Maryland University College (M,D)
University of Memphis (B)
University of St. Francis (B,M)
The University of Tennessee at Martin (B)
University of Wisconsin–Stout (B)
Upper Iowa University (B)
Walden University (M,D)
Wayland Baptist University (M)
Western International University (B,M)
Worcester Polytechnic Institute (GC,M)

MANAGEMENT (HYBRID)

Baldwin-Wallace College (M)

MANAGEMENT ACCELERATED BBA/MBA

Dallas Baptist University (M)

MANAGEMENT ACCELERATED BBS/MBA

Dallas Baptist University (M)

MANAGEMENT ACCOUNTING

Minnesota School of Business–Online (A)
Minnesota School of Business–Richfield (A)

MANAGEMENT AND BUSINESS ETHICS

Laurel University (B)

MANAGEMENT AND ETHICS

Dallas Christian College (B)
Williamson Christian College (B)

MANAGEMENT AND HUMAN RESOURCE SKILLS FOR PHARMACISTS

Oregon State University (UC)

MANAGEMENT AND LEADERSHIP

Bluefield College (B)
Judson University (B)
Liberty University (M)
Tarleton State University (M)
Webster University (M)

MANAGEMENT AND ORGANIZATIONAL DEVELOPMENT

Bethel University (B)

MANAGEMENT AND ORGANIZATIONAL LEADERSHIP

St. Petersburg College (B)

MANAGEMENT AND ORGANIZATIONAL LEADERSHIP–ADULT DEGREE COMPLETION

George Fox University (B)

MANAGEMENT AND SUPERVISION (IN STATE)

Daytona State College (B)

MANAGEMENT AND SUPERVISION (OUT OF STATE)

Daytona State College (B)

MANAGEMENT AND SUPERVISION CERTIFICATE IN CRIMINAL JUSTICE

Kaplan University Online (UC)

MANAGEMENT AND SUPERVISORY DEVELOPMENT

Portland Community College (A)

MANAGEMENT APPLICATION AND PRINCIPLES

Pitt Community College (UC)

MANAGEMENT APPLICATIONS

Athabasca University (UC)

MANAGEMENT BASICS

Front Range Community College (UC)

MANAGEMENT COMMUNICATION

Amridge University (B)

MANAGEMENT CONCENTRATION

Andrew Jackson University (M)
Colorado Technical University Colorado Springs (B)

MANAGEMENT DEVELOPMENT

Alvin Community College (A)
College of Southern Maryland (UC,A)

MANAGEMENT DEVELOPMENT–MARKETING

College of Southern Maryland (UC)

MANAGEMENT FOUNDATIONS

Athabasca University (UC)

MANAGEMENT IN THE INCLUSIVE CLASSROOM

Graceland University (M)

MANAGEMENT INFORMATION SYSTEMS

Champlain College (B)
Columbia College (B)
Dakota State University (B)
Dallas Baptist University (B,M)
Excelsior College (B)
Florida State University (M)
Fort Hays State University (GC,B)
Friends University (M)
Liberty University (A,B)
Minot State University (B)
Montgomery County Community College (A)
National-Louis University (B)
University of Atlanta (B,M)
University of Illinois at Springfield (M)
Upper Iowa University (B)

MANAGEMENT INFORMATION SYSTEMS (MIS)

University of Memphis (B)

MANAGEMENT INFORMATION SYSTEMS ACCELERATED BBS/MBA

Dallas Baptist University (M)

MANAGEMENT INFORMATION SYSTEMS DUAL DEGREE PROGRAM

Auburn University (M)

MANAGEMENT OF ANIMAL HEALTH RELATED ORGANIZATIONS

Kansas State University (GC)

MANAGEMENT OF HUMAN RESOURCES

Excelsior College (B)

MANAGEMENT OF INFORMATION SYSTEMS

Ellis University (B)

MANAGEMENT OF PROJECTS AND PROGRAMS

Brandeis University (M)

MANAGEMENT OF TECHNOLOGY

University of Waterloo (M)

MANAGEMENT ONLINE

Kirkwood Community College (A)
Lesley University (B)

MANAGEMENT POST-DIPLOMA (3 YEAR)

Athabasca University (B)

MANAGEMENT POST-DIPLOMA (4 YEAR)

Athabasca University (B)

MANAGEMENT PRACTICES

Dallas Baptist University (UC)

MANAGEMENT SPECIALTY

San Jacinto College District (UC)

MANAGEMENT STUDIES

University of Maryland University College (B)

MANAGEMENT WITH FIRE SERVICES ELECTIVES

Spartanburg Community College (A)

MANAGEMENT WITH MARKETING ELECTIVES

Spartanburg Community College (A)

MANAGEMENT–ACQUISITION AND CONTRACT MANAGEMENT CONCENTRATION

Florida Institute of Technology (M)

MANAGEMENT–EBUSINESS CONCENTRATION

Florida Institute of Technology (M)

MANAGEMENT–HUMAN RESOURCES CONCENTRATION

Fort Hays State University (B)

MANAGEMENT–HUMAN RESOURCES MANAGEMENT CONCENTRATION

Florida Institute of Technology (M)

MANAGEMENT–INFORMATION SYSTEMS

Indiana Tech (B)

MANAGEMENT–INFORMATION SYSTEMS CONCENTRATION

Florida Institute of Technology (M)

MANAGEMENT–LOGISTICS MANAGEMENT CONCENTRATION

Florida Institute of Technology (M)

MANAGEMENT–TRANSPORTATION MANAGEMENT CONCENTRATION

Florida Institute of Technology (M)

MANAGEMENT, GENERAL

Dallas Baptist University (M)
The University of Texas at Arlington (M)

MANAGERIAL SCIENCE

University of Atlanta (D)

MANAGING APPLIED RESEARCH

University of Colorado Boulder (GC)

MANAGING INNOVATION AND INFORMATION TECHNOLOGY

Champlain College (M)

MANAGING RESEARCH AND DEVELOPMENT

University of Colorado Boulder (GC)

MANUFACTURING ENGINEERING

Columbia University (UC)
Missouri University of Science and Technology (M)
University of Michigan (M)
University of Wisconsin–Stout (B,M)
Western Michigan University (B)

MANUFACTURING ENGINEERING (INDUSTRIAL AND MANUFACTURING ENGINEERING CONCENTRATION)

Kettering University (M)

MANUFACTURING ENGINEERING CONCENTRATION

Kettering University (M)

MANUFACTURING ENGINEERING TECHNOLOGY

Oregon Institute of Technology (M)
Thomas Edison State College (A,B)

MANUFACTURING LEADERSHIP

Rochester Institute of Technology (M)

MANUFACTURING MANAGEMENT (BMM)

University of Minnesota, Crookston (B)

MANUFACTURING OPERATIONS

Kettering University (M)

MANUFACTURING SYSTEMS ENGINEERING

Lehigh University (M)
University of Wisconsin–Madison (M)

MANUFACTURING SYSTEMS MANAGEMENT

Southern Methodist University (M)

MANUFACTURING SYSTEMS TECHNOLOGY

Jacksonville State University (M)

MANUFACTURING TECHNOLGY

Quinsigamond Community College (A)

MARITIME STUDIES

University of West Florida (B)

MARITIME STUDIES–BACHELOR OF MARITIME STUDIES (BMS)

Memorial University of Newfoundland (B)

MARKETING

Athabasca University (UC)
Caldwell College (B)
Central Pennsylvania College (A)
City University of Seattle (UC,GC)
Columbia Southern University (B,M)
Columbus State Community College (A)
Dakota State University (B)
Dallas Baptist University (GC,B,M)
Excelsior College (B)
Florida Tech University Online (A)
Fort Hays State University (UC,B)
Franklin Pierce University (UC,A,B)
Greenville Technical College (A)
Indiana Wesleyan University (B)
James A. Rhodes State College (A)
Lasell College (GC,M)
Lynn University (M)
Minot State University (B)
Montgomery County Community College (A)
Mount Saint Vincent University (B)
National University (B)
New Mexico State University (B)
Nichols College (B)
Northern State University (B)
Piedmont Community College (UC)
Pitt Community College (UC)
Regent University (A)
Saint Leo University (GC)
Saint Mary-of-the-Woods College (B)
Seminole State College of Florida (UC)
Southern New Hampshire University (GC,A,B,M)
Southwestern Oklahoma State University (B)
Texas Woman's University (B)
Thomas Edison State College (B)
University of Colorado at Colorado Springs (M)
University of Houston–Downtown (B)
University of Houston–Victoria (B)
University of Maine at Machias (UC)
University of Mary (B)
University of Maryland University College (B)
University of Minnesota, Crookston (B)
University of Wisconsin–Platteville (UC)
Upper Iowa University (UC,B)
Western International University (M)
Western Wyoming Community College (A)
West Los Angeles College (A)
Wisconsin Indianhead Technical College (A)

MARKETING ACCELERATED BBS/MBA

Dallas Baptist University (M)

MARKETING AND E-BUSINESS OPTION

Clark State Community College (A)

MARKETING AND INNOVATION MANAGEMENT

Concordia University, St. Paul (B)

MARKETING AND MANAGEMENT

Butler Community College (A)

MARKETING AND SUPPLY CHAIN MANAGEMENT

University of Memphis (B)

MARKETING AND TECHNOLOGY INNOVATION

Worcester Polytechnic Institute (M)

MARKETING BASICS

Front Range Community College (UC)

MARKETING CONCENTRATION

Andrew Jackson University (M)
Colorado Technical University Colorado Springs (B,M)
Saint Leo University (M)

MARKETING MANAGEMENT

Hope International University (M)
University of Management and Technology (B)

MARKETING PRE-ASSOCIATE CERTIFICATE

Thomas Edison State College (UC)

MARKETING, ELECTRONIC COMMERCE SPECIALIZATION

Danville Community College (A)

MARRIAGE AND FAMILY

Eastern University (D)

MARRIAGE AND FAMILY THERAPY

Amridge University (M)
Liberty University (M)
Mercy College (M)

MARRIAGE EDUCATION (FOR CREDIT)

University of Bridgeport (UC)

MARRIAGE EDUCATION (NON-CREDIT)

University of Bridgeport (UC)

MARRIAGE, COUPLE, AND FAMILY COUNSELING

Walden University (M)

MASS COMMUNICATION

North Dakota State University (M)

MASS COMMUNICATION AND MEDIA MANAGEMENT

Lynn University (M)

MASS MEDIA ARTS AND JOURNALISM

Clarion University of Pennsylvania (M)

MASTER OF APPLIED INDUSTRIAL/ORGANIZATIONAL PSYCHOLOGY

Colorado State University (M)

MASTER OF APPLIED SCIENCE IN ENVIRONMENTAL POLICY AND MANAGEMENT

University of Denver (M)

MASTER OF APPLIED SCIENCE IN INFORMATION AND COMMUNICATIONS TECHNOLOGY

University of Denver (M)

MASTER OF APPLIED SCIENCE IN SECURITY MANAGEMENT

University of Denver (M)

MASTER OF ARCHITECTURE

Lawrence Technological University (M)

MASTER OF BIOMEDICAL IMAGING AND SIGNALS

Illinois Institute of Technology (M)

MASTER OF DISTANCE EDUCATION AND E-LEARNING

University of Maryland University College (M)

MASTER OF ENTREPRENEURSHIP (ME PROGRAM)

Western Carolina University (M)

MASTER OF HEALTH AND HUMAN SERVICES

Youngstown State University (M)

MASTER OF INTEGRATED MANUFACTURING SYSTEMS ENGINEERING

North Carolina State University (M)

MASTER OF LETTERS

Faulkner University (M)

MASTER OF MANUFACTURING ENGINEERING VIA THE INTERNET

Illinois Institute of Technology (M)

MASTER OF NATURAL RESOURCES

Oregon State University (M)

MASTER OF NETWORK ENGINEERING

Illinois Institute of Technology (M)

MASTER OF NUCLEAR ENGINEERING

North Carolina State University (M)

MASTER OF POWER ENGINEERING

Illinois Institute of Technology (M)

MASTER OF SCIENCE IN APPLIED SCIENCE AND TECHNOLOGY IN CLINICAL TRIALS (MSAST)

Thomas Edison State College (M)

MASTER OF SCIENCE IN APPLIED SCIENCE AND TECHNOLOGY IN TECHNICAL STUDIES (MSAST)

Thomas Edison State College (M)

MASTER OF SCIENCE IN INTERIOR ARCHITECTURE

Chatham University (M)

MASTER OF TELECOMMUNICATIONS AND SOFTWARE ENGINEERING

Illinois Institute of Technology (M)

MASTER OF THEOLOGY

Campbellsville University (M)

MASTER OF VLSI AND MICROELECTRONICS

Illinois Institute of Technology (M)

MASTER READING TEACHER

Stephen F. Austin State University (GC)

MASTER TEACHER ELEMENTARY

Emporia State University (M)

MASTER TECHNOLOGY TEACHER

The University of Texas at Brownsville (UC)

MASTERS IN EDUCATION LEADERSHIP

Wheeling Jesuit University (M)

MASTERS IN TEACHING EXCELLENCE

The Sage Colleges (M)

MASTERS OF STRATEGIC LEADERSHIP

LeTourneau University (M)

MASTERY IN PRIOR LEARNING ASSESSMENT

DePaul University (UC)

MATERIAL ACQUISITION MANAGEMENT

Florida Institute of Technology (M)

MATERIAL AND CHEMICAL SYNTHESIS

Illinois Institute of Technology (M)

MATERIALS ENGINEERING

Auburn University (M)
Colorado State University (M)
University of Illinois at Urbana–Champaign (GC)
University of Southern California (M)

MATERIALS FAILURE ANALYSIS

University of Illinois at Urbana–Champaign (GC)

MATERIALS SCIENCE AND ENGINEERING

Columbia University (UC,M,D)
North Carolina State University (M)
University of Florida (M)
University of Florida (M)

MATH AND SCIENCE (K-8)

Slippery Rock University of Pennsylvania (M)

MATH LEARNING AND TEACHING

Drexel University (M)

MATHEMATICAL SCIENCES

University of Illinois at Springfield (B)

MATHEMATICS

Mayville State University (B)
Mercy College (B)
Ohio University (A)
Regent University (B)
Saint Mary-of-the-Woods College (B)
Thomas Edison State College (A,B)
University of Arkansas at Little Rock (B)
University of Central Florida (GC)
University of Houston (M)
University of Houston–Downtown (B)
The University of Texas at Brownsville (M)
University of West Florida (M)

MATHEMATICS EDUCATION

Georgia State University (M)
Mayville State University (B)
Western Kentucky University (M)

MATHEMATICS EDUCATION (1-8)

Lesley University (M)

MATHEMATICS FOR TEACHERS

University of Waterloo (M)

MATHEMATICS LEARNING AND TEACHING

Drexel University (GC)

MEASUREMENT AND STATISTICS

Georgia State University (M)

MEASUREMENT, EVALUATION, STATISTICS AND ASSESSMENT

University of Illinois at Chicago (M)

MECHANICAL AND AEROSPACE ENGINEERING

University of Florida (M)

MECHANICAL AND AEROSPACE ENGINEERING (DYNAMICS AND CONTROL TRACK)

University of Florida (M)

MECHANICAL AND AEROSPACE ENGINEERING (FUNDAMENTALS OF THERMAL FLUIDS TRANSPORT TRACK)

University of Florida (M)

MECHANICAL AND AEROSPACE ENGINEERING (SOLID MECHANICS AND DESIGN TRACK)

University of Florida (M)

MECHANICAL COGNATE

Kettering University (M)

MECHANICAL DESIGN (ME CONCENTRATION)

Kettering University (M)

MECHANICAL DESIGN CONCENTRATION

Kettering University (M)

MECHANICAL DRAFTING TECHNOLOGY

Wake Technical Community College (UC)

MECHANICAL ENGINEERING

Auburn University (M)
Bradley University (M)
Columbia University (M,D)
Georgia Institute of Technology (M)
Kansas State University (M)
Michigan Technological University (M,D)
Missouri University of Science and Technology (M)
North Carolina State University (M)
Purdue University (M)
Southern Methodist University (M)
Trine University (M)
University of Central Florida (M)
University of Idaho (M)
University of Illinois at Urbana–Champaign (M)
University of Michigan–Dearborn (M)
University of North Dakota (B)
University of Southern California (M)
The University of Texas at Arlington (M)

MECHANICAL ENGINEERING (ENGINEERING MANAGEMENT)

Colorado State University (M)

MECHANICAL ENGINEERING (MS OR MENG)

Lehigh University (M)

MECHANICAL ENGINEERING TECHNOLOGY

Indiana State University (B)
Thomas Edison State College (A,B)
Wake Technical Community College (A)
Wayne Community College (A)

MECHANICAL ENGINEERING TECHNOLOGY–ENGINEERING FUNDAMENTALS

Wake Technical Community College (UC)

MECHANICAL ENGINEERING TECHNOLOGY–ENGINEERING MANAGEMENT

Wake Technical Community College (UC)

MECHANICAL ENGINEERING TECHNOLOGY–MATERIALS ENGINEERING

Wake Technical Community College (UC)

MECHANICAL ENGINEERING TECHNOLOGY–MECHANICAL DESIGN

Wake Technical Community College (UC)

MECHANICAL ENGINEERING TECHNOLOGY–THERMAL MECHANICS

Wake Technical Community College (UC)

MECHANICAL ENGINEERING/ MATERIALS

University of Illinois at Urbana–Champaign (GC)

MECHANICAL ENGINEERING/ MATERIALS FAILURE ANALYSIS

University of Illinois at Urbana–Champaign (GC)

MECHANICS AND MAINTENANCE

Thomas Edison State College (A)

MEDIA ACTIVISM

Burlington College (B)

MEDIA BUSINESS

Minnesota School of Business–Online (B)

MEDIA COMMUNICATIONS

Webster University (M)

MEDIA MAJOR (SCHOOL LIBRARY MEDIA AND INSTRUCTIONAL TECHNOLOGY TRACKS)

University of West Georgia (M)

MEDIA PSYCHOLOGY

Fielding Graduate University (D)

MEDIA PSYCHOLOGY AND SOCIAL CHANGE

Fielding Graduate University (M)

MEDIATION

Colorado State University (UC)

MEDIATION AND APPLIED CONFLICT STUDIES

Champlain College (M)

MEDIATION AND DISPUTE RESOLUTION CONCENTRATION

Colorado Technical University Colorado Springs (M)

MEDICAL ADMINISTRATION

Monroe College (A)

MEDICAL ADMINISTRATIVE ASSISTANT

Bryant & Stratton Online (A)
Dakota College at Bottineau (A)

MEDICAL ADMINISTRATIVE SPECIALIST

Wisconsin Indianhead Technical College (A)

MEDICAL AND HEALTHCARE INFORMATION TECHNOLOGIES

University of Denver (UC)

MEDICAL ASSISTANT

Dakota College at Bottineau (UC,A)

MEDICAL ASSISTING

Kaplan University Online (A)
Midway College (A)
Mountain State University (A)
Portland Community College (UC)
Southeast Community College Area (UC,A)
Wayne Community College (A)

MEDICAL ASSISTING SERVICES

Herzing University Online (UC,A)

MEDICAL ASSISTING/ADVANCED STANDING ALTERNATIVE FOR MEDICAL OFFICE ADMIN OR MEDICAL TRANSCRIPTION

Wayne Community College (A)

MEDICAL BILLER/CODER

University of Cincinnati (UC)

MEDICAL BILLING AND CODING

California State University, Dominguez Hills (GC)
Drexel University (UC)
Montana State University–Great Falls College of Technology (A)
Wake Technical Community College (UC)

MEDICAL BILLING SPECIALIST

Montana State University–Great Falls College of Technology (UC)

MEDICAL CODER

St. Petersburg College (UC)

MEDICAL CODER/ TRANSCRIPTIONIST

Herkimer County Community College (UC)

MEDICAL CODING

Columbus State Community College (GC)
Dakota College at Bottineau (UC)
Midway College (A)
Pittsburgh Technical Institute (UC)
Presentation College (UC)

MEDICAL CODING AND BILLING

Grantham University (A)
Mountain State University (UC)

MEDICAL CODING AND BILLING SPECIALIST

Sinclair Community College (UC)

MEDICAL CODING SPECIALIST

Southwest Wisconsin Technical College (UC)

MEDICAL DEVICE AND DIAGNOSTIC ENGINEERING

University of Southern California (M)

MEDICAL DEVICES REGULATORY AFFAIRS

Northeastern University (GC)

MEDICAL DIAGNOSTIC IMAGING

Fort Hays State University (B)

MEDICAL DOCUMENT SPECIALIST

Wake Technical Community College (UC)

MEDICAL DOSIMETRY

University of Wisconsin–La Crosse (UC,M)

MEDICAL FAMILY THERAPY

Drexel University (GC)

MEDICAL IMAGING

Clarion University of Pennsylvania (B)
Clarkson College (B)
Thomas Edison State College (A,B)

MEDICAL IMAGING POST-BACCALAUREATE CERTIFICATE

MGH Institute of Health Professions (UC)

MEDICAL LAB TECH

Hibbing Community College (A)

MEDICAL LABORATORY SCIENCE

Allen College (B)

MEDICAL LABORATORY TECHNICIAN

Harcum College (A)

MEDICAL LABORATORY TECHNOLOGY

Clark State Community College (A)
Columbus State Community College (A)
J. Sargeant Reynolds Community College (A)
Portland Community College (A)
St. Petersburg College (A)
University of Maine at Augusta (A)

MEDICAL OFFICE ADMINISTRATION

Haywood Community College (A)
Herzing University Online (UC,A)
Pitt Community College (A)
Presentation College (A)
Wake Technical Community College (A)

MEDICAL OFFICE ADMINSTRATION

Wayne Community College (A)

MEDICAL OFFICE ASSISTANT

Edison State Community College (A)

MEDICAL OFFICE ASSISTANT DEGREE D190

Illinois Eastern Community Colleges, Olney Central College (A)

MEDICAL OFFICE MANAGEMENT

Broward College (UC)
Kaplan University Online (A)
Tyler Junior College (UC)

MEDICAL OFFICE SPECIALIST

Central Texas College (UC)
Wake Technical Community College (UC)

MEDICAL PHYSICS

Georgia Institute of Technology (M)

MEDICAL RECORD CODING CERTIFICATE

Central Carolina Technical College (UC)

MEDICAL REIMBURSEMENT AND CODING

Bryant & Stratton Online (A)

MEDICAL SUPPORT SPECIALIST, MEDICAL ASSISTING OPTION

Quinsigamond Community College (A)

MEDICAL TRANSCRIPTION

California State University, Dominguez Hills (GC)
Central Texas College (UC)
Dakota College at Bottineau (UC)
Kaplan University Online (A)
Montana State University–Great Falls College of Technology (UC,A)
Moraine Park Technical College (UC)
North Dakota State College of Science (UC)
Southwest Wisconsin Technical College (UC)

MEDICINE

Saint Francis University (M)

MENTAL HEALTH AND HUMAN SERVICES

University of Maine at Augusta (A,B)

MENTAL HEALTH AND REHABILITATION SERVICES

Thomas Edison State College (B)

MENTAL HEALTH COUNSELING

Prescott College (M)
University of Massachusetts Boston (M)
Walden University (M)

MERCHANDISING

Colorado State University (M)
Framingham State University (GC)
Kansas State University (M)
North Dakota State University (GC,M)

MICROCOMPUTER OFFICE SPECIALIST

Lake Superior College (UC)

MICROELECTRONICS MANUFACTURING ENGINEERING

Rochester Institute of Technology (M)

MICROFINANCE MANAGEMENT

Southern New Hampshire University (GC)

MICROSOFT APPLICATION SPECIALIST

Wake Technical Community College (UC)

MICROSOFT CERTIFIED SYSTEMS ADMINISTRATOR

Seminole State College of Florida (UC)
Wake Technical Community College (UC)

MICROSOFT CERTIFIED SYSTEMS ENGINEER

Seminole State College of Florida (UC)

MICROSOFT INFORMATION TECHNOLOGY SERVER ADMINISTRATOR

Central Texas College (UC)

MICROSOFT OFFICE SPECIALIST CERTIFICATION PREPARATION

Lansing Community College (UC)

MICROSOFT SYSTEMS ADMINISTRATOR

Lake Superior College (UC)

MIDDLE CHILDHOOD EDUCATION AND STUDENTS WITH DISABILITIES

Mercy College (M)

MIDDLE CHILDHOOD EDUCATION, GRADES 5-9

Mercy College (M)

MIDDLE GRADES

Brenau University (M)
University of Illinois at Urbana–Champaign (UC)

MIDDLE GRADES AND SECONDARY EDUCATION

The University of North Carolina at Charlotte (M)

MIDDLE GRADES EDUCATION

Brenau University (M)

MIDDLE GRADES MATH AND SCIENCE

North Georgia College & State University (M)

MIDDLE/SECONDARY EDUCATION IN BIOLOGY (7-12), ENGLISH (5-12), OR SOCIAL STUDIES (5-12)

Franklin Pierce University (M)

MIDDLE/SECONDARY TEACHING

Indiana State University (UC)

MIDWIFERY

Philadelphia University (M)
University of Minnesota, Twin Cities Campus (D)

MILD/MODERATE 7-12 (UG AND G)

University of Nebraska at Kearney (UC)

MILD/MODERATE INTERVENTION SPECIALIST LICENSE

Baldwin-Wallace College (UC)

MILD/MODERATE K-6 (UG AND G)

University of Nebraska at Kearney (UC)

MILD/MODERATE SPECIAL EDUCATION, 5-12

Graceland University (M)

MILD/MODERATE SPECIAL EDUCATION, K-8

Graceland University (M)

MILITARY HISTORY

Austin Peay State University (M)

MILITARY LEADERSHIP

San Diego Community College District (A)

MILITARY SPECIALTIES

Fort Hays State University (B)

MILITARY STUDIES

Columbia College (M)
Luna Community College (A)

MINING ENGINEERING

Missouri University of Science and Technology (M)

MINISTERIAL EDUCATION

God's Bible School and College (A,B)

MINISTERIAL LEADERSHIP

Amridge University (M)

MINISTERIAL STUDIES

Hobe Sound Bible College (B)

MINISTERIAL STUDIES LEVEL ONE (CERTIFIED MINISTER)

Global University (UC)

MINISTERIAL STUDIES LEVEL THREE (ORDAINED MINISTER)

Global University (UC)

MINISTERIAL STUDIES LEVEL TWO (LICENSED MINISTER)

Global University (UC)

MINISTERIAL STUDIES–BROAD FIELD PLAN

Global University (M)

MINISTERIAL STUDIES–EDUCATION CONCENTRATION

Global University (M)

MINISTERIAL STUDIES–INTERCULTURAL STUDIES

Global University (M)

MINISTERIAL STUDIES–LEADERSHIP CONCENTRATION

Global University (M)

MINISTRY

Amridge University (M)
Anderson University (M)
Baptist Bible College of Pennsylvania (M)
Clear Creek Baptist Bible College (B)
Free Will Baptist Bible College (A)
Global University (UC)
Indiana Wesleyan University (M)
Laurel University (A)
Liberty University (D)

MINISTRY (MINISTERIAL LEADERSHIP AND YOUTH MINISTRY CONCENTRATIONS)

Indiana Wesleyan University (M)

MINISTRY AND LEADERSHIP

Dallas Christian College (B)

MINISTRY AND LEADERSHIP DEGREE COMPLETION PROGRAM

Life Pacific College (B)

MINISTRY LEADERSHIP

Crown College (M)
George Fox University (M)
Moody Bible Institute (B)
Toccoa Falls College (B)

MINISTRY LEADERSHIP IN BUSINESS MINISTRY

Dallas Baptist University (GC)

MINISTRY STUDIES

The Baptist College of Florida (B)
Grace College (M)
Judson College (B)

MINISTRY–LEADERSHIP AND RENEWAL

Regent University (D)

MINISTRY/BIBLE

Amridge University (B)

MIS CONCENTRATION, SAP EMPHASIS
Central Michigan University (M)

MISSILE SYSTEMS ENGINEERING
The University of Alabama in Huntsville (M)

MISSIONAL CHRISTIANITY
University of Dubuque (M)

MISSIONS
City Vision College (B)

MISSIONS STUDIES
Taylor University (UC)

MISSIONS/INTERCULTURAL STUDIES
Hope International University (M)

MOBILE PROGRAMMING
Champlain College (UC)

MODELING AND SIMULATION
The University of Alabama in Huntsville (M)
University of Central Florida (M)

MOLECULAR BIOLOGY
Lehigh University (M)

MOLECULAR BIOSCIENCES
Washington State University (GC)

MONTESSORI INTEGRATIVE LEARNING
Endicott College (M)

MORTGAGE BANKING
North Lake College (A)

MORTUARY SCIENCE
Arapahoe Community College (A)

MOTION MEDIA DESIGN
Savannah College of Art and Design (M)

MOTION PICTURES AND TELEVISION
Academy of Art University (A,B,M)

MS AGRIBUSINESS/MBA BUSINESS
Purdue University (M)

MULTI-CULTURAL INTERNATIONAL STUDIES
Labette Community College (A)

MULTICULTURAL EDUCATION WITH ESL OR TESOL
Eastern University (M)

MULTIDISCIPLINARY STUDIES
Grantham University (A,B)
Siena Heights University (B)
West Virginia University (B)

MULTIDISCIPLINARY STUDIES/ HUMANITIES
Caldwell College (B)

MULTIDISCIPLINARY STUDIES/ SOCIAL SCIENCE/FIRE SCIENCE
Caldwell College (B)

MULTIDISCIPLINARY STUDIES/ SOCIAL SCIENCE/PHARMACY MANAGEMENT
Caldwell College (B)

MULTIDISCIPLINARY STUDIES/ SOCIAL SCIENCES
Caldwell College (B)

MULTIMEDIA APPLICATIONS
University of Massachusetts Lowell (UC)

MULTIMEDIA COMMUNICATIONS
Academy of Art University (B,M)

MULTIMEDIA DESIGN AND DEVELOPMENT
DeVry University Online (B)

MULTIMEDIA NETWORKING
Columbia University (UC)

MULTIPLE MAJORS
Union Institute & University (B)

MUSEUM STUDIES
Prescott College (M)
Southern University at New Orleans (M)

MUSIC
Auburn University (M)
Judson College (B)
Prescott College (B)
Thomas Edison State College (B)
Valley City State University (B)

MUSIC EDUCATION
Boston University (M)
New Mexico State University (M)
Stephen F. Austin State University (M)
University of Nebraska at Kearney (M)

MUSIC EDUCATION–MASTERS IN MUSIC EDUCATION
Duquesne University (M)
University of Southern Mississippi (M)

MUSIC FOR VISUAL MEDIA
Academy of Art University (A,B,M)

MUSIC THERAPY
Colorado State University (M)
Georgia College & State University (M)
Saint Mary-of-the-Woods College (M)

MUTUAL FUNDS AND INVESTMENTS
New England College of Business and Finance (GC)

NANOTECHNOLOGY
Columbia University (UC)

NATIONAL SECURITY ADMINISTRATION POST-BACCALAUREATE CERTIFICATE
Kaplan University Online (UC)

NATURAL RESOURCE MANAGEMENT
University of Denver (UC)

NATURAL RESOURCES
Oregon State University (B)

NATURAL RESOURCES AND CONSERVATION
Prescott College (B,M)

NATURAL RESOURCES AND ENVIRONMENTAL SCIENCES
University of Illinois at Urbana–Champaign (M)

NATURAL RESOURCES AND THE ENVIRONMENT
Colorado State University (UC)

NATURAL SCIENCE
College of the Humanities and Sciences, Harrison Middleton University (M)
Ohio University (A)

NATURAL SCIENCES EDUCATION
Colorado State University (M)

NATURAL SCIENCES, SOCIAL SCIENCE, AND HUMANITIES

College of San Mateo (A)

NATURAL SCIENCES/ MATHEMATICS

Thomas Edison State College (B)

NEGOTIATION, CONFLICT RESOLUTION, AND PEACEBUILDING

California State University, Dominguez Hills (M)

NETMATH

University of Illinois at Urbana–Champaign (UC)

NETWORK ADMINISTRATION

Lake Superior College (A)

NETWORK AND COMMUNICATIONS MANAGEMENT

DeVry University Online (B,M)

NETWORK AND INFORMATION SECURITY

University of Louisville (GC)

NETWORK AND INTERNET ADMINISTRATION

Southwest Virginia Community College (UC)

NETWORK AND SYSTEM ADMINISTRATION

Dakota State University (A)

NETWORK ARCHITECTURE

University of Colorado Boulder (GC)

NETWORK CENTRIC SYSTEMS

University of Southern California (GC)

NETWORK ENGINEERING AND MANAGEMENT

DePaul University (M)

NETWORK MANAGEMENT

Colorado Technical University Colorado Springs (M)

NETWORK PLANNING AND DESIGN

Rochester Institute of Technology (GC)

NETWORK SECURITY

University of Massachusetts Lowell (GC)

NETWORK SECURITY AND ADMINISTRATION

Champlain College (B)

NETWORK SERVICES TECHNOLOGY

Seminole State College of Florida (A)

NETWORK SPECIALIST

Central Texas College (UC)

NETWORK SYSTEMS ADMINISTRATION

DeVry University Online (A)

NETWORK SYSTEMS ADMINISTRATOR

Central Texas College (A)

NETWORK TECHNOLOGY

Stanly Community College (A)

NETWORK+ CERTIFICATION AND COMPUTER TECHNOLOGY

Cleveland Institute of Electronics (UC)

NETWORKING AND SYSTEMS

Columbia University (UC)

NETWORKING AND SYSTEMS ADMINISTRATION

Rochester Institute of Technology (GC,M)

NETWORKING TECHNOLOGY

Wayne Community College (A)

NETWORKING/ TELECOMMUNICATIONS

City University of Seattle (UC)

NETWORKS AND DISTRIBUTED SYSTEMS

University of Illinois at Urbana–Champaign (GC)

NEURODIAGNOSTIC TECHNOLOGY

Harcum College (A)

NEW MEDIA ENGINEERING

Columbia University (UC)

NEW TESTAMENT

Johnson University (M)

NEW TESTAMENT CONCENTRATION

Global University (M)

NEWFOUNDLAND STUDIES

Memorial University of Newfoundland (UC)

NON-CERTIFICATION

The University of West Alabama (M)

NON-PROFIT MANAGEMENT

Hope International University (M)
Lasell College (GC,M)
University of Florida (GC)

NON-PROFIT MANAGEMENT AND LEADERSHIP

Lawrence Technological University (GC)

NONPROFIT ADMINISTRATION

Lindenwood University (M)

NONPROFIT AND ASSOCIATION FINANCIAL MANAGEMENT

University of Maryland University College (GC)

NONPROFIT BUSINESS ADMINISTRATION

Toccoa Falls College (B)

NONPROFIT MANAGEMENT

City Vision College (B)
Columbus State Community College (GC)
DePaul University (M)
Eastern University (M)
Northeastern University (GC,M)
Thomas Edison State College (M)
University of Central Florida (GC,M)
West Virginia University (GC)

NONPROFIT MANAGEMENT AND LEADERSHIP

Walden University (M)

NONPROFIT MANAGEMENT POST-BACHELOR'S

Walden University (GC)

NONWOVEN SCIENCE AND TECHNOLOGY

North Carolina State University (GC)

NUCLEAR ENGINEERING TECHNOLOGY

Excelsior College (A,B)
Thomas Edison State College (A,B)

NUCLEAR ENGINEERING UNDERGRADUATE MINOR

Kansas State University (UC)

NUCLEAR MEDICINE TECHNOLOGY

Ferris State University (B)
Thomas Edison State College (A,B)

NURSE ADMINISTRATION

Western Carolina University (M)

NURSE ADMINISTRATOR

Kaplan University Online (GC)
University of Mary (M)

NURSE AIDE

Columbus State Community College (GC)

NURSE ANESTHESIA

Oakland University (M)
University of Minnesota, Twin Cities Campus (D)

NURSE ANESTHESIA CONCENTRATION

Mountain State University (GC,M)

NURSE ANESTHESIA POST-GRADUATE CERTIFICATE

Oakland University (GC)

NURSE EDUCATOR

Alcorn State University (M)
Florida State University (M)
Graceland University (GC,M)
Kaplan University Online (GC)
Southern Illinois University Edwardsville (M)
The University of Toledo (M)

NURSE EDUCATOR POST-GRADUATE PROGRAM

Western Carolina University (GC)

NURSE EDUCATOR TRACK

Western Carolina University (M)

NURSE EDUCATOR, PEDIATRIC NURSE PRACTITIONER, WOMEN'S HEALTH NURSE PRACTITIONER, OR NEONATAL NURSE PRACTITIONER EMPHASIS

University of Missouri–Kansas City (M)

NURSE INFORMATICS

Kaplan University Online (GC)

NURSE MIDWIFERY

Philadelphia University (UC)
University of Cincinnati (M)
University of Minnesota, Twin Cities Campus (M)
Vanderbilt University (M)

NURSE PRACTICE

Concordia University Wisconsin (D)

NURSE PRACTITIONER

University of St. Francis (M)

NURSE PRACTITIONER ADVANCEMENT

Northern Kentucky University (UC)

NURSE PRACTITIONER AND CLINICAL SPECIALIST

University of Colorado at Colorado Springs (M)

NURSING

Allen College (M)
Athabasca University (M)
Ball State University (M)
Boise State University (M)
California State University, Chico (B,M)
California State University, Dominguez Hills (M)
California State University, San Bernardino (M)
Chamberlain College of Nursing (M)
Clarion University of Pennsylvania (B)
Colorado Technical University Colorado Springs (B)
Columbus State Community College (A)
Concordia University Wisconsin (M)
Duquesne University (M,D)
Eastern Illinois University (B)
Excelsior College (A,B,M)
Ferris State University (B,M)
Frostburg State University (B)
Gannon University (B)
Georgia State University (D)
Gonzaga University (M)
Graceland University (B)
Hannibal-LaGrange University (B)
Jacksonville State University (M)
Kaplan University Online (A,B,M)
Lakehead University (M)
La Roche College (B,M)
Lewis-Clark State College (B)
Lewis University (M)
Liberty University (M)
McKendree University (M)
McNeese State University (M)
Medical University of South Carolina (M,D)
Memorial University of Newfoundland (M)
Mercy College (B)
Mesa State College (B)
Middle Tennessee State University (B,M)
Motlow State Community College (A)
National University (B)
New Mexico State University (B,D)
Northeastern University (B)
Northern Kentucky University (M)
North Georgia College & State University (B)
Northwestern Michigan College (A)
Oakland University (D)
Oregon Health & Science University (B)
Pennsylvania College of Technology (B)
Rivier College (B)
Saint Louis University (GC,M,D)
Samuel Merritt University (M)
Shawnee State University (B)
Slippery Rock University of Pennsylvania (B)
Spring Arbor University (M)
State University of New York at Plattsburgh (B)
State University of New York College of Technology at Canton (B)
State University of New York Empire State College (B)
State University of New York Institute of Technology (B)
Texas A&M University–Corpus Christi (B)
Texas Christian University (M,D)
Texas Woman's University (D)
Thomas Edison State College (B,M)
Union University (B)
The University of Akron (M)
University of Arkansas at Little Rock (B)
University of Central Florida (B,M)
University of Colorado at Colorado Springs (D)
University of Illinois at Chicago (D)
University of Mary (B)
University of Maryland, Baltimore (M,D)
University of Michigan–Flint (B)
University of North Dakota (D)
University of St. Francis (D)
University of South Alabama (B,M,D)
The University of South Dakota (B)
The University of Tennessee at Martin (B)
The University of Texas at Brownsville (B)
University of West Florida (M)
University of Wisconsin–Madison (B)
Walden University (B)
Wayland Baptist University (B)
West Virginia University (M)
Wheeling Jesuit University (M)

NURSING (HEALTH SYSTEMS MANAGEMENT)

Texas Woman's University (M)

NURSING (RN COMPLETION)

University of Southern Mississippi (B)

NURSING ADMINISTRATION

Fort Hays State University (M)
Indiana Wesleyan University (M)
Mercy College (M)
State University of New York Institute of Technology (M)
Texas A&M University–Corpus Christi (M)
University of Cincinnati (M)
The University of North Carolina at Charlotte (GC,M)
The University of Texas at Arlington (M)
University of West Florida (M)

NURSING ADMINISTRATION AND LEADERSHIP

Saint Joseph's College of Maine (GC)

NURSING AND ADULT NURSE PRACTITIONER

Clarkson College (M)

NURSING AND HEALTH ADMINISTRATION

Saint Joseph's College of Maine (M)

NURSING AND HEALTH CARE EDUCATION

Saint Joseph's College of Maine (GC)

NURSING AND RN TO BS

University of Southern Maine (B)

NURSING BRIDGE PROGRAM

Herzing University Online (B)

NURSING COMPLETION PROGRAM

California State University, Dominguez Hills (B)

NURSING EDUCATION

Andrews University (M)
Clarkson College (M)
Fort Hays State University (M)
Grantham University (M)
Indiana State University (M)
Indiana Wesleyan University (M)
Jacksonville State University (GC)
Mansfield University of Pennsylvania (M)
Mercy College (M)
Oakland University (M)
Pace University (M)
State University of New York Institute of Technology (M)
Texas Woman's University (M)
University of Central Florida (GC)
University of Colorado at Colorado Springs (GC)
The University of North Carolina at Charlotte (GC,M)
The University of Toledo (GC)
University of West Georgia (GC)
Walden University (UC)

NURSING EDUCATION AND FACULTY ROLE

Drexel University (UC,GC,M)

NURSING EDUCATION OR LEADERSHIP (HYBRID PROGRAM)

Framingham State University (M)

NURSING EDUCATION POST-BACCALAUREATE CERTIFICATE

Oakland University (GC)

NURSING EDUCATION POST-GRADUATE CERTIFICATE

Oakland University (GC)

NURSING FAST TRACK

University of St. Francis (B)

NURSING FOR REGISTERED NURSES

Minot State University (B)

NURSING HEALTH CARE ADMINISTRATION

Clarkson College (M)

NURSING HOME ADMINISTRATION

Southeast Community College Area (UC)

NURSING INFORMATICS

Grantham University (M)
Vanderbilt University (M)
Walden University (UC)

NURSING LEADERSHIP AND MANAGEMENT

Walden University (UC)

NURSING LEADERSHIP IN HEALTH SYSTEMS MANAGEMENT

Drexel University (UC,M)

NURSING MANAGEMENT

Penn State University Park (UC)

NURSING MANAGEMENT AND ORGANIZATIONAL LEADERSHIP

Grantham University (M)

NURSING MANAGEMENT, POLICY, AND LEADERSHIP PROGRAM

Yale University (M)

NURSING PRACTICE

Ball State University (D)
Chatham University (D)
Drexel University (D)
Indiana State University (D)
Northern Kentucky University (D)
University of Central Florida (D)
University of Michigan–Flint (D)
University of Missouri–Kansas City (D)
University of Nevada, Reno (D)
The University of Toledo (D)
Vanderbilt University (D)
West Virginia University (D)

NURSING PRACTICE DOCTORATE

The Ohio State University (D)

NURSING RN/BSN

Southwestern Oklahoma State University (B)

NURSING RN/MSN

Oakland University (M)

NURSING SCIENCE

University of Missouri–Kansas City (D)
Vanderbilt University (D)

NURSING–AAS NURSING, HEALTH CARE PROVIDER TO RN ARTICULATION

St. Clair County Community College (A)

NURSING–ACCELERATED BACHELOR OF SCIENCE IN NURSING

Medical University of South Carolina (B)

NURSING–ACUTE CARE NURSE PRACTITIONER

Drexel University (M)
Vanderbilt University (M)

NURSING–AD-LPN TO BSN NURSING COMPLETION

Presentation College (B)

NURSING–ADULT NURSE PRACTITIONER

Clarkson College (M)
Kaplan University Online (UC)
State University of New York Institute of Technology (M)
University of Cincinnati (M)
Vanderbilt University (M)

NURSING–ADULT PSYCHIATRIC MENTAL HEALTH NURSE PRACTITIONER

Drexel University (GC,M)

NURSING–ADULT/ GERONTOLOGICAL NURSE PRACTITIONER

University of Minnesota, Twin Cities Campus (D)
Vanderbilt University (M)

NURSING–ADULT/PALLIATIVE CARE NURSE PRACTITIONER

Vanderbilt University (M)

NURSING–ADULT/WOMEN'S HEALTH NURSE PRACTITIONER

University of Minnesota, Twin Cities Campus (D)

NURSING–ADVANCED PRACTICE FORENSIC NURSE

University of Illinois at Chicago (UC)

NURSING–BACHELOR OF SCIENCE IN NURSING
Allen College (B)

NURSING–BACHELOR OF SCIENCE IN NURSING (BSN)
The University of Texas at Arlington (B)

NURSING–BRIDGE TO ASN NURSING
North Dakota State College of Science (A)

NURSING–BSN COMPLETION
Crown College (B)

NURSING–BSN COMPLETION FOR RN'S
Concordia University Wisconsin (B)

NURSING–BSN COMPLETION PROGRAM FOR RNS
University of Illinois at Chicago (B)

NURSING–BSN TRACK
Walden University (M)

NURSING–BSN-RN ON LINE PROGRAM
Alcorn State University (B)

NURSING–CLINICAL NURSE LEADER
University of Central Florida (GC)

NURSING–CLINICAL NURSE SPECIALIST (CNS) POST-MASTERS
University of Massachusetts Boston (GC)

NURSING–CLINICAL NURSE SPECIALIST OPTION
Murray State University (M)

NURSING–CLINICAL NURSE SPECIALIST/NURSE EDUCATOR
University of Cincinnati (M)

NURSING–CLINICAL NURSING
University of North Florida (D)

NURSING–DOCTOR OF NURSING PRACTICE
Duquesne University (D)
Simmons College (D)

NURSING–EDUCATION SPECIALIZATION
University of North Dakota (M)

NURSING–FAMILY NURSE PRACTITIONER
Clarion University of Pennsylvania (M)
Clarkson College (M)
Fort Hays State University (M)
Graceland University (GC,M)
Kaplan University Online (UC)
Prairie View A&M University (M)
Southern Illinois University Edwardsville (M)
State University of New York Institute of Technology (M)
University of Cincinnati (M)
University of Mary (M)
University of Minnesota, Twin Cities Campus (D)
Vanderbilt University (M)

NURSING–FAMILY NURSE PRACTITIONER SPECIALIZATION
University of North Dakota (M)

NURSING–FAMILY NURSE PRACTITIONER TRACK
Fort Hays State University (M)

NURSING–FAST TRACK RN TO BSN DEGREE COMPLETION PROGRAM
Chamberlain College of Nursing (B)

NURSING–FORENSIC NURSING
Duquesne University (M)
University of Colorado at Colorado Springs (GC)

NURSING–GERIATRIC NURSING EDUCATION
Penn State University Park (GC)

NURSING–GERONTOLOGICAL NURSE PRACTITIONER
State University of New York Institute of Technology (M)

NURSING–GERONTOLOGICAL NURSING
University of Colorado at Colorado Springs (GC)

NURSING–GERONTOLOGICAL NURSING SPECIALIZATION
University of North Dakota (M)

NURSING–GERONTOLOGICAL/ ADULT AND FAMILY NURSE PRACTITIONER
University of Massachusetts Boston (GC)

NURSING–HOLISTIC NURSING
University of Colorado at Colorado Springs (GC)

NURSING–INNOVATION AND INTRA/ENTREPRENEURSHIP IN ADVANCED NURSING PRACTICE
Drexel University (UC,M)

NURSING–LPN CERTIFICATE TO BSN NURSING COMPLETION
Presentation College (B)

NURSING–LPN TO BSN
North Dakota State University (B)

NURSING–LPN TO RN
Kirtland Community College (A)

NURSING–LPN-BS
Indiana State University (B)

NURSING–MASTER OF SCIENCE IN FORENSIC NURSING
Fitchburg State University (M)

NURSING–NEONATAL NURSE PRACTITIONER
Vanderbilt University (M)

NURSING–NURSING ADMINISTRATION SPECIALIZATION
Indiana State University (M)

NURSING–NURSING EDUCATION SPECIALIZATION
Indiana State University (M)

NURSING–NURSING FOR REGISTERED NURSES
Northeastern State University (B)

NURSING–NURSING PRACTICE, ADVANCED
Athabasca University (GC)

NURSING–ONLINE RN TO BSN
California State University, San Bernardino (B)

NURSING–ONLINE RN-TO-BSN TRACK
Mississippi College (B)

NURSING–PARISH NURSING
Indiana Wesleyan University (UC)

NURSING–PEDIATRIC CNS
University of Minnesota, Twin Cities Campus (D)

NURSING–PEDIATRIC NURSE PRACTITIONER

University of Minnesota, Twin Cities Campus (D)
Vanderbilt University (M)

NURSING–POST-BSN

Duquesne University (UC)

NURSING–POST-LPN

Athabasca University (B)

NURSING–POST-MASTER'S DNP

University of Minnesota, Twin Cities Campus (D)

NURSING–POST-MASTERS

Duquesne University (GC)

NURSING–POST-MASTERS CERTIFICATE IN NURSE EDUCATOR

Thomas Edison State College (GC)

NURSING–POST-MASTERS DOCTOR OF NURSING PRACTICE

University of Massachusetts Boston (D)

NURSING–POST-MASTERS NURSING ADMINISTRATION

Fort Hays State University (UC)

NURSING–POST-MASTERS NURSING EDUCATION

Fort Hays State University (UC)

NURSING–POST-MASTERS PRIMARY CARE NURSING

Indiana Wesleyan University (GC)

NURSING–POST-RN

Athabasca University (B)
Memorial University of Newfoundland (B)

NURSING–PRIMARY CARE NURSING

Indiana Wesleyan University (M)

NURSING–PROFESSIONAL PROGRAM IN NURSING

University of Wisconsin–Green Bay (B)

NURSING–PSYCHIATRIC CLINICAL NURSE SPECIALIST

University of Cincinnati (M)

NURSING–PSYCHIATRIC MENTAL HEALTH CNS

University of Minnesota, Twin Cities Campus (D)

NURSING–PSYCHIATRIC MENTAL HEALTH NURSE PRACTITIONER

Vanderbilt University (M)

NURSING–PSYCHIATRIC NURSE PRACTITIONER

University of Cincinnati (M)

NURSING–PUBLIC HEALTH NURSING

University of Minnesota, Twin Cities Campus (M,D)

NURSING–PUBLIC HEALTH NURSING-ADOLESCENT HEALTH

University of Minnesota, Twin Cities Campus (D)

NURSING–REGISTERED NURSE FIRST ASSISTANT

Columbus State Community College (GC)

NURSING–REGISTERED NURSING

Clark State Community College (A)

NURSING–RN

Prairie View A&M University (B)

NURSING–RN TO BACHELOR OF SCIENCE IN NURSING

Ball State University (B)
University of Louisville (B)

NURSING–RN TO BS

Indiana State University (B)
University of Massachusetts Boston (B)

NURSING–RN TO BS COMPLETION

The College of St. Scholastica (B)
Indiana Wesleyan University (B)

NURSING–RN TO BS IN NURSING

Texas Woman's University (B)

NURSING–RN TO BS ONLINE DEGREE COMPLETION OPTION

Boise State University (B)

NURSING–RN TO BS OPTION

Southern Illinois University Edwardsville (B)

NURSING–RN TO BSN

Angelo State University (B)
Blessing-Rieman College of Nursing (B)
Brenau University (B)
Chatham University (B)
Clarkson College (B)
Drexel University (B)
Florida Hospital College of Health Sciences (B)
Fort Hays State University (B)
Illinois State University (B)
Liberty University (B)
Loyola University New Orleans (B)
Mansfield University of Pennsylvania (B)
Marymount University (B)
Misericordia University (B)
North Carolina Central University (B)
North Dakota State University (B)
Northern Kentucky University (B)
Ohio University (B)
Penn State University Park (B)
Pittsburg State University (B)
Saint Joseph's College of Maine (B)
Saint Louis University (B)
Southwestern College (B)
University of Colorado at Colorado Springs (B)
University of Maine at Fort Kent (B)
University of Maryland, Baltimore (B)
University of Memphis (B)
University of North Alabama (B)
University of North Dakota (B)
The University of Toledo (B)
Washington State University (B)
Webster University (B)
Western Carolina University (B)
West Virginia University (B)
Youngstown State University (B)

NURSING–RN TO BSN COMPLETION

Presentation College (B)
Southeast Missouri State University (B)
The University of North Carolina at Charlotte (B)
West Texas A&M University (B)

NURSING–RN TO BSN COMPLETION PROGRAM

Temple University (B)

NURSING–RN TO BSN COMPLETION TRACK

Austin Peay State University (B)

NURSING–RN TO BSN DEGREE COMPLETION PROGRAM

Grantham University (B)

NURSING–RN TO BSN STEP PROGRAM

Jacksonville State University (B)

NURSING–RN TO BSN TO MSN STEP PROGRAM

Jacksonville State University (M)

NURSING–RN TO BSN TRACK

Ashland University (B)

NURSING–RN TO BSN TRANSITION PROGRAM

Stephen F. Austin State University (B)

NURSING–RN TO BSN, REGISTERED NURSE TO BACHELOR OF SCIENCE IN NURSING

The University of Texas at Arlington (B)

NURSING–RN TO BSN/MSN

Duquesne University (B)

NURSING–RN TO MS

University of North Dakota (M)

NURSING–RN TO MSN

Angelo State University (M)
Wheeling Jesuit University (B)

NURSING–RN TO MSN DEGREE COMPLETION PROGRAM

Grantham University (M)

NURSING–RN TRACK

Walden University (M)

NURSING RN/BSN

Oakland University (B)
University of Missouri–Kansas City (B)
Winston-Salem State University (B)

NURSING–RN-BSN COMPLETION PROGRAM

Miami University–Regional Campuses (B)

NURSING–RN-MSN BRIDGE PROGRAM

Drexel University (M)

NURSING–RN/BSN COMPLETION

Bowling Green State University (B)

NURSING–SCHOOL NURSE

University of Illinois at Chicago (UC)

NURSING–SCHOOL NURSE LICENSURE

Ashland University (UC)

NURSING–WOMEN'S HEALTH CARE NURSE PRACTITIONER

University of Minnesota, Twin Cities Campus (M)

NURSING–WOMEN'S HEALTH NURSE PRACTITIONER

Drexel University (M)

NURSING, BSN

New Mexico Highlands University (B)

NURSING, NURSING EDUCATION CONCENTRATION

Herzing University Online (M)

NURSING, NURSING MANAGEMENT CONCENTRATION

Herzing University Online (M)

NURSING/FAMILY NURSE PRACTITIONER

Saint Joseph's College of Maine (M)

NUTRITION

Huntington College of Health Sciences (A)
North Carolina State University (M)
Texas Woman's University (M)

NUTRITION AND DIETETICS

Central Michigan University (M)
State University of New York College at Oneonta (M)

NUTRITION EDUCATION

Framingham State University (GC)

NUTRITION EDUCATION–NUTRITION EDUCATION SPECIALIST

Framingham State University (M)

NUTRITION EDUCATION–SCHOOL NUTRITION SPECIALIST

Framingham State University (M)

NUTRITION SCIENCE

Kaplan University Online (B)

NUTRITION–MASTER OF SCIENCE OF NUTRITION

Huntington College of Health Sciences (M)

OBJECT-ORIENTED PROGRAMMING

Pitt Community College (UC)

OCCUPATIONAL AND ENVIRONMENTAL HYGIENE, PART-TIME/INTERNET-BASED MASTER OF SCIENCE IN PUBLIC HEALTH (MSPH)

The Johns Hopkins University (M)

OCCUPATIONAL HEALTH AND SAFETY CERTIFICATE

Columbus State Community College (GC)

OCCUPATIONAL HEALTH PSYCHOLOGY

Kansas State University (GC)

OCCUPATIONAL SAFETY

Eastern Kentucky University (B)

OCCUPATIONAL SAFETY AND HEALTH

Columbia Southern University (B,M)
Oakland University (B)

OCCUPATIONAL SAFETY AND HEALTH TECHNOLOGY

Odessa College (A)

OCCUPATIONAL SAFETY AND HEALTH/ENVIRONMENTAL MANAGEMENT

Columbia Southern University (M)

OCCUPATIONAL SAFETY AND HEALTH/FIRE SCIENCE

Columbia Southern University (B)

OCCUPATIONAL STUDIES

Thomas Edison State College (A)

OCCUPATIONAL THERAPY

Boston University (D)
Misericordia University (D)
Temple University (D)
Texas Woman's University (D)
University of Florida (M)

OCCUPATIONAL THERAPY (ADVANCED MASTERS OF SCIENCE)

A.T. Still University of Health Sciences (M)

OCCUPATIONAL THERAPY ASSISTANT

James A. Rhodes State College (A)
Wisconsin Indianhead Technical College (A)

OCEANOGRAPHY

University of West Florida (B)

OFFICE ADMINISTATION

Pitt Community College (A)

OFFICE ADMINISTRATION

Central New Mexico Community College (A)
Clark State Community College (A)
Haywood Community College (A)
Montgomery County Community College (UC,A)
Nashville State Technical Community College (A)
Seminole State College of Florida (A)
Wake Technical Community College (UC,A)

OFFICE ADMINISTRATION (IN STATE)

Daytona State College (A)

OFFICE ADMINISTRATION (OUT OF STATE)

Daytona State College (A)

OFFICE ADMINISTRATION (SPECIALTY CERTIFICATE)

Montgomery County Community College (UC)

OFFICE ADMINISTRATION TECHNOLOGY

Wayne Community College (A)

OFFICE ADMINISTRATION–LEGAL

Haywood Community College (A)
Wake Technical Community College (A)

OFFICE APPLICATIONS SPECIALIST

Northwestern Michigan College (UC)

OFFICE ASSISTANT

Bellevue College (UC)
Central Texas College (UC)

OFFICE INFORMATION SYSTEMS

Spokane Community College (A)
Western Wyoming Community College (A)

OFFICE MANAGEMENT

Broward College (UC)
Central Texas College (A)
Seminole State College of Florida (UC)

OFFICE MANAGEMENT LEVELS 1 AND 2

Central Texas College (UC)

OFFICE PROFESSIONAL

Union County College (UC)

OFFICE SOFTWARE APPLICATIONS

Seminole State College of Florida (UC)

OFFICE SPECIALIST

Broward College (UC)
Columbus State Community College (GC)
Seminole State College of Florida (UC)
Wake Technical Community College (UC)

OFFICE SUPPORT

Broward College (UC)
Seminole State College of Florida (UC)

OFFICE SUPPORT SPECIALIST

Wisconsin Indianhead Technical College (UC)

OFFICE SYSTEMS TECHNOLOGY

Atlantic Cape Community College (A)
Randolph Community College (A)
Western Kentucky University (A)

OFFICE TECHNOLOGY SKILLS, BASIC

Pitt Community College (UC)

OHIO READING ENDORSEMENT PROGRAM

Bowling Green State University (GC)

ONCOLOGY REHABILITATION CERTIFICATE

Oakland University (GC)

ONLINE ASSOCIATE OF ARTS DEGREE

East Georgia College (A)

ONLINE BUSINESS ADMINISTRATION–MANAGEMENT

Pittsburgh Technical Institute (A)

ONLINE EXECUTIVE MBA

California State University, Monterey Bay (M)
University of Nevada, Reno (M)

ONLINE GLOBAL

Anaheim University (M)

ONLINE INSTRUCTIONAL DESIGN

North Carolina Central University (M)

ONLINE LEARNING AND TEACHING POST-BACCALAUREATE CERTIFICATE

Thomas Edison State College (UC)

ONLINE MASTER IN EDUCATION

LeTourneau University (M)

ONLINE MASTER OF SCIENCE IN LITERACY

Canisius College (M)

ONLINE MASTER OF SCIENCE IN PHYSICAL EDUCATION

Canisius College (M)

ONLINE MASTER OF SCIENCE IN SPORT ADMINISTRATION

Canisius College (M)

ONLINE MASTERS OF EDUCATION

University of St. Thomas (M)

ONLINE MBA

The University of Scranton (M)

ONLINE MBA IN HEALTH CARE MANAGEMENT

The University of Scranton (M)

ONLINE SAFETY AND SECURITY ADMINISTRATION

Pittsburgh Technical Institute (A)

ONLINE TEACHING

Boise State University (GC)

ONLINE TEACHING AND LEARNING

New Mexico State University (UC)
Webster University (UC)

ONLINE TEACHING AND LEARNING OPTION

California State University, East Bay (M)

ONLINE TEACHING EMPHASIS

New Mexico State University (M)

OPERATIONS AND PROJECT MANAGEMENT

Southern New Hampshire University (M)

OPERATIONS DESIGN AND LEADERSHIP

Worcester Polytechnic Institute (M)

OPERATIONS MANAGEMENT

Excelsior College (B)
Fort Hays State University (UC)
Kettering University (M)
Oregon Institute of Technology (B)
Southern New Hampshire University (GC)

Southwestern College (B)
Thomas Edison State College (B)
The University of Scranton (M)

OPERATIONS MANAGEMENT CONCENTRATION

Colorado Technical University Colorado Springs (M)

OPERATIONS MANAGEMENT PRE-ASSOCIATE CERTIFICATE

Thomas Edison State College (UC)

OPERATIONS RESEARCH

Columbia University (UC,M)
Florida Institute of Technology (M)
Georgia Institute of Technology (M)
Kansas State University (M)
Southern Methodist University (M)
The University of Alabama in Huntsville (M)

OPERATIONS RESEARCH ENGINEERING

University of Southern California (M)

OPERATIONS RESEARCH–METHODS IN FINANCE

Columbia University (M)

OPERATIONS TECHNOLOGY

Northeastern University (B)

OPTICAL SCIENCES

The University of Arizona (GC,M)

OPTICIANRY

J. Sargeant Reynolds Community College (A)

OPTICIANS APPRENTICE

J. Sargeant Reynolds Community College (UC)

ORACLE DATABASE ADMINISTRATION POST-BACCALAUREATE CERTIFICATE

Kaplan University Online (UC)

ORACLE DBA PROGRAMMING

Wake Technical Community College (UC)

ORACLE DEVELOPER

Wake Technical Community College (UC)

OREGON TRANSFER

Chemeketa Community College (A)

OREGON TRANSFER MODULE

Chemeketa Community College (UC)

ORGANIC AGRICULTURE

Washington State University (UC)

ORGANIZATION MANAGEMENT AND DEVELOPMENT

Fielding Graduate University (UC,M)

ORGANIZATION MANAGEMENT AND LEADERSHIP

Friends University (B)

ORGANIZATIONAL ADMINISTRATION

Southeast Missouri State University (B)

ORGANIZATIONAL AND HUMAN RESOURCE DEVELOPMENT (OHRD)

Abilene Christian University (M)

ORGANIZATIONAL AND PROFESSIONAL COMMUNICATION

University of Denver (M)

ORGANIZATIONAL AND PROFESSIONAL DEVELOPMENT

Eastern Illinois University (B)

ORGANIZATIONAL BEHAVIOR

National University (B)

ORGANIZATIONAL COMMUNICATION

Penn State University Park (UC)

ORGANIZATIONAL COMMUNICATION COMPREHENSIVE OPTION

University of Nebraska at Kearney (B)

ORGANIZATIONAL COMMUNICATIONS

Northeastern University (GC,B)
Pace University (B)
Upper Iowa University (UC)

ORGANIZATIONAL DEVELOPMENT

Champlain College (UC)
Colorado State University (UC)
University of the Incarnate Word (B,M)

ORGANIZATIONAL DEVELOPMENT AND LEADERSHIP

Widener University (B)

ORGANIZATIONAL DEVELOPMENT AND TRAINING

University of Denver (UC)

ORGANIZATIONAL LEADERSHIP

Baldwin-Wallace College (B)
Brenau University (B)
Columbia Southern University (B,M)
Crown College (M)
Eastern University (B,M,D)
Fort Hays State University (GC,B)
Gonzaga University (M)
Indiana Tech (B,M)
Indiana Wesleyan University (M,D)
Judson University (M)
Kansas State University (GC)
Lewis University (M)
Lincoln Christian University (M)
Mansfield University of Pennsylvania (M)
Mercy College (M)
Mountain State University (B)
National University (M)
Nichols College (M)
Northern Kentucky University (B)
Penn State University Park (B)
Quinnipiac University (B)
Regent University (M,D)
Southern New Hampshire University (M)
University of Mary (B)
University of St. Francis (B)
Upper Iowa University (UC)

ORGANIZATIONAL LEADERSHIP (BSOL)

Thomas Edison State College (B)

ORGANIZATIONAL LEADERSHIP AND CHANGE

Colorado Technical University Colorado Springs (M)

ORGANIZATIONAL LEADERSHIP AND MANAGEMENT

Regent University (B)

ORGANIZATIONAL LEADERSHIP IN ANIMAL ADVOCACY

Duquesne University (GC)

ORGANIZATIONAL LEADERSHIP–BUSINESS STUDIES, COMMUNICATIONS STRATEGIES, LIBERAL STUDIES, OR SOCIAL STUDIES FOCUS

Rogers State University (B)

ORGANIZATIONAL LEADERSHIP, CRIMINAL JUSTICE ADMINISTRATION CONCENTRATION

Mountain State University (B)

ORGANIZATIONAL LEADERSHIP, GENERAL DEGREE

Quinnipiac University (M)

ORGANIZATIONAL LEADERSHIP, HOSPITALITY LEADERSHIP CONCENTRATION

Mountain State University (B)

ORGANIZATIONAL LEARNING AND PERFORMANCE

Colorado State University (UC)

ORGANIZATIONAL MANAGEMENT

Mercy College (B)
Misericordia University (M)
St. Joseph's College, Long Island Campus (B)
St. Joseph's College, New York (B)
Spring Arbor University (B)
University of Great Falls (M)
Wayne State College (M)

ORGANIZATIONAL MANAGEMENT AND LEADERSHIP

Concordia University, St. Paul (B)

ORGANIZATIONAL MANAGEMENT AND LEADERSHIP POST-BACCALAUREATE CERTIFICATE

Thomas Edison State College (UC)

ORGANIZATIONAL PERFORMANCE AND CHANGE (OPC)

Colorado State University (M,D)

ORGANIZATIONAL PSYCHOLOGY AND DEVELOPMENT POST-BACHELOR'S SPECIALIZED LEARNING CERTIFICATE

Walden University (UC)

ORGANIZATIONAL SECURITY

University of Denver (UC)

ORGANIZATIONAL STUDIES

Robert Morris University (B,M)

ORIENTATION AND MOBILITY

University of Arkansas at Little Rock (M)
Western Michigan University (M)

PAINTING

Savannah College of Art and Design (M)

PALLIATIVE CARE INTERDISCIPLINARY CERTIFICATE

Lakehead University (UC)

PARAEDUCATION

Dakota College at Bottineau (UC,A)

PARALEGAL

Boston University (GC)
Franklin Pierce University (UC)
Herkimer County Community College (A)
Minnesota School of Business–Online (A,B)
Minnesota School of Business–Richfield (A,B)
The Paralegal Institute, Inc. (A)

PARALEGAL CERTIFICATE

California State University, Dominguez Hills (GC)

PARALEGAL CERTIFICATE, ADVANCED

California State University, Dominguez Hills (GC)

PARALEGAL ONLINE

Bryant & Stratton Online (A)

PARALEGAL STUDIES

Ellis University (A,B)
Hodges University (A)
Kaplan University Online (A,B)
Lake Superior College (A)
Liberty University (A,B)
Peirce College (UC,A,B)
Roger Williams University (B)
Saint Mary-of-the-Woods College (UC,A,B)
Tompkins Cortland Community College (A)
University of Great Falls (A,B)
University of Massachusetts Lowell (UC)

PARALEGAL STUDIES (PLD)

Mount Wachusett Community College (A)

PARALEGAL–CREDIT

Northeastern University (UC)

PARALEGAL–NONCREDIT

Northeastern University (UC)

PARAMEDIC TECHNICIAN

Wisconsin Indianhead Technical College (A)

PARAMEDIC TECHNOLOGY

Quinsigamond Community College (A)

PARAMEDICINE COMPLETION

Western Kentucky University (A)

PARK AND RECREATION RESOURCE MANAGEMENT

Frostburg State University (M)

PARK AND RESOURCE MANAGEMENT

Slippery Rock University of Pennsylvania (M)

PARKS, RECREATION, TOURISM AND SPORT MANAGEMENT

North Carolina State University (M)

PASTORAL COUNSELING

Amridge University (M)
Liberty University (M)

PASTORAL MINISTRIES

Laurel University (B)

PASTORAL MINISTRY

Summit Pacific College

PASTORAL STUDIES

Aquinas Institute of Theology (M)
Southwestern College (B)

PASTORAL THEOLOGY

Saint Joseph's College of Maine (M)
Saint Mary-of-the-Woods College (M)

PATHWAY TO PARALEGAL (POST-BACCALAUREATE)

Kaplan University Online (UC)

PATHWAY TO PARALEGAL POST-BACCALAUREATE CERTIFICATE

Kaplan University Online (UC)

PATIENT ADVOCATE

The University of Toledo (GC)

PATIENT AND PRODUCT SAFETY

University of Southern California (GC)

PATIENT CARE SKILLS

Columbus State Community College (GC)

PATIENT SAFETY LEADERSHIP

University of Illinois at Chicago (M)

PATIENT SAFETY, ERROR SCIENCE, AND FULL DISCLOSURE

University of Illinois at Chicago (UC)

PAYROLL ACCOUNTING CLERK

Wake Technical Community College (UC)

PEACE STUDIES
Prescott College (M)

PEDIATRIC PRIMARY CARE
Drexel University (M)

PERFORMANCE EXCELLENCE
University of Colorado Boulder (GC)

PERFORMANCE IMPROVEMENT
Grantham University (M)

PERFORMANCE MANAGEMENT
Colorado State University (UC)

PERSONAL FINANCIAL PLANNING
Kansas State University (GC,M,D)

PEST CONTROL TECHNOLOGY
University of Florida (UC,GC)

PEST MANAGEMENT
University of Florida (M)

PETROLEUM ENGINEERING
University of Southern California (M)

PETROLEUM ENGINEERING (SMART OILFIELD TECHNOLOGIES)
University of Southern California (GC,M)

PHARMACEUTICAL BUSINESS
University of the Sciences in Philadelphia (M)

PHARMACEUTICAL CHEMISTRY
University of Florida (GC,M)

PHARMACEUTICAL ENGINEERING
University of Michigan (M)

PHARMACEUTICAL MANAGEMENT
Drexel University (M)

PHARMACEUTICAL OUTCOMES AND POLICY
University of Florida (M)

PHARMACEUTICAL SCIENCE–FORENSIC DNA AND SEROLOGY
University of Florida (M)

PHARMACEUTICAL SCIENCE–FORENSIC DRUG CHEMISTRY
University of Florida (M)

PHARMACEUTICAL SCIENCE–FORENSIC SCIENCE
University of Florida (M)

PHARMACEUTICAL SCIENCES, COSMETIC SCIENCE EMPHASIS
University of Cincinnati (M)

PHARMACY
Auburn University (D)
University of Wisconsin–Madison (D)

PHARMACY TECHNICIAN
North Dakota State College of Science (A)
Sinclair Community College (UC)
Vincennes University (A)

PHARMACY, FIRST PROFESSIONAL DEGREE
University of Florida (D)

PHARMACY, WORKING PROFESSIONAL
University of Florida (D)

PHILANTHROPY AND NONPROFIT DEVELOPMENT
University of Northern Iowa (M)

PHILOSOPHY
Holy Apostles College and Seminary (M)
Labette Community College (A)
Prescott College (M)
Thomas Edison State College (B)
University of Illinois at Springfield (B)
University of Memphis (B)
University of Waterloo (B)

PHILOSOPHY AND RELIGION
Butler Community College (A)
College of the Humanities and Sciences, Harrison Middleton University (M)

PHILOSOPHY, POLITICS, AND ECONOMICS
Eastern Oregon University (B)

PHLEBOTOMY
Mountain State University (UC)

PHOTOGRAPHY
Academy of Art University (A,B,M)
Burlington College (B)
Columbus State Community College (GC)
Prescott College (M)
Savannah College of Art and Design (B)
Thomas Edison State College (B)

PHOTOSHOP FOR ILLUSTRATION AND DESIGN
Columbus State Community College (GC)

PHOTOSHOP FOR PHOTOGRAPHERS
Columbus State Community College (GC)

PHP PROGRAMMING
Champlain College (UC)

PHYSICAL ACTIVITY AND HEALTH
Eastern Oregon University (B)

PHYSICAL EDUCATION
Emporia State University (M)
Jacksonville State University (M)
Memorial University of Newfoundland (M)
University of Houston (M)

PHYSICAL EDUCATION PEDAGOGY
Western Kentucky University (M)

PHYSICAL EDUCATION STUDIES
Erie Community College (A)
Erie Community College, North Campus (A)
Erie Community College, South Campus (A)

PHYSICAL EDUCATION TEACHER EDUCATION
West Virginia University (M)

PHYSICAL EDUCATION, ADAPTED PHYSICAL EDUCATION TRACK (APE)
The University of Toledo (M)

PHYSICAL EDUCATION, COACHING SPECIALIZATION
Ball State University (M)

PHYSICAL EDUCATION, HEALTH EDUCATION, COACHING
Boston University (GC)

PHYSICAL EDUCATION, HEALTH, AND LEISURE STUDIES
Central Washington University (M)

PHYSICAL SCIENCES (EARTH SCIENCE EMPHASIS)
Emporia State University (M)

PHYSICAL THERAPIST ASSISTANT
Clark State Community College (A)
James A. Rhodes State College (A)

PHYSICAL THERAPIST ASSISTANT–MILITARY COMPLETER PROGRAM

Arapahoe Community College (A)

PHYSICAL THERAPY

Boston University (D)
Temple University (D)
The University of Tennessee at Chattanooga (D)

PHYSICAL THERAPY–POST-PROFESSIONAL DOCTOR OF PHYSICAL THERAPY

Rosalind Franklin University of Medicine and Science (D)

PHYSICAL THERAPY–TRANSITIONAL DOCTOR OF PHYSICAL THERAPY

MGH Institute of Health Professions (D)

PHYSICAL THERAPY–TRANSITIONAL DOCTORATE OF PHYSICAL THERAPY

Utica College (D)

PHYSICIAN ASSISTANT

Lock Haven University of Pennsylvania (M)

PHYSICIAN ASSISTANT POST-PROFESSIONAL PROGRAM

Drexel University (M)

PHYSICIAN ASSISTANT STUDIES

A.T. Still University of Health Sciences (M)
University of Wisconsin–Madison (M)

PHYSICIANS EXECUTIVE

Auburn University (M)

PHYSICIANS EXECUTIVE MBA

Auburn University (M)

PK-12 EDUCATIONAL ADMINISTRATION

New Mexico State University (M)

PLANT PESTS, PATHOGENS, AND PEOPLE

North Carolina State University (UC)

PLASTICS ENGINEERING FUNDAMENTALS

University of Massachusetts Lowell (GC)

PLAYWRITING AND SCREENWRITING

Prescott College (M)

POLICE ADMINISTRATION

Indiana Tech (M)

POLICE LEADERSHIP

University of Central Florida (GC)

POLICE STUDIES

Memorial University of Newfoundland (B)

POLICY ANALYSIS

University of North Dakota (GC)

POLICY AND MANAGEMENT IN DISTANCE EDUCATION AND E-LEARNING

University of Maryland University College (GC)

POLICY STUDIES

State University of New York Empire State College (M)

POLITICAL ECONOMY (3 YEAR)

Athabasca University (B)

POLITICAL ECONOMY (4 YEAR)

Athabasca University (B)

POLITICAL SCIENCE

Austin Peay State University (B)
Caldwell College (B)
Fort Hays State University (B)
Fort Valley State University (B)
Kaplan University Online (B)
Northeastern University (B)
Oregon State University (B)
Penn State University Park (B)
Prescott College (B)
Thomas Edison State College (B)
University of Central Florida (B)
University of Maryland University College (B)

POLITICAL SCIENCE (3 YEAR)

Athabasca University (B)

POLITICAL SCIENCE (4 YEAR)

Athabasca University (B)

POLITICAL SCIENCE AND PUBLIC ADMINISTRATION

Walden University (B)

POLITICAL SCIENCE–ONLINE

Oregon State University (B)

POLYMER SCIENCE AND ENGINEERING

Lehigh University (M)
University of Southern Mississippi (M)

POLYSOMNOGRAPHIC TECHNOLOGY

Oregon Institute of Technology (UC,A)

POLYSOMNOGRAPHY

The University of Texas at Brownsville (UC)

POLYSOMNOGRAPHY (ASAST)

Thomas Edison State College (A)

POST-BACCALAUREATE

University of Nebraska at Kearney (UC)

POST-BACCALAUREATE CERTIFICATE

Minnesota School of Business–Online (UC)

POST-DOCTORAL SPECIALIZED LEARNING CERTIFICATE

Walden University (UC)

POST-SECONDARY FACILITATOR

Indiana State University (UC)

POSTSECONDARY LITERACY INSTRUCTION

University of Cincinnati (UC)

POSTSECONDARY STUDIES

Memorial University of Newfoundland (M)

POSTSECONDARY TEACHING

Colorado State University (UC)

POWER ELECTRONICS

University of Colorado Boulder (GC)

POWER ELECTRONICS AND MACHINE DRIVES (EE CONCENTRATION)

Kettering University (M)

POWER SYSTEM PROTECTION AND RELAYING

University of Idaho (UC)

POWER SYSTEMS ENGINEERING

Worcester Polytechnic Institute (M)

PRACTICAL INTERNET MARKETING

DePaul University (UC)

PRACTICAL MINISTRY

Amridge University (M)

PRACTICAL THEOLOGY

Regent University (M)

PRE-BACHELOR OF ARTS

Miami Dade College (A)

PRE-KINDERGARTEN HANDICAPPED ENDORSEMENT

University of Central Florida (GC)

PRE-LAW

Broward College (A)
Fort Hays State University (UC)

PRE-MBA (BUSINESS MANAGEMENT)

Columbus State Community College (GC)

PRE-MBA (MARKETING)

Columbus State Community College (GC)

PRECLINICAL DRUG DEVELOPMENT

University of Southern California (GC)

PREDICTIVE ANALYTICS

DePaul University (M)

PREVENTION SCIENCE

Emory University (M)

PRIMARY HEALTH CARE AND HEALTH DISPARITIES

Oregon Health & Science University (M)

PRINCIPAL LICENSURE

University of Colorado at Colorado Springs (UC)

PRINCIPAL'S LICENSE

Ball State University (UC)

PRIOR LEARNING ASSESSMENT

DePaul University (UC)

PRIVATE SECURITY

Kaplan University Online (UC)

PRIVATE SECURITY AND LOSS PREVENTION

Indiana State University (UC)

PRIVATE SECURITY MANAGEMENT

Kaplan University Online (UC)

PROCUREMENT AND ACQUISITIONS MANAGEMENT

Webster University (M)

PRODUCT DEVELOPMENT

Rochester Institute of Technology (M)

PRODUCT DEVELOPMENT ENGINEERING

University of Southern California (M)

PRODUCTION AND INVENTORY CONTROL

California State University, Dominguez Hills (UC)

PROFESSIONAL AND TECHNICAL WRITING

Robert Morris University (B)

PROFESSIONAL AND TECHNICAL COMMUNICATION

Dakota State University (B)

PROFESSIONAL BOOKKEEPER

Lake Superior College (UC)

PROFESSIONAL COMMUNICATION

Valley City State University (B)

PROFESSIONAL COMMUNICATIONS

Western International University (B)

PROFESSIONAL COUNSELING

Amridge University (M)
Liberty University (M)

PROFESSIONAL DEVELOPMENT

Amberton University (M)

PROFESSIONAL DEVELOPMENT FOR TEACHERS

University of Northern Iowa (M)

PROFESSIONAL DEVELOPMENT IN CHURCH LEADERSHIP

Dallas Baptist University (M)

PROFESSIONAL DEVELOPMENT IN CRIMINAL JUSTICE

Dallas Baptist University (M)

PROFESSIONAL DEVELOPMENT IN FINANCE

Dallas Baptist University (M)

PROFESSIONAL DEVELOPMENT IN HIGHER EDUCATION

Dallas Baptist University (M)

PROFESSIONAL DEVELOPMENT IN LEADERSHIP STUDIES

Dallas Baptist University (M)

PROFESSIONAL DEVELOPMENT IN MANAGEMENT

Dallas Baptist University (M)

PROFESSIONAL DEVELOPMENT IN MANAGEMENT INFORMATION SYSTEMS

Dallas Baptist University (M)

PROFESSIONAL DEVELOPMENT IN MARKETING

Dallas Baptist University (M)

PROFESSIONAL DEVELOPMENT LEARNING COMMUNITY PROGRAM

University of Wisconsin–La Crosse (M)

PROFESSIONAL DEVELOPMENT POST-BACHELOR'S

Walden University (GC)

PROFESSIONAL DOCTOR OF OCCUPATIONAL THERAPY

Chatham University (D)

PROFESSIONAL IN HUMAN RESOURCES

DePaul University (UC)

PROFESSIONAL INVESTIGATION

Boston University (UC)

PROFESSIONAL PRACTICE

University of Wisconsin–Madison (M)

PROFESSIONAL SCIENCE

Washington State University (M)

PROFESSIONAL STUDIES

Drexel University (B,M)
Hodges University (M)
Johnson State College (B)
Kaplan University Online (B)
Misericordia University (B)
Rochester Institute of Technology (M)

Stony Brook University, State University of New York (M)
Widener University (B)

PROFESSIONAL STUDIES, APSU (ORGANIZATIONAL FORENSICS MINOR AVAILABLE)

Austin Peay State University (B)

PROFESSIONAL STUDIES, INFORMATION TECHNOLOGY CONCENTRATION

Middle Tennessee State University (B)

PROFESSIONAL STUDIES, ORGANIZATIONAL LEADERSHIP CONCENTRATION

Middle Tennessee State University (B)

PROFESSIONAL STUDIES, STRATEGIC LEADERSHIP CONCENTRATION

Middle Tennessee State University (M)

PROFESSIONAL TECHNOLOGY STUDIES

Pace University (B)

PROFESSIONAL WRITING

Chatham University (M)
Saint Mary-of-the-Woods College (B)
Taylor University (UC)
University of Central Florida (GC)
Washington State University (UC)

PROGRAM AND PROJECT MANAGEMENT

University of Michigan–Dearborn (M)

PROGRAM MANAGEMENT MASTER CERTIFICATE

University of Atlanta (GC)

PROGRAMMING

Front Range Community College (UC)

PROGRAMMING AND SOFTWARE DEVELOPMENT

The University of Toledo (A)

PROGRAMMING AND SYSTEMS DEVELOPMENT

Dakota State University (UC)

PROJECT ENGINEERING

University of Central Florida (GC)

PROJECT MANAGEMENT

Athabasca University (M)
Boston University (GC,M)
Brenau University (M)
City University of Seattle (UC,GC,M)
Colorado State University (UC)
Columbia Southern University (B,M)
Dallas Baptist University (GC,M)
DePaul University (UC)
DeVry University Online (M)
Drexel University (M)
Florida Institute of Technology (M)
Granite State College (M)
Grantham University (M)
Kaplan University Online (UC)
Lasell College (GC,M)
Lawrence Technological University (GC)
Lehigh University (UC)
Mississippi State University (M)
Northeastern University (GC,M)
Penn State University Park (GC,M)
Rochester Institute of Technology (GC)
University of Colorado at Colorado Springs (M)
University of Colorado Boulder (GC)
University of Denver (UC)
University of Management and Technology (GC,M)
University of Mary (M)
University of Maryland University College (GC)
The University of Texas at Dallas (M)
University of Wisconsin–Platteville (GC)
University of Wisconsin–Platteville (M)
Walden University (M)
Western Carolina University (M)

PROJECT MANAGEMENT ACCELERATED BBS/MBA

Dallas Baptist University (M)

PROJECT MANAGEMENT CONCENTRATION

Colorado Technical University Colorado Springs (B,M)

PROJECT MANAGEMENT POST-BACCALAUREATE

Western Carolina University (GC)

PROJECT MANAGEMENT POST-BACHELOR'S, ADVANCED

Walden University (GC)

PROJECT MANAGEMENT PREP

Auburn University (UC)

PROJECT MANAGEMENT–MASTER OF PROJECT MANAGEMENT

American Graduate University (M)

PROJECT MANAGEMENT, ADVANCED

University of Wisconsin–Platteville (GC)

PROJECT MANAGEMENT, INFORMATION SYSTEMS CONCENTRATION

Florida Institute of Technology (M)

PROJECT MANAGEMENT, OPERATIONS RESEARCH CONCENTRATION

Florida Institute of Technology (M)

PROPERTY MANAGEMENT

Drexel University (B,M)

PROPERTY MANAGEMENT CONCENTRATION

Colorado Technical University Colorado Springs (B)

PSYCH MENTAL HEALTH

University of Minnesota, Twin Cities Campus (M)

PSYCHOLOGICAL MEASUREMENT AND METHODOLOGIES

Colorado State University (UC)

PSYCHOLOGY

Andrew Jackson University (A)
Atlantic Cape Community College (A)
Baker College Online (B)
Barclay College (B)
Brookdale Community College (A)
Burlington College (B)
Caldwell College (B)
Colorado Technical University Colorado Springs (B)
Columbia College (B)
Columbia Southern University (B)
Dallas Baptist University (B)
Drexel University (B)
Drury University (A)
Eastern Oregon University (B)
Fort Valley State University (B)
Indiana Tech (B)
Judson College (B)
Kaplan University Online (B,M)
Lansing Community College (A)
Lesley University (B)
LeTourneau University (B,M)
Liberty University (A,B)
Limestone College (B)
Lynn University (B)
Mercy College (B,M)
Middlesex Community College (A)
Middle Tennessee State University (B)
Midway College (B)
Mountain State University (B,M)
National University (B)
North Carolina Wesleyan College (B)
Northeastern University (B)
Penn State University Park (B)
Peru State College (B)
Regent University (A,B)
Rivier College (B)
Saint Joseph's College of Maine (A,B)

Saint Leo University (B)
Saint Mary-of-the-Woods College (B)
San Diego Community College District (A)
Santa Rosa Junior College (A)
Southern New Hampshire University (B)
Southwestern Adventist University (B)
Thomas Edison State College (B)
Trine University (B)
Tyler Junior College (A)
Union College (M)
Union Institute & University (D)
University of Great Falls (B)
University of Houston (B)
University of Houston–Downtown (B)
University of Houston–Victoria (B)
University of Maryland University College (B)
University of Massachusetts Lowell (B)
University of Memphis (B)
University of North Dakota (B)
University of the Incarnate Word (B)
Upper Iowa University (B)
Utah State University (B)
Walden University (B,M,D)
West Hills Community College (A)

PSYCHOLOGY (3 YEAR)

Athabasca University (B)

PSYCHOLOGY (4 YEAR)

Athabasca University (B)

PSYCHOLOGY (CHILD AND ADOLESCENT DEVELOPMENT CONCENTRATION)

Southern New Hampshire University (B)

PSYCHOLOGY AND COMMUNITY STUDIES

University of Maine at Machias (B)

PSYCHOLOGY AND COUNSELING

Goddard College (M)

PSYCHOLOGY MAJOR

Central Michigan University (B)

PSYCHOLOGY OF THE WORKPLACE

Jamestown Community College (GC)

PSYCHOLOGY POST-DOCTORAL CERTIFICATE (RESPECIALIZATION)

Walden University (UC)

PSYCHOLOGY–APPLIED PSYCHOLOGY

City University of Seattle (B)

PSYCHOLOGY, INDUSTRIAL AND ORGANIZATIONAL PSYCHOLOGY EMPHASIS

Kansas State University (M)

PSYCHOLOGY/COUNSELING

Crown College (B)

PSYCHOLOGY/SOCIOLOGY

Alvin Community College (A)

PUBLIC ADMINISTRATION

Andrew Jackson University (M)
Athabasca University (UC)
Belhaven University (M)
California State University, Dominguez Hills (M)
California State University, San Bernardino (M)
Central Michigan University (M)
Clemson University (M)
Columbia Southern University (M)
DePaul University (M)
DeVry University Online (M)
Florida Institute of Technology (M)
Fort Hays State University (UC)
Gannon University (M)
Hodges University (M)
Indiana State University (GC,M)
Kansas State University (GC)
Kaplan University Online (A,M)
Marist College (M)
Memorial University of Newfoundland (UC)
National University (M)
Northeastern University (M)
Penn State University Park (M)
Roger Williams University (B,M)
Stephen F. Austin State University (M)
Thomas Edison State College (B)
University of Baltimore (M)
University of Central Florida (GC)
University of Colorado at Colorado Springs (M)
University of Illinois at Springfield (M)
University of Management and Technology (GC,M)
University of North Dakota (GC,M)
The University of Texas at Arlington (M)
University of West Florida (M)
Upper Iowa University (B)
Walden University (M)
Wayland Baptist University (M)
Western International University (M)

PUBLIC ADMINISTRATION AND POLICY

Kaplan University Online (B)

PUBLIC ADMINISTRATION PRE-ASSOCIATE CERTIFICATE

Thomas Edison State College (UC)

PUBLIC ADMINISTRATION–FIRE SCIENCE EMPHASIS

Upper Iowa University (B)

PUBLIC ADMINISTRATION–LAW ENFORCEMENT EMPHASIS

Upper Iowa University (B)

PUBLIC ADMINISTRATION, GENERAL STUDY EMPHASIS

Upper Iowa University (M)

PUBLIC ADMINISTRATION, GOVERNMENT ADMINISTRATION EMPHASIS

Upper Iowa University (M)

PUBLIC ADMINISTRATION, HEALTH AND HUMAN SERVICES EMPHASIS

Upper Iowa University (M)

PUBLIC ADMINISTRATION, INTERNATIONAL PUBLIC MANAGEMENT SPECIALIZATION

DePaul University (M)

PUBLIC ADMINISTRATION, JUSTICE AND HOMELAND SECURITY EMPHASIS

Upper Iowa University (M)

PUBLIC ADMINISTRATION, NONPROFIT ORGANIZATIONS EMPHASIS

Upper Iowa University (M)

PUBLIC ADMINISTRATION, PUBLIC PERSONNEL MANAGEMENT EMPHASIS

Upper Iowa University (M)

PUBLIC ADMINSTRATION/PUBLIC SAFETY

Mesa State College (B)

PUBLIC AFFAIRS

Northeastern University (B)

PUBLIC FINANCE

Thomas Edison State College (M)

PUBLIC HEALTH

A.T. Still University of Health Sciences (M)
Kaplan University Online (B,M)
Medical College of Wisconsin (GC,M)
Monroe College (B)
University of Florida (GC)
University of Illinois at Springfield (M)
University of Memphis (M)
University of Waterloo (M)
University of West Florida (M)
Walden University (M,D)

West Virginia University (M)
Youngstown State University (M)

PUBLIC HEALTH (BSAS)

Youngstown State University (B)

PUBLIC HEALTH GEOGRAPHIC INFORMATION SYSTEMS

University of Illinois at Chicago (UC)

PUBLIC HEALTH INFORMATICS

University of Illinois at Chicago (UC,M)

PUBLIC HEALTH MANAGEMENT

University of Illinois at Chicago (UC)

PUBLIC HEALTH PRACTICE TRAINING CERTIFICATE

The Johns Hopkins University (UC)

PUBLIC HEALTH SPECIALIZATION, ADVANCED

University of North Dakota (M)

PUBLIC HEALTH TRAINING CERTIFICATE

The Johns Hopkins University (UC)

PUBLIC HEALTH–FUNDAMENTALS AND PRINCIPLES

University at Albany, State University of New York (UC)

PUBLIC HEALTH, PART-TIME

The Johns Hopkins University (M)

PUBLIC HEALTH, PART-TIME/ INTERNET-BASED

The Johns Hopkins University (M)

PUBLIC HEALTH/PUBLIC POLICY

Thomas Edison State College (M)

PUBLIC JUSTICE

State University of New York at Oswego (B)

PUBLIC LIBRARIAN LEVEL IV

Indiana State University (GC)

PUBLIC MANAGEMENT AND LEADERSHIP POST-BACHELOR'S

Walden University (GC)

PUBLIC PERSONNEL ADMINISTRATION

Indiana State University (GC)

PUBLIC POLICY AND ADMINISTRATION

Walden University (D)

PUBLIC POLICY POST-BACHELOR'S

Walden University (GC)

PUBLIC RELATIONS

Ball State University (M)
Lasell College (GC,M)
University of Maryland University College (GC)
Webster University (M)

PUBLIC RELATIONS AND ADVERTISING

North Dakota State University (B)

PUBLIC RELATIONS AND MARKETING

University of Denver (UC)

PUBLIC RELATIONS COMMUNICATIONS–PROFESSIONAL WRITING

Rochester Institute of Technology (UC)

PUBLIC SAFETY

Herzing University Online (A)

PUBLIC SAFETY ADMINISTRATION

Lewis University (M)
St. Petersburg College (B)

PUBLIC SAFETY AND BUSINESS/ ORGANIZATION SECURITY

Amridge University (B)

PUBLIC SAFETY AND CRIMINAL JUSTICE

Amridge University (B)

PUBLIC SAFETY AND HOMELAND SECURITY

Amridge University (B)

PUBLIC SAFETY AND SECURITY MANAGEMENT

Western Carolina University (B)

PUBLIC SAFETY MANAGEMENT

Cardinal Stritch University (B)

PUBLIC SAFETY–CRIMINAL JUSTICE

Midway College (B)

PUBLIC SERVICE ADMINISTRATION AND LEADERSHIP

Thomas Edison State College (M)

PUBLIC SERVICE COMMUNITY AND ECONOMIC DEVELOPMENT

Thomas Edison State College (M)

PUBLIC SERVICE LEADERSHIP POST-BACCALAUREATE CERTIFICATE

Thomas Edison State College (UC)

PUBLIC SERVICE MANAGEMENT

DePaul University (M)

PUBLIC SERVICE MANAGEMENT (MPS) ONLINE

DePaul University (M)

PUBLISHING

Pace University (M)

PULMONARY SCIENCE

Concordia University, St. Paul (B)

PURCHASING

California State University, Dominguez Hills (UC)
Columbus State Community College (GC)

QA/RA PROGRAM

Temple University (M)

QUALITY ASSURANCE

California State University, Dominguez Hills (UC,B,M)
University of Central Florida (GC)

QUALITY LEADERSHIP

Saint Joseph's College of Maine (M)

QUALITY MANAGEMENT

Rochester Institute of Technology (UC)
University of Wisconsin–Stout (UC)

QUALITY SYSTEMS

Bowling Green State University (GC,B)

QUALITY SYSTEMS AND ENGINEERING

University of Colorado Boulder (GC)

QUANTITATIVE LITERACY

University of Illinois at Urbana–Champaign (M)

QUANTITATIVE METHODS IN PUBLIC HEALTH TRAINING CERTIFICATE

The Johns Hopkins University (UC)

RADIATION HEALTH PHYSICS

Oregon State University (M)

RADIATION PROTECTION

Thomas Edison State College (A,B)

RADIATION THERAPY

Thomas Edison State College (A,B)

RADIOGRAPHIC IMAGING

James A. Rhodes State College (A)

RADIOLOGIC PHYSICS

Illinois Institute of Technology (GC)

RADIOLOGIC SCIENCE ADMINISTRATION

Saint Joseph's College of Maine (A)

RADIOLOGIC SCIENCES

Florida Hospital College of Health Sciences (B)
Midwestern State University (B)

RADIOLOGIC SCIENCES (EDUCATION OR ADMINISTRATION MAJOR)

Midwestern State University (M)

RADIOLOGIC SCIENCES PREREQUISITE PROGRAM

Clarion University of Pennsylvania (UC)

RADIOLOGIC TECHNOLOGY

Mesa State College (B)

RADIOLOGIC TECHNOLOGY COMPLETION PROGRAM

Presentation College (B)

RADIOLOGIC TECHNOLOGY PROGRAM

Southeast Community College Area (A)

RADIOLOGICAL SCIENCE ADMINISTRATION

Saint Joseph's College of Maine (B)

RADIOLOGICAL SCIENCE–RADIOLOGICAL SCIENCE DEGREE COMPLETION

Oregon Institute of Technology (B)

RADIOLOGIST ASSISTANT

Bloomsburg University of Pennsylvania (M)

RANGELAND ECOSYSTEM SCIENCE

Colorado State University (M)

READING

Concordia University Wisconsin (M)
New Mexico State University (UC)
West Texas A&M University (M)

READING AND LANGUAGE

University of Massachusetts Lowell (M)

READING AND LITERACY

City University of Seattle (M)

READING AND LITERACY K-12

Central Michigan University (M)

READING EDUCATION

Texas Woman's University (M)

READING INSTRUCTION FOR SPECIAL EDUCATION (RISE)

Penn State University Park (GC)

READING PK-12

University of Nebraska at Kearney (M)

READING SPECIALIST

Fort Hays State University (UC)
Kansas State University (UC)
Pittsburg State University (M)
University of South Alabama (UC,M)

READING TEACHER CERTIFICATION

University of Wisconsin–Stout (UC)

READING TEACHER EDUCATION

Youngstown State University (UC)

READING, LANGUAGE, AND LITERACY

The University of North Carolina at Charlotte (M)

READING, LANGUAGE, AND LITERACY EDUCATION

Georgia State University (M)

REAL ESTATE

Drexel University (GC)
Marylhurst University (B)
North Lake College (A)
Santa Rosa Junior College (A)
Thomas Edison State College (B)
West Los Angeles College (UC,A)

REAL ESTATE PROFESSIONAL CERTIFICATE

University of Memphis (UC)

RECEPTION SERVICES

Dakota College at Bottineau (UC)

RECREATION

California State University, East Bay (B)

RECREATION ADMINISTRATION

The University of Toledo (M)

RECREATION AND TOURISM

California State University, East Bay (M)

RECREATION MANAGEMENT

Dakota College at Bottineau (UC,A)
North Carolina Central University (UC)

RECREATION SERVICES

Thomas Edison State College (B)

RECREATION, SPORT, AND TOURISM

University of Illinois at Urbana–Champaign (M)

REGENTS BACHELOR OF ARTS

Marshall University (B)
West Virginia University (B)

REGENTS ONLINE DEGREE PROGRAM

Austin Peay State University (B)

REGISTERED EMPLOYEE BENEFITS CONSULTANT(R) (REBC(R)) DESIGNATION

The American College (UC)

REGISTERED HEALTH UNDERWRITER(R) (RHU(R)) DESIGNATION

The American College (UC)

REGULARY AFFAIRS

Colorado State University (UC)

REGULATORY AFFAIRS

Lehigh University (GC)
San Diego State University (M)

REGULATORY AFFAIRS FOR DRUGS, BIOLOGICS, AND MEDICAL DEVICES

Northeastern University (M)

REGULATORY AND CLINICAL AFFAIRS

University of Southern California (GC)

REGULATORY SCIENCE

University of Southern California (M)

REHABILITATION COUNSELING

Assumption College (M)
Auburn University (M)
Salve Regina University (M)
San Diego State University (M)
University of Arkansas at Little Rock (M)
University of Massachusetts Boston (M)
Utah State University (M)
West Virginia University (M)

REHABILITATION COUNSELING AND CASE MANAGEMENT

Fort Valley State University (M)

REHABILITATIVE SCIENCE

Clarion University of Pennsylvania (M)

RELIGION

Liberty University (A,B,M)
Southwestern Adventist University (B)
Thomas Edison State College (B)

RELIGIOUS EDUCATION

Global University (B)
Newman Theological College (GC)

RELIGIOUS EDUCATION THREE-YEAR BA DEGREE

Global University (B)

RELIGIOUS STUDIES

Global University (A)
Indiana Wesleyan University (UC)
Judson College (B)
North Carolina Wesleyan College (B)
Prairie Bible Institute (A)
Prescott College (M)
Regent University (B)
University of the Incarnate Word (B)

REMOTE SENSING

Northeastern University (GC)

RENEWAL STUDIES

Regent University (D)

RESEARCH ADMINISTRATION

Medical University of South Carolina (M)

RESIDENTIAL INTERIORS

Colorado State University (UC)

RESOURCE INTERPRETATION

Stephen F. Austin State University (M)

RESPIRATORY CARE

James A. Rhodes State College (A)
Oregon Institute of Technology (B)
Southeast Community College Area (A)
Thomas Edison State College (A,B)

RESPIRATORY CARE DEGREE COMPLETION PROGRAM

Boise State University (B)

RESPIRATORY CARE LEADERSHIP

Northeastern University (M)

RESPIRATORY THERAPY

J. Sargeant Reynolds Community College (A)
The University of North Carolina at Charlotte (B)

RESPIRATORY THERAPY–ADVANCED PRACTICE

J. Sargeant Reynolds Community College (UC)

RETAIL LEADERSHIP

Drexel University (UC)

RETAIL MANAGEMENT

Columbus State Community College (A)
Southern New Hampshire University (B)

RETAILING AND CONSUMER SCIENCE

University of Houston (B)

RHIM-HIM ONLINE SEQUENCE

Illinois State University (B)

RICH MEDIA COMMUNICATION

Columbus State Community College (GC)

RISK MANAGEMENT AND INSURANCE

Excelsior College (B)

RISK MANAGEMENT AND ORGANIZATIONAL CONTINUITY

Boston University (GC)

RISK MANAGEMENT/INSURANCE

Florida State University (M)

ROTORCRAFT SYSTEMS ENGINEERING

The University of Alabama in Huntsville (M)

ROYAL RANGERS ORGANIZATIONAL LEADERS–BRONZE TIER

Global University (UC)

ROYAL RANGERS ORGANIZATIONAL LEADERS–GOLD TIER

Global University (UC)

ROYAL RANGERS ORGANIZATIONAL LEADERS–PLATINUM TIER

Global University (UC)

ROYAL RANGERS ORGANIZATIONAL LEADERS–SILVER TIER

Global University (UC)

RURAL PUBLIC SAFETY ADMINISTRATION

University of Maine at Fort Kent (B)

SAFETY MANAGEMENT

Oakland University (M)
University of Houston–Downtown (B)
West Virginia University (M)

SAFETY SCIENCE

Indiana University of Pennsylvania (M)

SAFETY SCIENCES

Indiana University of Pennsylvania (GC)

SAFETY, SECURITY, AND EMERGENCY MANAGEMENT

Eastern Kentucky University (M)

SALES AND MARKETING

Minnesota School of Business–Online (A)

SALES MANAGEMENT CONCENTRATION

Andrew Jackson University (M)

SAP (SYSTEMS, APPLICATIONS AND PRODUCTS IN DATA PROCESSING)

Penn State University Park (UC)

SCHOOL ADMINISTRATION

Appalachian State University (UC)
Indiana State University (UC)
Southwestern Oklahoma State University (M)

SCHOOL ADMINISTRATION PROGRAM

Western Carolina University (M)

SCHOOL ADMINISTRATION/ EDUCATIONAL LEADERSHIP

Wayne State College (M)

SCHOOL AND CHURCH ADMINISTRATION

Shasta Bible College (M)

SCHOOL AND PUBLIC LIBRARY

Appalachian State University (M)

SCHOOL BUILDING LEADER IN EDUCATIONAL ADMINISTRATION AND SUPERVISION

St. John's University (M)

SCHOOL BUILDING LEADERSHIP

Mercy College (M)

SCHOOL BUSINESS ADMINISTRATION

University of the Southwest (M)

SCHOOL COUNSELING

Seton Hall University (M)
Southwestern Oklahoma State University (M)
University of Massachusetts Boston (M)
University of the Southwest (M)
The University of West Alabama (M)

SCHOOL COUNSELING (K-12)

Emporia State University (M)

SCHOOL COUNSELING (POST-MASTERS)

The University of North Carolina at Charlotte (GC)

SCHOOL COUNSELOR

Fort Hays State University (UC)

SCHOOL DISTRICT LEADER ADVANCED CERTIFICATE

St. John's University (GC)

SCHOOL HEALTH EDUCATION

West Virginia University (M)

SCHOOL IMPROVEMENT

University of West Georgia (D)

SCHOOL LEADERSHIP

University of North Florida (M)

SCHOOL LIBRARIAN (GRADUATE)

University of Nebraska at Kearney (UC)

SCHOOL LIBRARY CERTIFICATION

McNeese State University (UC)

SCHOOL LIBRARY MEDIA ADD-ON

University of West Georgia (GC)

SCHOOL LIBRARY MEDIA SERVICES

Indiana State University (GC)

SCHOOL LIBRARY MEDIA SPECIALIST

New Mexico State University (UC)

SCHOOL MEDIA

Syracuse University (GC)

SCHOOL PRINCIPALSHIP

Central Michigan University (M)
Dallas Baptist University (GC)

SCHOOL PRINCIPALSHIP–PREK-8 OR 7-12

University of Nebraska at Kearney (M)

SCHOOL SUPERINTENDENCY

Ball State University (M)

SCHOOL SYSTEMS, SUPERINTENDENCY, AND LEADERSHIP

Webster University (M)

SCHOOL TECHNOLOGY COORDINATION

Boise State University (GC)

SCIENCE

Excelsior College (A,B)
Oakton Community College (A)

SCIENCE AND ARTS TRANSFER DEGREE D111

Illinois Eastern Community Colleges, Frontier Community College (A)
Illinois Eastern Community Colleges, Lincoln Trail College (A)
Illinois Eastern Community Colleges, Olney Central College (A)
Illinois Eastern Community Colleges, Wabash Valley College (A)

SCIENCE EDUCATION

Georgia State University (M)
Western Michigan University (M)

SCIENCE IN A CHANGING WORLD

University of Massachusetts Boston (GC,M)

SCIENCE IN EDUCATION

Lesley University (M)

SCIENCE INSTRUCTION, ADVANCED

Colorado State University (GC)

SCIENCE, MATH, AND TECHNOLOGY

State University of New York Empire State College (A,B)

SCIENCE, TECHNOLOGY, ENGINEERING, AND MATH 1-6 (HYBRID)

Framingham State University (M)

SECONDARY EDUCATION

Ball State University (M)
Fitchburg State University (M)
Lewis-Clark State College (UC)
Mississippi State University (M)
Montgomery County Community College (A)
University of Memphis (M)
The University of West Alabama (M)

SECONDARY EDUCATION SCIENCE EMPHASIS

West Virginia University (M)

SECONDARY EDUCATION SOCIAL STUDIES EMPHASIS

West Virginia University (M)

SECONDARY EDUCATION–COMPOSITE SOCIAL SCIENCE

Dickinson State University (B)

SECONDARY EDUCATION–ENGLISH

Dickinson State University (B)
Saint Mary-of-the-Woods College (B)

SECONDARY EDUCATION–HISTORY

Dickinson State University (B)

SECONDARY EDUCATION–MATH

Dickinson State University (B)

SECONDARY EDUCATION–MATHEMATICS
Saint Mary-of-the-Woods College (B)

SECONDARY EDUCATION–SOCIAL STUDIES
Saint Mary-of-the-Woods College (B)

SECONDARY EDUCATION, ENGLISH SPEAKING OTHER LANGUAGE (ESOL) MAJOR
University of South Alabama (M)

SECONDARY MATH AND SCIENCE EDUCATION
Columbus State University (M)

SECONDARY TEACHING
University of Great Falls (M)

SECURE AND DEPENDABLE COMPUTING SYSTEMS
University of Idaho (UC)

SECURITY ADMINISTRATION
Southwestern College (M)

SECURITY ENGINEERING
Southern Methodist University (M)

SECURITY MANAGEMENT
Colorado Technical University Colorado Springs (M)
Nichols College (M)
Southwestern College (B)

SECURITY MANAGEMENT AND HOMELAND SECURITY
University of Massachusetts Lowell (UC)

SECURITY MANAGEMENT CERTIFICATE
University of Calgary (UC)

SECURITY POLICY STUDIES
Notre Dame College (M)

SECURITY STUDIES
University of Massachusetts Lowell (GC)

SEED TECHNOLOGY EDUCATION
Colorado State University (UC)

SELF-DESIGNED MAJOR
Burlington College (B,M)

SELF-DESIGNED PROGRAM
St. Cloud State University (B)

SEMICONDUCTOR THEORY AND DEVICES
University of Idaho (UC)

SENIOR LIVING MANAGEMENT
Rochester Institute of Technology (GC)

SEPSIS AWARENESS AND EDUCATION
St. Petersburg College (UC)

SEQUENTIAL ART
Savannah College of Art and Design (B)

SERVICE LEADERSHIP AND INNOVATION
Rochester Institute of Technology (M)

SINGLE DISCIPLINE TRACK–CHRISTIAN MINISTRY
Dallas Baptist University (M)

SIX SIGMA INNOVATION AND DESIGN
University of Idaho (UC)

SLEEP AND SLEEP DISORDERS IN HEALTH AND DISEASE
University of Massachusetts Lowell (GC)

SLEEP STUDY
Columbus State Community College (GC)

SLEEP TECHNOLOGY FOR POLYSOMNOGRAPHY
J. Sargeant Reynolds Community College (UC)

SMALL BUSINESS ADMINISTRATION
Middlesex Community College (A)

SMALL BUSINESS AND ENTREPRENEURSHIP
Champlain College (UC)

SMALL BUSINESS MANAGEMENT
Herkimer County Community College (UC)
Middlesex Community College (UC)
Rochester Institute of Technology (UC)

SOCIAL AND BEHAVIORAL SCIENCES
San Diego Community College District (A)
Santa Rosa Junior College (A)

SOCIAL AND HEALTH SERVICES
Roger Williams University (B)

SOCIAL DEVELOPMENT STUDIES
University of Waterloo (B)

SOCIAL RESPONSIBILITY AND SUSTAINABLE COMMUNITIES
Western Kentucky University (M)

SOCIAL SCIENCE
Atlantic Cape Community College (A)
California State University, Chico (B)
Central Texas College (A)
College of the Humanities and Sciences, Harrison Middleton University (M)
Lansing Community College (A)
Mesa State College (A)
Montgomery County Community College (A)
Southern New Hampshire University (B)
University of Maryland University College (B)
University of North Dakota (B)
West Hills Community College (A)

SOCIAL SCIENCE EDUCATION
Webster University (M)

SOCIAL SCIENCE/HISTORY
Saint Mary-of-the-Woods College (B)

SOCIAL SCIENCES
Brookdale Community College (A)
Ohio University (A)
Rose State College (A)
Southwestern Adventist University (B)
Syracuse University (M)
Thomas Edison State College (B)
Upper Iowa University (B)
Washington State University (B)

SOCIAL SERVICES
Thomas Edison State College (B)

SOCIAL SERVICES ADMINISTRATION
Thomas Edison State College (B)

SOCIAL SERVICES FOR SPECIAL POPULATIONS
Thomas Edison State College (B)

SOCIAL THEORY, SOCIAL STRUCTURE, AND CHANGE
State University of New York Empire State College (A,B)

SOCIAL WORK
Boston University (M)
Colorado State University (M)
Florida State University (M)
Memorial University of Newfoundland (M)
New Mexico State University (M)
Tyler Junior College (A)
The University of Akron (M)

University of Manitoba (B)
University of North Dakota (M)
University of Southern California (M)
Vincennes University (A)
Wayne State University (B)

SOCIAL WORK SPECIALIZATION

Central Texas College (A)

SOCIETY OF HUMAN RESOURCE MANAGEMENT LEARNING SYSTEM (SHRM)

Colorado State University (UC)

SOCIOLOGY

Adams State College (B)
Appalachian State University (GC)
Brookdale Community College (A)
Caldwell College (B)
California State University, Chico (B)
Columbia College (B)
Dallas Baptist University (B)
Fort Hays State University (B)
Lansing Community College (A)
McNeese State University (B)
Mercy College (B)
National University (B)
New Mexico State University (B,M)
North Dakota State University (B)
Northeastern University (B)
Oregon State University (B)
Saint Leo University (B)
Thomas Edison State College (B)
Tyler Junior College (A)
University of Nebraska at Kearney (B)
University of North Alabama (B)
The University of Texas of the Permian Basin (B)
The University of Western Ontario (B)
Western Kentucky University (B)

SOCIOLOGY (3 YEAR)

Athabasca University (B)

SOCIOLOGY (4 YEAR)

Athabasca University (B)

SOCIOLOGY OF MEDICINE AND AGING

Fort Hays State University (UC)

SOFTWARE APPLICATIONS FOR THE PROFESSIONAL

Sinclair Community College (UC)

SOFTWARE APPLICATIONS SPECIALIST

Central Texas College (UC)

SOFTWARE DESIGN AND PROGRAMMING

University of Denver (UC)

SOFTWARE DEVELOPMENT

Butler Community College (A)
Champlain College (UC,A,B)
Herzing University Online (B)

SOFTWARE DEVLEOPMENT

Herzing University Online (A)

SOFTWARE ENGINEERING

Brandeis University (M)
Cleveland Institute of Electronics (A)
Colorado State University (GC)
Colorado Technical University Colorado Springs (M)
DePaul University (M)
Drexel University (M)
Florida State University (B)
Kansas State University (M)
National University (B)
North Dakota State University (GC,M)
Penn State University Park (M)
Southern Methodist University (M)
The University of Alabama in Huntsville (M)
University of Colorado Boulder (GC)
University of Illinois at Urbana–Champaign (GC)
University of Management and Technology (M)
University of Maryland University College (GC)
University of Michigan–Dearborn (M)
West Virginia University (GC,M)

SOFTWARE ENGINEERING ADMINISTRATION

University of West Florida (M)

SOFTWARE PRODUCTIVITY

University of Cincinnati (UC)

SOIL AND WATER SCIENCE, ENVIRONMENTAL SCIENCE

University of Florida (M)

SOIL ECOSYSTEMS SERVICES

University of Florida (GC)

SOIL SCIENCE

North Carolina State University (UC)

SPACE OPERATIONS

University of Colorado at Colorado Springs (M)

SPACE STUDIES

University of North Dakota (M)

SPACE SYSTEMS MANAGEMENT

University of Colorado at Colorado Springs (M)

SPANISH

New Mexico State University (M)

SPANISH TRANSLATION

The University of Texas at Brownsville (UC)

SPECIAL EDUCATION

Ball State University (M)
Campbellsville University (M)
Cardinal Stritch University (M)
Drexel University (M)
Florida State University (M)
Fort Hays State University (M)
Oakland University (M)
Prescott College (B)
St. Cloud State University (B,M)
Southern Oregon University (M)
University of Central Florida (GC)
University of Colorado at Colorado Springs (M)
University of Florida (M)
University of Houston–Victoria (M)
University of Illinois at Urbana–Champaign (M)
University of Maine at Machias (B)
University of Memphis (M)
University of North Dakota (M)
University of Southern Mississippi (B,M)
The University of Texas of the Permian Basin (M)
University of the Southwest (M)
The University of West Alabama (M)
University of West Florida (M)
University of West Georgia (M)
Walden University (M)
Western Carolina University (M)
West Virginia University (M)

SPECIAL EDUCATION (ADAPTIVE)

Emporia State University (M)

SPECIAL EDUCATION (GIFTED, ADVANCED PRACT., MILD/ MODERATE DISABILITIES)

University of Nebraska at Kearney (M)

SPECIAL EDUCATION (K-12)–GENERAL CURRICULUM

The University of North Carolina at Charlotte (M)

SPECIAL EDUCATION ALTERNATIVE LICENSURE

New Mexico State University (UC)

SPECIAL EDUCATION AND LEVEL I SPECIALIST CREDENTIAL MILD/ MODERATE

National University (M)

SPECIAL EDUCATION CERTIFICATION

Drexel University (GC)

SPECIAL EDUCATION EARLY CHILDHOOD

The University of Toledo (M)

SPECIAL EDUCATION ENDORSEMENT

University of Colorado at Colorado Springs (UC)

SPECIAL EDUCATION ENDORSEMENT PROGRAMS (WITH MS EDUCATION)

Walden University (M)

SPECIAL EDUCATION LEADERSHIP

Regent University (M)

SPECIAL EDUCATION SPECIALIZATION

Northeastern University (M)

SPECIAL EDUCATION SUPERVISORY CERTIFICATE

Penn State University Park (UC)

SPECIAL EDUCATION–LEVEL II CREDENTIAL ESPE

California State University, San Bernardino (M)

SPECIAL EDUCATION–ORIENTATION AND MOBILITY

University of Massachusetts Boston (GC,M)

SPECIAL EDUCATION–SIGN LANGUAGE INTERPRETING TRACK (BACHELOR COMPLETION PROGRAM)

University of Cincinnati (B)

SPECIAL EDUCATION–TEACHING OF STUDENTS WITH VISUAL IMPAIRMENTS

University of Massachusetts Boston (M)

SPECIAL EDUCATION, ADAPTED CURRICULUM

The University of North Carolina at Charlotte (GC)

SPECIAL EDUCATION, AMERICAN SIGN LANGUAGE (ASL)/ENGLISH INTERPRETING CONCENTRATION

University of North Florida (M)

SPECIAL EDUCATION, ASSISTIVE TECHNOLOGY SPECIALIZATION

Bowling Green State University (M)

SPECIAL EDUCATION, AUTISM SPECTRUM DISORDER CERTIFICATION

West Virginia University (M)

SPECIAL EDUCATION, EARLY INTERVENTION/EARLY CHILDHOOD CERTIFICATION

West Virginia University (M)

SPECIAL EDUCATION, GENERAL CURRICULUM TEACHER LICENSURE

The University of North Carolina at Charlotte (GC)

SPECIAL EDUCATION, GIFTED EDUCATION CERTIFICATION

West Virginia University (M)

SPECIAL EDUCATION, LOW VISION/BLINDNESS CERTIFICATION

West Virginia University (M)

SPECIAL EDUCATION, MASTER TEACHER OR SUPERVISION

Slippery Rock University of Pennsylvania (M)

SPECIAL EDUCATION, MULTICATEGORICAL CERTIFICATION

West Virginia University (M)

SPECIAL EDUCATION, SEVERE/ MULTIPLE DISABILITIES CERTIFICATION

West Virginia University (M)

SPECIAL EDUCATION/AUTISM TRACK

Monmouth University (M)

SPECIALIZED MINISTRIES–YOUTH AND YOUNG ADULT MINISTRY

Southwestern College (M)

SPECIALIZED STUDIES

Ohio University (B)

SPEECH COMMUNICATION

North Dakota State University (M)

SPEECH-LANGUAGE PATHOLOGY

Florida State University (M)
James Madison University (M)
Texas Woman's University (M)

SPEECH/LANGUAGE PATHOLOGY ASSISTANT

Chemeketa Community College (UC,A)

SPIRITUAL FORMATION

George Fox University (M)

SPIRITUAL FORMATION AND LEADERSHIP

Spring Arbor University (M)

SPORT ADMINISTRATION

Central Michigan University (M)

SPORT BUSINESS CONCENTRATION

Saint Leo University (M)

SPORT COACHING EDUCATION

University of Southern Mississippi (M)

SPORT HOSPITALITY MANAGEMENT

Lasell College (GC)

SPORT LEADERSHIP

Lasell College (GC)

SPORT MANAGEMENT

Columbia Southern University (B)
Drexel University (M)
Jacksonville State University (M)
Mesa State College (A,B)
Missouri Baptist University (M)
Nichols College (M)
Southern New Hampshire University (GC,M)
University of Southern Mississippi (M)

SPORT MANAGEMENT–SPORT HOSPITALITY MANAGEMENT

Lasell College (M)

SPORT MANAGEMENT–SPORT LEADERSHIP

Lasell College (M)

SPORT MANAGEMENT–SPORT NON-PROFIT MANAGEMENT

Lasell College (M)

SPORT NON-PROFIT MANAGEMENT

Lasell College (GC)

SPORTS AND ATHLETICS ADMINISTRATION

Lynn University (M)

SPORTS AND EVENT MANAGEMENT

AIB College of Business (A)

SPORTS AND TOURISM

Finger Lakes Community College (A)

SPORTS COACHING

United States Sports Academy (UC,B,M)

SPORTS COACHING (INTERNATIONAL CERTIFICATION)

United States Sports Academy (UC)

SPORTS COMMERCE

University of Memphis (M)

SPORTS FITNESS

United States Sports Academy (M)

SPORTS LEADERSHIP

Duquesne University (M)
Northeastern University (M)

SPORTS MANAGEMENT

Concordia University, St. Paul (M)
Franklin Pierce University (M)
United States Sports Academy (UC,B,M,D)
University of Florida (B)
West Virginia University (M)

SPORTS MANAGEMENT (INTERNATIONAL CERTIFICATION)

United States Sports Academy (UC)

SPORTS MANAGEMENT–OLYMPIC EMPHASIS

United States Sports Academy (D)

SPORTS MEDICINE

United States Sports Academy (UC,M)

SPORTS NUTRITION

Simmons College (GC)

SPORTS STUDIES

United States Sports Academy (B,M)

SPREADSHEET MANAGEMENT

Wake Technical Community College (UC)

STATISTICAL METHODS FOR PRODUCT AND PROCESS IMPROVEMENT

Rochester Institute of Technology (GC)

STATISTICAL QUALITY

Rochester Institute of Technology (GC)

STATISTICAL THEORY AND METHOD

Colorado State University (UC)

STATISTICS

Colorado State University (M)
University of Idaho (UC)
Youngstown State University (M)

STENO TRANSCRIPTION

AIB College of Business (A)

STRATEGIC BUSINESS MANAGEMENT

Hofstra University (M)

STRATEGIC COMMUNICATION

Crown College (B)

STRATEGIC COMMUNICATION AND LEADERSHIP

Seton Hall University (M)

STRATEGIC COMMUNICATION MANAGEMENT

Concordia University, St. Paul (M)

STRATEGIC FORESIGHT

Regent University (M)

STRATEGIC HUMAN RESOURCE MANAGEMENT

University of Denver (M)

STRATEGIC INNOVATION AND CHANGE

University of Denver (UC)

STRATEGIC LEADERSHIP

Mountain State University (M)
Regent University (D)
Southwestern College (B)
University of Mary (M)

STRATEGIC LEADERSHIP CONCENTRATION

Andrew Jackson University (M)

STRATEGIC LEADERSHIP, MINISTRY EMPHASIS

Life Pacific College (M)

STRATEGIC MANAGEMENT INFORMATION SYSTEMS

Cardinal Stritch University (B)

STRATEGIC MANAGEMENT OF HEALTHCARE

University of Denver (UC)

STRATEGIC PLANNING AND PUBLIC POLICY POST-BACHELOR'S

Walden University (GC)

STRATEGIC PROCUREMENT

Columbus State Community College (GC)

STRATEGIC TECHNOLOGY MANAGEMENT

University of Illinois at Urbana–Champaign (GC)

STRATEGIC TRAINING

Rochester Institute of Technology (GC)

STRUCTURAL ENGINEERING

University of Central Florida (GC)
University of Idaho (UC)
University of Wisconsin–Platteville (GC)

STRUCTURAL/GEOTECHNICAL ENGINEERING

University of Wisconsin–Platteville (GC)

STRUCTURED LEARNING

Heritage College (A)

STUDENT AFFAIRS

Regent University (M)

STUDENT AFFAIRS ADMINISTRATION IN HIGHER EDUCATION

University of Wisconsin–La Crosse (M)

STUDENT AFFAIRS AND HIGHER EDUCATION

Indiana State University (M)

STUDENT AFFAIRS IN HIGHER EDUCATION

Colorado State University (GC,M)

STUDENT DEVELOPMENT AND AFFAIRS

Drexel University (GC)

STUDENT DEVELOPMENT COUNSELING AND ADMINISTRATION

Indiana Wesleyan University (M)

STUDENT MINISTRY (YOUTH AND COLLEGIATE)

Dallas Baptist University (M)

STUDIES OF CHILD ABUSE

University of Waterloo (UC)

SUBSTANCE ABUSE COUNSELING

University of Cincinnati (B)

SUPERINTENDENCY

The University of Texas of the Permian Basin (M)

SUPERINTENDENT CERTIFICATION

Abilene Christian University (UC)

SUPERVISORY MANAGEMENT

Mid-State Technical College (A)
Wisconsin Indianhead Technical College (A)

SUPPLY CHAIN LOGISTICS MANAGEMENT

Vincennes University (A)

SUPPLY CHAIN MANAGEMENT

Columbus State Community College (GC,A)
Fontbonne University (M)
Kettering University (M)
Lehigh University (UC)
National University (GC)
Penn State University Park (GC,M)
University of Houston–Downtown (B)

SUPPLY MANAGEMENT

American Graduate University (M)

SURGICAL TECHNOLOGY

Southeast Community College Area (A)

SURGICAL TECHNOLOGY COMPLETION PROGRAM

Presentation College (A)

SURVEY RESEARCH METHODS

University of Illinois at Chicago (UC)

SURVEYING

Thomas Edison State College (A,B)

SUSTAINABILITY

Goddard College (B)

SUSTAINABILITY AND GREEN CONSTRUCTION

Drexel University (GC)

SUSTAINABILITY EDUCATION

Prescott College (M,D)

SUSTAINABILITY LEADERSHIP

Fielding Graduate University (GC)

SUSTAINABILITY MANAGEMENT

St. Petersburg College (B)

SUSTAINABILTY TECHNOLOGY

Wayne Community College (A)

SUSTAINABLE BUILDING

Columbus State Community College (GC)

SUSTAINABLE BUSINESS

City University of Seattle (GC)
Marylhurst University (M)

SUSTAINABLE BUSINESS AND COMMUNITIES

Goddard College (M)

SUSTAINABLE COMMUNITY DEVELOPMENT

Prescott College (B,M)

SUSTAINABLE CONSTRUCTION

University of Florida (GC)

SUSTAINABLE DESIGN

Boston Architectural College (UC,M)

SUSTAINABLE ENERGY AND HYBRID TECHNOLOGY

Kettering University (M)

SUSTAINABLE ENTERPRISE MANAGEMENT

University of Wisconsin–Stout (UC)

SUSTAINABLE LAND RESOURCES AND NUTRIENT MANAGEMENT

University of Florida (GC)

SUSTAINABLE MANAGEMENT

Anaheim University (M)
University of Wisconsin–Parkside (B)
University of Wisconsin–Stout (B)
University of Wisconsin–Superior (B)

SUSTAINABLE MANAGEMENT SCIENCE

University of Wisconsin–Stout (UC)

SUSTAINABLE MILITARY LAND MANAGEMENT

Colorado State University (UC)

SUSTAINABLE NATURAL RESOURCES

Oregon State University (GC)

SUSTAINABLE PRACTICES

Philadelphia University (GC)

SYNTHESIS AND CHARACTERIZATION OF INORGANIC AND ORGANIC MATERIALS

Illinois Institute of Technology (GC)

SYNTHESIS AND CHARACTERIZATION OF INORGANIC MATERIAL

Illinois Institute of Technology (GC)

SYNTHESIS AND CHARACTERIZATION OF ORGANIC MATERIALS

Illinois Institute of Technology (GC)

SYSTEM ADMINISTRATION

Champlain College (UC)

SYSTEM DYNAMICS

Worcester Polytechnic Institute (M)

SYSTEM SOFTWARE

University of Illinois at Urbana–Champaign (GC)

SYSTEM Z

Columbus State Community College (GC)

SYSTEMS ANALYSIS

University of Maryland University College (GC)

SYSTEMS ARCHITECTING AND ENGINEERING

University of Southern California (GC,M)

SYSTEMS ENGINEERING

Colorado State University (UC,M)
Colorado Technical University Colorado Springs (M)
Columbia University (UC)
The Johns Hopkins University (M)

Missouri University of Science and Technology (M)
New Mexico State University (UC)
Penn State University Park (M)
Southern Methodist University (M)
The University of Alabama in Huntsville (M,D)
University of Central Florida (GC)
University of Colorado at Colorado Springs (GC,M)
University of Florida (M)
University of Illinois at Urbana–Champaign (GC)
Worcester Polytechnic Institute (M)

SYSTEMS ENGINEERING (INDUSTRIAL AND MANUFACTURING ENGINEERING CONCENTRATION)

Kettering University (M)

SYSTEMS MANAGEMENT

Florida Institute of Technology (M)

SYSTEMS MANAGEMENT, OPERATIONS RESEARCH CONCENTRATION

Florida Institute of Technology (M)

SYSTEMS MODELS AND MANAGEMENT

University of Massachusetts Lowell (GC)

SYSTEMS SIMULATION FOR ENGINEERS

University of Central Florida (GC)

TAKING INITIATIVE FOR MANAGEMENT EFFECTIVENESS

Lansing Community College (UC)

TAXATION

California State University, East Bay (M)
DePaul University (M)

TAXATION SPECIALIST

Columbus State Community College (GC)

TEACHER AS LEADER

Northern Kentucky University (M)

TEACHER ASSISTANT

University of Calgary (UC)

TEACHER CERTIFICATION

Prescott College (UC)

TEACHER EDUCATION

Baptist Bible College of Pennsylvania (M)
LeTourneau University (B)
Marygrove College (M)

TEACHER EDUCATION CERTIFICATION PROGRAM

Marian University (M)

TEACHER EDUCATION TRANSFER

Genesee Community College (A)

TEACHER LEADER

The University of West Alabama (M)

TEACHER LEADERSHIP

Oakland University (M)
Rowan University (M)
University of Illinois at Springfield (M)
University of the Incarnate Word (M)
Walden University (M)

TEACHER OF BLIND AND/OR VISUALLY IMPAIRED

Dominican College (M)

TEACHER PREPARATION POST-BACCALAUREATE

Walden University (M)

TEACHING

Friends University (M)
Kaplan University Online (M)
La Sierra University (M)
Liberty University (M)
National University (M)
North Carolina State University (M)
Ozarks Technical Community College (A)
Southwestern College (M)
State University of New York Empire State College (M)
Texas Woman's University (M)
University of Houston–Downtown (M)
University of Maryland University College (M)
University of Southern California (M)
West Texas A&M University (M)

TEACHING (MOST)

Florida State University (M)

TEACHING AND LEARNING

Bob Jones University (M)
Lock Haven University of Pennsylvania (M)
University of St. Francis (M)
University of Southern Maine (M)

TEACHING AND LEARNING, ADVANCED STUDIES

Middle Tennessee State University (M)

TEACHING AND TRAINING AT A DISTANCE

University of Maryland University College (GC)

TEACHING ASSISTANT

Herkimer County Community College (UC)

TEACHING CERTIFICATION

The University of West Alabama (M)

TEACHING CERTIFICATION, ACCELERATED

Wheeling Jesuit University (GC)

TEACHING CHILDREN WHO ARE VISUALLY IMPAIRED

Western Michigan University (M)

TEACHING CHILDREN WHO ARE VISUALLY IMPAIRED/ ORIENTATION AND MOBILITY–MA/MA DUAL DEGREE

Western Michigan University (M)

TEACHING CHILDREN WITH DISABILITIES IN CHILDHOOD EDUCATION

St. John's University (M)

TEACHING ENGLISH AS A SECOND LANGUAGE

St. Cloud State University (M)

TEACHING ENGLISH AS A SECOND LANGUAGE (TESL)

Drexel University (UC)

TEACHING ENGLISH AS A SECOND LANGUAGE/FOREIGN LANGUAGE

University of Colorado at Colorado Springs (GC)

TEACHING ENGLISH AS A SECOND OR FOREIGN LANGUAGE

Indiana State University (GC)

TEACHING ENGLISH IN SECONDARY SCHOOLS (TESS)

University of Northern Iowa (M)

TEACHING ENGLISH LANGUAGE LEARNERS

Valley City State University (GC)

TEACHING ENGLISH TO SPEAKERS OF OTHER LANGUAGES

Emporia State University (M)
Mercy College (M)
Murray State University (M)
Southeast Missouri State University (M)

TEACHING ENGLISH TO SPEAKERS OF OTHER LANGUAGES (TESOL)

Anaheim University (M)
California State University, San Bernardino (M)
Lincoln Christian University (M)
University of Northern Iowa (M)

TEACHING IN SECONDARY MATHEMATICS AND SCIENCE

University of West Georgia (M)

TEACHING IN THE VIRTUAL CLASSROOM

Fielding Graduate University (UC)

TEACHING LITERACY, BIRTH TO GRADE 12

Mercy College (M)

TEACHING MATHEMATICS

University of Idaho (M)

TEACHING OF ENGLISH TO SPEAKERS OF OTHER LANGUAGES (TESOL)

University of Southern California (M)

TEACHING OF LANGUAGES (MATL)

University of Southern Mississippi (M)

TEACHING OF READING

Fontbonne University (M)

TEACHING OF SCIENCE

New Mexico State University (M)

TEACHING ONLINE CONCENTRATION

Franciscan University of Steubenville (M)

TEACHING ONLINE POST-MASTERS SPECIALIZED LEARNING CERTIFICATE

Walden University (UC)

TEACHING SECOND LANGUAGE

University of Calgary (UC)

TEACHING WITH TECHNOLOGY

Kaplan University Online (UC)

TEACHING WITH TECHNOLOGY AND DISTANCE LEARNING

Colorado State University (UC)

TEACHING–CURRICULUM AND INSTRUCTION

The University of Tennessee at Martin (M)

TEACHING, LEARNING, AND CURRICULUM

Drexel University (M)

TEACHING/LEARNING IN NURSING AND HEALTH SCIENCES

University of Illinois at Chicago (UC)

TECHNICAL AND APPLIED STUDIES

Ohio University (B)

TECHNICAL COMMUNICATION, BASIC

Rochester Institute of Technology (UC)

TECHNICAL COMMUNICATIONS

Northeastern University (B,M)

TECHNICAL COMMUNICATIONS, ADVANCED

Rochester Institute of Technology (UC)

TECHNICAL EDUCATION AND INDUSTRY TRAINING

University of Central Florida (B)

TECHNICAL INFORMATION DESIGN

Rochester Institute of Technology (GC)

TECHNICAL JAPANESE

University of Wisconsin–Madison (M)

TECHNICAL MANAGEMENT

DeVry University Online (B)
Southern New Hampshire University (B)

TECHNICAL STUDIES

Excelsior College (A)
Thomas Edison State College (B)

TECHNICAL STUDIES (ASAST)

Thomas Edison State College (A)

TECHNICAL WRITING

California State University, Dominguez Hills (GC)

TECHNOLOGICAL EDUCATION, ADVANCED

Bowling Green State University (B)

TECHNOLOGY

Central Michigan University (M)
Excelsior College (A,B)
The University of West Alabama (B)

TECHNOLOGY APPRENTICESHIP

Vincennes University (A)

TECHNOLOGY APPRENTICESHIP–GENERAL STUDIES OPTION

Vincennes University (A)

TECHNOLOGY COMMERCIALIZATION

Northeastern University (M)

TECHNOLOGY EDUCATION

Ball State University (M)
Valley City State University (B)

TECHNOLOGY FACILITATOR

Ashland University (UC)

TECHNOLOGY FOR EDUCATION AND TRAINING

The University of South Dakota (M)

TECHNOLOGY IN DISTANCE EDUCATION AND E-LEARNING

University of Maryland University College (GC)

TECHNOLOGY IN EDUCATION

Lesley University (M)
National-Louis University (M)

TECHNOLOGY IN EDUCATION (GLOBAL)

University of Michigan–Flint (M)

TECHNOLOGY INTEGRATION

Boise State University (GC)
Graceland University (M)

TECHNOLOGY LEADERSHIP

Fort Hays State University (B)
Webster University (M)

TECHNOLOGY LEADERSHIP AND MANAGEMENT

Roger Williams University (B)

TECHNOLOGY MANAGEMENT

Bowling Green State University (D)
City University of Seattle (GC,M)
Herzing University Online (B)
Indiana State University (B,D)
Kansas State University (B)
Marist College (M)
National University (M)

Pennsylvania College of Technology (B)
St. Petersburg College (B)
State University of New York Institute of Technology (M)
University of Bridgeport (M)
University of Colorado at Colorado Springs (M)
University of Denver (UC)
University of Maryland University College (M)
University of Wisconsin–Stout (M)
Western Kentucky University (B,M)

TECHNOLOGY MANAGEMENT CONCENTRATION

Colorado Technical University Colorado Springs (M)

TECHNOLOGY MANAGEMENT, COMPUTER SCIENCE MINOR

Herzing University Online (B)

TECHNOLOGY VENTURES AND PRODUCT MANAGEMENT

University of Colorado Boulder (GC)

TECHNOLOGY–BACHELOR TECHNOLOGY (BTECH)

Memorial University of Newfoundland (B)

TELECOMMUNICATIONS

Bossier Parish Community College (A)
Columbia University (UC)
Pace University (GC,B)
Southern Methodist University (M)
University of Colorado Boulder (M)

TELECOMMUNICATIONS AND NETWORK MANAGEMENT

Syracuse University (M)

TELECOMMUNICATIONS AND SOFTWARE ENGINEERING

Illinois Institute of Technology (M)

TELECOMMUNICATIONS ENGINEERING TECHNOLOGY

Rochester Institute of Technology (M)

TELECOMMUNICATIONS MANAGEMENT

University of Denver (UC)
University of Maryland University College (GC)

TELECOMMUNICATIONS POLICY

University of Colorado Boulder (GC)

TELECOMMUNICATIONS SYSTEMS MANAGEMENT

Murray State University (B,M)

TELECOMMUNICATIONS TECHNOLOGY

Quinsigamond Community College (A)
University of Denver (UC)

TELECOMMUNICATIONS TECHNOLOGY–VERIZON

Erie Community College (A)
Erie Community College, North Campus (A)
Erie Community College, South Campus (A)

TELEVISION ARTS

Regent University (M)

TESOL

Northeastern University (GC)
Regent University (UC,M)

TEXTILE CHEMISTRY

North Carolina State University (M)

TEXTILES FUNDAMENTALS

North Carolina State University (UC)

TEXTILES OFF-CAMPUS PROGRAMS (TOP)

North Carolina State University (M)

THE ARTS

Central Carolina Technical College (A)
Greenville Technical College (A)
Iowa Valley Community College District (A)
Lenoir Community College (A)
Pasco-Hernando Community College (A)
State University of New York Empire State College (A,B)
Wake Technical Community College (A)

THE HEALTH SYSTEMS LEADERSHIP TRACK–LEADER/MANAGER, CLINICAL NURSE LEADER, NURSING EDUCATION TRACK

University of West Georgia (M)

THEATER

Regent University (B)
Thomas Edison State College (B)

THEATER ARTS

Regent University (M)

THEOLOGICAL STUDIES

Andrews University (B)
George Fox University (M)
Laurel University (M)
Liberty University (M)
Newman Theological College (UC)
Prairie Bible Institute (GC)

THEOLOGICAL STUDIES (GRADUATE)

Prairie Bible Institute (UC)

THEOLOGY

Caldwell College (B)
The Catholic Distance University (B,M)
Franciscan University of Steubenville (M)
Global University (UC)
Heritage Christian University (A,B)
Holy Apostles College and Seminary (M)
Saint Mary-of-the-Woods College (B)
Southwestern Adventist University (B)

TOURISM AND HOSPITALITY LEADERSHIP

Fort Hays State University (UC)

TOURISM AND HOSPITALITY LEADERSHIP (GRADUATE/INDUSTRY)

Fort Hays State University (GC)

TOURISM AND HOSPITALITY MANAGEMENT

Fort Hays State University (UC,B)
Mount Saint Vincent University (B)

TOURISM AND HOSPITALITY MARKETING

Fort Hays State University (UC)

TOURISM AND TRAVEL MANAGEMENT

Chemeketa Community College (UC,A)

TOURISM MANAGEMENT

Finger Lakes Community College (A)

TRAFFIC SAFETY EDUCATION

University of Wisconsin–Stout (UC)

TRAINING AND DEVELOPMENT

North Carolina State University (GC,M)
Southern New Hampshire University (GC)
University of St. Francis (M)
University of Wisconsin–Stout (M)

TRANSFER DEGREE

Bellevue College (A)
NorthWest Arkansas Community College (A)

TRANSFER DEGREE D110

Illinois Eastern Community Colleges, Frontier Community College (A)
Illinois Eastern Community Colleges, Lincoln Trail College (A)
Illinois Eastern Community Colleges, Olney Central College (A)
Illinois Eastern Community Colleges, Wabash Valley College (A)

TRANSFER DEGREE FOR BUSINESS STUDENTS

Bellevue College (A)

TRANSFER STUDIES

Anne Arundel Community College (A)
Lansing Community College (UC)

TRANSFORMATIONAL LEADERSHIP

Crown College (GC)

TRANSITION DOCTOR OF PHYSICAL THERAPY

The University of Scranton (D)

TRANSITION TO TEACHING

Indiana Wesleyan University (UC)

TRANSITIONAL DOCTOR OF OCCUPATIONAL THERAPY

University of St. Augustine for Health Sciences (D)

TRANSITIONAL DOCTOR OF PHYSICAL THERAPY

A.T. Still University of Health Sciences (D)
The College of St. Scholastica (D)
Dominican College (D)
Northeastern University (D)
University of Michigan–Flint (D)
University of St. Augustine for Health Sciences (D)

TRANSITIONAL DOCTORATE OF PHYSICAL THERAPY

The Sage Colleges (D)
The University of South Dakota (D)

TRANSITIONAL DOCTORATE OF PHYSICAL THERAPY (TDPT)

Misericordia University (D)

TRANSPERSONAL PSYCHOLOGY

Burlington College (B)
Naropa University (M)

TRANSPERSONAL PSYCHOLOGY, ECOPSYCHOLOGY CONCENTRATION

Naropa University (M)

TRANSPORTATION AND URBAN SYSTEMS

North Dakota State University (GC,M)

TRANSPORTATION BUSINESS

Minnesota School of Business–Online (A)
Minnesota School of Business–Richfield (A)

TRANSPORTATION ENGINEERING

Kansas State University (UC)
University of Central Florida (GC)

TRANSPORTATION LEADERSHIP

North Dakota State University (GC)

TRAVEL

West Los Angeles College (A)

TRAVEL AND TOURISM–HOSPITALITY AND EVENTS MANAGEMENT

Herkimer County Community College (A)

TRAVEL, BASIC

West Los Angeles College (UC)

TURFGRASS MANAGEMENT

Penn State University Park (UC,M)

TURFGRASS MANAGEMENT TECHNOLOGY

Wayne Community College (A)

TURFGRASS MANAGEMENT, ADVANCED

Penn State University Park (UC)

TURFGRASS SCIENCE

Penn State University Park (B)

TURFGRASS SCIENCE AND MANAGEMENT

Penn State University Park (A)

TWO-YEAR COMMUNITY COLLEGE ADMINISTRATION PROGRAM

Western Carolina University (M)

TYPEFACE DESIGN

Savannah College of Art and Design (GC)

ULTRASOUND–DEGREE COMPLETION IN ULTRASOUND, ECHOCARDIOGRAPHY OPTION

Oregon Institute of Technology (B)

ULTRASOUND–DEGREE COMPLETION IN ULTRASOUND, VASCULAR TECHNOLOGY OPTION

Oregon Institute of Technology (B)

UNCLASSIFIED STUDENT STATUS

University of Dubuque (M)

UNDERGRADUATE DEGREE COMPLETION PROGRAM

Boston University (B)

UNIVERSITY PARALLEL

Nashville State Technical Community College (A)

UNIVERSITY STUDIES

Brigham Young University–Idaho (B)
Dickinson State University (B)
North Dakota State University (B)
University of Maine (B)
University of Maine at Fort Kent (B)
The University of Tennessee at Martin (B)

UNIVERSITY TRANSFER

Central Carolina Community College (A)
Clark State Community College (A)
Cossatot Community College of the University of Arkansas (A)
Piedmont Community College (A)

UNIVERSITY TRANSFER PROGRAM (LIBERAL ARTS)

Spartanburg Community College (A)

UNIVERSITY TRANSFER PROGRAM (SCIENCE)

Spartanburg Community College (A)

UNIX

University of Massachusetts Lowell (UC)

UPWARD MOBILITY NURSING PROGRAM

Lamar State College–Port Arthur (A)

URBAN BIBLE TRAINING

Global University (UC)

URBAN EDUCATION

University of Central Florida (GC)

URBAN FORESTRY TECHNOLOGY

Dakota College at Bottineau (UC)

URBAN PEST MANAGEMENT

University of Florida (UC,GC)

URBAN STUDIES

Eastern University (M)

VALUE DRIVEN ORGANIZATION

Central Michigan University (M)

VARIOUS PROGRAMS

Spencerian College (UC,A)

VARIOUS SUBJECTS–BIOQUALITY, ENTREPRENEUR, HUMAN RESOURCES MANAGEMENT
Central Carolina Community College (UC)

VARIOUS SUBJECTS–INCOME TAX PREPARER, LIBRARY SERVICES, MANAGER TRAINEE
Central Carolina Community College (UC)

VARIOUS SUBJECTS–MEDICAL TRANSCRIPTION, NETWORKING
Central Carolina Community College (UC)

VARIOUS SUBJECTS–PAYROLL ACCOUNTING, SMALL BUSINESS FINANCIAL ADVISOR I AND II
Central Carolina Community College (UC)

VET HOMELAND SECURITY
Purdue University (GC)

VETERINARIAN TECHNICIAN
Purdue University (A)

VETERINARY HOSPITAL MANAGEMENT
St. Petersburg College (UC)

VETERINARY MEDICAL SCIENCES–FORENSIC TOXICOLOGY
University of Florida (M)

VETERINARY MEDICINE ONLINE
Colorado State University (UC)

VETERINARY SERVICES MANAGEMENT
State University of New York College of Technology at Canton (B)

VETERINARY TECHNOLOGY
St. Petersburg College (A,B)

VICTIM ADVOCACY
Fort Hays State University (UC)

VICTIM STUDIES
University of Massachusetts Lowell (GC)

VIRTUAL MBA (EXECUTIVE MANAGEMENT)
Indiana Wesleyan University (M)

VIRTUAL MBA (INTERNATIONAL BUSINESS)
Indiana Wesleyan University (M)

VIRTUAL TEAM MANAGEMENT AND COMMUNICATION
Brandeis University (M)

VISION REHABILITATION THERAPY
Western Michigan University (M)

VISION REHABILITATION THERAPY SPECIALIZATION
University of Massachusetts Boston (GC,M)

VISION SPECIALIST
Mississippi State University (GC)

VISUAL ART AND DESIGN
University of Denver (UC)

VISUAL C# PROGRAMMING
Wake Technical Community College (UC)

VISUAL COMMUNICATION
Columbus State Community College (GC)

VISUAL IMPAIRMENT
Indiana State University (UC)

VOCATIONAL DIVERSIFIED OCCUPATIONS (UG & G)
University of Nebraska at Kearney (UC)

VOCATIONAL REHABILITATION COUNSELING
University of Wisconsin–Stout (M)

VOCATIONAL REHABILITATION–REHABILITATION COUNSELING
University of Wisconsin–Stout (M)

VOCATIONAL TEACHER PREPARATION
State University of New York at Oswego (B,M)

VOICE CAPTIONING
AIB College of Business (A)

VOICE COURT REPORTING
AIB College of Business (A)

VOICE TRANSCRIPTION
AIB College of Business (A)

WASTEWATER OPERATOR CERTIFICATE
Central Carolina Technical College (UC)

WATER CONFLICT MANAGEMENT
Oregon State University (GC)

WATER OPERATOR CERTIFICATE
Central Carolina Technical College (UC)

WATER QUALITY
Moraine Park Technical College (A)

WATER RESOURCES
Colorado State University (GC)

WATER RESOURCES ENGINEERING
University of Idaho (UC)

WATER RESOURCES PLANNING AND MANAGEMENT
University of Florida (M)

WATER, WASTEWATER, AND STORMWATER ENGINEERING
University of Florida (M)

WATER/WASTEWATER SPECIALIZATION
Mountain Empire Community College (A)

WEALTH MANAGEMENT
DePaul University (UC)

WEATHER FORECASTING
Penn State University Park (UC)

WEB AUTHORING
Front Range Community College (UC)

WEB COMMUNICATION
Columbus State Community College (GC)

WEB DESIGN
Champlain College (UC)
Sessions College for Professional Design (A)

WEB DESIGN AND DEVELOPMENT
Champlain College (A,B)
University of Denver (UC)

WEB DESIGN AND MULTIMEDIA
Pennsylvania College of Technology (B)

WEB DESIGN AND NEW MEDIA
Academy of Art University (A,B,M)

WEB DESIGN BASICS

Central Texas College (UC)

WEB DESIGNER

Wake Technical Community College (UC)

WEB DEVELOPER

College of Southern Maryland (UC)
Wake Technical Community College (UC)

WEB DEVELOPER (LEMOORE CAMPUS-BASED)

West Hills Community College (UC)

WEB DEVELOPMENT

Fort Hays State University (UC)
Lewis-Clark State College (A,B)
Minot State University (GC)
North Shore Community College (UC)
Seminole State College of Florida (UC)

WEB GRAPHIC DESIGN

DeVry University Online (A)

WEB INFRASTRUCTURE

Champlain College (UC)

WEB MBA

Georgia College & State University (M)

WEB PROGRAMMING

Champlain College (UC)

WEB SERVICES

Webster University (GC)

WEB SITE DESIGN

Webster University (UC)

WEB SITE DEVELOPER

Lansing Community College (UC)

WEB SITE DEVELOPMENT

Webster University (UC)

WEB SITE DEVELOPMENT CERTIFICATE

Western Wyoming Community College (UC)

WEB STRATEGY AND DESIGN

Mercy College (M)

WEB TECHNOLOGIES

Piedmont Community College (A)
Wake Technical Community College (A)

WEB TECHNOLOGIES–E-COMMERCE PROGRAMMING

Wake Technical Community College (UC)

WEB TECHNOLOGY

Motlow State Community College (A)
Pellissippi State Technical Community College (A)

WEBSITE DESIGN AND DEVELOPMENT

University of Massachusetts Lowell (UC)

WELDING ENGINEERING

The Ohio State University (M)

WESTERN AMERICAN STUDIES

Western Wyoming Community College (UC)

WETLAND AND WATER RESOURCE MANAGEMENT

University of Florida (GC)

WETLANDS MANAGEMENT

Prescott College (M)

WILDLIFE MANAGEMENT

Mountain State University (A)
Prescott College (M)

WIRELESS AND ADVANCED

Seminole State College of Florida (UC)

WIRELESS AND ELECTRONIC COMMUNICATIONS

Cleveland Institute of Electronics (UC)

WIRELESS AND MOBILE NETWORKING

Columbia University (UC)

WIRELESS COMMUNICATIONS TECHNOLOGY

University of Illinois at Chicago (UC)

WIRELESS NETWORK AND TECHNOLOGIES

University of Colorado Boulder (GC)

WOMEN STUDIES

Oregon State University (B)

WOMEN'S AND GENDER STUDIES

Fort Hays State University (UC)

WOMEN'S HEALTH

Rosalind Franklin University of Medicine and Science (GC,M)

WOMEN'S HEALTH NURSE PRACTITIONER

University of Cincinnati (M)
Vanderbilt University (M)

WOMEN'S IMAGING

Fort Hays State University (UC)

WOMEN'S STUDIES

Western Kentucky University (GC)

WOMEN'S STUDIES (3 YEAR)

Athabasca University (B)

WOMEN'S STUDIES (4 YEAR)

Athabasca University (B)

WOMEN'S STUDIES CERTIFICATE

Bowling Green State University (GC)

WORD PROCESSING AND PUBLICATIONS

Wake Technical Community College (UC)

WORKFORCE EDUCATION LEADERSHIP

Mississippi State University (M)

WORKFORCE EDUCATION LEADERSHIP (MSN)

Alcorn State University (M)

WORKFORCE LEADERSHIP

University of Louisville (B)

WORKFORCE LEADERSHIP AND SUPERVISION

The University of Texas at Brownsville (B)

WORKFORCE TRAINING AND DEVELOPMENT

University of Southern Mississippi (M)

WORKPLACE E-LEARNING AND PERFORMANCE SUPPORT

Boise State University (GC)

WORKPLACE INSTRUCTIONAL DESIGN

Boise State University (GC)

WORKPLACE LEARNING AND PERFORMANCE

Colorado State University (GC)

WORKPLACE TECHNOLOGIES

Lawrence Technological University (GC)

WORLD HISTORY AND CULTURE

University of Denver (UC)

WORSHIP

Hope International University (M)

WORSHIP LEADERSHIP

Dallas Baptist University (M)

WORSHIP MINISTRY CONCENTRATION

Dallas Baptist University (M)

WORSHIP STUDIES

Liberty University (M)

WRITING

Lindenwood University (M)
Perelandra College (B)
The University of Western Ontario (UC)

WRITING AND LITERATURE

Burlington College (B)

XPRESS

Indiana Wesleyan University (M)

YOUTH DEVELOPMENT

Clemson University (M)
Kansas State University (GC,M)

YOUTH MINISTRIES

Toccoa Falls College (B)

YOUTH MINISTRY

Southwestern College (B)

YOUTH MINISTRY LEADERSHIP

Defiance College (UC)

YOUTH SERVICES SPECIALIST

Drexel University

NON-DEGREE-RELATED COURSE SUBJECT AREAS

Index of individual courses offered by institutions, arranged by subject. U=Undergraduate; G=Graduate; N=Noncredit

ACCOUNTING AND COMPUTER SCIENCE

Acadia University (U)
Albertus Magnus College (U)
Alcorn State University (U)
Allen Community College (U)
Arapahoe Community College (U)
Arkansas State University–Mountain Home (U)
Ashland University (U)
Athabasca University (U)
Austin Peay State University (N,U)
Baker College Online (U)
Belmont Technical College (U)
Bridgewater State University (U)
Brigham Young University–Idaho (U)
Bronx Community College of the City University of New York (U)
Bryant University (N)
Burlington County College (U)
Butler Community College (U)
Cabrillo College (U)
California State University, San Bernardino (U)
California State University, San Marcos (N,U)
Carroll University (U)
Cascadia Community College (U)
Cedarville University (U)
Central Michigan University (U,G)
Central Pennsylvania College (U)
Central Texas College (U)
Cerritos College (U)
Chattanooga State Community College (U)
Citrus College (U)
City Colleges of Chicago System (U)
Clackamas Community College (U)
Clark State Community College (U)
Cleveland Community College (U)
Cleveland Institute of Electronics (N)
Cleveland State Community College (N)
Clovis Community College (U)
Community College of Allegheny County (U)
Community College of Beaver County (N,U)
Corning Community College (U)
Dabney S. Lancaster Community College (N,U)
Dakota College at Bottineau (U)
Dallas Baptist University (U)
Daytona State College (U)
Delgado Community College (U)
Dickinson State University (U)
Drake University (G)
Drexel University (N)
D'Youville College (U)
East Central Community College (U)
Eastern Kentucky University (U)
Eastern West Virginia Community and Technical College (U)
East Los Angeles College (U)
Enterprise State Community College (U)
Excelsior College (U)
Ferris State University (U)
Finger Lakes Community College (U)
Fitchburg State University (U,G)
Fort Hays State University (N,U)
Fort Valley State University (U)
Franklin Pierce University (G)
Gadsden State Community College (U)
Greenville Technical College (U)
Harcum College (U)
Hocking College (U)
Hofstra University (U)
Holyoke Community College (U)
Hopkinsville Community College (U)
Illinois Eastern Community Colleges, Frontier Community College (U)
Illinois Eastern Community Colleges, Lincoln Trail College (U)
Illinois Eastern Community Colleges, Olney Central College (U)
Indiana State University (U)
Inter American University of Puerto Rico, San Germán Campus (U)
Iowa Lakes Community College (U)
Jacksonville State University (U,G)
Jamestown Community College (U)
John A. Logan College (U)
Johnston Community College (U)
Kansas State University (U)
Keystone College (U)
Kilian Community College (U)
Lackawanna College (U)
Lipscomb University (U)
Luna Community College (U)
Macon State College (U)
Mansfield University of Pennsylvania (N)
Marlboro College Graduate College (U)
Maryville University of Saint Louis (U)
McKendree University (U)
Miami Dade College (U)
Middlesex Community College (U)
Middle Tennessee State University (U)
Minnesota School of Business–Online (U)
Mississippi State University (U)
Monroe College (U)
Moorpark College (U)
Mount Olive College (U)
Mount Wachusett Community College (N)
Murray State College (U)
Nashville State Technical Community College (U)
Naugatuck Valley Community College (U)
New Mexico Junior College (U)
Nichols College (G)
North Central State College (N,U)
North Hennepin Community College (N)
North Seattle Community College (U)
Northwestern Oklahoma State University (U)
Northwest-Shoals Community College (U)
Northwest State Community College (U)
Notre Dame College (U)
Oakland Community College (U)
Oklahoma Panhandle State University (U)
Oregon Coast Community College (U)
Ozarks Technical Community College (U)
Pacific States University (G)
Pamlico Community College (U)
Paris Junior College (N)
Peru State College (U)
Piedmont Community College (U)
Portland Community College (N,U)
Prairie View A&M University (U)
Pulaski Technical College (U)
Quinebaug Valley Community College (N)
Quinnipiac University (U,G)
Quinsigamond Community College (U)
Rend Lake College (U)
The Richard Stockton College of New Jersey (U)
Richmond Community College (U)
Rose State College (U)
Sacramento City College (U)
Saint Francis University (U)
St. Gregory's University (U)
St. Louis Community College (U)
Saint Paul College–A Community & Technical College (U)
St. Petersburg College (N)
St. Philip's College (U)
San Diego Community College District (N,U)
Santa Fe Community College (U)
Santa Monica College (U)
Seton Hill University (U)
Sinclair Community College (U)
Southern Arkansas University–Magnolia (U)
Southern New Hampshire University (U,G)
Southern Union State Community College (U)
South Piedmont Community College (U)
South Suburban College (U)
Spokane Community College (U)
Spring Arbor University (U)
State University of New York at Oswego (U)
State University of New York College of Agriculture and Technology at Morrisville (U)
State University of New York Institute of Technology (G)
Sullivan County Community College (N,U)
Toccoa Falls College (U)
Union University (U)
University of Alaska Fairbanks (U)
University of Alaska, Prince William Sound Community College (U)
The University of Arizona (U)
University of Cincinnati (N)
University of Colorado at Colorado Springs (N)
University of Evansville (N)
University of Idaho (U,G)
University of Maine at Machias (U)
University of Management and Technology (U,G)
University of Minnesota, Crookston (U)
University of Missouri–Kansas City (U)
The University of South Dakota (U,G)

University of Southern Maine (U)
The University of Texas at Arlington (U)
The University of Texas at Dallas (G)
University of West Florida (G)
University of West Georgia (U)
University of Wisconsin–Superior (U)
Upper Iowa University (N)
Wayne Community College (N)
Webber International University (U)
Western Kentucky University (U)
West Los Angeles College (U)
West Texas A&M University (G)
West Virginia Northern Community College (N)
Wharton County Junior College (U)
Windward Community College (U)
Yavapai College (U)
Youngstown State University (U)

ACCOUNTING AND RELATED SERVICES

Acadia University (U)
Adams State College (N,U)
Alcorn State University (U)
Amberton University (U)
American Graduate University (G)
Angelina College (U)
Anne Arundel Community College (U)
Antelope Valley College (U)
Arapahoe Community College (U)
Arizona Western College (U)
Arkansas State University (U)
Arkansas State University–Beebe (U)
Athabasca University (N,U,G)
Auburn University (G)
Austin Peay State University (U)
Baker College Online (G)
Bellevue College (U)
Belmont Technical College (U)
Big Bend Community College (U)
Blackhawk Technical College (U)
Bloomfield College (U,G)
Bob Jones University (U)
Boise State University (U)
Brazosport College (U)
Brenau University (U,G)
Brewton-Parker College (U)
Brigham Young University (U)
Brigham Young University–Idaho (U)
Bronx Community College of the City University of New York (U)
Brookdale Community College (U)
Bryant University (N)
Buena Vista University (U)
Burlington County College (U)
Butler Community College (U)
Butler County Community College (U)
Cabrillo College (U)
Caldwell College (U,G)
California State University, Dominguez Hills (N)
California State University, Sacramento (U)
California State University, San Bernardino (U)
Cape Fear Community College (U)
Capital Community College (U)
Carleton University (U)
Carl Sandburg College (U)
Cascadia Community College (U)
Cayuga County Community College (U)
Cedarville University (U)
Central Carolina Community College (U)
Central Carolina Technical College (U)
Centralia College (U)
Central New Mexico Community College (U)
Central Texas College (U)
Central Virginia Community College (U)
Central Washington University (U,G)
Central Wyoming College (U)
Cerritos College (U)
Champlain College (U)
Charter Oak State College (U)
Chatham University (U,G)
Chattanooga State Community College (U)
Chemeketa Community College (U)
Cincinnati State Technical and Community College (U)
City Colleges of Chicago System (U)
City University of Seattle (U)
Clackamas Community College (U)
Clatsop Community College (U)
Clemson University (N)
Cleveland Community College (U)
Cleveland State Community College (N,U)
Clinton Community College (U)
Coleman University (U)
College of San Mateo (U)
College of Southern Maryland (U)
College of the Siskiyous (U)
Colorado Mountain College (U)
Columbia Basin College (U)
Columbia College (U)
Columbus State Community College (U)
Concordia University Wisconsin (U)
Corning Community College (U)
Cossatot Community College of the University of Arkansas (N,U)
Crown College (U)
Culver-Stockton College (U)
Dabney S. Lancaster Community College (U)
Dakota College at Bottineau (U)
Dakota State University (U)
Dallas Baptist University (U,G)
Dallas Christian College (U)
Danville Community College (U)
DePaul University (G)
DeVry University Online (U,G)
Dickinson State University (U)
Drake University (U)
Drexel University (U,G)
Drury University (U)
D'Youville College (U)
Eastern Oregon University (U)
Eastern Washington University (U)
Eastern Wyoming College (U)
Edgecombe Community College (N,U)
Edison State Community College (U)
Elaine P. Nunez Community College (U)
Enterprise State Community College (U)
Erie Community College (U)
Erie Community College, North Campus (U)
Erie Community College, South Campus (U)
Fort Hays State University (N)
Fort Valley State University (U)
Franklin Pierce University (U)
Front Range Community College (U)
Frostburg State University (U)
Gannon University (U)
Gaston College (U)
Genesee Community College (U)
Governors State University (U)
Grand Valley State University (U,G)
Grantham University (U,G)
Hagerstown Community College (N)
Harrisburg Area Community College (U)
Haywood Community College (U)
Heartland Community College (U)
Herkimer County Community College (U)
Hibbing Community College (N,U)
Hofstra University (G)
Hopkinsville Community College (N)
Houston Community College System (U)
Illinois Eastern Community Colleges, Olney Central College (U)
Illinois Eastern Community Colleges, Wabash Valley College (U)
Illinois Valley Community College (U)
Indiana State University (U)
Indiana University of Pennsylvania (U)
Indiana University–Purdue University Fort Wayne (U)
Inter American University of Puerto Rico, San Germán Campus (G)
Iowa Lakes Community College (U)
Iowa Valley Community College District (U)
Jacksonville State University (U,G)
James A. Rhodes State College (U)
James Madison University (U)
Jamestown Community College (N,U)
Jefferson Community College (U)
John A. Logan College (U)
Johnston Community College (U)
J. Sargeant Reynolds Community College (U)
Kansas State University (U)
Kauai Community College (U,G)
Kean University (N,U,G)
Kirkwood Community College (U)
Kirtland Community College (U)
Lake Superior College (U)
Lansing Community College (U)
Lawrence Technological University (G)
Lehman College of the City University of New York (U)
Lewis-Clark State College (U)
Liberty University (U,G)
Lindenwood University (U)
Lipscomb University (U,G)
Long Beach City College (U)
Los Angeles Harbor College (U)
Louisiana State University and Agricultural and Mechanical College (U)
Macon State College (U)
Maharishi University of Management (N,U,G)
Mansfield University of Pennsylvania (N,U)
Marist College (U,G)
Marshall University (U,G)
Mary Baldwin College (U)
Maryville University of Saint Louis (N)
Mayville State University (U)
McDowell Technical Community College (U)
McKendree University (G)
McNeese State University (N)
Medical College of Wisconsin (G)
Mercer County Community College (U)
Mesa State College (U)
Metropolitan Community College–Penn Valley (U)
Miami Dade College (U)
Middlesex Community College (U)
Middle Tennessee State University (U)
Midland College (U)
Midstate College (U)
Midway College (U)
Minnesota School of Business–Online (U)
Minnesota School of Business–Richfield (U)

Minot State University (U)
Mississippi College (U)
Mississippi State University (U)
Monroe Community College (U)
Montcalm Community College (N,U)
Montgomery Community College (U)
Montgomery County Community College (N,U)
Moorpark College (U)
Mountain Empire Community College (U)
Mountain State University (U)
Murray State University (U)
Nassau Community College (U)
National University (U,G)
Naugatuck Valley Community College (N,U)
New England College of Business and Finance (N,U)
New Mexico Highlands University (U,G)
New Mexico State University (U)
New Mexico State University–Grants (U)
New River Community College (U)
Nichols College (U)
Nicolet Area Technical College (U)
Nipissing University (U)
North Arkansas College (U)
North Carolina State University (U)
North Central State College (N)
North Dakota State College of Science (U)
North Dakota State University (U)
Northeastern State University (U)
Northern State University (U)
North Hennepin Community College (N,U)
North Iowa Area Community College (U)
North Lake College (U)
North Seattle Community College (U)
NorthWest Arkansas Community College (U)
Northwestern Michigan College (U)
Northwestern Oklahoma State University (U)
Oakton Community College (U)
Ocean County College (U)
Odessa College (U)
Ohio University (N,U)
Oklahoma Panhandle State University (U)
Olympic College (U)
Orange Coast College (U)
Oregon Institute of Technology (U)
Oxnard College (U)
Pace University (U)
Pacific States University (U)
Palm Beach State College (U)
Pamlico Community College (U)
Pasco-Hernando Community College (U)
Pellissippi State Technical Community College (U)
Peninsula College (U)
Pennsylvania College of Technology (U)
Philadelphia University (U,G)
Phoenix College (N,U)
Pikes Peak Community College (U)
Pitt Community College (U)
Pittsburg State University (U)
Portland Community College (N)
Pratt Community College (U)
Pulaski Technical College (U)
Quincy University (U)
Quinnipiac University (G)
Quinsigamond Community College (N)
Randolph Community College (N,U)
Rappahannock Community College (U)
Reading Area Community College (U)
Regent University (U,G)
Reinhardt University (U)
Rend Lake College (N,U)
The Richard Stockton College of New Jersey (N)
Rio Hondo College (U)
Riverside Community College District (U)
Robert Morris University (U)
Rogers State University (U)
Rose State College (U)
Rowan-Cabarrus Community College (N,U)
Sacramento City College (U)
St. Ambrose University (U)
St. Clair County Community College (U)
Saint Francis University (U)
St. John's University (U)
Saint Joseph's College of Maine (G)
Saint Leo University (U)
Saint Mary-of-the-Woods College (U)
St. Petersburg College (U)
St. Philip's College (U)
Sampson Community College (U)
San Bernardino Valley College (U)
San Diego Community College District (U)
San Jacinto College District (U)
Santa Monica College (U)
Santa Rosa Junior College (U)
Sauk Valley Community College (U)
Seminole State College of Florida (U)
Seton Hill University (G)
Shippensburg University of Pennsylvania (U,G)
Sinclair Community College (U)
Slippery Rock University of Pennsylvania (U)
Southeast Community College Area (U)
Southeastern Community College (U)
Southeastern Oklahoma State University (N,U,G)
Southern New Hampshire University (U,G)
Southern Oregon University (U,G)
Southern Union State Community College (U)
South Piedmont Community College (U)
Southwestern Community College (U)
Southwest Wisconsin Technical College (U)
Spartanburg Community College (N,U)
Spoon River College (U)
Stanly Community College (U)
State University of New York at Oswego (G)
State University of New York College at Potsdam (N)
State University of New York College of Agriculture and Technology at Morrisville (U)
State University of New York College of Technology at Canton (U)
State University of New York Empire State College (U)
State University of New York Institute of Technology (U,G)
Stephen F. Austin State University (U)
Stephens College (U,G)
Suffolk University (G)
Sullivan County Community College (U)
Taft College (U)
Tarleton State University (N,U)
Temple University (G)
Texas A&M University–Corpus Christi (U,G)
Thiel College (U)
Three Rivers Community College (U)
Tompkins Cortland Community College (U)
Trident Technical College (U)
Trine University (U)
Tyler Junior College (N,U)
Union County College (U)
The University of Akron (U,G)
The University of Alabama in Huntsville (G)
University of Alaska Fairbanks (U)
University of Arkansas at Little Rock (U)
University of Cincinnati (N,U)
University of Colorado at Colorado Springs (N)
University of Evansville (U)
The University of Findlay (U,G)
University of Houston–Downtown (U)
University of Houston–Victoria (U,G)
University of Idaho (U)
University of Illinois at Chicago (G)
University of Illinois at Springfield (U)
University of Maine (U)
University of Maine at Augusta (U)
University of Mary (U)
University of Mary Washington (U)
University of Michigan–Flint (N,U,G)
University of Minnesota, Crookston (U)
University of Nevada, Reno (U)
University of New Haven (U,G)
University of North Alabama (U,G)
The University of North Carolina at Chapel Hill (U)
University of North Dakota (U)
University of Northern Iowa (U)
University of North Florida (U)
University of Oregon (U)
University of St. Francis (U)
University of South Carolina Sumter (U)
University of Southern Maine (U)
University of Southern Mississippi (U)
The University of Tennessee at Martin (N)
The University of Texas at Arlington (U)
The University of Texas at Brownsville (N)
The University of Texas at Dallas (G)
The University of Texas of the Permian Basin (G)
University of the Southwest (U)
University of Toronto (N)
University of Virginia (U)
University of Waterloo (N,U)
University of Windsor (U)
The University of Winnipeg (U)
University of Wisconsin–La Crosse (G)
University of Wisconsin MBA Consortium (G)
Upper Iowa University (N,U,G)
Utah State University (U)
Vincennes University (U)
Wake Technical Community College (N,U)
Wayland Baptist University (U,G)
Wayne State University (G)
Webber International University (U)
Westchester Community College (U)
Western Wyoming Community College (U)
Westmoreland County Community College (U)
Wilfrid Laurier University (U)
Wilkes Community College (U)
Wisconsin Indianhead Technical College (N,U)
York College of Pennsylvania (N)
York County Community College (U)
York Technical College (U)
York University (U)
Youngstown State University (N)

AEROSPACE, AERONAUTICAL AND ASTRONAUTICAL ENGINEERING

Auburn University (G)
Georgia Institute of Technology (N,G)
Indiana State University (U)
Middle Tennessee State University (U,G)
Missouri University of Science and Technology (N)
Naugatuck Valley Community College (U)
The University of Alabama in Huntsville (G)
University of Colorado at Colorado Springs (G)
University of Colorado Boulder (N,G)
University of Florida (N)
The University of Tennessee Space Institute (G)
The University of Texas at Arlington (G)

AGRICULTURAL AND DOMESTIC ANIMAL SERVICES

Auburn University (G)
Butler Community College (U)
Central Wyoming College (N,U)
Dickinson State University (U)
Kansas State University (N,U)
Minnesota School of Business–Online (U)
North Carolina State University (U)
Nova Scotia Agricultural College (U)
Oklahoma State University (U)
University of Florida (U)
Yavapai College (U)

AGRICULTURAL AND FOOD PRODUCTS PROCESSING

Auburn University (G)
Butler Community College (U)
Fort Valley State University (U)
Kansas State University (N,U,G)
Mansfield University of Pennsylvania (N)
North Carolina State University (U,G)
NorthWest Arkansas Community College (U)
Oklahoma State University (U)
The Richard Stockton College of New Jersey (N)
Sampson Community College (U)
University of Florida (U)
University of Illinois at Urbana–Champaign (G)
University of Minnesota, Crookston (U)
Wisconsin Indianhead Technical College (N,U)

AGRICULTURAL BUSINESS AND MANAGEMENT

Adams State College (U)
Allen Community College (U)
Arkansas State University (U)
Arkansas State University–Beebe (U)
Athabasca University (G)
Austin Peay State University (U)
Blackhawk Technical College (U)
Butler Community College (U)
Central Virginia Community College (U)
Clark State Community College (U)
Cossatot Community College of the University of Arkansas (U)
Dawson Community College (U)
Eastern Oregon University (U)
Eastern Wyoming College (U)
Fort Valley State University (U)
Hope International University (G)
Iowa Lakes Community College (U)
Kansas State University (N,U,G)
Luna Community College (U)
Middle Tennessee State University (U)
Minnesota School of Business–Online (U)
Mitchell Technical Institute (N)
North Central Texas College (U)
Nova Scotia Agricultural College (U)
Oregon State University (U)
Sam Houston State University (U)
Southern Illinois University Carbondale (U)
State University of New York College of Agriculture and Technology at Morrisville (U)
The University of British Columbia (U)
University of Florida (U,G)
University of Illinois at Urbana–Champaign (U)
University of Saskatchewan (N,U)
Wayne Community College (U)
Wisconsin Indianhead Technical College (N,U)

AGRICULTURAL ENGINEERING

Fort Valley State University (U)
Southern Illinois University Carbondale (U,G)
University of Idaho (U,G)

AGRICULTURAL MECHANIZATION

Southern Illinois University Carbondale (U)
University of Florida (G)

AGRICULTURAL PRODUCTION

Auburn University (G)
Kansas State University (N,U)
Murray State University (U)
North Carolina State University (U)
Nova Scotia Agricultural College (U)
Oklahoma State University (U)
Sampson Community College (U)
University of Florida (U)
Wayne Community College (U)

AGRICULTURAL PUBLIC SERVICES

Kansas State University (N,G)
University of Florida (U,G)

AGRICULTURE

Allen Community College (U)
Arkansas State University (U,G)
Arkansas Tech University (U)
Auburn University (U)
Austin Peay State University (U)
California State University, Chico (U)
Central Carolina Community College (U)
Central Carolina Technical College (U)
Clemson University (G)
Dawson Community College (U)
Dickinson State University (U)
Eastern Wyoming College (U)
Illinois State University (G)
Kansas State University (N,U,G)
Louisiana State University at Eunice (U)
Luna Community College (U)
Mid-State Technical College (U)
Mississippi State University (G)
Murray State University (U,G)
North Carolina State University (U,G)
NorthWest Arkansas Community College (U)
Nova Scotia Agricultural College (N,U)
The Ohio State University (U)
Oregon State University (U)
Paris Junior College (U)
Purdue University (N)
Southern Arkansas University–Magnolia (G)
Southern Illinois University Carbondale (U)
State University of New York College of Agriculture and Technology at Morrisville (U)
Stephen F. Austin State University (U)
The University of Arizona (U)
The University of British Columbia (U)
University of Florida (U,G)
University of Illinois at Urbana–Champaign (G)
University of Saskatchewan (U)
Western Texas College (U)
Wisconsin Indianhead Technical College (N,U)
Yavapai College (U)

AGRICULTURE AND AGRICULTURE OPERATIONS RELATED

Alcorn State University (U)
Austin Peay State University (U)
Iowa Lakes Community College (U)
Kansas State University (N,U,G)
Louisiana State University at Eunice (U)
Mitchell Technical Institute (N)
North Carolina State University (G)
Oregon State University (U)
Portland Community College (N)
Sampson Community College (U)
Tarleton State University (U)
The University of Arizona (U)
University of California, Riverside (N)
University of Florida (U)
University of Illinois at Urbana–Champaign (U)
University of Saskatchewan (N)
Utah State University (G)

AIR FORCE ROTC

Austin Peay State University (U)
California State University, San Bernardino (U)

AIR TRANSPORTATION

Central Oregon Community College (U)
Central Wyoming College (N)
Community College of Beaver County (U)
Portland Community College (U)
St. Petersburg College (N)
San Diego Community College District (U)
San Jacinto College District (U)
Southeastern Oklahoma State University (U)
University of Dubuque (U)
West Los Angeles College (U)

ALLIED HEALTH AND MEDICAL ASSISTING SERVICES

Allen Community College (U)
Angelina College (U)
Anne Arundel Community College (U)
Arapahoe Community College (U)
Austin Peay State University (N,U)
Big Bend Community College (U)
Blackhawk Technical College (U)
Blackstone Career Institute (N,U)
Boise State University (U,G)
Bossier Parish Community College (U)
Brenau University (U)
Bronx Community College of the City University of New York (U)
Butler Community College (U)
Butler County Community College (U)
Cabrillo College (U)
California State University, San Bernardino (U)
California State University, San Marcos (U)
Carl Sandburg College (U)
Central Carolina Technical College (U)
Central Michigan University (U)
Central Oregon Community College (U)
Central Texas College (U)
Central Virginia Community College (U)
Chattanooga State Community College (U)
Chemeketa Community College (U)
Cincinnati State Technical and Community College (U)
Clackamas Community College (U)
Clarion University of Pennsylvania (U)
Clark State Community College (U)
Clemson University (N)
Cleveland State Community College (U)
Columbus State Community College (U)
Dakota College at Bottineau (U)
Danville Community College (U)
Daytona State College (U)
Dominican College (G)
East Central Community College (U)
Eastern Washington University (N)
Edison State Community College (U)
Ferris State University (U)
Franklin Pierce University (G)
Front Range Community College (U)
Gaston College (U)
Georgia Highlands College (U)
Hagerstown Community College (N)
Harcum College (U)
Harrisburg Area Community College (U)
Hocking College (U)
Illinois Eastern Community Colleges, Frontier Community College (U)
Indiana University–Purdue University Fort Wayne (N)
James A. Rhodes State College (U)
John A. Logan College (U)
Kirtland Community College (U)
Lamar State College–Orange (U)
Lamar State College–Port Arthur (N)
Lansing Community College (U)
Lenoir Community College (U)
Lewis-Clark State College (N)
Lock Haven University of Pennsylvania (N)
Louisiana State University at Eunice (U)
Luna Community College (U)
Mansfield University of Pennsylvania (N)
McDowell Technical Community College (U)
McNeese State University (N)
Mercy College of Northwest Ohio (N,U)
Middle Tennessee State University (N)
Midstate College (U)
Mid-State Technical College (U)
Minnesota School of Business–Online (U)
Monroe College (U)
Montgomery Community College (N,U)
Moorpark College (U)
Murray State College (U)
Nashville State Technical Community College (N,U)
National University (U)
New Mexico Junior College (U)
New Mexico State University (U)
New Mexico State University–Carlsbad (U)
Nicolet Area Technical College (U)
North Arkansas College (U)
North Central State College (N,U)
North Dakota State College of Science (U)
North Dakota State University (N)
North Seattle Community College (U)
Northwestern Connecticut Community College (U)
Northwest State Community College (U)
Odessa College (U)
The Ohio State University (U,G)
Okefenokee Technical College (N,U)
Orange Coast College (U)
Oregon Coast Community College (U)
Ozarks Technical Community College (U)
Pamlico Community College (U)
Paris Junior College (N,U)
Pellissippi State Technical Community College (U)
Peninsula College (N,U)
Pratt Community College (U)
Pulaski Technical College (U)
Quinebaug Valley Community College (N)
Quinsigamond Community College (U)
Randolph Community College (N)
Rappahannock Community College (U)
Reading Area Community College (N)
The Richard Stockton College of New Jersey (N,G)
Richmond Community College (N,U)
Rose State College (U)
Sacramento City College (U)
San Diego Community College District (U)
San Jacinto College District (U)
Santa Fe Community College (U)
Santa Rosa Junior College (U)
Sinclair Community College (U)
Southeastern Community College (U)
Southern Maine Community College (U)
South Piedmont Community College (U)
Southwest Wisconsin Technical College (U)
Spokane Community College (N,U)
Spoon River College (U)
Texas State University–San Marcos (U)
Three Rivers Community College (N)
Union County College (U)
The University of Akron (N,U)
University of Alaska Fairbanks (U)
University of Alaska, Prince William Sound Community College (U)
University of California, Davis (N)
University of Cincinnati Raymond Walters College (U)
University of Colorado at Colorado Springs (N)
University of Evansville (N)
University of Illinois at Chicago (N)
Valencia College (U)
Vermont Technical College (U)
Vincennes University (U)
Wake Technical Community College (U)
Wayne Community College (N)
West Los Angeles College (U)
West Virginia Northern Community College (U)
Wharton County Junior College (U)
Winston-Salem State University (U)
Yavapai College (U)
Youngstown State University (N)

ALLIED HEALTH DIAGNOSTIC, INTERVENTION, AND TREATMENT PROFESSIONS

Arapahoe Community College (U)
Austin Peay State University (U)
Boise State University (U)
Brenau University (G)
Bronx Community College of the City University of New York (U)
Burlington County College (U)
Butler Community College (U)
California State University, San Bernardino (G)
Capital Community College (U)
Columbus State Community College (U)
Danville Community College (U)
Dominican College (U)
Eastern Washington University (N,U)
Erie Community College (U)
Erie Community College, North Campus (U)
Erie Community College, South Campus (U)
Ferris State University (U)
Harcum College (U)
Labette Community College (U)
Lamar State College–Port Arthur (N)
McKendree University (U,G)
Mercer County Community College (U)
Moorpark College (U)
North Carolina Central University (N)
North Seattle Community College (U)
NorthWest Arkansas Community College (U)
The Ohio State University (G)
Randolph Community College (N)
Rockingham Community College (N)
Rose State College (U)
Sacramento City College (U)
St. Petersburg College (U)
San Diego Community College District (U)
Santa Fe Community College (U)
Santa Monica College (U)
South Piedmont Community College (U)
Stanly Community College (U)
The University of Akron (U)
University of Alaska Fairbanks (U)
University of Alaska, Prince William Sound Community College (U)
The University of British Columbia (U)
University of Michigan–Flint (U)
University of the Sciences in Philadelphia (G)
University of West Florida (G)
Valencia College (U)

ALTERNATIVE AND COMPLEMENTARY MEDICAL SUPPORT SERVICES

Austin Peay State University (N)
DePaul University (N)

Drexel University (G)
Kean University (N)
Lamar State College–Port Arthur (N)
Prescott College (N)
Rose State College (U)
Sacramento City College (U)
Western Michigan University (U,G)

ALTERNATIVE AND COMPLEMENTARY MEDICINE AND MEDICAL SYSTEMS

California State University, Dominguez Hills (N)
Dabney S. Lancaster Community College (U)
Drexel University (G)
Front Range Community College (U)
Lamar State College–Port Arthur (N)
Lewis University (U)
Maharishi University of Management (U)
North Central State College (N)
Rose State College (U)
Western Michigan University (U)

AMERICAN SIGN LANGUAGE (ASL)

Austin Peay State University (N)
Cascadia Community College (U)
Chattanooga State Community College (U)
John A. Logan College (U)
Laurel University (U)
New River Community College (U)
Oregon State University (U)
Paris Junior College (N)
Pine Technical College (U)
Presentation College (U)
Riverside Community College District (U)
Sacramento City College (U)
San Diego Community College District (U)
Santa Fe Community College (U)
Spartanburg Community College (U)
Spokane Community College (U)
Union County College (U)
University of Arkansas at Little Rock (U)
University of Cincinnati Raymond Walters College (U)
University of Maine at Augusta (U)
University of Maine at Machias (U)
University of North Florida (U)
University of Southern Maine (U)
Utah State University (U)

ANIMAL SCIENCES

Auburn University (N,U)
Baptist Bible College of Pennsylvania (U,G)
Bronx Community College of the City University of New York (U)
Central Wyoming College (N)
Clemson University (G)
Duquesne University (N)
Fort Valley State University (U,G)
Haywood Community College (U)
Kansas State University (N,U,G)
Minnesota School of Business–Richfield (U)
North Carolina State University (U,G)
North Dakota State University (U)
Nova Scotia Agricultural College (N,U)
Oklahoma State University (U)
Portland Community College (U)
Purdue University (U)
Sampson Community College (U)
State University of New York College of Technology at Canton (U)
The University of Arizona (U)
The University of British Columbia (U)
University of Maine (G)
University of Southern Maine (U)
Windward Community College (U)

ANTHROPOLOGY

Allen Community College (U)
Alvin Community College (U)
American University (U)
Arapahoe Community College (U)
Athabasca University (N,U)
Bellevue College (U)
Big Bend Community College (U)
Boise State University (U)
Brenau University (U)
Bridgewater State University (U)
Brigham Young University (U)
Bronx Community College of the City University of New York (U)
Brookdale Community College (U)
Broward College (U)
Buffalo State College, State University of New York (U)
Burlington County College (U)
Butler Community College (U)
Cabrillo College (U)
California State University, Chico (U)
California State University, East Bay (U)
California State University, Sacramento (U)
Cascadia Community College (U)
Cayuga County Community College (U)
Cedarville University (U)
Central Carolina Community College (U)
Centralia College (U)
Central Texas College (U)
Central Washington University (U)
Cerritos College (U)
Chemeketa Community College (U)
Citrus College (U)
City Colleges of Chicago System (U)
College of the Siskiyous (U)
Colorado Mountain College (U)
Columbia Basin College (U)
Columbia College (U)
Columbia International University (N,G)
Columbus State Community College (U)
Community College of Allegheny County (U)
Cornell University (U,G)
Dawson Community College (U)
Eastern Kentucky University (U)
Eastern Oregon University (U)
Eastern Wyoming College (U)
East Los Angeles College (U)
Edison State Community College (U)
El Camino College (U)
Erie Community College (U)
Erie Community College, North Campus (U)
Erie Community College, South Campus (U)
Framingham State University (U)
Front Range Community College (U)
Genesee Community College (U)
Goddard College (U,G)
Governors State University (U,G)
Harrisburg Area Community College (U)
Haywood Community College (U)
Heartland Community College (U)
Hibbing Community College (U)
Hofstra University (U)
Hope International University (U)
Houston Community College System (U)
Indiana University of Pennsylvania (U,G)
Indiana University–Purdue University Fort Wayne (U)
Ithaca College (U)
Jacksonville State University (U)
Jefferson Community College (U)
John A. Logan College (U)
Johnson State College (U)
Kirkwood Community College (U)
Lakehead University (U)
Lake Superior College (U)
Lansing Community College (U)
Lassen Community College District (U)
Laurel University (U)
Lewis-Clark State College (U)
Lock Haven University of Pennsylvania (U)
Long Beach City College (U)
Los Angeles Trade-Technical College (U)
Louisiana State University and Agricultural and Mechanical College (U)
Mansfield University of Pennsylvania (U)
Marquette University (U)
Marshall University (U)
Memorial University of Newfoundland (U)
Mercer County Community College (U)
Middlesex Community College (U)
Minot State University (U)
Montgomery County Community College (U)
Moorpark College (U)
Murray State University (U)
Nassau Community College (U)
New Mexico State University (U)
New Mexico State University–Carlsbad (U)
North Arkansas College (U)
North Carolina State University (U)
North Dakota State University (U)
Northeastern State University (U)
North Seattle Community College (U)
Northwestern Michigan College (U)
Oakton Community College (U)
The Ohio State University (U)
Oklahoma State University (U)
Olympic College (U)
Orange Coast College (U)
Oregon Institute of Technology (U)
Oregon State University (U)
Oxnard College (U)
Ozarks Technical Community College (U)
Pace University (U)
Palm Beach State College (U)
Pellissippi State Technical Community College (U)
Peninsula College (U)
Phoenix College (U)
Pikes Peak Community College (U)
Prairie Bible Institute (U,G)
Providence College and Theological Seminary (U)
Pulaski Technical College (U)
Quinebaug Valley Community College (U)
Rend Lake College (U)
The Richard Stockton College of New Jersey (U)
Rio Hondo College (U)
Riverside Community College District (U)
Rochester Institute of Technology (U)
Rockland Community College (U)
Sacramento City College (U)
St. Cloud State University (U)

St. John's University (U)
St. Louis Community College (U)
Saint Paul College–A Community & Technical College (U)
St. Petersburg College (U)
Sam Houston State University (U)
San Bernardino Valley College (U)
San Diego Community College District (U)
San Diego State University (U)
San Jacinto College District (U)
Santa Fe Community College (U)
Santa Rosa Junior College (U)
Seminole State College of Florida (U)
Southeast Arkansas College (U)
Southern Illinois University Carbondale (U,G)
Spokane Community College (U)
State University of New York at New Paltz (U)
State University of New York at Oswego (U,G)
State University of New York at Plattsburgh (U)
State University of New York College at Potsdam (U)
Syracuse University (G)
Temple University (U)
Toccoa Falls College (U)
Tunxis Community College (U)
University at Albany, State University of New York (U)
The University of Akron (U)
University of Alaska Fairbanks (U)
The University of Arizona (U)
University of Arkansas at Little Rock (U)
University of Cincinnati (U)
University of Florida (U)
University of Hawaii at Hilo (U)
University of Houston (U)
University of Idaho (U)
University of Illinois at Urbana–Champaign (U)
The University of Kansas (U)
University of Louisville (U)
University of Maine (G)
University of Maine at Augusta (U)
University of Maine at Fort Kent (U)
University of Mary (U)
University of Massachusetts Boston (U)
University of Minnesota, Duluth (U)
University of Nevada, Reno (U)
The University of North Carolina at Chapel Hill (U)
University of North Dakota (U)
University of North Florida (U)
University of Pittsburgh at Bradford (U)
University of Saskatchewan (U)
University of Southern Maine (U)
The University of Texas at Arlington (U)
University of Utah (U)
University of Waterloo (U)
University of West Florida (U)
University of West Georgia (U)
University of Wisconsin Colleges (U)
Utah State University (U)
Valencia College (U)
Wake Technical Community College (U)
Washington State University (U)
Wayne State University (U,G)
Westchester Community College (U)
Western Michigan University (U)
Western Wyoming Community College (U)
West Los Angeles College (U)
Wichita State University (U)
Wilfrid Laurier University (U)
Windward Community College (U)
Yavapai College (U)

APPAREL AND TEXTILES

Academy of Art University (U,G)
Arapahoe Community College (U)
Blackhawk Technical College (N)
Drexel University (U)
Kansas State University (N,U,G)
Nassau Community College (U)
North Carolina Central University (U)
North Carolina State University (U)
North Dakota State University (U,G)
NorthWest Arkansas Community College (U)
Philadelphia University (G)
Portland Community College (N)
Rose State College (U)
San Diego Community College District (N,U)
Santa Fe Community College (U)

APPLIED HORTICULTURE AND HORTICULTURAL BUSINESS SERVICES

Central Wyoming College (N)
Clark State Community College (U)
Dakota College at Bottineau (U)
Haywood Community College (U)
Kansas State University (N,U)
Oklahoma State University (U)
Oregon State University (U)
Spokane Community College (U)
University of California, Riverside (N)
University of Florida (U)
University of Saskatchewan (N)

APPLIED MATHEMATICS

Alvin Community College (U)
Anne Arundel Community College (U)
Arapahoe Community College (U)
Austin Peay State University (U)
Baldwin-Wallace College (U)
Beulah Heights University (U)
Bossier Parish Community College (U)
Butler Community College (U)
Butler County Community College (U)
California State University, San Marcos (U)
Central Texas College (U)
Central Virginia Community College (U)
Chemeketa Community College (U)
Cleveland State Community College (N)
Clinton Community College (U)
Columbia University (N,G)
Corning Community College (U)
Dabney S. Lancaster Community College (U)
Danville Community College (U)
East Los Angeles College (U)
Enterprise State Community College (U)
Friends University (U)
Georgia Institute of Technology (G)
Harrisburg Area Community College (U)
Hillsborough Community College (U)
Holyoke Community College (U)
Jacksonville State University (U)
The Johns Hopkins University (G)
Johnson State College (U)
Lock Haven University of Pennsylvania (U)
Macon State College (U)
Mansfield University of Pennsylvania (N)
Marquette University (U)
Midstate College (U)
Murray State College (U)
Murray State University (U)
Naugatuck Valley Community College (U)
New Mexico State University–Alamogordo (U)
New Mexico State University–Carlsbad (U)
North Dakota State College of Science (U)
North Dakota State University (U)
North Iowa Area Community College (U)
North Seattle Community College (U)
NorthWest Arkansas Community College (U)
Northwest State Community College (U)
Notre Dame College (U)
Oakton Community College (U)
Oklahoma State University (U)
Oregon State University (U)
Oxnard College (U)
Pamlico Community College (U)
Portland Community College (U)
Pulaski Technical College (U)
Quinnipiac University (U)
Quinsigamond Community College (U)
The Richard Stockton College of New Jersey (U)
Sacramento City College (U)
San Diego Community College District (U)
San Jacinto College District (U)
Sinclair Community College (U)
Southeast Arkansas College (U)
Southern Union State Community College (U)
South Piedmont Community College (U)
Southwest Wisconsin Technical College (U)
Spartanburg Community College (N,U)
Spokane Community College (U)
Stanly Community College (U)
State University of New York at Oswego (U)
Taft College (U)
Tarleton State University (U)
The University of Akron (G)
University of Alaska Fairbanks (U)
University of Florida (U)
University of Idaho (U,G)
University of Maine at Augusta (U)
University of Management and Technology (U)
University of Southern Maine (U)
The University of Texas of the Permian Basin (U)
University of West Georgia (U,G)
Utah State University (U)
Vincennes University (U)
Western Wyoming Community College (U)
West Los Angeles College (U)
Wisconsin Indianhead Technical College (N,U)
York County Community College (U)

ARCHEOLOGY

Alvin Community College (U)
Bellevue College (U)
Cascadia Community College (U)
Cedarville University (U)
Chemeketa Community College (U)
Erie Community College (U)
Erie Community College, North Campus (U)
Erie Community College, South Campus (U)
Pellissippi State Technical Community College (U)

Portland Community College (U)
Rio Hondo College (U)
St. Petersburg College (U)
State University of New York at Oswego (U)
The University of Akron (U)
University of Arkansas at Little Rock (U)
University of Louisville (U)
University of Massachusetts Boston (U)
University of Saskatchewan (U)
University of West Florida (U)

ARCHITECTURAL ENGINEERING

Boston Architectural College (N,U,G)
Georgia Institute of Technology (G)
Rochester Institute of Technology (U)

ARCHITECTURAL ENGINEERING TECHNOLOGIES

Boston Architectural College (N,U,G)
Hopkinsville Community College (U)
Indiana University–Purdue University Fort Wayne (U)

ARCHITECTURAL HISTORY AND CRITICISM

Goddard College (U)
Massachusetts College of Art and Design (U)
Riverside Community College District (U)
Santa Monica College (U)
Southern Illinois University Carbondale (U)

ARCHITECTURAL SCIENCES AND TECHNOLOGY

Boston Architectural College (N,U,G)
Santa Fe Community College (U)
Southern Illinois University Carbondale (U)
Wake Technical Community College (U)

ARCHITECTURE

Boston Architectural College (N,U,G)
Brigham Young University–Idaho (U)
City Colleges of Chicago System (U)
Columbus State Community College (U)
Lansing Community College (U)
Lawrence Technological University (U)
Massachusetts College of Art and Design (U)
Pennsylvania College of Technology (U)
Portland Community College (U)
Prairie View A&M University (U)
Riverside Community College District (U)
Santa Monica College (U)
Southern Illinois University Carbondale (U)
Temple University (U)

ARCHITECTURE RELATED

Arapahoe Community College (U)
Boston Architectural College (N,U,G)
Carleton University (G)
Central Michigan University (U)
Georgia Institute of Technology (G)
Lawrence Technological University (G)
Portland Community College (N)
University of Oregon (U,G)

AREA STUDIES

Andrews University (U)
Austin Peay State University (U)
Bowling Green State University (U,G)
Eastern Illinois University (U)
Goddard College (U)
Granite State College (U)
John Jay College of Criminal Justice of the City University of New York (U)
Naropa University (N)
Oakton Community College (U)
Oxnard College (U)
Paine College (U)
Paris Junior College (N)
The Richard Stockton College of New Jersey (U)
St. Petersburg College (U)
Southwestern Community College (U)
Taylor University (U)
The University of British Columbia (U)
University of Maine (U)
University of Nevada, Reno (U)
University of North Alabama (U,G)
The University of North Carolina at Chapel Hill (U)
University of Northern Iowa (U)
University of San Francisco (U)
University of Waterloo (U)

ARMY ROTC

Austin Peay State University (U)
The University of Akron (U)

ARTS, ENTERTAINMENT, AND MEDIA MANAGEMENT

Brigham Young University–Idaho (U)
Butler Community College (U)
California State University, East Bay (U,G)
Columbia College (U)
East Los Angeles College (U)
Hannibal-LaGrange University (U)
Hopkinsville Community College (U)
Indiana University of Pennsylvania (U)
Mercy College of Northwest Ohio (U)
Mesa State College (U)
Miami Dade College (U)
Michigan Technological University (U)
New Jersey City University (U)
North Dakota State University (U)
Reinhardt University (U)
Salem Community College (U)
Southern Union State Community College (U)
Spokane Community College (U)
State University of New York at Oswego (U)
University of Dubuque (U)
University of Lethbridge (U)
University of Mary (U)
University of Southern Maine (U)
University of Windsor (U)
Valencia College (U)
Webber International University (U)

ASTRONOMY AND ASTROPHYSICS

Acadia University (U)
Andrews University (U)
Antelope Valley College (U)
Arapahoe Community College (U)
Athabasca University (N,U)
Austin Peay State University (U)
Baptist Bible College of Pennsylvania (U,G)
Bellevue College (U)
Bowling Green State University (U)
Brenau University (U)
Brigham Young University (U)
Bronx Community College of the City University of New York (U)
Burlington County College (U)
Butler Community College (U)
California State University, San Bernardino (U)
Carleton University (U)
Cascadia Community College (U)
Central Virginia Community College (U)
Chemeketa Community College (U)
Citrus College (U)
Clackamas Community College (U)
Clemson University (U)
College of San Mateo (U)
College of Southern Maryland (U)
Colorado Mountain College (U)
Columbia College (U)
Columbus State Community College (U)
Eastern Illinois University (U)
El Camino College (U)
Greenville Technical College (U)
Harrisburg Area Community College (U)
Hillsborough Community College (U)
Hopkinsville Community College (U)
Houston Community College System (U)
Illinois Eastern Community Colleges, Lincoln Trail College (U)
Indiana University–Purdue University Fort Wayne (U)
John A. Logan College (U)
Judson University (U)
Lake Superior College (U)
Lansing Community College (U)
Lindenwood University (U)
Long Beach City College (U)
Los Angeles Trade-Technical College (U)
Michigan Technological University (U)
Middle Tennessee State University (U)
Montgomery County Community College (U)
Mountain Empire Community College (U)
Mountain State University (U)
Nassau Community College (U)
Naugatuck Valley Community College (U)
North Seattle Community College (U)
Oakton Community College (U)
Palm Beach State College (U)
Peninsula College (U)
Pikes Peak Community College (U)
Portland Community College (U)
Providence College (U)
Rappahannock Community College (U)
Riverside Community College District (U)
Rowan-Cabarrus Community College (U)
Sacramento City College (U)
St. Clair County Community College (U)
St. Cloud State University (U)
St. Petersburg College (U)
San Bernardino Valley College (U)
San Diego Community College District (U)
Santa Rosa Junior College (U)
Southeastern Oklahoma State University (U)
Spokane Community College (U)
Stephen F. Austin State University (U)
Sullivan County Community College (U)
Tyler Junior College (U)
Union County College (U)
University at Albany, State University of New York (U)
The University of Akron (U)
University of Alaska Fairbanks (U)

University of Arkansas at Little Rock (U)
University of Florida (U)
University of Louisville (U)
University of Maine at Fort Kent (U)
University of Minnesota, Duluth (U)
The University of North Carolina at Chapel Hill (U)
University of Oregon (U)
University of Pittsburgh at Bradford (U)
University of Waterloo (U)
University of Wisconsin–Superior (U)
Upper Iowa University (U)
Wake Technical Community College (U)
Wilfrid Laurier University (U)

ATMOSPHERIC SCIENCES AND METEOROLOGY

Austin Peay State University (U)
Bellevue College (U)
Bowling Green State University (U)
Butler Community College (U)
Clarion University of Pennsylvania (U)
Dallas Baptist University (U)
Jacksonville State University (U)
Miami Dade College (U)
Mountain Empire Community College (U)
Nassau Community College (U)
Oklahoma State University (U)
Oregon State University (U)
Santa Rosa Junior College (U)
The University of Arizona (U)
University of Arkansas at Little Rock (U)
University of California, Riverside (N)
University of Illinois at Urbana–Champaign (U)
The University of Kansas (U)

AUDIOVISUAL COMMUNICATIONS TECHNOLOGIES

Arapahoe Community College (U)
Austin Peay State University (U)
Boise State University (G)
Cincinnati State Technical and Community College (U)
Cleveland State Community College (N)
Lackawanna College (U)
McNeese State University (N)
Naugatuck Valley Community College (U)
Portland Community College (U)
Prescott College (N)
The Richard Stockton College of New Jersey (U)
Rose State College (U)
Sacramento City College (U)
San Diego Community College District (U)
San Jacinto College District (U)
Sessions College for Professional Design (N,U)
Sinclair Community College (U)
The University of Akron (U)
University of Cincinnati Raymond Walters College (U)
University of Florida (G)

BEHAVIORAL SCIENCES

Allen Community College (U)
Angelina College (U)
Anne Arundel Community College (U)
Arapahoe Community College (U)
Athabasca University (U)
Austin Peay State University (U)
Ball State University (G)
Barclay College (U)
Big Bend Community College (U)
Boise State University (U)
Bossier Parish Community College (U)
Brigham Young University–Idaho (U)
Butler Community College (U)
California State University, Chico (U)
Canisius College (G)
Capital Community College (U)
Cayuga County Community College (U)
Central Michigan University (U,G)
Charter Oak State College (U)
Chatham University (U)
Chattanooga State Community College (U)
Citrus College (U)
Clark State Community College (U)
Cleveland State Community College (N)
Columbia Basin College (U)
Columbia College (U)
Community College of Beaver County (U)
Dakota College at Bottineau (U)
Dallas Baptist University (U)
Danville Community College (U)
Daytona State College (U)
Dickinson State University (U)
Drury University (U)
East Los Angeles College (U)
Emory University (G)
Endicott College (G)
Excelsior College (U)
Fitchburg State University (U,G)
Florida Institute of Technology (N)
Fort Valley State University (U)
Franklin Pierce University (U)
Goddard College (U)
Graceland University (U)
Granite State College (U)
Harcum College (U)
Harrisburg Area Community College (U)
Haywood Community College (U)
Hofstra University (U)
Hope International University (U)
Inter American University of Puerto Rico, San Germán Campus (U)
Iowa Valley Community College District (U)
Jacksonville State University (U,G)
Jamestown College (U)
Jefferson Community College (U)
The Johns Hopkins University (G)
Johnson State College (U)
Judson College (U)
Kansas State University (U)
Keystone College (U)
Lackawanna College (U)
Lamar State College–Orange (U)
Lamar State College–Port Arthur (U)
Lenoir Community College (U)
Luna Community College (U)
Medical College of Wisconsin (G)
Miami Dade College (U)
Middlesex Community College (U)
Monroe College (U)
Moorpark College (U)
Murray State College (U)
Nassau Community College (U)
Naugatuck Valley Community College (U)
North Central State College (U)
NorthWest Arkansas Community College (U)
Notre Dame College (U)
Nyack College (U)
Oakton Community College (U)
The Ohio State University (U)
Oklahoma Panhandle State University (U)
Ouachita Technical College (U)
Ozarks Technical Community College (U)
Pamlico Community College (U)
Paris Junior College (N)
Pellissippi State Technical Community College (U)
Phoenix College (U)
Prescott College (N)
Quinnipiac University (U)
Quinsigamond Community College (U)
The Richard Stockton College of New Jersey (U)
Rivier College (U)
Rochester Institute of Technology (U)
Sacramento City College (U)
St. Cloud State University (G)
Saint Francis University (U)
St. Gregory's University (U)
Saint Joseph's College of Maine (U)
Saint Paul College–A Community & Technical College (U)
St. Petersburg College (U)
St. Philip's College (U)
Sampson Community College (U)
San Diego Community College District (U)
San Jacinto College District (U)
Santa Monica College (U)
Santa Rosa Junior College (U)
Sinclair Community College (U)
Southeastern Illinois College (U)
Southeastern Oklahoma State University (U)
Southern Illinois University Carbondale (U)
South Piedmont Community College (U)
South Suburban College (U)
Southwest Wisconsin Technical College (U)
State University of New York at Oswego (U)
State University of New York College at Potsdam (U)
Stephens College (U)
Sullivan County Community College (N,U)
Taylor University (U)
Texas State University–San Marcos (U)
Union University (U)
The University of Akron (U)
The University of Alabama in Huntsville (G)
University of Alaska Fairbanks (U)
University of Alaska, Prince William Sound Community College (U)
The University of Arizona (U)
University of Cincinnati Raymond Walters College (U)
University of Hawaii at Hilo (U)
University of Idaho (U)
The University of Kansas (G)
University of Louisville (U)
University of Maine at Augusta (U)
University of Maine at Fort Kent (U)
University of Maine at Machias (U)
University of Management and Technology (U)
The University of North Carolina at Asheville (U)
University of North Dakota (U)
The University of South Dakota (U)
University of Southern Maine (U)
The University of Texas at Brownsville (U)
The University of Texas of the Permian Basin (U)

University of the Pacific (N,U)
The University of West Alabama (U)
University of West Florida (G)
University of Wisconsin–Milwaukee (N)
Valencia College (U)
Vincennes University (U)
Webber International University (U)
Westchester Community College (U)
Western Kentucky University (U,G)
Western Texas College (U)
West Hills Community College (U)
West Los Angeles College (U)
Wharton County Junior College (U)
Winston-Salem State University (U)

BIBLICAL STUDIES

Abilene Christian University (U,G)
Acadia University (U)
Andover Newton Theological School (N,G)
Andrews University (U)
Asbury University (U)
Ashland University (G)
Austin Peay State University (U)
Bakke Graduate University (G)
Baptist Bible College of Pennsylvania (U,G)
The Baptist College of Florida (U)
Barclay College (U)
Beulah Heights University (U,G)
Bluefield College (U)
Bob Jones University (U,G)
Brigham Young University–Idaho (U)
Bryan College (U)
Cedarville University (U)
Central Bible College (U)
Central Carolina Community College (U)
Central Texas College (U)
Chattanooga State Community College (U)
Cincinnati Christian University (U,G)
Clear Creek Baptist Bible College (N,U)
Clovis Community College (U)
College of Emmanuel and St. Chad (G)
Columbia International University (N,U,G)
Covenant Theological Seminary (N,G)
Crown College (G)
Dallas Baptist University (U)
Dallas Christian College (U)
Defiance College (U)
Denver Seminary (G)
Earlham School of Religion (G)
East Central Community College (U)
Eastern Mennonite University (G)
Eastern University (N,U)
Edison State Community College (U)
Faulkner University (U)
Freed-Hardeman University (G)
Free Will Baptist Bible College (N,U)
Gannon University (U)
George Fox University (U)
Global University (N,U,G)
God's Bible School and College (U)
Hobe Sound Bible College (N,U)
Hope International University (N,U,G)
Indiana Wesleyan University (U,G)
Jamestown Community College (U)
Johnson University (U,G)
Judson College (U)
Judson University (U)
Lenoir Community College (U)
LeTourneau University (U)
Liberty University (U,G)
Life Pacific College (N,U)
Lincoln Christian University (N,U,G)
Lipscomb University (U,G)
Malone University (U,G)
Marylhurst University (U,G)
Master's College and Seminary (U)
McMurry University (U)
Miami Dade College (U)
Mid-Continent University (U)
Missouri Baptist University (U)
Montgomery Community College (N)
Moody Bible Institute (N,U,G)
Mount Olive College (U)
New Orleans Baptist Theological Seminary (N,U,G)
Nyack College (U,G)
Piedmont Baptist College and Graduate School (U,G)
Prairie Bible Institute (U,G)
Providence College and Theological Seminary (N,U,G)
Regent College (N,G)
Regent University (U,G)
Saint Francis University (U)
St. Petersburg College (U)
St. Stephen's College (G)
Shasta Bible College (N,U)
Southwestern Baptist Theological Seminary (U,G)
Summit Pacific College (N,U)
Taylor University (U)
Toccoa Falls College (U)
Trinity International University (G)
Unification Theological Seminary (N,G)
University of Dubuque (N)
The University of Findlay (U)
University of Florida (U)
University of the Southwest (U)
University of Waterloo (U)
Walla Walla University (U)
Western Kentucky University (U)
Western Seminary (N,G)
Williamson Christian College (U)

BILINGUAL, MULTILINGUAL, AND MULTICULTURAL EDUCATION

Acadia University (U)
Arkansas State University (U)
Austin Peay State University (N,U)
Brigham Young University–Idaho (U)
California State University, San Bernardino (U)
East Los Angeles College (U)
Indiana State University (G)
Lenoir Community College (U)
Middlesex Community College (U)
Middle Tennessee State University (N)
New Mexico Highlands University (U,G)
North Lake College (U)
Northwestern Oklahoma State University (G)
Oxnard College (U)
Pace University (U,G)
Paris Junior College (N)
Rockingham Community College (N)
Sacramento City College (U)
Sampson Community College (U)
San Jacinto College District (U)
Sinclair Community College (U)
Southern Union State Community College (U)
Texas Woman's University (G)
The University of Akron (U,G)
University of Alaska Fairbanks (U)
University of Illinois at Urbana–Champaign (G)
University of North Dakota (U)
University of Southern Maine (U)
The University of Texas at Brownsville (U)
The University of Texas of the Permian Basin (U)
University of the Southwest (U)
University of West Georgia (G)
Wayne Community College (N)
Wayne State University (G)
West Hills Community College (U)

BIOCHEMISTRY, BIOPHYSICS AND MOLECULAR BIOLOGY

Arapahoe Community College (U)
Austin Peay State University (U)
Chatham University (U)
Dabney S. Lancaster Community College (U)
Drake University (U)
Graceland University (U)
Hofstra University (U)
Huntington College of Health Sciences (U)
Kansas State University (U)
McMurry University (U)
Mountain State University (U)
North Seattle Community College (U)
Ozarks Technical Community College (U)
Peninsula College (U)
Pitt Community College (U)
Santa Monica College (U)
Southern Union State Community College (U)
State University of New York at Plattsburgh (U)
The University of Akron (U)
University of Florida (U)
University of New England (U)
University of Southern Mississippi (G)
University of Waterloo (U)

BIOETHICS/MEDICAL ETHICS

Arapahoe Community College (U)
Austin Peay State University (U)
Cedarville University (U)
Cincinnati State Technical and Community College (U)
Ferris State University (U)
Judson College (U)
Lamar State College–Orange (U)
Lock Haven University of Pennsylvania (U)
Medical College of Wisconsin (G)
Mercy College of Northwest Ohio (U)
North Carolina State University (U)
North Seattle Community College (U)
Saint Francis University (U,G)
Salem Community College (U)
University of Louisville (G)
University of Maine at Machias (U)

BIOLOGICAL AND BIOMEDICAL SCIENCES RELATED

Alcorn State University (G)
Athabasca University (U)
Austin Peay State University (U)
Bossier Parish Community College (U)
Brigham Young University (U)
Brigham Young University–Idaho (U)
Cabrillo College (U)
Cayuga County Community College (U)

Chemeketa Community College (U)
Columbia College (U)
Columbus State Community College (U)
Dakota College at Bottineau (U)
Danville Community College (U)
DeVry University Online (U)
D'Youville College (G)
Eastern Illinois University (U)
El Camino College (U)
Erie Community College (U)
Erie Community College, North Campus (U)
Erie Community College, South Campus (U)
Florida Hospital College of Health Sciences (U)
Gaston College (U)
Georgian Court University (G)
Hofstra University (U)
Iowa Lakes Community College (U)
Iowa Valley Community College District (U)
Jacksonville State University (U)
Kean University (N)
Lamar State College–Port Arthur (U)
Miami Dade College (U)
Michigan Technological University (G)
Middlesex Community College (U)
Nicolet Area Technical College (U)
North Georgia College & State University (U,G)
Oxnard College (U)
Pennsylvania College of Technology (U)
Robert Morris University (U)
Sacramento City College (U)
The Sage Colleges (U)
Saint Francis University (U)
Sinclair Community College (U)
Southeast Community College Area (U)
Southern Illinois University Carbondale (U)
Southern Union State Community College (U)
South Piedmont Community College (U)
Stanly Community College (U)
Stephens College (U)
University of Colorado at Colorado Springs (U)
University of Florida (G)
University of South Alabama (U)
The University of Texas at Arlington (U)
University of Waterloo (U)
University of West Florida (U)
Western Kentucky University (G)

BIOLOGICAL AND PHYSICAL SCIENCES

Allen Community College (U)
Anne Arundel Community College (U)
Ashland University (U)
Athabasca University (U)
Austin Peay State University (U)
Avila University (U)
Boise State University (U)
Bossier Parish Community College (U)
Brigham Young University–Idaho (U)
Burlington County College (U)
Butler Community College (U)
Cabrillo College (U)
Cascadia Community College (U)
Cayuga County Community College (U)
Cedarville University (U)
Central Bible College (U)
Central Carolina Community College (U)
Chemeketa Community College (U)
Citrus College (U)
Clark State Community College (U)
Clemson University (N,U,G)
Cleveland State Community College (N,U)
Clinton Community College (U)
Dallas Baptist University (U)
Davidson County Community College (U)
Daytona State College (U)
Delgado Community College (U)
D'Youville College (U,G)
East Central Community College (U)
Eastern Illinois University (U)
Eastern Kentucky University (U)
Ferris State University (U)
Fitchburg State University (U)
Fort Hays State University (U)
Front Range Community College (U)
Georgian Court University (U)
Harcum College (U)
Harrisburg Area Community College (U)
Hibbing Community College (U)
Huntington College of Health Sciences (U)
Illinois Valley Community College (U)
Indiana State University (U)
Jacksonville State University (U)
Jamestown College (U)
John A. Logan College (U)
Judson College (U)
Kansas State University (U)
Lake Superior College (U)
Lehigh University (G)
Lenoir Community College (U)
Lewis University (U)
Marquette University (U)
Mercy College of Northwest Ohio (N)
Miami Dade College (U)
Middlesex Community College (U)
Midway College (U)
Mississippi State University (U)
Moorpark College (U)
Murray State College (U)
National University (U)
New Mexico State University–Carlsbad (U)
New River Community College (U)
North Arkansas College (U)
North Carolina Central University (U)
North Carolina State University (U,G)
North Central State College (U)
Northern State University (U)
North Lake College (U)
North Seattle Community College (U)
Northwestern Connecticut Community College (U)
Oakton Community College (U)
Ohio University (U)
Oklahoma Panhandle State University (U)
Oregon Coast Community College (U)
Ouachita Technical College (U)
Ozarks Technical Community College (U)
Pace University (U)
Palm Beach State College (U)
Pamlico Community College (U)
Paris Junior College (U)
Peninsula College (U)
Pikes Peak Community College (U)
Quinebaug Valley Community College (U)
Quinnipiac University (U)
Quinsigamond Community College (U)
Sacramento City College (U)
Saint Francis University (U)
Saint Leo University (U)
St. Louis Community College (U)
Saint Paul College–A Community & Technical College (U)
St. Petersburg College (U)
Salem Community College (U)
San Diego Community College District (U)
Santa Monica College (U)
Seminole State College of Florida (U)
Sinclair Community College (U)
Southern Illinois University Carbondale (U)
Southern Union State Community College (U)
Stephens College (U)
Sullivan County Community College (N)
Syracuse University (U)
Taft College (U)
Taylor University (U)
Texas State University–San Marcos (U)
Union University (U)
The University of Akron (U)
University of Alaska Fairbanks (U)
University of Great Falls (U)
University of Waterloo (U)
Upper Iowa University (N)
Valencia College (U)
Westchester Community College (U)
Western Kentucky University (U,G)
Western Wyoming Community College (U)
West Hills Community College (U)
Winston-Salem State University (U)
York Technical College (U)

BIOLOGICAL/BIOSYSTEMS ENGINEERING

Cayuga County Community College (U)
Cornell University (U)

BIOLOGY

Acadia University (U)
Albertus Magnus College (U)
Allen Community College (U)
Alvin Community College (U)
Anderson University (U)
Angelina College (U)
Antelope Valley College (U)
Arapahoe Community College (U)
Arkansas State University–Mountain Home (U)
Arkansas Tech University (U)
Athabasca University (N,U)
Austin Peay State University (U)
Baptist Bible College of Pennsylvania (U,G)
Bellevue College (U)
Bethel University (U)
Boise State University (U)
Bowling Green State University (U)
Brazosport College (U)
Brigham Young University (U)
Brigham Young University–Idaho (U)
Bronx Community College of the City University of New York (U)
Brookdale Community College (U)
Broward College (U)
Bryan College (U)
Burlington County College (U)
Butler Community College (U)
Butler County Community College (U)
California State University, Dominguez Hills (U)
Canisius College (U)
Capital Community College (U)
Carleton University (U)

Cascadia Community College (U)
Cayuga County Community College (U)
Cedarville University (U)
Central New Mexico Community College (U)
Central Oregon Community College (U)
Central Virginia Community College (U)
Central Washington University (U)
Central Wyoming College (U)
Chatham University (U,G)
Chattanooga State Community College (U)
Chemeketa Community College (U)
Cincinnati State Technical and Community College (U)
Citrus College (U)
City Colleges of Chicago System (U)
Clackamas Community College (U)
Clarion University of Pennsylvania (U)
Clark State Community College (U)
Clemson University (N,U,G)
Cleveland Community College (U)
Clovis Community College (U)
Coastal Carolina University (U)
The College of St. Scholastica (U,G)
College of San Mateo (U)
College of Southern Maryland (U)
College of the Humanities and Sciences, Harrison Middleton University (U)
Colorado Mountain College (U)
Columbus State Community College (U)
Community College of Allegheny County (U)
Cossatot Community College of the University of Arkansas (U)
Culver-Stockton College (U)
Dakota State University (U)
Dallas Baptist University (U)
Danville Community College (U)
Dawson Community College (U)
Dickinson State University (U)
Dominican College (U)
Drury University (U)
Eastern Illinois University (U)
Eastern Kentucky University (U)
Eastern Oregon University (U)
Eastern Wyoming College (U)
East Georgia College (U)
Edison State Community College (U)
Elmira College (U,G)
Excelsior College (U)
Finger Lakes Community College (U)
Five Towns College (U)
Fort Valley State University (U)
Framingham State University (U)
Friends University (U)
Front Range Community College (U)
Gadsden State Community College (U)
Gannon University (U)
Georgia Highlands College (U)
Graceland University (U)
Hannibal-LaGrange University (U)
Harcum College (U)
Harford Community College (U)
Herkimer County Community College (U)
Hillsborough Community College (U)
Hofstra University (U,G)
Hopkinsville Community College (U)
Houston Community College System (U)
Huntington College of Health Sciences (U)
Indiana State University (U)
Indiana University–Purdue University Fort Wayne (U)
Iowa Lakes Community College (U)
Itasca Community College (U)
Ithaca College (U)
Jacksonville State University (U,G)
James Madison University (U)
Jefferson Community College (U)
John A. Logan College (U)
Johnston Community College (U)
J. Sargeant Reynolds Community College (U)
Kansas State University (U)
Keystone College (U)
Kirkwood Community College (U)
Kirtland Community College (U)
Lakehead University (U)
Lamar State College–Orange (U)
Lansing Community College (U)
Laurel University (U)
Lehman College of the City University of New York (U)
Lenoir Community College (U)
LeTourneau University (U)
Lewis-Clark State College (U)
Liberty University (U)
Lindenwood University (U)
Long Beach City College (U)
Louisiana State University and Agricultural and Mechanical College (N,U)
Louisiana State University at Eunice (U)
Macon State College (U)
Malone University (U)
Mayville State University (U)
McMurry University (U)
Memorial University of Newfoundland (U)
Mercy College of Northwest Ohio (U)
Mesa Community College (U)
Mesa State College (U)
Metropolitan Community College–Penn Valley (U)
Miami Dade College (U)
Middlesex Community College (U)
Mid-State Technical College (U)
Minnesota School of Business–Richfield (U)
Mississippi College (U,G)
Mississippi State University (U)
Missouri Baptist University (U)
Monroe Community College (U)
Montcalm Community College (U)
Montgomery County Community College (U)
Moorpark College (U)
Mountain Empire Community College (U)
Mountain State University (U)
Mount Allison University (U)
Mount Olive College (U)
Mount Wachusett Community College (U)
Murray State College (U)
Murray State University (U)
Nashville State Technical Community College (U)
Nassau Community College (U)
Naugatuck Valley Community College (U)
New Jersey City University (U)
New Mexico Junior College (U)
New Mexico State University (U)
New Mexico State University–Carlsbad (U)
New Mexico State University–Grants (U)
New River Community College (U)
North Carolina State University (U)
North Central Texas College (U)
North Dakota State College of Science (U)
North Dakota State University (U)
Northeastern State University (U)
Northern State University (U)
North Hennepin Community College (U)
North Iowa Area Community College (U)
North Lake College (U)
North Seattle Community College (U)
North Shore Community College (U)
NorthWest Arkansas Community College (U)
Northwestern Michigan College (U)
Oakland Community College (U)
Ocean County College (U)
Odessa College (U)
The Ohio State University (U)
Ohio University (U)
Oklahoma Panhandle State University (U)
Orange Coast College (U)
Ouachita Technical College (U)
Oxnard College (U)
Pace University (U)
Pamlico Community College (U)
Paris Junior College (U)
Pasco-Hernando Community College (U)
Pellissippi State Technical Community College (U)
Pennsylvania College of Technology (U)
Peru State College (U)
Phoenix College (U)
Piedmont Community College (U)
Pitt Community College (U)
Pittsburg State University (U)
Portland Community College (U)
Pratt Community College (U)
Providence College (U)
Pulaski Technical College (U)
Queen's University at Kingston (U)
Quinnipiac University (U)
Randolph Community College (N)
Riverside Community College District (U)
Rochester Institute of Technology (U)
Rockland Community College (U)
Rogers State University (U)
Rose State College (U)
Rowan-Cabarrus Community College (U)
Sacramento City College (U)
St. Cloud State University (U)
Saint Francis University (U)
St. John's University (U)
St. Joseph's College, Long Island Campus (U)
St. Joseph's College, New York (U)
Saint Paul College–A Community & Technical College (U)
St. Petersburg College (U)
St. Philip's College (U)
San Bernardino Valley College (U)
San Diego Community College District (U)
San Diego State University (U)
San Jacinto College District (U)
Santa Monica College (U)
Sauk Valley Community College (U)
Shippensburg University of Pennsylvania (U,G)
Sinclair Community College (U)
Southeastern Community College (U)
Southeastern Oklahoma State University (U)
Southern Illinois University Carbondale (U)
Southern Maine Community College (U)
Southern Union State Community College (U)
Southern University at New Orleans (U)
South Piedmont Community College (U)
South Suburban College (U)
Southwestern Community College (U)
Spartanburg Community College (U)
Spokane Community College (U)
Spoon River College (U)
Stanly Community College (U)

State University of New York at New Paltz (U)
State University of New York at Oswego (U)
State University of New York at Plattsburgh (U)
State University of New York College at Potsdam (U)
State University of New York Empire State College (U)
Stephens College (U)
Taylor University (U)
Texas State University–San Marcos (U)
Tyler Junior College (U)
Union County College (U)
The University of Akron (U)
University of Alaska Fairbanks (U)
University of Alaska, Prince William Sound Community College (U)
University of Arkansas at Little Rock (U,G)
The University of British Columbia (U)
University of Cincinnati Raymond Walters College (U)
University of Dubuque (U)
University of Florida (U)
University of Houston–Downtown (U)
University of Houston–Victoria (U)
University of Idaho (U)
University of Illinois at Springfield (U,G)
University of Illinois at Urbana–Champaign (U)
The University of Kansas (U)
University of Maine (U)
University of Massachusetts Boston (U)
University of Memphis (U)
University of Minnesota, Crookston (U)
University of New England (U)
The University of North Carolina at Asheville (U)
The University of North Carolina at Chapel Hill (U)
University of South Alabama (G)
The University of South Dakota (U)
University of Southern Mississippi (G)
The University of Texas at Arlington (U)
University of the Southwest (U)
University of Utah (U)
University of Waterloo (U)
The University of West Alabama (U)
University of West Florida (U)
University of West Georgia (U)
University of Windsor (U)
The University of Winnipeg (U)
University of Wisconsin Colleges (U)
University of Wisconsin–Superior (U)
Upper Iowa University (N,U)
Utah State University (U)
Utica College (U)
Valencia College (U)
Wake Technical Community College (U)
Westchester Community College (U)
Western Kentucky University (U,G)
Western Texas College (U)
West Hills Community College (U)
Westmoreland County Community College (U)
West Shore Community College (U)
West Virginia Northern Community College (U)
Wharton County Junior College (U)
Wichita State University (U)
Wilfrid Laurier University (U)
Wilkes Community College (U)
Yavapai College (U)

BIOLOGY/BIOTECHNOLOGY LABORATORY TECHNICIAN

Angelina College (N)
Austin Peay State University (U)
Charter Oak State College (U)
Clark State Community College (U)
Cleveland Community College (U)
Jacksonville State University (U)
University of Florida (G)

BIOMATHEMATICS, BIOINFORMATICS, AND COMPUTATIONAL BIOLOGY

Austin Peay State University (U)
Columbia University (N)

BIOMEDICAL/MEDICAL ENGINEERING

Austin Peay State University (U)
Cincinnati State Technical and Community College (U)
Columbia University (G)
Georgia Institute of Technology (G)
New Mexico State University–Alamogordo (U)
University of Colorado Boulder (N,G)
University of Illinois at Chicago (G)
Wayne State University (G)

BIOPSYCHOLOGY

Austin Peay State University (U)
Jacksonville State University (U)
Johnson State College (U)
State University of New York at Plattsburgh (U)
Wilfrid Laurier University (U)

BIOTECHNOLOGY

Austin Peay State University (U)
Central Carolina Community College (U)
Cleveland Community College (U)
Fort Valley State University (G)
Houston Community College System (U)
Piedmont Community College (U)
Southeastern Illinois College (U)
South Piedmont Community College (U)
Tompkins Cortland Community College (U)
Wake Technical Community College (U)

BOTANY/PLANT BIOLOGY

Bellevue College (U)
Brigham Young University (U)
Bronx Community College of the City University of New York (U)
Cascadia Community College (U)
Central Wyoming College (N)
Cossatot Community College of the University of Arkansas (U)
Dakota College at Bottineau (U)
Eastern Oregon University (U)
Indiana State University (U)
Kansas State University (N)
Mountain State University (U)
Nashville State Technical Community College (U)
North Carolina State University (U)
North Dakota State University (U)
Oregon State University (U)
Oxnard College (U)
Pellissippi State Technical Community College (U)
St. Cloud State University (U)
Santa Monica College (U)
The University of Akron (U)
University of Alaska Fairbanks (U)
University of Arkansas at Little Rock (U)
University of Florida (U)
University of Illinois at Urbana–Champaign (U)
University of Saskatchewan (N)
The University of West Alabama (U)
West Shore Community College (U)
Wilfrid Laurier University (U)

BUILDING/CONSTRUCTION FINISHING, MANAGEMENT, AND INSPECTION

Alpena Community College (N)
Athabasca University (N)
Boise State University (U)
Central Michigan University (N,U)
Central New Mexico Community College (U)
Chattanooga State Community College (U)
Clackamas Community College (U)
Clemson University (N)
Florida State University (N)
Georgia Institute of Technology (G)
National University (U)
New Mexico Junior College (N)
New Mexico State University–Carlsbad (U)
North Dakota State University (G)
North Hennepin Community College (U)
Pennsylvania College of Technology (U)
Pittsburg State University (U)
Portland Community College (N)
St. Petersburg College (N)
San Diego State University (U)
University of Arkansas at Little Rock (U)
University of Florida (G)
University of North Florida (U,G)

BUSINESS ADMINISTRATION, MANAGEMENT AND OPERATIONS

Acadia University (U)
Allen Community College (U)
Alvin Community College (U)
Amberton University (U,G)
The American College (U,G)
American Graduate University (G)
Anderson University (U,G)
Andrew Jackson University (U,G)
Anne Arundel Community College (U)
Antioch University Midwest (G)
Arapahoe Community College (U)
Arkansas State University (U)
Arkansas State University–Beebe (U)
Arkansas State University–Mountain Home (U)
Arkansas Tech University (U)
Athabasca University (N,U,G)
Auburn University (G)
Austin Peay State University (N)
Avila University (U)

Bakke Graduate University (G)
Baldwin-Wallace College (U,G)
Baptist Bible College of Pennsylvania (U)
The Baptist College of Florida (U)
Belhaven University (U,G)
Bellevue College (U)
Bethel University (U)
Beulah Heights University (G)
Blackhawk Technical College (U)
Bloomfield College (U)
Bob Jones University (U)
Boise State University (U)
Bowling Green State University (U)
Brazosport College (U)
Brenau University (U,G)
Brewton-Parker College (U)
Brigham Young University (U)
Brigham Young University–Idaho (U)
Brookdale Community College (U)
Bryant & Stratton Online (N,U)
Bryant University (N)
Buena Vista University (U)
Burlington County College (U)
Butler Community College (U)
Butler County Community College (U)
Caldwell College (U,G)
California State University, Monterey Bay (G)
California State University, San Bernardino (U)
California State University, San Marcos (U)
Campbellsville University (G)
Capital Community College (U)
Cardinal Stritch University (N)
Cascadia Community College (U)
Cayuga County Community College (U)
Central Carolina Technical College (U)
Centralia College (U)
Central Michigan University (U,G)
Central New Mexico Community College (U)
Central Oregon Community College (N,U)
Central Texas College (U)
Central Virginia Community College (U)
Central Washington University (U,G)
Chaminade University of Honolulu (U)
Champlain College (U)
Charter Oak State College (U)
Chatham University (G)
Chattanooga State Community College (U)
Chemeketa Community College (U)
Cincinnati State Technical and Community College (U)
City Colleges of Chicago System (U)
Clackamas Community College (U)
Clarion University of Pennsylvania (G)
Clark State Community College (U)
Clatsop Community College (U)
Clemson University (G)
Cleveland Community College (U)
Cleveland State Community College (N)
Clinton Community College (U)
Clovis Community College (U)
Coleman University (U,G)
The College at Brockport, State University of New York (U)
College of Southern Maryland (N)
Columbia Basin College (U)
Columbia College (U,G)
Columbia-Greene Community College (U)
Columbia University (N,G)
Columbus State Community College (U)
Columbus State University (G)
Community College of Allegheny County (U)
Community College of Beaver County (N,U)
Concordia University Wisconsin (G)
Corning Community College (U)
Cossatot Community College of the University of Arkansas (N)
Culver-Stockton College (U)
Dakota College at Bottineau (U)
Dakota State University (U)
Dakota Wesleyan University (U)
Dallas Baptist University (U,G)
Danville Community College (U)
Dawson Community College (U)
Delgado Community College (U)
Dickinson State University (U)
Drake University (U,G)
Drexel University (U,G)
D'Youville College (U)
East Central Community College (U)
Eastern Kentucky University (G)
Eastern Washington University (N)
Eastern West Virginia Community and Technical College (U)
Eastern Wyoming College (U)
East Georgia College (U)
East Los Angeles College (U)
Edgecombe Community College (N,U)
Edison State Community College (U)
Endicott College (U)
Excelsior College (U,G)
Fayetteville State University (G)
Ferris State University (U,G)
Fielding Graduate University (G)
Fitchburg State University (U,G)
Florida Institute of Technology (G)
Fontbonne University (U,G)
Fort Hays State University (N,U)
Framingham State University (U,G)
Franklin Pierce University (U,G)
Front Range Community College (U)
Frostburg State University (G)
Gadsden State Community College (U)
Genesee Community College (N)
George Fox University (U,G)
Georgian Court University (U)
Georgia State University (G)
Graceland University (U)
Grand Valley State University (U,G)
Granite State College (U)
Grantham University (U)
Harcum College (U)
Harrisburg Area Community College (U)
Haywood Community College (U)
Herkimer County Community College (U)
Hibbing Community College (U)
Hillsborough Community College (U)
Hofstra University (U)
Holyoke Community College (U)
Hope International University (G)
Hopkinsville Community College (N)
Houston Community College System (U)
Illinois Valley Community College (N)
Indiana State University (U)
Indiana University–Purdue University Fort Wayne (G)
Indiana Wesleyan University (U)
Inter American University of Puerto Rico, San Germán Campus (G)
Iona College (U,G)
Jacksonville State University (U,G)
James Madison University (N,G)
Jamestown College (U)
Jamestown Community College (N,U)
Jefferson Community College (U)
Johnson State College (U)
Johnston Community College (U)
Jones International University (U)
J. Sargeant Reynolds Community College (U)
Judson College (U)
Kansas State University (N,U,G)
Kauai Community College (U)
Kean University (N,U)
Kettering University (N)
Keystone College (U)
Kilian Community College (U)
Kirkwood Community College (U)
Kirtland Community College (U)
Lackawanna College (U)
Lake-Sumter Community College (U)
Lamar State College–Orange (U)
Lamar State College–Port Arthur (N,U)
Lansing Community College (U)
Lassen Community College District (U)
Lawrence Technological University (U,G)
Lehigh University (N,G)
Lehman College of the City University of New York (U)
LeTourneau University (U,G)
Lewis-Clark State College (U)
Liberty University (G)
Lipscomb University (U,G)
Long Beach City College (U)
Louisiana State University and Agricultural and Mechanical College (U)
Louisiana State University at Eunice (U)
Luna Community College (U)
Luzerne County Community College (U)
Malone University (U,G)
Mansfield University of Pennsylvania (U)
Marian University (U)
Marist College (G)
Marlboro College Graduate College (N,U)
Marshall University (U)
Mary Baldwin College (N,U)
Marymount University (G)
Maryville University of Saint Louis (N)
Mayville State University (U)
McDowell Technical Community College (U)
McKendree University (U)
McMurry University (U)
McNeese State University (U)
Memorial University of Newfoundland (U)
Mesa Community College (U)
Mesa State College (U,G)
Miami Dade College (U)
Miami University–Regional Campuses (U)
Mid-Continent University (U)
Middlesex Community College (U,N,U)
Middle Tennessee State University (N,U)
Midland College (N)
Mid-State Technical College (U)
Midway College (G)
Milwaukee School of Engineering (G)
Minnesota School of Business–Online (U)
Minnesota School of Business–Richfield (U,G)
Mississippi College (G)
Mississippi State University (G)
Missouri Baptist University (U)
Missouri University of Science and Technology (N,G)
Monroe College (U)
Montcalm Community College (N,U)
Montgomery Community College (N,U)
Montgomery County Community College (U)

Mountain State University (U)
Mount Olive College (U)
Mount Wachusett Community College (N,U)
Murray State College (U)
Murray State University (N,U,G)
Nassau Community College (U)
National University (U,G)
Naugatuck Valley Community College (U)
New England College of Business and Finance (N,U)
New Jersey City University (U,G)
New Mexico Highlands University (U,G)
New Mexico Junior College (U)
New Mexico State University (U)
New Mexico State University–Carlsbad (U)
New Mexico State University–Grants (U)
Nichols College (U,G)
Nicolet Area Technical College (U)
Nipissing University (U)
North Carolina State University (U,G)
North Central State College (U)
North Central Texas College (U)
North Dakota State College of Science (U)
North Dakota State University (N,G)
Northeastern State University (U,G)
Northern State University (U)
North Hennepin Community College (N)
North Seattle Community College (U)
NorthWest Arkansas Community College (U)
Northwestern Michigan College (U)
Northwestern Oklahoma State University (U,G)
Northwest-Shoals Community College (U)
Notre Dame College (U)
Nyack College (U,G)
Oakland Community College (U)
Ocean County College (U)
Odessa College (N)
The Ohio State University (G)
Ohio University (N)
Oklahoma Panhandle State University (U)
Oklahoma State University (U)
Olympic College (U)
Oregon Institute of Technology (U)
Ouachita Technical College (U)
Oxnard College (U)
Ozarks Technical Community College (U)
Pace University (U,G)
Pacific States University (G)
Pamlico Community College (U)
Paris Junior College (N)
Pasco-Hernando Community College (U)
Pellissippi State Technical Community College (U)
Peninsula College (U)
Penn State University Park (G)
Peru State College (U)
Philadelphia University (U)
Pikes Peak Community College (U)
Pittsburgh Technical Institute (U)
Portland Community College (N,U)
Pratt Community College (U)
Presentation College (U)
Providence College (U)
Providence College and Theological Seminary (U)
Pulaski Technical College (U)
Purdue University (G)
Rappahannock Community College (U)
Reading Area Community College (U)
Regent University (U,G)
Reinhardt University (U)
Rend Lake College (N,U)
The Richard Stockton College of New Jersey (U)
Richmond Community College (U)
Riverside Community College District (U)
Rivier College (U,G)
Rochester Institute of Technology (U,G)
Rockingham Community College (N)
Rogers State University (U)
Rose State College (U)
Rowan-Cabarrus Community College (U)
Rowan University (G)
Sacramento City College (U)
St. Ambrose University (G)
St. Clair County Community College (U)
Saint Francis University (U,G)
St. John's University (U)
St. Joseph's College, Long Island Campus (G)
St. Joseph's College, New York (G)
Saint Joseph's College of Maine (U,G)
Saint Leo University (U)
St. Louis Community College (N)
Saint Mary-of-the-Woods College (U,G)
St. Mary's University (G)
Saint Paul College–A Community & Technical College (U)
St. Petersburg College (U)
Salve Regina University (G)
Sampson Community College (U)
San Bernardino Valley College (U)
San Diego Community College District (U)
Santa Fe Community College (U)
Santa Monica College (U)
Santa Rosa Junior College (U)
Sauk Valley Community College (U)
Seminole State College of Florida (U)
Seton Hall University (G)
Shawnee State University (U)
Shippensburg University of Pennsylvania (G)
Siena Heights University (U)
Sinclair Community College (U)
Slippery Rock University of Pennsylvania (U)
Sonoma State University (N)
Southeast Arkansas College (U)
Southeast Community College Area (U)
Southeastern Community College (U)
Southeastern Oklahoma State University (U)
Southern Adventist University (G)
Southern Arkansas University–Magnolia (G)
Southern New Hampshire University (U,G)
Southern Oregon University (U,G)
South Piedmont Community College (U)
South Suburban College (U)
Spartanburg Community College (U)
Spokane Community College (U)
Spring Arbor University (U)
Stanly Community College (U)
State University of New York at Oswego (U,G)
State University of New York at Plattsburgh (U,G)
State University of New York College at Potsdam (N,U)
State University of New York College of Technology at Canton (U)
State University of New York Institute of Technology (U,G)
Stephen F. Austin State University (U)
Stephens College (U,G)
Sullivan County Community College (N,U)
Syracuse University (G)
Taft College (U)
Taylor University (U)
Temple University (U,G)
Texas Woman's University (N,U,G)
Three Rivers Community College (U)
Toccoa Falls College (U)
Trident Technical College (U)
Trine University (U)
Tunxis Community College (U)
Tyler Junior College (N,U)
Union County College (U)
United States Sports Academy (G)
University at Albany, State University of New York (U)
The University of Akron (N,U,G)
The University of Alabama in Huntsville (G)
University of Alaska Fairbanks (U)
University of Arkansas at Little Rock (U,G)
University of Denver (G)
University of Evansville (U)
The University of Findlay (U,G)
University of Florida (U)
University of Houston–Downtown (U)
University of Houston–Victoria (G)
University of Idaho (G)
University of Illinois at Chicago (N,U,G)
University of Illinois at Springfield (U,G)
University of Illinois at Urbana–Champaign (U)
University of Maine at Augusta (U)
University of Maine at Machias (U)
University of Management and Technology (U,G)
University of Mary (U)
University of Mary Washington (G)
University of Massachusetts Boston (U)
University of Massachusetts Lowell (N)
University of Memphis (U)
University of Michigan–Flint (N,G)
University of Minnesota, Crookston (U)
University of Missouri–Kansas City (N)
University of New Haven (U,G)
University of North Alabama (G)
The University of North Carolina at Chapel Hill (U)
The University of North Carolina Wilmington (U)
University of North Dakota (U,G)
University of Oregon (U,G)
University of St. Francis (U,G)
University of San Francisco (U)
The University of South Dakota (U,G)
University of Southern Maine (U)
The University of Tennessee at Martin (N)
The University of Texas at Brownsville (N)
The University of Texas at Dallas (G)
University of the Southwest (U,G)
University of Toronto (N)
University of Waterloo (N,G)
University of West Florida (G)
University of West Georgia (U,G)
University of Windsor (U)
University of Wisconsin–La Crosse (G)
University of Wisconsin–Parkside (U)
University of Wisconsin–Platteville (N)
University of Wisconsin–Stout (G)
University of Wisconsin–Superior (U)
Upper Iowa University (U,G)
Utah State University (U,G)
Valencia College (U)
Valley City State University (U)
Vincennes University (U)
Wake Technical Community College (N,U)

Wayland Baptist University (U,G)
Wayne Community College (U)
Wayne State College (U,G)
Wayne State University (G)
Webber International University (U)
Western Kentucky University (G)
Western Wyoming Community College (U)
West Hills Community College (U)
West Los Angeles College (U)
West Shore Community College (U)
West Virginia Northern Community College (U)
West Virginia State University (U)
Wharton County Junior College (U)
Wichita State University (U,G)
Wilkes Community College (U)
Winston-Salem State University (U)
Wisconsin Indianhead Technical College (N,U)
Worcester Polytechnic Institute (G)
Worcester State University (N,U)
Xavier University (G)
York College of Pennsylvania (N)
York County Community College (U)
York Technical College (U)
York University (U)
Youngstown State University (N)

BUSINESS/COMMERCE

Acadia University (U)
Adams State College (N,U)
Allen Community College (U)
The American College (U,G)
Angelina College (U)
Arizona Western College (U)
Athabasca University (N,U)
Austin Peay State University (N)
Bellevue College (U)
Berklee College of Music (N,U)
Big Bend Community College (U)
Bowling Green State University (N)
Brenau University (U,G)
Broward College (U)
Bryant & Stratton Online (N,U)
Bryant University (N)
Buena Vista University (U)
Burlington County College (U)
Cabrillo College (U)
California State University, San Marcos (N)
Cape Fear Community College (N)
Capital Community College (U)
Cayuga County Community College (U)
Central Carolina Community College (U)
Central Michigan University (N,U,G)
Central New Mexico Community College (U)
Central Washington University (U)
Cerritos College (U)
Champlain College (U,G)
Chattanooga State Community College (U)
Chemeketa Community College (U)
Cincinnati State Technical and Community College (U)
Citrus College (U)
City Colleges of Chicago System (U)
Clark State Community College (U)
Clemson University (N,U)
Cleveland Community College (U)
Cleveland State Community College (N,U)
Coleman University (G)
College of San Mateo (U)
College of Southern Maryland (U)
College of the Siskiyous (U)
Colorado Mountain College (U)
Columbia Basin College (U)
Columbia College (U)
Community College of Beaver County (N)
Concordia University, St. Paul (N,U,G)
Cossatot Community College of the University of Arkansas (N,U)
Dallas Baptist University (U,G)
Danville Community College (U)
DeVry University Online (U,G)
Drake University (U,G)
Drexel University (N,U,G)
D'Youville College (G)
Eastern Oregon University (U)
Eastern Washington University (N)
Eastern Wyoming College (U)
Edgecombe Community College (N,U)
Edison State Community College (U)
Elaine P. Nunez Community College (U)
Endicott College (N,U,G)
Fayetteville State University (U)
Finger Lakes Community College (U)
Five Towns College (U)
Florida Institute of Technology (G)
Gannon University (U,G)
Gaston College (U)
Gateway Community College (U)
Genesee Community College (U)
Grantham University (U)
Harrisburg Area Community College (U)
Haywood Community College (U)
Heartland Community College (N,U)
Herkimer County Community College (U)
Hillsborough Community College (U)
Illinois Eastern Community Colleges, Frontier Community College (U)
Illinois Eastern Community Colleges, Lincoln Trail College (U)
Illinois Eastern Community Colleges, Olney Central College (U)
Illinois Eastern Community Colleges, Wabash Valley College (U)
Indiana State University (U)
Indiana University–Purdue University Fort Wayne (U)
Iona College (G)
Jacksonville State University (U,G)
James A. Rhodes State College (U)
James Madison University (U)
Jamestown Community College (N,U)
Kansas State University (N,U,G)
Kirkwood Community College (N)
Kirtland Community College (U)
Lake-Sumter Community College (U)
Lake Superior College (U)
Lamar State College–Port Arthur (N)
Lansing Community College (U)
Liberty University (U)
Lock Haven University of Pennsylvania (N)
Los Angeles Harbor College (U)
Luna Community College (U)
Macon State College (U)
Malone University (U)
Marlboro College Graduate College (N)
Marymount University (G)
McDowell Technical Community College (U)
Mercer County Community College (U)
Middlesex Community College (N,U)
Middle Tennessee State University (N)
Midland College (U)
Midwestern State University (U)
Milwaukee School of Engineering (G)
Minnesota School of Business–Online (U)
Mississippi State University (G)
Monroe Community College (U)
Monroe County Community College (U)
Montcalm Community College (U)
Montgomery Community College (U)
Montgomery County Community College (U)
Moorpark College (U)
Mountain Empire Community College (U)
Mountain State University (U)
Mount Allison University (U)
Murray State University (G)
Nassau Community College (U)
National University (U,G)
New England College of Business and Finance (N)
New Mexico Highlands University (U,G)
New Mexico State University (U)
New Mexico State University–Carlsbad (U)
Nichols College (G)
Nicolet Area Technical College (U)
Nipissing University (U)
North Carolina Central University (U)
North Carolina State University (U)
North Central State College (N)
North Dakota State University (N)
Northern State University (U)
North Hennepin Community College (N,U)
North Iowa Area Community College (U)
North Lake College (U)
North Seattle Community College (U)
North Shore Community College (N,U)
Northwestern Oklahoma State University (U)
Oakton Community College (N,U)
Odessa College (U)
The Ohio State University (U)
Ohio University (N,U)
Oregon Institute of Technology (U)
Oregon State University (U)
Ozarks Technical Community College (U)
Pace University (N,U,G)
Pacific States University (G)
Palm Beach State College (U)
Pamlico Community College (U)
Paris Junior College (N,U)
Pellissippi State Technical Community College (U)
Peninsula College (U)
Pennsylvania College of Technology (U)
Pikes Peak Community College (U)
Portland Community College (N,U)
Pulaski Technical College (U)
Queen's University at Kingston (U)
Reading Area Community College (U)
Regent University (U,G)
Rend Lake College (N,U)
Riverside Community College District (U)
Rockingham Community College (N,U)
Rockland Community College (U)
Rose State College (U)
Rowan-Cabarrus Community College (N)
Sacramento City College (U)
Saint Francis University (U,G)
St. Louis Community College (N)
Saint Mary-of-the-Woods College (U)
St. Petersburg College (U)
St. Philip's College (U)
Salve Regina University (N,G)
San Diego Community College District (U)
San Diego State University (N,U)
San Jacinto College District (U)

Santa Monica College (U)
Santa Rosa Junior College (U)
Sauk Valley Community College (U)
Seton Hill University (U)
Sinclair Community College (U)
Southeast Arkansas College (U)
Southeast Community College Area (U)
Southeastern Community College (U)
Southeastern Illinois College (U)
Southeastern Oklahoma State University (U)
Southern Illinois University Carbondale (U)
Southern New Hampshire University (U,G)
Southern Union State Community College (U)
South Piedmont Community College (U)
Spartanburg Community College (U)
State University of New York at Oswego (U)
State University of New York College at Potsdam (N)
State University of New York College of Agriculture and Technology at Morrisville (U)
State University of New York Empire State College (G)
State University of New York Institute of Technology (U,G)
Stephens College (U,G)
Taft College (U)
Tarleton State University (N,U)
Taylor University (U)
Temple University (G)
Texas State University–San Marcos (U)
Texas Woman's University (G)
Tompkins Cortland Community College (U)
Trident Technical College (U)
Trine University (U)
Tunxis Community College (N)
Tyler Junior College (N,U)
The University of Akron (N,U)
University of Alaska Fairbanks (U)
University of Bridgeport (U)
University of Cincinnati (N,U)
University of Cincinnati Raymond Walters College (U)
University of Colorado at Colorado Springs (G)
The University of Findlay (U)
University of Florida (U)
University of Houston (G)
University of Idaho (U)
University of Illinois at Chicago (N,G)
University of Maine (G)
University of Maine at Augusta (U)
University of Maine at Fort Kent (U)
University of Maine at Machias (U)
University of Management and Technology (G)
University of Michigan–Flint (N,U)
University of Nevada, Reno (U)
University of New Haven (U)
University of North Alabama (G)
The University of South Dakota (U)
The University of Texas at Dallas (G)
University of Wisconsin Colleges (U)
Vincennes University (U)
Wayne Community College (U)
Webber International University (U)
Westchester Community College (U)
Western Wyoming Community College (U)
West Los Angeles College (U)
Westmoreland County Community College (U)
Wharton County Junior College (U)
Wilfrid Laurier University (U)
Wilkes Community College (U)
Winston-Salem State University (U)
Wisconsin Indianhead Technical College (N,U)
York College of Pennsylvania (N,U,G)
York County Community College (U)
York Technical College (U)

BUSINESS/CORPORATE COMMUNICATIONS

Abilene Christian University (U)
Acadia University (U)
Adams State College (U)
American Graduate University (G)
Angelina College (U)
Arapahoe Community College (U)
Arkansas State University (U)
Arkansas State University–Beebe (U)
Athabasca University (N,U,G)
Austin Peay State University (N)
Bellevue College (U)
Boise State University (U)
Brenau University (U,G)
Bridgewater State University (U)
Brigham Young University (U)
Bryant & Stratton Online (N,U)
Bryant University (N)
Buena Vista University (U)
Burlington County College (U)
California State University, Dominguez Hills (N)
California State University, Sacramento (U)
Cayuga County Community College (U)
Cedarville University (U)
Central Michigan University (U,G)
Central Oregon Community College (N)
Central Texas College (U)
Central Washington University (U)
Champlain College (U)
Chemeketa Community College (U)
Cincinnati State Technical and Community College (U)
Clinton Community College (U)
Coleman University (G)
College of San Mateo (U)
College of Southern Maryland (U)
College of the Siskiyous (U)
Colorado Mountain College (U)
Columbus State Community College (U)
Community College of Beaver County (N)
Cossatot Community College of the University of Arkansas (N,U)
Dallas Baptist University (U,G)
Dickinson State University (U)
Drexel University (G)
Eastern Washington University (N)
East Los Angeles College (U)
Edgecombe Community College (N,U)
Edison State Community College (U)
Finger Lakes Community College (U)
Gannon University (U)
Gaston College (U)
Herkimer County Community College (U)
Illinois Valley Community College (U)
Iona College (U,G)
Jacksonville State University (U,G)
Jamestown Community College (N,U)
Jones International University (U,G)
Lake-Sumter Community College (U)
Lake Superior College (U)
Lehigh University (N)
Lewis-Clark State College (U)
Liberty University (U)
Macon State College (U)
Mansfield University of Pennsylvania (N,G)
Marlboro College Graduate College (U)
Marylhurst University (U)
Maryville University of Saint Louis (N)
Middlesex Community College (U)
Middle Tennessee State University (N,U)
Midland College (U)
Midwestern State University (U)
Minnesota School of Business–Online (U)
Montgomery Community College (N)
Murray State College (U)
Murray State University (U)
New Mexico Junior College (N)
Nichols College (G)
North Arkansas College (U)
North Central State College (U)
North Dakota State University (N,G)
North Hennepin Community College (N)
NorthWest Arkansas Community College (U)
Northwestern Michigan College (U)
Northwestern Oklahoma State University (U)
Oakton Community College (U)
Oklahoma State University (U)
Olympic College (U)
Oregon State University (U)
Oxnard College (U)
Ozarks Technical Community College (U)
Pasco-Hernando Community College (N)
Pennsylvania College of Technology (U)
Pikes Peak Community College (U)
Purdue University (U)
Quinebaug Valley Community College (N)
Rappahannock Community College (U)
Rend Lake College (U)
Rochester Institute of Technology (U)
Rockingham Community College (N)
Rose State College (U)
Sacramento City College (U)
St. Clair County Community College (U)
Saint Francis University (U,G)
Saint Paul College–A Community & Technical College (U)
St. Petersburg College (N,U)
San Diego Community College District (U)
Santa Monica College (U)
Santa Rosa Junior College (U)
Seton Hall University (G)
Sonoma State University (N)
Southeast Arkansas College (U)
Southeast Community College Area (U)
Southern New Hampshire University (U,G)
Southern Union State Community College (U)
Southwest Wisconsin Technical College (U)
Spokane Community College (U)
Stephen F. Austin State University (U)
Stephens College (U)
Tarleton State University (N)
Temple University (N)
Tompkins Cortland Community College (U)
Tyler Junior College (U)
The University of Akron (U)
University of Colorado at Colorado Springs (N)
University of Denver (U)
The University of Findlay (G)
University of Illinois at Urbana–Champaign (U)
University of Maine at Augusta (U)

University of Mary Washington (G)
University of Memphis (U)
University of Michigan–Flint (N)
The University of North Carolina at Chapel Hill (N,U)
The University of South Dakota (G)
University of Toronto (N)
University of Waterloo (N)
University of West Florida (U)
University of Wisconsin–Milwaukee (N)
Upper Iowa University (U)
Wayne Community College (N)
Webber International University (U)
Western Kentucky University (G)
York College of Pennsylvania (N)
York County Community College (U)
York University (U)

BUSINESS, MANAGEMENT, AND MARKETING RELATED

Acadia University (U)
Adams State College (U)
Albertus Magnus College (U,G)
Alcorn State University (U,G)
Allen Community College (U)
Anaheim University (G)
Angelo State University (U)
Anne Arundel Community College (N,U)
Antelope Valley College (U)
Arapahoe Community College (U)
Arkansas State University (U,G)
Arkansas State University–Beebe (U)
Asbury University (U)
Ashland University (U)
Athabasca University (N,U,G)
Austin Peay State University (N)
Avila University (U)
Baker College Online (G)
Baldwin-Wallace College (U)
Ball State University (U)
Bellevue College (U)
Bethel University (G)
Blackhawk Technical College (U)
Bloomfield College (U)
Bloomsburg University of Pennsylvania (U,G)
Boise State University (U)
Boston University (G)
Bradley University (U)
Brazosport College (U)
Brenau University (U,G)
Brewton-Parker College (U)
Brigham Young University (U)
Brigham Young University–Idaho (U)
Bryant University (N)
Buena Vista University (U)
Buffalo State College, State University of New York (U)
Burlington County College (U)
Butler Community College (U)
Butler County Community College (U)
California State University, Dominguez Hills (N)
California State University, Sacramento (U,G)
California State University, San Bernardino (U)
Campbellsville University (U)
Canisius College (U)
Cape Fear Community College (U)
Capital Community College (U)
Carroll University (U)
Cayuga County Community College (U)
Central Carolina Community College (U)
Centralia College (U)
Central Michigan University (U,G)
Central New Mexico Community College (U)
Central Oregon Community College (N)
Central Texas College (U)
Champlain College (G)
Charter Oak State College (U)
Chatham University (U)
Chattanooga State Community College (U)
Chemeketa Community College (U)
Cincinnati State Technical and Community College (U)
City Colleges of Chicago System (U)
Clackamas Community College (U)
Clemson University (N)
Cleveland Community College (U)
Cleveland State Community College (N)
College of Saint Mary (U)
Columbia College (U,G)
Community College of Beaver County (N,U)
Concordia University Wisconsin (U)
Cossatot Community College of the University of Arkansas (N)
Dabney S. Lancaster Community College (U)
Dakota College at Bottineau (U)
Dallas Baptist University (U,G)
Dallas Christian College (U)
Danville Community College (U)
Daytona State College (U)
Delgado Community College (U)
Dickinson State University (U)
Dominican College (U)
Drexel University (U,G)
Drury University (U)
D'Youville College (U)
Eastern Washington University (N)
Eastern West Virginia Community and Technical College (U)
East Los Angeles College (U)
Edgecombe Community College (N,U)
Edison State Community College (U)
Elmira College (G)
Endicott College (U)
Enterprise State Community College (U)
Excelsior College (U)
Ferris State University (U)
Five Towns College (U)
Fort Valley State University (U)
Framingham State University (G)
Front Range Community College (U)
Gaston College (U)
Genesee Community College (U)
Georgian Court University (G)
Glenville State College (U)
Granite State College (U)
Grantham University (U)
Greenville Technical College (U)
Hagerstown Community College (N)
Harcum College (U)
Harrisburg Area Community College (U)
Hibbing Community College (U)
Hofstra University (U,G)
Holyoke Community College (U)
Hope International University (U)
Hopkinsville Community College (U)
Illinois State University (U)
Illinois Valley Community College (U)
Indiana State University (U)
Indiana University of Pennsylvania (U,G)
Indiana University–Purdue University Fort Wayne (N)
Inter American University of Puerto Rico, San Germán Campus (G)
Iona College (U,G)
Iowa Lakes Community College (U)
Iowa Valley Community College District (U)
Jacksonville State University (U,G)
Jamestown Community College (N,U)
Jefferson Community College (U)
John A. Logan College (U)
Johnson State College (U)
Johnston Community College (U)
Jones International University (G)
J. Sargeant Reynolds Community College (U)
Kansas State University (N,U,G)
Kean University (N)
Kettering University (N)
Keystone College (U)
Kirtland Community College (U)
Lake-Sumter Community College (U)
Lamar State College–Orange (U)
Lamar State College–Port Arthur (N)
Lansing Community College (U)
La Roche College (U)
Lehman College of the City University of New York (U)
Lenoir Community College (U)
Lesley University (U)
Lewis-Clark State College (U)
Liberty University (U,G)
Lincoln Christian University (U)
Lock Haven University of Pennsylvania (U)
Long Beach City College (U)
Los Angeles Trade-Technical College (U)
Louisiana State University at Eunice (U)
Lourdes College (U)
Macon State College (U)
Maharishi University of Management (G)
Marist College (U,G)
Marlboro College Graduate College (U)
Marquette University (U)
Marylhurst University (U)
Marymount University (G)
Maryville University of Saint Louis (U)
McKendree University (U,G)
Mercer County Community College (U)
Miami Dade College (U)
Michigan Technological University (U,G)
Middlesex Community College (U)
Middle Tennessee State University (N)
Midstate College (U)
Midway College (G)
Milwaukee School of Engineering (U)
Minnesota School of Business–Online (U)
Missouri University of Science and Technology (N,G)
Mitchell Technical Institute (N)
Monroe College (U)
Montgomery Community College (U)
Moorpark College (U)
Mountain State University (U)
Mount Wachusett Community College (N)
Murray State University (U,G)
Nashville State Technical Community College (N,U)
Naugatuck Valley Community College (U)
New England College of Business and Finance (N,U)
New Mexico Highlands University (U,G)
New Mexico Junior College (N)
New Mexico State University (U)
New Mexico State University–Carlsbad (U)
New River Community College (U)

Nichols College (U,G)
Nipissing University (U)
North Carolina State University (U)
North Central Texas College (U)
North Dakota State College of Science (U)
North Dakota State University (N,G)
Northern State University (U)
North Georgia College & State University (U)
North Hennepin Community College (N)
North Iowa Area Community College (U)
North Lake College (U)
North Seattle Community College (U)
NorthWest Arkansas Community College (U)
Northwestern Connecticut Community College (U)
Northwestern Michigan College (U)
Odessa College (N,U)
Ohio University (N)
Okefenokee Technical College (N,U)
Oklahoma Panhandle State University (U)
Oklahoma State University (U)
Olympic College (U)
Orange Coast College (U)
Oregon State University (N)
Oxnard College (U)
Ozarks Technical Community College (U)
Pacific States University (U)
Pamlico Community College (U)
Pellissippi State Technical Community College (U)
Peninsula College (U)
Penn State University Park (G)
Peru State College (U,G)
Phoenix College (N,U)
Pine Technical College (U)
Pittsburg State University (U)
Portland Community College (N,U)
Prairie View A&M University (U)
Prescott College (N)
Quincy University (U)
Quinebaug Valley Community College (U)
Quinnipiac University (G)
Quinsigamond Community College (N,U)
Reading Area Community College (N)
Regent University (U,G)
Reinhardt University (U)
Rend Lake College (U)
The Richard Stockton College of New Jersey (G)
Rio Hondo College (U)
Robert Morris University (U)
Rochester Institute of Technology (U,G)
Rockingham Community College (N)
Rosemont College (U)
Rose State College (U)
Sacramento City College (U)
The Sage Colleges (U)
Saint Francis University (U,G)
St. John Fisher College (G)
St. John's University (G)
Saint Joseph's College of Maine (G)
St. Louis Community College (N,U)
Saint Mary-of-the-Woods College (G)
Saint Paul College–A Community & Technical College (U)
Sam Houston State University (U)
San Bernardino Valley College (U)
San Diego Community College District (U)
San Diego State University (U)
San Jacinto College District (U)
Santa Monica College (U)
Seton Hall University (G)
Shawnee State University (U)
Siena Heights University (U)
Sinclair Community College (U)
Sonoma State University (N)
Southeast Arkansas College (U)
Southeastern Oklahoma State University (U)
Southern Adventist University (G)
Southern Arkansas University–Magnolia (U)
Southern Illinois University Carbondale (U)
Southern New Hampshire University (U,G)
Southern Oregon University (U)
Southern Union State Community College (U)
Southern University at New Orleans (G)
South Piedmont Community College (U)
Southwestern Adventist University (G)
Southwest Wisconsin Technical College (U)
Spartanburg Community College (N,U)
Spokane Community College (U)
State University of New York College at Cortland (G)
State University of New York College at Potsdam (U)
State University of New York Institute of Technology (U,G)
Stephens College (U,G)
Suffolk University (G)
Sullivan County Community College (U)
Syracuse University (U)
Tarleton State University (U)
Taylor University (U)
Thiel College (U)
Toccoa Falls College (U)
Tompkins Cortland Community College (N)
Union County College (U)
Union University (U)
United States Sports Academy (N,U)
The University of Akron (U)
The University of Alabama in Huntsville (G)
University of Alaska Fairbanks (U)
University of Arkansas at Little Rock (U,G)
University of Bridgeport (U)
University of Cincinnati Raymond Walters College (U)
University of Dubuque (U)
The University of Findlay (N)
University of Florida (U,G)
University of Houston–Downtown (U)
University of Idaho (G)
University of Illinois at Chicago (N,G)
University of Illinois at Springfield (U)
University of Illinois at Urbana–Champaign (U)
University of Louisville (N)
University of Maine at Augusta (U)
University of Maine at Fort Kent (U)
University of Maine at Machias (U)
University of Management and Technology (U)
University of Mary (U)
University of Mary Washington (U,G)
University of Massachusetts Boston (N)
University of Massachusetts Lowell (N)
University of Michigan–Flint (N)
The University of Montana Western (U)
University of New Haven (U)
University of North Alabama (U)
The University of North Carolina at Chapel Hill (N)
University of North Dakota (U)
University of Pittsburgh at Bradford (U)
The University of South Dakota (U,G)
The University of Texas at Arlington (U)
The University of Texas at Dallas (G)
The University of Texas of the Permian Basin (U)
University of the Southwest (U)
University of Toronto (N)
University of West Florida (N)
University of West Georgia (U)
University of Wisconsin–Milwaukee (G)
University of Wisconsin–Platteville (N)
University of Wisconsin–Stout (U)
Upper Iowa University (U,G)
Utah State University (U)
Valencia College (U)
Valley City State University (U)
Vincennes University (U)
Walden University (G)
Wayne Community College (N)
Wayne State University (G)
Webber International University (U)
Webster University (G)
Westchester Community College (U)
Western Kentucky University (G)
West Hills Community College (U)
West Los Angeles College (U)
West Shore Community College (U)
West Virginia University (N)
Wharton County Junior College (U)
Wilkes Community College (U)
Winston-Salem State University (N)
Yavapai College (U)
York College of Pennsylvania (N,G)
York County Community College (U)
Youngstown State University (N,U)

BUSINESS/MANAGERIAL ECONOMICS

Acadia University (U)
Adams State College (U)
Allen Community College (U)
American Graduate University (G)
Anne Arundel Community College (U)
Athabasca University (N,U,G)
Austin Peay State University (N)
Bellevue College (U)
Bloomfield College (U)
Boise State University (U)
Brenau University (U,G)
Bridgewater State University (U)
Bryant University (N)
Buena Vista University (U)
Burlington County College (U)
Capital Community College (U)
Cayuga County Community College (U)
Central Michigan University (U,G)
Central New Mexico Community College (U)
Central Texas College (U)
Champlain College (G)
Chatham University (U)
Cleveland Community College (U)
Columbia College (G)
Community College of Beaver County (N,U)
Corning Community College (U)
Cossatot Community College of the University of Arkansas (N,U)
Dallas Baptist University (U,G)
Delgado Community College (U)
Drake University (U)
Drexel University (U,G)
D'Youville College (G)
Edgecombe Community College (N)
Elmira College (G)

Ferris State University (U)
Fort Valley State University (U)
Franklin Pierce University (U,G)
Gadsden State Community College (U)
Grantham University (U,G)
Harcum College (U)
Harrisburg Area Community College (U)
Hofstra University (U)
Inter American University of Puerto Rico, San Germán Campus (U,G)
Iona College (G)
Iowa Lakes Community College (U)
Jacksonville State University (U,G)
James Madison University (N)
Jamestown Community College (U)
John A. Logan College (U)
Kansas State University (N,G)
Labette Community College (U)
Lamar State College–Port Arthur (N)
La Roche College (U)
Lewis-Clark State College (U)
Liberty University (U)
Louisiana State University at Eunice (U)
Luna Community College (U)
Marist College (G)
Marshall University (U)
McKendree University (G)
McMurry University (U)
Mercer County Community College (U)
Miami Dade College (U)
Middlesex Community College (U)
Middle Tennessee State University (N)
Midland College (U)
Midway College (G)
Milwaukee School of Engineering (G)
Minnesota School of Business–Online (U)
Mississippi State University (G)
Monroe College (U)
Montgomery Community College (U)
Murray State University (U)
Naugatuck Valley Community College (U)
New England College of Business and Finance (N)
New Mexico Highlands University (U,G)
Nichols College (U,G)
Olympic College (U)
Pacific States University (G)
Pamlico Community College (U)
Pikes Peak Community College (U)
Portland Community College (U)
Quinnipiac University (U,G)
Rend Lake College (U)
Richmond Community College (U)
Rockingham Community College (N)
Rose State College (U)
Sacramento City College (U)
Saint Francis University (U,G)
Sampson Community College (U)
San Diego Community College District (U)
Sinclair Community College (U)
Southeast Arkansas College (U)
Southeastern Community College (U)
Southern Union State Community College (U)
Southern University at New Orleans (U)
South Piedmont Community College (U)
Southwest Wisconsin Technical College (U)
Spokane Community College (U)
State University of New York at Oswego (U)
State University of New York College at Potsdam (U)
State University of New York Institute of Technology (G)
Stephens College (G)
Tarleton State University (U)
Taylor University (U)
Trident Technical College (U)
The University of Akron (U)
The University of Alabama in Huntsville (G)
University of Alaska Fairbanks (U)
The University of Findlay (N,U,G)
University of Illinois at Chicago (G)
University of Maine at Augusta (U)
University of Nevada, Reno (U)
University of North Dakota (U)
University of San Francisco (U)
University of South Carolina Sumter (U)
The University of South Dakota (U,G)
University of Southern Maine (U)
The University of Texas at Dallas (G)
University of Toronto (N)
University of Waterloo (U)
Upper Iowa University (G)
Wayne State University (G)
Webber International University (U)
West Hills Community College (U)
West Los Angeles College (U)
Wilkes Community College (U)
York University (U)
Youngstown State University (N)

BUSINESS OPERATIONS SUPPORT AND ASSISTANT SERVICES

Alvin Community College (N,U)
Athabasca University (N)
Austin Peay State University (N)
Bellevue College (U)
Blackhawk Technical College (N,U)
Boise State University (U)
Burlington County College (U)
California State University, San Marcos (U)
Cayuga County Community College (U)
Central Carolina Community College (U)
Central Carolina Technical College (U)
Central Michigan University (U)
Central New Mexico Community College (U)
Central Oregon Community College (N)
Central Texas College (U)
Central Virginia Community College (U)
Central Wyoming College (N)
Cerritos College (U)
Chatham University (G)
Chemeketa Community College (U)
Cincinnati State Technical and Community College (U)
Clemson University (N)
Columbia Basin College (U)
Columbia University (G)
Columbus State Community College (U)
Community College of Beaver County (N)
Corning Community College (U)
Cossatot Community College of the University of Arkansas (N)
Dakota College at Bottineau (U)
Danville Community College (U)
Eastern West Virginia Community and Technical College (U)
Edgecombe Community College (N)
Edison State Community College (U)
Erie Community College (U)
Erie Community College, North Campus (U)
Erie Community College, South Campus (U)
Front Range Community College (U)
Indiana State University (U)
Iona College (U)
James A. Rhodes State College (U)
Jamestown Community College (N,U)
J. Sargeant Reynolds Community College (U)
Kansas State University (G)
Kirkwood Community College (U)
Kirtland Community College (U)
Lake Superior College (U)
Lamar State College–Port Arthur (N)
Lansing Community College (U)
Lewis-Clark State College (U)
Louisiana State University at Eunice (U)
Maryville University of Saint Louis (U)
Mercy College of Northwest Ohio (N)
Midland College (N,U)
Minnesota School of Business–Online (U)
Mitchell Technical Institute (N)
Montgomery Community College (U)
Montgomery County Community College (N)
Mount Wachusett Community College (N)
Nashville State Technical Community College (N)
Naugatuck Valley Community College (U)
New England College of Business and Finance (N,U)
Nichols College (G)
North Central Texas College (U)
North Dakota State University (N)
North Shore Community College (N)
NorthWest Arkansas Community College (U)
Odessa College (U)
Ohio University (U)
Olympic College (U)
Oxnard College (U)
Paris Junior College (N)
Phoenix College (N)
Piedmont Community College (U)
Pikes Peak Community College (U)
Pulaski Technical College (U)
Randolph Community College (N)
Reinhardt University (U)
Rend Lake College (N,U)
Richmond Community College (N)
Rockingham Community College (N)
Sacramento City College (U)
Saint Francis University (U)
Saint Paul College–A Community & Technical College (U)
San Diego Community College District (U)
Santa Rosa Junior College (U)
Sauk Valley Community College (U)
Southern Union State Community College (U)
Spokane Community College (U)
Sullivan County Community College (U)
Tarleton State University (N)
Tompkins Cortland Community College (N)
Trident Technical College (U)
Tyler Junior College (U)
The University of Akron (U)
University of Alaska Fairbanks (U)
University of Cincinnati (N)
University of Evansville (N)
University of Maine at Augusta (U)
The University of South Dakota (U)
Utah State University (U)
Vincennes University (U)
Wake Technical Community College (N,U)
Western Wyoming Community College (U)
West Los Angeles College (U)
Westmoreland County Community College (U)

Wisconsin Indianhead Technical College (N,U)
York County Community College (U)
Youngstown State University (N)

CARPENTRY

Austin Peay State University (U)
Bossier Parish Community College (N)
South Piedmont Community College (U)
Wayne Community College (N)

CELL BIOLOGY AND ANATOMICAL SCIENCES

Allen Community College (U)
Austin Peay State University (U)
Baptist Bible College of Pennsylvania (U,G)
Cabrillo College (U)
Carl Sandburg College (U)
Cayuga County Community College (U)
Cincinnati State Technical and Community College (U)
Clark State Community College (U)
Columbus State Community College (U)
Edison State Community College (U)
Hocking College (U)
Huntington College of Health Sciences (U)
Lehigh University (G)
Louisiana State University and Agricultural and Mechanical College (U)
Mountain State University (U)
New Mexico State University–Carlsbad (U)
Ozarks Technical Community College (U)
Queen's University at Kingston (U)
Sacramento City College (U)
Saint Francis University (U)
Saint Paul College–A Community & Technical College (U)
Santa Monica College (U)
South Piedmont Community College (U)
Southwestern Community College (U)
Texas State University–San Marcos (U)
Tyler Junior College (U)
The University of Akron (U)
The University of Arizona (U)
University of Waterloo (U)
Wayne State University (U,G)
Western Kentucky University (U,G)

CERAMIC SCIENCES AND ENGINEERING

Columbia University (G)

CHEMICAL ENGINEERING

Austin Peay State University (U)
Brigham Young University (U)
Columbia University (G)
The Johns Hopkins University (G)
Kansas State University (U,G)
Lehigh University (N,G)
Michigan Technological University (U)
Mississippi State University (G)
University of Illinois at Chicago (G)
University of North Dakota (U)

CHEMISTRY

Acadia University (U)
American University (U)
Anne Arundel Community College (U)
Antelope Valley College (U)
Arapahoe Community College (U)
Ashland University (U)
Athabasca University (N,U)
Austin Peay State University (U)
Bellevue College (U)
Big Bend Community College (U)
Boise State University (U)
Brazosport College (U)
Brigham Young University (U)
Bronx Community College of the City University of New York (U)
Brookdale Community College (U)
Butler Community College (U)
Butler County Community College (U)
Carleton University (U)
Cascadia Community College (U)
Central Carolina Community College (U)
Centralia College (U)
Central Virginia Community College (U)
Central Washington University (U)
Central Wyoming College (U)
Champlain College (U)
Chatham University (U)
Chattanooga State Community College (U)
Chemeketa Community College (U)
Clackamas Community College (U)
Clarion University of Pennsylvania (U)
Clark State Community College (U)
Cleveland State Community College (N)
Clovis Community College (U)
Colorado Mountain College (U)
Columbia College (U)
Columbus State Community College (U)
Corning Community College (U)
Dakota College at Bottineau (U)
Drury University (U)
East Central Community College (U)
Eastern Oregon University (U)
Edison State Community College (U)
Erie Community College (U)
Erie Community College, North Campus (U)
Erie Community College, South Campus (U)
Fort Valley State University (U)
Front Range Community College (U)
Gadsden State Community College (U)
Gaston College (U)
Graceland University (U)
Grantham University (U)
Harford Community College (U)
Hibbing Community College (U)
Hopkinsville Community College (U)
Houston Community College System (U)
Huntington College of Health Sciences (U,G)
Illinois Eastern Community Colleges, Wabash Valley College (U)
Illinois State University (G)
Indiana State University (U)
Indiana University–Purdue University Fort Wayne (U)
Iowa Lakes Community College (U)
Jacksonville State University (U,G)
Jamestown College (U)
Jefferson Community College (U)
Johnston Community College (U)
J. Sargeant Reynolds Community College (U)
Kansas State University (U)
Kirkwood Community College (U)
Lakehead University (U)
Lansing Community College (U)
Lehigh University (N,G)
Lehman College of the City University of New York (U)
Marshall University (U)
Mayville State University (U)
McMurry University (U)
Mercy College of Northwest Ohio (U)
Mesa State College (U)
MGH Institute of Health Professions (U)
Miami University–Regional Campuses (U)
Michigan Technological University (U)
Middlesex Community College (U)
Missouri Baptist University (U)
Missouri University of Science and Technology (N)
Mountain State University (U)
Murray State University (U)
Naugatuck Valley Community College (U)
New Mexico State University–Alamogordo (U)
New River Community College (U)
North Carolina State University (U)
North Dakota State College of Science (U)
North Dakota State University (U)
North Hennepin Community College (U)
North Iowa Area Community College (U)
North Lake College (U)
North Seattle Community College (U)
NorthWest Arkansas Community College (U)
Northwestern Michigan College (U)
Oakton Community College (U)
The Ohio State University (U)
Oklahoma Panhandle State University (U)
Olympic College (U)
Oregon State University (U)
Oxnard College (U)
Pace University (U)
Palm Beach State College (U)
Pamlico Community College (U)
Peninsula College (U)
Pennsylvania College of Technology (U)
Phoenix College (U)
Portland Community College (U)
Portland State University (U)
Pratt Community College (U)
Queen's University at Kingston (U)
Quinnipiac University (U)
Rochester Institute of Technology (U)
Rockland Community College (U)
Sacramento City College (U)
St. Clair County Community College (U)
St. Cloud State University (U)
Saint Francis University (U)
Saint Paul College–A Community & Technical College (U)
St. Petersburg College (U)
St. Philip's College (U)
Sam Houston State University (U)
San Bernardino Valley College (U)
San Diego Community College District (U)
Sauk Valley Community College (U)
Sinclair Community College (U)
Slippery Rock University of Pennsylvania (U)
Southeastern Community College (U)
Southern Adventist University (U)
Southern University at New Orleans (U)
South Piedmont Community College (U)
Spartanburg Community College (U)
Spokane Community College (U)
Spoon River College (U)
State University of New York at Oswego (U)
Union County College (U)
The University of Akron (U)

University of Colorado at Colorado Springs (U)
The University of Findlay (U)
University of Florida (U)
University of Houston–Downtown (U)
University of Illinois at Springfield (U)
University of Illinois at Urbana–Champaign (U)
University of Mary (U)
University of Massachusetts Boston (U)
University of New England (U)
The University of North Carolina at Chapel Hill (U)
The University of North Carolina Wilmington (G)
University of North Dakota (U)
University of Pittsburgh at Bradford (U)
The University of South Dakota (U)
The University of Texas of the Permian Basin (U)
University of Utah (U)
University of Waterloo (N,U)
The University of Winnipeg (U)
University of Wisconsin Colleges (U)
University of Wisconsin–Green Bay (U)
University of Wisconsin–Stout (U)
Utah State University (U)
Valencia College (U)
Vincennes University (U)
Wake Technical Community College (U)
Westchester Community College (U)
Western Kentucky University (U)
Western Texas College (U)
West Virginia Northern Community College (U)
West Virginia State University (U)
Windward Community College (U)

CITY/URBAN, COMMUNITY AND REGIONAL PLANNING

Athabasca University (N)
Austin Peay State University (U)
Eastern Washington University (U)
Goddard College (U)
Middle Tennessee State University (N)
North Dakota State University (G)
The Ohio State University (G)
The University of Akron (U)
University of Southern Mississippi (G)

CIVIL ENGINEERING

Auburn University (G)
Brigham Young University (U)
Columbia University (N,G)
Georgia Institute of Technology (N,G)
Kansas State University (U,G)
Mid-State Technical College (U)
Mississippi State University (G)
Missouri University of Science and Technology (N,G)
Sinclair Community College (U)
Southern Methodist University (G)
The University of Akron (U)
The University of Alabama in Huntsville (G)
The University of British Columbia (U)
University of Colorado Boulder (N,G)
University of Florida (N,G)
University of Idaho (U,G)
University of Illinois at Urbana–Champaign (G)
University of Maine (G)
University of North Dakota (U)
University of Wisconsin–Platteville (N)

CIVIL ENGINEERING TECHNOLOGIES

Auburn University (G)
Cincinnati State Technical and Community College (U)
James A. Rhodes State College (U)
Kansas State University (U,G)
Mid-State Technical College (U)
Missouri University of Science and Technology (N,G)
North Dakota State College of Science (U)
Southern Methodist University (G)
The University of Akron (U)
The University of Alabama in Huntsville (G)
The University of Arizona (U)
University of Maine (U)
Wake Technical Community College (U)

CLASSICAL AND ANCIENT STUDIES

Austin Peay State University (U)
Boise State University (U)
Bowling Green State University (U)
Brigham Young University–Idaho (U)
Columbus State Community College (U)
Florida State University (U)
Front Range Community College (U)
Goddard College (U)
Hopkinsville Community College (U)
The Ohio State University (U)
Oklahoma State University (U)
Queen's University at Kingston (U)
Sacramento City College (U)
Sinclair Community College (U)
University of Florida (G)
University of Illinois at Urbana–Champaign (U)
The University of Kansas (U)
University of Massachusetts Boston (U,G)
University of Northern Iowa (G)
University of Pennsylvania (U)
University of Southern Maine (U)
West Hills Community College (U)

CLINICAL, COUNSELING AND APPLIED PSYCHOLOGY

Malone University (G)
Southern Arkansas University–Magnolia (G)
University of Alaska Fairbanks (U)
The University of Texas at Dallas (N)

CLINICAL/MEDICAL LABORATORY SCIENCE/ RESEARCH

Arapahoe Community College (U)
Austin Peay State University (U)
Blackhawk Technical College (U)
California State University, Sacramento (U)
Central Carolina Community College (N)
Central New Mexico Community College (U)
Clarion University of Pennsylvania (U)
Dakota College at Bottineau (U)
Drexel University (G)
D'Youville College (U)
Erie Community College (U)
Erie Community College, North Campus (U)
Erie Community College, South Campus (U)
Hibbing Community College (U)
Randolph Community College (N)
Sacramento City College (U)
University of Illinois at Chicago (G)
University of Illinois at Springfield (U)

COGNITIVE SCIENCE

Austin Peay State University (U)
Boise State University (G)
D'Youville College (G)
Queen's University at Kingston (U)
San Diego Community College District (U)
University of Alaska Fairbanks (U)

COMMUNICATION AND JOURNALISM RELATED

American University (U,G)
Angelo State University (U,G)
Arapahoe Community College (U)
Ashland University (U)
Athabasca University (U)
Austin Peay State University (U,G)
Ball State University (N,G)
Bloomfield College (U)
Bluefield College (U)
Bridgewater State University (U)
Brigham Young University–Idaho (U)
Buena Vista University (U)
Burlington College (U)
Butler Community College (U)
Cabrillo College (U)
Caldwell College (U)
California State University, Dominguez Hills (N)
California State University, San Bernardino (U)
California State University, San Marcos (N)
Cascadia Community College (U)
Cayuga County Community College (U)
Cedarville University (U)
Central Michigan University (G)
Central Washington University (U)
Champlain College (U)
Chatham University (U)
City Colleges of Chicago System (U)
City University of Seattle (U)
Clarion University of Pennsylvania (G)
Cleveland State Community College (N)
Coastal Carolina University (U)
The College at Brockport, State University of New York (U)
College of Southern Maryland (N)
Columbus State Community College (U)
Dallas Baptist University (U)
Drake University (U)
Eastern Illinois University (U)
Eastern Kentucky University (U)
Ferris State University (U)
Finger Lakes Community College (U)
Fort Hays State University (N,U)
Front Range Community College (U)
Goddard College (U)
Hofstra University (U)
Hopkinsville Community College (U)
Illinois State University (U)
Indiana University–Purdue University Fort Wayne (U)

Iona College (U,G)
Jones International University (G)
Kean University (N)
Keystone College (U)
Lackawanna College (U)
La Roche College (U)
Malone University (U)
Mansfield University of Pennsylvania (N,U)
Marquette University (U)
Marshall University (U)
Middlesex Community College (U)
Minnesota School of Business–Online (U)
Mississippi State University (U)
Moorpark College (U)
Mount Wachusett Community College (U)
Murray State University (U)
Naugatuck Valley Community College (U)
New Mexico Junior College (U)
North Carolina Central University (U)
North Carolina State University (U)
North Dakota State University (N,U,G)
North Hennepin Community College (N)
Oakton Community College (N,U)
Odessa College (U)
Orange Coast College (U)
Pace University (U)
Paris Junior College (U)
Peninsula College (U)
Pittsburg State University (U,G)
Prairie View A&M University (U)
Purdue University (U)
Quincy University (U)
Quinnipiac University (U,G)
Regent University (U,G)
Robert Morris University (U)
Rochester Institute of Technology (U)
Rockingham Community College (N)
Rose State College (U)
Sacramento City College (U)
St. Clair County Community College (U)
St. John's University (U)
St. Louis Community College (U)
Saint Paul College–A Community & Technical College (U)
San Bernardino Valley College (U)
San Diego Community College District (U)
Santa Monica College (U)
Santa Rosa Junior College (U)
Seton Hill University (U)
Sinclair Community College (U)
Southeastern Community College (U)
Southeastern Illinois College (U)
Southern New Hampshire University (U)
Southern University at New Orleans (U)
South Piedmont Community College (U)
Southwest Wisconsin Technical College (U)
Spoon River College (U)
Spring Arbor University (U)
State University of New York at Oswego (U)
State University of New York College at Potsdam (U)
Stephens College (U)
Sullivan County Community College (N)
Taylor University (U)
Thiel College (U)
University at Albany, State University of New York (U)
The University of Akron (U)
University of Alaska Fairbanks (U)
University of Arkansas at Little Rock (U)
University of Colorado at Colorado Springs (N)
The University of Findlay (U)
University of Florida (U)
University of Houston–Victoria (U)
University of Illinois at Springfield (U)
University of Illinois at Urbana–Champaign (U)
University of Mary (U)
University of Michigan–Flint (U)
University of Missouri–Kansas City (U)
University of New Haven (U)
University of North Dakota (U)
University of South Alabama (U)
The University of Texas at Arlington (U)
The University of Texas of the Permian Basin (U)
The University of West Alabama (U)
University of Wisconsin Colleges (U)
University of Wisconsin–Superior (U)
Utah State University (U)
Valencia College (U)
Valley City State University (U)
Webster University (G)
Western Wyoming Community College (U)
Westmoreland County Community College (U)
West Virginia State University (U)
Yavapai College (U)
Youngstown State University (U)

COMMUNICATION AND MEDIA

Abilene Christian University (U)
Academy of Art University (U,G)
Albertus Magnus College (U)
Andrew Jackson University (U)
Anne Arundel Community College (U)
Arapahoe Community College (U)
Arkansas State University–Beebe (U)
Ashland University (U)
Athabasca University (N,U)
Auburn University (U)
Austin Peay State University (U)
Bellevue College (U)
Beulah Heights University (U)
Bowling Green State University (U)
Bradley University (U)
Brenau University (U)
Bridgewater State University (U,G)
Brigham Young University (U)
Brigham Young University–Idaho (U)
Bronx Community College of the City University of New York (U)
Buena Vista University (U)
Buffalo State College, State University of New York (U)
Burlington College (U)
Burlington County College (U)
Butler County Community College (N,U)
California State University, Chico (U)
California State University, San Bernardino (U,G)
Canisius College (U)
Capital Community College (U)
Carlow University (U)
Carroll University (U)
Cascadia Community College (U)
Cayuga County Community College (U)
Central New Mexico Community College (U)
Central Texas College (U)
Central Wyoming College (U)
Champlain College (U)
Charter Oak State College (U)
Chattanooga State Community College (U)
Cincinnati State Technical and Community College (U)
Citrus College (U)
City University of Seattle (U)
Clarion University of Pennsylvania (U,G)
Clark State Community College (U)
Clemson University (N,U,G)
Cleveland Institute of Electronics (U)
Cleveland State Community College (N)
Clovis Community College (U)
The College at Brockport, State University of New York (U)
College of Southern Maryland (U)
College of the Siskiyous (U)
Columbia Basin College (U)
Columbus State Community College (U)
Concordia University, St. Paul (N)
Cossatot Community College of the University of Arkansas (U)
Dallas Baptist University (U)
Danville Community College (U)
Dawson Community College (U)
DeVry University Online (U,G)
Dickinson State University (U)
Drake University (U)
Drury University (U,G)
Eastern Washington University (U)
Eastern Wyoming College (U)
Edgecombe Community College (N)
Edison State Community College (U)
Enterprise State Community College (U)
Fitchburg State University (U,G)
Five Towns College (U)
Florida State University (U)
Fontbonne University (U)
Fort Valley State University (U)
Framingham State University (U)
Franklin Pierce University (U)
Friends University (U)
Front Range Community College (U)
Gaston College (U)
Georgian Court University (U)
Goddard College (U)
Governors State University (N,U)
Grand Valley State University (G)
Granite State College (U)
Heartland Community College (U)
Hillsborough Community College (U)
Hocking College (U)
Hofstra University (U)
Holyoke Community College (U)
Illinois Eastern Community Colleges, Olney Central College (U)
Illinois State University (U)
Indiana University of Pennsylvania (U)
Indiana University–Purdue University Fort Wayne (U)
Indiana Wesleyan University (U)
Iona College (U)
Iowa Valley Community College District (U)
Ithaca College (U)
James A. Rhodes State College (U)
James Madison University (U)
Jamestown Community College (N,U)
Judson University (U)
Keystone College (U)
Kirkwood Community College (U)
Labette Community College (U)
Lackawanna College (U)
Lake Superior College (U)
Lewis-Clark State College (U)

Liberty University (U)
Lock Haven University of Pennsylvania (U,G)
Louisiana State University and Agricultural and Mechanical College (U)
Luna Community College (U)
Macon State College (U)
Malone University (U)
Marquette University (U)
Marshall University (U)
Mary Baldwin College (U)
Marylhurst University (U)
Maryville University of Saint Louis (U)
McDaniel College (U)
McNeese State University (U)
Mercer County Community College (U)
Mesa Community College (U)
Michigan Technological University (U)
Middlesex Community College (U)
Middle Tennessee State University (U)
Midwestern State University (U)
Minnesota School of Business–Online (U)
Minnesota School of Business–Richfield (U)
Mississippi State University (U)
Monroe Community College (U)
Moorpark College (U)
Mountain Empire Community College (U)
Naugatuck Valley Community College (U)
New Mexico Junior College (U)
Nicolet Area Technical College (U)
North Carolina Central University (U)
North Carolina State University (U)
North Dakota State University (N,U,G)
Northern Kentucky University (U)
North Hennepin Community College (U)
North Shore Community College (N)
NorthWest Arkansas Community College (U)
Northwestern Oklahoma State University (U)
Nyack College (U)
Oakton Community College (U)
Ohio University (U)
Olympic College (U)
Oregon State University (N,U)
Oxnard College (U)
Ozarks Technical Community College (U)
Pace University (U)
Palm Beach State College (U)
Pellissippi State Technical Community College (U)
Pratt Community College (U)
Prescott College (N,G)
Providence College (U)
Providence College and Theological Seminary (U)
Quinnipiac University (U,G)
Regent University (U,G)
The Richard Stockton College of New Jersey (U)
Richmond Community College (U)
Riverside Community College District (U)
Rivier College (U)
Rochester Institute of Technology (U,G)
Rockingham Community College (N)
Sacramento City College (U)
St. Cloud State University (U)
Saint Paul College–A Community & Technical College (U)
St. Petersburg College (N,U)
San Diego Community College District (U)
Santa Monica College (U)
Santa Rosa Junior College (U)
Seton Hall University (G)
Shippensburg University of Pennsylvania (U,G)
Sinclair Community College (U)
Slippery Rock University of Pennsylvania (U)
Southeastern Community College (U)
Southeastern Oklahoma State University (U)
Southern Connecticut State University (U)
Southern New Hampshire University (U)
South Piedmont Community College (U)
Southwest Wisconsin Technical College (U)
Spokane Community College (U)
Spoon River College (U)
State University of New York at New Paltz (U)
State University of New York at Oswego (U,G)
State University of New York College at Cortland (U)
State University of New York College at Potsdam (N)
State University of New York Empire State College (U)
State University of New York Institute of Technology (U,G)
Stephens College (U)
Syracuse University (G)
Temple University (U,G)
Thiel College (U)
Tompkins Cortland Community College (U)
Tunxis Community College (U)
Union County College (U)
University at Albany, State University of New York (U)
The University of Akron (U)
University of Alaska Fairbanks (U)
University of Alaska, Prince William Sound Community College (U)
University of Arkansas at Little Rock (U)
University of Colorado at Colorado Springs (U)
University of Denver (G)
University of Dubuque (U)
University of Evansville (U)
University of Florida (U,G)
University of Houston (U)
University of Houston–Downtown (U)
University of Illinois at Springfield (U,G)
University of Illinois at Urbana–Champaign (U)
University of Louisville (G)
University of Maine at Augusta (U)
University of Maine at Fort Kent (U)
University of Maine at Machias (U)
University of Massachusetts Boston (U)
University of Memphis (G)
University of Missouri–Kansas City (U)
University of Nevada, Reno (U)
University of New Haven (U)
University of North Alabama (U)
The University of North Carolina at Chapel Hill (U)
University of North Dakota (U)
University of Northern Iowa (U)
University of Pittsburgh at Bradford (U)
University of Southern Maine (U)
The University of Texas at Arlington (U)
The University of Texas of the Permian Basin (U)
University of the Pacific (U)
University of Toronto (N)
University of Waterloo (N)
University of West Florida (U)
University of West Georgia (U)
University of Wisconsin–Superior (U)
Upper Iowa University (N,U)
Wayland Baptist University (U)
Wayne State University (U,G)
Westchester Community College (U)
West Virginia State University (U,G)
Wichita State University (U)
Wilfrid Laurier University (U)
Wilkes Community College (U)
Wisconsin Indianhead Technical College (N,U)
Worcester State University (N,U)
York College of Pennsylvania (N)
York University (U)

COMMUNICATION DISORDERS SCIENCES AND SERVICES

Athabasca University (N,U)
Auburn University (U)
Bowling Green State University (U)
Bridgewater State University (U)
Brigham Young University (U)
Eastern Illinois University (G)
Eastern Washington University (U)
Florida State University (G)
Fontbonne University (G)
Fort Hays State University (U)
Franklin Pierce University (G)
Hofstra University (U)
Illinois State University (U)
MGH Institute of Health Professions (U,G)
North Carolina Central University (G)
State University of New York at New Paltz (U)
Texas Woman's University (G)
The University of Akron (G)
University of Alaska, Prince William Sound Community College (U)
University of Cincinnati (U,G)
University of Maine (U)
Utah State University (U)

COMMUNICATIONS TECHNOLOGIES AND SUPPORT SERVICES RELATED

Austin Peay State University (U)
Bloomsburg University of Pennsylvania (N)
Boise State University (G)
Bowling Green State University (U)
Dallas Baptist University (U)
Drexel University (U)
Iona College (G)
La Roche College (U)
Marlboro College Graduate College (N)
Quinnipiac University (G)
Sacramento City College (U)
University of Alaska Fairbanks (U)
Wayne State College (G)

COMMUNICATIONS TECHNOLOGY

Arapahoe Community College (U)
Athabasca University (N,U)
Austin Peay State University (U)
Ball State University (G)
Boise State University (G)
Bossier Parish Community College (U)

California State University, San Bernardino (U,G)
Cayuga County Community College (U)
Central Michigan University (G)
Dabney S. Lancaster Community College (N)
Dakota State University (U)
Dallas Baptist University (U)
DeVry University Online (G)
Franklin Pierce University (G)
Gaston College (U)
Grantham University (G)
Hofstra University (U)
Iowa Lakes Community College (U)
James Madison University (U)
Jones International University (U)
Mansfield University of Pennsylvania (N)
Marlboro College Graduate College (N)
Maryville University of Saint Louis (N)
Middlesex Community College (U)
National University (U)
New England Institute of Technology (U)
North Dakota State University (N,G)
North Lake College (U)
Pamlico Community College (U)
Paris Junior College (N)
Regent University (U,G)
Rockingham Community College (N)
Sacramento City College (U)
San Diego Community College District (U)
Santa Rosa Junior College (U)
Seton Hill University (G)
Sinclair Community College (U)
South Piedmont Community College (U)
State University of New York Institute of Technology (G)
Syracuse University (G)
Temple University (U,G)
The University of Akron (N)
University of Alaska Fairbanks (U)
University of Florida (G)
University of Illinois at Urbana–Champaign (G)
University of Missouri–Kansas City (U)
University of New Haven (G)
University of Waterloo (N)
University of West Florida (N,U)
Valencia College (U)
Westmoreland County Community College (U)
Wilkes Community College (U)
Yavapai College (U)

COMMUNITY ORGANIZATION AND ADVOCACY

Athabasca University (N,U,G)
Austin Peay State University (U)
Burlington College (U)
Central Michigan University (U)
DePaul University (G)
Goddard College (U,G)
Kansas State University (U,G)
Lewis-Clark State College (U)
Medical College of Wisconsin (G)
Murray State University (U)
Pace University (U,G)
Penn State University Park (G)
Prescott College (N,G)
The University of Akron (U)
University of Massachusetts Boston (U)
University of Waterloo (U)
Western Kentucky University (U)

COMPUTATIONAL SCIENCE

Antelope Valley College (U)
Luna Community College (U)
University of Alaska Fairbanks (U)

COMPUTER AND INFORMATION SCIENCES

Acadia University (U)
Allen Community College (U)
Alvin Community College (N,U)
Anderson University (U)
Angelina College (U)
Angelo State University (U)
Anne Arundel Community College (N,U)
Antelope Valley College (U)
Arapahoe Community College (U)
Arizona Western College (U)
Arkansas State University–Beebe (U)
Arkansas Tech University (U)
Athabasca University (N,U,G)
Austin Peay State University (N,U)
Bellevue College (U)
Belmont Technical College (U)
Bloomfield College (U)
Bossier Parish Community College (N,U)
Bradley University (U)
Brazosport College (U)
Brenau University (U,G)
Brigham Young University (N)
Bronx Community College of the City University of New York (U)
Burlington County College (U)
Cabrillo College (U)
California State University, Dominguez Hills (N)
California State University, Sacramento (U)
California State University, San Marcos (N)
Campbellsville University (U)
Cape Fear Community College (U)
Capital Community College (U)
Cayuga County Community College (U)
Central Carolina Community College (N)
Centralia College (N)
Central Michigan University (G)
Central New Mexico Community College (U)
Central Oregon Community College (U)
Central Texas College (U)
Central Virginia Community College (U)
Central Wyoming College (U)
Champlain College (U)
Charter Oak State College (U)
Chattanooga State Community College (U)
Chemeketa Community College (U)
Cincinnati State Technical and Community College (U)
Citrus College (U)
City Colleges of Chicago System (U)
Clark State Community College (N)
Clemson University (N)
Cleveland Community College (U)
Cleveland State Community College (N,U)
Clinton Community College (U)
Clovis Community College (U)
Coleman University (U)
The College of St. Scholastica (U)
College of San Mateo (U)
Colorado State University (G)
Columbia College (U)
Columbia University (N,G)
Columbus State Community College (U)
Community College of Beaver County (N,U)
Cossatot Community College of the University of Arkansas (N,U)
Dabney S. Lancaster Community College (N)
Dakota College at Bottineau (U)
Dakota State University (U,G)
Dallas Baptist University (U,G)
Delgado Community College (U)
DeVry University Online (U,G)
Drake University (U)
Drexel University (U,G)
Drury University (U)
Duquesne University (N)
D'Youville College (U)
East Central Community College (U)
Eastern West Virginia Community and Technical College (U)
Eastern Wyoming College (U)
East Los Angeles College (U)
Edgecombe Community College (N,U)
Edison State Community College (N,U)
Endicott College (G)
Enterprise State Community College (U)
Excelsior College (U)
Faulkner University (U)
Finger Lakes Community College (U)
Five Towns College (U)
Florida State University (G)
Fontbonne University (U)
Fort Hays State University (U)
Fort Valley State University (U)
Franklin Pierce University (U,G)
Front Range Community College (U)
Frostburg State University (U)
Gaston College (U)
Genesee Community College (U)
Georgia Institute of Technology (G)
Georgia State University (U)
Graceland University (U)
Grantham University (U)
Harford Community College (N)
Haywood Community College (U)
Herkimer County Community College (U)
Hibbing Community College (N,U)
Hillsborough Community College (U)
Hofstra University (U,G)
Hopkinsville Community College (N)
Illinois Eastern Community Colleges, Olney Central College (U)
Indiana Wesleyan University (U)
Inter American University of Puerto Rico, San Germán Campus (U)
Iona College (G)
Jacksonville State University (U,G)
James Madison University (N)
Jamestown Community College (N,U)
John A. Logan College (U)
The Johns Hopkins University (G)
Johnston Community College (U)
Kansas State University (U,G)
Kean University (N)
Kilian Community College (U)
Kirkwood Community College (N)
Lake Superior College (U)
Lamar State College–Port Arthur (N,U)
Lansing Community College (U)
La Roche College (U)
Lenoir Community College (U)
Long Beach City College (U)
Los Angeles Harbor College (U)
Luna Community College (U)
Macon State College (U)

Maharishi University of Management (G)
Mansfield University of Pennsylvania (N,U)
Marian University (U)
Marlboro College Graduate College (N,U)
Marquette University (G)
Marshall University (U,G)
Maryville University of Saint Louis (N,U)
McKendree University (U)
McNeese State University (U)
Mercer County Community College (U)
Miami Dade College (U)
Michigan Technological University (N,U)
Middlesex Community College (U)
Middle Tennessee State University (N,U)
Midland College (N,U)
Midstate College (U)
Mid-State Technical College (U)
Midwestern State University (U)
Milwaukee School of Engineering (U)
Minnesota School of Business–Online (U)
Mississippi State University (U)
Missouri Baptist University (U)
Missouri University of Science and Technology (N,G)
Mitchell Technical Institute (N)
Monroe College (U)
Monroe County Community College (U)
Montcalm Community College (N)
Montgomery Community College (N,U)
Montgomery County Community College (U)
Moorpark College (U)
Motlow State Community College (U)
Mountain Empire Community College (U)
Mount Wachusett Community College (N)
Murray State University (U)
Nashville State Technical Community College (N)
Nassau Community College (U)
National University (G)
Naugatuck Valley Community College (U)
New England College of Business and Finance (U)
New England Institute of Technology (U)
New Mexico State University (U)
New Mexico State University–Alamogordo (U)
New Mexico State University–Carlsbad (U)
Nichols College (U)
North Central State College (N)
North Central Texas College (U)
North Dakota State College of Science (U)
North Dakota State University (N,U)
Northern State University (U)
North Georgia College & State University (U)
North Hennepin Community College (N,U)
North Lake College (U)
North Shore Community College (N)
NorthWest Arkansas Community College (U)
Northwestern Connecticut Community College (N,U)
Northwestern Michigan College (U)
Northwest-Shoals Community College (U)
Oakland Community College (U)
Oakton Community College (N,U)
Ocean County College (U)
Odessa College (U)
The Ohio State University (U)
Okefenokee Technical College (N,U)
Oklahoma Panhandle State University (U)
Olympic College (U)
Orange Coast College (U)
Ouachita Technical College (U)
Oxnard College (U)
Ozarks Technical Community College (U)
Pace University (N,G)
Palm Beach State College (U)
Pamlico Community College (U)
Paris Junior College (N)
Pasco-Hernando Community College (N,U)
Pellissippi State Technical Community College (U)
Peninsula College (N,U)
Penn State University Park (G)
Pennsylvania College of Technology (U)
Pittsburg State University (U)
Pulaski Technical College (U)
Quinnipiac University (G)
Quinsigamond Community College (U)
Randolph Community College (N,U)
Reading Area Community College (U)
Rio Hondo College (U)
Riverside Community College District (U)
Robert Morris University (G)
Rochester Institute of Technology (G)
Rockingham Community College (N)
Rowan-Cabarrus Community College (N,U)
Sacramento City College (U)
The Sage Colleges (U)
St. Clair County Community College (U)
Saint Francis University (U)
St. Louis Community College (N,U)
Saint Mary-of-the-Woods College (U)
St. Petersburg College (N)
Sampson Community College (N,U)
San Diego Community College District (N,U)
San Jacinto College District (U)
Santa Rosa Junior College (U)
Sauk Valley Community College (N,U)
Seton Hill University (U)
Sinclair Community College (U)
Slippery Rock University of Pennsylvania (U)
Southeastern Community College (U)
Southeastern Illinois College (U)
Southeastern Oklahoma State University (U)
Southern Arkansas University–Magnolia (G)
Southern Illinois University Carbondale (U)
Southern Methodist University (G)
Southern New Hampshire University (U)
South Piedmont Community College (U)
South Suburban College (U)
Southwest Wisconsin Technical College (U)
Spartanburg Community College (N,U)
Spokane Community College (U)
Stanly Community College (U)
State University of New York at Oswego (U)
State University of New York College at Potsdam (N)
State University of New York College of Technology at Canton (U)
Stephens College (U)
Sullivan County Community College (U)
Syracuse University (U,G)
Tarleton State University (G)
Taylor University (U)
Texas State Technical College West Texas (U)
Texas Woman's University (U)
Three Rivers Community College (U)
Tompkins Cortland Community College (U)
Trident Technical College (U)
Tunxis Community College (N,U)
Tyler Junior College (N,U)
Union County College (U)
University at Albany, State University of New York (U,G)
The University of Akron (N,U,G)
University of Alaska Fairbanks (U,G)
University of Alaska, Prince William Sound Community College (U)
The University of British Columbia (U)
University of Cincinnati (N,U)
University of Denver (G)
University of Dubuque (U)
University of Florida (G)
University of Great Falls (U)
University of Houston–Victoria (U,G)
University of Illinois at Chicago (G)
University of Illinois at Urbana–Champaign (N,G)
University of Maine at Augusta (U)
University of Maine at Fort Kent (U)
University of Management and Technology (U)
University of Mary Washington (G)
University of Massachusetts Boston (U)
University of Memphis (N,U)
University of Michigan–Dearborn (U,G)
University of Minnesota, Crookston (U)
University of Missouri–Kansas City (U)
University of Nevada, Reno (U)
University of North Alabama (U)
The University of North Carolina at Chapel Hill (U)
University of North Dakota (U)
University of North Florida (U)
University of St. Francis (U)
University of South Alabama (U)
The University of Tennessee at Martin (N)
The University of Texas of the Permian Basin (U)
University of the Southwest (U)
University of Waterloo (U)
University of West Georgia (U,G)
University of Wisconsin–Milwaukee (U,G)
Valencia College (U)
Vincennes University (U)
Wayne State University (U,G)
Webber International University (U,G)
Webster University (U)
Westchester Community College (U)
Western Kentucky University (U)
West Hills Community College (U)
West Los Angeles College (U)
Westmoreland County Community College (N)
West Shore Community College (U)
West Virginia Northern Community College (N)
Wharton County Junior College (U)
Wilkes Community College (U)
Windward Community College (U)
Wisconsin Indianhead Technical College (N,U)
Worcester State University (N,U)
York County Community College (U)
Youngstown State University (N)

COMPUTER AND INFORMATION SCIENCES AND SUPPORT SERVICES RELATED

Acadia University (U)
Alvin Community College (N)
Antelope Valley College (U)
Arapahoe Community College (U)
Athabasca University (U,G)
Austin Peay State University (N,U)

Baptist Bible College of Pennsylvania (G)
Bellevue College (U)
Belmont Technical College (U)
Blackhawk Technical College (U)
Boise State University (U)
Bossier Parish Community College (U)
Bowling Green State University (N)
Caldwell College (U)
California State University, San Marcos (U)
Cascadia Community College (U)
Cayuga County Community College (U)
Central Michigan University (G)
Central Texas College (U)
Champlain College (U)
Chatham University (U)
Chemeketa Community College (U)
Cincinnati State Technical and Community College (U)
Cleary University (U)
Cleveland State Community College (N)
Colorado State University (G)
Columbia Basin College (U)
Cossatot Community College of the University of Arkansas (N)
Dakota College at Bottineau (U)
Dakota State University (U,G)
Dallas Baptist University (U)
DePaul University (U)
Drexel University (G)
East Los Angeles College (U)
Edgecombe Community College (N,U)
Elaine P. Nunez Community College (U)
Enterprise State Community College (U)
Genesee Community College (N)
Iona College (U)
Jacksonville State University (U,G)
Jamestown Community College (N,U)
John A. Logan College (U)
John Jay College of Criminal Justice of the City University of New York (U)
Kansas State University (U,G)
Lansing Community College (U)
Lewis-Clark State College (U)
Lock Haven University of Pennsylvania (N)
Long Beach City College (U)
Mansfield University of Pennsylvania (N)
Marlboro College Graduate College (N)
Marshall University (U)
McNeese State University (N)
Mercer County Community College (U)
Middlesex Community College (U)
Midland College (N)
Mid-State Technical College (U)
Minnesota School of Business–Online (U)
North Central State College (N)
North Dakota State College of Science (U)
North Hennepin Community College (N)
NorthWest Arkansas Community College (U)
Northwestern Michigan College (U)
Odessa College (U)
Ohio University (N)
Olympic College (U)
Pace University (U,G)
Pamlico Community College (U)
Peninsula College (N)
Phoenix College (N)
Pikes Peak Community College (U)
Quinebaug Valley Community College (N)
Quinsigamond Community College (N)
Sacramento City College (U)
Saint Francis University (U)
St. Louis Community College (U)
Sampson Community College (U)
San Diego Community College District (U)
Santa Rosa Junior College (U)
Sauk Valley Community College (U)
Sinclair Community College (U)
Southern Methodist University (G)
South Piedmont Community College (U)
Southwest Virginia Community College (N)
Stanly Community College (U)
Stephens College (U)
Tarleton State University (G)
Tyler Junior College (U)
University at Albany, State University of New York (G)
The University of Akron (N)
University of Alaska Fairbanks (U)
University of Colorado at Colorado Springs (N)
University of Denver (G)
University of Evansville (N)
University of Maine (U)
University of Maine at Augusta (U)
University of Missouri–Kansas City (U)
Wake Technical Community College (N,U)
Wayne Community College (N)
Webber International University (U)
Webster University (G)
Westchester Community College (U)
Western Kentucky University (U)
West Hills Community College (U)
Wilkes Community College (U)
York Technical College (N)

COMPUTER ENGINEERING

Austin Peay State University (U)
Cleveland Institute of Electronics (U)
Columbia University (N,G)
Cossatot Community College of the University of Arkansas (N)
Drexel University (G)
Edison State Community College (U)
Georgia Institute of Technology (N,G)
Grantham University (U)
Hopkinsville Community College (U)
Jacksonville State University (G)
Jamestown Community College (U)
The Johns Hopkins University (G)
Kansas State University (U,G)
Marshall University (U)
Mississippi State University (G)
North Dakota State University (G)
Oxnard College (U)
Sacramento City College (U)
San Diego State University (U)
Shippensburg University of Pennsylvania (U)
Southern Methodist University (G)
The University of Alabama in Huntsville (G)
University of Alaska Fairbanks (U)
University of Colorado Boulder (N,G)
University of Florida (N,G)
University of Idaho (U,G)
University of Michigan–Dearborn (G)
University of Missouri–Kansas City (U)
University of North Florida (U)
University of West Florida (N)

COMPUTER ENGINEERING TECHNOLOGIES

Austin Peay State University (N,U)
Cape Fear Community College (U)
Columbia University (N,G)
Drexel University (G)
Georgia Institute of Technology (G)
Grantham University (U)
Haywood Community College (U)
Iona College (G)
Jamestown Community College (U)
Kansas State University (U,G)
Lenoir Community College (U)
Prairie View A&M University (U)
Sacramento City College (U)
Southern Methodist University (G)
The University of Alabama in Huntsville (G)
University of Missouri–Kansas City (U)
Wake Technical Community College (U)
West Virginia University (G)

COMPUTER/INFORMATION TECHNOLOGY ADMINISTRATION AND MANAGEMENT

Alpena Community College (U)
Alvin Community College (U)
Arapahoe Community College (U)
Arkansas State University (U)
Ashland University (U)
Athabasca University (N,U,G)
Auburn University (N)
Austin Peay State University (U)
Bridgewater State University (U)
California State University, Dominguez Hills (N)
Capital Community College (U)
Central Carolina Technical College (U)
Central Washington University (U)
Champlain College (U)
Cincinnati State Technical and Community College (U)
Cleveland Community College (U)
Cleveland Institute of Electronics (N)
Coleman University (U)
College of Southern Maryland (N)
Cossatot Community College of the University of Arkansas (N)
Dakota State University (U)
Dallas Baptist University (G)
Drexel University (G)
D'Youville College (U)
Eastern Illinois University (G)
Eastern West Virginia Community and Technical College (U)
Edgecombe Community College (N,U)
Edison State Community College (N,U)
Erie Community College (U)
Erie Community College, North Campus (U)
Erie Community College, South Campus (U)
Ferris State University (G)
Finger Lakes Community College (U)
Florida State University (N)
Franklin Pierce University (G)
Granite State College (U)
Grantham University (U)
Haywood Community College (U)
Hillsborough Community College (U)
Houston Community College System (U)
Illinois Valley Community College (U)
Iona College (G)
Jacksonville State University (U,G)
Jamestown Community College (U)
The Johns Hopkins University (G)
Jones International University (U)
Kansas State University (U,G)

Kettering University (N)
Keystone College (U)
Lamar State College–Port Arthur (N)
Lansing Community College (U)
Lawrence Technological University (U,G)
Liberty University (U)
Macon State College (U)
Marlboro College Graduate College (N,U)
Maryville University of Saint Louis (U)
McKendree University (U)
McMurry University (U)
Mercer County Community College (N)
Mesa Community College (U)
Middle Tennessee State University (N)
Minnesota School of Business–Online (U)
Monroe College (U)
Murray State University (G)
New Mexico State University (U)
North Arkansas College (U)
North Central Texas College (U)
North Dakota State College of Science (U)
NorthWest Arkansas Community College (U)
Orange Coast College (U)
Oregon Institute of Technology (U)
Oxnard College (U)
Pace University (G)
Pamlico Community College (U)
Peru State College (U)
Pittsburgh Technical Institute (U)
Prairie View A&M University (G)
Rend Lake College (U)
Rochester Institute of Technology (G)
Rogers State University (U)
Rose State College (U)
Rowan-Cabarrus Community College (U)
Sacramento City College (U)
Saint Francis University (U)
Saint Leo University (U)
Saint Paul College–A Community & Technical College (U)
St. Petersburg College (N)
Salem Community College (U)
San Diego Community College District (U)
Sauk Valley Community College (U)
Seminole State College of Florida (U)
Sonoma State University (N)
Southeast Arkansas College (U)
Southern Illinois University Carbondale (U)
Southern Methodist University (G)
South Piedmont Community College (U)
Spokane Community College (U)
State University of New York College of Agriculture and Technology at Morrisville (U)
State University of New York Empire State College (U)
Syracuse University (G)
Tarleton State University (G)
Taylor University (U)
Trident Technical College (U)
Tyler Junior College (U)
University at Albany, State University of New York (U,G)
The University of Akron (N)
University of Cincinnati Raymond Walters College (U)
University of Denver (G)
University of Dubuque (U)
University of Houston–Downtown (U)
University of Illinois at Urbana–Champaign (G)
University of Management and Technology (U)
University of Mary (U)
University of Mary Washington (G)
University of Massachusetts Boston (U)
University of Memphis (U)
University of Missouri–Kansas City (U)
University of North Florida (U)
The University of Texas at Arlington (U)
University of Toronto (N)
University of Virginia (U)
Valencia College (U)
Vincennes University (U)
Wayne Community College (U)
Webber International University (U)
Western Kentucky University (U)
West Hills Community College (U)
West Los Angeles College (U)
Yavapai College (U)
York County Community College (U)
Youngstown State University (U)

COMPUTER PROGRAMMING

Acadia University (U)
Alvin Community College (U)
Angelina College (U)
Arapahoe Community College (U)
Arkansas State University–Beebe (U)
Athabasca University (N,U)
Austin Peay State University (U)
Bellevue College (U)
Belmont Technical College (U)
Blackhawk Technical College (U)
Bossier Parish Community College (N)
Butler Community College (U)
Butler County Community College (U)
California State University, San Marcos (U)
Cayuga County Community College (U)
Central Carolina Community College (U)
Centralia College (N)
Central New Mexico Community College (U)
Central Texas College (U)
Champlain College (U)
Chemeketa Community College (U)
Citrus College (U)
Clemson University (N)
Cleveland Community College (U)
Cleveland Institute of Electronics (N)
Clinton Community College (U)
Coleman University (U)
College of San Mateo (U)
Columbia Basin College (U)
Columbia-Greene Community College (U)
Columbia University (N,G)
Columbus State Community College (U)
Columbus State University (G)
Community College of Beaver County (U)
Corning Community College (U)
Cossatot Community College of the University of Arkansas (N,U)
Dakota State University (U)
Danville Community College (U)
Daytona State College (U)
DePaul University (U,G)
Edgecombe Community College (N,U)
Edison State Community College (U)
Finger Lakes Community College (U)
Front Range Community College (U)
Gaston College (U)
Granite State College (U)
Grantham University (U)
Greenville Technical College (U)
Hagerstown Community College (N)
Harford Community College (N)
Harrisburg Area Community College (U)
Haywood Community College (U)
Hibbing Community College (U)
Hillsborough Community College (U)
Indiana State University (U)
Iona College (U)
Jacksonville State University (U,G)
James A. Rhodes State College (U)
Jamestown Community College (U)
The Johns Hopkins University (G)
Kansas State University (U,G)
Kean University (N)
Labette Community College (U)
Lamar State College–Orange (U)
Lamar State College–Port Arthur (N,U)
Lansing Community College (U)
Lenoir Community College (U)
Lewis-Clark State College (U)
Lock Haven University of Pennsylvania (U)
Long Beach City College (U)
Los Angeles Harbor College (U)
Macon State College (U)
Mansfield University of Pennsylvania (N)
Marlboro College Graduate College (U)
Maryville University of Saint Louis (U)
McKendree University (U)
McNeese State University (N)
Mercer County Community College (U)
Mesa Community College (U)
Miami Dade College (U)
Middlesex Community College (U)
Middle Tennessee State University (N)
Minnesota School of Business–Online (U)
Minot State University (U)
Monroe College (U)
Montcalm Community College (U)
Montgomery County Community College (U)
Mount Wachusett Community College (U)
Murray State University (N)
Nashville State Technical Community College (U)
National University (G)
New River Community College (U)
North Arkansas College (U)
North Carolina State University (U)
North Central State College (N)
North Dakota State College of Science (U)
North Dakota State University (N,U,G)
North Lake College (U)
North Seattle Community College (U)
NorthWest Arkansas Community College (U)
Northwestern Michigan College (U)
Oakland Community College (U)
Olympic College (U)
Orange Coast College (U)
Oxnard College (U)
Pace University (U,G)
Pamlico Community College (U)
Pasco-Hernando Community College (N)
Piedmont Community College (U)
Pikes Peak Community College (U)
Pine Technical College (U)
Portland Community College (U)
Quinsigamond Community College (U)
Rend Lake College (U)
Rio Hondo College (U)
Rockingham Community College (N)
Rose State College (U)
Sacramento City College (U)

Saint Paul College–A Community & Technical College (U)
San Diego Community College District (U)
San Diego State University (N)
Santa Monica College (U)
Santa Rosa Junior College (U)
Sauk Valley Community College (U)
Seminole State College of Florida (N,U)
Sinclair Community College (U)
Southeast Arkansas College (U)
South Piedmont Community College (U)
Southwest Wisconsin Technical College (U)
Spartanburg Community College (N)
Spokane Community College (U)
State University of New York College at Potsdam (N)
Sullivan County Community College (U)
Tarleton State University (N,U,G)
Tompkins Cortland Community College (U)
Trident Technical College (U)
Tyler Junior College (N,U)
University at Albany, State University of New York (U)
The University of Akron (N)
University of Alaska Fairbanks (U)
University of Cincinnati (N)
University of Colorado at Colorado Springs (N)
University of Florida (G)
University of Idaho (U)
University of Management and Technology (U)
University of Missouri–Kansas City (U)
University of North Dakota (N)
University of North Florida (U)
University of Waterloo (N)
University of West Florida (U)
Utah State University (G)
Valencia College (U)
Wake Technical Community College (N,U)
Wayne State University (U,G)
Webber International University (U)
Westchester Community College (U)
Wilkes Community College (U)
Winston-Salem State University (U)
Wisconsin Indianhead Technical College (N,U)
York County Community College (U)

COMPUTER SCIENCE

Acadia University (U)
Alvin Community College (U)
Angelo State University (U)
Anne Arundel Community College (U)
Arapahoe Community College (U)
Arkansas State University–Mountain Home (U)
Ashland University (U)
Athabasca University (N,U,G)
Auburn University (U,G)
Austin Peay State University (U)
Baker College Online (U)
Baldwin-Wallace College (U)
Ball State University (U)
Bellevue College (U)
Belmont Technical College (U)
Beulah Heights University (U)
Bossier Parish Community College (U)
Bowling Green State University (U)
Bronx Community College of the City University of New York (U)
Broward College (U)
Buffalo State College, State University of New York (U)
Butler Community College (U)
Butler County Community College (U)
Cabrillo College (U)
California State University, Monterey Bay (U)
Carl Sandburg College (U)
Carroll University (U,G)
Cayuga County Community College (U)
Central Carolina Community College (U)
Central Texas College (U)
Central Wyoming College (U)
Chattanooga State Community College (U)
Chemeketa Community College (U)
City Colleges of Chicago System (U)
Clackamas Community College (U)
Clarion University of Pennsylvania (U)
Cleveland Institute of Electronics (N)
Coastal Carolina University (U)
The College at Brockport, State University of New York (U)
College of the Siskiyous (U)
Colorado Mountain College (U)
Columbia Basin College (U)
Columbia University (N,U,G)
Columbus State University (U)
Community College of Allegheny County (U)
Community College of Beaver County (N,U)
Concordia University Wisconsin (U)
Corning Community College (U)
Cossatot Community College of the University of Arkansas (N)
Dakota State University (U)
Dallas Baptist University (U)
Danville Community College (U)
DePaul University (U,G)
Dickinson State University (U)
Drexel University (U,G)
Eastern Oregon University (U)
Edgecombe Community College (N)
Edison State Community College (U)
Enterprise State Community College (U)
Erie Community College (U)
Erie Community College, North Campus (U)
Erie Community College, South Campus (U)
Fayetteville State University (U)
Ferris State University (U)
Fitchburg State University (U,G)
Fort Valley State University (U)
Framingham State University (U)
Friends University (U)
Front Range Community College (U)
Gadsden State Community College (U)
Georgia Institute of Technology (G)
Grantham University (U)
Harrisburg Area Community College (U)
Haywood Community College (U)
Heartland Community College (U)
Hibbing Community College (U)
Hillsborough Community College (U)
Hofstra University (N,U,G)
Holyoke Community College (U)
Hopkinsville Community College (U)
Houston Community College System (U)
Indiana State University (U)
Indiana University of Pennsylvania (U)
Indiana University–Purdue University Fort Wayne (U)
Inter American University of Puerto Rico, San Germán Campus (U)
Iona College (G)
Itasca Community College (U)
Jacksonville State University (U,G)
James Madison University (G)
Jamestown College (U)
Jamestown Community College (U)
John A. Logan College (U)
J. Sargeant Reynolds Community College (U)
Kansas State University (U,G)
Labette Community College (U)
Lamar State College–Orange (U)
Lamar State College–Port Arthur (N,U)
Lansing Community College (U)
Lehman College of the City University of New York (U)
Lewis-Clark State College (U)
Long Beach City College (U)
Marlboro College Graduate College (U)
Marymount University (G)
McKendree University (U)
Memorial University of Newfoundland (U)
Mesa Community College (U)
Metropolitan Community College–Penn Valley (U)
Miami Dade College (U)
Middlesex Community College (U)
Middle Tennessee State University (N)
Midway College (U)
Minnesota School of Business–Online (U)
Minnesota School of Business–Richfield (U)
Minot State University (U)
Mississippi College (U)
Mississippi State University (U,G)
Missouri University of Science and Technology (N,G)
Montgomery County Community College (U)
National University (G)
Naugatuck Valley Community College (U)
New Jersey City University (U)
New Mexico Highlands University (U)
New Mexico State University (U)
New Mexico State University–Grants (U)
New River Community College (U)
North Dakota State University (N,U,G)
North Hennepin Community College (N)
North Shore Community College (U)
Notre Dame College (U)
Oakton Community College (U)
Odessa College (U)
Oxnard College (U)
Pace University (U)
Peru State College (U)
Phoenix College (U)
Pikes Peak Community College (U)
Portland Community College (U)
Quinnipiac University (U)
Rend Lake College (U)
Richmond Community College (U)
Riverside Community College District (U)
Rockingham Community College (N)
Rockland Community College (U)
Rose State College (U)
Sacramento City College (U)
Saint Francis University (U)
St. John's University (U)
Saint Paul College–A Community & Technical College (U)
St. Petersburg College (U)
San Diego Community College District (N,U)
San Jacinto College District (U)
Santa Monica College (U)
Santa Rosa Junior College (U)
Shippensburg University of Pennsylvania (U)

Sinclair Community College (U)
Southeast Arkansas College (U)
Southeastern Community College (U)
Southeastern Oklahoma State University (U)
Southern Illinois University Edwardsville (U)
Southern Methodist University (G)
Southern Oregon University (U)
Southern Union State Community College (U)
South Piedmont Community College (U)
South Suburban College (U)
Spokane Community College (U)
State University of New York at New Paltz (U,G)
State University of New York at Oswego (U)
Taft College (U)
Tarleton State University (G)
Taylor University (U)
Tyler Junior College (U)
Union County College (U)
Union University (U)
University at Albany, State University of New York (U)
The University of Akron (N,U)
The University of Alabama in Huntsville (G)
University of Alaska Fairbanks (U)
The University of Arizona (U)
University of Colorado Boulder (N,G)
The University of Findlay (U)
University of Florida (G)
University of Great Falls (U)
University of Houston (G)
University of Houston–Downtown (U)
University of Idaho (U,G)
University of Illinois at Chicago (G)
University of Illinois at Springfield (U,G)
University of Illinois at Urbana–Champaign (G)
University of Management and Technology (U)
University of Mary Washington (U)
University of Michigan–Dearborn (U,G)
University of Michigan–Flint (U)
University of Missouri–Kansas City (U)
University of Saskatchewan (U)
The University of Tennessee at Chattanooga (U)
The University of Texas at Brownsville (U)
The University of Texas of the Permian Basin (U)
University of Waterloo (U)
University of West Florida (U,G)
University of West Georgia (U)
University of Windsor (U)
University of Wisconsin–Parkside (U)
Utah State University (G)
Valencia College (U)
Vermont Technical College (U)
Wayne State University (U)
Webber International University (U)
Westchester Community College (U)
Western Kentucky University (U)
Western Texas College (U)
Western Wyoming Community College (U)
West Los Angeles College (U)
West Virginia University (G)
Wharton County Junior College (U)
Wilkes Community College (U)
Worcester State University (N)
York Technical College (U)

COMPUTER SOFTWARE AND MEDIA APPLICATIONS

Adams State College (N)
Allen Community College (U)
Alvin Community College (U)
Angelina College (U)
Arapahoe Community College (U)
Athabasca University (N,U)
Austin Peay State University (N,U)
The Baptist College of Florida (U)
Bellevue College (U)
Belmont Technical College (U)
Blackhawk Technical College (N)
Bossier Parish Community College (N,U)
Bowling Green State University (N)
Brigham Young University (N)
Brigham Young University–Idaho (U)
Burlington County College (U)
Butler Community College (U)
Butler County Community College (N)
California State University, Sacramento (U)
Capital Community College (U)
Cardinal Stritch University (N)
Carl Sandburg College (U)
Carroll University (G)
Cascadia Community College (U)
Cayuga County Community College (U)
Centralia College (N,U)
Central Oregon Community College (N)
Central Texas College (U)
Central Virginia Community College (U)
Central Washington University (U)
Central Wyoming College (N)
Champlain College (U)
Chatham University (N)
Chemeketa Community College (U)
Cincinnati State Technical and Community College (U)
Clark State Community College (N,U)
Clemson University (N)
Cleveland Community College (U)
Cleveland Institute of Electronics (N)
Cleveland State Community College (N)
The College at Brockport, State University of New York (U)
College of San Mateo (U)
Colorado Mountain College (U)
Columbia Basin College (U)
Columbia University (N,G)
Columbus State Community College (U)
Community College of Beaver County (N,U)
Corning Community College (U)
Cossatot Community College of the University of Arkansas (N)
Dallas Baptist University (U,G)
Danville Community College (U)
Dawson Community College (U)
DePaul University (U,G)
Dickinson State University (U)
Eastern Wyoming College (U)
Edgecombe Community College (N,U)
Edison State Community College (N,U)
Enterprise State Community College (U)
Erie Community College (U)
Erie Community College, North Campus (U)
Erie Community College, South Campus (U)
Excelsior College (U)
Finger Lakes Community College (N)
Florida State University (N)
Front Range Community College (U)
Gaston College (U)
Glenville State College (U)
Grantham University (U)
Hagerstown Community College (N)
Harrisburg Area Community College (U)
Haywood Community College (U)
Heartland Community College (N)
Herkimer County Community College (U)
Hibbing Community College (N,U)
Hillsborough Community College (U)
Illinois Eastern Community Colleges, Lincoln Trail College (U)
Illinois Valley Community College (U)
Indiana Wesleyan University (U)
Iona College (U,G)
Iowa Lakes Community College (N,U)
Jacksonville State University (U,G)
James A. Rhodes State College (U)
Jamestown Community College (N,U)
Jefferson Community College (N)
John A. Logan College (U)
Jones International University (U,G)
J. Sargeant Reynolds Community College (U)
Judson University (U)
Kansas State University (U,G)
Kean University (N)
Kirkwood Community College (N,U)
Labette Community College (U)
Lake-Sumter Community College (U)
Lake Superior College (U)
Lamar State College–Port Arthur (N,U)
Lansing Community College (U)
Long Beach City College (U)
Los Angeles Trade-Technical College (U)
Louisiana State University at Eunice (U)
Luzerne County Community College (N)
Macon State College (U)
Mansfield University of Pennsylvania (N)
Marlboro College Graduate College (N,U)
Maryville University of Saint Louis (N,U)
McNeese State University (N)
Mercer County Community College (U)
Mesa Community College (U)
Miami Dade College (U)
Middlesex Community College (N,U)
Middle Tennessee State University (N)
Midland College (U)
Midstate College (U)
Minnesota School of Business–Online (U)
Mitchell Technical Institute (N)
Monroe County Community College (U)
Montgomery Community College (N,U)
Montgomery County Community College (U)
Mount Wachusett Community College (N,U)
Murray State College (U)
National University (U,G)
Naugatuck Valley Community College (U)
New Mexico Junior College (U)
New Mexico State University–Carlsbad (U)
Nicolet Area Technical College (U)
North Central Texas College (U)
North Dakota State University (N,U,G)
North Hennepin Community College (N)
North Iowa Area Community College (N)
North Seattle Community College (U)
North Shore Community College (N)
NorthWest Arkansas Community College (U)
Northwestern Connecticut Community College (N)
Northwestern Michigan College (U)
Oakland Community College (U)
Oakton Community College (U)
Ocean County College (U)

Odessa College (N)
Orange Coast College (U)
Oregon State University (N)
Ouachita Technical College (U)
Oxnard College (U)
Pace University (U,G)
Pamlico Community College (U)
Pasco-Hernando Community College (N)
Pellissippi State Technical Community College (U)
Peninsula College (N,U)
Pikes Peak Community College (U)
Portland Community College (U)
Quinebaug Valley Community College (N)
Randolph Community College (N,U)
Rend Lake College (N,U)
Richmond Community College (N)
Rockingham Community College (N,U)
Rose State College (U)
Rowan-Cabarrus Community College (N,U)
Sacramento City College (U)
St. Louis Community College (U)
Saint Paul College–A Community & Technical College (U)
St. Philip's College (U)
San Diego Community College District (N,U)
San Diego State University (N)
San Jacinto College District (U)
Santa Fe Community College (U)
Santa Rosa Junior College (U)
Sauk Valley Community College (U)
Sinclair Community College (U)
Sonoma State University (N)
Southeast Arkansas College (U)
Southeastern Community College (U)
Southeastern Illinois College (U)
Southeastern Oklahoma State University (N)
Southern Methodist University (G)
South Piedmont Community College (U)
Southwest Wisconsin Technical College (U)
Spartanburg Community College (N,U)
Spokane Community College (U)
Spring Arbor University (U)
State University of New York College at Cortland (U)
State University of New York College at Potsdam (N)
State University of New York College of Agriculture and Technology at Morrisville (U)
Stephens College (U)
Sullivan County Community College (N)
Syracuse University (G)
Tarleton State University (N,U,G)
Texas Woman's University (N)
Thiel College (U)
Three Rivers Community College (N)
Tompkins Cortland Community College (N,U)
Trident Technical College (U)
Tyler Junior College (N,U)
The University of Akron (N,U,G)
University of Alaska Fairbanks (U)
University of California, Riverside (N)
University of Cincinnati (U)
University of Cincinnati Raymond Walters College (U)
University of Colorado at Colorado Springs (N)
University of Florida (G)
University of Great Falls (U)
University of Illinois at Urbana–Champaign (N,G)
University of Lethbridge (U)
University of Maine at Augusta (U)
University of Management and Technology (U)
University of Michigan–Flint (N)
The University of Montana Western (N,U)
University of North Dakota (N)
The University of Tennessee at Chattanooga (N)
The University of Texas at Brownsville (N)
University of Waterloo (N)
University of West Florida (U)
Utah State University (G)
Wake Technical Community College (N,U)
Wayne Community College (N,U)
Wayne State University (U,G)
Webber International University (U)
Western Wyoming Community College (U)
Westmoreland County Community College (U)
West Virginia Northern Community College (U)
West Virginia University (N)
Wharton County Junior College (U)
York County Community College (U)
Youngstown State University (N)

COMPUTER SYSTEMS ANALYSIS

Albertus Magnus College (U)
Arapahoe Community College (U)
Athabasca University (N,U,G)
Austin Peay State University (N,U)
Bloomfield College (U)
Bossier Parish Community College (N)
Cayuga County Community College (U)
Centralia College (N)
Central Michigan University (G)
Central Texas College (U)
College of Southern Maryland (U)
Columbia University (N,G)
Dakota State University (U)
Dallas Baptist University (U,G)
Edgecombe Community College (U)
Edison State Community College (U)
Erie Community College (U)
Erie Community College, North Campus (U)
Erie Community College, South Campus (U)
Georgia Institute of Technology (G)
Granite State College (U)
Grantham University (U)
Haywood Community College (U)
Iona College (G)
Jacksonville State University (U,G)
Jamestown Community College (U)
Kirkwood Community College (N)
Lamar State College–Port Arthur (N)
Lansing Community College (U)
Lewis-Clark State College (U)
Macon State College (U)
Mansfield University of Pennsylvania (N)
Marlboro College Graduate College (U)
Maryville University of Saint Louis (N)
McNeese State University (N)
Middlesex Community College (N)
Midland College (N)
Minnesota School of Business–Online (U)
Monroe College (U)
National University (G)
North Dakota State University (U,G)
Oakland Community College (U)
Oxnard College (U)
Pace University (G)
Portland Community College (U)
Rend Lake College (U)
Robert Morris University (U)
Rockingham Community College (N)
Rose State College (U)
Sacramento City College (U)
Southeast Arkansas College (U)
Southern University at New Orleans (U)
Syracuse University (G)
Tarleton State University (G)
Tyler Junior College (U)
The University of Akron (N)
University of California, Davis (U)
University of Florida (G)
University of Illinois at Urbana–Champaign (G)
University of Management and Technology (U)
University of North Dakota (U)
Utah State University (G)
Wake Technical Community College (U)
Webber International University (U)
Westchester Community College (U)

COMPUTER SYSTEMS NETWORKING AND TELECOMMUNICATIONS

Alpena Community College (U)
Arapahoe Community College (U)
Athabasca University (U)
Austin Peay State University (N,U)
Blackhawk Technical College (U)
Bloomfield College (U)
Bossier Parish Community College (U)
Boston University (G)
Butler Community College (U)
Butler County Community College (U)
California State University, East Bay (U)
Cape Fear Community College (U)
Carl Sandburg College (U)
Cayuga County Community College (U)
Central Texas College (U)
Champlain College (U)
Charter Oak State College (U)
Chemeketa Community College (U)
Cincinnati State Technical and Community College (U)
City University of Seattle (U)
Clemson University (N)
Cleveland Community College (U)
College of Southern Maryland (U)
Columbia University (N,G)
Columbus State Community College (U)
Corning Community College (U)
Dallas Baptist University (U,G)
DePaul University (U,G)
DeVry University Online (G)
Edgecombe Community College (U)
Edison State Community College (U)
Franklin Pierce University (G)
Gaston College (U)
Grantham University (U)
Hagerstown Community College (N)
Harford Community College (N)
Haywood Community College (U)
Herkimer County Community College (U)
Illinois Eastern Community Colleges, Lincoln Trail College (U)
Iona College (G)
Jacksonville State University (U,G)

Jamestown Community College (N,U)
John A. Logan College (U)
The Johns Hopkins University (G)
Johnston Community College (U)
Jones International University (U,G)
Kirkwood Community College (N)
Labette Community College (U)
Lamar State College–Orange (U)
Lamar State College–Port Arthur (N,U)
Long Beach City College (U)
Macon State College (U)
Mansfield University of Pennsylvania (N)
Marlboro College Graduate College (U)
Maryville University of Saint Louis (N)
McDowell Technical Community College (U)
McNeese State University (N)
Mercer County Community College (N)
Middle Tennessee State University (N)
Midland College (N)
Minnesota School of Business–Online (U)
Monroe College (U)
Nashville State Technical Community College (N)
Naugatuck Valley Community College (U)
Northeastern State University (U)
North Hennepin Community College (N)
North Lake College (U)
North Seattle Community College (U)
North Shore Community College (N)
NorthWest Arkansas Community College (U)
Northwestern Michigan College (U)
Ouachita Technical College (U)
Oxnard College (U)
Pace University (U,G)
Pamlico Community College (U)
Pikes Peak Community College (U)
Portland Community College (U)
Pratt Community College (U)
Pulaski Technical College (U)
Rend Lake College (U)
Riverside Community College District (U)
Rockingham Community College (N)
Rose State College (U)
Rowan-Cabarrus Community College (N)
Sacramento City College (U)
Sampson Community College (U)
San Diego Community College District (U)
Santa Rosa Junior College (U)
Seminole State College of Florida (U)
Sinclair Community College (U)
Sonoma State University (N)
Southeast Arkansas College (U)
Southeastern Community College (U)
Southeastern Oklahoma State University (N)
Southern Methodist University (G)
South Piedmont Community College (U)
Southwest Wisconsin Technical College (U)
Spokane Community College (U)
Stanly Community College (U)
State University of New York at Oswego (U)
Sullivan County Community College (N)
Syracuse University (G)
Tarleton State University (G)
Tompkins Cortland Community College (N)
Trident Technical College (U)
Tunxis Community College (U)
Tyler Junior College (U)
The University of Akron (N,U)
University of Colorado Boulder (N,G)
University of Denver (G)
University of Florida (G)
University of Idaho (U)
University of Illinois at Urbana–Champaign (G)
University of Management and Technology (U)
University of Missouri–Kansas City (U)
The University of Texas at Brownsville (N)
University of Waterloo (N)
University of West Florida (U)
Utah State University (G)
Wake Technical Community College (U)
Wayne Community College (U)
Wayne State University (U)
Westchester Community College (U)
Western Kentucky University (U)
Westmoreland County Community College (U)
Wharton County Junior College (U)
Youngstown State University (N)

CONSTRUCTION ENGINEERING

Austin Peay State University (U)
Columbia University (N,G)
Haywood Community College (U)
Southern Methodist University (G)

CONSTRUCTION ENGINEERING TECHNOLOGIES

Austin Peay State University (U)
Clemson University (N)
Columbia University (N,G)
Indiana State University (U)
Mansfield University of Pennsylvania (N)
National University (U)
North Hennepin Community College (U)
Pennsylvania College of Technology (U)
Pittsburg State University (U)
Sonoma State University (N)
University of Southern Mississippi (G)

CONSTRUCTION MANAGEMENT

Arapahoe Community College (U)
Auburn University (N)
Austin Peay State University (N,U)
Central Michigan University (U)
Clemson University (U,G)
Columbia University (N,G)
Columbus State Community College (U)
Drexel University (G)
Haywood Community College (U)
Indiana State University (U)
North Dakota State University (U)
Pittsburg State University (G)
Rochester Institute of Technology (G)
Sonoma State University (N)
University of Arkansas at Little Rock (U)
University of Florida (G)
Wake Technical Community College (U)

CONSTRUCTION TRADES

Austin Peay State University (U)
Central Michigan University (N,U)
College of Southern Maryland (N)
Haywood Community College (U)
Lock Haven University of Pennsylvania (N)
Los Angeles Trade-Technical College (U)
Mansfield University of Pennsylvania (N)
Oakland Community College (U)
Peninsula College (N)
Phoenix College (U)
Wake Technical Community College (U)
Wayne Community College (N)

CONSTRUCTION TRADES RELATED

Alpena Community College (N,U)
Austin Peay State University (N,U)
Bowling Green State University (N)
Haywood Community College (U)
James A. Rhodes State College (U)
Paris Junior College (N)
Peninsula College (N)
Sullivan County Community College (N)
University of Arkansas at Little Rock (U)
University of California, Davis (N)

COSMETOLOGY AND RELATED PERSONAL GROOMING SERVICES

Clary Sage College (U)
Davidson County Community College (U)
Gadsden State Community College (U)
Haywood Community College (U)
Midland College (N)
Mid-State Technical College (U)
Minnesota School of Business–Online (U)
Northwest-Shoals Community College (U)
Pamlico Community College (U)
Sacramento City College (U)
Southwest Wisconsin Technical College (U)
Wake Technical Community College (U)
Wayne Community College (N)

CRAFTS, FOLK ART AND ARTISANRY

Austin Peay State University (N)
Big Bend Community College (U)
Blackhawk Technical College (N)
Bossier Parish Community College (N)
Burlington College (U)
Butler County Community College (N)
Lamar State College–Orange (U)
Middle Tennessee State University (N)
Naugatuck Valley Community College (N)
Peninsula College (N)
Prescott College (N)
Southeastern Oklahoma State University (N)
Temple University (U)
The University of Tennessee at Martin (N)
Wayne Community College (N)
Western Kentucky University (U)

CRIMINAL JUSTICE AND CORRECTIONS

Adams State College (U)
Albertus Magnus College (U)
Allen Community College (U)
Alpena Community College (U)
Anderson University (U)
Andrew Jackson University (U,G)
Angelina College (U)
Anne Arundel Community College (U)
Arapahoe Community College (U)
Arizona Western College (U)
Arkansas State University (U)
Arkansas State University–Beebe (U)
Athabasca University (N,U)
Austin Peay State University (N,U)
Ball State University (U)

Bellevue College (U)
Bethel University (U)
Blackhawk Technical College (N,U)
Boise State University (U,G)
Bossier Parish Community College (U)
Brazosport College (U)
Brenau University (U)
Bridgewater State University (U)
Bronx Community College of the City University of New York (U)
Brookdale Community College (U)
Buena Vista University (U)
Buffalo State College, State University of New York (U)
Burlington College (U)
Burlington County College (U)
Butler Community College (U)
Cabrillo College (U)
Caldwell College (U)
California State University, Sacramento (U)
California State University, San Bernardino (U,G)
Cape Fear Community College (U)
Cayuga County Community College (U)
Central Carolina Community College (N,U)
Central Carolina Technical College (U)
Centralia College (U)
Central New Mexico Community College (U)
Central Texas College (U)
Central Washington University (U)
Chaminade University of Honolulu (U,G)
Chemeketa Community College (U)
Citrus College (U)
City University of Seattle (U)
Clackamas Community College (U)
Clatsop Community College (U)
Cleveland Community College (U)
Clinton Community College (U)
Clovis Community College (U)
College of Southern Maryland (U)
Columbia College (U,G)
Community College of Allegheny County (U)
Community College of Beaver County (U)
Corning Community College (U)
Dabney S. Lancaster Community College (U)
Dallas Baptist University (U,G)
Danville Community College (U)
Davidson County Community College (U)
Dawson Community College (U)
Daytona State College (U)
Delgado Community College (U)
Drury University (N)
Eastern Wyoming College (U)
East Los Angeles College (U)
Edison State Community College (U)
Erie Community College (U)
Erie Community College, North Campus (U)
Erie Community College, South Campus (U)
Excelsior College (U)
Faulkner University (G)
Fayetteville State University (U,G)
Ferris State University (U)
Finger Lakes Community College (U)
Fort Hays State University (U)
Fort Valley State University (U)
Franklin Pierce University (U)
Front Range Community College (U)
Frostburg State University (U)
Gadsden State Community College (U)
Gannon University (U)
Gaston College (U)
Genesee Community College (U)
Glenville State College (U)
Governors State University (N)
Grand Valley State University (U)
Granite State College (U)
Grantham University (U)
Harrisburg Area Community College (U)
Haywood Community College (U)
Herkimer County Community College (U)
Hibbing Community College (U)
Hillsborough Community College (U)
Holyoke Community College (U)
Hopkinsville Community College (U)
Huston-Tillotson University (U)
Illinois State University (U)
Indiana State University (U,G)
Indiana University of Pennsylvania (G)
Indiana Wesleyan University (U)
Iowa Lakes Community College (U)
Iowa Valley Community College District (U)
Jacksonville State University (U,G)
James A. Rhodes State College (U)
James Madison University (U)
Jamestown Community College (U)
Johnston Community College (U)
J. Sargeant Reynolds Community College (U)
Judson College (U)
Kansas State University (U)
Keystone College (U)
Kirkwood Community College (U)
Lackawanna College (U)
Lander University (U)
Lansing Community College (U)
Lenoir Community College (U)
Lewis-Clark State College (U)
Liberty University (U)
Lindenwood University (U)
Los Angeles Harbor College (U)
Los Angeles Trade-Technical College (U)
Louisiana State University at Eunice (U)
Loyola University New Orleans (U)
Mansfield University of Pennsylvania (N,U)
Marian University (U)
Marquette University (U)
Mary Baldwin College (U)
McNeese State University (U)
Mesa Community College (U)
Mesa State College (U)
Metropolitan Community College–Penn Valley (U)
Miami Dade College (U)
Miami University–Regional Campuses (U)
Middlesex Community College (U)
Middle Tennessee State University (U)
Midland College (N)
Midwestern State University (U)
Minnesota School of Business–Online (U)
Minot State University (U)
Mississippi College (U,G)
Monmouth University (G)
Monroe College (U)
Monroe Community College (U)
Montcalm Community College (U)
Montgomery Community College (U)
Moorpark College (U)
Mountain Empire Community College (U)
Mountain State University (U,G)
Mount Olive College (U)
Mount Wachusett Community College (U)
Murray State College (U)
Murray State University (U)
Nashville State Technical Community College (N)
National University (U)
Naugatuck Valley Community College (U)
New Jersey City University (U)
New Mexico Junior College (U)
New Mexico State University (U,G)
New Mexico State University–Grants (U)
New River Community College (U)
Nichols College (U,G)
North Carolina Central University (U)
North Central State College (U)
North Central Texas College (U)
North Dakota State University (U)
Northeastern State University (U)
Northern Kentucky University (U)
NorthWest Arkansas Community College (U)
Northwestern Michigan College (U)
Northwestern Oklahoma State University (U)
Northwest-Shoals Community College (U)
Oakland Community College (U)
Ohio University (U)
Ouachita Technical College (U)
Oxnard College (U)
Ozarks Technical Community College (U)
Pace University (U)
Pamlico Community College (U)
The Paralegal Institute, Inc. (U)
Paris Junior College (U)
Peninsula College (U)
Penn State University Park (U)
Peru State College (U)
Phoenix College (U)
Piedmont Community College (U)
Pikes Peak Community College (U)
Pittsburg State University (U)
Portland Community College (U)
Portland State University (U)
Prairie View A&M University (G)
Pratt Community College (U)
Quinsigamond Community College (U)
Randolph Community College (U)
Rappahannock Community College (U)
Regent University (U)
Rend Lake College (U)
The Richard Stockton College of New Jersey (U)
Richmond Community College (N,U)
Rio Hondo College (U)
Rogers State University (U)
Roger Williams University (U)
Rose State College (U)
Rowan-Cabarrus Community College (U)
Sacramento City College (U)
St. Cloud State University (U,G)
St. John's University (U,G)
Saint Joseph's College of Maine (U)
Saint Leo University (U)
St. Petersburg College (U)
Sampson Community College (U)
San Bernardino Valley College (U)
San Diego Community College District (U)
San Diego State University (U)
San Jacinto College District (U)
Santa Fe Community College (U)
Santa Rosa Junior College (U)
Sauk Valley Community College (U)
Shippensburg University of Pennsylvania (U,G)
Slippery Rock University of Pennsylvania (U,G)
Southeast Arkansas College (U)
Southeastern Community College (U)
Southeastern Oklahoma State University (U)

Southern Illinois University Carbondale (U)
Southern New Hampshire University (G)
Southern Oregon University (U)
Southern University at New Orleans (G)
South Piedmont Community College (U)
Spartanburg Community College (N)
Spokane Community College (U)
Spring Arbor University (U)
Stanly Community College (U)
State University of New York at Oswego (U)
State University of New York College of Technology at Canton (U)
State University of New York Empire State College (U)
Taft College (U)
Taylor University (U)
Tompkins Cortland Community College (U)
Trident Technical College (U)
Tunxis Community College (N,U)
Tyler Junior College (U)
Union County College (U)
University at Albany, State University of New York (U)
The University of Akron (U)
University of Alaska Fairbanks (U)
University of Arkansas at Little Rock (U,G)
University of Cincinnati (U,G)
University of Colorado at Colorado Springs (G)
The University of Findlay (U)
University of Florida (U)
University of Great Falls (U,G)
University of Houston–Downtown (U,G)
University of Houston–Victoria (U)
University of Illinois at Springfield (U)
University of Maine at Augusta (U)
University of Maine at Fort Kent (U)
University of Management and Technology (U,G)
University of Massachusetts Boston (U,G)
University of Memphis (U)
University of Nevada, Reno (U)
University of New Haven (U,G)
University of North Alabama (U)
The University of North Carolina at Chapel Hill (U)
The University of North Carolina Wilmington (U)
University of North Dakota (U)
University of North Florida (U)
University of Pittsburgh at Bradford (U)
The University of South Dakota (U,G)
The University of Tennessee at Chattanooga (U)
The University of Tennessee at Martin (N)
The University of Texas at Brownsville (N)
The University of Texas of the Permian Basin (U)
University of the Southwest (U)
University of West Georgia (U)
The University of Winnipeg (U)
University of Wisconsin–Platteville (N)
Upper Iowa University (U)
Valencia College (U)
Vincennes University (U)
Wake Technical Community College (U)
Wayland Baptist University (U)
Wayne Community College (N,U)
Wayne State College (U,G)
Wayne State University (U)
Westchester Community College (U)
Western Kentucky University (U,G)
West Hills Community College (U)
West Los Angeles College (U)
West Shore Community College (U)
West Texas A&M University (U)
West Virginia Northern Community College (U)
West Virginia State University (G)
Wharton County Junior College (U)
Wichita State University (U,G)
Winston-Salem State University (U)
Worcester State University (U)
Yavapai College (U)
York Technical College (U)
Youngstown State University (U)

CRIMINOLOGY

Adams State College (U)
American University (U,G)
Athabasca University (N,U)
Atlantic Cape Community College (U)
Austin Peay State University (U)
Bellevue College (U)
Boise State University (U,G)
Brenau University (U)
Bryant & Stratton Online (N,U)
Burlington College (U)
Burlington County College (U)
Butler Community College (U)
Butler County Community College (U)
California State University, East Bay (U)
Capital Community College (U)
Carleton University (U)
Cayuga County Community College (U)
Central Pennsylvania College (U)
Central Texas College (U)
Charter Oak State College (U)
Chemeketa Community College (U)
Dallas Baptist University (U,G)
Danville Community College (U)
Dominican College (U)
Drury University (U,G)
Eastern Oregon University (U)
East Los Angeles College (U)
Edison State Community College (U)
Florida State University (U)
Front Range Community College (U)
Gannon University (U)
Gaston College (U)
Haywood Community College (U)
Holyoke Community College (U)
Houston Community College System (U)
Indiana State University (U,G)
Indiana University of Pennsylvania (U,G)
Jacksonville State University (U,G)
Jamestown Community College (U)
Kansas State University (U)
Keystone College (U)
Kirkwood Community College (U)
Labette Community College (U)
Lansing Community College (U)
Lewis-Clark State College (U)
Lindenwood University (U)
Lock Haven University of Pennsylvania (U)
Los Angeles Harbor College (U)
Louisiana State University and Agricultural and Mechanical College (U)
Marquette University (U)
Memorial University of Newfoundland (G)
Mercer County Community College (U)
Miami Dade College (U)
Middlesex Community College (U)
Minnesota School of Business–Online (U)
Monroe College (U)
Montgomery County Community College (U)
Mountain Empire Community College (U)
Mountain State University (U)
Mount Olive College (U)
Mount Wachusett Community College (U)
National University (G)
New Mexico Highlands University (U)
North Central Texas College (U)
Northwest-Shoals Community College (U)
Ohio University (U)
Ozarks Technical Community College (U)
Pace University (U)
Pamlico Community College (U)
Pikes Peak Community College (U)
The Richard Stockton College of New Jersey (U)
Riverside Community College District (U)
Roger Williams University (U)
Rowan-Cabarrus Community College (U)
St. Philip's College (U)
San Jacinto College District (U)
Santa Rosa Junior College (U)
Sauk Valley Community College (U)
Seminole State College of Florida (U)
Slippery Rock University of Pennsylvania (U,G)
Southeast Arkansas College (U)
Southeastern Oklahoma State University (U)
Southern Illinois University Carbondale (U)
Southern Maine Community College (U)
Southern Oregon University (U)
Texas State University–San Marcos (U)
Tunxis Community College (U)
University at Albany, State University of New York (U)
The University of Akron (U)
University of Alaska Fairbanks (U)
University of Arkansas at Little Rock (U)
University of Dubuque (U)
The University of Findlay (U)
University of Florida (U)
University of Maine at Augusta (U)
University of Maine at Machias (U)
University of Management and Technology (U,G)
University of Minnesota, Duluth (U)
University of Northern Iowa (U,G)
The University of South Dakota (U)
University of Southern Maine (U)
The University of Texas at Arlington (U)
University of the Southwest (U)
University of Wisconsin–Platteville (N)
Upper Iowa University (U)
Valencia College (U)
Western Kentucky University (U,G)
West Virginia State University (U)
York Technical College (U)

CULINARY ARTS AND RELATED SERVICES

Austin Peay State University (U)
Blackhawk Technical College (U)
Bossier Parish Community College (N)
Burlington County College (U)
Butler County Community College (N)
Cabrillo College (U)
Central New Mexico Community College (U)
Central Texas College (U)
Central Wyoming College (N)

Columbus State Community College (U)
Dabney S. Lancaster Community College (N)
Erie Community College (U)
Erie Community College, North Campus (U)
Erie Community College, South Campus (U)
Ferris State University (U)
Hagerstown Community College (N)
Hibbing Community College (U)
Middle Tennessee State University (N)
Naugatuck Valley Community College (U)
NorthWest Arkansas Community College (U)
Oakton Community College (N)
Ozarks Technical Community College (U)
Prescott College (N)
Saint Paul College–A Community & Technical College (U)
San Jacinto College District (U)
Santa Rosa Junior College (U)
Southeastern Oklahoma State University (N)
Southern Maine Community College (U)
Southwest Wisconsin Technical College (U)
Spartanburg Community College (N,U)
Spokane Community College (U)
State University of New York College at Potsdam (N)
The University of Texas at Brownsville (N)
Valencia College (U)
Wake Technical Community College (U)
Westchester Community College (U)

CULTURAL STUDIES/CRITICAL THEORY AND ANALYSIS

Bowling Green State University (U)
Columbia College (U)
East Los Angeles College (U)
Faulkner University (U)
Providence College (U)
Queen's University at Kingston (U)
Sacramento City College (U)
Sinclair Community College (U)

CURRICULUM AND INSTRUCTION

Alvin Community College (U)
Arkansas State University (U,G)
Athabasca University (G)
Austin Peay State University (U)
Bloomsburg University of Pennsylvania (G)
Boise State University (U)
Bossier Parish Community College (U)
Boston University (G)
Bowling Green State University (U)
Brenau University (U)
Bridgewater State University (U)
Brigham Young University (U)
Brigham Young University–Idaho (U)
Buena Vista University (U,G)
California State University, Chico (U)
Canisius College (G)
Central Michigan University (G)
Cerritos College (U)
Chemeketa Community College (U)
The College of St. Scholastica (G)
Columbia College (U)
Columbia International University (G)
Concordia University Wisconsin (G)
Dallas Baptist University (U,G)
Drexel University (G)
Duquesne University (G)
Eastern Kentucky University (U,G)
Fort Valley State University (U)
Frostburg State University (G)
Global University (G)
Goddard College (U)
Granite State College (U)
Illinois State University (U,G)
Indiana State University (U,G)
Jacksonville State University (U,G)
Kansas State University (N,U,G)
Lenoir Community College (U)
Lesley University (G)
LeTourneau University (U)
Liberty University (G)
Lock Haven University of Pennsylvania (G)
Louisiana State University and Agricultural and Mechanical College (U)
Luna Community College (U)
Marian University (G)
McMurry University (U)
Minot State University (U)
Misericordia University (G)
Mississippi State University (U,G)
Murray State University (U)
New Mexico Highlands University (U,G)
New Mexico State University (U)
North Carolina State University (G)
North Dakota State University (G)
Northwestern Oklahoma State University (U)
Pace University (G)
Penn State University Park (G)
Pittsburg State University (U,G)
Portland Community College (U)
Purdue University (G)
The Richard Stockton College of New Jersey (U)
Robert Morris University (G)
Southern Arkansas University–Magnolia (U,G)
Southwest Wisconsin Technical College (U)
State University of New York at New Paltz (U)
State University of New York at Oswego (G)
Stephen F. Austin State University (U)
Stephens College (G)
Tarleton State University (U,G)
University at Albany, State University of New York (U)
The University of Akron (N,U,G)
University of Alaska Fairbanks (U,G)
University of Cincinnati (G)
University of Evansville (U)
University of Florida (G)
University of Illinois at Urbana–Champaign (G)
The University of Kansas (U,G)
University of Maine at Machias (U)
University of Mary Washington (G)
University of Memphis (U)
University of Nevada, Reno (U,G)
University of Northern Iowa (G)
University of Oregon (U,G)
University of Saskatchewan (U)
University of Southern Mississippi (G)
The University of Texas at Arlington (G)
The University of Texas at Brownsville (U)
The University of Texas of the Permian Basin (U,G)
University of the Pacific (G)
University of the Southwest (G)
University of Waterloo (G)
University of West Georgia (U,G)
University of Wisconsin–Superior (U)
Utah State University (G)
Vanguard University of Southern California (U)
Western Kentucky University (U,G)
Western Michigan University (G)
Winston-Salem State University (U)

DANCE

Austin Peay State University (U)
Bossier Parish Community College (N)
Brigham Young University (U)
California State University, Chico (U)
Central Wyoming College (N)
Goddard College (G)
Lehman College of the City University of New York (U)
Long Beach City College (U)
Mesa State College (U)
Naugatuck Valley Community College (N)
New Mexico Junior College (N)
North Central Texas College (U)
Prescott College (N)
Southeastern Oklahoma State University (N)
Texas State University–San Marcos (U)
University of Houston (U)
University of Illinois at Urbana–Champaign (U)
The University of Texas at Brownsville (N)
University of the Pacific (U)
Wayne State University (U)
Western Kentucky University (U)

DATA ENTRY/MICROCOMPUTER APPLICATIONS

Allen Community College (U)
Arkansas State University–Beebe (U)
Athabasca University (N)
Austin Peay State University (U)
Butler Community College (U)
Butler County Community College (U)
Cape Fear Community College (U)
Cayuga County Community College (U)
Central Carolina Technical College (U)
Centralia College (N)
Central Michigan University (N)
Central Wyoming College (N,U)
Cerritos College (U)
Chemeketa Community College (U)
Clemson University (N)
Cleveland Institute of Electronics (N)
Cleveland State Community College (U)
Dakota College at Bottineau (U)
Davidson County Community College (U)
Dickinson State University (U)
East Los Angeles College (U)
Edgecombe Community College (N,U)
Enterprise State Community College (U)
Erie Community College (U)
Erie Community College, North Campus (U)
Erie Community College, South Campus (U)
Front Range Community College (U)
Grantham University (U)
Haywood Community College (U)
Hibbing Community College (U)
Holyoke Community College (U)
Judson University (U)
Kirkwood Community College (N)
Lamar State College–Port Arthur (N,U)
Lansing Community College (U)
Lewis-Clark State College (U)
Lewis University (U)

Mansfield University of Pennsylvania (N)
Maryville University of Saint Louis (N,U)
Mercy College of Northwest Ohio (N,U)
Miami Dade College (U)
Middlesex Community College (U)
Minnesota School of Business–Online (U)
Mitchell Technical Institute (N)
Montcalm Community College (U)
Naugatuck Valley Community College (N,U)
North Central Texas College (U)
North Dakota State University (N,U)
Northwest-Shoals Community College (U)
Oakton Community College (N,U)
Oxnard College (U)
Pamlico Community College (U)
Peninsula College (N)
Pulaski Technical College (U)
Rockingham Community College (N,U)
Sacramento City College (U)
Saint Francis University (U)
St. Louis Community College (U)
St. Petersburg College (N)
Sampson Community College (U)
San Diego Community College District (U)
Sinclair Community College (U)
Southeast Arkansas College (U)
Southeastern Illinois College (U)
Spartanburg Community College (U)
Spokane Community College (U)
State University of New York College at Potsdam (N)
Stephens College (U)
Tarleton State University (N)
Trident Technical College (U)
The University of Akron (N)
University of Alaska Fairbanks (U)
University of Arkansas at Little Rock (U)
University of Evansville (N)
University of Minnesota, Crookston (U)
University of West Florida (U)
Utah State University (U)
Valencia College (U)
Wake Technical Community College (N,U)
Western Kentucky University (U)
West Los Angeles College (U)

DATA PROCESSING

Adams State College (N)
Athabasca University (N,U)
Auburn University (N)
Austin Peay State University (U)
Bronx Community College of the City University of New York (U)
Central New Mexico Community College (U)
Cincinnati State Technical and Community College (U)
Clemson University (N)
Front Range Community College (U)
Jacksonville State University (U)
John A. Logan College (U)
Kirkwood Community College (N)
Lamar State College–Port Arthur (N)
Lansing Community College (U)
Lewis-Clark State College (U)
Mansfield University of Pennsylvania (N)
Maryville University of Saint Louis (N,U)
Minnesota School of Business–Online (U)
Naugatuck Valley Community College (N)
Northwest-Shoals Community College (U)
Ozarks Technical Community College (U)
Pulaski Technical College (U)
Rockingham Community College (N)
St. Petersburg College (N)
Sinclair Community College (U)
Southeastern Community College (U)
Spokane Community College (U)
State University of New York College at Potsdam (U)
Syracuse University (G)
Tompkins Cortland Community College (N)
The University of Akron (N)
University of Alaska Fairbanks (U)
University of Illinois at Urbana–Champaign (G)
University of Minnesota, Crookston (U)
University of Southern Maine (U)
University of Waterloo (N)
Utah State University (U)
Wake Technical Community College (N,U)
Wayne Community College (U)
Westchester Community College (U)
Western Kentucky University (U)
Wilkes Community College (U)

DEMOGRAPHY AND POPULATION

Athabasca University (U)
The Johns Hopkins University (G)
Western Kentucky University (U)

DENTAL SUPPORT SERVICES AND ALLIED PROFESSIONS

Austin Peay State University (N)
Blackhawk Technical College (U)
Chattanooga State Community College (U)
Clarion University of Pennsylvania (U)
Columbus State Community College (U)
Danville Community College (U)
James A. Rhodes State College (U)
John A. Logan College (U)
Mansfield University of Pennsylvania (N)
McNeese State University (N)
Middlesex Community College (U)
Monroe Community College (U)
Montgomery County Community College (U)
The Ohio State University (U)
Peninsula College (U)
Pennsylvania College of Technology (U)
Phoenix College (U)
Portland Community College (U)
Quinebaug Valley Community College (N)
Sacramento City College (U)
Santa Fe Community College (U)
Spartanburg Community College (U)
Spokane Community College (U)
Tunxis Community College (U)
University of Bridgeport (U)
The University of British Columbia (U)
University of Missouri–Kansas City (N)
University of New Haven (U)
Wake Technical Community College (U)
Wayne Community College (N)
West Los Angeles College (U)
Wichita State University (U)

DENTISTRY AND ORAL SCIENCES (ADVANCED/GRADUATE)

Danville Community College (U)
University of Missouri–Kansas City (G)
West Los Angeles College (U)

DESIGN AND APPLIED ARTS

Academy of Art University (U,G)
Austin Peay State University (N,U)
Bossier Parish Community College (N)
Brenau University (U)
Buffalo State College, State University of New York (U)
Burlington College (U)
Butler County Community College (N)
California State University, Dominguez Hills (N)
Central Wyoming College (N)
Columbus State Community College (U)
Corning Community College (U)
Danville Community College (U)
Edison State Community College (U)
Hopkinsville Community College (N)
James A. Rhodes State College (U)
John A. Logan College (U)
Lansing Community College (U)
Long Beach City College (U)
Massachusetts College of Art and Design (U)
Minneapolis College of Art and Design (N,U,G)
New Mexico Junior College (U)
North Carolina State University (U)
Paris Junior College (N)
Pikes Peak Community College (U)
Pittsburg State University (U,G)
Prescott College (N)
Rockingham Community College (N)
Sacramento City College (U)
Santa Fe Community College (U)
Sessions College for Professional Design (N,U)
The University of Akron (U)
University of Alaska Fairbanks (U)
University of Dubuque (U)
The University of North Carolina at Asheville (U)
Western Kentucky University (G)
Western Texas College (U)
West Los Angeles College (U)

DIETETICS AND CLINICAL NUTRITION SERVICES

Austin Peay State University (U)
Big Bend Community College (U)
Buffalo State College, State University of New York (U)
California State University, Dominguez Hills (N)
Central Michigan University (G)
Cincinnati State Technical and Community College (U)
Community College of Allegheny County (U)
Erie Community College (U)
Erie Community College, North Campus (U)
Erie Community College, South Campus (U)
Kansas State University (N,U,G)
Miami Dade College (U)
North Dakota State University (G)
Quinebaug Valley Community College (N)
Rend Lake College (U)
Southern Maine Community College (U)
South Piedmont Community College (U)
University of New Haven (U)
University of North Dakota (U)
University of North Florida (U,G)
Wayne State University (U)
Westchester Community College (U)

DISPUTE RESOLUTION

Austin Peay State University (N)

DRAFTING/DESIGN ENGINEERING TECHNOLOGIES

Blackhawk Technical College (N)
Butler Community College (U)
Cedarville University (U)
Chemeketa Community College (U)
Columbus State Community College (U)
Danville Community College (U)
Illinois Valley Community College (U)
Indiana State University (U)
Long Beach City College (U)
North Dakota State College of Science (U)
Oakland Community College (U)
Orange Coast College (U)
Pittsburgh Technical Institute (U)
Sacramento City College (U)
San Jacinto College District (U)
Sinclair Community College (U)
Union County College (U)
University of Alaska Fairbanks (U)
Wake Technical Community College (U)
Wayne Community College (N,U)

DRAMA/THEATRE ARTS AND STAGECRAFT

Angelina College (U)
Arkansas State University–Mountain Home (U)
Austin Peay State University (U)
Brigham Young University (U)
Brigham Young University–Idaho (U)
Brookdale Community College (U)
California State University, San Marcos (N)
Carl Sandburg College (U)
Cascadia Community College (U)
Central Carolina Community College (U)
Central Wyoming College (N)
Columbus State Community College (U)
Eastern Oregon University (U)
Edison State Community College (U)
Erie Community College (U)
Erie Community College, North Campus (U)
Erie Community College, South Campus (U)
Fort Valley State University (U)
Goddard College (U,G)
Graceland University (U)
Lamar State College–Orange (U)
Long Beach City College (U)
Louisiana State University and Agricultural and Mechanical College (U)
McMurry University (U)
North Seattle Community College (U)
Oakton Community College (U)
Ohio University (U)
Ozarks Technical Community College (U)
Paris Junior College (U)
Pellissippi State Technical Community College (U)
Pikes Peak Community College (U)
Reading Area Community College (U)
Regent University (U)
Sacramento City College (U)
Sinclair Community College (U)
Southeastern Oklahoma State University (N)
Southern Illinois University Carbondale (U)
State University of New York at Oswego (U)
The University of Akron (U,G)
University of Alaska Fairbanks (U)
University of Houston–Downtown (U)
University of Louisville (U)
The University of North Carolina at Chapel Hill (U)
The University of South Dakota (U)
The University of Texas at Arlington (U)
Wake Technical Community College (U)
West Los Angeles College (U)
Wilkes Community College (U)

ECOLOGY, EVOLUTION, SYSTEMATICS, AND POPULATION BIOLOGY

Arkansas State University–Beebe (U)
Austin Peay State University (U)
Bellevue College (U)
Boston Architectural College (N,U,G)
Burlington County College (U)
Cascadia Community College (U)
Duke University (G)
Edison State Community College (U)
Judson College (U)
Kansas State University (U)
Louisiana State University and Agricultural and Mechanical College (U)
Miami Dade College (U)
Mountain State University (U)
The Ohio State University (U)
Oregon State University (U)
Santa Monica College (U)
Slippery Rock University of Pennsylvania (U)
Spoon River College (U)
University of Florida (U,G)
University of Waterloo (U)
The University of Winnipeg (U)
Western Kentucky University (U,G)

ECONOMICS

Abilene Christian University (U)
Acadia University (U)
Allen Community College (U)
Alvin Community College (U)
Angelina College (U)
Angelo State University (U,G)
Anne Arundel Community College (U)
Antelope Valley College (U)
Arapahoe Community College (U)
Arkansas State University (U)
Arkansas State University–Beebe (U)
Arkansas State University–Mountain Home (U)
Asbury University (U)
Ashland University (U)
Athabasca University (N,U,G)
Austin Peay State University (U)
Avila University (U)
Bellevue College (U)
Big Bend Community College (U)
Bloomfield College (U)
Boise State University (U)
Brazosport College (U)
Brenau University (U,G)
Bridgewater State University (U,G)
Brigham Young University (U)
Brigham Young University–Idaho (U)
Broward College (U)
Bryant University (G)
Buffalo State College, State University of New York (U)
Burlington County College (U)
Butler Community College (U)
Butler County Community College (U)
Caldwell College (U)
California State University, Sacramento (U)
California State University, San Bernardino (U)
Cape Fear Community College (U)
Capital Community College (U)
Carleton University (U)
Carlow University (U)
Carroll University (U)
Cascadia Community College (U)
Cayuga County Community College (U)
Central Carolina Community College (U)
Central Carolina Technical College (U)
Central Michigan University (U,G)
Central New Mexico Community College (U)
Central Texas College (U)
Central Virginia Community College (U)
Central Washington University (U)
Central Wyoming College (U)
Champlain College (U)
Chatham University (U)
Chattanooga State Community College (U)
Chemeketa Community College (U)
Citrus College (U)
City Colleges of Chicago System (U)
City University of Seattle (U)
Clarion University of Pennsylvania (U)
Clatsop Community College (U)
Clemson University (U)
Cleveland Community College (U)
Cleveland State Community College (N)
Clinton Community College (U)
Clovis Community College (U)
College of Saint Mary (U)
The College of St. Scholastica (U)
College of Southern Maryland (U)
Colorado Mountain College (U)
Columbia Basin College (U)
Columbia College (U)
Columbus State Community College (U)
Community College of Allegheny County (U)
Community College of Beaver County (U)
Concordia University Wisconsin (U)
Cornell University (U)
Corning Community College (U)
Cossatot Community College of the University of Arkansas (U)
Culver-Stockton College (U)
Dabney S. Lancaster Community College (U)
Dakota College at Bottineau (U)
Dakota State University (U)
Dallas Baptist University (U,G)
Daytona State College (U)
Delgado Community College (U)
DePaul University (G)
DeVry University Online (U,G)
Dickinson State University (U)
Drake University (U,G)
Drexel University (N)
D'Youville College (U)
East Central Community College (U)
Eastern Illinois University (U)
Eastern Kentucky University (U)
Eastern Oregon University (U)
Eastern West Virginia Community and Technical College (U)
Eastern Wyoming College (U)
East Georgia College (U)
Edison State Community College (U)

Elaine P. Nunez Community College (U)
El Camino College (U)
Endicott College (U)
Enterprise State Community College (U)
Erie Community College (U)
Erie Community College, North Campus (U)
Erie Community College, South Campus (U)
Ferris State University (U)
Finger Lakes Community College (U)
Florida State University (U)
Fontbonne University (U)
Fort Hays State University (N,U)
Framingham State University (U)
Franklin Pierce University (U)
Friends University (U)
Front Range Community College (U)
Gadsden State Community College (U)
Gannon University (U)
Genesee Community College (U)
Georgia Highlands College (U)
Glenville State College (U)
Goddard College (U)
Grantham University (U)
Greenville Technical College (U)
Harcum College (U)
Harrisburg Area Community College (U)
Haywood Community College (U)
Heartland Community College (U)
Hibbing Community College (U)
Hillsborough Community College (U)
Hocking College (U)
Holyoke Community College (U)
Hope International University (U)
Hopkinsville Community College (U)
Houston Community College System (U)
Illinois Eastern Community Colleges, Olney Central College (U)
Illinois Valley Community College (U)
Indiana State University (U)
Indiana University–Purdue University Fort Wayne (U)
Iona College (U,G)
Iowa Valley Community College District (U)
Ithaca College (U)
Jacksonville State University (U,G)
Jefferson Community College (U)
Johnston Community College (U)
J. Sargeant Reynolds Community College (U)
Judson College (U)
Kansas State University (U)
Keystone College (U)
Kirkwood Community College (U)
Lackawanna College (U)
Lake-Sumter Community College (U)
Lake Superior College (U)
Lamar State College–Orange (U)
Lamar State College–Port Arthur (U)
Lansing Community College (U)
Lehman College of the City University of New York (U)
Lenoir Community College (U)
LeTourneau University (U)
Lewis-Clark State College (U)
Liberty University (U)
Long Beach City College (U)
Los Angeles Harbor College (U)
Louisiana State University and Agricultural and Mechanical College (U)
Luna Community College (U)
Mansfield University of Pennsylvania (U)
Marist College (U)
Marshall University (U)
Mary Baldwin College (U)
McKendree University (U)
Memorial University of Newfoundland (U)
Mercer County Community College (U)
Mesa Community College (U)
Metropolitan Community College–Penn Valley (U)
Miami Dade College (U)
Michigan Technological University (G)
Middlesex Community College (U)
Middle Tennessee State University (U,G)
Midway College (U)
Minot State University (U)
Mississippi College (U)
Monroe College (U)
Monroe County Community College (U)
Montcalm Community College (U)
Montgomery County Community College (U)
Moorpark College (U)
Motlow State Community College (U)
Mountain Empire Community College (U)
Mountain State University (U)
Mount Allison University (U)
Mount Olive College (U)
Mount Wachusett Community College (U)
Murray State University (U)
Nassau Community College (U)
Naugatuck Valley Community College (U)
New England College of Business and Finance (U)
New Jersey City University (U)
New Mexico Junior College (U)
New Mexico State University (U)
New Mexico State University–Alamogordo (U)
New Mexico State University–Carlsbad (U)
New River Community College (U)
Nichols College (U,G)
Nicolet Area Technical College (U)
Nipissing University (U)
North Arkansas College (U)
North Carolina State University (U)
North Central Texas College (U)
North Dakota State College of Science (U)
North Dakota State University (U,G)
Northern State University (U)
North Hennepin Community College (U)
North Iowa Area Community College (U)
North Lake College (U)
North Seattle Community College (U)
NorthWest Arkansas Community College (U)
Northwestern Michigan College (U)
Notre Dame College (U)
Oakton Community College (U)
Ocean County College (U)
Odessa College (U)
Ohio University (U)
Oklahoma Panhandle State University (U)
Olympic College (U)
Oregon Institute of Technology (U)
Oregon State University (U)
Oxnard College (U)
Ozarks Technical Community College (U)
Pace University (U)
Pacific States University (U,G)
Palm Beach State College (U)
Paris Junior College (U)
Peirce College (U)
Peninsula College (U)
Peru State College (U)
Philadelphia University (U)
Phoenix College (U)
Pikes Peak Community College (U)
Pittsburg State University (U)
Portland Community College (U)
Portland State University (U)
Prairie View A&M University (U,G)
Pratt Community College (U)
Pulaski Technical College (U)
Queen's University at Kingston (U)
Quinsigamond Community College (U)
Randolph Community College (U)
Reading Area Community College (U)
Reinhardt University (U)
Rend Lake College (U)
Richmond Community College (U)
Rio Hondo College (U)
Riverside Community College District (U)
Rivier College (U)
Rockingham Community College (U)
Rockland Community College (U,G)
Rose State College (U)
Rowan-Cabarrus Community College (U)
Sacramento City College (U)
St. Ambrose University (U)
St. Clair County Community College (U)
St. Cloud State University (U)
St. John Fisher College (U)
St. John's University (U,G)
Saint Leo University (U)
Saint Paul College–A Community & Technical College (U)
St. Petersburg College (U)
St. Philip's College (U)
Sam Houston State University (U)
San Bernardino Valley College (U)
San Diego Community College District (U)
San Diego State University (U)
San Jacinto College District (U)
Santa Fe Community College (U)
Santa Monica College (U)
Santa Rosa Junior College (U)
Sauk Valley Community College (U)
Seminole State College of Florida (U)
Shippensburg University of Pennsylvania (U)
Sinclair Community College (U)
Southeast Arkansas College (U)
Southeast Community College Area (U)
Southeastern Community College (U)
Southeastern Illinois College (U)
Southeastern Oklahoma State University (U)
Southern Illinois University Edwardsville (U)
Southern Maine Community College (U)
Southern New Hampshire University (U)
Southern Oregon University (U)
Southern University at New Orleans (U)
South Piedmont Community College (U)
Southwest Wisconsin Technical College (U)
Spokane Community College (U)
Spoon River College (U)
Spring Arbor University (U)
Stanly Community College (U)
State University of New York at New Paltz (U)
State University of New York at Oswego (U)
State University of New York College at Potsdam (U)
State University of New York College of Technology at Canton (U)
State University of New York Institute of Technology (G)
Stephen F. Austin State University (U)
Sullivan County Community College (U)
Taft College (U)

Tarleton State University (U)
Taylor University (U)
Temple University (N,U,G)
Texas A&M University–Corpus Christi (G)
Trident Technical College (U)
Trine University (U)
Tyler Junior College (U)
Union County College (U)
The University of Akron (U,G)
The University of Alabama in Huntsville (G)
University of Alaska Fairbanks (U)
University of Arkansas at Little Rock (U,G)
University of Bridgeport (U)
University of Cincinnati (U)
University of Colorado at Colorado Springs (U)
The University of Findlay (U)
University of Florida (U)
University of Houston–Downtown (U)
University of Idaho (U)
University of Illinois at Chicago (G)
University of Illinois at Springfield (U)
University of Illinois at Urbana–Champaign (U)
The University of Kansas (U)
University of Maine at Augusta (U)
University of Maine at Fort Kent (U)
University of Maine at Machias (U)
University of Management and Technology (U,G)
University of Mary Washington (U)
University of Massachusetts Boston (U)
University of Minnesota, Crookston (U)
University of Missouri–Kansas City (U)
University of Nevada, Reno (U)
University of New Haven (U)
University of North Alabama (U)
The University of North Carolina at Chapel Hill (U)
University of North Dakota (U,G)
University of Northern Iowa (U)
University of Oregon (U)
University of Pittsburgh at Bradford (U)
University of Saskatchewan (U)
The University of South Dakota (G)
University of Southern Maine (U)
University of Southern Mississippi (U)
The University of Texas at Arlington (U)
The University of Texas at Dallas (G)
University of the Southwest (U)
University of Toronto (N)
University of Utah (U)
University of Waterloo (U)
The University of West Alabama (U)
University of West Florida (U)
University of West Georgia (U)
University of Windsor (U)
University of Wisconsin Colleges (U)
University of Wisconsin–La Crosse (G)
University of Wisconsin MBA Consortium (G)
University of Wisconsin–Stout (U)
Utah State University (U)
Utica College (U)
Valencia College (U)
Vincennes University (U)
Wake Technical Community College (U)
Washington State University (U)
Wayland Baptist University (U,G)
Wayne Community College (U)
Wayne State College (U,G)
Wayne State University (U)
Webber International University (U)
Westchester Community College (U)
Western Kentucky University (U,G)
Western Wyoming Community College (U)
West Hills Community College (U)
West Los Angeles College (U)
West Virginia Northern Community College (U)
West Virginia State University (U)
Wilfrid Laurier University (U)
Windward Community College (U)
Worcester State University (U)
York Technical College (U)
York University (U)
Youngstown State University (U)

EDUCATION

Abilene Christian University (U,G)
Acadia University (U)
Adams State College (G)
Albertus Magnus College (G)
Alcorn State University (G)
American University (U,G)
Anderson University (U,G)
Andrews University (G)
Antioch University Midwest (G)
Arapahoe Community College (U)
Arkansas State University (U)
Asbury University (G)
Ashland University (U,G)
Athabasca University (U)
Atlantic Cape Community College (U)
Auburn University (G)
Austin Peay State University (N,U)
Ball State University (G)
Belhaven University (G)
Bellevue College (U)
Bennington College (G)
Bethel University (U,G)
Bloomfield College (U)
Bob Jones University (G)
Boise State University (U)
Bossier Parish Community College (N,U)
Bowling Green State University (U)
Bradley University (U,G)
Brazosport College (U)
Brenau University (U,G)
Brewton-Parker College (U)
Bridgewater State University (U)
Brigham Young University (U)
Brigham Young University–Idaho (U)
Brock University (U)
Bronx Community College of the City University of New York (U)
Buena Vista University (U,G)
Buffalo State College, State University of New York (U,G)
Burlington County College (U)
Butler Community College (U)
Butler County Community College (U)
California State University, Chico (U,G)
California State University, Dominguez Hills (N,U)
California State University, Monterey Bay (G)
California State University, San Bernardino (U,G)
Canisius College (G)
Cape Fear Community College (U)
Cardinal Stritch University (G)
Carl Sandburg College (U)
Cedarville University (U,G)
Central Bible College (U)
Central Carolina Community College (U)
Centralia College (U)
Central Michigan University (N)
Central Texas College (U)
Central Washington University (U,G)
Chaminade University of Honolulu (U,G)
Chatham University (U,G)
Chattanooga State Community College (U)
Chemeketa Community College (U)
Cincinnati Christian University (U,G)
Clackamas Community College (U)
Clarion University of Pennsylvania (U,G)
Cleveland Community College (U)
Cleveland State Community College (U)
Coastal Carolina University (U,G)
The College at Brockport, State University of New York (U)
College of Southern Maryland (N)
College of the Siskiyous (U)
Columbia College (U,G)
Columbia International University (N,G)
Columbus State University (U)
Community College of Allegheny County (U)
Community College of Beaver County (U)
Concordia University, St. Paul (U,G)
Corning Community College (U)
Cossatot Community College of the University of Arkansas (U)
Crown College (G)
Culver-Stockton College (U)
Cumberland University (G)
Dakota College at Bottineau (U)
Dakota Wesleyan University (U)
Dallas Baptist University (U,G)
Danville Community College (U)
Davidson County Community College (U)
Daytona State College (U)
DePaul University (U)
Dickinson State University (U)
Dominican College (U,G)
Drake University (U,G)
Drexel University (G)
Drury University (G)
Duquesne University (G)
D'Youville College (U,G)
East Central Community College (U)
Eastern Illinois University (U)
Eastern Washington University (N,U)
Eastern Wyoming College (U)
East Georgia College (U)
Elmira College (G)
Endicott College (U,G)
Erie Community College (U)
Erie Community College, North Campus (U)
Erie Community College, South Campus (U)
Fayetteville State University (G)
Ferris State University (U,G)
Fielding Graduate University (G)
Finger Lakes Community College (U)
Fitchburg State University (U,G)
Five Towns College (U,G)
Fontbonne University (G)
Framingham State University (G)
Franciscan University of Steubenville (G)
Franklin Pierce University (G)
Front Range Community College (U)
Gannon University (U,G)
Genesee Community College (U)
Georgia College & State University (G)
Georgian Court University (U,G)
Global University (U,G)

Goddard College (U,G)
Goucher College (G)
Governors State University (N)
Graceland University (G)
Grand Valley State University (G)
Haywood Community College (U)
Heartland Community College (U)
Hobe Sound Bible College (N)
Hofstra University (N,U,G)
Hope International University (G)
Hopkinsville Community College (U)
Huston-Tillotson University (U)
Illinois State University (U)
Illinois Valley Community College (U)
Indiana State University (U,G)
Indiana University of Pennsylvania (U,G)
Indiana University–Purdue University Fort Wayne (U)
Iona College (G)
Iowa Valley Community College District (U)
Jacksonville State University (U,G)
John A. Logan College (U)
Johnson State College (U)
Johnston Community College (U)
J. Sargeant Reynolds Community College (U)
Judson College (U)
Kansas State University (N,U,G)
Kauai Community College (U)
Kean University (N)
Lackawanna College (U)
Lake-Sumter Community College (U)
Lansing Community College (U)
Lenoir Community College (U)
Lesley University (G)
Lewis-Clark State College (U)
Liberty University (U)
Lincoln Christian University (U)
Lindenwood University (G)
Lipscomb University (U,G)
Lock Haven University of Pennsylvania (N,U,G)
Louisiana State University and Agricultural and Mechanical College (U)
Louisiana State University at Eunice (U)
Lourdes College (U)
Luna Community College (U)
Macon State College (U)
Mansfield University of Pennsylvania (U,G)
Marian University (U,G)
Marlboro College Graduate College (N)
Marquette University (U,G)
Mary Baldwin College (U,G)
Marylhurst University (G)
Marymount University (G)
Mayville State University (U)
McDowell Technical Community College (U)
McKendree University (U,G)
McMurry University (U)
McNeese State University (U,G)
Memorial University of Newfoundland (U)
Mercer County Community College (U)
Mesa State College (U,G)
Metropolitan Community College–Penn Valley (U)
Miami Dade College (U)
Middlesex Community College (U)
Middle Tennessee State University (U)
Midwestern State University (U)
Midwives College of Utah (N,U,G)
Minot State University (U)
Misericordia University (G)
Mississippi College (G)
Monmouth University (U,G)
Montgomery County Community College (U)
Mount Mary College (U,G)
Mount Olive College (U)
Murray State University (U)
Naropa University (N,G)
National University (U,G)
Naugatuck Valley Community College (N)
New Jersey City University (U,G)
New Mexico Highlands University (U,G)
New Mexico State University (U)
New Mexico State University–Carlsbad (U)
New Mexico State University–Grants (U)
North Carolina Central University (U)
North Carolina State University (G)
North Central Texas College (U)
North Dakota State University (U,G)
Northeastern State University (U)
Northern State University (U,G)
North Georgia College & State University (N,G)
North Hennepin Community College (U)
North Iowa Area Community College (U)
North Lake College (U)
Northwestern Oklahoma State University (U)
Northwest-Shoals Community College (U)
Notre Dame College (N)
Nyack College (U,G)
The Ohio State University (U,G)
Oregon State University (U,G)
Ozarks Technical Community College (U)
Pace University (N,U,G)
Palm Beach State College (U)
Pamlico Community College (U)
Paris Junior College (U)
Pasco-Hernando Community College (N)
Peninsula College (U)
Peru State College (U,G)
Phoenix College (U)
Pittsburg State University (U,G)
Portland Community College (U)
Prairie View A&M University (G)
Pratt Community College (U)
Prescott College (G)
Providence College (U)
Pulaski Technical College (U)
Quincy University (U,G)
Quinebaug Valley Community College (U)
Quinnipiac University (N)
Rappahannock Community College (U)
Regent University (U,G)
Rend Lake College (U)
The Richard Stockton College of New Jersey (U)
Richmond Community College (N,U)
Rivier College (G)
Robert Morris University (U)
Rowan-Cabarrus Community College (U)
Rowan University (G)
The Sage Colleges (U,G)
St. John's University (U,G)
Saint Joseph's College of Maine (G)
Saint Leo University (U)
Saint Mary-of-the-Woods College (U,G)
Saint Paul College–A Community & Technical College (U)
St. Petersburg College (N,U)
Saint Vincent College (U)
San Diego Community College District (U)
San Diego State University (N,U)
San Jacinto College District (U)
Santa Monica College (U)
Seton Hill University (G)
Shippensburg University of Pennsylvania (U,G)
Sinclair Community College (U)
Slippery Rock University of Pennsylvania (U,G)
Southeastern Community College (U)
Southeastern Illinois College (U)
Southern Adventist University (G)
Southern Arkansas University–Magnolia (G)
Southern Connecticut State University (G)
Southern Illinois University Carbondale (G)
Southern Illinois University Edwardsville (U,G)
Southern Oregon University (U,G)
South Piedmont Community College (U)
Southwestern Adventist University (G)
Spartanburg Community College (U)
Spoon River College (U)
State University of New York at New Paltz (G)
State University of New York at Oswego (G)
State University of New York at Plattsburgh (U,G)
State University of New York College at Cortland (G)
State University of New York College at Oneonta (G)
State University of New York Empire State College (U,G)
Stephens College (U,G)
Stony Brook University, State University of New York (G)
Sullivan County Community College (N)
Tarleton State University (U,G)
Taylor University (U)
Temple University (U,G)
Texas Woman's University (G)
Toccoa Falls College (U)
Tyler Junior College (U)
Union Institute & University (G)
Union University (U,G)
The University of Akron (U,G)
University of Alaska Fairbanks (U)
University of Arkansas at Little Rock (U,G)
University of Calgary (G)
University of California, Davis (N,U)
University of Cincinnati (U)
University of Dubuque (U)
University of Florida (U,G)
University of Hawaii at Hilo (U)
University of Houston–Downtown (U)
University of Houston–Victoria (U,G)
University of Idaho (U)
University of Illinois at Urbana–Champaign (U,G)
University of Lethbridge (G)
University of Louisville (G)
University of Maine (G)
University of Maine at Machias (U)
University of Mary Washington (G)
University of Massachusetts Boston (G)
University of Michigan–Flint (U,G)
University of Minnesota, Duluth (N)
University of Minnesota, Morris (U)
University of Missouri–Kansas City (N,G)
The University of Montana Western (U)
University of Nevada, Reno (G)
University of New Haven (G)
University of North Alabama (U,G)
The University of North Carolina at Asheville (N,U)

The University of North Carolina at Charlotte (U,G)
University of North Dakota (U,G)
University of Northern Iowa (U,G)
University of North Florida (U,G)
University of Pittsburgh at Bradford (U)
University of St. Francis (U)
University of St. Thomas (G)
University of South Alabama (U)
University of South Carolina Sumter (U)
The University of South Dakota (U,G)
University of Southern California (G)
University of Southern Maine (G)
University of Southern Mississippi (G)
The University of Tennessee at Chattanooga (U,G)
The University of Tennessee at Martin (N)
The University of Texas of the Permian Basin (U,G)
University of the Southwest (U,G)
University of Virginia (G)
The University of West Alabama (U)
University of West Georgia (U,G)
University of Wisconsin–Stout (U,G)
University of Wisconsin–Superior (U,G)
Utah State University (G)
Valencia College (U)
Valley City State University (U)
Vanguard University of Southern California (U)
Vincennes University (U)
Walden University (G)
Walla Walla University (G)
Wayne State College (U,G)
Wayne State University (U,G)
Webster University (G)
Western Carolina University (U)
Western Kentucky University (U,G)
Western Michigan University (U,G)
Western Texas College (U)
West Hills Community College (U)
West Los Angeles College (U)
West Texas A&M University (U)
West Virginia State University (U)
West Virginia University (N)
Wheeling Jesuit University (U,G)
Wichita State University (U,G)
Winston-Salem State University (U,G)
Worcester State University (G)
Xavier University (G)
Yavapai College (U)

EDUCATIONAL/INSTRUCTIONAL MEDIA DESIGN

Acadia University (U,G)
Arkansas Tech University (U,G)
Athabasca University (N)
Austin Peay State University (U)
Bloomsburg University of Pennsylvania (G)
Boise State University (U,G)
Boston University (G)
Bowling Green State University (G)
Brenau University (U)
California State University, Sacramento (G)
California State University, San Bernardino (U,G)
Central Washington University (U)
Charter Oak State College (U)
Dakota State University (G)
Dallas Baptist University (G)
Danville Community College (U)
Daytona State College (U)
Drexel University (G)
Duquesne University (G)
Florida State University (G)
Franciscan University of Steubenville (G)
Gannon University (U)
Georgia State University (G)
Indiana State University (G)
Iona College (G)
Jacksonville State University (U,G)
Jones International University (G)
Kansas State University (U,G)
La Sierra University (G)
Lawrence Technological University (G)
Lesley University (G)
Liberty University (G)
Lindenwood University (G)
Malone University (U)
Marian University (G)
Marlboro College Graduate College (N)
McDaniel College (G)
Mississippi State University (U,G)
National University (G)
New Mexico State University (U)
North Carolina Central University (G)
North Carolina State University (G)
North Dakota State University (G)
Northeastern State University (U)
Ozarks Technical Community College (U)
Pace University (G)
Penn State University Park (G)
St. John's University (G)
St. Petersburg College (N,U)
San Diego State University (U,G)
Seton Hill University (G)
Sonoma State University (U)
Southern Adventist University (G)
Southwestern Baptist Theological Seminary (G)
Southwest Wisconsin Technical College (U)
State University of New York at Plattsburgh (G)
State University of New York Institute of Technology (G)
Tarleton State University (U)
Taylor University (U)
Temple University (U)
Tyler Junior College (N,U)
The University of Akron (N,U,G)
University of Arkansas at Little Rock (G)
University of Calgary (G)
The University of Findlay (G)
University of Florida (G)
University of Illinois at Urbana–Champaign (N,G)
University of Massachusetts Boston (G)
University of Massachusetts Lowell (N)
University of Memphis (G)
University of Michigan–Flint (N)
The University of North Carolina at Charlotte (G)
University of North Dakota (G)
University of North Florida (G)
University of Saskatchewan (N,U)
University of South Alabama (G)
University of West Florida (G)
University of West Georgia (U,G)
Utah State University (G)
Western Kentucky University (G)
Western Michigan University (U,G)
Youngstown State University (G)

EDUCATIONAL ADMINISTRATION AND SUPERVISION

Arapahoe Community College (U)
Arkansas State University (U,G)
Arkansas Tech University (G)
Asbury University (G)
Athabasca University (N,G)
Austin Peay State University (U)
Bob Jones University (G)
Brenau University (U,G)
Bridgewater State University (U,G)
Brigham Young University (U)
Caldwell College (G)
California State University, Dominguez Hills (N,U)
Campbellsville University (G)
Cardinal Stritch University (G)
Charter Oak State College (U)
Columbia International University (G)
Concordia University Wisconsin (G)
Crown College (G)
Dakota Wesleyan University (G)
Dallas Baptist University (G)
DePaul University (G)
Dickinson State University (U)
Drexel University (G)
Eastern Illinois University (G)
Eastern Kentucky University (U,G)
Ferris State University (G)
Fitchburg State University (G)
Fort Hays State University (U)
Frostburg State University (G)
Gannon University (U)
George Fox University (G)
Georgian Court University (U)
Global University (G)
Hofstra University (G)
Illinois State University (G)
Indiana State University (G)
Indiana University–Purdue University Fort Wayne (G)
Iona College (G)
Jacksonville State University (U,G)
Kansas State University (N,U,G)
Kean University (G)
Lesley University (G)
Liberty University (G)
Lindenwood University (G)
Lipscomb University (G)
Lock Haven University of Pennsylvania (G)
Marlboro College Graduate College (N)
Marshall University (G)
McKendree University (G)
McNeese State University (U,G)
Mississippi State University (G)
Missouri Baptist University (U,G)
National University (G)
New Jersey City University (G)
New Mexico Highlands University (U,G)
North Carolina Central University (U)
North Carolina State University (G)
North Dakota State University (G)
Northeastern State University (U,G)
Northern State University (U)
Northwestern Oklahoma State University (G)
The Ohio State University (G)
Oregon State University (G)
Pace University (G)
Pittsburg State University (G)
Regent University (G)
St. Cloud State University (U)

St. John's University (G)
Saint Joseph's College of Maine (G)
St. Petersburg College (N)
San Diego State University (G)
Seton Hall University (G)
Shasta Bible College (G)
Southeastern Oklahoma State University (G)
Southern Adventist University (G)
Southern Arkansas University–Magnolia (G)
Southern Illinois University Carbondale (U)
South Piedmont Community College (U)
Southwestern Baptist Theological Seminary (G)
State University of New York at Oswego (G)
State University of New York at Plattsburgh (G)
Stephen F. Austin State University (G)
Stony Brook University, State University of New York (G)
Tarleton State University (U,G)
Temple University (G)
Union University (G)
The University of Akron (U,G)
University of Alaska Fairbanks (U,G)
University of Arkansas at Little Rock (G)
University of Calgary (G)
University of Colorado at Colorado Springs (G)
University of Florida (G)
University of Illinois at Urbana–Champaign (G)
The University of Kansas (G)
University of Lethbridge (G)
University of Louisville (G)
University of Memphis (G)
University of Michigan–Flint (N,G)
University of Missouri–Kansas City (G)
The University of North Carolina at Charlotte (G)
University of North Dakota (G)
University of North Florida (G)
The University of Scranton (G)
University of South Alabama (G)
University of Southern Mississippi (U,G)
The University of Texas of the Permian Basin (G)
University of the Southwest (G)
University of West Georgia (G)
University of Wisconsin–Superior (G)
Utah State University (G)
Vanguard University of Southern California (U)
Wayne State College (G)
Wayne State University (G)
Webster University (G)
Western Carolina University (N,U,G)
Western Kentucky University (G)
Western Michigan University (G)
Youngstown State University (G)

EDUCATIONAL ASSESSMENT, EVALUATION, AND RESEARCH

Acadia University (G)
Athabasca University (N,U,G)
Austin Peay State University (U)
Boise State University (U)
Brenau University (U,G)
Bridgewater State University (U)
California State University, Sacramento (G)
Canisius College (G)
College of Saint Mary (U)
Columbia College (G)
Corning Community College (U)
Dallas Baptist University (U,G)
Drexel University (G)
Frostburg State University (G)
George Fox University (G)
Global University (G)
Governors State University (N)
Indiana State University (G)
Iona College (G)
Jacksonville State University (U,G)
Kansas State University (N)
Lewis-Clark State College (U)
Liberty University (G)
Lindenwood University (G)
Lipscomb University (G)
Louisiana State University and Agricultural and Mechanical College (U)
Mansfield University of Pennsylvania (G)
Marlboro College Graduate College (N)
Marshall University (G)
McDaniel College (G)
McKendree University (G)
Medical College of Wisconsin (G)
Middle Tennessee State University (G)
Mississippi State University (G)
New Mexico State University (U)
North Carolina Central University (U)
North Dakota State University (G)
Northeastern State University (U)
Pace University (G)
Penn State University Park (G)
St. John's University (G)
St. Petersburg College (N,U)
Southeastern Oklahoma State University (G)
Southern Adventist University (G)
Southwestern Baptist Theological Seminary (G)
Tarleton State University (G)
Union University (G)
The University of Akron (U,G)
University of Alaska Fairbanks (U)
University of Arkansas at Little Rock (G)
University of Calgary (G)
University of Evansville (U)
The University of Findlay (G)
University of Florida (U,G)
University of Illinois at Chicago (G)
University of Illinois at Urbana–Champaign (G)
University of Lethbridge (G)
University of Louisville (G)
University of Michigan–Flint (N)
University of Missouri–Kansas City (G)
University of North Dakota (G)
University of St. Francis (G)
University of Southern Maine (G)
University of Southern Mississippi (U,G)
University of West Georgia (G)
Utah State University (G)
Wayne State University (G)
Western Kentucky University (G)
Western Michigan University (G)
West Texas A&M University (G)

EDUCATION RELATED

Acadia University (U,G)
Arapahoe Community College (U)
Arkansas Tech University (U,G)
Athabasca University (N,G)
Auburn University (G)
Austin Peay State University (N,U)
Ball State University (G)
Barclay College (U)
Boise State University (N,U,G)
Bossier Parish Community College (U)
Bowling Green State University (U)
Brenau University (U,G)
Brigham Young University (U)
Brock University (U)
Broward College (U)
Buffalo State College, State University of New York (U,G)
Burlington County College (U)
California State University, Dominguez Hills (U)
California State University, Monterey Bay (U)
California State University, San Bernardino (N,U)
California State University, San Marcos (G)
Canisius College (G)
Cascadia Community College (U)
Cayuga County Community College (U)
Central Michigan University (N)
Central Virginia Community College (U)
Chemeketa Community College (U)
Clarion University of Pennsylvania (U)
Cleveland Community College (U)
Cleveland State Community College (N)
College of Southern Maryland (U)
College of the Humanities and Sciences, Harrison Middleton University (G)
Colorado Mountain College (U)
Columbia International University (G)
Concordia University Wisconsin (G)
Crown College (G)
Dakota College at Bottineau (U)
Dakota State University (U,G)
Dakota Wesleyan University (G)
Dallas Baptist University (U,G)
Dickinson State University (U)
Drake University (U)
Drexel University (G)
Eastern Oregon University (G)
Elaine P. Nunez Community College (U)
Elmira College (G)
Erie Community College (U)
Erie Community College, North Campus (U)
Erie Community College, South Campus (U)
Fitchburg State University (U,G)
Fort Hays State University (U,G)
Fort Valley State University (N)
Gadsden State Community College (U)
Genesee Community College (U)
Georgia State University (U)
Global University (G)
Goddard College (U,G)
Governors State University (N)
Granite State College (N)
Haywood Community College (U)
Hopkinsville Community College (U)
Illinois State University (U)
Indiana State University (U,G)
Institute for Christian Studies (G)
Iona College (G)
Jacksonville State University (U,G)
John A. Logan College (U)
Jones International University (G)
Kansas State University (N,G)
Lansing Community College (U)
La Sierra University (G)
Lenoir Community College (U)
Lesley University (G)

LeTourneau University (U)
Lewis-Clark State College (U)
Liberty University (G)
Lindenwood University (U,G)
Louisiana State University and Agricultural and Mechanical College (U)
Mansfield University of Pennsylvania (N)
Marlboro College Graduate College (N)
Marshall University (G)
Mary Baldwin College (G)
Marylhurst University (G)
McDaniel College (G)
Memorial University of Newfoundland (U,G)
Miami Dade College (U)
Midway College (U)
Midwestern State University (G)
Mississippi State University (U)
Moorpark College (U)
Murray State University (U)
Naropa University (N)
New Mexico Highlands University (U,G)
New Mexico Junior College (U)
New Mexico State University (G)
North Arkansas College (U)
North Central State College (N)
North Dakota State University (U,G)
Northern Kentucky University (G)
Northwestern Oklahoma State University (G)
Nyack College (U,G)
Ocean County College (U)
The Ohio State University (U,G)
Ohio University (N)
Oklahoma State University (U)
Oregon State University (U,G)
Ozarks Technical Community College (U)
Pace University (G)
Pamlico Community College (U)
Paris Junior College (N,U)
Pasco-Hernando Community College (N,U)
Portland Community College (U)
Prescott College (N)
Providence College and Theological Seminary (N,U,G)
Pulaski Technical College (U)
Quinnipiac University (G)
Rio Hondo College (U)
Rowan-Cabarrus Community College (N)
St. John's University (G)
Saint Mary-of-the-Woods College (U,G)
San Diego Community College District (U)
San Diego State University (U)
Seton Hill University (U)
Shasta Bible College (N,U,G)
Slippery Rock University of Pennsylvania (U,G)
Sonoma State University (U)
Southeastern Oklahoma State University (N,U,G)
Southern Adventist University (U)
Southern Arkansas University–Magnolia (U,G)
Southern Illinois University Carbondale (U)
South Piedmont Community College (U)
Southwestern Baptist Theological Seminary (G)
Spartanburg Community College (N)
State University of New York at Plattsburgh (U,G)
State University of New York College of Environmental Science & Forestry, Ranger School (G)
Stephen F. Austin State University (G)
Stephens College (U,G)
Sullivan County Community College (N)
Tarleton State University (G)
Taylor University (U)
Texas A&M University–Corpus Christi (G)
Texas Woman's University (G)
Tunxis Community College (N)
The University of Akron (N,U,G)
University of Alaska Fairbanks (U,G)
University of Arkansas at Little Rock (U,G)
University of California, Davis (N)
University of California, Riverside (N)
University of Cincinnati (G)
University of Florida (G)
University of Idaho (U)
University of Illinois at Springfield (U,G)
University of Illinois at Urbana–Champaign (U,G)
University of Lethbridge (U,G)
University of Louisville (G)
University of Maine at Fort Kent (U)
University of Maine at Machias (U)
University of Massachusetts Boston (U)
University of Massachusetts Lowell (N)
University of Minnesota, Duluth (N)
University of Missouri–Kansas City (G)
University of Nevada, Reno (U,G)
The University of North Carolina at Asheville (G)
University of North Dakota (U,G)
University of Northern Iowa (U,G)
University of North Florida (G)
University of Saskatchewan (N,U,G)
The University of South Dakota (G)
University of Southern Mississippi (U)
The University of Texas at Brownsville (G)
The University of Texas of the Permian Basin (U,G)
University of the Pacific (G)
University of the Southwest (G)
University of West Florida (N,G)
University of West Georgia (U,G)
Valencia College (U)
Vanguard University of Southern California (U)
Wake Technical Community College (N)
Wayland Baptist University (U,G)
Wayne Community College (U)
Western Carolina University (U)
Western Kentucky University (U,G)
Western Michigan University (G)
West Hills Community College (U)
Westmoreland County Community College (U)
West Virginia University (N)
Wilkes Community College (U)
York College of Pennsylvania (G)

EDUCATION (SPECIFIC LEVELS AND METHODS)

Arapahoe Community College (U)
Arkansas Tech University (U)
Asbury University (G)
Auburn University (G)
Austin Peay State University (U)
Blackhawk Technical College (U)
Boise State University (U)
Brenau University (U)
Canisius College (U,G)
Central Michigan University (N,G)
Central Washington University (U)
Dallas Baptist University (U,G)
Dickinson State University (U)
Drexel University (G)
Eastern Wyoming College (U)
Fayetteville State University (U)
Franklin Pierce University (G)
Georgia Highlands College (U)
Georgia State University (G)
Goddard College (U,G)
Granite State College (U)
Hobe Sound Bible College (U)
Indiana State University (G)
Inter American University of Puerto Rico, San Germán Campus (U)
Iona College (G)
Jacksonville State University (U,G)
James A. Rhodes State College (U)
James Madison University (U)
Johnston Community College (U)
Judson College (U)
Kansas State University (N,U,G)
Kean University (U,G)
Lamar State College–Orange (U)
Lander University (G)
La Sierra University (U,G)
Lesley University (G)
LeTourneau University (U)
Lewis-Clark State College (U)
Liberty University (G)
Louisiana State University and Agricultural and Mechanical College (U)
Macon State College (U)
Mary Baldwin College (G)
McDowell Technical Community College (U)
McMurry University (U)
Middlesex Community College (U)
Midland College (U)
Minot State University (U)
Mississippi State University (U)
North Dakota State University (G)
Northwestern Connecticut Community College (U)
Notre Dame College (N)
Nyack College (U)
The Ohio State University (U)
Oregon State University (G)
Pamlico Community College (U)
Paris Junior College (U)
Peru State College (U)
Pittsburg State University (G)
St. Clair County Community College (U)
St. John's University (G)
Saint Mary-of-the-Woods College (U)
St. Petersburg College (U)
San Diego State University (U,G)
Seminole State College of Florida (N)
Sonoma State University (U)
Southern Adventist University (G)
Southern Arkansas University–Magnolia (U,G)
Southern Oregon University (U)
South Piedmont Community College (U)
State University of New York College at Potsdam (G)
Stephen F. Austin State University (G)
Stephens College (U,G)
Tarleton State University (U,G)
Tompkins Cortland Community College (U)
The University of Akron (N,U,G)
University of Alaska Fairbanks (G)
The University of Arizona (G)
University of Arkansas at Little Rock (U,G)

University of Calgary (N)
University of California, Davis (N)
University of Florida (G)
University of Great Falls (G)
University of Idaho (U)
University of Maine at Fort Kent (U)
University of Maine at Machias (U)
University of Minnesota, Duluth (U)
University of Missouri–Kansas City (G)
The University of Montana Western (U)
University of North Dakota (U)
University of Northern Iowa (U,G)
University of Oregon (U,G)
University of Saskatchewan (U)
University of South Alabama (G)
The University of South Dakota (G)
The University of Tennessee at Chattanooga (U)
The University of Tennessee at Martin (N)
The University of Texas of the Permian Basin (U,G)
University of the Southwest (U)
University of West Georgia (N,U,G)
University of Windsor (N)
University of Wisconsin–Milwaukee (N)
University of Wisconsin–Stout (N)
Utah State University (G)
Wake Technical Community College (U)
Western Carolina University (N,U,G)
Western Kentucky University (U,G)
Western Michigan University (G)
Western Wyoming Community College (U)
West Los Angeles College (U)

EDUCATION (SPECIFIC SUBJECT AREAS)

Arapahoe Community College (U)
Arkansas Tech University (U,G)
Auburn University (G)
Austin Peay State University (U)
Boise State University (U)
Brenau University (U)
California State University, San Bernardino (U,G)
California State University, San Marcos (U,G)
Canisius College (G)
Carlow University (U)
Carroll University (G)
Central Michigan University (N,G)
Central Washington University (U)
Central Wyoming College (U)
Cincinnati State Technical and Community College (U)
Columbus State University (G)
Dallas Baptist University (U)
DePaul University (G)
Dickinson State University (U)
Drake University (U,G)
Drexel University (G)
D'Youville College (U)
Eastern Illinois University (U)
Eastern Washington University (U)
Edgecombe Community College (U)
Erie Community College (U)
Erie Community College, North Campus (U)
Erie Community College, South Campus (U)
Fort Hays State University (G)
Framingham State University (G)
Franklin Pierce University (G)
Gaston College (U)
Georgia State University (G)
Glenville State College (U)
Goddard College (G)
Granite State College (G)
Hannibal-LaGrange University (U)
Harford Community College (U)
Indiana State University (G)
Iona College (G)
Jacksonville State University (U,G)
James Madison University (N)
Judson College (U)
Kansas State University (N,U,G)
Kauai Community College (G)
Kean University (U)
Keystone College (U)
Kirkwood Community College (U)
La Sierra University (U,G)
Lesley University (G)
LeTourneau University (U)
Lewis-Clark State College (U)
Liberty University (G)
Louisiana State University and Agricultural and Mechanical College (U)
Mansfield University of Pennsylvania (U)
Mary Baldwin College (U,G)
Marygrove College (U,G)
McNeese State University (G)
Michigan Technological University (G)
Middlesex Community College (U)
Minneapolis College of Art and Design (G)
Mississippi State University (U,G)
Missouri Baptist University (U,G)
Nashville State Technical Community College (N,U)
National University (G)
New Mexico Highlands University (G)
North Carolina State University (U,G)
North Dakota State University (G)
Northeastern State University (U)
North Georgia College & State University (N)
Northwest-Shoals Community College (U)
The Ohio State University (U)
Olympic College (U)
Oregon State University (G)
Pace University (U)
Pasco-Hernando Community College (N)
Penn State University Park (G)
Randolph Community College (U)
St. Ambrose University (U,G)
St. John's University (G)
Saint Mary-of-the-Woods College (U)
San Diego State University (U)
Santa Fe Community College (U)
Sioux Falls Seminary (G)
Slippery Rock University of Pennsylvania (G)
Southeast Arkansas College (U)
Southeastern Oklahoma State University (G)
Southern Adventist University (G)
Southern Arkansas University–Magnolia (U,G)
Southern Illinois University Carbondale (U)
Southern Oregon University (G)
South Piedmont Community College (U)
Spring Arbor University (U)
State University of New York at Oswego (U)
State University of New York College at Cortland (G)
State University of New York College at Potsdam (U)
Stony Brook University, State University of New York (G)
Tarleton State University (G)
Three Rivers Community College (U)
The University of Akron (U,G)
University of California, Davis (U)
University of Florida (U,G)
University of Illinois at Chicago (G)
University of Illinois at Urbana–Champaign (U,G)
University of Maine (U)
University of Maine at Machias (U)
University of Massachusetts Boston (G)
University of Michigan–Flint (N)
University of Minnesota, Duluth (N,U,G)
University of Minnesota, Morris (U)
University of New Haven (G)
The University of North Carolina Wilmington (U,G)
University of North Dakota (U,G)
University of Northern Iowa (U,G)
University of Saskatchewan (N,U)
The University of South Dakota (G)
The University of Tennessee at Martin (G)
The University of Texas of the Permian Basin (U,G)
University of the Pacific (G)
University of the Southwest (U,G)
University of Utah (U)
University of West Florida (N)
University of Wisconsin–Superior (G)
Utah State University (G)
Valley City State University (U)
Wayne Community College (U)
Wayne State College (U,G)
Western Carolina University (N)
Western Kentucky University (U,G)
West Los Angeles College (U)
West Texas A&M University (G)
West Virginia University (N)

ELECTRICAL AND POWER TRANSMISSION INSTALLATION

Austin Peay State University (U)
Central Wyoming College (N)
Cleveland Institute of Electronics (N)
Cossatot Community College of the University of Arkansas (N)
Mitchell Technical Institute (U)
Pratt Community College (U)

ELECTRICAL, ELECTRONICS AND COMMUNICATIONS ENGINEERING

Arkansas Tech University (U)
Austin Peay State University (U)
California State University, Sacramento (G)
Columbia University (N,U,G)
Cossatot Community College of the University of Arkansas (N)
Drexel University (G)
Frostburg State University (U)
Grantham University (U)
Indiana State University (G)
The Johns Hopkins University (G)
Kansas State University (U,G)
Kettering University (N)
Michigan Technological University (N,U,G)
Mississippi State University (G)
Missouri University of Science and Technology (G)
Mitchell Technical Institute (U)
Pittsburgh Technical Institute (U)
Sacramento City College (U)

Southern Methodist University (G)
University of Idaho (U)
University of Illinois at Chicago (G)

ELECTRICAL/ELECTRONICS MAINTENANCE AND REPAIR TECHNOLOGY

Austin Peay State University (U)
Central Wyoming College (N)
Cleveland Community College (U)
Cleveland Institute of Electronics (N)
Clovis Community College (U)
Cossatot Community College of the University of Arkansas (N)
James A. Rhodes State College (U)
Long Beach City College (U)
Missouri University of Science and Technology (N)
Pamlico Community College (U)
Sacramento City College (U)
St. Petersburg College (N)
South Piedmont Community College (U)
Wake Technical Community College (U)
Wayne Community College (N)

ELECTRICAL ENGINEERING TECHNOLOGIES

Alpena Community College (U)
Angelina College (U)
Arapahoe Community College (U)
Austin Peay State University (U)
Boise State University (U)
Bradley University (G)
Central Carolina Community College (U)
Clemson University (U,G)
Cleveland Institute of Electronics (U)
Columbia University (N,G)
Cossatot Community College of the University of Arkansas (N)
Drexel University (G)
Fort Valley State University (U)
Grantham University (U)
Indiana State University (U,G)
The Johns Hopkins University (G)
Kansas State University (U,G)
McNeese State University (U)
Miami University–Regional Campuses (U)
Missouri University of Science and Technology (N,G)
Palm Beach State College (U)
Pamlico Community College (U)
Sacramento City College (U)
St. Clair County Community College (U)
Southern Methodist University (G)
Sullivan County Community College (N)
University of Colorado Boulder (N,G)
University of Idaho (U,G)
University of Illinois at Chicago (G)
University of Illinois at Urbana–Champaign (U)
Wake Technical Community College (U)
Wayne Community College (U)
Wayne State University (U)
Wichita State University (U)

ELECTROMECHANICAL ENGINEERING

Columbia University (G)
Sacramento City College (U)

ELECTROMECHANICAL INSTRUMENTATION AND MAINTENANCE TECHNOLOGIES

Austin Peay State University (U)
Blackhawk Technical College (U)
Columbia University (N,G)
Cossatot Community College of the University of Arkansas (N)
Indiana State University (G)
Miami University–Regional Campuses (U)
Sacramento City College (U)
Southeast Arkansas College (U)

ENERGY AND BIOLOGICALLY BASED THERAPIES

Austin Peay State University (U)

ENGINEERING

Alcorn State University (U)
Auburn University (N)
Chatham University (U)
Cleveland Institute of Electronics (U)
Columbia University (N,G)
Danville Community College (U)
Drexel University (G)
Frostburg State University (U)
Georgia Institute of Technology (U)
Grantham University (U)
Harrisburg Area Community College (U)
Haywood Community College (U)
Indiana University–Purdue University Fort Wayne (U)
Inter American University of Puerto Rico, San Germán Campus (U)
Jacksonville State University (U)
Kansas State University (U,G)
Kettering University (N)
Lawrence Technological University (G)
LeTourneau University (G)
McNeese State University (U)
Memorial University of Newfoundland (U)
Metropolitan Community College–Penn Valley (U)
Mississippi State University (G)
Missouri University of Science and Technology (N,G)
North Carolina State University (G)
North Hennepin Community College (U)
Oakton Community College (U)
Purdue University (N,G)
Quinebaug Valley Community College (U)
Rowan University (G)
Southern Illinois University Edwardsville (U)
State University of New York College of Technology at Canton (U)
Sullivan County Community College (N)
Temple University (U)
Texas Woman's University (N)
Union County College (U)
The University of Akron (G)
The University of Alabama in Huntsville (G)
The University of Arizona (G)
University of Florida (N,G)
University of Idaho (U,G)
University of Illinois at Chicago (U,G)
University of Illinois at Urbana–Champaign (N,G)
University of Mary Washington (G)
University of Michigan–Dearborn (G)
University of New Haven (U)
The University of North Carolina at Charlotte (G)
University of North Dakota (U)
University of North Florida (U)
University of South Alabama (U)
University of Southern California (G)
University of Wisconsin–Platteville (N)
Worcester Polytechnic Institute (G)

ENGINEERING MECHANICS

Columbia University (N,G)
Columbus State Community College (U)
Kansas State University (U,G)
Missouri University of Science and Technology (G)
Southern Methodist University (G)
The University of Alabama in Huntsville (G)
The University of Arizona (G)
University of North Florida (U)
The University of Texas at Arlington (G)

ENGINEERING RELATED

Arkansas State University (U)
Boise State University (U)
Columbia University (N)
Danville Community College (U)
Drexel University (G)
Inter American University of Puerto Rico, San Germán Campus (U)
Kansas State University (U,G)
Kettering University (N)
Missouri University of Science and Technology (N)
The Ohio State University (U,G)
San Diego Community College District (U)
Southern Methodist University (G)
The University of Akron (U)
University of Cincinnati (U,G)
University of Colorado Boulder (N,G)
University of Illinois at Chicago (G)
University of Illinois at Urbana–Champaign (U)
Walden University (G)
West Virginia University (N)
Youngstown State University (U)

ENGINEERING-RELATED FIELDS

Auburn University (G)
Columbia University (N)
Danville Community College (U)
Drexel University (G)
Indiana University of Pennsylvania (G)
The Johns Hopkins University (G)
Kansas State University (U,G)
Kettering University (N)
Missouri University of Science and Technology (N)
Southern Methodist University (G)
University of Illinois at Urbana–Champaign (G)
Wayne State University (U)

ENGINEERING-RELATED TECHNOLOGIES

Columbia University (N,G)
Drexel University (G)
Indiana State University (U)
Kansas State University (U,G)

Missouri University of Science and Technology (N,G)
North Central State College (N)
Rogers State University (U)
Shawnee State University (U)
Southern Methodist University (G)

ENGINEERING SCIENCE

Auburn University (G)
Drexel University (G)
The Johns Hopkins University (G)
Kansas State University (U,G)
Metropolitan Community College–Penn Valley (U)
Missouri University of Science and Technology (G)
Southern Methodist University (G)
University of Idaho (U)
University of Illinois at Urbana–Champaign (G)
University of Michigan–Dearborn (N,G)

ENGINEERING TECHNOLOGIES RELATED

Alcorn State University (G)
Arapahoe Community College (U)
Cincinnati State Technical and Community College (U)
Columbia University (N)
Columbus State Community College (U)
Drexel University (G)
Haywood Community College (U)
James A. Rhodes State College (U)
Kansas State University (U)
Miami University–Regional Campuses (U)
Mississippi State University (G)
Missouri University of Science and Technology (G)
Pittsburg State University (U,G)
Southern Methodist University (G)
University of Southern Mississippi (U)
University of West Florida (U)
West Virginia University (G)

ENGINEERING TECHNOLOGY

Drexel University (G)
Kansas State University (U,G)
Naugatuck Valley Community College (U)
New England Institute of Technology (U)
Southern Methodist University (G)
State University of New York College of Technology at Canton (U)
The University of Akron (U)
University of Houston–Downtown (U)
University of Idaho (U,G)
University of Illinois at Chicago (G)
The University of North Carolina at Charlotte (U)
Wayne State University (U)

ENGLISH

Abilene Christian University (U)
Acadia University (U)
Allen Community College (U)
Alpena Community College (U)
Alvin Community College (U)
Anderson University (U)
Angelo State University (U,G)
Antelope Valley College (U)
Arapahoe Community College (U)
Arizona Western College (U)
Arkansas State University–Beebe (U)
Athabasca University (N,U)
Austin Peay State University (U)
Barclay College (U)
Bellevue College (U)
Belmont Technical College (U)
Beulah Heights University (U)
Big Bend Community College (U)
Bloomfield College (U)
Bluefield College (U)
Bob Jones University (U,G)
Boise State University (U)
Bossier Parish Community College (U)
Bradley University (U)
Brenau University (U)
Brigham Young University–Idaho (U)
Bronx Community College of the City University of New York (U)
Brookdale Community College (U)
Buena Vista University (U)
Buffalo State College, State University of New York (U)
Burlington College (U)
Burlington County College (U)
Butler Community College (U)
Cabrillo College (U)
California State University, Chico (U)
California State University, San Bernardino (U)
Canisius College (U)
Capital Community College (U)
Carleton University (U)
Carlow University (U)
Carl Sandburg College (U)
Carroll University (U)
Cascadia Community College (U)
Cayuga County Community College (U)
Cedarville University (U)
Central Carolina Community College (U)
Central Carolina Technical College (U)
Centralia College (U)
Central New Mexico Community College (U)
Central Texas College (U)
Central Virginia Community College (U)
Central Washington University (U)
Chaminade University of Honolulu (U)
Champlain College (U)
Chatham University (U)
Chattanooga State Community College (U)
Citrus College (U)
City University of Seattle (U)
Clark State Community College (U)
Clemson University (G)
Cleveland Community College (U)
Clinton Community College (U)
Clovis Community College (U)
Coastal Carolina University (U)
Coleman University (U)
Columbia Basin College (U)
Columbia College (U)
Columbus State Community College (U)
Community College of Allegheny County (U)
Community College of Beaver County (U)
Corning Community College (U)
Culver-Stockton College (U)
Dabney S. Lancaster Community College (U)
Dakota State University (U)
Dallas Baptist University (U)
Danville Community College (U)
Daytona State College (U)
Delgado Community College (U)
Dickinson State University (U)
Dominican College (U)
Drake University (U)
Drury University (U)
East Central Community College (U)
Eastern Oregon University (U)
Eastern Washington University (U)
Eastern West Virginia Community and Technical College (U)
Eastern Wyoming College (U)
East Georgia College (U)
Edgecombe Community College (N)
Edison State Community College (U)
Elaine P. Nunez Community College (U)
Endicott College (U)
Enterprise State Community College (U)
Erie Community College (U)
Erie Community College, North Campus (U)
Erie Community College, South Campus (U)
Excelsior College (U)
Faulkner University (U)
Ferris State University (U)
Fitchburg State University (U)
Fort Hays State University (U)
Framingham State University (U)
Friends University (U)
Front Range Community College (U)
Frostburg State University (U)
Gadsden State Community College (U)
Gannon University (U)
Gaston College (U)
George Fox University (U)
Georgia Highlands College (U)
Glenville State College (U)
Goddard College (U)
Granite State College (U)
Hannibal-LaGrange University (U)
Harcum College (U)
Harford Community College (U)
Harrisburg Area Community College (U)
Haywood Community College (U)
Heartland Community College (U)
Herkimer County Community College (U)
Hillsborough Community College (U)
Hocking College (U)
Hofstra University (U)
Huntington College of Health Sciences (U)
Huston-Tillotson University (U)
Illinois State University (U)
Illinois Valley Community College (U)
Indiana State University (U)
Indiana University of Pennsylvania (U,G)
Indiana University–Purdue University Fort Wayne (U)
Jacksonville State University (U)
James Madison University (U)
Jamestown College (U)
Jamestown Community College (U)
Jefferson Community College (U)
John A. Logan College (U)
Johnson State College (U)
Johnston Community College (U)
Judson College (U)
Judson University (U)
Kansas State University (U)
Keystone College (U)
Lackawanna College (U)
Lakehead University (U)
Lamar State College–Port Arthur (U)
Lansing Community College (U)
Lassen Community College District (U)

Lehman College of the City University of New York (U)
Lenoir Community College (U)
LeTourneau University (U)
Lewis-Clark State College (U)
Liberty University (G)
Lipscomb University (U)
Long Beach City College (U)
Los Angeles Harbor College (U)
Los Angeles Trade-Technical College (U)
Louisiana State University and Agricultural and Mechanical College (N,U)
Loyola University New Orleans (U)
Luna Community College (U)
Macon State College (U)
Mansfield University of Pennsylvania (U)
Marian University (U)
Marquette University (U)
Mary Baldwin College (U)
Marylhurst University (U)
McKendree University (U)
McMurry University (U)
McNeese State University (U)
Memorial University of Newfoundland (U)
Mercer County Community College (U)
Mesa Community College (U)
Mesa State College (U)
Miami Dade College (U)
Middlesex Community College (U)
Middle Tennessee State University (U)
Midland College (U)
Minot State University (U)
Monroe College (U)
Montcalm Community College (U)
Montgomery Community College (N,U)
Moorpark College (U)
Mount Allison University (U)
Mount Marty College (U)
Murray State University (U,G)
Naropa University (G)
Nassau Community College (N)
National University (U)
Naugatuck Valley Community College (U)
New England College of Business and Finance (U)
New Jersey City University (U)
New Mexico State University–Carlsbad (U)
New River Community College (U)
Nichols College (U)
Nipissing University (U)
North Carolina Central University (U)
North Carolina State University (U)
North Central Texas College (U)
North Dakota State College of Science (U)
North Dakota State University (U)
Northeastern State University (U,G)
Northern State University (U)
North Hennepin Community College (U)
North Lake College (U)
North Seattle Community College (U)
NorthWest Arkansas Community College (U)
Northwestern Oklahoma State University (U)
Northwest-Shoals Community College (U)
Notre Dame College (U)
Nyack College (U)
Oakton Community College (U)
Ocean County College (U)
Odessa College (U)
Ohio University (U)
Oklahoma Panhandle State University (U)
Olympic College (U)
Orange Coast College (U)
Oregon State University (N,U)
Oxnard College (U)
Ozarks Technical Community College (U)
Pace University (U)
Pamlico Community College (U)
Paris Junior College (U)
Pasco-Hernando Community College (N)
Peirce College (U)
Pellissippi State Technical Community College (U)
Perelandra College (U,G)
Peru State College (U)
Phoenix College (U)
Pikes Peak Community College (U)
Pittsburg State University (U)
Portland Community College (U)
Portland State University (U)
Providence College (U)
Pulaski Technical College (U)
Quinsigamond Community College (U)
Regent University (U)
Reinhardt University (U)
Rend Lake College (U)
Richmond Community College (U)
Rio Hondo College (U)
Riverside Community College District (U)
Rivier College (U)
Robert Morris University (U)
Rockland Community College (U)
Rogers State University (U)
Rose State College (U)
Rowan-Cabarrus Community College (U)
Sacramento City College (U)
St. Ambrose University (U)
St. Cloud State University (U)
Saint Francis University (U)
St. Gregory's University (U)
St. John Fisher College (U)
St. John's University (U)
St. Joseph's College, Long Island Campus (U)
St. Joseph's College, New York (U)
Saint Leo University (U)
Saint Paul College–A Community & Technical College (U)
St. Philip's College (U)
Sam Houston State University (U)
San Bernardino Valley College (U)
San Diego Community College District (U)
San Diego State University (U)
San Jacinto College District (U)
Santa Monica College (U)
Santa Rosa Junior College (U)
Seminole State College of Florida (U)
Shippensburg University of Pennsylvania (U,G)
Sinclair Community College (U)
Southeast Arkansas College (U)
Southeast Community College Area (U)
Southeastern Community College (U)
Southeastern Illinois College (U)
Southern Adventist University (U)
Southern Illinois University Carbondale (U)
Southern Illinois University Edwardsville (U)
Southern Maine Community College (U)
Southern University at New Orleans (U)
South Piedmont Community College (U)
Southwestern Adventist University (U)
Spartanburg Community College (U)
Spokane Community College (U)
Spoon River College (U)
Spring Arbor University (U)
State University of New York at Oswego (U)
State University of New York at Plattsburgh (U)
State University of New York College of Technology at Canton (U)
Stephens College (U)
Sullivan County Community College (N,U)
Taft College (U)
Tarleton State University (U)
Taylor University (U)
Texas State University–San Marcos (U)
Texas Woman's University (N,U)
Tompkins Cortland Community College (U)
Tunxis Community College (U)
Union County College (U)
University at Albany, State University of New York (U)
The University of Akron (U,G)
University of Alaska Fairbanks (U)
University of Arkansas at Little Rock (U,G)
The University of British Columbia (U)
University of Cincinnati (U)
University of Florida (U)
University of Great Falls (U)
University of Houston (U)
University of Houston–Downtown (U)
University of Idaho (U)
University of Illinois at Springfield (U)
University of Illinois at Urbana–Champaign (U)
The University of Kansas (U)
University of Louisville (U)
University of Maine at Augusta (U)
University of Maine at Fort Kent (U)
University of Maine at Machias (U)
University of Management and Technology (U)
University of Massachusetts Boston (U,G)
University of Memphis (U,G)
University of Minnesota, Morris (U)
University of Missouri–Kansas City (U)
University of Nevada, Reno (U)
University of New Haven (U)
University of North Alabama (U,G)
The University of North Carolina at Asheville (U)
The University of North Carolina Wilmington (U)
University of North Dakota (U)
University of Northern Iowa (U)
University of Pennsylvania (U)
University of Pittsburgh at Bradford (U)
University of St. Francis (U)
University of Saskatchewan (U)
The University of South Dakota (U)
University of Southern Maine (U)
University of Southern Mississippi (U)
The University of Texas of the Permian Basin (U)
University of the Pacific (U)
The University of West Alabama (U)
University of West Florida (U)
University of West Georgia (U)
The University of Winnipeg (U)
University of Wisconsin Colleges (N,U)
University of Wisconsin–Superior (U)
Upper Iowa University (U)
Utah State University (U,G)
Utica College (U)
Valencia College (U)
Vermont Technical College (U)
Washington State University (U)
Wayne Community College (U)

Wayne State College (U)
Wayne State University (U)
Webber International University (U)
Westchester Community College (U)
Western Kentucky University (U)
Western Texas College (U)
West Hills Community College (U)
West Los Angeles College (U)
West Virginia State University (U)
Wharton County Junior College (U)
Wichita State University (U)
Wilfrid Laurier University (U)
Wilkes Community College (U)
Windward Community College (U)
Winston-Salem State University (U)
Worcester State University (U,G)
Yavapai College (U)
York Technical College (U)

ENGLISH LANGUAGE AND LITERATURE RELATED

Acadia University (U)
Adams State College (U)
Alpena Community College (U)
American University (U,G)
Antelope Valley College (U)
Arapahoe Community College (U)
Arkansas Tech University (U)
Asbury University (U)
Ashland University (U)
Athabasca University (U)
Austin Peay State University (U)
Avila University (U)
Bellevue College (U)
Belmont Technical College (U)
Big Bend Community College (U)
Bloomfield College (U)
Boise State University (U)
Bowling Green State University (U)
Brenau University (U)
Brigham Young University (N)
Brigham Young University–Idaho (U)
Bryan College (U)
Burlington College (U)
Burlington County College (U)
California State University, East Bay (U)
Capital Community College (U)
Cascadia Community College (U)
Cayuga County Community College (U)
Cedarville University (U)
Central Texas College (U)
Charter Oak State College (U)
Clatsop Community College (U)
The College at Brockport, State University of New York (U)
College of Saint Mary (U)
College of the Humanities and Sciences, Harrison Middleton University (G)
College of the Siskiyous (U)
Columbus State Community College (U)
Corning Community College (U)
Cossatot Community College of the University of Arkansas (U)
Dabney S. Lancaster Community College (U)
Dakota State University (U)
Dallas Baptist University (U)
Danville Community College (U)
Daytona State College (U)
Eastern Illinois University (U)
Eastern Oregon University (U)
Erie Community College (U)
Erie Community College, North Campus (U)
Erie Community College, South Campus (U)
Ferris State University (U)
Friends University (U)
Gateway Community College (U)
Genesee Community College (U)
Georgia Highlands College (U)
Goddard College (U)
Granite State College (U)
Greenville Technical College (U)
Haywood Community College (U)
Hofstra University (U)
Holyoke Community College (U)
Hopkinsville Community College (U)
Inter American University of Puerto Rico, San Germán Campus (U)
Iowa Lakes Community College (U)
Jacksonville State University (U)
Jamestown Community College (U)
John A. Logan College (U)
John Jay College of Criminal Justice of the City University of New York (U)
Johnson State College (U)
Johnston Community College (U)
Judson University (U)
Kean University (N)
Lakehead University (U)
Lake-Sumter Community College (U)
Lamar State College–Orange (U)
Laurel University (U)
Lewis-Clark State College (U)
Lindenwood University (U)
Lock Haven University of Pennsylvania (U)
Los Angeles Harbor College (U)
Los Angeles Trade-Technical College (U)
Louisiana State University and Agricultural and Mechanical College (U)
Mansfield University of Pennsylvania (U)
Marylhurst University (U)
McDowell Technical Community College (U)
Mercy College of Northwest Ohio (U)
Mesa State College (U)
Miami Dade College (U)
Middlesex Community College (U)
Misericordia University (U)
Mountain State University (U)
Mount Olive College (U)
Murray State University (G)
Nassau Community College (U)
Naugatuck Valley Community College (U)
New England Institute of Technology (U)
Nicolet Area Technical College (U)
North Carolina State University (U)
North Central Texas College (U)
North Dakota State University (U)
North Iowa Area Community College (U)
North Seattle Community College (U)
NorthWest Arkansas Community College (U)
Northwestern Michigan College (U)
Nyack College (U)
Oakland Community College (U)
Ohio University (U)
Oklahoma Panhandle State University (U)
Oklahoma State University (U)
Olympic College (U)
Oregon State University (U)
Paine College (U)
Pamlico Community College (U)
Pennsylvania College of Technology (U)
Perelandra College (U,G)
Prairie View A&M University (U)
Providence College and Theological Seminary (U)
Queen's University at Kingston (U)
Quinebaug Valley Community College (U)
Reading Area Community College (U)
Rose State College (U)
The Sage Colleges (U)
Saint Francis University (U)
San Diego Community College District (U)
San Jacinto College District (U)
Sinclair Community College (U)
Southeast Arkansas College (U)
Southern New Hampshire University (U)
South Piedmont Community College (U)
South Suburban College (U)
Spokane Community College (U)
State University of New York College at Cortland (U)
State University of New York College of Agriculture and Technology at Morrisville (U)
Stephens College (U)
Stony Brook University, State University of New York (G)
Syracuse University (U)
Taft College (U)
Texas State University–San Marcos (U)
The University of Akron (U,G)
University of Alaska Fairbanks (U)
University of Alaska, Prince William Sound Community College (U)
University of Arkansas at Little Rock (U)
University of Colorado at Colorado Springs (N)
University of Dubuque (U)
University of Florida (U)
University of Idaho (U)
University of Illinois at Urbana–Champaign (U)
University of Maine at Machias (U)
University of Mary (U)
University of Minnesota, Crookston (U)
University of New Haven (U)
University of North Florida (U)
University of Southern Maine (U)
The University of Texas of the Permian Basin (U,G)
University of the Southwest (U)
Walla Walla University (U)
Westchester Community College (U)
Western Kentucky University (U,G)
West Hills Community College (U)
West Los Angeles College (U)
Wharton County Junior College (U)
Wilkes Community College (U)
York County Community College (U)
York University (U)
Youngstown State University (N,U)

ENGLISH OR FRENCH AS A SECOND OR FOREIGN LANGUAGE (TEACHING)

Acadia University (U)
Anaheim University (N,G)
Athabasca University (N)
Austin Peay State University (N,U)
Bob Jones University (U,G)
Buena Vista University (G)
The College at Brockport, State University of New York (G)
Columbus State Community College (U)

Dallas Baptist University (U,G)
Drexel University (G)
Heartland Community College (N)
Indiana State University (G)
Johnson University (U)
Kansas State University (U,G)
Kean University (N)
Lesley University (G)
Lincoln Christian University (U,G)
Long Beach City College (U)
Murray State University (G)
New Mexico Highlands University (G)
North Carolina State University (U)
North Hennepin Community College (N)
Northwestern Connecticut Community College (U)
Oregon State University (G)
Providence College and Theological Seminary (U)
Sacramento City College (U)
Southern Arkansas University–Magnolia (G)
Spokane Community College (U)
The University of Akron (U)
University of Florida (U)
University of Maine (U)
University of Nevada, Reno (U)
University of North Dakota (G)
University of Saskatchewan (N,U)
The University of Tennessee at Martin (G)
The University of Texas of the Permian Basin (U)
University of West Georgia (G)
Webber International University (U)
Western Kentucky University (U)

ENTREPRENEURIAL AND SMALL BUSINESS OPERATIONS

Adams State College (N)
Andrew Jackson University (U,G)
Arapahoe Community College (U)
Austin Peay State University (N,U)
Bakke Graduate University (G)
Bellevue College (U)
Boise State University (U)
Boston University (G)
Bridgewater State University (U)
Broward College (U)
Butler Community College (U)
Cayuga County Community College (U)
Central Michigan University (G)
Central New Mexico Community College (U)
Central Texas College (U)
Champlain College (U)
Cleveland Community College (U)
Columbia College (U)
Columbia University (G)
Community College of Beaver County (N)
Dallas Baptist University (G)
DeVry University Online (G)
Dickinson State University (U)
Drexel University (N,U,G)
Eastern West Virginia Community and Technical College (U)
Eastern Wyoming College (U)
Front Range Community College (U)
Genesee Community College (N)
Goddard College (G)
Haywood Community College (U)
Herkimer County Community College (U)
Iona College (U)
Jamestown Community College (N,U)
Jones International University (U,G)
Lamar State College–Port Arthur (N)
Lewis-Clark State College (U)
Marlboro College Graduate College (U)
Maryville University of Saint Louis (N)
Minnesota School of Business–Richfield (U)
Minot State University (U)
Missouri University of Science and Technology (N)
Mitchell Technical Institute (N)
Monroe College (U)
Mount Wachusett Community College (N)
Nashville State Technical Community College (U)
Nassau Community College (U)
New Mexico Junior College (N)
New River Community College (U)
North Central State College (N)
Northern Kentucky University (U)
North Shore Community College (N)
NorthWest Arkansas Community College (U)
Olympic College (U)
Peninsula College (U)
Piedmont Community College (U)
Prescott College (N)
Quinsigamond Community College (N)
Rend Lake College (N)
Rockingham Community College (N)
St. Petersburg College (U)
Santa Monica College (U)
Seminole State College of Florida (N)
Shippensburg University of Pennsylvania (G)
Sinclair Community College (U)
Southeast Arkansas College (U)
Southern New Hampshire University (U)
South Piedmont Community College (U)
State University of New York at Plattsburgh (U,G)
State University of New York College at Potsdam (N,U)
State University of New York College of Agriculture and Technology at Morrisville (U)
Stephens College (U,G)
Suffolk University (G)
Sullivan County Community College (N)
United States Sports Academy (G)
The University of Akron (N)
University of Alaska Fairbanks (U)
University of Bridgeport (U)
University of Florida (U)
University of Houston–Victoria (G)
University of Illinois at Urbana–Champaign (G)
University of Maine at Machias (U)
University of Minnesota, Crookston (U)
The University of Texas at Dallas (G)
University of the Pacific (N)
Upper Iowa University (U)
Vincennes University (U)
Wake Technical Community College (N)
West Hills Community College (U)
Worcester State University (N)
Youngstown State University (N)

ENVIRONMENTAL CONTROL TECHNOLOGIES

Athabasca University (N,U)
Austin Peay State University (U)
California State University, Dominguez Hills (N)
Columbia University (N,G)
Columbus State Community College (U)
Jacksonville State University (U,G)
Lamar State College–Orange (U)
Odessa College (U)
Oxnard College (U)
Sullivan County Community College (N)
The University of British Columbia (U)
The University of Findlay (G)
University of Florida (N,G)
The University of Texas of the Permian Basin (U)

ENVIRONMENTAL DESIGN

Boston Architectural College (N,U,G)
Bowling Green State University (U)
Central Michigan University (N)
Chatham University (U)
Columbia University (N,G)
Cornell University (U)
Goddard College (G)
Mount Wachusett Community College (N)
Philadelphia University (G)
Prescott College (N)
St. Petersburg College (N)
Santa Fe Community College (U)
Sonoma State University (N,U)
Southern Methodist University (G)
Sullivan County Community College (N)
University of Oregon (U,G)

ENVIRONMENTAL/ ENVIRONMENTAL HEALTH ENGINEERING

Central Carolina Technical College (U)
Clackamas Community College (U)
Columbia University (N,G)
Fort Valley State University (G)
Georgia Institute of Technology (N,G)
Harrisburg Area Community College (U)
The Johns Hopkins University (G)
Johnson State College (U)
Medical College of Wisconsin (G)
Missouri University of Science and Technology (N)
New York Medical College (G)
North Carolina State University (U)
Odessa College (U)
Oregon State University (G)
Pennsylvania College of Technology (U)
Robert Morris University (U)
Rochester Institute of Technology (G)
St. Cloud State University (U)
Southern Methodist University (G)
State University of New York College of Environmental Science & Forestry, Ranger School (U)
Three Rivers Community College (U)
The University of Alabama in Huntsville (G)
University of Colorado Boulder (N,G)
University of Dubuque (U)
University of Florida (N,G)
University of Idaho (U,G)
University of Illinois at Springfield (G)
University of Illinois at Urbana–Champaign (G)
University of Massachusetts Boston (U)
The University of North Carolina at Asheville (U)
University of North Dakota (G)

The University of Texas at Arlington (G)
The University of Winnipeg (U)
Worcester Polytechnic Institute (G)
York Technical College (U)

ETHNIC, CULTURAL MINORITY, GENDER, AND GROUP STUDIES

Arapahoe Community College (U)
Athabasca University (N)
Austin Peay State University (U)
Bellevue College (U)
Beulah Heights University (U)
Bowling Green State University (U)
Bridgewater State University (U)
Burlington College (U)
California State University, Chico (U)
California State University, East Bay (U)
California State University, San Bernardino (U)
Cayuga County Community College (U)
Central Texas College (U)
Chemeketa Community College (U)
Columbia Basin College (U)
Columbus State Community College (U)
Eastern Washington University (U)
Edgecombe Community College (U)
Ferris State University (U)
Global University (U)
Goddard College (U)
Hope International University (N)
Illinois Valley Community College (U)
Kansas State University (U)
Louisiana State University and Agricultural and Mechanical College (U)
Middlesex Community College (U)
Naropa University (N,U)
Nicolet Area Technical College (U)
North Carolina State University (U)
North Dakota State University (U)
Ohio University (U)
Oregon State University (U)
Pace University (U)
Prairie View A&M University (G)
Prescott College (N,G)
Queen's University at Kingston (U)
Randolph Community College (U)
The Richard Stockton College of New Jersey (U)
Sacramento City College (U)
Saint Paul College–A Community & Technical College (U)
Salem Community College (U)
San Diego State University (U)
Santa Rosa Junior College (U)
Seminole State College of Florida (N)
Sinclair Community College (U)
Southwest Wisconsin Technical College (U)
State University of New York at Plattsburgh (U)
State University of New York College at Oneonta (U)
Stephens College (U)
Syracuse University (U,G)
Tompkins Cortland Community College (U)
The University of Akron (U)
University of Alaska Fairbanks (U)
University of Arkansas at Little Rock (U)
The University of British Columbia (U)
The University of Findlay (U)
University of Illinois at Urbana–Champaign (U)
The University of Kansas (U)
University of Louisville (U)
University of Maine (U)
University of Nevada, Reno (G)
University of New Haven (U)
The University of North Carolina at Asheville (U,G)
The University of North Carolina at Chapel Hill (N,U)
University of Oregon (U)
University of Southern Maine (U)
University of Waterloo (U)
University of Wisconsin Colleges (U)
University of Wisconsin–Green Bay (U)
Webber International University (U)
Western Kentucky University (U,G)
Western Michigan University (U)
Western Wyoming Community College (U)
West Hills Community College (U)
Wichita State University (U)
Wilkes Community College (U)
Yavapai College (U)

FAMILY AND CONSUMER ECONOMICS

Austin Peay State University (N,U)
Brigham Young University–Idaho (U)
California State University, San Marcos (N)
Cleveland State Community College (N)
College of the Siskiyous (U)
Eastern Illinois University (U,G)
East Los Angeles College (U)
Hopkinsville Community College (U)
Illinois State University (U)
Jacksonville State University (U)
Kansas State University (N)
McNeese State University (U)
Minnesota School of Business–Online (U)
North Dakota State University (U,G)
Oakton Community College (N)
The Ohio State University (U)
Oregon State University (N)
Ozarks Technical Community College (U)
Pasco-Hernando Community College (N)
Pulaski Technical College (U)
Rend Lake College (U)
Sacramento City College (U)
Sam Houston State University (U)
Southeastern Oklahoma State University (N)
Southern University at New Orleans (U)
Stephen F. Austin State University (U)
Texas Woman's University (U,G)
The University of Arizona (G)
University of Idaho (U)
University of Northern Iowa (U)
Utah State University (U)
Valencia College (U)
Wake Technical Community College (N)
Western Kentucky University (G)
Western Michigan University (U,G)
Wichita State University (U)

FAMILY AND CONSUMER SCIENCES/HUMAN SCIENCES

Antelope Valley College (U)
Austin Peay State University (U)
Bowling Green State University (U)
Bradley University (U)
Brigham Young University–Idaho (U)
Central Michigan University (U)
Central Texas College (U)
Eastern Washington University (U)
Eastern Wyoming College (U)
Erikson Institute (N,G)
Fontbonne University (U,G)
Granite State College (N)
Jacksonville State University (U)
Kansas State University (N,U,G)
Kean University (N)
Liberty University (G)
Middle Tennessee State University (U)
Minnesota School of Business–Online (U)
North Carolina Central University (U)
North Carolina State University (G)
North Central State College (N)
North Dakota State University (U,G)
Ohio University (U)
Sacramento City College (U)
Santa Rosa Junior College (U)
The University of Akron (U)
The University of Arizona (U)
University of Maine at Augusta (U)
Utah State University (U,G)
Western Kentucky University (U)
Western Michigan University (U,G)
Windward Community College (U)

FAMILY AND CONSUMER SCIENCES/HUMAN SCIENCES BUSINESS SERVICES

Cardinal Stritch University (N)
Jacksonville State University (U)
Minnesota School of Business–Online (U)
North Dakota State University (G)
Pittsburg State University (U)
Rend Lake College (U)
Sacramento City College (U)
The University of Arizona (U)
Western Kentucky University (U)

FAMILY AND CONSUMER SCIENCES/HUMAN SCIENCES RELATED

Central Michigan University (U)
Central Washington University (U)
Jacksonville State University (U,G)
Kansas State University (N,U,G)
Mesa Community College (U)
Minnesota School of Business–Online (U)
North Dakota State University (U,G)
The Ohio State University (U)
Sacramento City College (U)
Sinclair Community College (U)
Southeastern Illinois College (U)
Tarleton State University (U)
University of Idaho (U)
Western Kentucky University (U)
Western Michigan University (U)

FILM/VIDEO AND PHOTOGRAPHIC ARTS

Academy of Art University (U,G)
Antelope Valley College (U)
Arapahoe Community College (U)
Auburn University (U)
Austin Peay State University (U)
Blackhawk Technical College (N)
Bossier Parish Community College (N,U)

Bowling Green State University (U)
Burlington College (U)
Burlington County College (U)
Butler County Community College (N)
Cabrillo College (U)
California State University, Dominguez Hills (N)
California State University, Monterey Bay (U)
Cape Fear Community College (U)
Cayuga County Community College (U)
Central Wyoming College (N)
Chatham University (U,G)
Cleveland State Community College (N)
College of San Mateo (U)
Columbus State Community College (U)
Hofstra University (U)
Houston Community College System (U)
Illinois Valley Community College (U)
John A. Logan College (U)
Kean University (N)
Kirkwood Community College (U)
Lock Haven University of Pennsylvania (U)
Long Beach City College (U)
Los Angeles Trade-Technical College (U)
Mansfield University of Pennsylvania (N)
Marylhurst University (U)
Minneapolis College of Art and Design (N,U)
Mount Wachusett Community College (N,U)
New Mexico State University (U)
North Dakota State University (N,U)
North Shore Community College (U)
Oakland Community College (U)
Oakton Community College (U)
Orange Coast College (U)
Oregon State University (N)
Peninsula College (N)
Prescott College (N)
Reading Area Community College (U)
Regent University (U,G)
Rend Lake College (U)
The Richard Stockton College of New Jersey (N,U)
Riverside Community College District (U)
Sacramento City College (U)
St. Petersburg College (N)
Sam Houston State University (U)
San Diego State University (N)
Sessions College for Professional Design (N,U)
Southeastern Oklahoma State University (N)
Temple University (U)
University of Alaska Fairbanks (U)
The University of British Columbia (U)
University of Cincinnati Raymond Walters College (U)
University of Maine at Machias (U)
University of North Alabama (U)
Valencia College (U)
Wake Technical Community College (N)
Wayne State University (U)
Webber International University (U)
Westmoreland County Community College (U)
West Virginia State University (U,G)
Worcester State University (N)
York University (U)

FINANCE AND FINANCIAL MANAGEMENT SERVICES

Adams State College (U)
Albertus Magnus College (U)
Alcorn State University (U,G)
The American College (U,G)
American University (U)
Andrew Jackson University (G)
Anne Arundel Community College (N,U)
Arapahoe Community College (U)
Athabasca University (N,U)
Austin Peay State University (U)
Baker College Online (U,G)
Baldwin-Wallace College (U)
Boston University (N)
Brenau University (G)
Bryant & Stratton Online (N,U)
Bryant University (N)
Buena Vista University (U)
Butler County Community College (N,U)
California State University, Dominguez Hills (N)
California State University, San Bernardino (U)
Carroll University (U)
Cedarville University (U)
Central Michigan University (G)
Central Wyoming College (N)
Champlain College (U)
Charter Oak State College (U)
Chattanooga State Community College (U)
Cleary University (G)
Cleveland Community College (U)
Cleveland State Community College (N)
Columbia College (U)
Columbia University (G)
Columbus State Community College (U)
Concordia University Wisconsin (U)
Dallas Baptist University (U,G)
Delgado Community College (U)
DePaul University (N,G)
DeVry University Online (G)
Drake University (G)
Drexel University (N,U,G)
Erie Community College (U)
Erie Community College, North Campus (U)
Erie Community College, South Campus (U)
Ferris State University (U)
Fitchburg State University (G)
Florida State University (N)
Framingham State University (G)
Gannon University (U)
Georgia State University (U)
Glenville State College (U)
Granite State College (U)
Grantham University (U,G)
Harrisburg Area Community College (U)
Haywood Community College (U)
Hillsborough Community College (U)
Indiana State University (U,G)
Indiana University of Pennsylvania (U)
Inter American University of Puerto Rico, San Germán Campus (U)
Iona College (U,G)
Jacksonville State University (U,G)
James A. Rhodes State College (U)
Jamestown Community College (N)
Kansas State University (N,U,G)
Kean University (N,U)
Labette Community College (U)
Lamar State College–Orange (U)
Lamar State College–Port Arthur (N)
La Roche College (U)
Lawrence Technological University (G)
Lewis-Clark State College (U)
Lipscomb University (G)
Long Beach City College (U)
Louisiana State University and Agricultural and Mechanical College (U)
Maharishi University of Management (N,U,G)
Marian University (U)
Marist College (U,G)
Marlboro College Graduate College (U)
Maryville University of Saint Louis (U)
Mercer County Community College (N)
Middlesex Community College (N)
Midway College (U)
Minot State University (U)
Monroe College (U)
Mountain State University (U)
Mount Wachusett Community College (N)
Murray State College (U)
New England College of Business and Finance (N,U)
New Mexico State University–Carlsbad (U)
New River Community College (U)
Nichols College (U)
Nipissing University (U)
North Dakota State University (N,G)
Northeastern State University (U)
North Georgia College & State University (U)
North Iowa Area Community College (U)
The Ohio State University (U)
Pace University (U)
Pacific States University (G)
Paris Junior College (N)
Pennsylvania College of Technology (U)
Philadelphia University (U,G)
Phoenix College (N)
Prairie View A&M University (U,G)
Quinnipiac University (G)
Randolph Community College (U)
Rend Lake College (U)
Robert Morris University (U)
Rockingham Community College (N)
Rockland Community College (U)
Roger Williams University (U)
Sacramento City College (U)
St. John's University (U,G)
St. Petersburg College (N,U)
Sam Houston State University (U)
Sampson Community College (U)
Shippensburg University of Pennsylvania (U)
Sinclair Community College (U)
Southeastern Oklahoma State University (U)
Southern Adventist University (U)
Southern Arkansas University–Magnolia (U)
Southern Illinois University Carbondale (U)
Southern New Hampshire University (U)
Southern Union State Community College (U)
South Piedmont Community College (U)
Southwest Wisconsin Technical College (U)
Spartanburg Community College (N)
Spring Arbor University (U)
Stanly Community College (U)
State University of New York College at Potsdam (N)
State University of New York Empire State College (U)
State University of New York Institute of Technology (G)
Stephen F. Austin State University (U)
Stephens College (U,G)
Suffolk University (G)
The University of Akron (U)
University of Alaska Fairbanks (U)
University of Arkansas at Little Rock (U,G)

University of Colorado at Colorado Springs (G)
University of Evansville (N)
University of Florida (U)
University of Houston–Downtown (U)
University of Idaho (U)
University of Illinois at Chicago (G)
University of Maine at Augusta (U)
University of Management and Technology (U)
University of Michigan (N)
University of North Alabama (U)
The University of Texas at Arlington (G)
The University of Texas at Dallas (G)
The University of Texas of the Permian Basin (G)
University of Toronto (N)
University of Utah (U)
University of Waterloo (U)
University of Wisconsin–La Crosse (G)
University of Wisconsin MBA Consortium (G)
Upper Iowa University (U)
Wake Technical Community College (N)
Wayland Baptist University (U)
Wayne State University (U,G)
Webber International University (U)
Webster University (G)
Western Carolina University (N)
West Virginia University (N)
Wilfrid Laurier University (U)
York College of Pennsylvania (N)

FINE AND STUDIO ARTS

Academy of Art University (U,G)
Alpena Community College (U)
Athabasca University (N,U)
Austin Peay State University (N,U)
Bluefield College (U)
Bossier Parish Community College (U)
Bowling Green State University (U)
Brazosport College (U)
Burlington College (U)
Burlington County College (U)
Butler Community College (U)
California State University, Dominguez Hills (N)
California State University, San Marcos (N)
Carl Sandburg College (U)
Central Texas College (U)
Central Wyoming College (N,U)
Chemeketa Community College (U)
City Colleges of Chicago System (U)
Clovis Community College (U)
Coastal Carolina University (U)
College of Southern Maryland (U)
Colorado Mountain College (U)
Columbia Basin College (U)
Community College of Beaver County (U)
Concordia University, St. Paul (N)
Corning Community College (U)
Cossatot Community College of the University of Arkansas (U)
Dakota State University (U)
Dallas Baptist University (U)
Dawson Community College (U)
Delgado Community College (U)
Duquesne University (U)
Eastern Kentucky University (U)
Eastern Washington University (U)
East Los Angeles College (U)
Edison State Community College (U)
Elaine P. Nunez Community College (U)
Erie Community College (U)
Erie Community College, North Campus (U)
Erie Community College, South Campus (U)
Friends University (U)
Georgian Court University (U)
Goddard College (U,G)
Governors State University (U,G)
Greenville Technical College (U)
Haywood Community College (U)
Hibbing Community College (U)
Houston Community College System (U)
Indiana University–Purdue University Fort Wayne (U)
Indiana Wesleyan University (U)
James Madison University (U)
Judson University (U)
Kean University (N,U)
Labette Community College (U)
Lake Superior College (U)
Lamar State College–Port Arthur (U)
Lenoir Community College (U)
Lewis University (U)
Lindenwood University (U)
Lock Haven University of Pennsylvania (U)
Louisiana State University and Agricultural and Mechanical College (U)
Lourdes College (U)
Malone University (U)
Mansfield University of Pennsylvania (N)
Mercy College of Northwest Ohio (U)
Mesa State College (U)
Middlesex Community College (N,U)
Middle Tennessee State University (N)
Minneapolis College of Art and Design (N,U,G)
Misericordia University (U)
Mississippi State University (U)
Mountain Empire Community College (U)
Mountain State University (U)
Mount Mary College (G)
Naugatuck Valley Community College (U)
North Arkansas College (U)
North Central Texas College (U)
North Hennepin Community College (U)
NorthWest Arkansas Community College (U)
Olympic College (U)
Oregon State University (N)
Oxnard College (U)
Pace University (U)
Peninsula College (N)
Pennsylvania College of Technology (U)
Phoenix College (N)
Rappahannock Community College (U)
Rio Hondo College (U)
Rockland Community College (U)
Rogers State University (U)
Saint Leo University (U)
St. Petersburg College (U)
San Bernardino Valley College (U)
San Diego Community College District (U)
San Jacinto College District (U)
Savannah College of Art and Design (U,G)
Sessions College for Professional Design (N,U)
Shippensburg University of Pennsylvania (U,G)
Sinclair Community College (U)
Southern University at New Orleans (U)
Southwestern Community College (U)
Spoon River College (U)
Taylor University (U)
Texas State University–San Marcos (U)
Tompkins Cortland Community College (U)
Trine University (U)
Tyler Junior College (U)
Union County College (U)
University of Alaska Fairbanks (U)
The University of Findlay (U)
University of Great Falls (U)
University of Houston–Downtown (U)
University of Illinois at Springfield (U)
University of Nevada, Reno (U)
The University of North Carolina at Chapel Hill (N,U)
The University of Texas at Arlington (U)
The University of Texas of the Permian Basin (U)
University of Utah (U)
University of West Florida (U)
University of Wisconsin–Green Bay (U)
University of Wisconsin–Superior (U)
Valencia College (U)
Western Kentucky University (U)
Westmoreland County Community College (U)
West Virginia State University (U)
Wichita State University (G)
Wilfrid Laurier University (U)
Wilkes Community College (U)

FIRE PROTECTION

Arizona Western College (U)
Bellevue College (U)
Blackhawk Technical College (N,U)
Bossier Parish Community College (U)
Bowling Green State University (N)
Butler Community College (U)
Butler County Community College (U)
Cabrillo College (U)
Carleton University (G)
Central New Mexico Community College (U)
Central Texas College (U)
Chattanooga State Community College (U)
Chemeketa Community College (U)
Cleveland Community College (N,U)
Cogswell Polytechnical College (U)
Columbus State Community College (U)
Community College of Allegheny County (U)
Cossatot Community College of the University of Arkansas (U)
Erie Community College (U)
Erie Community College, North Campus (U)
Erie Community College, South Campus (U)
Hillsborough Community College (U)
Houston Community College System (U)
Jacksonville State University (G)
Los Angeles Harbor College (U)
Luna Community College (U)
Metropolitan Community College–Penn Valley (U)
Middlesex Community College (U)
Midland College (N)
New Jersey City University (U)
New Mexico State University (U)
NorthWest Arkansas Community College (U)
Oklahoma State University (N,U)
Olympic College (U)
Pamlico Community College (U)
Pikes Peak Community College (U)
Portland Community College (U)
Quinsigamond Community College (U)

Rio Hondo College (U)
Rockingham Community College (N)
San Diego Community College District (U)
San Jacinto College District (U)
Santa Rosa Junior College (U)
Seminole State College of Florida (U)
Southeast Arkansas College (U)
State University of New York Empire State College (U)
Tyler Junior College (U)
The University of Akron (U)
University of Florida (U)
University of Memphis (U)
Vincennes University (U)
Wayne Community College (N)
West Los Angeles College (U)
Worcester Polytechnic Institute (G)
Yavapai College (U)

FISHING AND FISHERIES SCIENCES AND MANAGEMENT

Bossier Parish Community College (N)
Gadsden State Community College (U)
Oregon State University (U)
Peninsula College (N)
University of Alaska Fairbanks (U)

FOOD SCIENCE AND TECHNOLOGY

Austin Peay State University (U)
Bossier Parish Community College (U)
Brigham Young University (U)
Burlington County College (U)
Central Michigan University (G)
Central Wyoming College (N)
Jamestown Community College (N)
J. Sargeant Reynolds Community College (U)
Kansas State University (N,U,G)
Middle Tennessee State University (U)
North Carolina State University (G)
North Dakota State University (U,G)
NorthWest Arkansas Community College (U)
The Ohio State University (U)
Orange Coast College (U)
Sam Houston State University (U)
San Jacinto College District (U)
Santa Rosa Junior College (U)
University of Alaska Fairbanks (U)
University of California, Davis (N,U)
University of Florida (U,G)
Valencia College (U)
Wayne State University (U)
West Virginia University (N)

FOODS, NUTRITION, AND RELATED SERVICES

Acadia University (U)
Athabasca University (N,U)
Auburn University (N,G)
Austin Peay State University (U)
Blackhawk Technical College (N)
Brigham Young University–Idaho (U)
Burlington County College (U)
Butler County Community College (U)
Cabrillo College (U)
California State University, Sacramento (U)
Cascadia Community College (U)
Central Michigan University (G)
Central New Mexico Community College (U)
Central Texas College (U)
Central Wyoming College (N)
Charter Oak State College (U)
Chemeketa Community College (U)
Cleveland State Community College (N)
Columbus State Community College (U)
Community College of Allegheny County (U)
Dakota College at Bottineau (U)
Danville Community College (U)
Eastern Washington University (U)
East Los Angeles College (U)
Framingham State University (U,G)
Gannon University (U)
Harrisburg Area Community College (U)
Heartland Community College (U)
Hibbing Community College (U)
Houston Community College System (U)
Huntington College of Health Sciences (N,U,G)
Illinois Eastern Community Colleges, Frontier Community College (U)
Indiana University of Pennsylvania (U,G)
Jacksonville State University (U)
The Johns Hopkins University (G)
Kansas State University (N,U,G)
Lake-Sumter Community College (U)
Lamar State College–Port Arthur (U)
Lansing Community College (U)
Lewis-Clark State College (U)
Lock Haven University of Pennsylvania (U)
Long Beach City College (U)
Mansfield University of Pennsylvania (N)
Mesa Community College (U)
Miami Dade College (U)
Middlesex Community College (U)
Minnesota School of Business–Online (U)
Nassau Community College (U)
New Mexico State University (U)
North Carolina State University (U,G)
North Central State College (N)
North Dakota State College of Science (U)
North Dakota State University (U,G)
North Seattle Community College (U)
NorthWest Arkansas Community College (U)
Oklahoma State University (U)
Orange Coast College (U)
Oregon State University (G)
Ozarks Technical Community College (U)
Peninsula College (N)
Phoenix College (U)
Portland Community College (U)
Rend Lake College (U)
The Richard Stockton College of New Jersey (U)
Rose State College (U)
Sacramento City College (U)
Saint Paul College–A Community & Technical College (U)
Sam Houston State University (U)
Santa Fe Community College (U)
Santa Monica College (U)
Southeast Arkansas College (U)
Southeast Community College Area (U)
South Piedmont Community College (U)
Southwest Wisconsin Technical College (U)
State University of New York College at Oneonta (G)
Stephen F. Austin State University (U)
The University of Akron (U)
University of Alaska Fairbanks (U)
University of Arkansas at Little Rock (U)
University of Bridgeport (U,G)
The University of British Columbia (U)
University of Florida (N,U,G)
University of Idaho (U)
University of Maine at Machias (U)
University of Minnesota, Crookston (U)
University of North Alabama (U)
The University of North Carolina at Chapel Hill (U)
University of Northern Iowa (U)
University of Southern Mississippi (U)
The University of Texas at Brownsville (N)
University of Utah (U)
Valencia College (U)
Wayne State University (U)
Western Kentucky University (U)
West Los Angeles College (U)
West Virginia University (N)
Wisconsin Indianhead Technical College (N,U)
Youngstown State University (U)

FORESTRY

Central Carolina Technical College (U)
Dakota College at Bottineau (U)
Haywood Community College (U)
Michigan Technological University (N,U)
Mid-State Technical College (U)
Mississippi State University (U)
North Carolina State University (U)
The Ohio State University (U)
Oregon State University (U)
Stephen F. Austin State University (G)
The University of British Columbia (U)
University of Florida (U)
Wayne Community College (U)

FUNERAL SERVICE AND MORTUARY SCIENCE

Arapahoe Community College (U)
Arkansas State University (U)
St. Louis Community College (U)
St. Petersburg College (N,U)
Vincennes University (U)

GENETICS

Capital Community College (U)
Charter Oak State College (U)
Jacksonville State University (U)
The Johns Hopkins University (G)
Labette Community College (U)
North Carolina State University (U)
North Dakota State University (U)
Oakton Community College (U)
San Diego Community College District (U)
University of Arkansas at Little Rock (U)
University of Florida (G)
University of Illinois at Urbana–Champaign (N,G)

GEOGRAPHY AND CARTOGRAPHY

Acadia University (U)
Allen Community College (U)
Alvin Community College (U)
Andrews University (U)
Anne Arundel Community College (U)
Arapahoe Community College (U)
Arkansas State University–Beebe (U)

Athabasca University (U)
Austin Peay State University (U)
Bellevue College (U)
Bethel University (U)
Boise State University (U)
Bossier Parish Community College (U)
Bowling Green State University (U)
Brazosport College (U)
Brenau University (U)
Bridgewater State University (U)
Brigham Young University (U)
Bronx Community College of the City University of New York (U)
Broward College (U)
Cabrillo College (U)
California State University, Chico (U)
California State University, East Bay (U)
Carleton University (U)
Carl Sandburg College (U)
Cascadia Community College (U)
Cedarville University (U)
Centralia College (U)
Central Texas College (U)
Central Washington University (U)
Central Wyoming College (U)
Champlain College (U)
Chattanooga State Community College (U)
Chemeketa Community College (U)
City Colleges of Chicago System (U)
College of Southern Maryland (U)
Colorado Mountain College (U)
Columbia Basin College (U)
Columbia College (U)
Columbus State Community College (U)
Culver-Stockton College (U)
Danville Community College (U)
Drury University (U)
Eastern Kentucky University (U)
Eastern Oregon University (U)
Eastern Washington University (U)
Endicott College (U)
Erie Community College (U)
Erie Community College, North Campus (U)
Erie Community College, South Campus (U)
Ferris State University (U)
Florida State University (U)
Front Range Community College (U)
Gaston College (U)
Governors State University (U)
Harrisburg Area Community College (U)
Holyoke Community College (U)
Hopkinsville Community College (U)
Houston Community College System (U)
Illinois Eastern Community Colleges, Lincoln Trail College (U)
Illinois Valley Community College (U)
Indiana State University (U)
Jacksonville State University (U,G)
James A. Rhodes State College (U)
Johnston Community College (U)
Kansas State University (U)
Labette Community College (U)
Lakehead University (U)
Lake Superior College (U)
Lansing Community College (U)
Laurel University (U)
Lehman College of the City University of New York (U)
LeTourneau University (U)
Lock Haven University of Pennsylvania (U)
Long Beach City College (U)
Los Angeles Trade-Technical College (U)
Louisiana State University and Agricultural and Mechanical College (U)
Louisiana State University at Eunice (U)
Marshall University (U)
Metropolitan Community College–Penn Valley (U)
Middlesex Community College (U)
Midway College (U)
Midwestern State University (U)
Montgomery County Community College (U)
Moorpark College (U)
Mountain State University (U)
Murray State University (U)
New Mexico State University–Grants (U)
Nicolet Area Technical College (U)
North Carolina State University (G)
North Hennepin Community College (U)
North Iowa Area Community College (U)
NorthWest Arkansas Community College (U)
Northwestern Connecticut Community College (U)
Northwest-Shoals Community College (U)
Oakton Community College (U)
Ohio University (U)
Oklahoma State University (U)
Oregon State University (U,G)
Ozarks Technical Community College (U)
Penn State University Park (G)
Pikes Peak Community College (U)
Portland Community College (U)
Queen's University at Kingston (U)
Rend Lake College (U)
Riverside Community College District (U)
Rockland Community College (U)
Rose State College (U)
Sacramento City College (U)
St. Clair County Community College (U)
Saint Leo University (U)
St. Petersburg College (U)
San Diego State University (U)
San Jacinto College District (U)
Shippensburg University of Pennsylvania (U,G)
Slippery Rock University of Pennsylvania (U)
Southeast Arkansas College (U)
Southeastern Community College (U)
Southern Illinois University Carbondale (U)
Southern Illinois University Edwardsville (U)
Southern University at New Orleans (U)
South Piedmont Community College (U)
Southwestern Community College (U)
Spring Arbor University (U)
State University of New York at New Paltz (U)
State University of New York College at Potsdam (U)
Taylor University (U)
Trinidad State Junior College (U)
The University of Akron (U)
University of Alaska Fairbanks (U)
The University of Arizona (U)
University of Arkansas at Little Rock (U)
The University of British Columbia (U)
University of California, Riverside (N)
University of Cincinnati (U)
University of Colorado at Colorado Springs (U)
University of Florida (U)
The University of Kansas (U)
University of Louisville (U)
University of Maine at Fort Kent (U)
University of Massachusetts Boston (U)
University of Minnesota, Morris (U)
University of North Alabama (U,G)
The University of North Carolina at Chapel Hill (U)
University of North Dakota (U)
University of Northern Iowa (U,G)
University of Oregon (U,G)
University of Saskatchewan (U)
University of Southern California (G)
University of Southern Mississippi (U)
University of West Georgia (G)
The University of Winnipeg (U)
University of Wisconsin Colleges (U)
Utah State University (U)
Valencia College (U)
Wayland Baptist University (U)
Westchester Community College (U)
Western Kentucky University (U)
Wichita State University (U)
Wilfrid Laurier University (U)
York University (U)

GEOLOGICAL AND EARTH SCIENCES/GEOSCIENCES

Acadia University (U)
Alvin Community College (U)
Antelope Valley College (U)
Arapahoe Community College (U)
Arkansas State University–Beebe (U)
Athabasca University (N,U)
Auburn University (U)
Austin Peay State University (U)
Bellevue College (U)
Big Bend Community College (U)
Boise State University (U)
Bowling Green State University (U)
Bridgewater State University (U)
Brigham Young University (U)
Brigham Young University–Idaho (U)
Broward College (U)
Butler Community College (U)
Cabrillo College (U)
California State University, Chico (U)
California State University, East Bay (U)
California State University, Monterey Bay (U)
California State University, Sacramento (U)
Campbellsville University (U)
Cascadia Community College (U)
Cedarville University (U)
Centralia College (U)
Central Oregon Community College (U)
Charter Oak State College (U)
Chemeketa Community College (U)
Columbus State Community College (U)
Dallas Baptist University (U)
Dickinson State University (U)
Eastern Illinois University (U)
Eastern Wyoming College (U)
Edison State Community College (U)
El Camino College (U)
Fort Hays State University (U)
Framingham State University (U)
Gadsden State Community College (U)
Gaston College (U)
Harrisburg Area Community College (U)
Hillsborough Community College (U)
Illinois Valley Community College (U)
Indiana University–Purdue University Fort Wayne (U)
Jacksonville State University (U,G)
James Madison University (U)

Jefferson Community College (U)
Johnston Community College (U)
Kansas State University (U)
Keystone College (U)
Lake Superior College (U)
Lindenwood University (U)
Louisiana State University and Agricultural and Mechanical College (U)
McNeese State University (U)
Michigan Technological University (G)
Middle Tennessee State University (U)
Mississippi State University (U)
Missouri University of Science and Technology (N)
Montgomery County Community College (U)
Mountain Empire Community College (U)
Mount Allison University (U)
Nassau Community College (U)
New Jersey City University (U)
New Mexico Junior College (U)
New Mexico State University–Carlsbad (U)
Nicolet Area Technical College (U)
North Carolina State University (U)
North Seattle Community College (U)
NorthWest Arkansas Community College (U)
Oregon State University (U,G)
Oxnard College (U)
Peninsula College (U)
Penn State University Park (G)
Pennsylvania College of Technology (U)
Portland State University (U)
Rappahannock Community College (U)
Rend Lake College (U)
Rio Hondo College (U)
Rogers State University (U)
Rose State College (U)
Sacramento City College (U)
Sam Houston State University (U)
San Diego State University (N,U)
Santa Fe Community College (U)
Santa Monica College (U)
Santa Rosa Junior College (U)
Slippery Rock University of Pennsylvania (U,G)
Southern University at New Orleans (U)
State University of New York at New Paltz (U)
State University of New York at Oswego (U)
State University of New York at Plattsburgh (U)
State University of New York College at Potsdam (U)
Sullivan County Community College (U)
Taft College (U)
Trine University (U)
The University of Akron (U)
University of Alaska Fairbanks (U)
The University of Arizona (U,G)
University of Arkansas at Little Rock (U)
The University of British Columbia (U)
University of Cincinnati (U)
University of Florida (U)
University of Hawaii at Hilo (U)
The University of Kansas (U)
University of Maine at Fort Kent (U)
The University of Montana Western (U)
The University of North Carolina at Chapel Hill (U)
University of North Dakota (U)
University of Oregon (U)
University of Saskatchewan (U)
University of Southern Maine (U)
University of the Southwest (U)
University of Waterloo (U)
University of West Georgia (U,G)
University of Wisconsin Colleges (U)
Utah State University (U)
Wake Technical Community College (U)
Wayland Baptist University (U)
Wayne State University (U)
West Hills Community College (U)
West Shore Community College (U)
Wharton County Junior College (U)
Wilfrid Laurier University (U)
Winston-Salem State University (U)
Youngstown State University (U)

GEOLOGICAL/GEOPHYSICAL ENGINEERING

Arapahoe Community College (U)
Austin Peay State University (U)
Hillsborough Community College (U)
New Mexico State University–Carlsbad (U)
Rose State College (U)
University of Idaho (G)

GERONTOLOGY

Acadia University (U)
Adams State College (N)
The American College (U)
Ashland University (U)
Athabasca University (N)
Bowling Green State University (U)
Butler Community College (U)
California State University, Dominguez Hills (N)
California State University, Sacramento (U)
The College of St. Scholastica (U)
Dakota College at Bottineau (U)
Genesee Community College (U)
Harrisburg Area Community College (U)
Hofstra University (G)
Jacksonville State University (U)
Kansas State University (U,G)
Lewis-Clark State College (U)
Marylhurst University (U,G)
McDaniel College (G)
Middlesex Community College (N)
Midland College (N,U)
Misericordia University (G)
Mountain State University (U)
Mount Wachusett Community College (N)
North Central State College (N)
North Dakota State University (G)
Northern State University (U)
The Ohio State University (N)
Oklahoma State University (U)
Portland Community College (U)
Randolph Community College (N)
Sacramento City College (U)
Sam Houston State University (U)
San Diego State University (U)
Southeastern Oklahoma State University (U)
State University of New York at Oswego (G)
Sullivan County Community College (N)
University of Alaska Fairbanks (U)
The University of Arizona (G)
University of Arkansas at Little Rock (U,G)
University of Colorado at Colorado Springs (U,G)
University of Florida (N,U,G)
University of Massachusetts Boston (U,G)
University of North Alabama (U)
University of South Alabama (U,G)
University of Southern California (U)
University of Waterloo (U)
University of Wisconsin–Green Bay (U)
Utica College (U)
Wake Technical Community College (U)
Western Kentucky University (U)
West Virginia State University (U)
Wichita State University (U,G)
Winston-Salem State University (U)

GRAPHIC COMMUNICATIONS

Academy of Art University (U,G)
Arapahoe Community College (U)
Austin Peay State University (U)
Burlington College (U)
Butler County Community College (N)
California State University, Dominguez Hills (N)
Central Wyoming College (N)
Columbus State Community College (U)
Community College of Beaver County (N)
Corning Community College (U)
Dallas Baptist University (U)
Danville Community College (U)
Front Range Community College (U)
Lewis-Clark State College (U)
Long Beach City College (U)
Macon State College (U)
Oakton Community College (U)
Quinsigamond Community College (N)
Riverside Community College District (U)
Rochester Institute of Technology (U)
Rose State College (U)
Sacramento City College (U)
Saint Paul College–A Community & Technical College (U)
Santa Rosa Junior College (U)
Sessions College for Professional Design (U)
Spoon River College (U)
State University of New York Institute of Technology (G)
Texas State Technical College West Texas (N)
University of Colorado at Colorado Springs (N)
University of North Dakota (N)
University of Waterloo (N)
Wake Technical Community College (N)
Western Kentucky University (U)

GROUND TRANSPORTATION

Kansas State University (U,G)
St. Petersburg College (N)
The University of Texas at Brownsville (N)

HEALTH AIDES/ATTENDANTS/ORDERLIES

Allen Community College (U)
Arapahoe Community College (U)
Bossier Parish Community College (N)
Cincinnati State Technical and Community College (U)
Columbus State Community College (U)
Lamar State College–Port Arthur (N)
Pamlico Community College (U)
Paris Junior College (N)
South Piedmont Community College (N)

Southwest Wisconsin Technical College (U)
The University of Akron (N)

HEALTH AND MEDICAL ADMINISTRATIVE SERVICES

Alpena Community College (U)
Arapahoe Community College (U)
Arkansas Tech University (U)
Athabasca University (U)
Avila University (U)
Ball State University (G)
Blackhawk Technical College (U)
Boise State University (U,G)
Bossier Parish Community College (U)
Bradley University (G)
Brenau University (G)
Bryant & Stratton Online (N,U)
Burlington County College (U)
California State University, Chico (U)
California State University, Dominguez Hills (N)
Central Michigan University (N,U,G)
Champlain College (G)
Chattanooga State Community College (U)
Cincinnati State Technical and Community College (U)
The College of St. Scholastica (U,G)
College of Southern Maryland (N)
Colorado Mountain College (U)
Columbus State Community College (U)
Dakota College at Bottineau (U)
Dakota State University (U,G)
D'Youville College (G)
Eastern Washington University (U)
Edgecombe Community College (N,U)
Elaine P. Nunez Community College (U)
Elmira College (G)
Erie Community College (U)
Erie Community College, North Campus (U)
Erie Community College, South Campus (U)
Franklin Pierce University (G)
Granite State College (U)
Grantham University (U)
Iona College (U,G)
James Madison University (N,G)
Jamestown Community College (N)
The Johns Hopkins University (G)
Johnston Community College (U)
Lake-Sumter Community College (U)
Lewis-Clark State College (U)
Louisiana State University at Eunice (U)
Macon State College (U)
Mansfield University of Pennsylvania (N)
Marlboro College Graduate College (N)
Mary Baldwin College (U)
McNeese State University (N)
Medical College of Wisconsin (G)
Mercy College of Northwest Ohio (N)
Miami Dade College (U)
Midland College (U)
Minnesota School of Business–Online (U)
Minnesota School of Business–Richfield (U)
Monroe College (U)
Montgomery County Community College (N)
Mountain State University (U,G)
Murray State University (N,U)
North Dakota State College of Science (U)
North Seattle Community College (U)
Oakland Community College (U)
Oakton Community College (U)
Olympic College (U)
Oregon State University (N,U,G)
Pace University (G)
Pamlico Community College (U)
Pasco-Hernando Community College (N)
Presentation College (U)
Pulaski Technical College (U)
Quinebaug Valley Community College (N,U)
Rio Hondo College (U)
Robert Morris University (U)
Saint Joseph's College of Maine (G)
Saint Leo University (U)
Salve Regina University (N,G)
San Jacinto College District (U)
Seton Hall University (G)
Sinclair Community College (U)
Southeast Community College Area (U)
Southeastern Community College (U)
Spartanburg Community College (N)
Spokane Community College (U)
State University of New York College of Technology at Canton (U)
State University of New York Institute of Technology (U,G)
Stephens College (U)
Texas State University–San Marcos (U)
The University of Akron (N,U)
University of Alaska Fairbanks (U)
University of Baltimore (U,G)
University of Colorado at Colorado Springs (N,G)
University of Evansville (G)
University of Illinois at Urbana–Champaign (G)
University of Michigan (N)
University of Michigan–Flint (U,G)
University of Minnesota, Crookston (U)
University of North Dakota (N)
University of North Florida (U,G)
University of St. Francis (G)
The University of Texas at Dallas (G)
Wayland Baptist University (U,G)
Western Kentucky University (U)
Westmoreland County Community College (U)
Youngstown State University (N)

HEALTH AND PHYSICAL EDUCATION/FITNESS

Allen Community College (U)
American University (U,G)
Angelina College (U)
Anne Arundel Community College (U)
Antelope Valley College (U)
Arapahoe Community College (U)
Atlantic Cape Community College (U)
Auburn University (U)
Austin Peay State University (U,G)
Baldwin-Wallace College (U)
Bluefield College (U)
Bowling Green State University (U)
Brigham Young University (U)
Broward College (U)
Butler Community College (U)
Butler County Community College (U)
California State University, Sacramento (U)
Canisius College (G)
Cayuga County Community College (U)
Central Carolina Community College (U)
Centralia College (U)
Central Michigan University (U)
Central Oregon Community College (U)
Central Texas College (U)
Central Washington University (G)
Central Wyoming College (N,U)
Chemeketa Community College (U)
Clarion University of Pennsylvania (U)
Clatsop Community College (U)
Coastal Carolina University (U)
College of Southern Maryland (U)
College of the Siskiyous (U)
Columbia Basin College (U)
Columbus State Community College (U)
Community College of Allegheny County (U)
Corning Community College (U)
Cossatot Community College of the University of Arkansas (U)
Dakota College at Bottineau (U)
Dakota State University (U)
Dallas Baptist University (U)
Danville Community College (U)
Eastern Illinois University (U,G)
Eastern Oregon University (U)
Eastern Washington University (N,U)
Eastern Wyoming College (U)
East Los Angeles College (U)
El Camino College (U)
Erie Community College (U)
Erie Community College, North Campus (U)
Erie Community College, South Campus (U)
Finger Lakes Community College (U)
Fort Hays State University (U,G)
Fort Valley State University (U)
Gadsden State Community College (U)
Georgia College & State University (U)
Georgia Highlands College (U)
Georgia State University (G)
Haywood Community College (U)
Illinois Eastern Community Colleges, Frontier Community College (U)
Indiana State University (U)
Indiana University of Pennsylvania (U,G)
Inter American University of Puerto Rico, San Germán Campus (U)
Jacksonville State University (U,G)
James Madison University (U)
Jefferson Community College (U)
J. Sargeant Reynolds Community College (U)
Kean University (N)
Keystone College (U)
Labette Community College (U)
Lindenwood University (U)
Lock Haven University of Pennsylvania (U)
Long Beach City College (U)
Los Angeles Trade-Technical College (U)
Louisiana State University and Agricultural and Mechanical College (U)
Malone University (U)
McMurry University (U)
McNeese State University (U)
Mercer County Community College (U)
Mesa State College (U)
Middle Tennessee State University (U)
Midland College (U)
Minnesota School of Business–Online (U)
Mississippi College (U)
Mountain Empire Community College (U)
Mount Olive College (U)
Nassau Community College (U)
Naugatuck Valley Community College (N)
North Arkansas College (U)
North Carolina State University (U)
North Dakota State College of Science (U)
Northern State University (U)

North Hennepin Community College (U)
NorthWest Arkansas Community College (U)
Northwest-Shoals Community College (U)
Oakland Community College (U)
Ocean County College (U)
Orange Coast College (U)
Peninsula College (U)
Pittsburg State University (U)
Prescott College (N)
Rappahannock Community College (U)
Rend Lake College (U)
Rio Hondo College (U)
Rose State College (N,U)
Sacramento City College (U)
St. Petersburg College (N)
San Diego Community College District (N,U)
San Jacinto College District (U)
Santa Fe Community College (U)
Shawnee State University (U)
Southeast Arkansas College (U)
Southeastern Oklahoma State University (N,U,G)
Southern Oregon University (U)
Spokane Community College (U)
State University of New York at Plattsburgh (U)
Tarleton State University (U,G)
Texas Woman's University (U,G)
Thiel College (U)
United States Sports Academy (N,U,G)
The University of Akron (N)
University of Arkansas at Little Rock (U)
University of Great Falls (U)
University of Houston (U)
University of Louisville (U)
University of Maine at Machias (U)
University of Massachusetts Boston (U)
University of Memphis (U)
University of Minnesota, Duluth (U)
University of Northern Iowa (U)
University of Pittsburgh at Bradford (U)
The University of Tennessee at Chattanooga (U)
The University of Texas at Arlington (U)
The University of Texas of the Permian Basin (U,G)
Valley City State University (U)
Wake Technical Community College (N,U)
Wayne State University (U,G)
Westchester Community College (U)
Western Kentucky University (U)
Western Michigan University (G)
West Hills Community College (U)
West Los Angeles College (U)
West Virginia State University (U)
Winston-Salem State University (U)
Youngstown State University (U)

HEALTH/MEDICAL PREPARATORY PROGRAMS

Arapahoe Community College (U)
Athabasca University (U,G)
Austin Peay State University (U)
Boise State University (U)
Brenau University (U)
California State University, San Marcos (N)
Chattanooga State Community College (U)
Dakota College at Bottineau (U)
Edgecombe Community College (U)
Excelsior College (U,G)
Gateway Community College (U)
Hibbing Community College (U)
Hocking College (U)
Itasca Community College (U)
James A. Rhodes State College (U)
Kirkwood Community College (U)
Labette Community College (U)
Lake-Sumter Community College (U)
Lake Superior College (U)
Lamar State College–Orange (U)
Lewis-Clark State College (U)
Lock Haven University of Pennsylvania (U)
Long Beach City College (U)
Mercer County Community College (U)
Mesa Community College (U)
Miami Dade College (U)
Naugatuck Valley Community College (N)
Nicolet Area Technical College (U)
Pace University (G)
Rockland Community College (U)
Rose State College (U)
Saint Francis University (U,G)
Sinclair Community College (U)
Southern Arkansas University–Magnolia (U)
Southern Illinois University Carbondale (U)
Southwest Wisconsin Technical College (U)
Tabor College (U)
The University of Akron (N,U)
University of Alaska Fairbanks (U)
University of Evansville (U)
University of Florida (G)
University of Michigan–Flint (U)
University of New England (U)
University of North Florida (G)
University of West Georgia (G)
University of Wisconsin–Green Bay (U)
Western Kentucky University (U)
West Hills Community College (U)
West Los Angeles College (U)
Windward Community College (U)

HEALTH PROFESSIONS RELATED

Angelina College (U)
Arapahoe Community College (U)
Arkansas State University–Mountain Home (U)
Athabasca University (N,U,G)
A.T. Still University of Health Sciences (N)
Austin Peay State University (N,U)
Ball State University (G)
Bellevue College (U)
Bloomfield College (U)
Boise State University (U)
Bowling Green State University (N,U)
Brenau University (U,G)
Brigham Young University–Idaho (U)
Burlington County College (U)
Butler Community College (U)
Cabrillo College (U)
Carlow University (U,G)
Central Michigan University (N,U,G)
Central Texas College (U)
Central Virginia Community College (U)
Central Wyoming College (N)
Charter Oak State College (N)
Chattanooga State Community College (U)
Chemeketa Community College (U)
Cincinnati State Technical and Community College (U)
Clark State Community College (U)
The College at Brockport, State University of New York (U)
College of Saint Mary (U,G)
College of Southern Maryland (N)
Colorado Mountain College (U)
Columbus State Community College (U)
Cornell University (U)
Dakota College at Bottineau (U)
Dakota Wesleyan University (U)
Dallas Baptist University (U)
Danville Community College (U)
DeVry University Online (G)
Drake University (G)
Drexel University (U,G)
D'Youville College (U)
Eastern Kentucky University (U)
Florida Hospital College of Health Sciences (U)
Franklin Pierce University (G)
Front Range Community College (U)
Georgia College & State University (U,G)
Georgian Court University (G)
Georgia State University (U)
Governors State University (N)
Grantham University (U,G)
Hillsborough Community College (U)
Hofstra University (U)
Hopkinsville Community College (N)
Huntington College of Health Sciences (N,G)
Illinois Eastern Community Colleges, Lincoln Trail College (U)
Illinois State University (U)
Illinois Valley Community College (N,U)
Iona College (U,G)
Jacksonville State University (U,G)
James A. Rhodes State College (U)
James Madison University (U,G)
John Jay College of Criminal Justice of the City University of New York (G)
Kean University (N)
Lakehead University (U)
Lake Superior College (U)
Lamar State College–Port Arthur (U)
Lansing Community College (U)
Lock Haven University of Pennsylvania (G)
Louisiana State University at Eunice (U)
Macon State College (U)
Maharishi University of Management (G)
Marian University (N,G)
Marlboro College Graduate College (N)
Marshall University (U)
Mary Baldwin College (N)
Medical College of Wisconsin (G)
Mercy College of Northwest Ohio (U)
Mesa Community College (U)
MGH Institute of Health Professions (G)
Miami Dade College (N,U)
Midland College (N,U)
Midwestern State University (U,G)
Mississippi State University (G)
Mitchell Technical Institute (N)
Montcalm Community College (N)
Montgomery County Community College (N,U)
Mount Mary College (U,G)
Mount Wachusett Community College (N)
Naugatuck Valley Community College (U)
New Mexico State University (U)
New Mexico State University–Grants (U)
New York Medical College (G)
North Carolina State University (U)
North Central State College (N)
North Dakota State College of Science (U)
North Dakota State University (G)

Northern Kentucky University (U)
North Iowa Area Community College (N)
NorthWest Arkansas Community College (U)
Oakton Community College (U)
The Ohio State University (U,G)
Oregon State University (G)
Pasco-Hernando Community College (N)
Peninsula College (U)
Pennsylvania College of Technology (U)
Pine Technical College (N,U)
Pittsburgh Technical Institute (U)
Purdue University (U)
The Richard Stockton College of New Jersey (U)
Rochester Institute of Technology (G)
Rockland Community College (U)
Rogers State University (U)
Rose State College (U)
Sacramento City College (U)
The Sage Colleges (U,G)
Saint Francis University (U,G)
St. John Fisher College (G)
Saint Joseph's College of Maine (G)
Sam Houston State University (U)
San Diego Community College District (U)
San Jacinto College District (U)
Santa Rosa Junior College (U)
Seton Hall University (G)
Siena Heights University (U)
Slippery Rock University of Pennsylvania (U)
Southeast Arkansas College (U)
Southeast Community College Area (U)
Southeastern Illinois College (U)
Southern Arkansas University–Magnolia (U)
South Piedmont Community College (U)
Spartanburg Community College (N)
Spokane Community College (N)
Spoon River College (U)
State University of New York at Plattsburgh (U)
State University of New York Institute of Technology (U,G)
Stephens College (U)
Sullivan County Community College (N)
Tabor College (U)
Temple University (U,G)
Texas State University–San Marcos (U)
Trinity College of Nursing and Health Sciences (U)
Union University (G)
United States Sports Academy (G)
The University of Akron (N,U,G)
University of Alaska Fairbanks (U)
University of Arkansas at Little Rock (U)
University of Atlanta (U)
University of California, Davis (N,U)
University of Cincinnati Raymond Walters College (U)
University of Colorado at Colorado Springs (U,G)
University of Idaho (U)
University of Illinois at Chicago (N,U,G)
University of Illinois at Urbana–Champaign (G)
University of Maine at Augusta (U)
University of Maine at Fort Kent (U)
University of Management and Technology (U,G)
University of Michigan–Flint (U,G)
University of Nevada, Reno (U)
University of New England (U)
University of North Dakota (N,U,G)
University of North Florida (U)
University of St. Augustine for Health Sciences (N)
University of St. Francis (U)
The University of South Dakota (G)
University of Southern Maine (U)
University of Southern Mississippi (U)
University of the Sciences in Philadelphia (G)
University of Wisconsin–La Crosse (U)
Upper Iowa University (U)
Valencia College (U)
Wake Technical Community College (N)
Walden University (G)
Western Kentucky University (U)
West Hills Community College (U)
West Virginia State University (U)
West Virginia University (N)
Wheeling Jesuit University (U,G)
Worcester State University (U,G)
York University (U)
Youngstown State University (U,G)

HEALTH SERVICES/ALLIED HEALTH/HEALTH SCIENCES

Anderson University (U)
Anne Arundel Community College (N)
Arapahoe Community College (U)
Austin Peay State University (N,U)
Baker College Online (G)
Belmont Technical College (U)
Boise State University (U)
Bowling Green State University (U)
Bradley University (U,G)
California State University, Chico (U)
California State University, East Bay (U)
California State University, San Marcos (N)
Cape Fear Community College (U)
Capital Community College (U)
Carl Sandburg College (U)
Central Michigan University (U)
Central Oregon Community College (U)
Central Wyoming College (N)
Charter Oak State College (U)
Clarion University of Pennsylvania (U)
Clinton Community College (U)
The College at Brockport, State University of New York (G)
Columbus State Community College (U)
Dakota College at Bottineau (U)
Davidson County Community College (U)
Drake University (G)
Drexel University (U)
Eastern Illinois University (U)
Franklin Pierce University (G)
Gadsden State Community College (U)
Georgia State University (U,G)
Granite State College (N)
Heartland Community College (U)
Heritage College (N,U)
Illinois Valley Community College (U)
Iona College (U,G)
Ithaca College (U)
The Johns Hopkins University (G)
Lock Haven University of Pennsylvania (U)
Los Angeles Harbor College (U)
Louisiana State University at Eunice (U)
Luna Community College (U)
Macon State College (U)
Marlboro College Graduate College (N)
Marquette University (G)
Miami Dade College (U)
Mid-State Technical College (U)
Minnesota School of Business–Online (U)
Minot State University (U)
Monmouth University (G)
Moorpark College (U)
Nashville State Technical Community College (N)
New Jersey City University (U,G)
North Dakota State University (G)
Northern Kentucky University (G)
North Hennepin Community College (N,U)
NorthWest Arkansas Community College (U)
Northwest-Shoals Community College (U)
Oakton Community College (U)
Oregon State University (U)
Pamlico Community College (U)
Paris Junior College (U)
Pasco-Hernando Community College (N)
Penn State University Park (G)
Quinsigamond Community College (N)
Rend Lake College (U)
Rochester Institute of Technology (U,G)
Rose State College (U)
Sacramento City College (U)
Saint Francis University (U,G)
Saint Paul College–A Community & Technical College (U)
San Jacinto College District (U)
Santa Monica College (U)
Shawnee State University (U)
Sinclair Community College (U)
Southeast Arkansas College (U)
Southern Adventist University (U)
Southern Arkansas University–Magnolia (U)
South Piedmont Community College (U)
Spokane Community College (U)
State University of New York at Oswego (U)
State University of New York College at Cortland (G)
State University of New York Institute of Technology (U,G)
Tabor College (U)
Texas Woman's University (U,G)
Tyler Junior College (U)
The University of Akron (U)
University of Alaska Fairbanks (U)
University of Arkansas at Little Rock (U)
University of Hawaii at Hilo (U)
University of Illinois at Chicago (U,G)
University of Illinois at Urbana–Champaign (G)
The University of North Carolina at Asheville (G)
University of North Florida (U)
University of the Sciences in Philadelphia (G)
University of West Florida (G)
University of West Georgia (G)
University of Wisconsin–Green Bay (U)
Upper Iowa University (U)
Valencia College (U)
Wake Technical Community College (N,U)
Wayne State University (U,G)
Western Kentucky University (U)
West Hills Community College (U)
West Los Angeles College (U)
West Virginia University (N)
Wichita State University (U,G)

HEATING, AIR CONDITIONING, VENTILATION AND REFRIGERATION MAINTENANCE TECHNOLOGY

Austin Peay State University (N,U)
Blackhawk Technical College (U)
Boston Architectural College (N,U,G)
Ferris State University (U)
Los Angeles Trade-Technical College (U)
Mansfield University of Pennsylvania (N)
Mitchell Technical Institute (N)
Mount Wachusett Community College (N)
North Seattle Community College (U)
Pittsburgh Technical Institute (U)
Sacramento City College (U)
South Piedmont Community College (U)
University of North Dakota (N)
Wake Technical Community College (U)
Wayne Community College (U)

HEAVY/INDUSTRIAL EQUIPMENT MAINTENANCE TECHNOLOGIES

Alpena Community College (N)
Austin Peay State University (U)
Wake Technical Community College (U)

HISTORIC PRESERVATION AND CONSERVATION

Austin Peay State University (U)
Western Kentucky University (U,G)

HISTORY

Acadia University (U)
Adams State College (U)
Alcorn State University (U)
Allen Community College (U)
Alvin Community College (U)
American University (U)
Andover Newton Theological School (G)
Andrews University (U)
Angelina College (U)
Anne Arundel Community College (N,U)
Antelope Valley College (U)
Arapahoe Community College (U)
Arkansas State University–Beebe (U)
Arkansas State University–Mountain Home (U)
Arkansas Tech University (U)
Asbury University (U)
Ashland University (U)
Athabasca University (N,U,G)
Austin Peay State University (U)
Baldwin-Wallace College (U)
Baptist Bible College of Pennsylvania (U)
Bellevue College (U)
Big Bend Community College (U)
Bloomfield College (U)
Bluefield College (U)
Bob Jones University (U,G)
Boise State University (U)
Bossier Parish Community College (U)
Bowling Green State University (U,G)
Brazosport College (U)
Brenau University (U)
Brigham Young University (N,U)
Brigham Young University–Idaho (U)
Bronx Community College of the City University of New York (U)
Broward College (U)
Bryan College (U)
Buffalo State College, State University of New York (U)
Burlington College (U)
Burlington County College (U)
Butler Community College (U)
Butler County Community College (U)
Cabrillo College (U)
California State University, Chico (U)
California State University, Dominguez Hills (N)
California State University, East Bay (U)
California State University, Sacramento (U)
Capital Community College (U)
Carleton University (U)
Carlow University (U)
Carroll University (U)
Cascadia Community College (U)
Cayuga County Community College (U)
Cedarville University (U)
Central Bible College (U)
Central Carolina Community College (U)
Central Carolina Technical College (U)
Centralia College (U)
Central Oregon Community College (U)
Central Texas College (U)
Central Virginia Community College (U)
Central Washington University (U)
Central Wyoming College (N)
Cerritos College (U)
Chaminade University of Honolulu (U)
Champlain College (U)
Chatham University (U)
Chattanooga State Community College (U)
Chemeketa Community College (U)
Cincinnati Christian University (U,G)
Cincinnati State Technical and Community College (U)
Citrus College (U)
City Colleges of Chicago System (U)
City University of Seattle (U)
Clatsop Community College (U)
Clemson University (G)
Cleveland Community College (U)
Cleveland State Community College (U)
Clinton Community College (U)
Clovis Community College (U)
Coastal Carolina University (U)
Coleman University (U)
College of Southern Maryland (U)
College of the Humanities and Sciences, Harrison Middleton University (U)
College of the Siskiyous (U)
Colorado Mountain College (U)
Columbia Basin College (U)
Columbia College (U,G)
Columbia International University (G)
Columbus State Community College (U)
Community College of Allegheny County (U)
Community College of Beaver County (U)
Concordia University Wisconsin (U)
Corning Community College (U)
Cossatot Community College of the University of Arkansas (U)
Covenant Theological Seminary (N,G)
Culver-Stockton College (U)
Dabney S. Lancaster Community College (U)
Dakota College at Bottineau (U)
Dallas Baptist University (U,G)
Danville Community College (U)
Davidson County Community College (U)
Daytona State College (U)
Delgado Community College (U)
Denver Seminary (G)
Dickinson State University (U)
Dominican College (U)
Drake University (U)
Drury University (U)
D'Youville College (U)
East Central Community College (U)
Eastern Illinois University (U)
Eastern Kentucky University (U)
Eastern Washington University (U)
Eastern West Virginia Community and Technical College (U)
Eastern Wyoming College (U)
East Georgia College (U)
East Los Angeles College (U)
Edgecombe Community College (U)
Edison State Community College (U)
Elaine P. Nunez Community College (U)
Enterprise State Community College (U)
Erie Community College (U)
Erie Community College, North Campus (U)
Erie Community College, South Campus (U)
Excelsior College (U)
Faulkner University (U)
Fayetteville State University (G)
Ferris State University (U)
Finger Lakes Community College (U)
Fontbonne University (U)
Fort Hays State University (U)
Fort Valley State University (U)
Framingham State University (U)
Friends University (U)
Front Range Community College (U)
Frostburg State University (U)
Gadsden State Community College (U)
Gannon University (U)
Gateway Community College (U)
Genesee Community College (U)
George Fox University (U)
Georgia Highlands College (U)
Georgian Court University (U)
Glenville State College (U)
Global University (U,G)
Goddard College (U)
Graceland University (U)
Granite State College (U)
Grantham University (U)
Greenville Technical College (U)
Hannibal-LaGrange University (U)
Harford Community College (U)
Harrisburg Area Community College (U)
Haywood Community College (U)
Heartland Community College (U)
Hibbing Community College (U)
Hofstra University (U)
Holyoke Community College (U)
Hope International University (N,U)
Hopkinsville Community College (U)
Houston Community College System (U)
Illinois Eastern Community Colleges, Wabash Valley College (U)
Illinois State University (G)
Indiana State University (U)
Indiana University–Purdue University Fort Wayne (U)
Indiana Wesleyan University (U)
Inter American University of Puerto Rico, San Germán Campus (U)
Iona College (G)
Iowa Lakes Community College (U)

Iowa Valley Community College District (U)
Itasca Community College (U)
Jacksonville State University (U)
James Madison University (U)
Jamestown College (U)
Jamestown Community College (U)
Jefferson Community College (U)
John A. Logan College (U)
John Jay College of Criminal Justice of the City University of New York (U)
Johnson State College (U)
Johnston Community College (U)
J. Sargeant Reynolds Community College (U)
Judson College (U)
Judson University (U)
Kansas State University (U)
Kean University (U)
Keystone College (U)
Kirkwood Community College (U)
Labette Community College (U)
Lackawanna College (U)
Lakehead University (U)
Lake Superior College (U)
Lamar State College–Orange (U)
Lansing Community College (U)
La Roche College (U)
Lassen Community College District (U)
Lehman College of the City University of New York (U)
Lenoir Community College (U)
LeTourneau University (U)
Lewis-Clark State College (U)
Lewis University (U)
Liberty University (U)
Lincoln Christian University (U)
Lindenwood University (U)
Lock Haven University of Pennsylvania (U)
Long Beach City College (U)
Los Angeles Harbor College (U)
Los Angeles Trade-Technical College (U)
Louisiana State University and Agricultural and Mechanical College (U)
Louisiana State University at Eunice (U)
Lourdes College (U)
Loyola University New Orleans (U)
Luna Community College (U)
Macon State College (U)
Malone University (U)
Mansfield University of Pennsylvania (U)
Marquette University (U)
Marshall University (U,G)
Mary Baldwin College (U)
McMurry University (U)
McNeese State University (U)
Mercer County Community College (U)
Mesa Community College (U)
Mesa State College (U)
Metropolitan Community College–Penn Valley (U)
Miami Dade College (U)
Miami University–Regional Campuses (U)
Middlesex Community College (U)
Midland College (U)
Minot State University (U)
Mississippi College (U)
Montgomery County Community College (U)
Mountain Empire Community College (U)
Mountain State University (U)
Mount Mary College (U)
Mount Olive College (U)
Mount Wachusett Community College (U)
Murray State College (U)
Murray State University (U)
Nassau Community College (U)
National University (U)
New England College of Business and Finance (U)
New Jersey City University (U)
New Mexico Junior College (U)
New Mexico State University (U)
New Mexico State University–Carlsbad (U)
New Mexico State University–Grants (U)
New River Community College (U)
Nichols College (U)
Nicolet Area Technical College (U)
Nipissing University (U)
North Arkansas College (U)
North Carolina State University (U)
North Central Texas College (U)
North Dakota State College of Science (U)
North Dakota State University (U,G)
North Georgia College & State University (U,G)
North Iowa Area Community College (U)
North Lake College (U)
North Seattle Community College (U)
North Shore Community College (U)
NorthWest Arkansas Community College (U)
Northwestern Connecticut Community College (U)
Northwestern Michigan College (U)
Northwestern Oklahoma State University (U)
Northwest-Shoals Community College (U)
Notre Dame College (U)
Nyack College (U)
Oakland Community College (U)
Oakton Community College (U)
Ocean County College (U)
The Ohio State University (G)
Ohio University (U)
Oklahoma Panhandle State University (U)
Oklahoma State University (U)
Olympic College (U)
Orange Coast College (U)
Oregon Coast Community College (U)
Oregon State University (U)
Ouachita Technical College (U)
Oxnard College (U)
Ozarks Technical Community College (U)
Pace University (U)
Paine College (U)
Pamlico Community College (U)
Paris Junior College (U)
Peirce College (U)
Pellissippi State Technical Community College (U)
Peninsula College (U)
Pennsylvania College of Technology (U)
Peru State College (U)
Philadelphia University (U)
Phoenix College (U)
Piedmont Community College (U)
Pikes Peak Community College (U)
Pittsburg State University (U,G)
Portland Community College (U)
Portland State University (U)
Prairie Bible Institute (U)
Prairie View A&M University (U)
Pratt Community College (U)
Prescott College (G)
Providence College (U)
Providence College and Theological Seminary (U)
Pulaski Technical College (U)
Purdue University (U)
Queen's University at Kingston (U)
Quinebaug Valley Community College (U)
Quinnipiac University (U)
Quinsigamond Community College (U)
Randolph Community College (U)
Rappahannock Community College (U)
Regent University (U)
Reinhardt University (U)
Rend Lake College (U)
Rio Hondo College (U)
Riverside Community College District (U)
Rivier College (U)
Robert Morris University (U)
Rockland Community College (U)
Rogers State University (U)
Roger Williams University (U)
Rose State College (U)
Rowan-Cabarrus Community College (U)
Sacramento City College (U)
St. Ambrose University (U)
St. Clair County Community College (U)
St. Cloud State University (U)
Saint Francis University (U)
St. Gregory's University (U)
St. John's University (U)
St. Joseph's College, Long Island Campus (U)
St. Joseph's College, New York (U)
Saint Leo University (U)
St. Louis Community College (U)
Saint Mary-of-the-Woods College (U)
Saint Paul College–A Community & Technical College (U)
St. Petersburg College (U)
St. Philip's College (U)
Salem Community College (U)
Sam Houston State University (U)
Sampson Community College (U)
San Bernardino Valley College (U)
San Diego Community College District (U)
San Diego State University (N,U)
San Jacinto College District (U)
Santa Fe Community College (U)
Santa Monica College (U)
Sauk Valley Community College (U)
Seminole State College of Florida (U)
Seton Hill University (U)
Shippensburg University of Pennsylvania (U,G)
Sinclair Community College (U)
Southeast Arkansas College (U)
Southeast Community College Area (U)
Southeastern Community College (U)
Southeastern Illinois College (U)
Southeastern Oklahoma State University (U)
Southern Adventist University (U)
Southern Illinois University Carbondale (U)
Southern Maine Community College (U)
Southern Oregon University (U)
Southern Union State Community College (U)
Southern University at New Orleans (U)
South Piedmont Community College (U)
Southwest Virginia Community College (U)
Spartanburg Community College (U)
Spokane Community College (U)
Spring Arbor University (U)
State University of New York at New Paltz (U)
State University of New York at Oswego (U,G)
State University of New York at Plattsburgh (U)

State University of New York College of Technology at Canton (U)
State University of New York Empire State College (U)
Stephens College (U)
Sullivan County Community College (U)
Syracuse University (G)
Tabor College (U)
Taft College (U)
Tarleton State University (U,G)
Taylor University (U)
Texas State University–San Marcos (U)
Texas Woman's University (U)
Thiel College (U)
Three Rivers Community College (U)
Toccoa Falls College (U)
Trident Technical College (U)
Trine University (U)
Tunxis Community College (U)
Tyler Junior College (U)
Unification Theological Seminary (N,G)
Union County College (U)
University at Albany, State University of New York (U)
The University of Akron (U,G)
University of Alaska Fairbanks (U)
The University of Arizona (U)
University of Arkansas at Little Rock (U,G)
University of Bridgeport (U)
The University of British Columbia (U)
University of Central Florida (U)
University of Cincinnati (U)
University of Colorado at Colorado Springs (U)
University of Dubuque (U)
The University of Findlay (U)
University of Florida (U)
University of Great Falls (U)
University of Houston (U)
University of Houston–Downtown (U)
University of Houston–Victoria (U,G)
University of Idaho (U)
University of Illinois at Springfield (U,G)
University of Illinois at Urbana–Champaign (U)
The University of Kansas (U,G)
University of Maine at Augusta (U)
University of Maine at Fort Kent (U)
University of Maine at Machias (U)
University of Management and Technology (U)
University of Mary (U)
University of Massachusetts Boston (U,G)
University of Memphis (U)
University of Michigan–Flint (U)
University of Minnesota, Crookston (U)
University of Minnesota, Duluth (U)
University of Missouri–Kansas City (U)
The University of Montana Western (U)
University of Nevada, Reno (U)
University of New Haven (G)
University of North Alabama (U)
The University of North Carolina at Chapel Hill (N,U)
The University of North Carolina Wilmington (U)
University of North Dakota (U)
University of St. Francis (U)
University of Saskatchewan (U)
University of South Carolina Sumter (U)
The University of South Dakota (U)
University of Southern Maine (U)
The University of Texas of the Permian Basin (U)
University of the Pacific (U)
University of the Southwest (U)
University of Utah (U)
University of Waterloo (U)
The University of West Alabama (U)
University of West Florida (U)
University of West Georgia (U)
University of Windsor (U)
University of Wisconsin Colleges (U)
University of Wisconsin–La Crosse (U)
University of Wisconsin–Superior (U)
Upper Iowa University (N,U)
Utah State University (U)
Utica College (G)
Valencia College (U)
Vincennes University (U)
Wake Technical Community College (U)
Washington State University (U)
Wayland Baptist University (U)
Wayne Community College (U)
Wayne State University (U,G)
Westchester Community College (U)
Western Kentucky University (U,G)
Western Michigan University (U)
Western Texas College (U)
Western Wyoming Community College (U)
West Hills Community College (U)
West Los Angeles College (U)
West Shore Community College (U)
West Virginia Northern Community College (U)
Wharton County Junior College (U)
Wichita State University (U)
Wilfrid Laurier University (U)
Wilkes Community College (U)
Winston-Salem State University (U)
Worcester State University (U,G)
Yavapai College (U)
York Technical College (U)
York University (U)
Youngstown State University (U)

HOLOCAUST AND RELATED STUDIES

Austin Peay State University (U)
Cleveland Community College (U)
Dickinson State University (U)
Notre Dame College (U)
Oakton Community College (U)
The Richard Stockton College of New Jersey (G)
Seton Hill University (U,G)
University of Nevada, Reno (U)

HOMELAND SECURITY

Community College of Allegheny County (U)
Elmira College (G)
Long Island University at Riverhead (G)
Marian University (U)
Minnesota School of Business–Online (U)
Nashville State Technical Community College (U)
North Dakota State University (U)
Notre Dame College (N)
San Jacinto College District (U)
Vincennes University (U)

HOMELAND SECURITY, LAW ENFORCEMENT, FIREFIGHTING AND PROTECTIVE SERVICES RELATED

Arapahoe Community College (U)
Arkansas Tech University (U)
Austin Peay State University (N)
Bronx Community College of the City University of New York (U)
Cincinnati State Technical and Community College (U)
City Colleges of Chicago System (U)
Franklin Pierce University (U)
Jacksonville State University (U,G)
John Jay College of Criminal Justice of the City University of New York (U,G)
Long Island University at Riverhead (G)
Minnesota School of Business–Online (U)
Portland Community College (N)
The University of Akron (U)
Webster University (G)

HOSPITALITY ADMINISTRATION

Anne Arundel Community College (U)
Arkansas Tech University (U)
Atlantic Cape Community College (U)
Austin Peay State University (U)
Bossier Parish Community College (N)
Bowling Green State University (N)
Burlington County College (U)
Butler Community College (U)
Central Michigan University (G)
Central Texas College (U)
Chemeketa Community College (U)
Colorado Mountain College (U)
Columbus State Community College (U)
Corning Community College (U)
Drexel University (G)
Erie Community College (U)
Erie Community College, North Campus (U)
Erie Community College, South Campus (U)
Front Range Community College (U)
Genesee Community College (U)
Georgia State University (U)
Hocking College (U)
Holyoke Community College (U)
Indiana University of Pennsylvania (U)
Kansas State University (U,G)
Lansing Community College (U)
Lewis-Clark State College (U)
Louisiana State University at Eunice (U)
Mansfield University of Pennsylvania (N)
Miami Dade College (U)
Middlesex Community College (U)
Minnesota School of Business–Online (U)
Monroe College (U)
Mount Wachusett Community College (N)
Naugatuck Valley Community College (U)
North Dakota State University (U)
Northeastern State University (U)
NorthWest Arkansas Community College (U)
Orange Coast College (U)
Paris Junior College (N)
Riverside Community College District (U)
Rochester Institute of Technology (U,G)
Saint Paul College–A Community & Technical College (U)
St. Petersburg College (U)
Santa Fe Community College (U)
Southwest Wisconsin Technical College (U)

Spartanburg Community College (U)
Spring Arbor University (U)
State University of New York College of Agriculture and Technology at Morrisville (U)
Stephen F. Austin State University (U)
Tompkins Cortland Community College (U)
The University of Akron (U)
University of Houston (U,G)
The University of North Carolina at Chapel Hill (U)
Wake Technical Community College (U)

HOUSING AND HUMAN ENVIRONMENTS

Austin Peay State University (U)

HUMAN BIOLOGY

Angelina College (U)
Arapahoe Community College (U)
Boise State University (U)
Clovis Community College (U)
Illinois Eastern Community Colleges, Frontier Community College (U)
Iowa Lakes Community College (U)
The Johns Hopkins University (G)
Johnston Community College (U)
Lewis University (U)
Miami Dade College (U)
New Mexico State University–Carlsbad (U)
Sacramento City College (U)
Sinclair Community College (U)
University of Maine at Machias (U)

HUMAN COMPUTER INTERACTION

University of Michigan (N)

HUMAN DEVELOPMENT, FAMILY STUDIES, AND RELATED SERVICES

Abilene Christian University (G)
Antelope Valley College (U)
Arapahoe Community College (U)
Athabasca University (N,U,G)
Austin Peay State University (U)
Beulah Heights University (U)
Blackhawk Technical College (N)
Bloomfield College (U)
Boise State University (U)
Brenau University (U)
Brigham Young University (N)
Burlington College (U)
Burlington County College (U)
Butler Community College (U)
California State University, Chico (U)
California State University, Sacramento (U)
Capital Community College (U)
Centralia College (U)
Central Michigan University (U)
Central Washington University (U)
Chemeketa Community College (U)
Clackamas Community College (U)
Cleveland Community College (U)
Clinton Community College (U)
College of Southern Maryland (U)
Concordia University, St. Paul (U,G)
Cossatot Community College of the University of Arkansas (U)
Dabney S. Lancaster Community College (U)
Dallas Baptist University (U)
Danville Community College (U)
Eastern Illinois University (U,G)
Edgecombe Community College (U)
Edison State Community College (U)
El Camino College (U)
Endicott College (U)
Fielding Graduate University (G)
Front Range Community College (U)
Gaston College (U)
Granite State College (U)
Haywood Community College (U)
Heartland Community College (U)
Hillsborough Community College (U)
Hope International University (U)
Houston Community College System (U)
Jacksonville State University (U,G)
Jamestown Community College (U)
J. Sargeant Reynolds Community College (U)
Kansas State University (U,G)
LeTourneau University (U)
Long Beach City College (U)
Los Angeles Trade-Technical College (U)
Malone University (U)
Maryville University of Saint Louis (N)
Mayville State University (U)
Metropolitan Community College–Penn Valley (U)
Miami Dade College (U)
Middle Tennessee State University (U)
Minnesota School of Business–Online (U)
Mississippi State University (U)
Mountain Empire Community College (U)
Mount Wachusett Community College (U)
Murray State University (G)
Naropa University (N)
Naugatuck Valley Community College (U)
New Mexico State University–Carlsbad (U)
Nicolet Area Technical College (U)
North Dakota State University (N,U,G)
North Iowa Area Community College (N)
North Lake College (U)
North Seattle Community College (U)
Oakton Community College (U)
The Ohio State University (U)
Olympic College (U)
Orange Coast College (U)
Oregon State University (U)
Peninsula College (U)
Penn State University Park (U)
Portland Community College (U)
Prescott College (G)
Randolph Community College (U)
Reading Area Community College (U)
Rowan-Cabarrus Community College (U)
Sacramento City College (U)
Sampson Community College (U)
San Bernardino Valley College (U)
San Diego State University (U)
San Jacinto College District (U)
Santa Rosa Junior College (U)
South Piedmont Community College (U)
Southwestern Baptist Theological Seminary (G)
Spoon River College (U)
Stanly Community College (U)
State University of New York Empire State College (U)
Taft College (U)
Tarleton State University (N)
Trident Technical College (U)
Trinidad State Junior College (U)
University of Alaska Fairbanks (U,G)
University of Bridgeport (N,U)
University of Florida (U)
University of Idaho (U)
University of Illinois at Urbana–Champaign (U)
The University of Kansas (U)
University of Maine at Augusta (U)
University of Northern Iowa (U)
University of Southern Mississippi (U,G)
The University of Tennessee at Martin (N)
The University of Texas of the Permian Basin (U)
University of Waterloo (U)
University of Wisconsin–Green Bay (U)
University of Wisconsin–Stout (N)
Utah State University (U,G)
Vanguard University of Southern California (U)
Westchester Community College (U)
Western Kentucky University (U,G)
Western Michigan University (U)
West Hills Community College (U)
Westmoreland County Community College (U)
Wilkes Community College (U)
Wisconsin Indianhead Technical College (N,U)
Yavapai College (U)
York County Community College (U)
York University (U)

HUMAN RESOURCES MANAGEMENT

Adams State College (U)
Alcorn State University (U)
The American College (U,G)
Andrew Jackson University (G)
Arkansas State University (U)
Athabasca University (N,U,G)
Austin Peay State University (U)
Baker College Online (U,G)
Baldwin-Wallace College (U)
Bloomfield College (U)
Bob Jones University (U)
Boise State University (U,G)
Bossier Parish Community College (N)
Brenau University (U)
Brigham Young University–Idaho (U)
Bryant University (N)
Butler Community College (U)
Butler County Community College (U)
California State University, Dominguez Hills (N)
Cape Fear Community College (N)
Capital Community College (U)
Carlow University (G)
Central Michigan University (U,G)
Central Pennsylvania College (U)
Central Texas College (U)
Central Washington University (U)
Champlain College (U)
Clemson University (G)
Coleman University (U)
College of Southern Maryland (U)
Columbus State Community College (U)
Dakota College at Bottineau (U)
Dakota State University (U)

Dallas Baptist University (U,G)
DePaul University (N)
DeVry University Online (G)
Drake University (U,G)
D'Youville College (U)
Eastern Illinois University (U)
Eastern Washington University (N,U)
Edison State Community College (U)
Erie Community College (U)
Erie Community College, North Campus (U)
Erie Community College, South Campus (U)
Fitchburg State University (U)
Florida Institute of Technology (G)
Florida State University (G)
Franklin Pierce University (G)
Front Range Community College (U)
Gannon University (G)
Granite State College (U)
Grantham University (U,G)
Herkimer County Community College (U)
Holyoke Community College (U)
Houston Community College System (U)
Illinois Eastern Community Colleges, Wabash Valley College (U)
Indiana State University (U,G)
Iona College (G)
Jacksonville State University (G)
James Madison University (U)
Jamestown Community College (N,U)
Johnson State College (U)
Jones International University (U)
Kansas State University (U,G)
Keystone College (U)
Kilian Community College (U)
Kirkwood Community College (U)
Labette Community College (N,U)
Lamar State College–Port Arthur (N)
La Roche College (U,G)
Lawrence Technological University (U,G)
Lewis-Clark State College (U)
Mary Baldwin College (U)
Maryville University of Saint Louis (N)
Middlesex Community College (U)
Middle Tennessee State University (N,U)
Minnesota School of Business–Online (U)
Minot State University (U)
Monroe College (U)
Montgomery Community College (U)
Mount Wachusett Community College (N,U)
National University (G)
Nichols College (U,G)
Nipissing University (U)
North Arkansas College (U)
North Carolina State University (U)
North Dakota State University (N)
Northeastern State University (U)
North Iowa Area Community College (U)
Oakland Community College (U)
Ohio University (U)
Oklahoma State University (U)
Oregon State University (N)
Ouachita Technical College (U)
Ozarks Technical Community College (U)
Pacific States University (G)
Pellissippi State Technical Community College (U)
Penn State University Park (U,G)
Pittsburg State University (G)
Portland Community College (U)
Providence College and Theological Seminary (N)
Regent University (U)
Rend Lake College (N)
Riverside Community College District (U)
Rochester Institute of Technology (U)
Saint Francis University (U,G)
St. Joseph's College, Long Island Campus (G)
St. Joseph's College, New York (G)
Saint Leo University (U)
Saint Mary-of-the-Woods College (U)
Saint Paul College–A Community & Technical College (U)
Salve Regina University (N)
Seton Hill University (N,U)
Sinclair Community College (U)
Southern Maine Community College (U)
Southern New Hampshire University (U,G)
Southwest Wisconsin Technical College (U)
Spartanburg Community College (N)
Spring Arbor University (U)
State University of New York Institute of Technology (U,G)
Stephens College (U,G)
Stony Brook University, State University of New York (G)
Suffolk University (G)
Tarleton State University (N,G)
The University of Akron (N,U,G)
University of Alaska Fairbanks (U)
University of Arkansas at Little Rock (U,G)
The University of Findlay (U,G)
University of Florida (U)
University of Houston (G)
University of Illinois at Urbana–Champaign (G)
University of Louisville (N,G)
University of Maine at Augusta (U)
University of Maine at Machias (U)
University of Management and Technology (U)
University of Memphis (N)
University of Michigan–Flint (G)
University of New Haven (U,G)
University of North Dakota (N)
The University of South Dakota (G)
University of Southern Maine (U)
The University of Tennessee at Chattanooga (N)
University of Toronto (N)
University of Virginia (G)
University of Waterloo (N)
University of West Florida (N)
University of Wisconsin–Stout (U,G)
Upper Iowa University (U,G)
Utah State University (U,G)
Wake Technical Community College (U)
Wayland Baptist University (G)
Wayne State University (G)
Western Carolina University (G)
Western Kentucky University (U)
Worcester State University (N)
York University (U)

HUMAN SERVICES

Albertus Magnus College (G)
Amridge University (N,U,G)
Angelina College (U)
Athabasca University (N,U,G)
Austin Peay State University (U)
Bowling Green State University (U)
Bronx Community College of the City University of New York (U)
Burlington College (U)
Burlington County College (U)
Capital Community College (U)
Central Michigan University (U)
Chatham University (U)
City University of Seattle (U)
Clinton Community College (U)
Columbia College (U)
Corning Community College (U)
Dakota College at Bottineau (U)
DePaul University (G)
Edison State Community College (U)
Franklin Pierce University (U)
Gadsden State Community College (U)
Global University (U)
Greenville Technical College (U)
Herkimer County Community College (U)
Holyoke Community College (U)
Hopkinsville Community College (U)
Houston Community College System (U)
Indiana State University (U)
Indiana University–Purdue University Fort Wayne (U)
James A. Rhodes State College (U)
Jamestown Community College (N,U)
Judson University (U)
Kirkwood Community College (U)
Lackawanna College (U)
Middlesex Community College (U)
Mount Wachusett Community College (U)
New Mexico State University (U)
New Mexico State University–Carlsbad (U)
New River Community College (U)
Oxnard College (U)
Piedmont Community College (U)
Prescott College (G)
Quincy University (U)
Quinebaug Valley Community College (U)
Quinsigamond Community College (U)
Randolph Community College (N,U)
Rockingham Community College (N)
Sacramento City College (U)
St. Joseph's College, Long Island Campus (U)
Saint Joseph's College of Maine (U)
Saint Mary-of-the-Woods College (U)
Santa Fe Community College (U)
Sinclair Community College (U)
Southeast Community College Area (U)
Southern Oregon University (U)
South Piedmont Community College (U)
Stanly Community College (U)
Tompkins Cortland Community College (U)
Trident Technical College (U)
The University of Akron (G)
University of Alaska, Prince William Sound Community College (U)
University of Bridgeport (U)
University of Great Falls (U,G)
University of Illinois at Springfield (G)
University of Maine at Augusta (U)
University of Maine at Machias (U)
University of Massachusetts Boston (N)
University of Memphis (N)
University of Wisconsin–Milwaukee (N)
University of Wisconsin–Superior (U)
Upper Iowa University (U)
Wake Technical Community College (U)
Western Kentucky University (U,G)
West Virginia University (N)
Worcester State University (N)

INDUSTRIAL ENGINEERING

Austin Peay State University (U)
Columbia University (N,G)
Indiana University–Purdue University Fort Wayne (U)
Kansas State University (U,G)
Kettering University (N)
New Mexico State University (U,G)
Rochester Institute of Technology (G)
Rowan-Cabarrus Community College (U)
Southern Methodist University (G)
The University of Alabama in Huntsville (G)
The University of Arizona (G)
University of Florida (N,G)
University of Michigan (N)
University of Wisconsin–Platteville (N)
Western Michigan University (U)

INDUSTRIAL PRODUCTION TECHNOLOGIES

Austin Peay State University (U)
Brazosport College (U)
Eastern Illinois University (U)
Edison State Community College (U)
Elaine P. Nunez Community College (U)
Endicott College (U)
Fitchburg State University (U,G)
Itasca Community College (U)
Kansas State University (G)
Rockingham Community College (N)
University of Minnesota, Crookston (U)
The University of Texas of the Permian Basin (U)
Wayne Community College (U)
Wayne State College (U,G)

INFORMATION SCIENCE/STUDIES

Arapahoe Community College (U)
Athabasca University (G)
Austin Peay State University (U)
Ball State University (G)
Belmont Technical College (U)
Brenau University (U)
Brewton-Parker College (U)
Brigham Young University (U)
Caldwell College (U)
Carlow University (U)
Cayuga County Community College (U)
Central New Mexico Community College (U)
Central Virginia Community College (U)
Champlain College (G)
Chemeketa Community College (U)
Cincinnati State Technical and Community College (U)
College of Southern Maryland (U)
Dakota State University (U,G)
Dallas Baptist University (G)
DePaul University (U,G)
Drake University (U,G)
Drexel University (G)
D'Youville College (G)
Faulkner University (U)
Five Towns College (U)
Florida Institute of Technology (G)
Florida State University (G)
Fort Hays State University (U)
Franklin Pierce University (G)
Gaston College (U)
Graceland University (U)
Grantham University (U)
Harrisburg Area Community College (U)
Haywood Community College (U)
Hibbing Community College (U)
Indiana University of Pennsylvania (U)
Iona College (G)
Jacksonville State University (U,G)
The Johns Hopkins University (G)
J. Sargeant Reynolds Community College (U)
Kansas State University (U)
Lamar State College–Port Arthur (N)
Lawrence Technological University (G)
Louisiana State University at Eunice (U)
Macon State College (U)
Marlboro College Graduate College (U)
Marymount University (G)
McDowell Technical Community College (U)
Minot State University (U)
Missouri University of Science and Technology (G)
National University (U)
Nichols College (G)
Northern Kentucky University (U,G)
Pace University (U,G)
Peninsula College (U)
Penn State University Park (U)
Prairie View A&M University (U)
Regent University (U)
The Richard Stockton College of New Jersey (G)
Rose State College (U)
Sacramento City College (U)
Saint Francis University (U,G)
Saint Paul College–A Community & Technical College (U)
San Diego Community College District (U)
Santa Rosa Junior College (U)
Shippensburg University of Pennsylvania (U,G)
Southern Illinois University Carbondale (U)
Southern Illinois University Edwardsville (G)
Southern Methodist University (G)
Southern New Hampshire University (U)
State University of New York at Oswego (U)
State University of New York Institute of Technology (G)
Syracuse University (G)
Tarleton State University (G)
Taylor University (U)
Tunxis Community College (N)
Tyler Junior College (N)
University at Albany, State University of New York (G)
The University of Akron (N,G)
University of Alaska Fairbanks (U)
University of Atlanta (U)
University of Illinois at Chicago (G)
University of Maine at Augusta (U)
University of Michigan–Flint (U)
University of Minnesota, Crookston (U)
University of Nevada, Reno (U)
The University of North Carolina at Charlotte (G)
University of Oregon (G)
University of the Sciences in Philadelphia (U,G)
University of Virginia (G)
University of West Florida (G)
University of Wisconsin–Milwaukee (U,G)
Vincennes University (U)
Wayne State University (U,G)
Western Kentucky University (U)
West Hills Community College (U)
West Los Angeles College (U)

INSURANCE

The American College (U,G)
Arapahoe Community College (U)
Austin Peay State University (N)
Bryant University (N)
Drake University (G)
Hofstra University (N)
Indiana State University (U)
Mississippi State University (U)
Mountain State University (U)
Naugatuck Valley Community College (U)
New England College of Business and Finance (U)
North Iowa Area Community College (N,U)
Pasco-Hernando Community College (N)
St. Petersburg College (N)
Southeast Arkansas College (U)
Southern Illinois University Carbondale (U)
Texas Woman's University (N)
University of Florida (N,U)
University of Toronto (N)
University of Waterloo (U)
University of Wisconsin–La Crosse (U)

INTELLIGENCE, COMMAND CONTROL AND INFORMATION

Notre Dame College (N)

INTERCULTURAL/ MULTICULTURAL AND DIVERSITY STUDIES

Anne Arundel Community College (U)
Austin Peay State University (N,U)
Burlington College (U)
Cascadia Community College (U)
Columbus State Community College (U)
Crown College (G)
DePaul University (U)
Ferris State University (U)
Global University (U,G)
Goddard College (U)
Granite State College (N)
Hibbing Community College (U)
Hope International University (U)
Illinois State University (U)
Laurel University (U)
Lewis University (U)
Marylhurst University (U)
Mercy College of Northwest Ohio (U)
Ocean County College (U)
Portland Community College (U)
Saint Paul College–A Community & Technical College (U)
San Diego Community College District (U)
Santa Monica College (U)
Santa Rosa Junior College (U)
Sinclair Community College (U)
South Piedmont Community College (U)
University at Albany, State University of New York (U)
University of Alaska Fairbanks (U,G)
University of Illinois at Urbana–Champaign (U)
University of Nevada, Reno (U)
University of Wisconsin–Green Bay (U)

Western Kentucky University (G)
West Hills Community College (U)

INTERDISCIPLINARY STUDIES

Bowling Green State University (U)
Burlington College (U)
Dallas Christian College (U)
Keystone College (U)
Mercy College of Northwest Ohio (U)
Michigan Technological University (G)
North Dakota State University (U)
Providence College (U)
Providence College and Theological Seminary (U)
Sacramento City College (U)
Sinclair Community College (U)
University of Alaska Fairbanks (U)
University of Southern Maine (U)
Valencia College (U)
Winston-Salem State University (U)

INTERIOR ARCHITECTURE

Academy of Art University (U,G)
Boston Architectural College (N,U,G)
Brigham Young University–Idaho (U)
Chatham University (U,G)

INTERNATIONAL AGRICULTURE

Dallas Baptist University (U)

INTERNATIONAL AND COMPARATIVE EDUCATION

Crown College (G)
DePaul University (G)
Drexel University (G)
University of Minnesota, Morris (U)
Western Kentucky University (G)

INTERNATIONAL BUSINESS

American University (U)
Angelo State University (U)
Athabasca University (N,G)
Austin Peay State University (U)
Avila University (U)
Bradley University (U)
Brazosport College (U)
Brenau University (U,G)
Burlington County College (U)
Canisius College (G)
Central New Mexico Community College (U)
Champlain College (U)
Chatham University (U)
College of Southern Maryland (U)
Columbus State Community College (U)
Dallas Baptist University (G)
Dickinson State University (U)
Drexel University (N,G)
D'Youville College (U,G)
Eastern Washington University (N)
Gannon University (U,G)
Hofstra University (U)
Iona College (U,G)
Jacksonville State University (U)
Jones International University (U,G)
Lansing Community College (U)
Lawrence Technological University (G)
Long Beach City College (U)
Marist College (G)
Minnesota School of Business–Richfield (U)
Minot State University (U)
Monroe College (U)
Montcalm Community College (U)
Mountain State University (U)
New Mexico State University (U)
Nichols College (G)
Nipissing University (U)
North Central State College (U)
Northern State University (U)
North Seattle Community College (U)
NorthWest Arkansas Community College (U)
Oakton Community College (U)
Pace University (U)
Pacific States University (G)
Pennsylvania College of Technology (U)
Philadelphia University (G)
Pitt Community College (U)
Regent University (U,G)
The Richard Stockton College of New Jersey (U)
Rio Hondo College (U)
Rochester Institute of Technology (U)
Rockingham Community College (N)
Saint Paul College–A Community & Technical College (U)
Sauk Valley Community College (U)
Seminole State College of Florida (N)
Shippensburg University of Pennsylvania (U,G)
Sinclair Community College (U)
Southeast Arkansas College (U)
Southern New Hampshire University (G)
State University of New York at Oswego (U)
State University of New York Empire State College (U)
Suffolk University (G)
Tompkins Cortland Community College (U)
University of Alaska Fairbanks (U)
The University of Findlay (U)
University of Florida (U)
University of Management and Technology (U)
University of New Haven (G)
The University of Texas at Dallas (G)
Upper Iowa University (N,U)
Webber International University (G)
Western Kentucky University (U,G)

INTERNATIONAL/GLOBAL STUDIES

Austin Peay State University (U)
Bowling Green State University (U)
Burlington College (U)
Cascadia Community College (U)
Crown College (G)
DePaul University (G)
Drexel University (G)
D'Youville College (U)
Excelsior College (U)
Global University (G)
Goddard College (U)
Hofstra University (U)
James Madison University (N)
National University (U)
Rend Lake College (U)
St. Ambrose University (U)
Santa Rosa Junior College (U)
Sinclair Community College (U)
Southern New Hampshire University (G)
State University of New York at Oswego (U)
University of Illinois at Urbana–Champaign (U,G)
University of Management and Technology (U)
The University of Texas at Dallas (G)
University of Wisconsin–La Crosse (U)
Webber International University (G)
Webster University (G)
Western Kentucky University (U)

INTERNATIONAL RELATIONS AND NATIONAL SECURITY STUDIES

American University (U,G)
Athabasca University (N,U,G)
Austin Peay State University (U)
Columbus State Community College (U)
DePaul University (G)
Drake University (U)
Erie Community College (U)
Erie Community College, North Campus (U)
Erie Community College, South Campus (U)
Fort Valley State University (U)
Global University (U,G)
Miami Dade College (U)
Salve Regina University (G)
Southern New Hampshire University (U)
University of Massachusetts Boston (U,G)
University of Waterloo (U)
Webster University (G)
Western Kentucky University (U)
West Los Angeles College (U)

JOURNALISM

Arapahoe Community College (U)
Arkansas Tech University (U,G)
Athabasca University (N,U)
Austin Peay State University (U)
Ball State University (U)
Bowling Green State University (U)
Brenau University (U)
Burlington College (U)
Cabrillo College (U)
California State University, Sacramento (U)
Cerritos College (U)
Citrus College (U)
Coastal Carolina University (U)
Community College of Allegheny County (U)
Drake University (U,G)
Eastern Illinois University (U)
Eastern Kentucky University (U)
Eastern Washington University (U)
El Camino College (U)
Erie Community College (U)
Erie Community College, North Campus (U)
Erie Community College, South Campus (U)
Front Range Community College (U)
Hofstra University (U)
Indiana University of Pennsylvania (U)
Indiana University–Purdue University Fort Wayne (U)
Iona College (G)
Ithaca College (U)
Jamestown Community College (N)
Kirkwood Community College (U)
Lehman College of the City University of New York (U)
Long Beach City College (U)
Louisiana State University and Agricultural and Mechanical College (U)
Marshall University (U)

Maryville University of Saint Louis (N)
Middlesex Community College (U)
Middle Tennessee State University (U)
Midland College (U)
Moorpark College (U)
Mount Wachusett Community College (U)
Murray State University (U)
North Dakota State University (U,G)
Oakton Community College (U)
Ohio University (U)
Peninsula College (U)
Pikes Peak Community College (U)
Portland Community College (N)
Quinnipiac University (G)
Regent University (G)
Sacramento City College (U)
Saint Mary-of-the-Woods College (U)
San Diego Community College District (U)
San Diego State University (U)
Santa Monica College (U)
Santa Rosa Junior College (U)
Southern Illinois University Carbondale (U)
Southwestern Community College (U)
State University of New York at Oswego (U)
Taylor University (U)
Temple University (U,G)
Texas State University–San Marcos (U)
The University of Akron (U)
University of Alaska Fairbanks (U)
University of Arkansas at Little Rock (U)
University of Colorado at Colorado Springs (N)
University of Florida (U)
University of Idaho (U)
University of Illinois at Urbana–Champaign (U)
University of Memphis (U,G)
University of Michigan–Flint (U)
University of Nevada, Reno (U)
The University of North Carolina at Chapel Hill (U)
The University of Tennessee at Chattanooga (N)
University of the Pacific (U)
University of Wisconsin Colleges (U)
Utah State University (U)
Western Kentucky University (U)

LANDSCAPE ARCHITECTURE

California State University, Dominguez Hills (U)
Central Wyoming College (N)
Chatham University (G)
Columbus State Community College (U)
Mississippi State University (U)
North Carolina State University (U)
Oregon State University (U)
Penn State University Park (U)
Sonoma State University (N)
Southern Illinois University Carbondale (U)
Temple University (N)
The University of British Columbia (U)
University of Saskatchewan (N)
Wake Technical Community College (U)
Western Texas College (U)

LANGUAGES (AMERICAN INDIAN/NATIVE AMERICAN)

Central Wyoming College (U)
Southeastern Oklahoma State University (U)

LANGUAGES (CLASSICS AND CLASSICAL)

Austin Peay State University (U)
Columbia International University (N,G)
Dallas Baptist University (U)
Laurel University (U)
Louisiana State University and Agricultural and Mechanical College (U)
Moody Bible Institute (U)
Moorpark College (U)
New Orleans Baptist Theological Seminary (U)
Riverside Community College District (U)
Southern Union State Community College (U)
University of Alaska Fairbanks (U)
University of Florida (U)
University of Idaho (U)
University of Louisville (U)
University of Massachusetts Boston (U,G)
The University of North Carolina at Chapel Hill (U)
Youngstown State University (U)

LANGUAGES (EAST ASIAN)

Kean University (N)
Naropa University (G)
Southern Illinois University Carbondale (U)
Unification Theological Seminary (N,G)
The University of Akron (U)
The University of British Columbia (U)
University of Toronto (N)
West Los Angeles College (U)

LANGUAGES (FOREIGN LANGUAGES RELATED)

Acadia University (U)
Anne Arundel Community College (N)
Arkansas State University (U)
Auburn University (N)
Austin Peay State University (N,U)
Bellevue College (U)
Bennington College (G)
Blackhawk Technical College (N)
Boise State University (U)
Bowling Green State University (U)
Brigham Young University–Idaho (U)
Bronx Community College of the City University of New York (U)
California State University, San Bernardino (U)
California State University, San Marcos (N)
Central Carolina Community College (U)
Central Wyoming College (N)
City Colleges of Chicago System (U)
Clarion University of Pennsylvania (U)
College of the Humanities and Sciences, Harrison Middleton University (U)
Colorado Mountain College (U)
Columbus State Community College (U)
Dakota State University (U)
Daytona State College (U)
Eastern Washington University (N)
Ferris State University (U)
Fort Hays State University (U)
Fort Valley State University (U)
Georgian Court University (U)
Greenville Technical College (U)
Hofstra University (U)
Hopkinsville Community College (N)
Indiana Wesleyan University (U)
Iowa Lakes Community College (U)
Jacksonville State University (U)
Jamestown Community College (U)
Lansing Community College (U)
Lewis-Clark State College (U)
Luna Community College (U)
Maryville University of Saint Louis (N)
McMurry University (U)
McNeese State University (U)
Middlesex Community College (U)
Moorpark College (U)
Mount Wachusett Community College (N)
New Mexico Junior College (N)
New Mexico State University–Carlsbad (U)
Northern State University (U)
North Georgia College & State University (U)
North Hennepin Community College (N,U)
The Ohio State University (U)
Oregon State University (U)
Oxnard College (U)
Pace University (U)
Paris Junior College (N,U)
Phoenix College (U)
Portland Community College (N)
Prairie View A&M University (U)
Prescott College (N)
Pulaski Technical College (U)
Randolph Community College (N,U)
Rend Lake College (N)
Richmond Community College (N)
Riverside Community College District (U)
St. Petersburg College (N)
Santa Monica College (U)
Santa Rosa Junior College (U)
Seton Hill University (U)
Sinclair Community College (U)
Slippery Rock University of Pennsylvania (U)
Spokane Community College (U)
State University of New York College at Potsdam (U)
Tarleton State University (N)
Temple University (U)
University of Arkansas at Little Rock (U,G)
University of Houston–Downtown (U)
University of Illinois at Springfield (U)
University of Illinois at Urbana–Champaign (U)
University of Maine (U)
The University of North Carolina at Asheville (U)
The University of North Carolina at Chapel Hill (U)
University of Toronto (N)
University of Waterloo (N,U)
University of West Georgia (U)
University of Wisconsin–Parkside (U)
Wake Technical Community College (N)
Webster University (U)
Western Kentucky University (U)
West Los Angeles College (U)

LANGUAGES (GERMANIC)

Austin Peay State University (U)
Brigham Young University (U)
Columbus State Community College (U)
Lansing Community College (U)
Louisiana State University and Agricultural and Mechanical College (U)
North Carolina State University (U)
Northeastern State University (U)

Oakton Community College (U)
Oklahoma State University (U)
Oregon State University (U)
Ozarks Technical Community College (U)
Slippery Rock University of Pennsylvania (U)
The University of Akron (U)
University of Florida (U)
University of Idaho (U)
University of Toronto (N)
University of Waterloo (U)
Wilfrid Laurier University (U)

LANGUAGES (IRANIAN/PERSIAN)

Paine College (U)
Sacramento City College (U)

LANGUAGES (MIDDLE/NEAR EASTERN AND SEMITIC)

Brigham Young University (U)
Lincoln Christian University (G)
Riverside Community College District (U)
University of Colorado at Colorado Springs (U)

LANGUAGES (MODERN GREEK)

Austin Peay State University (U)
North Carolina State University (U)

LANGUAGES (ROMANCE LANGUAGES)

Andrews University (U)
Arapahoe Community College (U)
Austin Peay State University (N,U)
Boise State University (U)
Brigham Young University (U)
Brigham Young University–Idaho (U)
Broward College (U)
Cabrillo College (U)
California State University, Monterey Bay (U)
California State University, Sacramento (U)
Canisius College (U)
Cayuga County Community College (U)
Chatham University (U)
City Colleges of Chicago System (U)
Clemson University (N)
Clovis Community College (U)
College of San Mateo (U)
College of Southern Maryland (U)
College of the Humanities and Sciences, Harrison Middleton University (U)
Columbus State Community College (U)
Davidson County Community College (U)
Eastern Washington University (U)
Erie Community College (U)
Erie Community College, North Campus (U)
Erie Community College, South Campus (U)
Finger Lakes Community College (U)
Front Range Community College (U)
Georgia State University (U)
Hofstra University (U,G)
Houston Community College System (U)
Iona College (G)
Johnston Community College (U)
Kean University (N)
Lansing Community College (U)
Lehman College of the City University of New York (U)
Louisiana State University and Agricultural and Mechanical College (U)
Marian University (U)
Mercer County Community College (U)
Middlesex Community College (U)
Midland College (U)
Moorpark College (U)
Mountain Empire Community College (U)
Mount Allison University (U)
Nassau Community College (U)
New Mexico State University (U)
North Carolina State University (U)
North Central State College (N)
North Lake College (U)
North Shore Community College (U)
Oakton Community College (N,U)
Ohio University (N)
Oklahoma State University (U)
Oregon State University (N,U)
Pellissippi State Technical Community College (U)
Phoenix College (N)
Reading Area Community College (U)
Rio Hondo College (U)
Rogers State University (U)
Rowan-Cabarrus Community College (N)
St. John's University (U)
St. Louis Community College (U)
Santa Fe Community College (U)
Southeastern Oklahoma State University (N,U)
Southern Illinois University Carbondale (U)
Southwest Virginia Community College (U)
Spartanburg Community College (N)
Spokane Community College (U)
State University of New York at Plattsburgh (U)
State University of New York College at Potsdam (N)
Temple University (N)
Texas State University–San Marcos (U)
Tyler Junior College (U)
The University of Akron (U)
University of Alaska Fairbanks (U)
The University of British Columbia (U)
University of California, Davis (N,U)
University of Florida (U)
University of Idaho (U)
University of Illinois at Urbana–Champaign (U)
University of Maine at Augusta (U)
University of Massachusetts Boston (U,G)
University of Michigan–Flint (U)
University of Nevada, Reno (U)
The University of North Carolina at Asheville (U)
The University of North Carolina at Chapel Hill (U)
The University of Texas at Arlington (U)
University of Toronto (N)
Wake Technical Community College (N)
Wilfrid Laurier University (U)

LANGUAGES (SLAVIC, BALTIC, AND ALBANIAN)

The University of North Carolina at Chapel Hill (U)
University of Waterloo (U)
Wayne State University (U)

LANGUAGES (SOUTH ASIAN)

Arapahoe Community College (U)
North Carolina State University (U)
University of Toronto (N)
West Los Angeles College (U)

LANGUAGES (SOUTHEAST ASIAN AND AUSTRALASIAN/PACIFIC)

Oakton Community College (U)
West Los Angeles College (U)

LEATHERWORKING AND UPHOLSTERY

Blackhawk Technical College (N)

LEGAL PROFESSIONS AND STUDIES RELATED

Arapahoe Community College (U)
Austin Peay State University (N)
Burlington College (U)
Chatham University (U)
Clackamas Community College (U)
Clarion University of Pennsylvania (U)
Clemson University (N)
Erie Community College (U)
Erie Community College, North Campus (U)
Erie Community College, South Campus (U)
Front Range Community College (U)
Hopkinsville Community College (N)
Iona College (G)
John Jay College of Criminal Justice of the City University of New York (U)
Kansas State University (N)
Kean University (N)
Liberty University (G)
Lock Haven University of Pennsylvania (N)
Long Beach City College (U)
Mansfield University of Pennsylvania (N)
Michigan State University College of Law (N,G)
Middlesex Community College (U)
Minnesota School of Business–Richfield (U)
Mississippi College (U)
Mount Wachusett Community College (U)
Paris Junior College (N)
Penn State University Park (U)
Phoenix College (U)
Portland Community College (N)
Pulaski Technical College (U)
Quinebaug Valley Community College (N)
Quinsigamond Community College (N)
Regent University (G)
Rose State College (U)
Rowan-Cabarrus Community College (N)
The Sage Colleges (U)
Southern Union State Community College (U)
South Piedmont Community College (U)
South Suburban College (U)
Spokane Community College (U)
Sullivan County Community College (N)
Texas State University–San Marços (U)
Texas Woman's University (N)
University of Alaska Fairbanks (G)
University of Baltimore (G)
University of California, Davis (N,U)
University of Central Florida (U)
University of Illinois at Springfield (G)
The University of Montana Western (N)

University of the Incarnate Word (N)
University of the Pacific (N)
Valencia College (U)
Western Kentucky University (U)
West Los Angeles College (U)

LEGAL RESEARCH AND ADVANCED PROFESSIONAL STUDIES

Blackstone Career Institute (U)
Drake University (U)
Michigan State University College of Law (N,G)
Naugatuck Valley Community College (U)
Regent University (G)
Rose State College (U)
The University of Akron (G)
University of the Incarnate Word (N)
Wayne State University (G)

LEGAL STUDIES (NON-PROFESSIONAL GENERAL, UNDERGRADUATE)

Adams State College (U)
Angelina College (U)
Anne Arundel Community College (U)
Arapahoe Community College (U)
Athabasca University (U)
Austin Peay State University (U)
Brenau University (U)
Broward College (U)
Burlington College (U)
Burlington County College (U)
Cabrillo College (U)
Cape Fear Community College (U)
Carleton University (U)
Central Carolina Technical College (U)
Central New Mexico Community College (U)
Central Texas College (U)
Central Washington University (U)
Cerritos College (U)
Clovis Community College (U)
College of Southern Maryland (U)
Colorado Mountain College (U)
Columbus State Community College (U)
Delgado Community College (U)
DeVry University Online (U)
Drury University (U)
Finger Lakes Community College (U)
Fitchburg State University (U)
Florida Hospital College of Health Sciences (U)
Gannon University (U)
Gaston College (U)
Grantham University (U)
Hillsborough Community College (U)
Hofstra University (G)
Iona College (U)
James A. Rhodes State College (U)
Lansing Community College (U)
Lipscomb University (U)
Mansfield University of Pennsylvania (N)
Marist College (U)
McNeese State University (U)
Mercer County Community College (U)
Michigan State University College of Law (N)
Middlesex Community College (U)
Midland College (U)
Minnesota School of Business–Richfield (U)
Mountain Empire Community College (U)
Mountain State University (U)
Nassau Community College (U)
Naugatuck Valley Community College (U)
New Mexico State University–Alamogordo (U)
New River Community College (U)
Northeastern State University (U)
North Hennepin Community College (U)
North Shore Community College (U)
NorthWest Arkansas Community College (U)
Northwestern Michigan College (U)
Oakton Community College (U)
Oxnard College (U)
Pace University (U)
The Paralegal Institute, Inc. (U)
Pasco-Hernando Community College (N)
Penn State University Park (U)
Philadelphia University (U)
Pitt Community College (U)
Pulaski Technical College (U)
Randolph Community College (U)
Robert Morris University (U)
Roger Williams University (U)
Rose State College (U)
St. John's University (U)
Sam Houston State University (U)
San Diego Community College District (U)
Sinclair Community College (U)
State University of New York Empire State College (U)
State University of New York Institute of Technology (G)
Tompkins Cortland Community College (U)
Trine University (U)
Tyler Junior College (U)
University of Alaska Fairbanks (U)
University of Florida (U)
University of Great Falls (U)
University of Illinois at Springfield (U)
University of Mary Washington (U)
University of New Haven (U,G)
University of Waterloo (U)
University of Wisconsin–Superior (N,U)
Upper Iowa University (U)
Valencia College (U)
Wake Technical Community College (N)
Western Kentucky University (U)
West Los Angeles College (U)
Westmoreland County Community College (U)

LEGAL SUPPORT SERVICES

Anne Arundel Community College (U)
Arapahoe Community College (U)
Austin Peay State University (N,U)
Blackhawk Technical College (U)
Blackstone Career Institute (N,U)
Boston University (N)
Bryant & Stratton Online (N,U)
Burlington College (U)
Cape Fear Community College (U)
Columbus State Community College (U)
Community College of Allegheny County (U)
Duquesne University (N)
Eastern Illinois University (N)
Johnston Community College (U)
Kansas State University (N)
Michigan State University College of Law (N,G)
Minnesota School of Business–Online (U)
North Dakota State University (N)
Ohio University (N)
Pasco-Hernando Community College (U)
Randolph Community College (N)
Regent University (G)
Riverside Community College District (U)
San Jacinto College District (U)
Santa Fe Community College (U)
South Suburban College (U)
Spartanburg Community College (N)
Spokane Community College (U)
Tyler Junior College (U)
University of California, Davis (N,U)
University of North Dakota (N)
University of the Incarnate Word (N)
University of Wisconsin–Superior (N)
Wake Technical Community College (N)
Western Kentucky University (U)
West Los Angeles College (U)
West Virginia University (N)

LIBERAL ARTS AND SCIENCES, GENERAL STUDIES AND HUMANITIES

Acadia University (U)
Albertus Magnus College (U,G)
Alvin Community College (U)
Amridge University (N,U)
Angelina College (U)
Arapahoe Community College (U)
Arizona Western College (U)
Arkansas State University–Mountain Home (U)
Athabasca University (N)
Austin Peay State University (U)
Belhaven University (U)
Bellevue College (U)
Beulah Heights University (U)
Boise State University (U)
Bowling Green State University (U)
Brenau University (U)
Brigham Young University (U)
Burlington College (U)
Butler Community College (U)
California State University, Chico (U)
California State University, San Bernardino (U)
Cayuga County Community College (U)
Centralia College (U)
Central Oregon Community College (U)
Champlain College (U)
Chattanooga State Community College (U)
Chemeketa Community College (U)
Citrus College (U)
City Colleges of Chicago System (U)
Clinton Community College (U)
The College at Brockport, State University of New York (G)
College of the Siskiyous (U)
Colorado Mountain College (U)
Columbus State University (U)
Community College of Beaver County (U)
Dakota College at Bottineau (U)
Dallas Baptist University (U,G)
Dallas Christian College (U)
Danville Community College (U)
Delgado Community College (U)
DePaul University (U)
DeVry University Online (U)
Drake University (U)
Drury University (U)

Eastern Washington University (U)
Eastern West Virginia Community and Technical College (U)
East Los Angeles College (U)
Enterprise State Community College (U)
Erie Community College (U)
Erie Community College, North Campus (U)
Erie Community College, South Campus (U)
Excelsior College (U,G)
Faulkner University (U,G)
Finger Lakes Community College (U)
Five Towns College (U)
Florida Hospital College of Health Sciences (U)
Fort Hays State University (U,G)
Fort Valley State University (U)
Gaston College (U)
Georgian Court University (U)
Global University (U)
Goddard College (U,G)
Grand Valley State University (U)
Granite State College (U)
Harcum College (U)
Haywood Community College (U)
Herkimer County Community College (U)
Hibbing Community College (U)
Hocking College (U)
Hofstra University (U)
Hope International University (U)
Illinois Eastern Community Colleges, Olney Central College (U)
Illinois Eastern Community Colleges, Wabash Valley College (U)
Illinois Valley Community College (U)
Indiana University of Pennsylvania (G)
Indiana Wesleyan University (U,G)
Inter American University of Puerto Rico, San Germán Campus (U)
Iona College (U)
Iowa Lakes Community College (U)
Jacksonville State University (U,G)
James A. Rhodes State College (U)
Jamestown Community College (N,U)
John A. Logan College (U)
Judson University (U)
Kansas State University (U)
Keystone College (U)
Labette Community College (U)
Lake Superior College (U)
La Roche College (U)
Lewis-Clark State College (U)
Lewis University (U)
Lock Haven University of Pennsylvania (G)
Long Beach City College (U)
Los Angeles Trade-Technical College (U)
Luna Community College (U)
Luzerne County Community College (U)
Malone University (U)
Mansfield University of Pennsylvania (U)
Mary Baldwin College (U)
Marylhurst University (U,G)
Massachusetts College of Art and Design (U,G)
McDowell Technical Community College (U)
Mercy College of Northwest Ohio (U)
Miami Dade College (U)
Miami University–Regional Campuses (U)
Mid-Continent University (U)
Middlesex Community College (U)
Middle Tennessee State University (U)
Midwestern State University (U)
Minnesota School of Business–Richfield (U)
Minot State University (U)
Monroe Community College (U)
Montgomery Community College (U)
Montgomery County Community College (U)
Mountain State University (U)
Mount Olive College (U)
Naropa University (U,G)
Nashville State Technical Community College (N,U)
Naugatuck Valley Community College (U)
New Mexico State University (U)
New Mexico State University–Alamogordo (U)
Nicolet Area Technical College (U)
North Dakota State University (U,G)
Northern Kentucky University (U)
Northern State University (U)
North Georgia College & State University (U)
North Hennepin Community College (N,U)
North Seattle Community College (U)
NorthWest Arkansas Community College (U)
Oakton Community College (U)
Ocean County College (U)
Oklahoma State University (U)
Olympic College (U)
Oregon State University (U)
Ouachita Technical College (U)
Ozarks Technical Community College (U)
Pace University (N)
Peirce College (U)
Peninsula College (U)
Penn State University Park (U)
Peru State College (U)
Portland Community College (U)
Pratt Community College (U)
Providence College (U)
Pulaski Technical College (U)
Quinebaug Valley Community College (U)
Quinsigamond Community College (U)
Rend Lake College (U)
The Richard Stockton College of New Jersey (U)
Rockland Community College (U)
Rogers State University (U)
Rose State College (U)
Rowan University (U)
St. John's University (G)
St. Joseph's College, Long Island Campus (U)
St. Joseph's College, New York (U)
Saint Mary-of-the-Woods College (U)
Saint Paul College–A Community & Technical College (U)
St. Petersburg College (U)
San Bernardino Valley College (U)
San Diego Community College District (U)
Santa Rosa Junior College (U)
Seton Hill University (U)
Siena Heights University (U)
Sinclair Community College (U)
Southeast Community College Area (U)
Southern Arkansas University–Magnolia (U)
Southern New Hampshire University (U)
Spartanburg Community College (U)
Spokane Community College (U)
State University of New York at Oswego (U)
Stephens College (U)
Stony Brook University, State University of New York (G)
Sullivan County Community College (U)
Syracuse University (U)
Tabor College (U)
Taylor University (U)
Temple University (U)
Texas State University–San Marcos (U)
Toccoa Falls College (U)
Trine University (U)
Tyler Junior College (U)
Union County College (U)
Union Institute & University (U)
The University of Akron (U)
University of Alaska Fairbanks (U)
University of Alaska, Prince William Sound Community College (U)
University of Arkansas at Little Rock (U)
University of Bridgeport (U)
University of Cincinnati (U)
University of Denver (G)
University of Florida (U)
University of Great Falls (U)
University of Houston (U)
University of Houston–Downtown (U)
University of Idaho (U)
University of Illinois at Springfield (U)
University of Illinois at Urbana–Champaign (U,G)
The University of Kansas (U)
University of Maine (G)
University of Maine at Augusta (U)
University of Maine at Fort Kent (U)
University of Maine at Machias (U)
University of Massachusetts Boston (U)
University of Missouri–Kansas City (U,G)
The University of Montana Western (U)
University of Nevada, Reno (U)
The University of North Carolina at Asheville (G)
The University of North Carolina Wilmington (G)
University of Pennsylvania (U)
University of Saskatchewan (U)
The University of South Dakota (U,G)
University of Southern Maine (U)
University of Southern Mississippi (U)
The University of Texas of the Permian Basin (U)
University of Waterloo (U)
University of West Florida (U)
The University of Winnipeg (U)
University of Wisconsin–La Crosse (U)
Upper Iowa University (U)
Utah State University (U)
Utica College (U,G)
Valencia College (U)
Vincennes University (U)
Wake Technical Community College (U)
Wayne Community College (U)
Wayne State University (U)
Western Kentucky University (U)
West Hills Community College (U)
West Los Angeles College (U)
West Shore Community College (U)
Wharton County Junior College (U)
Winston-Salem State University (U)
York University (U)
Youngstown State University (U)

LIBRARY AND ARCHIVES ASSISTING

Austin Peay State University (U)
Belmont Technical College (U)
Oakland Community College (U)
Rose State College (U)

Sacramento City College (U)
Syracuse University (G)

LIBRARY SCIENCE AND ADMINISTRATION

Austin Peay State University (U)
Big Bend Community College (U)
Central Oregon Community College (U)
Central Wyoming College (U)
Clarion University of Pennsylvania (U,G)
Drexel University (G)
Eastern Kentucky University (G)
Fontbonne University (U)
Inter American University of Puerto Rico, San Germán Campus (G)
Kauai Community College (G)
Lake-Sumter Community College (U)
Long Beach City College (U)
Mansfield University of Pennsylvania (G)
Marshall University (U)
Mayville State University (U)
McNeese State University (U)
Memorial University of Newfoundland (U,G)
Middle Tennessee State University (G)
Missouri Baptist University (G)
New Mexico State University (U)
North Carolina Central University (G)
Northern State University (U)
North Seattle Community College (U)
Phoenix College (U)
Portland Community College (U)
The Richard Stockton College of New Jersey (N)
Rio Hondo College (U)
Riverside Community College District (U)
Rose State College (U)
Sacramento City College (U)
St. John's University (G)
San Diego Community College District (U)
Santa Monica College (U)
Santa Rosa Junior College (U)
Syracuse University (G)
Texas Woman's University (G)
Union University (U)
University of Alaska Fairbanks (U)
The University of Arizona (G)
University of Idaho (U,G)
University of Illinois at Urbana–Champaign (N,G)
University of Maine at Augusta (U)
University of Nevada, Reno (U,G)
University of West Georgia (U)
University of Wisconsin–Milwaukee (G)
University of Wisconsin–Superior (U,G)
Valley City State University (U)
Wayne State University (G)
Western Kentucky University (U,G)
West Los Angeles College (U)

LIBRARY SCIENCE RELATED

Antelope Valley College (U)
Austin Peay State University (U)
Belmont Technical College (U)
Boise State University (U)
Brigham Young University–Idaho (U)
Cabrillo College (U)
California State University, East Bay (U)
Central Carolina Community College (U)
Centralia College (U)
Central Virginia Community College (U)
The College of St. Scholastica (G)
Colorado Mountain College (U)
Drexel University (G)
Florida State University (G)
Harrisburg Area Community College (U)
Illinois State University (G)
Indiana State University (U,G)
Jones International University (G)
Los Angeles Harbor College (U)
Louisiana State University and Agricultural and Mechanical College (U)
Mercer County Community College (U)
Miami Dade College (U)
Northern Kentucky University (U)
North Seattle Community College (U)
Oakton Community College (U)
Pittsburg State University (G)
Reading Area Community College (U)
Rio Hondo College (U)
Rose State College (U)
Sacramento City College (U)
San Diego Community College District (U)
Santa Rosa Junior College (U)
Southern Arkansas University–Magnolia (G)
State University of New York at Plattsburgh (U)
Syracuse University (G)
University of Alaska Fairbanks (U)
The University of British Columbia (U,G)
University of Idaho (U,G)
University of Illinois at Urbana–Champaign (G)
University of Maine at Augusta (U)
The University of Montana Western (U)
University of Nevada, Reno (U)
University of Southern Mississippi (U)
University of Wisconsin–Milwaukee (U)
Utah State University (G)
Valley City State University (U)
Western Kentucky University (U,G)
West Los Angeles College (U)

LINGUISTIC, COMPARATIVE, AND RELATED LANGUAGE STUDIES

Acadia University (U)
Adams State College (N)
Athabasca University (N,U)
Austin Peay State University (U)
Bossier Parish Community College (U)
Brenau University (U)
Bridgewater State University (G)
California State University, Chico (U)
Columbia International University (G)
Dakota State University (U)
Davidson County Community College (U)
Goddard College (U)
Illinois State University (U)
James Madison University (U)
Jamestown Community College (N)
J. Sargeant Reynolds Community College (U)
Lansing Community College (U)
Lenoir Community College (U)
Los Angeles Harbor College (U)
Louisiana State University and Agricultural and Mechanical College (U)
Mesa Community College (U)
Middlesex Community College (U)
Middle Tennessee State University (N)
Mountain Empire Community College (U)
North Carolina Central University (N)
Northeastern State University (U)
Oakton Community College (U)
Odessa College (N)
The Ohio State University (U)
Ohio University (U)
Oregon State University (N)
Pace University (U)
Riverside Community College District (U)
St. Petersburg College (U)
Southwestern Baptist Theological Seminary (G)
State University of New York College at Potsdam (N)
Tarleton State University (N)
Tunxis Community College (U)
The University of Akron (U)
University of Alaska Fairbanks (U)
University of Denver (G)
University of Florida (U)
University of Management and Technology (G)
University of Massachusetts Boston (U,G)
University of Michigan–Flint (U)
University of Nevada, Reno (U)
University of North Dakota (U)
University of Oregon (U)
University of Southern Mississippi (U,G)
University of Waterloo (U)
University of Wisconsin–La Crosse (U)
Western Kentucky University (U)

LITERATURE

American University (U)
Arapahoe Community College (U)
Bluefield College (U)
Bowling Green State University (U)
Brigham Young University–Idaho (U)
Burlington College (U)
City Colleges of Chicago System (U)
Clatsop Community College (U)
Cleveland Community College (U)
East Georgia College (U)
Edison State Community College (U)
Gannon University (U)
John A. Logan College (U)
Johnston Community College (U)
Laurel University (U)
Lewis-Clark State College (U)
Lewis University (U)
Lindenwood University (U)
Loyola University New Orleans (U)
Minot State University (U)
North Dakota State University (N,U)
Northwest-Shoals Community College (U)
Ohio University (U)
Oklahoma State University (U)
Oregon Coast Community College (U)
Providence College (U)
Sacramento City College (U)
Sinclair Community College (U)
Slippery Rock University of Pennsylvania (U)
State University of New York at Oswego (U)
Sullivan County Community College (U)
Tabor College (U)
University of Alaska Fairbanks (U)
University of Maine at Machias (U)
University of Oregon (U)
Valencia College (U)

MANAGEMENT INFORMATION SYSTEMS

Arapahoe Community College (U)
Ashland University (U)
Athabasca University (N,U,G)
Austin Peay State University (U)
Baker College Online (U)
Ball State University (G)
Bellevue College (U)
Brenau University (U,G)
Brewton-Parker College (U)
Bryant University (N)
California State University, Sacramento (U)
Carlow University (U)
Cayuga County Community College (U)
Central Carolina Community College (N)
Centralia College (N,U)
Central Michigan University (G)
Central Texas College (U)
Central Washington University (U)
Cerritos College (U)
Charter Oak State College (U)
Chemeketa Community College (U)
Cincinnati State Technical and Community College (U)
Cossatot Community College of the University of Arkansas (N)
Culver-Stockton College (U)
Dallas Baptist University (U,G)
Drake University (U)
Drexel University (N,G)
Drury University (U)
Eastern Washington University (U)
East Los Angeles College (U)
Edgecombe Community College (N,U)
Edison State Community College (U)
Elmira College (U,G)
Endicott College (U)
Excelsior College (U)
Fort Hays State University (N)
Gaston College (U)
Granite State College (U)
Grantham University (U,G)
Haywood Community College (U)
Houston Community College System (U)
Indiana State University (U)
Indiana University of Pennsylvania (U)
Inter American University of Puerto Rico, San Germán Campus (U,G)
Iona College (U,G)
Jacksonville State University (U,G)
The Johns Hopkins University (G)
Kansas State University (U,G)
Kettering University (N)
Kirkwood Community College (U)
Labette Community College (U)
Lamar State College–Port Arthur (N)
Lawrence Technological University (G)
Louisiana State University and Agricultural and Mechanical College (U)
Luna Community College (U)
Mansfield University of Pennsylvania (N)
Marlboro College Graduate College (U)
Marshall University (U)
Maryville University of Saint Louis (N)
McMurry University (U)
Middlesex Community College (U)
Middle Tennessee State University (N)
Milwaukee School of Engineering (U)
Misericordia University (U)
Mississippi College (U,G)
Monroe College (U)
Motlow State Community College (U)
Mountain State University (U)
Mount Olive College (U)
Mount Wachusett Community College (U)
New Mexico Highlands University (U,G)
North Arkansas College (U)
North Carolina Central University (U)
Northern State University (U)
Notre Dame College (U)
Oklahoma State University (U)
Oregon Institute of Technology (U)
Pace University (G)
Penn State University Park (U)
Philadelphia University (U,G)
Prairie View A&M University (G)
Quinnipiac University (U,G)
Regent University (U)
Rend Lake College (U)
Robert Morris University (U,G)
Rockingham Community College (N)
St. Cloud State University (U)
Saint Francis University (U,G)
St. Louis Community College (N)
Saint Paul College–A Community & Technical College (U)
St. Petersburg College (N)
Shippensburg University of Pennsylvania (U,G)
Sinclair Community College (U)
Southern Arkansas University–Magnolia (U)
Southern Connecticut State University (U,G)
Southern University at New Orleans (U)
Southwest Wisconsin Technical College (U)
Stanly Community College (U)
State University of New York College at Potsdam (U)
State University of New York Empire State College (U)
State University of New York Institute of Technology (G)
Suffolk University (G)
Syracuse University (G)
Taylor University (U)
Trident Technical College (U)
Tunxis Community College (U)
Tyler Junior College (N)
Union University (U)
University of Alaska Fairbanks (U)
University of Arkansas at Little Rock (U)
University of Colorado Boulder (N)
The University of Findlay (N)
University of Houston–Downtown (U)
University of Illinois at Springfield (G)
University of Lethbridge (U)
University of Management and Technology (U,G)
University of Mary Washington (G)
University of Massachusetts Boston (U)
University of Michigan–Flint (N)
University of Minnesota, Crookston (U)
University of Oregon (G)
University of Southern Mississippi (U)
The University of Texas at Dallas (G)
University of Toronto (N)
University of Waterloo (G)
University of West Georgia (G)
University of Wisconsin MBA Consortium (G)
Upper Iowa University (N,U)
Wayland Baptist University (U,G)
Wayne Community College (U)
Webster University (G)
Westchester Community College (U)
Western Kentucky University (U)
West Hills Community College (U)
West Virginia University (N)
Wilkes Community College (U)
Xavier University (U)
York College of Pennsylvania (N)

MANAGEMENT SCIENCES AND QUANTITATIVE METHODS

Acadia University (U)
Athabasca University (N,G)
Austin Peay State University (U)
Boise State University (G)
Bowling Green State University (U)
Brenau University (U,G)
Bryant University (N)
Burlington County College (U)
Central Michigan University (G)
Columbia University (N)
Concordia University Wisconsin (U)
Cornell University (U)
Cossatot Community College of the University of Arkansas (N)
Dallas Baptist University (G)
DePaul University (N,G)
Drake University (U)
Drexel University (N,U,G)
Duke University (G)
Endicott College (U)
Franklin Pierce University (G)
Granite State College (U)
Iowa Valley Community College District (U)
Jacksonville State University (U,G)
The Johns Hopkins University (G)
Kettering University (N)
Louisiana State University and Agricultural and Mechanical College (U)
Marist College (G)
Mesa State College (U)
Miami Dade College (U)
National University (U)
New Mexico Highlands University (U)
Nichols College (G)
Nipissing University (U)
Philadelphia University (U,G)
Portland Community College (U)
Rockingham Community College (N)
St. Ambrose University (U)
Saint Francis University (G)
Saint Joseph's College of Maine (G)
Shippensburg University of Pennsylvania (U,G)
Southeast Community College Area (N)
Southern Illinois University Carbondale (U)
State University of New York College of Agriculture and Technology at Morrisville (U)
State University of New York Institute of Technology (G)
Tompkins Cortland Community College (U)
The University of Alabama in Huntsville (G)
University of Alaska Fairbanks (U)
University of California, Davis (U)
University of Colorado Boulder (G)
The University of Findlay (N)
University of Florida (U)
University of Illinois at Urbana–Champaign (N,U,G)
University of Lethbridge (U)

University of Maine at Augusta (U)
University of Management and Technology (U)
University of Mary Washington (G)
University of Michigan–Flint (U,G)
University of New Haven (U)
University of North Dakota (G)
The University of Texas at Dallas (N,G)
The University of Texas of the Permian Basin (U)
University of Toronto (N)
University of Wisconsin MBA Consortium (G)
Upper Iowa University (U)
Western Carolina University (N)
York University (U)

MANUFACTURING ENGINEERING

Columbia University (N,G)
Eastern Washington University (N)
Indiana University–Purdue University Fort Wayne (N,U)
James A. Rhodes State College (N)
James Madison University (N)
Kansas State University (U,G)
Kettering University (N)
Missouri University of Science and Technology (G)
New Mexico State University (G)
Portland Community College (U)
The University of Alabama in Huntsville (G)
University of Michigan (N)
University of Minnesota, Crookston (U)
The University of Texas at Dallas (N)
Western Michigan University (U)

MARINE SCIENCES

Coastal Carolina University (U)
Miami Dade College (U)
University of Alaska Fairbanks (U)
University of Hawaii at Hilo (U)

MARKETING

Acadia University (U)
Adams State College (U)
Alcorn State University (U,G)
Anne Arundel Community College (U)
Arapahoe Community College (U)
Arkansas State University (U)
Arkansas Tech University (U)
Athabasca University (N,U,G)
Austin Peay State University (N,U)
Baker College Online (U,G)
Bellevue College (U)
Blackhawk Technical College (U)
Bloomfield College (U)
Bob Jones University (U)
Boise State University (U)
Brenau University (U,G)
Bridgewater State University (U)
Brigham Young University (U)
Bronx Community College of the City University of New York (U)
Brookdale Community College (U)
Broward College (U)
Buena Vista University (U)
Burlington County College (U)
Butler Community College (U)
Butler County Community College (U)
Cape Fear Community College (U)
Capital Community College (U)
Cayuga County Community College (U)
Central Carolina Community College (U)
Central Carolina Technical College (U)
Central Michigan University (U,G)
Central Texas College (U)
Central Virginia Community College (U)
Central Washington University (U)
Charter Oak State College (U)
Chatham University (U)
Chattanooga State Community College (U)
City Colleges of Chicago System (U)
City University of Seattle (U)
Clemson University (U)
Coleman University (U,G)
College of Southern Maryland (U)
Columbia College (U)
Columbus State Community College (U)
Concordia University Wisconsin (U)
Cornell University (U,G)
Cossatot Community College of the University of Arkansas (N)
Dakota College at Bottineau (U)
Dallas Baptist University (U,G)
Danville Community College (U)
DePaul University (G)
DeVry University Online (U,G)
Dickinson State University (U)
Drake University (U)
Drexel University (U,G)
Drury University (U)
Eastern Kentucky University (U)
Eastern West Virginia Community and Technical College (U)
Eastern Wyoming College (U)
Edison State Community College (U)
Erie Community College (U)
Erie Community College, North Campus (U)
Erie Community College, South Campus (U)
Finger Lakes Community College (U)
Fort Hays State University (U)
Fort Valley State University (U)
Franklin Pierce University (U,G)
Front Range Community College (U)
Frostburg State University (G)
Gannon University (U)
Genesee Community College (U)
George Fox University (U)
Governors State University (U)
Graceland University (U)
Grantham University (U,G)
Greenville Technical College (U)
Harcum College (U)
Harrisburg Area Community College (U)
Hillsborough Community College (U)
Hofstra University (U,G)
Houston Community College System (U)
Huntington College of Health Sciences (U)
Illinois Eastern Community Colleges, Frontier Community College (U)
Illinois State University (G)
Indiana State University (U)
Indiana University of Pennsylvania (U)
Inter American University of Puerto Rico, San Germán Campus (U)
Iona College (U,G)
Ithaca College (U)
Jacksonville State University (U,G)
Jamestown Community College (N,U)
John A. Logan College (U)
Johnston Community College (U)
J. Sargeant Reynolds Community College (U)
Kansas State University (U)
Kean University (U)
Keystone College (U)
Lamar State College–Port Arthur (N)
Lansing Community College (U)
Lawrence Technological University (G)
Lewis-Clark State College (U)
Liberty University (U)
Lipscomb University (U,G)
Lock Haven University of Pennsylvania (U)
Long Beach City College (U)
Los Angeles Trade-Technical College (U)
Louisiana State University and Agricultural and Mechanical College (U)
Louisiana State University at Eunice (U)
Luna Community College (U)
Mansfield University of Pennsylvania (N,U)
Marian University (U)
Marist College (G)
Marlboro College Graduate College (U)
Marshall University (U,G)
Mary Baldwin College (U)
Maryville University of Saint Louis (N,U)
McKendree University (U)
McNeese State University (U)
Mercer County Community College (U)
Miami Dade College (U)
Middlesex Community College (U)
Middle Tennessee State University (U,G)
Minnesota School of Business–Online (U)
Minot State University (U)
Monroe College (U)
Montgomery County Community College (U)
Mountain Empire Community College (U)
Mountain State University (U)
Mount Wachusett Community College (N,U)
Murray State College (U)
Murray State University (G)
Nashville State Technical Community College (N,U)
Nassau Community College (U)
New Mexico State University (U)
New Mexico State University–Carlsbad (U)
New River Community College (U)
Nichols College (U,G)
Nipissing University (U)
North Carolina State University (U)
North Dakota State College of Science (U)
North Dakota State University (N,U)
Northeastern State University (U)
Northern State University (U)
North Georgia College & State University (U)
North Hennepin Community College (N,U)
North Iowa Area Community College (U)
North Shore Community College (U)
Notre Dame College (U)
Oakland Community College (U)
Oakton Community College (U)
Ocean County College (U)
Ohio University (U)
Oklahoma State University (U)
Olympic College (U)
Oxnard College (U)
Pace University (U,G)
Pacific States University (G)
Pamlico Community College (U)
Pellissippi State Technical Community College (U)
Pennsylvania College of Technology (U)
Philadelphia University (U,G)
Phoenix College (N,U)
Piedmont Community College (U)

Pikes Peak Community College (U)
Pitt Community College (U)
Pittsburg State University (U)
Portland Community College (U)
Prairie View A&M University (G)
Randolph Community College (U)
Reading Area Community College (U)
Regent University (U)
Rend Lake College (U)
The Richard Stockton College of New Jersey (N,U,G)
Rio Hondo College (U)
Riverside Community College District (U)
Robert Morris University (U)
Rockingham Community College (N)
Rockland Community College (U)
Rogers State University (U)
Rose State College (U)
Sacramento City College (U)
St. Ambrose University (U)
Saint Francis University (U,G)
St. John's University (U)
St. Joseph's College, New York (U)
Saint Leo University (U)
St. Louis Community College (U)
Saint Mary-of-the-Woods College (U)
Saint Paul College–A Community & Technical College (U)
Sam Houston State University (U)
San Diego Community College District (U)
San Diego State University (U)
San Jacinto College District (U)
Santa Monica College (U)
Santa Rosa Junior College (U)
Seminole State College of Florida (N,U)
Sessions College for Professional Design (N,U)
Shippensburg University of Pennsylvania (U,G)
Sinclair Community College (U)
Southeast Arkansas College (U)
Southeastern Community College (U)
Southeastern Oklahoma State University (U)
Southern Arkansas University–Magnolia (U)
Southern Illinois University Carbondale (N,U)
Southern New Hampshire University (U,G)
South Piedmont Community College (U)
Spokane Community College (U)
Spring Arbor University (U)
Stanly Community College (U)
State University of New York at Oswego (U)
State University of New York at Plattsburgh (U)
Stephens College (U,G)
Suffolk University (G)
Tarleton State University (G)
Taylor University (U)
Texas A&M University–Corpus Christi (G)
Tompkins Cortland Community College (U)
Trine University (U)
Union University (U)
United States Sports Academy (G)
The University of Alabama in Huntsville (G)
University of Alaska Fairbanks (U)
University of Arkansas at Little Rock (U,G)
University of Dubuque (U)
The University of Findlay (U,G)
University of Florida (U)
University of Idaho (U)
University of Illinois at Chicago (N,G)
University of Maine at Augusta (U)
University of Mary Washington (G)
University of Massachusetts Boston (U,G)
University of Michigan–Flint (U,G)
University of Minnesota, Crookston (U)
University of Nevada, Reno (U)
University of New Haven (U)
University of North Alabama (U)
University of Northern Iowa (U)
University of St. Francis (U)
University of Southern Maine (U)
University of Southern Mississippi (U,G)
The University of Texas at Dallas (N,G)
The University of Texas of the Permian Basin (G)
University of the Sciences in Philadelphia (G)
University of Toronto (N)
University of Virginia (G)
University of Waterloo (N)
The University of West Alabama (U)
University of West Georgia (U)
University of Wisconsin MBA Consortium (G)
Upper Iowa University (N,U)
Valencia College (U)
Valley City State University (U)
Wake Technical Community College (N,U)
Washington State University (U)
Wayland Baptist University (U)
Wayne State University (G)
Webber International University (U,G)
Webster University (G)
Westchester Community College (U)
Western Kentucky University (U)
West Los Angeles College (U)
West Shore Community College (U)
West Virginia University (G)
Wharton County Junior College (U)
Wilkes Community College (U)
Worcester Polytechnic Institute (G)
York Technical College (U)
York University (U)

MASONRY

Pamlico Community College (U)

MATERIALS ENGINEERING

Columbia University (N)
Missouri University of Science and Technology (N)
Prairie View A&M University (U)
University of Florida (N,G)
University of Idaho (U)
University of Illinois at Urbana–Champaign (G)
The University of Tennessee Space Institute (G)

MATERIALS SCIENCES

Columbia University (N,G)
Columbus State Community College (U)
Michigan Technological University (N,U,G)
Quinebaug Valley Community College (U)
The University of Alabama in Huntsville (G)
University of Florida (N,G)
University of Illinois at Urbana–Champaign (G)

MATHEMATICS

Acadia University (N)
Adams State College (U)
Albertus Magnus College (U)
Allen Community College (U)
Alpena Community College (U)
Alvin Community College (U)
Anderson University (U)
Angelo State University (U)
Antelope Valley College (U)
Arapahoe Community College (U)
Arkansas State University (U)
Arkansas State University–Beebe (U)
Arkansas State University–Mountain Home (U)
Arkansas Tech University (U)
Athabasca University (N,U)
Austin Peay State University (U)
The Baptist College of Florida (U)
Barclay College (U)
Bellevue College (U)
Beulah Heights University (U)
Big Bend Community College (U)
Bluefield College (U)
Bob Jones University (U)
Boise State University (U)
Bossier Parish Community College (U)
Bowling Green State University (U,G)
Brazosport College (U)
Brenau University (U)
Brigham Young University–Idaho (U)
Bronx Community College of the City University of New York (U)
Brookdale Community College (U)
Bryan College (U)
Burlington County College (U)
Butler Community College (U)
Butler County Community College (U)
Cabrillo College (U)
California State University, Dominguez Hills (N)
California State University, East Bay (U)
California State University, Sacramento (U)
California State University, San Bernardino (U)
California State University, San Marcos (N,U)
Cascadia Community College (U)
Cayuga County Community College (U)
Cedarville University (U)
Central Carolina Community College (U)
Central Carolina Technical College (U)
Centralia College (U)
Central New Mexico Community College (U)
Central Oregon Community College (U)
Central Texas College (U)
Central Virginia Community College (U)
Central Wyoming College (U)
Champlain College (U)
Charter Oak State College (U)
Chatham University (U)
Chattanooga State Community College (U)
Chemeketa Community College (U)
Citrus College (U)
City Colleges of Chicago System (U)
City University of Seattle (U)
Clackamas Community College (U)
Clatsop Community College (U)
Clemson University (N,U)
Cleveland Community College (U)
Cleveland State Community College (U)
Clovis Community College (U)
Coleman University (U)
College of San Mateo (U)
College of Southern Maryland (U)

College of the Humanities and Sciences, Harrison Middleton University (U,G)
College of the Siskiyous (U)
Columbia Basin College (U)
Columbia College (U)
Columbia University (U)
Columbus State Community College (U)
Community College of Allegheny County (U)
Community College of Beaver County (U)
Corning Community College (U)
Cossatot Community College of the University of Arkansas (U)
Culver-Stockton College (U)
Dabney S. Lancaster Community College (U)
Dakota College at Bottineau (U)
Dakota State University (U)
Dallas Baptist University (U)
Danville Community College (U)
Davidson County Community College (U)
Daytona State College (U)
Delgado Community College (U)
DeVry University Online (U,G)
Drury University (U)
East Central Community College (U)
Eastern Kentucky University (U)
Eastern West Virginia Community and Technical College (U)
Eastern Wyoming College (U)
East Georgia College (U)
East Los Angeles College (U)
Edison State Community College (U)
Elaine P. Nunez Community College (U)
Erie Community College (U)
Erie Community College, North Campus (U)
Erie Community College, South Campus (U)
Excelsior College (U)
Fitchburg State University (U)
Florida Hospital College of Health Sciences (U)
Fontbonne University (U)
Fort Valley State University (U)
Framingham State University (U)
Franklin Pierce University (U)
Friends University (U)
Front Range Community College (U)
Frostburg State University (U)
Gadsden State Community College (U)
Gannon University (U)
Gaston College (U)
Gateway Community College (U)
Genesee Community College (U)
George Fox University (U)
Georgia Highlands College (U)
Georgia Institute of Technology (N,U,G)
Georgian Court University (U)
Georgia State University (U)
Granite State College (U)
Grantham University (U)
Greenville Technical College (U)
Hannibal-LaGrange University (U)
Harcum College (U)
Harford Community College (U)
Harrisburg Area Community College (U)
Haywood Community College (U)
Heartland Community College (U)
Hibbing Community College (U)
Hocking College (U)
Holyoke Community College (U)
Houston Community College System (U)
Huntington College of Health Sciences (U)
Illinois Eastern Community Colleges, Lincoln Trail College (U)
Illinois Eastern Community Colleges, Olney Central College (U)
Illinois Eastern Community Colleges, Wabash Valley College (U)
Illinois State University (U,G)
Illinois Valley Community College (U)
Indiana State University (U)
Indiana University of Pennsylvania (U,G)
Indiana University–Purdue University Fort Wayne (U)
Indiana Wesleyan University (U,G)
Iona College (U)
Iowa Lakes Community College (U)
Iowa Valley Community College District (U)
Ithaca College (U)
Jacksonville State University (U)
Jamestown Community College (U)
John A. Logan College (U)
Johnston Community College (U)
J. Sargeant Reynolds Community College (U)
Judson University (U)
Kean University (N,U)
Keystone College (U)
Kirkwood Community College (U)
Labette Community College (U)
Lackawanna College (U)
Lakehead University (U)
Lake Superior College (U)
Lamar State College–Port Arthur (U)
Lansing Community College (U)
La Roche College (U)
Lesley University (G)
LeTourneau University (U)
Lewis-Clark State College (U)
Lincoln Christian University (U)
Long Beach City College (U)
Los Angeles Trade-Technical College (U)
Louisiana State University and Agricultural and Mechanical College (N,U)
Louisiana State University at Eunice (U)
Luna Community College (U)
Macon State College (U)
Mansfield University of Pennsylvania (U)
Marshall University (U)
Marylhurst University (U)
Mayville State University (U)
McMurry University (U)
McNeese State University (U)
Memorial University of Newfoundland (U)
Mercer County Community College (U)
Mercy College of Northwest Ohio (N,U)
Mesa Community College (U)
Mesa State College (U)
Metropolitan Community College–Penn Valley (U)
Miami Dade College (U)
Middlesex Community College (U)
Middle Tennessee State University (U,G)
Midway College (U)
Minnesota School of Business–Richfield (U)
Minot State University (U,G)
Mississippi College (U)
Mississippi State University (U)
Monroe College (U)
Monroe Community College (U)
Monroe County Community College (U)
Montgomery County Community College (U)
Moorpark College (U)
Motlow State Community College (U)
Mountain Empire Community College (U)
Mountain State University (U)
Mount Allison University (U)
Mount Marty College (U)
Mount Olive College (U)
Mount Wachusett Community College (U)
Murray State College (U)
Nashville State Technical Community College (U)
Nassau Community College (N,U)
Naugatuck Valley Community College (U)
New England Institute of Technology (U)
New Jersey City University (U,G)
New Mexico Junior College (U)
New Mexico State University (U)
New Mexico State University–Carlsbad (U)
New Mexico State University–Grants (U)
New River Community College (U)
Nichols College (U)
Nicolet Area Technical College (U)
Nipissing University (U)
North Arkansas College (U)
North Carolina Central University (N)
North Carolina State University (U)
North Central Texas College (U)
North Dakota State College of Science (U)
North Dakota State University (U)
Northern State University (U)
North Iowa Area Community College (U)
North Lake College (U)
North Seattle Community College (U)
North Shore Community College (U)
NorthWest Arkansas Community College (N,U)
Northwestern Connecticut Community College (U)
Northwest-Shoals Community College (U)
Notre Dame College (U)
Nyack College (U)
Oakland Community College (U)
Oakton Community College (U)
Ocean County College (U)
Odessa College (U)
The Ohio State University (U)
Ohio University (U)
Oklahoma Panhandle State University (U)
Oklahoma State University (U)
Olympic College (U)
Orange Coast College (U)
Oregon Coast Community College (U)
Oregon Institute of Technology (U)
Ouachita Technical College (U)
Oxnard College (U)
Ozarks Technical Community College (U)
Pace University (U)
Paine College (U)
Pamlico Community College (U)
Paris Junior College (N)
Peninsula College (U)
Pennsylvania College of Technology (U)
Peru State College (U)
Phoenix College (U)
Pine Technical College (U)
Pittsburgh Technical Institute (U)
Pittsburg State University (U)
Portland Community College (U)
Pratt Community College (U)
Presentation College (U)
Providence College and Theological Seminary (U)
Pulaski Technical College (U)
Quinsigamond Community College (U)
Randolph Community College (U)
Rappahannock Community College (U)
Reading Area Community College (U)

Regent University (U)
Rend Lake College (U)
Rio Hondo College (U)
Riverside Community College District (N,U)
Rochester Institute of Technology (G)
Rockland Community College (U)
Rogers State University (U)
Rose State College (U)
Sacramento City College (U)
St. Clair County Community College (U)
St. Cloud State University (U)
St. Gregory's University (U)
St. John's University (U)
Saint Leo University (U)
St. Louis Community College (U)
Saint Mary-of-the-Woods College (U)
Saint Paul College–A Community & Technical College (U)
St. Petersburg College (U)
St. Philip's College (U)
San Diego Community College District (U)
San Jacinto College District (U)
Santa Fe Community College (U)
Santa Rosa Junior College (U)
Shippensburg University of Pennsylvania (U)
Sinclair Community College (U)
Southeast Arkansas College (U)
Southeast Community College Area (N,U)
Southeastern Community College (U)
Southeastern Illinois College (U)
Southeastern Oklahoma State University (U)
Southern Arkansas University–Magnolia (G)
Southern Illinois University Carbondale (U)
Southern Illinois University Edwardsville (U)
Southern Maine Community College (U)
Southern Oregon University (U)
Southern Union State Community College (U)
Southern University at New Orleans (U)
South Piedmont Community College (U)
South Suburban College (U)
Southwest Wisconsin Technical College (U)
Spartanburg Community College (N,U)
Spokane Community College (U)
Stanly Community College (U)
State University of New York at New Paltz (U)
State University of New York at Oswego (U)
State University of New York at Plattsburgh (U)
State University of New York College of Agriculture and Technology at Morrisville (U)
Stephen F. Austin State University (U)
Sullivan County Community College (U)
Taft College (U)
Taylor University (U)
Texas State University–San Marcos (U,G)
Three Rivers Community College (U)
Toccoa Falls College (U)
Tompkins Cortland Community College (U)
Trident Technical College (U)
Trine University (U)
Union County College (U)
University at Albany, State University of New York (U)
The University of Akron (U,G)
University of Alaska Fairbanks (U)
The University of Arizona (U)
University of Arkansas at Little Rock (U,G)
University of Cincinnati (U)
University of Colorado at Colorado Springs (U)
University of Dubuque (U)
The University of Findlay (U)
University of Florida (U)
University of Great Falls (U)
University of Houston (G)
University of Houston–Downtown (U)
University of Idaho (U,G)
University of Illinois at Springfield (U)
University of Illinois at Urbana–Champaign (N,U,G)
The University of Kansas (U)
University of Maine at Augusta (U)
University of Maine at Machias (U)
University of Management and Technology (U)
University of Massachusetts Boston (U)
University of Michigan–Flint (U)
University of Minnesota, Crookston (U)
University of Minnesota, Morris (U)
University of Missouri–Kansas City (U)
The University of Montana Western (U)
University of Nevada, Reno (U)
University of North Alabama (U)
The University of North Carolina at Asheville (U)
University of North Dakota (N,U)
University of Northern Iowa (U)
University of Pennsylvania (U)
University of St. Francis (U)
University of Saskatchewan (U)
The University of South Dakota (U)
University of Southern Maine (U)
The University of Tennessee Space Institute (G)
The University of Texas at Brownsville (U)
The University of Texas of the Permian Basin (U)
University of Utah (U)
University of Waterloo (U)
University of West Florida (U)
University of West Georgia (U,G)
University of Wisconsin Colleges (N,U)
Upper Iowa University (U)
Utah State University (U)
Utica College (U)
Valencia College (U)
Vincennes University (U)
Wake Technical Community College (U)
Washington State University (U)
Wayne State College (G)
Webster University (U)
Westchester Community College (U)
Western Kentucky University (U,G)
Western Texas College (U)
West Hills Community College (U)
West Los Angeles College (U)
West Shore Community College (U)
Wichita State University (U)
Wilkes Community College (U)
Worcester State University (U)
Yavapai College (U)
York Technical College (U)
York University (U)
Youngstown State University (U)

MATHEMATICS AND COMPUTER SCIENCE

Acadia University (U)
Alvin Community College (U)
Arapahoe Community College (U)
Ashland University (U)
Athabasca University (N,U,G)
Austin Peay State University (U)
Bronx Community College of the City University of New York (U)
Burlington County College (U)
Caldwell College (U)
Cascadia Community College (U)
Cayuga County Community College (U)
Central Texas College (U)
Champlain College (U)
Chemeketa Community College (U)
City Colleges of Chicago System (U)
Columbia College (U)
Columbia University (N,U,G)
Concordia University, St. Paul (N)
Dakota College at Bottineau (U)
Danville Community College (U)
Drake University (U)
Edison State Community College (U)
Fitchburg State University (U)
Fort Hays State University (U)
Grantham University (U)
Harrisburg Area Community College (U)
Haywood Community College (U)
Herkimer County Community College (U)
Indiana State University (U)
Indiana Wesleyan University (G)
Jacksonville State University (U,G)
Jamestown Community College (U)
John A. Logan College (U)
Lansing Community College (U)
Laurel University (U)
Long Beach City College (U)
Macon State College (U)
Marquette University (U)
Marshall University (U)
Miami Dade College (U)
Middlesex Community College (U)
North Hennepin Community College (U)
Pamlico Community College (U)
Peninsula College (U)
Portland Community College (U)
Pulaski Technical College (U)
Sacramento City College (U)
San Diego Community College District (U)
Shippensburg University of Pennsylvania (U)
Sinclair Community College (U)
Southeast Arkansas College (U)
South Suburban College (U)
Spokane Community College (U)
Texas State University–San Marcos (U)
Union University (U)
The University of Akron (U,G)
University of Alaska Fairbanks (U)
University of Idaho (U,G)
University of Illinois at Urbana–Champaign (U)
The University of Texas of the Permian Basin (U)
University of Wisconsin Colleges (U)
University of Wisconsin–Superior (U)
Utah State University (U)
Valencia College (U)
Westchester Community College (U)
Western Kentucky University (U,G)
West Hills Community College (U)
Winston-Salem State University (U)

MATHEMATICS AND STATISTICS RELATED

Allen Community College (U)
Alvin Community College (U)
Andrews University (U)
Anne Arundel Community College (U)
Arapahoe Community College (U)
Austin Peay State University (U)
Baptist Bible College of Pennsylvania (U,G)
Bellevue College (U)
Bossier Parish Community College (U)
Brenau University (U)
Brigham Young University (U)
Brigham Young University–Idaho (U)
Broward College (U)
Burlington County College (U)
Butler Community College (U)
Cayuga County Community College (U)
Central Texas College (U)
Charter Oak State College (U)
Chattanooga State Community College (U)
Chemeketa Community College (U)
City Colleges of Chicago System (U)
City University of Seattle (U)
Clovis Community College (U)
College of Southern Maryland (U)
Colorado Mountain College (U)
Columbia Basin College (U)
Columbia University (U)
Dabney S. Lancaster Community College (U)
Dallas Baptist University (U)
Eastern Illinois University (U)
Eastern Kentucky University (U)
Eastern West Virginia Community and Technical College (U)
Ferris State University (U)
Finger Lakes Community College (U)
Fontbonne University (U)
Franklin Pierce University (U,G)
Front Range Community College (U)
Genesee Community College (U)
Glenville State College (U)
Granite State College (U)
Grantham University (U)
Heartland Community College (U)
Hopkinsville Community College (U)
Houston Community College System (U)
Illinois Eastern Community Colleges, Wabash Valley College (U)
Indiana State University (U)
Indiana Wesleyan University (G)
Jacksonville State University (U)
James Madison University (U)
Jefferson Community College (U)
The Johns Hopkins University (G)
Kettering University (N)
Keystone College (U)
Labette Community College (U)
Lansing Community College (U)
Lawrence Technological University (U)
Lenoir Community College (U)
Lewis-Clark State College (U)
Long Beach City College (U)
Los Angeles Trade-Technical College (U)
Louisiana State University and Agricultural and Mechanical College (U)
Macon State College (U)
Marshall University (U)
McDowell Technical Community College (U)
McKendree University (U)
Mercer County Community College (U)
Miami Dade College (U)
Michigan Technological University (U)
Middlesex Community College (U)
Midland College (U)
Minot State University (U)
Monroe College (U)
Mountain State University (U)
Mount Wachusett Community College (U)
Nassau Community College (U)
New England College of Business and Finance (U)
New Mexico Junior College (U)
New Mexico State University (U)
Nichols College (U,G)
Northern State University (U)
North Shore Community College (U)
Northwestern Michigan College (U)
Oakland Community College (U)
Odessa College (U)
Ohio University (U)
Oklahoma State University (U)
Oregon State University (U)
Pace University (U)
Pamlico Community College (U)
Pasco-Hernando Community College (U)
Peirce College (U)
Pellissippi State Technical Community College (U)
Peninsula College (U)
Piedmont Community College (U)
Portland Community College (U)
Portland State University (U)
The Richard Stockton College of New Jersey (U)
Robert Morris University (U)
Sacramento City College (U)
Sam Houston State University (U)
San Bernardino Valley College (U)
San Diego Community College District (U)
Sauk Valley Community College (U)
Seminole State College of Florida (U)
Seton Hill University (U)
Sinclair Community College (U)
Southeast Arkansas College (U)
Southern Adventist University (U)
Southern Illinois University Carbondale (U)
South Piedmont Community College (U)
Southwestern Community College (U)
Southwest Virginia Community College (U)
Southwest Wisconsin Technical College (U)
Spartanburg Community College (U)
Spokane Community College (U)
State University of New York Empire State College (U)
Stephens College (U)
Taft College (U)
Tarleton State University (U)
Thiel College (U)
Tyler Junior College (U)
The University of Akron (U,G)
The University of Alabama in Huntsville (G)
University of Alaska Fairbanks (U)
University of Arkansas at Little Rock (U)
University of Bridgeport (U)
University of Florida (U)
University of Great Falls (U)
University of Idaho (U,G)
University of Illinois at Urbana–Champaign (U)
University of Maine at Augusta (U)
University of Mary (U)
University of Michigan (N)
University of New Haven (U,G)
The University of North Carolina at Chapel Hill (U)
University of Northern Iowa (U)
University of Southern Maine (U)
University of Southern Mississippi (U)
The University of Texas at Brownsville (U)
University of Utah (U)
University of Waterloo (N,U,G)
University of West Florida (U)
University of Windsor (U)
University of Wisconsin Colleges (U)
Upper Iowa University (U)
Utah State University (U)
Valencia College (U)
Western Kentucky University (U)
West Hills Community College (U)
West Shore Community College (U)
West Virginia Northern Community College (U)
Youngstown State University (G)

MECHANICAL ENGINEERING

Columbia University (N,G)
Columbus State Community College (U)
Frostburg State University (U)
Georgia Institute of Technology (N,G)
Kansas State University (U,G)
Kettering University (N)
Louisiana State University and Agricultural and Mechanical College (U)
Michigan Technological University (N,U,G)
Missouri University of Science and Technology (G)
New Mexico State University (G)
Oakton Community College (U)
The Ohio State University (G)
Prairie View A&M University (U)
San Diego State University (U)
Southern Methodist University (G)
The University of Alabama in Huntsville (G)
The University of Arizona (G)
University of Colorado at Colorado Springs (U,G)
University of Colorado Boulder (N,G)
University of Florida (N,G)
University of Idaho (U,G)
University of Illinois at Urbana–Champaign (N,G)
University of Maine (U,G)
University of Michigan–Dearborn (G)
University of Missouri–Kansas City (G)
University of North Dakota (U)
University of North Florida (G)
The University of Tennessee Space Institute (G)
The University of Texas at Arlington (G)
University of Wisconsin–Platteville (N)
Westmoreland County Community College (U)

MECHANICAL ENGINEERING RELATED TECHNOLOGIES

Blackhawk Technical College (U)
Bronx Community College of the City University of New York (U)
Cincinnati State Technical and Community College (U)
Cleveland Institute of Electronics (N)
Columbia University (N,G)

Columbus State Community College (U)
Indiana State University (U)
Kansas State University (U,G)
Missouri University of Science and Technology (G)
Portland Community College (U)
Southern Methodist University (G)
University of Idaho (U,G)
Wayne Community College (U)

MECHANIC AND REPAIR TECHNOLOGIES RELATED

Arkansas Tech University (U)
Austin Peay State University (U)
Cleveland Institute of Electronics (N)
Oxnard College (U)
Portland Community College (N,U)
Wayne Community College (U)

MECHANICS AND REPAIR

Austin Peay State University (U)
Central Wyoming College (N,U)
Cleveland Institute of Electronics (N)

MEDICAL CLINICAL SCIENCES/ GRADUATE MEDICAL STUDIES

Bowling Green State University (U)
D'Youville College (G)
James Madison University (N)
Nova Southeastern University (N,G)
Union University (U)
The University of British Columbia (U,G)
University of Florida (N)
University of Southern California (G)
University of Wisconsin–Green Bay (U)

MEDICAL ILLUSTRATION AND INFORMATICS

Boise State University (U)
University of Illinois at Chicago (G)

MEDIEVAL AND RENAISSANCE STUDIES

Austin Peay State University (U)
Bellevue College (U)
Boise State University (U)
California State University, Sacramento (U)
Portland Community College (N,U)
Taylor University (U)
The University of British Columbia (U)
University of Waterloo (U)
Valencia College (U)
Western Michigan University (U)

MENTAL AND SOCIAL HEALTH SERVICES AND ALLIED PROFESSIONS

Athabasca University (N,U,G)
Central Texas College (U)
Central Wyoming College (N)
Columbus State Community College (U)
Fort Valley State University (G)
Granite State College (U)
The Johns Hopkins University (G)
Mount Wachusett Community College (U)
New Mexico State University (U)
New Mexico State University–Carlsbad (U)
The Ohio State University (N)
Pitt Community College (U)
Regent University (G)
Tompkins Cortland Community College (U)
University of Alaska Fairbanks (U)
University of Maine at Augusta (N,U)
Western Kentucky University (U)

METALLURGICAL ENGINEERING

The University of British Columbia (U)

MICROBIOLOGICAL SCIENCES AND IMMUNOLOGY

Acadia University (U)
Angelina College (N)
Austin Peay State University (U)
Brigham Young University (U)
Cayuga County Community College (U)
Central New Mexico Community College (U)
Gateway Community College (U)
Graceland University (U)
Harrisburg Area Community College (U)
MGH Institute of Health Professions (U)
Mid-State Technical College (U)
Mountain State University (U)
North Carolina State University (U)
North Dakota State College of Science (U)
North Dakota State University (G)
Notre Dame College (U)
Oxnard College (U)
Paris Junior College (U)
Quincy University (U)
Rend Lake College (U)
St. Petersburg College (U)
Spoon River College (U)
The University of Akron (U)
University of Idaho (U)
University of Minnesota, Crookston (U)
University of New England (U)
The University of South Dakota (U)
University of Southern Mississippi (U)
University of Waterloo (U)
University of Wisconsin–La Crosse (G)
Western Kentucky University (G)
West Hills Community College (U)
West Virginia Northern Community College (U)
Winston-Salem State University (U)

MILITARY SCIENCE, LEADERSHIP AND OPERATIONAL ART RELATED

Arkansas State University (U)
Luna Community College (U)

MINING AND MINERAL ENGINEERING

Missouri University of Science and Technology (N,G)

MISSIONARY STUDIES AND MISSIOLOGY

Amridge University (N,U,G)
Andover Newton Theological School (G)
Barclay College (U)
Central Bible College (U)
Columbia International University (N,U,G)
Covenant Theological Seminary (N,G)
Crown College (U,G)
Dallas Baptist University (U,G)
Eastern Mennonite University (G)
Fuller Theological Seminary (N,G)
Global University (N,U,G)
Hobe Sound Bible College (N,U)
Johnson University (U)
Lincoln Christian University (U)
Nyack College (G)
Prairie Bible Institute (U,G)
Providence College and Theological Seminary (N,G)
Regent University (G)
Taylor University (U)
Trinity International University (G)
University of Dubuque (G)

MOLECULAR MEDICINE

University of Maine at Machias (U)

MOVEMENT AND MIND-BODY THERAPIES AND EDUCATION

Boise State University (U)
Burlington College (U)
Central Wyoming College (N)
Goddard College (U,G)
Long Beach City College (U)
Prescott College (N,G)
University of Southern Maine (U)
University of the Pacific (U)

MULTI/INTERDISCIPLINARY STUDIES RELATED

Acadia University (U)
Austin Peay State University (U)
Avila University (U)
Burlington College (U,G)
California State University, San Bernardino (U)
Central Michigan University (U,G)
Central Texas College (U)
City Colleges of Chicago System (U)
Columbia College (U)
Fort Hays State University (U,G)
Global University (U)
Granite State College (U)
Hibbing Community College (U)
Indiana Wesleyan University (G)
John Jay College of Criminal Justice of the City University of New York (U)
Jones International University (U,G)
Kansas State University (U)
Lansing Community College (U)
La Roche College (U)
Mary Baldwin College (U)
Mississippi State University (U)
Mountain State University (G)
Naropa University (U,G)
North Carolina State University (U)
North Dakota State University (U)
Pace University (U)
Portland Community College (N)
Robert Morris University (U,G)
Rochester Institute of Technology (U)
Santa Rosa Junior College (U)
Tabor College (U)
Taylor University (U)

Temple University (U)
University of Arkansas at Little Rock (U)
University of Florida (U)
University of Illinois at Springfield (U)
University of Memphis (U)
University of Minnesota, Morris (U)
University of Oregon (U)
University of Waterloo (U)
Wayland Baptist University (G)
Wayne State College (U)
Western Kentucky University (U,G)
West Hills Community College (U)

MUSEUM STUDIES

Brenau University (U)
California State University, Dominguez Hills (N)
California State University, East Bay (G)
Chatham University (U)
Middlesex Community College (U)
Western Kentucky University (G)

MUSIC

Acadia University (U)
Alcorn State University (U)
Allen Community College (U)
Angelina College (U)
Angelo State University (U)
Arapahoe Community College (U)
Arkansas State University–Beebe (U)
Arkansas Tech University (U)
Athabasca University (N,U)
Atlantic Cape Community College (U)
Austin Peay State University (U)
Baldwin-Wallace College (U)
The Baptist College of Florida (U)
Bellevue College (U)
Berklee College of Music (N,U)
Boise State University (U)
Bowling Green State University (U,G)
Brazosport College (U)
Brenau University (U)
Bridgewater State University (U)
Brigham Young University (U)
Brigham Young University–Idaho (U)
Bronx Community College of the City University of New York (U)
Burlington County College (U)
Butler Community College (U)
Butler County Community College (U)
Cabrillo College (U)
California State University, Dominguez Hills (N,U)
California State University, Monterey Bay (U)
California State University, Sacramento (U)
Campbellsville University (U)
Carl Sandburg College (U)
Cascadia Community College (U)
Cayuga County Community College (U)
Central Carolina Technical College (U)
Central Texas College (U)
Central Virginia Community College (U)
Central Wyoming College (N,U)
Chatham University (U)
Chattanooga State Community College (U)
Chemeketa Community College (U)
Citrus College (U)
City Colleges of Chicago System (U)
Clackamas Community College (U)
Clarion University of Pennsylvania (U)
Clemson University (U)
Cleveland Community College (U)
Cleveland State Community College (U)
Clinton Community College (U)
The College of St. Scholastica (U,G)
Columbia College (U)
Columbus State Community College (U)
Dakota State University (U)
Daytona State College (U)
Dickinson State University (U)
Drury University (U)
Duquesne University (G)
East Central Community College (U)
Eastern Oregon University (U)
Eastern Washington University (U)
Eastern West Virginia Community and Technical College (U)
East Los Angeles College (U)
El Camino College (U)
Enterprise State Community College (U)
Erie Community College (U)
Erie Community College, North Campus (U)
Erie Community College, South Campus (U)
Fitchburg State University (U)
Five Towns College (U,G)
Fort Hays State University (U)
Framingham State University (U)
Front Range Community College (U)
Frostburg State University (U)
Gadsden State Community College (U)
Gannon University (U)
Genesee Community College (U)
George Fox University (U)
Goddard College (U)
Greenville Technical College (U)
Hannibal-LaGrange University (U)
Haywood Community College (U)
Heartland Community College (U)
Hibbing Community College (U)
Holyoke Community College (U)
Hopkinsville Community College (U)
Indiana State University (U)
Indiana University of Pennsylvania (U,G)
Indiana University–Purdue University Fort Wayne (U)
Indiana Wesleyan University (U,G)
Inter American University of Puerto Rico, San Germán Campus (U)
Iowa Lakes Community College (U)
Jacksonville State University (U)
James Madison University (U)
John A. Logan College (U)
Johnson University (U)
Johnston Community College (U)
Judson College (U)
Kansas State University (U)
Kean University (N)
Kirkwood Community College (U)
Labette Community College (U)
Lansing Community College (U)
Laurel University (U)
Lewis University (U)
Lipscomb University (U)
Lock Haven University of Pennsylvania (U)
Long Beach City College (U)
Louisiana State University and Agricultural and Mechanical College (U)
Mansfield University of Pennsylvania (U)
McNeese State University (U)
Mesa State College (U)
Miami Dade College (U)
Midland College (U)
Midway College (U)
Mississippi College (U)
Moorpark College (U)
Mountain Empire Community College (U)
Mountain State University (U)
Mount Olive College (U)
Mount Wachusett Community College (N)
Murray State College (U)
Nassau Community College (U)
Naugatuck Valley Community College (U)
New Mexico State University (U)
New River Community College (U)
Nichols College (U)
North Carolina State University (U)
North Central Texas College (U)
North Dakota State University (U,G)
Northern State University (U)
North Hennepin Community College (U)
North Lake College (U)
North Seattle Community College (U)
North Shore Community College (U)
NorthWest Arkansas Community College (U)
Northwestern Michigan College (U)
Northwest-Shoals Community College (U)
Notre Dame College (U)
Nyack College (U)
The Ohio State University (U)
Oklahoma Panhandle State University (U)
Oklahoma State University (U)
Orange Coast College (U)
Oxnard College (U)
Ozarks Technical Community College (U)
Paris Junior College (N)
Pellissippi State Technical Community College (U)
Peninsula College (U)
Peru State College (U)
Portland Community College (U)
Prairie Bible Institute (U)
Pratt Community College (U)
Prescott College (N)
Providence College and Theological Seminary (U)
Randolph Community College (U)
Rend Lake College (U)
Riverside Community College District (U)
Rogers State University (U)
Sacramento City College (U)
Saint Leo University (U)
Saint Mary-of-the-Woods College (G)
St. Petersburg College (U)
San Diego Community College District (N,U)
San Jacinto College District (U)
Santa Fe Community College (U)
Santa Monica College (U)
Shippensburg University of Pennsylvania (U)
Sinclair Community College (U)
Slippery Rock University of Pennsylvania (U)
Southeastern Community College (U)
Southeastern Illinois College (U)
Southeastern Oklahoma State University (U)
Southern Arkansas University–Magnolia (U)
Southern Illinois University Carbondale (U)
Southern Illinois University Edwardsville (U)
Southern Oregon University (U)
South Piedmont Community College (U)
Southwestern Community College (U)
Spartanburg Community College (N,U)
Spokane Community College (U)
Spring Arbor University (U)
State University of New York at Oswego (U)

State University of New York at Plattsburgh (U)
State University of New York College at Potsdam (U)
Stephen F. Austin State University (U,G)
Sullivan County Community College (U)
Taylor University (U)
Temple University (U,G)
Texas State University–San Marcos (U)
Tunxis Community College (U)
Tyler Junior College (U)
University at Albany, State University of New York (U)
The University of Akron (U)
University of Alaska Fairbanks (U)
University of Arkansas at Little Rock (U)
University of Bridgeport (U)
The University of British Columbia (U)
University of Dubuque (U)
University of Houston–Downtown (U)
University of Idaho (U)
University of Maine (U)
University of Maine at Augusta (U)
University of Maine at Fort Kent (U)
University of Massachusetts Boston (U)
University of Memphis (U)
University of Minnesota, Duluth (U)
University of Missouri–Kansas City (U)
University of Nevada, Reno (U)
The University of North Carolina at Chapel Hill (N,U)
University of Northern Iowa (U)
University of North Florida (U)
University of Pennsylvania (U)
University of Saskatchewan (U)
The University of South Dakota (U)
University of Southern Maine (U)
University of Southern Mississippi (U,G)
The University of Texas of the Permian Basin (U)
University of the Pacific (U)
University of Utah (U)
University of Wisconsin Colleges (U)
Utah State University (U)
Wake Technical Community College (U)
Walla Walla University (U)
Wayland Baptist University (U)
Wayne State University (U,G)
Westchester Community College (U)
Western Kentucky University (U)
Western Michigan University (U)
West Hills Community College (U)
West Los Angeles College (U)
West Shore Community College (U)
Wichita State University (U,G)
Winston-Salem State University (U)
Yavapai College (U)
York Technical College (U)

NANOTECHNOLOGY

Columbia University (N)
University of Michigan (N)

NATURAL RESOURCES AND CONSERVATION RELATED

Austin Peay State University (U)
Drury University (U)
Duke University (G)
Franklin Pierce University (G)
Goddard College (G)
Haywood Community College (U)
Kansas State University (U)
Lansing Community College (U)
Oakland Community College (U)
Oregon State University (U)
Pikes Peak Community College (U)
Prescott College (G)
Saint Mary-of-the-Woods College (G)
Spokane Community College (U)
University of Alaska Fairbanks (U)
University of California, Davis (U)
University of Florida (U,G)
University of Illinois at Urbana–Champaign (G)
University of Maine at Machias (U)
University of Massachusetts Boston (U)
Western Kentucky University (U)

NATURAL RESOURCES CONSERVATION AND RESEARCH

Athabasca University (U)
Austin Peay State University (U)
Central Carolina Technical College (U)
Duke University (G)
Erie Community College (U)
Erie Community College, North Campus (U)
Erie Community College, South Campus (U)
Goddard College (G)
Haywood Community College (U)
Kansas State University (U)
Lansing Community College (U)
Oregon State University (U,G)
Pikes Peak Community College (U)
University of Illinois at Urbana–Champaign (G)
University of Massachusetts Boston (G)
Western Kentucky University (U)

NATURAL RESOURCES MANAGEMENT AND POLICY

Athabasca University (U)
Austin Peay State University (U)
Bowling Green State University (N,U)
Duke University (G)
Franklin Pierce University (G)
Haywood Community College (U)
Kansas State University (U)
North Dakota State University (G)
Oregon State University (U,G)
Prescott College (G)
University of Alaska Fairbanks (U)
University of California, Davis (N,U)
University of Denver (G)
University of Florida (U,G)
University of Illinois at Urbana–Champaign (G)
Western Kentucky University (U)

NATURAL SCIENCES

Austin Peay State University (U)
Bellevue College (U)
Big Bend Community College (U)
Brigham Young University–Idaho (U)
Cascadia Community College (U)
City Colleges of Chicago System (U)
Columbus State Community College (U)
Culver-Stockton College (U)
Dakota College at Bottineau (U)
Dallas Baptist University (U)
Danville Community College (U)
Duke University (G)
D'Youville College (U)
Endicott College (U)
Franklin Pierce University (G)
Harcum College (U)
Haywood Community College (U)
Itasca Community College (U)
Kansas State University (U)
Lansing Community College (U)
Lewis-Clark State College (U)
Marylhurst University (U)
Miami Dade College (U)
Middlesex Community College (U)
North Carolina State University (U)
Northwest-Shoals Community College (U)
Notre Dame College (U)
Oklahoma Panhandle State University (U)
Peninsula College (U)
Pulaski Technical College (U)
Regent University (U)
Saint Leo University (U)
Saint Paul College–A Community & Technical College (U)
San Diego Community College District (U)
Sinclair Community College (U)
Stephens College (U)
University of Alaska Fairbanks (U)
University of Great Falls (U)
University of Houston–Downtown (U)
University of Windsor (U)
University of Wisconsin Colleges (U)
University of Wisconsin–Green Bay (U)
Upper Iowa University (U)
Wayne State College (U)
Westchester Community College (U)
Western Kentucky University (U)
Western Texas College (U)
West Hills Community College (U)
Youngstown State University (U)

NEUROBIOLOGY AND NEUROSCIENCES

Queen's University at Kingston (U)
Thiel College (U)

NUCLEAR AND INDUSTRIAL RADIOLOGIC TECHNOLOGIES

Austin Peay State University (U)
Columbus State Community College (U)
Ferris State University (U)
New Mexico Junior College (U)
Oregon State University (G)
University of Cincinnati Raymond Walters College (U)

NUCLEAR ENGINEERING

Kansas State University (U,G)
The Ohio State University (G)

NUCLEAR ENGINEERING TECHNOLOGIES

Bronx Community College of the City University of New York (U)
Excelsior College (U)

NUTRITION SCIENCES

Acadia University (U)
Allen Community College (U)

Antelope Valley College (U)
Austin Peay State University (U)
Bellevue College (U)
Boise State University (U)
Bowling Green State University (U)
Brazosport College (U)
Butler Community College (U)
Cascadia Community College (U)
Central Michigan University (G)
Central Virginia Community College (U)
Central Washington University (U)
Central Wyoming College (N)
City Colleges of Chicago System (U)
Clemson University (U,G)
College of San Mateo (U)
College of the Siskiyous (U)
Columbus State Community College (U)
Community College of Beaver County (U)
Dabney S. Lancaster Community College (U)
Dakota State University (U)
Danville Community College (U)
D'Youville College (G)
Eastern Wyoming College (U)
Elaine P. Nunez Community College (U)
Endicott College (U)
Erie Community College (U)
Erie Community College, North Campus (U)
Erie Community College, South Campus (U)
Finger Lakes Community College (U)
Front Range Community College (U)
Gadsden State Community College (U)
Georgia State University (U,G)
Hillsborough Community College (U)
Holyoke Community College (U)
Huntington College of Health Sciences (U,G)
Illinois Eastern Community Colleges, Frontier Community College (U)
Iowa Valley Community College District (U)
Jacksonville State University (U)
James Madison University (U,G)
Kansas State University (U)
Keystone College (U)
Lamar State College–Orange (U)
Lipscomb University (U)
Long Beach City College (U)
Luna Community College (U)
Mansfield University of Pennsylvania (N,U)
Mercer County Community College (U)
Mercy College of Northwest Ohio (U)
MGH Institute of Health Professions (U)
Middle Tennessee State University (U)
Montgomery County Community College (U)
Moorpark College (U)
Nassau Community College (U)
Naugatuck Valley Community College (U)
New Mexico State University (U,G)
North Carolina State University (U,G)
North Central Texas College (U)
North Dakota State University (G)
NorthWest Arkansas Community College (U)
Oakland Community College (U)
The Ohio State University (U,G)
Oklahoma State University (U)
Pasco-Hernando Community College (U)
Peninsula College (U)
Portland Community College (U)
Queen's University at Kingston (U)
Quinebaug Valley Community College (U)
Rend Lake College (U)
The Richard Stockton College of New Jersey (U)
Riverside Community College District (U)
Rogers State University (U)
Sacramento City College (U)
Saint Paul College–A Community & Technical College (U)
Sam Houston State University (U)
San Diego Community College District (U)
Santa Monica College (U)
Seminole State College of Florida (U)
Southeastern Oklahoma State University (N)
Texas Woman's University (G)
Three Rivers Community College (U)
University of Alaska Fairbanks (U)
University of Dubuque (U)
University of Florida (N,U)
University of Idaho (U)
University of Maine at Augusta (U)
University of Maine at Machias (U)
University of Massachusetts Boston (U)
University of New Haven (U)
University of North Florida (U,G)
Valencia College (U)
Wayne State University (U,G)
Westchester Community College (U)
Western Kentucky University (U,G)
West Hills Community College (U)
Youngstown State University (U)

OPERATIONS RESEARCH

Columbia University (G)
Drexel University (G)
Kansas State University (G)
Philadelphia University (U)
Southern New Hampshire University (G)
The University of Alabama in Huntsville (G)
The University of Texas at Dallas (G)

OPHTHALMIC AND OPTOMETRIC SUPPORT SERVICES AND ALLIED PROFESSIONS

Ferris State University (G)
Hillsborough Community College (U)
University of Wisconsin–La Crosse (U)

OUTDOOR EDUCATION

University of Alaska, Prince William Sound Community College (U)

PARKS, RECREATION AND LEISURE

Bowling Green State University (U)
California State University, Monterey Bay (U)
Clemson University (U)
The College at Brockport, State University of New York (G)
Dakota College at Bottineau (U)
Eastern Illinois University (U)
Eastern Washington University (U)
Haywood Community College (U)
Kean University (N)
Portland Community College (N)
St. Petersburg College (N)
United States Sports Academy (N)
University of Florida (U)
University of Illinois at Urbana–Champaign (U,G)
The University of North Carolina at Chapel Hill (U)
Webber International University (U)
Western Kentucky University (U)

PARKS, RECREATION AND LEISURE FACILITIES MANAGEMENT

Bowling Green State University (G)
The College at Brockport, State University of New York (G)
Dakota College at Bottineau (U)
Drexel University (G)
Franklin Pierce University (G)
Haywood Community College (U)
Kean University (U)
North Carolina Central University (G)
North Carolina State University (U,G)
Penn State University Park (U)
Prescott College (G)
Slippery Rock University of Pennsylvania (G)
United States Sports Academy (N)
University of Alaska, Prince William Sound Community College (U)
University of Florida (U,G)
University of Illinois at Urbana–Champaign (G)
University of Wisconsin–La Crosse (G)
Wayne State College (G)
Webber International University (U)
Western Kentucky University (U)

PARKS, RECREATION, LEISURE, AND FITNESS STUDIES RELATED

Dakota College at Bottineau (U)
Haywood Community College (U)
Mount Olive College (U)
North Carolina State University (U)
Oakland Community College (U)
Phoenix College (U)
Portland Community College (N)
San Diego State University (U)
United States Sports Academy (N)
University of Florida (U)
University of Illinois at Urbana–Champaign (G)
University of Southern Mississippi (G)
Western Kentucky University (U)

PASTORAL COUNSELING AND SPECIALIZED MINISTRIES

Amridge University (N,U,G)
Andover Newton Theological School (G)
Baptist Bible College of Pennsylvania (U)
Beulah Heights University (U,G)
Central Bible College (U)
Crown College (U)
Dallas Christian College (U)
Duquesne University (G)
Earlham School of Religion (G)
Eastern Mennonite University (G)
George Fox University (G)
Global University (N,U,G)
Hartford Seminary (G)
Hobe Sound Bible College (N,U)
Johnson University (U)
Master's College and Seminary (U)
Piedmont Baptist College and Graduate School (U)
Providence College and Theological Seminary (N,G)

Regent University (G)
St. Mary's University (G)
Southwestern Baptist Theological Seminary (G)
Summit Pacific College (U)
Taylor University (U)
Union Presbyterian Seminary (G)
University of Dubuque (N)

PEACE STUDIES AND CONFLICT RESOLUTION

Brenau University (U)
Burlington College (U)
Earlham School of Religion (G)
Eastern Mennonite University (G)
Global University (G)
Goddard College (U,G)
Jones International University (G)
Lipscomb University (G)
Portland Community College (U)
Prescott College (G)
Sonoma State University (U)
Taylor University (U)
The University of Akron (U)
University of California, Davis (U)
University of Waterloo (U)

PERSONAL AND CULINARY SERVICES RELATED

Austin Peay State University (U)
California State University, Dominguez Hills (N)
Central Wyoming College (N)
Kean University (N)
NorthWest Arkansas Community College (U)
Pace University (N)
Pasco-Hernando Community College (N)
Penn State University Park (U)
Portland Community College (N)
Quinebaug Valley Community College (N)
Valencia College (U)

PETROLEUM ENGINEERING

University of Pittsburgh at Bradford (U)

PHARMACOLOGY AND TOXICOLOGY

Arapahoe Community College (U)
Brenau University (U)
Cayuga County Community College (U)
Cleveland State Community College (U)
Columbus State Community College (U)
Dakota College at Bottineau (U)
Drexel University (G)
Front Range Community College (U)
Indiana University–Purdue University Fort Wayne (U)
Jacksonville State University (G)
Jamestown Community College (U)
Long Beach City College (U)
Middlesex Community College (U)
Naugatuck Valley Community College (U)
Northwestern Michigan College (U)
Oregon State University (N)
Peninsula College (U)
Queen's University at Kingston (U)
Research College of Nursing (G)
Saint Francis University (G)
Santa Monica College (U)
Sinclair Community College (U)
Stephens College (U)
University of Florida (N)
University of Maine at Machias (U)
University of North Dakota (U)
University of Wisconsin–Green Bay (U)

PHARMACY, PHARMACEUTICAL SCIENCES, AND ADMINISTRATION

Arapahoe Community College (U)
Auburn University (G)
Bossier Parish Community College (U)
Bronx Community College of the City University of New York (U)
Central Michigan University (N)
Charter Oak State College (N)
Davidson County Community College (U)
Drake University (U,G)
Indiana University–Purdue University Fort Wayne (N)
Mansfield University of Pennsylvania (N)
McNeese State University (N)
Mount Wachusett Community College (N)
Oakton Community College (U)
The Ohio State University (U)
Oregon State University (N)
Quinebaug Valley Community College (N)
Randolph Community College (N)
St. John's University (U)
Sinclair Community College (U)
The University of Akron (U)
University of Cincinnati (G)
University of Colorado at Colorado Springs (G)
University of Florida (N)
University of Illinois at Chicago (N,G)
University of Southern California (G)
Vincennes University (U)
West Virginia University (N)

PHILOSOPHY

Acadia University (U)
Allen Community College (U)
Alpena Community College (U)
Angelo State University (U)
Anne Arundel Community College (U)
Arapahoe Community College (U)
Arkansas State University–Beebe (U)
Asbury University (U)
Athabasca University (N,U,G)
Austin Peay State University (U)
Bellevue College (U)
Belmont Technical College (U)
Beulah Heights University (U)
Bob Jones University (U)
Boise State University (U)
Bowling Green State University (U)
Brenau University (U)
Brigham Young University (U)
Brigham Young University–Idaho (U)
Bronx Community College of the City University of New York (U)
Broward College (U)
Burlington College (U)
Butler Community College (U)
Butler County Community College (U)
Cabrillo College (U)
California State University, Chico (U)
California State University, San Marcos (N)
Campbellsville University (U)
Carlow University (U)
Carroll University (U)
Cascadia Community College (U)
Centralia College (U)
Central New Mexico Community College (U)
Central Texas College (U)
Central Virginia Community College (U)
Charter Oak State College (U)
Chattanooga State Community College (U)
Chemeketa Community College (U)
Citrus College (U)
City Colleges of Chicago System (U)
City University of Seattle (U)
Clarion University of Pennsylvania (U)
Coleman University (U)
College of San Mateo (U)
College of Southern Maryland (U)
College of the Humanities and Sciences, Harrison Middleton University (U)
Colorado Mountain College (U)
Columbia College (G)
Columbus State Community College (U)
Community College of Allegheny County (U)
Community College of Beaver County (U)
Corning Community College (U)
Culver-Stockton College (U)
Dakota Wesleyan University (U)
Dallas Baptist University (U)
Daytona State College (U)
Eastern Illinois University (U)
Eastern Kentucky University (U)
Eastern Mennonite University (G)
Eastern Oregon University (U)
Eastern Washington University (U)
Eastern West Virginia Community and Technical College (U)
East Los Angeles College (U)
Edison State Community College (U)
El Camino College (U)
Erie Community College (U)
Erie Community College, North Campus (U)
Erie Community College, South Campus (U)
Finger Lakes Community College (U)
Fontbonne University (U)
Fort Hays State University (U)
Framingham State University (U)
Franciscan University of Steubenville (N,U)
Friends University (U)
Front Range Community College (U)
Gadsden State Community College (U)
Gannon University (U)
Gateway Community College (U)
Georgian Court University (U)
Global University (U,G)
Goddard College (U)
Harrisburg Area Community College (U)
Hibbing Community College (U)
Hofstra University (U)
Hope International University (U)
Hopkinsville Community College (U)
Houston Community College System (U)
Indiana University of Pennsylvania (U)
Indiana University–Purdue University Fort Wayne (U)
Indiana Wesleyan University (U,G)
Institute for Christian Studies (G)
Iona College (U)
Ithaca College (U)
James Madison University (U)
Johnston Community College (U)
J. Sargeant Reynolds Community College (U)

Lamar State College–Port Arthur (U)
Lansing Community College (U)
Lewis-Clark State College (U)
Liberty University (U)
Lindenwood University (U)
Lipscomb University (U)
Long Beach City College (U)
Lourdes College (U)
Malone University (U)
Marian University (U)
Marquette University (U)
Marshall University (U)
Mary Baldwin College (U)
Memorial University of Newfoundland (U)
Mercer County Community College (U)
Metropolitan Community College–Penn Valley (U)
Miami Dade College (U)
Miami University–Regional Campuses (U)
Middlesex Community College (U)
Minot State University (U)
Misericordia University (U)
Monroe College (U)
Montgomery County Community College (U)
Moody Bible Institute (U)
Moorpark College (U)
Mountain State University (U)
Mount Mary College (U)
Murray State University (U)
Naropa University (N)
Nashville State Technical Community College (U)
Naugatuck Valley Community College (U)
New Mexico State University (U)
New Mexico State University–Alamogordo (U)
New River Community College (U)
Nipissing University (U)
North Arkansas College (U)
North Carolina State University (U)
North Hennepin Community College (U)
North Iowa Area Community College (U)
North Lake College (U)
North Seattle Community College (U)
NorthWest Arkansas Community College (U)
Northwestern Connecticut Community College (U)
Northwestern Michigan College (U)
Nyack College (U)
Oakland Community College (U)
Oakton Community College (U)
Ocean County College (U)
Ohio University (U)
Oregon State University (U)
Ouachita Technical College (U)
Oxnard College (U)
Ozarks Technical Community College (U)
Paine College (U)
Peirce College (U)
Pellissippi State Technical Community College (U)
Peninsula College (U)
Peru State College (U)
Phoenix College (U)
Pittsburg State University (U)
Portland Community College (U)
Providence College (U)
Providence College and Theological Seminary (U)
Pulaski Technical College (U)
Queen's University at Kingston (U)
Quincy University (U)
Rend Lake College (U)
Riverside Community College District (U)
Rivier College (U)
Rockland Community College (U)
Rogers State University (U)
Rose State College (U)
Sacramento City College (U)
The Sage Colleges (U)
St. Ambrose University (U)
St. Cloud State University (U)
Saint Francis University (U)
St. Gregory's University (U)
St. John's University (U)
Saint Leo University (U)
Saint Paul College–A Community & Technical College (U)
St. Petersburg College (U)
Salem Community College (U)
Sam Houston State University (U)
San Diego Community College District (U)
San Diego State University (U)
San Jacinto College District (U)
Santa Fe Community College (U)
Santa Rosa Junior College (U)
Seton Hill University (U)
Shippensburg University of Pennsylvania (U)
Sinclair Community College (U)
Slippery Rock University of Pennsylvania (U)
Southeast Community College Area (U)
Southeastern Community College (U)
Southeastern Illinois College (U)
Southern Illinois University Carbondale (U)
Southern Illinois University Edwardsville (U)
Southern Oregon University (U)
Southern University at New Orleans (U)
South Suburban College (U)
Spartanburg Community College (U)
Spokane Community College (U)
Spring Arbor University (U)
State University of New York at New Paltz (U)
State University of New York at Oswego (U)
Stephens College (U)
Taylor University (U)
Texas State University–San Marcos (U)
Toccoa Falls College (U)
Trident Technical College (U)
Tunxis Community College (U)
Unification Theological Seminary (N,G)
The University of Akron (U)
University of Arkansas at Little Rock (U)
University of Bridgeport (U)
The University of British Columbia (U)
University of Cincinnati (U)
University of Florida (U)
University of Houston–Downtown (U)
University of Idaho (U)
University of Illinois at Springfield (U)
University of Louisville (U)
University of Maine at Augusta (U)
University of Maine at Fort Kent (U)
University of Maine at Machias (U)
University of Mary (U,G)
University of Massachusetts Boston (U)
University of Minnesota, Crookston (U)
University of Minnesota, Duluth (U)
University of Missouri–Kansas City (U)
The University of Montana Western (U)
University of New Haven (U)
University of North Alabama (U)
The University of North Carolina at Chapel Hill (N,U)
University of North Florida (U,G)
University of Pittsburgh at Bradford (U)
University of Southern Maine (U)
University of Waterloo (U)
University of West Florida (U)
University of West Georgia (U)
University of Wisconsin Colleges (U)
University of Wisconsin–Green Bay (U)
Utah State University (U)
Utica College (G)
Wake Technical Community College (U)
Webster University (U)
Westchester Community College (U)
Western Kentucky University (U)
Western Michigan University (U)
Western Wyoming Community College (U)
West Hills Community College (U)
West Los Angeles College (U)
Westmoreland County Community College (U)
Wichita State University (U)
Wilfrid Laurier University (U)
Worcester State University (U)
York Technical College (U)
York University (U)
Youngstown State University (U)

PHILOSOPHY AND RELIGIOUS STUDIES

Atlantic Cape Community College (U)
Brigham Young University–Idaho (U)
Dallas Christian College (U)
Edison State Community College (U)
Elmira College (U)
Indiana Wesleyan University (G)
Iowa Lakes Community College (U)
Johnston Community College (U)
Kean University (U)
Lakehead University (U)
Lock Haven University of Pennsylvania (U)
Loyola University New Orleans (U)
Marshall University (U)
Mercer County Community College (U)
Notre Dame College (U)
Sacramento City College (U)
Sinclair Community College (U)
Southern Adventist University (U)
Winston-Salem State University (U)

PHILOSOPHY AND RELIGIOUS STUDIES RELATED

Albertus Magnus College (U)
Amridge University (N,U,G)
Ashland University (U)
Athabasca University (N,U)
Austin Peay State University (U)
Baptist Bible College of Pennsylvania (U,G)
The Baptist College of Florida (U)
Big Bend Community College (U)
Brigham Young University (U)
Brookdale Community College (U)
Broward College (U)
Burlington College (U)
Butler Community College (U)
Butler County Community College (U)
Cabrillo College (U)
The Catholic Distance University (N,U,G)
Central Bible College (U)
Central Texas College (U)
Central Washington University (U)

Charter Oak State College (U)
Chattanooga State Community College (U)
Chemeketa Community College (U)
City Colleges of Chicago System (U)
College of Southern Maryland (U)
College of the Humanities and Sciences, Harrison Middleton University (G)
Columbia College (U)
Columbus State Community College (U)
Crown College (U,G)
Dallas Baptist University (U,G)
Delgado Community College (U)
Denver Seminary (G)
Drury University (U)
Eastern Kentucky University (U)
Eastern Mennonite University (G)
Eastern Wyoming College (U)
Edison State Community College (U)
Front Range Community College (U)
Global University (N,U,G)
Greenville Technical College (U)
Hobe Sound Bible College (N,U)
Hofstra University (U)
Holy Apostles College and Seminary (G)
Indiana University–Purdue University Fort Wayne (U)
Indiana Wesleyan University (G)
Institute for Christian Studies (G)
Inter American University of Puerto Rico, San Germán Campus (U)
Iona College (U)
Iowa Valley Community College District (U)
Judson College (U)
Kirkwood Community College (U)
Lake Superior College (U)
Lamar State College–Port Arthur (U)
Lansing Community College (U)
La Roche College (U)
Lewis University (U)
Life Pacific College (U)
Maharishi University of Management (N)
Mary Baldwin College (U)
Marylhurst University (U)
Master's College and Seminary (U)
Miami Dade College (U)
Middlesex Community College (U)
Midland College (U)
Moody Bible Institute (U)
Moorpark College (U)
Mountain State University (U)
Murray State University (U)
Naropa University (N,U)
Nyack College (U)
Oakton Community College (U)
Ohio University (U)
Oregon State University (U)
Ozarks Technical Community College (U)
Pellissippi State Technical Community College (U)
Pennsylvania College of Technology (U)
Pitt Community College (U)
Portland Community College (N,U)
Prairie Bible Institute (U)
Prescott College (G)
Randolph Community College (U)
Rend Lake College (U)
Rose State College (U)
Rowan-Cabarrus Community College (U)
Sacramento City College (U)
Saint Francis University (U)
St. Louis Community College (U)
St. Stephen's College (G)
San Bernardino Valley College (U)
Siena Heights University (U)
Sinclair Community College (U)
Southeastern Community College (U)
Southern Illinois University Carbondale (U)
Southwestern Baptist Theological Seminary (G)
Southwestern Community College (U)
Spoon River College (U)
Stanly Community College (U)
State University of New York at Oswego (U)
Taylor University (U)
Unification Theological Seminary (N,G)
The University of Akron (U)
University of Alaska Fairbanks (U)
University of Arkansas at Little Rock (U)
University of Bridgeport (U)
University of Central Florida (U)
University of Cincinnati (U)
The University of Findlay (U)
University of Florida (U)
University of Great Falls (U)
University of Houston (U)
University of Idaho (U)
The University of North Carolina Wilmington (U)
University of North Dakota (U)
University of St. Francis (U)
University of Southern Mississippi (U)
University of Waterloo (U)
University of West Georgia (U)
Upper Iowa University (U)
Westchester Community College (U)
Western Kentucky University (U)
Wilkes Community College (U)
Youngstown State University (U)

PHYSICAL SCIENCES

Alcorn State University (U,G)
Allen Community College (U)
Arkansas State University–Beebe (U)
Arkansas Tech University (U)
Athabasca University (N,U)
Austin Peay State University (U)
Barclay College (U)
Bellevue College (U)
Belmont Technical College (U)
Big Bend Community College (U)
Brigham Young University (U)
Burlington County College (U)
Butler Community College (U)
Cabrillo College (U)
Champlain College (U)
Chatham University (G)
Chemeketa Community College (U)
City Colleges of Chicago System (U)
Coleman University (U)
College of Saint Mary (U)
Columbia College (U)
Dakota College at Bottineau (U)
Drury University (U)
East Central Community College (U)
Eastern Illinois University (U)
Enterprise State Community College (U)
Frostburg State University (U)
Gateway Community College (U)
Glenville State College (U)
Goddard College (U)
Harrisburg Area Community College (U)
Houston Community College System (U)
Jacksonville State University (U,G)
Kansas State University (U)
Labette Community College (U)
Lake-Sumter Community College (U)
Lake Superior College (U)
Lansing Community College (U)
Louisiana State University and Agricultural and Mechanical College (U)
Marian University (U)
Metropolitan Community College–Penn Valley (U)
Miami Dade College (U)
Middlesex Community College (U)
Moody Bible Institute (U)
Moorpark College (U)
Mountain State University (U)
Murray State College (U)
New Mexico State University–Carlsbad (U)
Nichols College (U)
North Carolina State University (U)
Oakton Community College (U)
Oklahoma Panhandle State University (U)
Oregon Coast Community College (U)
Oxnard College (U)
Pace University (U)
Pasco-Hernando Community College (U)
Peninsula College (U)
Peru State College (U)
Portland Community College (U)
Pulaski Technical College (U)
Regent University (U)
Robert Morris University (U)
Rockland Community College (U)
Rose State College (U)
Rowan-Cabarrus Community College (U)
Sacramento City College (U)
Saint Francis University (U)
San Diego Community College District (U)
Southeastern Oklahoma State University (U)
Southern Adventist University (U)
Southern Arkansas University–Magnolia (G)
Southern University at New Orleans (U)
State University of New York College at Potsdam (U)
State University of New York College of Technology at Canton (U)
Sullivan County Community College (U)
Tarleton State University (U,G)
Taylor University (U)
Temple University (G)
Union County College (U)
The University of Akron (U)
University of Alaska Fairbanks (U)
University of Arkansas at Little Rock (U)
University of Maine at Augusta (U)
University of North Dakota (U)
The University of South Dakota (U)
University of Waterloo (U)
University of West Florida (U)
University of Wisconsin–Superior (U)
Upper Iowa University (U)
Utah State University (U)
Valencia College (U)
Wayland Baptist University (U)
Wayne State College (U)
Wayne State University (U)
Western Kentucky University (U,G)
Western Texas College (U)
West Hills Community College (U)
Wilkes Community College (U)

PHYSICAL SCIENCES RELATED

Bellevue College (U)
Butler Community College (U)
Chemeketa Community College (U)
City Colleges of Chicago System (U)
Iowa Lakes Community College (U)
Kansas State University (U)
Lansing Community College (U)
Marylhurst University (U)
Miami Dade College (U)
Mississippi State University (U)
Nassau Community College (U)
Portland Community College (U)
Roger Williams University (U)
Rose State College (U)
Sacramento City College (U)
Saint Francis University (U)
San Diego Community College District (U)
Sinclair Community College (U)
Taylor University (U)
The University of Akron (U)
University of Alaska Fairbanks (U)
University of Arkansas at Little Rock (U)
University of West Florida (U)
Western Kentucky University (U)
West Hills Community College (U)

PHYSICAL SCIENCE TECHNOLOGIES

Columbia University (G)
Union University (U)
Western Kentucky University (U)

PHYSICS

Acadia University (U)
Arapahoe Community College (U)
Austin Peay State University (U)
Boise State University (U)
Bowling Green State University (U)
Brigham Young University (U)
Brigham Young University–Idaho (U)
Bronx Community College of the City University of New York (U)
Butler Community College (U)
California State University, Dominguez Hills (U)
California State University, East Bay (U)
Cascadia Community College (U)
Chatham University (U)
Chattanooga State Community College (U)
Clackamas Community College (U)
Clemson University (U)
Cleveland State Community College (U)
College of Southern Maryland (U)
Columbia University (N,G)
Columbus State Community College (U)
Community College of Allegheny County (U)
Dakota State University (U)
D'Youville College (U)
Eastern Illinois University (U)
Eastern Oregon University (U)
Edison State Community College (U)
Ferris State University (U)
Finger Lakes Community College (U)
Fort Hays State University (U)
Front Range Community College (U)
Grantham University (U)
Greenville Technical College (U)
Hopkinsville Community College (U)
Indiana University of Pennsylvania (U,G)
Indiana University–Purdue University Fort Wayne (U)
Jacksonville State University (U)
John A. Logan College (U)
Louisiana State University and Agricultural and Mechanical College (U)
Maharishi University of Management (N)
Miami Dade College (U)
Miami University–Regional Campuses (U)
Michigan Technological University (U)
Mississippi State University (U)
Mountain State University (U)
Mount Allison University (U)
New England Institute of Technology (U)
New Jersey City University (U)
New Mexico State University–Carlsbad (U)
Nipissing University (U)
North Carolina State University (U)
North Hennepin Community College (U)
North Lake College (U)
Northwestern Michigan College (U)
Ocean County College (U)
Ohio University (U)
Orange Coast College (U)
Oxnard College (U)
Pellissippi State Technical Community College (U)
Pittsburgh Technical Institute (U)
Portland Community College (U)
Queen's University at Kingston (U)
Rivier College (U)
St. Cloud State University (U)
Saint Francis University (U)
St. John's University (U)
San Diego Community College District (U)
Shippensburg University of Pennsylvania (U)
Sinclair Community College (U)
Southeastern Community College (U)
Temple University (U)
Union County College (U)
Union University (U)
University at Albany, State University of New York (U)
The University of Arizona (U)
University of Idaho (U)
University of Massachusetts Boston (U)
University of Minnesota, Crookston (U)
University of New England (U)
The University of North Carolina at Asheville (U)
The University of North Carolina at Chapel Hill (U)
University of North Dakota (U)
University of Oregon (U)
University of Pittsburgh at Bradford (U)
The University of Tennessee Space Institute (G)
University of Waterloo (N,U)
University of West Georgia (U)
The University of Winnipeg (U)
Utah State University (U)
Wake Technical Community College (U)
Wayne State College (U)
West Virginia Northern Community College (U)

PHYSIOLOGY, PATHOLOGY AND RELATED SCIENCES

Austin Peay State University (U)
Cincinnati State Technical and Community College (U)
Erie Community College (U)
Erie Community College, North Campus (U)
Erie Community College, South Campus (U)
Gateway Community College (U)
Huntington College of Health Sciences (U)
Illinois Eastern Community Colleges, Frontier Community College (U)
James A. Rhodes State College (U)
MGH Institute of Health Professions (U)
Mountain State University (U)
New England Institute of Technology (U)
Pittsburg State University (U)
Portland Community College (N)
Queen's University at Kingston (U)
Research College of Nursing (U,G)
Sacramento City College (U)
San Diego State University (U)
Stephens College (U)
University of Illinois at Urbana–Champaign (U)
University of Mary (U)
University of New England (U)
The University of South Dakota (U)
University of Waterloo (U)

PLANT SCIENCES

Athabasca University (U)
Auburn University (U)
Austin Peay State University (U)
Bellevue College (U)
Cascadia Community College (U)
Dakota College at Bottineau (U)
Haywood Community College (U)
Kansas State University (G)
Mercer County Community College (U)
Nashville State Technical Community College (N)
North Carolina State University (U,G)
North Dakota State University (U)
Nova Scotia Agricultural College (N,U)
The Ohio State University (U,G)
Oklahoma State University (U)
Oregon State University (U)
Paris Junior College (U)
Rend Lake College (U)
Southern Illinois University Carbondale (U)
Spartanburg Community College (U)
University of California, Riverside (N)
University of Illinois at Urbana–Champaign (U,G)
University of Maine (U)
Western Kentucky University (U,G)

PLUMBING AND RELATED WATER SUPPLY SERVICES

Austin Peay State University (U)

POLITICAL SCIENCE AND GOVERNMENT

Acadia University (U)
Albertus Magnus College (U)
Allen Community College (U)
Alpena Community College (U)
American University (U,G)
Anderson University (U)
Angelina College (U)
Angelo State University (U)

Anne Arundel Community College (U)
Antelope Valley College (U)
Arapahoe Community College (U)
Arkansas State University–Beebe (U)
Arkansas Tech University (U)
Athabasca University (N,U,G)
Austin Peay State University (U)
Baldwin-Wallace College (U)
Bellevue College (U)
Beulah Heights University (U)
Bloomfield College (U)
Bowling Green State University (U)
Bradley University (G)
Brazosport College (U)
Brenau University (U)
Bridgewater State University (U)
Brigham Young University (U)
Brigham Young University–Idaho (U)
Buena Vista University (U)
Buffalo State College, State University of New York (U)
Burlington College (U)
Burlington County College (U)
Butler Community College (U)
Butler County Community College (U)
Caldwell College (U)
California State University, Chico (U)
California State University, San Bernardino (U)
Capital Community College (U)
Carleton University (U)
Cascadia Community College (U)
Cayuga County Community College (U)
Centralia College (U)
Central Michigan University (U,G)
Central Texas College (U)
Central Virginia Community College (U)
Central Wyoming College (U)
Chaminade University of Honolulu (U)
Charter Oak State College (U)
Chatham University (U)
Chattanooga State Community College (U)
Chemeketa Community College (U)
Citrus College (U)
City Colleges of Chicago System (U)
Clinton Community College (U)
Clovis Community College (U)
Coastal Carolina University (U)
College of San Mateo (U)
College of Southern Maryland (U)
College of the Siskiyous (U)
Columbia Basin College (U)
Columbia College (U,G)
Columbus State Community College (U)
Community College of Allegheny County (U)
Culver-Stockton College (U)
Dakota State University (U)
Dallas Baptist University (U)
Danville Community College (U)
Dickinson State University (U)
Drake University (U,G)
Drury University (U)
D'Youville College (U)
Eastern Kentucky University (U)
Eastern Oregon University (U)
Eastern Washington University (U)
Eastern West Virginia Community and Technical College (U)
Eastern Wyoming College (U)
East Georgia College (U)
El Camino College (U)
Erie Community College (U)
Erie Community College, North Campus (U)
Erie Community College, South Campus (U)
Ferris State University (U)
Florida State University (U)
Fort Hays State University (U)
Fort Valley State University (U)
Framingham State University (U)
Friends University (U)
Frostburg State University (U)
Gadsden State Community College (U)
Genesee Community College (U)
Georgia State University (U)
Glenville State College (U)
Goddard College (U,G)
Greenville Technical College (U)
Haywood Community College (U)
Heartland Community College (U)
Hibbing Community College (U)
Hillsborough Community College (U)
Hofstra University (U)
Holyoke Community College (U)
Houston Community College System (U)
Illinois Valley Community College (U)
Indiana University of Pennsylvania (U,G)
Indiana University–Purdue University Fort Wayne (U)
Institute for Christian Studies (G)
Ithaca College (U)
Jacksonville State University (U,G)
John A. Logan College (U)
J. Sargeant Reynolds Community College (U)
Judson College (U)
Judson University (U)
Kansas State University (U)
Kean University (U)
Keystone College (U)
Labette Community College (U)
Lakehead University (U)
Lake Superior College (U)
Lander University (U)
Lansing Community College (U)
Lassen Community College District (U)
Lehman College of the City University of New York (U)
Lewis-Clark State College (U)
Lewis University (U)
Lindenwood University (U)
Lock Haven University of Pennsylvania (U)
Long Beach City College (U)
Los Angeles Harbor College (U)
Los Angeles Trade-Technical College (U)
Louisiana State University and Agricultural and Mechanical College (U)
Macon State College (U)
Malone University (U)
Mary Baldwin College (U)
Memorial University of Newfoundland (U)
Mesa Community College (U)
Mesa State College (U)
Miami Dade College (U)
Middlesex Community College (U)
Middle Tennessee State University (U)
Midwestern State University (U)
Minot State University (U)
Misericordia University (U)
Monroe College (U)
Monroe County Community College (U)
Moorpark College (U)
Mount Mary College (U)
Mount Wachusett Community College (U)
Murray State College (U)
New Jersey City University (U)
New Mexico State University–Carlsbad (U)
New Mexico State University–Grants (U)
Nichols College (U)
Nicolet Area Technical College (U)
North Carolina State University (U)
North Central Texas College (U)
North Hennepin Community College (U)
North Lake College (U)
NorthWest Arkansas Community College (U)
Northwest-Shoals Community College (U)
Nyack College (U)
Oakton Community College (U)
The Ohio State University (U)
Oklahoma Panhandle State University (U)
Oklahoma State University (U)
Olympic College (U)
Orange Coast College (U)
Oregon State University (U)
Ouachita Technical College (U)
Oxnard College (U)
Ozarks Technical Community College (U)
Pace University (U)
Paine College (U)
Peninsula College (U)
Peru State College (U)
Phoenix College (U)
Pikes Peak Community College (U)
Portland Community College (U)
Pratt Community College (U)
Pulaski Technical College (U)
Quinebaug Valley Community College (U)
Quinnipiac University (U)
Regent University (U,G)
Rend Lake College (U)
Rio Hondo College (U)
Riverside Community College District (U)
Rochester Institute of Technology (U)
Rockland Community College (U)
Rogers State University (U)
Rose State College (U)
Sacramento City College (U)
St. Clair County Community College (U)
Saint Francis University (U)
St. John's University (U)
Saint Leo University (U)
St. Louis Community College (U)
Saint Mary-of-the-Woods College (U)
Saint Paul College–A Community & Technical College (U)
St. Petersburg College (U)
Sam Houston State University (U)
San Bernardino Valley College (U)
San Diego Community College District (U)
Santa Fe Community College (U)
Seton Hill University (U)
Shippensburg University of Pennsylvania (U,G)
Sinclair Community College (U)
Slippery Rock University of Pennsylvania (U)
Southeastern Illinois College (U)
Southeastern Oklahoma State University (U)
Southern Connecticut State University (U)
Southern Illinois University Carbondale (U)
Southern Illinois University Edwardsville (U)
Southern Oregon University (U)
Southern University at New Orleans (U)
Stanly Community College (U)
State University of New York at Plattsburgh (U)
State University of New York College at Cortland (U)

State University of New York Empire State College (U,G)
Tarleton State University (U)
Taylor University (U)
Texas State University–San Marcos (U)
Tyler Junior College (U)
Union County College (U)
University at Albany, State University of New York (U)
The University of Akron (U,G)
University of Alaska Fairbanks (U)
The University of Arizona (U)
University of Arkansas at Little Rock (U,G)
University of Bridgeport (U)
The University of British Columbia (U)
University of Florida (U)
University of Houston–Downtown (U)
University of Idaho (U)
University of Illinois at Springfield (U,G)
University of Illinois at Urbana–Champaign (U)
The University of Kansas (U)
University of Louisville (U)
University of Maine at Augusta (U)
University of Maine at Fort Kent (U)
University of Maine at Machias (U)
University of Mary (U)
University of Massachusetts Boston (U)
University of Michigan–Flint (U)
University of Minnesota, Morris (U)
University of Missouri–Kansas City (U)
University of North Alabama (U)
The University of North Carolina at Asheville (U)
The University of North Carolina at Chapel Hill (N,U)
University of North Dakota (U)
University of Oregon (U)
University of Saskatchewan (U)
University of South Carolina Sumter (U)
University of Southern Maine (U)
The University of Tennessee at Chattanooga (G)
The University of Texas at Arlington (U,G)
The University of Texas of the Permian Basin (U)
University of Utah (U)
University of West Florida (U,G)
University of West Georgia (U)
University of Windsor (U)
University of Wisconsin Colleges (U)
Upper Iowa University (N,U)
Valencia College (U)
Wake Technical Community College (U)
Washington State University (U)
Wayland Baptist University (U)
Wayne State University (U)
Westchester Community College (U)
Western Kentucky University (U,G)
Western Michigan University (U)
West Hills Community College (U)
West Los Angeles College (U)
West Virginia Northern Community College (U)
Windward Community College (U)
Winston-Salem State University (U)
York University (U)

POLYMER/PLASTICS ENGINEERING

Lehigh University (N,G)
Quinebaug Valley Community College (N,U)
The University of Akron (U)

PRACTICAL NURSING, VOCATIONAL NURSING AND NURSING ASSISTANTS

Lewis-Clark State College (U)
North Central Texas College (U)
Olympic College (U)
Southwest Wisconsin Technical College (U)
University of Alaska Fairbanks (U)
Xavier University (G)

PRECISION METAL WORKING

Central Wyoming College (N)

PRECISION PRODUCTION RELATED

Portland Community College (N)

PSYCHOLOGY

Acadia University (U)
Allen Community College (U)
Alpena Community College (U)
Alvin Community College (U)
American University (U,G)
Anderson University (U)
Angelina College (U)
Angelo State University (U,G)
Antelope Valley College (U)
Arapahoe Community College (U)
Arkansas State University–Beebe (U)
Arkansas Tech University (U)
Asbury University (U)
Ashland University (U)
Athabasca University (N,U,G)
Austin Peay State University (U)
Avila University (U)
Barclay College (U)
Bellevue College (U)
Belmont Technical College (U)
Bloomfield College (U)
Boise State University (U)
Bowling Green State University (U)
Bradley University (U)
Brazosport College (U)
Brenau University (U)
Bridgewater State University (U,G)
Brigham Young University (U)
Brigham Young University–Idaho (U)
Bronx Community College of the City University of New York (U)
Broward College (U)
Bryan College (U)
Buena Vista University (U)
Burlington College (U)
Burlington County College (U)
Butler Community College (U)
Butler County Community College (U)
Caldwell College (U,G)
California State University, Chico (U)
California State University, Sacramento (U)
California State University, San Bernardino (U)
Capital Community College (U)
Carleton University (U)
Carlow University (U,G)
Carl Sandburg College (U)
Cascadia Community College (U)
Cayuga County Community College (U)
Central Carolina Technical College (U)
Centralia College (U)
Central Michigan University (U)
Central New Mexico Community College (U)
Central Texas College (U)
Central Virginia Community College (U)
Central Washington University (U)
Central Wyoming College (N,U)
Cerritos College (U)
Chaminade University of Honolulu (U)
Champlain College (U)
Charter Oak State College (U)
Chatham University (U)
Chattanooga State Community College (U)
Chemeketa Community College (U)
Cincinnati State Technical and Community College (U)
Citrus College (U)
City Colleges of Chicago System (U)
City University of Seattle (U)
Clarion University of Pennsylvania (U)
Clark State Community College (U)
Clatsop Community College (U)
Cleveland Community College (U)
Cleveland State Community College (U)
Clinton Community College (U)
Clovis Community College (U)
Coastal Carolina University (U)
Coleman University (U)
College of Saint Mary (U)
The College of St. Scholastica (U)
College of San Mateo (U)
College of Southern Maryland (U)
College of the Siskiyous (U)
Colorado Mountain College (U)
Columbia Basin College (U)
Columbia College (U)
Columbia-Greene Community College (U)
Columbus State Community College (U)
Columbus State University (U)
Community College of Allegheny County (U)
Community College of Beaver County (U)
Corning Community College (U)
Cossatot Community College of the University of Arkansas (U)
Culver-Stockton College (U)
Dabney S. Lancaster Community College (U)
Dakota College at Bottineau (U)
Dakota State University (U)
Dakota Wesleyan University (U)
Dallas Baptist University (U)
Danville Community College (U)
Davidson County Community College (U)
Dawson Community College (U)
DePaul University (U)
Dickinson State University (U)
Dominican College (U)
Drake University (U,G)
Drexel University (U)
Drury University (U)
East Central Community College (U)
Eastern Illinois University (U,G)
Eastern Oregon University (U)
Eastern Washington University (U)
Eastern West Virginia Community and Technical College (U)

Eastern Wyoming College (U)
East Los Angeles College (U)
Edgecombe Community College (U)
Edison State Community College (U)
Elaine P. Nunez Community College (U)
El Camino College (U)
Elmira College (G)
Endicott College (U)
Enterprise State Community College (U)
Erie Community College (U)
Erie Community College, North Campus (U)
Erie Community College, South Campus (U)
Excelsior College (U)
Faulkner University (U)
Fayetteville State University (U)
Fielding Graduate University (G)
Finger Lakes Community College (U)
Five Towns College (U)
Fontbonne University (U)
Fort Hays State University (U)
Fort Valley State University (U)
Framingham State University (U)
Franklin Pierce University (U)
Friends University (U)
Front Range Community College (U)
Frostburg State University (U,G)
Fuller Theological Seminary (G)
Gadsden State Community College (U)
Gannon University (U)
Gaston College (U)
Gateway Community College (U)
Genesee Community College (U)
George Fox University (U)
Georgia Highlands College (U)
Georgia State University (U)
Glenville State College (U)
Global University (U)
Goddard College (U,G)
Governors State University (U)
Graceland University (U)
Grantham University (U)
Greenville Technical College (U)
Hannibal-LaGrange University (U)
Harcum College (U)
Harford Community College (U)
Harrisburg Area Community College (U)
Haywood Community College (U)
Heartland Community College (U)
Herkimer County Community College (U)
Hibbing Community College (U)
Hillsborough Community College (U)
Hocking College (U)
Hofstra University (U)
Holyoke Community College (U)
Hope International University (N,U,G)
Houston Community College System (U)
Huntington College of Health Sciences (U)
Illinois Eastern Community Colleges, Lincoln Trail College (U)
Illinois Eastern Community Colleges, Olney Central College (U)
Illinois Eastern Community Colleges, Wabash Valley College (U)
Illinois Valley Community College (U)
Indiana State University (U)
Indiana University of Pennsylvania (U)
Indiana University–Purdue University Fort Wayne (U)
Indiana Wesleyan University (U,G)
Iona College (U,G)
Iowa Valley Community College District (U)
Jacksonville State University (U,G)
James Madison University (U)
Jamestown Community College (U)
Jefferson Community College (U)
John A. Logan College (U)
John Jay College of Criminal Justice of the City University of New York (U,G)
Johnson State College (U)
Johnston Community College (U)
J. Sargeant Reynolds Community College (U)
Judson College (U)
Judson University (U)
Kansas State University (U,G)
Kauai Community College (U)
Keystone College (U)
Kirkwood Community College (U)
Kirtland Community College (U)
Labette Community College (U)
Lackawanna College (U)
Lakehead University (U)
Lake-Sumter Community College (U)
Lake Superior College (U)
Lamar State College–Orange (U)
Lamar State College–Port Arthur (U)
Lansing Community College (U)
La Roche College (U)
Lassen Community College District (U)
Lenoir Community College (U)
Lesley University (U)
LeTourneau University (U,G)
Lewis-Clark State College (U)
Liberty University (U,G)
Lindenwood University (U)
Lipscomb University (G)
Lock Haven University of Pennsylvania (U)
Long Beach City College (U)
Los Angeles Harbor College (U)
Los Angeles Trade-Technical College (U)
Louisiana State University and Agricultural and Mechanical College (U)
Louisiana State University at Eunice (U)
Luna Community College (U)
Macon State College (U)
Malone University (U)
Mansfield University of Pennsylvania (U)
Marian University (U)
Marquette University (U)
Marshall University (U)
Mary Baldwin College (U)
Marylhurst University (U)
McKendree University (U)
McMurry University (U)
McNeese State University (U,G)
Memorial University of Newfoundland (U)
Mercy College of Northwest Ohio (U)
Mesa State College (U)
Metropolitan Community College–Penn Valley (U)
Miami Dade College (U)
Miami University–Regional Campuses (U)
Michigan Technological University (U)
Mid-Continent University (U)
Middlesex Community College (U)
Middle Tennessee State University (U)
Midstate College (U)
Midway College (U)
Minot State University (U)
Misericordia University (U)
Monmouth University (G)
Monroe College (U)
Monroe Community College (U)
Monroe County Community College (U)
Montcalm Community College (U)
Montgomery Community College (U)
Montgomery County Community College (U)
Moody Bible Institute (U)
Moorpark College (U)
Mountain Empire Community College (U)
Mountain State University (U,G)
Mount Allison University (U)
Mount Marty College (U)
Mount Olive College (U)
Mount Wachusett Community College (U)
Naropa University (N,U)
Nassau Community College (U)
National University (U)
Naugatuck Valley Community College (U)
New England Institute of Technology (U)
New Jersey City University (U)
New Mexico Junior College (U)
New Mexico State University (U)
New Mexico State University–Alamogordo (U)
New Mexico State University–Carlsbad (U)
New Orleans Baptist Theological Seminary (U,G)
New River Community College (U)
Nichols College (U)
Nicolet Area Technical College (U)
North Arkansas College (U)
North Carolina State University (U)
North Central Texas College (U)
North Dakota State College of Science (U)
North Dakota State University (U,G)
Northern State University (U)
North Georgia College & State University (U)
North Hennepin Community College (U)
North Iowa Area Community College (U)
North Lake College (U)
North Seattle Community College (U)
North Shore Community College (U)
NorthWest Arkansas Community College (U)
Northwestern Connecticut Community College (U)
Northwestern Michigan College (U)
Northwest-Shoals Community College (U)
Notre Dame College (U)
Nyack College (U)
Oakland Community College (U)
Oakton Community College (U)
Ocean County College (U)
The Ohio State University (U)
Ohio University (U)
Oklahoma Panhandle State University (U)
Oklahoma State University (U)
Orange Coast College (U)
Oregon Coast Community College (U)
Oregon Institute of Technology (U)
Oregon State University (N,U)
Ouachita Technical College (U)
Oxnard College (U)
Ozarks Technical Community College (U)
Pace University (U)
Paine College (U)
Pamlico Community College (U)
Paris Junior College (U)
Pasco-Hernando Community College (U)
Peirce College (U)
Pellissippi State Technical Community College (U)
Peninsula College (U)
Penn State University Park (U)
Peru State College (U)
Philadelphia University (U)
Phoenix College (U)

Piedmont Community College (U)
Pikes Peak Community College (U)
Pittsburg State University (U,G)
Portland Community College (U)
Portland State University (U)
Prairie Bible Institute (U)
Prairie View A&M University (G)
Pratt Community College (U)
Prescott College (G)
Presentation College (U)
Providence College (U)
Providence College and Theological Seminary (U)
Pulaski Technical College (U)
Queen's University at Kingston (U)
Quinsigamond Community College (U)
Randolph Community College (U)
Rappahannock Community College (U)
Reading Area Community College (U)
Regent University (U,G)
Rend Lake College (U)
The Richard Stockton College of New Jersey (U)
Richmond Community College (U)
Rio Hondo College (U)
Riverside Community College District (U)
Rivier College (U)
Robert Morris University (U)
Rochester Institute of Technology (U)
Rockland Community College (U)
Rose State College (U)
Rowan-Cabarrus Community College (U)
Sacramento City College (U)
The Sage Colleges (U)
St. Clair County Community College (U)
St. Cloud State University (U)
Saint Francis University (U)
St. Gregory's University (U)
St. John's University (U)
St. Joseph's College, Long Island Campus (U)
St. Joseph's College, New York (U)
Saint Joseph's College of Maine (U)
Saint Leo University (U)
Saint Mary-of-the-Woods College (U)
Saint Paul College–A Community & Technical College (U)
St. Petersburg College (U)
Sam Houston State University (U)
Sampson Community College (U)
San Diego Community College District (U)
San Diego State University (U)
San Jacinto College District (U)
Santa Fe Community College (U)
Santa Monica College (U)
Santa Rosa Junior College (U)
Sauk Valley Community College (U)
Seminole State College of Florida (U)
Seton Hill University (U)
Shawnee State University (U)
Shippensburg University of Pennsylvania (U,G)
Sinclair Community College (U)
Sonoma State University (G)
Southeast Arkansas College (U)
Southeast Community College Area (U)
Southeastern Community College (U)
Southeastern Illinois College (U)
Southeastern Oklahoma State University (U)
Southern Adventist University (U)
Southern Arkansas University–Magnolia (U)
Southern Connecticut State University (U)
Southern Maine Community College (U)
Southern New Hampshire University (U)
Southern Oregon University (U)
South Piedmont Community College (U)
Southwest Wisconsin Technical College (U)
Spartanburg Community College (U)
Spokane Community College (U)
Spring Arbor University (U)
Stanly Community College (U)
State University of New York at New Paltz (U)
State University of New York at Oswego (U,G)
State University of New York College at Cortland (U,G)
State University of New York College at Potsdam (U)
State University of New York College of Agriculture and Technology at Morrisville (U)
State University of New York College of Technology at Canton (U)
Stephen F. Austin State University (U,G)
Stephens College (U,G)
Sullivan County Community College (U)
Tabor College (U)
Taft College (U)
Tarleton State University (G)
Taylor University (U)
Temple University (U)
Texas State University–San Marcos (U)
Three Rivers Community College (U)
Toccoa Falls College (U)
Tompkins Cortland Community College (U)
Trident Technical College (U)
Trinidad State Junior College (U)
Tunxis Community College (U)
Tyler Junior College (U)
Union College (U,G)
Union County College (U)
Union Institute & University (G)
Union University (U)
The University of Akron (U,G)
The University of Alabama in Huntsville (G)
University of Alaska Fairbanks (U,G)
The University of Arizona (U)
University of Arkansas at Little Rock (U)
University of Bridgeport (U)
The University of British Columbia (U)
University of Central Florida (U)
University of Cincinnati (U)
University of Cincinnati Raymond Walters College (U)
University of Colorado at Colorado Springs (U)
University of Dubuque (U)
University of Florida (U)
University of Great Falls (U,G)
University of Hawaii at Hilo (U)
University of Houston–Downtown (U)
University of Houston–Victoria (U,G)
University of Idaho (U,G)
University of Illinois at Springfield (U)
University of Illinois at Urbana–Champaign (U)
The University of Kansas (U,G)
University of Louisville (U)
University of Maine (U)
University of Maine at Augusta (U)
University of Maine at Fort Kent (U)
University of Maine at Machias (U)
University of Management and Technology (U,G)
University of Mary (G)
University of Mary Washington (U)
University of Massachusetts Boston (U,G)
University of Memphis (U)
University of Minnesota, Crookston (U)
University of Minnesota, Duluth (U)
University of Minnesota, Morris (U)
The University of Montana Western (U)
University of Nevada, Reno (U)
University of New England (U)
University of North Alabama (U)
The University of North Carolina at Asheville (U)
The University of North Carolina at Chapel Hill (U)
The University of North Carolina Wilmington (U)
University of North Dakota (U,G)
University of Northern Iowa (U)
University of North Florida (U)
University of Pittsburgh at Bradford (U)
University of St. Francis (U)
University of Saskatchewan (U)
University of South Alabama (U)
The University of South Dakota (U)
University of Southern Maine (U)
The University of Texas of the Permian Basin (U,G)
University of the Southwest (U)
University of Utah (U)
University of Waterloo (U)
The University of West Alabama (U)
University of West Georgia (U)
University of Wisconsin Colleges (U)
University of Wisconsin–La Crosse (U)
Upper Iowa University (N,U)
Utah State University (U,G)
Utica College (U)
Valencia College (U)
Valley City State University (U)
Vincennes University (U)
Wake Technical Community College (U)
Walden University (G)
Walla Walla University (U)
Washington State University (U)
Wayland Baptist University (U)
Wayne State College (G)
Wayne State University (U,G)
Webber International University (U)
Westchester Community College (U)
Western Kentucky University (U,G)
Western Wyoming Community College (U)
West Hills Community College (U)
West Los Angeles College (U)
Westmoreland County Community College (U)
West Virginia Northern Community College (U)
Wharton County Junior College (U)
Wichita State University (U,G)
Wilfrid Laurier University (U)
Wilkes Community College (U)
Wisconsin Indianhead Technical College (N,U)
Worcester State University (U)
Yavapai College (U)
York County Community College (U)
York Technical College (U)

PSYCHOLOGY RELATED

Acadia University (U)
Allen Community College (U)

Alvin Community College (U)
Arapahoe Community College (U)
Athabasca University (U)
Austin Peay State University (U)
Bellevue College (U)
Bob Jones University (U)
Bossier Parish Community College (U)
Brenau University (U)
Burlington College (U)
Burlington County College (U)
California State University, Dominguez Hills (N)
California State University, San Marcos (N)
Cascadia Community College (U)
Cayuga County Community College (U)
Central Michigan University (U)
Central Texas College (U)
Central Virginia Community College (U)
Central Washington University (U)
Charter Oak State College (U)
Chemeketa Community College (U)
Citrus College (U)
City Colleges of Chicago System (U)
City University of Seattle (U)
Cleveland Community College (U)
The College at Brockport, State University of New York (U)
Columbia College (U)
Community College of Beaver County (U)
Dabney S. Lancaster Community College (U)
Dakota College at Bottineau (U)
Dallas Baptist University (U)
Drake University (U)
Edison State Community College (U)
Enterprise State Community College (U)
Faulkner University (G)
Florida Institute of Technology (N)
Franklin Pierce University (G)
Gaston College (U)
Genesee Community College (U)
Global University (U)
Goddard College (U,G)
Granite State College (U)
Grantham University (U)
Hopkinsville Community College (U)
Illinois Eastern Community Colleges, Lincoln Trail College (U)
Illinois Valley Community College (U)
Indiana Wesleyan University (G)
Iona College (U)
Iowa Lakes Community College (U)
Jacksonville State University (U,G)
James A. Rhodes State College (U)
Jamestown Community College (N,U)
Kansas State University (U,G)
Kirkwood Community College (U)
Lake-Sumter Community College (U)
Lansing Community College (U)
Lawrence Technological University (U)
Lewis-Clark State College (U)
Lindenwood University (G)
Louisiana State University and Agricultural and Mechanical College (U)
McDowell Technical Community College (U)
Mercer County Community College (U)
Miami Dade College (U)
Middlesex Community College (U)
Midwestern State University (U)
Minot State University (U)
Mountain State University (G)
Murray State University (G)
Naropa University (N,G)
Nashville State Technical Community College (U)
Nassau Community College (U)
Nichols College (U)
North Dakota State College of Science (U)
North Dakota State University (U)
NorthWest Arkansas Community College (U)
Northwestern Michigan College (U)
Ocean County College (U)
Olympic College (U)
Pamlico Community College (U)
Penn State University Park (U)
Portland Community College (N,U)
Rend Lake College (U)
The Richard Stockton College of New Jersey (U)
Rogers State University (U)
Rose State College (U)
Sacramento City College (U)
St. Cloud State University (G)
St. Louis Community College (U)
Saint Mary-of-the-Woods College (G)
St. Stephen's College (G)
San Bernardino Valley College (U)
San Diego Community College District (U)
San Jacinto College District (U)
Santa Rosa Junior College (U)
Simmons College (N)
Sinclair Community College (U)
Sonoma State University (G)
Southern Arkansas University–Magnolia (U)
South Piedmont Community College (U)
Southwestern Baptist Theological Seminary (G)
State University of New York at Plattsburgh (U)
Stephens College (U,G)
Taft College (U)
Tarleton State University (U)
Taylor University (U)
Texas State University–San Marcos (U)
Tompkins Cortland Community College (U)
Union College (U,G)
The University of Akron (G)
The University of Alabama in Huntsville (G)
University of Alaska Fairbanks (U,G)
University of Arkansas at Little Rock (U)
University of Florida (U)
University of Idaho (U)
University of Illinois at Springfield (U)
University of Illinois at Urbana–Champaign (U)
University of Maine at Machias (U)
University of Missouri–Kansas City (U)
University of Nevada, Reno (G)
University of North Dakota (U)
University of South Carolina Sumter (U)
University of Waterloo (U)
University of West Georgia (G)
Upper Iowa University (U)
Valencia College (U)
Western Kentucky University (U,G)
West Hills Community College (U)
West Virginia Northern Community College (U)
Wilfrid Laurier University (U)
Wilkes Community College (U)
York University (U)
Youngstown State University (U)

PUBLIC ADMINISTRATION

Andrew Jackson University (G)
Athabasca University (N,U,G)
Austin Peay State University (U)
Brenau University (U)
California State University, San Bernardino (G)
Central Michigan University (U,G)
Central Texas College (U)
Charter Oak State College (U)
Clemson University (N,U,G)
Cogswell Polytechnical College (U)
Dakota College at Bottineau (U)
DePaul University (G)
DeVry University Online (G)
Drake University (G)
Florida State University (U,G)
Grand Valley State University (G)
Indiana State University (G)
Jacksonville State University (U,G)
Kansas State University (U,G)
Kauai Community College (U)
Lackawanna College (U)
Lander University (U)
Midwestern State University (U)
Mississippi State University (G)
Murray State University (U,G)
National University (U,G)
Pace University (G)
Paris Junior College (N)
Regent University (G)
San Jacinto College District (U)
Sinclair Community College (U)
Southern Arkansas University–Magnolia (G)
Southern University at New Orleans (U)
Stephen F. Austin State University (G)
Stephens College (U)
The University of Akron (U,G)
University of Alaska Fairbanks (U)
University of Colorado at Colorado Springs (G)
The University of Findlay (G)
University of Florida (U)
University of Illinois at Chicago (G)
University of Illinois at Springfield (G)
University of Maine (U)
University of Maine at Fort Kent (U)
University of Management and Technology (U)
University of Memphis (U)
University of New Haven (U)
University of North Dakota (G)
The University of South Dakota (G)
University of Virginia (G)
Upper Iowa University (N,U)
Wayland Baptist University (G)
Western Kentucky University (U,G)
York University (U)
Youngstown State University (G)

PUBLIC ADMINISTRATION AND SOCIAL SERVICE PROFESSIONS RELATED

Athabasca University (N,G)
Austin Peay State University (U)
Brenau University (U)
Central Michigan University (U,G)
Charter Oak State College (U)
DePaul University (G)
Drake University (G)

Eastern Washington University (U)
Franklin Pierce University (G)
Indiana State University (G)
Indiana Wesleyan University (G)
Jacksonville State University (U,G)
John Jay College of Criminal Justice of the City University of New York (U,G)
Kansas State University (U,G)
Macon State College (U)
Pine Technical College (U)
Portland Community College (N)
San Diego Community College District (U)
Stephens College (U)
The University of Akron (U)
University of Alaska Fairbanks (U)
University of Illinois at Chicago (N)
University of Illinois at Springfield (G)
University of North Dakota (G)
The University of South Dakota (G)
University of West Florida (G)
Upper Iowa University (U)
Western Kentucky University (G)
York University (U)

PUBLIC HEALTH

Arapahoe Community College (U)
Athabasca University (N,U,G)
Austin Peay State University (U)
Ball State University (G)
Bowling Green State University (U)
Butler Community College (U)
Cornell University (U,G)
Dallas Baptist University (U)
Drake University (G)
Drexel University (G)
Eastern Kentucky University (G)
Emory University (G)
Goddard College (G)
Harrisburg Area Community College (U)
The Johns Hopkins University (G)
Kansas State University (U,G)
Kauai Community College (U)
Lock Haven University of Pennsylvania (G)
Macon State College (U)
Marlboro College Graduate College (N)
Medical College of Wisconsin (G)
Middlesex Community College (U)
Minot State University (U)
New Mexico State University (U,G)
New Mexico State University–Carlsbad (U)
New York Medical College (G)
Oakland Community College (U)
Oregon State University (G)
The Richard Stockton College of New Jersey (U)
Rockingham Community College (N)
Seminole State College of Florida (U)
The University of Akron (G)
University of Alaska Fairbanks (U)
The University of Arizona (G)
University of California, Davis (N,U)
University of Illinois at Chicago (N,G)
University of Illinois at Springfield (G)
University of Nevada, Reno (U)
University of New Haven (U)
University of North Dakota (G)
University of North Florida (U,G)
University of Southern Mississippi (G)
University of Waterloo (G)
University of Wisconsin–Green Bay (U)
Western Kentucky University (U,G)
Youngstown State University (G)

PUBLIC POLICY ANALYSIS

Athabasca University (N,U,G)
Austin Peay State University (U)
California State University, East Bay (U)
California State University, Sacramento (G)
Central Michigan University (U,G)
DePaul University (G)
Drexel University (G)
Duquesne University (G)
Goddard College (G)
Indiana Wesleyan University (G)
The Johns Hopkins University (G)
Regent University (G)
Sacramento City College (U)
University of Denver (U)
University of Maine at Fort Kent (U)
University of New Haven (U)
University of North Dakota (G)
University of Southern Maine (G)
Western Kentucky University (U)

PUBLIC RELATIONS, ADVERTISING, AND APPLIED COMMUNICATION RELATED

Arapahoe Community College (U)
Athabasca University (N,U,G)
Austin Peay State University (U)
Ball State University (G)
Brenau University (U)
Central Michigan University (G)
Champlain College (U)
City Colleges of Chicago System (U)
Columbus State Community College (U)
Drake University (U,G)
Edison State Community College (U)
Franklin Pierce University (G)
Indiana Wesleyan University (G)
Iona College (G)
Jones International University (G)
Judson University (U)
Lamar State College–Port Arthur (N)
Los Angeles Trade-Technical College (U)
Maryville University of Saint Louis (N)
Middlesex Community College (U)
Monroe Community College (U)
North Dakota State University (U,G)
Northwestern Oklahoma State University (U)
Oxnard College (U)
Pellissippi State Technical Community College (U)
Portland Community College (N)
San Jacinto College District (U)
State University of New York at New Paltz (U)
State University of New York at Oswego (U)
Stephens College (U)
University of Alaska Fairbanks (U)
University of Florida (U)
University of Illinois at Urbana–Champaign (U)
University of Memphis (U,G)
University of Michigan–Flint (U)
The University of South Dakota (U)
Upper Iowa University (U)
Webster University (U)
Western Kentucky University (U)
West Shore Community College (U)
Wilkes Community College (U)
Wisconsin Indianhead Technical College (N,U)
Worcester State University (N)
Youngstown State University (N)

PUBLISHING

Arapahoe Community College (U)
Brigham Young University–Idaho (U)
Clemson University (N)
Hagerstown Community College (N)
Mansfield University of Pennsylvania (N)
Middlesex Community College (U)
Pace University (G)
Rosemont College (G)
Sessions College for Professional Design (N,U)
University of Cincinnati (N)
University of Waterloo (N)
Wake Technical Community College (N)

QUALITY CONTROL AND SAFETY TECHNOLOGIES

California State University, Dominguez Hills (N)
Columbus State Community College (U)
Florida Institute of Technology (G)
Jacksonville State University (U,G)
James A. Rhodes State College (U)
Kansas State University (G)
Kettering University (N)
Lamar State College–Orange (U)
Missouri University of Science and Technology (N,G)
Mitchell Technical Institute (N)
Southeastern Oklahoma State University (U,G)
Southern Illinois University Carbondale (U)
Trident Technical College (U)
The University of Alabama in Huntsville (G)
University of Michigan (N)

RADIO, TELEVISION, AND DIGITAL COMMUNICATION

Athabasca University (N)
Austin Peay State University (U)
Brigham Young University–Idaho (U)
Cayuga County Community College (U)
Cerritos College (U)
Eastern Kentucky University (U)
Hofstra University (U)
Long Beach City College (U)
Middlesex Community College (U)
Middle Tennessee State University (U)
Oakton Community College (U)
Olympic College (U)
Oxnard College (U)
Pikes Peak Community College (U)
The Richard Stockton College of New Jersey (N)
Riverside Community College District (U)
San Bernardino Valley College (U)
State University of New York Institute of Technology (G)
University of Alaska Fairbanks (U)
Western Kentucky University (U)
Western Texas College (U)

REAL ESTATE

Angelo State University (U)
Antelope Valley College (U)

Arapahoe Community College (U)
Austin Peay State University (N)
Ball State University (G)
Blackhawk Technical College (N)
Bossier Parish Community College (N)
Butler County Community College (N)
Cabrillo College (U)
California State University, Sacramento (U)
Cayuga County Community College (U)
Centralia College (N,U)
Central New Mexico Community College (U)
Central Texas College (U)
Cerritos College (U)
Citrus College (U)
Clarion University of Pennsylvania (N,U)
Columbus State Community College (U)
Dickinson State University (U)
Drexel University (G)
Eastern Washington University (N)
Eastern West Virginia Community and Technical College (U)
Harford Community College (N)
Hibbing Community College (N)
Houston Community College System (U)
Jamestown Community College (N)
Lansing Community College (U)
Long Beach City College (U)
Los Angeles Harbor College (U)
Middle Tennessee State University (N)
Naugatuck Valley Community College (N,U)
North Iowa Area Community College (N)
North Lake College (N,U)
Orange Coast College (U)
Paris Junior College (N)
Pasco-Hernando Community College (N)
Phoenix College (N,U)
Portland Community College (N,U)
Quinebaug Valley Community College (N)
Rend Lake College (U)
The Richard Stockton College of New Jersey (N)
Riverside Community College District (U)
Sacramento City College (U)
St. Petersburg College (N)
San Bernardino Valley College (U)
San Diego Community College District (U)
San Jacinto College District (U)
Santa Rosa Junior College (U)
Southeast Arkansas College (U)
Southern Illinois University Carbondale (U)
Southern Union State Community College (U)
Spartanburg Community College (N)
Tarleton State University (N)
Texas Woman's University (N)
The University of Akron (U)
University of Alaska Fairbanks (U)
University of Arkansas at Little Rock (U,G)
University of Cincinnati (N)
University of Florida (U)
University of Idaho (U)
University of Maine at Fort Kent (U)
University of North Dakota (N)
The University of Texas at Brownsville (N)
University of Utah (N)
Wayne Community College (N)
Western Kentucky University (U)
West Los Angeles College (U)
Westmoreland County Community College (U)
West Virginia Northern Community College (N)

REAL ESTATE DEVELOPMENT

Cayuga County Community College (U)
Sacramento City College (U)
University of Alaska Fairbanks (U)

REGISTERED NURSING, NURSING ADMINISTRATION, NURSING RESEARCH AND CLINICAL NURSING

Arkansas State University (U)
Boise State University (U,G)
Erie Community College (U)
Erie Community College, North Campus (U)
Erie Community College, South Campus (U)
Ferris State University (G)
Indiana University–Purdue University Fort Wayne (U,G)
Long Beach City College (U)
North Central Texas College (U)
Rivier College (U)
Saint Joseph's College of Maine (U,G)
Southern Adventist University (U)
Tabor College (U)
University of North Florida (U,G)
University of Southern Maine (U)
Valencia College (U)
Winston-Salem State University (U)

REHABILITATION AND THERAPEUTIC PROFESSIONS

Arkansas Tech University (U)
Brenau University (G)
Clarion University of Pennsylvania (G)
Drake University (G)
Fort Valley State University (G)
Philadelphia University (G)
Salve Regina University (G)
Southern Illinois University Carbondale (G)
Texas Woman's University (G)
University of Alaska Fairbanks (U)
University of Arkansas at Little Rock (G)
The University of British Columbia (U)
University of Massachusetts Boston (G)
University of St. Augustine for Health Sciences (G)
Utah State University (G)
Vincennes University (U)
Wayne State University (G)
Western Michigan University (U)
Winston-Salem State University (G)

RELIGIOUS EDUCATION

Andover Newton Theological School (N,G)
Baptist Missionary Association Theological Seminary (U,G)
Beulah Heights University (U)
Bossier Parish Community College (N)
Brigham Young University (U)
Brigham Young University–Idaho (U)
Carroll University (U)
The Catholic Distance University (N,G)
Central Bible College (U)
Covenant Theological Seminary (N,G)
Crown College (U)
Dakota College at Bottineau (U)
Dallas Baptist University (U,G)
Defiance College (U)
Denver Seminary (G)
Earlham School of Religion (G)
Global University (N,U,G)
Hannibal-LaGrange University (U)
Indiana Wesleyan University (G)
Ithaca College (U)
Lincoln Christian University (G)
Master's College and Seminary (U)
Miami Dade College (U)
Missouri Baptist University (G)
Montgomery Community College (U)
Moody Bible Institute (U)
Mount Allison University (U)
Naropa University (N,G)
Newman Theological College (G)
New Orleans Baptist Theological Seminary (N,U,G)
Providence College (N)
Regent College (N,G)
Regent University (G)
St. Andrew's College (G)
Saint Francis University (N)
Seton Hill University (U)
Southwestern Baptist Theological Seminary (U,G)
Summit Pacific College (N,U)
Taylor University (U)
Toccoa Falls College (U)
Trinity International University (G)
Union Presbyterian Seminary (N,G)
University of Dubuque (N)
Wayland Baptist University (U,G)
Webster University (U)
Western Kentucky University (U)
Western Seminary (N,G)

RELIGIOUS/SACRED MUSIC

Barclay College (U)
Covenant Theological Seminary (N,G)
Global University (U)
Indiana Wesleyan University (G)
Naropa University (N)
New Orleans Baptist Theological Seminary (N,U,G)
Providence College and Theological Seminary (N)
Sioux Falls Seminary (G)
Southern Adventist University (U)
Southwestern Baptist Theological Seminary (G)
Taylor University (U)

RELIGIOUS STUDIES

Amridge University (N,U,G)
Anderson University (U,G)
Andover Newton Theological School (N,G)
Andrews University (U,G)
Asbury University (U)
Ashland University (U)
Bakke Graduate University (G)
Baptist Bible College of Pennsylvania (U,G)
Baptist Missionary Association Theological Seminary (U,G)
Beulah Heights University (G)
Bob Jones University (U,G)
Brewton-Parker College (U)
Brigham Young University (N,U)
Brigham Young University–Idaho (U)
Butler Community College (U)
Caldwell College (U)
California State University, Chico (U)

Campbellsville University (U,G)
Carleton University (U)
The Catholic Distance University (N,G)
Central Bible College (U)
Central Carolina Technical College (U)
Central Virginia Community College (U)
Central Wyoming College (U)
Chaminade University of Honolulu (G)
Chatham University (U)
Chattanooga State Community College (U)
Chemeketa Community College (U)
Cincinnati Christian University (G)
Clovis Community College (U)
Coastal Carolina University (U)
Columbia College (U)
Columbia International University (N,U,G)
Covenant Theological Seminary (N,G)
Crown College (U)
Culver-Stockton College (U)
Dallas Baptist University (U,G)
Davidson County Community College (U)
Denver Seminary (G)
DePaul University (U)
Drury University (U)
Earlham School of Religion (G)
Eastern Mennonite University (G)
Eastern Washington University (U)
Edison State Community College (U)
Erie Community College (U)
Erie Community College, North Campus (U)
Erie Community College, South Campus (U)
Fontbonne University (U)
Free Will Baptist Bible College (N,U)
Friends University (U)
Front Range Community College (U)
Fuller Theological Seminary (N,G)
Gannon University (U)
George Fox University (U)
Georgian Court University (U)
Global University (N,U,G)
Graceland University (G)
Hartford Seminary (N,G)
Haywood Community College (U)
Hope International University (N,U,G)
Indiana Wesleyan University (G)
John A. Logan College (U)
Johnson State College (U)
Johnson University (U)
Johnston Community College (U)
Kirkwood Community College (U)
Liberty University (U,G)
Life Pacific College (N)
Lincoln Christian University (N,U,G)
Mary Baldwin College (U)
Marylhurst University (U,G)
Master's College and Seminary (U)
McMurry University (U)
Memorial University of Newfoundland (U)
Mercy College of Northwest Ohio (U)
Mesa Community College (U)
Miami Dade College (U)
Midway College (U)
Misericordia University (U)
Missouri Baptist University (U,G)
Moody Bible Institute (N,U,G)
Mountain Empire Community College (U)
Mount Olive College (U)
Naropa University (N,U)
Nebraska Christian College (U)
New Orleans Baptist Theological Seminary (N,U,G)
Nichols College (U)
Northwest-Shoals Community College (U)
Nyack College (U,G)
Ozarks Technical Community College (U)
Phoenix College (U)
Piedmont Baptist College and Graduate School (U)
Presentation College (U)
Providence College (N)
Providence College and Theological Seminary (G)
Pulaski Technical College (U)
Rappahannock Community College (U)
Regent College (N,G)
Regent University (U,G)
Reinhardt University (U)
Rend Lake College (U)
Riverside Community College District (U)
Rivier College (U)
St. Andrew's College (G)
Saint Francis University (N,U)
St. Joseph's College, Long Island Campus (U)
St. Joseph's College, New York (U)
Saint Joseph's College of Maine (U)
Saint Leo University (U)
St. Stephen's College (G)
San Diego State University (U)
Seton Hill University (U)
Shasta Bible College (U)
Southeastern Illinois College (U)
Southern Illinois University Carbondale (U)
South Piedmont Community College (U)
Southwestern Baptist Theological Seminary (U,G)
Spring Arbor University (U)
Stanly Community College (U)
Summit Pacific College (N,U)
Taylor University (U)
Toccoa Falls College (U)
Trinity International University (G)
Union Presbyterian Seminary (N)
Union University (N,U,G)
University of Arkansas at Little Rock (U)
University of Bridgeport (U)
University of Dubuque (U)
The University of Findlay (U)
University of Florida (U)
The University of Kansas (U)
The University of North Carolina at Asheville (U)
The University of North Carolina at Chapel Hill (U)
University of North Dakota (U)
University of Northern Iowa (U,G)
University of North Florida (U)
University of Saskatchewan (U)
University of the Southwest (U)
University of Waterloo (U)
University of West Florida (U)
The University of Winnipeg (U)
Wake Technical Community College (U)
Wayland Baptist University (U,G)
Westchester Community College (U)
Western Kentucky University (U)
Western Michigan University (U)
Western Seminary (N,G)
Westmoreland County Community College (U)
Wilfrid Laurier University (U)
Wilkes Community College (U)
Williamson Christian College (U)
York County Community College (U)
York University (U)

RESEARCH AND EXPERIMENTAL PSYCHOLOGY

University of Alaska Fairbanks (U)

RHETORIC AND COMPOSITION/ WRITING STUDIES

Boise State University (U)
North Dakota State University (G)
Sacramento City College (U)
University of Alaska Fairbanks (U)
University of Dubuque (U)
Youngstown State University (U)

RURAL SOCIOLOGY

North Dakota State University (U,G)
University of Alaska Fairbanks (U)
University of Maine at Machias (U)

SALES MERCHANDISING, AND RELATED MARKETING OPERATIONS (GENERAL)

Adams State College (N)
Arapahoe Community College (U)
Athabasca University (N,U,G)
Austin Peay State University (N,U)
Ball State University (G)
Brenau University (G)
Brigham Young University–Idaho (U)
California State University, Dominguez Hills (N)
California State University, Sacramento (U)
Central Michigan University (G)
Central New Mexico Community College (U)
Chemeketa Community College (U)
Cleveland Community College (U)
Columbia College (U)
Columbus State Community College (U)
Cossatot Community College of the University of Arkansas (N)
Dallas Baptist University (U,G)
Drexel University (U,G)
Eastern Washington University (N)
Fort Hays State University (N)
Gateway Community College (U)
Genesee Community College (U)
Grantham University (U)
Indiana Wesleyan University (G)
Jacksonville State University (U,G)
James A. Rhodes State College (U)
Lamar State College–Port Arthur (N)
Lansing Community College (U)
Los Angeles Trade-Technical College (U)
Mansfield University of Pennsylvania (N)
Mary Baldwin College (N)
Maryville University of Saint Louis (U)
Middle Tennessee State University (U)
North Dakota State University (N,U,G)
Oakton Community College (U)
Oklahoma State University (U)
Oregon State University (U)
Pasco-Hernando Community College (N)
Phoenix College (N)
Quinebaug Valley Community College (N)
Quinsigamond Community College (N)
Rend Lake College (N)
The Richard Stockton College of New Jersey (N)
Rockingham Community College (N)

Rowan-Cabarrus Community College (U)
Southern Illinois University Carbondale (U)
Spartanburg Community College (N,U)
State University of New York Institute of Technology (G)
The University of Akron (U)
University of Alaska Fairbanks (U)
University of Bridgeport (U)
The University of Findlay (G)
University of Florida (U)
University of Wisconsin–La Crosse (G)
Wake Technical Community College (N)
Western Kentucky University (U)

SALES, MERCHANDISING AND RELATED MARKETING OPERATIONS (SPECIALIZED)

Adams State College (N)
The American College (U)
Andrew Jackson University (G)
Arapahoe Community College (U)
Athabasca University (N,G)
Austin Peay State University (N,U)
Blackhawk Technical College (N)
Bossier Parish Community College (N)
Brenau University (U,G)
California State University, Dominguez Hills (N)
Centralia College (N)
Central Texas College (U)
Chemeketa Community College (U)
Cossatot Community College of the University of Arkansas (N)
Drexel University (G)
Edgecombe Community College (N)
Finger Lakes Community College (U)
Herkimer County Community College (U)
Indiana Wesleyan University (G)
Jacksonville State University (U,G)
James A. Rhodes State College (U)
Kirtland Community College (U)
Lamar State College–Port Arthur (N)
Middle Tennessee State University (N)
Naugatuck Valley Community College (U)
Nicolet Area Technical College (U)
North Carolina Central University (G)
North Dakota State University (N,G)
Odessa College (N)
Ohio University (U)
Oklahoma State University (U)
Oregon State University (N)
Oxnard College (U)
Pasco-Hernando Community College (N)
Rockingham Community College (N)
Rowan-Cabarrus Community College (N)
Seton Hill University (N)
Southeast Community College Area (U)
State University of New York at Plattsburgh (U)
State University of New York College at Potsdam (N)
State University of New York Institute of Technology (G)
Stephen F. Austin State University (U)
Temple University (U)
The University of Akron (U)
University of Houston (U)
University of Michigan–Flint (N)
The University of Tennessee at Chattanooga (N)
Vincennes University (U)
Wake Technical Community College (N)
Westchester Community College (U)
West Los Angeles College (U)
Wilkes Community College (U)
Wisconsin Indianhead Technical College (N,U)
York College of Pennsylvania (N)
Youngstown State University (N)

SCIENCE TECHNOLOGIES

Bluefield College (U)
Indiana Wesleyan University (G)

SCIENCE TECHNOLOGIES RELATED

Athabasca University (N)
Austin Peay State University (U)
Cayuga County Community College (U)
Central Michigan University (N)
Columbus State Community College (U)
Dakota College at Bottineau (U)
Drexel University (G)
Indiana University of Pennsylvania (G)
Indiana Wesleyan University (G)
Iowa Lakes Community College (U)
Lansing Community College (U)
North Hennepin Community College (N)
Pamlico Community College (U)
Portland Community College (N)
St. John's University (U)
University of Management and Technology (U)
The University of North Carolina at Asheville (G)
University of Wisconsin–Milwaukee (N)
University of Wisconsin–Stout (G)
Western Kentucky University (U)

SCIENCE, TECHNOLOGY AND SOCIETY

Athabasca University (N)
Austin Peay State University (U)
DePaul University (U)
Goddard College (U,G)
Indiana Wesleyan University (G)
Iona College (U)
Jacksonville State University (U,G)
Lock Haven University of Pennsylvania (G)
North Carolina State University (U)
Northwestern Connecticut Community College (U)
Oregon State University (U)
Pace University (U)
Saint Paul College–A Community & Technical College (U)
Syracuse University (U)
University of Denver (U)
University of Illinois at Urbana–Champaign (N,G)
University of Management and Technology (U)
University of Oregon (U)
University of Windsor (U)
Wayne Community College (U)
Western Kentucky University (U,G)
Western Michigan University (G)

SECURITY POLICY AND STRATEGY

New Jersey City University (U,G)
University of Maine at Augusta (N)

SOCIAL AND PHILOSOPHICAL FOUNDATIONS OF EDUCATION

Arapahoe Community College (U)
Athabasca University (N)
Austin Peay State University (U)
Brenau University (U)
Burlington County College (U)
D'Youville College (G)
Global University (G)
Goddard College (G)
Jacksonville State University (U,G)
Lock Haven University of Pennsylvania (U)
Miami Dade College (U)
Sinclair Community College (U)
State University of New York at New Paltz (U)
The University of Akron (U,G)
University of Alaska Fairbanks (U)
University of Arkansas at Little Rock (G)
University of Florida (U)
University of Northern Iowa (U)
University of Southern Mississippi (G)
Western Kentucky University (U,G)
Winston-Salem State University (U)

SOCIAL SCIENCES

Acadia University (U)
Arapahoe Community College (U)
Athabasca University (N,U,G)
Austin Peay State University (U)
Bellevue College (U)
Bluefield College (U)
Bob Jones University (U)
Boise State University (U)
Bowling Green State University (U)
Brenau University (U)
Brigham Young University–Idaho (U)
Burlington College (U)
Burlington County College (U)
Butler Community College (U)
California State University, Chico (U)
California State University, Monterey Bay (U)
Capital Community College (U)
Carl Sandburg College (U)
Cascadia Community College (U)
Cayuga County Community College (U)
Cedarville University (U)
Centralia College (U)
Central Texas College (U)
Central Wyoming College (U)
Charter Oak State College (U)
Chemeketa Community College (U)
Citrus College (U)
City Colleges of Chicago System (U)
Cleveland Community College (U)
The College at Brockport, State University of New York (U)
College of the Humanities and Sciences, Harrison Middleton University (U)
College of the Siskiyous (U)
Community College of Beaver County (U)
Concordia University, St. Paul (N)
Dakota College at Bottineau (U)
Dallas Baptist University (U)

Danville Community College (U)
Drury University (U)
D'Youville College (U)
Eastern Illinois University (U)
Eastern Washington University (U)
Eastern West Virginia Community and Technical College (U)
Edison State Community College (U)
Endicott College (U)
Fitchburg State University (U,G)
Fuller Theological Seminary (N)
Gateway Community College (U)
Genesee Community College (U)
Global University (U)
Goddard College (U)
Granite State College (U)
Haywood Community College (U)
Hibbing Community College (U)
Hocking College (U)
Illinois Eastern Community Colleges, Olney Central College (U)
Illinois Valley Community College (U)
Indiana Wesleyan University (G)
Inter American University of Puerto Rico, San Germán Campus (U)
Iowa Lakes Community College (U)
Jacksonville State University (U,G)
Jefferson Community College (U)
John Jay College of Criminal Justice of the City University of New York (U)
Judson College (U)
Kansas State University (U)
Kauai Community College (U)
Lackawanna College (U)
Lansing Community College (U)
La Roche College (U)
Lewis-Clark State College (U)
Liberty University (U)
Lincoln Christian University (U)
Long Beach City College (U)
Louisiana State University and Agricultural and Mechanical College (U)
Loyola University New Orleans (U)
Massachusetts College of Art and Design (U,G)
McDowell Technical Community College (U)
Mercer County Community College (U)
Mercy College of Northwest Ohio (U)
Mesa State College (U)
Miami Dade College (U)
Middlesex Community College (U)
Middle Tennessee State University (U)
Minot State University (U)
Monroe College (U)
Monroe Community College (U)
Mountain State University (U)
Mount Wachusett Community College (U)
New Mexico Junior College (U)
New Mexico State University–Carlsbad (U)
Nicolet Area Technical College (U)
North Carolina State University (U)
North Central Texas College (U)
North Dakota State College of Science (U)
North Georgia College & State University (U)
North Iowa Area Community College (U)
NorthWest Arkansas Community College (U)
Oakland Community College (U)
Oakton Community College (U)
Ocean County College (U)
The Ohio State University (U)
Oklahoma Panhandle State University (U)
Oregon Coast Community College (U)
Oregon Institute of Technology (U)
Ouachita Technical College (U)
Ozarks Technical Community College (U)
Pace University (U)
Peninsula College (U)
Pittsburg State University (U)
Portland Community College (U)
Providence College and Theological Seminary (U)
Pulaski Technical College (U)
Quinebaug Valley Community College (U)
Regent University (U)
Rend Lake College (U)
Robert Morris University (U)
Rogers State University (U)
Rose State College (U)
Sacramento City College (U)
St. Clair County Community College (U)
St. Gregory's University (U)
St. Joseph's College, Long Island Campus (U)
St. Joseph's College, New York (U)
Saint Joseph's College of Maine (U)
Saint Leo University (U)
St. Philip's College (U)
San Diego Community College District (U)
Sinclair Community College (U)
Southeastern Community College (U)
Southern Illinois University Carbondale (U)
Southern Maine Community College (U)
Southern New Hampshire University (U)
South Piedmont Community College (U)
Southwest Wisconsin Technical College (U)
Spartanburg Community College (U)
Spoon River College (U)
Spring Arbor University (U)
State University of New York at Plattsburgh (U)
State University of New York College of Technology at Canton (U)
State University of New York Empire State College (G)
Stephens College (U)
Sullivan County Community College (U)
Syracuse University (U)
Tabor College (U)
Taft College (U)
Tarleton State University (G)
Taylor University (U)
Texas State University–San Marcos (U)
Trine University (U)
University at Albany, State University of New York (U)
The University of Akron (U)
University of Alaska Fairbanks (U)
University of Bridgeport (U)
The University of Findlay (U)
University of Great Falls (U)
University of Houston–Downtown (U)
University of Idaho (U)
University of Maine at Augusta (U)
University of Maine at Machias (U)
University of Mary (U)
University of Massachusetts Boston (U)
University of Michigan–Flint (U)
The University of North Carolina at Asheville (U)
University of North Dakota (U)
University of Pennsylvania (U)
University of St. Francis (U)
University of South Carolina Sumter (U)
University of Southern Maine (U)
University of Utah (U)
University of Waterloo (U)
The University of West Alabama (U)
University of West Georgia (G)
The University of Winnipeg (U)
University of Wisconsin Colleges (U)
University of Wisconsin–Superior (U)
Upper Iowa University (U)
Utah State University (U)
Valencia College (U)
Vincennes University (U)
Wayne State University (U)
Westchester Community College (U)
Western Kentucky University (U,G)
Western Texas College (U)
West Hills Community College (U)
West Los Angeles College (U)
West Virginia Northern Community College (U)
Wichita State University (G)
Winston-Salem State University (U)
York University (U)

SOCIAL SCIENCES RELATED

Acadia University (U)
Anne Arundel Community College (U)
Athabasca University (N,G)
Austin Peay State University (U)
Bellevue College (U)
Boise State University (U)
Brookdale Community College (U)
Burlington College (U)
Burlington County College (U)
Butler Community College (U)
Cayuga County Community College (U)
Central Texas College (U)
Central Virginia Community College (U)
Central Washington University (U)
Charter Oak State College (U)
Chemeketa Community College (U)
Cleveland Institute of Electronics (U)
College of the Humanities and Sciences, Harrison Middleton University (G)
Columbia College (U)
Columbus State Community College (U)
Community College of Beaver County (U)
Dallas Baptist University (U)
DePaul University (U)
Drake University (U)
Eastern Illinois University (U)
El Camino College (U)
Erie Community College (U)
Erie Community College, North Campus (U)
Erie Community College, South Campus (U)
Ferris State University (U)
Franklin Pierce University (U,G)
Fuller Theological Seminary (G)
Global University (U)
Goddard College (U,G)
Harford Community College (U)
Haywood Community College (U)
Indiana Wesleyan University (G)
James A. Rhodes State College (U)
J. Sargeant Reynolds Community College (U)
Kansas State University (N,U)
Keystone College (U)
Lansing Community College (U)
Lewis-Clark State College (U)
Louisiana State University and Agricultural and Mechanical College (U)
Malone University (U)
Mansfield University of Pennsylvania (G)

Marylhurst University (U)
Miami University–Regional Campuses (U)
Middlesex Community College (U)
Monroe College (U)
Mountain State University (U)
Murray State University (U)
North Arkansas College (U)
North Shore Community College (U)
NorthWest Arkansas Community College (U)
Oregon State University (U)
Pasco-Hernando Community College (U)
Portland Community College (N,U)
Pratt Community College (U)
Queen's University at Kingston (U)
Rockland Community College (U)
Rose State College (U)
Sacramento City College (U)
St. Cloud State University (U)
Saint Mary-of-the-Woods College (U)
San Bernardino Valley College (U)
San Diego Community College District (U)
San Jacinto College District (U)
Siena Heights University (U)
Sinclair Community College (U)
Spokane Community College (U)
Stephens College (U)
Taft College (U)
Taylor University (U)
Texas State University–San Marcos (U)
University at Albany, State University of New York (U)
University of Alaska Fairbanks (U)
University of Denver (U)
University of Florida (U)
University of Idaho (U)
University of Maine at Augusta (U)
University of Missouri–Kansas City (U)
The University of North Carolina at Asheville (U)
University of North Dakota (U)
University of Northern Iowa (U)
The University of South Dakota (U)
The University of Texas at Brownsville (U)
University of the Southwest (U)
University of Waterloo (U)
University of West Georgia (U)
University of Wisconsin–Green Bay (U)
Upper Iowa University (U)
Utah State University (G)
Western Kentucky University (U,G)
West Hills Community College (U)
West Los Angeles College (U)
Youngstown State University (U)

SOCIAL WORK

Arkansas State University (U)
Athabasca University (N,G)
Austin Peay State University (U)
Boise State University (U,G)
Bradley University (U)
Brigham Young University (U)
Brigham Young University–Idaho (U)
Burlington College (U)
Butler Community College (U)
California State University, Chico (U)
California State University, San Bernardino (U)
California State University, San Marcos (U)
Campbellsville University (U,G)
Canisius College (G)
Carleton University (U)
Cedarville University (U)
Central Texas College (U)
Chatham University (U)
The College at Brockport, State University of New York (U,G)
Dallas Baptist University (U)
Eastern Kentucky University (U)
Eastern Washington University (U,G)
Fayetteville State University (G)
Florida State University (G)
Fort Valley State University (U)
Governors State University (U,G)
Grand Valley State University (G)
Iona College (U)
Jacksonville State University (U,G)
Kauai Community College (G)
Lakehead University (U)
Lewis-Clark State College (U)
Lindenwood University (U)
Mansfield University of Pennsylvania (N)
Marian University (U)
Marshall University (U,G)
Mary Baldwin College (U)
Memorial University of Newfoundland (U,G)
Middlesex Community College (U)
Middle Tennessee State University (U)
Mountain State University (U)
Murray State University (U)
Nashville State Technical Community College (N,U)
Naugatuck Valley Community College (U)
New Mexico Highlands University (U)
New Mexico State University–Carlsbad (U)
New Mexico State University–Grants (U)
North Carolina State University (U,G)
Nyack College (U)
The Ohio State University (U,G)
Piedmont Community College (U)
Providence College and Theological Seminary (U)
Saint Francis University (U)
San Diego State University (U)
Santa Fe Community College (U)
Shippensburg University of Pennsylvania (U,G)
Slippery Rock University of Pennsylvania (U)
Southern Adventist University (U,G)
Southern Connecticut State University (G)
Southern University at New Orleans (U,G)
Spring Arbor University (U)
Stephen F. Austin State University (U)
Taylor University (U)
Temple University (G)
University at Albany, State University of New York (G)
The University of Akron (U,G)
University of Alaska Fairbanks (U)
University of Arkansas at Little Rock (U,G)
The University of British Columbia (U)
University of Calgary (U,G)
University of Illinois at Chicago (N,G)
University of Illinois at Springfield (U)
University of Illinois at Urbana–Champaign (G)
University of Louisville (G)
University of Maine (G)
University of Michigan–Flint (U)
University of Minnesota, Duluth (U)
University of Nevada, Reno (U)
University of North Alabama (U)
The University of North Carolina Wilmington (U)
University of North Dakota (U,G)
University of Northern Iowa (U,G)
University of North Florida (U)
University of Southern California (G)
University of Southern Maine (G)
University of Southern Mississippi (U,G)
The University of Texas at Arlington (N,U,G)
The University of Texas of the Permian Basin (U)
University of Waterloo (U)
University of Wisconsin–Platteville (N)
Utah State University (U,G)
Vincennes University (U)
Wake Technical Community College (U)
Walla Walla University (U)
Wayne State University (U,G)
Western Kentucky University (U,G)
Western Michigan University (U)
Western Wyoming Community College (U)
West Hills Community College (U)
West Virginia State University (U)
Wilfrid Laurier University (U)
York University (U)

SOCIOLOGY

Acadia University (U)
Adams State College (U)
Albertus Magnus College (U)
Allen Community College (U)
Alpena Community College (U)
Anderson University (U)
Andrews University (U)
Angelina College (U)
Angelo State University (U)
Anne Arundel Community College (U)
Antelope Valley College (U)
Arapahoe Community College (U)
Arkansas State University (U)
Arkansas State University–Beebe (U)
Asbury University (U)
Athabasca University (N,U,G)
Austin Peay State University (U)
Baldwin-Wallace College (U)
Barclay College (U)
Bellevue College (U)
Belmont Technical College (U)
Bloomfield College (U)
Boise State University (U)
Bossier Parish Community College (U)
Bowling Green State University (U)
Bradley University (U)
Brenau University (U)
Bridgewater State University (U)
Brigham Young University (U)
Brigham Young University–Idaho (U)
Bronx Community College of the City University of New York (U)
Brookdale Community College (U)
Broward College (U)
Burlington College (U)
Burlington County College (U)
Butler Community College (U)
Butler County Community College (U)
Cabrillo College (U)
Caldwell College (U)
California State University, Chico (U)
California State University, East Bay (U)
California State University, Sacramento (U)
Campbellsville University (U)
Capital Community College (U)
Carlow University (U)

Carl Sandburg College (U)
Carroll University (U)
Cascadia Community College (U)
Cayuga County Community College (U)
Cedarville University (U)
Central Carolina Community College (U)
Central Carolina Technical College (U)
Centralia College (U)
Central New Mexico Community College (U)
Central Texas College (U)
Central Virginia Community College (U)
Central Washington University (U)
Central Wyoming College (U)
Cerritos College (U)
Champlain College (U)
Charter Oak State College (U)
Chattanooga State Community College (U)
Chemeketa Community College (U)
Cincinnati State Technical and Community College (U)
Citrus College (U)
City Colleges of Chicago System (U)
Clark State Community College (U)
Clatsop Community College (U)
Clemson University (U)
Cleveland Community College (U)
Cleveland State Community College (U)
Clinton Community College (U)
Clovis Community College (U)
College of Saint Mary (U)
College of San Mateo (U)
College of Southern Maryland (U)
Colorado Mountain College (U)
Columbia Basin College (U)
Columbia College (U)
Columbia-Greene Community College (U)
Columbus State Community College (U)
Columbus State University (U)
Community College of Allegheny County (U)
Community College of Beaver County (U)
Concordia University, St. Paul (U,G)
Cornell University (U,G)
Corning Community College (U)
Cossatot Community College of the University of Arkansas (U)
Dakota State University (U)
Dakota Wesleyan University (U)
Dallas Baptist University (U)
Danville Community College (U)
Davidson County Community College (U)
Dawson Community College (U)
Dickinson State University (U)
Dominican College (U)
Drury University (U)
East Central Community College (U)
Eastern Washington University (U)
Eastern West Virginia Community and Technical College (U)
Eastern Wyoming College (U)
Edgecombe Community College (U)
Edison State Community College (U)
Elaine P. Nunez Community College (U)
El Camino College (U)
Enterprise State Community College (U)
Erie Community College (U)
Erie Community College, North Campus (U)
Erie Community College, South Campus (U)
Fayetteville State University (U)
Finger Lakes Community College (U)
Fitchburg State University (U)
Five Towns College (U)
Florida State University (U)
Fontbonne University (U)
Fort Hays State University (U)
Fort Valley State University (U)
Framingham State University (U)
Friends University (U)
Front Range Community College (U)
Frostburg State University (U)
Gadsden State Community College (U)
Gaston College (U)
Genesee Community College (U)
George Fox University (U)
Glenville State College (U)
Global University (U)
Goddard College (U,G)
Governors State University (U,G)
Graceland University (U)
Grand Valley State University (U,G)
Grantham University (U)
Greenville Technical College (U)
Harcum College (U)
Haywood Community College (U)
Heartland Community College (U)
Hibbing Community College (U)
Hillsborough Community College (U)
Holyoke Community College (U)
Hope International University (U)
Hopkinsville Community College (U)
Houston Community College System (U)
Huston-Tillotson University (U)
Illinois Valley Community College (U)
Indiana State University (U)
Indiana University–Purdue University Fort Wayne (U)
Indiana Wesleyan University (G)
Iowa Valley Community College District (U)
Ithaca College (U)
Jacksonville State University (U,G)
James Madison University (U)
Jamestown Community College (N)
Jefferson Community College (U)
Johnson State College (U)
Johnston Community College (U)
J. Sargeant Reynolds Community College (U)
Judson College (U)
Judson University (U)
Kansas State University (U)
Kean University (U)
Kirkwood Community College (U)
Labette Community College (U)
Lackawanna College (U)
Lake Superior College (U)
Lander University (U)
Lansing Community College (U)
Lassen Community College District (U)
Lewis-Clark State College (U)
Lewis University (U)
Lindenwood University (U)
Lock Haven University of Pennsylvania (U)
Long Beach City College (U)
Los Angeles Harbor College (U)
Los Angeles Trade-Technical College (U)
Louisiana State University and Agricultural and Mechanical College (U)
Lourdes College (U)
Malone University (U)
Mansfield University of Pennsylvania (U)
Marian University (U)
Marquette University (U)
Marshall University (U,G)
Mary Baldwin College (U)
McKendree University (U)
Memorial University of Newfoundland (U)
Mercer County Community College (U)
Mesa State College (U)
Metropolitan Community College–Penn Valley (U)
Miami Dade College (U)
Miami University–Regional Campuses (U)
Middlesex Community College (U)
Middle Tennessee State University (U)
Midland College (U)
Mid-State Technical College (U)
Midwestern State University (U)
Minot State University (U)
Misericordia University (U)
Monroe College (U)
Montgomery Community College (U)
Montgomery County Community College (U)
Moorpark College (U)
Mountain Empire Community College (U)
Mountain State University (U)
Mount Allison University (U)
Mount Marty College (U)
Mount Wachusett Community College (U)
Nashville State Technical Community College (U)
Nassau Community College (U)
Naugatuck Valley Community College (U)
New England Institute of Technology (U)
New Jersey City University (U)
New Mexico Junior College (U)
New Mexico State University (U,G)
New Mexico State University–Grants (U)
New River Community College (U)
Nichols College (U)
Nicolet Area Technical College (U)
North Carolina State University (U)
North Central Texas College (U)
North Dakota State College of Science (U)
North Dakota State University (U)
Northeastern State University (U)
Northern State University (U)
North Hennepin Community College (U)
North Lake College (U)
North Seattle Community College (U)
North Shore Community College (U)
NorthWest Arkansas Community College (U)
Northwestern Connecticut Community College (U)
Northwestern Michigan College (U)
Northwestern Oklahoma State University (U)
Northwest-Shoals Community College (U)
Notre Dame College (U)
Oakland Community College (U)
Oakton Community College (U)
Ocean County College (U)
Odessa College (U)
The Ohio State University (U)
Ohio University (U)
Oklahoma Panhandle State University (U)
Olympic College (U)
Oregon Coast Community College (U)
Oregon State University (U)
Ouachita Technical College (U)
Oxnard College (U)
Ozarks Technical Community College (U)
Pace University (U)
Pamlico Community College (U)
Paris Junior College (U)
Pasco-Hernando Community College (U)
Peirce College (U)
Pellissippi State Technical Community College (U)
Peninsula College (U)

Peru State College (U)
Philadelphia University (U)
Phoenix College (U)
Piedmont Community College (U)
Pikes Peak Community College (U)
Pitt Community College (U)
Portland Community College (U)
Portland State University (U)
Prairie View A&M University (U)
Pratt Community College (U)
Providence College (U)
Providence College and Theological Seminary (U)
Pulaski Technical College (U)
Purdue University (U)
Queen's University at Kingston (U)
Quinebaug Valley Community College (U)
Quinsigamond Community College (U)
Randolph Community College (U)
Rappahannock Community College (U)
Reading Area Community College (U)
Rend Lake College (U)
The Richard Stockton College of New Jersey (U)
Richmond Community College (U)
Rio Hondo College (U)
Riverside Community College District (U)
Rivier College (U)
Rochester Institute of Technology (U)
Rogers State University (U)
Roger Williams University (U)
Rose State College (U)
Rowan-Cabarrus Community College (U)
Sacramento City College (U)
St. Ambrose University (U)
St. Clair County Community College (U)
St. Cloud State University (U)
Saint Francis University (U)
St. John Fisher College (U)
St. John's University (U)
Saint Leo University (U)
St. Louis Community College (U)
Saint Paul College–A Community & Technical College (U)
Sam Houston State University (U)
Sampson Community College (U)
San Bernardino Valley College (U)
San Diego Community College District (U)
San Jacinto College District (U)
Santa Fe Community College (U)
Santa Monica College (U)
Santa Rosa Junior College (U)
Sauk Valley Community College (U)
Seminole State College of Florida (U)
Shippensburg University of Pennsylvania (U,G)
Sinclair Community College (U)
Southeast Arkansas College (U)
Southeastern Community College (U)
Southeastern Illinois College (U)
Southeastern Oklahoma State University (U)
Southern Adventist University (U)
Southern Connecticut State University (U,G)
Southern Illinois University Carbondale (U)
Southern Union State Community College (U)
South Piedmont Community College (U)
Southwestern Community College (U)
Southwest Virginia Community College (U)
Southwest Wisconsin Technical College (U)
Spartanburg Community College (U)
Spokane Community College (U)
Spring Arbor University (U)
Stanly Community College (U)
State University of New York at New Paltz (U)
State University of New York at Oswego (U)
State University of New York at Plattsburgh (U)
State University of New York College at Potsdam (U)
State University of New York Empire State College (U)
Syracuse University (G)
Tabor College (U)
Taft College (U)
Taylor University (U)
Texas State University–San Marcos (U)
Texas Woman's University (U,G)
Three Rivers Community College (U)
Tompkins Cortland Community College (U)
Trident Technical College (U)
Trinidad State Junior College (U)
Tunxis Community College (U)
Tyler Junior College (U)
Union County College (U)
University at Albany, State University of New York (U)
The University of Akron (U)
University of Alaska Fairbanks (U)
The University of Arizona (U)
University of Arkansas at Little Rock (U)
University of Bridgeport (U)
University of Central Florida (U)
University of Cincinnati Raymond Walters College (U)
University of Colorado at Colorado Springs (U)
University of Dubuque (U)
The University of Findlay (U)
University of Florida (U)
University of Great Falls (U)
University of Houston–Downtown (U)
University of Idaho (U)
University of Illinois at Springfield (U)
University of Illinois at Urbana–Champaign (U)
The University of Kansas (U)
University of Louisville (U)
University of Maine (U)
University of Maine at Augusta (U)
University of Maine at Fort Kent (U)
University of Maine at Machias (U)
University of Mary (U)
University of Massachusetts Boston (U,G)
University of Minnesota, Crookston (U)
University of Minnesota, Duluth (U)
University of Minnesota, Morris (U)
University of Missouri–Kansas City (G)
University of Nevada, Reno (U)
University of New Haven (U)
University of North Alabama (U)
The University of North Carolina at Chapel Hill (U)
University of North Dakota (U)
University of Northern Iowa (U,G)
University of North Florida (U)
University of Pittsburgh at Bradford (U)
University of Saskatchewan (U)
University of South Alabama (U,G)
University of South Carolina Sumter (U)
The University of South Dakota (U)
University of Southern Maine (U)
University of Southern Mississippi (U)
The University of Texas at Arlington (U)
The University of Texas of the Permian Basin (U)
University of the Southwest (U)
University of Waterloo (U)
The University of West Alabama (U)
University of West Georgia (U,G)
The University of Winnipeg (U)
University of Wisconsin Colleges (U)
Upper Iowa University (N,U)
Utah State University (U)
Valencia College (U)
Vincennes University (U)
Wake Technical Community College (U)
Washington State University (U)
Wayland Baptist University (U)
Wayne State University (U)
Webber International University (U)
Westchester Community College (U)
Western Kentucky University (U,G)
Western Michigan University (U)
Western Wyoming Community College (U)
West Hills Community College (U)
Westmoreland County Community College (U)
West Shore Community College (U)
West Virginia Northern Community College (U)
Wharton County Junior College (U)
Wichita State University (U)
Wilfrid Laurier University (U)
Wilkes Community College (U)
Windward Community College (U)
Winston-Salem State University (U)
Wisconsin Indianhead Technical College (N,U)
Worcester State University (U)
Yavapai College (U)
York County Community College (U)
York Technical College (U)
York University (U)

SOCIOLOGY AND ANTHROPOLOGY

Acadia University (U)
Arapahoe Community College (U)
Cayuga County Community College (U)
City Colleges of Chicago System (U)
Clovis Community College (U)
Harrisburg Area Community College (U)
Iowa Lakes Community College (U)
Lewis-Clark State College (U)
Lock Haven University of Pennsylvania (U)
Marquette University (U)
North Carolina State University (U)
North Dakota State University (U)
The Ohio State University (U)
Ohio University (U)
Sacramento City College (U)
Sinclair Community College (U)
Spokane Community College (U)
University of Alaska Fairbanks (U)
University of Illinois at Urbana–Champaign (U,G)
University of Maine at Machias (U)
University of North Florida (U)
University of Saskatchewan (U)
University of Wisconsin–La Crosse (U)
Wayne State University (U)

SOIL SCIENCES

Austin Peay State University (U)
Cedarville University (U)
Dakota College at Bottineau (U)
Haywood Community College (U)
North Carolina State University (U,G)
Oregon State University (U)
The University of British Columbia (U)
University of Florida (U,G)
University of Illinois at Urbana–Champaign (G)
University of Saskatchewan (N)
Western Kentucky University (U)

SOMATIC BODYWORK AND RELATED THERAPEUTIC SERVICES

Burlington College (U)
Goddard College (G)

SPECIAL EDUCATION

Acadia University (U)
Athabasca University (G)
Auburn University (G)
Austin Peay State University (U)
Baldwin-Wallace College (G)
Ball State University (G)
Boise State University (U)
Brenau University (U)
Bridgewater State University (U,G)
Brigham Young University (U)
California State University, Sacramento (U)
Campbellsville University (U,G)
Cedarville University (U)
College of Saint Mary (U,G)
Cossatot Community College of the University of Arkansas (N)
Dakota State University (U)
Dallas Baptist University (U)
Drake University (U)
D'Youville College (U,G)
Eastern Kentucky University (G)
Eastern Wyoming College (U)
Fayetteville State University (U,G)
Fitchburg State University (U)
Florida State University (G)
Fort Hays State University (U,G)
Framingham State University (G)
Gannon University (U)
Glenville State College (U)
Grand Valley State University (G)
Granite State College (G)
Hofstra University (G)
Holyoke Community College (U)
Illinois State University (G)
Indiana State University (G)
Jacksonville State University (U,G)
James Madison University (N,G)
Johnson State College (U)
Kean University (U,G)
La Sierra University (N)
Lesley University (G)
Lewis-Clark State College (U)
Liberty University (G)
McNeese State University (U)
Middlesex Community College (U)
Middle Tennessee State University (G)
Minot State University (U,G)
Mississippi State University (U)
Nashville State Technical Community College (U)
National University (G)
New Jersey City University (U,G)
New Mexico Highlands University (U,G)
New Mexico State University (G)
North Carolina Central University (G)
Northeastern State University (U)
The Ohio State University (N)
Penn State University Park (G)
Pittsburg State University (G)
The Richard Stockton College of New Jersey (U)
St. Cloud State University (U)
Saint Mary-of-the-Woods College (U)
St. Petersburg College (U)
San Diego State University (U)
Seton Hill University (U)
Shippensburg University of Pennsylvania (U,G)
Slippery Rock University of Pennsylvania (U,G)
Southeastern Oklahoma State University (G)
Southern Oregon University (U)
South Piedmont Community College (U)
Spring Arbor University (U)
State University of New York at Plattsburgh (G)
Stephen F. Austin State University (U,G)
Tarleton State University (G)
The University of Akron (U,G)
The University of Arizona (G)
University of Arkansas at Little Rock (G)
University of Dubuque (U)
University of Florida (G)
University of Illinois at Urbana–Champaign (U,G)
The University of Kansas (G)
University of Louisville (G)
University of Maine (U)
University of Maine at Fort Kent (U)
University of Mary Washington (G)
University of Massachusetts Boston (G)
University of Minnesota, Duluth (U,G)
University of North Dakota (G)
University of North Florida (U)
University of Oregon (U,G)
University of Saskatchewan (U)
University of South Alabama (G)
University of Southern Mississippi (U,G)
The University of Tennessee at Martin (G)
The University of Texas of the Permian Basin (G)
University of the Southwest (U)
University of Utah (U)
The University of West Alabama (U)
University of West Florida (G)
University of West Georgia (U,G)
Utah State University (U,G)
Wayne Community College (U)
Wayne State College (U,G)
Wayne State University (G)
Webster University (G)
Western Carolina University (U)
Western Kentucky University (G)

STATISTICS

Albertus Magnus College (U)
Allen Community College (U)
Anne Arundel Community College (U)
Arapahoe Community College (U)
Arkansas State University–Beebe (U)
Athabasca University (N,U)
Auburn University (U)
Austin Peay State University (U)
Baptist Bible College of Pennsylvania (U)
Bellevue College (U)
Belmont Technical College (U)
Bloomsburg University of Pennsylvania (U)
Boise State University (U)
Brenau University (U)
Brigham Young University (U)
Brigham Young University–Idaho (U)
Broward College (U)
Bryant University (G)
Burlington County College (U)
Butler Community College (U)
California State University, Sacramento (U)
Cascadia Community College (U)
Cayuga County Community College (U)
Centralia College (U)
Central Texas College (U)
Charter Oak State College (U)
Chattanooga State Community College (U)
Chemeketa Community College (U)
City Colleges of Chicago System (U)
Clatsop Community College (U)
Clemson University (G)
Cleveland Community College (U)
Cleveland State Community College (U)
Clinton Community College (U)
Clovis Community College (U)
Coleman University (U)
College of San Mateo (U)
College of Southern Maryland (U)
Colorado Mountain College (U)
Community College of Beaver County (U)
Cornell University (U,G)
Dallas Baptist University (U,G)
Dickinson State University (U)
Drexel University (N,G)
D'Youville College (U,G)
Eastern West Virginia Community and Technical College (U)
East Georgia College (U)
Edison State Community College (U)
Erie Community College (U)
Erie Community College, North Campus (U)
Erie Community College, South Campus (U)
Ferris State University (U)
Fitchburg State University (U)
Franklin Pierce University (G)
Front Range Community College (U)
Gannon University (U)
Genesee Community College (U)
Graceland University (U)
Harrisburg Area Community College (U)
Hofstra University (U,G)
Holyoke Community College (U)
Hopkinsville Community College (U)
Illinois Eastern Community Colleges, Wabash Valley College (U)
Indiana Wesleyan University (G)
Iowa Valley Community College District (U)
Jacksonville State University (U,G)
James Madison University (U)
Jamestown Community College (U)
The Johns Hopkins University (G)
Kansas State University (U)
Kirkwood Community College (U)
Lackawanna College (U)
Lansing Community College (U)
Lock Haven University of Pennsylvania (U)

Long Beach City College (U)
Los Angeles Trade-Technical College (U)
Louisiana State University and Agricultural and Mechanical College (U)
Macon State College (U)
Marist College (U)
Marshall University (U)
Memorial University of Newfoundland (U)
Mercy College of Northwest Ohio (U)
MGH Institute of Health Professions (U)
Miami Dade College (U)
Miami University–Regional Campuses (U)
Middlesex Community College (U)
Midland College (U)
Mid-State Technical College (U)
Minot State University (U)
Misericordia University (U)
Mississippi State University (U)
Monroe College (U)
Montgomery County Community College (U)
Moorpark College (U)
Motlow State Community College (U)
Mountain State University (U)
Mount Wachusett Community College (U)
Nassau Community College (U)
Naugatuck Valley Community College (U)
New England College of Business and Finance (U)
New England Institute of Technology (U)
New Mexico State University (U)
New Mexico State University–Carlsbad (U)
New River Community College (U)
Nichols College (U,G)
North Arkansas College (U)
North Carolina State University (U,G)
North Iowa Area Community College (U)
North Lake College (U)
North Seattle Community College (U)
North Shore Community College (U)
Northwestern Michigan College (U)
Northwest-Shoals Community College (U)
Notre Dame College (U)
Oakton Community College (U)
Ocean County College (U)
Oklahoma State University (U)
Oregon Coast Community College (U)
Oregon State University (U)
Pace University (U)
Pellissippi State Technical Community College (U)
Penn State University Park (G)
Pennsylvania College of Technology (U)
Philadelphia University (U,G)
Portland Community College (U)
Portland State University (U)
Presentation College (U)
Queen's University at Kingston (U)
Reading Area Community College (U)
The Richard Stockton College of New Jersey (U)
Rochester Institute of Technology (U,G)
Rockland Community College (G)
Sacramento City College (U)
St. Clair County Community College (U)
St. Cloud State University (U,G)
Saint Francis University (U)
Sam Houston State University (U)
San Diego Community College District (U)
San Jacinto College District (U)
Seton Hill University (U)
Simmons College (N)
Sinclair Community College (U)
Slippery Rock University of Pennsylvania (U)
Southeast Arkansas College (U)
Southeastern Illinois College (U)
Southeastern Oklahoma State University (U)
Southern Adventist University (U)
South Piedmont Community College (U)
Southwest Virginia Community College (U)
Southwest Wisconsin Technical College (U)
Spartanburg Community College (U)
Spoon River College (U)
State University of New York at Plattsburgh (U)
State University of New York Empire State College (U)
Stephens College (U)
Syracuse University (U)
Tabor College (U)
Taft College (U)
Texas A&M University–Corpus Christi (U)
Toccoa Falls College (U)
The University of Akron (U,G)
The University of Alabama in Huntsville (G)
University of Alaska Fairbanks (U)
University of Arkansas at Little Rock (U)
University of Central Florida (U)
The University of Findlay (U)
University of Florida (U,G)
University of Houston–Downtown (U)
University of Idaho (U,G)
University of Illinois at Chicago (G)
The University of Kansas (U)
University of Louisville (U)
University of Maine at Augusta (U)
University of Maine at Machias (U)
University of Management and Technology (U)
University of Massachusetts Boston (U,G)
University of Michigan–Flint (U)
University of Minnesota, Crookston (U)
University of Minnesota, Duluth (U)
University of Minnesota, Morris (U)
University of Nevada, Reno (U)
University of New England (U)
University of New Haven (G)
The University of North Carolina at Asheville (U)
The University of North Carolina at Chapel Hill (U)
University of North Dakota (U)
University of Northern Iowa (U)
The University of South Dakota (U)
University of Southern Maine (U)
University of Southern Mississippi (G)
The University of Texas at Dallas (G)
The University of Texas of the Permian Basin (G)
University of Utah (U)
University of Waterloo (U)
University of West Florida (U)
University of Wisconsin Colleges (U)
University of Wisconsin–Green Bay (U)
Upper Iowa University (N,U)
Utah State University (U)
Valencia College (U)
Western Kentucky University (U,G)
West Hills Community College (U)
West Virginia State University (U)
Wisconsin Indianhead Technical College (N,U)
Worcester State University (U)
York University (U)

STUDENT COUNSELING AND PERSONNEL SERVICES

Austin Peay State University (U)
Canisius College (G)
College of the Siskiyous (U)
Indiana State University (G)
Indiana University of Pennsylvania (G)
Jacksonville State University (U)
James Madison University (N)
Monroe College (U)
Pace University (G)
Seton Hall University (G)
Southern Arkansas University–Magnolia (G)
University of Massachusetts Boston (G)
University of North Dakota (G)
Western Kentucky University (U,G)

SURVEYING ENGINEERING

Auburn University (N)
Michigan Technological University (U,G)
Missouri University of Science and Technology (N)
Wake Technical Community College (U)

SUSTAINABILITY STUDIES

Austin Peay State University (N)
Cleary University (G)
Goddard College (U)
University of Waterloo (G)
Wayne Community College (U)

SYSTEMS ENGINEERING

Columbia University (N,G)
Grantham University (G)
Mid-State Technical College (U)
Missouri University of Science and Technology (N,G)
Penn State University Park (G)
Southern Methodist University (G)
The University of Alabama in Huntsville (G)
University of Florida (N,G)
University of Illinois at Urbana–Champaign (G)
Worcester Polytechnic Institute (G)

SYSTEMS SCIENCE AND THEORY

Florida Institute of Technology (G)
Syracuse University (G)
Western Kentucky University (G)
Worcester Polytechnic Institute (G)

TAXATION

Alcorn State University (U)
The American College (U,G)
Athabasca University (N,G)
Brenau University (U,G)
Bronx Community College of the City University of New York (U)
Bryant University (N)
Columbus State Community College (U)
Daytona State College (U)
DeVry University Online (G)
Miami Dade College (U)
Middlesex Community College (U)
Minnesota School of Business–Richfield (U)
Monroe College (U)
Slippery Rock University of Pennsylvania (U)

State University of New York Institute of Technology (G)
Suffolk University (G)
The University of Akron (U,G)
University of Maine at Augusta (U)
University of New Haven (G)
University of Toronto (N)

TEACHING ASSISTANTS/AIDES

Angelina College (N)
Arapahoe Community College (U)
Austin Peay State University (U)
Chatham University (G)
Clemson University (N)
Cleveland Community College (U)
College of the Siskiyous (U)
Dakota College at Bottineau (U)
Drexel University (G)
Haywood Community College (U)
Hopkinsville Community College (N)
Luna Community College (U)
Quinsigamond Community College (N)
The Richard Stockton College of New Jersey (N)
Southeast Arkansas College (N)
South Piedmont Community College (U)
University of Alaska Fairbanks (U)
University of Michigan–Flint (N)

TELECOMMUNICATIONS MANAGEMENT

Arapahoe Community College (U)
North Dakota State University (N)

TEXTILE SCIENCES AND ENGINEERING

North Carolina State University (U)
University of Florida (U)

THEOLOGICAL AND MINISTERIAL STUDIES

Amridge University (N,U,G)
Andover Newton Theological School (G)
Ashland University (G)
Bakke Graduate University (G)
Baptist Bible College of Pennsylvania (U,G)
Baptist Missionary Association Theological Seminary (N,U,G)
Barclay College (U)
Bob Jones University (U,G)
Bradley University (U)
The Catholic Distance University (N,U,G)
Central Bible College (U)
Clear Creek Baptist Bible College (N,U)
College of Emmanuel and St. Chad (G)
Columbia International University (N,U,G)
Covenant Theological Seminary (N,G)
Crown College (G)
Dallas Baptist University (U,G)
Dallas Christian College (U)
Danville Community College (U)
Defiance College (U)
Denver Seminary (G)
Drew University (N,G)
Duquesne University (U)
Earlham School of Religion (G)
Eastern Mennonite University (G)
Franciscan University of Steubenville (N,U,G)
Free Will Baptist Bible College (N,U)
Fuller Theological Seminary (N)
Global University (N,U,G)
God's Bible School and College (U)
Golden Gate Baptist Theological Seminary (G)
Hope International University (G)
Indiana Wesleyan University (G)
Institute for Christian Studies (G)
Liberty University (G)
Life Pacific College (U)
Lincoln Christian University (N,U,G)
Lourdes College (U)
Marian University (U)
Marylhurst University (U,G)
Master's College and Seminary (U)
Moody Bible Institute (N,U,G)
Naropa University (N)
Nebraska Christian College (U)
Newman Theological College (N,U)
Nyack College (U,G)
Piedmont Baptist College and Graduate School (U,G)
Prairie Bible Institute (U,G)
Providence College (U)
Providence College and Theological Seminary (N,U,G)
Regent College (N,G)
Regent University (U,G)
St. Andrew's College (G)
Saint Mary-of-the-Woods College (G)
St. Mary's University (G)
St. Stephen's College (G)
Sioux Falls Seminary (G)
Southwestern Adventist University (U)
Southwestern Baptist Theological Seminary (U,G)
Summit Pacific College (N,U)
Taylor University (U)
Toccoa Falls College (U)
Trinity International University (G)
Unification Theological Seminary (N,G)
University of Dubuque (G)
University of Great Falls (U)
University of Mary (U)
Western Seminary (N,G)
Williamson Christian College (U)

THEOLOGY AND RELIGIOUS VOCATIONS RELATED

Andover Newton Theological School (G)
Aquinas Institute of Theology (G)
Austin Peay State University (U)
Bakke Graduate University (G)
Baptist Bible College of Pennsylvania (U,G)
Baptist Missionary Association Theological Seminary (N,U,G)
Burlington College (U)
The Catholic Distance University (N,U,G)
Central Bible College (U)
Clear Creek Baptist Bible College (N,U)
College of Emmanuel and St. Chad (G)
Columbia International University (N,U,G)
Covenant Theological Seminary (N,G)
Dallas Baptist University (U)
Dallas Christian College (U)
Defiance College (U)
Duquesne University (U)
Earlham School of Religion (G)
Free Will Baptist Bible College (N,U)
Fuller Theological Seminary (G)
George Fox University (G)
Global University (N,U,G)
God's Bible School and College (U)
Golden Gate Baptist Theological Seminary (G)
Indiana Wesleyan University (G)
La Roche College (U)
Liberty University (U,G)
Lincoln Christian University (U)
Marquette University (U)
Marylhurst University (G)
Master's College and Seminary (U)
Moody Bible Institute (U,G)
Naropa University (N)
Nebraska Christian College (U)
Nyack College (U,G)
Ozarks Technical Community College (U)
Portland Community College (N)
Providence College and Theological Seminary (N,U,G)
Regent College (N,G)
Regent University (U,G)
St. Andrew's College (G)
St. John's University (U)
Saint Joseph's College of Maine (U,G)
Saint Mary-of-the-Woods College (U,G)
Sioux Falls Seminary (G)
Southwestern Baptist Theological Seminary (G)
Taylor University (U)
Union Presbyterian Seminary (N,G)
University of Dubuque (N)
Western Kentucky University (U)
Western Seminary (N,G)

TRANSPORTATION AND MATERIALS MOVING RELATED

Clark State Community College (N)
Florida Institute of Technology (G)
Minnesota School of Business–Online (U)
Missouri University of Science and Technology (N)
North Dakota State University (G)
North Lake College (U)
Riverside Community College District (U)
Sacramento City College (U)
Wake Technical Community College (U)

URBAN STUDIES/AFFAIRS

Bakke Graduate University (G)
DePaul University (G)
Eastern Washington University (G)
Florida State University (U)
Goddard College (G)
Hope International University (G)
Ozarks Technical Community College (U)
The University of Akron (U,G)
Wayne State University (U)

VEHICLE MAINTENANCE AND REPAIR TECHNOLOGIES

Arapahoe Community College (U)
Carl Sandburg College (U)
Central Wyoming College (N,U)
Columbus State Community College (U)
Midland College (N)
Naugatuck Valley Community College (U)
Sacramento City College (U)

St. Petersburg College (N)
Wayne Community College (N,U)

VETERINARY BIOMEDICAL AND CLINICAL SCIENCES

Auburn University (N)
Central Wyoming College (N)
Columbus State Community College (U)
Eastern Wyoming College (U)
Indiana Wesleyan University (G)
Kansas State University (N,U,G)
Kirkwood Community College (U)
Minnesota School of Business–Richfield (U)
Mount Wachusett Community College (N)
Purdue University (U)
Quinebaug Valley Community College (N)
Quinsigamond Community College (N)
University of Florida (G)
West Virginia University (N)

VISUAL AND PERFORMING ARTS

Academy of Art University (U,G)
Arapahoe Community College (U)
Arkansas State University–Beebe (U)
Austin Peay State University (U)
Berklee College of Music (N,U)
Burlington College (U)
California State University, San Bernardino (U)
Central Wyoming College (N)
Chatham University (U)
City Colleges of Chicago System (U)
Daytona State College (U)
East Los Angeles College (U)
George Fox University (U)
Goddard College (G)
Jacksonville State University (U)
Kean University (N)
Lakehead University (U)
Lansing Community College (U)
La Roche College (U)
Marshall University (U,G)
Massachusetts College of Art and Design (U,G)
Mesa State College (U)
Mississippi College (U)
North Georgia College & State University (U)
North Hennepin Community College (U)
North Iowa Area Community College (U)
Pace University (U)
Pulaski Technical College (U)
Regent University (U,G)
Riverside Community College District (U)
Sacramento City College (U)
Santa Rosa Junior College (U)
Sinclair Community College (U)
Southern Connecticut State University (U)
Spartanburg Community College (U)
State University of New York at Oswego (U)
Texas Woman's University (U,G)
Tompkins Cortland Community College (U)
Trident Technical College (U)
The University of Akron (U)
The University of Findlay (U)
University of Illinois at Springfield (U)
University of Illinois at Urbana–Champaign (U)
University of Maine (U)
University of Massachusetts Boston (U)
University of Michigan–Flint (U)
University of Missouri–Kansas City (U)
University of Pittsburgh at Bradford (U)
University of San Francisco (U)
The University of Texas of the Permian Basin (U)
Valencia College (U)
Wayne Community College (U)
Wayne State University (G)
Western Kentucky University (U)
West Los Angeles College (U)
Wilfrid Laurier University (U)
Worcester State University (U)

VISUAL AND PERFORMING ARTS RELATED

Angelina College (U)
Atlantic Cape Community College (U)
Austin Peay State University (U)
Bloomfield College (U)
Boise State University (U)
Brenau University (U)
Burlington College (U)
Cabrillo College (U)
Central Wyoming College (N)
Clarion University of Pennsylvania (U)
Columbus State Community College (U)
Drake University (U)
Enterprise State Community College (U)
Hocking College (U)
Jacksonville State University (U)
Lakehead University (N)
Lamar State College–Orange (U)
Lewis University (U)
Lock Haven University of Pennsylvania (U)
McNeese State University (U)
Minneapolis College of Art and Design (N,U,G)
Naugatuck Valley Community College (U)
The Ohio State University (U)
Ozarks Technical Community College (U)
Pellissippi State Technical Community College (U)
Portland Community College (N)
Sessions College for Professional Design (U)
Sinclair Community College (U)
Southern Oregon University (U)
Syracuse University (U,G)
University of Alaska Fairbanks (U)
University of Idaho (U)
University of Oregon (U)
University of Wisconsin Colleges (U)
Western Kentucky University (U)
West Virginia State University (U)
York University (U)

WILDLIFE AND WILDLANDS SCIENCE AND MANAGEMENT

Central Wyoming College (N)
Haywood Community College (U)
New Mexico State University (U)
Oregon State University (U)
Prescott College (G)
St. Petersburg College (U)
University of Alaska Fairbanks (U)
Western Kentucky University (U)

WOODWORKING

Blackhawk Technical College (N)
Burlington College (U)
Central Wyoming College (N)
Cerritos College (U)
Prescott College (N)

WORK AND FAMILY STUDIES

Alpena Community College (N)
Austin Peay State University (U)
Brigham Young University (U)
California State University, San Marcos (N)
Central Michigan University (U)
Goddard College (G)
Kansas State University (N,U)
Kean University (N)
McNeese State University (U)
Monroe County Community College (U)
North Carolina State University (G)
North Dakota State University (U,G)
Ozarks Technical Community College (U)
Portland Community College (U)
Rend Lake College (U)
Riverside Community College District (U)
St. Petersburg College (N)
State University of New York at Plattsburgh (U)
University of Alaska Fairbanks (U)
Wayne Community College (U)
Westchester Community College (U)
Western Kentucky University (U,G)
Western Michigan University (U,G)
West Los Angeles College (U)

ZOOLOGY/ANIMAL BIOLOGY

Austin Peay State University (U)
Cascadia Community College (U)
Central Wyoming College (U)
Cerritos College (U)
Eastern Wyoming College (U)
Kansas State University (N)
Mississippi State University (U)
North Carolina State University (U)
North Dakota State University (U)
Southeastern Community College (U)
Southern Illinois University Carbondale (U)
The University of Akron

GEOGRAPHICAL LISTING OF DISTANCE LEARNING PROGRAMS

U.S. and U.S. Territories

ALABAMA

Amridge University, 82
Andrew Jackson University, 83
Auburn University, 89
Columbia Southern University, 125
Enterprise State Community College, 142
Faulkner University, 144
Gadsden State Community College, 151
Heritage Christian University, 159
Jacksonville State University, 168
Judson College, 173
Northwest-Shoals Community College, 220
Southern Union State Community College, 261
United States Sports Academy, 279
The University of Alabama in Huntsville, 281
University of North Alabama, 301
University of South Alabama, 306
The University of West Alabama, 312

ALASKA

University of Alaska Fairbanks, 281
University of Alaska, Prince William Sound Community College, 282

ARIZONA

Arizona Western College, 86
College of the Humanities and Sciences, Harrison Middleton University, 122
Mesa Community College, 193
The Paralegal Institute, Inc., 227
Phoenix College, 230
Prescott College, 234
Sessions College for Professional Design, 253
The University of Arizona, 282
The University of Arizona, 282
Western International University, 324
Yavapai College, 331

ARKANSAS

Arkansas State University, 86
Arkansas State University–Beebe, 86
Arkansas State University–Mountain Home, 87
Arkansas Tech University, 87
Cossatot Community College of the University of Arkansas, 128
North Arkansas College, 213
NorthWest Arkansas Community College, 219
Ouachita Technical College, 225
Pulaski Technical College, 235
Southeast Arkansas College, 257
Southern Arkansas University–Magnolia, 259
University of Arkansas at Little Rock, 282

CALIFORNIA

Academy of Art University, 79
American Graduate University, 82
Anaheim University, 83
Antelope Valley College, 85
Cabrillo College, 103
California State University, Chico, 104
California State University, Dominguez Hills, 104
California State University, East Bay, 105
California State University, Monterey Bay, 105
California State University, Sacramento, 105
California State University, San Bernardino, 105
California State University, San Marcos, 106
Cerritos College, 113
Citrus College, 116
Cogswell Polytechnical College, 120
Coleman University, 120
College of San Mateo, 121
College of the Desert, 122
College of the Siskiyous, 122
East Los Angeles College, 140
El Camino College, 141
Fielding Graduate University, 145
Fuller Theological Seminary, 150
Golden Gate Baptist Theological Seminary, 155
Hope International University, 162
La Sierra University, 179
Lassen Community College District, 179
Life Pacific College, 182
Long Beach City College, 184
Los Angeles Harbor College, 184
Los Angeles Trade-Technical College, 185
Moorpark College, 203
National University, 208
Orange Coast College, 224
Oxnard College, 225
Pacific States University, 227
Perelandra College, 230
Rio Hondo College, 240
Riverside Community College District, 240
Sacramento City College, 243
Samuel Merritt University, 250
San Bernardino Valley College, 250
San Diego Community College District, 251
San Diego State University, 251
Santa Monica College, 252
Santa Rosa Junior College, 252
Shasta Bible College, 255
Sonoma State University, 257
Taft College, 272
University of California, Davis, 284
University of California, Riverside, 284
University of San Francisco, 305
University of Southern California, 307
University of the Pacific, 310
Vanguard University of Southern California, 319
West Hills Community College, 326
West Los Angeles College, 326

COLORADO

Adams State College, 80
Arapahoe Community College, 85
Colorado Mountain College, 123
Colorado State University, 123
Colorado Technical University Colorado Springs, 123
Denver Seminary, 133
Front Range Community College, 150
Heritage College, 159
Jones International University, 172
Mesa State College, 194
Naropa University, 207
Nazarene Bible College, 208
Pikes Peak Community College, 231
Trinidad State Junior College, 277
University of Colorado at Colorado Springs, 286
University of Colorado Boulder, 286
University of Denver, 286

CONNECTICUT

Albertus Magnus College, 80
Capital Community College, 107
Charter Oak State College, 114
Gateway Community College, 152
Hartford Seminary, 158
Holy Apostles College and Seminary, 161
Middlesex Community College, 195
Naugatuck Valley Community College, 208
Northwestern Connecticut Community College, 219
Quinebaug Valley Community College, 236
Quinnipiac University, 236
Southern Connecticut State University, 259
Three Rivers Community College, 276
Tunxis Community College, 278
University of Bridgeport, 283
University of New Haven, 301
Yale University, 331

DISTRICT OF COLUMBIA

American University, 82

FLORIDA

The Baptist College of Florida, 92
Broward College, 101
Daytona State College, 132
Everest University, 144
Florida Hospital College of Health Sciences, 146
Florida Institute of Technology, 146
Florida State University, 146
Florida Tech University Online, 147
Hillsborough Community College, 160
Hobe Sound Bible College, 160
Hodges University, 161
Kaplan University Online, 174

GEORGIA

HAWAII

IDAHO

ILLINOIS

INDIANA

IOWA

KANSAS

KENTUCKY

LOUISIANA

MAINE

MARYLAND

MASSACHUSETTS

MICHIGAN

MINNESOTA

MISSISSIPPI

MISSOURI

MONTANA

NEBRASKA

NEVADA

NEW HAMPSHIRE

NEW JERSEY

NEW MEXICO

NEW YORK

NORTH CAROLINA

NORTH DAKOTA

OHIO

OKLAHOMA

OREGON

PENNSYLVANIA

PUERTO RICO

RHODE ISLAND

SOUTH CAROLINA

SOUTH DAKOTA

TENNESSEE

TEXAS

UTAH

VERMONT

VIRGINIA

WASHINGTON

WEST VIRGINIA

WISCONSIN

WYOMING

Canada

ALBERTA

BRITISH COLUMBIA

MANITOBA

NEW BRUNSWICK

NEWFOUNDLAND AND LABRADOR

NOVA SCOTIA

ONTARIO

SASKATCHEWAN

ORGANIZATION	WEB SITE	INFORMATION PROVIDED
Interviewing Skills	**http://www.winway.com/ unlawful_questions.htm**	Includes advice for interviewees on how to react to and answer unlawful interview questions that violate EEOC regulations.
The Monster Board	**http://www.monster.com/**	A gathering place and information resource for HR professionals.
National Labor Relations Board (NLRB)	**http://www.doc.gov:80/nlrb/ homepg.html**	Home page of the National Labor Relations Board; includes an information locater and continuous updates of NLRB decisions.
Occupational Safety and Health Administration (OSHA)	**http://www.osha.gov/**	Home page of OSHA, which monitors many aspects of U.S. workplace safety and health.
Retirement Planning Associates, Inc.	**http://www.insworld.com/ Newsletter/index.html**	Articles from *Benefits Insights*, a nontechnical newsletter for managers who deal with retirement planning issues.
Society for Human Resource Management(SHRM)	**http://www.shrm.org/**	Home page of SHRM; summarizes the latest developments in HRM on a daily basis.
Thunderbird School of International Management	**http://www.t-bird.edu/**	Provides access to outstanding sources of international business and HR information.
Training Net	**http://www.trainingnet.com/**	An information resource for training professionals.
Workflow and Reengineering International Association (WARIA)	**http://vvv.com/waria/**	Provides information on workflow and reengineering publications and conferences.

Gómez–Mejía, Balkin, and Cardy's **HRM** Home Page

Be sure to check out this textbook's Web site at:

http://www.prenhall.com/gomez

*Please note that URLs (Web addresses) change frequently. If a URL does not work, try finding the site through an Internet search engine, such as Yahoo, Excite!, or Lycos.

Second Editon

MANAGING HUMAN RESOURCES

Luis R. Gómez-Mejía
Arizona State University

David B. Balkin
University of Colorado, Boulder

Robert L. Cardy
Arizona State University

PRENTICE HALL
UPPER SADDLE RIVER, NEW JERSEY 07458

Executive Editor: Natalie Anderson
Development Editor: Steven A. Rigolosi
Associate Editor: Lisamarie Brassini
Editorial Assistant: Crissy Statuto/Dawn-Marie Reisner
Editor-in-Chief: James Boyd
Director of Development: Steve Deitmer
Marketing Manager: Stephanie Johnson
Senior Production Editor: Cynthia Regan
Managing Editor: Dee Josephson
Manufacturing Buyer: Kenneth J. Clinton
Manufacturing Supervisor: Arnold Vila
Electronic Page Makeup Artist: Christy Mahon
Electronic Art Manager: Warren Fischbach
Electronic Art Specialist: Annie Bartell
Senior Manager of Production & Technology: Lorraine Patsco
Production Assistant: Theresa Festa
Senior Designer: Ann France
Design Director: Patricia Wosczyk
Interior & Cover Design: Ox and Company
Cover Art/Photo: Jude Maceren

A Simon & Schuster Company
Upper Saddle River, New Jersey 07458

Library of Congress Cataloging-in-Publication Data

Gómez-Mejía, Luis R.
Managing human resources / Luis R. Gómez-Mejía, David B. Balkin, Robert L. Cardy.—2nd ed.
p. cm.
Includes index.
ISBN 0-13-270943-0
1. Personnel management. I. Balkin, David B. II. Cardy, Robert L. III. Title.
HF5549.G64 1988 97-2384
658.3—dc21 CIP

Prentice-Hall International (UK) Limited, London
Prentice-Hall of Australia Pty. Limited, Sydney
Prentice-Hall Canada, Inc., Toronto
Prentice-Hall Hispanoamericana, S.A., Mexico
Prentice-Hall of India Private Limited, New Delhi
Prentice-Hall of Japan, Inc., Tokyo
Simon & Schuster Asia Pte. Ltd., Singapore
Editora Prentice-Hall do Brasil, Ltda., Rio de Janeiro

Printed in the United States of America
10 9 8 7 6 5 4 3 2

▶ *To my wife, Diane, and my two sons,*
Vince and Alex
—L.G.M.

▶ *To my parents, Daniel and Jeanne*
—D.B.B.

▶ *To my parents, Ralph and Dorothy; my wife, Laurel;*
and my two daughters, Lara and Emery
—R.L.C.

Brief Contents

▸ I. Introduction

▸ II. The Contexts of Human Resource Management

▸ III. Staffing

▸ IV. Employee Development

▸ V. Compensation

▸ VI. Governance

Contents

PART SIX ▸ GOVERNANCE 395

CHAPTER 13 DEVELOPING EMPLOYEE RELATIONS AND COMMUNICATIONS 395

CHAPTER 14 RESPECTING EMPLOYEE RIGHTS AND MANAGING DISCIPLINE 422

FEATURES

Issues + Applications **Highlighting Current Issues and Debates in Human Resource Management**

Manager's Notebooks

Tips, Procedures, and Strategies for Managing People in Organizations

Building Managerial Skills

Text Sections Focusing on the General Manager's Role in Managing Human Resources

Thematic Examples

Global HRM/Work Force Diversity

Chapter	Example	Page
1	Hong Kong jobs move to China as a cost-saving measure	4
	Diversity trends regarding minorities, women, and the age composition of the U.S. work force	4–5
	The globalization of the economy	5
2	Teams at GM's Opel plant in Eastern Germany	48
	Challenges to reengineering in Europe	53–54
	Use of general job descriptions at Nissan	68
	Guidelines for writing job descriptions so that women, minorities, and people with disabilities are not discriminated against	71
	Use of contingent workers in Japan, France, Britain, and Spain	72
	Outsourcing at Bennetton	73
	Internships at Seal Press, a woman-owned publishing company in Seattle, Washington	74
3	McDonald's socially responsible practice of hiring learning-disabled youth	86
	Anti-discrimination legislation, including the Equal Pay Act, Title VII, Age Discrimination in Employment Act, and Americans With Disabilities Act	89–100
	Affirmative action programs across the globe	103–104
4	Managing work force diversity: entire chapter (includes discussions of various minority groups and diversity awareness programs)	115–143
	Comparison of U.S. diversity efforts with those of other countries (Mexico and Japan)	122
	Global comparisons of day-care options provided to working mothers	134
5	Subordinates hire managers at Brazilian firm, Semco	153
	College recruitment practices in Japan	154
	Recruitment of protected classes	157
	Assessment centers at Mercury Communications, a British telecom company	167
	Use of graphology in Europe to screen applicants	168
6	Opportunity for greater diversity as a benefit of employee separations	183
	Japanese lifetime employment policies	188
	Use of variable pay policies as a hedge against the business cycle in Japan	190
	Requirements of advance notice for collective dismissals in European countries	192
	Tendency for minorities and women to be laid off under a seniority-based layoff criterion	192
	Global use of outplacement services	196
7	Employee diversity and conscious/unconscious bias in performance appraisal	213

Chapter	Example	Page
8	Delivering product and service quality consistently worldwide	237
	Use of apprenticeships in Europe	243
	Over-50 workers as cross-trainers	252
9	Management development programs in England	269
	Meeting the career development needs of a diverse work force	272–273
	Succession planning for a diverse work force	276
	Mentoring programs for female and minority employees	282
	Coaching programs for minority employees at Xerox	283
	Career development throughout the life cycle (younger, middle-aged, and older employees)	285–288
10	Fixed versus variable pay in the United States versus Japan	301
	Use of below-market wages in economically depressed areas with a higher proportion of women and minorities in the work force	304–305
	Job-based compensation systems biased against occupations traditionally filled by women	317
	Comparable worth legislation in Britain, Canada, and Australia	322
11	Individual pay-for-performance programs in the United States versus Japan	338
	International comparisons of executive compensation	348
	International comparisons of stock-based incentives for executives (United States, Germany, Japan)	350
12	The Canadian health care system	365
	Flexible benefits packages for a diverse work force	367–368
	Cross-country comparisons of health-care spending	374
	Women and defined contribution retirement plans	379
	Cross-country comparisons of vacation time	383
13	Male versus female communication styles	407
	Cross-cultural differences in meetings (United States, Japan, Italy)	407
	International comparisons of employee satisfaction	410
	Employee suggestion systems in Japan	415
14	Comparison of employment-at-will laws between the United States and other countries (Japan, France, Belgium, United Kingdom)	428–429
	Differing religious beliefs and family situations as reasons for absenteeism	442
	Use of probationary periods in Europe	443
	Including diverse employee groups in the recruitment and selection process	446
15	Reasons why Israeli workers join labor unions	456
	Canadian laws restricting employers from using permanent replacement workers	460
	Comparison of employee benefits systems in the United States versus Germany and Sweden	463–464

Chapter	Example	Page
15	Labor relations and unionism in Denmark, Great Britain, France, China, Sweden, Germany, and Japan	463–466
16	Controversy over genetic testing in high-paying jobs for women	503
	Death by overwork (*karoshi*) in Japan	506
17	Meeting the international HRM challenge (complete chapter, including the stages of international involvement, determining the mix of host-country and expatriate employees, managing expatriates, using HRM policies to enhance international operations, and developing HRM policies in a global context)	515–544

Managing Quality with Human Resources

Chapter	Example	Page
1	Introduction to and definition of total quality management (TQM)	8
2	Quality-based competition at Kodak	49
	Use of flat and boundaryless organization structures in organizations implementing a TQM strategy	51–52
	Work flow analysis in TQM programs	52
	Use of problem-solving teams in a TQM effort	56
	TQM as a reason for using general job descriptions	68
4	U.S. record of quality against that of other nations	120
	Diversity programs alongside TQM programs	131
5	Selection methods and TQM	169
7	Quality problems associated with outcome-based performance appraisal	211
	Performance appraisal at companies that have adopted TQM	216–217
8	Making a commitment to TQM before conducting training (Lantech, Inc.)	239–240
	Customer service training in TQM-oriented companies	256
9	Using management development and executive education programs to emphasize TQM	284
	Quality emphasis in University of Tennessee's management development program	285
11	Individual-based pay-for-performance plans and their effects on TQM programs	338
	Use of gainsharing plans in a quality environment	344
13	Bulletin board systems in a work team/TQM environment	402
	Use of voice mail in a Cadillac TQM program	404
	Employee recognition awards and TQM	415
15	Use of EI (employee involvement) groups to maintain or increase quality	468
16	Quality control and safety	489
17	Quality standards in McDonald's international operations	521

HRM in Small Businesses

CHAPTER	EXAMPLE	PAGE
1	The growth of small businesses as an organizational challenge in the twenty-first century	11–12
	The challenges of using subcontractors in a small business	14
	HR strategies at small high-tech firms	15
	Avoiding excessive concentration on the present, and planning for the future, at small companies	20
2	Fostering a small-business atmosphere within a larger company	51
3	Small business, the ADA, and reasonable accommodation	99
4	Diversity training programs in small businesses	133
5	Recruitment challenges faced by small businesses	154
6	Exit interviews at small companies (in Manager's Notebook)	183
	Nontraditional alternatives to layoff in small companies	190
7	Use of performance diaries at a small company (Azteca Foods, Inc.)	215
8	The manager's role in the training process at small companies	240
	Challenges in training at small companies (Minicase 2)	262
9	Succession planning in small businesses	277
	Mentoring programs at small businesses	282–283
10	Small businesses' use of variable pay	301
	Disadvantages of job-based compensation plans in small businesses	316
	Skill-based pay in small businesses and start-up companies	320
11	Intrapreneuring	342–343
	Team-based pay-for-performance plans at small businesses (The Published Image, Inc.)	343
	Executive/CEO compensation in small businesses	350
12	Provision of benefits in small companies (comparison with large and medium-sized businesses)	366
	Workers' compensation costs in small businesses	370
	Severance policies in small companies	384
13	Top-down and down-top communications in small businesses	399
	Nepotism in family businesses	400, 402
	Use of newsletters in a small-business environment	402
	Retreats in family businesses	408
14	Employment at will and the small business	428
15	Difficulty of organizing employees of small firms into a labor union	464
	Small businesses and union avoidance	467
16	OSHA's consultation services for small businesses	494
	Cost of proposed OSHA smoking regulations to small businesses	501
17	Opportunities for small exporting firms in the international arena	538

Technology (including Human Resource Information Systems)

Chapter	Example	Page
1	Strategic alliances in the technology industry (Figure 1-3)	10
	The rise of technology and the accompanying challenges for HRM (including a discussion of human resource information systems and the ethics of data access and use)	13–14
	Rise of the Internet	14
	Kodak's strategic approach to technology	18
2	Computer systems in the "minihospitals" at the Medical Center of Beaver (Beaver County, PA)	48
	Using computers to gather job information and conduct job analysis	62
	Technological developments as a reason for the growth of telecommuting	75
	Applications of and issues regarding human resource information systems (HRIS)	75–77
3	Enabling technologies for accommodating people with disabilities	99–100
	Using a HRIS to document decisions and comply with EEO laws	105
4	Technology helping workers with disabilities	126
5	Technology's role in forecasting productivity and labor demand	147
	HRIS in place in Wake County, North Carolina	149
6	Technology as one of the reasons behind layoffs	185
7	Computerized systems and naturally occurring outcomes	210
	Computerizing a 360° appraisal system	222
8	Virtual reality training at Motorola	236
	Use of computers and multimedia in training	244–245
9	Computer-based job posting systems, skills inventories, and career paths	278–280
10	Compensation in high-technology industries	301
	State of technology and job versus individual pay decisions	303
	Use of computers in developing a compensation plan	317
11	Technology's role in team-based pay-for-performance systems and gainsharing programs	342, 345
12	Use of computer software packages to administer flexible benefits programs	387
	Using computers to communicate benefits information to employees	388
13	Use of computers and networks to disseminate information among employees	397
	Audiovisual and electronic communication formats (including teleconferencing, voice mail, e-mail, and multimedia)	402–406
14	Computerized personnel files in an HRIS	427
	E-mail privacy controversy	427
	Computerized performance tests as an alternative to random drug testing	431–432
	Computer crime and its costs to the organization	432
	Electronic monitoring and computer security controls	432–434

CHAPTER	EXAMPLE	PAGE
15	Saturn's ability to change technology with the blessing of its labor union	466–467
16	Communicating safety programs with computers and other media	505
17	Use of telecommunications technology to keep expatriates in touch with the home office	525

Reengineering, Outsourcing, and Downsizing

CHAPTER	EXAMPLE	PAGE
1	Downsizing and layoffs at AT&T	2
	Weak response to international competition as a reason for layoffs in the United States	5
	Downsizing and restructuring as organizational challenges in the twenty-first century	9
2	Introduction to business process reengineering (BPR)	52–53
	Challenges to reengineering in Europe	54–55
	Downsizing of overly specialized jobs	60
	Increased use of managerial and professional temps as a result of downsizing	72
	Restructuring of core jobs into temporary positions as a result of downsizing	72
3	Affirmative action laws with regard to layoffs	88
4	Creative solutions of diverse task forces regarding downsizing	120
5	Effect of downsizing on recruitment efforts	154
6	Full chapter: "Managing Employee Separations, Downsizing, and Outplacement," including discussions of downsizing, rightsizing, and management of layoffs and early retirements	179–200
9	Workers' increased demands for career development as a result of downsizing and technological changes	269
	Layoffs/downsizing and self-development activities	270
	Middle-aged employees and plateauing as a result of downsizings and corporate restructuring	286
	Self-development in an age of downsizing and reorganizing	288
10	Using nonmonetary rewards during economic hard times	305, 316
11	Reorganizing an organizational structure into teams as a result of downsizing; use of team-based pay-for-performance programs	342
12	Relation of downsizing and layoffs to the unemployment tax rate levied on employers	371
	Use of severance packages following layoffs	384

Chapter	Example	Page
13	Communication efforts during downsizings, restructurings, and layoffs	398
	Use of videotapes to announce and explain a downsizing and layoff	402
	Use of employee assistance programs (EAPs) in a downsizing or restructuring effort	414
14	Implied contracts and the layoff decision	425
15	Unions' concerns with outsourcing and subcontracting	464
	German unions' use of codetermination to prevent layoffs	465
	Downsizings in Germany and Japan	466
	Layoff procedures in unionized companies (last-in, first-out rule)	480
	Xerox reserves the right to outsource in its agreement with unions (Minicase 2)	484
16	Layoffs or downsizings as a reason for violence in the workplace	499
17	How restructuring and downsizing have affected expatriates' compensation packages	530

PREFACE

The Plan of the Second Edition

Success in today's competitive business environment is increasingly a function of effective human resource management. Structure and technology can be easily duplicated. The factor that can set apart an organization—whether in manufacturing or services, or in the private or public sector—is its people. The quality of the organization's employees, their enthusiasm and satisfaction with their jobs, and their sense of fair treatment all impact the firm's productivity, level of customer service, reputation, and survival. In short, people make the difference.

Because all business students need to understand human resource issues, we adopted a managerial perspective in our first edition of *Managing Human Resources*. The managerial perspective means presenting and dealing with HR issues in a manner that is relevant to all students of business. We believe this approach works best because managers in all departments and functions confront HR issues daily. This means that an important part of the supervisor's job is dealing with people issues. Very few issues regarding the management of people can, or should, be routinely delegated to the HR department. For this reason, textbooks that approach HRM solely from the perspective of the HR department misrepresent how organizations deal with their HR issues. Such texts do not make the dynamic field of HRM relevant to students who do not plan to become HR specialists.

Since the first edition of *Managing Human Resources* was published in 1995, the general management perspective has become much more prevalent among practicing managers. Recent environmental and organizational forces have contributed greatly to this trend. Organizations are becoming flatter, and managers are expected to be generalists with a broad set of skills, including HRM skills. At the same time, fewer and fewer firms have a highly centralized and powerful HR department serving as a monitor, decision maker, and controller of HR practices throughout the organization. Indeed, international competition and a rapidly changing environment have made this type of organization almost obsolete.

The growing importance of a general management perspective to HRM has not lessened the importance of HR specialists, however. Many tools and techniques for selection, training, compensation, performance appraisal, and other traditional HR functions can greatly enhance the quality of hires, the skills of the work force, job satisfaction, and employee motivation. But HR specialists' focus has shifted from one of control to one of advice and support to line managers. The forces reinforcing this trend include downsizing, outsourcing of the HR function, and the inclusion of HR courses in masters', undergraduate, and executive education programs designed for the general manager (rather than the HR specialist).

Our goal for the second edition of *Managing Human Resources* is to emphasize general management applications even more than we did in the first edition. Among the innovative features of the second edition:

- A greater practical orientation—new material in every chapter on "Building Managerial Skills" and more Manager's Notebooks.
- Dozens of new examples, new art, and data updated using the most recent numbers available.
- The most up-to-date research from academic journals and the business press.
- An Internet site of interest to managers at the beginning of each chapter.

- A computer-based HRM simulation tied to each chapter's content.
- Almost 30 completely new minicases and case studies.

The response to the first edition has been very gratifying. Based on feedback we received, we have shortened the text to focus more tightly on general management issues. The second edition is 128 pages shorter than the first. We have preserved the core content of the HRM course, but some technical details and functional concerns (such as evaluation of the HR function and quality control) now appear in the Instructor's Manual.

Organization

Managing Human Resources includes an introductory chapter followed by 16 chapters. The book is divided into six parts.

Part One provides an overview of emerging challenges in the strategic management of human resources. We identified these challenges through an extensive analysis of the HR issues appearing in the business press over the past five years. We address these challenges in detail in later chapters. Part One also addresses the respective roles of and necessary collaboration between managers and the HR department.

Part Two considers the contexts in which HRM takes place. The contextual factors include work structures and work flows, the legal environment, and work force diversity. The chapter on work flows (2) discusses how a company can organize its business and its human resources to achieve its objectives. The chapter on legal issues (3) addresses the legal challenges and constraints facing organizations. The last chapter in this part (4) explores the challenges of effectively managing an increasingly diverse work force.

Part Three presents staffing issues and considers how organizations can effectively recruit, select, socialize, and phase out employees. The chapter on recruitment, selection, and socialization (5) examines the process by which organizations attract human resources and then effectively select among the applicants. The chapter on employee separations, downsizing, and outplacement (6) discusses the process of terminating the employment relationship, exploring alternatives to layoffs and different approaches to downsizing the work force.

Part Four addresses the development of human resources. The chapter on appraising and managing performance (7) focuses on the manager as both a judge and a coach. The chapter on training (8) presents training as an ongoing process and as a critical part of maintaining HR effectiveness. The chapter on career development (9) identifies the roles of the employee and the organization in the career development process.

Part Five examines compensation issues. The chapter on managing compensation (10) explains the important choices managers face when designing a compensation system and covers different approaches to salary management. The chapter on rewarding performance (11) examines the challenges of tying employees' pay to their performance. The benefits chapter (12) explains the significance of employee benefits programs and how managers are containing costs in this area.

Part Six looks at the governance of the workplace and the employer-employee relationship. The employee relations chapter (13) looks at how managers and the HR department can improve the quality of communications within the organization. The chapter on employee rights (14) examines the challenges of balancing those rights with the rights of managers. The chapter also offers guidelines for managing discipline and dealing with difficult employee problems such as chronic absenteeism and alcohol abuse. The organized labor chapter (15) examines why employees seek to be represented by unions and how unions alter the employer-employee relationship. The workplace safety and health chapter (16) explains the regulations that govern health and safety in the workplace and emerging health and safety issues. Finally, Chapter 17 focuses on how firms can meet global HR challenges. (Global issues are discussed throughout the book, but this chapter provides an integrated treatment of these issues.)

Two supplementary chapters, one on managing quality with human resources and the other on conducting an HR audit, are available in the Instructor's Manual.

Features

Managing Human Resources contains a number of innovative pedagogical features.

Chapter Organization

Each chapter contains a number of teaching tools:

- A set of learning objectives phrased as management challenges
- An opening vignette that draws students into the chapter
- A running marginal glossary of key terms
- A "Building Mangerial Skills" section outlining critical HRM skills
- A summary and conclusions section
- A list of key terms with page references
- Two minicases based on the experiences of small, medium-sized, and large businesses, with discussion questions
- Two case studies with critical thinking questions and cooperative learning exercises
- An exercise to accompany the computer-based *Human Resources Management Simulation* by Jerald R. Smith and Peggy Golden
- Notes and references

In addition, each chapter includes numerous examples of HRM practices at a wide variety of companies, from small, service-providing organizations to huge megacorporations. A concise dictionary of HRM terminology is provided at the end of the book, along with a subject index and a name, company, and product index.

Themes

In addition to the managerial perspective, we thread several themes throughout this book. These themes include:

- The need for proactive human resource management and cooperation between line managers and the HR department
- The importance of operating within the legal framework
- HRM in small businesses
- The effects of reorganization, outsourcing, and downsizing on HRM
- Work force diversity as a source of competitive advantage in the global economy
- The changing forces of technology and their implications for HRM
- The role of human resources in total quality management

A comprehensive, chapter-by-chapter list of the examples related to each of these themes appears after the detailed table of contents.

HRM on the Web

In just a few years, the Internet has become an essential component of business courses. Each chapter of the second edition begins with a description of a World Wide Web site maintained or sponsored by an HRM-oriented organization. Students should visit these sites at some point while studying the chapter. For example, Chapter 3 (on work force diversity) provides the URL for the Americans with Disabilities Document Center. Chapter

16 (on workplace safety and health) sends students to the home page of the Occupational Safety and Health Administration.

"Questions of Ethics"

Each chapter contains several questions aimed at generating classroom discussion of ethical issues. These are placed in the margins close to the text discussions of these issues.

Manager's Notebooks

To emphasize our managerial perspective, we've included at least one Manager's Notebook per chapter. These notebooks provide management tips on a variety of issues that managers confront daily, from reducing potential liability for sexual harassment, to managing telecommunications successfully, to conducting exit interviews.

Issues and Applications

Students enjoy reading additional examples and stories about HRM practices both in the United States and around the globe. They also enjoy sinking their teeth into current debates. To provide more information on hot topics in HRM, we've sprinkled "Issues and Applications" features throughout the text. For example, an Issues and Applications feature in Chapter 14 examines whether or not employers should have the right to deny jobs to people who smoke.

Building Managerial Skills

Because students want to take a set of skills into the workplace, each chapter includes a "Building Managerial Skills" section that provides detailed suggestions for the practice of HR management. For example, Chapter 14 provides suggestions for managing difficult employees, and Chapter 15 provides guidelines for managing integrative bargaining in a union setting.

Minicases

Each chapter includes two minicases based on the experiences of real-world companies. The discussion questions that accompany these brief exercises give students the opportunity to apply what they've learned in each chapter.

Case Studies with Critical Thinking Questions and Cooperative Learning Exercises

All chapters end with two case studies. We've developed these cases over the years and tested them in our classes, where they've generated excellent discussion. Critical thinking questions ask students to analyze the facts and situations presented in the case. Cooperative learning exercises ask students to work together, in pairs or in groups, to brainstorm ideas and arrive at solutions. Approximately 40% of the minicases and case studies are new to this edition.

HR Simulation Tie-In

Each chapter concludes with a tie-in to the *Human Resources Management Simulation*, by Jerald Golden and Peggy Smith. This computer simulation package and its accompanying workbook give student teams the opportunity to practice managing a company's HR functions in a dynamic business environment. After the team makes its decisions, the computer simulates the reaction of the firm and the labor market, then produces a report. Each team needs to consider the report's results and adjust its policies accordingly, if necessary, through several iterations.

Video Cases

Each of the six parts of the book concludes with a video case and discussion questions. The accompanying videos are included in the ABC News/Prentice Hall Video Library.

The Teaching and Learning Package

Each component of the teaching and learning package has been carefully crafted to ensure that the HRM course is rewarding for both instructors and students.

Instructor's Resource Manual with Video Guide

The IRM includes one chapter for every chapter in the student text. Each chapter includes:

- A chapter overview/lecture launcher
- Annotated outline (including all text features)
- Answers to all questions
- In-depth analysis of all in-text discussion questions, cooperative learning exercises, minicases, and case studies

The video guide includes for each clip:

- General information (title, source, air date, running time)
- A brief synopsis
- Tie-in to the text
- Suggestions for using the clip in class

The Instructor's Manual is also available on disk in ASCII format for instructors who would like to tailor the materials for their classroom needs.

Test Item File

The test item file includes 1,700 questions. Each chapter includes multiple choice, situational multiple choice, true/false, and essay questions. All questions are rated by level of difficulty (easy, moderate, challenging) and page-referenced to the text.

PH Custom Test

The test item file is designed for use with PH Custom Test, a computerized package that allows users to custom design, save, and generate classroom tests. Available in 3.5″, Windows version, PH Custom Test also permits professors to edit and add or delete questions from the test item file and to export files to various word processing programs, including WordPerfect and Microsoft Word.

For those with limited access to computers or clerical support, Prentice Hall's Telephone Testing Service allows instructors to order customized tests by calling a toll-free telephone number a few days before the test is to be administered. Please contact your Prentice Hall representative for more information.

Human Resources Simulation

The *Human Resources Management Simulation*, by Jerald R. Smith and Peggy Golden, is the first interactive, competitive business simulation game for HRM. The software and manuals realistically portray the HR department of a moderate size organization, focusing on the issues of daily HR work and asking students to make decisions that optimize the HR function. They are available as stand-alone items or shrinkwrapped to the text at a nominal fee.

Transparency Resource Package with Electronic Transparencies

There are more than 200 charts and figures in the second edition of *Managing Human Resources*. Of these, 100 have been prepared as full-color 8 1/2″ x 11″ acetates. Over 200 PowerPoint slides of figures and outlines are also available on disk.

Managing Human Resources *Web Site*

The Prentice Hall World Wide Web site devoted exclusively to this text, **http://www.prenhall.com/gomez**, is full of current examples relevant to each chapter of the book. Also visit Prentice Hall's unique PHLIP (Prentice Hall Learning on the Internet Partnership) Web site at **http://www.phlip.marist.edu** for links to "Management Web Site of the Week" and other HRM-related materials. This site has been developed *by* professors *for* professors and their students.

ABC News/Prentice Hall Video Library for Human Resource Management/Wall Street Journal/Wall Street Week in Review

ABC News and Prentice Hall have combined their experience in academic publishing and global reporting to provide a comprehensive video ancillary for the text. The library contains six news clips which correspond to the six parts of the text, from such ABC news programs as *Nightline, World News Tonight*, and *20/20*. Each clip has been chosen to illustrate the video cases that conclude each part of the text. A Video Guide is included in the Instructor's Resource Manual.

The New York Times *"Themes of the Times" Program*

The *New York Times* and Prentice Hall are sponsoring "Themes of the Times": a program designed to enhance student access to current information of relevance in the classroom.

Through this program, the core subject matter provided in the text is supplemented by a collection of time-sensitive articles from one of the world's most distinguished newspapers, the *New York Times*. These articles demonstrate the vital, ongoing connections between what is learned in the classroom and what is happening around us.

A new edition of the mini-newspaper is available semiannually. In addition, a reduced subscription rate to the *New York Times* is available in deliverable areas. For more information, call 1-800-631-1222.

Study Guide

Available to students, the Study Guide enhances and reinforces the text material. Each chapter corresponds to a text chapter and includes chapter objectives, study outline for notetaking, key terms for review, study questions, and important Internet sites.

Acknowledgments

The contributions of many people made this book possible. Steven Rigolosi, managing development editor, provided us with direction and expertise and, when needed, motivation to complete this project. He threw himself into this book and exhibited total commitment to this project. His effort and editing contributions were outstanding. We would also like to note the support and enthusiasm of Natalie Anderson, Crissy Statuto, Lisamarie Brassini, and Stephanie Johnson.

The production staff at Prentice Hall deserves special mention. Cynthia Regan did an expert job of turning the manuscript into a finished product. Teri Stratford's photo research skills greatly enhanced the book's visual appeal. We are also indebted to Ann France and Pat Wosczyk for supervising the design process.

Our experience in working with everyone at Prentice Hall has been superb. Everyone at PH approached this book with commitment and enthusiasm. We were partners with the PH staff and feel that we are part of a high-performance work team. We appreciate the commitment they displayed and would like to thank them for the experience.

We would also like to thank the many colleagues who reviewed the manuscript. Their comments were pivotal in the development of the text:

Uzo Anakwe—Pace University, New York, NY
D. Neil Ashworth—University of Richmond, Richmond, VA
Barry Axe—Barry University, Miami Shores, FL
Brendan Bannister—Northeastern University, Boston, MA
Karen Boroff—Seton Hall, South Orange, NJ
Ernie Bourgeois—Castleton College, Castleton, VT
Gene Brady—University of Bridgeport, Bridgeport, CT
John W. Budd—University of Minnesota, Minneapolis, MN
Janet Caruso—Briarcliff College, Woodbury, NY
J. Stephen Childers—East Carolina University, Greenville, NC
Catherine Clark—University of Rio Grande, Rio Grande, OH
Stephen Crow—University of New Orleans, New Orleans, LA
John Delery—University of Arkansas, Fayetteville, AR
Dennis Dossett—University of Missouri, St. Louis, MO
George Dreher—Indiana University, Bloomington, IN
Cathy DuBois—Kent State University, Kent, OH
Robert Eder—Portland State University, Portland, OH
Jiing-Lih Fahr—Louisiana State University, Baton Rouge, LA
Robert Figler—University of Akron, Akron, OH
James Harbin—Texas A&M University, Texarkana, TX
Marianne Koch—University of Oregon, Eugene, OR
John Kohl—University of Nevada, Las Vegas, NV
Elaine LeMay—Colorado State University, Fort Collins, CO
Stanley B. Malos—San Jose State University, San Jose, CA
Eilene D. Maupin—Spelman College, Atlanta, GA
Dominic Montileone—Delaware Valley College, Doylestown, PA
David Murphy—Madisonville Community College, Madisonville, NY
John Orife—Indiana University of Pennsylvania, Indiana, PA
Philip Quaglieri—University of Massachusetts, Boston, MA
Robert Scherer—Wright State University, Dayton, OH
Janice Smith—North Carolina Agricultural and Technical State University, Greensboro, NC
Howard Stanger—Buffalo State College, Buffalo, NY
Jeff Stauffer—Ventura College, Ventura, CA
Cynthia Sutton—Indiana University, South Bend, IN
Mary Ann Von Glinow—Florida International University, Miami, FL
Edward Ward—St. Cloud State University, St. Cloud, MN
Sandy Wayne—University of Illinois, Chicago, IL
Roger D. Weikle—Winthrop University, Rock Hill, SC
Teresa Welbourne—Cornell University, Ithaca, NY
Mark Wesolowski—Miami University, Oxford, OH
Carolyn Wiley—University of Tennessee, Chattanooga, TN

Finally, this book would not have been possible without the indulgence of family and friends. We sincerely appreciate the patience and tolerance that were extended to us as we wrote the second edition.

Luis R. Gómez-Mejía
David B. Balkin
Robert L. Cardy

About the Authors

Luis R. Gómez-Mejía is a Professor of Management in the College of Business at Arizona State University. He received his Ph.D. and M.A. in industrial relations from the University of Minnesota and a B.A. in economics from the University of Minnesota. Prior to entering academia, Professor Gómez-Mejía worked for eight years in human resources for the City of Minneapolis and Control Data Corporation. He has served as consultant to numerous organizations since then. Prior to joining ASU, he taught at the University of Colorado and the University of Florida. He has served two terms on the editorial board of the *Academy of Management Journal* and is editor and cofounder of the *Journal of High Technology Management Research.* He has published over 60 articles appearing in the most prestigious management journals including the *Academy of Management Journal, Administrative Science Quarterly, Strategic Management Journal, Industrial Relations,* and *Personnel Psychology*. He has also written and edited a dozen management books published by Prentice Hall, Southwestern Press, JAI Press, and Grid. He was ranked one of the top nine in research productivity based on the number of publications in the *Academy of Management Journal.* He has received numerous awards including "best article" in the *Academy of Management Journal* (1992) and *Council of 100 Distinguished Scholars* at Arizona State University (1994). Professor Gómez-Mejía's research focuses on macro HR issues, international HR practices, and compensation.

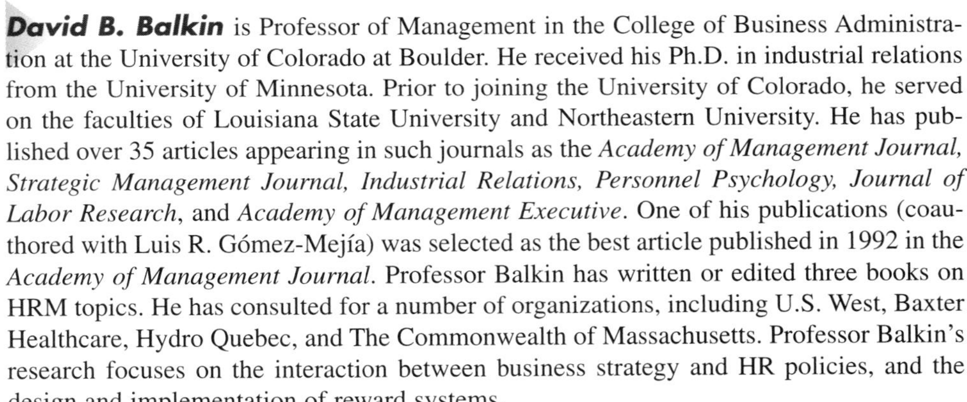

David B. Balkin is Professor of Management in the College of Business Administration at the University of Colorado at Boulder. He received his Ph.D. in industrial relations from the University of Minnesota. Prior to joining the University of Colorado, he served on the faculties of Louisiana State University and Northeastern University. He has published over 35 articles appearing in such journals as the *Academy of Management Journal, Strategic Management Journal, Industrial Relations, Personnel Psychology, Journal of Labor Research*, and *Academy of Management Executive*. One of his publications (coauthored with Luis R. Gómez-Mejía) was selected as the best article published in 1992 in the *Academy of Management Journal*. Professor Balkin has written or edited three books on HRM topics. He has consulted for a number of organizations, including U.S. West, Baxter Healthcare, Hydro Quebec, and The Commonwealth of Massachusetts. Professor Balkin's research focuses on the interaction between business strategy and HR policies, and the design and implementation of reward systems.

Robert L. Cardy is Professor of Management in the College of Business at Arizona State University. He received his Ph.D. in industrial/organizational psychology from Virginia Tech in 1982. He is an ad hoc reviewer for a variety of journals, including the *Academy of Management Journal* and the *Academy of Management Review*. He is editor and cofounder of the *Journal of Quality Management*. Professor Cardy has been recognized for this research, teaching, and service. He was ranked in the top 20 in research productivity for the decade 1980–89 based on the number of publications in the *Journal of Applied Psychology*. He was doctoral coordinator in ASU's management department for five years and received a University Mentor Award in 1993 for his work with doctoral students. He authors a regular column on current issues in HRM and received an Academy of Management certificate for outstanding service as a columnist for the HR division newsletter. Professor Cardy was a 1992 recipient of a certificate for significant contributions to the quality of life for students at ASU. His research focuses on performance appraisal and effective HRM practices in a quality-oriented organizational environment.

1 Meeting Present and Emerging Strategic Human Resource Challenges

The Downsizing Challenge. For years, AT&T was known for its commitment to lifetime job security. But as competition has increased, the company has announced wave after wave of layoffs. The challenges of managing layoffs and downsizings—and employee responses to those strategies—are some of the most important facing managers today.

CHALLENGES

After reading this chapter, you should be able to deal more effectively with the following challenges:

1 ▶ **Explain** how a firm's human resources influence its performance.

2 ▶ **Describe** how firms can use HR initiatives to cope with workplace changes and trends such as a more diverse work force, the global economy, downsizing, and new legislation.

3 ▶ **Distinguish** between the role of the HR department and the role of the firm's managers in utilizing human resources effectively.

4 ▶ **Indicate** how members of the HR department and managers within a company can establish a strong partnership.

5 ▶ **Formulate** and implement HR strategies that can help the firm achieve a sustained competitive advantage.

6 ▶ **Identify** HR strategies that fit corporate and business unit strategies.

http://www.shrm.org

Society for Human Resource Management (SHRM) Home Page

This Web site contains information on how to join the Society for Human Resource Management (SHRM) and provides access to *HR News Online,* which summarizes the latest developments in human resource management news. SHRM's home page also includes links to an HR Information Center that contains useful information about HRM practices.

American Telephone and Telegraph (AT&T) has been laying off an average of 900 people a month since 1984, with the pace quickening in the late 1990s. In 1996 alone, AT&T laid off 40,000 employees, or 13% of its entire staff. Why? Fierce new competition among "Ma Bell" and her children (the "Baby Bells") is forcing cost cuts achievable only through big layoffs.

AT&T's mass layoffs have come as a shock to many. Of all U.S. firms, AT&T probably came closest to a Japanese-style identification of worker with corporation. It was once common for AT&T employees to say "I work for the phone company" rather than "I'm an accountant" or "I'm an engineer."

In an interview with *Time* magazine, AT&T chairman Robert E. Allen expressed openly how much things have changed. Employment at AT&T, he remarks, "used to be a lifelong commitment on the employee's part and on our part. But our people now realize that the contract [the implied promise of lifetime job security in exchange for hard work and loyalty] does not exist anymore."[1]

human resources (HR)
People who work in an organization. Also called *personnel.*

human resource strategy
A firm's deliberate use of human resources to help it gain or maintain an edge against its competitors in the marketplace. The grand plan or general approach an organization adopts to ensure that it effectively uses its people to accomplish its mission.

human resource tactic
A particular HR policy or program that helps to advance a firm's strategic goal.

This book is about the people who work in an organization and their relationship with that organization. Different terms are used to describe these people: *employees, associates* (at Wal-Mart, for instance), *personnel, human resources.* None of these terms is better than the others, and they often are used interchangeably. The term we have chosen for the title of this text, and which we will use throughout, is **human resources (HR).*** It has gained widespread acceptance over the last decade because it expresses the belief that workers are a valuable and sometimes irreplaceable resource. Effective human resource management (HRM) is a major component of any manager's job.

A **human resource strategy** refers to a firm's deliberate use of human resources to help it gain or maintain an edge against its competitors in the marketplace.[2] It is the grand plan or general approach an organization adopts to ensure that it effectively uses its people to accomplish its mission. A **human resource tactic** is a particular policy or program that helps to advance a firm's strategic goal. Strategy precedes and is more important than tactics. The AT&T example illustrates how one company has been forced to develop a low-cost HR strategy to remain competitive, using as a tactic large-scale layoffs that many would consider unfair and leading to reduced employee loyalty.[3]

In this chapter, we focus on the general framework within which specific HR activities and programs fit. With the help of the company's human resources department (HR department, for short), managers implement the chosen HR strategies.[4] In subsequent chapters, we move from the general to the specific and examine in detail the spectrum of HR strategies (for example, those regarding work design, staffing, performance appraisal, career planning, and compensation).[5]

*All terms in boldface also appear in the Key Terms list at the end of the chapter.

▸ Human Resource Management: The Challenges

Before we take up the HR challenges that face managers, we need to define *manager* and say a word about where human resources fit into the organization. **Managers** are people who are in charge of others and are responsible for the timely and correct execution of actions that promote their units' successful performance. In this book, we use the term *unit* broadly; it may refer to a work team, department, business unit, division, or corporation.

manager
A person who is in charge of others and is responsible for the timely and correct execution of actions that promote his or her unit's success.

All employees (including managers) can be differentiated as line or staff. **Line employees** are directly involved in producing the company's good(s) or delivering the service(s). A *line manager* manages line employees. **Staff employees** are those who support the line function. For example, people who work in the HR department are considered staff employees because their job is to provide supporting services for line employees. Employees may also be differentiated according to how much responsibility they have. *Senior employees* are those who have been with the company longer and have more responsibility than *junior employees*. *Exempt employees* (sometimes called *salaried employees*) are those who do not receive extra pay for overtime work (beyond 40 hours per week). *Nonexempt employees* do receive overtime compensation. This text is written primarily to help students who intend to be managers deal effectively with the challenges of managing people.

line employee
An employee involved directly in producing the company's good(s) or delivering the service(s).

staff employee
An employee who supports line employees.

Figure 1-1 summarizes the major HR challenges facing today's managers. Firms that deal with these challenges effectively are likely to outperform those that do not. These challenges may be categorized according to their primary focus: the environment, the organization, or the individual.

Environmental Challenges

Environmental challenges are the forces external to the firm. They influence organizational performance but are largely beyond management's control. Managers, therefore, need to monitor the external environment constantly for opportunities and threats. They

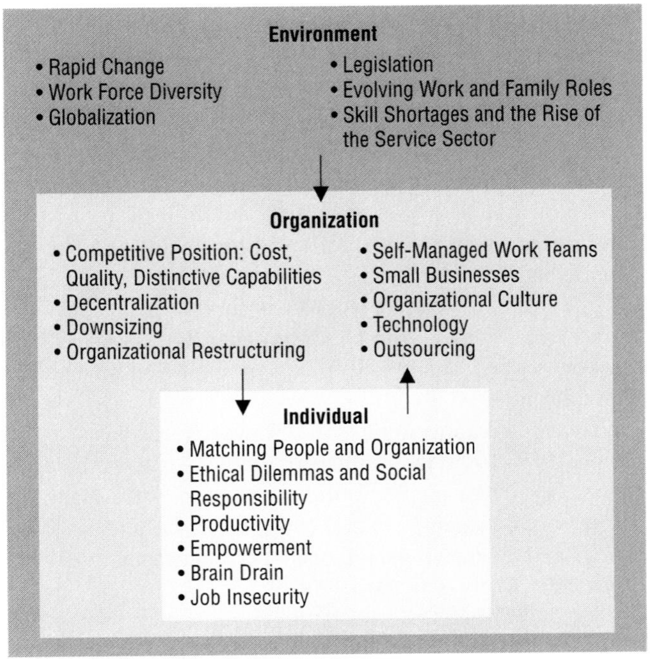

environmental challenges
Forces external to a firm that affect the firm's performance but are beyond the control of management.

Environment
- Rapid Change
- Work Force Diversity
- Globalization
- Legislation
- Evolving Work and Family Roles
- Skill Shortages and the Rise of the Service Sector

Organization
- Competitive Position: Cost, Quality, Distinctive Capabilities
- Decentralization
- Downsizing
- Organizational Restructuring
- Self-Managed Work Teams
- Small Businesses
- Organizational Culture
- Technology
- Outsourcing

Individual
- Matching People and Organization
- Ethical Dilemmas and Social Responsibility
- Productivity
- Empowerment
- Brain Drain
- Job Insecurity

FIGURE 1-1
Key HR Challenges for Today's Managers

must also maintain the flexibility to react quickly to challenges. One common and effective method for monitoring the environment is to read the business press, including *Business Week, Fortune,* and *The Wall Street Journal.* (Appendix A to this book provides an annotated listing of both general business publications and more specialized publications on HR management and related topics.)

Six important environmental challenges today are rapid change, work force diversity, globalization, legislation, evolving work and family roles, and skill shortages and the rise of the service sector.

A QUESTION OF ETHICS

How much responsibility does an organization have to shield its employees from the effects of rapid change in the environment? What risks does this type of "shock absorber" approach to management entail?

Rapid Change. Many organizations face a volatile environment in which change is nearly constant. If they are to survive and prosper, they need to adapt to change quickly and effectively. Human resources are almost always at the heart of an effective response system. Here are a few examples of how HR policies can help or hinder a firm grappling with external change:

- *Taking advantage of lower costs and job anxiety.* Hong Kong executives can't do without beepers to get important messages. The booming demand for paging services has created many jobs—more than 80,000 people in Hong Kong now work as paging company operators. But in 1996, the companies received permission to service local calls through lines to southern China, where wages are only $260 per month versus $1,100 in Hong Kong. "Nearly the whole industry will move to China," warns Wong Chimei, spokeswoman for the operators union. "And following pagers, others will move, too."[6]
- *Just-in-time hiring.* Hon Industries Inc., an office furniture maker, faces an unpredictable demand for factory workers at its plants in Muscaline, Iowa. Instead of waiting until the last minute to recruit, Hon has created a pool of "prequalified" candidates willing to wait for job openings. For example, out of 2,000 people who sought jobs in Hon's Muscaline plant, the company prequalified 109. It offered jobs to 48 of them almost immediately, and offered employment to the rest over the following months.[7]

Throughout this book we emphasize how HR practices can enable a firm to respond quickly and effectively to external changes.

Work Force Diversity. Managers across the United States are confronted daily with the increasing diversity of the work force. Approximately one third of the U.S. work force will be made up of African-Americans, Asian-Americans, Latinos, and other minorities by the year 2000. In many large urban centers, such as Miami, Los Angeles, and New York, the work force is already at least half composed of minorities; this figure may exceed three quarters by the end of the century. California is probably the most diverse state. Non-Latino whites now make up only 57% of its population. Latinos are the second largest group at 26%, followed by Asians and Pacific Islanders at 9% and African-Americans at 7%.[8]

The influx of women workers is another major change in the composition of the U.S. work force. Women with children under age six are now the fastest-growing segment of the work force.[9] In 1996, over 70% of employed men had employed wives. This compares with 54% in 1980.[10]

The age composition of the U.S. work force has also changed dramatically. During the period 1983–1995, the number of employees over the age of 45 increased nearly 25%.[11] In January 1996, the 76 million Americans who make up the "baby boom generation" (those born between 1946 and 1964) began turning 50. But as a result of corporate restructurings and downsizings, job displacement among workers 55 and older has surpassed that of younger workers in the 1990s.[12]

All these trends present both a significant challenge and a real opportunity for managers. Firms that formulate and implement HR strategies that capitalize on employee diversity are more likely to survive and prosper. Chapter 4 is devoted exclusively to the topic of managing employee diversity. This issue is also discussed in several other chapters throughout this book.

Globalization. One of the most dramatic challenges facing U.S. firms as they enter the twenty-first century is how to compete against foreign firms, both domestically and abroad. Many U.S. companies are already being compelled to think globally, something that doesn't come easily to firms long accustomed to doing business in a large and expanding domestic market with minimal foreign competition. For instance, it is estimated that only about 10% of U.S. firms are active exporters. This figure is closer to 80% for companies in Europe and in the Pacific Rim,[13] an area made up of the following countries: Japan, Korea, China, Taiwan, Hong Kong, Thailand, the Philippines, Malaysia, Singapore, Indonesia, Australia, and New Zealand.

Weak response to international competition may be resulting in upwards of 600,000 layoffs in the United States every year.[14] Human resources can play a critical role in a business's ability to compete head-to-head with foreign producers. The implications of a global economy on human resource management are many. Here are a few examples:

- *Worldwide company culture.* Some firms try to develop a global company identity to smooth over cultural differences between domestic employees and those in international operations. Minimizing these differences increases cooperation and can have a strong impact on the bottom line. For instance, the head of human resources at the European division of Colgate Palmolive notes, "We try to build a common corporate culture. We want them all to be Colgaters."[15]
- *Global alliances.* Some firms actively engage in international alliances with foreign firms or acquire companies overseas to take advantage of global markets. Making such alliances work requires a highly trained and devoted staff. For instance, Phillips (a German lighting and electronics firm) became the largest lighting manufacturer in the world by establishing a joint venture with AT&T and making several key acquisitions, including Magnavox, parts of GE Sylvania (which had been the lighting division of Westinghouse), and the largest lighting company in France.[16]

These illustrations show how firms can use HR strategies to gain a worldwide competitive advantage. An entire chapter of this book (Chapter 17) is devoted to the HR issues firms face as they expand overseas. In addition, most chapters address international concerns as they relate to the topic being discussed. We also include international examples throughout the book, in the text and in selected Issues and Applications features, to illustrate how firms in other countries manage their human resources.

Legislation. Much of the growth in the HR function over the past three decades may be attributed to its crucial role in keeping the company out of trouble with the law.[17] Most firms are deeply concerned with potential liability resulting from personnel decisions that may violate laws enacted by the U.S. Congress, state legislatures, and/or local governments.[18] These laws are constantly interpreted in thousands of cases brought before government agencies, federal courts, state courts, and the U.S. Supreme Court.

How successfully a firm manages its human resources depends to a large extent on its ability to deal effectively with government regulations. Operating within the legal framework requires keeping track of the external legal environment and developing internal systems (for example, supervisory training and grievance procedures) to ensure compliance and minimize complaints. Many firms are now developing formal policies on sexual harassment and establishing internal administrative channels to deal with alleged incidents before employees feel the need to file a lawsuit.

Legislation often has a differential impact on public- and private-sector organizations. (*Public sector* is another term for governmental agencies; *private sector* refers to all other types of organizations.) Some legislation applies only to public-sector organizations. For instance, affirmative action requirements (see Chapter 3) are typically limited to public organizations and to organizations that do contract work for them. However, much legislation applies to both public- and private-sector organizations. In fact, it's difficult to think of any HR practices that are *not* influenced by government regulations. For this reason, each chapter of this book addresses pertinent legal issues, and an entire chapter (Chapter 3) provides an overall framework that consolidates the main legal issues and concerns facing employers today.

Evolving Work and Family Roles. The proportion of *dual-career* families, in which both wife and husband (or both members of a couple) work, is increasing every year. Unfortunately, women face the double burden of working at home and on the job, devoting 42 hours per week on average to the office and an additional 30 hours at home to children. This compares to 43 hours spent working in the office and only 12 hours at home for men.[19]

More and more companies are introducing "family-friendly" programs that give them a competitive advantage in the labor market. These programs are HR tactics that companies use to hire and retain the best-qualified employees, male or female, and they are very likely to pay off. For instance, among the Big Six accounting firms, half of all recruits are women, but only 5% of partners are women. Major talent is being wasted as many women drop out after lengthy training because they have decided that the demanding 10- to 12-year partner track requires a total sacrifice of family life. These firms have started to change their policies and are already seeing gains as a result. KPMG and Ernst & Young, for example, have recently begun offering child-care and elder-care referral services. Ernst & Young and Coopers & Lybrand have introduced alternative scheduling to allow employees some flexibility in their work hours. The 50% increase in the number of women partners in Big Six firms in the 1990s is credited to such programs.[20]

Family-friendly policies are discussed in detail in Chapter 12 under the heading "Employee Services." Special issues that women confront in the workplace are discussed in Chapter 4.

Skill Shortages and the Rise of the Service Sector. As Figure 1-2 shows, the U.S. service sector has experienced much faster growth than the manufacturing sector over the past 40 years. Expansion of service-sector employment is linked to a number of factors, including changes in consumer tastes and preferences, legal and regulatory changes, advances in science and technology that have eliminated many manufacturing jobs, and changes in the way businesses are organized and managed.

Service, technical, and managerial positions that require college degrees will make up half of all manufacturing and service jobs by 2000. Unfortunately, most available workers will be too unskilled to fill those jobs. Even now, many companies complain that the supply of skilled labor is dwindling and that they must provide their employees with basic training to make up for the shortcomings of the public education system. For example, 84% of the 23,000 people applying for entry-level jobs at New York Telephone (now NYNEX) failed the qualifying test.[21] Chemical Bank reported that it had to interview 40 applicants to find one proficient teller.[22] David Hearns, chairman and CEO of Xerox, laments that "the American work force is running out of qualified people."[23]

To rectify these shortcomings, companies currently spend an estimated $55 billion a year on a wide variety of training programs. This is in addition to the $24 billion spent on training programs by the federal government each year.[24] Nonetheless, the skill shortage is likely to remain a major challenge for U.S. firms. Chapter 8 focuses directly on training, while Chapters 5 (staffing), 7 (appraising employee performance), and 9 (career development) discuss issues related to the skills and knowledge required to succeed on the job.

A QUESTION OF ETHICS

What is the ethical responsibility of an employer to employees who lack basic literacy and numeracy skills? Should companies be required by law to provide training opportunities for such employees, as some have proposed?

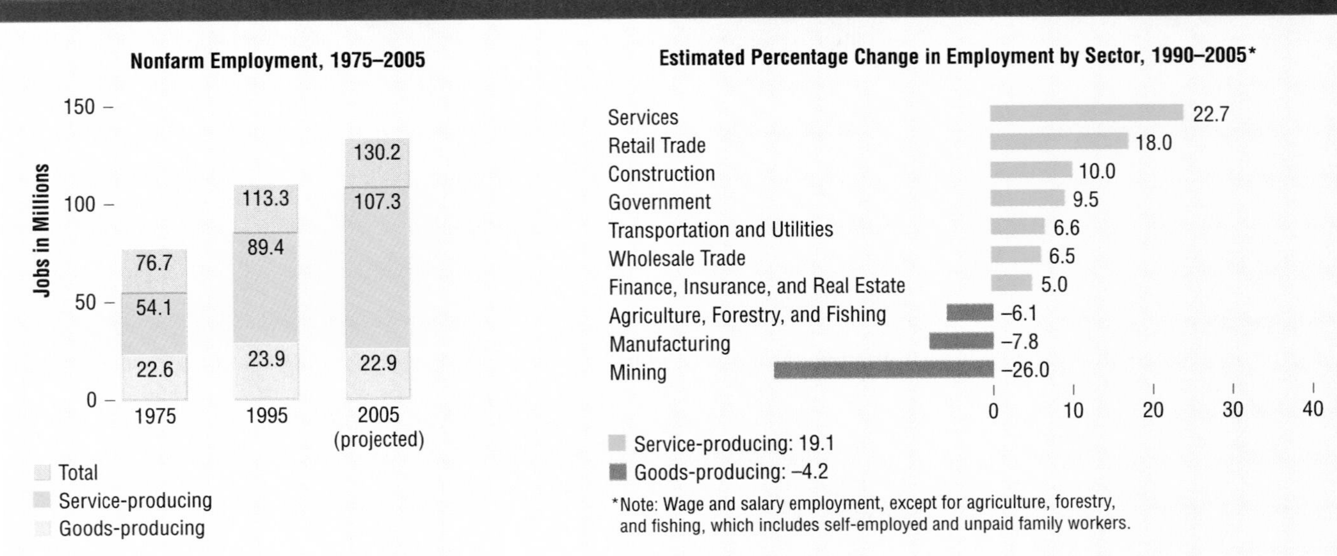

FIGURE 1-2

Where the Jobs Are: The Rise of the Service Sector

Source: Bureau of Labor Statistics. (1995, November). BLS perceptions to 2005. *Monthly Labor Review*. Washington, DC: U.S. Department of Labor.

Organizational Challenges

Organizational challenges are concerns or problems internal to a firm. They are often a byproduct of environmental forces because no firm operates in a vacuum. Still, managers can usually exert much more control over organizational challenges than over environmental challenges. Effective managers spot organizational issues and deal with them before they become major problems. One of the themes of this text is *proactivity:* the need for firms to take action before problems get out of hand. This can be done only by managers who are well informed about important HR issues and organizational challenges. These challenges include the need for a competitive position and flexibility, the problems of downsizing and organizational restructuring, the use of self-managed work teams, the rise of small businesses, the need to create a strong organizational culture, the role of technology, and the rise of outsourcing.

organizational challenges Concerns or problems internal to a firm; often a byproduct of environmental forces.

Competitive Position: Cost, Quality, or Distinctive Capabilities. Human resources represent the single most important cost in many organizations. Organizational labor costs range from 36% in capital-intensive firms like commercial airlines to 80% in labor-intensive firms like the U.S. Postal Service. How effectively a company uses its human resources can have a dramatic effect on its ability to compete (or even survive) in an increasingly competitive environment.

An organization will outperform its competitors if it effectively utilizes its work force's unique combination of skills and abilities to exploit environmental opportunities and neutralize threats. HR policies can influence an organization's competitive position by controlling costs, improving quality, and creating distinctive capabilities.

- *Controlling costs.* One way for a firm to gain a competitive advantage is to maintain low costs and a strong cash flow. A compensation system that uses innovative reward strategies to control labor costs can help the organization grow, as we discuss in Chapters 10 and 11. A well-designed compensation system rewards employees for behaviors that benefit the company.

  Other factors besides compensation policies can enhance a firm's competitiveness by keeping labor costs under control. These include: better employee selection so that workers are more likely to stay with the company and to perform better while they are there (Chapter 5); training employees to make them more efficient and productive (Chapter 8); attaining harmonious labor relations (Chapter 15); effectively managing health and safety issues in the workplace (Chapter 16); and structuring work to reduce the time and resources needed to design, produce, and deliver products or services (Chapter 2).
- *Improving quality.* The second way to gain a competitive advantage is to engage in continuous quality improvement. Many companies are implementing **total quality management (TQM)** initiatives, which are programs designed to improve the quality of all the processes that lead to a final product or service. In a TQM program, every aspect of the organization is oriented toward providing a quality product or service. Several chapters discuss how quality management should be integrated with specific HR programs such as pay-for-performance plans (Chapter 11) and employee appraisal (Chapter 7).[24a]
- *Creating distinctive capabilities.* The third way to gain a competitive advantage is to utilize people with distinctive capabilities to create unsurpassed competence in a particular area (for example, 3M's competence in adhesives, Carlson Corporation's leading presence in the travel business, and Xerox's dominance of the photocopier market). Chapter 5 (which discusses the recruitment and selection of employees), Chapter 8 (training), and Chapter 9 (the long-term grooming of employees within the firm) are particularly relevant to managers seeking to establish distinctive capabilities through the effective use of human resources.

total quality management (TQM)
An organizationwide approach to improving the quality of all the processes that lead to a final product or service.

Decentralization. In the traditional organizational structure, most major decisions are made at the top and implemented at lower levels. It is not uncommon for these organizations to centralize major functions, such as human resources, marketing, and production, in a single location (typically corporate headquarters) that serves as the firm's command center. Multiple layers of management are generally used to execute orders issued at the top and to control the lower ranks from above. Employees who are committed to the firm tend to move up the ranks over time in what some have called the *internal labor market.*[25] However, the traditional top-down form of organization is quickly becoming obsolete, both because it is costly to operate and because it is too inflexible to compete effectively. It is being replaced by **decentralization**, which transfers responsibility and decision-making authority from a central office to people and locations closer to the situation that demands attention.

decentralization
Transferring responsibility and decision-making authority from a central office to people and locations closer to the situation that demands attention.

HR strategies can play a crucial role in enhancing organizational flexibility by improving decision-making processes within the firm. The need for maintaining or creating organizational flexibility in HR strategies is addressed in several chapters of this book, including those dealing with work flows (Chapter 2), compensation (Chapters 10 and 11), training (Chapter 8), staffing (Chapter 5), and globalization (Chapter 17).

Downsizing. Periodic reductions in a company's work force to improve its bottom line—often called **downsizing**—are becoming standard business practice, even among firms that were once legendary for their "no layoff" policies, such as AT&T, IBM, Kodak, and Xerox.[26] A recent survey of 340 large U.S. firms indicated that nearly half had laid off workers in the year the survey was conducted.[27]

downsizing
A reduction in a company's work force to improve its bottom line.

In addition to fostering a lack of emotional commitment,[28] transient employment relationships create a new set of challenges for firms and people competing in the labor market, as well as for government agencies that must deal with the social problems associated with employment insecurity (including loss of health insurance and mental illness). However, the good news for laid-off employees is that the poor-performance stigma traditionally attached to being fired or laid off is fading.[29]

Chapter 6 of this book is devoted to downsizing and how to manage the process effectively. Other chapters of this book also shed light on this important issue, including the chapters on benefits (Chapter 12), the legal environment (Chapter 3), labor relations (Chapter 15), and employee relations and communications (Chapter 13).

Organizational Restructuring. The past two decades have witnessed a dramatic transformation in how firms are structured. Tall organizations that had many management levels are becoming flatter as companies reduce the number of people between the chief executive officer (CEO) and the lowest-ranking production employee in an effort to become more competitive.

This transformation has had enormous implications for the effective utilization of human resources. Since the late 1980s, many companies have instituted massive layoffs of middle managers, whose traditional role of planning, organizing, implementing, and controlling has come to be equated with the kind of cumbersome bureaucracy that prevents businesses from responding to market forces. It is estimated that two thirds of the jobs eliminated in the 1990s were supervisory/middle management jobs.[30] The newly emerging flatter form of organization has been labeled the *horizontal corporation*.[31] In this "delayered" corporate model, supervisors manage across, not up and down.

New relationships among firms are also fostering hybrid organizational structures and the blending of firms with diverse histories and labor forces. Mergers and acquisitions, in which formerly independent organizations come together as a single entity, represent two important sources of restructuring. Such transitions can present difficult challenges.[32] For example, Bank America's merger with Security Pacific in 1993 led to a clash of starkly different corporations—one (Bank America) centralized, rule bound, and conservative, and the other (Security Pacific) decentralized and freewheeling. When these two corporate styles couldn't be reconciled, many Security Pacific officials were forced out.

A newer and rapidly growing form of interorganizational bonding comes in the form of joint ventures, alliances, and collaborations among firms that remain independent, yet work together on specific products to spread costs and risks. For instance, Coca-Cola and Schweppes run a huge soft-drink bottling plant that has brought both companies tremendous cost savings. Ford and Nissan successfully designed a minivan together, and Ford has had a successful strategic alliance with Mazda for more than 20 years. Some alliances in the technology industry are illustrated in Figure 1-3 on page ten.

To be successful, organizational restructuring requires effective management of human resources. For instance, flattening the organization requires careful examination of staffing demands, work flows, communication channels, training needs, and so on. Likewise, mergers and other forms of interorganizational relations require the successful blending of dissimilar organizational structures, management practices, technical expertise, and so forth. Chapter 2 deals specifically with these issues. Other chapters that focus on related issues are Chapter 5 (staffing), Chapter 8 (training), Chapter 9 (career development), and Chapter 17 (international management).

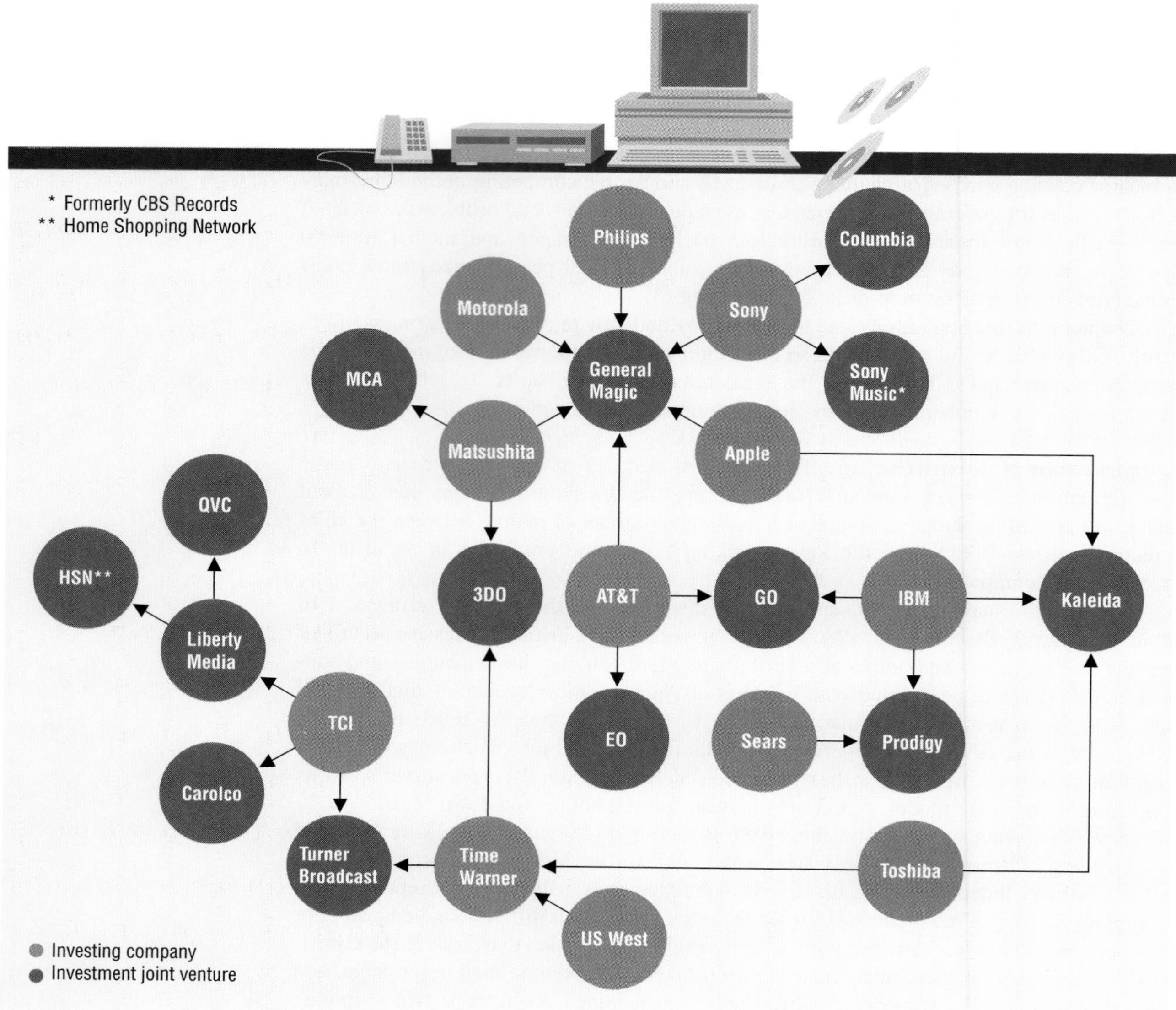

FIGURE 1-3

Examples of Alliances in the Technology Industry

Source: Reprinted from Yoder, S. K., and Zachary, G. P. (1993, July 14). Vague new world. *The Wall Street Journal,* A1. Reprinted by permission of *The Wall Street Journal*, © 1993 Dow Jones & Company, Inc. All rights reserved worldwide.

Self-Managed Work Teams. Another sweeping organizational change has been in the supervisor-worker relationship. The traditional system, in which individual employees report to a single boss (who oversees a group of three to seven subordinates), is being replaced in some organizations by the self-managed team system. In this system employees are assigned to a group of peers and, together, they are responsible for a particular area or task.[33] It has been estimated that by the year 2000, 40% of U.S. workers will be operating in some kind of team environment.[34]

According to two experts on self-managed work teams, "Today's competitive environment demands intense improvement in productivity, quality, and response time. Teams can deliver this improvement. Bosses can't.... Just as dinosaurs once ruled the earth and later faded into extinction, the days of bosses may be numbered."[35] Michael H. Walsh, CEO of

Tenneco Corporation, is even more blunt about the redundance of bosses: "In a hierarchical organization, bosses don't do much.... They just preside and take all the credit. It's criminal. A lot of good people are buried down there, and their bosses are happy to keep them buried."[36]

Very few rigorous scientific studies have been done on the effectiveness of self-managed work teams, mostly because these programs are so new. However, case studies do suggest that many firms that use teams enjoy impressive payoffs. For example, company officials at General Motors' Fitzgerald Battery Plant, which is organized in teams, report cost savings of 30% to 40% over traditionally organized plants. At Federal Express, a thousand clerical workers, divided into teams of five to ten people, helped the company reduce service problems by 13 percent.[37]

HR issues concerning self-managed work teams are discussed in detail in Chapter 2 (work flows), Chapter 10 (compensation), and Chapter 11 (rewarding performance).

The Growth of Small Businesses. According to the U.S. Small Business Administration (SBA), the precise definition of a small business depends on the industry in which it operates. For instance, to be considered "small" by the SBA, a manufacturing company may have a maximum of 500 to 1,500 employees (depending on the type of manufacturing). In wholesaling, a company is considered small if the number of its employees does not exceed 100.[38]

An increasing percentage of the 14 million businesses in the United States can be considered small. One study using tax returns as its source of data found that 99.8% of U.S. businesses have fewer than 100 employees and approximately 90% have fewer than 20 employees.[39] And, according to recent estimates, the percentage of total civilian employment in the mid-1990s represented by *Fortune* 500 companies is slightly more than half what it was in 1975.[40] However, the increase in jobs created by smaller firms has more than offset job losses among the large firms.

Several factors underlie the proliferation of small businesses in recent years. Among these factors are:[41]

- The increasing number of two-income, two-career families.
- The growing recognition that larger organizations do not always fulfill people's basic needs for autonomy and security.
- The shift in women's roles in economic life along with a parallel shift in the belief that women can be entrepreneurs. The current growth rate of new ventures created by women is considerably higher than the rate of new ventures created by men.
- A desire by local government officials to avoid falling hostage to larger corporations that become a city or town's dominant employer.
- A growing appreciation that entrepreneurship is not just the province of a few superstars or celebrity entrepreneurs.
- An understanding that owning one's own business is one of the few pathways left for the middle and lower classes to build wealth.
- A computer and information revolution that is presenting new opportunities while lowering entry costs and other startup barriers in many industries.
- The development of programs to study, teach, promote, and accelerate entrepreneurship, not only in the United States, but also in many nations around the world.

Unfortunately, small businesses face a high risk of failure. Although 1.3 million new businesses start every year, 40% of them fail in the first year, 60% of them fail before the start of the third year, and only 10% survive a decade.[42] To survive and prosper, a small business must manage its human resources effectively; the firm does not have the slack enjoyed by more mature, established firms. For instance, a mediocre performance by one person in a ten-employee firm can mean the difference between making a profit and losing money. In a company with 1,000 employees, one mediocre performance is so diluted that it is unlikely to exert much influence on the bottom line.

Most chapters in this book incorporate small-business examples to show how the HR practices discussed in that chapter relate to the special needs of small firms.

organizational culture
The basic assumptions and beliefs shared by members of an organization. These beliefs operate unconsciously and define in a basic taken-for-granted fashion an organization's view of itself and its environment.

Organizational Culture. The term **organizational culture** refers to the basic assumptions and beliefs shared by members of an organization. These beliefs operate unconsciously and define in a basic "taken for granted" fashion an organization's view of itself and its environment.[43] The key elements of organizational culture are:[44]

1. *Observed behavioral regularities* when people interact, such as the language used and the rituals surrounding deference and demeanor.
2. The *norms* that evolve in working groups, such as the norm of a fair day's work for a fair day's pay.
3. The *dominant values espoused* by an organization, such as product quality or low prices.
4. The *philosophy* that guides an organization's policy toward employees and/or customers.
5. The *rules of the game* for getting along in the organization—"the ropes" that a newcomer must learn to become an accepted member.
6. The *feeling* or *climate* that is conveyed in an organization by the physical layout and the way in which members of the organization interact with one another, customers, and outsiders.

Often a firm's culture hits you as soon as you walk into the company's building. In some firms a male "uniform" of white shirt, dark suit, and plain-color tie is prevalent; such a uniform projects a conservative company philosophy that emphasizes conformity. Employees in other firms may wear a wide array of clothing: The very lack of a uniform projects a company philosophy of individuality, autonomy, and low dependence on superiors. Even within an industry, organizational culture may differ greatly. Figure 1-4 compares the organizational culture at two computer firms, Hewlett-Packard and Apollo.

FIGURE 1-4

Cultural Differences Between Hewlett-Packard and Apollo

Cultural Element	Hewlett-Packard	Apollo
Behavioral regularities	• Planning and coordination • Professional orientation • People-minded style	• Crisis management • Entrepreneurial orientation • Rough-and-tumble style
Norms	• Carefully laid-out work objectives	• Pushing your own agenda
Dominant values	• Quality/reputation • Components company	• Time-to-market • Systems integrator
Philosophy	• Flexible bureaucracy • Functional/matrix structure	• "Ad-hoc-racy" • Functional/integrated structure
Rules of the game	• Problem solving • Specialize • Long tenure	• "Winning is everything" • Be a generalist • Job hoppers
Feeling or climate	• Strong engineering and marketing influence • Polite/congenial • Sing from the same hymnbook	• Strong R&D and engineering influence • Political/confrontational • Mixed bag/misfits

Source: Adapted with permission from Mirvis, P., and Marks, M. L. (1992). The human side of merger planning: Assessing and analyzing fit. *Human Resource Planning, 15*(3), 77. Copyright 1992 by The Human Resource Planning Society.

Firms that make cultural adjustments to keep up with environmental changes are likely to outperform those whose culture is rigid and unresponsive to external jolts. IBM's bureaucratic culture—with its emphasis on hierarchy, centralization of decisions, permanent employment, and strict promotion-from-within policy—has played a large role in its recent difficulties.[45] In contrast, Hewlett-Packard, named one of the best-managed new companies more than a decade ago, has retained its strong position through the 1990s. Many attribute Hewlett-Packard's continued success to the fact that the corporation divided into smaller sections in the mid-1980s, making it more nimble and able to bring new products to market quickly.[46]

Given its pervasiveness, we refer to organizational culture throughout this book—for instance, in discussing work design, performance appraisal, pay for performance, labor relations, and outplacement.

Technology. Technological advances are being introduced to organizations at an ever-increasing pace. At least half of all U.S. workers have experienced dramatic changes in their job duties in the last decade as a result of this trend.[47] Although technology is rapidly changing in many areas, such as robotics, one area in particular is revolutionizing human resources: information technology.[48] Computer systems that were state of the art three years ago are now obsolete and being replaced by faster, cheaper, more versatile systems. The *telematics technologies*—a broad array of tools including microcomputers (PCs) and word processors, networking programs, telecommunications, and fax machines—are now available and affordable to businesses of every size, even one-person companies. These new technologies have had multiple impacts on the management of human resources in organizations, specifically:

- *The rise of telecommuting.* Because the new technology makes information easy to store, retrieve, and analyze, the number of company employees working at home (*telecommuters*) at least part-time has been increasing by 15% annually. Recent estimates put the number at close to 8 million.[49] Because telecommuting arrangements are almost certain to continue growing in the future, they raise many important questions concerning such issues as performance monitoring, career planning, and overtime pay.
- *The ethics of proper data use.* Questions concerning data control, accuracy, right to privacy, and ethics are at the core of a growing controversy brought about by the new information technologies. Personal computers now make it possible to access huge databases containing information on credit files, work history, driving records, health reports, criminal convictions, and family makeup. It is tempting to access this type of data for personnel decisions such as hiring, promotions, international assignments, and the like. A critical observer notes: "The worst thing about this information blitzkrieg is that even though errors abound, what's said about us by computers is usually considered accurate, and significant decisions are made based on this information. Often those affected are unaware of the process and are given no chance to offer explanations."[50]
- *An increase in egalitarianism.* Because information is now available both instantaneously and broadly, organizational structures are becoming more *egalitarian,* meaning that power and authority are spread more evenly among all employees. In the words of noted HR consultant Randall Schuler, this means that "there is little need for layers of management between the top and first-line management. Automation also causes a significant change in organizational culture. It permits top management to bypass middle managers on their way to the first-line management."[51] In addition, groupware networks, which enable hundreds of workers to share information simultaneously, can give office workers intelligence previously available only to their bosses. They also enable the rank-and-file to join in online discussions with senior executives. In these kinds of interactions people are judged more by what they say than by their rank on the corporate ladder.[52]

- *The arrival of human resource information systems.* Technology has also had an impact on the HR department itself. The advent of personal computers and sophisticated database software has dramatically increased managers' ability to monitor the results of HR policies and to manage HR issues such as compensation and benefits more effectively. The same technology allows HR information to be widely distributed to managers. We discuss this technology in detail in Chapter 2.
- *The rise of the Internet.* The Internet started as a way for university scholars and government researchers to collaborate on projects and share research findings. Today, the Net and its multimedia offshot, the World Wide Web, are everywhere. Many companies have set up Internet sites or are in the process of doing so. As a result, they are creating departments and jobs that didn't exist only a few years ago.

The Internet contains a wealth of information for students in all disciplines, including HR managers and general managers. To acquaint you with some HRM-oriented Internet and Web sites, each chapter of this book begins with an "HRM on the Web" feature that refers you to a relevant site. For example, Chapter 10 on compensation directs you to the home page of the American Compensation Association.

The challenges and implications of rapidly changing technologies—especially information technologies—for human resources are discussed in several chapters of this book, including Chapter 13 (employee relations).

outsourcing
Subcontracting work to an outside company that specializes in and is more efficient at doing that kind of work.

Outsourcing. There is an ongoing movement at many large firms to shift work once performed internally to outside suppliers and contractors, a process called **outsourcing**. Their motivation is simple: Outsourcing saves money. *The Wall Street Journal* reports that more than 40% of *Fortune* 500 companies have outsourced some department or service—everything from HR administration to computer systems.[53] For example, American Airlines hires outsourced labor to work in its operations at 28 smaller airports. The savings are considerable. American pays its veteran agents up to $19 an hour, plus benefits. Subcontracted employees performing the same job earn only $7 to $9 an hour and receive minimal benefits.[54]

Outsourcing creates several HR challenges for firms. Although it often helps companies slash costs, employees may face layoffs when their jobs are farmed out to the lowest bidder. For instance, United Parcel Service (UPS) recently subcontracted 5,000 jobs at its 65 customer service centers.[55] In addition, the firm remains accountable for the actions of its subcontractors. Customer dissatisfaction can result if subcontractors are not carefully watched and evaluated. Finally, many believe that subcontractors tend to take on more work than they can handle.[56] When subcontractors are overloaded, small businesses may not receive the best available service and support from subcontractors.

We discuss outsourcing and its challenges for HRM throughout this book. Chapter 2 discusses subcontracting within the context of downsizing while Chapter 15 on labor relations discusses how outsourcing affects unions.

Individual Challenges

individual challenges
Human resource issues that address the decisions most pertinent to individual employees.

Human resource issues at the individual level address the decisions most pertinent to specific employees. These **individual challenges** almost always reflect what is happening in the larger organization. For instance, technology affects individual productivity; it also has ethical ramifications in terms of how information is used to make HR decisions (for example, use of credit or medical history data to decide whom to hire). How the company treats its individual employees is also likely to affect the organizational challenges we discussed earlier. For example, if many key employees leave the firm to join competitors, the organization's competitive position is likely to be affected. In other words, there is a two-way relationship between organizational and individual challenges. This is unlike the relationship between environmental and organizational challenges, in which the relationship goes only one way (see Figure 1-1); few organizations can have much impact on the environment. The most important individual challenges today involve matching people and organizations, ethics and social responsibility, productivity, empowerment, brain drain, and job security.

Matching People and Organizations. Research suggests that HR strategies contribute to firm performance most when the firm uses these strategies to attract and retain the type of employee who best fits the firm's culture and overall business objectives. For example, one study showed that the competencies and personality characteristics of top executives can hamper or improve firm performance, depending on what the firm's business strategies are. Fast-growth firms perform better with managers who have a strong marketing and sales background, who are willing to take risks, and who have a high tolerance for ambiguity. However, these managerial traits actually reduce the performance of mature firms that have an established product and are more interested in maintaining (rather than expanding) their market share.[57] Other research has shown that small high-tech firms benefit by hiring employees who are willing to work in an atmosphere of high uncertainty, low pay, and rapid change in exchange for greater intrinsic satisfaction and the financial opportunities associated with a risky but potentially very lucrative product launch.[58]

Chapter 5 deals specifically with the attempt to achieve the right fit between employees and the organization to enhance performance.

Ethics and Social Responsibility. People's expectations that their employers will behave ethically are increasing,[59] so much that many firms and professional organizations have created codes of ethics outlining principles and standards of personal conduct for their members. Figure 1-5 shows the code of ethics for members of the American Marketing Association. Unfortunately, these codes often do not meet employees' expectations of ethical employer behavior. These negative perceptions have worsened over the years.[60] In a recent poll of *Harvard Business Review* readers, almost half the respondents indicated their belief that managers do not consistently make ethical decisions.[61]

The widespread perceptions of unethical behavior may be attributed to the fact that managerial decisions are rarely clear-cut. Except in a few blatant cases (such as willful misrepresentation), what is ethical or unethical is open to debate. Even the most detailed codes of ethics are still general enough to allow much room for managerial discretion. In other words, many specific decisions related to the management of human resources are subject to judgment calls. Often these judgment calls constitute a Catch-22 because none of the alternatives is desirable.[62]

As a member of the American Marketing Association, I recognize the significance of my professional conduct and my responsibilities to society and to the other members of my profession:

1. By acknowledging my accountability to society as a whole as well as to the organization for which I work.
2. By pledging my efforts to assure that all presentations of goods, services, and concepts be made honestly and clearly.
3. By striving to improve marketing knowledge and practice in order to better serve society.
4. By supporting free consumer choice in circumstances that are legal and are consistent with generally accepted community standards.
5. By pledging to use the highest professional standards in my work and in competitive activity.
6. By acknowledging the right of the American Marketing Association, through established procedure, to withdraw my membership if I am found to be in violation of ethical standards of professional conduct.

FIGURE 1-5

Code of Ethics of the American Marketing Association

Source: O'Boyle, E. J., and Dawson, L. E., Jr. (1992, December). Code of ethics of the American Marketing Association. Reprinted by permission.

In recent years, the concept of social responsibility has been frequently discussed as a counterpart to ethics. A company that exercises *social responsibility* attempts to balance its commitments—not only to its investors, but also to its employees, its customers, other businesses, and the community or communities in which it operates. For example, McDonald's established Ronald McDonald houses several years ago to provide lodging for families of sick children hospitalized away from home. Sears and General Electric support artists and performers, and many local merchants support local children's sports teams.

An entire chapter of this book is devoted to employee rights and responsibilities (Chapter 13); it addresses important ethical issues in employer-employee relations. However, because most of the topics discussed in this book have ethical implications, each chapter includes (at selected points) pertinent ethical questions for which there are no absolute answers.

productivity
A measure of how much value individual employees add to the goods or services that the organization produces.

ability
Competence in performing a job.

Productivity. A prominent business concern over the past 20 years or so is that U.S. productivity is rising at a lower rate than it is in most other industrialized nations. **Productivity** is a measure of how much value individual employees add to the goods or services that the organization produces. The greater the output per individual, the higher the organization's productivity. Two important factors that affect individual productivity are ability and motivation.

Employee **ability,** competence in performing a job, can be improved through a hiring and placement process that selects the best individuals for the job; Chapter 5 specifically deals with this process. It can also be improved through training and career development programs designed to sharpen employees' skills and prepare them for additional responsibilities; Chapters 8 and 9 discuss these issues.

motivation
A person's desire to do the best possible job or to exert the maximum effort to perform assigned tasks.

Motivation refers to a person's desire to do the best possible job or to exert the maximum effort to perform assigned tasks. Motivation energizes, directs, and sustains human behavior. Several key factors affecting employee motivation are discussed in this book, including work design (Chapter 2), matching of employee and job requirements (Chapter 5), rewards (Chapters 11 and 13), and due process (Chapter 14).

quality of work life (QWL)
A measure of how safe and satisfied employees feel with their jobs.

A growing number of companies recognize that employees are more likely to choose a firm and stay there if they believe that it offers a high **quality of work life (QWL).** A high quality of work life is related to job satisfaction, which in turn is a strong predictor of absenteeism and turnover.[63] A firm's investments in improving the quality of work life also pay off in the form of better customer service.[64] We discuss issues covering job design and their effects on employee attitudes and behavior in Chapter 2.

empowerment
Providing workers with the skills and authority to make decisions that would traditionally be made by managers.

Empowerment. In recent years many firms have reduced employee dependence on superiors and placed more emphasis on individual control over (and responsibility for) the work that needs to be done. This process has been labeled **empowerment** because it transfers direction from an external source (normally the immediate supervisor) to an internal source (the individual's own desire to do well). In essence, the process of empowerment entails providing workers with the skills and authority to make decisions that would traditionally be made by managers. The goal of empowerment is an organization consisting of enthusiastic, committed people who perform their work ably because they believe in it and enjoy doing it (*internal control*). This situation is in stark contrast to an organization that gets people to work as an act of compliance to avoid punishment (for example, being fired) or to qualify for a paycheck (*external control*).

HR issues related to internal and external control of behavior are explicitly discussed in Chapter 2 (work flows).

brain drain
The loss of high-talent key personnel to competitors or startup ventures.

Brain Drain. With organizational success more and more dependent on knowledge held by specific employees, companies are becoming more susceptible to **brain drain**—the loss of intellectual property that results when competitors lure away key employees. High-tech firms are particularly vulnerable to this problem. Such important industries as semiconductors and electronics suffer from high employee turnover as key employees, inspired by the potential for huge profits, leave established firms to start their own businesses. This brain drain can negatively affect innovation and cause major delays in the introduction of new products.[65] To make matters worse, departing employees, particularly those in upper management, can wreak considerable havoc by taking other talent with them when they leave.

To combat the problem of defection to competitors, some firms are crafting elaborate antidefection devices. For example, Compaq computer has introduced a policy that revokes bonuses and other benefits to key executives if they take other employees with them when they quit. Micron Technology staggers key employees' bonuses; they lose unawarded portions when they leave.

Issues concerning brain drain and measures for dealing with it effectively are discussed in several chapters of this book, particularly in Chapter 3 (equal opportunity and the legal environment), Chapter 4 (managing diversity), Chapter 6 (employee separations and outplacement), and Chapter 11 (rewarding performance).

Job Insecurity. In this era of downsizing and restructuring, many employees fear for their jobs. For most workers, being able to count on a steady job and regular promotions is a thing of the past. Close to half a million U.S. jobs are being eliminated each year. Even the most profitable companies (including Procter & Gamble, American Home Products, Sara Lee, and Bank One) have laid off workers.

Companies argue that regardless of how well the firm is doing, layoffs have become essential in an age of cutthroat competition. In addition, the stock market often looks favorably on layoffs. For employees, however, chronic job insecurity is a major source of stress and can lead to lower performance and productivity. Reed Moskowitz, founder of a stress disorder center at New York University, notes that workers' mental health has taken a turn for the worse because "nobody feels secure any more."[66]

Though union membership has been declining in recent years, many workers still belong to unions, and job security is now a top union priority. In return for job security, though, many union leaders have had to make major concessions regarding pay and benefits.

We discuss the challenges of laying off employees, and making the remaining employees feel secure and valued, in Chapter 6. We discuss employee stress (and ways to relieve it) in Chapter 16. We explore union-management relations in Chapter 15.

▸ Planning and Implementing Strategic HR Policies

To be successful, firms must closely align their HR strategies and programs (tactics) with environmental opportunities, business strategies, and the organization's unique characteristics and distinctive competence. A firm with a poorly defined HR strategy or a business strategy that does not explicitly incorporate human resources is likely to lose ground to its competitors. Similarly, a firm may have a well-articulated HR strategy, yet fail if its HR tactics/policies do not help it implement its HR strategy effectively.

The Benefits of Strategic HR Planning

The process of formulating HR strategies and establishing programs or tactics to implement them is called **strategic human resource (HR) planning.** When done correctly, strategic HR planning provides many direct and indirect benefits for the company.

strategic human resource (HR) planning
The process of formulating HR strategies and establishing programs or tactics to implement them.

Encouragement of Proactive Rather Than Reactive Behavior. Being *proactive* means looking ahead and developing a vision of where the company wants to be and how it can use human resources to get there. In contrast, being *reactive* means responding to problems as they come up. Companies that are reactive may lose sight of the long-term direction of their business; proactive companies are better prepared for the future.

Explicit Communication of Company Goals. Strategic HR planning can help a firm develop a focused set of strategic objectives that capitalizes on its special talents and know-how. For instance, in an attempt to recover from more than a decade of failing at selling electronics, Kodak appointed George Fisher, who had headed Motorola, as its CEO in 1993.[67] Fisher is credited with the significant rebound in Kodak's stock price. He accomplished this by articulating Kodak's primary business goal as the successful blending of the company's image technology with wireless technology, using the accumulated knowledge of its human resources in both areas. Toward this end, Fisher channeled financial resources into the newly blended "digitized" technology and adopted HR strategies to hire, retain, train, and reward the employees needed to succeed in this focused business niche.

Stimulation of Critical Thinking and Ongoing Examination of Assumptions. Managers often depend on their personal views and experiences to solve problems and make business decisions. The assumptions on which they make their decisions can lead to success if they are appropriate to the environment in which the business operates. However, serious problems can arise when these assumptions no longer hold. For instance, in the 1980s IBM deemphasized sales of its personal computer because IBM managers were afraid that PC growth would decrease the profitability of the firm's highly profitable mainframe products. This decision allowed competitors to move aggressively into the PC market, eventually devastating IBM.[68]

The strategic HR planning process can help a company critically reexamine its assumptions and determine whether the programs that follow from these assumptions should be modified or discontinued. However, strategic HR planning can stimulate critical thinking and the development of new initiatives only if it is a continuing and flexible process rather than a rigid procedure with a discrete beginning and a specific deadline for completion. This is why many firms have formed an executive committee, which includes an HR professional and the CEO, to discuss strategic issues on an ongoing basis and periodically modify the company's overall HR strategies and programs.

Identification of Gaps Between Current Situation and Future Vision. Strategic HR planning can help a firm identify the difference between "where we are today" and "where we want to be." By forcing managers to think ahead, strategic planning can serve as a catalyst for change and mobilize the firm's resources to achieve or enhance a competitive edge in the future. For example, Textron, Inc. decided in 1985 that it had too many businesses to manage effectively. Its vision: to become a leaner, more focused firm with greater control over its assets. To this end, Textron sold 24 businesses between 1985 and 1994. Consistent with these changes, Textron's HR strategies began to emphasize cooperation among units. For example, to draw employees together the company created training programs and work teams consisting of people from different departments. It also began to encourage interunit transfers and frequent visits of employees from one plant to another. Textron credits this HR strategy with doubling its earnings and tripling its stock price.[69]

Encouragement of Line Managers' Participation. Like most HR activities, strategic HR planning will be of little value unless line managers are actively involved. Unfortunately, top management (including HR professionals) sometimes tends to see strategic planning as its domain, with line managers merely responsible for implementation. For HR strategy to be effective, line managers at all levels must buy into it. If they don't, it is likely to fail. For example, a large cosmetics manufacturing plant decided to introduce a reward program in which work teams would receive a large bonus for turning out high-quality products. The bonus was part of a strategic plan to foster greater cooperation among employees. But the plan, which had been developed by top executives in consultation with the HR department, backfired when managers and supervisors began hunting for individual employees responsible for errors. This created divisiveness within teams and conflict with supervisors. The plan was eventually dropped.

Identification of HR Constraints and Opportunities. Human resources play a major role in the eventual success or failure of any strategic business plan. When overall business strategy planning is done in combination with HR strategic planning, firms can identify the potential problems and opportunities with respect to the people expected to implement the business strategy.

Motorola is a good illustration of a highly successful firm that formulates HR strategies in tandem with its business strategies. A cornerstone of Motorola's business strategy is to identify, encourage, and financially support new-product ventures. To implement this strategy, Motorola relies on in-house venture teams, normally composed of five to six employees, one each from research and development (R&D), marketing, sales, manufacturing, engineering, and finance. Positions are broadly defined to allow all employees to use their creativity and to serve as champions of new ideas.

Creation of Common Bonds. A well-developed strategic HR plan with involvement at all levels can help the firm create a sense of shared values and expectations. This is important because a substantial amount of research shows that, in the long run, organizations that have a strong sense of "who we are" tend to outperform those that don't. A strategic HR plan that reinforces, adjusts, or redirects the organization's present culture can foster such values as a customer focus, innovation, fast growth, and cooperation.

The Challenges of Strategic HR Planning

In developing an effective HR strategy, the organization faces several important challenges.

Maintaining a Competitive Advantage. Any competitive advantage enjoyed by an organization tends to be short-lived because other companies are likely to imitate it. This is as true for HR advantages as for technological and marketing advantages. For example, many high-tech firms have "borrowed" reward programs for key scientists and engineers from other successful high-tech firms.

The challenge from an HR perspective is to develop strategies that offer the firm a sustained competitive advantage. For instance, a company may develop programs that maximize present employees' potential through carefully developed career ladders (see Chapter 9) while at the same time rewarding them generously with company stock with strings attached (for example, a provision that they will forfeit the stock if they quit before a certain date).

Reinforcing Overall Business Strategy. Developing HR strategies to support the firm's overall business strategy is a challenge for several reasons. First, top management may not always be able to enunciate clearly the firm's overall business strategy. Second, there may be much uncertainty or disagreement concerning which HR strategies should be used to support the overall business strategy. In other words, it is seldom obvious how particular HR strategies will contribute to the achievement of organizational strategies. Third, large corporations may have different business units, each with its own business strategies. Ideally, each unit should be able to formulate the HR strategy that fits its business strategy best. For instance, a division that produces high-tech equipment may decide to pay its engineering staff well above average to attract and retain the best people, while the consumer products division may decide to pay its engineers an average wage. Such differentials may cause problems if the engineers from the two divisions have contact with each other. Thus, diverse HR strategies may spur feelings of inequity and resentment.

Avoiding Excessive Concentration on Day-to-Day Problems. Some managers devote most of their attention to urgent problems. They are so busy putting out fires that they have no time to focus on the long term. Nonetheless, a successful HR strategy demands a vision tied to the long-term direction of the business. Thus, a major challenge of strategic HR planning is prodding people into stepping back and considering the big picture.

It takes considerable effort to detach oneself from current events and past history and trace a master plan for the organization's future direction. This is particularly true in many small companies, whose staffs are often so absorbed in growing the business today that they seldom pause to look at the big picture for tomorrow. Also, strategic HR planning in small companies is often synonymous with the whims of the company owner or founder, who may not take the time to formalize his or her plans.

Many companies today—both small and large—try to avoid excessive concentration on the present by creating a mission statement in which the company's purpose and goals are committed to paper. Alan Blazar, president of Blazing Graphics (a small graphics production company in Cranston, Rhode Island) believes that crafting a mission statement is "a very helpful process in that it makes you sit back and focus on things outside the day-to-day, filling-the-order kind of mentality."[70] Blazing Graphics' mission statement is reprinted in Figure 1-6.

Developing HR Strategies Suited to Unique Organizational Features. No two firms are exactly alike. Firms differ in history, culture, leadership style, technology, and so on. The chances are high that any ambitious HR strategy or program that is not molded to organizational characteristics will fail.[71] And therein lies one of the central challenges in formulating HR strategies: creating a vision of the organization of the future that does not provoke a destructive clash with the organization of the present.

Coping with the Environment. Just as no two firms are exactly alike, no two firms operate in an identical environment. Some must deal with rapid change, as in the computer industry; others operate in a relatively stable market, as in the market for food processors. Some face a virtually guaranteed demand for their products or services (for example, medical providers); others must deal with turbulent demand (for example, fashion designers). Even within a very narrowly defined industry, some firms may be competing in a market where customer service is the key (IBM's traditional competitive advantage), while others are competing in a market driven by cost considerations (the competitive advantage offered by the many firms producing IBM clones). A major challenge in developing HR strategies is crafting strategies that will work in the firm's unique environment to give it a sustainable competitive advantage.

Blazing Graphics will provide you with the most effective visual communication attainable. We will help you achieve all of your goals while providing you with the greatest value both seen and unseen.

Here at Blazing Graphics we will take the time to do things right. We do this by controlling the entire graphic arts process. This enables us to better coordinate each job while providing a higher level of service.

Our mission is to ensure exceptional quality by opening up communication between crafts normally separated and at times adverse to one another.

Here at Blazing Graphics we have committed ourselves and our resources to being on the forefront of technology.

Creative technical know-how is the single most critical determinant of economic competitiveness.

It's our real belief that together we can create an environment that will be both personally and professionally fulfilling for all the people who make up the Blazing Community.

FIGURE 1-6

Blazing Graphics' Mission Statement

Source: Nelton, S. (1994, February). Put your purpose in writing. *Nation's Business*, 61. Reprinted by permission. Copyright 1994, U.S. Chamber of Commerce.

Securing Management Commitment. HR strategies that originate in the HR department will have little chance of succeeding unless managers at all levels—including top executives—support them completely. To ensure managers' commitment, HR professionals must work closely with them when formulating policies. This is a point we emphasize again and again throughout this book.

Translating the Strategic Plan into Action. Often a strategic plan that looks great on paper fails because of poor implementation. The acid test of any strategic plan is whether or not it makes a difference in practice. If the plan does not affect practice, employees and managers will regard it as all talk and no action.

Cynicism regarding the strategic plan is practically guaranteed when a firm experiences frequent turnover at the top, with each new wave of high-level managers introducing their own freshly minted strategic plan. Perhaps the greatest challenge in strategic HR planning lies not in the formulation of strategy, but rather in the development of an appropriate set of programs that will make the strategy work.

Combining Intended and Emergent Strategies. There is a continuing debate over whether strategies are *intended* or *emergent*—that is, whether they are proactive, rational, deliberate plans designed to attain predetermined objectives (intended) or general "fuzzy" patterns collectively molded by the interplay of power, politics, improvisation, negotiation, and personalities within the organization (emergent).[72] Most people agree that organizations have intended *and* emergent strategies, that both are necessary, and that the challenge is to combine the best aspects of the two.

When based on a rigorous analysis of where the organization is and where it wishes to go, intended strategies can provide a sense of purpose and a guide for the allocation of resources. Intended strategies are also useful for recognizing environmental opportunities and threats and mobilizing top management to respond appropriately. On the downside,

A Company with a Vision.

Today's most successful firms have a written vision statement that clearly spells out the company's mission. Ortho Biotech's statement promises, "We will be the best in our business by providing customers with innovative solutions to significant medical problems through biotechnology and related science."

intended strategies may lead to a top-down strategic approach that squashes creativity and widespread involvement.

Emergent strategies also have their advantages and disadvantages. Among their benefits: (1) they involve everyone in the organization, which fosters grass-roots support; (2) they develop gradually out of the organization's experiences, and thus can be less upsetting than intended strategies; and (3) they are more pragmatic than intended strategies because they evolve to deal with specific problems or issues facing the firm. On the negative side, emergent strategies may lack strong leadership and fail to infuse the organization with a creative vision.[73]

Combining intended and emergent strategies effectively requires that managers blend the benefits of formal planning (to provide strong guidance and direction in setting priorities) with the untidy realities of dispersed employees who, through their unplanned activities, formulate emergent strategies throughout the firm.

Accommodating Change. Strategic HR plans must be flexible enough to accommodate change. A firm with an inflexible strategic plan may find itself unable to respond to changes quickly because it is so committed to a particular course of action. This may lead the organization to continue devoting resources to an activity of questionable value simply because so much has been invested in it already.[74] The challenge is to create a strategic vision and develop the plans to achieve it while staying flexible enough to adapt to change.

Strategic HR Choices

strategic HR choices
The options available to a firm in designing its human resources system.

A firm's **strategic HR choices** are the options it has available in designing its human resources system. Choices are strategic to the extent that they affect the firm's performance either favorably or unfavorably in the long run.

Figure 1-7 shows a sampling of strategic HR choices. At this point, it is important to keep three things in mind. First, the list of strategic HR choices in Figure 1-7 is not exhaustive. Second, many different HR programs or practices may be used separately or together to implement each of these choices. For example, if a firm chooses to base pay on performance, it can use many different programs to implement this decision, including cash awards, lump-sum annual bonuses, raises based on supervisory appraisals, and an employee-of-the-month award. Third, the strategic HR choices listed in Figure 1-7 represent two opposite poles on a continuum. Very few organizations fall at these extremes. Some organizations will be closer to the right end, some closer to the left end, and others closer to the middle.

A brief description of the strategic HR choices shown in Figure 1-7 follows. We will examine these choices and provide examples of companies' strategic decisions in these areas in later chapters.

Work Flows. Work flows refer to the ways tasks are organized to meet production or service goals. Organizations face several choices in what they emphasize as they structure work flows (Chapter 2). They can emphasize:

- efficiency (getting work done at minimum cost) or innovation (encouraging creativity, exploration, and new ways of doing things, even though this may increase production costs)
- control (establishing predetermined procedures) or flexibility (allowing room for exceptions and personal judgment)
- explicit job descriptions (in which each job's duties and requirements are carefully spelled out) or broad job classes (in which employees perform multiple tasks and are expected to fill different jobs as needed), and

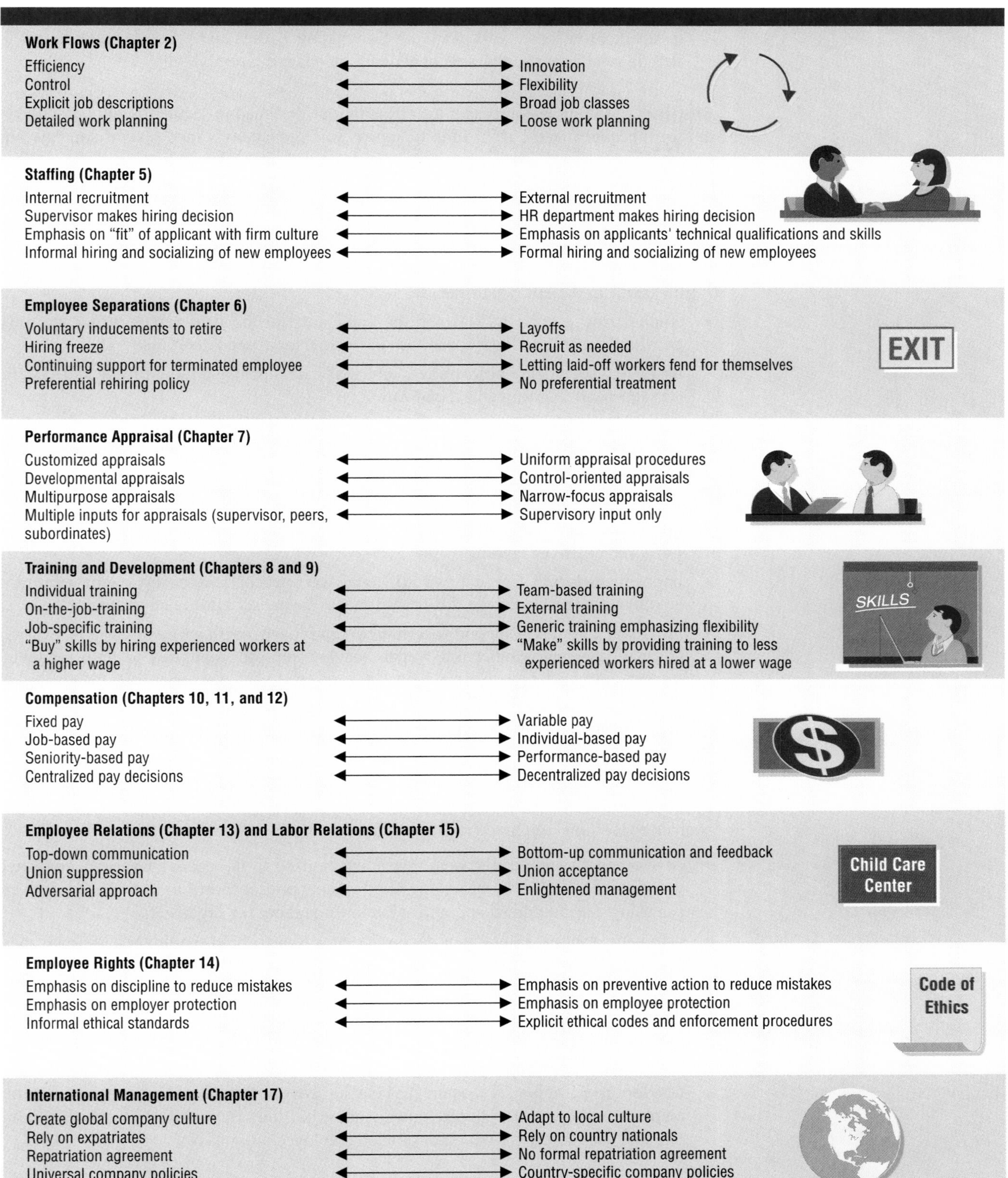

Work Flows (Chapter 2)	
Efficiency	Innovation
Control	Flexibility
Explicit job descriptions	Broad job classes
Detailed work planning	Loose work planning
Staffing (Chapter 5)	
Internal recruitment	External recruitment
Supervisor makes hiring decision	HR department makes hiring decision
Emphasis on "fit" of applicant with firm culture	Emphasis on applicants' technical qualifications and skills
Informal hiring and socializing of new employees	Formal hiring and socializing of new employees
Employee Separations (Chapter 6)	
Voluntary inducements to retire	Layoffs
Hiring freeze	Recruit as needed
Continuing support for terminated employee	Letting laid-off workers fend for themselves
Preferential rehiring policy	No preferential treatment
Performance Appraisal (Chapter 7)	
Customized appraisals	Uniform appraisal procedures
Developmental appraisals	Control-oriented appraisals
Multipurpose appraisals	Narrow-focus appraisals
Multiple inputs for appraisals (supervisor, peers, subordinates)	Supervisory input only
Training and Development (Chapters 8 and 9)	
Individual training	Team-based training
On-the-job-training	External training
Job-specific training	Generic training emphasizing flexibility
"Buy" skills by hiring experienced workers at a higher wage	"Make" skills by providing training to less experienced workers hired at a lower wage
Compensation (Chapters 10, 11, and 12)	
Fixed pay	Variable pay
Job-based pay	Individual-based pay
Seniority-based pay	Performance-based pay
Centralized pay decisions	Decentralized pay decisions
Employee Relations (Chapter 13) and Labor Relations (Chapter 15)	
Top-down communication	Bottom-up communication and feedback
Union suppression	Union acceptance
Adversarial approach	Enlightened management
Employee Rights (Chapter 14)	
Emphasis on discipline to reduce mistakes	Emphasis on preventive action to reduce mistakes
Emphasis on employer protection	Emphasis on employee protection
Informal ethical standards	Explicit ethical codes and enforcement procedures
International Management (Chapter 17)	
Create global company culture	Adapt to local culture
Rely on expatriates	Rely on country nationals
Repatriation agreement	No formal repatriation agreement
Universal company policies	Country-specific company policies

FIGURE 1-7

Strategic HR Choices

- detailed work planning (in which processes, objectives, and schedules are laid out well in advance) or loose work planning (in which activities and schedules may be modified on relatively short notice, depending on changing needs).

Staffing. Staffing encompasses the HR activities designed to secure the right employees at the right place at the right time (Chapter 5). Organizations face several strategic HR choices in recruiting, selecting, and socializing employees—all part of the staffing process. These include:

- promoting from within (*internal* recruitment) versus hiring from the outside (*external* recruitment)
- empowering immediate supervisors to make hiring decisions versus centralizing these decisions in the HR department
- emphasizing a good fit between the applicant and the firm versus hiring the most knowledgeable individual regardless of interpersonal considerations, and
- hiring and socializing new workers informally or choosing a more formal and systematic approach to hiring and socialization.

Employee Separations. Employee separations occur when employees leave the firm, either voluntarily or involuntarily (Chapter 6). Some strategic HR choices available to the firm for handling employee separations are:

- use of voluntary inducements (such as early retirement packages) to downsize a work force versus use of layoffs
- imposing a hiring freeze to avoid laying off current employees versus recruiting employees as needed, even if doing so means laying off current employees
- providing continuing support to terminated employees (perhaps by offering them assistance in securing another job) versus leaving laid-off employees to fend for themselves; and
- making a commitment to rehire terminated employees if conditions improve versus avoiding any type of preferential hiring treatment for ex-employees.

Performance Appraisal. Managers assess how well employees are carrying out their assigned duties by conducting performance appraisals (Chapter 7). Some strategic HR choices concerning employee appraisals are:

- developing an appraisal system that is customized to the needs of various employee groups (for example, by designing a different appraisal form for each job family) versus using a standardized appraisal system throughout the organization
- using the appraisal data as a developmental tool to help employees improve their performance versus using appraisals as a control mechanism to weed out low producers
- designing the appraisal system with multiple objectives in mind (such as training, promotion, and selection decisions) versus designing it for a narrow purpose (such as pay decisions only), and
- developing an appraisal system that encourages the active participation of multiple employee groups (for example, supervisor, peers, and subordinates) versus developing one that asks solely for the input of each employee's supervisor.

Training and Career Development. Training and career development activities are designed to help an organization meet its skill requirements and to help its employees realize their maximum potential (Chapters 8 and 9). Some of the strategic HR choices pertaining to these activities are:

- choosing whether to provide training to individuals or to teams of employees who may come from diverse areas of the firm
- deciding whether to teach required skills on the job or rely on external sources for training
- choosing whether to emphasize job-specific training or generic training, and
- deciding whether to hire at a high wage people from outside the firm who already have the required talents ("buy skills") or to invest resources in training the firm's own lower-wage employees in the necessary skills ("make skills").

Compensation. Compensation is the payment that employees receive in exchange for their labor. U.S. organizations vary widely in how they choose to compensate their employees (Chapters 10, 11, and 12). Some of the strategic HR choices related to pay are:

- providing employees with a fixed salary and benefits package that changes little from year to year (and therefore involves minimal risk) versus paying employees a variable amount subject to change
- paying employees on the basis of the job they hold versus paying them for their individual contributions to the firm
- rewarding employees for the time they've spent with the firm versus rewarding them for performance, and
- centralizing pay decisions in a single location (such as the HR department) versus empowering the supervisor or work team to make pay decisions.

Employee Rights. Employee rights concern the relationship between the organization and individual employees (Chapter 14). Some of the strategic choices that the firm needs to make in this area are:

- emphasizing discipline as the mechanism for controlling employee behavior versus proactively encouraging appropriate behavior in the first place
- developing policies that emphasize protecting the employer's interests versus policies that emphasize protecting the employees' interests, and
- relying on informal ethical standards versus developing explicit standards and procedures to enforce those standards.

Employee and Labor Relations. Employee and labor relations (Chapters 13 and 15) refer to the interaction between workers (either as individuals or as represented by a union) and management. Some of the strategic HR choices facing the firm in these areas are:

- relying on "top-down" communication channels from managers to subordinates versus encouraging "bottom-up" feedback from employees to managers
- actively trying to avoid or suppress union-organizing activity versus accepting unions as representatives of employees' interests, and
- adopting an adversarial approach to dealing with employees versus responding to employees' needs so that the incentive for unionization is removed (enlightened management).

International Management. Firms that operate outside domestic boundaries face a set of strategic HR options regarding how to manage human resources on a global basis (Chapter 17). Some of the key strategic HR choices involved in international management are:

A QUESTION OF ETHICS

Experts in career development note that in today's increasingly chaotic business and economic environment, individual employees need to prepare themselves for job and career changes. Does an employer have an ethical duty to help employees prepare for the change that is almost certain to come?

- creating a common company culture to reduce intercountry cultural differences versus allowing foreign subsidiaries to adapt to the local culture
- sending expatriates (domestic employees) abroad to manage foreign subsidiaries versus hiring local people to manage them
- establishing a repatriation agreement with each employee going abroad (carefully stipulating what the expatriate can expect upon return in terms of career advancement, compensation, and the like) versus avoiding any type of commitment to expatriates, and
- establishing company policies that must be followed in all subsidiaries versus decentralizing policy formulation so that each local office can develop its own policies.

Building Managerial Skills: Selecting HR Strategies to Increase Firm Performance

No HR strategy is "good" or "bad" in and of itself. Rather, the success of HR strategies depends on the situation or context in which they are used. In other words, an HR strategy's effect on firm performance is always dependent on how well it fits with other factors. This fact leads to a simple yet powerful prediction for HR strategies that has been widely supported by research: Fit leads to better performance, and lack of fit creates inconsistencies that reduce performance.[75] *Fit* refers to the consistency or compatibility between HR strategies and other important aspects of the organization.

Figure 1-8 depicts the key factors that firms should consider in determining which HR strategies will have a positive impact on firm performance: organizational strategies, environment, organizational characteristics, and organizational capabilities. As the figure shows, the relative contribution of an HR strategy to firm performance increases:

1. The greater the match between the HR strategy and the firm's overall organizational strategies.
2. The greater the extent to which the HR strategy is attuned to the environment in which the firm is operating.

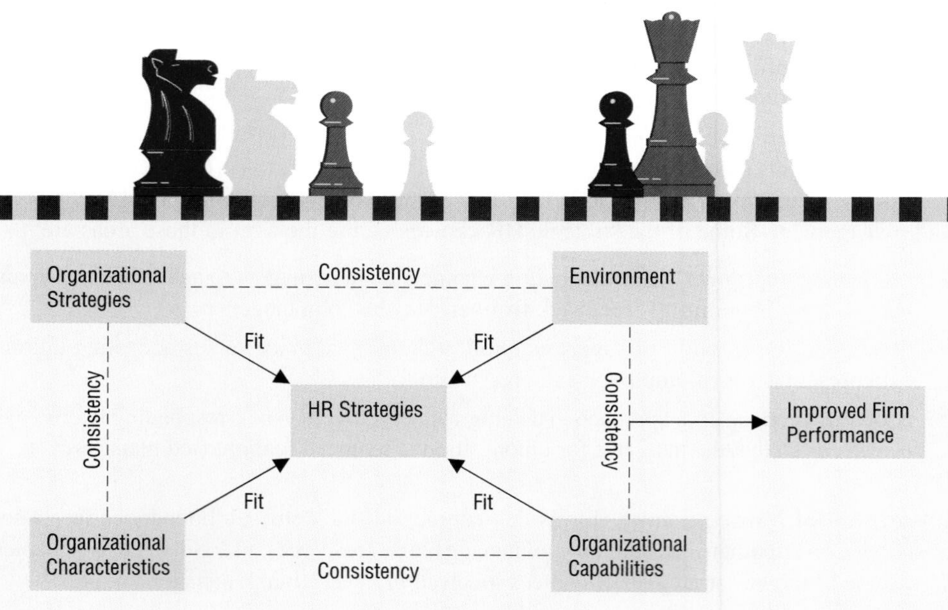

FIGURE 1-8

Effective HR Strategy Formulation and Implementation

3. The more the HR strategy is molded to unique organizational features.
4. The more the HR strategy enables the firm to capitalize on its distinctive competencies.
5. The more the HR strategies are mutually consistent or reinforce one another.

Fit with Organizational Strategies

Depending on the firm's size and complexity, organizational strategies may be examined at two levels: corporate or business. A corporation may have multiple businesses that are very similar to or completely different from one another. **Corporate strategy** refers to the mix of businesses a corporation decides to hold and the flow of resources among those businesses. The main strategic business decisions at the corporate level concern acquisition, divestment, diversification, and growth. **Business unit strategies** refer to the formulation and implementation of strategies by firms that are relatively autonomous, even if they are part of a larger corporation. For instance, until fairly recently, AT&T as a corporate entity owned hundreds of largely independent firms, including perfume makers and Hostess Twinkies, each with its own business strategy.[76] In the case of firms that produce a single product or highly related products or services (such as Compaq, a computer manufacturer), the business and corporate strategies are identical. For companies that have distinct corporate and business unit strategies, it is important to examine each in terms of its fit with HR strategies.

corporate strategy
The mix of businesses a corporation decides to hold and the flow of resources among those businesses.

business unit strategy
The formulation and implementation of strategies by a firm that is relatively autonomous, even if it is part of a larger corporation.

Corporate Strategies. There are two major types of corporate strategies and matching HR strategies. Corporations adopting an *evolutionary business strategy* engage in aggressive acquisitions of new businesses, even if these are totally unrelated to one another.[77] For example, before its reorganization, Gulf + Western was nicknamed "Engulf and Devour" because of its extensive purchasing and divesting of businesses in diverse markets and industries, including oil, agriculture, tourist attractions, and the arts.[78]

In evolutionary firms, the management of change is crucial to survival. Entrepreneurship is encouraged and control is deemphasized because each unit is relatively autonomous. Certain HR strategies fit best with an evolutionary strategy. HR strategies that foster flexibility, quick response, entrepreneurship, risk sharing, and decentralization are particularly appropriate. Because the evolutionary corporation is not committed to a particular business or industry, it may hire workers from the external market as needed and lay them off to reduce costs if necessary, with no promise of rehiring them. These HR strategies are appropriate because they "fit" with the organizational reality that change is the only constant.

At the other end of the spectrum, corporations adopting a *steady-state strategy* are very choosy about how they grow. They avoid acquiring firms outside their industry or even companies within the industry that are very different from them. Firms with a steady-state strategy have an inward focus. Top managers exercise a great deal of direct control over the company and prefer to promote employee dependence on supervisors rather than independent action or entrepreneurship. Internal development of new products and technologies and interunit coordination are very important to these firms.[79] This is the case at Rubbermaid, a company known for producing such mundane products as trash cans and dustpans. Yet, Rubbermaid's record for innovation is anything but mundane. The company brings out new products at the rate of one a day.[80] The HR strategies most appropriate to steady-state firms emphasize efficiency, detailed work planning, internal grooming of employees for promotion and long-term career development, centralization, and a paternalistic attitude (reflected, for example, in preferential recall of laid-off employees when the economic environment improves).

A QUESTION OF ETHICS

The dark side of strategic planning is that workers are sometimes thought of as numbers on a page or dollars in a budget rather than as flesh-and-blood human beings. When divisions are spun off or merged, individual employees are dramatically affected. What responsibility does the employer have toward its employees in situations like these?

Porter's Business Unit Strategies. Two well-known business unit strategies were formulated by Porter[81] and Miles and Snow.[82] Both of these may be used to analyze which HR strategies represent the best fit with a firm's business strategy.

Porter has identified three types of business unit strategies that help a firm cope with competitive forces and outperform other firms in the industry. For each of these strategies, outlined in Figure 1-9, a certain set of HR strategies would fit best.[83]

The *overall cost leadership strategy* is aimed at gaining a competitive advantage through lower costs. Financial considerations and budgetary constraints play a critical role here in shaping HR strategies. Cost leadership requires aggressive construction of efficient plant facilities (which requires sustained capital investment), intense supervision of labor, vigorous pursuit of cost reductions, and tight control of distribution costs and overhead. Firms that have successfully pursued a low-cost leadership strategy include Briggs and Stratton, Emerson Electric, Texas Instruments, Black and Decker, and Du Pont.[84]

Low-cost firms tend to emphasize structured tasks and responsibilities, products designed for easy manufacture, and the need to predict costs with minimal margin of error. The HR strategies that fit a low-cost orientation emphasize efficient, low-cost production; reinforce adherence to rational, highly structured procedures to minimize uncertainty; and discourage creativity and innovation (which may lead to costly experimentation and mistakes). Thus, effective HR strategies include carefully spelling out the work that each employee needs to do, job-specific training, hiring workers with the necessary technical qualifications and skills, paying employees on the basis of job held, and relying on performance appraisals as a control tool to weed out low performers.

A firm with a *differentiation business strategy* attempts to achieve a competitive advantage by creating a product or service that is perceived as unique. Some common charac-

FIGURE 1-9

Selected HR Strategies That Fit Porter's Three Major Types of Business Strategies

Source: Common organizational characteristics: Porter, M. E. (1980). *Competitive Strategy*, 40-41. New York: Free Press. HR Strategies: Prepared by the authors for this book.

Business Strategy	Common Organizational Characteristics	HR Strategies
Overall cost leadership	• Sustained capital investment and access to capital • Intense supervision of labor • Tight cost control requiring frequent, detailed control reports • Low-cost distribution system • Structured organization and responsibilities • Products designed for ease in manufacture	• Efficient production • Explicit job descriptions • Detailed work planning • Emphasis on technical qualifications and skills • Emphasis on job-specific training • Emphasis on job-based pay • Use of performance appraisal as a control device
Differentiation	• Strong marketing abilities • Product engineering • Strong capability in basic research • Corporate reputation for quality or technological leadership • Amenities to attract highly skilled labor, scientists, or creative people	• Emphasis on innovation and flexibility • Broad job classes • Loose work planning • External recruitment • Team-based training • Emphasis on individual-based pay • Use of performance appraisal as developmental tool
Focus	Combination of cost-leadership and differentiation strategy directed at a particular strategic target	Combination of HR strategies above

teristics of such firms are strong marketing abilities, an emphasis on product engineering and basic research, a corporate reputation for quality products, and amenities that are attractive to highly skilled labor. Approaches to differentiating can take many forms, among them: design or brand image (Fieldcrest in top-of-the-line towels and linens; Mercedes in automobiles); technology (Hyster in lift trucks; Fisher in stereo components; Coleman in camping equipment); features (Jenn-Air in electric ranges); customer service (IBM in computers); and dealer networks (Caterpillar Tractor in construction equipment).

Differentiation provides a competitive advantage because of the brand loyalty it fosters. Consumers who are brand loyal are less sensitive to changes in price. This enables the differentiator to enjoy higher profit margins, which in turn allow it to invest in activities that are costly and risky but that enhance the perceived superiority of its products or services. These activities include extensive research, experimentation with new ideas and product designs, catering to the needs of different customers, and supporting creative initiatives by managers and employees.

HR strategies that fit a differentiation strategy emphasize innovation, flexibility, renewal of the work force by attracting new talent from other firms, opportunities for mavericks, and reinforcement (rather than discouragement) of creative flair. The specific HR strategies that are likely to benefit differentiators include the use of broad job classes, loose work planning, external recruitment at all levels, team-based learning, emphasis on what the individual can do (rather than on the job title held) as a basis for pay, and reliance on performance appraisal as a developmental (rather than a control) device.

The *focus strategy* relies on both a low-cost position and differentiation, with the objective of serving a narrow target market better than other firms. The firm seeks to achieve differentiation either from better meeting the needs of the particular target, or from lowering costs in serving this target, or both.[85] Firms that have used this strategy successfully include Illinois Tool Works (in the specialty market for fasteners), Gymboree (a national franchise providing creative activities and accessories for children under the age of five), Fort Howard Paper (manufacturer of specialized industrial grade papers), and Porter Paint (producer of paints for professional housepainters).

The HR strategies likely to fit the focus strategy best would be somewhere in the middle of those described for low-cost producers and differentiators. At Illinois Tool Works (ITW), for instance, the chairman stresses working hand-in-hand with customers both to find out what they want and to learn how ITW can help them lower their operating costs. HR strategies reflect this focus by boosting efficiency to hold costs down. ITW's business is decentralized into 200 fairly small operating units, headed by managers whose pay is largely tied to sales and profits at their individual operations. The company's workers are nonunion, which helps to hold costs down. To keep ITW's products geared to customer needs, management puts heavy emphasis on R&D. ITW's R&D spending of almost $40 million a year keeps creativity high; ITW holds over 4,000 active patents.[86]

Miles and Snow's Business Strategies. Miles and Snow created another well-known classification of business unit strategies.[87] They characterize successful businesses as primarily adopting either a defender or a prospector strategy.

Defenders are conservative business units that prefer to maintain a secure position in relatively stable product or service areas instead of looking to expand into uncharted territory. Defenders attempt to protect their market share from competitors rather than engage in new-product development. Defenders tend to be highly formalized and centralized, to emphasize cost control, and to operate in a stable environment. Many defenders develop an elaborate internal system for promoting, transferring, and rewarding workers that is relatively isolated from the uncertainties of the external labor market. In exchange for a long-term commitment to the firm, employees are rewarded with job security and the expectation of upward mobility through the ranks. Defenders discourage risk-taking behaviors because they prefer reliability to innovation.

The HR strategies that best fit defenders' needs, categorized according to six major strategic HR choices we saw in Figure 1-7 earlier, are summarized in Figure 1-10. These strategies include work flows emphasizing managerial control and reliability, staffing and employee separation policies designed to foster long-term employee attachment to the firm, performance appraisals focused on managerial control and hierarchy, structured training programs, and compensation policies that emphasize job security.

Unlike defenders, whose success comes primarily from efficiently serving a stable market, the prospector's key objective is to find and exploit new product and market opportunities.[88] *Prospectors* emphasize growth and innovation, development of new products, and an eagerness to be the first in new product or market areas, even if some of these efforts fail. The prospector's strategy is associated with flexible and decentralized organizational structures, complex products (such as computers and pharmaceuticals), and unstable environments that change rapidly.

The HR strategies that match the strategic orientation of prospectors, also summarized in Figure 1-10, involve work flows that foster creativity and adaptability; staffing and employee separation policies that focus on the external labor market; customized, participative employee appraisals used for multiple purposes (including employee development); training strategies targeting broad skills; and a decentralized compensation system that

Strategic HR Area	Defender Strategy	Prospector Strategy
Work flows	• Efficient production • Control emphasis • Explicit job descriptions • Detailed work planning	• Innovation • Flexibility • Broad job classes • Loose work planning
Staffing	• Internal recruitment • HR department makes selection decision • Emphasis on technical qualifications and skills • Formal hiring and socialization process	• External recruitment • Supervisor makes selection decision • Emphasis on fit of applicant with culture • Informal hiring and socialization process of new employees
Employee separations	• Voluntary inducements to leave • Hiring freeze • Continuing concern for terminated employee • Preferential rehiring policy	• Layoffs • Recruit as needed • Individual on his/her own • No preferential treatment for laid-off workers
Performance appraisal	• Uniform appraisal procedures • Used as control device • Narrow focus • High dependence on superior	• Customized appraisals • Used as developmental tool • Multipurpose appraisals • Multiple inputs for appraisals
Training	• Individual training • On-the-job training • Job-specific training • "Make" skills	• Team-based or cross-functional training • External training • Generic training emphasizing flexibility • "Buy" skills
Compensation	• Fixed pay • Job-based pay • Seniority-based pay • Centralized pay decisions	• Variable pay • Individual-based pay • Performance-based pay • Decentralized pay decisions

FIGURE 1-10

Selected HR Strategies That Fit Miles and Snow's Two Major Types of Business Strategies

Source: Gómez-Mejía, L. R. (1997). Compensation strategies and Miles and Snow's business strategy taxonomy. Unpublished report. Management Department, Arizona State University.

rewards risk taking and performance. The Issues and Applications feature on page 32 titled "Lincoln Electric and Hewlett-Packard: Defender and Prospector" discusses how these two firms have successfully used HR strategies to support their opposite business strategies.

Fit with the Environment

In addition to reinforcing overall organizational strategies, HR strategies should help the organization better exploit environmental opportunities or cope with the unique environmental forces that affect it. The relevant environment can be examined in terms of four major dimensions: (1) *degree of uncertainty* (how much accurate information is available to make appropriate business decisions); (2) *volatility* (how often the environment changes); (3) *magnitude of change* (how drastic the changes are); and (4) *complexity* (how many different elements in the environment affect the firm, either individually or together). For example, much of the computer and high-tech industry is very high on all four of these dimensions:

- *Degree of uncertainty.* Compaq thought consumers would continue to pay a premium price for its high-performance computers. The company was proved wrong in the 1990s as low-cost competitors such as Dell, Packard Bell, and AST quickly cut into Compaq's market.
- *Volatility.* IBM paid dearly when demand for its mainframe computers declined drastically in the late 1980s and it was caught unprepared.
- *Magnitude of change.* The advent of each successive new generation of computer microprocessor chips (for example, Intel's 386, 486, Pentium) has almost immediately rendered all previously sold machines obsolete.
- *Complexity.* The number and variety of competitors in the computer industry, both domestically and overseas, have grown dramatically in recent years. The life of a product seldom extends more than three years now, as new innovations drive previous equipment and software out of the market.

Before formulating and implementing HR strategies, a firm needs to examine how low or high it is on each of these environmental dimensions. As Figure 1-11 shows, firms that

Environmental Dimension	Low	High
Degree of Uncertainty	• Detailed work planning • Job-specific training • Fixed pay • High dependence on superior	• Loose work planning • Generic training • Variable pay • Multiple inputs for appraisals
Volatility	• Control emphasis • Efficient production • Job-specific training • Fixed pay	• Flexibility • Innovation • Generic training • Variable pay
Magnitude of Change	• Explicit job descriptions • Formal hiring and socialization of new employees • "Make" skills • Uniform appraisal procedures	• Broad job classes • Informal hiring and socialization of new employees • "Buy" skills • Customized appraisals
Complexity	• Control emphasis • Internal recruitment • Centralized pay decisions • High dependence on superior	• Flexibility • External recruitment • Decentralized pay decisions • Multiple inputs for appraisals

FIGURE 1-11

Selected HR Strategies for Firms Low and High on Different Environmental Characteristics

Source: Based on Gómez-Mejía, L. R., and Balkin, D. B. (1992). *Compensation, organizational strategy, and firm performance.* Cincinnati, OH: South-Western; Gómez-Mejía, L. R., Balkin, D. B., and Milkovich, G. T. (1990). Rethinking your rewards for technical employees. *Organizational Dynamics, 18*(4), 62–75; Gómez-Mejía, L. R. (1992). Structure and process of diversification, compensation strategy, and firm performance. *Strategic Management Journal, 13*, 381–397; and Gómez-Mejía, L. R. (1994). *Fostering a strategic partnership between operations and human resources.* Scarsdale, NY: Work in America Institute.

Issues + Applications

Lincoln Electric and Hewlett-Packard: Defender and Prospector

To get a better idea of what it means for a company to be a defender or a prospector, let's look at the activities of two companies: Ohio-based Lincoln Electric, a manufacturer of electrical products; and Hewlett-Packard, the Palo Alto, California, electronics manufacturer that put Silicon Valley on the high-tech map.

LINCOLN ELECTRIC

Lincoln Electric is a classic defender. It has carved out a niche in the electrical products industry (the manufacture of electric arc-welding generators, welding equipment, and supplies) and has "defended" it for over 70 years through continuous efforts to improve production processes and product quality, cut costs, lower prices, and provide outstanding customer service. Lincoln is best known for its incentive system, which rewards high-quantity, high-quality output with wages and bonuses that average over *twice* the national average for comparable work classifications. Lincoln's HR strategies fit with the company's strategy because Lincoln has created a secure market share with moderate, steady growth. It relies heavily on internally developed human resources. Employees are carefully selected, placed, and trained, and they are expected to be with the company for much, if not all, of their careers.

The appropriate role for the HR department at Lincoln is clear. Selection, placement, appraisal, and long-term training assistance are key services. In addition, the HR department must constantly maintain the fit between job design and the incentive system. Lincoln is a tightly integrated company that requires predictable, planned HR inputs and regular maintenance.

HEWLETT-PACKARD

Hewlett-Packard (HP) began with the notion that high returns were possible from moving products as rapidly as possible from basic design to the market. It is a company well suited to the rapid expansion of a growing industry—a true prospector—with small, changing product divisions as its basic organizational building blocks. (The company has over 60,000 employees in more than 60 divisions or units.) A new-product idea or offshoot is evolved, a self-contained division created, and a market pursued as long as HP has a distinctive design or technological advantage. When products reach the stage where successful competition turns primarily on cost, HP may move out of the arena and turn its attention to a new design or an entirely new product.

HR units at both the division and the corporate level have the constant task of starting new groups, and finding and deploying managerial and technical resources. In this setting, HR departments perform an essentially entrepreneurial role, helping to identify and quickly develop (through rapid movement and alternative assignments) crucial human resources. Key human resources are brought in from the outside and invested in myriad units and divisions, as well as developed internally. Thus the overall HR strategy at Hewlett-Packard can be characterized as acquiring human resources.

Source: Based on Miles, R. E., and Snow, C. C. (1984). Designing strategic human resources systems. *Organizational Dynamics 13*(1), 43–46.

are high on these four dimensions are more likely to benefit from HR strategies that promote flexibility, adaptiveness, quick response, transferability of skills, the ability to secure external talent as needed, and risk sharing with employees through variable pay.

Conversely, firms facing environments that are low on uncertainty, volatility, magnitude of change, and complexity benefit from HR strategies that allow for an orderly, rational, and routine approach to dealing with a relatively predictable and stable environment. The "old" AT&T (before divestment), much of the airline and trucking industry before deregulation, utilities, and government bureaucracies fall at the low end of the scale on these four dimensions. Figure 1-11 shows that the HR strategies that fit firms operating under these conditions tend to be rather mechanistic: detailed work planning, job-specific training, fixed pay, explicit job descriptions, centralized pay decisions, and the like.

Fit with Organizational Characteristics

Every firm has a unique history and its own way of doing business. To be effective, HR strategies must be tailored to the organization's personality. The features of an organization's personality can be broken down into five major categories.

The Production Process for Converting Inputs into Output. Firms with a relatively routine production process (such as large-volume steel mills, lumber mills, and automobile plants) tend to benefit from HR strategies that emphasize control, such as explicit job descriptions and job-specific training. The opposite is true for firms with nonroutine production processes (such as advertising firms, custom printers, and biotechnology companies). These firms benefit from flexible HR strategies that support organizational adaptability, quick response to change, and creative decision making. These flexible strategies may include broad job classes, loose work planning, and generic training.

The Firm's Market Posture. Firms that experience a high rate of sales growth and engage in product innovation destined for a wide market segment tend to benefit from HR strategies that support growth and entrepreneurial activities. These HR strategies include external recruitment ("buying" skills), decentralized pay decisions, and customized appraisals. The opposite is true for firms with low rates of growth and limited product innovation destined for a narrow market segment. These firms tend to benefit more from HR strategies that emphasize efficiency, control, and firm-specific knowledge. Such strategies include internal recruitment ("making" skills), on-the-job training, and high dependence on superiors.

The Firm's Overall Managerial Philosophy. Companies whose top executives are averse to risk, operate with an autocratic leadership style, establish a strong internal pecking order, and are inwardly rather than outwardly focused may find that certain HR practices match this outlook best. The HR strategies most often used in these kinds of firms include seniority-based pay, formal hiring and socializing of new employees, selection decisions made by the HR department, and use of top-down communication channels. The HR strategies that fit a managerial philosophy high on risk taking, participation, egalitarianism, and an external, proactive environmental orientation include variable pay, giving supervisors a major role in hiring decisions, up-and-down communication channels, and multiple inputs for performance appraisals.

The Firm's Organizational Structure. Some HR strategies fit very well with highly formalized organizations that are divided into functional areas (for example, marketing, finance, production, and so on) and that concentrate decision making at the top. The HR strategies appropriate for this type of firm include a control emphasis, centralized pay decisions, explicit job descriptions, and job-based pay. Firms whose organizational structures are less regimented will benefit from a different set of HR strategies, including informal hiring and socializing of new employees, decentralized pay decisions, broad job classes, and individual-based pay.

The Firm's Organizational Culture. Two important dimensions of a firm's culture should be considered when formulating and implementing HR strategies: entrepreneurial climate and moral commitment. Companies that foster an *entrepreneurial climate* benefit from such supporting HR strategies as loose work planning, informal hiring and socializing of new employees, and variable pay. Firms that discourage entrepreneurship generally prefer a control emphasis, detailed work planning, formal hiring and socializing of new employees, and fixed pay.

A strong emphasis on *moral commitment*—the extent to which a firm tries to foster a long-term emotional attachment between the firm and its employees—is also associated with certain supporting HR strategies. These include an emphasis on preventive versus remedial disciplinary action to handle employee mistakes, employee protection, and explicit ethical codes to monitor and guide behavior. Firms that are low on moral commitment usually rely on an authoritarian relationship between employee and company. HR strategies consistent with this orientation include an emphasis on discipline or punishment to reduce employee mistakes, employment at will (discussed in Chapters 3 and 14), and informal ethical standards.

Fit with Organizational Capabilities

distinctive competencies
The characteristics that give a firm a competitive edge.

A firm's organizational capabilities include its **distinctive competencies,** those characteristics (such as technical ability, management systems, and reputation) that give the firm a competitive edge. For instance, Mercedes-Benz automobiles are widely regarded as superior because of the quality of their design and engineering. Wal-Mart's phenomenal success has been due, at least in part, to its ability to track products from supplier to customer better than its competitors can.

Following the fit logic, HR strategies make a greater contribution to firm performance the greater the extent to which (1) they help the company exploit its specific advantages or strengths while avoiding weaknesses, and (2) they assist the firm in better utilizing its own unique blend of human resource skills and assets.

The following examples illustrate how one type of HR strategy—compensation strategy—may be aligned with organizational capabilities.[89]

- Firms known for excellence in customer service tend to pay their sales force only partially on commission, thereby reducing their sales employees' potential for abrasive behaviors and overselling.
- Smaller firms can use compensation to their advantage by paying low wages but being generous in stock offerings to employees. This strategy allows them to use more of their scarce cash to fuel future growth.
- Organizations may take advantage of their unused capacity in their compensation strategies. For example, most private universities offer free tuition to faculty and their immediate family. With average tuition at private colleges exceeding $11,000 a year, this benefit represents a huge cash savings to faculty members, thereby allowing private universities to attract and retain good faculty with minimal adverse impact on their cost structure.

Manager's Notebook

But Will It Work? Questions for Testing the Appropriateness of HR Programs Before Implementation

HR programs that look good on paper may turn out to be disasters when implemented because they conflict too much with company realities. To avoid this kind of unpleasant surprise, it's important to ask the following questions *before* implementing a new HR program.

1. **Are the HR Programs Effective Tools for Implementing HR Strategies?**
   - Are the proposed HR programs the most appropriate ones for implementing the firm's HR strategies?
   - Has an analysis been done of how each of the past, current, or planned HR programs contributes to or hinders the successful implementation of the firm's HR strategies?
   - Can the proposed HR programs be easily changed or modified to meet new strategic considerations without violating either a "psychological" or a legal contract with employees?
2. **Do the HR Programs Meet Resource Constraints?**
   - Does the organization have the capacity to implement the proposed HR programs? In other words, are the HR programs realistic?
   - Are the proposed programs going to be introduced at a rate that can be easily absorbed, or will the timing and extent of changes lead to widespread confusion and strong employee resistance?
3. **How Will the HR Programs Be Communicated?**
   - Are the proposed HR programs well understood by those who will implement them (for example, line supervisors and employees)?
   - Does top management understand how the proposed programs are intended to affect the firm's strategic objectives?
4. **Who Will Put the HR Programs in Motion?**
   - Is the HR department playing the role of an internal consultant to assist employees and managers responsible for carrying out the proposed HR programs?
   - Is top management visibly and emphatically committed to the proposed programs?

Choosing Consistent and Appropriate HR Tactics to Implement HR Strategies

As noted earlier, even the best-laid strategic HR plans may fail when specific HR programs are poorly chosen or implemented.[90] In addition to fitting with each of the four factors just described (organizational strategy, environment, organizational characteristics, and organizational capabilities), a firm's HR strategies must be mutually consistent. That is, HR strategies are more likely to be effective if they reinforce one another rather than work at cross-purposes. For instance, many organizations are currently trying to improve their performance by structuring work in teams. However, these same organizations often continue to use a traditional performance appraisal system in which each employee is evaluated individually. The appraisal system needs to be overhauled to make it consistent with the emphasis on team performance.

Because it is not always possible to know beforehand if an HR program will meet its objectives, a periodic evaluation of HR programs is necessary. The Manager's Notebook titled "But Will It Work?" lists a series of important questions that should be raised to examine the appropriateness of HR programs. These questions should be answered as new programs are being chosen and while they are in effect. (A Manager's Notebook feature appears in every chapter in this book.) ▼

▸ The HR Department and Managers: An Important Partnership

This book takes a managerial approach to human resources and HR strategy. All managers—regardless of their functional area, their position in the hierarchy, and the size of the firm for which they work—must effectively deal with HR issues because these issues are at the heart of being a good manager.

The role of a company's human resources department is to support, not to supplant, managers' HR responsibilities. For instance, the HR department may develop a form to help managers measure the performance of subordinates, but it is the managers who conduct the actual evaluation. Stated another way, the HR department is primarily responsible for helping the firm meet its business objectives by designing HR programs, but managers must carry out these programs. This means that every manager is a human resource manager.

There is widespread consensus that HR professionals need to know their organization's business thoroughly—not only in terms of people, but also in terms of the economic, financial, environmental, and technological forces affecting it.[91] Rather than playing a staff role, they should become internal consultants known for their expertise and ability to help solve the HR problems faced by line managers. They should also be able to merge HR activities effectively with the firm's business needs.[92]

For the sake of the firm, managers and the HR department need to work together closely. Unfortunately, lack of cooperation has traditionally been a problem, and even today it is not uncommon for managers and HR professionals to view each other negatively. These negative perceptions often create a communication gap and hinder the establishment of an effective partnership between the two groups. Figure 1-12 on page 36 lists the five sets of competencies HR professionals need to be considered full strategic partners in running the business.

Companies can take certain steps to foster an effective partnership between managers and the HR department.[93] Specifically, companies should:

- Analyze the people side of productivity rather than depend solely on technical solutions to problems. This requires that managers be trained in certain HR skills. It also requires encouraging managers to value human resources as a key element in organizational effectiveness and performance.
- View HR professionals as internal consultants who can provide valuable advice and support that improve the management of operations. In other words, rather than thinking of the HR department as a group responsible for enforcing bureaucratic procedures, view it as a source of expertise capable of assisting managers in solving personnel-related problems, planning for the future, and improving utilization of productive capacity.
- Instill a shared sense of common fate in the firm rather than a win/lose perspective among individual departments and units. This means developing incentives for managers and HR professionals to work together to achieve common goals.
- Require some managerial experience as part of the training of HR professionals. This requirement should make HR staff more sensitive to and cognizant of the problems managers face.

Leadership
- Understand the nature and styles of leadership, and display appropriate leadership characteristics in performance of professional responsibilities.
- Demonstrate leadership at multiple performance levels:
  - Individual
  - Team
  - Unit or organization

Knowledge of the Business
- Understand corporate business (structure, vision and values, goals, strategies, financial and performance characteristics).
- Understand the unit's business, including special knowledge of competitors, products, technology, and sources of competitive advantage.
- Understand internal and external customers.
- Understand the environment (external and internal) of corporation and individual businesses.
- Understand:
  - Key business disciplines
  - Nature, scope, and HR implications of business globalization
  - Information technology as it affects competitiveness and business processes

HR Strategic Thinking
- Understand the strategic business planning process.
- Understand and be able to apply a systematic HR planning process.
- Be able to select, design, and integrate HR systems or practices to build organizational mindset, capability, and competitive advantage for the business.
- Be able to develop and integrate business unit HR strategies within framework of corporate HR strategies.

Process Skills
- All HR professionals should be competent in key corporate processes and understand management processes critical to particular business units.
- Understand key process skills such as consulting, problem solving, evaluation/diagnosis, workshop design, and facilitation.
- Understand the basic principles, methodologies, and processes of organizational change and development. Facilitate and manage organizational change.
- Balance, integrate, and manage under conditions of uncertainty and paradox.

HR Technologies
- All HR professionals should have a generalist perspective on HR systems and practices as they relate to achievement of business competitive advantage.
- Generalists are capable of designing, integrating, and implementing HR systems to build organizational capability and create business competitive advantage.
- Specialists are capable of designing/delivering leading-edge practices to meet competitive business needs.
- All HR professionals are capable of measuring effectiveness of HR systems and practices.

FIGURE 1-12

Competencies Required of HR Department to Become a Full Strategic Partner

Source: Adapted with permission from Boroski, J. W. (1990). Putting it together: HR planning in "3D" at Eastman Kodak, *Human Resource Planning, 13*(1), 54. Copyright 1990 by The Human Resource Planning Society.

- Actively involve top corporate and divisional managers in formulating, implementing, and reviewing all HR plans and strategies in close collaboration with the HR department. This should increase top management's commitment to the effective implementation of these plans.
- Require senior HR executives to participate on an equal basis with other key managers from the various functional areas (marketing, finance) involved in charting the enterprise's strategic direction.

HR audit
A periodic review of the effectiveness with which a company uses its human resources. Frequently includes an evaluation of the HR department itself.

Companies should also periodically conduct an **HR audit** to evaluate how effectively they are using their human resources. The audit, which is typically conducted by the HR department, deals with a broad set of questions, including:

- Is the turnover rate exceptionally low or high?
- Are the people quitting good employees who are frustrated in their present job, or are they marginal performers?
- Is the firm receiving a high return on the money it spends on recruitment, training, and pay-for-performance plans?

- Is the firm complying with government regulations?
- How well is the company managing employee diversity?
- Is the HR department providing the services that line managers need?
- Are HRM policies and procedures helping the firm accomplish its long-term goals?

The HR audit addresses these and other important issues systematically so that effective programs can be maintained and ineffective programs corrected or eliminated.

Specialization in Human Resource Management

Over the past three decades, the size of the typical HR department has increased considerably. This increase reflects both the growth and complexity of government regulations and a greater awareness that HR issues are important to the achievement of business objectives.

Many colleges and universities now offer specialized degrees in human resources at the associate, bachelor's, master's, and doctoral levels. The Society for Human Resource Management (SHRM), which has almost 60,000 members, has set up a certification institute to offer HR professionals the opportunity to be certified officially at the PHR (Professional Human Resources) or SPHR (Senior Professional Human Resources) level. SHRM certification requires a certain amount of experience and mastery of a body of knowledge as indicated by successful completion of a comprehensive examination. (For additional information and application materials, write to the Society at 606 North Washington Street, Alexandria, VA 22314.) Other organizations whose members specialize in a particular area of HRM are the American Compensation Association, the Human Resource Planning Society, and the American Society for Training and Development.[94]

As Figure 1-13 shows, the earnings of HR professionals are substantial. This is particularly true for those who work in larger firms. The average salary of the top HR professionals among *Fortune* 500 firms is close to $200,000, with more than 100 earning approximately $300,000.[95]

	Median Earnings
HR Directors	
• Firms with revenues over $1 billion	$250,000
• Top 20 companies	400,000
• All companies	58,953
HR Specialists (All firms)	
Training directors	70,000
Corporate benefits directors	61,388
Employee/community relations directors	57,117
Plant/location personnel directors	54,500
Recruitment/interviewing managers	49,731
Employment/interviewing supervisors	44,052
Employee assistance/counseling specialist	42,263
Equal employment opportunity/affirmative action specialists	37,354
Job evaluation specialist	28,392
Personnel records secretaries	19,547

FIGURE 1-13

Earnings of HR Professionals

Source: American Management Association. (1994, January). *Compensation Trends*, 3.

Summary and Conclusions

Human Resource Management: The Challenges. The major HR challenges facing managers today can be divided into three categories: environmental challenges, organizational challenges, and individual challenges.

The environmental challenges are: rapid change, work force diversity, economic globalization, legislation, evolving work and family roles, skill shortages, and the rise of the service sector.

The organizational challenges are: choosing a competitive position, decentralization, downsizing, organizational restructuring, the rise of self-managed work teams, the increased number of small businesses, organizational culture, advances in technology, and the rise of outsourcing.

The individual challenges involve matching people with the organization, treating employees ethically and engaging in socially responsible behavior, increasing individual productivity, deciding whether or not to empower employees, taking steps to avoid brain drain, and dealing with issues of job insecurity.

Planning and Implementing Strategic HR Policies. Correctly done, strategic HR planning provides many direct and indirect benefits for a company. These include: the encouragement of proactive (rather than reactive) behavior; explicit communication of company goals; stimulation of critical thinking and ongoing examination of assumptions; identification of gaps between the company's current situation and its future vision; the encouragement of line managers' participation in the strategic planning process; the identification of HR constraints and opportunities; and the creation of common bonds within the organization.

In developing an effective HR strategy, an organization faces several challenges. These include: putting in place a strategy that creates and maintains a competitive advantage for the company and reinforces the overall business strategy; avoiding excessive concentration on day-to-day problems; developing strategies suited to unique organizational features; coping with the environment in which the business operates; securing management commitment; translating the strategic plan into action; combining intended and emergent strategies; and accommodating change.

A firm's strategic HR choices are the options available to it in designing its human resources systems. Firms must make strategic choices in many HR areas, including work flows, staffing, employee separations, performance appraisal, training and career development, compensation, employee rights, employee and labor relations, and international management.

Selecting HR Strategies to Increase Firm Performance. To be effective, HR strategies must fit with overall organizational strategies, the environment in which the firm is operating, unique organizational characteristics, and organizational capabilities. HR strategies should also be mutually consistent and reinforce one another.

The HR Department and Managers: An Important Partnership. Responsibility for the effective utilization of human resources lies primarily with managers. Hence all managers are personnel managers. HR professionals' role is to act as internal consultants or experts, assisting managers to do their jobs better.

Over the past three decades, the size of the typical HR department has increased considerably. This increase reflects both the growth and complexity of government regulations and a greater awareness that HR issues are important to the achievement of business objectives.

Key Terms

Discussion Questions

1. Can well-meaning HR programs have negative effects on a firm? If so, how?
2. Which of the environmental, organizational, and individual challenges identified in this chapter will be most important for human resource management in the twenty-first century, in your opinion? Which will be least important? Use your own experiences in your answer.
3. In a recent national survey of HR executives in more than 400 companies, most respondents reported that the priorities of top management at their firms are to counter competition, cut costs, and improve performance. Yet only 12% of these HR executives said that their department had a major responsibility for improving productivity, quality, and customer service in their companies. What do you think are some of the reasons for this gap between top management's priorities and the responsibility of the HR department? What are some of the consequences of this gap? Outline several ways in which HR departments can align themselves with their company's strategic goals. How do you think an HR department can gain top management's support for *its* programs and goals?
4. In 1995, Procter & Gamble, a very profitable company, announced that it would be slashing 13,000 of its 106,000 jobs. Chairman Edwin C. Arzt emphasized that the layoffs weren't the result of financial difficulties: "We must slim down to stay competitive. The consumer wants better value. Our competitors are getting leaner and quicker, and we are simply going to have to run faster to stay ahead.... The public has come to think of corporate restructuring as a sign of trouble, but this is definitely not our situation." To what types of challenges is Procter & Gamble responding by cutting almost 13% of its work force? What challenges will Procter & Gamble's HR department face in carrying out these layoffs? Do you see the justification given by Arzt as ethical?
5. Many countries have government regulations that make it very difficult to lay off employees unless the layoff can be justified for business reasons. Do you think that local, state, and federal governments in the United States should develop a similar policy? Why or why not?
6. 3M's competitive business strategy is based on innovation. 3M requires that at least 25% of its annual sales come from products introduced over the previous five years, a goal it often exceeds. Specific HR programs adopted to implement this strategy include the creation of a special fund that allows employees to start new projects or follow up on ideas. 3M's "release time" program, in which workers are given time off during the day to pursue their own interests, is given credit for the creation of new products that management would not have thought of by itself. In addition, 3M's appraisal process encourages risk taking. A senior manager at 3M says, "If you are threatened with dismissal after working on a project that fails, you will never try again." What other types of HR policies might 3M institute to spur product innovation?
7. When some former A&P supermarkets reopened as Super Fresh Food Stores, many of the old unionized A&P employees got their jobs back. Today these workers contribute ideas for the success of their stores through a formalized system of union-management-worker interaction set up to carry out a quality of work life (QWL) initiative. However, Super Fresh Food Stores uses a top-down management approach, so union members have no influence over such management strategies as personnel assignment, buying policies, and operating logistics. How effective do you think Super Fresh Foods' QWL strategy is likely to be?
8. Many believe that top managers care little about human resources compared to such areas as marketing, finance, production, and engineering. What might account for this perception, and what would you do to change it?

MINICASE 1 *Flexible Programs Versus Inflexible Culture*

When Charlotte, North Carolina-based NationsBank launched a pilot program for employees who wanted to work part-time, the program was so successful that the company extended it throughout the company, renaming it SelectTime. The program has helped the company retain valuable employees. (Two thirds of the associates said they would have left the bank rather than continue full-time.) Nearly all the participants say that the program reduces stress. Furthermore, most associates and their managers say that they are more efficient and effective now than they were when they worked full-time.

Flexible scheduling success stories, like that of NationsBank, are legion. However, a survey of 80 *Fortune* 500 companies revealed that although 85% of these companies say they offer flexible work programs, less than 2% of their employees use telecommuting, job sharing, and part-time schedules.

What challenges face the growing number of companies that are initiating flexible work programs? HR experts say that in many companies, the corporate culture just hasn't caught up with the programs. For instance, the notion that productivity and loyalty

continued

Flexible Programs Versus Inflexible Culture continued

can be measured by how many hours a day you work at the office is still strongly held. Appraisal systems, compensation systems, and career management systems often reinforce this attitude. Others say that companies need to make their new family-friendly policies formal. The fact that flexible work benefits are subject to managerial discretion in many cases remains one of the major stumbling blocks to employees' use of flexible programs.

Discussion Questions

1. In what type of organizational culture do flexible scheduling programs have the highest chance of success? What aspects of a company's culture might make it difficult for employees to take advantage of flexible benefits?
2. What do you think the HR department and top management can do to ensure that employees take advantage of—and benefit from—flexible schedules?
3. Suppose a company has initiated a flexible scheduling program, but has no formal policy regarding its use—it's left up to individual employees and their supervisors to determine whether their jobs lend themselves to part-time work or telecommuting. Do you think this arrangement would discourage employees from telecommuting?

Source: Adapted from Solomon, C. M. (1994, May). Work/family's failing grade: Why today's initiatives aren't enough. *Personnel Journal*, 72–87.

MINICASE 2 *IBM's Wandering Tribe*

An important trend in business today is the "virtual office," or office without walls. Thanks to the new technologies, even such traditional companies as IBM are saving on office costs by making their employees work out of their homes:

> Out in the heartland of America, IBM has eviscerated that most sacred of corporate perks: the corner office. Today, all the company's salespeople and sales managers in the midwestern region, as well as in other locations, are no longer assigned specific offices. They work from home, where extra phone lines, computer, fax equipment, desks and chairs have been provided at IBM expense. And they work from their cars, with cellular phones and laptops. None of the sales teams, a total of 15,000 employees and growing, have fixed work locations provided by IBM.
>
> If they need an office for the day they go to one of a series of "office hotels," as John Frank, a manager for work force mobility for IBM, describes it. These are scattered throughout the region of eight (plus portions of three more) midwestern states. Each has been designed to be nearly interchangeable "to minimize disruption on the road."... Check in for the day, get an assigned cubicle or team or conference room, have all your telephone calls routed automatically to your new desk and get to work.
>
> "We've saved the corporation $12 million a year in reduced physical space costs," Frank says. "And we're helping push our sales folks out into the field so they're with customers more often." Virtual office workers? At IBM?
>
> In the 1950s, '60s, and '70s, Big Blue fielded the most famous salespeople the technology world has seen. White-shirted IBM recruits sang the corporate song. Team spirit was cemented by promise of lifelong employment. At its peak IBM employed more than 400,000 people worldwide. Advancing up the organization meant angling for tiny advantages; a leading form of one-upmanship was office size and location....
>
> "We needed to change the entire way we did business," says Susan Whitney, general manager for IBM, North America's midwestern region. "Coming back to a desk with a brass plate on it is a lot less important than keeping a customer satisfied."

Discussion Questions

1. Which of the key HR challenges identified in this chapter is IBM facing?
2. Basing your analysis on Miles and Snow's business strategies, describe IBM's strategy before and after the change described in this minicase.
3. How do you think the employees involved react to being part of IBM's "wandering tribe"?

Source: "Hit the Road, Jack: IBM'S Wandering Tribe," *Forbes ASAP*, August 28, 1995, p. 93.

Managers and HR Professionals at Sands Corporation: Friends or Foes?

Sands Corporation is a medium-sized company located in the Midwest. It manufactures specialized computer equipment used in cars, serving as a subcontractor to several automobile manufacturers as well as to the military. Federal contracts are an important part of Sands' total sales. In 1965 the firm had 130 employees. At that time, the personnel department had a full-time director (who was a high school graduate) and a part-time clerk. The department was responsible for maintaining files, placing recruitment ads in the newspaper at management's request, processing employment applications and payroll, answering phones, and handling other routine administrative tasks. Managers and supervisors were responsible for most personnel matters, including whom to hire, whom to promote, whom to fire, and whom to train.

Today Sands employs 700 people. Personnel, now called the human resources department, has a full-time director with a master's degree in industrial relations, three specialists (with appropriate college degrees and certifications: one in compensation, one in staffing, and one in training and development), and four personnel assistants. Sands' top management believes that a strong HR department with a highly qualified staff can do a better job of handling most personnel matters than line supervisors can. It is also convinced that a good HR department can keep line managers from inadvertently creating costly legal problems. One of Sands' competitors recently lost a $5 million sex discrimination suit, which has only strengthened Sands' resolve to maintain a strong HR department.

Some of the key responsibilities the company assigns to its HR department are:

- *Hiring*. The HR department approves all ads, screens all applicants, tests and interviews candidates, and so forth. Line supervisors are given a limited list of candidates (usually no more than three) per position from which to choose.
- *Work force diversity*. The HR department ensures that the composition of Sands' work force meets the government's diversity guidelines for federal contractors.
- *Compensation*. The HR department sets the pay range for each job based on its own compensation studies and survey data of salaries at similar companies. The department must approve all pay decisions.
- *Employee appraisal*. The HR department requires all supervisors to complete annual appraisal forms on their subordinates. The department scrutinizes these appraisals of employees' performance closely; it is not uncommon for supervisors to be called on the carpet to justify performance ratings that are unusually high or low.
- *Training*. The HR department conducts several training programs for employees, including programs in improving human relations, quality management, and the use of computer packages.
- *Attitude surveys*. The HR department conducts an in-depth attitude survey of all employees each year, asking them how they feel about various facets of their job, such as satisfaction with supervisor and working conditions.

Over the past few weeks several supervisors have complained to top executives that the HR department has taken away many of their management rights. Some of their gripes are:

- The HR department ranks applicants based on test scores or other formal criteria (for example, years of experience). Often the people they pick don't fit well in the department and/or don't get along with the supervisor and coworkers.
- Excellent performers are leaving because the HR department will not approve pay raises exceeding a fixed limit for the job title held, even when a person is able to perform duties beyond those specified in the job description.
- It takes so long to process the paperwork to hire new employees that the unit loses good candidates to competitors.
- Much of the training required of employees is not focused on the job itself. These "canned" programs waste valuable employee time and provide few benefits to the company.
- Supervisors are afraid to be truthful in their performance ratings for fear of being investigated by the HR department.
- Attitude survey data are broken down by department. The HR department then scrutinizes departments with low scores. Some supervisors feel that the attitude survey has become a popularity contest that penalizes managers who are willing to make necessary (but unpopular) decisions.

The HR department director rejects all of these accusations, arguing that supervisors "just want to do things their way, not taking into account what is best for the company."

Critical Thinking Questions

1. What seems to be the main source of conflict between supervisors and the HR department at Sands Corporation? Explain.
2. Do you believe that managers should be given more autonomy to make personnel decisions such as hiring, appraising, and compensating subordinates? If so, what are some potential drawbacks to granting them this authority? Explain.
3. How should Sands' top executives deal with the complaints expressed by supervisors? How should the director of the HR department deal with the situation? Explain.

continued

Cooperative Learning Exercise

4. The CEO of Sands Corporation has called a meeting of four managers, all of whom have lodged some of the complaints noted in the case, and four members of the HR department (the director and three specialists). The instructor or a student acts as the CEO in that meeting. The exercise is carried out as follows: (a) Each side presents its case, with the CEO acting as moderator. (b) The two groups then try to agree on how Sands' HR department and managers can develop a closer working relationship in the future. The two groups and the CEO may conduct this exercise in separate groups or in front of the classroom.

CASE 2 *How Hampton Inn Guarantees "100% Satisfaction"*

Hampton Inn, a national hotel chain with over 7,000 employees, recently introduced a "100% Satisfaction Guarantee" policy to help it gain a distinctive advantage in a highly competitive industry where customers have little allegiance to any particular hotel. When guests walk away from a hotel dissatisfied, chances are that they will relate their unhappy experience to friends and business associates, who might spread the story around even further. Thus are hotel reputations lost. Hampton Inn decided to take advantage of this informal communication chain with its new policy. The company believes that guests who go away impressed with the way Hampton Inn handled a problem will spread the word and generate additional business for the chain.

The guarantee is simple: Guests who are not completely satisfied with every aspect of their stay are not expected to pay. The guarantee allows every Hampton Inn employee to do whatever it takes to satisfy guests—including giving them their money back. Rhonda Thompson, one of Hampton Inn's employees, describes the 100% Satisfaction Guarantee policy in terms of its supporting HR strategies:

> While working as guest services representative at a Hampton Inn hotel, I overheard a guest at our complimentary continental breakfast complaining quite loudly that his favorite cereal was not available. Rather than dismiss the person as just another disgruntled guest, I looked at the situation and saw an opportunity to make this guest happy. I gave him his money back—not for the continental breakfast, but for the cost of one night's stay at our hotel. And I did it on the spot, without checking with my supervisor or the general manager of the hotel, and without making the guest fill out a long complaint form.
>
> Some people might be surprised to hear this story, or they might not believe it could happen. After all, how could a front-desk employee give a guest his money back without getting permission from the boss? And why would the hotel support this action for something simple like a bowl of cereal?
>
> Before the 100% Satisfaction Guarantee was introduced, my job was like most other jobs in the hotel industry. My responsibilities were outlined in my job description, and I was evaluated on how well I fulfilled those duties. There wasn't much room to express my own ideas, and I wasn't really expected to come up with any. Most people I worked with liked it this way because they knew what their jobs entailed and what to expect. When the 100% Satisfaction Guarantee policy was first announced, many employees thought this program would have very little effect on their jobs. But when we learned that every employee would go through a three-day training program, we knew that the guarantee was something special. It became more and more apparent that the new Hampton Inn guarantee would affect all of our jobs, and we would have to change the way we thought about performing our routine duties. The company scheduled a series of training sessions at every hotel, involving videos, classroom-style teaching, open discussions and role playing. Through this training, we learned what to do if a guest asks to invoke the guarantee. We also learned how to identify situations when we, as employees, should invoke the guarantee for guests before they even complain. This training reinforced the message that employees at every level should use this responsibility to make sure guests are satisfied.
>
> Many employees—including myself—were skeptical at first. Although we were proud of our hotels and the service that we offered, we thought that guests might take advantage of the guarantee as a way to get something for free. But the training emphasized that, although any reason given by a guest is a valid reason to invoke the guarantee, most guests would not take advantage of us. Hampton Inn basically threw out its old job descriptions. Of course, a housekeeper's duties still include cleaning and preparing guest rooms. But the housekeeper's real job is to satisfy guests and this typically is accomplished by cleaning the room to perfection. For example, if a housekeeper sees a guest having a problem with the lock on her room door, the housekeeper has the authority to stop what he or she is doing and take whatever action is necessary to correct the situation. While the goal of the 100% Satisfaction Guarantee is to give every guest a satisfying stay, the

guarantee has made employees' jobs more satisfying as well. When Hampton Inn tells employees that they can do whatever it takes to make a guest happy—without needing approval from a manager—they're telling employees that they trust them to do their jobs. Most employees have never worked for a company that will unconditionally back them up for refunding a guest's money, no matter how small the problem was to begin with.

This type of trust motivates employees to do a better job, and makes them try harder to deliver excellent customer service. Employees know that they don't have to wait for their once-a-year review to find out if they're doing a good job; they find out every day from guests staying at the hotel.

Critical Thinking Questions

1. How would you describe the new HR strategy adopted by Hampton Inn? How does it compare with Hampton's previous HR strategy?
2. Distinguish between Hampton's HR strategy and the HR program used to implement it. Is the HR program Hampton chose an effective mechanism for implementing its HR strategy?
3. Does Hampton's new HR strategy fit with the hotel's business strategy? Explain.
4. How does Hampton's new HR strategy allow the hotel to deal with environmental threats more effectively?
5. What risks may Hampton Inn incur by adopting its new HR strategy? Explain.

Cooperative Learning Exercise

6. Students form groups of five and role-play the following situation: A major stockholder has complained that Hampton Inn's new HR strategy will lead to higher costs. According to this stockholder, customers will take advantage of the employees, who will be unable to protect the hotel's interests. This stockholder is calling for tighter controls to prevent abuses of the 100% Satisfaction Guarantee. Hampton's CEO has called a meeting in response to the stockholder's complaint. The meeting is attended by the complaining stockholder, two workers (who will provide the employee perspective of the situation), and the HR director (who will discuss the business rationale for the new HR strategy). Each of these parties presents its view of the situation to the CEO, who then makes a decision concerning the new HR strategy based on the arguments advanced in the meeting.

Source: Reprinted by permission of the publisher, from *HRFocus*, July 1993,

HRM Simulation 

One of the supplementary manuals available with this book is the *Human Resources Management Simulation* by Gerald R. Smith and Peggy Golden. This computer simulation package and its accompanying workbook give you the opportunity to practice managing a company's HR functions in a dynamic business environment. Using the simulation, you can make important HR decisions and see the results of those decisions in both the short run and the long run.

How does the package work? Student teams manage the HR department of a medium-sized organization that will be competing with up to 20 other teams/organizations. The program can simulate a profit or nonprofit company in a manufacturing or service industry. Each team establishes objectives, plans a strategy, and makes the decisions dictated by these plans. Each decision set represents a quarter of a year (three months).

After the team makes its decisions, the computer simulates the reaction of the firm and the labor market, then produces a report for each team. Each team needs to consider the report's results and adjust its policies accordingly, if necessary, through several iterations. There are no right or wrong answers, just as in the real world.

Each chapter in this book concludes with an exercise based on the HR Simulation. Enjoy the experience, and good luck!

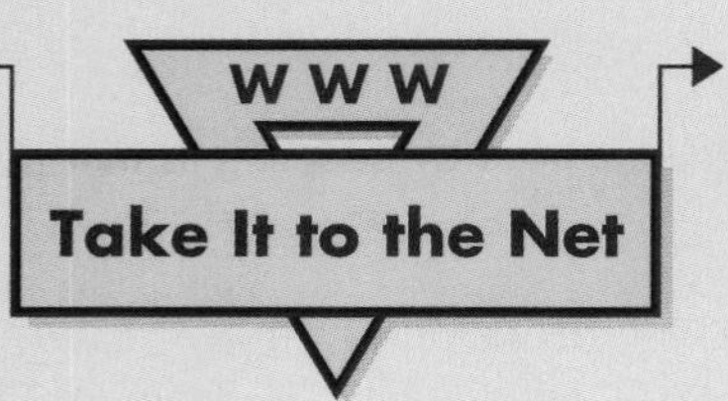

We invite you to visit the Gómez-Mejía/Balkin/Cardy page on the Prentice Hall Web site:

http://www.prenhall.com/gomez

You can also visit the Web sites for these companies, featured within this chapter:

Coca-Cola	http://www.cocacola.com
Coopers & Lybrand	http://www.coopers&lybrand.com
Du Pont	http://www.DuPont.com
General Motors	http://www.gm.com
Intel	http://www.intel.com
Wal-Mart	http://www.walmart.com
Xerox	http://www.xerox.com

Endnotes

1. Adapted from Church, G. J. (1996, January 15). Disconnected: How AT&T is planning to put 40,000 members of its work force out of service. *Time*, 44–45.
2. Butler, J. E., Ferris, G. R., and Napier, N. K. (1991). *Strategy and human resources management.* Cincinnati, OH: South-Western; and Dyer, L. (1984). Linking human resources and business strategies. *Human Resource Planning, 7*(2), 79–84.
3. Berstein, A. (1995, July 17). The wage squeeze. *Business Week*, 54–60; Murray, M. (1995, May 4). Thanks, goodbye. *The Wall Street Journal*, A-1; Murray, M. (1995, May 4). Among record profits companies continue to lay off employees. *The Wall Street Journal*, A-1.
4. Golden, K., and Ramanujan, V. (1985). Between a dream and a nightmare: On the integration of the human resource function and the strategic business planning process. *Human Resource Management, 24,* 429–451; and Dyer, 1984. See also Huselid, M.A. (1995). The impact of human resource management on turnover, productivity, and corporate financial performance. *Academy of Management Journal, 38*, 635–672.
5. Bailey, B. (1991). Ask what HR can do for itself. *Personnel Journal, 70*(7), 35–39; Filipowski, D. (1991, June). Life after HR. *Personnel Journal*, 64–71.
6. Einhorn, B. (1995, July 24). This tiger has a thorn in its paw. *Business Week*, 48.
7. *The Wall Street Journal*. (1995, May 2). Hiring pools make a big splash at an Iowa furniture maker, A-1.
8. Pinkerton, J. P. (1995, November 13). Why affirmative action won't die. *Fortune*, 191.
9. Elliott, V., and Orgera, A. (1993, June). Competing for and with workforce 2000. *HR Focus,* 3.
10. Edmonson, B. (1996, January 8). Women are slowly approaching majority of U.S. labor force. *The Wall Street Journal*, A11.
11. Graham, E. (1995, October 31). Their careers: Count on nothing and work like a demon. *The Wall Street Journal*, B-1.
12. *Id.*
13. Gómez-Mejía, L. R. (1988). The role of human resources strategy in export performance. *Strategic Management Journal, 9*(3), 493–505.
14. Greenwald, J. (1994, January 10). Picking up speed. *Time,* 18.
15. Hagerty, B. (1993, June 14). Trainers help expatriate employees. *The Wall Street Journal,* B1, B3.
16. Walker, J. (1992). *Human resource strategy.* New York: McGraw-Hill.
17. Gómez-Mejía, L. R. (1994). *Fostering a strategic partnership between operations and human resources.* Scarsdale, NY: Work in America Institute.
18. Ledvinka, J., and Scarpello, V. G. (1991). *Federal regulation of personnel and human resource management.* Boston: Kent.
19. *The Wall Street Journal.* (1993, June 21). Work and family, R5.
20. Shellenbarger, S. (1993b, August 10). More women become partners in accounting. *The Wall Street Journal*, B1.
21. Perry, N. (1988, November 7). Saving the schools: How business can help. *Fortune*, 42–52.
22. Nussbaum, B. (1988, September 19). Needed: Human capital. *Business Week*, 100–103.
23. Miller, W. H. (1988, July 4). Employers wrestle with "dumb" kids. *Industry Week*, 4.
24. Salwen, K. G., and Thomas, P. (1993, December 16). Job programs flunk at training but keep Washington at work. *The Wall Street Journal*, A1.

24a. For research on the relationship between HRM and quality, see Cowherd, D. M. and Levine, D. (1992). Product quality and pay equity between lower-level employees and top management: An investigation of distributive justice theory. *Administrative Science Quarterly 37*, 302–320.

25. Doeringer, P. B., and Piore, M. J. (1971). Theories of low-wage labor workers. In L. G. Reynolds, S. H. Masters, and C. H. Moser (Eds.), *Readings in labor economics and labor relations,* 15–31. Englewood Cliffs, NJ: Prentice Hall; and Pinfield, L. T., and Berner, M. F. (1994). Employment systems: Toward a coherent conceptualization of internal labor markets. In G. Ferris (Ed.), *Research in Personnel and Human Resources Management, 12,* 50–81.
26. Lublin, J. S. (1994b, February 9). Before you take that great job, get it in writing. *The Wall Street Journal*, B1.
27. Deters, B. (1994a, March 7). Cut to the bone: Valley firms drop incentives, reduce work force by layoffs. *Arizona Republic,* E1.
28. See, for example, De Meuse, K. P., and Tornow, W. W. (1990). The tie that binds has become very, very frayed. *Human Resource Planning, 13*(3), 203–213.
29. Salwen, K. G. (1994, February 8). Decades of downsizing eases stigma of layoffs. *The Wall Street Journal*, B1.
30. Stewart, T. A. (1995, March 20). World without managers. *Fortune*, 72.
31. Marcus, S. (1991). Delayering: More than meets the eye. *Perspectives, 3*(1), 22–26; Byrne, J. A. (1993, December 20). The horizontal corporation. *Business Week*, 76–81; Tully, S. (1993, February 8). The modular corporation. *Fortune*, 106–111; Brown, T. (1994, March 7). The rise of the intelligent organization. *Industry Week*, 17–21; and Brown, T. (1993, November 1). Future organizations. *Industry Week*, 22–28.
32. Zweig, P. L., Perlman, K., Anderson, S., and Gudridge, K. (1995, October 30). The case against mergers. *Business Week*, 124.
33. Hackman, J. R. (1986). The psychology of self-management in organizations. In M. S. Pollack and R. O. Perloff (Eds.), *Psychology and work: Productivity change and employment,* 85–136. Washington, DC: American Psychological Association; and Walton, R. E. (1985). From control to commitment in the workplace. *Harvard Business Review, 63*, 77–84.
34. Manz, C. C. (1992). *Mastering self-leadership: Empowering yourself for personal*

excellence. Englewood Cliffs, NJ: Prentice Hall.
35. Manz, C. C., and Sims, H. P., Jr. (1993). *Business without bosses: How self-managing teams are building high performance companies*. New York: Wiley.
36. *Id.*
37. *Id.*
38. U.S. Small Business Administration. (n.d.). *SBA Loan Programs*. Washington, DC: U.S. Small Business Administration.
39. Fry, F. L. (1993). *Entrepreneurship: A planning approach*. St. Paul, MN: West.
40. Case, J. (1995, August). *The state of small business*, 14–29.
41. Adapted from Fry, 1993.
42. Adapted from Timmons, J. A. (1990). *New venture creation: Entrepreneurship in the 1990s*. Homewood, IL: Irwin.
43. Adapted from Schein, E. H. (1986). *Organizational culture and leadership*. San Francisco, CA: Jossey Bass.
44. Adapted from *Id.*
45. Drucker, P. F. (1993, October 21). The five deadly business sins. *The Wall Street Journal*, A1.
46. Odom, M. (1994, February 23). Management guru preaches to choir. *Arizona Republic*, E2.
47. Doeringer, P. B. (1991). *Turbulence in the American workplace*. New York: Oxford University Press.
48. *The Wall Street Journal*. (1994, February 11). Special report on telecommunications. B1.
49. Shellenbarger, S. (1993c, December 14). Some thrive, but many wilt working at home. *The Wall Street Journal*, B1.
50. Rothfeder, J. (1994, January). Dangerous things strangers know about you. *McCall's*, 88–94.
51. Schuler, 1989, p. 265.
52. Wilke, J. R. (1993, December 9). Computer links erode hierarchical nature of workplace culture. *The Wall Street Journal*, A10.
53. Lancaster, H. (1995, September 12). Saving your career when your position has been outsourced. *The Wall Street Journal*, B-1.
54. Berstein, A., and Zellner, A. (1995, July 17). Outsourced—and out of luck, 61.
55. *Id.*
56. Melcher, R. A. (1996, January 8). Who says you can't find good help? *Business Week*, 107.
57. Gupta, A. K., and Govindarajan, V. (1984). Business unit strategy, managerial characteristics, and business unit effectiveness at strategy implementation. *Academy of Management Journal*, 27, 25–41.
58. Balkin, D. B., and Gómez-Mejía, L. R. (1985). Compensation practices in high tech industries. *Personnel Administrator, 30*(6), 111–123.
59. Associated Press. (1994, March 3). Women win discrimination case against Honeywell after 17 years. *Arizona Republic,* A17.
60. Pastin, M. (1986). *The hard problems of management: Giving the ethics edge*. San Francisco: Jossey Bass.
61. Noe, R., Hollenbeck, J. R., Gerhart, G., and Wright, P. M. (1994). *Human resource management: Gaining a competitive advantage*. Homewood, IL: Austen.
62. Mathieu, J. E., and Zajac, D. M. (1990). A review and meta-analysis of the antecedents, correlates, and consequences of organizational commitment. *Psychological Bulletin, 108*, 171–194.
63. Hom, P., and Griffeth, R. (1994). *Employee turnover.* Cincinnati, Ohio: South-Western.
64. Campion, M. A., and McClelland, C. L. (1991). Interdisciplinary examination of the costs and benefits of enlarged jobs. *Journal of Applied Psychology, 76,* 186–198.
65. Gómez-Mejía, L. R., Balkin, D. B., and Milkovich, G. T. (1990). Rethinking your rewards for technical employees. *Organizational Dynamics 18*(4), 62–75.
66. Murray, 1995.
67. Rigdon, J. C., Hill, G. C., and Naik, G. (1993, October 21). Turbulent film market. *The Wall Street Journal*, A1.
68. Drucker, P. (1993, October 21). The five deadly business sins. *The Wall Street Journal*, R2.
69. Bulkeley, W. M. (1994, March 1). Conglomerates make a surprising comeback—with a '90s twist. *The Wall Street Journal*, A1.
70. Nelton, S. (1994, February). Put your purpose in writing. *Nation's Business,* 61–64.
71. Butler, J. E., Ferris, G. R., and Napier, N. K. (1991). *Strategy and human resources management.* Cincinnati, OH: South-Western.
72. Mintzberg, H. (1990). The design school: Reconsidering the basic premises of strategic management. *Strategic Management Journal, 11*, 171–196; Walker, J. (1992). *Human resource management strategy,* Chapter 1. New York: McGraw-Hill.
73. *Id.*
74. Brockner, J. (1992). The escalation of commitment to a failing course of action: Toward theoretical progress. *Academy of Management Review, 17*(1), 39–61; and Staw, B. (1976). Knee-deep in Big Muddy: A study of escalating commitment to a chosen course of action. *Organizational Behavior and Human Performance, 16,* 27–44.
75. See the following reviews: Dyer, L., and Holder, G. W. (1988). A strategic perspective of human resource management. In L. Dyer (Ed.), *Human resource management: Evolving roles and responsibilities.* Washington, DC: Bureau of National Affairs; and Gómez-Mejía, L. R., and Balkin, D. B. (1992). *Compensation, organizational strategy, and firm performance.* Cincinnati, Ohio: South-Western.
76. Bulkeley, 1994.
77. Kerr, J. (1985). Diversification strategies and managerial rewards: An empirical study. *Academy of Management Journal, 28*, 155–179; Leontiades, M. (1980). *Strategies for diversification and change.* Boston: Little, Brown; and Pitts, R. A. (1974, May). Incentive compensation and organization design. *Personnel Journal, 20*(5), 338–344.
78. Bulkeley, 1994.
79. Gómez-Mejía, L. R. (1992). Structure and process of diversification, compensation strategy, and firm performance. *Strategic Management Journal, 13,* 381–397; and Kerr, 1985.
80. Farnam, A. (1994, February 7). Corporate reputations. *Fortune*, 50–54.
81. Porter, M. E. (1980). *Competitive strategy.* New York: Free Press; Porter, M. E. (1985). *Competitive advantage.* New York: Free Press; and Porter, M. E. (1990). *The competitive advantage of nations.* Boston: Free Press.
82. Miles, R. E., and Snow, C. C. (1978). *Organizational strategy, structure, and process.* New York: McGraw-Hill; and Miles, R. E., and Snow, C. C. (1984). Designing strategic human resources systems. *Organizational Dynamics, 13*(1), 36–52.
83. Montemayor, E. F. (1994). Pay policies that fit organizational strategy: Evidence from high-performing firms. Unpublished paper. East Lansing, MI: School of Industrial and Labor Relations, Michigan State University.
84. Porter, 1980.
85. *Id.*
86. Byrne, H. S. (1992, November 16). Illinois Tool Works: Satisfying customers...and investors. *Barron's*, 51–52.
87. Miles and Snow, 1984, 1978.
88. Miles, R. E., Snow, C. C., Meyer, A. D., and Coleman, H. J. (1978). Organizational strategy, structure, and process. *Academy of Management Review, 3,* 546–562.
89. Gómez-Mejía, L. R. and Balkin, D. B. (1992). *Compensation, organizational strategy, and firm performance.* Cincinnati, OH: South-Western, p. 125.
90. For another example, see Corden, R., Elmer, M., Knudsen, J., Mountain, R., Rider, M., and Ross, W. (1994, March-April). When a new pay plan fails: The case of Beta Corporation. *Compensation & Benefits Review,* 26–32.
91. Jones, G., and Wright, P. (1992). An economic approach to conceptualizing the utility of human resource management practices. *Research in Personnel/Human Resources, 10,* 271–299; Schuler, R., and Walker, J. (1990, Summer). Human resources strategy: Focusing on issues and actions. *Organizational Dynamics,* 5–19; and Wright, P., and Snell, S. (1991). Toward an integrative view of strategic human resource management. *Human Resource Management Review,* 203–225.
92. Gómez-Mejía, 1994.
93. Bailey, B. (1991, July). Ask what HR can do for itself. *Personnel Journal,* 35–39.
94. For more information, see Wiley, C. (1992, August). The certified HR professional. *HRMagazine 37*(8), 77–79, 82–84; and Wiley, C., and Goff, E. F. (1994). Trends, strategies, objectives, linkages, and professionalism. *Compensation Guide* (New York: Warren Gorham and Lamont).
95. Solomon, J. (1990, March 9). People power. *The Wall Street Journal*, R33.

The End of Job Security and Loyalty?

ABCNEWS

Seniority—the amount of time a person works for a company—used to be an important consideration in many employment decisions. For example, seniority might play a major role in determining salary increases, vacation time, and work schedules. The longer employees worked for a company, the better off they usually were. The implicit message to many workers was that loyalty had its benefits. If workers stuck by their company, the company would stick by them. Things are very different today.

Job security is now all but gone from most organizations. Downsizing has made it clear to many workers that their jobs are anything but secure thanks to changes in economic conditions, technology, and organizational structure, jobs that exist one day may be gone the next. The implicit message to workers is clear: Your job future is uncertain, not secure. Announcement of a downsizing could sweep away your job at any time. Unfortunately, a climate of uncertainty is generally not a climate of efficiency and high morale.

An alternative approach to downsizing involves communicating with workers, explaining to them the pressures the organization is facing, and giving them the opportunity to demonstrate that they can contribute to the organization. Seniority, tenure, and loyalty don't have much to do with this approach, which emphasizes partnership between management and employees.

Pinnacle Brands is one company that has taken this contribution approach. When the company fell on hard times, it did not inform its workers that they would lose their jobs, as other companies in the industry did. Instead, Pinnacle gave its workers the opportunity to demonstrate that they could achieve important results for the company.

The Pinnacle approach doesn't necessarily build employee loyalty to the organization, but it does push workers to build their skills, achieve outcomes, and improve their résumés.

Discussion Questions

1. What are the benefits of the traditional job security/loyalty exchange between employees and organizations? What are the costs?
2. Do you think that the contribution approach used by Pinnacle Brands is preferable to the loyalty approach? Why or why not?
3. What can you do to maximize your personal employment security? Do you think job security is a concept of the past?
4. Identify some of the key things a company must do to implement a contribution approach as a successful alternative to downsizing. Are there circumstances under which downsizing might be preferable? Describe.

2

Managing Work Flows and Conducting Job Analysis

A Bunch of Cards. The past decade has been characterized by the rise of team-based organizations. At Hallmark Cards, cross-functional teams now work together to produce a steady stream of greeting cards for all occasions. In the past, artists, designers, printers, and financial people had been located as much as a city block apart—even though they were all working on the same card.

CHALLENGES

After reading this chapter, you should be able to deal more effectively with the following challenges:

1 ▶ **Describe** bureaucratic, flat, and boundaryless organizational structures and the business environments in which each is most appropriate.

2 ▶ **List** the factors influencing worker motivation that are under managers' control.

3 ▶ **Conduct** job analysis and prepare job descriptions and specifications.

4 ▶ **Apply** flexible work designs to situations in which employees have conflicts between work and family, or employers face fluctuating demand for their products.

5 ▶ **Develop** policies and procedures to protect human resource information system data so that employees' privacy rights are maintained.

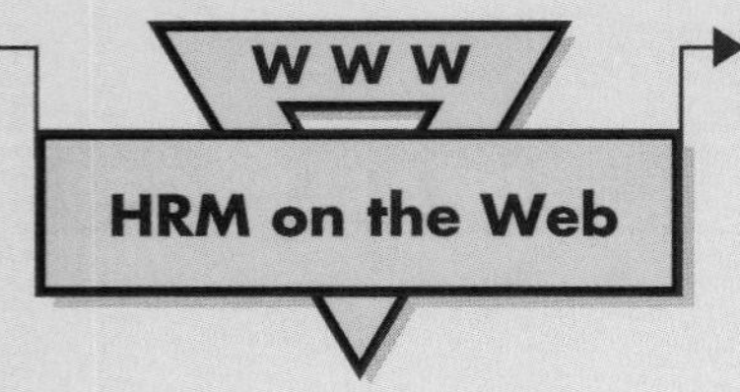

http://vvv.com/waria/

Workflow and Reengineering International Association (WARIA)

WARIA's Web site provides information on work flow and reengineering publications and conferences. It also identifies vendors of work flow software and has a list of consultants who provide reengineering services. Other Web sites on work flow and reengineering are listed, and a job exchange is available.

The powerful forces of technology and global competition are forcing managers to rethink all aspects of business. Work is in a state of flux as companies change basic work processes and structures to focus more on customers' needs.

One important change is the fairly recent practice of using work teams instead of individual workers as the basic work unit. Today many workers spend much of their time on a team established to satisfy customers' needs. For example:

- The Medical Center of Beaver in Beaver County, Pennsylvania, uses multiskilled worker teams to increase hospital efficiency and customer satisfaction. Teams of nurses, doctors, and technicians dispense medical care to patients. Each ward in the hospital is a self-contained minihospital with its own administration, pharmacy, lab, and x-ray department linked by a large computer network. Sophisticated computer systems allow medical staff to track a patient's medical history and current medical status without generating massive amounts of paper. Doctors and nurses have cellular phones and pagers that link them to the computer terminals located in each hospital room.[1]
- Xerox develops new products using teams that work together instead of in separate departments. These product development teams—which include workers who represent marketing, research, engineering, and manufacturing—can develop new products much faster than workers could under the company's previous division of labor.[2]
- The use of teams at GM's Opel plant in Eisenach, Eastern Germany, has made it a model of efficiency. Workers in the former Communist state find the team structure to be similar to working in the "brigade" they knew in Communist days.[3]

Like work teams, organizations are fundamentally groups of people. The relationships among these people can be structured in different ways. In this chapter we describe how top managers decide on the most appropriate structure for the organization as a whole and for the flow of work within the organization. While you may never be asked to redesign your organization, it is likely that your company will eventually undergo structural change because such change is necessary for survival. It is important that you understand structural issues so that you can see the big picture and take an active role in implementing changes.

Work can be viewed from three different perspectives: that of the entire organization, that of work groups, and that of individual employees. We examine each of these perspectives, and their implications for human resource management, in turn. We also discuss job analysis (a critical HR activity) and the use of contingent workers and alternative work schedules to create a flexible work force. We conclude the chapter with a discussion of human resource information systems.

Work: The Organization Perspective

organizational structure
The formal or informal relationships between people in an organization.

work flow
The way work is organized to meet the organization's production or service goals.

Organizational structure refers to the formal or informal relationships between people in an organization. **Work flow** refers to the way work is organized to meet the organization's production or service goals. In this section we discuss the relationship between strategy and organizational structure, the three basic organizational structures, and the uses of work flow analysis.

Strategy and Organizational Structure

An organization develops a business strategy by establishing a set of long-term goals based on (1) an analysis of environmental opportunities and threats, and (2) a realistic appraisal of how the business can deploy its assets to compete most effectively. The business strategy selected by management determines the structure most appropriate to the organization.[4] Whenever management changes its business strategy, it should also reassess its organizational structure.

Recall from Chapter 1 that a company would select a *defender strategy* when it is competing in a stable market and has a well-established product. For example, a regulated electric utility company might adopt such a strategy. Under a defender strategy, work can be efficiently organized into a structure based on an extensive division of labor, with hierarchies of jobs assigned to functional units such as customer service, power generation, and accounting. Management is centralized and top management has the responsibility for making key decisions. Decisions are implemented from the top down via the chain of command. Workers are told what to do by supervisors, who in turn are handed directions from middle managers, who take orders from the company's top executives.

A company would select a *prospector strategy* when operating in uncertain business environments that require flexibility. Companies that are experiencing rapid growth and launching many new products into a dynamic market are likely to select such a strategy. In companies with a prospector strategy, control is decentralized so that each division has some autonomy to make decisions that affect its customers. Workers who are close to the customer are allowed to respond quickly to customers' needs without having to seek approval from supervisors.

Management selects HR strategies to fit and support its business strategies and organizational structure. Here are some examples of strategic HR choices regarding structure and work flows that companies have made to achieve cost efficiency and product quality.

- In 1994 Xerox signed a ten-year agreement with EDS Corporation and Andersen Consulting to provide Xerox's computer operations. The contract was designed to help Xerox cut costs. Xerox management decided that outsourcing its computer operations (which have an annual budget of $670 million) would help it focus on its core business, document processing.[5]
- Kodak in the early 1990s eliminated several layers of middle management through early retirements, then delegated these laid-off managers' responsibilities to teams of engineers and technicians. Kodak management wanted to differentiate its product from the competition based on quality and believed that a reorganized product development process could help it reach that goal.[6]

A QUESTION OF ETHICS

Implicit in this chapter is the view that organizational change is necessary for survival. However, organizational change often places individual employees under considerable stress, particularly the stress resulting from job loss. Is the organization ethically responsible for protecting employees from these stressful changes?

Designing the Organization

Designing an organization involves choosing an organizational structure that will help the company achieve its goals most effectively. There are three basic types of organizational structure: bureaucratic, flat, and boundaryless (Figure 2–1, page 50).

Bureaucratic Organization. Companies that adopt a defender business strategy are likely to choose the **bureaucratic organizational structure.** This pyramid-shaped structure consists of hierarchies with many levels of management. It utilizes a top-down or "command and control" approach to management in which managers provide considerable direction to and have considerable control over their subordinates. The classic example of a bureaucratic organization is the military, which has a long pecking order of intermediate officers between the generals (who initiate combat orders) and the troops (who do the fighting on the battlefield).

bureaucratic organizational structure
A pyramid-shaped organizational structure that consists of hierarchies with many levels of management.

A bureaucratic organization is based on a *functional division of labor*. Employees are divided into divisions based on their function. Thus production employees are grouped in

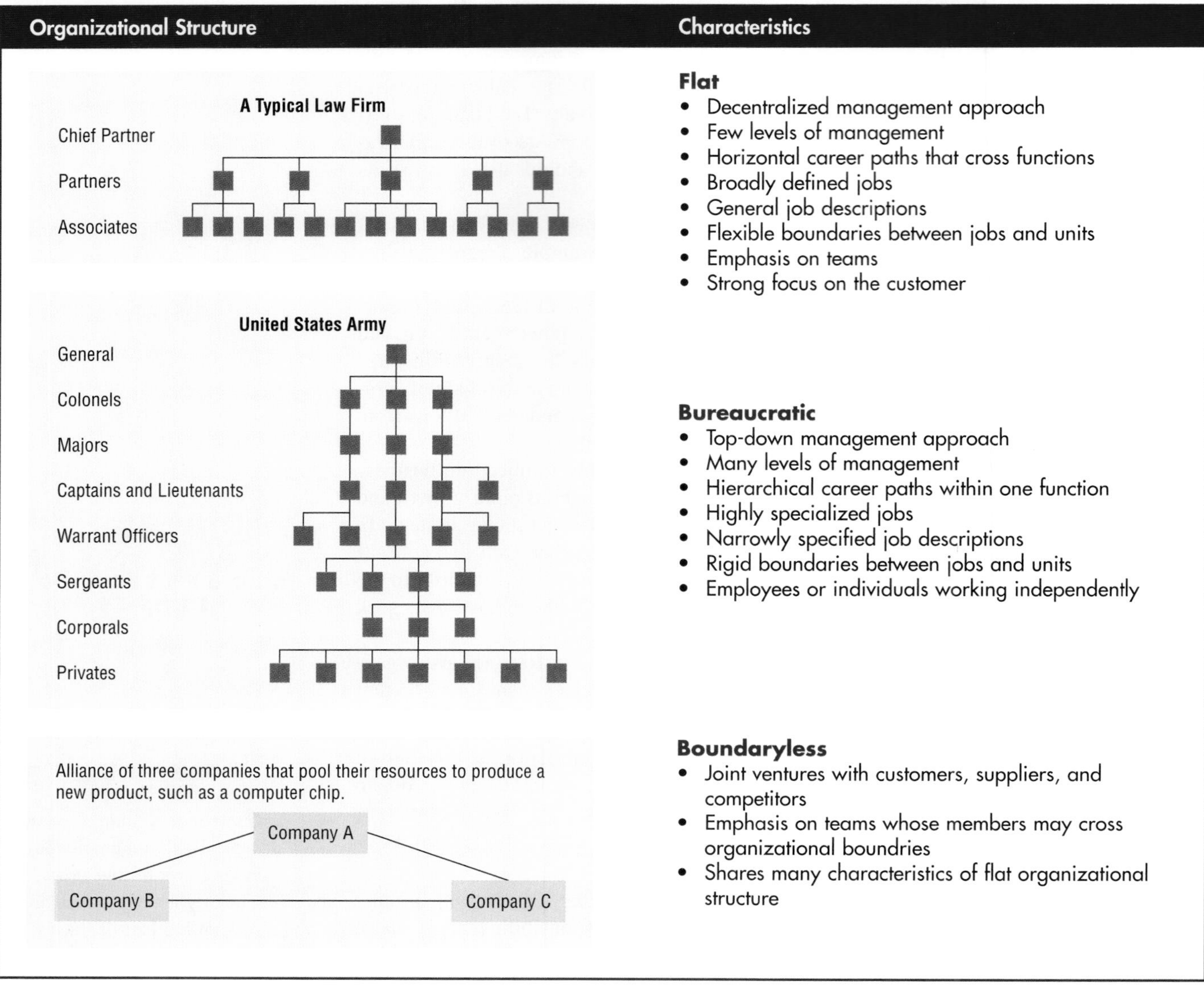

FIGURE 2-1
Organizational Structures

one division, marketing employees in another, engineering employees in a third, and so on. Rigid boundaries separate the functional units from one another. At a bureaucratic auto parts company, for instance, automotive engineers would develop plans for a new part and then deliver its specifications to the production workers.

Rigid boundaries also separate workers from one another and from their managers because the bureaucratic structure utilizes *work specialization*. Narrowly specified job descriptions clearly mark the boundaries of each employee's work. Employees are encouraged to do only the work specified in their job description—no more and no less. They spend most of their time working individually at specialized tasks and usually advance only within one function. For example, employees who begin their career in sales can advance to higher and higher positions in sales or marketing, but cannot switch into production or finance.

The bureaucratic structure works best in a predictable and stable environment. It is highly centralized and depends on front-line workers performing repetitive tasks according to managers' orders. In a dynamic environment, this structure is less efficient, and sometimes it is disastrous.

Flat Organization. A company that selects the prospector business strategy is likely to choose the **flat organizational structure.** A flat organization has only a few levels of managers and emphasizes a decentralized approach to management. Flat organizations encourage high employee involvement in business decisions. Nucor (a Charlotte, North Carolina, steel company) has a flat organizational structure. Though Nucor has over 5,000 employees, only three levels separate the front-line steel workers from the president of the company. Headquarters staff consists of a mere 30 people in a modest cluster of offices.[7]

flat organizational structure
An organizational structure that has only a few levels of management and emphasizes decentralization.

Flat organizations are likely to be divided into units or teams that represent different products, services, or customers. The purpose of this structure is to create independent small businesses that can respond rapidly to customers' needs or changes in the business environment. For example, Hewlett-Packard (HP), a large manufacturer of computers and electronic instruments, is organized into about 60 different product-based business units. Each HP unit behaves like a minibusiness that is responsible for generating a profit for the overall company, and employees within each unit feel as if they are working for a small company. The flat organizational structure has fostered an entrepreneurial culture that has enabled HP to innovate and sustain itself at the cutting edge of technology.

The flat organizational structure reduces some of the boundaries that isolate employees from one another in bureaucratic organizations. Boundaries between workers at the same level are reduced because employees are likely to be working in teams. In contrast to workers at bureaucratic organizations, employees of a flat organization can cross functional boundaries as they pursue their careers (for instance, starting in sales, moving to finance, and then into production). In addition, job descriptions in flat organizations are more general and encourage employees to develop a broad range of skills (including management skills). Boundaries that separate employees from managers and supervisors also break down in flat organizations, where employees are empowered to make more decisions.

Flat organizational structures can be useful for organizations that are implementing a total quality management (TQM) strategy that emphasizes customer satisfaction. Implementing a TQM strategy may require changing work processes so that customers can receive higher-quality products and better service. For example, an auto insurance company may change its claims adjustment process to speed up reimbursement to customers. Rather than using 25 employees who take 14 days to process a claim, the company may create a claims adjustment team that works closely with the customer to take care of all the paperwork within three days.

The flat structure works best in rapidly changing environments because it enables management to create an entrepreneurial culture that fosters employee participation.

Boundaryless Organization. A **boundaryless organizational structure** enables an organization to form relationships with customers, suppliers, and/or competitors, either to pool organizational resources for mutual benefit or to encourage cooperation in an uncertain environment. Such relationships often take the form of joint ventures, which let the companies share talented employees, intellectual property (such as a manufacturing process), marketing distribution channels (such as a direct sales force), or financial resources. Boundaryless organizational structures are most often used by companies that select the prospector business strategy and operate in a volatile environment.

boundaryless organizational structure
An organizational structure that enables an organization to form relationships with customers, suppliers, and/or competitors, either to pool organizational resources for mutual benefit or to encourage cooperation in an uncertain environment.

Boundaryless organizations share many of the characteristics of flat organizations. They break down boundaries between the organization and its suppliers, customers, or competitors. They also strongly emphasize teams, which are likely to include employees representing different companies in the joint venture. For example, a quality expert from an automobile manufacturing company may work closely with employees at one of the company's auto parts suppliers to train them in specific quality management processes.

Companies often use a boundaryless organizational structure when they (1) are adopting a total quality management strategy, (2) are entering foreign markets that have entry barriers to foreign competitors, or (3) need to manage the risk of developing an expensive new technology. The boundaryless organization is appropriate in these situations because it is open to change, facilitates the formation of joint ventures with foreign companies, and reduces the financial risk to any one organization. Here are some examples of boundaryless organizational structures:

- Many Hollywood movies are produced by networks of small business and freelance contributors who provide services such as special effects, set design, payroll, and security. These boundaryless organizations are rapidly replacing the bureaucratic structures used by the old Hollywood studios.[8]
- Apple Computer, IBM, and Motorola formed a strategic alliance in 1991 to develop the PowerPC microprocessor used in the Power Macintosh. The alliance links a supplier of integrated circuits (Motorola) with customers (Apple and IBM) that will use the circuits in the designs of their latest personal computers.[9]
- MCI (the long-distance telephone company) and Rupert Murdoch's News Corp. (a provider of video programming) have joined forces to build a direct broadcast satellite television network. Each partner is providing both financial resources and competencies in the different technologies necessary to develop the network.[10]

Work Flow Analysis

work flow analysis
The process of examining how work creates or adds value to the ongoing processes in a business.

We said earlier that work flow is the way work is organized to meet the organization's production or service goals. Managers need to do **work flow analysis** to examine how work creates or adds value to the ongoing business processes. (*Processes* are value-adding, value-creating activities such as product development, customer service, and order fulfillment.[11]) Work flow analysis looks at how work moves from the customer (who initiates the need for work) through the organization (where employees add value to the work in a series of value-creating steps) to the point at which the work leaves the organization as a product or service for the customer.

Each job in the organization should receive work as an input, add value to that work by doing something useful to it, and then move the work on to another worker. Work flow analysis usually reveals that some steps or jobs can be combined, simplified, or even eliminated. In some cases, it has resulted in the reorganization of work so that teams rather than individual workers are the source of value creation.

Work flow analysis can be used in TQM programs to tighten the alignment between employees' work and customers' needs. It can also help a company make major performance improvements through another program called *business process reengineering*.

Business Process Reengineering. The term *reengineering* was coined by Michael Hammer and James Champy in their pioneering book *Reengineering the Corporation.* Hammer and Champy emphasize that reengineering should not be confused with restructuring or simply laying off employees in an effort to eliminate layers of management.[12] **Business process reengineering (BPR)** is not a quick fix but rather a fundamental rethinking and radical redesign of business processes to achieve dramatic improvements in cost, quality, service, and speed.[13] Reengineering examines the way a company does its business by closely analyzing the core processes involved in producing its product or delivering its service to the customer. By taking advantage of computer technology and different ways of organizing human resources, the company may be able to reinvent itself.[14]

business process reengineering (BPR)
A fundamental rethinking and radical redesign of business processes to achieve dramatic improvements in cost, quality, service, and speed.

BPR uses work flow analysis to identify jobs that can be eliminated or recombined to improve company performance. Figure 2–2 shows the steps involved in processing a loan

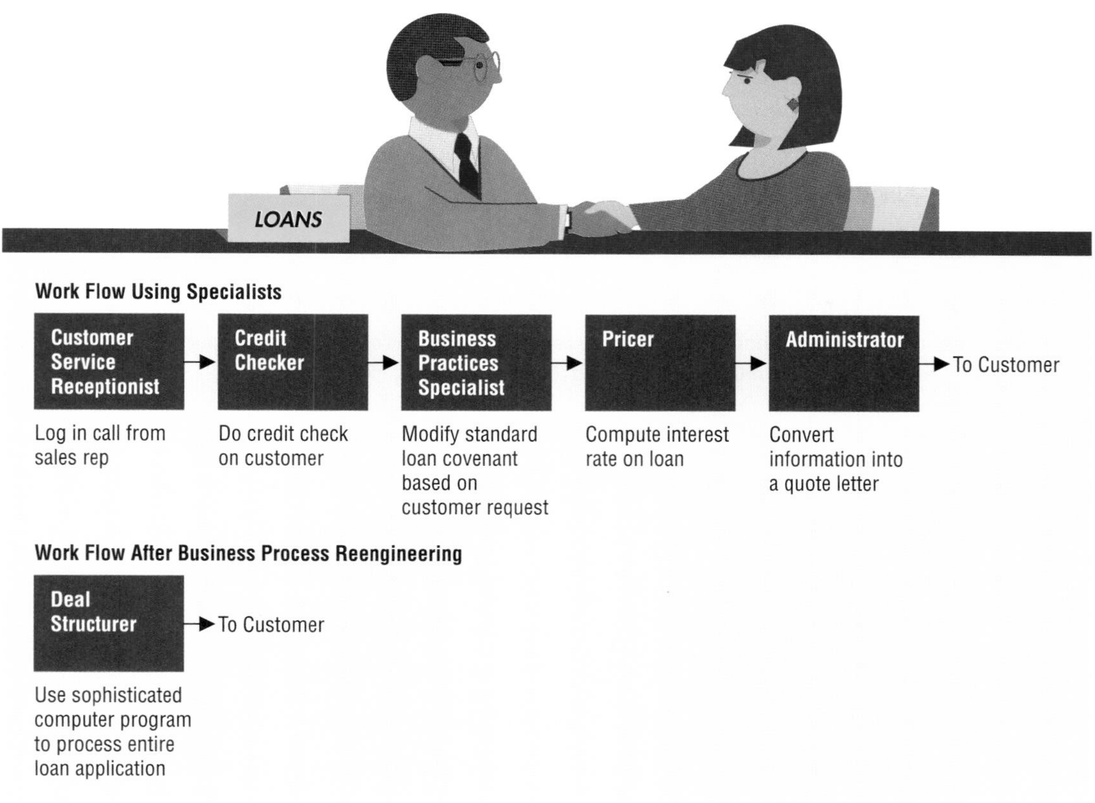

FIGURE 2-2

Processing a Loan Application at IBM Credit Corporation Before and After Business Process Reengineering

application at IBM Credit Corporation before and after business process reengineering. Before the BPR effort, work flow analysis showed that loan applications were processed in a series of five steps by five loan specialists, each of whom did something different to the loan application. The entire process took an average of six days to complete, which gave customers the opportunity to look elsewhere for financing.[15] For much of that time, the application was either in transit between the loan specialists or sitting on someone's desk waiting to be processed.

Using BPR, the jobs of the five loan specialists were reorganized into the job of just one generalist called the deal structurer. The deal structurer uses a new software program to print out a standardized loan contract, access different credit checking databases, price the loan, and add boilerplate language to the contract. With the new process, loan applications can be completed in four hours instead of six days.[16]

Critics of reengineering claim that over half of reengineering projects fail to meet their objectives while causing pain to companies and employees in the form of layoffs and disruptions to established work patterns.[17] However, a recent survey by CSC Index, a leading reengineering consulting firm, reported that reengineering is very popular in both the United States and Europe. The survey of 621 large European and U.S. companies found that 69% of U.S. firms and 75% of European firms are already engaged in reengineering and over half of the remaining companies are thinking about embarking on a reengineering project.[18] For a look at some of the barriers Europe faces in reengineering its business processes, see the Issues and Applications feature on the next page titled "Roadblocks to Reengineering Europe."

Roadblocks to Reengineering Europe

Issues + Applications

European companies looking to reengineer their business processes are confronting several challenges:

- *An abiding belief in social rights.* In its initial phase, reengineering usually means heavy layoffs and substantial job reorganization. Member countries of the European Union that already have a high average unemployment rate are loath to do anything that will cost jobs in such alarming numbers. The opposition of organized labor is also a factor. Trade unions in Europe tend to be much stronger than in the United States. Particularly in Germany, Holland, and Italy, they have a powerful voice in policy making.
- *Corporate culture.* The overall corporate culture in Europe is significantly different from that in the United States. Consider Germany. According to Gunter Conrad, a partner at Andersen Consulting in Munich, pride in their craft keeps German workers from embracing radical change. Says Conrad, "When you used to be the best manufacturers in the world, it is sometimes difficult to admit that other ways of doing things might be better."
- *Nationalism.* While 15 West European countries form a single market today, a residual nationalism keeps companies in those countries from reducing bureaucracy and eliminating costly duplication. Companies usually find it prudent to keep a few managers in each country in the European Union to untangle local laws and sweet-talk local politicians.

Still, several have already made significant strides, including Britain's Reuters Holdings and Rolls-Royce Motor Cars and Switzerland's Union Bank and Ciba Geigy. Rolls-Royce actually started redesigning itself in 1990, before the term *reengineering* was coined. The company simplified its management structure, eliminated foremen and shop stewards, and handed decision-making responsibilities over to teams of workers.

Sources: *The Economist.* (1994, February 26). Re-engineering Europe, 63–64; and Guterl, F. (1993, June 14). On the Continent, a new era is also dawning. *Business Week*, 61.

Work: The Group Perspective

We turn now to an examination of work from the perspective of employee groups. In the flat and boundaryless organizational structures, teamwork is an imperative. Indeed, as we've seen, teams are the basic building blocks of both types of structures.

team
A small number of people with complementary skills who work toward common goals for which they hold themselves mutually accountable.

What exactly is a team and how does it operate? A **team** is a small number of people with complementary skills who work toward common goals for which they hold themselves mutually accountable.[19] The size of most teams ranges from 6 to 18 employees.[20] Unlike *work groups,* which depend on a supervisor for direction, a team depends on its own members to provide leadership and direction.[21] Teams can also be organized as departments. For example, a company may have a product development team, a manufacturing team, and a sales team.

Several types of teams are used in organizations today. The type that is having the most impact on U.S. companies is the self-managed team.

Self-Managed Teams

self-managed team (SMT)
A team responsible for producing an entire product, a component, or an ongoing service.

Organizations are implementing self-managed work teams primarily to improve quality and productivity and to reduce operating costs. **Self-managed teams (SMTs)** are responsible for producing an entire product, a component, or an ongoing service. In most cases, SMT members are cross-trained on the different tasks assigned to the team. Some SMTs have members with a set of complex skills—for example, scientists and engineers with training in different disciplines. Members of the SMT have many managerial duties, including work scheduling, selecting work methods, ordering materials, evaluating performance, and disciplining team members.[22]

One company that has switched over to SMTs is the San Diego Zoo. The zoo's employees traditionally had very narrow and well-defined job responsibilities: Keepers did the keeping and gardeners did the gardening. Then, in 1988, the zoo decided to develop bioclimatic zones, in which plants and animals are grouped together in cageless enclosures that resemble their native habitats. Because the zones themselves are interdependent, the employees who manage them must work together. For instance, the humid 3.5-acre Tiger River exhibit is run by a seven-member team of mammal and bird specialists, horticulturists, and maintenance and construction workers.[23]

HRM practices are likely to change in the following ways when SMTs are established:[24]

- Peers, rather than a supervisor, are likely to evaluate individual employee performance.
- Pay practices are likely to shift from pay based on seniority or individual performance to pay focused on team performance (for example, team bonuses).
- Rather than being based solely on input from managers and HR staff, team members may have a decisive amount of input in the hiring of new employees.

Self-managed teams have made some impressive contributions to the bottom lines of companies that have used them. For instance, after implementing SMTs, Shenandoah Life found it could process 50% more applications and customer service requests with 10% fewer employees.[25] Xerox plants using SMTs are 30% more productive than Xerox plants organized without them.[26] Boeing used SMTs to reduce the number of engineering problems in the development of the new 777 passenger jet by more than half.[27]

Because team members often initially lack the skills necessary for the team to function successfully, it may take several years for an SMT to become fully operational. A company can hasten this evolution by using its HR department to train employees in the skills required of team members. Three areas are important:[28]

Manager's Notebook

Five Common Misconceptions About Self-Managed Teams

1. **Self-managed teams do not need leaders.** The opposite is true. Teams definitely need some type of leader (who may be called a "coach" or "facilitator") to transfer what has traditionally been called "leadership responsibility" to team members. The role of the leader will vary from team to team, but leaders definitely have a role to play.
2. **Leaders lose power in the transition to teams.** Power is a flexible resource. Instead of exercising power within the group to control people, leaders of self-managed teams turn their power outward and use it to break down barriers in the organization that prevent the team from being effective.
3. **Newly formed teams are automatically self-managing.** Team development takes time. Describing new teams as self-managed by definition may establish unrealistic expectations.
4. **Employees are eager to be empowered.** Some consultants have estimated that 25% to 30% of working Americans—regardless of their position in the organization—don't want to be empowered.
5. **If you group employees in a team structure, they will function as a team, and the organization will reap the benefits of teamwork.** Unfortunately, it doesn't always work that way. Groups must go through a developmental process before they can function successfully as teams.

Source: Excerpt from Caudron, S. (1993, December). Are self-directed teams right for your company? *Personnel Journal*, 81. Copyright December 1993. Reprinted with the permission of *Personnel Journal*, ACC Communications, Inc., Costa Mesa, California; all rights reserved.

1. *Technical skills.* Team members must be cross-trained in new technical skills so that they can rotate among jobs as necessary. Team members who are cross-trained give the team greater flexibility and allow it to operate efficiently with fewer workers.
2. *Administrative skills.* Teams do much of the work done by supervisors in organizations that don't have teams. Therefore, team members need training in such management/administrative skills as budgeting, scheduling, monitoring and evaluating peers, and interviewing job applicants.
3. *Interpersonal skills.* Team members need good communication skills to form an effective team. They must be able to express themselves effectively in order to share information, deal with conflict, and give feedback to one another.

In addition to training employees in the skills needed for teamwork, companies would be wise to debunk some of the myths managers commonly hold about SMTs and how they work. For more on this topic, see the Manager's Notebook above titled "Five Common Misconceptions About Self-Managed Teams."

Other Types of Teams

problem-solving team
A team consisting of volunteers from a unit or department who meet one or two hours per week to discuss quality improvement, cost reduction, or improvement in the work environment.

special-purpose team
A team consisting of workers who span functional or organizational boundaries and whose purpose is to examine complex issues.

In addition to the SMT, businesses use two other types of teams: the problem-solving team and the special-purpose team.[29] The **problem-solving team** consists of volunteers from a unit or department who meet one or two hours per week to discuss quality improvement, cost reduction, or improvement in the work environment. The formation of problem-solving teams does not affect an organization's structure because these teams exist for only a limited period; they are usually disbanded after they have achieved their objectives. Problem-solving teams are often used when organizations decide to pursue a TQM effort; the teams focus on making improvements in the quality of a product or service.

The **special-purpose team** consists of members who span functional or organizational boundaries and whose purpose is to examine complex issues—for example, introducing a new technology, improving the quality of a work process that spans several functional units, or encouraging cooperation between labor and management in a unionized setting. An example of a special-purpose team is the quality of work life (QWL) program, which consists of team members (including union representatives and managers) who collaborate on making improvements in all aspects of work life, including product quality. The QWL program at Ford and General Motors has focused on improving product quality, while the QWL program between the United Steel Workers of America and the major steel companies has concentrated on developing new ways to improve employee morale and working conditions.[30]

▸ Work: The Individual Perspective

The third and final perspective from which we will examine work flows and structure is that of the individual employee and job. We look first at the various theories of what motivates employees to achieve higher levels of performance, and then at different ways jobs can be designed to maximize employee productivity. In the next section we look at job analysis, the gathering and organization of information concerning the tasks and duties of specific jobs. The section concludes with a discussion of job descriptions, which are one of the primary results of job analysis.

Motivating Employees

motivation
That which energizes, directs, and sustains human behavior. In HRM, a person's desire to do the best possible job or to exert the maximum effort to perform assigned tasks.

Motivation can be defined as that which energizes, directs, and sustains human behavior.[31] In HRM, the term refers to a person's desire to do the best possible job or to exert the maximum effort to perform assigned tasks. An important feature of motivation is that it is behavior directed toward a goal.

Motivation theory seeks to explain why employees are more motivated by and satisfied with one type of work than another. It is essential that managers have a basic understanding of work motivation because highly motivated employees are more likely to produce a superior-quality product or service than employees who lack motivation.

Two-Factor Theory. The *two-factor theory of motivation,* developed by Frederick Herzberg, attempts to identify and explain the factors that employees find satisfying and dissatisfying about their jobs.[32] The first set of factors, called *motivators,* are internal job factors that lead to job satisfaction and higher motivation. In the absence of motivators, employees will probably not be satisfied with their work or motivated to perform up to their potential. Some examples of motivators are:

- The work itself
- Achievement
- Recognition
- Responsibility
- Opportunities for advancement

Notice that salary is not included in the motivator list. Herzberg contends that pay belongs among the second set of factors, which he calls *hygiene* or *maintenance factors.* Hygiene factors are external to the job; they are located in the work environment. The absence of a hygiene factor can lead to active dissatisfaction and demotivation and, in extreme situations, to avoidance of the work altogether. Hygiene factors include the following:

- Company policies
- Working conditions
- Job security
- Salary
- Employee benefits
- Relationships with supervisors and managers
- Relationships with coworkers
- Relationships with subordinates

According to Herzberg, if management provides the appropriate hygiene factors, employees will not be dissatisfied with their jobs, but neither will they be motivated to perform at their full potential. To motivate workers, management must provide some motivators.

Two-factor theory has two implications for job design:

- Jobs should be designed to provide as many motivators as possible.
- Making (external) changes in hygiene factors such as pay or working conditions is not likely to sustain improvements in employee motivation over the long run unless (internal) changes are also made in the work itself.

Work Adjustment Theory. Every worker has unique needs and abilities. *Work adjustment theory* suggests that employees' motivation levels and job satisfaction depend on the fit between their needs and abilities and the characteristics of the job and the organization.[33] A poor fit between individual characteristics and the work environment may lead to reduced levels of motivation. Work adjustment theory proposes that:

- A job design that one employee finds challenging and motivating may not motivate another employee. For example, a mentally disabled employee may find a repetitive job at a fast-food restaurant highly motivating and challenging, but a college graduate may find the same job boring.
- Not all employees want to be involved in decision making. Employees with low needs for involvement may fit poorly on a self-managed team because they may resist managing other team members and taking responsibility for team decisions.

Goal-Setting Theory. *Goal-setting theory,* developed by Edwin Locke, suggests that employees' goals help to explain motivation and job performance.[34] The reasoning is as follows: Because motivation is goal-directed behavior, goals that are clear and challenging will result in higher levels of employee motivation than goals that are ambiguous and easy.

Because it suggests that managers can increase employee motivation by managing the goal-setting process, goal-setting theory has some important implications for managers:[35]

- Employees will be more motivated to perform when they have clear and specific goals. A store manager whose specific goal is to "increase store profitability by 20% in the next six months" will exert more effort than one who is told to "do the best you can" to increase profits.
- Employees will be more motivated to accomplish difficult goals than easy goals. Of course, the goals must be attainable; otherwise the employee is likely to become frustrated. For example, an inexperienced computer programmer may promise to deliver a program in an unrealistic amount of time. The programmer's manager may work with her to establish a more realistic, yet still challenging, deadline for delivering the program.
- In many (but not all) cases, goals that employees participate in creating for themselves are more motivating than goals that are simply assigned by managers. Managers may

establish mutually agreed-upon goals with employees through a management by objectives (MBO) approach (discussed in Chapter 7) or by creating self-managed teams that take responsibility for establishing their own goals.

- Employees who receive frequent feedback on their progress toward reaching their goals sustain higher levels of motivation and performance than employees who receive sporadic or no feedback. For example, a restaurant manager can motivate servers to provide better service by soliciting customer feedback on service quality and then communicating this information to employees.

Job Characteristics Theory. Developed by Richard Hackman and Greg Oldham, *job characteristics theory* states that employees will be more motivated to work and more satisfied with their jobs to the extent that jobs contain certain core characteristics.[36] These core job characteristics create the conditions that allow employees to experience critical psychological states that are related to beneficial work outcomes, including high work motivation. The strength of the linkage among job characteristics, psychological states, and work outcomes is determined by the intensity of the individual employee's need for growth (that is, how important the employee considers growth and development on the job).

There are five core job characteristics that activate three critical psychological states. The core job characteristics are:[37]

1. *Skill variety.* The degree to which the job requires the person to do different things and involves the use of a number of different skills, abilities, and talents.
2. *Task identity.* The degree to which a person can do the job from beginning to end with a visible outcome.
3. *Task significance.* The degree to which the job has a significant impact on others—both inside and outside the organization.
4. *Autonomy.* The amount of freedom, independence, and discretion the employee has in areas such as scheduling the work, making decisions, and determining how to do the job.
5. *Feedback.* The degree to which the job provides the employee with clear and direct information about job outcomes and performance.

The three critical psychological states affected by the core job characteristics are:[38]

1. *Experienced meaningfulness.* The extent to which the employee experiences the work as important, valuable, and worthwhile.
2. *Experienced responsibility.* The degree to which the employee feels personally responsible or accountable for the results of the work.
3. *Knowledge of results.* The degree to which the employee understands on a regular basis how effectively he or she is performing the job.

Skill variety, task identity, and task significance are all linked to experienced meaningfulness of work, as Figure 2–3 shows. Autonomy is related to experienced responsibility and feedback to knowledge of results.

A job with characteristics that allow an employee to experience all three critical psychological states provides internal rewards that sustain motivation. These rewards come from having a job where the person can learn (knowledge of results) that he or she has performed well on a task (experienced responsibility) that he or she cares about (experienced meaningfulness).[39] In addition, this situation results in certain outcomes that are beneficial to the employer: high-quality performance, higher employee satisfaction, and lower turnover and absenteeism. Job characteristics theory maintains that jobs can be designed to contain the characteristics that employees find rewarding and motivating.

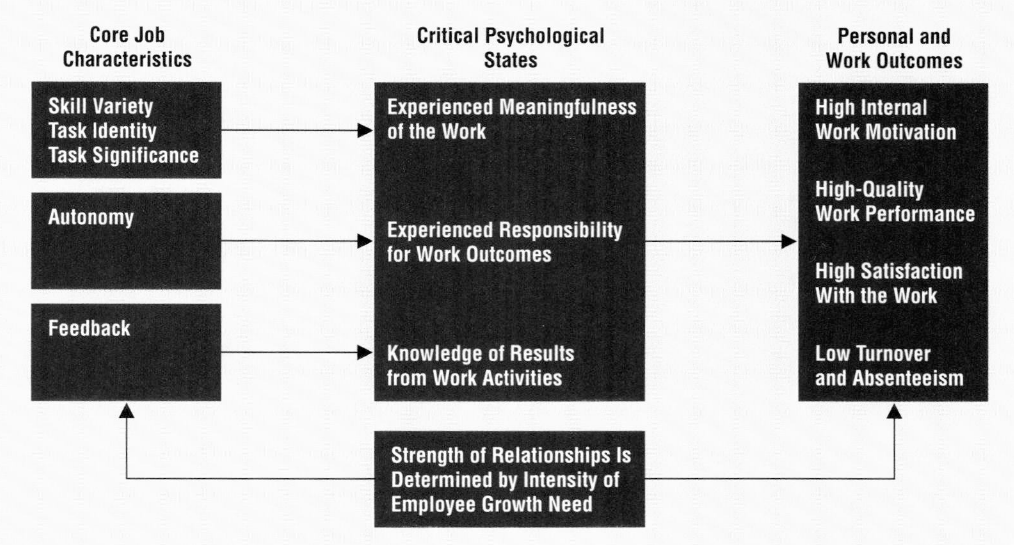

FIGURE 2-3

The Job Characteristics Theory of Work Motivation

Building Managerial Skills: Designing Jobs and Conducting Job Analysis

All the theories of employee motivation suggest that jobs can be designed to increase motivation and performance. **Job design** is the process of organizing work into the tasks required to perform a specific job.

job design
The process of organizing work into the tasks required to perform a specific job.

Job Design

There are three important influences on job design. One is work flow analysis, which (you will recall) seeks to ensure that each job in the organization receives work as an input, adds value to that work, and then passes it on to another worker. The other two influences are business strategy and the organizational structure that best fits that strategy. For example, an emphasis on highly specialized jobs could be expected in a bureaucratic organizational structure because work in bureaucratic organizations is built around the division of labor.

We will examine five approaches to job design: work simplification, job enlargement, job rotation, job enrichment, and team-based job design.

Work Simplification. *Work simplification* assumes that work can be broken down into simple, repetitive tasks that maximize efficiency. This approach to job design assigns most of the thinking aspects of work (such as planning and organizing) to managers and supervisors, while giving the employee a narrowly defined task to perform. Work simplification can utilize labor very effectively to produce a large amount of a standardized product. The automobile assembly line, where workers engage in highly mechanical and repetitive tasks, exemplifies the work simplification approach.

Although work simplification can be efficient in a stable environment, it is less effective in a changing environment where customers demand custom-built products of high quality. Moreover, work simplification often leads to high levels of employee turnover and low levels of employee satisfaction. (In fact, where work simplification is used, employees may feel the need to form unions to gain some control over their work.) Finally, higher-level professionals subjected to work simplification may become so specialized in what they do that they cannot see how their job affects the organization's overall product or service. The result can be employees doing work that has no value to the customer. This is a discovery organizations suddenly made in the 1990s. Hence, many professional employees in highly specialized jobs have become casualties of corporate restructurings in recent years.

Work simplification is not to be confused with *work elimination.* Companies trying to eliminate work challenge every task and every step within a task to see if there is a better way to get the work done. Even if parts of the work cannot be eliminated, some aspect of the job may be simplified or combined with another job. Oryx—a Dallas, Texas–based oil and gas producer—saved $70 million in operating costs in one year after it set up teams to take a fresh look at operation. The teams discovered many procedures, reviews, reports, and approvals that had little to do with Oryx's business and could easily be eliminated. Work elimination is similar to business process reengineering, though it differs in that work elimination typically focuses on particular jobs and processes rather than on overhauling the entire company.[40]

job enlargement
The process of expanding a job's duties.

job rotation
The process of rotating workers among different narrowly defined tasks without disrupting the flow of work.

Job Enlargement and Job Rotation. Job enlargement and job rotation are used to redesign jobs to reduce fatigue and boredom among workers performing simplified and highly specialized work. **Job enlargement** expands a job's duties. For example, auto workers whose specialized job is to install carpets on the car floor may have their job enlarged to include the extra duties of installing the car's seats and instrument panel.[41]

Job rotation rotates workers among different narrowly defined tasks without disrupting the flow of work. On an auto assembly line, for example, a worker whose job is installing carpets would be rotated periodically to a second workstation where she would install only seats in the car. At a later time period she might be rotated to a third workstation, where her job would be to install only the car's instrument panels. During the course of a day on the assembly line, the worker might be shifted at two-hour intervals among all three workstations.

Both job enlargement and job rotation have limitations because these approaches focus mainly on eliminating the demotivating aspects of work and thus improve only one of the five core job characteristics that motivate workers (skill variety).

job enrichment
The process of putting specialized tasks back together so that one person is responsible for producing a whole product or an entire service.

Job Enrichment. Job enrichment is an approach to job design that directly applies job characteristics theory (see Figure 2–3) to make jobs more interesting and to improve employee motivation. **Job enrichment** puts specialized tasks back together so that one person is responsible for producing a whole product or an entire service.[42]

Job enrichment expands both the horizontal and the vertical dimensions of a job. Instead of people working on an assembly line at one or more stations, the entire assembly line process is abandoned to allow workers to assemble an entire product, such as a kitchen appliance or radio.[43] For example, at Motorola's Communications Division, individual employees are now responsible for assembling, testing, and packaging the company's pocket radio-paging devices. Previously, these products were made on an assembly line that broke the work down into 100 different steps and used as many workers.[44]

Job enrichment gives employees more opportunities for autonomy and feedback. It also gives them more responsibilities that require decision making, such as scheduling work, determining work methods, and judging quality.[45] However, the successful implementation of job enrichment is limited by the production technology available and the capabilities of the employees who produce the product or service. Some products are highly complex and require too many steps for one individual to produce them efficiently. Other products require the application of so many different skills that it is not feasible to train employees in all of them. For example, it could take an employee a lifetime to master all the skills necessary to assemble a Boeing 747 jet aircraft.

Team-Based Job Designs. *Team-based job designs* focus on giving a team, rather than an individual, a whole and meaningful piece of work to do.[46] Team members are empowered to decide among themselves how to accomplish the work.[47] Team members are cross-trained in different skills, then rotated to do different tasks within the team. Team-based job designs match best with flat and boundaryless organizational structures.

One company that emphasizes team-based job design is General Motors' Saturn division, located in Spring Hill, Tennessee. The process of assembling the Saturn car is accomplished by self-managed teams of 8 to 15 workers. Each team takes responsibility for managing itself. It interviews and hires new team members, manages its own budget, and receives reports on the amount of waste it generates so that it can develop plans to utilize its materials more effectively.[48]

Job Analysis

After a work flow analysis has been done and jobs have been designed, the employer needs to define and communicate job expectations for individual employees. This is best done through **job analysis,** which is the systematic gathering and organization of information concerning jobs. Job analysis puts a job under the microscope to reveal important details about it. Specifically, it identifies the tasks, duties, and responsibilities of a particular job.

job analysis
The systematic process of collecting information used to make decisions about jobs. Job analysis identifies the tasks, duties, and responsibilities of a particular job.

- A *task* is a basic element of work that is a logical and necessary step in performing a job duty.
- A *duty* consists of one or more tasks that constitute a significant activity performed in a job.
- A *responsibility* is one or several duties that identify and describe the major purpose or reason for the job's existence.

Thus, for the job of administrative assistant, a task might be completing a travel authorization form, which is part of the duty to keep track of the department's travel expenses, which is part of the responsibility to manage the departmental budget.

The Great Unveiling.

Teams at GM's Saturn division take responsibility for managing themselves. Each team interviews and hires team members, manages its own budget, keeps track of the waste it generates, and seeks ways to increase its own efficiency. The public unveiling of the first Saturn was a celebration for all Saturn workers, who are known for their dedication to their product.

Job analysis provides information to answer the following questions: Where does the work come from? What machines and special equipment must be used? What knowledge, skills, and abilities (KSAs) does the job holder need to perform the job? How much supervision is necessary? Under what working conditions should this job be performed? What are the performance expectations for this job? On whom must the job holders depend to perform this job? With whom must they interact?

Who Performs Job Analysis? Depending on the technique selected, job analysis is performed either by a member of the HR department or by the *job incumbent* (the person who is currently assigned to the job in question). In some businesses a manager may perform the job analysis.

Methods of Gathering Job Information. Companies use several methods to gather job information: interviews, observation, diaries, and questionnaires. Factors such as cost and job complexity will influence the choice of method.

- *Interviews.* The interviewer (usually a member of the HR department) interviews a representative sample of job incumbents using a structured interview. The structured interview includes a series of job-related questions that are presented to each interviewee in the same order.
- *Observation.* An individual observes the job incumbent actually performing the job and records the core job characteristics from observation. This method is used in cases where the job is fairly routine and the observer can identify the job essentials in a reasonable amount of time. The job analyst may videotape the job incumbent in order to study the job in greater detail.
- *Diaries.* Several job incumbents may be asked to keep diaries or logs of their daily job activities and record the amount of time spent on each activity. By analyzing these diaries over a representative period of time (perhaps several weeks), a job analyst is able to capture the job's essential characteristics.
- *Questionnaires.* The job incumbent fills out a questionnaire that asks a series of questions about the job's duties, responsibilities, and knowledge, skill, and ability requirements. Each question is associated with a quantitative scale that measures the importance of the job factor or the frequency with which it occurs. A computer can then tally the scores on the questionnaires and create a printout summarizing the job's characteristics. The computerized method of gathering job information with questionnaires is the most expensive method.

The Uses of Job Analysis. Job analysis measures job content and the relative importance of different job duties and responsibilities. Having this information helps companies comply with government regulations and defend their actions from legal challenges that allege unfairness or discrimination. As we will see in Chapter 3, the generic defense against a charge of discrimination is that the contested decision (to hire, to give a raise, to terminate) was made for job-related reasons. Job analysis provides the documentation for such a defense. For instance:

- A company may be able to defend its policy of requiring sales representatives to have a valid driver's license if it can show via job analysis that driving is an essential activity in the sales rep's job. Otherwise, under the Americans with Disabilities Act (see Chapter 3), the employer may be asked to make a reasonable accommodation for a blind job applicant who asserts his rights to be considered for the job.
- The owner of a fast-food restaurant who pays an assistant manager a weekly salary (without any overtime pay) may be able to defend herself from charges of an overtime pay violation with a job analysis proving that the assistant manager job is exempt from the overtime provisions of the Fair Labor Standards Act (see Chapter 10). The owner can

prove this by showing that most of the job duties and responsibilities involve supervising and directing others rather than preparing food and providing service to customers.

In addition to establishing job relatedness for legal purposes, job analysis is also useful for the following HR activities:

- *Recruitment.* Job analysis can help the HR department generate a higher-quality pool of job applicants by making it easy to describe a job in newspaper ads that can be targeted to qualified job applicants. Job analysis also helps college recruiters screen job applicants because it tells them what tasks, duties, and responsibilities the job entails.
- *Selection.* Job analysis can be used to determine whether an applicant for a specific job should be required to take a personality test or some other kind of test. For example, a personality test that measures extroversion (the degree to which someone is talkative, sociable, active, aggressive, or excitable) may be justified for selecting a life insurance sales representative. (Such a job is likely to emphasize customer contact, which includes making "cold calls" on potential new accounts.) Job analysis may also reveal that the personality test measuring extroversion has a weak relationship to the job content of other jobs (for example, lab technician) and should not be used as part of the selection process for those jobs.
- *Performance appraisal.* The performance standards used to judge employee performance for purposes of promotion, rewards, discipline, or layoff should be job related. Under federal law, a company is required to defend its appraisal system against lawsuits and prove the job relatedness of the performance criteria used in the appraisal.
- *Compensation.* Job analysis information can be used to compare the relative worth of each job's contributions to the company's overall performance. The value of each job's contribution is an important determinant of the job's pay level. In a typical pay structure, jobs that require mastery of more complex skills or that have greater levels of responsibility pay more than jobs that require only basic skills or have low amounts of responsibility.
- *Training and career development.* Job analysis is an important input for determining training needs. By comparing the knowledge, skills, and abilities that employees bring to the job with those that are identified by job analysis, managers can identify their employees' skill gaps. Training programs can then be put in place to improve job performance.

The Techniques of Job Analysis. Figure 2–4 on page 64 lists the major techniques of job analysis. Detailed descriptions of these techniques are beyond the scope of this book. However, a brief description of four of them—task inventory analysis, the critical incident technique, the position analysis questionnaire, and functional job analysis—will provide you with a sense of what job analysis entails. For a set of general guidelines on conducting a job analysis effectively, see the Manager's Notebook on page 66 titled "Guidelines for Conducting a Job Analysis."

Task Inventory Analysis. *Task inventory analysis* is actually a collection of methods that are offshoots of the U.S. Air Force task inventory method.[49] The technique is used to determine the **knowledge, skills, and abilities (KSAs)** needed to perform a job successfully. The analysis involves three steps: (1) interview, (2) survey, and (3) generation of a task by KSA matrix.

KSAs
The knowledge, skills, and abilities needed to perform a job successfully.

The interview step focuses on developing lists of tasks that are part of the job. Interviews are conducted both with workers who currently hold the job and with their managers. The goal of the interviews is to generate specific descriptions of individual tasks that can be used in the task inventory survey.

The survey step involves generating and administering a survey consisting of task statements and rating scales. The survey might ask respondents—the current job holders—to rate each task on importance, frequency, and training time needed. Whether the survey

Technique	Employee Group Focused On	Data-Collection Method	Analysis Results	Description
1. Task Inventory Analysis	Any—large number of workers needed	Questionnaire	Rating of tasks	Tasks are rated by job incumbent,* supervisor, or job analyst. Ratings may be on characteristics such as importance of task and time spent doing it.
2. Critical Incident Technique	Any	Interview	Behavioral description	Behavioral incidents representing poor through excellent performance are generated for each dimension of the job.
3. Position Analysis Questionnaire (PAQ)	Any	Questionnaire	Rating of 194 job elements	Elements are rated on six scales (for example, extent of use, importance to job). Ratings are analyzed by computer.
4. Functional Job Analysis (FJA)	Any	Group interview/ Questionnaire	Rating of how job incumbent relates to people, data, and things	Originally designed to improve counseling and placement of people registered at local state employment offices. Task statements are generated and then presented to job incumbents to rate on such dimensions as frequency and importance.
5. Methods Analysis (Motion Study)	Manufacturing	Observation	Time per unit of work	Systematic means for determining the standard time for various work tasks. Based on observation and timing of work tasks.
6. Guidelines-Oriented Job Analysis	Any	Interview	Skills and knowledge required	Job incumbents identify duties as well as knowledge, skills, physical abilities, and other characteristics needed to perform the job.
7. Management Position Description Questionnaire (MPDQ)	Managerial	Questionnaire	Checklist of 197 items	Managers check items descriptive of their responsibilities.
8. Hay Plan	Managerial	Interview	Impact of job on organization	Managers are interviewed regarding such issues as their responsibilities and and accountabilities. Responses are analyzed according to four dimensions: objectives, dimensions, nature and scope, accountability.

*The term *job incumbent* refers to the person currently filling a particular job.

FIGURE 2-4

The Techniques of Job Analysis

is sent to a sample of the workers or to all of them will depend on the number of workers and the economic constraints on the job analysis.

The final step is the creation of a task by KSA matrix, which is used to rate the extent to which a variety of KSAs are important for the successful completion of each task. An abbreviated example of a KSA rating matrix is presented in Figure 2–5. Ratings in the matrix are usually determined by subject matter experts, who might include supervisors, managers, consultants, and job incumbents.

Task inventory analysis has two major advantages. First, it is a systematic means for analyzing the tasks in a particular situation. Second, it uses a tailor-made questionnaire rather than an already-prepared stock questionnaire. The technique can be used to develop job descriptions and performance appraisal forms, as well as to develop or identify appropriate selection tests.

Rating Scale Importance of characteristics for successful performance of task				
1 Very Low	2 Low	3 Medium	4 High	5 Very High

	Worker Characteristics									
Job Task	Mathematical Reasoning	Analytical Ability	Ability to Follow Directions	Memory	Comprehension—Oral	Comprehension—Written	Expression—Oral	Expression—Written	Problem-Solving Ability	Clerical Accuracy
1. Reviews production schedules to determine correct job sequencing										
2. Identifies problem jobs and takes corrective action										
3. Determines need for and provides special work orders										
4. Maintains log book and makes required assignments										
5. Negotiates with foremen to determine critical dates for emergency situations										
6. Analyzes material availability and performs order maintenance										
7. Prepares job packets										
8. Maintains customer order file										
9. Negotiates with Purchasing to ensure material availability										
10. Determines product availability for future customer orders										
11. Determines promise dates and provides to customers										
12. Determines adequacy of materials given document forecast										

FIGURE 2-5
Sample Task by KSA Matrix

Critical Incident Technique. The *critical incident technique (CIT)*[50] is used to develop behavioral descriptions of a job. In CIT, supervisors and workers generate behavioral incidents of job performance. The technique involves the following four steps: (1) generate dimensions, (2) generate incidents, (3) retranslate, and (4) assign effectiveness values. In the generating dimensions step, supervisors and workers identify the major dimensions of a job. "Dimensions" are simply aspects of performance. For example, interacting with customers, ordering stock, and balancing the cash drawer are the major dimensions of a retail job. Once they have agreed on the job's major dimensions, supervisors and workers generate "critical incidents" of behavior that represent high, moderate, and low levels of per-

Manager's Notebook

Guidelines for Conducting a Job Analysis

Conducting a job analysis requires managers to take five steps:

1. *Determine the desired applications of the job analysis.* For example, if used as a basis for performance appraisal, job analysis should collect data that are representative of differing levels of job performance. If used as a basis for determining training needs, then job analysis should collect information on the necessary knowledge, skills, and abilities that lead to effective job performance.
2. *Select the jobs to be analyzed.* Factors that make specific jobs appropriate for job analysis include the stability or obsolescence of job content (rapidly changing jobs require more frequent job analysis). Entry-level jobs (which require selection tools that determine who gets hired and who gets rejected) are also analyzed regularly.
3. *Gather the job information.* Within budget constraints, collect the desired information using the most appropriate job analysis technique.
4. *Verify the accuracy of the job information.* Both the job incumbents and their immediate supervisors should review the job information to ensure that it is representative of the actual job.
5. *Document the job analysis by writing a job description.* Document the job analysis information in a job description that summarizes the job's essential duties and responsibilities, as well as the knowledge, skills, and abilities necessary for the job. This document allows managers to compare different jobs on various dimensions and is an important part of many HR programs.

Source: Adapted from Gatewood, R. D., and Feild, H. S. (1987). *Human resource selection.* Chicago: The Dryden Press.

formance on each dimension. An example of a critical incident of high performance on the dimension "interacting with customers" might be:

> When a customer complained to the clerk that she could not find a particular item, seeing no one else was in line, this clerk walked with the customer back to the shelves to find the item.

An example of low performance on the same dimension might be:

> When a customer handed the clerk a large number of coupons, the clerk complained out loud to the bagger that he hated dealing with coupons.

The last two steps, retranslation and assigning effectiveness values, involve making sure that the critical incidents generated in the first two steps are commonly viewed the same way by other employees.

The CIT provides a detailed behavioral description of jobs. It is often used as a basis for performance appraisal systems and training programs, as well as to develop behaviorally based selection interview questions. The appendix to Chapter 7 gives you the opportunity to develop critical incidents.

Position Analysis Questionnaire (PAQ). The PAQ is a job analysis questionnaire that contains 194 different items. Using a five-point scale, the PAQ seeks to determine the degree to which the different items, or job elements, are involved in performing a particular job.[51] The 194 items are organized into six sections:

1. *Information input.* Where and how a worker gets information needed to perform the job.
2. *Mental processes.* The reasoning, decision-making, planning, and information-processing activities involved in performing the job.
3. *Work output.* The physical activities, tools, and devices used by the worker to perform the job.
4. *Relationships with other persons.* The relationships with other people required in performing the job.
5. *Job context.* The physical and social contexts in which the work is performed.
6. *Other characteristics.* The other activities, conditions, and characteristics relevant to the job.

A computer analyzes the completed PAQ and generates a score for the job and a profile of its characteristics.

Functional Job Analysis. Functional job analysis, a technique used in the public sector, can be done by either interview or questionnaire.[52] This technique collects information on the following aspects of the job:

1. What the job incumbent does to people, data, and things.
2. The methods and techniques the job incumbent uses to perform the job.
3. The machines, tools, and equipment used by the job incumbent.
4. The materials, projects, or services produced by the job incumbent.

The results of functional job analyses are published by the U.S. federal government in the *Dictionary of Occupational Titles (DOT)*.[53] The DOT contains standard and comprehensive descriptions of about 20,000 jobs, and has helped to bring about more uniformity in the job titles used in different sections of the country. The DOT listings also facilitate the exchange of statistical information about jobs.

Job Analysis, the Legal Environment, and Organizational Flexibility. Because job analysis can be the basis on which a firm wins or loses a lawsuit over how it selects or appraises employees, it is important that organizations carefully document their job-analysis efforts.

There are two important questions regarding job analysis. First: Which job analysis method is best? Although there are many job-analysis techniques, there is no clear choice as to which is best. Some, like task inventory analysis and Guidelines-Oriented Job Analysis, were developed to satisfy legal requirements, but there is no legal basis to prefer one to another. The *Uniform Guidelines* published by the Equal Employment Opportunity Commission state that a job analysis should be done but do not specify a preferred technique.

As a general rule, the more concrete and observable the information, the better. Thus, job-analysis approaches that provide specific task or behavioral statements, such as task inventory analysis or CIT, may be preferable. CIT can be very expensive because of the time commitment required of supervisors and workers.

Given the lack of a single best technique, the choice of job-analysis technique should, within economic constraints, be guided by the purpose of the analysis. For example, if the major purpose for the analysis is the redesign of jobs, then an analysis focusing on tasks would probably be best. But if the major purpose is the development of a training program, a behaviorally focused technique would probably be best.

The second question regarding job analysis is: How does detailed job-analysis information fit into today's organizations, which need to be flexible and innovative to remain competitive?

Whatever technique is used, job analysis is a static view of the job as it currently exists, and a static view of jobs is at odds with current organizational trends emphasizing flexibility and innovativeness. For instance, America West Airlines attempts to keep labor costs down by having employees do a variety of tasks. The same person may be a flight attendant, ticket agent, and baggage handler all in the same week. And almost all jobs today are affected by the constant advances in information and communication technologies. Such factors can render even the most thorough job analysis virtually useless after a very short time.

In an organizational environment of change and innovation, it is better to focus job analyses on *worker* characteristics than on *job* characteristics. The tasks involved in jobs may change, but such employee characteristics as innovativeness, team orientation, interpersonal skills, and communication skills will likely remain critical to organizational success. Unfortunately, most job-analysis techniques are not focused on discovering worker characteristics not directly related to the immediate tasks. But, because the importance of fit with the organization is being increasingly recognized as a factor that should be considered in selection,[54] job analysis may become more focused on underlying employee factors.[55] Sun Microsystems, Toyota (USA), and AFG Industries are some of the organizations that have expanded job analysis to emphasize fit between prospective employees and the organization.

Job Descriptions

A **job description** is a summary statement of the information collected in the job-analysis process. It is a written document that identifies, defines, and describes a job in terms of its duties, responsibilities, working conditions, and specifications. There are two types of job descriptions: specific job descriptions and general job descriptions.

job description
A written document that identifies, describes, and defines a job in terms of its duties, responsibilities, working conditions, and specifications.

A *specific job description* is a detailed summary of a job's tasks, duties, and responsibilities. This type of job description is associated with work flow strategies that emphasize efficiency, control, and detailed work planning. It fits best with a bureaucratic organizational structure with well-defined boundaries that separate functions and the different levels of management. Figure 2–6 shows an example of a specific job description for the job of service and safety supervisor. Note that this job description closely specifies the work that is unique to a person who will supervise *safety* employees. The specific job knowledge of safety regulations and Red Cross first-aid procedures included in this job description make it inappropriate for any other type of supervisor (for example, a supervisor at a local supermarket).

The *general job description,* which is fairly new on the scene, is associated with work flow strategies that emphasize innovation, flexibility, and loose work planning. This type of job description fits best with a flat or boundaryless organizational structure where there are few boundaries between functions and levels of management.

Only the most generic duties and responsibilities for a position are documented in the general job description.[56] Figure 2–7 on page 70 shows a general job description for the job of "supervisor." Note that all the job duties and responsibilities in Figure 2–7 apply to the job of *any* supervisor—one who supervises accountants, engineers, or even the safety employees managed by the service and safety supervisor in Figure 2–6.

The driving force behind a move toward general job descriptions may be a TQM program or business process reengineering.[56a] For example, the Arizona Public Service (APS), a public utility, moved toward general job descriptions after discovering that it had 1,000 specific job descriptions for its 3,600 workers.[57] This massive number of specific job descriptions erected false barriers among work functions, choked off change, and prevented APS from providing high levels of customer service. By using general job descriptions, APS was able to reduce the number of its job descriptions to 450.

An even more impressive application of general job descriptions is seen at Nissan, the Japanese auto manufacturer. Nissan has only one general job description for all its hourly-wage production employees.[58] By comparison, some of the divisions of General Motors have hundreds of specific job descriptions for their hourly production work force. This fact is partially explained by the vigilance of the United Auto Workers' Union (UAW) in defending the rights of its members to work in specific jobs.

Elements of a Job Description. Job descriptions have four key elements: identification information, job summary, job duties and responsibilities, and job specifications and minimum qualifications.[59] Figures 2-6 and 2-7 show how this information is organized on the job description.

To comply with federal law, it is important that job descriptions document only the essential aspects of a job. Otherwise, qualified women, minorities, and persons with disabilities may be unintentionally discriminated against for not meeting specified job requirements. For example, a valid driver's license should not be put in the job description if the job can be modified so that it can be performed by a physically disabled person without a driver's license.

Identification Information. The first part of the job description identifies the job title, location, and source of job-analysis information; who wrote the job description; the dates of the job analysis and the verification of the job description; and whether the job is exempt from the overtime provision of the Fair Labor Standards Act or subject to overtime pay rates. To be certain that the identification information ensures equal employment opportunities, HR staff should:

- Make sure the job titles do not refer to a specific gender. For example, use the job title "sales representative" rather than "salesman."
- Make sure job descriptions are updated regularly so that the date on the job description is current. Job descriptions more than two years old have low credibility and may provide flawed information.

Job Title: Service and Safety Supervisor
DIVISION: Plastics
DEPARTMENT: Manufacturing
SOURCE(S): John Doe — WAGE CATEGORY: Exempt
JOB ANALYST: John Smith — VERIFIED BY: Bill Johnson
DATE ANALYZED: 12/26/97 — DATE VERIFIED: 1/5/98

Job Summary
The SERVICE AND SAFETY SUPERVISOR works under the direction of the IMPREGNATING & LAMINATING MANAGER: **schedules** labor pool employees; **supervises** the work of gardeners, cleaners, waste disposal and plant security personnel; **coordinates** plant safety programs; **maintains** daily records on personnel, equipment, and scrap.

Job Duties and Responsibilities

1. **Schedules** labor employees to provide relief personnel for all manufacturing departments; **prepares** assignment schedules and **assigns** individuals to departments based on routine as well as special needs in order to maintain adequate labor levels through the plant; **notifies** Industrial Relations Department weekly about vacation and layoff status of labor pool employees, contractual disputes, and other employment-related developments.
2. **Supervises** the work of gardeners, cleaners, waste disposal and plant security personnel; **plans** yard, clean-up, and security activities based on weekly determination of needs; **assigns** tasks and responsibilities to employees on a daily basis; **monitors** progress or status of assigned tasks; **disciplines** employees.
3. **Coordinates** plant safety programs; **teaches** basic first-aid procedures to security, supervisory, and lease personnel in order to maintain adequate coverage of medical emergencies; **trains** employees in fire fighting and hazardous materials handling procedures; **verifies** plant compliance with new or changing OSHA regulations; **represents** division during company-wide safety programs and meetings.
4. **Maintains** daily records on personnel, equipment, and scrap; **reports** amount of waste and scrap to cost accounting department; **updates** personnel records as necessary; **reviews** maintenance checklists for tow-motors.
5. **Performs** other miscellaneous duties as assigned.

Job Requirements

1. Ability to apply basic principles and techniques of supervision.
   a. Knowledge of principles and techniques of supervision.
   b. Ability to plan and organize the activities of others.
   c. Ability to get ideas accepted and to guide a group or individual to accomplish the task.
   d. Ability to modify leadership style and management approach to reach goal.
2. Ability to express ideas clearly both in written and oral communications.
3. Knowledge of current Red Cross first-aid operations.
4. Knowledge of OSHA regulations as they affect plant operations.
5. Knowledge of labor pool jobs, company policies, and labor contracts.

Minimum Qualifications
Twelve years of general education or equivalent; one year supervisory experience; and first-aid instructor's certification.

OR

Substitute 45 hours classroom supervisory training for supervisory experience.

FIGURE 2-6

Example of a Specific Job Description

Source: Excerpt from Jones, M. A. (1984, May). Job descriptions made easy. *Personnel Journal*. Copyright May 1984. Reprinted with the permission of *Personnel Journal*, ACC Communications, Inc., Costa Mesa, California; all rights reserved.

- Ensure that the supervisor of the job incumbent(s) verifies the job description. This is a good way to ensure that the job description does not misrepresent the actual job duties and responsibilities. (A manager who is familiar with the job may also be used to verify the description.)

Job Title: Supervisor
DIVISION: Plastics
DEPARTMENT: Manufacturing
SOURCE(S): John Doe, S. Lee — WAGE CATEGORY: Exempt
JOB ANALYST: John Smith — VERIFIED BY: Bill Johnson
DATE ANALYZED: 12/26/97 — DATE VERIFIED: 1/5/98

Job Summary
The SUPERVISOR works under the direction of the MANAGER: **plans** goals; **supervises** the work of employees; **develops** employees with feedback and coaching; **maintains** accurate records; **coordinates** with others to achieve optimal use of organizational resources.

Job Duties and Responsibilities

1. **Plans** goals and allocates resources to achieve them; **monitors** progress toward objectives and adjusts plans as necessary to reach them; **allocates** and **schedules** resources to assure their availability according to priority.
2. **Supervises** the work of employees; **provides** clear instructions and explanations to employees when giving assignments; **schedules** and assigns work among employees for maximum efficiency; **monitors** employees' performance in order to achieve assigned objectives.
3. **Develops** employees through direct performance feedback and job coaching; **conducts** performance appraisals with each employee on a regular basis; **provides** employees with praise and recognition when performance is excellent; **corrects** employees promptly when their performance fails to meet expected performance levels.
4. **Maintains** accurate records and documents actions; **processes** paper work on a timely basis, and with close attention to details; **documents** important aspects of decisions and actions.
5. **Coordinates** with others to achieve the optimal use of organizational resources; **maintains** good working relationships with colleagues in other organizational units; **represents** others in unit during division or corporatewide meetings.

Job Requirements

1. Ability to apply basic principles and techniques of supervision.
   a. Knowledge of principles and techniques of supervision.
   b. Ability to plan and organize the activities of others.
   c. Ability to get ideas accepted and to guide a group or individual to accomplish the task.
   d. Ability to modify leadership style and management approach to reach goal.
2. Ability to express ideas clearly in both written and oral communications.

Minimum Qualifications
Twelve years of general education or equivalent; and one year supervisory experience.

OR

Substitute 45 hours classroom supervisory training for supervisory experience.

FIGURE 2-7

Example of a General Job Description

Source: Excerpt from Jones, M. A. (1984, May). Job descriptions made easy. *Personnel Journal*. Copyright May 1984. Reprinted with the permission of *Personnel Journal*, ACC Communications, Inc., Costa Mesa, California; all rights reserved.

Job Summary. The job summary is a short statement that summarizes the job's duties, responsibilities, and place in the organizational structure.

Job Duties and Responsibilities. Job duties and responsibilities explain what is done on the job, how it is done, and why it is done.[60]

Each job description typically lists the job's three to five most important responsibilities. Each responsibility statement begins with an action verb. For example, the job of supervisor in Figure 2–7 has five responsibilities that start with the following action verbs: plans, supervises, develops, maintains, and coordinates. Each responsibility is associated with one or more job duties, which also start with action verbs. For example, the supervisor job in Figure 2–7 has two job duties associated with the responsibility of "plans goals": (1) monitors progress toward objectives, and (2) allocates and schedules resources. The job duties and responsibilities statement is probably the most important section of the job description because it influences all the other parts of the job description. Therefore, it must be comprehensive and accurate.

Job Specifications and Minimum Qualifications. The **job specifications** section lists the worker characteristics (KSAs) needed to perform a job successfully. The KSAs represent the things that an employee who has mastered the job can do.

job specification
The worker characteristics needed to perform a job successfully.

When documenting KSAs it is important to list only those that are related to successful job performance. It is inappropriate to list what a specific job incumbent knows that is not related to the job. For example, a current computer programmer may have mastered some programming languages that are not necessary for job performance. These should not be included in the job description.

The *minimum qualifications* are the basic standards a job applicant must have achieved to be considered for the job. These can be used to screen job applicants during the recruiting and selection process. Minimum requirements must be carefully specified to avoid discriminating against job applicants. Here are some things to watch for when documenting minimum qualifications:

- A college degree should be used as a minimum qualification only if it is related to the successful performance of the job. For example, a bachelor's degree may be a minimum qualification for an accountant in a major accounting firm, but it is not likely to be necessary for the job of shift supervisor in a fast-food restaurant. The same logic applies to requirements for all other education standards, including a high school diploma or an advanced college degree.
- Work experience qualifications should be carefully specified so that they do not discriminate against minorities or persons with disabilities. For example, the job description in Figure 2–7 provides for a substitute of 45 classroom hours of supervisory training for the one year of work experience minimum qualification. This provision allows people who have been excluded from employment opportunities in the past to be considered for the position. This flexibility allows the company to consider diverse job applicants, who are less likely to meet the work experience qualification. ▼

The Flexible Work Force

One of the imperatives for many modern organizations is flexibility. We have seen how organizations can be structured and jobs designed to maximize this flexibility. In this section we examine two additional strategies for ensuring flexibility. First, we look at the practice of using contingent workers. Second, we examine flexible work schedules. Flexible work schedules let employers utilize talented employees who might otherwise be unavailable for employment.

Contingent Workers

core workers
An organization's full-time employees.

contingent workers
Workers hired to deal with temporary increases in an organization's workload or to do work that is not part of its core set of capabilities.

There are two types of workers: core workers and contingent workers. A company's **core workers** have full-time jobs and enjoy privileges not available to contingent workers. Many core workers expect a long-term relationship with the employer that includes a career in the organization, a full array of benefits, and job security. In contrast, the jobs of **contingent workers** are based on the employer's convenience and efficiency needs. Firms hire contingent workers to help them deal with temporary increases in their workload or to do work that is not part of their core set of capabilities. Contingent workers are easily dismissed when an organization no longer needs their services. When the business cycle moves into a downturn, the contingent workers are the first employees to be discharged. They thus provide a buffer zone of protection for the core workers. For example, in some large Japanese corporations core workers' jobs are protected by a large contingent work force that can be rapidly downsized when business conditions change.

Contingent workers include temporary employees, part-time employees, outsourced subcontractors, contract workers, and college interns. In the United States, contingent workers made up 27% of the total labor force in 1995. This number includes approximately 22 million part-time employees, 10.2 million contract workers, and 2.2 million temporary employees.[61] The jobs held by contingent workers are diverse, ranging from secretaries, security guards, sales clerks, and assembly-line workers to doctors, college professors, engineers, managers, and even chief executives.[61a]

Temporary Employees. Temporary employment agencies provide companies with *temporary employees* (or "temps") for short-term work assignments. Temps work for the temporary employment agency and are simply reassigned to another employer when their current job ends. Temporary employees are used to fill in for employees who are sick or on family leave. They can also be used to increase output when demand is high and to do work that is peripheral to the core employees' work. Manpower, the largest of the 7,000 U.S. temporary employment agencies, is also the nation's largest private employer, with almost 750,000 people on its payroll.[62]

Temporary employees provide employers with two major benefits:

- Temps on average receive less compensation than core workers. Temporary employees are not likely to receive health insurance, retirement, or vacation benefits from the company that uses their services. They generally do not receive these benefits from the temporary agency either. For example, as layoffs have mounted in the 1990s, the total payroll for professionals and managers employed by temporary firms has more than tripled.[63] However, many managers working at temp jobs earn 50% less than they earned as core workers.[64]
- Temporary employees may be highly motivated workers since many employers choose full-time employees from the ranks of the top-performing temps. Because temps can be screened for long-term career potential in an actual work setting and be easily dismissed if the company determines that they have low potential, hiring temps helps employers reduce the risk of selecting employees who prove to be a poor fit.

Temporary employees are being used with increasing regularity throughout the world. In France, one in five workers is on a temporary or part-time contract, and in Britain more than 30% of the work force is temporary or part-time. Almost 70% of the new jobs created in Spain in 1995 were for temporary workers.[65]

Part-Time Employees. *Part-time employees* work fewer hours than full-time core employees. Employers have the flexibility to schedule these people for work when they are needed. Part-time jobs offer far fewer employee benefits than full-time jobs, thus providing substantial savings to employers. Traditionally, part-timers have been employed by service businesses that have a high variance in demand between peak and off-peak times. For example, restaurants and markets hire many part-time employees to provide service to customers during peak hours (usually evenings and weekends).

Companies are finding many new applications for part-time workers. For example, United Parcel Service has created 25-hour-per-week part-time jobs for shipping clerks and supervisors who sort packages at its distribution centers. Companies that downsize their work forces to reduce payroll costs have been known to restructure full-time core jobs into part-time positions.

In a special type of part-time employment called **job sharing,** a full-time job is divided between two or more people to create two part-time jobs. The people in the job-sharing arrangement divide the job's responsibilities, hours, and benefits among themselves. During a recent downscaling of its work force, Du Pont used job sharing between employees in its management, research, and secretarial areas to avoid layoffs.[66]

job sharing
A work arrangement in which two or more employees divide a job's responsibilities, hours, and benefits among themselves.

Outsourcing/Subcontracting. As we saw in Chapter 1, outsourcing (sometimes called *subcontracting*) is the process by which employers transfer routine or peripheral work to another organization that specializes in that work and can perform it more efficiently. Employers that outsource some of their nonessential work gain improved quality and cost savings. Outsourcing agreements may result in a long-term relationship between an employer and the subcontractor, though it is the employer who has the flexibility to renew or end the relationship at its convenience.[67]

Many employees and union representatives complain bitterly about the practice of outsourcing work, particularly to foreign countries. Part of the complaint is that companies do this to avoid paying fair wages and providing employee benefits that U.S. workers expect. Is this an ethical issue? If so, on what basis should companies make outsourcing decisions?

Outsourcing is the wave of the future as more and more companies look to the "virtual corporation" as an organizational model.[68] A *virtual company* consists of a small core of permanent employees and a constantly shifting work force of contingent employees. A recent survey found that 32% of employers already outsource some or all of the administration of their human resources and benefit programs.

Establishing the right relationship with service vendors is very important for companies that decide to outsource. While some companies view their outsourced vendors as strategic partners, others caution that, ultimately, company and vendor do not have identical interests. For example, one petroleum company that outsourced its information systems function in the late 1980s, found itself paying $500,000 in excess fees the first month into the contract—a full 50% more than it expected—because managers had erroneously assumed that certain services were covered by the contract. The lesson is that it pays to communicate clearly and specifically with vendors from the beginning.[69]

One company that relies on outsourcing as a source of competitive advantage is Benetton, the Italian multinational corporation that makes clothing sold in 110 countries. Benetton views itself as a "clothing services" company rather than as a retailer or manufacturer.[70] The company outsources a large amount of clothes manufacturing to local suppliers but makes sure to provide its subcontractors with the clothes-making skills that Benetton views as crucial to maintaining quality and cost efficiency.[71]

Contract Workers. *Contract workers* are employees who develop work relationships directly with an employer (instead of with a subcontractor through an outsourcing arrangement) for a specific piece of work or time period.[72] Contract workers are likely to be self-employed, supply their own tools, and determine their hours of employment. Sometimes contract workers are called *consultants* or *freelancers.* Because contract workers are not part of the company headcount, managers can rely on their services to get around company restrictions on staffing policies intended to avoid payroll costs.

Many professionals with specialized skills become contract workers. Hospitals use contract workers as emergency room physicians. Universities use them as adjunct professors to teach basic courses. U.S. West, one of the Baby Bell telecommunications companies, uses contract workers for many of its HR jobs.

Contract workers can often be more productive and efficient than in-house employees because freelancers' time is usually not taken up with the inevitable company bureaucracy and meetings. They can also give companies a fresh outsider's perspective. However, for all the benefits of using contract workers, they do pose some administrative challenges. It's not always easy to motivate a freelancer for whom you are one of several clients, each with urgent projects and pressing deadlines.

The rise of outsourcing and contract workers has led some to predict the death of the traditional job. Such predictions seem extreme, but they do mirror the fact that the job market has changed greatly as a result of the contingent work force. For more details, see the Issues and Applications feature titled "Are Jobs Obsolete?"

College Interns. One of the newest developments in the contingency work area is the use of *college interns,* college students who work on full-time or part-time assignments of short duration (usually for one academic semester or summer) to obtain work experience. Some interns are paid, some are not. Employers use interns to provide support to professional staff. Sometimes interns work a trial run for consideration as a potential core employee after graduation from college. Large companies that use college interns include IBM and General Electric (which have internships for electrical engineers), the Big 6 accounting firms (which use interns on auditing engagements with clients), and Procter & Gamble (which uses interns in its sales and marketing areas).

College interns are also used extensively by small companies that want to attract employees who will grow with the company. For instance, at Seal Press, a small and women-owned publishing company in Seattle, Washington, a woman who started as a marketing intern went on to become marketing assistant and is now marketing director. Editorial interns log in and read unsolicited manuscripts, write detailed reader's reports, and sometimes attend staff meetings. Because the work is challenging, there is a long waiting list of applicants.

Flexible Work Schedules

Flexible work schedules alter the scheduling of work while leaving intact the job design and the employment relationship. Employers can use flexible work schedules to modify the traditional 9-to-5 Monday-through-Friday work schedule to provide advantages for both themselves and employees. Employers may get higher levels of productivity and job satisfaction.[73] Employees may feel that they are trusted by management, which can improve the quality of employee relations (see Chapter 13).[74] Employees with flexible work schedules may also experience less stress by avoiding rush hour traffic.

The three most common types of flexible work schedules are flexible work hours, condensed workweeks, and telecommuting.

Flexible Work Hours. Flexible work hours give employees control over the starting and ending times of their daily work schedules. Employees are required to put in a full 40-hour workweek at their onsite workstation, but have some control over the hours when they perform the work. **Flexible work hours** divide work schedules into **core time,** when all employees are expected to be at work, and *flexible time* (**flextime**), when employees can choose to organize work routines around personal activities.

flexible work hours
A work arrangement that gives employees control over the starting and ending times of their daily work schedules.

core time
Time when all employees are expected to be at work. Part of a flexible work hours arrangement.

flextime
Time during which employees can choose not to be at work. Part of a flexible work hours arrangement.

Companies that use flexible work hours vary in the degree of flexibility they offer to employees. Hewlett-Packard's policy gives workers the flexibility to arrive at work between 6:30 a.m. and 8:30 a.m. and leave after they put in eight hours of work. Hewlett-Packard's core hours are between 8:30 a.m. and 2:30 p.m.[75] Meetings and team activities take place in this core time.

Compressed Workweeks. *Compressed workweeks* alter the number of workdays per week by increasing the length of the workday to ten or more hours. One type of compressed workweek schedule consists of four ten-hour workdays. Another consists of four 12-hour workdays in a four days on/four days off schedule. This schedule gives workers two four-day blocks of time off every 16 days.[76]

Compressed workweeks provide employers with two main advantages. First, they create less potential for disruptions to businesses that provide 24-hour-per-day services, such as hospitals and police forces. Second, they lower absenteeism and tardiness rates at companies with work sites in remote locations that require long commutes to work (for example, off-shore oil drilling platforms).

Issues + Applications

Are Jobs Obsolete?

Not too long ago, most people worked 40 hours a week, 50 weeks a year. But such traditional jobs are becoming increasingly scarce in an era of downsizing, reengineering, outsourcing, and part-time employment.

Does the rise of a contingent work force mean that traditional jobs, in which workers can expect a long-term relationship with their employer, will soon be obsolete? Probably not, although there are likely to be many fewer traditional jobs than in the past. Rather, the trend toward a flexible work force is leading to a redefinition of the term *job*. Jobs are increasingly seen as arrangements in which people sell their services to employers in a variety of ways, often starting as contingency workers and being promoted into full-time positions later on. For example, new entrants to the labor market may work first as temporary employees, then move into traditional jobs with clients who hired their services and were pleased with their work.

The evolution of the job requires a corresponding evolution in employees' approach to work. Just as employers are transforming themselves to get closer to their market and their customers, employees must get closer to the reality of the labor market. Employees should think of themselves as entrepreneurs who own a bundle of skills and competencies, which they can market to their "clients." Thus workers need to continuously update their skill bundles to remain attractive to employers. The best way to do this: Look for work arrangements that offer good training opportunities and the chance to work with the latest equipment or technology.

Source: Adapted from Bridges, W. (1994, September 19). The end of the job. *Fortune*, 62–74.

Compressed workweeks offer both advantages and disadvantages to employees. The major advantage is that they give employees three- or four-day weekends to spend with their families or engage in personal interests. However, employees who work a compressed workweek may experience increased levels of stress and fatigue.[77] Employers should select employees for whom a longer workday will not interfere with job performance.

Telecommuting. **Telecommuting** provides flexibility in both the hours and the location of work. Personal computers, modems, fax machines, e-mail, and the Internet (which connects computers in an international network) have created the opportunity for millions of people in the United States to work out of a home office.[78] Telecommuting allows employees to cultivate tailored lifestyles while working a full-time job.

telecommuting
A work arrangement that allows employees to work in their homes full-time, maintaining their connection to the office through phone, fax, and computer.

Telecommuting gives employers the flexibility to hire talented employees who might not otherwise be able to offer their services. For instance, it lets workers with child-rearing responsibilities work out of their homes. Employers also save on office space costs with telecommuting. However, telecommuting does present several challenges to managers. We discuss these in detail in Chapter 13.

▸ Human Resource Information Systems

As we have seen, many organizations are choosing nontraditional structures, designing work to break down barriers among employees, and using a variety of techniques to ensure work force flexibility. While these strategies are very potent for increasing organizational effectiveness, they can make it difficult to keep track of all the people who work for the organization. Fortunately, computer hardware and software have made keeping track of human resources much easier.

Human resource information systems (HRIS) are systems used to collect, record, store, analyze, and retrieve data concerning an organization's human resources.[79] Most of today's HRIS are computerized, so we will focus on these. While it is beyond the scope of

human resource information system (HRIS)
A system used to collect, record, store, analyze, and retrieve data concerning an organization's human resources.

this book's managerial approach to discuss the technical details of the HRIS, it is worth briefly exploring two relevant issues: the applications of HRIS and the management of security and privacy issues related to HRIS.

HRIS Applications

A computerized HRIS contains computer hardware and software applications that work together to help managers make HR decisions.[80] The hardware may be a mainframe computer or a fairly inexpensive personal computer. The software may be a custom-designed program or an off-the-shelf (prepackaged) applications program. (The latter is more likely to be used on personal computers.) Figure 2–8 shows some HRIS software applications currently available to business. These include:

- *Employee information.* An employee information program sets up a database that provides basic employee information: name, sex, address, phone number, date of birth, race, marital status, job title, and salary. Other applications programs can access the data in the employee information database for more specialized HR uses.
- *Applicant tracking.* An applicant tracking program can automate some of the labor-intensive activities associated with recruiting job applicants. These activities include storing job applicant information so that multiple users can access it and evaluate the applicant, scheduling interviews with different managers, updating the status of the job applicant (such as whether the applicant has received other job offers or has special personal circumstances such as a dual-career marriage), generating correspondence (for example, a job offer or a rejection letter), and producing the necessary equal employment opportunity (EEO) records required by the government.
- *Skills inventory.* A skills inventory keeps track of the supply of job skills in the employer's work force and searches for matches between skill supply and the organization's demand for job skills. The skills inventory can be used to support a company's policy of promotion from within.
- *Payroll.* A payroll applications program computes gross pay, federal taxes, state taxes, Social Security, other taxes, and net pay. It can also be programmed to make other deductions from the paycheck for such items as employee contributions to health insurance, employee contributions to a tax-deferred retirement plan, and union dues.
- *Benefits administration.* A benefits application program can automate benefits record-keeping, which can consume a great deal of time if done manually. It can also be used to administer various benefit programs or to provide advice about benefit choices (for example, determining when an employee will have enough deferred compensation in his or her retirement fund to be able to consider early retirement). Benefits software can also provide an annual benefits statement for each employee.

FIGURE 2-8

Selected Human Resource Information Systems Applications

Source: Kavanagh, M., Gueutal, H., and Tannenbaum, S. (1990). *Human resource information systems: Development and application,* 50. Boston: PWS-Kent. Reproduced with the permission of South-Western College Publishing.

- Applicant tracking
- Basic employee information
- Benefits administration
- Bonus and incentive management
- Career development/planning
- Compensation budgeting
- EEO/AA compliance
- Employment history
- Health and safety
- Health insurance utilization
- HR planning and forecasting
- Job descriptions/analysis
- Job evaluation
- Job posting
- Labor relations planning
- Payroll
- Pension and retirement
- Performance management
- Short- and long-term disabilities
- Skills inventory
- Succession planning
- Time and attendance
- Turnover analysis

HRIS Security and Privacy

The HR department must develop policies and guidelines to protect the integrity and security of the HRIS. Unauthorized users of HRIS can create havoc. In one case, an executive who worked for a brokerage house tapped into her company's HRIS to get employee names and addresses for her husband, a life insurance agent who used the information to mail solicitations to his wife's colleagues. The solicited employees brought a million-dollar class-action suit against the company for invasion of privacy.[81] In another case, a computer programmer tapped into a computer company's HRIS, detected the salaries of a number of employees (including top managers and executives), and disclosed this information to other employees. The situation became very disruptive as angry employees demanded to know why large pay discrepancies existed.[82]

To maintain the security and privacy of HRIS records, companies should:

- Limit access to the HRIS by controlling access to the computer and its data files. Rooms that house computers and sensitive databases should be locked. Sometimes the data can be encoded so that they are not understandable to an unauthorized user.
- Permit access to different portions of the database with the use of passwords and special codes. For example, a manager may receive authorization and a special code to tap into the skills inventory database, but may not be granted permission to access sensitive medical information in the benefits database.
- Grant permission to access employee information only on a need-to-know basis.
- Develop policies and guidelines that govern the utilization of employee information and notify employees how this policy works.
- Allow employees to examine their personal records to verify their accuracy and make corrections if necessary.

Summary and Conclusions

Work: The Organizational Perspective. A firm's business strategy determines how it structures its work. Under a defender strategy, work can be efficiently organized into a functional structure based on division of labor, with hierarchies of jobs assigned to functional units. Under a prospector strategy, decentralization and a low division of labor are more appropriate. The bureaucratic organizational structure is likely to be most effective when an organization is operating in a stable environment. The flat and the boundaryless organizational structures are more likely to be effective when organizations operate in uncertain environments that require flexibility.

Work flow analysis examines how work creates or adds value to ongoing business processes. It helps managers determine if work is being accomplished as efficiently as possible. Work flow analysis can be very useful in TQM programs and business process reengineering.

Work: The Group Perspective. Flat and boundaryless organizational structures are likely to emphasize the use of self-managed teams (SMTs), small work units (between 6 and 18 employees) that are responsible for producing an entire product, a component, or an ongoing service. Businesses also use two other types of team designs. Problem-solving teams consist of volunteers from a unit or department who meet one or two hours per week to discuss quality improvement, cost reduction, or improvement in the work environment. Special-purpose teams consist of members who span functional or organizational boundaries and whose purpose is to examine complex issues.

Work: The Individual Perspective. Motivation theory seeks to explain how different job designs can affect employee motivation. Four important work motivation theories are the two-factor, work adjustment, goal-setting, and job characteristics theories.

Designing Jobs and Conducting Job Analysis. Job design is the process of organizing work into the tasks required to perform a specific job. Different approaches to job design are work simplification, job enlargement, job rotation, job enrichment, and team-based job designs.

Job analysis is the systematic process of gathering and organizing information concerning the tasks, duties, and responsibilities of jobs. It is the basic building block of many important HR activities. Job analysis can be used for purposes of legal compliance, recruitment, selection, performance appraisal, compensation, and training and career development.

Given the lack of a single best job-analysis technique, the choice of technique should be guided by the purposes of the analysis.

Job descriptions are statements of a job's essential duties, responsibilities, working conditions, and specifications. They are derived from job analysis. Job descriptions, which can be specific or general, have four elements: identification information, job summary, job duties and responsibilities, and job specifications and minimum qualifications.

The Flexible Work Force. Flexible work designs help managers deal with unexpected jolts in the environment and accommodate the needs of a diverse work force. To maintain flexibility in the work force, employers can use contingent workers (temporary employees, part-time employees, outsourced subcontractors, contract workers, and college interns). They can also alter work with flexible work schedules (flexible work hours, compressed workweeks, and telecommuting).

Human Resource Information Systems. Human resource information systems (HRIS) are systems used to collect, record, store, analyze, and retrieve relevant HR data. HRIS data matched with the appropriate computer software have many applications that support HR activities. These include applicant tracking, skills inventories, payroll management, and benefits administration. It is important that the HR department develop policies to protect the security of the HRIS data and the privacy rights of its employees.

Key Terms

boundaryless organizational structure, 51
bureaucratic organizational structure, 49
business process reengineering (BPR), 52
contingent workers, 71
core time, 74
core workers, 71
flat organizational structure, 51
flexible work hours, 74
flextime, 74
human resource information system (HRIS), 75
job analysis, 61
job description, 67
job design, 59
job enlargement, 60
job enrichment, 60
job rotation, 60
job sharing, 73
job specification, 71
knowledge, skills, and abilities (KSAs), 63
motivation, 56
organizational structure, 48
problem-solving team, 55
self-managed team (SMT), 54
special-purpose team, 56
team, 54
telecommuting, 75
work flow, 48
work flow analysis, 52

Discussion Questions

1. When American Greetings Corporation, the Cleveland greeting card and licensing company, redesigned about 400 jobs in its creative division, it asked workers and managers to reapply for the new jobs. Everyone was guaranteed a position and no one took a pay cut. Employees now develop products in teams instead of in assembly-line fashion, and are free to transfer back and forth among teams that make different products instead of working on just one product line, as they did in the past. Give some reasons that you think American Greetings restructured its work to be performed in teams. Would the teams at American Greetings be considered self-managed work teams? Why or why not?
2. Why is it so difficult to predict whether a new employee will be a highly motivated employee? What factors can influence employee motivation?
3. Motivating employees saddled with routine work has become a significant challenge for information systems (IS) managers. In the 1970s IS jobs were very exciting because IS managers were creating systems. Today more and more companies are buying applications programs rather than developing them in-house. This means that between 70% and 75% of systems work is now maintenance. In addition, IS departments at many companies are still regarded as an expense rather than a strategic investment and get little recognition for their efforts. What types of job design strategies would you suggest to motivate underappreciated IS workers?
4. Are job descriptions really necessary? What would happen if a company decided not to use any job descriptions at all?
5. Are managers likely to question the work commitment of their contingent workers? What might be the consequences for management when the majority of a company's work force consists of temporary employees and contract workers?
6. What are the drawbacks to using flexible work hours from the organization's perspective? Compressed workweeks? Telecommuting? How should the HR department deal with these challenges?

MINICASE 1 *Food Lion, Inc., and Maids International: Working Smarter or Harder?*

Companies design jobs and work flow with many different goals in mind, from maximizing efficiency and profits to motivating employees to stay at the company longer. The following examples show how management ideas impact workers in a grocery chain and house-cleaning franchise—for better and for worse.

- Maids International, a franchised house-cleaning service, employs mainly women part-timers with young children. These women earn from $4.25 to $7.50 an hour. To avoid high turnover rates, CEO Dan Bishop studied how his employees worked. His goal: to redesign the job to make it both more efficient and more satisfying. Now his maids wind a vacuum cord in 3 seconds (versus the previous 8) and bend over 30 times while cleaning the average house (versus the previous 72). The maids work in groups of four and rotate jobs. The maid who cleans the kitchen in one house does the bedroom in another. There's even a scheduled time to chat—during drives between customers' houses. Turnover at Maids International is nine months, compared to five months at places such as McDonald's.
- In the 1990s Food Lion, Inc. was one of the faster-growing supermarket chains in the country, partly because of a brainchild CEP Patrick Smith called "effective scheduling." This system mandates the work each department should do in 40 hours, based on anticipated sales and on the number of items scanned at the cash register the week before. The result: Baggers pack with two hands at once and stockers are expected to reload shelves at the rate of 50 cases an hour. Managers who run out of allocated hours have to pitch in themselves to meet the mandate. Smith's goal is to make sure there's "an hour's worth of work for an hour's worth of labor." Former employee Francis C. Carpenter routinely put in 60- to 70-hour weeks during his seven years at the nonunionized grocery chain in order to meet productivity goals. Yet he didn't see a penny of overtime pay.

Discussion Questions

1. The emphasis on "lean and mean" corporations in recent years has led to various efforts to speed up work to get costs down. How effective do you think the speeding-up policies at Food Lion and at Maids International are in terms of motivating employees? How do these management initiatives differ?
2. Why do you think former Food Lion workers are supporting the United Food & Commercial Workers' drive to unionize the 730-store chain? What job design steps could Food Lion take to keep workers from quitting or to convince current workers not to vote for unionization?

Sources: Stewart, T. (1990, October). Do you push your people too hard? *Fortune*, 121–128; Denton, D.K. (1994, January–February) !#*@#! I hate this job! *Business Horizons*, 46–52; and Konrad, W. (1991, September 23). Much more than a day's work—for just a day's pay? *Business Week*, 40.

MINICASE 2 *No Job Descriptions: Prescription for Quality or Recipe for Disaster?*

At a recent HRM conference, the keynote speaker—a well-known consultant and HR professor—described a situation he had encountered in his consulting practice. The story went as follows:

Silica, Inc. (name disguised) is a computer components manufacturer in Silicon Valley, California. The electronic components manufactured by Silica require advanced technologies that change rapidly, and have short product life cycles before they become obsolete (about 18 months). The company does not use job descriptions and has no intentions of doing so. A high priority for the company is manufacturing quality parts that are as defect-free as possible. In speaking with Silica's general manager, the consultant noted that without job descriptions the company would find it difficult to defend its employment practices in a court of law. The general manager replied that he agreed with the consultant's observation, but implied that job descriptions would likely reduce the company's flexibility to deploy its human resources to their full potential in a highly competitive environment.

Discussion Questions

1. Are there some business situations in which it is better to not use any job descriptions? Do you think the situation described in this minicase is one such situation? If you were the consultant, what further advice would you give to the manager concerning the use of job descriptions?
2. Other than written job descriptions, are there alternative ways of finding out what people are doing on their jobs?

Source: Author's files.

CASE 1 *Temps on the Team*

Techno Toys, located in Omaha, Nebraska, produces electronic toys for children between the ages of 6 and 12. The toy industry is a cyclical business with peak demand for its products during the Christmas season. Management at Techno Toys anticipates a strong demand for its toys this Christmas season and has added 50 temporary toy assemblers for its four-month peak production period (September through December). Techno management chose to hire these workers through temporary employment agencies rather than directly recruit full-time workers. It did so for two important reasons. First, the temps can be easily dismissed after the four-month peak production season ends. Second, given the seasonal time constraints, it is difficult to locate and hire 50 full-time assemblers from the Omaha labor market, which currently has a very low unemployment rate of only 3.5 percent.

The 50 temporary toy assemblers were assigned to work side by side with the 50 full-time assemblers on self-managed work teams. Dave Smith, the plant manager, organized the assemblers into ten teams. Each assembly team was assigned an equal number of temps and full-time employees. Each team must decide how to schedule its work, choose the appropriate methods and tools for assembling the toys, and control for the quality of the toys that it produces.

After about a month of experience with the self-managed toy assembly teams, Dave Smith noticed a higher-than-acceptable rate of return from retailers with complaints about the toys' reliability and quality. These problems could be traced to the assembly process. After investigating, Dave discovered the following facts:

- The temporary employees were hired through two different temporary employment agencies, and each agency paid its temps a different rate. All the temps were paid lower wages than the full-time employees. The temps knew about these pay disparities.
- All the temporary employees anticipated being reassigned to work at a different company after the Christmas toy season. They knew they had no future at Techno Toys.
- The full-time employees on each team tended to act as supervisors to the temps, closely monitoring their work. The temps tended to comply with directions given by the full-timers but showed little initiative in doing their jobs.

After reviewing this information, Dave wondered whether he should recommend reorganizing the toy assembly operation and terminating all the temps or try to improve the teams' effectiveness by making some changes in the teams.

Critical Thinking Questions

1. What do you think of the practice of mixing temporary employees with full-time employees on teams? Do you see any problems in how the temps are being used at Techno Toys?
2. Is there a better way to utilize temporary employees in the toy assembly process?
3. How can the HR department help Dave solve his problem of getting the self-managed teams to produce high-quality toys?

Cooperative Learning Exercise

4. In groups of five, rethink how Techno Toys can better manage its flexible work force. Should Dave terminate all the temps and start over with a totally new approach, or is there a way to improve the performance of the self-managed teams as they are now constituted? Each group should elect a spokesperson to provide a recommendation to the instructor.

CASE 2 *How Flexible Is Too Flexible?*

Manager Barbara Reed has a big problem. Actually, four of the seven tellers at the small branch bank she runs have the problems. Barbara has the challenge of dealing with them.

One teller is on maternity leave. Nearly three months ago, she gave birth to a very premature one-pound baby. She's due back soon, but she is unwilling to leave her baby, who is still in the neonatal unit of a big-city hospital 90 miles away. She wants to extend her leave.

Another teller has just informed Barbara that his elderly mother, who has been living by herself in a distant town, fell and broke her hip. The teller, an only child, wants at least a month off to tend to his mother and find a new living arrangement for her.

A new teller has asked to cut back her hours slightly so that she can be home with her children after school. The next-door neighbor who had been caring for them will be moving soon, and the teller—who is new in town—can't find anyone she trusts to watch them.

Barbara's best teller, one who she thinks could be a manager someday, has just asked to pare her hours so she can begin taking courses for her MBA. Barbara sorely wants to grant this request because her own performance is judged in part by her skill in developing and promoting women and minorities.

In the past, Barbara wouldn't have agonized over any of these decisions. She simply would have said no, instructed all her tellers to stay at their posts, and replaced any who didn't. But Barbara's company recently adopted a policy saying it would do whatever it could to accommodate employees with conflicts between work and family responsibilities. Barbara is now supposed to be a flexible manager, which means that she has to try to satisfy her employees' requests. But how can she do that and still run the bank?

Barbara is considering an array of flexible work options, including regular part-time and temporary part-time work, flexible work hours, compressed workweeks, job sharing, leaves of absence, and telecommuting.

Critical Thinking Questions

1. Do all these tellers have good reasons to modify their work schedules? How can Barbara determine which tellers' requests should receive priority, which should be taken into consideration, and which should be turned down?
2. What might happen if Barbara tries to satisfy every employee's request for a modified work schedule?
3. What implementation guidelines should Barbara put in place so that the bank branch will operate smoothly without disruption of service to its customers? For example, how much flexibility in hours should the flex program provide? Who should be eligible for it? How much advance notice should a manager require to change an employee's work schedule?

Cooperative Learning Exercise

4. With a partner or small group, decide on some programs that would enable Barbara to respond to the four tellers' needs for modified work schedules from the array of flexible work options. Can Barbara satisfy all four of these requests simultaneously with the program(s) you have selected? If not, what should she do?

Source: Adapted with permission from Geber, B. (1993, February). The bendable, flexible, open-minded manager. *Training*, 46–48.

HRM Simulation 

The company is considering the installation of a human resource information system (HRIS). (Refer to pages nine and ten of the players' manual.) What benefits would the company receive from the HRIS? Do these benefits justify the expense of $5,000 per quarter to install and maintain the HRIS? What HRIS applications should receive the highest priority?

The installation of an HRIS creates the potential for the disclosure of sensitive personnel information to unauthorized users. What do you recommend that the company do to ensure that employees' privacy rights are not violated?

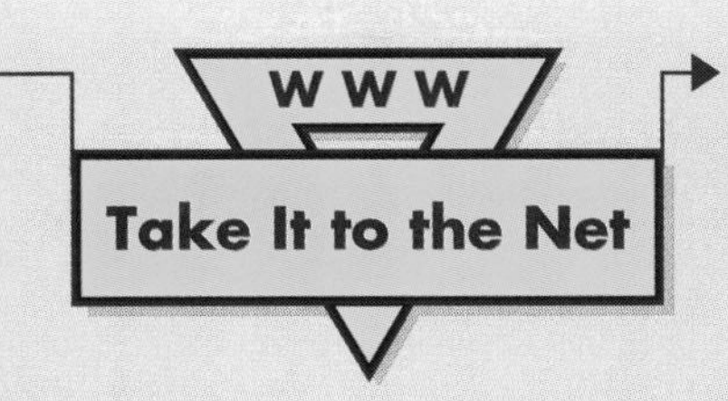

We invite you to visit the Gómez-Mejía/Balkin/Cardy page on the Prentice Hall Web site:

http://www.prenhall.com/gomez

You can also visit the Web sites for these companies, featured within this chapter:

America West Airlines	http://www.americawest.com
Ciba Geigy	http://www.ciba.com
IBM	http://www.ibm.com
Kodak	http://www.kodak.com
MCI	http://www.mci.com

Endnotes

1. Baker, S. (1994, February 21). How one medical center is healing itself. *Business Week*, 106.
2. Byrne, J. (1993, December 20). The horizontal corporation. *Business Week*, 76–81.
3. Bennet, J. (1994, October 31). GM success in an unlikely place. *The New York Times*, C1, C5.
4. Thompson, A., and Strickland, A. (1993). *Strategic management* (7th ed.). Homewood, IL: Irwin.
5. Caldwell, B. (1994, March 14). *Information Week*, 12–13.
6. Hammer, M., and Champy, J. (1993). *Reengineering the corporation.* New York: HarperCollins.
7. Lawler, E. (1992). *The ultimate advantage.* San Francisco, CA: Jossey-Bass.
8. Kotkin, J. (1995, March). Why every business will be like show business. *Inc.*, 64–77.
9. Rebello, K. (1994, March 7). A juicy apple? *Business Week*, 88–90.
10. Arnst, C. (1996, February 19). MCI is swarming over the horizon. *Business Week*, 68–69.
11. Hammer, M., and Champy, J. (1994, April). Avoiding the hottest new management cure. *Inc.*, 25–26.
12. Hammer, M., and Champy, J. (1993). *Reengineering the corporation.* New York: HarperCollins.
13. *Id.*
14. Greengard, S. (1993, December). Reengineering: Out of the rubble. *Personnel Journal*, 48B–48O; and Verity, J. (1993, June 21). Getting work to go with the flow. *Business Week*, 156–161.
15. Hammer and Champy, 1993.
16. *Id.*
17. Hammer, M. (1995, May 15). Beating the risks of reengineering. *Fortune*, 105–114.
18. *The Economist.* (1994, July 2). Re-engineering reviewed, 66.
19. Katzenback, J., and Smith, D. (1993, March–April). The discipline of teams. *Harvard Business Review,* 111–120.
20. Orsburn, J., Moran, L., Musselwhite, E., and Zenger, J. (1990). *Self-directed work teams.* Homewood, IL: Business One Irwin.
21. Katzenback and Smith, 1993.
22. Hoerr, J. (1989, July 10). The payoff from teamwork. *Business Week*, 56–62.
23. Caudron, S. (1993, December). Are self-directed teams right for your company? *Personnel Journal,* 76–84.
24. Bassin, M. (1996, January). From team to partnerships. *HRMagazine*, 86–92.
25. Orsburn, Moran, Musselwhite, and Zenger, 1990.
26. *Id.*
27. Dumaine, B. (1994, September 5). The trouble with teams. *Fortune*, 86–92.
28. Orsburn, Moran, Musselwhite, and Zenger, 1990.
29. Hoerr, 1989.
30. Lawler, 1992.
31. Steers, R. (1984). *Introduction to organizational behavior* (2nd ed.). Glenview, IL: Scott, Foresman.
32. Herzberg, F. (1968, January–February). One more time: How do you motivate employees? *Harvard Business Review,* 52–62.
33. Lofquist, L., and Dawis, R. (1969). Adjustment to work: A psychological view of man's problems in a work-oriented society. Englewood Cliffs, NJ: Prentice Hall.
34. Locke, E. (1968). Toward a theory of task motives and incentives. *Organizational Behavior and Human Performance, 3*, 157–189.
35. Pinder, C. (1984). *Work motivation.* Glenview, IL: Scott, Foresman.
36. Hackman, J., and Oldham, G. (1976). Motivation through the design of work: Test of a theory. *Organizational Behavior and Human Performance, 16,* 250–279.
37. Nadler, D. A., Hackman, J. R., and Lawler, E. E. (1979). *Managing organizational behavior.* Boston: Little, Brown.
38. *Id.*
39. Hackman, J. (1976). Work design. In Hackman, J., and Suttle, J. (Eds.). *Improving life at work,* 96–162. Santa Monica, CA: Goodyear.
40. Denton, D. K. (1992, August). Redesigning a job by simplifying every task and responsibility. *Industrial Engineering,* 46–48.
41. Szilagyi, A., and Wallace, M. (1980). *Organizational behavior and performance* (2nd ed.). Santa Monica, CA: Goodyear.
42. Lawler, E. (1986). *High involvement management.* San Francisco, CA: Jossey-Bass.
43. *Id.*
44. Steers, 1984.
45. Lawler, 1986.
46. Campion, M. A., and Higgs, A. C. (1995, October). Design work teams to increase productivity and satisfaction. *HRMagazine*, 101–107.
47. Lawler, 1992.
48. Geber, B. (1992, June). Saturn's grand experiment. *Training,* 27–35.
49. Drauden, G. M. (1988). Task inventory analysis in industry and the public sector. In S. Gael (Ed.), *The job analysis handbook for business, industry, and government,* 105–171. New York: Wiley and Sons.
50. Flanagan, J. C. (1954). The critical incident technique. *Psychological Bulletin, 51,* 327–358.
51. McCormick, E., and Jeannerette, R. (1988). The position analysis questionnaire. In S. Gael (Ed.), *The job analysis handbook for business, industry, and government,* 880–901. New York: John Wiley and Sons.
52. Fine, S. A. (1992). *Functional job analysis: A desk aid.* Milwaukee, WI: Sidney A. Fine.
53. U.S. Department of Labor. (1991). *Dictionary of occupational titles* (4th ed.). Washington, DC: U.S. Government Printing Office.
54. Chatman, J. A. (1989). Improving interaction organizational research: A model of person-organization fit. *Academy of Management Review, 14*, 333–349.
55. Cardy, R. L., and Dobbins, G. H. (1994). *Performance appraisal: Alternative perspectives*. Cincinnati, OH: South-Western.
56. Sunoo, B. P. (1996, February). Generic or non-generic job descriptions. *Personnel Journal,* 102.

56a. Cardy, R. L. and Dobbins, G. H. (1995). Human resources, high technology, and a quality organizational environment: Research agendas. *Journal of High Technology Management Research, 6*(2), 261–279.

57. Cardy, R., and Dobbins, G. (1992, Fall). Job analysis in a dynamic environment. *Human Resources Division News,* 4–6.
58. *Id.*
59. Jones, M. (1984, May). Job descriptions made easy. *Personnel Journal,* 31–34.
60. Fierman, J. (1994, January 24). The contingent work force. *Fortune,* 30–36.
61. Castro, J. (1993, March 29). Disposable workers. *Time,* 43–47.

61a. *Monthly Labor Review.* (1995, July). Selected employment indicators, 97; Aley, J. (1995, October 16). The temp biz boom: Why it's good. *Fortune*, 53–55.

62. Hershey, R. D. (1995, August 19). Survey finds 6 million, fewer than thought, in impermanent jobs. *The New York Times*, 1, 17; Melcher, R. A. (1996, June 10). Manpower upgrades its résumé. *Business Week*, 81+.
63. Stewart, T. A. (1995, March 20). World without managers. *Fortune*, 72.
64. Uchitelle, L., and Kleinfield, N. R. (1996, March 3). The downsizing of America. *The New York Times*, special report.
65. Templeman, J. (1996, April 8). A continent swarming with temps. *Business Week*, 54; Overman, S. (1993, August). Temporary services go global. *HRMagazine,* 72–74.
66. Rogers, B. (1992, May). Companies develop benefits for part timers. *HRMagazine,* 89–90.
67. Sunoo, B. P., and Laabs, J. J. (1994, March). Winning strategies for outsourcing contracts. *Personnel Journal,* 69–78.
68. *The Economist.* (1995, October 25). The outing of outsourcing, 57–58.
69. Sunoo and Laabs, 1994.
70. *The Economist.* (1994, April 23). Benetton: The next era, 68.
71. For information on a new twist on outsourcing, see Semler, R. (1993). *Maverick.* New York: Warner Books.
72. Pearce, J. (1993). Toward an organizational behavior of contract laborers: Their psychological involvement and effects on employee co-workers. *Academy of Management Journal, 36,* 1082–1096.
73. Sheppard, E. M., Clifton, T. J., and Kruse, D. (1996). Flexible work hours and productivity: Some evidence from the pharmaceutical industry. *Industrial Relations, 35,* 123–129.

74. Denton, D. (1993, January–February). Using flextime to create a competitive workplace. *Industrial Management,* 29–31.
75. *Id.*
76. Pierce, J., and Dunham, R. (1992). The 12-hour work day: A 48-hour, eight-day week. *Academy of Management Journal,* 1086–1098.
77. Sunoo, B. P. (1996, January). How to manage compressed workweeks. *Personnel Journal*, 110.
78. *Forbes ASAP*. (1995, August 28). Their private Idaho, 20–25.
79. Kavanaugh, M., Gueutal, H., and Tannenbaum, S. (1990). *Human resource information systems: Development and application.* Boston, MA: PWS-Kent.
80. Townsend, A. M., and Hendrickson, A. R. (1996, February). Recasting HRIS as an information resource. *HRMagazine*, 91–94.
81. Leonard, B. (1991, July). Open and shut HRIS. *Personnel Journal*, 59–62.
82. *Id.*

CHALLENGES

After reading this chapter, you should be able to deal more effectively with the following challenges:

1 ▶ **Explain** why compliance with HR law is an important part of doing business.

2 ▶ **Follow** changes in HR law, regulation, and court decisions.

3 ▶ **Manage** within equal employment opportunity laws and understand the rationale and requirements of affirmative action.

4 ▶ **Make** managerial decisions that will avoid legal liability.

5 ▶ **Know** when to seek the advice of legal counsel on HRM matters.

3 Understanding Equal Opportunity and the Legal Environment

Equal Justice Under Law. Hundreds of laws and legal rulings regulate the practice of human resource management. The goal of most of these laws and rulings is simple: to guarantee that employees do not face workplace-related discrimination on the basis of color, religion, sex, national origin, age, or disability.

http://www.winway.com/unlawful_questions.htm

Handling Unlawful Questions

This Web site includes advice for interviewees on how to react to, and answer, unlawful interview questions that violate EEOC regulations. The site also includes links to a job finder's toolkit and other career planning materials.

WHICH COMPANY WOULD YOU RATHER WORK FOR?

Company A: Coworkers [sexually] harassed an employee for a period of nearly four years in a manner a judge termed "malevolent" and "outrageous." Despite many complaints by the victim, her supervisor took no action other than to hold occasional meetings at which employees were reminded of the company policy against harassment. The supervisor never conducted an investigation or disciplined any employees until the victim filed a complaint.[1]

Company B: An employee complained that her coworker had talked to her about sexual activities and touched her in an offensive manner. Within four days of receiving the complaint, the employer investigated the charges, reprimanded the guilty employee, placed him on probation, and warned him that further misconduct would result in discharge.[2]

* * *

IF YOU WERE A JUDGE, WHICH EMPLOYER WOULD YOU FIND GUILTY OF DISCRIMINATION?

Company X: Michael, an African-American employee, was discharged because of his repeated tardiness. Michael identified two coworkers who had been repeatedly tardy, but were not discharged. His manager countered that Michael was discharged for unexcused tardiness. The two employees Michael had singled out had permission to arrive late for work because of family emergencies. The manager also identified several employees of different races who were discharged because of unexcused tardiness.[3]

Company Y: A manufacturer requires newly hired machine repairpersons to have a minimum of four years' work experience. An African-American applicant who did not have this experience was denied employment. At the time, only one of the 31 machine repairpersons was an African-American. On investigation, you learn that the company had previously hired machine repairpersons without this experience on an emergency basis, and that these employees had worked out just fine.[4]

The government regulates the practice of human resource management at many levels. Which employees are selected to work for a firm, how they are compensated, what benefits they are offered, how the firm must accommodate them when they have children, and how and when they can be terminated are all managerial decisions that are constrained to some extent by law.

In this chapter we examine the various aspects of HR law and regulation. First, we look at why understanding the legal environment is important. Next we explore several challenges to legal compliance. Then we discuss *equal employment opportunity (EEO)* law, the enforcement mechanisms in place to ensure compliance, and several other laws that affect HRM. Finally, we describe ways for the effective manager to avoid the many potential pitfalls in this area.

We need to start with a caveat. As with any legal issue you face, you should seek the advice of a qualified attorney when faced with specific legal questions or problems relating to HRM. There are many lawyers and law firms specializing in labor law. However, you should not feel that you cannot make *any* decisions without specific legal counsel, and it is a mistake to let legal considerations become so important that you end up making poor business decisions. One goal of this chapter is to give you enough information to know when it is necessary to seek legal counsel.

▸ Why Understanding the Legal Environment Is Important

Understanding and complying with HR law is important for three reasons. It helps you do the right thing, realize the limitations of your firm's HR and legal departments, and minimize your firm's potential liability.

Doing the Right Thing

First and foremost, compliance with the law is important because it is the right thing to do. While you may disagree with the specific applications of some of the laws we will discuss, the primary requirement of all these laws is to mandate good management practice. The earliest of the EEO laws requires that male and female employees who do the same job for the same organization receive the same pay. This is the right thing to do. The most recent EEO law requires that applicants or employees who are able to perform a job should not be discriminated against because of a disability. This, too, is the right thing to do.

Operating within these laws has benefits beyond simple legal compliance. Compensation practices that discriminate against women not only create potential legal liability but also lead to poor employee morale and low job satisfaction, which can in turn lead to poor job performance. Discriminating against qualified disabled employees makes no sense; in discriminating, the organization hurts itself by not hiring and retaining the best employees. McDonald's has taken the lead in hiring learning-disabled youth. This is socially responsible, and has created a positive impression among many customers.[5]

Realizing the Limitations of the HR and Legal Departments

A firm's HR department has considerable responsibilities with respect to HR law. These include keeping records, writing and implementing good HR policies, and monitoring the firm's HR decisions. However, if managers make poor decisions, the HR department will not always be able to resolve the situation. For instance, if a manager gives a poor employee an excellent performance rating, the HR department cannot undo the damage and provide the documentation necessary to support a decision to terminate the employee.

Nor can a firm's legal department magically solve problems created by managers. The primary function of legal counsel, whether internal or external, is to try to limit damage after it has occurred. The manager's job is to prevent the damage from happening in the first place.

Members of the HR department support managers who have to make HR decisions with legal implications. In acting as internal consultants, HR staff may monitor managers' decisions or act as consultants to managers. For example:

- A supervisor wants to discharge an employee for unexcused absences and consults the HR department to determine if there is enough evidence to discharge this person for "just cause." The HR department can help the manager and the company avoid a lawsuit for "wrongful discharge."
- A manager receives a phone call from a company that is inquiring about the qualification of a former employee. The manager is not sure how much information in the former employee's work history to reveal, so she seeks the HR department's advice. HR can help the manager and the company avoid a lawsuit for defamation (damage to an employee's reputation as a result of giving out false information to a third party).

Limiting Potential Liability

Considerable financial liabilities can occur when HR laws are broken or perceived to be broken. One recent report analyzed the awards given to employees who won discrimination suits between 1988 and 1992. Broken down by type of case, the average awards were as follows:

Age bias	$302,914
Sex bias	$255,734
Race bias	$176,578
Disability claims	$151,421[6]

These are just averages; individual awards can be much larger.

Organizations may also face a public relations nightmare when discrimination charges are publicized. In a series of highly publicized cases from late 1991 through 1993, several individual store managers and employees of Denny's restaurant chain were alleged to have discriminated against African-American customers. Not only did the company subsequently have to pay $46 million to African-American patrons and $8.7 million in legal fees to settle these complaints, but the company's image with customers was damaged as well.[7] In recent years, though, Denny's has made major strides: In 1996, 27 of the chain's 600 franchises were owned by African-Americans, compared to only one in 1993.[8]

▸ Challenges to Legal Compliance

Several challenges confront managers attempting to comply with HR law. These include a dynamic legal landscape, the complexity of regulations, conflicting strategies for fair employment, and unintended consequences.

A Dynamic Legal Landscape

The appendix to this chapter contains a table listing all the laws discussed throughout this text. A quick scan of that table clearly demonstrates that many laws affect the practice of human resource management. Several of these laws have been passed since 1990.

The opinions handed down in court cases add to this dynamic environment. For example, in 1971 the Supreme Court handed down a landmark civil rights decision in a case titled *Griggs v. Duke Power*.[9] Among other things, this decision placed a heavy burden of proof on the employer in an employment discrimination case. Normally, a Supreme Court decision sets a precedent that the Court is then very reluctant to overturn. However, in a 1989 case, the Court revised the standard it had set in *Griggs*, making it more difficult for an employee to win a discrimination case.[10] Then, in 1991, Congress passed a lengthy amendment to the Civil Rights Act of 1964 (discussed later in this chapter) that returned to the burden-of-proof standard established in the *Griggs* decision.

These fast-paced changes are not limited to issues of courtroom procedure. Sexual harassment has been a topic of major concern since it was propelled into the national spotlight by the 1991 Clarence Thomas–Anita Hill confrontation. Sexual harassment regulations were adopted by the Equal Employment Opportunity Commission (EEOC) in the early 1980s, and accepted by the Supreme Court in 1986. Since then, companies, lawyers, and judges have been attempting to figure out just what they mean and require. Opinions on these issues vary widely, which means that different courts have made differing decisions about what constitutes sexual harassment. Until the Supreme Court makes several more rulings, or Congress clarifies the underlying law, managers will need to pay close attention to the unfolding developments.

The Complexity of Laws

HR law, like most other types of law, is very complex. Each individual law is accompanied by a set of regulations that can be quite lengthy. For instance, the Americans with Disabilities Act (1990) is spelled out in a technical manual that is several hundred pages in length. To make matters even more complex, one analysis has concluded that there may be as many as 1,000 different disabilities affecting over 43 million Americans.[11] It is very difficult for an expert in HR law, much less a manager, to understand all the possible implications of a particular law.

Nonetheless, the gist of most HR law is fairly straightforward. Managers should be able to understand the basic intention of all such laws without too much difficulty, and can easily obtain the working knowledge they need to comply with those laws in the vast majority of situations.

Conflicting Strategies for Fair Employment

fair employment
The goal of EEO legislation and regulation: a situation in which employment decisions are not affected by illegal discrimination.

affirmative action
A strategy intended to achieve fair employment by urging employers to hire certain groups of people who were discriminated against in the past.

Society at large, political representatives, government employees, and judges all have different views regarding the best ways to achieve equitable HR laws. One of the major debates in this area centers on the competing strategies used to further the goal of **fair employment**—the situation in which employment decisions are not affected by illegal discrimination. The plain language of most civil rights law prohibits employers from making decisions about employees (hiring, performance appraisal, compensation, and so on) on the basis of race, sex, or age. Thus, one strategy to reach the goal of fair employment is for employment decisions to be made without regard to these characteristics. A second strategy, **affirmative action**, aims to accomplish the goal of fair employment by urging employers to hire certain groups of people who were discriminated against in the past. Thus, affirmative action programs require that employment decisions be made, at least in part, on the basis of characteristics such as race, sex, or age. Obviously, there is a conflict between these two strategies—one proposing that only "blind" hiring practices are fair, the other proposing that fairness requires organizations to make an effort to employ certain categories of people (Figure 3–1).

A QUESTION OF ETHICS

Is it ethical to refuse to give preferential treatment to minorities and women, who have been widely discriminated against in the past?

While the battle resulting from these competing strategies is being played out throughout society, the main legal struggle has occurred in the Supreme Court. Based on a series of Supreme Court decisions, the following conclusions seem warranted:

- The affirmative action strategy has been upheld. Specifically, employers are permitted to base employment decisions, in part, on a person's race, sex, age, and certain other characteristics.
- To be permissible, the employment decision cannot be made *solely* on the basis of these characteristics. Further, the people considered for the position should be "essentially equally qualified" on job-relevant characteristics before these other characteristics are permitted to play a role in the employment decision.
- The one situation in which affirmative action is not permitted is during layoffs. For instance, a white teacher should not be laid off to save the job of a Latino teacher, even if this means that minorities will be underrepresented in the postlayoff work force.

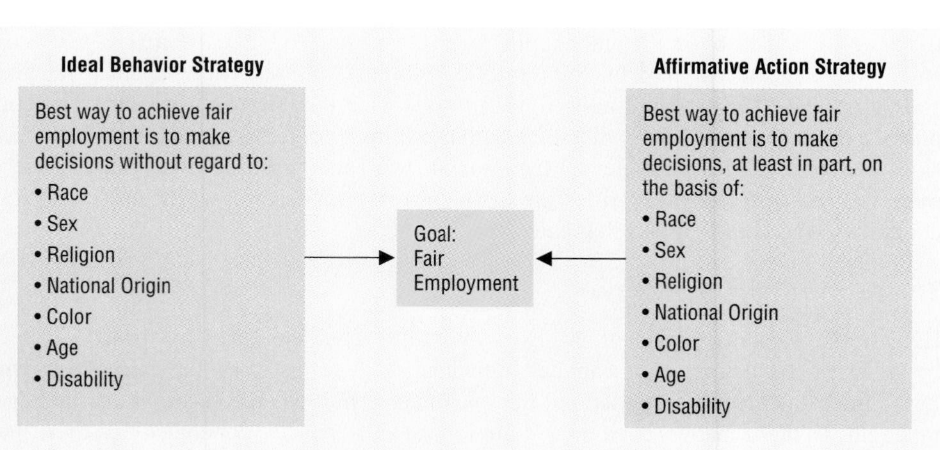

FIGURE 3–1
Competing Strategies for Fair Employment

- Courts may order an affirmative action program with specific quotas when an organization has a history of blatant discrimination.

Unintended Consequences

It is very common for a law, a government program, or an organizational policy to have numerous unanticipated consequences, some of which turn out to be quite negative. HR law is certainly not immune to this phenomenon. For example, the Americans with Disabilities Act (ADA) was primarily intended to increase the possibility of employment for people with physical and/or mental disabilities. However, during the first two years the law was in effect, very few of the complaints filed under it were made by job applicants. Rather, the large majority was made by current employees who were injured on the job—a situation traditionally covered by state workers' compensation laws (see Chapter 12). Nobody intended the ADA to become a national workers' compensation law, but that appears to be just what is happening. The challenge to managers is to anticipate and deal with both the intended and unintended consequences of law.

Equal Employment Opportunity Laws

The laws that affect HR issues can be divided into two broad categories: (1) equal employment opportunity laws and (2) everything else. We will spend the bulk of this chapter on the EEO laws because these are the ones that most affect a manager's day-to-day behavior. In addition, the EEO laws cut across almost every other issue that we discuss in this text. The other laws tend to be more specifically focused, and we discuss them in the context in which they apply. For instance, we discuss the laws governing union activities in Chapter 15 and the Occupational Safety and Health Act (OSHA) in Chapter 16.

The major EEO laws are the Equal Pay Act of 1963, Title VII of the Civil Rights Act of 1964, the Age Discrimination in Employment Act of 1967, and the Americans with Disabilities Act of 1990. The Civil Rights Act of 1964 has been amended through the years, most recently in 1991. The theme that ties these laws together is simple: Employment decisions should not be based on such characteristics as race, sex, age, or disability.

The Equal Pay Act of 1963

The first of the civil rights laws was the **Equal Pay Act**, which became law in 1963. It requires that men and women who do the same job in the same organization should receive the same pay. "Same pay" means that no difference is acceptable.

Equal Pay Act (1963)
The law that requires the same pay for men and women who do the same job in the same organization.

Determining whether or not two employees are doing the same job can be difficult. The law specifies that jobs are the same if they are equal in terms of skill, effort, responsibility, and working conditions. Thus, it is permissible to pay one employee more than another if the first employee has significant extra job duties, such as supervisory responsibility. Pay can also be different for different work shifts. The law also specifies that equal pay is required only for jobs held in the same geographical region. This allows an organization to make allowances for the local cost of living and the fact that it might be harder to find qualified employees in some areas.

The law contains several explicit exceptions. First, it does not prohibit the use of a merit pay plan. That is, an employer can pay a man more if he is doing a better job than his female coworker. In addition, companies are permitted to pay for differences in quantity and quality of production. Seniority plans also are exempted; a company that ties pay rates to seniority can pay a man more if he has been with the company longer than a female employee. Finally, the law indicates that any factor other than sex may be used to justify different pay rates.[12]

When the Equal Pay Act was passed, the average female employee earned only about 59 cents for each dollar earned by the average male worker. While this gap has narrowed in the intervening years, to about 74 cents in 1995,[13] this average differential remains troubling, and in some jobs it is much higher. For instance, in 1994 men in insurance sales positions earned $37,960 on average, while the average insurance saleswoman earned only $24,128.[14] Some states, such as Washington and Illinois, have responded to this issue by requiring that civil service employers pay equally for work of comparable worth.[15] Understanding equal pay and comparable worth requires more knowledge of compensation decisions, so we will return to these issues in Chapter 10.

Title VII of the Civil Rights Act of 1964

Title VII
Section of the Civil Rights Act of 1964 that applies to employment decisions; mandates that employment decisions not be based on race, color, religion, sex, or national origin.

While not the oldest of the civil rights laws, **Title VII of the Civil Rights Act of 1964** is universally seen as the most important passed to date. This law was enacted in the midst of the seething civil rights conflicts of the 1960s, one year after the civil rights march on Washington at which Dr. Martin Luther King, Jr., delivered his "I Have a Dream" speech.

Prior to the passage of the Civil Rights Act of 1964, open and explicit discrimination based on race, particularly against African-Americans, was widespread. *Jim Crow laws* legalized racial segregation in many southern states. The act itself had several sections, or titles, all of which aim at prohibiting discrimination in various parts of society. For instance, Title IX applies to educational institutions. Title VII applies to employers who have 15 or more employees, as well as to employment agencies and labor unions.

General Provisions. Title VII prohibits employers from basing employment decisions on a person's race, color, religion, sex, or national origin. The heart of the law, Section 703(a), is reprinted in Figure 3–2. Note that employment decisions include "compensation, terms, conditions, or privileges of employment."

protected class
A group of people who suffered discrimination in the past and who are given special protection by the judicial system.

Title VII clearly covers persons of any race, any color, any religion, both sexes, and any national origin. However, as court cases and regulations have grown up around this law, so has the legal theory of a **protected class**. This theory states that groups of people who suffered discrimination in the past require, and should be given, special protection by the judicial system. Under Title VII, the protected classes are African-Americans, Asian-Americans, Latinos, Native Americans, and women. While it is not impossible for a nonprotected-class plaintiff to win a Title VII case, it is highly unusual.

discrimination
The making of distinctions. In HR context, the making of distinctions among people.

Discrimination Defined. Despite the negative connotation the word has acquired, **discrimination** simply means making distinctions—in the HR context, distinctions among people. Therefore, even the most progressive companies are constantly discriminating when they decide who should be promoted, who should receive a merit raise, and who should be laid off. What Title VII prohibits is making discriminations among people based on their race, color, religion, sex, or national origin. Specifically, it makes two types of discrimination illegal.

FIGURE 3–2
Title VII of the Civil Rights Act of 1964

Section 703. (a) It shall be an unlawful employment practice for an employer—

(1) to fail or refuse to hire or to discharge any individual, or otherwise to discriminate against any individual with respect to his compensation, terms, conditions, or privileges of employment, because of such individual's race, color, religion, sex, or national origin; or

(2) to limit, segregate, or classify his employees or applicants for employment in any way which would deprive or tend to deprive any individual of employment opportunities or otherwise adversely affect his status as an employee, because of such individual's race, color, religion, sex, or national origin.

The first type of discrimination, **disparate treatment**, occurs when an employer treats an employee differently because of his or her protected-class status. Disparate treatment is the kind of treatment that you probably first think of when considering discrimination. For instance, Robert Frazier, who is a bricklayer's assistant and an African-American, was fired after quarreling with a white bricklayer. However, Frazier's employer did not discipline the white bricklayer at all, even though he had injured Frazier by throwing a broken brick at him. A federal court judge ruled that Frazier had been treated more harshly because of his race, and thus suffered from disparate treatment discrimination.[16]

disparate treatment
Discrimination that occurs when individuals are treated differently because of their membership in a protected class.

The second type of discrimination, **adverse impact** (also called *disparate impact*), occurs when the same standard is applied to all applicants or employees, but that standard affects a protected class more negatively (adversely). For example, most police departments around the United States have dropped their former requirement that officers be of a minimum height because the equal application of that standard has an adverse impact on women, Latinos, and Asian-Americans (that is, any given height standard will rule out more women than men, and more Latinos and Asian-Americans than African-American and nonminority individuals). Figure 3–3 summarizes the distinctions between disparate treatment and adverse impact.

adverse impact
Discrimination that occurs when the equal application of an employment standard has an unequal effect on one or more protected classes. Also called *disparate impact*.

The adverse impact definition of discrimination was confirmed in a very important 1971 Supreme Court case that we've already discussed, *Griggs v. Duke Power*.[17] Griggs was an African-American employee of the Duke Power Company in North Carolina. He and other African-American employees were refused promotions because Duke Power, on the day that Title VII took effect, had implemented promotion standards that included a high school diploma and passing scores on two tests, one of general intellectual ability and one of mechanical ability. The Supreme Court ruled that such standards, even though applied equally to all employees, were discriminatory because (1) they had an adverse impact on a protected class (in this case, African-Americans) and (2) Duke Power was unable to show that the standards were related to subsequent job performance.

Griggs v. Duke Power is an important case because it means that a company may be judged to be discriminating even when it pays scrupulous attention to ensuring that an HR decision process is equally applied. If the outcome is such that a protected class suffers from adverse impact, then the organization may be required to demonstrate that the standards used in the decision process were related to the job. In October 1993, Domino's Pizza lost a case in which it attempted to defend a "no-beard policy." The appellate court ruled that the policy had an adverse effect on African-Americans because almost half of male African-Americans suffer from a genetic condition that makes shaving very painful or impossible. Almost no white men suffer from this malady. Therefore, African-Americans are more adversely affected by this requirement than whites are.[18] Domino's could have won this case if it had shown that not having a beard was necessary for good job performance. It could not, so the court ruled the no-beard policy a violation of Title VII.

Disparate Treatment	Adverse Impact
Direct discrimination	Indirect discrimination
Unequal treatment	Unequal consequences or results
Decision rules with a racial/sexual premise or cause	Decision rules with racial/sexual consequences or results
Intentional discrimination	Unintentional discrimination
Prejudiced actions	Neutral actions
Different standards for different groups	Same standards, but different consequences for different groups

FIGURE 3–3

Two Kinds of Discrimination

Source: Adapted from Ledvinka, J., and Scarpello, V. G. (1991). *Federal regulation of personnel and human resource management* (2nd ed.). Boston: PWS-Kent. Reproduced with the permission of South-Western College Publishing. Copyright 1991 by PWS-Kent. All rights reserved.

In an earlier (1975) case, *Albemarle Paper Company v. Moody*, the Supreme Court established procedures to help employers determine when it is appropriate to use employment tests as a basis for hiring or promoting employees. The Court ruled that employers can use an employment test only when they can demonstrate that the test is a valid predictor of job performance. Thus, *Albemarle* places the burden of proof on the employer to prove that a contested test (for example, a test that has an adverse impact on a protected class) or other selection tool is a valid predictor of job success.[19]

Defense of Discrimination Charges. When a discrimination case makes it to court, it is the responsibility of the plaintiff (the person bringing the complaint) to show reasonable evidence that discrimination has occurred. The legal term for this type of evidence is *prima facie*, which means "on its face." In a disparate treatment lawsuit, to establish a prima facie case the plaintiff only needs to show that the organization did not hire her (or him), that she appeared to be qualified for the job, and that the company continued to try to hire someone else for the position after rejecting her. This set of requirements, which originated from a court case brought against the McDonnell-Douglas Corporation, is often called the *McDonnell-Douglas test*.[20] In an adverse impact lawsuit, the plaintiff only needs to show that a restricted policy is in effect—that is, that a disproportionate number of protected-class individuals were affected by the employment decisions.

four-fifths rule
An EEOC provision for establishing a prima facie case that an HR practice is discriminatory and has an adverse impact. A practice has adverse impact if the hiring rate of a protected class is less than four-fifths the hiring rate of a majority group.

One important EEOC provision for establishing a prima facie case that an HR practice is discriminatory and has an adverse impact is the **four-fifths rule**. The four-fifths rule comes from the EEOC's *Uniform Guidelines on Employee Selection Procedures*, an important document that informs employers how to establish selection procedures that are valid and therefore legal.[21]

The four-fifths rule compares the hiring rates of protected classes to those of majority groups (such as white men) in the organization. It assumes that an HR practice has an adverse impact if the hiring rate of a protected class is less than four-fifths of the hiring rate of a majority group. For example, assume that an accounting firm hires 50% of all its white male job applicants for entry-level accounting positions. Also assume that only 25% of all African-American male job applicants are hired for the same job. Applying the four-fifths rule, there is prima facie evidence that the accounting firm has discriminatory hiring practices because $50\% \times 4/5 = 40\%$, and 40% exceeds the 25% hiring rate for African-American men.

Once the plaintiff has established a prima facie case, the burden of proof switches to the organization. In other words, the employer is then placed in a position of proving that illegal discrimination did not occur. This can be very tough to prove. Suppose that a sales manager interviews two applicants for a sales position, a man and a woman. Their qualifications look very much the same on paper. However, in the interview the man comes across as more motivated. He is hired, and the rejected female applicant files a disparate treatment discrimination suit. She can, almost automatically, establish a prima facie case (she was qualified, she was not hired, the company did hire someone else). Now the sales manager has to prove that the decision was based on a judgment about the applicant's motivation, not on the applicant's sex.

While these cases can be difficult, employers do win their share of them. There are four basic defenses that an employer can use:

bona fide occupational qualification (BFOQ)
A characteristic that must be present in all employees for a particular job.

- *Job relatedness.* The employer has to show that the decision was made for job-related reasons. This is much easier to do if the employer has written documentation to support and explain the decision. In our example, the manager will be asked to give specific job-related reasons for the decision to hire the man for the sales job. As we noted in Chapter 2, job descriptions are particularly useful for documenting the job-related reasons for any particular HR decision.
- *Bona fide occupational qualification.* A **bona fide occupational qualification (BFOQ)** is a characteristic that must be present in all employees for a particular job.

For instance, a film director is permitted to consider only females for parts that call for an actress.

- *Seniority.* Employment decisions that are made in the context of a formal seniority system are permitted, even if they discriminate against certain protected-class individuals. However this defense requires the seniority system to be well established and applied universally, not just in some circumstances.
- *Business necessity.* The employer can use the business necessity defense when the employment practice is necessary for the safe and efficient operation of the organization, and that there is an overriding business purpose for the discriminatory practice. For example, an employee drug test may adversely impact a disadvantaged minority group, but the need for safety (to protect other employees and customers) may justify the drug-testing procedure.

Of these four defenses, the job-relatedness defense is the most common because of the strict limitations courts have placed on the BFOQ, seniority, and business necessity defenses.

Title VII and Pregnancy. In 1978 Congress amended Title VII to state explicitly that women are protected from discrimination based either on their ability to become pregnant or on their actual pregnancy. The *Pregnancy Discrimination Act of 1978* requires employers to treat an employee who is pregnant in the same way as any other employee who has a medical condition. The law also states that a company cannot design an employee health benefit plan that provides no coverage for pregnancy. These are strict requirements, as evidenced by the following case.

Johnson Controls manufactures batteries. In 1977, in response to increasing medical evidence that the lead levels to which some of its workers were exposed could harm fetuses (but not adults), Johnson asked its female employees not to work in particular jobs if they were planning to become pregnant. Between 1979 and 1983, eight female employees became pregnant even though they had levels of lead in their blood that were potentially dangerous to the fetuses. The company therefore adopted a policy that excluded all women capable of becoming pregnant from jobs in which they would be exposed to unsafe lead levels. The unions to which these women belonged sued the company. In 1991 the

The Laws of Pregnancy.

U.S. law requires employers to treat pregnant employees in the same way as any other employees with a medical condition. In addition, the Family and Medical Leave Act of 1993 requires certain employers to provide up to 12 weeks' unpaid leave to eligible employees who adopt a child or need to care for a sick parent, child, or spouse.

Supreme Court ruled that this exclusionary policy was a violation of Title VII. In effect, the Court ruled that decisions about health concerns such as this were the employee's, not the employer's, responsibility.[22]

But what if a female employee at Johnson Controls has a child with a birth defect? Can she then sue the company for allowing her to work in a job that exposed her fetus to harm? The justices considered this issue and, in fact, carried on a debate about it in the written opinion. The majority of the justices ruled that, as long as employees are given adequate notice of the substance's potential to harm fetuses, the employer would be protected from such a suit. Other justices, while agreeing with the main decision, questioned the extent of this legal protection. In addition, they pointed out that the child could potentially bring a suit against the company, for (obviously) the child could not have been warned in advance.[23] So managers who find this issue confusing can take some comfort in knowing that some of the brightest legal minds have struggled with the same issue and were unable to resolve it.

Sexual Harassment. The Title VII prohibition of sex-based discrimination has also been interpreted to prohibit sexual harassment. In contrast to the protection for pregnancy, the sexual harassment protection was not an amendment to the law but rather a 1980 EEOC interpretation of the law. This interpretation has since been validated by two Supreme Court decisions. The EEOC's definition of sexual harassment is given in Figure 3–4. Also shown in the figure is the definition of general harassment issued by the EEOC in 1993. The vast majority of harassment cases filed to date have dealt with sexual harassment, but this may change in the future.[24]

quid pro quo sexual harassment
Harassment that occurs when sexual activity is required in return for getting or keeping a job or job-related benefit.

hostile work environment sexual harassment
Harassment that occurs when the behavior of anyone in the work setting is sexual in nature and is perceived by an employee as offensive and undesirable.

There are two broad categories of sexual harassment. The first, **quid pro quo sexual harassment**, covers the first two parts of the EEOC's definitions. It occurs when sexual activity is demanded in return for getting or keeping a job or job-related benefit. For instance, a buyer for the University of Massachusetts Medical Center was awarded $1 million in 1994 after she testified that her supervisor had forced her to engage in sex once or twice a week over a 20-month period as a condition of keeping her job.[25]

The second category, **hostile work environment sexual harassment**, occurs when the behavior of coworkers, supervisors, customers, or anyone else in the work setting is sex-

1980 Definition of Sexual Harassment
Unwelcome sexual advances, requests for sexual favors, and other verbal or physical conduct of a sexual nature constitute sexual harassment when:

1. submission to such conduct is made either explicitly or implicitly a term or condition of an individual's employment;
2. submission to or rejection of such conduct by an individual is used as a basis for employment decisions affecting such individual; or
3. such conduct has the purpose or effect of unreasonably interfering with an individual's work performance or creating an intimidating, hostile, or offensive working environment.

1993 Definition of Harassment
Unlawful harassment is verbal or physical conduct that denigrates or shows hostility or aversion toward an individual because of his or her race, color, religion, gender, national origin, age or disability, or that of his/her relatives, friends, or associates, and that:

1. has the purpose or effect of creating an intimidating, hostile, or offensive working environment;
2. has the purpose or effect of unreasonably interfering with an individual's work performance; or
3. otherwise adversely affects an individual's employment opportunities.

FIGURE 3–4
EEOC Definitions of Harassment

ual in nature and the employee perceives the behavior as offensive and undesirable. Consider this example from a Supreme Court case decided in 1993.[26]

Teresa Harris was a manager at Forklift Systems, Inc., an equipment rental firm in Nashville, Tennessee. Her boss was Charles Hardy, the company president. Throughout the two and one-half years that Harris worked at Forklift, Hardy made such comments to her as "You're a woman, what do you know?" and "We need a man as the rental manager." He suggested in front of other employees that the two of them "go to the Holiday Inn to negotiate her raise." When Harris asked Hardy to stop, he expressed surprise at her annoyance, but did not apologize. Less than one month later, after Harris had negotiated a deal with a customer, Hardy asked her in front of other employees, "What did you do, promise the guy . . . some [sex] Saturday night?" Harris quit her job at the end of that month.

The issue the Court had to decide was whether Hardy violated the sexual harassment regulations based on Title VII. Lower courts had held that Hardy's behavior was certainly objectionable, but that Harris had not suffered serious psychological harm and that Hardy had not created a hostile work environment. The Supreme Court disagreed, holding that the behavior only needed to be such that a "reasonable person" would find it to create a hostile or abusive work environment. Figure 3–5 lists the tests that the Supreme Court said should be considered by judges and juries in deciding whether certain conduct creates a "hostile work environment" and is thus prohibited by Title VII.

Men may be the victims of sexual harassment as well as women. In 1995 a federal judge awarded a man $237,257 for being sexually harassed by a female supervisor at a Domino's Pizza restaurant. The female supervisor made unwelcome sexual advances to the male subordinate, creating a hostile work environment. When the man threatened to report the supervisor's inappropriate conduct to top management, he was fired.[27]

Sexual harassment has become a major EEO issue for employers. A recent Harris survey found that 31% of women reported that they had been sexually harassed in the workplace.[28] The Manager's Notebook on page 96 titled "Reducing Potential Liability for Sexual Harassment" spells out some ways to prevent or correct instances of sexual harassment.

A QUESTION OF ETHICS

Some businesses thrive on a sexual theme. For example, "Hooters" attracts customers by marketing a sexual environment. Many ad campaigns have explicit sexual themes. Are such marketing efforts ethical? What effect might these public images have on the working environment at the company that uses them?

The Civil Rights Act of 1991. In 1991, believing that the Supreme Court was beginning to water down Title VII, Congress passed a comprehensive set of amendments to Title VII. Together, these amendments are known as the *Civil Rights Act of 1991*. While the legal aspects of these amendments are fairly technical, their impact is very real for many organizations. Among the most important effects of the 1991 amendment are:

- *Burden of proof.* As we noted earlier, the employer bears the burden of proof in a discrimination case. Once the applicant or employee files a discrimination case and shows some justification for it, the organization has to defend itself by proving that it had a good job-related reason for the decision it made. This standard was originally established in the *Griggs v. Duke Power* decision in 1971. Then a 1989 Supreme Court case, *Wards Cove Packing Co. v. Antonio*, had the effect of placing more of the burden of proof on the plaintiff.[29] The 1991 law reinstates the *Griggs* standard.
- *Quotas.* To avoid adverse impact, many organizations (including the Department of Labor) had developed a policy of adjusting scores on employment tests so that a cer-

The Supreme Court listed these questions to help judges and juries decide whether verbal and other nonphysical behavior of a sexual nature create a hostile work environment.

- How frequent is the discriminatory conduct?
- How severe is the discriminatory conduct?
- Is the conduct physically threatening or humiliating?
- Does the conduct interfere with the employee's work performance?

FIGURE 3–5

Do You Have a Hostile Work Environment?

Manager's Notebook

Reducing Potential Liability for Sexual Harassment

To reduce the potential liability of a sexual harassment suit, managers should:

- ✔ Establish a written policy prohibiting harassment.
- ✔ Communicate the policy and train employees in what constitutes harassment.
- ✔ Establish an effective complaint procedure.
- ✔ Quickly investigate all claims.
- ✔ Take remedial action to correct past harassment.
- ✔ Make sure that the complainant does not end up in a less desirable position if he or she needs to be transferred.
- ✔ Follow up to prevent continuance of harassment.

Source: Commerce Clearing House. (1991). *Sexual harassment manual for managers and supervisors*. Chicago: Commerce Clearing House.

tain percentage of protected-class applicants would be hired. The 1991 law amending Title VII prohibits **quotas**, which are employer adjustments of hiring decisions to ensure that a certain number of people from a certain protected class are hired. Thus, quotas, which had received mixed reviews in Supreme Court decisions prior to 1991, are now explicitly forbidden. Employers who have an affirmative action program that gives preference to protected-class candidates have to walk a very fine line between "giving preference" (which is permissible) and "meeting a quota" (which is forbidden).

- *Damages and jury trials.* The original Title VII law allowed successful plaintiffs to collect only back pay awards. However, racial minorities were also able to use an 1866 law to collect punitive and/or compensatory damages. **Punitive damages** are fines awarded to a plaintiff in order to punish the defendant. **Compensatory damages** are fines awarded to a plaintiff to compensate for the financial or psychological harm the plaintiff has suffered as a result of the discrimination. The 1991 law extended the possibility of collecting punitive and compensatory damages to persons claiming sex, religious, or disability-based discrimination. Such damages are capped at $50,000 to $300,000, depending on the size of the employer.[30] In addition, the law allows plaintiffs to request a trial by jury.

quotas
Employer adjustments of hiring decisions to ensure that a certain number of people from a certain protected class are hired.

punitive damages
Fines awarded to a plaintiff in order to punish the defendant.

compensatory damages
Fines awarded to a plaintiff to compensate for the financial or psychological harm the plaintiff has suffered.

Some believe that by expressly forbidding quotas, the Civil Rights Act of 1991 has prohibited a very useful mechanism for reducing discrimination in employment decisions. Many organizations had found that the best way to prevent adverse impact was to use a combination of quotas and cognitive ability testing. That is, the employer would select a certain percentage of applicants from various groups, and then choose the highest performers on cognitive ability tests from each group. This employment strategy resulted in both the maintenance of a quality work force and the greater participation of minorities in that work force. Yet, by outlawing quotas, the Civil Rights Act of 1991 has prohibited this option.[31]

executive order
A presidential directive that has the force of law. In HR context, a policy with which all federal agencies and organizations doing business with the federal government must comply.

Executive Order 11246. **Executive orders** are policies that the president establishes for the federal government and organizations that contract with the federal government. Executive Order 11246 (as amended by Executive Order 11375), issued by President Johnson in 1965, is *not* part of Title VII. It does, however, prohibit discrimination against the same categories of people that Title VII protects. In addition, it goes beyond the Title VII requirement of no discrimination by requiring covered organizations (firms with government contracts over $50,000 and 50 or more employees) to develop affirmative action programs to promote the employment of protected-class members. For instance, government contractors such as Northrup and Martin Marietta are required to have active affirmative action programs.

The Age Discrimination in Employment Act of 1967

Age Discrimination in Employment Act (1967)
The law prohibiting discrimination against people who are 40 or older.

The **Age Discrimination in Employment Act (ADEA)** prohibits discrimination against people who are 40 or older. When first enacted in 1967, it protected people aged 40 to 65. Subsequently, it was amended to raise the age to 70, and in 1986 the upper age limit was removed entirely.

The large majority of ADEA complaints is filed by employees who have been terminated. For instance, a 57-year-old computerized control salesman for GE Fanuc Automation was the only employee terminated during a "reduction in force"; he was replaced by six younger sales representatives. He brought a lawsuit, claiming that he was fired because of his age, and a Detroit jury awarded him $1.1 million in damages and lost wages and benefits.[32] Employers can also lose lawsuits as a result of ill-informed workplace humor. Employers have lost several age discrimination cases because terminated employees had evidence that supervisors had told jokes about old age.[33]

An important amendment to the ADEA is the *Older Workers Protection Act (OWPA)* of 1990, which makes it illegal for employers to discriminate in providing benefits to employees based on age. For example, it would be illegal for employers to provide disability benefits only to employees who are age 60 or less, or to require older disabled employees to take early retirement. Another OWPA provision makes it more difficult for firms to ask older workers in downsizing and layoff situations to sign waivers in which they give up their right to any future age-discrimination claims in exchange for a payment.[34]

The Americans with Disabilities Act of 1990

The most recent of the major EEO laws is the **Americans with Disabilities Act (ADA).** Signed into law in 1990 and gradually implemented since then, ADA has three major sections. Title I contains the employment provisions; Titles II and III concern the operation of state and local governments and places of public accommodation such as hotels, restaurants, and grocery stores. The employment provisions began to be enforced for the approximately 264,000 U.S. employers with 25 or more employees on July 26, 1992, and for the approximately 666,000 U.S. employers with 15 or more employees on July 26, 1994.[35]

Americans with Disabilities Act (1990)
The law forbidding employment discrimination against people with disabilities who are able to perform the essential functions of the job with or without reasonable accommodation.

The central requirement of Title I of the ADA is as follows:

> Employment discrimination is prohibited against *individuals with disabilities* who are able to perform the *essential functions* of the job with or without *reasonable accommodation.*

Three parts of this requirement need definition.

Individuals with Disabilities. For the purposes of ADA, **individuals with disabilities** are people who have a physical or mental impairment that substantially affects one or more major life activities. Some examples of major life activities are:[36]

individuals with disabilities
Persons who have a physical or mental impairment that substantially affects one or more major life activities.

- walking
- speaking
- breathing
- performing manual tasks
- sitting
- lifting
- seeing
- hearing
- learning
- caring for oneself
- working
- reading

Obviously, persons who are blind, hearing impaired, or wheelchair bound are individuals with disabilities. But the category also includes people who have a controlled impairment. For instance, a person with epilepsy is disabled even if the epilepsy is controlled through medication. The impairment must be physical or mental, and not due to environmental, cultural, or economic disadvantages. For example, a person who has difficulty reading due to dyslexia is considered disabled, but a person who cannot read because he or she dropped out of school is not. Persons with communicable diseases, including those who are HIV-positive (infected with the virus that causes AIDS), are included in the definition of individuals with disabilities.

In addition, the ADA protects persons who are *perceived* to be disabled. For instance, an employee might suffer a heart attack. When he tries to return to work, his boss may be scared that the workload will be "too much" and refuse to let him come back. The employer would be in violation of the ADA because he perceives the employee as disabled and is discriminating against him on the basis of that perception.

Two particular classes of people are explicitly *not* considered disabled: individuals whose current use of alcohol is affecting their job performance and those who use illegal drugs (whether they are addicted or not). However, those who are recovering from their former use of either alcohol or drugs are covered by ADA.

essential functions
Job duties that each person in a certain position must do or must be able to do to be an effective employee.

Essential Functions. The EEOC separates job duties and tasks into two categories: essential and marginal. **Essential functions** are job duties that every employee must do or must be able to do to be an effective employee. *Marginal functions* are job duties that are required of only some employees or are not critical to job performance. The following examples illustrate the difference between essential and marginal functions:

- A company advertises a position for a "floating" supervisor to substitute when regular supervisors on the day, night, and graveyard shifts are absent. The ability to work any time of the day or night is an essential job function.
- A company wishes to expand its business with Japan. In addition to sales experience, it requires all new hires to speak fluent Japanese. This language skill is an essential job function.
- In any job requiring computer use, it is essential that the employee have the ability to access, input, or retrieve information from the computer terminal. However, it may not be essential that the employee be capable of manually entering or visually retrieving information because technology exists for voice recognition input and auditory output.

Apple Solutions.

Apple Computer has created many technologies to help accommodate the needs of workers with disabilities. Apple's World Wide Web site **(http://www.apple.com/disability)** explains these enabling technologies in detail. (The actual Disability Solutions Store no longer exists, but the products are still available from Apple.)

- A group of chemists working together in a lab may occasionally need to answer the telephone. This is considered a marginal job duty if not every one of the chemists can answer the phone because the other chemists can do so.

ADA requires that employers make decisions about applicants with disabilities solely on the basis of their ability to perform essential job functions.

Reasonable Accommodation. Organizations are required to take some reasonable action to allow disabled employees to work for them. The major aspects of this requirement are:

- Employers must make **reasonable accommodation** for the known disabilities of applicants or employees so that disabled people enjoy equal employment opportunity. For example, an applicant who uses a wheelchair may need accommodation if the interviewing site is not wheelchair accessible.
- Employers cannot deny a disabled person employment to avoid providing the reasonable accommodation, unless providing the accommodation would cause an "undue hardship." Undue hardship is a highly subjective determination, based on the cost of the accommodation and the employer's resources. For instance, an accommodation routinely provided by large employers (such as specialized computer equipment) may not be required of small employers because the small employers do not have the large employer's financial resources.
- No accommodation is required if the individual is not otherwise qualified for the position.
- It is usually the obligation of the disabled individual to request the accommodation.
- If the cost of the accommodation would create an undue hardship for the employer, the disabled individual should be given the option of providing the accommodation. For instance, if a visually impaired person applies for a computer operator position in a small company that cannot afford to accommodate the applicant, then the applicant should be given the option to provide the accommodating technology. (It should be noted, though, that the Job Accommodation Network reports that 31% of accommodations do not cost anything at all, and less than 1% cost more than $5,000.[37]) The Manager's Notebook titled "Designing Flexible Work Areas to Accommodate Employees with Disabilities" describes some of the ways that employers can design flexible work areas to accommodate employees with disabilities.

Manager's Notebook

Designing Flexible Work Areas to Accommodate Employees with Disabilities

By planning ahead when designing work areas, employers can easily accommodate employees with disabilities. Here are some tips for designing flexible work areas:

- ✔ Use panel systems so that work spaces can be easily modified and work surface heights can be raised or lowered as needed.
- ✔ Install electronically controlled work surfaces and tables.
- ✔ Lower storage areas or install storage areas that are mobile.
- ✔ Install adjustable keyboard pads that adjust easily with little hand pressure.
- ✔ Install adjustable lighting with variable intensity that can add more or less light to the work space as needed.

Source: Reprinted, by permission of publisher, from *HR Focus*. (1992, July). Some quick tips to make workspaces more flexible, *69*, 12–14.

reasonable accommodation
An action taken to accommodate the known disabilities of applicants or employees so that disabled persons enjoy equal employment opportunity.

A wide variety of accommodations is possible, and they can come from some surprising sources. For example, Kreonite, Inc., a small family-owned business (about 250 employees) that manufactures specialized photographic film, has been committed to employing persons with disabilities. Several of Kreonite's employees are deaf. Kreonite turned to a local not-for-profit training center for someone to teach its hearing employees sign language. The training was free, and 30 Kreonite employees volunteered to attend.[38]

Some additional examples of potential reasonable accommodations that the EEOC has suggested are:[39]

- Reassigning marginal job duties.
- Modifying work schedules.

- Modifying examinations or training materials.
- Providing qualified readers and interpreters.
- Permitting use of paid or unpaid leave for treatment.

As we noted earlier in the chapter, the main focus of the ADA and its accompanying regulations is the hiring process. However, the large majority of complaints filed so far involves situations in which current employees have become disabled on the job. The single largest category of complaints is back injuries, which are notoriously difficult to diagnose and treat. Managers need to be prepared to deal with a set of issues not anticipated by the lawmakers and regulators who created and passed the ADA.

The Vocational Rehabilitation Act of 1973. The *Vocational Rehabilitation Act* is the precursor to the ADA. However, this act applied only to the federal government and its contractors. Like Executive Order 11246, the Vocational Rehabilitation Act not only prohibits discrimination (in this case, on the basis of disability) but also requires that the covered organizations have an affirmative action plan to promote the employment of disabled individuals. Familiarity with this law is useful to organizations attempting to comply with the ADA because it has led to over 20 years' worth of court and regulatory decisions based on the same central prohibition against disability-based discrimination.

The Vietnam Era Veterans Readjustment Act of 1974

One additional EEO law deserves brief mention. The *Vietnam Era Veterans Readjustment Act of 1974* prohibits discrimination against Vietnam-era veterans (those who served in the military between August 5, 1964, and May 7, 1975) by federal contractors. It also requires federal contractors to take affirmative action to hire Vietnam-era veterans.

EEO Enforcement and Compliance

The enforcement of EEO laws is the responsibility of the executive branch of government, which is headed by the president. In this section we describe the regulatory agencies that enforce the various EEO laws, as well as some of the plans that have been used to comply with affirmative action requirements.

Regulatory Agencies

Two agencies are primarily responsible for the enforcement of EEO law: the Equal Employment Opportunity Commission (EEOC) and the Office of Federal Contract Compliance Programs (OFCCP).

Equal Employment Opportunity Commission (EEOC)
The federal agency responsible for enforcing EEO laws.

Equal Employment Opportunity Commission (EEOC). The **Equal Employment Opportunity Commission (EEOC)**, which was created by Title VII, has three major functions. The first is processing discrimination complaints. The second is issuing written regulations. The third is information gathering and dissemination.[40]

In processing discrimination complaints, the EEOC follows a three-step process:

- *Investigation.* An applicant or employee who thinks that he or she has been discriminated against begins the process by filing a complaint with the EEOC. The EEOC then notifies the company that a complaint has been filed, and the company becomes responsible for ensuring that any records relating to the complaint are kept safe. The EEOC usually finds itself with a backlog, so it may take up to two years to begin investigating the complaint. And the number of cases is rapidly accelerating, increasing 4.6% from 1989 to 1990 and 21.6% from 1992 to 1993.[41] In 1994, 91,200 cases were filed with the EEOC, compared to 62,100 in 1990.

After conducting the investigation, the EEOC determines if it is likely that the company did in fact violate one or more EEO laws. Complainants are always free to file a lawsuit, but the courts are unlikely to rule in their favor without the EEOC's backing.

- *Conciliation.* If the EEOC finds that an EEO law was likely violated, it attempts to resolve the case through conciliation. **Conciliation** consists of negotiation among the three parties involved: the complainant, the employer, and the EEOC. The goal of conciliation is to reach a fair settlement while avoiding a trial.
- *Litigation.* If conciliation is not possible, the EEOC can choose between two courses of action. The EEOC does not have the power to compel an employer to pay compensation or any other kind of damages; this can be done only as the result of a court's decision. Because pursuing a lawsuit is very expensive, the EEOC takes this course of action only in a relatively small percentage of cases. If the EEOC chooses not to pursue the case, it issues a right-to-sue letter to the complainant, who is then free to pursue court action with the blessing (if not the financial or legal support) of the EEOC.

conciliation
An attempt to reach a negotiated settlement between the employer and an employee or applicant in an EEO case.

In addition to resolving complaints, the EEOC is responsible for issuing regulations and guidelines. These documents put "meat on the bones" of the individual laws. For instance, when the EEOC decided that sexual harassment was prohibited by Title VII, it issued regulations defining what sexual harassment is (see Figure 3–4) and what it expects employers to do in response to employee complaints of harassment. Similarly, when the ADA was signed into law in 1990, the EEOC was given the responsibility of issuing regulations that would inform employers exactly what they would (and would not) be expected to do to comply with the law. Figure 3–6 lists some of the most prominent EEOC regulations.

The EEOC also gathers information to monitor the hiring practices of organizations. It does this by requiring organizations with 100 or more employees to file an annual report (EEO-1) indicating the number of women and minorities who hold jobs in nine different job categories. The EEOC examines this information to identify patterns of discrimination that may exist in organizations.

Finally, the EEOC disseminates posters to employers. These posters explain to workers how to protect themselves from employment discrimination and how to file a com-

Sex discrimination guidelines
Questions and answers on pregnancy disability and reproductive hazards
Religious discrimination guidelines
National origin discrimination guidelines
Interpretations of the Age Discrimination in Employment Act
Employee selection guidelines
Questions and answers on employee selection guidelines
Sexual harassment guidelines
Record keeping and reports
Affirmative action guidelines
EEO in the federal government
Equal Pay Act interpretations
Policy statement on maternity benefits
Policy statement on relationship of Title VII to 1986 Immigration Reform and Control Act
Policy statement on reproductive and fetal hazards
Policy statement on religious accommodation under Title VII
Disability discrimination guidelines

FIGURE 3–6

Principal EEOC Regulations

Source: Adapted from Ledvinka, J., and Scarpello, V. G. (1991). *Federal regulation of personnel and human resource management* (2nd ed.). Boston: PWS-Kent. Reproduced with the permission of South-Western College Publishing.

plaint. The EEOC requires employers to display the posters in a prominent place (such as the company cafeteria).

Office of Federal Contract Compliance Programs (OFCCP)
The federal agency responsible for monitoring and enforcing the laws and executive orders that apply to the federal government and its contractors.

Office of Federal Contract Compliance Programs (OFCCP). The **Office of Federal Contract Compliance Programs (OFCCP)** is responsible for enforcing the laws and executive orders that apply to the federal government and its contractors. Specifically, it enforces Executive Order 11246 and the Vocational Rehabilitation Act, which both go beyond prohibiting discrimination to requiring affirmative action programs by covered employers.

Many of the regulations written by the OFCCP are very similar to those issued by the EEOC. However, there are two major differences between the enforcement activities of the two agencies. First, in contrast to the EEOC, the OFCCP actively monitors compliance with its regulations. That is, it does not wait for an employee or applicant to file a complaint. Rather, it requires covered employers to submit annual reports on the state of their affirmative action program. Second, unlike the EEOC, the OFCCP has considerable enforcement power. Being a government contractor is considered a privilege, not a right. The OFCCP can take away that privilege if it determines that an employer is not complying with the law. It can also levy fines and other forms of punishment.

Affirmative Action Plans

An affirmative action plan is required of all government agencies and businesses that do a significant amount of work for the government. There are three steps to developing an affirmative action plan: conducting a utilization analysis, establishing goals and timetables, and determining action options.

Utilization Analysis. The first step in developing an affirmative action plan is conducting a *utilization analysis* to describe the organization's current work force relative to the pool of qualified workers in the labor force. There are two parts to conducting this analysis. The first involves determining the demographic composition of the current work force by dividing all the jobs in the organization into classifications. For instance, all management jobs are placed in one classification, all clerical and secretarial jobs in a second, all sales positions in a third, and so on. The percentage of persons from each protected class working in each of these classifications is then determined.

The second part is determining the percentage of those same protected classes in the available labor market. In gathering this information, organizations need to consider the eight different pieces of information listed in Figure 3–7. For instance, what percentage of qualified and available managers are women? What percentage are African-Americans? What percentage are Asian-Americans? The OFCCP offers guidelines for determining

FIGURE 3–7

Components of an Eight-Factor Availability Analysis

Determine the percentage of protected-class members for each of the following groups of people:

- Local population
- Local unemployed workers
- Local labor force
- Qualified workers in the local labor market
- Qualified workers in the labor market from which you recruit
- Current employees who might be promoted into the job classification
- Graduates of local education and training programs that prepare people for this job classification
- Participants in training programs sponsored by the employer

these figures. If the available figures are significantly higher than the currently employed in any category, the protected groups are said to be underutilized in that job category.

Goals and Timetables. The second step is setting goals and timetables for correcting underutilization. The OFCCP explicitly requires that rigid numerical quotas *not* be set. Rather, the employer should take into consideration the size of the underutilization, how fast the work force turns over, and whether the work force is growing or contracting. Another consideration in setting goals and timetables is the types of actions the employer intends to take.

Action Plans. The final step in developing an affirmative action plan is deciding exactly what affirmative actions to take. The OFCCP suggests the following guidelines:

- Recruiting protected-class members.
- Redesigning jobs so that the underrepresented workers are more likely to be qualified.
- Providing specialized training sessions for underprepared applicants.
- Removing any unnecessary barriers to employment. For instance, a company located in an area not served by public transportation might consider providing van service from certain areas so that potential applicants who do not have reliable transportation can become employees.

The central concern for organizations is determining how much (if any) preference they should give to applicants who belong to an underutilized protected class. For instance, a few years back there was a job opening in the transportation department of Santa Clara County, California. After going through the normal selection process, the candidates for promotion were ranked according to their performance on tests and in interviews. County rules allowed any of the top seven candidates to be chosen. The supervisors were poised to choose the employee ranked second—Paul Johnson, a white man. Diane Joyce, a white woman who was ranked fourth, called the county's affirmative action officer and ended up with the job.

Johnson filed suit. His argument was straightforward: Title VII prohibits discrimination based on sex, and he did not get the job because he is a man. This is a classic case of **reverse discrimination**, discrimination that occurs as the result of an attempt to recruit and hire more people from the protected classes. In this case, the job classification to which the person was to be promoted had 238 positions, none of which were held by women. Johnson pursued his case all the way to the U.S. Supreme Court. In 1987 the Court ruled that Santa Clara County's decision was permissible.[42]

reverse discrimination Discrimination against a nonprotected-class member resulting from attempts to recruit and hire members of protected classes.

The Supreme Court has decided over a dozen reverse discrimination cases since the first one in 1977.[43] Although the Court has favored the affirmative action strategy side of the tension outlined in Figure 3–1, almost all of these cases were decided by 6–3 or 5–4 margins. Because new justices are added to the Supreme Court fairly regularly, how these kind of cases will be decided in the future is very much an open question.

The United States is not the only country with affirmative action. Other countries have created similar policies to provide employment or educational opportunities for disadvantaged groups. For example, India has tried to improve the status of the untouchables, the lowest caste in its society, by providing them with preferential treatment in employment and education. This policy has had mixed results because it has enraged some members of the higher castes. Malaysia has favored the Islamic Malays over the Chinese (who on average are wealthier and more highly educated than the Malays) for jobs and higher education opportunities. Significant numbers of Chinese Malaysians have responded to this policy by emigrating to Asia and North America.[44] Other countries have disadvantaged groups in their population but have decided not to create employment policies favorable to these groups. For example, France has a large population of Algerians who have been historically disadvantaged, but it has avoided remedying the high Algerian unemployment rate with a policy similar to affirmative action in the United States. In Great Britain, the government's Commission for Racial Equality concluded that most British firms do little to ensure equal employment opportunity beyond verbal support for the idea.[44a]

Other Important Laws

We have concentrated on equal employment opportunity laws in this chapter because they have a broad effect on almost all HR issues and, as such, are highly likely to influence managers' behavior. The other HR laws, listed in the appendix to this chapter and discussed elsewhere in the book, are much more narrowly focused. These include laws that affect compensation and benefit plans (state workers' compensation laws, the Social Security Act, the Fair Labor Standards Act, the Employee Retirement and Income Security Act, the Consolidated Omnibus Budget Reconciliation Act, and the Family and Medical Leave Act), union-management relations (the Wagner Act, the Taft-Hartley Act, and the Landrum-Griffin Act), safety and health issues (the Occupational Safety and Health Act), and layoffs (the Worker Adjustment and Retraining Act).

A QUESTION OF ETHICS

Is it ethical for an employer to require all employees to speak only English at the workplace?

Four laws not addressed elsewhere deserve brief mention. The *Immigration Reform and Control Act of 1986* was intended to reduce the inflow of illegal immigrants to the United States. The law has one provision that affects employers. To discourage the hiring of illegal immigrants, the law mandates that employers hire only people who can document that they are legally permitted to work in the United States. The Employment Eligibility Verification (I-9) form specifies which documents employers need to see from new employees. It appears that the major impact of the Immigration Reform and Control Act has been the creation of a market for fake documents.

The *Immigration Act of 1990* was legislated to make it easier for skilled immigrants to enter the United States. This law represents a modification of previous U.S. immigration policy, which favored immigrants who either (1) had family members who are U.S. citizens or (2) were leaving a country that was assigned a large quota of immigrants to the United States based on historical trends.[45]

The *Drug Free Workplace Act of 1988* requires that government contractors try to ensure that their workplaces are free from drug use. Employers are required to prevent the use of illegal drugs at their work sites and to educate their employees about the hazards of drug use. While the law does not mandate drug testing, it—along with other more narrowly focused laws and regulations—has led to a general acceptance of drug testing, both of current employees and applicants, across the United States.[46] About 98% of *Fortune* 200 companies now conduct some form of drug testing.[47]

The *Uniformed Services Employment and Reemployment Rights Act of 1994* protects the rights of people who take short leaves from a private-sector employer to perform military service (such as reserve duty). The law protects these employees' seniority rights and benefits. It also protects them from employer discrimination in hiring, promotion, or layoff decisions.

Building Managerial Skills: Avoiding Pitfalls in EEO

The great majority of employees and job applicants in the United States fall into one or more protected classes. This means that almost any decision made by a manager that affects a worker's employment status can be challenged in a court of law. In most cases, sound management practices will not only help managers avoid EEO lawsuits but will also contribute to the organization's bottom line. Five specific management practices are recommended: providing training, establishing a complaint resolution process, documenting your decisions, being honest, and asking applicants only for information that you need to know.

Provide Training

One of the best ways to avoid EEO problems is to provide training. Two types of training are appropriate. First, the HR department should provide supervisors, managers, and executives with regular updates on EEO and other labor issues, since this area of law is in a constant state of flux.[48] The Supreme Court regularly decides cases that impact HR practice. While managers can try to read periodicals to stay current, most find their everyday demands too taxing to allow time for this. Regular, focused training sessions conducted by the HR department are the most efficient method of communicating this information to managers.

Second, employers should focus on communicating to employees their commitment to a discrimination-free work environment. For instance, all employees need to be instructed in what sexual harassment is, how to stop it before it becomes a problem, and what to do if it does become a problem. Honeywell has a council of employees with disabilities, one function of which is to promote awareness of disability issues throughout the company.[49]

Establish a Complaint Resolution Process

Every organization should establish a process for the internal resolution of EEO and other types of employee complaints. It is much less expensive to resolve these concerns if the EEOC, OFCCP, and legal counsel are not involved. More importantly, employee morale and satisfaction can be improved when employees are able to pass along their concerns to upper-level management. (We describe complaint resolution systems in detail in Chapters 13 and 15).

Once in place, the complaint resolution process should be followed correctly. AT&T avoided liability in a sexual harassment case because it was able to show that it had acted promptly to remedy the problem once management had been informed of it.[50] The Issues and Applications feature on page 106 titled "Alternative Dispute Resolution Methods at Marriott" describes how Marriott has taken the lead in experimenting with new ways to resolve employee complaints, many of which are EEO related.

Document Decisions

It is widely understood and accepted that all financial transactions and decisions need to be well documented. Documentation is necessary so that these decisions can be audited and summarized, problem areas identified, and solutions implemented. The same rationale can be applied to decisions made about employees. The nature of any HR decision, and the rationale for it, should be clearly documented. Both the EEOC and OFCCP have certain reporting requirements. Employers that have a sound human resource information system in place do not find it difficult to comply with these requirements. One important type of documentation is performance appraisal. As we will see in Chapter 7, there are many good reasons for conducting appraisals, only one of which is to provide documentation in case of a lawsuit.

Nonetheless, the legal reason is an important one. In a discrimination case the generic charge is that the employer has based a decision in whole or in part on a non–job-related characteristic (age, sex, race, religion, and so on). The employer's generic defense is that it had a job-related reason for its decision. This defense is much easier to establish if the employer can provide written documentation to support its claim.

Be Honest

Typically, applicants and employees will not file an EEO complaint unless they think they have been mistreated. Perceptions of mistreatment often result from situations in which

Alternative Dispute Resolution Methods at Marriott

Issues + Applications

Ron Wilensky, vice president for employee relations for Marriott International, was not satisfied with the company's "Guarantee of Fair Treatment" program, which instructed employees with complaints to go first to their immediate supervisor, then to the supervisor's manager, and so on up the ladder if necessary. Based on his experience with three *Fortune* 500 companies that had similar policies, he estimated that 75% of employees bypass such a policy and consult an attorney. To verify his hunch, he established a committee to examine employee satisfaction with the Guarantee of Fair Treatment. The results indicated that employees did not trust the policy. Instead, they wanted a system that would give those with grievances a chance to air their concerns before impartial listeners and have those concerns addressed promptly—without fear of retribution.

To give employees what they want, Wilensky and his committee have been experimenting with three dispute resolution systems.

1. *Mutual agreement through mediation.* A neutral person, typically an expert in dispute resolution, meets with both parties to the conflict and tries to arrange a negotiated settlement. Since 80% to 90% of litigation is settled out of court anyway, the goal is to reduce attorney fees and other associated costs.
2. *A helping hotline.* Wilensky found that it was difficult to track employee grievances across so many different geographical locations, so Marriott uses a toll-free 800-number hotline at 300 of its food service locations. Available 24 hours a day, 7 days per week, the hotline is intended to be used only to report cases of perceived wrongful discharge, discrimination, and harassment. Marriott promises to initiate an investigation within three days of receiving the complaint.
3. *A panel of peers.* In 50 Marriott locations, employees have an opportunity to air their grievance before a panel of their peers. The panel is chosen at random from a group of specially trained volunteers. The panel has the authority to make final, binding decisions on all grievances brought before it.

While the effectiveness of these systems remains to be seen, the panel of peers has shown some positive early results. Although the number of EEO complaints at work sites without peer review increased from 1992 to 1993, sites with peer review saw EEO complaints drop 50% in 1992 and 83% in 1993.

Source: Wilensky, R., and Jones, K. M. (1994, March). Quick response key to resolving complaints. *HRMagazine*, 42–47. Reprinted with the permission of *HRMagazine*, published by the Society for Human Resource Management, Alexandria, VA.

employees' or applicants' expectations have not been met. Imagine the following scenario: A 50-year-old employee has consistently received excellent performance evaluations over a 20-year period. He is then abruptly terminated by his manager for poor work performance. This employee is likely to file a lawsuit because over time he has developed the expectation that he is a valued employee, and he now believes that the only possible reason for his termination is his age. While it may be painful in the short term, providing honest feedback to employees is a good management practice that may reduce legal problems in the long run.

Ask Only for Information You Need to Know

Major sources of potential lawsuits are the application and interview phases of the hiring process. The general rule is that companies should ask only for information that is related to job performance. For instance, you should not ask about an applicant's religious affiliation, although you may ask if a person can work on specific days of the week. Similarly, you can ask if the applicant is capable of performing the essential physical aspects of the job (preferably specifically listed), but asking general questions about health would probably be interpreted as a violation of the ADA. Figure 3–8 gives several more examples of appropriate and inappropriate questions to ask on an application form or during an interview. ▼

Subject of Question	Examples of Acceptable Questions	Examples of Unacceptable Questions	Comments
Name	"What is your name?" "Have you worked for this company under another name?"	"What was your maiden name?"	Questions about an applicant's name that may indicate marital status or national origin should be avoided.
Age	"Are you at least 18 years old?" "Upon employment, all employees must submit legal proof of age. Can you furnish proof of age?"	"What is your date of birth?" "What is your age?"	A request for age-related data may discourage older workers from applying.
Race, Ethnicity, and Physical Characteristics	"After employment, the company must have a photograph of all employees. If employed, can you furnish a photograph?" "Do you read, speak, or write a foreign language?"	"What is your race?" "What are your height and weight?" "Would you please submit a photograph with your application for identification purposes?" "What is the color of your hair? Your eyes?" "What language do you commonly use?" "How did you acquire your ability to read, write, or speak a foreign language?"	Information relative to physical characteristics may be associated with sexual or racial group membership.
Religion	A statement may be made by the employer of the days, hours, and shifts worked.	"What is your religious faith?" "Does your religion keep you from working on weekends?"	Questions that determine applicants' availability have an exclusionary effect because of some people's religious practices.
Gender, Marital Status, and Family	"If you are a minor, please list the name and address of a parent or guardian." "Please provide the name, address, and telephone number of someone who should be contacted in case of an emergency."	"What is your sex?" "Describe your current marital status." "List the number and ages of your children." "If you have children, please describe the provisions you have made for child care." "With whom do you reside?" "Do you have any dependents or relatives who should be contacted in case of an emergency?" "Do you prefer being referred to as Miss, Mrs., or Ms.?"	Direct *or* indirect questions about marital status, children, pregnancy, and childbearing plans frequently discriminate against women and may be a violation of Title VII.

(continued on page 108)

FIGURE 3–8

Examples of Acceptable and Unacceptable Questions Asked on Application Forms or During Interviews

Source: Adapted from Gatewood, R. D., and Feild, H. S. (1994). *Human resource selection*, 3rd ed. Fort Worth, TX: Dryden.

Subject of Question	Examples of Acceptable Questions	Examples of Unacceptable Questions	Comments
Physical Conditions	"Are you willing to take a physical exam if the nature of the job for which you are applying requires one?"	"Do you have any physical disabilities, defects, or handicaps?" "How would you describe your general physical health?" "When was your last physical exam?"	A blanket policy excluding the disabled is discriminatory. Where physical condition is a requirement for employment, employers should be able to document the business necessity for questions on the application form relating to physical condition.
Military Service	"Please list any specific educational or job experiences you may have acquired during military service that you believe would be useful in the job for which you are applying."	"Please list the dates and type of discharge you may have received from military service."	Minority service members have a higher percentage of undesirable military discharges. A policy of rejecting those with less than an honorable discharge may be discriminatory.
Hobbies, Clubs, and Organizations	"Do you have any hobbies that are related to the job for which you are making application?" "Please list any clubs or organizations in which you are a member that relate to the job for which you are applying."	"Please list any hobbies you may have." "Please list all clubs and other organizations in which you are a member."	If questions on club/organization memberships are asked, a statement should be added that applicants may omit those organizations associated with age, race, sex, or religion.
Credit Rating	None.	"Do you own your own car?" "Do you own or rent your residence?"	Use of credit rating questions tends to have an adverse impact on minority group applicants and has been found unlawful. Unless shown to be job-related, questions on car ownership, home ownership, length of residence, garnishments of wages, etc., may violate Title VII.

FIGURE 3-8
continued

Summary and Conclusions

Why Understanding the Legal Environment Is Important. Understanding and complying with human resource law is important because (1) it is the right thing to do, (2) it helps you realize the limitations of your firm's HR and legal departments, and (3) it helps you minimize your firm's potential liability.

Challenges to Legal Compliance. HR law is challenging for four reasons. Laws, regulations, and court decisions are all part of a dynamic legal landscape. The laws and regulations are complex. The strategies for fair employment required by the laws and regulations sometime compete with, rather than reinforce, one another. And laws often have unanticipated or unintended consequences.

Equal Employment Opportunity Laws. The following are the most important EEO laws: (1) Equal Pay Act of 1963—Prohibits discrimination in pay between men and women performing the same job in the same organization. (2) Title VII of the Civil Rights Act of 1964—Prohibits employers from basing employment decisions on a person's race, color, religion, sex, or national origin. It has been amended or interpreted to prohibit discrimination based on pregnancy (the Pregnancy Discrimination Act of 1978) and sexual harassment. Most recently, it has been amended by the Civil Rights Act of 1991, which places the burden of proof in a discrimination case squarely on the defendant (employer), prohibits the use of quotas, and allows for punitive and compensatory damages as well as jury trials. Executive Order 11246 prohibits discrimination against the same categories of people that Title VII protects, but also requires that government agencies and contractors take affirmative action to promote the employment of persons in protected classes. (3) Age Discrimination in Employment Act of 1967—Prohibits discrimination against employees who are 40 years old or older. (4) Americans with Disabilities Act of 1990—Prohibits discrimination against individuals with disabilities who can perform the essential functions of a job with or without reasonable accommodation. The Vocational Rehabilitation Act of 1973, the precursor to ADA, applied only to government agencies and contractors. (5) Vietnam Era Veterans Readjustment Act of 1974—prohibits discrimination against Vietnam-era veterans by federal contractors and requires federal contractors to take affirmative action to hire Vietnam-era veterans.

EEO Enforcement and Compliance. Two main agencies are responsible for enforcing EEO laws. The Equal Employment Opportunity Commission (EEOC) enforces EEO laws. It processes discrimination complaints, issues written regulations, and gathers and disseminates information. The Office of Federal Contract Compliance Programs (OFCCP) enforces the laws and executive orders that apply to the federal government and its contractors. The OFCCP also monitors the quality and effectiveness of affirmative action plans.

Other Important Laws. The Immigration Reform and Control Act of 1986 requires employers to document the legal work status of their employees. The Immigration Act of 1990 makes it easier for skilled immigrants to enter the United States. The Drug-Free Workplace Act of 1988 requires that government contractors try to ensure that their workplaces are free of drug use. The Uniformed Services Employment and Reemployment Act of 1994 protects the rights of private-sector employees who take short leaves to perform military service.

Avoiding Pitfalls in EEO. Employers can avoid many pitfalls associated with HR law by engaging in sound management practices. Among the most important of these practices are training, establishing an employee complaint resolution system, documenting decisions, communicating honestly with employees, and asking job applicants only for information the employer needs to know.

Key Terms

adverse impact, 91
affirmative action, 88
Age Discrimination in Employment Act (1967), 96
Americans with Disabilities Act (1990), 97
bona fide occupational qualification (BFOQ), 92
compensatory damages, 96
conciliation, 101
discrimination, 90
disparate treatment, 91
Equal Employment Opportunity Commission (EEOC), 100
Equal Pay Act (1963), 89
essential functions, 98
executive order, 96
fair employment, 88
four-fifths rule, 92
hostile work environment sexual harassment, 94
individuals with disabilities, 97
Office of Federal Contract Compliance Programs (OFCCP), 102
protected class, 90
punitive damages, 96
quid pro quo sexual harassment, 94
quotas, 96
reasonable accommodation, 99
reverse discrimination, 103
Title VII (Civil Rights Act of 1964), 90

Discussion Questions

1. Why should managers be concerned with understanding HR law instead of leaving it to the experts?
2. Explain why HR decisions are heavily regulated. Based on your analysis of current social forces, what new laws or regulations do you think will be passed or issued in the next few years?
3. You own a small construction business. One of your workers is 55 years old and had heart bypass surgery about six months ago. He wants to come back to work, but you are concerned that he will not be able to handle the job's physical tasks. What should you do? What are you prohibited from doing? What laws apply in this case?
4. What three steps are involved in developing an affirmative action program? How much flexibility does an employer have in developing the specific points in such a program?
5. Why do so many organizations use drug testing? Do you think that drug testing will be as common in ten years as it is today?
6. Should employers have a policy that prevents employees from dating each other? Would such a policy be legal? Would it be ethical?
7. How can an individual show prima facie evidence for adverse impact discrimination? How would an employer defend itself from this evidence?

MINICASE 1 *Disaccommodating an Employee and Inviting a Lawsuit*

Thomas Peterson began providing telephone counseling to small businesses at the University of Wisconsin–Madison Small Business Development Center in 1988. In December of 1991 he had a malignant brain tumor removed. On returning to work two months later, he asked for and received a 20% reduction in work and pay. He was fired in June 1992, after receiving a letter from the College of Business's associate dean asking him to work more hours—a request he declined.

Peterson filed suit under the ADA and reached a settlement with the university in February 1994. In addition to receiving a $200,000 payment, he was reinstated to a different job in the university, working about 13 hours a week (for an annual total of $11,667) and receiving full benefits.

Discussion Questions

1. What responsibility did Peterson's employer have under the ADA?
2. What should the university have done differently to avoid litigation?
3. How might an alternative dispute resolution service have helped to alter the outcome of this case?

Source: Adapted from *BNA's Employee Relations Weekly.* (1994, March 7). University worker to receive $200,000, reinstatement under settlement terms, *12,* 249–250.

MINICASE 2 *Wanted: Young, Male, Physically Fit Employees*

The New England Apple Council, Inc., a consortium of apple growers, submitted an "employee profile" to the Labor Department as part of an application to hire alien workers for seasonal picking jobs in 1994. The application was necessary because employers wishing to hire temporary alien workers must first describe their efforts to recruit U.S. citizens. The profile said that the growers "prefer male workers aged 22–40" who are "free from physical impairments of backs, limbs, eyes, ears, or any other condition which would make the individual unable to meet quality or quantity standards."

Discussion Questions

1. Which laws does the apple growers' statement of hiring preference appear to violate?
2. What were the apple growers trying to ensure with their statement? How could they have worded the statement to accomplish their goal while operating within EEO laws?

Source: Adapted from *BNA's Employee Relations Weekly.* (1994, April 4). New England apple growers warned on discriminatory hiring preferences, *12,* 369.

CASE 1 *Discrimination at Gemco, Inc.?*

Several African-American employees of Gemco, Inc., an electronics assembly and distribution facility, have filed a complaint with the EEOC because they feel that the company's promotion practices are racially biased.

Jeanne Phillips, the plant manager, is taken aback by the complaint. She was in charge when the current promotion policy was put in place, and she knows that it was carefully crafted to ensure equal employment opportunity. Employees are chosen for a supervisory training program based on their supervisors' evaluations. The performance appraisal form on which these evaluations are recorded asks supervisors to rate employees on each of the following ten dimensions on a five-point scale from "outstanding" to "unsatisfactory."

- Knowledge of work
- Dependability
- Productivity
- Safety
- Quality of output
- Cooperation
- Relationships with others
- Initiative
- Organizing and planning
- Judgment

The assumption behind the company's promotion policy—that supervisors are the people most qualified to decide which employees might make a good supervisor—has always seemed fair and reasonable to Phillips. However, she has to admit that only a very small percentage of the plant's African-American employees has been selected to enter the training program under this policy.

Critical Thinking Questions

1. What type of discrimination is being alleged by the African-American employees at Jeanne Phillips's plant?
2. If this case were to go to litigation, what features of the promotion decision process will the court be most likely to scrutinize?
3. How can the company defend itself in this discrimination case?

Cooperative Learning Exercise

4. Students form groups of six. Each group is given the task of suggesting ways to change the promotion decision process so that it is more legally defensible. Present the best suggestions to the class.

Source: Ledvinka, J., and Scarpello, V. G. (1991). *Federal regulation of personnel and human resource management* (2nd ed.). Boston: PWS Kent.

CASE 2 *An Ethical and Legal Dilemma*

Sheila Smith is the HR director for a medium-sized producer of sports apparel: T-shirts, sweats, shorts, and so on. The majority of the firm's 1,000 employees works at sewing machines, but the firm also employs designers, engineers, buyers, warehouse personnel, and the full complement of office and business personnel necessary to support the production operation.

Smith is concerned about her company's ability to comply adequately with the Americans with Disabilities Act. Her immediate concern deals with a request she just received from a local not-for-profit organization that provides vocational training to people with a wide variety of physical disabilities, including those who are blind, deaf, or wheelchair bound. Smith wants very much to explore the possibility of employing some of the graduates of this training program. But she is concerned that if she begins a relationship, she will saddle her company with ever-increasing and expensive accommodation demands from disabled applicants. If she opens the doors to persons who are disabled now, she wonders, will she be inviting ADA-related lawsuits later on?

Critical Thinking Questions

1. Are Sheila Smith's concerns justified?
2. What should Smith do now? What programs or activities should she initiate? What would be the HR department's responsibility in this situation?

Cooperative Learning Exercises

3. Students form groups of five and role-play a task force put together by Sheila Smith. This task force consists of employees from each of the company's major departments. Its purpose is to (1) explore ways in which the company can make itself more accessible to persons with disabilities and (2) air concerns about the new law.
4. Students form into pairs. One takes the role of Sheila Smith, the other the role of the director of the not-for-profit training center. Smith expresses her worries about getting the company into a situation that it may find difficult and expensive. The director tries to alleviate some of these concerns and to explain the responsibilities that ADA places on employers. Role-play the discussion between these two people.

HRM Simulation 

The company may select one of two strategies to achieve fair employment. In the first approach, the *ideal behavior strategy,* the company follows the guidelines in Equal Employment Opportunity law. In the second approach, the *affirmative action strategy,* the company takes a proactive stance in hiring women and minorities, including the establishment of hiring goals for these groups. (Refer to page 10 of the players' manual.) What are the costs and benefits of each approach? Which approach would you recommend for your company?

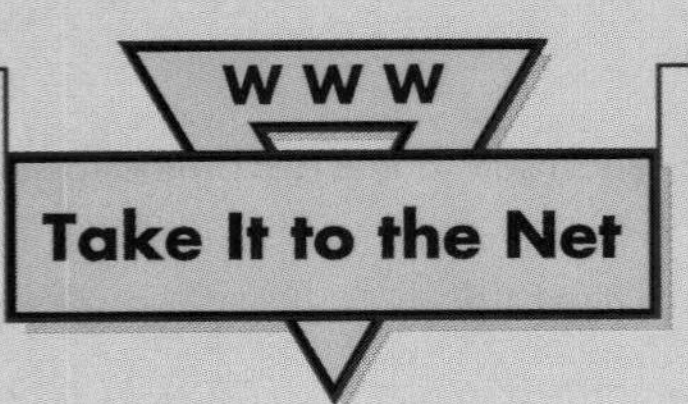

We invite you to visit the Gómez-Mejía/Balkin/Cardy page on the Prentice Hall Web site:

http://www.prenhall.com/gomez

You can also visit the Web sites for these companies, featured within this chapter:

Domino's Pizza	http://www.dominos.com
Honeywell	http://www.honeywell.com
Marriott	http://www.marriott.com
McDonald's	http://www.mcdonalds.com
McDonnell-Douglas	http://www.mdc.com

Endnotes

1. Commerce Clearing House. (1991). *Sexual harassment manual for managers and supervisors*. Chicago, IL.
2. *Id.*
3. Adapted from Commerce Clearing House. (1992). *Equal employment opportunity manual for managers and supervisors* (2nd ed.). Chicago, IL.
4. Adapted from *id.*
5. Hall, F. S., and Hall, E. L. (1994). The ADA: Going beyond the law. *Academy of Management Executive, 8*, 17–26.
6. Geyelin, M. (1993, December 17). Age-bias cases found to bring big jury awards. *The Wall Street Journal*, B1.
7. Serwer, A. E. (1993, July 12). What to do when race charges fly. *Fortune*, 95–96; Levinson, M. (1993, July 19). Always open to customers? *Newsweek*, 36; and Sniffen, M. J. (1994, May 25). Denny's will pay a record amount. *The Chattanooga Times*, A16.
8. Harris, N. (1996, March 25). A new Denny's—diner by diner. *Business Week*, 166–167.
9. *Griggs v. Duke Power Co.*, 401 U.S. 424 (1971).
10. *Wards Cove v. Antonio*, 109 S.Ct. 2115, 49 FEP CASES 1523 (1989).
11. Hall and Hall, 1994.
12. Greenlaw, P. S., and Kohl, J. P. (1995). The equal pay act: Responsibilities and rights. *Employee Responsibilities and Rights Journal, 8*, 295–307.
13. Harris, D. (1996, February). How does your pay stack up? *Working Woman*, 27–44.
14. *Id.*, 27.
15. Ledvinka, J., and Scarpello, V. G. (1991). *Federal regulation of personnel and human resource management*. (2d ed.). Boston: PWS-Kent; and Twomey, D. P. (1990). *Equal employment opportunity* (2nd ed.). Cincinnati, OH: South-Western.
16. *BNA's Employee Relations Weekly*. (1993, September 13). EEOC meets new, higher burden of proof in race bias case in California court. *11*, 1991.
17. *Griggs v. Duke Power Co.*, 401 U.S. 424 (1971).
18. *HR News*. (1994, February). No beard rule found to have disparate impact, 17.
19. *Albemarle Paper Co. v. Moody*, 422 U.S. 405 (1975).
20. *McDonnell Douglas Corp. v. Green*, 411 U.S. 792 (1973).
21. Equal Employment Opportunity Commission. (1978). *Uniform Guidelines on Employee Selection Procedures*, 29 Code of Federal Regulations, Part 1607, Sec. 6.A.
22. *Auto Workers v. Johnson Controls*, 1991, 55 FEP Cases 365–382.
23. *Id.*
24. Platt, H. A. (1994, March). Nonsexual harassment claims hit HR's desk. *HR Magazine*, 29–34.
25. *BNA's Employee Relations Weekly*. (1994, January 31). Medical center employee awarded $1 million in Massachusetts suit, *12*, 111–112.
26. *Harris v. Forklift Systems, Inc.* 114 S. Ct. 367 (1993).
27. *Human Resource Management Ideas and Trends*. (1996, February 14). Sexual harassment complaints no longer limited to women, 30.
28. *BNA's Employee Relations Weekly*. (1994, April 4). Survey finds 31 percent of women report having been harassed at work, *12*, 367.
29. *Wards Cove Packing Co. v. Antonio*, 409 U.S. 642 (1989).
30. Bureau of National Affairs. (1991, November 11). Civil rights act of 1991. *Employee Relations Weekly* (special supplement).
31. Carson, K. P. (1991, November 22). New civil rights law shoots itself in the foot. *The Wall Street Journal*, A10.
32. Geyelin, 1993.
33. Harper, L. (1994, April 5). Labor letter. *The Wall Street Journal*, A1.
34. Milkovich, G. T., and Newman, J. M. (1996). *Compensation* (5th ed.). Chicago: Irwin.
35. Sharpe, R. (1994, April 19). Labor letter. *The Wall Street Journal*, A1.
36. EEOC. (1992, January). *A technical assistance manual on the employment provisions of the Americans with Disabilities Act.*
37. Martinez, M. N. (1990, November). Creative ways to employ people with disabilities. *HRMagazine*, 40–44, 101.
38. *Id.*
39. EEOC, 1992.
40. Ledvinka and Scarpello, 1991.
41. Evans, S. (1994, March). Doing mediation to avoid litigation. *HRMagazine*, 48–51.
42. *Johnson v. Santa Clara County, Transportation Agency, Santa Clara County*, 107 S.Ct. 1442, 43 FEP Cases 411 (1987). See also Nazario, S. L. (1989, June 27). Many minorities feel torn by experience of affirmative action. *The Wall Street Journal*, A1; Roberts, S. V. (1995, February 13). Affirmative action on the edge. *U.S. News & World Report*, 32–38.
43. *Regents of the University of California v. Bakke*, 438 U.S. 265 (1978).
44. *The Economist* (1995, April 15). A question of colour, 13–14.

44a. Wynter, L. (1996, February 7). Business and race. *The Wall Street Journal*, B1.

45. Sovereign, K. L. (1994). *Personnel Law* (2nd ed.). Englewood Cliffs, NJ: Prentice Hall.
46. Ledvinka and Scarpello, 1991.
47. *BNA's Employee Relations Weekly*. (1994, March 28). Testing programs deter abuse, are cost effective, report says, *12*, 349.
48. *HR News*. (1994, March). Washington scorecard, *13*, 4.
49. Hall and Hall, 1994.
50. *HR News*. (1994, March). Legal report, 18.

Appendix to Chapter 3

Human Resource Legislation Discussed in This Text

The laws are listed in chronological order.

LAW	YEAR	DESCRIPTION	CHAPTER(S)
Workers' Compensation Laws	Various	State-by-state laws that establish insurance plans to compensate employees injured on the job	12, 15, 16
Social Security Act	1935	Payroll tax to fund retirement benefits, disability and unemployment insurance	12
Wagner Act	1935	Legitimized labor unions and established the National Labor Relations Board	14, 15
Fair Labor Standards Act	1938	Established minimum wage and overtime pay	10, 15
Taft-Hartley Act	1947	Provided some protections for employers and limited union power; permitted states to enact right-to-work laws	15
Landrum-Griffin Act	1959	Protects union members' right to participate in union affairs	15
Equal Pay Act	1963	Prohibits unequal pay for same job	3, 10
Title VII of Civil Rights Act	1964	Prohibits employment decisions based on race, color, religion, sex, and national origin	3, 4, 5, 7, 14, 16, 17
Executive Order 11246	1965	Same as Title VII; also requires affirmative action	3, 5
Age Discrimination in Employment Act	1967	Prohibits employment decisions based on age when person is 40 or older	3, 5
Occupational Safety and Health Act	1970	Establishes safety and health standards for organizations to protect employees	14, 16
Employee Retirement Income Security Act	1974	Regulates the financial stability of employee benefit and pension plans	12, 16
Job Training Partnership Act	1982	Provides block money grants to states, which pass them on to local governments and private entities that provide on-the-job training	8
Vietnam-Era Veterans Readjustment Act	1974	Prohibits federal contractors from discriminating against Vietnam-era veterans and encourages affirmative action plans to hire Vietnam veterans	3
Pregnancy Discrimination Act	1978	Prohibits employers from discriminating against pregnant women	3, 16
Consolidated Omnibus Budget Reconciliation Act	1985	Requires continued health insurance coverage (paid by employee) following termination	12
Immigration Reform and Control Act	1986	Prohibits discrimination based on citizenship status; employers required to document employees' legal work status	3, 17
Worker Adjustment and Retraining Act (WARN)	1988	Employers required to notify workers of impending layoffs	6
Drug-Free Workplace Act	1988	Covered employers must implement certain policies to restrict employee drug use	3, 16

(continued on page 114)

LAW	YEAR	DESCRIPTION	CHAPTER(S)
Americans with Disabilities Act	1990	Prohibits discrimination based on disability	3, 4, 5, 14, 16
Civil Rights Act	1991	Amends Title VII; prohibits quotas, allows for monetary punitive damages	3, 5
Family and Medical Leave Act	1993	Employers must provide unpaid leave for childbirth, adoption, illness	12, 15
Uniformed Services Employment and Reemployment Rights Act	1994	Employers must not discriminate against individuals who take leave from work to fulfill military service obligations	3

Laws discussed briefly:

Byrnes Antistrikebreaking Act—Chapter 15
Coal Mine Health and Safety Act—Chapters 4, 16
Employee Polygraph Protection Act—Chapter 5
Immigration Act of 1990—Chapter 3
Norris-LaGuardia Act—Chapter 15
Older Workers Protection Act of 1990—Chapter 3
Railway Labor Act—Chapter 15
Job Training Partnership Act of 1982—Chapter 8

4 Managing Diversity

CHALLENGES

After reading this chapter, you should be able to deal more effectively with the following challenges:

1 ▶ **Link** affirmative action programs to employee diversity programs to ensure that the two support each other.

2 ▶ **Identify** the forces that contribute to the successful management of diversity within the firm.

3 ▶ **Reduce** potential conflict among employees resulting from cultural clashes and misunderstandings.

4 ▶ **Draw** a profile of employee groups that are less likely to be part of the corporate mainstream and develop policies specifically targeted to these groups' needs.

5 ▶ **Implement** HR systems that assist the firm in successfully managing diversity.

Celebrating Diversity. The U.S. work force grows more diverse with each passing year. Progressive and effective companies recognize that this diversity can be the source of greater creativity, better problem solving, and increased enthusiasm in the workplace.

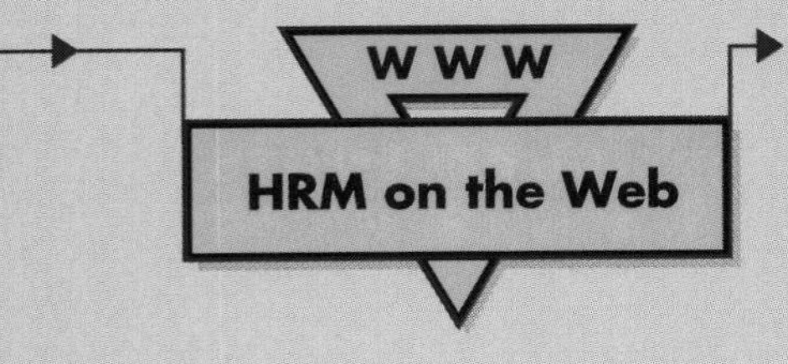

http://janweb.icdi.wvu.edu/kinder/

The Americans with Disabilities Act (ADA) Document Center

This home page provides links to numerous ADA resources, including sites concerned with specific disabilities such as HIV/AIDS, cancer, hearing impairment, visual impairment, mobility impairment, and alcohol and drug-related issues. The site also includes links to the Job Accommodation Network (JAN), which provides free technical support and assistance to people with disabilities and to businesses regarding how to fashion job site accommodations.

The second-grade schoolteacher posed a simple problem to the class: "There are four blackbirds sitting in a tree. You take a slingshot and shoot one of them. How many are left?"

"Three," answered the seven-year-old European with certainty. "One subtracted from four leaves three."

"Zero," answered the seven-year-old African with equal certainty. "If you shoot one bird, the others will fly away."

Which child answered correctly? Clearly, the answer depends on your cultural point of view. For the first child, the birds in the problem represented a hypothetical situation that required a literal answer. For the second child, the birds in the problem had a relationship to known behavior that could be expected to occur.[1]

The blackbird story clearly illustrates one of the most important truths of HRM: People with different life experiences may interpret reality very differently. By the time people enter an organization, their *cognitive structure*—the way they perceive and respond to the world around them—has been largely determined. This cognitive structure is shaped both by unique personal experiences (with family, peers, school system) and by the socializing influences of the person's culture, and it operates both at home and in the workplace.

Managing work force diversity in a way that both respects the employee and promotes a shared sense of corporate identity and vision is one of the greatest challenges facing organizations today. Most U.S. firms now have diverse work forces. In this chapter we examine the issues that diversity raises for managers. By the end of the chapter, you will understand diversity issues better and have some idea of how to handle them successfully.

What Is Diversity?

diversity
Human characteristics that make people different from one another.

Although definitions vary, **diversity** simply refers to human characteristics that make people different from one another. The English language has well over 23,000 words to describe personality[2] (such as "outgoing," "intelligent," "friendly," "loyal," "paranoid," and "nerdy"). The sources of individual variation are complex, but they can generally be grouped into two categories: those over which people have little or no control and those over which they have some control.[3]

Individual characteristics over which a person has little or no control include biologically determined characteristics such as race, sex, age, and certain physical attributes, as well as the family and society into which he or she is born. These factors exert a powerful influence on individual identity and directly affect how a person relates to other people.

In the second category are characteristics that people can adopt, drop, or modify during their lives through conscious choice and deliberate efforts. These include work background, income, marital status, military experience, political beliefs, geographic location, and education.

It is important to keep in mind the distinction between the sources of diversity and the diversity itself. Without this distinction, stereotyping tends to occur. Essentially, stereotyping is assuming that group averages or tendencies are true for each and every member of that group. For instance, employees who have had significant military experience are generally more accepting of an authoritarian management style than those who have not had such experience. However, if you conclude that *all* veterans favor authoritarian leadership, you will be wrong. While veterans *on average* are more accepting of authority, there may be, as Figure 4–1 shows, very wide differences among veterans on this score. True, veterans *on the whole* show this characteristic to a greater degree than nonveterans, but the differences *within* each group are far greater than the average difference between groups. In fact, many veterans develop a distaste for authoritarian management *because* of their military experience, and many nonveterans prefer an authoritarian leadership style.

If you take this example and substitute any two groups (male-female, young-old, and so on) and any individual characteristic (aggressiveness, flexibility, amount of education), you will find in the vast majority of cases that the principle illustrated by Figure 4–1 holds true. In fact, it is very difficult to identify individual characteristics that do *not* have a substantial overlap between two groups. The main point of this discussion is to emphasize that while employees are diverse, a relatively small amount of this diversity is explained by their group membership.

As we proceed through this chapter, we will point out some characteristics that are typical of specific groups. Such depictions are both valuable and dangerous. They are valuable because they alert managers to diversity in their employees. But they are dangerous because it is very easy to fall into the trap of assuming that a group tendency is true of all individual employees. The effective manager sees his or her employees as individuals, not as members of a particular group. As we saw in Chapter 3, it is illegal to base employment decisions on certain group characteristics. These laws merely codify an important principle of effective management: Treat people as individuals, not as representatives of a group.

Why Manage Employee Diversity?

Unless effectively managed, the presence of diversity among employees may create misunderstandings that have a negative impact on productivity and teamwork. It may also result in overt or subtle discrimination by those who control organizational resources against those who do not fit into the dominant group.

In addition to being illegal, excluding certain people from participation in an organization because of their group membership is counterproductive because it prevents effective people from contributing to or remaining with the organization. Consider Chris Powell, a young African-American man. After graduating from college, he landed a sales job at Ford Motor Company. Eager to advance, he often asked his supervisors for feedback. "I'd go and

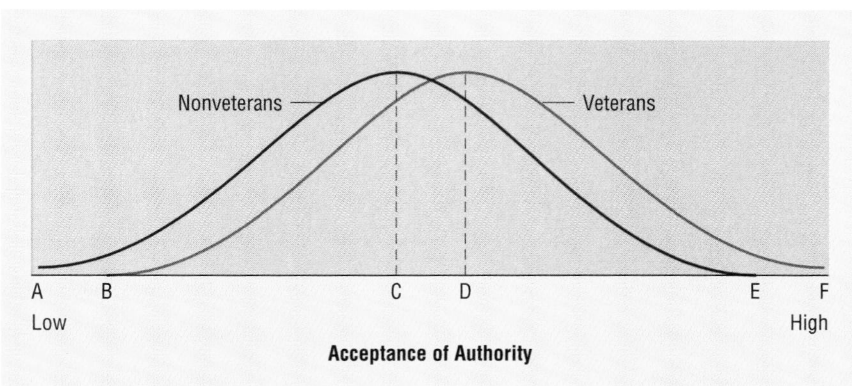

FIGURE 4-1

Group versus Individual Differences on Acceptance of Authoritarian Leadership

seek their counsel, but they would just say I was doing a fine job and should keep on doing it," Powell says. "No one offered any advice on how to get to the next step."

Then Powell's division was asked to push a slow-selling car. One of Powell's white coworkers learned that Ford was offering some promotion money to help salespeople with the sales pitch. The coworker tapped into the fund and won the contest. "That information came from someone who was watching out for him—and it gave him the edge," says a disappointed Mr. Powell. After three years at Ford, with no promotion in sight, Powell quit.[4]

To survive and prosper in an increasingly heterogeneous society, organizations must capitalize on employee diversity as a source of competitive advantage. For example, at Levi Strauss—one of the most ethnically and culturally diverse companies in the United States—promoting and valuing diversity not only makes good ethical sense but good financial sense as well. Levi Strauss executives say it's easier to develop and design merchandise for diverse markets when you understand them, and that understanding begins in the workplace.

Affirmative Action versus Managing Employee Diversity

Many people perceive *management of diversity* as a new label for affirmative action. In reality, these are two very distinct concepts. *Affirmative action* first emerged from government pressures on business to provide greater opportunities for women and minorities. **Management of diversity,** in contrast, recognizes that traditional firms, where white men are the majority, are becoming a thing of the past. There is a growing awareness that a key factor in corporate performance is how well *nontraditional employees* such as women and minorities can be fully integrated and work effectively with one another and with their white male counterparts.

management of diversity
The set of activities involved in integrating nontraditional employees (women and minorities) into the work force and using their diversity to the firm's competitive advantage.

The push behind managing employee diversity originated and found its strongest advocates among private corporations in the 1980s. It has continued today as the government's commitment to affirmative action has waned. Most corporations now see diversity management as a business necessity rather than a means to achieve social goals or meet government requirements (as many saw affirmative action). Several factors provide a rationale for diversity management. These include demographic trends, the need to view diversity as an asset, and marketing concerns.

Demographic Trends. The changing composition of the labor force is altering the employee landscape at a very rapid pace. Figure 4–2 presents data on the growth rates of various demographic groups and on their relative participation in the work force. Historical data are given for 1982 through 1993; projections are used for 1994 through 2005. We will refer to the data in this figure when we discuss specific groups later in this chapter. At this point, note the figures given in boldface type, which reflect the more startling changes. In the next decade or so, we will see a dramatic growth rate in people aged 55 or older (42.2%), though their rate of relative participation in the work force will rise far more modestly. Asian-Americans, Hispanic-Americans, and other ethnic minorities have shown very rapid growth rates since 1982, and these are projected to continue (at somewhat lower rates) into the next century. Both groups have registered increases in work force participation in recent years, and these are also expected to continue. White Americans will still make up a substantial majority of the work force in the year 2005 (73.7%), but less of a majority than in 1992 (76.7%). Women's participation rates are expected to keep rising and men's to go on declining.

Note that the data contained in the figure are national. If we focus on the larger metropolitan areas, where most large employers are located, the changes have been even more dramatic. Of the top 25 markets, "minorities" now make up a majority of the population in 16.[5] Figure 4–3 maps U.S. counties in which various minorities constitute from 25% to 75% of the population. In some states—most notably California, where nonwhites account for more than half of the population—the future is already here.

	GROWTH Actual 1982–1993	GROWTH Projected 1994–2005	PARTICIPATION Actual 1994	PARTICIPATION Projected 2005
AGE				
16–24	−17.2	11.0	16.5	16.3
25–54	30.9	7.6	71.6	68.7
55 and older	1.9	42.2	11.9	16.0
SEX				
Men	11.5	8.5	54.0	52.2
Women	22.3	16.6	46.0	47.8
RACE				
African-Americans	23.1	14.6	11.1	11.3
Asian-Americans and Other*	73.8	39.4	4.2	5.2
Hispanic-Americans	54.1	36.4	9.1	11.1
Non-Hispanic White Americans	13.7	7.8	76.7	73.7

*"Other" includes Asians, Pacific Islanders, Native Americans, and Alaskan Natives.

FIGURE 4-2

Growth and Participation in the U.S. Labor Force (Actual and Projected), 1982–2005

Source: *Monthly Labor Review*. (1995, November), 5.

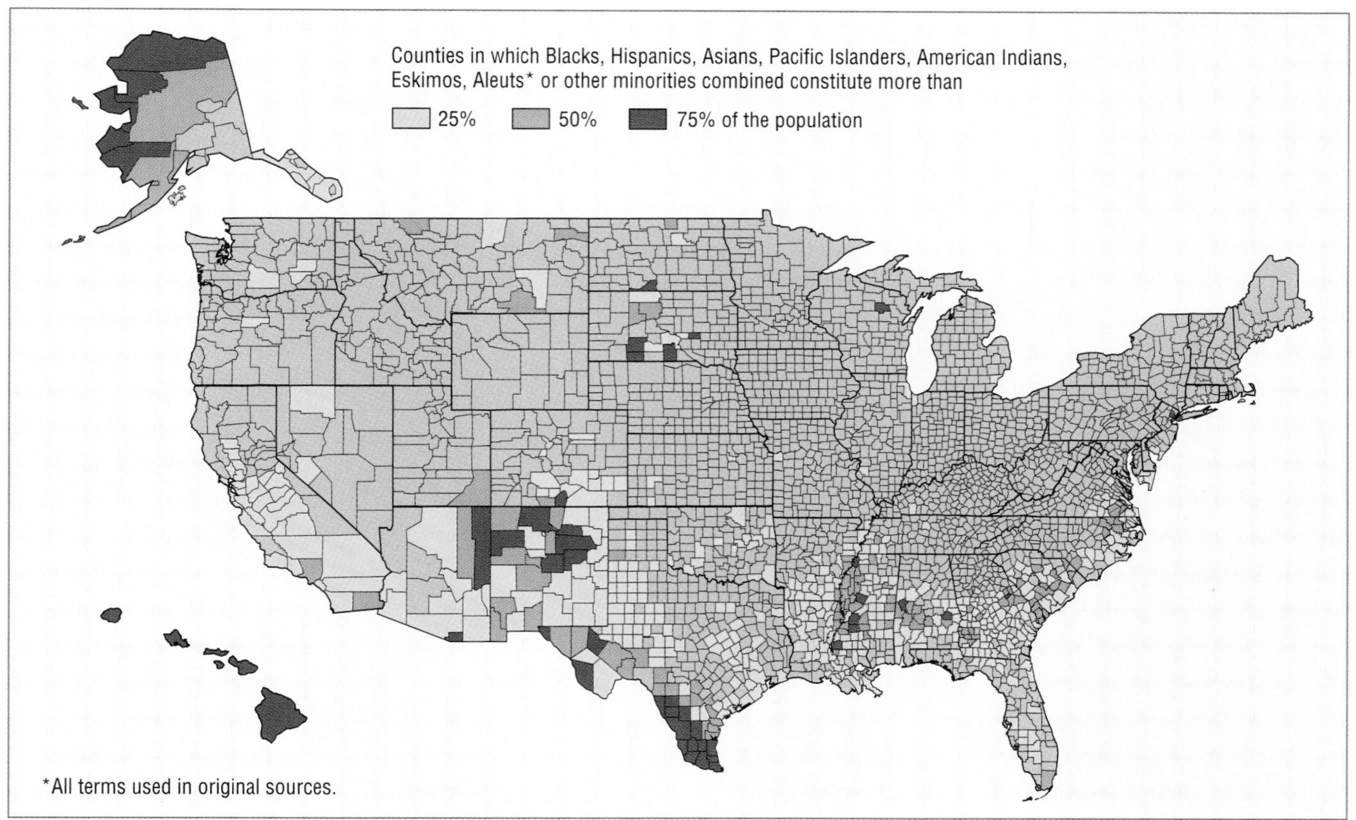

FIGURE 4-3

Diversity Map of the United States

Source: *Time* (1993, July 12), p. 15. Copyright 1993 Time Inc. Reprinted by permission.

Many Americans think of employee diversity in terms of poor minorities and women occupying relatively unskilled and low-paying positions, with professional and managerial jobs held by white men. This stereotype, while true in the past, is rapidly eroding. At Bell Laboratories, for instance, American-born physicists are in the minority. At Schering-Plough's research labs, the first language of biochemists is less likely to be English than Korean, Hindi, Chinese, Japanese, German, Russian, Vietnamese, or Spanish. Most U.S. doctorates in engineering are granted to people whose native language is not English and who came to the United States from non-European countries. Approximately 40% of corporate managers in the rapidly growing service sector are now women, almost twice as many as in 1976. Similarly, the percentage of these jobs held by minorities has almost doubled over the past 20 years, reaching approximately 12% in 1995.[6]

Of the 20-million-plus jobs projected to be created over the next decade, 75% will be filled by women and minorities. This means that firms must actively compete to attract and retain educated and talented workers from those groups. At Levi Strauss, for example, 56% of the company's 23,000 U.S. employees belong to minority groups—a far cry from 1908, when the company brochure advertised "none but white women and girls are employed."[7] Merck, Xerox, Corning, Chrysler, Philip Morris, Salomon Brothers, Sara Lee, Sears, Coca-Cola, IBM, Prudential, Digital, Syntex, and Hewlett-Packard are eagerly trying to create receptive environments for nontraditional employees.

Together, all these demographic changes are making it imperative that employers plan for the central role that diversity management will play in the twenty-first century. The forces of international competition (discussed in Chapter 17) are putting increased pressure on U.S. corporations to produce higher-quality products and services at reasonable prices and to accelerate the rate of technical innovations. The U.S. record against some foreign competition during the past quarter-century has been unimpressive.[8] U.S. corporations can help reverse this trend by viewing diversity as an asset and capitalizing on the different strengths it brings to the work force.

Diversity as an Asset. Once, diversity in the work force was thought to lead to garbled communications and conflict, and thus a less efficient workplace. Today, many firms realize that diversity can actually enhance organizational effectiveness. Employee diversity can improve organizational functioning by stimulating greater creativity, better problem solving, and greater system flexibility.[9] Rosabeth Kanter, a well-known business consultant based at Harvard University, notes that most innovative firms purposely establish heterogeneous work groups "to create a marketplace of ideas, recognizing that a multiplicity of points of views need to be brought to bear on a problem."[10]

- *Greater creativity.* Employee diversity can stimulate consideration of less obvious alternatives. Consider the following true story:

  > A Hispanic man and a white woman were members of a task force advising the CEO on a planned organizational downsizing. These two people suggested that the recommendation of the task force majority to lay off 10% of the work force would devastate morale. The majority, who were white men, initially felt that these two members were allowing their "soft hearts" to interfere with the need to make a hard-nosed business decision. Upon further consideration, the CEO decided not to lay off employees and opted instead for a plan proposed by these two dissenters. The plan proposed to reduce labor costs by offering early retirement, unpaid vacations, and stock in the firm to employees in exchange for a 5% salary cut. Most employees reacted very positively to the plan, with many reporting that it increased their loyalty and commitment to the firm.[11]

- *Better problem solving.* Homogeneous groups are prone to a phenomenon called *groupthink,* in which all members quickly converge on a mistaken solution because they share the same mindset and view the problem through the lens of conformity.[12] In a heterogeneous group with a broader and richer reservoir of experiences and cultural perspectives, the potential for groupthink shrinks.

- *Greater system flexibility.* In today's rapidly changing business environments, flexibility is an important characteristic of successful firms. If properly managed, employee diversity can infuse more flexibility into the firm. The existence of diversity at different levels generates more openness to new ideas in general and greater tolerance for different ways of doing things.

Marketing Concerns. It is easier for an organization to market products to a multicultural, multiethnic population when its own work force mirrors that diversity. For example, Equitable's Suquet Agency in Miami has 240 employees, 40% of whom are Latinos representing 12 different countries in a city where people of Hispanic descent are in the majority. According to Suquet's district manager, Alfredo Cepero, "It is essential that managers look beyond cloning themselves when hiring associates." He adds, "They should look for people that reflect the market. People with similar frames of mind, similar values and principles have a strong basis for communication, and communication is the art of sales."[13] This strategy has worked for Avon Corporation, which reports that its most profitable markets are in the inner city, where African-American and Latino managers and sales employees are Avon's top producers.[14]

Challenges in Managing Employee Diversity

Although employee diversity offers opportunities that can enhance organizational performance, it also presents managers with a new set of challenges. These challenges include appropriately valuing employee diversity, balancing individual needs with group fairness, dealing with resistance to change, ensuring group cohesiveness and open communication, avoiding employee resentment and backlash, retaining valued performers, and maximizing opportunity for all.

Valuing Employee Diversity

In some ways, the idea that diversity is good runs counter to the "melting pot" tradition—the notion that individuals should assimilate into the U.S. mainstream. The melting pot tradition makes some people uncomfortable with differences.[15] According to consultant Jo Vanderkloot, a major obstacle to managing diversity is embedded in "one of the hidden rules in American culture…that you don't comment on differences, because the differences mean a deficiency."[16]

In recent years the *"difference as deficiency" perspective* (which assumes that everyone, regardless of culture or race, should strive to be alike) has given way to *"difference as better" advocacy* in many quarters. Indeed, much of the rationale behind affirmative action in the 1970s and 1980s was based on the melting pot principle: Opening the corporate doors to women and minorities would give them the chance to assimilate into the existing corporate culture and learn the behaviors, skills, and strategies of the white men who had created and still maintained that culture.[17]

Recently the difference debate has become highly charged and politicized. Those who oppose diversity argue that the United States is losing the common ground necessary to a viable society, while those who advocate diversity argue that assimilation wrongly assumes a hierarchy of skills and behaviors with white men at the top and women and minorities below them. Organizations often find themselves attacked from both sides and frustrated in their attempts to manage employee diversity effectively. As one divisional manager of a major corporation says:

Many organizations have policies requiring that members of certain demographic groups (such as women and African-Americans) sit on certain (or all) committees. Are there any dangers to such a policy? Could the potential benefits outweigh the potential costs?

> I feel like as a company we are walking on eggshells all the time. No matter what we do someone will find it offensive. If we use the term "diversity" some people accuse us of trying to enforce political correctness. If we don't openly celebrate diversity, others will accuse us of being sexists and racists. This is a no-win proposition.[18]

Nonetheless, the United States has made more progress on the diversity front than other countries have. In Mexico, for example, management positions are reserved for Mexicans of European descent. In Japan it took an AT&T manager months to get Japanese managers to talk to key East Indian employees.[19]

Individual versus Group Fairness

An issue closely related to the "difference is divisive/better" debate is how far management should go in adapting HR programs to diverse employee groups. Should the company make the ability to speak Spanish a condition of employment for first-line supervisors who manage a large number of Latino employees? Should management require that appraisals of all African-American employees be reviewed by an African-American manager? Should the firm be more lenient about punctuality and deadlines for employees whose cultures are not time sensitive? Should management make dress code exceptions for employees who view coats and ties as European customs that do not fit their lifestyles? These questions are not hypothetical; in some organizations, they are being seriously debated.

universal concept of management
The management concept holding that all management practices should be standardized.

cultural relativity concept of management
The management concept holding that management practices should be molded to the different sets of values, beliefs, attitudes, and behaviors exhibited by a diverse work force.

The extent to which a **universal concept of management,** which leads to standardized management practices, should be replaced by a **cultural relativity concept of management,** which calls for molding management practices to the work force's different sets of values, beliefs, attitudes, and patterns of behaviors, is an extraordinarily complex question. The proponents of universalism believe that fitting management practices to a diverse work force sows the seeds for a permanent culture clash in which perceived inequities lead to intense workplace conflict. For instance, when the Lotus software company extended benefits coverage to homosexual couples, unmarried heterosexual employees living with a partner felt that they had been unfairly left out. Conversely, the proponents of relativity argue that failure to adapt HR practices to the needs of a diverse population may alienate much of the work force and reduce their potential contributions.

Resistance to Change

Although employee diversity is a fact of life, the dominant groups in organizations are still composed of white men. Some argue that a long-established corporate culture is very resistant to change, and that this resistance is a major roadblock for women and minorities seeking to survive and prosper in a corporate setting.

Group Cohesiveness and Interpersonal Conflict

Although employee diversity can lead to greater creativity and better problem solving, it can also lead to open conflict and chaos if there is mistrust and lack of respect among groups. This means that as organizations become more diverse, they face greater risks that employees will not work together effectively. Interpersonal friction rather than cooperation may become the norm.

Segmented Communication Networks

Shared experiences are often strongly reinforced by *segmented communication channels* in the workplace. One study found that most communication within organizations occurs between members of the same sex and race. This was found to be true across all professional categories, even at the top, where the number of women and minorities is very small.[20]

The presence of segmented communication poses three major problems to businesses. First, the organization cannot fully capitalize on the perspectives of diverse employees if they remain confined to their own groups. Second, segmented communication makes it more difficult to establish common ground across various groups. Third, women and minorities often miss opportunities or are unintentionally penalized for not being part of the mainstream communication networks.

A QUESTION OF ETHICS

Many managers and executives use golfing as an opportunity to combine business and pleasure. How could this practice damage an organization's diversity efforts?

Resentment

Although affirmative action is now decades old, it remains clouded in controversy. At the heart of this debate is the fact that equal employment opportunity (EEO) was imposed by government rather than self-initiated. In the vast majority of U.S. organizations, it was a forced change rather than a voluntary one. The response to this forced change was, in many cases, grudging compliance.[21]

One side effect of forced compliance has been the reinforcement of a belief among some managers and mainstream employees that organizations have to compromise their standards to comply with EEO laws. Some have seen EEO laws as legislating a "forced diversity" that favors political solutions over performance and/or competence.

Given this background, it is perhaps not surprising that twice as many white men as women and minorities feel that promotions received by the latter groups can be attributed to affirmative action.[22] This belief presents two problems. First, women and minorities in positions of authority and responsibility may not be taken as seriously as white men are. Second, the belief that white men are getting the short end of the stick may provoke some of them to vent their frustration against those employees (women and minorities) whom they believe are getting an unfair advantage.

It is important that managers deal with these issues because affirmative action is here to stay. A recent poll conducted by *Fortune* magazine found that 96% of CEOs would not change their affirmative action efforts, even if all federal enforcement was abolished.[23]

Backlash

Some white men feel that they have been made the scapegoats for society's ills, and that they have to defend themselves against encroachments by those using their gender or ethnicity to lay claim to organizational resources (such as promotions, salaries, and job security). Thus, while women and minorities may view a firm's "cultural diversity policy" as a commitment to improving their chances for advancement, white men may see it as a threat. Derogatory phrases such as "white male bashing" are often used by those who feel threatened by the diversity concept. Clearly, firms face a major challenge in trying to grapple with this backlash—which may be unwarranted, for white men still enjoy considerable advantages.[24] It is doubtful that a firm can effectively manage employee diversity if its white male employees (some of whom may be in positions of power) are hostile toward the concept.

Retention

The job satisfaction levels of women and minorities are often lower than those of white men. The main complaint among female and minority employees is that they lack career growth opportunities. This perception that their upward mobility is thwarted grows stronger at higher levels as women and minorities bump up against the **glass ceiling,** an intangible barrier within the organization that prevents them from rising to any higher position. Lower job satisfaction translates into higher resignation rates, with a resulting loss of valuable talent and greater training costs because of high turnover. At all organizational levels and ages, the turnover rate for African-Americans is approximately 40% higher than it is for whites. For women, the rate is more than twice as high as it is for white men.[25]

glass ceiling
The intangible barrier within an organization that prevents female and minority employees from rising to positions above a certain level.

The glass ceiling is not just a catch phrase; it reflects an undeniable reality. Women hold only 5% of the senior-level jobs in organizations, and African-Americans and other minorities fare even worse. They account for less than 3% of top jobs (which are defined as vice president and above.)[26]

A QUESTION OF ETHICS

What ethical problems might arise from giving preferential treatment to certain employees based on their group membership?

Competition for Opportunities

As minorities grow both proportionately and absolutely in the U.S. population, competition for jobs and opportunities is likely to become much stronger. Already there are rising tensions among minorities jockeying for advancement. Employers are being put into the uncomfortable position of having to decide which minority is most deserving.[27] Consider the following examples:

- "Blacks have been too successful at the expense of everyone else," grumbles Peter Rogbal, a Mexican-American captain in the San Francisco Fire Department. "Other groups have been ignored to placate the black community."
- In Los Angeles, black and white members of the Laborers Local 300 are suing to overturn a plan giving Latinos preference in winning unskilled construction work.
- In 1995 the Justice Department defended a black-only scholarship program at the University of Maryland. The plaintiff in the case was a Hispanic-American.[28]

There are no fail-proof techniques for effectively handling these challenges. There is, however, one principle that managers should always keep in mind: Treat employees as individuals, not as members of a group. With this principle as a guide, many of these challenges become much more manageable.

We now turn to a discussion of the concerns of specific employee groups. As you read this material; remember that discussions such as these necessarily make broad generalizations that can easily be misused. Our purpose is to give you some idea of the complexity of employee diversity, not to stereotype individuals.

▸ Diversity in Organizations

The elements of diversity—such as race, ethnicity, and gender—tend to have a profound impact on how people relate to one another. In this section we discuss (in alphabetical order) the groups that are most likely to be "left out" of the corporate mainstream. Of course, one individual may belong to several of these groups. For instance, a person could be an Amerasian (of American and Vietnamese parentage) woman who is legally blind (disabled) and who came to the United States five years ago (foreign born). This example highlights the limitations of group-based descriptions.

African-Americans

African-Americans constitute approximately 11% of the U.S. work force (see Figure 4–2) and about 11.5% of the U.S. population. After enduring centuries of forced slavery, they continued to experience outright discrimination until the 1960s. While there are still significant barriers to black advancement—including both blatant and subtle discrimination—many improvements have taken place in the last three decades. Since the passage of the Civil Rights Act of 1964, the number of African-American officials, managers, technicians, and skilled craftspeople has tripled, while the number in clerical positions has quadrupled and the number in professional jobs has doubled.[29] However, a significant percentage of African-Americans (perhaps as high as 25%) are among the "hardcore" unemployed.

African-Americans face two major problems in organizations. First, explicit, intentional racism still exists some 40 years after the first civil rights victories. African-Americans are not the only group to suffer from blatant racism, but it is safe to say that they are the group that suffers the most. The persistence of the Ku Klux Klan and other white supremacy organizations serves as a constant reminder, to both African-Americans and U.S. society as a whole, that the struggle for civil rights is not over. Managers need to be careful to reassure their African-American employees, and the entire organization, that racist views will not be tolerated in the workplace.

The second problem African-Americans face as a group is less educational preparation than whites. This is not an issue unique to blacks. As Figure 4–4 shows, people of Hispanic origin also have less educational preparation for the workplace than whites do. Because of the increasing importance of technology and information in the U.S. economy, the discrepancy between the wage rates of college-educated and non-college-educated workers is growing. Therefore, the differential in educational preparation between African-Americans (and Hispanic-Americans) and whites puts the former at a severe disadvantage in the labor market. The poverty rate among African-Americans is twice that of whites.[30] The typical college-educated African-American worker making $25,000–$50,000 a year has a net worth of $17,000; the typical white college-educated worker earning the same salary has a net worth of $74,000.[31]

Still, there is some reason for optimism. A 1995 survey of large employers shows that African-Americans' share of management jobs has increased fivefold since 1966.[32] Before World War II, just 5% of African-Americans were in the middle class. Today, that number is close to 60 percent.[33] Finally, the percentage of African-Americans completing four or more years of college has quadrupled since 1950.[34]

Asian-Americans

Americans of Asian descent constitute approximately 4.2% of the U.S. work force and approximately 3.6% of the U.S. population. Their representation in the labor force almost doubled from 1982 to 1993, and is projected to increase by another 39.4% by 2005 (see Figure 4–2). Although Asian-Americans have done well in technical fields and are very well represented in institutions of higher education, they are underrepresented in top corporate positions. Employer discrimination probably accounts for this to some extent, for Asian-Americans are often stereotyped as being too cautious and reserved to lead.[35] They also suffer from the belief held in some quarters that, because of their educational attainments, they are an advantaged group and therefore do not deserve special consideration in hiring and promotion decisions. As a result, they are less likely to benefit from programs intended to improve the employment conditions of women and other minorities. Finally, one survey found that 40% of African-Americans and Hispanic-Americans and 27% of whites saw Asian-Americans as "unscrupulous, crafty, and devious in business."[36] For all these reasons, some Asian-Americans are relegated to technical and support positions that require minimal interpersonal interactions and offer limited opportunities for advancement.

Percent distribution of young workers aged 14 to 22 by sex, race, or Hispanic origin, and educational attainment in 1990

Worker Characteristic	Less Than High School	High School Graduate	Some College	College Graduate
Total	12.7	45.4	20.7	21.2
Men	13.9	45.7	19.5	20.9
Women	11.1	44.8	22.3	21.8
White	10.6	44.8	20.4	24.2
Black	16.7	46.2	20.4	11.7
Hispanic	22.6	47.8	21.2	8.4

FIGURE 4-4

Educational Preparation of Selected Worker Groups

Source: Veum, J. R., and Weiss, A. B. (1993, April). Education and the work histories of young adults. *Monthly Labor Review*, 14.

Most Asian immigrants to the United States today are from the Philippines, Indonesia, Sri Lanka, and Thailand. At least half of these immigrants are women, many of whom end up working for very low wages in high-pressure industries like the garment business.[37]

People with Disabilities

There are approximately 43 million people with disabilities in the United States, 15 million of whom are actively employed and six million of whom subsist on social security payments and disability insurance.[38] The remainder are either unemployed (presumably supported by their families) or under working age. People who are physically disabled face four main problems at work.

First, social acceptance of disabilities hasn't advanced much since the dark ages.[39] Many people still view people with disabilities with suspicion, even scorn, feeling that those who are physically impaired should stay away from the work world and let "normal" people assume their duties. At a more subtle level, coworkers may not befriend employees with disabilities because they simply don't know how to relate to them. Even extroverts can suddenly become shy in front of the disabled.

Second, people with disabilities are often seen as being less capable than others. This misconception persists even though the legally blind and deaf can perform many tasks just as well as those with normal sight and hearing, and modern technology allows many paralyzed people to run computers.

Third, many employers are afraid to hire people with disabilities or put them in responsible positions for fear that they may quit when work pressures mount. This myth persists despite the fact that absenteeism and turnover among such employees are only a fraction of those of other employees. For instance, Marriott Corporation reports that turnover among employees with disabilities is only 8% annually, compared to 105% among workers in general.[40] Pizza Hut has also found a huge difference in turnover rates: 20% for employees with disabilities versus more than 200% for employees without disabilities.[41]

Fourth, many employers have overestimated the costs of accommodating employees with disabilities ever since the passage of the Americans with Disabilities Act in 1990. In fact, employers have found that accommodations are usually simple and quite cheap. For instance, Griener Engineering, Inc., in Irving, Texas, installed a lighter-weight door on the

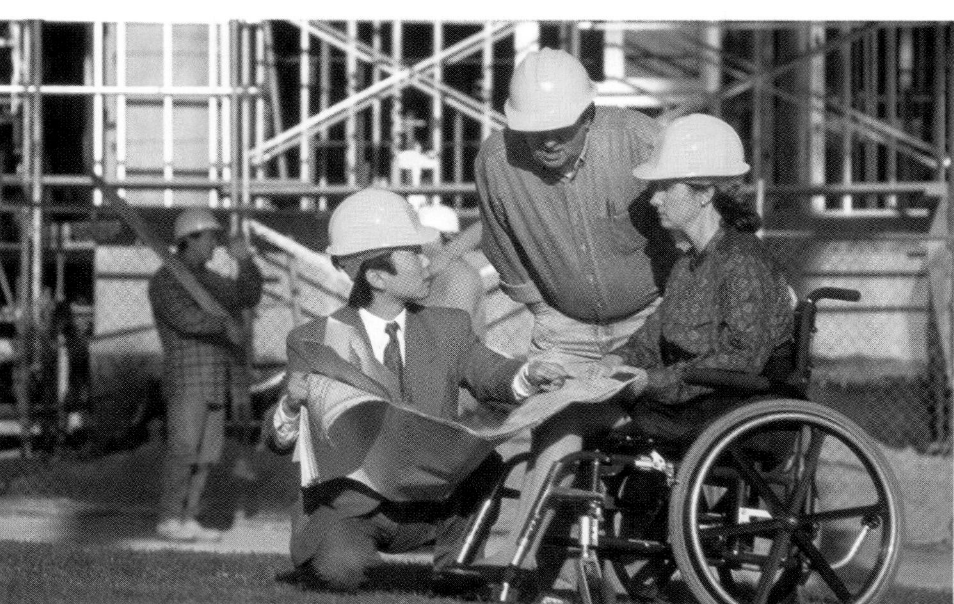

Accomodating People with Diasabilities.

Many employers have overestimated the costs of accommodating employees with disabilities. One report indicates that 31% of all accommodations cost nothing at all, and fewer than 1% cost more than $5,000.

women's restroom and raised a drafting table by putting bricks under its legs. The HR director at Exabyte, a manufacturer of computer storage tape drives in Boulder, Colorado, said that the accommodations the company has made for its five deaf workers are "things you'd have to be a Scrooge not to do." They include hiring a translator for meetings and offering sign language classes to other staffers.[42]

The Foreign Born

At least 10% of the U.S. population is foreign born. Reliable statistics are hard to come by because of illegal immigration and census undercounts (fearing legal reprisal, many undocumented workers wish to remain incognito), but at least 25 million immigrants have come to the United States over the past 25 years.[43] In addition, half a million foreign students on temporary visas are attending U.S. universities at any one time, and many of these people remain in the United States after obtaining their degrees. Regardless of their parents' legal status, all children born in the United States are automatically U.S. citizens under the U.S. Constitution.

The United States is a nation of immigrants, and those coming to the country increase the U.S. supply of labor. Most of the world continues to view the United States as a land of opportunity because political barriers are low and opportunities for advancement are great. Nonetheless, many immigrants face significant barriers because of their language difficulties, race or ethnicity (most are non-Europeans), and cultural differences. Many illegal immigrants work very hard in jobs with low wages, and often do not collect benefits. In addition, they often meet with resentment from whites and other minorities who feel that the newcomers are taking jobs away from them.

Certain myths about foreign-born workers need to be debunked. First, it is not true that all immigrants are uneducated. An Urban Institute study, which screened newcomers from such countries as Mexico and El Salvador, found that 79% of adult immigrants had high school diplomas and 33% had college degrees.[44] Second, there is not a higher proportion of immigrants on public assistance today than at the beginning of the century. In 1909, more than 50% of welfare recipients were immigrants; today only 9% of immigrant families receive public assistance. This figure compares to 7.4% of households headed by the native-born.[45]

Homosexuals

While early research dating to the 1940s suggested that about 10% of the population is gay, there is considerable debate about the true percentage, with estimates ranging from 1–2% to 10%.[46] In recent years gay advocacy groups have become very outspoken about their rights, arguing that sexual preference should not be a criterion for personnel-related decisions. But homosexuality is still taboo in many workplaces.

Gays have little legal protection at present. There is no federal law to prevent overt discrimination against homosexuals, and only six states (Connecticut, Massachusetts, Minnesota, New Jersey, Wisconsin, and Hawaii) have such antidiscrimination laws on their books. Currently, the U.S. military has a controversial "don't ask, don't tell" policy that prevents gay soldiers from openly discussing their sexual orientation, but also prohibits inquiries about the sexual orientation of new or current enlistees. Many other organizations have explicit or implicit policies against the hiring or retention of homosexuals, even if they do not discuss their homosexuality.

Homosexuals face three problems in the workplace. The first is outright refusal to hire or retain homosexual employees (which is not illegal in 44 states). The second is intolerance from workers or managers in companies that do not have explicit policies forbidding discrimination against gays. Third, AIDS is adding fear to prejudice. These problems have a chilling effect that causes many gay people to stay in the closet for fear of being fired or ostracized at work.

In most jobs sexual preference per se is not likely to affect work performance, so companies that practice discrimination in hiring or promotion may be robbing themselves of valuable employees. Still, in firms that do not practice discrimination or have explicit policies against it (such as Apple Computer), managers may face difficulties in integrating openly gay employees into heterosexual teams that are intolerant of homosexuals.

Latinos (Hispanic-Americans)

The label Hispanic is of recent vintage, encompassing those individuals whose declared ancestors or who themselves came from Latin American countries. The label Latino is the term that these groups (both in the United States and abroad) have traditionally used for cultural self-definition and to distinguish their cultural identity from that of non-Latino North Americans. The label Hispanic, the official label used by the U.S. government, is "essentially a term of convenience for administrative agencies and researchers."[47]

A mistake people sometimes make is to equate the term Hispanic with race, something that many Latinos find offensive. Latinos include people of European descent (there are at least 70 million of them in Latin America) and African descent (there are at least 25 million living in the Spanish-speaking Antilles and the Caribbean basin), as well as Latin Indians (who make up a very large proportion of the Mexican and Andean population), Asians (there are probably 10 million Asians of Hispanic descent), and a very large number of people of mixed origin. In fact, most Latinos do not divide people into exclusive racial categories (for example, white or black), but see them as a blend of various racial traits. In some Spanish-speaking Caribbean countries like Cuba, Puerto Rico, and the Dominican Republic, there may be as many as ten different terms to designate people of mixed African and European descent based on physical features. In short, it is very difficult to draw a portrait of a "typical" Latino.[48]

There are at least 25 million Latinos in the United States. Their current rate of work force participation is 9.1%, and the projected rate for 2005 is 11.1% (see Figure 4–2). The U.S. Latino population is very diverse. Under this umbrella one finds individuals whose families were in the United States prior to the country's independence and others who arrived a month ago. Many Latinos are professionals and entrepreneurs; others are unskilled laborers and farmers. One also finds large differences in income. At the high end of the scale are upper- and middle-class Cubans who came to the United States in the aftermath of the 1959 Cuban Revolution; on the low end are migrant workers.

Latinos face a number of problems in the U.S. workplace. One is language.[49] More than any other immigrant group (perhaps because of their segregated urban enclaves, large numbers, and geographical proximity to Latin America), Latinos tend to retain their native language as the primary language at home. As a result, many have a limited proficiency in English, which hinders employment opportunities and can be a source of discrimination at work. Second, cultural clashes may occur because of value differences. Some Latinos see non-Latino North Americans as unemotional, insensitive, self-centered, rigid, and ambitious to the point where they live to work rather than the other way around. Meanwhile, non-Latinos often complain that with Latinos "punctuality, absenteeism, planning, and scheduling can be a lot more loose than one would expect."[50]

Third, Latinos of African or Latin American Indian descent (many of whom migrate to the United States because of their extreme poverty at home) often face an additional hurdle: racial discrimination because of their skin color. This may occur both within the Latino community and in the larger society.

All of these challenges do not negate the noteworthy progress that Latinos have made in recent years. The largest 500 Latino-owned firms in the United States export more than $1 billion worth of goods each year, generating many U.S. jobs in the process.[51] In 1996, there were 217 Latino senior executives at *Fortune* 1000 firms, a 28% increase over two years earlier.[52] A Latino, Roberto Goizueta, is CEO of one of the world's most profitable companies: Coca-Cola.

Older Workers

The U.S. work force is getting older. The average U.S. worker is 38 and 45% of employees are over the age of 40. Older workers face several important challenges in the workplace. First, the United States is a youth-oriented culture that has not yet come to terms with its changing demographics. Starting around the age of 40, but particularly after the age of 50, employees encounter a number of stereotypes that may block their career advancement. Among the most common negative assumptions about older workers are that they are:

- Less motivated to work hard.
- "Dead wood."
- Resistant to change and can't learn new methods.
- "Fire proof."[53]

These negative characterizations are not supported by research. In fact, one of the most stunning economic achievements in U.S. business in the last decade—the turnaround of manufacturing productivity and growth—has been accomplished at plants staffed predominantly by older assembly-line workers.[54]

Second, *generational conflict* may arise. Older workers sometimes feel that their position and status are threatened by "young bucks" eager to push "over-the-hill" employees out of the way. This tension can negatively affect the cohesiveness of teams and work units. It can also sour the relationship between boss and subordinate.

Third, although many older workers are in good health, this group is more susceptible to physical problems. Often they are forced to step down from their jobs because the firm cannot and/or will not find appropriate opportunities for them to use their seasoned judgment, knowledge, and ability to serve as mentors for new workers.

Many companies find that accommodating the physical problems and limitations of aging workers pays off. At Alcoa's plant in Davenport, Iowa, where the average age of workers is 47, strains and sprains were becoming a chronic problem. Since the company asked all 2,500 workers to attend a "back class," injuries have declined.[55] It is important to point out, however, that most older workers, particularly those in nonphysical jobs, function as well as they did 20 or 30 years ago. This fact underscores our general theme that it is necessary for managers to treat employees as individuals, not as members of a group or class.

Women

One of the most important U.S. demographic changes over the past 30 years has been the influx of women into the work force. Since 1970, the percentage of women in the labor force has doubled. Women now make up 46% of the U.S. work force, and that percentage is expected to rise to nearly 48% by 2005 (see Figure 4–2).[56] Unfortunately, women's earnings have not mirrored this participation trend. After falling to a low of 59% of male earnings in 1975, the female-to-male earnings ratio rose slowly and is now 71%, just a few points above its level in 1920 (63%), when only 20% of women were in the labor force.[57]

There may be reason for optimism, however. A recent survey showed that women's share of management jobs has increased threefold since 1966.[58] The number of women and minorities on corporate boards of directors jumped 29% between 1992 and 1994.[59] And 55% of employed women bring in half or more of their total household income.[60]

Still, there is no doubt that most women still earn considerably less than their male counterparts. Other than overt sex discrimination (which is, of course, illegal), several factors may account for the earnings differential between women and men and women's lack of upward mobility. These include biological constraints and social roles, a male-dominated corporate culture, exclusionary networks, and sexual harassment.

Biological Constraints and Social Roles. Obviously, only women can become pregnant and give birth. But even after three decades of feminism, women continue to encounter a fairly rigid set of expectations regarding their roles and behavior that extend far beyond these biological constraints. Women are still primarily responsible for taking care of the children and performing most household duties, while men are still expected to "bring home the bacon" and handle yard work. In survey after survey, men say a woman's place is in the home.[61]

Perhaps reflecting these societal norms, organizations have traditionally failed to be flexible enough to meet the needs of working women. Only a tiny proportion of companies provide day care and other support options (such as job sharing and reduced work hours for employees with young children). For this reason, many talented and highly educated women are forced to curtail their career aspirations and/or quit the organization in their late 20s or early to mid-30s—crucial years in one's career—if they wish to have a family. Practically all male top managers are married and have children, while the majority of women who make it to the top are single and childless.

A Male-Dominated Corporate Culture. Most women perceive a male-dominated corporate culture as an obstacle to their success.[62] However, most gender differences are not related to performance, particularly in white-collar occupations, where sheer physical strength is seldom required.

A number of studies have shown that men tend to emerge in leadership positions in U.S. culture because they are more likely than women to exhibit traits that are believed to "go hand in hand" with positions of authority. These traits include: (1) more aggressive behaviors and tendencies; (2) initiating more verbal interactions; (3) focusing remarks on "output" (as opposed to "process") issues; (4) less willingness to reveal information and expose vulnerability; (5) a greater task (as opposed to social) orientation; and (6) less sensitivity, which presumably enables them to make tough choices quickly.[63] Thus, cultural expectations may create a self-fulfilling prophecy, with individuals exhibiting the "female traits" of focusing on process, social orientation, and so on more likely to be relegated to operational and subordinate roles.

old boys' network
An informal social and business network of high-level male executives that typically excludes women and minorities. Access to the old boys' network is often an important factor in career advancement.

Exclusionary Networks. Many women are hindered by lack of access to the **old boys' network,** the informal relationships formed between male managers and executives. As we noted earlier in this chapter, most communication at work takes place within groups of members of the same sex. This happens even at the highest organizational levels. Because most high-level positions are filled by men, women are often left out of the conversations that help men get ahead.[64] During a gender-awareness workshop at Corning, for example, women executives complained that their male colleagues never invited them to lunch. These women felt that they were missing out on the opportunity to get vital insider gossip, such as news of an employee's imminent transfer or of the boss's interest in a new product category.[65]

Sexual Harassment. Women have to confront sexual harassment to a much greater extent than men do. Women have had to forfeit promising careers because they would not accept the sexual advances of men in positions of power and did not feel they had any recourse but to quit their jobs. Anita Hill's testimony at the Clarence Thomas Supreme Court confirmation hearings in October 1991 was a national turning point on this issue. Since the hearing, many more women have come forward with complaints about sexual harassment in the workplace.

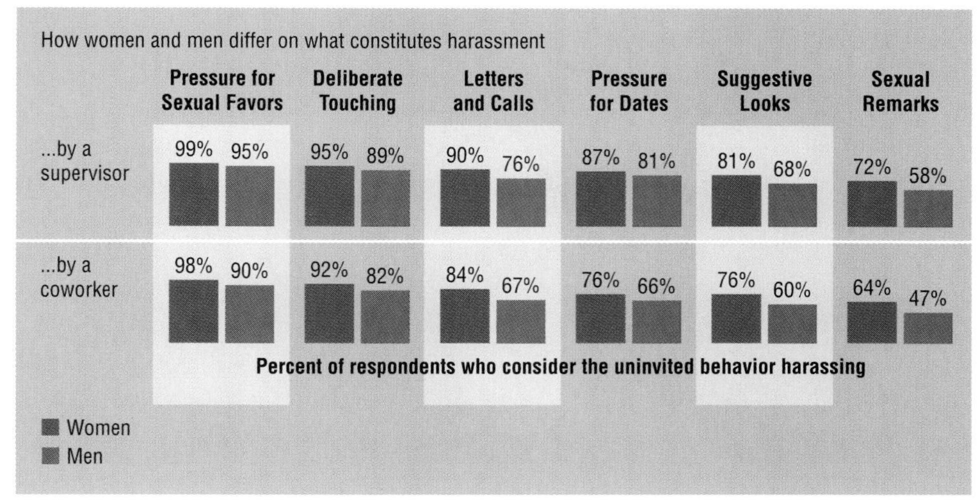

FIGURE 4-5

Male and Female Views of Sexual Harassment

Source: Deutschman, A. (1991, November). Dealing with sexual harassment. *Fortune*, 145.

Businesses have been getting tougher on this issue by crafting stronger sexual harassment policies and setting up intensive seminars for employees. These educational efforts are particularly important because men and women often have different notions of what kind of behavior constitutes sexual harassment (see Figure 4–5). Du Pont's anti-sexual harassment program, titled "A Matter of Respect," uses video scenes of sexual harassment to get male and female employees to discuss specific actions. For instance, in one scene a woman sales representative is ready to close an important deal with a client in a hotel dining room when the client asks, "Why don't we go upstairs and talk about this some more?" At this point the trainer stops the video and encourages the group to discuss what the woman should do.[66]

Building Managerial Skills: Improving the Management of Diversity

Organizations that have made the greatest strides in successfully managing diversity tend to share a number of characteristics. These are a commitment from top management to valuing diversity, diversity training programs, employee support groups, accommodation of family needs, senior mentoring and apprenticeship programs, communication standards, organized special activities, diversity audits, and a policy of holding management responsible for the effectiveness of diversity efforts.

Top-Management Commitment to Valuing Diversity

It is unlikely that division managers, middle managers, supervisors, and others in positions of authority will become champions of diversity unless they believe that the chief executive officer and those reporting to the CEO are totally committed to valuing diversity. Xerox, Du Pont, Corning, Procter & Gamble, Avon, the *Miami Herald,* Digital Equipment Corporation, U.S. West, and other pacesetters in the successful management of diversity all have CEOs who are fully dedicated to putting this ideal into practice. For example, Avon has established a multicultural participation council (which includes the CEO) that meets regularly. Similarly, in a startling ten-page color brochure, the CEO of Corning announced that management of diversity is one of Corning's three top priorities, alongside total quality management and a higher return to shareholders. Figure 4–6 on page 132 shows an advertisement used by The Quaker Oats Company to signal top management's commitment to diversity.

FIGURE 4-6
Quaker Diversity Ad
Source: © The Quaker Oats Company. Reprinted with permission.

Diversity Training Programs

diversity training programs Programs that provide diversity awareness training and educate employees on specific cultural and gender differences and how to respond to these in the workplace.

Supervisors need to learn new skills that will enable them to manage and motivate a diverse work force. Ortho Pharmaceuticals, Hewlett-Packard, Wells Fargo, Kaiser Permanente, and other companies have developed extensive in-house **diversity training programs** that provide awareness training and workshops to educate managers and employees on specific cultural and gender differences and how to respond to these in the workplace.[67] A recent survey of CEOs found that the most common reason for implementing diversity training programs was "tapping diverse customers and markets" (44%). Only 2.9% of respondents indicated the avoidance of litigation as a reason.[68]

Much experimentation in this type of training is occurring around the United States. Du Pont has sponsored an all-expense-paid conference for African-American managers to discuss the problems they encounter and how they can contribute more to the firm. AT&T has offered homophobia seminars designed to help straight employees feel comfortable working alongside openly gay employees and to eliminate offensive jokes and insults from the workplace.[69] Corning has introduced a mandatory four-day awareness training program for some 7,000 salaried employees—a day and a half for gender awareness, two and a half days for ethnic awareness.[70] In one of the most creative programs of this kind, Ethicon, Inc., a subsidiary of Johnson & Johnson that makes sutures, requires each supervisor to assume the identity of an employee of different ethnicity or gender and role-play accordingly.

Diversity training is also gaining a toehold in smaller companies, where managing diversity is not a "frill" or an "extra" but a survival tactic. At Cardiac Concepts, a Texas outpatient laboratory, most of the 11 employees are women and minority members representing half a dozen different religious faiths. At one time, religious squabbles were common. Owner Emma Colquitt did what many large companies are doing: She hired a consultant to give her diverse workers a course on how to get along.

Large companies may pay $50,000 and upward for outside diversity trainers, depending on the number of employees included in the training and the length of the sessions. Companies that are known for their success at diversity management generally do not rely on one-shot workshops. Rather, they use these as part of an ongoing effort. "The biggest myth is that we [give] the training, we hold hands and sing 'We are the World,' and things are all better—but that's not true," says Hattie Hill-Storks, a copartner at the International Productivity Institute. "If the boss uses diversity training as a Band-Aid, the problems often recur."[71]

Support Groups

Some employees perceive corporate life as insensitive to their culture and background, perhaps downright hostile. The perception of an attitude that says "You don't belong here" or "You are here because we need to comply with government regulations" is largely responsible for the high turnover of minorities in many corporations.

To counteract these feelings of alienation, top management at many firms has been setting up **support groups**. These groups are designed to provide a nurturing climate for diverse employees who would otherwise feel shut out. These groups also provide a way for employees with the same ethnic or racial background or sexual orientation to find one another in the vast corporate bureaucracy. The following examples illustrate how these employee support groups operate:

support group
A group established by an employer to provide a nurturing climate for employees who would otherwise feél isolated or alienated.

- Allstate employees from Spanish-speaking backgrounds in Miami can join a support group called HOY (translated as "today" in English), or Hispanics Organized for You. Members meet monthly to socialize, build internal networks and contacts with other Hispanics at Allstate, and serve as a "sounding board" for new ideas.[72]
- In addition to having their own in-house support groups, Digital Equipment Corporation's DEC PLUS (for People Like Us)—whose members are gay and lesbian employees—communicate openly with one another through an electronic bulletin board, with management approval. Likewise, Xerox's gay computer bulletin board might include a note cautioning members that it is less acceptable to be openly gay when visiting Rank Xerox, the company's British arm, or a greeting from an employee new to the group.[73]

Accommodation of Family Needs

Firms can dramatically cut the turnover rate of their female employees if they are willing to help women handle a family and career simultaneously. Employers can use the following options to assist women in this endeavor. Unfortunately, most organizations do not yet offer these services.[74]

To what extent should employers be responsible for the appropriate care of their employees' children?

Day Care. Perhaps the best way to make it easier for women to keep their jobs after starting a family is to provide day care. Yet only about 6% of the nation's major employers provide any sort of day-care assistance.[75] Even among this group of firms, only a handful (including Merck and Campbell's Soup) have day-care centers at the workplace. The U.S. government has a "hands off" policy on day care. This is in sharp contrast with most other industrialized countries, where the government takes an active role in the provision of day care. (For more details, see the Issues and Applications feature on page 134 titled "What European Countries Do for Mum, Maman, Mütter, and More...").

Issues + Applications

What European Countries Do for Mum, Maman, Mütter, and More...

When it comes to creating a family-friendly workplace, more than an ocean separates U.S. and European companies. Unlike the United States, many European countries have provisions for maternity leave, child care, and flexible schedules—and they've had them in place for years. For example:

- Germany adopted its maternity leave law back in 1878. German women receive six weeks' prenatal leave at full pay and eight weeks postnatal leave, also at full pay. After mothers return to work, they get time off to breastfeed. In addition, there is a three-year parental leave for all working parents, both male and female.
- Sweden was the first nation to broaden extended postnatal maternity leave to "parental leave," for either the mother or the father, or for both alternately. Today Swedish parents are guaranteed a one-year leave of absence after childbirth. The first half is reserved for the mother, who receives 90% of her salary from social security.
- Denmark, with the highest level of publicly funded services in Europe, offers women 18 weeks' maternity leave, four weeks before the birth and 14 weeks afterward. Men can take ten days' leave after their baby is born, and parental leave policy allows either the mother or the father to take an additional ten weeks off after the birth.
- France leads the pack in day-care support. In addition to getting at least 16 weeks' maternity leave at 84% of their salaries, working mothers can bring their children to state-run day-care centers called *crèches,* which are open 11 hours a day and cost between $3.00 and $17.50 daily.
- Some European companies, such as National Westminster Bank (NWB) in London, have career break policies that allow employees to take a multiyear leave following the birth of a child. During that period the employee remains in contact with the company, fills in for vacationing employees, and participates in training. At NWB, career breaks of six months to seven years are available to staff at all grades.

"What we tend to find in Europe," says a coordinator of Daycare Trust in London, "is that the more government involvement there is in these issues, the more likely there is to be involvement by employers." In the United States it is up to individual companies to provide family-friendly programs. This creates some packets of work-family innovation, but to the chagrin of many dual-earner families, there is no national trend toward providing these kinds of services.

Alternative Work Patterns. Employers like Quaker Oats, IBM, Ciba-Geigy, and Pacific Telesis Group have been willing to experiment with new ways to help women balance career goals and mothering, and thereby have retained the services of many of their top performers. As we saw in Chapter 2, these programs come in a variety of forms, including flexible work hours, flextime, telecommuting, and job sharing. Another option is extended leave. A rare benefit, **extended leave** allows employees to take a sabbatical from the office, sometimes up to three years, with benefits and the guarantee of a comparable job on return. Some companies require leave-takers to be on call for part-time work during their sabbatical.[76]

extended leave
A benefit that allows an employee to take a long-term leave from the office, while retaining benefits and the guarantee of a comparable job on return.

These alternative work patterns are often collectively labeled the *mommy track.* This term can be negative or positive, depending upon how the company views its female employees who need assistance in combining a career with motherhood.[77] The less common term *daddy track* has arisen to describe the career paths of men who opt to spend some time raising their children. A recent survey conducted for the benefits consulting firm Robert Half International indicated that 74% of the men surveyed would accept slower career development in exchange for more time to spend with their families.[78] In addition, 21% of men report that they would prefer to stay home caring for family members if they didn't need a paycheck.[79]

senior mentoring program
A support program in which senior managers identify promising women and minority employees and play an important role in nurturing their career progress.

Senior Mentoring Programs

Some companies encourage **senior mentoring programs,** in which senior managers identify promising women and minority employees and play an important role in nurturing their career progress. At Marriott, for instance, newly hired employees with disabilities are paired with Marriott managers who serve as their coaches. Honeywell and 3M team up experienced executives with young women and minorities to give them advice on career strategies and corporate politics, as do Xerox and DQE Corporation, a Pittsburgh utilities firm.[80]

Apprenticeships

apprenticeship
A program in which promising prospective employees are groomed before they are actually hired on a permanent basis.

Apprenticeships are similar to senior mentoring programs, except that promising prospective employees are groomed before they are actually hired on a permanent basis. As with senior mentoring, company managers are encouraged to become actively involved in apprenticeship programs. For example, Sears has established an apprenticeship program that gives students hands-on training in skills like basic electronics and appliance repair. The best students are hired for ten hours a week to work at a Sears Service Center. This on-the-job training is integrated into the school curriculum, and the most talented students are hired upon completion of the program.

Communication Standards

Certain styles of communication may be offensive to women and minority employees. Examples are the use of "he" when referring to managers and "she" when referring to secretaries; inadequately representing or ignoring minorities in annual reports; failure to alphabetize ethnic groups' titles (Asian, Latino, etc.); and using terms, such as protected classes and alien, that may have a precise legal meaning but are offensive to those being described. To avoid these problems, organizations should set *communication standards* that take into account the sensitivities of a diverse employee population. Some companies, like Control Data Corporation, have a centralized publications office that establishes corporatewide communication standards and reviews and approves all documents before they are released.

IBM: "None of Us Is as Strong as All of Us."

IBM—some of whose employees are pictured here—has diversity firmly rooted in its heritage. Its first disabled employee was among the first group of people the company hired upon its founding in 1914. In fact, IBM has had a department dedicated to diversity since 1967. The company's director of work force diversity explains: "We must view every citizen in every country as a potential consumer. Consumers must be able to look in at the IBM company and see people like them."

Organized Activities

diversity audit
A review of the effectiveness of an organization's diversity management program.

All the programs we have discussed here may be supplemented by social events that celebrate diversity. For instance, Pillsbury regularly offers ethnic cuisine and specialty events in the Pillsbury cafeteria. Likewise, Valley Bank (now Bank of America, the largest bank in Phoenix, Arizona) sponsors an annual ethnic Easter egg exhibit.

Manager's Notebook

Preventing Diversity Backlash

Many organizations that have instituted diversity programs have experienced adverse reactions from employee groups, particularly white men. Here are some guidelines for HR professionals and company managers who are attempting to manage diversity without adversity.

1. Adopt an inclusive definition of diversity that addresses all kinds of differences among employees, including (but not limited to) race and gender. A broader definition of diversity will invite participation and lower resistance.
2. Make sure that top management is not only committed to establishing a diversity program but also communicates that commitment directly to all employees. Top executives should also let managers know why diversity is important to the company's bottom line and global competitiveness.
3. Involve everyone, including white men, in designing the diversity program. White men will be less resistant to these programs if they are included on the task forces, panels, and other groups the company sets up to look at diversity issues and decide how the company should handle them.
4. Avoid stereotyping groups of employees, such as white men, when explaining cultural or ethnic differences. While the airing of stereotypes is a common facet of diversity training workshops, trainers should direct trainees away from focusing on any group as "the culprit" and affirm the value of each person's individual experience and viewpoint.
5. Recognize and reward white men who are part of the solution rather than blaming men who are part of the problem. Many white men who have long been advocates for diversity feel they aren't being recognized for it.
6. Avoid one-shot training efforts that stir up emotions without channeling them in productive directions. Use ongoing training that encompasses diversity as only one facet of needed change in the corporate culture.

Sources: Mobley, M. (1992, December). Backlash! The challenge to diversity training. *Training & Development*, 45–52; Nelton, S. (1992, September). Winning with diversity. *Nation's Business*, 18–24; Galen, M. (1994, January 31). Taking adversity out of diversity. *Business Week*, 54–55.

Diversity Audits

Often the roots of an employee diversity problem (such as high turnover of minority employees) are not immediately evident. In these instances, research in the form of a **diversity audit** may be necessary to uncover possible sources of bias. When Xerox discovered that women and minorities early in their careers with the company were less likely to hold positions that successful managers had held when they were at lower levels, the company concentrated on assigning promising women and minorities to jobs with greater fast-track potential.

Management Responsibility and Accountability

Management of diversity will not be a high priority and a formal business objective unless managers and supervisors are held accountable for implementing diversity management and rewarded for doing so successfully. At the very minimum, successful diversity management should be one of the factors in the performance appraisal system for those in positions of authority. For instance, at Garrett Company, a manufacturer of jet engines, bonus pay is tied to a supervisor's record on managing diversity. ▼

▸ Some Warnings

Two potential pitfalls must be avoided if diversity management programs are to be successful. These are (1) avoiding the appearance of "white male bashing" and (2) avoiding the promotion of stereotypes.

Avoiding the Appearance of "White Male Bashing"

Disproving the accusation that managing diversity is just another catchphrase for providing opportunities for women and minorities *at the expense of white men* is crucial to the successful management of diversity programs. Otherwise, these programs are likely to engender resentment, heighten anxieties, and inflame the prejudices of those who feel threatened. A delicate balancing act is required because, given limited resources, some competition is inevitable. At the very least, management should continually emphasize the positive aspects of capitalizing on employee diversity by framing it as something that (1) must be done to gain a competitive advantage and (2) is in the best interests of all employees. Training programs, if properly designed, may be used as efficient vehicles to convey these messages. Another approach is to use rewards. For instance, Whirlpool distributed an extra $2,700 to each employee in its Benton Harbor, Michigan, plant in a single year in response to productivity and quality improvements. The plant has a significant minority population, and the group incentive induced all employees to work closely together in what they saw as a win-win effort.[81]

For some guidelines on what HR professionals and company managers can do to avoid the appearance of "white male bashing" and increase the positive response to the firm's diversity program, see the Manager's Notebook titled "Preventing Diversity Backlash."

Avoiding the Promotion of Stereotypes

As we discussed earlier, an inherent danger in diversity programs is inadvertent reinforcement of the notion that one can draw conclusions about a particular person based simply on his or her group characteristics. Remember, differences between individuals *within* any given group are almost always greater than the "average" or typical differences *between* any two groups. **Cultural determinism**—promoting the idea that one can infer an individual's motivations, interests, values, and behavioral traits based on that individual's group memberships—robs employees of their individuality and creates a divisive mindset of "them versus us."

cultural determinism
The idea that one can successfully infer an individual's motivations, interests, values, and behavioral traits based on that individual's group memberships.

Unfortunately, cultural awareness programs and other diversity training activities tend (unintentionally) to overdramatize diversity. This may lead participants to hold assumptions regarding groups that are totally incorrect (and most likely offensive) when applied to specific employees.[82]

Every employee deserves to be treated as an individual who has a unique set of needs, experiences, motivations, interests, and capabilities. The result of diversity efforts should always be to promote the value of individuals. It may be necessary to discuss group differences and characteristics as a means to that end, but those discussions should never be the stopping point. Managers who remember and apply this basic tenet will be able to take full advantage of the abilities of all their employees.

Summary and Conclusions

What Is Diversity? Diversity refers to human characteristics that make people different from one another. Today's labor force is highly diverse. If effectively managed, this diversity can provide the organization with a powerful competitive edge because it stimulates creativity, enhances problem solving by offering broader perspectives, and infuses flexibility into the firm.

Challenges in Managing Employee Diversity. An organization confronts significant challenges in making employee diversity work to its advantage. These include: (1) genuinely valuing employee diversity; (2) balancing individual needs with group fairness; (3) coping with resistance to change; (4) promoting group cohesiveness; (5) ensuring open communication; (6) avoiding employee resentment; (7) preventing backlash; (8) retaining valued performers; and (9) managing competition for opportunities.

Diversity in Organizations. Some groups are likely to be left out of the corporate mainstream. African-Americans still face a certain amount of explicit racism and tend to be less educationally prepared for the workplace. Asian-Americans confront two stereotypes—one saying they are too cautious and reserved to lead, and another saying they are unscrupulous in business—as well as the feeling that they are too educated to merit special consideration as a minority. Full social acceptance is still denied to people with disabilities, who are often incorrectly perceived as being less capable than others, more prone to quit their jobs under pressure, and costly to accommodate in the workplace.

Foreign-born workers face language and cultural barriers and sometimes ethnic/racial prejudice. They are often resented by Americans of all races, who believe they are taking their jobs. Homosexuals sometimes confront outright discrimination (the refusal to hire or retain them as employees), and sometimes ostracism from coworkers or managers. Latinos face language and cultural difficulties and, in some cases, racial discrimination.

Older workers encounter negative stereotypes about their abilities, energy, and adaptability, as well as some physical problems and resentment from younger workers. Women often fare badly in male-dominated corporate cultures that display masculine leadership biases and have old boys' networks that exclude women. They are also subject to sexual harassment to a much greater degree than men.

Improving the Management of Diversity. Organizations that have capitalized the most on their diverse human resources to gain a competitive advantage tend to have top management committed to valuing diversity; solid, ongoing diversity training programs; support groups that nurture nontraditional employees; and policies that accommodate employees' family needs. They also have senior mentoring and apprenticeship programs to encourage employees' career progress, set communication standards that discourage discrimination, celebrate diversity through organized activities, use diversity audits to uncover bias, and hold their managers responsible for effectively implementing diversity policies.

Some Warnings. There are two pitfalls in diversity management programs that managers must be careful to avoid: (1) giving the appearance of "white male bashing" and (2) unintentionally promoting stereotypes.

Key Terms

apprenticeship, 135
cultural determinism, 137
cultural relativity concept of management, 122
diversity, 116
diversity audit, 136
diversity training programs, 132
extended leave, 134
glass ceiling, 123
management of diversity, 118
old boys' network, 130
senior mentoring program, 134
support group, 133
universal concept of management, 122

Discussion Questions

1. Why is management of diversity acquiring such a central role in HRM? Is this a temporary or a long-term phenomenon? Explain.
2. For more than a decade, Monsanto's Chocolate Bayou chemical plant in southeast Texas used affirmative action programs to boost the number of minority and women workers at the plant. But even as the company was accelerating the hiring of women and minorities, it noticed that these employees were leaving Monsanto at a disproportionately rapid rate. In conducting exit interviews, the company found that departing women and minority employees felt they were being treated unfairly in pay and promotion decisions. This information convinced top management to begin a series of diversity management programs. What is the connection, if any, between affirmative action and the management of diversity? Why did Monsanto start its diversity programs, and how do you think the company should link these programs to its affirmative action policy?
3. Women and ethnic minorities are often lumped together as a single class. What do these two groups have in common? What are the major differences between them? Explain.
4. Conflicts among minority groups may arise as they compete for a limited number of jobs and promotion opportunities. What can firms do to avoid these kinds of conflict?
5. Some people still believe that the best way—and perhaps the only fair way—to manage is to treat all employees equally regardless of their gender, race, ethnicity, physical impairment, and other personal characteristics. Do you agree? Explain.
6. When a long-time contract employee for Pacific Gas & Electric in Tracy, California, was the first in his unit to be laid off, he claimed that the others—an African-American woman and a man of Indian descent—had been kept on (even though they were less qualified than he was) because PG&E was intent on creating a more diverse workplace. "I feel like I'm losing out," this white male employee said. PG&E claimed his race and sex had nothing to do with his being laid off. What can companies do to keep white males from feeling victimized by diversity efforts and training programs instead of valued as "diverse" employees in their own right?
7. James L. Schneider, owner of a small computer design and software consulting company in San Francisco, complains that he has a difficult time competing with firms that bring foreign software engineers into the United States to do similar work for one third the price Schneider charges. "American citizens are out on the street," Schneider says. "In the competitive world, it is difficult to bid against people who work at substantially lower rates."

   On the other side of the coin, many U.S. computer companies fear that if they don't hire foreign talent, then competitors in other countries will. What is your position on these opposite views? Explain.
8. Doug Dokolosky, a former IBM executive who specializes in coaching women, argues that "to reach the top requires sacrifice and long hours. If that is your ambition, forget things like balancing work and family...." Do you agree with Dokolosky that most U.S. firms just pay lip service to family accommodation policies? Can you think of any noteworthy exceptions?

MINICASE 1 *Diversity Training Backfires at Lucky Stores*

A common way trainers get managers to banish stereotypes is to air them at diversity training workshops. Percy Thomas, president of the National Diversity Institute, writes the stereotypes that managers hold on large flip charts. "I discuss with the group how these characteristics are garbage. 'And what do we do with garbage?' I ask them. 'Throw it away.'" At which point Thomas promptly rips off the page of offending stereotypes and tosses it into the trash. Managers in a Lucky Stores diversity training workshop would have been wise to take Thomas's approach.

In 1988 managers at Lucky Stores, a Dublin, California-based grocery store chain, attended a workshop designed to increase sensitivity to women and minority group employees. When the trainer asked supervisors to mention stereotypes they'd heard about women and minority group members, one manager said, "Women cry more." Another manager said, "Black females are aggressive." To management's horror, notes containing these comments and others like them were found by an employee, and they turned up later as evidence in a sex-discrimination lawsuit claiming that female employees were not being fairly promoted by the Lucky Stores chain. The employees won in court. Although the judge's ruling wasn't based solely on the training notes, they did contribute to the guilty verdict. "We hadn't known what went on at the meetings, but hearing them say this confirmed that's what they thought of us," said one bookkeeper at Lucky's, who shared more than $90 million in damages with about 20,000 other women.

Discussion Questions

1. What are the implications of the Lucky Stores case for other employers who provide, or would like to provide, diversity training?
2. What do you think of the practice of airing stereotypes at diversity training workshops?
3. What can employers do to protect themselves from potential litigation resulting from diversity training?

Sources: Caudron, S. (1993, April). Employees use diversity-training exercise against Lucky Stores in intentional-discrimination suit. *Personnel Journal*, 52; and Murray, K. (1993, August 1). The unfortunate side effects of "diversity training." *The New York Times*, 3, 511.

MINICASE 2 *Diversity Training Helps Denny's Turn Over a New Leaf*

In the early 1990s, managers of several Denny's restaurants were accused of discriminating against African-Americans. Now, in the late 1990s, Denny's franchise owners are dealing with the aftermath and trying to get Denny's back on track.

> When Charles E. Davis [an African-American man] bought a Denny's Inc. restaurant in Syracuse, N.Y., last year, he knew many blacks wouldn't readily stroll through the door. Denny's, everyone assumed, was racist. So Davis traveled the city's bars and churches and got a well-connected black public-relations man to introduce him to local Urban League and NAACP officials. He bought airtime on black radio stations, set up a youth mentoring program, and ran ads in fraternity and sorority publications—and black business has more than doubled. "Every opportunity I got, I was telling people that Denny's was in town with a new attitude," he says.
>
> That's for sure. Just two years ago, Denny's Inc. still was a snow-white export of the Old South. Some managers routinely barred black customers; others required African-Americans to prepay dinner bills. Just one of the chain's 512 franchises was minority-owned. Denny's money-losing parent, Flagstar Cos., paid $54 million in 1994 to settle two civil rights class actions.
>
> But a sweeping cultural overhaul has transformed the restaurant company. Senior management no longer is the exclusive preserve of white men. Store managers' pay is linked to diversity goals, and African-Americans own 27 franchises. Flagstar chairman and CEO James B. Adamson has consolidated authority for restaurant operations, setting strict rules and sending a clear warning to employees and franchisees alike: "If you discriminate," he says, "you're history."

Discussion Questions

1. Should managers' pay be linked to meeting diversity goals, as Denny's has done? What problems might such a policy create? Explain.
2. A recent study conducted by Denny's indicated that sales have significantly increased in the two years since the implementation of the employee diversity program, while sales at Denny's competitors have dropped. Denny's uses these figures to show that diversity training makes good business sense. Do you agree? Why or why not?
3. Critics argue that Denny's diversity programs are designed solely to eliminate further litigation. Advocates argue that diversity programs are valuable, regardless of the motivation behind their implementation. Where do you stand on this issue? Are the benefits of diversity training somehow lessened if the motivation behind it is purely monetary?

Source: Reprinted from March 25, 1996 issue of *Business Week* by special permission,

E 1 Conflict at Northern Sigma

...igma, a hypothetical high-technology firm head-...ed in New York, develops and manufactures advanced ...ronic equipment. The company has 20 plants around the ...nited States and 22,000 employees, 3,000 of whom work at a single site in Chicago that is responsible for research and development. About half of the employees at that facility are scientists and engineers. The other half are support personnel, managers, and market research personnel. Corporate executives are strongly committed to hiring women and minorities throughout the entire organization, but particularly at the Chicago site. The company has adopted this policy for two reasons: Women and minorities are severely underrepresented in the Chicago plant (making up only about 13% of the work force), and it is becoming increasingly difficult to find top-notch talent in the dwindling applicant pool of white men.

Phillip Wagner is the general manager of the Chicago plant. In his most recent performance evaluation he was severely criticized for not doing enough to retain women and minorities. For the past two years, the turnover rate for these groups has been three times higher than that for other employees. Corporate executives estimate that this high turnover rate is costing at least $1 million a year in training costs, lost production time, recruitment expenses, and so forth. In addition, more than 70 charges of discrimination have been filed with the EEOC during the past three years alone—a much higher number of complaints than would be expected given the plant's size and demographic composition.

Under pressure from headquarters, Wagner has targeted the turnover and discrimination problems as among his highest priorities for this year. As a first step, he has hired a consulting team to interview a representative sample of employees to find out (1) why the turnover rate among women and minorities is so high and (2) what is prompting so many complaints from people in these groups. The interviews were conducted in separate groups of 15 people each. Each group consisted either of white men or a mix of women and minorities. A summary of the report prepared by the consultants follows.

WOMEN AND MINORITY GROUPS

A large proportion of women and minority employees expressed strong dissatisfaction with the company. Many felt they had been misled when they accepted employment at Northern Sigma. Among their most common complaints:

- Being left out of important task forces.
- Personal input not requested very often—and when requested, suggestions and ideas generally ignored.
- Contributions not taken very seriously by peers in team or group projects.
- Need to be ten times better than white male counterparts to be promoted.
- Lack of respect and lack of acknowledgment for work experience.
- A threatening, negative environment that discourages open discussion of alternatives.
- Supervisors often arrogant, insensitive, domineering, and patronizing.
- Frequent use of demeaning ethnic- or gender-related jokes.
- Minimal career support once hired.

WHITE MALE GROUPS

Most white men, particularly supervisors, strongly insisted that they were interested solely in performance and that neither race nor sex had anything to do with how they treated their staff members or fellow employees. They often used such terms as equality, fairness, competence, and color-blindness to describe their criteria for promotions, assignments, selection for team projects, and task force membership. Many of these men felt that, rather than being penalized, women and minorities were given "every conceivable break."

The consulting team asked this group of white men specific questions concerning particular problems they may have encountered at work with women and the three largest minority groups in the plant (African-Americans, Asian-Americans, and Latinos). The most common comments regarding the white men's encounters with each of these groups follow.

African-Americans

- Frequently overreact.
- Expect special treatment because of their race.
- Unwilling to blend in with the work group, even when white colleagues try to make them feel comfortable.
- Like to do things on their own terms and schedules.
- Do not respond well to supervision.

Asian-Americans

- Difficult to figure out what they really think; very secretive.
- Passive-aggressive: One can never tell when they are upset, but they have their way of getting back at you when you least expect it.
- Very smart with numbers, but have problems verbalizing ideas.
- Stoic and cautious; will not challenge another person even when that person is blatantly wrong.

- Like to be left alone; don't want to become supervisors even if this means an increase in pay.
- Prone to express agreement or commitment to an idea or course of action, yet are uncommitted to it in their hearts.

Latinos

- Many can barely speak English.
- Often volatile and emotional.
- More concerned with their extended family than with work; work is often incidental to them and they exhibit little attachment to the firm.
- Often have a difficult time handling structured tasks as employees, yet become dogmatic and authoritarian in supervisory positions.
- Have a difficult time at work dealing with women, whom they expect to be submissive and passive.
- Very lax about punctuality and schedules.
- Difficult to tell when they really mean "yes" because they have many ways of saying "yes"; quite often "yes" really means "maybe" or "no," but they just don't want to offend you. Yet you are still expected to figure out their true response.
- Tend to be verbal rather than analytical.

Women

- Most are not very committed to work and are inclined to quit when things don't go their way.
- Often more focused on interpersonal relationships than on work performance.
- Respond too emotionally when frustrated by minor problems, thus unsuited for more responsibility.
- Sensitive and unpredictable.
- Moody.
- Tend to misinterpret chivalry as sexual overtures.
- Indecisive.
- Cannot keep things confidential and enjoy gossip.

Phillip Wagner was shocked at many of these comments. He had always thought of his plant as a friendly, easygoing, open-minded, liberal, intellectual place because it has a highly educated work force (most employees have college degrees, and a significant proportion have advanced graduate degrees). He is now trying to figure out what to do next.

Critical Thinking Questions

1. What consequences are likely to result from the problems at the Northern Sigma plant? Explain your answer.

2. Should Wagner be held responsible for these problems? Explain.

3. What specific recommendations would you offer Wagner to improve the management of diversity at the Chicago plant?

Cooperative Learning Exercise

4. The class divides into groups of three to five students. Each group should discuss what recommendations it would make to Wagner. After 10 to 15 minutes, each group should present its recommendations to the class. How different are the recommendations from group to group? What principles from the chapter were you able to apply to this problem?

CASE 2 *The Crying Game?*

Read the following excerpt from *Time* describing the efforts to keep the Virginia Military Institute an all-male institution, then answer the questions that follow.

> Do you ever get the feeling that the men in the world might not care if the door closed and there were no women in the room? Ever suspect many men still think that when a woman argues a point she's being combative, while a man is being analytic; that women are motivated by emotions and the need to be loved, while men are driven by facts; that when a woman asks for a raise, if she has the temerity to do so, she is grasping, unlike male breadwinners, who are simply collecting their due?...
>
> Several of the country's most powerful lawyers, in briefs and in oral argument before the Supreme Court last week, trotted out those stereotypes and more in a last-ditch attempt to save the 157-year-old, state-supported Virginia Military Institute as an all-male preserve. According to VMI's argument, women respond more naturally to an "ethic of care" than to an egalitarian "ethic of justice," and those few women who are confident need to go to a women's school to be "reminded" that female "leadership" carries "the hazard of being oppressive." In lower court, VMI had solicited the expert testimony of retired Harvard sociology professor David Riesman, who warned that a young woman's "aspira-

continued

...me? continued

...y are "still in the South very common," and that ...vide women into the "good girls and the bad girls"— ... know which kind would want to attend a single-sex ...l. Besides, noted Riesman, even "macho" women cry.

VMI also argued that a leadership program it set up at Mary Baldwin College in Staunton, Virginia, although separate, is entirely equal. A traditional women's school that features Apple Day and genteel residence halls with brass chandeliers, carpeting, cable TV and microwaves, Baldwin offers two hours of ROTC a week for freshmen, but none of the character-building deprivation or bonding possibilities of barracks life. There is also no Bachelor of Science degree or alumni network similar to VMI's, which has always been touted as the key to cracking the Virginia establishment. Last week VMI put itself in the ridiculous position of lowballing its worth, pointing out that only one member of the Virginia general assembly was a grad and, in effect, questioning why any woman would want to go to such a dump.

Critical Thinking Questions

1. How might you explain the Virginia Military Institute's strong opposition to accepting female students?
2. Are the stereotypes expressed in this case prevalent in other organizational settings? If so, to what degree?
3. Should VMI be legally forced to admit women? If so, what approach should it take to handle diversity problems that may ensue? Explain your answer.

Cooperative Learning Exercise

4. The class splits into two groups. The first group identifies reasons why VMI should not admit women. The second group focuses on why VMI should accept women. Each group chooses one member to represent its position in a debate on the issue.

Source: Excerpted with permission from Carlson, M. (1996, January 29). *Time*, 34.

HRM Simulation 

A crucial mechanism to achieve greater employee diversity within the firm is the staffing process, which includes both the selection of employees from the labor market and the promotion of employees internally. Women and minorities are underrepresented at all job levels in your firm (see work force demographics, page 4 of the players' manual). In the simulation, you will be making decisions about whom to select (Incident D) and whom to promote (Incident N). How could you consider diversity factors when making those decisions?

Another important consideration in the management of diversity is how employees are appraised. What would you do to ensure that the performance appraisal process helps create a company climate in which diversity is valued and respected?

Finally, several requests for training and management development are on your desk (Incident 6). Should you support the implementation of a diversity training program for supervisors? Why or why not?

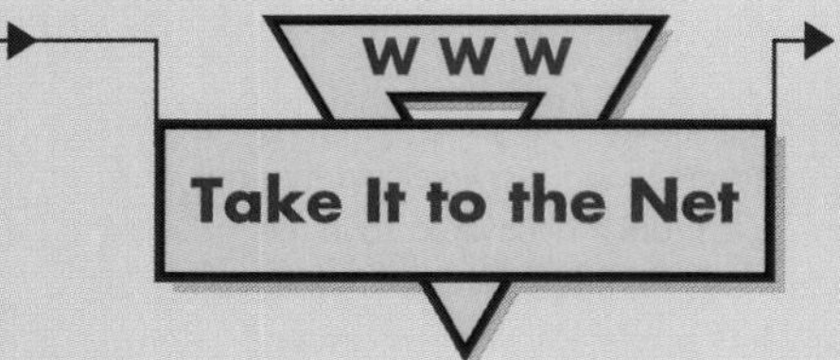

We invite you to visit the Gómez-Mejía/Balkin/Cardy page on the Prentice Hall Web site:

http://www.prenhall.com/gomez

You can also visit the Web sites for these companies, featured within this chapter:

Allstate	http://www.allstate.com
Avon Corporation	http://www.avon.com
Campbell's Soup	http://www.campbells.com
Corning	http://www.corning.com
Levi Strauss	http://www.levi.com
Procter and Gamble	http://www.pg.com
Quaker	http://www.quakeroats.com
Sara Lee	http://www.saralee.com

Endnotes

1. Edwards, A. (1991, January). The enlightened manager. *Working Woman*, 45–51 (p. 45).
2. Allport, G. W., and Odbert, H. S. (1933). Trait-names: A psycho-lexical study. *Psychological Monographs, 47*, 171–220.
3. Loden, M., and Rosener, J. B. (1991). *Workforce America*, 18. Homewood, IL: Irwin.
4. Hymowitz, C. (1995, April 24). How a dedicated mentor gave momentum to a woman's career. *The Wall Street Journal*, B1.
5. Loden and Rosener, 1991.
6. Kaufman, J. (1996, January 29). Passing the plate. *The Wall Street Journal*, A1.
7. Cuneo, A. (1992, October 23). Diverse by design. *Business Week*, 72.
8. Morrow, L. (1992, February 10). Japan in the mind of America. *Time*, 16–23.
9. Cox, T. H., and Blake, S. (1991). Managing cultural diversity: Implications for organizational competitiveness. *Academy of Management Executive, 5*(3), 45–46.
10. Kanter, R. M. (1983). *The change masters*, 52. New York: Simon & Schuster.
11. Author's files.
12. Sheppard, C. R. (1964). *Small groups*, 118. San Francisco: Chandler.
13. Lindenberg, S. (1991, January 7). Managing a multi-ethnic field force. *National Underwriter*, 16–17 (p. 16).
14. Cox and Blake, 1991.
15. Duke, L. (1991, January 1). Cultural shifts bring anxiety for white men: Growing diversity imposing new dynamic in work force. *Washington Post*, A1.
16. Edwards, 1991, p. 46.
17. Fine, M. C., Johnson, P. L., and Ryan, S. M. (1990). Cultural diversity in the workplace. *Public Personnel Management, 19*(3), 305–319 (p. 307).
18. Author's files.
19. Wynkter, L. E. (1994, January 19). Business and race: Multi-culturalism stalls at the national divide. *The Wall Street Journal*, 81–82.
20. Fine et al., 1990.
21. Loden and Rosener, 1991.
22. Fine et al., 1990.
23. Pinkerton, J. P. (1995, November 23). Why affirmative action won't die. *Fortune*, 191–198.
24. Fernandez, J. P. (1991). *Managing a diverse work force*. Lexington, MA: Lexington Books.
25. Cox and Blake, 1991.
26. Kaufman, J. (1995, March 20). How workplaces may look without affirmative action. *The Wall Street Journal*, B1.
27. Dwyer, P., and Cuneo, A. (1991, July 8). The "other minorities" demand their due. *Business Week*, 60.
28. Pinkerton, 1995.
29. Gleckman, H., Smart, T., Dwyer, P., Segal, T., and Weber, J. (1991, July 8). Race in the workplace. *Business Week*, 50–63.
30. Koretz, G. (1995, October 23). A smidgen of Black progress. *Business Week*, 26.
31. Kaufman, 1995.
32. Yang, C., and McNamee, M. (1995, March 27). A hand up but not a handout. *Business Week*, 70.
33. Allis, S., Blackman, A., Dowell, W., and McDowel, J. (1995, October 30). I, too, sing America. *Time*, 35–37.
34. Pinkerton, 1995.
35. Loden and Rosener, 1991.
36. L H Research national phone poll. (1994, March 4). *Chattanooga Times*, 1.
37. Wong, J. (1996, February 9). Asian women migrant workers suffering abuse. *The Wall Street Journal*, A7a.
38. Weber, J. (1988, June 6). Social issues: The disabled. *Business Week*, 140.
39. *Id.*
40. Perry, N. J. (1991, June 10). The workers of the future. *Fortune*, 51–58.
41. Briefs. (1993, February 22). *Workforce Strategies, 4*(2), WS-12.
42. Yang, C. (1993, April 12). Business has to find a new meaning for "fairness." *Business Week*, 72.
43. Pinkerton, 1995.
44. Yang, C. (1995, May 29). Immigration: You can't test for drive and ambition. *Business Week*, 35–36.
45. Rose, F. (1995, April 22). Muddled masses. *The Wall Street Journal*, A1.
46. For a critical discussion of the higher figure, see Muir, J. G. (1993, March 31). Homosexuals and the 10% fallacy. *The Wall Street Journal*, A13.
47. Portes, A., and Truelove, L. (1987). Making sense of diversity: Recent research on Hispanic minorities in the U.S. *American Review of Sociology, 13*, 359–385 (p. 360).
48. Wynter, L. (1996, February 7). Business and race. *The Wall Street Journal*, B1.
49. Templin, N. (1996, January 2). Targeting English-speaking Hispanics. *The Wall Street Journal*, B1.
50. Banach, E. (1990, September). Today's supply of entry level workers reflects diversity. *Savings Institution*, 74–75.
51. Russel, J. (1995, September). Trading with the world. *Hispanic Business*, 26–27.
52. Zate, M. (1996, January–February). Breaking through the glass ceiling. *Hispanic Business*, 30.
53. Loden and Rosener, 1991, 65.
54. Levin, D. P. (1994, February 20). The graying factory. *The New York Times*, 3: 1, 6.
55. *Id.*
56. Other estimates place the figure at 50%. See Edmonson, B. (1996, January 8). Women are approaching majority of the U.S. labor force. *The Wall Street Journal*, A11a.
57. Marini, M. M. (1989). Sex differences in earnings in the U.S. *American Review of Sociology, 15*, 343–380.
58. Yang and McNamee, 1995.
59. McMenamin, B. (1995, March 22). *Forbes*, 176–177.
60. Shellenbarger, S. (1995, May 11). Women indicate satisfaction with role of breadwinner. *The Wall Street Journal*, B6–B7.
61. Dwyer, P. (1996, April 15). Out of the typing pool, into career limbo. *Business Week*, 92–94.
62. (1990, August 6). *Business Week*, 53.
63. Baird, J. E., Jr., and Bradley, P. H. (1979, June). Styles of management and communication: A comparative study of men and women. *Communication Monographs, 46*, 101–110.
64. DePalma, A. (1991, November 12). Women can be hindered by lack of "boys" network. *Boulder Daily Camera*, Business Plus Section, 9.
65. Castro, L.L. (1992, January 2). More firms "gender train" to bridge the chasms that still divide the sexes. *The Wall Street Journal*, 7–11.
66. NiCarthy, G., Gottlieb, N., and Coffman, S. (1993). *You don't have to take it! A woman's guide to confronting emotional abuse at work*. Seattle: Seal Press; Deutschman, A. (1991, November 4). Dealing with sexual harassment. *Fortune*, 147–148; and Meyer, A. (1992, July). Getting to the heart of sexual harassment. *HRMagazine*, 82–84.
67. *HRFocus* (1993, November). Diversity-related training sessions gain popularity, 12.
68. Wynter, 1996.
69. Stewart, T. A. (1991, December 10). Gay in corporate America. *Fortune*, 42–50 (p. 43).
70. Thomas, R. F (1990, March–April). From affirmative action to affirming diversity. *Harvard Business Review*, 107–119.
71. Lee, M. (1993, September 2). Diversity training brings unity to small companies. *The Wall Street Journal*, B, 2–3.
72. Williams, M. (1990, January). *TABC Communication World*, 16–17.
73. Stewart, 1991, p. 42.
74. *Compflash*. (1994, January). Benefits flash. American Management Association, 5.
75. Hamilton, J. O. C., and Weiner, E. (1987, June 8). Day care. *Business Week*, 100.
76. Goodstein, J. D. (1994). Institutional pressures and strategic responsiveness: Employer involvement in work-family issues. *Academy of Management Journal 37*(2), 350–383.
77. Kantrowitz, B., and Wingert, P. (1993, February). Being smart about the mommy track. *Working Woman*, 49–51, 80–81.
78. Hammonds, K. H. (1991, April 15). Taking baby steps toward a daddy track. *Business Week*, 90–92.
79. Shellenbarger, 1995.
80. Hymowitz, 1995.
81. Wartzman, R. (1992, May 4). A Whirlpool factory raises productivity and pay of workers. *The Wall Street Journal*, A1.
82. Njeri, I. (1989, April 2). When different groups convene, the ignorant and the curious can be unexpectedly rude. *Los Angeles Times*, Part 6, p. 1.

VIDEO CASE

ABCNEWS

Sexual Harassment—Still Going Strong

Sexual harassment became illegal in 1980, when the Equal Employment Opportunity Commission interpreted the 1964 Civil Rights Act prohibition of sex-biased discrimination to prohibit sexual harassment (see chapter 4). However, organizations continue to pay millions of dollars each year to victims of harassment.

What exactly constitutes sexual harassment remains unclear, and there is uncertainty regarding the line that separates the legal from the illegal. To complicate matters further, men and women may differ in their standards and in how they interpret behavior.

Probably the clearest form of sexual harassment involves the request of sexual favors in return for job-related benefits. This *quid pro quo* (something for something) form of harassment is easy to recognize. A second form of sexual harassment, creating a hostile work enviroment, is probably more common but more difficult to recognize. Hostile-environment sexual harassment involves unwelcome sexual behavior that creates an intimidating or offensive work environment, or interferes with job performance. Does telling an off-color joke constitute harassment? How about hugging your coworkers or subordinates to celebrate a job well done? There can be uncertainty here because the presence of a hostile environment is based on the perception of the harassed person, and knowing how someone else will interpret a situation can be very tricky.

Charges of sexual harassment can have unexpected consequences. Consider the following cases:

- Linda Noble, an employee at Bath Iron Works, took a job in the traditionally male arena of shipbuilding. In addition to receiving good pay, she received unwelcome attention from her male coworkers. Linda endured comments about her body and menstrual cycle. She finally filed a harassment suit against the company and settled it out of court. Now she thinks that bringing her case forward wasn't worth it. Some coworkers won't talk to her and others are openly hostile.
- Stanford Medical School experienced a sexual harassment controversy when a neurosurgeon publicly charged that her department had a climate of sexism. The department head was removed and the school instituted sensitivity training for faculty and students.
- A male administrator at a community college was accused of harassment by a female subordinate and lost his job. However, other workers claim that there was no harassment, only jealousy of the man's success and an attempt to politically destroy him.

Despite being illegal for nearly 20 years, sexual harassment doesn't seem to be going away any time soon. Perhaps part of the reason is our basic gender-based instincts. According to anthropologist Helen Fisher, men and women unconsciously send out sexually charged messages. The modern way of putting men and womwn together in the workplace may simply be asking for difficulties, such as sexual harassment. Signals may be unwittingly sent and other behaviors may be misinterpreted as signals.

Discussion Questions

1. Do you think that people who have experienced sexual harassment should report their harassers? Why or why not? Would you recommend performing a risk-benefit analysis before coming forward? Why or why not?
2. What can you do to make sure the workplace is free of sexual harassment? Would you hug a worker for a job well done?
3. What can you do to protect yourself against charges of sexual harassment?
4. Do you agree with Helen Fisher's assertion that it is difficult for men and women to work together? What can be done about unconscious signals and the problems they can cause?

5 Recruiting, Selecting, and Socializing Employees

Career Expo. A great number of recruitment sources are available to organizations. These include current employees, referrals from employees, advertisements, employment and temporary-help agencies, and (pictured here) college career expositions.

CHALLENGES

After reading this chapter, you should be able to deal more effectively with the following challenges:

1 ▶ **Understand** the human resource planning process.

2 ▶ **Weigh** the advantages and disadvantages of internal and external recruiting.

3 ▶ **Distinguish** among the major selection methods and use the most legally defensible of them.

4 ▶ **Make** staffing decisions that minimize the hiring and promotion of the wrong people.

5 ▶ **Provide** reasonable job expectations to new recruits.

6 ▶ **Understand** the legal constraints on the hiring process.

http://www.monster.com/

The Monster Board

For HR professionals, The Monster Board offers a gathering place and an information resource. It includes several topic areas related to recruitment, including articles that describe effective recruitment practices, listings of job fairs, layoff notices, advertising agencies, and international recruiting suggestions.

Acme Publishing Company was looking to replace Jerry Rogers, a manager who left to take a job with a competitor. After a few months of interviewing and testing, the HR department announced that a new manager had been hired.

The new hire, George Agros, turned out to be too gruff and distant for most of the workers. At first, they were relieved that a manager was finally in place, even if he wouldn't win any personality awards. But this relief soon changed to resentment. The workers disliked George's style and often disagreed with his decisions, which seemed to depend more on Acme's internal politics than on its clients' needs. Since George's past managerial experience was in another industry, they also doubted his ability to make the best decisions for the unit.

Six months after arriving, George met with Acme's HR director. She asked him how things were going and mentioned that she'd been hearing complaints from the employees in George's unit. George couldn't believe his ears. He had agreed to take this position in a new field at a very modest salary because he'd been promised a promotion and a salary increase after two months. Both were four months overdue. He knew that he didn't fit into the company's culture, he said, but it wasn't his fault. Acme had hired him and Acme should have known what it was getting. After the meeting, the director wondered whether George would have to be transferred or terminated, and George wondered whether he should quit and sue Acme for misrepresenting the job and his promotion and salary opportunities. Meanwhile, the workers in George's unit wondered how they would survive another hiring process if George left or was forced out.

The experience of the Acme Publishing Company illustrates several important questions that firms face when hiring employees:

- Who should make hiring decisions?
- Should applicants' "fit" with the firm's culture be considered in addition to their skills?
- How can a firm give applicants realistic expectations so that new hires don't become disillusioned?
- What characteristics should the firm look at when deciding whom to hire, and how should these characteristics be measured?

The way firms handle these and other staffing questions directly affects the quality of the people hired and the retention rate of skilled workers. Hiring (and promoting) the right people is critical to effective operations and organizational potential. In addition, because there are many barriers to terminating employees, firms often have to live with their hiring mistakes.

In this chapter we focus on staffing, perhaps one of the most important HR activities in which line managers are involved. First, we define and discuss the human resource planning process. Second, we examine the hiring process in detail. Third, we look at the major challenges managers face in hiring and promoting. Fourth, we recommend a set of procedures for dealing with these challenges and avoiding potential problems. Finally, we describe and evaluate specific methods for making hiring decisions and briefly discuss the legal issues involved in staffing.

▸ Human Resource Planning

Human resource planning (HRP) is the process an organization uses to ensure that it has the right amount and the right kinds of people to deliver a particular level of output or services in the future. Firms that do not conduct HR planning may not be able to meet their future labor needs (a labor shortage) or may have to resort to layoffs (in the case of a labor surplus).

human resource planning (HRP) The process an organization uses to ensure that it has the right amount and the right kind of people to deliver a particular level of output or services in the future.

A failure to plan can lead to significant financial costs. For instance, firms that lay off large numbers of employees are required to pay higher taxes to the unemployment insurance system, while firms that ask their employees to work overtime are required to pay them a wage premium. (We discuss both of these issues in detail in Chapter 2.) In addition, firms sometimes need to do HR planning to satisfy legally mandated affirmative action programs (see Chapter 3). In large organizations HR planning is usually done centrally by specially trained HR staff.

Figure 5–1 summarizes the HRP process. The first HRP activity entails forecasting *labor demand*, or how many workers the organization will need in the future. Labor demand is likely to increase as demand for the firm's product or services increases and to decrease as labor productivity increases (because more output can be produced with fewer workers, usually because of the introduction of new technology).

The second part of the HRP process entails estimating *labor supply*, or the availability of workers with the required skills to meet the firm's labor demand. The labor supply may

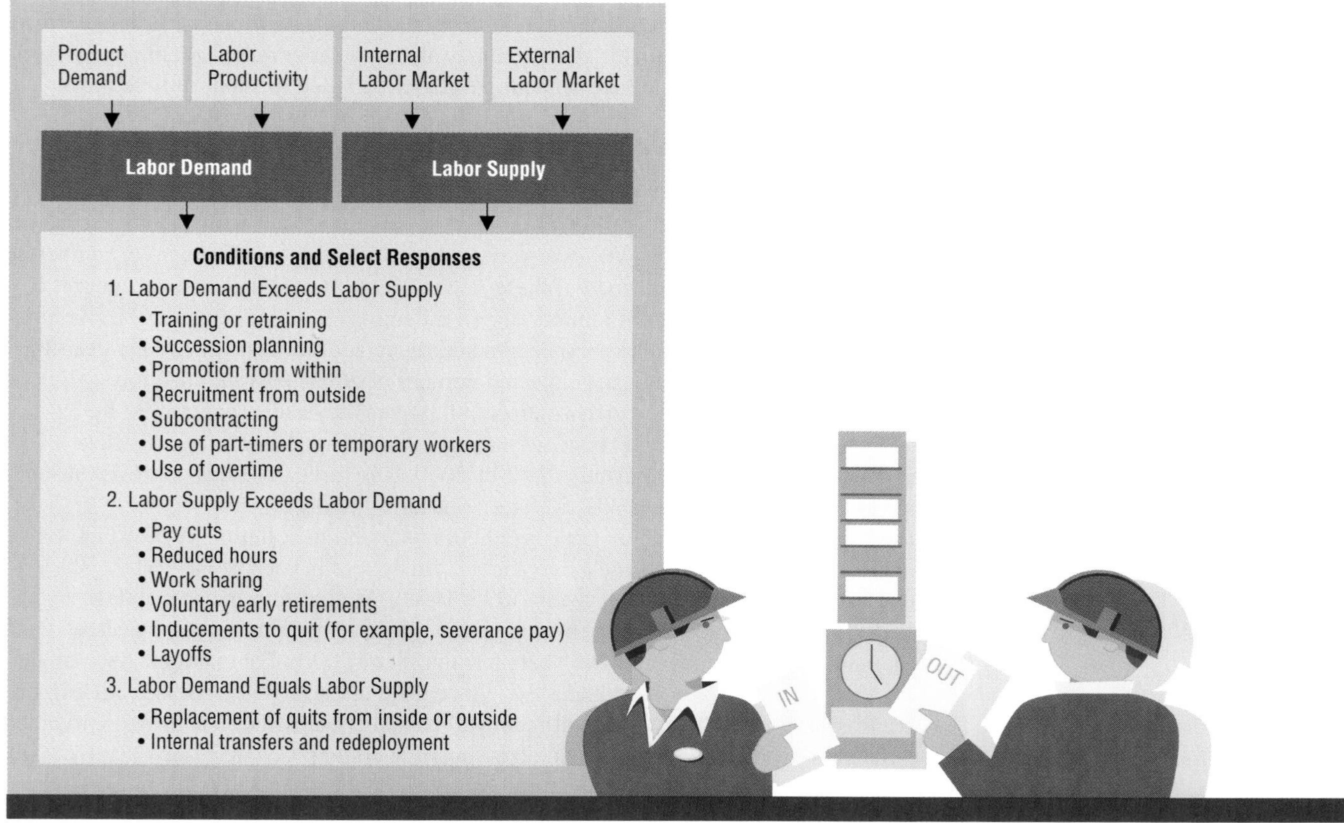

FIGURE 5–1

Human Resource Planning

come from existing employees (the *internal* labor market) or from outside the organization (the *external* labor market).

After estimating labor demand and supply for a future period, a firm faces one of three conditions, each of which requires a different set of responses. In the first scenario, the firm will need more workers than will be available. A variety of approaches can then be used to increase the labor supply available to a specific firm. These include training or retraining existing workers, grooming current employees to take over vacant positions (*succession planning*), promoting from within, recruiting new employees from outside the firm, subcontracting part of the work to other firms, hiring part-timers or temporary workers, and paying overtime to existing employees. Which approach or approaches are appropriate will depend on their relative costs and how long the labor shortage is expected to last. For instance, if demand exceeds supply by only a small amount and this situation is deemed temporary, paying overtime may be less expensive than hiring new workers, which entails extra costs in terms of training and legally mandated benefits (such as Social Security payments and workers' compensation insurance).

In the second scenario, labor supply is expected to exceed labor demand. This means that the firm will have more employees than it needs. Firms may use a variety of measures to deal with this situation. These include pay cuts, reducing the number of hours worked, and work sharing (all of which may save jobs). In addition, the firm may eliminate positions through a combination of tactics, including early retirement incentives, severance pay, and outright layoffs. (We discuss these issues in detail in Chapter 6 and Chapter 13.) If the labor surplus is expected to be modest, the firm may be better off reducing the number of hours worked instead of terminating employees (which, under federal law, would force the firm to pay more into the unemployment compensation insurance program).

In the third scenario, labor demand is expected to match labor supply. The organization can deal with this situation by replacing employees who quit with people promoted from the inside or hired from the outside. The firm may also transfer or redeploy employees internally, with training and career development programs designed to support these moves.

A Simplified Example of Forecasting Labor Demand and Supply

Figure 5–2 shows an example of how a large national hotel chain with 25 units forecasts its labor demand for 16 key jobs two years ahead. Column A indicates the number of employees who currently hold each of these jobs. Column B calculates the present ratio of employees to hotels—that is, the number of current employees divided by the current number of hotels (25). The hotel chain expects to add seven additional hotels by the year 2000 (for a total of 32). In column C, the expected number of employees for each job in 2000 is calculated by multiplying the current ratio of employees to hotels (column B) by 32. For instance, in 1998 there were nine resident managers for 25 hotels, or a ratio of .36 (9 ÷ 25). When the number of hotels expands to 32 in 2000, it is forecasted that 12 resident managers will be needed (.36 × 32 = 11.52, or 12.0 after rounding).

The same hotel chain's labor supply prediction is found in columns A–D of Figure 5–3 on page 150. Column A shows the percentage of employees in each of the 16 key jobs who left the firm during the past two years (1995–1998). Multiplying this percentage by the number of present employees in each of these key jobs produces an estimate of how many current employees will have quit two years from now (by 2000). For example, 38% of general managers quit between 1995 and 1998. Since there are now 25 employees holding this job, it is forecasted that by 2000, ten of them will have left the firm (.38 × 25 = 9.5, rounded to 10). The projected turnover for each job is shown in column C. This means that by 2000, 15 of the current general managers (25 minus 10; see column D) will still be working for the company. Since the projected labor demand for general managers in 2000 is 32 (see Figure 5–2), 17 new general managers (32 minus 15) will have to be hired by 2000.

	A Number of Employees (1998)	B Ratio of Employees/Hotels (Calculated as Column A ÷ 25)	C Projected 2000 Labor Demand for 32 Hotels (Calculated as Column B × 32)*
Key Positions			
General Manager	25	1.00	32
Resident Manager	9	.36	12
Food/Beverage Director	23	.92	29
Controller	25	1.00	32
Assistant Controller	14	.56	18
Chief Engineer	24	.96	31
Director of Sales	25	1.00	32
Sales Manager	45	1.80	58
Convention Manager	14	.56	18
Catering Director	19	.76	24
Banquet Manager	19	.76	24
Personnel Director	15	.60	19
Restaurant Manager	49	1.96	63
Executive Chef	24	.96	31
Sous Chef	24	.96	31
Executive Housekeeper	25	1.00	32
Total	379		486

*These figures are rounded.

FIGURE 5-2

Example of Predicting Labor Demand for a Hotel Chain with 25 Hotels

In the past, many firms avoided human resource planning, simply because their staffs were too swamped with everyday paperwork to manage the planning process effectively. For example, the personnel department in Wake County, North Carolina could barely keep up with the paperwork tracking who had been interviewed, what their qualifications were, and who had been offered a job. All of this changed when the county put a computerized human resources information system (HRIS) in place. The HRIS tracks all applicants and generates paperwork automatically, so that HR staff members can now focus more on planning for the county's future HR needs.[1] In fact, many software companies now offer sophisticated and powerful computer-based HRP programs.

Forecasting Techniques

There are two basic categories of forecasting techniques, quantitative and qualitative. The example we have just discussed is a highly simplified version of a *quantitative technique*. A variety of mathematically sophisticated quantitative techniques has been developed to estimate labor demand and supply.[2] Although used more often, quantitative forecasting models have two main limitations. First, most rely heavily on past data or previous relationships between staffing levels and other variables, such as output or revenues. Relationships that held in the past may not hold in the future, and it may be better to change previous staffing practices than to perpetuate them. Second, most of these forecasting techniques were created during the 1950s, 1960s, and early 1970s, and were appropriate for the large firms of that era, which had stable environments and work forces. They are less appropriate today, when firms are struggling with such destabilizing forces as rapid technological change and intense global competition. These forces are creating major organizational changes that are difficult to predict from past data.

	Supply Analysis				Supply-Demand Comparison	
	A % Quit* (1996–1998)	B Number of Present Employees (See Figure 5–2,Column A)	C Projected Turnover by 2000 (Column A × Column B)	D Employees Left by 2000 (Column B – Column C)	E Projected Labor Demand in 2000 (See Figure 5–2, Column C)	F Projected New Hires in 2000 (Column E – Column D)
Key Positions						
General Manager	38	25	10	15	32	17
Resident Manager	77	9	7	2	12	10
Food/Beverage Director	47	23	11	12	29	17
Controller	85	25	21	4	32	28
Assistant Controller	66	14	9	5	18	13
Chief Engineer	81	24	16	8	31	23
Director of Sales	34	25	9	16	32	16
Sales Manager	68	45	30	15	58	43
Convention Manager	90	14	13	1	18	17
Catering Director	74	19	14	5	24	19
Banquet Manager	60	19	12	7	24	17
Personnel Director	43	15	6	9	19	10
Restaurant Manager	89	49	44	5	63	58
Executive Chef	70	24	17	7	31	24
Sous Chef	92	24	22	2	31	29
Executive Housekeeper	63	25	16	9	32	23
Total Employees		379	257	122	486	364

*These figures are rounded.

FIGURE 5–3

Example of Predicting Labor Supply and Required New Hires for a Hotel Chain

Unlike quantitative techniques, *qualitative* techniques rely on experts' qualitative judgments or subjective estimates of labor demand or supply. The experts may include top managers, whose involvement in and support of the HR planning process is a worthwhile objective in itself. One advantage of qualitative techniques is that they are flexible enough to incorporate whatever factors or conditions the expert feels should be considered. In other words, unlike quantitative methods, qualitative techniques are not constrained by past relationships. However, a potential drawback of these techniques is that subjective judgments may be less accurate or lead to rougher estimates than those obtained through quantitative methods.

For those interested in learning more about quantitative and qualitative forecasting techniques, Appendix B at the end of this book contains tables outlining both groups of techniques and their major advantages and disadvantages.

▸ The Hiring Process

recruitment
The process of generating a pool of qualified candidates for a particular job; the first step in the hiring process.

Once the firm has determined its staffing needs, it needs to hire the best employees to fill the available positions. As Figure 5–4 shows, the hiring process has three components: recruitment, selection, and socialization.

Recruitment is the process of generating a pool of qualified candidates for a particular job. The firm must announce the job's availability to the market and attract qualified candidates to apply. The firm may seek applicants from inside the organization, outside the organization, or both.

Selection is the process of making a "hire" or "no hire" decision regarding each applicant for a job. The process typically involves determining the characteristics required for effective job performance and then measuring applicants on those characteristics. The characteristics required for effective job performance are typically based on a job analysis (see Chapter 2). Depending on applicants' scores on various tests and/or the impressions they have made in interviews, managers determine who will be offered a job. This selection process often involves the establishment of *cut scores*; applicants who score below these levels are considered unacceptable.

selection
The process of making a "hire" or "no hire" decision regarding each applicant for a job; the second step in the hiring process.

Socialization involves orienting new employees to the organization and to the units in which they will be working. It is important that new employees be familiarized with the company's policies, procedures, and performance expectations. Socialization can make the difference between a new worker's feeling like an outsider and feeling like a member of the team.

socialization
The process of orienting new employees to the organization or the unit in which they will be working; the third step in the hiring process.

Challenges in the Hiring Process

Most people would agree that the best-qualified candidates should be hired and promoted. In the long run, hiring the best candidates makes a tremendous contribution to the firm's performance. It has been estimated that above-average employees are worth about 40% of their salary more to the organization than average employees.[3] Thus, an above-average new hire in a sales job with a $40,000 salary would be worth $16,000 more to the organization than an average employee hired for the same position. Over ten years, the above-average employee's added value to the company would total $160,000!

The potential negative consequences of poor hiring decisions are equally graphic. Poor hiring decisions are likely to cause problems from day one. Unqualified or unmotivated workers will probably require closer supervision and direction. They may require additional training yet never reach the required level of performance. They may also give customers inaccurate information or make customers go to competitors.

All of this underscores a simple point: If a company makes the right hiring decision to begin with, it will be far better off. For this reason, it is essential that line managers be involved in the hiring process. While the HR department has an active role to play in recruiting, selecting, and socializing new employees, managers also need to be active in this process. In the end, it is the managers who will actively be supervising the new hires, and line managers often have job-related insights that members of the HR department may lack.

Despite the obvious importance of selecting the best available talent, the hiring process is fraught with challenges. The most important of these are:

- Determining which characteristics that differentiate people are most important to performance.
- Measuring those characteristics.
- Evaluating applicants' motivation levels.
- Deciding who should make the selection decision.

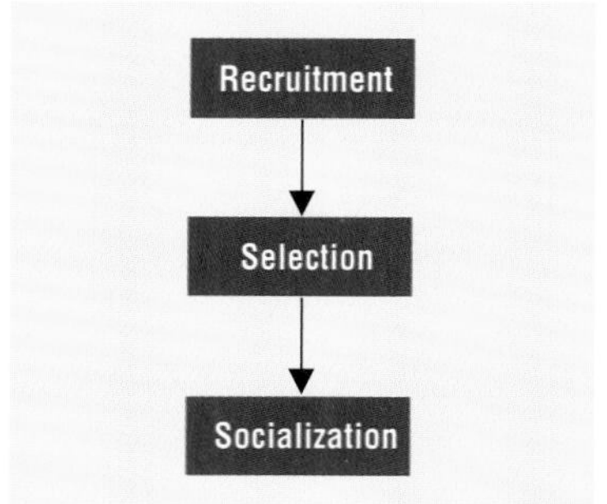

FIGURE 5–4
The Hiring Process

Determining the Characteristics Most Important to Performance

For several reasons, the characteristics a person needs to perform a job effectively are not necessarily obvious. First, the job itself is very often a moving target. For instance, the knowledge, skills, and abilities (KSAs—see Chapter 2) necessary for a good computer programmer right now are certainly going to change as hardware and software continue evolving. Second, the organization's culture may need to be taken into account. Sun

Microsystems, a fast-growing computer company, interviews up to 20 applicants between four and seven times before it makes a hiring decision because it is very concerned that new hires fit in with Sun's dynamic, growth-oriented culture.[4] Third, different people in the organization often want different characteristics in a new hire. For example, upper-level managers may want the new manager of an engineering group to be financially astute, while the engineers in the group may want a manager with technical expertise.

Measuring the Characteristics That Determine Performance

Once it is determined that a set of characteristics is important for job performance, how are those characteristics to be measured? Suppose that mathematical ability is considered critical. You can't infer from looking at someone what level of mathematical ability he or she possesses. Rather, you must administer some test of mathematical ability. Some tests are better than others at predicting job performance, and they can vary widely in cost.

The Motivation Factor

Most of the measures used in hiring decisions focus on *ability* rather than *motivation*. There are countless tests of mathematical ability, verbal ability, and mechanical ability. But as the following equation makes clear, motivation is also critical to performance:

$$\text{Performance} = \text{Ability} \times \text{Motivation}$$

This equation shows that a high ability level can yield poor job performance if it is combined with low motivation. Likewise, a high level of motivation cannot offset a lack of ability. (We will discuss another influence on performance, system factors, in Chapter 7.)

Unfortunately, motivation is very difficult to measure. Many employers try to assess motivation during the employment interview, but (as we will see later in this chapter) there are numerous problems with this method. In addition, motivation seems to be much more dependent on context than ability is. If you are a typical student, your motivation to work hard in a class depends to a large extent on whether you like the course content, how much you like and respect your instructor, and how grades are determined. Your academic ability is fairly stable from course to course, but your motivation level is much more variable. Work situations are just as variable: How much you like your job responsibilities, how well you get along with your boss, and how you are compensated all affect your level of effort.

Who Should Make the Decision?

In many organizations, staffing decisions are routinely made by the HR department, particularly for entry-level jobs. There are two good reasons for letting the HR department run the staffing process. The first (and more important) is that the organization must ensure that its employment practices comply with the legal requirements described in Chapter 3, and making HR staff responsible for all hiring decisions can help avoid problems in this area. The second reason is convenience. Since the HR staff is usually responsible for processing initial contacts with applicants, and is often the repository of information about applicants, many organizations find it easier to let the HR department follow through and make hiring decisions.

However, having the HR department play the central role in hiring has one obvious drawback: This system leaves the line personnel out of a process that is critical to the operation's effectiveness. It is the line personnel, after all, who are intimately familiar with the line jobs and who must work with the candidates selected in the hiring process.

If an organization decides to involve line employees in hiring decisions, which ones should it consult? There are at least three separate groups. The first, and most obvious, are the managers who will be supervising the new hire. The second group consists of the new hire's coworkers. The third group, where applicable, is the new hire's subordinates. As we saw in the Acme Publishing example that opened this chapter, these groups do not necessarily share the same view of what characteristics are important in the new employee.

An interesting example of a company that heavily involves subordinates in hiring decisions is Semco, a Brazilian manufacturing firm. Semco is well known for its egalitarian culture and policies. The company has no receptionists, secretaries, standard hierarchies, or executive privileges. It lets workers set their own hours and salary, and asks subordinates to help hire their own managers. In his book *Maverick*, Semco's owner, Ricardo Semler, describes a group "grilling" of a Semco manager being considered for promotion to general manager of another unit:

> Anatoly Timoshenko was going into the arena, and the lions were hungry. Gathered in a meeting room at Santo Amaro was as antagonistic a group of people as he was likely to face in peacetime. If he was lucky, they would be his future subordinates.[5]

Building Managerial Skills: Meeting the Challenges of Effective Staffing

As we noted earlier, choosing the right person for a job can make a tremendous positive difference in productivity and customer satisfaction. Choosing the wrong person can result in sluggish operations and lost customers. For these reasons it is important that each step of the staffing process—recruitment, selection, and socialization—be managed carefully. We discuss each of these steps in turn.

Recruitment

Recruitment aims to attract *qualified* job candidates. We stress the word *qualified* because attracting applicants who are unqualified for the job is a costly waste of time. Unqualified applicants need to be processed and perhaps even tested or interviewed before it can be determined that they are not qualified. To avoid these costs, the recruiting effort should be targeted solely at applicants who have the basic qualifications for the job.

Sources and Costs of Recruiting. A great number of recruitment sources are available to organizations.[6] The most prominent of these are:

- *Current employees.* Many companies have a policy of informing current employees about job openings before trying to recruit from other sources. Internal job postings give current employees the opportunity to move into the firm's more desirable jobs. However, an internal promotion automatically creates another job opening that has to be filled.
- *Referrals from current employees.* Studies have shown that employees who were hired through referrals from current employees tend to stay with the organization longer and display greater loyalty and job satisfaction than employees who were recruited by other means.[7] However, current employees tend to refer people who are demographically similar to themselves, which can create EEO problems.
- *Former employees.* A firm may decide to recruit employees who previously worked for the organization. Typically, these are people who were laid off, though they may also be people who have worked seasonally (during summer vacations or tax season, for example). Because the employer already has experience with these people, they tend to be very safe hires.
- *Advertisements.* Advertisements can be used both for local recruitment efforts (newspapers) and for targeted regional, national, or international searches (trade or professional publications). For instance, clinical psychologists often find jobs through listings in the American Psychology Association's monthly newspaper.

- *Employment agencies.* Many organizations use external contractors to recruit and screen applicants for a position. Typically, the employment agency is paid a fee based on the salary offered to the new employee. Agencies can be particularly effective when the firm is looking for an employee with a specialized skill. Another advantage of employment agencies: They often seek out candidates who are presently employed and not looking for a new job, which indicates that their current employer is satisfied with their performance.
- *Temporary help agencies.* An increasing number of organizations are turning to temporary workers as a source of labor. Temporary workers allow an organization to get through the ups and downs of the business cycle without making permanent hiring decisions.
- *College recruiting.* Your school probably has a job placement office that helps students make contacts with employers. Many larger employers have college recruiting programs that target certain colleges and universities and/or certain majors. Accounting, engineering, and computer programming majors at the undergraduate level and those with graduate degrees in business and law are often considered the most desirable candidates because of the applied training they have received. Dayton, Ohio–based NCR Corporation, a computer manufacturer, maintains a visible presence on college campuses even when it is doing little or no hiring. It does this through its college scholarship and internship programs and its award-winning publication *Career Contact*, which is aimed at college students.[8]

  In Japan, where some large companies offer lifetime employment, college recruitment is practically the only way employers can bring in new blood. Competition among college students to gain access to the largest companies is fierce. For instance, college students routinely send "information request postcards" to prospective employers beginning in December of their junior year. A student may mail well over 1,000 cards to prospective employers, with 40 to 50 cards sent to employers the student really wants to impress. The companies send the students information, including an invitation to come to the company's "information sessions."[9]
- *Customers.* One innovative recruitment source is the organization's customers, who are already familiar with the organization and what it offers.[10] These people, who must be happy with the organization's product or service because they've remained customers, may bring more enthusiasm to the workplace than other applicants who are less familiar with the organization. Also, customers have been the recipients of the firm's product or service and therefore may have valuable insights into how the organization could be improved.

The appropriateness of these sources depends on the type of job to be filled and the state of the economy. When the unemployment rate is high, companies find it easy to attract qualified applicants. When it is low, organizations need to be more resourceful in locating qualified applicants. For some years now, the unemployment rate has been higher than normal for the post–World War II period and companies have scaled back their college recruiting efforts. As U.S. firms continue to downsize and restructure, recruitment efforts continue to diminish.

Small U.S. firms often find it difficult to recruit qualified applicants even when the unemployment rate is high. In a recent survey of 519 small businesses, more than a quarter of the respondents said finding qualified and motivated employees was among their top three business worries.[11] Bad hires can be catastrophic for small businesses, which don't have the luxury of being able to reassign workers who are not well suited for their positions.[12]

How do employers evaluate the effectiveness of different recruitment sources? One way is to look at how long employees recruited from different sources stay with the company. Studies show that employees who know more about the organization and have realistic expectations about the job tend to stay longer than other applicants.[13] For instance, potential flight attendants who are familiar with the job realize that the position's glamorous, jet-setting image is offset by its many not-so-attractive aspects: dealing with difficult passengers, flying the same route over and over, living out of a suitcase, and working odd schedules. The first three recruitment sources we discussed—current employees, employee referrals, and former employees—are likely to turn up applicants with realistic expectations of the job.

Another way of evaluating recruitment sources is by their cost. The organization should carefully consider the most cost-effective recruiting method for a particular situation. As Figure 5–5 on page 156 shows, there are substantial cost differences between advertising and using cash awards to encourage employee referrals, and between hiring locally and hiring beyond the local area (which entails relocating the new employee). When it is necessary to go outside the local area to get employees it may make sense for company managers to travel to other cities and conduct employment interviews there rather than to pay transportation expenses for applicants to visit the company site.

Line managers can increase the effectiveness of the HR department by providing HR personnel with continuous feedback on the quality of the various recruitment sources. For example, managers can set up a simple spreadsheet with recruiting sources in the rows and effectiveness measures (say, on a scale of 1 to 10) in the columns. Alternatively, the columns might track various outcomes from each of the recruitment sources, such as number of employment offers, number of acceptances, turnover at one year, and employee performance ratings at one year:

Source	Number of employment offers	Number of acceptances	Total cost	Turnover after one year	Average performance rating at one year
Referrals					
Ads					
Agencies					
College Recruitment					
Customers					

Managers themselves might update the grid periodically, or delegate this task to individuals or team members, who will then interpret the grid and provide recommendations to the HR department. (Some data, such as performance ratings, may be confidential and appropriate only for management consideration.)

External versus Internal Candidates. External and internal candidates both have benefits and drawbacks. Hiring externally gives the firm the advantage of fresh perspectives and different approaches. In fact, several major organizations have even gone outside their industries to find CEOs capable of forging a new vision. A case in point is IBM's selection of Louis Gerstner, former CEO of RJR Nabisco, to spearhead IBM's massive reorganization. RJR Nabisco then picked an outsider to take Gerstner's place: Charles M. Harper, former chairman of ConAgra, Inc.[14] Sometimes it also makes economic sense to search for external specialists rather than bear the expense of training current workers in a new process or technology.

On the downside, current employees may see externally recruited workers as "rookies," and therefore discount their ideas and perspectives. When this is the case, people brought in to rejuvenate a department or firm will have only a limited impact. Another disadvantage: External workers need time to become familiar with the firm's policies and procedures. It

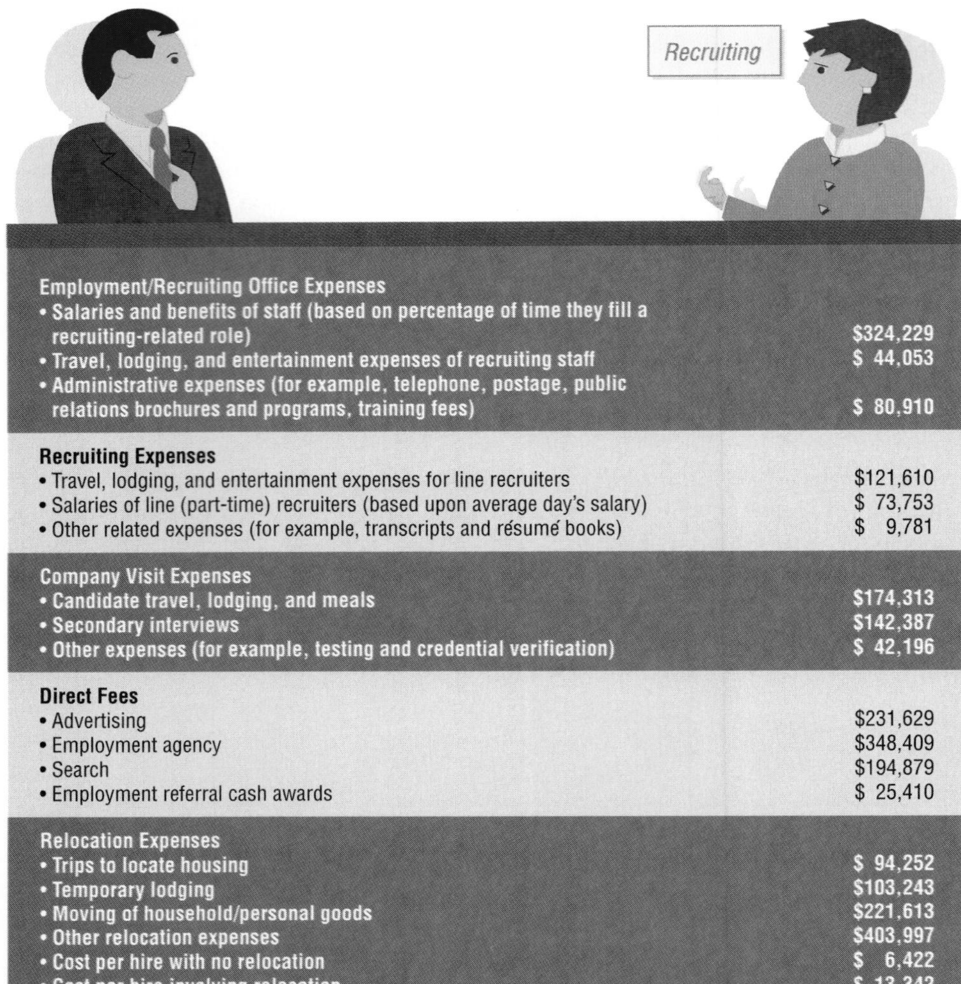

Employment/Recruiting Office Expenses	
• Salaries and benefits of staff (based on percentage of time they fill a recruiting-related role)	$324,229
• Travel, lodging, and entertainment expenses of recruiting staff	$ 44,053
• Administrative expenses (for example, telephone, postage, public relations brochures and programs, training fees)	$ 80,910
Recruiting Expenses	
• Travel, lodging, and entertainment expenses for line recruiters	$121,610
• Salaries of line (part-time) recruiters (based upon average day's salary)	$ 73,753
• Other related expenses (for example, transcripts and résumé books)	$ 9,781
Company Visit Expenses	
• Candidate travel, lodging, and meals	$174,313
• Secondary interviews	$142,387
• Other expenses (for example, testing and credential verification)	$ 42,196
Direct Fees	
• Advertising	$231,629
• Employment agency	$348,409
• Search	$194,879
• Employment referral cash awards	$ 25,410
Relocation Expenses	
• Trips to locate housing	$ 94,252
• Temporary lodging	$103,243
• Moving of household/personal goods	$221,613
• Other relocation expenses	$403,997
• Cost per hire with no relocation	$ 6,422
• Cost per hire involving relocation	$ 13,342

FIGURE 5-5

Average Annual Costs for Recruiting Salaried Employees

Sources: Cost estimates based on Employee Management Association National Cost Per Hire Survey—1984, adjusted by the authors for inflation through 1996. Survey sample included 70 employers. Survey results reported in Norback, C. T. (Ed.), (1986), *The human resources yearbook*. Englewood Cliffs, NJ: Prentice Hall.

may take weeks before a new recruit is up and running. Bringing in someone from the outside can also cause difficulties if current workers resent the recruit for filling a job they feel should have gone to a qualified internal worker. Finally, as we saw in the example of Acme Publishing Company, the outsider's style may clash with the work unit's culture.

Internal recruiting, usually in the form of promotions and transfers, also has its advantages and disadvantages. On the positive side, it is usually less costly than external recruiting. It provides a clear signal to the current work force that the organization offers opportunities for advancement. And internal recruits are already familiar with the organization's policies, procedures, and customs.

3M has a particularly effective internal recruiting system. The company's Job Information System helps managers identify suitable internal candidates and employees identify skills they need to prepare for different jobs. More than 98% of all jobs available at 3M are listed on this job-posting system. Employees may apply for any listed job for which they feel qualified.[15]

One drawback of internal recruiting is that it reduces the likelihood of innovation and new perspectives. Another is that workers being promoted into higher-level jobs may be undercut in their authority because they are so familiar with their subordinates. For example, former coworkers may expect special treatment from a supervisor or manager who used to be a colleague.

Recruiting Protected Classes. An integral part of many organizations' recruitment efforts, both externally and internally, involves attracting women, minorities, people with disabilities, and other employees in the protected classes. While the Equal Employment Opportunity Commission guidelines stipulate only that government employers and government contractors must have written affirmative action policies, many private-sector employers believe that such policies make good business sense for them. It stands to reason, for instance, that newspapers with diverse readerships would want to increase the diversity of their editorial and reporting staffs.

A good rule of thumb for companies wanting to increase the diversity of their work force is to target their audience through the media or recruitment avenue rather than through their message. When a company puts too much emphasis on minority hiring in ads, candidates may feel resentful or believe they are being hired simply to fill a quota. Recruitment experts say that minority candidates should be addressed in the same way all candidates are.[16] Figure 5–6 shows effective recruiting ads for the Orange, California–based Hospital

FIGURE 5–6

Effective Recruiting Advertisements

When the Hospital Council of Southern California wanted to recruit among teens and second-career adults in Los Angeles minority communities, it printed ads in English and Spanish and posted them in metro-area buses over a six-month period. The ad said, "If you would like to earn $25,000–$50,000 a year after only 2–6 years of education, consider health care—a career that never goes out of style," and featured a "take-one" card with a toll-free number. The council got 929 calls, 399 of which were from Latinos.

FIGURE 5–7

Sources for Recruiting Minorities

Source: Laabs, J. J. (1991, May). Affirmative outreach. *Personnel Journal*, 91.

- State Fair Employment Agency
- Regional Equal Employment Opportunity office
- Small Business Administration
- Local chamber of commerce
- Community organizations
- City council office
- County human rights commission
- State Department of Rehabilitation
- Historically black colleges and universities
- Hispanic Association of Colleges and Universities
- Professional associations
- Student associations
- Alumni associations
- Church organizations

Council of Southern California. Some other potential sources for minority recruitment are listed in Figure 5–7.

Planning the Recruitment Effort. To be effective, recruitment should be tied to human resource planning.[17] As we saw early in this chapter, human resource planning involves a comparison of present work force capabilities with future demands. The analysis might indicate, for example, a need for ten more staff personnel given the firm's expansion plans and anticipated market conditions. This information should play a key role in determining the level of the recruitment effort.

Once HRP has been performed, an important question remains: How many candidates should the recruitment effort attempt to attract for each job opening? The answer depends on *yield ratios*, which relate recruiting input to recruiting output. For example, if the firm finds that it has to make two job offers to get one acceptance, this offer-to-acceptance ratio indicates that approximately 200 offers will have to be extended to have 100 offers accepted. Perhaps the interview-to-offer ratio has been 3:1. This ratio indicates that the firm will have to conduct at least 600 interviews to make 200 offers. Other ratios to consider are the number of invitations-to-interview ratio and the number of advertisements or contacts-to-applicant ratio. Each firm sets its own number of candidates to number of job openings ratio. The desired level of recruitment effort may be higher if the firm wishes to be particularly selective in making employment offers.

While most companies focus their recruitment and interviewing efforts domestically, some multinational firms cast their nets wider in their search for talent. For more details, see the Issues and Applications feature titled "Global Recruiting at Gillette and Coca-Cola."

Selection

Given the pool of candidates that results from the recruitment effort, selection is the mechanism that determines the overall quality of an organization's human resources. To understand the impact of selection practices, consider what happens when the wrong person is hired or promoted. How do you, as a customer, like being served by someone who is slow and inept? How would you, as a line supervisor, like to deal with the problems caused by a worker who cannot perform necessary tasks on a production line? These direct effects of poor selection practice are only the beginning. Hiring the wrong person can also cause friction among staff as other workers become resentful of having to pick up the slack for inept employees. Inappropriate hires may even lead better employees to seek employment elsewhere.

All of these effects have economic ramifications.[18] In fact, the economic value of good selection procedures is higher than most people realize. For example, the federal government's use of ability testing for entry-level jobs has been estimated to save the government over $15 billion per year.[19] This amazing figure is derived from the cumulative effects of modest job-performance increases by people hired because they scored better than average on the selection test. Continually hiring people who perform, say, 20% above average can make a tremendous difference to an organization that hires many workers.

Global Recruiting at Gillette and Coca-Cola

Issues + Applications

Organizations that conduct business globally often face the challenge of integrating different (and sometimes conflicting) cultural characteristics and languages. In these situations, choosing employees who demonstrate high levels of cultural awareness and sensitivity can make a major contribution to the bottom line.

In practice, most international recruitment efforts focus on high-level managerial and executive positions rather than shop-floor and entry-level positions. Nevertheless, some companies have taken steps toward developing a complete work force with a global perspective. For example, Gillette International actively recruits foreign talent from the pool of business school graduates in foreign countries. Gillette subsidiaries in various developing nations target the top business students from prestigious local universities. Gillette then offers students the opportunity to train in their home countries for six months. After six months, the candidates are transferred to Gillette headquarters in Boston for 18 more months of training. If trainees are successful, and about 80% of them usually are, they are typically offered entry-level management positions in their home countries.

Coca-Cola has an international recruiting program similar to Gillette's, but targets foreign students studying at top U.S. universities. The company also has an internship program for foreign students and is particularly impressed with students who are multilingual.

Source: Laabs, J. J. (1991, August). The global talent search. *Personnel Journal*, 38–44.

A variety of tools can be used in the selection process. Before we consider these techniques, though, it is important for you to be aware of two important concepts important to selection tools: reliability and validity.

Reliability and Validity. Reliability refers to consistency of measurement, usually across time, but also across judges. Put differently, reliability is a measure of how much error is present in a measure. There are many sources of error in measurement. Consider the typical employment interview. After the interview is over, the interviewer has an overall impression of the job candidate. This overall impression is the measurement that results from the interview. It is hoped that the candidate's job-related qualifications have had a large impact on that measurement. But, almost certainly, other factors not related to the job have also influenced the measure. These other factors may include:

reliability
Consistency of measurement, usually across time but also across judges.

- *Comparison to other candidates.* If the other candidates have been pretty bad, a mediocre candidate will probably impress the interviewer as strong. The reverse also holds: If the other candidates have been exceptionally strong, a well-qualified candidate may seem merely mediocre.
- *Time pressures.* The interviewer may be distracted during the interview by other pressing job demands and therefore unable to evaluate accurately the candidate's strengths and weaknesses.
- *Impression management.* Some interviewees are skillful at creating a very positive first impression, but this favorable impression does not carry over to actual job performance. (Of course, some jobs, like sales, are probably best filled by people who are good at impression management.)

The job interview is supposed to measure job-related qualifications. The more factors influencing the interview impression, the more errors there are likely to be in that particular measure. Reliability is an index of how much these errors have influenced the measure.

Validity is the extent to which scores on a test or interview correspond to actual job performance. Validity is at the heart of effective selection. It represents how well the technique used to assess candidates for a certain job is related to performance in that job. A

validity
The extent to which scores on a test or interview correspond to actual job performance.

technique that is not valid is useless, and may even present legal problems. In fact, documentation of the validity of a selection technique is central to that technique's legal defensibility. When discrimination in hiring practices is charged, the critical evidence will be the job relatedness (validity) of the selection technique.[20]

There are two strategies for demonstrating the validity of selection methods: content and empirical. A *content validity* strategy assesses the degree to which the content of the selection method (say, an interview or a test) is representative of job content. Job-knowledge tests are often validated using a content validation strategy. For instance, applicants for the job of commercial airline pilot are required to take a series of exams administered by the Federal Aviation Administration. These exams assess whether the candidates have the necessary knowledge to pilot safely and effectively. However, passing these tests does not guarantee that the applicant has the other abilities necessary to perform well in the cockpit.

An *empirical validity* strategy demonstrates the relationship between the selection method and job performance. Scores on the selection method (say, interview judgments or test scores) are compared to ratings of job performance. If applicants who receive higher scores on the selection method also turn out to be better job performers, then empirical validity has been established.

Before we proceed to examine specific selection methods, we need to emphasize an important point concerning reliability and validity. Selection methods can be reliable, but not valid; however, selection methods that are not reliable cannot be valid. This fact has a great deal of practical significance. Whether someone has an MBA or not can be measured with perfect reliability. But if having an MBA is not associated with improved job performance, attainment of an MBA is not a valid selection criterion for that job. It seems clear that more highly motivated applicants make better employees, but if the selection method used to measure motivation is full of errors (not reliable), then it cannot be a valid indicator of job performance.

A QUESTION OF ETHICS

Suppose you are asked to write a recommendation letter for a friend whom you like but consider unreliable. Would it be ethical for you to write a positive reference even though you anticipate that your friend will not be a good employee? If not, would it be ethical for you to agree to write the letter knowing that you will not be very positive in your assessment of your friend's abilities?

Selection Tools as Predictors of Job Performance. In this section we look at the most commonly used methods of selection, in no particular order. Each approach has its limitations as well as its advantages.

Letters of Recommendation. In general, letters of recommendation are not highly related to job performance because most are highly positive.[21] This doesn't mean that *all* letters of recommendation are poor indicators of performance, however. A poor letter of recommendation may be very predictive and shouldn't be ignored.

A content approach to considering letters of recommendation can increase the validity of this selection tool. This approach focuses on the content of the letters rather than on the extent of their positivity.[22] Assessment is done in terms of the traits the letter writer ascribed to the job candidate.[23] For example, two candidates may produce equally positive letters, but the first candidate's letter may describe a detail-oriented person, while the second candidate's letter describes someone who is outgoing and helpful. The job to be filled may require one type of person rather than the other. For example, customer relations calls for an outgoing and helpful person, while clerical work requires someone who is good at details. Desired personal characteristics should be identified through job analysis prior to any recruitment efforts.

Application Forms. Organizations often use application forms as screening devices to determine if a candidate satisfies minimum job specifications, particularly for entry-level jobs. The forms typically ask for information regarding past jobs and present employment status.

A recent variation on the traditional application form is the *biodata form*.[24] This is essentially a more detailed version of the application form in which applicants respond to a series of questions about their background, experiences, and preferences. Responses to these questions are then scored. For instance, candidates might be asked how willing they are to travel on the job, what leisure activities they prefer, and how much experience they have had with computers. As with any selection tool, the biodata most relevant to the job should be identified through job analysis before the application form is created. Biodata have moderate validity in predicting job performance.

Ability Tests. Various tests measure a wide range of abilities, from verbal and qualitative skills to perceptual speed. *Cognitive ability tests* measure a candidate's potential in a certain area, such as math, and are valid predictors of job performance when the abilities tested are based on a job analysis.

A number of studies have examined the validity of *general cognitive ability (g)* as a predictor of job performance. General cognitive ability is typically measured by summing the scores on tests of verbal and quantitative ability. Essentially, *g* measures general intelligence. A higher level of *g* indicates a person who can learn more and faster and who can adapt quickly to changing conditions. People with higher levels of *g* have been found to be better job performers, at least in part because few jobs are static today.[25]

Some more specific tests measure physical or mechanical abilities. For example, the *physical ability tests* used by police and fire departments measure strength and endurance. The results of these tests are considered indicators of how productively and safely a person could perform a job's physical tasks. However, companies can often get a more direct measure of applicants' performance ability by observing how well they perform on actual job tasks. These types of direct performance tests, called *work sample tests*, ask applicants to perform the exact same tasks that they'll be performing on the job. For example, one of Levi Strauss's work sample tests asks applicants for maintenance and repair positions to disassemble and reassemble a sewing machine component.[26]

Work sample tests are widely viewed as fair and valid measures of job performance, as long as the work samples adequately capture the variety and complexity of tasks in the actual job. Work sample test scores have even been used as criteria for assessing the validity of general mental ability selection measures.[27] However, physical ability measures have been found to screen out more women and minorities than white men. Physical preparation prior to the testing has been found to reduce this adverse impact significantly.[28]

Personality Tests. Personality tests assess *traits*, individual workers' characteristics that tend to be consistent and enduring. Personality tests were widely used to make employee selection decisions in the 1940s and 1950s,[29] but today they are rarely used to predict job-related behaviors.[30] The arguments against using personality tests revolve around questions of reliability and validity. It has been argued that traits are subjective and unreliable,[31] unrelated to job performance,[32] and not legally acceptable.[33]

Perhaps the major reason personality tests fell out of favor is that there is no commonly agreed-upon set of trait measures. Many traits can be measured in a variety of ways, and this lack of consistency produces problems with reliability and validity. However, recent research on personality measurement has demonstrated that personality can be reliably measured[34] and summarized as being composed of five dimensions.[35] These "Big Five" factors, now widely accepted in the field of personality psychology, are:[36]

- Extroversion—the degree to which someone is talkative, sociable, active, aggressive, and excitable.
- Agreeableness—the degree to which someone is trusting, amiable, generous, tolerant, honest, cooperative, and flexible.
- Conscientiousness—the degree to which someone is dependable and organized and conforms and perseveres on tasks.
- Emotional stability—the degree to which someone is secure, calm, independent, and autonomous.
- Openness to experience—the degree to which someone is intellectual, philosophical, insightful, creative, artistic, and curious.

Of the five factors, conscientiousness appears to be most related to job performance.[37] It is hard to imagine a measure of job performance that would not require dependability or an organization that would not benefit from employing conscientious workers. Conscientiousness is thus the most generally valid personality predictor of job performance.

The validity of the other personality factors seems to be more job specific, which brings us to two warnings about personality tests. First, whether or not personality characteristics are valid predictors of job performance depends on both the job and the criteria used to measure job performance. As in all selection techniques, a job analysis should be done first to identify the personality factors that enhance job performance. Second, personality may play little or no role in predicting performance on certain measures, such as the number of pieces produced on a factory line (which may depend largely on such factors as speed of the production line). However, personality factors may play a critical role in jobs that are less regimented and demand teamwork and flexibility. Clearly, then, selection procedures should take both personality and the work situation into account.[38] Some types of people may be better suited for some work situations than for others.

The Meyers-Brigg Type Indicator, a popular personality test favored by such companies as Allied Signal, Apple, AT&T, Citicorp, Exxon, GE, Honeywell, and 3M, has been used primarily in management development programs. Further recent studies have found that personality can be an accurate predictor of the performance of not only job candidates[39] but also college students.[40]

Psychological Tests. Retail chains, banks, and other service-sector companies have long used pencil-and-paper psychological tests to weed out applicants who might steal on the job. Today, there are broader psychological tests designed to gauge, for example, whether a job applicant has a strong work ethic or will be motivated or defeated by the challenges of the job. These broad tests attempt to uncover likely behavior with such questions as: "Would you agree that to be successful, luck is more important than hard work?" Wet Seal, Inc. (a women's wear retailer in Irvine, California) has since 1990 spent $100,000 a year on psychological testing developed to select more motivated employees. Within the first six months of using these tests, store managers were reporting that newer hires seemed "more willing to go the extra mile" for customers.[41] While Wet Seal and other employers, including Burger King and JPFood Services,[42] have had success in using psychological tests as selection instruments, employers need to be careful in using these types of exams.

The Second Step.

After sending in a résumé or completing a qualifying test, qualified candidates are often called in for a face-to-face interview. Many candidates are chosen only after a series of interviews with managers and employees from across the company.

The questions and scoring methods must be the same for all applicants, and they must be job related rather than general inquisitions into employees' personal lives.

Interviews. Although the job interview is probably the most common selection tool, it has often been criticized for its poor reliability and low validity.[43] Countless studies have found that interviewers do not agree with one another on candidate assessments. Other criticisms include human judgment limitations and interviewer biases. For example, one early study found that most interviewers make decisions about candidates in the first two or three minutes of the interview.[44] Snap decisions can adversely affect an interview's validity because they depend on very limited information. More recent research, however, indicates that interviewers may not make such hasty decisions.[45]

Another criticism is that traditional interviews are conducted in such a way that the interview experience is very different from interviewee to interviewee. For instance, it is very common for the interviewer to open with the following question: "Tell me about yourself." The interview then proceeds in a haphazard fashion depending on the applicant's answer to that first question. Essentially, each applicant experiences a different selection method. Thus, it is not surprising that traditional interviews have very low reliability. However, it is possible to increase the effectiveness of traditional, unstructured job interviews by following the guidelines presented in the Manager's Notebook titled "Unstructured Doesn't Mean Unprepared: Making the Most of the Hiring Interview."

Dissatisfaction with the traditional unstructured interview has led to an alternative approach called the structured interview.[46] The **structured interview** is based directly on a thorough job analysis. It applies a series of job-related questions with predetermined answers consistently across all interviews for a particular job.[47] Figure 5–8 on page 164 gives examples of the three types of questions commonly used in structured interviews:[48]

- *Situational questions* try to elicit from candidates how they would respond to particular work situations. These questions can be developed from the critical incident technique of job analysis: Supervisors and workers rewrite critical incidents of behavior as situational interview questions, then generate and score possible answers. During the interview, candidates' answers to the situational questions are scored on the basis of the possible answers already generated.[48a]
- *Job-knowledge questions* assess whether candidates have the basic knowledge needed to perform the job.
- *Worker-requirements questions* assess candidates' willingness to perform under prevailing job conditions.

Structured interviews are quite valid predictors of job performance.[49] A number of factors are probably responsible for this high level of validity. First, the content of a structured

Manager's Notebook

Unstructured Doesn't Mean Unprepared: Making the Most of the Hiring Interview

Managers can increase the effectiveness of unstructured interviews by focusing on six simple tasks.

- ✔ **Be prepared.** The Boy Scouts' motto could just as well be the interviewer's. Lack of preparation is the most common and costly mistake interviewers make. At least a day in advance, use the interviewee's résumé and discussions with key personnel to create an interview agenda, and take at least 15 minutes to review this agenda before the appointment.
- ✔ **Put applicants at ease in the first few minutes.** Few things are more unsettling to an interviewee than being ushered into an office and watching his or her interviewer make business phone calls or have an impromptu meeting with a colleague. Take care of business before greeting interviewees, and put them at ease with some pleasant small talk before rushing into the interview questions.
- ✔ **Don't be ruled by snap judgments or stereotypes.** Stereotyping is bad for the manager and bad for the company. Curb your tendency to rush to judgment and always keep in mind that you are dealing with an individual, not a type.
- ✔ **Ask results-oriented questions.** Ask questions that are designed to uncover not only what the job candidate has done but also what the results of the person's actions have been.
- ✔ **Don't underestimate the power of silence.** Many interviewers make the mistake of jumping in during any pause in the dialogue to discuss their own views on management and the company. Silences can be a time when the interviewee is absorbing information and forming a question or comment, and these are usually worth waiting for.
- ✔ **Close the interview with care.** Some interviewers let the session drift on until both parties begin to flounder about or lose interest. Others close an interview abruptly when interrupted by a phone call or a colleague. It's best to plan a time limit for the interview and to bring it to a natural close rather than let an outside event terminate the conversation prematurely.

Source: Excerpted, with permission of the publisher, from Uris, A. (1988). *88 mistakes interviewers make and how to avoid them.* New York: Amacom Books.

structured interview
Job interview based on a thorough job analysis, applying job-related questions with predetermined answers consistent across all interviews for a job.

Type	Example
Situational	You're packing things into your car and getting ready for your family vacation when it hits you that you promised to meet a client this morning. You didn't pencil the meeting into your calendar and it slipped your mind until just now. What do you do?
Job Knowledge	What is the correct procedure for determining the appropriate oven temperature when running a new batch of steel?
Worker Requirements	Some periods are extremely busy in our business. What are your feelings about working overtime?

FIGURE 5-8

Examples of Structured Interview Questions

interview is, by design, limited to job-related factors. Second, the questions asked are consistent across all interviewees. Third, all responses are scored the same way. Finally, a panel of interviewers is typically involved in conducting the structured interview; this limits the impact of individual interviewers' idiosyncrasies and biases.

Structured interviews have been used very successfully at several large companies, including Philip Morris U.S.A. and Virginia Natural Gas Company. At these companies interviewing panels range from two to six members and typically include an HR professional, the hiring manager, and the person who will be the candidate's manager. The panels often also include key people from other departments who have to work very closely with the new hire. The usual practice is to interview all candidates over a one- or two-day period. This makes it easier to recall interviewee responses and compare them equitably. Immediately after an interview, panel members rate the interviewee using a one- to two-page sheet that lists important job dimensions along with a five-point rating scale. After each interviewer has rated the candidate, one member of the panel—usually either the HR professional or the hiring manager—facilitates a discussion in which the panel arrives at a group rating for the candidate. After all applicants have been interviewed, the panel creates a rank order of acceptable job candidates.[50]

If the structured interview is so effective, why is the traditional interview much more popular? One reason is that many equate the panel format of structured interviews with a stress test. Another is that organizations find the traditional interview quite useful, probably because it serves more functions than just selection.[51] For example, it can be an effective public relations tool in which the interviewer gives a positive impression of the organization. Even a candidate who isn't hired may retain this positive impression. In addition, the unstructured interview may be a valid predictor of the degree to which a candidate will fit with the organization. While the concept of "fit" is somewhat ambiguous,[52] we are referring here to the match between the candidate's values and traits and the chemistry of the organization or work unit. A good fit helps make things run smoothly and efficiently and is related to job satisfaction and intention to stay with the organization.[53] Fit with the organization can be particularly important in team situations, which is why some companies have started to conduct "team interviews." For more details, see the Issues and Applications feature on page 166 titled "Hiring for Teamwork: What to Look For."

Finally, unstructured interviews may be better than structured interviews at screening out unsuitable applicants.[54] Many times a candidate who seemed "fine" on paper reveals some disturbing qualities during an unstructured interview (see Figure 5–9). Human judgment may be subject to error and bias, but people can be quite good at assessing a candidate's fit with their organization.

Whether employers choose to use structured or unstructured interviews, they need to make sure their interview questions are not illegal. Companies that ask job applicants cer-

Based on a nationwide survey of 200 executives conducted by Accountemps, the world's largest temporary personnel service for accounting, bookkeeping, and information technology, the interview behavior of some jobseekers today can only be described as bizarre. Here are some of the more unusual behaviors respondents witnessed or heard of happening during a job interview:

- "Left his dry cleaner tag on his jacket and said he wanted to show he was a clean individual."
- "After a difficult question, she wanted to leave the room momentarily to meditate."
- "Applicant walked in and inquired why he was here."
- "Said that if I hired him, I'd soon learn to regret it."
- "Said if he was hired, he'd teach me ballroom dancing at no charge, and started demonstrating."
- "Arrived with a snake around her neck. Said she took her pet everywhere."
- "Woman brought in a large shopping bag of canceled checks and thumbed through them during the interview."
- "When asked about loyalty, showed a tattoo of his girlfriend's name."
- "Applicant indicated that if he wasn't hired, the future of the company would be jeopardized for confidential reasons."
- "Took three cellular phone calls. Said she had a similar business on the side."
- "She returned that afternoon asking if we could redo the entire interview."

FIGURE 5–9

Unusual Job Interview Behaviors

Source: Survey reveals unusual job interview behavior. *Human Resource Measurements by Wonderlic Personnel Test, Inc.* (a supplement to the September 1992 issue of *Personnel Journal*), 7.

tain questions (for example, their race, creed, sex, national origin, marital status, or number of children) either on application forms or in the interview process run the risk of being sued. To operate within the limits of the law, interviewers should remember the nine don'ts of interviewing:[55]

1. Don't ask applicants if they have children, plan to have children, or what child-care arrangements they have made.
2. Don't ask an applicant's age.
3. Don't ask whether or not the candidate has a physical or mental disability that would interfere with doing the job. The law allows employers to explore the subject of disabilities only *after* making a job offer that is conditioned on satisfactory completion of a required physical, medical, or job-skills test.
4. Don't ask for such identifying characteristics as height or weight on an application.
5. Don't ask a female candidate for her maiden name. Some employers have asked this in order to ascertain marital status, another topic that is off-limits in interviewing both men and women.
6. Don't ask applicants about their citizenship.
7. Don't ask applicants about their arrest records. You are, however, allowed to ask whether the candidate has ever been convicted of a crime.
8. Don't ask if a candidate smokes. Because there are numerous state and local ordinances that restrict smoking in certain buildings, a more appropriate question is whether the applicant is aware of these regulations and is willing to comply with them.
9. Don't ask a job candidate if he or she has AIDS or is HIV-positive.

Issues + Applications

Hiring for Teamwork: What to Look For

Teamwork situations require team members to communicate and work toward common goals. Specific technical skills, which are often the central concern when selecting people to work in individual jobs, may be much less important in team situations. What characteristics, then, should employers look for when hiring people who will work on a team? While much research remains to be done, preliminary findings indicate that effective team members should be able to:

- *Recognize and resolve conflict.* Conflict can destroy a team's effectiveness. Team members must have the ability to deal with and resolve the disagreements and clashes that are bound to occur.
- *Participate and collaborate in problem solving.* Teams are often expected to solve their own problems rather than look to supervisors for answers.
- *Communicate openly and supportively.* Teams need open communication, and team members need to support one another. The inability to communicate, or a tendency to communicate negatively, could be very detrimental to team effectiveness.
- *Coordinate and synchronize activities.* Team operations require the cooperation of all team members and the coordination of various tasks.

In addition, effective team members usually have the following personality characteristics:

- *Conscientiousness.* Team members must be able to depend on one another. Someone who doesn't follow through can cause problems for the entire group effort.
- *Agreeableness.* Team members need to be flexible and tolerant if they are to meld into an effective unit.

Because current team members are often very sensitive to the requirements for success on their team, a number of companies are now conducting "team interviews" to determine whether job candidates possess the necessary skills and traits. Such interviews are likely to become more popular as the emphasis on teamwork increases.

Source: Cardy, R. L., and Stewart, G. L. (1997). Quality and teams: Implications for HRM theory and research. In D. B. Fedor & S. Ghosh (Eds.), *Advances in the Management of Organization Quality*, 2. Greenwich, CT: JAI Press; Stevens, M. J., and Campion, M. A. (1994). The knowledge, skill, and ability requirements for teamwork: Implications for human resource management. *Journal of Management*, *20*, 503–530.

The key point to remember is not to ask questions that are peripheral to the work itself. Rather, interviewers should stay focused on the objective of hiring someone who is qualified to perform the tasks required by the job.

assessment center
A set of simulated tasks or exercises that candidates (usually for managerial positions) are asked to perform.

Assessment Centers. An **assessment center** is a set of simulated tasks or exercises that candidates (usually for managerial positions) are asked to perform. Observers rate performance on these simulations and make inferences regarding each candidate's managerial skills and abilities. More than 2,000 organizations, including AT&T, Pepsico, IBM, Rubbermaid, Diamond Star Motors, Motorola, Toyota Motor Manufacturing, the Tennessee Valley Authority, and the FBI, use assessment centers to select and promote managers.[56]

While expensive, the assessment center appears to be a valid predictor of managerial job performance.[57] Assessment centers may be well worth the price when the costs of poor hiring or promotion decisions are high, as in the hiring of police officers or firefighters.[58] Assessment centers are usually conducted off premises, last from one to three days, and may include up to six candidates at a time. Most assessment centers evaluate each candidate's abilities in four areas: organizing, planning, decision making, and leadership. However, there is considerable variability in what exercises an assessment center includes, how these are conducted, and how they are scored.[59]

The *in-basket exercise* is probably the exercise most widely associated with assessment centers. An in-basket exercise includes the kinds of problems, messages, reports, and so on that might be found in a manager's in-basket. The candidates are asked to deal with these issues as they see fit, and then are assessed on how well they prioritized the issues, how creative and responsive they were in dealing with each one, the quality of their decisions, and other factors. Performance on an in-basket exercise can be highly revealing. Often it points up the skills of a candidate who might otherwise have appeared average.[60]

Assessment centers have been used to help select front-line workers as well as managers. For instance, the British telecommunications firm Mercury Communications used assessment centers to recruit 1,000 customer service assistants for its new site near Manchester. The assessment center activities involved simulated call-handling and decision-making exercises. Mercury's managers believe these assessment centers are very effective in screening for the skills important to customer-service reps. These include listening skills, sensitivity to customers, and the ability to cope in a high-pressure environment.[61]

Drug Tests. Preemployment drug testing typically involves asking job applicants to undergo urinalysis as part of routine selection procedures. Applicants who test positive are usually eliminated from further consideration. Alternatively, they may be given the option of taking another test at their own expense if they challenge the test's outcome.[62]

The purpose of preemployment drug testing is to avoid hiring people who may become problem workers. However, applicants may avoid detection of drug use if they remain drug-free for a sufficient period of time prior to taking the test. The extent to which this type of cheating occurs is not known, but a significant percentage of applicants (about 12%) do test positive in drug tests.

An important issue in preemployment drug testing is its effectiveness. Does testing applicants for drugs really have an effect on job performance? The answer is yes. In one study done by the U.S. Postal System, urine samples were taken from over 5,000 job applicants, but the results were not used in hiring. Six months to one year later, it was found that the applicants who had tested positive were absent 41% more often and fired 38% more often than those who had not tested positive. It appears that drug testing is a valid predictor of job performance.[63]

Honesty Tests. Each year U.S. businesses lose an estimated $6 billion to $200 billion to employee theft.[64] In the past, companies often used polygraph tests as part of the preemployment screening process. The polygraph measures the interviewee's pulse, breathing rate, and galvanic skin response (perspiration) while he or she is asked a series of questions. The theory is that these physiological measures will change when the interviewee is not telling the truth. However, the passage of the federal *Employee Polygraph Protection Act* in 1988 has eliminated the use of polygraph tests by most employers. Paper-and-pencil honesty tests are an increasingly popular alternative. It has been estimated that between 5,000 and 6,000 organizations use integrity testing in the hiring process, with as many as five million people tested annually.[65] The typical test measures attitudes toward honesty, particularly whether the applicant believes that dishonest behavior is normal and not criminal.[66] For example, the test might measure the applicant's tolerance for theft by other people and the extent to which the applicant believes most people steal regularly.

A recent study by independent researchers appears to confirm the validity of honesty testing.[67] It found that scores on the honesty test taken by applicants for positions at a retail convenience store chain were moderately tied to actual incidences of theft. Specifically, those who scored more poorly on the honesty test were more likely to steal from their employer.

Nevertheless, honesty tests are controversial. Most of the arguments against integrity testing center on the issue of false positives: people who are honest but score poorly on the tests. Typically, at least 40% of the test takers receive failing marks.[68] To see how you might score on such a test, answer the sample honesty test questions in the Issues and Applications feature on page 168 titled "Your Answers Could Win—or Cost—You Your Job."

Reference Checks. One of the best methods of predicting the future success of prospective employees is to look at their past employment record. Fear of defamation suits has

A QUESTION OF ETHICS

Some contend that urinalysis is an invasion of privacy and therefore should be prohibited unless there is reasonable cause to suspect an employee of drug use. Is it ethical for companies to insist that applicants undergo urinalysis? Suppose a company that wants to save on health insurance costs decides to test the cholesterol levels of all job applicants to eliminate those susceptible to heart attacks. Would this practice be ethical? Would it be legal?

Issues + Applications

Your Answers Could Win — or Cost — You Your Job

The following are typical questions used in integrity tests prepared by the Chicago-based test publisher Reid Psychological Systems.

- Do you believe a person who writes a check for which he knows there is no money in the bank should be refused a job in which honesty is important?
- Do you think a person should be fired by a company if it is found that he helped the employees cheat the company out of overtime once in a while?
- If you found $100 that was lost by a bank truck on the street yesterday, would you turn the money over to the bank, even though you knew for sure that there was no reward?
- Do you think it is all right for one employee to give another employee a discount even though the company does not allow it?
- Do you believe that an employee who regularly borrows small amounts of money from the place where he works without permission, but always pays it back, is honest?
- Do you think that the way a company is run is more responsible for employee theft than the attitudes and tendencies of employees themselves?
- On the 20th of each month, an old employee took company money to pay on his mortgage. On the 30th of each month—payday—he paid it back. After 15 years the man finally was seen by his boss putting the money back. No shortage was found, but the boss fired him anyway. Do you think the boss was right?
- Would you ever consider buying something from somebody if you knew the item had been stolen?

Source: Adapted from Budman, M. (1993, November–December). Your answers could win—or cost—your job. *Across the Board*, 35.

often caused companies to keep mum about job-related information on former employees. However, checking employees' references is an employer's best tactic for avoiding negligent hiring suits, in which the employer is held liable for injuries inflicted by an employee while on the job. What should companies do? Courts in almost every state have held that employers—both former and prospective—have a "qualified privilege" to discuss an employee's past performance. But to enjoy that privilege, a company must follow three rules. First, it must determine that the inquirer has a job-related need to know. Second, the former employer must release only truthful information. Third, EEO-related information (such as an employee's race or age) should not be released.[69]

graphology
The study of handwriting for the purpose of measuring personality or other individual traits.

Handwriting Analysis. **Graphology**, the study of handwriting for the purpose of measuring personality or other individual traits, is routinely used to screen job applicants in Europe, the birthplace of the technique. Analysis can involve assessment of over 300 aspects of handwriting, including the slope of the letters, the height at which the letter *t* is crossed, and the pressure of the writing. Although graphology is not as widely used in the United States as it is in Europe, it is estimated that over 3,000 U.S. organizations use the procedure as part of their screening process. Furthermore, the covert and occasional use of graphology may be even more widespread and may be growing.[70] The important question, of course, is whether handwriting is a valid predictor of job performance. Research on this issue indicates that the answer is no.

One study collected handwriting samples from 115 real estate associates and gave them to 20 graphologists, who scored each sample on a variety of traits, such as confidence, sales drive, and decision making.[71] Later, these results were compared with the subject's actual performance ratings as well as with objective performance measures such as total sales volume. There was a fair amount of consistency across graphologists' judgments of the handwriting samples (reliability). However, none of the judgments made by the graphologists correlated with any of the performance measures, so graphology cannot be considered a valid measure. This conclusion is echoed by other research on graphology.[72]

Thus, it should not be used as an employment screening device, and you should be wary when you see graphology touted as a valuable selection tool in magazines and other popular press outlets.[73]

Combining Predictors. Organizations often use multiple methods to collect information about applicants. For instance, managers may be selected on the basis of past performance ratings, an assessment center evaluation, and an interview with the manager to whom they will be reporting. How should these pieces of information be combined to make an effective selection decision? There are three basic strategies. The first requires making a preliminary selection decision following the administration of each method. This approach is called *multiple hurdle strategy* because an applicant has to clear each hurdle before moving on to the next one. Those who do not clear the hurdle are eliminated from further consideration.

Both of the remaining approaches require collecting all the information before making any decision; the difference is in how that information is combined. In a *clinical strategy* the decision maker subjectively evaluates all of the information and comes to an overall judgment. In a *statistical strategy* the various pieces of information are combined according to a mathematical formula, and the job goes to the candidate with the highest score.

The multiple hurdle strategy is often the choice when a large number of applicants must be considered. Usually, the procedure is to use the less expensive methods first to screen out clearly unqualified applicants. Research studies indicate that a statistical strategy is generally more reliable and valid than a clinical strategy,[74] but many people—and probably most organizations—prefer a clinical strategy.

Selection and Total Quality Management. Many companies have successfully used the various selection tools to hire above-average employees who've made a significant contribution to the firm's bottom line.[75] However, the traditional approach to selection may not be appropriate for organizations that have embraced a total quality management (TQM) philosophy. In many companies emphasizing TQM, activities and decisions are decentralized, and workers find themselves working in cross-functional teams.[76] In these situations, candidates' job skills (as measured by selection tests) may not be as important as their ability to perform effectively in a continuous-improvement, high-involvement environment.

For this reason, some companies have been searching for a way to measure the degree of "fit" between job candidates and the organization.[77] However, at this point it seems unlikely that these types of tests will achieve widespread use, for two reasons. First, it is not clear that an organization could defend a discrimination lawsuit by pointing to "lack of fit" instead of "lack of job-specific skills." Second, most research has validated selection methods by using supervisor evaluations of job performance on specific job-relevant characteristics. Thus, while we know which selection tools predict job-specific performance, we do not know how well they predict organizational fit.

Reactions to Selection Devices. In the last several pages we've discussed how well the various selection tools predict job performance. Before we turn to the third phase of the hiring process—socialization—we need to consider one final topic: reactions to selection tools. How do applicants and managers respond to the selection methods we've discussed? The answer is clearly important, since these responses may be the determining factor in a decision to file a lawsuit.

Applicant Reactions to Selection Devices. Applicants are a major customer of selection systems; they want and may demand fair selection devices. Moreover, applicants' reactions to selection methods can influence their attraction to and opinions of an organization, and their decision to accept or reject an offer of employment.[78] Applicants' reactions to selection tools also influence their willingness to purchase the company's products.[79]

To which selection tests do applicants respond most favorably and least favorably? Some interesting findings have emerged. For example, despite the increasing use of personality assessment devices as predictors, many job applicants believe that personality traits are "fakeable" and not job relevant. In addition, applicants perceive biodata, which have substantial validity, as irrelevant and invasive; they generally respond negatively to cognitive ability measures also. They respond most favorably to job simulations (for example, assessment center exercises) and interviews.

Manager Reactions to Selection Systems. Managers need selection systems that are quick and easy to administer and that deliver results that are easy to understand. However, very little research has considered manager reactions to selection systems. One recent study surveyed 635 managers from 38 agencies in state government.[80] The study assessed the managers' perceptions of various factors related to the selection process, including selection methods. These findings were used to revise selection systems and other HR practices in those agencies.

A central issue is the extent to which an organization should balance the traditional measures of reliability and validity with the measures of applicants' and managers' reactions in determining which selection methods to use. Clearly, reliability and validity cannot be jettisoned completely. A reasonable balance between the traditional criteria of reliability and validity and the quality criteria of applicants'/managers' reactions needs to be maintained.

Socialization

The staffing process isn't, and shouldn't be, complete once applicants are hired or promoted. To retain and maximize the human resources who were so carefully selected, organizations must pay careful attention to socializing them.

The socialization process is often informal and, unfortunately, informal can mean poorly planned and haphazard. A thorough and systematic approach to socializing new employees is necessary if they are to become effective workers. Without a socialization program, new employees may misunderstand the company's mission and reporting relationships, and may get inaccurate views of how things work and why.

Socialization can be divided into three phases: (1) anticipatory, (2) encounter, and (3) settling in.[81] At the *anticipatory stage*, applicants generally have a variety of expectations about the organization and job based on accounts provided by newspapers and other media, word of mouth, public relations, and so on. A number of these expectations may be unrealistic and, if unmet, can lead to dissatisfaction, poor performance, and high turnover.

realistic job preview (RJP)
Realistic information given to new hires about the demands of the job, the organization's expectations of the job holder, and the work environment.

A **realistic job preview (RJP)** is probably the best method of creating appropriate expectations about the job.[82] As its name indicates, an RJP presents realistic information about the demands of the job, the organization's expectations of the job holder, and the work environment. This presentation may be made either to applicants or to newly selected employees before they start work. For example, a person applying for a job selling life insurance should be told up front about the potentially negative parts of the job, such as the uncertain commission-based income and the need to try to sell insurance to personal acquaintances. Of course, the positive parts of the job, such as personal autonomy and high income potential, should also be mentioned. RJPs can be presented orally, in written form, on videotape, or, occasionally, in a full-blown work sample. For instance, at Toyota USA's Georgetown (Kentucky) plant, job simulations and work samples are used to demonstrate to applicants the repetitive nature of manufacturing work and the need for teamwork.

In the *encounter phase*, the new hire has started work and is facing the reality of the job. Even if an RJP was provided, new hires need information about policies and procedures, reporting relationships, rules, and so on. This type of information is helpful even for new employees who've had substantial experience elsewhere because the organization or work unit often does things somewhat differently than these employees are used to. In addition, providing systematic information about the organization and job can be a very positive signal to new workers that they are valued members of the organization. We discuss this *orientation period* for employees as a training opportunity in detail in Chapter 8.

During the *settling-in phase*, new workers begin to feel like part of the organization. If the settling in is successful, the worker will feel comfortable with the job and his or her role in the work unit. If it is unsuccessful, the worker may feel distant from the work unit and fail to develop a sense of membership in the organization. An *employee mentoring program*, in which an established worker serves as an adviser to the new employee, may help ensure that settling in is a success.[83] (We talk about mentoring programs at length in Chapter 9.)

Even the most extensive socialization program won't make new hires feel at ease if their immediate supervisors are not supportive during their adjustment period. See the Manager's Notebook titled "Building New Workers' Confidence" for a list of actions managers can take to make new employees feel at home in the organization. ▼

Manager's Notebook

Building New Workers' Confidence

Although there is no universally effective set of practices for helping new workers get into the swing of things, the following actions tend to work well with most people and in most situations.

✔1. **Delegate noncritical tasks that are challenging yet achievable.** Letting new people test their wings on a series of challenging tasks where mistakes can't do too much damage is always a good idea. As they experience success incrementally, their confidence will grow.

✔2. **Sandwich criticism between praise.** When something the new employee does causes things to go haywire, try not to blow the error out of proportion. Start by praising positive accomplishments, then discuss what needs correcting and close the conference on a note of praise.

✔3. **Express confidence in the person's abilities.** It's a real ego boost to hear someone say "I think you can do it."

✔4. **Share early job experiences and self-doubts.** Hearing about the boss's days as a new recruit makes employees realize that their anxiety is natural.

✔5. **Acknowledge the value of previous experience.** Ask new workers with previous experience to compare your company's systems and procedures with those of other employers.

✔6. **Emphasize potential.** Emphasizing potential encourages new workers to focus their energy on growth and development.

Source: Reprinted by permission of the publisher, from *Supervisory Management*, May 1993, ©1993. American Management Association, New York. All rights reserved.

▸ Legal Issues in Staffing

Legal concerns can play an exceptionally important role in staffing, particularly in selection. Selection is affected by a number of legal constraints, most notably federal legislation and its definition of illegal discrimination.

The Civil Rights Act of 1964 and its extension, the Civil Rights Act of 1991, provide broad prohibition against discrimination based on race, color, sex, religion, and national origin. These laws, which state that such discrimination in *all terms and conditions* of employment is illegal, affect selection as well as many other organizational programs, including performance appraisal and training.

To lower the chances of lawsuits claiming discrimination, firms should ensure that selection techniques are job-related. In other words, the best defense is evidence of the validity of the selection process. For example, if a minority group member turned down for a job claims discrimination, the organization should have ample evidence to document the job-relatedness of its selection process. This evidence should include job-analysis information and evidence that test scores are valid predictors of performance.

The Age Discrimination in Employment Act of 1967 and the 1978 amendments to the act prohibit discrimination against people age 40 and over. Again, the organization needs evidence of the validity of the selection process if older applicants are turned away—particularly if comparable but younger applicants are hired.

The Americans with Disabilities Act (ADA) of 1991 extends the Vocational Rehabilitation Act of 1973 and provides legal protection for people with physical or mental disabilities. ADA requires employers to provide reasonable accommodations for people whose disabilities may prevent them from adequately performing essential job functions, unless doing so will create an undue hardship for the organization. Thus, employers need to determine what constitutes a job's essential functions. Though the law does not clearly define "reasonable accommodation," the courts may deem reasonable such actions as modifications in schedules, equipment, and facilities. In terms of selection, ADA prevents employers from asking applicants if they have a disability and prohibits the requirement of medical examinations prior to making job offers. However, an employer can ask applicants if they can perform a job's essential functions. Also, job offers can be made contingent on the results of a medical examination.

Affirmative action must also be considered. Federal Executive Order 11246 requires organizations that are government contractors or subcontractors to have affirmative action programs in place. These programs are designed to eliminate any underutilization that might occur in an organization's employment practices (see Chapter 3). Affirmative action is not the same as the equal employment opportunity required by the Title VII of Civil Rights Act and related legislation. Making job-related selection decisions while not discriminating against subgroups is not the same as setting utilization goals. However, organizations that are not government contractors or subcontractors can lose the privilege of selecting employees solely on the basis of expected job performance if they are found guilty of discrimination. In that case, they can be ordered to put an affirmative action program in place.

Negligent Hiring

The final legal issue in staffing concerns claims of *negligent hiring*. Negligent hiring refers to a situation in which an employer fails to use reasonable care in hiring an employee, who then commits a crime while in his or her position in the organization. Because claims of negligent hiring have increased over the years,[84] managers need to be particularly sensitive to this issue. For example, Avis Rent-A-Car hired a man without thoroughly checking his background; the man later raped a female coworker. Avis was found guilty of negligent hiring and had to pay damages of $800,000. Had the company carefully checked the information provided in the man's job application, it would have discovered that he was in prison when he claimed he was attending high school and college. Employers are responsible for conducting a sound investigation into applicants' backgrounds. Factors such as gaps in employment or admission of prior criminal convictions should prompt closer investigation. To avoid liability for negligent hiring, employers should:[85]

- Develop clear policies on hiring as well as on disciplining and dismissing employees. The hiring policy should include a thorough background check of applicants, including verification of educational, employment, and residential information.
- Check state laws regarding hiring applicants with criminal records. States vary widely in what is legal in this area.
- Learn as much as possible about applicants' past work-related behavior, including violence, threats, lying, drug or alcohol abuse, carrying of weapons, and other problems. Keep in mind that privacy and discrimination laws prohibit inquiries into an applicant's personal, non–work-related activities. Behavioral problems may be investigated only in the context of their possible effect on job performance.

Summary and Conclusions

Human Resource Planning. HR planning is the process an organization uses to ensure that it has the right amount and right kinds of people to deliver a particular level of output or services at some point in the future. HR planning entails using a variety of qualitative or quantitative methods to forecast labor demand and labor supply, and then taking actions based on those estimates.

The Hiring Process. The hiring process consists of three activities: recruitment, selection, and socialization.

Challenges in the Hiring Process. The hiring process is filled with challenges. These include (1) determining which characteristics are most important to performance, (2) measuring these characteristics, (3) evaluating applicants' motivation, and (4) deciding who should make hiring decisions.

Meeting the Challenge of Effective Staffing. Because choosing the right person for a job can make a tremendous positive difference to productivity and customer satisfaction, it is important that each step of the hiring process be managed carefully.

Recruiting should focus on attracting qualified candidates, internally and/or externally. Recruiting efforts should be tied to the firm's human resource planning efforts. To ensure proper fit between hires and their jobs, and to avoid legal problems, firms should conduct job analyses.

Many selection tools are available. These include letters of recommendation, application forms, ability tests, personality tests, psychological tests, interviews, assessment centers, drug tests, honesty tests, reference checks, and handwriting analysis. The best (and most legally defensible) selection tools are both reliable and valid.

Socialization takes place in three stages: anticipatory, encounter, and settling in. Good socialization procedures ensure that new employees fit into the organization and work productively and effectively.

Legal Issues in Staffing. Several federal legal issues govern staffing practices. The Civil Rights Act, the Age Discrimination Act, and the Americans with Disabilities Act all prohibit various forms of discrimination. Executive Order 11246 spells out affirmative action policies. Employers must also take steps to protect themselves from negligent hiring litigation.

Key Terms

assessment center, 166
graphology, 168
human resource planning (HRP), 147
realistic job preview (RJP), 170
recruitment, 150
reliability, 159
selection, 151
socialization, 151
structured interview, 163
validity, 159

Discussion Questions

1. Smith & Nephew DonJoy, Inc., is a small but fast-growing manufacturer of medical devices in the north end of San Diego County. Because of the recent downsizing of Southern California's aerospace and defense industries, each job opening at DonJoy draws five times more applications than it did just a few years ago. An engineering position is likely to pull in as many as 300 applicants. You'd think that under these conditions, finding employees would be easy, but the selective layoffs made during the downsizings and the need for people to seek new career paths has created a glut of less-than-qualified applicants. What selection tool(s) can DonJoy use to get the most qualified employees from its huge pool of applicants? In general, which selection tool(s) do you think are the best predictors of job performance?
2. Should applicants be selected primarily on the basis of ability or on personality/fit? How can fit be assessed?
3. After returning to Los Angeles from Montana, a former LA police officer thought it would be relatively simple to gain reinstatement in the police force. After all, he had served on the LAPD for 10 years, and won commendations and the respect of his peers and supervisors. Yet two years after his return, this former officer still had not regained his job. Why? Because he is a white man and scored 98 on his oral exam. As of August 1993, the only way for a white man to land a job with the LAPD was to score a perfect 100. The lowest eligible score for a Latino man was 96, for an African-American man 95, and for all female candidates 94. This scoring was established when the city agreed to establish goals for minority and female officer recruiting.

   Do you think there are other ways the LAPD can recruit qualified minority and female employees that will not negatively affect white male recruits? Explain. In general, how would you design a selection process to achieve a diverse work force and hire the most qualified workers?
4. Julie Watkins has worked in her new position writing software documentation for three months. At first, she was excited about joining the fast-paced, growing software industry, but now she's having doubts. She keeps hearing about how important her job is to the company, but she doesn't understand how her work contributes to the whole. Her exposure to the company is limited to her department colleagues (other technical writers), the employee cafeteria, and the payroll office. What could Watkins's company have done to make her see the whole picture and gain an understanding of and commitment to how the company works?
5. Interviewing unqualified applicants can be a frustrating experience and a waste of time for managers, peers, or whoever is responsible for interviewing. How can the HR department minimize or eliminate this problem?
6. You work for a medium-sized, high-tech firm that faces intense competition on a daily basis. Change seems to be the only constant in your workplace, and each worker's responsibilities shift from project to project.

   Suppose you have the major responsibility for filling the job openings at your company. How would you go about recruiting and selecting the best people? How would you identify the best people to work in this environment?

MINICASE 1 *A Target for Lawsuits?*

As you read in this chapter, some companies use psychologically based selection tools to help choose employees who have a strong work ethic and are stable, motivated, and likely to stick with a job. However, some companies—including Minneapolis-based Target Stores—have run into trouble through their use of personal questions on their testing instruments, as the following excerpt from the *Los Angeles Times* explains:

> George Hite, a vice president for [Target] said the tests are widely used by police agencies to detect emotional instability.
>
> Target Stores required the tests for 300 security posts among 20,000 California employee positions to eliminate guard applicants who might pose risks, Hite said. The tests involved 700 true or false questions, among them:
>
> - I believe in the second coming of Christ.
> - I believe there is a devil and a hell in afterlife.
> - I have never indulged in any unusual sex practices.
>
> The case arose from a lawsuit filed by Sibi Soroka of Lafayette and other applicants required to take the tests for security guard jobs with Target in 1989.

Discussion Questions

1. What do you think are the advantages and disadvantages of using psychological tests to screen job applicants?
2. How do psychological tests like the one used by Target Stores differ from integrity tests?
3. Are there certain types of jobs for which the use of psychological tests is more justified than it is for other jobs?

Source: Reprinted from Hager, P. (1991, October 29). Court bars psychological tests in hiring. *The Los Angeles Times*, A20.

MINICASE 2 *Picking Employees By Phone*

When Pic 'n Pay Stores, Inc. had a problem with turnover, the Matthews, North Carolina–based shoe retailer decided on a radical solution. It replaced its old hiring system, which relied on more than 900 store managers—many of whom lacked HR expertise—with a centralized electronic hiring process called HR Easy. Now the company interviews people for positions in all its stores via telephone from headquarters.

First, applicants complete an application in the store where they wish to work and submit it to the manager, who checks it for any obvious inconsistencies. If the application passes muster, the store manager gives the candidate an 800 number to call for an interview. An electronic voice leads the candidate through a battery of yes/no questions about honesty, drug use, and personal habits. Applicants enter their answers on a touch-tone phone and computers record responses and response times. Then interviewers at corporate headquarters review the record and design questions for a follow-up live telephone interview, in which applicants get a chance to explain their answers to interviewers who are trained by psychologists to interpret pauses, changes of tone, and speech patterns.

Local store managers can challenge central decisions, but so far challenges have been rare. The company estimates that it's saved over $1 million through reduced turnover and theft by using HR Easy. It also plans to market its new system to fast-food chains, convenience stores, and other high-turnover businesses.

Discussion Questions

1. Do you think Pic 'n Pay's hiring process is more reliable for recruiting qualified employees than unstructured interviews and paper-and-pencil honesty tests?
2. How would you feel about being interviewed by "voice mail"? Do you think qualified people might be passed over by such an electronic screening process? Why or why not?
3. Do you think electronic screening is better at ruling out bias and stereotyping in the selection process than the traditional person-to-person interview?
4. How does Pic 'n Pay's HR Easy hiring program change the role of local store managers? Do you think this change is for the better? Explain.

Source: Adapted from Nhan, T. (1994, March 7). Turning a problem into profit. *The Charlotte Observer*, Section D, 1.

CASE 1 Making the Grade at Grade 1 Tools

The Grade 1 Company manufactures hand tools, from screwdrivers and hammers to various types of wrenches. The company takes pride in producing the highest-quality tools for craftspeople worldwide, and has exacting specifications for both mass production and custom runs of tools. However, Grade 1 has realized that it is no longer competitive in terms of getting its product to customers in a timely fashion. Timing can be a critically important issue in this industry, and Grade 1 is losing orders and clients.

A study of the issue didn't take long to uncover the source of Grade 1's difficulties. While the quality of Grade 1's products is not an issue, the company still relies on a labor-intensive production system that is not computerized. Other tool companies have long since switched to computerized production and production-control systems that deliver comparable quality in shorter times. Furthermore, those companies can give definite promises regarding delivery dates. Grade 1's delivery data system consists of educated guesses and, too often, missed deadlines and new promises.

As a result of the study, Grade 1 has made a commitment to computerizing its operations. Over the last six months, the production control system has been computerized and everyone at Grade 1 is excited about the new system's potential. Production and scheduling are now done by computer, and software accurately forecasts delivery dates. However, management's excitement over the new system's potential is tempered by the realization that it requires a new set of employee skills to be utilized effectively. Grade 1 has offered an early retirement option to its work force, and a number of workers have taken it. There is now room in the production area to hire a significant number of new workers.

Critical Thinking Questions

1. Design a selection system for staffing Grade 1's production department. What knowledge, skills, and abilities should the qualified candidates possess?
2. How large a role do you think personality or fit issues should play in Grade 1's selection system? How much of a role should tool production experience play? Explain your answer.
3. The Grade 1 workers who did not take or were not eligible for early retirement may or may not be acceptable workers under the new selection system. How should the company determine what to do with its current workers?
4. How could you collect evidence regarding the validity, or lack of validity, for the various predictors that Grade 1 could use?

Cooperative Learning Exercises

5. With your partner or a small group, identify the characteristics that might be most important to job performance in Grade 1's computerized production area. Prepare a list of the best ideas, and present these to the class.
6. Which selection tools should Grade 1 use in its staffing process? Consider the possibilities with your partner or team and present your conclusions to the class. If more than one predictor should be used, should one precede the others?

CASE 2 Wanted: Enthusiastic Employees to Grow with Growing Minds, Inc.

Growing Minds, Inc. is a national chain of retail outlets specializing in creative toys and innovative learning materials for children. The company caters to the upper end of the market and focuses on customer service for competitive advantage. It provides workshops for parents and children on such topics as learning with the computer and indoor gardening, and offers crafts classes ranging from papier-mâché to pottery.

Growing Minds plans to expand and open five new retail outlets in the coming quarter. This may mean up to 200 new hires, and the executive team wants to make sure that the best people are hired and retained. It has issued a challenge to its retail management personnel to design a staffing process that will accomplish these goals.

The children's market in which Growing Minds operates demands service personnel who are endlessly patient; knowledgeable about children, toys, and learning; and, perhaps most important, sociable, enthusiastic, and engaging. Excellent customer service is the top priority at Growing Minds, and obtaining the desired performance from personnel has meant a major investment in training. Unfortunately, new workers often leave within a year of being hired. This means that the company barely gets an adequate return on the training it has invested in its new hires. Apparently, turnover is due (at least in part) to the demanding nature of the job.

Recently, Growing Minds has been emphasizing the establishment of work teams to improve the quality of its services, iden-

continued

Wanted: Enthusiastic Employees to Grow with Growing Minds, Inc. continued

tify and fix any problems in service delivery, and brainstorm new opportunities. This approach has yielded better-than-anticipated results, so the team concept will be central to the new outlets.

Critical Thinking Questions

1. How can Growing Minds attract the best applicants for jobs at its new retail outlets? On what groups, if any, should the company's recruiting efforts focus? How should the recruiting be done?
2. How should Growing Minds select the best candidates? What type of characteristics and measures should be used? Why?
3. How might Growing Minds address its retention problem?
4. How might Growing Minds socialize its employees so that they are attuned to the firm's culture and plans for the future?

Cooperative Learning Exercises

5. Students who have worked in a retail setting, particularly one focusing on children and/or excellent customer service, share with the class the worker characteristics they found most important in that experience.
6. Divide into groups of three or four to identify possible sources of Growing Minds' employee retention problem. What could be done in the staffing process to address this problem? Each person in the group should list at least one possibility. Compile the best ideas produced by the group and present them to the class.

HRM Simulation 

Recruitment and selection are key HRM activities. In the simulation, your company needs to recruit 50 employees (Incident C) and you need to determine whom to hire for a supervisory position (Incident D). An important issue in both these decisions is whether employees should be brought in from outside or promoted from inside the company. Of course, you must keep in mind that employee diversity and ability to perform the job are also important in recruitment and selection. What are your decisions regarding recruitment and selection? What are the pros and cons of your decisions?

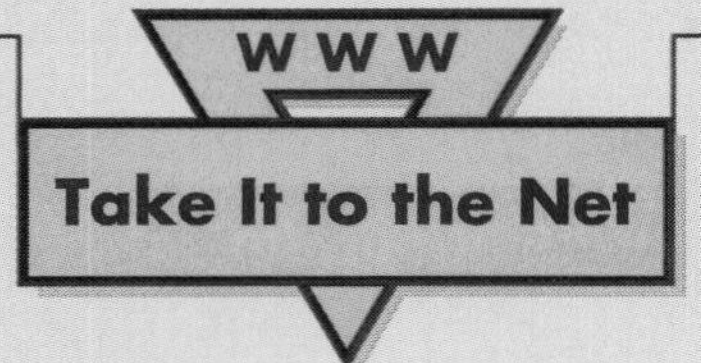

We invite you to visit the Gómez-Mejía/Balkin/Cardy page on the Prentice Hall Web site:

http://www.prenhall.com/gomez

You can also visit the Web sites for these companies, featured within this chapter:

3M	http://www.3m.com
Apple	http://www.apple.com
Rubbermaid	http://www.rubbermaid.com
Sun Microsystems	http://www.sun.com
Toyota Motor Manufacturing	http://www.toyota.com

Endnotes

1. Flynn, G. (1994, May). A new HRIS in Wake County streamlines HR. *Personnel Journal*, 137–142.
2. See, for example, Rothwell, W. J., and Kazanas, H. C. (1988). *Strategic human resources planning and management.* Englewood Cliffs, NJ: Prentice Hall; Bartholomew, D. J., and Forbes, A. F. (1979). *Statistical techniques for manpower planning.* Chichester, England: Wales Heneman, H. G. III, and Sandver, M. G. (1977). Markov analysis in human resource administration: Applications and limitations. *Academy of Management Review, 2*(4), 535–542; and Burack, E. H., and Mathys, N. J. (1987). *Human resource planning: A pragmatic approach to manpower staffing and development.* Lake Forest, IL: Brace-Park.
3. Cardy, R. L., and Carson, K. P. (1996). Total quality and the abandonment of performance

appraisal: Taking a good thing too far? *Journal of Quality Management, 1*, 193–206.
4. Bowen, D. E., Ledford, G. E., and Nathan, B. R. (1991). Hiring for the organization, not the job. *Academy of Management Executive, 5* (4), 35–51.
5. Semler, R. (1993). *Maverick*, 169–177. New York: Warner Books.
6. Rynes, S. L. (1991). Recruitment, job choice, and post-hire consequences: A call for new research directions. *Handbook of industrial and organizational psychology* (2nd ed.), Vol. 2, 399–444.
7. *Id.*
8. Gunsch, D. (1993, September). Comprehensive college strategy strengthens NCR's recruitment. *Personnel Journal*, 58–62.
9. Yamamoto, T. (1993, October). Recruiting system badly designed, badly run, unlikely to change. *Tokyo Business Today*, 52–54.
10. Posner, B. G. (1990). Putting customers to work. *Inc., 12*, 111–112.
11. Klein, E. (1993, January–February). Heroes for hire. *D&B Reports*, 26–28.
12. Sackett, P. R., and Arvey, R. D. (1993). Selection in small settings. In N. Schmitt, W. C. Borman (Eds.). *Personnel selection in organizations.* San Francisco: Jossey-Bass.
13. Wanous, J. P. (1992). *Organizational entry* (2nd ed.). Reading, MA: Addison-Wesley.
14. Lesly, E. (1993, October 11). CEOs with the outside edge. *Business Week*, 60–62.
15. *Training & Development*. (1993, November). Catalysts for career development: Four case studies, 26–27.
16. Laabs, J. J. (1991, May). Affirmative outreach. *Personnel Journal*, 86–93.
17. Walker, J. W. (1990, December). Human resource planning, 1990s style. *Human Resource Planning*, 229–230.
18. Hunter, J. E., and Hunter, R. F. (1984). Validity and utility of alternative predictors of job performance. *Psychological Bulletin, 96*, 72–98; Hunter, J. E., and Schmidt, F.L. (1982). The economic benefits of personnel selection using psychological ability tests. *Industrial Relations, 21*, 293–308; and Schmidt, F. L., and Hunter, J. E. (1983). Individual differences in productivity: An empirical test of the estimate derived from studies of selection procedure utility. *Journal of Applied Psychology, 68*, 407–414.
19. Hunter and Hunter, 1984.
20. Kleiman, L. S., and Faley, R. H. (1985). The implications of professional and legal guidelines for court decisions involving criterion-related validity: A review and analysis. *Personnel Psychology, 38*, 803–833.
21. Muchinsky, P. M. (1979). The use of reference reports in personnel selection: A review and evaluation. *Journal of Occupational Psychology, 52*, 287–297.
22. Aamodt, M. G., Bryan, D. A., and Whitcomb, A. J. (1993). Predicting performance with letters of recommendation. *Public Personnel Management, 22*, 81–90.
23. Peres, S. H., and Garcia, J. R. (1962). Validity and dimensions of descriptive adjectives used in reference letters for engineering applicants. *Personnel Psychology, 15*, 279–296.
24. Russell, C. J., Mattson, J., Devlin, S. E., and Atwater, D. (1990). Predictive validity of biodata items generated from retrospective life experience essays. *Journal of Applied Psychology, 75*, 569–580.
25. Hunter, J. E. (1986). Cognitive ability, cognitive aptitudes, job knowledge, and job performance. *Journal of Vocational Behavior, 29*, 340–362.
26. Bounds, G. M., Dobbins, G. H., and Fowler, O. S. (1995). *Management: A total quality perspective.* Cincinnati, OH: South-Western.
27. Harville, D. L. (1996). Ability test equity in predicting job performance work samples. *Educational and Psychological Measurement, 56*, 344–348.
28. Hogan, J., and Quigley, A. (1994). Effects of preparing for physical ability tests. *Public Personnel Management, 23*, 85–104.
29. Guion, R. M., and Gottier, R. F. (1965). Validity of personality measures in personnel selection. *Personnel Psychology, 18*, 135–163.
30. Bernardin, H. J., and Beatty, R. W. (1984). *Performance appraisal: Assessing human behavior at work.* Boston: Kent.
31. Landy, F. J. (1989). The psychology of work behavior (4th ed.). Pacific Grove, CA: Brooks/Cole.
32. Guion and Gottier, 1965.
33. Kleiman and Faley, 1985.
34. Funder, D. C., and Dobroth, J. M. (1987). Difference between traits: Properties associated with inter-judge agreement. *Journal of Personality and Social Psychology, 52*, 409–418.
35. Digman, J. M. (1990). Personality structure: Emergence of the five-factor model. *Annual Review of Psychology, 41*, 417–440; and Goldberg, L. R. (1993). The structure of phenotypic personality traits. *American Psychologist, 48*, 26–34.
36. Barrick and Mount, 1991; Digman, 1990; Hogan, R. (1991). Personality and personality measurement. In M. D. Dunnette & L. M. Hough (Eds.), *Handbook of industrial and organizational psychology* (2nd ed.), Vol. 1. Palo Alto, CA: Consulting Psychologists.
37. Barrick and Mount, 1991.
38. House, R. J., Shane, S. A., and Herold, D. M. (1996). Rumors of the death of dispositional research are vastly exaggerated. *Academy of Management Review, 21*, 203–224.
39. Dunn, W., Mount, M. K., Barrick, M. R., and Ones, D. S. (1995). Relative importance of personality and general mental ability in managers' judgments of applicant qualifications. *Journal of Applied Psychology, 80*, 500–509.
40. Wolfe, R. N., and Johnson, S. D. (1995). Personality as a predictor of college performance. *Educational and Psychological Measurement, 55*, 177–185.
41. Lublin, S. (1992, February 13). Trying to increase worker productivity, more employers alter management style. *The Wall Street Journal*, B1, B3.
42. Martin, S. I., and Lehnen, L. P. (1992, June). Select the right employees through testing. *Personnel Journal*, 46–51.
43. Arvey, R. D., and Campion, J. E. (1982). The employment interview: A summary and review of recent research. *Personnel Psychology, 35*, 281–322; and Harris, M. M. (1989). Reconsidering the employment interview: A review of recent literature and suggestions for future research. *Personnel Psychology, 42*, 691–726.
44. Springbett, B. M. (1958). Factors affecting the final decision in the employment interview. *Canadian Journal of Psychology, 12*, 13–22.
45. Buckley, M. R., and Eder, R. W. (1988). B. M. Springbett and the notion of the "snap decision" in the interview. *Journal of Management, 14*, 59–67.
46. Campion, M. A., Pursell, E. D., and Brown, B. K. (1988). Structured interviewing: Raising the psychometric properties of the employment interview. *Personnel Psychology, 41*, 25–42.
47. Pursell, E. D., Campion, M. A., and Gaylord, S. R. (1980). Structured interviewing: Avoiding selection problems. *Personnel Journal, 59*, 907–912.
48. Wright, P. M., Licthenfels, P. A., and Pursell, E. D. (1989). The structured interview: Additional studies and a meta-analysis. *Journal of Occupational Psychology, 62*, 191–199.
48a. See Pulakos, E. D., and Schmitt, N. (1995). Experience-based and situational interview questions: Studies of validity. *Personnel Psychology, 48*, 289–308.
49. Hunter and Hunter, 1984.
50. Warmke, D. L., and Weston, D. J. (1992, April). Success dispels myths about panel interviewing. *Personnel Journal*, 120–126.
51. Harris, 1989.
52. Kerr, J. (1982). Assigning managers on the basis of the life cycle. *Journal of Business Strategy, 2*, 58–65; Olian, J. D., and Rynes, S. L. (1984). Organizational staffing: Integrating practice with strategy. *Industrial Relations, 23*, 170–183; and Rynes, S., and Gerhart, B. (1990). Interviewer assessments of applicant "fit": An exploratory investigation. *Personnel Psychology, 43*, 13–35.
53. Chatman, J. A. (1989). Improving interaction organizational research: A model of person-organization fit. *Academy of Management Review, 14*, 333–349.
54. *Id.*
55. Pouliot, J. S. (1992, July). Topics to avoid with applicants. *Nation's Business*, 57–59.
56. Bounds, Dobbins, and Fowler, 1995; Gaugler, B. B., Rosenthal, D. B., Thornton, G. C., and Bentson, C. (1987). Meta-analysis of assessment center validity. *Journal of Applied Psychology, 72*, 493–511.
57. McEvoy, G. M., and Beatty, R. W. (1989). Assessment centers and subordinate appraisals of managers: A seven-year study of predictive validity. *Personnel Psychology, 42*, 37–52.

58. Coulton, G. F., and Feild, H. S. (1995). Using assessment centers in selecting entry-level police officers: Extravagance or justified expense? *Public Personnel Management, 24*, 223–254.
59. Bender, J. M. (1973). What is "typical" of assessment centers? *Personnel, 50*, 50–57.
60. Lopez, J. A. (1993, October 6). Firms force job seekers to jump through hoops. *The Wall Street Journal*, B1, B6.
61. Thatcher, M. (Ed.). (1993, November). "Front-line" staff selected by assessment centre. *Personnel Management*, 83.
62. Cowan, T. R. (1987). Drugs and the workplace: To drug test or not to test? *Public Personnel Management, 16*, 313–322.
63. Wessel, D. (1989, September 7). Evidence is skimpy that drug testing works, but employers embrace practice. *The Wall Street Journal*, B1, and B9.
64. Murphy, K. R. (1993). *Honesty in the workplace*. Belmont, CA: Brooks/Cole.
65. Bernardin, H. J., and Cooke, D. K. (1993). Validity of an honesty test in predicting theft among convenience store employees. *Academy of Management Journal, 36*, 1097–1108.
66. Terris, W., and Jones, J. W. (1982). Psychological factors relating to employees' theft in the convenience store industry. *Psychological Reports, 51*, 1219–1238.
67. Bernardin and Cooke, 1993.
68. Budman, M. (1993, November–December). The honesty business. *Across the Board*, 34–37.
69. Brown, M. (1991, December). Reference checking: The law is on your side. *Human Resource Measurements* (a supplement to *Personnel Journal*), 4–5.
70. Fowler, A. (1991). An even-handed approach to graphology. *Personnel Management, 23*, 40–43.
71. Rafaeli, A., and Klimoski, R. J. (1983). Predicting sales success through handwriting analysis: An evaluation of the effects of training and handwriting sample content. *Journal of Applied Psychology, 68*, 212–217.
72. Cox, A., and Tapsell, J. (1991). Graphology and its validity in personnel assessment. Paper presented at the British Psychological Society.
73. Bianchi, A. (1996, February). The character-revealing handwriting analysis. *Inc.*, 77–79.
74. Kleinmutz, B. (1990). Why we still use our heads instead of formulas: Toward an integrative approach. *Psychological Bulletin*, 107, 296–310.
75. For a review, see Gatewood, R. D., and Feild, H. S. (1994). *Human Resource Selection*. Orlando, FL: Harcourt, Brace and Company.
76. Cardy, R. L., and Stewart, G. (1997). Quality and teams: Implications for HRM theory and research. In D. B. Fedor and S. Ghosh (Eds.), *Advance in the Management of Organization Quality, 2*, Greenwich, CT: JAI Press, in press.
77. Kristof, A. L. (1996). Person-organization fit: An integrative review of the conceptualizations, measurement, and implications. *Personnel Psychology, 49*, 1–49; Barrett, R. S. (1995). Employee selection with the performance priority survey. *Personnel Psychology, 48*, 653–662.
78. Rynes, S. L. (1992). Recruitment, job choice, and post-hire consequences: A call for new research directions. In M. D. Dunnett and L. M. Hugh (Eds.), *Handbook of industrial and organizational psychology* (Vol. 2). CA: Consulting Psychologists Press, 399–444.
79. Macan, T. H., Avedon, M. J., Paese, M., and Smith, D. (1994). The effects of applicants' reactions to cognitive ability tests and an assessment center. *Personnel Psychology, 47*, 715–738.
80. Heneman, H. G., Huett, D. L., Lavigna, R. J., and Oston, D. (1995). Assessing managers' satisfaction with staffing service. *Personnel Psychology, 48*, 163–172.
81. Wanous, J. P., Reichers, A. E, and Malik, S. D. (1984). Organizational socialization and group development: Toward an integrative perspective. *Academy of Management Review, 9*, 670–683.
82. Breaugh, J. A. (1983). Realistic job previews: A critical appraisal and future research directions. *Academy of Management Review, 8*, 612–623.
83. Bragg, A. (1989, September). Is a mentor program in your future? *Sales & Marketing Management*, 54–63.
84. Cook, S. H. (1988, November). Playing it safe: How to avoid liability for negligent hiring. *Personnel*, 32–36.
85. *Id.*

CHALLENGES

After reading this chapter, you should be able to deal more effectively with the following challenges:

1 ▶ **Identify** the costs and benefits associated with employee separations.

2 ▶ **Understand** the differences between voluntary and involuntary separations.

3 ▶ **Avoid** problems in the design of early retirement policies.

4 ▶ **Design** HRM policies for downsizing the organization that are alternatives to a layoff; and, when all else fails, develop a layoff program that is effective and fair to the firm's stakeholders.

5 ▶ **Understand** the significance and value of outplacement programs.

6 Managing Employee Separations, Downsizing, and Outplacement

Out of Business. As the economy has become more globally competitive, more companies have found themselves unable to compete. When businesses downsize or close and people lose their jobs, the surrounding community is negatively affected also.

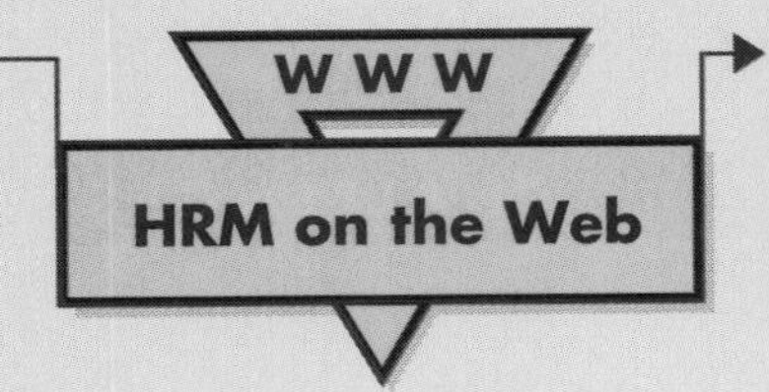

http://www.insworld.com/Newsletter/index.html

Retirement Planning Associates, Inc.

This Web site contains articles from *Benefits Insights,* a nontechnical newsletter for managers who deal with retirement planning issues. Such information is valuable for managers who plan to use early retirement incentives as an alternative to layoffs.

Imagine yourself in the following situation:

You are a division manager at AT&T in 1996 when the company's CEO, Robert E. Allen, announces a massive downsizing strategy that will eliminate 40,000 jobs. As a result of deregulation, the Baby Bells are now free to invade AT&T's long-distance stronghold, and to remain competitive AT&T must reduce its bloated staff of middle managers and other white-collar employees. Top executives have generated a plan for your division requiring you to develop and implement a layoff policy immediately. In drafting the policy, you are considering the following questions:[1]

- *What criteria should we use to determine who will be laid off?* Should we base the layoff decision on seniority? If so, would we lose some of the top-performing employees we recently hired? But if we base the layoff on merit, do we have an accurate system to measure performance? Will this system be defensible if angry employees challenge it in court?
- *How much notice should we give to employees who will be laid off?* Should we give them several years' notice, as General Motors did in 1992 when it announced future plant closings in advance? Or would giving advance notification create performance problems as current employees search for new jobs?
- *How will we provide security to our remaining employees and protect our business from sabotage or theft by employees who are losing their jobs?* Will we have to deal with disgruntled former employees? Should we hire armed guards to escort laid-off employees out of the building? What message would that send to remaining employees and the media?
- *How should we communicate news of the layoff to the employees who will be let go?* Should we tell them about the layoff in a memo or let them read about it in the newspaper? Should we hold a general meeting to inform the affected employees? Who should be responsible for telling employees that they have been selected for discharge?
- *When should we tell the media about the layoffs?* How do we control rumors that may appear in the media? How do we let our investors, our suppliers, and our customers know that we are committed to doing business with them and that the layoff will not hurt our relationship with them?
- *How will our remaining work force, the "survivors," feel about working for our company after the layoff?* Will they still be motivated to perform? Will they remain committed to our company? How should we deal with the anger and grief they will be feeling?
- *What kind of services can we provide to laid-off employees to help them find other jobs?* Should we retain a company that can supply these services? Can we extend the laid-off employees' benefits for a certain period of time to help ease the pain?

These are just some of the questions that managers face in trying to implement a layoff effectively. While the previous chapter discussed the management aspects of employee *inflow* into an organization (HR planning, recruitment, selection, and placement decisions), this chapter deals with the sometimes more unpleasant task of managing an organization's outflow of human resources. This is a particularly pressing issue in today's business environment, where downsizing and layoffs have become the norm.

employee separation
The termination of an employee's membership in an organization.

turnover rate
The rate of employee separations in an organization.

What Are Employee Separations?

An **employee separation** occurs when an employee ceases to be a member of an organization. The **turnover rate** is a measure of the rate at which employees leave the firm.

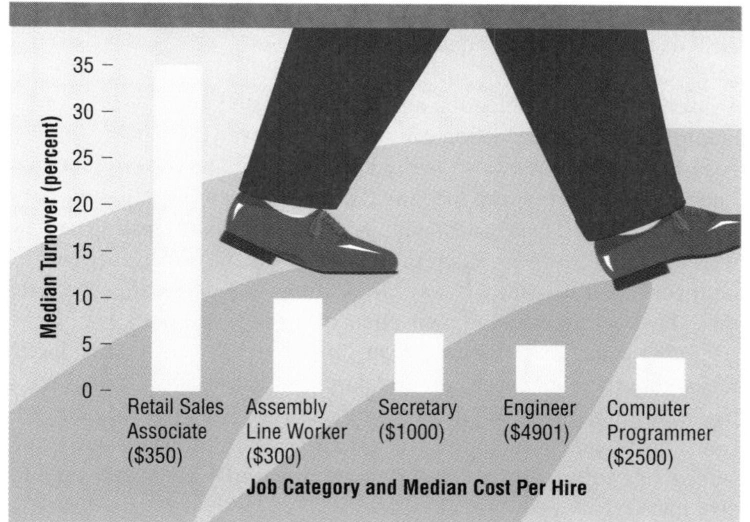

FIGURE 6-1

Turnover Rates and Costs for Specific Job Categories

Source: Adapted with permission from *Journal of Accountancy* (1992, October), p. 18. Copyright © 1992 by American Institute of Certified Public Accountants, Inc.

Companies try to monitor and control their turnover rate so that they can, in turn, monitor and control the costs of replacing employees. For example, replacing a U.S. Navy fighter pilot may cost over $1,000,000.[2] Figure 6–1 shows turnover rates and the costs of replacing employees in some other specific job categories. An excessively high turnover rate compared to the industry standard is often a symptom of problems within the organization.

Employee separations can and should be managed. Before we discuss the management of separations, however, it is beneficial to examine both the costs and the benefits of separations.

The Costs of Employee Separations

The costs of employee separations depend on whether managers intend to eliminate the position or to replace the departing employee. By eliminating positions, the company can reduce costs in the long run. This is why many companies in the 1990s have downsized their labor forces. However, even when positions are eliminated, the separation costs can be considerable. For example, IBM's 1991 decision to reduce its staff through early retirement incentives is costing hundreds of millions of dollars a year.

Figure 6–2 shows some of the costs involved in replacing an employee. These costs can be categorized as *recruitment costs, selection costs, training costs,* and *separation costs.*

Recruitment Costs. The costs associated with recruiting a replacement may include advertising the job vacancy and using a professional recruiter to travel to various locations (including college campuses). To fill executive positions or technologically complex openings, it may be necessary to employ a search firm to locate qualified individuals, who most

Recruitment Costs	Selection Costs	Training Costs	Separation Costs
• Advertising • Campus visits • Recruiter time • Search firm fees	• Interviewing • Testing • Reference checks • Relocation	• Orientation • Direct training costs • Trainer's time • Lost productivity during training	• Separation pay • Benefits • Unemployment insurance cost • Exit interview • Outplacement • Vacant position

FIGURE 6-2

Human Resource Replacement Costs

likely are already employed. A search firm typically charges the company a fee of about 30% of the employee's annual salary.

Selection Costs. Selection costs are associated with selecting, hiring, and placing a new employee in a job. Selection can involve interviewing the job applicant, which includes the costs associated with travel to the interview site and the productivity lost in organizing the interviews and arranging meetings to make selection decisions. For example, a law firm's decision to hire a new associate may involve the participation of many junior associates as well as senior partners. Each of these lawyers may charge clients hundreds of dollars per hour for his or her time. If several meetings are called after the interviews are completed, these lawyers may charge their clients for fewer hours.

Other selection costs involve testing the employee and conducting reference checks to make sure the applicant's qualifications are legitimate. Finally, the company may have to pay relocation costs, which include the costs of moving the employee's personal property, travel costs, and sometimes even housing costs. Housing costs may include the costs of selling one's previous house and the transaction costs of buying a house in a more expensive market.

Training Costs. Organizations incur costs in providing new employees with the knowledge necessary to perform on the job. Most new employees need some specific training to do their job. For example, sales representatives need training on the company's line of products. Training costs also include the costs associated with an orientation to the company's values and culture. Also important are direct training costs—specifically, the cost of instruction, books, and materials for training courses. Finally, while new employees are being trained, they are not performing at the level of fully trained employees, so some productivity is lost. For example, new computer programmers may write fewer lines of code in a given amount of time than experienced programmers do.

Separation Costs. A company incurs separation costs for all employees who leave, whether or not they will be replaced. The largest separation cost involves compensation in terms of pay and benefits. Most companies provide *severance pay* (also called *separation pay*) for laid-off employees. Severance pay may add up to several months' salary for an experienced employee. For example, IBM recently laid off 170 employees in its San Jose, California, disk drive plant. The affected workers were given 8 to 26 weeks of separation pay, depending on their length of service.

Less frequently, employees may continue to receive health benefits until they find a new job. In addition, employers who lay off employees may also see their unemployment insurance rates go up. Companies are penalized with a higher tax if more of their former employees draw benefits from the unemployment insurance fund in the states in which they do business.

Other separation costs are associated with the administration of the separation itself. Administration often includes an **exit interview** to find out the reasons why the employee is leaving (if he or she is leaving voluntarily) or to provide counseling and/or assistance in finding a new job. It is now common practice in larger firms to provide departing employees with **outplacement assistance,** which helps them find a job more rapidly by providing them with training in job-search skills. Finally, employers incur a cost if a position remains vacant and the work does not get done. The result may be a reduction in output or quality of service to the firm's clients or customers.

Conducting exit interviews is a challenge because it's often difficult to get departing employees to speak honestly about the company, usually because they don't want to "burn their bridges behind them." The Manager's Notebook titled "Excelling at Exit Interviews" gives some tips for eliciting truthful responses.

exit interview
An employee's final interview following separation. The purpose of the interview is to find out the reasons why the employee is leaving (if the separation is voluntary) or to provide counseling and/or assistance in finding a new job.

outplacement assistance
A program in which companies help their departing employees find jobs more rapidly by providing them with training in job-search skills.

The Benefits of Employee Separations

Although many people see separations negatively, they have several benefits. When turnover rates are too low, few new employees will be hired and the number of opportunities for promotion is sharply curtailed. A persistently low turnover rate may have a negative effect on performance if the work force becomes complacent and fails to generate innovative ideas. A certain level of employee separations is a good and necessary part of doing business, and the benefits of employee separations to the organization include the following: Labor costs are reduced; poor performers are replaced; innovation is increased; and opportunities for greater diversity are enhanced.

Employees may receive some potential benefits from a separation, too. An individual may escape from an unpleasant work situation and eventually find one that is less stressful or more personally and professionally satisfying.

Reduced Labor Costs. An organization can reduce its total labor costs by reducing the size of its work force. Although separation costs in a layoff can be considerable, the salary savings resulting from the elimination of some jobs can easily outweigh the separation pay and other expenditures associated with the layoff.

Replacement of Poor Performers. An integral part of management is identifying poor performers and helping them improve their performance. If an employee does not respond to coaching or feedback, it may be best to terminate him or her so that a new (and presumably more skilled) employee can be brought in. The separation of poor performers creates the opportunity to hire good performers in their place.

Manager's Notebook

Excelling at Exit Interviews

1. Start with the assumption that open and honest responses will not be easily obtained.
2. Use skilled interviewers, preferably from the HR department. In very small or family-run companies where this is impossible, paper-and-pencil questionnaires can be mailed to an ex-employee's home. This may not be a disadvantage because these kinds of surveys tend to produce more candid answers.
3. Assure departing employees that any comments they make will be held confidential (except those that concern potential legal issues) and that their responses won't endanger their chances of getting a good job reference.
4. Start with routine departure basics, such as when benefits will end, before moving to the heart of the interview: why the employee is leaving.
5. Ask open-ended questions and avoid coming across as the company's interrogator or defender.
6. Before taking any action, make sure the feedback from exit interviews correlates with other available information, such as employee surveys or peer and supervisor reviews.
7. Take action. People are more likely to feel their comments make a difference at companies that have a history of responding to ex-employees' perspectives.

Sources: Messmer, H. (1993, September). Parting words. *Small Business Reports*, 9–12; Pearl, J. (1993, June). Exit interviews: Getting the truth. *Working Woman*, 16–17; and Drost, D. A. (1987, February). Exit interviews: Master the possibilities. *Personnel Administrator*, 104–110.

Increased Innovation. Separations create advancement opportunities for high-performing individuals. They also open up entry-level positions as employees are promoted from within. An important source of innovation in companies is new people hired from the outside who can offer a fresh perspective. Such individuals may be entry-level college graduates armed with the latest research methods, or they may be experienced managers or engineers hired from leading research laboratories.

The Opportunity for Greater Diversity. Separations create opportunities to hire employees from diverse backgrounds and to redistribute the cultural and gender composition of the work force. Increasing its work force diversity allows an organization to take advantage of a diverse work force (see Chapter 4) while maintaining control over its hiring practices and complying with the government's EEOC policies.

▸ Types of Employee Separations

Employee separations can be divided into two categories. Voluntary separations are initiated by the employee. Involuntary separations are initiated by the employer. When employees leave voluntarily, they are less likely to take their former employers to court for "wrongful discharge." To protect themselves against legal challenges by former employees, employers must manage involuntary separations very carefully with a well-documented paper trail.

Voluntary Separations

voluntary separation
A separation that occurs when an employee decides, for personal or professional reasons, to end the relationship with the employer.

Voluntary separations occur when an employee decides, for personal or professional reasons, to end the relationship with the employer. The decision could be based on the employee's obtaining a better job, changing careers, or wanting more time for family or leisure activities. Alternatively, the decision could be based on the employee's finding the present job unattractive because of poor working conditions, low pay or benefits, a bad relationship with a supervisor, and so on. In most cases, the decision to leave is a combination of having attractive alternatives and being unhappy with aspects of the current job. There are two types of voluntary separations: quits and retirements.

Quits. The decision to *quit* depends on (1) the employee's level of dissatisfaction with the job and (2) the number of attractive alternatives the employee has outside the organization.[3] The employee can be dissatisfied with the job itself, the job environment, or both. For example, if the hours and location of a job are unattractive, an employee may look for a job with better hours and a location closer to home.

In recent years some employers have been using pay incentives to encourage employees to quit voluntarily. Employers use these *voluntary severance plans,* or *buyouts,* to reduce the size of their work force while avoiding the negative factors associated with a layoff. The pay incentive may amount to a lump-sum cash payment of six months to two years of salary, depending on the employee's tenure with the company and the plan's design. In 1995 Connecticut Mutual Life Insurance Company used an employee buyout to reduce the size of its work force after it merged with Massachusetts Mutual Life Insurance. Workers with three years or more were given three weeks of pay for each year of service, with a minimum of 26 weeks of pay and a maximum of 76 weeks.[4]

Retirements. Like a quit, a *retirement* is initiated by the employee. However, a retirement differs from a quit in a number of respects. First, a retirement usually occurs at the end of an employee's career. A quit can occur at any time. (In fact, it is in the early stages of one's career that a person is more likely to change jobs.) Second, retirements usually result in the individual's receiving retirement benefits from the organization. These may include a retirement income that is supplemented with personal savings and Social Security benefits. People who quit do not receive these benefits. Finally, the organization normally plans retirements in advance. HR staff can help employees plan their retirement, and managers can plan in advance to replace retirees by grooming current employees or recruiting new ones. Quits are much more difficult to plan for.

Most employees postpone retirement until they are close to 65 because that is the age at which they are entitled to full Social Security and Medicare benefits from the government (see Chapter 12). Without these benefits, many workers would find it difficult to retire. It is illegal for an employer to force an employee to retire on the basis of age.

Many *Fortune* 500 companies have found *early retirement incentives* an effective way to reduce their work force. These incentives make it financially attractive for senior employees to retire early. Along with buyouts, they are used as alternatives to layoffs because they are seen as a gentler way of downsizing. We discuss the management of early retirements in detail later in this chapter.

Involuntary Separations

involuntary separation
A separation that occurs when an employer decides to terminate its relationship with an employee due to (1) economic necessity or (2) a poor fit between the employee and the organization.

An **involuntary separation** occurs when management decides to terminate its relationship with an employee due to (1) economic necessity or (2) a poor fit between the employee and the organization. Involuntary separations are the result of very serious and painful decisions that can have a profound impact on the entire organization, especially the employee who loses his or her job.

Although managers implement the decision to dismiss an employee, the HR staff makes sure that the dismissed employee receives "due process" and that the dismissal is performed within the letter and the spirit of the company's employment policy. Cooperation and teamwork between managers and HR staff are essential to effective management of the dismissal process. HR staff can act as valuable advisers to managers in this arena by helping them avoid mistakes that can lead to claims of wrongful discharge. They can also help protect employees whose rights are violated by managers. There are two types of involuntary separations: discharges and layoffs.

Discharges. A *discharge* takes place when management decides that there is a poor fit between an employee and the organization. The discharge is a result of either poor performance or the employee's failure to change some unacceptable behavior that management has tried repeatedly to correct. Sometimes employees engage in serious misconduct, such as theft or dishonesty, which may result in immediate termination.

Managers who decide to discharge an employee must make sure they follow the company's established discipline procedures. Most nonunion companies and all unionized firms have a *progressive discipline procedure* that allows employees the opportunity to correct their behavior before receiving a more serious punishment. For example, an employee who violates a safety rule may be given a verbal warning, followed by a written warning within a specified period of time. If the employee does not stop breaking the safety rule, the employer may choose to discharge the employee. Managers must document the occurrences of the violation and provide evidence that the employee knew about the rule and was warned that its violation could lead to discharge. In this way, managers can prove that the employee was discharged for just cause. Chapter 14 details the criteria that managers can use to determine if a discharge meets the standard of just cause.*

Layoffs. A *layoff* differs from a discharge in several ways. In a layoff, employees lose their jobs because a change in the company's environment or strategy forces it to reduce its work force. Global competition, reductions in product demand, changing technologies that reduce the need for workers, and mergers and acquisitions are the primary factors behind most layoffs. In contrast, most discharged employees have usually been a direct cause of their separation.

Layoffs have a powerful impact on the organization. They can affect the morale of the organization's remaining employees, who may fear losing their jobs in the future. In addition, layoffs can affect a region's economic vitality, including the merchants who depend on the workers' patronage to support their businesses. When layoffs happen, the entire community may suffer. This was the case when National Cash Register (NCR) closed many plants in the Dayton, Ohio area in the 1990s. Dayton's economic prosperity collapsed when it lost 20,000 high-paying jobs due to a failed merger between NCR and AT&T.[5]

Investors may be affected by layoffs as well. The investment community may interpret a layoff as a signal that the company is having serious problems. This, in turn, may lower the price of the company's stock on the stock market. Finally, layoffs can change a company's image. They can hurt a company's standing as a good place to work and make it difficult to recruit highly skilled employees who can choose among numerous employers. For example, the recent layoffs of thousands of aerospace engineers from defense contractors such as General Dynamics, Lockheed, and Northrup may make it difficult for these companies to attract the best new engineering graduates.

What can a company do to help a community when it decides to close a plant that is important to the community's economic prosperity?

*In some jurisdictions, it is possible for management to discharge an employee based on evidence that does not meet the standard of just cause. However, the authors recommend meeting this standard as a good business practice.

downsizing
A company strategy to reduce the scale (size) and scope of its business in order to improve the company's financial performance.

rightsizing
The process of reorganizing a company's employees to improve their efficiency.

Layoffs, Downsizing, and Rightsizing. It is appropriate at this point to clarify the difference between a layoff and two concepts that are frequently (but sometimes mistakenly) associated with it: downsizing and rightsizing. A company that adopts a **downsizing** strategy reduces the scale (size) and scope of its business in order to improve its financial performance.[6] When a company decides to downsize, it may choose layoffs as one of several ways of reducing costs or improving profitability.[7] In recent years many firms have done exactly this, but we want to emphasize that companies can take many other measures to increase profitability without resorting to layoffs. We discuss these measures later in this chapter.

Rightsizing involves reorganizing a company's employees to improve their efficiency.[8] An organization needs to rightsize when it becomes bloated with too many management layers or too many bureaucratic work processes that add no value to its product or service. For example, companies that reconfigure their front-line employees into self-managed work teams may find that they are overstaffed and need to reduce their headcount to take advantage of the efficiencies provided by the team structure. The result may be layoffs, but layoffs are not always necessary. As with downsizing strategy, management may have several alternatives to layoffs available when it rightsizes its work force.

Managing a layoff is an extremely complex process. Before we examine the specifics, however, it is useful to examine an important alternative to layoffs: early retirements.

Building Managerial Skills: ▸ Managing Early Retirements

When a company decides to downsize its operation, its first task is to examine alternatives to layoffs. As we mentioned earlier, one of the most popular of these methods is early retirement. In recent years such companies as IBM, Exxon, Du Pont, AT&T, Hewlett-Packard,[9] NYNEX,[10] and GTE[11] have used early retirement to reduce the size of their work force.

The Features of Early Retirement Policies

Early retirement policies consist of two features: (1) a package of financial incentives that makes it attractive for senior employees to retire earlier than they had planned and (2) an *open window* that restricts eligibility to a fairly short period of time. After the window is closed, the incentives are no longer available.[12]

The financial incentives are usually based on a formula that accelerates senior employees' retirement eligibility and increases their retirement income. It is not unusual for companies to provide a lump-sum payment as an incentive to leave. Many companies also offer the continuation of health benefits so that early retirees enjoy coverage until they are eligible for Medicare at age 65. However, as companies have opened the early retirement window to more and more employees in recent years, they have had to scale back once-generous severance packages. For instance, when IBM announced its early retirement policy in 1991, it allowed any employee with 30 years of service to retire with full retirement benefits regardless of age. Employees who accepted the offer received a lump sum of one year's salary. By 1993 departing employees got a maximum of 26 weeks' pay plus only six months' paid medical coverage.[13]

Early retirement policies can reduce the size of a company's work force substantially. Du Pont experienced a 10% reduction and Exxon experienced a 15% reduction in their work forces with early-retirement policies.[14]

Avoiding Problems with Early Retirements

Managing early retirement policies requires careful design, implementation, and administration. When not properly managed, early retirement policies can give rise to a host of

Out of the Rat Race.

After 13 years as a fuels buyer with BP America, Inc., Ron Colvin started his own business as a chimney sweep. Colvin is happy to be out of corporate life and is making decent money. The only problem: "It gets lonely, working by yourself," he says.

problems. Too many employees may take early retirement, the wrong employees may leave, and employees may perceive that they are being forced to leave, which may result in age discrimination complaints.

Du Pont was surprised in 1985 when 12,000 of its employees, about twice as many as expected, elected to take advantage of the company's early retirement incentives.[15] One way to avoid excess resignations is to restrict eligibility to divisions that have redundant employees with high levels of seniority (instead of making the policy available to all employees throughout the corporation). Another way is to ask senior employees how they would respond to a specific early retirement plan. This survey could then be used to predict the number of senior employees who would retire if the incentives were made available. If the survey shows that too many would leave, the incentives could be fine-tuned so that a controlled number of employees take early retirement.

Sometimes the most marketable employees with the best skills can easily find another job and decide to "take the money and run." To avoid this situation and keep its most valuable people, the company can develop provisions to hire back retired employees as temporary consultants until suitable replacements can be promoted, hired, or trained.

Early retirement programs must be managed so that eligible employees do not perceive that they are being forced to retire and consequently file age discrimination charges. Situations that could be interpreted as coercive include the following:

- A longtime employee who has performed satisfactorily over many years suddenly receives an unsatisfactory performance evaluation.
- A manager indicates that senior employees who do not take early retirement may lose their jobs anyway because a layoff is likely in the near future.
- Senior employees notice that their most recent pay raises are quite a bit lower than those of other, younger workers who are not eligible for early retirement.

A recent example from the business pages illustrates how a lack of sensitivity on the part of management can result in litigation. A former employee who sued IBM for age discrimination was awarded $315,000 in compensatory damages because he convinced the jury that he was forced to take early retirement.[16] The employee introduced evidence showing that his job had been reclassified after he voiced some reservations about taking early retirement. Shortly after that, he claimed, he received a warning that his next performance evaluation would be considered unsatisfactory.

Managers can avoid lawsuits by following one simple guideline: All managers with senior employees should make certain that they do not treat senior employees any differently than other employees. HR staff members play an important role here by keeping managers aware of the letter and the spirit of the early retirement policy so that they do not (consciously or unconsciously) coerce senior employees during the open window period. ▼

Building Managerial Skills: ▸ Managing Layoffs

Typically, an organization will institute a layoff when it cannot reduce its labor costs by any other means. Figure 6–3, which presents a model of the layoff decision and its alternatives, shows that managers should first try to reduce their labor costs by using alternatives to layoffs, such as early retirements and other voluntary work force reductions. After managers make the decision to implement a layoff, they must concern themselves with the outplacement of the former employees.

An important influence on the likelihood of a layoff is the business's HR strategy (see Chapter 1). Companies with a lifelong employment HR strategy are less likely to lay off employees because they have developed alternative policies to protect their permanent employees' job security. The best-known examples of firms with lifelong employment policies are the large Japanese corporations, which employ about one third of Japanese workers. In the United States a few companies (such as Hewlett-Packard and IBM) have used lifelong employment policies, but most firms have market-driven HR strategies that permit layoffs when alternatives are not available. It is interesting to note that by the mid-1990s even IBM had been forced to modify its commitment to lifelong job security and to institute its first layoffs.

Alternatives to Layoffs

Figure 6–4 shows the alternatives to layoffs. These include employment policies, changes in job design, pay and benefits policies, and training. Managers can use these alternatives both to reduce labor costs and to protect the jobs of full-time employees.

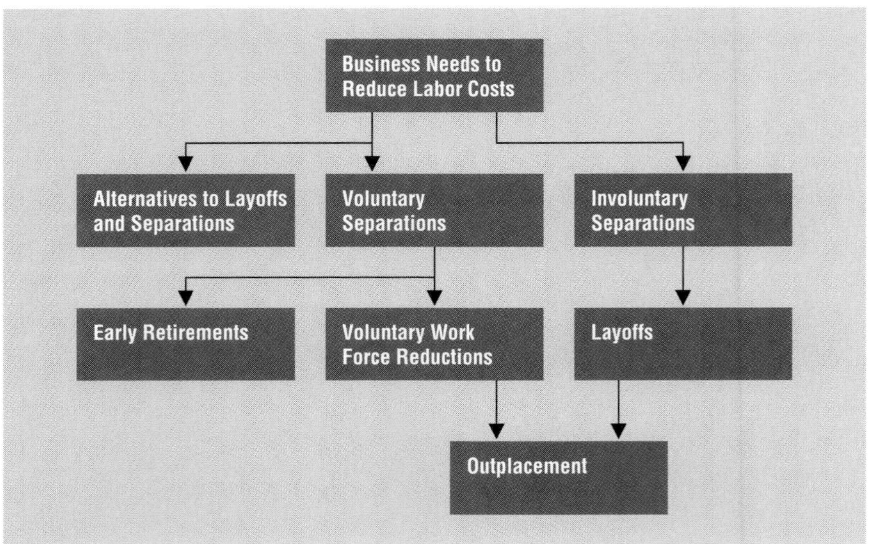

FIGURE 6-3
The Layoff Decision and Its Alternatives

Employment Policies	Changes in Job Design	Pay and Benefits Policies	Training
• Reduction through attrition • Hiring freeze • Cut part-time employees • Cut internships or co-ops • Give subcontracted work to in-house employees • Voluntary time off • Leaves of absence • Reduced work hours	• Transfers • Relocation • Job sharing • Demotions	• Pay freeze • Cut overtime pay • Use vacation and leave days • Pay cuts • Profit sharing or variable pay	• Retraining

FIGURE 6-4
Alternatives to Layoffs

Employment Policies. The first alternatives to layoffs that managers are likely to consider are those that intrude the least on the day-to-day management of the business. These alternatives usually focus on adjustments to employment policies.

The least disruptive way to cut labor costs is through **attrition.** By not filling job vacancies that are created by turnover, improvements can be made on the bottom line. When greater cost reductions are needed, a **hiring freeze** may be implemented. Many universities have used hiring freezes to balance their budgets in years of fiscal restraint. Temporary employees, part-time employees, student interns, co-ops, and subcontracted employees may also be eliminated to protect the jobs of permanent full-time employees.

attrition
An employment policy designed to reduce the company's work force by not refilling job vacancies that are created by turnover.

hiring freeze
An employment policy designed to reduce the company's work force by not hiring any new employees into the company.

Other employment policies are aimed at decreasing the number of hours worked and, therefore, the number of hours for which the company must pay its employees. Workers may be encouraged to take voluntary (unpaid) time off or leaves of absence, or they may be asked to put in a shorter workweek (for example, 35 hours rather than 40).

The strategic application of employment policies to provide job security for a firm's full-time, core employees is called a *rings of defense* approach to job security. Under this approach, headcounts of full-time employees are purposely kept low. An increase in the demand for labor will be satisfied by hiring part-time and temporary employees or subcontracting work to freelancers. These people can be easily dismissed when business conditions worsen.[17]

Changes in Job Design. Managers can use their human resources more cost-effectively by changing job design and transferring people to different units of the company. Alternatively, they may relocate people to jobs in different parts of the country where the cost of living and salaries are lower. The cost of relocating an employee plus the fact that some employees do not want to move sometimes make this alternative problematic. Another practice, common in unionized companies, allows a senior employee whose job is eliminated to take a job in a different unit of the company from an employee with less seniority. This practice is called *bumping.*

Companies can also use *job sharing* (which we discussed in Chapter 2) when it is possible to reconfigure one job into two part-time jobs. The challenge here is to find two people willing to share the job's hours and pay. Finally, as a last resort, highly paid workers may be demoted to lower-paying jobs.

A QUESTION OF ETHICS

Is it ethical for top managers to receive cash bonuses while at the same time asking lower-level employees to accept a pay freeze?

Pay and Benefits Policies. As one way of reducing costs, managers can enforce a *pay freeze* during which no wages or salaries are increased. Pay freezes should be done on an across-the-board basis to avoid accusations of discrimination. These policies can be augmented by reductions in overtime pay and policies that ask employees to use up their vacation and leave days. Many state governments have enforced annual pay freezes on their employees. Unfortunately, pay freezes often cause some top-performing, highly marketable employees to leave the company.

A more radical and intrusive pay policy geared toward reducing labor costs is a *pay cut*. This action can be even more demoralizing to the work force than a pay freeze, and should be used only if employees are willing to accept it voluntarily as an alternative to layoffs. Recently, unions in several U.S. industries have accepted wage reductions in return for job security. For example, in 1994 the unions that represent the pilots and machinists at United Airlines accepted a 15% pay cut in exchange for 55% of the company stock and three out of 12 seats on the board of directors.[18] The impetus for this innovative agreement was the employees' desire for job security, since United Airlines management had been considering a major downsizing that would include layoffs of union members. By 1996 United Airlines reported healthy profits that were well received by the investment community and resulted in a doubling of the value of its stock.

A long-term pay policy that may protect workers from layoffs entails structuring compensation so that profit sharing (the sharing of company profits with employees) or variable pay (pay contingent on meeting performance goals) makes up a significant portion of employees' total compensation (around 15 to 20%). When the business cycle hits a low point, the company can save up to about 20% of the payroll by not paying out profit sharing or variable pay, but still retain its employees by paying them the salary portion of their total compensation. Few companies in the United States use this approach, but it is very common in Japan.

Training. By retraining employees whose skills have become obsolete, a company may be able to match newly skilled workers with available job vacancies. Without this retraining, the workers might have been laid off. For example, IBM has retrained some of its production workers in computer programming and placed them in jobs requiring this skill.

Nontraditional Alternatives to Layoffs. In their attempt to avoid layoffs, some companies have come up with innovative alternatives.

- Hugh Aaron's small East Coast plastics company had been plagued by cyclical layoffs for years. Finally Aaron took a daring step. He promised employees he would eliminate all future layoffs if they agreed to work overtime or take on new job tasks whenever necessary. To avoid burnout and understaffing when business was strong, Aaron called in retirees who were happy to mix with the old gang, and he relied on college students to fill in during the busy summer months. As a result of the program, employee morale reached new heights.
- Sidney Harman, chairman of Harman International Industries, Inc., employs 1,500 production workers in California's San Fernando Valley. Harman has succeeded in creating an internal labor buffer for periods of slack demand. He has dubbed his idea *OLE*, an acronym for off-line employment. Production workers who would otherwise be idle during downturns are employed making clock faces from scrap wood or working in one of Harman's new outlet stores. More work has been brought back inside the plants (rather than jobbed out to outside companies). In addition, Harman regularly pulls workers off the line and puts them into training programs.

Implementing a Layoff

Once the layoff decision is made, managers must implement it carefully. A layoff can be a traumatic event that affects the lives of thousands of people. As the Issues and Applications feature "Layoffs at General Motors: Strategically Sound or a Quick Fix?" shows, General Motors' 1992 announcement that it was closing 21 plants had a major effect on all associated with the company.

Issues + Applications

Layoffs at General Motors: Strategically Sound or a Quick Fix?

The following announcement appeared in February 1992:

DETROIT—General Motors Corp. reported a record $4.5 billion 1991 loss yesterday and identified some of the plants it will close to try to restore profits at the world's largest industrial corporation.

It was the worst annual loss for an American corporation in history.

GM Chairman Robert Stempel announced the closings of two assembly plants—one each in Michigan and New York—and the shuttering of operations in 10 of GM's supplier complexes, affecting 16,000 workers.

He also described a long-range plan to eliminate redundancies in nearly all areas of the company's operations, including vehicle design and marketing, technical research, and support operations.

"We must accelerate the fundamental changes," Stempel told a news conference.

The details answered some of the questions left when the automaker announced a broad restructuring program last December. The overall plan calls for 21 plant closings and 74,000 job cuts by the middle of the decade.

Analysts have said slow vehicle development, generous labor contracts, and the recession have combined to force GM to shrink....

Stempel is imparting to GM's struggling North American car and truck operations some of the structural changes the company instituted in its European operations.

GM said that overseas operations earned $2.1 billion last year, much of it coming from Europe.

Prime among the European changes is workers opting for more flexible work rules that have boosted productivity.

"If you look at what we've been doing in Europe, one of the things we've done over there is used fixed facilities literally 24 hours a day," Stempel said. "We know where we are and we know what's happening to our costs over there.

"Obviously, it's the way we're going to have to go."

UAW [United Auto Workers] President Owen Bieber and Vice President Stephen P. Yokich accused GM of "closing its eyes to the misery inflicted on its workers and their communities."

"They have failed to inform us of significant decisions, disregarded major cost-saving proposals on sourcing and employee efficiency and, contrary to their official rhetoric, pitted plant against plant and community against community," the labor leaders said in a statement.

Reprinted with permission from Standish, F. (1992, February 25). *Denver Post*, 1C, 3C.

The key issues that managers must settle are notifying employees, developing layoff criteria, communicating to laid-off employees, coordinating media relations, maintaining security, and reassuring survivors of the layoff.

Notifying Employees. The **Worker Adjustment and Retraining Notification Act (WARN)** requires U.S. employers with 100 or more employees to give 60 days' advance notice to employees who will be laid off as a result of a plant closing or a mass separation of 50 or more workers.[19] This law, passed in 1988, was designed to give workers more time to look for a new job. Employers who do not notify their employees must give them the equivalent of 60 working days of income. Employers who lay off fewer than 50 employees have greater flexibility as to when they can notify the affected employees.

Worker Adjustment and Retraining Notification Act (WARN) of 1988
A federal law requiring U.S. employers with 100 or more employees to give 60 days' advance notice to employees who will be laid off as a result of a plant closing or a mass separation of 50 or more workers.

There are several arguments in favor of giving at least several weeks' notice prior to a layoff. It is socially and professionally correct to extend employees this courtesy. Also, this treatment is reassuring to the employees who will remain with the company. But there are also arguments in favor of giving no notification. If the labor relations climate is poor, there is the potential for theft or sabotage to company equipment. In addition, the productivity of employees who are losing their jobs may decline.[20]

The requirements for layoff notification tend to be more restrictive in European countries than in the United States. For example, in Sweden management must give at least 60 days' advance notice in layoffs of five or more workers, while in France as few as two workers must get at least 45 days' notification.[21] Figure 6–5 on page 192 lists advance notice requirements in several other European nations.

Developing Layoff Criteria. In planning and implementing a layoff, it is essential that the criteria for dismissal be clear. When the criteria are clearly laid out, the managers responsible for determining who will be laid off can make consistent, fair decisions. The

FIGURE 6-5

Requirements of Advance Notice for Collective Dismissals in Selected European Countries

Source: Ehrenberg, R. G., and Jakubson, G. H. (1988). *Advance notice provisions in plant closing legislation.* Kalamazoo, MI: W.E. Upjohn Institute for Employment Research.

Country	Notice Requirements
Belgium	30 days
Denmark	30 days
Germany	30 days
Greece	30 days
Ireland	30 days
Italy	22 to 32 days
Luxembourg	60 to 75 days
Netherlands	2 to 6 months
United Kingdom	30 to 90 days (if at least ten workers are involved)

A QUESTION OF ETHICS

How much notice of a layoff is a company obligated to give?

two most important criteria used as the basis for layoff decisions are seniority and employee performance.

Seniority, the amount of time an employee has been with the firm, is by far the most commonly used layoff criterion. It has two main advantages. First, seniority criteria are easily applied; managers simply examine all employees' dates of hire to determine the seniority of each (in years and days). Second, many employees see the seniority system as fair because (1) managers cannot play "favorites" under a seniority-based decision and (2) the most senior employees have the greatest investment in the company in terms of job rights and privileges (they have accrued more vacation and leave days, and have more attractive work schedules, for example).

There are disadvantages to using the "last in, first out" method, however. The firm may lose some top performers, as well as a disproportionate amount of women and minorities—who are more likely to be recent hires in certain jobs. Nonetheless, the courts have upheld seniority as the basis for layoff as long as all employees have equal opportunities to obtain seniority.

When the work force is unionized, layoff decisions are usually based on seniority. This provision is written into the labor contract. However, when the work force is nonunion and especially when cuts must be made in professional and managerial employees, it is not unusual for companies to base layoff decisions on performance criteria or a combination of performance and seniority. Using performance as the basis for layoffs allows the company to retain its top performers in every work unit and eliminate its weakest performers. Unfortunately, performance levels are not always clearly documented, and the company may be exposed to wrongful discharge litigation if the employee can prove that management discriminated or acted arbitrarily in judging performance. Because of these legal risks, many companies avoid using performance as a basis for layoff.

If a company has taken the time to develop a valid performance appraisal system that accurately measures performance and meets government guidelines, then there is no reason why appraisal data cannot be used as the basis for layoff. For example, IBM used performance as the basis for layoffs of its professional work force in a 1990s downsizing effort.[22] When using this criterion, managers should take the employee's total performance over a long period of time into account. Managers who focus on one low performance appraisal period and ignore other satisfactory or exceptional performance appraisals could be viewed as acting arbitrarily and unfairly. We discuss this topic in detail in the next chapter.

Communicating to Laid-off Employees. It is crucial to communicate with the employees who will be laid off as humanely and sensitively as possible. No employee likes being told he or she will be discharged, and the way a manager handles this unpleasant task can affect how the employee and others in the organization accept the decision. Some general guidelines on how to lay off an employee are given in the Manager's Notebook.

Laid-off employees should first learn of their fate from their supervisor in a face-to-face private discussion. Employees who learn about their dismissal through a less personal form of communication (for example, a peer or a memo) are likely to be hurt and angry. The information session between supervisor and employee should be brief and to the point. The manager should express appreciation for what the employee has contributed, if appropriate, and explain how much severance pay and what benefits will be provided and for how long. This information can be repeated in greater detail at a group meeting of laid-off employees and should be documented in a written pamphlet handed out at the meeting.

The best time to hold the termination session is in the middle of the workweek. It is best to avoid telling workers they are being laid off during their vacation or right before a weekend, when they have large blocks of time on their hands.[23]

One example of how *not* to communicate a layoff is provided by the following example: A petroleum company brought employees together for a rather unsettling meeting. Each employee was given an envelope with the Letter A or B on it. The A's were told to stay put while the B's were ushered into an adjacent room. Then, en masse, the B's were told that they were being laid off.

Manager's Notebook

The Dos and Don'ts of Terminating/Laying Off Employees

Consulting firms offer the following advice for telling employees that they will be terminated or laid off.

DOs

- Give as much warning as possible for mass layoffs.
- Sit down one-on-one with the individual, in a private office.
- Complete a firing session within 15 minutes.
- Provide written explanations of severance benefits.
- Provide outplacement services away from company headquarters.
- Be sure the employee hears about his or her termination from a manager, not a colleague.
- Express appreciation for what the employee has contributed, if appropriate.

DON'Ts

- Don't leave room for confusion. Tell the individual in the first sentence he or she is terminated.
- Don't allow time for debate.
- Don't make personal comments; keep the conversation professional.
- Don't rush the employee off-site unless security is really an issue.
- Don't fire or lay people off on significant dates, like the twenty-fifth anniversary of their employment or the day their mother died.
- Don't fire employees when they are on vacation or have just returned.

Source: Adapted with permission from Alexander, S. (1991, October 4). *The Wall Street Journal*, p. B1.

Coordinating Media Relations. Rumors of an impending layoff can be very dangerous to the work force's morale as well as to the organization's relations with customers, suppliers, and the surrounding community. Top managers, working with HR staff members, should develop a plan to provide accurate information about the layoff to external clients (via the media) as well as the work force (via internal communications).[24] In this way, managers can control and put to rest rumors that may exaggerate the extent of the firm's downsizing efforts. It is also important that direct communication take place with the employees directly affected by the layoff *and* the surviving employees, and that all communication be coordinated with press releases to the media. In addition, HR staff must prepare to answer any questions that employees or the media may have regarding outplacement, severance pay, or the continuation of benefits.

Maintaining Security. In some situations a layoff may threaten company property. Laid-off employees may find themselves rushed out of the building, escorted by armed guards, and their personal belongings delivered to them later in boxes. Although such treatment may seem harsh, it may be necessary in certain industries (such as banking and computer software) where sabotage could result in substantial damage. Security was given high priority when *The Record,* a newspaper based in Hackensack, New Jersey, discharged several of its employees. Employees indicated that the newspaper cut off their access to computers before they learned about their terminations so that they would not be able to sabotage the computer system.[25]

In most cases security precautions are probably not necessary when implementing a layoff, and using armed guards and other heavy-handed tactics will only lead to hard feelings and resentment. Treating laid-off employees with dignity and respect generally reduces the potential for sabotage.

Reassuring Survivors of the Layoff. A sometimes neglected aspect of layoff implementation is developing plans to deal with the layoff's survivors. An organization may lose the cost savings of a layoff if survivor productivity drops as a result of the layoff.[26] Survivors of a layoff initially have low morale and experience stress. Many will have lost important friendships in the layoff. Some may feel the same emotions experienced by survivors of tragedies: guilt ("Why not me?"), anger ("This is not fair"), and anxiety ("Am I next?").[27] The following reactions of layoff survivors express some of the feelings of anger and depression that are very common:

- "Stop telling us to work smarter. Show us how. . . .Stop blaming us! We've been loyal to the company. We've worked hard, and did everything we were told. We've moved for the company; we've traveled for the company; and we've taken on extra work for the company. And now you say we did wrong. You told us to do it. Management told us to do it! And the company did pretty well while we did it. Stop blaming us!"[28]
- "You see a lot of good people being let go and that's very demoralizing, to know that an excellent person is being let go."
- "They're padding their pockets. In the good times the bonuses and everything go to the top executives, and during the bad times the workers get cut out. The company hasn't shown me that they care as much about me."[29]

To cope with these feelings, the survivors may try to "escape." It is not unusual to see a sharp increase in absenteeism as well as turnover of key people who leave to work for competitors.

Companies can minimize problems in this arena by developing special programs for survivors. For example, Duracell developed a survivor program that consisted of two parts: (1) information releases to keep survivors informed about the reasons for the layoff and how it worked, and (2) emotional support for survivors to help them deal with their emotions and get on with their jobs.[30] Some ways to help survivors cope are small-group discussions with the supervisor a day or two after the layoff, pep talks to larger groups of employees given by top executives, and sometimes a party at which people can reminisce.[31] It is also important to tell employees what their new workloads will be in the post-layoff environment. Managers should also make survivors aware of the new opportunities available in the changed work environment.[32]

Finally, managers can solicit survivors' input during the transition period. At Eastman Kodak, for instance, the postlayoff environment became fertile ground for redesigning the work survivors do and making it more interesting for them (*job enrichment*). Before the layoff, Kodak employee Daniel Cardinale operated a punch press eight hours a day. Now he coaches fellow team members, meets with suppliers, interviews prospective recruits, and helps manage inventory.[33] ▼

▸ Outplacement

As we mentioned at the beginning of this chapter, outplacement is an HR program created to help separated employees deal with the emotional stress of job loss and provide assistance in finding a new job.[34] Outplacement activities are often handled by consulting firms retained by the organization, which pays a fee based on the number of outplaced employees. Companies are often willing to pay for outplacement because it can reduce some of the risks associated with layoffs, such as negative publicity or an increased likelihood that unions will

Issues + Applications

Saving Face While Saving the Company

These days, a layoff of a few dozen employees from a huge U.S. company wouldn't raise many reporters' eyebrows. However, when Japan's Pioneer Electronics announced a layoff of 35 workers in 1993, the news sparked headlines both in Japan and the United States. In a culture famous for its lifetime employment policies, layoffs used to be avoided at all costs—even if it meant Tokyo paying companies to retain redundant workers. Now, with an estimated one million "in-house unemployed" on company payrolls, surging manufacturing costs, and economic downturn, the threat of layoffs looms in many of Japan's largest companies.

To avoid the stigma of announcing layoffs, many Japanese companies are resorting to transfers and early retirement. And, to ease the transition for workers who get the dreaded *kata-tataki*, or tap on the shoulder, more Japanese firms are relying on U.S.-style outplacement firms to counsel workers and find new jobs for them. The sole U.S.-based outplacement firm in Japan, Drake Beam Morin Inc., grew fivefold between 1991 and 1993 and now serves 500 Japanese companies.

Yet few Japanese companies will admit publicly that they use outplacement firms. Most are embarrassed about being unable to honor the promise of lifetime employment. Some workers are optimistic, though, about hints of more freedom in the workplace. "The company isn't a god any more," says one software salesman who was advised by his company to start looking for a new job.

Sources: Based on Miller, K. L. (1993, January 11). Land of the rising jobless. *Business Week*, 47. Schlesinger, J. M. (1993), September 16). Japan begins to confront job insecurity. *The Wall Street Journal*, A10.

attempt to organize the work force.[35] Employers who provide outplacement services tend to give the goal of social responsibility a high priority as part of their HR strategy.

The Goals of Outplacement

The goals of an outplacement program reflect the organization's need to control the disruption caused by layoffs and other employee separations. The most important of these goals are (1) reducing the morale problems of employees who are about to be laid off so that they remain productive until they leave the firm; (2) minimizing the amount of litigation initiated by separated employees; and (3) assisting separated employees in finding comparable jobs as quickly as possible.[36]

Outplacement Services

The most common outplacement services are emotional support and job-search assistance. These services are closely tied to the goals of outplacement.

Emotional Support. Outplacement programs usually provide counseling to help employees deal with the emotions associated with job loss—shock, anger, denial, and lowered self-esteem. Because the family may suffer if the breadwinner becomes unemployed, sometimes family members are included in the counseling as well.[37] Counseling also benefits the employer because it helps to defuse some of the hostility that laid-off employees feel toward the company.

Job-Search Assistance. Employees who are outplaced often do not know how to begin the search for a new job. In many cases, these people have not had to look for a job in many years.

An important aspect of this assistance is teaching separated employees the skills they need to find a new job. These skills include résumé writing, interviewing and job search techniques, career planning, and negotiation skills.[38] Outplaced employees receive instruction in these skills from either a member of the outplacement firm or the HR department. In addition, the former employer sometimes provides administrative support in the form of clerical help and phone answering and fax services.[39] These services allow laid-off employees to use computers to prepare résumés, copiers to copy them, and fax machines to send them out.

The use of outplacement has become a global management practice. Several large corporations in Great Britain have recently restructured their operations, eliminating thousands of jobs. British Telecom has cut its work force by 40,000, and Midland Bank has eliminated 10,000 jobs over the past decade.[40] An important part of these downsizing strategies is the use of outplacement services to smooth the affected employees' transition to a new job. Similarly, Japanese corporations have started to use outplacement firms to find jobs for surplus workers.[41] The Issues and Applications feature on page 195 titled "Saving Face While Saving the Company" shows why Japanese firms have started to use outplacement—which in Japan is viewed as an American management practice.

Summary and Conclusions

What Are Employee Separations? Employee separations occur when employees cease to be members of an organization. Separations and outplacement can be managed effectively. Managers should plan for the outflow of their human resources with thoughtful policies. Employee separations have both costs and benefits. The costs include (1) recruitment costs, (2) selection costs, (3) training costs, and (4) separation costs. The benefits are (1) reduced labor costs, (2) replacement of poor performers, (3) increased innovation, and (4) the opportunity for greater diversity.

Types of Employee Separations. Employees may leave either voluntarily or involuntarily. Voluntary separations include quits and retirements. Involuntary separations include discharges and layoffs. When an employee is forced to leave involuntarily, a much greater level of documentation is necessary to show that a manager's decision to terminate the employee was fair and consistent.

Managing Early Retirements. When downsizing an organization, managers may elect to use voluntary early retirements as an alternative to layoffs. Early retirement programs must be managed so that eligible employees do not perceive that they are being forced to retire.

Managing Layoffs. Layoffs should be used as a last resort after all other cost-cutting alternatives have been exhausted. Important considerations in developing a layoff policy include (1) notifying employees, (2) developing layoff criteria, (3) communicating to laid-off employees, (4) coordinating media relations, (5) maintaining security, and (6) reassuring survivors of the layoff.

Outplacement. No matter what policy is used to reduce the work force, it is a good idea for the organization to use outplacement services to help separated employees cope with their emotions and minimize the amount of time they are unemployed.

Key Terms

attrition, 189
downsizing, 186
employee separation, 180
exit interview, 182
hiring freeze, 189
involuntary separation, 184
outplacement assistance, 182
rightsizing, 186
turnover rate, 180
voluntary separation, 184
Worker Adjustment Act and Retraining Notification (WARN), 191

Discussion Questions

1. After eight years as marketing assistant for the New York office of a large French bank, Sarah Schiffler was told that her job, in a non-revenue-producing department, was being eliminated. Her choices: She could either be laid off (with eight months' severance pay) or stay on and train for the position of credit analyst, a career route she had turned down in the past. Nervous about making mortgage payments on her new condo, Sarah agreed to

stay, but after six months of feeling miserable in her new position, she quit. Was her separation from the bank voluntary or involuntary? Can you think of situations in which a voluntary separation is really an involuntary separation? What are the managerial implications of such situations?

2. What are the advantages and disadvantages of using seniority as the basis for layoff? What alternatives to seniority are available as layoff criteria?
3. Would an employer ever want to increase the rate of employee turnover in a company? Why or why not?
4. What role does the HR department play in employee separations and outplacement?
5. In an age when more and more companies are downsizing, an increasingly important concept is "the virtual corporation." The idea is that a company should have a core of owners and managers, but that, to the greatest degree possible, workers should be contingent—temporary, part-time, or on short-term contracts. This gives the corporation maximum flexibility to shift vendors, cut costs, and avoid long-term labor commitments. What are the advantages and disadvantages of the virtual corporation from the point of view of both employers and workers?
6. Under what circumstances might a company's managers prefer to use layoffs instead of early retirements or voluntary severance plans as a way to downsize the work force?
7. Under what set of conditions should a company lay off employees without giving them advance notice?
8. "The people who actually have the face-to-face contact with the person who is being laid off aren't the ones who made the decision. They often didn't have any input into which of their people would go," says a technician at a firm that experienced large-scale layoffs. What role should managers—who have the "face-to-face" contact with employees—play in implementing a layoff? Do you think managers and HR staff members always agree on how employee separations should be handled? Why or why not?

MINICASE 1 *Managing the Turnover of Key Employees with Noncompete Agreements*

Companies in high-technology and creative industries (such as publishing and advertising) often worry about the turnover of high-potential employees. *High-potential* employees (sometimes called *key employees*) are people who have rare and special talents and who provide valuable contributions that can directly affect the firm's performance. Some well-known examples of high-potential people are film director Steven Spielberg (whose films are more profitable than those of any other director) and superstar Michael Jordan of the Chicago Bulls basketball team. Because most organizations have only a few high potentials, retaining these employees has important strategic implications for the business.

To protect themselves against the loss of high potential employees and the intellectual property (such as trade secrets) that they may take with them, some companies are requiring all employees to sign *noncompete* agreements that restrict their freedom to work for a competitor after quitting the organization. For example, Career Track, a Colorado company that provides professional training seminars on business-related topics, took a former star trainer and workshop developer to court to enforce a noncompete agreement, after this high-potential employee quit to work for a competitor in California. The company wanted to avoid losing business to a competitor; it also wanted to let other high potentials know that the company is prepared to defend its rights if someone decides to challenge the noncompete agreement.

Discussion Questions

1. Do you think noncompete agreements are ethical? Should a company require all employees to sign them, or only high-potential employees? What problems could arise from the use of noncompete agreements?
2. Are there other human resource management practices that could be substituted for noncompete agreements that would be likely to improve the retention of high-potential employees? Which one would you recommend?

MINICASE 2 A Valid Explanation?

David M. Noer, vice president for training and education for the Center for Creative Leadership, has conducted extensive studies on the effects of layoffs on survivors and the organizations that employ them. "If I were to compile a composite of all the speeches I have heard executives present to layoff survivors," says Noer, "it would go like this":

> Our ROI has eroded to the point where the security analysts have expressed concern over the value of our stock to the shareholders. As you may know, our gross margins have also been declining over the past six quarters and reached a point last quarter where we suffered a pre-tax loss. Based on recent market research, we have confirmed the fact we are losing market share in the U.S. and are facing increasingly stiff competition in Europe. The quality indicators we installed last year show that we are not making the gains we had planned and our revenue per employee has declined. We have no alternative but to implement a downsizing effort at this time if this organization is to remain a viable economic entity. It is a straightforward economic decision. Any questions?

Discussion Questions

1. Imagine you have just survived a layoff in which some of your coworkers have been let go. What is your reaction to this speech?

2. Put yourself in the employer's shoes and try to write a brief speech that addresses how survivors might be feeling.

Source: Noer, David M. (1993). *Healing the wounds: Overcoming the trauma of layoffs and revitalizing downsized organizations.* San Francisco: Jossey-Bass, pp. 103–104.

CASE 1 A Layoff at Wilson Industrial

Wilson Industrial is a small auto parts manufacturer located in Ohio. It employs 100 people and its work force is nonunion. Due to increased competition in the automobile industry, the company's managers anticipate a permanent reduction in the demand for Wilson Industrial's products. They have decided to lay off 15 production workers. The company has never experienced layoffs and at present has no policy that governs how a layoff should be conducted.

Top managers have told Joe McGuire, the manager of the production department, to retain the best performers. McGuire examined the performance appraisals and production records of all 60 employees in his department and drew up a list of 15 employees to lay off. Many of the top performers have been working for Wilson Industrial for only one or two years.

Sam Kowalski has been employed as a lathe operator for 20 years. Although McGuire has always given Kowalski good performance evaluations, he now informs Kowalski that he is on the layoff list and that his job performance is marginal. McGuire also explains that he gave good evaluations to Kowalski in the past only so that he could receive higher pay increases. Kowalski is very upset about losing his job and is thinking about taking legal action against Wilson Industrial.

Critical Thinking Questions

1. Does Kowalski have good reason to take his case to court?

2. Did top management handle the layoff correctly?

3. What could Joe McGuire have done differently to avoid potential litigation?

Cooperative Learning Exercise

4. Students form pairs and take the roles of Kowalski and McGuire. The student with the McGuire role explains to Kowalski that he is about to be laid off. Kowalski reacts to this news. How could the HR department support McGuire in his unpleasant task?

CASE 2 Managing Outplacement at Rocky Mountain Oil

Rocky Mountain Oil has announced that it will reduce the scale of its U.S. operations and eliminate several hundred administrative positions at its Denver headquarters. The organization wants to provide outplacement assistance to the employees who will lose their jobs. However, it does not want to spend much money on outplacement.

The company has formed an outplacement committee consisting of top managers, most of whom come from the operations and financial units of the business. The committee has provided a recommendation for an outplacement program that has been accepted by Rocky Mountain's CEO, Barbara Robinson. This program consists of two parts. First, each laid-off employee's immediate supervisor will provide counseling and emotional support to his or her laid-off employees. All supervisors will receive an outplacement counseling packet that includes the recent article "Ten Easy Steps to Help Employees Deal With Losing Their Jobs." Trailers will be placed at the far end of the company parking lot to serve as temporary offices for former employees, who can use them while searching for jobs and receiving counseling from their former supervisors.

Second, the outplacement program will help former employees develop job-search skills. Each employee will be given a copy of the book *What Color Is Your Parachute?*, which provides tips on how to conduct a job search. In addition, each employee will be offered the opportunity to take a course at nearby Black Rock Junior College called "Introduction to Personnel Management," in which students learn to write a résumé, gain information about the labor market, and gather tips on how to interview. Rocky Mountain Oil will pick up the cost of tuition (about $100 per employee) for the course.

Shortly after the CEO approved the outplacement program, Rocky Mountain Oil's director of human resources, Karen Sinclair, read a copy of the memo announcing the program. Sinclair had not been invited to be a member of the outplacement committee. After she finished reading the memo, Ms. Sinclair thought to herself, "That's what happens when you let accountants design a human resource program."

Critical Thinking Questions

1. Do you see any problems with the outplacement program at Rocky Mountain Oil?
2. What did Karen Sinclair mean by her statement?
3. What improvements to the design of the outplacement program do you think need to be made?

Cooperative Learning Exercise

4. Students form pairs, one role-playing Barbara Robinson and the other playing Karen Sinclair. Each tries to convince the other of the advantages of the outplacement program she prefers.

HRM Simulation 

In Incident K you are considering the use of outplacement services provided by a national counseling firm to handle the termination of Kathleen Jordan. What is the purpose of outplacement? Does the case of Ms. Jordan require outplacement? If yes, what kind of outplacement services would you advise for Ms. Jordan? If not, how should management handle her situation? What general guidelines would you recommend for the use of outplacement services?

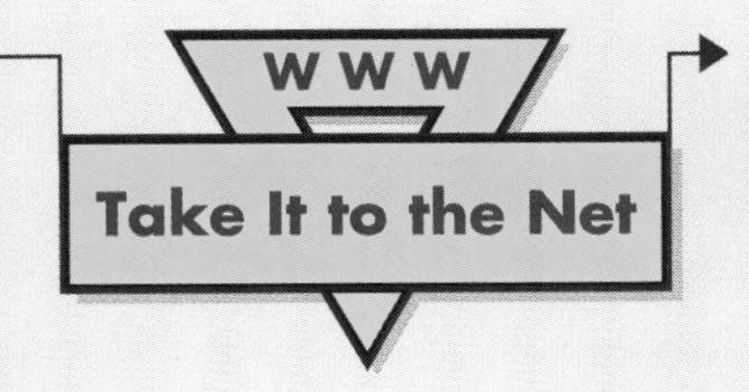

We invite you to visit the Gómez-Mejía/Balkin/Cardy page on the Prentice Hall Web site:

http://www.prenhall.com/gomez

You can also visit the Web sites for these companies, featured within this chapter:

British Telecom	http://www.bt.com
GTE	http://www.gte.com
Hewlett-Packard	http://www.hp.com
National Cash Register (NCR)	http://www.ncr.com
NYNEX	http://www.nynex.com
United Airlines	http://www.ual.com

Endnotes

1. Uchitelle, L., and Kleinfield, N. (1996, March 3). The downsizing of America (part 1 of a 7-part series). *The New York Times*, A1.
2. Cascio, W. F. (1991). *Costing human resources: The financial impact of behavior in organizations*. Boston: PWS-Kent.
3. Mobley, W. H. (1982). *Employee turnover: Causes, consequences, and control.* Reading, MA: Addision-Wesley.
4. Quint, M. (1995, December 15). Company buyout: Was it that good? *The New York Times*, C1, C2.
5. Rimer, S. (1996, March 6). The downsizing of America (part 4 of a 7-part series). *The New York Times*, A1, A8–A10.
6. Robbins, D. K., and Pearce, J. A. (1992). Turnaround: Retrenchment and recovery. *Strategic Management Journal, 13*, 287–309.
7. McKinley, W., Sanchez, C. M., and Schick, A. G. (1995). Organizational downsizing: Constraining, cloning, learning. *Academy of Management Executive, 9*(3), 32–42.
8. Messmer, M. (1991, October). Right-sizing reshapes staffing strategies. *HRMagazine*, 60–62.
9. Balkin, D. B. (1992). Managing employee separations with the reward system. *Academy of Management Executive, 6*(4), 64–71.
10. Byrne, J. (1994, May 9). The pain of downsizing. *Business Week*, 60–68.
11. Hill, R. E., and Dwyer, P. C. (1990, September). Grooming workers for early retirement. *HRMagazine*, 59–63.
12. Grant, P. B. (1991). The "open window"—Special early retirement plans in transition. *Employee Benefits Journal, 16*(1), 10–16.
13. Lopez, J. A. (1993, October 25). Out in the cold: Many early retirees find the good deals not so good after all. *The Wall Street Journal*, B1.
14. Tomasko, R. (1991). Downsizing: Layoffs and alternatives to layoffs. *Compensation and Benefits Review, 23*(4), 19–32.
15. Grant, 1991.
16. Beck, M. (1991, December 9). Old enough to get fired. *Newsweek*, 64.
17. Bolt, J. F. (1983, November/December). Job security: Its time has come. *Harvard Business Review*, 115–123.
18. Bernstein, A. (1996, March 18). United we own. *Business Week*, 96–102.
19. Ehrenberg, R. G., and Jakubson, G. H. (1989). Advance notification of plant closing: Does it matter? *Industrial Relations, 28*, 60–71.
20. Brockner, J., Grover, S., Reed, T. F., and DeWitt, R. L. (1992). Layoffs, job insecurity, and survivors' work effort: Evidence of an inverted-U relationship. *Academy of Management Journal, 35,* 413–425.
21. Ehrenberg, R. G., and Jakubson, G. H. (1988). *Advance notice provisions in plant closing legislation.* Kalamazoo, MI: W.E. Upjohn Institute for Employment Research.
22. Eisman, R. (1992, May). Remaking a corporate giant. *Incentive*, 57–63.
23. Alexander, S. (1991, October 14). Firms get plenty of practice at layoffs, but they often bungle the firing process. *The Wall Street Journal*, B1.
24. Bunning, R. L. (1990). The dynamics of downsizing. *Personnel Journal, 69*(9), 69–75.
25. Alexander, 1991.
26. Brockner, J. (1992). Managing the effects of layoffs on survivors. *California Management Review, 34*(2), 9–28.
27. Reibstein, L. (1988, December 5). Survivors of layoffs receive help to lift morale and reinstate trust. *The Wall Street Journal*, 31.
28. O'Neil, H. M., and Lenn, D. J. (1995). Voices of survivors: Words that downsizing CEOs should hear. *Academy of Management Executive, 9*(4), 23–34.
29. Noer, David M. (1993). *Healing the wounds: Overcoming the trauma of layoffs and revitalizing downsized organizations.* San Francisco, CA: Jossey-Bass.
30. Feldman, L. (1989). Duracell's first aid for downsizing survivors. *Personnel Journal, 68*(8), 91–94.
31. Reibstein, 1988.
32. Brockner, 1992.
33. *Id.*
34. Sweet, D. H. (1989). Outplacement. In W. Cascio (Ed.), *Human resource planning, employment and placement,* Washington, DC: Bureau of National Affairs.
35. Newman, L. (1988). Goodbye is not enough. *Personnel Administrator, 33*(2), 84–86.
36. *Id.*
37. Sweet, 1989.
38. Gibson, V. M. (1991). The ins and outs of outplacement. *Management Review, 80*(10), 59–61.
39. Burdett, J. O. (1988). Easing the way out. *Personnel Administrator, 33*(6), 157–166.
40. Crofts, P. (1991). Helping people face up to redundancy. *Personnel Management, 23*(12), 24–27.
41. Rudolph, B. (1986, December 8). The sun also sets. *Business Week,* 60–61.

The Ugly Truth

ABCNEWS

It is against the law to make employment decisions based on factors such as race, sex, or national origin. And, legality aside, it just isn't good business practice to base hiring, compensation, and training decisions on anything other than ability to perform the job. However, could it be that we let other people's looks determine whether they will get a job or how much salary they will earn? Unfortunatley, the answer appears to be a clear "yes."

In one experiment, two female actors, differing in terms of good looks but with similar education and work experience, applied for the same job at numerous organizations. Each time, the more attractive candidate was offered the job. She also was likely to be offered higher pay than the less attractive candidate.

The effect of looks on employment decisions doesn't happen only with women. Tests with male actors found the same bias for good looks. And this bias appears pervasive and begins to occur at a very early age. For example, first-grade children claim that good-looking teachers are smarter and listen better. The effect works in the opposite direction, too. Research indicates that good-looking children get more attention from teachers and enjoy the benefit of the doubt if a problem occurs. Perhaps most surprising, by 12 months of age, infants show a preference for more attractive faces. A bias based on looks has been found in courtrooms, where better-looking defendents are less likely to be convicted and more likely to receive lenient sentences than more homely defendants.

We all abhor racism amd sexism, but most of us might be guilty of an unconscious attractiveness bias. Perhaps the bias is partly innate and partly learned. Whatever the cause, we tend to equate good looks with a host of positive characteristics, such as intelligence, competence, and "niceness." But can we base such conclusions on looks alone? The rational answer, of course, is that we can't but that we do so on a regular basis.

Discussion Questions

1. Is bias based on attractiveness illegal? Explain.
2. If an attractiveness bias is partly innate in how we make judgments about other people, how can we combat it? Describe the steps you would take to eliminate or reduce the influence of attractiveness on hiring, compensation, and other job-related outcomes.
3. Do you think the attractiveness bias will become irrevelant over time as the actual job performance of a worker is observed? Why or why not?

After reading this chapter, you should be able to deal more effectively with the following challenges:

1 ▶ **Explain** why performance appraisal is important and describe its components.

2 ▶ **Discuss** the advantages and disadvantages of different performance rating systems.

3 ▶ **Manage** the impact of rating errors and bias on performance appraisals.

4 ▶ **Discuss** the potential role of emotion in performance appraisal and how to manage its impact.

5 ▶ **Identify** the major legal requirements for appraisal.

6 ▶ **Use** performance appraisals to manage and develop employee performance.

7 Appraising and Managing Performance

The Value of Feedback. Although some managers consider performance appraisal a time-consuming chore, many realize that periodic reviews can help employees improve their performance over time. The best managers both appraise their workers' performance and act as coaches, encouraging employees to learn new skills and expand their responsibilities.

http://www.shrm.org/docs/HRmagazine.html

HRMagazine

HRMagazine is a monthly magazine published by the Society for Human Resource Management (SHRM). Articles from the current issue of the magazine on performance appraisal and management (as well as other HR topics) are available at this Web site.

CASE 1:

Bob has just come out of his annual feedback session with his manager. He feels great. True, his manager did not give him the highest possible ratings. However, she spent time reviewing the areas in which he excelled as well as those in which he could improve. Best of all, she gave him the opportunity to express his frustrations with the way his work is organized. He feels he can do a much better job if some minor changes are made. He has the sense that his manager is "in his corner," sincerely hoping he will do a great job so that his ratings will be even higher next year.

* * *

CASE 2:

The company's annual appraisal period has just ended, and it has done so with the usual mix of worker anxieties and complaints. What a process!

Several issues came up this year. Many workers charged their supervisors with bias, complaining that performance ratings are a function of "how much a supervisor likes you." Others complained that their managers handed down annual ratings without giving employees any feedback on how to improve their performance. Another prickly issue was the apparent conflict between the appraisal system and the organization's team structure. The team structure requires cooperation, but the appraisal system seems to focus on individual achievement. Managers overheard some workers saying that they are going to "take care of number one" for the next appraisal period and not concern themselves so much with the team.

Supervisors raised another troublesome issue. Jobs are so much in flux, they argued, that by the time the appraisal period comes around, they are rating workers on things they are no longer doing.

Which of these stories reflects most people's experience? Unfortunately, the second story seems more representative of U.S. organizations than the first. The measurement and management of performance are two of the most difficult issues a manager faces.

It is widely accepted that accurate measurement of employee performance is necessary for effective management. Our first goal in this chapter is thus to acquaint you with the foundation, design, and implementation of performance measurement systems. Our second is to describe the principles of effective performance management.

What Is Performance Appraisal?

Performance appraisal (Figure 7–1 on page 204) involves the *identification, measurement,* and *management* of human performance in organizations.[1]

performance appraisal
The identification, measurement, and management of human performance in organizations.

- *Identification* means determining what areas of work the manager should be examining when measuring performance. Rational and legally defensible identification requires a measurement system based on job analysis (Chapter 2). Thus, the appraisal system should focus on performance that affects organizational success rather than performance-irrelevant characteristics such as race, age, or gender.

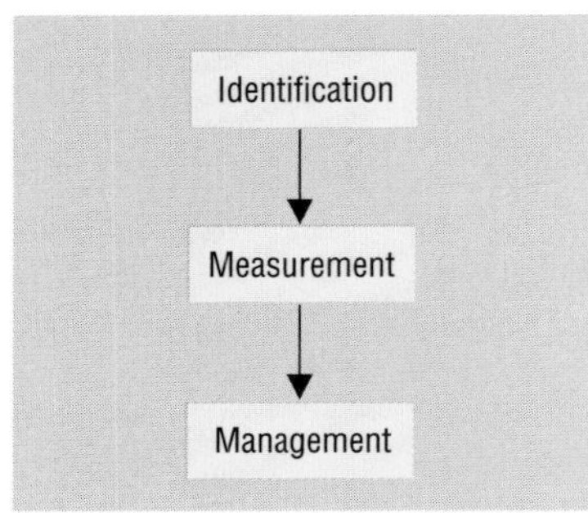

FIGURE 7-1

A Model of Performance Appraisal

- *Measurement,* the centerpiece of the appraisal system, entails making managerial judgments of how "good" or "bad" employee performance was. Good performance measurement must be consistent throughout the organization. That is, all managers in the organization must maintain comparable rating standards.[2]
- *Management* is the overriding goal of any appraisal system. Appraisal should be more than a past-oriented activity that criticizes or praises workers for their performance in the preceding year. Rather, appraisal must take a future-oriented view of what workers can do to achieve their potential in the organization. This means that managers must provide workers with feedback and coach them to higher levels of performance.

The Uses of Performance Appraisal

Organizations usually conduct appraisals for *administrative* and/or *developmental* purposes.[3] Performance appraisals are used administratively whenever they are the basis for a decision about the employee's work conditions, including promotions, termination, and rewards. Developmental uses of appraisal, which are geared toward improving employees' performance and strengthening their job skills, include counseling employees on effective work behaviors and sending them for training.

Appraisals are typically done once a year, and are often based on supervisors' subjective judgments[4] rather than on objective indicators of performance, such as number of units produced. This has led many to conclude that appraisals are full of errors. For example, annual appraisals can place an excessive burden on the memory of a person who has to rate multiple workers. Also, supervisors' judgments may be influenced by stereotypes and other personal beliefs or perceptions.[5]

For these and other reasons, dissatisfaction with appraisal is rampant. One survey found that the majority of HR professionals are dissatisfied with their current appraisal system.[6] Some companies have even decided to do away with traditional appraisal systems altogether. For instance, some Cigna divisions have dropped numerical ratings and written appraisals in favor of more verbal communications.[7]

Nonetheless, written appraisal remains an important activity in most organizations. The challenge is to manage the appraisal system so that it furthers the goals of performance improvement and worker development. In the next two sections, we explain the issues and challenges involved in the first two steps of performance appraisal, identification and measurement. We conclude the chapter by discussing how managers can use the results of appraisal to improve employee performance.

▸ Identifying Performance Dimensions

The first step in the performance appraisal process (see Figure 7–1) is identifying what is to be measured. This process seems fairly simple at first glance. In practice, however, it can be quite complicated. Consider the following example:

dimension
An aspect of performance that determines effective job performance.

Nancy manages a group of computer programmers. She needs to evaluate each to determine who should receive the largest raise. Before she can decide which programmer is most effective, she must identify the aspects, or **dimensions,** of performance that determine effective job performance. Whether or not the computer programs work well is one appropriate dimension. This aspect of performance might be labeled *quality of programs written.* But Nancy also realizes that David, one of the programmers, always does very good work—but takes three times as long to write a program as the other programmers. So she includes a dimension called *quantity of programs written* on her list of things to assess. Unfortunately, Luis, the programmer with the best mix of quantity and quality, also constantly berates his coworkers. So Nancy adds a third dimension labeled *interpersonal effectiveness.*

This process might continue until Nancy has identified eight or ten dimensions. As you have probably realized, the process of identifying performance dimensions is very much like the job-analysis process described in Chapter 2. In fact, job analysis is the mechanism by which performance dimensions should be identified.

Identification of performance dimensions is the very important first step in the appraisal process. If a significant dimension is missed, employee morale is likely to suffer because employees who do well on that dimension will not be recognized or rewarded. If an irrelevant or trivial dimension is included, employees may perceive the whole appraisal process as meaningless.

Measuring Performance

Measuring employee performance involves assigning a number to reflect an employee's performance on the identified characteristics or dimensions.[8] Technically, numbers are not mandatory. Labels such as "excellent," "good," "average," and "poor" might be used instead. But these grades could just as well be numbered 1 through 4, and you would still need to decide what grade is appropriate for a given employee.

It is often difficult to quantify performance dimensions. For example, "creativity" may be an important part of the advertising copywriter's job. But how exactly does one measure creativity—by the number of ads written per year, by the number of ads that win industry awards, or by some other criterion? These are the issues that managers face when trying to evaluate an employee's performance.

Measurement Tools

Numerous techniques for measuring performance have been developed over the years. Today managers have a wide array of appraisal formats from which to choose. Here we discuss the formats that are most common and legally defensible. These formats can be classified in two ways: (1) the type of judgment that is required (relative or absolute), and (2) the focus of the measure (trait, behavior, or outcome).

Relative and Absolute Judgments. Measures of employee performance can be classified on the basis of whether the type of judgment called for is relative or absolute.

Relative Judgments. Appraisal systems based on **relative judgment** ask supervisors to compare an employee's performance to the performance of other employees doing the same job. Providing a *rank order* of workers from best to worst is an example of a relative approach. Another type of relative judgment format classifies employees into groups, such as top third, middle third, or lowest third.

relative judgment
An appraisal format that asks supervisors to compare an employee's performance to the performance of other employees doing the same job.

Relative rating systems have the advantage of forcing supervisors to differentiate among their workers. Without such a system, many supervisors are inclined to rate everyone the same, which destroys the appraisal system's value. For example, one study that examined the distribution of performance ratings for more than 7,000 managerial and professional employees in two large manufacturing firms found that 95% of employees were crowded into just two rating categories.

Most HR specialists believe that the disadvantages of relative rating systems outweigh their advantages, however.[9] First, relative judgments (such as ranks) do not make clear how great or small the differences between employees are. Second, such systems do not provide any absolute information, so managers cannot determine how good or poor employees at the extreme rankings are. For example, relative ratings do not reveal whether the top-rated worker in one work team is better or worse than an average worker in another work team. The worst-rated worker in one team may be a better performer than the average-rated workers in another team that has a poorer overall level of performance. This problem is illustrated in Figure 7–2 on page 206. Mark, Jill, and Frank are the highest-ranked performers in their respective work teams. However, Jill, Frank, and Gary are actually the best overall performers.

Actual	Ranked Work	Ranked Work	Ranked Work
10 (High)		Jill (1)	Frank (1)
9			Gary (2)
8		Tom (2)	Lisa(3)
7	Mark (1)	Sue (3)	
6	Pam (2)		
5			
4	Joyce (3)	Greg (4)	
3	Bill (4)	Ken (5)	Cindy (4)
2	Richard (5)		Steve (5)
1 (Low)			

FIGURE 7-2

Rankings and Performance Levels Across Work Teams

Third, relative ranking systems force managers to identify differences among workers where none may truly exist.[10] This can cause conflict among workers if and when ratings are disclosed. Finally, relative systems typically require assessment of overall performance. The "big picture" nature of relative ratings makes performance feedback ambiguous and of questionable value to workers who would benefit from specific information on the various dimensions of their performance. For all these reasons, there is a growing trend to use relative rating systems only when there is an administrative need (for example, to make decisions regarding promotions, pay raises, or termination).[11]

absolute judgment
An appraisal format that asks supervisors to make judgments about an employee's performance based solely on performance standards.

Absolute Judgments. Unlike relative judgment appraisal formats, **absolute judgment** formats ask supervisors to make judgments about an employee's performance based solely on performance standards. Comparisons to the performance of coworkers are not made. Typically, the dimensions of performance deemed relevant for the job are listed on the rating form, and the manager is asked to rate the employee on each dimension. An example of an absolute judgment rating scale is shown in Figure 7–3.

Theoretically, absolute formats allow employees from different work groups, rated by different managers, to be compared to one another. If all employees are excellent workers, they all can receive excellent ratings. Also, because ratings are made on separate dimensions of performance, the feedback to the employee can be more specific and helpful.

Although often preferable to relative systems, absolute rating systems have their drawbacks. One is that all workers in a group can receive the same evaluation if the supervisor is reluctant to differentiate among workers. Another is that different supervisors can have markedly different evaluation standards. For example, a rating of 6 from an "easy" supervisor may actually be lower in value than a rating of 4 from a "tough" supervisor. But when the organization is handing out promotions or pay increases, the worker who received the 6 rating would be rewarded.

Nonetheless, absolute systems do have one distinct advantage: They avoid creating conflict among workers. This, plus the fact that relative systems are generally harder to defend when legal issues arise, may account for the prevalence of absolute systems in U.S. organizations.

It is interesting to note, though, that most people *do* make comparative judgments among both people and things. That is, they tend to make evaluative judgments in relative rather than absolute terms. A political candidate is better or worse than opponents, not good or bad in an absolute sense. Your favorite brand is better than others, not a 5.6 on some scale of brand quality. If comparative judgments are the common and natural way of making judgments, it may be that supervisors can be more accurate when making relative ratings than when making absolute ratings.[12]

Trait, Behavioral, and Outcome Data. In addition to relative and absolute judgments, performance measurement systems can be classified by the type of performance data on which they focus: trait data, behavioral data, or outcome data.

PERFORMANCE REVIEW

Three-month (H&S) ☐ Annual (H-Only) ☐
Six-month (H&S) ☐ Special (H&S) ☐
H = Hourly S = Salaried

Employee Name: ______________________

Social Security # ☐☐☐☐☐☐☐☐☐ Hourly ☐ Salaried ☐

For probationary employee review: Do you recommend that this employee be retained? Yes ☐ No ☐

Classification/Classification Hire Date: ______________________

Review period: From __________ To __________

Department/Division: ______________________

For each applicable performance area, mark the box that most closely reflects the employee's performance.
1 = unacceptable; 2 = needs improvement; 3 = satisfactory; 4 = above average; 5 = outstanding.

PERFORMANCE AREA	1	2	3	4	5
Ability to make job-related decisions					
Accepts change					
Accepts direction					
Accepts responsibility					
Attendance					
Attitude					
Compliance with rules					
Cooperation					
Cost consciousness					
Dependability					

PERFORMANCE AREA	1	2	3	4	5
Effective under stress					
Initiative					
Knowledge of work					
Leadership					
Operation and care of equipment					
Planning and organizing					
Quality of work					
Quantity of acceptable work					
Safety practices					
SUPERVISOR'S OVERALL APPRAISAL					

For overall appraisals at the 1 or 2 level: Is the employee to remain or be placed on probationary status? Yes ☐ No ☐

If yes, what is the approximate date of next performance review? __________

JOB STRENGTHS AND SUPERIOR PERFORMANCE INCIDENTS: __________

AREAS FOR IMPROVEMENT: __________

PROGRESS ACHIEVED IN ATTAINING PREVIOUSLY SET GOALS: __________

SPECIFIC OBJECTIVES TO BE UNDERTAKEN PRIOR TO NEXT REVIEW FOR IMPROVED WORK PERFORMANCE: __________

SUPERVISOR COMMENTS: __________

EMPLOYEE COMMENTS: __________

Use separate sheet, if necessary, for additional comments by supervisor or employee. Please note on form if separate sheet is used.

Signing a review does not indicate agreement, only acknowledgment of being reviewed.

Employee's Signature ______ Date ______ Rating Supervisor's Signature ______ Social Security # ☐☐☐☐☐☐☐☐☐ Date ______

Second Level Supervisor's Signature ______ Date ______ Department Head's Signature ______ Date ______

FIGURE 7-3

Sample of Absolute Judgment Rating Scale

trait appraisal instrument
An appraisal tool that asks a supervisor to make judgments about worker characteristics that tend to be consistent and enduring.

Trait Data. **Trait appraisal instruments** ask the supervisor to make judgments about *traits*, worker characteristics that tend to be consistent and enduring. Figure 7–4 presents four traits that are typically found on trait-based rating scales: decisiveness, reliability, energy, and loyalty. While a number of organizations use trait ratings, current opinion is against them. Trait ratings have been criticized for being much too ambiguous[13] as well as for leaving the door open for conscious or unconscious bias. In addition, trait ratings (because of their ambiguous nature) are less defensible in court than other types of ratings.[14] Definitions of reliability, for example, can differ dramatically across supervisors, and the courts seem to be sensitive to the "slippery" nature of traits as criteria. Another difficulty with trait formats is choosing from among the hundreds of possible traits those that should be included in the rating instrument.

Assessment of traits also focuses on the *person* rather than on the *performance,* which can make employees defensive. Trait ratings imply that poor performance resides within the person and, therefore, are equivalent to ratings of the person's worth. From the limited research done in this area, it seems that this type of person-focused approach is not conducive to performance development. Measurement approaches that focus more directly on performance, either by evaluating behaviors or results, are generally more acceptable to workers and more effective as development tools.

Despite these problems, trait ratings may be more effective than many believe. After all, traits are simply a shorthand way of describing a person's behavioral tendencies. Thus, trait judgments can be based on behavior, which would make them less error laden than critics suggest. We routinely make trait judgments about others, and it is rare for someone to be described other than through his or her traits. If you doubt this, perform the following experiment:

Let's say a classmate has asked you to describe one of your professors. Let's also imagine that this professor does magic tricks to maintain class interest and to accentuate lecture points, sparks lively discussion, and is known for wearing outrageous costumes. Would your initial response to your classmate consist of a list of behaviors that you've seen the professor engage in? Not likely! You'd more likely use the words "lively," "wild," "entertaining," "engaging," "crazy"—all trait terms. You might follow up this assessment with some behavioral description, but probably more for the purpose of enjoyable storytelling than anything else. The point is that we routinely make trait judgments about others; they are a powerful way of describing people. Because we do it all the time, we also may be quite good at it.

Rate each worker using the scales below.

Decisiveness:						
1	2	3	4	5	6	7
Very low			Moderate			Very high
Reliability:						
1	2	3	4	5	6	7
Very low			Moderate			Very high
Energy:						
1	2	3	4	5	6	7
Very low			Moderate			Very high
Loyalty:						
1	2	3	4	5	6	7
Very low			Moderate			Very high

FIGURE 7-4
Sample Trait Scales

Behavioral Data. **Behavioral appraisal instruments** focus on assessing a worker's behaviors. That is, instead of ranking leadership ability (a trait), the rater is asked to assess whether an employee exhibits certain behaviors (for example, works well with coworkers, comes to meetings on time). In one type of behavioral instrument, Behavioral Observation Scales, supervisors record how frequently the various behaviors listed on the form occurred.[15] However, ratings assessing the value rather than the *frequency* of specific behaviors are more commonly used in organizations. Probably the best-known behavioral scale is the Behaviorally Anchored Rating Scale (BARS). Figure 7–5 is an example of a BARS scale used to rate the effectiveness with which a department manager supervises his or her sales personnel.

behavioral appraisal instrument An appraisal tool that asks managers to assess a worker's behaviors.

The main advantage of a behavioral approach is that the performance standards are concrete. Unlike traits, which can have many facets, behaviors across the range of a dimension are included directly on the behavioral scale. This concreteness makes BARS and

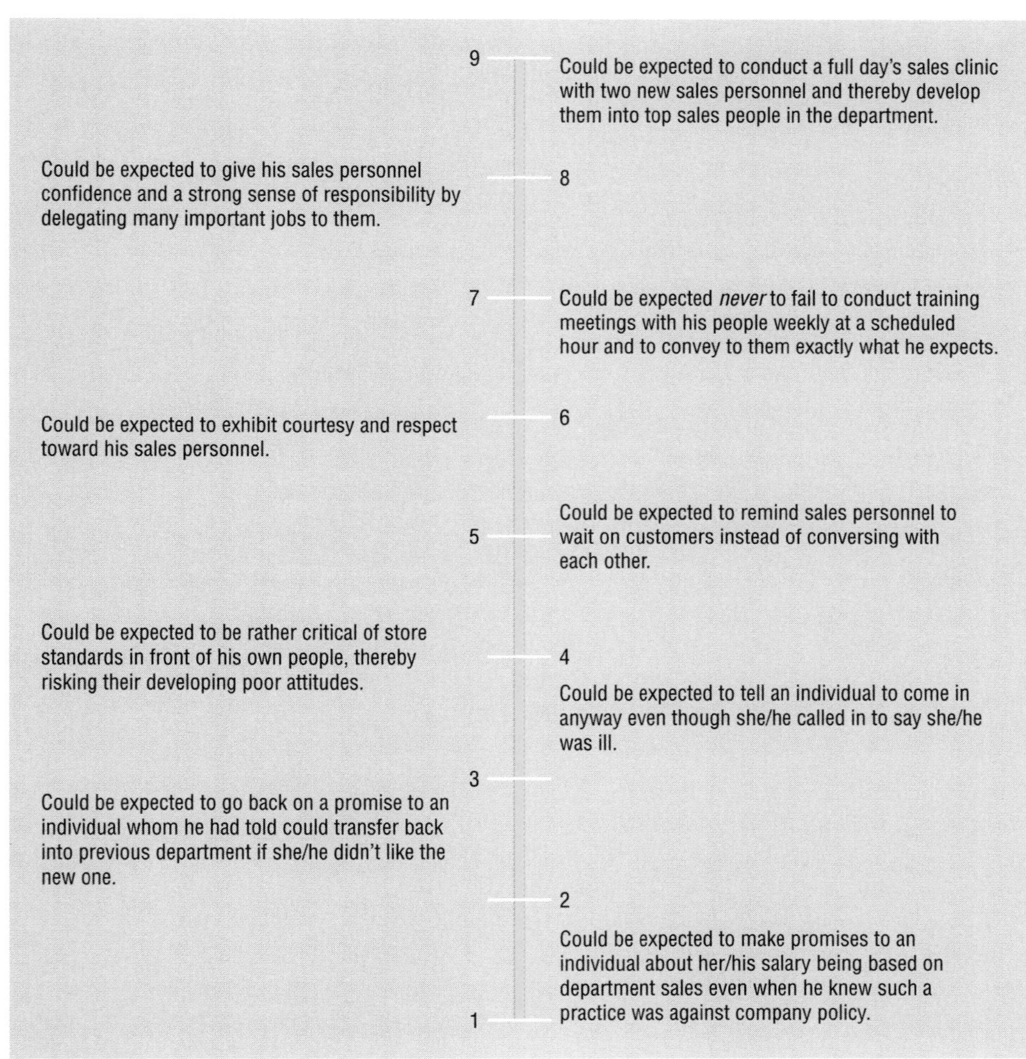

FIGURE 7-5

Sample BARS Used to Rate a Sales Manager

Source: Campbell, J.P., Dunnette, M.D., Arvey, R.D., and Hellervik, L.V. (1973). The Development and Evaluation of Behaviorally Based Rating Scales. *Journal of Applied Psychology*, 15–22. ©1973 by the American Psychological Association. Reprinted with permission.

other behavioral instruments more legally defensible than trait scales, which often use such hard-to-define adjectives as "poor" and "excellent." Behavioral scales also provide employees with specific examples of the types of behaviors to engage in (and to avoid) if they want to do well in the organization. In addition, behavioral scales encourage supervisors to be specific in their performance feedback. Finally, both workers and supervisors can be involved in the process of generating behavioral scales.[16] This is likely to increase understanding and acceptance of the appraisal system.

Behavioral systems are not without disadvantages, however. Most notably, the development of behavioral scales can be very time consuming, easily taking several months. Another disadvantage of behavioral systems is their specificity. The points, or *anchors,* on behavioral scales are clear and concrete, but they are only examples of behavior a worker *may* exhibit. Employees may never exhibit some of these anchor behaviors, which can cause difficulty for supervisors at appraisal time. Also, significant organizational changes can invalidate behavioral scales. For example, computerization of operations can dramatically alter the behaviors that workers must exhibit to be successful. Thus, the behaviors painstakingly developed for the appraisal system could become useless or, worse, operate as a drag on organizational change and adaptation. Workers will be unwilling to make changes in their work behaviors when the criteria by which their performance is judged aren't changed as well.

Another potential difficulty is many supervisors' belief that a behavioral focus is an unnatural way of thinking about and evaluating workers. As we discussed earlier, traits are a more natural way to think about others. Supervisors required to make behaviorally based evaluations may merely translate their trait impressions into behavioral judgments. Thus, although a behavioral approach seems less ambiguous, it may require mental gymnastics that can introduce error into ratings. No research has directly examined this issue, but one study has found a preference among both supervisors and workers for a trait-based system over a behaviorally based system.[17] The "unnaturalness" of a behavioral orientation may underlie this preference.

outcome appraisal instrument An appraisal tool that asks managers to assess the results achieved by workers.

management by objectives (MBO) A goal-directed approach to performance appraisal in which workers and their supervisors set goals together for the upcoming evaluation period.

Outcome Data. **Outcome appraisal instruments** ask managers to assess the results achieved by workers, such as total sales or number of products produced. The most prevalent outcome approaches are **management by objectives (MBO)**[18] and naturally occurring outcome measures. MBO is a goal-directed approach in which workers and their supervisors set goals together for the upcoming evaluation period. The rating then consists of deciding to what extent the goals have been met. With *naturally occurring outcomes,* the performance measure isn't so much discussed and agreed to as it is handed to supervisors and workers. For example, a computerized production system used to manufacture cardboard boxes may automatically generate data regarding the number of pieces produced, the amount of waste, and the defect rate.

The outcome approach provides clear and unambiguous criteria by which worker performance can be judged. It also eliminates subjectivity and the potential for error and bias that goes along with it. In addition, outcome approaches provide increased flexibility. For example, a change in the production system may lead to a new set of outcome measures and, perhaps, a new set of performance standards. With an MBO approach, a worker's objectives can easily be adjusted at the beginning of a new evaluation period if organizational changes call for new emphases.

Are outcome-based systems, then, the answer to the numerous problems with the subjective rating systems discussed earlier? Unfortunately, no. Although objective, outcome measures may give a seriously deficient and distorted view of worker performance levels. Consider an outcome measure defined as follows: "the number of units produced that are within acceptable quality limits." This performance measure may seem fair and acceptable. But consider further that production involves the use of some complex equipment that not everyone is good at troubleshooting. As long as the equipment is running fine, even an inexperienced worker can attend the machine and accrue handsome production numbers.

However, when the machine is not running properly, it can take several hours—sometimes an entire shift—to locate the problem and resolve it. If you were a manager faced with this situation, wouldn't you put your best workers on the problem? Of course you would. But consider what would happen to those workers' performance records. Your best workers could actually end up looking like the worst workers in terms of the amount of product produced.

This situation actually occurred at a manufacturer of automobile components.[19] To resolve the issue, management concluded that supervisors' subjective performance judgments were superior to objective outcome measures. The subjective ratings differed radically from the outcome measures. But in this case, the subjective ratings were found to be related to workers' scores on job-related tests while no such relationship was found for the outcome measures. Clearly, in some situations human judgment is superior to objective measures.

Another potential difficulty with outcome-based performance measures is the development of a "results at any cost" mentality.[20] Using objective measures has the advantage of focusing workers' attention on certain outcomes, but this focus can have negative effects on other facets of performance. For example, an organization may use the number of units produced as a performance measure because it is fairly easy to quantify. Workers concentrating on quantity may neglect quality and follow-up service to the long-term detriment of the organization. Although objective goals and other outcome measures are effective at increasing performance levels, these measures may not reflect the entire spectrum of performance.[21]

Measurement Tools: Summary and Conclusions. Our discussion so far makes it clear that there is no single best appraisal format. Each approach has positive and negative aspects. Figure 7–6 summarizes the strengths and weaknesses of each approach in the areas of administration, development, and legal defensibility. The choice of appraisal system should rest largely on the appraisal's primary purpose.

Most appraisal systems were developed on the premise that companies could reduce or eliminate rater errors by using the right appraisal format. However, rating formats make little difference in the actual ratings that are obtained. In fact, empirical evidence suggests that the type of tool doesn't make that much difference in the accuracy of ratings.[22]

If formats don't have much impact on ratings, what does? Not surprisingly, the supervisor. Characteristics such as the rater's intelligence, familiarity with the job,[23] and ability to separate important from unimportant information[24] influence rating quality. A number of studies indicate that raters' ability and motivation levels are the critical factors in rating employees effectively.

A QUESTION OF ETHICS

Is it appropriate for organizations to evaluate and compensate employees according to objective measures of performance, even though performance is at least partially determined by factors beyond their control? Should a salesperson, for instance, be paid completely on commission even in the midst of a recession that makes it practically impossible to sell enough to make a decent living?

Challenges to Effective Performance Measurement

How can managers ensure accurate measurement of worker performance? The primary means is to understand the barriers that stand in the way. Managers confront five challenges in this area:

	Criteria		
Appraisal Format	**Administrative Use**	**Developmental Use**	**Legal Defensibility**
Absolute	0	+	0
Relative	++	–	–
Trait	+	–	– –
Behavior	0	+	++
Outcome	0	0	+

– – Very poor   – Poor   0 Unclear or mixed   + Good   ++ Very good

FIGURE 7-6

Evaluation of Major Appraisal Formats

- Rater errors and bias
- The influence of liking
- Organizational politics
- Whether to focus on the individual or the group
- Legal issues

rater error
An error in performance appraisals that reflects consistent biases on the part of the rater.

Rater Errors and Bias. A **rater error** is an error in performance appraisals that reflects consistent biases on the part of the rater. One of the most prominent rater errors is *halo error*, the tendency to rate similarly across dimensions.[25] Suppose you are buying a refrigerator. If you are most interested in one particular feature—say, the versatility of shelving arrangements—you would commit a halo error if you allowed a particular model's shelving versatility to influence your ratings of its other features (appearance, energy efficiency, and so on). Similarly, raters commit halo errors in performance measurement when they allow the rating they give on one performance dimension to influence the ratings they give on other dimensions. Despite the word's angelic connotations, "halo" can cause uniformly negative ratings as well as uniformly positive ones.

There are at least two causes of halo error:[26] (1) A supervisor may make an overall judgment about a worker and then conform all dimensional ratings to that judgment, and/or (2) a supervisor may make all ratings consistent with the worker's performance level on a dimension that is important to the supervisor. To return to the computer programmer example we used earlier: If Nancy rates Luis low on all three performance dimensions (quality of programs written, quantity of programs written, and interpersonal effectiveness) even though his performance on quality and quantity is high, then she has committed a halo error.

Another type of rater error is *restriction of range error*, which occurs when a manager restricts all of his or her ratings to a small portion of the rating scale. A supervisor who restricts ranges tends to rate all workers similarly. Three different forms of range restriction are common: *leniency errors,* or restricting ratings to the high portion of the scale; *central tendency errors,* or using only the middle points of the scale; and *severity errors,* or using only the low portion of the rating scale.

Suppose that you are an HR manager reviewing the performance ratings given by the company's supervisors to their subordinates. The question is: How can you tell how accurate these ratings are? In other words, how can you tell what types of rating error, if any, have colored the ratings? The answer is that it is very difficult to tell. Let's say that a supervisor has given one of her subordinates the highest possible rating on each of five performance dimensions. There are at least three possible explanations. The employee may actually be very good on one of the dimensions and has been rated very high on all because of this (halo error). Or the rater may only use the top part of the scale (leniency error). Or the employee may be a very good all-around worker (accurate). Although sophisticated statistical techniques have been developed to investigate these possibilities, none is practical for most organizations or managers.

comparability
In performance ratings, the degree to which the performance ratings given by various supervisors in an organization are similar.

This problem is of more than academic interest. A major difficulty in performance measurement is ensuring comparability in ratings across raters.[27] **Comparability** refers to the degree to which the performance ratings given by various supervisors in an organization are similar. In essence, the comparability issue is concerned with whether or not supervisors use the same measurement yardsticks. What one supervisor considers excellent performance, another may view as only average.

Personal Bias. Personal bias may also cause rater error. Consciously or unconsciously, a supervisor may systematically rate certain workers lower or higher than others on the basis of race, national origin, gender, age, or other factors. Conscious bias is extremely difficult, if not impossible, to eliminate. Unconscious bias can be overcome once it is brought to the rater's attention. For example, a supervisor might be unconsciously giving higher evaluations to employees who went to his alma mater. When made aware of this leaning, however, he may correct it.

Blatant, systematic negative biases should be recognized and corrected within the organization. Negative bias became an issue at the U.S. Drug Enforcement Agency (DEA) in the early 1980s when a lawsuit, *Segar v. Civiletti,* established that African-American agents were systematically rated lower than white agents and thus were less likely to receive promotions and choice job assignments. The DEA failed to provide supervisors with any written instructions on how to evaluate agents' performance, and virtually all the supervisors conducting the evaluations were white.[28]

One of the most effective ways to deal with errors and bias is to develop and communicate evaluation standards via **frame-of-reference (FOR) training,**[29] which uses fictitious examples of performance that a worker might exhibit. These performance examples are presented to supervisors, either in writing or on videotape. After rating the performance of the person in the example, the supervisors are told what their ratings should have been. Discussion of which worker behaviors represent each dimension (and why) follows. This process of rating, feedback, and discussion is succeeded by the presentation of another example. Again, rating, feedback, and discussion follow. The process continues until the supervisors develop a common frame of reference for performance evaluation.

frame-of-reference (FOR) training
A type of training that presents supervisors with fictitious examples of worker performance (either in writing or on videotape), asks the supervisors to evaluate the workers in the examples, and then tells them what their ratings should have been.

FOR training is the only type of rater training that increases the accuracy of performance ratings.[30] Perhaps even more important, it develops common evaluation standards among supervisors. This makes comparability among various supervisors' ratings possible and is critical to lowering bias in ratings.

The FOR training procedure does have a number of drawbacks, though. One glaring problem is the expense, which can be prohibitive thanks to the amount of time and number of people involved. (The appendix to this chapter presents an abbreviated and less costly approach called the *critical incident technique*.) Another drawback of the FOR approach is that it can be used only with behaviorally based appraisal systems.

The Influence of Liking. *Liking* can cause errors in performance appraisals when raters allow their like or dislike of an individual to influence their assessment of that person's performance. Liking plays a potent role in performance measurement because both liking and ratings are person-focused. The two may be at odds, however. Liking is emotional and often unconscious, whereas formal ratings are—or should be—nonemotional and conscious. Because liking is unconscious, it seems to be established very quickly,[31] which puts it in a good position to influence (bias) more conscious evaluations that occur later.

Although there is much to be learned in this area, one study found that liking may be a more important determinant of performance ratings than actual worker performance.[32] This provocative finding can be interpreted in two ways. One possibility is that performance ratings have little, if anything, to do with worker performance and instead are based largely on how much a supervisor likes the employee. The second possibility is that objective performance indicators are seriously deficient as indicators of worker performance. Objective measures may miss a number of important characteristics of job performance that supervisors pick up. Furthermore, good supervisors may tend to like good performers and dislike poor performers. Thus, it would be no surprise to find performance ratings related to supervisory liking but not related to objective measures of worker performance.

The fundamental question, of course, is whether the relationship between liking and performance ratings is appropriate or biased.[33] It is appropriate if supervisors like good performers better than poor performers. It is biased if supervisors like or dislike employees for reasons other than their performance and allow these feelings to contaminate their ratings. It is often very difficult to separate these two possibilities.[34] Nonetheless, most workers appear to believe that their supervisor's liking for them influences the performance ratings they receive.[35] The perception of bias can cause communication problems between workers and supervisors and lower supervisors' effectiveness in managing performance.

Precautions. Given the potentially biasing impact of liking, it is critical that supervisors manage their emotional reactions to workers. The first step in managing any emotional reaction is recognizing the presence of the emotion. Managers should be aware of their emotional reactions to workers so that they can guard against their influence.

To ensure that they evaluate workers on performance rather than liking, managers should keep a performance diary on each worker.[36] This diary, which should record behavioral incidents observed by the supervisor, can serve as the basis for evaluation and other managerial actions. An external record of worker behaviors can dramatically reduce error and bias in ratings.

Recordkeeping should be done routinely—for example, daily or weekly. This may seem like a time-consuming task, but the time spent keeping such records may be less than anticipated and the benefits greater. In one field study of such recordkeeping, supervisors reported that the task took five minutes or less per week.[37] More important, the majority of supervisors reported that they would prefer to continue, rather than discontinue, the recording of behavioral incidents. This preference for additional paperwork may seem unusual until one considers the benefits derived from the process. By compiling a weekly record, they did not have to rely much on general impressions and possibly biased memories when conducting appraisals. In addition, the practice signaled workers that appraisal wasn't a personality contest. Finally, the diaries provided a legal justification for the appraisal process: The supervisor could cite concrete behavioral examples that justified the rating.

Two warnings are in order here. First, performance diaries are not guarantees against bias due to liking, because supervisors can be biased in the type of incidents they choose to record. However, short of intentional misrepresentation, the keeping of such records should go a long way toward reducing both actual bias and the perception of bias.

Second, some managers use performance diaries in place of intervention and discussion because it is less uncomfortable, initially, to record a performance problem than to discuss it with the employee. Documenting problems is fine, and even useful for creating a legally defensible case in the event that the employee must be terminated. However, it is unfair to keep a secret running list of "offenses" and then suddenly unveil it to the

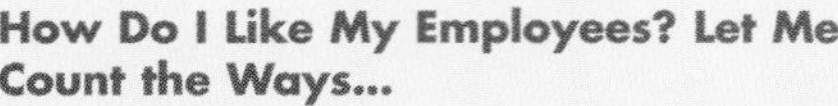

How Do I Like My Employees? Let Me Count the Ways...

While liking can be a source of bias in performance appraisals, it can also be the direct result of good performance. Managers tend to like employees who have a positive attitude, who get along well with their coworkers, and who perform consistently well.

employee when he or she commits an infraction that can't be overlooked. The message for managers is simple: If an employee's behavior warrants discussion, the discussion should take place immediately.[38]

Here's how one company used performance diaries both to aid performance appraisal and to enhance employee coaching:

> In its drive to revamp its performance appraisal system, Azteca Foods, Inc., a 125-employee company, asked its 25 managers to begin keeping a daily log of each employee's performance. Every time an employee did something negative (like arriving late to work or missing an assignment deadline) or something positive (like making a notable contribution) the manager was expected to write it down and give immediate feedback. While this procedure may sound time-consuming, the company found the payback worth the extra effort. At appraisal time managers were able to bring up concrete examples of what an employee did instead of saying "You've done a good (or inadequate) job." The procedure also fosters communication between managers and subordinates and motivates workers to continuously improve performance.[39]

Organizational Politics. Thus far we have taken a *rational perspective* on appraisal.[40] In other words, we have assumed that the value of each worker's performance can be estimated. Unlike the rational approach, the *political perspective* assumes that the value of a worker's performance depends on the agenda, or goals, of the supervisor.[41] In other words, the political approach to appraisal holds that performance measurement is a goal-oriented activity and that the goal is seldom accuracy. Consider the following quote from an executive with extensive experience in evaluating his subordinates:

> As a manager, I will use the review process to do what is best for my people and the division.... I've got a lot of leeway—call it discretion—to use this process in that manner.... I've used it to get my people better raises in lean years, to kick a guy in the pants if he really needed it, to pick up a guy when he was down or even to tell him that he was no longer welcome here.... I believe that most of us here at ___ operate this way regarding appraisals.[42]

The distinction between the rational and political approaches to appraisal can best be understood by examining how they differ on various facets of the performance appraisal process.

- The *goal* of appraisal from a rational perspective is accuracy. The goal of appraisal from a political perspective is *utility,* the maximization of benefits over costs given the context and agenda. The value of performance is relative to the political context and the supervisor's goals. For example, a supervisor may give a very poor rating to a worker who seems uncommitted in the hopes of shocking that worker into an acceptable level of performance. Or the supervisor may give positive ratings to workers in an attempt to reduce complaints and conflict. In these circumstances, it is clear that the goal of appraisal is not accuracy.
- The *roles* played by supervisors and workers also differ in the rational and political approaches. The rational approach sees supervisors and workers largely as passive agents in the rating process: Supervisors simply notice and evaluate workers' performance. Thus, the accuracy of supervisors is critical to the attainment of accurate evaluations. In contrast, the political approach views both supervisors and workers as motivated participants in the measurement process. Workers actively try to influence their evaluations, either directly or indirectly.

The various persuasion techniques that workers use to alter the supervisor's evaluation are direct forms of influence. For example, just as a student tells a professor that he needs a higher grade to keep his scholarship, a worker might tell her boss that she needs an above-average rating to get a promotion. Indirect influences on ratings include a variety of behaviors in which workers engage to influence how supervisors notice, interpret, and recall events.[43] Behaviors ranging from flattery to excuses to apologies all are examples of how workers attempt to influence supervisors' impressions.

- From a rational perspective, the *focus* of appraisal is measurement. Supervisors are flesh-and-blood instruments[44] who must be carefully trained to measure performance meaningfully. The evaluations are used in decisions regarding pay raises, promotions, training, and termination. The political perspective sees the focus of appraisal as management, not accurate measurement. Appraisal isn't so much a test that should be fair and accurate as a management tool with which to reward or discipline workers.
- *Assessment criteria,* the standards used to judge worker performance, also differ between the rational and political approaches. The rational approach holds that a worker's performance should be defined as clearly as possible. Without a clear definition of what is being assessed and clear standards for its assessment, accurate assessment is impossible. In the political approach, the definition of what is being assessed is left ambiguous so that it can be bent to the current agenda. Thus, ambiguity ensures the necessary flexibility in the appraisal system.
- Finally, the *decision process* involved in performance assessment differs between the rational and political approaches. In the rational approach, supervisors make dimensional and overall assessments based on specific behaviors they've observed. For instance, in the computer programmer example we've been using, Nancy would rate each programmer on each dimension, and then combine all the dimensional ratings into an overall evaluation. In the political approach, it is the other way around: Appropriate assessment of specifics follows the overall assessment. Thus, Nancy would first decide who in her group should get the highest rating (for whatever reason), and then justify that overall assessment by making appropriate dimensional ratings.

A QUESTION OF ETHICS

Is it right to give someone a higher (or lower) rating than you think that person deserves because you are trying to "send a message," or is this sort of behavior simply lying and therefore wrong?

Appraisal in most organizations seems to be a political rather than a rational exercise.[45] It appears to be used as a tool for serving various and changing agendas; accurate assessment is seldom the real goal. But should the rational approach be abandoned because appraisal is typically political? No! Politically driven assessment may be common, but that doesn't make it the best approach to assessment. Accuracy may not be the main goal in organizations, but it is the theoretical ideal behind appraisal.[46] Accurate assessment is necessary if feedback, development, and HR decisions are to be based on employees' actual performance levels. Basing feedback and development on managerial agendas is an unjust treatment of human resources. Careers have been ruined, self-esteem lost, and productivity degraded because of the political use of appraisal. Such costs are difficult to assess and to ascribe clearly to politics. Nonetheless, they are very real and important for workers.

Individual or Group Focus. Just as we have assumed throughout this chapter that the performance measurement process is rational, we have also assumed that the appropriate focus is the individual employee. This is largely a reflection of our Western culture. We value the rugged individual, the superstar, the person who stands out from the crowd. Our entire economic system is based on competition and survival of the fittest. However, in organizations, teamwork and cooperation are necessary for the achievement of common goals. Indeed, as we've seen in earlier chapters, teams are becoming increasingly common in the U.S. workplace. It has been estimated that 50% of all U.S. organizations will have teams in at least one part of their operations by the year 2000.[47]

Performance appraisal that focuses solely on individual achievement can create serious morale problems among employees working in teams.[48] One person may be an excellent team player who spends time helping coworkers, only to get penalized at appraisal time for not reaching individual objectives. W. Edwards Deming, a founder of the quality movement, went so far as to suggest that individually focused performance assessment is a "deadly management disease" that is killing organizations, and he recommended that appraisal be eliminated!

In practice, most companies have not followed this extreme advice.[48a] (Figure 7–7 lists several reasons, from both the employer's and employee's perspective, why appraisal is still valuable, despite the criticisms that have been leveled against it.) However, many quality-oriented companies have changed their appraisal practices to make them more compatible with a quality environment. Eastman Chemical Company, for example, emphasizes self- and peer assessment using a nonnumerical approach.[49] Workers and their peers identify their relative strengths and weaknesses, then meet with their team members to identify how they can improve their performance. By not using numbers on the rating form, which sometimes creates competition and divisiveness among workers, Eastman hopes to maintain the cohesive team environment it has developed. Other companies, such as the Cadillac division of General Motors, have made similar changes in their appraisal systems.[50] (We discuss self- and peer review in detail later in this chapter.)

In their quest for team cohesion, quality-oriented organizations have also turned to using "coarser" rating scales. St. Luke's Hospital's MeritCare, a 2,100-employee hospital, designed a new appraisal system that is in sync with its commitment to excellent customer service.[51] There are only three rating levels in the new system ("at standards," "above standards," or "below standards"), compared to five in the previous system. This coarse rating scale means fewer distinctions among workers and therefore a less competitive rating environment. Like Eastman and other quality-oriented organizations (including Federal Express and Digital Equipment Corporation), MeritCare has shifted to using multiple sources of appraisal. In addition to traditional supervisory sources, these companies ask the employees themselves, peers, subordinates, and internal and external customers to rate the employees' effectiveness.[52]

Two final points: First, experts recommend that individual performance still be assessed, even within a team environment, because U.S. society is so strongly focused on individual performance.[53] Second, there is no consensus as to what type of appraisal instrument should be used for team evaluations. The best approach may include internal and external customers making judgments across both behavioral and outcome criteria.[54]

Employer Perspective

1. Despite imperfect measurement techniques, individual differences in performance can make a difference to company performance.
2. Documentation of performance appraisal and feedback may be needed for legal defense.
3. Appraisal provides a rational basis for constructing a bonus or merit system.
4. Appraisal dimensions and standards can help to implement strategic goals and clarify performance expectations.
5. Providing individual feedback is part of the performance management process.
6. Despite the traditional focus on the individual, appraisal criteria can include teamwork and the teams can be the focus of appraisal.

Employee Perspective

1. Performance feedback is needed and desired.
2. Improvement in performance requires assessment.
3. Fairness requires that differences in performance levels across workers be measured and have an effect on outcomes.
4. Assessment and recognition of performance levels can motivate workers to improve their performance.

FIGURE 7-7

The Benefits of Performance Appraisal

Source: Cardy, R.L., and Carson, K.P. (1996). Total quality and the abandonment of performance appraisal: Taking a good thing too far? *Journal of Quality Management*, 193-206.

Legal Issues. The major legal requirements for performance appraisal systems are set forth in Title VII of the Civil Rights Act of 1964, which prohibits discrimination in all terms and conditions of employment (see Chapter 3). This means that performance appraisal must be free of discrimination at both the individual and group levels. Some courts have also held that performance appraisal systems should meet the same *validity* standards as selection tests (see Chapter 5). As with selection tests, *adverse impact* may occur in performance evaluation when members of one group are promoted at a higher rate than members of another group based on their appraisals.

Probably the most significant court test of discrimination in performance appraisal is *Brito v. Zia Company,* a 1973 U.S. Supreme Court case. In essence, the Court determined that appraisal is legally a test and must therefore meet all the legal requirements regarding tests in organizations. In practice, however, court decisions since *Brito v. Zia* have employed less stringent criteria when assessing charges of discrimination in appraisal.

A review of appraisal-related court cases since *Brito v. Zia* shows that the courts do not wish to rule on whether appraisal systems conform to all accepted professional standards (such as whether employees were allowed to participate in developing the system).[55] Rather, they simply want to determine if discrimination occurred. The essential question is whether individuals who have similar employment situations are treated differently. The courts look favorably on a review system in which a supervisor's manager reviews appraisals to safeguard against the occurrence of individual bias. In addition, the courts take a positive view of feedback and employee counseling to help improve performance problems.

One of the reasons the courts have been favorably disposed toward organizational discretion in performance appraisal is found in a very old legal doctrine called *employment at will.* This doctrine states that unless there is an employment contract (such as a union contract or an implied contract), both the employer and the employee are free to end the employment relationship whenever and for whatever reason they choose. This is good for employees because it means that if they go out for lunch and decide never to return to work, their employer has no legal recourse against them. The converse is also true, however. A boss can say, "Why don't you take a long lunch...like for the rest of your life," and just like that, the person is out of a job.

Recently, however, many state courts have been ruling that there are exceptions to the general employment-at-will doctrine.[56] One of these exceptions is when an employee is terminated for refusing to do something that is contrary to public policy, such as lie under oath or disrobe in public. Another exception occurs when an employer has promised something to employees, then fails to live up to this promise. For instance, if an organization states that employees will be fired only after being given a warning, then failure to follow this procedure may be an exception.

Employment at will is a very complex legal issue that depends on laws and rulings that vary from state to state. We discuss employment at will fully in Chapter 14. Here, it is enough to say that managers can protect themselves from lawsuits by following good professional practice. If they provide subordinates with honest, accurate, and fair feedback about their performance, and then make decisions consistent with that feedback, they will have nothing to fear from ongoing questions about employment at will.

Building Managerial Skills: Managing Performance

The effective management of human performance in organizations requires more than formal reporting and annual ratings. A complete appraisal process includes informal day-to-day interactions between managers and workers as well as formal face-to-face interviews. Although the ratings themselves are important, even more critical is what managers do with them. In this section we discuss the third and final component of performance appraisal, performance management.

Performance Diagnosis and Feedback

Upon completing the performance rating, the supervisor usually conducts an interview with the worker to provide feedback—one of the most important parts of the appraisal process. Many managers dread the performance appraisal, particularly if they do not have good news to impart. The HR department can help managers by training them in conducting interviews, giving them practice in role-playing, and offering them advice on thorny issues.

It has been common practice to conduct performance appraisals in two separate sessions: one to discuss performance, the other to discuss salary.[57] (This practice remains the norm in Great Britain, where 85% of large companies split the appraisal meeting.) The logic behind this system was based on two assumptions. First, managers cannot simultaneously be both a coach and a judge. Thus, the manager was expected to play the coach role during the performance development meeting and the judge role during the salary meeting. Second, if performance and salary discussions were combined, employees probably wouldn't listen to their performance feedback because their interest would be focused on salary decisions.

However, research has found that discussion of salary in an appraisal session has a *positive* impact on how employees perceive the appraisal's usefulness.[58] There are at least two reasons for this. First, when money is at stake, the manager is much more likely to take the tasks of appraisal and feedback seriously. Managers who have to justify a low salary increase will likely take time to carefully support their performance assessments, and this more detailed feedback should make the appraisal session more valuable to the employee. Second, including the salary discussion can energize the performance discussion. Feedback, goal setting, and making action plans can become a hollow and meaningless exercise when salary implications are divorced from the session.

In sum, it appears that the best management practice is to combine development and salary discussion into one performance review. Informal performance management throughout the appraisal period requires a combination of judgment and coaching. To be most effective, judgment and coaching should also be used together in the formal review session.

Performance Improvement

Because formal appraisal interviews typically are conducted only once a year,[59] they may not always have substantial and lasting impact on worker performance.[60] Much more important than the annual interview is informal day-to-day performance management. Supervisors who manage performance effectively generally share four characteristics. They:

- Explore the causes of performance problems.
- Direct attention to the causes of problems.
- Develop an action plan and empower workers to reach a solution.
- Direct communication at performance and emphasize nonthreatening communication.[61]

Each of these characteristics is critical to achieving improved and sustained performance levels.

Exploring the Causes of Performance Problems. Exploring the causes of performance problems may sound like an easy task, but it is often quite challenging. Performance can be the result of many factors, some of which are beyond the worker's control. In most work situations, though, observers tend to attribute the causes to the worker.[62] That is, supervisors tend to blame the worker when they observe poor performance, while workers tend to blame external factors. This tendency is called *actor/observer* *bias*.[63] The experience of baseball teams provides an analogy. When a team is losing, the players (workers/actors) point to external causes such as injuries, a tough road schedule, or bad weather. The manager (supervisor/observer) blames the players for sloppy execution in the field. And the team's owner and the sportswriters (top management/higher observers) hold the manager responsible for the team's poor performance.

It is important that managers determine the causes of performance deficiencies accurately for three reasons. First, determination of causes can influence how performance is evaluated. For example, a manager is likely to evaluate an episode of poor performance very differently if he thinks it was due to low effort than if he thinks it was due to poor materials. Second, causal determination can be an unspoken and underlying source of conflict between supervisors and their workers. Supervisors often act on what they believe are the causes of performance problems. This is only rational. But when the supervisor's perception significantly differs from the worker's, the difference can cause tension. Third, causal determinations affect the type of remedy selected; what is thought to be the cause of a performance problem determines what is done about it. For instance, very different actions would be taken if poor performance was thought to be the result of inadequate ability rather than inadequacies in the raw materials.

How can the process of determining the causes of performance problems be improved? A starting point is to consider the possible causes consciously and systematically. Traditionally, performance has been thought to be caused by two primary factors: ability and motivation.[64] A major problem with this view is that situational factors external to the worker, such as degree of management support, also affect worker performance.[65] A more inclusive version of the causes of performance embraces three factors: ability, motivation, and situational factors. The *ability* factor reflects the worker's talents and skills, including such characteristics as intelligence, interpersonal skills, and job knowledge. *Motivation* can be affected by a number of external factors (such as rewards and punishments) but is ultimately an internal decision: It is up to the worker to determine how much effort to exert on any given task. **Situational factors** (or, in TQM terminology, **system factors**) include a wide array of organizational characteristics that can positively or negatively influence performance. System factors include quality of materials, quality of supervisor, and the other factors listed in Figure 7–8.[66]

situational factors or system factors
A wide array of organizational characteristics that can positively or negatively influence performance.

Performance depends on all three factors. The presence of just one cause is not sufficient for high performance to occur; however, the absence or low value of one factor can result in poor performance. For example, making a strong effort will not result in high performance if the worker has neither the necessary job skills nor adequate support in the workplace. But if the worker doesn't put forth any effort, low performance is inevitable, no matter how good that worker's skills and how much support is provided.

- Poor coordination of work activities among workers.
- Inadequate information or instructions needed to perform a job.
- Low-quality materials.
- Lack of necessary equipment.
- Inability to obtain raw materials, parts, or supplies.
- Inadequate financial resources.
- Poor supervision.
- Uncooperative coworkers and/or poor relations among people.
- Inadequate training.
- Insufficient time to produce the quantity or quality of work required.
- A poor work environment (for example, cold, hot, noisy, frequent interruptions).
- Equipment breakdown.

FIGURE 7-8

Situational (System) Factors to Consider in Determining the Causes of Performance Problems

In determining the causes of performance problems, managers should carefully consider situational factors. The factors in Figure 7–8 are only a starting point; they are too generic for use in some situations. For best results, supervisors should use this list as a basis for generating their own job-specific lists of factors. Involving workers in creating the lists will both produce examples of which supervisors may not have been aware and send a signal that managers are serious about considering workers' input. The supervisor and worker (or work team) can go over the list together to isolate the causes of any performance difficulties.

Finally, supervisors should also consider using self-, peer, and subordinate reviews on an annual or semiannual basis. **Self-review,** in which workers rate themselves, allows employees input into the appraisal process and can help them gain insight into the causes of performance problems. For example, there may be a substantial difference in opinion between a supervisor and an employee regarding one area of the employee's evaluation. Communication and possibly investigation are warranted in such a case.

self-review
A performance appraisal system in which workers rate themselves.

When a supervisor and a worker cannot resolve their disagreement, performance assessments from additional sources, such as peers and subordinates, may be useful. In a **peer review,** workers at the same level of the organization rate one another. In a **subordinate review,** workers review their supervisors. Figure 7–9 shows that such upward appraisal is being used by some of America's most respected companies. If peers' and subordinates' judgments converge with the supervisor's, then it is likely that the supervisor's judgment is correct. If peers' and subordinates' judgments do not match the supervisor's, it may be that the supervisor is not aware of or sensitive to the impact of certain factors on the worker's performance.

peer review
A performance appraisal system in which workers at the same level in the organization rate one another.

subordinate review
A performance appraisal system in which workers review their supervisors.

More and more companies are using peer review as a performance appraisal system. W. L. Gore & Associates, the company known by outdoors enthusiasts for its Gore-Tex fabric, has used peer review since its founding over 30 years ago. At Gore, every employee is ranked by peers on the basis of his or her contributions to the company's goals. The peers in this case are committees of six to ten coworkers. Because W. L. Gore limits the size of its 40-odd plants to fewer than 200 people, coworkers tend to be familiar with one another's work. The rankings, called "contribution lists," may be compiled several times a year. They begin at the team level, asking about each group, "Who is the most valuable contributor to this function? Who is the next most valuable?" and so on.

Alcoa (metals)
Amoco (petroleum refining)
AT&T (diversified service)
BellSouth (utilities)
Burlington Resources (mining, crude oil production)
Du Pont (chemicals)
Eaton (motor vehicles, parts)*
Federal Express (delivery services)
General Mills (food)
Hewlett-Packard (computers, office equipment)
Massmutual (life insurance)
Merck (pharmaceuticals)*
Herman Miller (furniture)
J.P. Morgan (commercial banking)
Morgan Stanley Group (diversified financial)
Motorola (electronics, electrical equipment)
Northwestern Mutual Life (life insurance)*
Procter & Gamble (soaps, cosmetics)
Reader's Digest (publishing, printing)
WH Smith (news and retail)
Levi Strauss Associates (apparel)
3M (scientific, photographic, and control equipment)
United Parcel Service (transportation)

*Limited program.

FIGURE 7-9

Companies Where Employees Rate Executives

Sources: List compiled from Romano, C. (1994). Conquering the fear of feedback, (March, 9-10); Thatcher, M. (1996). Allowing everyone to have their say. *People Management, 21*, 28-30; *Fortune*. (1993, December 27). Companies where employees rate executives, 128.

360° feedback
The combination of peer, subordinate, and self-review.

The combination of peer, subordinate, and self-review, termed **360° feedback**, is rapidly becoming important and may someday be the rule rather than the exception. One reason for the rise of 360° feedback is the trend to fewer management layers. With so many more employees reporting to one supervisor, it's just not possible for the supervisor to gauge everyone's work accurately. Another reason is that the old system where the supervisor alone reviews performance is out of sync with today's emphasis on teamwork and participative management.[67]

The shift to a 360° system can be a major change that requires careful planning to be successful. The Manager's Notebook on page 224 titled "Key Steps in Implementing 360° Appraisal" provides steps to follow that should result in an effective and acceptable system.

Collecting performance appraisals from multiple sources can be time consuming and expensive. Consider the costs that a 360° system can involve:

Situation: 400 employees each receive feedback from 12 raters using a questionnaire that takes, on average, 30 minutes to fill out.

Total Time Calculation: 30 minutes × 12 raters per ratee = 6 rater hours
6 rater hours × 400 ratees = 2,400 hours
2,400 hours ÷ 8 hours per workday = 300 workdays

If the average daily salary is $200, then the rater-time cost for administering the 360° system would be $60,000.

Companies can significantly reduce the time need for 360° appraisal by putting the appraisal system online. Computerizing the system can streamline the process and reduce the amount of time raters need to devote to the evaluation task. For example, with an automated system a 90-item questionnaire may take only 30 minutes to complete, compared to 45 minutes for a paper questionnaire. The evaluations may also be better because the rating task demands less time from the raters.

Computerizing the 360° system can reduce many other costs as well. These include:

- *Paper costs.* In a computerized system, the costs of paper and paper handling are trivial. In a traditional system, they are quite high. For example, at one airline that conducts 360° appraisal each rater receives 47 pieces of paper (including instructions, rating forms, and envelopes). Each of the 16,000 employees also receives 9 to 21 pages of feedback on their own performance. The paper costs certainly add up. By computerizing its appraisal system, this airline could save nearly one million pages of paper per year.
- *Administrative overhead.* Going online can greatly reduce administrative overhead. One expert has estimated that computerizing the 360° system decreases the number of people dedicated to managing the system from three full-time employees per 1,000 participants to one employee per 2,000 participants.[68]

Customer Appraisals. In addition to feedback from within the organization, companies are increasingly looking to customers as a valuable source of appraisal. Traditional top-down appraisal systems may encourage employees to perform only those behaviors that supervisors see or pay attention to. Thus, behaviors that are critical to customer satisfaction may be ignored.[69]

Indeed, customers are often in a better position to evaluate the quality of a company's products or services than supervisors are. Supervisors may have limited information or a limited perspective, while internal and external customers often have a wider focus or greater experience with more parts of the business. Figure 7–10 presents an example of a customer appraisal form.

Directing Attention to the Causes of Problems. After supervisor and worker have discussed and agreed on the causes of performance problems, the next step is to take steps

Name: ______________________________

This survey asks your opinion about specific aspects of the products and services you received. Your individual responses will remain confidential and will be compiled with those of other customers to improve customer service. Please use the following scale to indicate the extent to which you agree with the statement. Circle one response for each item.

1 = Strongly Disagree
2 = Disagree
3 = Neutral
4 = Agree
5 = Strongly Agree
? = Unsure

If you feel unable to adequately rate a specific item, please leave it blank.

QUALITY

I had to wait an unreasonable amount of time for my requests to be met .... 1 2 3 4 5 ?

The products I have received have met my expectations.................... 1 2 3 4 5 ?

My requests were met on or before the agreed upon deadline................................. 1 2 3 4 5 ?

The products I have received have generally been error free........... 1 2 3 4 5 ?

SERVICE/ATTITUDE

When serving me, this person:

Was helpful....................... 1 2 3 4 5 ?

Was cooperative in meeting my requests......... 1 2 3 4 5 ?

Communicated with me to understand my expectations for products........................... 1 2 3 4 5 ?

Was uncooperative when I asked for revisions/additional information....................... 1 2 3 4 5 ?

Told me when my requests would be filled................................. 1 2 3 4 5 ?

When necessary, sufficiently explained to me why my expectations could not be met.................................. 1 2 3 4 5 ?

Kept me informed about the status of my request............................ 1 2 3 4 5 ?

CUSTOMER SATISFACTION

How would you rate your overall level of satisfaction with the *service* you have received?

1 = Very Dissatisfied
2 = Dissatisfied
3 = Neutral
4 = Satisfied
5 = Very Satisfied

What specifically could be done to make you more satisfied with the *service*?

____
____
____

How would you rate your overall level of satisfaction with the *products* you have received?

1 = Very Dissatisfied
2 = Dissatisfied
3 = Neutral
4 = Satisfied
5 = Very Satisfied

What specifically could be done to make you more satisfied with the *products*?

____
____
____

FIGURE 7-10

Customer Appraisal Form

Source: Cardy, R. L., and Dobbins, G. H. (1994). *Performance appraisal: Alternative perspectives*. Cincinnati, OH: South-Western.

to control them. If certain factors affect performance positively, managers should try to ensure that those factors are present as much as possible. In the more common case of constraining factors, managers should try to reduce or eliminate them. Depending on whether the cause of performance problems is related to ability, effort, or situational characteristics, very different tactics are called for. As Figure 7–11 on page 224 makes clear, different remedies are required for different categories of performance shortfalls. Leaping to a remedy like training (a common reaction) will not fix a problem that is not ability caused and will be a waste of the organization's resources.[70]

Developing an Action Plan and Empowering Workers to Reach a Solution. Effective performance management requires empowering workers to improve their performance. The traditional management approach of supervisors giving orders and workers following them usually does not lead to maximum performance levels. The newer empowerment approach requires supervisors to take on the role of coach rather than director and controller.[71] As in a sports team, the supervisor-as-coach assists workers in interpreting and reacting to the work situation. The role is not necessarily one of mentor, friend, or counselor. Rather, it is that of enabler. The supervisor-as-coach works to ensure that the necessary resources are available to workers and helps employees identify an action plan to solve performance problems. For example, the supervisor may suggest ways for the worker to eliminate, avoid, or get around situational obstacles to performance. In addition to creating a supportive, empowered work environment, coach/supervisors clarify performance expectations; provide immediate feedback; and strive to eliminate unnecessary rules, procedures, and other constraints.[72]

Directing Communication at Performance. Communication between supervisor and worker is critical to effective performance management. Exactly what is communicated and how it is communicated can determine whether performance improves or declines. The Manager's Notebook on page 226 titled "Providing Constructive Feedback" provides 12 recommendations for communicating and maximizing the effectiveness of performance feedback.

It is important that communication regarding performance be directed at the performance and not at the person. For example, a worker should not be asked why he's such a jerk! It is usually much more effective to ask the worker why his performance has been ineffective lately. Open-minded communication is more likely to uncover the real reason for a performance problem and thus pave the way for an effective solution.

Communication to workers regarding performance should be probing but nonevaluative to avoid evoking a defensive reaction. Figure 7–12 presents some examples of good and bad forms of supervisory coaching communications. ▼

Manager's Notebook

Key Steps in Implementing 360° Appraisal

To create a successful 360° appraisal program, companies should proceed as follows:

1. Top management communicates the goals of and need for 360° appraisal.
2. Employees and managers are involved in the development of the appraisal criteria and appraisal process.
3. Employees are trained in how to give and receive feedback.
4. Employees are informed of the nature of the 360° appraisal instrument and process.
5. The 360° system undergoes pilot testing in one part of the organization.
6. Management continuously reinforces the goals of the 360° appraisal and is ready to change the process when necessary.

Source: Adapted from Milliman, J. F., Zawacki, R. A., Norman, C., Powell, L., and Kirksey, J. (1994). Companies evaluate employees from all perspectives. *Personnel Journal*, November, 99–103.

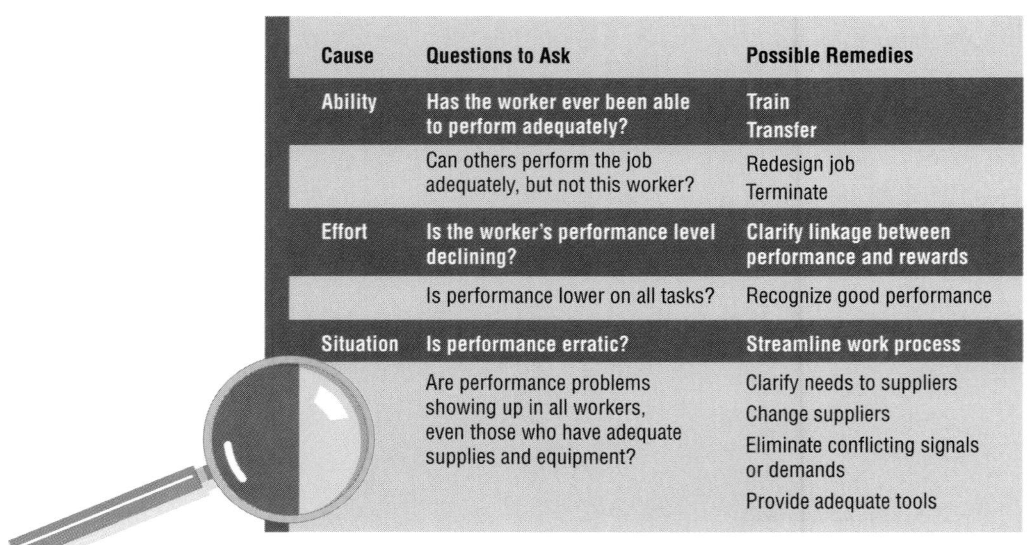

Cause	Questions to Ask	Possible Remedies
Ability	Has the worker ever been able to perform adequately?	Train Transfer
	Can others perform the job adequately, but not this worker?	Redesign job Terminate
Effort	Is the worker's performance level declining?	Clarify linkage between performance and rewards
	Is performance lower on all tasks?	Recognize good performance
Situation	Is performance erratic?	Streamline work process
	Are performance problems showing up in all workers, even those who have adequate supplies and equipment?	Clarify needs to suppliers Change suppliers Eliminate conflicting signals or demands Provide adequate tools

FIGURE 7-11

How to Determine and Remedy Performance Shortfalls

Source: Adapted from Schermerhorn, J. R., Gardner, W. I., and Martin, T. N. (1990). Management dialogues: Turning on the marginal performer. *Organizational Dynamics, 18*, 47–59; and Rummler, G. A. (1972). Human performance problems and their solutions. *Human Resource Management, 19*, 2–10.

The communication approaches suggested here are designed to reduce ratee defensiveness. All of these approaches emphasize analysis rather than evaluation of employee problems.

I. Evaluation vs. Description

Rather than evaluate the employee's behavior, try describing the problem so that you and the ratee can jointly arrive at a solution.

Evaluation	Description
1. You simply can't keep making these stupid mistakes.	1. We're still having a problem reducing the amount of waste produced.
2. Bob, you're tactless and undiplomatic.	2. Some people interpret your candor as hostility.
3. The accident was your fault.	3. This accident appears to involve some differences in interpreting the safety regulations.

II. Control vs. Problem Orientation

Control communications emphasize the supervisor's power over the ratee. Problem orientation conveys respect for the ratee's ability to solve the problem and is more likely to generate useful options.

EXAMPLES

Control	Problem Orientation
1. Bob, I'd like to see you doing X, Y, and Z over the next week.	1. Bob, what sort of things might we do here?
2. I think my suggestions are clear, so why don't you get back to work?	2. Let's both think about these possibilities and get back together next week to discuss them.
3. I've decided what you must do to reduce mistakes.	3. Have you thought about what we might do to reduce mistakes?

III. Neutrality vs. Empathy

Raters often interpret a supervisor's neutrality as lack of interest in the problem and its impact on them. Empathy signals concern for the ratee and his or her situation.

EXAMPLES

Neutrality	Empathy
1. I really don't know what we can do about it.	1. At this point I can't think of anything, but I know where we might look for help.
2. Too bad, but we all go through that.	2. I think I know how you're feeling. I can remember a similar experience I had...
3. I didn't know that.	3. I wasn't aware of that. Let me make sure I understand.

IV. Superiority vs. Equality

EXAMPLES

Superiority	Equality
1. Bob, I've worked with this problem for ten years and I know what will work.	1. This idea has worked before. Do you think it might work in this case?
2. Look, I'm being paid to make these decisions, not you.	2. I'll have to make the final decision, Bob, but why don't you get your suggestions in to me as soon as possible?
3. The management staff has thought this policy through pretty thoroughly.	3. We've discussed this policy at the management meeting, but I'm interested in your thoughts since you're the one who has to deal with it on the front line.

FIGURE 7-12

Suggestions for Coaching Communications

Source: Reprinted by permission of the publisher, from *Supervisory Management,* March, 1978,

Manager's Notebook

Providing Constructive Feedback

To maximize the effectiveness of the performance appraisal, managers should:

1. Conduct the appraisal in private and allow enough time for the employee to discuss issues important to him or her.
2. Present perceptions, reactions, and opinions as such and *not* as facts.
3. Refer to the relevant performance, behavior, or outcomes, not to the individual as a person.
4. Provide feedback in terms of specific, observable behavior, not general behavior.
5. Talk in terms of established criteria, probable outcomes, or possible improvement, as opposed to such judgments as "good" or "bad."
6. Discuss performance and the specific behaviors that appear to be contributing to or limiting full effectiveness.
7. Suggest possible means of improving performance in discussing problem areas that contain technical or established procedures for achieving solutions.
8. Avoid loaded terms (for example, "crabby," "mess-up," "rip-off," or "stupid"), which produce emotional reactions and defensiveness.
9. Concentrate on those things over which an individual can exercise some control, and focus on ways that indicate how the employee can use the feedback to improve performance.
10. Deal with defensiveness or emotional reactions rather than trying to convince, reason, or supply additional information.
11. Give feedback in a manner that communicates acceptance of the appraisee as a worthwhile person and of that person's right to be an individual.
12. Keep in mind that feedback is intended to be helpful and, therefore, should be tied to specific development plans to capitalize on strengths and minimize performance weaknesses.

Source: Adapted from Gómez-Mejía, L.R. (1990). Increasing productivity: Performance appraisal and reward systems. *Personnel Journal, 19*(2).

Summary and Conclusions

What Is Performance Appraisal? Performance appraisal is the identification, measurement, and management of human performance in organizations. Appraisal should be a future-oriented activity that provides workers with useful feedback and coaches them to higher levels of performance. Appraisal can be used administratively or developmentally.

Identifying Performance Dimensions. Performance appraisal begins by identifying the dimensions of performance that determine effective job performance. Job analysis is the mechanism by which performance dimensions should be identified.

Measuring Performance. The methods used to measure employee performance can be classified in two ways: (1) whether the type of judgment called for is relative or absolute, and (2) whether the measure focuses on traits, behavior, or outcomes. Each measure has its advantages and disadvantages. But it is clear that the overall quality of ratings is much more a function of the rater's motivation and ability than of the type of instrument chosen.

Managers face five challenges in managing performance: rater errors and bias; the influence of liking; organizational politics; whether to focus on the individual or the group; and legal issues (including discrimination and employment at will).

Managing Performance. The primary goal of any appraisal system is performance management. To manage and improve their employees' performance, managers must explore the causes of performance problems, direct manager and employee attention to those causes, develop action plans and empower workers to find solutions, and use performance-focused communication.

Key Terms

absolute judgment, 206
behavioral appraisal instrument, 209
comparability, 212
dimension, 204
frame-of-reference (FOR) training, 213
management by objectives (MBO), 210
outcome appraisal instrument, 210
peer review, 221
performance appraisal, 203
rater error, 212
relative judgment, 205
self-review, 221
situational factor or system factors, 220
subordinate review, 221
360° feedback, 222
trait appraisal instrument, 208

Discussion Questions

1. At ARCO Transportation, a $1 billion division of Atlantic Richfield, employees are hired, promoted, and appraised according to how they fulfill the performance dimensions most valued by the company. One of these performance dimensions is "communication"—specifically, "listens and observes attentively, allowing an exchange of information" and "speaks and writes clearly and concisely, with an appropriate awareness of the intended audience." Would you say that ARCO appraises performance based on personality traits, job behavior, or outcome achieved? On which of these three aspects of performance do you think workers should be appraised?
2. Superficially, it seems preferable to use objective performance data (such as productivity figures), when available, rather than subjective supervisory ratings to assess employees. Why might objective data be less effective performance measures than subjective ratings?
3. How important are rating formats to the quality of performance ratings? What is the most important influence on rating quality?
4. What is comparability? How can it be maximized in performance appraisal?
5. "Occasionally an employee comes along who needs to be reminded who the boss is, and the appraisal is an appropriate place for such a reminder." Would the manager quoted here be likely to use a rational or a political approach to appraisal? Contrast the rational and political approaches. To what extent is it possible to separate the two?
6. Do you think performance appraisal should still be done in quality-oriented organizations? If so, what should be measured and how?
7. What criteria do you think should be used to measure team performance? What sources should be used for the appraisal? Should individual performance still be measured? Why or why not?
8. You're the owner of a 25-employee company that has just had a fantastic year. Everyone pulled together and worked hard to achieve the boost in company profits. Unfortunately, you need to sink most of those profits into paying your suppliers. All you can afford to give your workers is a 3% pay raise across the board. At appraisal time, how would you communicate praise for a job well done coupled with your very limited ability to reward such outstanding performance? Now assume you can afford to hand out some handsome bonuses or raises. What would be the best way to evaluate employees when *everyone* has done exceptional work?

MINICASE 1 *Two Approaches to 360° Appraisal*

A number of companies are turning to 360° appraisal systems as a means of providing performance information to employees and making them accountable to their customers. However, 360° appraisal can involve some difficult choices.

Johnson & Johnson Advanced Behavioral Technology uses a 360° approach that asks internal customers, external customers, and peers to rate each employee. Each Johnson & Johnson employee compiles a list of five to ten people who could serve as his or her raters. However, the supervisor has final authority over who will be selected as each employee's raters, and may choose to remove some people from the employee's list while adding others. The employee's supervisor is also responsible for summarizing the judgments and determining the final performance rating. Supervisors are encouraged to look for trends in the ratings, rather than overinterpret one rater's particularly positive or negative evaluation. After compiling the ratings, the supervisor conducts a formal performance review session with the employee. Johnson &

continued

Johnson also provides raters the option of making ratings anonymously or providing the ratee with his or her identity.

Appraisal at Digital Equipment Corporation is very different. In Digital's 360° system, the employee has the primary responsibility for selecting raters. A random sample of the people nominated by each employee is then asked to serve as raters. The ratee is also responsible for summarizing his or her own feedback from the raters. Employees throw out the lowest and highest ratings to ensure the least biased set of judgments. Digital also has a rule that no rater can give negative feedback in the appraisal unless he or she has previously given that feedback directly to the ratee.

Discussion Questions

1. How do you think raters should be selected in a 360° appraisal system? Should the supervisor or the ratee have primary control over this factor? What are the advantages and disadvantages of each approach?
2. Should the ratee be trusted with the responsibility of summarizing his or her own feedback, or should the Johnson & Johnson approach of having supervisors do this task be followed? Why or why not? What are the advantages and disadvantages of each approach?
3. Should feedback from the various sources in a 360° appraisal system be anonymous? What problems or benefits might result from each approach?

Source: Adapted from Milliman, J. F., Zawack, R. A., Norman, C., Powell, L., and Kirksey, J. (1994). Companies evaluate employees from all perspectives. *Personnel Journal*, November, 99–103.

MINICASE 2 *Internal Appraisal and Goal Setting at Federal Express*

Appraisal ratings from multiple sources can provide a rich source of feedback to employees. However, translating this feedback into concrete objectives that will guide and improve performance in the next appraisal period may be difficult. To improve its internal operations, Federal Express is shifting to a future-oriented approach and piloting a 360° "goal-setting system."

How does this system work? Departments at Federal Express assess how well other departments are providing needed inputs to their internal customers. Based on the ratings it receives, each department summarizes the goals of its internal customers and then provides those customers with a service guarantee. For example, Fed Ex's HR department has provided the following guarantee to its internal customers:

- Timely response
- A 24-hour turnaround for feedback on important requests
- Two-hour response time to emergency calls
- Critical feedback on EEO and employee grievances
- Semiannual training sessions on topical subjects
- Updates on employee relations issues
- Meetings with managers to review recruitment, plans, goals, and results
- Bimonthly meetings with employees.

These goals set a clear foundation for future customer assessment of how well HR employees are performing.

Discussion Questions

1. A potential problem with 360° goal setting is that various internal customers may have unrealistic and conflicting performance expectations. What actions could managers take to avoid this problem?
2. It is possible for a business to be overly concerned with satisfying customers. For example, giving away products for free might delight customers but would put the company out of business. How could a company use customer-driven goal setting to avoid this problem?

Source: Adapted from Milliman, J. F., Zawacki, R. A., Schulz, B., Wiggins, S., and Norman, C. A. (1995). Customer service drives 360 degree goal setting. *Personnel Journal*, June, 136–141.

CASE 1 An Unexpected Problem

Ron Moore has worked for Assessment Systems, Inc., for five years. In his third year with the company, he was recognized as a top performer because of his outstanding enthusiasm and reliability, his team orientation, and his dedication to charitable activities. Don Madison, his manager, was very proud of Moore's performance and often held him up as a model employee. A little over a year ago, Madison left to direct an overseas arm of Assessment Systems, Inc., and another manager, Paul Adams, took his place. Shortly afterward, Moore's performance began to decline.

When Adams arrived, Madison told him that Moore was an excellent performer. Adams met with Moore and told him that he felt fortunate to have such a good performer under his direction.

At first, things went well. Adams found he could even count on Moore to take responsibility when Adams was called away for meetings and other duties. Then Adams started to notice a dip in Moore's performance. At first this consisted of avoiding responsibility in Adams's absence and responding to other employees' requests by telling them to wait for Adams to deal with the issue. Then Moore started calling in sick and showing up late for work. This pattern was unprecedented in Moore's work record, and Adams thought that Moore might be having some personal problems. He decided not to confront him about the change in his performance, but rather to cut him some slack so he could work out whatever problems he was having.

When the performance problems continued for more than a month, Adams felt compelled to confront Moore. The following conversation occurred at Moore's workstation after he arrived late yet again.

Adams: About time you rolled in, Ron. I've been waiting for you since 8 A.M., and it's now 12 minutes after. I don't have time for this and you, award-winning performer or not, have no business showing up here late.

Moore: Well, good morning, Paul. It's nice to see you.

Adams: Listen, don't give me that nonchalant stuff. Your whole attitude has become too nonchalant. It's time you turned things around.

Moore: Hey, what's the big deal? Other people come in late and don't have you jumping on them for it.

Adams: I know what you're capable of, Ron. You owe it to yourself and the company to perform to the best of your potential. I'm going to be watching you closely from now on, and another string of absences or late arrivals is going to get you a verbal warning.

Adams walked away. He hated making threats, and the confrontation had gone even worse than he had anticipated. But, he told himself, he couldn't just let things go on as they were. He hoped he would see Moore's performance jump back to what it had been when he first arrived at the unit.

Two weeks later, Adams was examining performance records and noticed that Moore was tardy only one day. "What an improvement," he thought. "I guess our little talk did some good after all." But his positive feeling soon disappeared when he noticed Moore's productivity. Although Moore had routinely performed at or near the top, he was now in the average range. Another talk with Moore was definitely in order.

Adams: Ron, your performance over the past few weeks hasn't been up to par. You can do better if you apply yourself. I know you can.

Moore: What do you mean, my performance hasn't been up to par?

Adams: It looks like you've licked the problem of getting here on time, but your productivity is off. You're only hitting the average for your group.

Moore: So, what's so bad about average?

Adams: You know the answer to that. You're capable of doing better. Let me give you some advice. I've had rough periods, too. The key is to just knuckle down and do it. When the going gets tough, the tough get going, and all that sort of thing. OK?

Moore: Yeah, I'll see what I can do.

Moore's performance problems continued and so did Adams's frustration. Every performance record gave Adams a reason to confront Moore. The confrontations accomplished nothing, and Adams was feeling increasingly frustrated. The annual appraisal was coming around, and Adams was considering giving Moore a low rating so that he would get the message that his performance was unacceptable.

Critical Thinking Questions

1. What is wrong with Adams's approach to managing Moore's performance problem?
2. What do you think might be causing Moore's performance difficulties? How should Adams go about identifying the cause(s)?
3. Once Adams has explored the causes, how should he approach the issue of improving Moore's performance?
4. Do you agree with Adams's decision to give Moore a low rating to send him a message? Why or why not?

Cooperative Learning Exercises

5. Form groups of three students each. One student in each group takes the role of Ron Moore and the other two play Ron's coworkers. The role-play begins with Ron describing his recent run-ins with Paul Adams, perhaps over lunch. The coworkers should react as they think coworkers would react in such a situation.
6. Form pairs of students. One student takes the role of Paul Adams, the second the role of Don Madison. Paul has placed an overseas call to Ron Moore's former boss because he is very frustrated by his inability to reach Ron. Role-play the resulting phone conversation.
7. Form into groups of four students each. One student assumes the role of Ron and another plays Paul Adams. The situation is the performance review session that has followed the interactions described in the case. As the two students role-play that session, the other two students observe and then critique the interaction. What alternate approaches might Adams take?

CASE 2 *Changing the Appraisal System at Southeastern University*

The staff at Southeastern University has expressed a number of complaints regarding performance appraisal over the past couple of years. The system was put in place more than 12 years ago, and a number of people on staff believe it is time for a change. Staff positions run the gamut from janitors and plumbers to secretaries. The staff has its own council and has appointed a committee to study the appraisal issue. One of the committee's more interesting findings was that the university is using more than a dozen different rating forms. This discovery has only added to employees' perceptions of inequitable appraisal, and soon there were a number of charges of discrimination in appraisal.

These problems attracted the attention of Southeastern University's president, who appointed a task force to study the issue and to recommend a new appraisal system. In the course of its study, the task force surveyed other universities' staff appraisal systems. It found every type of approach, ranging from the simple to the highly sophisticated. Some were based on traits, others on outcomes, still others on behaviors. There seemed to be no consistency across universities.

With the assistance of a management professor, the task force also conducted a survey of staff workers and their supervisors. Here are some of the major findings of this survey:

1. The majority of supervisors and staff (60%) view the purpose of the current system as administrative rather than developmental. The percentages are reversed (40/60) in regard to what staff would prefer the purpose of appraisal to be. A more developmental system seems to be desired.
2. Approximately two thirds of the staff believe that supervisory liking influences performance appraisal. One third of the supervisors concur.
3. Both supervisors and workers believe that situational factors place constraints on performance. For example, more than half of those surveyed indicated that budget constraints and equipment availability adversely affected performance.
4. Many workers believe that their supervisor does not provide adequate feedback. Overall, there seems to be dissatisfaction with supervision and a belief that favoritism and bias are commonplace.

The task force needs to make recommendations to the university president, and the chair of the task force is looking for direction.

Critical Thinking Questions

1. What kind of staff appraisal system would you recommend for Southeastern University? Why?
2. How can managers address the issues raised in the staff survey? Explain.
3. Describe how the new system should be implemented.

Cooperative Learning Exercises

4. Form pairs of students. Each pair spends 5 to 10 minutes discussing the recommendations they think the task force should make to the president and then writes down the three best recommendations. Recommendations are exchanged with a second group. All four students from both groups then present the reasoning behind their recommendations to the class, explaining why they chose the particular approach they did.
5. The entire class discusses recommendations until the students reach a consensus on four or five that the task force should present to the university president. Then students form groups of three. One student assumes the role of the task force chair, another that of the university president, and a third that of the management professor who assisted the committee. Role-play the meeting at which the task force informs the president of its recommendations.

HRM Simulation

Your company currently has no formal appraisal system, and some employees have complained that rewards go to those who are popular with supervisors rather than to those who do the best work (see Performance Appraisal Program, page 10 of the players' manual). Two important decisions regarding appraisal systems are the sources for the ratings (such as self, supervisor, peer, and/or subordinate) and the rating format used (such as a checklist or a behaviorally anchored rating scale). Of the choices offered in Incident E, which sources and format do you recommend? Why?

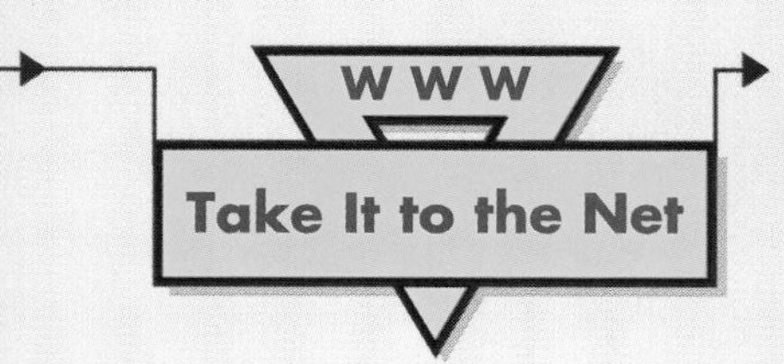

We invite you to visit the Gómez-Mejía/Balkin/Cardy page on the Prentice Hall Web site:

http://www.prenhall.com/gomez

You can also visit the Web sites for these companies, featured within this chapter:

Cigna	http://www.cigna.com
Federal Express	http://www.fedex.com
General Mills	http://www.genmills.com
Merck	http://www.merck.com
Northwestern Mutual Life	http://www.northwesternmutual.com
United Parcel Service (UPS)	http://www.ups.com

Endnotes

1. Carroll, S. J., and Schneir, C. E. (1982). *Performance appraisal and review systems: The identification, measurement, and development of performance in organizations.* Glenview, IL: Scott, Foresman.
2. Banks, C. G., and Roberson, L. (1985). Performance appraisers as test developers. *Academy of Management Review, 10,* 128–142.
3. Cleveland, J. N., Murphy, K. R., and Williams, R. E. (1989). Multiple uses of performance appraisals: Prevalence and correlates. *Journal of Applied Psychology, 74,* 130–135.
4. Landy, F. J., and Farr, J. L. (1980). Performance ratings. *Psychological Bulletin, 87,* 72–107.
5. Bureau of National Affairs. (1975). Employee performance: Evaluation and control. *Personnel Policies Forum.* Survey No. 8. Washington, DC: Bureau of National Affairs.
6. Bernardin, H. J., and Klatt, L. A. (1985). Managerial appraisal systems: Has practice "caught up" to the state of the art? *The Personnel Administrator, 30,* 79–86.
7. Odom, M. (1992, October 18). From tough to tender, firms reconsider employee appraisals. *The Washington Post,* H2.
8. Nunnally, J. C. (1978). *Psychometric theory.* New York: McGraw-Hill.
9. Bernardin, H. J., and Beatty, R. W. (1984). *Performance appraisal: Assessing human behavior at work.* Boston, MA: Kent; Latham, G. P., and Wexley, K. N. (1981). *Increasing productivity through performance appraisal.* Reading, MA: Addison-Wesley; Miner, J. B. (1988). Development and application of the rated ranking technique in performance appraisal. *Journal of Occupational Psychology, 6,* 291–305.
10. Miner, 1988.
11. Bernardin, H. J., Kane, J. S., Ross, S., Spina, J. D., and Johnson, D. L. (1995). Performance appraisal design, development, and implementation. In G. R. Ferris, S. D. Rosen, and D. T. Barnum (eds.), *Handbook of human resources management,* Cambridge, MA: Blackwell.
12. Cardy, R. L., and Sutton, C. L. (1993). *Accounting for halo-accuracy paradox: Individual differences.* Paper presented at the Annual Conference of the Society for Industrial and Organizational Psychology, 1993, San Francisco.
13. Bernardin and Beatty, 1984.
14. *Id.*
15. Latham and Wexley, 1981.
16. Blood, M. R. (1973). Spin-offs from behavioral expectation scale procedures. *Journal of Applied Psychology, 59,* 513–515.
17. Harris, C. (1988). A comparison of employee attitudes toward two performance appraisal systems. *Public Personnel Management, 17,* 443–456.
18. Drucker, P. F. (1954). *The practice of management.* New York: Harper.
19. Cardy, R. L., and Krzystofiak, F. J. (1991). Interfacing high technology operations with blue collar workers: Selection and appraisal in a computerized manufacturing setting. *Journal of High Technology Management Research, 2,* 193–210.
20. Bernardin and Beatty, 1984.
21. See, for example, Smith, R. W. (1992, Fall). Moving managers to a higher plane of performance. *Business Forum, 17,* 5–6.
22. Cardy, R. L., and Dobbins, G. H. (1994). *Performance appraisal: Alternative perspectives.* Cincinnati, OH: South-Western Publishing Co.
23. Borman, W. C. (1979). Individual difference correlates of rating accuracy using behavior scales. *Applied Psychological Measurement, 3,* 103–115.
24. Cardy, R. L., and Kehoe, J. F. (1984). Rater selective attention ability and appraisal effectiveness: The effect of a cognitive style on the accuracy of differentiation among ratees. *Journal of Applied Psychology, 69,* 589–594.
25. Thorndike, E. L. (1920). A constant error in psychological ratings. *Journal of Applied Psychology, 4,* 25–29.
26. Cooper, W. H. (1981). Ubiquitous halo. *Psychological Bulletin, 90,* 218–244.
27. Edwards, M. R., Wolfe, M. E., and Sproull, J. R. (1983). Improving comparability in performance appraisal. *Business Horizons, 26,* 75–83.
28. Rosen, D. I. (1992, November). Appraisals can make—or break—your court case. *Personnel Journal,* 113–116.
29. Bernardin, H. J., and Buckley, M. R. (1981). Strategies in rater training. *Academy of Management Review, 6,* 205–212.
30. Bernardin, H. J., and Pence, E. C. (1980). Rater training: Creating new response sets and decreasing accuracy. *Journal of Applied Psychology, 65,* 60–66; Cardy, R. L., & Keefe, T. J. (1994). Observational purpose and valuative articulation in frame-of-reference training: The effects of alternative processing models on rating accuracy. *Organizational Behavior and Human Decision Processes 57,* 338–357.
31. Zajonc, R. B. (1980). Feeling and thinking: Preferences need no inferences. *American Psychologist, 35,* 151–175.
32. Alexander, E. R., and Wilkins, R. D. (1982). Performance rating validity: The relationship between objective and subjective measures of performance. *Group and Organization Studies, 7,* 485–496.
33. Cardy and Dobbins, 1994.
34. Cardy, R. L., and Dobbins, G. H. (1986). Affect and appraisal: Liking as an integral dimension in evaluating performance. *Journal of Applied Psychology, 71,* 672–678.
35. Cardy and Dobbins, 1994.
36. Bernardin, H. J., and Walter, C. S. (1977). Effects of rater training and diary keeping on psychometric error in ratings. *Journal of Applied Psychology, 62,* 64–69; and Flanagan, J. C. (1954). The critical incident technique. *Psychological Bulletin, 51,* 327–358.

37. Flanagan, J. C., and Burns, R. K. (1955, September–October). The employee performance record: A new appraisal and development tool. *Harvard Business Review,* 95–102.
38. Day, D. (1993, May). Training 101: Help for discipline dodgers. *Training & Development,* 19–22.
39. Jacobs, H. (1993, October). The rating game. *Small Business Reports,* 21–25.
40. Ferris, G. R., and Judge, T. A. (1991). Personnel/human resources management: A political influence perspective. *Journal of Management, 17,* 1–42.
41. Murphy, K. R., and Cleveland, J. N. (1991). *Performance appraisal: An organizational perspective.* Boston: Allyn & Bacon.
42. Adapted from C. O. Longenecker, H. P. Sims, Jr., and D. A. Gioia. Behind the mask: The politics of employee appraisal. Copyright © by the Academy of Management. Reprinted by permission of the publisher. *Academy of Management Executive 1* (3), August 1987, 183–193.
43. Ferris and Judge, 1991; Ferris, G. R., Judge, T. A., Rowland, K. M., and Fitzgibbons, D. E. (1993). Subordinate influence and the performance evaluation process: Test of a model. *Organizational Behavior and Human Decision Processes, 58,* 101–135.
44. Banks and Roberson, 1985.
45. Longenecker, Sims, and Gioia, (1987)
46. Cardy and Dobbins, 1993.
47. Stewart, G. L. and Manz, C. C. (1995). Leadership for self-managing work teams: A topology and integrative model. *Human Relations, 48,* 747–770.
48. Cardy, R. L., and Dobbins, G. H. (1994). Performance appraisal: Alternative perspectives. Cincinnati, OH: South-Western.
48a. Cardy, R. L. and Carson, K. P. (1996). Total quality and the abandonment of performance appraisal: Taking a good thing too far? *Journal of Quality Management, 1,* 193-206.
49. Cardy, R. L. (1992). Employee empowerment and HRM. Column in *Personnel/Human Resources Division of the Academy of Management Newsletter, XV,* Spring.
50. Bounds, G. M., Dobbins, G. H., and Fowler, O. S. (1995). *Management: A total quality perspective.* Cincinnati, OH: South-Western.
51. Fleury, L., Hanson, R., and McCaul, J. H. (1994). Review system supports customer focus. *HRMagazine,* January, *39,* 66–69.
52. Milliman, J. F., Zawacki, R. A., Norman, L., Powell, L., and Kirksey, J. (1994, November). Companies evaluate employees from all perspectives. *Personnel Journal,* 99–103.
53. Cardy, R. L., and Stewart, G. L. (1997). Quality and teams: Implications for HRM theory and research. In D.B. Fedor and S. Ghosh (Eds.), *Advances in the management of organization quality, 2,* Greenwich, CT: JAI Press.
54. *Id.*
55. Barrett, G. V., and Kernan, M. C. (1987). Performance appraisal and terminations: A review of court decisions since *Brito v. Zia* with implications for personnel practices. *Personnel Psychology, 40,* 489–503.
56. Koys, D. J., Briggs, S., and Grenig, J. (1987). State court disparity on employment-at-will. *Personnel Psychology, 40,* 565–577.
57. Meyer, H. H., Kay, E., and French, J. R. P., Jr. (1965, March). Split roles in performance appraisal. *Harvard Business Review,* 9–10.
58. Prince, J. B., and Lawler, E. E. (1986). Does salary discussion hurt the development appraisal? *Organizational Behavior and Human Decision Processes, 37,* 357–375.
59. Landy and Farr, 1980.
60. Bernardin and Beatty, 1984.
61. Dobbins, G. H., Cardy, R. L., and Carson, K. P. (1991). Perspectives on human resource management: A contrast of person and system approaches. In G. R. Ferris and K. M. Rowland (Eds.), *Research in personnel and human resources management, 9.* Greenwich, CT: JAI Press; and Ilgen, D. R., Fisher, C. D., and Taylor, S. M. (1979). Consequences of individual feedback on behavior in organizations. *Journal of Applied Psychology, 64,* 347–371.
62. Carson, K. P., Cardy, R. L., and Dobbins, G. H. (1991). Performance appraisal as effective management or deadly management disease: Two initial empirical investigations. *Group and Organization Studies, 16,* 143–159.
63. Kelly, H. H. (1973). The processes of causal attribution. *American Psychologist, 28,* 107–128.
64. Cascio, W. F. (1998). *Applied psychology in human resource management* (5th ed.). Upper Saddle River, NJ: Prentice Hall.
65. Blumberg, M., and Pringle, C. D. (1982). The missing opportunity in organizational research: Some implications for a theory of work performance. *Academy of Management Review, 7,* 560–569; Carson, Cardy, and Dobbins, 1991; and Schermerhorn, J. R., Jr., Gardner, W. L., and Martin, T. N. (1990). Management dialogues: Turning on the marginal performers. *Organizational Dynamics, 18,* 47–59.
66. Blumberg and Pringle, 1982; and Rummler, G. A. (1972). Human performance problems and their solutions. *Human Resource Management, 19,* 2–10.
67. *Small Business Reports.* (1993, July). A twist on performance reviews, 27–28.
68. Edwards, M., and Ewen, A. (1996, March). Automating 360 degree feedback. *HR Focus, 70,* 3.
69. Cardy and Dobbins, 1994.
70. Rummler, 1972.
71. Evered, R. D., and Selman, J. C. (1989). Coaching and the art of management. *Organizational Dynamics, 18,* 16–33.
72. Schermerhorn, Gardner, and Martin, 1990.

Appendix to Chapter 7

The Critical Incident Technique: A Method for Developing a Behaviorally Based Appraisal Instrument

The critical incident technique (CIT) is one of many types of job-analysis procedures. The CIT is often used because it produces behavioral statements that make explicit to an employee what is required, and to a rater what the basis for an evaluation should be.

CIT Steps

The following steps are involved in a complete CIT procedure:

1. *Identify the major dimensions of job performance.*
   This can be done by asking a group of raters and ratees to brainstorm and generate dimensions relevant to job performance. Each person lists, say, three dimensions. The group members then combine their lists and eliminate redundancies.

2. *Generate "critical incidents" of performance.*
For each dimension, the group members should list as many incidents as they can think of that represent effective, average, and ineffective performance levels. Each person should think back over the past 6 to 12 months for examples of performance-related behaviors that they have witnessed. Each incident should include the surrounding circumstances or situation.
If you are having trouble generating incidents, you might want to think of the following situation:
Suppose someone said that person A, whom you feel is the most effective person in the job, is a poor performer. What incidents of person A's behavior would you cite to change the critic's opinion?
Try to make sure that the incidents you list are observable *behaviors* and not *personality characteristics* (traits).
3. *Double-check that the incidents represent one dimension.*
This step is called *retranslation*. Here you are trying to make sure there is clear agreement on which incidents represent which performance dimension. If there is substantial disagreement among group members, this incident may need to be clarified. Alternatively, another dimension may need to be added or some dimensions may need to be merged.
In the retranslation process, each person in the group is asked to indicate what dimension each incident represents. If everyone agrees, the group moves on to the next incident. Any incidents on which there is disagreement are put to the side for further examination at the end of the process. At that time they may be discarded or rewritten.
4. *Assign effectiveness to each incident.*
Effectiveness values are assigned to all the incidents that survived retranslation. How much is incident "A" worth in our organization, on, say, an effectiveness scale of 1 (unacceptable) to 7 (excellent)? All group members should rate each incident. If there is substantial disagreement regarding the value of a certain behavior, that behavior should be discarded.

Note: Disagreement on incident values indicates differences in valuative standards or lack of clarity in organizational policy. Differences in valuative standards can be a fundamental problem in appraisal. The CIT procedure can help to reduce these differences.

The following are some CIT worksheets for you to try your hand at. The dimensions included are a subset of those generated in a research project conducted for a hospital that wanted a common evaluation tool for all nonnursing employees.*

Critical Incidents Worksheet
Job Title:
Job Dimension: Knowledge of Job—Understanding of the position held and the job's policies, techniques, rules, materials, and manual skills.
Instructions: Provide at least one behavioral statement for each performance level.

1. Needs improvement:
2. Satisfactory:
3. Excellent:
4. Outstanding:

Critical Incidents Worksheet
Job Title:
Job Dimension: Initiative—The enthusiasm to get things done, energy exerted, willingness to accept and perform responsibilities and assignments; seeks better ways to achieve results.
Instructions: Provide at least one behavioral statement for each performance level.

1. Needs improvement:
2. Satisfactory:
3. Excellent:
4. Outstanding:

*Goodale, J. G., and Burke, R. J. (1975). Behaviorally based rating scales need not be job specific. *Journal of Applied Psychology, 60*, 389–391.

Critical Incidents Worksheet
Job Title:
Job Dimension: Personal Relations—Attitude and response to supervision, relationships with coworkers, flexibility in working as part of the organization.
Instructions: Provide at least one behavioral statement for each performance level.

1. Needs improvement:
2. Satisfactory:
3. Excellent:
4. Outstanding:

Critical Incidents Worksheet
Job Title:
Job Dimension: Dependability—Attention to responsibility without supervision, meeting of deadlines.
Instructions: Provide at least one behavioral statement for each performance level.

1. Needs improvement:
2. Satisfactory:
3. Excellent:
4. Outstanding:

The jobs covered ranged from floor sweeper and clerical worker to laboratory technician and social worker. Of course, the behavioral standards for each dimension differed across jobs—an excellent floor sweeper behavior would not be the same as an excellent lab technician behavior. The dimensions included in the worksheets appear fairly generic, though, and are probably applicable to jobs in most organizations. You may want to develop more specific dimensions, or other dimensions altogether.

Remember, after generating incidents, your group should determine agreement levels for the dimension and value for each incident. An easy way to do this is for one person to recite an incident and have everyone respond with dimension and value. This process could be informal and verbal, or formal and written.

8 Training the Work Force

After reading this chapter, you should be able to deal more effectively with the following challenges:

1 ▶ **Determine** when employees need training and the best type of training given a company's circumstances.

2 ▶ **Recognize** the characteristics that make training programs successful.

3 ▶ **Weigh** the costs and benefits of a computer-based training program.

4 ▶ **Design** job aids as complements or alternatives to training.

Training the Troops. For most workers, an important part of the job involves training in the latest technology. At Motorola's Illinois learning center, trainees practice operating assembly lines on virtual-reality computer programs that let them "stop" production, troubleshoot, and restart when the problem is solved.

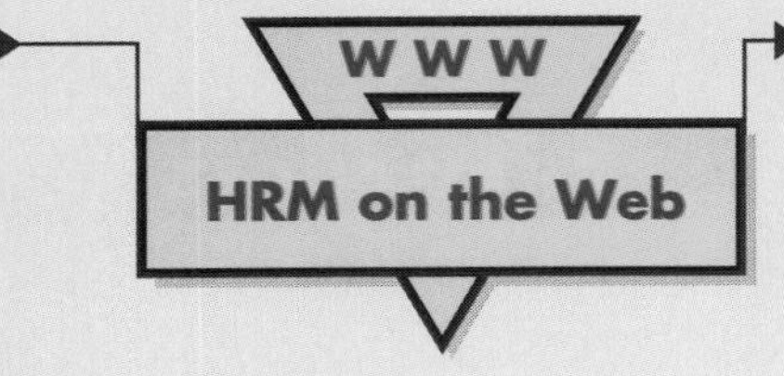

http://www.trainingnet.com/

The Training Net

The Training Net is an information resource for training professionals. It contains archives that can locate in-depth articles and books on training; provides links to other Internet sites on specific training topics; and includes a chat forum where training professionals can discuss their views and experiences on various training topics (such as computer training, just-in-time training, diversity training, and managing change in the workplace). The site also contains a jobs database and a training products database.

It's impossible to pick up a magazine or newspaper today without reading about *virtual reality (VR)*, a computer-based technology that replicates the real world. Using special gloves and headsets, users of VR programs can interact with virtual worlds and manipulate objects in real time.

Many companies have been exploring the "fun side" of virtual reality, creating adventure games for adults. But virtual reality holds promise in many other areas of business, particularly in training. Indeed, at high-tech companies like Motorola, the future of VR training is already here.[1]

Motorola manufactures a variety of communication and computer equipment, including pagers, semiconductors, and cellular telephones. The company employs approximately 60,800 manufacturing workers worldwide and uses cutting-edge robotic machinery in its many manufacturing plants. Of course, all of these employees must be trained to run and troubleshoot the robotic assembly lines effectively. Because technology advances so quickly, the need for training is ongoing.

In the past, Motorola trained its employees in a classroom setting. The company equipped each classroom with duplicates of the machinery found in its manufacturing sites. However, duplicating the ever-evolving equipment was expensive and difficult. Sending workers for three-day training sessions was also costly and inefficient. Furthermore, continued company growth meant an ever-increasing demand for training—a demand that was becoming increasingly difficult to meet. The company needed a more efficient way of delivering the training while retaining the relevance of a hands-on environment.

To meet these challenges head on, Motorola decided to try VR technology to replicate its assembly-line equipment. While the cost of program development and equipment for the virtual reality training could range from $30,000 to over $100,000, Motorola's managers realized, the cost of duplicating manufacturing equipment was even higher. VR seemed worth a shot.

The results of early VR training efforts, based on a comparison of three separate training groups, have been stunning. One group was trained on real equipment, Motorola's traditional training method. Another group was given computer-based training using a computer screen and mouse. The third group was given virtual reality training. Following the training, the trainees were asked to start, run, and shut down the actual equipment. Training managers tallied the number of errors made in each of these steps. The first two groups averaged six mistakes in each step. The group trained in three-dimensional virtual worlds averaged only one mistake per step!

otorola's experience illustrates some of the important training issues facing today's organizations. Specifically:

- *How can training keep pace with a changing organizational environment?* Motorola confronts this challenge by using computer software that can be updated as manufacturing equipment and techniques change. However, the computerized approach may not be the answer for all organizations. For example, many companies operate in fast-paced service-oriented environments rather than assembly-line environments. Training in these situations might be better focused on improving employees' customer-service skills.
- *Should training take place in a classroom setting or on the job?* Classroom training may lack realism and not be as effective as training that occurs while on the job. However,

on-the-job training can cause slowdowns that decrease production or irritate customers. Motorola's solution maximizes the relevance of classroom training by using virtual reality technology. However, this approach may not be applicable or cost-effective in other organizations. For example, virtual reality cannot be used to improve teamwork or people skills because VR training is, by its nature, an individual experience.

- *How can training be effectively delivered worldwide?* Many of today's organizations conduct operations around the world. Consistent quality of products or service is critical to organizational survival in today's competitive markets. Unfortunately, achieving uniformity worldwide can be difficult. Virtual reality training provides Motorola with a realistic and effective training tool that can easily be deployed worldwide. Solutions for companies that cannot afford VR training might include teleconference- or video-based training.
- *How can training be delivered so that trainees are motivated to learn?* Lectures and workbooks may have outstanding content but be totally ineffective if they do not engage the trainees or motivate them to learn. Motorola's virtual reality training appears to get past this problem; in many cases, its trainees have decided to skip lunch rather than take a break from the training. Other engaging delivery mediums might include videos and multimedia displays.

In this chapter we discuss how organizations confront the challenges of training. First, we distinguish between training and development. Then we discuss the major challenges managers face in trying to improve workers' performance through training. Next we offer some suggestions on managing the three phases of the training process, explore selected types of training, and consider ways to maximize and evaluate training's effectiveness. We close the chapter with a section on what is arguably the most important training opportunity: the orientation of new employees.

Training versus Development

Although training is often used in conjunction with development, the terms are not synonymous. **Training** typically focuses on providing employees with specific skills or helping them correct deficiencies in their performance.[2] For example, new equipment may require workers to learn new ways of doing the job, or a worker may have a deficient understanding of a work process. In both cases, training can be used to correct the skill deficit. In contrast, **development** is an effort to provide employees with the abilities the organization will need in the future.

training
The process of providing employees with specific skills or helping them correct deficiencies in their performance.

development
An effort to provide employees with the abilities the organization will need in the future.

Figure 8–1 summarizes the differences between training and development. In training, the focus is solely on the current job; in development, the focus is on both the current job and jobs that employees will hold in the future. The scope of training is on individual employees, while the scope of development is on the entire work group or organization. That is, training is job-specific and addresses particular performance deficits or problems, while development is concerned with the work force's skills and versatility.[3] Training tends to focus on immediate organizational needs, while development tends to focus on

	Training	Development
Focus	Current job	Current and future jobs
Scope	Individual employees	Work group or organization
Time Frame	Immediate	Long term
Goal	Fix current skill deficit	Prepare for future work demands

FIGURE 8-1
Training versus Development

long-term requirements. The goal of training is a fairly quick improvement in workers' performance, while the goal of development is the overall enrichment of the organization's human resources. Training strongly influences present performance levels, while development pays off in terms of more capable and flexible human resources in the long run.

It is essential to remember these differences when generating and evaluating training programs. For example, using a training approach to affect a long-range issue is likely to be futile. Similarly, taking a development approach to improve current job performance problems will probably prove ineffective. In this chapter we focus on training. Development is the subject of Chapter 9.

▸ Challenges in Training

The training process brings with it a number of questions that managers must answer. These are:

- Is training the solution to the problem?
- Are the goals of training clear and realistic?
- Is training a good investment?
- Will the training work?

Is Training the Solution?

A fundamental objective of training is the elimination or improvement of performance problems. However, not all performance problems call for training. Performance deficits can have several causes, many of which are beyond the worker's control and would therefore not be affected by training.[4] For example, unclear or conflicting requests, morale problems, and poor-quality materials cannot be improved through training.

Before choosing training as the solution, managers should carefully analyze the situation to determine if training is the appropriate response.

Are the Goals Clear and Realistic?

To be successful, a training program must have clearly stated and realistic goals. These goals will guide the program's content and determine the criteria by which its effectiveness will be judged. For example, management cannot realistically expect one training session to make everyone a computer expert. Such an expectation guarantees failure because the goal is unattainable.

Unless the goals are clearly articulated before training programs are set up, the organization is likely to find itself training employees for the wrong reasons and toward the wrong ends. A recent survey of 200 companies in the United States and Canada found that while most information systems (IS) managers have no trouble naming the challenges faced by their organization, few have training programs that address those challenges. Managers said that the most pressing skills needed by their staffs were nontechnical skills such as communications, management, and teamwork, but the survey found that the goals of current IS training programs were geared more toward improving technical skills such as programming and analysis.[5]

Some companies reimburse the educational expenses of employees who take classes on their own. In an era when people can count less and less on a single employer to provide them with work over the course of their careers, do you think employers have a responsibility to encourage their employees to pursue educational opportunities?

Is Training a Good Investment?

Training can be quite expensive. To get an idea of how expensive, look at Figure 8–2. The total amount U.S. companies spent on training in 1995 was $55 billion, up from $50 billion in 1994. Organizations with 100 to 499 employees spent an average of $8,735 on conferences alone in 1995, and organizations with 10,000 or more employees spent an average of $622,516.[6]

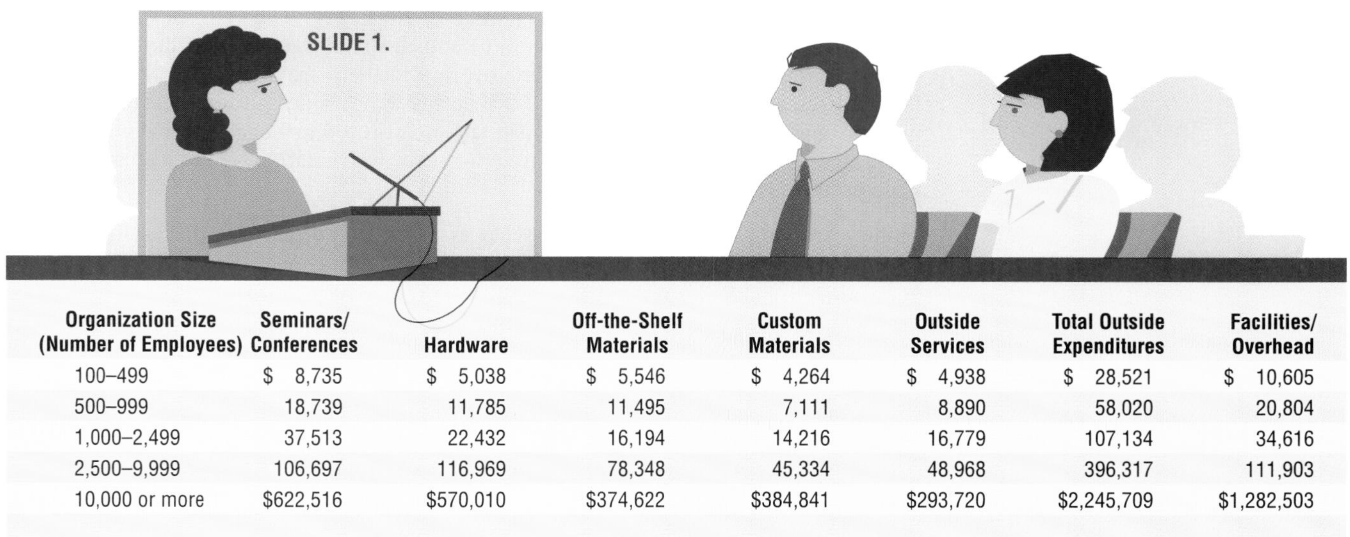

Organization Size (Number of Employees)	Seminars/ Conferences	Hardware	Off-the-Shelf Materials	Custom Materials	Outside Services	Total Outside Expenditures	Facilities/ Overhead
100–499	$ 8,735	$ 5,038	$ 5,546	$ 4,264	$ 4,938	$ 28,521	$ 10,605
500–999	18,739	11,785	11,495	7,111	8,890	58,020	20,804
1,000–2,499	37,513	22,432	16,194	14,216	16,779	107,134	34,616
2,500–9,999	106,697	116,969	78,348	45,334	48,968	396,317	111,903
10,000 or more	$622,516	$570,010	$374,622	$384,841	$293,720	$2,245,709	$1,282,503

FIGURE 8-2

Average 1995 Training Budgets per Organization by Size

Source: *Training*. (1995). Training budgets. *32*, 44.

In addition to the cost of delivering the training program, there are costs associated with analyzing and evaluating the program's effectiveness. In some cases, training may be appropriate but not cost-effective. Before beginning a training program, managers must weigh how much the current problem costs against how much the training to eliminate it will cost. It could be that the training cure is more costly than the performance ailment—in which case alternatives to training must be considered.

Determining whether training is a good investment requires measuring the training's potential benefits in dollars. Training that focuses on "hard" areas (such as the running and adjustment of machines) that have a fairly direct impact on outcomes (such as productivity) can often be easily translated into a dollar value. Estimating the economic benefits of training in "softer" areas—such as teamwork and diversity training—is much more challenging.

Will Training Work?

There are many types of training programs in widespread use. Some are computerized, others use simulations, and still others use the traditional lecture format. Some types of training are more effective than others for some purposes and in some situations. Designing effective training remains as much an art as a science, however, because no single type of training has proved most effective overall.

Beyond the type of training and its content, a number of contextual issues can determine a training program's effectiveness. For example, an organizational culture that supports change, learning, and improvement can be a more important determinant of a training program's effectiveness than any aspect of the program itself. Participants who view training solely as a day away from work are unlikely to benefit much from the experience. Furthermore, if participants' managers do not endorse the content and purpose of the training, it is unlikely that the training program will have any influence on work processes. Consider the following example of a training program that worked:

> At Lantech, a stretch-wrap machine manufacturer based in Louisville, Kentucky, the president spent an entire year building employee commitment to total quality management before buying training. Teams of employees, including the president, held

many discussions about the company's vision and strategy and how its production quality could be improved. Only then did Lantech spend thousands of dollars—and hours—training its more than 300 employees with help from two outside training firms. Seven years after the training, TQM seems to be working well at Lantech. It's unlikely that the training would have had any effect if top management had not been gung-ho every step of the way. TQM training at Lantech clearly was not just an academic exercise.[7]

Finally, training will not work unless it is related to organizational goals. A well-designed training program flows from the company's strategic goals; a poorly designed one has no relationship to—or even worse, is at cross-purposes with—those goals. It is the manager's responsibility to ensure that training is linked with organizational goals.

Building Managerial Skills: Managing the Training Process

Effective training can raise performance, improve morale, and increase an organization's potential. Poor, inappropriate, or inadequate training can be a source of frustration for everyone involved. To maximize the benefits of training, managers must closely monitor the training process.

As Figure 8–3 shows, the training process consists of three phases: (1) needs assessment, (2) development and conduct of training, and (3) evaluation. In the *needs assessment phase,* the problems or needs that the training must address are determined. In the *development and conduct phase,* the most appropriate type of training is designed and offered to the work force. In the *evaluation phase,* the training program's effectiveness is assessed. In the pages that follow, we provide recommendations for maximizing the effectiveness of each of these phases.

In large organizations, managers are very important for determining what training is needed (phase 1), but the actual training (phase 2) is usually provided by either the organization's own training department or an external resource (such as a consulting firm or a local university). After the training program is completed, managers are often called upon to determine whether or not the training has been useful (phase 3). In small businesses, the manager may be responsible for the entire process, although external sources of training may still be used.

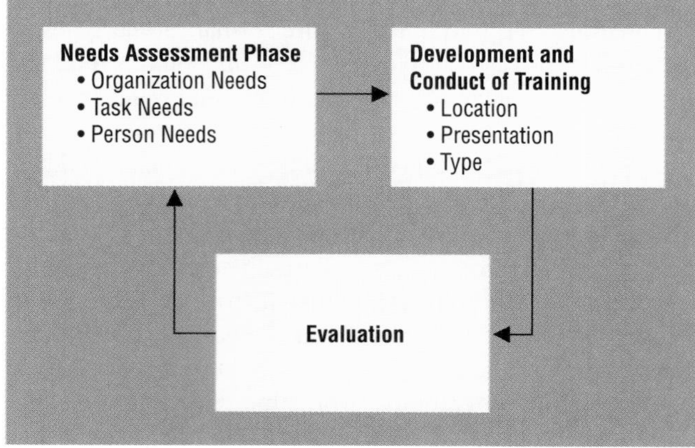

FIGURE 8-3
The Training Process

The Assessment Phase

The overall purpose of the assessment phase is to determine if training is needed, and if so, to provide the information required to design the training program. Assessment consists of three levels of analysis: organizational, task, and person.

The Levels of Assessment. *Organizational analysis* examines such broad factors as the organization's culture, mission, business climate, long- and short-term goals, and structure. Its purpose is to identify both overall organizational needs and the level of support for training. Perhaps the organization lacks the resources needed to support a formal training program, or perhaps the organization's strategy emphasizes innovation. In both cases, the organizational analysis that reveals such information plays a major role in determining whether training will be offered and the type of training (or alternative to training) that would be most appropriate. If a lack of resources prevents formal training, a mentoring program might be used as an alternative. An innovative environment may call for a training program focused on encouraging workers' creativity.

Task analysis is an examination of the job to be performed. It focuses on the duties and tasks of jobs throughout the organization to determine which jobs require training. A recent and carefully conducted job analysis should provide all the information needed to understand job requirements. These duties and tasks are then used to identify the knowledge, skills, and abilities (KSAs) required to perform the job adequately (see Chapter 2). Then the KSAs are used to determine the kinds of training needed for the job.

Person analysis determines which employees need training by examining how well employees are carrying out the tasks that make up their jobs.[8] Training is often necessary when there is a discrepancy between a worker's performance and the organization's expectations or standards. Often, a person analysis entails examining worker performance ratings, then identifying individual workers or groups of workers who are weak in certain skills. The source of most performance ratings is the supervisor, but (as we saw in Chapter 7) a more complete picture of workers' strengths and weaknesses may be obtained by expanding the sources to include self-assessment by the individual worker and performance assessments by the worker's peers.[9]

As we noted in Chapter 4, performance problems can come from numerous sources, many of which would not be affected by training. The only source of a performance problem that training can address is a deficiency that is under the trainee's control.[10] Because training focuses on changing the worker, it can improve performance only when the worker is the source of a performance deficiency. For example, sales training will improve sales only if poor sales techniques are the source of the problem. If declining sales are due to a poor product, high prices, or a faltering economy, sales training is not going to help.

It's important to note that when we talk about the worker as the source of performance problems, we are not referring only to deficiencies in such hard areas as knowledge, skills, and abilities directly connected to the job. Sometimes the deficiencies occur in such soft areas as diversity, ethics, and AIDS awareness, and they, too, require training to correct. For instance, if workers erroneously believe that they will "catch" AIDS by working alongside someone they know to be HIV positive, they will obviously not work effectively and the disruption could cause performance problems. This was the case at Prudential Insurance Company's Western Home Office. The medical director remembers that the first time it became known an employee had AIDS, fearful coworkers streamed into her office posing hypothetical questions about contagion. Emotions ran high and productivity suffered. Prudential has had AIDS awareness training in place since 1987.[11] (We discuss the development and implementation of AIDS awareness programs in Chapter 16.)

Training is not the only option available for responding to a worker deficiency. For example, if it is determined that the training needed to bring workers up to desired levels would be too costly, transferring or terminating the deficient workers may be the more cost-effective course. Strict KSA requirements can then be used to select new employees and eliminate the performance gap. The obvious drawbacks of terminating or replacing employees deemed deficient is that these options are likely to harm commitment and morale in the work force. For this reason, managers should consider training preferable to transfer or termination.

Clarifying the Objectives of Training. The assessment phase should provide a set of objectives for any training program that might be developed following the assessment. Each objective should relate to one or more of the KSAs identified in the task analysis, and should be challenging, precise, achievable, and understood by all.[12]

Whenever possible, objectives should be stated in behavioral terms and the criteria for judging the training program's effectiveness should flow directly from the behavioral objectives. Suppose the cause of a performance deficiency is poor interpersonal sensitivity. The overall objective of the training program designed to solve this problem, then, would be to increase interpersonal sensitivity. Increasing "interpersonal sensitivity" is a noble training goal, but the term is ambiguous and doesn't lead to specific content for a training program or to specific criteria by which the training's effectiveness can be judged. Stating this objective in behavioral terms requires determining what an employee will know, do, and not do after training. For example, the employee will greet customers and clients by name, refrain from sexual humor that could be perceived as harassing, and show up for all meetings on time.[13]

Figure 8–4 shows how the overall objective of sensitivity training provides a starting point that can be broken down into dimensions (specific aspects of job performance) for which specific behavioral goals can then be developed. The overall objective in the figure is to increase the interpersonal sensitivity of supervisors in their relations with production employees. First, this overall objective is divided into two dimensions: listening and feedback skills. Then specific behaviors that are part of these dimensions are identified, both to guide the training effort and to help evaluate whether the training has been successful.

The Training and Conduct Phase

The training program that results from assessment should be a direct response to an organizational problem or need. Training approaches vary by location, presentation, and type.

Location Options. Training can be carried out either on the job or off the job. In the very common *on-the-job training (OJT)* approach, the trainee works in the actual work setting, usually under the guidance of an experienced worker, supervisor, or trainer. At the Los

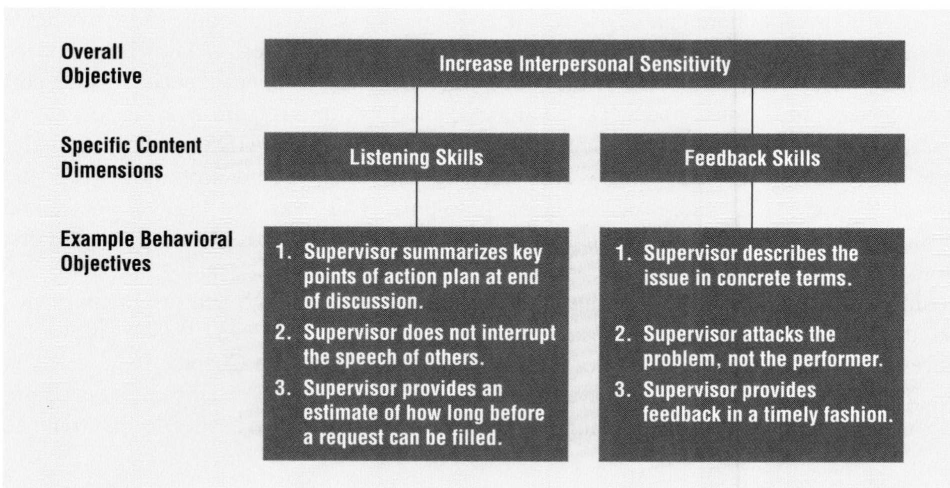

FIGURE 8-4

Example of Development of Behavioral Training Objectives

Alamos National Laboratory of the U.S. Department of Energy, for instance, training often relies on one-on-one coaching, hands-on demonstrations, and practice. Before setting the training in motion, however, management at this New Mexico-based facility carefully considers the task employees are being trained for, the level of training needed, the number of trainees, and the availability of instructional settings and resources. The Manager's Notebook titled "Guidelines for Using On-the-Job Training" provides a list of the factors that HR professionals and managers need to consider when developing an OJT program.[14]

Job rotation, apprenticeships, and internships are all forms of OJT.

- *Job rotation,* as we saw in Chapter 2, allows employees to gain experience at different kinds of narrowly defined jobs in the organization. It is often used to give future managers a broad background.
- *Apprenticeships,* OJT programs typically associated with the skilled trades, derive from the medieval practice of having the young learn a trade from an experienced worker. In Europe, apprenticeships are still one of the major ways for young men and women to gain entry to skilled jobs. In the United States, apprenticeships are largely confined to adults looking to work in certain occupations, such as carpentry and plumbing. These apprenticeships generally last four years, and the apprentice's pay starts at about half that of the more experienced "journey workers." While there are some shining examples of youth apprenticeship programs, such as the Cornell University–funded youth Apprenticeship Demonstration Project, only 27 states have apprenticeship agencies and only 2% of U.S. high school graduates enter apprenticeships for skilled jobs. One of the consequences of this lack of youth apprenticeship programs is the rapidly shrinking pool of skilled labor in the United States.[15]
- Just as apprenticeships are a route to certain skilled blue-collar jobs, *internships* are a route to white-collar or managerial jobs in a variety of fields. Internships are opportunities for students to gain real-world job experience, often during summer vacations from school. Although most internships offer very low or no pay, student interns can often gain college credits and, possibly, the offer of a full-time job after graduation.

Manager's Notebook

Guidelines for Using On-the-Job Training

The following checklist is useful for determining when OJT is appropriate and what it should cover.

Managers Should Select OJT When:

- Participatory learning is essential.
- One-on-one training is necessary.
- Five or fewer employees need training.
- Taking employees out of the work environment for training is not cost-effective.
- Classroom instruction is not appropriate.
- Equipment and safety restrictions make other training methods ineffective.
- Frequent changes in standard operating procedures allow minimal time for retraining.
- Work in progress cannot be interrupted.
- The task for which the training is designed is infrequently performed.
- Immediate changes are necessary to meet new safety requirements.
- A defined proficiency level or an individual performance test is required for certification or qualification.

What OJT Should Cover:

- Large or secured equipment.
- Delicate or calibrated instruments.
- Tools and equipment components of a complex system.
- Delicate or dangerous procedures.
- Classified information retained in a secured area.

Source: Mullaney, C. A., and Trask, L. D. (1992, October). Show them the ropes. *Technical & Skills Training*, 8–11. Copyright 1992 by American Society for Training and Development, 1640 King St., Box 1443, Alexandria, VA 22313.

OJT has both benefits and drawbacks. This type of training is obviously relevant to the job because the tasks confronted and learned are generated by the job itself. Very little that is learned in the context of OJT would not transfer directly to the job. OJT also spares the organization the expense of taking employees out of the work environment for training and usually the cost of hiring outside trainers, since company employees generally are capable of doing the training. On the negative side, OJT can prove quite costly to the organization in lost business when on-the-job trainees cause customer frustration. (Have you ever been caught in a checkout line that moves like molasses because a trainee is operating the cash register?) Even if only a handful of customers switch to a competitor because of dissatisfaction with service provided by trainees, the cost to the organization can be substantial. Errors and damage to equipment that occur when a trainee is on the job may also prove costly. Another potential drawback is that trainers might be top-notch in terms of their skills but inadequate at transferring their knowledge to others. In other words, those who can, can't always teach.

Off-the-job training is an effective alternative to OJT. Common examples of off-the-job training are formal courses, simulations, and role-playing exercises in a classroom setting. One advantage of off-the-job training is that it gives employees extended uninterrupted periods of study. Another is that a classroom setting may be more conducive to learning and retention because it avoids the distractions and interruptions that commonly occur in an OJT environment. The big disadvantage of off-the-job training is that what is learned may not transfer back to the job. After all, a classroom is not the workplace, and the situations simulated in the training may not closely match those encountered on the job. Also, if employees view off-the-job training as an opportunity to enjoy some time away from work, not much learning is likely to take place.

Presentation Options. A variety of presentation techniques can be employed in training. The most common presentation techniques are slides and videotapes, teletraining, computers, simulations, virtual reality, and classroom instruction and role-plays.

Slides and Videotapes. Slides and videotapes can be used either off-the-job or in special media rooms in an organization's facility. Slides and videotapes provide consistent information and, if done well, can be interesting and thought provoking. However, these presentation media do not allow trainees to ask questions or receive further explanation (although new advances in videotape technology are permitting some interaction between the observer and the medium). Many companies prefer to use slides, film, or tapes to supplement a program led by a trainer, who can answer individuals' questions and flesh out explanations when necessary.

Teletraining. A training option that is particularly useful when trainees are dispersed across various physical locations is teletraining.[15a] Satellites are used to beam live training broadcasts to employees at different locations. In addition to the video reception, the satellite link can allow trainees to ask questions of the instructor during the broadcast.

Two disadvantages of teletraining are the need for an expensive satellite connection and the difficulty of scheduling the broadcast so that everyone will be able to attend. An innovative solution to these drawbacks was developed at AT&T Productivity Training.[16] The satellite broadcast of a training program is put on videotape, and the video is edited to eliminate the live questions and discussion. The video is then made available at sites where people still need to receive the training. At a specified delivery time the training instructor is available via conference call to introduce the sections of the videotape and to respond to questions. This method makes the trainer's expertise available to trainees without requiring her to redeliver the entire training program.

Computers. With the widespread availability of personal computers brought about by falling prices, both small and large businesses are finding computers a cost-effective training medium. Figure 8–5 summarizes some of the advantages of computer-based training, which is sometimes called *computer-assisted interaction (CAI).* If a job requires extensive use of computers, then computer-based training is highly job related and provides for a high degree of transfer of training back to the job. Computers also have the advantage of allowing trainees to learn at a comfortable pace. As a trainer, the computer never becomes tired, bored, or short-tempered. Finally, advancing technology is making the computer a truly multimedia training option in which text can be combined with film, graphics, and audio components.

Indeed, many organizations are successfully using computer-based multimedia approaches to training. For example, Texaco recently developed a multimedia training and evaluation program for new owner/operators of Texaco service stations.[17] The program covers all the important aspects of running a gas station, including advertising, accounting, merchandising, and handling of hazardous materials. The program includes graphics, audio,

Content	
1. Job-related	For jobs that involve computer duties, the training may match the work situation. For jobs that aren't computer intensive, the computer training medium can still closely match the actual work environment.
2. Flexible	Changes in procedure or equipment can be easily accommodated with a computer program. With training based on written materials, such changes may make the package obsolete.
Process	
3. Self-paced	Trainees can learn at their own pace. Those who are slower and more methodical in their approach to learning won't be rushed and those who are faster won't be bored.
4. Easily distributed	Computer-based training can easily be distributed electronically over a network or on disks. It is easier and cheaper to distribute the training than it is to bring all the trainees to one location.
5. Standardized	Computer-based training means that the material is covered in a uniform way regardless of time, place, instructor, and so on.
6. Available	Trainees can start a computerized session whenever they want to.
7. Self-sufficient	Trainees control the learning process without direction from supervisors, peers, or others.
8. Individualized	Computerized training can be programmed so that trainees can skip sections that they have already mastered. This means training time should be maximally effective for each trainee.
Outcomes	
9. Learning	Computer-based training has been found to result in levels of learning that are equal to or higher than more traditional approaches to training.
10. Costs	Computerized training costs more to develop but is much cheaper to deliver than traditional training (due mainly to reduced training time and the elimination of travel).
11. Time	Time savings of 40 to 60% are commonly reported with computerized training. The time savings are primarily due to tighter instructional design and the ability to focus on sections yet to be mastered.

FIGURE 8-5

Potential Advantages of Computer-Based Training

Source: Adapted from Granger, R. E. (1989). Computer-based training improves job performance. *Personnel Journal, 68*, 116–123. Hall, B. (1996, March). Lessons in corporate training: Multimedia's big payoff. *NewMedia*, 40–45.

and video and is distributed over a national network from the company's mainframe. It takes new operators about three hours to complete the program and complete a final quiz. The quizzes are automatically scored, and the scores are added to an operator database.

Computer-based training may pose disadvantages in some circumstances, however. The most obvious drawback is the fact that an adequate number of computers must be available for training. Otherwise the experience can be an exercise in frustration as people crowd around the available machines and fight for their turn. Also, although computers connote cutting-edge technology and precision, the quality of the medium is not necessarily an indicator of the quality of the training content. Whether utilizing computers or some other medium, the content of a training program requires careful preparation. Further, the learning of some areas—particularly complex and conceptual issues—may best be accomplished through interaction with peers or supervisors who have developed expertise through experience. Finally, using computers for training makes most sense when the trainee's job duties require interaction with a computer. When a job's duties do not entail the use of a computer, the computerization aspect may interfere with transference of what is learned back to the job.[17a]

Simulations. Particularly effective in training are **simulations,** devices or situations that replicate job demands at an off-the-job site. Organizations often use simulations when the information to be mastered is complex, the equipment used on the job is expensive, and/or

simulation
A device or situation that replicates job demands at an off-the-job site.

the cost of a wrong decision is quite high. A dramatic example of a training simulation program is FATS, developed by FireArms Training Systems of Duluth, Georgia, and now used by more than 300 law enforcement agencies in the United States.[18] The FATS program uses a microcomputer (a PC) and a 10-foot video screen to confront police-officers-in-training with the sights and sounds of a number of situations commonly encountered in police work. For example, a dangerous suspect is fleeing on a crowded street. Should the officer shoot at the suspect and risk injuring or killing innocent bystanders? FATS gives police trainees the opportunity to practice making such snap decisions in a safe but realistic setting.

The airline industry has long used simulators to train pilots. Unlike FATS, flight simulations often include motion in addition to visual and auditory realism. This aspect substantially increases the cost of the simulation but makes the training even more realistic.

Simulating the Workplace.

(top) More than 300 law enforcement agencies across the United States use the simulation package developed by FireArms Training Systems to train police officers. (bottom) Many newly hired pilots are instructed by seasoned professionals using a flight simulation program. The new pilots gain valuable experience while putting nobody's life in danger.

Another type of simulation confronts trainee doctors with an accident victim arriving at the emergency room. The trainees choose from a menu of options, with the patient dying if the decision is delayed too long or is incorrect.

Traditionally, simulators have been considered separate from computer-based training. With recent advances in multimedia technology, however, the distinctions between these two methods have blurred considerably. In fact, as the technology develops, simulators are becoming more affordable, and hence accessible, for a wider range of organizations.

Few studies have been done on the effectiveness of simulations, but the limited data available indicate that this training method does have a positive impact on job performance. For example, one study found that pilots who trained on simulators become proficient at flight maneuvers nearly twice as fast as pilots who trained only in the air.[19] The importance of this difference is underscored by the fact that the cost of simulator training is only about 10% of the cost of using the real equipment to train pilots.

Virtual Reality. As we saw in the Motorola example at the beginning of the chapter, **virtual reality (VR)** uses a number of technologies to replicate the entire real-life working environment rather than just several aspects of it, as in simulations. Within these three-dimensional environments, a user can interact with and manipulate objects in real time.

virtual reality (VR)
The use of a number of technologies to replicate the entire real-life working environment in real time.

Tasks that are good candidates for VR training are those that require rehearsal and practice, working from a remote location, or visualizing objects and processes that are not usually accessible. VR training is also excellent for tasks in which there is a high potential for damage to equipment or danger to individuals. One such task is marshaling, an Air Force operational job in which a person on the ground uses hand and arm signals to help a plane land. Imagine the stress you'd feel the first time you rehearsed these maneuvers with a multiton aircraft approaching you at high speed! It's easy to see why VR training is used to prepare people to handle the real situation.[20]

Early studies have indicated a great deal of success with VR training. The immersion of trainees in a virtual world may be the key to this success.[21] The VR experience provides a sense of self-location in a simulated environment in which objects appear solid and can be navigated around, touched, lifted, and so on. This sense of immersion is probably connected to the excitement and motivation often reported by VR trainees. For example, following VR training of space shuttle flight control and engineering personnel at NASA, trainees commented on how much fun the training was and how it was the "neatest" training experience they'd ever had.[22] Such trainee experiences can only add to the effectiveness of VR training.

One drawback of VR training is that the technology is meant for one individual user at a time rather than multiple participants. Thus, VR training has not been applicable to team training situations. This limitation may soon be overcome, however. The U.S. military is currently developing a VR training system that allows for the cooperative efforts of multiple trainees.[23] The system includes over 50 different human-computer interfaces and can use one of three simulated terrains, with each terrain representing over 15,000 square kilometers of virtual space. The training exercises are based on scenarios used with combat units in field training. While the system is still being refined, it may represent the next wave of VR training. The prevalence of teams in the workplace demands effective techniques for improving cooperation among people and work groups. VR training may soon be able to meet this need.

Classroom Instruction and Role-Plays. Classroom lectures are used in many organizations to impart information to trainees. Although widely viewed as "boring," classroom instruction can be exciting if other presentation techniques are integrated with the lecture. For example, a videotape could complement the discussion by providing realistic examples of the lecture material. In-class case exercises and role-plays (both of which are found throughout this book) provide an opportunity for trainees to apply what is being taught in the class and increase transfer back to the job. Solving and discussing case problems helps trainees learn technical material and content, and role-plays are an excellent way of applying the interpersonal skills being emphasized in the training. If done well, role-plays give trainees the opportunity to integrate new information with job behavior.[24]

Types of Training. As we noted earlier, there are many approaches to training. We focus here on the types of training that are commonly used in today's organizations: skills, retraining, cross-functional, team, creativity, literacy, diversity, crisis, and customer service training.

Skills Training. When we think of training, most of us probably envision a program that focuses on particular skill needs or deficits. Indeed, this type of training is probably the most common in organizations. The process is fairly simple: The need or deficit is identified via a thorough assessment. Specific training objectives are generated, and training content is developed to achieve those objectives. The criteria for assessing the training's effectiveness are also based on the objectives identified in the assessment phase.

To understand how skills training programs are developed, let's examine a classic example of skills training. In 1992, 10% of all complaints to IBM's CEO centered on the handling of telephone calls. Since customer service is one of IBM's top priorities, the CEO knew he had to take action. He appointed a project team composed of both line managers and trainers to investigate the situation. This arrangement was designed to ensure that line personnel would take the project team's recommendations and actions seriously. (Programs that come out of the "black box" of the HR department are sometimes discounted by line managers.)

The project team did a careful assessment. A survey of IBM customers revealed that 70% of customer contact was via telephone.[25] Additionally, a formal survey of over 10,000 IBM customers revealed that shoddy phone handling was the biggest complaint. As Figure 8–6 shows, analysis of the survey responses indicated that customers' most frequent complaints were that they could not reach a knowledgeable person and that their calls were not being returned. The project team then conducted a survey of IBM employees and found that while over 75% knew how to put a customer on hold, fewer than 5% knew how to forward a call. The team also found that most professional employees felt that they didn't need telephone skills because calls from customers should be handled by the secretarial staff. Based on these survey results, the team categorized the telephone interaction problem into two broad categories: (1) not using phone features and (2) not treating customers with professional courtesy.

The team presented its findings and recommended a training strategy to senior management. The senior vice president in charge of the team, who agreed that telephone inter-

FIGURE 8-6

Sources of Customer Dissatisfaction with IBM Telephone Service

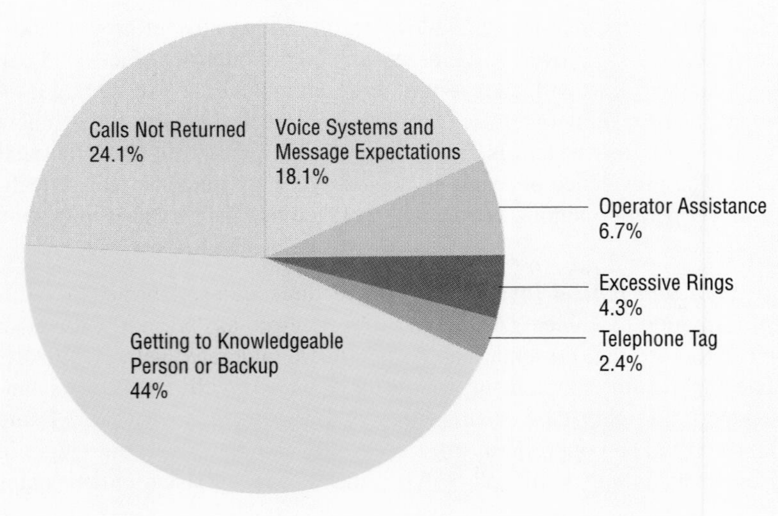

Source: Estabrooke, R. M., and Fay, N. F. (1992). Answering the call of "tailored training," *Training, 29*, 85–88. Reprinted with permission from the October 1992 issue of *Training*. Copyright 1992. Lakewood Publications, Minneapolis, MN. All rights reserved. Not for resale.

actions were a problem to be taken seriously, issued the stern memo reprinted in Figure 8–7. Any employee receiving this memo clearly got the message that telephone skills were now a main issue at IBM. The strong support of top management forced line employees to take the issue seriously and helped the project team obtain funds for the training program.

The project team divided employees into two groups on the basis of how often they used the phone system and then tailored the training to each group. The "intensive" group was composed of such employees as secretaries and operators, the "casual" group of engineers, managers, and other professionals. The intensive group was relatively small in number but accounted for most of the phone interaction with customers. It was important that this group be both courteous and well acquainted with the phone system. The casual group needed only to understand the basics of the phone system, but also had to be trained in telephone etiquette.

Training for the intensive user group involved broad-based coverage of expected behaviors and instruction in the phone system's specific operational features. Among the training program's features: a videotape of good and poor role models of phone interaction shown to secretaries and switchboard operators, a computer-based training program that covered details of the phone system as well as courtesy skills, and pamphlets and other reference materials. Depending on their current levels of skill and knowledge, trainees took from three to nine hours to complete the program.

The casual users required a substantially different approach, for three reasons. First, they did not need the same level of knowledge as the intensive group because they had much less phone interaction with customers. Second, the cost of intensive training for the approximately 150,000 professional employees who fell into the casual group would be prohibitive. Third, the casual users were not motivated to improve their telephone skills because they didn't see a problem in their phone performance. These employees' training package, then, was designed to be brief and entertaining. A videotape shown at departmental meetings provided an overview of the topic. In addition, a brief and humorous audiotape that could be played in the car or on the job emphasized the desired behaviors. An abbreviated version of the computer-based training program focusing on only the key elements of phone operation was included in the casual users' package. Pamphlets and other reference sources were also provided. The project team assumed that most casual users would select the product they preferred and spend perhaps an hour with the material.

Other HR activities focused on motivating employees to solve the phone communication problem. For example, the senior vice president selected telephone effectiveness as one of five key annual performance measures. Additionally, the project team's staff made random calls monthly to assess each business unit's phone effectiveness. Figure 8–8, which can serve as a model for any kind of skill improvement training program, summarizes the process followed by the training project team at IBM.

INTEROFFICE MEMO

Overall, the rating of our telephone service by customers and internal users is poor. Together, we are going to fix this problem, and fix it fast.

FIGURE 8-7

IBM Senior Vice President's Memo to All Managers

Source: Estabrooke, R. M., and Fay, N. F. (1992). Answering the call of "tailored training." *Training, 29,* 85–88. Reprinted with permission from the October 1992 issue of *Training*. Copyright 1992. Lakewood Publications. Minneapolis, MN. All rights reserved. Not for resale.

1. Build in commitment.
   - Gain support of management.
2. Thoroughly analyze the problem.
   - Is it important?
   - What is the real problem?
3. Gain line support.
4. Develop training strategies.
   - Is there more than one group of employees that needs training?
   - Design materials appropriate to each group's needs and motivation levels.
5. Develop motivational strategies.
   - Take steps to heighten awareness of issue.
   - Signal importance of issue through measurement and recognition programs.

FIGURE 8-8

Steps to Skill Improvement at IBM

The program was quite successful. After one year, customer satisfaction with IBM's telephone responsiveness increased by nearly 10%. While the long-term goal is 100% satisfaction, a 10% increase in the first year of a program is certainly a healthy improvement.

IBM's program offers several lessons:

- In some organizational settings, the most important step in building commitment to training may be the inclusion of people who have a great deal of informal or political power in the organization. If someone is politically strong enough to torpedo an instructional effort, it may be best to include him or her in the program's training design from the outset.
- The idea of beginning a training program with assessments at the organizational, task, and person levels may be more academic than realistic. In reality, problems often suddenly come to light in organizations, and something must be done about them quickly if the organization is to remain competitive.
- Multiple forms of a training package may be needed for different groups of trainees. Some employee groups may need detailed knowledge and a high level of skills in a particular area, while others may need only broad familiarity and basic skills. Tailoring the training to each group's skill requirements maximizes the training's effectiveness.
- Providing trainees with materials such as pamphlets and reference guides can help to ensure that the training results in improved performance. These sorts of materials, **job aids,** are external sources of information that workers can access quickly when they need help in making a decision or performing a specific task.[26] Their use is growing rapidly for a few reasons. First, job aids reduce the need to memorize many details and therefore decrease errors and bolster efficiency. Second, although job aids can't replace formal training programs, they can supplement training and help ensure that the training transfers back to the job. Third, they are relatively inexpensive and can be developed and delivered quickly.

job aids
External sources of information, such as pamphlets and reference guides, that workers can access quickly when they need help in making a decision or performing a specific task.

Retraining. A subset of skills training, *retraining* focuses on giving employees the skills they need to keep pace with their job's changing requirements. For instance, however proficient garment workers may be at a traditional skill such as sewing, they will need retraining when the company invests in computerized sewing equipment. Unfortunately, even though retraining is much cited in the media as an item at the top of the corporate agenda, many companies rush to upgrade their equipment without taking comparable steps to upgrade their employees' skills. They erroneously believe that automation means a lower-skilled work force when, in fact, it often requires a more highly skilled one.

One company that takes retraining seriously is RJR Nabisco. It gives workers faced with new technology the option of accepting early retirement or receiving retraining. Other significant developments on the retraining front have been spearheaded by creative partnerships between labor unions and employers. For instance, the Garment Industry Development Corporation, founded in 1984, consolidates union and industry efforts. Its Super Sewer program teaches a worker all the operations necessary to make a garment using computerized pattern making.[27]

Retraining not only involves getting the presently employed up to speed but also providing training assistance to displaced (laid-off) and unemployed workers. Retraining can be particularly important to these workers, since one study found that laid-off workers earn an average of $6,000 per year less in their new jobs.[28] In the past decade several government initiatives have provided funding for retraining, so there is a vast pool of job candidates available to companies that may not be able to launch their own skills training programs. *The Job Training Partnership Act (JTPA) of 1982* is the largest single training program financed by the federal government; its annual budget exceeds $4 billion.[29] JTPA gives block grants to states, which pass them on to local governments and private entities that provide on-the-job training. The state of Missouri, for example, received $4 million through the JTPA to help more than 2,000 workers who were laid off from McDonnell Douglas Corporation as a result of Defense Department budget cuts.[30]

Unfortunately, retraining efforts do not appear to be as effective as some would hope. Government statistics show that only 7 to 12% of dislocated workers take advantage of JTPA retraining programs. Furthermore, not all the people who go through retraining complete the program or benefit from it.[31] Critics also point out that the JTPA's placement rate is a disappointing 50%, and argue that government retraining efforts are reactive rather than proactive in that they deal with people only after they lose their jobs. On the positive side, some employers who obtain workers through the JTPA claim that these workers stay longer.[32]

Cross-Functional Training. Traditionally, organizations have developed specialized work functions and detailed job descriptions. However, today's organizations are emphasizing versatility rather than specialization. For example, the restructuring and upgraded technology at USX prompted a need for upgraded and broader skills in the company's work force.[33] Many companies need workers who can quickly change job assignments, help out where needed, and respond rapidly to changing conditions.[34] Training workers in multiple functions or disciplines is thus becoming increasingly popular.

Cross-functional training involves training employees to perform operations in areas other than their assigned job. There are many approaches to cross-functional training. For example:

cross-functional training
Training employees to perform operations in areas other than their assigned job.

- Job rotation can be used to provide a manager in one functional area with a broader perspective than he or she would otherwise have.
- Departments can trade personnel for periods of time so that each worker or set of workers develops an understanding of the other department's operation.
- **Peer trainers,** high-performing workers who double as internal on-the-job trainers, can be extraordinarily effective in helping employees develop skills in another area of operation.[35]

peer trainers
High-performing workers who double as internal on-the-job trainers.

Peer trainers must be selected carefully. Aside from having top-notch skills, they must be patient and motivated to teach others. An effective way to choose motivated people is simply to ask workers if they would like to be a peer trainer and then select the best volunteers. Some organizations promote the peer-trainer role as an honor and offer a tangible reward to sweeten the added responsibility. At Walt Disney's parks, peer trainers are paid extra while they're instructing and bear a trainer designation on their name badges as they move around the park.

Volunteers often need to undergo a formal training program to become successful peer trainers. At T.J. Maxx, the national retail chain, peer trainers receive five days of training at national headquarters. The course includes discussions of adult learning theory, questioning skills, facilitation skills, and the technical skills involved in running cash registers and managing inventory.[36]

Since some workers, and even some managers, balk at the idea of cross-functional training, it is important that they be instructed in the necessity for such training and the benefits it can provide. Among these benefits:

- The more adaptable workers are, the more valuable they become to the organization. Adaptability increases both workers' job security and the organization's "depth on the bench." The analogy to baseball is apt. Suppose a baseball team does not have a trained replacement for a particular player. When that player is injured, the coach has a problem because there is no one on the bench who can effectively play that position. Similarly, an organization is in trouble if a worker who leaves, is promoted, or becomes ill cannot quickly be replaced with someone else who can do the job. Cross-functional training can provide the talent base that ensures operations will continue to run smoothly.
- Versatile employees can better engineer their own career paths.

- When promotions aren't available, broader exposure and responsibility can motivate workers.
- Training coworkers can clarify a worker's own job responsibilities.
- A broader perspective increases workers' understanding of the business and reduces the need for supervision.[37] This broader understanding allows workers to anticipate the effects of possible actions on the entire operation and to use cross-departmental ties to solve problems collectively.
- When workers can fill in for other workers who are absent, it is easier to use flexible scheduling, which is increasingly in demand as more employees want to spend more time with their families. Often the absence of one skilled worker can disrupt production and increase costs for the company.

Employees 50 years or older may be particularly valuable when it comes to cross-functional versatility.[38] Older workers have often performed a variety of jobs, which will have naturally provided them with a good amount of cross-functional experience. They also tend to have a broader perspective on the organization's operations. For these reasons, older workers are often quick studies in a cross-functional training program and make effective peer trainers.

Team Training. Many organizations are organizing more and more of their work around teams. Companies are realizing increased productivity, effectiveness, and efficiency through work teams.[39] Team training can be divided into two areas based on the two basic team operations: content tasks and group processes.[40] *Content tasks* directly relate to a team's goals—for example, cost control and problem solving. *Group processes* pertain to the way members function as a team—for example, how team members behave toward one another, how they resolve conflicts, and extent of members' participation. Unlike traditional individual training, team training goes beyond the content skills and includes group processes.[41]

Surprisingly, little is known about how to train teams most effectively. The following initial findings can be used to guide team training efforts:

- Team members should be trained in communication skills (both speaking and listening) that encourage respect for all team members.
- Training should emphasize the interdependence of team members.
- Instruction should instill the recognition that team goals and individual goals are not always the same, and provide strategies for dealing with conflicts that will inevitably arise between the two.
- Flexibility should be emphasized because teamwork almost always gives rise to unexpected situations.[42]

One type of training that has become increasingly popular for developing teamwork, particularly among managerial and supervisory employees, is outdoor experiential training. Companies such as IBM, General Electric, and Du Pont periodically take hundreds of employees out of the office and into the woods in hopes of building teamwork, increasing communication skills, and boosting self-esteem. Many of these experiential training programs resemble Outward Bound, the rigorous outdoor adventure course, though they are less physically demanding.

Creativity Training. As a means of tapping their workers' innovative potential, many organizations have been turning to creativity training. According to *Training* magazine, the number of organizations with 100 or more employees that offer creativity training doubled from 16% in 1986 to 32% in 1990.[43] In 1995 this figure was 35%.[44]

Creativity training is based on the assumption that creativity can be learned. There are several approaches to teaching creativity, all of which attempt to help people solve problems in new ways.[45] One common approach is the use of **brainstorming,** in which participants are given the opportunity to generate ideas as wild as they can come up with, without fear of judgment. Only after a good number of ideas have been generated are they individually submitted to rational judgment in terms of their cost and feasibility. Creativity is generally viewed as having two phases: imaginative and practical.[46] Brainstorming followed by rational consideration of the options it produces satisfies both of these phases. Figure 8–9 presents some other approaches to increasing creativity.

brainstorming
A creativity training technique in which participants are given the opportunity to generate ideas openly, without fear of judgment.

Since people often find it difficult to break out of their habitual ways of thinking, creativity trainers provide exercises designed to help them see things in a new way. In one innovative program provided by a Dallas-based creativity consultant, half a dozen gifted, outgoing youngsters from a Dallas school are cloistered with up to 30 top managers in daylong sessions. The adults vent their business problems—and the kids give them advice. The adult participants have found talking to kids about these problems helpful because, as an executive from Texas Utilities Mining put it, "They didn't have any preconceived ideas."[47]

Skeptics criticize creativity training, saying there is no way to measure its effectiveness. They also say that training in a soft skill like creativity might make people feel good but does not produce any lasting change in their work performance. It's true that documenting the bottom-line results of creativity training is nearly impossible. Yet some companies have found impressive results. For example, Frito-Lay says a cost-management program done in conjunction with creative problem-solving training saved more than $500 million in the five years from 1983 through 1987. And when a team of Du Pont's top engineers was stumped at why new technology worked in the lab but faltered in a manufacturing plant, creativity trainers came to the rescue. After employees at the plant were trained in creative thinking techniques, the technology worked as planned.

Of course, creativity training is not a magic solution to all problems. No training program is. And while a training program can help stimulate creativity, the more important factor in generating creative solutions is an organizational environment that supports creativity.[48]

Literacy Training. The abilities to write, speak, and work well with others are critical in today's business environment. Unfortunately, as Figure 8–10 on page 254 shows, many workers do not meet employer requirements in these areas. For example, although most workplace materials require a tenth- or eleventh-grade reading level, about 20% of Americans between the ages of 21 and 25 cannot read at even an eighth-grade level.[49] The American Management Association reported that one in three job applicants tested for jobs in 1995 lacked sufficient reading or math skills to perform the job he or she was seeking. In a recent survey of manufacturers, over half of the responding companies indicated serious worker deficiencies in such basic skills as math, reading, and problem solving. In the face of these problems, it is surprising that less than 20% of U.S. companies offer literacy training of any kind.[50]

Creativity can be learned and developed. The following techniques can be used to improve a trainee's skill in generating innovative ideas and solutions to problems.

1. **Analogies and Metaphors**—drawing comparisons or finding similarities can improve insight into a situation or problem.
2. **Free Association**—freely associating words to describe a problem can lead to unexpected solutions.
3. **Personal Analogy**—trying to see oneself as the problem can lead to fresh perspectives and, possibly, effective solutions.
4. **Mind Mapping**—generating topics and drawing lines to represent the relationships among them can help to identify all the issues and their linkages.

FIGURE 8-9

Techniques to Increase Creativity

Source: Adapted from Higgins, J. M. (1994). *101 creative problem solving techniques: The handbook of new ideas for business.* Winter Park, FL: New Management Publishing Company.

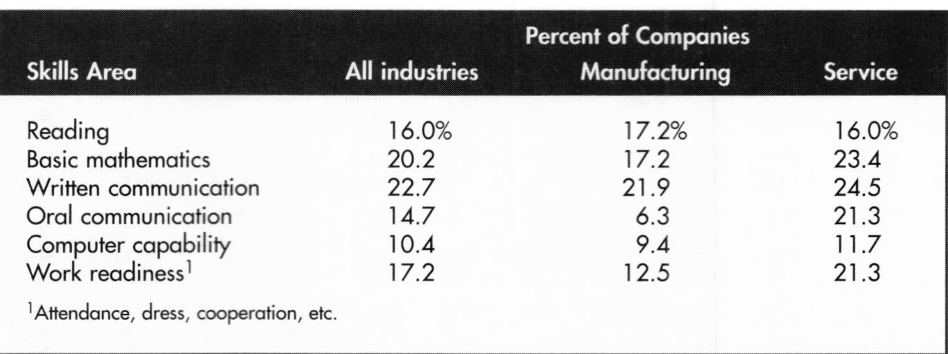

Skills Area	Percent of Companies All industries	Manufacturing	Service
Reading	16.0%	17.2%	16.0%
Basic mathematics	20.2	17.2	23.4
Written communication	22.7	21.9	24.5
Oral communication	14.7	6.3	21.3
Computer capability	10.4	9.4	11.7
Work readiness[1]	17.2	12.5	21.3

[1]Attendance, dress, cooperation, etc.

FIGURE 8-10

Basic Skill Deficits in Workers That Cause Difficulties for Employers

Source: Lund, L., and McGuire, E. P. (1990). *Literacy in the work force*. New York: The Conference Board.

literacy
The mastery of basic skills (reading, writing, arithmetic, and their uses in problem solving).

Before proceeding further, it is important to clarify some definitions. The term **literacy** is generally used to mean the mastery of *basic skills*—that is, the subjects normally taught in public schools (reading, writing, arithmetic, and their uses in problem solving). It is important to distinguish between general literacy and functional literacy. *General literacy* is a person's general skill level, while *functional literacy* is a person's skill level in a particular content area. An employee is functionally literate if he or she can read and write well enough to perform important job duties (reading instruction manuals, understanding safety messages, filling out order slips). The most pressing issue for employers is not the general deficiencies in the work force but rather their workers' ability to function effectively in their jobs. For example, a generally low level of reading ability may be cause for societal concern, but it is workers' inability to understand safety messages or fill out order slips that is the immediate concern for business. Functional illiteracy can be a serious impediment to an organization's productivity and competitiveness. It has been estimated that over 30 million workers in the United States are functionally illiterate.[51]

While it is difficult to put a dollar figure on how much functional illiteracy costs U.S. companies, these are some of the consequences of illiteracy:

- Accounting clerks bill customers incorrectly, and thousands of dollars in accounts receivable are lost.
- Production workers incorrectly measure raw materials because of an inability to read, and these errors result in production waste.
- Plant workers unable to read manuals maintain machinery inadequately, causing breakdowns.
- Order clerks misinterpret customers' instructions and send the wrong product or incorrect amounts.[52]

Illiteracy is also a real threat to the safety of other workers. The Occupational Safety and Health Administration (see Chapter 16) believes that there is a direct correlation between illiteracy and some workplace accidents.

Functional literacy training programs focus on the basic skills required to perform a job adequately and capitalize on most workers' motivation to get help or advance in a particular job. These programs use materials drawn directly from the job. For example, unlike a reading comprehension course (which teaches general reading skills), functional training teaches employees to comprehend manuals and other reading materials they must use on the job.

Working in concert with unions, government agencies, and schools, companies have devised a number of programs to remedy deficiencies in basic skills. These programs fall into three basic categories:

- *Company in-house programs.* These programs are conducted solely or primarily for company employees. One of the earliest in-house programs was begun in the 1960s at Polaroid Corporation. Polaroid's program focuses on a range of basic literacy and

A QUESTION OF ETHICS

Are companies ethically responsible for providing literacy training for workers who lack basic skills? Why or why not?

arithmetic skills. Employees are assessed by their supervisors and the HR department, and those with reading skills below the fourth-grade level enter a tutorial program that takes four hours per week. Instruction is tailored to the individual's job.

Companies that offer literacy training must vigorously advertise and promote their programs in order to reach the employees who need them. Many firms do this through company newsletters or the sort of bulletin-board announcement shown in Figure 8–11, which was used by Murray Ohio, a bicycle manufacturer.

- *Company/local schools programs.* Many companies join with a local high school or community college in a partnership aimed at improving workers' literacy. In these partnerships, companies and/or unions pay the tuition for workers to attend classes at local schools. Some companies allow workers up to six hours off per week to attend classes. Sometimes several companies are involved in the partnership, as in the Newark Literacy Campaign, the Alliance for Education in Worcester, Massachusetts, and the Memphis Literacy Coalition.
- *Company/local or state government programs.* In some areas, local or state government has supplied the major initiative for literacy programs. The South Carolina Institute for Work Force Excellence is one of the most extensive partnership programs between state government and the state's leading employers. In the first year after the South Carolina legislature passed a broad education reform measure, 338 initiative programs enrolling more than 3,000 people were held across the state. A third of the people enrolled work for Springs Industries, Inc., the state's largest employer. Other major participating companies are Campbell's Soup, Digital Equipment, and Sun Oil.[53]

Diversity Training. Ensuring that the diverse groups of people working in a company get along and cooperate is vital to organizational success. As we saw in Chapter 4, *diversity training programs* are designed to educate employees on specific cultural and gender differences and how to respond to these in the workplace. Diversity training is particularly important when team structures are used. In 1994, 53% of organizations with 100 or more employees offered diversity training.[54] (See Chapter 4 for additional information about this type of training.)

Crisis Training. Unfortunately, accidents, disasters, and violence are part of life. Events such as plane crashes, chemical spills, and workplace violence can wreak havoc on organizations. Yet many companies are ill prepared to deal with the tragedies and their aftermath. Consider the case of Pan Am, which made one mistake after another when trying to cope with a terrorist attack that resulted in the death of everyone aboard one of its flights. The following are just some of the mistakes Pan Am made:[55]

To All Employees

Murray Ohio will begin offering Adult Basic Education classes on three levels at the Training Center on Monday, March 13th. Classes will range from learning to read to studying for the GED test.

1st Shift: 3:45–5:15 p.m.
2nd Shift: 1:30–3:00 p.m.
3rd Shift: Either Session
Mon–Tues–Wed–Thurs
Classes Are Free And Are Open To All
Murray Ohio
Employees And Their Families!

FIGURE 8-11

Bulletin Board Announcement of Literacy Programs Offered by Murray Ohio

Source: Lund, L., and McGuire, E. P. (1990). *Literacy in the work force*, 18, New York: The Conference Board.

Customer Service Training at Federal Express

Issues + Applications

Federal Express has more than 35,000 customer-contact employees and prides itself on outstanding service. The core of customer-service training at FedEx is interactive video. Employees use the system to learn about policies and procedures and to become familiar with customer-service issues. The company has over 1,200 interactive video instruction units at various locations, all of them linked to a central mainframe. This system virtually eliminates travel costs and ensures that all information is standardized. In addition, no trainers are needed. Employees use the system to study topics and complete a series of "courses."

At the end of each course, the program generates an "interactive assessment score." Employees need a score of 90% or higher to be considered competent in that area. Following the test, each employee receives a *test score report* and a *student prescription*. The test report provides the score and a breakdown of performance in various areas covered by the test. The prescription provides suggestions for how the trainee can improve his or her understanding of the topic, and may refer the trainee to other video instruction courses and manuals.

Federal Express pays its employees for two hours of study time prior to each test. The company also pays for the two hours of test-taking time and two hours of remediation time after the test. The company makes this investment because of the benefits it receives from the training and testing program. Federal Express is held up as a model of customer service, and the company is consistently profitable.

Source: Wilson, W. (1994). Video training and testing supports customer service goals. *Personnel Journal, 73,* 47–51.

- The airline informed one family of their daughter's death by leaving a message on their answering machine.
- A family awaiting the arrival of their only child's body was told that their "shipment" had arrived. At the local airport the family was met by a forklift driver at a building marked "livestock."
- A flight attendant who was supposed to work on the doomed flight was so upset that she asked to be excused from her next flight. She was told that if she didn't fly she would be fired.

Ironically, Pan Am had practiced responding to a mock crash only two months earlier. As is too often the case, however, the crisis management training didn't address the human elements of a crisis.

In addition to after-the-fact crisis management, *crisis training* can focus on prevention. For example, organizations are becoming increasingly aware of the possibility of workplace violence, such as attacks by disgruntled former employees or violence against spouses. Prevention training often includes seminars on stress management, conflict resolution, and team building.[56]

Customer Service Training. Organizations are increasingly recognizing the importance of meeting customers' expectations, particularly those companies that have a TQM system in place. In addition to establishing philosophies, standards, and systems that support customer service, these companies often provide customer service training to give employees the skills they need to meet and exceed customer expectations. The customer service training program at Federal Express provides an example of an effective program.[57] (For more details, see the Issues and Applications feature titled "Customer Service Training at Federal Express.")

The Evaluation Phase

In the evaluation phase of the training process, the effectiveness of the training program is assessed. Effectiveness can be measured in monetary or nonmonetary terms. However it's measured, it is important that the training be judged on how well it addresses the needs it was designed to address. For example, a training program designed to increase workers' efficiency might justifiably be evaluated in terms of its effects on productivity or costs, but not in terms of employee satisfaction.

All too often the evaluation phase of the training process is neglected. This is tantamount to making an investment without ever determining if you're receiving an adequate (or any) return on it. Granted, it is sometimes difficult to collect the necessary data and find the time to analyze training results. But at the very least, companies should estimate the costs and benefits of a training program, even if these cannot be directly measured. Without such information, training's value cannot be demonstrated, and upper management may feel there is no compelling reason to continue the training effort.

The evaluation process followed by Allied Signal's Garrett Engine Division provides an excellent illustration of how to measure training's effectiveness. Personnel responsible for training at Garrett Engines assessed its effectiveness at the four levels presented in Figure 8–12. At level 1, trainees rated the course and instructor at the time of training. At level 2, participants were given an after-training test. The results of these tests were compared against scores on a pretest and against the scores achieved by a group of workers who did not go through the training (the *control group*). At level 3, trainees' use of their new skills and knowledge back on the job were compared against the job performance of the control group. At level 4, the evaluation team examined the critical issue of whether the training made a real difference to the company's bottom line.

In general, the outcomes of the first three levels of measurement were positive. At level 1, trainees gave high ratings to the course and instructor. The test at level 2 indicated that the performance of employees who had received training was higher than that of the employees who had not. The same result was achieved at level 3. Nonetheless, the big question remained: Did the training have a positive dollar impact on the company?

To answer this question, the Garrett training team measured performance before and after training for both trained and untrained groups of maintenance workers in terms of response time to job requests and job-completion time. It was assumed that if the maintenance teams were responding and completing jobs more quickly, the equipment would be down less time and Garrett Engine Division would save money. The maintenance department had already calculated the cost of equipment downtime, and this figure was used to translate downtime into dollar amounts. As Figure 8–13 on page 258 shows, the after-training downtime for the training group, at $1,156, was $55 less than that for the control group, at $1,211. This $55 value appears to be the monetary benefit of the training experience. While this may seem like a small amount, it represents the savings *per job,* and the team completed on average 55 jobs per week. The total cost of the team-building training was estimated at $5,355. A monthly return on investment (ROI) calculation using these figures is presented in Figure 8–14 on the next page. While the training's long-term effectiveness is not yet known, in the short run the training certainly appears to be paying off.

Level	Type of Measurement
1	Participants' reaction to the training at the time of the training.
2	Participants' learning of the content of the training.
3	Participants' use of their new skills and knowledge back on the job.
4	Company's return on the training investment.

FIGURE 8-12

Four Measurement Levels Employed by Garrett Engine Division

Source: Pine, J., and Tingley, J. C. (1993). ROI of soft skills training. *Training, 30*, 55–60. Reprinted with permission from the February 1993 issue of *Training*. Copyright 1993. Lakewood Publications, Minneapolis, MN. All rights reserved. Not for resale.

FIGURE 8-13

Performance Levels of Training and Control Groups at Garrett Engine Division

Source: Pine, J., and Tingley, J. C. (1993). ROI of soft skills training. *Training, 30*, 55–60. Reprinted with permission from the February 1993 issue of *Training*. Copyright 1993. Lakewood Publications, Minneapolis, MN. All rights reserved. Not for resale.

	Response Time	Completion Time	Total Down Time	Estimated Cost
Training Group				
Before training	4.8 hours	13.6 hours	18.4 hours	$1,341
After training	4.1 hours	11.7 hours	15.8 hours	$1,156
Control Group[1]				
Before training	4.4 hours	11.6 hours	16.0 hours	$1,165
After training	4.4 hours	11.7 hours	16.1 hours	$1,211

[1]The control group was not trained. The numbers cited here for the control group were compiled before and after the training group underwent training.

FIGURE 8-14

ROI After Four Average Workweeks at Garrett Engine Division

Source: Pine, J., and Tingley, J. C. (1993). ROI of soft skills training. *Training, 30*, 55–60. Reprinted with permission from the February 1993 issue of *Training*. Copyright 1993. Lakewood Publications, Minneapolis, MN. All rights reserved. Not for resale.

	$55 (average savings per job)
×	55 (jobs per week)
×	4 (number of weeks)
=	$12,100 (benefits)
−	$5,355 (cost of training)
=	$6,745 (net benefits)

$\frac{6,745}{5,355} = 1.26 =$ **126% ROI**

Legal Issues and Training

Like all other HRM functions, training is affected by legal regulations. The major requirement here is that employees must have access to training and development programs in a nondiscriminatory fashion. Equal opportunity regulations and antidiscrimination laws apply to the training process, just as they do to all other HR functions.

As we discussed in Chapter 3, determining whether a training program has adverse impact is a primary means of deciding if a process is discriminatory. If relatively few women and minorities are given training opportunities, it would appear that there is discrimination in terms of development offered to different groups of employees. This situation could trigger an investigation and the company may have to demonstrate that development opportunities are offered on a job-relevant and nondiscriminatory basis. ▼

▸ A Special Case: Employee Orientation

orientation
The process of informing new employees about what is expected of them in the job and helping them cope with the stresses of transition.

It is possible, though difficult to prove, that the most important training opportunity occurs when employees start with the firm. At this time managers have the chance to set the tone for new employees through **orientation,** the process of informing new employees about what is expected of them in the job and helping them cope with the stresses of transition. Orientation is an important aspect of the socialization stage of the staffing process discussed in Chapter 5. Perhaps no organization accomplishes orientation quite as effectively as the military. As soon as new recruits step off the bus, they are confronted by the stereotypical "in your face" drill sergeant. The recruits know immediately who is in charge and that only absolute, unquestioning obedience is acceptable.

Do not misunderstand our example. We are not suggesting that other organizations should copy the military and demand unquestioning obedience from new employees. What we are saying is that new recruits are informed immediately about what is expected of them, and that this expectation is consistent throughout their military career. What other organizations can learn from the military is that the optimal time to establish expectations about appropriate behavior is at the beginning of the employee's tenure with the organization. Metropolitan Property and Casualty Insurance Company has taken this lesson to heart with its Focus from the Start program. Figure 8–15 details what this MetLife division does to let new employees know about the company's expectations.[58]

Orientation is important not just for the firm, but also for the new employee. Several studies indicate that starting a new job is a very stressful event for many people.[59] In addition, employees often start a new job around the time that other stressful events are occurring in their lives: loss of previous job, marriage, or moving into a new area. One important function of orientation is to provide new workers with the tools to manage and control stress. John Wanous suggests that companies use an orientation approach that he calls Realistic Orientation Programs for new Employee Stress, or *ROPES*.[60] A good ROPES program does all of the following:

- *Provides realistic information.* Orientation should include realistic information about the job and the organization. While sugarcoated information may postpone stress for a little while, the stress will be magnified later when employees' expectations are not met.
- *Gives general support and reassurance.* The orientation program should let new employees know that the stress they are experiencing is normal. Also, it should provide managers with training in how to support their new employees.

Metropolitan Property and Casualty Insurance Company's Focus from the Start Program combines several elements to provide a high level of support to the new employee during his or her first six to nine months with the company. The key components of this intensive orientation program are:

- **Supervisor's role.** A four-page guide is given to each new employee's supervisor; it may be individualized for each employee. The guide includes topics for dialogue and a discussion of expectations, and encourages the supervisor to provide ongoing feedback to support the employee's adjustment and shorten the learning curve.
- **Mentor's role.** Each employee is assigned a mentor—a coworker selected by the supervisor.
- **Partnership of peers.** The program sensitizes all employees to the needs of new associates by providing their coworkers with "A Guide for Peers."
- **Self-development.** The employee is responsible for working through an employee *Orientation Workbook,* which includes self-paced activities, discussion topics for the employee to pursue, a list of educational programs, and a six-month planner.
- **Feedback.** The system is intended to encourage ongoing informal dialogue and feedback. During the third month on the job, the employee completes a feedback form and meets with the supervisor.
- **Videos.** The new employee views two videos: *Looking Back to See Ahead* (a history of the parent company, MetLife) and *Focus from the Start* (which highlights teamwork and creativity).
- **Vision.** Each new employee receives a copy of the company vision statement, which discusses mission, philosophy, and goals.
- **Values.** Each new employee receives an employee handbook that covers key corporate policies and core values.

FIGURE 8-15

Orientation Program at Metropolitan Property and Casualty Insurance Company

Source: Adapted from McCarthy, J. P. (1992, September). Focus from the start. *HRMagazine*, 77–83. Reprinted with the permission of *HRMagazine* (formerly *Personnel Administrator*) published by the Society for Human Resource Management, Alexandria, VA.

- *Demonstrates coping skills.* As part of an orientation program, new employees should be trained to cope with the stresses of the new job. For instance, the training situation might include a role-play in which a new employee asks his or her new manager for advice. Or the trainer might describe a stressful event and demonstrate by "thinking out loud" how new employees can control the stress by managing their own thoughts. In this type of training practice, called *behavior modeling,* the trainees model, or copy, the behavior demonstrated by the trainer.
- *Identifies specific potential stressors.* The organization should try to identify specific stressors that new employees might face. For instance, Texas Instruments found that its current employees tended to initiate new employees by telling them exaggerated horror stories from the company's past. To counteract this influence, the company included a segment warning of this behavior in its new-employee orientation.

The ROPES approach to orientation helps new employees cope with the transition to a new job and reduces turnover, which saves the company both time and money.[61] We discuss more techniques for reducing employees' stress levels in Chapter 16.

Summary and Conclusions

Training versus Development. Though training and development often go hand in hand, the terms are not synonymous. Training typically focuses on providing employees with specific skills and helping them correct deficiencies in their performance. Development is an effort to provide employees with the abilities that the organization will need in the future.

Challenges in Training. Before embarking on a training program, managers must answer several important questions: (1) Is training the solution to the problem? (2) Are the goals of training clear and realistic? (3) Is training a good investment? and (4) Will the training work?

Managing the Training Process. The training process consists of three phases: assessment, development and conduct of training, and evaluation. In the assessment phase, organizational, task, and person needs are identified and the goals of training are clarified. Several options are available during the training phase. Training can take place either on the job or off the job, and can be delivered through a variety of techniques (slides and videotapes, teletraining, computers, simulations, virtual reality, classroom instruction, and role-plays). The most appropriate type of training (for example, skills, retraining, cross-functional, team, creativity, literacy, diversity, crisis, or customer service) should be chosen to achieve the stated objectives. In the evaluation phase, the costs and benefits of the training program should be assessed to determine its effectiveness.

A Special Case: Employee Orientation. Organizations should pay particular attention to orientation, or informing new employees about what is expected of them in the job and helping them cope with the inevitable stresses of transition. The ROPES method of orientation can help companies orient employees successfully.

Key Terms

brainstorming, 253
cross-functional training, 251
development, 237
job aids, 250
literacy, 254
orientation, 258
peer trainers, 251
simulation, 246
training, 237
virtual reality (VR), 247

Discussion Questions

1. Performance problems seem all too common in your workplace. People don't seem to be putting forth the needed effort, and interpersonal conflict on the work teams seems to be a constant. Is training the answer? If so, what kind of training should be done? What other actions may be appropriate?
2. How effective do you think training can be in raising employee motivation?
3. An HR manager recalls a longtime employee who came to her in tears because she heard a rumor that workers would soon be required to use new equipment with a video screen that provided information in text form. The worker knew her inability to read would be discovered and feared she would lose her job.

   Many workers who are illiterate would not be so forthright—partly out of embarrassment, partly out of fear. Another HR manager notes, "They will ask for directions many times, even though the instruction manual is alongside their machine....Some workers always seem to be having problems with their eyesight or their glasses.... The truth is that they simply cannot read." How would you go about identifying workers who should receive literacy training? Discuss the differences between general illiteracy and functional illiteracy and how you would decide which of these issues a training program should address.
4. How important is it that the effectiveness of a training program be measured in dollar terms? Why is it important to measure training effectiveness in the first place?
5. Training provides workers with skills needed in the workplace. However, many organizations have dynamic environments in which change is the norm. How can training requirements be identified when job duties are a moving target?
6. Simuflite, a Texas aviation training company, expected to whip the competition with FasTrak, its computer-based training (CBT) curriculum for corporate pilots. Instead, the new venture sent Simuflite into a nose dive. In traditional ground-school training, pilots ask questions and learn from "war stories" told by classmates and instructors. With FasTrak, they sat in front of a computer for hours absorbing information. Their only interaction was in tapping the computer screen to provide answers to questions, and that novelty wore off very quickly. Pilots grew bored with the CBT ground school.

   What does Simuflite's experience suggest about the limitations of interactive media and CBT? In what situations is CBT most likely to be beneficial to trainees?
7. According to one survey, trainees list the following as some of the traits of a successful trainer: knowledge of the subject, adaptability, sincerity, and sense of humor. What other traits do you think trainers need to be successful in the training situation?

MINICASE 1 *Team Training at Coca-Cola: Keeping a Classic on Top*

For a long time, the corporate culture at Coca-Cola was largely driven by the individualistic values of U.S. culture. But today Coke is committed to shifting its culture toward a team orientation. The team training process developed at Coke's Baltimore Syrup Operation is a good example of an effective approach to developing team skills simultaneously with other important job-related skills.

The Baltimore syrup plant trains its employees in three skill areas: technical job skills, interpersonal skills, and team-action skills.

- The *technical job skills* training consists of training in the job-related knowledge and skills trainees need to be good performers. In addition, Coca-Cola encourages its associates to complete "four-deep training." *Four-deep training* means learning at least four different jobs. This depth of technical training provides flexibility and the ability to cover tasks when people are absent.
- *Interpersonal skills* training focuses on listening skills, handling conflict, and influencing and negotiating with internal and external customers. Trainees need these skills to be effective team members.
- *Team-action skills* training addresses such skills as team leadership, meeting management, team member roles and responsibilities, group dynamics, and problem solving. Team members need these skills to work together effectively.

The team focus seems to be working quite well at the Baltimore plant. Associates have participated in thousands of hours of training, and the majority have received training in areas outside their normal work duties. Productivity has increased. Employees are satisfied because they are finding that the team training gives them skills that widens their career choices.

Discussion Questions

1. Of the three categories of training at the Baltimore plant, do you think one is more important than the others? Why or why not?
2. Coca-Cola had to overcome an individualistic culture. How can resistance to a team orientation be reduced? What steps would you take to make sure teams become recognized as the best way of doing things? How can training help here?

Source: Phillips, S. N. (1996). Team training puts fizz in Coke plant's future. *Personnel Journal, 75*, 87–92.

MINICASE 2 *Partners International: "Train Thy Neighbor"*

Small companies face a common challenge: how to train employees without a training budget. After installing a new computer system for its 50 employees, Partners International, a small nonprofit organization that provides counseling services for Protestant churches, found a way to get the right training to the right people without additional expense:

Installing the system was one thing; using it effectively was another. Very few people knew how to operate a computer-based information system. Partners International got the equipment for a bargain, but the vendor contract didn't include much training. If people couldn't use the system, it obviously would be no bargain at all.

As support services manager, [Diane] Mundy was responsible for training—though she had no previous experience in either computer systems or training. Fortunately, she had a few things going for her: a teachable spirit, a genuine interest in helping people succeed, and the good sense to trust others with responsibility.

"Before the computer system was installed," Mundy says, "I recruited a few key staff people to learn the system with me. At first we learned the basics and took all the training the vendor offered. When that was exhausted, we participated in training seminars outside the organization. Then the money ran out, so we continued learning through self-teaching and by collaborating on problems as they arose." To gain the expertise the organization needed without waiting for everyone to keep up, Mundy assigned each staff member to learn a special application. In this way, every major functional area of the organization developed its own in-house expert. The purpose of involving those key staff members from the outset was, of course, to develop a team of amateur trainers. Through them every computer user in the organization had access to timely, well-informed help.

Discussion Questions

1. In Partners International's OJT of computer users there were no scheduled classes and no instructional materials. The computer manuals served as textbooks and the work to be done as the course outline. What do you think are the potential benefits and drawbacks of this type of approach?
2. Partners International is a small company without a training department. Do you think its unstructured approach to peer training could work in a larger company with, say, 500 employees? Why or why not?

Source: Adapted from Rickett, D. (1993, February). Peer training: Not just a low-budget answer. *Training*, 70–72. Reprinted with permission from the February 1993 issue of *Training*.

CASE 1 *Rough Edges at Central Lumber*

Central Lumber Company is a retail lumber and home improvement operation that caters to both contractors and do-it-yourselfers. The company has outlets across the United States, with each outlet under the direction of a general manager. One of the largest outlets, Bloomfield Central, is located on the outskirts of a rapidly growing city and employs 22 salespeople. The home office wants to improve customer service and its outlets' sales performance, and intends to use Bloomfield Central as a model operation.

Given these aspirations, Central's regional manager, Ann Henry, has been instructed to assess the current situation at Bloomfield Central. To scope the place out, Ann sent some of her employees to Bloomfield Central. These "spotters" were to pose as customers and provide her with reports on what they observed and experienced.

The reports did not make Ann happy. A central complaint was the salespeople's behavior. They seemed to treat contractors much better than they treated do-it-yourselfers. Several of the spotters saw salespeople leave the service counter to carry on extended conversations with people who appeared to be their personal friends. In addition, salespeople were several times heard using crude and vulgar language in front of customers.

Ann summarized these problems in a memo and sent it to Les Giacomo, Bloomfield Central's general manager, along with a description of headquarters' plans for the operation. Shortly after, she paid a personal visit to Bloomfield Central.

"Listen, Les," she said, "this is a second-rate operation and headquarters wants to move it up to world class. Frankly, I doubt that can be done with your current work force. I think you should seriously consider getting rid of most of your salespeople and bringing in higher quality."

"Oh, come on," responded Les. "You know that these guys know their stuff. They're just a little rough around the edges—same as the sales staff at all our outlets. It comes with the lumber territory. Besides, I could hire a new set of salespeople who have great manners but don't know the difference between a two-by-four and a one-by-two. Then where would we be?"

Ann knew Les was right. Nonetheless, something had to be done about the sales force's attitude toward customer service. "That may be true, Les, but we can't capitalize on the do-it-yourself market until we turn around the behavior of our people. Bloomfield Central isn't going to be a model of customer service and sales performance until we smooth out those rough edges. How you do it is up to you. Just do it! I'll check back with you in three months."

Les was worried about the ultimatum. His salespeople weren't perfect, but they knew the lumber business, and some of them had been with the company for more than 10 years. What could he do?

Critical Thinking Questions

1. Do you think Bloomfield Central's problem should be solved through training or replacement? Should an assessment phase be carried out? Why?
2. Describe the kind of training you think would be effective in this situation. How would you go about developing such a training program for the sales staff?
3. What criteria could be used to determine the effectiveness of a new training program at Bloomfield Central?

Cooperative Learning Exercises

4. What types of location and presentation options could be used for a training program at Bloomfield Central? Brainstorm the possibilities with your partner or team and present your best idea to the class.

CASE 2 *Virtual Teams: A Special Case For Team Training?*

Pulling together a diverse group of people from various functional and geographic areas sounds like the beginning of a great "virtual team." Indeed, many organizations are finding that much of their teamwork is taking place through telephone, fax, and computer connections, not through face-to-face contact. There is concern, however, over how to get everyone working together compatibly and productively because electronic communications may not always be efficient. Differences in time zones, telephone tag, and different work styles can all be sources of frustration to team members—especially when these people have never met face-to-face.

Most companies believe that a crucial step in making a geographically dispersed team work is to provide time for initial face-to-face interaction among team members. However, there is great variance across organizations in terms of how much introductory time is needed. For example, virtual teams at Price Waterhouse usually do not meet physically before being put on projects. In contrast, the research and education operation of Lotus Development Corporation always sponsors at least a one-day videoconference for team members to see and meet one another. Other companies bring remote team members together for weeks or months before they separate and become a virtual team.

Critical Thinking Questions

1. How important do you think initial face-to-face contact is to the effectiveness of virtual teams? What characteristics of an organization or team assignment may make "team bonding" more or less important?
2. What type(s) of training do you think virtual team members should be given? How would you go about delivering this training? What delivery formats would you use?

Cooperative Learning Exercises

3. With your partner or group, brainstorm the skills particularly important for virtual team members. Based on your list, suggest the types of training that would best provide those skills. Share the list and suggested training approaches with the rest of the class.
4. With your partner or group, survey local companies to get a sense of how often they use virtual teams. How do these companies approach bonding and training of virtual teams? Report your findings to the class.

Source: Geber, B. (1995). Virtual teams. *Training, 32*, 36–40.

HRM Simulation 

Your company does not currently have any training programs (see Training, page 8 of the players' manual). However, training can provide employees with needed skills, resulting in better performance, improved morale, and decreased turnover. Training is not free and you must determine which training requests in Incident F should be funded. Which training programs do you think the company should offer? Explain the rationale behind your selections.

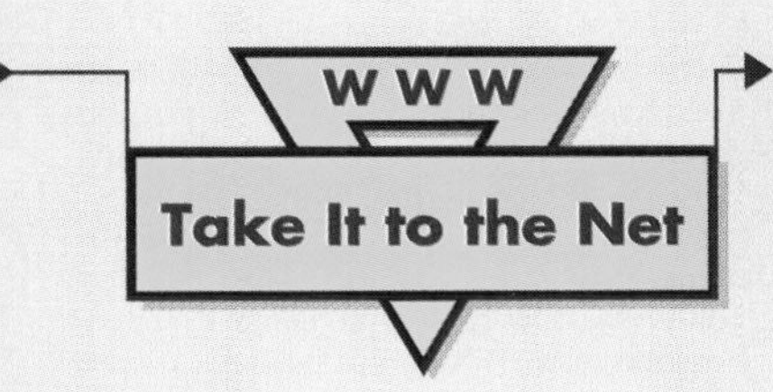

We invite you to visit the Gómez-Mejía/Balkin/Cardy page on the Prentice Hall Web site:

http://www.prenhall.com/gomez

You can also visit the Web sites for these companies, featured within this chapter:

American Management Association	http://www.tregisty.com/ttr/ama.htm
Disney	http://www.disney.com
Frito-Lay	http://www.fritolay.com
Motorola	http://www.motorola.com
Polaroid Corporation	http://www.polaroid.com
Prudential Insurance Company	http://www.prudential.com

Endnotes

1. Adams, N. (1995). Lessons from the virtual world. *Training, 32,* 45–47.
2. Fitzgerald, W. (1992). Training versus development. *Training & Development, 46,* 81–84.
3. Bartz, D. E., Schwandt, D. R., and Hillman, L. W. (1989). Differences between "T" and "D." *Personnel Administrator, 34,* 164–170.
4. Rummler, G. A. (1972). Human performance problems and their solutions. *Human Resource Management, 19,* 2–10.
5. Cummings, J. (1993, February 15). Survey finds managers lack focus on training goals. *Network World,* 75.
6. *Training*. (1995a). Training budgets. *32,* 44.
7. Galagan, P. A. (1992, October). How to get your TQM training on track. *Nation's Business,* 24–28.
8. Goldstein, I. L. (1986). *Training in organizations: Needs assessment, development, and evaluation* (2nd ed.). Monterey, CA: Brooks-Cole.
9. Mirabile, R. J. (1991). Pinpointing development needs: A simple approach to skills assessment. *Training & Development, 45,* 19–25.
10. Mager, R. F., and Pipe, P. (1984). *Analyzing performance problems: Or, you really oughta wanna.* Belmont, CA: Lake and Rummler, 1972.
11. Breuer, N. L. (1992, January). AIDS issues haven't gone away. *Personnel Journal,* 47–49.
12. Nowack, K. M. (1991). A true training needs analysis. *Training & Development, 45,* 69–73; and Phillips, J. J. (1983, May). Training programs: A results-oriented model for managing the development of human resources. *Personnel,* 11–18.
13. *Id.*
14. Mullaney, C. A., and Trask, L. D. (1992, October). Show them the ropes. *Technical & Skills Training,* 8–11.
15. McKenna, J. F. (1992, January 20). Apprenticeships: Something old, something new, something needed. *Industry Week,* 14–20.

15a. Gupta, U. (1996, January 3). TV seminars and CD-ROMs train workers. *The Wall Street Journal,* B1, B8.

16. Sickler, N. G. (1993). Synchronized videotape teletraining: Efficient, effective and timely. *Tech Trends, 38,* 23–24.
17. Hall, B. (1996, March). Lessons in corporate training: Multimedia's big payoff. *New-Media,* 40–45.

17a. For more on CD-ROM training, see Murphy, K. (1996, May 6). Pitfalls vs. promise in training by CD-ROM. *The New York Times,* D3.

18. Geber, B. (1990). Simulating reality. *Training, 27,* 41–46.
19. Geber, B. (1990).
20. Middleton, T. (1992, Spring). The potential of virtual reality technology for training. *Journal of Interactive Instructional Development,* 8–11.
21. Psotka, J. (1995). Immersive training systems: Virtual reality and education and training. *Instructional Science, 23,* 405–431.
22. *Id.*
23. Mastaglio, T. W., and Callahan, R. (1995). A large scale complex virtual environment for team training. *Computer, 28,* 49–56.
24. Swink, D. F. (1993). Role-play your way to learning. *Training & Development, 47,* 91–97.
25. Estabrooke and Foy, 1992.
26. Patterson, P. A. (1991). Job aids: Quick and effective training. *Personnel, 68,* 13.
27. Overman, S. (1993, October). Retraining our work force. *HRMagazine,* 40–44.
28. Stamps, D. (1994). Reinventing retraining. *Training, 31,* 43–50.
29. Laabs, J. J. (1992, March). How federally funded training helps business. *Personnel Journal,* 35–39.
30. Overman, 1993.
31. Simmons, D. L. (1995). Retraining dislocated workers in the community college: Identifying factors for persistence. *Community College Review, 23,* 47–58.
32. Stamps, 1994; Laabs, 1992.
33. Case, S., and Szakacs, B. (1993). Taking control of maintenance costs through training. *Industrial Engineering, 25,* 36–37.
34. Challenger, J. E. (1993). Two or more for one: A new way of looking at employment. *Industry Week, 242,* 25.
35. Nilson, C. (1990). How to use peer training. *Supervisory Management, 35,* 8.
36. Filipczak, B. (1993, June). Frick teaches Frack. *Training,* 30–34.
37. Messmer, M. (1992). Cross-discipline training: A strategic method to do more with less. *Management Review, 81,* 26–28.
38. Fyock, C. D. (1991). Teaching older workers new tricks. *Training & Development, 45,* 21–24.
39. Ludeman, K. (1995). Motorola's HR learns the value of teams firsthand. *Personnel Journal, 74,* 117–123.
40. Burns, G. (1995). The secrets of team facilitation. *Training & Development, 49,* 46–52.
41. Phillips, S. N. (1996). Team training puts fizz in Coke plant's future. *Personnel Journal, 75,* 87–92.
42. Goldstein, I. L. (1993). *Training in organizations* (3rd ed.). Pacific Grove, CA: Brooks-Cole.

43. Hequet, M. (1992, February). Creativity training gets creative. *Training,* 41–46.
44. *Training*. (1995b). Vital statistics. *32,* 55–66.
45. Wise, R. (1991). The boom in creativity training. *Across the Board, 28,* 38–42.
46. Solomon, C. M. (1990). Creativity training. *Personnel Journal, 69,* 65–71.
47. Hequet, 1992.
48. Wise, 1991.
49. Koretz, G. (1996, May 20). A crash course in the 3R's? *Business Week*, 26. Educational Testing Service (1990). *From school to work.* Princeton, NJ: Educational Testing Service.
50. Rosow, J. M., and Zager, R. (1992). *Job-linked literacy: Innovative strategies at work.* Part II. *Meeting the challenges of change: Basic skills for a competitive workforce.* Scottsdale, NY: Work in America Institute.
51. Rosow and Zager, 1992.
52. Lund, L., and McGuire, E. P. (1990). *Literacy in the work force.* New York: The Conference Board.
53. Lund and McGuire, 1990.
54. *Training*. 1995b.
55. Nelms, D. W. (1993). Managing the crisis. *Air Transport World, 30*, 62–65.
56. Bensimon, H. F. (1994). Crisis and disaster management: Violence in the workplace. *Training and Development, 48*, 27–32.
57. Wilson, W. (1994). Video training and testing supports customer service goals. *Personnel Journal, 73*, 47–51.
58. McCarthy, J. P. (1992, September). Focus from the start. *HRMagazine,* 77–83.
59. Wanous, J. P. (1992). *Organizational entry* (2nd ed.). Reading, MA: Addison-Wesley.
60. Wanous, 1992.
61. *Id.*

9 Developing Careers

CHALLENGES

After reading this chapter, you should be able to deal more effectively with the following challenges:

1 ► **Establish** a sound process for helping employees develop their careers.

2 ► **Understand** how to develop your own career.

3 ► **Identify** the negative aspects of an overemphasis on career development.

4 ► **Understand** the importance of dual-career issues in career development.

5 ► **Develop** a skills inventory and a career path.

6 ► **Establish** an organizational culture that supports career development.

Climbing the Ladder. For most employees, career development is a priority—understandably so, because salaries increase as one climbs the corporate ladder. Progressive companies sponsor active career development programs for their employees, but in today's competitive enviroment workers must take responsibility for their own career advancement.

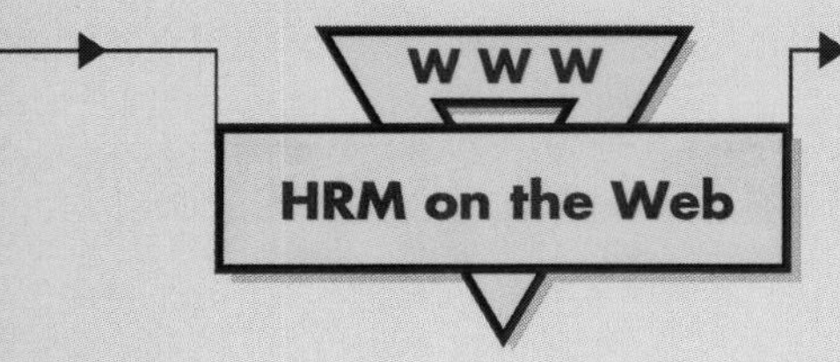

http://www.careermosaic.com/

Career Mosaic

The Career Mosaic Web site contains a wealth of career and job information, including a large database of current job opportunities at hundreds of companies.The site also provides a career resource center with tips on job hunting and résumé writing, and links to major employers and professional trade associations.

Steve, a technician at GCX for the past six years, was once an excellent performer. Over the past couple of years, however, he has grown increasingly frustrated and disillusioned. He expected to move up in the company and it isn't happening.

When his department supervisor retired last year, Steve thought that he would be promoted into the position. He told Natalie, the unit manager, of his interest, and she assured him that he would be given every consideration. The next thing Steve knew, someone from outside the company had been offered the job.

Steve was disappointed and angry, and the lack of an explanation didn't help. He didn't understand why he had been passed over. He had consistently been a top performer. He knew the technical end of the business as well as anyone, and he always achieved his performance objectives. What did he have to do to get into management?

After a couple of weeks of quietly seething, Steve decided to ask Natalie point blank why he had not been offered the supervisor's job. Natalie seemed quite surprised at Steve's eagerness to be promoted. She told him that she hadn't thought his interest in the supervisory position was very strong and that an outsider got the job simply because he had better credentials. She advised Steve to keep trying; sooner or later, something would open up.

Steve was no closer to understanding what he needed to do to get promoted. When he got home that night, he made some phone calls about job openings he had seen advertised. Maybe he could advance faster somewhere else. Even if he didn't leave GCX, he thought, he sure wasn't going to go out of his way for the company anymore. He had some sick days coming and he planned on using them soon.

* * *

Barbara relaxed at home after two long, interesting days. Her company, a large telecommunications firm, had sent her to an assessment center for an evaluation of her strengths and weaknesses as a potential middle-level manager. Currently, she was the head of a sales office located in Des Moines, Iowa, and was responsible for the surrounding metropolitan area.

Her experience at the assessment center could not have been better. After a day and a half of various activities, she had met with the consultants who operate the center. They told her that she definitely had the characteristics her company was looking for in a future manager. She had a few weak areas—most notably, confidence in pushing her ideas in the face of opposition—but she already knew this and was working on overcoming her timidity. They told her that the report she received would also be given to her boss, as well as to the HR manager responsible for management development activities. She knew that while it might take a year or two for a position to become available, she was on her way up.

Steve's experience, unfortunately, is much more common than Barbara's. Workers often have goals and aspirations that their organizations do not know about. Whether these goals are reasonable or unrealistic, lack of progress toward them can have a strongly negative effect on performance.

An active career development program can lead to a win-win scenario for both worker and organization. In this chapter we consider the various facets of career development. First, we define career development. Second, we explore some of the major challenges connected with career development and offer some approaches to help managers avoid problems in this area. We conclude the chapter by discussing three special issues in career development: managerial development, development through the life cycle, and self-development.

▸ What Is Career Development?

As we noted in Chapter 8, career development is different from training. Career development has a wider focus, longer time frame, and broader scope. The goal of training is improvement in performance; the goal of development is enriched and more capable workers. **Career development** is not a one-shot training program or career-planning workshop. Rather, it is an ongoing organized and formalized effort that recognizes people as a vital organizational resource.[1]

career development
An ongoing and formalized effort that focuses on developing enriched and more capable workers.

The field of career development is quite young—most career development programs were initiated only in the 1970s—but it has grown rapidly over the last two decades. The companies that have had the most success with career development are those that have integrated it with other HRM programs, such as performance appraisal and training.[2] Recent studies of organizational career development have identified the following companies as outstanding or innovative in this area:

- 3M has actively addressed its employees' career development needs since the mid-1980s. While the company has historically focused more on appraisal and HR planning, it is now trying, with its relatively new career resources department, to strike a better balance between organizational and employee needs. The new department systematizes and coordinates career development through such programs as supervisor and employee workshops, career counseling, and partner relocations for dual-career couples.[3]
- Sun Microsystems found that career concerns can be a great source of stress for employees. To combat this problem, Sun now offers every employee two hours of free career counseling per year. The company also encourages employees to think of themselves as "self-employed" within the organization,[4] and to pursue all opportunities to advance their careers.
- The English company Lex Service has banded together with other English firms to create a development program that challenges their senior managers. Managers from similar functional areas regularly get together to share their experiences. One manager presents a description of what he or she is attempting to accomplish in his or her organization, and the rest of the group provides feedback and shares relevant experiences with the goal of helping the speaker set up an action plan.[5]

Initially, most organizations instituted career development programs to help meet organizational needs (such as preparing employees for anticipated management openings) rather than to meet employees' needs.[6] More recently, career development has come to be seen as a way of meeting both. Figure 9–1 on page 270 shows how organizational and individual career needs can be linked to create a successful career development program. Organizations now view career development as a way of preventing job burnout (see Chapter 16), improving the quality of employees' work lives, and meeting affirmative action goals.[7] This changed emphasis has largely resulted from a combination of competitive pressures (such as downsizing and technological changes) and workers' demands for more opportunities for growth and skill development.[8] This combination has made career development a more difficult endeavor than it used to be. There is no longer a strict hierarchy of jobs from which a career path can easily be constructed. Career development today involves workers' active participation in thinking through the possible directions their careers can take.

An organization must make career development a key business strategy if it intends to survive in an increasingly competitive and global business environment.[9] In the information age, companies will compete more on their workers' knowledge, skill, and innovation levels than on the basis of labor costs or manufacturing capacity.[10] Because career development plays a central role in ensuring a competitive work force, it cannot be a low-priority program offered only during good economic times.

Organizational Needs

What are the organization's major strategic issues over the next two to three years?

- What are the most critical needs and challenges that the organization will face over the next two to three years?
- What critical skills, knowledge, and experience will be needed to meet these challenges?
- What staffing levels will be required?
- Does the organization have the strength necessary to meet the critical challenges?

Issue:

Are employees developing themselves in a way that links personal effectiveness and satisfaction with the achievement of the organization's strategic objectives?

Individual Career Needs

How do I find career opportunities within the organization that:

- Use my strengths
- Address my developmental needs
- Provide challenges
- Match my interests
- Match my values
- Match my personal style

FIGURE 9-1

Career Development System: Linking Organizational Needs with Individual Career Needs

Source: Gutteridge, T. G., Leibowitz, Z. B., and Shore, J. E. (1993). *Organizational career development: Benchmarks for building a world-class workforce.* Reprinted with permission from *Conceptual Systems*, Silver Springs, MD.

Challenges in Career Development

While most businesspeople today agree that their organizations should invest in career development, it is not always clear exactly what form this investment should take. Before putting a career development program in place, management needs to consider three major challenges.

Who Will Be Responsible?

A QUESTION OF ETHICS

How much responsibility does a company have for managing its employees' careers? Can a company take too much responsibility for employee career development? In what ways might this be harmful to employees?

The first challenge is deciding who will be ultimately responsible for career development activities. In traditional, bureaucratic organizations development was something done "for" individual employees. For instance, the organization might have an assessment center to identify employees who have the characteristics necessary to hold middle- and upper-management positions. Once identified, these individuals would be groomed through a variety of programs: special-project assignments, positions in international divisions, executive training programs, and so on. The individual employee, while certainly not kept in the dark about the company's plans, would not actively participate in the development decisions.

In contrast, many modern organizations have concluded that employees must take an active role in planning and implementing their own personal development plans. The mergers, acquisitions, and downsizings of the 1980s and 1990s have led to layoffs in managerial ranks and managers' realization that they cannot depend on their employers to plan their careers for them. Added to this economic turmoil is the empowerment movement, which shifts decision-making responsibility down through the organizational hierarchy. Both of these trends have led companies to encourage their employees to take responsibility for their own development. We will look at strategies for personal development at the end of this chapter.

One company known for encouraging employees to develop their own careers is British Petroleum Exploration (BPX), the arm of British Petroleum that finds and develops oil and gas reserves.[11] BPX provides its employees with a personal development program that they can use to improve their skills, performance, and job satisfaction. Employees go through five phases in this do-it-yourself development process:

1. In the first phase, they complete self-assessment exercises that help them determine which skills, interests, and values they already have and which they need to develop.
2. In the second phase, they are encouraged to ask for feedback from their supervisors, peers, subordinates, family, and friends.
3. In the third phase, they establish goals both for their current jobs and for future positions. Employees may decide to improve their performance in their present job, take on new responsibilities, do something to enhance their core skills, or volunteer for lateral moves. They turn this blueprint into an action plan by specifying development and improvement activities, setting target dates for completing these activities, and identifying the resources required to complete them.
4. In the fourth phase, employees and supervisors agree on assessments, goals, and action plans. Together, they do a "reality check," asking such questions as: How can the employee reach this goal within BPX, and what job qualifications does the employee need to meet?
5. The process doesn't end when the employee and supervisor agree on a course of action. Personal development plans are updated as employees increase their skills and knowledge, as they complete items on their action plans, or as business needs change.[12]

It is probably a mistake for companies to take the employee responsibility perspective too far, though. Giving employees total responsibility for managing their own careers can create problems in today's flatter organizations, where opportunities to move up through the hierarchy are far fewer than in traditional bureaucratic organizations. Employees need at least general guidance regarding the steps they can take to develop their careers, both within and outside the company.

How Much Emphasis Is Appropriate?

So far, we have presented career development as a positive way for companies to invest in their human resources. However, too great an emphasis on career enhancement can be detrimental to organizational effectiveness.[13] Employees with an extreme careerist orientation can become more concerned about their image than their performance.

It is difficult to pinpoint where an employee's healthy concern for his or her career becomes excessive. However, there are certain warning signs managers should watch for:

- Is the employee more interested in capitalizing on opportunities for advancement than in maintaining adequate performance?
- Does the employee devote more attention to managing the impressions he or she makes on others than to reality?
- Does the employee emphasize networking, flattery, and being seen at social functions over job performance? In the short run, people who engage in these tactics often enjoy advancement. However, sooner or later they run into workplace duties or issues they are not equipped to deal with.
- For better or for worse, studies have found that such strategies are effective in helping employees advance through the organization.[14]

Managers should also be aware that a career development program can have serious side effects—including employee dissatisfaction, poor performance, and turnover—if it fosters unrealistic expectations for advancement.

How Will the Needs of a Diverse Work Force Be Met?

To meet the career development needs of today's diverse work force, companies need to break down the barriers some employees face in achieving advancement. In 1991 the first major government study of the glass ceiling revealed that women and minorities are held back not only from top executive positions but also from lower-level management positions and directorships. The study revealed that women and minorities are frequently excluded from such informal career development activities as networking, mentoring, and participation in policy-making committees. In addition to outright discrimination, some of the practices that contribute to their exclusion are informal word-of-mouth recruitment, companies' failure to sensitize and instruct managers about equal employment opportunity requirements, lack of mentoring, and the too-swift identification of high-potential employees.[15]

Because the barriers to advancement of women and minorities tend not to be obvious, they are difficult to identify and remove. Perhaps the best course a company can take is to design a broad-based approach to employee development that is anchored in education and training. For instance, in an industry long dominated by men, the accounting firm Deloitte and Touche launched a long-term initiative to lower the rate of turnover among female managers and to encourage the promotion of more women to partnership ranks. The initiative, prompted by the company's Task Force on the Retention and Recruitment of Women, features companywide training in workplace gender dynamics along with structured career planning for women, succession planning, networking opportunities, and family-friendly work options.[16]

Despite such programs, a 1995 study by the Federal Glass Ceiling Commission found the continued existence of barriers to the advancement of women in business. However, substantial progress has been made in this area. The Issues and Applications feature titled "Cracks in the Glass Ceiling?" discusses this progress.

dual-career couple
A couple whose members both have occupational responsibilities and career issues at stake.

Another employee group that may need special consideration is **dual-career couples.** When both members of a couple have career issues at stake, personal lives can complicate and become intertwined with occupational lives. A career opportunity for one member that demands a geographic move can produce a crisis for both the couple and their companies. Rather than waiting until they reach such a crisis point to resolve competing career issues, it is better for the couple to plan their careers and discuss how they will proceed if certain options become available. This approach also reduces the possibility of abrupt personnel losses for organizations.

The most common organizational approaches to dealing with the needs of dual-career couples are flexible work schedules and telecommuting (both discussed in Chapter 4) and the offering of child-care services (see Chapter 12). These practices are not prevalent, but they are increasing. For example, survey results indicate that family-friendly benefits increased significantly from 1990 to 1995. The number of employers offering child-care assistance increased from 64% to 85%, and the number offering elder-care programs increased from 12% to 26%. The number of companies offering flextime scheduling also increased, from 54% to 67%.[17]

Some companies have also begun counseling couples in career management. These proactive programs, which involve both the employee and his or her spouse or significant other, are usually reserved for executives and others who are considered key personnel in the organization.[18] First, each partner individually comes up with his or her goals and action plans. Then the partners are brought together to share their agendas and work through any conflicts. Professional counselors offer possible solutions and alternatives.[19] The result of the process—a joint career plan—is then provided to the organization. Employees and their partners benefit from this approach by formulating a mutually agreeable plan, and the organization benefits by increasing the probability of retaining key employees. While career management for couples is fairly new and costly, it is a very promising approach whose use is expected to increase. Indeed, recent findings underscore

Cracks in the Glass Ceiling?

Issues + Applications

In 1995, only 5% of senior managers (those with a rank of vice president or above) in *Fortune* 1000 firms were women. While this figure may seem discouraging, it represents a substantial improvement: In the mid-1980s, only 1.5% of senior managers were women. In addition, the 5% figure may be an underestimate because it is based on surveys done in 1989 and 1990. More current surveys and estimates put the figure between 7 and 10%.

The following are some other positive indicators that the glass ceiling may be breaking:

- **There are many women managers outside the Fortune 1000.** The 5% figure cited above is based on the small and select group of *Fortune* 1000 companies. However, only about 20% of U.S. workers are employed by *Fortune* 1000 firms. If the entire national labor market is considered, 43% of managers are women. This figure is higher in certain industries, such as insurance and nonprofit social services, which are predominantly female.
- **Many women are self-employed.** Women are increasingly choosing to become their own bosses. As of 1995, there were over 6.5 million women-owned businesses.
- **Many women are receiving advanced degrees in business.** Currently, about one third of business school students are female. As the percentage of women obtaining MBAs and other advanced degrees increases, the percentage who makes it to the top rungs of business should also increase.
- **Workplace changes may favor female managers.** Some business researchers have argued that organizations may find that women make better managers. This argument is based on the notion that women's natural leadership styles may be more effective in today's collaborative and empowered work environments.

Sources: Kaufman-Rosen, L., and Kalb, C. (1995). Holes in the glass ceiling theory. *Newsweek, 125,* 24–25; Bass, B. M., and Avalio, B. J. (1994). Shatter the glass ceiling: Women may make better managers than men. *Human Resource Management, 33,* 549–560.

the importance of and potential benefits of dual-career counseling and spousal support services.[20] The levels of work stress and job satisfaction experienced by dual-career workers are significantly influenced by the spouse's level of support; over the long term, lack of spousal support can have a negative influence on job performance and even cause a worker to leave his or her job.

Building Managerial Skills: ▸ Meeting the Challenges of Effective Career Development

Creating a development program almost always consists of three phases: the assessment phase, the direction phase, and the development phase (Figure 9–2). Although presented separately in Figure 9–2, the phases of development often blend together in a real-life program.

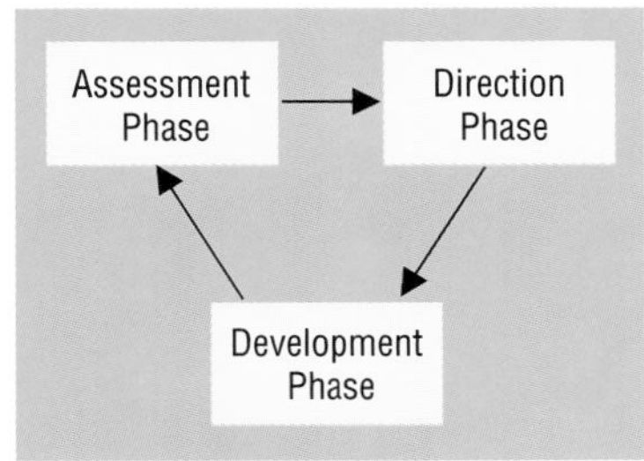

FIGURE 9-2

The Career Development Process

The Assessment Phase

The *assessment phase* of career development involves activities ranging from self-assessment to organizationally provided assessment. The goal of assessment, whether performed by employees themselves or by the organization, is to identify employees' strengths and weaknesses. This kind of clarification helps employees (1) to choose a career that is realistically obtainable and a good fit and (2) to determine the weaknesses they need to overcome to achieve their career goals. Figure 9–3 on the next page lists some tools that are commonly used for self-assessment and for organizational assessment.

Self-Assessment	Organizational Assessment
Career workbooks Career-planning workshops	Assessment centers Psychological testing Performance appraisal Promotability forecasts Succession planning

FIGURE 9-3
Common Assessment Tools

Self-Assessment. Self-assessment is increasingly important for companies that want to empower their employees to take control of their careers. The major tools used for self-assessment are workbooks and workshops.

Career workbooks have been very popular for decades. Generic workbooks were commonly used in the 1970s, but tailored workbooks gained in popularity in the 1980s.[21] In addition to the exercises included in a generic career workbook, tailored workbooks might contain a statement of the organization's policies and procedures regarding career issues as well as descriptions of the career paths and options available in the organization.

Career-planning workshops, which may be led either by the company's HR department or by an external provider such as a consulting firm or local university, give employees information about career options in the organization. They may also be used to provide participants with feedback on their career aspirations and strategy. Participation in most workshops is voluntary, and some organizations hold these workshops on company time to demonstrate their commitment to their work force.

Whether done through workbooks or workshops, self-assessment usually involves doing skills assessment exercises, completing an interests inventory, and clarifying values.[22]

- As their name implies, *skills assessment exercises* are designed to identify an employee's skills. For example, a workbook exercise might ask the employee to compile a brief list of his or her accomplishments. Once the employee has generated a set of, say, five accomplishments, he or she then identifies the skills involved in making each accomplishment a reality. In a workshop situation, people might share their accomplishments in a group discussion, and then the entire group might help identify the skills underlying the accomplishments.

  Another skills assessment exercise presents employees with a list of skills they must rate on two dimensions: their level of proficiency at that skill and the degree to which they enjoy using it. A total score is then generated for each skill area—for example, by multiplying the proficiency by the preference rating. Figure 9–4 shows an example of this approach to skills assessment. Scores below 6 indicate areas of weakness or dislike, while scores of 6 or above indicate areas of strength. The pattern of scores can guide employees regarding the type of career for which they are best suited.
- An *interest inventory* is a measure of a person's occupational interests. Numerous off-the-shelf inventories can give employees insight into what type of career will best fit their interests. One of the best-known inventories is the Strong Vocational Interest Inventory.[23] The interest inventory asks people to indicate how strong or weak an interest they have in such activities as dealing with very old people, making a speech, and raising money for charity. Responses to items on the inventory are then scored to identify the occupations in which the individual has the same interests as the professionals employed in those fields.
- *Values clarification* involves prioritizing personal values. The typical values-clarification exercise presents employees with a list of values and asks them to rate how important each value is to them. For example, employees may be asked to prioritize security, power, money, and family in their lives. Knowing their priority values can help employees make satisfying career choices.

Use the scales below to rate yourself on each of the following skills. Rate each skill area both for your level of proficiency and for your preference.

Proficiency:

1	2	3
Still learning	OK—competent	Proficient

Preference:

1	2	3
Don't like to use this skill	OK—Don't particularly like or dislike using this skill	Really enjoy using this skill

Skill Area	Proficiency	×	Preference	=	Score
1. Problem solving	______		______		______
2. Team presentation	______		______		______
3. Leadership	______		______		______
4. Inventory	______		______		______
5. Negotiation	______		______		______
6. Conflict management	______		______		______
7. Scheduling	______		______		______
8. Delegation	______		______		______
9. Participative management	______		______		______
10. Feedback	______		______		______
11. Planning	______		______		______
12. Computer	______		______		______

FIGURE 9-4
Sample Skills Assessment Exercise

Organizational Assessment. Some of the tools traditionally used by organizations in selection (see Chapter 5) are also valuable for career development. Among these are assessment centers, psychological testing, performance appraisal, promotability forecasts, and succession planning.

- *Assessment centers* are situational exercises—such as interviews, in-basket exercises, and business games—that are often used to select managerial talent. While assessment centers have traditionally been used for selection, companies are increasingly using them as a developmental tool. A recent survey of the development efforts of 256 U.S. companies found that 43% of respondent companies use assessment centers as part of their career development programs.[24] Assessment centers provide participants with feedback on their strengths and weaknesses as uncovered in the exercises. This feedback increases employees' understanding of their skills and helps them develop realistic career goals and plans.

  Somewhat surprisingly, there have been few empirical studies of the effectiveness of assessment centers for developmental purposes.[25] However, the limited number of studies do indicate that assessment centers have significant and positive impacts on participants, even months after the assessment center exercise.

- Some organizations also use *psychological testing* to help employees better understand their skills and interests. Tests that measure personality and attitudes, as well as interest inventories, fall into this category.[26]

- Performance appraisal is another source of valuable career development information. Unfortunately, appraisals are frequently limited to assessment of past performance rather than oriented toward future performance improvements and directions. Future-oriented performance appraisal can give employees important insights into their strengths, their weaknesses, and the career paths available to them.

promotability forecast
A career development activity in which managers make decisions regarding the advancement potential of subordinates.

- **Promotability forecasts** are decisions made by managers regarding the advancement potential of their subordinates. These forecasts allow the organization to identify people who appear to have high advancement potential.[27] The high-potential employees are then given developmental experiences (such as attending an executive training seminar) to help them achieve their advancement potential.

  For example, in 1988 AT&T launched a companywide computerized program to track high-potential managers and equip them with the right experiences to face business challenges in the years ahead. The emphasis in this Leadership Continuity Program (LCP) is on development, not promotion in the near term. Participants accept assignments that will prepare them for increased responsibilities. Candidates are selected for LCP on the basis of three criteria: sustained strong performance, overall high standing in relation to peers, and a demonstrated potential to perform at least four salary levels above their current level.[28]

succession planning
A career development activity that focuses on preparing people to fill executive positions.

- **Succession planning** focuses on preparing people to fill executive positions. Formally, succession planning means examining development needs given a firm's strategic plans. Informally, it means high-level managers identifying and developing their own replacements. Most succession planning is informal. The employees identified as having upper-management potential may then be given developmental experiences that will help prepare them for the executive ranks, such as workshops on the organization's values and mission.

  Succession planning is one of the trickiest challenges in the area of career development. Organizations have often been accused of discriminating against women and minorities when filling high-level positions. Rather than outright discrimination, it is usually the informality of much succession planning that makes companies unwittingly exclude these groups as candidates. Formal succession planning programs, such as those in place at 3M and Westpac Banking Corporation (Australia's largest bank), can make the identification of high-potential employees and replacement candidates a more egalitarian procedure.

What employee characteristics and experiences predict success at the managerial and executive levels? The earliest work in this area was done by researchers at AT&T.[29] For example, one study examined the influence of various educational characteristics on management performance two decades later. The study found that college major and extent of extracurricular activities were significantly related to later management performance. Grades were found to predict managers' overall motivation levels, with the grades themselves reflecting more the manager's work ethic than the degree of skill or knowledge obtained in various courses.

A more recent study examined the extent to which demographic, human capital, motivational, and organizational variables predict executive career success.[30] The researchers divided career success into objective (for example, pay level) and subjective (for example, job satisfaction) components. The researchers concluded that educational level, quality and prestige of the university, and major were all related to the pay levels of a sample of 1,388 executives. Interestingly, ambition was negatively related to job satisfaction, with the more ambitious executives indicating less satisfaction in their current positions.

Personality characteristics are also a determinant of success in higher-level management jobs. For example, one study examined the effects of both personality and cognitive abilities on the current earnings of managers, and concluded that such characteristics as creativity, sociability, self-reliance, and self-control are strongly related to managers' suc-

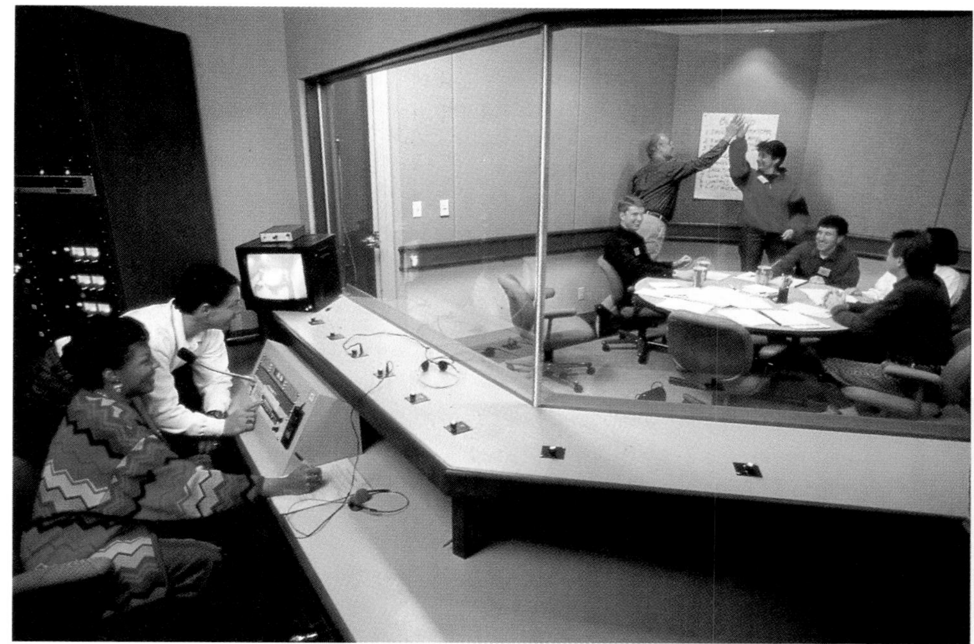

Assessing Management Potential.

Some companies ask outside consultants to evaluate their internal candidates for promotion. Here, psychologists at the Center for Creative Leadership assess candidates' leadership skills through one-way glass.

cess as determined by pay level.[31] Thus, managers should consider these characteristics, as well as level of technical knowledge and motivation, when preparing their promotability forecasts and conducting succession planning.

In small companies succession planning is crucial because the sudden departure or illness of a key player can set the business floundering. Yet just as some people shy away from drafting a will for fear of recognizing their own mortality, some small-business owners shy away from succession planning for fear of recognizing that they won't always be in control of their business. Other small-business owners are too caught up in the daily pressures of running a business to plan for the future. A recent poll of 800 business owners revealed that only about one fourth of small-business owners have a succession plan, and just half of those owners have formalized the plan by committing it to paper.[32]

In doing succession planning, small-business owners—whether aged 20 or 50—should consider whether they want to keep the business in the family, recruit an outside manager to run it, sell it to a key executive, or put it on the market. At Lavelle Company (a building materials company in Fargo, North Dakota), founder George Lavelle used these considerations as a starting point for fleshing out a detailed succession plan. He wanted to involve all six of his sons who worked in the business in succession planning, so he took them to a succession program at The Center for Family Business in Cleveland in 1980, 13 years before he retired in 1993. Shortly after, he also decided to hire and groom an outsider to serve as president when he retired. He made this move because he thought that none of his sons should be pressured to assume the top leadership role before he was ready. Lavelle also avoided the emotional task of choosing which son to appoint as successor. Instead he left the decision to an executive committee, which includes the new president and several of Lavelle's sons. In praise of his father's deliberate planning, the eldest son acknowledges, "We are probably the envy of other companies in our position."[33]

The Direction Phase

The *direction phase* of career development involves determining the type of career that employees want and the steps they must take to realize their career goals. Appropriate

Manager's Notebook

Making Career Development an Organizational Priority

1. Stress commitment to career growth and development in formal communications with employees.
2. Make career development a priority at all levels of the organization, starting at the top.
3. Provide managers with the people skills they need to develop their subordinates.
4. Emphasize that career development is a collaborative effort and that the employee must take primary responsibility for his or her own career.
5. Require managers to meet with their subordinates regularly to review personal career goals and objectives.
6. Ask managers to outline employee achievements and strengths when conducting an appraisal review session.
7. Encourage managers to collaborate with subordinates to develop a career vision.
8. Emphasize that part of the manager's job is helping employees develop career action plans.
9. Encourage employees to take advantage of continuing education and other development activities.
10. Require managers to develop collaborative rather than top-down, control-oriented working relationships with their subordinates.

Source: Adapted from Koonce, R. (1991, January–February). Management development: An investment in people. *Credit Magazine*, 16–19.

direction requires an accurate understanding of one's current position. Unless the direction phase is based on a thorough assessment of the current situation, the goals and steps identified may be inappropriate. The two major approaches to career direction are individual counseling and various information services.

Individual Career Counseling. *Individual career counseling* refers to one-on-one sessions with the goal of helping employees examine their career aspirations.[34] Topics of discussion might include the employee's current job responsibilities, interests, and career objectives. Although career counseling is frequently conducted by managers or HR staff members, some organizations, such as Coca-Cola and Disneyland, use professional counselors.[35] When line managers conduct the career counseling sessions, the HR department generally monitors the sessions' effectiveness and provides assistance to the managers in the form of training, suggested counseling formats, and the like.

There are several advantages to having managers conduct career counseling sessions with their employees. First, managers are probably more aware of their employees' strengths and weaknesses than anyone else. Second, knowing that managers understand their employees' career development concerns can foster an environment of trust and commitment.

Unfortunately, assigning career counseling responsibility to managers does not guarantee that the task will be carried out carefully. As with performance appraisal and many other important HR activities, managers may treat employee career development simply as a paper-shuffling exercise unless top management signals its strong support for development activities. If managers only go through the motions, there is likely to be a negative impact on employee attitudes, productivity, and profits.

The Manager's Notebook titled "Making Career Development an Organizational Priority" lists ten actions that organizations and managers can take to ensure that employees see career development as an important activity. Together, these actions create an organizational culture that places a priority on development. The first step—emphasizing commitment to development in formal communications—can be a refreshing change for employees, many of whom are accustomed to formal communications that deal only with what is expected of them.

Information Services. As their name suggests, information services provide career development information to employees. Determining what to do with this information is largely the employee's responsibility. This approach makes sense given the diversity of interests and aspirations in today's organizations.

The most commonly provided information services are job-posting systems, skills inventories, career paths, and career resource centers.

job-posting system
A system in which an organization announces job openings to all employees on a bulletin board, in a company newsletter, or through a phone recording or computer system.

- **Job-posting systems** are a fairly easy and direct way of providing employees with information on job openings. The jobs available in an organization are announced ("posted") on a bulletin board, in a company newsletter, or through a phone recording or computer system. This is the practice at 3M and at NCR, the AT&T company that develops information systems and products.[36] Whatever the media used for the posting, it is important that all employees have access to the list. All postings should include clear descriptions of both the job's specifications and the criteria that will be used to select among the applicants. Such information helps employees determine whether they are qualified for the position. In addition, information on how the criteria will be applied to fill the position should be supplied. Doing so alleviates employees' fears that selection may be a political process.

Job-posting systems have the advantage of reinforcing the notion that the organization promotes from within.[37] This belief not only motivates employees to maintain and improve their performance but also tends to reduce turnover.

- **Skills inventories** are company-maintained records with such information as employees' abilities, skills, knowledge, and education.[38] The company can use this comprehensive, centralized HR information system to get an overall picture of its work force's training and development needs, as well as to identify existing talent in one department that may be more productively employed in another.

  Skills inventories can prove valuable for employees as well. Feedback regarding how they stack up against other employees can encourage them to improve their skills or seek out other positions that better match their current skill levels.

skills inventory
A company-maintained record of employees' abilities, skills, knowledge, and education.

- **Career paths** provide valuable information regarding the possible directions and career opportunities available in an organization. A career path presents the steps in a possible career and a plausible timetable for accomplishing them. Just as a variety of paths may lead to the same job, so may starting from the same job lead to very different outcomes. Figure 9–5 provides an example of alternative career paths that a busperson in the hotel business might follow.

  To be realistic, career paths must specify the qualifications necessary to proceed to the next step and the minimum length of time employees must spend at each step to obtain the necessary experience. This information could be generated by computer.

  Figure 9–6 on page 280 presents examples of two survey forms that might be used to collect career path information. Form A asks employees to indicate how important certain

career path
A chart showing the possible directions and career opportunities available in an organization; it presents the steps in a possible career and a plausible timetable for accomplishing them.

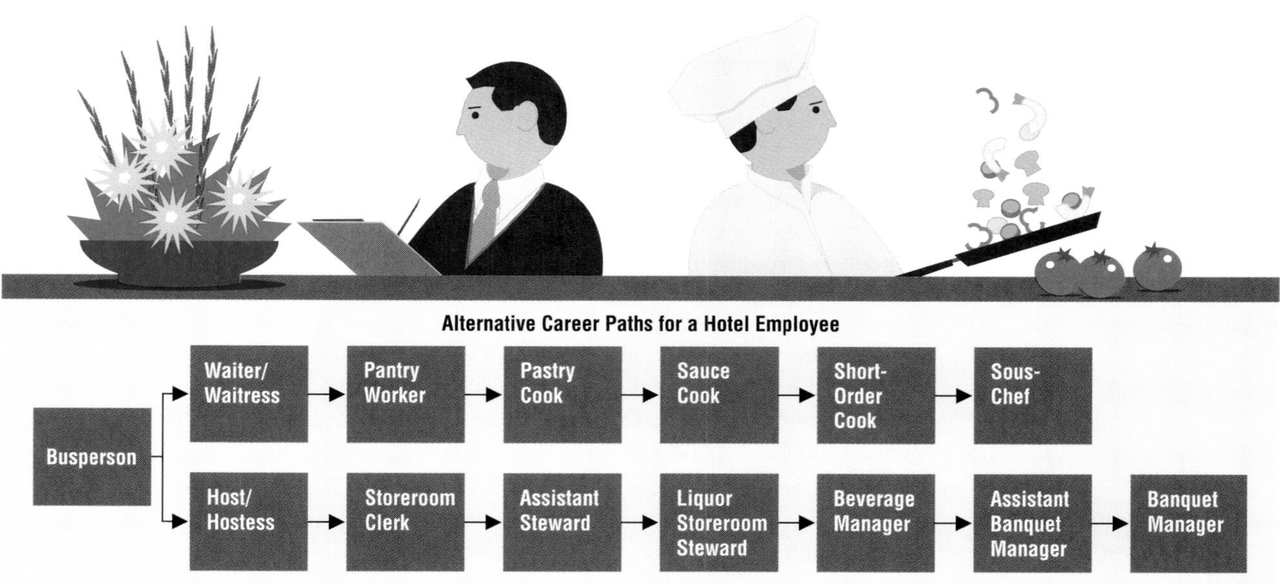

FIGURE 9-5

Alternative Career Paths for a Hotel Employee

This is a generic example of alternative career paths. Actual career paths should specify a time frame for each job.

Form A: Skill Requirements

Instructions: A list of various skills that apply to various jobs is presented below. Use the scale provided to indicate the extent to which each skill is applicable to your current position.

	Circle the Most Appropriate Number			
Skills	**Not applicable**	**Somewhat desirable/ useful at times**	**Very desirable but not essential**	**Critical—could not perform job without it**
1. Determine daily/forecasted production and service equipment requirements.	1	2	3	4
2. Clean guest rooms.	1	2	3	4
3. Set up, break down, and change over function rooms.	1	2	3	4
4. Handle security problems.	1	2	3	4
5. Clean public areas/restrooms.	1	2	3	4
6. Assist in menu development.	1	2	3	4
7. Register/preregister guests into hotel.	1	2	3	4
8. Participate in the preparation of sauces, soups, stews, and special dishes.	1	2	3	4
9. Prepare and serve salads, fruit cocktails, fruits, juices, and so on.	1	2	3	4
10. Participate in the rating of meats and other dishes.	1	2	3	4
11. Care for, clean, and distribute laundry items.	1	2	3	4

(continued)

FIGURE 9-6
Two Career Path Information Forms

skills are for the performance of their job. The skills included on the form can be determined by examining job-analysis information and by interviewing individual employees. Employee responses can then be used to develop lists of critical and desirable skills for each job. The abbreviated list of skills in Form A is based on jobs in the hotel industry.

Form B asks employees to judge the extent to which experience in other jobs in the organization is needed to perform their current job adequately. The lowest-level jobs, which still involve the skill requirements uncovered with the use of Form A, would not require previous job experience within the organization. Higher-level or more complex jobs would likely require more job experience.

career resource center
A collection of career development materials such as workbooks, tapes, and texts.

A **career resource center** is a collection of career development materials such as workbooks, tapes, and texts. These resources might be maintained by the HR department, either in its offices or in an area that is readily accessible to employees. Companies with many locations might publicize the availability of these materials and lend them to employees who express interest. Some colleges and universities maintain career resource centers, and many consulting firms (particularly those specializing in employee outplacement) provide career development materials as well. Career resource centers can help people identify for themselves their strengths and weaknesses, career options, and educational and training opportunities.

Form B: Experience Requirements

Instructions: A list of work experience by job titles is presented below. Use the scale provided to indicate for each item: (a) how important previous experience in this work is for the successful performance of your current job duties; and (b) the amount of experience that constitutes adequate training or exposure so that you are able to function efficiently in your current position.

	Circle the Most Appropriate Number							
	Importance of Requirement			**Minimium Experience**				
Work Experience	Not very important	Very desirable but not essential	Critical—could not perform job without it	0–6 months	7–11 months	1–2 years	3–5 years	6+ years
1. *Storeroom Clerk*: Accurately compute daily food costs by assembling food invoices, totaling food requisitions, taking monthly inventory of food storeroom, and so on.	1	2	3	1	2	3	4	5
2. *Liquor Storeroom Steward*: Maintain adequate levels of alcoholic beverages and related supplies; properly receive, store, and issue them to user departments.	1	2	3	1	2	3	4	5
3. *Pantry Worker:* Prepare and serve to waiters salads, fruit cocktails, fruit juices, and so on.	1	2	3	1	2	3	4	5
4. *Pastry Cook:* Prepare mixes for baking cakes, pies, soufflés, and so on.	1	2	3	1	2	3	4	5
5. *Short-Order Cook:* Prepare short-order foods in assigned restaurant areas.	1	2	3	1	2	3	4	5
6. *Sous Chef:* Assist Executive Chef in all areas of kitchen production; directly supervise the operations of the kitchen in his or her absence.	1	2	3	1	2	3	4	5
7. *Waiter or Waitress:* Take food and beverage orders from customers and serve them in a restaurant or lounge.	1	2	3	1	2	3	4	5
8. *Beverage Manager:* Supervise and schedule personnel as required and maintain budgeted liquor cost and supplies for the lounge and/or banquet functions.	1	2	3	1	2	3	4	5
9. *Assistant Banquet Manager:* Assist in the coordination and successful completion of all banquet functions, such as coordinating staffing requirements, ensuring that function room is properly set and tidied, and keeping banquet manager fully informed of all problems or unusual matters.	1	2	3	1	2	3	4	5

FIGURE 9-6
continued

The Development Phase

Meeting the requirements necessary to move up in an organization can require a great deal of growth and self-improvement. The *development phase,* which involves taking actions to create and increase skills to prepare for future job opportunities, is meant to foster this growth and self-improvement. The most common development programs offered by organizations are mentoring, coaching, job rotation, and tuition assistance.

mentoring
A developmentally oriented relationship between senior and junior colleagues or peers that involves advising, role modeling, sharing contacts, and giving general support.

Mentoring. **Mentoring** is a developmentally oriented relationship between senior and junior colleagues or peers. Mentoring relationships, which can occur at all levels and in all areas of an organization, generally involve advising, role modeling, sharing contacts, and giving general support. Mentoring can be either voluntary and informal or involuntary and formal. Informal mentoring is generally more effective than mentoring done solely as a formal responsibility,[39] though there are situations in which a formal mentoring program may be the better choice.

Mentoring has been found to make a real difference in careers, with executives who were mentored early in their careers tending to make more money at a younger age and more likely to follow a career plan than those who were not mentored. For mentors, particularly those nearing retirement, the mentoring role can offer new challenges and reignite enthusiasm and motivation.

There are, it should be noted, some problems with this kind of development program. Women employees are often reluctant to initiate a relationship with a potential male mentor because such an appeal may be misconstrued as a sexual advance. And with the increasing attention being paid to sexual harassment in the workplace, male managers may be even more hesitant to take on a female protégé. Formal mentoring programs can help counter this reluctance.

Formal programs may also offer advantages to minority employees. When the American Society of Association Executives (ASAE) found it faced an uphill battle attracting racial and ethnic minority members, it launched a mentoring program to augment the association's diversity program. The ASAE invited chief executives in the Washington, DC area to nominate minority colleagues in the developmental stages of their careers as candidates for a pilot mentoring program. Fourteen finalists were selected from among 54 applicants, then paired off with ASAE fellows and former members of the ASAE board of directors. One of the finalists, Reuben Blackwell IV, noted, "The best encouragement for young African-Americans and people of color is to see men and women like themselves succeeding in their careers." Successful formal mentoring programs, such as the ASAE's, involve much more than simply bringing mentor and protégé together. See the Manager's Notebook titled "A Short Course in Mentoring Management" for guidelines on how to increase the value of a mentoring program.[40]

While formal mentoring programs are more likely to be found at large companies, some small companies have developed more informal, but equally intensive, mentoring programs. Ed Fu, the owner of a growing computer consulting firm, Fu Associates, takes a personal interest in training a select group of talented employees. He calls it "Fu-izing." Each new hire starts out working directly with a mid-level

Manager's Notebook

A Short Course in Mentoring Management

1. Establish a clear set of goals and objectives. Mentoring goals may emphasize vocational or educational outcomes and/or social outcomes such as working with a role model or receiving support.
2. Orient the participants. Discuss the roles, responsibilities, and qualifications of both the mentor and the protégé.
3. Evaluate and match mentor personal characteristics, skills, and goals with the characteristics and needs of the protégés.
4. To increase the immediate effectiveness and subsequent value of a mentoring program, train mentors. Many people have not naturally developed the skills required for being a good mentor and thus require training in interpersonal communication.
5. Allow the mentor-protégé pair to work together on a trial or preparatory basis for a brief period. This gives them the opportunity to get acquainted and resolve logistical problems such as scheduling conflicts. After this trial period, it's important to review the roles, responsibilities, expectations, and goals of the association.
6. Monitor, evaluate, and make adjustments over the duration of the mentoring relationship.
7. Encourage protégé independence. The mentor must guide the protégé to become more and more independent and self-reliant.

Source: Adapted from Timothy J. Newby and Ashlyn Heide, The value of mentoring, *Performance Improvement Quarterly, 54,* 2–15. Copyright © 1992 by The Learning Systems Institute, Florida State University, Suite 4600, University Center, Bldg. C, Tallahassee, FL 32306-4041. Reprinted by permission from *Performance Improvement Quarterly.*

employee. After new hires have been on the job a couple of months, Fu chooses from among them designers to serve on projects for which he is the senior systems analyst.

Group Mentoring: Professional and Trade Associations. Like women and minorities in large firms, people who work for a small business or are self-employed may find it difficult to find a mentor. These people can benefit from membership in professional and trade associations. This form of "group mentoring" may complement individual mentoring or serve as a substitute for it.

Membership in professional organizations is an effective career development tool. While research is limited, it is clear that association membership provides important networking opportunities, and many a career has been advanced as a result of networking. Interestingly, skill development does not appear to be an important benefit of trade group membership, probably because most people look to their workplaces for skill development. Even though most professional organizations emphasize the educational content of their functions, the social process and networking opportunities seem to be much more important to members.[41]

Coaching. Employee *coaching* consists of ongoing, sometimes spontaneous, meetings between managers and their employees to discuss the employee's career goals and development. Working with employees to chart and implement their career goals enhances productivity and can spur a manager's own advancement. Then why do so many managers give short shrift to employee coaching? For one thing, in today's flatter organizations managers have more people under their supervision and less time to spend on developing each employee. For another, as we noted earlier, managers tend to view "employee development" as a buzz phrase unless top management clearly and strongly supports it. Finally, most managers are ill-prepared to coach employees and feel uncomfortable in the role.[42]

Coaching need not be the ordeal many managers think it is. The secret is to take advantage of what some HR consultants have called "coachable moments"—opportunities that occur in the midst of ongoing work for valuable, if brief, career counseling. Here are five common cues from employees that can open the door to coachable moments:

1. An employee demonstrates a new skill or interest.
2. An employee seeks feedback.
3. An employee expresses an interest in a change in the organization.
4. An employee is experiencing a poor job fit.
5. An employee mentions a desire for development opportunities.[43]

Sometimes employees coach one another. This was what ten African-American sales reps in Xerox's Washington, DC office began doing in 1971. One of the company's few African-American sales reps had left the company abruptly, and his colleagues, fearing that his departure had to do with race, banded together to form a survival network they called the Corporate Few. Meeting in each other's apartments, they coached one another on presentation skills, sales techniques, and pricing strategies. The three most senior sales reps tutored the others on the nuances of Xerox's culture. When the network widened and spawned similar groups at other Xerox offices, Xerox's top brass took notice. Then-president David T. Kearns learned about the network and openly supported it. Today Xerox is widely acclaimed for its acceptance and advancement of minorities. Ten percent of the company's vice presidents are African-American and the internal African-American network is thriving.[44]

Job Rotation. *Job rotation* involves assigning employees to various jobs so that they acquire a wider base of skills. Broadened job experience can give workers more flexibility to choose a career path. And, as we discussed in Chapter 8, employees can gain an even wider and more flexible experience base through cross-functional training.

In addition to offering more career options for the employee, job rotation results in a more broadly trained and skilled work force for the employer. However, job rotation programs have some disadvantages. They do not suit employees who want to maintain a narrow and specialized focus. From the organization's perspective, they can slow down operations as workers learn new skills. While the development benefits of job rotation may be high in the long run, firms should be aware of the short run and intermediate costs.

Tuition Assistance Programs. Organizations offer *tuition assistance programs* to support their employees' education and development. Tuition and other costs of educational programs (ranging from seminars, workshops, and continuing education programs to degree programs) may be entirely covered, partially covered, or covered contingent upon adequate performance in the program.

A recent survey of educational reimbursement programs revealed that 43% of these plans reimbursed less than 100% of tuition. Typically, there is a fixed limit—such as 75% of tuition—for all courses. Some companies vary the percentage of tuition funds reimbursed according to the relevance of the course to organizational goals. For instance, a business-book publishing company might encourage its editors to take professional courses related to the business, such as economics and marketing, by reimbursing these courses at 100%. However, if editors want to take courses on sign language interpretation, art history, or English literature, the company might reimburse only 50% of the tuition. 3M is an exceptional employer in this area. The company provides tuition assistance not only for courses related to an employee's current job, but also for any courses in a job-related or career-related degree program. This policy is a powerful incentive for employees to stay with 3M.[45] ▼

▸ Special Issues in Career Development

We conclude this chapter by examining three special issues related to career development. The first concerns the components of a management development program, the second pertains to development issues specific to particular age groups, and the third to the management of your personal career.

Management Development

With the urgent need for U.S. companies to become more globally competitive, management development has taken on major importance and undergone a shift in emphasis. Historically, companies viewed management development purely as a means of bringing managers up to speed on fundamental management skills (such as the basics of finance and marketing and techniques for supervising employees). A former professor comments that this approach is now "as outmoded as rear-wheel-drive V8-engine cars." Today companies are crafting *executive education* programs intended to teach the more intangible aspects of leadership. They are also using executive education to spur organizational change. For instance, an education program might be designed to transform a traditional organizational culture into one that emphasizes continuous improvement and total quality management.[46]

The general development issues we have already discussed also apply to the special case of management development. However, there are several types of programs specifically associated with managerial development. Management development systems usually incorporate more than one of these programs.

- *Company schools.* Several large companies have their own "universities" for managers. Among the most notable of these are the $10 million Galvin Center for Continuing Education in Schaumberg, Illinois, which is informally known as "Motorola University," and McDonald's "Hamburger University," located in Oak Brook, Illinois.

Company schools educate both current and potential managers in the corporate culture, management philosophy and skills, and methods of doing business.

- *University-based programs.* Many business schools offer education programs designed specifically for managers and executives. The Ivy League schools such as Harvard, Dartmouth, and Cornell have the most famous programs. Harvard's program relies heavily on the **case study method,** in which students do in-depth analyses of real-life companies. Other universities, lacking the name recognition and prestige of the Ivy League schools, often try to develop a particular emphasis that will appeal to clients. For example, the management development program at the University of Tennessee's School of Business in Knoxville is well known for its focus on quality issues.

case study method
A business school teaching method in which students do in-depth analyses of real-life companies.

- *Management training.* We looked at general training programs in Chapter 8. Management training, whether provided in a company school, university business school, or (as is most often the case) a less formal setting, often utilizes special techniques. One such technique is **role-playing,** in which participants adopt the role of a particular manager placed in a specific situation—for instance, a manager who has to give a negative performance review to an employee. **Management games** are elaborate role-playing exercises in which multiple participants enact a management situation. For instance, the Center for Creative Leadership conducts the Looking Glass simulation, in which 20 participants "manage" the Looking Glass Company over a three-day period. The participants interact with one another, both face-to-face and by phone, write memos and reports, and make decisions.

role-playing
A management development technique in which participants adopt the role of a particular manager placed in a specific situation.

management games
Elaborate role-playing exercises in which multiple participants enact a management situation.

Development through the Life Cycle

As we discussed in Chapter 4, age is a source of diversity in organizations. Like all other HR initiatives, career development programs need to be flexible enough to deal with employees at different stages of life.

Younger Employees. Younger employees starting their careers have different development needs than do middle-aged employees or employees approaching retirement. For instance, the group of approximately 50 million people who are approaching or in their 20s—the so-called baby busters—have a different attitude toward work and its significance than older people do. "The quality of working life as a career objective is far higher on the priority list [for younger workers] than in the past," says Eleanor Haller-Jorden, founder of the Paradigm Group, a Brooklyn, New York–based international HR consulting firm. This attitude may stem from the experience of looking for work in a recessionary economy, in which monetary rewards are lower. Also important to baby busters is quality of family life. In a recent survey, 62% of the 25- to 35-year-old respondents cited family-related issues as their single most important concern over the next three years.[47]

One company that has done an excellent job of recruiting and developing younger workers is Lost Arrow Corporation, parent of the outdoor outfitter Patagonia. Based in Ventura, California, Patagonia employs 450 workers, 40% of whom are in their 20s. Patagonia has a nontraditional office environment where everyone works out in the open. Employees develop their own schedules under a flexible work hours policy and can take personal leaves of absence for as long as four months each year. Patagonia believes its personal leave policy helps retain baby-buster employees who want to take extended time off in the summer for such activities as working as guides on river expeditions.[48]

Whether or not a company can offer these kinds of policies, managers should follow certain guidelines in supervising and developing younger workers:

- Do not treat younger employees as children. Instead, empower them and ask them to contribute to the organization as adults. At Patagonia, for instance, younger employees are involved in decision making, allowed to develop and implement new ideas, and encouraged to take calculated risks.

- Spend a lot of time early on with younger employees, keeping them informed, including them in meetings, taking them out to lunch, and generally showing them the ropes. Making younger workers participants in the company's mission can increase loyalty in an age group in which job hopping is the norm.
- Don't assume that baby busters have the same values or point of view as older workers. For example, traditionalists—members of the World War II generation—are very loyal to their jobs and see work as a key part of their identities. The same goes for the baby-boom generation (those born between 1946 and 1964), many of whom became workaholics in the 1980s.

Middle-Aged Employees. While younger employees are learning the ropes and trying new experiences, many baby boomers are feeling stymied in their careers. With the elimination of whole layers of management in many companies in the 1980s and 1990s, employees caught between youth and old age are facing a new type of midlife crisis. These midlifers may be competing without much hope against 30 other employees for the same promotion, but fear to leave the company because of the tight job market. This unanticipated and unwanted leveling of careers is known as **plateauing.** A typical reaction to this dilemma is that of a 46-year-old geologist who had spent 11 years with a major Houston oil company when the industry suddenly collapsed. Instructed to fire half of her close-knit team of 12 geologists, she began to fear getting the ax herself. In the weak oil market, job hopping wasn't an option, and she recalls, "I felt trapped. I would come home and go to bed earlier and earlier so I wouldn't have to think about my job."[49]

plateauing
The unanticipated and unwanted leveling of careers due to the elimination of management layers through corporate restructuring.

Some companies are taking measures to reinvigorate their diminished and demoralized ranks of midlife management employees. These measures include additional training, lateral moves, sabbaticals, and compensation based on people's contribution and skills rather than on the job they hold. We discuss the new types of compensation plans in Chapters 10 and 11, but here's one story about a worker who used a sabbatical to recharge her career:

> Helen Wilkinson had worked her way up at the BBC (British Broadcasting Corporation) to become a producer of her own half-hour films. She worked long hours for seven years to get where she was, but she wondered where her career was heading. She wanted time to recharge and a change in her environment, so she took an unpaid one-year leave from her job.
>
> During her sabbatical, Wilkinson directed a research project examining the attitudes and aspirations of young people in Great Britain. She found that many of the people she interviewed did not want to dedicate themselves to a corporate career that may not exist in the near future. The sabbatical gave Wilkinson a change of pace and an opportunity to use and develop different skills, and she ultimately decided that she could be much more creative outside a corporation rather than inside one. She is now working as a freelance writer and writing a book based on the research project she directed.[50]

Although Wilkinson decided to leave her company as a result of her sabbatical, many workers return from sabbatical feeling refreshed, recharged, and ready to take on new challenges.

Older Employees. As middle-aged employees struggle to keep their careers afloat, older workers face employment-related decisions such as whether to retire, whether to return to the work force after retirement, and if so, whether to do so as a full- or part-time employee. Labor statistics indicate that older people are staying in the work force longer than ever before, probably as a result of the protection afforded by the Age Discrimination in Employment Act.[51] Technological advances also play a role here, in that many jobs are becoming less physically demanding, allowing people to work longer. Finally, many older

Never Left the Work Force.

Labor statistics indicate that older people are staying in the work force longer than ever before. It has been estimated that one in four workers will be age 55 or older within the next 20 years.

workers need to work for financial reasons. According to the American Association of Retired Persons, nearly one fifth of the older population (those age 55 and over) are below the poverty line.

There are strong reasons for employers to retain and hire older workers.[52] One is the sheer numbers of older workers available. There are 76 million baby boomers, but only 56 million baby busters. Employers can use older workers to fill some of the jobs that normally go to younger workers. In addition, older people tend to be good workers. They often have lower accident rates, good interpersonal skills, and a strong work ethic.

Older workers will remain an important part of the employment landscape in the years to come. It has been estimated that one in four workers will be age 55 or older within the next 20 years. The following suggestions can help managers supervise an older work force effectively:[53]

- *Provide flexible work schedules and part-time jobs.* Many older workers do not want a full-time job and do not want to lose Social Security benefits. (Social Security rules set a limit on how much people can earn per year without reducing or losing their Social Security benefits.) Restructuring a job into a part-time situation may make the difference between losing the valuable experience of older workers and retaining (or hiring) them.
- *Making training relevant to older workers.* Older workers want to learn and are just as capable of learning as any other employee group. However, older workers may have a greater need to see the direct relevance of the training they're receiving. McDonald's has a McMasters program (active in California and Washington, DC) that provides hands-on, relevant training to older workers.
- *Sensitize managers and other employees to older workers.* Younger managers may be uncomfortable directing older workers. Also, other employees may have negative stereotypes about older people and their capabilities in the workplace. McDonald's and Home Shopping Network, two companies that employ many older people, provide sensitivity training to managers and other workers. These sessions focus on dispelling myths and answering questions about older employees.
- *Tailor career opportunities.* Some older workers are satisfied with a part-time job and limited responsibility, while other older workers want a challenge or a change from a career that no longer interests them. Managers need to know older workers' aspirations and preferences, then act accordingly.

- *Ask older workers to consider being mentors.* Older workers often have a wealth of valuable experience and breadth of vision. These characteristics can make them excellent mentors. Sharing their experiences and insights can be a rewarding experience for older employees, while providing younger workers with excellent development opportunities.

Self-Development

When an employer does not routinely offer development programs, it is essential that employees work out their own development plan. Employees who neglect to do this risk stagnation and obsolescence.

Figure 9-7 lists a set of suggestions to help employees enhance their own development and increase their opportunities for advancement. The *development suggestions* focus on personal growth and direction, while the *advancement suggestions* focus on the steps employees can take to improve their promotability in the organization.

Development Suggestions. The development suggestions in Figure 9–7 are based on the assumption that the organization does not offer development programs. However, these suggestions are relevant even when the company provides development activities.

1. *Create your own personal mission statement.* Like an organizational mission statement, a *personal mission statement* should indicate the business you'd like to be in and the role you'd like to play.[54] You should see the statement as changeable over time, not a commandment to which you must blindly adhere regardless of situational or personal factors.

   The process of developing the statement can reveal personal values and preferences you may not have realized you have. Once completed, the mission statement should help you set your strategic direction, clarify your priorities, and avoid investing time and energy in pursuits that are not instrumental to achieving your mission.
2. *Take responsibility for your own direction and growth.* You should not place all of your hopes in a company-provided development program. Things change, and steps in a career path can be eliminated as a result of downsizing or reorganizing. Organizations may also eliminate or replace development programs. Such changes could be devastating for people who place their future entirely in the hands of their organization.
3. *Make enhancement, rather than advancement, your priority.* Organizational flattening and downsizing mean that there will be fewer opportunities for advancement in the coming years. Even today direct upward paths to desired higher-level positions are

Development	Advancement
1. Create your own personal mission statement. 2. Take responsibility for your own direction and growth. 3. Make enhancement your priority, rather than advancement. 4. Talk to people in positions to which you aspire and get suggestions on how to proceed. 5. Set reasonable goals. 6. Make investment in yourself a priority.	1. Remember that performance in your function is important, but interpersonal performance is critical. 2. Set the right values and priorities. 3. Provide solutions, not problems. 4. Be a team player. 5. Be customer-oriented. 6. Act as if what you're doing makes a difference.

FIGURE 9-7

Suggestions for Self-Development

Source: Advancement suggestions adapted from Matejka, K., and Dunsing, R. (1993). Enhancing your advancement in the 1990s. *Management Decision, 31*, 52–54.

rare. It is best to accept this reality and search for opportunities to broaden your skills in the short term. Enhancing your skills in the short run should lead to advancement in the longer run.

4. *Talk to people in positions to which you aspire and get their suggestions on how to proceed.* People who are currently in the kind of job you desire can give you valuable insight into the job and what you must do to make it to that level. Talking to people is also a good way of networking and keeping your name on people's lips.
5. *Set reasonable goals.* As with any major undertaking, it is best to set reasonable goals along the way to your ultimate goal. Breaking your career aspirations into smaller, more manageable goals can help you take the necessary steps toward accomplishing your ultimate goal. It is important to make these minigoals reasonable and achievable. Expecting too much too soon can lead to disillusionment and frustration.
6. *Make investment in yourself a priority.* When multiple demands are made on your time and attention, it is easy to neglect self-development activities. It's important to remind yourself that these activities are actually investments in yourself and your future, and that no one else is likely to make those investments for you.

Advancement Suggestions. The advancement suggestions in Figure 9–7 focus on the steps you can take to improve your chances of being considered for advancement. The development suggestions are fundamental and provide the necessary base, but the advancement suggestions provide the necessary attitudes and organizational presence.

1. *Remember that performance in your function is important, but interpersonal performance is critical.* Advancing in an organization requires excellent interpersonal skills. The abilities to communicate (both one-on-one and to groups), to collaborate, to listen, to summarize, and to write concise reports and memos are essential to being considered a viable candidate for advancement.
2. *Set the right values and priorities.* Your worth to an organization increases after you have discovered the organization's values and priorities and aligned yourself with them. For example, some organizations place a high value on collaboration and teamwork, while others emphasize independence and individual contribution. Aligning your behavior with the organization's values improves your chances for advancement.[55]
3. *Provide solutions, not problems.* Nobody likes to hear complaints. So, rather than voicing complaints and pointing out problems, take some time to think issues through and offer potential solutions. You'll be perceived as a much more valuable member of the organization.
4. *Be a team player.* You should not try to steal the limelight for your work group's accomplishments. Rather, you should try to shine the spotlight on the group's efforts. When you do, you'll be viewed as a facilitator rather than a grandstander. However, you should be sure that those responsible for evaluating your performance know of your personal accomplishments. One way to balance these concerns is to refuse to seek public praise for your performance but not be afraid to call attention to your successes when appropriate.
5. *Be customer oriented.* Always keep in mind that anyone with whom you have an exchange is your "customer." Whether these interactions are internal or external, understanding and satisfying customer needs should be a top priority. When you take a customer-orientation approach to your job, the organization will recognize you as a high-quality representative who can be expected to accomplish things.
6. *Act as if what you're doing makes a difference.* A sure way to be overlooked for advancement is to display an apathetic or negative attitude. Not all tasks or projects to which you're assigned will spur your interest, but if you approach these activities with a positive attitude, others will see you as a contributor and a valuable team player.

Summary and Conclusions

What Is Career Development? Career development is an ongoing organized and formalized effort that focuses on developing enriched and more capable workers. It has a wider focus, longer time frame, and broader scope than training. Development must be a key business strategy if an organization is to survive in today's increasingly competitive and global business environment.

Challenges in Career Development. Before putting a career development program in place, management needs to determine (1) who will be responsible for development, (2) how much emphasis on development is appropriate, and (3) how the development needs of a diverse work force (including dual-career couples) will be met.

Meeting the Challenges of Effective Development. Career development is a continuing cycle of three phases: an assessment phase, a direction phase, and a development phase. Each phase is an important part of developing the work force.

In the assessment phase, employees' skills, interests, and values are identified. These assessments may be carried out by the workers themselves, by the organization, or by both. Self-assessment is often done through career workbooks and career-planning workshops. Organizational assessment is done through assessment centers, psychological testing, performance appraisal, promotability forecasts, and succession planning.

The direction phase involves determining the type of career that employees want and the steps they must take to make their career goals a reality. In this phase workers may receive individual career counseling or information from a variety of sources, including a job-posting system, skills inventories, career paths, and career resource centers.

The development phase involves taking actions to create and increase employees' skills and promotability. The most common development programs are mentoring, coaching, job rotation, and tuition assistance programs.

Special Issues in Career Development. Management development is a high priority in today's intensely competitive business environment. Organizations use company schools, university-based programs, and management training programs to provide employees with the skills they need to be effective managers.

Career development programs must be flexible enough to deal with employees at different stages of the life cycle. Younger employees place great importance on quality of work life and on having time off for family life. Midlife employees are subject to plateauing, the unanticipated leveling of careers that is the result of corporate restructuring and downsizing. Many older workers have entered the work force, and managers need to be aware of these workers' scheduling and training needs.

In situations where the employer does not routinely offer development programs, employees must take an active role in their own development. To do otherwise is to risk stagnation and obsolescence.

Key Terms

career development, 269
career path, 279
career resource center, 280
case study method, 285
dual-career couple, 272
job-posting system, 278
management games, 285
mentoring, 282
plateauing, 286
promotability forecast, 276
role-playing, 285
skills inventory, 279
succession planning, 276

Discussion Questions

1. Retention of top talent is a critical element in the strategy of today's leaner organizations. How can career development activities contribute to retention?
2. How would you go about retaining older workers and utilizing them to their highest potential?
3. Today's organizations are flatter and offer fewer opportunities for advancement. How do you think careers should be developed in this type of organizational environment?
4. In a recent survey of 925 men and women MBAs, it was found that "traditional" married men—those who have children and whose wives don't work—earn on average 20% more per year than family men without children and employed wives. Yet only 21% of the managers surveyed said they were in this type of traditional family structure. By contrast, 39% are in "posttraditional" family units, and these workers express greater satisfaction with their careers. What challenges do these posttraditional family units pose to company career development plans? How can companies meet these challenges?
5. People who adopt a careerist strategy focus on career advancement through political machinations rather than excellent performance. Experts have pointed out four

ways in which workers try to influence their superiors' opinions of them: favor doing (doing a favor for a superior in hopes that the favor will someday be returned), opinion conformity (agreeing with superiors in order to build trust and a relationship), other enhancement (flattery), and self-presentation (portraying oneself as having very desirable traits and motives).

In what other ways might employees try to influence their superiors' opinions of them? How can managers tell when an employee is sincere? What criteria should be used when deciding which employees to promote?

6. Companies use various tactics to encourage managers to make employee development a top priority. At Honeywell, for instance, a prestigious award worth $3,000 is given to those managers who contribute strongly to their unit's profitability, who assist the career development of at least three people, and who have excellent records as mentors of diverse employee groups. Winners gain companywide recognition as well as the financial reward. What do you think of this policy of tying financial rewards to people development? What are some other ways companies can hold managers accountable for developing those they supervise?

MINICASE 1 *Go Abroad to Get Ahead*

Gary Ellis works at Medtronic, Inc., a major producer of pacemakers and other medical devices. Gary had advanced quickly at Medtronic and everyone recognized him as someone on the management fast track. Why, then, did Medtronic ship him off to Brussels to head the company's European operations? Because global experience is increasingly part of the fast track at Medtronic and other corporations. Medtronic's CEO believes that living and working abroad for several years will be a prerequisite for successful executives in the future.

While on his assignment in Europe, Gary quickly gained a great deal of management experience. He had to confront a variety of situations and effectively deal with a wide assortment of people, including factory managers, labor leaders, and government ministers. After a couple of years Medtronic needed a corporate comptroller back in the United States and—you guessed it—Gary got the job.

Discussion Questions

1. Overseas assignments were once considered career-ending experiences, but they're now viewed as a very useful, perhaps essential, step in the development of a managerial career. However, the risk still exists that managers will be forgotten once they've been shipped overseas. What steps can managers take to minimize this risk and keep abreast of developments back home?
2. Global experiences may be a key career development experience that leads to advancement. How could you go about landing an overseas assignment for yourself? What qualities do you think a manager needs to be successful abroad?

Source: Adapted from Loeb, M. (1995). The real fast track is overseas. *Fortune, 132,* 129.

MINICASE 2 *A Résumé on the Screen*

One of the supreme on-the-job fears is having your boss come into your office while your résumé is on the computer screen. Of course, employees shouldn't conduct job-hunting activities during office hours. But should they always keep their outside job-hunting efforts secret from their employers? What happens when companies find out about concealed efforts to search for opportunities outside the company walls? The fallout can range from awkwardness and tension to firing, as this incident shows:

...Though he kept his quest secret, a job search nearly cost Christopher Hunt his post as credit manager for MLC Financial, a medical-equipment leasing company in Ridgefield, Conn. A potential employer told MLC about Mr. Hunt's search.

The division president became angry and wanted to fire Mr. Hunt for disloyalty. MLC had spent "a lot of time and effort to bring me up to speed," says Mr. Hunt, "...But I had every right to look around." He escaped the ax after his immediate supervisor pleaded with the division president. Mr. Hunt says he quit anyway a month later to take a credit director's job that paid 15% more.

Discussion Questions

1. Should companies encourage employees to tell them about their efforts to seek employment elsewhere, or should they

continued

punish employees whose job-hunting activities come to light? Explain your answer.

2. MLC's division head believed that Hunt's job search revealed disloyalty. What career development tactics could MLC have deployed to retain Hunt and win his loyalty?
3. Many of the companies discussed in this chapter have internal career resource centers in which employees can discuss their career plans with professional career counselors. Should these discussions be kept confidential or should they be made known to employees' immediate supervisors? How do you think companies can employ the services of career counselors to meet both individual and organizational needs?

Source: Reprinted from Lublin, J. S. (1993, July 28). Managing your career: A good boss may even help you find a greener pasture. *The Wall Street Journal*, B1.

CASE 1 *Family versus Career—And a Company Caught in the Middle*

Dave and Nora live in the Los Angeles area, where Dave works for a major software company. He is very motivated to put in whatever time and effort are needed to complete tasks and projects successfully. Top management recognizes his contributions as important and his prospects at the company are excellent.

Nora has been married to Dave for five years and knows how devoted he is to his career. Both of them want to start a family and agree that Los Angeles isn't where they want to raise their children. Nora, feeling that she can't wait forever to have kids, has been pressuring Dave to find a job in a more congenial area.

Understanding Nora's concerns, Dave made a couple of discreet phone calls and was soon called for an interview by a company located in a small city in the Midwest. Dave didn't know what to say when the company made him an offer. The job pays less than his present job and offers fewer opportunities for advancement, but the area is the kind of environment he and Nora want. He knows Nora is thrilled at the prospect of the move, yet he can't help feeling sad. How can he simply walk away from all he has invested in his career at his present company? Maybe there is more to life than his career, but he is already depressed and he hasn't even quit yet.

When Dave told his boss, Terri, about the new job offer, Terri was shocked. Dave is a central figure in the company's plans for the next couple of years, and his expertise is indispensable on a couple of important projects. Terri feels that Dave has blindsided the company. Things will be a mess for a long while if he leaves. But what can the company do to keep him if money isn't the issue?

Critical Thinking Questions

1. What preventive measures could Dave's company have taken to avoid the crisis it is faced with? What can the company do now?
2. Should Dave's company involve Nora in any of its attempts to retain Dave? How?
3. Should Dave's company implement any career development programs after this crisis passes? What kind would you recommend? Why?

Cooperative Learning Exercises

4. Ask students who have seen someone in their family leave a job because of dual-career or family issues to describe the circumstances to the class and address what the organization could have done to avoid losing the person.
5. Besides a husband or wife, who else can have a significant influence on a person's career decision? Brainstorm the possibilities with your partner or team and share your ideas with the class. How might the organization deal with these people?

CASE 2 *Stuck at the Bottom?*

Sam has been an employee at Consumer Electronics for three years. He has worked in the warehouse since his first day with CE and has seen most of his coworkers get promoted to sales and beyond. Consumer Electronics has a promotion-from-within policy. All of the current sales staff started working in the warehouse. Before they moved into sales, though, most of them took courses at a local community college in sales and marketing, and some even took courses in electronics repair and maintenance. The company does not formally require such courses of its salespeople and does not reimburse them for their tuition costs.

Sam does not think he needs these courses. He has tinkered with electronic devices since he was in grade school, so he is sure the electronics courses would be a waste of time. Furthermore, he worked in sales at a furniture retailer for a year and a half before he got this job and was the top seller during his last quarter there. He feels he is qualified for a sales job right now.

When he was given the opportunity to work on the loading dock, Sam turned it down because it was still a warehouse job. He also applied for higher-level jobs in the company but never got them. He had hoped to be a sales manager by now, but here he is, still in the warehouse. Now he finds it hard to care much about his job or the organization, and he keeps wondering if he will be fired.

Critical Thinking Questions

1. What do you think Consumer Electronics should do about Sam's career aspirations?
2. If you were Sam's supervisor, what would you say to him and what would you do?
3. If you were a consultant to Consumer Electronics, what advice would you give top management about the company's lack of a formal development program for employees?

Cooperative Learning Exercises

4. At least part of the problem appears to be that Sam isn't taking responsibility for his own development and advancement. With your partner or group, identify how Sam can do more to advance his own career. Select the best ideas generated and share them with the class.
5. Do you think it's possible for all people to learn the skills necessary to develop and advance themselves? Or is this an area in which some people excel and others don't? Have the class choose sides on this issue and select teams to debate the question.

HRM Simulation 

As discussed in the chapter, development tends to be a long-term issue. Which training and development choices in the simulation (Incident F) tend to be development issues? Which ones do you think the company should provide?

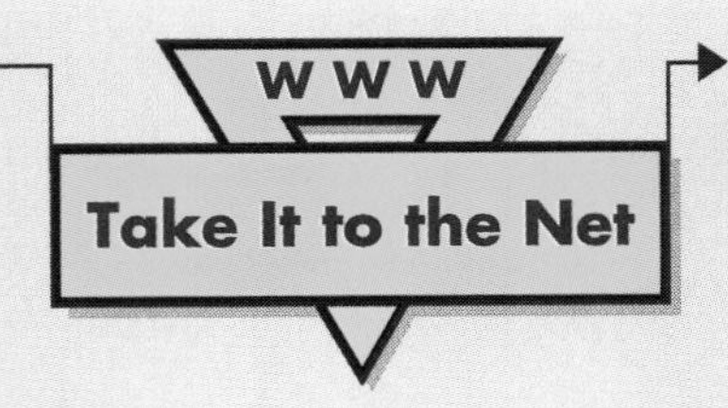

We invite you to visit the Gómez-Mejía/Balkin/Cardy page on the Prentice Hall Web site:

http://www.prenhall.com/gomez

You can also visit the Web sites for these companies, featured within this chapter:

Bell Labs	http://www.bellLabs.com
British Broadcasting Company	http://bbc.co.uk
British Petroleum	http://www.bp.com
Coca-Cola	http://www.cocacola.com

Endnotes

1. Leibowitz, Z. B. (1987). Designing career development systems: Principles and practices. *Human Resource Planning, 10,* 195–207.
2. *Id.*
3. Gutteridge, T. G., Leibowitz, Z. B., and Shore, J. E. (1993). *Organizational career development: Benchmarks for building a world-class workforce.* San Francisco: Jossey-Bass.
4. Breuer, N. L. (1995). Minimize distractions for maximum output. *Personnel Journal, 74,* 71–76.
5. Arkin, A. (1996). Lessons from life. *People Management, 2,* 41.
6. Morgan, D. C. (1977). Career development programs. *Personnel, 54,* 23–27.
7. Gutteridge, T., and Otte, F. (1983). Organizational career development: What's going on out there? *Training and Development, 37,* 22–26; Hall, D. T. (1986). An overview of current career development, theory, research, and practice. In D. T. Hall & Associates (Eds.), *Career development in organizations,* 1–20, San Francisco: Jossey-Bass; and Leibowitz, Z. B., and Schlossberg, N. K. (1981). Designing career development programs in organizations: A systems approach. In D. H. Montross and C. J. Shinkman (Eds.), *Career development in the 1980s,* 277–291, Springfield, IL: Charles C. Thomas.
8. Russell, J. E. A. (1991). Career development interventions in organizations. *Journal of Vocational Behavior, 38,* 237–287.
9. Koonce, R. (1991, January–February). Management development: An investment in people. *Credit Magazine,* 16–19.
10. Steele, B., Bratkovich, J. R., and Rollins, T. (1990). Implementing strategic redirection through the career management system. *Human Resource Planning, 13,* 241–263.
11. Tucker, R., and Moravec, M. (1992, February). Do-it-yourself career development. *Training Magazine,* 48–52.
12. *Id.*
13. Feldman, D. C., and Weitz, B. A. (1991). From the invisible hand to the gladhand: Understanding a careerist orientation to work. *Human Resource Management, 30,* 237–257.
14. Aryee, S., Wyatt, T., and Stone, R. (1996). Early career outcomes of graduate employees: The effect of mentoring and ingratiation. *Journal of Management Studies, 33,* 95–118.
15. Kalish, B. B. (1992, March). Dismantling the glass ceiling. *Management Review,* 64; and Hawkins, B. (1991, September 8). Career-limiting bias found at low job levels. *Los Angeles Times Magazine,* 33.
16. *Training & Development.* (1993, September). Advancing women in the workplace, 9–10.
17. Lopez, J. A. (1996, May 5). New era for working parents. *Arizona Republic,* AI, 30.
18. Bourne, K. (1992). Companies offer career management for couples. *Journal of Compensation and Benefits, 7,* 32–36.
19. *Id.*
20. Bures, A. L., Henderson, D., Mayfield, J., Mayfield, M., and Worley, J. (1995). The effects of spousal support and gender on workers' stress and job satisfaction: A cross national investigation of dual career couples. *Journal of Applied Business Research, 12,* 52–58.
21. Scarpello, V. G., and Ledvinka, J. (1988). *Personnel/human resource management: Environment and functions.* Boston: PWS-Kent; and Russell, 1991.
22. Haskell, J. R. (1993, February). Getting employees to take charge of their careers. *Training & Development,* 51–54.
23. Anastasi, A. (1976). *Psychological testing* (4th ed.). New York: Macmillan.
24. Gutteridge, Leibowitz, and Shore, 1993.
25. Engelbrecht, A. S., and Fischer, A. H. (1995). The managerial performance implications of a developmental assessment center process. *Human Relations, 48,* 387–404.
26. Scarpello and Ledvinka, 1988.
27. Morgan, M. A., Hall, D. T., and Martier, A. (1979). Career development strategies in industry—Where are we and where should we be? *Personnel, 56,* 13–30.
28. Rocco, J. (1991, August). Computers track high-potential managers. *HRMagazine,* 66–68.
29. Howard, A. (1986). College experiences and managerial performance. *Journal of Applied Psychology, 71,* 530–552.
30. Judge, T. A., Cable, D. M., Boudreau, J. W., and Bretz, R. D. (1995). An empirical investigation of the predictors of executive career success. *Personnel Psychology, 48,* 485–519.
31. Baehr, M. E., and Orban, J. A. (1989). The role of intellectual abilities and personality characteristics in determining success in higher-level positions. *Journal of Vocational Behavior, 35,* 270–287.
32. Garrett, E. M. (1994, April). Going the distance. *Small Business Reports,* 22–30.
33. *Id.*
34. Russell, 1991.
35. Gutteridge, T. (1986). Organizational career development systems: The state of the practice. In D. T. Hall & Associates (Eds.), *Career development in organizations,* 50–94. San Francisco: Jossey-Bass.
36. Gutteridge, Leibowitz, and Shore, 1993.
37. Gutteridge, 1986.
38. Russell, 1991.
39. Noe, R. A. (1988). An investigation of the determinants of successful assigned mentoring relationships. *Personnel Psychology, 41,* 457–479.
40. *Association Management.* (1993, May). Mentor program promotes opportunity for all, 166.
41. Dansky, K. H. (1996). The effect of group mentoring on career outcomes. *Group & Organization Management, 21,* 5–21.
42. Kaye, B. (1993, December). Career development—Anytime, anyplace. *Training & Development,* 46–49.
43. *Id.*
44. Lesly, E. (1993, November 29). Sticking it out at Xerox by sticking together. *Business Week,* 77.
45. Georgemiller, D. (1992, Winter). Making the grades: The ABC's of educational reimbursement. *The Human Resources Professional,* 16–19.
46. O'Reilly, B. (1993, April 8). How executives learn now. *Fortune,* 52–58.
47. Solomon, C. M. (1992, March). Managing the baby busters. *Personnel Journal, 52,* 54–59.
48. *Id.*
49. Bryant, M. (1990, August). When employees "plateau." *Business & Health,* 46–47.
50. Wilkinson, H. (1995). Looking down the road not taken. *Working Woman, 20,* 45, 60.
51. Solomon, C. M. (1995). Unlock the potential of older workers. *Personnel Journal, 74,* 56–66.
52. *Id.*
53. Adapted from *id.*
54. Morrisey, G. L. (1992, November). Your personal mission statement: A foundation for your future. *Training & Development,* 71–74.
55. Matejka, K., and Dunsing, R. (1993). Enhancing your advancement in the 1990s. *Management Decision, 31,* 52–54.

VIDEO CASE

Emotional Intelligence: Success Takes More Than Academic Intelligence

ABCNEWS

To become successful, people need more than academic intelligence. For example, very bright people can be utter failures when it comes to interacting with others in a group or team situation. Very often, "smart" may not make up for a lack of social skills.

The concept of "emotional intelligence" is based on the recent work of Daniel Goleman, who published a book on the subject in 1994. According to Goleman, there are four basic "people skills" that are separate from academic intelligence but important to success. These components of emotional intelligence are:

- Delaying your gratification.
- Controlling your emotions.
- Dealing constructively with your anger.
- Reading other people's feelings.

A very simple test used to assess the ability to delay gratification has been found to relate to success 25 years later. Children are left alone in a room with marshmallows or M&Ms. They can either wait five minutes or eat the candy immediately. They are told that if they wait, they will get more candy. Those children who weren't able to control their impulses and ate the candy immediately were more likely to be in jail 25 years later.

Like the ability to delay gratification, the ability to control our emotions and deal with anger constructively is critical to success. Some people aren't able to control their anger and are prone to fits of temper. However, emotional outbursts usually aren't very adaptive and can cause problems when interacting with others.

While we may not reflect on it much, the ability to read other's feelings is also a critical skill. People who are better able to correctly read the emotions displayed in the faces of others are more successful in the workplace and tend to have more friends.

Emotional intelligence is a necessary qualification for being a good team player in today's business enviroment. For example, emotional intelligence made an important difference in the performance of Bell Labs in New Jersey. Bell engineers whose performance was rated the highest by their peers were found to have high levels of emotional intelligence. The highly rated engineers were simply better at relating to others.

Can emotional intelligence be learned? The answer seems to be "yes." Emotional intelligence seems to be more of a set of skills than an innate capacity. As such, it should be something that people can learn and develop.

Discussion Questions

1. How important do you think emotional intelligence is in the workplace?
2. Do you think organizations should be concerned with their employees' emotional intelligence? What steps should an organization take to increase the level of emotional intelligence in its work force?
3. Do you think emotional intelligence can be measured in the workplace? How? Should it be included in the appraisal of workers? Why or why not?

After reading this chapter, you should be able to deal more effectively with the following challenges:

1 ▶ **Identify** the compensation policies and practices that are most appropriate for a particular firm.

2 ▶ **Weigh** the strategic advantages and disadvantages of the different compensation options.

3 ▶ **Establish** a job-based compensation scheme that is internally consistent and linked to the labor market.

4 ▶ **Understand** the difference between a compensation system in which employees are paid for the skills they use and one in which they are paid for the job they hold.

5 ▶ **Make** compensation decisions that comply with the legal framework.

10 Managing Compensation

Money, Moola, Dinero, Dough, Legal Tender. While money is not the only part of an employee's total compensation package, it is the main component. Money is not the *only* thing that motivates employees, but many studies have shown that it is indeed a very important motivator. Employees work harder, and are more dedicated to their jobs, when they perceive their compensation to be fair and competitive.

http://www.ahrm.org/aca/aca.htm

American Compensation Association

The American Compensation Association is a professional organization composed of practitioners, consultants, and academics engaged in the design, implementation, and management of employee compensation and benefits programs. The ACA's Web site provides information on compensation-related publications, workshops, conferences, satellite broadcasts, and opportunities to receive professional certification.

Sigma, Inc. is a medium-sized biotechnology firm specializing in genetic engineering. The firm was founded in 1993 by a college professor, Dr. Roger Smith, who left academia to start a new company in a promising young field. The venture has been a resounding success, with Sigma's stock price increasing a hundredfold over its original value and its number of employees reaching 350. Smith is still Sigma's chief executive officer and continues to be actively involved in all hiring and pay decisions. He repeatedly tells his line managers that Sigma "will pay whatever it takes to hire the best talent in the market."

During the past year Smith has noticed an erosion in Sigma's "family atmosphere" and an increase in the number of dissatisfied employees. Despite Sigma's generous compensation package, pay appears to be a major concern. There have been three pay-related complaints during the past week alone, and Smith suspects this is only the tip of the iceberg. The first complaint came from a computer programmer who has been with Sigma for five years. He is upset that another programmer was recently hired at a salary 15% higher than his. Smith explained that such starting salaries are necessary to attract top experienced programmers from other firms. The second complaint came from a software engineer who feels that Sigma's best technical people—the lifeblood of a biotechnology firm—are discriminated against in pay because supervisors (who, in his words, are often "failed engineers") receive 30% more pay. The third complaint was filed by a head secretary who has been with Sigma from the start. She is angry that janitors are getting more money than she is, and she is not satisfied with Smith's explanation that it is difficult to hire and retain reliable people who are willing to clean up and dispose of dangerous chemicals.

Sigma's experience raises several important questions that firms face in designing and administering compensation programs. Among these questions:

- Who should be responsible for making salary decisions?
- Should pay be dictated by what other employers are paying?
- What types of activities should be rewarded with higher salaries?
- What criteria should be used to determine salaries?
- Which employee groups should receive special treatment when scarce pay resources are allocated?

The way a firm handles these and other compensation-related questions has a direct impact on its ability to attract, retain, and motivate employees. It also has a direct bearing on the extent to which labor costs detract from or contribute to business objectives and profitability.

Managers need to understand the issues related to the design and management of a compensation system. In the first part of this chapter, we define the components of compensation and present the nine criteria used in developing a compensation plan. Next, we describe the process of designing a compensation plan. We conclude the chapter with a discussion of the legal and regulatory influences on employee compensation.

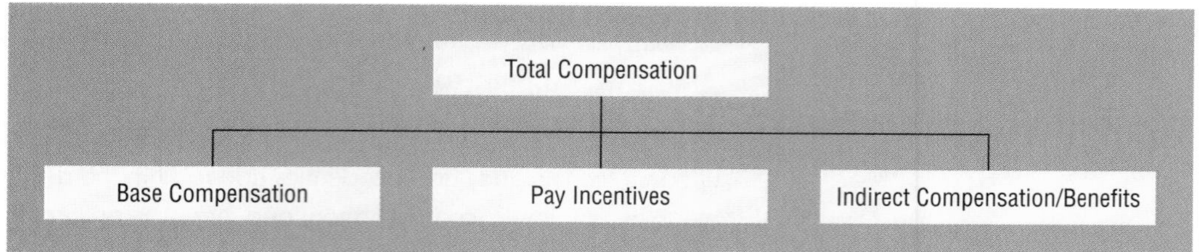

FIGURE 10–1

The Elements of Total Compensation

▸ What Is Compensation?

total compensation
The package of quantifiable rewards an employee receives for his or her labors. Includes three components: base compensation, pay incentives, and indirect compensation/benefits.

base compensation
The fixed pay an employee receives on a regular basis, either in the form of a salary or as an hourly wage.

pay incentive
A program designed to reward employees for good performance.

As Figure 10–1 shows, an employee's **total compensation** has three components. The relative proportion of each (known as the *pay mix*) varies extensively by firm.[1] The first and (in most firms) largest element of total compensation is **base compensation**, the fixed pay an employee receives on a regular basis, either in the form of a salary (for example, a weekly or monthly paycheck) or as an hourly wage. The second component of total compensation is **pay incentives**, programs designed to reward employees for good performance. These incentives come in many forms (including bonuses and profit sharing) and are the focus of Chapter 11. The last component of total compensation is *benefits*, sometimes called *indirect compensation*. Benefits encompass a wide variety of programs (for example, health insurance, vacations, and unemployment compensation), the costs of which averaged 41% of workers' compensation packages in 1994.[2] A special category of benefits called *perquisites*, or perks, are available only to employees with some special status in the organization, usually upper-level managers. Common perks are a company car, a special parking place on company grounds, and company-paid country club memberships. Chapter 12 discusses benefit programs in detail.

Compensation is the single most important cost in most firms. Personnel costs are as high as 60% of total costs in certain types of manufacturing environments, and even higher in some service organizations (for example, labor costs amount to approximately 80% of the U.S. Postal Service's budget). This means that the effectiveness with which compensation is allocated can make a significant difference in gaining or losing a competitive edge. For instance, a high-tech firm that provides generous compensation to managerial and marketing personnel but underpays its research and development staff may lose its ability to innovate because competitors constantly pirate away its best talent. Thus, *how much* is paid and *who* gets paid what are crucial strategic issues for the firm; they affect the cost side of all financial statements and determine the extent to which the firm realizes a low or high return on its payroll dollars.[3]

Building Managerial Skills: ▸ Designing a Compensation System

An employee's paycheck is certainly important for its purchasing power. In most societies, however, a person's earnings also serve as an indicator of power and prestige and are tied to feelings of self-worth. In other words, compensation affects a person economically, sociologically, and psychologically.[4] For this reason, mishandling compensation issues is likely to have a strong negative impact on employees and, ultimately, on the firm's performance.[5]

The wide variety of pay policies and procedures presents managers with a two-pronged challenge: to design a compensation system that (1) enables the firm to achieve its strategic objectives and (2) is molded to the firm's unique characteristics and environment.[6] We discuss the criteria for developing a compensation plan in the sections that follow and summarize these options in Figure 10–2. Although we present each of these as an either/or choice for the sake of simplicity, most firms institute policies that fall somewhere between the two poles.

Internal versus External Equity

Fair pay is pay that employees generally view as equitable. There are two forms of pay equity. **Internal equity** refers to the perceived fairness of the pay structure within a firm. **External equity** refers to the perceived fairness of pay relative to what other employers are paying for the same type of labor.

internal equity
The perceived fairness of the pay structure within a firm.

external equity
The perceived fairness in pay relative to what other employers are paying for the same type of labor.

In considering internal versus external equity, managers can use two basic models: the distributive justice model and the labor market model.

The Distributive Justice Model. The *distributive justice model* of pay equity holds that employees exchange their contributions or input to the firm (skills, effort, time, and so forth) for a set of outcomes. Pay is one of the most important of these outcomes, but nonmonetary rewards like a company car may also be significant. This social-psychological perspective suggests that employees are constantly (1) comparing what they bring to the firm to what they receive in return and (2) comparing this input/outcome ratio with that of other employees within the firm. Employees will think they are fairly paid when the ratio of their inputs and outputs is equivalent to that of other employees whose job demands are similar to their own.

Some employees compare their input/outcome ratio to that of employees in other firms, but most compare themselves to their peers in the same organization. From this perspective, then, the compensation system's key task is to ensure that salaries and wages are set so that employees perceive a fair input/outcome balance within the firm and, to a lesser extent, outside it.

1. **Internal versus External Equity** Will the compensation plan be perceived as fair within the company, or will it be perceived as fair relative to what other employers are paying for the same type of labor?
2. **Fixed versus Variable Pay** Will compensation be paid monthly on a fixed basis—through base salaries—or will it fluctuate depending on such preestablished criteria as performance and company profits?
3. **Performance versus Membership** Will compensation emphasize performance and tie pay to individual or group contributions, or will it emphasize membership in the organization—logging in a prescribed number of hours each week and progressing up the organizational ladder?
4. **Job versus Individual Pay** Will compensation be based on how the company values a particular job, or will it be based on how much skill and knowledge an employee brings to that job?
5. **Egalitarianism versus Elitism** Will the compensation plan place most employees under the same compensation system (egalitarianism), or will it establish different plans by organizational level and/or employee group (elitism)?
6. **Below-Market versus Above-Market Compensation** Will employees be compensated at below-market levels, at market levels, or at above-market levels?
7. **Monetary versus Nonmonetary Awards** Will the compensation plan emphasize motivating employees through monetary rewards like pay and stock options, or will it stress nonmonetary rewards such as interesting work and job security?
8. **Open versus Secret Pay** Will employees have access to information about other workers' compensation levels and how compensation decisions are made (open pay), or will this knowledge be withheld from employees (secret pay)?
9. **Centralization versus Decentralization of Pay Decisions** Will compensation decisions be made in a tightly controlled central location, or will they be delegated to managers of the firm's units?

FIGURE 10–2
The Nine Criteria for Developing a Compensation Plan

The Labor Market Model. According to the *labor market model* of pay equity, the wage rate for any given occupation is set at the point where the supply of labor equals the demand for labor in the marketplace (W_1 in Figure 10–3). In general, the less employers are willing to pay (low demand for labor) and the lower the pay workers are willing to accept for a given job (high supply of labor), the lower the wage rate for that job.[7]

The actual situation is a great deal more complicated than this basic model suggests, however. People base their decisions about what jobs they are willing to hold on many more factors than pay. The organization's location and the job's content and demands are just two of these factors. Moreover, the pay that an employer offers is based on many factors besides the number of available people with the skills and abilities to do the job. These factors include historical wage patterns, the presence or absence of unions, and internal organizational politics. A complete exploration of this topic is beyond the scope of this book. However, the basic point of the labor market model is that external equity is achieved when the firm pays its employees the "going rate" for the type of work they do.[8] A firm cannot stray too far in either direction from the market wage. If it offers pay much below the going rate, it may be unable to attract and retain qualified workers. If it pays much more than the going rate, it may be unable to charge competitive prices for its product because its labor costs are too high.

Balancing Equity. Ideally, a firm should try to establish both internal and external pay equity, but these objectives are often at odds. For instance, universities sometimes pay new assistant professors more than senior faculty who have been with the institution for a decade or more,[9] and firms sometimes pay recent engineering graduates more than engineers who have been on board for many years.[10]

You may wonder why the senior employees accept lower pay instead of leaving and competing for higher-paying positions elsewhere. Senior faculty are usually tenured, which means they would give up job security if they went to another university. Furthermore, both college professors and engineers work in fields where the knowledge base is constantly changing, making recent graduates (who are more likely to be aware of new developments in their field) somewhat more valuable employees.

In addition to balancing internal and external equity, many firms have to determine which employee groups' pay will be adjusted upward to meet (or perhaps exceed) market rates and which groups' pay will remain at or under market. This decision is generally based on each group's relative importance to the firm. For example, marketing employees tend to be paid more in firms that are trying to expand their market share and less in older firms that have a well-established product with high brand recognition.

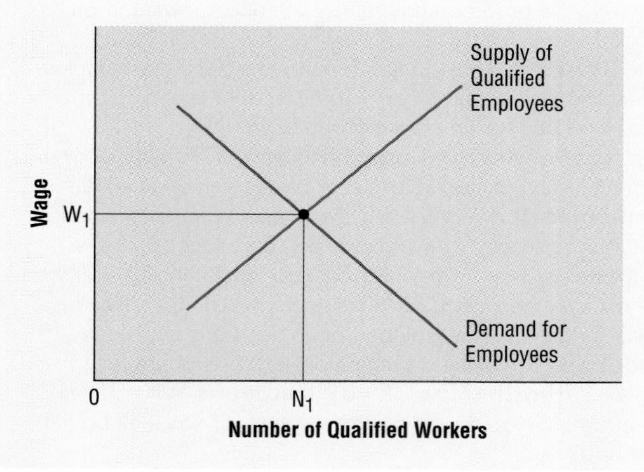

FIGURE 10–3
The Labor Market Model

In general, emphasizing external equity is more appropriate for newer, smaller firms in a rapidly changing market. These firms often have a high need for innovation to remain competitive and are dependent on key individuals to achieve their business objectives.[11] Much of the relatively new high-tech industry fits this description. A greater emphasis on internal equity is more appropriate for older, larger, well-established firms. These firms often have a mature product, employees who plan to spend most of their career with the firm, and technology and jobs that don't change often. Much of the utilities industry fits this description.

Fixed versus Variable Pay

Firms can choose to pay a high proportion of total compensation in the form of base pay (for example, a predictable monthly paycheck) or in the form of variable pay that fluctuates according to some preestablished criterion. For example, CitiBank pays its employees (except for those at the highest executive ranks) almost exclusively in the form of fixed compensation or base pay. In contrast, Anderson Windows pays its employees up to 50% of their total compensation in the form of a bonus based on company profits for the year.

There is a great deal of variation in the way firms answer the fixed versus variable pay question. On average, 5% of an employee's pay in the United States is variable. This compares to 20% in Japan. However, the range is huge in both countries—from 0% up to 70%. For select employee groups (such as sales), variable pay can be as high as 100%.[12]

As we discuss in Chapter 11, variable compensation takes many forms, including individual bonuses, team bonuses, profit sharing, and stock ownership programs. The higher the proportion of variable pay, the more *risk sharing* there is between the employee and the firm. This means a trade-off between income security and the potential for higher earnings.[13]

Fixed pay is the rule in the majority of U.S. organizations largely because it reduces the risk to both employer and employee. However, variable pay can be used advantageously in smaller companies, firms with a product that is not well established, companies with a young professional work force that is willing to delay immediate gratification in hopes of greater future returns, firms supported by venture capital, organizations going through a prolonged period of cash shortages, and companies that would otherwise have to institute layoffs because their revenues are volatile.

Apple Computer provides an excellent example of a young firm that used variable pay to its own and its employees' advantage. Employees were willing to work for low salaries for several years in exchange for company stock; many of those who persevered became millionaires after Apple's stock went sky high in the mid-1980s. Similarly, many Wal-Mart store managers who worked for years at a low salary plus Wal-Mart stock became wealthy when the company's stock soared.

Not all variable-pay plans work out well for employees, however. Employees at two airlines, People Express and America West, found that the stock they received in lieu of a higher salary was almost worthless when they tried to cash it in.

Performance versus Membership

A special case of fixed versus variable compensation involves a choice between performance and membership.[14] A company emphasizes performance when a substantial portion of its employees' pay is tied to individual or group contributions and the amount received can vary significantly from one person or group to another. The most extreme forms of *performance-contingent compensation* are traditional piece-rate plans (pay based on units produced) and sales commissions. Other performance-contingent plans use awards for cost-saving suggestions, bonuses for perfect attendance, or merit pay based on supervisory appraisals. All these options are provided on top of an individual's base pay (see Chapter 11).

Firms that emphasize *membership-contingent compensation* provide the same or a similar wage to every employee in a given job, as long as the employee achieves at least satisfactory performance. Employees receive a paycheck for logging in a prescribed num-

Performance-Contingent Compensation.

Clothing manufacturers around the world have traditionally paid their employees on piece-rate plans. Workers receive a specific amount for each piece produced. While piecework systems can motivate employees to produce more, they can also lead to "sweatshops" where people work long hours for low pay. For this reason, piecework systems are not often used in the United States.

ber of hours of work per week (normally 40). Typically, salary progression occurs by moving up in the organization, not by doing the present job better.

The relative emphasis placed on performance versus membership depends largely on the organization's culture and the beliefs of top managers or the company's founder. For instance, 3M's CEO has noted that the most important managerial value at 3M is that "human beings are endowed with the urge to create, to bring into being something that has never existed before…[therefore] rewards have to be tied directly to successful innovation…the worst thing we could do with [innovators] is to base their rewards on how well they fit into some preconceived management mold."[15] 3M's encouragement of innovation has paid off. In what has become a legend in the field of product development, one of its chemists developed the immensely popular adhesive Post-It™ Notes after getting tired of having bookmarks fall out of his hymnal at church. It took a year of tinkering to develop the final product, but 3M provided the chemist with the time to tinker and a handsome bonus for the final result.[16]

Most companies that emphasize performance tend to be smaller than 3M. They are usually characterized by fewer management levels, rapid growth, internal competition among people and groups, readily available performance indicators (see Chapter 7), and strong competitive pressures.[17]

Job versus Individual Pay

Most traditional compensation systems assume that in setting base compensation a firm should evaluate the value or contributions of each job, not how well the employee performs it.[18] Under this system, the job becomes the unit of analysis for determining base compensation, not the individual(s) performing that job. This means that the minimum and maximum values of each job are set independently of individual workers, who must be paid somewhere in the range established for that job. For instance, an unemployed Ph.D. in chemistry may accept a job as a janitor and do an outstanding job of keeping the building clean and well organized. Yet he may be paid $4.85 an hour—not because he doesn't deserve more, given his credentials and janitorial performance, but because this is the maximum hourly pay set for this job. He can get paid more only by being promoted, and this could take years.

Rather than basing pay on a narrowly defined job, companies may choose to emphasize an individual's abilities, potential, and flexibility to perform multiple tasks in setting his or her pay. For example, the chemistry Ph.D. may be offered a job at $20 per hour because he can do many things that are as necessary to the organization as cleaning, such as helping in the lab and drafting reports. In this type of **knowledge-based pay** or **skill-based pay** system, employees are paid on the basis of the jobs they *can* do or the talents they have that can be successfully applied to a variety of tasks and situations.[19] Thus, the more hats an individual can wear, the more pay he or she will receive. Employees' base compensation increases as they become able to perform more duties successfully.

knowledge-based pay or **skill-based pay**
A pay system in which employees are paid on the basis of the jobs they can do or talents they have that can be successfully applied to a variety of tasks and situations.

While the traditional job-centered pay system is still predominant, more and more firms are opting for a knowledge-based approach. Proponents argue that knowledge-based pay provides greater motivation for employees, makes it easier to reassign workers to where they are most needed, reduces the costs of turnover and absenteeism because other employees can assume missing employees' duties, and provides managers with much more staffing flexibility. However, critics maintain that a skill-based system may lead to higher labor costs, loss of labor specialization, greater difficulty in selecting applicants because the qualifications are less specific, and a chaotic workplace where "the left hand doesn't know what the right hand is doing."[20]

How, then, should managers approach the job versus individual pay option? Research suggests that neither approach is always preferable; the better choice depends on the prevailing conditions at the firm. A job-based pay policy tends to work best in situations where:

- Technology is stable.
- Jobs don't change often.
- Employees do not need to cover for one another frequently.
- Much training is required to learn a given job.
- Turnover is relatively low.
- Employees are expected to move up through the ranks over time.
- Jobs are fairly standardized within the industry.

The automobile industry fits most of these criteria. Individual-based compensation programs are more suitable when:

- The firm has a relatively educated work force with both the ability and the willingness to learn different jobs.
- The company's technology and organizational structure change frequently.
- Employee participation and teamwork are encouraged throughout the organization.
- Opportunities for upward mobility are limited.
- Opportunities to learn new skills are present.
- The costs of employee turnover and absenteeism in terms of lost production are high.[21]

Individual-based pay plans are common in manufacturing environments that rely on continuous-process technologies.[22]

Elitism versus Egalitarianism

Firms must decide whether to place most of their employees under the same compensation plan (an **egalitarian pay system**) or to establish different compensation plans by organizational level and/or employee group (an **elitist pay system**). For example, in some firms only the CEO is eligible for stock options. In other companies even the lowest-paid worker is offered stock options. Some companies offer a wide menu of pay incentives only to specific employee groups (such as salespeople), while others make these available to most employees. At Ben & Jerry's Homemade, Inc., the Vermont–based ice cream company, the compensation system is linked to company prosperity. When the company does well, everyone does well. The profit-sharing plan awards the same percentage to all employees, from the top to the bottom.[23]

egalitarian pay system
A pay plan in which most employees are part of the same compensation system.

elitist pay system
A pay plan in which different compensation systems are established for employees or groups at different organizational levels.

The egalitarianism versus elitism choice is important because it creates an impression of what it takes to succeed in the firm and the type of work managers value. A traditional organizational hierarchy is reinforced if compensation plans and perks vary with one's place in the hierarchy.[24] For instance, in one large computer firm based in the Midwest, average compensation was perfectly correlated with the floor on which one worked in corporate headquarters: the higher the floor, the higher the pay. In addition, there were four dining rooms in the building and employees could use only the one assigned to them; an observer could immediately tell a person's rank (and prestige level) by where he or she had lunch.

The trend in recent years has been toward more egalitarian compensation systems.[25] Why? A company that has fewer differences between employee levels and fewer compensation plans, allows employees to increase their earnings without moving into management, and keeps status-related perks to a minimum enjoys distinct benefits. The most significant of these are a focus on joint-task accomplishment, more consultation between subordinates and supervisors, and better cooperation among employees.

Nonetheless, both systems have their advantages and disadvantages. Egalitarianism gives firms more flexibility to deploy employees in different areas without having to change their pay levels. It can also reduce barriers between people who need to work closely together. Elitist pay structures tend to result in a more stable work force because employees make more money only by moving up through the company.

Elitist compensation systems are more prevalent among older, well-established firms with mature products, a relatively unchanging market share, and limited competition. Egalitarian compensation systems are more common in highly competitive environments, where firms frequently take business risks and try to expand their market share by continually investing in new technologies, ventures, and products.

Below-Market versus Above-Market Compensation

Some people argue that it is wrong for CEOs to earn multimillion-dollar salaries while some of their employees are earning the minimum wage or even being laid off. Some suggest that a firm's top earner should earn no more than 20 times what the lowest-ranked employee earns. What do you think?

The below-market versus above-market compensation decision is crucial for two reasons.[26] First, employees' pay relative to alternative employment opportunities directly impacts the firm's ability to attract workers from other companies. Pay satisfaction is very highly correlated with pay level, and dissatisfaction with pay is one of the most common causes of employee turnover. Second, the choice has an important cost component. The decision to pay above market for all employee groups allows the firm to hire the "cream of the crop," minimize voluntary turnover, and create a climate that makes all employees feel they are part of an elite organization. This has traditionally been the choice for "blue-chip" firms like IBM, 3M, and Procter & Gamble. However, few companies can afford such a policy. Instead, most firms recognize the importance of certain groups explicitly by paying them above market, and cover these costs by paying other groups below market. For example, many high-tech firms compensate their R&D workers quite well while paying their manufacturing employees below-market wages.

In general, above-market pay policies are more prevalent among larger companies in less competitive industries (like utilities) and among companies that have been performing well and therefore have the ability to pay more. In addition, companies starting up in some overseas areas must consider paying above-market wages. Demi Lloyd found this out when she and her husband set up DD Traders, Inc., a buying agency for Christmas decorations in Hong Kong, and within six months experienced a 100% staff turnover. Since Hong Kong's unemployment rate is below 2%, employees have the upper hand. To attract and retain the best and most experienced workers, Lloyd found she had to offer salaries 10% to 20% above the market levels.[27] Unions, which we discuss in detail in Chapter 15, also contribute to above-market pay. Unionized workers receive approximately 9% to 12% higher wages than similar nonunionized workers do.[28]

At-market wages are typical in industries that are both well established and highly competitive (for example, grocery store and hotel chains). Firms paying below market tend to be small, young, and nonunionized. They often operate in economically depressed areas and have a higher proportion of women and minorities in the work force. Growing firms making risky business decisions that leave them short of cash may also offer a lower base salary relative to the market.

Monetary versus Nonmonetary Rewards

One of the oldest debates about compensation concerns monetary versus nonmonetary rewards. Unlike cash or payments that can be converted into cash in the future (such as stocks or a retirement plan), nonmonetary rewards are intangible. Such rewards include interesting work, challenging assignments, and public recognition.[29]

Many surveys have shown that employees rank pay low in importance. For example, in a recent large-scale survey only 2% of Americans declared that pay is a very important aspect of a job.[30] This finding should be viewed with skepticism, however. As two well-known commentators note, pay "may rank higher than people care to admit to others—or to themselves. In practice, it appears that good old-fashioned cash is as effective as any reward that has yet been invented."[31]

Most HRM researchers and practitioners agree that pay symbolizes what the organization values and signals the activities it wants to encourage. For instance, most research-oriented universities base faculty pay primarily on the number of papers a faculty member has published in leading academic journals. The result: Teachers at these universities spend a great deal of time writing papers for publication. Furthermore, employees at all levels do those things that they believe will be rewarded with pay raises.

Nonetheless, organizations do face a choice concerning how much emphasis to place on money and how much to place on other rewards such as high job security. For instance, Amway, a distributor of cleaning products through home-based franchises, is well known for emphasizing monetary rewards, while companies such as Xerox and Texas Instruments are pacesetters in providing nonmonetary rewards. However, these firms also provide strong monetary incentives.

In general, companies that emphasize monetary rewards want to reinforce individual achievement and responsibility. Those that emphasize nonmonetary rewards prefer to reinforce commitment to the organization. Thus, a greater emphasis on monetary rewards is generally found among firms facing a volatile market with low job security, firms emphasizing sales rather than customer service, and firms trying to foster a competitive internal climate rather than long-term employee commitment. A greater reliance on nonmonetary rewards is usually found in companies with a relatively stable work force, those that emphasize customer service and loyalty rather than fast sales growth, and those that want to create a more cooperative atmosphere within the firm.[32]

It should also be noted that in the midst of an economic recession or a downturn in company profits, some companies offer nonmonetary rewards as a way to retain employees for whom getting a new job is the only way to get a raise. Financially squeezed by the recession of the early 1990s, some companies developed creative nonmonetary ways to reward employees. For instance, to avoid a brain drain of its scientists, Hewlett-Packard set up a technical track to let scientists advance without taking on the managerial tasks they dislike. Other companies provided flexible work arrangements, overseas transfers, or educational sabbaticals.[33]

Open versus Secret Pay

Firms vary widely in the extent to which they communicate openly about workers' compensation levels and company compensation practices. At one extreme, some firms require employees to sign an oath that they will not divulge their pay to coworkers; the penalty for breaking the oath is termination. At the other extreme, every employee's pay is a matter of public record; in public universities this information may even be published in the student newspaper. Many organizations are somewhere in between: They do not publish individual data but they do provide information on pay and salary ranges.

Open pay has two advantages over secret pay.[34] First, limiting employees' access to compensation information often leads to greater pay dissatisfaction because employees tend to overestimate the pay of coworkers and superiors. In other words, when compensation is secret, people tend to feel more underpaid than they really are. Second, open pay forces managers to be more fair and effective in administering compensation because bad decisions cannot be hidden and good decisions can serve as motivators to the best workers.

But open pay has a downside. First, it forces managers and supervisors to defend their compensation decisions publicly. As we will see later in this chapter, personal judgments play a major role in deciding who gets paid what in any pay system. Regardless of good-faith attempts to explain these judgments, it may be impossible to satisfy everyone (even those who are doing very well may feel that they should be doing better). Second, the cost of making a mistake in a pay decision increases when pay is open. Third, to avoid time-consuming and nerve-wracking arguments with employees, managers may eliminate pay differences among subordinates despite differences in performance levels. The result may be turnover of the better performers, who feel underpaid.

So, despite its potential benefits, open pay is not appropriate for every organization. Recent research suggests that greater pay openness is more likely to be successful in organizations with extensive employee involvement and an egalitarian culture that engenders trust and commitment.[35] This is because open pay can foster perceptions of fairness and greater motivation only in a climate that nurtures employee relations. In more competitive climates, it may unleash a destructive cycle of conflict and hostility that is difficult to stop.

Centralization versus Decentralization of Pay Decisions

Organizations must decide where pay decisions will be made. In a centralized system, pay decisions are tightly controlled in a central location, normally the HR department at corporate headquarters. In a decentralized system, pay decisions are delegated deep down into the firm, normally to managers of each unit. What are the advantages of centralization versus decentralization of pay decisions?

Centralized pay is more appropriate when it is cost-effective and efficient to hire compensation specialists who can be located in a single place and made responsible for salary surveys, benefits administration, and recordkeeping.[36] If the organization faces frequent legal challenges, it may also be prudent to centralize major compensation decisions in the hands of professionals. In addition, companies tend to centralize the compensation function during periods of decline to control expenses.

There are some potential negative consequences of too much centralized control. A centralized system maximizes internal equity, but does not handle external equity (market) concerns very well. Thus, large and diverse organizations are better served by a decentralized pay system. For example, Mars, Inc., a worldwide leader in the candy market with estimated annual revenues of $11 billion and 30,000 employees, has only two HR people at corporate headquarters. Each Mars unit is responsible for its own pay decisions. This system is part of Mars's HR resource strategy to minimize corporatewide rules, regulations, and red tape.[37]

HR professionals at large companies like Monsanto are soliciting more and more input on compensation from managers, supervisors, and even employees. The Manager's Notebook, "Checklist for Planning a New Way to Pay," lists some crucial questions managers should consider when helping to devise a new compensation program.

Summary. Compensation is a complex topic that has a significant impact on organizational success. You may be feeling a bit overwhelmed by the number of decisions that companies need to make in designing and implementing a compensation system. In practice, however, the nine issues we have discussed are not independent of one another. For instance, if circumstances dictate that paramount attention be given to external equity, then decisions on the other issues will follow from that. Pay for the job (as opposed to the individual) will be necessary because the job is the basis of the external comparison and market wages are by definition associated with external equity. Monetary rather than nonmonetary rewards will probably be used because money is the usual measure of external equity. And, as we have just seen, external equity is easier to manage in a decentralized system.

In short, the good news is that there are not as many separate compensation systems as the nine options might suggest. The bad news is that none of these options is a simple either/or decision. Rather, each pair of criteria defines two end points on a continuum, with many possibilities between them.

One final note: We will discuss the role of unions in detail in Chapter 15. However, it is important to note here that compensation policies that apply to a unionized work force are subject to negotiation and bargaining. Thus, managers in union shops are often severely restricted in what they can and cannot do with regard to compensation issues. ▼

Manager's Notebook

Checklist for Planning a New Way to Pay

- ✔ Are we currently able to attract the caliber of employees we need in our work unit?
- ✔ What are the strengths and deficiencies of our current salary program?
- ✔ In what areas are my needs as supervisor not being met? Are these shortfalls due to the compensation program design?
- ✔ What components of the program seem to be out of sync with my understanding of our compensation philosophy and program objectives? Does this mean we need to replace these components or can we fix them?
- ✔ Are we communicating to employees appropriately? Do they understand our objectives and the program's rationale? Can we fine-tune the program to correct the message?

Source: Excerpted from Risher, H. (1993, January–February). Strategic salary planning. *Compensation and Benefits Review*, 46–50. Reprinted by permission of the publisher. American Management Association, NY.

Compensation Tools

For the past 100 years, companies have used numerous techniques to decide who should get paid what. The goal of all these tools is to produce pay systems that are equitable and that allow the firm to attract, retain, and motivate workers while keeping labor costs under control. Despite their diversity, compensation tools can be grouped into two broad categories depending on the unit of analysis used to make pay decisions: job-based approaches and skill-based approaches.

The first category, *job-based approaches*, includes the most traditional and widely used types of compensation programs.[38] These plans assume that work gets done by people who are paid to perform well-defined jobs (for example, secretary, bookkeeper). Each job is designed to accomplish specific tasks (for example, typing, recordkeeping) and is normally performed by several people. Because all jobs are not equally important to the firm and the labor market puts a greater value on some jobs than on others, the compensation system's primary objective is to allocate pay so that the most important jobs are paid the most.

A simplified example of a typical job-based pay structure appears in Figure 10–4 on page 308. It shows the pay structure of a hypothetical large restaurant with 87 employees performing 18 different jobs. These 18 jobs are grouped into six **pay grades**, with pay levels ranging from $4.50 an hour for jobs in the lowest grades to a maximum of $30.00 an hour for the job in the highest grade (chef). Employees are paid within the range established for the grade at which their job is classified. Thus, a dishwasher or a busser would be paid between $4.50 and $5.25 an hour (Grade 1).

pay grades
Groups of jobs that are paid within the same pay range.

The second type of pay plan, the *skill-based approach*, is far less common. It assumes that workers should be paid not according to the job they hold, but rather by how flexible or capable they are at performing multiple tasks. Under this type of plan, the greater the variety of job-related skills workers possess, the more they are paid. Figure 10–5 on the next page shows a simple example of a skill-based approach that could be used as an alternative to the job-based approach depicted in Figure 10–4. Workers who master the first set of skills (Block 1) receive $5 an hour; those who learn the skills in Block 2 (in addition to those in Block 1) receive $6.50 an hour; those who acquire the skills in Block 3 (in addition to those in Blocks 1 and 2) are paid $9.50 an hour; and so on.

In the sections that follow, we discuss these two major types of compensation programs in greater depth. Because compensation tools and pay plans can be very complex,

	Jobs	Number of Positions	Pay
GRADE 6	Chef	2	$19.50–$30.00/hr.
GRADE 5	Manager	1	$10.50–$20.00/hr.
	Sous-Chef	1	
GRADE 4	Assistant Manager	2	$6.50–$11.00/hr
	Lead Cook	2	
	Office Manager	1	
GRADE 3	General Cook	5	$5.50–$7.00/hr.
	Short-Order Cook	2	
	Assistant to Lead Cook	2	
	Clerk	1	
GRADE 2	Server	45	$5.00–$6.00/hr.
	Hostess	4	
	Cashier	4	
GRADE 1	Kitchen Helper	2	$4.50–$5.25/hr.
	Dishwasher	3	
	Janitor	2	
	Busser	6	
	Security Guard	2	

FIGURE 10–4

Pay Structure of a Large Restaurant Developed Using a Job-Based Approach

Skill Block	Skills	Pay
5	• Create new items for menu • Find different uses for leftovers (e.g., hot dishes, buffets) • Coordinate and control work of all employees upon manager's absence	$22.00/hr.
4	• Cook existing menu items following recipe • Supervise kitchen help • Prepare payroll • Ensure quality of food and adherence to standards	$16.00/hr.
3	• Schedule servers and assign workstations • Conduct inventory • Organize work flow on restaurant floor	$9.50/hr.
2	• Greet customers and organize tables • Take orders from customers • Bring food to tables • Assist in kitchen with food preparations • Perform security checks • Help with delivery	$6.50/hr.
1	• Use dishwashing equipment • Use chemicals/disinfectants to clean premises • Use vacuum cleaner, mop, waxer, and other cleaning equipment • Clean and set up tables • Perform routine kitchen chores (e.g., making coffee)	$5.00/hr.

FIGURE 10–5

Pay Schedule of a Large Restaurant Designed Using a Skill-Based Approach

we avoid many of the operational details, focusing instead on these programs' intended uses and their relative strengths and weaknesses. Excellent sources that provide step-by-step procedures of how to implement such programs are available elsewhere.[39]

Job-Based Compensation Plans

There are three key components of developing job-based compensation plans: achieving internal equity, achieving external equity, and achieving individual equity. Figure 10–6 summarizes how these are interrelated and the steps involved in each component. The large majority of U.S. firms rely on this or a similar scheme to compensate their work force.[40]

Achieving Internal Equity: Job Evaluation. Job-based compensation assesses the relative value or contribution of different jobs (*not* individual employees) to an organization. The first part of this process, referred to as **job evaluation**, is composed of six steps intended to provide a rational, orderly, and systematic judgment of how important each job is to the firm. The ultimate goal of job evaluation is to achieve internal equity in the pay structure.

job evaluation
The process of evaluating the relative value or contribution of different jobs to an organization.

Step 1: Conduct Job Analysis. As we discussed in Chapter 2, job analysis is the gathering and organization of information concerning the tasks, duties, and responsibilities of specific jobs. In this first step in the job-evaluation process, information is gathered about the duties, tasks, and responsibilities of all jobs being evaluated. Job analysts may use personal interviews with workers, questionnaires completed by employees and/or supervisors, and business records (for example, cost of equipment operated and annual budgets) to study the what, how, and why of various tasks that make up the job. Sample items from a commonly used job analysis questionnaire, the Position Analysis Questionnaire, appear in

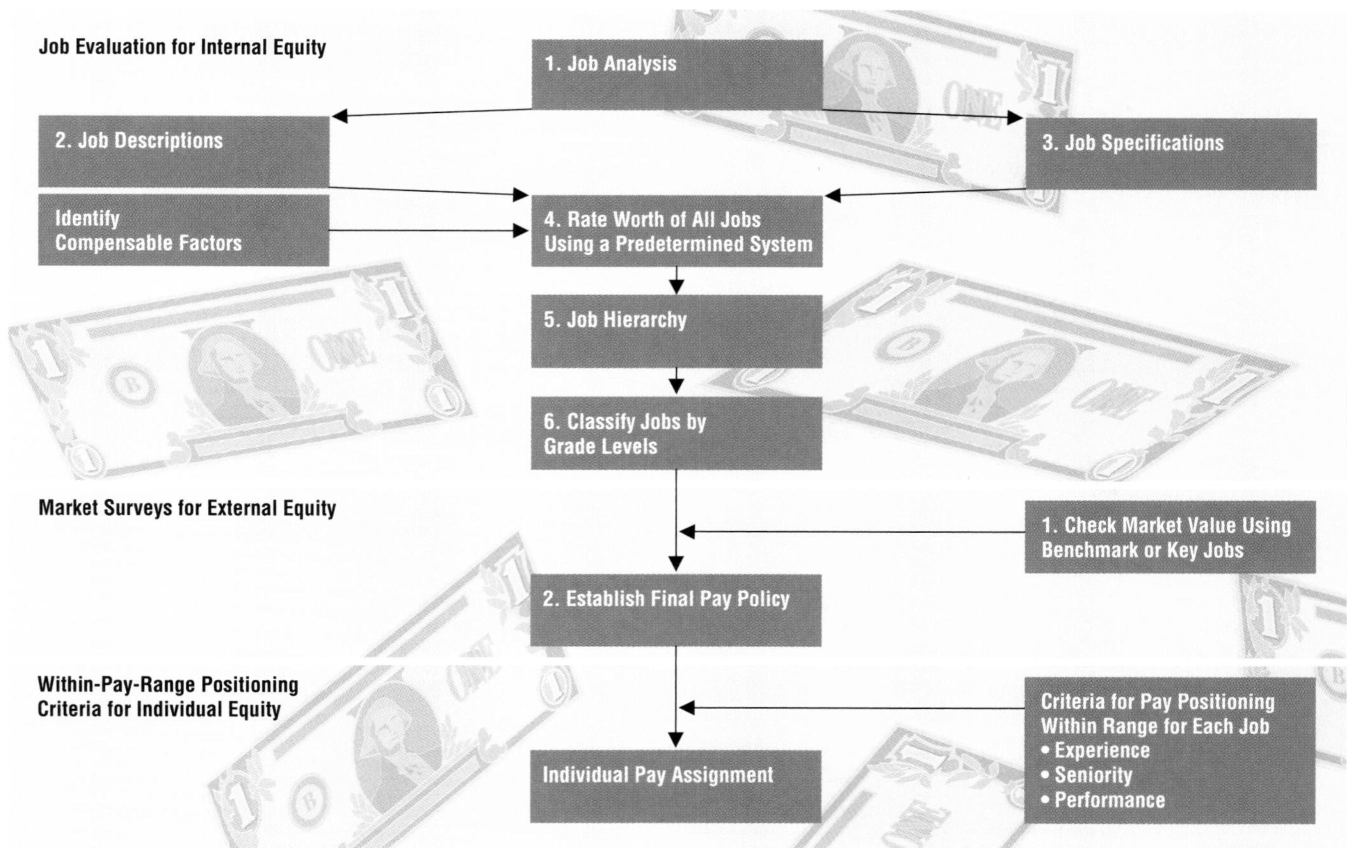

FIGURE 10–6

The Key Steps in Creating Job-Based Compensation Plans

Figure 10–7. For each question, the job analyst considers what is known about the job and decides which of the five descriptions is most appropriate.

Step 2: Write Job Descriptions. In the second step in the job-evaluation process, the job-analysis data are boiled down into a written document that identifies, defines, and describes each job in terms of its duties, responsibilities, working conditions, and specifications. This document is called a *job description*. (You will recall this term from Chapter 2.)

Step 3: Determine Job Specifications. *Job specifications* consist of the worker characteristics that an employee must have to perform the job successfully. These prerequisites are

Mental Processes

Decision Making, Reasoning, and Planning/Scheduling

36. Decision making
Using the response scale below, indicate the level of decision making typically involved in the job, considering the number and complexity of the factors that must be taken into account, the variety of alternatives available, the consequences and importance of the decisions, the background experience, education, and training required, the precedents available for guidance, and other relevant considerations.

Level of Decision

1 *Very limited*
(e.g., decisions such as those in selecting parts in routine assembly, shelving items in a warehouse, cleaning furniture, or handling automatic machines)

2 *Limited*
(e.g., decisions such as those in operating a wood planer, dispatching a taxi, or lubricating an automobile)

3 *Intermediate*
(e.g., decisions such as those in setting up machines for operation, diagnosing mechanical disorders of aircraft, reporting news, or supervising auto service workers)

4 *Substantial*
(e.g., decisions such as those in determining production quotas or making promoting and hiring decisions)

5 *Very substantial*
(e.g., decisions such as those in approving an annual corporate budget, recommending major surgery, or selecting the location for a new plant)

37. Reasoning in problem solving
Using the response scale below, indicate the level of reasoning required in applying knowledge, experience, and judgment to problems.

Level of Reasoning in Problem Solving

1 *Very limited*
(use of common sense to carry out simple or relatively uninvolved instructions, e.g., hand assembler or mixing machine operator)

2 *Limited*
(use of some training and/or experience to select from a limited number of solutions the most appropriate action or procedure in performing the job, e.g., sales clerk, electrician apprentice, or library assistant)

3 *Intermediate*
(use of relevant principles to solve practical problems and to deal with a variety of concrete variables in situations where only limited standardization exists, such as that used by supervisors or technicians)

4 *Substantial*
(use of logic or scientific thinking to define problems, collect information, establish facts, and draw valid conclusions, such as that used by petroleum engineers, personnel directors, or chain store managers)

5 *Very substantial*
(use of logical or scientific thinking to solve a wide range of intellectual and practical problems, such as that used by research chemists, nuclear physicists, corporate presidents, or managers of a large branch or plant)

FIGURE 10–7

Sample Items from Position Analysis Questionnaire

Source: Purdue Research Foundation, West Lafayette, IN 47907-1650. Used with permission.

drawn from the job analysis, although in some cases they are legally mandated (for example, plumbers must have a plumbing license). Job specifications are typically very concrete in terms of necessary years and type of prior work experience, level and type of education, certificates, vocational training, and so forth. They are usually included on job descriptions.

Step 4: Rate Worth of all Jobs Using a Predetermined System. After job descriptions and job specifications are finalized, they are used to determine the relative value or contributions of different jobs to the organization. This job evaluation is normally done by a three- to seven-person committee that may include supervisors, managers, HR department staff, and outside consultants. Several well-known evaluation procedures have evolved over the years, but the *point factor system* is used by the vast majority of firms.[41]

The point factor system uses **compensable factors** to evaluate jobs. Compensable factors are work-related criteria that the organization considers most important in assessing the relative value of different jobs. One commonly used compensable factor is knowledge. Jobs that require more knowledge (acquired either through formal education or through informal experience) receive a higher rating, and thus more compensation. While each firm can determine its own compensable factors, or even create compensable factors suitable to various occupational groups or job families (clerical, technical, managerial, and so on), most firms adopt compensable factors from well-established job-evaluation systems. Two point factor systems that are almost universally accepted are the *Hay Guide Chart Profile Method* and the Management Association of America (MAA) *National Position Evaluation Plan* (formerly known as the NMTA point factor system). The Hay Method, which is summarized in Figure 10–8, uses three compensable factors to evaluate jobs: know-how, problem solving, and accountability. The MAA (NMTA) plan has three separate units: Unit I for

compensable factors
Work-related criteria that an organization considers most important in assessing the relative value of different jobs.

KNOW-HOW

Know-how is the sum total of every kind of skill, however acquired, necessary for acceptable job performance. This sum total, which comprises the necessary overall "fund of knowledge" an employee needs, has three dimensions:

- • Knowledge of practical procedures, specialized techniques, and learned disciplines.
- •• The ability to integrate and harmonize the diversified functions involved in managerial situations (operating, supporting, and administrative). This know-how may be exercised consultatively as well as executively and involves in some combination the areas of organizing, planning, executing, controlling, and evaluating.
- ••• Active, practicing skills in the area of human relationships.

PROBLEM SOLVING

Problem solving is the original "self-starting" thinking required by the job for analyzing, evaluating, creating, reasoning, and arriving at conclusions. To the extent that thinking is circumscribed by standards, covered by precedents, or referred to others, problem solving is diminished and the emphasis correspondingly is on know-how.

Problem solving has two dimensions:

- • The environment in which the thinking takes place.
- •• The challenge presented by the thinking to be done.

ACCOUNTABILITY

Accountability is the answerability for an action and for the consequences thereof. It is the measured effect of the job on end results. It has three dimensions:

- • Freedom to act—the degree of personal or procedural control and guidance.
- •• Job impact on end results.
- ••• Magnitude—indicated by the general dollar size of the areas(s) most clearly or primarily affected by the job (on an annual basis).

FIGURE 10–8

Hay Compensable Factors

Source: Courtesy of The Hay Group, Boston, MA.

hourly blue-collar jobs; Unit II for nonexempt clerical, technical, and service positions; and Unit III for exempt supervisory, professional, and management-level positions. The MAA (NMTA) plan includes 11 factors divided into four broad categories (skill, effort, responsibility, and working conditions). The Unit I plan is summarized in Figure 10–9.[42]

In both systems each compensable factor is assigned a scale of numbers and degrees. The more important factors are given higher point values, the less important factors lower values. For instance, as Figure 10–10 shows, the highest possible points under the MAA (NMTA) system are for experience, with each degree of experience worth 22 points. The value of the other two MAA (NMTA) skill factors is 14 points per degree. All other factors are worth either 5 or 10 points per degree.

This scale allows the evaluation and compensation committee to assign a number of points to each job on the basis of each factor degree. For example, using the MAA (NMTA) table in Figure 10–10, let's assume that job X is rated at the fifth degree for physical demand (50 points), equipment or process (25 points), material or product (25 points), safety of others (25 points), and work of others (25 points); at the fourth degree for mental or visual demand (20 points), working conditions (40 points), and hazards (20 points); at the second degree for experience (44 points); and at the first degree for knowledge (14 points) and initiative and ingenuity (14 points). The total points for this job across all 11 MAA (NMTA) compensable factors is thus 302.

Skill

1. *Knowledge.* Measures the level of learning or equivalent formal training applied in a given type of work.
2. *Experience.* Measures the amount of time usually needed before being able to perform a job's duties with no more than normal supervision.
3. *Initiative and ingenuity.* Indicates the extent to which independent judgment and decision making are exercised on the job.

Effort

4. *Physical demand.* Measures how much and how often duties include lifting heavy materials, moving them, and working in difficult positions.
5. *Mental attention or visual demand.* Measures how much fatigue occurs from work that is visually or mentally intense, concentrated, and exacting.

Responsibility

6. *Equipment or process.* Measures the damage to equipment or process that would probably result from error or carelessness.
7. *Material, product, or service quality.* Refers to losses that would likely occur through spoilage, waste, and negligence in processing, inspection, testing, or delivery of service.
8. *Safety of others.* Measures the extent to which a job involves protecting others from injury or health hazards.
9. *Work of others or as a member of quality/process team.* Refers to the extent of responsibility for assisting, instructing, or directing others or involvement in quality or process teams which impact other operations within the company.

Job Conditions

10. *Working conditions.* Measures the degree of exposure to such elements as dust, heat, noise, or fumes.
11. *Hazards.* Concerns the risk of injury from materials, tools, equipment, and locations that remains even after protective and safety measures have been taken.

FIGURE 10–9

MAA National Position Evaluation Plan's 11 Compensable Factors (Unit I—The Manufacturing, Maintenance, Warehousing, Distribution, and Service Positions)

Source: MAA (formerly NMTA) National Position Evaluation Plan.

Points Assigned to Factor Degrees					
Factor	**1st Degree**	**2nd Degree**	**3rd Degree**	**4th Degree**	**5th Degree**
Skill					
1. Knowledge	14	28	42	56	70
2. Experience	22	44	66	88	110
3. Initiative and ingenuity	14	28	42	56	70
Effort					
4. Physical Demand	10	20	30	40	50
5. Mental or Visual Demand	5	10	15	20	25
Responsibility					
6. Equipment or Process	5	10	15	20	25
7. Material or Product	5	10	15	20	25
8. Safety of Others	5	10	15	20	25
9. Work of Others	5	10	15	20	25
Job Conditions					
10. Working Conditions	10	20	30	40	50
11. Hazards	5	10	15	20	25

FIGURE 10–10

MAA National Position Evaluation Plan: Points Assigned to Factor Degrees

Source: MAA (formerly NMTA) National Position Evaluation Plan.

Step 5: Create a Job Hierarchy. The four steps described thus far produce a **job hierarchy**, a listing of jobs in terms of their relative assessed value (from highest to lowest). Figure 10–11 on page 314 illustrates a job hierarchy for office jobs in a typical large organization. Column 1 of the figure shows the total points assigned to each job in descending order. These range from a high of 300 for customer service representative to a low of 60 for receptionist.

job hierarchy
A listing of jobs in order of their importance to the organization, from highest to lowest.

Step 6: Classify Jobs by Grade Levels. For the sake of simplicity, most large organizations classify jobs into grades as the last step in the job-evaluation process. For instance, at Control Data Corporation, a manufacturer of computer equipment, thousands of jobs have been grouped into fewer than 20 grades.[43] Typically, the job hierarchy is reduced to a manageable number of grade levels, with the assigned points used to determine where to set up dividing lines between grades. For example, column 2 in Figure 10–11 shows how the hierarchy of 18 clerical jobs is divided into five grade levels. All jobs in a given grade are judged to be essentially the same in terms of importance because the points assigned to each are very close in number.

Other job-evaluation systems are the *ranking system* (in which the evaluation committee puts together a hierarchy of job descriptions from highest to lowest based on an overall judgment of value); the *classification system* (in which the committee sorts job descriptions into grades without using a point system, as in the federal civil service job classification system); *factor comparison* (a complex and seldom-used variation of the point and ranking systems); and *policy capturing* (in which mathematical analysis is used to estimate the relative value of each job based on the firm's existing practices).

You should keep two key aspects of our discussion so far in mind. First, job evaluation is performed internally and does not take into account the wage rates in the marketplace or what other firms are doing. Second, job evaluation focuses only on the value of the tasks

	1 Points	2 Grade	3 Weekly Pay Range
Customer Service Representative	300	5	$500–$650
Executive Secretary/Administrative Assistant	298		
Senior Secretary	290		
Secretary	230	4	$450–$550
Senior General Clerk	225		
Credit and Collection	220		
Accounting Clerk	175	3	$425–$475
General Clerk	170		
Legal Secretary/Assistant	165		
Senior Word Processing Operator	160		
Word Processing Operator	125	2	$390–$430
Purchasing Clerk	120		
Payroll Clerk	120		
Clerk-Typist	115		
File Clerk	95	1	$350–$400
Mail Clerk	80		
Personnel Clerk	80		
Receptionist	60		

FIGURE 10-11

Hierarchy of Clerical Jobs, Pay Grades, and Weekly Pay Range for a Hypothetical Office

that make up each job, not the people performing them. The MAA (NMTA) booklet distributed to all employees whose jobs are evaluated under that system makes this very explicit: "The plan does not judge anyone as an individual; it does not rate anyone's ability to perform a job. It [evaluates] each job according to a simple set of [compensable] factors...that are applied in exactly the same way to all jobs."[44]

Achieving External Equity: Market Surveys. To achieve external equity, firms often conduct *market surveys*. The purpose of these surveys is to determine the pay ranges for each grade level. An organization may conduct its own salary surveys, but most purchase commercially available surveys. Consulting firms conduct literally hundreds of such surveys each year for almost every type of job and geographical area. Some widely used surveys are summarized in Figure 10–12.

Why spend time and money on internal job evaluations when market data can be used to determine the value of jobs? There are two reasons. First, most companies have jobs that are unique to the firm and therefore cannot be easily matched to market data.[45] For instance, the job of "administrative assistant" in Company Y may involve supporting top management in important tasks (for example, making public appearances for an executive when he or she is not available), while in Company Z it may involve only routine clerical duties. Second, the importance of a job can vary from firm to firm. For example, the job of "scientist" in a high-tech firm (where new-product creation is a key to competitive advantage) is usually far more important than in a mature manufacturing company (where scientists are often expected to perform only routine tests).

Using market surveys to link job-evaluation results to external wage/salary data generally involves two steps: benchmarking and establishing a pay policy.

benchmark job or **key job**
A job that is similar or comparable in content across firms.

Step 1: Identify Benchmark or Key Jobs. To link the internal job-evaluation hierarchy or grade-level classification to market salaries, most firms identify **benchmark** or **key jobs**—that is, jobs that are similar or comparable in content across firms—and check salary surveys to determine how much these key jobs are worth to other employers. The

Abbott, Langer & Associates Compensation in the Accounting/Financial Field. Covers 18 jobs broken down by type and size of employer, functional area, supervisory responsibility, and geographic location.

Bureau of Labor Statistics Occupational Compensation Survey Program. Covers earnings for white- and blue-collar office and factory workers, based on occupation and locality.

Coopers & Lybrand Compensation in Emerging Businesses. Covers top executive compensation in companies with sales of under $50 million.

D. Dietrich Associates Scientific and Lab Technician Surveys. Covers eight scientist and five lab technician levels plus a lab supervisor position.

Management Compensation Services International Study. Covers executive compensation in 56 countries.

Organization Resource Counselors, Inc. Salary Information Retrieval System Survey. Covers 360 nonexempt positions and 6,767 exempt positions in the aerospace/defense, airline, biotechnology, chemical, computer/software, consumer products, electronics, financial, health care, pharmaceutical, and semiconductor industries.

FIGURE 10–12

Examples of Labor Market Surveys

Source: Reprinted, by permission of publisher, from Solomon, B. (1993, October). A shopper's guide to salary surveys. *CompFlash*, 5–8.

company then sets pay rates for nonkey jobs (for which market data are *not* available) by assigning them the same pay range as key jobs that fall into the same grade level.

An example will help here. Let's say five of the jobs in our office example in Figure 10–11 are identified as key. (These are briefly described in Figure 10–13.) The company purchases a salary survey for office workers in the area showing both average weekly pay and the 25th, 50th, and 75th percentiles in weekly pay for these key jobs. For example, Figure 10–14 on page 316 shows that 25% of the customer service representatives in organizations included in the survey earn $400 per week or less, 50% earn $500 or less, and 75% earn $650 or less. The average weekly salary in the area for this job is $495. The company uses these market data to assign a pay range for all jobs that were evaluated as at the same grade level as the key job of customer service representative—in this case, executive secretary and senior secretary. But first it needs to establish a pay policy.

Step 2: Establish a Pay Policy. Because market wages and salaries vary widely (look again at Figure 10–14), the organization needs to decide whether to lead, lag, or pay the

Customer Service Representative—Establishes and maintains good customer relations and provides advice and assistance on customer problems.

Credit and Collection Clerk—Performs clerical tasks related to credit and collection activities; performs routine credit checks, obtains supplementary information, investigates overdue accounts, follows up by mail and/or telephone to customers on delinquent payments.

Accounting Clerk—Performs a variety of routine accounting clerical work such as maintaining journals, subsidiary ledgers, and related reports according to well-defined procedures or detailed instructions.

Word Processing Operator—Operates word processing equipment to enter or search, select, and merge text from a storage device or internal memory for continuous or repetitive production of copy.

Clerk-Typist—Performs routine clerical and typing work; follows established procedures and detailed written or oral instructions; may operate simple types of office machines and equipment.

FIGURE 10–13

Sample Benchmark Jobs for Office Personnel

Source: 1994 AMS Foundation *Office, Secretarial, Professional, Data Processing and Management Salary Report*, AMS Foundation, 550 W. Jackson Blvd., Suite 360, Chicago, IL 60661.

FIGURE 10–14

Market Salary Data for Selected Benchmark Office Jobs

Benchmark Jobs	Weekly Pay Percentile 25th	50th	75th	Weekly Pay Average
1. Customer Service Representative	$400	$500	$650	$495
2. Credit and Collection Clerk	$400	$450	$550	$455
3. Accounting Clerk	$370	$425	$475	$423
4. Word Processing Operator	$380	$390	$430	$394
5. Clerk-Typist	$330	$350	$400	$343

pay policy
A firm's decision to pay above, below, or at the market rate for its jobs.

going rate (which is normally defined as the midpoint of the wage/salary distribution in the survey). A firm's **pay policy** is determined by how it chooses to position itself in the pay market. The hypothetical firm shown in Figure 10–11, for example, decided to set a pay policy pegging the minimum pay for each grade to the 50th percentile and the maximum pay to the 75th percentile in the market (see column 3 of Figure 10–11). Some firms use more complex methods to achieve the same objective.

Achieving Individual Equity: Within-Pay-Range Positioning Criteria. After the firm has finalized its pay structure by determining pay ranges for each job, it must perform one last task: Assign each employee a pay rate within the range established for his or her job. Companies frequently use previous experience, seniority, and performance appraisal ratings to determine how much an employee is to be paid within the stipulated range for his or her job. The objective of this last step is to achieve individual equity. **Individual equity** refers to fairness in pay decisions for employees holding the same job.

individual equity
The perceived fairness of individual pay decisions.

Evaluating Job-Based Compensation Plans. As we noted earlier, job-based compensation programs are widely used. These systems are rational, objective, and systematic, all features that minimize employee complaints. They are also relatively easy to set up and administer. However, they have several significant drawbacks, specifically:

- Job-based compensation plans do not take into account the nature of the business and its unique problems. For example, jobs are harder to define and change more rapidly in small, growing companies than in larger, more stable companies (such as those in the insurance industry). Heavy reliance on job-evaluation procedures and surveys assumes a universal perspective that may not be relevant to the firm.
- The process of establishing job-based compensation plans is much more subjective and arbitrary than its proponents suggest. These plans may provide a facade of objectivity to cover what is essentially a series of judgment calls.
- Job-based systems are less appropriate at higher levels of an organization, where it is more difficult to separate individual contributions from the job itself. At managerial and professional levels, the employee helps define the job. To force people to conform to a narrowly defined job description robs the organization of much-needed creativity.
- As the economy has become more service oriented and the manufacturing sector has continued to shrink, jobs have become more broadly defined. As a result, job descriptions are often awash in generalities. This makes it more difficult to evaluate the relative importance of jobs.
- Job-based compensation plans tend to be bureaucratic, mechanistic, and inflexible. Once an internal pay structure is put in place, it is difficult to change. Thus, firms cannot easily adapt their pay structure to a rapidly changing economic environment. In addition, because they rely on fixed salary and benefits associated with each level in the hierarchy, these plans tend to result in layoffs to save on costs during economic downturns. Japanese firms, which rely less on job-based compensation plans and often

provide 20% to 30% of their employees' pay in variable form, have greater flexibility to absorb the economy's ups and downs.

- The job-evaluation process is biased against those occupations traditionally filled by women (clerical, elementary school teaching, nursing, and the like). Although empirical studies are inconclusive on this issue, critics often use vivid examples to make their point, such as sanitation jobs (garbage collectors) in New York City being evaluated higher than teaching jobs.
- Wage and salary data obtained from market surveys are not definitive. After adjusting for job content, company size, firm performance, and geographic location, differences ranging from 35% to 300% in the pay of identical jobs within the same industry are not uncommon.[46] One researcher has concluded: "Clearly, the pay practices of firms in the same industry are often widely divergent.... No doubt, this means that employers, on the basis of a carefully selected survey sample, can justify widely divergent pay practices (a point frequently ignored when competitive pay is analyzed and discussed)."[47]
- In determining internal and external equity, it is the employees' perceptions of equity that count, not the assessments of job-evaluation committees and paid consultants. Job-based compensation plans assume that the employer can decide what is equitable for the employee. Because equity is in the eye of the beholder, this approach may simply rationalize an employer's pay practices rather than compensate employees according to their contributions.

Despite all these criticisms, job-based compensation plans continue to be widely used, probably because there are no alternative systems that are both cost efficient and generally applicable. Skill-based pay, which we describe later in this chapter, offers an alternative approach, but it is costly and its uses are limited.

Suggestions for Practice. Rather than dismissing job-based compensation plans completely, it is more realistic to take steps to reduce the potential problems associated with them. In developing a job-based pay plan, the firm should take the following recommendations into account:

- *Think strategically in making policy decisions concerning pay.* Tools are a means to an end, not an end in themselves. For example, it may be in the firm's best interests to design a certain number of jobs very broadly and flexibly. The firm may also find it advantageous to pay at the top of the market for critical jobs that are central to its mission and at the low end of the market for jobs it considers less important. In short, the firm's business and HR strategy should drive the use of compensation tools rather than the other way around.
- *Secure employee input.* Employee dissatisfaction will be reduced to the extent that employees have a voice in the design and management of the compensation plan. A simple, straightforward way to solicit employee input is to use computers. Computer-assisted job-evaluation systems allow employees to describe their jobs in a way that can be synthesized, displayed, rearranged, and easily compared. This approach offers two benefits. First, it gives employees a chance to describe what they do. This tends to improve the acceptability of job-evaluation results (although it does not eliminate the need for evaluative judgments to develop a job hierarchy). Second, it offers an inexpensive way to update job descriptions and to incorporate these changes into the system regularly (for example, yearly).
- *Increase each job's range of pay while expanding its scope of responsibility.* For instance, instead of setting the difference between the low and high ends of the pay range at 15% on average, the firm might increase the difference to 50 percent. This approach, commonly called **job banding**, entails replacing narrowly defined job descriptions with broader categories (bands) of related jobs.[47a] Job banding allows the firm to cut back the

job banding
The practice of replacing narrowly defined job descriptions with broader categories (bands) of related jobs.

number of job titles and permits employees to receive a substantial pay raise without having to change jobs or get promoted. Banding has three potential benefits. First, it gives the firm more flexibility because jobs are not narrowly defined. Second, during periods of slow growth, the firm can reward top performers without having to promote them. Third, the firm may save on administrative costs because with banding there are fewer layers of staff and management. For more details on how one company instituted a successful job banding system, see the Issues and Applications feature titled, "Banding at Fine Products: A Boost in Competitive Advantage," on page 319.

- *Conduct pay equity audits periodically to ensure that the gender composition of a job does not affect its position in the hierarchy or the interpretation of salary survey data.* Several procedures have been suggested for accomplishing this.[48] One approach uses computer-generated data to examine the extent to which job-evaluation results reflect differences in job content rather than the proportion of women in a given job.[49]
- *Expand the proportion of employees' pay that is variable (bonuses, stock plans, and so forth).* Variable-pay programs provide the firm with the flexibility to reduce costs without resorting to layoffs. A large firm may prevent thousands of layoffs by devoting as little as 10% of an employee's pay to a variable-pay pool that rewards workers during good times and serves as a "shock absorber" during bad times.
- *Establish dual-career ladders for different types of employees so that moving into management ranks or up the organizational hierarchy is not the only way to receive a substantial increase in pay.* In some situations, such as in a large organization with multiple business units and several layers of management, a tall job hierarchy is appropriate; in others, a relatively flat hierarchy with much room for salary growth (based, for instance, on performance and seniority) makes more sense. Figure 10–15 is an example of a dual-career ladder.

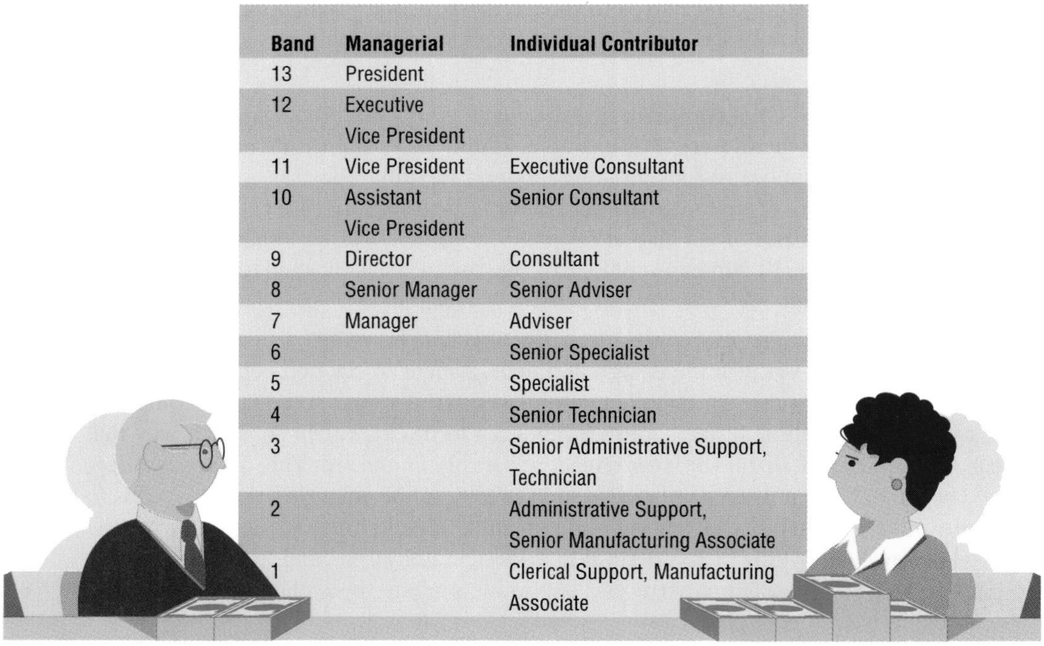

Band	Managerial	Individual Contributor
13	President	
12	Executive Vice President	
11	Vice President	Executive Consultant
10	Assistant Vice President	Senior Consultant
9	Director	Consultant
8	Senior Manager	Senior Adviser
7	Manager	Adviser
6		Senior Specialist
5		Specialist
4		Senior Technician
3		Senior Administrative Support, Technician
2		Administrative Support, Senior Manufacturing Associate
1		Clerical Support, Manufacturing Associate

FIGURE 10–15

Example of a Dual-Career Ladder

Source: LeBlanc, P. (1992). Banding the new pay structure for the transformed organization. *Perspectives in Total Compensation, 3*(8). American Compensation Association, Scottsdale, AZ. Used with permission of the author, Peter V. LeBlanc, of Sibson & Company.

Issues + Applications

Banding at Fine Products: A Boost in Competitive Advantage

Fine Products, Inc., a highly profitable consumer products company, found itself faced with increasing competition from lower-cost producers and consumer demand for greater product variety. An executive task force identified the company's compensation system for managers and professionals as a major impediment to dealing with these competitive challenges. Separate pay programs for different employee groups promoted a feeling of "class distinction"; workers could obtain significant pay increases only by moving up through a hierarchy of 20 levels; and a large number of job titles with narrow salary ranges prevented effective teamwork. In addition, managers were being rewarded for "empire building" rather than performance because their pay was linked to the number of people reporting to them. To solve these problems the company implemented a broadbanding system, reducing the company's overloaded job structure to six broadbands and collapsing many managerial and professional job titles. For example, the company collapsed 13 separate plant, regional, and production manager job titles down to four jobs with increased responsibility. The pay differential between bands was set at approximately 30%, with the range within each band set at approximately 90% (from $28,500 to $54,500 for "Band C," for instance).

Fine Products' new compensation system has given it the competitive advantage it needed. Broader salary bands have offered more room to reward sustained contributions, skills acquisition, and effective involvement in task force or project team assignments. The decreased emphasis on job levels has encouraged employees to make cross-functional moves to jobs that were at the same or a lower level in the old system. The new program has also facilitated job flexibility and cross-training because the broad bands can accommodate workers' current pay levels. Only a significant increase in an employee's accountability now justifies moving that employee to a new band.

Source: Based on Haslett, S. (1995, November/December). Broadbanding: A strategic tool for organizational change. *Compensation and Benefits Review,* 40–43. Reprinted by permission of the publisher. American Management Association, N.Y.

Skill-Based Compensation Plans

Unlike job-based compensation plans, skill-based compensation plans use skills as the basis of pay.[50] All employees start at the same pay rate and advance one pay level for each new skill they master.[51]

Three types of skills may be rewarded. Employees acquire *depth skills* when they learn more about a specialized area or become expert in a given field. They acquire *horizontal* or *breadth skills* when they learn more and more jobs or tasks within the firm, and *vertical skills* when they acquire "self-management" abilities, such as scheduling, coordinating, training, and leadership. Skill-based pay has been adopted by a wide range of industries, such as telecommunications (AT&T and Northern Telecom), insurance (Shenandoah Life Insurance), hotels (Embassy Suites), and retailing (Dayton Hudson). While it is used by only a relatively small proportion (5 to 7%) of all firms, skill-based pay is one of the fastest-growing innovations in the United States.[52]

Skill-based pay offers several potential advantages to the firm.[53] First, it creates a more flexible work force that is not straitjacketed by job descriptions specifying work assignments for a given job title. Second, it promotes cross-training, thus preventing absenteeism and turnover from disrupting the work unit's ability to meet deadlines. Third, it calls for fewer supervisors, so management layers can be cut to produce a leaner organization. Fourth, it increases employees' control over their compensation because they know in advance what it takes to receive a pay raise (learning new skills).

Skill-based pay does pose some risks to the organization. First, it may lead to higher compensation and training costs that are not offset by greater productivity or cost savings. This can happen when many employees master many or all of the skills and thus receive a higher wage than they would under a job-based pay rate. Second, unless employees have the opportunity to use all the skills they've acquired, they may become "rusty." Third, when employees hit the top of the pay structure, they may become frustrated and leave the firm because they have no further opportunity to receive a pay raise. Fourth, attaching monetary values to skills can become a guessing game unless external comparable pay data are available. Finally, skill-based pay may become part of the problem it is intended to solve (extensive bureaucracy and inflexibility) if an elaborate and time-consuming process is required to monitor and certify employee skills.

In short, skill-based pay is no panacea. To avoid cost overruns, perceptions of unfairness, and a highly regimented system, managers must carefully fit a skill-based pay system into their entire HR strategy. For example, to justify the additional training expenditures associated with skill-based pay, HR development should receive high priority in the firm's strategic plan. Such programs are more likely to work in organizations staffed with employees who are interested in learning multiple jobs rather than in beating the game to receive higher pay.

One final observation about skill-based pay: This is the pay system that many new and small businesses use by default. An entrepreneur who needs additional help hires people because of what they can do. Those who can do more things are more valuable to a growing business. Because flexibility is crucial for continued growth, flexible employees are more highly valued and paid accordingly. When a business is fairly new, of course, there is no formalized system relating specific skills to specific compensation values. However, at some point the company must systematize its compensation structure. It is then that the design issues described earlier become critical.

▸ The Legal Environment and Pay System Governance

The legal framework exerts substantial influence on the design and administration of compensation systems. The key federal laws that govern compensation criteria and procedures are the Fair Labor Standards Act, the Equal Pay Act, and the Internal Revenue Code. In addition to these, each state has its own sets of regulations that complement federal law. Labor laws may also limit managerial discretion in setting pay levels.

The Fair Labor Standards Act

Fair Labor Standards Act (FLSA)
The fundamental compensation law in the United States. Requires employers to record earnings and hours worked by all covered employees and to report this information to the U.S. Department of Labor. Defines two categories of employees: exempt and nonexempt.

exempt employee
An employee who is not covered by the provisions of the Fair Labor Standards Act. Most professional, administrative, executive, and outside sales jobs fall into this category.

nonexempt employee
An employee who is covered by the provisions of the Fair Labor Standards Act.

The **Fair Labor Standards Act (FLSA)** of 1938 is the compensation law that affects most pay structures in the United States. To comply with the FLSA, employers must keep accurate records of earnings and hours worked by all covered employees, and must report this information to the Wage and Hour Division of the U.S. Department of Labor. Most businesses are covered by the FLSA, except those with only one employee or annual gross sales under $500,000.

The FLSA defines two categories of employees: exempt and nonexempt. **Exempt employees** are not covered by the provisions of the act; **nonexempt employees** are. Exempt categories include professional, administrative, executive, and outside sales jobs. The Department of Labor provides guidelines to determine if a job is exempt or nonexempt. Managers are often tempted to classify as many jobs as possible as exempt to avoid some of the costs associated with nonexempt status, principally the minimum wage and overtime payments. However, there are heavy penalties for employers who unfairly classify nonexempt jobs as exempt.

Minimum Wages. The minimum wage set by the FLSA is currently $4.75 per hour ($5.15 per hour, effective September, 1997). Minimum wage legislation is controversial. Those in favor believe that it raises the standard of living for the poorest members of society. Those who oppose it argue that it results in higher levels of unemployment and poverty among low-skilled workers because it discourages firms from hiring and/or retaining workers. Opponents also claim that minimum wages encourage U.S. firms to open overseas plants in low-wage countries (such as Mexico and the Philippines), thereby creating more unemployment at home. This debate has not yet been resolved, probably because the minimum wage is set at a much lower level than most U.S. firms are willing to pay.

In a phenomenon known as *pay compression*, the minimum wage sometimes narrows differences in pay between levels in the firm, particularly at the lowest ranks. For example, the minimum wage increased by 27% in 1991, after being frozen since 1981. This was a much larger increase than those granted to employees at higher levels in the typical firm in 1991. An increase in the minimum wage may be quite costly if firms decide to restore the original pay differences by making pay adjustments in non–minimum-wage positions.

Overtime. The FLSA requires that nonexempt employees be paid one and a half times the standard wage for each hour they work over 40 hours a week. This provision was intended to stimulate hiring by making it more costly to expand production using existing employees. In fact, however, many firms would rather pay overtime than incur the costs associated with hiring additional employees (recruitment, training, benefits, and so on).

The Equal Pay Act

The Equal Pay Act (EPA) was passed in 1963 as an amendment to the FLSA. As we discussed in Chapter 3, it requires that men and women be paid the same amount of money if they hold similar jobs that are "substantially equal" in terms of skill, effort, responsibility, and working conditions. The EPA includes four exceptions that allow employers to pay one gender more than the other: (1) more seniority; (2) better job performance; (3) greater quantity or quality of production; and (4) certain other factors, such as paying extra compensation to employees for working the night shift. If there is a discrepancy in the average pay of men and women holding similar jobs, managers should ensure that at least one of the four exceptions to the EPA applies. If none of the four applies, the company may face stiff penalties in the form of legal costs and back pay to affected employees.

Comparable Worth. Equal pay should not be confused with comparable worth, a much more stringent form of legislation enacted in some countries and used in a few public jurisdictions in the United States. **Comparable worth** calls for comparable pay for jobs that require comparable skills, effort, and responsibility and have comparable working conditions, even if the job content is different. For instance, if a company using the point factor

comparable worth
A pay concept or doctrine that calls for comparable pay for jobs that require comparable skills, effort, and responsibility and have comparable working conditions, even if the job content is different.

Woman's Work.

As more women move into jobs traditionally filled by men, the issue of comparable worth has entered the spotlight.

job-evaluation system we described earlier finds that the administrative assistant position (held mostly by women) receives the same number of points as the shift supervisor position (held mostly by men), comparable worth legislation would require paying employees in these jobs equally, even though they might be exercising very different skills and responsibilities.

The considerable controversy surrounding comparable worth legislation centers mainly on how it should be implemented rather than on its main goal of pay equity between the sexes. Supporters of comparable worth legislation favor using job-evaluation tools to advance pay equity, pointing out that many private firms already use this method to set wages. Opponents argue that job evaluations are inherently arbitrary and that they do not take sufficient account of jobs' market value. For example, comparable worth proponents have often said that markets treat nurses unfairly because society links the profession to women's unpaid nurturing role in the family. Yet, in response to shortages, U.S. registered nurses' salaries rose 27.7% from 1981 to 1990, while the average salary paid to men declined by 2.8% (both figures are adjusted for inflation). In Minnesota's public sector, where comparable worth legislation is in place, nursing job evaluations showed nurses to be overpaid, and their salaries were lowered accordingly. Today many public health directors complain that they cannot afford to pay rates established by comparable worth legislation for nurses in the private sector. Despite all the problems with implementation, comparable worth is already being used in many countries, including Britain, Canada, and Australia.[54]

The Internal Revenue Code

Internal Revenue Code (IRC) The code of tax laws that affects how much of their earnings employees can keep and how benefits are treated for tax purposes.

The **Internal Revenue Code (IRC)** affects how much of their earnings employees can keep. It also affects how benefits are treated for tax purposes, as we discuss in Chapter 12. The IRC requires the company to withhold a portion of each employee's income to meet federal tax obligations (and, indirectly, state tax obligations, which in most states are set as a percentage of the federal tax deduction).

Tax laws change from time to time, and these changes affect an employee's take-home pay as well as what forms of compensation can be sheltered from taxes. An employer's failure to take advantage of IRC legislation may result in wasted payroll dollars. For instance, the tax laws currently treat capital gains (profits) on the sale of stock as ordinary income. This reduces the motivational value of stock as a long-term pay incentive because employees bear more risk with stock than with a cash-based form of pay. However, setting the capital gains tax below the tax on ordinary income could make stock more attractive to employees as a pay incentive.

Summary and Conclusions

What Is Compensation? Total compensation has three components: (1) base compensation, the fixed pay received on a regular basis; (2) pay incentives, programs designed to reward good performance; and (3) benefits or indirect compensation, including health insurance, vacations, and perquisites.

Designing a Compensation System. An effective compensation plan enables the firm to achieve its strategic objectives and is suited to the firm's unique characteristics as well as to its environment. The pay options managers need to consider in designing a compensation system are: (1) internal versus external equity, (2) fixed versus variable pay, (3) performance versus membership, (4) job versus individual pay, (5) egalitarianism versus elitism, (6) below-market versus above-market compensation, (7) monetary versus nonmonetary rewards, (8) open versus secret pay, and (9) centralization versus decentralization of pay decisions. In all situations, the best choices depend on how well they "fit" with business objectives and the individual organization.

Compensation Tools. There are two broad categories of compensation tools: job-based approaches and skill-based approaches. The typical job-based compensation plan has three components. (1) To achieve internal equity, firms use job evaluation to assess the relative value of jobs throughout the firm. (2) To achieve external equity, they use salary data on benchmark or key jobs obtained from market surveys to set a pay policy. (3) To achieve individual equity, they use a combination of experience, seniority, and performance to establish an individual's position within the pay range for his or her job.

Skill-based compensation systems are more costly and more limited in use. Skill-based pay rewards employees for acquiring depth skills (learning more about a specialized area), horizontal or breadth skills (learning about more areas), and vertical skills (self-management).

The Legal Environment and Pay System Governance. The major federal laws governing compensation practices are the Fair Labor Standards Act (which governs minimum wage and overtime payments and provides guidelines for classifying employees as exempt or nonexempt); the Equal Pay Act (which prohibits pay discrimination based on gender); and the Internal Revenue Code (which specifies how various forms of employee pay are subject to taxation). Some countries and municipalities have comparable worth legislation, which calls for comparable pay for jobs that require comparable skills, effort, and responsibility and have comparable working conditions, even if the job content is different.

Key Terms

base compensation, 298
benchmark job or key job, 314
comparable worth, 321
compensable factors, 311
egalitarian pay system, 303
elitist pay system, 303
exempt employee, 320
external equity, 299
Fair Labor Standards Act (FSLA), 320
individual equity, 316
internal equity, 299
Internal Revenue Code (IRC), 322
job banding, 317
job evaluation, 309
job hierarchy, 313
knowledge-based pay or skill-based pay, 303
nonexempt employee, 320
pay grades, 307
pay incentive, 298
pay policy, 316
total compensation, 298

Discussion Questions

1. Some companies have a policy of selectively matching external offers to prevent employees from leaving the company. What are the pros and cons of such a policy? Explain.
2. In 1996, the wealthiest 5% of Americans earned more than 20% of total household income, up from about 15% in 1970. Salaries for the top 5% of the work force have increased dramatically in recent years while those for the lowest 33% have decreased after adjusting for inflation. For example: The average physician in private practice in the United States nets $218,000 per year; the average orthopedic surgeon earns $364,000 per year. Nine medical professors at Cornell, Columbia, and Stanford Universities earn more than $1 million each per year. The typical partner in a law firm receives annual pay of $168,000. At last count, 5,043 professors in the United States were receiving over $100,000 for a nine-month academic year salary.

   Some people believe that these large salaries and growing inequalities in the labor market are unfair and show that the labor market doesn't work. Do you agree? Explain your answer.
3. Seventeen years ago a brash young engineer in a large chemical company handed her boss a four-page list of the promotions she expected to gain every two years as she rose through the ranks. She hoped for a vice presidency eventually, which would put her only half a dozen rungs below chairman at this title-stingy company. The engineer has held nine jobs so far, but the last three have kept her at the director's level. The company is restructuring and this talented 48-year-old woman is getting discouraged. What kind of nonmonetary rewards can the company offer to keep her from leaving?
4. One observer argues that external equity should always be the primary concern in compensation, noting that it attracts the best employees and prevents the top performers from leaving. Do you agree?
5. For jobs in Minnesota's public sector, compensation is based on job-evaluation systems. Several of these evaluation systems award high points, and thus high pay, for decision making, but their definition of "decision" is controversial. For instance, one sign language interpreter told a legislative committee that she had to make four decisions at the same time in her work, but under her jurisdiction's evaluation system, these types of decisions did not count. Do you agree with those, like the sign language interpreter, who argue that job evaluation is unfair? What are its advantages and disadvantages?
6. Recall the woman in question 3 who has been stuck at the director's level for several years. She is one of the few female engineers in the company, and she just found out through the grapevine that a male engineer at her rank is getting paid 25% more than she is. How would you determine if this pay difference meets at least one of the four exceptions to the Equal Pay Act?

MINICASE 1 *Aetna Finds Strength in Fewer Numbers—Of Job Descriptions*

Like many large firms, Aetna Life and Casualty Company has always relied on a highly stratified job-classification system in which everything, from salary levels and promotional opportunities to job descriptions and supervisory responsibilities, is connected to job class. "You know your job class, you know everything," explains Aetna's director of base-salary development.

Since it became a diversified financial services company, Aetna has been operating in a fast-changing and increasingly competitive business environment. But its employees are not accustomed to responding to market changes unless new tasks are written into their job descriptions. Since the old job-classification system isn't working in the new climate, Aetna is in the process of changing it. The company now defines work by the actual functions performed, gives information on market compensation levels to managers, and lets them make pay decisions based on an individual's performance. Major skills and competencies needed by employees are being identified and grouped into a broad job-family structure. With fewer job levels, employees may no longer be able to rely on promotions to get ahead. Instead they will earn bonuses for performing better. When Aetna completes this process, it expects to have just 200 job families instead of 7,000 job descriptions covering its 42,000 employees.

Discussion Questions

1. How would you describe Aetna's new system in terms of the following compensation criteria laid out in this chapter: job-based versus individual pay, centralized versus decentralized pay decisions?
2. Why does Aetna think that having broad rather than narrow job classifications is a motivating force? What kind of employees do you think will do best under the new system?

Source: Adapted from Caudron, S. (1993, June). Master the compensation maze. *Personnel Journal*, 64B–64O. Copyright June 1993. Reprinted with the permission of *Personnel Journal*, ACC Communications, Inc., Costa Mesa, CA (714) 751-1883; all rights reserved.

MINICASE 2 *Compensation and the New Economics of Mental Health*

Psychotherapists are complaining about a growing drug problem among their patients. But in this new wave of apparent drug abuse, it isn't the users who are responsible.

Marge Wertlieb, a Dix Hills, NY, psychotherapist, says she detected signs of heavy drug use in a troubled 10-year-old boy she saw earlier this year. "He looked like someone on heroin," Ms. Wertlieb says. "This child was clearly not in this world. I couldn't treat the child while he was in that state."

The twist was that the boy's pill-popping wasn't his idea, but rather that of a psychiatrist working for a managed health care company.

Managed-care companies, with their mandate to cut costs, often prefer to treat mental health problems with drugs. Not only do they limit coverage for psychotherapy, they often pay psychiatrists more per hour to supervise drug treatment than to provide counseling. "The pay premium has an enormous influence on how therapists practice," says Chicago psychiatrist John Gottlieb, "because it makes a significant difference in yearly income."

Executives at managed-care firms respond that traditional psychotherapists have financial incentives to favor months or even years of talk therapy, which can cost patients (or their insurers) as much as $100 a session. As Ian Shaffer, Chief Medical Officer of Value Behavioral Health Inc. in Falls Church, VA, puts it, the goal of cost-effective managed care (which saves employers as much as 30% in treatment cost per patient) is to "get as many [patients] better as fast as you can."

Discussion Questions

1. Do you think it is appropriate and ethical for managed-care companies to give doctors pay incentives to control costs? Why or why not?
2. How might a managed-care company structure its compensation system so that both doctors and patients benefit?

Source: Adapted from Pollock, E. J. (1995, December 1). Side effects. *The Wall Street Journal*, A-1.

CASE 1 Scott Paper: A Miracle or a Hoax?

After less than two years as CEO of Scott Paper, in 1996 Albert J. Dunlap, nicknamed "chainsaw Al," walked away with nearly $100 million in salary, bonus, stock gains, and other perks. Kimberly-Clark (which recently purchased Scott Paper) had agreed to pay Dunlap and a corps of his loyal lieutenants an extraordinary $41 million in the most lucrative noncompete agreement ever crafted in U.S. business. Dunlap alone got $20 million in exchange for his agreement not to work for a rival for five years, while five senior executives pocketed $4.2 million each.

Critics argue that Dunlap and other former Scott Paper executives were being rewarded for doing all the wrong things. Soon after taking over, critics say, Dunlap's team began making moves that suggested their time horizons weren't very long. In late 1994, Scott's R&D budget was slashed in half, to about $35 million, and 60% of the R&D was eliminated. At the request of Dunlap's team, the marketing department began to generate weekly volume forecasts rather than monthly reports.

The cost cutters didn't go after just R&D, according to detractors. They also forbade managers from being involved in community activities because that would take away from their business duties. They banned memberships in industry organizations that allowed managers to network with competitors. They also scrapped a yearly event at which Scott met with its leading suppliers to improve relationships and get better prices. As a result of these policies, several communities lost a generous corporate citizen—especially in the Philadelphia area, where the company was headquartered from its founding in 1879 until 1995. Before moving the world headquarters to Boca Raton, Florida—just after buying an $18 million house there—Dunlap eliminated all corporate gifts to charities, even reneging on the final $50,000 payment of a $250,000 pledge to the Philadelphia Museum of Art. More than 11,000 of Scott's employees (71% of headquarters staff, 50% of managers, 20% of hourly workers) lost their jobs during Dunlap's brief tenure.

Scott's earnings more than doubled during Dunlap's tenure as CEO, but critics claim that Dunlap engineered these illusory gains to maximize his pay and that of his close colleagues. They argue that Dunlap cut plenty of muscle along with the fat, pumping up short-term results at the expense of long-term health and destroying employees' commitment to the firm. To bolster their claim, Dunlap's critics point out that Scott actually lost market share in the three major product fields (paper towels, bathroom tissue, and facial tissue) during Dunlap's tenure.

Critical Thinking Questions

1. What problems may arise when pay is based on "objective" performance results?
2. What are some of the pros and cons of Scott's compensation policies for top managers and executives? Are these attuned to Scott's goal of increasing profits and competitiveness in an increasingly crowded market? Explain.
3. Under Dunlap's leadership, Scott's stock rose 22.5%, making shareholders very happy. Many financial experts believe that maximizing shareholders' welfare must be a corporation's overriding objective in a free market economy. Do you agree that managers' pay should be closely tied to the pursuit of this goal? Explain.

Cooperative Learning Exercise

4. Students divide into groups of five. Some groups are asked to defend Dunlap's actions at Scott Paper, while other groups are asked to argue the opposite side. The instructor will play the role of moderator in an open debate.

Sources: Byrne, J. A., and Weber, J. (1996, January 15) *Business Week*, 44–49; Reinhard, B. (1995, July 19). Scott CEO reaps millions from turnaround merger. *Palm Beach Post* (Internet site); and Reinhard, B. (1995, July 20). Scott's second quarter earnings triple to record $145.5 million. *Palm Beach Post* (Internet site).

CASE 2 An Academic Question

Mountain States University is a medium-sized public university with 21,000 students and 1,200 faculty members. The College of Business Administration is the largest one on campus, with 8,000 students and 180 faculty members. For the past few years, the dean has had to deal with a large number of dissatisfied faculty who complain that they are underpaid relative to newly hired faculty. Many of the complainants are senior tenured professors who refuse to engage in committee activities beyond the minimum service requirements and who are seldom in their offices because they feel aggrieved. They teach six hours a week, spend two hours in the office, and then disappear from campus. Recently, the head of the college's faculty council compiled some statistics and sent these to the dean, demanding "prompt action to create more equity in the faculty

continued

Rank	1980 New Hires	1980 Current	1986 New Hires	1986 Current
Full professors	$30,200	$33,200	$47,000	$42,000
Associate professors	$25,100	$29,100	$39,000	$36,000
Assistant professors	$18,000	$20,000	$34,000	$30,000

Rank	1992 New Hires	1992 Current	Now New Hires	Now Current
Full professors	$68,000	$56,000	$79,000	$62,000
Associate professors	$62,000	$51,000	$73,000	$61,000
Assistant professors	$52,000	$48,000	$61,000	$59,000

pay structure." The average salary statistics are shown in the table above.

The dean replied that he has little choice but to make offers to new faculty that are competitive with the market and that the university will not give him enough funds to maintain equitable pay differences between new and current faculty or between higher and lower ranks.

Critical Thinking Questions

1. Based on the data collected by the faculty council, name three compensation problems that exist at Mountain States University.
2. Is the dean's explanation for decreased pay differences by rank and/or seniority justifiable?
3. How would you suggest the dean deal with senior faculty who feel underpaid?

Cooperative Learning Exercise

4. A group of six faculty members has come to see the dean to express dissatisfaction with pay compression at the college. All six represent current faculty; two are assistant professors, two are associate professors, and two are full professors. Students divide into groups of seven and role-play this situation as the dean attempts to deal with the pay complaints raised by the faculty. The dean doesn't have the money to correct the pay-compression problem, yet he can't afford to alienate the faculty.

HRM Simulation 

Your firm pays somewhat below the local market, which may account for the firm's high turnover rate. This high turnover rate is expensive because of the costs associated with selecting and training new employees, and disruptions in the work flow. What makes your problem more serious is the fact that the more experienced employees (those who are the hardest to replace) are quitting at a higher rate. Your team faces a dilemma here: Increasing wages will increase costs, but turnover is also expensive. Either option may put you at a competitive disadvantage. Given that the CEO has given you authority for making compensation decisions, subject to certain constraints, what would you recommend? What are the pros and cons of your recommendations?

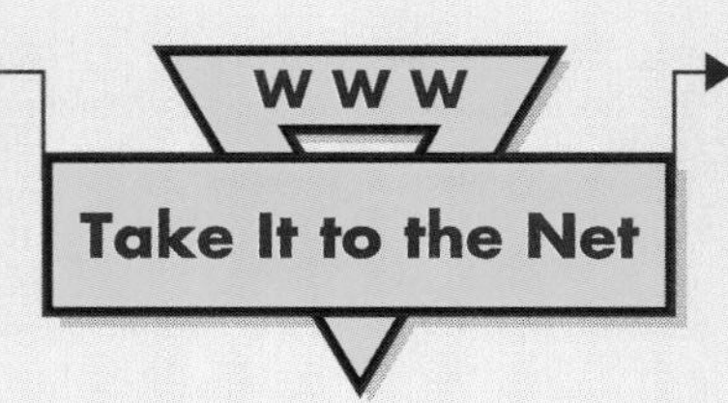

We invite you to visit the Gómez-Mejía/Balkin/Cardy page on the Prentice Hall Web site:

http://www.prenhall.com/gomez

You can also visit the Web sites for these companies, featured within this chapter:

Amway	http://www.amway.com
Ben and Jerry's Homemade, Inc.	http://www.benjerry.com
Citibank	http://www.citibank.com
Texas Instruments	http://www.ti.com
U.S. Postal Service	http://www.usps.com

Endnotes

1. Milkovich, G. T., and Newman, J. M. (1996). *Compensation* (4th ed.). Homewood, IL: Irwin.
2. U.S. Chamber of Commerce (1994). *Employee Benefits*. Washington, DC: U.S. Chamber of Commerce; and Salisbury, D. (1996, May). Reforming social security and other public entitlements. *ACA News*, 6–9.
3. Gómez-Mejía, L. R., and Balkin, D. B. (1992a). The determinants of faculty pay: An agency theory perspective. *Academy of Management Journal, 35*(5), 921–955.
4. Duff, C. (1996, February 14). Wage-benefit increase sets 14-year low. *The Wall Street Journal*, A-2; Church, G. J. (1996, January 20). Are we better off? *Time*, 37–45; Lancaster, H. (1995, November 7). Experts won't say it, but that counteroffer may be your best bet. *The Wall Street Journal*, B-1; Wallace, M. J., and Fay, C. H. (1983). *Compensation theory and practice*. Boston: PWS-Kent.
5. Platt, R. K. (1996, January). Driving change. *ACA News*, 1; Wallace, M. J. (1991). Sustaining success with alternative rewards. In M. L. Rock and L. A. Berger (Eds.), *The compensation handbook*. New York: McGraw-Hill.
6. Hugessen, K. (1996, January). Strategic compensation: A new compensation model for a new age. *ACA News*, 3; Carroll, S. J. (1987). Business strategies and compensation systems. In D. B. Balkin and L. R. Gómez-Mejía (Eds.), *New perspectives on compensation*. Englewood Cliffs, NJ: Prentice Hall; and Milkovich, G. T., and Broderick, R. F. (1991). Developing a compensation strategy. In M. L. Rock and L. A. Berger (Eds.), *The compensation handbook*. New York: McGraw-Hill.
7. Case, K. and Fair, R. (1996). *Principles of economics*, (4th ed.), Upper Saddle River, NJ: Prentice Hall.
8. Wallace, M. J., and Fay, C. H. (1983). *Compensation theory and practice* (1st ed.). Boston: Kent Publishing Co., 41.
9. Gómez-Mejía and Balkin, 1992a.
10. Cascio, W. F. (1990). Strategic human resource management in high technology industry. In L. R. Gómez-Mejía and M. Lawless (Eds.), *Organizational issues in high technology management*. Greenwich, CT: JAI Press; and Kail, J. C. (1987). Compensating scientists and engineers. In D. B. Balkin and L. R. Gómez-Mejía (Eds.), *New perspectives on compensation*. Englewood Cliffs, NJ: Prentice Hall.
11. Gómez-Mejía, L. R., and Welbourne, T. M. (1988). Compensation strategy: An overview and future steps. *Human Resource Planning, 11*(3), 173–189.
12. Desmond, E. W. (1996, April 22). The failed miracle. *Time*, 61–64; and Gómez-Mejía, L. R., and Balkin, D. B. (1992b). *Compensation, organizational strategy, and firm performance*. Cincinnati, OH: South-Western.
13. Lancaster, H. (1996, January 27). Chasing start ups may not always lead to a pot of gold. *The Wall Street Journal*, B-1; Milkovich, G. T., Gerhart, B., and Hannon, J. (1991). The effects of research and development intensity on managerial compensation in large organizations. *Journal of High Technology Management Research, 2*(1), 133–150.
14. Plachy, R., and Schroeder, L. (1996, January). Pay for results—New philosophy rewards accomplishments. *ACA News*, 5; Mahoney, T. A. (1989). Employment compensation planning and strategy. In L. R. Gómez-Mejía (Ed.), *Compensation and benefits*. Washington, DC: Bureau of National Affairs.
15. Lehr, L. W. (1986, Winter). The care and flourishing of entrepreneurs at 3M. *Directors and Boards*, 18–20.
16. Bylinsky, G. (1990, July 2). Turning R&D into real products. *Fortune*, 72.
17. Platt, 1996; and Lawler, E. E., III. (1991). Paying the person: A better approach to management. *Unpublished technical report*, Center for Effective Organizations, University of Southern California, Los Angeles.
18. Wolf, M. G. (1991). Theories, approaches, and practices of salary administration. In M. L. Rock and L. A. Berger (Eds.), *The compensation handbook*. New York: McGraw-Hill.
19. Tosi, H., and Tosi, L. (1986). What managers need to know about knowledge-based pay. *Organizational Dynamics, 14*(3), 52–64; and Wallace, 1991.
20. Dewey, B. J. (1994, January–February). Changing to skill-based pay. *Compensation and Benefits Review*, 38–43; Ledford, L. W. (1991). The design of skill-based plans. In M. L. Rock and L. A. Berger (Eds.), *The compensation handbook*. New York: McGraw-Hill.
21. Gómez-Mejía and Balkin, 1992b.
22. Caudron, S. (1993, June). Master the compensation maze. *Personnel Journal*, 64B-64O.
23. Laabs, J. (1992, November). Ben and Jerry's caring capitalism. *Personnel Journal*, 50–57.
24. Gómez-Mejía, L. R., Balkin, D. B., and Malkovich, G. T. (1990). Rethinking your rewards for technical employees. *Organizational Dynamics, 1*(1), 107–118; and Lawler, E. E., III. (1990). *Strategic Pay*. San Francisco: Jossey-Bass.
25. Lawler, 1991.
26. Fay, C. H. (1987). Using the strategic planning process to develop a compensation strategy. *Topics in Total Compensation, 2*(2), 117–129.
27. Lloyd, D. (1994, January 24). Manager's journal: Beating the Hong Kong hiring blues. *The Wall Street Journal*, A12.
28. Jarrel, S. B., and Stanley, T. D. (1990). A meta-analysis of the union-nonunion wage gap. *Industrial and Labor Relations Review, 44*(1), 54–67.
29. Hambrick, D. C., and Snow, C. C. (1989). Strategic reward systems. In C. C. Snow (Ed.), *Strategy, organization design, and human resources management*. Greenwich, CT: JAI Press.
30. Associated Press. (1991, April 4). What matters to Americans. *Arizona Republic*, A7.
31. Seidman, W. L., and Skancke, S. L. (1989). *Competitiveness: The executive's guide to success*. New York: M.E. Sharpe.
32. Werner, S., and Gemeinhardt, G. (1995, September/October). Nonprofit organizations: What factors determine pay level? *Compensation and Benefits Review*, 53–60; and Gómez-Mejía and Balkin, 1992b.
33. Weber, J. (1990, December 10). Farewell fast track: Promotions and raises are scarcer—So what will energize managers? *Business Week*, 192–200.
34. Lawler, 1990.

35. Gómez-Mejía and Balkin, 1992a.
36. Balkin, D. B., and Gómez-Mejía, L. R. (1990). Matching compensation and organizational strategies. *Strategic Management Journal, 11*, 153–169; and Carroll, 1987.
37. Cantoni, C. J. (1995, May 15). A waste of human resources. *The Wall Street Journal*, B-1.
38. Kanin-Lovers, J. (1991). Job evaluation technology. In M. L. Rock and L. A. Berger (Eds.), *The compensation handbook*. New York: McGraw-Hill.
39. Milkovich and Newman, 1996; Rock, M. L., and Berger, L. A. (Eds.) (1991). *The compensation handbook*. New York: McGraw-Hill; and issues of *Compensation & Benefits Review* and *American Compensation Association Journal*.
40. Gómez-Mejía, Balkin, and Milkovich, 1990.
41. Milkovich and Newman, 1996.
42. Additional information on the criteria, conventions, interpretation, and application of the MAA (NMTA) plan can be obtained by contacting the nearest MAA association office:

    AAIM Management Association, St. Louis, MO; AAIM, The Management Association, North Haven, CT; American Society of Employers, Southfield, MI; Capital Associated Industries, Inc., Raleigh, NC; CMEA The Employers Association, Worcester, MA; Employers Association, Inc., Minneapolis, MN; Employers Association of Western Massachusetts, Inc., Ludlow, MA; TEA–The Employers Association, Inc., Braintree, MA; The Employers Association, Lincoln, RI; Employers Resource Council, Seven Hills, OH; IMA Management Association, Inc., Clifton, NJ; IMC–Industrial Management Council, Rochester, NY; The Management Association of Illinois, Broadview, IL; MidAtlantic Employers' Association, Valley Forge, PA; MRA–The Management Association, Inc., Brookfield, WI.
43. Gómez-Mejía, L.R., Page, R. C., and Tornow, W. (1987). Computerized job evaluation systems. In D. B. Balkin and L. R. Gómez-Mejía (Eds.), *New perspectives on compensation*. Englewood Cliffs, NJ: Prentice Hall.
44. NMTA Associates. (1992). National position evaluation plan, 3. Clifton, NJ.
45. Lichty, D. T. (1991). Compensation surveys. In M. L. Rock and L. A. Berger (Eds.), *The compensation handbook*. New York: McGraw-Hill.
46. Dunlop, J. T. (1957). The task of contemporary wage theory. In G. W. Taylor and F. C. Pierson (Eds.), *New concepts in wage determination*. New York: McGraw-Hill; Gerhart, B., and Milkovich, G. T. (1993). Employee compensation: Research and practice. In M. D. Dunnette and L. M. Hough (Eds.), *Handbook of industrial and organizational psychology* (Vol. 3). Palo Alto, CA: Consulting Psychologists Press; and Treiman, D. J., and Hartmann, H. I. (Eds.). (1981). *Women, work, and wages: Equal pay for jobs of equal value*. Washington, DC: National Academy Press.
47. Foster, K. E. (1985, September). An anatomy of company pay practices. *Personnel*, 66–72.

47a. LeBlanc, P. V., and Ellis, G. M. (1995, Winter). The many faces of banding. *ACA Journal*, 52–62; *ACA Journal* (1995, Autumn). Clark refining and marketing broadbands: Annual pay rates, 57.

48. See, for example, Balkin, D. B., and Gómez-Mejía, L. R. (1996). Determining faculty pay equity by gender. Paper presented at Academy of Management National Convention, Cincinnati, OH; Balkin, D. B., and Miller, J. (1996). The influence of comparable worth in Ontario. *Unpublished paper*, University of Colorado, Boulder.
49. Gómez-Mejía, Page, and Tornow, 197.
50. Ledford, 1991; Zingheim, P. K., Ledford, G. E., and Schuster, J. R. (1996, Spring). Competencies and competency models: Does one size fit all? *ACA Journal, 5*(1), 56–65.
51. Wallace, M. J. (1990). *Rewards and renewal: America's search for competitive advantage through alternative pay strategies*. Scottsdale, AZ: American Compensation Association.
52. Barton, P. (1996, February). Team-based pay. *ACA Journal, 5* (1), 15-30; Watson Wyatt Data Services (1996). The 1995–1996 ECS surveys of middle management and office personnel compensation. Rochelle Park, NJ.
53. Gupta, N., Ledford, G. E., Jenkins, G. D., and Doty, D. (1992). Survey-based prescriptions for skill-based pay. *American Compensation Association Journal, 1*(1), 48–59; Ledford, L. W. (1990). The effectiveness of skill-based pay. *Perspectives in total compensation, 1*(1), 1–4; Ledford, 1991; and Tosi and Tosi, 1986.
54. Aaron, H. J., and Lougy, C. M. (1986). *The comparable worth controversy*. Washington, DC: The Brookings Institution, 3–4; Rhoads, S. E. (1993, July–August). Pay equity won't go away. *Across the Board*, 37–41; and Balkin and Hiller, 1996.

11 Rewarding Performance

A Job Well Done. The positive psychological effects of recognition for a job well done are substantial. For this reason, many companies offer their employees not only annual raises and bonuses, but also prizes and awards ceremonies.

CHALLENGES

After reading this chapter, you should be able to deal more effectively with the following challenges:

1 ▶ **Recognize** individual and group contributions to the firm by rewarding high performers.

2 ▶ **Develop** pay-for-performance plans that are appropriate for different levels in an organization.

3 ▶ **Identify** the potential benefits and drawbacks of different pay-for-performance systems and choose the plan that is most appropriate for a particular firm.

4 ▶ **Design** an executive compensation package that motivates executives to make decisions that are in the firm's best interests.

5 ▶ **Weigh** the pros and cons of different compensation methods for sales personnel and create an incentive plan that is consistent with the firm's marketing strategy.

6 ▶ **Design** an incentive system to reward excellence in customer service.

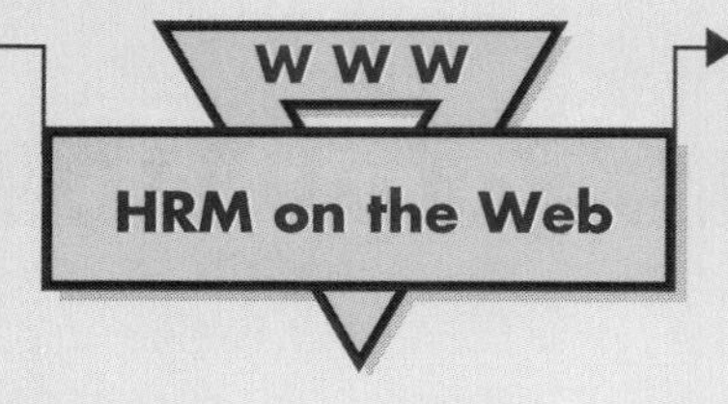

http://www.fed.org/library.html

Equity Compensation Strategies

This Web site contains a variety of materials focusing on performance-based compensation. The site provides information on such topics as developing an equity-based compensation strategy, stock bonus awards, stock option plans, employee stock ownership plans (ESOPs), and 401(k) and other qualified retirement plans. Many of these plans are used to reward employees and managers for their long-term performance.

Century Telephone Company bases its employees' annual pay raises on how well they perform their job duties. For the past ten years, these "merit raises" have averaged 4.5% of base pay. About two years ago the HR department conducted an employee attitude survey. One of its most striking findings: More than 75% of employees felt that pay raises and performance were unrelated. In response, top managers asked the HR staff to determine if pay raises were indeed based on performance (as required by policy) or on some other unrelated factors. Surprisingly, the data showed that employees were right: Supervisors rated more than 80% of their workers as "excellent," and there was only minimal differentiation in the percentage raises received by individual employees.

Top management concluded that supervisors were equalizing performance ratings and raises, sidestepping their responsibility to reward employees on the basis of performance.

To remedy the situation, Century instituted a new procedure a year ago. Under this new system, supervisors must distribute employee performance ratings as follows: excellent (top 15%), very good (next 20%), good (next 20%), satisfactory (next 35%), marginal or unsatisfactory (lowest 10%). Pay raises are pegged to these performance classifications, with employees at the top receiving a 10% raise and those at the bottom receiving nothing.

Shortly after the system was put in place, it became obvious that something had gone wrong. A large number of employees could not understand how or why their performance had "dropped" compared to the previous year. Many believed that favoritism played a big role in who received pay increases. Irate employees hounded their supervisors, who in turn complained that increased tension was poisoning interpersonal relationships and interfering with performance.

The experience of Century Telephone (a real company here given a fictitious name) shows how well-meaning attempts to motivate employees with pay incentives can backfire. Nonetheless, the use of pay incentives is clearly on the rise. Between 1988 and 1995 the number of U.S. companies offering pay for performance (chiefly in the form of bonuses) to all salaried employees jumped from 47% to 77%.[1] At the extreme end of this scale is Levi Strauss, which recently promised all its employees in 60 countries a full year's pay as bonus, if the company hits a target cash-flow level over the next several years. This program could cost Levi Strauss an estimated $750 million.[1a]

In this chapter we discuss the design and implementation of pay-for-performance (incentive) systems. First, we address the major challenges facing managers in their attempts to link pay and performance. Second, we offer a set of general recommendations to deal with these challenges. Third, we describe specific types of pay-for-performance programs and the advantages and disadvantages of each. We conclude with a discussion of unique pay-for-performance plans for two important employee groups, executives and sales personnel.

▸ Pay for Performance: The Challenges

Most workers believe that those who work harder and produce more should be rewarded accordingly. If employees see that pay is not distributed on the basis of merit, they are more likely to lack commitment to the organization, decrease their level of effort, and look for employment opportunities elsewhere.[2]

In Chapter 10, we examined the process of classifying jobs into hierarchies. Jobs at the top of the hierarchy contribute more to the organization and, therefore, receive higher compensation than jobs at the bottom of the hierarchy. In this chapter, we are concerned with how effectively employees within the same job classification perform their tasks. **Pay-for-performance systems**, also called **incentive systems**, reward employee performance on the basis of three assumptions:[3]

pay-for-performance system or **incentive system**
A system that rewards employees on the assumptions that: (1) individual employees and work teams differ in how much they contribute to the firm; (2) the firm's overall performance depends to a large degree on the performance of individuals and groups within the firm; and (3) to attract, retain, and motivate high performers and to be fair to all employees, the firm needs to reward employees on the basis of their relative performance.

1. Individual employees and work teams differ in how much they contribute to the firm—not only in what they do, but also in how well they do it.
2. The firm's overall performance depends to a large degree on the performance of individuals and groups within the firm.
3. To attract, retain, and motivate high performers and to be fair to all employees, a company needs to reward employees on the basis of their relative performance.

These assumptions seem straightforward and acceptable. However, it is widely recognized that incentive systems can create negative consequences for firms. Thus, before talking about specific types of pay-for-performance plans, we will discuss eight challenges facing organizations that want to adopt an incentive system.

The "Do Only What You Get Paid For" Syndrome

To avoid the charge that pay is distributed on the basis of subjective judgments or favoritism, pay-for-performance systems tend to rely on objective indicators of performance.[4] This may lead some managers to use whatever "objective" data are available to justify pay decisions. Unfortunately, the closer pay is tied to particular performance indicators, the more employees tend to focus on those indicators and neglect other important job components that are more difficult to measure. Consider the following examples:

- In some school systems where teachers' pay has been linked to students' scores on standardized tests, teachers spend more time helping students do well on the tests than helping them understand the subject matter. As one expert has noted, "When you interview the teachers, they tell you they would like to teach other things, but they feel they have to teach to the test [because] they are afraid that a poor showing by their pupils will result in negative evaluations for themselves or their schools."[5]
- Administrators in many colleges and universities rely on student ratings to evaluate faculty performance, even though many people believe that this measure reflects popularity more than quality of instruction.
- Many brokerage houses pay more than 50% of a broker/analyst's compensation in the form of commissions generated on the stocks they pick. This sometimes leads analysts to push stocks that pay the highest commissions, even if these are a poor investment for clients. This potential conflict of interest has exposed brokerage houses to significant legal risks and, in some cases, costly court settlements in favor of customers.[6]

Negative Effects on the Spirit of Cooperation

The experiences of Century Telephone Company clearly show that pay-for-performance systems may provoke conflict and competition while discouraging cooperation.[7] For instance, employees may withhold information from a colleague if they believe that it will

Issues + Applications

Incentives That Backfired: The Case of Lantech

Lantech, a small manufacturer of machinery in Kentucky, learned through firsthand experience how incentive plans can backfire:

> Incentive pay encourages workers to improve quality, cut costs, and otherwise enhance the corporate good. Right? Well, that's the way it's supposed to work. In the real world, pay for performance can also release passions that turn workers into rival gangs, so greedy for extra dollars they will make another gang's numbers look bad to make their own look good. Such was the experience of Pat Lancaster, the chairman of Lantech.…To his dismay, Lancaster discovered that the lust for bonus bucks grew so overheated and so petty that one of his workers tried to stiff a competing division for the toilet paper bill.
>
> "Incentive pay is toxic," says Lancaster, "because it is so open to favoritism and manipulation."
>
> At one point, each of the company's five manufacturing divisions was given a bonus determined by how much profit it made. An individual worker's share of the bonus could amount to as much as 10% of his or her regular pay. But the divisions are so interdependent, it was very difficult to sort out which division was entitled to what profits. "That led to so much secrecy, politicking, and sucking noise that you wouldn't believe it," says CEO Jim Lancaster, Pat's son. For example, the division that built standard machines and the one that added custom design features to those machines depended on each other for parts, engineering expertise, and such. So inevitably the groups clashed, each one trying to assign costs to the other and claim credit for revenues.
>
> "I was spending 95% of my time in conflict resolution instead of on how to serve our customers," recalls Pat. The divisions wrangled so long over who would get charged for overhead cranes to haul heavy equipment around the factory floor that Lantech couldn't install those useful machines until 1992, several years later than planned. At the end of each month, the divisions would rush to fill orders from other parts of the company. Such behavior created profits for the division filling the order but, unfortunately, generated piles of unnecessary and costly inventory in the receiving division. Some employees even argued over who would have to pay for the toilet paper in the common restrooms.
>
> So Lantech has finally abandoned individual and division performance pay, and relies instead on a profit-sharing system in which all employees get bonuses based on salary. Furious passions have subsided, and the company is doing just fine now, says the senior Lancaster.

Source: Reprinted from Nulty, P. (1995, November 13). Incentive pay can be crippling. *Fortune*, 235.

help the other person get ahead. Those who are receiving less than they feel they deserve may try to "get back" at those who are receiving more, perhaps by sabotaging a project or spreading rumors. Internal competition may set off rivalries that lead to quality problems or even cheating.

Lack of Control

As we noted in Chapter 7, employees often cannot control all of the factors affecting their performance. Some examples of factors beyond an employee's control are the supervisor, performance of other work group members, the quality of the materials the employee is working with, working conditions, the amount of support from management, and environmental factors.[8] For instance, the sales generated by a particular salesperson may be more a function of the territory than of the person's sales ability. Linking pay to performance in such a situation is inequitable and demoralizing.

Difficulties in Measuring Performance

As we saw in Chapter 7, assessing employee performance is one of the thorniest tasks a manager faces, particularly when the assessments are used to dispense rewards.[9] At the employee level, the appraiser must try to untangle individual contributions from those of the work group while avoiding judgments based on a personality bias (being a strict or a lenient rater), likes and dislikes, and political agendas. At the group or team level, the rater must try to isolate the specific contributions of any given team when all teams are interdependent.[10] Appraisers experience the same difficulties in attempting to determine the performance of plants or units that are interrelated among themselves and with corporate headquarters. In short, accurate measures of performance are not easy to achieve, and tying pay to inaccurate measures is likely to create problems.

Psychological Contracts

Once implemented, a pay-for-performance system creates a psychological contract between the employee and the firm.[11] A *psychological contract* is a set of expectations based on prior experience, and it is very resistant to change.

Breaking a psychological contract can have damaging results. For instance, when a computer products manufacturer changed the terms of its pay-for-performance program three times in a two-year period, the result was massive employee protests, the resignation of several key managers, and a general lowering of employee morale.

Two other problems may arise with respect to the psychological contract. First, because employees feel entitled to the reward spelled out in the pay-for-performance plan, it is difficult to change the plan even when conditions call for a change. Second, it is sometimes hard to come up with a formula that is fair to diverse employee groups.

The Credibility Gap

Employees often do not believe that pay-for-performance programs are fair or that they truly reward performance, a phenomenon called the *credibility gap*.[12] Some studies indicate that as many as 75% of a typical firm's employees question the integrity of pay-for-performance plans.[13] If employees do not consider the system legitimate and acceptable, it may well have negative rather than positive effects on their behavior. For instance, merit pay for teachers has been a favorite topic of political candidates over the past 20 years, but the merit pay systems that have been implemented have generally received low marks from teachers. In one North Carolina pilot project, outsiders sat in on classes three times a year to review teachers' performance. Teachers complained that the reviews were subjective and that bad teachers just cleaned up their act for the evaluation.[14]

Job Dissatisfaction and Stress

Pay-for-performance systems may lead to greater productivity but lower job satisfaction.[15] Some research suggests that the more pay is tied to performance, the more the work unit begins to unravel and the more unhappy employees become.[16] The Issues and Applications feature describing what happened at Lantech illustrates how incentives can raise stress along with productivity.

How much consideration should the organization give to the psychological health of its employees when designing a pay-for-performance system?

Potential Reduction of Intrinsic Drives

Pay-for-performance programs may push employees to the point of doing whatever it takes to get the promised monetary reward, in the process stifling their talents and creativity. Thus, an organization that puts too much emphasis on pay in attempting to influence behaviors may reduce employees' *intrinsic drives*. One expert argues that the more a firm stresses pay as an incentive for high performance, the less likely it is that employees will engage in activities that benefit the organization (such as overtime and extra special service) unless they are promised an explicit reward.[17]

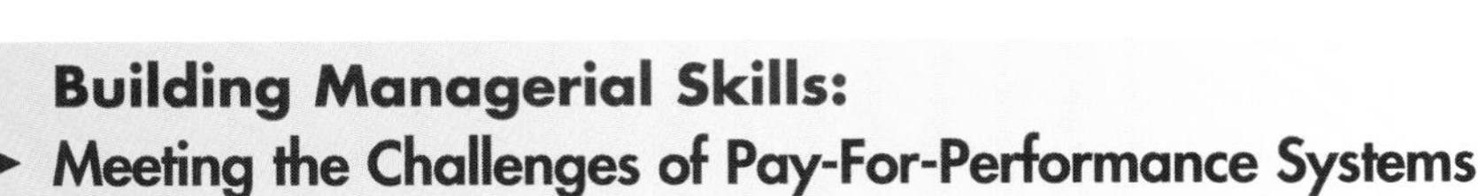

Building Managerial Skills: ▸ Meeting the Challenges of Pay-For-Performance Systems

Properly designed pay-for-performance systems present managers with an excellent opportunity to align employees' interests with those of the organization. The following recommendations can help to enhance the success of performance programs and avoid the pitfalls we just discussed.

Link Pay and Performance Appropriately

piece-rate system
A compensation system in which employees are paid per unit produced.

There are few cases in which managers can justify paying workers according to a preestablished formula or measure. Traditional **piece-rate systems**, in which workers are paid per unit produced, represent the tightest link between pay and performance. Many piece-rate systems have been abandoned because they tend to create the kinds of problems discussed earlier, but there are situations in which piece-rate plans are appropriate. The primary requirement is that the employee has complete control over the speed and quality of the work. For example, it is appropriate to pay typists for the number of pages they type *if* they can work at their own pace. However, most typists should not be paid on a piece-rate basis because they often have other responsibilities (for example, handling telephone calls) and are subject to constant interruptions.

Use Pay for Performance as Part of a Broader HRM System

Pay-for-performance programs are not likely to achieve the desired results unless they are accompanied by complementary HRM programs. For instance, performance appraisals and supervisory training usually play a major role in the eventual success or failure of a pay-for-performance plan. As we saw in Chapter 7, performance ratings are often influenced by factors other than performance. Since a defective appraisal process can undermine even the most carefully conceived pay plan, supervisors should be rigorously trained in correct rating practice.

Poor staffing practices can also damage the credibility of a pay-for-performance program. For instance, if employees are hired because of their political connections rather than for their skills and abilities, other employees will get the message that good performance is not that important to the organization.

Build Employee Trust

Even the best-conceived pay-for-performance program can fail if managers have a poor history of labor relations or if the organization has a cutthroat culture. Under these conditions, employees are not likely to attribute rewards to good performance, but rather to chance or good impression management. If a pay-for-performance program is to have a chance of succeeding, managers need to build employee trust, which may require making major changes in the organization's climate.

Building trust can be a tall order, particularly in companies where cynicism rules. Managers should start by answering these questions from their employees' perspective:

- Does it pay for me to work longer, harder, or smarter?
- Does anyone notice my extra efforts?

If the answers are no, managers need to go all out to show that they care about employees and are aware of the work they do. Even more important, they need to keep employees informed and involved when making any changes in management or the compensation plan.[18]

Promote the Belief that Performance Makes a Difference

Because of the problems noted earlier, managers may shy away from using pay to reward performance.[19] However, unless an organization creates an atmosphere in which performance makes a difference, it may end up with a low-achievement organizational culture. In a sense, then, pay-for-performance systems are the lesser of two evils because without them, performance may drop even lower.[20]

Use Multiple Layers of Rewards

All pay-for-performance systems have advantages and disadvantages. For instance, bonuses or pay raises given to individual employees are more motivating than some other incentives because they allow employees to see how their personal contributions led to a direct reward. At the same time, though, they tend to create more internal competition, which leads to less cooperation. Bonuses given to teams or work units promote cooperation (because they foster a sense of common interest), but they also prevent individual employees from linking the reward to their own efforts and thus reduce the reward's motivational impact.

Since all pay-for-performance systems have positive and negative features, providing different types of pay incentives for different work situations is likely to produce better results than relying on a single type of pay incentive. With a multiple-layers-of-rewards system, the organization can realize the benefits of each incentive plan while minimizing its negative side effects. For instance, at AT&T Credit, variable pay (in the form of bonuses) is based on 12 measures reflecting the performance of both regional teams and the entire business unit. Team members must meet their individual performance goals to qualify for variable pay.[21]

Increase Employee Involvement

An old saying among compensation practitioners is: "Acceptability is the ultimate determinant of success in any compensation plan." When employees do not view a compensation program as legitimate, they will usually do whatever they can to subvert the system—from setting maximum production quotas for themselves to shunning coworkers who receive the highest rewards. The best way to increase acceptance is to have employees participate in the design of the pay plan.[22] Employee involvement will result in a greater understanding of the rationale behind the plan, greater commitment to the pay plan, and a better match between individual needs and pay-plan design.[23]

At B.F. Goodrich's plant in Terre Haute, Indiana, employee involvement is an integral part of a plantwide pay-for-performance plan called PLUS (Performance Lets Us Share). When the plant (which used to manufacture the compound for phonograph records) switched to producing a variety of plastic compounds, it had to put in place new processes, new goals, and new pay plans for its work force. From the beginning, a task force of employees was involved in crafting a plan that would reward workers for achieving the new performance goals. Management was so pleased with the task force's work that it adopted a formal employee-involvement structure that encourages employees to make and carry out their own suggestions. In the first year PLUS was implemented, the plant averaged five ideas per employee and workers earned bonuses in nine out of 12 months.[24]

Employee participation in designing the plan is not the same as employee dispensation of the rewards. Managers should still control and allocate rewards because employees may not be able to separate self-interest from effective pay administration. Managers can, however, solicit employee input by instituting an appeal mechanism that allows workers to voice their complaints about how rewards have been distributed. Such a mechanism is likely to enhance the perceived fairness of the system, particularly if a disinterested third party acts as an arbitrator and is empowered to take corrective actions.[25] A good appeals system may also help the organization avoid the costly legal fees and penalties in back pay that may result when disputes are resolved through litigation.

Use Motivation and Nonfinancial Incentives

This chapter focuses on financial awards, which are managers' biggest concern in administering incentive plans. However, nonfinancial rewards can be used effectively to motivate employee performance. One of the most basic facts of motivation is that people are driven to obtain the things they need or want. While pay is certainly a strong motivator, it is not an equally strong motivator for everyone. Some people are more interested in the nonfinancial aspects of their work.

Nonfinancial rewards include public and nonpublic praise, honorary titles, and expanded job responsibilities. Even if it is impossible to provide a financial reward for a job well done, many employees appreciate overt recognition of excellent performance. ▼

▸ Types of Pay-For-Performance Plans

A firm may use a variety of approaches to reward performance. As Figure 11–1 shows, pay-for-performance plans can be designed to reward the performance of the individual, team, business unit or plant, entire organization, or any combination of these. All of these plans have advantages and disadvantages, and each is more effective in some situations than in others. Most organizations are best served by using a variety of plans to counterbalance the potential drawbacks of any single plan.

Individual-Based Plans

At the most micro level, firms attempt to identify and reward the contributors of individual employees. *Individual-based pay plans* are the most widely used pay-for-performance plans in industry.[26]

merit pay
An increase in base pay, normally given once a year.

Of the individual-based plans commonly used, merit pay is by far the most popular; its use is almost universal.[27] **Merit pay** consists of an increase in base pay, normally given once a year. Supervisors' ratings of employees' performance are typically used to determine the amount of merit pay granted. For instance, subordinates whose performance is rated "below expectations," "achieved expectations," "exceeded expectations," and "far exceeded expectations" may receive 0%, 3%, 6%, and 9% pay raises, respectively. Once a merit pay increase is given to an employee, it remains a part of that employee's base salary for the rest of his or her tenure with the firm (except under extreme conditions, such as a general wage cut or a demotion).

bonus program or **lump-sum payment**
A financial incentive that is given on a one-time basis and does not raise the employee's base pay permanently.

Individual **bonus programs** (sometimes called **lump-sum payments**) are similar to merit pay programs but differ in one important respect. Bonuses are given on a one-time basis and do not raise the employee's base pay permanently. Bonuses tend to be larger than merit pay increases because they involve lower risk to the employer (the employer is not

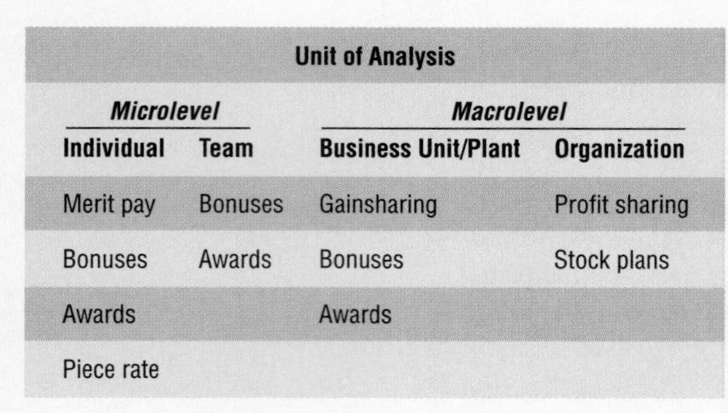

Unit of Analysis			
Microlevel		*Macrolevel*	
Individual	**Team**	**Business Unit/Plant**	**Organization**
Merit pay	Bonuses	Gainsharing	Profit sharing
Bonuses	Awards	Bonuses	Stock plans
Awards		Awards	
Piece rate			

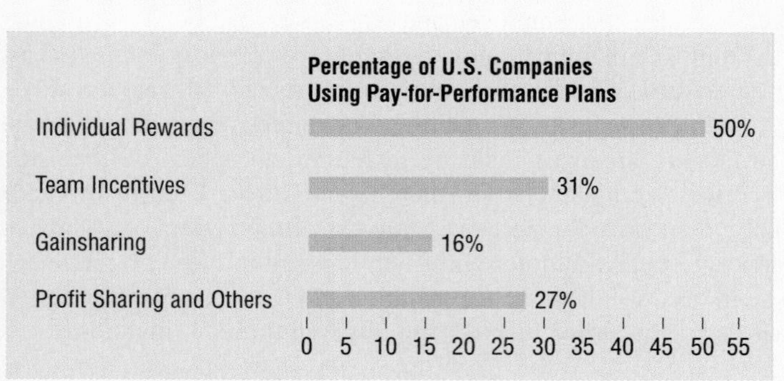

FIGURE 11-1

Pay-for-Performance Programs

Source: Hansen, F. (1995, December). Variable pay: Still a select program. *CompFlash*, 5–7.

making a permanent financial commitment). Bonuses can also be given outside the annual review cycle when employees achieve certain milestones (for example, completing a challenging project early and under budget) or offer a valuable cost-saving suggestion. A recent survey of 2,719 midsize companies shows that 30% of the companies provide lump-sum payments to their employees, most commonly to those at the upper end of the salary range. The lump-sum payments averaged 3.5% of annual salary.[28]

Awards, like bonuses, are one-time rewards, but tend to be given in the form of a tangible prize, such as a paid vacation, a television set, or a dinner for two at a fancy restaurant.

award
A one-time reward, usually given in the form of a tangible prize.

Perhaps the oldest and most extreme individual-based pay incentive is the piece-rate system we discussed earlier. The piece-rate system is less often used today because it does not fit with the greater interdependencies in modern production processes, rapid technological changes, and the increased emphasis on quality and service rather than on raw quantity.[29]

Advantages of Individual-Based Pay-for-Performance Plans. There are four major advantages to individual-based plans:

expectancy theory
A theory of behavior holding that people tend to do those things that are rewarded.

- *Performance that is rewarded is likely to be repeated.* **Expectancy theory**, a widely accepted theory of motivation, is often used to explain why higher pay leads to higher performance. People tend to do those things that are rewarded. Money is an important reward to most people, so individuals tend to improve their work performance when a strong performance-pay linkage exists.[30] In other words, because employees value money as a reward, they will work harder to achieve or exceed a performance level if they believe that they will receive money for doing so.
- *Individuals are goal-oriented and financial incentives can shape an individual's goals over time.* Every organization is interested not only in the level at which employees perform but also in the focus of their efforts. A pay incentive plan can help make employees' behavior consistent with the organization's goals.[31] For instance, if an automobile dealer has a sales employee who sells a lot of cars, but whose customers rarely return to the dealership, the dealer might implement a pay incentive plan that gives a higher sales commission for cars sold to repeat buyers. This plan would encourage the sales staff to please the customer rather than just sell the car.

Pink Cadillacs, Plush Velvet Seats.

Mary Kay Ash, founder of Mary Kay Cosmetics, knows how to motivate her salespeople. She gives them prizes and recognition, not just cash. These Mary Kay sales directors drive the company's coveted pink Cadillacs. Mary Kay's Cadillac fleet includes over 6,500 cars and is worth more than $90 million.

- *Assessing the performance of each employee individually helps the firm achieve individual equity.* An organization must provide rewards in proportion to individual efforts. Individual-based plans do exactly this. If individuals are not rewarded, high performers may leave the firm or reduce their performance level to make it consistent with the payment they are receiving.
- *Individual-based plans fit in with an individualistic culture.* National cultures vary in the emphasis they place on individual achievement versus group achievement (see Chapter 17). The United States is at the top of the list in valuing individualism, and U.S. workers expect to be rewarded for their personal accomplishments and contributions. This cultural orientation is likely to enhance the motivational value of a pay-for-performance system designed for U.S. employees.

  In contrast, the Japanese don't tend to reward individual performance. "It's against their ethic," says a consultant with Tasa, Inc., which has conducted executive searches for the U.S. offices of many Japanese concerns. That ethic has its costs outside Japan. Japanese banks in New York, for instance, often have trouble recruiting and keeping first-rate U.S. managers, who are used to reaping rewards for their accomplishments.[32]

Disadvantages of Individual-Based Pay-for-Performance Plans. Many of the pitfalls of pay-for-performance programs are most evident at the individual level. Two particular dangers are that individual plans may (1) create competition and destroy cooperation among peers and (2) sour working relationships between subordinates and supervisors. And because many managers believe that below-average raises are demoralizing to employees and discourage better performance, they tend to equalize the percentage increases among employees, regardless of individual performance. This, of course, defeats the very purpose of an incentive plan.

Other disadvantages of individual-based plans include the following:

- *Tying pay to goals may promote single-mindedness.* Linking financial incentives to the achievement of goals may lead to a narrow focus and the avoidance of important tasks, either because goals are difficult to set for these tasks or because their accomplishment is difficult to measure at the individual level. For instance, if a grocery store sets a goal of happy and satisfied customers, it would be extremely difficult to link achievement of this goal to individual employees. Individual-based plans have a tendency to focus on goals that are easy to measure even if these goals are not very important to the organization. They also tend to encourage people to "play it safe" by choosing to accomplish more modest goals instead of riskier goals that are harder to achieve.
- *Many employees do not believe that pay and performance are linked.* Although practically all organizations claim to reward individual performance, it is difficult for employees to determine to what extent their companies really do so. As we saw in Chapter 7, many managers use the performance appraisal process for reasons other than accurately measuring performance.[33] So it should come as no surprise that many surveys over the past three decades have found that up to 80% of employees do not see a connection between personal contributions and pay raises.[34] The beliefs underlying this perception, many of which have proved very resistant to change, are summarized in Figure 11–2.
- *Individual pay plans may work against achieving quality goals.* Individuals rewarded for meeting production goals often sacrifice attention to product quality. Individual-based plans also work against TQM programs that emphasize teamwork because individual programs generally do not reward employees for helping other workers or coordinating work activities with other departments.
- *Individual-based programs promote inflexibility in some organizations.* Because supervisors generally control the rewards, individual-based pay-for-performance plans promote dependence on supervisors. Thus these plans tend to prop up tradi-

- Performance appraisal is inherently subjective, with supervisors evaluating subordinates according to their own preconceived biases.
- Regardless of the appraisal form used, rating errors are rampant.
- Merit systems emphasize individual rather than group goals, and this may lead to dysfunctional conflict in the organization.
- The use of a specified time period (normally one year) for the performance evaluation encourages a short-term orientation at the expense of long-term goals.
- Supervisors and employees seldom agree on the evaluation, leading to interpersonal confrontations.
- Increments in financial rewards are spaced in such a way that their reinforcement value for work behaviors is questionable. For example, becoming twice as productive now has little perceived effect on pay when the employee must wait a whole year for a performance review.
- Individual merit pay systems are not appropriate for the service sector, where many people in the United States work. In knowledge-based jobs (such as "administrative assistant"), it is even difficult to specify what the desired product is.
- Supervisors typically control a rather limited amount of compensation, so merit pay differentials are normally quite small and therefore of questionable value.
- A number of bureaucratic factors that influence the size and frequency of merit pay (for example, position in salary range, pay relationships within the unit and between units, and budgetary limitations) have little to do with employee performance.
- Performance appraisals are designed for multiple purposes (training and development, selection, work planning, compensation, and so forth). When a system is used to accomplish so many objectives, it is questionable whether it can accomplish any of them well. It is difficult for the supervisor to play the role of counselor or adviser and evaluator at the same time.

FIGURE 11–2

Factors Commonly Blamed for the Failure of Individual-Based Pay-for-Performance Systems

Source: Balkin, D. B., and Gómez-Mejía, L. R. (Eds.). (1987). *New perspectives on compensation*, 159. Englewood Cliffs, NJ: Prentice Hall.

tional organizational structures, which make them particularly ineffective for firms trying to take a team approach to work.

Conditions Under Which Individual-Based Plans Are Most Likely to Succeed. Despite the challenges they present to managers, rewards based on individual performance can be highly motivating. Individual-based pay-for-performance plans are most likely to be successful under the following conditions:

- *When the contributions of individual employees can be accurately isolated.* Identifying any one person's contributions is generally difficult, but it is more easily done for some jobs than for others. For instance, a strong individual incentive system can work well with salespeople because it is relatively easy to measure their accomplishments in a timely manner. In contrast, research scientists in industry are generally not offered individual-based performance incentives because they typically work so closely together that individual contributions are hard to identify.
- *When the job demands autonomy.* The more independently employees work, the more it makes sense to assess and reward the performance of each individual. For example, the performance of managers of individual stores in a large retail chain like The Gap can be rated fairly easily, whereas the performance of the HR director in a large company is much more difficult to assess.
- *When cooperation is less critical to successful performance or when competition is to be encouraged.* Practically all jobs require some cooperation, but the less cooperation needed, the more successful an individual-based pay program will be. For example, less employee cooperation is expected of a stockbroker than of a pilot in an Air Force squadron.

Team-Based Plans

In an attempt to increase the flexibility of their work forces, a growing number of firms are redesigning work to allow employees with unique skills and backgrounds to tackle projects or problems together. For instance, at Compaq Computer Corp., as many as 25% of the company's 16,000 employees are on teams that develop new products and bring them to market.[35] Employees in this new system are expected to cross job boundaries within their team and to contribute in areas in which they have not previously worked. Other companies that have implemented a team approach to job and work design are Clairol/Bristol-Myers, Squibb, Hershey's Chocolate, Newsday/Times Mirror, Pratt & Whitney/United Technologies, General Motors, TRW, Digital Equipment, Shell Oil, and Honeywell.[36] A team-based compensation system can provide integral support for effective team arrangements. Based on his experience at Kraft General Foods, one observer has noted that "in terms of support for team activity, nothing is symbolically more important than compensation."[37]

Team-based pay plans normally reward all team members equally based on group outcomes. These outcomes may be measured objectively (for example, completing a given number of team projects on time or meeting all deadlines for a group report) or subjectively (for example, using the collective assessment of a panel of managers). The criteria for defining a desirable outcome may be broad (for example, being able to work effectively with other teams) or narrow (for example, developing a patent with commercial applications). As in individual-based programs, payments to team members may be made in the form of a cash bonus or in the form of noncash awards such as trips, time off, or luxury items.

Some firms allow the team to decide how its bonus will be distributed within the group. One such firm is Johnsonville Foods (JF), which produces specialty sausage products. JF's monthly bonus program, Great Performance Shares, provides bonuses to teams whose contributions have helped the company achieve "great performance." Work crews (rather than the supervisor) decide the amount team members should receive based on their contributions. At Texas Instruments, teams get a lump-sum amount to divide among members.[38]

Low on Calories, Big on Business.

A team of young managers at Yoplait Yogurt has built the company into a thriving business by setting tougher goals for themselves than the parent company, General Mills, set for them. When the team exceeded these goals, its managers collected bonuses of $30,000 to $50,000, about half their annual salaries.

Advantages of Team-Based Pay-for-Performance Plans. When properly designed, team-based incentives have two major advantages.

- *They foster group cohesiveness.* To the extent that team members have the same goals and objectives, work closely with one another, and depend on one another for the group's overall performance, team-based incentives can motivate group members to behave and think as a unit rather than as competing individuals. In this situation, each worker is more likely to act in a way that benefits the entire group.[39]
- *They facilitate performance measurement.* A number of studies have shown that performance can be measured more accurately and reliably for an entire team than for individuals.[40] This is true because less precise measurement is required when an individual's performance does not need to be identified and evaluated in relation to others in a group.

Disadvantages of Team-Based Pay-for-Performance Plans. Managers need to be aware of potential pitfalls with team-based plans. These are:

- *Possible lack of fit with individualistic cultural values.* Because most U.S. workers expect to be recognized for their personal contributions, they may not react well to an incentive system in which individual efforts take a back seat to the group effort, with all team members rewarded equally. On the other side of the coin, individual incentives are likely to fail in societies with a collective orientation. The Japanese, for example, are far less comfortable with individual risk than Americans are. Nonetheless, in a striking display of cultural insensitivity, many U.S. companies have introduced high-risk individual incentives to their Japanese subsidiaries. These plans have generally failed.[41]
- *The free-riding effect.* In any group, some individuals put in more effort than others. In addition, ability levels differ from one person to the next. Those who contribute little to the team—either because of low effort or limited ability—are *free riders*.[42]

  When all team members (including free riders) are rewarded equally for a group outcome, there are likely to be complaints of unfairness. (Think what would happen in a classroom study group if the same grade were given to all group members.) The result may be conflict rather than the cooperation the plan was intended to foster, with supervisors having to step in to judge who is contributing what.[43] Supervisory intercession, of course, negates the worth of team-based incentives and may produce a very negative climate of accusation and infighting.

  To minimize the free-riding effect, some companies have been adjusting pay incentives to encourage individual performance within teams. Unisys sets annual base pay raises on performance reviews by a team coach and three peers chosen by the employee. All team members can also receive up to 20% of base pay as a team bonus. AT&T Universal Card has created wider differences in base salaries after employees in a 200-member team demanded greater recognition of their individual performances.[44]
- *Social pressures to limit performance.* Although group cohesiveness may motivate all team members to increase their effort and work to their full potential—both positively through encouraging a supportive team spirit and negatively through reproaching those who don't carry their share of the weight—it can also dampen team productivity. When the labor relations climate is hostile or the firm has a history of broken promises, group dynamics may result in the setting of artificial performance limits. When commercial airline pilots want to express a grievance, for instance, they sometimes agree among themselves to fly "by the book." This means that they follow every rule without exception, leading to an overall work slowdown. This is a very effective strategy because the airline can hardly complain publicly that its pilots are following the rules. Group dynamics may also encourage team members to try to beat the game—cheating to get the reward, for instance—as a way to get back at management.[45]
- *Difficulties in identifying meaningful groups.* Before they decide how to distribute rewards based on team performance, managers must define a *team*. Coming up with a

definition can be tricky because various groups may be highly interdependent, making it difficult to identify which ones did what. Also, a person may be a member of more than one team, and teams may change members frequently. For instance, while the editor of the book you are reading now is a member of the editorial team, he works closely with the production team (to produce the book), the art team (to develop the art program and design), the photo team (to research and get permission to reprint the photos in the book), the marketing team (to make the book meet its audience's expectations and demands) and, finally, the sales force (to sell the book to your instructor and help with customer service).

- *Intergroup competition leading to a decline in overall performance.* A team may become so focused on maximizing its own performance that it ends up competing with other teams. The results can be quite undesirable. For instance, the manufacturing group may produce more units than the marketing group can possibly sell, or the marketing group may make sales commitments that manufacturing is hard pressed to meet on schedule.[46]

Conditions Under Which Team-Based Plans Are Most Likely to Succeed. While managers need to be aware of the potential disadvantages of team-based plans, they should also be on the lookout for situations conducive to their successful use. Such plans are likely to be successful under the following circumstances:

- *When work tasks are so intertwined that it is difficult to single out who did what.* This is often the case in research and development labs, where scientists and engineers work in teams. It is also the case with firefighter crews and police units, which often think of themselves as one indivisible entity.
- *When the firm's organization facilitates the implementation of team-based incentives.* Team-based incentives are appropriate when:
  1. *There are few levels in the hierarchy, and teams of individuals at the same level are expected to complete most of their work with little dependence on supervisors or upper management.* Both public-sector and private-sector organizations that have had to lay off workers to maintain efficiency and profitability have found that teamwork becomes a necessity. For instance, when the city of Hampton, Virginia underwent a massive downsizing and restructuring that resulted in the loss of several layers of supervision, it had to redesign its work. The city created self-managed teams and incorporated team-based pay into a multilayered pay-for-performance plan.[47]
  2. *Technology allows for the separation of work into relatively self-contained or independent groups.* This can be done more easily in a service unit (such as a telephone repair crew) than in a large manufacturing operation (such as a traditional automobile assembly line).
  3. *Employees are committed to their work and are intrinsically motivated.* Such workers are less likely to shirk responsibility at the expense of the group, so free riding is not a serious concern. Intrinsic motivation is often found in not-for-profit organizations, whose employees are emotionally committed to the organization's cause.
  4. *The organization needs to insist on group goals.* In some organizations this is a paramount need. For example, high-tech firms often find that their research scientists have their own research agendas and professional objectives—which are frequently incompatible with those of the firm or even their peers. Team-based incentives can focus such independent-minded employees' efforts on a common goal.[48]
- *When the objective is to foster entrepreneurship in self-managed work groups.* Sometimes, to encourage innovation and risk taking within employee groups, a firm will give certain groups extensive autonomy to perform their task or achieve certain objectives. This practice is often referred to as *intrapreneuring* (a term coined by Gifford

Pinchot, who published a book with that title in 1985). Intrapreneuring means creating and maintaining the innovation and flexibility of a small-business environment within the confines of a large bureaucratic structure.[49] In an intrapreneuring environment, management often uses team-based incentives as a hands-off control mechanism that allows each group to assume the risk of success or failure, as entrepreneurs do.

The formation of self-managed teams and the use of team-based pay plans are not limited to large companies. When The Published Image, a custom newsletter publisher with 26 employees, experienced extremely rapid growth at the expense of low quality, low employee morale, and high turnover, the firm's founder, Eric Gershman, decided on a radical reorganization. To combat employees' belief that their job was to please the boss instead of the customer, he divided employees into four largely autonomous teams, each with its own clients and staff of sales, editorial, and production workers. Published Image managers-turned-coaches field questions and rate the teams for timeliness and accuracy. A monthly score of 90 or higher entitles team members to biannual bonuses, which can add up to 15% to their base pay.[50]

Plantwide Plans

Plantwide pay-for-performance plans reward all workers in a plant or business unit based on the performance of the entire plant or unit. Profits and stock prices are generally not meaningful performance measures for a plant or unit because they are the result of the entire corporation's performance. Most corporations have multiple plants or units, which make it difficult to attribute financial gains or losses to any single segment of the business. Therefore, the key performance indicator used to distribute rewards at the plant level is plant or business unit efficiency, which is normally measured in terms of labor or material cost savings compared to an earlier period.

Plantwide pay-for-performance programs are generally referred to as **gainsharing** programs because they return a portion of the company's cost savings to the workers, usually in the form of a lump-sum bonus. Three major types of gainsharing programs are used. The oldest is the *Scanlon Plan*, which dates back to the 1930s. It relies on committees of employees, union leaders, and top managers to generate and evaluate cost-saving ideas. If actual labor costs are lower than expected labor costs over an agreed-upon period (normally one year), the difference is shared between the workers (who, as a group, usually receive 75% of the savings) and the firm (which usually receives 25% of the savings). A portion of the savings may also be set aside in a rainy day fund.

gainsharing
A plantwide pay-for-performance plan in which a portion of the company's cost savings is returned to workers, usually in the form of a lump-sum bonus.

The second gainsharing program, the *Rucker Plan*, uses worker-management committees to solicit and screen ideas. These committees are less involved and simpler in structure than those used by the Scanlon Plan. But the cost-saving calculation in the Rucker Plan tends to be more complex because the formula encompasses not only labor costs but also other expenses involved in the production process.

The last type of gainsharing program, *Improshare* ("*Im*proved *pro*ductivity through *shar*ing"), is a relatively new plan that has proved easy to administer and communicate. First, a standard is developed—based on either studies by an industrial engineering group or some set of base-period experience data—that identifies the expected number of hours required to produce an acceptable level of output. Any savings arising from production of this agreed-on output in fewer than the expected hours are shared between the firm and the workers.

Although gainsharing plans have been used mostly in the manufacturing sector, many service-sector companies are developing their own versions of gainsharing. A number of hospitals, for instance, are starting to use gainsharing. Sutter Health Services, a not-for-profit corporation that operates 12 hospitals throughout California, was a gainsharing pioneer in its field. The SutterShare program, instituted in 1985, has been enthusiastically received by employees and has yielded significant productivity gains.[51]

Advantages of Plantwide Pay-for-Performance Plans. The primary rationale for gainsharing programs can be traced to the early work of Douglas McGregor,[52] a colleague and collaborator of Joseph Scanlon, founder of the Scanlon Plan. According to McGregor, a firm can be more productive if it follows a participative approach to management—that is, if it assumes that workers are intrinsically motivated, can show the company better ways of doing things if given the chance, and enjoy being team players.

In contrast to individual-based incentive plans, gainsharing does not embrace the idea that pay incentives motivate people to produce more. Rather, gainsharing suggests that cost savings result from treating employees better and involving them intimately in the firm's management. The underlying philosophy is that competition between individuals and teams should be avoided, that all workers should be encouraged to use their talents for the plant's common good, that employees are willing and able to contribute good ideas, and that the financial gains generated when those ideas are implemented should be shared with employees.

Gainsharing plans can provide a vehicle to elicit active employee input and improve the production process. They can also increase the level of cooperation across workers and teams by giving everyone a common goal. In addition, gainsharing plans are subject to fewer measurement difficulties than individual- or team-based incentives. Because gainsharing plans do not require managers to sort out the specific contributions of individuals or interdependent teams, it is easier both to formulate bonus calculations and to achieve worker acceptance of these plans.

Gainsharing plans have been lauded not only for increasing organizational productivity but also for improving quality in manufacturing firms that previously relied on individual-incentive or piece-rate plans. When Tech Form Industries (TFI), a Shelby, Ohio–based producer of tubular exhaust systems, realized that its individual-based incentive plans were driving quality—and its business—down the tubes, it discontinued its piece-rate system and, with employee involvement, developed a companywide gainsharing plan. Within three years, returns of defective products went down by 83%, direct labor hours spent on repairs decreased by 50%, and grievances declined by 41%. The transition from an individual-based incentive system to gainsharing required many steps, the first of which was to negotiate with the United Steel Workers union to fashion salary packages that were at least comparable to the piecework plan.[53]

Disadvantages of Plantwide Pay-for-Performance Plans. Like all other pay-for-performance plans, plantwide gainsharing programs may suffer from a number of difficulties, among them:

- *Protection of low performers.* The free-rider problem can be very serious in plants where rewards are spread across a large number of employees. Because so many people work together in a plant, it is less likely that peer pressure will be used to bring low performers into the fold.
- *Problems with the criteria used to trigger rewards.* Although the formulas used to calculate bonuses in gainsharing plans are generally straightforward, four problems may arise. First, once the formula is determined, employees may expect it to remain the same forever. A too-rigid formula can become a management straitjacket, but managers may not want to risk employee unrest by changing it. Second, improving cost savings will not necessarily improve profitability because the latter depends on many uncontrollable factors (such as consumer demand). For example, an automobile production facility can operate at high efficiency, but if it is producing a car that is in low demand, that plant's financial performance will not look good. Third, when gainsharing is first instituted, it is easier for inefficient than for efficient plants or business units to post a gain. This is because opportunities for dramatic labor-cost savings are much higher in the less efficient units.[54] Thus, gainsharing programs may seem to penalize

already efficient units, which can be demoralizing to those who work in them. Fourth, there may be only a few labor-saving opportunities in a plant. If these are quickly exhausted, further gains will be difficult to achieve.

- *Management-labor conflict.* Many managers feel threatened by the concept of employee participation. When the gainsharing program is installed, they may be reluctant to give up their authority to committees, thus creating conflict and jeopardizing the program's credibility. In addition, only hourly workers are included in many gainsharing plans. The exclusion of salaried employees may foster hard feelings among them.

Conditions Favoring Plantwide Plans. A number of factors affect the successful implementation of gainsharing programs.[55] These are:

- *Firm size.* Gainsharing is more likely to work well in small to mid-size plants, where employees can see a connection between their efforts and the unit's performance.
- *Technology.* When technology limits improvements in efficiency, gainsharing is less likely to be successful.
- *Historical performance.* If the firm has multiple plants with varying levels of efficiency, the plan must take this variance into account so that efficient plants are not penalized and inefficient plants rewarded. It is difficult to do this where there are scanty historical records. In these cases, past data are insufficient for establishing reliable future performance standards, making it difficult to implement a gainsharing program.
- *Corporate culture.* Gainsharing is less likely to be successful in firms with a traditional hierarchy of authority, heavy dependence on supervisors, and a value system that is antagonistic to employee participation. Gainsharing can be used effectively in a firm that is making the transition from a more autocratic to a more participative management style, but it probably cannot lead the charge as a stand-alone program.
- *Stability of the product market.* Gainsharing is most appropriate in situations where the demand for the firm's product or service is relatively stable. Under these circumstances, historical data may be used to forecast future sales reliably. When demand is unstable, the formulas used to calculate bonuses may prove unreliable and force management to change the formula, which is likely to lead to employee dissatisfaction. For example, increases in total output that occur as efficiency improves may create an inventory surplus that the market cannot absorb. When this happens, management may have little money to distribute or, even worse, may have to lay off employees as a cost-cutting measure.

Corporatewide Plans

The most macro type of incentive programs, *corporatewide pay-for-performance plans*, reward employees based on the entire corporation's performance. The most widely used program of this kind is **profit sharing**, which differs from gainsharing in several important ways:[56]

profit sharing
A corporatewide pay-for-performance plan that uses a formula to allocate a portion of declared profits to employees. Typically, profit distributions under a profit-sharing plan are used to fund employees' retirement plans.

- In a profit-sharing program, no attempt is made to reward workers for productivity improvements. Many factors that affect profits (such as luck, regulatory changes, and economic conditions) have little to do with productivity, and the amount of money employees receive depends on all of these factors.
- Profit-sharing plans are very mechanistic. They make use of a formula that allocates a portion of declared profits to employees, normally on a quarterly or annual basis, and do not attempt to elicit worker participation.
- In the typical profit-sharing plan, profit distributions are used to fund employees' retirement plans. As a result, employees seldom receive profit distributions in cash. (This

Issues + Applications

Newly Rich at Oregon Steel

One advantage of ESOPs in small companies is that if the stock soars, there are fewer people to share in the bonanza. This came as a pleasant surprise to workers at Oregon Steel:

> PORTLAND, Ore.—After an Oregon Steel Mills Inc. board meeting this year, Jackie Williams walked up to C. Lee Emerson, the company's retiring chairman, and kissed him.
>
> "Lee," she told him, "I just want to say thank you for making me a millionaire."
>
> Her gratitude is understandable. When Ms. Williams took a bookkeeping job with the company 17 years ago, she was a young divorcee raising her son in a mobile home. Now she's worth some $1.3 million and has just built a half-million dollar house on the 16th hole of the Club Green Meadows golf course near here.
>
> Ms. Williams is one of the nearly 100 Oregon Steel employees whose shares in the company, once nearly worthless, reached a value of more than $1 million in three years after the company went public. Seventy percent of the 517 people who worked for the company at the time of its initial public offering had holdings that eventually reached over $100,000. It all happened when an Employee Stock Ownership Plan and an unusual profit-sharing program, which the company adopted in desperation during a leverage buyout, turned into a bonanza.

Source: Reprinted by permission of *The Wall Street Journal* (1992, October 27), A1.

deferral of profit-sharing payments is commonly done for tax reasons.) Profit sharing that is distributed via a retirement plan is generally viewed as a benefit rather than an incentive. Some companies do have profit-sharing programs that are true incentives, however. A notable case is Andersen Corporation, the Minnesota-based manufacturer of windows and patio doors. Employees have received up to 84% of their annual salary in a lump-sum check at the end of the year from Andersen's profit-sharing pool.[57]

employee stock ownership plan (ESOP)
A corporatewide pay-for-performance plan that rewards employees with company stocks, either as an outright grant or at a favorable price that may be below market value.

Like profit sharing, **employee stock ownership plans (ESOPs)** are based on the entire corporation's performance—in this case, as measured by the firm's stock price. ESOPs reward employees with company stock, either as an outright grant or at a favorable price that may be below market value.[58] Employers often use ESOPs as a low-cost retirement benefit for employees because stock contributions made by the company are nontaxable until the employee redeems the stock. Employees whose retirement plans are based on ESOPs are exposed to risk, however, because the price of the company's stock may fluctuate as a result of general stock market activity or mismanagement of the firm. The Issues and Applications feature titled "Newly Rich at Oregon Steel" provides an example of one particularly successful ESOP.

Advantages of Corporatewide Pay-for-Performance Plans. Corporatewide pay-for-performance plans have distinct advantages, several of which are economic rather than motivational. These are:

- *Financial flexibility for the firm.* Both profit sharing and ESOPs are variable compensation plans: Their cost to the firm is automatically adjusted downward during economic downturns. This feature allows the firm to retain a larger work force during a recession. In addition, these plans allow employers to offer lower base compensation in exchange for company stock or a profit-sharing arrangement. This feature gives the firm "float," or flexibility to direct scarce cash where it is most needed. ESOPs may also be used to save a foundering company—one whose cash is running out or is facing a hostile takeover bid. Weirton Steel, Hyatt Clark, Polaroid, and Chevron have effectively used ESOPs for this purpose.[59]
- *Increased employee commitment.* Employees who are entitled to profit sharing and ESOPs are more likely to identify themselves with the business and increase their commitment to it. Many consider the sharing of profits between the firm's owners and workers as a just distribution of income in a capitalistic society.

- *Tax advantages.* As noted earlier, both profit sharing and ESOPs enjoy special tax privileges. In essence, they allow the firm to provide benefits (discussed in detail in Chapter 12) that are subsidized in part by the federal government. Although these types of plans are sometimes blamed for the loss of enormous amounts in tax revenues, it can be argued that they let firms that cannot afford to pay employees high salaries grow and prosper, thereby creating more jobs and tax revenues in the long run. Apple Computer, Sun Microsystems, Oracle Corporation, Quantum Corporation, and Software Publishing might not be around today were it not for tax-subsidized ESOPs and profit-sharing plans.

Disadvantages of Corporatewide Pay-for-Performance Plans. Like all other pay-for-performance programs, corporatewide plans have their drawbacks:

- *Employees may be at considerable risk.* Under profit sharing or ESOP plans, workers' financial well-being may be threatened by factors beyond their control. Often workers are not fully aware of how much risk they face because the factors affecting profits or stock prices can be very complex. The more reliant long-term employees are on these programs for savings (for their children's college tuition, their own retirement, or some other purpose), the more vulnerable they are to the firm's fate. For example, many IBM employees lost about half the value of their stock holdings when the company suffered a severe setback in the early 1990s. And when ailing America West Airline underwent an extensive reorganization in 1992, it wiped out the equity of its stockholders, a significant portion of whom were company employees.[60]
- *Limited effect on productivity.* Because the connection between individual goal achievement and firm performance is small and difficult to measure, corporatewide programs are not likely to improve productivity. However, they should reduce turnover if seniority strongly affects how much an employee is entitled to under the plan.
- *Long-run financial difficulties.* Both profit sharing and ESOPs often appear painless to the company in the short run, either because funds are not paid out to employees until retirement or because employees are paid in "paper" (company stock). This illusion may induce managers to be more generous with these types of compensation than they should be, leaving future management generations with less cash available, lower profits to distribute to investors, and a firm that has decreased in value.

Conditions Favoring Corporatewide Plans. A number of factors influence the successful implementation of corporatewide pay-for-performance plans:

- *Firm size.* Although they may be used at firms of any size, profit sharing and ESOPs are the plans of choice for larger organizations, in which gainsharing is less appropriate.[61]
- *Interdependence of different parts of the business.* Corporations with multiple interdependent plants or business units often find corporatewide plans most suitable because it is difficult to isolate the financial performance of any given segment of the corporation.
- *Market conditions.* Unlike gainsharing, which requires relatively stable sales levels, profit sharing and ESOP programs are attractive to firms facing highly cyclical ups and downs in the demand for their product. The structuring of these incentives helps the firm cut costs during downturns. (This is why these programs are often called "shock absorbers.") Employees are not immediately affected by these fluctuations in short-term earnings because most profit-sharing benefits are deferred until retirement.
- *The presence of other incentives.* Because corporatewide pay-for-performance plans are unlikely to have much motivational impact on individuals and teams within the firm, they should not be used on their own. When used in conjunction with other incentives (for example, individual and team bonuses), corporatewide programs can promote greater commitment to the organization by creating common goals and a sense of partnership among managers and workers.

▸ Designing Pay-for-Performance Plans for Executives and Salespeople

Executives and salespeople are normally treated very differently than most other types of workers in pay-for-performance plans. Because pay incentives are an important component of these employees' total compensation, it is useful to examine their special compensation programs in some detail. It is also useful to examine how companies are rewarding excellence in customer service—a key source of competitive advantage today.

Executives

Is anyone worth $76 million a year? That's how much Walt Disney Company's CEO, Michael D. Eisner, earned on average per year during 1993–1995 when you add up his salary, bonuses, and long-term compensation. Assuming Eisner worked 50 hours a week and took four weeks of vacation, he pulled in $31,667 an hour—or $527.78 for every minute he was running the company.

Much of Eisner's earnings came from cashing in stock options granted a decade earlier. Still, the total pay of the average CEO in the United States was about $3,746,392 in 1995—a sizable 30% increase over the previous year and 185 times what the average employee makes (up from 143 times in 1992 and 42 times in 1980).[62] In comparison, the average Japanese CEO was paid $895,648 in 1995, less than 33 times what the average Japanese worker was paid.[63]

On average, 37% of CEO pay is in the form of base salary, 24% is in the form of annual bonuses, and 39% is in the form of long-term incentives. These percentages tend to vary by firm size and type of industry. For example, annual bonuses represent 18% of total CEO compensation in small financial firms, yet they reach 85% and 132% for large high-tech and insurance firms respectively.[64]

A large number of plans are used to link executives' pay to firm performance, but there is little agreement on which is best. The disagreement is only heightened by the huge sums of money involved and the weak or inconsistent correlation between executive earnings and firm performance.[65]

Do you think it is ethical for a company to give its CEO and its other top executives multimillion-dollar pay packages that are not closely tied to the company's performance?

Salary and Short-Term Incentives. The amount of executives' base pay increases as firms get larger[66]—practically all CEOs of *Fortune* 500 firms earn a base of at least half a million dollars a year. Executives' bonuses are usually short-term incentives linked to the firm's specific annual goals. More than 90% of U.S. firms reward executives with year-end bonuses, but the criteria used to determine these bonuses vary widely.

Two major concerns are often expressed regarding executives' annual bonuses. First, because executives are likely to maximize whatever criteria are used to determine their bonuses, they may make decisions that have short-term payoffs at the expense of long-term performance. For instance, long-term investments in research and development may be crucial to the firm's success in introducing new products over time. Yet if bonus calculations treat such investments as costs that reduce net income, executives may be tempted to scale back R&D. Second, many bonus programs represent salary supplements that the CEO can expect to receive regardless of the firm's performance. For instance, a survey of 1,300 companies during the 1990–1991 recession found that only 13% of firms offering such programs failed to pay a bonus to their CEOs.[67]

The almost automatic payment of lavish bonuses to top executives has led to much resentment among middle managers. One vice president at a major bank expressed a common middle-management frustration: "It disturbs me when someone on high dictates that no matter how hard you work or what you do, you're only going to get a 6% increase, and if you don't like it, you can take a hike. Yet whatever they've negotiated for themselves—10%, 20%, or 30%—is a different issue from the rest of the staff."

Even among the most progressive firms such as Green Tree Finance, executive bonuses can be controversial. Imagine how Green Tree's workers felt in 1995 when its CEO, Lawrence M. Coss, garnered $65.6 million, while 118 other executives and managers divvied up a $7.2 million bonus pool. Less than half as much ($3.5 million) was distributed in bonuses to Green Tree's other 2,300 workers.[68]

Long-Term Incentives. Most executives also receive long-term incentives, either in the form of equity in the firm (stock-based programs) or a combination of cash awards and stock. A brief description of the most commonly used executive long-term incentive plans appears in Figure 11–3.

Stock-Based Programs

Stock Options. Allow the executive to acquire a predetermined amount of company stock within a stipulated time period (which may be as long as ten years) at a favorable price.

Stock Purchase Plans. Provide a very narrow time window (usually a month or two) during which the executive can elect to purchase the stocks at a cost that is either less than or equal to fair market value. (Stock purchase plans are commonly available to all employees of the firm.)

Restricted Stock Plans. Provide the executive with a stock grant requiring little, if any, personal investment in return for remaining with the firm for a certain length of time (for example, four years). If the executive leaves before completing the specified minimum length of service, all rights to the stock are forfeited.

Stock Awards. Provide the executive with "free" company stock, normally with no strings attached. Often used as a one-time-only "sign-on" bonus for recruitment purposes.

Formula-Based Stock. Stock provided to the executive either as a grant or at a stipulated price. Unlike other stock-based programs, the value of the stock to the executive when he or she wishes to redeem it is not its market price, but one calculated according to a predetermined formula (normally book value, which is assets minus liabilities divided by the number of outstanding shares). Used when the board believes that the market price of an organization's stock is affected by many variables outside the control of the top-management team.

Junior Stock. Stock whose value is set at a lower price than common stock, so that the executive is required to spend less cash up front to acquire it. Unlike the owners of common stock, the owners of junior stock have limited voting and dividend rights. However, junior stock can be converted to common stock upon achievement of specific performance goals.

Programs That Combine Cash Awards and Stocks

Stock Appreciation Rights (SARs). Provide the executive with the right to cash or stocks equal to the difference between the value of the stock at the time of the grant and the value of that same stock when the right is exercised. Thus, the executive is rewarded for any increase in the value of the stock, although no stock was actually granted by the firm. No investment on the executive's part is required. May be offered alone or mixed with stock options.

Performance Plan Units. Under this plan, the value of each share is tied to a measure of financial performance such as earnings per share (EPS). For example, for every 5% increase in EPS, the firm may provide the executive with $1,000 for every share he or she owns. Therefore, if EPS increases by 15%, the executive will receive $3,000 for each share owned. The payment may be made in cash or common stocks.

Performance Share Plans. Offer the executive a number of stocks based on profitability figures using a predetermined formula. The actual compensation per share depends on the market price per share at the end of the performance or award period.

Phantom Stock. Pays executives a bonus proportional to the change in prices of company stocks, rather than changes in profitability measures. A phantom stock is only a bookkeeping entry because the executive does not receive any stock per se. The executive is awarded a number of shares of phantom stock to track the cash reward that will be received upon attaining the performance objectives. The award may be equal to the appreciation or the value of the share of phantom stock.

FIGURE 11–3

Commonly Used Long-Term Executive Incentive Plans

Source: Reproduced with the permission of South-Western College Publishing from Gómez-Mejía, L. R., and Balkin, D. B. (1992). *Compensation, organizational strategy, and firm performance*, 219. Cincinnati, OH: South-Western.

The primary criticism of long-term incentive plans is that they are not very closely linked with executive performance. There are three reasons for this. First, even executives themselves rarely know how much their equity in the firm is worth because its value depends on stock prices at redemption. Second, the executive is likely to have very little control over the value of a company's stock (and thus the worth of his or her own long-term income) because stock prices tend to be highly volatile. (This can work to the executive's benefit or detriment. For example, the stock market's record gains in 1995 gave a big boost to CEO pay. By 1996, Disney's Michael Eisner was sitting on a $317.9 million paper gain on his stock options, while PepsiCo's chairman Wayne Calloway's stock options were worth nearly $120 million.[69]) Third, designing long-term incentive plans involves many judgment calls, and these are not always addressed in a manner consistent with achieving the firm's long-term strategic objectives. The major questions that firms should address in designing executive long-term programs are listed in Figure 11–4.

It is interesting that stock options for executives are almost unheard of in Asia and most parts of Europe. In fact, the countries most admired for their long-term business vision—Germany and Japan—do not have any long-term financial incentives for CEOs.[70]

It should be noted that smaller U.S. companies tend to show restraint on CEO pay. Among companies recently studied by the New York consulting firm William M. Mercer, Inc., the small and mid-size concerns were curbing pay increases even though their median profits had shot up by 21%. In contrast, the big companies were granting hefty raises even as their median net income declined by 6.4%. Many small-business CEOs have a big stake in their company. Rather than take huge compensation packages now, they prefer to plow profits back into the company in hopes of reaping a bigger payoff in the long run.[71]

perquisites ("perks") Noncash incentives given to a firm's executives.

Perks. In addition to cash incentives, many executives receive a large number of **perquisites** or **"perks."** These may keep the executive happy, but they are seldom linked to business objectives.[71a] They are also an easy target of criticism for those who feel that executive compensation is already excessive. Figure 11–5 shows the most common perks received by U.S. executives.

There are no easy answers to these criticisms. Executive compensation will probably always be more an art than a science because of all the factors that must be considered and each firm's unique conditions. Nonetheless, it is safe to say that an executive compensation plan is more likely to be effective if: (1) it adequately balances rewarding short-term accomplishments with motivating the executive to consider the firm's long-term performance; (2) the incentives provided are linked to the firm's overall strategy (for example, fast growth and risky investments versus moderate growth and low business risks); (3) the board of directors can make informed judgments about how well the executive is fulfilling his or her role; and (4) the executive has some control over the factors used to calculate the incentive amount.[72]

FIGURE 11–4

Key Strategic Pay Policy Questions in the Design of Executive Long-Term Income Programs

Source: Gómez-Mejía, L. R., and Balkin, D. B. (1992). *Compensation, organizational strategy, and firm performance*, 225. Cincinnati, OH: South-Western.

1. How long should the time horizon be for dispensing rewards?
2. Should length of service be considered in determining the amount of the award?
3. Should the executive be asked to share part of the costs and, therefore, increase his or her personal risk?
4. What criteria should be used to trigger the award?
5. Should there be a limit on how much executives can earn or a formula to prevent large unexpected gains?
6. How often should the awards be provided?
7. How easy should it be for the executive to convert the award into cash?

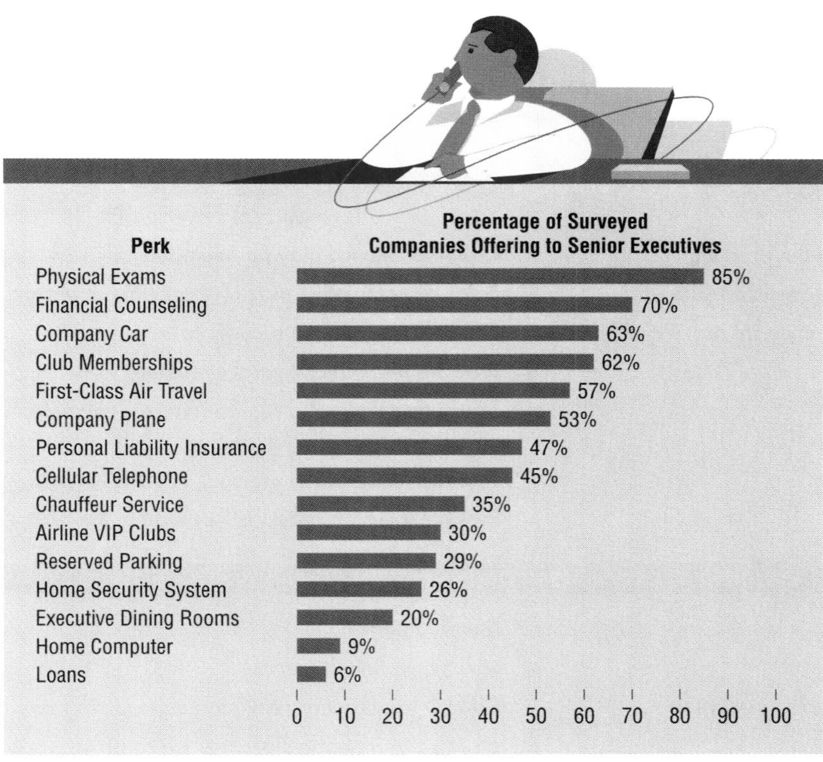

FIGURE 11-5

Most Common Perks Received by U.S. Senior Executives

Source: Adapted from Schellhardt, T. D. (1994, April 13). Passing of perks. *The Wall Street Journal*, R4. Reprinted by permission of *The Wall Street Journal*, © 1994 Dow Jones & Company, Inc. All rights reserved worldwide.

Salespeople

Sales professionals, working with the marketing staff, are responsible for bringing revenues into the company. There are several reasons why setting up a compensation program for salespeople is so much different from setting up compensation programs for other types of employees.[73]

- The spread in earnings between the lowest- and highest-paid salespeople is usually several times greater than the earnings spread in any other employee group within the company.
- The reward system for salespeople plays a supervisory role because these employees generally operate away from the office and may not report to the boss for weeks at a time.
- Perceptions of pay inequity are a lesser concern with this group than with others because few employees outside the company's marketing organization have knowledge of either sales achievement or rewards.
- Sales compensation is intimately tied to business objectives and strategies.
- The performance variation among salespeople tends to be quite large. Most organizations rely on relatively few stars to generate most of the sales.
- The salesperson generally works alone and is personally accountable for results.
- Accurate market data on pay practices and levels are extremely difficult to find for salespeople, and commercial salary surveys are usually unreliable.

Sales professionals may be paid in the form of *straight salary* (with no incentives), *straight commission* (in which all earnings are in the form of incentives), or a *combination plan* that mixes the two. Straight salary is most appropriate when maintaining good customer relations and servicing existing accounts are the key objectives, with increased sales

Manager's Notebook

Salary? Commission? Or Both? A Guide to Compensating Salespeople

STRAIGHT-COMMISSION SALES COMPENSATION PLAN

Advantages

- Effective for generating new accounts
- Sales force is highly motivated to sell the product
- High performers' contributions are recognized with pay
- Sales representatives become entrepreneurial and require minimal supervision
- Selling costs are efficiently controlled
- Plan administration is simple

Disadvantages

- Sales volume is emphasized over profits
- Customer service may be neglected
- Sales representative may overstock the customer
- Offers less economic security to sales force
- Provides less direct control over sales force
- Top-performing sales representatives may outearn other employees, including executives
- Possible resistance to changes in sales territories
- Possible focus on products that require the least effort to sell

STRAIGHT-SALARY SALES COMPENSATION PLAN

Advantages

- Secure income
- Sales force is willing to perform nonselling activities
- Plan administration is simple
- Sales force is less likely to overstock customers
- Low resistance to change in sales territories
- Low employee turnover rates
- Sales force treated as salaried professionals

Disadvantages

- Low motivational impact
- Difficult to attract or retain top sales performers
- More sales managers are needed to provide supervision
- Sales representatives may focus on products that require least effort to sell

COMBINATION SALES COMPENSATION PLAN

Advantages

- Incorporates advantages of both straight-salary and straight-commission plans
- Recognizes both selling and nonselling activities with pay
- Can offer both economic security and monetary incentives to sales representatives
- Greater variety of marketing goals can be supported with plan

Disadvantages

- Plan is more complicated to design
- Sales force may become confused and try to accomplish too many objectives
- Plan is more difficult and costly to administer
- Sales representatives may receive unanticipated windfall earnings

Source: Adapted from Gómez-Mejía, L. R., and Balkin, D. B. (1992). *Compensation, organizational strategy, and firm performance.* Cincinnati, OH: South-Western. Reproduced with the permission of South-Western College Publishing.

a secondary goal. Straight commission is most appropriate when the key objective is to generate greater sales volume through new accounts. Only one fourth of all firms use either a straight-salary or straight-commission method. Three quarters use a combination of the two, though the relative proportion of salary versus incentives varies widely across firms. The recent trend is to put more emphasis on commissions in a mixed plan; more than 36% of companies changed their salary/incentive mix in this direction during 1993–1995.[74]

As the Manager's Notebook shows, all three sales compensation methods have their pros and cons. The main criterion that should determine the type of plan chosen is overall marketing philosophy, which is derived from the firm's business strategies.[75] If increased sales is the major goal and these sales involve a one-time transaction with the customer and little expectation of a continuing relationship, then a greater proportion of incentives in the pay mix is appropriate. If customer service is crucial and the sales representative is expected to respond to clients' needs on a long-term basis, then greater reliance on straight salary is appropriate. For example, used car salespeople are often paid in the form of straight commission, while sales representatives for highly technical product lines (which often require extensive customer service) tend to be paid on straight salary.

Rewarding Excellence in Customer Service

More and more companies are using incentive systems to reward and encourage better customer service. A recent survey of 1,400 employers revealed that 35% of the respondents factor customer satisfaction into their formula for determining incentive payments. Another third are considering doing so. Common measures of customer satisfaction used to determine incentive payments are customer surveys, records of on-time delivery of products and services, and number of complaints received.[76]

Customer service rewards may be individual-, team-, or plant-based. For example, Storage Technology in Louisville, Colorado, uses customer service as part of its formula to distribute gainsharing monies to all employees covered by the plan. To ensure that sales reps and managers don't shortchange the customer for the sake of increasing sales and short-term profits, IBM introduced a plan where 40% of incentive earnings are tied to customer satisfaction. IBM uses a survey to determine if buyers are happy with the local sales team.[77] AT&T Cards Company provides a $200 on-the-spot bonus for employees who deal effectively with customers' complaints on the phone; phone calls are randomly monitored for this purpose.[78]

Summary and Conclusions

Pay-for-Performance: The Challenges. Pay-for-performance (incentive) programs can improve productivity, but managers need to consider several challenges in their design and implementation. Employees may be tempted to do only what they get paid for, ignoring those intangible aspects of the job that are not explicitly rewarded. Cooperation and teamwork may be damaged if individual merit pay is too strongly emphasized. Individual merit systems assume that the employee is in control of the primary factors affecting his or her work output, an assumption that may not be true. Individual performance is difficult to measure, and tying pay to inaccurate performance measures is likely to create problems. Pay incentive systems can be perceived as an employee right and can be difficult to adapt to the organization's changing needs. Many employees do not believe that good performance is rewarded (the credibility gap). Emphasizing merit pay can place employees under a great deal of stress and lead to job dissatisfaction. Finally, merit pay may decrease employees' intrinsic motivation.

Meeting the Challenges of Pay-for-Performance Systems. To avoid the problems sometimes associated with pay-for-performance systems, managers should: (1) link pay and performance appropriately, (2) use pay for performance as part of a broader HRM system, (3) build employee trust, (4) promote the belief that performance makes a difference, (5) use multiple layers of rewards, (6) increase employee involvement, and (7) consider using nonfinancial incentives. Employee participation in the design of the plan can enhance its credibility and long-term success.

Types of Pay-for-Performance Plans. There are four types of incentive programs. At the level of individual employees, merit pay (which becomes part of base salary) and bonuses and awards (given on a one-time basis) determined via supervisory appraisals are most common. At the next level, team-based plans reward the performance of groups of employees who work together on joint projects or tasks, usually with bonuses and noncash awards. At the level of the plant or business unit, gainsharing is the program of choice. Gainsharing rewards workers based on cost savings, usually in the form of a lump-sum bonus. At the fourth and highest level of the organization—the entire corporation—profit sharing and employee stock option plans (ESOPs) are used to link the firm's performance with employees' financial rewards. Both plans are commonly used to fund retirement programs.

Designing Pay-for-Performance Plans for Executives and Salespeople. Two employee groups, top executives and sales personnel, are normally treated very differently than most other workers in pay-for-performance plans. Short-term annual bonuses, long-term incentives, and perks may be used to motivate executives to make decisions that help the firm meet its long-term strategic goals. Sales employees are revenue generators, and their compensation system is normally used to reinforce productive behavior. A reliance on straight salary for salespeople is most appropriate where maintaining customer relations and servicing existing accounts are the key objectives. A heavy reliance on straight commission is most appropriate if the firm is trying to increase sales. Most firms use a combination of the two plans. In today's globally competitive marketplace, many firms are also using incentive programs to reward customer service.

Key Terms

award, 337
bonus program or lump-sum payment, 336
employee stock ownership plan (ESOP), 346
expectancy theory, 337
gainsharing, 343
merit pay, 336
pay-for-performance system or incentive system, 331
perquisites ("perks"), 350
piece-rate system, 334
profit sharing, 345

Discussion Questions

1. This chapter identifies three assumptions underlying pay-for-performance plans. Do you believe these assumptions are valid?
2. How can a pay-for-performance system increase the motivation of individual employees and improve cooperation at the same time?
3. One observer notes that "the problem with using pay as an incentive is that it is such a powerful motivational weapon that management can easily lose control of the situation." Do you agree? Why or why not?
4. A growing trend in compensation is "on-call" pay plans, which reward employees for simply being available to work outside their regular shifts. Employees are free to sleep or conduct personal activities during their scheduled on-call period, but they must be reachable and able to respond within a specified amount of time. Some people are very concerned with this trend (on-call plans were almost nonexistent in 1994, but were used by approximately one third of firms in 1996) because these incentives can greatly increase stress levels and disrupt employees' family life. What are some other possible disadvantages of these plans? What are some possible advantages?
5. An insurance company compensates its work teams by awarding an annual bonus based on three factors: productivity, customer satisfaction, and quality of work. In one of its teams, four members came up with a way to speed up claims payments that boosted customer satisfaction and productivity and also satisfied quality goals. In this situation, is a bonus for the entire ten-member team justified? How can the insurance company make sure that free riders (low performers) don't benefit from the productivity of others in the group, and that those who do the most work will be rewarded appropriately?
6. Some people believe that it is unfair to pay executives the lion's share (in some cases all) of the bonus money distributed by the firm as performance improves, simply because much of what happens inside the company is beyond executives' control. According to this argument, more bonus money should be allocated to those who make performance improvement possible—midlevel managers, supervisors, and employees. Do you agree with this argument? Why or why not? Can you think of any examples where extremely high levels of CEO pay would be justified?
7. Incentive systems for top executives are often criticized for filling the pockets of these individuals, with little benefit (and sometimes even negative results) to stockholders and the company in general. Using the latest annual listing of the highest-paid executives from *Fortune* magazine or *Business Week*, pick five CEOs and try to determine which CEO gave shareholders the most for his or her pay.
8. A customer survey for Landmark Company reports that people don't trust what sales representatives say about their firm's products. How might you use the compensation system to help change this negative image?

MINICASE 1 *At Battelle Labs, R&D Means Royalties and Development*

A research scientist for a large pharmaceutical corporation develops and patents a successful new drug that produces $100 million in revenue during its first year in the market. The executives of the division receive large cash bonuses and the salespeople enjoy windfall commissions, but the scientist walks away with a $500 honorarium.

Contrast this scenario, a common one at many U.S. companies, with what happens at Battelle Pacific Northwest Laboratory in Richland, Washington. At Battelle, researchers develop technologies that the company then licenses to private industry. The company receives licensing fees for the technology, as well as royalties on any products using it. Key researchers share a pool of funds worth 10% of gross royalties or other proceeds derived from the licensing fees. On average, four to six employees share royalties on any given technology patent, and in the last three years key contributors have received approximately $200,000 through the royalty program. There is a catch, though. Employees don't receive royalties unless they're still at Battelle when the technology achieves commercialization. After that, royalties continue even if the employee leaves the company.

Discussion Questions

1. What are the advantages and disadvantages of rewarding technology developers or research scientists with royalties from the sale or licensing of products they develop?
2. Do you think there would be any difference in team dynamics between Battelle and a company where researchers work together to develop a product without getting a share in the profits? Explain.

Source: Adapted from Caudron, S. (1993, September 6). Share the wealth. *Personnel Journal*, 45–46.

MINICASE 2 *Bad Marks for School Cash Incentives?*

It seemed like a promising idea: rewarding teachers with more pay if their students' performance improves. But according to a recent Urban Institute study, the idea looks better on paper than in the classroom. In a follow-up of merit-pay incentive plans implemented by school districts around the United States in the 1980s and 1990s, the institute researchers found that almost all merit plans had been terminated by the mid-1990s.

Most school districts trying merit-pay plans did report some positive effects, such as declines in teacher absenteeism, improved teacher motivation, and increased attention to teaching. But these were often offset by morale problems stemming from increased rivalry among teachers and resentment when teachers were denied rewards they felt they deserved. High program costs and heavy demands on administrators also eroded community support for the plans. The bottom line: Despite high hopes, none of the districts studied was able to use teacher pay incentives to achieve significant, lasting gains in student performance.

For this reason, focus is now shifting to school administrators. Many school systems are now linking school administrators' pay to performance indicators such as raising scores in state tests, reducing the reading gap between white and minority students, increasing attendance rates, and the like. In Minneapolis, for example, a school superintendent may receive up to $470,000 in incentive pay for achieving quantitative performance goals, while in Philadelphia the superintendent may take an $8,000 pay cut for failing to attain numeric goals. These programs, implemented for the first time in the mid-1990s, are quite controversial. Superintendents simply aren't analogous to corporate executives, says Pam Houston, executive director of the Washington-based American Association of School Administrators. "We're not making widgets here. There are a lot of factors superintendents don't have control over," she says, listing poverty, violence, and school funding as examples. Others warn that pay incentives could encourage districts to alter teaching to play to the tests or fudge test scores.

Discussion Questions

1. Do you think linking pay to performance for teachers and school administrators is a good idea? Why or why not?
2. What criteria or system would you use to reward the performance of teachers and school administrators that may prevent some of the problems noted in this minicase? Explain.

Sources: Koretz, G. (1995, September 4). Bad mark for pay by results. *Business Week*, 28; and Lubman, S. (1995, March 15). Schools tie salaries to pupil performance. *The Wall Street Journal*, B1.

CASE 1 *Loafers at Lakeside Utility Company*

Lakeside Utility Company provides electrical power to a county with 50,000 households. Pamela Johnson is the manager in charge of all repair and installation crews. Each crew consists of approximately seven employees who work closely together to respond to calls concerning power outages, fires caused by electrical malfunctions, and installation of new equipment or electric lines. Fourteen months ago Johnson decided to implement a team-based incentive system that will award an annual bonus to each crew that meets certain performance criteria. Performance measures include such indicators as average length of time needed to restore power, results of a customer satisfaction survey, and number of hours required to complete routine installation assignments successfully. At the end of the first year, five crews received an average cash bonus of $12,000 each, with the amount divided equally among all crew members.

Soon after Johnson announced the recipients of the cash bonus, she began to receive a large number of complaints. Some teams not chosen for the award voiced their unhappiness through their crew leader. The two most common complaints were that the teams working on the most difficult assignments were penalized (because it was harder to score higher on the evaluation) and that crews unwilling to help out other crews were being rewarded.

Ironically, members of the crews that received the awards also expressed dissatisfaction. A surprisingly large number of confidential employee letters from the winning teams reported that the system was unfair because the bonus money was split evenly among all crew members. Several letters named loafers who received "more than their share" because they were frequently late for work, took long lunches and frequent smoking breaks, and lacked initiative. Johnson is at a loss about what to do next.

Critical Thinking Questions

1. What major issues and problems concerning the design and implementation of pay-for-performance systems does this case illustrate? Explain.
2. Are team-based incentives appropriate for the type of work done by Johnson's crews?
3. Might it be desirable to use a combination of team-based and individual incentives at Lakeside Utility Company? How might such a plan be structured?

Cooperative Learning Exercises

4. Students form pairs. One student takes the role of Pamela Johnson, the other the role of an HRM consultant Johnson has hired to help her decide what to do next. Role-play the meeting between the two. Johnson explains what has happened and the consultant reacts.
5. The class divides into groups of five students each. One of the students takes the role of a consultant hired by Pamela Johnson to help her decide what to do. The remaining four students take the roles of line workers, each from a different crew. The consultant is gathering information from the crews about how they feel about the bonus system and what changes they would like to see.

CASE 2 *Too Good to Be True: You Get What You Pay For*

During the late 1980s and early 1990s, Hong Kong was the star of Bausch & Lomb's (B&L's) international division, often racking up annual growth of 25% as it rocketed to about $100 million in revenues in the mid-1990s.

Trouble was, in recent years, some of the reported sales were fake. Under heavy pressure to maintain its phenomenal record, the Hong Kong unit would pretend to book big sales of Ray-Ban sunglasses to distributors in Southeast Asia. But the goods would not be shipped. Rather, staffers were instructed to send the goods to an outside warehouse in Hong Kong. Later, some of B&L's sales managers would try to persuade distributors to buy the excess. Some of the glasses were also funneled into the *gray market*; buyers could profit by reselling them in Europe or the Middle East, where wholesale prices were higher. But Hong Kong began to have trouble keeping up its juggling act. Tipped off by falling revenues and soaring receivables—since no one was paying for many of the glasses booked as sales—B&L sent a team of auditors to Hong Kong. The auditors discovered significant irregularities, including half a million pairs of sunglasses stashed in a warehouse.

Investigation revealed that these events were hardly isolated. They were also evident in many other B&L locations. Dan Gill, CEO of B&L, managed by the numbers. "Each year, the top executives would agree on what number they wanted to make," recalls Harold O. Johnson, the longtime head of the contact lens unit. "The numbers would be divided out by operating units and then assigned. The president would come to me and say, 'Here's your number.'" Once the goals were set, Gill and other top executives rarely accepted excuses for shortfalls; even Gill's backers agree that "making the numbers was key." This was often accomplished at the expense of sound business practice or ethical behavior. B&L's operating units gave customers extraordinarily long payment periods and threatened to cut off distributors unless they took on huge quantities of unwanted products. Some also shipped goods before customers ordered them and booked the shipments as sales. The compensation system, which emphasized sales growth and deemphasized customer satisfaction, played a major role in B&L's troubles. The compensation signals from the top down led some to cut corners, several former managers say. As a result, some divisional managers began using tactics that were costly for the company but which maximized reported earnings and thus their own bonuses.

Critical Thinking Questions

1. Bausch & Lomb's intense focus on the bottom line and quarterly results is hardly unique. Many of corporate America's most successful companies have a similar focus. What do you think went wrong at B&L? Explain.
2. Some experts believe that managerial incentives should be exclusively based on the price of the company's stock because it is determined by the "invisible hand" of the market and can't be manipulated (unlike reported earnings, which can be manipulated, as described above). Do you agree? Why or why not?

Cooperative Learning Exercises

3. The class divides into groups of six members each. Each group prepares a series of recommendations to change B&L's culture to prevent the problems described in this case. The groups will then debate their recommendations in front of the class, with the instructor serving as moderator.
4. Students form into groups of three and spend about five minutes brainstorming the advantages and disadvantages of linking top management's pay to accounting performance measures (such as sales growth, earnings, total revenues, and the like), and then about five minutes brainstorming the advantages and disadvantages of linking top executives' pay incentives to the price of the company's stock. Does either of these plans emerge as clearly superior?

Sources: Barnathan, J. (1995, October 23). *Business Week*, 78–92; Reuters News Service (1996; April 23), Bausch & Lomb, Inc. absolves executives in probe; Maremont, M., and DeGeorge, G. (1995, October 23). Money laundering in Miami? *Business Week*, 89.

HRM Simulation 

The simulation presents you with several options to reward employees for their performance (Incident 6). These include individual-based plans such as bonuses and merit increases linked to individual contributions; group-based plans (in which workers would receive a base hourly wage plus a bonus based on team performance); and aggregate incentive plans, such as profit sharing/gainsharing and employee stock ownership plans. Which of these plans would you choose? Would you consider a mix of them? What factors would you take into account when choosing among these plans? What are the advantages and disadvantages of each?

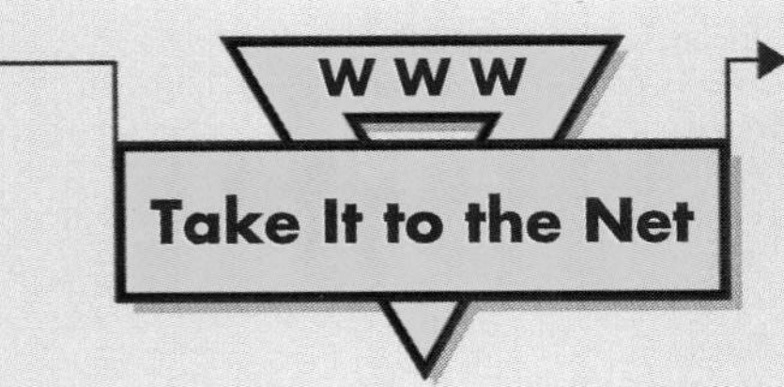

We invite you to visit the Gómez-Mejía/Balkin/Cardy page on the Prentice Hall Web site:

http://www.prenhall.com/gomez

You can also visit the Web sites for these companies, featured within this chapter:

Bausch and Lomb	http://www.bausch.com
Compaq Computer Corp.	http://www.compaq.com
The Gap	http://www.gap.com
Hershey's Chocolate	http://www.hersheys.com
Kraft General Foods	http://www.kraftfoods.com
Mary Kay Cosmetics	http://www.marykay.com
Pepsico	http://www.pepsico.com
Unisys	http://www.unisys.com

Endnotes

1. *CompFlash* (1995, October). American Management Association, 2.

1a. Hamilton, J. O. (1996, June 24). Levi's pot o' gold. *Business Week*, 44.

2. Milkovich, G. T., and Newman, J. (1996). *Compensation*. Homewood, IL: Irwin.
3. Gómez-Mejía, L. R., and Balkin, D. B. (1992). *Compensation, organizational strategy, and firm performance.* Cincinnati, OH: South-Western.
4. Milkovich, G. T., Wigdor, A. K., Broderick, R. F., and Mavor, A. S. (Eds.) (1991). *Pay for performance: Evaluating performance appraisal and merit pay.* Washington, DC: National Academy Press; Barton, R. (1996, February). Pay plans must be well designed because "you get what you pay for." *ACA News*, 1–3; O'Neal, S. (1996, Spring). Reengineering and compensation: An interview with Michael Hammer. *ACA Journal, 5*(1), 8–11.
5. *Boston Globe* (1992, October 16). Teaching to the test shortchanges pupils. *Arizona Republic*, A4.
6. Spiro, L. N., and Schoeder, M. (1995, February 20). Can you trust? *Business Week*, 70–76.
7. Pearce, J. L. (1987). Why merit pay doesn't work: Implications from organizational theory. In D. B. Balkin and L. R. Gómez-Mejía (Eds.), *New perspectives on compensation.* Englewood Cliffs, NJ: Prentice Hall.
8. Gabor, A. (1991). *The man who discovered quality.* New York: Time Books; Scholtes, P. R. (1987). *An elaboration on Deming's teachings on performance appraisal.* Madison, WI: Joiner Associates; Walton, M. (1991). Deming management at work. New York: G. P. Putnam's Sons; Edwards, M. and Ewen, A. J. (1995, Winter). Moving multisource assessment beyond development. *ACA Journal, 5* (1), 82–87; Bors, K. K., Clark, A. W., Power, V., Seltz, J. C., Scwartz, R. B., and Turbridy, G. S. (1996, Spring). Multiple perspectives: Essays on implementing performance measures. *ACA Journal*, *5*(1), 40–55.
9. Lord, R. G. (1985). Accuracy in behavioral measurement: An alternative definition based on raters' cognitive schema and signal detection theory. *Journal of Applied Psychology, 70*, 66–71; Murphy, W., and Cleveland J. (1991). *Performance appraisal: An organizational perspective,* Boston: Allyn and Bacon; Tsui, A. S., and Ohlott, P. (1988). Multiple assessment of managerial effectiveness: Interrater agreement and consensus in effectiveness models. *Personnel Psychology, 41*, 779–802; Edwards, M., and Ewen, A. J. (1995, Winter). Moving multisource assessment beyond development. *ACA Journal*, 82–87; Bors, K. K., Clark, A. W., Power, V., Seltz, J. C., Schwartz, R. B., and Tubridy, G. S. (1996, Spring). Multiple perspectives: Essays on implementing performance measures. *ACA Journal, 5*(1), 40–55.
10. Lawler, E. E. III, and Cohen, S. G. (1992). Designing a pay system for teams. *American Compensation Association Journal, 1*(1), 6–19.
11. Gómez-Mejía, L. R., and Welbourne, T. M. (1988). Compensation strategy: An overview and future steps. *Human Resource Planning, 11*(3), 173–189.
12. Hills, F. S., Scott, D. K., Markham, S. E., and Vest, M. J. (1987). Merit pay: Just or unjust desserts? *Personnel Administrator, 32*(9), 53–64; and Hughes, C. L. (1986). The demerit of merit. *Personnel Administrator, 31*(6), 40.
13. Gómez-Mejía and Balkin, 1992.
14. *Business Week* (1992, July 6), 38.
15. Schwab, D. P. (1974). Conflicting impacts of pay on employee motivation and satisfaction. *Personnel Journal, 53*(3), 190–206.
16. Gómez-Mejía and Balkin, 1992.
17. Deci, E. L. (1972). The effects of contingent and non-contingent rewards and controls on intrinsic motivation. *Organizational Behavior and Human Performance, 8*, 15–31.
18. *Profit-Building Strategies for Business Owners* (1992, December), *22*(12), 23–24.
19. Greeley, T. P., and Oshsner, R. C. (1986). Putting merit pay back into salary administration. *Topics in Total Compensation, 1*(1), 14–30; and Smith, J. M., President of American Compensation Association. (1990, July 9). *Arizona Republic*, B-6.
20. Gómez-Mejía and Balkin, 1992.
21. (1991, October). AT&T credit: Continuous improvement as a way of life. *Work in America Institute, 16*(10), 2.
22. Gómez-Mejía, L. R., Page, R. C., and Tornow, W. (1982). A comparison of the practical utility of traditional, statistical, and hybrid job evaluation approaches. *Academy of Management Journal, 25*, 790–809.
23. McAdams, J. L., and Hawk, E. J. (1992). Capitalizing on human assets through performance based rewards. *American Compensation Association Journal, 1*(1), 60–71.
24. Masternak, R. L., and Ross, T. L. (1992, January–February). A bonus plan for employee involvement. *Compensation and Benefits Review*, 46–54.
25. Greenberg, J. (1990). Looking fair vs. being fair: Managing impressions of organizational justice. In L. Cummings and B. M. Staw (Eds.), *Research in organizational behavior* (Vol. 2). Greenwich, CT: JAI Press.
26. Milkovich, G. T., and Newman, J. M. (1994). *Compensation* (3d ed.). Plano, TX: B.P.I.
27. Gómez-Mejía, L. R., and Balkin, D. B. (1989). Effectiveness of individual and aggregate compensation strategies. *Industrial Relations, 28*, 431–445.
28. William Mercer Inc. (1996). Compensation planning survey. *Unpublished technical report.*
29. Lawler, E. E. III. (1989). The strategic design of pay-for-performance programs. In L. R. Gómez-Mejía (Ed.), *Compensation and benefits*. Washington, DC: Bureau of National Affairs; and Lawler, E. E. III. (1990). *Strategic pay*. San Francisco: Jossey-Bass.
30. Mount, M. K. (1987). Coordinating salary action and performance appraisal. In D. B. Balkin and L. R. Gómez-Mejía, *New perspectives on compensation*. Englewood Cliffs, NJ: Prentice Hall.
31. Locke, E. A., Shaw, K., Saari, L. M., and Latham, G. P. (1981). Goal setting and task performance: 1969–1980. *Psychological Bulletin, 90*, 125–152.
32. Fuchsberg, G. (1990, April 18). Culture shock. *The Wall Street Journal*, R5:1.
33. See Longenecker, C. O., Sims, H. P., and Gioia, D. A. (1987). Behind the mask: The politics of employee appraisal. *Academy of Management Executive, 1*, 183–193, for appraisal issues; see Bartol, K. M., and Martin, D. C. (1989). Influences on managerial pay allocations: A dependency perspective. *Personnel Psychology, 41*, 361–378, for a discussion specific to pay decisions.
34. Gómez-Mejía and Balkin, 1992; Walsh, B. (1995, October 9). Managing the monster. *Forbes ASAP*, 17.
35. Hewitt Associates, Lincolnshire, IL, reported in *The Wall Street Journal* (1995, November 28), A1.
36. Welbourne, T. M., and Gómez-Mejía, L. R. (1991). Team incentives in the workplace. In L. Berger (Ed.), *Handbook of wage and salary administration*, 236–247. New York: McGraw-Hill; and Zingheim, P. K. and Schuster, J. R. (1995, November/December). The team pay research study. *Compensation and Benefits Review*, G-9.
37. Bassim, M. (1988). Teamwork at General Foods: New and improved. *Personnel Journal, 67*(5), 62–70.
38. *ACA News*, (1992, October) 1; Hewitt Associates, 1995.
39. Lawler and Cohen, 1992; Gross, S., and Blair, J. (1995, September/October). Reinforcing team effectiveness through pay. *Compensation and Benefits Review*, 34–36; Zigon, J. (1996). How to measure the results of work teams. Zigon Performance Group, Media, PA; and Zingheim and Schuster, 1995.
40. Liden, R. C., and Mitchell, T. R. (1983). The effects of group interdependence on supervisor performance evaluations. *Personnel Psychology, 36*, 289–299.
41. Reynolds, C. (1992). Developing global strategies in total compensation. *American Compensation Association Journal, 1*(1), 74–85.
42. Heneman, F., and Von Hippel, C. Interview appearing in *The Wall Street Journal* (1995, November 28), A1; Dalton, 1996; and Lawler, 1996.
43. Albanese, R., and VanFleet, D. D. (1985). Rational behavior in groups: The freeriding tendency. *Academy of Management Review, 10*, 244–255.

44. Heneman and Von Hippel, 1995.
45. Gordon, D. M., Edwards, R., and Reich, M. (1982). *Segmented work, divided workers: The historical transformation of labor in the United States*. London: Cambridge University Press.
46. Mohrman, A. M., Mohrman, S. A., and Lawler, E. E. (1992). *Performance measurement, evaluation and incentives*. Boston: Harvard Business School.
47. Hogarty, D. B. (1994, January). New ways to pay. *Management Review*, 34–36.
48. Martell, K., Carroll, S. J., and Gupta, A. K. (1992). What executive human resource management practices are most effective when innovativeness requirements are high? In L. R. Gómez-Mejía and M. W. Lawless (Eds.), *Top management and effective leadership in high technology*. Greenwich, CT: JAI Press; and Hewitt Associates (1996, February). Companies advance in supporting teams through pay. *ACA News*, 6.
49. Pinchot, G. (1985). *Intrapreneuring*. New York: Harper & Row.
50. Selz, M. (1994, January 11). Testing self-managed teams, entrepreneur hopes to lose job. *The Wall Street Journal*, B1–B2.
51. Gross, S. E., and Bacher, J. P. (1993, January–February). The new variable pay programs: How some succeed, why some don't. *Compensation and Benefits Review*, 51–56.
52. McGregor, D. (1960). *The human side of enterprise*. New York: McGraw-Hill.
53. Ross, T. L., Hatcher, L., and Ross, R. A. (1989, May). The incentive switch: From piecework to companywide gainsharing. *Management Review*, 22–26.
54. Sullivan, J. F. (1988). The future of merit pay programs. *Compensation and Benefits Review, 20*(3), 22–30.
55. Gómez-Mejía and Balkin, 1992; Welbourne, T., and Gómez-Mejía, L. R. (1995). Gainsharing: A critical review. *Journal of Management, 21*(3), 559–609; Welbourne, T., Balkin, D., and Gómez-Mejía, L. R. (1995). Gainsharing and mutual monitoring. *Academy of Management Journal, 38*(3), 818–834; and Altmansberger, H. N., and Wallace, M. J. (1995, Winter). Strategic use of gainsharing at Corning. *ACA Journal*, 64–69.
56. Florkowski, G. W. (1987). The organizational impact of profit sharing. *Academy of Management Review, 12*, 622–636.
57. *Time*. (1988, February 1), 13.
58. Edelman, R. (1996, February). Record amount of stock awards allocated for compensation plans. *ACA News*, 5; Bennett, M. A. (1995, December). Building ownership. *ACA News*, 1; and Cook, F. (1996, Spring). A step toward fairness to employees requiring shareholders to accept more dilution from stock options. *ACA Journal, 5*(1), 26–30.
59. Bureau of National Affairs Special Report. (1988). *Changing pay practices: New developments in employee compensation*. Washington, DC: The Bureau of National Affairs.
60. Gillespie, P. (1992, March 15). America West Workers take stock loss in stride. *Arizona Republic*, A1.
61. Cheadle, A. (1989). Explaining patterns of profit sharing activity. *Industrial Relations, 28*, 387–401.
62. Smolowe, J. (1996, February 5). Reap as ye shall sow. *Time*, 45.
63. Asquith, N. (1995, November). Executive pay. *Compflash Metric*, 2.
64. *Id.*
65. Hyman, J. S. (1991). Long term incentives. In M. L. Rock and L. A. Berger (Eds.), *The compensation handbook*. New York: McGraw-Hill; Gómez-Mejía, L. R., and Wiseman, R. Executive compensation. *Journal of Management* (in press); Marquardt, E. P. (1996, Spring). Executive pay plans: Sharpening the focus on strategy execution. *ACA Journal, 5*(1), 32–39.
66. Crystal, G. S. (1990, June 18). The great CEO pay sweepstakes. *Fortune*, 99–102; and Kerr, J., and Bettis, R. A. (1987). Boards of directors, top management compensation and shareholder returns. *Academy of Management Journal, 30*, 745–664.
67. ECS, Wyatt Data Services Company. (1992). *The 1991/1992 top management report*. Ft. Lee, NJ.
68. Bryne, J. A. (1996, April 22). How high can CEO pay go? *Business Week*, 100–120.
69. *Id.*
70. Reynolds, 1992.
71. Bowers, B., and Gupta, U. (1993, October 15). Survey finds small firms show restraint on CEO pay. *The Wall Street Journal*, B2.
71a. *The Wall Street Journal News Roundup*. (1995, March 7). In a cost-cutting era, many CEOs enjoy imperial perks, B-1.
72. Gómez-Mejía, L. R. (1994). Executive compensation. In Ferris, R. *Advances in personnel/human resource management* (6th ed.). Cincinnati, OH: JAI Press, 25–50.
73. Gómez-Mejía and Balkin, 1992
74. *Id.*; Watson Wyatt Data Services. (1996). *The 1995–1996 Sales and Marketing Personnel Report*. New York, New York.
75. Colletti, J. A. (1986). Job evaluation and pay plans: Field sales representatives. In J. Famularo (Ed.), *Handbook of human resources administration*. New York: McGraw-Hill; Colletti, J. A., and Cichelli, D. J. (1991). Increasing sales force effectiveness through the compensation plan. In M. L. Rock and L. A. Berger (Eds.), *The compensation handbook*. New York: McGraw-Hill; and Stanton, W. J., and Buskirk, R. H. (1987). *Management of the sales force* (7th ed.). Homewood, IL: Irwin.
76. *HR Focus* (1993, July). Incentive pay focuses on quality, 15.
77. Sager, I., McWilliams, G., and Hof, D. (1994, Feb. 7). IBM leans on its salesforce. *Business Week*, 110.
78. *Forbes* (1994, February 28), 15-20.

CHALLENGES

After reading this chapter, you should be able to deal more effectively with the following challenges:

1 ▶ **Understand** the significance of employee benefits to both employers and employees.

2 ▶ **Design** a benefits package that supports the firm's overall compensation strategy and other HRM policies.

3 ▶ **Distinguish** between a defined benefit retirement plan and a defined contribution retirement plan and recognize the situations in which each is most appropriate.

4 ▶ **Explain** how traditional health insurance plans and managed-care health insurance plans work and the advantages and disadvantages of each.

5 ▶ **Develop** cost-containment strategies for the different types of employee benefits.

6 ▶ **Understand** the administrative complexities of providing a full array of benefits to the work force and suggest ways to deliver benefits effectively.

7 ▶ **Recognize** the HR department's key role in keeping accurate records of employee benefits and informing employees about their benefits.

12 Designing and Administering Benefits

A Day at the Beach. Employers provide their employees with paid vacations to give them time away from the stresses and strains of the daily work routine. Vacation time is an important benefit that allows employees to recharge themselves psychologically and emotionally, and can lead to improved job performance.

http://www.magicnet.net/benefits/index.html

Benefits Link

This Web site provides a wealth of information on employee benefit plans, including articles and government publications. It also includes discussion groups, a "yellow pages" listing of benefits service providers, and a comprehensive index of benefits-related legislation.

Today's HR managers face a number of challenges that did not exist a decade ago. One of these challenges is managing the rapidly increasing costs of employee benefits. Although health-care costs have received the most attention, the costs of many other employee benefits are also on the rise. At the same time, benefits have become crucial to attracting, retaining, and motivating employees. A recent report by the National Study of the Changing Work Force found that 43% of employees who changed jobs rated employee benefits as "very important" in their decision, while only 35% said the same for salary or wages.

The following examples give some idea of the many ways companies are managing employee benefits in difficult times. Some companies are:

- *cutting benefits costs wherever they can.* Because of a new accounting regulation requiring companies to report the cost of future retiree benefits on their balance sheets, hundreds of firms have reduced health insurance coverage for retirees, whom they had previously covered in full. When Unisys was staring at a $700 million benefits liability, it told most of its 25,000 retirees that they must start bearing the entire cost of their health insurance. Other companies have cut retirees' health benefits to avoid decreasing benefits for currently employed workers.[1]
- *providing more flexible benefits.* When Chicago-based Quaker Oats decided to update its benefits program, top management concluded that the company was spending money on benefits that weren't valuable to all employees. The company decided to offers its work force a flexible benefits program, one that provides a menu of items from which employees can choose to meet their individual and family needs. Quaker employees now buy and sell vacation days and choose between such options as healthy lifestyle credits and dependent-care spending accounts.[2] At Hi-Tech Hose, in Newburyport, Massachusetts, employees make use of paid time-off (PTO) banks. PTO banks pool time off into a bank of days that employees may use for vacation, sick, or personal days. PTO programs allow employees to choose how they will use their time off without feeling the pressure to justify their absence to the boss.[3]

Offering benefits that give employees a sense of security while containing costs might seem to be mutually exclusive goals. The challenge is for managers and HR professionals to work together to (1) give employees meaningful benefit choices that match their needs, (2) keep the costs of these benefits under control, and (3) ensure that employees are fully informed of their benefit options.

In this chapter we explain benefits in detail. We begin with an overview of employee benefits and the relationship of benefits to the rest of the compensation package. Second, we examine strategies for designing benefits programs. Next, we describe the scope and significance of two categories of employee benefits programs: legally required benefits and voluntary benefits. Finally, we discuss some important issues in benefits administration.

▸ An Overview of Benefits

Employee benefits are group membership rewards that provide security for employees and their family members. They are sometimes called **indirect compensation** because they are given to employees in the form of a plan (such as health insurance) rather than cash. A benefits package complements the base-compensation and pay-incentives components of total compensation. According to a recent U.S. Chamber of Commerce study, ben-

employee benefits or **indirect compensation**
Group membership rewards that provide security for employees and their family members.

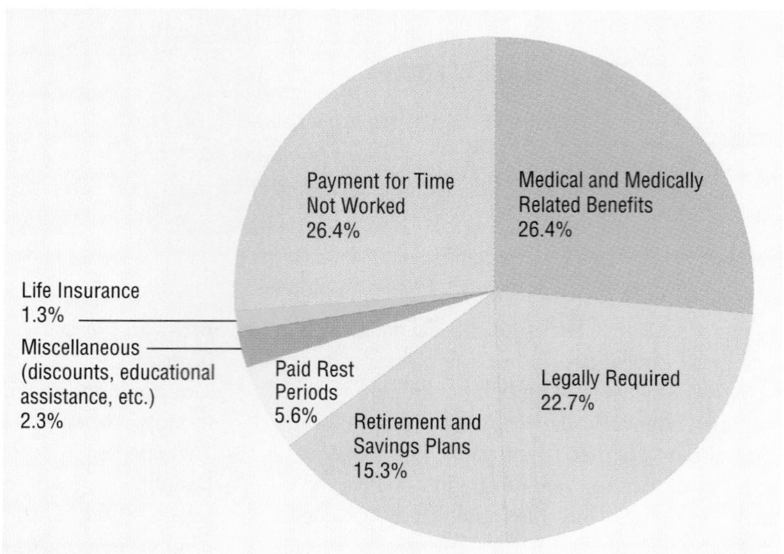

FIGURE 12-1

How the Benefit Dollar Is Spent

Source: U.S. Chamber of Commerce (1992). *1992 Employee benefits report.* Washington, DC: U.S. Chamber of Commerce.

efits cost U.S. companies about $14,807 per year for the average employee.[4] Figure 12–1 shows how the benefit dollar is divided in the average firm.

Employee benefits protect employees from risks that could jeopardize their health and financial security. They provide coverage for sickness, injury, unemployment, and old age and death. They may also provide services or facilities that many employees find valuable, such as child-care services or an exercise center.

In the United States the employer is the primary source of benefits coverage. The situation is quite different in other countries, where many benefits are sponsored by the government and funded with taxes. For example, in the United States employers voluntarily provide their employees with health insurance, while in Canada health insurance is a right bestowed on all citizens by the country's national health system. For a brief summary of Canada's health-care policy, see the Issues and Applications feature on page 365 titled "Benefits Across the Border: A Look at Canada's Health-Care System."

The benefits package offered by a firm can support management's efforts to attract employees. When a potential employee is choosing among multiple job offers with similar salaries, a firm offering an attractive benefits package will be ahead of the pack. For example, Swedish Medical Center, a hospital in Denver, Colorado, uses its on-site child-care center as a recruiting tool to attract high-quality staff.[5] It is one of only two hospitals in its region that offer this benefit.

Benefits can also help management retain employees. Benefits that are designed to increase in value over time encourage employees to remain with their employer. For instance, many companies make contributions to employees' retirement funds, but these funds are available only to employees who stay with the company for a certain number of years. For this reason, benefits are sometimes called "golden handcuffs." An excellent example of the power of benefits to retain employees is the U.S. military, which provides early retirement benefits to personnel who put in 20 years of service. This "20 years and out" retirement provision allows retired military people to start a second career at a fairly young age with the security of a lifelong retirement income to supplement their earnings. These generous benefits help the armed forces retain valuable officers and professionals who would otherwise be attracted to higher-paying civilian jobs.[6]

Basic Terminology

Before we proceed, it is necessary to define some basic terms we will use throughout this chapter:

- **Contributions:** All benefits are funded by contributions from the employer, the employee, or both. For example, vacations are an employer-provided benefit: The salary or wages paid to the employee during the vacation period come entirely from the employer. Premiums for health-care insurance are often paid partly by the employer and partly by the employee.
- **Copayments:** Payments made to cover health-care expenses that are split between the employer's insurance company and the employee. For instance, under an 80/20 insurance plan, the employer's insurance company would pay 80% of the employee's health-care costs and the employee would pay the remaining 20%.
- **Deductible:** An annual out-of-pocket expenditure that an insurance policyholder must make before the insurance plan makes any reimbursements. For instance, the 80/20 plan described previously may also have a $500 deductible, in which case the employee would be responsible for the first $500 of medical expenses before the insurance company begins to make the 80% copayment.
- **Flexible benefit programs:** A **flexible benefits program,** also called a **cafeteria benefits program,** allows employees to select the benefits they need most from a menu of choices. Unlike employers that try to design a one-size-fits-all benefits package, employers with a flexible benefits program recognize that their employees have diverse needs that require different benefits packages. A 30-year-old married female employee with a working spouse and small children is likely to need child-care benefits and may be willing to forgo extra paid vacation days in exchange for this benefit. A 50-year-old married male employee with grown children may prefer a larger employer contribution to his retirement plan.

contributions
Payments made for benefits coverage. Contributions for a specific benefit may come from the employer, employee, or both.

copayments
Payments made to cover health-care expenses that are split between the employer's insurance company and the insured employee.

deductible
An annual out-of-pocket expenditure that an insurance policyholder must make before the insurance plan makes any reimbursements.

flexible or **cafeteria benefits program**
A benefits program that allows employees to select the benefits they need most from a menu of choices.

The Cost of Benefits in the United States

The cost of employee benefits in the United States has increased dramatically over the decades as businesses have offered more and more benefits. As Figure 12–2 shows, the cost of employee benefits as a percentage of an employer's payroll increased from 3% in 1929 to about 41% in 1993.[7] This growth can be explained by a combination of factors,

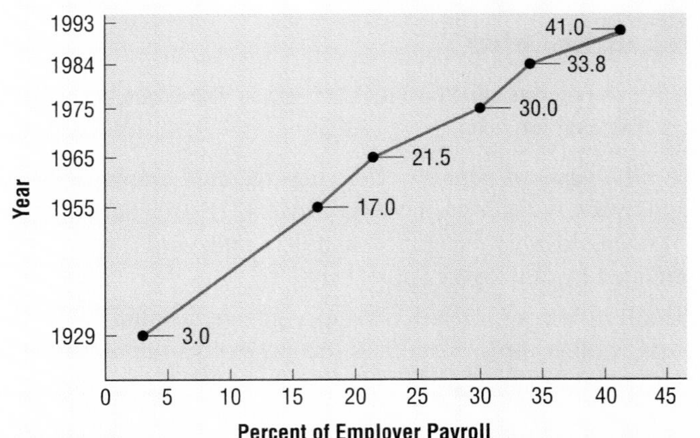

FIGURE 12-2

Cost of Employee Benefits in the United States, 1929–1993

Source: U.S. Chamber of Commerce, 1994. *Employee benefits 1993*, Washington, DC: U.S. Chamber of Commerce.

including federal tax policy, federal legislation, the influence of unions, and the cost savings of group plans.

Federal Tax Policy. Since the 1920s, the federal government has provided favorable tax treatment for group benefit plans that meet certain standards (discussed later in this chapter).[8] Employers who meet the tax policy guidelines receive tax deductions for their benefits expenditures.

Employees also receive favorable treatment under the tax policy because they receive many of their benefits on a *tax-free* basis. For example, employees receive their employer's contribution to a health insurance plan tax-free. In contrast, self-employed individuals have to pay for health insurance out of their taxable income. Other benefits are received on a *tax-deferred* basis. For example, employee contributions to a qualified retirement plan (up to a maximum amount) may be tax-deferred until the employee retires, at which time the person may be taxed at a lower rate. Federal tax policy on benefits has encouraged employees to demand additional benefits because each additional dollar a company allocates for benefits has more value than a dollar allocated as cash compensation, which is taxed as ordinary income.

Federal Legislation. In 1935, federal legislation decreed that all employers must provide Social Security and unemployment insurance benefits to their employees. We take a closer look at these benefits later in this chapter. At this point, we only wish to make the point that federal law requires some benefits, and that federal legislation will probably continue to cause significant growth in the cost of benefits.

Union Influence. Unions have been in the forefront of the movement to expand employee benefits for the last half century. In the 1940s, powerful unions such as the United Auto Workers and the United Mine Workers obtained pensions and health insurance plans from employers. In recent years, unions have been asking for dental-care coverage, extended vacation periods, and unemployment benefits beyond those required by federal law.

Once benefit patterns are established in unionized firms, these same benefits tend to spread to nonunionized companies, which often wish to avoid union organization drives (see Chapter 15).

Cost Savings of Group Plans. Employers can provide benefits for much less money than employees would pay to obtain them on their own. When insurance companies can spread risk over a large group of individuals, they can reduce the cost of benefits per person. This fact causes employees to put considerable pressure on their employers to provide certain benefits.

Types of Benefits

Benefits can be organized into six categories. These categories, which we examine in detail later in this chapter, are:

1. *Legally required benefits:* U.S. law requires employers to give four benefits to all employees, with only a few exceptions: (1) Social Security, (2) workers' compensation, (3) unemployment insurance, and (4) family and medical leave. All other benefits are provided by employers voluntarily.
2. *Health insurance:* Health insurance covers hospital costs, physician charges, and the costs of other medical services. Because of its importance, health insurance is usually considered separately from other types of insurance.
3. *Retirement:* Retirement benefits provide income to employees after they retire.
4. *Insurance:* Insurance plans protect employees or their dependents from financial difficulties that can arise as a result of disability or death.

Issues + Applications

Benefits Across the Border: A Look at Canada's Health Care System

When Tommy Bettis from Arkansas broke his arm and cut his head while helping to repair the garage of his Ontario friend, Kristopher Goering, Bettis received emergency care at a Canadian hospital by presenting Goering's health card. While this case involved an emergency occurring in Canada, thousands of Americans are routinely borrowing Canadian health cards to get medical care.

Why are ailing Americans going to another country and using illegal means to get health care there? Because in Canada health care is free. In the debate on U.S. health-care reform, the U.S. media have alternately portrayed Canada's national health-care system as a medical miracle or as a bureaucratic nightmare. The truth seems to be somewhere in between. Yet, from the vantage point of 37 million uninsured residents of the United States—many of whom are employed full- or part-time—Canada's system is more in the miracle category.

Canada's national system covers all residents' medical and hospital bills and is funded through income taxes (top bracket: 48% on income over $50,000) and through a payroll tax on employers. Doctors and hospitals are reimbursed directly by provincial governments according to a negotiated schedule of fees, while patients pay nothing—except higher taxes than U.S. citizens. (In fact, Americans take home the largest percentage of their gross pay among all industrialized nations.) Health-care expenditures are 40% lower per capita than in the United States, however, and the burden is lighter for employers, too. Consider Ford Motor Company of Canada. In 1990 it spent $41 million on coverage for its 22,000 workers, or about $65 per vehicle produced—many times less than what its U.S. parent pays for health coverage for U.S. employees. But does Canada get more out of its health system for less? Statistics seem to say so: Canada boasts the eighth-highest life expectancy in the world, 77.03 years as opposed to 75.22 for the United States, which ranks thirty-third. Canada's infant mortality rate of 7.9 per 1,000 live births is the tenth lowest in the world, while the U.S. rate of 10 per 1,000 is twenty-first.

Is there a catch in the Canadian system? Canadians sometimes have to wait for nonemergency procedures, but rarely for run-of-the-mill services. Also, in Canada, recession has cut into tax revenues, so the system is facing a financial crunch. But there is one rising cost Canada can do something about: the cost of Americans using the system illegally. Canadian officials are cracking down on health-care fraud, seizing the cards of ineligible users and making a bigger effort to collect for medical services provided to nonresidents.

Sources: Multinational Division, Sedwick Noble Lowndes (1996). *The 1995 guide to pensions and labor law in Europe, Japan, and the U.S.A.* Chicago, IL. Farnsworth, C. H. (1993, December 20). Americans filching free health care in Canada. *The New York Times*, A1; *Money* (1993, June). How to get medical care for all. 22, 87ff; and Symonds, W. C. (1992, March 9). It's not perfect, but it sure works. *Business Week*, 54.

5. *Paid time off:* Time-off plans give employees time off with or without pay, depending on the plan.
6. *Employee services:* Employee services are tax-free or tax-preferred services that enhance the quality of employees' work or personal life.

Figure 12–3 on page 366 shows the percentage of full-time U.S. employers providing selected benefits plans. As the figure makes clear, large- and medium-sized private firms (those that employ more than 100 individuals) and state and local governments offer a wider variety of benefits than small businesses do.

The growth of benefits over the years, coupled with increased benefits costs, has encouraged employers to hire more part-time or temporary employees when their business grows. Companies often do not provide benefits to part-time employees and temporary employees.

The Role of the Manager

More than almost any other issue addressed in this text, benefits programs are centrally controlled by an organization's HR department. Nonetheless, it is important that line managers be familiar with benefits, for several reasons:

FIGURE 12-3

Percentage of Employers Providing Selected Benefit Plans

Source: U.S. Department of Labor, Bureau of Labor Statistics, (1993, July). *Monthly Labor Review*, 93; U.S. Department of Labor, Bureau of Labor Statistics (1995).

	Medium and Large Private Firms[1] 1993	Small Private Firms[2] 1994	State and Local Governments[3] 1990
Health Insurance	82	66	93
Retirement Plans			
Defined Benefit Plans	56	15	90
Defined Contribution Plans	49	34	9
Insurance Plans			
Life Insurance	91	61	88
Long-term Disability Insurance	41	20	27
Time-off Plans			
Paid Vacations	97	88	67
Paid Holidays	91	82	74
Paid Sick Leave	65	50	95
Flexible Benefits Plans	12	3	5

[1]Firms employing 100 workers or more.
[2]Firms employing fewer than 100 workers.
[3]Data for 1990 are the most recent available.

- *Benefits are important to employees.* Benefit issues are often extremely important to employees. For instance, if an employee has a child who needs urgent medical attention, that employee's manager should be able to explain what the firm offers in terms of medical benefits. The manager needs to understand both generic benefits issues and the specifics of the company plan to counsel employees effectively.
- *Benefits can be a powerful recruiting tool.* Managers at companies that offer attractive benefits can use this advantage to recruit high-quality applicants.
- *Certain benefits play a part in managerial decisions.* Some benefits (such as vacations, family and medical leave, and sick days) give employees scheduling flexibility. Managers need to be aware of these benefits to effectively manage work schedules.
- *Benefits are important to managers.* Managers need to be aware of their own benefit options. Some decisions, particularly those concerning retirement plans, have long-term consequences. Good decisions in this area made early in a career will make life easier down the road.

The Benefits Strategy

To design an effective benefits package, a company needs to align its benefits strategy with its overall compensation strategy. The benefits strategy requires making choices in three areas: (1) benefits mix, (2) benefits amount, and (3) flexibility of benefits. These choices provide a blueprint for the design of the benefits package.

The Benefits Mix

benefits mix
The complete package of benefits that a company offers its employees.

The **benefits mix** is the complete package of benefits that a company offers its employees. There are at least three issues that should be considered when making decisions about the benefits mix: the total compensation strategy, organizational objectives, and the characteristics of the work force.[9]

The total compensation strategy issue corresponds to the "below-market versus above-market compensation" decision we discussed in Chapter 10. The company must choose the market in which it wants to compete for employees and then provide a benefits package attractive to the people in that market. In other words, management tries to answer the question: Who are my competitors for employees and what kinds of benefits do they provide?

For example, a high-tech firm may want to attract people who are risk takers and innovators. The firm's management may decide not to offer retirement benefits because high-tech companies are usually considered desirable places to work by people in their 20s, and people this young are generally not concerned about retirement. As an upstart challenger to IBM, Apple Computer chose not to offer retirement benefits because management did not think this benefit would attract the entrepreneurial employees it wanted.[10]

Most larger employers provide some sort of retirement fund for their employees. Do you think that companies are ethically bound to offer this benefit? Does the financial condition of the firm (good or poor) make any difference to your analysis?

The organization's objectives also influence the benefits mix. For instance, if the company philosophy is to minimize differences between low-level employees and top management, the benefits mix should be the same for all employees. If the organization is growing and needs to retain all its current personnel, it needs to ensure that it offers the benefits its work force desires.

Finally, the characteristics of the work force must be considered when choosing the benefits mix. If the firm's work force consists largely of young women, it is likely that child-care benefits will be important. A professional work force will probably want more say in decisions about its retirement funds. A unionized work force is likely to demand a guaranteed retirement plan.

Benefits Amount

The benefits amount choice governs the percentage of the total compensation package that will be allocated to benefits compared to the other components of the package (base salary and pay incentives). This choice corresponds to the "fixed versus variable pay" decision covered in Chapter 10. Once management determines the amount of money available for all benefits, it can establish a benefits budget and decide on the level of funding for each part of the benefits program. Management will then know how much it can contribute for each benefit and how much it will need to ask employees to pay toward that benefit. In larger companies these calculations are usually performed by the benefits administrator, while smaller companies often hire a benefits consultant to do the math.

A company that focuses on providing job security and long-term employment opportunities is likely to devote a large portion of its compensation dollars to benefits. One company that prides itself on its excellent employee benefits is Procter & Gamble (P&G). Its profit-sharing plan—the oldest such plan in continuous operation in the United States—was started in 1887. P&G was also one of the first companies to offer all its employees comprehensive sickness, disability, and life insurance programs.[11] Figure 12–4 lists the ten U.S. companies that provide the most generous benefits, including extensive medical coverage, lengthy vacations, and lavish pension and profit-sharing plans.

1. Xerox*
2. Quaker Oats*
3. John Hancock
4. Chrysler
5. Merck*
6. Bell Atlantic
7. AT&T*
8. Citibank
9. Johnson & Johnson
10. Hewlett-Packard

*Company offers a flexible benefits plan.

FIGURE 12-4

Companies with the Best Benefits

Source: Alderman, L., and Kim, J. (1996, January). Get the most from your company benefits. *Money*, 102–106.

Flexibility of Benefits

The *flexibility of benefits choice* concerns the degree of freedom employees have to tailor the benefits package to their personal needs. This choice corresponds to the "centralization versus decentralization of pay" decision described in Chapter 10. Some organizations have a relatively standardized benefits package that gives employees few options. This system makes sense in organizations that have a fairly homogeneous work force, such as a logging firm or a law firm. In these firms a standardized benefits package can be designed for a "typical" employee. However, because of the changing demographics of the U.S. work force—more women working full-time, dual-career marriages, and single-parent families—there is now a greater variety of employee needs. In organizations that cannot develop a "typical" employee profile, a decentralized benefits package that emphasizes choice will probably be more effective. We discuss flexible benefits packages in detail at the end of this chapter.

▸ Legally Required Benefits

With only a few exceptions, all U.S. employers are legally required to provide Social Security, workers' compensation, and unemployment insurance coverage for their employees—benefits that are designed to give the work force a basic level of security. The employer pays a tax on an employee's earnings for each of these three required benefits. In the case of Social Security, the employee also pays a tax to fund the benefit. A fourth legally required benefit has been added in recent years: Employers must offer unpaid leave to employees in certain family and medical circumstances.

Social Security

Social Security
A government program that provides income for retirees, the disabled, and survivors of deceased workers, and health care for the aged through the Medicare program.

Social Security provides (1) income for retirees, the disabled, and survivors of deceased workers, and (2) health care for the aged through the Medicare program. Established by the Social Security Act in 1935, Social Security is funded through a payroll tax paid in equal amounts by the employer and the employee. The Social Security tax in 1997 was 7.65% of an employee's annual earnings on the first $65,400 of income. This means that both the employer and employee pay a tax of 7.65% on the employee's earnings. The Social Security tax actually has two components: a tax of 6.2% to fund the retirement, disability, and survivor benefits, and a tax of 1.45% to fund Medicare. Employees who earn above $65,400 are taxed at 1.45% of all their additional earnings. This 1.45% tax is also matched by the employer.

To be eligible for full Social Security benefits, a person must have worked 40 quarter-year periods (which equals ten years of total employment) and have earned a minimum of $620 per quarter. Figure 12–5 spells out the provisions of the four Social Security benefits—retirement income, disability income, Medicare, and survivor benefits—and who is eligible to receive them.

Retirement Income. Social Security provides retirement income to people who retire at age 65. Workers who retire between ages 62 and 64 receive benefits reduced by as much as 20%.

The retirement income provided by Social Security averages about 30% of one's earnings in the final year before retirement at age 65. This means that people need to develop other sources of postretirement income if they want to maintain a lifestyle similar to the one they enjoyed prior to retirement. These sources might include a company-provided pension plan, personal savings, or another job. According to the Social Security Administration, people who retired at age 65 in 1996 could expect a monthly Social Security check ranging from $750 to $1,150, depending on their preretirement earnings. In the future the minimum age for receiving Social Security benefits will increase. For people born after 1950, the minimum retirement age for full benefits will be 66, and for individuals born in 1960 or later, it will be age 67.

Disability Income. For people who become disabled and cannot work for at least 12 months, Social Security provides a monthly income comparable to retirement benefits. Because the level of disability income averages only about 30% of one's earnings from the job, workers need to derive disability income from other sources. These sources include short- and long-term disability insurance and personal savings and investments.

Benefit	Eligibility	Provisions
Retirement income	• Age 65 (full benefits) *or* • Age 62–64 (benefits reduced up to 20%)	Monthly payments for life beginning at retirement. Average benefit provides about 30% of earnings prior to retirement.
Disability income	• Totally and continuously disabled for 5 months. • Disability should be expected to last at least 12 months or result in death.	Monthly payments comparable to retirement benefits as long as totally disabled. Provisions for payments to dependents.
Medicare	• Age 65 *or* • Receiving Social Security disability payments for 24 months.	Covers hospital expenses, nursing home and home health agency expenses, subject to a deductible payment. Medical expenses are covered, subject to monthly premium.
Survivor benefits	• Family members of the deceased person, including widow or widower age 60 or over, child or grandchild under age 18, or dependent parent age 62 or over.	Monthly payments related to the deceased worker's primary Social Security retirement benefit.

FIGURE 12-5

Social Security Benefits

Source: Adapted from McCaffery, R. M. (1992). *Employee benefit programs: A total compensation perspective* (2nd ed.), 50–51. Boston, MA: PWS Kent.

Medicare. **Medicare** provides health insurance coverage for people 65 and older. Medicare has two parts. Part A covers hospital costs. People who pay an annual deductible ($736 in 1996) receive up to 60 days of hospital expenses covered under Medicare. Part B, for which individuals pay a monthly fee ($142.50 in 1996), covers medical expenses such as doctors' fees and the cost of medical supplies. The deductibles and monthly fees for Medicare are adjusted periodically as the cost of medical care increases.

Medicare
A part of the Social Security program that provides health insurance coverage for people aged 65 and over.

Survivor Benefits. A deceased employee's surviving family members may receive a monthly income if they qualify. Survivor benefits are related to the deceased worker's primary retirement benefit. Those eligible to receive survivor benefits are (1) widows and widowers age 60 and over, and (2) widows and widowers of any age who care for a child age 16 or younger, an unmarried child or grandchild younger than age 18, or a dependent parent age 62 or over.

Workers' Compensation

Workers' compensation provides medical care, income continuation, and rehabilitation expenses for people who sustain job-related injuries or sickness. "Workers' comp" also provides income to the survivors of an employee whose death is job-related.

workers' compensation
A legally required benefit that provides medical care, income continuation, and rehabilitation expenses for people who sustain job-related injuries or sickness. Also provides income to the survivors of an employee whose death is job-related.

Workers' compensation is designed to provide a *no-fault remedy* to workers who are injured on the job. This means that even workers who were wholly at fault for their accidents can still receive a benefit. Employers who provide workers' compensation coverage cannot be sued by injured employees.

Workers' compensation is administered by state governments and is required by 47 out of 50 states for all employees, including part-time workers. In South Carolina, Texas, and New Jersey, workers' comp is elective. It is funded by a payroll tax, the proceeds of which go to a state workers' compensation fund or to a private insurance company. Only the employer pays for workers' compensation. While the average workers' compensation cost is only about 1% of total payroll expense, companies in accident-prone industries may pay over 25% of their payroll in workers' compensation taxes.[12]

The rates that employers pay for workers' compensation are based on three factors: (1) the risk of injury for an occupation, (2) the frequency and severity of the injuries sustained by a company's work force (called the company's injury *experience rating*), and (3) the level of benefits provided for specific injuries within the state where the company is located. Because the company's experience rating is based on its own safety record, managers have an incentive to design and promote a safe work environment: A better safety record leads directly to a lower payroll tax rate. Some states offer greater benefits to injured workers, which leads to higher workers' comp taxes assessed on employers in those states.

Small businesses in industries like construction and food service have had great difficulty dealing with cost increases in workers' compensation taxes resulting from increasing claims. Consider the following examples:

- Workers' compensation costs for William Solburg, the owner of a small construction company near Tallahassee, Florida, have skyrocketed. Over 25% of his total payroll costs go to cover workers' compensation insurance, and he foresees a significant increase in the near future. Solburg is uncertain whether or not his business can survive much longer with workers' compensation costs rising so quickly.[13]
- At Olsten Corporation, a Westbury, New York, temporary employee service firm, workers' compensation costs tripled in a recent four-year period. Some of these cost increases came about because certain Olsten employees filed fraudulent claims for alleged long-term disabilities. When Olsten hired a detective agency to monitor a worker out on disability for a back injury, the camera caught him changing a tire on his car, a job that required bending over and heavy lifting.[14]

Some small companies are fighting back by banding together to form *self-insurance* pools. L.E. Mason Company, a Boston maker of lighting fixtures and other construction materials, joined a self-insurance group because its rates were 40% below Mason's alternatives. Here's how a self-insurance fund works: A fund's member companies, often in the same industry, band together and hire an administrator. The administrator contracts with actuaries, investment managers, health-care providers, and anyone else necessary to perform the functions of an insurance company. Fund members share one another's risk, paying losses out of premiums and investment returns. A typical fund member has between 60 and 100 employees and pays between $50,000 and $100,000 a year for coverage. As of 1996, 35 states allowed self-insurance funds, up from 20 in 1986.

Self-insurance funds are not the answer for all companies. In firms that go it alone, HR staff can help managers control workers' compensation costs in several important ways:

- The HR department should stress safe work procedures by impressing upon employees the importance of safety (see Chapter 16). Many accidents are caused by carelessness, ignorance of safe work practices, personal problems, or the use of alcohol or drugs. HR staff should train managers and supervisors to communicate and enforce the company's safety program. Employees who disregard safe work practices should be disciplined.[15]
- The HR department should audit workers' compensation claims. Managers should challenge any claim they suspect is fraudulent or not job-related.
- HR should manage how workers' comp benefits work with employers' health insurance benefits when workers sustain job-related injuries. HR should establish controls so that duplicate medical benefits are not paid out to employees.
- HR staff should design jobs and work assignments so that there are fewer risks of such injuries as back strain and repetitive motion injuries. For example, employees can have their video display terminals adjusted daily to avoid strain on the arms and wrists.[16]

A QUESTION OF ETHICS

One way for companies to lower their workers' compensation costs is to move from a state with a high workers' compensation tax rate to one with a lower rate. Is this a legitimate reason for moving a business? What other ethical issues should employers think about when trying to decrease workers' comp costs?

- HR can encourage workers who are partially disabled to return to work under a *modified duty plan*. Under such a plan, a manager or HR staff member works with injured employees to develop modified tasks that they can perform until they are ready to handle their regular job. For instance, a maintenance worker with a back injury might be assigned to help schedule the work orders. Modified duty plans can save the company money on benefits that provide income continuation for employees who may be needlessly postponing the return to employment.

Unemployment Insurance

unemployment insurance
A program established by the Social Security Act of 1935 to provide temporary income for people during periods of involuntary unemployment.

The Social Security Act of 1935 established **unemployment insurance** to provide temporary income for people during periods of involuntary unemployment. The program is part of a national wage stabilization policy designed to stabilize the economy during recessionary periods. The logic underlying this policy is fairly simple: If unemployed workers have enough income to maintain their consumption of basic goods and services, the demand for these products will be sustained, which ultimately will preserve the jobs of many people who might otherwise be added to the ranks of the unemployed.

Unemployment insurance is funded by a tax paid by employers on all employees' earnings. The tax averages 6.2% on the first $7,000 earned by each employee.[17] The proceeds of the tax are split between the state government and the federal government, which provide different services for the unemployed. The federal government levies a tax of 0.8%, a rate that does not change from employer to employer. In contrast, the state's assessment ranges from at or near zero to over 10% (the average is about 5.4%). All the states give employers an experience rating comparing the employer's contributions to the unemployment insurance fund against the benefits drawn by the employer's workers from the fund over a period of time. This system allows the state to lower the unemployment tax rate for employers that discharge only a small number of employees, and raise it for those that discharge large numbers of employees for any reason (including layoffs).

To be eligible for unemployment insurance, employees must meet several qualifications. First, they must be available for and actively seeking employment. Second, they must have worked a minimum of four quarter-year periods out of the last five quarter-year periods and have earned at least $1,000 during those four quarter-year periods combined. Finally, they must have left their job involuntarily.

Employees may be disqualified for unemployment insurance benefits for several reasons. The following people are not eligible for unemployment insurance:

- An employee who quits voluntarily.
- An employee who is discharged for gross misconduct (for example, for failing a drug test).
- An employee who refuses an offer of suitable work (that is, a job and pay level comparable to the employee's previous position).
- An employee who participates in a strike (48 out of 50 states deny benefits to strike participants).
- A person who is self-employed.[18]

Unemployment benefits were designed to cover an employee's basic living expenses but not to be a disincentive against actively seeking employment. For this reason, unemployment benefits seldom cover more than 50% of lost earnings, and people discharged from high-paying jobs generally receive only a small fraction of their lost earnings. States have developed their own schedules for unemployment benefits and cap them at a maximum level that ranges from about $100 to $400 per week. Unemployment benefits last for 26 weeks, although in states with persistently high unemployment rates, extensions of benefits in 13-week periods may be given. In addition, some companies provide **supplemental unemployment benefits (SUB)** to their laid-off employees. These benefits are most often written into the union contract.

supplemental unemployment benefits (SUB)
Benefits given by a company to laid-off employees over and above state unemployment benefits.

Containing the costs of unemployment insurance is an important priority for management. The HR department can make important contributions here by establishing practices that lower the firm's experience rating. Here are some useful HR practices in this area:

- HR planning can tell management whether an increase in the company's workload is due to short-term or long-term causes. Short-term increases in the workload should be handled by hiring temporary employees or consultants rather than by creating full-time positions. Since neither temporary employees nor consultants can claim unemployment benefits, it costs the company nothing to let them go when the workload decreases. If the increased workload appears to be long-term, however, the company may decide to hire more full-time employees.
- The employee benefits administrator should audit all unemployment claims filed by former employees. Employers have the right to appeal these claims, and in about half the cases they win.
- Managers or members of the HR department should conduct exit interviews with all discharged employees to (1) come to a mutual understanding on the reason for termination and (2) advise them that the company will fight unemployment claims not made for good reason. For example, if an employee discharged for theft makes a claim for unemployment benefits, the company will contest the claim.

Unpaid Leave

Family and Medical Leave Act of 1993 (FMLA)
A federal law that requires employers to provide up to 12 weeks' unpaid leave to eligible employees for the birth or adoption of a child; to care for a sick parent, child, or spouse; or to take care of health problems that interfere with job performance.

Employees occasionally need long periods of time off to take care of their families or their own health problems. Until recently, most employers refused to give workers unpaid leaves for any reason other than the birth of a child. The **Family and Medical Leave Act of 1993 (FMLA),** enacted under the Clinton administration, now requires most employers to provide up to 12 weeks' unpaid leave to eligible employees for the following reasons:[19]

- The birth of a child.
- The adoption of a child.
- To care for a sick spouse, child, or parent.

A Family Friendly Act.

The Family and Medical Leave Act of 1993 requires most employers to provide up to 12 weeks' unpaid leave to eligible employees who adopt a child; who need to care for a sick spouse, parent, or child; or who must take care of their own serious health problems that interfere with job performance.

- To take care of the employee's own serious health problems that interfere with effective job performance.

The FMLA applies only to businesses with 50 or more employees and to employers with multiple facilities that have 50 workers within a 75-mile radius. The law requires employers to give employees returning from FMLA leave the same job they held prior to taking the leave or an equivalent job. Employers must maintain coverage of health insurance and other employee benefits while the employee is on FMLA leave.[20] Employees are eligible to take FMLA leave after accumulating one year of service with their employer. "Highly compensated" employees—those at the top 10% of the pay scale and who tend to be the company's top managers—are not eligible for FMLA leave because it may be a hardship for the employer to replace them for a 12-week period.

The FMLA forces companies to develop contingency plans to keep their operations running with a minimum of disruption and added cost when employees are on leave. Managers may want to consider (1) cross-training some workers to cover for employees on leave or (2) hiring temporary workers.[21]

Mandatory unpaid leave also forces companies to confront some troublesome issues, such as:

- Can employees substitute accrued sick days for unpaid leave?
- What sort of illnesses are serious enough to justify a leave?
- How can FMLA leave be coordinated with other laws such as ADA?
- Just what constitutes an "equivalent" job when a leavetaker returns and finds his or her job filled?

The last question was the subject of a Wisconsin lawsuit filed well before the FMLA was passed. Elizabeth Marquardt returned from maternity leave to find that her Milwaukee-based employer, Kelley Company, had eliminated her job as credit manager during a restructuring. Kelley gave Marquardt a new job with the same pay and benefits. However, the new job involved supervising one employee instead of four, and unlike the old position, it included about 25% clerical work. Marquardt resigned the next day. Kelley claimed that the reassignment was intended to sidestep Marquardt's longstanding problems with customers. But a Wisconsin appeals court ruled that the jobs were not equivalent because Marquardt's "authority and responsibility were greatly reduced in the new position." HR professionals and line managers will have to work together to avoid such court challenges.[22]

What effects has the FMLA had on business operations? In 1996 the Commission on Family and Medical Leave published a report examining the FMLA's impact on U.S. industry during an 18-month period in 1994 and 1995. The key findings were: (1) fewer than 4% of eligible workers took FMLA leave during this 18-month period; (2) approximately 90% of employers reported no change or only small changes in operating costs due to FMLA; and (3) most people who took leave (about 60%) did so for their health problems, and only 13% used FMLA leave for child-care issues.[23]

Voluntary Benefits

The benefits provided voluntarily by employers include health insurance, retirement benefits, other types of insurance plans, time off, and employee services. Future legislation may move some of these benefits from the voluntary category to the legally required category.

Health Insurance

Health insurance provides health-care coverage for both employees and their dependents, protecting them from financial disaster in the wake of a serious illness. Because the cost of individually obtained health insurance is much higher than that of an employer-sponsored group health plan, many people could not afford health insurance if it were not provided by their employer. As Figure 12–3 shows, 82% of large- and medium-sized private businesses in the United States offer health insurance to their employees. However, only 66% of small firms (those with fewer than 100 employees) do so. It has been estimated that about 41 million people in the United States do not have any health insurance coverage.

During the early 1990s, U.S. health-care costs increased at an astonishing 10% to 20% per year. By 1996, spending on health care accounted for about 14% of the U.S. gross domestic product (GDP). This is the highest percentage found in any country in the world.[24] For example, per capita health spending in the United States exceeds that of Canada by 40%, of Germany by 91%, and of the United Kingdom by 182%.[25] And unlike the United States, these countries provide health-care coverage for all their citizens. Figure 12–6 compares health-care expenditures across the 24 countries that are members of the Organization for Economic Cooperation and Development (OECD). The data in the figure are for 1990. Note that the U.S. expenditure grew in six years from 12.2% to 14% of GDP.[26]

Obviously, cost containment of health spending will be an important issue for companies and the nation for many years. The benefits specialist in the HR department can make an important contribution to the bottom line by keeping spending on health insurance under control. For example, many companies are now requiring employees to make larger contributions toward the cost of their health insurance.

Consolidated Omnibus Budget Reconciliation Act of 1985 (COBRA)
Legislation that gives employees the right to continue their health-insurance coverage for 18 to 36 months after their employment has terminated.

The health insurance benefits that a company offers are significantly affected by the **Consolidated Omnibus Budget Reconciliation Act (COBRA) of 1985,** which gives employees the right to continue their health insurance coverage after their employment has terminated. Employees and their dependents are entitled to 18 to 36 months' additional coverage from the group health insurance plan after separation from the organization. The former employee (or relative of the employee) must pay the full cost of coverage at the group rate, which is still considerably less than the individual rate that could be purchased from a health insurance company on the open market. All employees who are covered by an organization's health-care plan are also covered by COBRA provisions.

There are three common types of employer-provided health insurance plans: (1) traditional health insurance, (2) health maintenance organizations (HMOs), and (3) preferred provider organizations (PPOs). Figure 12–7 summarizes the differences among these plans.

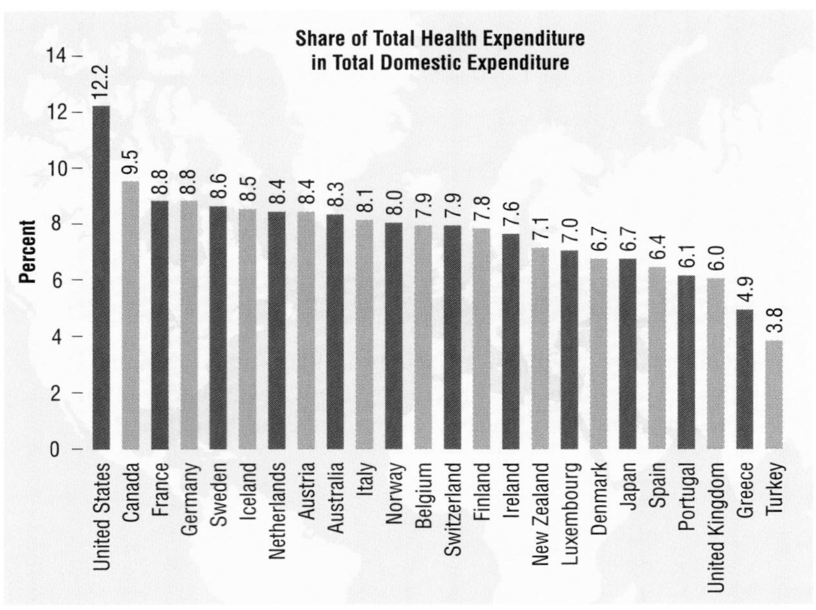

FIGURE 12-6

Health Spending in Various Countries, 1990

Source: OECD. (1993). *OECD health systems: facts & trends, 1960–1991*. Vol. 1. Paris: OECD.

Issue	Traditional Coverage	Health Maintenance Organization (HMO)	Preferred Provider Organization (PPO)
Where must the covered parties live?	May live anywhere.	May be required to live in an HMO-designated service area.	May live anywhere.
Who provides health care?	Doctor and health-care facility of patient's choice.	Must use doctors and facilities designated by HMO.	May use doctors and facilities associated with PPO. If not, may pay additional copayment/ deductible.
How much coverage of routine/preventive medicine?	Does not cover regular checkups and other preventive services. Diagnostic tests may be covered in part or full.	Covers regular checkups, diagnostic tests, and other preventive services with low or no fee per visit.	Same as HMO if doctor and facility are on approved list. Copayment and deductibles are much higher for doctors and facilities not on list.
What hospital care costs are covered?	Covers doctors' and hospitals' bills.	Covers doctors' bills; covers bills of HMO-approved hospitals.	Covers bills of PPO-approved doctors and hospitals.

FIGURE 12-7

Employer-Provided Health Insurance Plans

Source: Milkovich, G., and Newman, J. (1996). *Compensation* (5th ed.), 466. Homewood, IL: Irwin.

Traditional Health Insurance. Provided by an insurance company that acts as an intermediary between the patient and health-care provider, *traditional health insurance plans* (also called *fee-for-service plans*) develop a fee schedule based on the cost of medical services in a specific community. They then incorporate these fees into the costs of insurance coverage. The best-known examples of traditional health insurance plans are the Blue Cross and Blue Shield organizations. Traditional health insurance covers hospital and surgical expenses, physicians' care, and a substantial portion of expenses for serious illnesses.

Traditional health insurance plans have several important features. First, they include a deductible that a policyholder must meet before the plan makes any reimbursements. Second, they require a monthly group rate (also called a **premium**) paid to the insurance company. The premium is usually paid partially by the employer and partially by the employee. Third, they provide for a copayment. The typical copayment allocation is 80/20 (80% of the cost is covered by the insurance plan and 20% is picked up by the employee). The deductible, premium, and copayment can be adjusted, so the employer's and employee's costs of health care insurance vary depending on how the parties agree to allocate the costs.

premium
The money paid to an insurance company for coverage.

Traditional plans give employees the greatest amount of choice in selecting a physician and a hospital. However, these plans have several disadvantages. First, they often do not cover regular checkups and other preventive services. Second, calculating the deductible and copayment requires a significant amount of paperwork. Each time they visit a physician, employees must fill out claims forms and obtain bills with long, itemized lists of services. This can be frustrating for patients and costly to physicians, who often need to hire clerical workers solely to process forms.

Health Maintenance Organizations (HMOs). A **health maintenance organization (HMO)** is a health-care plan that provides comprehensive medical services for employees and their families at a flat annual fee. People covered by an HMO have unlimited access to medical services because the HMO is designed to encourage preventive health care to reduce ultimate costs. (The "stitch in time saves nine" analogy applies here.) HMO members pay a monthly premium, plus a small copayment or deductible. Some HMOs have no

health maintenance organization (HMO)
A health-care plan that provides comprehensive medical services for employees and their families at a flat annual fee.

copayment or deductible. The HMOs' annual flat fee per member acts as a monetary disincentive to the HMOs' participatory doctors, who might otherwise be tempted to give patients unnecessary medical tests or casually refer them to expensive medical specialists. In 1994 HMOs provided health care to about 50 million people in the United States.[27]

HMOs have two major advantages. First, for a fixed fee, people covered by the HMO receive most of their medical services (including preventive care) without incurring large copayments or deductibles or having to fill out claims forms. Second, HMOs encourage preventive health care and healthier lifestyles.

The major disadvantage of HMOs is that they restrict people's ability to select their physicians and the hospitals at which they receive medical services. The HMO may service a limited geographic area, which may restrict who can join the plan. People may be forced to leave their existing doctor and choose one from a list of those who belong to the HMO. In the case of serious illnesses, the specialists consulted must also belong to the HMO, even if there are doctors in the area with better reputations and stronger qualifications. In addition, some consumer groups have criticized HMOs for skimping on patient care to save money on medical costs.

preferred provider organization (PPO)
A health-care plan in which an employer or insurance company establishes a network of doctors and hospitals to provide a broad set of medical services for a flat fee per participant. In return for the lower fee, the doctors and hospitals who join the PPO network expect to receive a larger volume of patients.

Preferred Provider Organizations (PPOs). A **preferred provider organization (PPO)** is a health-care plan in which an employer or insurance company establishes a network of doctors and hospitals to provide a broad set of medical services for an annual flat fee per participant. The fee is lower than that which doctors and hospitals normally charge their customers for the bundle of services, and the monthly premium is lower than that charged by a traditional plan for the same services. In return for charging a lower fee, the doctors and hospitals who join the PPO network expect to receive a larger volume of patients. Members of the PPO can use it for preventive health care (such as checkups) without paying a doctor's usual fee for the service. PPOs collect information on the utilization of their health services so that employers can periodically improve the plan's design and reduce costs.

PPOs combine some of the best features of HMOs (managed health care and a wide array of medical services for a fixed fee) with the flexibility of the traditional health insurance plan. They include provisions that allow their members to go outside the PPO network and use non-PPO doctors and medical facilities. People who select non-PPO doctors and hospitals pay additional fees in the form of deductibles and copayments determined by the PPO. Because PPOs have few of the disadvantages of traditional health insurance plans or HMOs, they are expected to continue growing rapidly.

Health Insurance Coverage of Employees' Partners. Traditionally, health insurance benefits have been offered only to employees and their spouses or dependents. Today, however, employers are being asked to offer the same health insurance benefits to employees' domestic partners—that is, unmarried heterosexual or homosexual partners.

So far, only a handful of companies and municipalities allow employees to include domestic partners in their health insurance coverage, and most of these limit coverage to gay and lesbian employees. But among the firms that offer such benefits are some of the most prestigious names in U.S. business: Lotus Development, Silicon Graphics, MCA, Microsoft, Viacom, Apple Computer, and Warner Bros. Companies that also cover unmarried heterosexual couples include Ben & Jerry's Homemade, Levi Strauss, and the Federal National Mortgage Association.

Most of corporate America, however, is resisting the pressure to extend health insurance benefits to domestic partners for a number of reasons. First, some companies fear that they will end up footing the bill for more AIDS-related expenses if they offer health benefits to gay partners. Second, companies fear that employees will abuse the domestic partner benefits by signing up a friend or a string of partners. Finally, companies worry about pitting gay and straight employees against each other, since most current plans offer benefits only to same-sex couples.

Most of these fears seem unfounded. Research shows that, in fact, health-care costs for gay partners and unmarried heterosexual couples are often lower than those for married couples. Moreover, many homosexual employees don't sign up for the benefits because they want to keep their sexual orientation private. Employers can protect themselves against abuse by asking eligible employees to file affidavits of "spousal equivalency" showing a history of living together and sharing assets. The question of pitting heterosexual employees against gay and lesbian employees may become moot because the growing threat of discrimination lawsuits may force employers to offer coverage to all domestic partners in the near future.[28]

Health-Care Cost Containment. A company's HR benefits manager can control health-care costs by designing (and modifying) health insurance plans carefully and developing programs that encourage employees to adopt healthier lifestyles. Specifically, HR staff can:

- *Develop a self-funding arrangement for health insurance.* A company is self-funding when it puts the money it would otherwise pay in insurance premiums into a fund to pay employee health-care expenses. Under this type of plan, the employer has an incentive to assume some responsibility for employees' health. Self-funding plans can be designed to capture administrative efficiencies that translate into lower costs for the same services provided by a traditional health insurance plan.[28a]
- *Coordinate health insurance plans for families with two working spouses.* HR staff can encourage spouses who have duplicate coverage under two different insurance plans to establish a cost-sharing arrangement. Many companies, such as General Electric, require employees whose working spouses decline their own employers' health insurance to pay a significantly higher premium than nonworking spouses or those who can't get insurance elsewhere.[29]
- *Develop a wellness program for employees.* A *wellness program* assesses employees' risk of serious illness (for example, heart disease or cancer) and then teaches them how to reduce that risk by changing some of their habits (such as diet, exercise, and avoidance of harmful substances like alcohol, tobacco, and caffeine). Adolph Coors Company, the Colorado-based beer producer, has a wellness program composed of six areas: health hazard appraisal, exercise, smoking cessation, nutrition and weight loss, physical and cardiovascular rehabilitation, and stress and anger management. It has been estimated that Coors' wellness program returns $3.37 to the company for each dollar spent on it.[30]

Retirement Benefits

After retiring, people have three main sources of income: Social Security, personal savings, and retirement benefits. Because Social Security can be expected to provide only about one fourth of preretirement earnings, retirees must rely on retirement benefits and personal savings to maintain their standard of living. Retirement benefits support an employee's long-term financial goal of achieving a planned level of retirement income.

An important service that the HR department can provide to employees nearing retirement is preretirement counseling. *Preretirement counseling* sessions give employees information about their retirement benefits so that they can plan their retirement years accordingly.[31] A benefits specialist can answer questions like:

- What will my total retirement income be when Social Security is added to it?
- Would I be better off taking my retirement benefits in the form of a lump sum or as an annuity (a fixed amount of income each year)?
- What would be the tax effects on my retirement benefits if I earn additional income from a part-time job?

Retirement benefit plans that are "qualified" by the Internal Revenue Service receive favorable tax treatment under the Internal Revenue Code. To qualify, the retirement plan must be available to broad classes of employees and must not favor highly compensated workers over lower-paid workers. Under a qualified retirement plan, employees pay no taxes on the contributions made to the plan until these funds are distributed at retirement. Also, the earnings on the fund's investments accumulate without being taxed each year. Employers may also take a tax deduction for the annual contributions they make to a qualified retirement plan.

Employee Retirement Income Security Act (ERISA)
A federal law established in 1974 to protect employees' retirement benefits from mismanagement.

ERISA. The major law governing the administration of retirement benefits in the United States is the **Employee Retirement Income Security Act (ERISA).** Passed in 1974, ERISA protects employees' retirement benefits from mismanagement. The key provisions of ERISA cover who is eligible for retirement benefits, vesting, and funding requirements.

- *Eligibility for retirement benefits:* ERISA requires that the minimum age for participation in a retirement plan cannot be greater than 21. However, employers may restrict participation in the retirement plan to employees who have completed one year of service with the company.

vesting
A guarantee that accrued retirement benefits will be given to retirement plan participants when they retire or leave the employer.

- *Vesting:* **Vesting** is a guarantee that accrued retirement benefits will be given to retirement plan participants when they retire or leave the employer. Under current ERISA rules, employee vesting rules must conform to one of two schedules: (1) full vesting after five years of service; or (2) 20% vesting after three years of service and a further 20% vesting each year thereafter, until the employee is fully vested at seven years of service. Employers are allowed to vest employees faster than this if they wish. Vesting pertains only to employer contributions to the retirement plan. Any contributions the employee has made to the plan are always the employee's property, along with any earnings that have accumulated on those contributions. These employee-provided funds, and any employer contributions that are vested, are said to be **portable**—that is, they stay with the employee as he or she moves from one company to another.

portable benefits
Employee benefits, usually retirement funds, that stay with the employee as he or she moves from one company to another.

- *Funding requirements and obligations:* In addition to establishing guidelines for a retirement plan's minimum funding requirements, ERISA requires that retirement plan administrators act prudently in making investments with participants' funds. Plans that do not meet ERISA funding standards are subject to financial penalties from the Internal Revenue Service.

To protect employees from an employer's possible failure to meet its retirement obligations, ERISA requires employers to pay for plan termination insurance, which guarantees the payment of retirement benefits to employees even if the plan terminates (either because of poor investment decisions or because the company has gone out of business) before they retire. Termination insurance for defined benefit plans (discussed next) is provided by the **Pension Benefit Guaranty Corporation (PBGC)**, a government agency.

Pension Benefit Guaranty Corporation (PBGC)
The government agency that provides plan termination insurance to employers with defined benefit retirement programs.

defined benefit plan or **pension**
A retirement plan that promises to pay a fixed dollar amount of retirement income based on a formula that takes into account the average of the employee's last three to five years' earnings prior to retirement.

Defined Benefit Plans. A **defined benefit plan,** also called a **pension,** is a retirement plan that promises to pay a fixed dollar amount of retirement income based on a formula that takes into account the average of the employee's last three to five years' earnings prior to retirement. The amount of annual income provided by defined benefit plans increases with the years of service to the employer. For example, based on a final five-year preretirement average salary of $50,000, Eastman Kodak's pension plan pays a retired employee with 30 years of service $20,523 per year at age 65. Merck, the pharmaceutical giant, pays an employee with the same salary and 30 years of service $24,000 per year at age 65.[32] Medium and large companies are more likely to provide a pension plan for their workers: 56% of these firms offer a defined contribution plan, compared to only 15% of small businesses (see Figure 12–3).

Under a defined benefit plan, the employer assumes all the risk of providing the promised income to the retiree and is likely to make all of the financial contributions to the plan. Defined benefit plans are most appropriate for firms that want to provide a secure and predictable retirement income for employees. Michigan-based Dow Chemical is one such company.[33] They are less appropriate for firms that stress risk taking and want employees to share in the risk and responsibility of managing their retirement assets.

Defined Contribution Plans. A **defined contribution plan** is a retirement plan in which the employer promises to contribute a specific amount of funds into the plan for each participant. For example, a defined contribution plan may require the employer to contribute 6% of the employee's salary into the plan each pay period. Some defined contribution plans also allow or require employees to make additional contributions to the plan. The retirement income that the participants receive depends on the success of the plan's investments and therefore cannot be known in advance.[34] Companies that value employee risk taking and participation are likely to offer defined contribution plans. Under these plans, employees and employers share both risk and responsibility for retirement benefits. Employees may need to decide how to allocate their retirement funds from different investment choices that represent various levels of risk. Because they require fewer obligations from employers than defined benefit plans, most of the new retirement plans established in recent years have been defined contribution plans.

defined contribution plan
A retirement plan in which the employer promises to contribute a specific amount of funds into the plan for each participant. The final value of each participant's retirement income depends on the success of the plan's investments.

There is a dark side to this trend toward defined contribution plans. While highly educated and highly paid employees may benefit from such risk-taking arrangements, defined contribution plans are likely to be devastating for low-wage workers, according to a report by the Senate Labor and Human Resources Committee. By the year 2020, more than 50 million U.S. men and women will be of retirement age, but many won't be able to retire because as low-wage earners, they could not afford to invest in the defined contribution plans established by their employers. Many of these low-wage workers are women.[35]

Figure 12–8 summarizes the most common defined contribution retirement plans: the 401(k) plan, the individual retirement account (IRA), the simplified employee pension

Plan	Available to	Appropriate for	Maximum Contribution	Tax Break on Contributions/Earnings
401(k)	Employees of for-profit businesses	Everyone who qualifies	15% of salary up to $9,500 in 1996	Yes/Yes
IRA	Anyone with earned income	Those without company pension plans or who have put the maximum into their company plan	100% of salary up to $2,000; $2,250 if joint with spouse	Sometimes/Yes
SEP	The self-employed and employees of small businesses	Self-employed person who is a sole proprietor	15% of gross self-employment income or $22,500, whichever is less	Yes/Yes
Profit-Sharing Keogh	The self-employed and employees of unincorporated small businesses	Small-business owner who is funding a plan for self and employees	Same as SEP	Yes/Yes

FIGURE 12-8

A Comparison of Defined Contribution Retirement Plans

Source: Adapted from Stark, E. (1993). Supercharge your retirement savings. *Money, 22* (13), 75. Reprinted from the *Money, Forecast 1994* issue by special permission; copyright 1993, Time Inc.; and Teitelbaum, R. (1995, December 25). Getting the most from your 401(k). *Fortune*, 183–184.

(SEP), and the profit-sharing Keogh. These plans all have tax benefits that can prove very valuable in the long run.

401(k) Plan. To understand the features and benefits of a *401(k) plan* (as well as other tax-deferred retirement plans), consider the following situation. Suppose you want to save $100 per month for your retirement, you are in the 28% federal income tax bracket, and the money you invest will earn 8% per year. If you save the money out of your salary and put it into a personal savings account, the $1,200 that you set aside each year would, in effect, be reduced to $864 because of taxes (Figure 12–9). With one year's interest, that $864 would grow to $891. Each year the investment earnings would also be taxed at the 28% rate. If you continue to set aside $1,200 each year in a personal account, your retirement fund would grow to $67,514 in 30 years.

With tax-deferred retirement plans like the 401(k), the money you save each month is not taxed. Therefore, each year you are saving the full $1,200 you put into your retirement account. In addition, the earnings on your investment are not taxed. After the first year, the value of your account would be $1,251 (compared to $864 under the personal account scenario). After 30 years, the value would grow to $141,761, more than twice the size of the personal account. When you retire and draw down the funds, your withdrawals will be taxed at your retirement tax rate.

Anyone who works for a for-profit business is eligible to participate in a 401(k) plan. Most companies that establish 401(k) plans will match 25% to 100% of employee contributions up to 6% of the employee's salary.[36] In 1996 the maximum annual employee contribution that could be made to a 401(k) plan was 15% of salary up to a limit of $9,500 per year.[37]

The 401(k) plan's matching feature makes it attractive to both employers and employees. Employees benefit by accumulating tax-deferred retirement funds; employers benefit by reducing their risk, since there is no payment required when the employee leaves or retires. Usually, employees are free to decide individually how they wish to invest their

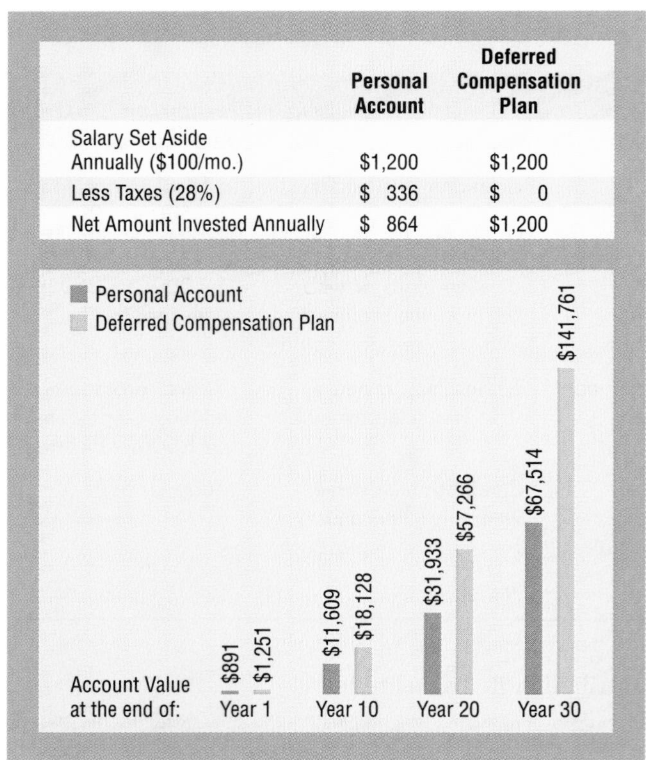

	Personal Account	Deferred Compensation Plan
Salary Set Aside Annually ($100/mo.)	$1,200	$1,200
Less Taxes (28%)	$ 336	$ 0
Net Amount Invested Annually	$ 864	$1,200

FIGURE 12-9

Personal Account versus Deferred Compensation Plan

Source: State of Tennessee. *Introduction to the deferred compensation programs.*

funds. The basic choice is between an investment strategy with a high potential return, but the risk of a low or even a negative return, and a strategy with low risk and a low to moderate return. Investing in the stock market is an example of the first investment strategy; investing in a savings account is an example of the second.

IRA. An *individual retirement account (IRA)* allows people to contribute up to $2,000 per year tax-free (or $2,250 per year into a joint account with a spouse). Unlike the other defined contribution plans, IRAs are personal savings plans—that is, employers do not contribute to them. As with the 401(k) plan, the interest on an IRA account is tax-deferred until the employee cashes it in at retirement. This tax-free benefit is eliminated for employees who participate in a qualified retirement plan with their employer and/or employees who have an adjusted gross income of at least $35,000 (single people) or $50,000 (married people filing a joint return). However, there are no such restrictions on the IRA's tax-deferred earnings. IRAs are available to both those without company pension plans and those who have contributed the maximum to their company plan.

SEP. A *simplified employee pension (SEP)* is similar to an IRA, but while IRAs are available to people who also participate in a retirement fund through their employer (subject to the limits described earlier), SEPs are available only to people who are self-employed or who work for small businesses that do not have a retirement plan. Those who are eligible for an SEP can invest up to 15% of their annual income or $22,500 (whichever is less) on a tax-deferred basis.

Profit-Sharing Keogh Plan. A *profit-sharing Keogh plan* provides for the same maximum contribution as an SEP but allows the employer to contribute to an employee's retirement account on the basis of company performance as measured by profits. Profit-sharing Keogh plans allow employers to make smaller contributions when profits are modest and larger contributions when profits are high. Keogh plans have three main advantages. First, because they allow employees to share in the company's success, they foster a sense of teamwork. Second, they let employers make contributions to the retirement plan that reflect their ability to pay. Third, their tax benefits are similar to those of SEPs.

Hybrid Pension Plans. Several hybrid pension plans have sprung up to address the limitations of both defined benefit plans and defined contribution plans. Defined benefit plans reward long-term service in a world in which employees are more and more mobile. And while defined contribution plans offer greater portability than defined benefit plans, defined contribution plans are tied more to investment returns than to job performance. Thus, fast-trackers who move from job to job may end up with less retirement income than those who work in a company with a traditional pension plan. One of the most popular hybrid plans developed to bridge these two types of pensions is the *cash balance plan*, which works like this: Employees are credited with a certain amount of money for their tax-deferred retirement account each year, based on their annual pay. These contributions are compounded using an agreed-upon interest rate (such as the interest rate on five-year Treasury bills). The employees take the cash balances with them when they change jobs. One drawback of cash balance plans is the time-consuming and expensive recordkeeping required for individual accounts. However, they are becoming popular because they are effective for retaining younger employees. Duracell International and Bank of America are two companies that have cash balance plans.[38]

Insurance Plans

A wide variety of insurance plans can provide financial security for employees and their families. Two of the most valued company-provided insurance benefits are life insurance and long-term disability insurance.

Life Insurance. Basic *term life insurance* pays a benefit to the survivors of a deceased employee. The typical benefit is one or two times the employee's annual income. For example, both Citicorp and AT&T offer their employees life insurance that will pay one year's salary to their survivors. In most cases, company-provided term life insurance policies cover workers only while they are employed by the organization. Companies with a flexible benefits policy may allow employees to purchase insurance beyond the basic level. An employee with a nonworking spouse, for example, may need a benefit of three to five years' salary to provide for his or her survivors. Approximately 91% of medium and large businesses provide a life insurance benefit to full-time employees.

Long-Term Disability Insurance. Employees who experience a serious injury away from the job (for example, in an auto accident) may not be able to perform their job duties for a long period of time. These employees need replacement income to cover the earnings lost while they are recovering from the accident or, if they are permanently disabled, for the rest of their lives. Workers' compensation does not provide disability income for people who have had off-duty accidents, and Social Security provides only a modest level of disability income to cover the most basic needs.

Long-term disability insurance provides replacement income to disabled employees who cannot perform their essential job duties. An employee is eligible to receive disability benefits after being disabled for six months or more. These benefits range from 50% to 67% of the employee's salary.[39] For example, Xerox provides 60% replacement income under its long-term disability insurance plan, while IBM provides 67 percent.[40] Employees who are disabled for less than six months are likely to receive replacement income under a sick leave policy (discussed later in this chapter). Employees can also purchase short-term disability insurance, which provides coverage until the long-term coverage takes over.

With Social Security benefits added to long-term disability insurance benefits, an employee's total replacement income is likely to be 70% to 80% of his or her salary. Long-term disability insurance plans usually take Social Security into account and are designed so that disabled employees do not receive more than 80% of their salary from these combined sources—the theory being that a higher percentage might be a disincentive to return to work. Approximately 41% of medium and large companies offer long-term disability insurance benefits to their workers (see again Figure 12–3).

Paid Time Off

Paid time off provides breaks from regularly scheduled work hours so that employees can pursue leisure activities or take care of personal or civic duties. Paid time off includes sick leave, vacations, severance pay, and holidays. Paid time off is one of the most expensive benefits for the employer. A recent survey by the U.S. Chamber of Commerce found that paid time off costs U.S. employers 13.1% of total payroll.[41]

Sick Leave. *Sick leave* provides full pay for each day that an employee experiences a short-term illness or disability that interferes with his or her ability to perform the job. Employees are often rewarded with greater amounts of sick leave in return for long-term service to the company. According to the U.S. Bureau of Labor Statistics, employers with sick leave benefits provide an average of 15 days of sick leave for employees with one year of full-time service to the company. Many employers allow employees to accumulate sick leave over time. For example, an employee with ten years on the job may accumulate 150 sick days if he or she has not used any sick time (10 years × 15 days per year of sick leave = 150 days). This accumulated sick leave coverage would be more than enough to give the employee full replacement income for the first six months of a serious illness, after which long-term disability coverage takes over.

Some companies allow retiring employees to collect pay for accumulated sick leave and vacation time. For example, when John Young retired as the CEO of Hewlett-Packard, he collected $937,225 in lieu of unused sick pay and vacation leave accumulated during his 34 years with the company.[42]

An HR benefits specialist must monitor and control sick leave benefits to prevent employees from using sick leave to take care of personal business or to reward themselves with a "mental health day" off from work. The HR department should consider instituting the following guidelines:

- Set up a "wellness pay" incentive program that monetarily rewards employees who do not use any sick days. Wellness programs may also encourage employees to adopt healthier lifestyles and file for fewer health benefits. For example, Quaker Oats provides bonuses of as much as $500 for employees who exercise, shun smoking, and wear seat belts.[43]
- Establish flexible work hours so that employees can take care of some personal business during the week, thereby decreasing their need to use sick days for this reason.
- Reward employees with a lump sum that represents their unused sick days when they leave or retire from the organization. Alternatively, give employees the chance to accrue vacation days as a percentage of unused sick leave.
- Allow employees to take one or two personal days each year. This helps to discourage employees from regarding sick days as time off to which they are entitled even if they do not get sick.

Vacations. Employers provide paid vacations to give their employees time away from the stresses and strains of the daily work routine. Vacation time allows employees to recharge themselves psychologically and emotionally and can lead to improved job performance.[44] Many companies reward long-term service to the company with more vacation time. For example, Hewlett-Packard employees with one year of service are eligible for 15 days' vacation; after 30 years of service, they are entitled to 30 days.

Figure 12–10 is an international comparison of the annual number of paid vacation days that employees receive from their companies after one year of service. U.S. employees average about ten days (two weeks) of paid vacation. This is the same as in Japan, but far less than in most European Union nations. For example, French workers receive 25 days (five weeks) and Swedish workers receive 30 days (six weeks) of paid vacation. Many European countries have laws stipulating the number of paid vacation days that workers must receive, but the United States has no such laws.

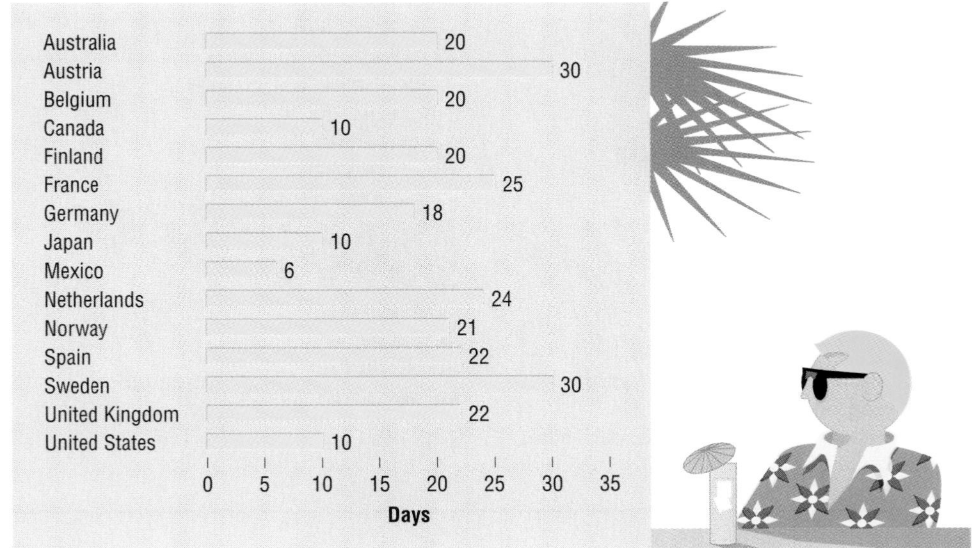

FIGURE 12-10

Annual Number of Vacation Days in Various Countries for Employees with One Year of Service

Source: Reprinted, by permission of the publisher, from *HR Focus*, May 1992, © 1992. American Management Association, New York. All rights reserved.

Some U.S. businesses are starting to offer employees *sabbatical leave,* which is an extended vacation with pay. Sabbaticals, which can be considered a vacation with a purpose, help employees improve their skills or provide a service to the community. Sabbaticals are very common for college and university faculty, for whom they are a tradition. In the business world, where they are much newer, they are most likely to be found in the high-tech industries, where employee skills become obsolete rapidly and need to be renewed. At Intel, for example, engineers and technical employees who have worked for the company for seven years are entitled to an eight-week paid sabbatical in addition to their annual paid vacation. Employees have used these sabbaticals to continue their education, teach in public schools or colleges, or do volunteer work for nonprofit organizations.[45]

Severance Pay. While not typically thought of as a benefit, the severance pay given to laid-off employees is also a form of paid time off. The type of severance pay offered varies widely. Some organizations offer one month's pay for each year the employee has worked for them, often capped at one year's salary. Severance pay is provided to cushion the shock of termination and to finance the employee's search for a new position.

Severance policies are not limited to large companies. In a recent survey, 66% of all companies with fewer than 100 employees said they had a severance policy.[46]

Holidays and Other Paid Time Off. Many employers give their employees paid holidays or pay extra to employees who are required or volunteer to work on holidays. While they are not required to, many employers also provide paid leave for jury duty. In manufacturing environments where employees work on tight time schedules, many employers provide (either voluntarily or through a union contract) time for employees to eat, clean up, and get dressed. Some union contracts (particularly those in railroad and other transportation firms) also stipulate that employees will be paid if they are scheduled for work even though no work is available.

Employee Services

The last category of employee benefits is *employee services,* which employers provide on a tax-free or tax-preferred basis to enhance the quality of employees' work or personal life. Figure 12–11 lists some well-known employee services. These include child care, health

FIGURE 12-11

Selected Tax-Free or Tax-Preferred Employee Benefits or Services

Source: Henderson, R. (1989). *Compensation management*, 443. Englewood Cliffs, NJ: Prentice Hall.

1. Charitable contributions
2. Counseling
   - Financial
   - Legal
   - Psychiatric/psychological
3. Tax preparation
4. Education subsidies
5. Child adoption
6. Child care
7. Elder care
8. Subsidized food service
9. Discounts on merchandise
10. Physical awareness and fitness programs
11. Social and recreational opportunities
12. Parking
13. Transportation to and from work
14. Travel expenses
    - Car reimbursement
    - Tolls and parking
    - Food and entertainment reimbursement
15. Clothing reimbursement/allowance
16. Tool reimbursement/allowance
17. Relocation expenses
18. Emergency loans
19. Credit union
20. Housing
21. Employee assistance programs
22. On-site health services
23. Credit unions

Issues + Applications

Children: On-Site at Stride Rite

The following excerpt describes the origins of Stride Rite's on-site day-care center a quarter of a century ago.

In the early 1970s the neighborhood surrounding Stride Rite's corporate headquarters and factory on Harrison Avenue in Boston's Roxbury neighborhood was showing signs of decay. Crime was common, housing was in disrepair, and business was leaving the area for more stable surroundings. Each time the then-chairman, Arnold Hiatt, looked out his office window, he noticed small children wandering in the streets unattended, with little to occupy their time.

Hiatt decided that it would make sense to convert some of the company's empty manufacturing space into a child-care center so the neighborhood children would have somewhere to go and something constructive to do. Under his direction and vision, corporate America's first on-site day-care center was born in 1971—years before most companies even considered the idea—as Hiatt offered employees the opportunity to bring their own children to the center. Hiatt's vision set the tone for the company's corporate culture, which is based on respect for workers and maintaining working conditions that demonstrate that respect.

When the company's headquarters moved to Cambridge, Massachusetts in 1981, the child-care center moved with it. The facility has expanded into an intergenerational center, in which youngsters and seniors can spend their time together while family members work.

Fees are set at 14% of income with a maximum of $140 a week for child care and $100 a week for elder care. These care facilities have a positive effect on the retention and morale of current employees and on the community at large.

Good child care is so tied to the company's commitment to employees' quality of life that when it entered into a joint manufacturing venture with Thailand-based Bangkok Rubber Co. three years ago, Stride Rite insisted that its new Thai partner open a day-care center for employees there, too.

Source: Excerpted from *Personnel Journal.* (1993, January). Benefits built on base of on-site care, 60.

club memberships, subsidized company cafeterias, parking privileges, and discounts on company products.

Companies are taking a fresh look at employee services and their value to employees. For years, employers offered services tentatively and experimentally, often as kind of a side dish to the main course of medical and health insurance and pension plans. But today companies are using a wide array of services to attract and retain employees, particularly if they cannot offer competitive salaries or raises. John Hancock Mutual Life Insurance of Boston recruits prospective employees with a heavy emphasis on its variety of benefits, including flexible scheduling, dependent-care services, fitness center, and take-home food from the company cafeteria.[47]

Some companies offer unconventional services. For example, one increasingly popular employee service is free self-defense classes. Model Muggings of Boston, a firm that specializes in teaching self-defense techniques, has seen considerable growth in the demand for its on-site classes. When book publisher Houghton Mifflin began offering Model Muggings classes at its Boston site, 210 out of 800 workers signed on immediately.[48]

One of the most valued employee services today is child care. Currently, about 5% of U.S. employers provide some child-care benefits, and this percentage is likely to increase because of the growing number of single parents and dual-career households with children.

Companies that decide to offer child-care services have several options. The most expensive is an on-site child-care center. The Issues and Applications feature titled "Children: On-Site at Stride Rite" explores how this system works at the Massachusetts shoe manufacturer. Other child-care options include subsidizing employee child-care costs at off-site child-care centers and establishing a child-care referral service for working parents.[49] Because child care is expensive, employers usually subsidize 50% to 75% of the costs and require employees to pay the rest.[50]

Building Managerial Skills: Administering Benefits

We conclude this chapter by examining two critical issues in the administration of employee benefits: (1) the use of flexible benefits and (2) the importance of communicating benefits to employees. The HR department usually takes the lead in administering benefits, but managers need to help communicate options to employees, provide advice occasionally, keep records (vacation time, sick days), and be prepared to call on the HR department if disputes arise.

Flexible Benefits

As we have seen, employees have different benefits needs, depending on a number of factors: age, marital status, whether the employee's spouse works and has duplicate benefits coverage, and the presence and ages of children in the household. A flexible benefits program allows employees to choose from a selection of such employer-provided benefits as vision care, dental care, health insurance coverage for dependents, additional life insurance coverage, long-term disability insurance, child care, elder care, more paid vacation days, legal services, and contributions to a 401(k) retirement plan.

As Figure 12–3 shows, 12% of large- and medium-sized U.S. employers have a flexible benefits plan in place, among them TRW Systems, Educational Testing Services, Chrysler, and Bell Atlantic.[51] In the future, as the work force becomes even more diverse, it is likely that more companies will implement flexible benefits plans.

Types of Flexible Benefits Plans. The three most popular flexible benefits plans are modular plans, core-plus options plans, and flexible spending accounts.[52]

Modular plans consist of a series of different bundles of benefits or different levels of benefits coverage designed for different employee groups. For example, Module A might be the basic package paid for entirely by employer contributions. It would include only the most essential benefits and would be designed for single employees. Module B might include everything in Module A plus such additional benefits as family coverage under the health insurance plan, dental care, and child care. This module might be designed for married employees with young children and could require both employer and employee contributions.

Core-plus options plans consist of a core of essential benefits and a wide array of other benefits options that employees can add to the core. The core is designed to provide minimum economic security for employees, and usually includes basic health insurance, life insurance, long-term disability insurance, retirement benefits, and vacation days. Core-plus options plans give employees "benefits credits" that entitle them to "purchase" the additional benefits that they want. In most cases, all employees receive the same number of credits and may use them either to purchase higher levels of coverage in the core benefits package or to purchase additional benefits such as dental care or child care.

Flexible spending accounts are individual employee accounts funded by the employer, the employee (with pretax dollars), or both. Employees "pay" for the combination of benefits from their accounts. The result can be added take-home pay because employees do not pay taxes on the dollars that they have spent on benefits from their flexible spending accounts. Employee benefits administrators must design flexible spending accounts that conform to the rules specified in Section 125 of the Internal Revenue Code, which governs which benefits are exempt from taxes and which are not. For example, educational benefits and van pooling cannot be included in a flexible spending account because they are taxable benefits.

Challenges with Flexible Benefits. Flexible benefits offer employees the opportunity to tailor a benefits package that is meaningful to them at a reasonable cost to the company. However, they do pose some challenges to benefits administrators. These are:

1. *Adverse selection.* The *adverse selection* problem occurs when enough employees use a specific benefit more than the average employee does. Intensive use of a benefit can drive up the benefit's cost and force the employer either to increase spending on benefits or reduce the amount of coverage it provides. For example, employees who know they will need expensive dental work may select a dental-care option instead of some other benefit. Or employees who know they have a high probability of an early death (due to a health condition such as high blood pressure or even a terminal condition such as cancer) may choose extra life insurance coverage. In both cases, the cost of the insurance coverage will eventually be driven up.

   Benefits administrators can deal with the adverse selection problem by placing restrictions on benefits that are likely to result in adverse selection problems. For instance, the company might require those applying for higher life insurance coverage to successfully pass a physical exam. They can also bundle a broad package of benefits together into modules to ensure a more balanced utilization of each benefit.[53]

2. *Employees who make poor choices.* Sometimes employees make a poor choice of benefits and later regret it. For example, an employee who selects additional vacation days instead of long-term disability insurance is likely to regret his choice if he experiences a long-term illness that exceeds his accumulated amount of sick leave. Benefits administrators can manage this problem by (1) establishing core benefits that minimize an employee's risks and (2) communicating benefits choices effectively so that employees make appropriate choices.

3. *Administrative complexity.* A flexible benefits program is difficult to administer and control. Employees must be kept informed of changes in the cost of benefits, the coverage of benefits, and their utilization of benefits. They must also be given the opportunity to change their benefits selection periodically. In addition, the potential for errors in recordkeeping is high. Fortunately, computer software packages can help the HR department manage the recordkeeping aspect of benefits administration. Benefits consultants can assist HR staff in selecting and installing these software programs.

Manager's Notebook

Eight Ways to Save a Bundle on Benefits

Companies can save thousands of dollars by administering the basics of benefits well. Here are eight practical ways to save big benefit dollars:

1. Grant vacation and personal time on a pro rata basis (for example, one day of vacation per four weeks worked) instead of giving employees lump-sum amounts at the beginning of a year to be used by the end of that year. A pro rata system can prevent employees from using a full year's vacation quota in their first three months of employment and then resigning.
2. Enforce use of vacation time with a "use it or lose it" policy. Don't allow the time to accrue indefinitely.
3. Companies that give new hires a probationary period might consider not granting health-care benefits until the probationary period is over.
4. Use a no-fault absence approach to counter sick time abusers. Under a no-fault system, the reason for an unscheduled absence is irrelevant. After a specified number of unscheduled absences, formal discipline occurs, leading up to termination.
5. Reward employees for wellness. Rewards might include granting bonuses when an employee reaches the ideal cholesterol count or paying for health club memberships.
6. Pay employees a bonus if they find errors in benefits bills.
7. Demand employee utilization data from health and dental carriers. Information is power, and utilization data help identify underutilized services that, if managed properly, will lower the company's costs.
8. Consider offering long-term disability coverage no higher than 60% of salary. Lowering the benefit payment from 66.67% to 60%, for instance, can significantly reduce the premium.

Source: Adapted from Markowich, M. M. (1992, October). 25 ways to save a bundle. *HRMagazine*, 48–57. Reprinted with the permission of *HRMagazine* (formerly *Personnel Administrator*), published by the Society for Human Resource Management, Alexandria, VA.

For details on some other ways to control the costs of benefits, see the Manager's Notebook titled "Eight Ways to Save a Bundle on Benefits."

Benefits Communication

Benefits communication is a critical part of administering an employee benefits program. Many employees in companies with excellent benefits packages have never been informed of the value of these benefits and are therefore likely to underestimate their worth.[54] The two major obstacles to effective benefits communication are (1) the increasing complexity of benefits packages and (2) employers' reluctance to devote enough resources to explain these complex packages to employees.

Colorful Fliers or Newsletters
Can be mailed to employees' homes so they can read them at leisure.

Payroll Stickers or Posters
Stimulate employees' curiosity, and are especially good for calling attention to an enrollment period.

Wallet Cards
Provide important numbers, such as a toll-free employee assistance program number.

Audio-Visual Presentations
Slides and videos that present concepts in an upbeat fashion can ensure that employees at different locations receive the same information.

Toll-Free Number
Lets employees call to enroll in a benefits program or hear automated information about these programs 24 hours a day.

Computer Software Package
Allows employees to play "what-if" scenarios with their benefits. For example, they can determine the amount that will be deducted from their paychecks if they enroll in medical plan A as opposed to plan B, or how much money they would save by age 60 if they contribute 6% a year to the 401(k) plan.

FIGURE 12-12

Selected Methods of Employee Benefits Communication

Source: Families and Work Institute, 1992. Reprinted by permission.

Traditionally, benefits have been communicated via a group meeting during new-employee orientation or a benefits handbook that describes each benefit and its level of coverage. In today's dynamic world of employee benefits, however, more sophisticated communication media (such as videotape presentations and computer software that generates personalized benefits status reports for each employee) are needed. Here are a few of the approaches employers are taking to inform employees about additions to or changes in their benefits:

- In its innovative 15½-minute video, the Los Angeles County Employees Retirement Association (LACERA) uses a Sam Spade–type detective character to "crack the case" of confusing retirement plans. During the course of the video the animated detective discovers what confusing terms like *noncontributory* and *defined benefits* mean—and so do LACERA's 500 new hires each month.[55]
- When it changed its benefits plan, oil field equipment maker Baker Hughes, Inc., of Houston, Texas, issued each employee a 26-page booklet titled *Your Decisions Guide,* which contained four pages of personalized information for each of the company's 13,500 employees spread across 35 states. Baker Hughes wanted to take extra care to explain how the plan changes would affect employees individually.[56]

Figure 12–12 lists some of the ways a company can keep its employees informed about their benefits or answer questions about coverage. ▼

Summary and Conclusions

An Overview of Benefits. Benefits are group membership rewards that provide security for employees and their families. Benefits cost companies about $14,807 per year for the average employee. The cost of employee benefits has increased dramatically in recent years. Although benefits programs are usually centrally controlled in organizations, line managers need to be familiar with them so they can counsel employees, recruit job applicants, and make effective managerial decisions.

The Benefits Strategy. The design of a benefits package should be aligned with the business's overall compensation strategy. The benefits strategy requires making choices in three areas: (1) benefits mix, (2) benefits amount, and (3) flexibility of benefits.

Legally Required Benefits. The four benefits that almost all employers must provide are Social Security, workers' compensation, unemployment insurance, and unpaid family and medical leave. These benefits form the core of an employee's benefits package. All other employer-provided benefits are designed to either complement or augment the legally required benefits.

Voluntary Benefits. Businesses often provide five types of voluntary benefits to their employees: (1) Health insurance provides health care for workers and their families. The major types of health insurance plans are traditional health insurance, health maintenance organizations (HMOs), and preferred provider organizations (PPOs). (2) Retirement benefits consist of deferred compensation set aside for an employee's retirement. Funds for retirement benefits can come from employer contributions, employee contributions, or a combination of the two. The Employee Retirement Income Security Act (ERISA) is the major law governing the management of retirement benefits. There are two main types of retirement benefit plans: defined benefit plans and defined contribution plans. In a defined benefit plan, the employer promises to provide a specified amount of retirement income to an employee. A defined contribution plan requires employees to share with their employer some of the risk of and responsibility for managing their retirement assets. The most popular defined contribution plans are 401(k) plans, individual retirement accounts (IRAs), simplified employee pension plans (SEPs), and profit-sharing Keogh plans. (3) Insurance plans protect employees or their survivors from financial disaster in the case of untimely death, accidents that result in disabilities, and serious illnesses. Two kinds of insurance likely to be included in a benefits package are life insurance and long-term disability insurance. (4) Paid time off, which gives employees a break to pursue leisure activities or take care of personal and civic duties, includes sick leave, vacations, severance pay, and holidays and other paid time off. (5) Employee services consist of a cluster of tax-free or tax-preferred services that employers provide to improve the quality of their employees' work or personal life. One of the most valued employee services is child-care benefits.

Administering Benefits. Two important issues involving benefits administration are the use of flexible benefits and communicating benefits to employees. Though the benefits administration is likely to be performed by an HR benefits specialist, managers need to understand their companies' benefits package well enough to help communicate benefits to their employees and keep records.

Key Terms

benefits mix, 366
Consolidated Omnibus Budget Reconciliation Act of 1985 (COBRA), 374
contributions, 363
copayments, 363
deductible, 363
defined benefit plan or pension plan, 378
defined contribution plan, 379
employee benefits or indirect compensation, 361
Employee Retirement Income Security Act (ERISA), 378
Family and Medical Leave Act of 1993 (FMLA), 372
flexible or cafeteria benefits program, 363
health maintenance organization (HMO), 375
Medicare, 369
Pension Benefit Guaranty Corporation (PBGC), 378
portable benefits, 378
preferred provider organization (PPO), 376
premium, 375
Social Security, 368
supplemental unemployment benefits (SUB), 371
unemployment insurance, 371
vesting, 378
workers' compensation, 369

Discussion Questions

1. How might the increasing diversity of the work force affect the design of employee benefits packages in large companies?
2. The United States mandates only four benefits, yet U.S. employers provide many other benefits—such as health insurance, retirement benefits, and paid vacations—voluntarily. Why do so many employers provide these benefits even though they are not legally required to do so?
3. What are the advantages and disadvantages of enacting a federal law that requires all employers to provide health insurance for their workers?
4. How do managed-care health insurance plans (HMOs and PPOs) differ from traditional fee-for-service health insurance plans? What are the costs and benefits of each to the employer? To the employee?
5. Why should younger employees (those in their 20s and 30s) care about retirement benefits?

6. Why is cost containment such an important issue in employee benefit programs?
7. As pointed out in the chapter, some countries legislate the provision of more generous employment benefits than the United States does. What are the pros and cons of such an approach?
8. A growing trend in the United States is outsourcing the administration of employee benefits to a company that specializes in this area. What are the advantages and disadvantages of outsourcing benefits administration?
9. Should HR staff recommend particular investments (such as mutual funds) to employees for their 401(k) plans? Why or why not?

MINICASE 1 *Companies Face Hidden Benefits Costs in Mexico*

Companies that build factories in Mexico with the expectation of cheap labor costs may be in for a surprise when they consider total compensation expenses. While base pay in the United States accounts for 71% of total hourly labor costs, in Mexico base pay accounts for less than 30% of labor costs. Benefits account for the remaining 70%. This means that a company that focuses on the average Mexican hourly wage of $1.80 in its cost planning is really paying about $6.00 per hour to its Mexican workers after adding the cost of benefits to the wage bill.

Mexican labor law requires employers to provide supplemental benefits to all their employees. For example, employers must give Mexican workers one month's pay as a bonus at Christmas. Private companies are required to share a portion of their profits with their workers in the form of a profit-sharing bonus. In addition, Mexican workers are entitled to a vacation pay premium of 80% added to regular pay rates during vacations. The law also requires employers to pay employees for 365 days a year, even though they may take the weekends off from work.

Discussion Questions

1. In Mexico workers' wages are a much smaller portion of total compensation than in the United States. How could this system affect the types of HRM practices that managers would select to use in Mexico?
2. Do you think that a company that does business in both Mexico and the United States (such as McDonald's and Wal-Mart) should offer the same benefits to its Mexican and U.S. workers, such as the Christmas bonus and the vacation pay premium? Why or why not?

Source: Alley, J. (1994, October 17). Mexican labor's hidden costs. *Fortune*, 32.

MINICASE 2 *Manor Care Changes Its Benefits and Reduces Turnover*

When Manor Care, Inc. set out to become one of the world's great service organizations, it decided to find out what would motivate its front-line service employees to stay with the company. At 72%, employee turnover was a big problem for the Springfield, Maryland–based parent company of Choice Hotels International and Manor HealthCare Corporation. After conducting extensive surveys and studies, the company concluded that to reduce turnover, it needed to offer its lower-paid front-line employees a benefits program they could afford. For instance, while Manor Care's 401(k) plan was a good one, only 20% of employees making $12,000 a year were participating in it.

The company decided to redesign its benefits program, and the result was a program unlike any before it. For instance, in contrast to most defined contribution pension plans, which make contributions based on a uniform percentage for all participants, Manor Care adjusts its contribution percentages according to employee salaries, paying proportionately higher amounts at the lower salary ranges. But Manor Care didn't stop there. It also revamped its medical benefits in a similar manner, so that the more an employee earns, the higher his or her deductible and copayments are. Long-term employees pay less for their benefits as their years of service increase. Since the company redesigned its benefits package, turnover among front-line employees has declined by 25%. In turn, customer service quality has increased, according to surveys completed by 10,000 of Manor Care's health-care customers.

Discussion Questions

1. Do you think Manor Care could have reduced turnover just as much by raising front-line service employees' compensation? Why or why not?
2. What other steps might Manor Care take to reduce turnover?

Source: Gunsch, D. (1993, February). Benefits program helps retain front-line workers. *Personnel Journal*, 88–94. Copyright February 1993. Adapted with the permission of *Personnel Journal*, ACC Communications, Inc., Costa Mesa, CA; all rights reserved.

CASE 1 *Keeping Workers' Compensation Costs Under Control*

Oregon Retirement Apartments is an apartment complex in Portland, Oregon that provides housing, meals, and some assisted living services for its residents. Approximately 300 residents live in the facility. Fifty people work for the complex: a professional staff of administrators and social workers and an operations staff consisting of food service employees, housekeepers, building and maintenance workers, and night managers. Oregon Retirement Apartments tries to provide a rich social and cultural life for its residents (most of whom are in their 70s and 80s) so that they can live independently in a pleasant environment.

Barbara Spector, the facility's executive director, is very concerned about employees who abuse workers' compensation. This concern results from an incident involving Pat O'Toole, a housekeeping employee who filed a claim for workers' compensation benefits for a work-related back injury. Barbara suspected that Pat's injury did not occur on the job and therefore contested the claim. The investigation that followed showed that the claim was indeed false; Pat had sustained her back injury in a skiing accident, not during work hours. The investigation also revealed Pat's long history of filing workers' compensation claims with previous employers. According to files maintained by the state government, Pat has filed a total of 12 workers' compensation claims over her employment life.

After the incident with Pat, Barbara decided to establish a new hiring policy: People with a high likelihood of filing workers' compensation claims will not be hired. She justifies this policy change by citing her responsibility for containing the cost of workers' compensation insurance (which is adjusted according to the safety record of a company's work force). The new policy requires Oregon Retirement's HR staff to examine the workers' compensation records of all job applicants at the same time that their references are checked. The services of a local HR consulting firm are used to scan the workers' compensation database for evidence of an applicant's previous claims. Job applicants who have filed three or more workers' compensation claims are considered a "high risk" and dropped from the applicant pool.

Critical Thinking Questions

1. Is Barbara Spector's policy of rejecting job applicants who have filed three or more workers' compensation claims fair? Is it ethical?
2. What impact does the Americans with Disabilities Act (see Chapter 3) have on an employment practice that rejects applicants who have previously filed workers' compensation claims? Could this practice discriminate against people with disabilities?

Cooperative Learning Exercises

3. With a partner or a small group, develop some alternative employment practices to help Barbara Spector avoid hiring people who are likely to misuse workers' compensation benefits.
4. Discuss the following situation with your partner or group: During a job interview, an applicant reports that he has never applied for workers' compensation benefits. After hiring the applicant, the employer checks on this information and finds out that the employee lied. What should the company do?

CASE 2 *Managing Sick Leave at Lutheran Hospital*

Lutheran Hospital, located in St. Cloud, Minnesota, is the major hospital serving the north-central region of the state. It employs 850 full-time health-care professionals. The hospital's executive team has asked Peter Hanson, the director of human resources, to look for ways to reduce employee benefits expenses in order to improve efficiency and profitability.

One benefit that Peter believes is used inefficiently is sick leave. Under the hospital's current sick leave policy, all full-time employees earn one day of paid sick leave per month. Sick leave accumulates for as long as an employee works at the hospital. When employees leave the hospital, they forfeit their accrued sick leave. In 1996 each employee used an average of six days' sick leave. These absences forced the hospital to hire additional staff to cover for the absent employees. Informal focus groups of employees organized by Mary Rasmussen, the manager of employee benefits, have revealed that at least half of the sick days taken are used by employees to recover from the stressful working conditions at Lutheran Hospital.

Peter has asked Mary to develop some recommendations for reducing the cost of sick leave benefits. After much discussion with her staff, Mary has submitted three recommendations, all based on approaches adopted by other local companies:

1. A "use it or lose it" plan that prevents employees from accumulating sick days beyond one year. At the end of

continued

Managing Sick Leave at Lutheran Hospital continued

the year, employees forfeit all sick days that they have not utilized.

2. A requirement that employees obtain a doctor's note for each sick day taken. The note must indicate that the employee was too sick to perform the job on the day in question.
3. A "wellness pay" incentive program that rewards employees who do not use any of their annual sick leave days with a bonus of $300 and recognition in the employee newsletter.

Mary thinks all of these plans will prove very cost-effective, but warns Peter that each has some disadvantages.

Critical Thinking Questions

1. Which of Mary's three recommendations for managing sick leave would be most appropriate for hospital staff?
2. Might one or more of these approaches encourage employees to go to work when they are sick? If so, should the hospital be concerned about the effect that might have on patients' welfare?

Cooperative Learning Exercise

3. With a partner or small group, try to develop a better approach to managing sick leave at Lutheran Hospital. What criteria could be used to judge whether or not your group's sick leave policy is effective in cutting costs?

HRM Simulation 

Your company has a substandard benefits package (11% of base wages), as indicated on pages 6 and 7 of the players' manual. How will a noncompetitive benefits package affect the company over the long run? Which benefits (if any) do you think are most important to add to the benefits package? Why? (Refer to Table 2 on page 7 of the players' manual.) What procedure would you implement to learn the employees' benefits preferences? Do you think it is reasonable to ask employees to share the cost of some of the additional benefits they request? What would be a fair way to ask the employees to share these costs?

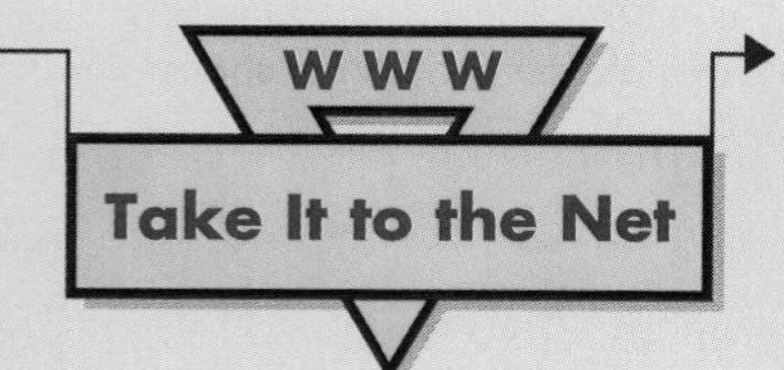

We invite you to visit the Gómez-Mejía/Balkin/Cardy page on the Prentice Hall Web site:

http://www.prenhall.com/gomez

You can also visit the Web sites for these companies, featured within this chapter:

Ford Motor Company	http://www.ford.com
Johnson and Johnson	http://www.jnj.com
Microsoft	http://www.microsoft.com
Silicon Graphics	http://www.sgi.com
Warner Bros. Companies	http://www.warnerbrothers.com

Endnotes

1. Luciano, L. (1993, May). How companies are slashing benefits. *Money,* 128–129
2. Santora, J. E. (1994, April). Employee team designs flexible benefits program. *Personnel Journal,* 30–39.
3. *Inc.* (1995, February). Time off you can bank on, 112.
4. U.S. Chamber of Commerce. (1994). *Employee benefits 1993.* Washington, DC: U.S. Chamber of Commerce.
5. Lieb, J. (1990, March 19). Day-care demand creates new perk. *Denver Post,* 1C, 5C.
6. Gómez-Mejía, L. R., and Balkin, D. B. (1992). *Compensation, organizational strategy and firm performance.* Cincinnati, OH: South-Western.
7. U.S. Chamber of Commerce. (1994). *Employee Benefits 1993.* Washington, DC: U.S. Chamber of Commerce.
8. McCaffery, R. M. (1992). *Employee benefit programs: A total compensation perspective* (2nd ed.). Boston, MA: PWS-Kent.
9. McCaffery, R. M. (1989). Employee benefits and services. In L. R. Gómez-Mejía (Ed.), *Compensation and benefits.* Washington, DC: The Bureau of National Affairs.
10. Lawler, E. E. III. (1990). *Strategic pay.* San Francisco, CA: Jossey-Bass.
11. Levering, R., Moskowitz, M., and Katz, M. (1984). *The 100 best companies to work for in America.* Reading, MA: Addison-Wesley.
12. U.S. Chamber of Commerce. (1991). *Employee benefits 1990.* Washington, DC: U.S. Chamber of Commerce.
13. Thompson, R. (1990, March). Fighting the high cost of workers' compensation. *Nation's Business,* 20–29.
14. Light, L. (1992, October 5). When injured employees act anything but. *Business Week,* 120.
15. Lorenz, C. (1995, May–June). Nine practical suggestions for streamlining workers' compensation costs. *Compensation and Benefits Review,* 40–44.
16. Fefer, M. D. (1994, October 3). Taking control of your workers' comp costs. *Fortune,* 131–136.
17. Milkovich, G. T., and Newman, J. M. (1996). *Compensation* (5th ed.). Homewood, IL: Irwin.
18. Richman, L. S. (1995, April 17). Getting past economic insecurity. *Fortune,* 161–168.
19. Snarr, B. (1993, May–June). The Family and Medical Leave Act of 1993. *Compensation and Benefits Review,* 6–9.
20. Crampton, S. M., and Mishra, J. M. (1995). Family and medical leave legislation: Organizational policies and strategies. *Public Personnel Management, 24*(3), 271–289.
21. Gunsch, D. (1993, September). The Family Leave Act: A financial burden? *Personnel Journal,* 48–57.
22. McNamee, M. (1993, August 9). Sure, "unpaid leave" sounds simple, but... *Business Week,* 32–33.
23. Meckler, L. (1996, May 2). Family leave not shown to hurt business. *Boulder Daily Camera,* 4B.
24. Pear, R. (1993, May–June). The Family and Medical Leave Act of 1993. *Compensation and Benefits Review,* 6–9.
25. Becher, G. (1993, March). European health issues. *Employees Benefits Journal,* 34–45.
26. *Business Week.* (March 27, 1995). The health-care gap widens, 28.
27. Pear, R. (1994, August 23). Once in forefront, HMOs lose their luster in health debate. *The New York Times,* A10; Larson, E. (1996, January 22). The soul of an HMO. *Time,* 44–52; and Magnusson, P., and Hammonds, K. (1996, April 8). Health care: The quest for quality. *Business Week,* 104–106.
28. Jefferson, D. J. (1994, March 8). Family matters: Gay employees win benefits for partners at more corporations. *The Wall Street Journal,* A1, A6; and Jenner, L. (1994, January). Domestic partner update: Awareness and resistance. *HR Focus,* 10.

28a. Fenn, D. (1996, July). Health insurance: Cost cutting strategies, 91.

29. Bernstein, A. (1991, August 19). Playing "Pin the insurance on the other guy." *Business Week,* 104–105.
30. Bunch, D. K. (1992, March). Coors Wellness Center—Helping the bottom line. *Employee Benefits Journal,* 14–18.
31. Wiley, J. L. (1993, August). Preretirement education: Benefits outweigh liability. *HR Focus,* 11.
32. *Money* (1993, May). The best benefits. 130–31.
33. Murray, K. A. (1993, July). For some companies, portable pensions aren't practical. *Personnel Journal,* 38–39.
34. Rotello, P., and Cornwell, R. (1994, February). Is it time to rethink your retirement program? *HR Focus,* 4–5.
35. Dimeo, J. (1992, October). Women receive the short end when it comes to their retirement pension incomes. *Pension World,* 28, 30.
36. Hogan, M. C. (1992, December). Educating the 401(k) investor. *Employee Benefits Journal,* 18–22.
37. Teitelbaum, R. (1995, December 25). Getting the most from your 401(k). *Fortune,* 183–184.
38. Murray, K. A. (1993, July). How HR is making pensions portable. *Personnel Journal,* 36–46; Tobin, V. M. (1992). Beyond defined contribution or defined benefit pension plans. In *The Conference Board report 1004: Controlling the costs of employee benefits,* New York: The Conference Board; and Snell, N. W. (1992). Pension plan modifications. In *The Conference Board report 1004: Controlling the costs of employee benefits,* New York: The Conference Board.
39. DeCenzo, D. A., and Holoviak, S. J. (1990). *Employee benefits.* Englewood Cliffs, NJ: Prentice Hall.
40. *Money.*
41. U.S. Chamber of Commerce, 1991.
42. Eckhouse, J. (1993, March 24). Retired exec at HP received $937,225 for unused sick leave. *San Francisco Chronicle,* C1, C40.
43. Tully, S. (1995, June 12). America's healthiest companies. *Fortune,* 98–106.
44. Matthes, K. (1992, May). In pursuit of leisure: Employees want more time off. *HR Focus,* 1.
45. Gómez-Mejía, L. R., Balkin, D. B., and Milkovich, G. T. (1990). Rethinking your rewards for technical employees. *Organizational Dynamics, 1*(1), 62–75.
46. *Inc.* (1996, July). Severance policies, 92.
47. Fuchsberg, G. (1992, April 22). What is pay, anyway? *The Wall Street Journal,* R3.
48. BNA. (1994, January 31). Self-defense classes for employees becoming popular. *Workforce Strategies* (published with *BNA's Employee Relations Weekly*), 5, 3.
49. *The Conference Board.* (1995). Child care services. *The Conference Board,* 5(4) 3–12.
50. Henderson, R. (1989). *Compensation management* (5th ed.). Englewood Cliffs, NJ: Prentice Hall.
51. Alderman, L., and Kim, S. (1996, January). Get the most from your company benefits. *Money,* 102–106.
52. DeCenzo and Holoviak, 1990.
53. McCaffery, 1992.
54. Wilson, M., Northcraft, G. R., and Neale, M. A. (1985). The perceived value of fringe benefits. *Personnel Psychology, 38,* 309–320.
55. Shalowitz, D. (1992, October 12). Cracking the case of the confusing retirement plan. *Business Insurance,* 22.
56. Johnson, N. P. (1993, November 8). Baker Hughes keeps it simple. *Business Insurance,* 4.

VIDEO CASE *Will You Have Enough Money for Your Old Age?*

Advances in medical science have resulted in a higher life expectancy for all of us. We expect to enjoy our retirement for many years, perhaps decades. But are we putting away enough money to see us through this increased period of retirement? The answer for most people appears to be "no."

A retirement pension used to be considered the part of an employee's compensation package that would take care of him in his retirement years. Social Security payments were a "safety net" used to supplement pension payments. But times have changed. Many of today's workers do not stay with one organization long enough to become vested in a pension fund. Furthermore, companies are increasingly shifting the responsibility of saving for retirement to employees. There is also concern that the Social Security system will go bankrupt, be dismantled, or provide inadequate benefits in the future.

Maintaining a standard of living into retirement can be difficult when that standard of living is beyond what the person can afford. Saving for retirement can also seem all but impossible when workers' compensation packages don't seem to cover all their needs today, let alone tomorrow. What can and should be done to counter these problems?

Some companies have begun to educate workers about investing for retirement. Workers need to understand the importance of retirement planning and be aware of their investment options. Furthermore, the U.S. Labor Department has information that may help small businesses set up simple pension plans. This is important because many workers are employed by small businesses and earn modest incomes.

Unfortunately, many companies are not educating their workers in retirement planning at all. Those who have considered such education claim that they are reluctant to offer the training because they don't want to get into the investment-advice business. In addition, many smaller companies don't seem to give the retirement issue much attention at all.

Discussion Questions

1. Do you think most people's retirement savings are inadequate? Why or why not?
2. Responsibility for retirement planning is increasingly being shifted from employers to individual employees. How could you go about implementing a retirement planning education program in your organization? Do you think steps other than education should be taken? If so, identify them.
3. To what extent should organizations be responsible for employee education and choices regarding retirement planning? Should employers be expected to take the time and absorb the cost of educating workers in this area? Why or why not?

CHALLENGES

After reading this chapter, you should be able to deal more effectively with the following challenges:

1 ▶ **Understand** how good employee relations and communications can contribute to business goals.

2 ▶ **Describe** the three types of programs used to facilitate employee communications.

3 ▶ **Explain** the various appeals procedures through which employees can challenge management actions.

4 ▶ **Understand** how employee assistance programs can help employees deal with personal problems that may interfere with job performance.

5 ▶ **Be aware** of the technological innovations that allow managers to disseminate information quickly and how information dissemination influences an organization's employee relations.

13

Developing Employee Relations and Communications

Their Job's a Picnic. Good employee relations involve making employees feel like valued members of the organization. As part of their employee relations programs, many companies hold annual picnics and holiday parties. Pictured here is the annual summer picnic of the Prentice Hall Business Publishing team—the people who worked with the authors of this text to edit, produce, and distribute the textbook you are now reading.

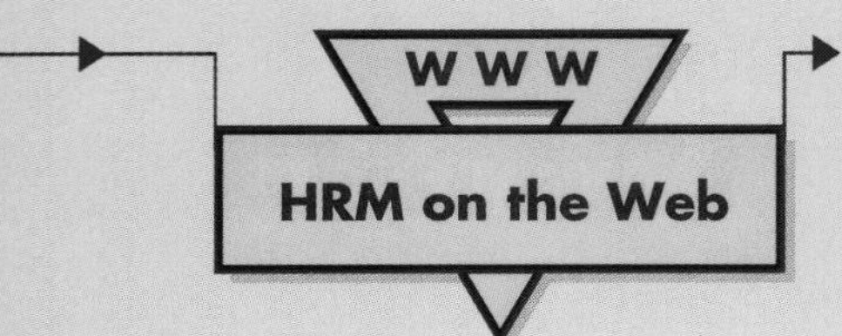

http://www.nyper.com/

Employee Relations Web Picks

This site identifies e-mail newsgroups of interest to HRM professionals, offers resources on legal rulings, and lists publications on employee relations.

Nancy is a customer service manager for a copier company. She started about four years ago as a customer service representative. In her job she occasionally came into contact with customers who would "hit" on her or make suggestive comments, but she was always able to handle those situations. Usually, a diplomatic brush-off was enough. Now, however, she faces a situation that she does not know how to handle.

It all began six months ago when she was promoted to her current position of customer service manager. She really likes the job and the company, and hopes to be promoted further. The problem is her boss. Steve was largely responsible for her promotion, and Nancy feels indebted to him. But after about two months, she realized that his attention to her went beyond work. He began to tell her about his marriage problems and commented that he found her very attractive. After all the help he'd given her, Nancy hesitated to tell him directly that she wasn't interested in him romantically. But after he started sending flowers and asking her out, she finally asked him to stop.

That didn't work. In fact, things got much worse. Steve's requests became more direct, and now they had threats attached. Specifically, he told her that if she did not begin a relationship with him, he would not only not recommend her for any further promotions, he would try to get her terminated. Nancy feels trapped. She knows that Steve is well liked by his colleagues, and she is afraid that if she complains about him, she will only lose her job faster.

Then she read in the monthly newsletter about the company's employee relations program. One of the program's goals is to give employees confidential access to an employee relations specialist who can help them resolve interpersonal problems on the job. Nancy called the confidential hotline and set up an appointment with a counselor. She is looking forward to explaining her dilemma to someone who is impartial and in a position to help her.

Dealing successfully with a problem like Nancy's requires effective employee relations— the subject of this chapter. First, we explore the roles of managers and employee relations specialists, describing how they should work together to coordinate an employee relations program. Next, we present a model of communication and explore specific policies that give employees access to important information. Finally, we examine some programs for recognizing employees' individual and team contributions to company goals.

The Roles of the Manager and the Employee Relations Specialist

Good *employee relations* involve providing fair and consistent treatment to all employees so that they will be committed to the organization. Companies with good employee relations are likely to have an HR strategy that places a high value on employees as stakeholders in the business. Employees who are treated as *stakeholders* have certain rights within the organization and can expect to be treated with dignity and respect. For example, IBM—a company known for its excellent employee relations—is committed to a philosophy articulated more than 50 years ago by its founder, Tom Watson: respect for the individual. To foster good employee relations, managers must listen to and understand what employees are saying and experiencing, keep them informed about what management plans to do with the business, and tell them how those plans may affect their jobs. They should also give employees the freedom to air grievances about management decisions. There may be good reasons for not changing the decision, but management should at least listen to the grievances.

Effective employee relations require cooperation between managers and **employee relations representatives.** These specialists are members of the HR department who act as internal consultants to the business. They try to ensure that company policies and procedures are followed and advise both supervisors and employees on specific employee relations problems. **Employee relations policies** provide channels to resolve such problems before they become more serious.

employee relations representative
A member of the HR department who ensures that company policies are followed and consults with both supervisors and employees on specific employee relations problems.

employee relations policy
A policy designed to communicate management's thinking and practices concerning employee-related matters and prevent problems in the workplace from becoming more serious.

For example, an employee whose supervisor has denied her request for two weeks' vacation (to which she is entitled according to the employee handbook) may ask the employee relations representative to speak to her supervisor and clarify why she is being denied her preferred vacation time. Or a supervisor may request assistance because he suspects that one of his subordinates has an alcohol abuse problem that is affecting job performance. In both these cases, the employee relations representative will try to resolve the problem within the letter and spirit of the appropriate employment policy, while carefully balancing the interests of the supervisor, the employee, and the company.

Employee relations representatives may also develop new policies that help maintain fairness and efficiency in the workplace. The client in this situation may be a top manager who needs assistance in drafting a new policy on smoking in the workplace or the hiring of employees' spouses and other relatives.

▸ Developing Employee Communications

Many companies have found that the key to a good employee relations program is a *communication channel* that gives employees access to important information and an opportunity to express their ideas and feelings. When supervisors are familiar with employment policies and employees are aware of their rights, there is less opportunity for misunderstandings to arise and productivity to drop.

Because corporations are very complex, they must develop numerous communication channels to move information up, down, and across the organizational structure. For instance, IBM provides many communication channels that allow employees and managers to speak with one another and share information. Managers communicate with their employees by walking around and talking to them informally, sponsoring newsletters, and maintaining a cable TV channel that broadcasts information to the entire IBM community. They also solicit employee feedback through opinion surveys. As today's organizations have delegated more responsibilities and decision-making authority to employees, the importance of making more information available to employees has increased substantially.[1]

Types of Information

Two forms of information are sent and received in communications: facts and feelings. *Facts* are pieces of information that can be objectively measured or described. Examples are the cost of a computer, the daily defect rate in a manufacturing plant, and the size of the deductible payment in the company-sponsored health insurance policy. Recent technological advances have made factual information more accessible to more employees than ever before. Facts can be stored in databases and widely distributed to employees by networks of personal computers.

Feelings are employees' emotional responses to the decisions made or actions taken by managers or other employees. Managers who implement decisions must be able to anticipate or respond to the feelings of the employees who are affected by those decisions. If they cannot or do not, the plan may fail. For example, a public university changed its health insurance coverage without consulting the employees affected by the change. When these employees learned of their diminished coverage, they responded so negatively that the manager of employee benefits resigned. (The health insurance policy was subsequently changed to be more favorable to the employees.)

A company must be especially careful of employees' feelings when it is restructuring or downsizing and laying off a considerable portion of its work force. A production employee at a large East Coast manufacturing firm remembers how top management kept issuing memos that said, in effect, "we're doing fine, we're doing fine," and then suddenly announced layoffs. Survivors of the layoff were shocked and hurt and became highly distrustful of management.[2]

Organizations need to design communication channels that allow employees to communicate facts and feelings. In many cases, these channels must provide for face-to-face communication because many feelings are conveyed nonverbally. Employees cannot write on a piece of paper or record on a computer database their complex emotional reactions to a decision that they fear will cost them their jobs.

How Communication Works

Figure 13–1 is a simple representation of the communications process within an organization. Communication starts with a *sender*, who has a message to send to the *receiver*. The sender must *encode* the message and select a *communication channel* that will deliver it to the receiver. In communicating facts, the message may be encoded with words, numbers, or digital symbols; in communicating feelings, it may be encoded as body language or tone of voice.

Some communication channels are more appropriate than others for sending certain messages. For example, memos are usually not very effective for sending information that has a lot of feeling in it. A more effective channel for conveying strong emotions is a meeting or other form of face-to-face communication.

Communication is not effective unless the receiver is able to *decode* the message and understand its true meaning. The receiver may misinterpret a message for many reasons. For example, the message may be filled with technical jargon that makes it difficult to decode, the receiver may misinterpret the sender's motives for sending the message, or the sender may send a message that lends itself to multiple interpretations.

Because of the strong possibility of miscommunication, important communications should include opportunities for *feedback* from the receiver. This way the sender can clar-

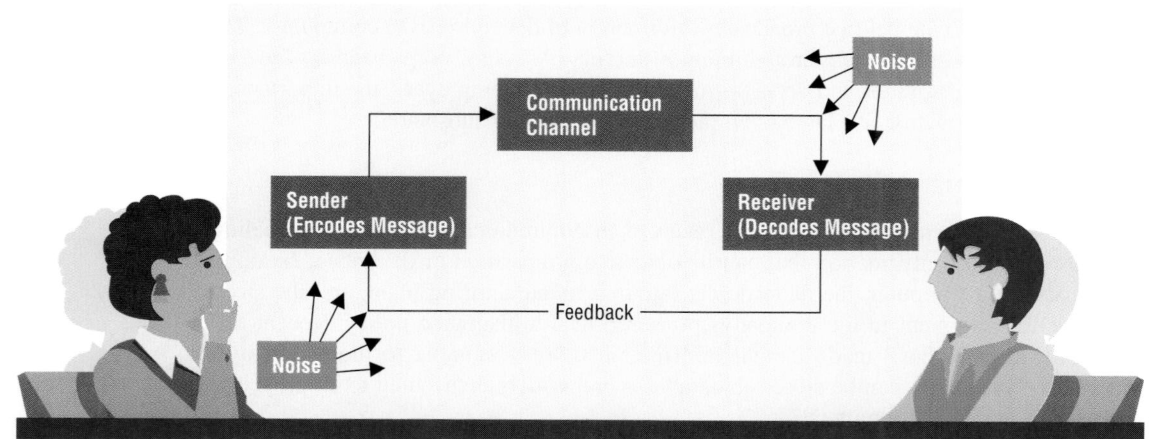

FIGURE 13-1

The Communications Process within an Organization

ify the message if its true meaning is not received. In addition, noise in the sender's or receiver's environment may block or distort the message. *Noise* is anything that disrupts the message: inaccurate communication by the sender, fatigue or distraction on the part of the receiver, or actual noise that distorts the message (other people talking, traffic, telephone ringing). Very often noise takes the form of information overload. For example, if the receiver gets 65 memos in one week, she may not read the most important one very carefully because she is overwhelmed by the barrage of paper.

Communications that provide for feedback are called *two-way communications* because they allow the sender and receiver to interact with each other. Communications that provide no opportunity for feedback are one-way. Although ideally all communications should be interactive, this is not always possible in large organizations, where large amounts of information must be distributed to many employees. For example, top executives at large companies do not usually have the time to speak to all the employees they need to inform about a new product about to be released. Instead, they may communicate with the employees via a memo or report. In contrast, top executives at small businesses have much less difficulty communicating with their employees.

Downward and Upward Communication. Employee relations specialists help to maintain both downward communication and upward communication in an organization. **Downward communication** allows managers to implement their decisions and to influence employees lower in the organizational hierarchy. It can also be used to disperse information controlled by top managers. **Upward communication** allows employees at lower levels to communicate their ideas or feelings to higher-level decision makers. Unfortunately, many organizations erect serious barriers in their upward communication channels. For example, in many companies it is considered disloyal for an employee to go "over the head" of an immediate supervisor and communicate with a higher-level executive about a problem.

downward communication Communication that allows managers to implement their decisions and to influence employees lower in the organizational hierarchy.

upward communication Communication that allows employees at lower levels to communicate their ideas and feelings to higher-level decision makers.

One final but very important note concerning communication in general: The U.S. economy is shifting from an industrial base to an information base. This revolution is as significant as the move from an agrarian to an industrial economy over a century ago. In an industrial economy, production processes are the focus of concern. In an information economy, communication (the production and transmission of information) is the focus. How information is communicated, both internally and externally, is becoming more and more important to organizational success. A strong symbol of this transition is the rise of Microsoft, the software giant. Software is almost pure information; it has no tangible aspect. Yet the man who supplies most of the world's operating system software (the kind that controls a computer's operation and directs the processing of programs) and application software (the specific programs run on the computer)—Bill Gates, the founder and CEO of Microsoft—is reportedly the wealthiest man in the United States.

Building Managerial Skills: ▸ Facilitating Effective Communications

Working with supervisors and managers, employee relations representatives can facilitate effective communications by developing and maintaining three types of programs: information dissemination, employee feedback, and employee assistance.

Information Dissemination Programs

Information is a source of power in organizations. In traditional top-down hierarchies, top managers zealously guard information as their special preserve. But the information age has forced many businesses to forge a new set of rules. Today organizations depend more

knowledge worker
A worker who transforms information into a product or service.

information dissemination
The process of making information available to decision makers, wherever they are located.

and more on knowledge workers to produce their product or service. **Knowledge workers** (for example, programmers, writers, educators) transform information into a product or service and need large amounts of information to do their jobs effectively. For these workers, the dissemination of information throughout the organization is critical to providing high-quality service and products to the organization's customers.

Information dissemination involves making information available to decision makers, wherever they are located. Employees who have access to abundant information are more likely to feel empowered and are better able to participate in decision making. Information dissemination also helps managers adopt more participative leadership styles and work configurations, leading to greater employee involvement and, ultimately, to better employee relations.

The most important methods of disseminating information to employees are employee handbooks, written communications, audiovisual communications, electronic communications, meetings, retreats, and informal communications.

The Employee Handbook. The *employee handbook* is probably the most important source of information that the HR department can provide. It sets the tone for the company's overall employee relations philosophy,[3] informing both employees and supervisors about company employment policies and procedures and communicating employees' rights and responsibilities. The handbook lets employees know that they can expect consistent and uniform treatment on issues that affect their job or status in the company. It also tells supervisors how to evaluate, reward, and discipline their employees. It can protect supervisors and the company from making uninformed and arbitrary decisions that may hurt the work force's morale or lead to litigation from angry employees.

A QUESTION OF ETHICS

Some companies attempt to restrict the behavior of employees while they are off the job. The most common restriction is a prohibition against smoking. Less common is a prohibition against public drinking. Is it ethical for a company to try to control its employees' behavior while they are not on the job?

Employee handbooks contain information on such issues as employee benefits, performance evaluation, dress codes, employment of family members, smoking, probationary employment periods, drug-testing procedures, family leave policies, sexual harassment, discipline procedures, and safety rules.[4] Handbooks need to be updated annually to reflect the current legal environment and to remain consistent with the company's overall employee relations philosophy.

Recent court interpretations in some states have suggested that employee handbooks may constitute an implied contract between employer and employee that restricts the employer's freedom to discharge employees without just cause. To avoid such restrictive interpretations by the courts, employers should include at the end of their handbook a disclaimer stating that employees can be discharged for any reason or no reason and that the handbook does not constitute an employment contract.[5] Some firms go even further to protect themselves: They ask all new employees to sign an employee handbook acknowledgment form stating they have received the handbook; will refer to it for company rules, regulations, and policies; and understand that it is in no way a contract. Figure 13–2 shows a sample employee handbook acknowledgment form.[6] Not surprisingly, such forms have been controversial because the legal protection they provide the employer also tends to undermine the goodwill the handbook was designed to foster.

nepotism
The practice of favoring relatives over others in the workplace.

Still, employee handbooks can help prevent or solve problems in the work force. Figure 13–3 shows how a firm might communicate an enlightened nepotism policy through its employee handbook. (**Nepotism** is the practice of favoring relatives over others in the workplace.) The policy communicated in Figure 13–3 protects the rights of family members but balances those rights with the company's need to avoid conflicts of interest that could affect the efficiency of its business.

In family-owned businesses where owners often groom sons, daughters, or other family members to take over the company, nepotism is taken for granted. In these situations, the question becomes: How much nepotism is okay? It is not uncommon for company owners to put their children in positions of power and grant them pay, titles, and privileges denied to more experienced or qualified company employees. Naturally, this antagonizes nonfamily employees. Family business consultants Craig E. Aronoff and John L. Ward rec-

TJP INC. EMPLOYEE HANDBOOK ACKNOWLEDGMENT FORM

This employee handbook has been given to ______________________

on (date) ______________________

by ______________ (title) ______________

Employee's effective starting date ______________________

Employee's pay period ______________________

Employee's hours and workweek are ______________________

Welcome to TJP Inc. Below is a list of your benefits with their effective date:

Benefit	**Effective Date**
Hospitalization ______________________	________
Life insurance ______________________	________
Retirement ______________________	________
Vacation ______________________	________
Sick leave ______________________	________
Holidays ______________________	________
Personal days ______________________	________
Bereavement ______________________	________
Workers' compensation ______________________	________
Social Security ______________________	________
Your first performance appraisal will be on ____________	________

I understand that my employee handbook is for informational purposes only and that I am to read and refer to the employee handbook for information on employment work rules and company policies. TJP Inc. may modify, revoke, suspend or terminate any and all policies, rules, procedures and benefits at any time without prior notice to company employees. This handbook and its statements do not create a contract between TJP Inc. and its employees. This handbook and its statements do not affect in any way the employment-at-will relationship between TJP Inc. and its employees.

(Employee's signature) ______________________

(Date) ______________________

FIGURE 13–2

Sample Employee Handbook Acknowledgment Form

Source: Reprinted, by permission of the publisher, from *Management Review,* June 1993, © 1993. American Management Association, New York. All rights reserved.

NEPOTISM POLICY

Section 1. **Family Member Employment.** The company considers it an unlawful employment practice regarding a member of an individual's family working or who has worked for the Company to:

a. Refuse to hire or employ that individual;
b. Bar or terminate from employment that individual; or
c. Discriminate against that individual in compensation or in terms, conditions, or privileges of employment.

Section 2. **Conflict of Interest.** The Company is not required to hire or continue in employment an individual if it:

a. Would place the individual in a position of exercising supervisory, appointment, or grievance adjustment authority over a member of the individual's family, or in a position of being subject to the authority that a member of the individual's family exercises; or
b. Would cause the Company to disregard a bona fide occupational requirement reasonably necessary to the normal operation of the Company's business.

Section 3. **Member of an Individual's Family.** Member of an individual's family includes wife, husband, son, daughter, mother, father, brother, brother-in-law, sister, sister-in-law, son-in-law, daughter-in-law, father-in-law, mother-in-law, aunt, uncle, niece, nephew, stepparent, or stepchild of the individual.

FIGURE 13–3

Sample Nepotism Policy Statement from an Employee Handbook

Source: Adapted from Decker, K. H. (1989). *A manager's guide to employee privacy: Policies and procedures,* 231–232. New York: Wiley.

ommend that family members meet the following three qualifications before making the family business a permanent career:

- Get an education appropriate for the job sought.
- Work three to five years outside the family business.
- Start in an existing, necessary job within the family business and honor precedents for pay and performance.[7]

Written Communications: Memos, Financial Statements, Newsletters, and Bulletin Boards. There are many other forms of written communication besides the employee handbook. *Memos* are useful for conveying changes in policies or procedures. For example, when there is a change in coverage of a specific type of medical procedure, the affected group of employees can be notified by written memo. In addition, the company should disseminate *financial reports* to make employees knowledgeable about the company's performance. Shareholders are routinely given this information, but employees should receive it too because it is an important source of feedback on their aggregate performance.

One activity for which the HR department is likely to have direct responsibility is the production and distribution of an employee newsletter. The *newsletter* is usually a short monthly or quarterly publication designed to keep employees informed of important events, meetings, and transitions and to provide inspirational stories about employee and team contributions to the business (Figure 13–4).[8] Newsletters help foster community spirit in a company or unit. The advent of desktop publishing packages for personal computers has made newsletter production and distribution feasible for even the smallest of companies. For example, Valleylab, a medical instruments manufacturer in Colorado, started a newsletter to inform its employees about quality improvements made by various employee teams under its total quality management (TQM) program.

Two important components of a TQM program are ongoing information about rivals and feedback on team members' performance from managers.[9] Some managers use a simple *bulletin board* to post current team performance data and comparisons with outside competitors or other teams with the company.

Audiovisual Communications. New technologies have made it possible to disseminate information that goes beyond the printed word. Visual images and audio information are powerful communication tools. The widespread use of videocassette recorders (VCRs) in the home allows companies to distribute videotapes to employees when they need to convey important information. Managers at the Rocky Flats Nuclear Weapons Arsenal in Denver used prerecorded videotapes quite successfully to announce a downsizing (due to defense cuts) that would result in the layoff of several thousand employees. Each employee received a videotape containing a message from top executives explaining the reasons for the work force reduction and the company's new mission. The tape also included a personal message from then-President George Bush explaining why the end of the Cold War meant a change in the U.S. government's spending priorities. In this case, audiovisual communication helped to maintain employee morale despite all the changes and uncertainty at the company.

teleconferencing
The use of audio and video equipment to allow people to participate in meetings even when they are a great distance away from the conference location or one another.

A recent technological advance, **teleconferencing,** allows people with busy schedules to participate in meetings even when they are a great distance away from the conference location (or one another). Through video cameras and other sophisticated equipment, teleconferencing makes it possible for employees at remote locations to interact with one another as if they were all seated in the same conference room. One four-hour video conference that keeps five people off an airplane and out of hotels and restaurants could save a company at least $5,000. With teleconferencing systems ranging in price from $20,000 to $40,000, however, the costs are still prohibitive for many companies. Fortunately, advances in computers and phone networks may soon make it possible to equip desktop

2 Animation appeals to adults and kids alike. Even if some ARE little *Rugrats!*

3 Making our mark on the global map: a special International Insert.

7 Keying in on Nickelodeon Movies' *Harriet the Spy.*

8 *VH1 Honors* the global rights organization, Witness.

A PUBLICATION FOR VIACOM EMPLOYEES WORLDWIDE JUNE 1996

VIACOMMENTS

Mission: Impossible Smashes Box-Office Records $75 Million Largest 6-Day Gross In History!

A MARKETING MISSION

A former Russian spy selling international intelligence on the black market...a spy agency ready to disavow the actions or existence of any of its members captured or killed...and one man on a mission that seems impossible.

Paramount Pictures' Memorial Day Weekend release of *Mission: Impossible* enjoyed a blast of promotional exposure under the Viacom umbrella and with outside marketing partners. The first film from the Cruise/Wagner production team, *Mission: Impossible* had the marketing advantages of its history as the well-known Bruce Geller television show from the late '60s and '70s in addition to the enormous box-office draw and popularity of its star, Tom Cruise.

Viacom businesses supported the film through a variety of promotions and sneak previews to help build on the excitement. ▪ Paramount Television's *Entertainment Tonight* gave the movie extensive coverage including a special lead segment the day after the premiere, interviews with the stars, and exclusive teasers about the movie and the soundtrack months before *Mission: Impossible* was released. ▪ MTV heavily promoted the movie through a global viewer sweepstakes awarding winners from around the world a trip to the LA premiere and a chance to meet Tom Cruise. Additionally, the network produced global coverage and specials, including one on the worldwide premiere. ▪ VH1 also did specials and featured the *Mission: Impossible* theme song music video on the air. ▪ Simon & Schuster's Pocket Books novelized the screenplay. ▪ Viacom Radio stations aired the *Mission: Impossible* theme song. ▪ Viacom Consumer Products has developed a variety of licensed items including a disguisable action figure. *Mission: Impossible* is the first title published under the *Marvel Presents: Paramount Comics* imprint.

Many promotions with outside partners also helped establish consumer awareness about the movie. ▪ Apple joined Paramount Pictures in promoting *Mission: Impossible* through a marketing push unprecedented in the technology industry. Apple borrowed the movie's tagline, "Expect the impossible," for its innovative television and print ads and for its promotions, which included merchandising, in-theater programs, an Internet Web adventure and tie-ins with Apple dealers. ▪ Kellogg's Corn Pops is sponsoring the *Mission: Impossible Talking Chip Sweepstakes* on 23 million custom packages, with select ones featuring a light-activated sound chip that plays the movie's theme song if the customer wins one of the Sweepstakes' many prizes. ▪ TNT Sports, TBS Sports and Foot Locker developed cross-promotions on Turner's CNN, Headline News and Airport channels during the NBA playoffs and 1,400 Foot Locker stores had a 30-minute, NBA *Mission: Impossible* videotape, in-store signage displays and 3 million bag stuffers for the duration of the play-off series.

The Marketing Mission is certainly paying off. *Mission: Impossible* set the record for the biggest Memorial Day Weekend box-office and became the largest six-day grossing film in movie history. Not bad for one man on a mission that seems impossible. ■

MISSION: IMPOSSIBLE

At top, Tom Cruise and Emmanuelle Beart heat up summer screens in Paramount Pictures' *Mission: Impossible*. Above, Cruise as Ethan Hunt drops in on the CIA.

going global in a big way

SUMNER REDSTONE CALLS "GLOBALIZATION" THE ONE BUZZWORD OF RECENT VINTAGE THAT CARRIES WITH IT DEEP MEANING AND IMPACT. ALREADY A MAJOR GLOBAL PLAYER, VIACOM DEVELOPS, CREATES, PACKAGES AND DISTRIBUTES SOME OF THE WORLD'S MOST RECOGNIZED BRANDS. BUT THERE'S MORE TO COME. REDSTONE SAYS, "PHENOMENAL GROWTH LIES BEYOND OUR BORDERS."

In its biggest move towards global expansion yet, Viacom struck a far-reaching and lucrative foreign television alliance with KirchGroup, the major German media company, to distribute Paramount Pictures' and Paramount Television product to German-speaking territories in Europe. KirchGroup also has agreed to carry MTV Europe, VH-1 Germany, a Nickelodeon programming block and certain future Viacom programming networks for its new digital pay TV service. This alliance with KirchGroup is an important turning point for Viacom, as the Company plans to follow it up with other arrangements in Europe and around the world.

Simon & Schuster became the first American publisher to co-publish a book in mainland China. The *Ten Minute Guide to Windows 95*, published in Mandarin, is the first of more than 100 computer book titles that Simon & Schuster will co-publish locally in China this year. This relationship with Beijing-based China Science Press marks the continuation of an Asian publishing initiative that focuses on computer, education and trade publishing in both local languages and English-language translations.

MTV, the world's largest network, boosted its global presence by a recent investment in state-of-the-art technology, including digital compression, to introduce new services within its European, Latin American and Asian networks and to increase the amount of regionalized programming it produces in each of these regions, including Japan.

Today about 50 percent of film box-office revenues come from overseas markets and by the year 2000 that number could reach 70 percent. In addition, tremendous investment is taking place in the building and refurbishment of motion picture theaters. The growth of exhibition will have an enormous impact on the motion picture business throughout the world.

Blockbuster Video, already the unrivaled leader in the U.S., has tremendous opportunities for growth in international marketplaces where there is basically no such thing as a neighborhood Blockbuster store...yet.

Save this issue's special insert that shares senior management's international strategy and highlights the Company on the global map. ■

1

FIGURE 13–4

Sample Employee Newsletter

Source: VIACOM, Inc. and design by The Barnett Group, Inc.

computers with a camera and videoconferencing circuit board for as little as $1,000 to $1,500. Besides making videoconferencing more affordable, desktop systems promise to make the technology less intimidating to managers and employees.[10]

Electronic Communications

Advances in electronic communications have made interactive communications possible even when the sender and receiver are separated by physical distance and busy schedules. With **voice mail,** an employee can avoid playing "telephone tag" with busy managers and instead leave a detailed voice message for them. The sender can also transmit a prerecorded voice mail message to some or all the people within the company's telephone network. For example, an executive can send a personalized greeting to a large group of employees. In addition, the receiver can leave different voice mail messages for different types of callers

voice mail
A form of electronic communication that allows the sender to leave a detailed voice message for a receiver.

by creating a menu of messages. Voice mail can also be used strategically by companies engaged in quality management efforts. While Cadillac was in the process of applying for the Malcolm Baldrige National Quality Award, its employees got updates and answers to oft-asked questions via "The Baldrige Minute" on the company's voice mail system.[11]

Like any technology, voice mail has some drawbacks. Many people still dislike speaking to a machine. And this machine has plenty of potential for misuse. People often use it to screen calls, avoiding callers they don't want to talk to by pretending they're not there. This is fine in private life, but screening too many calls at the office can create problems. The following guidelines can help managers cut down on potential abuses of the voice mail system:[12]

- *Limit message capacity.* To discourage long-winded voice mail messages, set the individual message capacity for 60 seconds.
- *Don't leave people in limbo.* Sometimes it's necessary to screen calls. However, screening doesn't mean not returning calls for five or six days. To prevent the screening habit, some companies have a policy stipulating that answering machines cannot be turned on when employees are in their offices.
- *Don't allow voice mail to be used as a crutch.* Senders who are supposed to phone someone with unpleasant news should not wait until the person is out to lunch so they can leave the message on voice mail.
- *Make sure everyone understands the system.* This includes temporary employees, people from other departments, and new hires.
- *Respect the caller.* Employees who will be away from the office on business, or on vacation and not checking their messages, should leave a message for the callers telling them how to reach a colleague who is taking their calls.[13]

electronic mail (e-mail) A form of electronic communication that allows employees to communicate with each other via electronic messages sent through personal computer terminals linked by a network.

Electronic mail, or **e-mail,** allows employees to communicate with each other via written electronic messages sent through personal computer terminals linked by a network. E-mail is a very fast way to convey important business results or critical events to a large number of employees.[14] It also permits the sharing of large information databases among employees and even members of different organizations. E-mail has made it possible for professors at different universities worldwide to collaborate on research studies, write manuscripts, and share data as quickly as if they were working next door to each other at the same university. Interorganizational electronic communication is likely to increase significantly in the coming years, thanks to the rise of the Internet. For more details on how the Internet works and the opportunities it offers for improved HRM services, see the Issues and Applications feature.

Despite its many advantages, e-mail has created some problems for managers. One problem is that, through ease of use, e-mail contributes to information overload. "Fifty percent of e-mail is a complete waste of time," says the assistant director of fire and aviation at the U.S. Forestry Service. "People create mailing lists and send one document to 50 people when only five people need to see it." To combat this problem, the U.S. Forestry Service's system typically allows space for only 30 to 50 messages; senders often have their memos sent back to them if the receiver's mailbox is full. Another problem is people's tendency to print out every message they get, causing exactly the kind of paper blitz that e-mail is supposed to prevent.[15]

Firms that set up e-mail systems with the idea of boosting productivity are sometimes dismayed to find that they are actually *lowering* productivity. Ira Chaleff, president of International Business Technology U.S., a Washington, DC–based management consulting firm, recommends the following guidelines for using e-mail productively:

- Establish an e-mail improvement team to develop protocols and procedures for getting the most out of the system.
- Create electronic files for messages that need to be saved and organize them in subject folders for quick retrieval.

Opportunities Galore on the Internet

Issues + Applications

The Internet, a worldwide network of linked computers that allows people to exchange text, data, and graphics, provides many opportunities for enhanced communication. Many organizations have developed home pages on the World Wide Web (a part of the Internet with multimedia capabilities) that offer a wealth of information about the organization's products and services.

For example, many universities are now listing the details of their educational programs on the Internet to attract students from other countries.

The Internet offers many opportunities for improved HRM services. New businesses post résumés on an online Internet site that employers can access as they seek to fill positions. For example, Actors Pavilion provides a Web site on which actors can post their résumés and photographs, which can be downloaded by casting directors who are seeking actors to fill parts in films, plays, or commercials.

The Net also offers a variety of *newsgroups,* "virtual communities" of people who share professional or personal interests. Newsgroup subscribers converse on an Internet "party line" that makes the content accessible to all group members. The HRNet newsgroup, sponsored by the Academy of Management's Human Resource Management Division, has over 3,000 members, mostly academics and HRM practitioners. A practitioner may post a question about an HRM practice that the company is considering, such as a casual dress code, and quickly get feedback from other members of the HRNet who have experience with casual dress codes. Such information can be invaluable when it comes time to make the final decision.

Sources: Sprout, A. (1995, November 27). The Internet inside your company. *Fortune,* 161–168; Kirkpatrick, D. (1995, May 1). As the Internet sizzles, online services battle for stakes. *Fortune,* 86–96; and Grusky, S. (1996, February). Winning resume. *Internet World,* 58–64.

- Set up a common folder or electronic bulletin board to which senders can route reports and memos intended for general distribution. An electronic bulletin board can save considerable system space and time.[16]
- Shut off the computer beep that alerts the receiver to incoming messages to prevent constant interruptions of work.
- Do not send all kinds of documents through e-mail. Regular interoffice mail should be used most of the time; avoid the bureaucratic tendency to upgrade most e-mail messages to "certified" and "confidential."

The thorniest problem managers confront with e-mail requires consultation with HR professionals. This is the tendency of employees to view their e-mail messages as private property, sacrosanct from employer inspection. This assumption can lead them to use e-mail to communicate about off-hours activities or to spread rumors, misinformation, and complaints speedily throughout the organization. Some managers have been shocked to find "gripe-nets" formed by disgruntled workers who use e-mail to sabotage managers' plans.[17] For these reasons, employers sometimes decide to monitor their employees' e-mail. Employees usually resent this, regarding it as an invasion of their privacy.[18] For example, when setting up Epson America's e-mail system, e-mail administrator Alana Shoars reassured 700 nervous Epson employees that their e-mail would be private. When Shoars found out that her supervisor was copying and reading employees' e-mail messages, she complained—and lost her job. She filed suit, but the judge agreed with the company. Because state privacy statutes didn't make specific reference to e-mail or the workplace, the judge said, the law didn't protect electronic messages in the office. Epson has since notified employees that it cannot guarantee e-mail privacy, citing in part its need to protect itself from computer crime. Unless HR staff members develop e-mail policies that are explicit and reasonable, employee relations may suffer.[19]

Should companies have the right to read and monitor their employees' e-mail?

multimedia technology
A form of electronic communication that integrates voice, video, and text, all of which can be encoded digitally and transported on fiber optic networks.

The future will bring even more powerful communication technologies into organizations. Soon **multimedia technology**—integrating voice, video, and text, all of which are encoded digitally and can be transported on fiber optic networks—will make it possible to interact with video images of employees located across the country or around the world as if they were in the same room.

Multimedia technology has potential applications in many areas. One is in employee training programs (see Chapter 8). For example, pilots can develop aviation skills on a multimedia flight simulator without risking an accident to the plane. Many textbooks now offer multimedia disks that help students learn skills and apply the information they've learned from the text.[20] These multimedia programs include voice and video clips and ask the student to make a decision from a menu of possible choices. After making a decision, the student can see the outcome on video.

Another application of multimedia technology is in telecommuting, a trend that is already changing the face of companies across the nation. More and more employees are working with company-equipped computer systems and faxes in their homes.[21] The accompanying Manager's Notebook, "Five Keys to Managing Telecommuters," addresses the managerial implications of this new workplace development.

Manager's Notebook

Five Keys to Managing Telecommuters

Telecommuting must be carefully planned. The following suggestions can make managing telecommuters a little easier:

- Select telecommuters with care, considering the work habits of the employee and the type of work involved. People who are not very self-motivated may not be able to manage their time well at home.
- Maintain schedules and make sure telecommuters stick to deadlines. While it's okay for telecommuters to work off-hours, they should be available for consultation when the company needs them.
- Make sure the technology works. Without the right compatibility between employers' and telecommuters' computer systems, there will be delays in communication and traffic tie-ups on the electronic highway.
- Have home-based workers come in to the office on a regular basis so they can attend meetings and interact with managers. Doing so not only keeps these employees in the flow but also helps combat their feelings of isolation.
- Don't discriminate against telecommuters. These employees should receive the same pay, benefits, and promotion opportunities as in-house employees.

Sources: Based on Caudron, S. (1992, November). Working at home pays off. *Personnel Journal,* 40–49; Broadwell, L. (1993, August). Long-distance employees. *Small Business Reports,* 44–48; and *Information Management Forum* (1993, February). Telecommuting: Pros and cons. An insert in *Management Review,* 3.

Meetings. Formal meetings are opportunities for face-to-face communication between two or more employees and are guided by a specific agenda. Formal meetings facilitate dialogue and promote the nurturing of personal relationships, particularly among employees who may not interact frequently because they are separated by organizational or geographic barriers.

Meetings take place at different organizational levels. For example, staff meetings allow managers to coordinate activities with subordinates in their units. Division or corporate meetings involve issues that have a larger impact, and may include managers or employees from all divisions across the corporation. For instance, when a company like Microsoft decides to unveil a new product, organization-

Making Meetings Work.

Meetings can be extremely productive or a major drain on workers' time. The best meetings have a specific agenda, are scheduled at an appropriate place and time, and encourage active participation.

wide meetings are sometimes used to make sure that everyone in the organization is communicating the same message. Task force meetings may be called to discuss specific goals such as a change in marketing strategy or compensation policies.

It has been estimated that managers and executives spend as much as 70% of their time in meetings.[22] Poorly managed meetings can be a colossal waste of time that lower a company's productivity. Think about what it might cost for several highly paid executives to spend three hours at a meeting without accomplishing their objectives—and then multiply that amount by 260 workdays a year. Yet meetings don't have to be a necessary evil. Here are some guidelines for making meetings more productive:

1. Decide whether it's even necessary to hold a meeting. If a matter can be handled by a phone call or memo, don't schedule a meeting.
2. Make meeting participation match the meeting's purpose. For instance, if a meeting is being held for the purpose of sharing information, a large group might be appropriate. For a problem-solving session, a smaller group is usually more productive.
3. Distribute a carefully planned agenda before the meeting. This will provide participants with purpose and direction and give them a chance to plan their own contributions.
4. Choose an appropriate meeting space and time. It's difficult for people to accomplish much when they're crowded into a small room with notepads balanced on their laps. Holding a meeting in a room that's too large may encourage participants to spread out and not develop the necessary cohesion. Timing is crucial, too. At meetings scheduled in the hour before lunch, attendees may be listening to their stomachs growl rather than to their colleagues. Some managers like to schedule meetings in the morning, when people are more alert. To encourage promptness, they set a time that is not exactly on the hour—such as 10:10 instead of 10:00 A.M.
5. In the case of a problem-solving or policy-setting meeting, close with an action plan and follow up with a memo outlining what happened at the meeting and what steps need to be taken.[23]

Skillful management of the dynamics among meeting participants is even more important than logistics. It is inevitable that some participants will attempt to dominate the proceedings with either helpful or negative contributions. Meeting leaders must strive to establish an atmosphere in which everyone feels at ease—one in which differences of opinion are encouraged and treated with respect.

Further clouding the air in the conference room are gender differences. Women often complain that they find it difficult to get, and hold, the floor in meetings with male colleagues. Sociolinguist Deborah Tannen has found that women and men have different communication styles that lead to misunderstandings both at work and at home.[24] Cultural differences also crop up in the meeting room. In a U.S. business meeting, the focus tends to be on action. In contrast, the objective of Japanese business meetings is to gather information or to analyze data before planning action. In Italy, meetings are often a way for managers to demonstrate their authority and power.[25]

In addition to scheduled formal meetings with specific work-related goals, managers can use informal meetings to build personal relationships among employees. Friday social hours have become a regular part of business at Silicon Valley's high-technology companies, including Apple Computer and Sun Microsystems. At these social hours, technical employees talk among themselves and with managers and marketing staff about projects and share information that may not be communicated through formal channels. This practice has spread to many other businesses outside California.

Retreats. One type of meeting that has gained popularity with U.S. businesses in recent years is the *retreat*. The company takes employees to a relaxing location such as a mountain lodge or an oceanside resort, where they mix business with recreational activities like golf, tennis, or sailing. Some retreats are designed to develop creative ideas for long-term planning or for implementing changes in business practices. Others, such as the outdoor adventures organized by Outward Bound, encourage employees to develop interpersonal skills by involving them in such activities as mountain climbing or whitewater rafting, where they are forced to be interdependent. These intense shared experiences can foster mutual appreciation among coworkers. A retreat can also be an excellent way of improving employee relations. For example, one medium-sized law firm in the Denver area used a retreat to improve relations between partners and associates. All the firm's members spent two days at a mountain lodge talking in small groups about ways to improve their relationships with one another. These discussions brought into the open many touchy issues that had been simmering. In the retreat setting, the firm's members could deal with them constructively.

Many family businesses are discovering the value of retreats. Two brothers, Steve and Elliott Dean, bought all the stock in their father's company, Dean Lumber Company in Gilmer, Texas. Three years later Steve realized that he'd been so busy with day-to-day affairs that he hadn't spoken with family members about his plans for the company's future. The solution: a family retreat at which all 15 members of the Dean clan gathered for two days to discuss Steve's vision for Dean Lumber, helped by a facilitator from the Family Business Institute at Baylor University in Waco, Texas. The retreat, which included a preretreat screening, facilities with meals, the facilitator, and guest speakers, cost the Deans $5,000.

Most family business consultants recommend using a nonfamily facilitator at the first retreat, to get the process going and keep emotions from running too high. Later on the role of facilitator can be rotated among family members. To help the Dean family get a grip on the issue of succession, for example, the facilitator asked the group to pretend that Steve and Elliott had been killed in a plane crash and asked what they would do. This proved a shocking exercise for the brothers because it made them realize how very little short- or long-term planning they had done.[26]

In addition to using retreats to air important issues, many family businesses use them to set up a *family council*, an organizational and strategic planning group whose members regularly meet to decide values, policy, and direction.

informal communications
Also called "the grapevine." Information exchanges without a planned agenda that occur informally among employees.

Informal Communications. Sometimes called the "grapevine," **informal communications** consist of information exchanges without a planned agenda that occur informally among employees. Many informal communications take place among employees who form friendships or networks of mutual assistance at the water fountain or in the hallway, company cafeteria, offices, or parking lot. Informal communications pass along information that is usually not available through more formal communication channels—for example, the size of upcoming merit pay increases, who is in line for a big promotion, who has received an outside job offer, and who has gotten a low performance evaluation and is upset about it.

Informal communications can be the source of creative ideas. US West, a regional telecommunications company, has designed a new research facility to take advantage of the benefits of informal communication. The architect designed "breakout rooms" and hallways to optimize spontaneous interactions between technicians and scientists so that informal groups can brainstorm together to solve technical problems and generate ideas.

management by walking around (MBWA)
A technique in which managers walk around and talk to employees informally to monitor informal communications, listen to employee grievances and suggestions, and build rapport and morale.

When organizations allow too much information to be communicated informally, there is a good chance that it will be distorted by rumor, gossip, and innuendo. The result may be poor employee morale and poor employee relations. To guard against this, the HR department and managers need to monitor informal communications and, when necessary, clarify them through more formal channels. One effective way to monitor informal communications is through **management by walking around (MBWA).** MBWA, championed by Tom Peters and Robert Waterman in their wildly successful book *In Search of Excellence*, is a management technique in which the manager walks around the company so that employees at all levels have an opportunity to offer suggestions or voice grievances. This management style is used to build rapport with employees and monitor morale at IBM and many other companies.

Employee Feedback Programs

To provide upward communications channels between employees and management, many organizations offer **employee feedback programs.** These programs are designed to improve management-employee relations by (1) giving employees a voice in decision making and policy formulation and (2) making sure that employees receive due process on any complaints they lodge against managers. The HR department not only designs and maintains employee feedback programs but is also expected to protect employee confidentiality in dealing with sensitive personal issues. HR personnel are also charged with ensuring that subordinates are not subject to retaliation from angry managers.

employee feedback program
A program designed to improve employee communications by giving employees a voice in policy formulation and making sure that they receive due process on any complaints they lodge against managers.

The most common employee feedback programs are employee attitude surveys, appeals procedures, and employee assistance programs. Here we discuss the first two kinds of programs, which are intended to resolve work-related problems. We discuss employee assistance programs (EAPs), which are designed to help employees resolve personal problems that are interfering with their job performance, later in this chapter.

Employee Attitude Surveys. Designed to measure workers' likes and dislikes of various aspects of their jobs, **employee attitude surveys** are typically formal and anonymous. They ask employees how they feel about the work they do, their supervisor, their work environment, their opportunities for advancement, the quality of the training they received, the company's treatment of women and minorities, and the fairness of the company's pay policies. An excerpt from an employee attitude survey is reproduced in Figure 13–5. The survey responses of various subgroups can be compared to those of the total employee population to help managers identify units or departments that are experiencing poor employee relations.

employee attitude survey
A formal anonymous survey designed to measure employee likes and dislikes of various aspects of their jobs.

Making specific improvements in employee relations can avert acts of sabotage or labor unrest (such as strikes, absenteeism, and turnover) that are directly attributable to strains between subordinates and managers. For example, in analyzing attitude survey

To what extent am I satisfied with...

	Highly Satisfied		Satisfied		Highly Dissatisfied
1. my pay and bonus	1	2	3	4	5
2. my benefits—overall	1	2	3	4	5
3. my chance to get a promotion or a better job	1	2	3	4	5
4. having a sense of well-being on the job	1	2	3	4	5
5. the respect and recognition I receive from management	1	2	3	4	5
6. my job security	1	2	3	4	5
7. the morale of my division	1	2	3	4	5
8. the degree of responsibility and autonomy I have in doing my work	1	2	3	4	5
9. the opportunity to have my ideas adopted	1	2	3	4	5
10. working with highly talented and capable people	1	2	3	4	5
11. interdivisional cooperation and communication	1	2	3	4	5

FIGURE 13–5

Excerpt from an Employee Attitude Survey

Source: Goodrich & Sherwood Company, 521 Fifth Avenue, New York, NY 10175. Used with permission.

data, a chain of retail stores in the Midwest found that employees at one store had much lower levels of satisfaction than the employees at any other store in the chain. The chain's top managers immediately realized this was the same store that had experienced several serious acts of sabotage. Instead of retaliating against employees, corporate management set out to solve the store's supervision problems with training and mediation.

To manage an employee attitude survey effectively, managers should follow three rules. First, they should tell employees what they plan to do with the information they collect and then inform them about the results of the survey. There is no point in surveying opinions unless the firm intends to act on them. Second, managers should use survey data ethically to monitor the state of employee relations, both throughout the company and within employee subgroups (such as women, accountants, or newly hired workers), and to make positive changes in the workplace. They should not use the information they collect to fire someone (for example, a supervisor whose workers are unhappy) or to take away privileges. Finally, to protect employee confidentiality and maintain the integrity of the data, the survey should be done by a third party, such as a consulting firm.

In which countries are workers the most satisfied with their jobs and their employers? According to a recent survey (Figure 13–6), Swiss workers are the happiest, while Japanese workers are the least happy. The United States falls in the middle range—at about the same level as Germany and Sweden, two countries known for their enlightened approaches to management.[27]

Appeals Procedures. Providing a mechanism for employees to voice their reactions to management practices and challenge management decisions will enhance employees' perception that the organization has fair employment policies. Organizations without an effective set of **appeals procedures** increase their risk of litigation, costly legal fees, and back-pay penalties to employees who use the courts to obtain justice.[28] Effective appeals procedures give individual employees some control over the decisions that affect them and help to identify managers who are ineffective or unfair.

appeals procedure
A procedure that allows employees to voice their reactions to management practices and to challenge management decisions.

Some of the most common management actions appealed by employees are:

- The allocation of overtime work
- Warnings for safety rule violations
- The size of merit pay increases
- The specification of job duties
- The employer's reimbursement for medical expense claims filed by employees
- Performance evaluations

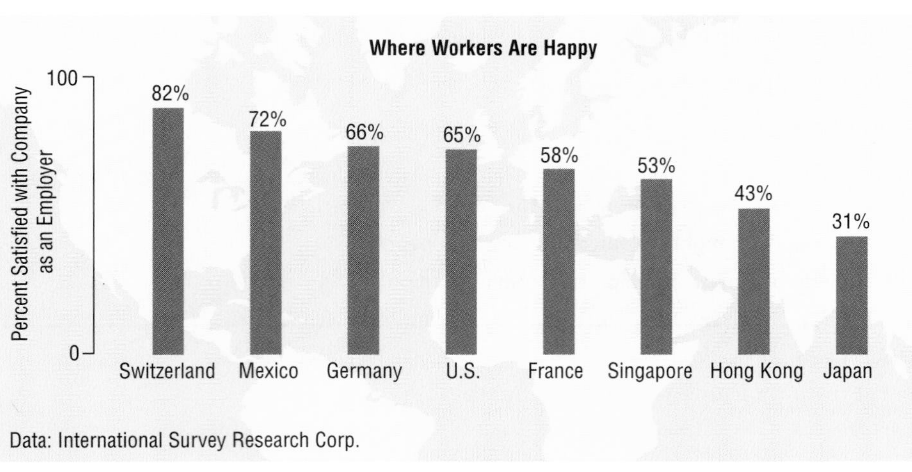

FIGURE 13–6

International Comparisons of Employee Satisfaction

Source: Reprinted from June 24, 1996 issue of *Business Week* by special permission, copyright © by The McGraw-Hill Companies, Inc.

Managers may choose from several different types of appeals procedures that vary in formality.[29] The most informal is an *open door program*. While the specifics of open door programs vary from company to company, the common theme is that all employees have direct access to any manager or executive in the organization. IBM's open door policy has been much admired and imitated. An IBM employee can walk into the office of any manager, up to and including the CEO, and ask for an opinion on a complaint or any other problem worrying the employee. The manager consulted must conduct a fair investigation into both sides of the issue and provide an answer within a specified period of time. For example, an employee who is dissatisfied with his or her performance evaluation may seek a second opinion from another manager. The open door policy has two major benefits: It makes employees feel more secure and committed to IBM, and it makes managers less likely to act arbitrarily.

Like the open door policy, a *speak-up program* is informal and flexible. It differs in that it prescribes specific steps for the employee to take in bringing a work problem to management's attention. CIGNA, a financial services and insurance company, has a speak-up program called Speak Easy that guarantees employees access to higher levels of management, but only after they bring their problems to the attention of their immediate supervisor (Figure 13–7).

Speak Easy

Speak Easy is a special program which gives you the opportunity to talk to management about work-related concerns. Speak Easy, with the support of CIGNA Corporation management, ensures an open line of communication and guarantees a timely response.

Through the Speak Easy Program, you may want to:

- Comment on your treatment as an employee;
- Describe a specific situation that is affecting your performance or the way you feel about your job.

Management wants to hear what you have to say…so Speak Easy.

Hear's how the program works:

Phase I. This is the first and most direct way to raise issues about your job or work situation. Go to your supervisor or manager and ask to talk over problems or questions. He or she is committed to listen and give you a fair and honest answer.

But if your supervisor or manager disagrees, cannot correct the situation, or is unwilling to change an earlier decision, Phase I offers you another step.

At your request, your supervisor will arrange interview(s) with additional levels of your management, including the top company official of your department or location. You will be invited to present your concerns, and every effort will be made to resolve your issue.

Phase II. Phase II has been designed for privately raising the matters not resolved in Phase I. You may be unhappy with the course of action taken or feel the matter is too touchy to go through your supervisor. Phase II will give you another audience—someone not directly involved in the situation. But it's important to note that this phase is normally **not a replacement for Phase I employee-management discussions.**

In Phase II of the program, your issues will be kept strictly confidential and reviewed impartially by the Speak Easy Coordinator. Only the coordinator will know your identity if you choose.

All you do is pick up a Speak Easy envelope located in holders throughout your office and fill in the pertinent information.… Then drop the completed form and envelope in the mail. You can expect a prompt response from the coordinator, so long as your signature, home address, and phone number are on the form. Otherwise, you cannot be contacted and advised of the results of the coordinator's review.

If, for some reason, the review cannot be continued without revealing your name, the coordinator will tell you. It will be your decision whether or not to continue.

Please remember the sole responsibility of the Speak Easy Coordinator is to make sure that your situation is dealt with fairly and equitably.

Phase III. This is the final step if you still aren't completely satisfied with the decision. This phase gives you direct access to the Head of your Operating Group or Staff Organization.

If after using Phases I and II, you are not satisfied with the decision about your situation, you may send a Speak Easy form or a letter fully stating the issue to the Head of your Operating Group or Staff Organization with a copy to your Speak Easy Coordinator.

The situation will be immediately reviewed and you will be informed promptly of the final resolution of your appeal. If the review supports the previous opinions or decisions, these will be upheld; if not, the prior decision will be modified.

FIGURE 13–7

Excerpt from CIGNA's Speak Easy Brochure

Source: Excerpt from CIGNA's "Speak Easy" Brochure. Reprinted with permission of the CIGNA Corporation.

The grievance panel and the union grievance procedure are the most formal mechanisms used by organizations to handle employee complaints. *Grievance panels* are used in nonunion firms. They are composed of the complaining employee's peers and managers other than the employee's direct manager. The grievance panel conducts an investigation into the grievance brought before it. Grievance panels are typically the last step in the appeal process. For example, Honeywell's grievance panel, called the Management Appeals Committee, is asked to resolve a grievance only if solutions have not been found at earlier steps involving, first, the employee's supervisor and, second, an employee relations representative.

The *union grievance procedure* is the appeals procedure used by all employees working under a union contract. Like the grievance panel procedure, it entails multiple steps leading to a final and binding decision made by a neutral decision maker called an arbitrator. The union grievance procedure is an important feature of labor contracts, and we will explain it in greater detail in Chapter 15.

Organizations should use a mix of appeals procedures. For instance, a company might implement an open door policy to deal with fairly simple problems that can be resolved quickly (such as determining whether an employee violated a safety rule). Next, it might institute an employee assistance program to deal with sensitive problems that involve an employee's privacy (such as a terminal illness). Finally, it might set up a grievance panel to examine complex problems affecting employee relations within a group or organizational unit (such as the definition of a fair production quality standard).

Employee Assistance Programs

employee assistance program (EAP)
A company-sponsored program that helps employees cope with personal problems that are interfering with their job performance.

Employee assistance programs (EAPs) help employees cope with personal problems that are interfering with their job performance. These problems may include alcohol or drug abuse, domestic violence, elder care, AIDS and other diseases, eating disorders, and compulsive gambling.[30] Organizations with EAPs publicize the programs to employees and assure them that their problems will be handled confidentially. When an employee's personal problem interferes with job performance, the individual is considered a *troubled employee*.[31] In a typical company about 10% of the total employee population at any given time is troubled.

Figure 13–8 shows some of the symptoms of a troubled employee. A troubled employee generally behaves inconsistently in terms of attendance, quality of work, atten-

1. Excessive absenteeism patterns: Mondays, Fridays, days before and after holidays
2. Unexcused absences
3. Frequent absences
4. Tardiness and early departures
5. Altercations with coworkers
6. Causing injuries to other employees through negligence
7. Poor judgment and bad decisions
8. Unusual on-the-job accidents
9. Increased spoilage and breaking of equipment through negligence
10. Involvements with the law—for example, a DWI (driving while intoxicated) conviction
11. Deteriorating personal appearance

FIGURE 13–8

Symptoms of a Troubled Employee

Source: Adapted from Filipowicz, C. A. (1979). The troubled employee: Whose responsibility? *Personnel Administrator, 24*(6), 8. Reprinted with the permission of *HRMagazine* (formerly *Personnel Administrator*) published by the Society for Human Resource Management, Alexandria, VA.

tion to detail, and concern for personal appearance. A great deal of the person's energy is devoted to coping with a personal crisis that he or she may want to keep secret from the company. Until this personal problem is resolved, the employee will be in emotional and/or physical pain and the company will be deprived of the full benefit of his or her skills. It is therefore in the interests of both the troubled employee and the employer to resolve the problem.

Four steps are involved in the operation of an EAP (Figure 13–9):

1. The first step is identifying troubled employees and referring them for counseling. About half of all referrals are self-referrals by employees who realize they are in a crisis and need help, but want to keep their problem confidential. The other half are made by supervisors who observe some of the symptoms of a troubled employee. When job performance is deficient, the EAP referral is usually linked to the company's discipline procedure—it may be the last step taken before the employee is dismissed. Employees have the right to refuse to participate in the EAP, but refusal may mean termination if the problem has a significant negative impact on their work. In fact, though, many employees appreciate the company's willingness to help them through EAP counseling.
2. The second step after referral is a visit with an EAP counselor, who interviews the employee to help identify the problem. In the case of a complex personal problem like alcohol abuse, employees may strongly deny having a problem. The counselor, however, is trained to identify the problem and arrange for treatment.
3. The third step is to solve the problem. Sometimes the EAP counselor is able to help the employee do this in a short time (three sessions or fewer). For example, an employee in financial difficulty may need only short-term counseling in how to manage personal finances. Some problems, however, take longer to resolve. For these, the EAP counselor will send the troubled employee to an outside agency equipped to provide the necessary treatment. The counselor will try to find a service that best fits the employee's needs and is also cost-effective. For example, an EAP counselor who determines that an employee needs treatment for alcoholism must decide if the employee should receive inpatient residential treatment, receive outpatient treatment, or attend Alcoholics Anonymous (AA) meetings.[32] Inpatient residential treatment may require a 30-day hospitalization period that costs about $15,000. The other two alternatives cost much less.
4. The fourth and final step depends on the outcome of the treatment. If the employee has been placed on leave and the treatment is successful, the employee is allowed to return

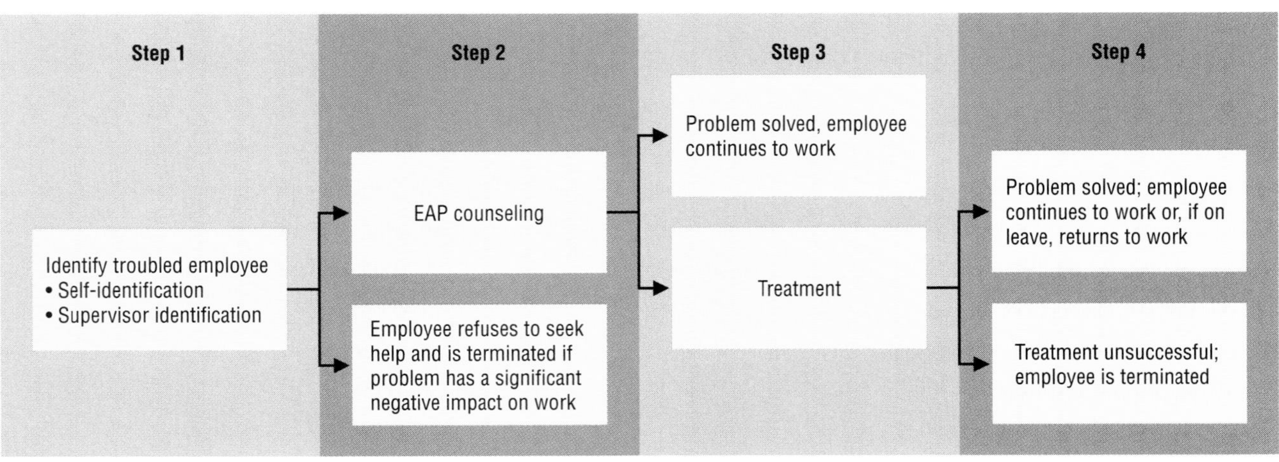

FIGURE 13–9

An Employee Assistance Program

to work. In some cases, treatment does not require the employee to take a leave of absence; the employee remains on the job while being treated and continues after treatment has been successfully concluded. If the treatment is unsuccessful and the difficulty continues to disrupt the employee's work performance, the employer usually terminates the employee.

EAPs can help employees suffering from anxiety and stress due to restructurings or downsizings. The EAP at Rohm & Haas, a specialty chemical company headquartered in Philadelphia, played an important role in easing the effects of downsizing the company's production facility. When employment was cut from 800 to about 550, the company negotiated with its EAP vendor for an on-site psychologist who, in addition to maintaining office hours at the plant, sat in on management meetings and walked around the plant talking to employees. At GTE, EAPs are used to identify and provide support for managers who are dealing with people who are being let go or transferred.[33]

In the United States there are more than 12,000 EAPs; 75% of *Fortune* 500 companies use them[34] to deal with a wide variety of problems. Gambling casinos in the Atlantic City, New Jersey area have used EAPs to deal with the high incidence of alcohol- and drug-related performance problems that employees in the gambling industry experience. The EAP for the Association of Flight Attendants, which represents flight attendants from 19 airlines, has an unusually large number of individuals seeking help for weight loss.[35]

EAPs contribute to effective employee relations because they represent a good-faith attempt by management to support and retain employees who might otherwise be dismissed because of poor performance. The annual cost per employee of an EAP runs about $30 to $40.[36] However, employers gain financial benefits that outweigh their out-of-pocket EAP expenses in terms of savings on employee turnover, absenteeism, medical costs, unemployment insurance rates, workers' compensation rates, accident costs, and disability insurance costs. One study showed that the rate of problem resolution for EAPs is about 78%.[37] ▼

▸ Employee Recognition Programs

employee recognition program A program that rewards employees for their ideas and contributions.

Companies operating in global markets need employees who continuously improve the way they do their jobs to keep the company competitive. Employees are more likely to share their ideas for work improvements when managers give them credit for their contributions. **Employee recognition programs** can enhance employee relations by communicating that the organization cares about its employees' ideas and is willing to reward them for their efforts. The HR department can help here by developing and maintaining formal employee recognition programs such as suggestion systems and recognition awards.

Suggestion Systems

A *suggestion system* is designed to solicit, evaluate, and implement suggestions from employees, and then reward the employees for worthwhile ideas.[38] Although the reward is often monetary, it does not have to be. It might instead be public recognition, extra vacation time, a special parking spot, or some other benefit. Suggestion systems have been successfully implemented in such diverse organizations as hospitals, universities, the U.S. Postal Service and other branches of government, and private-sector companies such as Amoco, Eastman Kodak, Black & Decker, Simon & Schuster, and Lincoln Electric Company.[39] The Issues and Applications feature titled "The Suggestion System at American Airlines: A Win-Win Situation" shows how both a company and its employees can benefit from a well-designed suggestion system.

Managers should adhere to three guidelines when designing a suggestion system. They should:

Issues + Applications

The Suggestion System at American Airlines: A Win-Win Situation

A well-designed suggestion system can be profitable for both a company and its employees. In three months, the American Achievers suggestion program at American Airlines inspired nearly 3,500 seven-person teams to provide more than 1,600 suggestions that the company adopted. These suggestions resulted in more than $20 million in cost-saving or revenue-generating improvements for the company. Employees earned more than $4.7 million in merchandise prizes, with each prize based on the cash value of the idea that was implemented. In addition, the employees enthusiastically supported the policy changes derived from the suggestions because they had designed them. The success of the suggestion program has led to a continuing system called AAchievers, which provides instant rewards for excellent individual or team contributions.

How does the AAchievers program work? Managers, crew chiefs, and other supervisors can award Achiever points at any time for any reason to any employee or team. For example, points can be awarded to employees for helping a passenger with an emergency or for bringing in new business. These points are issued on certificates that can be exchanged for travel benefits or merchandise from a catalog compiled for the program.

Source: Adapted from Nelson, B. (1994). *1001 ways to reward employees,* New York: Workman Publishing, 104.

- Use a suggestion evaluation committee to evaluate each suggestion fairly and provide an explanation to employees why their suggestions have not been used.
- Implement accepted suggestions immediately and give credit to the suggestion's originator. The company newsletter can be used to publicly recognize employees whose suggestions have resulted in improvements.
- Make the value of the reward proportional to the suggestion's benefit to the company. For example, a loan manager at Bank of America who made a suggestion that saved the bank $363,520 a year received a cash award of $36,520 for her idea.[40]

Suggestion systems, long a part of U.S. business, have become more popular globally in recent years. For example, Japanese companies have successfully gathered numerous suggestions from their employees, resulting in significant improvements in their products (including automobiles).

Recognition Awards

Recognition awards give public credit to people or teams that make outstanding contributions to the organization. These people or teams may become role models for others by communicating what behaviors and accomplishments the company values. McDonald's Employee of the Month award consists of a notice posted in each restaurant for all employees and customers to see. IBM employees who make major contributions are recognized in a host of different ways, ranging from a simple thank-you letter from a division manager to a cash award of $150,000 (recently given to two company scientists who won the Nobel Prize in science).

The recognition of teams and people who make important quality contributions is an important component of a total quality management (TQM) program. The recognition awards associated with TQM can be either monetary or nonmonetary. For example, Federal Express allows supervisors to confer instant cash awards to employees for quality efforts.[41] Fed Ex has earned the Malcolm Baldrige National Quality Award, the highest recognition of quality that a U.S. company can receive.

A recognition award can be initiated by a manager or by an internal customer of an individual or a team, with nominees evaluated by a recognition and awards committee. To emphasize that quality improvement should be continuous, there should be no limit on the number of times that a person or team can receive a recognition award.

A recognition award should be a celebration of the team or individual's success that encourages all organization members to work toward the organization's goals.[42] Recognition awards that focus attention on team or individual accomplishments include:

- A company-paid picnic to which all team members and their families are invited.
- T-shirts, coffee mugs, or baseball caps with a team insignia encouraging team commitment.
- A company-paid night on the town (such as dinner at a nice restaurant or tickets to a concert or sports event) for an employee and his or her spouse.
- A plaque engraved with the names of individuals or teams that have made outstanding contributions.

Recognition programs can serve purposes other than providing positive feedback to employees. A Phoenix area hotel rewarded employees who made outstanding contributions with a free night's stay at the hotel. Not only was this a valued prize, but it also gave employees the chance to view their organization from the customer's perspective. Management hoped that this experience would prompt new suggestions for improving customer service.

Summary and Conclusions

The Roles of the Manager and the Employee Relations Specialist. Good employee relations involve providing fair and consistent treatment to all employees so that they will be committed to the organization. The backbone of an effective employee relations program is the manager, who is expected to evaluate, reward, and discipline employees in line with the company's employee relations philosophy. Employee relations representatives from the HR department ensure that employment policies are being fairly and consistently administered within the company. They often consult with both supervisors and employees on specific employee relations problems.

Developing Employee Communications. To develop effective employee relations, a company needs communication channels to move information up, down, and across the organization. Effective communications in an organization involve (1) a sender who encodes the message, (2) a communication channel that transmits the message, (3) a receiver who decodes the message, and (4) provisions for feedback because noise in the environment may distort the message's true meaning.

Facilitating Effective Communications. Working with supervisors and managers, employee relations representatives can facilitate effective communications by developing provisions for (1) information dissemination, (2) employee feedback, and (3) employee assistance programs.

Information dissemination involves making information available to decision makers, wherever they are located. Employee handbooks, written communications (memos, financial statements, newsletters, and bulletin boards), audiovisual communications, electronic communications (voice mail, e-mail, and multimedia applications), meetings, retreats, and informal communications are some of the choices available for disseminating information to employees.

Employee feedback programs are designed to improve communications by giving employees a voice in decision making and policy formulation and making sure they receive due process on any complaints they lodge against managers. Two programs that the HR department can establish to solicit employee feedback are (1) employee attitude surveys and (2) appeals procedures.

Employee assistance programs are designed to help employees whose emotional or psychological troubles are affecting their work performance. The employee is given the opportunity and resources to resolve the problem. Successful resolution of personal problems benefits both the employer and the employee.

Employee Recognition Programs. Employee recognition programs can enhance communications and employee relations by recognizing and rewarding employees who make important contributions to the organization's success. Recognition programs often use suggestion systems and recognition awards. The rewards given to individuals or teams may be monetary or nonmonetary.

Key Terms

appeals procedure, 410
downward communication, 399
electronic mail (e-mail), 404
employee assistance program (EAP), 412
employee attitude survey, 409
employee feedback program, 409
employee recognition program, 414
employee relations policy, 397
employee relations representative, 397
informal communications, 408
information dissemination, 400
knowledge worker, 400
management by walking around (MBWA), 408
multimedia technology, 405
nepotism, 400
teleconferencing, 402
upward communication, 399
voice mail, 403

Discussion Questions

1. List three ways the HR department can contribute to positive employee relations in a company.
2. Employee privacy has been called "today's most important workplace issue." What kinds of dilemmas have the new technologies created regarding employee privacy? What other kinds of problems have the new technologies created in employee relations and communications, and how might managers deal with them?
3. Bob Allenby's company handbook states that employees will be fired only if they violate the company's listed reasons for termination. Bob is fired, yet his conduct did not match any of the reasons outlined in the handbook. He has decided to file a lawsuit against his company for wrongful dismissal. Can an employee handbook be considered an employment contract, and if so, is Bob's company liable in this case? What can HR specialists do to protect a company against such lawsuits?
4. What are the advantages and disadvantages of telecommuting employees from the company's perspective?
5. Why do employees not take suggestion systems seriously in some companies? What can management do to improve the credibility of its employee suggestion system?
6. Shelly Wexler tells her supervisor, Rob Levine, that having to care for her aging mother is forcing her to leave work early and is making her feel increasingly "stressed out." While Rob refers her to the company's EAP, he also tries to convince her to put her mother in a home for the aged and even gives her some information about nursing homes in the area. Do you think Rob is just showing ordinary concern for his employee, or do you think he is overstepping managerial boundaries? Discuss the supervisor's role in implementing an EAP. Should a supervisor try to diagnose an employee's personal problem? Why or why not?
7. Do you think most employees have reservations about using an appeals procedure such as an open door policy? What can managers do to convince employees that the available procedures are fair and effective?

MINICASE 1 A Publisher Opens Its Books

Many companies talk about sharing financial information with employees, but McDougal Littel, a publisher of educational materials in Evanston, Illinois, has gone a step further. To help its employees understand the monthly financial reports it distributes, the company sends all of its employees to a day-long accounting class and a customized seminar that explains a year's worth of company financials. And because all kinds of training need to be reinforced, the company holds monthly budget meetings that all managers are required to attend but that are also open to everyone else in the company. "This is to reinforce the notion that the company financials are not a secret," stresses the company's controller.

The financial lessons are paying off. A case in point: When several inventory control managers were preparing for a quarterly budget meeting, they grew concerned that the distribution center was spending $13,000 to store excess inventory in an outside facility. So they devised a way to use their existing warehouse space better by timing the purchasing of materials to keep inventory down. Other payoffs: More sales reps are booking lower air fares by taking advantage of Saturday night stayovers and customer service reps are questioning expensive priority mail shipments.

Discussion Questions

1. Can you think of situations in which a company should withhold financial information from its employees?
2. Do you think knowledge of the company's financial situation is enough to motivate employees to trim costs? What type of compensation system might be implemented to motivate employees to cut costs?

Source: Adapted, by permission of the publisher, from Livingston, A. (1993, November). There are no secrets here. *Small Business Report*, 9–13.

MINICASE 2 Does E-Mail Decrease Employee Productivity?

A recent study by EdWel & Co., a Chicago-based consulting firm, examined the use of e-mail at *Fortune* 500 companies. The study revealed high levels of inefficiency in both message quality and usage patterns in company e-mail systems. Some people received 80 to 100 e-mail messages per day, and the average e-mail user received about 15 messages per day and spent almost 50 minutes merely reading the messages. Because half of the messages were likely to require a response, it was not uncommon for e-mail users to spend one quarter of the workday reading and responding to e-mail communications.

The study also found a disturbingly high percentage of ineffective, poorly written e-mail messages. More than 65% of all e-mail messages failed to give receivers enough information to allow them to act effectively on the message. Lack of organization and clarity, poor grammar, and misinformation were all cited as common problems. The constant barrage of less-than-useful e-mail messages disrupts work flows and robs employees of productive time.

Discussion Questions

1. Management has asked you to develop a set of e-mail guidelines that addresses the problems identified in the EdWel study. What are your recommendations?
2. Do you think employees should be trained in the use of e-mail? What should be the goals of the training? How might the training be delivered to employees?

Source: Adapted from Frazee, V. (1996, May). Is e-mail doing more harm than good? *Personnel Journal*, 23.

CASE 1 Casual Dress at Digital Devices

Digital Devices designs and manufactures custom integrated circuits for electronic consumer products such as pocket pagers, electronic calculators, and cellular phones. Based on the results of an employee attitude survey, the company's top executives decided to implement a casual dress code policy for Digital employees. Management announced the casual dress policy in the employee newsletter and in an e-mail message sent to all employees. The policy stated simply that employees are encouraged to come to work in casual clothes except on days when they have meetings with clients (on those days, appropriate business attire is required).

There are several advantages of casual dress for both the company and employees. Casual dress improves employee morale by reducing status barriers that tend to separate managers (who are likely to wear suits and ties) from nonmanagement personnel. There is likely to be better communication and collaboration throughout the organization when status barriers are reduced. Casual dress is a good recruiting tool for top technical people, who tend to be young engineering graduates who want to work in a progressive company with a "fun" atmosphere. Employees also like the fact that casual dress is more comfortable and saves them money—they don't have to buy more expensive business clothes or use dry cleaning services to maintain the clothing.

Six months after the casual dress policy was announced, Sharon Greene, Digital's manager of human resources, noticed that the casual dress policy was a mixed blessing. Several unanticipated problems cropped up with employees' misuse of the policy, including the following:

- Some employees try to test the limits of casual dress. Computer programmers have come to work in T-shirts displaying their favorite rock bands, such as the Grateful Dead, that may have references to drug use or sexual innuendoes that may offend other employees or clients.
- Employees' behavior has become more casual, and in phone conversations with clients they often refer to customers or prospects as "buddies." This casuality has resulted in some complaints to the sales manager.
- The HR department is now referred to as the "fashion police" because it is expected to uphold dress standards when employees wear inappropriate dress (tank tops, bicycle shorts, jeans with holes in them, and so on). This new role has undermined some of HR's credibility.

Greene is now contemplating ways to improve the casual dress policy at Digital Devices.

Critical Thinking Questions

1. Do you think Digital Devices should abandon its casual dress policy? Why or why not?
2. Suppose that Digital decides to revise its casual dress policy. Should the revised policy list approved types of clothing and unacceptable types of clothing so that employees know exactly what they can and cannot wear to work? Are there any potential problems with this approach?
3. How should the company communicate the revised casual dress policy to its employees?

Cooperative Learning Exercise

4. The class divides into groups of four or five students each. Each group develops a new casual dress code policy for Digital Devices. One representative of each group presents the group's recommended policy to the class. Other students and the instructor may ask questions or comment on the features of each group's policy.

CASE 2 Was the Loader Loaded?

Bill Slater is the operations manager of a distribution center for a national auto parts retailer. The distribution center has 65 employees, mostly inventory clerks, truck loaders, and forklift operators.

Slater suspects that Phil McCoy, one of the truck loaders, has a drinking problem, and he is concerned that this problem could lead to an accident and/or hurt the morale of the other loaders, all of whom work in teams. Slater is considering a confrontation with McCoy before the problem turns into a disaster.

Slater's suspicion about McCoy arose from McCoy's behavior both at work and off the job. Slater and some of the distribution center's other employees usually go out for drinks on Fridays after work to celebrate the end of the week. Slater has noticed that McCoy drinks as many as four or five bottles of beer on Fridays, while Slater and the others drink no more than two. McCoy, normally a quiet man, becomes loud and animated at these get-togethers. One Friday night, McCoy

continued

Was the Loader Loaded? continued

made some critical comments about Slater's leadership style, indicating that Slater is not a very good listener.

The incident that convinced Slater he must deal with McCoy immediately happened just yesterday. McCoy had come to work with his hair uncombed and a day's growth of stubble on his face. When Slater greeted McCoy on the loading dock, McCoy's words were so slurred that his response was barely understandable. Later that day, Kathy Jaworski, one of the other loaders on McCoy's loading team, told Slater that she saw at least six empty beer cans in the back seat of McCoy's car as she passed it in the company parking lot that morning.

Critical Thinking Questions

1. Do you think Slater should confront McCoy about his drinking problem? Or should he let it go until something serious happens?
2. How convincing is the evidence that McCoy has a drinking problem?
3. What advice would an employee relations representative be likely to give Slater about handling this problem?

Cooperative Learning Exercises

4. One student plays the role of Slater and another the role of McCoy at a meeting Slater has set up to confront McCoy with the evidence of his drinking problem. The class should evaluate Slater's effectiveness at this meeting. What has he done well? How could his effectiveness in this situation be improved?
5. One student plays Slater and another an employee relations representative to whom Slater has gone for advice about how to handle the situation described in this case. What specific advice would be appropriate in this situation?

HRM Simulation

Do you think your company needs a formal grievance procedure? Refer to page 9 of the players' manual. Are there any alternatives to the grievance procedure that may be appropriate for the company? Who in the company should handle the grievances—department heads, a representative from the HR department, or someone else? Since this is a nonunion company, is it possible to have a fair grievance procedure even though employees do not have the benefit of union representation?

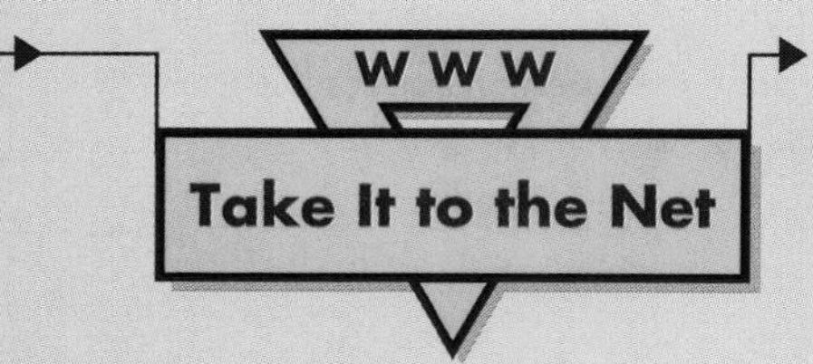

We invite you to visit the Gómez-Mejía/Balkin/Cardy page on the Prentice Hall Web site:

http://www.prenhall.com/gomez

You can also visit the Web sites for these companies, featured within this chapter:

Bank of America	http://www.BankAmerica.com
Black and Decker	http://www.blackanddecker.com
Cadillac	http://www.cadillac.com
Epson	http://www.epson.com
Outward Bound	http://www.outwardbound.org
Rohm and Haas	http://www.rohmhaas.com
Simon & Schuster	http://www.simonandschuster.com

Endnotes

1. Lawler, E. E. III (1992). *The ultimate advantage*. San Francisco: Jossey-Bass.
2. Noer, D. M. (1993). *Healing the wounds: Overcoming the trauma of layoffs and revitalizing downsized organizations*, 103–104. San Francisco: Jossey-Bass.
3. Johnson, P. R., and Gardner, S. (1989). Legal pitfalls of employee handbooks. *SAM Advanced Management Journal, 54*(2), 42–46.
4. Hesser, R. G. (1991, July). Watch your language. *Small Business Reports*, 45–49.
5. Johnson and Gardner, 1989.
6. Brady, T. (1993, June). Employee handbooks: Contracts or empty promises? *Management Review*, 33–35.
7. Aronoff, C. E., and Ward, J. L. (1993, January). Rules for nepotism. *Nation's Business*, 64–65.
8. Sosnin, B. (1996, June). Corporate newsletters improve employee morale. *HRMagazine*, 106–110.
9. Lawler, 1992.
10. Flanagan, P. (1994, February). Videoconferencing changes the corporate meeting. *Management Review*, 7; and Bhargava, S. W., and Coy, P. (1991, November 12). Videoscreen meetings: Still out of sight. *Business Week*, 162E.
11. Blackburn, R., and Rozen, B. (1993, August). Total quality and human resources management: Lessons learned from Baldrige Award–winning companies. *Academy of Management Executive*, 49–66.
12. *Information Management Forum*. (1993, January). Voice mail or voice pony express, insert into *Management Review*, 3.
13. Weeks, D. (1995, February). Voice mail: Blessing or curse? *World Traveler*, 51–54.
14. Lawler, 1992.
15. Pearl, J. A. (1993, July). The e-mail quandary. *Management Review*, 48–51.
16. *Id.*
17. Crawford, M. (1993, May). The new office etiquette. *Canadian Business*, 22–31.
18. Brady, R. (1995, October). Electronic mail: Drafting a policy. *HR Focus*, 19; Daniel, T. (1995, Summer). Electronic and voice mail monitoring of employees: A practical approach. *Employee Relations Today*, 1–10; and Weiss, B. (1996, January). Four black holes in cyberspace. *Management Review*, 30–32.
19. *Information Management Forum*. (1993, July). Who's reading your e-mail? an insert into *Management Review*, 1, 4; and Casarez, N. B. (1993, Summer), Electronic mail and employee relations: Why privacy must be considered. *Public Relations Quarterly*, 37–39.
20. *Economist*. (1996, April 20). Textbooks on CD-ROM, 11.
21. Kugelmass, J. (1995). *Telecommuting*. New York: Lexington Books.
22. Mintzberg, H. (1975, July–August). The manager's job: Folklore or fact. *Harvard Business Review, 53*, 69–71.
23. Michaels, E. A. (1989, February). Business meetings. *Small Business Reports*, 82–88.
24. Interview of Deborah Tannen by L. A. Lusardi (1990, July). Power talk. *Working Woman*, 92–94.
25. Elashmawi, F. (1991, November). Multicultural business meetings and presentations. *Tokyo Business Today, 59*(11), 66–68.
26. Montgomery, E. (1993, October). A family affair. *Small Business Reports*, 10–14; and Jaffe, D. T. (1992, June). How to create a family council. *Nation's Business*, 54–55. For more on succession planning, see *Inc*. (1996, July). Three ways to plan ahead, 96.
27. Mandel, M. J. (1996, June 24). Satisfaction at work. *Business Week*, 28.
28. Gómez-Mejía, L. R., and Balkin, D. B. (1992). *Compensation, organizational strategy, and firm performance*. Cincinnati, OH: South-Western.
29. Aram, J. D., and Salipante, P. F., Jr. (1981). An evaluation of organizational due process in the resolution of employee/employer conflict. *Academy of Management Review, 16*, 197–204.
30. Kirrane, D. (1990). EAPs: Dawning of a new age. *HRMagazine,* 35(1), 30–34.
31. Filipowicz, C. A. (1979). The troubled employee: Whose responsibility? *Personnel Administrator, 24*(6), 5–10.
32. Carson, K. D., and Balkin, D. B. (1992). An employee assistance model of health care management for employees with alcohol-related problems. *Journal of Employment Counseling, 29,* 146–156.
33. Wise, D. (1993, April). Employee assistance programs expand to fit companies' needs. *Business & Health*, 40–45.
34. Feldman, S. (1991, February). Today's EAPs make the grade. *Personnel*, 3.
35. Fisher, C., Schoenfeldt, L., and Shaw, J. (1996). *Human Resource Management*, 3rd ed. Boston, MA: Houghton Mifflin.
36. Cascio, W. F. (1991). *Costing human resources: The financial impact of behavior in organizations* (Vol. 6) (3rd ed.). Boston: PWS-Kent.
37. Luthans, F., and Waldersee, R. (1989). What do we really know about EAPs? *Human Resource Management, 28,* 385–401.
38. Meyers, D. W. (1986). *Human resources management*. Chicago: Commerce Clearing House.
39. Nelson, B. (1994). *1001 ways to reward employees*. New York: Workman Publishing.
40. Trunko, M. E. (1993). Open to suggestions. *HRMagazine, 38*(2), 85–89.
41. Knouse, S. (1995). *The reward and recognition process*. Milwaukee, WI: ASQC Quality Press.
42. Orsburn, J. D., Moran, L., Musselwhite, E., and Zenger, J. H. (1990). *Self-directed work teams*. Homewood, IL: Business One Irwin.

14 Respecting Employee Rights and Managing Discipline

CHALLENGES

After reading this chapter, you should be able to deal more effectively with the following challenges:

1 ▶ **Understand** the origins and the scope of employee rights and management rights.

2 ▶ **Explain** why the HR department must balance management's rights and employees' rights when designing employment policies.

3 ▶ **Describe** the employment-at-will doctrine.

4 ▶ **Distinguish** between progressive discipline procedures and positive discipline procedures.

5 ▶ **Apply** fair standards to a case of employee misconduct and justify the use of discipline.

6 ▶ **Manage** difficult people who challenge their supervisors with such problems as poor attendance, low performance, insubordination, and substance abuse.

7 ▶ **Avoid** disciplinary actions by taking a proactive and strategic approach to HRM.

A Problem Employee? Managers need to be trained to recognize the symptoms of troubled employees and potential disciplinary problems. In addition to dealing with drug- and alcohol-related problems in the workplace, managers must often confront employees who exhibit poor attendance, insubordination, or poor performance.

http://www.doc.gov:80/nlrb/homepg.html

National Labor Relations Board

This Web site is the home page of the National Labor Relations Board (NLRB), the independent federal agency that administers U.S. labor law. The NLRB's Web site includes an information locater and summaries of its recent decisions.

All employees have rights that are based on laws, company employment policies, and traditions. Employers also have rights that support their authority and what they can expect from their employees. Sometimes these two sets of rights conflict. Consider the following situations:

- Hooters, a chain of sports bars, makes its waitresses wear a uniform of tight-fitting shorts and a low-cut blouse. How strictly could managers enforce this dress code for women who want to wear more modest clothing?
- A few weeks after James Russell Wiggins accepted a job with District Cablevision in Washington, DC, the company performed a background check on Wiggins. The check indicated that he had been previously convicted of cocaine possession. Wiggins protested that the information was wrong, but to no avail—District Cablevision fired him. Later, it was discovered that James *Russell* Wiggins's identity had been confused with that of James *Ray* Wiggins. The unemployed Wiggins now has a $10 million lawsuit against Equifax and Cablevision tied up in the courts. Do employees have privacy rights that limit how employers can use information from background checks?[1]
- Like many other companies, the Turner Broadcasting Company has a "no-smoker" policy that forbids its employees to smoke either on or off the job. Managers justify strict no-smoking policies because smokers raise the cost of health benefits for all employees. Employees have lost their jobs for violating a no-smoker policy. Do no-smoker policies infringe on an employee's right to engage in legal behavior (smoking) during nonwork hours?[2]

These examples suggest that the rights of both employees and employers should be clearly spelled out in every employment relationship. The HR department can help by (1) developing and enforcing policies that inform employees of their rights and responsibilities and (2) making managers aware of their employees' rights and managers' obligations to employees. But it is the manager who can make the difference here. Managers who respect employees' rights are more likely to have subordinates with high levels of morale and job satisfaction than managers who ignore these rights. Respecting employees' rights also lessens the likelihood of a costly grievance procedure or lawsuit.

In this chapter, we examine employee rights and employee discipline. These two issues are closely related to the quality of employee relations (discussed in the preceding chapter). Organizations with effective employee relations ensure that their managers respect employees' rights and use fair and consistent discipline procedures.

First, we examine the concepts of employee rights, management rights, and the employment-at-will doctrine that governs many nonunion employers. Second, we explore some challenges that managers encounter in balancing employee rights with the rights of management. Next, we discuss employee discipline and offer some suggestions for managing difficult employees. We conclude by examining how the HR department can support managers with proactive policies that minimize the need for disciplinary procedures.

▸ Employee Rights

right
The ability to engage in conduct that is protected by law or social sanction, free from interference by another party.

A **right** is the ability to engage in conduct that is protected by law or social sanction, free from interference by another party (such as an employer). For example, employees have the legal right to form a union. It is illegal for an employer to discourage employees from exercising their right to form a union by withholding pay increases from those who support the union.

The scope of *employee rights* has broadened in the last 35 years as the federal and state governments have enacted laws giving employees specific protections. Additionally, in the last decade courts have been more willing to protect employees from wrongful discharge than they were in the past. Many believe that the courts have been more proactive in protecting employees' rights because of the shrinking proportion of the labor force that is protected by union contracts.

Figure 14–1 shows the three different categories of employee rights that managers must consider: (1) statutory rights, (2) contractual rights, and (3) other rights.

Statutory Rights

statutory right
A right protected by specific laws.

Employees' **statutory rights** are protected by specific laws enacted by government. Employees' key statutory right is protection from discrimination based on race, sex, religion, national origin, age, handicap, or other protected status under Title VII of the Civil Rights Act of 1964 and other equal employment opportunity laws (see Chapter 3). The *Equal Employment Opportunity Commission (EEOC)* regulates employer conduct to ensure that employees are not discriminated against.

Another important employee statutory right is protection from unsafe or unhealthy working conditions. The Occupational Safety and Health Act (OSHA) requires employers to provide safe working conditions for workers and has established the *Occupational Safety and Health Administration* to regulate health and safety practices at companies (see Chapter 16).

Employees also have the legal right to form unions and participate in union activities (see Chapter 15). The *National Labor Relations Board* (NLRB) regulates employer and employee conduct to ensure fair labor practices.

Contractual Rights

contractual right
A right based on the law of contracts.

contract
A legally binding promise between two or more competent parties.

employment contract
A contract that spells out explicitly the terms of the employment relationship for both employee and employer.

Contractual rights are based on the law of contracts. A **contract** is a legally binding promise between two or more competent parties.[3] A breach of contract, in which one of the parties does not perform his or her promised duty to the other party, is subject to legal remedy.

Both employers and employees have rights and obligations to each other when they enter into a contract. An **employment contract** spells out explicitly the terms of the employment relationship for both employee and employer. In general, such contracts state that the employee is expected to work competently over a stipulated period of time and that the employer is expected to provide a mutually agreed upon amount of pay, as well as specific working conditions, over this time period.[4] Employees covered by employment con-

Statutory Rights	Contractual Rights	Other Rights
• Protection from discrimination • Safe working conditions • Right to form unions	• Employment contract • Union contract • Implied contracts/ employment policies	• Ethical treatment • Privacy (limited) • Free speech (limited)

FIGURE 14–1
Categories of Employee Rights

tracts include nonunionized public school teachers, college football coaches, actors in film and television, and top-level executives. Only a very small percentage of the labor force works under employment contracts.

The provisions of the employment contract give the employee job security and are, at least theoretically, negotiated individually. We say "theoretically" because there are cases in which contracts are so similar as to be standard. For instance, many public school teachers not covered by union contracts are hired on a year-to-year basis by the school district. In theory, each teacher negotiates his or her own contract. In practice, because of the volume of contracts that must be written, the vast majority of these contracts follow a standard pattern. For some high-profile jobs, such as top-level executives, the contract will not follow the standard pattern and will, in fact, be negotiated individually. An employee under contract may be fired for reasons other than nonperformance, but he or she is then entitled to compensation for the life of the contract.

A significant percentage of employees in the U.S. labor force (around 15%) are covered by *union contracts*, which protect groups of unionized workers. Union contracts do not provide as much job security as individually negotiated employment contracts do, but they do provide some job security through seniority and union grievance procedures. Seniority provisions protect the jobs of the most senior workers through the "last in, first out" layoff criterion that is commonly written into the union contract (see Chapter 6). Union grievance procedures subject all disciplinary actions (including discharge) to **due process,** which requires a fair investigation and a showing of just cause to discipline employees who have not performed according to expectations. An arbitrator who is empowered to decide discipline and rights cases can restore the job rights and back pay of an employee who has been wrongfully discharged. (**Wrongful discharge** is discharge for reasons that are either illegal or inappropriate, such as age or the refusal to engage in illegal activities.)

due process
Equal and fair application of a policy or law.

wrongful discharge
Termination of an employee for reasons that are either illegal or inappropriate.

Sometimes employers and employees enter into a contract even though no formal contract exists. In this case, the employer and the employee are said to have entered into an *implied contract.* Certain employment policies and practices may unintentionally create an implied contract. The courts have interpreted statements made by an interviewer or manager such as "You will always have a job as long as you do your work" as a promise of job security.[5] Employees who lost their jobs because of layoffs have successfully obtained legal remedies when such promises were made.

Employee handbooks can be another source of implied employment contracts if they offer job security. Some courts have interpreted statements like "Employees will be dismissed only for just cause" as placing the burden of proof on the company for a termination decision.[6] In addition, when an employee handbook or employment policy makes a distinction between "probationary" and "permanent" employees, the courts have held that employers are promising continued employment to workers who successfully complete the probationary period and become permanent employees. To date, at least 30 state supreme courts have ruled that employee handbooks can be interpreted as enforceable contracts.[7]

Other Rights

Employees often expect certain other rights in addition to statutory and contract rights. These include a right to ethical treatment and limited rights to free speech and privacy. These rights differ from the first two categories of rights in an important way: While employees may expect these rights, they may have no legal recourse if they feel that these rights have been violated. Even though the law does not require employers to extend these other rights to employees, doing so is likely to result in more satisfied workers who are willing to go the extra mile for the organization.

Right to Ethical Treatment. Employees expect to be treated fairly and ethically in return for providing their employer with a fair and reasonable amount of work. This expectation is called the *psychological contract*.[8] Employers who uphold the psychological contract generally have more productive employees. In contrast, those who violate the psychological contract may cause employees to quit or to form a union. Because employee turnover is costly and unionization results in some loss of control over the business, managers should be aware of the importance of the psychological contract to employees.[9] One way of sealing the psychological contract is to develop and publicize a code of ethics.[10] Figure 14–2 reproduces an excerpt from one company's ethical code.

Managers and supervisors can influence their companies' climate of fairness and ethical behavior by the tone they set for employees in their work units. Specifically, managers and supervisors should:

- Take actions that develop trust, such as sharing useful information and making good on commitments.
- Act consistently so that employees are not surprised by unexpected management actions or decisions.
- Be truthful and avoid white lies and actions designed to manipulate others by giving a certain (false) impression.
- Demonstrate integrity by keeping confidences and showing concern for others.
- Meet with employees to discuss and define what is expected of them.
- Ensure that employees are treated equitably, giving equivalent rewards for similar performance and avoiding actual or apparent special treatment of favorites.
- Adhere to clear standards that are seen as just and reasonable—for example, neither praising accomplishments nor imposing penalties disproportionately.
- Demonstrate respect toward employees, showing openly that they care about employees and recognize their strengths and contributions.[11]

Limited Right to Privacy. The right to privacy protects people from unreasonable or unwarranted intrusions into their personal affairs. While this right is not explicitly stated in the U.S. Constitution, the Supreme Court found in a 1965 ruling that it is implicit in the Constitution. For instance, the Constitution does explicitly prohibit unreasonable searches and seizures, and this prohibition is consistent with a more general right to privacy.

Ethics is a matter of choices. Every employee of Ball Aerospace & Technologies Corp. (BATC) is faced with ethical choices daily. In making these choices, it is imperative that each employee act with the highest standards of integrity and honor.

We at BATC strive to:

- Conduct our business with a strong commitment to quality, reliability, technical excellence, and cost effectiveness;
- Perform our activities with honesty and fairness and in compliance with all applicable government laws, rules, and regulations, as well as all company policies, procedures, and guidelines.
- Avoid all conflicts of interest or self-dealing that could improperly influence decisions or actions within BATC and with our customers and suppliers; and
- Encourage and support voluntary disclosure of unethical conduct to the company.

It is the duty and obligation of all employees to adhere to these ethical principles. In doing so, we will perpetuate BATC's legacy of uncompromising dedication to integrity and pride in excellence.

FIGURE 14–2

Ball Aerospace & Technologies Corp. Code of Ethics (Excerpt)

Source: Ball Aerospace & Technologies Corp. (1996). Aerospace Ethics Program, *Employee Handbook*, 9. Boulder, CO: Ball Publications. Reprinted with permission of Ball Aerospace & Technologies Corp.

There are two additional legal bases for privacy rights. First, several state constitutions (including those of Arizona and California) contain an explicitly stated right to privacy. Second, several federal laws protect specific aspects of an employee's privacy. For instance, the Crime Control and Safe Streets Act of 1968 has a provision that prevents employers from viewing or listening to an employee's private communications without obtaining prior consent.

Because the U.S. and state constitutions limit the powers of the government, federal and state employees' privacy rights are protected, though not absolutely. For instance, under a program mandated by Congress, employees whose jobs in U.S. aviation are directly related to safety must undergo periodic blood alcohol testing.[12] However, the same constitutional protections do not apply to private employee arrangements. For instance, government employers are typically prohibited from searching their employees' personal work space (desks, lockers, etc.) unless they have reasonable cause, but private employers typically are not prohibited from this kind of activity. Still, because employees expect certain privacy rights, it is almost always good policy for an employer to respect employee privacy.

A sensitive issue involving employee privacy rights is the maintenance of personnel files. Each worker's **personnel file** contains the documentation of critical information, such as performance appraisals, salary history, disciplinary actions, and career milestones. Access to the personnel file should be denied to all people except managers who have a job-related "need to know" certain information. Employees should be able to review the information in their personnel file periodically to ensure its accuracy. If personnel files are stored in a human resource information system (HRIS), access to this sensitive information should be controlled by the use of passwords or special codes to protect employees' privacy rights.

personnel file
A file, maintained for each employee, containing the documentation of critical HR-related information, such as performance appraisals, salary history, disciplinary actions, and career milestones.

Employees of the U.S. federal government have the privacy of their personnel files protected under the **Privacy Act of 1974**. The act requires federal agencies to permit employees to examine, copy, correct, or amend employee information in their personnel file. The act also includes provisions for an appeal procedure if there is a dispute over the accuracy of the information or what is to be included in the file.[13]

Privacy Act of 1974
Guarantees the privacy of personnel files for employees of the U.S. federal government.

Limited Right to Free Speech. The First Amendment to the U.S. Constitution guarantees all U.S. citizens the right to free speech. This right is therefore more explicit than the right to privacy. However, it too is limited. Again, government employees are more fully protected than those who work for private employers. For instance, an IRS agent who disagrees with the current president's tax policies is perfectly free to say so publicly without fear of official retribution. However, if a Sears store manager publicly disagrees with corporate pricing strategy, Sears is free to discipline or terminate that manager. Thus, managers in the private sector can legally discipline employees who say something damaging to the company or its reputation. There are important exceptions to this situation, however. When employees reveal management misconduct to outsiders, they are engaging in whistleblowing, which is a legal right under federal and some state laws. We discuss whistleblowing in detail later in this chapter.

As with the right to privacy, managers should interfere as little as possible with employees' free speech because this right is so deeply ingrained in U.S. culture. Managers need to balance the costs and benefits of extending versus not extending privacy and speech rights. For instance, we saw in Chapter 13 that e-mail is becoming a very popular method of communication. Should companies establish a policy allowing managers to read all their employees' electronic communications? Employees who know that managers are looking at their communications are likely to "censor" them to some degree, and the loss of candor may lead to less-than-optimal decisions. In addition, such a policy would injure the trust relationship between employees and their employer. Thus, any theoretical benefit

A computer programming manager suspects that one of her programmers is sharing programming information with a competitor through electronic mail. Is it appropriate for the manager to examine her employee's e-mail files without the suspected programmer's permission?

a company might gain from such a policy—like guarding against criminal activity—would almost certainly be offset by work-related and psychological costs.

▸ Management Rights

management rights
Management's rights to run the business and retain any profits that result.

The rights of the employer, usually called **management rights,** can be summed up as the rights to run the business and to retain any profits that result. In the United States, management rights are supported by property laws, common law (a body of traditional legal principles, most of which originated in England), and the values of a capitalistic society that accepts the concepts of private enterprise and the profit motive.[14] The stockholders and owners who control a firm through their property rights delegate the authority to run the business to managers.

Management rights include the right to manage the work force and the rights to hire, promote, assign, discipline, and discharge employees. Management's right to direct the work force is moderated by the right of employees (at least those who have not signed an employment contract) to quit their jobs at any time. Thus, it is in management's interest to treat employees fairly.

Management rights are influenced by the rights of groups who have an interest in decisions made in the workplace. For example, managers have the right to hire the employees they wish to hire, but this right is affected by EEOC laws that prevent the employer from discriminating on the basis of certain applicant characteristics (age, race, sex, and so on). Furthermore, managers have the right to set pay levels for their employees, but the presence of a union labor contract with a pay provision requires managers to pay employees according to the contract's terms.

Management rights are often termed *residual rights* because they pertain to the remaining rights that are not affected by contracts or laws that represent the interests of employees or other parties (such as a union).[15] According to the residual rights perspective, managers have the right to make decisions that affect the business and the work force except where limited by laws or contract provisions.

One of the most important employer rights is employment at will.

Employment at Will

employment at will
A common-law rule used by employers to assert their right to end an employment relationship with an employee at any time for any cause.

Employers have long used **employment at will,** a common-law rule, to assert their right to end their employment relationship with an employee at any time for any cause. U.S. courts adopted the rule in the nineteenth century to promote flexibility in the labor market by acknowledging the existence of a symmetrical relationship between employer and employee. Because workers were free to terminate their relationship with their employer for any reason, the courts deemed it fair for employers to be able to end their relationship with employees whenever they see fit to do so. Employment at will can be a particularly important management right in small business, where a low-performing employee can make the difference between a healthy profit and an unhealthy loss.

Although the courts originally assumed that employment at will would give both parties equal footing in the employment relationship, it is apparent that employment at will has stacked the deck in favor of employers. Because of the employment-at-will doctrine, many employees who are wrongfully discharged each year have no legal remedies.[16] One labor relations expert has estimated that approximately 150,000 employees are wrongfully discharged by their employers each year.[17] Virtually all of these wrongful discharges occur in the 70% of the U.S. labor force that is not protected by either a union contract or *civil service rules,* which guarantee government employees the right of due process in termination procedures. Employment at will is not accepted in other parts of the world, including Japan and the nations of the European Union. These countries have enacted laws that make it difficult for employers to discharge a worker without good cause. In

France, Belgium, and the United Kingdom, the only grounds for immediate dismissal are criminal behavior.[18]

Legal Limitations to Employment at Will. For the past 15 years or so, state courts have been ruling that employment at will is limited in certain situations. Because these are state rather than federal cases, they have varied widely. In general, however, employment-at-will limitations can be grouped into three categories: public policy exceptions, implied contracts, and lack of good faith and fair dealing. In some states plaintiffs have received sizable settlements for punitive damages as well as back pay. In one wrongful discharge case, a plaintiff was awarded $102,000, of which $88,000 was for emotional distress.[19]

Public Policy Exceptions. The courts have ruled that an employee may not be discharged for engaging in activities that are protected by law. Examples are:

- Filing a legitimate workers' compensation claim
- Exercising a legal duty, such as jury duty
- Refusing to violate a professional code of ethics
- Refusing to lobby for a political candidate favored by the employer[20]

Implied Contracts. As we saw earlier in this chapter, the courts have determined that an implied contract may exist when an employee handbook promises job security for good performance, or when an employee is guaranteed a permanent position after the successful completion of a probationary period.

Lack of Good Faith and Fair Dealing. Courts in some jurisdictions expect each party in the employment relationship to treat the other in good faith. If one party acts with malice or bad faith, the courts may be willing to provide a remedy to the injured party. For example, the courts may reason that firing a worker shortly before he or she becomes eligible for a retirement plan indicates bad faith. In this situation, the burden of proof may be on the employer to show that the discharge was for just cause.

The following case makes it plain how costly it can be for an employer to act in bad faith in discharging employees:

> In 1987 two employees of a New Jersey real estate management firm took maternity leave. One was dismissed after she returned to work; the other was fired seven weeks before her planned return. Both women sued, and in 1992 a jury awarded them $210,000 and $225,000, respectively, in compensatory damages. They were awarded another $250,000 each in punitive damages, and on top of that the judge added another $374,000 in interest and legal fees. Total cost to the employer: $1.3 million.[21]

To minimize the risk of wrongful discharge lawsuits, many employers have drawn up employment-at-will statements that all new employees must sign, acknowledging their understanding that the employer can terminate their employment at any time for any reason.

A QUESTION OF ETHICS

Is it ethical to require all employees to sign an employment-at-will statement acknowledging that they understand that the employer can terminate their employment at any time for any reason?

▸ Employee Rights Challenges: A Balancing Act

Three workplace issues are particularly challenging to HR professionals and managers because they require walking a thin line between the rights of employees and those of management: (1) random drug testing, (2) electronic monitoring, and (3) whistleblowing.

Random Drug Testing

The practice of random drug testing pits management's duty to protect the safety of its employees and customers against an employee's right to privacy. *Random drug testing* screens employees for the use of drugs randomly, without suspicion or cause. The test usually involves the analysis of a urine specimen provided by the employee.

Many employees consider random drug testing an unreasonable and illegal invasion of their privacy.[22] Although random drug testing is required by law for specific occupations where safety is critical, such as airline pilots and military personnel, it has been challenged in cases where the employer has other methods available to ensure a drug-free work environment. For example, the International Association of Fire Fighters will permit clauses in its labor contracts that allow drug testing based on "probable cause," but will not agree to random drug testing.

Because no employee groups have succeeded in stopping drug testing under the U.S. Constitution, the legal battle between employee privacy and employer-mandated drug testing is being played out at the state level.[23] Not only do state constitutions vary widely in their protections of employee privacy—for example, New Jersey and California have added employee privacy provisions to their state constitutions, while Utah and Texas have not[24]—but the courts' interpretation of these protections has veered from one side to the other as well. For instance, the California Supreme Court dealt what was considered a death blow to random drug testing in that state when it ruled in 1990 that an employer must have a "compelling interest" to require employees not in safety-sensitive positions to submit to random drug tests.[25] Pro-employee groups cheered the ruling, but four years later the California Supreme Court allowed the National Collegiate Athletic Association to conduct random drug testing of student athletes. The court said that the private sector, like the government, must abide by the state constitution's right of privacy, but that the private sector can invade privacy for "legitimate" interests.[26]

Designing a random drug-testing policy poses numerous challenges. The HR staff can be helpful in counseling management on how to deal with some of the following issues:

- How should employees who test positive in the drug test be treated? Should the manager discharge them or attempt to rehabilitate them?
- Sometimes drug-testing procedures generate a false-positive outcome. If an employee tests positive for a legitimate reason, such as using a prescription drug or eating a poppy seed bagel (poppy seeds are the source of opium), how can the employer ensure that the employee is not charged with using illegal drugs? How can an employer protect employees from false positives in general?
- What can managers do to maintain security over urine specimens provided for the drug test so that they are free from adulteration designed to alter the results? Should managers require that employees be monitored while providing the urine sample to ensure its authenticity? Or does such monitoring violate the employee's privacy rights?

Motorola's random drug-testing policy was designed specifically to deal with these issues. It is administered by the company's HR department and is described in detail in the Issues and Applications feature, titled "How Motorola's Random Drug-Testing Policy Works." Motorola decided to implement random drug testing after it estimated the cost of employees' drug use in terms of lost time, reduced productivity, and health care and workers' compensation claims at $190 million annually. This amounted to 40% of the company's net profits.[27]

The jury is still out on whether the benefits of random drug testing outweigh the resentment and mistrust this policy often generates. A survey of workers at one of the nation's largest railroads found that only 57 out of 174 respondents expressed support for periodic drug testing—and all stipulated that it was justifiable only for safety reasons. Many commented that drug testing undermined their loyalty to the company. One worker wrote:

> I am a faithful and loyal employee. I felt like a common criminal, and I didn't even do anything wrong.…I happen to have bashful kidneys. The first time I took a drug test it took me almost three hours of drinking water and coffee before I could give a sample. Needless to say I was upset, angry, humiliated, defensive, etc.…[28]

Issues + Applications

How Motorola's Random Drug-Testing Policy Works

Companies that wish to implement a random drug-screening process face many challenges. The following is a description of Motorola's well-thought-out policy statement.

Motorola's drug policy is stated simply: "No use of illegal drugs; no use of legal drugs illegally." To enforce the policy, the Schaumburg, Illinois–based electronics manufacturer instituted a universal drug-testing program on January 1, 1991. HR administers the program. Here's how it works.

Every employee's name—including that of the chairman and the contractors who remain on company premises for longer than 30 days—becomes part of a database. A specially designed computer program selects from each Motorola site employee names to be tested each day. The computer program ensures that every employee is selected at least once in three years for a drug test. It's possible, however, for some employees to be selected more than once during that period. This is designed to prevent an employee's feeling safe from testing after taking one test. When the computer selects names of workers who are sick, on vacation, or away from the job site for any other legitimate reason, those names are put into a pool to be selected again randomly within 90 days.

After selecting the names of individuals to be tested on a particular day, an HR clerk informs the employees' supervisors, who are responsible for relaying the information to the employees. This serves two purposes. Not only does it get the information to the employees who will be tested, but it also allows the supervisors to prepare for those employees' brief absences. The employees whose names are selected must report at their designated times. Failure to do so results in disciplinary action.

The collection area prepares split samples for the Motorola employees, allowing for analyses from two different labs if the employees request it. If an employee's test comes out positive, the company's medical review officer is contacted. The medical review officer discusses the situation with the employee to determine if there's some legitimate reason—such as a prescription drug that the employee forgot to mention—for a positive result. Except in security-sensitive positions, it's up to the employee to decide whether or not his or her supervisor should be notified of the results.

If it's determined that a drug-abuse problem exists, the next step for the employee is to report to HR to set a meeting with an EAP adviser and plan a rehabilitation method. The company pays for the employee's rehabilitation. "We're trying to do as much as we can on the rehabilitation side, as opposed to the discipline or punitive side," says Motorola's assistant corporate director of employee relations.

All employees, except some in safety-sensitive or security-clearance positions, continue working in their jobs during rehabilitation. (An exception is when the rehabilitation requires an extended stay at an in-patient treatment center.) The government requires that the organization report any positive tests of individuals who work in clearance-type operations. If the government deems it appropriate to suspend the employee's safety clearance, Motorola will have to remove the employee from that position. The company will try to place that employee in another position temporarily.

Similarly, if an employee who tests positive works in a safety-sensitive position, the organization will place the employee in another job during rehabilitation, if recommended by the EAP. Removal from the position is contingent on circumstances.

After employees complete their rehabilitation program, their names go into a special random pool. Motorola tests these employees once every 120 days for a one-year period.

If during this one-year period an employee again tests positive, the organization terminates him or her. If, however, all tests following rehabilitation come out negative, the employee's name goes back into the three-year pool, and he or she begins the testing process again.

Source: Adapted from Gunsch, D. (1993, May). Training prepares workers for drug testing. *Personnel Journal*, 54.

Employees' anger and humiliation at random drug testing is compounded by the evidence that it doesn't help deter accidents: In 1991 a Federal Railroad Administration report found that only 3.2% of workers involved in railroad accidents tested positive for drugs.[29]

Fortunately, there is an alternative to drug testing that does not invade employee privacy and that is much more reliable for determining an employee's fitness for work: the performance test. For example, there are computer-based performance tests that test work-

Can an Employer Deny Jobs to People Who Smoke?

Issues + Applications

In one of the first court cases dealing with off-the-job smoking as part of the screening and selection process, the U.S. Supreme Court refused to hear the appeals of job applicants who were rejected from consideration for employment with the City of North Miami, Florida, because they are smokers. The denied appeal leaves in place an earlier Florida Supreme Court decision in favor of a city regulation requiring that all job applicants sign an affidavit stating that they have not used any tobacco products for one year before seeking a job with the city.

Arlene Kurtz, a cigarette smoker who applied for a job as a clerk-typist, filed suit, claiming that the city's action interfered with her privacy rights to smoke during her time away from the job. Kurtz offered to comply with any reasonable on-the-job smoking restrictions, but indicated that she had smoked for 30 years and had tried to quit smoking without success. The city argued that it established the policy because employees who use tobacco cost as much as $4,611 per year more than nonsmokers. The court noted that the regulation was the least intrusive way to accomplish the city's interest because it does not affect current employees, only job applicants.

Outside of Florida, a number of other states have recently enacted laws that protect employees' legal off-duty activities such as smoking or skiing (a high-risk leisure activity that an employer might also object to because of higher insurance costs). These state laws prohibit employers from using an applicant's off-the-job smoking as a basis for hiring or continuing the employment relationship.

Source: Adapted from Barlow, W., Hatch, D., and Murphy, B. (1996, April). Employer denies jobs to smoker applicants. *Personnel Journal*, 142.

ers' hand-eye coordination to measure their ability to do their jobs. Every morning at Silicon Valley's Ion Implant Services, Inc., delivery drivers line up in front of a computer console to "play" a short video game. Unless the machine spits out a receipt confirming they have passed the test, they can't climb behind the wheel of their trucks. What happens to workers who fail their performance tests? Some companies refer them to a supervisor, others to an employee assistance program. Besides being both more reliable and less invasive of employees' privacy, performance testing has another advantage over random drug testing: It's cheaper. Performance tests cost from 60 cents to $1 per employee compared with the $10 per employee that the cheapest drug test costs.[30]

Many employers justify random drug testing on the grounds that drug use is illegal. In recent years, however, some companies have also begun testing employees who engage in *legal* activities, such as smoking. The Issues and Applications feature titled "Can an Employer Deny Jobs to People Who Smoke?" examines the controversy surrounding employer policies that reject all applicants who smoke on or off the job.

Electronic Monitoring

It has been estimated that employee theft costs U.S. business between $120 billion and $200 billion a year.[31] "Theft" includes theft of merchandise, embezzlement, industrial espionage, computer crime, acts of sabotage, and misuse of time on the job. While the average annual loss a bank suffers from embezzlement is $42,000, the average computer crime costs around $400,000.[32] Industrial spies who steal competitive trade secrets, such as software codes or plans for a microprocessor chip, may take property so valuable that its theft threatens the very existence of the business. Employees' theft of time from employers can also be costly. Employees steal time when they take long lunches, use the telephone for private conversations, misuse sick leave for extra vacation time, or moonlight for another employer on their principal employer's time.

Companies are attempting to fight these various forms of theft by using electronic surveillance devices to monitor employees.[33] In industries like telecommunications, banking, and insurance, as many as 80% of employees are subject to some form of electronic monitoring.[34] To eavesdrop on employees, companies use hidden microphones and transmitters attached to telephones and tiny fish-eye video lenses installed behind pinholes in walls and ceilings. In a recent survey published by *Macworld* magazine, over 21% of respondents said they have "engaged in searches of employee computer files, voice mail, electronic mail or other networking communications." Most said they were monitoring work flow or investigating thefts or espionage.[35]

The increased sophistication of computer and telephone technology now makes it possible for employers to track employees' job performance electronically—for example, to count the number of keystrokes an employee makes on a computer terminal or determine how many reservations a travel agent books in a given time period.[36] This use of electronic monitoring has raised concerns not only about employee privacy but also about the dehumanizing effect such relentless monitoring can have on employees. Many employees whose work is tracked electronically feel that monitoring takes the human element out of their work and causes too much stress. One recent study comparing monitored and nonmonitored clerical workers showed that 50% of monitored workers felt stressed, compared with 33% of nonmonitored workers; and that 34% of monitored workers lost work time because of stress-induced illness, compared with 20% of nonmonitored workers.[37] Some research suggests that there is a higher incidence of headaches, backaches, and wrist pains among monitored employees.[38]

Employees are most likely to see electronic monitoring as legitimate when management uses it to control theft. But even in this area some managers have exceeded reasonable standards. For example, a 1988 study by the Office of Technology Assessment estimated that more than 10 million U.S. workers were subjected to secret electronic monitoring that year.[39] (This number is expected to grow to 30 million by the year 2000.[40]) In

The Hidden Camera.

Video surveillance has become very common, but it can be a source of friction between management and employees. To maintain good employee relations, managers should make employees aware of any video surveillance cameras in the workplace.

one case, the nurses at Holy Cross Hospital in Silver Spring, Maryland, became quite upset after discovering that a silver box hanging on the locker room wall was a video camera monitored by the hospital security chief—who was a man.[41]

To use electronic monitoring devices to control theft while not intimidating or invading the privacy of honest employees (who make up the majority of the work force), managers should:

- Make employees aware of any electronic surveillance devices that are being used to monitor their behavior. Secret monitoring should be avoided, except with specific individuals whom managers have reason to believe are stealing from the company. In those cases, management should obtain a court order to perform the secret surveillance.
- Find positive uses for electronic monitoring devices that are beneficial to employees as well as to the employer. Avis Car Rentals, for example, has used monitoring devices to provide feedback on employee performance. This practice has been accepted as a valuable training tool.
- Develop a systematic antitheft policy and publicize it throughout the company. Also establish other practices to discourage theft, such as reference checks, pencil-and-paper honesty or integrity tests that screen out employees who are likely to behave dishonestly, and internal controls that control the use of cash (accounting controls), merchandise (inventory controls), computers and databases (computer security controls), and company trade secrets (security badges and clearance procedures).

Whistleblowing

whistleblowing
Employee disclosure of an employer's illegal, immoral, or illegitimate practices to persons or organizations that may be able to take corrective action.

Whistleblowing occurs when an employee discloses an employer's illegal, immoral, or illegitimate practices to persons or organizations that may be able to take corrective action.[42] Whistleblowing can result in effective solutions, but it can also disrupt the organization's operations.

Whistleblowing is risky because managers and other employees sometimes deal harshly with the whistleblower.[43] Although whistleblowers often have altruistic motives, they may be shunned, harassed, and even fired for their efforts. For example:

- When Margot O'Toole, an MIT scientist, exposed fabricated research data for a scientific article authored by Nobel laureate David Baltimore, she lost her job. It took five years before she was vindicated when Baltimore admitted that his research was flawed.[44]
- A manager at MCA, a large entertainment conglomerate, suspected some executives of ordering large shipments of free record albums for recipients not entitled to them. He notified his supervisor three times of a possible kickback scheme. Instead of receiving thanks, he was fired, ostensibly for not performing his job adequately.[45]
- Mark Whitacre, an executive at Archer Daniels Midland (ADM), a U.S. agribusiness firm, spent three years helping an FBI probe into alleged price fixing conducted by the company's top executives. When ADM discovered Whitacre's connection to the FBI, it accused him of stealing $2.5 million and fired him.[46]

You discover that your supervisor has been billing the company for business trips that he never took. When you ask him about it, he says this is common practice throughout the company, the other department heads do the same thing, and corporate headquarters has set reimbursement rates so low that employees have to pad their expense accounts to be fairly reimbursed. What should you do?

Dealing with whistleblowing involves balancing employees' right to free speech with the employer's right to prevent employees from disregarding managers' authority or disclosing sensitive information to outsiders. Although whistleblowers who work for the federal government and some state and local governments have certain legal protections, there is far less protection for private-sector employees, except in states that have enacted whistleblower laws. Many times the whistleblower is subject to the employment-at-will rule and may be discharged in retaliation for going public about an illegal or unethical company activity. As Figure 14–3 indicates, a potential whistleblower should have good documentation of the evidence of wrongdoing before disclosing it to others. The whistleblower should also be prepared to deal with employer retaliation and have a contingency plan, which may include lining up another job in case the worst happens.

Despite all these risks, many employees have used whistleblowing to call their employers to account. For this reason many companies have realized that it is in their best interests to establish a whistleblowing policy that encourages people to reveal misconduct internally instead of exposing it externally. This way the company can avoid negative publicity and all the investigative, administrative, and legal actions associated with it.[47] Figure 14–4 lists some of the most important elements of an effective whistleblowing policy.

DO make sure your allegation is correct. Something may look fishy but be allowable under a technicality you don't understand.

DO keep careful records. Document what you've observed—and your attempt to rectify the problem or alert a supervisor. Keep copies outside the office.

DO research on whether or not your state provides protection for whistleblowers. It may require that you follow special procedures.

DO be realistic about your future. Talk to your family and make sure you're prepared for a worst-case scenario, which can include a loss of job, severe financial burdens, and blacklisting in your field. Even if you're not fired, you may be treated with suspicion by colleagues and management.

DON'T assume a federal or state law will protect you. Legal protection for private-sector workers is often inadequate and varies widely from state to state. Most federal protections cover only government workers.

DON'T run to the media. You may be giving up certain rights or risking a defamation suit. Check with an attorney before contacting any reporters.

DON'T expect a windfall if you're fired. Although some states allow punitive damages, you may be eligible only for back pay and reinstatement—in a place you probably don't want to work anyway.

FIGURE 14–3

Dos and Don'ts for Whistleblowers

Source: Reprinted from June 3, 1991 issue of *Business Week* by special permission, copyright © 1991 by The McGraw-Hill Companies, Inc.

1. Develop the policy in written form.
2. Seek input from top management in developing the policy, and obtain approval for the finished work.
3. Communicate the policy to employees using multiple media. Inclusion in the employee handbook is not sufficient. Active communication efforts such as ethics training, departmental meetings, and employee seminars will increase awareness of the policy and highlight the company's commitment to ethical behavior.
4. Provide a reporting procedure for employees that does not require them to go to their supervisor first. Instead, designate a special office or individual to hear initial employee complaints. Streamline the process and cut the red tape. Make it easy for employees to use the procedure.
5. Make it possible for employees to report anonymously, at least initially.
6. Guarantee employees who report suspected wrongdoing in good faith that they will be protected from retaliation by any member of the organization. Make this guarantee stick.
7. Develop a formal investigative process and communicate to employees exactly how their reports will be handled. Use this process to investigate all reported wrongdoing.
8. If the investigation reveals that the employee's suspicions are accurate, take prompt action to correct the wrongdoing. Employees will quickly lose confidence in the policy if disclosed wrongdoing is allowed to continue. Whatever the outcome of the investigation, communicate it quickly to the whistleblowing employee.
9. Provide an appeals process for employees dissatisfied with the outcome of the initial investigation. Provide an advocate (probably from the HR department) to assist the employee who wishes to appeal an unfavorable outcome.
10. Finally, a successful whistleblowing policy requires more than a written procedure. It requires a commitment from the organization, from top management down. This commitment must be to create an ethical work environment.

FIGURE 14–4

Developing an Effective Whistleblowing Policy

Source: Adapted from Barrett, T. and Cochran, D. (1991). Making room for the whistleblower. *HRMagazine, 36*(1), 59. Reprinted with the permission of *HRMagazine* (formerly *Personnel Administrator*) published by the Society for Human Resource Management, Alexandria, VA.

Probably the most important is support by top management, including the chief executive officer. Other important elements of a whistleblowing policy are provisions for the whistleblower to remain anonymous initially and to be protected from retribution. Some companies that have effective whistleblowing policies are Bank of America, Pacific Gas & Electric, McDonald's, and General Electric.[48]

Building Managerial Skills: Disciplining Employees

Managers have traditionally recognized the need to control and change employees' behavior when it does not meet their expectations. *Employee discipline* is a tool that managers rely upon to communicate to employees that they need to change a behavior. For example, some employees are habitually late to work, ignore safety procedures, neglect the details required for their job, act rude to customers, or engage in unprofessional conduct with coworkers. Employee discipline entails communicating the unacceptability of such behavior along with a warning that specific actions will follow if the employee does not change the behavior.[49]

Employee discipline is usually performed by supervisors, but in self-managed work teams employee discipline may be a team responsibility. For instance, at Hannaford Bros., a food distribution center outside Albany, New York, the 120 warehouse employees are divided into five teams, each of which has a serious conduct committee. The committee handles employee discipline and makes recommendations to management, including counseling and even termination. Management usually adopts these recommendations. The committees generally come up with creative solutions for handling discipline problems. In fact, it has rarely proved necessary to terminate an employee.[50]

Employee and employer rights may come into conflict over the issue of employee discipline. Sometimes employees believe they are being disciplined unfairly. In such situations, a company's HR staff may help sort out disputed rights. This HR contribution is particularly valuable because it can enable the employee and the supervisor to maintain an effective working relationship.

Two different approaches to employee discipline are widely used: (1) progressive discipline and (2) positive discipline. In both these approaches, it is necessary that supervisors discuss the behavior in question with their employees. Managers almost invariably find it difficult to confront an employee for disciplinary purposes. Reasons for their discomfort range from not wanting to be the bearer of bad news, to not knowing how to start the discussion, to a fear that the discussion will get out of control. The Manager's Notebook titled "Ten Steps for Effective Disciplinary Sessions" offers some guidelines that should make it easier for managers to handle an admittedly distasteful task.

Progressive Discipline

progressive discipline
A series of management interventions that gives employees opportunities to correct undesirable behaviors before being discharged.

The most commonly used form of discipline, progressive discipline, consists of a series of management interventions that gives employees opportunities to correct their behavior before being discharged. **Progressive discipline** procedures are warning steps, each of which involves a punishment that increases in severity the longer the undesirable behaviors persist.[51] If the employee fails to respond to these progressive warnings, the employer is justified in discharging the individual.

Progressive discipline systems usually have three to five steps, although a four-step system is the most common. Minor violations of company policy involve using all the steps in the progressive discipline procedure. Serious violations, sometimes referred to as *gross misconduct,* can result in the elimination of several steps and sometimes even begin at the last step, which is discharge. Examples of gross misconduct are assaulting a supervisor and falsifying employment records. However, most applications of discipline involve minor rule infractions like violating a dress code, smoking at an inappropriate time or place, or being habitually late. Figure 14–5 on page 438 shows more examples of minor and serious violations.

A four-step progressive discipline procedure includes the following steps:

1. *Verbal Warning*
   An employee who commits a minor violation receives a verbal warning from the supervisor and is told that if this problem continues within a specific time period, harsher punishment will follow.
2. *Written Warning*
   The employee violates the same rule within the specified time period and now receives a written warning from the supervisor. This warning goes into the employee's records. The employee is told that failure to correct the violation within a certain time period will result in more severe treatment.
3. *Suspension*
   The employee still fails to respond to warnings and again violates the work rule. The employee is now suspended from employment without pay for a specific amount of time. He or she receives a final warning from the supervisor, indicating that discharge will follow upon violating the rule within a specified time period.
4. *Discharge*
   The employee violates the rule one more time within the specified time period and is discharged.[52]

   Figure 14–6 on page 438 illustrates how an employer would use progressive discipline with an employee who has a pattern of unexcused absences from work.

For infractions that fall between the categories of minor violation and serious violation, one or two steps in the procedure are skipped. These infractions are usually handled by supervisors, who give the employees an opportunity to correct the behavior before discharging them. For example, two employees get into a fistfight at work, but there are mitigating circumstances (one employee verbally attacked the other). In this situation, both employees may be suspended without pay and warned that another such violation will result in discharge.

Positive Discipline

In many situations punishment does not motivate an employee to change a behavior. Rather, it only teaches the person to fear or resent the allocator of punishment—that is, the supervisor. This emphasis on punishment in progressive discipline may encourage employees to deceive their supervisor rather than correct their actions. To avoid this outcome, some companies have replaced progressive discipline with

Manager's Notebook

Ten Steps for Effective Disciplinary Sessions

1. Determine whether discipline is called for. Is the problem an isolated infraction or part of a pattern?
2. Have clear goals for the discussion with the poor performer. Many times a manager meets with an employee to discuss a performance problem, but by the end of the session, the employee still has no clear idea of the manager's expectations for improvement. Managers need to be specific; they should not rely on indirect comments.
3. Hold the discussion in private. Anyone who has ever witnessed a public reprimand knows full well that it embarrasses not only the employee but his or her coworkers as well. The result: The manager loses the trust and respect of all who observe the public reprimand.
4. Be calm. A manager who approaches a performance discussion calmly is more likely to remain objective and undistracted by irrelevant problems.
5. Time the discussion carefully. The manager who at 8 a.m. announces a 2:30 p.m. meeting is likely to destroy most of the employee's day. If the problem isn't obvious, the employee will spend the intervening time worrying about what is wrong. Conversely, if the problem is obvious, the employee will have plenty of time to prepare defensive arguments.
6. Prepare effective opening remarks. To make sure the meeting is effective, a manager needs to be absolutely confident about his or her opening remarks. These should be thought out in advance, even rehearsed.
7. Avoid beating around the bush. Too much small talk at the beginning will actually raise the employee's anxiety level rather than getting the employee to relax.
8. Ensure two-way communication. The most helpful disciplinary meeting is a discussion, not a lecture; a manager can't get to the bottom of a performance problem if the employee isn't allowed to speak. The objective of the meeting, after all, is to come up with a solution, not to berate the employee.
9. Establish a follow-up plan. The agreement to a follow-up plan is crucial in both the progressive and positive disciplinary procedures. It's particularly important to establish the time frame in which the employee's behavior is to improve.
10. End on a positive note. This may be a time for the manager to emphasize the employee's strengths so that the employee can leave the meeting believing that the manager—and the company—wants him or her to succeed.

Source: Adapted from Day, D. (1993, May). Training 101: Help for discipline dodgers. *Training & Development*, 19–22.

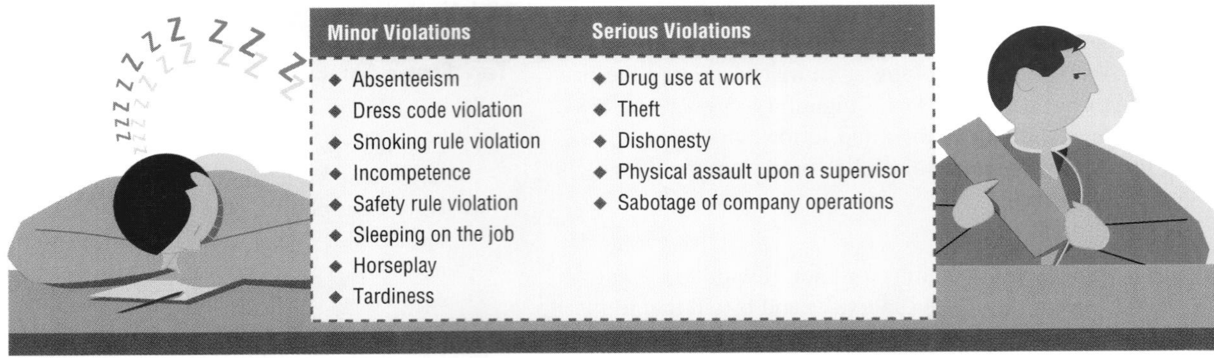

FIGURE 14-5

Categories of Employee Misconduct

positive discipline
A discipline procedure that encourages employees to monitor their own behaviors and assume responsibility for their actions.

positive discipline, which encourages employees to monitor their own behaviors and assume responsibility for their actions.

Positive discipline is similar to progressive discipline in that it too uses a series of steps that increase in urgency and severity until the last step, which is discharge. However, positive discipline replaces the punishment used in progressive discipline with counseling sessions between employee and supervisor. These sessions focus on getting the employee to learn from past mistakes and initiate a plan to make a positive change in behavior. Rather than depending on threats and punishments, the supervisor uses counseling skills to motivate the employee to change. Rather than placing blame on the employee, the supervisor emphasizes collaborative problem solving. In short, positive discipline alters the supervisor's role from adversary to counselor.

To ensure that supervisors are adequately prepared to counsel employees, companies that use positive discipline must see that they receive appropriate training either from the

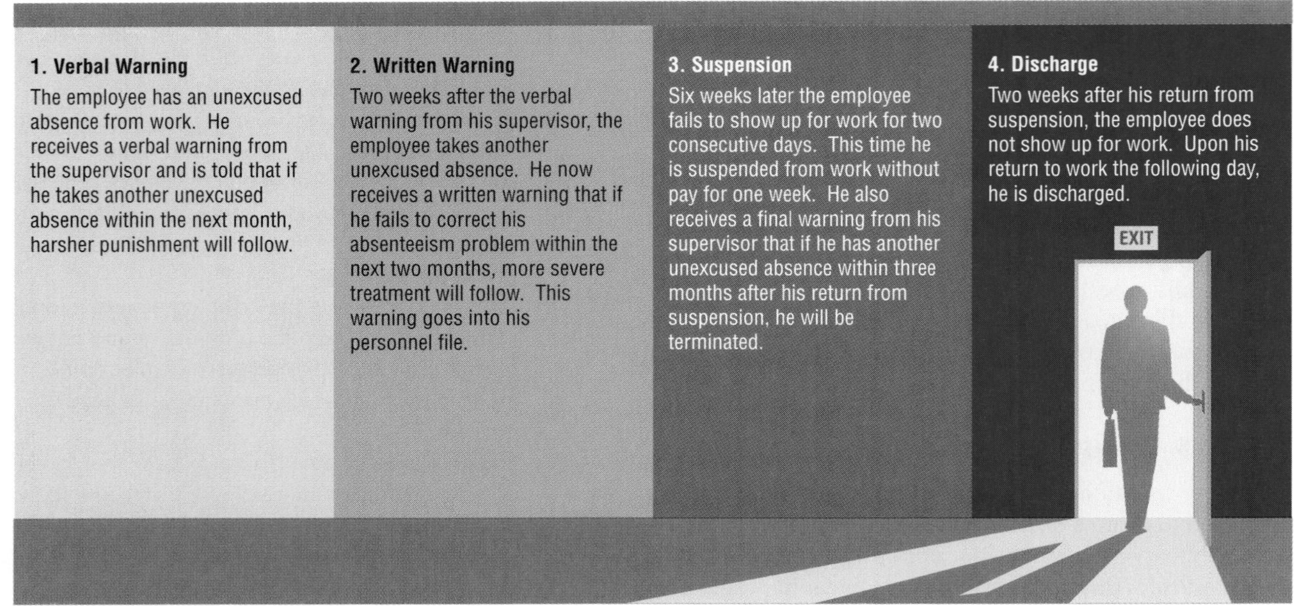

FIGURE 14-6

Four Steps in a Progressive Discipline Procedure

company's own HR department or from outside professional trainers. At Union Carbide, which began using positive discipline in the late 1970s, managers attend a two-day training program to gain familiarity with positive discipline policies and practices. Because Union Carbide had long used a progressive discipline approach, a key element of the training is helping managers abandon their tendency to respond to performance problems in a punitive way. Managers also receive training in documenting their discussions specifically, factually, and defensibly.[53]

A four-step positive discipline procedure starts with a first counseling session between employee and supervisor that ends with a verbal solution that is acceptable to both parties. If this solution does not work, the supervisor and employee meet again to discuss why it failed and to develop a new plan and timetable to solve the problem. At this second step, the new agreed-upon solution to the problem is written down.

If there is still no improvement in performance, the third step is a final warning that the employee is at risk of being discharged. Rather than suspend the employee without pay (as would happen under progressive discipline), this third step gives the employee some time to evaluate his or her situation and come up with a new solution. In doing so, the employee is encouraged to examine why earlier attempts to improve performance did not work. Some companies even give the employee a "decision-making day off" with pay to develop a plan for improved performance.[54]

Managers often resist this aspect of positive discipline because they feel that it rewards employees for poor performance. Some suspect that employees intentionally misbehave to get a free day off. According to the employee relations director of Union Carbide, which uses a paid decision-making day off as part of its disciplinary procedure, this isn't so. The company believes a paid day off is more effective than the unpaid suspension used in progressive discipline procedures because (1) workers returning from an unpaid suspension often feel anger or apathy, which may lead to either reduced effectiveness on the job or subtle sabotage; (2) paying the employee for the decision-making day off avoids making the employee a martyr in the eyes of coworkers; and (3) paying for the decision-making day off underscores management's "good faith" toward the employee and probably reduces the chances that the employee will win a wrongful discharge suit if he or she is eventually terminated.[55]

Failure to improve performance after the final warning results in discharge, the fourth step of the positive discipline procedure. Incidents of gross misconduct (such as theft) are treated no differently under a positive discipline procedure than under a progressive discipline procedure. In both systems, theft will most likely result in immediate discharge.

In addition to the costs of training managers and supervisors in appropriate counseling skills and approaches, progressive discipline has another drawback. Counseling sessions require a lot of time to be effective, and this is time that both the supervisor and employee are not working on other tasks. Nonetheless, positive discipline offers considerable benefits to both employees and managers. Employees prefer it because they like being treated with respect by their supervisors. Counseling generally results in a greater willingness to change undesirable behaviors than discipline does. Supervisors prefer it because it does not demand that they assume the role of disciplinarian. Counseling makes for better-quality working relationships with subordinates than discipline does. In addition, under a system of positive discipline, managers are much more likely to intervene early to correct a problem.

Finally, positive discipline can have positive effects on a company's bottom line, as evidenced at Union Carbide. Studies in five of the company's facilities have shown an average decline in absenteeism of 5.5% since the company switched from punitive to positive discipline procedures. Moreover, in one unionized facility at the company, disciplinary grievances went down from 36 in one year to 8 in the next. Since Union Carbide executives estimate that taking an employee complaint through all steps of the grievance procedure (short of arbitration) costs approximately $400 at this facility, the switch in discipline procedures saved the company over $11,000 per year.[56] Pennzoil, General Electric, and Procter & Gamble also have adopted the positive discipline procedure and have reported successful outcomes with it.[57] In addition, many city police forces use positive discipline. For example, a junior police officer who inappropriately takes his or her weapon out of its holster in the line of duty would receive a counseling session with a superior officer. The two officers would work together to develop a plan of improvement for the junior officer. ▼

▸ Administering and Managing Discipline

Managers must ensure that employees who are disciplined receive due process. In the context of discipline, *due process* means fair and consistent treatment. If an employee challenges a disciplinary action under the EEO laws or a union grievance procedure, the employer must prove that the employee engaged in misconduct and was disciplined appropriately for it. Thus, supervisors should be properly trained in how to administer discipline. Two important elements of due process that managers need to consider in this area are (1) the standards of discipline used to determine if the employee was treated fairly and (2) whether or not the employee has a right to appeal a disciplinary action.

Basic Standards of Discipline

Some basic standards of discipline should apply to all rule violations, whether major or minor. All disciplinary actions should include the following procedures at a minimum:

- *Communication of rules and performance criteria.* Employees should be aware of the company's rules and standards and the consequences of violating them. Every employee and supervisor should understand the company's disciplinary policies and procedures fully. Employees who violate a rule or do not meet performance criteria should be given the opportunity to correct their behavior.
- *Documentation of the facts.* Managers should gather a convincing amount of evidence to justify the discipline. This evidence should be carefully documented so that it is difficult to dispute. For example, time cards could be used to document tardiness; videotapes could document a case of employee theft; the written testimony of a witness could substantiate a charge of insubordination. Employees should have the opportunity to refute this evidence and provide documentation in self-defense.
- *Consistent response to rule violations.* It is important for employees to believe that discipline is administered consistently, predictably, and without discrimination or favoritism. If they perceive otherwise, they will be more likely to challenge discipline decisions. This does not mean that every violation should be treated exactly the same. For example, an employee with many years of seniority and an excellent work record who breaks a rule may be punished less harshly than a recently hired employee who breaks the same rule. However, two recently hired employees who break the same rule should receive the same punishment.

hot-stove rule
A model of disciplinary action: Discipline should be immediate, provide ample warning, and be consistently applied to all.

The **hot-stove rule** provides a model of how a disciplinary action should be administered. The rule suggests that the disciplinary process is similar to touching a hot stove: (1) Touching a hot stove results in an immediate consequence, which is a burn. Discipline should also be an immediate consequence that follows a rule infraction. (2) The hot stove provides a warning that one will get burned if one touches it. Disciplinary rules should inform employees of the consequences of breaking the rules as well. (3) A hot stove is consistent in administering pain to anyone who touches it. Disciplinary rules should be consistently applied to all.[58]

The Just Cause Standard of Discipline

In cases of wrongful discharge that involve statutory rights or exceptions to employment at will, U.S. courts require the employer to prove that an employee was discharged for *just cause*. This exacting standard, which is written into union contracts and into some nonunion companies' employment policies and employee handbooks, consists of seven questions that must be answered in the affirmative for just cause to exist.[59] Failure to answer "yes" to one or more of these questions suggests that the discipline may have been arbitrary or unwarranted.

1. *Notification*
   Was the employee forewarned of the disciplinary consequences of his or her conduct? Unless the misconduct is very obvious (for example, theft or assault), the employer should make the employee aware, either verbally or in writing, that he or she has violated a rule.
2. *Reasonable Rule*
   Was the rule the employee violated reasonably related to safe and efficient operations? The rule should not jeopardize an employee's safety or integrity in any way.
3. *Investigation Prior to Discipline*
   Did managers conduct an investigation into the misconduct before administering discipline? If immediate action is required, the employee may be suspended pending the outcome of the investigation. If the investigation reveals no misconduct, all of the employee's rights should be restored.
4. *Fair Investigation*
   Was the investigation fair and impartial? Fair investigations allow the employee to defend himself or herself.
5. *Proof of Guilt*
   Did the investigation provide substantial evidence or proof of guilt? Management may need a "preponderance of evidence" to prove serious charges of gross misconduct, and a less stringent (but still substantial) amount of evidence to prove minor violations.
6. *Absence of Discrimination*
   Were the rules, orders, and penalties of the disciplinary action applied evenhandedly and without discrimination? It is not acceptable for managers to go from lax enforcement of a rule to sudden rigorous enforcement of that rule without notifying employees that they intend to do so.
7. *Reasonable Penalty*
   Was the disciplinary penalty reasonably related to the seriousness of the rule violation? The employer should consider related facts, such as the employee's work record, when determining the severity of punishment. There might be a range of penalties for a given rule infraction that depend on the length and quality of the employee's service record.

Because the just cause standard is fairly stringent and can prove unwieldy in cases of minor infractions that require immediate supervisory attention, nonunion employers who believe that their employees work under employment at will may choose a less demanding discipline standard.

The Right to Appeal Discipline

Sometimes employees believe they have been disciplined unfairly, either because their supervisors have abused their power or because their supervisors are biased in dealing with individuals whom they like or dislike. For a disciplinary system to be effective, employees must have access to an appeals procedure in which others (who are perceived to be free from bias) can examine the facts. As we discussed in Chapter 13, good employee relations requires establishing appeals procedures that employees can use to voice their disagreement with managers' actions. For challenging disciplinary actions, two of the most useful appeals procedures are the open door policy and the use of employee relations representatives. These two methods are attractive because of their flexibility and their ability to reach quick resolutions.

Building Managerial Skills: Managing Difficult Employees

Thus far we've focused on the challenges of administering discipline. We now turn to some common problems that managers are likely to encounter. All of the problems we discuss here—poor attendance, poor performance, insubordination, and substance abuse—often lead to disciplinary actions. Managing the discipline of difficult employees requires good judgment and common sense.

Poor Attendance

The problem of poor attendance includes absenteeism and/or tardiness. Poor attendance can become a serious problem that leads to discharge for just cause. If poor attendance is not managed properly, employee productivity can decline and group morale can suffer as those with good attendance are forced to increase their efforts to compensate for people who shirk their responsibilities.

Sometimes employees are absent or tardy for legitimate reasons—for example, sickness, child-care problems, inclement weather, or religious beliefs. Managers should identify those employees who have legitimate reasons and treat them differently than they treat those who are chronically absent or tardy.

When disciplining an employee for poor attendance, managers need to consider several factors:

- *Is the attendance rule reasonable?* Attendance rules should be flexible enough to allow for the emergencies or unforeseen circumstances that most employees experience from time to time, including religious or cultural holidays celebrated by a diverse work force. Most companies deal with this issue by showing leniency when an employee gives notice that he or she is sick or experiencing an emergency. For instance, an increasingly likely emergency for many employees is providing care for an aging parent. Some companies require documentation, such as a doctor's note, in support of the incident.
- *Has the employee been warned of the consequences of poor attendance?* This could be particularly important when an employee is unaware of how much time flexibility is possible in reporting to the job.
- *Are there any mitigating circumstances that should be taken into consideration?* Sometimes special circumstances need to be considered. These circumstances include work history, length of service, reason for absence, and likelihood of improved attendance.[60]

Managers should be aware of patterns of poor attendance within a work unit. Systemic absenteeism or tardiness may be a symptom of job avoidance. Employees may dread coming to work because coworkers are unpleasant, the job has become unchallenging, they are experiencing conflicting demands from job and family, or supervision is poor. A disciplinary approach is not the best way to deal with this type of absenteeism. It would be better for the manager or company to look for ways to change the work environment. Possible solutions to job avoidance are redesigning jobs and, when the problem is widespread, restructuring the organization.

For employees whose absences are due to overwhelming family demands, flexible work schedules or permission to work at home (telecommuting) may be desirable. Flexible work schedules are gaining popularity at companies both large and small. Ten months into Xerox Corporation's experiment with flexible work schedules, absences had fallen by one third, teamwork had improved, and worker surveys showed that morale had risen.[61]

Poor Performance

Every manager must deal with employees who perform poorly and who do not respond to coaching or feedback. In most cases, the performance appraisal (see Chapter 7) can be used to turn around poor performers by helping them develop an action plan for improvement. Sometimes, however, the poor performance is so serious that it requires immediate intervention. Consider the following situations:

- A restaurant manager receives daily complaints from angry customers about the quality of one waitress's service.
- A partner's poor interpersonal skills affect his working relationships with the other two partners in his firm. The firm is now failing to meet its goals because of the severe conflicts and disruptions instigated by this one person.

These examples suggest a glaring need for progressive or positive discipline procedures. If these employees failed to improve their performance after receiving some warnings or counseling, dismissal would be justified.

Companies and managers should follow three guidelines when applying discipline for poor performance:

1. The company's performance standards should be reasonable and communicated to all employees. Job descriptions can be used for this purpose.
2. Poor performance should be documented and poor performers should be told how they are not meeting the expected standards. One source of documented evidence can be the pattern of the employee's performance appraisals over a period of time.
3. Managers should make a good-faith attempt to give employees an opportunity to improve their performance before disciplining them.

Sometimes poor performance is the result of factors beyond the employee's control. In these cases, managers should avoid using discipline except as a last resort. For example, an employee may be unable to perform at expected standards because of incompetence. An *incompetent employee* (one who is lacking in ability, not effort) may be given remedial training (see Chapter 8) or transferred to a less demanding job rather than be dismissed. An incompetent employee's poor performance may be the result of a flaw in the organization's selection system that caused a poor match between the employee's skills and the job requirements.

Some organizations use a *probationary employment period* (a period of time that allows the employer to discharge any employee at will) to weed out incompetent employees early. Probationary employment periods typically last one to three months. In Europe, where permanent employment is the norm, many companies insist on a six-month trial period as part of the employment contract. However, this policy can present a problem when recruiting executives, who understandably want to be guaranteed a permanent position before leaving their current job.

It is not only inappropriate but also illegal to use discipline to correct poor performance when an employee has a physical or mental disability. The Americans with Disabilities Act (ADA, see Chapter 3) requires employers to make reasonable accommodation for disabled employees who cannot perform the job as it is structured. Accommodation may include redesigning the job or modifying policies and procedures. For example, an employee who is diagnosed with a terminal illness may request a change from a full-time job to a part-time job or one with a more flexible work schedule. The EEOC, which regulates how employers respond to the needs of employees with disabilities, would probably consider this a reasonable request, so failure to make such an accommodation could lead to government sanctions.

Unfortunately, many myths hinder firms' compliance with the ADA. One myth is that reasonable accommodation always involves prohibitive expense. Actually, accommodation is not necessarily costly, and more often than not, the money spent to accommodate a disabled individual is minor compared with the cost of litigation. Samsonite Corporation, a luggage company located in Denver, has employed deaf production workers for years. The only accommodation necessary—beyond an accommodating attitude and the willingness of many employees to learn some sign language—has been the use of lights in the production area in addition to the standard beepers alerting employees to the presence of forklifts.[62]

Insubordination

The willingness of employees to carry out managers' directives is essential to a business's effective operations. For example, consider the case of a sales representative who refuses to submit the weekly activity reports requested by his manager.[63] How should the sales manager react to the sales representative's behavior?

insubordination
Either refusal to obey a direct order from a supervisor or verbal abuse of a supervisor.

Insubordination, which involves an employee's refusal to obey a direct order from a supervisor, is a direct challenge of management's right to run the company. Insubordination also occurs when an employee is verbally abusive to a supervisor. The discipline for insubordination usually varies according to the seriousness of the insubordination and the presence or absence of mitigating factors. Mitigating factors include the employee's work history and length of service and whether or not the employee was provoked by a supervisor's verbal abuse.

To justify disciplining an employee for insubordination, managers should document the following: (1) The supervisor gave a direct order to a subordinate, either in writing or orally; and (2) the employee refused to obey the order, either by indicating so verbally or by not doing what was asked. The discipline for a first insubordination offense ranges from applying the first step of the progressive discipline procedure to immediate suspension or discharge.

Two exceptions allow an employee to disobey a direct order: illegal activities and safety considerations. For instance, a California court found that an employer had violated public policy when it fired an employee who refused to commit perjury. Other illegal orders that employees can refuse with legal protection are participation in price-fixing and improper bookkeeping.[64] The whistleblowing laws passed in some states provide further protection to employees who can prove they were discharged for refusing to break the law. The Occupational Safety and Health Administration protects the rights of employees who refuse to expose themselves to serious jeopardy. For insubordination to be acceptable, the employee should have "reasonable cause" to fear for his or her safety—for example, knowing that a truck the worker is ordered to drive has defective brakes.

Because the penalties for insubordination are severe, companies should create internal systems and cultures (open door policies, appeal systems) that allow employees to appeal charges of insubordinate behavior. The legal and monetary penalties to companies for refusing to hear an employee's reasons for insubordination can be severe. Managers should be sure that insubordination charges are not being used to protect their own illegal or unethical behavior. For instance, a supervisor who charges an employee with insubordination may be attempting to force out someone who objects to the supervisor's illegal behavior. Companies that ignore such signs of trouble may find that a small problem has escalated into a very difficult and/or expensive situation.

Alcohol-Related Misconduct

Employees' use of alcohol presents two separate challenges to managers. First, there is the challenge of managing an employee who is an alcoholic. Second, there is the challenge of managing an employee who uses alcohol or is intoxicated on the job. Each of these employees should be disciplined differently.

Alcoholic employees are generally viewed sympathetically because alcoholism is an illness and medical treatment is the generally accepted remedy for it. However, as we mentioned in Chapter 13, some alcoholic employees have a strong denial mechanism that prevents them from admitting that they are alcoholics. Others may not view them as alcoholics either because alcoholism is often masked by such behavioral symptoms as poor attendance. Thus, a supervisor may perceive an alcoholic employee as someone who has an attendance or performance problem rather than an alcohol problem, and discipline the employee accordingly. Organizations with employee assistance programs give employees the opportunity to visit a counselor as the last step in progressive discipline prior to discharge. This is where the alcoholism may finally be discovered and the employee referred to an alcohol rehabilitation facility.

Sometimes employees claim to be alcoholic to cover up their misconduct. If the EAP counselor determines that the individual is not an alcoholic, the discipline procedure is the appropriate managerial response to the problem.

Using alcohol on the job and coming to work intoxicated are both considered serious misconduct and can lead to harsh discipline. Organizations that have job-related reasons to restrict alcohol use at work or working "under the influence" should have clearly stated and reasonable policies. For example, it is reasonable to restrict the alcohol use, on or off the job, of heavy equipment operators at a construction site. It is more difficult to forbid a sales representative to drink alcohol when entertaining a prospective client at a lunch.

The best way to prove that an employee has come to work intoxicated is to administer a blood alcohol content test. A supervisor can ask an employee to submit to this test if there is a reasonable suspicion that the worker is intoxicated. Supervisors may suspect an individual is intoxicated if he or she engages in unusual behavior (talking particularly loud or using profanity), has slurred speech, or has alcohol on the breath.

A first intoxication offense may result in suspension or discharge because of the potential for damage that an alcohol-impaired employee can create. An extreme example of an alcohol-impaired employee's cost to an organization is the accident in which the Exxon *Valdez* oil tanker spilled oil off the coast of Alaska in March 1989. A blood alcohol test revealed that the ship's captain was intoxicated at the time of the oil spill, which cost Exxon over $1 billion to clean up.

Illegal Drug Use and Abuse

Drug use and abuse by employees also presents a serious challenge to managers. "Illegal drug use" refers to any use of prohibited substances such as marijuana, heroin, and cocaine as well as the illegal use of prescription drugs such as Valium. The problems associated with drug use are very similar to those associated with the use of alcohol. The primary difference is that the use of illegal drugs is prohibited by law and is socially unacceptable, while the use of alcohol in moderation is socially acceptable.

We examined the specifics of drug-use detection systems earlier in this chapter, and we will address the health aspects of drug use in Chapter 16. Here we note only that illegal drug use is often masked by symptoms such as inattention and unexplained absences. Managers who suspect that drug use or addiction is the source of a performance problem should refer the employee to EAP counseling if the organization has such a program. Simultaneously, they should document performance problems and begin disciplinary procedures. These will prove valuable should it be necessary to terminate the employee because of failure to overcome the substance abuse problem after counseling and treatment. ▼

Preventing the Need for Discipline with Human Resource Management

By taking a strategic and proactive approach to the design of HRM systems, managers can eliminate the need for a substantial amount of employee discipline. HR programs designed to use employees' talents and skills effectively, reduce the need to resort to discipline to shape employee behavior. In this section we briefly revisit some of the functional areas of HR we discussed in earlier chapters to show how each can be designed to prevent problem employees.[65]

Recruitment and Selection

By spending more time and resources on recruiting and selection, managers can make better matches between individuals and the organization.

- Workers can be selected for fit in the organization as well as the job. Choosing applicants who have career potential in the company decreases the likelihood that employees will exhibit performance problems later.
- Checking references and gathering background information on applicants' work habits and character are useful preliminaries to making a job offer.
- Multiple interviews that involve diverse groups in the company can reduce biases that lead to poor hiring decisions. When women, minorities, peers, and subordinates, as well as senior people, are involved in the interviewing process, companies stand a better chance of obtaining an accurate portrait of the applicant.

Training and Development

Investing in employees' training and development now saves a company from having to deal with incompetents or workers whose skills are obsolete down the road.

- An effective orientation program communicates to new employees the values important to the organization. It also teaches employees what is expected from them as members of the organization. These insights into the company can help employees manage their own behavior better. Federal Express, for instance, has an extensive orientation program to communicate company values to employees.[66]
- Training programs for new employees can reduce skill gaps and improve competencies.
- Retraining programs can be used for continuing employees whose skills have become obsolete. For example, employees may need periodic retraining on word processing software as the technology changes and more powerful programs become available.
- Training supervisors to coach and provide feedback to their subordinates encourages supervisors to intervene early in problem situations with counseling rather than discipline.
- Career ladders can be developed to give employees incentives to develop a long-term commitment to the organization's goals. When employees know that the organization has a long-term use for their contributions, they are more likely to engage in acts of good citizenship with their coworkers and customers.

Human Resource Planning

Jobs, job families, and organizational units can be designed to motivate and challenge employees. Highly motivated workers seldom need to be disciplined for inadequate performance.

- Jobs should be designed to utilize the best talents of each employee. It may be necessary to build some flexibility into job designs to put an employee's strengths to best use. One way companies are creating greater job flexibility is through *job banding*. Discussed in Chapter 10, this system replaces traditional narrowly defined job descriptions with broader categories, or bands, of related jobs. By putting greater variety into jobs, job banding makes it less likely that employees will feel so underchallenged or bored that they start avoiding work through absences or tardiness. Job banding has been implemented successfully by such companies as Aetna, General Electric, and Harley Davidson.[67]

- Job descriptions and work plans should be developed to communicate effectively to employees the performance standards to which they will be held accountable.

Performance Appraisal

Many performance problems can be avoided by designing effective performance appraisal systems. An effective performance appraisal system lets people know what is expected of them, how well they are meeting those expectations, and what they can do to improve on their weaknesses.

- The performance appraisal criteria should set reasonable standards that employees understand and have some control over.
- Supervisors should be encouraged to provide continuous feedback to subordinates. Many problems can be avoided with early interventions.
- Performance evaluations for supervisors should place strong emphasis on their effectiveness at providing feedback and developing their subordinates.
- Employee appraisals should be documented properly to protect employers against wrongful discharge or discrimination suits.

Compensation

Employees who believe that rewards are allocated unfairly (perhaps on the basis of favoritism) are likely to lose respect for the organization. Worse, employees who believe that pay policies do not recognize the value of their contributions are more likely to withhold future contributions.

- Pay policies should be perceived as fair by all employees. Employees deserve rewards for their contributions. It is important to explain to them the procedures used to establish their compensation level.
- An appeal mechanism that gives employees the right to challenge a pay decision should be established. Employees who can voice their frustration with a pay decision through a legitimate channel are less likely to engage in angry exchanges with supervisors, coworkers, or customers.

Summary and Conclusions

Employee Rights. In the employment relationship, both employees and employers have rights. Employee rights fall into three categories: statutory rights (protection from discrimination, safe work conditions, the right to form unions), contractual rights (as provided by employment contracts, union contracts, and employment policies), and other rights (the rights to ethical treatment, privacy, and free speech).

Management Rights. Employers have the right to run their business and make a profit. These rights are supported by property laws, common law, and the values of a society that accepts the concepts of private enterprise and the profit motive. Management rights include the right to manage the work force and to hire, promote, assign, discipline, and discharge employees. Another important management right is employment at will, which allows an employer to dismiss an employee at any time for any cause. There are three key exceptions to the employment-at-will doctrine: public policy exceptions, implied contracts, and lack of good faith and fair dealing.

Employee Rights Challenges: A Balancing Act. Sometimes the rights of the employer and employees are in conflict. For example, a random drug-testing policy can create a conflict between an employer's responsibility to provide a safe workplace and employees' rights to privacy. HR professionals need to balance the rights of the employee with those of the employer when designing policies that address workplace issues like random drug testing, electronic monitoring of employees, and whistleblowing.

Disciplining Employees. Managers rely on discipline procedures to communicate to employees the need to change a behavior. There are two approaches to discipline. The progressive discipline procedure relies on increasing levels of punishment leading to discharge. The positive discipline procedure uses counseling sessions between supervisor and subordinate to encourage the employee to monitor his or her own behavior. Both procedures are designed to deal with forms of misconduct that are correctable.

Administering and Managing Discipline. To avoid conflict and lawsuits, managers must administer discipline properly. This entails ensuring that disciplined employees receive due process. Managers need to be aware of the standards used to determine if an employee was treated fairly and whether or not the employee has a right to appeal disciplinary action. For a disciplinary system to be effective, an appeal mechanism must be in place.

Managing Difficult Employees. It is often necessary to discipline employees who exhibit poor attendance, poor performance, insubordination, or substance abuse. Managing the discipline process in these situations requires a balance of good judgment and common sense. Discipline may not be the best solution in all cases.

Preventing the Need for Discipline with Human Resource Management. The need for discipline can often be avoided by a strategic and proactive approach to HRM. A company can avoid discipline by recruiting and selecting the right employees for current positions as well as future opportunities, by training and developing workers, by designing jobs and career paths that best utilize people's talents, by designing effective performance appraisal systems, and by compensating employees for their contributions.

Key Terms

contract, 424
contractual right, 424
due process, 425
employment at will, 428
employment contract, 424
hot-stove rule, 440
insubordination, 444
management rights, 428
personnel file, 427
positive discipline, 438
Privacy Act of 1974, 427
progressive discipline, 436
right, 424
statutory right, 424
whistleblowing, 434
wrongful discharge, 425

Discussion Questions

1. Why have managers needed to place greater emphasis on employee rights in recent years?
2. Do employers have rights? If so, what are these rights?
3. In a highly publicized court case in 1988, *Foley v. Interactive Data Corp.,* the plaintiff was fired two months after he told a company vice president that his supervisor, a recent hire, was under investigation by the FBI for embezzlement from his previous employer. (The supervisor pleaded guilty in court six months after Foley was fired.) In his more than six years of employment at Interactive Data, Foley had received a steady stream of raises, promotions, and superior performance reviews. Based on his performance reviews and the company's written termination policy (which prescribed a seven-step termination procedure), Foley believed that Interactive Data could not dismiss him. He sued the company on the basis of three theories, or causes, of action. What do you think these three causes of action were? Could any of these be considered exceptions to employment at will?
4. Recently National Medical Enterprises, Inc., a $4 billion operator of hospitals and psychiatric treatment centers, faced criminal probes for such practices as widespread overbilling and fraudulent diagnoses to extend patients' hospital stays. Investigators found that NME's top management urged hospital administrators to adopt "intake" goals designed to lure patients into hospitals for lengthy and unnecessary treatments. Hospital staffers were also urged to admit fully half of all patients who came in for an evaluation. Suppose a hospital staffer at NME refused to admit patients for whom she felt treatment was unnecessary. Could her refusal be considered insubordination? If the same staffer considered exposing fraudulent diagnoses to an

outside agency, what whistleblowing precautions would she be wise to consider before going public with her case?

5. Compare and contrast the progressive and positive discipline procedures.
6. Total Recall Corporation of Spring Valley, New York, has developed a camouflaged video surveillance system called Babywatch, designed for parents who are concerned about the quality of child care they are receiving from their babysitters. The small inconspicuous device operates under low light and is capable of recording up to five hours of video and audio material. Do you think that parents using this system secretly would be invading the babysitter's privacy, or do you think they have a legitimate reason for monitoring the babysitter?
7. What are the advantages and disadvantages of letting the team administer discipline to a team member?
8. What alternatives to electronic monitoring could an employer use to effectively control employee theft?

MINICASE 1 *Documenting Performance: Doing the Right Thing ...*

CASE 1

The following facts came to light in *Palmer v. Director* (1983): The Office of Personnel Management (OPM) provided extensive documentation of performance problems over the three-year period during which a discharged minority male employee worked for the agency. Evidence showed that the employee was informed of his performance shortcomings verbally and in writing, received unsatisfactory ratings on performance appraisals, was given two opportunities to perform in other types of positions, and even was suspended in an attempt to get him to improve his performance. The court, in finding no evidence of racial discrimination, commented that OPM had "exercised great patience in tolerating plaintiff's ineptitude and misconduct for so long."

CASE 2

The following is a summary of *Dominic v. Consolidated Edison Co. of New York:*

While still employed, an employee complained to his immediate supervisor that he was the victim of age discrimination. Within a few months, the supervisor fired the employee for unsatisfactory job performance. Just before the employee's dismissal, his supervisor evaluated his job performance negatively, causing the company to believe that it would have an ironclad defense in an age-discrimination suit. Testimony at trial, however, revealed that the supervisor had lowered the worker's performance appraisal deliberately without his knowledge after he had complained about age discrimination, and subsequently deluged the employee with job assignments. The judge, in refusing to overturn a $450,000 jury verdict, concluded that the jury could have reasonably inferred that the supervisor had purposely set up the employee for failure, hoping to create a pretext for firing him.

Discussion Questions

1. In *Palmer v. Director*, why did the court rule in favor of the employer?
2. What caused the court to rule in the employee's favor in *Dominic v. Consolidated Edison Co. of New York*? What could Consolidated Edison's HR department have done to prevent the supervisor's discriminatory actions?
3. Keeping both of these cases in mind, what guidelines would you suggest for documenting employee performance during the appraisal or discipline process?

Sources: Case #1 based on Goddard, R. W. (1989, January). Is your appraisal system headed for court? *Personnel Journal,* 114–118; Posen, D. I. (1992, November). Appraisals can make—or break—your court case. *Personnel Journal,* 113–116.

MINICASE 2 *Blowing the Whistle on Big Tobacco*

Read the following excerpt from *Time* about one former executive's battle against a major tobacco company:

> One night a few months ago, Carl Alfarano returned to his Westchester, New York, home after work to discover that he had just missed a visit from two private detectives. They told his wife they wanted his help with a "personality sketch" of Alfarano's old friend Jeffrey Wigand. The pair claimed they had come in person only because they did not have Alfarano's telephone number—something Alfarano insists is not true. "I found it rather unnerving," says Alfarano, who worked with Wigand at two medical-device

continued

Blowing The Whistle on Big Tobacco continued

companies in the 1980s and who gave the men no information. But when he learned about the thick dossier the detectives had managed to compile about Wigand, a former vice president of Brown & Williamson [a large tobacco company] and the highest-ranking tobacco executive ever to turn whistleblower, he was appalled. "It hit me like a silver bullet," says Alfarano. "[B&W] can deal with one or two defectors, but I think [they wanted] to send a signal to anybody else who's thinking about testifying."

To date, no one has ever bested the nearly $50 billion-a-year tobacco industry, which historically has been willing to spend whatever it takes to neutralize its enemies. In all the years of litigation against cigarette makers, they have yet to pay out even a nickel in damages.

But Wigand, with his allegations that B&W manipulated nicotine levels in cigarettes, knowingly used a carcinogenic additive to make pipe tobacco taste better and covered up research into "safer" cigarettes, has begun talking to lawyers, grand juries, and the media at an inopportune moment for tobacco. The Food and Drug Administration has proposed to regulate nicotine as a drug in cigarettes; teen smoking rates have taken an alarming jump; and five grand juries are looking into possible perjury and malfeasance by industry executives. At the same time, a novel legal strategy which would hold the tobacco industry responsible to taxpayers rather than individual smokers, is gaining momentum around the country. "The current round of attacks on the tobacco industry is better thought out, better funded and better organized than at any time in history," says Matthew Myers, a Washington lawyer who has spent 14 years litigating cases on behalf of the Coalition on Smoking or Health. "And it comes at a time when the tobacco industry is more vulnerable than ever, given the disclosures from inside the industry."

So far, no B&W colleagues have jumped the wall to support Wigand; in fact, none have even contacted him to offer words of encouragement. That is understandable: Wigand, who says he received two telephone death threats after he began cooperating with investigators, has been reduced to traveling with a security guard, and another guard watches over his two young daughters. His corporate career in the biomedical field, which until he worked at B&W had been on a steady upward trajectory ("I wanted to be CEO of a company," he confesses), has foundered. His marriage hit the rocks owing, he says, to the stress of battling his former employer. Nevertheless, Wigand, 53, tells TIME [magazine] that now that he has begun to talk, he has no plans to stop.

Discussion Questions

1. What do you see as the key environmental, organizational, and individual HR challenges in this case?
2. To what extent is the tobacco company's response to Jeffrey Wigand's threat appropriate or inappropriate? Explain.
3. What are the most important ethical and social responsibility issues in this case? Does the tobacco company have a responsibility to protect the interest of employees, the public, and shareholders? What kinds of trade-offs do you see in this case?
4. If you had been in the shoes of Jeffrey Wigand, would you have blown the whistle on Brown & Williamson? Explain.
5. The public has read the *Time* magazine article, and it is calling B&W to account for its actions. The CEO of Brown & Williamson has appointed a five-member advisory committee to provide recommendations on how B&W should respond to the present situation. The committee consists of the human resource manager, a corporate lawyer, the director of public relations, the marketing director, and chief corporate security officer. The class divides into groups of five. Each group presents its recommendations to the CEO, represented by the instructor.

Source: Adapted from Gleick, E. (1996, March 11). Tobacco blues. *Time*, pp. 54–55.

CASE 1 A Loose Cannon at Great Lakes University

Kate Murphy, the chair of the Marketing Department at Great Lakes University, and Carl Wharton, the dean of the College of Business Administration, have scheduled a meeting to discuss Professor Vladimir Badenov. Great Lakes University is a large publicly funded university with a prominent faculty noted for its excellence in research. Professor Badenov is one of the top marketing scholars on the faculty; his research is highly respected and widely cited. However, because of his outrageous behavior, Badenov is regarded as a "loose cannon" by both his colleagues and the administration.

Professor Badenov has embarrassed and intimidated Chairwoman Murphy during faculty meetings by interrupting her with loud and boisterous comments. Badenov has told graduate students not to work with one junior faculty member because he is a "loser" and does bad research. He has sent hundreds of e-mail messages to colleagues in different universities complaining that Dean Wharton is incompetent because Wharton would not provide funds for Badenov's trip to Paris to present a research paper. A faculty member who makes the mistake of offending Professor Badenov usually receives a barrage of obscenities in response. Badenov's antics have hurt the morale at the College of Business. Most faculty members go out of their way to avoid him.

Professor Badenov is a full professor with tenure. A tenured professor cannot be discharged for any reason other than "moral turpitude," which is usually defined as "base or depraved acts." The administration does not regard his outrageous conduct as coming under that definition. Tenure is intended to protect freedom of speech, but faculty members sometimes see it as a way to engage in controversial conduct without fear of retribution. Both Murphy and Wharton agree that something must be done about Professor Badenov's conduct.

Critical Thinking Questions

1. What are the likely consequences of doing nothing about Professor Badenov's conduct?
2. The administration cannot discharge Professor Badenov because he is protected by tenure. What kind of discipline could be used to discourage him from being a "loose cannon"?
3. Do you consider Professor Badenov's behavior unethical? How can a professional who behaves unethically be discouraged from mistreating his or her colleagues?

Cooperative Learning Exercise

4. In small groups, develop an action plan that describes what the chair should do when a faculty member engages in disruptive behavior. What conduct would justify the discharge of a tenured faculty member?

CASE 2 *Stealing a Smoke, Losing a Job*

Health Unlimited is a store in Jacksonville, Florida, that sells health foods to the general public. It offers organically grown produce, meat that is raised without chemical additives, vitamins, and a health food restaurant with a salad and sandwich bar. As a condition of employment, each employee is required to sign a statement that he or she is a nonsmoker and will not smoke either at work or away from work. Smoking at any time is considered a violation of this no-smoker policy and is enforced with immediate discharge. The company justifies this policy by saying that smokers are generally less healthy than nonsmokers and raise the health insurance rates it must pay for all employees. Many of the store's customers and employees are as adamantly opposed to smoking as the company is.

Lisa DeMarco is the produce manager of Health Unlimited. She was an ex-smoker at the time of her initial employment. In recent months, though, because she is experiencing stress over her separation from her husband, Lisa has started smoking again. She restricts her smoking to off-duty hours away from the market. However, one of Lisa's coworkers spotted her smoking in a local bar and informed the store's manager, Ellen Guidry.

The next day Ellen Guidry confronted Lisa, who admitted to smoking and explained her situation. Ellen said she was sorry, but the no-smoker policy had to be enforced. She had no recourse but to discharge Lisa immediately. Lisa felt that her discharge was not fair because she was honest with her boss and had a good work record. She also believed she deserved some consideration for the difficulties she was going through in her personal life.

Critical Thinking Questions

1. Is it legal for a business to institute a no-smoking policy that restricts smoking during off-duty hours as well as at work? If legal, is such a policy ethical?
2. Do you think Ellen treated Lisa fairly by discharging her for violating the no-smoker policy? Should the mitigating circumstances Lisa cited have entered into Ellen's decision? How would you have handled this case?

Cooperative Learning Exercise

3. In a small group, discuss why it is difficult to discipline employee off-duty conduct. Develop some general guidelines that managers should use to decide when and how to discipline employees' off-duty conduct.

HRM Simulation 

In Incident M, do you think Tom Clark deserves to be disciplined? If so, what work rule or company policy do you think he violated in his pay negotiations with his supervisor? Does the discipline given to Tom Clark meet the "just cause" standard? Suppose management decides to rehire Tom Clark. Will doing so create a precedent for future cases similar to this one? If an employee says he or she quits one day and then has a change of heart the next day, should management be required to discharge the employee? What factors might influence this decision?

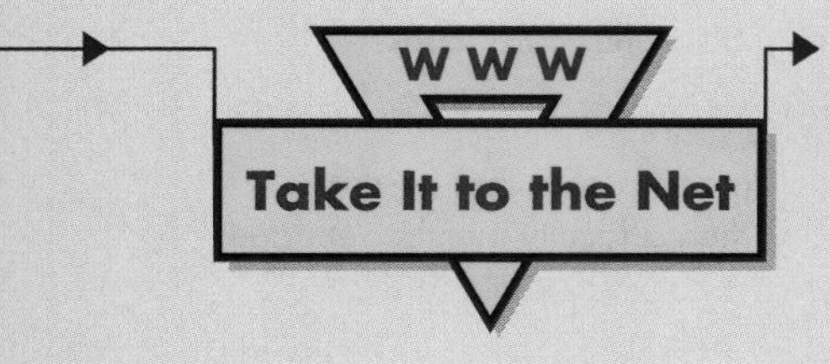

We invite you to visit the Gómez-Mejía/Balkin/Cardy page on the Prentice Hall Web site:

http://www.prenhall.com/gomez

You can also visit the Web sites for these companies, featured within this chapter:

Aetna	http://www.aetna.com
Avis Car Rental	http://www.avis.com
General Electric	http://www.ge.com
Harley Davidson	http://www.harleydavidson.com
MCA	http://www.mca.com

Endnotes

1. Greengard, S. (1996, May). Privacy: Entitlement or illusion? *Personnel Journal,* 74–88.
2. Miller, J. L., Balkin, D. B., and Allen, R. (1993). Employer restrictions on employees' legal off-duty conduct. *Labor Law Journal, 44*(4), 208–219.
3. Cheeseman, H. (1997). *Contemporary Business Law*, (2nd ed.) Upper Saddle River, NJ: Prentice Hall.
4. Egler, T. (1996, May). A manager's guide to employment contracts. *HRMagazine*, 28–33.
5. Gullett, C. R., and Greenwade, G. D. (1988). Employment at will: The no fault alternative. *Labor Law Journal, 39*(6), 372–378.
6. *Id.*
7. McWhirter, D. (1989). *Your rights at work.* New York: Wiley.
8. Brett, J. M. (1980, Spring). Why employees want unions. *Organizational Dynamics, 8,* 316–332.
9. Rousseau, D. (1995). *Psychological contracts in organizations.* Thousand Oaks, CA: Sage Publications.
10. Lynn, J. (1995, August). A matter of principle: An ethics policy helps your company maintain its integrity and its customers. *Entrepreneur*, 59.
11. Sashkin, M., and Kiser, K. J. (1993). *Putting total quality management to work.* San Francisco, CA: Berrett-Koehler.
12. Otto, J. (1993, January 11). Random alcohol test proposed. *Aviation Week & Space Technology, 138*(2), 33.
13. Sovereign, K. (1994). *Personnel law,* (3rd ed.) Englewood Cliffs, NJ: Prentice Hall.
14. Holley, W. H., and Jennings, K. M. (1991). *The labor relations process* (4th ed.). Chicago, IL: Dryden.
15. Elkouri, F., and Elkouri, E. A. (1973). *How arbitration works* (3rd ed.). Washington, DC: Bureau of National Affairs.
16. Brown, D. R., and Gray, G. R. (1988, Summer). A positive alternative to employment at will. *SAM Advanced Management Journal, 53,* 13–16.
17. Maltby, L. L. (1990). The decline of employment at will—a quantitative analysis. *Labor Law Journal, 41*(1), 51–54.
18. Utroska, D. R. (1992, November). Management in Europe. *Management Review,* 21–24.
19. Hunt, J. W. (1989). *The law of the workplace.* Washington, DC: Bureau of National Affairs.
20. Buckley, M. R., and Weitzel, W. (1988). Employing at will. *Personnel Administrator, 33*(8), 78–80.
21. Bordwin, M. (1993, November). Timing is everything. *Small Business Reports,* 43–51.
22. Rosse, J., Miller, J., and Ringer, R. (1996, Summer). The deterrent value of drug and integrity testing. *Journal of Business and Psychology, 10*, 477–485.
23. Zigarelli, M. (1995). Drug testing litigation: Trends and outcomes. *Human Resource Management Review, 5,* 245–265; and Flynn, G. (1996, April). Will drug testing pass or fail in court? *Personnel Journal*, 141–144.
24. Green, W. E. (1989, November 21). Drug testing becomes corporate mine field. *The Wall Street Journal,* B1, B8.
25. Verespoj, M. A. (1990, July 2). Death blow for random testing. *Industry Week,* 47–48.
26. *The Wall Street Journal.* (1994, February 8). Drug testing gets big boost from the California Supreme Court, A1.
27. Gunsch, D. (1993, May). Training prepares workers for drug testing. *Personnel Journal,* 52–59.
28. Hanson, A. (1990, July). What employees say about drug testing. *Personnel,* 32–36.
29. Maltby, L. (1990, July). Put performance to the test. *Personnel,* 30–31.
30. Hamilton, J. O. (1991, June 3). A video game that tells if employees are fit for work. *Business Week,* 36; and Maltby, 1990.
31. Kleiman, C. (1996, April 14). Treating workers fairly may reduce employee theft. *The Denver Post*, J1.
32. Willis, R. (1986, January). White collar crime. *Management Review, 75,* 22–30.
33. Aiello, J. (1993). Computer-based work monitoring: Electronic surveillance and its effects. *Journal of Applied Social Psychology, 23*, 499–507.
34. DeTienne, K., and Flint, R. (1996, Spring). The boss's eyes and ears: A case study of electronic monitoring and the privacy for consumers and workers act. *The Labor Lawyer*, 93–115.
35. *USA Today.* (1993, May 24). Bosses peek at e-mail, B, 1:2.

36. *Business Week.* (1990, January 15). Is your boss spying on you?, 74–75.
37. See Garson, B. (1988). The electronic sweatshop: How computers are transforming the office of the future into the factory of the past. New York: Penguin Books; and Piturro, M. (1989, May). Employee performance monitoring…or meddling? *Management Review,* 31–33.
38. DeTienne and Flint, 1996.
39. Laabs, J. J. (1992). Surveillance: Tool or trap? *Personnel Journal, 71,* 96–104.
40. Bates, R., and Holton, E. (1995). Computerized performance monitoring: A review of human resource issues. *Human Resource Management Review, 5,* 267–288.
41. *Business Week,* 1990.
42. Near, J., and Miceli, M. (1985). Organizational dissidence: The case of whistleblowing. *Journal of Business Ethics, 4,* 1–16.
43. Near, J., and Miceli, M. (1995). Effective whistle-blowing. *Academy of Management Review, 20,* 679–708.
44. Hamilton, J. (1991, June 3). Blowing the whistle without paying the piper. *Business Week,* 138–139.
45. *Id.*
46. *The Economist.* (1995, August 19). The uncommon good, 55–56.
47. Boyle, R. D. (1990). A review of whistleblower protection and suggestions for change. *Labor Law Journal, 41*(12), 821–828.
48. Miceli, M., and Near, J. (1994). Whistleblowing: Reaping the benefits. *Academy of Management Executive, 8*(3), 65–72.
49. Trevino, L. (1992). The social effects of punishment in organizations: A justice perspective. *Academy of Management Review, 17,* 647–676.
50. Weinstein, S. (1992, September). Teams without managers. *Progressive Grocer,* 101–104.
51. Redeker, J. R. (1989). *Employee discipline.* Washington, DC: Bureau of National Affairs.
52. *Id.*
53. Osigweh, C., Yg, A. B., and Hutchison, W. R. (1989, Fall). Positive discipline. *Human Resource Management, 28*(3), 367–383.
54. Bryant, A. W. (1984). Replacing punitive discipline with a positive approach. *Personnel Administrator, 29*(2), 79–87.
55. Osigweh et al., 1989.
56. *Id.*
57. Harvey, E. L. (1987, March). Discipline vs. punishment. *Management Review, 76,* 25–29.
58. Sherman, C. V. (1987). *From losers to winners.* New York: American Management Association.
59. Bureau of National Affairs. (1987). *Grievance guide* (7th ed.). Washington, DC: Bureau of National Affairs.
60. Redeker, 1989.
61. Shellenbarger, S. (1994, January 13). More companies experiment with workers' schedules. *The Wall Street Journal,* B1–3.
62. Breuer, N. L. (1993, September). Resources can relieve ADA fears. *Personnel Journal,* 131–142.
63. Mamis, R. (1995, January). Employees from hell. *Inc.,* 50–57.
64. Sculnick, M. W. (1990, Spring). Key court cases. *Employee Relations Today, 17*(1), 53–59.
65. Sherman, 1987.
66. Denton, D. K. (1992, Summer). Keeping employees: The Federal Express approach. *SAM Advanced Management Journal, 57*(3), 10–13.
67. Leblanc, P. V., and McInerney, M. (1994, January). Need a change? Jump on the banding wagon. *Personnel Journal,* 72–78.

CHALLENGES

After reading this chapter, you should be able to deal more effectively with the following challenges:

1 ▶ **Understand** why employees join unions.

2 ▶ **Understand** the National Labor Relations (Wagner) Act and how the National Labor Relations Board regulates labor practices and union elections.

3 ▶ **Describe** labor relations in the United States and other parts of the world.

4 ▶ **Identify** labor relations strategies and describe how they affect operational and tactical labor relations decisions.

5 ▶ **Describe** the three phases of the labor relations process: union organizing, collective bargaining, and contract administration.

6 ▶ **Explain** how the union grievance procedure works and why the supervisor's role is critical in achieving sound labor relations with a union.

7 ▶ **Identify** the ways in which a union can affect a company's entire pattern of human resource management, including its staffing, employee development, compensation, and employee relations policies.

15 Working with Organized Labor

A Happy Ending. Although some U.S. companies have adopted an anti-labor-union stance, many firms enjoy amicable relations with their employees' labor unions. Here, managers and labor representatives shake hands on a mutually agreeable labor contract—the final stage in the negotiation process.

WWW

HRM on the Web

http://www.aflcio.org/

The AFL-CIO Home Page

This is the home page of the AFL-CIO, a federation to which most U.S. unions belong. The site covers topics of interest to managers and employees who work with organized labor, and includes (1) labor news on line, (2) press releases about union activities, (3) union policy statements, and (4) information about the AFL-CIO Organizing Institute.

Few institutions illustrate the power of people banding together for a common cause more effectively than labor unions. Unions can change the policies and practices of management profoundly. Consider the following situation:[1]

In 1989, after 17 years of organizing and negotiating, the Harvard Union of Clerical and Technical Workers (HUCTW) signed its first contract with Harvard University. The union had its genesis in the early 1970s, when a small group of women employed as support staff began to meet occasionally to share their personal and professional concerns. After discovering that they were not alone in feeling undervalued and overburdened in their jobs, these women decided to try to organize the 3,000 office workers in over 400 buildings across the campus. Finally, in 1987, their campaign came to the attention of the American Federation of State, County, and Municipal Employees (AFSCME). With AFSCME's support, HUCTW intensified its organizing efforts and pursued a very different strategy from that taken by traditional unions. For instance, it highlighted the gains unionization would bring in personal autonomy and human dignity, and refused to assail the university administration. In fact, a popular button read "It's not anti-Harvard to be pro-union."

Victory came at last in May 1988, when the National Labor Relations Board certified HUCTW after employees voted 1,530 to 1,486 in favor of the union. The contract that was signed in 1989 included the following provisions:

- Average wage increases of 32% over the next three years.
- A $50,000 a year scholarship fund.
- Eight weeks' leave at 70% of salary for mothers after giving birth and one week at full salary for fathers and adoptive parents.
- Joint union-management planning and problem-solving councils in each area of the university.
- Major improvements in pension benefits.
- An increase in the share of health insurance costs paid for by Harvard.
- Strong language regarding affirmative action.
- A joint union-management committee to address long-term needs.[2]

HUCTW's chief negotiator, Kristine Rondeau, hailed the contract as proof that labor could "win strong economic improvements and simultaneously develop a promising and forward-thinking relationship between the union and the university."[3] For Harvard management, which had vigorously fought the union, the contract mandated major changes in management policies and practices. The formation of management-labor "work councils" meant that the university would have to give its clerical and technical workers more say in the way things were done. Still, on the day the contract was signed, Harvard University president Derek Bok said, "We look forward with increasing confidence to a positive relationship between Harvard and the union."[4]

In this chapter we explore the labor-management relationship between companies and unions. We begin by examining why employees join unions and why some employers prefer the workplace not to be unionized. We then briefly review the history of U.S. labor unions. Next, we discuss the role of the manager in labor relations, outline the major U.S. legislation that governs labor issues, and describe the current labor-relations climate in the United States and in some other countries. We then examine the different labor relations strategies available to employers and explore the rules and procedures that govern union activities. Finally, we address the impact of unions on a variety of HR practices.

▸ Why Do Employees Join Unions?

union
An organization that represents employees' interests to management on such issues as wages, work hours, and working conditions.

A **union** is an organization that represents employees' interests to management on such issues as wages, work hours, and working conditions. Employees participate in administering the union and support its activities with *union dues*, fees they pay for the union's services. The law protects employees' rights to join and participate in unions. The law also requires employers to bargain and confer with the union over certain employment issues that affect unionized employees.

Employees join unions for different reasons. For example, in Israel, employees join unions because of their belief in the social justice represented by the union.[5] Employees in the United States seek union representation when they (1) are dissatisfied with certain aspects of their job, (2) feel that they lack influence with management to make the needed changes, and (3) see unionization as a solution to their problems.[6] The union's best ally is bad management. If managers listen to employees, give them some say in the policies that affect their jobs, and treat them fairly, employees usually will not feel the need to organize. Managers who ignore their workers' interests and treat them inconsistently often end up having to deal with a union.

Companies usually prefer a nonunion work force. The primary reason is that wages are typically higher for union employees, which puts unionized companies at a competitive disadvantage if their competitors are not unionized. In addition, unions constrain what managers can and cannot do with a particular employee. For instance, a unionized employee who is doing a particularly good job usually cannot be given a merit raise or promoted over someone who has greater seniority. And many labor agreements spell out the specific work responsibilities of certain employees, which reduces flexibility in work assignments. Of course, many unionized companies flourish, and unions have some very positive social benefits. For example, a recent study reported that unions boosted productivity at hospitals by 16% compared to nonunion hospitals.[7] But given the choice, most managers would prefer a nonunion environment.

The Origins of U.S. Labor Unions

Unions, as we think of them today, were largely unprotected by law in the United States until 1935. Certainly there were labor organizations prior to that time that attempted, with varying degrees of success, to influence and control the terms and conditions of their members' employment. The approach of the U.S. government to unions prior to 1935 was simple: In a free market economy the employment relationship is essentially a private one, and both employee and employer are free to accept or reject this relationship if they find it unsatisfactory. (See the discussion of employment at will in Chapter 14.)

This thinking regards the employer and the employee as in similar positions of power: Employees who find their compensation unfair or working conditions unreasonable are free to find another job; employers who are unhappy with an employee's performance can fire that employee. In practice, of course, employers have considerably more power than individual employees. A large steel manufacturer does not miss one employee who quits because there is usually a ready supply of applicants to replace that person. However, a large employer can so dominate a neighborhood, city, or region that there are few or no other employment alternatives. The large steel mills in Pittsburgh, the auto manufacturers in Detroit, the coal mine operators in Appalachia, and the tire companies in Akron are examples of employers and industries that have dominated their respective regions.

Early in this century, some of these large industrial employers created horrendous working conditions. Many of their employees were recent immigrants to the United States who had few skills, limited English, and no financial resources to cushion an employment interruption. Others were rural Americans who were part of the huge population shift from rural to urban areas. They, too, had few skills and financial resources. Employers were free to exploit both sets of workers because there was always a ready supply of replacements.

For instance, steel workers in Pittsburgh worked just inches away from molten iron and razor-sharp, fast-moving ribbons of steel.

In the Great Depression of the 1930s millions of workers lost their jobs as employers came under tremendous pressure to cut production costs. These cutbacks put even more pressure on the working class. It was in this environment that union activity as we know it was legalized by the Wagner Act (1935), which attempted to equalize the power of employers and employees. In fact, this goal explains much of the governmental and societal response to union activity during the Depression and in the years following World War II. Unions were widely supported because of the public perception that working people had little power.

In recent years, however, the public perception has changed. When President Reagan ordered the firing of striking air traffic controllers on August 5, 1981, two days after they began an illegal strike, the terminated employees received little sympathy from society at large, probably because unions were widely perceived to have become too powerful. This action took place in the middle of a period of dramatic decline in strikes in the United States: From a peak of 424 in 1974, strikes decreased to 45 in 1994.

The Role of the Manager in Labor Relations

The manager is on the front line in all labor-management relations. However, when a union represents a group of employees in a company, the company needs a staff of specialists who can represent management's interests to the union. These **labor relations specialists**, who are often members of the HR department, help resolve grievances, negotiate with the union over changes in the labor contract, and provide advice to top management on a labor relations strategy.

labor relations specialist
Someone, often a member of the HR department, who is knowledgeable about labor relations and can represent management's interests to a union.

Still, it is managers who bear the major responsibility for day-to-day labor-management relations. Thus, it is important that they understand the workplace issues associated with unions. First, as we noted earlier, unions generally take hold only in firms where employees are dissatisfied with their jobs, and managers greatly influence how employees perceive their work environment. Second, where there is a union, managers are responsible for the day-to-day implementation of the terms of the labor agreement. The more effectively they carry out this responsibility, the less time the company will spend resolving labor conflicts. Third, managers need to have a basic understanding of labor law so that they do not unintentionally create a legal liability for the company. Well-meaning managers can very easily do something illegal if they do not understand the law. Finally, individual managers are often asked to serve on committees to hear grievances brought by union members against the company. A manager who understands general labor issues will be better prepared to hear and decide such cases.

In this text we have generally saved the discussion of legal issues until later in the chapter. However, because the nature and function of unions are so dependent on legislation, we will look at the specifics of that legislation first.

▸ Labor Relations and the Legal Environment

The key labor relations legislation in the United States consists of three laws enacted between the 1930s and 1950s: the Wagner Act (1935), the Taft-Hartley Act (1947), and the Landrum-Griffin Act (1959). These laws regulate labor relations in the private sector. Public-sector labor relations are covered by federal or state laws that are patterned after these laws.

The history of labor relations law in the United States can be described as a balancing act. The government has tried to balance (1) employers' rights to operate their businesses free from unnecessary interference, (2) unions' rights to organize and bargain for their members, and (3) individual employees' rights to choose their representatives or to decide that they do not want or need union representation. Balancing these three sets of rights has been an extremely complex task. Before 1935, employer rights were essentially unchecked by federal legislation. After passage of the Wagner Act, however, many felt that union rights were too strongly protected, relative to both employer and individual employee rights. This sentiment led Congress to pass two laws—the Taft-Hartley Act and the Landrum-Griffin Act—in an attempt to achieve balance. Commentators differ as to the effectiveness of these laws in achieving the correct balance of employer, union, and employee rights.

The Wagner Act

Wagner Act/National Labor Relations Act (1935)
A federal law designed to protect employees' rights to form and join unions and to engage in such activities as strikes, picketing, and collective bargaining.

National Labor Relations Board (NLRB)
The independent federal agency created by the Wagner Act to administer U.S. labor law.

The **Wagner Act**, also known as the **National Labor Relations Act**, was passed during the Great Depression in 1935. It was designed to protect employees' rights to form and join unions and to engage in such activities as strikes, picketing, and collective bargaining. It is interesting to note that when Congress passed the Wagner Act, the Supreme Court upheld its constitutionality by the narrowest of margins (5–4).

The Wagner Act created the **National Labor Relations Board (NLRB)**, an independent federal agency charged with administering U.S. labor law. The NLRB's primary functions are: (1) to administer *certification elections*, secret ballot elections that determine whether employees want to be represented by a union, and (2) to prevent and remedy unlawful acts called *unfair labor practices*. The NLRB remedies an unfair labor practice by issuing a *cease and desist order*, which requires the guilty party to stop engaging in the unlawful labor practice. The Wagner Act established five illegal labor practices that can be remedied by the National Labor Relations Board:

1. Interfering with, restraining, or coercing employees to keep them from exercising their rights to form unions, bargain collectively, or engage in concerted activities for mutual protection.
2. Dominating or interfering with the formation or administration of a union or providing financial support for it.
3. Discriminating against an employee to discourage union membership. Discrimination can include not hiring a union supporter, or not promoting, firing, or denying a pay raise to an employee who is a union member or who favors union representation.
4. Discharging or otherwise discriminating against an employee who has filed charges or given testimony under the act's provisions.
5. Refusing to bargain collectively with the union that employees chose to represent them.

The Taft-Hartley Act

Taft-Hartley Act (1947)
A federal law designed to limit some of the power acquired by unions under the Wagner Act by adjusting the regulation of labor-management relations to ensure a level playing field for both parties.

The **Taft-Hartley Act**, enacted in 1947 shortly after the end of World War II, was designed to limit some of the power that unions acquired under the Wagner Act and to protect the rights of management and employees. Although the Taft-Hartley Act was basically favorable to management's interests, its goals were to adjust the regulation of labor-management relations to ensure a level playing field for both parties.

Taft-Hartley included remedies from the National Labor Relations Board for six unfair union labor practices:

1. Restraining or coercing employees in the exercise of their rights guaranteed under the act, and/or coercing an employer's choice of a representative in collective bargaining.
2. Causing or attempting to cause an employer to discriminate against an employee who is not a member of a labor union for any reason other than failure to pay the union dues and initiation fees uniformly required as a condition of acquiring or retaining membership in the union.

3. Refusing to bargain in good faith with an employer after a majority of the employees in a unit have elected the union as their representative.
4. Asking or requiring its members to boycott products made by a firm engaged in a labor dispute with another union (*secondary boycott*). However, a union can call a boycott of products produced by its own firm (*primary boycott*).
5. Charging employees excessive or discriminatory union dues as a condition of membership in a union under a union shop clause. (A **union shop clause** requires employees to join the union 30 to 60 days after their date of hire.)
6. Causing an employer to pay for services that are not performed. This practice, often called *featherbedding*, is technically illegal, but the definition of unnecessary or unperformed work is often murky. For example, railroad unions continued to require the presence of firemen on engines long after their main duty (taking care of the fire on a steam engine) was eliminated by the advent of diesel engines.

union shop clause
A union arrangement that requires new employees to join the union 30 to 60 days after their date of hire.

Twelve years later, the Landrum-Griffin Act added a seventh unfair union labor practice: It is illegal for a union to picket an employer for the purpose of union recognition (a practice known as *recognitional picketing*).

Perhaps the most controversial provision of the Taft-Hartley Act is Section 14b, which gives permission to the states to enact right-to-work laws. A state **right-to-work law** makes it illegal within that state for a union to include a union shop clause in its contract. Unions negotiate union shop clauses into their contracts to provide greater security to union employees and prevent nonunion employees from receiving union services without paying union dues. A less restrictive arrangement called the *agency shop clause* requires employees to pay a union service fee (about equal to union dues) but does not require them to join the union. Currently, 21 states have right-to-work laws, which make it more difficult to organize and sustain unions in those states. Most of these states are located in the southern or western United States, away from major industrial centers.

right-to-work law
A state law that makes it illegal within that state for a union to include a union shop clause in its contract.

Several other provisions of Taft-Hartley are noteworthy. First, the act made *closed shops*, which require an employee to be a union member as a condition of being hired, illegal. This provision was modified 12 years later by the Landrum-Griffin Act to allow a closed shop in the construction industry as the only exception. Second, Taft-Hartley allowed employees to get rid of a union they no longer want through a *decertification election* and charged the NLRB with regulating decertification elections. Finally, Taft-Hartley created a new agency, the *Federal Mediation and Conciliation Service*, to help mediate labor disputes so that economic disruptions due to strikes and other labor disturbances would be fewer and shorter.

The Landrum-Griffin Act

The **Landrum-Griffin Act** was enacted in 1959 to protect union members and their participation in union affairs. To protect this right, Landrum-Griffin allows the government, through the Department of Labor, to regulate union activities. Landrum-Griffin was enacted because a few unions experienced problems with corrupt leadership and the misuse of funds for illegal activities.

Landrum-Griffin Act (1959)
A law designed to protect union members and their participation in union affairs.

The Landrum-Griffin Act includes the following key provisions:

1. Each union must have a bill of rights for union members to ensure minimum standards of internal union democracy.
2. Each union must adopt a constitution and provide copies of it to the Department of Labor.
3. Each union must report its financial activities and the financial interests of its leaders to the Department of Labor.
4. Union elections are regulated by the government, and union members have the right to participate in secret ballot elections.

5. Union leaders have a fiduciary responsibility to use union money and property for the benefit of the membership and not for their own personal gain. Members can sue and recover damages from union leaders who fail to exercise their fiduciary responsibilities.

Other laws that affect labor relations include the Railway Labor Act (1926, last amended in 1970), the Norris-LaGuardia Act (1932), and the Byrnes Antistrikebreaking Act (1938). Of course, the equal employment opportunity laws discussed in Chapter 3 also apply to unionized workers.

While much of U.S. labor relations law is over four decades old, it would be a mistake to assume that nothing new is happening in this area. As this text was being written, Congress was considering the Teamwork for Employees and Management Act, which would amend the Wagner Act to ensure that employers are permitted to establish and maintain employee involvement programs.[8] Another set of amendments under consideration would eliminate an employer's right to use permanent replacements during an economic strike or work stoppage.[9] In Canada, several provinces have recently enacted laws that restrict employers from using replacement workers during strikes.[10] Clearly, the struggle to find the correct balance of employer, union, and employee rights is ongoing.

We now turn to a description of the current state of labor relations in the United States.

▸ Labor Relations in the United States

Labor relations in the United States evolved from the philosophy of the U.S. labor movement, which accepted the country's capitalist economic structure and wanted to operate within it.[11] U.S. unions have avoided a permanent affiliation with a political party and have focused on improving their members' welfare through dealing directly with the companies that employ their members. The key factors that characterize labor relations in the United States are: (1) business unionism, (2) unions structured by type of job, (3) a focus on collective bargaining, (4) labor contracts, (5) the adversarial nature of labor-management relations and shrinking union membership, and (6) the growth of unions in the public sector.

Business Unionism

business unionism
A form of unionism that focuses on improving workers' economic well-being.

U.S. unions put a high priority on improving the economic welfare of their members. **Business unionism** is unionism that focuses on "bread-and-butter" issues (such as wages, benefits, and job security) so that workers get a larger slice of the economic pie. U.S. unions, which practice business unionism, have traditionally avoided trying to influence the running of the company, and they provide little input to management on such strategic decisions as how to market a product or what types of new business to enter. It is rare to see U.S. union members on a company's board of directors. The key concerns of U.S. unions are shop-floor issues that relate directly to workers. U.S. labor laws reinforce this tendency by making wages, hours, and working conditions mandatory topics for bargaining. This means that management is obligated to bargain on these issues in good faith. Other issues, such as how to run the business, are not mandatory bargaining topics.

Unions Structured by Type of Job

In contrast to unions in some other countries, U.S. unions tend to be organized by type of job. For instance, truck drivers are often members of the Teamsters Union, many public school teachers are members of the National Education Association, and most auto workers belong to the United Auto Workers no matter which auto manufacturer employs them. Because most unions represent employees from multiple employers, they are typically arranged into *locals* governed by a national body. Each local consists of the union members in a particular geographical location. The local has its own officers and is generally concerned with day-to-day labor practices and disputes. The national organization ties these locals together, governs how locals are organized and operated, and, most importantly, establishes policy for contract negotiations.

The *AFL-CIO*, formed by the merger of the old American Federation of Labor and the Congress of Industrial Organizations, is a confederation of many different unions. Because it represents so many workers (approximately 14 million), the AFL-CIO has a tremendous influence on federal labor policies. It also provides support to individual national unions and mobilizes support for laws that are beneficial to working people. Finally, the AFL-CIO resolves disputes between national unions.[12]

Focus on Collective Bargaining

Unions and management are the dominant players in the U.S. labor relations system. Generally, the U.S. government takes a neutral role, allowing the players to make the rules that govern their particular workplace. The mechanism of choice for developing these rules is collective bargaining. Under a **collective bargaining** system, unions and management negotiate with each other to develop the work rules under which union members will work for a stipulated period of time, usually two or three years. **Work rules** include any terms or conditions of employment, including pay, work breaks and lunch periods, vacation, work assignments, and grievance procedures.

collective bargaining
A system in which unions and management negotiate with each other to develop the work rules under which union members will work for a stipulated period of time.

work rules
Any terms or conditions of employment, including pay, work breaks and lunch periods, vacation, work assignments, and grievance procedures.

Unions that are legally elected by workers in the United States act as the sole representative of those workers' concerns to management. While unions may compete for recognition, once one is recognized, individual employees cannot choose to be represented by another union.

Labor Contracts

The product of collective bargaining is a **labor contract** that spells out the conditions of employment and work rules that affect employees in the unit represented by the union. Because both parties enter into the contract voluntarily, one party can use the legal system to enforce the terms of the contract if the other party does not fulfill its responsibilities.

labor contract
A union contract that spells out the conditions of employment and work rules that affect employees in the unit represented by the union.

Labor contracts are an important feature of the U.S. labor relations system. In many other countries, such as Germany and Sweden, working conditions and employee benefits are codified into labor laws, but in the United States labor and management have historically established workers' economic benefits without government interference. Increasingly, however, the United States is following the lead of other countries in this respect. The most recent example is the Family and Medical Leave Act of 1993 (see Chapter 3), which grants employees many protections that had previously been available only to employees covered by a union contract. Current health reform proposals also seek to mandate certain health insurance benefits that until now have been the subject of labor-management negotiation.

The Adversarial Nature of Labor-Management Relations and Shrinking Union Membership

U.S. labor laws view labor and management as natural adversaries who will disagree over the distribution of the firm's profits. For this reason, rules have been put in place so that the pie is distributed peacefully.

In a sense, the U.S. labor relations system is modeled on the U.S. court system. In a court, "justice" may be considered the result of the clash of adversaries, with the district attorney representing the plaintiff's interests and the defense attorney representing the defendant's interests. Similarly, "economic justice" may be considered the result of negotiations between the union (the advocate of the employees) and management (the advocate of the firm's owners). While this adversarial model worked well for many years in the United States, it has recently become an obstacle to union-management cooperation, which has grown in importance as both labor markets and product markets have become more globally competitive.

As Figure 15–1 shows, 15.5% of the U.S. labor force is unionized. This is down from a peak of about 35% in 1945. There are several reasons for this decline: the shrinking base of blue-collar industrial jobs (the traditional area of unionization) due to automation and foreign competition; the increase in employment legislation that provides workers with remedies that address their needs; and the aggressively hostile labor relations strategies of many companies, which have made it difficult for unions to organize workers.[13] Other possible reasons for declining union membership are an increasingly educated work force, as well as the highly publicized legal problems of some union leaders.

Despite shrinking union membership, unions continue to be an important part of the U.S. labor relations system because they establish wage and benefit patterns that influence nonunion employers. In this way, unions indirectly affect about 40% to 50% of the U.S. labor force. In fact, many employees of nonunion firms benefit from the upward adjustments in their wages and benefits that their employers make to prevent a union from organizing their workers. Unions have also pioneered worker safety measures and antidiscriminatory labor practices. Unless the underlying causes that gave birth to unions are abolished—low wages, unsafe working conditions, health hazards, arbitrary firings and layoffs—it's a safe bet that unions will not disappear.

The Growth of Unions in the Public Sector

As the percentage of unionized workers in the private sector has declined, the percentage of unionized workers in the public sector has increased substantially. This increase is due in part to the expansion of local government in the 1980s and in part to organizing efforts that have targeted both public-sector and service-sector employees.[14]

Unions in the public sector are in many ways a special case of labor relations because although public-sector employees are more likely to be organized than private-sector

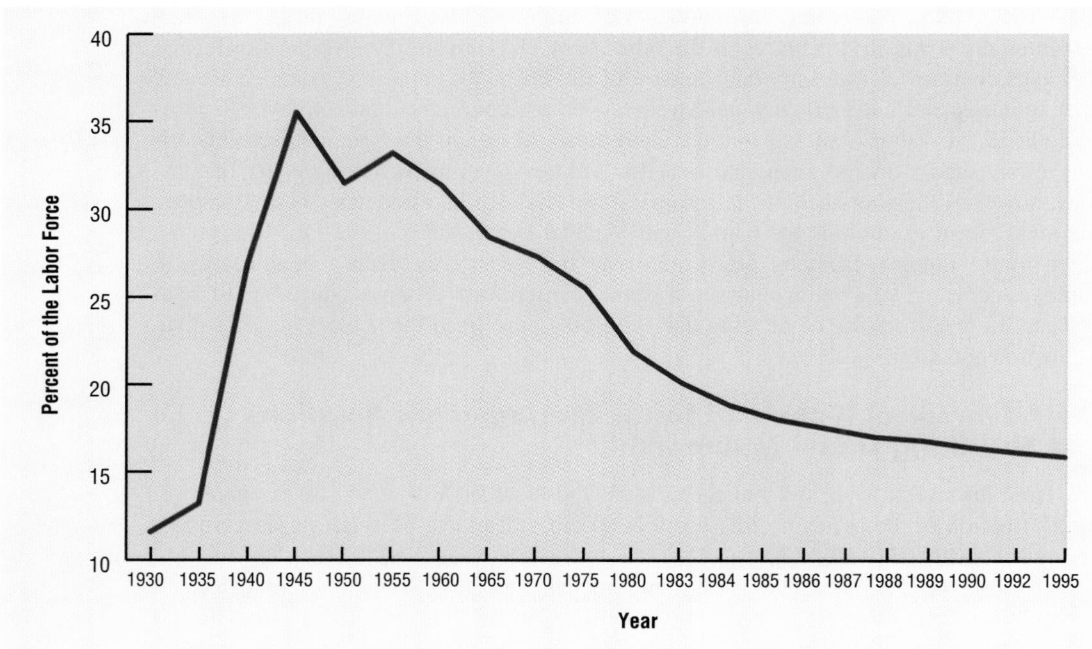

FIGURE 15–1

Union Membership in the United States, 1930–1995

Source: Bureau of Labor Statistics, Department of Labor.

employees, public-sector workers tend to have less bargaining power. There are two main reasons for this difference.

First, governmental power is diffuse. The typical private-sector firm is hierarchically organized so that there is one individual at the top who is in charge. However, governmental bodies in the United States have been intentionally structured so that power is divided among the legislative, executive, and judicial branches. This makes it more difficult for public-sector unions to negotiate and bargain collectively because the employer's representative often has only limited authority. For instance, a city employees' union may bargain with the mayor's office for higher pay, but the money for the higher salaries has to be appropriated by the city council, which may not concur with the mayor.

The second reason public-sector unions have less power is that many governmental entities severely restrict their employees' right to strike. The reasoning is that the government is a monopoly provider of essential services like police protection, garbage collection, and highway maintenance. If its employees were to go on strike, there would be no one else to provide these essential services. States differ in restrictiveness on this issue. For instance, Colorado forbids strikes by any state employees, including teachers. In contrast, New York, Michigan, Wisconsin, and some other states give some of their employees the right to strike in certain circumstances.

Because their right to strike is limited, public-sector unions have taken the lead in devising and experimenting with new ways to negotiate, including mandated arbitration and mediation. Their limited economic power has also made public-sector unions less likely than private-sector unions to put pay issues at the top of their agendas. For instance, teachers' unions often focus on such issues as class size, job security, and academic freedom rather than straight salary issues.

While having government as an employer can present difficulties to unionized workers, it also brings certain advantages. One is that union members, by virtue of the fact that they are also voters, have some political power over their employer. Because voter participation in nonfederal elections is often low in the United States, a well-organized public-sector union can be a powerful force in local politics. In fact, even national candidates court public-sector union support. A second advantage stems from the very diffusion of power we discussed earlier. This makes it possible for the union to play one branch of government against the other in certain circumstances. For instance, a union may be able to achieve a bargaining victory because it has the support of a city council member whose vote the mayor needs on some unrelated issue.

▸ Labor Relations in Other Countries

Labor relations systems vary from country to country because unions mean different things in different countries. In the United States labor relations involves collective bargaining and labor contracts, but in Sweden and Denmark it involves national wage setting, in Japan it involves enterprise unions that cooperate with company management, in Great Britain it involves union affiliation with the Labor Party, and in Germany it involves union representation on the company's board of directors.[15] Moreover, the shrinking percentage of private-sector employees represented by unions in the United States is not a world trend. Unions not only represent a large portion of the labor force in most other industrialized countries but are also important factors in the labor relations systems of many of those countries.

Figure 15–2 on page 464 compares union membership as a percentage of the labor force in 12 industrialized countries, including the United States. Union membership as a percentage of the labor force is higher in most European countries, with Denmark and Sweden having, respectively, 88% and 95% of their workers represented by unions in 1990. Although unionism declined in Great Britain in the 1980s, British unions still rep-

Year	United States	Canada	Austria	Aust-ralia	Japan	Den-mark	France	Ger-many	Italy	Nether-lands	Sweden	Switzer-land	United Kingdom
				Percent of Total Civilian Wage and Salary Employees									
1955	33	31	64	—	36	59	21	44	57	41	62	32	46
1960	31	30	61	—	33	63	20	40	34	42	62	33	45
1965	28	28	46	—	36	63	20	38	33	40	68	32	45
1970	30	31	43	—	35	64	22	37	43	38	75	31	50
1975	29	34	48	—	35	72	23	39	56	42	83	35	53
1980	25	35	47	—	31	86	19	40	62	41	88	35	56
1985	17	36	47	—	29	92	17	40	61	34	95	32	51
1990	16	36	43	34	25	88	—	—	—	28	95	31	46

FIGURE 15-2

Union Membership in Selected Countries, 1955–1990

Source: Chang, C., and Sorrentino, C. (1991, December). Union membership statistics in 12 countries. *Monthly Labor Review*, 48.

resented 46% of the work force in 1990, almost triple the percentage of U.S. workers. Even in Japan, whose firms seek to avoid unions when they locate factories in the United States, 25% of workers are unionized. This is significantly higher than the U.S. percentage.[16]

How Unions Differ Internationally

One analysis of unionism around the globe suggests that unions in different countries have different priorities.[17] Unions in different nations can be classified according to whether they emphasize economic issues, political issues, neither, or both. As we have seen, U.S. unions place a very strong emphasis on economic issues, particularly pay, benefits, and (more recently) job security. For example, in recent years outsourcing has become a major concern of U.S. unions because the first jobs to be subcontracted tend to be blue-collar jobs, the union's mainstay.[18] Compared to unions in other countries, U.S. unions place much less emphasis on political issues. True, some U.S. unions and union leaders are involved in political life, but their involvement tends to be less ideological than pragmatic. That is, political involvement is just another means to address economic concerns.

At the other end of the spectrum, unions in France tend to be much more politically involved and less concerned with economic issues. The two largest labor confederations in France have clear political orientations, and one is even religiously oriented. Strikes in France tend to focus on political change as the primary means of protecting or improving conditions for union members.

In China, unions are low in both economic and political involvement, primarily because of the pervasive control of the Chinese Communist Party over both political and economic affairs. A secondary reason is that the large majority of Chinese employees work for very small firms, which are notoriously difficult to organize.

Finally, Swedish unions tend to have a high degree of economic and political involvement. Swedish trade unions are often represented on governmental commissions in addition to actively representing their workers in economic affairs.[19]

We now turn our attention to two labor relations systems that have achieved high productivity and cooperation between unions and management: those of Germany and Japan.

Labor Relations in Germany

German law requires that all corporations involve workers in decisions at both the plant and the corporate level. This system is sometimes called *industrial democracy*. As practiced in Germany, industrial democracy means workers are represented at the plant level in works councils and at the corporate level through codetermination.

works council
A committee composed of both worker representatives and managers who have responsibility for governing the workplace; used in Germany.

Works councils are committees composed of both worker representatives and managers who have responsibility for governing the workplace. They are involved in operational decisions, such as the allocation of overtime, the discipline and discharge of workers, the hiring of new workers, and training.[20] At the plant level, works councils make many decisions on which unions would bargain with management in the United States. German unions focus on bargaining across industries on such issues as wages, rather than on bargaining within an industry, as is typical in the United States.

codetermination
The representation of workers on a corporation's board of directors; used in Germany.

Codetermination involves worker representation on a corporation's board of directors. German workers are well represented on boards of directors because it is assumed that labor and capital should form a partnership in governing the enterprise. With one third to one half of their boards of directors representing workers, German companies are likely to give employees' needs a high priority.[21] (The other board members represent the shareholders.) Not surprisingly, codetermination has fostered a spirit of cooperation between workers and managers. For the German economy, the results have been fewer strikes and higher productivity. For workers, the results have been both greater responsibility and greater security. For example, IG Metall, Germany's largest union, has taken the lead on a number of important issues instead of merely reacting to company proposals. The union's group-work policies, the product of nearly two decades of research and activism, are designed to protect workers from layoff or transfer to lower-paying jobs.

Labor Relations in Japan

enterprise union
A labor union that represents workers in only one large company rather than in a particular industry; used in Japan.

Japan has developed a successful labor relations system characterized by a high degree of cooperation between unions and management. A key factor in this success has been the Japanese enterprise union. The **enterprise union**, which represents Japanese workers in large corporations such as Toyota, Toshiba, and Hitachi, organizes the workers in only one company. This practice ensures that the union's loyalty will not be divided among different companies. The enterprise union negotiates with management with an eye on the company's long-term prosperity. This labor relations system was long reinforced by large Japanese corporations' offer of lifelong employment, which allowed Japanese workers to feel secure and unthreatened by changes in technology or job characteristics.[22]

Givebacks from the French.

In recent years, increased international competition has forced many U.S. unions to accept layoffs and other givebacks. The same is now happening in Europe. Here, French workers protest against proposed cuts in their pensions.

The traditional lifelong employment policy has encouraged cooperation between the enterprise unions and management. Many Japanese executives started their careers as union members right out of school, advanced to a leadership position in the union, and then got promoted into management, all within the same company. This type of labor relations system leads to close personal relationships among managers, union leaders, and workers that would be impossible under the more adversarial U.S. labor relations system. Because the enterprise union's legitimacy is unchallenged by management, there is a degree of trust and respect between the union and management in Japan that would be unthinkable in the United States. This fact helps to explain the behavior of Japanese executives who cooperate with a union in Japan but try at all costs to avoid unionization in their U.S. plants.

Unfortunately, there are signs that the labor relations systems in both Germany and Japan are in danger. In Germany, high labor costs for the average factory worker ($24 per hour versus $15 per hour in the United States in 1994) and the economic costs of unification with East Germany are forcing companies to drive a harder bargain with unions. Competition in global markets has led to downsizings in some of Germany's largest companies and has strained labor relations. For example, Daimler-Benz, Germany's largest industrial company, has reduced its work force by 70,000 jobs and announced expansion of a new automobile plant in Alabama, where labor costs are much lower than in Germany.[23] And in Japan, a closer look at lifelong employment policies shows that they have always been restricted to the largest companies, applied only to men, and end at age 55. Moreover, downsizing in Japan has made it difficult to sustain lifelong employment policies. NTT, Japan's giant telecommunications company, announced in 1996 plans to reduce its work force by 45,000 jobs, a quarter of its total number of employees. Nissan, the auto maker, is planning to lay off 7,000 of its workers and close one of its auto assembly plants.[24]

▸ Labor Relations Strategy

labor relations strategy
A company's overall plan for dealing with labor unions.

A company's **labor relations strategy** is its management's overall plan for dealing with unions. As Figure 15–3 shows, a company's labor relations strategy sets a tone that can range from open conflict with the union to labor-management cooperation.

The most important choice affecting a company's labor relations strategy is management's decision to accept or to avoid unions.[25]

Union Acceptance Strategy

union acceptance strategy
A labor relations strategy in which management chooses to view the union as its employees' legitimate representative and accepts collective bargaining as an appropriate mechanism for establishing workplace rules.

Under a **union acceptance strategy**, management chooses to view the union as its employees' legitimate representative and accepts collective bargaining as an appropriate mechanism for establishing workplace rules. Management tries to obtain the best possible labor contract with the union, and then governs employees according to the contract's terms. The labor relations policy shown in Figure 15–4 is an example of a union acceptance strategy.

A union acceptance strategy is likely to result in labor relations characterized by labor-management cooperation or working harmony. The relationship between General Motors and the United Auto Workers (UAW) union at the Saturn auto plant in Tennessee is an example of such a strategy. The union negotiated a very flexible contract with management at this plant in exchange for union recognition and job security for its workers. Management can redesign jobs, change technology, and streamline work rules—a degree of flexibility unknown in other unionized General Motors auto plants.[26] In turn, labor is involved in decision making to a degree that is rare in unionized companies. Groups of 5 to 15 workers perform managerial tasks such as hiring. They also elect representatives to higher-level teams that make joint decisions with management on every aspect of the business from car design to marketing to sticker price.[27]

Unfortunately, the road to union-management cooperation can be rocky. Even at Saturn, which is often held up as a model of cooperative labor relations, there are signs of trouble: Recent hires are frequently less committed to the employee participation idea than those who have been at the plant from the beginning, and some distrust the union's close ties with management. In fact, worker distrust of union-management cooperation threatens to derail teamwork initiatives at an increasing number of companies, especially since the NLRB ruled that management-led employee teams can violate the Wagner Act.[28] For management guidelines in this area, see the Manager's Notebook on page 468 titled "When Is a Team Not a Team?"

For smaller companies in particular, the adversarial model of management-labor relations has been slow to give way to a cooperative model. Although many small-business owners do work closely with their workers, they tend to regard such concepts as worker-management teams as a big company's game. "For the smallest firms, you start talking about things like that and they die laughing," says a research fellow at the National Federation of Independent Business, a small-business lobbying group. According to the NLRB, two thirds of unfair labor practice complaints are filed against employers with fewer than 100 workers. Since the great majority of small businesses are nonunionized, this record has encouraged unions to target small firms for membership expansion. In 1992 unions won certification at firms with fewer than 50 workers at twice their rate of success at companies employing more than 500 workers.[29] To avoid the loss of management control caused by unionization, many small companies have chosen to pursue a union avoidance strategy.

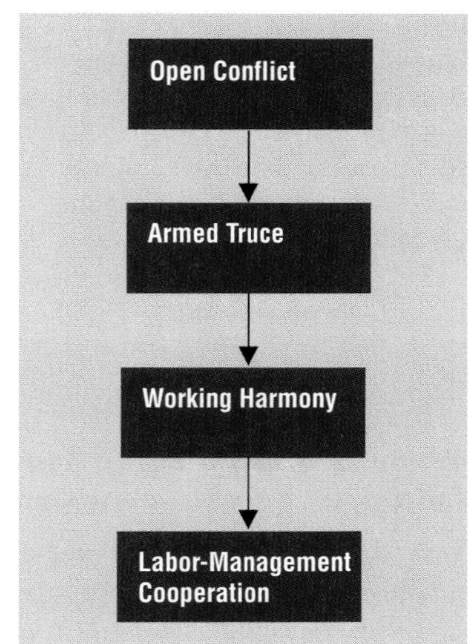

FIGURE 15–3

Types of Labor-Management Relations

Source: Mills, D. O. (1989). *Labor-management relations*, (4th ed.), 222. New York: McGraw-Hill.

Union Avoidance Strategy

Management selects a **union avoidance strategy** when it fears the union will have a disruptive influence on its employees or fears losing control of its workers to a union. Companies that choose a union avoidance strategy are likely to be, at best, in an armed truce with unions and, at worst, in open conflict with them (see Figure 15–3).

union avoidance strategy
A labor relations strategy in which management tries to prevent its employees from joining a union, either by removing the incentive to unionize or by using hardball tactics.

There are two different approaches to union avoidance: union substitution and union suppression.[30] Which approach a company pursues usually depends on the values of top management.

Our objective is to establish a labor policy that is consistent and fair. The purpose is to develop an agreeable working relationship with the union while retaining our full management rights. The rationale behind our labor relations policy is consistency, credibility, and fairness to union representatives and the workers who are in the union. In order to make our policy effective, the Company will:

- Accept union representation of employees in good faith, provided the union represents the majority of our employees;
- Maintain the right of management to manage;
- Adopt procedures by which top management continuously supports the positions of its representatives in implementing the firm's policies and practices in the area of industrial relations;
- Enforce disciplinary policies in a fair, firm, and consistent manner;
- See to it that union representatives follow all Company rules except those from which they are exempted under specific provisions of the labor contract;
- Handle all employee complaints fairly, firmly, and without discrimination;
- See that every representative of management exercises a maximum effort to follow Company policies fairly and consistently; and
- See to it that all decisions and agreements pertaining to the present contract are documented in writing.

FIGURE 15–4

Labor Relations Policy: Union Acceptance Strategy

Source: (1990). *The company policy manual*, 332, New York: Harper Business Division of HarperCollins Publishers.

union substitution/proactive human resource management A union avoidance strategy in which management becomes so responsive to employees' needs that it removes the incentives for unionization.

Union Substitution. In the **union substitution** approach, also known as the **proactive human resource management approach**, management becomes so responsive to employees' needs that it removes the incentive for unionization. Using this approach, IBM, Hewlett-Packard, Eli Lilly, Eastman Kodak, and Gillette avoided unionization and simultaneously developed a reputation as good places to work. All these companies have instituted a number of policies that lead to employees' feeling generally satisfied with their jobs and their ability to participate in management decisions. Some of the policies used by companies that take the union substitution approach are:

- Job security policies that protect the jobs of full-time workers. Among these is a policy that subcontracted, temporary, and part-time workers must be discharged before permanent employees can be laid off.
- Promoting-from-within policies that encourage the training and development of employees.
- Profit-sharing and employee stock ownership plans (see Chapter 11) that share the company's success with its employees.
- High-involvement management practices that solicit employee input into decisions.
- Open door policies and grievance procedures that try to give workers the same sense of empowerment that they would have under a union contract.[31]

Manager's Notebook

When Is a Team Not a Team? Guidelines for Employee Involvement Committees

Two conditions determine whether or not a company's employee involvement (EI) group violates the Wagner Act. A group is illegal if it can be proved to be *both* "employer dominated" and a "labor organization" under the law. Though it's often unclear which category a specific condition or action falls under, here are some general guidelines to help managers steer clear of illegalities:

- Determine whether the issues addressed by an EI team clearly constitute "conditions of employment." Until legal developments shed new light on the situation, experts say EI groups should be limited to addressing production, quality, and safety matters.
- Employer domination can be construed if any group of employees is perceived as constituting a "select" group empowered to speak to management on behalf of all employees. Managers can guard against such a charge by periodically rotating employee participants on EI teams.
- In light of the NLRB's recent ruling, grievance committees, especially in a nonunion setting, can easily come under fire. Managers must make sure that any such group functions in a way that is strictly independent of management influence. If disputes are settled by means of a negotiation process between employer and employee, employer dominance is often readily established. But if management delegates the authority to resolve grievances to the group and the group resolves such problems on its own, the group is likely to be seen as benign, despite the fact that management played a key role in establishing and encouraging it.
- In a unionized setting, getting union participation in EI committees is virtually a surefire way to avoid litigation.
- If the company is nonunion, the situation can be trickier. Managers must be sure to get visible employee input and make the venture a cooperative and voluntary one.
- *Never* start up an EI group during a union-organizing campaign. Such activity can readily be seen as union busting.

Source: Adapted, by permission of the publisher, from *Management Review Forum*, February 1994, © 1994. American Management Association, New York. All rights reserved.

Union Suppression. Management uses the **union suppression** approach when it wants to avoid unionization at all costs and does not make any pretense of trying "to do the right thing" for its employees. Under this approach, management employs hardball tactics, which may be legal or illegal, to get rid of a union or to prevent the union from organizing its workers.

For example, in the mid-1980s, Continental Airlines' CEO Frank Lorenzo used the U.S. bankruptcy courts to reorganize Continental and escape the company's obligations to employees under its labor contracts with its unions. When the airline emerged from bankruptcy, it had a nonunion work force with pay levels about 40% lower than had prevailed under the union contracts. In another case at about the same time, the *Chicago Tribune* bargained aggressively with its production unions and, when the union workers went out on strike, substituted permanent replacement workers. The result was a completely nonunionized work force at the newspaper.

Sometimes the union suppression approach backfires and management reaps nothing but an angry union, bitter employees, and the worst kind of public relations. In 1990, management at the New York *Daily News*, which was then owned by the Chicago Tribune Company, tried to use replacement workers to intimidate its striking unions, but lost the battle because the media and the public sympathized with the union cause. J. P. Stevens, a textile manufacturer with plants in the southern United States, illegally tried to intimidate its workers by firing union organizers before a union certification election. The National Labor Relations Board intervened on behalf of the union and ordered J. P. Stevens to recognize and bargain with the union.

In general, the union suppression approach is a higher-risk strategy than the union substitution approach and for this reason is used less frequently. Hardball tactics not only entail legal risks but can also come back to haunt management. Frank Lorenzo's use of the bankruptcy courts to break the company's unions looked like a great success at the time. However, in 1994 Lorenzo's bid to start a new low-fare airline was rejected by the Department of Transportation because of safety and regulatory compliance problems during Lorenzo's stewardship of Eastern and Continental Airlines. The DOT said that both of these airlines "experienced operational, maintenance, and labor-related problems that were among the most serious in the history of aviation."[32]

union suppression
A union avoidance strategy in which management uses hardball tactics to prevent a union from organizing its workers or to get rid of a union.

One strategy for suppressing union activity is to ask certain workers to report to management any union-organizing activities that are taking place at the company. Is this strategy legal? Is it ethical? If you answered yes to both questions, do you think it is good management practice? Why or why not?

Building Managerial Skills: Managing the Labor Relations Process

Now that you have some grounding in the history of management-labor relations and relevant law, as well as a sense of the current state of labor relations and corporate strategies in this area, we can examine the specific components of the labor relations process. As Figure 15–5 shows, there are three phases of labor relations that managers and labor relations specialists must deal with: (1) union organizing, in which employees exercise their right to form a union; (2) collective bargaining, in which union and management representatives negotiate a labor contract; and (3) contract administration, in which the labor contract is applied to specific work situations on a daily basis.

Union Organizing

Union organizing takes place when employees work with a union to form themselves into a cohesive group. The key issues that managers confront in a union organizing campaign are union solicitation, preelection conduct, and the certification election.

Union Solicitation. Before it will order a union certification election, the National Labor Relations Board requires a union to show that there is significant interest in unionization among a company's employees. To meet this requirement, a minimum of 30% of the employees in the relevant work unit must sign an authorization card indicating that they want to be represented by a specific union for collective bargaining purposes. A sample union authorization card is shown in Figure 15–6 on page 470.

Unions often conduct the early stages of their solicitation effort in private homes or public facilities so that management will not be aware of the organizing drive until the required percentage of workers has signed authorization cards. However, sometimes the union finds it necessary to solicit on company property, which alerts management and gives it the opportunity to respond.

Management's choice of labor relations strategy guides a company's response to union solicitation. Companies with a union avoidance strategy usually have a "no solicitation" policy that restricts all solicitations to nonwork areas (for example, solicitation may take place in lunch or break rooms, but not in offices) and nonwork times. A no-solicitation policy makes it more difficult for the union to influence workers' attitudes toward the union and persuade them to sign authorization cards. However, companies that have a no-solicitation policy must be careful to enforce it consistently so that *all* solicitations (including those for charitable causes) are restricted. Singling out union-organizing activities for restriction is an unfair labor practice that can result in an NLRB order to cease and desist the discriminatory policy.

Consistent enforcement of a no-solicitation policy was one of the key factors that led the Supreme Court to rule in favor of Lechmere, Inc., a Newington, Connecticut, store that

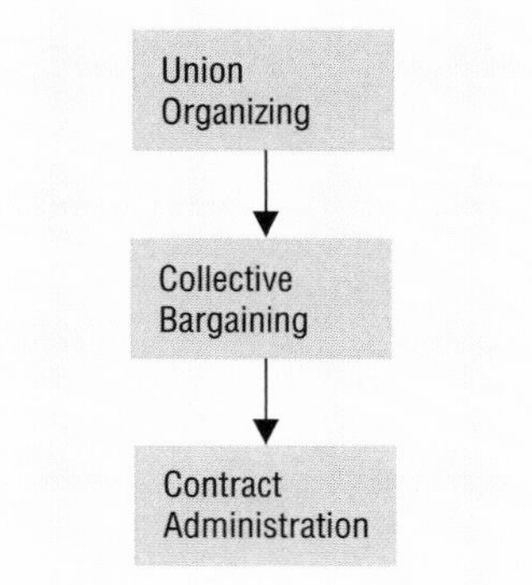

FIGURE 15–5
The Three Phases of the Labor Relations Process

Date .... 19 ....

STRICTLY CONFIDENTIAL

Office & Professional Employees International Union, Local 153, AFL-CIO
265 West 14th Street, New York, NY 10011   741-8282

I hereby authorize Office & Professional Employees International Union, Local 153, AFL-CIO, to represent me and to petition the National Labor Relations Board to conduct a secret ballot election among the staff.

Name .... Tel. No. ....
(Please print)

Address ....
(Zip Code No.)

Present Employer ....

Present Employer's Address ....

Position .... Dept. ....

Signature ....

CONFIDENTIAL

FIGURE 15-6

Sample Union Authorization Card

Source: Office & Professional Employees Union, New York, NY.

had banned unions from its premises. The court found that Lechmere did not violate the Wagner Act largely because it had consistently enforced its no-solicitation policy against all organizations, including the Girl Scouts and the Salvation Army. The court also found that the store's 200 workers were otherwise accessible to the union's nonemployee organizers.[33]

Preelection Conduct. If the union can show sufficient employee interest in forming a union, the NLRB will schedule a certification election. During the period before the election, management and union leaders should allow employees to freely exercise their right to vote for or against representation. It is the NLRB's policy to provide an environment in which employees can make an uncoerced choice in their selection of a bargaining agent—or, alternatively, an uncoerced choice not to be represented by any union.

During the preelection period, managers must avoid treating employees in a manner that could be interpreted as using their position to influence the outcome of the election. The NLRB "Notice to Employees" shown in Figure 15–7 indicates some types of conduct that are unacceptable before an election. Managers are prohibited from threatening employees with the loss of their jobs or benefits if they vote for the union. They must also avoid promising employees benefits (such as pay raises or promotions) if they vote against the union. On their side, unions must avoid threatening workers with harm if they do not vote for unionization. While the NLRB's rules for permissible conduct during a union election campaign are exceedingly complex and constantly changing, the Manager's Notebook titled "Quick TIPS for Preelection Conduct" provides some general guidelines for managers.

It *is* permissible for managers to try to persuade employees before a representation election that they would be better off without a union. Some of the methods that managers can legally use to do this are:

Manager's Notebook

Quick TIPS for Preelection Conduct

The acronym TIPS is a quick way to remember the following guidelines developed by labor lawyers and consultants to guide managers' preelection conduct.

Threats. It is unlawful to threaten employees with theoretical dire consequences should the union win the election.

Intimidation. Employers by law cannot intimidate or coerce employees to vote against the union.

Promises. Management cannot promise employees benefits or rewards if they vote against the union.

Surveillance. It is unlawful to secretly or overtly spy on organizing meetings.

Source: Reprinted by permission of the publisher, from *HR Focus*, January 1992,

NOTICE TO EMPLOYEES

FROM THE

National Labor Relations Board

A PETITION has been filed with this Federal agency seeking an election to determine whether certain employees want to be represented by a union.

The case is being investigated and NO DETERMINATION HAS BEEN MADE AT THIS TIME by the National Labor Relations Board. IF an election is held Notices of Election will be posted giving complete details for voting.

It was suggested that your employer post this notice so the National Labor Relations Board could inform you of your basic rights under the National Labor Relations Act.

YOU HAVE THE RIGHT under Federal Law

- **To self-organization**
- **To form, join, or assist labor organizations**
- **To bargain collectively through representatives of your own choosing**
- **To act together for the purposes of collective bargaining or other mutual aid or protection**
- **To refuse to do any or all of these things unless the union and employer, in a state where such agreements are permitted, enter into a lawful union-security agreement requiring employees to pay periodic dues and initiation fees. Nonmembers who inform the union that they object to the use of their payments for nonrepresentational purposes may be required to pay only their share of the union's costs of representational activities *(such as collective bargaining, contract administration, and grievance adjustments).***

It is possible that some of you will be voting in an employee representation election as a result of the request for an election having been filed. While NO DETERMINATION HAS BEEN MADE AT THIS TIME, in the event an election is held, the NATIONAL LABOR RELATIONS BOARD wants all eligible voters to be familiar with their rights under the law IF it holds an election.

The Board applies rules that are intended to keep its elections fair and honest and that result in a free choice. If agents of either unions or employers act in such a way as to interfere with your right to a free election, the election can be set aside by the Board. Where appropriate the Board provides other remedies, such as reinstatement for employees fired for exercising their rights, including backpay from the party responsible for their discharge.

NOTE:

The following are examples of conduct that interfere with the rights of employees and may result in the setting aside of the election.

- **Threatening loss of jobs or benefits by an employer or a union**
- **Promising or granting promotions, pay raises, or other benefits to influence an employee's vote by a party capable of carrying out such promises**
- **An employer firing employees to discourage or encourage union activity or a union causing them to be fired to encourage union activity**
- **Making campaign speeches to assembled groups of employees on company time within the 24-hour period before the election**
- **Incitement by either an employer or a union of racial or religious prejudice by inflammatory appeals**
- **Threatening physical force or violence to employees by a union or an employer to influence their votes**

Please be assured that IF AN ELECTION IS HELD every effort will be made to protect your right to a free choice under the law. Improper conduct will not be permitted. All parties are expected to cooperate fully with this Agency in maintaining basic principles of a fair election as required by law. The National Labor Relations Board, as an agency of the United States Government, does not endorse any choice in the election.

NATIONAL LABOR RELATIONS BOARD
an agency of the
UNITED STATES GOVERNMENT

THIS IS AN OFFICIAL GOVERNMENT NOTICE AND MUST NOT BE DEFACED BY ANYONE

FORM NLRB-666 (5-90) ★U.S. GOVERNMENT PRINTING OFFICE: 1991-312-471/51356

FIGURE 15-7

NLRB Representation Election Notice to Employees

Source: National Labor Relations Board.

- Making speeches to groups of employees emphasizing why they do not need a union (legal up to 24 hours before the election).
- Employing a labor relations consultant to assist with the antiunion strategy.
- Sending a personal letter to employees.
- Showing movies that view unions in an unfavorable light.
- Writing memos to employees that summarize all the good things that the employer has provided for them.

Organizing Campaigns: A New Priority

Issues + Applications

In recent years, many unions have started to pour significant resources into their organizing campaigns. In some cases they are targeting workers they have long ignored: the low-wage service workers on the bottom rung of the U.S economic ladder. In other cases, they are appealing to high-wage professional workers who until recently had not seen a need for union representation. Here are some examples of recent successful union-organization activities:

- At Case Foods, Inc., a poultry plant in Morgantown, North Carolina, workers were required to pay for gloves and hairnets and had to ask permission to use the restroom. The workers were paid only $6.15 per hour. After three men were denied permission to use the restroom, the workers (most of whom spoke Spanish as their native language) walked off their jobs in protest. After the walkout, Spanish-speaking organizers from the Laborers Union successfully organized the company.
- Flight attendants at Atlanta-based ValueJet, a regional airline, were upset about company regulations that required them to buy their own uniforms and pay for airport parking. In addition, the flight attendants—who earned about $12 per hour—spent 14 hours traveling but were paid for only eight. The Association of Flight Attendants organized the employees in secret, fearing that the airline would retaliate against prounion workers. Caught off guard, ValueJet mounted its opposition too late to prevent 58% of its flight attendants from voting for the union.
- Disa Sacks, a Florida rheumatologist, found that her medical practice could not survive if she did not sign on to insurance companies' managed-care networks. Sacks resented the interference of the networks, which cap doctors' fees and monitor the tests and operations they can prescribe. So she joined a union, the Federation of Physicians & Dentists, which has signed up 500 private practitioners in Florida. Doctors join unions in the hope that collective strength will give them the clout they need to deal on a more equal basis with the Aetnas and Prudentials of the world.

Sources: Adapted from Zachery, G. (1995, September 1). Some unions step up organizing campaigns and get new members. The *Wall Street Journal*, A1, A2; Valez-Dapena, P. (1995, January 23). Doctors with union cards. *Business Week*, 101; and Levinson, M. (1996, July 8). It's hip to be union. *Newsweek*, 44-45.

Certification Election. The NLRB supervises the certification election, determining who is eligible to vote and counting the ballots. The voting is done by secret ballot, and the outcome is determined by the participating voters.

If the union receives a majority of the votes, it becomes the certified bargaining agent for all of the unit's employees. This means that it becomes the exclusive agent for both union and nonunion employees in collective bargaining with the employer. The *bargaining unit* consists of all the employees who are represented by a union that engages in collective bargaining with the employer.

If the majority of voters vote against the union, NLRB policy states that no other representation election may be held for a 12-month period. In recent years unions have been losing more than half of the representation elections held in the United States.[34] Because of this trend, unions have begun to devote more resources to organizing activities.[34a] The Issues and Applications feature titled "Organizing Campaigns: A New Priority" gives some examples of successful attempts by U.S. unions to organize diverse groups of employees.

Collective Bargaining

If union organizing results in certification, the next step in the labor relations process is collective bargaining that results in a labor contract. Most labor contracts last for two to three years, after which they are subject to renegotiation.

Four of the most important issues related to collective bargaining are bargaining behavior, bargaining power, bargaining topics, and impasses in bargaining. In all of these areas, managers must monitor their behavior carefully.

Bargaining Behavior. Once the NLRB certifies a union as the bargaining agent for a unit of employees, both management and the union have a duty to bargain with each other in "good faith." Refusing to bargain in good faith can result in an NLRB cease and desist order that is enforced in the courts. The parties are showing good faith in collective bargaining when:

- Both parties are willing to meet and confer with each other at a reasonable time and place.
- Both parties are willing to negotiate over wages, hours, and conditions of employment (the mandatory bargaining topics).
- The parties sign a written contract that formalizes their agreement and binds them to it.
- Each party gives the other a 60-day notice of termination or modification of the labor agreement before it expires.

In general, *good faith bargaining* means treating the other party reasonably even when disagreements arise. To show good faith, management should develop different proposals and suggestions for negotiating with the union instead of simply rejecting all union proposals. For example, in the early 1960s a negotiator for General Electric made a single proposal to the union on a take-it-or-leave-it basis, and then refused to negotiate on any of the union's counteroffers. The NLRB interpreted this inflexible approach to bargaining as an unfair labor practice that did not show good faith.

A QUESTION OF ETHICS

Suppose at a prebargaining meeting between the company's negotiating team and top management it is decided that the company will give up to a 4% raise. When negotiations start, however, the lead management negotiator states that the company cannot afford more than a 2% raise, and will go no higher. Is this ethical behavior? What if the situation were reversed and it was the union negotiator who stated an absolute minimum demand, knowing that the union leadership will accept less? Would that be ethical?

Bargaining Power. In collective bargaining sessions, both parties are likely to take opening positions that favor their goals while indicating that they are prepared to make some concessions to reach a satisfactory outcome. In other words, the parties select initial positions that leave them some room to negotiate. For example, on the topic of pay raises, the union may initially ask for 8% but be willing to go as low as 5%. Management may initially offer the union 2% but be willing to go as high as 6%.

At which point will the parties reach agreement, 5% or 6%? The party that understands how to use its bargaining power will probably be able to achieve settlement closer to its initial bargaining position. *Bargaining power* is one party's ability to get the other party to agree to its terms. If management has greater bargaining power than the union, it is likely to get the union to agree to a 5% pay increase.

An important aspect of a party's bargaining power is how it is perceived by the other party. Each party can engage in behaviors that shape the other party's perceptions. Management that acts in a powerful and intimidating manner may influence the union to make additional concessions. However, aggressive posturing by management may backfire and cause union negotiators to make fewer concessions.

Parties in negotiations have several tactical alternatives. Two bargaining tactics are often used to increase bargaining power: distributive bargaining and integrative bargaining.[35]

Distributive Bargaining. **Distributive bargaining** focuses on convincing your counterpart in negotiations that the cost of disagreeing with your terms would be very high. In collective bargaining the cost of disagreement is often a strike. Strikes usually occur in the United States when a labor contract expires without both sides reaching a new agreement. Distributive bargaining tactics tend to be used when the two sides are competing for very limited resources.

distributive bargaining
Bargaining that focuses on convincing the other party that the cost of disagreeing with the proposed terms would be very high.

Labor uses distributive bargaining when it attempts to convince management that it is willing and able to sustain a long strike that will severely damage the company's profits and weaken the company's position against its competitors. For example, in its 1993 negotiations with United Parcel Service, the Teamsters Union presented the company with several key bargaining demands, including substantial pay and benefit increases, improved job security, conversion of part-time jobs to full-time jobs, and less stringent productivity standards. When UPS, after intense contract talks and contract extensions, presented the

Manager's Notebook

Guidelines for Integrative Bargaining

Integrative bargaining is the process of identifying a common, shared, or joint goal and developing a process to achieve it. An emphasis on integrative bargaining can lead to cooperation between union and management and the possibility of mutual gains for both. To achieve integrative bargaining, both parties should:

- *Attempt to understand the other negotiator's real needs and objectives.* To this end, the parties should engage in a dialogue in which both sides disclose preferences and priorities, rather than disguise or manipulate them.
- *Create a free flow of information.* Negotiators must be willing to listen to the other negotiator carefully, and to accept a joint solution that incorporates both parties' needs.
- *Emphasize the commonalities, and minimize the differences, between the parties.* Specific goals should be reframed to be considered part of a larger, collaborative goal. For example, a safe workplace may be a goal on which both the union and management agree, although they may differ on a specific approach to achieve this goal.
- *Search for solutions that meet both parties' goals and objectives.* When parties are combative or competitive, they are more likely to focus only on their own objectives and ignore those of the other party. Integrative bargaining is successful only when both parties' needs are met.

Source: Adapted from Lewicki, R., and Litterer, J. (1985). *Negotiation.* Homewood, IL: Irwin.

Teamsters with a contract that did not come close to meeting the union's demands, the Teamsters suspended negotiations and set a strike date. A national strike against United Parcel Service could have crippled the company at a time when it was facing stiff competition from nonunion rivals, like Federal Express and Roadway Package Services. Before this happened, however, Ron Carey, the Teamsters' new reformist president, hammered out a contract that provided a good economic package and an end to some of the stringent work rules that had long irked union members.[36]

Management uses distributive bargaining when it tries to convince the union that it can sustain a long strike much better than union members, who will have to survive without their paychecks. For example, in 1975 management at the *Washington Post* tried to persuade the newspaper's unions that it could sustain a strike and still get the paper out because it had cross-trained managers to do the jobs of union workers. In this instance, management was able to pull it off.

Integrative Bargaining. **Integrative bargaining** focuses on convincing your counterpart in negotiations that the benefits of agreeing with your terms would be very high. Integrative bargaining is similar to a problem-solving session in which both parties are seeking mutually beneficial alternatives. Recently U.S. West and the Communication Workers of America (CWA) negotiated an agreement that illustrates the benefits of integrative bargaining. Because of the new technologies being used in the telecommunications industry, U.S. West needed to reduce the size of its unionized work force. In exchange for the union's agreement to eliminate some jobs, the company offered to pay for retraining the affected union employees. Realizing that it was in both parties' best interests to keep the company competitive in its industry, the union accepted the company's terms. The Manager's Notebook titled "Guidelines for Integrative Bargaining" shows what both parties need to do to achieve integrative bargaining.

integrative bargaining
Bargaining that focuses on convincing the other party that the benefits of agreeing with the proposed terms would be very high.

It is not unusual in collective bargaining for both sides to use both distributive and integrative bargaining tactics. However, the firm's overall labor relations strategy generally determines what type of bargaining it adopts. Firms with a union acceptance strategy are more likely to mix integrative and distributive bargaining, while those with a union avoidance strategy are more likely to focus solely on distributive bargaining. In addition, the strategies selected by the union will influence a firm's bargaining strategies and tactics because collective bargaining is a dynamic process.

Bargaining Topics. The NLRB and courts classify bargaining topics into three categories: mandatory, permissive, and illegal.

As mentioned earlier, *mandatory bargaining topics* are wages, hours, and employment conditions. These are the topics that both union and management consider fundamental to the organization's labor relations. Some examples of each of these mandatory topics are shown in Figure 15–8.

The NLRB and courts have interpreted wages, hours, and employment conditions fairly broadly. "Wages" can mean any type of compensation, including base pay rates, pay incentives, health insurance, and retirement benefits. "Hours" can mean anything to do with work scheduling, including the allocation of overtime and the amount of vacation

Wages	Hours	Employment Conditions
Base pay rates	Overtime	Layoffs
Overtime pay rates	Holidays	Promotions
Retirement benefits	Vacation	Seniority provisions
Health benefits	Shifts	Safety rules
Travel pay		Work rules
Pay incentives		Grievance procedures
		Union shop
		Job descriptions

FIGURE 15-8

Mandatory Bargaining Topics

time granted. "Employment conditions" can mean almost any work rule that affects the employees represented by the union. These include grievance procedures, safety rules, job descriptions, and the bases for promotions.

Permissive bargaining topics may be discussed during collective bargaining if both parties agree to do so, but neither party is obligated to bargain on these topics. Some permissive bargaining topics are provisions for union members to serve on the company's board of directors and benefits for retired union members. In the recessionary economy of the early 1990s, some unions swapped wage concessions for equity in the company and a stronger voice in how it is run. Management-labor agreements in the airline industry have incorporated some novel approaches to rescue faltering airlines and thousands of jobs. For instance:

- Financially beleaguered Northwest Airlines and its three major unions—the Machinists, the Air Line Pilots Association, and the International Brotherhood of Teamsters—reached an agreement in 1993 on contract concessions to keep the carrier flying. The unions consented to over $700 million worth of concessions in return for 30% of Northwest's preferred stock, three seats on the company's 15-member board, enhanced job security, and a significant voice in company operations.[37]
- At United Airlines, the unions that represent pilots and machinists traded 15% in pay cuts for 55% of the company stock and three of 12 board seats in 1994. By 1996 United's stock price had more than doubled and the employee-owned airline was outperforming most of its rivals.[38]

Illegal bargaining topics may not be discussed in collective bargaining. Examples of illegal topics are closed shop agreements, featherbedding, and discriminatory employment practices. The NLRB considers the discussion of illegal bargaining topics an unfair labor practice.

Impasses in Bargaining. A labor contract cannot be finalized until the bargaining representatives on both sides go back to their organizations and obtain approval of the contract. Union negotiators typically ask the members to vote on the contract. Most unions require a majority of union members to approve the contract. Management's negotiating team may need approval from the company's top executives. If the parties cannot agree on one or more mandatory issues, they have reached an *impasse* in bargaining. A party that insists on bargaining over a permissive topic to the point of impasse engages in an unfair labor practice.

If the impasse persists because the parties have taken rigid positions, a strike may result. Before a strike is called, either party may ask a mediator to help resolve the impasse. Mediators are trained in conflict resolution techniques and are sometimes able to improve communication so that the impasse is resolved. The Federal Mediation and Conciliation Service (FMCS), established by the Taft-Hartley Act, monitors labor disputes and (under certain circumstances) mediates disputes. In addition, the FMCS maintains a list of impartial mediators and arbitrators who are qualified to assist with contract disputes.

If the contract's expiration date approaches, and the parties are still at an impasse, the union may ask its members to vote on a strike. If members approve, the strike will start the day after the current labor contract expires. Striking union members withhold their labor from the employer and often publicize their dispute by picketing in front of the employer's buildings. A strike imposes costs on both parties. Striking union members receive no wages or benefits until they return to work, although they may draw some money from the union's strike fund, which is set up to give a small allowance to cover the striking members' basic expenses. However, a long strike may exhaust the strike fund, putting pressure on the union to make concessions in order to get its members back to work.

Workers on strike also face the risk of losing their jobs to permanent replacement workers. Caterpillar, Inc., the world's largest manufacturer of construction equipment, used the threat of hiring permanent replacement workers to win a heated dispute with the United Auto Workers. The company set a deadline and told striking workers, "Go back to work or lose your job." The strikers were scared off the picket line and returned to work on management's terms.[39] The use of permanent replacement workers is very controversial, and organized labor is trying to get Congress to pass legislation restricting it.[40] See the Issues and Applications feature titled "Permanent Replacement Workers: A Strike Against Labor or an Economic Necessity?" for more on this issue.

Sometimes unions are legally bound by their contracts to honor another union's picket line, which makes it more difficult for the company to hire replacement workers. For example, during a strike by the screenwriters at the three major U.S. television networks, all the other television production workers left their jobs in a *sympathy strike*. The solidarity of the unions forced the television studios to abandon all production work until they could reach a settlement with the screenwriters.

Management also faces significant strike costs. A strike can force a company to shut down operations and lose customers. In a highly competitive market such actions may plunge the company into bankruptcy. This is exactly what happened at Eastern Airlines when the International Association of Machinists and Aerospace Workers (IAM) struck the air carrier in a contract dispute in 1989.

Despite the negative outcomes sometimes associated with strikes, they are an important feature of the collective bargaining process. The pressure of an impending strike deadline forces both union and management negotiators to make concessions and resolve their differences. In the United States less than 0.2% of total working time lost is lost because of strikes. Put another way, less working time is lost because of strikes than because of the common cold.[41] Without the potential for strikes, there would undoubtedly be more unresolved impasses in collective bargaining.

economic strike
A strike that takes place when an agreement is not reached during collective bargaining.

wildcat strike
A spontaneous work stoppage that happens under a valid contract and is usually not supported by union leadership.

lockout
Occurs when an employer shuts down its operations before or during a labor dispute.

There are several different kinds of strikes. The type of strike we have been discussing thus far, which takes place when an agreement is not reached during collective bargaining, is called an **economic strike**. Another type of strike, called the **wildcat strike**, is a spontaneous work stoppage that happens under a valid contract and is usually not supported by union leadership. Wildcat strikes generally occur when workers are angered by a disciplinary action taken by management against one of their colleagues. This type of strike is designed to draw management's attention to an issue that the strikers want settled. Some contracts forbid wildcat strikes and penalize workers who participate in them, sometimes by termination. The preferred method of resolving disputes between unionized workers and management is the grievance procedure. One tool that employers can use against workers is the lockout. A **lockout** occurs when the employer shuts down its operation before or during a labor dispute. Employers may use a lockout during a bargaining impasse to protect themselves from unusual economic hardship when the timing of a srike may ruin critical materials. For example, a brewer must bottle beer by a certain date or the entire batch can be ruined. Because employers have other alternatives to influence the union to make concessions, such as the use of replacement workers, lockouts are rarely used.

Issues + Applications

Permanent Replacement Workers: A Strike Against Labor or an Economic Necessity?

When over 6,300 drivers abandoned Greyhound buses during a bitter strike in 1989, the company had 700 new recruits on hand to drive the fleet and 900 more in training. And after the strike ended, most of the new hires remained on the job. Replacement workers also remained on the job after bitter protracted strikes at International Paper and Eastern and Continental Airlines.

Replacing striking workers has been a legal employer option for about 60 years, but it wasn't until 1981, when President Ronald Reagan fired striking air traffic controllers and kept the air traffic system going with replacements, that employers began using this tactic regularly. And with the economy slowing and high-paying industrial jobs difficult to get, it hasn't been hard for employers to draw replacement workers from the swelling ranks of the unemployed.

To organized labor, the hiring of permanent replacement workers undermines the bargaining power granted to unions under the Wagner Act's guaranteed right to strike. Once the unions' trump card, the strike has become a card many unions are afraid to play in an era when strikers fear losing their jobs. Labor advocates argue that permanent replacement is the same as firing striking workers, which is illegal.

The current law on replacement workers derives from a 1938 case, *NLRB v. Mackay Radio & Telegraph Co.*, in which the court declared that while the company in this case (Mackay) was guilty of firing strikers, in other cases where management has committed no illegal practices, the company is not bound to discharge replacement workers and hire back strikers when they wish to return to work. Labor advocates insist that "not hired back" equals "fired." On their side, employers argue that the ability to hire permanent replacements is necessary to ensure the survival of companies. Jack Schwartz, the labor counsel for National Tea, a New Orleans–based company, echoed the views of many employers when he said that legislation banning permanent replacement workers will encourage companies to relocate to "Mexico or another country where they don't have to worry about that risk."

Sources: Budd, J. (1996). Canadian strike replacement legislation and collective bargaining: Lessons for the United States. *Industrial Relations, 35,* 245–260; (1994, January 24). *BNA's Employee Relations Weekly.* Negotiators for management and labor gauge impact of striker replacements, *12* (4), 87–88; Bernstein, A. (1991, August 5). You can't bargain with a striker whose job is no more. *Business Week,* 27; and Kilborn, P. T. (1990, March 13). Replacement workers: Management's big gun. *The New York Times,* A24.

Contract Administration

The last phase of labor relations is contract administration, which involves application and enforcement of the labor contract in the workplace. Disputes occasionally arise between labor and management over such issues as who should be promoted or whether an employee has abused sick leave privileges. The steps taken to resolve such disputes are spelled out in the labor contract.

The mechanism preferred by most unions and managements to settle disputes is the grievance procedure. A **grievance procedure** is a systematic step-by-step procedure designed to settle disputes regarding the interpretation of the labor contract.

grievance procedure
A systematic step-by-step process designed to settle disputes regarding the interpretation of a labor contract.

Although employees may attempt to settle their grievances through such alternatives as an open door policy or a meeting with an employee relations representative in the HR department (see Chapter 13), grievance procedures under union contracts have two significant advantages for employees that no other HRM program can provide:

union steward
An advocate dedicated to representing an employee's case to management in a grievance procedure.

arbitration
The last step in a grievance procedure. The decision of the arbitrator, who is a neutral individual selected from outside the firm, is binding on both parties.

1. The grievance procedure provides the employee with an advocate dedicated to representing the employee's case to management. This representative is called the **union steward**. Under any other system used to handle grievances, the employee is represented by someone who is either a manager or an agent of management. Such people obviously cannot be entirely dedicated to the employee's position.
2. The last step in the grievance procedure is **arbitration**, a quasi-judicial process that is binding on both parties. The arbitrator is a neutral person selected from outside the firm and compensated by both the union and management (who split the fee). Unlike

grievance panels, which are composed of people on the company payroll, the arbitrator has no personal stake in the outcome and can make a tough decision without worrying about how it will affect his or her career.[42]

Steps in the Grievance Procedure. Most union grievance procedures have three or four steps leading up to arbitration, the final step. Figure 15–9 illustrates a four-step union grievance procedure. Usually a time limit is set for resolution of the grievance at each step. Later steps in the procedure require more time than earlier steps, and the degree of formality increases with each step. Because the grievance procedure is time consuming and distracts several people from their regular job duties, it is generally advantageous for the company to resolve disputes as early as possible.

The key to an effective grievance procedure is training supervisors to understand the labor contract and to work with union stewards to settle grievances at the first step. The labor relations staff in the HR department can make an important contribution here by training and consulting with supervisors.

The first step of the grievance procedure is taken when an employee tells the union steward about his or her grievance. In our example in Figure 15–9, the employee must make the dispute known to the steward and/or the supervisor within five working days of

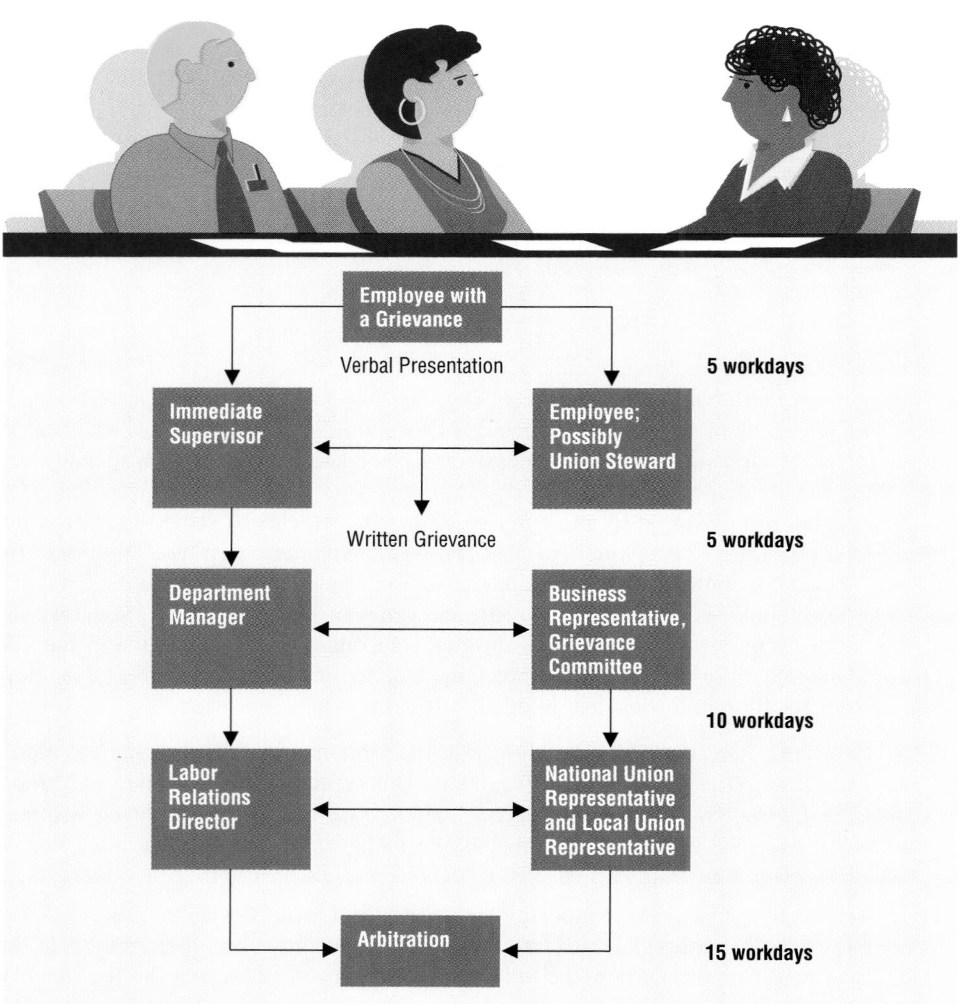

FIGURE 15–9

A Union Grievance Procedure

Source: Adapted from Allen, R., and Keavany, T. (1988). *Contemporary labor relations* (2nd ed.), 530. Reading, MA: Addison-Wesley. Reprinted by permission of Robert Allen.

its occurrence. The steward refers to the labor contract to determine if the grievance is valid and, if it is, tries to work with the employee's supervisor to settle it. The grievance may or may not be put in writing. Most grievances (about 75%) are settled at this first step.

If the dispute cannot be resolved at this first step, the grievance is put into writing, and, in our example, the department or plant manager and a union official (such as the union's business representative) have an additional five working days to resolve the issue. At this second step, a formal meeting is usually held to discuss the grievance.

If the second step is unsuccessful at resolving the grievance, the parties move on to the third step. This step usually involves both a corporate manager (for example, the company's director of labor relations) and a local and national union representative. In our example, the labor agreement gives these people 10 days to respond to and resolve the grievance. Grievances that have the potential to set precedents affecting employment policy may get "kicked up" to this level because it is inappropriate for plant supervisors or managers to settle them. For example, a grievance concerning production standards may have widespread implications for all workers if a corporatewide labor contract is in effect. Because the third step is the last step prior to arbitration, it is management's final opportunity to negotiate a settlement with the union. It is common for management to try to "cut a deal" with the union at this step.

The final step of the grievance procedure is arbitration. Only about 1% of grievances get as far as arbitration; the rest are settled at the earlier steps. Both parties select the arbitrator, before whom the union and management advocates present their case and evidence at a hearing with a quasi-judicial format. The arbitrator then examines the evidence and makes a ruling. Most arbitrators also write an opinion outlining their reasoning and the sections of the labor contract that influenced their decision. This opinion can serve as a guideline for dealing with similar disputes in the future. The arbitrator's decision is final and binding on both parties.

Types of Grievances. Employees initiate two types of grievances. The first is a *contract interpretation grievance* based on union members' rights under the labor contract. If the contract's language is ambiguous, this type of grievance may go to arbitration for clarification. For example, suppose that a labor contract allows workers two 10-minute coffee breaks per day. If management decides it would be more efficient to get rid of coffee breaks, employees may file a contract interpretation grievance to get this privilege restored.

The second type of grievance involves employee discipline. In such cases, the grievance procedure examines whether the employee in question was disciplined for just cause, and management has the burden of proof. An important aspect of these cases is determining whether the disciplined employee received due process. For minor infractions, management is expected to give employees the opportunity to correct their behavior via the progressive discipline procedure (verbal warning, written warning, suspension, discharge). For more serious charges (such as theft), management must provide strong evidence that the discipline was warranted.

Benefits of Union Grievance Procedures. Union grievance procedures provide benefits to both management and employees. Specifically:

- The grievance procedure protects union employees from arbitrary management decisions; it is the mechanism for organizational justice.
- The grievance procedure helps management quickly and efficiently settle conflicts that could otherwise end up in the courts or result in work stoppages.
- Management can use the grievance procedure as an upward communications channel to monitor and correct the sources of employee dissatisfaction with jobs or company policies. ▼

▸ The Impact of Unions on Human Resource Management

A union can significantly alter a company's HRM policies because of its bargaining power, which is supported by labor law. In the absence of a union, management is more likely to develop HRM policies based on the principle of efficiency. For example, a nonunion company is more likely to adopt a meet-the-market pay policy because the market wage is the most efficient way to allocate labor costs (see Chapter 10). But when a union enters the picture, management must develop policies that reflect the preferences of the majority of workers who are represented by the union.[43] In this case, management is more likely to adopt an above-the-market pay policy because union members have strong preferences for higher wages. In this section, we look at the changes in staffing, employee development, compensation, and employee relations practices that are likely under unionization.

Staffing

seniority
The length of time a person works for an employer.

Under a labor contract, job opportunities are allocated to people on the basis of seniority. **Seniority** is the length of time a person works for an employer. In a unionized company, promotions, job assignments, and shift preferences are given to the employee with the most seniority in the unit.[44] Layoffs in unionized firms are also governed according to the last in, first out rule (see Chapter 6).[45]

Work rules tend to be less flexible in a unionized workplace because they are likely to be formalized in the labor agreement. When labor relations are adversarial, labor contracts are more likely to have inflexible work rules written into them. When labor relations are more cooperative, work rule specifications may purposely be left out of the contract. In certain industries, this gives management the flexibility to adjust to the rapidly changing technological requirements of producing a product or service. For instance, under the terms of the contract between Inland Steel and the United Steelworkers, the union agreed that the company not only could cut its work force by 25% through attrition but also that it could eliminate certain restrictive work rules, such as those dealing with staffing levels, job assignments, and job descriptions. In return, Inland Steel agreed to adhere to a no-layoff clause, unless it experiences a major financial crisis.[46] The UAW and Saturn, and the CWA and the Baby Bell phone systems, have also negotiated provisions for flexible work rules.

In the absence of a union, the employer is more likely to allocate job opportunities to employees on the basis of merit.[47] In most cases, merit is determined by a supervisor's judgment of the employee's performance. Supervisors in a nonunion workplace have more power and influence because of their authority to reward employees' efforts with promotions, attractive job assignments, and preferred work schedules. Layoff decisions in nonunion firms are more likely to take both merit and seniority into consideration. Finally, work rules are often more flexible in a nonunion firm because the employer is not tied to a contract and is, therefore, not required to justify to employees any changes made in the way work is done. In nonunion firms it is management alone that determines the most efficient way to produce a product or service and deliver it to the customer.

Employee Development

In unionized companies, the uses of performance appraisal are very limited because the appraisal data usually come from the supervisor, a source that many unions find problematic. Unions tend to balk at using performance appraisal as the basis for making pay and staffing decisions. If performance appraisal is done at all for union employees, it is used simply to provide some feedback on their performance. In a nonunion workplace, however, the performance appraisal is likely to have a broad set of uses for HR decisions. It is used to determine pay raises, promotions, job assignments, career planning, training needs, and layoff or discharge.[48]

Unionized firms tend to retain their employees longer than nonunion firms do.[49] There are a few reasons for the lower quit rates in unionized firms. First, unionized employees are more likely to express their dissatisfaction through the grievance procedure, so this channel may become an alternative to quitting. Second, unionized firms on average pay their employees a higher wage, which may make it more difficult for them to find an equally high-paying job if they leave. The higher employee retention rates at unionized companies provide an incentive for those companies to make greater investments in training because they can expect a longer payback on their training investment.[50]

Unions themselves have become far more interested in worker training and development in recent years. The 1990 contract between General Motors and the UAW, for instance, specified that the company will create Skills Centers (adult educational facilities) for union workers. So far, 36 GM plants in the United States have set up these centers. As unions have stepped up their organizing efforts (see the Issues and Applications feature on page 472), many have offered to fund worker training programs. In New York City, for instance, locals of the Amalgamated Labor and Textile Workers Unions, the International Ladies Garment Workers Union, and other major unions work with a Center for Worker Education to provide English as a Second Language and high school equivalency classes for their members and for worker groups they are trying to organize.[51]

Compensation

A company experiences an increase in total compensation costs when a union organizes its employees. On average, union employees earn 10% to 20% higher wages than comparable nonunionized employees.[52]

The presence of a union also affects the company's policy on pay raises. Unionized firms avoid using merit pay plans and are likely to give across-the-board pay raises to employees based on market considerations.[53] Across-the-board pay plans are often based on **cost-of-living adjustments (COLAs)** that are tied to such inflation indicators as the Consumer Price Index. About 16% of U.S. workers received COLAs in 1995, down from 60% in 1983[54]. Unions prefer across-the-board pay raises to merit pay plans because they see the latter as undermining union solidarity by encouraging employees to compete against one another to win higher pay increases. Furthermore, unions are often skeptical of the fairness of merit pay increases because of the potential for favoritism on the part of supervisors (see Chapter 7). Unions apply this same logic to the use of individual pay incentives such as lump-sum bonuses. In contrast, nonunion firms tend to use merit pay and bonuses to encourage competition and recognize their top performers.

cost-of-living adjustment (COLA) Pay raises, usually made across the board, that are tied to such inflation indicators as the Consumer Price Index.

Unions are less likely to object to group pay incentives because group plans (such as gainsharing or profit sharing) tend to reinforce group cohesion. Each of the Big Three automakers in the United States has negotiated a profit-sharing plan with the UAW. It is not unusual to find gainsharing plans in both union and nonunion companies.[55] However, nonunion firms generally have more flexibility to use both individual and group pay incentives to reward different types of work outcomes.

Unions have generally influenced employers to offer a more valuable benefits package to each employee.[56] Through collective bargaining, they have been able to negotiate packages with a broader array of benefits than nonunion workers receive.

In unionized firms the employer pays for most benefits, while in nonunion firms employer and employee share the costs.[57] The result is better health benefits for unionized employees than for their nonunion counterparts. As U.S. health-care costs have soared over the last decade, nonunionized companies have begun asking their employees to pay a greater share of these costs through both higher monthly premiums and higher deductibles. Although unionized employers face the same rising health-care costs, unions have used collective bargaining to persuade many employers to pursue alternative cost-saving methods such as managed health care, second opinions, and audits.[58]

In terms of retirement benefits, unions have been able to provide more security for employees by influencing employers to adopt a defined benefit plan, which provides a fixed amount of income to employees upon retirement. Nonunion employers are more likely to adopt a defined contribution plan, which requires only that the employer set aside a fixed portion of the employee's income each month in a plan that meets the ERISA (Employee Retirement Income Security Act) standards for these plans. Under a defined contribution plan, employees do not know how much total income will be available for their retirement until they actually retire (see Chapter 12).

Employee Relations

The union is an empowerment mechanism that gives employees a voice in the development of work rules that affect their jobs. The labor contract gives employees specific rights. Nonperformance by the employer of an employee right guaranteed in the contract can be remedied under the grievance procedure. For example, an employee overlooked for promotion may file a grievance and be reconsidered for the promotion if the contract stipulates that the employee has a right to that promotion.

Nonunion employers tend to document their employees' basic rights in an employee handbook (see Chapter 13). However, employee handbooks provide fewer employee rights than labor contracts do. In fact, many of them contain only general guidelines and specifically state that supervisors may need to make exceptions to the written policy from time to time. For example, employees may have the right to bid on a promotion posted on a job board, but the handbook usually states that management reserves the right to determine which employee will ultimately get the job.

The appeals mechanism that a nonunion employer is most likely to use is the open door policy.[59] Unlike the grievance procedure, which is administered by both the union and management, the open door policy is controlled by management. It gives management the opportunity to resolve an employee's complaint while balancing both parties' interests. The only recourse open to employees who are unhappy with the resolution of a complaint under the open door policy is to find legal counsel and go to court to obtain justice—an option more employees are pursuing every year. Under the union grievance procedure, it is much less likely that an employee will take a case to court because judges are usually unwilling to challenge the results of arbitration.

Summary and Conclusions

Why Do Employees Join Unions? U.S. employees generally seek representation from a union because they (1) are dissatisfied with certain aspects of their job, (2) lack influence with management to make the needed changes, and (3) see the union as a solution to their problems.

Labor unions were largely unprotected by law in the United States until 1935. Economic conditions during the Great Depression led Congress to try to equalize the power of employers and employees. After several decades of widespread support, unions are today widely perceived as too powerful.

Managers strongly affect how employees perceive the work environment and thus whether they will be susceptible to unionization. Managers must possess enough knowledge of basic labor law to (1) avoid creating a legal liability for the company, (2) implement the terms of labor agreements fairly and impartially, and (3) hear and resolve employee grievances.

Labor Relations and the Legal Environment. The most important laws governing labor relations in the United States are the Wagner Act (1935), the Taft-Hartley Act (1947), and the Landrum-Griffin Act (1959). The Wagner Act created the National Labor Relations Board, which administers union certification elections and prevents and remedies unfair labor practices.

Labor Relations in the United States. Labor relations in the United States are characterized by (1) business unionism, (2) unions structured by type of job, (3) a focus on collective bargaining, (4) the use of labor contracts, (5) the adversarial nature of labor-management relations and shrinking union membership, and (6) the growth of unions in the public sector.

Labor Relations in Other Countries. The labor relations systems of two key global competitors of the United States, Germany and Japan, have achieved a greater degree of cooperation between unions and management than the U.S. system has. The German system uses works councils and codetermination to involve workers in decisions at all levels of the organization. In Japan, enterprise unions have worked closely with companies for the mutual benefit of both parties. Some believe that economic pressures are straining labor-management relations in these countries today.

Labor Relations Strategy. A labor relations strategy is a company's overall plan for dealing with unions. Companies that choose a union acceptance strategy view unions as their employees' legitimate representatives and accept collective bargaining as an appropriate mechanism for establishing workplace rules. Companies that choose a union avoidance strategy use either union substitution or union suppression to keep unions out of the workplace.

Managing the Labor Relations Process. The labor relations process has three phases: (1) union organizing, (2) collective bargaining, and (3) contract administration. In the union organizing phase, management must confront the issues involved with union solicitation, preelection conduct, and the certification election. In the collective bargaining phase, union and management representatives negotiate workplace rules that are formalized in a labor contract. The contract administration phase starts after the labor contract is settled and deals with day-to-day administration of the workplace. A key feature of the contract administration phase is the grievance procedure, a step-by-step process for settling employee disputes about contract interpretations or disciplinary actions.

The Impact of Unions on Human Resource Management. The impact of a union on the way a company manages its human resources is significant. Management can expect that the union will affect virtually every major area of HRM. In a unionized workplace, staffing decisions will be heavily influenced by seniority rather than by merit. Individually focused performance appraisals are severely curtailed, while training programs are emphasized. Unionized employees tend to receive larger compensation and benefit packages. Finally, employee relations processes in a union shop are by definition highly structured.

Key Terms

arbitration, 477
business unionism, 460
codetermination, 465
collective bargaining, 461
cost-of-living adjustment (COLA), 481
distributive bargaining, 473
economic strike, 476
enterprise union, 465
grievance procedure, 477
integrative bargaining, 474
labor contract, 461
labor relations specialist, 457
labor relations strategy, 466
Landrum-Griffin Act (1959), 459
lockout, 476
National Labor Relations Board (NLRB), 458
right-to-work law, 459
seniority, 480
Taft-Hartley Act (1947), 458
union, 456
union acceptance strategy, 466
union avoidance strategy, 467
union shop clause, 459
union steward, 477
union substitution/proactive human resource management, 468
union suppression, 469
Wagner Act/National Labor Relations Act (1935), 458
wildcat strike, 476
works council, 465
work rules, 461

Discussion Questions

1. Why have labor and management tended to treat each other as adversaries in the U.S. labor relations system?
2. What factors are encouraging unions and management in the United States to adopt more cooperative strategies today?
3. What factors explain why unions in the United States have been losing more than 50% of all certification elections?
4. Suppose a goal of management is to reduce the number of grievances filed by union employees each year. What are some ways that the HRM staff can contribute to this goal?
5. How can management's collective bargaining tactics be influenced by the company's labor relations strategy? Provide examples.
6. What are some advantages and disadvantages of a strike from management's perspective? From the union's perspective?
7. What, in your opinion, is the most significant impact of a union on the management of human resources? Explain.
8. It is often said that "good pay and good management" are the keys to successful union avoidance. Spell out the kind of policies and practices companies should develop if they want to keep their workers from unionizing. Do you think the employee relations practices you've mentioned are less costly or more costly than working with unionized labor?

MINICASE 1 *Should Union Organizers Be Hired?*

The U.S. Supreme Court concluded in 1995 that an employer violates the National Labor Relations Act (NLRA) when it refuses to interview or discharges people who seek to organize a union at the company. Town & Country Electric, Inc., a nonunion electrical contractor, advertised for several licensed electricians for construction work. The company refused to interview ten applicants who were union organizers. It also terminated a union organizer it had recently hired after only a few days on the job.

When these workers filed suit, NLRB concluded that the employer violated the NLRA. The Eighth Circuit Court of Appeals disagreed, concluding that paid union organizers who sought employment solely to organize the company's employees were not covered under the NLRA because they did not meet the act's definition of an "employee."

The Supreme Court reversed the appeals court's decision. It broadly interpreted the definition of an employee under the NLRA to include paid union organizers. This means that all job applicants and individuals who work for an employer for pay are protected by the law from employment discrimination. In particular, union organizers have the same rights and protection from arbitrary treatment as any other employee.

Discussion Questions

1. Do you agree or disagree with the Supreme Court's position that paid union organizers who seek employment should be treated just like any other job applicant or employee? Explain your answer.
2. Suppose you are a nonunion employer and you learn that one of the employees in your company is attempting to organize a union. Would you treat this employee any differently after you learn about his or her organizing activities? What would you do?

Source: Adapted from Barlow, W., Hatch D., and Murphy, B. (1996, February). Paid union organizers have "employee" rights. *Personnel Journal*, 86.

MINICASE 2 *Xerox and the ACTWU: Keeping Jobs in the United States*

Xerox became the first major U.S. firm to win back market share from the Japanese without government intervention, thanks in large part to cooperative initiatives with the Amalgamated Labor and Textile Workers Unions. The ACTWU represents 4,200 Xerox workers at the company's high-tech manufacturing center near Rochester, New York, and almost 2,000 Xerox workers in other areas of the country. Here's how Xerox and the ACTWU worked together to keep jobs in the United States:

> One area of cooperation at Xerox developed as a response to management's realization that it could save money by moving production of the wire harness—the configuration of strands of wires that delivers the current throughout the copier—to the company's plant near Mexico City. This would mean eliminating 182 jobs at its Webster, New York, plant....The union urged management to give workers a chance to bring costs down at the Webster plant to make it competitive with the Mexico operation. A study team found $2.9 million in potential savings, which management accepted as close enough to the $3 million that it said it needed to stay in the U.S.
>
> The same situation arose a few years later. This time the study team was unable to get as close to the figure as needed. The team pointed out, however, that it could reduce the quality and attain sufficient cost reductions. Management recognized that the quality of the harnesses produced in Mexico was not as high. In fact, it had moved some operations back to the U.S. because of quality problems in Mexico. In the end, managers decided that the higher quality, along with the reduced shipping cost, was enough to make the difference. The jobs have stayed in the U.S.—for now....Perhaps the most unusual union-management cooperative effort [at Xerox] is the subcontracting provision that provides that if the work isn't performed competitively in terms of cost, then the organization reserves the right to subcontract or outsource that work...but only after a joint company-union team has had an opportunity to bring the cost of that business to within acceptable norms.

Discussion Questions

1. What benefits result from Xerox and the ACTWU's cooperative efforts? Can you think of any disadvantages to this arrangement?
2. How do you think the knowledge that their work may be outsourced will affect productivity of the ACTWU workers at Xerox?

Sources: *Workforce Strategies.* (1993, August 30). New Xerox plant is product of cooperative efforts, 4 (8), 47. Excerpt reprinted from Stuart, P. (1993, August). Labor unions become business partners. *Personnel Journal*, 54–63.

CASE 1 *Union Avoidance at Sid's Market*

Sid's Market is an upscale supermarket that caters to a clientele living in the prosperous suburbs of Chicago's North Shore. Although most of the supermarkets in the Chicago area are unionized, Sid's Market has been able to avoid unions by matching unionized markets' pay and benefits. Sid Clark, founder and owner of Sid's, has told store manager Lee Shaw that one of her top priorities should be discouraging union organization at the market. Clark is convinced that if the store is unionized, it will lose its "family" environment and become a bureaucratic, impersonal market like the other major food chains in Chicago.

Recently, Shaw became aware that the United Food and Commercial Workers (UFCW) union is attempting to organize Sid's Market. In trying to discourage the UFCW, she took the following actions to implement Sid's union avoidance strategy:

- She monitored all employees to make sure they were not soliciting for the union on company time. She disciplined two courtesy clerks who were wearing UFCW buttons on their clothing and told them to remove the buttons. Another courtesy clerk in the store was wearing a button that said "Go Bulls" in support of the Chicago basketball team, but Shaw did not reprimand him.
- The UFCW wrote to Shaw and asked her to provide a list of the names and addresses of all the employees who work at Sid's Market. Shaw refused to do so.
- Shaw set up small group meetings of store employees on company time to explain why Sid's Market would be much better off without a union.
- Shaw instructed the market's security guards to ask the union organizers who are not employees at Sid's to stop handing out union literature to employees as they enter and leave the market. When the union organizers ignored this request, the guards escorted them off the market property and confiscated their literature.

A few weeks after these four incidents, Shaw received a letter from the National Labor Relations Board indicating that the UFCW had accused Sid's Market of engaging in unfair labor practices designed to prevent employees from forming a union.

Critical Thinking Questions

1. Which of these four incidents is the NLRB most likely to view as unfair labor practices? Why?
2. Which of these four incidents is the NLRB not likely to consider unfair labor practices? Why?
3. What could Lee Shaw have done differently to operate within the law that governs union-organizing activities?

Cooperative Learning Exercises

4. Students divide into groups of four to five. Assume that you are employees at Sid's Market. Would you support the formation of a union? Why or why not? Compare your reasons with those of other groups.
5. The class divides into six groups. Three of the groups identify reasons to support a union, with one group taking the perspective of employees, another the perspective of customers, and another the perspective of management. The remaining three groups identify reasons not to support the union, with each group taking one of the three different perspectives. Six students, one from each group, should debate the value of unions, with each maintaining his or her group's perspective, positive or negative.

CASE 2 *When Is a Team a Union?*

Amalgamated Tool, a nonunion manufacturer of auto parts in Michigan, suffered such significant financial losses in 1997 that it froze the pay of all its employees to conserve cash. The company also asked its employees to pay a larger share of their health insurance costs. The employees were extremely upset by these actions, and both morale and productivity declined.

To improve morale, Amalgamated's management decided to form several problem-solving employee teams. After meeting to discuss the problems at Amalgamated, the teams presented management with suggestions on how to provide pay raises and health insurance to employees fairly and efficiently. Each problem-solving team had a leader elected by the other team members to present the team's suggestions, but only about 20% of Amalgamated's employees were asked to serve on a team. The teams' suggestions were largely adopted by management, and morale and efficiency went up the next year.

On behalf of some dissatisfied Amalgamated employees, a local union filed an unfair labor practice claim stating that management had illegally used the problem-solving teams to

continued

When Is a Team a Union? continued

form a management-dominated union, in violation of a provision of the Wagner Act that states: "It is an unfair labor practice for an employer to dominate or interfere with the formation of any labor organization or contribute financial support to it."

The National Labor Relations Board sustained the union's position and ordered Amalgamated to cease and desist using its problem-solving teams.

Critical Thinking Questions

1. Why did the local union object to the way Amalgamated's management used problem-solving teams?
2. What is the difference between a team and a union?
3. To avoid the NLRB's cease and desist order, what should Amalgamated's management have done differently in using problem-solving teams?

Cooperative Learning Exercise

4. Students form into groups of four to six members and role-play National Labor Relations Board members. Each group discusses whether or not Amalgamated violated the Wagner Act's prohibition of a company "dominating a union or providing financial support to it." Compare conclusions and arguments across groups.

HRM Simulation 

Suppose the Amalgamated Workers Union (AWU) organizes the employees at your company (Incident L in the players' manual). What changes in HRM policies are likely to take place at the company after the union negotiates a labor contract with management? How would these changes affect managers' jobs? How would they affect the company's cost structure and ability to compete? If the union wins the election, should the company select a cooperative or adversarial labor relations strategy? Explain your answer.

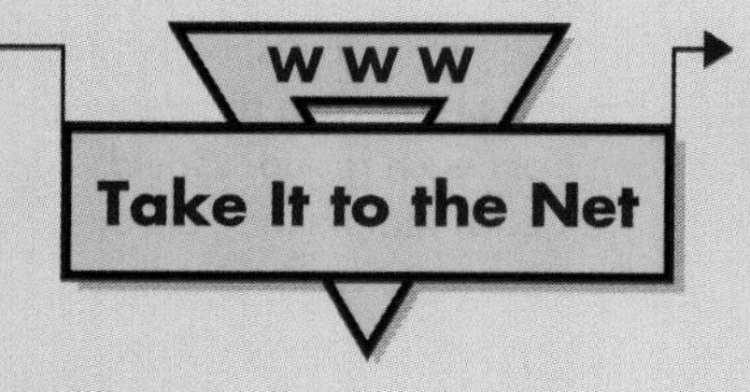

We invite you to visit the Gómez-Mejía/Balkin/Cardy page on the Prentice Hall Web site:

http://www.prenhall.com/gomez

You can also visit the Web sites for these companies, featured within this chapter:

Caterpillar, Inc.	http://www.caterpillar.com
Daimler-Benz	http://www.daimler-benz.com
Hitachi	http://www.hitachi.com
International Paper	http://www.ipaper.com
Eli Lilly	http://www.lilly.com
Nissan	http://www.nissan.com
Teamsters Union	http://www.teamsters.org
Toshiba	http://www.toshiba.com
U.S. West	http://www.uswest.com

Endnotes

1. Based on Shostak, A. B. (1991). *Robust unionism*, 94–100. Ithaca, NY: ILR Press; Weinstein, H. (1989, June 17). Union reaches agreement on Harvard pact. *Los Angeles Times*, I15; and (1989, June 17). Harvard reaches accord with union. *The New York Times*, A13.
2. Shostak, 1991.
3. Weinstein, 1989.
4. *The New York Times*, June 17, 1989.
5. Haberfeld, Y. (1995). Why do workers join unions? The case of Israel. *Industrial and Labor Relations Review, 48*, 656–670.
6. Brett, J. M. (1980). Why employees want unions. *Organizational Dynamics, 9*, 316–332.
7. Bernstein, A. (1994, May 23). Why America needs unions. *Business Week*, 70–82.
8. Flynn, G. (1996, February). TEAM Act: What it is and what it can do for you. *Personnel Journal*, 85–87.
9. *HR News*. (1994, February). Washington scorecard. *13*(2), 5.
10. Budd, J. (1996). Canadian strike replacement legislation and collective bargaining: Lessons for the United States. *Industrial Relations, 35*, 245–260.
11. Holley, W. H., and Jennings, K. M. (1991). *The labor relations process*. Chicago: Dryden.
12. Fossum, J. (1995). *Labor relations* (6th ed.). Chicago, IL: Irwin.
13. Lawler, E. E., and Mohrman, S. A. (1987). Unions and the new management. *Academy of Management Executive, 1*, 293–300.
14. Overman, S. (1991, December). The union pitch has changed. *HRMagazine*, 44–46.
15. Freeman, R. B. (1989). The changing status of unionism around the world. In W. C. Huang (Ed.), *Organized labor at the crossroads*. Kalamazoo, MI: W. E. Upjohn Institute for Employee Research.
16. Chang, C., and Sorrentino, C. (1991, December). Union membership statistics in 12 countries. *Monthly Labor Review*, 46–53.
17. Ofori-Dankwa, J. (1993). Murray and Reshef revisited: Toward a typology/theory of paradigms of national trade union movements. *Academy of Management Review, 18*, 269–292.
18. Husain, I. (1995, January). Fresh start: Laid off workers need somewhere to turn. *Entrepreneur*, 306.
19. Ofori-Dankwa, 1993.
20. Mills, D. Q. (1989). *Labor-management relations*. New York: McGraw-Hill.
21. Wilpert, B. (1975). Research in industrial democracy and the German case. *Industrial Relations Journal, 6*(1), 53–64.
22. Marsland, S. E., and Beer, M. (1985). Note on Japanese management and employment systems. In M. Beer and B. Spector (Eds.), *Readings in human resource management*. New York: The Free Press.
23. *The Economist*. (1996, February 10). Stakeholder capitalism: Unhappy families, 23–25.
24. *Id.*
25. Delaney, J. T. (1991). Unions and human resource policies. In K. Rowland and G. Ferris (Eds.) *Research in personnel and human resources management*. Greenwich, CT: JAI Press.
26. Lawler and Mohrman, 1987.
27. Bernstein, A. (1993, January 25). Making teamwork work—and appeasing Uncle Sam. *Business Week*, 101.
28. Woodruff, D. (1993, February 8). Saturn: Labor's love lost? *Business Week*, 122, 124.
29. Salwen, K. G. (1993, July 27). Workplace friction: To some small firms, idea of cooperating with labor is foreign. *The Wall Street Journal*, A1.
30. Kochan, T. A., and Katz, H. C. (1988). *Collective bargaining and industrial relations*. Homewood, IL: Irwin.
31. Foulkes, F. (1980). *Personnel policies in large nonunion companies*. Englewood Cliffs, NJ: Prentice Hall.
32. Bryant, A. (1994, April 6). Lorenzo plan for airline rejected. *The New York Times*, D53.
33. *Small Business Reports*. (1933, March). Unions vs. private property, 25.
34. Rose, J., and Chaison, G. (1996). Linking union density and union effectiveness: The North American experience. *Industrial Relations, 35*, 78–105.

34a. Bernstein, A. (1997, February). Sweeney's bitz. *Business Week*, 56–62.

35. Walton, B., and McKersie, R. (1965). *A behavioral theory of labor negotiations*. New York: McGraw-Hill.
36. Cimini, M. H., Behrmann, S. L., and Johnson, E. M. (1994, January). Labor-management bargaining in 1993. *Monthly Labor Review*, 20–35.
37. *Id.*; and Kelly, K. (1993, August 2). Labor deals that offer a break from "us vs. them." *Business Week*, 30.
38. Bernstein, A. (1995, March 18). United we own. *Business Week*, 96-102.
39. Cook, M. (Ed.). (1993). *The human resources yearbook: 1993/1994 Edition*, 16.2. Englewood Cliffs, NJ: Prentice Hall.
40. BLS Reports. (1994, February 14). Record low number of strikes continues into 1993. *BNA's Employee Relations Weekly, 12*(7), 167.
41. Freeman, R. B., and Medoff, J. L. (1984). What do unions do? New York: Basic Books.
42. Holley, W., and Jennings, K. (1994). *The labor relations process* (5th ed.). Fort Worth, TX: The Dryden Press; and Fossum, J. (1995). *Labor relations* (6th ed.). Chicago, IL: Irwin.
42. Peterson, R. B., and Lewin, D. (1990). The nonunion grievance procedure: A viable system of due process? *Employee Responsibility and Rights Journal, 3*, 1–18.
43. Freeman, R. B., and Medoff, J. L. (1979). The two faces of unionism. *The Public Interest, 57*, 69–93.
44. Abraham, K. G., and Medoff, J. L. (1985). Length of service and promotions in union and nonunion work groups. *Industrial and Labor Relations Review, 38*, 408–420.
45. Abraham, K. G., and Medoff, J. L. (1984). Length of service and layoffs in union and nonunion work groups. *Industrial and Labor Relations Review, 38*, 87–97.
46. Cimini, Behrmann, and Johnson, 1994.
47. Foulkes, 1980.
48. Bernardin, J., and Beatty, R. (1984). *Performance appraisal: Assessing human behavior at work*. Boston: Kent.
49. Abraham, K. G., and Farber, H. S. (1988). Returns to seniority in union and nonunion jobs: A new look at evidence. *Industrial and Labor Relations Review, 42*, 3–19; and Freeman & Medoff, 1984.
50. Bartel, A. P. (1989). *Formal employee training programs and their impact on labor productivity: Evidence from a human resources survey*. National Bureau of Economic Research Working Paper No. 3026.
51. Gunsch, D. (1993, March). On-site schools are required by a UAW contract. *Personnel Journal*, 43.
52. Stevens, C. (1995). The social cost of rent seeking by labor unions in the United States. *Industrial Relations, 34*, 190–202; Jarrel, S., and Stanley, T. (1990). A meta analysis of the union-nonunion wage gap. *Industrial and Labor Relations Review*, *44*, 54–67; and Freeman, R. B. (1982). Union wage practices and wage dispersion within establishments. *Industrial and Labor Relations Review 36*, 3–21.
53. Freeman, 1982.
54. Wasilewski, E. (1996, January). Bargaining outlook for 1996. *Monthly Labor Review*, 10–24.
55. Driscoll, J. W. (1979). Working creatively with a union: Lessons from the Scanlon Plan. *Organizational Dynamics*, *8*, 61–80.
56. Freeman, R. B. (1981). The effect of unionism on fringe benefits. *Industrial and Labor Relations Review*, *34*, 489–509.
57. Fosu, A. G. (1984). Unions and fringe benefits: Additional evidence. *Journal of Labor Research*, *5*, 247, 254.
58. Gómez-Mejía, L. R., and Balkin, D. B. (1992). *Compensation, organizational strategy and firm performance*. Cincinnati: South-Western.
59. Foulkes, 1980.

CHALLENGES

After reading this chapter, you should be able to deal more effectively with the following challenges:

1 ▶ **Describe** the extent of the employer's responsibility to maintain a safe and healthy work environment.

2 ▶ **Explain** the reasons for safety and health laws and the costs and obligations they impose on employers.

3 ▶ **Identify** the basic provisions of workers' compensation laws and the Occupational Safety and Health Act.

4 ▶ **Develop** an awareness of contemporary health and safety issues, including AIDS, workplace violence, smoking in the workplace, cumulative trauma disorders, fetal protection, hazardous chemicals, and genetic testing.

5 ▶ **Describe** the features of safety programs and understand the reasons for and the effects of programs designed to enhance employee well-being.

16

Managing Workplace Safety and Health

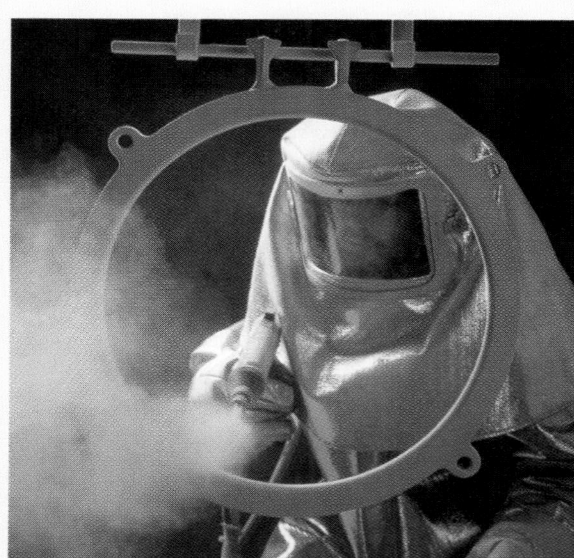

Keeping Healthy in the Workplace. The U.S. government has passed legislation regulating almost every aspect of workplace safety and health, from requiring protective gear in certain situations to providing a workers' compensation system. Still, each year about 5,000 workers die in work-related accidents and another 3.5 million suffer disabling injuries.

http://www.osha.gov/

Occupational Safety and Health Administration

This is the home page of the U.S. Department of Labor's Occupational Safety and Health Administration (OSHA). OSHA's Web site covers many aspects of workplace safety and health including OSHA publications, news releases, programs and services, standards, and statistics. The page also includes frequently asked questions about safety and health and links to other U.S. government Internet sites.

In early 1996, the Federal Aviation Administration (FAA) issued a memo recommending that ValuJet airlines be relicensed, a process that would temporarily shut down the business.[1] The relicensing never took place. Rather, FAA executives launched a 12-day review of the airline.

The FAA review was close to completion when ValuJet Flight 592 crashed in the Florida Everglades. The swampy crash site, west of Miami International Airport, engulfed the plane and all of its 110 passengers were killed. The cause of the crash has not yet been determined, and the airplane's debris and cargo may never be recovered from the mire. However, it is clear that the FAA had serious concerns about the safety of ValuJet's flights.

ValuJet is just one of a growing number of low-fare airlines that use price to compete in the marketplace. Like its rivals, ValuJet keeps fares low by outsourcing the expensive functions that established airlines do themselves. For example, ValuJet pilots must pay for their own training. Furthermore, the aircraft are maintained by outside repair shops. Even its reservations clerks are hired by an employment agency. The major airlines do not make such broad use of outsourcing, but when they do outsource they have their own auditors, mechanics, and engineers to ensure that the outside work meets the airline's standards. Most startup airlines do not have this quality control capability.

The FAA can do only so much to guarantee air safety. The agency currently has 2,600 inspectors to monitor flight crews, maintenance, instruments, and so on. While this number may seem large, there has been tremendous growth in the airline industry, with the number of annual passengers now exceeding 50 million. The FAA's inspection force is being strained by this growth. Furthermore, the computer system that FAA inspectors use to enter their reports is so unreliable that some refuse to use it.[2]

The crash of ValuJet flight 592 dramatically illustrates the devastating consequences of paying insufficient attention to safety concerns and social responsibility. As more companies rely on outsourcing to remain competitive, do consumers need to worry more about the safety of those companies' products and services?

In this chapter we discuss workplace safety and health in detail. First, we deal with the legal issues of workplace safety and health by exploring management's legal obligations to fund a workers' compensation system and to provide a safe and healthy workplace. Next we present and discuss a variety of contemporary safety and health issues, including AIDS, violence in the workplace, cumulative trauma disorders, fetal protection, dangerous chemicals, and the use of genetic testing on employees. Finally, we describe and evaluate programs designed to maintain employee safety and health.

▸ Workplace Safety and the Law

Each year in the United States, about 5,000 employees die in work-related accidents and another 3.5 million suffer disabling injuries. The National Safety Council reports that workplace accidents resulted in 125 million lost workdays in 1994 and cost U.S. businesses $60.9 billion.[3]

To address this problem, all levels of government have passed numerous laws to regulate workplace safety. Many of these laws include detailed regulations dealing with work hazards in specific industries such as coal mining and railroads. However, there are two basic sets of workplace safety laws that affect most workers: the various workers' compensation laws at the state level and the Occupational Safety and Health Act of 1970 (OSHA) at the federal level. The objectives, policies, and operations of these two sets of laws are very different.

Each state has its own workers' compensation law, so the provisions for funding and enforcing the law differ by state. As we discussed in Chapter 12, the main goal of the workers' compensation system is to provide compensation to workers who suffer job-related injuries or illnesses. Workers' compensation laws have no safety regulations or mandates, but they do require employers to pay for workers' compensation insurance. Because insurance costs are higher for employers with more workplace accidents and injuries, employers have a financial incentive to create and maintain a safe work environment.

In contrast, OSHA is a federal law designed to make the workplace safer by ensuring that the work environment is free from hazards. The act mandates numerous safety standards and enforces these standards through a system of inspections, citations, and fines. Unlike the workers' compensation laws, however, OSHA does not provide for the compensation of accident victims.[4]

Workers' Compensation

In the early 1800s, people injured on the job went without medical care unless they could afford to pay for it themselves, and rarely received any income until they could return to work. Employees who sued their employers for negligence had little hope of winning, for under U.S. common law the courts habitually ruled that employees assumed the usual risks of a job in return for their pay. In addition, under the *doctrine of contributory negligence* employers were not liable for an employee's injuries when that employee's own negligence contributed to or caused the injury. And under the *fellow-servant rule*, employers were not responsible for an employee's injury when the negligence of another employee contributed to or caused the injury.

In the early years of the twentieth century—after a host of workplace disasters including a 1911 fire in a New York shirt factory that killed more than 100 women—public opinion pressured several state legislatures to enact *workers' compensation* laws. The workers' compensation concept is based on the theory that work-related accidents and illnesses are costs of doing business that the employer should pay for and pass on to the consumer.[5] Since 1948, all states have had workers' compensation programs, though workers' comp is mandatory in only 47 states. These state-administered and employer-funded programs are designed to provide financial and medical assistance to employees injured on the job.

The stated goals of the workers' compensation laws are:[6]

- Providing prompt, sure, and reasonable medical care to victims and income to both victims and their dependents.
- Providing a "no-fault" system in which injured workers can get quick relief without undertaking expensive litigation and suffering court delays.
- Encouraging employers to invest in safety.
- Promoting research on workplace safety.

The Benefits of Workers' Compensation. Workers' compensation benefits compensate employees for injuries or illnesses occurring on the job. These benefits are:[7]

- *Total disability benefits.* Partial replacement of income lost as the result of a work-related total disability.

- *Impairment benefits.* Benefits for temporary or permanent partial disability, based on the degree and duration of the impairment. Injuries are classified as scheduled or nonscheduled. Scheduled injuries are those in which a body part (such as an eye or a finger) is lost; there is a specific schedule of payments for these injuries. Unscheduled injuries are all other injuries (such as back injuries); these are dealt with on a case-by-case basis.
- *Survivor benefits.* In cases of work-related deaths, the worker's survivors receive a burial allowance and income benefits.
- *Medical expense benefits.* Workers' compensation provides medical coverage, normally without dollar or time limitations.
- *Rehabilitation benefits.* All states provide medical rehabilitation for injured workers, and many states provide vocational training for employees who can no longer work at their previous occupation as the result of a job-related injury or illness.

The Costs of Workers' Compensation. While the costs of workers' compensation doubled during the 1980s,[8] recent figures indicate that these costs may be leveling off.[9] Approximately $43 billion was paid out under workers' compensation in 1993, the most recent year for which data are available. While this is a substantial number, it is a 4% decrease from the 1992 costs.

Nonetheless, the costs of workers' comp remain an important issue. Fraudulent claims drive up the costs of workers' compensation.[10] To keep their workers' comp rates under control, companies are becoming more aware of fraud and many are contesting claims they believe to be fraudulent. Furthermore, the courts are becoming stingier in allowing claims for workers' compensation.

The Occupational Safety and Health Act (OSHA)

Changing political and social values during the 1960s added considerable momentum to the movement to regulate workplace safety. In 1969, the death of 78 coal miners in a mine explosion galvanized public opinion and led to the passage of the Coal Mine Health and Safety Act to regulate mine health and safety.[11] While no single event is responsible for the passage of the **Occupational Safety and Health Act of 1970 (OSHA)**, the dramatic increase in reported injury rates and workplace deaths during the 1960s (reflecting the inability of workers' compensation laws to give employers adequate incentives to maintain a safe work environment) was probably the major impetus.[12] During the latter part of that decade, the federal government reported that job-related accidents killed more than 14,000 workers and disabled nearly two and a half million workers annually. In addition, an estimated 300,000 new cases of occupational diseases were being reported every year. OSHA was passed to address the staggering economic and human costs of workplace accidents and health hazards.[13]

Occupational Safety and Health Act of 1970 (OSHA)
A federal law that requires employers to provide a safe and healthy work environment, comply with specific occupational safety and health standards, and keep records of occupational injuries and illnesses.

OSHA's Provisions. OSHA is fairly straightforward. It imposes three major obligations on employers:

- *To provide a safe and healthy work environment.* Each employer has a general duty to provide a place of employment free from recognized hazards that are likely to cause death or serious physical harm. This *general duty provision* recognizes that not all workplace hazards can be covered by a set of specific standards. The employer is obligated to identify and deal with safety and health hazards not covered by specific regulations.[14]
- *To comply with specific occupational safety and health standards.* Each employer must become familiar with and comply with specific occupational standards (OSHA's rules

deal with specific occupations rather than with industries), and must make certain that employees comply as well.

- *To keep records of occupational injuries and illnesses.* Under OSHA, employers must record and report work-related accidents and injuries. Organizations with eight or more employees must keep records of any occupational injury or illness resulting in death, lost work time, or medical treatment and retain these records for five years. The injuries and illnesses must be recorded on OSHA forms and posted annually on an employee bulletin board for all to see. The records must also be made available to OSHA compliance officers, and annual summaries must be prepared.[15]

Employees also have responsibilities under OSHA. Although they cannot be cited for violations, they must comply with the relevant safety and health standards. They should also report all hazardous conditions, injuries, or work-related illnesses to their employer. Employee rights under OSHA include the right to file safety or health grievances and complaints to the government, participate in OSHA inspections, and request information on safety and health hazards without fear of discrimination or retaliation by their employer.[16] Under both OSHA and state *right-to-know regulations*, employers must provide employees with information about hazardous substances in the workplace.[17] OSHA's hazardous substance regulation, known as the *Hazard Communication Standard*, is explained in the pamphlet excerpt reproduced in Figure 16-1. In addition, the U.S. Supreme Court has upheld an employee's right to refuse to work under conditions where the employee reasonably believes there is an immediate risk of injury or death.[18]

Three agencies administer and enforce OSHA: the *Occupational Safety and Health Administration* (the OSH Administration, also known by the acronym OSHA), the *Occupational Safety and Health Review Commission (OSHRC)*, and the *National Institute for Occupational Safety and Health (NIOSH)*. States with federally approved safety plans have their own regulatory apparatus.

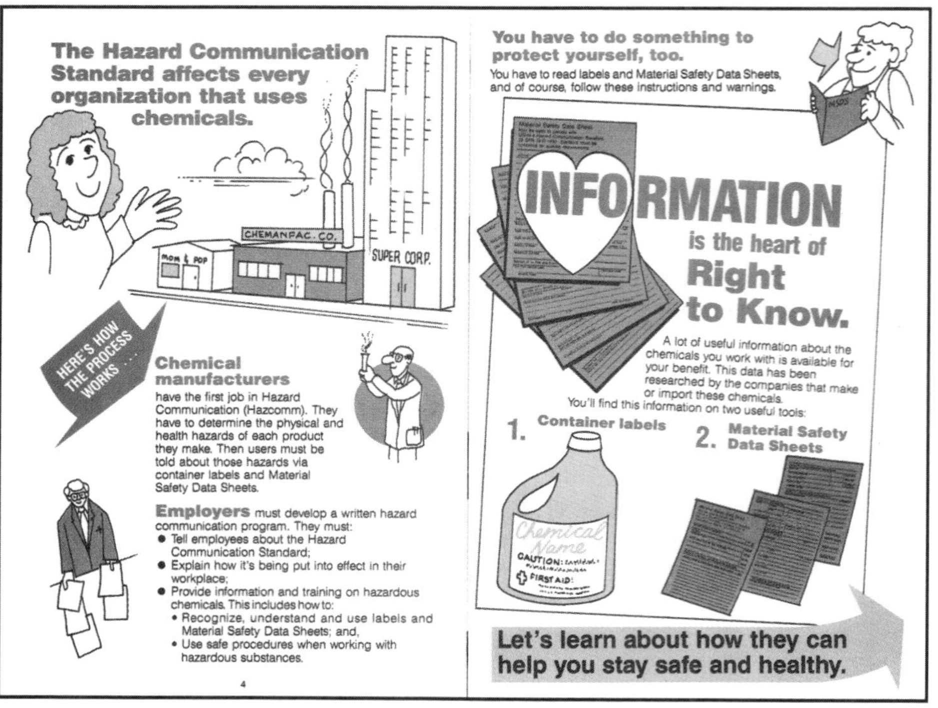

FIGURE 16-1

OSHA's Hazard Communication Standard

This excerpt from an employee pamphlet explains that employers must tell their employees how OSHA's hazardous communication standard is being put into effect in their workplace and train them in (1) how to recognize and understand U.S. government-required labels on hazardous substances and (2) how to use safety procedures when working with these substances.

Source: Business and Legal Reports, Inc. (1985, revised 1991). *Hazards in the workplace: Your right to know.* Madison, CT: Business and Legal Reports, Inc. To obtain the full booklet, request order no. 200 031 from Business and Legal Reports, Inc., 39 Academy Street, P.O. Box 1513, Madison, CT 06443-1513.

The Occupational Safety and Health Administration. The Occupational Safety and Health Administration has the primary responsibility for enforcing OSHA. It develops occupational standards, grants variances to employers, conducts workplace inspections, and issues citations and penalties.

- *Occupational standards.* Occupational standards, which cover hazards ranging from tools and machinery safety to microscopic airborne matter, can be exceedingly complex and detailed. While many standards are clearly reasonable and appropriate, OSHA has frequently been criticized for adopting infeasible standards or standards whose costs exceed their benefits. The courts, however, generally do not require the OSH Administration to balance the costs and benefits of particular standards, only to demonstrate their feasibility.[19]

  The development of occupational standards can begin with the OSH Administration, NIOSH, state and local governments, or a variety of other sources, including industry groups and labor organizations. Proposed new standards are published in the *Federal Register*, the official legal news publication of the U.S. government. Comments from interested parties are sought, and hearings regarding the standards may be held. The full text of any adopted standard and the implementation date are then reported in the *Federal Register*.[20]
- *Variances.* Employers may ask the OSH Administration for a temporary (up to one year) variance from a standard when they cannot comply with a new standard by its effective date. The OSH Administration may grant a permanent variance from a particular standard when an employer can demonstrate that it has in place alternatives that protect employees as effectively as compliance with the standard would.[21]
- *Workplace inspections.* The OSH Administration has the power to conduct workplace inspections to make sure that organizations are complying with OSHA standards. Since it would be impossible to inspect each of the hundreds of thousands of affected workplaces each year, OSHA has established an inspection priority system that calls for inspections to be made in the following order:[22] (1) situations involving "imminent danger" in the workplace, (2) incidents resulting in fatalities or hospitalization of five or more employees, (3) follow-up of employee complaints of unsafe or unhealthful working conditions, and (4) "high-hazard" industries and occupations (for example, mining, farming, construction, and transport).

OSHA inspectors have the right to enter an establishment without notice to examine work environment, materials, and equipment, and to question both employers and employees. However, this right conflicts with the employer's constitutional protection from warrantless searches. In a 1978 case involving a company's refusal to allow an OSHA inspection until the agency could produce a search warrant, the Supreme Court ruled that the employer does have a right to demand a search warrant before the OSH Administration can make an inspection. While the OSH Administration can generally obtain a search warrant based on an employee complaint or on the agency's own inspection priority system, some argue that forfeiting the element of surprise makes inspection less effective because it gives employers leeway to alter unsafe conditions or practices (for example, erratically using safety equipment) until the inspection is complete.[23]

- *Citations and penalties.* The OSH Administration may issue citations and impose penalties for any violations of OSHA standards. The exact penalty varies with the employer's good faith attempts to comply with OSHA regulations, its history of previous violations, the seriousness of the infraction, and the size of the business. These penalties may include criminal penalties as well as substantial fines. In fact, executives of firms that recklessly endanger workers are becoming increasingly likely to spend time in jail.[24] In 1987 five senior executives of Chicago Magnet Wire Company were prosecuted for causing workers' illnesses by allowing them to be exposed to hazardous chemicals. In 1989 a supervisor at Jackson Enterprises in Michigan was convicted of involuntary manslaughter in an employee's work-related death.[25]

Fines for violations of OSHA standards may range from no fine for minor violations to megafines of several million dollars for companies guilty of numerous, repeated, and willful infractions. A recent study of OSHA fines found the mean (average) fine to be $875,000 but the median fine to be greater than $3 million.[26] Thus, there are more fines of relatively smaller amounts, but the fines seem to be of substantial size nonetheless. An important question is whether or not these fines have any meaningful impact on organizations. One approach to answering this question is to see if the announcement of fines levied by the OSH Administration has any impact on the value of the firm's stock. If there is no impact on the stock, there would be little pressure on top executives to improve safety and health conditions and avoid future fines. It has been found that the announcement of OSHA penalties does have a significant negative impact on the firm's stock.[27] However, the downturn in stock prices is a short-term effect that occurs only in the day or two following the announcement of the penalties. Furthermore, it appears that it is simply the announcement of a violation, not the amount of the fine, that impacts the company's stock price. Figure 16-2 defines the various types of violations and their associated penalties.

OSHA funds a free consultation service that works with businesses to help them identify potential workplace hazards and improve safety management systems. This service is especially useful for small businesses. It provides for a confidential inspection, completely separate from the OSH Administration's inspection program, that does not result in penalties or fines. However, the employer is obligated to correct serious safety and health hazards found in the inspection.

The procedure works as follows:[28]

1. The employer must contact the OSH Administration consultant to get things started.
2. An opening conference is scheduled at the work site to discuss the consultant's role and the employer's obligations under the service.
3. Employer and consultant examine workplace conditions together. The consultant may talk to employees, discuss OSHA standards with them, and point out safety problems.
4. In a closing conference the consultant reviews the findings of the inspection with the employer, detailing both what the employer is doing right and where improvement is needed.

FIGURE 16-2

Penalties for Violations of OSHA Standards

Source: U.S. Department of Labor, Occupational Safety and Health Administration. (1985). *All about OSHA* (rev. ed.). Washington, DC: U.S. Government Printing Office.

Violation	Description	Penalty
Other than serious violation	No direct relationship to job safety or health; probably not capable of causing death or serious physical harm.	Discretionary fine of up to $1,000 for each violation.
Serious violation	Serious probability of death or serious injury could result and employer knew, or should have known, of the hazard.	Mandatory $1,000 penalty for each violation.
Willful violation	Intentionally or knowingly committing a violation.	Fine of up to $10,000 per violation. Possible criminal penalties.
Repeated violation	Reinspection reveals a substantially similar violation.	Fine of up to $10,000 per violation.
Failure to correct prior violation	Failure to correct a violation for which the company was previously cited.	Fine of up to $1,000 for every day the violation continues.

5. Following the closing conference, the consultant provides a written report explaining the findings and confirming proposed times within which the employer is to remedy hazards found in the inspection. (These are known as *abatement periods*.)

The Occupational Safety and Health Review Commission (OSHRC). OSHRC operates independently of the OSH Administration, and reviews its citations. An employer can appeal an OSHA citation, an abatement period, or a penalty to OSHRC. Rulings made by this commission can be appealed only through the federal court system.[29]

The National Institute for Occupational Safety and Health (NIOSH). NIOSH exists mainly to research safety and health problems and to assist the OSH Administration in the creation of new health and safety standards. Like the OSH Administration, NIOSH may inspect the workplace and gather information from employers and employees about hazardous materials. In addition, NIOSH trains inspectors and others associated with the enforcement of OSHA.[30]

State Programs. OSHA permits states to create their own occupational safety and health programs, and almost half of the states have chosen to do so. OSHA will approve a state plan if the state shows that it is able to set and enforce standards, provide and train competent enforcement personnel, and give educational and technical assistance to business. Upon approval of a state program, the OSH Administration funds 50% of that program's operating costs and passes primary enforcement responsibility to the state. The OSH Administration continually monitors and evaluates state programs, and may withdraw approval if it determines that a state is failing to maintain an effective program.[31]

Opponents of "Big Government" claim that excessive regulation of workplace safety hurts productivity and increases costs. They argue that in a free market, employees should be responsible for their own health and safety—that they should be free to choose between taking a wage premium for hazardous work and accepting lower pay for safer work. Would such a policy be ethical? What are its pros and cons?

The Effectiveness of OSHA. Has OSHA been an effective tool for creating a safer and healthier workplace? OSHA's critics suggest that its detailed and expansive regulations produce costs that exceed their benefits. However, many other people feel that while the OSHA-related costs borne by employers are direct and easy to measure, the benefits of an accident-free workplace are not. They point out that it is accident victims—employees—who bear the costs of an absence of health and safety regulations, not the employer.

Indeed, the costs of accidents and illness can be immense. For example, the cost of work-related injuries in 1994 was approximately $121 billion.[32] The good news is that there is evidence that the regulations, penalties, and increased awareness brought about by OSHA have significantly reduced workplace accidents. For example, between 1912 and 1994, deaths in the workplace per 100,000 people decreased from 21 to 2.[33] In 1912 there were between 18,000 and 21,000 workplace deaths, while in 1994, with a work force more than three times the size and producing 12 times the goods and services, there were only 5,000 deaths. Nonetheless, some occupations remain dangerous. For more information on two such occupations, see the Issues and Applications feature on page 496 titled "The Most Dangerous Games."

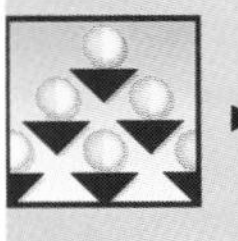

Building Managerial Skills: Managing Contemporary Safety, Health, and Behavioral Issues

Effectively managing workplace safety and health requires far more than reducing the numbers of job-related accidents and injuries. In practice, managers must deal with a variety of practical, legal, and ethical issues, many of which involve a careful balancing of individual rights (particularly the right to privacy) with the needs of the organization (see Chapter 14). Because these issues often give rise to legal questions, HR professionals are frequently called upon to develop and implement policies to deal with them. Among the

The Most Dangerous Games

Issues + Applications

What is the most dangerous occupation in the United States? There is some dispute over this dubious designation, but many claim that it belongs to logging. With three serious injuries per day for every 1,000 workers in the U.S. logging industry, logging has the highest documented risk among blue-collar workers. This is despite increased training and the use of more protective equipment and safer machinery in recent years. Industry experts suggest the high accident rate is due both to the mystique of the job (the logger as "rugged individualist" who disdains safety) and to the more mundane fact that few logging companies initiate or enforce safety rules.

Others claim that workers in the Alaskan fishing industry face the most dangerous working conditions in the United States. According to NIOSH, while the current accidental death rate for all U.S. occupations is 2 per 100,000 workers, Alaskan fishermen have a death rate of 200 per 100,000. The figure rises to 660 per 100,000 for crab fishermen (which is more than 300 times the national average). The reason for this extraordinarily high fatality rate? Few safety or labor regulations are in force when boats are at sea, and the combination of inexperienced, overworked crews and naturally hazardous work makes the occupation deadly.

Sources: National Safety Council. (1995). *Accident facts*, 1995 edition. Itsaca, IL: National Safety Council; Ewing, Lance J. (1992, July). Logging industry: Safety deep in the woods. *Professional Safety 37*(7), 30–31; and Saporito, B. (1993, May 31). The most dangerous job in America. *Fortune 127*(11), 130–140.

weightiest issues facing employers today are dealing with AIDS in the workplace, workplace violence, smoking in the workplace, cumulative trauma disorders, fetal protection, hazardous chemicals, and genetic testing.

It is important to recognize that, in addition to these direct challenges, there is also the challenge of employee commitment to safety and health programs. Many organizations face the problem of employees ignoring and even being hostile to safety and health measures. The reason: Employees often view safety and health measures as intrusive and inefficient.

Top managers can generate commitment to safety and health programs by explaining to supervisors and others the rationale for the relevant safety and health practices. For example, it is important that everyone understand the cost of accidents to the organization. Furthermore, the costs (such as fines) for violating safety and health standards should be clearly explained to employees at all levels. Once people understand the linkage between safety measures and the business's bottom line, resistance to safety programs should largely disappear. Of course, removing human resistance to any kind of program can be a difficult and delicate process that requires time and commitment.

AIDS

Dealing effectively with workplace concerns that arise when an employee contracts acquired immunodeficiency syndrome (AIDS) will be one of the most important workplace health challenges of the next decade. In the early 1980s AIDS was scarcely known, but by 1996, the Center for Disease Control reported that two thirds of organizations with more than 2,500 employees had already experienced an employee with this disease or HIV (the human immunodeficiency virus that leads to AIDS[34]).

Today, approximately 1 million people in North America are infected with HIV. This number corresponds to one in every 290 people.[35] Among people of prime working age (25 to 44 years), HIV infection is now the leading cause of death in men and the third leading cause in women.[36] Given these numbers, organizations in the United States and across the world are being increasingly forced to deal with AIDS in the workplace.

While some U.S. companies (such as Digital Equipment Corporation, Levi Strauss, and Wells Fargo Bank) have corporate policies regarding the treatment of employees with AIDS that reflect a strong sense of social responsibility, other companies have been reluctant even to acknowledge the issue.[37] A recent survey found that only one third of large and mid-size companies have formal HIV and AIDS policies.[38] In light of the public attention AIDS has received, the unwillingness of the majority of companies to formulate a formal AIDS policy is surprising. As the manager of Digital Equipment's HIV/AIDS program, Paul A. Ross, has stated, "Waiting for the first case of AIDS before starting an education program is like waiting to create a fire evacuation program until you smell smoke."[39]

Some companies are reluctant to come to grips with the AIDS issue because of the fear and anxiety it provokes. Failure to deal with the issue proactively, however, is a prescription for crisis because AIDS carries high economic and morale costs. The estimated treatment cost of a single case of HIV from diagnosis to death ranges from $90,000 to $120,000; annual productivity losses from all AIDS cases could be more than $50 billion per year.[40] AIDS can also have indirect costs in the form of disruption of the workplace. When an employee of an Atlanta Toys 'Я' Us store died of AIDS in 1992, misinformed employees refused to use water fountains and restrooms, and morale and performance suffered dramatically.[41] Fear may lead some employees to refuse to work with infected coworkers, even though the law gives them no protection for such a refusal and they can be disciplined or discharged.[42] Others may come to resent an infected coworker during the advanced stages of AIDS if the productivity of that coworker suffers and they have to pick up the slack.[43]

It is clear that AIDS contagion is a primary health concern of U.S. workers. A recent Center for Disease Control and Prevention survey of 2,000 adults found that 67% would have "some misgivings" about working near someone with AIDS, and 26% would feel "uncomfortable." And while 90% of the respondents said that HIV-positive employees should be treated like any other employee, this result was tempered by the fact that more than half of the respondents said their companies have no written policy to do so.[44]

While companies may prefer to sweep the topic of AIDS under the rug, there are federal guidelines regarding AIDS that require organizational compliance. The major sources of these guidelines are OSHA and the Americans with Disabilities Act (ADA).

OSHA. In 1992 OSHA issued the Bloodborne Pathogens Standards, which must be followed in all workplaces where employees can reasonably be expected to come in contact with blood or other body fluids. OSHA takes these standards very seriously, both in health-care and non-health-care organizations. Between 1993 and 1994, it issued over 1,000 violation citations and nearly $1 million in fines to organizations in the Midwest.[45] Figure 16-3 summarizes the key points of the OSHA standards.

- *Exposure Control Plan* — Outline the procedures to identify workers at risk and specify methods for complying with standards.
- *Universal Precautions* — Follow the Center for Disease Control and Prevention's recommendations for handling all blood and body fluid as though they are contaminated.
- *Personal Protective Equipment* — Provide all necessary personal protection equipment, such as gloves and masks.
- *Cleaning Protocols* — Identify the methods of decontamination and the procedures for handling waste.
- *Hazard Communication* — Use warning labels and signs to identify restricted areas.
- *Information and Training* — Educate employees regarding AIDS and the OSHA standards.
- *Recordkeeping* — Document efforts relating to the standards and keep the medical records of employees exposed to risk for the duration of their employment plus 30 years.

FIGURE 16-3

Key Components of OSHA's Bloodborne Pathogens Standards

Source: Adapted from Oswald, E. M. (1996). No employer is immune: AIDS exposure in the workplace. *Risk Management, 43*, 18–21.

ADA. According to ADA guidelines, having HIV or AIDS would not prevent people from performing the essential functions of most jobs.[46] Thus, organizations must make reasonable accommodations for infected employees. Reasonable accommodation might include adjustments to work schedules or workstation modifications. For example, one company gave a manager with AIDS a chair that converted into a sleeping recliner and allowed a 90-minute break in the afternoon.[47] The chair allowed the manager to deal with the drop in his energy level in the afternoon. The manager scheduled all meetings in the morning and came into work extra hours on evenings and weekends, if needed. This arrangement was reasonable and provided an important accommodation for the manager at minimal cost.

ADA guidelines also affect the hiring process. Employers cannot ask job candidates about their HIV or AIDS status or require job candidates to take an HIV test before making a job offer. Testing *can* be done and questions posed after a job offer is made. However, test results must be kept confidential. The job offer cannot be withdrawn on the basis of a positive HIV test unless the employer can demonstrate that the person would pose a direct threat to coworkers or customers, and that this threat could not be eliminated through reasonable accommodation. Such demonstration would be all but impossible in most jobs.

In addition to simply complying with the guidelines issued by federal agencies, organizations should proactively address the AIDS issue by developing an AIDS policy. Figure 16-4 outlines some of the issues that employers must consider when developing an AIDS policy. Such a policy sends a clear signal of the importance the company places on its human resources and the support it provides to AIDS victims.

An effective AIDS policy should not only outline the procedures to be followed when an employee contracts HIV, but also educate the work force. Many employees fear that they can contract the disease by working alongside someone who has AIDS. Educational programs can eliminate these fears by providing accurate information about the disease and how it is transmitted.

The Manager's Role. What is the role of managers and supervisors in dealing with AIDS in the workplace? Managers should be able to answer employee questions about AIDS and effectively deal with any AIDS-related issues that arise. For this reason, the educational effort should involve familiarizing supervisors and managers with the organization's AIDS policy and training them in how to deal with AIDS issues.[48]

Violence in the Workplace

On January 28, 1993, a man in a business suit entered the cafeteria of Fireman's Fund Insurance Company in Tampa, Florida, then walked up to a table where managers, super-

FIGURE 16-4

Issues in the Development and Implementation of an AIDS Policy

Sources: Fremgen, B., and Whitty, M. (1992, December). How to avoid a costly AIDS crisis in the organization. *Labor Law Journal*, 751–758; Smith, J. M. (1993, March). How to develop and implement an AIDS workplace policy. *HR Focus*, 15; and Stodghill, R. (1993, February). Why AIDS policy must be a special policy. *Business Week, 3303*, 53–54.

- Who is responsible for development and implementation of the policy?
- What are the objectives of the AIDS policy?
- What is covered under the AIDS policy?
- What rights will covered employees have, particularly in terms of workplace accommodation and confidentiality?
- What benefits will victims receive?
- Who is in charge of administering the policy?
- What kind of training should supervisors and managers have, particularly to prepare them to manage coworkers' concerns and fears?
- How does the company deal with job restructuring issues, accommodation, and requests for transfers by AIDS victims and coworkers?
- How should the AIDS policy be communicated to employees?
- How should organizations deal with affected workers' productivity problems?
- How can organizations help victims cope by providing support and referral services?

visors, and executives were seated. He pulled a gun from beneath his suit jacket and opened fire. Three men were killed in the attack and two women were injured.

The gunman was a former employee named Paul Calden who had been discharged about eight months earlier. Witnesses later recalled hearing him say, "This is what you get for firing me!" Police said that Calden had a longstanding and very bitter grudge against Fireman's Fund managers, and he appeared to have plotted his revenge for several weeks. Two hours after the shootings, Calden was found dead from a self-inflicted gunshot wound.[49]

Unfortunately, this scenario is not uncommon. In 1994, homicide was the second leading cause of job-related deaths for all workers, accounting for a total of 1,071 deaths (16% of all workplace fatalities).[50] Homicide was the leading cause of death for female workers, accounting for 35% of their fatal work injuries.

While homicides have received the most attention, workplace violence can take a variety of forms, including harassment, assault, and threats. In a recent survey of corporate security directors conducted by the National Safe Workplace Institute, 94% of respondents ranked domestic violence as a high security problem, and 88% reported that more than five incidents of domestic violence (for example, husbands assaulting their wives) had occurred in their companies.[51] Over 60% reported that their companies do not have procedures that allow victims or potential victims to report threats of domestic violence and do not have procedures to protect potential victims.[52]

The possibility of becoming a victim of workplace violence is among the highest in the health-care industry. In 1993 the Bureau of Labor Statistics reported that health-care workers had the highest incidence of assault injuries. For example, homicide was the leading cause of traumatic occupational death among those working in nursing homes and personal care facilities, and 26% of nurses have been victims of physical assault.[53] The cause of this relatively high degree of violence in the health-care field is unclear, but it may have something to do with the close physical proximity that nursing involves and the possibility that clients and visitors may include those who engage in criminal and violent behavior. Regardless of the causes, it is important that health-care organizations take steps to reduce the incidence of violence. A set of OSHA guidelines released in 1995, "Guidelines for Preventing Workplace Violence for Health Care and Social Service Workers," requires health-care providers to have a written workplace violence prevention program as part of their overall safety and health program.[54] Figure 16-5 presents some of the guidelines' main requirements.

- Establish a policy of zero tolerance for workplace violence.
- Encourage reporting of incidents of workplace violence.
- Develop a plan for workplace security.
- Appoint a person with program responsibility and provide adequate resources.
- Ensure management commitment to employee safety.
- Hold employee meetings on safety issues.

FIGURE 16-5

OSHA Violence Prevention Program Requirements

Source: Adapted from Epstein, B. D. (1996). *Preventing workplace violence: Agency issues guidelines for providers. Provider* 6, 71–72.

Whether or not an organization is in the health-care field, it is important from both a legal and a social responsibility perspective that managers deal with workplace violence proactively. Under **negligent hiring** laws, employers can be held responsible for their employees' violent acts on the job, particularly when the employer knows, or should know, that an employee has a history of violent behavior (see Chapter 5). In one California case, for example, a temporary help agency employed a man who subsequently stabbed a woman coworker to death. The man was a paroled murderer with a five-year gap in his résumé that the agency failed to investigate. A state court ordered the temporary agency to pay the dead woman's relatives $5.5 million. These types of cases are still uncommon, but their numbers appear to be increasing.[55]

negligent hiring
Hiring an employee with a history of violent or illegal behavior without conducting background checks or taking proper precautions.

The Manager's Role. Managers need to take responsibility for reducing or eliminating violence in the workplace. To this end, they must be sensitive to the causes of workplace violence. Many people feel pressured in their jobs and fear layoffs. Add to this stress level such workplace events as negative performance appraisals, personality conflicts with coworkers or managers, or personal problems such as a divorce, and a potentially dangerous person may emerge.

Certainly, managers cannot eliminate all these pressures, which are realities of everyday life in modern organizations. However, they can make sure that employees are treated fairly. Treating employees as though they are expendable will not create commitment to

Manager's Notebook

Profile of People Prone to Workplace Violence and Warning Signs

Profile of Characteristics:

- White men between 30 and 40 years of age.
- Socially isolated—a "loner," who may avoid socializing during breaks or work functions.
- Experiencing stress in personal life, such as divorce or death in the family.
- Low self-esteem with no healthy outlet for anger.
- Work is the person's primary, or sole, activity and it provides him with the opportunity to be "somebody."
- Difficulty dealing with criticism or frustration.
- Difficulty dealing with authority.
- Fascinated with weapons and the military.
- Temper-control problems.
- May abuse alcohol or drugs.
- History of conflict with others.

Warning Signs:

- May blame others for problems.
- A behavioral change, such as becoming withdrawn, depressed, or irritable.
- May hold a grudge over a termination, lost promotion, performance feedback, or some other outcome.
- May make threats and intimidate other workers.
- May exhibit paranoia and believe that management or other employees are out to get him.
- May test the limits of policies.

Sources: Adapted from Missouri Capitol Police (1996). Violence in the workplace... http://www.dps.state.mo.us.DPS/MCP/STUDY/WKVIOLNC.HTM, June 7, 1996, 1–6; and Bensimon, H. F. (1994). Crisis and disaster management: Violence in the Workplace. *Training and Development, 48*, 27–32.

the company and could be enough to trigger a violent reaction. Managers should deal with performance problems by focusing on the behavior and future improvement, rather than condemning the person for past performance problems (see Chapter 7 on performance appraisal). Managers should never discipline employees in front of coworkers; doing so can humiliate the person and incite a violent reaction.[56]

Managers should also take steps to reduce the possibility of hiring workers who might be prone to violence. For example, interviewers might ask job candidates to describe how they reacted to a past management decision they didn't agree with and why.[57] The responses to this question and follow-up questions could be quite revealing. Also, interviewers should check for evidence of substance abuse or emotional problems, which might be indicated by careless driving or DWI (driving while intoxicated) entries on driving records. Unexplained gaps in a person's employment history should be carefully examined. The Manager's Notebook presents a profile of the characteristics of those who commit violence and a list of some warning signs.

Smoking in the Workplace

In 1994 Melvin Simon and Associates, owners of 85 large shopping malls throughout the United States, announced that smoking would no longer be allowed in any of its facilities. This announcement closely followed decisions by two major fast-food chains, McDonald's and Arby's, to eliminate smoking in their restaurants.[58] Since these actions, many organizations have enacted smoking elimination policies.

The push to restrict workplace smoking has come largely in the last decade. As far back as 1964, the U.S. Surgeon General published the initial government report on the health consequences of smoking. By 1981, however, a Bureau of National Affairs survey revealed that only 8% of U.S. companies restricted smoking. In the mid-1980s a report from Surgeon General C. Everett Koop asserted that smokers create health risks for nonsmoking coworkers and customers.[59] By 1986, 36% of all organizations restricted smoking in the workplace.[60] Over two thirds of U.S. employers now have smoke-free workplaces.[61]

Recent public opinion and demographics provide support for restrictions, if not outright bans, on smoking. A recent Gallup poll found that 63% of smokers believe that secondhand smoke is harmful to adults. In addition, 38% of the respondents in a 1994 poll wanted to ban smoking in restaurants and 32% favored total workplace bans.[62] Many cities and states have enacted regulations regarding smoking.[63] For example, Aspen, Colorado has had a smoking ban in effect for restaurants for a number of years. San Francisco and San Jose, among other cities, have banned smoking in nearly all nonresidential indoor spaces.

The state of New York has one of the most comprehensive laws protecting the rights of nonsmoking employees in the workplace. It requires each employer to adopt a written smoking policy, post the policy prominently in the workplace, and supply written copies to employees upon request. Requirements include:[64]

- A smoke-free work area for nonsmoking employees.
- A work area set aside for smoking if all working in the area agree.
- Contiguous nonsmoking areas in cafeterias and break rooms.
- A prohibition against smoking in auditoriums, gymnasiums, restrooms, elevators, hallways, and other common areas.
- A prohibition against smoking in company vehicles and meeting rooms unless all present agree that smoking be permitted.

More controversial than workplace restrictions on smoking is employers' refusal to hire or retain smokers. Most companies base this decision on the fact that smokers raise health-care costs for all workers, not just the smokers themselves.

Indeed, it is fairly well established that employer costs associated with employee smoking are substantial. A study of 46,000 Du Pont workers in the late 1980s found that the average smoker costs $960 more in medical costs and sick days than nonsmokers.[65] Smoking employees are absent 50% more than nonsmokers, use health insurance 50% more often, and take more time per day in breaks.[66] Relative to nonsmokers, smokers are absent from work 34% longer, are 29% more likely to be involved in a work-related accident, are 40% more likely to suffer an occupational injury, and are 55% more likely to be disciplined.[67]

As more companies have begun to introduce stringent off-duty tobacco use rules, individual smokers have begun to press claims of discrimination against their "right to smoke" and to accuse companies of violating their privacy rights. However, the courts have consistently refused to recognize on-the-job smoking as a right and have denied unemployment compensation claims to employees who resigned because they could not quit smoking. Nonetheless, despite the fact that on-the-job smoking is not a legal right, a growing number of states have enacted legislation that restricts employers from discriminating against individuals for off-the-job use of lawful products, particularly tobacco. The laws vary considerably in terms of exemptions and penalties. Many exempt specific organizations (for example, hospitals and religious organizations) allow exceptions where not smoking is shown to be a bona fide occupational qualification (for example, working for an organization, like the American Cancer Society, whose goal is to promote health), and require smokers to conform to on-the-job smoking rules. Many of these state laws, however, do allow employers to charge smoking employees higher health insurance rates.[68]

OSHA proposed federal regulations regarding the regulation of smoking in the workplace in 1994. This set of rules would limit worker exposure to secondhand smoke by requiring employers to provide enclosed smoking lounges with separate ventilation systems.[69] Installing a ventilated lounge can be a costly proposition, particularly for smaller businesses that cannot afford the expense. Thus, many businesses could be forced to eliminate smoking altogether as a means of complying with the regulations. However, it is unknown when, if ever, OSHA's proposed regulations will become law. The current congressional sentiment is that businesses and local governments should develop their own smoking policies without interference from the federal government.[70]

While OSHA does not as yet have specific workplace standards regarding smoking, the act's general duty clause does require a work environment free from recognized hazards.[71] In a 1976 case involving New Jersey Bell Telephone, the court applied the general duty provision by recognizing that secondhand smoke is a preventable recognized hazard and ordering a smoking ban in working areas in response to an employee's suit.

Another complication for employers could be the application of the Americans with Disabilities Act to the workplace smoking issue. It is clear that employees sensitive to smoke are qualified disabled employees under the ADA and must be accommodated. However, a reasonable accommodation for these employees need not mean a smoke-free workplace; other types of accommodation, such as fans, ventilation, and separate work areas, might suffice. Finally, while some employees have tried to claim that habitual smoking is a disability under the ADA and have asked for accommodation, this type of claim generally has not been very successful.

The Manager's Role. Managers need to be aware of any local or state regulations regarding smoking and ensure that employees understand and abide by these rules. While some smokers may still resent such regulations, smoking bans have been in effect for a number of years now, and the issue has been widely discussed in the media. Thus, smoking in the workplace is probably not as volatile a management issue as it once was. Nonetheless, managers should not overlook problems that arise over smoking policies because the feelings of both smokers and nonsmokers can be deeply held. It is important that managers approach any problems in this area fairly and quickly, ensuring that all parties abide by legal and company regulations.

Cumulative Trauma Disorders

cumulative trauma disorder (CTD)
An occupational injury that occurs from repetitive physical movements, such as assembly-line work or data entry.

Cumulative trauma disorders (CTDs) are also called repetitive stress (or motion or strain) injuries (or illnesses or syndromes). CTDs do not refer to one disorder but rather to a wide array of maladies from *carpal tunnel syndrome (CTS)*, which often afflicts the wrists of computer keyboard users, to tennis elbow and forearm and shoulder complaints.[72] The number of workers with CTDs has risen dramatically in recent years. In 1983 there were fewer than 50,000 U.S. workers diagnosed with CTDs. By 1993, that number had reached 302,000.

ergonomics
The science of adapting working conditions to employee safety and comfort needs.

OSHA has proposed ergonomic workplace standards as a means of reducing CTDs. **Ergonomics** is a young science that focuses on adapting working conditions to employee safety and comfort needs. OSHA's proposed standards would require education of workers in the warning signs of CTDs, establishment of a process for reporting symptoms, and the institution of engineering controls to reduce the incidence of CTDs.[73] For example, companies may need to make tools of various sizes available so that workers can choose the one most suited to their working style. Many businesspeople have severely criticized these proposed standards, estimating the costs of compliance at $21 billion a year. This price tag is very high, and businesses worry that compliance with the standards will adversely affect U.S. productivity and competitiveness. Given business opposition and the current congressional focus on keeping government out of business, it is unlikely that the ergonomic standards will become federal law in the near future.

Indeed, there may be other good reasons to delay OSHA's proposed regulations. The prevalence of CTDs is a very controversial issue. A recent medical publication asserts that CTDs account for 30 to 50% of workplace injuries and cost employers $150 billion a year.[74] However, CTDs accounted for only 4.5% of the total number of workplace injuries and illnesses in 1993. In addition, there is much debate over the accuracy of such statistics. Labor advocates contend that the numbers underrepresent the true extent of the problem because many workers are misdiagnosed or continue working as best they can. Business lobbyists contend that the problem is overstated, partially as a result of media hype. Interestingly, there is similar controversy in the medical community. For example, one medical doctor who has treated over 900 workers complaining of CTDs claims that only about 20% of these patients present the symptoms of a neuromuscular disorder. He contends that the other 80% may have the symptoms but the cause is not the physical workplace.[75] Likewise, a hand surgeon has stated that many workers complaining of a CTD are not model employees and that a precipitating event, such as a reprimand or negative performance feedback, often precedes the medical complaint. It is also interesting to note that numerous suits have been filed against computer keyboard makers, but that no plaintiff had won a judgment until 1996.[76]

In December of 1996, Digital Equipment Company became the first employer to lose a case of disabling arm and wrist injuries blamed on their keyboards.[77] The three workers who filed suit worked for other companies but used the keyboards made by Digital. The workers were awarded a total of $6 million. Digital had been cited by OSHA in 1989 for similar injuries among its own workers. The company put in a program that reduced the incidence of the problem eightfold in its own workforce. However, the computer manufacturer did not inform its customers of the potential for repetitive stress syndrome problems by the use of their product or how the problems might be avoided. These facts were used against Digital in the court case and a federal jury was persuaded that Digital knew of the problem but failed to inform customers.

The Manager's Role. While legal compliance may not be an issue right now, socially responsible organizations should be aware of CTDs and their likely causes. Managers should take steps to reduce CTDs by educating workers and altering the physical arrangement of the workplace if necessary. Figure 16-6 presents a set of do's and don'ts to help workers avoid CTDs. Managers should also remember that posting these tips prominently can decrease the likelihood that workers will develop a CTD.

Reducing CTDs could be part of an organization's *voluntary protection program.* OSHA recognizes that simple compliance with federal standards does not mean that a company is truly oriented toward employee safety and health. OSHA started the Voluntary Protection Program in 1982 as a way of recognizing organizations with outstanding safety and health programs. Figure 16-7 on page 504 describes this program.

Fetal Protection, Hazardous Chemicals, and Genetic Testing

During the 1970s and 1980s, a handful of large U.S. firms developed workplace policies designed to prevent pregnant employees from exposure to hazardous chemicals that might damage the fetus. These policies were controversial because they tended to restrict women's access to some of industry's better-paying jobs. For example, in 1978 several women working for American Cyanamid underwent sterilization rather than risk losing highly paid jobs.

The fetal protection controversy came to national attention in 1982 when Johnson Controls, a battery manufacturer, prevented women of childbearing age from working in jobs involving contact with lead. The union sued Johnson Controls for sex discrimination because the company's policy restricted only female employees. The Supreme Court ruled against the company, finding it guilty of illegal sex bias.[78]

This decision caused great concern among companies like General Motors, Du Pont, Olin, Monsanto, and others with fetal protection policies. These companies argue that their only

DO:

- Take breaks (every 20 minutes).
- Stretch and relax at your work area (once per hour).
- Maintain and build your physical fitness.
- Maintain good posture when working at a computer/terminal:
- Sit erect.
- Feet flat on floor.
- Bend elbows at a comfortable angle.
- Sit about 18-28 inches from the screen.
- Place documents at the same height and angle as the monitor

DON'T:

- Engage in a lot of repetitive motion with your hands and arms.
- Bend your wrists continuously.
- Grasp or pinch objects continuously.
- Work in an awkward position.
- Exert a lot of force with your arms and hands.

FIGURE 16-6

Avoiding CTDs: The Do's and Don'ts

Source: Adapted from Worsnop, R. L. (1995). Repetitive stress injuries. *The CQ Researcher, 5,* 537–560.

OSHA's Voluntary Protection Program recognizes excellence in safety and health programs provided by employers.

The Application:
Organizations need to apply to OSHA to be considered for recognition. The application is very detailed and time consuming. On the application, employers must provide:

- A statement of management's commitment to worker safety and health.
- Details of health surveys, hazard analyses, and accident investigations conducted by the company.
- Description of hazard prevention and control programs.
- Description of the safety and health training provided to employees.
- Description of the safety committees and safety-related employee involvement activities at the company.

The OSHA Consideration Process:
If viewed positively, the application will be followed by an onsite visit of up to three OSHA compliance officers, who will hold a conference with management and employees.

Level of Recognition
OSHA will make a formal decision regarding whether or not to recognize the organization for its voluntary health and safety efforts. There are three levels of recognition:

1. STAR—STAR program status is reserved for work sites that provide outstanding safety and health protection to their employees.
2. MERIT—Merit status is a stepping-stone to the STAR level and is given to work sites that are committed to providing the best worker protection.
3. DEMONSTRATION—This status is reserved for work sites that are pilot-testing cutting-edge safety and health strategies that may eventually alter the STAR program requirements.

FIGURE 16-7

OSHA's Voluntary Protection Program

Sources: Adapted from Lawrence, K. L. (1995, Fall/Winter). Voluntary protection programs praised for accomplishments. *Job Safety & Health Quarterly*, 18-19; Swartz, G. (1995). OSHA's voluntary protection program. *Professional Safety*, *40*, 21-23.

alternative is to reduce the use of certain substances greatly. But reducing the use of these compounds, they claim, would be both difficult and costly. Critics counter that these companies should do more to protect *all* workers, not simply remove some from the workplace.[79]

Reproductive health concerns are an important workplace issue with the potential to impact thousands of employers and millions of workers. For example, one study of 1,600 pregnant women showed that those who use video display terminals heavily have a miscarriage rate double that of women who do not use VDTs. A study of pregnant women at a Digital Equipment plant in Houston reached a similar conclusion. Clearly, the implications of this type of problem are substantial when one considers the number of VDTs currently in use.[80] The fetal health issue is compounded by the fact that only a handful of companies have comprehensive fetal health policies, and research about the effects of many industrial compounds on reproductive health is inconclusive or incomplete. While some substances (for example, lead) represent clear health threats to fetuses, exposure to many other compounds may not cause problems. These compounds may also prevent significant reproductive hazards to *both* sexes, not just women.

Hazardous Chemicals. Many thousands of workplace accidents and injuries reported each year have been attributed to exposure to toxic chemicals. In the past, workers were often required to handle chemicals without being fully informed of the hazards involved. In 1983, however, OSHA's hazard communication standard gave employees the right to know about hazardous chemicals in the workplace (see Figure 16-1). The current standard requires manufacturers and users of hazardous chemicals to identify the chemicals, provide employees with information about them, and train employees in the dangers and handling of them.[81]

Genetic Testing. A new and controversial tool used to deal with exposure to workplace substances is **genetic testing**, which identifies employees who are genetically susceptible to specific occupational substances. The goal is to avoid placing at-risk employees in dangerous jobs. Very few organizations use genetic testing at present (1% or fewer), but advances in genetic research may make this screening device more attractive in years to come. Critics question the predictive ability of genetic screening and criticize it from both legal and ethical perspectives because it has significant potential to discriminate. Indeed, heavy use of genetic screening may conflict with both Title VII of the Civil Rights Act and the Americans with Disabilities Act. An additional argument against genetic screening is similar to that raised against fetal protection policies: It is the work environment that is the problem, not the worker, and organizations should remove the hazard, not the person.[82]

genetic testing
A form of biological testing that identifies employees who are genetically susceptible to specific occupational substances.

The Manager's Role. Line managers have the obligation to stay informed and to help the HR department develop policies that balance employees' rights with the organization's needs. Because they are on the front line, managers are responsible for directly communicating information about hazards to employees in a clear and timely manner. They should also make sure the employees understand the risks involved in working with hazardous substances and take all appropriate precautions. They should also inform employees of their rights, responsibilities, and alternatives, handling each situation with respect and fairness. ▼

▸ Safety and Health Programs

We have devoted most of the chapter thus far to discussing physical hazards in the workplace and their impact on both workers and the organization. However, there are other hazards that have major effects on workers, including stress, unsafe behaviors, and poor health habits. To cope with both types of hazards, companies often design comprehensive safety and health programs.

Safety Programs

A safe working environment does not just happen; it has to be created. The organizations with the best reputations for safety have developed deliberate, well-planned, and thorough safety programs. Concern for safety should begin at the highest level within the organization, and managers and supervisors at all levels should be charged with demonstrating safety awareness, held responsible for safety training, and rewarded for maintaining a safe workplace. Typically, however, the safety director and most safety programs are part of the HR function. HR managers are often responsible for designing and implementing safety programs, as well as for training supervisors and managers in the administration of workplace safety rules and policies.

Effective safety programs share the following features:

- They include the formation of a safety committee and participation by all departments within the company. Employees participate in safety decisions and management carefully considers employee suggestions for improving safety.
- They communicate safety with a multimedia approach that includes safety lectures, films, posters, pamphlets, and computer presentations.
- They instruct supervisors in how to communicate, demonstrate, and require safety, and they train employees in the safe use of equipment.

Manager's Notebook

Ten Ways That Managers Can Help Employees Reduce Stress

1. *Allow employees to talk freely with one another.* This not only reduces stress but also enhances productivity and problem solving.
2. *Reduce personal conflicts on the job.* To minimize conflicts: work with employees to resolve conflicts through communication, negotiation, and respect; treat employees fairly; and define job expectations clearly.
3. *Give employees adequate control over how they do their work.* Workers are more productive and better able to deal with stress if they have some control over how they perform their work.
4. *Ensure that staffing budgets are adequate.* Heavier workloads can increase illness, turnover, and accidents and decrease productivity. Therefore, a new project may not be worth taking on if staffing and funding are inadequate.
5. *Talk openly with employees.* Keep employees informed about bad news as well as good news. Give them opportunities to air their concerns.
6. *Support employees' efforts.* Workers are better able to cope with heavy workloads if managers are sympathetic, understanding, and encouraging. Listening to employees and addressing issues they raise are also helpful.
7. *Provide competitive personal leave and vacation benefits.* Workers who have time to relax and recharge after working hard are less likely to develop stress-related illnesses.
8. *Maintain current levels of employee benefits.* Workers' stress levels increase when their benefits are reduced. Employers must weigh carefully the savings gained from reducing benefits with the potentially high costs of employee burnout.
9. *Reduce the amount of red tape for employees.* Managers can lower burnout rates by ensuring that employees' time isn't wasted on unnecessary paperwork and procedures.
10. *Recognize and reward employees for their accomplishments and contributions.* Ignoring employees' accomplishments can lower morale and encourage talented and experienced employees to seek work elsewhere.

Source: Adapted with permission from Solomon, C. M. (1993, June). Working smarter: How HR can help. *Personnel Journal, 72,* 54–64.

- They use incentives, rewards, and positive reinforcement to encourage safe behavior. They reward employee complaints or suggestions about safety. They may also provide rewards (such as safe driving awards given to truck drivers) to employees with exceptional safety records.
- They communicate safety rules and enforce them. They know that OSHA obligates employees to adhere to safety rules, and they are willing to use the disciplinary system to penalize unsafe work behavior.
- They use safety directors and/or the safety committee to engage in regular self-inspection and accident research to identify potentially dangerous situations, and to understand why accidents occur and how to correct them.

Companies with comprehensive safety programs are likely to be rewarded with fewer accidents, fewer workers' compensation claims and lawsuits, and lower accident-related costs.

Employee Assistance Programs (EAPs)

As we saw in Chapter 13, *employee assistance programs (EAPs)* are programs designed to help employees whose job performance is suffering because of physical, mental, or emotional problems. Originating in the 1940s in firms like Du Pont and Eastman Kodak as programs to treat alcoholism, EAPs now address a variety of employee problems ranging from drug abuse to marital problems. Recent surveys indicate that EAPs are generally quite prevalent, but tend to be more common in larger organizations. For example, 45% of full-time employees have an EAP available to them, but EAPs are available to over 70% of employees in organizations employing between 1,000 to 5,000 workers.[83]

Many organizations create EAPs because they recognize their ethical and legal obligations to protect not only their workers' physical health but their mental health as well. The ethical obligation stems from the fact that the causes of organizational stress—climate, change, rules, work pace, management style, work group characteristics, and so forth—are also frequently the causes of behavioral, psychological, and physiological problems for employees.[84] Ethical obligation becomes legal obligation when employees sue the company or file workers' compensation claims for stress-related illnesses. In fact, much of the heightened concern about dealing with the consequences of workplace stress stems from the increasing incidence and severity of stress-related workers' compensation claims and their associated costs.[85] In Japan work-related stress (*karoshi*) has come to be seen as a deadly national problem. The Manager's Notebook titled "Ten Ways That Managers Can Help Employees Reduce Stress" gives valuable pointers on how managers can prevent stress from turning into a serious health problem.

burnout
A stress syndrome characterized by emotional exhaustion, depersonalization, and reduced personal accomplishment.

Stress often results in **burnout**, a syndrome characterized by emotional exhaustion, depersonalization, and reduced personal accomplishment.[86] People who experience burnout may dread returning to work for another day, treat coworkers and clients callously, withdraw from the organization, and feel less competent in their jobs. Some of the factors that may lead to burnout include ambiguity and conflict regarding how to deal with various job-related issues and problems.[87] A lack of social support can aggravate these effects.

Burnout can lead to serious negative consequences for the individual and for the organization. Mental and physical health can be negatively impacted by burnout.[88] Mental health problems resulting from burnout can include depression, irritability, lowered self-esteem, and anxiety. Physical problems can include fatigue, headaches, insomnia, gastrointestinal disturbances, and chest pains. Organizational outcomes associated with burnout include turnover, absenteeism, and a decrease in job performance.[89] In addition, sometimes burnout leads to increased drug and alcohol use.[90]

Many organizations perceive EAPs as being cost-effective solutions to performance, stress, and burnout problems. In fact, although U.S. businesses spend as much as $750 million per year on EAPs, many see this as an investment rather than a cost. EAP professionals claim that for every dollar invested in EAP programs, employers recover three to five dollars.[91] The savings come from lower insurance costs, reduced sick time, and better job performance.

The success of EAPs depends on how well they are planned and implemented. There is also some evidence that they are more effective at dealing with certain types of problems than others. For instance, EAPs appear to be more effective at dealing with alcoholism than with drug addiction.[92]

Wellness Programs

As health-care costs have skyrocketed over the last two decades, organizations have become more interested in preventive programs. Recognizing that they can have an effect on their employees' behavior and lifestyle off the job, companies are encouraging employees to lead more healthy lives. They are also attempting to reduce health-care costs through formal employee wellness programs. Where EAPs focus on *treating* troubled employees, **wellness programs** focus on *preventing* health problems. A recent survey of employer coalitions found that 75% sponsored wellness programs.[93]

wellness program
A company-sponsored program that focuses on preventing health problems in employees.

Staying Healthy, Staying Happy.

American Airlines offers a variety of activities designed to help employees stay happy, healthy, and productive. Here, food-service workers take a lunchtime aerobics class.

A complete wellness program has three components:

- It helps employees identify potential health risks through screening and testing.
- It educates employees about such health risks as high blood pressure, smoking, poor diet, and stress.
- It encourages employees to change their lifestyles through exercise, good nutrition, and health monitoring.

Wellness programs may be as simple and inexpensive as providing information about stop-smoking clinics and weight-loss programs or as comprehensive and expensive as providing professional health screening and multimillion-dollar fitness facilities.

Some feel that wellness and employee assistance programs should be evaluated on a cost-benefit basis and discontinued if these programs' benefits do not exceed their costs. Others feel that since companies create many of the stressful conditions that contribute to employee health problems, they are ethically bound to continue providing these types of programs. What do you think?

Rewarding Good Health Habits. Should managers attempt to change employees' bad health habits through a "carrot" or a "stick" approach? That is, should employees be rewarded for healthy behaviors (the carrot) or penalized for unhealthy behaviors (the stick)? Some companies prefer the stick approach. For example, Atlanta's Turner Broadcasting refuses to hire workers who smoke, and Best Lock of Indianapolis has fired workers for drinking excessively *after* their shift. Both companies claim their actions are justified by higher health-care costs for smokers and drinkers. A number of organizations charge smokers more for health insurance. U-Haul and International Paper impose fines on employees with unhealthy lifestyles, as well as make them pay more for insurance.[94]

In contrast, General Mills uses a carrot approach that includes lowering insurance premiums for workers with healthy lifestyles (including those who control their weight and blood pressure and do not smoke.) Grand Rapids, Michigan's Butterworth Hospital uses both carrot and stick by providing financial incentives for employees who lead healthy lifestyles ($25 every other week) and imposing financial penalties in the form of higher health insurance premiums on those who do not. Mesa Limited Partnership pays employees to get a computerized health-risk appraisal and awards them up to almost $1,000 per year for participating in weight-loss and exercise plans.[95] Employees at Quaker Oats Company in Chicago can participate in a health incentive plan that provides an annual medical expense allowance of $300 to each participating employee. Employees can use the $300 to pay health insurance deductibles or health-care expenses, or can simply take a cash refund at the end of the year. Employees can also participate in a flexible benefits plan in which they can earn $140 each year by pledging to engage in certain healthy behaviors.[96]

Evidence suggests that wellness programs can save companies money. For example, the Adolph Coors Company estimates that its cardiac rehabilitation program alone earned more than $2.3 million in wages ordinarily lost to missed work time and replacement hiring salaries. Steelcase, Inc., the office-furniture manufacturer, found that the average medical costs for inactive employees (i.e., those without a fitness regimen) was $869.98 but only $478.61 for active employees, a difference of 46%.[97] Employees who took advantage of General Electric's fitness centers cut their per capita medical costs by 27% in one year.[98] However, other studies of wellness programs show mixed results, and the cost-effectiveness of wellness plans varies with the type of plan. For instance, one study found that fitness plans by themselves were not cost-effective compared with wellness programs that included screening for at-risk employees along with counseling.[99]

Summary and Conclusions

Workplace Safety and the Law. There are two sets of workplace safety laws: (1) workers' compensation, an employer-funded insurance system that operates at the state level, and (2) the Occupational Safety and Health Act (OSHA), a federal law that mandates safety standards in the workplace.

Workers' compensation—which consists of total disability, impairment, survivor, medical expense, and rehabilitation benefits—is intended to ensure prompt and reasonable medical care to employees injured on the job, as well as income for them and their dependents or survivors. It also encourages employers to invest in workplace safety by requiring higher insurance premiums from employers with numerous workplace accidents and injuries.

OSHA compels employers to provide a safe and healthy work environment, to comply with specific occupational safety and health standards, and to keep records of occupational injuries and illnesses. Its safety standards are enforced through a system of inspections, citations, fines, and criminal penalties.

Managing Contemporary Safety, Health, and Behavioral Issues. The most significant safety, health, and behavioral issues for employers are AIDS, violence in the workplace, cumulative trauma disorders, fetal protection, hazardous chemicals, and genetic testing. In all of these areas line managers must deal with a variety of practical, legal, and ethical questions that often demand a careful balancing of individual rights (especially privacy rights) with the needs of the organization.

Safety and Health Programs. Comprehensive safety programs are well-planned efforts in which management (1) involves employees and carefully considers their suggestions, (2) communicates safety rules to employees and enforces them, (3) invests in training supervisors to demonstrate and communicate safety on the job, (4) uses incentives to encourage safe behaviors and discipline to penalize unsafe behaviors, and (5) engages in regular self-inspection and accident research to identify and correct potentially dangerous situations.

Employee assistance programs (EAPs) are designed to help employees cope with physical, mental, or emotional problems (including stress) that are undermining their job performance.

Wellness programs are preventive efforts designed to help employees identify potential health risks and deal with them before they become problems.

Key Terms

burnout, 506
cumulative trauma disorder (CTD), 502
ergonomics, 502
genetic testing, 505
negligent hiring, 499
Occupational Safety and Health Act of 1970 (OSHA), 491
wellness program, 507

Discussion Questions

1. What is the difference between the objectives of workers' compensation and the objectives of OSHA?
2. What kind of policies do you think would work best to prevent workplace violence?
3. Should CTDs be the subject of federal regulations? Why or why not?
4. If a job is potentially hazardous to the fetus of a pregnant employee, should it be legal for the company to restrict the job to men?
5. How could genetic testing be used to discriminate?
6. How can managers use the discipline system and the organization's reward system to encourage workplace safety?
7. *Karoshi*, a term coined by the Japanese, means "death from overwork." Karoshi is now the second leading cause of death, after cancer, among Japanese workers. Put yourself in the place of a Japanese manager. What could you do to reduce the risk of *karoshi* in your workers?

MINICASE 1 *Back to School*

Martin Marietta Energy Systems, Inc. employs approximately 20,000 people in the south central United States. For years the company consistently experienced annual costs of nearly $1 million as a result of employees' lower back injuries. In response, the company started an onsite physical therapy program. The program, which includes a staff of physical therapists, physicians, nurses, laboratory technicians, and an x-ray technician, is called the Back School and is taught as part of general employee training. The Back School staff also offers programs on fitness, stretching, flexibility, posture, and lifting. When all costs are considered, Martin Marietta's management estimates that the program has saved the company over $800,000 per year—a whopping 9:1 benefit-to-cost ratio.

Lower back injuries are a serious workplace problem, accounting for one third of all workers' compensation lost-time cases in 1993. In addition, these cases are about 33% more expensive and last longer than other claims. A national health objective is to have at least 59% of work sites offering back injury prevention programs by the year 2000. The number of work sites with 50 or more employees that offer such programs increased slightly from 29% to 32% between 1985 and 1992.

Discussion Questions

1. Statistics indicate that lower back problems are a serious workplace issue but, like CTDs, are not directly observable and often defy diagnosis of specific physical cause. How could you convince your organization to establish a "Back School" program similar to Martin Marietta's, particularly when the costs are certain and benefits may not be so visible or immediate?
2. How might managers help workers prevent back injuries while keeping costs to a minimum?

Sources: Anspaugh, D. J., Hunter, S., and Mosley, J. (1995). The economic impact of corporate wellness programs. *AAOHN Journal, 43*, 203–210; Karas, B. E., & Conrad, K. M. (1996). Back injury prevention interventions in the workplace. *AAOHN Journal, 44*, 189–196.

MINICASE 2 *Developing an AIDS Policy at Burroughs Wellcome*

Survey after survey has revealed that even though the number of AIDS cases continues to increase, few large companies and virtually no small organizations have established formal AIDS policies. While top managers realize that AIDS could become a serious problem in their organization, most have no plan to deal with it. In contrast, management at Burroughs Wellcome realized early on that their corporate culture dictated a proactive stance toward the AIDS issue. They felt that Burroughs had the social responsibility to provide not only medical benefits but also support, compassion, and understanding to employees with AIDS.

In 1987 Burroughs became a pioneer when it announced that it would not discriminate against AIDS victims—that, on the contrary, it would provide them with health benefits and counseling. The company articulated a policy to educate *all* employees about the effects of AIDS and provided a mechanism to deal with safety questions. Burroughs used its own employees to prepare an educational video on AIDS. It also set up training sessions using the video, educational brochures, and scientific and medical staff to train managers on how to deal with employees with AIDS. Burroughs feels that its program is responsible for the fact that the company has experienced no AIDS-related problems.

Discussion Questions

1. What can companies that fail to develop an AIDS policy expect when, for the first time, an employee reveals that he or she has the AIDS virus? Why must an AIDS policy stress education?
2. To what lengths should an organization go to help prevent employees from contracting HIV or AIDS? Should training include materials on "safe sex" or healthy lifestyles?

Source: Adapted, by permission of the publisher, from Bradley, J. (1990, February). Developing and implementing a policy on AIDS. *Management Review, 79(2)*, 64.

CASE 1 *Panic on the Assembly Line*

Joe Wilson, the director of human resources at Realgood Snack Foods, is sitting in plant manager Bill Stone's office, stunned. Just 20 minutes ago the production supervisor, Max Jones, had been in Wilson's office describing what sounded like an employee revolt. Jones said that several people on his team had discovered this morning that a coworker, Robert Carter, has AIDS. Not only were they refusing to work alongside Carter, they were also threatening to go "public" with the news that the company was allowing someone with AIDS to work on the assembly line.

Wilson knows that Realgood has a written policy on how to deal with an employee who has AIDS. His boss at headquarters mailed everyone a copy of the policy last year, but never said much about it. Wilson himself had never given much thought to the possibility that he would have to deal with an AIDS-related problem until today. He doesn't quite know why the line employees are so upset and wonders what he can do to mollify them.

The plant, one of several of Realgood's manufacturing facilities scattered around the Midwest, employs about 800 people engaged in manufacturing potato chips and corn chips. It is located in a medium-sized conservative community. The company was unionized several years earlier, so all production employees are union members. The relations between union and management are generally good, and the company offers above-average pay for the area and equally good benefits.

As Wilson sits in Stone's office, he remembers some of the facts that led to the present crisis. Carter is a good production worker who, up until a few months ago, had an excellent attendance record. Since August, however, he has missed work several times, with each episode lasting several days. Jones felt that the morale of Carter's work team had diminished considerably over the last two months, and part of the reason was Carter's behavior. Carter had recently become somewhat withdrawn and prone to anger easily. Additionally, some team members had begun to gripe about having to cover for his continued absences.

When Carter returned to work this morning from his most recent absence, he looked terrible. A member of his team asked him sarcastically, "What's wrong, Carter, you got AIDS?" The laughter abruptly died when Carter replied that, indeed, he did have AIDS. After several minutes of discussion, several team members came to Jones with their ultimatum.

Stone immediately realized the seriousness of the situation, particularly the employees' threat to go to the press. He is certain that the public will react to the disclosure by refusing to buy Realgood's products. As plant manager, he feels the only reasonable solution is to remove Carter from the work group. Since Carter's recent attendance has been poor and his behavior hostile, Stone believes that it would save the company a lot of trouble to simply fire him and be done with it. He is looking to Wilson for advice on the best way to handle the situation.

Critical Thinking Questions

1. Based on what you know about this situation, could Realgood have done anything to prevent the employees' reaction to Carter's illness?
2. What legal action might Carter take if he is fired? What might be the union's role in this issue?
3. Suppose that Wilson advises Stone to order the team members back to work and they refuse to go. What actions should management take?
4. Compare Realgood's legal obligations to its social responsibility in this situation. Is there a conflict between Stone's duty to Realgood's shareholders and the company's ethical obligation to Carter? How would you handle this situation if you were Wilson?

Cooperative Learning Exercises

5. Students form into groups of four or five. Each group should develop a sample AIDS policy that meets the criteria described in the chapter and present it to the class.
6. Form into pairs to survey local organizations to see if they have developed formal AIDS policies. Each pair should go to one or two organizations and report back to the class. The class then discusses any common features found in these policies, especially in how they are communicated (to employees or only to supervisors and managers?) and whether or not they include AIDS education.

CASE 2 Refusing to Perform a Hazardous Task at Whirlpool

At the Whirlpool appliance plant in Marion, Ohio, overhead conveyors were used to transport appliance components from one area of the plant to another. To prevent workers from being harmed by falling parts, the company had installed a horizontal wire mesh screen secured to angle iron frames beneath the conveyor belts. The mesh was about 20 feet above the plant floor.

Part of regular maintenance at the plant included spending several hours each week removing parts from the screen and replacing paper used to catch grease that dropped from the conveyor. Maintenance employees had to stand on the angle frames, or on the mesh itself, to perform the work.

In 1973 the company began to replace the mesh with a heavier mesh because of safety concerns. Several employees had fallen partway through the mesh, and one had even fallen to the floor below, but had survived. When employees brought complaints about the unsafe conditions to the foreman, they were instructed to walk on the iron beams only, not the mesh.

In June 1974, a maintenance employee fell through the old mesh to his death. The next week two maintenance employees, Virgil Deemer and Thomas Cornwell, again complained about safety issues. Two days later, they asked the plant safety director to provide them with a phone number of the area OSH Administration office. They were told to think about what they were doing, but were given the number. They subsequently called an OSH Administration inspector.

The next day, the foreman instructed Deemer and Cornwell to walk on the mesh screen to perform regular maintenance. They refused to comply with the foreman's order, claiming that the work was unsafe. Both employees were told to go to the personnel office. They were then instructed to punch out for the remainder of the day, and were subsequently given a written reprimand for insubordination.

This case eventually made its way to the U.S. Supreme Court. The Court upheld the rights of workers under the Occupational Safety and Health Act to choose not to perform their assigned task because of a reasonable apprehension of death or serious injury, when no other alternative is available to them.

Critical Thinking Questions

1. Was the refusal by Deemer and Cornwell to perform their assigned tasks justified by a reasonable apprehension of death or injury?
2. If you were the safety director at Whirlpool, what would you have done when the employees came to you with questions about how to contact the OSH Administration?
3. The HR manager has the responsibility to protect employees, but at the same time does not want to be perceived as undermining a supervisor's authority. Why is this balancing act so difficult in the type of situation discussed in this case?
4. What unanticipated and damaging results could an organization suffer if it forces workers to do what they perceive as dangerous work?

Cooperative Learning Exercises

5. Students form into groups of four or five. Each group should develop criteria for "reasonableness" by which to judge refusal to perform job tasks perceived as dangerous. The leader of each group should then present its set of criteria to the class.
6. Identify people in the class who have worked on dangerous jobs and ask them how dangerous tasks are assigned. Has anyone ever refused to perform, or been in a situation where they have seen others refuse to perform, dangerous work? If so, what was the result of the refusal?
7. Students form into groups of three or four to discuss the effects on individuals of asking them to choose between their livelihood (their job) and their safety. Each group should elect a leader to present its conclusions to the class.

Source: *Whirlpool Corp. v. Marshall*, 100 S. Ct. 883 (1980).

HRM Simulation 

The accident rate in your company is higher than it should be, probably due to high turnover and poor morale (see Safety, page 8 of the players' manual). Incident J offers you a number of approaches to dealing with the safety issue. Which approach would you recommend? Why?

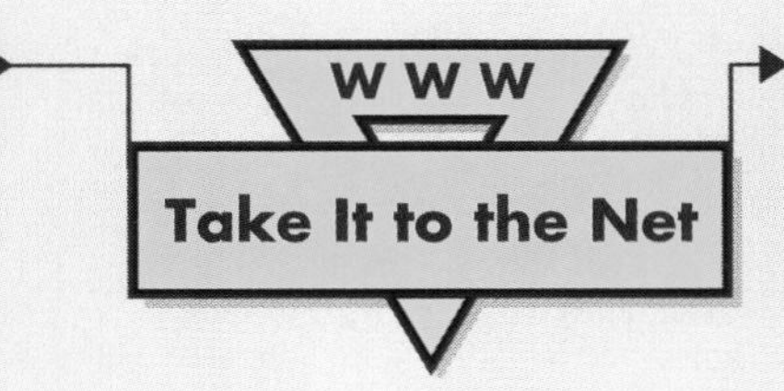

We invite you to visit the Gómez-Mejía/Balkin/Cardy page on the Prentice Hall Web site:

http://www.prenhall.com/gomez

You can also visit the Web sites for these companies, featured within this chapter:

Digital Equipment Corporation	http://www.dec.com
Johnson Controls	http://www.jci.com
Monsanto	http://www.monsanto.com
National Safety Council	http://www.nsc.org
Steelcase, Inc.	http://www.steelcase.com
Toys 'Я' Us	http://www.toysrus.com
Wells Fargo Bank	http://picasso.wellsfargo.com
Whirlpool	http://www.WhirlpoolAppliances.com

Endnotes

1. Hedges, S. J., Cary, P., Cohen, G., and Loeb, P. (1996). The mystery of flight 592. *U.S. News & World Report, 120*, 35–37.
2. *Id.*
3. National Safety Council (1995). *Accident facts, 1995 Edition.* Itasca, IL: National Safety Council.
4. Ledvinka, J., and Scarpello, V. G. (1991). *Federal regulation of personnel and human resource management* (2nd ed.), 209. Boston: PWS-Kent.
5. Sherman, A.W., and Bohlander, G.W. (1996). *Managing human resources* (10th ed.). Cincinnati, OH: South-Western.
6. McCaffery, R. M. (1992). *Employee benefit programs: A total compensation perspective*, 57–58. Boston: PWS-Kent.
7. *Id.*, 59–60.
8. Pritula, M. (1992, January 13). Workers' comp: Tranquilizing a benefit gone mad. *The Wall Street Journal*, A14.
9. National Safety Council, 1995.
10. Colburn, L. E. (1995). Defending against workers' compensation fraud. *Industrial Management, 37*, 1–2.
11. French, W. L. (1994). *Human resources management* (3rd ed.), 529. Boston: Houghton Mifflin.
12. Ashford, N. A. (1976). *Crisis in the workplace: Occupational disease and injury*, 3. Cambridge, MA: MIT Press.
13. U.S. Department of Labor, Occupational Safety and Health Administration. (1985). *All about OSHA* (rev. ed.), 1. Washington, DC: U.S. Government Printing Office.
14. Ledvinka and Scarpello, 1991, p. 215.
15. Anthony, W. P., Perrewe, P. L., and Kacmar, K. M. (1993). *Strategic human resource management*, 514. Fort Worth, TX: Dryden; and Cascio, W. F. (1989). *Managing human resources: Productivity, quality of work life, profits* (2nd ed.), 554–556. New York: McGraw-Hill.
16. *All about OSHA*, 1985, pp. 43–46.
17. May, B. D. (1986, August). Hazardous substances: OSHA mandates the right to know. *Personnel Journal, 65*, 128.
18. See *Whirlpool Corporation v. Marshall*, 445 U.S. 1, 10–12 (1980).
19. Ledvinka and Scarpello, 1991, pp. 221–224.
20. *All about OSHA*, 1985, p. 8.
21. *Id.*, 10.
22. *Id.*, 19–22.
23. Ledvinka and Scarpello, p. 224; see also *Marshall v. Barlow's, Inc.*, 436 U.S. 307 (1978).
24. Garland, S. B. (1989, February 20). This safety ruling could be hazardous to employer's health. *Business Week*, 34.
25. Garland, 1989; and Bureau of National Affairs. (1989, July 24). *BNA's Employee Relations Weekly*. Michigan Supreme Court rules OSH Act does not preempt state proceedings, *7*, 945.
26. Davidson, W. N., Worrell, D., and Cheng, L. T. W. (1994). The effectiveness of OSHA penalties: A stock-market-based test. *Industrial Relations, 33*, 283–296.
27. *Id.*
28. U.S. Department of Labor. (1989). *Fact sheet no. OSHA 89–04*. Washington, DC: U.S. Government Printing Office.
29. *All about OSHA*, 1985, pp. 31–32.
30. *Id.*, 8; Ledvinka and Scarpello, 1991, p. 220.
31. *All about OSHA*, 33–34.
32. National Safety Council, 1995.
33. *Id.*
34. Oswald, E. M. (1996). No employer is immune: AIDS in the workplace. *Risk Management, 43*, 18–21.
35. *Id.*
36. Center for Disease Control and Prevention (1996, June 7). HIV/AIDS surveillance report, *7*, 1–8, http://cdcnac.org:72/0/4/yearend95/intro95.txt.
37. Fremgen and Whitty, 1992, p. 751; and Stodghill II, R. (1993a, February 1). Managing AIDS: How one boss struggled to cope. *Business Week, 3303*, 48.
38. Smith, J. M. (1993, March). How to develop and implement an AIDS workplace policy. *HR Focus*, 15.
39. Woolsey, C. (1993, February 1). Ensuring proper AIDS treatment: Employer drafts standards for HMOs. *Business Insurance*, 17.
40. Fremgen and Whitty, 1992, p. 752; Harris, D. (1987, November). AIDS: We'll all pay. *Money*, 109–34; and Woolsey, 1993, p. 17.
41. Stodghill II, R. (1993b, February 1). Why AIDS policy must be a special policy. *Business Week, 3303*, 33.
42. Berger, R. S., and Lewis, G. L. (1992). AIDS and employment: Judicial and arbitral responses. *Labor Law Journal, 43*, 259–280.
43. Stodghill, 1993a, pp. 48–52.
44. Bureau of National Affairs. (1993, April 5). AIDS ranks as chief health concern of half of U.S. workers, survey says. *BNA Employee Relations Weekly, 11*, 4.
45. Oswald, 1996.
46. *Id.*
47. *Id.*

48. *Id.*
49. Associated Press. (1993, January 28). Ex-employee opens fire on former bosses, kills 3. *Arizona Republic*, A2; and Associated Press. (1993, January 29). Firings, stress fuel workplace violence. *Arizona Republic*, A2.
50. Tuscano, G., and Windau, J. (1995). National census of fatal occupational injuries, 1994. *Job Safety & Health Quarterly, 6*, 28–34.
51. Bureau of Labor Statistics (1994). *Issues in labor statistics: Violence in the workplace comes under closer scrutiny (Summary 94–10)*. Washington, DC: United States Department of Labor.
52. Family Violence Prevention Fund (1996, June 20). Domestic violence—A workplace security problem, 1–4, http://www.igc.apc.org/fund/the__facts/security.html.
53. Williams, M. F. (1996). Violence and sexual harassment: Impact on registered nurses in the workplace. *AAOHN Journal, 44*, 73–77.
54. Epstein, B. D. (1996). Preventing workplace violence. *Provider, 22*, 71–72.
55. Bureau of National Affairs. (1993, April 26). Preventing workplace violence: Legal imperatives can clash. *Employee Relations Weekly, 11*(17), 451–452.
56. Missouri Capitol Police. (1996, June 6). Violence in the workplace..., 1–6. http://www.dps.state.mo.us/DPS/MCP/STUDY/WKVIOLNC.HTM.
57. *Id.*
58. Boddenhausen, K. G. (1994, March 3). It's...becoming a fact of life. *Springfield News-Leader*, B3.
59. Rudolph, B. (1987, May 18). Thou shalt not smoke. *Time, 129*, 58–59.
60. Prewitt, E. (1986, September 15). The drive to kick smoking at work. *Fortune, 114*, 42–43.
61. Marley, S. (1992, February 10). Employers pay when workers smoke: Study. *Business Insurance, 26*(6), 3, 22.
62. Robinson, J. P., and Speer, T. L. (1995). The air we breathe. *American Demographics, 17*, 24–32.
63. Litvan, L. M. (1994). A smoke-free workplace? *Nation's Business, 82*, 65.
64. New York Public Health Law, Section 1399 (Consol. 1993).
65. Smith, L. (1993, August 9). Can smoking or bungee jumping get you canned? *Fortune, 128*(3), 92.
66. Fry, E. H. (1990, November–December). Not smoking in the workplace: The real issue. *Business Horizons, 33*(6), 13–17.
67. Marley, 1992, pp. 3, 22.
68. Drake, J. (1994). The dynamics of the rights and privileges of smoking and non-smoking employees. *Unpublished master's thesis*, Southwest Missouri State University.
69. Litvan, 1994.
70. Robinson and Speer, 1995.
71. Davenport, F. C. (1989, May–June). The legal aspects of a smoking policy in the workplace. *Industrial Management, 31*(3), 25–32.
72. Worsnop, R. L. (1995). Repetitive stress injuries. *CQ Researcher, 5*, 539–556.
73. *Id.*
74. Schwartz, R. G., and Weinstein, S.M. (1996). Getting a handle on cumulative trauma disorders. *Patient Care, 30*, 118–120; Gangemi, R. A. (1996, July). Ergonomics: Reducing workplace injuries. *Inc.*, 92.
75. Voiss, D. V. (1995). What a little brain work can do: Rethinking workers' compensation problems. *Compensation & Benefits Review, 27*, 30–32.
76. Worsnop, 1995.
77. Associated Press (1996). Digital equipment loses case on keyboard injuries. *Arizona Republic*, December 10, 1996. E1.
78. Wermiel, S. (1991, March 21). Justices bar "fetal protection" policies. *The Wall Street Journal*, B1, B5.
79. Trost, C. (1990, October 8). Business and women anxiously watch suit on "fetal protection." *The Wall Street Journal*, 1.
80. Altman, L. E. (1988, June 5). Pregnant women's use of VDT's is scrutinized. *The New York Times*, 22; Meier, B. (1987, February 5). Companies wrestle with threats to reproductive health. *The Wall Street Journal*, 23.
81. Jacob, S. L. (1988, November 22). Small business slowly wakes to OSHA hazard rule. *The Wall Street Journal*, B2; and Myers, D.W. (1992). *Human resource management* (2nd ed.), 717. Chicago: Commerce Clearing House.
82. Bureau of National Affairs (1991, November 18). Value of genetic testing said minimal for gauging workplace risks. *BNA's Employee Relations Weekly*, 1235; Draper, E. (1991). *Risky business: Genetic testing and exclusionary practices in the hazardous workplace*. Cambridge, England: Cambridge University Press; Olian, J. D. (1984). Genetic screening for employment purposes. *Personnel Psychology, 37*, 423–438; and Schuler, R. S., and Huber, V. L. (1993). *Personnel and human resource management* (5th ed.), 251. Minneapolis: West.
83. Johnson, A. T. (1995). Employee assistance programs and employee downsizing. *Employee Assistance Quarterly, 10*, 13–27.
84. Fisher, C. C., Schoenfeldt, L. F., and Shaw, J. B. (1996). *Human resource management* (3rd ed.). Boston: Houghton Mifflin; and Schuler & Huber, 1993, pp. 667–669.
85. Thompson, R. (1990). Fighting the high cost of workers' comp. *Nation's Business, 78*(3), 28.
86. Maslach, C., and Jackson, S. E. (1981). The measurement of experienced burnout. *Journal of Occupational Behavior, 2*, 99–113.
87. Gordes, C. L., and Dougherty, T. W. (1993). A review and integration of research on job burnout. *Academy of Management Review, 18*, 621–656.
88. Kahill, S. (1988). Symptoms of professional burnout: A review of the empirical evidence. *Canadian Psychology, 29*, 284–297.
89. Cordes and Dougherty, 1993.
90. Jackson, S. E., and Maslach, C. (1982). After effects of job-related stress: Families as victims. *Journal of Occupational Behavior, 3*, 63–77.
91. Kirrane, D. (1990, January). EAPs: Dawning of a new age. *HRMagazine*, 34.
92. Anthony, Perrewe, & Kacmar, 1993, 535–536; and Pesternak, C. (1990, August). HRM update. *HRMagazine*, 24.
93. Helmer, D. C., Dunn, L. M., Eaton, K., Macedonio, C., and Lubritz, L. (1995). Implementing corporate wellness programs. *AAOHN Journal, 43*, 558–563.
94. Bernstein, A. (1990, May 21). Health care costs: Trying to cool the fever. *Business Week*, 46–47; and Feinstein, S. (1990, July 30). Companies target catastrophic illnesses in bid to curb soaring health costs. *The Wall Street Journal*, A1.
95. Keaton, P. N., and Semb, M. J. (1990, September). Shaping up the bottom line. *HRMagazine*, 81–86; and Smith, 1993, p. 92.
96. Anspaugh, D. J., Hunter, S., and Mosley, J. (1995). The economic impact of corporate wellness programs. *AAOHN Journal, 43*, 203–210.
97. *Id.*
98. *CompFlash* (1994, February). Fitness center users cut their healthcare costs by 27% in GE study, 8.
99. Erfurt, J. C., Foote, A., and Heirich, M. A. (1992). The cost-effectiveness of worksite wellness programs for hypertension control, weight loss, smoking cessation, and exercise. *Personnel Psychology, 45*, 5–27.

CHALLENGES

17

Meeting the International HRM Challenge

After reading this chapter, you should be able to deal more effectively with the following challenges:

1 ▶ **Specify** the HRM strategies that are most appropriate for firms at different stages of internationalization.

2 ▶ **Identify** the best mix of host-country and expatriate employees given the conditions facing a firm.

3 ▶ **Explain** why international assignments often fail and the steps a firm can take to ensure success in this area.

4 ▶ **Reintegrate** returning employees into the firm after they complete an international assignment.

5 ▶ **Develop** HRM policies and procedures that match the needs and values of different cultures.

Brave New World. Countries no longer conduct business in a vacuum; they face competition from all over the world. As firms expand their operations beyond their national borders, they encounter a host of challenges, among them cultural differences that affect the way they manage their human resources.

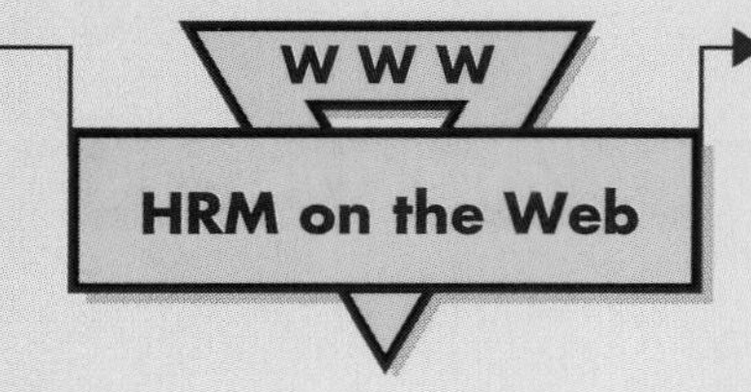

http://www.t-bird.edu/

Thunderbird School of International Management

This Web site provides access to Dom Pedro II International Studies Research Center, which is an outstanding source of international business and HR information. Thunderbird's home page provides links to files on more than 200 countries, as well as information on the European Union (EU) and the North American Free Trade Association (NAFTA). The sources of this information include economic reports, articles from international journals, and news clippings that pertain to business in many different countries and cultures.

"Every major [aero]space contractor who wants to be cost-effective should be thinking about relations with Russian partners," maintains David Williams, country coordinator for Russia at Rockwell International. Rolls-Royce, United Technology, and Rockwell, among others, are now heavily investing in Russian avionic firms.

From a U.S. perspective, the strongest attraction of Russian science and technology is bargain prices. Most Russian Ph.D.'s will work for $300 per month. Thus, when McDonnell Douglas needed a new liquid oxygen tank on its DC-X rocket (an experimental reusable spacecraft), it turned to Moscow's Mechanical Engineering Research Institute. The Russians happened to be experimenting with a suitable aluminum-lithium alloy capable of withstanding temperatures below −150° C. The Russians went from drawing board to finished tank within eight months at a cost of only $1 million.

Another attraction is that the Russians are innovative in ways unknown in the West. For decades, Soviet scientists were cut off from many discoveries and new methods of doing research. "Western programmers can afford to be sloppy because they have so much computing power to work with," explains Tony Loeb, who heads Sun Microsystems' very active Moscow office. "Here they had to squeeze the last drop of performance out of every bit and byte of power." Sun is employing the workshop of Boris Babaian, the man known as the father of Soviet supercomputing, to get the most out of Sun's new 64-bit Sparc microprocessor. Motorola, whose chips govern the inner workings of everything from Sony camcorders to BMW engines, has homegrown its Russian research team, hiring several hundred physicists and mathematicians in both Moscow and St. Petersburg.[1]

A**s we've stressed throughout this book, countries no longer conduct business in a** vacuum. Virtually every U.S. company now faces competition from abroad, and the fortunes of most U.S. firms, large and small, are inextricably bound to the global economy. In this chapter we demonstrate how managers can use HRM practices to enhance their firms' competitiveness in an era of international opportunities and challenges. First, we cover the stages of international involvement, the challenges of expatriate job assignments, and ways to make those assignments more effective. We then discuss the development of HRM policies in a global context and the specific HR concerns of exporting firms.

The Stages of International Involvement

As Figure 17–1 shows, firms progress through five stages as they internationalize their operations.[2] The higher the stage, the more HR practices must be adapted to diverse cultural, economic, political, and legal environments.

- In *Stage 1*, the firm's market is exclusively domestic. Prior to World War II, most U.S. firms fell into this category. One firm at this stage today is Boulder Beer, which pro-

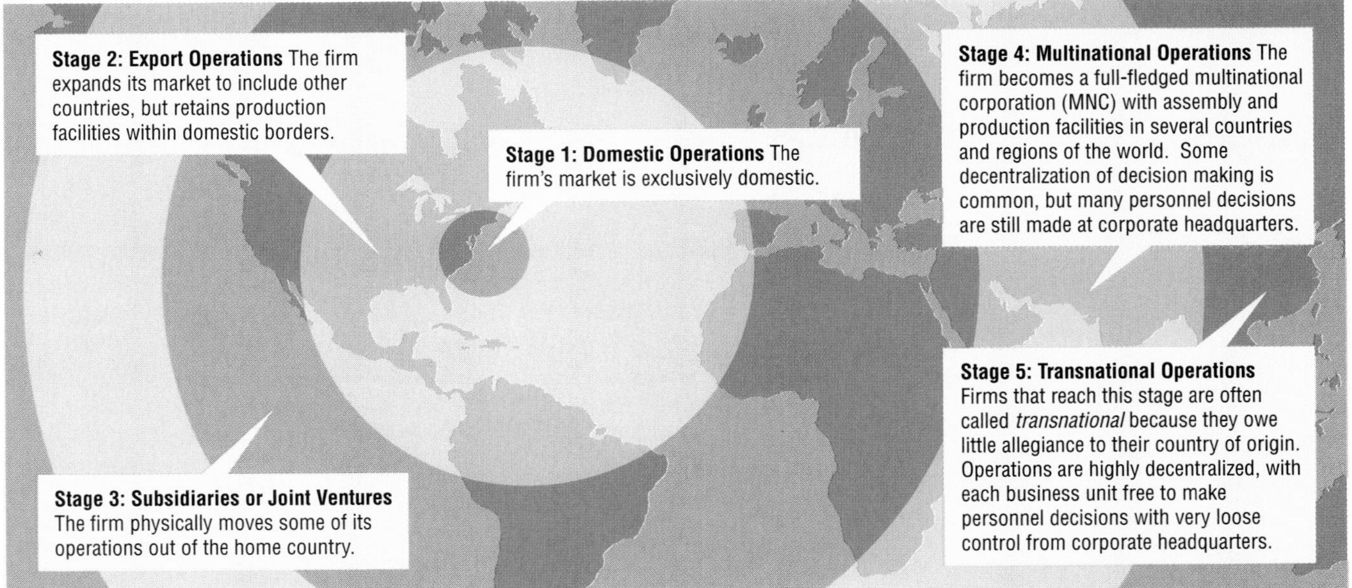

FIGURE 17-1

The Stages of Internationalization

duces its ales in the Boulder, Colorado area and seldom sells them outside the Mountain States region. Many other U.S. firms are still at this stage, but their number is diminishing, particularly in manufacturing. Staffing, training, and compensation for firms at Stage 1 are dictated primarily by local and/or national forces. The only sites considered for plant locations are in the United States, and only the national or regional market is considered in strategic business decisions about production and marketing issues.

- In *Stage 2*, the firm expands its market to include foreign countries, but retains its production facilities within domestic borders. HRM practices at this stage should facilitate exporting of the firm's products through managerial incentives, appropriate training, and staffing strategies that focus on the demands of international customers.

  An example of a Stage 2 firm is Turbo-Tek Enterprises, Inc., located in Los Angeles. It generates \$50 million a year in revenues, 38% of which come from overseas sales. The firm's single product is Turbo Wash, a water-spraying attachment for common household hoses. Turbo-Tek's entire manufacturing, packaging, and distribution system is designed with international markets in mind, and the firm's HRM practices play a crucial role in this system. Turbo Wash is produced in Los Angeles, but the product is repackaged in the Netherlands for European markets. Managerial bonuses are substantially based on foreign sales. Turbo-Tek rewards its employees for developing innovative ideas to increase exports. For instance, the firm's marketing department translated user instructions into 11 languages; production made changes to meet local tastes and needs, such as including a special adapter to fit English hoses; and research and development ensured that the exact chemical composition of the shampoo included with Turbo Wash would comply with strict governmental regulations in Finland, France, and other European countries.

  Falling trade barriers are greatly increasing the number of U.S. firms that fall into Stage 2. A recent survey of 750 U.S. companies found that 20% of companies with fewer than 500 employees exported products and services in 1995, almost double the 1992 amount. For instance, Jeff A. Victor, who is general manager of \$6 million

Treatment Products Ltd., credits NAFTA (the North American Free Trade Agreement) for his firm's surging export volume. The company, which makes car cleaners and waxes, had been trying to expand its small presence in Mexico since 1990. But stiff Mexican tariffs made that impossible. Six months after NAFTA went into effect in January 1993, Victor landed contracts with almost every major retail chain in Mexico. His shipments to Mexico have tripled, to roughly $300,000, about 20% of the company's total current exports.[3]

- In *Stage 3*, the firm physically moves some of its operations out of the home country. These facilities are primarily used for parts assembly, although some limited manufacturing may take place. For instance, many U.S. apparel manufacturers have opened facilities throughout the Caribbean to assemble a wide variety of garments. The foreign branches or subsidiaries tend to be under close control of corporate headquarters at this stage, and a high proportion of top managers are **expatriates** (employees who are citizens of the corporation's home country). HRM practices at Stage 3 need to focus on the selection, training, and compensation of expatriates, as well as on the development of personnel policies for local employees where the foreign facilities are located.

expatriate
A citizen of one country living and working in another country.

multinational corporation (MNC)
A firm with assembly and production facilities in several countries and regions of the world.

- In *Stage 4*, the firm becomes a full-fledged **multinational corporation (MNC),** with assembly and production facilities in several countries and regions of the world. Strategic alliances between domestic and foreign firms, such as that between Ford Motor Company and Mazda Motor Corp. to build trucks in Thailand, are very common.[4] While there is usually some decentralization of decision making for firms at Stage 4, many personnel decisions affecting foreign branches are still made at corporate headquarters, typically by an international personnel department. In addition, foreign operations are still managed by expatriates. Amoco, IBM, Rockwell, General Motors, General Electric, and Xerox are all at Stage 4. HRM practices at these companies are quite complex because they must deal with large numbers of expatriates and their families in overseas assignments, and diverse ethnic and cultural groups in multiple countries. They must also facilitate the control of overseas subsidiaries from corporate headquarters.

transnational corporation
A firm with operations in many countries and highly decentralized operations. The firm owes little allegiance to its country of origin and has weak ties to any given country.

- In *Stage 5*, the most advanced stage of internationalization, firms are often called **transnational corporations** because they owe little allegiance to their country of origin and have weak ties to any given country. Operations are highly decentralized; each business unit is free to make personnel decisions with very loose control from corporate headquarters. The board of directors is often composed of people of different nationalities, and the firm tries hard to develop managers who see themselves as citizens of the world. These firms freely hire employees from any country. For example, Olivetti, the large Italian-based conglomerate, has an extensive "no frontiers" recruitment program to hire managers and professionals from around the world.

A QUESTION OF ETHICS

U.S. law does not prohibit selection decisions based on marital status, as long as they are applied equally to men and women. Why might a company have such a policy? Is it ethical? Is it in the best long-term interests of the company?

HRM practices at Stage 5 companies are designed to blend individuals from diverse backgrounds to create a shared corporate (rather than national) identity and a common vision. For instance, Gillette (which develops and manufactures personal care products) has developed an extensive program in which local personnel offices in 48 countries search for the best young university graduates who are single and fluent in English. The individuals selected are given six months of training in the home country, and those who come through this probationary period successfully travel to Gillette's headquarters in Boston to begin 18 months of management training. They are then sent on one- to three-year assignments overseas to gain greater international exposure. In the words of Gillette's international personnel director, "The person we are looking for is someone who says, 'Today, it's Manila. Tomorrow, it's the U.S. Four years from now, it's Peru or Pakistan.'...We really work hard at finding people who aren't parochial and who want international careers."[5]

▸ Determining the Mix of Host-Country and Expatriate Employees

Once a firm passes from the exporting stage (Stage 2) to the stage in which it opens a foreign branch (Stage 3)—either a **wholly owned subsidiary** (the foreign branch is fully owned by the home office) or a **joint venture** (part of the foreign branch is owned by a host country entity: another company, a consortium of firms, an individual, or the government)—it must decide who will be responsible for managing the unit. This decision is important because in most cases the investment required for plant and equipment is enormous, and the success of the foreign venture (like that of any other business) depends largely on who is in charge. A recent survey of 151 executives representing 138 large companies identified the choice of management for overseas units as one of their most crucial business decisions.[6]

wholly owned subsidiary
In international business, a foreign branch owned fully by the home office.

joint venture
In international business, a foreign branch owned partly by the home office and partly by an entity in the host country (a company, a consortium of firms, an individual, or the government).

There are three approaches to managing an international subsidiary: ethnocentric, polycentric, and geocentric.[7]

- In the **ethnocentric approach** to managing international operations, top management and other key positions are filled by people from the home country. For instance, Fluor Daniel, Inc., has 50 engineering and sales offices on five continents and concurrent construction projects in as many as 80 countries at any given time. The firm uses a large group of expatriate managers, including 500 international HRM professionals who are involved in recruitment, development, and compensation worldwide and who report directly to a corporate vice president. The vice president himself is a roving expatriate who spends at least two months a year abroad supervising international operations.
- In the **polycentric approach,** international subsidiaries are managed and staffed by personnel from the host country. For instance, General Electric's Tungsram subsidiary in Hungary runs eight factories and employs 8,000 people, almost all of whom are Hungarian nationals.[8] Coca-Cola, which has been global for most of its 100-year history, currently operates in 160 countries, employing about half a million workers worldwide.
- In the **geocentric approach,** nationality is deliberately downplayed and the firm actively searches on a worldwide or regional basis for the best people to fill key positions. Transnational firms (those in Stage 5) tend to follow this approach. For example, Electrolux (the vacuum cleaner company) has for many years attempted to recruit and develop a group of international managers from diverse countries. These people constitute a mobile pool of managers who are used in a variety of facilities as the need arises. Rather than representing a particular country, they represent the organization wherever they are. Most important to Electrolux is the development of a common culture and an international perspective, and the expansion of its international networks.[9]

ethnocentric approach
An approach to managing international operations in which top management and other key positions are filled by people from the home country.

polycentric approach
An approach to managing international operations in which subsidiaries are managed and staffed by personnel from the host country.

geocentric approach
An approach to managing international operations in which nationality is downplayed and the firm actively searches on a worldwide or regional basis for the best people to fill key positions.

As Figure 17–2 on page 520 shows, there are both advantages and disadvantages to using local nationals and expatriates in foreign subsidiaries. Most firms use expatriates only for such key positions as senior managers, high-level professionals, and technical specialists. Because expatriates tend to be very costly (approximately \$80,000–\$230,000 per person per year, with some expatriates in Tokyo costing \$430,360 a year), it makes little financial sense to hire expatriates for positions that can be competently filled by foreign nationals. It has been estimated that an expatriate costs 2000% to 4000% more than a local employee.[10] In addition, many countries require that a certain percentage of the work force be local citizens, with exceptions usually made for upper management. In general, reliance on expatriates increases when:[11]

Locals	
Advantages • Lowers labor costs • Demonstrates trust in local citizenry • Increases acceptance of the company by the local community • Maximizes the number of options available in the local environment • Leads to recognition of the company as a legitimate participant in the local economy • Effectively represents local considerations and constraints in the decision-making process	**Disadvantages** • Makes it difficult to balance local demands and global priorities • Leads to postponement of difficult local decisions (such as layoffs) until they are unavoidable, when they are more difficult, costly, and painful than they would have been if implemented earlier • May make it difficult to recruit qualified personnel • May reduce the amount of control exercised by headquarters

Expatriates	
Advantages • Cultural similarity with parent company ensures transfer of business/management practices • Permits closer control and coordination of international subsidiaries • Gives employees a multinational orientation through experience at parent company • Establishes a pool of internationally experienced executives • Local talent may not yet be able to deliver as much value as expatriates can	**Disadvantages** • Creates problems of adaptability to foreign environment and culture • Increases the "foreignness" of the subsidiary • May involve high transfer, salary, and other costs • May result in personal and family problems • Has disincentive effect on local-management morale and motivation • May be subject to local government restrictions

FIGURE 17–2

Advantages and Disadvantages of Using Local and Expatriate Employees to Staff International Subsidiaries

Sources: Locals: Adapted from Doz, Y., and Prahalad, C. K. (1986). Controlled variety: A challenge for human resource management in MNC. *Human Resource Management, 21*(1), 57; Expatriates: Adapted from Hamil, J. (1989). Expatriate policies in British MNNs. *Journal of General Management, 14*(4), 20; Sheridan, W. R., and Hansen, P. T. (1996, Spring). Linking international business and expatriate compensation strategies. *ACA Journal*, 66–78; and Warner, J., Templeman, J., and Horn, R. (1995, October 30). The world is not always your oyster. *Business Week*, 132–133.

- *Sufficient local talent is not available.* This is most likely to occur in firms operating in developing countries. For instance, top managers of Falcombridge and Alcoa (both mining companies operating in Latin America and Africa) are almost always expatriates.
- *An important part of the firm's overall business strategy is the creation of a corporatewide global vision.* Some firms prefer to make subsidiaries part of an international network with a shared corporate identity. When this is the case, expatriates are used to link the organization's international subsidiaries. (Locals are generally more concerned with their own unit than with the organization as a whole.) For example, Whirlpool Corporation, the world's largest home appliance manufacturer, has operations in 40 countries and is deeply committed to the notion of one global company with one global vision. The company has a worldwide leadership program involving extensive use of expatriates, conferences that bring together top executives from different subsidiaries around the world, and global project teams that tackle common problems and facilitate a total international integration process.[12]
- *International units and domestic operations are highly interdependent.* In some cases, the production process requires that all divisions of a corporation, both international

and domestic, work closely with one another. This is particularly necessary when the output of one business unit is needed as an input by another business unit of the same corporation. For example, IBM, Hewlett-Packard, and Xerox have specialized manufacturing facilities in different parts of the United States and the world. The outputs of these different facilities (computer chips, software) must be closely monitored and integrated to produce such highly sophisticated products as computers, medical equipment, and photocopying machines. Linking production processes generally calls for greater reliance on expatriate managers and specialists, who can bridge the gaps and tie the units of the organization together.

This policy is not necessary in corporations with primarily stand-alone operations with low interdependence across units. For instance, McDonald's Corporation operates in more than 50 countries; approximately 3,000 of its 12,000 restaurants are located overseas. The primary involvement of corporation headquarters in Oak Brook, Illinois, is to train restaurant managers from all over the world in McDonald's Hamburger University. The company also has five international personnel directors who serve as internal consultants. Thus, although McDonald's demands strict product quality standards across countries, expatriates play a minor role in this process because each restaurant functions as a highly autonomous unit.

- *The political situation is unstable.* Corporations tend to rely on expatriates for top-management positions when the risk of government intervention in the business is high, when actual or potential turmoil within the country is serious, when the threat of terrorism exists, and when there has been a recent history of social upheaval in the country. Although expatriate top managers may increase tensions between nationalistic groups and a foreign firm, they do provide some assurance to the home office that its interests are well represented locally. Expatriates are also less susceptible to the demands of local political forces.

  Most Western ventures in the new republics of Eastern Europe and the former Soviet Union are run by expatriates. The same is true in the few remaining communist countries, where political instability remains high.

- *There are significant cultural differences between the host country and the home country.* The more dissimilar the culture where the subsidiary is located to that of the home office (in terms of language, religion, customs, and so forth), the more important it is to appoint expatriates who can serve as interpreters or go-betweens for the two cultures. Since this boundary-spanning role demands much cross-cultural sensitivity, the MNC needs to select and carefully train individuals suitable for these positions. This may require considerable career planning.

  Researchers have identified nations and world regions where dissimilarities with U.S. culture are great and the expatriate needs exceptional skills to be successful. Cultural barriers are lowest in European countries, Canada, Australia, and New Zealand; midrange in most of Latin America; and greatest in India/Pakistan, Southeast Asia, the Middle East, North Africa, East Africa, and Liberia.[13]

The Challenges of Expatriate Assignments

One of the most challenging tasks for any international firm is to manage its expatriate work force effectively. The statistics, unfortunately, are not encouraging. The failure of U.S. expatriates—that is, the percentage who return prematurely, without completing their assignment—is estimated to be in the 20%–40% range. This failure rate is three to four times higher than the failure rates experienced by European and Asian companies. One reason for the high U.S. failure rate: Two generations of economic dominance and a strong domestic market have contributed to the creation of a colonial mentality in many U.S. companies.[14]

Failures can be very expensive. Premature returnees cost $70,000 to $210,000 each in 1993 dollars, which translates into $2.7 billion per year in direct costs to U.S. firms. The more intangible costs of failure include business disruptions, lost opportunities, and negative impact on the firm's reputation and leadership, and are probably many times greater. In addition, the personal hardship on the people involved and their families, including diminished self-image, marital strife, uprooted children, lost income, and tarnished career reputation, can be substantial.[15]

Why International Assignments End in Failure

It is important to understand the reasons behind expatriates' high failure rates so that preventive measures can be taken. Six factors account for most failures, although their relative importance varies by firm.[16] These are career blockage, culture shock, lack of cross-cultural training, an overemphasis on technical qualifications, a tendency to use international assignments as a way to get rid of problem employees, and family problems.

Career Blockage. Initially, many employees see the opportunity to work and travel abroad as exciting. But once the initial rush wears off, many feel that the home office has forgotten them and that their career has been sidetracked while their counterparts at home are climbing the corporate ladder. Some recent statistics indicate that less than one half of 1% of U.S. expatriates view international assignments as a career route to the top.[17] In fact, although U.S. companies give themselves high marks for career planning for their expatriate employees, most of their employees don't, according to a recent survey by the Society for Human Resources Management. Only 14% of the 209 expatriate managers who completed the society's questionnaire said their firm's career planning for them was sufficient.[18] In addition, only about 50% of firms have identified the technical, managerial, and interpersonal competencies that contribute to the success of expatriates in international assignments,[19] and only 32% of firms have linked international competencies and experiences to career planning.

culture shock
The inability to adjust to a different cultural environment.

Culture Shock. Many people who take international assignments cannot adjust to a different cultural environment, a phenomenon called **culture shock.** Instead of learning to work within the new culture, the expatriate tries to impose the home office's or home country's values on the host country's employees. This practice may trigger cultural clashes and misunderstandings that escalate until the expatriate decides to return home to more familiar surroundings—perhaps leaving a mess behind.

In his book *Going International*, coauthor and consultant Lewis Griggs recounts the culture shock experienced by a female vice president of a U.S. company doing business in Saudi Arabia. She was invited to dinner at the home of a Saudi businessman, and, upon entering the home, was escorted to a room set aside for women. Feeling that she was not being accorded proper respect, she joined the men in their dining room. Dinner and business discussion ended abruptly.

Firms can help employees avoid culture shock by using selection tools to choose the employees with the highest degree of cultural sensitivity. However, research indicates that few companies are doing so. For example, only 18% of the companies in a recent survey use structured interviews, only 12% use candidate/spouse self-assessment, only 6% use psychological and cognitive testing, and only 2% use a formal assessment center.[20]

Lack of Predeparture Cross-Cultural Training. Surprisingly, only about one third of multinationals provide *any* cross-cultural training to expatriates, and those that do tend to offer rather cursory programs.[21] Often the expatriate and his or her family literally pack their bags and travel to their destination with only a U.S. passport and whatever information they could cull from magazines, tourist brochures, and the library. This is a recipe for trouble, as the following example illustrates:

> I once attended a business meeting in Tokyo with a senior U.S. executive. The Japanese go through a very elaborate ritual when exchanging business cards, and the American didn't have a clue. She just tossed some of her business cards across the table at the stunned Japanese executives. One of them turned his back on her and walked out. Needless to say, the deal never went through.[22]

Overemphasis on Technical Qualifications. The person chosen to go abroad may have impressive credentials and an excellent reputation in the home office for getting things done. He or she may seem like the natural choice to start a new international facility, to manage a subsidiary that needs tightening up, or to act as a troubleshooter when technical difficulties arise. Unfortunately, the same traits that led to success at home can be disastrous in another country. Consider the experience of one executive from a large U.S. electronics firm who spent only three months of what was supposed to be a two-year assignment in Mexico:

> I just could not accept the fact that my staff meetings would always start at least a half hour late and that schedules were treated as flexible guidelines with much room to spare. Nobody seemed to care but me! I also could not understand how many of the first-line supervisors would hire their friends and relatives, regardless of competence. What I viewed as nepotism of the worst kind was seen by them as an honorable obligation to their extended families, and this included many adopted relatives or compadres who were not even related by blood.[23]

In a recent survey, 96% of respondents rated the technical requirements of a job as the most important selection criteria for international assignments, largely ignoring cultural sensitivity.[24] This outlook is a recipe for failure. In more enlightened companies, such as Prudential Relocation (an arm of Prudential Insurance), nearly 35% of managers cite "cultural adaptability" as the most important trait for overseas success. Only 22% of Prudential managers cite technical skills as the most important.[25]

Getting Rid of a Troublesome Employee. International assignments may seem to be a convenient way of dealing with managers who are having problems in the home office. By sending these managers abroad, the organization is able to resolve difficult interpersonal situations or political conflicts at the home office, but at a significant cost to its international operations. Although the number of people in this category is difficult to assess, the "let's find an out-of-the-way place for So-and-So" syndrome is not unusual. The following true story was told to one of the authors:

> Joe and Paul were both competing for promotion to divisional manager. The corporate vice president responsible for making the selection decision felt that Joe should get the promotion but also believed that Paul would never be able to accept the decision and would actively try to undermine Joe's authority. Paul also had much support from some of the old-timers, so the only way to avoid the dilemma was to find a different spot for Paul where he could not cause any trouble. The vice president came up with the idea of promoting Joe to divisional manager while appointing Paul as a senior executive at the Venezuelan subsidiary. Paul (who had seldom been out of the country and who had taken introductory Spanish in high school 20 years earlier) took the job. It soon became obvious that the appointment was a mistake. Two months after being assigned to the Venezuelan post there was a major wildcat strike attributed to Paul's heavy-handed style in dealing with the labor unions, and he had to be replaced.

Family Problems. The inability or unwillingness of the expatriate's spouse and children to adapt to life in another country is one of the most important reasons for failure. In fact, more than half of all early returns can be attributed to family problems.[26] Given the stress the employee usually experiences in trying to function in unfamiliar surroundings, trouble at home can easily become the proverbial straw that breaks the camel's back.

It is surprising that most firms do not anticipate these problems and develop programs to prevent them from happening. Indeed, few companies consider the feelings of the spouses of those they've selected for international assignments.[27] One expatriate's wife comments:

> A husband who is racked by guilt over dragging his wife halfway around the world, or distracted because she is ill-equipped to handle a foreign assignment, is not a happy or productive employee.…Most women actually start out all right. The excitement quickly fades for a traveling wife, though, when her husband abandons her for a regional tour immediately upon arrival and she's left behind with the moving boxes and the responsibility of finding good schools. Or when she is left to hire servants to set up a household without knowing the language…[Often] they are asked to jump off their own career paths and abandon healthy salaries…just so that they can watch their self-esteem vanish somewhere over the international date line.[28]

The expectations of dual-career couples are another cause of failure in expatriate assignments. MNCs are increasingly confronted with couples who expect to work in the same foreign location—at no sacrifice to either's career. Yet one spouse usually has to sacrifice, and this often leads to dissatisfaction. When ten-year AT&T veteran Eric Phillips was asked to move to Brussels, his wife, Angelina, had to give up her well-paying job as a market researcher. While the move represented a terrific career opportunity for Phillips, his wife recalls finding it very difficult to adjust.[29]

Difficulties upon Return

Although the failure of expatriates abroad has received the most attention in research journals, a number of studies suggest that expatriates' return home may also be fraught with difficulties. It is estimated that 20% to 40% of returning expatriates (called *repatriates*) leave the organization shortly after returning home.[30] Four common problems confronting returning expatriates are their company's lack of respect for the skills they acquired while abroad, loss of status, poor planning for the expatriate's return, and reverse culture shock. This chapter's Manager's Notebook, titled "Communicate to Repatriate," summarizes some of the practices companies can use to counter these problems. We discuss these practices in greater detail later in this chapter.

Lack of Respect for Acquired Skills. Most U.S. firms are still heavily oriented toward the domestic market. This is true even of those that have a long history of operating internationally. As a result, international experience is not highly valued. The expatriate who has gathered a wealth of information and valuable skills on a foreign assignment may be frustrated by the lack of appreciation shown by peers and supervisors at corporate headquarters. Some in the organization even see the expatriate as out of touch, particularly if the international assignment lasted several years. According to recent data, only 12% of expatriates felt that their overseas assignment had enhanced their career development, and almost two thirds reported that their firm did not take advantage of what they had learned overseas.[31]

Loss of Status. Returning expatriates often experience a substantial loss of prestige, power, independence, and authority. This *status reversal* affects as many as three fourths of repatriated employees.[32] It is common to respond to this situation with bitterness, as the following example illustrates:

> When I was in Chile, I had occasions to meet various ministers in the government and other high-ranking industry officials. Basically my word was the final one. I had a lot of latitude because the home office didn't really want to be bothered with what was happening in Chile and therefore was uninformed anyway. I made decisions in Chile that only our CEO would make for the domestic operation. When I returned, I felt as though all the training and experience I had gotten in Chile was totally useless. The position I had seemed about six levels down as far as I was concerned. I had to get

approval for hiring. I had to get my boss's signature for purchases worth one tenth of the values of ones I approved in Chile. To say I felt a letdown would be a significant understatement.[33]

Poor Planning for Return Position. Often management repatriates an employee with no idea of what position this person should hold in the home office. Uncertainties regarding their new career assignment may provoke much anxiety in returning employees. One survey suggests that more than half of expatriates were unaware of what job awaited them at home.[34] The following story is typical of returning expatriates:

> I received a letter from the home office three months prior to the expiration of my assignment in Hungary (where I was responsible for a team of engineers developing a computerized system for handling inventories in four new joint ventures). I was told that I would be assuming the position of Supervisor of Technical Services in corporate headquarters. It sounded impressive enough. I was astonished to find out upon return, however, that I was given the honorary title of supervisor with nobody under my command. It smelled like a dead rat to me so I jumped ship as soon as I could.[35]

Reverse Culture Shock. Most firms assume the returning expatriate will be happy to be back home. But this is not always true, particularly for those returning from extended international assignments. Living and working in another culture for a long time changes a person, especially if he or she has internalized some of the foreign country's norms and customs. Because much of this internalization occurs subconsciously, expatriates are usually unaware of how much psychological change they have undergone until they return home. It has been reported that as many as 80% of returning expatriates experience *reverse culture shock,* which sometimes leads to alienation, a sense of uprootedness, and even disciplinary problems.[36] One expatriate who had worked in Spain notes:

> I began to take for granted the intense camaraderie at work and after hours among male friends. Upon returning to the U.S. I realized for the first time in my life how American males are expected to maintain a high psychological distance from each other, and their extremely competitive nature in a work environment. My friendly overtures were often misperceived as underhanded maneuvers for personal gain.[37]

Despite all these difficulties, many managers today are lining up for international assignments as companies gradually realize that employees with international experience can be a valuable asset. One recent survey showed that a majority of companies have increased their expatriate populations since 1989 and expect to increase or maintain that volume.[38] The "out of sight—out of mind" mentality that has long governed international assignments is being replaced at some companies by the notion that these assignments should be structured to enhance the firm's global efforts. For instance, Gerber Products, which is busily building markets in Latin America and Central and Eastern Europe, has announced that from now on, international assignments will be emphasized as part of normal career development for com-

Manager's Notebook

Communicate to Repatriate

Companies that have relatively low repatriation failure rates attribute their success to intensive interactions with the individual and his or her family before, during, and after the international assignment. Here are some of the practices and programs that have been found to increase organizational commitment among expatriate employees:

- *Advance career planning helps expatriates know what to expect when they return to the United States.* Management needs to sit down with HR professionals and the employee to lay out a potential career path before the employee goes abroad.
- *Mentors can make expatriates feel they are vital members of the organization.* At Nashville-based Northern Telecom, Inc., for instance, senior managers and vice presidents correspond regularly with expatriate employees and meet with them periodically either at the home office or on location. The reentry process is much easier for employees who do not feel they were forgotten while they were away.
- *Opening global communication channels keeps expatriates up-to-date on organizational developments.* Some companies do this through newsletters and briefings. And, of course, telecommunications technology enables expatriates to stay in constant touch with the home office through faxes and e-mail.
- *Recognizing the contributions of repatriated employees eases their reentry.* Repatriated employees whose accomplishments abroad are acknowledged are more likely to stay with the company.

Source: Adapted from Shilling, M. (1993, September). How to win at repatriation. *Personnel Journal*, 40.

pany executives. As a result, Gerber's country manager in Poland feels he has an edge over many of his colleagues. "My overseas experience sets me apart from the rest of the MBA bunch," he says. "I'm not just one of hundreds of thousands."[39]

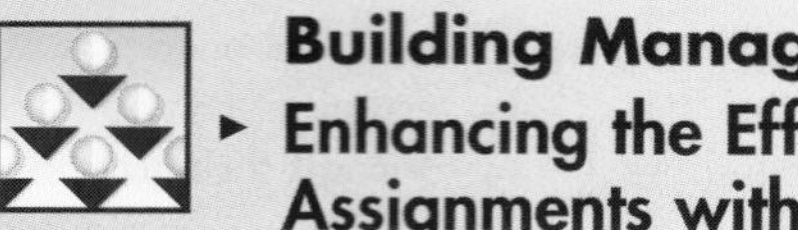

Building Managerial Skills: Enhancing the Effectiveness of Expatriate Assignments with HRM Policies and Practices

Although expatriate assignments will probably always be more problematic than domestic transfers, companies can minimize the chances of failure by creating a sensible set of HRM policies and practices that get to the root of the problems we've discussed. In this section we look at how selection, training, career development, and compensation policies can help companies avoid these problems.

Selection

The choice of an employee for an international assignment is a critical decision. Because most expatriates work under minimal supervision in a distant location, mistakes in selection are likely to go unnoticed until it is too late. To choose the best employee for the job, management should:

- *Emphasize cultural sensitivity as a selection criterion.* The firm should assess the candidate's ability to relate to people from different backgrounds. For instance, one large electronics manufacturing firm conducts in-depth interviews with the candidate's supervisors, peers, and subordinates, particularly those whose gender, race, and ethnic origin are different from the candidate's. Personal interviews with the candidate and written tests that measure social adjustment and adaptability should also be part of the selection process.
- *Establish a selection board of expatriates.* Some HRM specialists strongly recommend that all international assignments be approved by a selection board consisting of managers who have worked as expatriates for a minimum of three to five years.[40] This kind of board should be better able to detect potential problems than managers with no international background. For instance, an employee may express the desire to work in South America where "maids are cheap." This kind of remark may be regarded as inconsequential or humorous by the HR director, but would probably raise a red flag among managers with international experience.
- *Require previous international experience.* While not always feasible, it is highly desirable to choose candidates who have already spent some time in a different country. The major reason the state of Utah is in the forefront of international business is its large Mormon population, whose church requires them to spend a minimum of two years as missionaries in another country. Some schools (such as the American School of International Management in Phoenix, Arizona) and some multinationals offer overseas internships. In this way, candidates acquire some knowledge of a country's language and customs before taking on a full-blown expatriate assignment.
- *Explore the possibility of hiring foreign-born employees who can serve as "expatriates" at a future date.* Japanese companies have been quite successful at hiring young foreign-born (non-Japanese) employees straight out of college to work in the home office in Japan. These recruits enter the firm with little experience and exposure to work in their host country, and thus are blank slates on which the Japanese multinational can write its own philosophy and values.[41] Some U.S. companies, such as Coca-Cola, have been following a similar practice for years.

- *Screen candidates' spouses and families.* Because the unhappiness of expatriates' family members plays such a large role in the failure of international assignments, some companies are screening candidates' spouses. For instance, Ford formally assesses spouses on such qualities as flexibility, patience, and adaptability, asking such questions as: "How do you feel about this assignment? Do you feel you can adjust?" Exxon, too, meets with spouses and children during the selection process.[42]

Training

The assumption that people everywhere respond in similar fashion to the same images, symbols, and slogans has hurt U.S. companies offering their products in international markets. Consider the following examples:

- An international division of a U.S. airline translated its slogan, "Travel on leather," for the Latin American market. Unfortunately, the literal translation, *viaje en cuero*, means "travel naked." The advertisements had to be pulled.
- In 1990 Procter & Gamble's commercial for Camay soap worked wonders in Europe but bombed in Japan. The image of a husband barging into the bathroom as his wife lathered up with Camay in the bathtub struck Japanese consumers as rude. P&G changed the commercial to show a European woman alone in a European-style bath, and now deems the ad a success in Japan.
- Choice Hotels now makes sure the suitcase it depicts in the German version of its international commercial is the hard-sided kind after discovering that, for Germans, a cloth suitcase conjures up images of job-seeking immigrants rather than upscale travelers.
- John P. Woolley, general manager of PC Industries, shipped a $10,000 replacement computer component to a French customer and was stunned when he was billed $2,500 for value-added tax. The company had to absorb the unexpected bill.[43]

Cultural Sensitivity for Customer Satisfaction.

Some companies need to make only language adjustments in packaging, signs, and logos when attempting to sell their products in international markets. Coca-Cola (right) is exactly the same whether it is sold in Seattle or Moscow—except for the lettering on the bottle. In contrast, McDonald's restaurants in Saudi Arabia (left) have had to adjust their menus, ingredients, and hours of operation to suit Arabian culture.

If these companies had given their expatriate executives appropriate cross-cultural training before their departure, these blunders would never have been committed. Cross-cultural training sensitizes candidates for international assignment to the local culture, customs, language, tax laws, and government.[44]

Because insensitivity to the local culture can have severe financial consequences, cross-cultural training seminars are on the rise in global-minded companies. While these seminars cost $1,000 and upward per manager, many companies feel the expense is minor compared to the huge cost of failed expatriate stints. For instance, despite massive cost-cutting moves at General Motors, the auto giant still spends nearly $500,000 a year on cross-cultural training for about 150 Americans and their families headed abroad. GM's general director of international personnel attributes the very low (less than 1%) premature return rate of GM expatriates to this training. The experience of a Cortland, Ohio, family transferred to Kenya by GM is typical. The family members underwent three days of cross-cultural training that consisted of a crash course in African political history, business practices, social customs, and nonverbal gestures. The family's two teenagers, who were miserable about moving to Africa, sampled Indian food (popular in Kenya) and learned how to ride Nairobi public buses, speak a little Swahili, and even how to juggle.[45]

Another type of cross-cultural training is designed not to address the cultural and political realities of a particular country but rather to give executives the skills to deal with a wide range of people with different values. For instance, Motorola has opened a special center for cultural training at its headquarters in Schaumburg, Illinois, with the goal of making Motorola managers "transculturally competent."[46]

While all employees embarking on an international assignment would benefit from extensive training, economic sense dictates that the more rigorous and lengthy training be reserved for expatriates whose stay abroad will exceed one year and whose job assignment requires a good deal of knowledge of the local culture. Figure 17–3 shows three approaches to cross-cultural training. The least expensive type, the *information-giving approach*, lasts less than a week and merely provides indispensable briefings and a little language training. The *affective approach* (one to four weeks) focuses on providing the psychological and managerial skills the expatriate will need to perform effectively during a moderate-length assignment. The most extensive training, the *impression approach* (one to two months), prepares the manager for a long assignment with greater authority and responsibility by providing, for instance, field experiences and extended language training. Ideally, at least a portion of these training programs should be targeted to the expatriate's family. Although Figure 17–3 is concerned with predeparture training, it is also possible (indeed desirable) to use similar "decompression" training programs for returning expatriates to help them cope with reverse culture shock.

Career Development

The expatriate's motivation to perform well on an international assignment, to remain in the post for the duration of the assignment, and to be a high performer upon returning to the home office will depend to a large extent on the career development opportunities offered by the employer. At a minimum, successful career planning for expatriates requires the firm to do two things:

- *Position the international assignment as a step toward advancement within the firm.* The firm should explicitly define the job, the length of the assignment, and the expatriate's reentry position, level, and career track upon return. Companies with successful expatriate programs, such as Dow Chemical and Arthur Andersen, have practiced this policy for years. At Whirlpool, a person's career may be planned for up to 25 years into the future through positioning in critical international locations that are clearly marked as posts along a career path leading to top management.

Length of Stay	Length and Level of Training	Cross-Cultural Training Approach
1–3 years	1–2 months + High	**Impression Approach** Assessment center Field experiences Simulations Sensitivity training Extensive language training
2–12 months	1–4 weeks Moderate	**Affective Approach** Language training Role-playing Critical incidents Cases Stress-reduction training Moderate language training
1 month or less	Less than a week Low	**Information-Giving Approach** Area briefings Cultural briefings Films/books Use of interpreters "Survival-level" language training

FIGURE 17-3

Three Approaches to Cross-Cultural Training

Source: Adapted from Mendenhall, M., and Oddou, G. (1986). Acculturation profiles of expatriate managers: Implications for cross-cultural training. *Columbia Journal of World Business*, 78. Copyright 1986. *Columbia Journal of World Business*. Reprinted with permission.

- *Provide support for expatriates.* To prevent expatriates from feeling isolated and disconnected, the home office should stay in regular touch with them. Maintaining contact can be accomplished in a number of ways.[47] A popular method is the buddy system, in which a manager or mentor at the home office is appointed to keep in touch with the expatriate and to provide assistance wherever necessary. Another approach has the expatriate employee come back to the home office occasionally to foster a sense of belonging to the organization and to reduce reentry shock. A third approach offers mini-sabbaticals in the home office at specified intervals (for example, for two weeks every six months) to keep the expatriate tuned in to current happenings and future plans at the corporate base. Some firms will pay for the expatriate's family to return home with him or her during this time.

Compensation

Firms can use compensation packages to enhance the effectiveness of expatriate assignments. However, compensation policies can create conflict if locals compare their pay packages to the expatriate's and conclude that they are being treated unfairly.

Planning compensation for expatriates requires management to follow three important guidelines:

- *Provide the expatriate with a disposable income that is equivalent to what he or she would receive at home.* This usually requires granting expatriate employees an allowance for price differences in housing, food, and other consumer goods. Allowances for children's schooling and the whole family's medical treatment may also be necessary. The best-known cost-of-living index for world locations is published by Corporate Resources Group, a Geneva-based consulting firm that surveys 97 cities worldwide twice a year. Using New York as a base of 100, Tokyo (at 171) and Osaka (at 157) are the most expensive cities in the world for expatriates, with Bombay (at 61) the least costly.[48] Maintaining income equality with the home office is not an exact science (for example, finding housing in Japan comparable to that available in U.S. suburbs is nearly impossible), but as a general rule, it is better to err on the side of generosity. See Figure 17–4 for a comparative list of housing costs in various cities around the world.

- *Provide an explicit "add-on" incentive for accepting an international assignment.* This incentive may take several forms. The company may provide a sign-on bonus prior to departure. Or it may offer the employee a percentage increase over his or her home base salary; the standard increase is 15% of the base salary.[49] Or it may provide a lump-sum payment upon successful completion of the foreign assignment. Some firms offer a combination of these incentives. Generally, the greatest incentives are reserved for the least desirable locations. For instance, multinationals hoping to lure Western managers to Eastern Europe, where poor air quality, political instability, and a shortage of quality housing make assignments unattractive, often offer packages that include company-paid housing, subsidized shipment of scarce consumer goods, up to four trips home a year, and weekend getaways to Western Europe.[50]
- *Avoid having expatriates fill the same jobs held by locals or lower-ranking jobs.* This is to prevent perceptions of inequity. Local employees tend to compare their pay and living standards to those of expatriates, and feelings of unfairness are more likely to surface if an expatriate at the same or lower rank than the local is receiving greater pay.

Calculating compensation packages for expatriate employees is one of the most difficult tasks facing multinationals.[51] Compensation used to be a relatively simple issue: Low-level local hirees got paid in the local currency, while expatriate managers' pay was pegged to U.S. salaries. However, in an era of dramatic corporate restructuring to cut costs, expatriate packages based on U.S. salaries are increasingly being considered too expensive. Moreover, as companies move into the later stages of internationalization, they work with a team of international employees operating out of the home office rather than just expatriates. As it has become more costly to maintain salary equity between these two groups of employees, more U.S. companies have been devising pay packages like the one created by Oklahoma-based Phillips Petroleum Company. When a British geophysicist first went abroad to work for Phillips in the mid-1970s, he was paid in dollars and his salary was equivalent to that of someone in the United States doing a similar job. Today, under Phillips' third-party nationals program, he gets the same housing allowance, home leave, and educational assistance for his children. However, his salary is now pegged to the more modest level at which he would be paid in his home country rather than to the U.S. salary for that job.[52]

Still, some companies continue to compensate their expatriates generously. To avoid potential pay inequities when employees are transferred from one international post to another, 3M compares net salaries in both the old and the new country and provides the transferred employee with whichever pay package is higher.[53] And Seagram Spirits and Wine Group has come up with an "international cadre policy" for those expatriates who work abroad permanently (as opposed to expatriates who will return to the United States

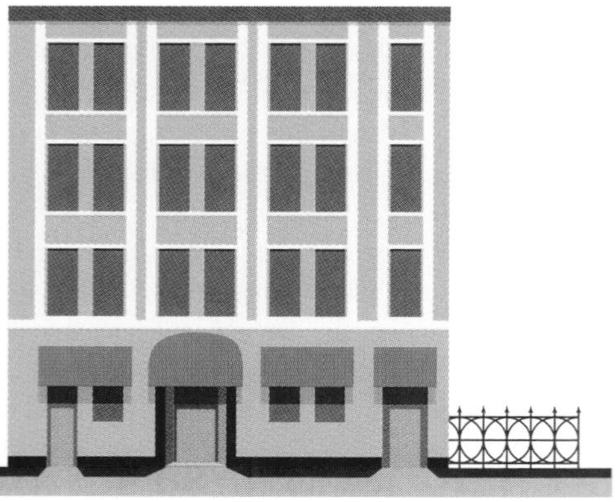

FIGURE 17–4

What It Costs to House Expatriates Worldwide

Source: Runzheimer International, cited in Laabs, J. J. (1993, July). For your information. *Personnel Journal*, 16; data updated and adjusted by authors.

Location	Total Annual Housing Cost
Tokyo	$130,020
Hong Kong	93,110
Paris	78,495
London	56,797
Caracas	50,884
Frankfurt	50,691
Mexico City	49,287
Rio de Janeiro	42,015
Chicago	31,783

in the future). The package features a standardized cost-of-living adjustment and a global standard employee housing contribution that is the same regardless of location. For temporary U.S. expatriates, Seagram maintains what it terms a "pure expatriate" package that keeps people up to par with U.S. compensation standards.[54] ▼

▸ Developing HRM Policies in a Global Context

Firms operating in multiple countries need to worry not just about meeting the special needs of expatriate employees but also about the design and implementation of HRM programs in diverse cross-cultural settings. One company that is widely viewed as exceptional in its achievement of a unified global HRM program—even with two thirds of its employees working overseas—is Coca-Cola.

In many countries reliance on U.S., or Western, managerial practices is likely to clash with deeply ingrained norms and values.[55] For instance, the open door style of management, which works well in a culture that readily accepts questioning of authority, will probably not work in countries where such behavior is considered unacceptable—for example, China. Effectively meeting the multinational challenge requires a sophisticated HRM system that can be adapted to a variety of cultural conditions. In other words, rather than simply transferring abroad HRM practices that are based on the home country's social and cultural standards, managers should mold these practices to the cultural environment in which a particular facility is located. If there is too much inconsistency between a nation's culture and a company's HRM practices, the company is likely to face noncompliance at best, and acts of open hostility at worst.

National Culture, Organizational Characteristics, and HRM Practices

"Culture is important to HRM practices." This statement may seem obvious, but its relevance may be lost in a country like the United States, where many of the best-known theories of management practice are firmly rooted in Western culture. Geert Hofstede, a Dutch professor, has spent the better part of his professional life studying the similarities and differences among cultures. He has concluded that there are five major dimensions to culture:

1. *Power distance*, the extent to which individuals expect a hierarchical structure that emphasizes status differences between subordinates and superiors.
2. *Individualism*, the degree to which a society values personal goals, autonomy, and privacy over group loyalty, commitment to group norms, involvement in collective activities, social cohesiveness, and intense socialization.
3. *Uncertainty avoidance*, the extent to which a society places a high value on reducing risk and instability.
4. *Masculinity/femininity*, the degree to which a society views assertive or "masculine" behavior as important to success and encourages rigidly stereotyped gender roles.
5. *Long-term/short-term orientation*, the extent to which values are oriented toward the future (saving, persistence) as opposed to the past or present (respect for tradition, fulfilling social obligations).[56]

Although Hofstede's research has been criticized for being based largely on the experiences of employees working for only one company (IBM) and for downplaying the importance of cultural differences within countries, other evidence suggests that the five dimensions are a fair summary of cultural differences.[57] These dimensions have proved useful for examining how cultural factors affect organizations. Most important, they provide clues regarding the general configuration of HRM strategies that are most likely to mesh with a particular culture's values. Figure 17–5 on pages 532-535 outlines the char-

Power Distance, Organizational Characteristics, and Selected HR Practices

Power Distance	Dominant Values	Sample Countries	Organizational Features	Reward Practices	Staffing/Appraisal Practices
HIGH	• Top-down communications • Class divisions seen as natural • Authoritarianism • High dependence on superiors • Power symbols • White-collar jobs valued more than blue-collar jobs	• Malaysia • Philippines • Mexico • Arab nations • Venezuela • Spain	• Centralization and tall organizational structures • Traditional line of command	• Hierarchical compensation system • Differences in pay and benefits reflect job and status differences; large differential between higher- and lower-level jobs • Visible rewards that project power, such as a large office or company car	• Limited search methods in recruitment; emphasis on connections and "whom you know" • Few formal mechanisms of selection • Superior makes selection choice for his or her sphere of influence • Personal loyalty to superior is crucial trait for advancement • Social class and extended family may play a role in personnel decisions • Nepotism may be commonly practiced • Formal appraisals lacking; more "verbal" or "psychological contracts" between supervisor and subordinate
LOW	• Egalitarianism • Status based on achievement • Joint decision making • High value placed on participation • Low dependence on superiors • Disdain for power symbols • Hard work valued even if manual in nature	• The Netherlands • Australia • Switzerland • Sweden	• Flatter organizational structures • Decentralized control • Greater reliance on matrix-type networks • Great degree of worker involvement	• Egalitarian-based compensation systems • Small differences in pay and benefits between higher- and lower-level jobs • Participatory pay strategies (such as gainsharing) more prevalent	• Multiple search methods; extensive advertisement • Formalized selection methods "to give everyone a fair chance" • Superior constrained in making selection choices • Selection based on merit; loyalty to superiors deemphasized • Contextual non–job-related factors (such as social class) ignored • Nepotism viewed as conflict of interest and even unethical • Formal appraisals based on notion of joint planning, two-way feedback, and performance documentation

(continued)

FIGURE 17–5

Cultural Characteristics and Dominant Values

Source: This is an updated and expanded version of an earlier chart appearing in Gómez-Mejía, L. R., and Welbourne, T. (1991). Compensation strategies in a global context. *Human Resource Planning, 14*(1), 38.

acteristics of cultures ranking high or low on each of Hofstede's dimensions, lists sample countries falling at each end of the spectrum, and summarizes the organizational features and HRM practices that work best at each end of the scale.

The information in Figure 17–5 has enormous implications for international firms. As businesses move out of their home countries and employ people with potentially very different cultural values, it is essential that corporations consider the inevitable clash between their "exported" HRM practices and the national culture.

Individualism, Organizational Characteristics, and Selected HR Practices					
INDIVIDUALISM	**Dominant Values**	**Sample Countries**	**Organizational Features**	**Reward Practices**	**Staffing/Appraisal Practices**
HIGH	• Personal accomplishment • Selfishness • Independence • Belief in individual control and responsibility • Belief in creating one's own destiny • Business relationship between employer and employee	• United States • Great Britain • Canada • New Zealand	• Organizations not compelled to care for employees' total well-being • Employees look after their own individual interests • Explicit systems of control necessary to ensure compliance and prevent wide deviation from organizational norms	• Performance-based pay • Individual achievement rewarded • External equity emphasized • Extrinsic rewards are important indicators of personal success • Attempts made to isolate individual contributions (i.e., who did what) • Emphasis on short-term objectives	• Emphasis on credentials and visible performance outcomes attributed to individual • High turnover; commitment to organization for career reasons • Performance rather than seniority as criterion for advancement • "Fitting in" deemphasized; belief in performance as independent of personal likes and dislikes • Attempts at ascertaining individual strengths and weaknesses and providing frequent feedback to employee
LOW	• Team accomplishment • Sacrifice for others • Dependence on social unit • Belief in group control and responsibility • Belief in the hand of fate • Moral relationship between employer and employee	• Singapore • South Korea • Indonesia • Japan • Taiwan	• Organizations committed to high-level involvement in workers' personal lives • Loyalty to the firm is critical • Normative, rather than formal, systems of control to ensure compliance	• Group-based performance is important criterion for rewards • Seniority-based pay utilized • Intrinsic rewards essential • Internal equity guides pay policies • Personal needs (such as number of children) affect pay received	• Value of credentials and visible performance outcomes depends on perceived contributions to team efforts • Low turnover; commitment to organization as "family" • Seniority plays an important role in personnel decisions • "Fitting in" with work group crucial; belief that interpersonal relations are important performance dimension • Limited or no performance feedback to individual to prevent conflict and defensive reactions

(continued)

FIGURE 17–5
continued

As a general principle, *the more an HRM practice contradicts the prevailing societal norms, the more likely it will fail.* For instance, Hofstede describes management by objectives (MBO) as "perhaps the single most popular management technique 'made in the U.S.A.'"[58] because it assumes (1) negotiation between the boss and employee, or a not-too-large power distance; (2) a willingness on the part of both parties to take risks, or weak uncertainty avoidance; and (3) that both supervisors and subordinates see performance and its associated rewards as important. Because all three assumptions are prominent features of U.S. culture, MBO "fits" the United States. But in other countries — France, for example — MBO has generally run into problems because of cultural incompatibility:

> The high power distance to which the French are accustomed from childhood ultimately has thwarted the successful utilization of MBO as a truly participative process.... The problem is not necessarily with MBO per se but the French managers...who are

Uncertainty Avoidance, Organizational Characteristics, and Selected HR Practices

UNCERTAINTY AVOIDANCE	Dominant Values	Sample Countries	Organizational Features	Reward Practices	Staffing/Appraisal Practices
HIGH	• Fear of random events and the unknown • High value placed on stability and routine • Low tolerance for ambiguity • Low risk propensity • Comfort in security, lack of tension, and lack of contradictions	• Greece • Portugal • Italy	• Mechanistic structures • Written rules and policies guide the firm • Organizations strive to be predictable • Management avoids making risky decisions • Careful delineation of responsibilities and work flows	• Bureaucratic pay policies utilized • Compensation programs tend to be centralized • Fixed pay more important than variable pay • Little discretion given to supervisor in dispensing pay	• Bureaucratic rules/procedures to govern hiring and promotion • Seniority an important factor in hiring and promotions • Government/union regulations limit employer discretion in recruitment, promotion, and terminations • Limited external hires • Limited use of appraisals requiring judgment
LOW	• Unexpected viewed as challenging and exciting • Stability and routine seen as boring • Ambiguity seen as providing opportunities • High risk propensity • Tensions and contradictions spur innovation, discovery, and mastery of change	• Singapore • Denmark • Sweden • Hong Kong	• Less-structured activities • Fewer written rules to cope with changing environmental forces • Managers are more adaptable and tend to make riskier decisions	• Variable pay a key component in pay programs • External equity emphasized • Decentralized pay program is the norm • Much discretion given to supervisors and business units in pay allocation	• Fewer rules/procedures to govern hiring and promotions • Seniority deemphasized in personnel decisions • Employer provided much latitude in recruitment, promotion, and terminations • External hiring at all levels • Extensive use of appraisals requiring judgment

(continued)

FIGURE 17-5
continued

unaware that they are trying to exert control through the implementation of the objectives of MBO almost by fiat.[59]

EEO in the International Context

As you well know by now, employee selection in the United States is highly regulated by federal and state equal employment opportunity (EEO) legislation. The globalization of industry raises numerous EEO issues, some of which the U.S. courts have addressed and others of which they have not. Several texts devoted solely to employment law do not deal explicitly with international issues, indicating that this is not a well-developed area of employment law.[60] However, the following principles seem clear:

- U.S. companies are prohibited from basing employment decisions on such employee characteristics as race, sex, and age. This prohibition applies to international assignments, with the single exception that companies are not required to violate a host nation law. Thus, if a nation prohibits women from working in a specific business context, a U.S. company doing business in that nation is free to offer the particular international assignment covered by this host country law only to men. However, it should

Masculinity/Femininity, Organizational Characteristics, and Selected HR Practices

MASCULINITY	Dominant Values	Sample Countries	Organizational Features	Reward Practices	Staffing/Appraisal Practices
HIGH	• Material possessions important • Men given higher power and status than women • Rigid gender stereotypes • Gender inequities in pay accepted as a given	• Austria • Mexico • Germany • United States	• Some occupations labeled as "male," others as "female" • Fewer women in higher-level positions	• Differential pay policies that allow for gender inequities • Tradition an acceptable basis for pay decisions • "Male" traits rewarded in promotions and other personnel decisions • Paternalistic benefits for women (such as paid maternity leave, day care, special work hours)	• De facto preferential treatment for men in hiring/promotion decisions into higher-level jobs (even if it is illegal) • "Glass ceiling" for women • Occupational segregation • Only small proportion of men supervised by women • "Male" traits (such as aggressiveness, initiative, leadership) highly valued in appraisals
LOW	• Quality of life valued more than material gain • Men not believed to be inherently superior • Minimal gender stereotyping • Strong belief in equal pay for jobs of equal value, regardless of workers' gender	• The Netherlands • Norway • Sweden • Finland • Denmark	• More flexibility in career choice for men and women • More women in higher-level jobs	• Jobs evaluated without regard for gender of job holders • Focus on work content rather than tradition to assess value of different jobs • Well-developed "equity goals" for pay determination • "Masculine" traits carry no special value for promotions and other personnel decisions • Few perks based on gender	• Gender deemphasized in hiring/promotion decisions for any job • More women in upper-level positions • Occupational integration between the sexes • Little stigma for men to be supervised by women • Appraisals not biased in favor of male-oriented characteristics

Long-Term/Short-Term Orientation, Organizational Characteristics, and Selected HR Practices

LONG-TERM/SHORT-TERM ORIENTATION	Dominant Values	Sample Countries	Organizational Features	Reward Practices	Staffing/Appraisal Practices
HIGH	• Future-oriented • Delayed gratification • Persistence • Long-term goals	• Japan • Hong Kong • China	• Stable organizations • Low employee turnover • Strong company culture	• Long-term rewards • Seniority as basis for pay • Managers rewarded for multiyear accomplishments • Reliance on qualitative measures to distribute rewards • No expectation of frequent pay adjustments	• Slow promotions • Promotions from within • High employment security • Minimal feedback • High emphasis on saving employees' face • High emphasis on coaching versus evaluation • High investment in training and employee development
LOW	• Past- or present-oriented • Immediate gratification • Change course of action as necessary • Short-term goals	• United States • Indonesia	• Changing organization • High employee turnover • Weak company culture	• Short-term rewards • Recent performance as a basis for pay • Managers rewarded for annual accomplishments • Reliance on quantitative measures to distribute rewards • High expectation of frequent pay adjustments	• Fast promotions • Internal and external hires • Low employment security • High appraisal feedback • Low emphasis on saving employees' face • High emphasis on evaluation versus coaching • Low investment in training and employee development

FIGURE 17–5

continued

be noted that most countries that openly discriminate against their own female citizens are quite flexible in dealing with U.S. companies' female employees. Therefore, companies should not make exclusions automatically.

- Foreign national employees of U.S. companies working in their own country or in some other foreign country are not covered by U.S. employment law. For instance, the U.S. Supreme Court ruled that a Saudi Arabian citizen working for an American oil company in Saudi Arabia could not sue his employer under Title VII.[61]
- Under the Immigration Control and Reform Act of 1986, people who are not U.S. citizens but who are living, and have legal work status, in the United States may not be discriminated against.

Important Caveats

The effectiveness of an HRM practice depends on how well it matches a culture's value system. Even so, managers need to keep several caveats in mind.

- *"National culture" may be an elusive concept.* For this reason, managers should be careful not to be guided by stereotypes that hold some truth but may not apply to very many people in a culture. Stereotyping is a great danger in large, heterogeneous countries like the United States, where cultural differences are often huge, but it can also cause problems even in relatively homogeneous nations. For instance, Western German firms hiring Eastern German workers frequently found that the latter reacted negatively to incentive systems that had been used successfully with their Western German counterparts—despite the fact that the two groups shared the same language, ethnicity, and cultural background. The Eastern Germans distrusted such incentive schemes, reported they felt manipulated by management, and shunned those workers who outproduced others.[62]
- *Corporate headquarters sometimes blame international personnel problems on cultural factors without careful study.* Often personnel problems have little to do with cultural values and much to do with poor management. For example, a U.S. company introduced individual incentives for R&D employees at its English subsidiary. This policy created intense conflict, lack of cooperation, and declining performance. Top managers blamed the strong role of labor unions in England for these disappointing results. In fact, a large amount of evidence indicates that individual-based incentives are counterproductive when the nature of the task requires extensive teamwork (as is the case in R&D). The outcome in this case had nothing to do with national culture.[63]
- *Hard data on the success or failure of different HRM practices as a function of national culture are practically nonexistent.* This means that judgment calls, gut feeling, and some trial and error based on a fine-tuned cultural sensitivity and openmindedness are mandatory in international HRM.
- *Different cultures often have very different notions of right and wrong.* In many cases, corporate headquarters may have to impose its own value system across multiple nations with conflicting value structures. For example, child labor is common in many Asian and African countries. The corporation may choose to avoid such practices on ethical grounds, but it must recognize that doing so can put it at a competitive disadvantage because local firms that have no qualms about using child labor will have lower labor costs.

A QUESTION OF ETHICS

In some areas of the world business practices that are contrary to Western values—such as child labor, payment of bribes to government officials, and sex or race discrimination in hiring and promotion—are common. Should U.S. corporations and their expatriate representatives refuse to engage in such practices even if doing so would put the firm at a competitive disadvantage?

Finally, in this chapter we have focused on the HR challenges faced by U.S. companies doing business abroad. But it is also true that foreign companies face many challenges when setting up operations in the United States. For example, cultural and social differences have been the source of great tension at the Mitsubishi Motors plant in Illinois, where a group of women has filed sexual harassment charges against plant management. For background and more details, see the Issues and Applications feature titled "Culturally Accepted Sexual Harassment at Mitsubishi?"

Issues + Applications

Culturally Accepted Sexual Harassment at Mitsubishi?

Sometimes cultural differences can lead to litigation. Consider the experience of Mitsubishi:

Citizens of Normal, Illinois, were thrilled when Mitsubishi Motors opened a $650 million assembly plant in their town in the late 1980s. The plant employs some 4,000 people, including 70 Japanese nationals—all of them managers—and almost 900 women. Assembly-line and maintenance workers make about $18 an hour and, with overtime and shift-preference pay, can earn annual incomes as high as $50,000 to $60,000.

For that kind of paycheck, many of the women who work at this and other auto plants are willing to shoulder some boorish behavior in addition to the tough, sometimes monotonous job on the line. Others are not. As early as 1992, female employees at Mitsubishi began to complain of sexual misbehavior on the factory floor. They reported obscene, crude sketches of genital organs and sex acts, and names of female workers scratched into unpainted car bodies moving along the assembly line....Women were called various obscene names, and explicit sexual graffiti were scrawled on rest-area and bathroom walls.

After repeated appeals to management and to their United Auto Workers local brought no relief, a group of 29 women filed a private suit against Mitsubishi charging "relentless sex discrimination, sexual harassment, sexual abuse from male colleagues and, in many cases, from their male supervisors." The suit charges that Mitsubishi's Japanese managers were complicitious by their complacency. This is because, they allege, Japan's manager society is far more sexist than America's. For instance, in Japan women are almost unheard of in management.

Mitsubishi's American managers—all men—got a first-hand glimpse of this male-dominated culture when they spent time in Japan training. After work, the men were routinely taken to clubs where sexually explicit entertainment was available—a practice that was to be repeated in Normal. This kind of behavior, the complaint declared, has "contributed to an atmosphere in which males in the plant widely believe that management will tolerate abusive activities toward women."

After the EEOC investigators interviewed more than 100 current and former female employees at the plant, it brought a separate suit against the company in 1996, charging that the Japanese-managed plant created a "hostile and abusive work environment" and not only failed to take appropriate action in cases where the complaints were made, but actually retaliated against the women who made them.

Source: Excerpted from Jaroff, L. (1996, June 6). Assembly-line sexism? *Time*, pp. 56–57.

▸ Human Resource Management and Exporting Firms

Our discussion so far has focused on larger firms with international facilities (that is, those in Stages 3–5 of internationalization). However, the practices we've discussed are also relevant to smaller firms that are interested solely in exporting their products. It is estimated that only about 20% of U.S. firms with fewer than 500 employees have ever been active exporters, a percentage that lags way behind that found in most industrialized nations. At least 30,000 small firms in the United States have the potential to export competitively but do not do so.[64]

A number of studies have shown that the key impediments to exporting are (1) lack of knowledge of international markets, business practices, and competition and (2) lack of management commitment to generating international sales.[65] These impediments can be largely attributed to poor utilization of human resources within U.S. firms rather than to external factors. There is some evidence that a company that clearly reinforces international activities in its HRM practices is more likely to fare better in its export attempts.[66] Reinforcing international activities in HRM practices requires a company to:

- Explicitly consider international experience when making promotion and recruitment decisions, particularly to the senior management ranks.
- Provide developmental activities designed to equip employees with the skills and knowledge necessary to carry out their jobs in an international context. Developmental activi-

ties that enhance a firm's ability to compete globally include (1) programs designed to provide specific job skills and competencies in international business, (2) opportunities for development and growth in the international field, and (3) the use of appraisal processes that explicitly consider international activities as part of performance reviews.

- Create career ladders that take into account short- and long-term international strategies.
- Design a reward structure that motivates key organizational players to take full advantage of the company's export potential. Reinforcing desired export-related behaviors is likely to increase commitment to foreign sales as managers devote greater attention to skill development, information gathering, and scanning the environment for international opportunities.

The decision to export will require CEOs and senior marketing personnel to spend a significant time away from the office attending trade shows and developing relationships with distributors and companies abroad. Particularly in small companies, this means that the staff back home must be empowered to make decisions regarding the running of the business, with the traveling CEOs and executives keeping in touch via phone or fax.

The process of making the right export connections and establishing relationships can be slow and painstaking, but for many small firms, patience has paid off. Hurley Chicago, Inc., of Alsip, Illinois, a 12-employee manufacturer of water filtration systems, now sells 62% of its products overseas, with 15% going to Japan. Hurley's president makes annual trips to Tokyo to visit the president of James Corporation, the largest distributor of Hurley water systems worldwide. The two executives had to surmount language barriers before they could work together to overcome the obstacles to marketing Hurley products in Japan: Japanese government sanctions, differences between Japanese and U.S. plumbing, and resistance to direct marketing. Eventually the obstacles were overcome, and today Hurley Chicago encourages other businesses to be patient and flexible in their exporting efforts because the payoff is worth it.[67]

Summary and Conclusions

The Stages of International Involvement. Firms progress through five stages as they internationalize their operations: (1) domestic operations, (2) export operations, (3) subsidiaries or joint ventures, (4) multinational operations, and (5) transnational operations. The higher the stage, the more HR practices need to be adapted to diverse cultural, economic, political, and legal environments.

Determining the Mix of Host-Country and Expatriate Employees. In managing its overseas subsidiaries, a firm can choose an ethnocentric, polycentric, or geocentric approach. Firms tend to rely on expatriates more when sufficient local talent is unavailable, the firm is trying to create a corporatewide global vision, international and domestic units are highly interdependent, the political situation is unstable, and there are significant cultural differences between the host country and the home country.

The Challenges of Expatriate Assignments. An important part of international HRM is managing expatriate employees, both during their international assignments and when they return home. International assignments fail because of career blockage, culture shock, lack of predeparture cross-cultural training, an overemphasis on technical qualifications, the use of such assignments to get rid of troublesome employees, and family problems. Upon returning, expatriates may meet with a lack of respect for their acquired skills, a loss of status, poorly planned jobs, and reverse culture shock.

Enhancing the Effectiveness of Expatriate Assignments. To avoid problems in the international arena, a sensible set of HR policies should be put in place. In selecting people for international assignments, employers should emphasize cultural sensitivity, establish a selection board of expatriates, require previous international experience when possible, explore the possibility of hiring the foreign-born who can later serve as "expatriates," and screen candidates' spouses and families. Cross-cultural training programs of various lengths and levels of rigor can be implemented to prepare employees for their assignments. In terms of career development for expatriates, companies should position international assignments as a step toward advancement within the firm and provide support for expatriates. To avoid problems in the compensation area, companies should provide expatriates with enough disposable income and incentive bonuses, and avoid having expatriates fill the same or lower-ranking jobs than locals hold in the international operation.

Developing HRM Policies in a Global Context. Managers should not simply transfer abroad HRM practices based on the home country's social and cultural standards. Rather, they should mold these practices to the cultural environments in which the international facilities are located. In general, the more an HRM practice contradicts prevailing societal norms, the more likely it will fail.

Human Resource Management and Exporting Firms. Many firms have the potential to export profitably. A company is more likely to fare better in its export attempts when it clearly reinforces international activities by (1) explicitly considering international experience in hiring decisions, (2) providing developmental activities to equip employees with international skills, (3) creating career ladders for internationally experienced employees, and (4) designing a reward structure that motivates employees to begin export activities.

Key Terms

culture shock, 522
ethnocentric approach, 519
expatriate, 518
geocentric approach, 519
joint venture, 519
multinational corporation (MNC), 518
polycentric approach, 519
transnational corporation, 518
wholly owned subsidiary, 519

Discussion Questions

1. Some low-wage developing countries are finding profitable ways to produce and export illegal versions of music cassettes, computer software, and CD-ROMs at a fraction of the U.S. cost. For instance, CDs made in China at 36 cents each are sold in Hong Kong for $4.30 each. Local governments' attempts to crack down on these producers (usually as a result of U.S. pressure) have generally been unsuccessful. From a human resource perspective, what can U.S. firms and their foreign subsidiaries do to meet this challenge?
2. How might an international firm trying to adapt HRM practices to the local culture produce worse results than it would produce by "exporting" HRM practices from the home office?
3. Under what specific conditions would you recommend an ethnocentric, a polycentric, and a geocentric approach to interternational staffing?
4. U.S. multinationals experience a much higher rate of early returns with their expatriate employees than European and Japanese MNCs do. What explains this difference? What HRM policies and procedures would you develop to reduce this problem?
5. Expatriates frequently complain that when they accept an international assignment they put their career on hold while their peers in the home office continue to climb the corporate ladder. To what would you attribute this perception? What recommendations would you make to change it?
6. Some people believe that U.S. multinationals should serve as vehicles for cultural change in developing countries by introducing modern U.S. HRM practices and instilling values (such as punctuality and efficiency) in the work force that are necessary for industrialization. Do you agree with this assertion? Explain your position.
7. The recent history of law and business ethics shows that, to remain competitive, a number of U.S. MNCs are willing to engage in bribery in foreign countries where bribes are the custom. Similarly, a few years back, many U.S. MNCs acquiesced in the policy of apartheid in South Africa, despite the fact that such behavior would not be tolerated in the United States. Some argue that a multinational company should be able to use whatever HRM practices produce the most profits at the lowest costs, as long as these practices comply with the labor codes and laws of each country in which the MNC operates. Do you agree or disagree? State your reasons.
8. Some studies indicate that U.S. firms do not exploit international markets for their products as well as firms in other industrialized nations do. How can a firm use its human resources to change this disparity?

MINICASE 1 "The Saudis Made Us Do It"

The Civil Rights Act of 1991 extended coverage of EEO laws and regulations to U.S. citizens working abroad for U.S.-controlled companies. However, the act states that where the foreign country's laws conflict with U.S. EEO laws, the foreign laws will apply. In the following court case, reported in the *Bureau of National Affairs Employee Relations Weekly*, a U.S. company was found not liable under the Age Discrimination in Employment Act for firing two older, Saudi Arabia–based American workers:

> ...The U.S. Court of Appeals for the Tenth Circuit recently ruled that an American company doing contract work in Saudi Arabia was not liable for discharging two older workers at the request of the Saudi government (*Brownlee v. Lear Siegler Management Services Corp.*)....
>
> In early 1990 Harry Brownlee and Roy Waddell signed three-year employment contracts with Lear Siegler to work in Saudi Arabia under the direction of the Royal Saudi Air Force....Sometime after Brownlee and Waddell arrived in Saudi Arabia, air force personnel insisted that they were unsuitable for their assigned duties, allegedly because of their age, which was not specified in the decision. When Lear's efforts to dissuade the Saudi air force from its position failed, the company capitulated and discharged Brownlee and Waddell. The two men filed suit, charging breach of contract and age discrimination. A federal magistrate rejected the claims, finding that Lear Siegler "only terminated the plaintiffs because of directions by the RSAF and not because of their age."...The magistrate concluded that Brownlee and Waddell had "failed to prove any obligation" on the part of Lear Siegler "for the actions, deeds or thoughts" of the Saudi air force or the Saudi Arabian government.

Discussion Questions

1. What are the implications of this court case for U.S. multinational companies? For their expatriate employees?
2. What can U.S. multinationals do to prepare expatriate employees for encountering age, gender, or racial discrimination in host countries?

Source: (1994, March 7). *BNA's Employee Relations Weekly*. U.S. company not liable for firing older workers at Saudi Arabia's request. *12* (10), 255.

MINICASE 2 The Mark of Tiny Fingerprints

How should multinational firms behave regarding child labor laws in other countries? Consider the following:

> Kathie Lee Gifford tearfully confessed on her morning talk show in the summer of 1996 that her Wal-Mart outfits were made by Honduran girls paid 31 cents an hour—"but she didn't know, she didn't know." Made in the U.S.A., a lobbying group, soon after reminded consumers that Michael Jordan reportedly earns $20 million a year endorsing Nike sneakers, claiming that this is more than the total annual payroll for the thousands of Indonesians who help make them.
>
> The flaying of celebrities like Gifford and Jordan made it easy to miss the point. For years children have been sold as slaves, blinded or maimed for crying or rebelling, or trying to return home, ill-fed, bone-weary, short-lived. They file the scissors blades, mix the gunpowder for the firecrackers, knot the carpets, stitch the soccer balls with needles longer than their fingers. Human-rights groups guess there may be 200 million children around the world, from China to South America, working full time—no play, no school, no chance. All of which raises the question, once the news lands on the front page: How much are we willing to sacrifice the children of other countries to give our children what they want?
>
> Americans search for bargains with enduring passion, but it is hard to find them—such as a handmade rug for only $700—without tiny fingerprints on them somewhere. If child-labor and safety laws were truly enforced, trade experts say, whole industries in many countries would collapse, at great cost to both developing and developed economies.

Discussion Questions

1. Do you think U.S. companies have a moral responsibility to fight exploitative practices in foreign countries, even if doing so means putting the company at a competitive disadvantage?
2. Nike's Indonesian workers are paid about 50 cents an hour. While that amount may seem like slave wages, it is twice the country's minimum wage and workers are eager to work for that price. Is Nike being fair? Why or why not?

Source: Adapted from Dickerson, J. F., Rivera, E., and Shari, M. (1996, June 17). Cause celebre. *Time*, 28–30.

CASE 1 *Two Sides to Every Story*

Four years ago Pressman Company, a U.S.-based firm, entered into a joint venture with a Polish firm to manufacture a variety of plumbing supplies, both for the internal Polish market and for export to neighboring countries. Last week Pressman received the resignation of Jonathan Smith, an expatriate from the home office who nine months ago was appointed general manager of the Polish subsidiary for a four-year term. In the previous 39 months, two other expatriate general managers had also decided to call it quits long before their foreign assignments expired. In addition, 13 of the 28 U.S. technicians sent to work in the Polish facility returned home early. George Stevens, a senior vice president in corporate headquarters, estimates that these expatriates' resignations and early returns have cost the company at least $4 million in direct expenses and probably three times as much in lost production and delayed schedules.

When he heard rumors of widespread discontent in the work force and a threatened strike, Stevens decided to travel to the Polish facility to find out what was happening. In the course of interviewing five local supervisors and ten workers with the help of a translator, he repeatedly heard three complaints: first, the American managers and technicians thought they "knew it all" and treated their Polish counterparts with contempt; second, the American employees had unrealistic expectations of what could be accomplished within the stipulated deadlines established at corporate headquarters; and third, American employees were making three times more money than their Polish counterparts and enjoyed looking down their noses at locals by driving fancy cars, living in expensive homes, and hiring an army of maids and helpers.

When he arrived back in the States, Stevens also interviewed Jonathan Smith and five of the technicians who returned early. Some common reasons for their early resignations emerged from these interviews. First, they described their Polish colleagues as "lazy" and "just doing the minimum to get by while keeping a close eye on the clock for breaks, lunches, and go-home time." Pushing them to work harder only provoked anger. Second, they indicated that the Polish workers and managers had a sense of entitlement with little intrinsic motivation and initiative. Third, they complained of loneliness and their inability to communicate in Polish. Finally, most reported that their spouses and children were homesick and longing to return to the States after the first month or so. As he sits in his office, George Stevens is staring blankly out the window, trying to decide what to do.

Critical Thinking Questions

1. Based on what you have learned in this chapter, what do you think are the underlying problems in the Polish subsidiary of Pressman Company?
2. How would you account for the sharp differences in the perceptions of the Polish locals and U.S. expatriates?
3. If you were hired as a consultant by Pressman Company, what steps would you recommend that Stevens take?

Cooperative Learning Exercises

4. Students form pairs. One student plays Stevens, the other an HRM consultant. Role-play the initial meeting between these two, with Stevens explaining the problems at the Polish plant and the consultant identifying the additional information that will be needed to get to the root of the difficulties, and how this information might be collected.
5. Students form into groups of four or five. Each group's task is to make suggestions for the content of a training program for the next group of employees to be sent to Pressman's Polish plant. Besides information from this chapter, use principles you learned from Chapters 4 (Managing Diversity) and 8 (Training the Work Force) to develop these programs. When the task is finished (approximately 20 minutes), a member from each group should present the group's recommendations to the class. How similar or dissimilar are the groups' recommendations? Why? Which recommendations are likely to be most effective?

CASE 2 *Are Culture-Specific HR Policies a Good Idea?*

Over the past ten years, East Computer Company has grown from a domestic producer of IBM clones in Boston to a multinational company with assembly plants in four foreign locations. The company's personnel policies were developed five years ago, prior to East Computer's international expansion, by a task force headed by the vice president for HRM in Boston. The company's CEO has just appointed a new task force to examine the extent to which current domestic personnel policies can be "exported" to East's new international locations. The essential elements of these policies are the following:

1. All job openings are posted to allow any employee to apply for a position.
2. Selection is based on merit. Appropriate selection devices (for example, tests, structured interviews, and the like) are used to ensure proper implementation of this policy.
3. Nepotism is expressly forbidden.
4. Promotion from within is the norm whenever feasible.
5. Equal employment opportunities are available to all, regardless of sex, race, national origin, or religion.
6. Pay for various positions is established through a rational process that includes both job evaluation and market survey data.
7. There is equal pay for equal work, regardless of sex, race, national origin, or religion.
8. Goals are jointly set by supervisor and subordinate, with an annual formal appraisal session at which both parties have the chance to discuss progress toward goal achievement. The appraisal is used both to provide performance feedback to the employee and as a basis for merit pay decisions.

As a first step in evaluating these policies, the vice president for HRM classified the countries where East's facilities are located according to Hofstede's dimensions. She came up with the matrix below.

You have been hired by East Computer Company to help management develop personnel policies for each of the four international facilities. Ideally, management would prefer to use the same policies that it uses in the United States to maintain consistency and reduce administrative problems. However, the vice president for HRM has made a strong case for "tailor-made" personnel policies that are suitable to each facility's cultural environment.

CULTURAL DIMENSIONS

Facility Location	Power Distance	Individualism	Uncertainty Avoidance	Masculinity	Long-Term Orientation
Australia	Low	High	Medium	Medium	Low
Mexico	High	Low	High	High	Medium
England	Low	High	Low	High	Low
Norway	Low	Medium	Medium	Low	High

Critical Thinking Questions

1. Given East Computer Company's present personnel policies, what problems is the company likely to face in each facility if it transports its domestic policies abroad?
2. How would you change or adapt each of the company's current personnel policies to better fit the cultural environment of each international facility?
3. What could go wrong if your recommendations are implemented? In other words, what warnings would you give to East's management along with your recommendations?

Cooperative Learning Exercises

4. Students break into groups of five. One student role-plays a consultant who is conducting an exercise to uncover possible problems in uniform application of the company's current policy. Each of the other four students takes the role of advocate for one of the four international locations. Each advocate should make an argument for or against keeping specific parts of East's existing HR policies.
5. Students form groups of four students, with each group acting as the advocate for one of the four international locations. After deciding which policies to keep and which to change, a representative from each group presents the group's recommendations to the class. Following these brief presentations, the class discusses the costs and benefits of culture-specific HR policies.

HRM Simulation

Right now, your company is selling its products in the domestic market. However, over the next ten years, it will be important for the firm to start entering international markets in order to grow. To save on labor costs and compete more effectively with other firms, it may also be necessary to open some facilities overseas, either as wholly owned subsidiaries or joint ventures. While this is a long-term scenario, the CEO believes that it is now time to begin thinking about these issues and to develop the necessary human resources to support these efforts. Given all the decisions that your team is making as part of the simulation, in which areas (for example, performance appraisal, selection, compensation) would you start preparing the company for an international future? How? Explain.

We invite you to visit the Gómez-Mejía/Balkin/Cardy page on the Prentice Hall Web site:

http://www.prenhall.com/gomez

You can also visit the Web sites for these companies, featured within this chapter:

Amoco	http://www.amoco.com
Electrolux	http://www.electrolux.com
James River Corporation	http://www.jamesrivercorp.com
Mazda Motor Corporation	http://www.mazda.com
Nike	http://www.nike.com
Olivetti	http://www.olivetti.com
Rockwell International	http://www.rockwell.com

Endnotes

1. Adapted from Mellow, C. (1996, June 6). Brain rush: Why western business is investing in Russian R&D. *Fortune*, 83–84.
2. Deans, C. P., and Kane, M. J. (1992). *International dimensions of information systems and technology.* Boston, MA: PWS-Kent.
3. Barrett, A. (1995, April 17). It is a small business world. *Business Week*, 96–97.
4. Naughton, K., Horn, R., and Hill-Updike, E. (1996, June 3). GM starts up a long hill in Asia. *Business Week*, 56.
5. Laabs, J. J. (1991, August). The global talent search. *Personnel Journal,* 39.
6. *ACA News* (1996, June). International, 32.
7. Dowling, P., and Welch, D. E. (1991). The strategic adaptation process in international human resource management: A case study. *Human Resource Planning, 14*(1), 61–69.
8. Beck, E. (1995, May 1). Foreign companies in Hungary concerned about wage increase. *The Wall Street Journal*, B13(1).
9. Hardy, L., and Barham, K. (1990). International management development in the 1990s. *Journal of European Industrial Training, 14*(6), 31.
10. Swaak, R. A. (1995, September-October). Role of human resources in China. *Compensation and Benefits Review*, 39–46; Sheridan, W. R. and Hansen, P. T. (1996, Spring). Linking International business and expatriate compensation strategies. *ACA Journal*, 66–78.
11. Boyacigiller, N. (1990). Role of expatriates in the management of interdependence, complexity, and risk of MNNs. *Journal of International Business Studies,* 3rd quarter, 357–378.
12. Dunn, E. (1991, January). Global outlook: Whirlpool Corporation. *Personnel Journal,* 52.
13. Mendenhall, M., and Oddou, G. (1985). Dimensions of expatriate acculturation. *Academy of Management Review, 10*(1), 39–47.
14. *Fortune* (1995, October 16). From the front, 225.
15. *ACA News* (1996, June). International, 32; *Fortune* (1995, October 16). From the front. 225; Swaak, R. (1995, November-December). Expatriate failures: Too many, too much cost, too little planning. *Compensation and Benefits Review*, 47–75; Stephens, G. K., and Black, S. (1991). The impact of spouse's career-orientation on managers during international transfers. *Journal of Management Studies, 28*(4), 417–429; and Tung, R. (1988). *The new expatriates: Managing human resources abroad.* Cambridge, MA: Bellinger.
16. Gómez-Mejía, L. R., and Balkin, D. B. (1987). The determinants of managerial satisfaction with the expatriation and repatriation process. *Journal of Management Development, 6,* 7–18; Hamill, J. (1989). Expatriate policies in British multinationals. *Journal of General Management, 14*(4), 19–26; and Hixon, A. L. (1986, March). Why corporations make haphazard overseas staffing decisions. *Personnel Administrator,* 91–94.
17. Fuchsberg, G. (1992, January 9). As costs of overseas assignments climb, firms select expatriates more carefully. *The Wall Street Journal,* B1.
18. Rowland, M. (1993, December 5). Thriving in a foreign environment. *The New York Times,* Sect. 3, 17.
19. Swaak, 1995.
20. *Id.*
21. Dunbar, E., and Katcher, A. (1990, September). Preparing managers for foreign assignments. *Training and Development Journal,* 45–47.

22. *Fortune*, 1995.
23. *Personal interview* conducted by authors.
24. Swaak, 1995.
25. Dallas, S. (1995, May 15). Working overseas: Rule no. 1: Don't diss the locals. *Business Week*, 8.
26. Tung, 1988.
27. Swaak, 1995.
28. Pascoe, R. (1992, March 2). Employers ignore expatriate wives at their own peril. *The Wall Street Journal,* A10.
29. Oster, P. (1993, November 1). The fast track leads overseas. *Business Week,* 64–68.
30. Oddou, G. R., and Mendenhall, M. E. (1991, January–February). Succession planning for the 21st century: How well are we grooming our future business leaders? *Business Horizons,* 26–35.
31. *Id.*
32. Gómez-Mejía and Balkin, 1987.
33. Oddou and Mendenhall, 1991, 29.
34. Gómez-Mejía and Balkin, 1987.
35. *Personal interview* conducted by authors.
36. Gómez-Mejía and Balkin, 1987.
37. *Personal interview* conducted by authors.
38. *CompFlash.* (1994, March). Expatriate numbers should continue to rise, 9.
39. Oster, P. (1993). The fast track leads overseas.
40. Hixon, 1986.
41. Bird, A., and Makuda, M. (1989). Expatriates in their own home: A new twist in the human resource management strategies of Japanese MNCs. *Human Resource Management, 28*(4), 437–453.
42. Shellenbarger, S. (1991, September 6). Spouses must pass test before global transfers. *The Wall Street Journal,* B1.
43. Barrett, A., 1995, 96–98.
44. Beamish, P. W., Killing, J. P., Secraw, D. J., and Morrison, A. J. (1994). *International Management.* Burr Ridge, FL: Irwin.
45. Lublin, J. S. (1992, August 4). Companies use cross-cultural training to help their employees adjust abroad. *The Wall Street Journal,* B1, B3.
46. Hagerty, B. (1993a, June 14). Trainers help expatriate employees build bridges to different cultures. *The Wall Street Journal,* B1, B3.
47. Kendall, D. W. (1981). Repatriation: An ending and a beginning. *Business Horizons, 24*(6), 21–25.
48. *The Wall Street Journal.* (1991, December 6). Expensive cities for expatriates, R1.
49. Fuchsberg, 1992.
50. Lublin, J. S. (1993, March 12). Jobs in Eastern Europe demand more goodies. *The Wall Street Journal,* B1.
51. Healey, M. A. (1996, July-August). Managing compensation in a globalizing market. *ACA News*, 16–17; and Reynolds, C. (1994). *Compensation basics for North American expatriates.* Scottsdale, AZ: American Compensation Association.
52. Bennett, A. (1993, April 21). What's an expatriate? *The Wall Street Journal,* R5.
53. *Id.*
54. Cook, M. (Ed.). (1993). *The human resources yearbook, 1993–1994 Edition,* 3.14–3.16.
55. *Business Week.* (1990, May 14). The stateless corporation, 98–105.
56. Hofstede, G. (1980). *Culture's consequences.* Beverly Hills, CA: Sage, and (1993). Cultural constraints in management theories. *Academy of Management Executive, 7,* 81–94.
57. Jaeger, A. (1986). Organization development and national culture: Where's the fit? *Academy of Management Review, 11*(1), 178–190.
58. Hofstede, 1980, 58.
59. Jaeger, 1986, 180.
60. Player, M. A. (1991). *Federal law of employment discrimination.* St. Paul, MN: West Publishing; Twomey, D. P. (1994), (3rd ed.). *Equal employment opportunity.* Cincinnati, OH: South-Western; and Ledvinka, J., and Scarpello, V. G. (1991). *Federal regulation of personnel and human resource management,* (2nd ed.). Boston: PWS-Kent.
61. Player, 1991, 28.
62. Gómez-Mejía, L. R., and Welbourne, T. (1991). Compensation strategies in a global context. *Human Resource Planning, 14*(1), 38; see also Woodruff, D., and Widman, M. (1996, June 17). East Germany is still a mess—$580 billion later. *Business Week,* 58.
63. Gómez-Mejía and Welbourne, 1991.
64. Barrett, 1995.
65. Cavusgil, T. S. (1984). Organizational characteristics associated with export activity. *Journal of Management Studies, 24*(1), 3–21.
66. Gómez-Mejía, L. R. (1988). The role of human resources strategy in export performance: A longitudinal study. *Strategic Management Journal, 9*(3), 493–505.
67. *Business America.* (1993, November 1). Exporting pays off, 28.

VIDEO CASE

The Changing Face of Labor

ABCNEWS

Technology, the changing nature of work, downsizing, outsourcing, and other characteristics of today's workplace have all had important effects on labor—the human resource of organizations. It used to be that unions set the tone in many industries. Strikes and the threat of strikes were often part of the negotiation and power struggle between labor and management. Better wages, better benefits, and job security were typical outcomes of the adversarial relationship between labor and management. Workplaces are changing, however. Many organizations are much flatter than before and make much less distinction between labor and management. Key words in today's workplace are *cooperation* and *teamwork* rather than *confrontation* and *collective bargaining agreement.* In addition, the dynamic new nature of the workplace means that workers need to be flexible and adaptable to a variety of situations. In turn, this means that employees must learn new skills to remain vital contributors. However, these contributions are increasingly made without assurance of job security. American workers are now more educated but less secure in their jobs than ever before.

Unions are not as powerful a force as they used to be, and they represent a decreasing percentage of the labor force. When unions do strike, their members might lose their jobs to replacement workers. Air-traffic controllers went on strike about 15 years ago, and President Reagan fired them. Their union was destroyed. Union leaders view this presidential action as the beginning of the "dark ages" for organized labor, and claim that the labor picture today is bleak. There is limited or no job security, wages are generally flat, and most of the increase in jobs is taking place in the lower-paid service sector. These characteristics describe the general conditions in today's labor market, but things look much more positive in some organizations.

For example, in some organizations, such as United Airlines, the employees have a controlling interest in the firm. Such employee ownership can certainly align the interests of workers and management. As owners, employees don't want to strike or take other action to reduce the organization's effectiveness. A partnership rather than an adversarial relationship can be beneficial to both labor and management.

Discussion Questions

1. Is the current situation for labor better or worse today than it used to be? Explain.
2. The history of the relationship between labor and management in the United States has been one of shifting power between the two parties. Does the current labor situation as described in the video mean that management has won and labor has lost the power struggle?
3. Do you think organizations should be responsible for educating and retraining workers? If not, who should be responsible?
4. Evaluate the change from an adversarial to a partnership relationship with management. How can managers help to successfully and smoothly implement this change?

Appendix A

HRM and Business Periodicals

The following is an annotated listing of general business publications and specialized HRM publications. Many of these resources may prove helpful to you, not only in your study of HRM but also in your own career development. As we noted in the text, more and more companies are shifting career development responsibilities onto their employees, while providing them with tools for career planning. These tools can be the first in your career-planning toolkit.

General Business Periodicals

Across the Board. Conference Board. 845 Third Avenue, New York, NY 10022. Provides articles that present business topics in nontechnical terms. Articles range from discussions of general business issues to examinations of specific companies and industries.

Black Enterprise. Earl G. Graves Publishing Co. 130 Fifth Avenue, New York, NY 10011. *Black Enterprise* focuses on business, jobs, career potential, and financial opportunities as they relate to African, Caribbean, and African-American consciousness. Its annual list of the nation's top black businesses and financial institutions is considered an invaluable accounting of African-American business enterprises.

Business Week. McGraw-Hill, Inc. 1221 Avenue of the Americas, New York, NY 10020. The leading general business magazine, *Business Week* offers comprehensive coverage of the news and developments affecting the business world. It includes information on computers, finance, labor, industry, marketing, science, and technology.

Fast Company. P.O. Box 52760, Boulder, CO 80321-2760. Fairly new on the scene, *Fast Company* focuses on a wide variety of business topics and is geared toward giving companies an edge in a very competitive marketplace. The magazine's subtitle is "How smart business works."

Forbes. Forbes, Inc. 60 Fifth Avenue, New York, NY 10011. A general business magazine that celebrates capitalism. Short articles report on company activities, industry developments, economic trends, and investment tips.

Fortune. Time, Inc. Time & Life Building, Rockefeller Center, New York, NY 10020. *Fortune* reports on companies and industries, developments and trends. Its articles tend to be longer than those in other business magazines, and its frequent use of sidebars allows readers to learn more about corollary issues.

Harvard Business Review. Graduate School of Business Administration, Harvard University. Boston, MA 02163. This well-known product of Harvard Business School publishes articles in the areas of business and management. Topics include planning, manufacturing, and innovation. Each issue includes a case study.

Hispanic Business. P.O. Box 469038, Escondido, CA 92046-9038. A general business magazine focusing on a variety of business issues (including career opportunities, entrepreneurial ventures, and legislation) as they relate to Latino workers and Latino-owned businesses in the United States.

Inc.: The Magazine for Growing Companies. Goldhirsch Group, Inc. 38 Commercial Wharf, Boston, MA 02110. *Inc.* is targeted to the person involved in managing new, small, or growing companies. Articles focus on entrepreneurial ventures, general business topics, and profiles of successful managers.

Journal of Business Ethics. Kluwar Academic Publishers. 101 Philip Dr., Norwell, MA 02061. This journal publishes scholarly articles dealing with the ethical issues confronted in business. It is clearly written, free of technical jargon, and contains articles on such topics as ethics and business schools, competitor intelligence, corporate executives, and disasters.

Management Review. American Management Association. 135 West 50th St., New York, NY 10020. This monthly publication describes management trends, techniques, and issues for middle- and upper-level managers in the corporate and public sector.

Nation's Business: U.S. Chamber of Commerce. 1615 H St. N.W., Washington, DC 20062. *Nation's Business* reports on current business activities and topics such as quality, entrepreneurship, and going public. It is directed mainly to entrepreneurs and small business owners and managers. Each issue contains a feature on issues affecting family businesses.

Small Business Reports. American Management Association. 135 West 50th St., New York, NY 10020. Articles in this monthly magazine tend to offer practical advice for small business owners and managers. However, topics are of interest to all business managers.

The Wall Street Journal. Dow Jones & Co., Inc. 200 Liberty St., New York, NY 10281. With a greater circulation than either *The New York Times* or *USA Today*, this comprehensive national newspaper offers in-depth coverage of national and international finance and business. A must for anyone interested in the business of business.

Working Woman. Working Woman, Inc. 230 Park Avenue, New York, NY 10169. Geared toward the white-collar career woman interested in advancing in her field. Articles focus on career advancement, management, communicaiton skills, money management, and investment information. Features items on new technology, changing demographics, and profiles of successful businesswomen. Of special interest is the annual "Hottest Careers" issue featuring listings of up-and-coming occupations.

HRM Periodicals

ACA News. American Compensation Association, 14040 N. Northsight Blvd., Scottsdale, AZ 58260. Published monthly, this newsletter includes articles of interest to compensation practitioners. It also reports on the resources available to practitioners, as well as positions available in the field.

Academy of Management Executive. Pace University, P.O. Box 3020, Briarcliff Manor, NY 10510. Published quarterly and geared toward executives and students of business, this journal presents straightforward practical articles, many of them written by leading management scholars.

American Compensation Association (ACA) Journal. 14040 N. Northsight Blvd., Scottsdale, AZ 85260. The *ACA Journal* is a specialized publication of the American Compensation Association. Issues appear quarterly and feature six to eight articles on such compensation-related topics as pay for performance, compensation strategy, tax considerations, executive pay, and benefits.

Compensation & Benefits Review. American Management Association. 135 West 50th St., New York, NY 10020. A specialized publication of the American Management Association, this journal contains four to six articles in each issue, covering compensation management and strategy and such diverse topics as job evaluation as a barrier to excellence and compensating overseas executives. One invaluable feature is its condensations of noteworthy articles appearing in other business publications.

CompFlash. American Compensation Association, 14040 N. Northsight Blvd., Scottsdale, AZ 58260. Published monthly, this newsletter includes short articles and information on the latest trends/statistics useful for compensation management, including the most recent surveys.

Employee Relations Law Journal. Executive Enterprises, Inc. 22 West 21st St., New York, NY 10010. While geared toward attorneys specializing in employment law, in-house counsel, and HR executives, this journal contains practical advice that is not highly technical. Articles deal with such topics as personnel management techniques, legal compliance, and court cases, and such issues as sex discrimination, privacy in the workplace, and drug testing. Features up-to-date coverage of federal regulatory agency actions.

Employee Relations Weekly. Bureau of National Affairs. 1231 25th Street, N.W. Washington, DC 20037. This government publication covers such workplace issues as EEO developments, health and safety, pay and benefits, and policy and practices. Recent articles have touched on employee committees, domestic partner benefits, and sexual harassment. Useful for discussions of court cases relevant to employee relations.

HRMagazine. Society for Human Resource Management. 606 N. Washington St., Alexandria, VA 22314. Formerly called *Personnel Administrator*, this magazine offers in-depth coverage of all areas of HRM.

International Journal of Human Resource Management. Routledge Journals, 11 New Fetter Lane, London EC4P 4EE. Published monthly, this journal covers research on international HRM issues and trends.

Labor Notes. Labor and Education Research Project. 7435 Michigan Avenue, Detroit, MI 48210. This workers' magazine is as critical of big labor as it is of management. It features nationwide coverage of such issues as contracts, ongoing negotiation, boycotts, working conditions, and problems confronting women and minority workers. Useful for its "shop-floor" view and as counterbalance to the management perspective.

Monthly Labor Review. Bureau of Labor Statistics. U.S. Department of Labor, Washington, DC 20402. The source for U.S. labor statistics. Each issue carries four in-depth articles on labor-related topics.

Organizational Dynamics. American Management Association. 135 West 50th St., New York, NY 10020. Articles deal with appraisal systems and management systems in general, as well as with other relevant aspects of systems administration.

Personnel Journal. 245 Fischer Ave. B-2, Costa Mesa, CA 92626. *Personnel Journal* covers the full range of issues in human resources. There is extensive coverage of current HR policies and practices at actual companies, and each article contains company vital statistics. *Personnel Journal* also sponsors the annual Optimas Awards, which spotlight companies with excellent HR initiatives in a variety of categories.

Public Personnel Management. Personnel Management Association. 1617 Duke St., Alexandria, VA 22314. Research articles useful to personnel administrators in public-sector personnel management. Typical subjects are recruiting, interviewing, training, sick leave, and home-based employment.

Supervisory Management. American Management Association, 135 West 50th St., New York, NY 10020. Within its concise 12-page format, this magazine contains numerous brief articles offering practical advice on such topics as building quality awareness, handling problem employees, and conducting effective meetings.

Training & Development. American Society for Training & Development. 1640 King St., Alexandria, VA 22313. The official magazine of ASTD, *Training & Development* is directed toward HR professionals and other managers. It covers both practical issues and trends in training and development, including such topics as how to make a training video, how to train workers to write more clearly, and the ins and outs of successful diversity training.

Internet Resources

For the Internet addresses of companies and organizations relevant to the study of business in general and HRM in particular, see this book's endpapers.

APPENDIX B

QUANTITATIVE AND QUALITATIVE METHODS OF HR FORECASTING

This appendix provides a summary of various methods that may be used to forecast labor demand and supply. These methods are divided into two major groups: those that rely on statistical formulas (quantitative) and those that rely on expert judgments (qualitative).

Quantitative Methods of Forecasting HR Demand			
Method	***Description***	***Advantages***	***Disadvantages***
Moving Average	• Averages data about HR demand from recent periods and projects them into the future	• Simplicity. • Data easily available.	• Seasonal or cyclical patterns may be ignored. • Relies on past data.
Exponential Smoothing	• Forecasters can vary weights for HR demand assigned to different past time periods used to project future HR demand.	• May be used to take into account factors ignored by the moving average method (for example, cyclical patterns).	• Mathematical complexity. • Choice of weights may be arbitrary. • Relies on past data.
Trends Projections	• Numbers of people hired or requested placed on one axis; time is placed on the other axis. A straight line is plotted from past to future to predict HR demand.	• Easily explained to managers. • Easily prepared by HR planners.	• Rough estimates. • Relies on past data.
Regression	• Mathematical formula used to relate staffing to several variables (for example, output, product mix, per capita productivity).	• Can include many variables. • Efficient use of all available data.	• Mathematical complexity. • Requires large sample sizes. • Relies on past data.
Linear Programming	• Assesses required staffing level that matches desired output levels, subject to certain constraints (for example, budget, cost).	• Assesses what should be in the future, not what probably will be.	• Managers are skeptical of highly sophisticated methodology. • Numerous assumptions must be made.
Actuarial Models	• Relate turnover to such factors as age and seniority.	• Reflect past.	• May not be accurate in individual cases.
Simulations	• Use scenarios to test the effect of various personnel policies.	• Useful for considering alternative HR programs.	• Accuracy varies
Probability Matrixes	• Define "states" in the organization—such as strategy levels, performance ratings. • Identify time period.	• Help identify career patterns. • Help perform turnover analysis.	• Require some mathematical sophistication. • Accuracy varies.

Method	Description	Advantages	Disadvantages
First-Order Markov Model	• Multiply number of people in each job category by the probability of movement between job/position categories. Model assumes that current job/position category is the chief determinant of movement.	• Adequate for considering alternative effects of various HR strategies.	• Not adequate for long-term forecasts. • Requires mathematical sophistication.
Semi-Markov Model	• Same as first-order Markov model except that probability of movement is determined by (1) job/position category and (2) the individual's length of stay in the job class.	• More inclusive than a first-order Markov model.	• Not very useful for considering alternative effects of various HR strategies. • Requires mathematical sophistication.

Qualitative Methods of Forecasting HR Demand or Supply

Method	Description	Advantages	Disadvantages
Delphi Technique	• A group of experts exchanges several rounds of estimates of HR demand or supply, normally without meeting face to face. Feedback from other experts is used by each individual to "fine-tune" his or her independent estimate.	• Can involve key decision makers in process. • Can focus on what is expected or desired in future. • Not bound to the past.	• Highly subjective. • Judgments may not efficiently use objective data.
Nominal Group Technique	• A small group of experts meets face to face. Following a procedure that involves open discussion and private assessments, the group reaches a judgment concerning future HR demand or supply.	• Same as for Delphi technique. • Group discussions can facilitate exchange of ideas and greater acceptance of results by participants.	• Same as for Delphi technique. • Group pressure may lead to less accurate assessments that could be obtained through other means.

Source: Rothwell, W.J., and Kazanas, H.C. (1988). *Strategic human resources planning and management.* Englewood Cliffs, NJ: Prentice Hall.

Photo Credits

Chapter 1: Chapter Opener, A. Tannenbaum/Sygma; 21, Brain Smale/Brian Smale Photography.

Chapter 2: Chapter Opener, James Schnepf/James Schnepf Photography, Inc.; 61, Ted Thai/Time Picture Syndication.

Chapter 3: Chapter Opener, Adam Tanner/Comstock; 93, Jose L. Pelaez/The Stock Market; 98, Courtesy of Apple Computer, Inc.

Chapter 4: Chapter Opener, Ron Chapple/FPG International; 126, Esbin-Anderson/The Image Works; 135, John Abbott/John Abbott Photography.

Chapter 5: Chapter Opener, Dennis MacDonald/PhotoEdit; 157, The Center of Health Resources—Hospital Council of Southern California; 162, Bob Daemnwich/Stock Boston.

Chapter 6: Chapter Opener, John Giordano/SABA Press Photos, Inc.; 187, Roger Mastroianni.

Chapter 7: Chapter Opener, Jeff Greenberg/PhotoEdit; 214, Bruce Ayres/Tony Stone Images.

Chapter 8: Chapter Opener, Michael L. Abramson; 246, Mark L. Karwisch/Firearms Training Systems, Inc. (FATS); 246, Tom Sheppard/Tony Stone Images.

Chapter 9: Chapter Opener, Ron Lowery/Tony Stone Images; 277, Jay Dickman; 287, Walter Hodges/Tony Stone Images.

Chapter 10: Chapter Opener, Mark Harwood/Tony Stone Images; 302, Jim Leynse/SABA Press Photos, Inc.; 321, Andy Sacks/Tony Stone Images.

Chapter 11: Chapter Opener, Michael L. Abramson; 337, Nina Berman/SIPA Press; 340, James Schnepf/Gamma-Liaison, Inc.

Chapter 12: Chapter Opener, Ariel Skelley/The Stock Market; 372, Tom Stewart/The Stock Market.

Chapter 13: Chapter Opener, Simon & Schuster/PH College; 403, Viacom International Inc.; 406, Ron Chapple/FPG International.

Chapter 14: Chapter Opener, Bruce Ayres/Tony Stone Images; 433, Superstock, Inc.

Chapter 15: Chapter Opener, Skjold/The Image Works; 465, Valerie Macon/Rea/SABA Press Photos, Inc.

Chapter 16: Chapter Opener, Charlie Westerman/Gamma-Liaison, Inc.; 507, Michael Ainsworth/The Dallas Morning News.

Chapter 17: Chapter Opener, Charles Thatcher/Tony Stone Images; 527, Tom Hartwell/SABA Press Photos, Inc.; 527, Courtesy of Coca Cola.

Concise Dictionary of HR Terminology

ability Competence in performing a job. (16)

absolute judgment An appraisal format that asks supervisors to make judgments about an employee's performance based solely on performance standards. (206)

adverse impact Discrimination that occurs when the equal application of an employment standard has an unequal effect on one or more protected classes. Also called *disparate impact.* (91)

affirmative action A strategy intended to achieve fair employment by urging employers to hire certain groups of people who were discriminated against in the past. (88)

Age Discrimination in Employment Act (1967) The law prohibiting discrimination against people who are 40 or older. (96)

Americans with Disabilities Act (1990) The law forbidding employment discrimination against people with disabilities who are able to perform the essential functions of the job with or without reasonable accommodation. (97)

appeals procedure A procedure that allows employees to voice their reactions to management practices and to challenge management decisions. (410)

apprenticeship A program in which promising prospective employees are groomed before they are actually hired on a permanent basis. (135)

arbitration The last step in a grievance procedure. The decision of the arbitrator, who is a neutral individual selected from outside the firm, is binding on both parties. (477)

assessment center A set of simulated tasks or exercises that candidates (usually for managerial positions) are asked to perform. (166)

attrition An employment policy designed to reduce the company's work force by not refilling job vacancies that are created by turnover. (189)

award A one-time reward, usually given in the form of a tangible prize. (337)

base compensation The fixed pay an employee receives on a regular basis, either in the form of a salary or as an hourly wage. (298)

behavioral appraisal instrument An appraisal tool that asks managers to assess a worker's behaviors. (209)

benchmark job or **key job** A job that is similar or comparable in content across firms. (314)

benefits mix The complete package of benefits that a company offers its employees. (366)

bona fide occupational qualification (BFOQ) A characteristic that must be present in all employees for a particular job. (92)

bonus program or **lump-sum payment** A financial incentive that is given on a one-time basis and does not raise the employee's base pay permanently. (336)

boundaryless organizational structure An organizational structure that enables an organization to form relationships with customers, suppliers, and/or competitors, either to pool organizational resources for mutual benefit or to encourage cooperation in an uncertain environment. (51)

brain drain The loss of high-talent key personnel to competitors or startup ventures. (16)

brainstorming A creativity training technique in which participants are given the opportunity to generate ideas openly, without fear of judgment. (253)

bureaucratic organizational structure A pyramid-shaped organizational structure that consists of hierarchies with many levels of management. (49)

burnout A stress syndrome characterized by emotional exhaustion, depersonalization, and reduced personal accomplishment. (506)

business process reengineering (BPR) A fundamental rethinking and radical redesign of business processes to achieve dramatic improvements in cost, quality, service, and speed. (52)

business unionism A form of unionism that focuses on improving workers' economic well-being. (460)

business unit strategy The formulation and implementation of strategies by a firm that is relatively autonomous, even if it is part of a larger corporation. (27)

cafeteria benefits program See **flexible benefits program.** (363)

career development An ongoing and formalized effort that focuses on developing enriched and more capable workers. (269)

career path A chart showing the possible directions and career opportunities available in an organization; it presents the steps in a possible career and a plausible timetable for accomplishing them. (279)

career resource center A collection of career development materials such as workbooks, tapes, and texts. (280)

case study method A business school teaching method in which students do in-depth analyses of real-life companies. (285)

codetermination The representation of workers on a corporation's board of directors; used in Germany. (465)

collective bargaining A system in which unions and management negotiate with each other to develop the work rules under which union members will work for a stipulated period of time. (461)

comparability In performance ratings, the degree to which the performance ratings given by various supervisors in an organization are similar. (212)

comparable worth A pay concept or doctrine that calls for comparable pay for jobs that require comparable skills, effort, and responsibility and have comparable working conditions, even if the job content is different. (321)

compensable factors Work-related criteria that an

organization considers most important in assessing the relative value of different jobs. (311)

compensatory damages Fines awarded to a plaintiff to compensate for the financial or psychological harm the plaintiff has suffered. (96)

conciliation An attempt to reach a negotiated settlement between the employer and an employee or applicant in an EEO case. (101)

Consolidated Omnibus Budget Reconciliation Act of 1985 (COBRA) Legislation that gives employees the right to continue their health-insurance coverage for 18 to 36 months after their employment has terminated. (374)

contingent workers Workers hired to deal with temporary increases in an organization's workload or to do work that is not part of its core set of capabilities. (71)

contract A legally binding promise between two or more competent parties. (424)

contractual right A right based on the law of contracts. (424)

contributions Payments made for benefits coverage. Contributions for a specific benefit may come from the employer, employee, or both. (363)

copayments Payments made to cover health-care expenses that are split between the employer's insurance company and the insured employee. (363)

core time Time when all employees are expected to be at work. Part of a flexible work hours arrangement. (74)

core workers An organization's full-time employees. (71)

corporate strategy The mix of businesses a corporation decides to hold and the flow of resources among those businesses. (27)

cost-of-living adjustment (COLA) Pay raises, usually made across the board, that are tied to such inflation indicators as the Consumer Price Index. (481)

cross-functional training Training employees to perform operations in areas other than their assigned job. (251)

cultural determinism The idea that one can successfully infer an individual's motivations, interests, values, and behavioral traits based on that individual's group memberships. (137)

cultural relativity concept of management The management concept holding that management practices should be molded to the different sets of values, beliefs, attitudes, and behaviors exhibited by a diverse work force. (122)

culture shock The inability to adjust to a different cultural environment. (522)

cumulative trauma disorder (CTD) An occupational injury that occurs from repetitive physical movements, such as assembly-line work or data entry. (502)

decentralization Transferring responsibility and decision-making authority from a central office to people and locations closer to the situation that demands attention. (8)

deductible An annual out-of-pocket expenditure that an insurance policyholder must make before the insurance plan makes any reimbursements. (363)

defined benefit plan or **pension** A retirement plan that promises to pay a fixed dollar amount of retirement income based on a formula that takes into account the average of the employee's last three to five years' earnings prior to retirement. (378)

defined contribution plan A retirement plan in which the employer promises to contribute a specific amount of funds into the plan for each participant. The final value of each participant's retirement income depends on the success of the plan's investments. (379)

development An effort to provide employees with the abilities the organization will need in the future. (237)

dimension An aspect of performance that determines effective job performance. (204)

discrimination The making of distinctions. In HR context, the making of distinctions among people. (90)

disparate treatment Discrimination that occurs when individuals are treated differently because of their membership in a protected class. (91)

distinctive competencies The characteristics that give a firm a competitive edge. (34)

distributive bargaining Bargaining that focuses on convincing the other party that the cost of disagreeing with the proposed terms would be very high. (473)

diversity Human characteristics that make people different from one another. (116)

diversity audit A review of the effectiveness of an organization's diversity management program. (136)

diversity training programs Programs that provide diversity awareness training and educate employees on specific cultural and gender differences and how to respond to these in the workplace. (132)

downsizing A company strategy to reduce the scale (size) and scope of its business in order to improve the company's financial performance. (9, 186)

downward communication Communication that allows managers to implement their decisions and to influence employees lower in the organizational hierarchy. (399)

dual-career couple A couple whose members both have occupational responsibilities and career issues at stake. (272)

due process Equal and fair application of a policy or law. (425)

economic strike A strike that takes place when an agreement is not reached during collective bargaining. (476)

egalitarian pay system A pay plan in which most employees are part of the same compensation system. (303)

electronic mail (e-mail) A form of electronic communication that allows employees to communicate with each other via electronic messages sent through personal computer terminals linked by a network. (404)

elitist pay system A pay plan in which different compensation systems are established for employees or groups at different organizational levels. (303)

employee assistance program (EAP) A company-sponsored program that helps employees cope with personal problems that are interfering with their job performance. (412)

employee attitude survey A formal anonymous survey designed to measure employee likes and dislikes of various aspects of their jobs. (409)

employee benefits or **indirect compensation** Group membership rewards that provide security for employees and their family members. (361)

employee feedback program A program designed to improve employee communications by giving employees a voice in policy formulation and making sure that they receive due process on any complaints they lodge against managers. (409)

employee recognition program A program that rewards employees for their ideas and contributions. (414)

employee relations policy A policy designed to communicate management's thinking and practices concerning employee-related matters and prevent problems in the workplace from becoming more serious. (397)

employee relations representative A member of the HR department who ensures that company policies are followed and consults with both supervisors and employees on specific employee relations problems. (397)

Employee Retirement Income Security Act (ERISA) A federal law established in 1974 to protect employees' retirement benefits from mismanagement. (378)

employee separation The termination of an employee's membership in an organization. (180)

employee stock ownership plan (ESOP) A corporatewide pay-for-performance plan that rewards employees with company stocks, either as an outright grant or at a favorable price that may be below market value. (346)

employment at will A common-law rule used by employers to assert their right to end an employment relationship with an employee at any time for any cause. (428)

employment contract A contract that spells out explicitly the terms of the employment relationship for both employee and employer. (424)

empowerment Providing workers with the skills and authority to make decisions that would traditionally be made by managers. (16)

enterprise union A labor union that represents workers in only one large company rather than in a particular industry; used in Japan. (465)

environmental challenges Forces external to a firm that affect the firm's performance but are beyond the control of management. (3)

Equal Employment Opportunity Commission (EEOC) The federal agency responsible for enforcing EEO laws. (100)

Equal Pay Act (1963) The law that requires the same pay for men and women who do the same job in the same organization. (89)

ergonomics The science of adapting working conditions to employee safety and comfort needs. (502)

essential functions Job duties that each person in a certain position must do or must be able to do to be an effective employee. (98)

ethnocentric approach An approach to managing international operations in which top management and other key positions are filled by people from the home country. (519)

executive order A presidential directive that has the force of law. In HR context, a policy with which all federal agencies and organizations doing business with the federal government must comply. (96)

exempt employee An employee who is not covered by the provisions of the Fair Labor Standards Act. Most professional, administrative, executive, and outside sales jobs fall into this category. (320)

exit interview An employee's final interview following separation. The purpose of the interview is to find out the reasons why the employee is leaving (if the separation is voluntary) or to provide counseling and/or assistance in finding a new job. (182)

expatriate A citizen of one country living and working in another country. (518)

expectancy theory A theory of behavior holding that people tend to do those things that are rewarded. (337)

extended leave A benefit that allows an employee to take a long-term leave from the office, while retaining benefits and the guarantee of a comparable job on return. (134)

external equity The perceived fairness in pay relative to what other employers are paying for the same type of labor. (299)

fair employment The goal of EEO legislation and regulation: a situation in which employment decisions are not affected by illegal discrimination. (88)

Fair Labor Standards Act (FLSA) The fundamental compensation law in the United States. Requires employers to record earnings and hours worked by all covered employees and to report this information to the U.S. Department of Labor. Defines two categories of employees: exempt and nonexempt. (320)

Family and Medical Leave Act of 1993 (FMLA) A federal law that requires employers to provide up to 12 weeks' unpaid leave to eligible employees for the birth or adoption of a child; to care for a sick parent, child, or spouse; or to take care of health problems that interfere with job performance. (372)

flat organizational structure An organizational structure that has only a few levels of management and emphasizes decentralization. (51)

flexible or **cafeteria benefits program** A benefits program that allows employees to select the benefits they need most from a menu of choices. (363)

flexible work hours A work arrangement that gives employees control over the starting and ending times of their daily work schedules. (74)

flextime Time during which employees can choose not to be at work. Part of a flexible work hours arrangement. (74)

four-fifths rule An EEOC provision for establishing a prima facie case that an HR practice is discriminatory and has an adverse impact. A practice has adverse impact if the hiring rate of a protected class is less than four-fifths the hiring rate of a majority group. (92)

frame-of-reference (FOR) training A type of training that presents supervisors with fictitious examples of worker performance (either in writing or on videotape), asks the supervisors to evaluate the workers in the examples, and then tells them what their ratings should have been. (213)

gainsharing A plantwide pay-for-performance plan in which a portion of the company's cost savings is returned to workers, usually in the form of a lump-sum bonus. (343)

genetic testing A form of biological testing that identifies employees who are genetically susceptible to specific occupational substances. (505)

geocentric approach An approach to managing international operations in which nationality is downplayed and the firm actively searches on a worldwide or regional basis for the best people to fill key positions. (519)

glass ceiling The intangible barrier within an organization that prevents female and minority employees from rising to positions above a certain level. (123)

graphology The study of handwriting for the purpose of measuring personality or other individual traits. (168)

grievance procedure A systematic step-by-step process designed to settle disputes regarding the interpretation of a labor contract. (477)

health maintenance organization (HMO) A health-care plan that provides comprehensive medical services for employees and their families at a flat annual fee. (375)

hiring freeze An employment policy designed to reduce the company's work force by not hiring any new employees into the company. (189)

hostile work environment sexual harassment Harassment that occurs when the behavior of anyone in the work setting is sexual in nature and is perceived by an employee as offensive and undesirable. (94)

hot-stove rule A model of disciplinary action: Discipline should be immediate, provide ample warning, and be consistently applied to all. (440)

HR audit A periodic review of the effectiveness with which a company uses its human resources. Frequently includes an evaluation of the HR department itself. (36)

human resource information system (HRIS) A system used to collect, record, store, analyze, and retrieve data concerning an organization's human resources. (75)

human resource planning (HRP) The process an organization uses to ensure that it has the right amount and the right kind of people to deliver a particular level of output or services in the future. (147)

human resource strategy A firm's deliberate use of human resources to help it gain or maintain an edge against its competitors in the marketplace. The grand plan or general approach an organization adopts to ensure that it effectively uses its people to accomplish its mission. (2)

human resource tactic A particular HR policy or program that helps to advance a firm's strategic goal. (2)

human resources (HR) People who work in an organization. Also called *personnel.* (2)

incentive system See **pay-for-performance system.** (331)

indirect compensation See **employee benefits.** (361)

individual challenges Human resource issues that address the decisions most pertinent to individual employees. (14)

individual equity The perceived fairness of individual pay decisions. (316)

individuals with disabilities Persons who have a physical or mental impairment that substantially affects one or more major life activities. (97)

informal communications Also called "the grapevine." Information exchanges without a planned agenda that occur informally among employees. (408)

information dissemination The process of making information available to decision makers, wherever they are located. (400)

insubordination Either refusal to obey a direct order from a supervisor or verbal abuse of a supervisor. (444)

integrative bargaining Bargaining that focuses on convincing the other party that the benefits of agreeing with the proposed terms would be very high. (474)

internal equity The perceived fairness of the pay structure within a firm. (299)

Internal Revenue Code (IRC) The code of tax laws that affects how much of their earnings employees can keep and how benefits are treated for tax purposes. (322)

involuntary separation A separation that occurs when an employer decides to terminate its relationship with an employee due to (1) economic necessity or (2) a poor fit between the employee and the organization. (184)

job aids External sources of information, such as pamphlets and reference guides, that workers can access quickly when they need help in making a decision or performing a specific task. (250)

job analysis The systematic process of collecting information used to make decisions about jobs. Job analysis identifies the tasks, duties, and responsibilities of a particular job. (61)

job banding The practice of replacing narrowly defined job descriptions with broader categories (bands) of related jobs. (317)

job description A written document that identifies, describes, and defines a job in terms of its duties, responsibilities, working conditions, and specifications. (67)

job design The process of organizing work into the tasks required to perform a specific job. (59)

job enlargement The process of expanding a job's duties. (60)

job enrichment The process of putting specialized tasks back together so that one person is responsible for producing a whole product or an entire service. (60)

job evaluation The process of evaluating the relative value or contribution of different jobs to an organization. (309)

job hierarchy A listing of jobs in order of their importance to the organization, from highest to lowest. (313)

job-posting system A system in which an organization announces job openings to all employees on a bulletin board, in a company newsletter, or through a phone recording or computer system. (278)

job rotation The process of rotating workers among different narrowly defined tasks without disrupting the flow of work. (60)

job sharing A work arrangement in which two or more employees divide a job's responsibilities, hours, and benefits among themselves. (73)

job specification The worker characteristics needed to perform a job successfully. (71)

joint venture In international business, a foreign branch owned partly by the home office and partly by an entity in the host country (a company, a consortium of firms, an individual, or the government). (519)

knowledge-based pay or **skill-based pay** A pay system in which employees are paid on the basis of the jobs they can do or talents they have that can be successfully applied to a variety of tasks and situations. (303)

knowledge worker A worker who transforms information into a product or service. (400)

KSAs The knowledge, skills, and abilities needed to perform a job successfully. (63)

labor contract A union contract that spells out the conditions of employment and work rules that affect employees in the unit represented by the union. (461)

labor relations specialist Someone, often a member of the HR department, who is knowledgeable about labor relations and can represent management's interests to a union. (457)

labor relations strategy A company's overall plan for dealing with labor unions. (466)

Landrum-Griffin Act (1959) A law designed to protect union members and their participation in union affairs. (459)

line employee An employee involved directly in producing the company's good(s) or delivering the service(s). (3)

literacy The mastery of basic skills (reading, writing, arithmetic, and their uses in problem solving). (254)

lockout Occurs when an employer shuts down its operations before or during a labor dispute. (476)

management by objectives (MBO) A goal-directed approach to performance appraisal in which workers and their supervisors set goals together for the upcoming evaluation period. (210)

management by walking around (MBWA) A technique in which managers walk around and talk to employees informally to monitor informal communications, listen to employee grievances and suggestions, and build rapport and morale. (408)

management games Elaborate role-playing exercises in which multiple participants enact a management situation. (285)

management of diversity The set of activities involved in integrating nontraditional employees (women and minorities) into the work force and using their diversity to the firm's competitive advantage. (118)

management rights Management's rights to run the business and retain any profits that result. (428)

manager A person who is in charge of others and is responsible for the timely and correct execution of actions that promote his or her unit's success. (3)

Medicare A part of the Social Security program that provides health insurance coverage for people aged 65 and over. (369)

mentoring A developmentally oriented relationship between senior and junior colleagues or peers that involves advising, role modeling, sharing contacts, and giving general support. (282)

merit pay An increase in base pay, normally given once a year. (336)

motivation That which energizes, directs, and sustains human behavior. In HRM, a person's desire to do the best possible job or to exert the maximum effort to perform assigned tasks. (16, 56)

multimedia technology A form of electronic communication that integrates voice, video, and text, all of which can be encoded digitally and transported on fiber optic networks. (405)

multinational corporation (MNC) A firm with assembly and production facilities in several countries and regions of the world. (518)

Nation Labor Relations Act See **Wagner Act.** (458)

National Labor Relations Board (NLRB) The independent federal agency created by the Wagner Act to administer U.S. labor law. (458)

negligent hiring Hiring an employee with a history of violent or illegal behavior without conducting background checks or taking proper precautions. (499)

nepotism The practice of favoring relatives over others in the workplace. (400)

nonexempt employee An employee who is covered by the provisions of the Fair Labor Standards Act. (320)

Occupational Safety and Health Act of 1970 (OSHA) A federal law that requires employers to provide a safe and healthy work environment, comply with specific occupational safety and health standards, and keep records of occupational injuries and illnesses. (491)

Office of Federal Contract Compliance Programs (OFCCP) The federal agency responsible for monitoring and enforcing the laws and executive orders that apply to the federal government and its contractors. (102)

old boys' network An informal social and business network of high-level male executives that typically excludes women and minorities. Access to the old boys' network is often an important factor in career advancement. (130)

organizational challenges Concerns or problems internal to a firm; often a byproduct of environmental forces. (7)

organizational culture The basic assumptions and beliefs shared by members of an organization. These beliefs operate unconsciously and define in a basic taken-for-granted fashion an organization's view of itself and its environment. (12)

organizational structure The formal or informal relationships between people in an organization. (48)

orientation The process of informing new employees about what is expected of them in the job and helping them cope with the stresses of transition. (258)

outcome appraisal instrument An appraisal tool that asks managers to assess the results achieved by workers. (210)

outplacement assistance A program in which companies help their departing employees find jobs more rapidly by providing them with training in job-search skills. (182)

outsourcing Subcontracting work to an outside company that specializes in and is more efficient at doing that kind of work. (14)

pay-for-performance system or **incentive system** A system that rewards employees on the assumptions that: (1) individual employees and work teams differ in how much they contribute to the firm; (2) the firm's overall performance depends to a large degree on the performance of individuals and groups within the firm; and (3) to attract, retain, and motivate high performers and to be fair to all employees, the firm needs to reward employees on the basis of their relative performance. (331)

pay grades Groups of jobs that are paid within the same pay range. (307)

pay incentive A program designed to reward employees for good performance. (298)

pay policy A firm's decision to pay above, below, or at the market rate for its jobs. (316)

peer review A performance appraisal system in which workers at the same level in the organization rate one another. (221)

peer trainers High-performing workers who double as internal on-the-job trainers. (251)

pension See **defined benefit plan.** (378)

Pension Benefit Guaranty Corporation (PBGC) The government agency that provides plan termination insurance to employers with defined benefit retirement programs. (378)

performance appraisal The identification, measurement, and management of human performance in organizations. (203)

perquisites ("perks") Noncash incentives given to a firm's executives. (350)

personnel file A file, maintained for each employee, containing the documentation of critical HR-related information, such as performance appraisals, salary history, disciplinary actions, and career milestones. (427)

piece-rate system A compensation system in which employees are paid per unit produced. (334)

plateauing The unanticipated and unwanted leveling of careers due to the elimination of management layers through corporate restructuring. (286)

polycentric approach An approach to managing international operations in which subsidiaries are managed and staffed by personnel from the host country. (519)

portable benefits Employee benefits, usually retirement funds, that stay with the employee as he or she moves from one company to another. (378)

positive discipline A discipline procedure that encourages employees to monitor their own behaviors and assume responsibility for their actions. (438)

preferred provider organization (PPO) A health-care plan in which an employer or insurance company establishes a network of doctors and hospitals to provide a broad set of medical services for a flat fee per participant. In return for the lower fee, the doctors and hospitals who join the PPO network expect to receive a larger volume of patients. (376)

premium The money paid to an insurance company for coverage. (375)

Privacy Act of 1974 Guarantees the privacy of personnel files for employees of the U.S. federal government. (427)

proactive human resource management See **union substitutions.** (468)

problem-solving team A team consisting of volunteers from a unit or department who meet one or two hours per week to discuss quality improvement, cost reduction, or improvement in the work environment. (55)

productivity A measure of how much value individual employees add to the goods or services that the organization produces. (16)

profit sharing A corporatewide pay-for-performance plan that uses a formula to allocate a portion of declared profits to employees. Typically, profit distributions under a profit-sharing plan are used to fund employees' retirement plans. (345)

progressive discipline A series of management interventions that gives employees opportunities to correct undesirable behaviors before being discharged. (436)

promotability forecast A career development activity in which managers make decisions regarding the advancement potential of subordinates. (276)

protected class A group of people who suffered discrimination in the past and who are given special protection by the judicial system. (90)

punitive damages Fines awarded to a plaintiff in order to punish the defendant. (96)

quality of work life (QWL) A measure of how safe and satisfied employees feel with their jobs. (16)

quid pro quo sexual harassment Harassment that occurs when sexual activity is required in return for getting or keeping a job or job-related benefit. (94)

quotas Employer adjustments of hiring decisions to ensure that a certain number of people from a certain protected class are hired. (96)

rater error An error in performance appraisals that reflects consistent biases on the part of the rater. (212)

realistic job preview (RJP) Realistic information given to new hires about the demands of the job, the organization's expectations of the job holder, and the work environment. (170)

reasonable accommodation An action taken to accommodate the known disabilities of applicants or employees so that disabled persons enjoy equal employment opportunity. (99)

recruitment The process of generating a pool of qualified candidates for a particular job; the first step in the hiring process. (150)

relative judgment An appraisal format that asks supervisors to compare an employee's performance to the performance of other employees doing the same job. (205)

reliability Consistency of measurement, usually across time but also across judges. (159)

reverse discrimination Discrimination against a nonprotected-class member resulting from attempts to recruit and hire members of protected classes. (103)

right The ability to engage in conduct that is protected by law or social sanction, free from interference by another party. (424)

rightsizing The process of reorganizing a company's employees to improve their efficiency. (186)

right-to-work law A state law that makes it illegal within that state for a union to include a union shop clause in its contract. (459)

role-playing A management development technique in which participants adopt the role of a particular manager placed in a specific situation. (285)

selection The process of making a "hire" or "no hire" decision regarding each applicant for a job; the second step in the hiring process. (151)

self-managed team (SMT) A team responsible for producing an entire product, a component, or an ongoing service. (54)

self-review A performance appraisal system in which workers rate themselves. (221)

senior mentoring program A support program in which senior managers identify promising women and minority employees and play an important role in nurturing their career progress. (134)

seniority The length of time a person works for an employer. (480)

simulation A device or situation that replicates job demands at an off-the-job site. (246)

situational factors or system factors A wide array of organizational characteristics that can positively or negatively influence performance. (220)

skill-based pay See **knowledge-based pay.** (303)

skills inventory A company-maintained record of employees' abilities, skills, knowledge, and education. (279)

socialization The process of orienting new employees to the organization or the unit in which they will be working; the third step in the hiring process. (151)

Social Security A government program that provides income for retirees, the disabled, and survivors of deceased workers, and health care for the aged through the Medicare program. (368)

special-purpose team A team consisting of workers who span functional or organizational boundaries and whose purpose is to examine complex issues. (56)

staff employee An employee who supports line employees. (3)

statutory right A right protected by specific laws. (424)

strategic HR choices The options available to a firm in designing its human resources system. (22)

strategic human resource (HR) planning The process of formulating HR strategies and establishing programs or tactics to implement them. (17)

structured interview Job interview based on a thorough job analysis, applying job-related questions with predetermined answers consistent across all interviewers for a job. (163)

subordinate review A performance appraisal system in which workers review their supervisors. (221)

succession planning A career development activity that focuses on preparing people to fill executive positions. (276)

supplemental unemployment benefits (SUB) Benefits given by a company to laid-off employees over and above state unemployment benefits. (371)

support group A group established by an employer to provide a nurturing climate for employees who would otherwise feel isolated or alienated. (133)

Taft-Hartley Act (1947) A federal law designed to limit some of the power acquired by unions under the Wagner Act by adjusting the regulation of labor-management relations to ensure a level playing field for both parties. (458)

team A small number of people with complementary skills who work toward common goals for which they hold themselves mutually accountable. (54)

telecommuting A work arrangement that allows employees to work in their homes full-time, maintaining their connection to the office through phone, fax, and computer. (75)

teleconferencing The use of audio and video equipment to allow people to participate in meetings even when they are a great distance away from the conference location or one another. (402)

360° feedback The combination of peer, subordinate, and self-review. (222)

Title VII Section of the Civil Rights Act of 1964 that applies to employment decisions; mandates that employment decisions not be based on race, color, religion, sex, or national origin. (90)

total compensation The package of quantifiable rewards an employee receives for his or her labors. Includes three components: base compensation, pay incentives, and indirect compensation/benefits. (298)

total quality management (TQM) An organizationwide approach to improving the quality of all the processes that lead to a final product or service. (8)

training The process of providing employees with specific skills or helping them correct deficiencies in their performance. (237)

trait appraisal instrument An appraisal tool that asks a supervisor to make judgments about worker characteristics that tend to be consistent and enduring. (208)

transnational corporation A firm with operations in many countries and highly decentralized operations. The firm owes little allegiance to its country of origin and has weak ties to any given country. (518)

turnover rate The rate of employee separations in an organization. (180)

unemployment insurance A program established by the Social Security Act of 1935 to provide temporary income for people during periods of involuntary unemployment. (371)

union An organization that represents employees' interests to management on such issues as wages, work hours, and working conditions. (456)

union acceptance strategy A labor relations strategy in which management chooses to view the union as its employees' legitimate representative and accepts collective bargaining as an appropriate mechanism for establishing workplace rules. (466)

union avoidance strategy A labor relations strategy in which management tries to prevent its employees from joining a union, either by removing the incentive to unionize or by using hardball tactics. (467)

union shop clause A union arrangement that requires new employees to join the union 30 to 60 days after their date of hire. (459)

union steward An advocate dedicated to representing an employee's case to management in a grievance procedure. (477)

union substitution/proactive human resource management A union avoidance strategy in which management becomes so responsive to employees' needs that it removes the incentives for unionization. (468)

union suppression A union avoidance strategy in which management uses hardball tactics to prevent a union from organizing its workers or to get rid of a union. (469)

universal concept of management The management concept holding that all management practices should be standardized. (122)

upward communication Communication that allows employees at lower levels to communicate their ideas and feelings to higher-level decision makers. (399)

validity The extent to which scores on a test or interview correspond to actual job performance. (159)

vesting A guarantee that accrued retirement benefits will be given to retirement plan participants when they retire or leave the employer. (378)

virtual reality (VR) The use of a number of technologies to replicate the entire real-life working environment in real time. (247)

voice mail A form of electronic communication that allows the sender to leave a detailed voice message for a receiver. (403)

voluntary separation A separation that occurs when an employee decides, for personal or professional reasons, to end the relationship with the employer. (184)

Wagner Act/National Labor Relations Act (1935) A federal law designed to protect employees' rights to form and join unions and to engage in such activities as strikes, picketing, and collective bargaining. (458)

wellness program A company-sponsored program that focuses on preventing health problems in employees. (507)

whistleblowing Employee disclosure of an employer's illegal, immoral, or illegitimate practices to persons or organizations that may be able to take corrective action. (434)

wholly owned subsidiary In international business, a foreign branch owned fully by the home office. (519)

wildcat strike A spontaneous work stoppage that happens under a valid contract and is usually not supported by union leadership. (476)

work flow The way work is organized to meet the organization's production or service goals. (48)

work flow analysis The process of examining how work creates or adds value to the ongoing processes in a business. (52)

work rules Any terms or conditions of employment, including pay, work breaks and lunch periods, vacation, work assignments, and grievance procedures. (461)

Worker Adjustment and Retraining Notification Act (WARN) of 1988 A federal law requiring U.S. employers with 100 or more employees to give 60 days' advance notice to employees who will be laid off as a result of a plant closing or a mass separation of 50 or more workers. (191)

workers' compensation A legally required benefit that provides medical care, income continuation, and rehabilitation expenses for people who sustain job-related injuries or sickness. Also provides income to the survivors of an employee whose death is job-related. (369)

works council A committee composed of both worker representatives and managers who have responsibility for governing the workplace; used in Germany. (465)

wrongful discharge Termination of an employee for reasons that are either illegal or inappropriate. (425)

Company, Name, and Product Index

D

E

F

G

H

I

J

K

L

M

N

O

P

Q

R

S

T

U

V

W

SUBJECT INDEX

B

C

D

E

F

G

J

K

L

M

N

O

P

Q

R

T

U

Human Resource Management on the Internet

▶ Visit these HRM-oriented sites on the World Wide Web!

Organization	Web Site	Information Provided
AFL-CIO	**http://www.aflcio.org/**	Home page of the AFL-CIO, a labor federation to which most U.S. labor unions belong.
American Compensation Association	**http://www.ahrm.org/aca/aca.htm**	Home page of the American Compensation Association, an organization of professionals engaged in the design, implementation, and management of employee compensation programs.
Americans with Disabilities Act (ADA) Document Center	**http://janweb.icdi.wvu.edu/kinder/**	Provides numerous links to ADA resources, including sites regarding such specific disabilities as cancer, hearing impairment, and alcohol- and drug-related illnesses.
Benefits Link	**http://www.magicnet.net/benefits/index.html**	Provides information on a wide variety of employee benefits plans.
Career Mosaic	**http://www.careermosaic.com/**	Contains a wealth of career and job information, including a large database of current job opportunities.
Employee Relations Web Picks	**http://www.nyper.com/**	Identifies e-mail newsgroups of interest to HRM professionals, offers resources on legal rulings, and lists publications on employee relations.
Equity Compensation Strategies	**http://www.fed.org/library.html**	A wide variety of sources focusing on performance-based compensation, including employee stock ownership plans (ESOPs) and other forms of incentive compensation.
HRMagazine	**http://www.shrm.org/docs/Hrmagazine.html**	Articles from *HRMagazine*, published monthly by the Society for Human Resource Management.